TRAFFIC SAFETY AND HUMAN BEHAVIOR

SECOND EDITION

TRAFFIC SAFETY AND HUMAN BEHAVIOR

Second Edition

BY

David Shinar
Ben Gurion University of the Negev,
Beersheba, Israel

emerald
PUBLISHING

United Kingdom – North America – Japan
India – Malaysia – China

Emerald Publishing Limited
Howard House, Wagon Lane, Bingley BD16 1WA, UK

First edition 2007

British Library Cataloguing in Publication Data
A catalogue record for this book is available from the British Library

ISBN: 978-1-78635-222-4 (Print)
ISBN: 978-1-78635-221-7 (Online)
ISBN: 978-1-78714-633-4 (Epub)

ISOQAR REGISTERED
ISOQAR certified Management System, awarded to Emerald for adherence to Environmental standard ISO 14001:2004.
Certificate Number 1985
ISO 14001

FSC
www.fsc.org
MIX
Paper from responsible sources
FSC® C013604

INVESTOR IN PEOPLE

To

Naomi and Yuval, who contributed by just being and by giving me a new perspective on life. May all the safety issues raised here be resolved by the time they can read this.

Contents

Preface to the Second Edition ix

Part A - Background, Methods, and Models

1. Introduction and Background 3

2. Research Methods 41

3. Theories and Models of Driver Behavior 87

Part B - Driver Capacities and Individual Differences

4. Vision, Visual Attention, and Visual Search 137

5. Driver Information Processing: Attention, Perception, Reaction Time, and Comprehension 189

6. Young and Novice Drivers 257

7. Older Drivers 327

Part C - Driving Style

8. Speed and Safety 391

9. Personality and Aggressive Driving 459

10. Use of Occupant Restraints 513

Part D - Driver Temporary Impairments

11. Alcohol and Driving 563

12. Drugs and Driving 637

13. Distraction and Inattention 711

14. Fatigue and Driving 797

Part E - Vulnerable Road Users

15. Pedestrians 861

16. Motorcyclists and Riders of Other Powered Two-Wheelers (PTWs) 927

17. Bicyclists 983

Part F - Crash Causation and Countermeasures

18. Accident/Crash Causation and Analysis 1039

19. Crash Countermeasures and Design of Safety 1085

Glossary of Acronyms 1177

Author Index 1181

Subject Index 1235

Preface to the Second Edition

> "Understanding the human side of driving is critical for making large-scale improvements in traffic safety." (Njord and Steudle, 2015, p. 3).

This second edition came into being as a result of a confluence of three factors: the publisher's suggestion that it is time for an update, my entry into a new phase of my professional life (emeritus), and my realization that in the past 10 years there has been a most significant expansion in our knowledge about driving and safety. Much of the new research was spurred by changing cultural norms that emphasize sustainability (including sustainable safety), and from gradually evolving perceptions concerning the critical issues of safety and mobility. Let me elaborate here about the last – more substantive – factors: added knowledge, cultural change in our norms, and change in the critical issues of road users' behavior in the context of traffic safety.

In terms of cumulative knowledge, we have experienced (and are still experiencing) an explosion of interest and empirical research related to the safety of mobility: driving, riding, and walking. Prior to the first edition of this book, I was able to find only 17 books that were directly related to road safety. But in the 10 years since the publication of the first edition in 2007, 28 more book have been added to the list. The books, of course, only reflect the tip of the publications iceberg. There is a much greater increase in dedicated scientific conferences and refereed articles of original research. For example, Google Scholar lists approximately 62,000 articles containing all the words "road," "safety," "behavior," and "driving or riding" published prior to 2007, and over 70,000 in the 9 years since then. Narrowing the search scope to the combination of "traffic safety" and "human behavior" yields approximately 2,300 articles published prior to 2007, and over 3,000 since then. As cynical as one might be about the plethora of new and not-so-significant articles, with such a wealth of information there are bound to be some novel and unexpected findings. And there are. Consequently, each of the book chapters has been supplemented with new findings that either confirm previously drawn conclusions or refute them and merit new thinking.

The cultural shift was a gradual one that started in the last century and gained normative acceptance in this last decade. In the past, traffic crashes – invariably labeled as accidents – and injuries were accepted as part of the cost of mobility. But Sweden's 1997 policy shift to "Vision Zero" meaning striving toward zero traffic fatalities, was the harbinger of the new norm of zero tolerance for road fatalities. This has been translated to a practical yet aggressive goal for continued reduction traffic fatalities. This goal, common to both national and international institutions is to cut fatalities by 50 percent every 10 years. Commitment to such a demanding goal requires close cooperation among different agencies and careful considerations of the impact of changes in the traffic system on the behavior of its road users. These implications are discussed in nearly every chapter.

Finally, within the realm of traffic safety and human behavior the specific "hot" issues of concern, and approaches to crash prevention and injury reductions have also changed over the past decade. For example, interest and research in aggressive driving and its contribution to crashes peaked around 2004-2005 while I was writing the first edition of this book. But the interest in distracted driving was nearly nil before 2009 and has been rising fast since then with no signs of abatement as of this writing (based on Google Trends). Distracted driving research – or at least the focus on it – is fueled by the constantly expanding technological communications and advanced driver assistance systems. These are brought into the cars by their manufacturers or by their drivers, and can both aid and impede safety.

Instead of the behavioral crash countermeasures – such as education, public information, and enforcement – that starred in the early part of this century, we are now increasingly looking to technology to solve our problems of speeding, driving while impaired, and distraction. Technological innovations are a rapidly growing part of the arsenal of crash countermeasures and driver assistance systems designed to keep drivers safe in their lanes with safe headways to vehicles and obstacles ahead. But the acceptance, use, and utilization of the new technologies are human behavioral issues that are discussed throughout the book. And as always with people, when their environment changes, it is naïve to assume that "all other things" will stay the same. Behavior will not, and this is illustrated in current research on driver adaptation to new support systems.

Two issues that were hardly addressed in the first edition were bicycling and the emergence of autonomous vehicles; going back to basics (locomotion through pedaling) on the one hand and jumping into the future (commanding the car) on the other hand. Increasing congestion, the desire for environmental sustainability, and renewed interest in health have catapulted bicycling to the fastest growing mode of travel. Bicycling and the interactions of bicyclists with the rest of the traffic – drivers and pedestrians – have spawned many studies that are now discussed in a dedicated chapter on bicycling behavior and safety. A special emphasis in this chapter is how to integrate cyclists into the traffic system while ensuring their safety.

The second new issue is that of the autonomous vehicle. Though autonomous vehicles had been considered nearly a century ago, at the dawn of this century it was still, for most people, a speculative issue worthy of discussion by futurologists. But the vigorous entrance of high-tech companies and automotive manufactures into this arena have made the autonomous vehicle a reality that could change our mobility and life patterns as much as the introduction of the combustion engine changed it a century ago. Contrary to "common sense" the autonomous vehicle does not make driving a non-sequitur. Instead, the expected need of human control and rapid intervention in unforeseen critical situations make this a complex issue as far as human-vehicle interactions (and distraction) are concerned. This has significant implications for injury reduction and crash prevention, which are discussed in the last chapter.

Two significant research methods have contributed greatly to new knowledge and new conclusions concerning driving behavior and traffic safety: the use of naturalistic driving studies (NDS) and the technique of meta-analysis (MA). NDS is the ultimate ecologically valid study of road user behavior because it tracks road users as they move through traffic in their own vehicles going about their own business. Meta-analysis is a technique that synthesizes the results of multiple studies which have addressed the same issue using similar methods and outcome measures, to provide a robust measure of an effect or a countermeasure. As often happens in empirical research, the application of these methods – in different domains – either confirmed previous tentative less robust conclusions or actually debunked earlier misconceptions. The two techniques are described in Chapter 2, and results from their applications are evident in nearly every chapter of the book. Perhaps the most important finding from NDS, is the most recent conclusion emerging from the largest of its kind ever study of crash causation that demonstrated that even today the human factor is a critical element in over 90 percent of traffic crashes (Dingus *et al.*, 2016). In a way this provides prima facie justification for this updated text.

This second edition has the same organization as the previous one, but every chapter has been expanded to include the current relevant issues and the theoretical and empirical research to substantiate them. This edition has over 100 tables and over 200 figures, and cites over 2,500 research papers. Yet even this compendium of approximately 1,200 pages only provides a sample of the studies in this domain. The second edition provides updated research that supports and augments our knowledge of safety-relevant human limitations and capabilities (e.g., in terms of visual perception, and information processing), discusses new research methods and new findings that challenge our previous assumptions and conclusions (e.g., the nature and role of distraction, the risk of drugs, and the safety of older drivers), and discusses new topics that a decade ago did not seem as important (to me at least) as they are today (e.g., bicycling behavior and safety, and in-vehicle driver assistance systems and the autonomous vehicle). For this edition, I have significantly expanded all the chapters of the previous edition and added a chapter on bicycling. Although in the process some of the material of the previous edition was deleted, the new edition is still 50 percent longer than the first edition.

A work of this scope is rarely done without help, and this case was no exception. I would like to thank Tamar Ben-Bassat, John Eberhard, Tsippy Lotan, Ilit Oppenheim, Mike Perel, Edna Schechtman, and my wife Eva Shinar for reading and commenting on the drafts of one or more chapters. They were instrumental in forcing me to clarify some points and in uncovering and helping me correct multiple typographical, syntax, and substantive errors. The ones that remain are obviously mine to own. Finally, I thank the staff of Emerald Publishing, in particular Cristina Irving Turner, Emma Stevenson, Charlotte Hales, Nicki Dennis, and Jen McCall. Their consistent support over the past 3 years made this volume a reality.

References

Dingus, T. A., F. Guo, S. Lee, J. Antin, M. Perez, M. Buchanan-King, and J. Hankey (2016). Driver crash risk factors and prevalence evaluation using naturalistic driving data. *Proc. Natl. Acad. Sci., 113*, 2636-2641.

Njord, J., and K. Steudle (2015). Big data hit the road: The first year of use of the SHRP 2 safety databases. *TR News*, 300, pp. 3-8, November-December. Transportation Research Board, Washington, DC.

PART A
BACKGROUND, METHODS, AND MODELS

1

Introduction and Background

"Citizens care about safety. There was a time when we had to force people to be safe, when regulation was the only way. The failed Ford safety campaign of the 1950s is still cited as proof that 'safety doesn't sell', but I'm here to tell you that today safety does sell. We have moved on to market-driven development, with car makers now competing for top safety scores and consumers making real buying decisions based on these scores." (Claes Tingvall, President of European New Car Assessment Program – EuroNCAP – at Transport Research Area – TRA 2006 Conference Göteborg, Norway). (http://ec.europa.eu/research/transport/news/article_4271_en.html)

"Although road traffic injuries have been a leading cause of mortality for many years, most traffic crashes are both predictable and preventable." (WHO, 2015).

Background

On August 17, 1896, Bridget Driscoll, a 44-year-old mother of two, became the first road fatality in the world from a collision with a vehicle powered by an internal combustion engine. She was hit by a car that – according to witnesses – was going at a "tremendous speed" (reported to be 4 mph). The driver of the car was Arthur Edsell who had been driving for only 3 weeks (no driving tests or licenses existed at that time). He was also said to have been talking to the young lady passenger beside him. After a 6-hour inquest, the jury returned a verdict of "Accidental Death." At the inquest, the coroner said: "This must never happen again" (Road Peace, 2004).

Whether or not Bridget Driscoll was indeed the first (true) automobile crash victim is arguable (Fallon and O'Neill, 2005), as Mary Ward was killed 27 years earlier when she fell under the wheels of an experimental steam car in 1869 (Wikipedia, August 26, 2014). The important issue is that in the course of the past 120 years, highway traffic safety has come a long way. Or has it? The purpose of this book is to describe the complexity of the issue of highway safety and the advances and difficulties encountered in this area in the past half century, from the perspective of the driving task. As will be shown in the following chapters, issues that were brought out in the above description of the first traffic accident are remarkably similar to some of the issues plaguing highway safety today: inexperience of novice drivers, speeding, distraction from non-driving tasks, vulnerability of pedestrians, labeling traffic crashes as "accidental," and – most importantly – the desire of everyone involved to eradicate highway traffic injuries and fatalities.

Highway safety and driving behavior as topics of research are much younger than the history of traffic accidents or crashes. Crashes were a very early by-product of the automobile, as illustrated in Figure 1-1, for the first driver fatality crash in England. In fact, crashes and collisions were prophesied long before the automobile actually appeared on our streets. Nearly, 500 years ago the prophetess Mother Shipton proclaimed "A Carriage without a horse shall go/Disaster fill the world with woe" (Wikipedia, 2014). Some early analyses of traffic crashes were published already in the 1930s, but they were limited to technical reports of limited circulation and remained essentially obscured (e.g., Gilutz, 1937). Arguably, the first book on the topic of traffic psychology was the *Psychology and the Motorist* by Toops and Haven, published in 1938. This book cited only three references, and only two of those dealt with driving behavior. Yet, the situation as the authors noted was already alarming. In the U.S., the authors write "some thirty nine thousand Americans annually are killed by the auto." And this was at a time when the U.S. population was below 130 million. In contrast, in 2015 there were 35,200 traffic fatalities (NHTSA, 2016a), and the U.S. population doubled to more than

Figure 1-1. Wall plaque commemorating the site of the first motor vehicle accident in which the driver was fatally injured (courtesy of author).

322 million. Despite the magnitude of the problem, the issue was largely ignored by the academic world at that time. To wit, Toops and Haven's book has been cited only three times since its publication (according to Google Scholar).

Possibly, the first commercially published monograph to focus exclusively on driver and driving behavior was Lauer's (1960) book: *The Psychology of Driving: Factors of Traffic Enforcement.* Since then the number of books and articles have increased in an exponential manner. Books on traffic safety and various aspects of driver behavior that appeared since then include *Aggression on the Road* by Parry (1968), *Vision and Highway Safety* by Allen (1970), *Human Factors in Highway Traffic Safety Research* by Forbes (1972), *Road User Behavior and Traffic Accidents* by Näätänen and Summala (1976), *Psychology on the Road: The Human Factor in Traffic Safety* by Shinar (1978), *Human Behavior and Traffic Safety* by Evans and Schwing (1985), *Traffic Safety and the Driver* by Evans (1991), *Automotive Ergonomics* by Peacock and Karwowski (1993), *Ergonomics and Safety of Intelligent Driver Interfaces* by Noy (1997), *Forensic Aspects of Vision and Highway Safety* by Allen *et al.* (1998), *Understanding Driving: Applying Cognitive Psychology to a Complex Everyday Task* by Groeger (2000), *Human Factors for Highway Engineers* by Fuller and Santos (2002), *Traffic Safety* by Evans (2004), *Handbook of Road Safety Measures* by Elvik and Vaa (2004), *Human Factors of Transport Signs* by Castro and Horberry (2004), *Human Factors in Traffic Safety* by Dewar and Olson (2007), *Traffic Safety and Human Behavior by Shinar* (2007), *The Multisensory Driver: Implications for Ergonomic Car Interface Design* by Ho and Spence (2008), *In the Company of Cars: Driving as a Social and Cultural Practice* by Redshaw (2008), *The Handbook of Road Safety Measures* (2nd edition) by Elvik *et al.* (2009), *Human Factors of Visual and Cognitive Performance in Driving* by Castro (2009), *Maintaining Safe Mobility in an Aging Society* by Eby, Molnar, and Kartje (2009), *Driver Distraction: Theory, Effects, and Mitigation* by Regan, Lee, and Young (2009), *Driver Behaviour and Accident Research Methodology: Unresolved Problems* by Wåhlberg (2009), *Motorcycling and Leisure: Understanding the PTW Rider* by Broughton and Walker (2009), *Forensic Aspects of Driver Perception and Response* by Olson, Dewar, and Farber (2010), *Driver Behaviour and Training* by Dorn (2010), *Handbook of Traffic Psychology* by Porter (2011), *Human Modelling in Assisted Transportation* by Cacciabue *et al.* (2011), *The Safety of Intelligent Driver Support Systems* by Barnard, Risser, and Krems (2011), *The Fast and the Furious: Drivers, Speed Cameras and Control in a Risk Society* by Wells (2011), *Handbook of Driving Simulation for Engineering Medicine and Psychology* by Fisher, Rizzo, *et al.* (2011), *Ergonomics in the Automotive Design Process* by Bhise (2012), *Driver Behavior and Accident Research Methodology* by af Wåhlberg (2012), *Advances in Traffic Psychology* by Sullman and Dorn (2012), *Designing Safe Road Systems: a Human Factors Perspective* by Theeuwes, van der Horst, and Kuiken (2012), *Advances in Human Aspects of Road and Rail Transportation* by Stanton (2013), *Behavioural Adaptation and Road Safety* by Rudin-Brown and Jamson (2013), *Automotive Ergonomics: Driver-Vehicle Interactions* by Gkikas (2013), *Eliminating Serious Injury and Death from Road Transport* by Johnston, Muir, and Howard (2014), *Driver Acceptance of New Technology* by Regan, Horberry, and Stevens (2014), *Communication, Public Discourse, and Road Safety Campaigns* by Guttman (2014), *Driving with Music: Cognitive-Behavioral Implications* by Brodsky (2015), *Increasing Motorcycle Conspicuity* by Rößger, Lenné, and Underwood (2015), *Human Factors in*

Automotive Engineering and Technology by Walker, Stanton, and Salmon (2015), *Human Factors in Traffic Safety* (3rd edition) by Smiley (2015), *Handbook of Driver Assistance Systems* by Winner *et al.* (2016), and *Handbook of Teen and Novice Drivers: Research, Practice, Policy, and Directions* by Fisher, Caird, *et al.* (2016).

Thus, more books have been published in the past decade – since the publication of the first edition of this book – than in all of the previous century and first 7 years of this century! A similar trend also exists in the number of published scientific studies. In an interesting quantitative summary of articles published in the open literature, Hagenzieker, Commandeur, and Bijleveld (2014) found that up until 1950 the total number of journal articles on road safety research was in the single digit range. But since then, there has been an exponential explosion such that by 2010, there were over 2,000 articles in English language alone. Furthermore, the growth was accompanied by a shift in focus from that of accident prone drivers, through multiple crash causes and systems analysis, to today's focus on theories and models of driver behavior in the context of new intelligent transport systems (ITS) and autonomous driving. It is therefore not surprising that the role of psychology and psychological concepts such as risk taking and behavioral adaptation have assumed a central role in this area (Hakkert and Gitelman, 2014; Vaa, 2014).

Definitions: Safety, accidents, and crashes

It is interesting that safety in general and highway traffic safety, in particular, are most commonly defined by their negative outcomes: crashes or accidents. In this book, I will use the two terms interchangeably, though some researchers and safety organizations distinguish between the two and prefer the term "crashes." It appears that even the public – at least the American public – does not view accidents as random uncontrollable events as the word implies. In a national U.S. survey of the term "accident" (and not just traffic accidents), Girasek (2015) found that over 80 percent of the respondents thought that accidents are preventable. Yet, only 25 percent thought that they are predictable and a similar percentage thought that they are controlled by fate. Clearly, at least in the domain of traffic safety, there is a need to distinguish between a neutral and purely descriptive term, like a crash that does not convey any preconceptions about its causes, and an accident that is a random event or an act of God. The term accident is more loaded than a crash and implies a chance event, one that is out of the driver's control and in a sense almost an act of God. If a crash is a chance event ("there but for the grace of God…"), then by implication it cannot be foreseen, and therefore cannot be prevented. If traffic crashes are indeed accidents, then how can they be studied scientifically, and how can science improve traffic safety? As I hope to show in this book crashes most often are not accidents. A similar rationale led the U.S. National Highway Traffic Safety Administration (NHTSA) to replace the term "accident" with the term "crash" in all their official documents and communications in 1996 (NHTSA, 1996). According to the U.S. National HIghway Traffic Safety Administration (NHTSA) office of the Historian, "accidents imply random activity beyond human influence and control," whereas crashes are "predictable results of specific actions." Five years later the editors of the *British Journal of Medicine* declared: "we are banning the inappropriate use of 'accident' in our pages … in favor of the descriptive and more neutral terms 'crash' and 'collision'" (Davis, 2001). Thus, in the past 50 years the use of the term "accident" has been in constant decline in scientific papers, whereas the use of the term crash has been increasing consistently (Hagenzieker *et al.*, 2014). Nonetheless, since the term accident is still in common use, the two terms will be used interchangeably in this book.

Before we continue any further, we must agree on a definition of a crash or an accident. Unfortunately, this is very difficult. In the case of traffic accidents, perhaps the most commonly accepted definitions are the ones adopted by the U.S. NHTSA and the UN/ECE. According to NHTSA, a crash is "an unintended event resulting in injury or damage, involving one or more motor vehicles on a highway that is publicly maintained and open to the public for vehicular travel" (NHTSA, 1998). According to the UN/ECE accidents are events "which occurred or originated on a way or street open to public traffic; which resulted in one or more persons being killed or injured and in which at least one moving vehicle was involved" (Berns and Brühning, 1998). Although the definitions seem nearly identical, they are not, as each word that is in them – as well as every word that is not – is critical. For example, the NHTSA definition refers to "motor vehicles," whereas the OECD definition does not mention the word "motor" but does specify "moving vehicles." Thus, a collision between a bicyclist and a pedestrian would qualify as such for the OECD data, but not for the U.S. These kinds of differences create significant problems when we attempt to compare accident statistics across different countries, as done by the International Traffic Safety and Analysis Group that produces the International Road Traffic Accident Data Base (IRTAD) that includes data from all reporting OECD countries and some additional countries, which also vary slightly – but significantly – in their definitions (OECD, 1998). For example, most countries include only injury crashes in their database, but some include property damage crashes too (e.g., Denmark, Israel). However, these data are neither a complete census nor a representative sample. Also, even within countries there are inconsistencies in the inclusion criteria; for example, in cases of crashes resulting from police chases and suspected suicide or loss of consciousness prior to the crash. The similarity but non-identity in definitions means that when looking at international data, we may not be comparing apples and oranges, but we are definitely dealing with a wide variety of oranges (or apples). In addition, most countries do not include vehicle-related non-traffic fatalities on private properties. Thus, being crushed by a backing vehicle on a private driveway is not considered a traffic crash. Although, relative to other traffic crashes their number is small, they are still significant. In the U.S., for example, they claim the lives of approximately 500 people and injure over half a million people each year (NHTSA, 2015c). But because of their psychological impact – the victims being mostly small children – the NHTSA recently issued a regulation requiring a backup video camera and display in all vehicles produced after May 1, 2018.

Safety has come a long way in the past half century

In the western world, over the past 40 years the desire for greater traffic safety has fostered a dramatic social cultural change in norms. Forty years ago the U.S. nationwide front seat safety belt use was 15 percent, alcohol-related crashes accounted for over 50 percent of all fatal crashes, and safety was viewed by the automotive industry as something the public did not care about. In contrast, in 2012 the U.S. safety belt use in the front seats reached 86 percent (NHTSA, 2012), and in some countries (e.g., Australia, Canada, Czech Republic, France, Germany, Japan, Israel, New Zealand, Netherlands, Norway, Sweden, and the United Kingdom) it had reached 95 percent or higher (IRTAD, 2013). In 2012, in the U.S. alcohol impairment was responsible for 31 percent of traffic fatalities (NHTSA, 2013). Not surprisingly, the U.S. Centers for Disease Control listed "increased awareness and response for improving global road safety" as one of the "Ten great public health achievements worldwide: 2001–2010" (CDC, 2011). Perhaps, the most notable change has been in the regulatory and industrial emphasis on safety. In its Research, Development, and Technology Strategic Plan, the U.S. Department of Transportation listed safety as the #1 priority for the fiscal years 2013-2018, ahead of reducing congestion, improving mobility, and preserving the environment (DOT, 2013). On the automotive industry's front, Volvo has stated its safety goal as "no one should be killed or seriously injured in a new Volvo by 2020" (Eugensson, 2009; Eugensson *et al.*, 2011).

Yet, the public's attitude toward traffic safety is complex. A nationally representative survey conducted in the U.S. in 2005 (Mason-Dixon, 2005) found that safety is the single most important feature that Americans value in their personal car. At the same time the majority of the respondents in the same survey also felt that "driving today is less safe than five years ago," and that they are "more likely to be involved in a motor-vehicle collision today than five years ago." Thus, either way one looks at it – from the consumer's desires or the consumer's concerns – and despite the great advances just noted, traffic safety is of great interest to most drivers today. Similarly, in an earlier analysis of a decade of annual polls of the U.S. adult population health habits between the years 1985 and 1995, we found a steady improvement in driving-related safety habits that included significantly fewer people admitting to drinking and driving and significantly more people reporting that they regularly use safety belts (Shinar, Schechtman, and Compton, 1999). The result of all of these changes in driver attitudes and behaviors is reflected in the ever decreasing rate of traffic fatalities, which in the U.S., dropped in one decade, 2004-2014, from 1.44 to its lowest level ever of 1.08 fatalities per million vehicles miles of travel (NHTSA, 2015a, 2015b, 2016b). A similar dramatic trend of increasing highway safety has been observed in the European Union (EU) countries, as reflected in Figure 1-2, where the number of people killed in traffic accidents decreased by nearly 20 percent in the first half of this decade. Though this may be an impressive decline, it falls short of the rate of decline that is needed to meet the EU goal of a 50 percent reduction by the end of the decade.

Traffic safety must come at a cost. While we all want safer cars, safer roads, and safer road users, we often ignore the cost involved. The cost may be in terms of convenience, money, and mobility. From the perspective of driver behavior the cost is most often in terms of mobility and comfort. For example, we would like to "get there" "now" and we would like to get there safely. Well, there is a mathematically simple inverse relationship between speed and the time it takes to get from point "a" to point "b." And we are all aware of that. Unfortunately, there is also a relationship between speed and crash risk, and between speed and crash severity: the higher the speed, the higher the crash risk and crash severity (see Chapter 8). This relationship is more difficult to accept (or easier to

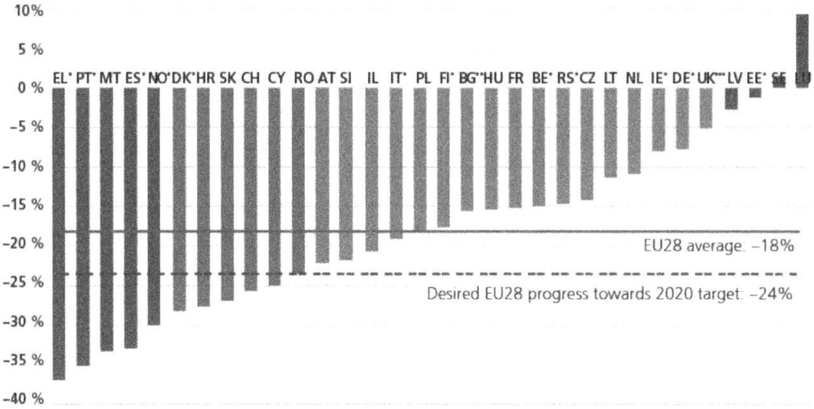

Figure 1-2. Percentage change in road traffic fatalities in 32 European Union and affiliated countries between 2010 and 2014. *Note*: Numbers for starred countries were based on estimates (from ETSC, 2015, with permission from the European Transport Safety Council, Brussels).

challenge) for many people. We can create safer cars with better energy absorption systems, better occupant protection devices (such as airbags), or occupant restraints (such as belts), but the first two cost more money and the third involves some inconvenience. Thus the claim that we all want maximum safety is really not tenable. Instead, what we all desire is to maximize other values, without exceeding a certain (hopefully low) level of crash risk (Evans, 2004; Wilde, 2002).

Scope and Measurement of Traffic Crashes and Injuries

The tremendous impact that crashes have on our society has attracted the attention of scientists, health officials, legislators, and policy makers to this issue, and in most countries significant advances have been made in curtailing accidents. However, to assess the scope of the problem and advances in safety, some standardized – or at least common – measures of the phenomenon must be agreed on.

The scope of the problem in terms of property-damage, injury, and fatal crashes

"Approximately 1.24 million people die every year on the world's roads, and another 20 to 50 million sustain nonfatal injuries as a result of road traffic crashes" (WHO, 2013a, 2013b). Unfortunately, this number has not changed significantly over the past 10 years (WHO, 2015). In contrast, in 2013 terrorists killed approximately 18,000 people worldwide or about 1.5 percent of the number killed by traffic (Kuper, 2015). World-wide traffic accidents are also the leading cause of death for people 15-29 years old, and the ninth leading cause of death across all age groups (WHO, 2015). Thus, there is an elephant in our lives that most people tend to ignore.

Defining severe injury: MAIS3+
In contrast to the specific number of traffic fatalities cited, injuries are expressed in terms of an enormous range of numbers: 20-50 million. This is because documenting and applying a standard common measure for injuries in all countries is a formidable challenge that still has to be met (Tingvall *et al.*, 2013) and because relative to fatalities they are quite poorly documented (WHO, 2013a, 2013b). As a start, the EU has embarked on an effort "to devise harmonised methodologies to produce comparable data on serious injuries in due time; (because) only when their true character and frequency is assessed in a sound and uniform way, can effective road safety management mechanisms be employed (such as target setting, implementation, monitoring and evaluation)" (IRTAD, 2014, p. 25). A review of the current practices for documenting injuries in the EU countries revealed that the 23 participating countries had nearly 23 different definitions. Most of these were based on administrative criteria such as hospitalization for 24 hours or more (e.g., Belgium, France, Germany, Ireland, Israel, Portugal, Spain, Switzerland, the United Kingdom), 48 hours or more (Hungary), or overnight (Greece). In very few cases the criteria were actually based on medically accepted measures for injury severity (Finland, Netherlands, and Romania). In short, international comparisons at this stage are practically meaningless. Realizing this, the EU has adopted a common criterion of serious injury: MAIS = 3+. The MAIS is a medically determined evaluation of the Maximum Abbreviated Injury Scale. AIS scores are determined by the injury severity to nine different body regions (head, face, neck, thorax, abdomen, spine, upper extremity, lower extremity, and unspecified) on a 6-level scale of severity, ranging from 1 (minor) to 6 (maximal), where each level corresponds to a probability of death (0 at AIS = 1 and 100 at AIS = 6). The MAIS is the AIS score of the most severely injured body region. MAIS3, the level agreed on by the EU as the threshold for serious injury is associated with an 8-10 percent likelihood of death. As of 2015, most European countries have accepted this new definition of serious injury and are working toward integrating it into their crash documentation (ETSC, 2013, 2015). Once this becomes the norm, comparisons will be meaningful, and the full and true medical, societal, and financial burden will be measurable – and probably very disturbing. Nonetheless, once measured objectively and systematically, a goal for its reduction can be stated.

Consequently, for now at least, we must settle on fatalities as the common comparable measure of national and international road safety. Also, often ignored, but very relevant is the death toll from traffic-based pollution. According to the World Bank (2014), when added to the death toll from road injuries, the total toll of traffic in 2010 was 1.33 million people, making it the sixth leading cause of death.

It is important to refrain from generalizing from fatal crashes to injury and non-injury crashes, as their characteristics are quite different in speed, location, time-of-day, and the people involved. This also means that efforts at reducing traffic fatalities will not necessarily reduce traffic injuries. Because most countries focus on reducing fatalities, the trends are also different. Over long periods of time, the difference is quite dramatic. In the U.S., in the past half century (1964-2013) the death rate per vehicle miles traveled decreased by 80 percent, whereas the number of people injured decreased by 50 percent. The differences in some of the European countries are even more dramatic. For example, in the two decades from 1990 to 2009 the number of fatalities in Spain decreased by approximately

65 percent whereas the number of injuries fluctuated greatly and decreased by approximately 25 percent. In Sweden, a country known for its excellent traffic safety record, over the same period fatalities decreased by approximately 45 percent, whereas the number of injuries actually *increased* by close to 10 percent (OECD, 2010).

As the world population grows, and as cars become more and more commonplace, the number of accidents worldwide increases. According to the World Health Organization (WHO, 2005), worldwide motor vehicle accidents are the second most frequent cause of death for people 5-29 years old and "projections indicate that these figures will increase by about 65 percent over the next 20 years unless there is new commitment to prevention" (WHO, 2004). Also because traffic crashes hit people of all ages, especially young inexperienced drivers, the rising cost of crashes is also reflected in the reduced quality of life as measured by disability-adjusted life years (DALYs – see Table 1-2 for a definition). Using this measure, traffic accidents were ranked as the ninth leading cause of this global burden of disease in 1990, but was projected to become the 3rd by the year 2020 if the trend is not changed (WHO, 2004). So far this prediction seems to be valid, as in 2010 road injuries were the eighth leading cause of deaths worldwide, responsible for the loss of over 75 million DALYs (World Bank, 2014). Furthermore, while the death rate from road crashes has been constantly decreasing in the developed world (Europe and Israel, North America), in the rest of the world it is either stable (Latin America, North Africa, and the Middle East – excluding Israel) or actually increasing (Southeast Asia, Sub-Saharan Africa), as can be gleaned from Figure 1-3.

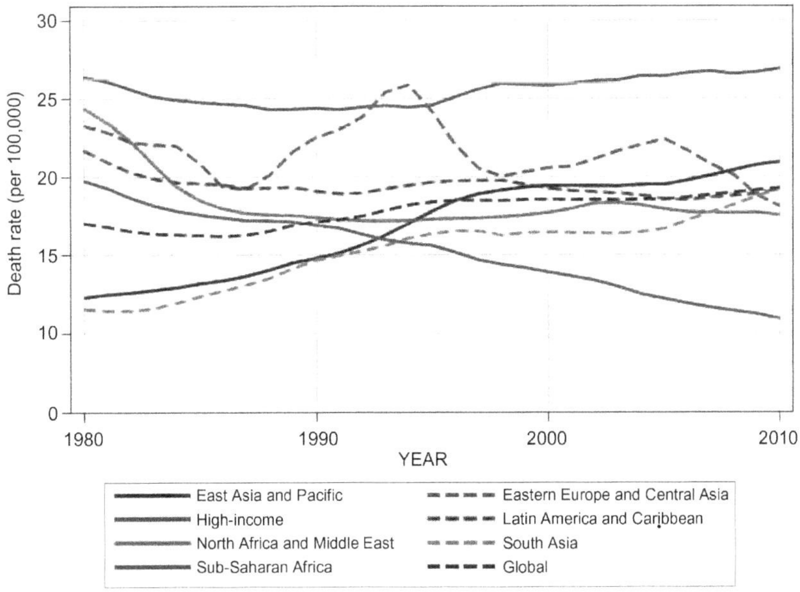

Figure 1-3. Worldwide trends in road injury death rates from 1980 to 2010 (from World Bank, 2014, p. 29, with permission from the World Bank).

Some people see this tremendous and increasing toll as an unavoidable cost of "progress." As the number of cars increases and as the world population increases, so will the number of crashes and victims. Thus, given the current trends, death from a motor vehicle crash worldwide was projected to become the fifth most common cause of death by 2030, versus its 10th place in 2015 (WHO, 2016). The data in Table 1-1, of the leading causes of death in the U.S., show that in the U.S., in terms of estimated years of life lost, this future is almost here. In fact, in 2011 motor vehicle crashes were the number one cause of death in the U.S. for people of ages 8-24 and the seventh leading cause in terms of years of life lost. The measure of "years of life lost" also has significant economic implications, especially when calculated in terms of composite measures that include the quality of life (such as DALY). Furthermore, when the analysis is restricted to unintentional injuries only, then death from motor vehicle crashes rises to the first or second leading cause of death for all age groups! (CDC, 2015).

Finally, though in this book the primary distinction is between crashes of different injury severities, it is important to acknowledge that there are other factors that define crashes, and they have critical implications for crash and injury reductions. Thus, the American National Standards Institute (ANSI, 2007) also classifies (and defines) motor vehicle traffic accidents in terms of damage severity, vehicle type, number of vehicles involved, first harmful event, location, and other variables.

Measuring safety

Since – all other things being equal – the absolute number of crashes is expected to increase over time (as the number of cars and drivers increase), trends in road fatalities are typically measured and tracked in terms of *rates* of crashes and injuries. When rates are used, the number of crashes or injuries is divided by some measure of exposure. Several different rates are often used to track changes in safety over time, each with a different exposure measure, and each providing a different measure of risk. Unfortunately, these measures of risk are often at variance with each other. This is where the use and abuse of statistics can come into play. A simple measure available in most countries is the number of crashes (or injuries or fatalities) divided by the size of the population. This measure gives the average risk per person. Another measure considers the risk per driver, and therefore uses only the number of licensed drivers in the population. However, because not all drivers have cars and by definition (in most countries at least) a traffic accident must involve a motor vehicle, a third exposure measure is the number of registered vehicles (after all, a driver without a car cannot cause a traffic accident). Finally, because only vehicles that are actually moving on the road can be involved in crashes, a fourth common measure of crash rate uses the total number of miles or kilometers driven as the denominator. With four potential denominators and at least three qualitatively different numerators – number of crashes, number of people injured, and number of fatalities – we now have 12 different indices with which we can describe the state of traffic safety in any one country. This gives policy makers a lot of room to either denounce the state of traffic safety or to congratulate themselves for the great improvements achieved on their watch. Table 1-2 provides a list of some of the

Table 1-1. Leading causes of death in the U.S. as a function of age, based on National Center for Health Statistics Mortality Data. Traffic Crashes are highlighted (from Liu, Singh, and Subramanian, 2015).

NHTSA
www.nhtsa.gov

Top 10 Leading Causes of Death in the United States in 2011, by Age Group[1]

National Highway Traffic Safety Administration's National Center for Statistics and Analysis

RANK	Cause and Number of Deaths											Years of Life Lost[2]
	Infants Under 1	Toddlers 1–3	Young Children 4–7	Children 8–15	Youth 16–20	Young Adults 21–24	Other Adults 25–34	Other Adults 35–44	Other Adults 45–64	Elderly 65+	All Ages	
1	Perinatal Period 11,931	Congenital Anomalies 448	Malignant Neoplasms 381	MV Traffic Crashes 785	MV Traffic Crashes 3,424	MV Traffic Crashes 3,300	Accidental Poisoning 7,652	Malignant Neoplasms 11,717	Malignant Neoplasms 161,469	Heart Disease 475,100	Heart Disease 596,577	Malignant Neoplasms 24% (9,188,476)
2	Congenital Anomalies 5,013	Accidental Drowning 308	MV Traffic Crashes 287	Malignant Neoplasms 693	Suicide 2,167	Homicide 2,449	Suicide 6,100	Heart Disease 10,635	Heart Disease 105,842	Malignant Neoplasms 397,107	Malignant Neoplasms 576,691	Heart Disease 19% (7,291,475)
3	Heart Disease 309	Homicide 363	Congenital Anomalies 158	Suicide 492	Homicide 2,154	Accidental Poisoning 2,301	MV Traffic Crashes 5,569	Accidental Poisoning 8,075	CLRD[6] 19,678	CLRD[6] 121,869	CLRD[6] 142,943	CLRD[6] 4% (1,714,895)
4	Homicide 290	Malignant Neoplasms 259	Accidental Drowning 151	Homicide 303	Accidental Poisoning 1,109	Homicide 2,300	Homicide 4,185	Suicide 6,599	Chronic Liver Disease 19,613	Stroke 109,323	Stroke 128,932	Stroke 4% (1,429,919)
5	Influenza/ Pneumonia 204	MV Traffic Crashes 247	Homicide 129	Congenital Anomalies 281	Malignant Neoplasms 690	Malignant Neoplasms 801	Malignant Neoplasms 3,499	MV Traffic Crashes 4,425	Diabetes 18,700	Alzheimer's 84,032	Alzheimer's 84,974	Accidental Poisioning 4% (1,394,750)
6	Septicemia 178	Heart Disease 138	Exposure to Smoke/Fire 96	Heart Disease 169	Heart Disease 403	Heart Disease 564	Heart Disease 3,301	Homicide 2,519	Stroke 16,910	Diabetes 52,402	Diabetes 73,831	Suicide 4% (1,393,748)
7	Stroke 134	Influenza/ Pneumonia 101	Heart Disease 92	Accidental Drowning 163	Accidental Drowning 173	Accidental Drowning 249	HIV 636	Chronic Liver Disease 2,449	Suicide 15,427	Influenza/ Pneumonia 45,363	Nephritis/ Nephrosis 53,609	MV Traffic Crashes 3% (1,297,257)
8	MV Traffic Crashes 93	Exposure to Smoke/Fire 89	Influenza/ Pneumonia 52	CLRD[6] 113	Congenital Anomalies 212	Congenital Anomalies 184	Diabetes 666	Diabetes 1,842	Accidental Poisoning 15,379	Nephritis/ Nephrosis 37,796	Nephritis/ Nephrosis 45,591	Diabetes 3% (1,119,576)
9	Nephritis/ Nephrosis 76	MV Nontraffic Crashes[4] 79	CLRD[6] 49	MV Nontraffic Crashes[4] 84	Accidental Falls 86	Pregnancy, Child Birth 119	Influenza/ Pneumonia 530	Stroke 1,718	MV Traffic Crashes 9,424	Septicemia 26,746	Suicide 39,518	Perinatal Period 2% (942,864)
10	Malignant Neoplasms 70	Septicemia 55	MV Nontraffic Crashes[4] 37	Influenza/ Pneumonia 79	Influenza/ Pneumonia[5] 81	Influenza/ Pneumonia 116	Stroke 505	HIV 1,619	Nephritis/ Nephrosis 7,414	Hypertension Renal Disease 23,272	Septicemia 36,280	Chronic Liver Disease 2% (761,320)
ALL[3]	23,985	3,572	2,205	4,885	12,983	15,669	43,748	69,893	505,562	1,831,844	2,515,458	All Causes 100% (38,536,588)

Table 1-2. Commonly used measures of crash and injury rates (from WHO, 2004, p. 57, with permission from the World Health Organization).

Measure	**Description**	**Use and Limitations**
Number of injuries	Absolute figure indicating the number of people injured in road traffic crashes. Injuries sustained may be serious or slight.	Useful for planning at the local level for emergency medical services. Useful for calculating the cost of medical care. Not very useful for making comparisons. A large proportion of slight injuries are not reported.
Number of deaths	Absolute figure indicating the number of people who die as a result of a road traffic crash.	Gives a partial estimate of magnitude of the road traffic problem, in terms of deaths. Useful for planning at the local level for emergency medical services. Not useful for making comparisons.
Fatalities per 10,000 vehicles	Relative figure showing ratio of fatalities to motor vehicles.	Shows the relationship between fatalities and motor vehicles. A limited measure of travel exposure because it omits non-motorized transport and other indicators of exposure. Useful for international caparisons.
Fatalities per 100,000 population	Relative figure showing ratio of fatalities to population.	Shows the impact of road traffic crashes on human population. Useful for international comparisons.
Fatalities per vehicle-km traveled	Number of road deaths per billion kilometers traveled.	Useful for international comparisons. Does not take into account non-motorized travel.
DALYs (Disability-Adjusted Life Years)	Healthy life years lost due to disability and mortality. 1 DALY lost = 1 year of healthy life lost, due to premature death/disability.	DALYs combine both mortality and disability.

more common measures and their uses. The important point is not that one measure is better than another, but that each statement of traffic safety has to specify the type of measure used. The intelligent reader can then interpret its meaning. This is not always easy because different measures are affected by different variables that by themselves have no bearing on safety policy. For example, O'Neill and Kyrychenko (2006), demonstrated that the number of deaths per distance traveled is greatly affected by the level of urbanization and demographic characteristics of the road users. Thus, in the U.S. where the fatality rates differ greatly among the 50 states, almost 70 percent of the variance is accounted for by differences in these two factors. The use of the different measures is illustrated below for crash and injury trends over time for specific countries, and at a given time for comparisons among countries.

The choice of a preferred rate goes beyond the immediate meaning of the measure. In recent years, with the dramatic increase in traffic accidents worldwide, traffic safety has come to the attention of health officials, who are now attempting to address it as they would any other disease. From the perspective of public health, traffic accidents are *the* disease of our time, and they are projected to remain in that dubious place of honor in the next few decades at least. As a public health issue the situation is not only grim, but has not improved at all over the past decades. An interesting illustration of this is provided by Sivak (1996) who notes, based on data provided by the U.S. National Safety Council, that between 1923 and 1994 the total number of people killed in the U.S. from traffic accidents annually more than doubled: from 18,400 to 43,000. However, the death rate per million vehicle kilometers decreased by 92 percent (!): from 13.4 to 1.1. During that time, at least part of the reason for the increase in the first measure and the decrease in the second measure was due to the increase in the size of the U.S. population, the number of licensed drivers, and the number of registered vehicles. With all these critical factors affecting the likelihood of traffic accidents, the fatality rate per 100,000 persons living in the U.S. remained essentially unchanged: at 16.5 in both periods. Thus, if we are to treat crashes as a modern day disease, we must look just as epidemiologists evaluate the risk of diseases and epidemics: at its impact relative to the number of people in the affected population; and the news concerning the traffic accident "disease" is not good. Incidentally, despite significant reductions in the U.S. traffic fatality rates, the U.S. is far from being a leader in this domain. Based on data collected by the IRTAD for 2013, the U.S. had 10.3 fatalities per 100,000 inhabitants while seven OECD countries – Denmark, Israel, Netherlands, Norway, Sweden, Switzerland, and the United Kingdom – led the pack with less than four fatalities per 100,000 inhabitants (IRTAD, 2015).

If we look at traffic accidents from the perspective of highway safety administrators and policy makers then we make allowance for all the factors for which the engineers – justifiably – cannot assume responsibility and these include the number of people and vehicles moving on the roads. The differences in philosophies concerning the place of traffic safety – as a unique safety phenomenon versus a public health concern – are also reflected in the different goals set by different countries. Of course, to be immune from criticism for biasing the safety picture, a country can strive to lead on all three rate measures of fatalities: per population, per vehicles, and per kilometers driven. Worldwide as of 2013, three countries excelled and led the rest of the world on all three measures: Sweden (with 27 fatalities per million inhabitants; 58 per million passenger cars, and 2.4 fatalities per billion vehicle kilometers), the United Kingdom (with 28, 59, and 2.8, respectively), and Netherlands (with 28, 60, and 3.3, respectively) (EC, 2015). By comparison, the U.S. which up to the 1970s led the world in traffic safety had 103.5 deaths per million inhabitants, 122.6 per million registered vehicles, and 17.5 per billion vehicle kilometers (NHTSA, 2015a).

The importance of setting measurable goals – regardless of the terms in which they are defined – is well established as a means of improving performance (Locke and Latham, 2002). Setting tough but achievable goals is a great motivating force. Once stated, a goal becomes a measure against which nations, governments, and other institutions can evaluate their performance, and be held accountable. Most European countries – where the population size is relatively stable – set their traffic safety goals in terms of reductions in either absolute number of fatalities or in terms of the rate of fatalities per population (IRTAD, 2015). The most ambitious and challenging goal phrased in absolute terms is the "Vision Zero" adopted by the Swedish parliament in 1997: "that no one would be killed or seriously injured in the road transportation system." This approach explicitly states that "the system designers are invariably ultimately responsible for the design, management and use of the road transport system and thus, they are jointly responsible for the level of safety of the whole system. The road users are obliged to abide by the rules that the system designers decide on for the use of the road transport system. If the road users fail to abide by the rules – for example, due to lack of knowledge, acceptance or ability – or if personal injuries occur, the system designers must take additional measures to prevent people from dying or being seriously injured" (Fahlquist, 2006, p. 1113, quoting the Swedish law).

In contrast, the U.S. Department of Transportation sets its safety goal in terms of the fatality rate per 100 million vehicle miles traveled. The strategic goal that was set in 2003 for 2008 was "not more than 1.0 per 100 million vehicle miles traveled" (U.S. DOT, 2003) or 0.62 deaths per 100 million vehicle kilometers traveled. Unfortunately, this goal was not achieved and instead a new more modest goal was set to "reduce the rate of roadway fatalities per miles traveled from 1.25 per million vehicle miles traveled (VMT) in 2008 to 1.03 per 100 million VMT in 2013" (i.e., 0.64 fatalities per 100 million vehicle kilometers traveled) (U.S. DOT, 2012), and that goal too has not been met (NHTSA, 2015a). In 2015, the fatality rate was 1.12 (NHTSA, 2016a) or 6.96 fatalities per billion kilometers traveled. Note that this is significantly worse than the rate of nearly all Western European countries (Figure 1-5).

Another caveat is the definition of a crash or an injury. For example, one of the more common definitions, used in the U.S. Fatal Analysis System, for a fatal traffic accident is "a police-reported crash involving a motor vehicle in transport on a trafficway in which at least one person dies within 30 days of the crash" (NHTSA, 2000). Not all countries limit recorded crashes in their data files to ones occurring on public roads (by including crashes off the road and on private roads) and motor vehicles in motion (by including crashes involving bicyclists and a parked car), and not all countries use the same time limit of 30 days (the range varies from 24 hours to no time limit at all) to note a fatality or a fatal crash. These differences in definitions make cross-cultural and international comparisons a little more uncertain than they appear. However, some approximations can be derived by factoring some of the differences. For example, the World Health Organization uses a 12-month rule for counting fatalities for vital statistics reporting. In the U.S. according to ANSI (2007) "experience indicates that, of the deaths from motor vehicle accidents which occur within 12 months of those accidents, about 99.5 percent occur within 90 days and about 98.0 percent occur within 30 days" (Section 3.1.3). This difference of 2.0 percent between 30 days and "anytime" (equivalent for all practical purposes to 1 year) has also been obtained for traffic fatalities in Israel (NRSA, 2010).

Perhaps, the most common rate used by traffic safety engineers and transportation experts is the number of crashes or fatalities per total vehicle miles (or kilometers) driven by all cars; that is, the risk per miles or kilometers of driving in any one country. Obviously, a registered vehicle that is not moving, cannot strike anyone, and the more time and distance a vehicle travels on the road the more it is at risk of being involved in an accident. But time-on-the-road is very difficult to evaluate, and we therefore resort to the estimate of total mileage driven. Unfortunately, the measure itself is not as accurate as we would like it to be because it typically depends on survey reports of people's estimates of their driving distances. Distance traveled can be accurate in countries with annual motor vehicle testing, where based on the odometer readings from all vehicles the aggregate measure of the total distance traveled by all vehicles can be calculated. However, this procedure is practiced in very few countries (e.g., Israel). Still, regardless of how it is calculated or estimated, when the change over time is great, the inherent inaccuracy of the measure is less important. Thus, as noted above, in the U.S. the risk of fatality per mile driven has decreased markedly over the half century by approximately 80 percent: from 5.5 fatalities per 100 million vehicle miles in 1966 to 1.1 fatalities per 100 million vehicle miles in 2012 (Figure 1-4). Statistically speaking, this means that in the U.S. a person would have to travel by car an average distance equivalent to over 460 round trips to the moon – which is on the average 238,855 miles from earth – before being killed in a traffic accident.

Using this rate, fatalities per total distance traveled, as a basis for international comparisons, it is easy to see from Figure 1-5 that, in general, the more developed, and more motorized, countries have lower fatality rates, with England and some of the Scandinavian countries leading the way. Note, however, that the U.S., the most motorized country in the world (with approximately eight vehicles for every 10 residents, including infants and children) does not fare well as these countries. This chart, however, does not include countries with fatality rates significantly above 100 such as China (126) and Russia (598).

The rate per miles driven is also oblivious to the impact of alternative modes of transportation on overall travel safety. Public transportation by train or bus is typically safer than travel by car and shifting the public's use to these modes can increase public safety without being reflected in the fatalities per miles driven. Thus, as comforting or disturbing as the rate of fatality per miles driven is (depending on where you live, of course),

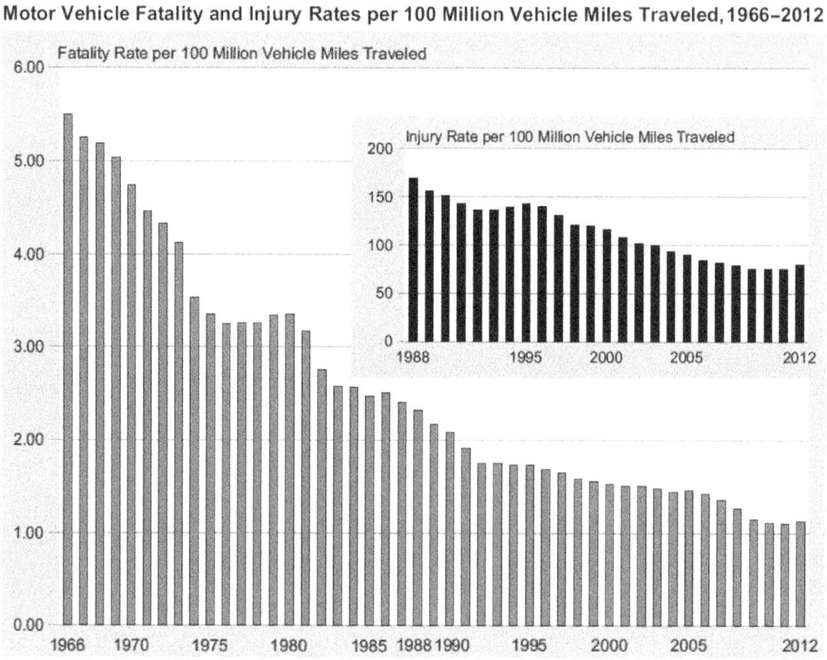

Figure 1-4. Trends in fatalities and injuries per 100 million vehicle miles of travel in the U.S., 1966-2012 (from NHTSA, 2014).

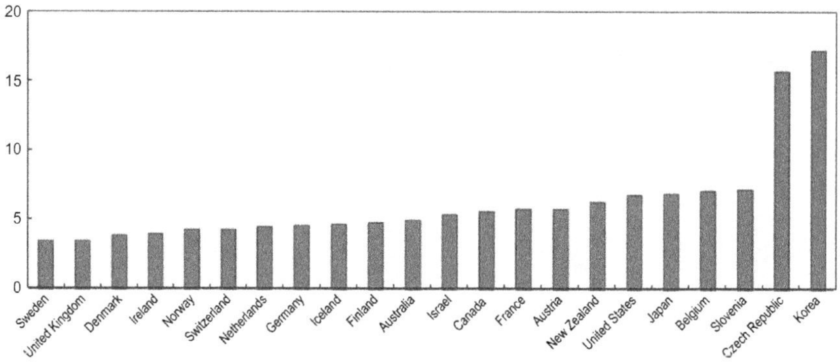

Figure 1-5. Fatalities per billion vehicle kilometers traveled in different countries in 2013. Data for Australia, Canada, Ireland, Lithuania and the U.S. is provisional. Data for the Czech Republic is from 2012 (from IRTAD, 2015, with permission from the OECD Publishing, Paris).

the state of traffic safety looks very different if we consider another common rate: the rate of fatalities per number of people in the population. This is the typical measure used in health statistics to estimate the risk of a person of contracting any disease in any one country.

Unlike the rate per miles driven, in the U.S. the rate of fatalities per population has stayed fairly constant with only a 5 percent drop from 1923 to 2000. Why the great disparity in the behavior of the two statistics? One possibility is that most of the improvement in the rate per miles driven is due to an increase in travel rather than due to a reduction in the number of crashes. Thus, a road segment may be equally safe (or unsafe) regardless of the number of cars traveling on it (within limits) and a car may be equally safe (or unsafe) regardless of the miles driven. Another possibility, raised by Sivak (2002) is that a society has a certain tolerance to traffic injuries, not in absolute terms (because the absolute numbers keep increasing) but relative to population size.

While the rate of involvement per population is a common rate used in the health area, it does not account for the number of drivers or vehicles running on the roads and potentially having the crashes. Obviously, the likelihood of being in a crash should be related to these. Also – especially from the perspective of policy makers – there is very little one can do to control all citizens, but there are a lot of actions that can be taken to regulate and improve the vehicles and the drivers. Therefore, two other common rates are the rate of crashes or fatalities per number of licensed drivers and the number of crashes or fatalities per number of registered vehicles (Figure 1-6). Figure 1-7 demonstrates the difference in the rates of fatalities relative to the number of people and relative to the number of registered vehicles in different countries. Although the data are somewhat dated, they still illustrate the importance of having both measures, and the differences between them. As can be seen from this figure, in the more developed countries of the Western world (in income per capita and the number of vehicles per person),

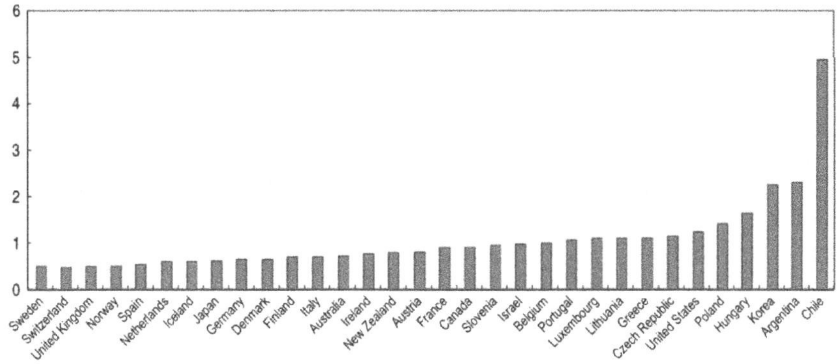

Figure 1-6. Road fatalities per 100,000 registered vehicles in 2013. (Total vehicles include mopeds for Argentina, Australia, Canada, Chile, Iceland, Ireland, Lithuania, and the U.S. Canada: 2012 data. Provisional data for Australia, Ireland, Lithuania, and the U.S.) (from IRTAD, 2015, with permission from the OECD Publishing, Paris).

both rates are relatively low, whereas in the less-developed countries such as Turkey and Korea, the rate per population is much lower than per vehicles. In general, the disparity between the two rates is even greater for poorer, less motorized countries. When we focus on rates per population only, finer distinctions among the countries become apparent, as can be seen for the EU countries in 2010 and 2014 (Figure 1-8).

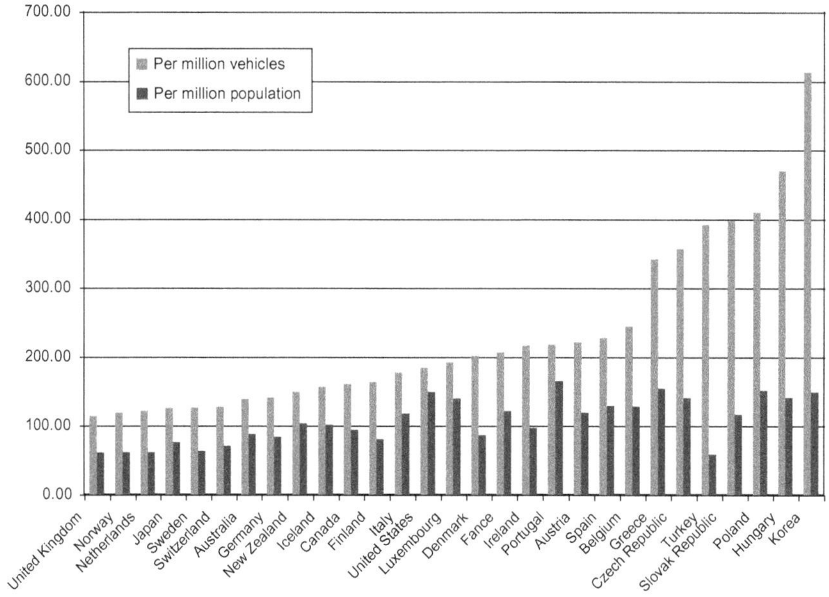

Figure 1-7. Traffic accident fatalities per population size and number of registered vehicles in different countries: 2002 (from OECD, 2006, with permission from the OECD Publishing, Paris).

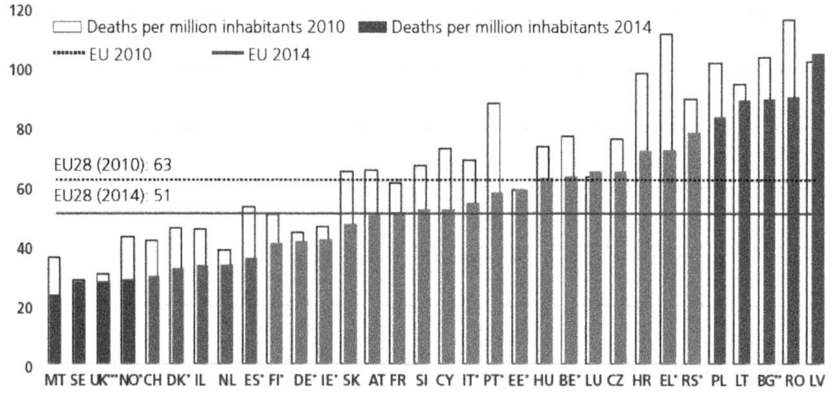

Figure 1-8. Road deaths per million inhabitants in 30 EU and affiliated countries in 2010 and in 2014. *Note*: Starred countries are estimates (from ETSC, 2015, with permission from the European Transport Safety Council).

Of the various measures described above, fatalities per vehicle miles/kilometers driven have evolved to become the gold standard of traffic safety measures. Yet, even for this measure (as well as the others) there are pitfalls in using aggregate data when comparing countries or states. The most common is the one known as "Simpson's Paradox," which states that "a trend that appears in different groups of data disappears when these groups are combined, and the reverse trend appears for the aggregate data" (Wikipedia). Stated with respect to international comparisons in fatality rates, it means that one country may appear safer than another when all of its regions are combined, whereas in fact, it is actually less safe when examined on a regional basis. An illustration from U.S. data is the comparison of the fatality rates of California and South Dakota (SD). California has a fatality rate of 1.27 fatalities per 100 million vehicle miles and SD has a fatality rate that is nearly 70 percent higher, 2.12 fatalities per 100 million vehicle miles. When the fatality rates are disaggregated by the types of roads, we get a completely different picture, as can be seen in Table 1-3. When the data are disaggregated into urban and rural roads, it is obvious that SD is safer on both. Yet, because most of the driving in California is on urban roads (where fatality rates are lower because of lower speeds), while most of the driving in SD is on rural roads, we actually get the misconception that driving on California roads is safer than driving on SD roads.

Given these large differences between the various measures, and the pitfalls that abound in interpreting the aggregate data on each measure, is there a simple way to describe safety levels? The answer is yes and no. Perhaps, the most common way to evaluate safety is to consider change over time in a given country, state, or locality, and then justify the particular measure used. The particular measure used will then depend on the nature, mission, and policy of the institution making the comparison. Health organizations would be more likely to evaluate safety in terms of rates relative to population size, whereas transportation organizations would be more likely to consider rates relative to drivers, vehicles, or total kilometers traveled. Still there remains one caveat: the change in safety may be due to exogenous reasons (confounding factors) that may only surface in comparisons to other locations.

Table 1-3. Demonstration of Simpson's paradox using California and South Dakota fatality rates (per 100 million vehicle miles of travel). Based on 2004 data (from Hedlund, 2008).

State	**Fatality Rate (per 100 Million? VMT)**			**Distribution of VMT**	
	Rural	Urban	Total	Rural	Urban
California	2.68	0.92	1.27	20%	80%
South Dakota	2.49	0.87	2.12	77%	23%

Motorization and Crashes – Smeed's Law

Contrary to appearance, the data in Figure 1-7 do not reflect independence of the two measures of safety. There is another measure that seems to mediate the relationship between safety per population size and safety per number of vehicles: the level of motorization. The level of motorization as an intervening variable was first proposed by Smeed in 1949 and is now known as Smeed's law. According to this "law" the rate of fatalities per number of vehicles decreases exponentially as a function of the number of vehicles per the size of the population. Stated in more intuitive terms, the involvement of each vehicle in a fatal crash decreases as the number of cars in a country increases. Although first formalized by Smeed on the basis of 1938 data from only 20 countries, it has since been validated repeatedly on more recent and larger samples of different countries based on annual statistics from different years (Adams, 1985; Evans, 2004; Smith, 1999). A relatively recent evaluation of this relationship is depicted in Figure 1-9, and it is based on mostly 2002 and 2003 data from 62 countries gathered by Link (2006). When Link's fatality rates (per million vehicles) are plotted relative to the level of motorization (vehicles per 1,000 people), we obtain the typical negative power relationship demonstrated by Smeed on data more than three quarters of a century ago. Further demonstration of the strength of this relationship was shown by Adams (1985) and Evans (2004) when they plotted the data for individual countries over the course of several years.

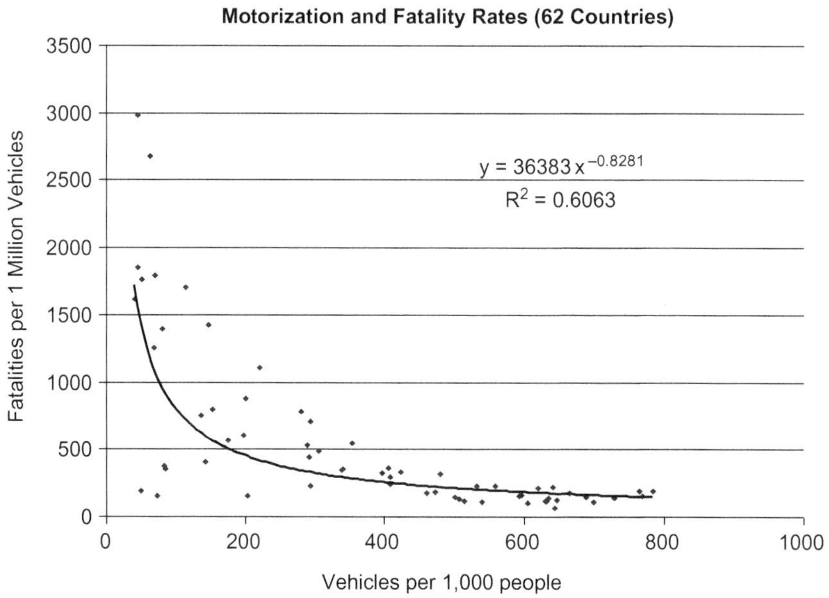

Figure 1-9. Smeed's Law based on data from 62 countries (collated by Link, 2006, with permission).

Various explanations have been offered for the relationship between fatalities per vehicles and the level of motorization (Näätänen and Summala, 1976). Because the relationship is one of association, it is likely that there are multiple factors that together contribute to this phenomenon, and it is their combined effects that are most likely responsible for the stability in this function across countries and across time. Other variables that covary with increasing motorization and that may directly or indirectly influence traffic safety include the increasing proportion of trips taken in motorized vehicles relative to trips taken by walking or bicycling (see Chapters 15 and 17); improvements in the transportation infrastructure (including divided highways, hard shoulders, barriers, etc.) that accompany the increase in vehicles; demographic shifts toward urbanization, where accidents are less severe; increasing traffic density and congestion, leading to reduction in high-speed crashes; improvements in emergency medical services; reductions in the exposure (kilometers driven) of each vehicle as the number of vehicles increases (we can accumulate vehicles, but we still cannot drive more than one vehicle at a time); increases in population risk awareness; and greater level of motorization due to greater government investment in safety in general, including education. Perhaps the most important implication of Smeed's law and the explanations offered for it is that because accidents and highway safety are affected by multiple factors, addressing any one of them without consideration for the others will only constitute a small part of the solution for a complex problem.

For example, we can illustrate the relationship between motorization and the mix of vehicles. The argument is that as the level of motorization increases, the mix of protective vehicles (cars), non-protective vehicles (motorcycles and bicycles), and vulnerable road users (pedestrians) changes, so that there are more of the former and fewer of the latter on the streets and highways. This is illustrated in Figure 1-10 that graphically displays the relative proportions of people killed in motor vehicle crashes as pedestrians, bicyclists, motorcyclists, and occupants of cars and trucks in different countries. Figure 1-11 displays the relevant data collapsed across countries but disaggregated by gross levels of income (which correlates highly with the level of motorization). The differences between highly motorized and high-income countries and the countries with low levels of motorization and income are striking. In motorized countries most of the people killed are car occupants. For example, in the EU countries the range is from close to 70 percent in Norway, Finland, and Sweden, to approximately 50 percent in Cyprus, Romania, and the Czech Republic (ETSC, 2011). In contrast, in low-income countries (especially in Sub-Saharan Africa), pedestrians account for more fatalities than any other mode of transportation (Figure 1-11). Obviously, once a collision occurs, the likelihood of an unprotected pedestrian being killed in a crash is much greater than that of a car driver or a passenger who is protected by their vehicle frame, a safety belt, and an airbag. For example, as detailed in Chapter 15, an analysis of the data from 62 countries revealed that the proportion of pedestrian fatalities is inversely related to the level of motorization ($r = -0.72$) and the level of affluence (gross domestic product/person, $r = -0.71$), which are positively related to each other ($r = 0.82$).

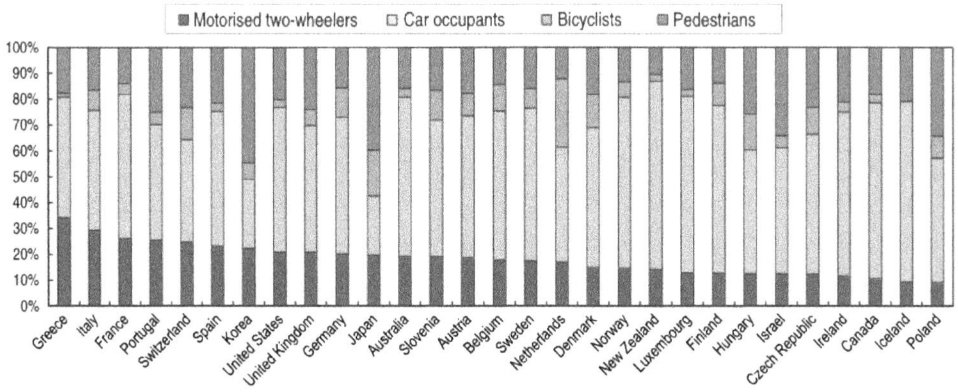

Figure 1-10. Percentage of different types of road users in fatalities (average 2009-2013) share of different road user classes in OECD countries. *Note*: in the U.S. sport utility vehicles are not included in the "car" category, and hence the large proportion of others (from IRTAD, 2015, with permission from the OECD Publishing, Paris).

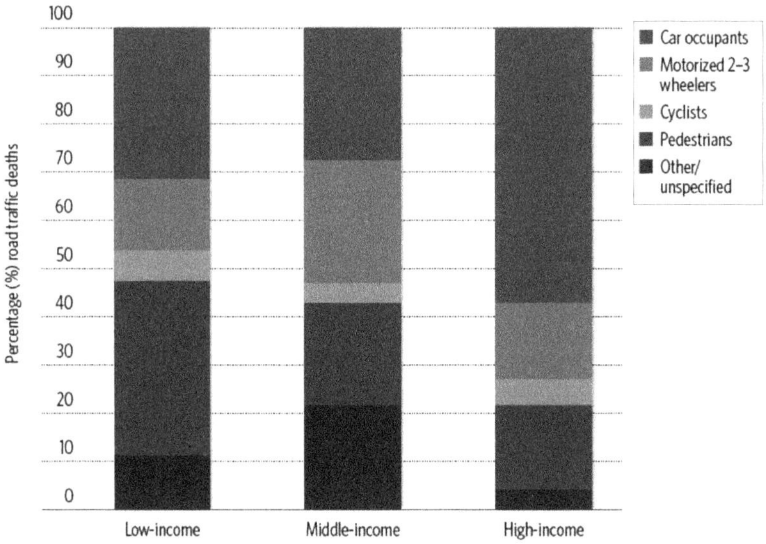

Figure 1-11. Percentages of road users killed as pedestrians, cyclists, mopeds and motorcycles, and cars and trucks, in different countries with different income levels (reprinted from Global Status Report on Road Safety 2013 (p. 7, Copyright World Health Organization, http://apps.who.int/iris/handle/10665/78256).

The Reliability and Validity of Crash Data

Even when crashes are well defined in identical terms, there are significant variations in crash data among sources. Various state agencies, such as police, licensing agencies, safety divisions, insurance companies, trauma centers, and bureaus of statistics do not always agree with each other. Furthermore, in many traffic safety studies, the crash data are based on the drivers' own reports. Needless to say there are many reasons for discrepancies between self-reports of crashes, reports from hospital trauma centers, and police reports.

The most ubiquitous source of crash data is police reports, which constitute the basis for national crash statistics in over 70 percent of the countries surveyed by the World Health Organization (WHO, 2013a, 2013b). However, for various reasons, listed in Table 1-4 (Elvik *et al.*, 2009), there are limitations to police reports.

It is worthwhile to dwell on the reasons for the data loss as they can introduce some significant biases in the data analysis, interpretation, and recommendations based on them. To start with, some accidents are simply not reported to the police for various reasons: poor communications (mostly in remote areas and in less-developed countries) and inadequate police force to record and investigate all crashes. Next, some accidents are "not reportable" according to the police definitions, such as minor injury and property-damage-only crashes. Some of these crashes are actually misclassified because of initial underestimation of injuries (such as those from internal bleeding). For these reasons and others, police records often underreport accidents relative to hospital records, especially pedestrian and bicycle accidents (Derriks and Mak, 2007). Thus, in a cross-country comparison, Elvik and Mysen (1999) estimated that global crash recording rates include only 95 percent of all fatal crashes, 70 percent of serious injury crashes (where at least one person was admitted to a hospital), 25 percent of slight injuries crashes (where no one was treated at a hospital), 10 percent of very slight injury crashes, and 25 percent of

Table 1-4. Reasons for incompleteness and inaccuracy of police accident data in the various stages of information transmission (from Elvik et al., 2009, with permission from Emerald Group Publishing).

Stages in the Recording of Accidents	**Reasons for Lost or Inaccurate Information**
All accidents on public roads	Not reported to the police
Accidents defined as reportable	Not reportable accidents
Accidents reported	Incomplete reporting
Data elements recorded	Missing data elements
Accuracy of recorded data	Inaccurate data

property-damage-only crashes. In fact in some countries and jurisdictions, police, as a matter of policy, do not become involved in the recording or investigation of property-damage-only crashes (e.g., Israel). Next, even when a crash is investigated some of the needed information may be missing. Finally, clerical and judgment errors often lead to inaccurate data in the final data set. Evaluations of the accuracy of police reports – even those of well-trained officers – often reveal some gross inaccuracies in data recording and interpretation of the evidence. Errors are most common when it comes to attributing the cause of the accident (Shinar, Treat, and McDonald, 1983), exact location, time, and speed (Chung and Chang, 2015). It is important to emphasize that underreporting and errors are not a random process or one that is the same for all countries. The greatest amount of underreporting occurs in the poorest countries where the death toll from road traffic crashes is the greatest (World Bank, 2014). But even in the developed world, underreporting is a significant problem for pedestrian and bicyclist crashes as these often occur on the sidewalk or on foot paths off the road and often do not involve a motorized vehicle (Turner, Roozenburg, and Francis, 2006).

Interestingly, there is no convincing argument for the preference of one data source over the other as they all have some advantages and disadvantages. The intuitive appeal of police reports as a data source for crash involvement is that they are based on police-observed facts. The appeal of self-reports is that they can supply details that police reports often lack. On the other hand, drivers suffer from memory failures and bias and are less reliable in recalling crashes from several years ago. Drivers are also probably less likely to report crashes in which they were culpable, especially if they involve socially unacceptable behaviors such as being intoxicated.

Overall, there is a moderate agreement between the total numbers of police-reported crashes and self-reported crashes, although the two definitely do not provide identical sets of cases. Marottoli, Cooney, and Tinetti (1997) consider the two sets complementary, but others are more skeptical. Owsley *et al.* (1991) compared crash frequencies in state records and self-reports and found a near zero correlation between the two sources ($r = 0.11$), although when the frequencies were grouped, and the measure of association was changed (to Kappa coefficient of agreement) a greater – although still low – level of agreement was obtained ($K = 0.40$). McGwin, Owsley, and Ball (1998) compared the two sources on a sample of 278 drivers 55+ years old and found a moderate agreement on whether or not the drivers had a crash in the past 5 years ($K = 0.45$), but poor agreement in terms of the number of crashes a driver had ($K = 0.25$). The discrepancies are not random, but biased in a specific manner. In their sample McGwin and his associates found that the amount of discrepancy depended on the driver demographics, driving exposure, and visual impairments. This creates a caveat that may account for some of the inconsistencies among studies and even within a single study. Thus, in their own study McGwin *et al.* (1998) found that performance on some driving-related skills (such as "useful field of view," discussed in Chapter 4) was associated with crashes on both data sets, whereas others (such as presence or absence of glaucoma) were significantly associated only with one only (police-reported crashes). In general, they also found that drivers tended to underreport crashes, omitting some of the crashes in the police-based files.

In many studies the source of the data is based on convenience. When available, police data are sought as the "more objective" source. But in some cases – such as the study by Maycock, Lockwood, and Lester (1991) on the relationship between age, experience, and crashes and the study by McCartt, Shabanova, and Leaf (2003) on the effects of graduated driver license on crash involvement – the researchers actually preferred to rely on drivers' self-reports because they are considered to be more valid for the specific issues examined in these studies (both studies are described in detail in Chapter 6 on young drivers).

A third source of crash data are hospital records. Obviously, this applies only to injury crashes above a certain level of severity. Also, because hospital injury records are not typically centralized in a national data file, an accurate comparison is difficult. Still, hospital records can be indicative of lacunas in police data. Studies conducted in several countries have consistently shown that when compared to hospital data, there is fairly a good agreement on fatalities, but an underreporting by the police, especially in accidents involving bicyclists (Amoros, Martin, and Laumon 2006; Broughton *et al.*, 2010; Rosman, 2001). Some of the underreporting stems from different definitions of "road accident" (police typically require the involvement of a motor vehicle) and injury severity (police use administrative criteria such as length of hospitalization, whereas hospitals use medical criteria such as the MAIS based on actual injury severity) (Broughton *et al.*, 2010). Still some of the discrepancies stem from differences in actual reporting where the driver fails to stop and the bicyclist is taken (or goes himself/herself) to the hospital without anyone notifying the police. These shortcomings of the police data relative to data from hospital records do not imply that the latter should substitute for the former, but that "because of underreporting problems and possible bias (e.g., with differing rates of reporting by vehicle type), police data should be complemented by hospital data, which are the next most useful source" (OECD, 2010, p. 8). Unfortunately, most countries do not have linked hospital, vital registry, and police data on traffic fatalities. When data from all sources are available, the police data often underestimate the scope of the problem (WHO, 2015).

The Concern for Traffic Safety

Despite the statement by Tingvall (quoted at the beginning of this chapter), the concern about traffic safety is not shared by all road users everywhere. A multi-nation Social Attitudes to Road Traffic Risk in Europe (SARTRE) (SARTRE 4, 2012) conducted in 2010 on a representative sample of 1,000 adults in 19 countries (17 European countries plus Cyprus, plus Israel) demonstrated very large differences among the people of different countries in their concern about traffic safety. Figure 1-12 shows the percentage of respondents who expressed different levels of concern about the road safety in their country. Although there were very large differences in the percentage of people who were "very concerned" – ranging from less than 20 percent in Germany to over 75 percent in Israel – only a very few people in all other countries stated that they were not concerned at all. Interestingly, the level of concern did not parallel the level of traffic

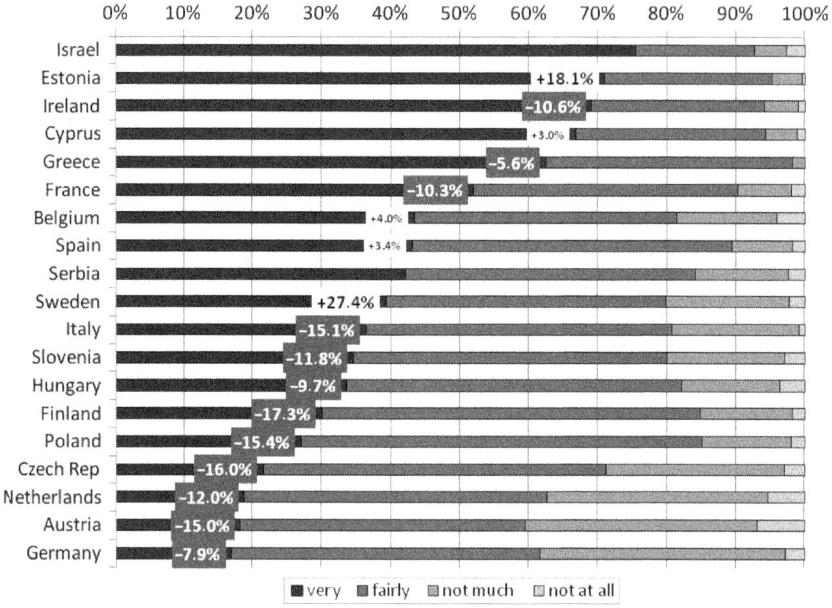

Figure 1-12. Concern about road safety in 2010. Frequency distribution in percentage of road users who are "very concerned" in 2010 (SARTRE 4) and the change from 2001 (SARTRE 3) noted in percentage points to SARTRE 4 (significant changes in bold) (from SARTRE, 2012, p. 47, with permission from J. Cestac, SARTRE 4 Coordinator and Final Report Editor).

safety: $r = 0.07$. It was highest (Israel) and lowest (Germany, Austria, Netherlands) in countries that rank quite high on most measures of traffic safety (as reflected in Figures 1-5 to 1-8). The absence of such a relationship is underscored when the concern for safety is plotted against the fatality rate relative to the number of people in the country (Figure 1-13). Sweden is quite consistently ranked as the safest country, yet it was in the middle in the ranking on "very concerned." Thus, it appears that concern for safety is not closely related to the actual level of safety. To the extent that being concerned drives the behavioral norms and the governments' investment in safety, it is a good thing to be very concerned. In Israel there is a false public perception – often shared by tourists who view Israelis as very aggressive drivers – that the road safety level in Israel is low, and definitely lower than it should be relative to other OECD countries, independently of all objective data (Figures 1-5 to 1-8). Relative to the previous SARTRE survey conducted in 2001, the change in the percentage of people who were "very concerned" was mostly negative (although not statistically significant). Thus, as road safety increased in nearly all EU countries over that period, the level of concern declined. The most notable exception is Sweden, where there was a statistically significant *increase* in concern despite its excellent road safety records. This supports the speculation that heightened concern is a good thing in a country where the government is attentive to the concern of its constituents. One of the most visible means of that attentiveness is the state of the country's roadway infrastructure. Thus, it should be no surprise that when

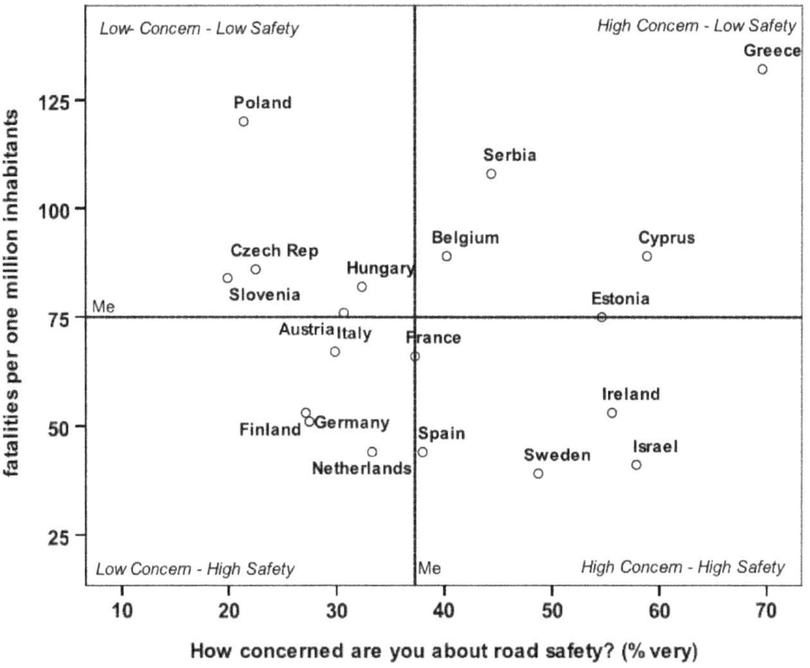

Figure 1-13. Personal concern about road safety versus fatality rate. The center lines indicate the medians of percentage of people who are "very concerned" and the fatality rate (from SARTRE 4, 2012, p. 49, with permission from J. Cestac, SARTRE 4 Coordinator and Final Report Editor).

the fatality rate was plotted relative to the percentage of people who rated the roads as "very" or "fairly" safe, a strong negative relationship emerged ($r = -0.72$). The higher the fatality rate the lower the percentage of people satisfied with their roads, with Sweden having the lowest fatality rate and highest level of satisfaction (Figure 1-14). It is probably also relevant to note that Volvo – that has always carved safety on its mission – is a dominant factor in the Swedish economy.

Organization of This Book, Additional Resources, and the Rationale for the New Edition

Book organization

In the remainder of the book, I will explore the reasons why highway safety is improving – and the reasons why it isn't, especially from the perspective of the road user behavior. Because the road user – driver, cyclist, or pedestrian – has been historically viewed as the only decision maker in the driver-vehicle-highway system, his or her role is critical. But the driver does not behave in vacuum. The roadway environment and the vehicle characteristics are crucial components in the highway traffic system as are other vehicles and road

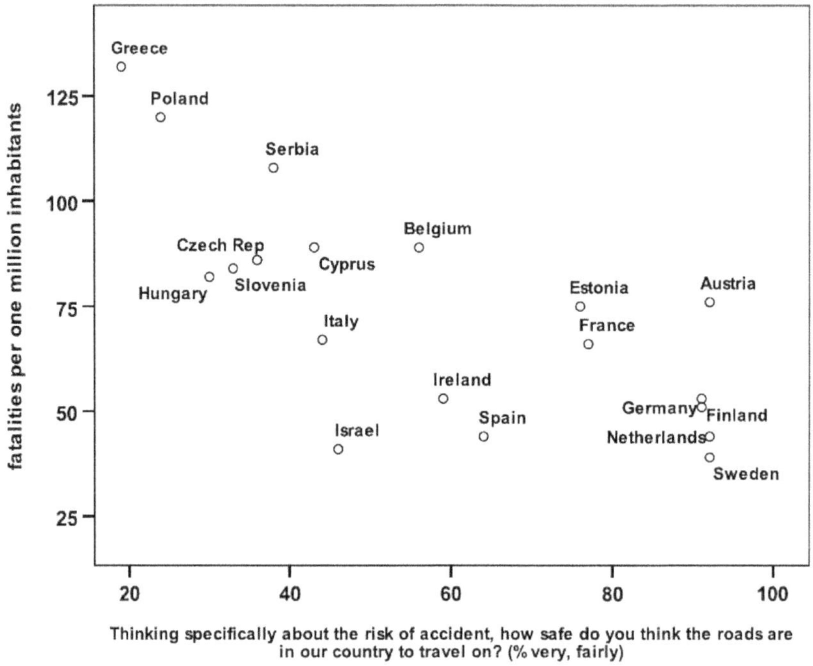

Figure 1-14. Perception of the safety of the roads versus the fatality rates (per one million in population) (from SARTRE 4, 2012, p. 51, with permission from J. Cestac, SARTRE 4 Coordinator and Final Report Editor).

users, the legal and social environment, and the enforcement that is or is not applied. When a crash occurs, it is not necessarily the "nut behind the wheel" that is responsible for it but many other "nuts and bolts" in this complex system that may be loose or missing at the critical moment. Nonetheless, the focus of this book will be on the driver and the driver's behavior as the significant element in highway safety.

The contents of the book are divided into six major parts, each further divided into 2-4 chapters, totaling 19 chapters. The first part, Background, Methods, Models (Chapters 1-3), essentially sets the stage for discussing the substantive issues of this book. Like any discipline, traffic safety has its own jargon, its own measures, and its own theoretical models within which the discussion of the issues is framed. The Methods chapter provides some very basic information on research design, independent and dependent measures, and statistics that are commonly used in behavioral research on highway safety.

The remainder of the book focuses on specific safety-related issues and, as much as possible, defines the nature of the issue, problem, or behavior, its scope and impact on traffic safety, and potential countermeasures that can reduce the magnitude of the problem.

The second part, Driver Capacities and Individual Differences (Chapters 4-7), focuses on four aspects of driver characteristics that have been studied extensively in their relation to safety: driver vision, driver information processing, and driver age. Age-wise the two groups that have received most of the attention – although they definitely constitute a minority of all drivers – are the young drivers (typically under 25 years) and the older drivers (typically 65 years old and older). Because the nature of their crash involvement differs and because they differ greatly in their experience, skills, and information processing abilities, they are treated separately in two chapters.

The third part, Driving Style, (Chapters 8-10) focuses on two aspects of driving style: speeding behavior and aggressive driving. Obviously, as most people would suspect, the two are related to other driver characteristics such as age and gender, and therefore the relationship of speeding and aggressive driving to age and gender is discussed in this context. In addition, this section also discusses the benefits of occupant protection and the road-users' tendencies to use them.

The fourth part, Driver Temporary Impairments (Chapters 11-14), focuses on the four types of impairments that most researchers associate with the greatest involvement in crashes: impairments from alcohol, impairments from (other) drugs, impairments from fatigue, and impairments from distraction and attentional lapses. Unlike the more stable individual differences of personality, gender, age, and visual and information processing abilities, these can change drastically within short intervals (on the order of minutes), and then their effects are often interactive with the person's more stable characteristics. When such interactions have been studied they will be discussed in these chapters.

The fifth part, Vulnerable Road Users (Chapters 15-17), implicitly acknowledges that most of the previous discussion was focused on car drivers and occupants. But these are not the only road users that contribute to and suffer from crashes. The others, often labeled as the "vulnerable" road users, consist of primarily riders of powered two-wheel vehicles (mopeds and motorcycles), bicyclists, and pedestrians. They are considered vulnerable for an obvious reason: They do not have the protective seat belts and shield of the car. Although most of the readers of this book probably think of themselves primarily as drivers of passenger cars, we are all at times vulnerable road users as well. In many countries the combined "contribution" of the vulnerable road users to the traffic death toll is greater than that of all car occupants (drivers and passengers). According to the World Health Organization "Half of the world's road traffic deaths occur among motorcyclists (23 percent), pedestrians (22 percent), and cyclists (5 percent)." Car occupants constitute (only) 31 percent of the deaths and the remaining 19 percent are "unspecified road users" (WHO, 2013a, 2013b, p. 6). The three groups making up the vulnerable road users are also distinctly different from each other on at least two dimensions. These include regulation: motorcyclists are regulated through licensing, whereas bicyclists and pedestrians are not, and age: motorcyclists essentially mimic the driver population in their age distribution (with greater frequencies of young riders), whereas bicyclists extend to much younger age groups (teens and preteens) and pedestrians – at least in terms of their crash involvement tend to concentrate on the very young and very old. Consequently, these three types of road users are treated in separate chapters.

The last part, Crash Causation and Countermeasures (Chapters 18 and 19), focuses on what we have learned over the past 100 years – and especially over the past few decades – about the causes of traffic accidents, their relative frequencies, and the means that have proven successful in combating accidents. The crash causation chapter also has a methodology component because often the relative frequency of various causes of traffic accidents is methodology-bound, meaning that different methods of analyses yield different conclusions. The countermeasures chapter is divided into four domains in which countermeasures can and have been applied: organizational actions (such as "Vision Zero" mentioned above), behavioral changes in drivers and other road users, environmental treatments of the roadway and its "furniture," and vehicular changes in both crash prevention and injury reduction. A significant conceptual change that has occurred over the past decade is reconsideration of the role of the driver as the controlling element in the vehicle. Recent innovations in in-vehicle safety systems transform the driver more and more into a monitor of the car and traffic and less of a continuous controller of the vehicle. In its most extreme form, we see the autonomous vehicle (often known as the Google Car, http://en.wikipedia.org/wiki/Google_driverless_car) that, within some limitations, can safely navigate itself in traffic. This approach involves numerous systems that regulate the speed and lateral control of the car while responding to various crash-related sensors that are sensitive to the prevailing roadway and traffic conditions. While autonomous vehicles would seem to negate even the presence of the driver (let alone the need to change the name), they do involve multiple aspects of the human driver and vehicle interactions that are critical to safety. These issues are discussed in the last part of Chapter 19.

Additional resources

Nearly 40 years ago, I published a small (212 pp.) book on this topic entitled *Psychology on the Road: The Human Factor in Traffic Safety*. At the time, the challenge was to find scientifically valid published research in this area. Ten years ago, while working on the first edition of this book, the challenge was to select the most pertinent research from a wealth of scientific reports published in refereed journals and other technical publications that cover the field. By that time the emphasis in reviewing the state-of-the-art shifted from searching for literature to selecting the most relevant literature. The emphasis in the current version was again on selection. But it was much more difficult now. As noted in the beginning of this chapter, in the last decade alone there were more books written on the topic of human behavior and traffic safety than in all the previous years since the appearance of the motorized vehicle. The same applies to refereed articles of original research and to technical reports. Although most of the studies have been published in a few journals that focus on safety and road user behavior (for example, *Accident Analysis and Prevention*, *Applied Ergonomics*, *Ergonomics*, *Human Factors*, *Injury Prevention*, *Journal of Safety Research*, *Journal of Traffic Medicine*, *Traffic Injury Prevention*, *Transportation Research Part F*, and *Transportation Research Record*), the internet search engines now reveal additional studies published in medicine, engineering, law, policy, and public administration journals. In addition much of the research is only published as technical reports of government and public research agencies, such as the NHTSA, the Federal Highway Administration (FHWA), and the Federal Motor Vehicle Carrier Safety Administration (FMVCSA) in the U.S.; the Road and Transport Research Institute (VTI) in Sweden; Institute for Transport Economics (TOI) in Norway; the Institute for Road Safety Research (SWOV) in Netherlands; the Department for Transport (DfT) in the United Kingdom; Institut Français Sciences et Technologies Transport a Ménagement Réseaux (IFSTAR) in France; and similar bodies.

There are also non-government organizations that are very active in research in this area such as the Insurance Institute of Highway Safety (IIHS) in the U.S., the Traffic Injury Research Foundation (TIRF) in Canada, and the Transport Research Laboratory (TRL) in England. Finally, there are university-based research centers that focus on highway safety such as the University of Michigan Transportation Research Institute, the Texas Transportation Institute at Texas A&M University, the Highway Safety Research Center of the University of North Carolina, the Institute of Transport Studies at the University of Leeds, the Monash University Accident Research Center, and the Centre for Accident Research and Road Safety at the Queensland University of Technology in Australia. All of these and many others have websites that describe their research activities and reports.

The rationale for a new edition

There were several reasons why I felt it was time to update the first edition of the book. First and foremost, the increasing interest in road safety beyond the domain of safety and into the domain of public health has generated an explosive growth in the number of research studies in this area. Second, the emergence of new study methods – specifically Field Operational Technique and Naturalistic Driving Studies – that brings research much closer to the actual driving context. Third, the plethora of electronic driver assistive systems that are designed to increase safety and infotainment systems that are designed to enhance the drivers' abilities to engage in non-driving tasks, at once improving and compromising driving safety. Fourth, the rapid shifting in urban transport from the car to the traditional and electric bicycles. Fifth, the shift toward sustainable lifestyle that is sweeping the world has also changed mobility patterns with a move toward cleaner vehicles, but more importantly with a shift toward alternative modes of transport such as bicycling, motorcycling, and walking, as well as combinations of the different modes of transport. All of these required updating all of the chapters in the first addition, as well as adding a chapter on the increasing role of bicycling (and electric bicycles) in the transportation system.

References

Adams, J. (1985). Smeed's law, seat belts and the emperor's new clothes. In: *Human Behavior and Traffic Safety* (L. Evans and R. Schwing eds.). Plenum Press, New York, NY.

af Wåhlberg, A. (2012). *Driver Behaviour and Accident Research Methodology: Unresolved Problems*. Ashgate Publishing, Farnham.

Allen, M. J. (1970). *Vision and Highway Safety*. Chilton Book Co., Philadelphia, PA.

Allen, M. J., B. S. Abrams, A. P. Ginsburg and L. Weintraub (1998). *Forensic Aspects of Vision and Highway Safety*. Lawyers and Judges Publishing Company, Inc., Tucson, AZ.

Amoros, E., J.-L.Martin and B. Laumon (2006). Under-reporting of road crash casualties in France. *Accid. Anal. Prev.*, *38*, 627-635.

ANSI (2007). *Manual on Classification of* Motor Vehicle Traffic Accidents (7th ed.). National Safety Council, Itasca, IL. http://www.atsip.org/images/uploads/d16.pdf.

Barnard, K., R. Risser and J. Krems (2011). *The Safety of Intelligent Driver Support Systems*. Ashgate, Farnham, England.

Berns, S., and E. Brühning (1998). Definitions and data availability Compilation and evaluation of A-level roads and hospitalised victims in OECD countries. Accident and injury definitions. IRTAD Special Report.

Bhise, V. D. (2012). *Ergonomics in the Automotive Design Process*. CRC Press, Taylor and Francis, Boca Raton, FL.

Brodsky, W. (2015). *Driving with Music: Cognitive-Behavioral Implilcations*. Ashgate, Farnham, Surrey.

Broughton, J., M. Keigan, G. Yannis, P. Evgenikos, A. Chaziris, E. Papadimitriou, ... J. Tecl (2010). Estimation of the real number of road casualties in Europe. *Safe. Sci.*, *48*, 365-371.

Broughton, P. and L. Walker (2009). *Motorcycling and Leisure: Understanding the Recreational PTW Rider*. Ashgate, Abingdon.

Cacciabue, P. C., M. Hjaldahl, A. Ludtke and C. Riccioli (2011). *Human Modelling in Assisted Transportation: Models, Tools, and Risk Methods*. Springer, Milan, IT.

Castro, C. (ed.) (2009). *Human Factors of Visual and Cognitive Performance in Driving*. RC Press, Taylor and Fracis, Boca Raton, FL.

Castro, C. and T. Horberry (eds.) (2004). *Human Factors of Transport Signs*. Taylor and Francis, CRC Press, Boca Raton, FL.

CDC (2011). Ten great public health achievements: Worldwide 2001–2010. *Morb. Mortal. Wkly Rep.*, *60*(24), 814-818.

CDC (2015). Ten leading causes of deaths and injuries. Centers for Disease Control and Prevention, Atlanta, GA. http://www.cdc.gov/injury/wisqars/leadingcauses.html.

Chung, Y. and I. Chang (2015). How accurate is accident data in road safety research? An application of vehicle black box data regarding pedestrian-to-taxi accidents in Korea. *Accid. Anal. Prev.*, *84*, 1-8.

Davis, R. (2001). Editorial: BMJ "bans" accidents. *Br. J. Med.*, *322*, 1320-1321.

Derriks, H. M. and P. M. Mak (2007). Underreporting of road traffic casualties. IRTAD Special Report. OECD, Paris, France.

Dewar, R. E. and P. Olson (eds.) (2007). *Human Factors in Traffic Safety* (2nd ed.). Lawyers and Judges Publishing Company, Inc., Tucson, AZ.

Dorn, L. (2010). *Driver Behaviour and Training*. Ashgate, Farnham, England.

DOT (2013). Research, technology, and development strategic plan, Fiscal years 2013–2018. U.S. Department of Transportation, Washington, DC.

Eby, D. W., L. J. Molnar and P. S. Kartje (2009). *Maintaining Safe Mobility in an Aging Society*. CRC Press, Francis and Taylor, Boca Raton, FL.

EC (2015). EU transport in figures: Statistical pocketbook 2015. European Commission, Brussels, Belgium.

Elvik, R. and A. B. Mysen (1999). Incomplete accident reporting: Meta-analysis of studies made in 13 countries. *Transport. Res. Rec.*, *1665*, 133-140.

Elvik, R. and T. Vaa (2004). *The Handbook of Road Safety Measures*. Elsevier, Oxford.

Elvik, R. A., T. V. Hoye and M. Sørensen (2009). *The Handbook of Road Safety Measures* (2nd ed.). Emerald, Bingley, UK.

ETSC (2011). 2010 road safety target outcome: 100,000 fewer deaths since 2001. 5th Road Safety PIN Report. European Transport Safety Council, Brussels BE. http://etsc.eu/projects/pin/

ETSC (2013). ETSC response to the European Commission staff working document "First Milestone towards a Serious Injury Strategy." European Transport Safety Council, Brussels, BE. http://archive.etsc.eu/documents/ETSC_Response_to_EC_First_Milestone_Towards_an_Injury__Strategy_May_2013.pdf

ETSC (2015). Ranking EU progress on road safety. 9th road safety pin report. European Transport Safety Council, Brussels BE. http://etsc.eu/projects/pin/

Eugensson, A. (2009). Volvo vision. https://www.unece.org/fileadmin/DAM/trans/roadsafe/unda/Sweden_Volvo_Vision_2020.pdf

Eugensson, A., J. Ivarsson, A. Lie and C. Tingvall (2011). Cars are driven on roads, joint visions and modern technologies stress the need for co-operation. 22nd ESV Conference. Washington, DC.

Evans, L. (1991). *Traffic Safety and the Driver*. Van Nostrand Reinhold, New York, NY.

Evans, L. (2004). *Traffic Safety*. Science Serving Society, Inc., Bloomfield Hills, MI.

Evans, L. and R. C. Schwing (eds.) (1985). *Human Behavior and Traffic Safety*. Plenum Press, New York, NY.

Fahlquist, J. N. (2006). Responsibility ascriptions and vision zero. *Accid. Anal. Prev.*, *38*, 1113-1118.

Fallon, I. and D. O'Neill (2005). The world's first automobile fatality. *Accid. Anal. Prev.*, *37*, 601-603.

Fisher, D., J. Caird, W. Horrey and L. Trick (2016). *Handbook of Teen and Novice Drivers: Research, Practice, Policy, and Directions*. CRC Press, Boca Raton, FL.

Fisher, D. L., M. Rizzo, J. Caird and J. D. Lee (eds.) (2011). *Handbook of Driving Simulation for Engineering, Medicine, and Psychology*. CRC Press, Boca Raton, FL.

Forbes, T. W. (ed.) (1972). *Human Factors in Highway Traffic Safety Research*. Wiley, New York, NY.

Fuller, R. and J. A. Santos (2002). *Human Factors for Highway Engineers*. Elsevier Science, London.

Gilutz, M. S. (1937). An investigation and a report on four years' fatal accidents in Oxfordshire. The Vincent Works, Ltd., Oxford.

Girasek, D. C. (2015). How members of the public interpret the word accident. *Inj. Prev.* *21*(3), 205-210.

Gkikas, N. (2013). *Automotive Ergonomics: Driver-Vehicle Interaction*. CRC Press, Boca Raton, FL.

Groeger, J. A. (2000). *Understanding Driving: Applying Cognitive Psychology to a Complex Everyday Task.* Psychology Press, Philadelphia, PA.

Guttman, N. (2014). *Communication, Public Discourse, and Road Safety Campaigns.* Routledge, New York, NY.

Hagenzieker, M. P., J. J. F. Commandeur and F. D. Bijleveld (2014). The history of road safety research: A quantitative approach. *Transport. Res. Part F, 25*, 150-162.

Hakkert, A. S. and V. Gitelman (2014). Thinking about the history of road safety research: Past achievements and future challenges. *Transport. Res. Part F, 25*, 137-149.

Hedlund, J. (2008). Traffic safety performance measures for states and federal agencies. National Highway Traffic Safety Administration. Report DOT HS 811 025. U.S. Department of Transportation, Washington, DC.

Ho, C. and C. Spence (2008). *The Multisensory Driver: Implications for Ergonomic Car Interface Design.* Ashgate, Hampshire.

IRTAD (International Road Traffic and Accident Data) (2013). *Road safety annual report. International Transport Form*, OECD, Paris, France.

IRTAD (International Road Traffic and Accident Data) (2014). *Road safety annual report. International Transport Form*, OECD, Paris, France.

IRTAD (International Road Traffic and Accident Data) (2015). Road safety annual report. International Transport Form, OECD, Paris, France.

Johnston, I. R., C. Muir and E. W. Howard (2014). *Eliminating Serious Injury and Death from Road Transport.* Taylor & Francis, CRC Press, Boca Raton, FL.

Kuper, S. (2015). Our deadliest problem not terrorism. *Financial Times*, July 13.

Lauer, A. R. (1960). *The Psychology of Driving: Factors of Traffic Enforcement.* Charles C. Thomas, Springfield, IL.

Link, D. (2006). International comparisons in traffic safety, based on IRTAD and IRF data. National Authority for Highway Safety, Jerusalem, Israel.

Liu, Y., S. Singh and R. Subramanian (2015). Motor vehicle traffc crashes as a leading cause of death in the United States, 2010 and 2011. Traffic Safety Facts Research Note. National Highway Traffic Safety Administration Report No. DOT HS 812 203. U.S. Department of Transportation, Washington, DC.

Locke, E. A. and G. P. Latham (2002). Building a practically useful theory of goal setting and task motivation. A 35-year odyssey. *Am. Psychol., 57*(9), 705-717.

Marottoli, R. A., L. M. Cooney and M. E. Tinetti (1997). Self-report versus state records for identifying crashes among older drivers. *J. Gerontol., 52A*, M184-M187.

Mason-Dixon Polling & Research (2005). Drive for life: Annual national driver survey. Mason-Dixon Polling & Research Inc., Washington, DC.

Maycock, G., C. R. Lockwood and J. F. Lester (1991). The accident liability of car drivers. Research Report 315. Transport and Road Research Laboratory, Crowthorne, England.

McCartt, A. T., V. I. Shabanova and W. A. Leaf (2003). Driving experience, crashes and traffic citations of teenage beginning drivers. *Accid. Anal. Prev., 35*, 311-320.

McGwin, G. Jr., C. Owsley and K. Ball (1998). Identifying crash involvement among older drivers: Agreement between self reports and state records. *Accid. Anal. Prev., 30*(6), 781-791.

Näätänen, R. and H. Summala (1976). *Road User Behaviour and Traffic Accidents*. North Holland Publishing Co., New York, NY.

NHTSA (1996). A chronology of dates significant in the background, history and development of the department of transportation. Office of the Historian, U.S. Department of Transportation, Washington DC. http://dotlibrary.dot.gov/Historian/chronology.htm#1994

NHTSA (1998). Highway safety program guideline no. 18: Accident investigation and reporting. Transportation Equity Act for the 21st century (TEA 21). U.S. Department of Transportation, Washington, DC. http://www.nhtsa.gov/nhtsa/whatsup/tea21/tea21programs/pages/AccidentInvest.htm

NHTSA (2000). Fatality Analysis Reporting System (FARS) web-based encyclopedia. U.S. Department of Transportation, Washington, DC. http://www-fars.nhtsa.dot.gov/terms.cfm?stateid=2&year=2000

NHTSA (2012). Safety belt use in 2012 – Overall results. National Highway Traffic Safety Administration, Traffic Safety Facts, Research Note DOT HS 811 691. U.S. Department of Transportation, Washington, DC.

NHTSA (2013). Alcohol impaired driving. Traffic Safety Facts, 2012 Data. National Highway Traffic Safety Administration Report DOT HS 811 870. U.S. Department of Transportation, Washington, DC.

NHTSA (2014). Traffic safety facts 2012. National Safety Administration Report DOT HS 812 032. U.S. Department of Transportation, Washington, DC.

NHTSA (2015a). Traffic safety facts: 2013 Data. National Highway Traffic Safety Administration Report DOT HS 812 169. U.S. Department of Transportation, Washington, DC.

NHTSA (2015b). Traffic safety facts. 2014 Crash data key findings. National Highway Traffic Safety Administration Report DOT HS 812 219. U.S. Department of Transportation, Washington, DC.

NHTSA (2015c). Not-in-traffic surveillance: Non-crash fatalities and injuries. Traffic safety facts. National Highway Traffic Safety Administration Report DOT HS 812 120. U.S. Department of Transportation, Washington, DC.

NHTSA (2016a). Traffic safety facts. Early estimates of motor vehicle traffic fatalities in 2105. National Highway Traffic Safety Administration Report DOT HS 812 269. U.S. Department of Transportation, Washington, DC.

NHTSA (2016b). Traffic safety facts 2014. National Highway Traffic Safety Administration Report DOT HS 812 261. U.S. Department of Transportation, Washington, DC.

Noy, Y. I. (1997). *Ergonomics and Safety of Intelligent Driver Interfaces*. Lawrence Erlbaum, New Jersey, NJ.

NRSA (2011). *Trends in Road Safety in Israel: 2010*. National Road Safety Authority, Jerusalem, Israel (Hebrew).

OECD (2006). OECD Factbook 2006 – Economic, Environmental and Social Statistics.

OECD (2010). Reporting on serious road traffic casualties. International Transport Forum, IRTAD, OECD, Paris, France.

Olson, P. L., R. Dewar and E. Farber (2010). *Forensic Aspects of Driver Perception and Response*. Lawyers and Judges, Tucson AZ.

O'Neill, B. and S. Kyrychenko (2006). Use and misuse of motor-vehicle crash death rates in assessing highway-safety performance. *Accid. Anal. Prev.*, *7*, 307-318.

Owsley, C., K. Ball, M. Sloane, D. L. Roenker and J. R. Bruni (1991). Visual/cognitive correlates of vehicle accidents in older drivers. *Psychol. Aging*, *6*, 403-415.

Parry, H. M. (1968). *Aggression on the Road*. Tavistock Ltd., London

Peacock, B. and W. Karwowski (eds.). (1993). *Automotive Ergonomics*. Taylor and Francis, London.

Porter, B. E. (Ed.). (2011). *Handbook of traffic psychology*. Elsevier, London.

Redshaw, S. (2008). *In the Company of Cars: Driving as a Social and Cultural Practice*. Ashgate, Abingdon.

Regan, M. A., T. Horberry and A. Stevens (2014). *Driver Acceptance of New Technology: Theory, Measurement, and Optimisation*. Ashgate, Oxon.

Regan, M. A., J. D.Lee and K. L. Young (eds.). (2009). *Driver Distraction: Theory, Effects and Mitigation*. CRC Press, Taylor and Francis, Boca Raton, FL.

Road Peace (2004). World's first road death. www.roadpeace.org/articles/worldfir.pdf. September 26.

Rößger, L., M. G. Lenné and G. Underwood (eds.) (2015). *Increasing Motorcycle Conspicuity*. Ashgate, Farnahm.

Rosman, D. L. (2001). The Western Australian road injury database (1987–1996): Ten years of linked police, hospital and death records of road crashes and injuries. *Accid. Anal. Prev.*, *33*, 81-88.

Rudin-Brown, C. M. and S. L. Jamson (eds.) (2013). *Behavioural Adaptation and Traffic Safety*. CRC Press, Taylor and Francis, London.

SARTRE 4 Report (2012). European road users' risk perception and mobility. (Contributors: D. Antov, A. Banet, C. Barbier, T. Bellet,Y. Bimpeh, A. Boulanger, C. Brandstätter, V. Britschgi, M. Brosnan, I. Buttler, J. Cestac, S. De Craen, P. Delhomme, E. Dogan, E. Drápela, S. Forward, R. Freeman, G. Furian, M. Gábor, C. Goldenbeld, P. Henriksson, H. Holte, S. Kraïem, E. Papadimitriou, A. Podlesek, M. Polič, F. Sánchez-Martín, G.-M. Sardi, E.-A. Schmidt, P. Silverans, T. Siska, P. Skládaná, A. Theofilatos, A. Von Below, G. Yannis, D. Zaidel, and N. Zavrides). European Commission: Directorate-general for mobility and transport, Paris. http://www.attitudes-roadsafety.eu/home/publications/

Shinar, D. (1978). *Psychology on the Road: The Human Factor in Traffic Safety*. Wiley and Sons, New York, NY.

Shinar, D., E. Schechtman and R. P. Compton (1999). Trends in safe driving behaviors and in relation to trends in health maintenance behaviors in the U.S.A.: 1985–1995. *Accid. Anal. Prev.*, *31*, 497-503.

Shinar, D., J. R. Treat and S. T. McDonald (1983). The validity of police reported accident data. *Accid. Anal. Prev.*, *15*, 175-191.

Sivak, M. (1996). Motor-vehicle safety in Europe and the USA: A public health perspective. *J. Safety Res.*, *27*(4), 225-231.

Sivak, M. (2002). How common sense fails us on the road: Contribution of bounded rationality to the annual worldwide toll of one million traffic fatalities. *Transport. Res. F*, *5*, 259-269.

Smeed, R. J. (1949). Some statistical aspects of road safety research. *J. R. Stat. Soc. Series A*, *62*(Part I, series 4), 1-24.

Smiley, A. (ed.) (2015). *Human Factors in Traffic Safety*. Lawyers & Judges, Tuscon, AZ.
Smith, I. (1999). Road fatalities, modal split, and Smeed's law. *Appl. Econ. Lett.*, *6*, 215-217.
Stanton, N. A. (2013). *Advances in Human Aspects of Road and Rail Transoportation*. CRC Press, Taylor and Francis, London.
Sullman, M., & Dorn, L. (eds.) (2012). *Advances in Traffic Psychology*. Ashgate, Abingdon.
Theeuwes, J. R., van der Horst and M. Kuiken (2012). *Designing Safe Road Systems: A Human Factors Perspective*. Ashgate, Abingdon.
Tingvall, C., J. Ifver, M. Krafft, A. Kullgren, A. Lie, M. Rizzi and Sternlund, S. (2013). The consequences of adopting a MAIS 3 injury target for road safety in the EU: A comparison with targets based on fatalities and long-term consequences. Paper IRC-13-10. IRCOBI Conference. Gothenburg, Sweden, September 11-13.
Toops, H. A. and S. E. Haven (1938). *Psychology and the Motorist*. R.G. Adams and Co., Columbus, OH.
Turner, S. A., A. P. Roozenburg and Francis, T. (2006). Predicting accident rates for cyclists and pedestrians. Land Transport New Zealand Research Report 289, p. 180.
U.S. DOT (2003). U.S. Department of Transportation Strategic Plan 2003–2008. U.S. Department of Transportation, Washington, DC.
U.S. DOT (2012). Transportation for a new generation: Strategic Plan 2012–2016. U.S. Department of Transportation, Washington, DC.
Vaa, T. (2014). From Gibson and Crooks to Damasio: The role of psychology in the development of driver behaviour models. *Transport. Res. F*, *25*, 112-119.
Wåhlberg, A. (2009). *Driver Behaviour and Accident Research Methodology: Unresolved Problems*. Ashgate, Farnham.
Walker, G. H., N. A. Stanton and P. M. Salmon (2015). *Human Factors in Automotive Engineering and Technology*. Ashgate Publishing, Abingdon.
Wells, H. (2011). *The Fast and the Furious: Drivers, Speed Cameras and Control in a Risk socieTy*. Ashgate, Farnham.
WHO (2004). World report on road traffic injury prevention. (M. Peden *et al.* ed.). World Health Organization. http://whqlibdoc.who.int/publications/2004/9241562609.pdf
WHO (2005). International travel and health. World Health Organization, Geneva. http://www.who.int/ith/en/. August 18.
WHO (2013a). The ten leading causes of deaths 2000 and 2011. Fact Sheet No. 310. http://who.int/mediacentre/factsheets/fs310/en/
WHO (2013b). Global status report on road safety: Supporting a decade of action. World Health Organization, Geneva, Switzerland.
WHO (2015). Global status report on road safety 2015: Supporting a decade of action. World Health Organization, Geneva, Switzerland.
WHO (2016). *The top 10 causes of death*. World Health Organization, Geneva, Switzerland. http://www.who.int/mediacentre/factsheets/fs310/en/index1.html
Wikipedia. (2014). Mother Shipton. http://en.wikipedia.org/wiki/Mother_Shipton
Wilde, G. J. S. (2002). Does risk homeostasis theory have implications for road safety: For. *Br. Med. J.*, *324*, 1149-1151.
Winner, H., S. Hakuli, F. Lotz and C. Singer (2016). *Handbook of Driver Assistance Systems*. SpringerNature, Switzerland.
World Bank (2014). Transport for health: The global burden of disease from motorized road transport. Report 83601. World Bank, Washington, DC.

2

Research Methods

"In God we trust. All others must bring data." (W. Edwards Deming).

The purpose of this chapter is to set a level field for all readers, by briefly describing the various methods used in driving and highway safety research. Most – but not all – of the methods and concepts described below should be familiar to anyone with behavioral research background or to an advanced student in the behavioral sciences background. Because the terms are repeatedly used in the following chapters, and some readers may not be familiar with all of them, they are defined here for reference.

Most people feel that they know a lot about driving. I am yet to encounter a taxi driver who does not have a "simple" solution to the "accident problem." Admittedly, most taxi drivers have extensive experience in driving, and may be more skillful than most non-professional drivers. Yet someone's personal feeling or idea is not a substitute for good research data. Interestingly, we feel that we can easily tell who is a good and who is a bad driver, who is an aggressive driver and who is a considerate driver, who is a careful and safe driver, and who is a reckless and dangerous driver. Many of us also feel they "know" the reason for most crashes, and what needs to be done (typically by the government) to "fix" the accident problem. Also, at one time or another most people had some formal driving instruction, have read some newspaper articles, or seen a television program about driving, and – most importantly – have been driving.

To support these gut-level convictions with good research is a lot more difficult. Research on driver, motorcyclist, bicyclist, and pedestrian behavior is complex because human behavior is complex and variable, and the driving context is complex and variable. For this reason, in order to understand road users' behavior we must conduct or rely on research at different levels of complexity – beginning with basic research on human behavior, in which the situation is quite simplified and well controlled, and ending with observational on-the-road studies where the situation is most complex and almost nothing is under the control of the researcher. Between the two extremes, there are laboratory studies with various levels of complexity that mimic the driving environment through the use of simulators, and there are controlled on-the-road studies with instrumented vehicles and drivers who are constantly aware of the fact that they are participating in a study.

The results of the various studies, when considered together can provide us with necessary insights and advances in highway safety. In brief, the main benefits of the laboratory studies are that they are safe, they can recreate many repetitions of situations that in real life occur rarely, and – most important of all – they afford us the opportunity to study the effects of specific factors on a person's response, without the presence of many other factors that may co-exist on the road. For example, a laboratory study can be designed to study the driver's reaction time to a brake light ahead in the absence of any distractions. In this case the driver (often referred to as subject) may be seated in front of a red light and asked to push a button whenever it goes on. The result – called simple reaction time – can be a good approximation of the minimum time a person needs to react to such a stimulus. Obviously, this minimum time is rarely achieved in a complex situation such as a real road with moving traffic and various sources of distraction. Therefore, it is not surprising that on the road we can observe reaction times to brake lights that are actually tenfold as long, such as when a tired driver is approaching a partially obscured traffic light while engaged in a conversation on the phone or attending to a pedestrian about to cross the street. Thus, a laboratory study has some use – because it provides us with a notion of "best possible" behavior under controlled conditions, but the ability to extrapolate its results to real life is limited. At the other extreme, on-the-road observational studies focus on driver behavior in the environment as it is. This makes the road study an obvious choice, except that the real environment changes all the time and a particular type of behavior obtained in one environment (e.g., on a rural road at night in England, with English drivers) may not be very relevant to the behavior of other drivers in countries with other driving cultures, on different types of roads, and at different hours of the day. Thus, an on-the-road study tells us a lot about behavior in the very specific environment in which it was tested, but very little about behavior in other environments. To complicate things, many factors – some of which are not even known to the researchers – are not controlled, and may account for the specific results that are obtained.

The remainder of this chapter defines some of the key terms that are relevant to behavioral research and the principal research methods. They are all illustrated with some examples from driving behavior research. Most of the concepts and methods are not restricted to driving or highway safety research, but they will be illustrated here with examples from highway safety research.

KEY CONCEPTS IN BEHAVIORAL RESEARCH

The purpose of this section is to present some concepts and terms that will be used in the rest of the book. They include various measures that relate to highway safety, validity and reliability of the measures, experimental versus observational studies, between-subject versus within-subject experimental designs, and statistical versus practical significance.

Variables of interest

Whenever we conduct a study we have at least two variables of interest: a predictor, or an independent variable (such as driving style or type of road), and a dependent variable, which is a behavior (such as violations) or a phenomena (such as crashes) that occurs and is assumed to be caused by it. But things are typically not that simple. Other variables – depicted in Figure 2-1, intervene in the process. They include control, confounding, moderating, and intervening variables that can either explain or complicate the results of most studies. Their definitions and effects are described below.

Independent and dependent variables
The goal of most studies is to determine how one factor affects another. We call the factors that are presumed to exercise an effect the independent variables, in the sense that they can be independently manipulated by the experimenter. The factor on which we examine the effects of the independent variable is called the dependent variable in the sense that its outcome depends on the independent variable or variables. For example, if

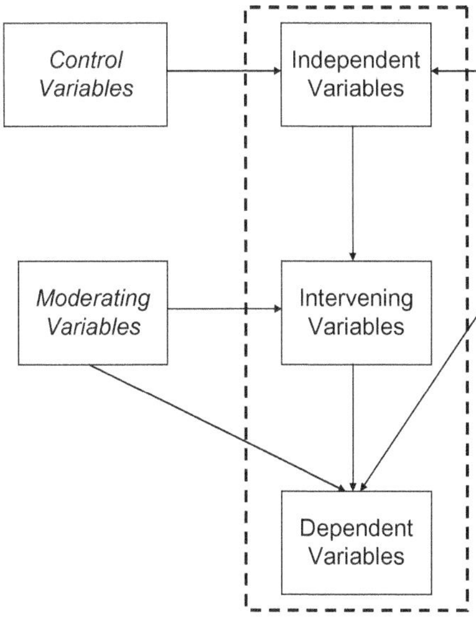

Figure 2-1. The relationships among various variables that are involved in empirical and experimental scientific research.

we wanted to study the effects of uncertainty on driver brake reaction time, we could set up mockup of a vehicle and then under various conditions turn the brake lights on and measure the driver reaction time. "Uncertainty" would be our independent variable and "reaction time" would be our dependent variable. We can vary the level of uncertainty by manipulating the predictability of the appearance of the light. Thus, in one situation, the timing of the onset of the lights would always be constant so the driver would know almost exactly when they will come on. In that case expectancy would be high and uncertainty would be minimal. This is the situation we have when the car ahead of us stops in response to a light that changed to red. In this situation the timing of the brake light onset is almost completely certain. In other situations the timing of the light could be highly variable so the driver would not know when to expect it. In that case the level of the independent variable – uncertainty – would be high. An example is an unexpected braking of a car ahead in stop-and-go traffic. It turns out that when such a study is conducted the level of uncertainty has a significant effect on reaction time: the greater the uncertainty the longer the reaction time (Warshawsky-Livne and Shinar, 2002). Similarly, we study the effects of alcohol blood concentrations, glare, drugs, hours of sleep, distractions from cell phones, and a host of other independent variables on dependent variables such as target detection, reaction time to obstacles, and crash involvement.

In highway safety, the dependent variable of greatest interest is some measure of crashes. We typically would like to know how everything affects safety and the ultimate measure of safety is a reduction in the number or rate of crashes. For various reasons measuring crashes (the dependent variable) is not always practical. Therefore, in many studies our dependent measures are intermediate or surrogate measures of safety that are related to accidents. For example, it is commonly accepted – at least by researchers in the area – that the risk of an accident and the level of injury in an accident (dependent variables) increase with increasing speed (independent variable). We may therefore decide to investigate means of reducing drivers' speed. We can then examine the effects of behavioral interventions (such as enforcement), environmental interventions (such as speed bumps), and in-vehicle devices (such as speed governors) on drivers' speed (which has now become the dependent variable).

When we cannot actually manipulate the independent variable, as when we wish to determine the effect of gender (independent variable) on crash involvement (dependent variable), we consider the first as the "predictor" variable and the latter as the "predicted" variable. The statistical relationship per se does not indicate causality, or which variable influences the other, but our basic understanding of human nature (or in some cases a theory that we have on human nature), indicates to us that gender is much more likely to affect crash involvement, than crash involvement can change gender.

Control variables

Control variables are factors that could affect the dependent measure, but for various reasons their level is held constant. In a typical controlled study when we focus on the effects of one or two independent variables (such as speed and headway) on one dependent variable (such as crash likelihood), we want to control all other variables that might increase the noise in the data; or technically speaking increase the variance. Thus, control variables are those variables that might have an effect on the dependent variables, but they are controlled by keeping their values constant and are not varied in the study. For example, in a driving simulation study on the effects of speed on crash likelihood, we may want to employ both male and female subjects. However, to reduce the noise/variance the researcher may decide to use gender as a control variable and include only males. The rationale would be that males are much more likely to speed and assume other risk-taking behaviors. Similarly the researcher can decide to control other variables that may increase the variance in the driving behavior and the effect on crash involvement such as driving experience, socio-economic level, the roads and traffic selected for the drive, the visibility, etc. The more variables that we can control, the more confident we are in our conclusions. So why not control for as many variables as we can? The reason is that as we add control variables we also limit the level of generalization of our findings to the particular driver and situational characteristics that were tested. For example, when we decide to restrict our study only to males, our conclusion must also be limited to males only. So, as often in life, we have a trade-off between the strength of our results in the situation in which they were obtained and the degree of generalization to other situations.

Intervening variables: Mediation between the independent and dependent variables

An intervening variable is one that – as its name implies – intervenes between the independent variables that we manipulate and the dependent variables that we measure. When I described the effects of uncertainty on reaction time, I also used the term expectancy. In fact, to understand the relationship we posit a psychological, latent (unobservable) term that we believe intervenes between the independent and dependent variables. We assume that the physical measure of uncertainty is related to the unobservable variable of expectancy. Expectancy, in turn, is assumed to directly affect the dependent variable. Thus, the vertical chain of independent → intervening → dependent variables in Figure 2-1 constitutes the basic relationships that are the focus of most experimental research.

Intervening variables – because they are not directly observed – are tricky. For example, there is currently overwhelming evidence that the use of cell phones while driving is dangerous. It impairs cognitive functioning and proper visual scanning of the road ahead, and increases the likelihood of crashes (Chapter 13 contains a detailed discussion of this area). But what is it about cell phones that make them so dangerous? What is the intervening variable? One possibility is that holding the phone limits the driver's control of the vehicle to the use of one hand. This implies that the intervening variable is the motor control of the vehicle. With this explanation in mind, many jurisdictions prohibit the use of hand-held cell phones. However, further research demonstrates that hands-free phones interfere with a host of driving tasks just as much as hand-held phones, and both increase the likelihood of a crash by similar degree. These findings have led many researchers to conclude that the intervening variable in this phone → driving performance → accidents chain is mediated by the intervening variable of attention: the phone, regardless of how it is used, simply creates a cognitive load that distracts too much attention from the road. However, "attention" is not an observable variable, and so we use surrogate measures to define the level of attention a task or a device requires, such as the amount of time drivers redirect their eye glances from the road ahead to the distracting (cell phone) task (Victor, Harbluk, and Engström, 2005), or performance on a secondary task (Strayer *et al.*, 2015). The plot does not end here, as studies using a new research methodology – namely naturalistic driving studies (see below) – that record driver behavior and glance behavior continuously, have shown that the only significant increase in the crash risk as a result of using a cell phone is during the brief periods when the driver's gaze is directed away from the road and the traffic (Fitch *et al.*, 2013; Klauer *et al.*, 2014). Thus, in the search for the intervening variable responsible for the deleterious effects of cell phones on driving safety, we have moved from an unobservable concept of cognitive distraction or overload to an observable variable of visual distraction.

The labels "independent," "intervening," and "dependent" are not part of a definition of a variable. Instead they represent the role that a variable plays in a particular experimental design. Occasionally, after we speculate about the role of an intervening variable in a particular relationship between independent and dependent variable, we can conduct another study to actually observe the effects of this variable. For example it has been repeatedly demonstrated that young novice drivers have the greatest crash risk. This is despite the fact that these drivers have the best vision and shortest reaction times. However, what these drivers do not have is the skill of effectively scanning their visual field in order to anticipate imminent accidents. To test for the effects of this intervening variable directly, Mourant and Rockwell (1972) compared the eye movement patterns of novice drivers as they accumulate more and more experience and showed that the visual search pattern becomes more efficient with increasing driving experience.

Confounding variables

A confounding variable is a variable that is not manipulated or controlled by the researcher and it is typically one of which the researcher is unaware at the time the study is designed. What makes one a confounding variable is that it behaves in a way that is similar to the independent variable, and thus, in retrospect, makes it impossible to determine whether the effect that was measured is due to the manipulation of the independent variable of interest or to the effect of the confounding variable that correlated with it. For example, if we measure the amount of ice cream sold on the beach and the number of drownings each day of the summer season, we may observe that the number of drownings is directly related to ice cream sales. We could then speculate on various intervening variables that would cause eating ice cream to drown (and many parents may already have that in their minds). In fact, a much simpler explanation is available: ice cream sales are directly related to the number of kids on the beach, and the more kids that there are on the beach, the more kids there are in the water, and the greater the number that may drown. Thus, the obviously confounding variable here is the number of kids in the water.

Confounding variables are actually not part of the study design, but they still have an effect on the results. They are less common in a laboratory setting where the situation is highly controlled, than in a field study where the researcher has very little control and a myriad of variables may be at work.

In highway safety research "exposure" or the extent to which a study group is exposed to a certain situation is a common confounding variable that always has to be considered. The literature is replete with examples, so we will pick three. The first example is a very costly one and stems from crash data obtained over 50 years ago. At that time some researchers and insurance actuaries noted that American teenagers who took formal driving instruction before getting their license were involved in fewer crashes than those who did not (meaning they were taught by their licensed family members or friends). This led to the premature conclusion that formal instruction improves safety and most insurance companies then offered reduced premiums to young drivers who took formal driving lessons. This resulted in an increase in demand to include driving instruction as part of the high school education program. A massive research effort was then launched by the U.S. National Highway Traffic Safety Administration to determine the actual benefits of structured instruction by professional instructors. The program, nicknamed Driver Education Evaluation Program (DEEP), randomly assigned teenagers to either formal training or not. Detailed tracking of the ensuing rates of violations and crashes failed to show the hoped-for benefits of the formal instruction. It turned out that the early findings were based on simple comparisons of crash and violation records of drivers who took driving instruction and drivers who did not take driving instruction. What these comparisons failed to take into account was the confounding variables of socio-economic status and safety orientation of the parents: the drivers who took the formal lessons came from families with lower crash rates, higher socio-economic levels, and greater concerns for safety than the ones who did not take the formal instruction (which, of course, cost money). Thus, the safety orientation of the young driver's family was suspected as a confounding variable that may have been responsible for the effect attributed to the driving instruction. Indeed, several evaluation studies of various driver education programs, where the allocation of teenagers to the instruction and non-instruction groups was randomized, failed to show any significant differences among the groups (see Chapter 6). Since then several studies have shown that the behavior of teen drivers is to a significant extent modeled after that of their parents (Bianchi and Summala, 2004; Miller and Taubman – Ben-Ari, 2010; Prato, Toledo, Lotan, and Taubman - Ben-Ari, 2010).

The second example is more recent and much less consequential. A study publicized in a daily newspaper in Israel claimed that young women are less careful when they drive close to home than when they drive further away, because they have more violations near their home than elsewhere (Barak, 2005). Unfortunately, the study did not control for exposure: the extent to which the women drove in the different vicinities. Since we spend more hours – in and out of our cars – in and close to home, it is obvious that we get more chances close to home for just about everything! This includes accidents, headaches, and misplacing our keys.

The third example is of a confounding variable that is well known but hard to control. It is almost axiomatic that young novice drivers are highly accident prone and that as they age and acquire more experience their crash risk diminishes. This is a statistical fact that insurance companies rely on when they set their higher premiums for young drivers. But is the effect due to age – or immaturity? Or is it due to the lack of safe driving skills that are acquired through experience? Thus, because in the general population age and driving experience are highly correlated, it appears that one of these two variables is a confounding variable, relative to the other. However, which is the true independent variable and which is the confounding one? The difficulty from the researcher's perspective is that age and experience greatly overlap since most drivers get their license almost as soon as they legally qualify. Nonetheless, a careful researcher will find a way to disentangle the two. When this is done, we find that the over-involvement of teenagers is actually due to both; indicating that neither is a confounding variable, and both actually affect the dependent variable (crashes) (Cooper, Pinili, and Wenjun, 1995; Maycock, Lockwood, and Lester, 1991; see also Chapter 6). These three examples demonstrate that the benefit of well-planned and carefully controlled research is that it considers potential confounding variables and tries to nullify or control for their effects by various experimental and statistical means.

Moderating variables
Moderating variables, as can be seen in Figure 2-1, are variables that affect the intervening variables, and therefore also affect the results observed on the dependent variables. These variables attenuate the effects of the independent variable by exerting an influence on – or moderating – the intervening variable. For example in the study cited above on the relationship between the uncertainty of a stimulus and the reaction time to it (Warshawsky-Livne and Shinar, 2002), the effects of the expectancy could be moderated by fatigue and motivation to excel. Therefore, the experimenter can control them by holding them constant or by experimentally manipulating them. For example, we can hold fatigue constant – meaning the same for everyone under all conditions – by making sure all participants had the same amount of sleep and the order of the different levels of uncertainty was randomly varied so that a given level of uncertainty would not always be at the end of the experiment when the participant is already tired. We can also manipulate the moderating variable and see its joint effects with expectancy. For example, we could run the same study twice: once in the morning and once in the evening and then see if the effects of expectancy are diminished or magnified at the end of the day when people are more fatigued.

Validity and reliability

Any time we do a study or read about a study there are two issues that determine our faith in the study's findings: (1) did the study actually and appropriately measure the things it reportedly measured, and (2) are the findings stable so that if other researchers in other places and other times were to replicate the study they would get the same results? These two issues define the study's validity – the extent to which the study actually measured what the researchers thought it did – and its reliability – the stability of the results across time and place. Thus, the early findings of the "effects" of driver education on driving safety mentioned above were actually quite reliable since the same results were obtained in several evaluations. However, as it turned out, the conclusions were not valid because the studies did not isolate the effects of the education program by themselves, but instead measured a host of other things that invalidated the early conclusions. Because most of the research in highway safety is of statistical nature, and the issue of confounding variables is always lurking in the background, we often seek more than one study to develop confidence in our conclusions. The ability to replicate a study by different researchers at different places around the globe gives the findings the needed reliability. This is critical in behavioral research – and that includes human factors in highway safety – because human behavior is quite variable, and often the results of a single study are not easily replicable. As an illustration, in a recent evaluation of the reliability of the results of 100 behavioral studies, in which 97 percent obtained statistically significant effects, 36 percent of the replications obtained statistically significant effects. In other words, nearly two-thirds of the findings could not be replicated (Open Science Collaboration, 2015).

But simply replicating the results does not validate them. The issue of validity is most often involved when we assume intervening variables and rely on surrogate measures of safety (rather than crash involvement). Thus, we should always question the validity of findings that are based on research in driving simulators and in studies relying on drivers' self-reports or responses to questionnaires. In neither instance do we measure actual driving behavior, and in neither case do we know how to consider the "accidents" relative to real ones.

Even the data we have on accidents should be examined for its validity. For example, given the proven effectiveness of seat belts and the overwhelming evidence for the effects of alcohol in crashes, we routinely accept the notion that an increase in seat belt use and a reduction in driving while intoxicated are intervening measures that mediate crash severity and involvement, respectively. The implication being that as seat belt use goes up and as driving under the influence of alcohol goes down, overall injury and crash rates should go down. Unfortunately, we often do not know the exact number of crashes a person had. The most common sources for data on crashes in every country are the police records. However, many crashes are not reported to the police, and many crashes that are reported do not merit a police investigation, and are therefore not recorded either (see discussion in Chapter 1). Most often these are crashes with either minor or no injuries and relatively little property damage. For example, repeated surveys conducted annually for three years on over 7,000 novice drivers in England revealed that only 35 percent of the accidents reported in the survey were also reported to the police, and even among the more serious accidents – the injury accidents – 10-20 percent were not reported to the police (Forsyth, Maycock, and Sexton, 1995). Detailed comparisons between records from trauma units in hospitals and police reports often show significant under-reporting by the police. This is especially so for non-fatal accidents. Furthermore, the under-reporting is not uniform across different variables. Police are less likely to report minor injury cases than severe injury cases, and less likely to report motorcycle and bicycle injury accidents than car accidents. (Amoros, Martin, and Laumon, 2006; Dhillon *et al.*, 2001; Janstrup *et al.*, 2016; Peleg and Aharonson-Daniel, 2004). This biased under-reporting then results not only in an unduly rosy picture of the level of traffic safety, but in incorrect proportion of different types of crashes, with potentially significant policy implications. Does that mean that we should rely on hospital records for all injury crashes? Not necessarily. Hospital staffs do not investigate crashes, and their records that a documented injury indeed was caused by a crash are not necessarily valid.

People may wish to report that injuries were incurred in a traffic accident in order to mask other kinds of violent events such as spouse abuse.

Given the shortcomings of police accident data, a significant body of research relies on self-reports to document crashes. Do self-reports and police reports reflect the same thing? The answer is a qualified yes. In terms of the number of crashes reported, people tend to report similar number of crashes as the police records reveal. However, these are not always the same crashes. As expected, people tend to report crashes that were not reported to or were not documented by the police, but then people sometime tend not to report significant crashes – such as ones involving driving under the influence of alcohol – even when these crashes were investigated and documented by the police.

When the criterion for validity is what happens in the "real world," it is often referred to as ecological validity. The results of two popular research methods that are often questioned in terms of their ecological validity are those based on self-reports and on behavior in driving simulators.

The ecological validity of self-reported behavior in general, not just with respect to crashes, is always suspect and cannot be assumed to reflect actual behavior. What people say they do and what people actually do may be slightly different, somewhat different, or even very different. However, the lure of using questionnaires and interviews to obtain information is great because they are both much cheaper, and often more detailed than obtaining similar information from direct objective observations or records. Furthermore, interviews can also provide insights to the respondents' reasons for their behavior.

The use of seat belts is a good example to demonstrate the complex issue of the validity of self-reports. To obtain an accurate observation-based estimate of belt use by front seat passengers under various conditions through a representative sample of observations in different parts of the U.S. is very expensive. To obtain responses over the phone from the same number of people in a representative sample of the U.S. driving population would cost a fraction of that. But are the two types of information the same? Obviously, the "socially desirable" answer to the direct question "do you use the seat belt when you drive?" is "yes." But is it the true answer? Several researchers in different parts of the world have compared the responses that people gave to this and similar questions after they were unobtrusively observed (Fahner and Hane, 1973, in Sweden; Stulginskas, Verreault, and Pless, 1985, in Canada; Streff and Wagenaar, 1989, in the U.S., and Özkan *et al.*, 2012, in Turkey). The results of all the studies were consistent in showing that although there is a significant correlation between the actual use and the reported use, the reported use was significantly higher than the actual use. In an attempt to improve the validity of reported belt use, Streff and Wagenaar from the University of Michigan Transportation Research Institute tried to provide a "correction factor" that could be applied to self-reports to obtain an estimate of actual belt use. They compared the results of unobtrusive observations with roadside interviews (with two different questionnaires) of the same drivers, and with the answers from a telephone survey of a similar sample. Their findings were somewhat complex. In essence they found that self-reports provide an over-estimate of the actual use, but there was no single correction factor that could be applied. This is because the similarity of the reported use to the actual use depended on the specific wording of the question asked and the circumstances. For example, the reported use in roadside interview was nearly identical to the observed use, when the percent of people responding that they "always" use seat belt was used as a comparison measure. In contrast, the same question in a telephone interview yielded a significant over-estimate of the belt use, relative to the observed, showing that the more dissimilar the situation (in time and place) the greater the disparity between the observed use and the reported use. Still, to provide an easy rule of thumb, at least with respect to the specific issue of estimating seat belt use, Streff and Wagenaar recommend that self-reported seat belt use be discounted by about 12 percent to approximate actual belt use. Thus, the implication from their finding and those of the other researchers is that because the two are correlated, and the gap can be estimated, reported use of seat belt can be a good and valid surrogate measure of actual belt use. Unfortunately that rule of thumb turns out to be inappropriate in some circumstances. Parada *et al.* (2001) compared the observed behavior of drivers entering various parking lots of gas stations' convenience stores in El Paso, Texas with the self-reported use based on a question imbedded in a driver opinion questionnaire on "drivers" opinions of Texas roadways." In their study, self-reports over-estimated the actual use by 27 percent for Hispanic drivers and by 21 percent for "white non-Hispanic" drivers. Such findings might suggest that under-reporting bias may be greater the lower the actual belt use (Türker *et al.*, 2012) and a valid correction factor would then be not a single number but a function.

Still, even with such gross correction factors, the results of these seat belt studies are important in two respects. First, they demonstrate the existence of a caveat that should be attached to self-reports. Second, they can provide specific correction factors once the relevant mediating variables (actual observed rate of the specific behavior, the population demographics, and the particular measure of interest – e.g., crashes versus seat belt usage) are established. Finally, in some evaluations self-reports are better than "objective" data. This was demonstrated by a study in Australia where performance of older drivers on a road test correlated with self-reports of past accidents but not with the police records of past accidents (Anstey *et al.*, 2009). This does not mean that self-reports are more accurate but only that the inaccuracies in one (poor memory and social desirability bias in self-reports) are still better than the inaccuracies in the other (non-reporting of less severe crashes in police records).

The second domain with serious concerns about its ecological validity is the use of simulators in research on driving behaviors (Shinar and Ronen, 2007). The need to validate measures obtained in a simulator against real world measures of driver behavior and crashes cannot be ignored, and as illustrated below is often addressed in simulation research. However, not all simulation measures can be validated. We can easily design situations that result in a crash in a simulator (for example by intoxicating people before they drive), but no one would consider replicating the same conditions in the true world to see if a crash will actually happen there. Thus, in interpreting the results of research reported in this book – or in any other venue, for that matter – a prudent reader should always ask whether or not the specific measure used warrants the conclusions drawn.

Obviously, it is best if we can combine multiple data sources to estimate an effect. For example, to obtain good crash data it would be desirable to combine police records, hospital records, and drivers' reports; desirable but prohibitively expensive and logistically complicated. Consequently, most studies use one of these sources and try to justify its validity. It is then up to the reader to judge whether or not the measures used are indeed valid or not. The rule of thumb here is "caveat emptor."

Study Design

The design of a study determines the conclusions that can be drawn from it. The ultimate study does not exist. Every study design is a compromise between the desirable and the practical, and it is important to understand what we can and cannot conclude from different study designs.

Experimental versus observational studies

In the best of all possible worlds we would very much like to be able to control all the independent variables and then be able to tell exactly how they affect the outcome measures or dependent variables. Unfortunately this is never the case. When we conduct an experimental evaluation we can control many of the variables, but not all of them. For example, to study the effects of drugs on driving we might consider two approaches. The first approach is to do a naturalistic study in which we stop drivers on the road, assess their driving and driving record, and test their blood and/or urine for illicit drugs. This study is more ethical and feasible than the second approach which involves a controlled study in which we actually administer drugs to some people (treatment group) and not to others (control group) and then test for differences between the two groups in their driving behavior. The first approach is an observational study because all it does is observe existing differences in the independent variable (presence/absence of drugs) and the dependent variable (driving behavior). The second approach is one that involves random drug administration to one of two groups that are matched on as many characteristics as possible. This is the experimental approach.

As one may easily surmise, the conclusions drawn from the experimental approach are much more valid than those drawn from observational research because in the former we actually control and manipulate the situation, whereas in the observational approach there may be many differences between those with drugs and those without drugs that may have nothing to do with the effects of drugs. These differences may be acting as confounding variables. For example, the drivers with drugs are more likely to be young males, who are more prone to risky behaviors to begin with (after all, they demonstrate that by taking drugs!), and be caught at night when driving is more dangerous to begin with, than the drivers not taking drugs. The disadvantage of the experimental approach is that it is impossible to simultaneously examine all the variables that actually operate in real life, and it is sometimes unethical to create the situations that occur "naturally" in real life. Very often a study will be mixed in the sense that some variables will be controlled and others will be observed. An example could be a study on the effects of varying amounts of alcohol on driving-related behaviors of male and female drivers. While we can experimentally control the amount of alcohol (making it an experimentally controlled independent variable), we cannot (at least in most situations) control the gender of the subjects, and so we select a group of males and a group of females as participants.

Between subjects versus within subjects study designs, and treatment versus control conditions

Within the controlled environment of experimental studies, one important distinction is between studies in which the different levels of the independent variables are administered to different people, versus the situation where all the different levels are administered to the same people but at different times. In the "between subjects" design we typically have one or more treatment groups (such as different groups of subjects each getting a different amount of alcohol) and one control group (people who are being given nothing or a placebo – a substance that appears like the treatment but does not contain its active ingredient; e.g., an alcohol-looking drink that has no alcohol in it). In the "within subjects" design instead of having several treatment groups we have one treatment group in which everyone is administered several treatment *conditions* so that all study participants get the same conditions (but typically in different order to cancel out "order" or "learning" effects), and one of the conditions, where the "treatment" is not administered at all is the control *condition*. The within-subject design in which the order of the conditions is counter-balanced is also called a cross-over design (for a detailed description of different cross-over designs, see Pocock, 1983). The benefits of the between subjects approach is that each person gets tested for a shorter period of time and there is no need to worry about the order effects. However, when the individual differences – the differences among the people in their reaction to the variable of interest – are high, as they are with alcohol, this creates a lot of "noise" in the data making it difficult to discern the effects of the independent variable. On the other hand, within subjects designs suffer from the need to control for order effects (e.g., would a person with three drinks perform any differently if he/she were previously evaluated after four drinks than if they previously had two drinks or none?), and from the fact that it is often impractical to have all the people experience all of the experimental conditions. The benefits of the within subjects design is that it actually enables us to see how changes in the level of the independent variable (such as the amount of alcohol) affect a person as he or she experiences more or less of that variable. In the context of studies of the effects of alcohol on driving we will often find both types of studies yielding similar results, thereby strengthening our conclusions (see Chapter 11).

There are some independent variables whose effects can be studied either in a within or a between-subject design, and others that must be studied only in a between subjects or a within subjects design, with different implications for each. If we wish to study the effect of learning, we can either study a single group who is exposed to training (e.g., looking at novice drivers immediately after receiving their license and then periodically every

2 months) or study the effect of training by observing different groups of drivers with various levels of training. In the latter case we must ensure that experience is not confounded with any other variables, and it is therefore less conclusive, so a preferred method would be to track a group of cohorts over a period of their first two years of driving (when most of the safety skills and habits are acquired). If we wanted to study the effects of age or aging on driving behavior and crash risk that would be a different story. Here the temporal sequence is much longer. To track the same drivers from their early teenage days of driving to their old age (whatever definition we use for "old") is very difficult for obvious reasons, so we often compare groups of drivers of different ages, trying to control for various generational differences, trying not to forget that the different generations also grew up under different social, health, demographic, and technological conditions.

One variation of the between subjects design that has some of the benefits of the within subjects design without its shortcomings is known as a "case control" design. In this case, instead of comparing two (or more) groups that are drawn at random from the same population, each subject in each group is matched with a specific subject (or subjects) in the other group. This method eliminates many potentially confounding variables that may otherwise distinguish between the groups and thus yield spurious results. As an example, in the fleet study described below that evaluated the crash reduction potential of an advance brake light system, for each vehicle (in the treatment group) equipped with the advance brake light system, another vehicle (in the control group) was selected that was of the same make and model, and driven for the same purpose in a similar environment. Thus, if an effect were to be found it would not be an artifact of any of these matching variables (though it could be due to unknown confounding variables). However, even in studies defined as case-control, the matching is not perfect and various sources of error that can affect the validity of the results have to be considered (see Houwing *et al.* (2013) for a review.

Statistical versus practical significance

Significance means different things to different people – especially statisticians. In everyday use, a "significant" finding is synonymous with an important, noteworthy, major, or momentous finding. In fact, these are the synonyms you will get if you use Microsoft, tools > language > thesaurus. We can consider that as a "practical" definition of significance. The statistical definition for a significant finding in the context of behavioral research is the degree to which this finding would not have been obtained by chance alone. In other words, if a given study were conducted repeatedly many times, in what percent of the trials would the same effect be obtained by chance; that is, when there is no real effect? How reliable is the initial finding? Thus, in the statistical sense significance is a measure of the reliability of the results.

We seek statistical significance because human behavior is very variable, and people do not consistently respond in the same way to the same stimulus. For example, do you always stop at an intersection when the "Don't Walk" red signal is on? To answer this question we use statistical tests of significance that tell us – for a given result – the likelihood of obtaining the same finding if the same study were run many times. A conventional rule of thumb is to consider a result as statistically significant if the likelihood of obtaining it by chance is five percent or less. Throughout this book, whenever a result will be reported, it will be implied that it was statistically significant at a level of 5 percent or less. What we strive for in research are results that have both statistical significance and practical significance; that is, they are both reliable and important. Statistical significance does not imply practical significance. Practical significance typically means that the size of the effect is large and not necessarily that it is consistent. When sample size in a study is large, we can find small differences that are highly reliable – therefore highly statistically significant – yet their size is small for all practical purposes (Hauer, 2004).

Research Methods: From Basic/Laboratory to Applied/Field

The most robust knowledge that we have about human behavior in highway safety comes from multiple studies employing multiple methods, all leading to the same conclusions. This means performing converging research operations to answer the same question. There are not many examples of this. Most often converging operations do not all support each other for various reasons, and often a promising idea that is based on one or two similar studies is not followed up with additional studies employing different methods or is simply not pursued further. However, occasionally a specific issue becomes sufficiently important that it is pursued by different researchers using different methods. A salient example, discussed in depth in Chapter 13, is the impact of cell phone use on driving performance and crash involvement. The remainder of this chapter will be devoted to demonstrating some of the research methods used in highway safety to evaluate the benefits of two different approaches to help drivers avoid rear-end collisions. These two approaches involve two different technologies: the center high-mounted stop lamp (CHMSL) and the advance brake warning (ABW) system.

A case in point: Reducing rear-end collisions

The most important cue that a driver has to indicate that the car ahead is braking is the onset of its brake lights. Regrettably, that cue may sometimes arrive too late, in the sense that by the time the following driver realizes that the car ahead is braking, he or she does not have enough time to brake in order to avoid a rear-end collision. The most dramatic and extreme situations of that type are the chain accidents on the high-speed freeways and motorways. The question is, is there a way to speed up that realization so that we can brake more rapidly in response to the lead car's deceleration?

The first approach, and one with which nearly all drivers are now familiar, is that of the Center High-Mounted Stop Lamp (CHMSL). The CHMSL is the product of years of research that culminated in a change in the U.S. Federal Motor Vehicle Safety Standard (NHTSA, 2004) that requires the addition of the CHMSL to all passenger cars registered in the U.S. as of 1986, and all vans and trucks as of 1994. Other countries followed suit with Canada requiring the CHMSL in 1986, Australia and New Zealand in 1990, Israel in 1994, and finally in Eurasia in 1998. The CHMSL is the red light located in the center rear of the car either just behind or in front of the rear windshield or at the top of the trunk, so it is higher than the two brake lights. It is connected to the brake pedal so that whenever the driver activates the brakes the light goes on. The goal of the various studies that led to the CHMSL was to improve communications among drivers so that the driver of a following car would be able to respond more quickly to the braking of the driver ahead, and even to the braking of drivers farther ahead. Prior to the introduction of the CHMSL, the following driver had to detect the onset of the two brake lights, which (as everyone knows) are located on the sides of the car near the ground and off the following driver's direct line of view. Thus, the standard brake lights are not in the center of the driver's field of view, but rather in the driver's visual periphery where target detection is poorer (see Chapter 4). Furthermore, the closer a driver is to the car ahead, the greater the angle between the gaze ahead and the location of the brake lights, and therefore the poorer the detection of the brake lights. Thus, the three benefits of the CHMSL are that (1) it is in the driver's direct line of sight, (2) it enables a following driver to see braking of several cars ahead (through the windshields), and (3) at night, it changes from being totally "off" to "on" (in contrast to the standard brake lights that from a distance appear to just make the rear lights brighter).

The time from the onset of the lead driver's brake lights till the activation of the brakes by the following driver is known as the brake reaction time. Obviously, the shorter the reaction time, the larger the gap between the cars when the lead car starts to brake, and the greater the safety margin to avoid a rear-end collision. When the brake reaction time exceeds the temporal gap between two cars (the distance between the cars divided by the speed of the following car), a collision is inevitable. So the goal of improving communications in this particular case was essentially one of reducing the brake reaction time by providing drivers with a brake light system that would be more conspicuous and quicker to detect than the standard configuration, thereby reducing the rate of rear-end collisions.

The second series of studies was designed to evaluate an innovative approach to reduce rear-end crashes by reducing the lag time between the lead driver's *decision* to brake and the response of the driver behind that car. The idea was that somehow the following driver would respond to the lead driver's decision rather than to the motor response (i.e., braking) that follows that decision. The concept behind the particular system, labeled an ABW (Advance Brake Warning) system – was based on an assumption that in case of emergency braking, the driver removes the foot from the accelerator pedal to the brake pedal in an automatic "reflexive" manner that is much quicker than in the case of the more typical premeditated controlled braking. It is well known, that automatic actions are generally much quicker than controlled actions (Shiffrin and Schneider, 1977). Given that, the technological challenge was to devise a sensor that would detect the speed of the retracting accelerator pedal, and whenever that speed exceeded a certain threshold, the sensor would trigger the onset of the brake lights. In that case the driver in the following car would see the brake lights of the lead car come on *before* they are actually activated by the brake pedals. In a sense the brake lights would come on in response to reading the driver's mind! This is an interesting idea but it requires answering a host of different questions. Is the release of the accelerator in an emergency braking situation really different from that involved in normal braking? If so, then what speed of accelerator release characterizes emergency braking? When the accelerator pedal is moved at that speed or faster, is it always followed by actual brake activation? If quick release of the accelerator pedal does not always involve braking, how often does it happen? Does this create a dangerous false alarm ("cry wolf") situation that may cause following drivers to habituate to the system and not respond to the onset of brake lights as a real braking of the lead drivers? If the quick release is always or almost always followed by actual braking, how much time does it take to move the foot from the accelerator to the brake pedal; that is, how much of an advance warning will that give the following driver relative to the current situation when he/she first sees the brake light after the brake pedal has been activated? Finally – and most important – given the advance warning, how many rear-end crashes are likely to be prevented by such a device? Several different studies, utilizing different approaches, are needed to answer all of these questions and several different methods were in fact employed to answer them.

The following sections briefly discuss the various research methods that are used to study human behavior in the context of highway safety, and each method is illustrated by a different study used to answer a different question related to the CHMSL or the ABW. The methods reviewed below include basic laboratory studies, digital simulations, physical simulations (also known as simulator studies), on-the-road experiments, and controlled field studies.

Laboratory "Basic" Research

The principal benefit of research conducted in the laboratory is that the experimenter has complete control of the situation. It is then easy to study the effect of one or more independent variables on one or more dependent variables, while controlling for potential confounding effects, and, if desired, manipulating various moderating variables. The flip side of this advantage is that we cannot control all of the variables that may be operating in the real world. Thus the ability to generalize from the lab to the real world may be quite limited, but that limited generalization is equally applicable to many different real situations. For example, to assess the advance warning time that can be provided by the ABW, we (Warshawsky-Livne and Shinar, 2002) designed a simple laboratory study in which a subject – representing a following driver – sat behind a mockup of a rear of a car with his or her right foot resting on an accelerator pedal. The subject's task was to release the accelerator and depress the brake pedal right next to it as soon as the red brake lights of the mockup car flashed. There were two dependent measures: (1) the reaction time to the light – measured in terms of the time from the onset of the brake lights until the start of the release of the accelerator pedal and (2) the movement time – measured as the time it took the subject to move the foot from the accelerator pedal to the brake pedal. The sum of the two times was the total brake reaction time.

The study involved four independent variables: the subject's gender and age, the number of times the task was performed, and the level of expectancy for the red brake lights.

Let's consider the definition and the rationale for each one in turn. Driver age was important because older drivers are susceptible to performance degradations in multiple driving-related manners: beginning with their vision (Shinar and Schieber, 1991) and ending with their motor responses and coordination (Seidler and Stelmach, 1995; Stelmach and Homberg, 1993). Thus, the study evaluated the performance of both young drivers (students ranging in age from 18 to 25) adult drivers (26-49), and older drivers (ranging in age from 50 to 82). Gender is always an interesting issue, especially since there are many differences between the amount, type, and style of driving of men and women. For obvious reasons both age and gender were between-subject variables (we still cannot manipulate age and – in most cases – gender).

The other two variables were manipulated in a within-subject design so each person experienced all of the different conditions. Because reaction time is not constant, and people's reaction times increase significantly when the stimulus is unexpected (Fitts and Posner, 1967), it was necessary to control the level of expectancy of the lights. This was done by having the people respond to the light under three conditions of temporal uncertainty (a more technical term for expectancy): (1) with the interval between the response and the beginning of the next trial short and constant (minimal level of uncertainty), (2) with the interval varying from 2 to 10 seconds in a random manner (intermediate level of uncertainty), and (3) with varying intervals and on a certain proportion of the trials the lights were not turned on at all (maximal level of uncertainty). These situations roughly correspond to actual driving situations with varying levels of uncertainty: (1) when a driver expects the car in front of him or her to brake as when it is close to a traffic light that has just turned yellow, (2) in a stop-and-go traffic when the car ahead brakes but it's braking action is not at a fixed pace, and (3) when the car ahead is close to a traffic signal so that it sometimes proceeds to cross the intersection and at other times it brakes (known as the amber light dilemma zone). The final independent variable was the learning process. It is well known that reaction time improves with practice, at least initially. This is also well known to most people from their own experience and it is supported by many controlled experimental studies (see Fitts and Posner, 1967, for a review). It is therefore common to examine the changes in reaction time as a function of the amount of practice, or in our case the number of trials. So each subject performed the task ten times in each of the three conditions of temporal uncertainty.

The results of the study are illustrated in Figure 5-2. In that figure the reaction times and movement times are plotted on the Y-axis and the trial number is presented on the X-axis. Several observations can be made from these results: movement time is much shorter than reaction time (approximately 0.17-0.18 seconds versus 0.36-0.43 seconds), and it is essentially unaffected by the temporal uncertainty, while reaction time is. It appears that the uncertainty affects the initial decision to brake, but once the brain issues a command to move the foot to the brake pedal, the movement itself is quite automatic. Thus, only the reaction time changes from approximately 0.36 seconds in the condition with least uncertainty to approximately 0.43 in the condition with the most uncertainty. Furthermore, it appears that both actions (the reaction and the movement) are so overlearned, that there is essentially no learning effect and the performance on the first trials is essentially the same as it is on the last trials. Not presented in the figure are the findings that the differences between the men and the women in the study were negligible (and statistically not significant), but the age effect was quite noticeable: the average reaction time of the young drivers was 0.35 seconds while the average reaction time of the oldest drivers was 0.43 seconds. Although these numbers appear very small, one should keep in mind that at a speed of 100 km/hr (62.5 mph) a car travels 27.8 meters/second (90 feet per second). This means that in the time that our average subject moved his or her foot from the accelerator pedal to the brake pedal a car going at 100 km/hr would travel an average of 4.8 meters (15 feet and 9 inches); a distance that may mean the difference between a near accident and a real accident or between a minor collision and a serious collision.

This simple laboratory study does tell us how much of an advance warning the ABW can provide, but it leaves many unanswered questions such as what headways do drivers maintain when traveling at different speeds? If the headways are always such that they exceed the total brake reaction time, then there is no benefit to the added warning. In a real world situation when a car brakes, its actual braking distance depends on the amount of friction between the tires and the road: good tires on dry road can provide a short stopping distance while bald tires on a wet road will result in much longer stopping distance. Also, in the real world driver reaction times are typically much longer; 3-5 times as long as those observed in the laboratory under optimal conditions (Johansson and Rumar, 1971). Furthermore, under conditions of low expectancy (surprise!) they may exceed two seconds (McGee *et al.*, 1983). So how do we evaluate the effects of all of these differences between the lab and the real world? One approach is to conduct a digital simulation, to which we now turn.

Digital Simulation Studies

A digital simulation study is a virtual study in the sense that we conjure up hypothetical situations and then let a computer program – based on previous mathematical and statistical functions – "run" the situation and determine its outcome. The benefit of a simulation study is that other than programming, it is free! Therefore simulation can be a great tool in exploring an issue "on the cheap." To illustrate the use of this approach we (Shinar, Rotenberg, and Cohen, 1997) used a simulation called Monte Carlo to estimate the potential benefits of the ABW with thousands of simulated runs of two vehicles following each other. Each run consisted of a pair of cars traveling in the same direction, one behind the other. At a certain point, the lead car braked as hard as possible, and the simulation program then determined whether or not the following car would hit the lead car or whether or not it would be able to brake in time to avoid it. In order to arrive at this conclusion, the simulation had to consider the reaction time of the following driver and the movement time to the brake. Reaction time distributions based on real-world driver braking reaction times were used, and on each run a data point from that distribution was sampled. The simulation also had to consider the conditions of the road (dry, wet, or icy), because they affect the coefficient of friction that determines the time it would take both vehicles to come to a stop. Finally, of course, it also had to consider the speed of the two cars and the headway (gap) between them at the time that the lead car started to brake. On half of the runs the lead car did not have an ABW and on half of the runs it had one and therefore the braking reaction time of the following driver was shortened by subtracting from it the movement time that would be saved. Thus, the study had four independent variables: the presence or absence of the ABW, the speed of the cars, the weather conditions, and the headway between the cars. The dependent variable was a dichotomous one: was a collision prevented or not. Some of the results of this study are presented in Table 2-1.

Table 2-1. Percent of rear-end crashes prevented with and without ABW at different vehicle headways (from Shinar *et al.*, 1997, reprinted with permission from the Human Factors and Ergonomics Society).

Private Headway	With ABWS	Without ABWS
0.50 seconds	50	0
0.75 seconds	95	32
1.00 seconds	100	50
Total	82	27

The table shows the percent of crashes prevented with the ABW and without the ABW as a function of the time headway (the temporal gap between the cars). The results are based on a total of 4,320 runs (720 in each cell) and are quite dramatic: with very short headways, none of the crashes would have been prevented without the ABW, while with the ABW 50 percent of the rear-end crashes would have been prevented. As the headway between the two cars increases, the overall number of crashes prevented in both situations increases, so that with ¾ of a second headway nearly all the crashes are prevented with the ABW and only 32 percent are prevented without it. If the headway is further increased to 1.0 second then all crashes are prevented with the ABW and 50 percent are prevented without it. When the headway is 1.5 seconds or higher (not included in the table) all crashes were prevented regardless of the presence or absence of the ABW.

Driving Simulator Studies

Physical simulation studies involve "driving" a mockup of a real vehicle inside a laboratory. This is achieved by projecting the driving scene on a screen in front of the car and by having the driver control the apparent movement of the scene via the vehicle's pedals and steering wheel. Most such simulators are based on computer-generated images. The rate and manner in which the projected images change are then determined by the activation of the pedals and steering wheel, which are also connected to the computer. The computer responds to the driver's actions by slowing down or speeding up the changes in the scene. Beyond this communality the differences among simulators are greater than the differences among cars.

But there is one other communality to all simulator studies – it is in their basic assumption that performance in a driving simulator is a good description of one or more aspects of real driving behavior. Given the discrepant results that are sometimes obtained with other methodologies, this assumption may not always be warranted; for example, in the case of distracted driving from cell phones when measured in naturalistic driving studies (see Chapter 13). A challenge to that assumption is the fact that unlike driving your own car, driving in a simulator is almost always a new experience. As such there is a learning or adaptation curve that must be considered, as driving in the first few minutes of a drive is probably very different than driving at the end of a drive. Obviously, it would be impractical to drive hundreds of hours before a person is considered equally familiar with the simulator as with his or her own car. So how much practice is enough? Most driving simulator research is done after a few minutes of practice or a few kilometers of driving, or until the driver "feels comfortable" with the task. However, recent studies (Ronen and Yair, 2013; Sahami and Sayed, 2013), have shown that the three criteria are very different from each other, and that the amount of practice at which performance on various indicators levels off is different for different measures of performance (such as stabilization of speed and lane position) and for different types of driving environments (such as rural versus urban, straight versus curved road). Thus, while simulators as a tool may be valid for comparisons among various conditions (relative validity), one must still be careful in interpreting the results given the many differences between driving a simulator and driving one's own car.

Despite the caveats listed above, there are different reasons why a study can best be conducted in a simulator. Some situations are dangerous to study in a controlled fashion on the road and are difficult to replicate in a valid manner in a rudimentary laboratory test. These include controlled studies of the effects of alcohol and drugs on driving or studies of drivers' reactions to unexpected obstacles to study the likelihood of collision. Other situations are the kinds that rarely occur on the road and collecting enough data may be prohibitively expensive. These include studies on the effects of extreme road, traffic, and weather conditions such as the behavior of drivers in fog and congestion (which, unfortunately, is not a very rare event in urban driving), or situations that are difficult to create on the road in a controlled manner even though they may occur quite frequently. To illustrate the latter, a study by Bar-Gera and Shinar (2005) sought to determine whether drivers tend to pass other vehicles because they impede their speed or because they do not like to drive behind another car and are therefore willing to increase their speed just in order to pass it. To determine this it was necessary to study the passing behavior of drivers, driving at different speeds, behind cars moving at different speeds relative to theirs. To manipulate and record the data from such situations on the actual road is quite difficult but to study it in a driving simulation is quite easy. In this particular example the simulation was designed so that while a driver drove down the road at a speed of his choice, a car appeared up ahead. That car then slowed down until it was closer to the driver and then it speeded up to a constant speed that was slightly below, at, or slightly above that of the driver. The results were quite surprising and they are reproduced in Figure 2-2. They show that the mere presence of a vehicle ahead causes some drivers to pass it, even if to do so they have to increase their speed. Thus, even when the vehicle ahead maintained a speed that was faster than that of the following driver by three km/hr, approximately 50 percent of the drivers still passed the car. Interestingly, on most of these occasions, after they passed the vehicle, the drivers slowed down to their previously preferred speed.

Another type of situations for which simulation studies are uniquely applicable is to evaluate systems that do not yet exist in the real-world, such as innovative safety devices. An example is the study of the effects of an innovative aid to keep safe headways while driving in long tunnels. Driving in tunnels is very different than driving on the open road: there are very few peripheral stimuli to give the driver an accurate sense of speed, there are no scenery to provide distraction and the darkness and proximity of the walls can give drivers a sense of claustrophobia. More important, perhaps, are the dangers of tunnel crashes. When a crash occurs in a tunnel, it often results in a fire and the fumes, flames, and smoke have no escape route other than up and down the tunnel. This, of course, poses a great risk to drivers and occupants of all vehicles who are often trapped inside the tunnel. One approach to reduce this risk is to require vehicles to maintain large headways. Unfortunately drivers are quite poor at estimating headways (Taieb-Maimon and Shinar, 2001). Therefore, as part of a European Union multi-national project we evaluated a technologically feasible – but non-existing – system in which a moving point of light would travel along the tunnel wall at a fixed distance behind each vehicle, and the task of a following driver would be to assure that he/she stayed behind

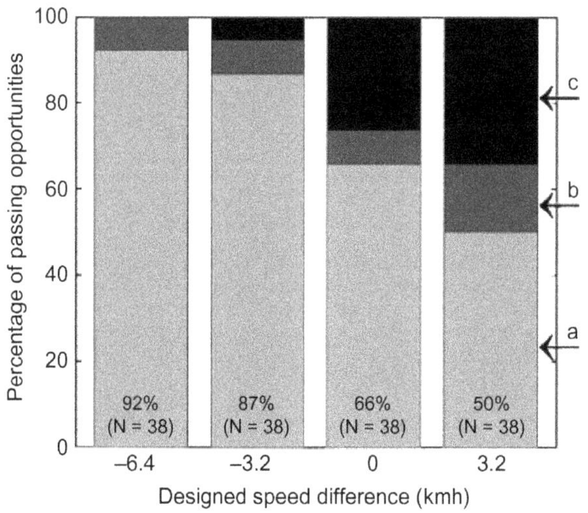

Figure 2-2. The distribution of drivers' actions as a function of designed speed difference between the lead car and the driver. Negative difference indicates that the lead car traveled at a lower speed when the driver (a) passed the lead car, (b) did not pass but wanted to, (c) did not pass (reprinted from Bar-Gera and Shinar, 2005, with permission from Elsevier).

that spot of light. A simulation study was designed in which the geometric features and dimensions of specific 13-kilometer Alpine tunnel connecting Leon in France with Bardonecchia in Italy was replicated and drivers were tested while driving the tunnel with this and other means of maintaining the desired headway. The system proved to be much better than no indicator and also significantly better than the traditional approach of painting equally-spaced markers on the road pavement or on the walls (Shinar and Shaham, 2003). With the rapid infusion of electronics into new vehicles, simulators are often utilized to guide and evaluate the design of advance driver support systems and minimize distraction from new infotainment systems (Boyle and Lee, 2010). The use of simulators in such cases is critical to safety because the effects of these technological innovations on actual crash data are slow and difficult to assess.

In general we distinguish between two types of simulators: fixed base and moving base. In a fixed base simulator the driver and vehicle are stationary and only the scene on the screen moves. Thus, there is only an apparent movement effect provided by the changing visual sense. Figure 2-3 is a schematic drawing and picture of the fixed base simulator at Ben Gurion University of the Negev, Israel. In contrast, a moving base simulator is designed to provide the additional cues of actual movement that we get when we move in a real car. These include the effects of the movement on our sense of equilibrium (generated by organs in the inner ear) that is affected by the pitch of the vehicle (the forward lurching when we brake and the backward lurching when we accelerate), proprioceptive stimulation caused by the yaw of the car (when it takes a curve), and the vibrations

Figure 2-3. A fixed base simulator at the Ben Gurion University Ergonomics Laboratory. Clockwise from top left: partial view of a simulated street scene, the full-size car and the 140-degree curved screen, driver connected to EEG electrodes, monitors in the control room, and steering and dashboard console.

caused by deformation in the road and the type of the road pavement (heave). To provide the driver with all of these cues moving base simulators consist of a vehicle cab that actually moves within a limited space so as to provide the "driver" with the non-visual cues of the movement. The most advanced moving base simulator – the U.S. National Advanced Driving Simulator (NADS), housed at the University of Iowa – is shown in Figure 2-4. This simulator is currently promoted as "the world's highest fidelity simulator" (NADS, 2014). It consists of a large building that houses a moveable 24 feet diameter dome. Inside the dome is a full-size vehicle that the driver "drives." The visual scene is projected on a circular 360-degree screen via 15 computer-synchronized projectors. The visual scene is interactive and can be designed to show various environments under various roads, time of day, precipitation, and traffic conditions. More complicated are the non-visual cues that are provided to the driver, including sound, and vehicle movements in response to speed, acceleration and deceleration, and turning curves. Studies with the NADS enable recording of a multiple array of driver behaviors, eye movements, speed, and lane keeping performance. To appreciate the level of sophistication and complexity of this simulation, take a virtual tour that is available on the web (http://www.nads-sc.uiowa.edu/sim_nads1.php).

While it would be nice to conduct all simulation studies in NADS-like simulators, the difference in cost between a rudimentary fixed base simulator and a moving base simulator such as the NADS is over 1,000 fold! Thus, research with a driving simulator has to consider the ecological validity of the simulator relative to the task that the driver has to perform. To measure reaction time to a traffic light that turns red directly in front of a driver it is probably sufficient to simply present a light that changes from green to red on a computer screen, but to measure a driver's reaction to a light that changes from red to green while the driver is moving in traffic approaching an intersection at various

Figure 2-4. The U.S. National Advanced Driving Simulator (NADS) at the University of Iowa. The left panel shows the moving dome that contains the vehicle and driver and the right panel shows a scene on the front screen as seen by the driver (from NHTSA, 2007).

speeds and may be at different distances from the intersection when the light changes – for this a more sophisticated simulator is needed.

Validity of driving simulators

Regardless of the level of sophistication of the simulator, its use always raises the question of its validity: how relevant are the results obtained with it to results that would be obtained in a similar task on the real road. Because each simulation is unique in some aspects, each simulator must be validated independently. One feature that is relatively easy to evaluate is the sense of speed in a simulator versus the real road. To evaluate the validity of speed perception in the fixed base driving simulator at Ben Gurion University of the Negev, drivers drove in both the simulator and on the road. For that particular evaluation, licensed drivers were asked to drive a car on a rural road outside the city, and while their view of the speedometer was occluded they were given two types of tasks. In one type – speed production – the task was to drive at different speeds ranging from 40 to 100 km/hr. Once the driver said that he or she reached designated speed, the actual speed was recorded. The second type – speed estimation – involved having the drivers accelerate or decelerate until they were told to maintain that speed, and then they were asked to estimate that speed. For the simulator validation, a scenario consisting of a road with identical geometric properties (width, lanes, and curves) and similar roadside features was designed and the drivers were asked to perform the identical speed production and speed estimation tasks in the simulator. Figure 2-5 shows the results from the speed estimation task. The Y-axis shows the estimated speeds and the X-axis shows the actual speeds. As can be easily seen there is a very strong linear relationship between the estimated speed and the actual speed. This is not surprising on the road where people have thousands of hours of driving experience, but it is gratifying to obtain in the simulator: in both cases, the faster one drives, the faster the perceived speed. More important perhaps is the similarity of the simulator estimation to the actual speed. The dashed line indicates a perfect identity relationship. In the simulator the rate of change in speed is very similar

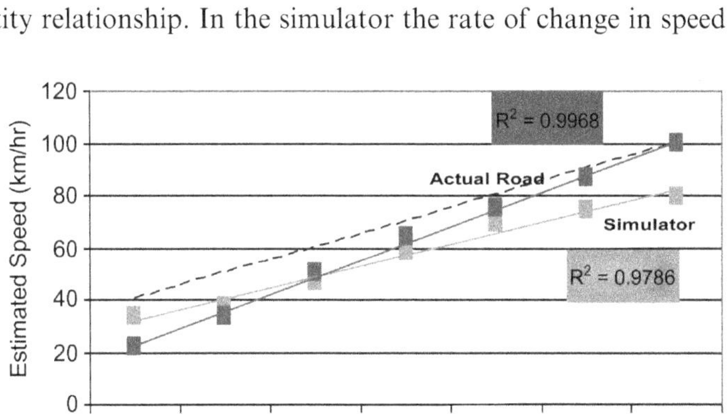

Figure 2-5. The relationship between actual speed and estimated/perceived speed in Ben Gurion University's simulator and on the road (from Shinar and Ronen, 2007).

to that on the road (represented by the similar slopes of the lines), but the simulated speed appears lower than the real one by approximately 10-20 km/hr. This difference can then be used to adjust the simulation speed in order to provide a sensation of the actual speed on the road. Interestingly, even on the road, the estimated speed was lower than the true speed, though as the speed increased, the estimate became closer to the actual speed. In the simulator the relationship was actually "cleaner" in the sense that the estimated speed was almost a constant underestimate of approximately 7 km/hr. Thus, these results demonstrate that studies with this particular simulator are valid as far as the drivers' relative speed perceptions are concerned. Furthermore, these results can also be applied to other studies with the same simulator, by supplying a transfer function to use in order to achieve any perceived speed. Similar results – demonstrating the relative – but not the absolute – validity of perceived speed in a simulator relative to real-world driving were obtained in an Australian simulator (Godley, Triggs, and Fildes, 2002).

In another type of simulator validation, McGehee, Mazzaae, and Baldwin (2000) compared the brake and steering reaction times of drivers when they encountered an unexpected vehicle that crossed their path as they approached an intersection. The simulator used was a highly advanced moving base simulator with six degrees of movement, and with 190 degrees visual field in front and 60 degrees visual field in the rear-view mirrors. Thus, the simulator provided the driver with both a visual and a kinesthetic environment that are nearly identical to that experienced in real driving. The validation evaluation revealed that in the sophisticated simulator the average steering reaction times were 1.64 seconds and on the road they were 1.67 seconds. The average brake reaction times were 2.2 seconds in the simulator and 2.3 seconds on the road. Thus, on both measures the simulator provided a highly valid simulation of real driving. On the other hand performance on another related measure – the throttle release time in response to the sudden appearance of the car – was significantly faster in the simulator (0.96 seconds) than on the road (1.28 seconds).

Other studies have demonstrated that while the simulator does not replicate the effects found on the road at an absolute level there is often a strong relative validity, meaning that the same relationships observed in the simulator are observed on the road even if the absolute magnitudes are different. Thus, different studies have demonstrated the relative validity of the simulation for degraded lateral control under the influence of alcohol (Helland *et al.*, 2013), the response to rumble strips (Godley*et al.*, 2002), different measures of fatigue (Hallvig *et al.*, 2013), and braking responses to avoid collisions (Hoffman *et al.*, 2002; Donkor, Burnett, and Sharples, 2014). Recent research has even demonstrated the relative validity of driving simulators in inducing and testing the effects of emotions such as anger (Abdu *et al.*, 2012; Donkor *et al.*, 2014) It is important to note that these behaviors were always tested within a particular context and the degree of validity can change with the changing context, such as when tested at night versus during the day (Hallvig *et al.*, 2013). Taken together, these results and many others obtained in different simulators indicate that and moderate to high levels of relative validity can be achieved (Mullen *et al.*, 2011).

One study evaluated the validity of four different simulators, in different locations in the U.S. with different degrees of physical reality, on the same driving simulation task, and yielded some unexpected results. In this study by Lee *et al.* (2013) different drivers drove through the same scenarios in the NADS, in a fixed base simulator with three degrees of movement and a 240-degree horizontal field of view, in a fixed base simulator without any movement and a somewhat similar visual field, and in a mini-NADS that is a fixed base simulator with three small front screens providing a total of 132-degree horizontal visual field. The general conclusion was that all simulators had good relative fidelity for speed. More surprising was the finding that all simulators – regardless of their physical realism provided similar perception of "overall feel and similarity to driving" and similar levels of simulator sickness (a plague of driving simulation studies that seems to affect approximately 10 percent of the potential participants). It is important to note that each simulator was driven by different drivers, and thus a direct comparison of the four simulators by the same drivers was impossible. It would be puzzling (and disappointing to those who have invested so much in moving simulators) if the NADS and the mini-NADS provided the same feel of realism.

The primary objective of simulation-based studies is to predict on-road performance from simulator data. This can be accomplished without absolute validity if a transformation equation can be developed. For example, drivers in a simulator typically drive faster than on the road, probably because the optical flow in a simulator is less than in the real world. Thus, there is no absolute validity for speed. But as long as there is some mathematical, and hopefully linear, equation that relates simulator speed to road speed (as in Figure 2-5), it is easy to use simulator data to predict road behavior. Because it is less expensive to "build" new roads in a simulator, different geometries can be efficiently compared in a simulator before they are actually implemented. Finally, no one has ever died in a simulator crash so research that might be high risk on a road can still be conducted in a simulator. A good use of the simulator is demonstrated in a study by Jamson, Lai, and Jamson (2010) that compared the utility of different engineering treatments for speed abatement in a moving-base simulator. In total there were 20 different treatments including various types of peripheral hatchings of the lane markers, rumble strips, vehicle-activated electronic speed signs, and speed limit signs. Various alternative treatments were evaluated in terms of their effectiveness at speed reductions on urban (straight segments and junctions) and rural segments (straight, curved, junctions, and entry to built-up areas). The important differences between these treatments are that they affect different driver information processing and decision functions such as alerting and risk perception. Controlling all other conditions would be impossible in the real driving environment, yet easy to accomplish in the simulator. The results showed, to quote the authors that "whilst straight sections of road are difficult to treat, speed reductions can be obtained by increasing risk perception. In contrast, alerting treatments had more effect at junctions, particularly in an urban environment; drivers approaching curves demonstrated improved speed adaptation if the curve radius was highlighted (either implicitly or explicitly)" (p. 961).

The significant improvements in digital computing have brought about a change in the perception of the utility of simulators. In the U.S. driving simulators are used mostly for the evaluation of drivers' behavior in situations that would be difficult or unethical or unsafe to study on the roads, but in Europe simulators are also used as tools in roadway design. This use can range all the way from informal evaluations of alternative designs to formal experimental studies of drivers' responses to alternative designs. Informal evaluations use the simulator as a means of visualizing designs before they are implemented. Thus, in the Netherlands, highway engineers rely on the Organization for Applied Scientific Research (TNO) simulator, to view dynamic presentations of their planned designs (from the driver's perspective) before finalizing them (Keith *et al.*, 2005). Formal experimental studies have been conducted with the Norwegian Institute of Technology (SINTEF) simulator to evaluate alternative lighting designs for Europe's longest tunnel (24.5 km!). The eventual design that consists of a changing light pattern improved drivers' comfort and reduced drivers' fatigue and anxiety as they drove through this long tunnel (Lotsberg, 2001). In Florida results from a driving simulation were used to demonstrate drivers' sensitivity to the speed of opposing traffic when they had to make a left turn, and thus cross the street between the moving cars. It turned out that drivers crossed with smaller gaps (averaging 5.8 seconds) when the traffic speed was high (55 mph), and higher gaps (averaging 7.3 seconds) when the traffic speed was low (25 mph). Thus, the behavioral data cast some doubt on the U.S. federal recommendations that assume a constant minimum gap of 7.5 seconds regardless of the traffic speed (Klee, 2004).

On-the-Road Studies

On the road studies fall into two general types: experimental studies that involve some manipulation of the situation, and thus an independent variable is actually manipulated, and observational studies that simply observe behavior of unsuspecting drivers under various naturally occurring situations, and thus all variables – independent and dependent – are not under direct control of the researcher. A special and relatively new type of observational studies is the naturalistic driving studies that merit a separate discussion below.

Experimental studies

As dramatic as the results from digital simulation of the ABW were, they still did not answer two critical questions. First, do drivers in fact always brake when they release the accelerator rapidly? If they do not, then how often will the activation of the ABW create a "false alarm" – a situation when the following driver sees the rear brake lights go on despite the fact that the lead driver does not brake. Second, how often do these conditions occur in real-life? For example, are drivers always attentive to the car ahead? Both of these questions were answered in partially controlled, experimental, on-the-road studies.

To minimize the potential harm from false alarms, the ABW was designed so that the accelerator release activated the brake light for only one second – ample time to move the foot to the brake pedal (given the movement times reported above). If in that interim the driver does not brake, then the brake lights go off. To determine the potentially dangerous likelihood of false alarms, five ABWs and monitors were installed in five different vehicles that belonged to a car pool used by members of a kibbutz (a communal settlement where much of the property – such as cars – is shared). This way, the individual drivers who drove the cars were not aware that the ABWs were installed in the cars and that their driving was being monitored. All together over a period of three months these five vehicles covered a distance of nearly 62,000 kilometers, and the drivers braked approximately 95,000 times. False alarms constituted a significant 23 percent of all ABW activations, but in reality were quite rare: approximately once every 250 kilometers. Furthermore, since these false alarms appeared as 1.0 second brake lights, it was interesting to compare them to the frequency of brief braking actions lasting one second or less. It turned out that drivers actually activated their brakes for brief periods quite often: approximately 40 times for every 250 kilometers. Thus, relative to these brief actual brakes, the false alarms were nearly zero (Shinar, 1995).

The ultimate test of any safety device is its ability to prevent crashes, or reduce crash severity, or both. The problem with the evaluation of any new system – such as the ABW or the CHMSL – before it is actually implemented – is that it does not yet exist in the cars on the road, and therefore the ability to directly assess its actual safety benefit is difficult. In the case of the ABW, a "fleet study" was designed in which a fleet of cars – consisting of 764 government vehicles – were included in the study. ABWs were installed in one half of the cars, and in a matching half of the study sample no ABWs were installed. The matching consisted of making sure that for each car with an ABW, a car of identical make and model, for use in the same government department and with a similar purpose, was selected for not installing the ABW. During the study period of 23 months the cars with the ABW accumulated a total of 44.6 million (!) kilometers while the control group accumulated a total of 42.1 million kilometers. During this period the ABW-equipped cars were actually involved in slightly more rear-end collisions than the control group: 75 versus 67. After adjustments for exposure (crashes per kilometers driven) all the analyses indicated that the two groups did not differ significantly from each other in terms of their crash involvement. Thus, despite the laboratory demonstration of the time needed to move the foot to the accelerator, despite the digital simulation demonstrating a very large benefit under various hypothetical conditions, and despite the field study conducted to allay fears of excessive false alarms, the bottom line from this study was that the ABW is not a significant safety device. Why then was this field study not conducted initially? The answer is simple and pragmatic. Controlled fleet studies are very time consuming, logistically and administratively complicated, and eventually very expensive. Thus, they are typically justified only when small-scale studies looking at parts of the issue point out to a probable benefit of a system. Then a large fleet study justifies the expense.

A similar methodological approach was applied in the evaluation of the CHMSL, but the outcome was totally different as can be surmised by anyone traveling in most of the world where the CHMSL is ubiquitous. After years of various small-scale studies on different configurations, colors, and brightness levels of the rear brake lights, beginning in the late 1950s and ending with three large fleet studies (Digges, Nicholson, and Rouse, 1985, for a review of the history of the CHMSL), the U.S. National Highway Traffic Safety Administration initiated a change in the Federal Motor Vehicle Safety Codes that required all passenger cars from 1986 and onward to have a CHMSL. Then, over a period of a little more than a decade the CHMSL became standard in the rest of the world.

The "acid test" of the CHMSL's effectiveness consisted of three independent studies, conducted on fleets of taxis and utility vehicles. In all three studies this particular configuration of the two traditional side lights plus the center high light proved to be very effective in preventing rear-end crashes. The research method was the same in all studies: a fleet of cars was identified and half of the cars in each fleet had the CHMSL installed and half did not. All cars were then tracked for their involvement in rear-end crashes for a period of approximately one year. The results of the three independent fleet studies conducted at different times and at three different sites yielded remarkably similar results: a fifty percent reduction in "relevant" rear-end collisions. The analyses in all studies involved a detailed reconstruction of every rear-end collision to determine if the CHMSL was "relevant" or not. A crash was considered "relevant" – whether or not a CHMSL was installed on the vehicles involved – if the following driver collided with a lead car that was in the process of braking or had just braked. Thus, all rear-end collisions with a parked car or with a car that has been stopped for more than a few seconds were considered irrelevant. Under these circumstances it turned out that in all three studies the CHMSL-equipped vehicles had approximately 50 percent fewer "relevant" rear-end collisions than the non-CHMSL vehicles. Since "relevant" collisions constituted approximately 65 percent of all rear-end crashes, the CHMSL was associated with an overall reduction of approximately 35 percent of all rear impact crashes (Kahane and Hertz, 1998).

A few years later, McKnight and Shinar (1992) demonstrated the effectiveness of the CHMSL in trucks and vans. In this study a research vehicle moving on the road cut in front of an unsuspecting driver. Then at a certain point, the driver of the research vehicle braked, and the time for the following driver to brake was measured. Thus, this study was similar to the laboratory study used to evaluate the brake reaction time for the ABW, but it was conducted under naturalistic conditions and the subjects were drivers who were actually responding to the real braking of a vehicle, without being aware that they were participating in a study. The independent variable of main interest in that study was the presence or absence of a CHMSL on the research vehicle. Thus, everything about the research vehicle was the same on all trials, except for the presence or absence of the CHMSL. Furthermore, the tests with and without the CHMSL were carried out on the same road, same days of the week, and same times of the day. The results indeed demonstrated a small saving of 0.06 seconds to 0.12 seconds, depending on the particular configuration of the CHMSL. With these additional data, in 1994 the NHTSA extended the requirement for a CHMSL to trucks and vans. In summary, the development and evaluation of both the ABW and the CHMSL through progressive research provide a good demonstration of the criticality of well-designed human factors research for improvements in highway safety through judicious and empirically supported changes in-vehicle design.

On-road experimental studies have also benefitted from technological innovations that enable driver monitoring to an extent never available. Instrumented vehicles can now be equipped to study driver glance behavior using in-vehicle cameras that track the eye fixations in the car and out on the road and relate these fixations to the specific devices in the car and specific objects on the road, respectively. Eye movement tracking and analysis has been applied to understanding the cognitive demands that driving places on young/novice and old drivers, hazard perception and the acquisition of hazard perception skills, distraction from in-vehicle devices, external sources, and even cognitive distraction such as using hands-free phones (Taylor *et al.*, 2013). Experimental vehicles can also be employed with devices that detect extreme behavior such as sudden acceleration or braking and sudden lane changes. Coupled with algorithms that relate these to dangerous driving, these technologies have been used to classify drivers (as aggressive or not), and feedback from such devices has been successfully used to reduce aggressive driving of young drivers (Farah *et al.*, 2014; Toledo and Lotan, 2007; Toledo, Musicant, and Lotan, 2008).

Field operational test (FOT) – A quasi-experimental method

An increasingly popular type of on-road quasi-experimental studies is that of the field operational test (FOT): a study undertaken to evaluate an existing or proposed system, under normal operating conditions, in environments typically encountered by the host vehicle(s) using quasi-experimental methods (FESTA, 2011). FOTs have been used to evaluate various driver support, information, communication, assistance, and crash avoidance systems. In FOTs volunteer participants are recruited and provided with cars that are fitted with the systems to be evaluated and with a host of (hopefully) unobtrusive sensors and recording instruments. The drivers then drive the vehicles as they would their own car: to the same places in the same times as they normally drive. Because the driving route is idiosyncratic and varies from one driver to the other, the study is not strictly experimental but quasi-experimental. The participants' driving behavior is then recorded continuously, first without the activation of the system being tested, and then with it. Any differences in behavior are then attributed to the system. The benefits of this approach – assuming that the monitoring equipment is sufficiently unobtrusive and inconspicuous – is that the systems are being evaluated under the typical conditions of everyday driving. However, as most often the vehicle is not the driver's own car, it can only be hoped that after a short period of adjustment, the participants drive these cars as they drive their own cars; for better or for worse, similarly to the way people drive rental cars. When the costs of instrumenting the vehicle are not prohibitive, the FOTs are conducted with the drivers' own personal or leased vehicle. This was effectively done in a study by Shinar and Schechtman (2002) to demonstrate the impact of a headway alerting device in changing drivers' car-following behavior. In these studies there is no control group (as there is in controlled field experiments such as the ABW fleet study), and instead each driver serves as his/her own control when the monitoring equipment is turned on but the system that is being evaluated is not. One drawback of this design is that it must assume that any change in behavior is attributed to the system being evaluated and not to any other factors such as seasonal changes or changes in driving patterns and environments that coincide with the activation of the system (i.e., potential confounding variables). However, to the extent that such changes happen they can be noted and with highly experienced drivers it is safe to assume that the typical driving style does not change throughout the duration of the study.

Several FOTs have been conducted in the U.S. in Europe, Australia, and Israel to evaluate current and emerging electronic driver assistance systems such as adaptive cruise control, forward collision warning, lane departure warning, curve speed warning, blind spot monitoring, speed limiting, and "intelligent speed adaptation" (see Chapters 8 and 19). According to Carsten, Kircher, and Jamson (2013) "FOTs provide almost the only sensible methodology for assessing long-term driver behaviour with new in-vehicle systems" (p. 165). However, their usefulness is limited because they typically focus on the effects of one or very few devices, involve small sample sizes (a bi-product of the cost of such studies), and the participants are still aware that they are in a study. Consequently, their results are often inconclusive (see Carsten *et al.*, 2013, for a review of FOTs). A research paradigm that addresses these three concerns is the Naturalistic Driving Study (NDS), a variation of the observational studies discussed below.

Observational/correlational/associational studies

Almost all of the studies described so far were experimental studies. That means that in each case an experiment was set up – whether in the laboratory or on the road – in which the independent variable was manipulated by the experimenter. In the laboratory study this was done by controlling the uncertainty of the timing of the stop light, in the road studies it was done by giving the ABW and the CHMSL to predetermined groups of drivers/cars, and *not* giving the ABW and CHMSL to a *matched* sample of control drivers/cars. In these situations the experimenter creates a difference in the manipulation of the independent variable between the groups or conditions (as in the FOTs where the study is within subjects and each driver serves as his/her own control). The effects are then observed on the dependent variables.

In many situations the experimental approach is impossible. This is most often the case in medical studies that attempt to assess the effects of various substances on humans. For example, it is ethically unthinkable of giving cigarettes to one group of people and withholding them from a matched group in order to study the effects of smoking on lung cancer. We can do it in the laboratory with mice, but when it comes to people we have to find the ones who already smoke and compare them to those who don't. Similarly it would be unthinkable to design a study in which drugs are administered to drivers who are then set loose on the road. And so, instead we resort to the epidemiological approach: we try to observe people on the road who already – of their own free will – are under the influence of drugs, and compare them to other drivers who are not. In that case the possibility of many confounding variables is very real and must be considered. Potential confounding variables that can account for differences between the two groups can be differences in the tendency for risk-taking behaviors, exercising, dieting, socio-economic class, regularity of medical check-ups, attitudes towards health and safety, and (of course) age and gender. Analysis of crash data basis is fraught with other potential random and systematic errors and a good description of these in the case of assessing drug effects on crash involvement is provided by Houwing *et al.* (2013).

In the realm of highway safety, to study the actual crash savings of the CHMSL in "real life," once it became a standard on all cars in the U.S., repeated analyses were conducted in which the U.S. National Highway Traffic Safety Administration tracked the effectiveness of the CHMSL in actually preventing rear-end collisions. The police-reported crash data from eight states were used for the data base. In each state and calendar year of data, the ratio of rear impacts to non-rear impacts for model year 1986-1989 cars (all CHMSL equipped) was compared to the corresponding ratio in 1982-1985 cars (mostly without the CHMSL). Statistical methods were used to control for the potential confounding effects of vehicle age (because it may be argued that older vehicles with older and less efficient braking systems may be involved in more rear-end crashes, regardless of the presence or absence of a CHMSL). These evaluations demonstrated a positive but diminishing contribution of the CHMSL to roadway safety. The field observational studies yielded effects that were significantly smaller than the 35 percent savings in rear-end crashes that were obtained in the early experimental studies. In 1987 the overall reduction in rear-end crashes that could be attributed to the CHMSL was 8.5 percent, and it diminished in the following two years and then stabilized at about 4.3 percent, with the last evaluation made in 1995 (Kahane and Hertz, 1998). As these vintage vehicles became older fewer of them remained on the road and it became more difficult to make meaningful comparisons to assess the effects of the CHMSL in the U.S. Nonetheless, even at the 4.3 percent savings in crashes the CHMSL was estimated by NHTSA to prevent approximately 100,000 crashes, 50,000 injuries, and over 0.5 billion dollars in property damage and associated costs across the whole U.S. on an annual basis. An extremely good return on a $15 investment in each car!

How reliable are the results obtained in the U.S.? How well do they translate to other countries? Most European countries did not implement the CHMSL as a safety standard until 1998 so its effectiveness with European drivers could not be evaluated before that time. However, in Israel the CHMSL was introduced as a mandatory standard in 1994. Bar-Gera and Schechtman (2005) evaluated its effectiveness there by comparing the crash involvement of passenger cars of model years 1994-1996 (that are all equipped with CHMSL) with the crash involvement of passenger cars of model years 1991-1993 (with almost no cars equipped with CHMSL). Their measure of effectiveness was different than that used by Kahane and Hertz (1998). It was the ratio of number of involvements as the struck vehicle in a rear-end accident relative to the number of involvements as the striking vehicle in a rear-end accident. The initial analysis indicated that the CHMSL was responsible for a seven percent decrease in police-reported accidents. However, the statistical strength of the finding was marginal and there were confounding variables (unrelated to the CHMSL) that could have accounted for the positive effect. This led the authors to conclude that "it is therefore not at all clear whether it is appropriate to attribute this specific difference to the CHMSL contribution to safety."

The history of the research on the CHMSL illustrates the importance of conducting converging operations to the study of almost any simple device, let alone any applied complex issue. Despite the overwhelming evidence in favor of the CHMSL from the early results that prompted its required installation in all cars traveling on the U.S. highways, its lasting effectiveness still remains in doubt. When the evidence must rely on observational studies there is always the fear that some confounding yet-to-be-discovered variable may actually account for the effect observed. Thus, while the results of any one study may be valid in and of themselves, the conclusions based on that study – especially an observational study – must be taken with a grain of salt.

The analyses of the actual on-the-road effectiveness of the CHMSL also illustrate another important highway safety issue. There is no single solution to the problem of highway crashes. Even a device originally estimated to be 35 percent effective in all rear-end crashes, was eventually demonstrably effective in only four percent of them, and that too only in the U.S. There are no panaceas in this area. As we add new crash prevention measures – be they through vehicle improvement, driver regulation and behavior modification, or safer and more forgiving highways – drivers adapt their behavior, and the long-term effects of any one improvement are typically much less than its initial estimated effects.

Naturalistic driving studies

An NDS is a hybrid of epidemiological and empirical methods (Dingus *et al.*, 2006). In NDS volunteer drivers have their cars fitted with multiple sensing and recording instruments that typically include several video cameras that record the roadway, surrounding areas, and the vehicle's interiors that include the driver and passengers. Electronic sensors also record longitudinal and lateral vehicle movements, pedals activation, and steering wheel movements, as well as combined vehicle-road data such as lane position, and headway to a car ahead. Additional background – presumably stable – information is also collected on the drivers that may include attitude questionnaires, psycho-motor tests, and biographical details. Once instrumented, the drivers fairly quickly adapt to the instrumentation and presumably drive their cars as they normally would, while massive amounts of data are recorded continuously and then downloaded to and analyzed by a central computer. So far the NDS is very similar to the FOT. However, unlike the FOT, here the purpose is not to evaluate a particular (innovative) system, but to obtain a record of typical driving behaviors in various situations, especially near crashes, conflicts with other vehicles, and actual crashes. Because a primary goal is to understand the causes and variables associated with crashes, and because crashes are (thankfully) relatively rare events, a lot of data has to be collected in order to analyze these "needles in the haystack" of normal uneventful driving. One way to circumvent this dearth of crash data, is to examine "near crashes" – events that involve a last-minute evasive maneuver on the part of the participating driver. Near crashes are ten times as common as crashes, and arguably share the same characteristics of real crashes (Guo *et al.*, 2010). In addition, "uneventful" driving data are also useful as they provide exposure data for the safety-critical events. Thus we can, for the first time, under naturalistic driving conditions study how the crash or near crash events differ from the "normal" driving in similar situations. All in all, collecting and analyzing these data make such studies quite expensive; in fact, extremely expensive.

The first large scale NDS was conducted by Virginia Tech Transportation Institute and it involved instrumenting and tracking 100 vehicles. In this "100 Car Study," as it came to be known, there were a total of 241 primary and secondary drivers who drove the cars for 12-13 months, accumulating approximately 3.2 million vehicle kilometers (two million vehicle miles) and approximately 43,000 hours of driving. The data included five channels of video recording and multiple vehicle state and kinematic variables. Yet, when all these data were examined there were a total of only 69 crashes most of them so minor as to hardly be noticed and labeled as such by the driver (Neale *et al.*, 2005).

In order to increase the sample size, real crashes are often combined with near crashes and critical incidents (of which there were 761 in the 100-car study). This combination does have some validity. In fact, Guo *et al.* (2010) have argued that the combination actually underestimates the risk of contributing factors relative to looking at the crashes only. Regardless of this tendency and justification of combining real crashes with near crashes, the wealth of driving data served as an excellent proof of concept, showing that it is feasible to collect and analyze such data to arrive at conclusions concerning the involvement of various factors such as visual distraction and fatigue in crashes.

Other studies initiated since the 100-car study have selectively focused on motorcycles (McLaughlin, 2010), trucks (Dingus *et al.*, 2006; Olson *et al.*, 2009), and novice drivers (Klauer *et al.*, 2014). The NDS approach has also spread to other countries such as Japan (Uchida *et al.*, 2010), European Union countries such as The Netherlands, the United Kingdom, Sweden, Germany, Spain, and others (Twisk, Van Nes, and Haupt, 2012), and Australia (Grzebieta, 2015; Regan *et al.*, 2013). Small-scale demonstration projects of the NDS approach have also been conducted in the United Kingdom, Greece, and Spain (Valero-Mora *et al.*, 2013). The largest European study of this kind, UDRIVE, with researchers from over 20 European organizations – is being conducted right now and is scheduled for completion in 2017. It examines driving and crashes of car drivers as well as truck drivers and motorcycle riders. In addition to crash causation, risk, and driving style, the study is also focusing on the effects of distraction, and on interactions with pedestrians and bicyclists (Eenink *et al.*, 2014).

An impressive demonstration of some of the unique capabilities of the NDS approach is contained in two recent studies that evaluated the role of cell-phone based distractions in crashes and other safety-critical events (Fitch *et al.*, 2013; Klauer *et al.*, 2014). Because of the ability of these studies to collect continuous data at high rates they were able to demonstrate that safety-critical events are due primarily to visual-manual distractions, especially those associated with texting and handling of cell phone conversation. In contrast, the cognitive distraction associated with the conversation phase of the phone call was not associated with an increase in crash or near crash risk. Yet, as naturalistic as the NDS and FOT studies are, they still have their shortcomings, as they are not able to isolate the role of various individual factors, collect data that might be intrusive (such as physiological or controlled secondary task performance), thereby contaminating the naturalistic aspect of the driving and determine causal relationships (see Carsten *et al.*, 2013, for a critical review of these methods). Also, the never-before amounts of data come with a very big catch: how to analyze and make sense of it. As these data are being gathered a major effort is being dedicated to defining new algorithms for reducing tera-bytes of data into fewer manageable chunks of more comprehensible information (Dozza, Bärgman, and Lee, 2013).

A very recently completed and by far the most ambitious NDS is the U.S. congressionally mandated study known as the SHRP2 (Strategic Highway Research Program-2) NDS. This study was initiated in 2006 and by the time data collection ended in November 2013, the SHRP2 NDS had logged in-vehicle data from 3,152 consenting drivers who together drove 3,958 vehicle years, logging one million hours of driving video, in six sites across the U.S. The data base has 5.5 million trips covering approximately 35 million vehicle miles, and – most importantly – 1,541 crashes and 2,705 near-crashes. Most of the crashes were very minor, but 250 crashes were severe enough to be "police-reportable." Interestingly, there was not a single fatal crash in all the 35 million miles traveled (Figure 2-6 contains a snapshot of a combined video image from the four cameras installed in each vehicle (Council, 2013; Kidd and McCartt, 2015; Njord and Steudle, 2015). In designing the study a very serious consideration was given to what questions it can answer. Despite the huge cost of such a data collection effort, not all questions could be answered within the budget. Still over 400 research questions were defined and it is expected that over the next 10-30 years different researchers using the data will answer all of these – and some more – questions. This unprecedented effort was aptly summarized by Council (2013, p. 34) who wrote that "Never before has the science of highway safety had such a rich resource, which will not only make roads safer, but will support researchers in road safety disciplines, as well as in other disciplines related to surface transportation…" (p. 38). A few small demonstration studies based on partial SHRP2 NDS data have already been published (Hedlund, 2015), and one analysis of the role of distraction in crashes of various types and severities has already been released (Kidd and McCartt, 2015; Njord and Steudle, 2015). However, these are only the initial fruits of this huge labor, and we must now patiently wait to see how many of the anticipated benefits of this grand study will materialize.

Cost notwithstanding, NDS is often considered an ecologically attractive improvement over driving simulation studies. But contrary to the impression that may have been

Figure 2-6. Video data collected in the SHRP 2 NDS from four cameras documenting (clockwise from top left) the view of the road and traffic ahead, the driver's face and right side, the rear view, and the driver's hands and steering wheel (from Campbell, 2012. Employee demonstration, courtesy of the Virginia Tech Transportation Institute).

created in the above description of the NDS, it is not a panacea. When compared to simulated driving studies both have advantages and disadvantages that make them more complementary than competitive. Table 2-2 summarizes the differences between the two approaches along 12 dimensions. While most entries in that table are self-explanatory, one dimension needs further explanation: the representation of crashes (#5). Because real crashes are rare, as mentioned above, an NDS typically pools together near crashes,

Table 2-2. Similarities and differences between simulation studies and naturalistic driving studies along 12 dimensions (from Shinar, 2015).

	Issue	**Simulation**	**NDS**
1	Sample size	Typically small	Typically large
2	Sample representativeness	Biased toward convenience within selected groups	Biased toward safety/research oriented drivers
3	Immersion	Partial – with by-product of simulator sickness	Practically total
4	Stimulus representation	Controlled and artificial	Uncontrolled and real
5	Response representation of crashes	Mostly surrogate measures of driver performance – not all valid predictors of safety	Surrogate and outcome measures of Safety-Critical Events – but small Ns
6	Study design	Experimental	Descriptive/associational
7	Driver demand characteristics	At forefront (based on instructions)	Over time become minimal
8	Exposure duration/repetition	Typically one trial	Extended – over multiple trips and long periods
9	Cost	Low	Very high
10	Driver's level of control	Operational only	Strategic, tactical, and operational
11	Ecological validity	Measures performance: what drivers can do	Measures behavior: what drivers typically do
12	Impact of new technologies	Can be assessed relative to workload and risk	Difficult to assess – as only very few vehicles have them

critical events, and actual crashes. While there is a similarity in the frequency of the events that contribute to crashes and near crashes (Guo *et al.*, 2010), the few crashes that are captured by NDS are predominantly very minor property-damage crashes. Extrapolating from these to serious injury and fatal crashes is probably not warranted because minor non-injury crashes differ from serious and fatal crashes, but near crashes differ from actual crashes in even more ways. As Knipling (2015) points out, crashes are defined by their outcome, whereas near crashes are defined by the driver behaviour, two very different aspects of safety. In contrast, a significant strength of simulation is that it can create the conditions that increase the likelihood of high-impact or severe crashes (though its generalizability to real-life remains an issue).

Meta-analysis – Quantitative synthesis of the results of multiple studies

"Meta-analysis is a quantified synthesis of results of several studies that have evaluated the same road safety measure stated in the form of a weighted mean estimate of effect" (Elvik *et al.*, 2009, p. 20). With the rapid explosion of information, there is a parallel explosion of studies that evaluate various crash countermeasures; including behavioral (such as education and enforcement strategies), environmental (such as roadway illumination, signage, and delineation), and vehicular (such as in-vehicle safety technologies including forward crash avoidance, lane departure warning, and intelligent speed adaptation). Meta-analysis is a statistical technique that pools together the results of several independent studies that focus on the same issue using the same dependent variables of safety (e.g., crashes, violations) and the same independent variable (e.g., automated enforcement, cell phones) to provide a combined measure of effectiveness. An extensive compilation of meta-analyses of various safety-related measures is provided by Elvik *et al.* (2009) in their *Handbook of Road Safety Measures*. Because combining data obtained at different times, in different places, and by varying methods is fraught with pitfalls, Elvik and his associates correct for some biases by estimating a *weighted* mean effect; that is, giving more weight to recent studies, giving more weight to findings based on larger sample sizes, giving less weight the greater the dispersion of the results of a study, adjusting for skewed data points in each study, and adjusting for "publication bias" (the tendency of journals not to publish "negative" results). Following these adjustments, a mean weighted odds ratio is derived. The odds ratio is the ratio between the odds of a given independent measure (e.g., cell phone use) versus (non-use) in the crash data, divided by the odds of the same variable in the non-crash control data. When the two odds are identical the odds ratio $OR = 1.0$ and there is no significant effect of the independent variable (e.g., cell phone use) on crash risk. When the $OR > 1.0$ it means that the crash risk from the independent variable (cell phone use) is significant.

For those readers not familiar with odds ratios and relative risk, a short explanation is needed here. The odds ratio is a somewhat difficult concept to grasp. A much easier concept is that of relative risk. The similarity and difference between the two measures is demonstrated in Table 2-3 for cell-phone use.

Table 2-3. The calculation of odds ratio and relative risk.

	Crash sample	**Non-Crash sample**	**Total**
Using the phone	a	b	a + b
Not using the phone	c	d	c + d
Total	a + c	b + d	a + b + c + d

Odds ratio (OR) = (a/b)/(c/d).
Relative risk (RR) = [a/(a + b)]/[c/(c + d)].

While odds ratio compares the odds of an event relative to another, the risk compares directly by how much the risk is increased or reduced. Although the calculation is different, when the critical event (a – e.g., use of phone in crash sample and c – use of phone in the non-crash sample) is rare, the numerical values tend to become very similar. We can then get a rough estimate of the relative risk of an event (e.g., using the phone) directly from the odds ratio. Because the critical event (e.g., using the phone, taking a drug) is often confounded by other factors that are crash-related (e.g., age and gender), when data on the confounding factors is available we use an adjusted odds ratio which is the odds ratio that remains after the effects of the confounding factors are accounted for.

Some of the results of meta-analysis reported by Elvik and his associates are included in their book (in the relevant chapters), including the effects of bicycle lanes, setting speed limits, traffic controls for pedestrians, bicycle and motorcycle helmets, and public information and education. Other, meta-analyses include the evaluation of the effectiveness of graduated driver licensing programs (Vanlaar *et al.*, 2014, see Chapter 6), red light cameras (Erke, 2009, see Chapter 20), and road safety campaigns (Phillips, Ullenberg, and Vaa, 2011, see Chapter 19), and the impact of cell phones on driving behavior (Caird *et al.*, 2008) and crash risk (Elvik, 2011, see Chapter 13).

As appealing as meta-analysis is, it cannot replace a focused qualitative review of the literature that it purports to summarize for the simple fact that the process of combining the results of various studies ignores the many subtle differences among them in the design, the procedure, the participants, and the techniques used to obtain the results that are eventually pooled. Thus, while meta-analysis can provide a quantitative estimate of the effect of a countermeasure or a risk factor based on results pooled from similar studies, the strength of a more qualitative literature synthesis and review is that it can provide an appreciation of the different effects from widely different studies, include insights concerning the processes underlying these effects, and include studies that do not meet the quantitative requirements of a meta-analysis (Caird *et al.*, 2014).

Concluding Remarks

The study of human behavior in highway safety is challenging because it presents the researcher with many complex methodological difficulties. Because there is no single golden rule to the design and analysis of all issues, multiple methods should be considered. Though each method may have its own limitation, effects that are repeatedly obtained by multiple study designs are most likely to be ecologically valid. The two current approaches involving experimental manipulation of multiple factors with simulators, and observational naturalistic driving studies that examine actual driving in the real environment should be considered complementary approaches to common issues. Together they can provide us with reliable and valid conclusions. Also, given the limited scope and samples involved in individual studies, the best method to overcome reliability and validity issues associated with different approaches is to address each issue from a variety of perspectives, and with different research methods. Finally, as the number of studies that have examined specific issues – and especially crash countermeasures – has increased in recent years, we can now use a quantitative method – known as meta-analysis – to gain more confidence in our conclusions concerning different safety issues. Thus, in evaluating the research presented in the following chapters it would be judicious to consider the conclusions presented as strong as the number of different studies, employing different methodologies that yield the same results.

References

Abdu, R., D. Shinar and N. Meiran (2012). Situational anger and driving. *Transport. Res. F*, *15*, 575-580.

Amoros, E., J.-L. Martin and B. Laumon (2006). Under-reporting of road crash casualties in France. *Accid. Anal. Prev.*, *38*(4), 627-635.

Anstey, K. J., J. Wood, H. Caldwell, G. Kerr and S. R. Lord (2009). Comparison of self-reported crashes, state crash records and an on-road driving assessment in a population-based sample of drivers aged 69 95 years. *Traffic Inj. Prev.*, *10*, 84-90.

Barak, B. (2005). Research: Young female drivers are not so careful. YNET. http://www.ynet.co.il/articles/0,7340,L-3118184,00.html. July 26.

Bar-Gera, H. and E. Schechtman (2005). The effect of Center High Mounted Stop Lamp on rear-end accidents in Israel. *Accid. Anal. Prev.*, *37*, 531-536.

Bar-Gera, H. and D. Shinar (2005). The tendency of drivers to pass other vehicles. *Transport. Res. F*, *8*, 429-439.

Bianchi, A. and H. Summala (2004). The "genetics" of driving behavior: parents' driving style predicts their children's driving style. *Accid. Anal. Prev.*, *36*, 655-659.

Boyle, L. N. and J. D. Lee (2010). Using driving simulators to assess driving safety. *Accid. Anal. Prev.*, *42*, 785-787 (Prologue to special issue on driving simulation).

Caird, J., C. R. Willness, P. Steel and C. Scialfa (2008). A meta-analysis of the effects of cell phones on driver performance. *Accid. Anal. Prev.*, *40*, 1282-1293.

Caird, J. K., K. A. Johnston, C. R. Willness and M. Asbridge (2014). The use of meta-analysis or research synthesis to combine driving simulation or naturalistic study results on driver distraction. *J. Safety Res.*, *49*, 91-96.

Campbell, K. L. (2012). The SHRP 2 naturalistic driving study: Addressing driver performance and behavior in traffic safety. *TR News*, p. 282. Transportation Research Board, Washington, DC.

Carsten, O., K. Kircher and S. Jamson (2013). Vehicle-based studies of driving in the real world: the hard truth? *Accid. Anal. Prev.*, *58*, 162-174.

Cooper, P. J., M. Pinili and C. Wenjun (1995). An examination of the crash involvement rates of novice drivers aged 16 to 55. *Accid. Anal. Prev.*, *27*, 89-104.

Council, F. (2013). This ain't your grandma's safety research: Naturalistic driving study yields long-sought data. TR News, No. 289, pp. 36-39.

Dhillon, P. K., A. S. Lightstone, C. Peek-Asa and J. F. Kraus (2001). Assessment of hospital and police ascertainment of automobile versus childhood pedestrian and bicyclist collisions. *Accid. Anal. Prev.*, *33*(4), 529-537.

Digges, K. H., R. N. Nicholson and E. J. Rouse (1985). The technical basis for the Center High-Mounted Stop Lamp. SAE Technical Series, No. 851240. Society of Automotive Engineering, Detroit, MI.

Dingus, T. A., V. L. Neale, S. G. Klauer, A. D. Petersen and R. J. Carroll (2006). The development of a naturalistic data collection system to perform critical incident analysis: An investigation of safety and fatigue issues in long-haul trucking. *Accid. Anal. Prev.*, *38*, 1127-1136.

Donkor, R. A., G. A. Burnett and S. Sharples (2014). Measuring the emotional validity of driving simulators. *Adv. Transport. Studies Int. J.*, *1*(Special Issue), 51-64.

Dozza, M., J. Bärgman and J. D. Lee (2013). Chunking: A procedure to improve naturalistic data analysis. *Accid. Anal. Prev.*, *53*(4), 309-317.

Eenink, R., Y. Barnard, M. Baumann, X. Augros and F. Utesch (2014). UDRIVE: The European naturalistic driving study. In Transport Research Arena (TRA) 5th Conference: Transport Solutions from Research to Deployment, Paris, France.

Erke, A. (2009). A red light for red light cameras? A meta-analysis of the effects of red-light cameras on crashes. *Accid. Anal. Prev.*, *41*, 897-905.

Elvik, R. (2011). Effects of mobile phone use on accident risk. *Transport. Res. Record.*, *No. 2236*, 20-26.

Elvik, R., A. Høye, T. Vaa and M. Sørensen (2009). *The Handbook of Road Safety Measures* (2nd Ed.). Emerald, Bingley, UK.

Farah, H., O. Musicant, Y. Shimshoni, T. Toledo, E. Grimberg, H. Omer and T. Lotan (2014).Can providing feedback on driving behavior and training on parental vigilant care affect male teen drivers and their parents? *Accid. Anal. Prev.*, *69*, 62-70.

Fahner, G. and M. Hane (1973). Seat belts: The importance of situational factors. *Accid. Anal. Prev.*, *5*, 267-285.

Fitch, G. A., S. A. Soccolich, F. Guo, J. McClafferty, Y. Fang, R. L. Olson, M. A. Perez, R. J. Hanowski, J. M. Hankey and T. A. Dingus (2013). The impact of hand-held and hands-free cell phone use on driving performance and safety-critical event risk. NHTSA Report No. DOT HS 811 757. U.S. Department of Transportation, Washington, DC.

Fitts, P. M. and M. I. Posner (1967). *Human Performance*. Brooks/Cole, Belmont, CA.

FESTA (2011). *FESTA Handbook*. Version 4. Revised by FOT-Net. http://www.fot-net.eu/download/festa handbook rev4.pdf

Forsyth, E., G. Maycock and B. Sexton (1995). Cohort study of learner and novice drivers: Part 3, accidents, offences, and driving experience in the first three years of driving. Research Report 111. Transport Research Laboratory, Crowthorne, England.

Godley, S. T., T. J. Triggs and B. N. Fildes (2002). Driving simulator validation for speed research. *Accid. Anal. Prev.*, *34*(5), 589-600.

Grzebieta, R. (2015). Australia's naturalistic driving study. *J. Australas. Coll. Road. Safety*, *26*(1), 46-47.

Guo, F., S. G. Klauer, J. M. Hankey and T. A. Dingus (2010). Near crashes as crash surrogate for naturalistic driving studies. Transportation Research Record, No. 2147, pp. 66-74.

Hallvig, D., A. Anund, C. Forsb, G. Kecklundd, J. G. Karlssonc , M. Wahdea and T. Åkerstedt (2013). Sleepy driving on the real road and in the simulator—A comparison. *Accid. Anal. Prev.*, *50*, 44-50.

Hauer, E. (2004). The harm done by tests of significance. *Accid. Anal. Prev.*, *36*(3), 495-500.

Hedlund, J. (2015). SHRP 2 naturalistic driving study: the first data analysis studies (Editorial). *J. Safety Res.*, *54*, 3-4.

Helland, A., G. D. Jenssenc, L.-E. Lervågc, A. A. Westina, T. Moenc, K. Sakshaugc, S. Lydersend, J. Mørlande and L. Slørdala (2013). Comparison of driving simulator performance with real driving after alcohol intake: A randomised, single blind, placebo-controlled, cross-over trial. *Accid. Anal. Prev.*, *53*, 9-16.

Houwing, S., M. Hagenzieker, R. P. M. Mathijssen, S.-N. Legrand, A. G. Verstraete, T. Hels, I. M. Bernhoft, K. W. Simonsen, P. Lillsunde, D. Favretto, S. D. Ferraraf, M. Caplinskiene, K. L. L. Movig and K. A. Brookhuis (2013). Random and systematic errors in case–control studies calculating the injury risk of driving under the influence of psychoactive substances. *Accid. Anal. Prev.*, *52*, 144-153.

Jamson, S., F. Lai and H. Jamson (2010). Driving simulators for robust comparisons: A case study evaluating road safety engineering treatments. *Accid. Anal. Prev.*, *42*, 961-971.

Janstrup, K. H., S. Kaplan, T. Hels, J. Lauritsen and C. G. Prato (2016). Understanding traffic crash under-reporting: linking police and medical records to individual and crash characteristics. *Traffic Inj. Prev.*, *19*, 580-584.

Johansson, G. and K. Rumar (1971). Drivers' brake reaction times. *Hum. Fact.*, *13*(1), 23-27.

Kahane, C. J. and E. Hertz (1998). The long-term effectiveness of the Center High Mounted Stop Lamp in passenger cars and light trucks. NHTSA Technical Report No. DOT HS 808 696. U.S. Department of Transportation, Washington, DC.

Keith, K., M. Trentacoste, L. Depue, T. Granda, E. Huckaby, B. Ibarguen, B. Kantowitz, W. Lum and T. Wilson (2005). Roadway human factors and behavioral safety in Europe. Federal Highway Administration Report FHWA-PL-05-005. U.S. Department of Transportation, Washington, DC.

Kidd, D. G. and McCartt, A. T. (2015). The relevance of crash ype and sevfeirty when estimating cfrash risk using the SHRP2 naturalistic driving data. International Driver Distraction and Inattention Conference. Sydney, Australia.

Klee, H. (2004). Assessment of the use of a driving simulator for traffic engineering and human factors studies. Final Report No. BC096/RPWO#18. Center for Advanced Transportation Systems Simulation, University of Central Florida, Orlando, FL.

Klauer, S. G., F. Guo, B. G. Simons-Morton, M. C. Ouimet, S. E. Lee and T. A. Dingus (2014). Distracted driving and risk of road crashes among novice and experienced drivers. *New Eng. J. Med.*, *370*(1), 54-59.

Knipling, R. R. (2015). Naturalistic driving events: no harm, no foul, no validity. Paper presented at the 2015 Driver Assessment conference. Salt Lake, UT.

Lee, J. D., J. D. Hoffman, T. L. Brown and D. V. McGehee (2002). *Comparison of Driver Braking Responses in a High Fidelity Driving Simulator and on a Test Track.* NHTSA Report No. DOT HS 809 447. U.S. Department of Transpoortation, Washington, DC.

Lee, J. D., N. Ward, E. Boer, T. L. Brown, S. A. Balk and O. Ahmad (2013). Exploratory advanced research: Making driving simulators more useful for behavioral research – Simulator characteristics comparison and model-based transformation. Report by the NADS, University of Iowa to the FHWA U.S. Department of Transportation, Washington, DC.

Lotsberg, G. (2001). Safety design of the 24.5 km long Laerdal tunnel in Norway. International Conference on Traffic and Safety in Road Tunnels 28/29 May 2001 in Hamburg. Norwegian Public Roads Administration, Oslo.

Maycock, G., C. R. Lockwood and J. F. Lester (1991). The accident liability of car drivers. Research Report 315. Transport and Road Research Laboratory, Crowthorne, England.

McGee, H. W., K. G. Hooper, W. E. Hughes and W. Benson (1983). Highway design and operations standards affected by driver characteristics. Volume II of Fedreal Highway Administration Report FHWA-RD-83-015. U.S. Department of Transportation, Washington, DC.

McGehee, D. V., E. N. Mazzaae and G. H. S. Baldwin (2000). Driver reaction time in crash avoidance research: validation of a driving simulator study on a test track. Proceedings of the International Ergonomics Association Conferencc.

McKnight, A. J. and D. Shinar (1992). Brake reaction time to center high-mounted stop lamps on vans and trucks. *Hum. Fact.*, *34*(2), 205-213.

Miller, G. and O. Taubman - Ben-Ari (2010). Driving styles among young novice drivers—The contribution of parental driving styles and personal characteristics. *Accid. Anal. Prev.*, *42*, 558-570.

Mourant, R. R. and T. H. Rockwell (1972). Strategies of visual search by novice and experienced drivers. *Hum. Fact.*, *14*, 325-335.

Mullen, N., J. Charlton, A. Devlin and M. Bédard (2011). Simulator validity: Behaviors observed on the simulator and on the road. In: *Handbook of Driving Simulation for Engineering, Medicine, and Psychology* (Fisher, D., M. Rizzo, J. K. Caird and J. D. Lee eds.) CRC Press, Taylor and Francis, Boca Raton, FL.

McLaughlin, S. (2010). Ongoing naturalistic driving studies and field operational tests and utility in ADAS development. Presentation at the 17th ITS World Congress. Busan, Korea. http://www.fot-net.eu/download/internationalworkshops/Busan2010/ss61/vtti naturalistic and fots.Pdf

NADS (2014). The National Advanced Driving Simulator. The University of Iowa. http://www.nads-sc.uiowa.edu/overview.php. Accessed February 9, 2014.

Neal, V. L., T. A. Dingus, S. G. Klauer, J. Sudweeks and M. Goodman (2005). An overview of the 100-car naturalistic study and findings. Proceedings of the Enhanced Safety Vehicles Conference, Paper No. 05-0400. NHTSA, Washington, DC.

NHTSA (2004). U.S. Code of Federal Regulations, Volume 49, Chapter 5, Section 571.108 (10-1-04 Edition). U.S. Department of Transportation, Washington, DC.

NHTSA (2007). National advance driving simulator (NADS). http://www-nrd.nhtsa.dot.gov/departments/nrd-12/NADS/. Accessed March 25, 2007.

Njord, J. and K. Steudle (2015). Big data hit the road: the first year of use of the SHRP2 safety databases. *TR News*, No. 300, November-December 3-7. Transportation Research Board, Washington, DC.

Olson, R. L., R. J. Hanowski, J. S. Hickman and J. Bocanegra (2009). Driver distraction in commercial vehicle operations: Final report. Report No. FMCSA-RRR-09-042. Federal Motor Carrier Safety Administration, Washington, DC. www.distraction.gov/download/research-pdf/Driver-Distraction-Commercial-Vehicle-Operations.pdf

Open Science Collaboration (2015). Estimating the reproducibility of psychological science. *Science, 349*, 6251. http://www.sciencemag.org/content/349/6251/aac4716.full#aff-1

Özkan, T., P. Puvanachandra, T. Lajunen, C. Hoe and A. Hyder (2012). The validity of self-reported seatbelt use in a country where levels of use are low. *Accid. Anal. Prev., 47*, 75-77.

Parada, M. A., L. D. Cohn, E. Gonzlez, T. Byrd and M. Cortes (2001). The validity of self-reported seat belt use: Hispanic and non-Hispanic drivers in El Paso. *Accid. Anal. Prev., 33*, 139-143.

Peleg, K. and L. Aharonson-Daniel (2004). Road Traffic Accidents – Severe injuries??? How missing data can impair decision making. *Harefuah, J. Israeli Med. Assoc., 143*(2), 111-115 (Hebrew).

Phillips, R. O., P. Ullenberg and T. Vaa (2011). Meta-analysis of the effect of road safety campaigns on accidents. *Accid. Anal. Prev., 43*, 1204-1218.

Pocock, S. J. (1983). *Clinical Trials: A Practical Approach*. Wiley, New York, NY.

Prato, C. G., T. Toledo, T. Lotan and O. Taubman - Ben-Ari (2010). Modeling the behavior of novice young drivers during the first year after licensure. *Accid. Anal. Prev., 42*, 480-486.

Regan, M. A., A. Williamson, R. Grzebieta, J. Charlton, M. Lenne, B. Watson, N. Haworth, A. Rakotonirainy, J. Woolley, R. Anderson, T. Senserrick and K. Young (2013). The Australian 400-car naturalistic driving study: Innovation in road safety research and policy. Paper 12 of the Proceedings of the 2013 Australasian Road Safety Research, Policing & Education Conference, Brisbane, Queensland, August 28-30.

Ronen, A. and N. Yair (2013). The adaptation period to a driving simulator. *Transport. Res. F, 18*, 94-106.

Sahami, S. and T. Sayed (2013). How drivers adapt to drive in driving simulator, and what is the impact of practice scenario on the research? *Transport. Res. F, 16*, 41-62.

Seidler, R. D. and G. E. Stelmach (1995). Reduction in sensorimotor control with age. *Quest, 47*, 386-394.

Shiffrin, R. M. and W. Schneider (1977). Controlled and automatic human information processing: Perceptual learning, automatic attending, and a general theory. *Psychol. Rev.*, *84*, 127-190.

Shinar, D. (1995). Field evaluation of an advance brake warning system. *Hum. Fact.*, *37*, 746-751.

Shinar, D. (2015). Naturalistic driving studies vs. simulated driving: Complementary or competitive approaches? Presentation at the Annual Meeting of the Transportation Research Board, Washington, DC, January 11.

Shinar, D. and A. Ronen (2007). Validation of speed perception and production in STI- SIM single screen simulator. *Adv. Transport. Studies Int. J.*, *5* (Special Issue), 51-56. (http://host.uniroma3.it/riviste/ats/)

Shinar, D. and E. Schechtman (2002). Headway feedback improves inter-vehicular distance: a field study. *Hum. Fact.*, *44*(3), 474-481.

Shinar, D. and F. Schieber (1991). Visual requirements for safety and mobility of older drivers. *Hum. Fact.*, *33*, 507-520.

Shinar, D. and M. Shaham (2003). Benefits of a moving point-of-light (POL) as a means to maintaining safe headways in tunnels. Proceedings of the 3rd Driving Simulation Conference – North America, Dearborn, MI, October 10.

Shinar, D., E. Rotenberg and T. Cohen (1997). Crash Reduction with an advance brake warning system: A digital simulation. *Hum. Fact.*, *39*, 296-302.

Stelmach, G. E., V. Homberg (1993). *Sensorimotor impairment in the elderly*. Kluwer Academic, Norwell MA.

Strayer, D. L., J. Turrill, J. M. Cooper, J. R. Coleman and N. Medeiros-Ward (2015). Assessing cognitive distraction in the automobile. *Hum. Fact.*, *75*, 1300-1324.

Streff, F. M. and A. C. Wagenaar (1989). Are there really shortcuts? Estimating seat belt use with self-report measures. *Accid. Anal. Prev.*, *21*, 509-516.

Stulginskas, J. V., R. Verreault and I. B. Pless (1985). A comparison of observed and reported restraint use by children and adults. *Accid. Anal. Prev.*, *17*, 381-386.

Taieb-Maimon, M. and D. Shinar (2001). Minimum and comfortable driving headways: reality versus perception. *Hum. Fact.*, *43*(1), 159-172.

Taylor, T., A. K. Pradhan, G. Divekar, M. Romoser, J. Muttart, R. Gomez, A. Pollatsek and D. L. Fisher (2013). The view from the road: The contribution of on-road glance-monitoring technologies to understanding driver behavior. *Accid. Anal. Prev.*, *58*, 175-186.

Toledo, T. and T. Lotan (2007). In-vehicle data recorder for evaluation of driving behav-ior and safety. *Transport. Res. Record J. Transport. Res. Board*, No. 1953, 112-119.

Toledo, T., O. Musicant and T. Lotan (2008). In-vehicle data recorder for monitoringand feedback on drivers' behavior. *Transport. Res. C Emerg. Technol.*, *16*(3), 320-331.

Türker, Ö., P. Puvanachandra, T. Lajunen, C. Hoe and A. Hyder (2012). The validity of self-reported seatbelt use in a country where levels of use are low. *Accid. Anal. Prev.*, *47*, 75-77.

Twisk, D., N. Van Nes and J. Haupt (2012). Understanding safety critical interactions between bicycles and motor vehicles in Europe by means of naturalistic driving techniques. Proceedings of the International Cycling Safety Conference, Helmond, The Netherlands, November 7-8.

Uchida, N., M. Kawakoshi, T. Tagawa and T. Mochida (2010). An investigation of factors contributing to major crash types in Japan based on naturalistic driving data. *IATSS Res.*, *34*, 22-30.

Valero-Mora, P. M., A. Tontsch, R. Welsh, A. Morris, S. Reed, K. Touliou and D. Margaritis (2013). Is naturalistic driving research possible with highly instrumented cars? Lessons learnt in three research centres. *Accid. Anal. Prev.*, *58*, 187-194.

Vanlaar, W. A., McKiernan, H., McAteer, R., Robertson, D., Mayhew, D., Carr, S. B., & Holmes, E. (2014). *A meta-analysis of cognitive screening tools for drivers aged 80 and over*. Traffic Injury Research Foundation, Ottawa, Canada.

Victor, T. W., J. L. Harbluk and J. A. Engström (2005). Sensitivity of eye-movement measures to in-vehicle task difficulty. *Transport. Res. F*, *8*, 167-190.

Warshawsky-Livne, L. and D. Shinar (2002). Effects of uncertainty, transmission type, and driver age and gender on brake reaction and movement time. *J. Safety Res.*, *33*, 117-128.

3

Theories and Models of Driver Behavior

> "The society which scorns excellence in plumbing as a humble activity and tolerates shoddiness in philosophy because it is an exalted activity will have neither good plumbing nor good philosophy: neither its pipes nor its theories will hold water." (Gardner, 1961).

> "The increasing stress involved in motoring nowadays makes the psychological efficiency of the driver a more important factor than the mechanical efficiency of the vehicle he drives." (Parry, 1968).

The purpose of this chapter is to present some theories and conceptual models that have been offered to describe, explain, predict, and affect driver behavior. In our attempt to understand this behavior, predict it in different circumstances, and if possible control or modify it (e.g., discourage drivers from using the phone while driving, respect the speed limits, be defensive rather than aggressive), it is necessary to have some kind of a theoretical framework as a starting point. A valid theory or model of human behavior enables us not only to better understand why we behave on the road the way we do, but also to predict drivers' reactions to many potential safety measures, and to develop quantitative driver guidance systems (Donges, 1978), user-oriented highways and vehicle designs, and better driver training programs. This is because the introduction of a safety measure into the vehicle or highway – such as electronic stability control and programmable signs, respectively – not only changes the vehicle and roadway characteristics, but also changes driver behavior in response to them. Sometimes, the behavioral change may actually negate the expected benefits, and we need to understand why and when that may happen and how to avoid it.

Why We Need Driver Theories and Models

The argument for the need for theories and models of human behavior for highway safety was made very succinctly by Kantowitz *et al.* (2004): "Absent the theories, it is almost impossible to specify what new countermeasures might emerge. Thus, what is a standard operating procedure for many human factors researchers (using models) might require an act of faith from practicing highway engineers who do not normally invoke theories of human behavior. If aviation, nuclear power, and human-computer interaction can create better countermeasures through models, so can driving" (pp. 85-86).

A theory is the best practical human factors tool, because, as Kantowitz (2000) notes:

1. It fills in where data are lacking. No handbook or guideline has all the necessary data.
2. Computational theories provide quantitative predictions needed by engineers.
3. It prevents us from reinventing the wheel by allowing us to recognize similarities among problems, such as the tendency of drivers to adopt inappropriate decision criteria in many situations.
4. It is reusable. Once the investment has been made to build a model for a particular domain, the theory can be recycled inexpensively to answer many system-design questions.

The body of research that has accumulated on driving behavior is not just a collection of findings and conclusions but hopefully more like a jigsaw puzzle in which many pieces are made to fit together to form a coherent picture. That picture is our theory of driving behavior. Once we have a theory we can better direct our search at gathering additional "facts" to fill the remaining gaps. In short, the purpose of the models or theories of driver behavior are to make sense of it all.

A theory and a model are not synonymous terms. A theory is a conceptual organization of concepts, mechanisms, and processes that are involved in the operation of a system, such as the atoms in a molecule or – of greater relevance here – driver in traffic. A model is less presumptive in the sense that it does not presume that these mechanisms and processes actually exist, but only that if we posit them then we can explain human behavior. Often after a model of human behavior is developed and validated, a search is done to see if some of its mechanisms actually exist. An example of this is the formulation of the human memory in terms of two distinct mechanisms: short-term memory and long-term memory. The two different mechanisms were first defined and proposed in order to explain various phenomena associated with learning, memorizing, and forgetting. Only after their "invention," did scientists find physiological evidence for the existence of two such distinct information storage areas in the brain (in the hippocampus for short-term memory and the frontal lobes for long-term memory; Costandi, 2009). Thus, a model can often serve as a basis for a theory. In general, unless there is independent evidence for the existence of specific processes and mechanisms, it is safer to talk of models of driver behavior than theories of driver behavior.

Unlike the physical sciences, where a single model is typically the working model for all (until it is replaced by a more general, parsimonious, or valid one), in behavioral interdisciplinary sciences we often have multiple models often using the same terms inconsistently (Hughes *et al.*, 2015). Therefore, laying a unitary theoretical foundation for the discussion in the rest of the book is not practical or efficient. Instead, this chapter discusses several theories and models of driver behavior, broadly defined as theories or models of driver *performance* or driver *behavior*. The different models that are considered below can be described as belonging to one of two categories or attempts to combine both. Models designed to predict driver *performance* most often depict the driver as a limited-capacity information processor, and models designed to explain and predict the more complex real on-road *behavior* assume that actual driving behavior represents the style and strategy the driver adopts to achieve his/her goals. In the broadest sense, the models are actually complementary: the first describe *performance* – or the best the driver can do in a given situation – and the second describe *behavior* – or what a driver tends to do in the typical situation, within his or her limits of performance. Driver performance is the end product of what a driver can do, given the human limitations and given the vehicle and environmental constraints. Driver behavior is what the driver actually does given the limitations and constraints *and* given the driver's needs, motivation, and goals that can be achieved through the driving task. The foundations for the first kind of models are in cognitive and physiological psychology, whereas the foundations for the second kind of models are in theories of personality, social psychology, and organizational behavior. The performance models are used to predict the limits of maximal behavior, while the motivational models are best at predicting typical behavior.

In reality our behavior on the road is a combination of both typical behavior (most of the time we drive) and maximal performance (when we find ourselves in very demanding situations). Thus, both approaches are useful, but in slightly different contexts. This being the case, many models try to incorporate both aspects of our driving: our typical behaviors and our maximal performance or ability. Another approach to classifying models of driving behavior is to distinguish between descriptive models that focus on describing *what* the driver does in various situations, and functional models that focus on *why* the driver does what he or she does. Thus the former can serve as good prescriptive guidelines to what a driver must do to accomplish the driving task, while the latter focuses on the mechanisms and motivations that drive (no pun intended) the different behaviors. Within each class there are further distinctions based on how the different components are organized. Descriptive models can be formulated in a hierarchical fashion (as detailed below) (Michon, 1985) or in terms of feedback control loops (McRuer and Weir, 1969). Functional models are often centered on the driver's information processing system (Rasmussen, 1986) or on motivational concepts (Wilde, 1998), or both (Fuller, 2011).

Obviously, models of driver behavior should always be regarded as work in progress: they either replace one another, or supplement each other, or are updated and modified as new data on driver behavior and driver adaptation accumulate and as the driving environment and vehicles change. An excellent summary of the evolution of driver models up to the early 1990s of the last century is provided by Ranney (1994), and up to the end of the first decade of this century by Vaa (2014). The models described below were picked because they were either widely cited or because they exemplify some of the more pertinent issues that driving research addresses.

The Context of Driving: Hierarchical Decision-Making

Driving is a task that is conducted within a larger framework of mobility. The mobility task – and challenge – is to safely get from one place to another. The decisions a driver has to make in order to achieve that can be described in a hierarchical system such as the one proposed by Janssen (1979) and Michon (1985) and illustrated in Figure 3-1. The system has three levels: the top level consists of the strategic decisions, the intermediate level consists of the navigational decisions, and the lowest level consists of the operational control.

The decisions at the highest – strategic/planning – level include the decision to drive (versus to take a bus or a train or to postpone the trip), the route to choose, the time to leave, etc. The variables that moderate such decisions include the joy or distaste of driving, the need to hurry, the economy of travel mode, the time available, and the latest traffic reports. These are all issues that have to be resolved before the person gets into the car. Once a decision to drive has been made, the second-level decisions – at the tactical/navigation level – must be made. These decisions are made while driving and include how to best avoid obstacles, when and how to change lanes to gain a maneuvering advantage or in preparation for a turn, whether to slow down or speed up at a certain distance from a light that has turned yellow, etc. Finally, at the lowest – control/automatic – level the decisions are mostly unconscious and reflexive and they involve the moment-to-moment actions in response to various stimuli. These include acceleration and deceleration, signaling, changing gears, checking mirrors prior to lane changes, stopping at traffic lights and accelerating from a stop, braking and swerving response to

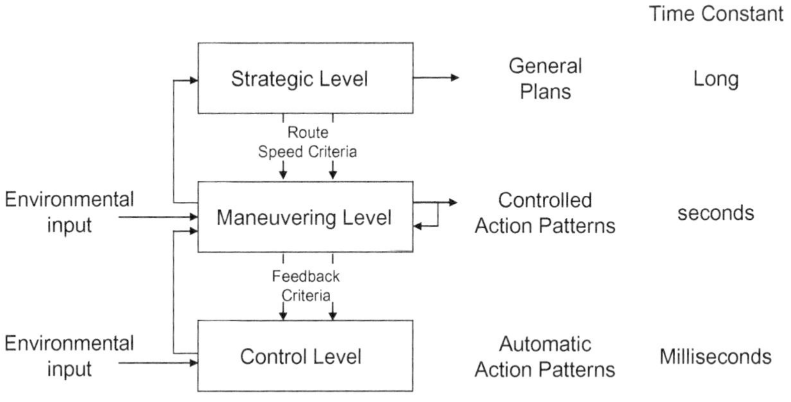

Figure 3-1. The hierarchical structure of the mobility/driving task (from Michon, 1985, based on Janssen, 1979, with kind permission of Springer Science and Business Media).

sudden emergencies, etc. Driving skills and habits play a major role in our behavior at the control level, and much of the driver instruction and initial learning is concerned with the acquisition of these skills. While these skills may not always play a role in safe driving, they often play a crucial role in the avoidance of collisions once a driver has entered a dangerous situation. The decisions a person makes at each level are very important because – among other things – when combined with the driver's specific skills and deficiencies, they directly affect his or her level of risk of being involved in a crash on a given trip (Hakamies-Blomqvist, 2006).

The decisions we make at each level of the hierarchy are based on some criteria of what we would like to achieve. Thus, if at the strategic level we wish to reach our goal with minimum time, this may imply that (1) at the strategic level we choose a certain mode of transportation (drive rather than take public transportation), (2) at the maneuvering level we decide to drive at the high-speed lane at maximum acceptable speed, and (3) at the operational level we minimize braking activities and weave between vehicles. These goals and criteria that dictate behavior then yield various performance outcomes as illustrated in Table 3-1 for a driver whose strategic goal is to reach the destination quickly.

How we perform the tasks at each level – what biases, constraints, desires, limits, and skills govern our behavior – is the subject matter of the theories and models researchers have proposed to explain on-the-road behavior. Note that our behavior does not occur in a vacuum, but has "environmental inputs." These include not only the visible and immediate inputs from the roadway, the traffic, the weather, and the lighting conditions, but also the less tangible environment consisting of traffic laws, norms of behavior, and culture that govern the way we drive. For example, it is the latter that are responsible for stereotypes of "New York drivers," "Italian drivers," "Israeli drivers," and "English drivers."

The hierarchy and time scale associated with each of the three tasks also implies a temporal sequence. When we embark on a trip, we first decide how to get there, when to leave, and by what route (strategic decisions). If we choose to drive, then once on the road we decide on a lane of travel, whether to track a car ahead or pass it (navigational decisions), and then we perform the skilled motor behaviors that govern our safe movement on a moment-to-moment basis such as accelerating, decelerating, and braking, in response to specific stimuli such as the brake lights of the car ahead (control decisions). However, note that the model has both top-to-bottom arrows and bottom-up feedback loops. Thus, repeated agitating control actions in stop-and-go traffic may make us reconsider some of the navigation decisions, and we may decide to change lanes to what appears a faster one (always the one we are not on), and eventually we may also decide to change strategies, and possibly stop for an early meal in the hope that when we resume driving the congestion will have dissipated. Thus, decisions at all levels may actually be carried out at all times, and variables that govern each level may operate at all times. This of course makes behavior quite complex to describe, and even more difficult to understand on the part of other drivers on the road. An example is a driver who suddenly cuts across our lane dangerously close to the front of our car in order to exit the motorway at the last minute.

Table 3-1. The interaction between travel related criteria, driving behaviors, and driving performance at the strategic, tactical, and operational levels of a hierarchical driver model for a driver whose goal is to reach the destination quickly (from Östlund *et al.*, 2006, with permission from VTI).

	Criteria	Behavior	Performance
Strategic	1. Reach the destination quickly. 2. Stay clear of oncoming traffic and other objects.	1. Chooses a high-speed route. 2. Aims at driving fast. 3. Accepts high risks.	1. Does not reach the destination quickly enough.
Tactical	1. Drive as fast as other vehicles, the environment and the vehicle permits. 2. Overtake slow going vehicles.	1. Tailing vehicles and prone to overtake. 2. Cuts curves. 3. Drives at yellow light. 4. Drives fast.	1. Does not manage to overtake the slow vehicles as quickly as desired. 2. Tailgating.
Operational	1. Stay within accepted headway to the lead vehicle. 2. Follow the desired path of travel, e.g. when overtaking. 3. Keep vehicle within road boundaries.	1. High lateral position variation. 2. High-speed variation.	1. Occasionally less headway than accepted. 2. Occasionally departures from the desired path of travel. 3. Vehicle occasionally partly exceeds lane boundaries.

To make the hierarchical model more useful it has to be more detailed. An example of one such elaboration is provided in Figure 3-2. This model is more specific than the one in Figure 3-1 and Table 3-1, both in terms of specifying variables that can affect actions at each level and in terms of the time frame that is relevant to each level. There can be many applications of the general model, and the one in Figure 3-2 illustrates the application of the hierarchical model to evaluation of the potential impact of one of today's most heatedly debated vehicle-roadway features: telematics – an integration of wireless communications, vehicle monitoring systems and location devices (Braddy, 2006). As can be seen from Figure 3-2, the availability of on-line information transmission about the road and other traffic can initiate various types of responses at all three levels. At the strategic level, predicted levels of congestion can assist a person on deciding on what mode of transportation to take and what route to choose. At the tactical level telematics can aid a person in driving-related decisions, but they can also constitute a distraction. At the operational level, too, they can serve as an aid or as an impediment. For example,

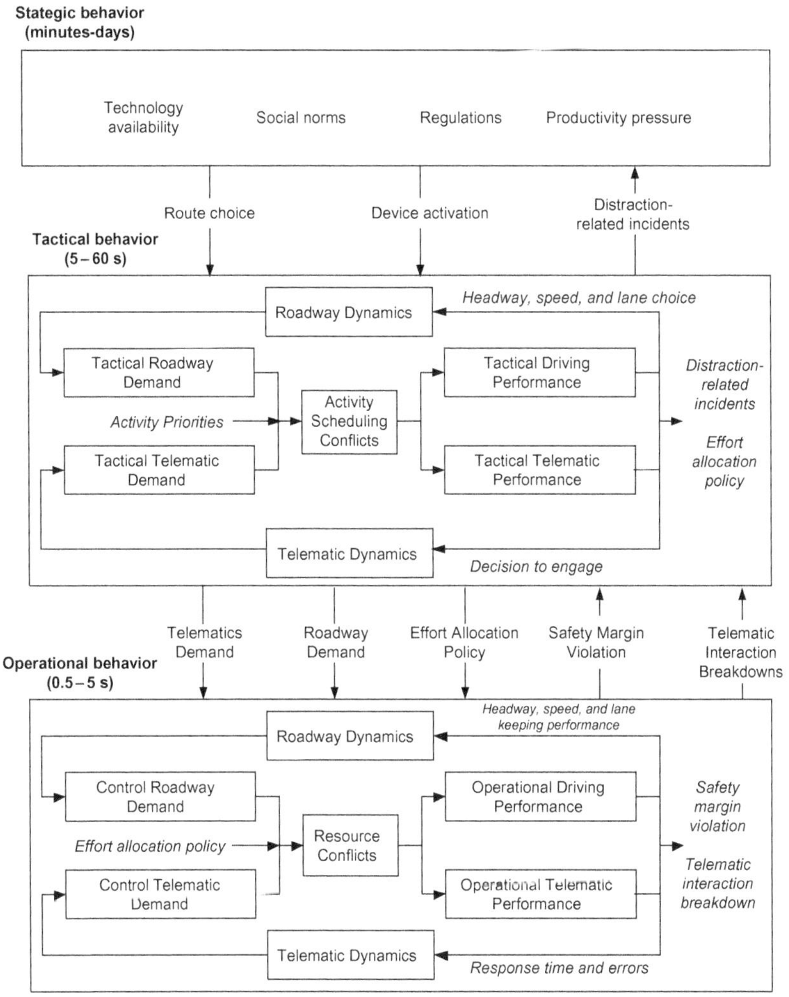

Figure 3-2. A detailed control theory-based hierarchical model of driving behavior (with application to telematics systems) (from Lee and Strayer, 2004, reprinted with permission from the Human Factors and Ergonomics Society).

consider an advance in-vehicle collision-avoidance warning system. Such systems are already installed in many new cars either as original equipment or as after-market safety devices (see e.g., http://www.mobileye.com/products/mobileye-5-series/), and their basic function is to warn a driver whenever his or her vehicle gets too close to another vehicle or object, and when the vehicle deviates from the lane. These devices can be a great aid in avoiding crashes, but reliance on an imperfect system – with some inevitable errors – can also lead to reduced attention and to crashes that would otherwise be avoided (Maltz and Shinar, 2004) or to greater risk taking due to reliance on these systems (LeBlanc *et al.*, 2013).

Still, even at the level of detail presented in Figure 3-2, the hierarchical model is insufficient to predict specific outcomes in specific situations. However, it is sufficient to demonstrate the role and potential impact of various factors in both crash prevention and crash occurrence. To be useful as a predictive model for specific situations, quantitative data has to be fed into the various functions of the model. Work in this direction has already yielded initial encouraging results that are applicable to well-defined specific situations such as the impact of forward collision warning (Barnard, Carsten, and Lai, 2014) and to specific behaviors such as visual scanning (Horrey, Wickens, and Vonsalus, 2006).

To move from the hierarchical structure of the driver task to working models of driver behavior, we now need to consider the variables that affect these decisions, the limitations placed on us as decision makers, and the needs and biases that we bring into the driving situation. That is the role of driving models: to explain and predict driver behavior in the context of the driver's environment, personal goals, and information processing limitations.

The two classes of models that are described below approach the issue from different perspectives, but they supplement each other more than conflict with each other, and both are useful for understanding driver behavior.

Attention and Information Processing Models

The common – though incorrect – notion that we cannot do more than one thing at a time is based on the fact that our capacity to process information is limited. In the context of driving, the typical limiting factor is the need to process information under severe temporal constraints. Driving is not so much a motor task – though autonomous vehicles notwithstanding we still need to employ our hands and feet to drive – as it is an information processing task in which most of the information is received through the visual channel. The typical limit on our capacity is not in the amount of information we have to see or attend to, but in the *rate* at which we can process that information. Because driving is a temporal task, we have limited *time* to identify the relevant information, attend to it, decide how to act on it, and actually perform the needed maneuver. Often the time limits for multiple driving-related tasks can be on the order of seconds, and sometimes even fractions of a second. As we drive, the roadway ahead and the traffic around us present a stream of stimuli to which we attend (or not) and respond (or not). While the total amount of information that a driver has to process between two points on the road is constant, the rate at which we have to process it varies as a function of our speed and the speed of other traffic on the road: the faster we drive, the more vehicles we have to consider, and the faster they move, the greater the rate of information flow. When critical information flows at a rate that is greater than our capacity, we experience a failure. That failure can take the form of missing some information, misperceiving information we attend to, or not considering all the information needed to make a decision. If any of these failures are critical to making the right decision at the appropriate time, then the situation can lead to a crash.

To better understand these limits on our processing capability, several information processing models have been proposed. One generally accepted model, proposed by Wickens (1992), is depicted in Figure 3-3. The model is a general one, not specific to driving behavior, but as applicable to it as to any other time-dependent task. According to this model our contact with the external world is through the sensory receptors. The amount of information that impinges on these sensors is staggering, and the first task of the human operator is to select from this array pertinent items of information. The information in the sensory receptors is there only briefly – stored in a short-term sensory storage (STSS) where it decays within a few seconds. Thus, before the infinite information is lost it must be scanned and its relevant and salient features must be extracted. This is the first stage of information filtering and selection, and it corresponds closely to attention. This means that information that we do not attend to is eternally lost to us. For all intents and purposes, transient unattended events never enter our consciousness and are as if they never happened. Events that we attend to are perceived, in the sense that we actually process them in an active manner. The perception is not an all-or-none process: we can process different items with varying degrees of attention, and consequently become aware of them at varying levels of consciousness. In routine driving much of the information that we process is done at a minimal level and consequently we are barely aware of it, despite the fact that we respond appropriately to it. This can include many of our reactions to traffic signs and signals as well as cars ahead and next to us. Most of the time – almost as soon as we pass these stimuli and they are no longer relevant – we cannot remember them. For example, several studies have demonstrated that immediately after passing a sign that was clearly unobstructed and often responded to, most drivers cannot recall what that sign was (Costa *et al.*, 2014; Martens, 2000; Milosevic and Gajic, 1986; Näätänen and Summala, 1976; Shinar and Drory, 1983), possibly because it was barely looked at or attended to begin with (Costa *et al.*, 2014).

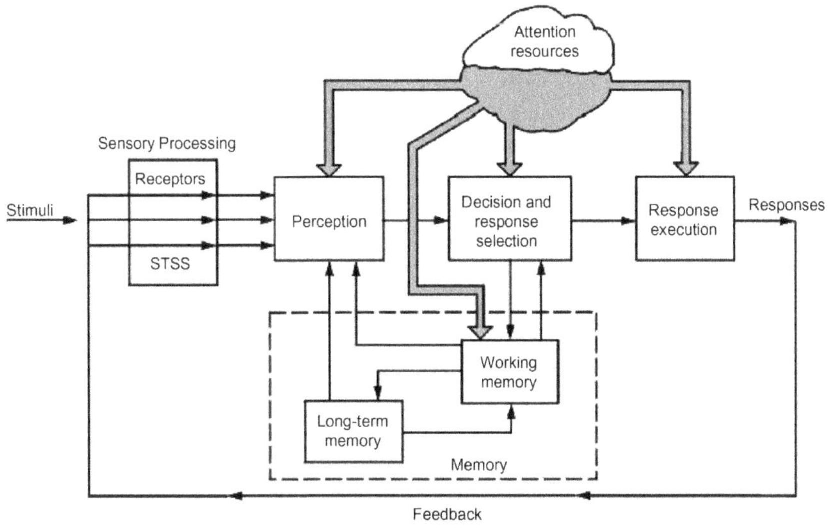

Figure 3-3. A general limited-capacity human information processing model (from Wickens, 1992).

Thus, perception is the process by which we become aware of the world around us. However, that awareness is not simply due to the stimuli impinging on our eyes, ears, nose, and proprioceptive receptors, but also due to how we interpret them with the aid of our memory of previous relevant experiences. In the model, memory is represented by two distinct storage mechanisms: short-term memory (STM) also known as working memory and long-term memory (LTM) also known as permanent storage. In many ways this distinction parallels the distinction between the working memory of a computer (RAM – random access memory) and the hard disk storage space (ROM – read only memory): the first is the one we constantly use and it is quite limited and the second is the one we occasionally refer to, in order to retrieve information, and it is bigger by several orders of magnitude. Very briefly, the two human memory systems are very different in the following respects:

1. Storage capacity: STM is extremely limited; to approximately seven unrelated pieces of information (such as the digits in an unfamiliar telephone number, and hence the typical string of digits in a phone number is seven). LTM is essentially limitless, and the implication is that we can continue to accrue new pieces of information forever, without forgetting any of the old ones.
2. Storage mechanism: Perceived information enters STM and may or may not be transferred to LTM. The transfer typically happens through rehearsal or repetition (such as recitation of a poem or a phone number, or route guidance directions), or by linking to other information by association.
3. Nature of information: The immediate information stored in STM is typically visual or acoustic in its nature while the information in LTM is typically semantic or conceptual. You tend to recall the actual words or image on a billboard off the road immediately after viewing it as they appeared, but you tend to recall – if at all – the "message" and not the specific words of the sign later on. Similarly, when we listen to a speech or try to take notes in class, our immediate memory (STM) is of the actual sounds and words. But after a short while, all we can recall is the part of the message that was transferred to LTM and not the specific words.
4. Decay of information: Information in STM can remain there indefinitely, but only as long as it is not "bumped off" by another piece of information. Thus, retention of a new phone number is lost if you are disrupted by an unrelated question. One means of preventing interference from new coming information is rehearsing it – repeating it over and over so that no other information can displace it. We often do that when we want to dial a phone number. Once we have dialed the number we allow other information to enter, only to be frustrated and needing to look the number up again if we get a busy signal. Information in LTM is practically permanent, but not always accessible or retrievable. It is analogous to a book in a library. Even if it is in the library, if it is misplaced in a wrong shelf it is as good as gone, even though physically it – and the information in it – are still in the library. Thus, the limits on LTM are mostly due to our inadequate search and retrieval. The information we are seeking may or may not be where we are searching, but it is still there "somewhere."
5. Retrieval of information: Retrieval from STM, which only contains a few items, is immediate. On the other hand, retrieval from LTM may take a long time depending on the efficiency of our search for that information.

The nature of the process so far is simple to illustrate with an example of a driver approaching and then stopping at a stop sign. The sensory information consists of a pattern of different colored dots in an octagonal shape that fall on our eyes, and our past experience helps us interpret that pattern – by retrieving the information that is already coded in LTM – as a "stop" sign. Once we obtain a match between the information that stimulates our eyes and the information retrieved from LTM, we perceive (i.e., comprehend) the image as a "stop" sign.

The next phase is the decision process. As the model shows, this phase is also heavily influenced by memory. The memory of a novice driver may be different from that of an experienced driver, and they may respond differently to the sign. To begin with, the experienced driver already has some schema (a set of experiences and relevant rules of behavior) in LTM that assist him or her in a more efficient scanning of the scene, and is therefore a priori more likely to direct the eyes toward the stop sign and detect it. This is best demonstrated when experience is actually a hindrance. For example, when a traffic sign is placed in an unexpected place, the experienced driver is less likely to detect it, while the novice driver is unaffected by the change (Borowsky, Shinar, and Parmet, 2008). Second, the experienced driver will probably know when is the best time to initiate a braking action and at what level of deceleration to do it. An experienced driver may decide to first slow down by removing the foot off the accelerator and only then brake gradually. A novice driver may continue to drive and then brake from a higher speed. An interesting example of how experience can shape behavior was provided by Routledge, Repetto-Wright, and Howarth (1976). They noted that while adults teach children to stop before they cross the street, look right-left-right (in England where cars drive on the left side of the street), and only then cross; the adults themselves do not manifest this behavior. Instead, the experienced adult pedestrian evaluates the traffic situation well before crossing the street and then adjusts the walking pace and selects the specific location of crossing so that he or she will not have to stop at all.

Once information is perceived and relevant decisions have been made, we either modify or not modify our overt response to the situation. Up to this point the process has been inferred and unobservable. The response, however, is observable and may or may not be appropriate. This is the motor aspect of behavior, and it is the one that much of the early driver training focuses on: how to brake and accelerate appropriately, how to shift gears, when to start signaling, how to negotiate a passing or turning maneuver smoothly, etc. A person can decide to make the right response, but its execution may be faulty. Because the instructor sitting next to a learner can only observe the driver's responses, it is much easier to correct the motor behavior aspects of driving than to guide the attentional and decision-making parts of the information processing sequence.

As described so far, the model is very limited. It describes the human operator as a passive information transmission channel, who performs various actions within the limits of his or her capacities. But the system has two more crucial components: the attention allocation mechanism itself and a feedback loop. The feedback loop indicates that the process we just described is a recursive ongoing one that is continuously modified in accordance with new stimuli. For example, in driving we visually perceive the rate at which we approach a car that may have stopped ahead of us, and based on that perception we modify our own braking behavior. Also, the stimuli are not limited to the road environment, the other drivers and the pedestrians, but also include our own car and the changes brought on by our own behavior. Furthermore, the stimuli to which we respond are not only visual. Our sense of proprioception – that informs us of the relative position of different parts of our body – provides us with feedback on our rate of deceleration as we stop, and if it is too abrupt we ease our foot off the brake pedal; if it is not sufficient we press harder. Our sense of proprioception is also a key factor in our speed selection and modification when we negotiate curves, and in fact is responsible for preventing us from potential rollover crashes in such circumstances (Herrin and Neuhardt, 1974), and recent research shows that it can be utilized to provide the driver with haptic steering support whenever the vehicle approaches its handling limits (Katzourakis *et al.*, 2014). In short, we constantly focus on critical stimuli which we sense, perceive, analyze, and act upon in order to continue driving safely.

Arguably the most critical component of the information processing model, in the context of driving, is the attention (Klauer *et al.*, 2006). Attention is the resource of psychic energy that we devote to the task at any time. It is a central capacity that is not specific to the individual senses. Thus, in a demanding driving situation – such as entering a congested highway – we often block irrelevant sensory information in order to devote all of our attention to the driving task. For example, we cease to hear the radio or a passenger sitting next to us until we relocate ourselves in the traffic stream and the lane of choice. In this case, all of our attention was diverted to the visual inputs for the driving task, and none was left to direct to the auditory inputs. Once in the lane, the rate of flow of visual information that we have to process is greatly diminished and we can once again divide our attention between the auditory and visual channels. We may then direct our gaze toward the road ahead of us, while being oblivious to many of the non-essential stimuli there.

Attentional capacity and distribution of attention

There are two critical aspects to the allocation of attention: the total amount of attentional capacity that we have at any one time and the distribution of that amount among various driving and non-driving tasks. The amount is finite, but it is not constant, and the distribution of attention is possible, but within limits.

From our own experience we know that we can be and generally are more attentive after a good night sleep than at the end of a long working day. But our level of available attention to the driving task varies even more dramatically from moment to moment as we divert resources from one task to another. Here, we have good and bad news. The good news is that we can allocate the total capacity that we have to different tasks at the same time. The bad news is that we don't always do it appropriately. Two advantages of a skilled and experienced driver over a novice one is that the skilled driver is both much more adaptive in the allocation of attention, and requires less attention for the driving task. The ability to adapt the allocation of attention is achieved by the experienced driver through the complementary processes of focusing attention on selected sources of information and dividing attention among several sources of interest. The efficiency is achieved through reliance on automated rather than controlled processes (discussed below).

Let us first consider the use of focused and divided attention. Much of the time that we drive we divide our attention between the driving task and various non-driving tasks. For example, while driving home from work, we may be preoccupied at processing some events from a meeting we just ended (diverting much of our attentional resources to decision-making and memory that is not related to the driving task), and only minimally paying attention to the visual stimuli from the road and traffic – but enough to manage the drive on most days most of the time. Similarly, we may be almost totally absorbed in a phone conversation or a radio broadcast while driving and unequally dividing our attention between the two tasks. Extensive research in cognitive psychology has revealed that although the process of dividing attention itself requires some attentional resources, we are generally quite good in the allocation of attention to various simultaneous tasks (Wickens and Hollands, 2000).

An interesting aspect of our ability to divide attention among multiple sources of information is that this ability is not constant but depends on the amount of resources the multiple tasks demand and extent to which these demands are placed on the same or different dimensions of the information processing resources. In a well validated model known as the "Theory of Multiple Resources" Wickens (1984) showed that these different dimensions include (1) the stages of processing (perception + memory versus response selection + execution), (2) the input modalities (visual versus auditory, though there could be more), and (3) the response modalities (manual/spatial versus verbal/auditory). In experiments designed to validate the model, Wickens and his colleagues (Horrey *et al.*, 2006) noted that within the perceptual dimension, inputs to the peripheral and focal system do not conflict with each other and so the model was modified to include these as independent inputs. An example of such non-interfering dual processing is the management of the car position within the lane by relying on peripheral stimulation of lane markers while focusing on objects ahead that could turn into safety-critical events such as a change in the signal light. The model predicts that multiple tasks that load on different components of the three dimensions interfere less with each other than multiple tasks that load on the same ones. This makes the model extremely important for predicting the impact of various tasks and for designing various in-vehicle systems. For example, it predicts that texting while driving should be much more demanding and detrimental to driving than talking on the phone while driving, as the former competes for the same inputs and responses as the driving (visual and manual) while the latter employs different inputs (auditory) and responses (verbal). Recent research in this area provides strong support for this prediction (Fitch *et al.*, 2013; Klauer *et al.*, 2013; see Chapter 13 for a detailed discussion of the distraction issue).

In a complementary process to multi-tasking or the division of attention, we can also focus our attention on selected sources of information and ignore irrelevant stimuli (that constitute noise). This is classically demonstrated by the "cocktail party phenomenon" where we are able to maintain a conversation with one person while ignoring the many other conversations going on around us, even if their volume levels exceed ours (Cherry, 1953). In general, division of attention is more difficult than focusing attention. We are much less efficient in our attempts to simultaneously attend to multiple sources (divided attention) than in our attempts to focus on specific stimuli while ignoring others (selective or focused attention).

The limits of attention are one of the primary reasons for accidents, as illustrated in Figure 3-4, which is based on an early cognitive model of driving proposed by Blumenthal (1968). In this simplistic and intuitively appealing model the X-axis represents travel time and the Y-axis represents the attentional energy allocated to and required by the driving task. The two curves represent the moment-to-moment variations in the attention demanded by the road and the traffic (dashed line) and the energy, or attentional resources, allocated by the driver to the road and the traffic (continuous line). If we think of the demands in terms of the rate of information that the road and traffic present to us, then it is easy to accept that this rate varies greatly. It is very low when we drive slowly down a deserted rural road. It increases as we increase our speed; it increases further as more traffic joins the road; and it can become quite high in specific situations such as high-speed merging maneuvers on motorways. Fortunately, most of the time we can anticipate the attentional requirements and the energy we allocate to the driving task is above the level that is required. We manage to do this because part of the driving skill that we have all acquired is good situation awareness (SA) (discussed below): the rapid comprehension of the driving situation and the ability to predict events. For example, we know that a light that has just turned red will typically stay that way for the next 20-40 seconds and we can relax our attention while we wait for it to change – to the point of quickly reading some newspaper

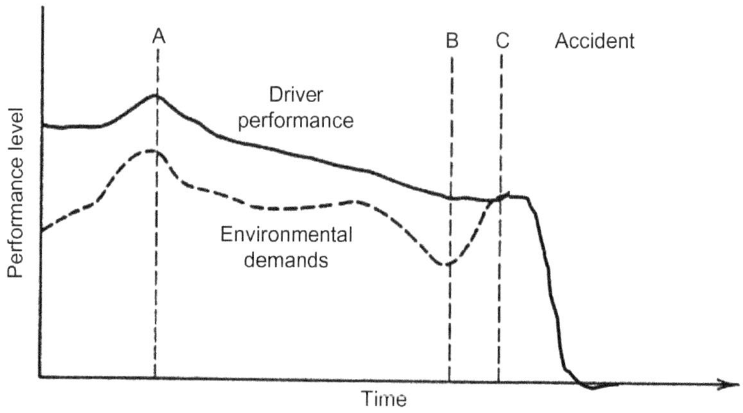

Figure 3-4. A simple model depicting the relationship between the temporal changes in the attention demands of the drive and the attention levels allocated by the driver. A is a typical situation when the amount allocated is greater than the amount needed. B is a situation with a sudden increase in demand that is not perceived by the driver. C is the situation when the demand exceeds the attention allocated and a crash results (adapted from Blumenthal, 1968).

headlines. We also know that at the end of the green phase, a brief (typically 3 seconds in Israel) yellow phase will be followed by a red light. So when approaching a green light we have to allocate more attention in order to analyze our situation and take an immediate action (to speed or to brake) if the green phase ends. However, every once in a while – fortunately quite rarely – the demand suddenly and unexpectedly increases to a level beyond the level of allocated attention – while we are distracted by a pedestrian on the curb or by a phone conversation – as when the car ahead suddenly stops. It is then that we have a crash!

The distinction between controlled and automated processes was first defined and studied by Schneider and Shiffrin (1977). In a series of laboratory studies they demonstrated that the process by which we learn to deal with complex situations involves the "automation" of various sequences of behavior. Prior to automation each component in that behavior is controlled through monitoring and feedback. This process is relatively slow, requires much attention, and prevents us from doing other tasks simultaneously. As we repeatedly perform some of these sequences, the process becomes automated, in the sense that once it is initiated, the sequence of actions is hardly monitored, requires minimal attention, and is performed more or less unconsciously. Changing manual gears has often been used as an example of a controlled process that through repeated experience becomes automated (Shinar, Meir, and Ben-Shoham, 1998). The concepts of controlled and automated processes are discussed in more details in Chapter 5 on Information Processing.

A driver information processing model

We can now consider Wickens' model in light of Blumenthal's focus on the importance of allocating attentional resources, and apply both to a driver information processing model, such as the one described in Figure 3-5. I proposed this model nearly 40 years ago (Shinar, 1978), and it is sufficiently general that it is still valid today. In fact, a similar model is one of the models currently used to guide the human factors research on driving safety at the Netherlands' Organization for Applied Scientific Research (TNO) (Keith *et al.*, 2005). This model presents the driver as a limited-capacity controlling element in the driver-vehicle-roadway system. This limited capacity is used to perceive the driving-related (and distracting) cues, make instantaneous decisions, and act on them through the vehicle controls. Because the central processing capacity is quite limited, the first step the driver must take is to filter much of the stimulation that impinges on his or her senses. This includes visual inputs from other drivers, pedestrians, traffic signs and signals, and his or her vehicle's own displays such as the speedometer and the mirrors. There are also auditory inputs from other vehicles, other drivers and pedestrians, the driver's own car and proprioceptive inputs from the driver's own body when he or she accelerates, decelerates, or turns a corner. And these are only the driving-relevant stimuli. In addition there are irrelevant stimuli such as billboards (including dynamic electronic billboards) and scenery outside the car as well as in-vehicle distractions from stereo systems, cellular phones, navigation systems, and passengers; distractions that can be auditory, visual, or both. All of these can have a significant impact on the driver's allocation of attention, behavior, and crash rates, as described in the following chapters.

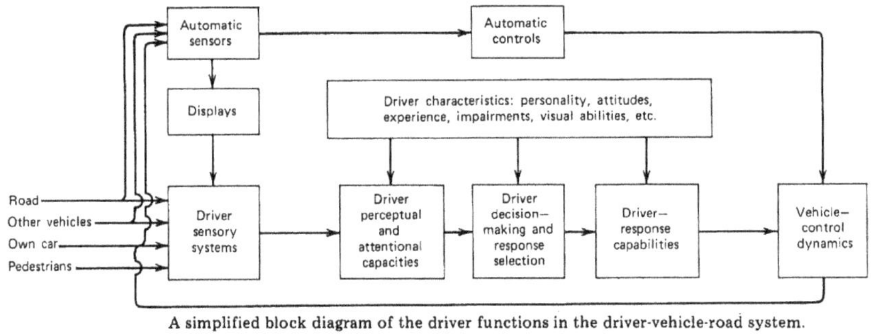

Figure 3-5. A limited-capacity model of driver information processing (from Shinar, 1978).

To alleviate some of the demands on the driver's limited information processing capabilities, a plethora of driver aids have been proposed, tested, and in some cases implemented in many new vehicles. These have included automatic sensing devices that act to either alert drivers to impending crashes (such as in-vehicle crash avoidance warnings – IVCAW; Maltz and Shinar, 2004; Wege, Will, and Victor, 2013) or actually intervene in the vehicle control (such as adaptive cruise control systems, anti-lock braking systems, and electronic stability control; often referred to as ACC, ABS, and ESC, respectively; see Chapter 19).

The efficiency and appropriateness of the selection of the information and its processing depend on many factors too. They are listed in Figure 3-5 under the general heading of driver characteristics. Although most of these factors are unobservable, they are very real: they include the driver's level of fatigue, possible intoxication, amount of experience, familiarity with the vehicle and the road, and various motivations and needs that govern the way the driver drives. By any criterion this is indeed a complex process. Given that complexity, it is actually amazing that most of the time, most of the drivers manage to drive within inches of each other (in parallel and opposing lanes) at speeds that are definitely greater than those for which humans were designed (i.e., walking and running speeds), without repeatedly colliding with each other.

Blumenthal's, Shinar's, and Wickens' models leave a most important issue unanswered: what determines the driver's attention allocation strategy? Once we can answer this question, we can design effective countermeasures to increase and properly direct the driver's attention to the relevant sources of information; and also – in some situations – redesign the environment so that its attentional demands will not overwhelm the drivers. This issue is addressed by motivational models described later in this chapter.

Measuring mental task load

Given the predominance of the information processing approach to assessing driver behavior, it is worthwhile to briefly describe the main methods that have been developed to measure it. In general three approaches have been used to assess mental task load: performance based measures using a secondary task, physiological measures of stress, and subjective evaluations of mental load.

Performance on a secondary task

The use of a secondary task derives directly from the information processing model. If a primary task – such as driving – does not require all of our processing capacities, then when another task – such as a phone conversation – is added, it is difficult to assess the added load that it imposes. One way to solve this problem is to give the driver an additional task that is difficult enough so that the driver cannot perform it perfectly. With two tasks – the driving task and the secondary task – the driver is then already overloaded in the sense that despite all the attentional capacity allocated, performance falls short of perfect. We then introduce the task whose demands we would like to assess, such as a distracting phone task, and measure by how much the secondary task performance is degraded. The rationale for this approach is illustrated in Figure 3-6. We can illustrate the application of this model to driver behavior with a study conducted by Patten *et al.* (2004) on the effects of a cell phone task on driving. Consider driving without talking on the phone the easy primary task in Figure 3-6, and driving while talking on the phone the more difficult task. Because in both situations the driver's maximum capacity is not exceeded, it is impossible to tell how taxing the added phone task is. To assess the mental load imposed by the cell phone task, we now add a "secondary task" (though it is already a third task, after driving and talking on the phone) – such as detecting visual targets presented in the peripheral visual field.

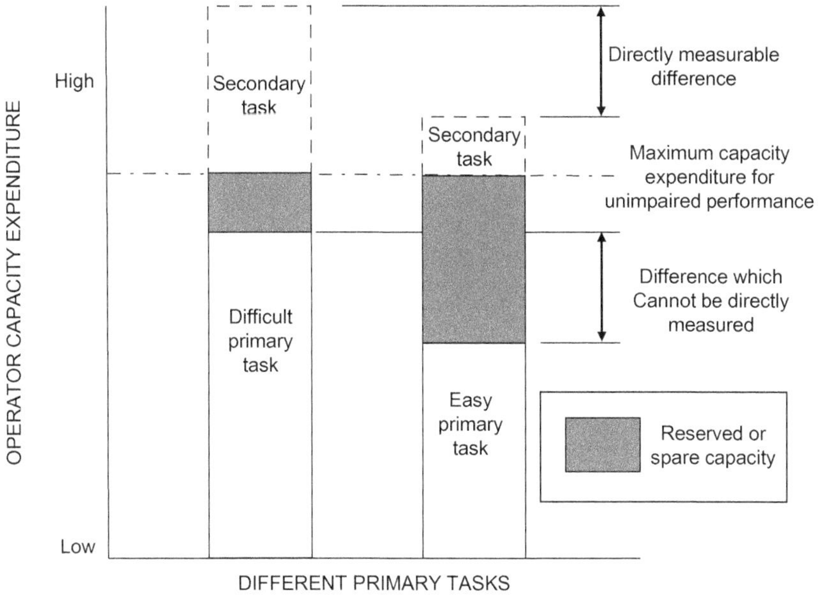

Figure 3-6. The subsidiary task paradigm (from O'Donnel and Eggemeier, 1986, with permission from Wiley-Liss, Inc., a subsidiary of John Wiley & Sons, Inc.).

With this additional task, we now exceed the driver's maximum capacity as indicated in Figure 3-6. The difference in performance on the detection task between the driving task alone and the driving task while talking on the phone can now be estimated directly from the difference in the performance on the target detection task. The secondary task method has also been used to demonstrate that novice drivers experience a much greater mental load than experienced drivers even when they drive in the same environments (Patten *et al.*, 2004).

Physiological indicators of stress
There are various physiological indicators of stress that are used to measure mental task load. One of the more popular measures that have been related to driver task load in particular is heart rate variability (HRV – the variability around the mean heart rate). While the mean level of heart rate is primarily sensitive to physical – and not mental – stress, the variability of the heart rate around the mean level is sensitive to mental load. During rest, the heart rate is quite variable. As the level of stress or mental task load increases, the HRV decreases, and the relative change from a relaxed or resting position can then serve as a reliable indicator of stress and workload (Brookhuis and de Waard, 1993; 2001). Average heart rate is much more sensitive to physical workload, but it too has been used to measure mental stress or task load (Liu and Lee, 2006). Other measures include electrical evoked brain potentials (Gopher and Donchin, 1986) and pupil diameter (the larger the pupil the greater the load – Kahneman and Beatty 1966; Kahneman, Beatty, and Pollack 1967).

Subjective scales of mental load
The most direct way of assessing mental load is simply asking people how loaded they feel. Because "mental load" may be a multi-dimensional concept, different indices have been developed in which people are asked to rate their level of load on different dimensions. Perhaps the most popular of all subjective mental task load indices is the one developed by the U.S. National Aeronautical and Space Administration: the NASA-TLX. This measure is based on questions pertaining to six self-reported different dimensions of stress: mental demands, physical demands, temporal demands, performance (the perceived task accomplishment), effort exerted, and frustration felt. A composite measure based on all dimensions is also calculated to give the total task load index. Other measures of subjective task load have also been used, including a multi-dimensional scale known as Subjective Workload Assessment Scale (SWAT), and even a simple one-question of "overall task load experienced." Interestingly, in a study that compared the scores people gave to the same tasks with the different scales, the correlations among all subjective ratings were quite high, indicating that for a single one-dimensional assessment of workload the single "overall workload" question may be just as good as the more complicated tests (Hill *et al.*, 1992). The NASA-TLX has been extensively used to assess the workload imposed by the use of in-vehicle technologies, such as cell phones, on driving (see Chapter 13).

Endsley's situation awareness model and efficient information processing

Responding to all the inputs in a timely manner while driving at high speeds would be close to impossible if in fact we had no way of streamlining the information processing task. Automatic processing goes a long way toward that goal, but not enough. There are simply too many stimuli to attend to, too many alternatives to consider, and not enough time to make proper rational decisions based on unbounded knowledge of all the relevant information. So we have to devise a method of making rational decisions that are limited to or "bounded" by our past experience. We do that through a process known as Situation Awareness (SA).

SA has been studied extensively by researchers of human behavior in complex systems. It refers to an ability of an operator to effectively filter information in a data-rich environment. Driving, being a very rich environment, easily lends itself to this need to filter information, and so the issue becomes one of how to filter the information effectively. Endsley, one of the leading researchers in this area, defines SA as "the perception of the elements in the environment within a volume of time and space, the comprehension of their meaning, and the projection of their status to the near future" (Endsley, 1995, p. 36). Thus, the concept involves three hierarchical levels: perception, comprehension of meaning, and projection to the future. Applied to the driving environment, at the perceptual level the driver would have to perceive among other things, the roadway geometry, other vehicles and road users, their relation relative to his or her vehicle, and the speed and acceleration of all vehicles, including the driver's own. At the comprehension level the driver has to understand the "significance of those elements in light of (his or her) goals." To do so, the driver has to create a "holistic picture of the environment comprehending the significance of objects and events" (Endsley, 1995, p. 37). Finally, at the highest level the driver must perceive the implications of this pattern of events and objects for the near and the immediate future in order to take the most appropriate action. For example, an experienced driver approaching a traffic signal that has just turned green will typically also observe the behavior of the cross traffic, and project the slowing down or speeding up of a crossing car to the next few seconds, in order to decide if to slow down to accommodate it or to ignore it and accelerate into the intersection.

In layman's terms, Endsley suggests that SA basically means "knowing what is going on." She also distinguishes among three mechanisms involved in SA: (1) short-term sensory storage, (2) working memory that includes perception, interpretation of the situation, and projection from it to the future, decision-making, and action guidance – all of which are affected by attention allocation, and (3) long-term memory that includes various schemata – experience-based frameworks for understanding various patterns of elements and events; and scripts – schemata for sequences of appropriate actions – that guide the operator's decisions and actions. The model, presented in Figure 3-7, has many similarities to Wickens' and Shinar's models of information processing. This is not by chance. SA builds on the information processing model, and attempts to define how we actually use these mechanisms in the process of highly learned, but complex, skills like driving. In such situations with information overload from high rate of information presentation and the need to rapidly make complex decisions and perform multiple tasks, the needed capacity can easily exceed that of the driver, and unless the driver can adjust the rate of information input (e.g., by slowing down), an accident can occur. This in fact is a relatively rare occasion because in the course of gaining experience we learn

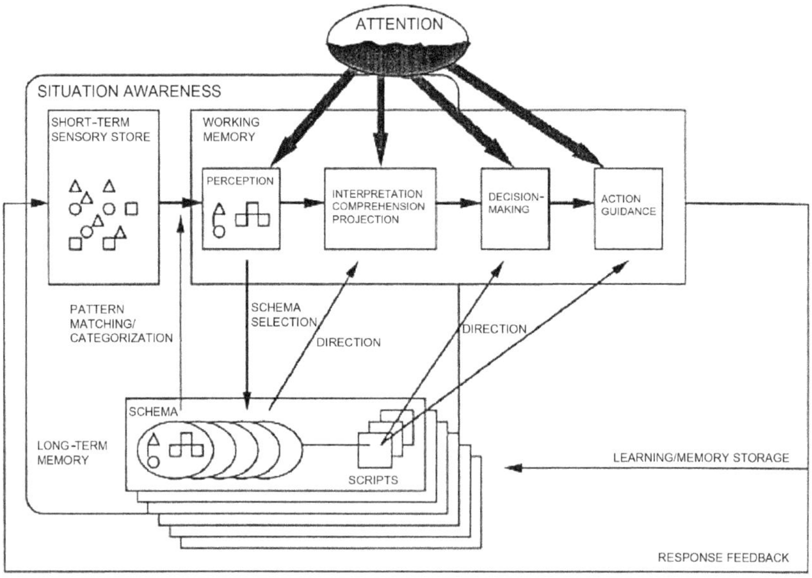

Figure 3-7. The mechanisms involved in situation awareness (from Endsley, 1995, reprinted with permission from the Human Factors and Ergonomics Society).

to select cues from our environment more efficiently, perceive the relevant ones more quickly, utilize various remembrances (schemas) in long-term memory, to identify their implications, and to retrieve effective appropriate action plans (scripts) in a timely fashion to deal with the situation.

To illustrate the relevance of SA for driving, let us consider the case of hazard perception and hazard avoidance for a novice and an experienced driver. Hazard perception is a critical skill that correlates with crash involvement (Horswill, Hill, and Wetton, 2015) and distinguishes skilled drivers from novice drivers (Horswill and McKenna, 2004). To develop the three levels of SA – perceive, comprehend, and project – for any given situation, a novice driver must, under the time constraints of driving, be able to quickly select the cues that are indicative of a hazard, integrate them into holistic patterns, comprehend their implications, project how the situation may evolve into a potential accident, and select the necessary action from his or her repertoire of driving behaviors. The more experience a driver has, the greater the repertoire of situations and schemata he or she has in long-term memory. Thus, with experience the driver learns to effectively select the cues to attend to, quickly perceive their meanings, and on the basis of these cues quickly identify the situation and project its implications into the immediate future (Borowsky, Shinar, and Oron-Gilad, 2010; 2012; Lim, Sheppard, and Crundall, 2014). Using scripts built through past experience this driver then controls the vehicle in a very effective manner. This mode of driving is very effective because behaviors are guided by partial information that has been previously organized into complete situations which in turn are linked to pre-established behavior sequences. Thus, much of the driving can be automated, and when a totally unexpected hazard (e.g., one never encountered before) is encountered the driver still has spare capacity to deal with it. The novice driver, in contrast, does not have all of these benefits of experience and therefore must attend to more stimuli, which necessitate slower driving in environments that are not as complex in order to build up the necessary skills and repertoire of experiences. As this driver accumulates experience, more and more of the driving scene is recognized through schemata and more and more of the behavior is automated; allowing the driver to better attend to other driving tasks, or to time-share the driving with non-driving tasks (such as talking on the phone). This in fact is the rationale behind the controlled gradual exposure in the graduated driving licensing paradigm (see Chapter 6). Results of driver eye movement research support this model and show that novice drivers are less efficient in their visual scanning (Borowsky *et al.*, 2010; Konstantopoulos, Chapman, and Crundall, 2010; Mourant and Rockwell, 1972); that experienced drivers adapt their scanning to the various environments more readily than novice drivers (Crundall, Underwood, and Chapman, 1998); that older drivers are better than novice drivers at detecting far hazards (Brown, 1982) and can be trained to improve that skill (Horswill *et al.*, 2010); and that advance police training in hazardous driving leads to both faster hazard perception reaction times (McKenna and Crick, 1994), and more appropriate speed adjustments in hazardous situations (McKenna, Horswill, and Alexander, 2006).

Automation is also involved in driving on familiar roads. Charlton and Starkey (2013) had drivers drive the same route for 20 sessions over a period of three months in a driving simulator. While the road geometry remained the same, there were occasional slight variations in the scenery and occasional targets that had to be detected. As expected, they found that driving effort declined over the repeated exposure and people started to describe the experience as "driving without thinking about it" or "going on autopilot." However, when familiar landmarks or critical driving cues (such as lane markers) were removed the rated difficulty increased. Thus, even when driving without awareness, changes in the scenery caught the drivers' attention and resulted in a shift from mostly automated driving to largely controlled driving.

The concepts of SA, schemata, and scripts all have uses in understanding driver behavior, and in developing driver education and training programs to make driving safe and efficient. Drivers can be trained to develop schematas and scripts that can help them recognize and respond appropriately to hazards. Knowledge of schematas and scripts that drivers have can enable us to estimate what we can and cannot expect from drivers with particular levels and types of experience in particular environments. This knowledge can also serve highway and vehicle designers in their quest for reducing the driver information load. In all of these respects the SA theory is a very good theory: it is practical.

Rational Decision-Making Models

Many of us like to think that we behave in a rational manner. This is not always the case, and economists often use the "rational man" model only as a straw man, to demonstrate and understand biases in the actual behavior of people, especially in their purchasing decisions. Our decisions are biased in many ways, and only recently have some of the psychological biases been understood (Kahneman, 2013; Tversky and Kahneman, 1992). Still, there is reason to our behavior; at least on many occasions and at least within limits of the information available to us. The challenge to the rational model of driver behavior is to allow for all our limitations and biases. Conceptual approaches to explaining and predicting driver behavior in the context of a process of "rational" decisions have been offered by Sivak (2002), Fuller (2005), and Parker and her associates (1992).

Application of "bounded rationality" to driver behavior

In the context of driving, Sivak (2002) and Elvik (2016) suggest that we consider the economic concepts of "bounded" and "unbounded" rationality as tools to understand driver and pedestrian behavior. Decisions based on unbounded rationality consider all of the alternative options, the use of all the information needed to select among them, unlimited processing capabilities to analyze them, and no restriction of time. Obviously, in driving when decisions often have to be made almost instantaneously this is not the case. Bounded rationality is what we use when we do not have all the information, processing capacity, and time to consider all of the options. Our rationality is then "bounded" or restricted by some limits of knowledge and time, and our decisions are further biased by needs and misperceptions. Thus, bounded rationality is a form of experience-based behavior modification. This is the typical situation we have in driving. Sivak (2002) provides an example of a driver waiting at a stop sign to cross the street. Unbounded rationality would suggest that the driver first calculate the temporal gap needed to cross the street and then observe the opposing traffic for the first opportunity of such a gap based on the speed and distance between cars in the crossing traffic. With bounded rationality, we set a criterion gap that we consider safe, based on our past experience (which may or may not be totally safe), and then observe the traffic for such a gap. However, our estimates of the gaps are actually flawed, and the longer we wait, the greater the risk we might assume by adding other considerations, such as an expectation that a crossing driver will slow down once he or she sees us entering his or her path. By simply observing the behavior of a driver stopped at an intersection we cannot know how flawed the bounded rationality of the driver is until we observe a collision – something that would never occur with unbounded rationality, because no driver would voluntarily enter the intersection knowing that a collision would result. If we now add the limits of bounded rationality to the hierarchical models in Figures 3-1 and 3-2, we can see how the bounded rationality can affect all three decision levels of this hierarchy, leading to potentially very dangerous behaviors on the road. For example, bounded rationality can account for a driver's speed choice between the two alternatives of speeding up and slowing down. If the goal is to arrive at the destination as quickly as possible without being in a crash or being stopped for speeding then the past experiences in these domains can account for the speed chosen (Schmidt-Daffy, 2014). Elvik (2016) argues that within limits the theory of bounded rationality can account for the success of some safety communication campaigns, and can serve as a guide to better campaigns that can affect road users' bounded rationality.

Ajzen's theory of planned behavior (TPB)

The theory of planned behavior (TPB), proposed by Ajzen, is an attempt to explain behavior in a social context. It was derived from an earlier formulation of a social behavior model – that of reasoned behavior – proposed approximately 40 years ago by Fishbein and Ajzen (Ajzen and Fishbein, 1980; Fishbein and Ajzen, 1975). According to the theory of reasoned behavior, when people are in full control of their behavior, it can be easily tracked to their intentions, which in turn are based on their attitudes and subjective (internalized) norms. In short, we are responsible for our actions and we supposedly behave as we planned. In reality, in most social contexts we do not have full control of our behavior. In that respect, driving definitely occurs in a social context much of the time (even when other drivers are not present we stop at a stop light because we have internalized the prevailing social norm – or, in some parts of the world – such as New York City at 3 am – some drivers do *not* stop for the same reason). To account for this, Ajzen (1991) proposed the TPB that is schematically illustrated in Figure 3-8. This figure illustrates how we formulate our intentions to commit any behavior (e.g., speeding) on the basis of the attitude we have toward that behavior (e.g., we enjoy speed, believe it is safe, and tend to do it in the absence of constraints), the subjective norm we embrace (e.g., all of our friends do it, except for the "sissies" and the "nerds"), and the perceived

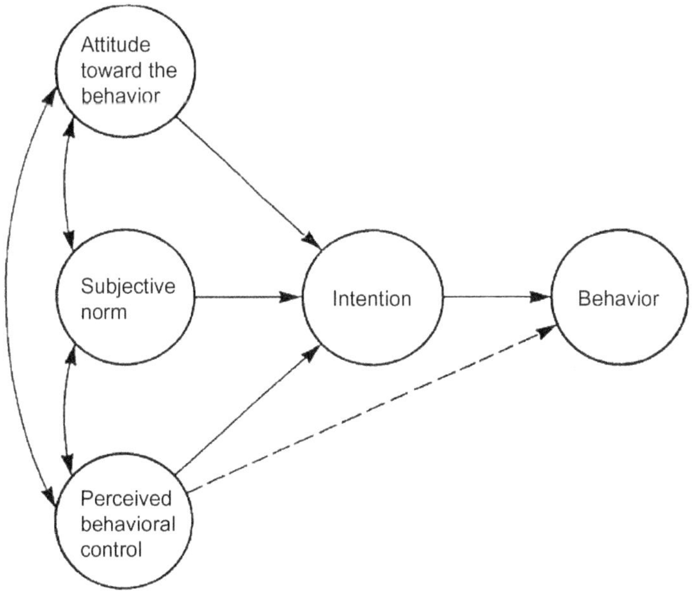

Figure 3-8. Schematic representation of Ajzen's theory of planned behavior (from Ajzen, 1991, with permission from Elsevier).

control on this behavior (e.g., there is a speed camera immediately up the road or the road is straight and empty and there is no enforcement in sight). The three factors may provide us with consistent information (e.g., there is no enforcement in sight) in which case the intention and the behavior follow in a very predictable manner (we intend to and we speed). But often the information from the three sources is not consistent (e.g., there is a speed camera ahead), and then the resulting behavior is a resolution of the relative risks involved in the alternative behaviors (e.g., we might restrain ourselves from speeding or we might take a risk and speed in the hope that the camera is inoperative).

Ajzen's TPB has been extremely fertile in spawning hypotheses and predicting multiple aspects of health-related behaviors (McEachan *et al.*, 2011). In the context of driving, it has been successfully applied to explain and predict risky driving that involves conscious violations (rather than unintended errors) (Parker *et al.*, 1992), aggressive driving (Efrat and Shoham, 2013; Özkan and Lajunen, 2005), driver education programs for young drivers (Brijs *et al.*, 2014), effects of peer pressure on young drivers (Møller and Haustein, 2014), speeding in general (Elliott and Armitage, 2009) and of young drivers in particular (Cestac, Paran, Delhomme, 2011; 2014); pedestrians' street-crossing behavior (Holland and Hill, 2007; Zhou and Horrey, 2010); mobile phone use (Waddell and Wiener, 2014; Zhou *et al.*, 2012), and drinking and driving (Castanier and Woodman, 2013; Elias *et al.*, 2016; Johnson and Voas, 2004).

To illustrate, how the theory is useful we can consider the study by Iversen and Rundmo (2004). They demonstrated the utility of the model in a survey of the attitudes of a nationally representative sample of Norwegian drivers. In their study they examined the correlation between drivers' self-reported attitudes and near accidents and their accidents and violations history. The results, reproduced in part in Figure 3-9 demonstrate how attitudes toward violations and speeding, careless driving, and drinking and driving related to risky driving behaviors, and how the latter are significantly associated with crash involvement. In this schematic representation, attitudes were based on the drivers' tendencies to violate traffic rules and to speed, including the overtaking of others even when they keep appropriate speed, and ignoring and breaking traffic rules to proceed

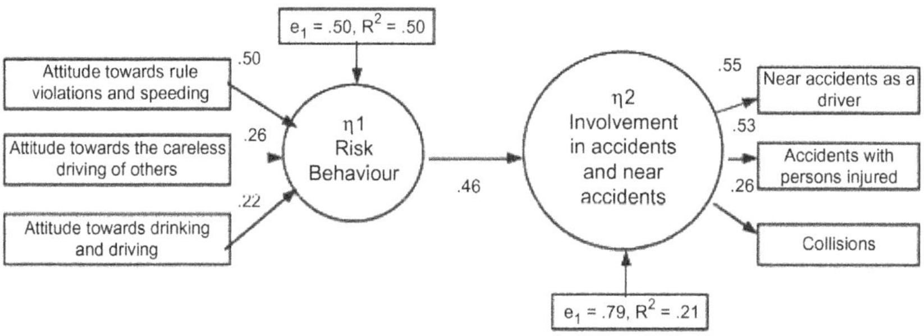

Figure 3-9. The associations between attitudes toward safe driving behaviors, risky behaviors, and accident involvement (from Iversen and Rundmo, 2004, with permission from Taylor and Francis, Ltd. http://www.informaworld.com).

faster. Reckless driving attitudes included driving too close to the car in front, creating dangerous situations caused by lack of attention, and driving without any or enough safety margins. Drinking and driving included attitudes toward driving after drinking more than one glass of beer or wine, and attitudes toward riding with someone who the respondent knows has been drinking too much. Together, these variables accounted for 50 percent of the variance in the respondents' inclinations toward engaging in risky behaviors. These behavioral inclinations, in turn, correlated quite highly with the combined measure of accident involvement. In assessing the predictive power of the TPB, it is important to note that the predictive power cannot be higher than the reliability of the predicting measures. This is a serious limitation because questionnaire-based assessments of attitudes, subjective norms, and perceived behavioral control rarely exceed $r = 0.80$ (Ajzen, 2011). In addition, the strength of the predictive power is moderated by the time interval between the stated intentions and the measured behaviors (McEachan *et al.*, 2011), and this is often a significant interval.

Fuller's task-capability interface (TCI) model and risk allostasis theory (RAT) of driving behavior

How is attention allocated within the maximal performance limits of each function specified in Wickens' model (Figure 3-3)? The answer is that it depends on a variety of things. Fortunately, we are fairly flexible in our allocation, and seem to be able to change allocation of attention fairly quickly. The change is determined by multiple factors – both endogenous (such as an individual driver's experience, skills, attitudes, etc.), and exogenous (such as the road, weather, and traffic conditions). An attempt to address that issue is made in a model that focuses on the relationship between the driving demands and the driver's capacities to handle them. The Task-Capability interface model was first proposed by Fuller in 2005, who later revised it slightly and renamed it risk allostasis theory (Fuller, 2011). The schematic representation of the earlier model is depicted in Figure 3-10.

In this model the main diagonal line represents the crossover point from a non-collision situation (control) to one involving a collision. Whenever the task demands (denoted as D) exceed the driver's capabilities (denoted as C) we enter the situation of "loss of control" which may turn into a collision or – when we are lucky because other drivers compensate for our mistakes or a forgiving highway is there for us – a "lucky escape." The added value of this model to that of Blumenthal's (1968) is in the additional boxes that specify the sources of the task demands on the one hand and the limits on the driver's capabilities – the "human factors" – on the other hand. The shortcoming of this model is that it does not address the time-dependent contingencies that are so critical to driving and that are a focus of attention in the previous models.

An interesting concept that ties this model to Blumenthal's early model is "task difficulty." Task difficulty is the driver's subjective appraisal of the disparity between the capabilities allocated to the task of driving and the demands placed on performing the task successfully. When the capabilities allocated greatly exceed the demands the task is

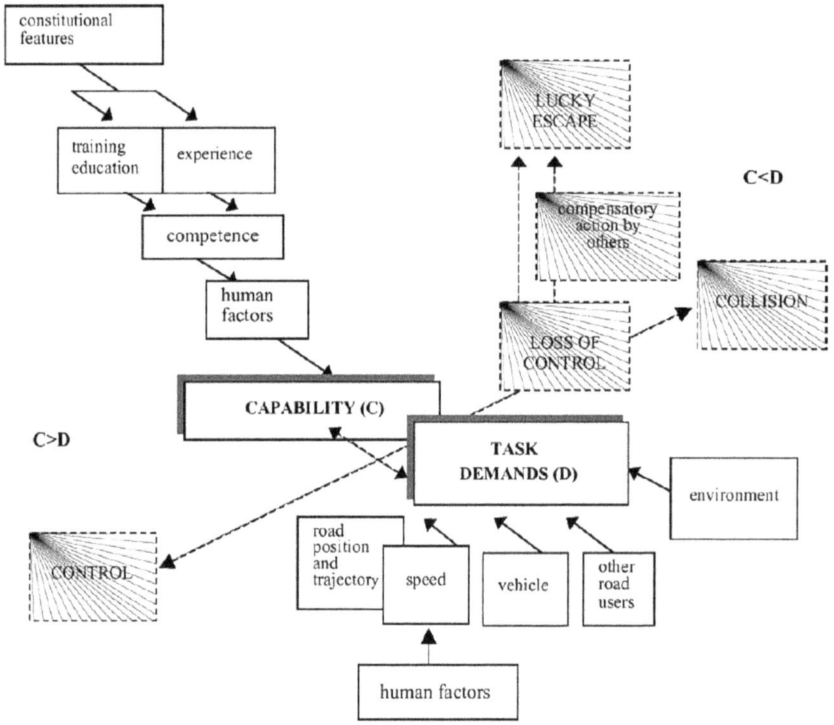

Figure 3-10. Driver capacity versus driving demands model (reprinted from Fuller, 2005, with permission from Elsevier).

easy. When the capabilities allocated match the demands the task, the safe control of the vehicle is maintained but the task is perceived as difficult. However, when the demands exceed the capabilities, the driver loses control, and – depending on the forgiveness of the roadway and compensation by other road users – may or may not have an accident. Loss of control may be limited to forgoing some safe behaviors and not necessarily to total loss of control. For example, an experienced driver would check the rear-view mirror before braking abruptly to verify that he or she is not being tailgated. However, in a very demanding situation – such as the unexpected and abrupt braking of a car ahead – this precautionary behavior may be omitted. A rear end collision is then avoided only if there are no cars immediately behind the driver. Chain collisions on motorways are typical of such situations when all the drivers are proceeding at high speed and short headways, assuming that no one will brake suddenly. Once the first driver violates this assumption, the drivers behind often lose control in the sense that they cannot reallocate their attention and respond appropriately in sufficient time given the short headways and long stopping distances.

In Fuller's model, the driving demands are quite easy to assess and quantify. They consist of the vehicle dynamics and characteristics (e.g., acceleration, field of view), the roadway characteristics (e.g., shoulders, lane markings, potholes, signs, and signals), and other road users (e.g., other drivers and pedestrians). Fuller also includes speed as a demand. This is because once a driver selects a speed – although it is a "human factor" that we can select to fit our capabilities, it becomes part of the driving conditions, with implications for the task demands. For example, to respond to a change in a traffic signal light when the driver is at a given distance from the intersection, the faster a driver is driving the faster he or she must respond to the changing light. This makes driving very different from externally paced tasks (such as working on a production line). Because driving most often is self-paced, we have a significant control over the task demands. This is an essential characteristic of driving that complicates much of the research in this area. For example, elderly drivers (see Chapter 8) whose driving skills are often impaired, control their safety by driving at low speeds and in low risk situations. Similar speed compensations have also been noted for drivers under the influence of marijuana (see Chapter 12) and drivers talking on their cell phones (see Chapter 13).

On the driver capabilities side of the equation, Fuller notes that our long-term capabilities are based on the competence that we bring to the driving situation. This, in turn, is based on our experience, driver education, and training, which are discussed in detail in Chapter 6. Beyond these human factors, the model also acknowledges the driver's "constitutional features." These include various personality attributes, attitudes, and cognitive style that are discussed in Chapter 9. They also include various states of consciousness that can reduce overall capabilities such as alcohol impairment, drug impairment, distraction, and fatigue (discussed in Chapters 11-14, respectively). The inclusion of the constitutional features is a significant addition to Blumenthal's and Wickens' models, because it acknowledges motivational factors that affect our driving style, with implications for our information processing capabilities that affect our driving performance.

Given all these human factors, we can now see that the task difficulty varies not only as a function of the changing road demands, but also as a function of fluctuating capabilities allocated to the driving task. How then does the driver adjust the gap between the two? According to Fuller, "drivers are motivated to maintain a preferred level of task difficulty," and "speed choice is the primary solution to the problem of keeping task difficulty within selected boundaries" (2005, p. 467).

In its revised version, as Risk Allostasis Theory (RAT), Fuller notes that two emotions that drive speed choice are fear (when it is perceived as too high) and frustration (when it is perceived as too low) (Fuller, 2011). The concept of allostasis implies that the risk the driver selects is not a statistical constant but an equilibrium that is sought in a constantly changing driving situation. Furthermore, the notion of risk here is a subjective one – the feeling of risk – rather than an objective risk tied to empirical data (as in Wilde's theory below). To illustrate, if we perceive the driving task demands as low (such as when driving within a posted low speed limit zone on a deserted rural road), then rather than increase the gap between demands and capabilities, we instead reduce the capabilities allocated to the task and end up with "spare" capacity that may be allocated to non-driving tasks such as talking on the phone or listening to the radio. In a corresponding manner, if for some reason we decide to allocate some of our attention to a non-driving task (such as talking on the phone), we can maintain the desired task difficulty or risk by reducing the task demands through a reduction in speed (Lansdown, Brook-Carter, and Kersloot, 2004; Shinar, Tractinsky, and Compton, 2005) or an increase in headways (Jamson *et al.*, 2004). This, in fact, has been demonstrated in controlled studies where people were required to share the driving with phone tasks (Brookhuis, De Vries, and de Waard, 1991; Recarte and Nunes, 2003; Shinar *et al.*, 2005 – see Chapter 13).

The hypothesized desire to maintain a constant level of task difficulty has two critical implications: The first is that when the demands are perceived as low and the attention allocated is correspondingly low, we may not have enough time to adjust to a sudden increase in the demands (as illustrated in Point C in Blumenthal's model in Figure 3-4). The second implication is that as highway and automotive engineers design safer roads and vehicles, we adjust to that by allowing ourselves to devote less and less of our capacity to the task, and thus the overall safety is not improved. This brings forth the issue of motivation. What motives play a part in the way we transport ourselves from one place to another? Do we strive to maximize safety (obviously not)? Minimize time (not always)? Maximize pleasure or comfort (sometimes)? Are there other motives that come into play? The obvious answer is that we try to do it all. This is where motivational models come into play.

Motivational Models

Motivational models of driver behavior are labeled as such because they emphasize the driver motivations – rather than the driver capacity – as a key determinant of the driving style and safety. Fuller's model incorporates the motivational aspect through the driver's "constitutional features" but certainly does not make that the heart of the model. Motivational models assume that most of the time we do not allocate all of our attentional capacities to the safe negotiation of our car. Safety is just one motive, and – judging by the marketing strategies of the automotive industry (Ferguson, Hardy, and Williams, 2003; Schonfeld, Sheehan, and Steinhardt, 2005; Shin *et al.*, 2005), with some exceptions such as Volvo's – is not even an important one. Based on content analyses of new car advertisements in Australia (Schonfeld *et al.*, 2005), and in North America (Ferguson *et al.*, 2003; Shin *et al.*, 2005), marketing gurus believe that the primary motives behind the choice of the car we buy are related to the car's performance (including high-risk speeding) and looks. This is despite the fact that at least according to one survey, 40 percent of the U.S. drivers rate "safety" as the single most important feature that they look for in a car. However, in the same survey significant numbers of drivers rated economic/fuel efficiency as the most important feature is selecting a car (31 percent), or seating and cargo space (13 percent), or speed/performance (8 percent), or appearance (6 percent) (Mason-Dixon, 2005). Nonetheless, much of the automobile industry's advertising focuses on vehicle performance, and – when targeting the younger consumers – speed (Donovan *et al.*, 2011) and aggressive driving (Shin *et al.*, 2005). Once we drive the car we bought, we also try to satisfy various needs and desires, other than safety (thrill and aggression?). If safety is not the key determinant of our driving behavior, then how do we incorporate it into our driving utility function?

The most common of all the motivations considered by driving researchers is risk: the minimization of risk or the compensation for risk. The minimization models assume that we do not drive to maximize safety, but we drive to minimize risk. An early approach offered by Näätänen and Summala (1976) and later revised by Summala (1985, 1988) argued that drivers adjust their driving in order to maintain a zero – or some minimal – risk level. In other words, most drivers behave as if most of the time there is no risk at all (a perception often not shared by their passengers; Dillon and Dunn, 2005). To modify the driving, the perceived risk has to exceed the zero level by some threshold amount. Thus, most of the time drivers are assumed to be driving with a perceived level of zero risk, or very slightly above it. Only when that level is seriously compromised do they change their behavior. In Fuller's model, perceived risk is also a primary factor in the determination of the safety margin between the task demands and the capabilities allocated to it.

It is important to note that risk perception may differ greatly among people. Risk is relative, and people are likely to behave in accordance with the way they perceive their risk (Yates and Chua, 2002). To illustrate, safety belts reduce the risk of fatal injury by approximately 45 percent (Evans, 2004). This is a huge effect, and one that should motivate all safety organizations to promote safety belts. On the other hand, from an individual person's perspective, the first question may be "45 percent of what?" In other words, "what is the risk of my dying in a crash when not using a safety belt?" That risk, in the Western world is infinitesimal. For example, in the U.S. in 2014 a person's probability of dying in a crash from driving or riding in a car in one year was 0.000102. If that person then considers the probability of dying in a crash on any given trip – each trip constituting an event for which the decision to buckle up or not to buckle up has to be made – then that number should further be divided by the number of trips taken in one year. In short, for all practical purposes, a person's risk of being killed in a car whenever he or she takes a trip is essentially zero (approximately 10^{-6}, assuming 100 trips per year). In that context the appeal of reducing this "zero" risk by close to 50 percent is inconsequential. [Interestingly, that same person may very religiously buy a lottery ticket every week, in which the likelihood of winning the jackpot is on the same order of magnitude. That is because our risk perception for negative and positive outcomes – with the same objective probabilities – is very different (Tversky and Kahneman, 1992)]. The different perspectives on the safety benefits of seat belts are illustrated in Figure 3-11.

Behavioral adaptation

If risk governs our driving behavior, then when risk changes, we should adjust our behavior accordingly. This process is called behavioral adaptation. Behavioral adaptation is our response to the world around us as a means for survival. In the context of

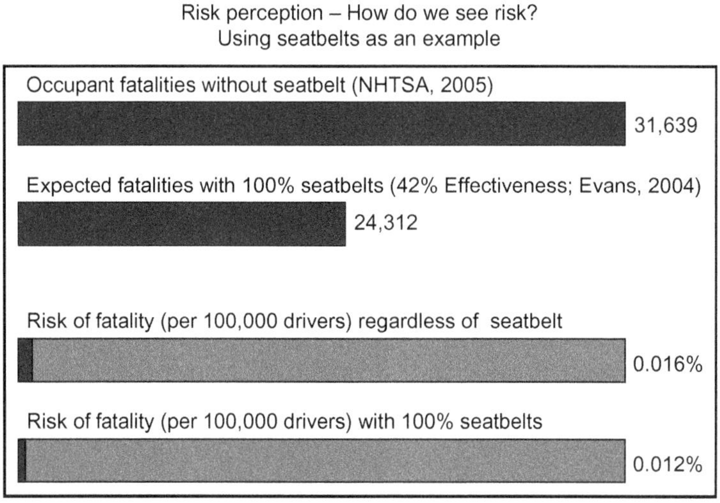

Figure 3-11. Bar graphs of risk displays (top) versus stacked bar displays (bottom). Top bars show reduction in occupant fatalities with 100 percent belt use. Bottom graphs show change in risk of fatality for an individual licensed driver. (Numbers are based on NHTSA, 2005, fatality data with 45 percent belt use among fatally injured, 45 percent belt effectiveness in fatality reduction.)

driving it reflects our adjustments to the changes in the driving environment. This environment includes our own car, the physical infrastructure of streets and roads, the traffic, and the laws and norms that are designed to affect our driving style. The term "adaptation" already implies change. Thus, as any aspect of our environment changes, we consider an adaptive change in our behavior. This change "reflects the independence of the road user in the face of regulators and engineers and the complexity and oft times unpredictability of human nature" (Smiley, 2013). Behavioral adaptation flies in the face of the ubiquitous qualifying statement "all other things remaining the same." In our different roles – drivers, occupants, pedestrians, bicyclists, and motorcyclists – we tend to change our behavior whenever our environment is perceptibly changed. Thus, to mitigate the dangers of speeding on dangerous roads, the highway engineers improve them, but only to discover that people then drive faster. While this is fairly easily predictable, other modifications may not be. The installation of highly reflective delineators along the road is designed to give drivers a farther preview of the road ahead, to better predict the vehicle control needs at night. Yet an evaluation of their impact in Finland (Kallberg, 1993), and a more recent simulator study in Israel (Sharfi and Shinar, 2014), showed that these roadway "improvements" were actually associated with more crashes. Similarly, the introduction of anti-lock brake systems (ABS) was heralded with great expectations that they would reduce crashes as they significantly reduced braking distances on slippery roads and enabled drivers to retain control of their steering while braking sharply. Yet crash analysis by the U.S. Insurance Institute for Highway Safety showed that their impact on fatal crashes is questionable (Farmer 2001; Farmer *et al.*, 1997).

In all of these examples, the driver is aware of the enhanced safety margins and thus can adapt to them if he or she wishes to retain the same risk level. However, when improvements to safety are not demonstrably perceptible – as when air bags are added and collapsible steering columns replace the old rigid ones – there is a possibility that they will not induce a negative behavioral adaptation and therefore their actual positive effects on injury reduction may equal the expected benefits and not be diminished. Elvik (2004) suggested that the extent of behavioral adaptation to a new crash countermeasure depends on six factors: (1) how noticeable the measure is, (2) the extent to which the driver has already adapted to the risk factor (e.g., reduced visibility at night; the more the driver has already adapted the less likely he or she are to adapt further), (3) the estimated magnitude of the engineering effect on generic risk factors (the greater the estimated benefit the more likely the compensatory behavior), (4) the extent to which the measure primarily reduces injury severity (rather than the likelihood of a crash; adaptation being less likely to injury reduction than to crash prevention), (5) the expected damage in case of an accident, and (6) the overall utility of behavioral adaptation (the more a measure decreases it the less likely adaptation will occur). As some of these conditions are hard to quantify, and their relative weights probably differ among individuals, the ability to predict the impact of perceptible countermeasures remains quite elusive. Still the argument of behavioral adaptation has a great intuitive appeal as most of us can probably identify with it based on our own driving experience. The motivational models described below are probably a good step in assisting us in such predictions.

Risk homeostasis model of driver behavior

The best-known motivational model – and the one that has been most frequently challenged – is the risk homeostasis theory of driving behavior. The first formulation of this model was probably Taylor's (1964) "risk-speed compensation model," which postulated that drivers adjust their speeds in accordance with the perceived risk. Näätänen and Summala (1976), suggested that we strive to drive with (perceived) zero risk. The model was later expanded by Wilde (1998, 2002) to include and account for a host of driver behaviors. Because of the controversy it has generated and the research that it has spurred, it will be described here in some detail. According to Wilde, we strive not to minimize risk (or maximize safety), but to reduce (or increase) it to a non-zero level with which we feel comfortable. Because different driving situations have different levels of inherent dangers, we constantly strive to adjust our behavior to maintain a relatively constant risk level. The continuous adjustment process, similar to that of a room thermostat, is displayed in Figure 3-12.

The central adjustment processor – labeled "comparator" in Figure 3-12 – weighs the inputs from the driver's desired risk level and the perceived level of risk posed by the immediate situation. The comparator is part of a feedback loop where the perceived level of risk is continuously revised, based on the crash experience and the driver's contribution to it at each location. Note that both inputs are affected by some personal factors. The perceived level of risk is a function that is affected not only by the objective danger in a situation, but also by the driver's skills at handling it. Thus, a given driving task or

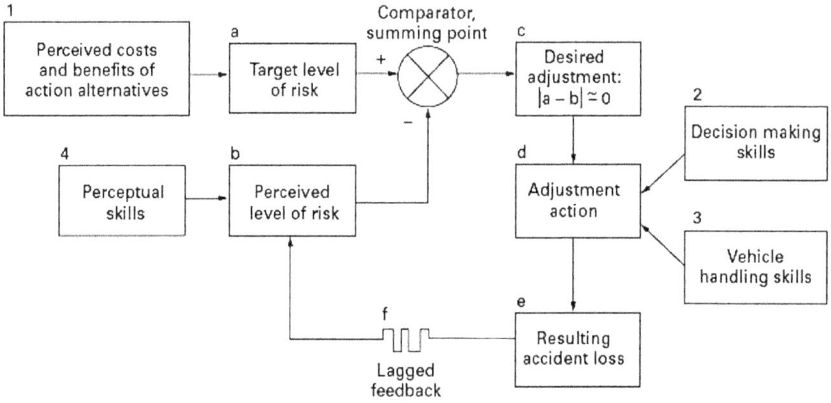

Figure 3-12. A schematic representation of Wilde's risk homeostasis theory relating driver behavior to the gap between the driver target risk level and the perceived risk based on actual crash history at the site (from Wilde, 1998; 2002; with permission from BMJ Publishing Group, Ltd.).

situation may be perceived as very risky to an old driver who is conscious of his or her reduced skills, much less risky to an experienced younger driver, but hardly risky to a novice driver who may be oblivious to some inherent dangers. The "target level of risk" also varies among drivers. Some drivers – especially young drivers – are more risk or sensation seeking oriented than other drivers (Zuckerman, 1979, 1983, 1994; Jonah, 1997), and they probably set a higher level of risk that they will tolerate (or even seek) in order to satisfy other needs that are fulfilled by driving. Perhaps the most important aspect of the theory is that the level of risk assumed by a particular driving style is dependent mostly on the perceived danger of the specific driving situation. This is because for a given person at a given phase in life the target level of risk and the perceptual skills are fairly constant.

Wilde's model leads to the somewhat surprising conclusion that most vehicle and highway improvements in safety will have little or no long-term effects on the driver's actual safety since they will change the perceived level of risk (by reducing it), which in turn will make the driver assume greater risk (e.g., by speeding) in order to maintain the same target level of risk. In short, behavioral adaptation will prevail to undo the potential benefits of the improvements. Vehicle and highway improvements will have short-term effects because it takes time for the drivers to realize that the inherent danger associated with the old driving style has now been significantly reduced. This also leads Wilde to conclude that the only effective means of long-term improvements in safety is through a change in the target level of risk; that is, in having people shift toward a lower risk level than they currently assume. This, according to Wilde, can be achieved only through behavior modification: either by positively reinforcing safe behaviors or by punishing unsafe behaviors. Most societies attempt to increase safety through increased enforcement as a means of punishing drivers for unsafe actions. Wilde (2002) argues, with the support of some examples, that the alternative approach – of reinforcing safe driving

– when it has been tried, has yielded much more dramatic improvements. Examples cited by Wilde for the positive approach include crash reductions in California following renewal of driving license by mail for crash-free drivers, and crash reductions of novice drivers in Norway following a promise to reimburse crash-free novice drivers in the amount of young driver insurance surcharge. A more recent demonstration of the potential of positive reinforcement for safe driving was made by Reagan *et al.* (2013) when they gave drivers a monitory incentive to remain within 5 mph of the speed limit. Although the amount was small (maximal earning of $25 if they never exceeded the speed limit in two weeks of driving) and the deduction was very little for every minute that they exceeded the limit, the effect was quite dramatic: the incentive increased the percent time below the speed limit +5 from 70 percent to over 80 percent. Of course applying such a strategy on a national basis can turn out to be an expensive proposition. However, a fuel savings on-line monitor may be able to accomplish the same goal.

The theory of risk homeostasis has a very intuitive appeal. Many living systems – including ourselves – constantly strive to maintain a prescribed level of homeostasis, a gentle balance among the various forces that act on us. We also know that people are adaptive. They change in response to changes in their environment. In the context of driving this should be obvious from the driver-vehicle-roadway system depicted in Figure 3-5. Drivers respond to roadway and vehicle characteristics, and they respond to *changes* in road and vehicle characteristics. The critical issue is not whether the drivers change their behavior, but whether the net result following the change is a positive one or a negative one. According to Wilde we adjust our driving to actually maintain a certain significant level of risk, and any vehicle-based or road-based change to reduce it is negated by our behavioral adaptation. To illustrate, one factor that greatly affects our collision avoidance capability is the friction between the tires and the road: the greater the coefficient of friction, the shorter the stopping distance when we brake. Thus, the introduction of studded tires – before radial tires became commonplace – was considered a great safety device because it significantly increased the coefficient of friction on icy and snow-covered roads. The actual benefits were tested in several studies, and were somewhat disappointing. A study conducted in Norway – a country that definitely has its share of snow-covered roads – on the accident experience of four major cities over a ten years period revealed that "studded tires are shown to have a very modest overall safety effect when behavioral adaptation is taken into account" (Fridestroem, 2001). In another study, based on analyses of crashes in Reykjavik, Iceland (where snow is just as abundant), drivers with studded tires were much safer than drivers with non-studded winter tires, especially in the winter. But – and this is a very important "but" – the researchers concluded that most of the 28 percent reduction in accidents was due more to the drivers' characteristics than to the tire characteristics: the former being responsible for over 20 percent of the improvement and the latter being responsible for less than 5 percent of the improvement (Thigthorsson, 1998). As a group, the drivers using studded tires were older than those without them, and a greater proportion of them used seat belts. Thus, the drivers with studded tires were essentially more safety conscious to begin with than the ones without them. However, a more recent analysis of loss-of-control crashes in Sweden (Strandroth *et al.*, 2012), using induced exposure for control, found that studded tires were responsible for an enormous drop of 42 percent in fatal crashes on roads covered by snow or ice. Thus, even if there is some risk compensation on the part of the driver, the net effect of the vehicle control improvement is very high.

Assessments of the benefits of various vehicle-based safety systems also fly in the face of the risk homeostasis theory. A recent assessment (Kahane, 2015) of the impacts of various vehicle-based safety standards that were introduced in the U.S. over the past 50 years, including safety belts and air bags, greater impact absorption of the vehicle structure and interiors, and electronic stability control concluded that all of them contributed significantly to the reduction of fatalities (see Chapter 19).

Despite its intuitive appeal, the theory has been challenged by many researchers in the field (Evans, 2004; Fuller, 2005; Haight, 1986; O'neill and Williams, 1998; Robertson, 2002), to the extent of being "ludicrous" (Robertson, 2002). In brief, the main criticisms of the risk homeostasis theory, summarized by Robertson (2002) are that:

1. Only a small percent of the drivers in every country actually experience a crash, and so most drivers never accumulate the personal experience with crashes in different situations to assess the differential risk or a crash in different situations.
2. The actual risk of a crash may change momentarily and independently of a driver's actions (for example when another driver in an opposing lane suddenly drifts across the median). There is almost no way to adjust for that.
3. Most of the research that supports the risk homeostasis theory is flawed in its design or analysis, and "overwhelming contrary findings" negate its results.
4. In nearly all of the industrial countries motor-vehicle death rates per distance traveled have declined dramatically over the past 30-50 years. If as drivers we were to adjust the risk over time of travel, then the more we drive the more crashes and fatalities we should see. (Wilde's argument that the risk level per capita has remained relatively constant does not counter that argument, unless one assumes that people lower the risk level for every additional kilometer that they drive in order to adjust for their expected total annual mileage, a somewhat difficult assumption to swallow).
5. Crash data indicate that the risk of a crash varies by a factor of over 100 among different countries, and within a given country the rate diminishes greatly when various improvements are made to the infrastructure. If drivers were to adjust for these differences then the crash rates would be similar in all countries and would remain the same over time (Evans, 2004).

But the fact remains that we do adapt ourselves to our environment. If we don't adjust our driving to a certain risk level, then is there another factor that is responsible for our behavioral adaptation? According to Fuller (2005; 2011) there is, and it is the task difficulty. In fact, Fuller also found that the perceived difficulty of the driving task correlates very highly with the perceived risk, but the perceived risk is hardly correlated with the actual risk of a crash. Thus, the contribution of the risk homeostasis is not so much in its specific formulation of how we adjust our driving but in the explicit statement that an improvement in non-driver components of the driver-vehicle-roadway system are likely to change driver behavior as well. The primary goal of driving for most people is mobility, and when safety improvements can actually enhance mobility at the cost of some of the potential safety benefits, drivers may opt for the mobility benefits. Limited-access divided highways ("motorways" and "freeways") are much safer than two-lane rural roads, and that safety benefit remains even after the increase in speed on the freeway. It is likely that if drivers drove on freeways at the speeds they drive on winding rural roads, the safety benefits of the freeways would be even greater ... but that will simply not happen.

However, the model does suggest two approaches to modifying driver behavior. The most obvious and direct approach is to increase the perceived risk of apprehension for violating the traffic laws. Not surprising, there are ample data to show that increased speed enforcement is almost invariably accompanied by reduced speeds (see Chapter 8). In fact, it has been shown that excessive speeding can be reduced even without increasing actual levels of enforcement, by managing to increase the *perceived* level of enforcement (Shinar and McKnight, 1986). Another, more sophisticated approach to increase the perceived risk is by directly affecting the driver's perception of the risk. Three studies, spanning over 30 years and three continents (by Denton, 1973, in England; by Shinar, Rockwell, and Malecki, 1980, in the U.S.; and by Godley, Triggs, and Fildes, 2004, in Australia) have demonstrated that manipulation of driver's perceptions through changes in the pavement markings can affect driver behavior. The changes were such that they created visual illusions of a narrowing lane or an increasing speed, and in both cases they caused a significant reduction of speed, especially at the high end of the speed distribution (for details see Chapter 19).

The motivational approach to understanding (and affecting) driver behavior does not begin and end with risk and task difficulty or demands. These are just two of the potential motivating (or deterring) factors, albeit the ones discussed most often. For example, in the case of speed selection, other factors that have been identified include the achievement of pleasure, risks posed by the surrounding traffic, time, and expenses (Rothengatter, 1988; Shinar, 2001), tendency toward higher speeds, reluctance to reduce speed, conservation of effort (Summala, 1988), desire for comfort (Ohta, 1993; Shinar, 2001), and presence of passengers in the car (Shinar, 2001). Regardless of the motive, it is important to keep in mind that changes in any component of the driving system will most likely be accompanied by changes in the driving behavior (Elvik, 2004).

A functional model of driving behavior must allow for interactions among the system's components and be able to predict how changes in roadways and vehicles will affect driver behavior. This is very pertinent to the plethora of in-vehicle devices that are currently being introduced into our vehicles (Barnard *et al.*, 2014). As a general rule of thumb, models that do not allow for such interactions will overestimate the expected utility of safety improvements, whereas models that allow for the interaction will typically be much more conservative in their prediction, but also much more accurate. Evans (2004) typifies the former as being naïve because they are non-interactive, zero feedback, and engineering-oriented models. In contrast, the interactive models include behavior feedback and behavior change. In that respect the Risk Homeostasis Model is definitely one of the latter, but – because of its many shortcomings noted above – it is more useful as a stimulus to more research and as a post hoc explanatory model than as a model to predict behavior.

Integrative Models: Information Processing in the Context of Motivational Factors

It is obvious that our on-road behavior is determined by both motivational factors – long-term and short-term – and information processing limits. Both types of models acknowledge the existence of the other factors, and therefore to truly understand behavior and design safety features we must consider both.

An interesting insight into how both factors operate was offered by Reason and his associates (Reason *et al.*, 1990). They suggest that one way of observing both aspects is to look at drivers' "aberrant behaviors"; behaviors that deviate from the norms and put the drivers at risk. Reason then distinguishes between two types of aberrant behaviors: violations and errors. Violations are typically – but not always – deliberate actions that are considered to be unsafe behaviors and often are illegal (such as speeding or passing on the right or on the left in the United Kingdom). They can be observed, measured, and documented. Errors, on the other hand, are failures of "planned actions to achieve their intended consequences." Errors can be further categorized into slips, lapses, and mistakes. Reason *et al.* (1990) also provide some examples of the different types of errors and violations, and these are reproduced in Table 3-2. The importance in distinguishing

Table 3-2. Types of undesirable driver behaviors classified in terms of errors and violations (based on Reason *et al.*'s, 1990, model, with permission from Taylor & Francis Ltd.).

Aberrant Behaviors	**Examples**
Slips – misapplication of automated behaviors	Misreading road sign, depressing brakes pedal instead of accelerator pedal
Lapses – loss of situational awareness	Forgetting car is in high gear when starting in intersection; no recollection of road just traveled
Mistakes – decision-making errors	Underestimating gaps between cars, selecting wrong lane for planned route
Unintended violations – loss of situational awareness	Unintended speeding, forgetting to renew license
Deliberate violations – risk taking decisions	Speeding, running red lights

between errors and violations is that errors are primarily due to failures in information processing of the individual drivers. In contrast, violations are primarily driven by motivational factors and must be described relative to the context in which they occur: be it social norms or enforced traffic laws.

Using the statistical procedure of factor analysis, Reason *et al.* (1990), further demonstrated that the two types of behaviors are fairly independent, in the sense that people who are likely to commit violations are not necessarily likely to commit errors, and vice versa. They also found that the tendency to commit violations is greater for men than for women, and that this tendency decreases with increasing age. On the other hand, the tendency to commit errors was the same for men and women and remained quite constant across all age groups. More recent studies and meta-analysis tended to confirm these early conclusions (De Winter and Dodou, 2010). The Driver Behavior Questionnaire (DBQ) that Reason and his associates developed to distinguish between errors and violations has been validated by different researchers in countries with widely different infrastructure and driving cultures such as France (Guého, Granie, and Abric, 2014), Denmark (Martinussen *et al.*, 2013), and China (Qu *et al.*, 2014). Most notably, younger people are typically fast information processors who intend and do commit violations such as speeding, and consequently their crashes often involve excessive speed as the cause of their crashes. Older drivers' crashes are typically linked to errors due to slips, lapses, and unintended violations such as failing to correctly estimate gaps or detect other traffic when crossing intersections (see Chapters 6 and 7).

Even among young drivers, Fergenson (1971) demonstrated that high violations drivers are not necessarily high accident drivers. Using self-reports Fergenson first identified four groups of college age drivers: high violations-high accidents, high violations-low accidents, low violations-high accidents, and low violations-low accidents drivers. He then measured their reaction time to simple and complex stimuli, and showed that the high accidents-high violations drivers had the slowest information processing rates while the low accidents-high violations drivers had the fastest rates. Thus, the crash risk was highest for the drivers who were motivated to commit violations, but unable to cope with their potential consequences, while the high violations drivers who had fast information processing rates were probably able to extricate themselves from many dangerous situations that they encountered due to their information processing skills. In a somewhat similar vein, Qu *et al.* (2015) surveyed drivers in Beijing and found that while male drivers had slightly more violations (in terms of penalty points and fines) than females, they were slightly less likely to be involved in accidents, again demonstrating the questionable assumption that violations can be used as surrogate measures of accidents.

An attempt to integrate the information processing and motivational aspects in a single model was made by Vaa (2011) in his Risk Monitor Model. Vaa's point of departure is a very general evolutionary one that assumes that our primary motive is survival. To survive we must monitor risk on a continuous basis; while driving too. In driving we seek "the *bestfeeling* which can be established in any given situation." Unlike Wilde's risk monitor these feelings can be derived from both unconscious and conscious emotions.

Practical Implications of Theoretical Considerations

Unlike the elegance of some of the models and theories in the physical sciences, no aspects of human behavior in general or of driver behavior in particular can be distilled to a simple mathematical equation with a high level of predictive validity. Early attempts to develop a human transfer function in tracking tasks (considered at the time as representative of steering in driving) largely failed when it turned out with practice people not just became better at the task, but also changed their strategies, implying that the people were responding not just to the displacement of the target but also its derivatives: velocity and acceleration (Poulton, 1969). This is because human behavior is governed by learning and a multitude of factors and their interactions, and many of these operate at subconscious levels. Consequently, it takes a significant leap of faith to predict driver behavior from a multi-variable theoretical model – as detailed and complex as it may be. Still theories and models of driver behavior are essential if we are to understand how changes in vehicle, roadway, social, and legal environment can affect driver behavior (Gielen and Sleet, 2003).

The significant contribution of theories and models of driver behavior is in describing these behaviors within a framework of concepts that appear reasonable (i.e., they have face validity), and are useful (i.e., they have at least moderate predictive validity). Thus, driver behavior models can be useful tools to evaluate potential accidents and violations countermeasures. They can be utilized in two ways: by generating countermeasures that emerge from the model and by evaluating proposed countermeasures relative to the model. A countermeasure that makes no sense in light of any of the models above would probably not be an effective countermeasure. On the other hand, a countermeasure that is consistent with one or more of the above models would probably have some degree of effectiveness, though in the long run, given behavioral adaptation it may not be cost/effective.

The potential applications of the above models to traffic safety programs are infinite. By simply considering some of the key concepts reviewed above, we can generate and evaluate the potential benefits of a myriad of programs. Some of the key concepts that should be considered include driver attention with its limitations and biases, the roles of controlled and automated processes in affecting behavior in different situations, the training of drivers to have appropriate schemata and scripts to correctly identify their situations, the drivers' perceived risk levels as a means of modifying their behavior, and the biases drivers may have when they make rational – but bounded – decisions. Most importantly, in the current world of rapid technological innovations models can be extremely useful in initial evaluations of many of the emerging driver assistive crash avoidance systems prior to their implementation.

Driver behavior models have also had a significant impact on vehicle and roadway designs. By incorporating various parameters of driver information processing, we can optimize the timing of the transition phase of a traffic signal (i.e., the amber light), alert the driver to changing road conditions in time for him or her to respond, and design programmable highway signs that are consistent with the drivers' schemata, and thus raise SA. From within the vehicle we can reduce the driver's workload by monitoring the driver's and vehicle's actions (such as speed, steering inputs, and speed of windshield wipers) and based on these parameters limit the availability of in-vehicle distracting devices such as cell phones or inputs to a navigation system (Green, 2004). By understanding the manifestations and effects of fatigue on driver visual search behavior and vehicle control, we can design in-vehicle monitoring systems that can alert drivers to their fatigue-related impairments (Hermann, 2004). Thus, as our models become more quantitative and accurate, we can apply emerging technologies in a manner that is smarter and friendlier to the drivers (Cacciabue *et al.*, 2011).

References

Ajzen, I. (1991). The theory of planned behavior. *Org. Behav. Hum. Dec. Pro.*, *50*, 179-211.

Ajzen, I. (2011). The theory of planned behaviour: Reactions and reflections (Editorial). *Psych. Health*, *26*, 1113-1127.

Ajzen, I. and M. Fishbein (1980). *Understanding Attitudes and Predicting Social Behavior*. Prentice-Hall, Englewood Cliffs, NJ.

Barnard, Y., O. M. J. Carsten and F. C. H. Lai (2014). From a theoretical model to a predictive simulation model of operator interaction with support systems: Designing experiments to build the numerical simulation. *Cog. Tech. Work*, *16*, 117-129.

Blumenthal, M. (1968). Dimensions of the traffic safety problem. *Traff. Safe. Res. Rev.*, *12*, 7-12.

Borowsky, A., T. Oron-Gilad, A. Meir and Y. Parmet (2012). Drivers' perception of vulnerable road users: A hazard perception approach. *Accid. Anal. Prev.*, *44*, 160-166.

Borowsky, A., D. Shinar and T., Oron-Gilad (2010). Age, skill, and hazard perception in driving. *Accid. Anal. Prev.*, *42*, 1240-1249.

Borowsky, A., D. Shinar and Y. Parmet (2008). The relationship between driving experience and road signs relative to their location. *Hum. Fact.*, *50*(2), 173-182.

Braddy (2006). http://www.braddye.com/glossary.html. April 20.

Brijs, K., A. Cuenen, T. Brijs, R. A. C. Ruiter and G. Wets (2014). Evaluating the effectiveness of a post-license education program for young novice drivers in Belgium. *Accid. Anal. Prev.*, *66*, 62-71.

Brookhuis, K. A., G. De Vries and D. de Waard (1991). The effects of mobile telephoning on driving performance. *Accid. Anal. Prev.*, *23*, 309-316.

Brookhuis, K. A. and D. de Waard (1993). The use of psychophysiology to assess driver status. *Ergonomics*, *36*, 1099-1110.

Brookhuis, K. A. and D. de Waard (2001). Assessment of drivers' workload: Performance and subjective and physiological indexes. In: *Stress, Workload, and Fatigue* (P. A. Hancock and P. A. Desmond, eds.). pp. 321-333. Erlbaum, Mahwah, NJ.

Brown, I. D. (1982). Exposure and experience are a confounded nuisance in research on driver behavior. *Accid. Anal. Prev.*, *14*, 345-352.

Cacciabue, P. C., M. Hjälmdahl, A. Lüdtke and C. Riccioli (eds.) (2011) *Human Modelling in Assisted Transportation*. Springer, Milan.

Castanier, C. and T. T. Woodman (2013). Theory of planned behaviour and road violations: The moderating influence of perceived behavioural control. *Transport. Res. F, 18*, 148-158.

Cestac, J., F. Paran and P. Delhomme (2011). Young drivers' sensation seeking, subjective norms, and perceived behavioral control and their roles in predicting speeding intention: How risk-taking motivations evolve with gender and driving experience. *Safe. Sci., 49*, 424-432.

Cestac, J., F. Paran and P. Delhomme (2014) Drive as I say, not as I drive: Influence of injunctive and descriptive norms on speeding intentions among young drivers. *Transport. Res. F, 14*, 44-56.

Charlton, S. G. and N. J. Starkey (2013). Driving on familiar roads: Automaticity and inattention blindness. *Transport. Res. F, 19*, 121-133.

Cherry, E. C. (1953). Some experiments on the recognition of speech, with one and two ears. *J. Acoust. Soc. Am., 25*, 975-979.

Costa, M., A. Simone, V. Vignali, C. Lantieri, A. Bucchi and G. Dondi (2014). Looking behavior for vertical road signs. *Transport. Res. F, 23*, 147-155.

Costandi, M. (2009). Where are old memories stored in the brain? *Sci. Am.* http://www.scientificamerican.com/article/the-memory-trace/. February, 10.

Crundall D. E., G. Underwood and P. R. Chapman (1998). How much do novice drivers see? The effects of demand on visual search strategies in novice and experienced drivers. In: *Eye Guidance in Reading and Scene Perception* (G. Underwood, ed.), pp. 395-418. Elsevier, Oxford, England.

De Winter, J. C. F. and D. Dodou (2010). The driver behaviour questionnaire as a predictor of accidents: A meta-analysis. *J Safe. Res., 41*, 463-470.

Denton, G. G. (1973). The influence of visual pattern on perceived speed at Newbridge MB Midlothian. Report LR531. Transport and Road Research Laboratory, Crowthorne, Berkshire.

Dillon, K. M. and D. L. Dunn (2005). Passenger complaints about driver behavior. *Accid. Anal. Prev., 37*, 1012-1018.

Donges, E. (1978). A two-level model of driver steering behavior. *Hum. Fact., 20*, 691-707.

Donovan, R. J., L. J. Fielder, R. Ouschan and M. Ewing (2011). Self-regulation of motor vehicle advertising: Is it working in Australia? *Accid. Anal. Prev., 43*, 631-636.

Efrat, K. and A. Shoham (2013). The theory of planned behavior, materialism, and aggressive driving. *Accid. Anal. Prev., 59*, 459-465.

Elias, W., O. Baron-Epel, S. Bord, A. Gesser-Edelsburg and Y. Shiftan (2016). Factors influencing the decision to engage in alcohol-impaired driving among Arab-Israeli youths. *Transport. Res. F, 44*, 180-191.

Elliott, M. A. and C. J. Armitage (2009). Promoting drivers' compliance with speed limits: Testing an intervention based on the theory of planned behavior. *Br. J. Psych., 100*, 111-132.

Elvik, R. (2004). To what extent can theory account for the findings of road safety evaluation studies? *Accid. Anal. Prev., 36*, 841-849.

Elvik, R. (2016). A theoretical perspective on road safety communication campaigns. *Accid. Anal. Prev.*, *97*, 292-297.

Endsley, M. R. (1995). Toward a theory of situation awareness in dynamic systems. *Hum. Fact.*, *37*(1), 32-64.

Evans, L. (2004). *Traffic Safety*. Science Serving Society, Bloomfield Hills, MI.

Farmer, C. M. (2001). New evidence concerning fatal crashes of passenger vehicles before and after adding antilock braking systems. *Accid. Prev. Anal.*, *33*, 361-369.

Farmer, C. M., A. Lund, R. Trempel and E. Braver (1997). Fatal crashes of passenger vehicles before and after adding antilock braking systems. *Accid. Anal. Prev.*, *29*, 745-757.

Fergenson, O. E. (1971). The relationship between information processing and driving accident and violations record. *Hum. Fact.*, *13*, 173-176.

Ferguson, S. A., A. P. Hardy and A. F. Williams (2003). Content analysis of television advertising for cars and minivans: 1983–1998. *Accid. Anal. Prev.*, *35*, 825-831.

Fishbein, M. and I. Ajzen (1975). *Belief, Attitude, Intention and Behavior*. Addison-Wesley, New York, NY.

Fitch, G. M., S. A. Soccolich, F. Guo, J. McClafferty, Y. Fang, R. L. Olson, M. A. Perez, R. J. Hanowski, J. M. Hankey and T.s A. Dingus (2003) The impact of hand-held and hands-free cell phone use on driving performance and safety-critical event risk. National Highway Traffic Safety Administration Report No. DOT HS 811 757. U.S. Depatment of Transportation, Washington, DC.

Fridestroem, L. (2001). The safety effect of studded tyres in Norway. Report No. TOI-RAP-493/2000. Norwegian Institute of Transport Economics, Oslo (TOI).

Fuller, R. (2005). Towards a general theory of driver behavior. *Accid. Anal. Prev.*, *37*, 461-472.

Fuller, R. (2011). Driver control theory from task difficulty homeostasis to risk allostasis. In: *Handbook of Traffic Psychology* (B. E. Porter, ed.), pp. 13-26. Elsevier, Amsterdam.

Gardner, J. W. (1961). *Excellence* – Can We be Equal and Excellent Too? Harper, New York, NY.

Gielen, A. C. and D. Sleet (2003). Application of behavior-change theories and methods to injury prevention. *Epidemiol. Rev.*, *25*, 65-76.

Godley, S. T., T. J. Triggs and B. N. Fildes (2004). Perceptual lane width, wide perceptual road centre markings and driving speeds. *Ergonomics*, *47*(3), 237-256.

Gopher, D. and E. Donchin (1986). Workload: An examination of the concept. In: *Handbook of Perception and Human Performance: Vol. II. Cognitive Processes and Performance* (K. R. Boff, L. Kaufman and J. P. Thomas, eds.), pp. 41/1-41/49. Wiley Interscience, New York, NY.

Green, P. A. (2004). Driver distraction, telematics design, and workload managers: Safety issues and solutions. Soc. Automot. Eng. (SAE). Paper No. 2004-21-0022.

Guého, L., M. A. Granie and J. C. Abric (2014). French validation of a new version of the Driver Behavior Questionnaire (DBQ) for drivers of all ages and level of experiences. *Accid. Anal. Prev.*, *63*, 41-48.

Haight, F. A. (1986). Risk, especially risk of traffic accidents. *Accid. Anal. Prev.*, *18*, 359-366.

Hakamies-Blomqvist, L. (2006). Are there safe and unsafe drivers? *Transport. Res. F.*, *9*, 347-352.

Hermann, S. (2004). Driver monitoring – New challenges for smart sensor-based systems. In: *Wearable eHealth Systems for Personalised Health Management* (A. Lymberis, D. De Rossi, eds.), pp. 103-110. IOS Press, Amsterdam.

Herrin, G. D. and J. B. Neuhardt (1974). An empirical model for automobile driver horizontal curve negotiation. *Hum. Fact.*, *16*, 129-133.

Hill, S. G., H. P. Iavecchia, A. C. Bittner Jr., J. C. Byers, A. L. Zacklad and R. C. Christ (1992). Comparison of four subjective workload rating scales. *Hum. Fact.*, *34*(4), 429-439.

Holland, C. and R. Hill (2007). The effects of age, gender and driver status on pedestrians' intentions to cross the road in risky situations. *Accid. Anal. Prev.*, *39*, 224-237.

Horrey, W. J., C. D. Wickens and K. P. Vonsalus (2006). Modeling drivers' visual attention allocation while interacting with in-vehicle technologies. *J. Exp. Psych. Appl.*, *12*, 67-78.

Horswill, M. S., A. Hill and M. Wetton (2015). Can a video-based hazard perception test used for driver licensing predict crash involvement?. *Accid. Anal. Prev.*, *82*, 213-219.

Horswill, M. S. and F. P. McKenna (2004). Drivers' hazard perception ability: Situation awareness on the road. In: *A Cognitive Approach to Situation Awareness: Theory and Application* (S. Banbury and S. Tremblay, eds.), pp. 155-175. Ashgate Publishing, Aldershot.

Horswill, M. S., C. N. Kemala, M. Wetton, C. T. Scialfa and N. A. Pachana (2010). Improving older drivers' hazard perception ability. *Psychol. Aging*, *25*, 464-469.

Hughes, B. P., S. Newstead, A. Anund, C. C. Shu and T. Falkmer (2015). A review of models relevant to road safety. *Accid. Anal. Prev.*, *74*, 250-270.

Iversen, H. and T. Rundmo (2004). Attitudes towards traffic safety, driving behaviour and accident involvement among the Norwegian public. *Ergonomics*, *47*(5), 555-572.

Jamson, A. H., S. J. Westerman, G. R. J. Hockey and O. M. J. Carsten (2004). Speech-based e-mail and driver behavior: Effects of an in-vehicle message system interface. *Hum. Fact.*, *46*(4), 625-939.

Janssen, W. H. (1979). Routeplanning en geleiding: Een literatuurstudie. Report IZF 1979 C-13. Soesterberg (The Netherlands). Institute for Perception TNO (As cited by Michon, 1985).

Johnson, M. B. and R. B. Voas (2004). Potential risks of providing drinking drivers with bac information. *Traffic Inj. Prev.*, *5*, 42-49.

Jonah, B. A. (1997). Sensation seeking and risky driving: A review and synthesis of the literature. *Accid. Anal. Prev.*, *29*, 651-665.

Kahane, C. J. (2015). Lives saved by vehicle safety technologies and associated Federal Motor Vehicle Safety Standards, 1960 to 2012 – Passenger cars and LTVs – With reviews of 26 FMVSS and the effectiveness of their associated safety technologies in reducing fatalities, injuries, and crashes. NHTSA Report No. DOT HS 812 069. U.S. Department of Transportation, Washington, DC.

Kahneman, D. (2013). The marvels and the flaws of intuitive thinking. In *Thinking: The New Science of Decision-Making, Problem-Solving, and Prediction* (J. Brockman ed.). Harper Perennial, New York, NY.

Kahneman, D. and J. Beatty (1966). Pupil diameter and load on memory. *Science, 154*, 1583-1585.

Kahneman, D., J. Beatty and I. Pollack (1967). Perceptual deficit during a mental task. *Science, 157*, 218-219.

Kallberg, V. (1993). Reflector posts-signs or danger? Transportation Research Record 1403. Transportation Research Board of the National Academies, Washington, C.

Kantowitz, B. H. (2000). In-vehicle information systems: Premises, promises, and pitfalls. *Transport. Hum. Fact. J., 2*(4), 359-379.

Kantowitz B. H., J. P. Singer, N. D. Lerner, H. W. McGee, W. E. Hughes, W. A. Perez and G. L. Ullman (2004). Development of critical gaps and knowledge base in support of the safety R & T partnership agenda. University of Michigan, Transportation Research Institute. Contract # DTFH61-01-C-00049. Report to the Federal Highway Administration, Washington, DC.

Katzourakis, D., E. Velenis, E. Holweg and R. Happee (2014). Haptic steering support for driving near the vehicle's handling limits: Test-track case. *IEEE Transport. Intelligent Tran. Syst., 15*(4), 1781-1789.

Keith, K., M. Trentacoste, L. Depue, T. Granada, E. Huckaby, B. Ibarguen, B. Kantowitz, W. Lum and T. Wilson. (2005). Roadway Human Factors and behavioral safety in Europe. Federal Highway Administration. Report No. FHWA-PL-05-005. U.S. Department of Transportation, Washington, DC.

Klauer, S. G., T. A. Dingus, V. L. Neale, J. D. Sudweeks and D. J. Ramsey (2006). The impact of driver inattention on near-crash/crash risk: An analysis using the 100-car naturalistic driving study data. National Highway Traffic Safety Administration Report No. DOT HS 810 594. U.S. Department of Transportation, Washington, DC.

Klauer, S. G., F. Guo, B. G. Simons-Morton, M. C. Ouimet, S. E. Lee and T. A.. Dingus (2013) Distracted driving and risk of road crashes among novice and experienced drivers. *N. Engl. J. Med., 370*, 54-59.

Konstantopoulos, P., P. Chapman and D. Crundall (2010). Driver's visual attention as a function of driving experience and visibility. Using a driving simulator to explore drivers' eye movements in day, night and rain driving. *Accid. Anal. Prev., 42*, 824-827.

Lansdown, T. C., N. Brook-Carter and T. Kersloot (2004). Distraction from multiple in-vehicle secondary tasks: Vehicle performance and mental workload implications. *Ergonomics, 47*(1), 91-104.

LeBlanc, D. J., S. Bao, J. R. Sayer and S. Bogard (2013). Longitudinal driving behavior with integrated crash-warning system: Evaluation from naturalistic driving data. *Transportation Research Record*, No. 2365. Transportation Research Board, Washington, DC.

Lee, J. D. and D. L. Strayer (2004). Preface to a special section on driver distraction. *Hum. Fact., 46*, 583-586.

Lim, P. C., E. Sheppard and D. Crundall (2014). A predictive hazard perception paradigm differentiates driving experience cross-culturally. *Transport. Res. F*, *26*, 210-217.

Liu, B.-S. and Y.-H. Lee (2006). In-vehicle workload assessment: Effects of traffic situations and cellular telephone use. *J. Safe. Res.*, *37*, 99-105.

Maltz, M. and D. Shinar (2004). Imperfect in-vehicle collision avoidance warning systems can aid drivers. *Hum. Fact.*, *46*, 357-366.

Martens, M. H. (2000). Assessing road sign perception: A methodological review. *Trans. Hum. Fact.*, *2*(4), 347-357.

Martinussen, L. M., T. Lajunen, M. Møller and T. Özkan (2013). Short and user-friendly: The development and validation of the Mini-DBQ. *Accid. Anal. Prev.*, *50*, 1259-1265.

Mason-Dixon Polling & Research (2005). *Drive for Life: Annual National Driver Survey*. Mason-Dixon Polling & Research Inc., Washington, DC.

McKenna, F. P. and J. Crick (1994). Hazard perception for drivers: A methodology for testing and training. TRL Report 313. Transport Research Laboratory, Crowthorne, UK.

McKenna, F. P., M. S. Horswill and J. L. Alexander (2006). Does anticipation training affect drivers' risk perception? *J. Exp. Psychol. Appl.*, *12*(1), 1-10.

McEachan, R. R. C., M. Conner, N. J. Taylor and R. J. Lawton (2011). Prospective prediction of health-related behaviours with the theory of planned behaviour: A meta-analysis. *Health Psych. Rev.*, *5*, 97-144.

McRuer, D. T. and D. H. Weir (1969). Theory of manual vehicular control. *Ergonomics*, *12*, 599-633.

Michon, J. A. (1985). A critical view of driver behavior models: What do we know, what should we do? In: *Human Behavior and Traffic Safety* (L. Evans and R. Schwing eds.). Plenum Press, New York, NY.

Milosevic, S. and R. Gajic (1986). Presentation factors and driver characteristics affecting road-sign registration. *Ergonomics*, *29*(6), 807-815.

Møller, M. and S. Haustein (2014). Peer influence on speeding behaviour among male drivers aged 18 and 28. *Accid. Anal. Prev.*, *64*, 92-99.

Mourant, R. R. and T. H. Rockwell (1972). Strategies of visual search by novice and experienced drivers. *Hum. Fact.*, *14*, 325-335.

Näätänen, R. and H. Summala (1976). *Road User Behavior And Traffic Accidents*. North-Holland, Amsterdam.

NHTSA (2005). Traffic safety facts 2004. National Highway Traffic Safety Administration Report No. DOT HS 809 919. U.S. Department of Transportation, Washington, DC.

O'Donnel, R. D. and F. T. Eggemeier (1986). Workload assessment methodology. In: *Handbook of Perception and Human Performance* (K. R. Boff, L. Kaufman and J. P. Thomas, eds.), Vol. 2. pp. 1-42 to 42-49. Wiley-Interscience, New York, NY.

Ohta, H. (1993). Individual differences in driving distance headway. In: *Proceedings of Vision in Vehicles* (A. G. Gale, I. D. Brown, C. M. Haslegrave, I. Moorhead and S. P. Taylor, eds.). pp. 91-100. Elsevier, Amsterdam.

O'neill, B. and A. Williams (1998). Risk homeostasis: A rebuttal. *Inj. Prev.*, *4*, 92-93.

Östlund, J., L. Nilsson, J. Törnros and Å. Forsman (2006). Effects of cognitive and visual load in real and simulated driving. VTI Report 533A for the EC Project HASTE. Linköping, Sweden, VTI.

Özkan, T. and T. Lajunen (2005). Why are there sex differences in risky driving? the relationship between sex and gender-role on aggressive driving, traffic offences, and accident involvement among young turkish drivers. *Aggress. Behav.*, *31*(6), 547-558.

Parker D., A. S. Manstead, S. G. Stradling and J. T. Reason (1992). Determinants of intention to commit driving violations. *Accid. Anal. Prev.*, *24*(2), 117-121.

Parry, M. H. (1968). *Aggression on the Road.* Tavistock, London.

Patten, C. J. D., A. Kircher, J. Östlund and L. Nilsson (2004). Using mobile telephones: Cognitive workload and attention resource allocation. *Accid. Anal. Prev.*, *36*, 341-350.

Poulton, E. C. (1969). Tracking. In: *Principles of Skill Acquisition* (E. A. Bilodeau and I.McD. Bilodeau eds). Academic Press, New York.

Qu, W., Y. Ge, C. Jiang, F. Du and K. Zhang (2014). The Dula dangerous driving index in China: An investigation of reliability and validity. *Accid. Anal. Prev.*, *64*, 62-68.

Qu, W., Y. Ge, Y. Xiong, R. Carciofo, W. Zhao and K. Zhang (2015). The relationship between mind wandering and dangerous driving behavior among Chinese drivers. *Safety Sci.*, *78*, 41-48.

Ranney, T. A. (1994). Models of driving behavior: A review of their evolution. *Accid. Anal. Prev.*, *26*, 733-750.

Rasmussen, J. (1986). *Information Processing and Human-Machine Interaction. An Approach to Cognitive Engineering.* North-Holland, Amsterdam.

Reagan, I. J., J. P. Bliss, R. Van Houten and B. W. Hilton (2013). The effects of external motivation and real-time automated feedback on speeding behavior in a naturalistic setting. *Hum. Fact.*, *55*, 218-230.

Reason, J., A. S. Manstead, S. Stradling, J. Baxter and K. Campbell (1990). Errors and violations on the roads: A real distinction? *Ergonomics*, *33*(10/11), 1315-1332.

Recarte, M. A. and L. Nunes (2003). Mental workload while driving: Effects on visual search, discrimination and decision making. *J. Exp. Psychol. Appl.*, *9* (2), 119-137.

Robertson, L. S. (2002). Does risk homeostasis theory have implications for road safety: Against. *Br. Med. J.*, *324*, 1151-1152.

Rothengatter, T. (1988). Risk and the absence of pleasure: A motivational approach to modeling road user behavior. *Ergonomics*, *31*(4), 599-607.

Routledge, D. A., R. Repetto-Wright and C. I. Howarth (1976). The development of road crossing skill by child pedestrians. Proceedings of the International Conference on Pedestrian Safety. Michlol, Haifa, Israel.

Schmidt-Daffy, M. (2014). Prospect balancing theory: Bounded rationality of drivers' speed choice. *Accid. Anal. Prev.*, *63*, 49-64.

Schneider W. and R. M. Shiffrin (1977). Controlled and automatic human information processing: I. Detection, search and attention. *Psychol. Rev.*, *84*(1), 1-66.

Schonfeld, C., M. Sheehan and D. Steinhardt (2005). A content analysis of Australian Motor Vehicle Advertising: Effects of the 2002 voluntary code on restricting the use of unsafe driving themes. Proceedings Australasian Road Safety Research, Policing and Education Conference, pp. 1-5, Wellington, NZ.

Sharfi, T. and D. Shinar (2014). Enhancement of road delineation can reduce safety. *J. Safety Res.*, *49*, 61-68.

Shin, P. C., D. Hallett, M. L. Chipman, C. Tator and J. T. Granton (2005). Unsafe driving in North American automobile commercials. *J. Pub. Health*, *27*(4), 318-325.

Shinar, D. (1978). *Psychology on the Road: The Human Factor in Traffic Safety*. Wiley, New York, NY.

Shinar, D. (2001). Driving speed relative to the speed limit and relative to the perception of safe, enjoyable, and economical speed. Proceedings of the Conference on Traffic Safety on Three Continents. Moscow, Russia, September.

Shinar, D. and A. Drory (1983). Sign registration in daytime and nighttime driving. *Hum. Fact.*, *25*(1), 117-122.

Shinar, D. and A. J. McKnight (1986). The combined effects of enforcement and public information campaigns on compliance. In: *Human Behavior and Traffic Safety* (L. Evans and R. Schwing eds.). Plenum Press, New York, NY.

Shinar, D., M. Meir and I. Ben-Shoham (1998). How automatic is manual gear shifting? *Hum. Fact.*, *40*, 647-654.

Shinar, D., T. H. Rockwell and J. Malecki (1980). The effects of changes in driver perception on rural curve negotiation. *Ergonomics*, *23*, 263-275.

Shinar, D., N. Tractinsky and R. P. Compton (2005). Effects of practice, age, and task demands, on interference from a phone task while driving. *Accid. Anal. Prev.*, *37*, 315-326.

Sivak, M. (2002). How common sense fails us on the road: Contribution of bounded rationality to the annual worldwide toll of one million traffic fatalities. *Transport. Res. F*, *5*, 259-269.

Smiley, A. (2013). Forward to C. Rudin-Brown and S. Jamson (Eds.), *Behavioarl Adaptation and Road Safety: Theory, Evidence, and Action*. CRC Press, Taylor and Francis, Boca Raton, FL.

Strandroth, J., M. Rizzi, M. Olai, A. Lie and C. Tingvall (2012). The effects of studded tires on fatal crashes with passenger cars and the benefits of electronic stability control (ESC) in Swedish winter driving. *Accid. Anal. Prev.*, *45*, 50-60.

Summala, H. (1985). Modeling driver behavior: A pessimistic prediction? In: *Human Behavior and Traffic Safety* (L. Evans and R. C. Schwing, eds.). Plenum Press, New York, NY.

Summala, H. (1988). Risk control is not risk adjustment: The zero-risk theory of driver behavior and its implications. *Ergonomics*, *31*, 491-506.

Taylor, D. H. (1964). Drivers' Galvanic skin response and the risk of accidents. *Ergonomics*, *7*, 439-451.

Thigthorsson, H. (1998). Studded winter tyres and traffic safety. Nordic Road and Transport Research, No. 3, 4-7.

Tversky, A. and D. Kahneman (1992). Advances in prospect theory: Cumulative representation of uncertainty. *J. Risk Uncertainty*, *5*, 297-323.

Vaa, T. (2011). Drivers' information processing, decision-making, and the role of emotions: Predictions of the Risk Monitor Model. In: *Human Modelling in Assisted*

Transportation (P. C. Cacciabue, M. Hjälmdahl, A. Lüdtke and C. Riccioli eds.). pp. 23-32. Springer, Milan.

Vaa, T. (2014). From Gibson and Crooks to Damasio: The role of psychology in the development of driver behaviour models. *Transport. Res. F.*, *25*, 112-119.

Waddell, L. P. and K. K. K. Wiener (2014). What's driving illegal mobile phone use? Psychosocial influences on drivers' intentions to use hand-held mobile phones. *Transport. Res. F*, *22*, 1-11.

Wege, C., S. Will and T. Victor (2013). Eye movement and brake reactions to real world brake-capacity forward collision warnings—A naturalistic driving study. *Accid. Anal. Prev.*, *58*, 259-270.

Wickens, C. D. (1984). Processing resources in attention. In: *Varieties of Attention* (R. Parasuraman and R. Davies eds.). pp. 63-101. Academic Press, New York, NY.

Wickens, C. D. (1992). *Engineering Psychology and Human Performance* (2nd ed.) Harper-Collins, New York, NY.

Wickens, C. D. and J. G. Hollands (2000). *Engineering Psychology and Human Performance* (3rd ed.). Prentice Hall, Upper Saddle River, NJ.

Wilde, G. J. S. (1998). Risk homeostasis theory: An overview. *Inj. Prev.*, *4*, 89-91.

Wilde, G. J. S. (2002). Does risk homeostasis theory have implications for road safety: For. *Br. Med. J.*, *324*, 1149-1151.

Yates, J. F. and H. F. Chua (2002). Risky driving from a decision making perspective. Proceedings of the 16th Conference of the International Council on Alcohol, Drugs, & Traffic Safety, Montreal, August 4-9.

Zhou, R. and W. J. Horrey (2010). Predicting adolescent pedestrians' behavioural intentions to follow the masses in risky crossing situations. *Transport. Res. F.*, *13* (3), 153-163.

Zhou, R., P.-L. P. Rau, W. Zhang and D. Zhuang (2012). Mobile phone use while driving: Predicting drivers' answering intentions and compensatory decisions. *Safe. Sci.*, *50*, 138-149.

Zuckerman, M. (1979). *Sensation Seeking: Beyond the Optimal Level of Arousal.* Lawrence Erlbaum Associates, Hillsdale, NJ.

Zuckerman, M. (1983). A biological theory of sensation seeking. In: *Biological Bases of Sensation Seeking, Impulsivity, and Anxiety Sensation Seeking: Beyond the Optimal Level of Arousal* (M. Zuckerman ed.). pp. 37-76. Lawrence Erlbaum Associates, Hillsdale, NJ.

Zuckerman, M. (1994). *Behavioral Expressions and Biosocial Bases of Sensation Seeking.* University of Cambridge Press, Cambridge.

PART B
DRIVER CAPACITIES AND INDIVIDUAL DIFFERENCES

4

Vision, Visual Attention, and Visual Search

– Keep it straight.
– No fun just to keep it straight. You've got to move a little bit, feel the road.
– Please?
– Just like this. All right?
– There you go. Take it nice and easy.
– Do you like this?
– Slow it down a little. You goin' a little fast. Colonel, slow it down.
– Something's happened to my foot!
– Slow it down, please.
– Hold on, Charlie. I think I've got another gear.
– Colonel Slade?
– Whoo-ah!
– Watch out!
– Hah-hah!
– You'll get us killed!
– Don't blame me, Charlie. I can't see!

Dialog from the 1992 movie "Scent of a Woman" in which the blind Colonel Slade test-drives a Ferrari, as his friend and protégé, Charlie, reluctantly guides him while the panic-stricken car dealer cringes in the back seat.

You can see a lot by just looking. (Yogi Berra, NY Yankees manager).

Fact: the blind cannot drive. Most of the information we use to drive is visual, and consequently vision is the most important sense needed for driving. In fact, loss of vision is the only sensory loss that warrants universal denial of a license. But how much of driving is vision dependent? And exactly what kind and level of vision is needed for safe driving? A common response to the first question is that 90-95 percent of the information needed for driving is visual (e.g., Chun *et al.*, 2013; Kline *et al.*, 1992; Sojourner and Antin, 1990; Wood and Troutbeck, 1992). However, in an interesting search for the source of this claim, Sivak (1996) discovered that this estimate has no scientific basis at all. Nonetheless, such a high "guesstimate" reflects the intuition of many researchers that vision plays a very important role in driving, by far more important than any other sensory input. It is obvious that we need to see in order to drive, but it is not at all obvious how well we need to see in order to drive. The second question – what kind of vision do we need for safe driving – can be answered once we establish what it is exactly that we need to see to drive safely.

Many people when asked what constitutes good vision reflexively reply 6/6 (or 20/20 in the U.S.), without quite knowing what it means. As discussed in more detail below, this is a measure of visual acuity: a person's ability to resolve small details. But visual acuity is not the only visual skill needed for driving. As typically measured and defined, visual acuity is a measure of a person's ability to resolve details when they are presented under optimal illumination (meaning high levels of illumination, high contrast, and no glare), in the middle of the observer's visual field (meaning when the observer is directly staring at it), with both the target and the observer being static (meaning neither one of them is moving), and under no time constraints (meaning the person can take as long as he or she needs to decide what the detail is). This highly constrained measure of visual performance is very relevant to reading from the board in a classroom (for which it was originally created by Snellen) or to deciphering the name of a street when standing during the daylight hours at some distance from it. But driving involves a very different visual task. In driving *none* of the above conditions apply most of the time: the driver is moving relative to the visual environment, the lighting conditions are often far from optimal (night, fog, and glare), emerging dangers typically first appear off to the side of the visual field and not where the driver is looking (as when a pedestrian darts into the street or a car converges from an adjacent lane), and the driver has very little time to perceive and respond to many hazardous situations. Finally, seeing small details may not be the skill we need at all. Pedestrians and vehicles that we might collide with are not small details, and we do not collide with them because we are unable to read the words on a t-shirt or the make of the car.

The goal of this chapter is to demonstrate that there is a lot more to vision – as needed for driving – than just visual acuity as tested for licensing. However, before we can discuss the role of vision in driving, it is necessary to briefly describe the capabilities and limits of our visual system.

Our Visual System

Our visual system consists of more than just our eyes. Information from the eyes is transmitted to our brain where the visual stimuli are analyzed and given a meaning. The eye does not see words on this page, but we do. The eye only sees a pattern of black and white dots, which are interpreted by our brain as letters and words that have meanings. Interestingly, we are conscious of the end product (our perceptions of the words, the meanings), and not of the pattern of the physical stimuli (the different colored lights) that hit the eye. A detailed discussion of the higher – perceptual – processes is postponed to the next chapter, and the discussion below is limited to the process that the light entering the eye undergoes, and its implications for our vision.

Our eyes are sensitive to a very narrow band of the electromagnetic waves that impinge on them: 400-700 nanometers (billionths of a meter) long. We call radiation within that range light. Within that range, different wavelengths are associated with different colors: the blue colors are in the short range, the green are in the middle, and the red hues are toward the end. Radiation that is slightly longer than 700 nanometers is what we label infrared, and radiation that is slightly shorter than 400 nanometers is ultra violet. Although our body can respond to these and other radiation wavelengths, they cannot be "seen" by our eyes. To be seen, the light reflected from objects around us must first hit our eye, and then it continues through its hard transparent cover, the cornea. Behind the cornea is a partially exposed lens that focuses the light on a photosensitive layer of cells – the retina – that sends signals to the brain where we finally interpret the patterns of nerve excitations as visual images. The opening that exposes the lens to light is the pupil. When we move from a brightly lit place to a dim place (as when we enter a tunnel) the pupillary constrictor muscles relax to expand the size of the opening, and when we move from a dimly lit place to a bright one (as when we exit the tunnel) the pupillary constrictor muscles constrict to shrink the size of the pupil. This reduces the amount of light entering the eye through the lens. The function of the lens is to bend the light rays so that they converge to a point on the inner surface of the eyeball, known as the retina. The retina is the tissue that converts the light stimulation to signals to the brain. If the lens focuses the light rays at some point inside the eye before the retina, we suffer myopia (near vision), and if the lens focuses the image beyond the retina we suffer from hyperopia (far vision). In either case we suffer from blurred vision that can be corrected with glasses, contact lenses, or surgery that essentially add a correction to our existing lens or reshape the lens curvature, so that the image is now focused on the retina. This simple procedure enables almost all people to achieve good acuity – or at least acuity that is good enough to qualify for a driver license.

The most interesting mechanism in the eye is the retina. It consists of light sensitive cells that respond differentially to the different wavelengths in the 400-700 nanometers range. It is at that surface that photochemical reactions take place, and it is from the retina that information is transferred to the brain to be interpreted. The anatomy and physiology of the retina are quite complex, and they are two of the primary determinants of how and what we see. The discussion here is quite simplistic and more detailed information can be found in various books on vision (e.g., Cornsweet, 1970). There are two types of light sensitive cells in the retina: rods and cones. There are approximately 120 million rods in each eye, they are sensitive to low levels of light, but they do not provide a good resolution of the image detail. They are also not sensitive to color. The cones on the other hand, of which we have "only" about six millions in each eye, are color sensitive and provide us with good resolution, but they are not as sensitive to low levels of light. Furthermore, the rods and cones are not evenly distributed on the retina. The distribution of the rods and cones is illustrated in Figure 4-1. In this figure, the X-axis represents the location on the retina (in this case of the left eye) along the horizontal meridian. The zero point is the center of the visual field – the direction of the viewer's gaze – and points to the right and left of the zero point represent the angular distance from the center of the visual field. For example, the location of 45 to the right of zero indicates the location of an object that is 45 degrees to the *left* of the visual gaze. Similarly an object that is located 45 degrees to the right of the visual gaze would reflect the light rays to the point indicated as 45 degrees to the *left* of zero. As can be seen from this figure, the cones are located primarily in the center of the eye – called the fovea. This is where the gaze is directed. As we move further and further from the direction of the gaze, the number and density of the cones quickly diminish. The rods are totally absent in the fovea and their density first increases toward the periphery, then reach a maximum at about 20 degrees from the fovea, and then gradually decrease toward the periphery of the retina and the visual field.

The most interesting aspect of vision is in the physiology – the way the system functions. One simplifying analogy is to think of the retina as a screen, with rods and cones as pixels on that screen. When you consider that a standard computer monitor has approximately one million pixels (e.g., 1280X800), then the potential resolution of a "monitor" with 126 million pixels – all on a screen (retina) that is a few centimeters square – becomes

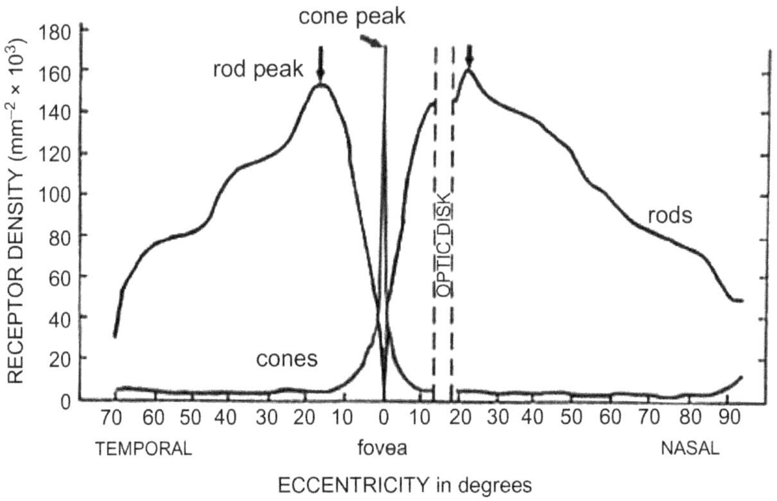

Figure 4-1. The distribution of the light sensitive cells – the rods and cones – in the retina. The center of the retina – the fovea – is the location of the direct gaze of the eye. The narrow band, marked as the optic disc, is the location of the blind spot, which is approximately 15 degrees toward the nose on the horizontal plane of each eye (the left eye in this drawing) (from Osterberg, 1935, with permission from Blackwell Publishing).

readily apparent. However, the actual resolution is significantly lower. That is because in their pathway to the brain, multiple cells are integrated into single neurons. The integration is much greater for the rods than for the cones, and that is one reason the rods are more sensitive to low light levels while the cones are more discriminating for details. The cones are more sensitive during the day, and the level of resolution that they provide is much greater than that of the rods. Thus, our ability to resolve details is greatest at the center of the visual field where the cones are most closely packed and diminishes toward the periphery. If a person has 6/6 acuity in the center of the visual field, that acuity drops to approximately 6/9 2.5 degrees away from the center, to 6/18 5 degrees away, to 6/30 10 degrees away, and to 6/60 20 degrees away (Linksz, 1952). Snellen acuity of 6/60 is the threshold for legal blindness in most countries. This rapid deterioration is illustrated in Figure 4-2. The rods cannot provide us with as detailed a picture of our environment, but they are much more sensitive to low lights, thus, in reduced illumination – as in a moonlit night – we are deprived of the benefits of the less sensitive cones and rely mostly on our rods. Because only the cones are differentially sensitive to the different wavelengths, color vision is enabled only by the cones, and therefore is greatly impaired at night. You can experience this if you ever try to find your car at night at an unlit parking lot. The only distinguishing characteristics among the cars are their shapes and their brightness (on a black-white continuum). Given all this, how well can we see objects in the center of the visual field, or in low levels of illumination, or in glare, and all of this while in

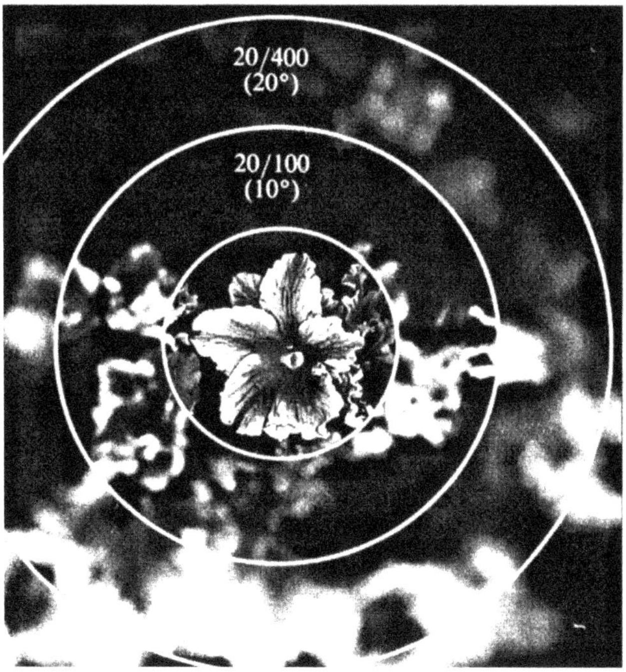

Figure 4-2. The blurring of an image as a function of the angular distance from the center of the visual field (i.e., from the direction of the visual gaze), in degrees (from Allen *et al.*, 2001, with permission from Lawyers and Judges Publishing Co.).

motion? We obviously need to perform such functions for safe driving, and the role of the different functions has been the focus of extensive investigations in the context of assessing driver visual capabilities and determining driver visual needs. The following is a brief review of the primary functions that have been studied relative to the visual needs in driving.

Driving-Related Visual Functions

There are many ways to measure vision. Visual acuity is the most common one. Other familiar ones include color vision, and visual field. Less common measures that may be more closely associated with the visual needs in driving include dynamic visual acuity, visual acuity in reduced illumination and under the presence of glare, contrast sensitivity, stereopsis (the ability to see depth of field with the aid of two eyes), motion detection (the ability to distinguish very slow movement from lack of movement), and *effective* (or useful) visual field. The relevance of all of these functions for driving has been evaluated extensively, and each of these functions and the evidence for their relevance is discussed below.

Visual acuity

Definition of visual acuity
There are various reasons why we think of visual acuity, our ability to resolve small details in the center of the visual field, as a generic measure of the quality of vision: it is the one test that kids get at an early age, especially if they have trouble reading from the board in class; it is most often the source of referral for correction with glasses; and when it is corrected we experience a sense of suddenly seeing a lot more of the world than before. It is also the only test that is common to all licensing tests anywhere in the world. It is the one test that we need to take, no matter where we are in the world, in order to get a driver license.

Good visual acuity is typically labeled 6/6 (or 20/20 in the U.S.). The literal meaning of that ratio is that a person, standing 6 meters (or 20 feet) away from a target is able to perceive a detail that a '"normally sighted' person can also perceive from a distance of 6 meters (or 20 feet). A person who can see from 6 meters what a "normally" sighted individual can see from 12 meters has a visual acuity of 6/12, and can resolve details only if they are twice as large as those that can be resolved by a person with 6/6 vision. This metric also implies that some people can have vision that is better than 6/6, such as 6/5 or even 6/4. But what *is* the acuity of someone with 6/6? How fine a detail can that person see? Well, it is the ability to discern a detail that subtends only 1 minute of arc-angle, or 1/60 of one degree in space. This is roughly the ability to detect an object that is slightly smaller than 2 millimeters from a distance of 6 meters, or the ability to detect a small coin (say a Euro-cent) from a distance of roughly 35 meters. This level of acuity is much more than is needed to discern the presence of a vehicle or a pedestrian 1 kilometer away!

Standards of visual acuity

For licensing purposes, most countries will grant a license to any one with binocular visual acuity of at least 6/12 (people with less than 6/12 vision in their better eye are considered "low vision" people). This is the European standard (EEC, 1991) and the standard adopted by 40 states in the U.S., though exceptions – especially for older drivers – are not rare (NHTSA, 2003). However, there is no compelling scientific basis for this standard (though highway signs are designed for that level in mind), and some U.S. states have more lenient requirements. For example, in the U.S., Florida, that has a large percentage of older people, requires only 6/21 (or 20/70 in feet) in the better eye (Peli, 2002). Despite the "lax" requirement, its fatality rate in 2011 was 1.25 fatalities per 100 million vehicle miles. While this rate was above the U.S. average of 1.10, it was still lower than the rate of nine states – all with more stringent visual acuity requirements (NHTSA, 2013). Another indication of the arbitrariness of the visual Snellen acuity standard of 6/12 comes from a small but detailed study that examined actual driving performance in Helsinki, Finland. The study compared responses, of five male drivers with impaired acuity (of 6/30 Snellen acuity) and five normally sighted male drivers (with 6/12 or better Snellen acuity) to experimentally manipulated hazards. All the drivers in both groups had normal contrast sensitivity and peripheral vision, and the two groups were matched for age, driving experience, and safety record. The results failed to show any significant difference between the two groups in actual driving behaviors, except that the visually impaired drivers were slightly slower in responding to the brake lights of a car ahead by an average of 0.2 seconds. Based on these results the authors concluded that the European and U.S. standard of 6/12 "is not a necessary prerequisite for safe driving" (Lamble, Summala, and Hyvarinen, 2002, p. 711).

An interesting exception to the 6/6 acuity standard is the UK criterion, which requires drivers to be able to read the characters on a license plate (where the height of the characters is 79.4 millimeters) from a distance of 20.5 meters (Young *et al.*, 2012). This translates to a visual acuity of roughly 6/15; meaning a slightly more liberal requirement than in most of the rest of the world. The appeal of the British approach is that a person can easily test his/her visual acuity at any time to see if they meet the licensing requirements simply by testing his or her ability to see the numerals on a license plate from 20 meters. Regardless of the specific requirement, fortunately most of the impairments in visual acuity can be corrected with glasses, contact lenses, or laser surgery. For example, in the U.S., until the age of 60, after correction, less than one half of one percent of the people has less than 6/12 acuity. Less than two percent of the people under 70 years old and less than four percent of the people under 80 years old have visual acuity of less than 6/12 in their better eye (National Eye Institute, 2004). This means that at least as far as vision, nearly everyone is able to achieve the minimum required level of visual acuity to be licensed to drive. Once we get past the age of 80 the situation is different. At the age of 80+ nearly 40 percent suffer from "low vision," or visual acuity of less than 6/12 in the better eye.

Visual acuity and driving performance

The relevance of visual acuity to safe driving is hardly ever questioned by anyone applying for a license. This provides the test of vision with "face validity" for licensing: a perception that it is a relevant and valid measure of safe driving. In fact, the relevance of visual acuity to driving can be, and has been, demonstrated experimentally by blurring people's vision and then measuring their driving performance. Higgins, Wood, and Tait (1998) gave drivers glasses with different amounts of blurring that artificially reduced their vision from 6/6 to 6/12, 6/30, or 6/60 (the level considered "legally blind" in most countries). They then had the people drive on a 5.1 kilometer closed course with the different levels of blur. The results showed that performance on visual tasks deteriorated significantly as the amount of blur increased. The percent of signs detected decreased from 81 percent with 6/6 vision, to 63 percent with 6/30 vision, to only 44 percent with 6/60 vision. With blurred vision the drivers also hit more "road hazards" that consisted of gray foam rubber speed bumps: from nearly zero (two percent) with 6/6, to 28 percent with 6/30, to 59 percent with 6/60. The driving degradation due to the blurring was actually even greater than indicated by the above numbers, because the drivers also drove significantly slower with increasing amounts of blur (slowing from an average of 54 km/hr with 6/6 to an average of 44 km/hr with 6/60). In a later study, Higgins and Wood (2005) replicated some of the earlier findings, demonstrating a relationship between acuity and total time needed to complete the drive, hazard avoidance performance, and sign recognition. However, in their second study they also added a condition that simulated mild cataract (with frosted lenses) and measured contrast sensitivity as well. When the effects of the cataracts and the scoring on the contrast sensitivity tests were added to the prediction of the driving performance measure, the effects of the visual acuity all but disappeared. Thus, while the early results provided some empirical scientific validity for the importance of visual acuity for driving, the more recent and sophisticated study did not. In fact, based on both studies Higgins and Wood concluded that "static acuity can only predict variations in closed road driving performance measured under degraded conditions that include simulated mild cataracts when it is combined with supplementary vision tests." Young *et al.* (2012) also examined the effect of reduced acuity using blurring lenses in a driving simulator and they too obtained minimal effects on only few of the driving measures (speed variance and lane excursions). On the other hand, Wood *et al.* (2012) found that even slight blurring (that reduced visual acuity to approximately 6/9) was sufficient to impair the identification of signs and detection of a dark clothed pedestrian at night, while driving on a closed course. However, as both of these measures are exclusively visual, and sign identification requires resolution of details, this is not very surprising,

In addition to Higgins and Wood's qualification about the relevance of acuity, there is also a problem with accepting their results and those of Young *et al.* (2012) at face value. The problem is that in all of these studies the impaired acuity was artificially induced. This is significant, because it is likely that people with non-induced reduced acuity adapt to their limitation, and may find a variety of ways to compensate for it. This is something that the people in these studies had no time to do. Some support for that adaptation process comes from a study by Wood and Owens (2005), who measured the visual acuity (and contrast sensitivity) of drivers, and then had them drive on a closed course with various signs and obstacles, in daytime and nighttime conditions (with high-beams headlamps with various amounts of light power). The drivers' task was to avoid the obstacles and report on each sign that they passed. Although sign recognition deteriorated from day to night and as the headlight power was decreased, no relation was found between the daytime acuity and the sign recognition performance under any level of illumination. However, when performance on daytime acuity test was combined with performance on tests of either contrast sensitivity or low-luminance acuity (both discussed below) a significant relationship was obtained. These results suggest that while no single measure of visual performance is very strongly related to driving performance, some combinations of visual skills may be quite relevant. This conclusion is supported by a later study by Wood *et al.* (2013). In this study they administered multiple functional vision tests (including visual acuity, visual field and contrast sensitivity) to elderly drivers (65 + years old) who were classified as safe or unsafe based on the ratings they obtained in an on-road in-traffic driving test by a professional examiner. They found that although no single functional test provided adequate sensitivity and specificity, the complete battery together with some cognitive tests was useful in predicting on-road driving performance, with a sensitivity (correct detections) of 80 percent and specificity of 73 percent (correct rejections).

If one stops to actually consider it, most of the "targets" that are relevant to safe driving – including cars and pedestrians with which we might collide – are quite big and their detection or identification must often be performed under severe time constraints. One qualification to this generalization is that in some situations while the "target" on the road is quite large, the cues needed to avoid a crash with it may be small and within the range of good visual acuity. Thus, Lacherez, Au, and Wood (2014) found that visual acuity is weakly correlated ($r = .32$) with the reaction time to suddenly emerging hazards, and Anstey *et al.* (2012) and Wood *et al.* (2013) found that acuity *when combined with contrast sensitivity* was weakly correlated with hazard perception.

Visual acuity and crash involvement

On-the-road performance is just one of many intervening variables that mediate between driver skills and limitations and crash involvement. Therefore, it should not be surprising that the relationship between acuity and crash involvement is conceptually more tenuous than between acuity and on-the-road visual performance. Nearly all of the studies that attempted to relate visual acuity to crash involvement failed to find any practically significant relationships between the two (e.g., Cross *et al.*, 2009; Green, McGwin, and Owsley, 2013; Rubin *et al.*, 2007). For reviews of the many earlier studies see DfT, 2005; Owsley and McGwin, 1999; Shinar, 1977; Shinar and Schieber, 1991).

There are several reasons why more than 100 independent studies failed to find a significant association between visual acuity and driving. The first is that crashes are caused by multiple factors (see Chapter 18 on crash causation), and impaired vision may be confounded by other crash-related variables (such as age and co-morbidity). For example, on the one hand the people with the best visual acuity are typically the young drivers, who are also the highest-risk drivers on the road. On the other hand, the people with the worst visual performance are the old drivers who are probably the most cautious on the road both in the way they drive and in selecting the times and places to drive (see Chapter 7). However, even after age is controlled for, the magnitude of the relationship between visual acuity (after correction with glasses, lenses, or surgery) and crashes remains close to zero (Burg, 1967; Shinar, 1977, 1978).

A second possible reason for the lack of empirical association between visual acuity and crash involvement is that – by necessity – all the studies that investigated this relationship were conducted on licensed drivers, and these people already had corrected visual acuity of 6/12 or better (at least at one time) (Higgins *et al.*, 1998). This is known as a "restriction of range" effect: when the range of score on one or both variables is small, the correlation between the two variables cannot be high (Heiman, 2000). In our case, a potentially strong relationship between visual acuity and crashes may be masked because the range of visual acuity scores is restricted, because applicants with poor visual acuity have already been screened out of the driving population. But to see the true strength of the relationship we would have to allow everyone to drive, regardless of their acuity. It is impossible to imagine a licensing agency that would assume this risk to public health just in order to satisfy some researcher's scientific curiosity. The restricted range effect is partially overcome in a study conducted on 399 commercial intercity Nigerian drivers where 2.8 percent had less than 5/18 (= 20/60) acuity, and 11 percent had less than the 6/9 required for commercial license. Yet in that sample too, there was no relationship between visual acuity and accident involvement (Adekoya *et al.*, 2009).

A third reason is that crashes occur in the context of very specific conditions, while visual acuity is measured in a sterile environment under optimal conditions that may be irrelevant to the crash situation (Sivak, 1981). This argument is a little complicated, but what it essentially means is that if vision (or any other personal attribute) is not consistently affected to the same extent in all people by different situations (for example in the presence of glare from the sun), then it is unlikely that its measurement under the standardized and optimal conditions will be related to the specific crash characteristics. For example, older people are more affected by glare than young people with the same acuity as measured in the doctor's office under optimal illumination. Therefore, in the presence of glare an older person's acuity would be worse than that of a young person with the same acuity as measured in the absence of glare (e.g., as it is measured in the optometrist's office or the licensing bureau).

Despite all of these post hoc explanations, a few studies have found significant relationships between visual acuity and crash involvement (e.g., Hofstetter, 1976; Davison, 1985), but they are by far a small fraction of the studies conducted to test this relationship. Thus, already 40 years ago the weight of the evidence suggested that if there is a relationship, it is quite weak; and more recent research from the past three decades has not changed that fact. Studies by Owsley and her colleagues found a slight trend suggesting that people with less than 6/12 Snellen acuity might have more crashes, but these relationships were not statistically significant (Green *et al.*, 2013; Owsley *et al.*, 1998; Sims *et al.*, 2000). In an extensive analysis of the relationship between visual acuity and crashes on a sample of 30,000 70-year-old Quebec drivers, Gresset and Meyer (1994) failed to find an effect, as long as the acuity was not extremely degraded or the driver was monocular (having the benefit of only one functioning eye, in which case the visual field is also reduced). More recently, Woolnough and his associates (2013) analyzed the relationship between the two-year crash history of over 1,200 Canadian, Australian, and New Zealand drivers and many of the medically assessed driving-related skills, including visual acuity. They found no relationship between the two (though there was a statistically significant relationship between the combined impairment of visual acuity and hearing and crash involvement).

These repeated findings of a lack of strong relationship between visual acuity and crash involvement prompted Gresset and Meyer more than 20 years ago (1994) to propose that the licensing criterion be made more liberal and reset at 6/15 rather than 6/12. Such a proposal is actually very practical because with the present visual acuity requirement of 6/12 most license applicants eventually get the license, but those who initially fail the test have to appeal and engage the licensing authorities in more paper work. This was most convincingly demonstrated by Zaidel and Hocherman (1986) who tracked the license renewal process of 10,022 65+years old Israeli passenger vehicle drivers. The licensing visual acuity requirement in Israel, as in most of the world is 6/12 or better in the better eye. Approximately 92 percent of the drivers returned the completed medical forms. In 54 percent of these cases there were no visual problems that precluded license renewal, and in 19 percent there were correctable vision problems. The remaining 27 percent were forwarded to the National Medical Institute for Road Safety for evaluation. The Institute either placed restrictions on the license (mostly a requirement to use corrective lenses), or invited the applicants for re-evaluation. At the end of the process, of those invited for further evaluation, not a single license was eventually denied (though in some cases the license was restricted to wearing corrective lenses or use of panoramic mirrors). It is of course possible that the eight percent who did not return the application form in order to renew their license did so as a self-selection process because their vision or medical condition had deteriorated. To check for this possibility, Zaidel and Hocherman contacted a random sample of the families of these drivers. It turned out that in about half the cases the drivers had died since their last license renewal, and in the rest of the cases non-renewal was due to non-medical and non-vision problems, but to a "host of economic and health factors." Interestingly, despite the marginal (if at all) relationship to crashes, reduced visual acuity appears to be weakly associated with older drivers' decision to hang up their keys and cease driving (Emerson *et al.*, 2012). Thus, even subjectively the loss of visual acuity may lead to reduced confidence in one's driving.

To detect potential hazards on the roads we need other skills. For example, to detect a child who is about to jump into the lane requires the detection of a peripheral target well before it enters our line of vision. To detect the braking of a car ahead in order to prevent a rear-end collision requires motion detection capability. A similar capability is needed to determine if a car on a crossroad is on a collision path with us. To respond to visual emergencies at night or in glare requires good contrast sensitivity, and adequate dark adaptation and light adaptation. Even if we do need to detect and identify small targets, we need to do that under conditions of movement, and hence we need to resort to dynamic acuity.

How do these visual requirements relate to visual acuity that is tested under static conditions with optimal illumination? Apparently not very well. An interesting demonstration of the relative independence of the different visual skills, and the fallacy of relying on one (such as static acuity under optimal illumination) as a surrogate for all others (such as nighttime acuity or acuity in the presence of glare) is provided in two studies by Sivak and his associates (Sivak, Olson, and Pastalan, 1981; and Sivak and Olson, 1982). In the first study they recruited young (under 25 years old) and old (over 61 years old) drivers who had identical daytime visual acuity (as measured under optimal illumination). They then measured their nighttime legibility distance (distance from which they could distinguish among different letters). The driver's task was to drive at night toward a retroreflective sign that contained the letter E in either its normal orientation or its mirrored image. The legibility distance was the distance at which the driver was able to identify the orientation of the letter. They found that despite the identical daytime acuity, the older drivers' sign legibility distances were 65-75 percent (depending on the particular letter/background color combination) lower than the legibility distance of the young drivers. This meant that factors other than daytime acuity were responsible for the difference between the age groups. In the next study, they again compared the performance of younger and older drivers, but this time they matched the two groups on their nighttime acuity by having them take an acuity test under low-luminance conditions (after giving each person 10 minutes to adapt to the dark). This time there were no significant differences between the two groups in the sign legibility distance. Together, the two experiments demonstrate two important characteristics of visual performance. First they show how specific but different visual skills are responsible for seemingly identical tasks (sign reading in daytime and nighttime), and how screening for one skill may totally miss the mark if another skill is needed. Second, they illustrate the interaction between age and vision. Even when static visual acuity is the same, there are significant age-related deteriorations that vary from one skill to another, making prediction of performance for older people even more difficult. With such findings in mind, let us review the evidence for the involvement of visual skills other than daytime acuity in driving. The discussions below will focus on "night vision" and vision in glare, dynamic visual acuity, motion detection, contrast sensitivity, and visual field.

Visual acuity under degraded conditions: Low illumination and glare

Under low levels of illumination, that is typical of night driving, the amount of light is insufficient for the color-sensitive cones. We must also rely on our rods, which are essentially inactive in high levels of illumination. The process of adjustment, however, takes time. We are aware of this whenever we enter a darkened theater after the movie has started. At first we feel totally blind, and then gradually we are able to see the rows of seats and eventually the seats that are occupied and the ones that are empty.

This process is called dark adaptation. The adaptation of the cones to their maximal sensitivity takes approximately 8 minutes, but to achieve the maximal sensitivity of the rods we need upwards of 20 minutes! Fortunately, the rate of diminishing light at dusk is slower than our dark adaptation, and at most times we can operate with maximal visual efficiency. Interestingly, it takes much less time to adjust from darkness to light. In that case we are initially blinded by the light, but we typically need less than a minute to achieve full light adaptation.

When we drive at night we are actually operating with mesopic acuity: acuity at light levels that are between those of light adaptation (known as photopic acuity) and dark adaptation (known as scotopic acuity). As one would expect and as can be seen in Figure 4-3, our mesopic acuity and our acuity in the presence of glare are significantly poorer than our acuity under optimal illumination. Perhaps more important, while daylight acuity is correctable and once corrected remains relatively stable even beyond the age of 60, that is not the case for nighttime acuity and acuity under glare. They are not correctable and start to deteriorate significantly at that age, so that a slight deterioration in daylight acuity is accompanied by a very large deterioration in mesopic acuity and acuity under glare. Thus, while daytime visual acuity may be relevant to our ability to read signs in daylight, it is apparently totally unrelated to our ability to recognize roadway signs as we drive by them under reduced levels of illumination (Wood and Owens, 2005). Also, corrected visual acuity – which is the basis for licensing – may be due to near-sightedness (myopia) or far-sightedness (hyperopia), and night vision, glare sensitivity, and glare recovery time are different for people with the two types of degraded acuity. Myopic people are likely to perform worse under low levels of illumination and glare than hyperopic people. For example, in one study the glare recovery time of myopic

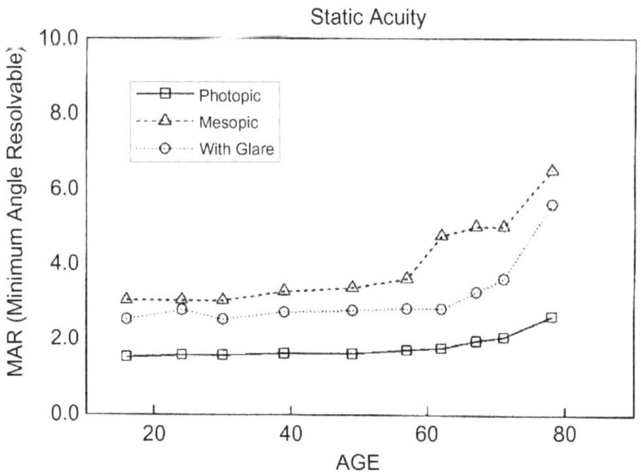

Figure 4-3. Acuity of drivers in optimal illumination (photopic), nighttime illumination (mesopic), and in the presence of glare. Acuity is noted in minimum resolvable angle, where 1.0 is equivalent to Snellen acuity of 6/6, 2.0 is equivalent to 6/12, 4.0 is equivalent to 6/24, etc. (from Shinar, 1977).

people was 40 percent longer than that of hyperopic people, and the greater the myopia the longer the recovery time (Mashige, 2010).

The different dark and light adaptation times have significant implications for driving. We need to be dark-adapted in order to drive without headlights on an unlit rural road at night. Fortunately our vision is aided by our vehicle headlights, and sometimes by additional streetlights. Several studies have shown that stationary road lights can reduce crashes with pedestrians by over 50 percent (Pegrum, 1972; Polus and Katz, 1978) and other crashes and fatalities to a slightly lesser degree (Bullough, Donnel, and Rea, 2013; Elvik, *et al.*, 2009). As we drive along, we typically encounter approaching cars that create transient glare. This is where the asymmetry in the dark adaptation and light adaptation becomes critical. The effect of an approaching car's headlights is to initiate the process of light adaptation. Because the process is relatively quick, it takes only a few seconds to start to lose our dark adaptation. So while we are still trying to adapt to the new bright visual environment, the car passes us by. This puts us back in the relative darkness but this time it is without the benefit of our dark adaptation. We experience this in the few seconds after the car passes us when we feel we are still "blinded" and cannot see the road. The glare recovery time is dependent on our glare vision threshold, and may last anywhere from one second to over 6 seconds (Mashige, 2010). During that interval we drive on faith alone. The situation is, of course, more complicated for older drivers, who because of their poorer nighttime vision also require more time to recover from glare (Schieber, 1994).

An interesting study that demonstrated drivers' inappropriate handling of glare was conducted by Pulling *et al.* (1980). In their study they first measured drivers' acuity in the presence of glare and noted the minimal amount of glare needed for each person to lose some of the acuity. They then had the same people drive in a simulator, on a round track, toward a car with its high beams on. They were instructed to drive "as fast as considered comfortable and safe and slow down when the varying brightness of the headlights on oncoming cars became so great that potential hazards on the highway could not be distinguished in time to drive around them or avoid a collision by stopping." As they drove, the experimenter varied the brightness of the lights of the oncoming car until they produced a glare level that caused the drivers to either slow or change their steering behavior. When Pulling *et al.* (1980) compared the tolerable glare levels in the acuity test and the tolerable glare levels in driving they found that drivers' "subjective glare tolerance" was above their visual threshold for glare, meaning that drivers tolerated higher levels of glare on the road before they changed their behavior, than would be predicted from their visual performance under glare. Furthermore, young drivers were willing to tolerate a greater disparity between the two, indicating a greater level of risk taking. One possible explanation for the difference between young and old drivers in this behavior is that older drivers feel the discomfort from glare before young drivers do.

Evidence concerning the relationship between mesopic acuity and glare sensitivity is relatively scarce (possibly because these tests are not commonly administered), but at least two studies that evaluated it directly (Shinar, 1977; von Hebenstreit, 1984), and other studies that evaluated it indirectly (van den Berg *et al.*, 2009) have found that people with reduced mesopic acuity and increased glare sensitivity are more likely to be involved in nighttime crashes than those without these impairments. Gruber *et al.* (2013) reviewed the empirical literature on the relationship between various visual skills of older drivers and their night driving performance and nighttime crashes. They found that reduced mesopic acuity and heightened glare sensitivity impair nighttime driving performance and increase nighttime crash likelihood. Though many of the studies were not able to control for various confounding variables, the weight of the evidence does show that older drivers who are in general more prone to reduced mesopic acuity and greater glare sensitivity are at a greater risk when driving at night.

Dynamic visual acuity

Dynamic visual acuity is a measure of our acuity when we are in relative motion to the target of observation. Whereas good static acuity only depends on the refraction of the lens and the health of the retina, dynamic visual acuity also depends on the observer's ability to move the eyes in order to track a moving target in such a way that the target remains projected in the center of the visual field where our ability to resolve details is the greatest. Obviously, this situation is much more applicable to the driving environment than the static visual acuity that is measured in a doctor's office or in a driver licensing station. With this argument in mind, Burg (1966) devised an apparatus that consisted of a black box with an opening through which a person viewed a target that moved across the horizontal visual field at different rates. The target was a Landolt Ring, which is essentially a circle with an opening that could appear in one of four different orientations (when the opening is to the right, the target looks like the letter C). The observer's task was to determine the location of the opening. Burg then projected the moving target on a circular screen at different rates, and for each rate determined the smallest target that the observer could see clearly enough to determine the location of the gap in the circle. This test was then administered to 17,000 California residents who came to apply for a new license or for a license renewal.

The first part of the results of Burg's extensive tests is reproduced in Figure 4-4, where the mean acuity for each target speed (in degrees per second) is noted in terms of the arc-angle that could be resolved. An arc angle of 1 minute is equivalent to 6/6, 2 minutes are equivalent to 6/12, 3 minutes are equivalent to 6/18, etc. Three important conclusions emerge from these results. First, corrected average static acuity (the bottom-most curve) is hardly affected by age. Acuity (often with corrective lenses) remains quite constant until the age of 40 and then it diminishes slightly. But even at the age of 80, most of the license applicants could resolve a detail smaller than needed for 6/12. Second, acuity for moving targets was worse than it was for the static targets, and it worsened as the targets moved faster and faster. Third – and most important – the decrement in dynamic visual acuity worsened significantly with age, starting as early as age 40. This is demonstrated by the increasing gaps between the curves as age increases.

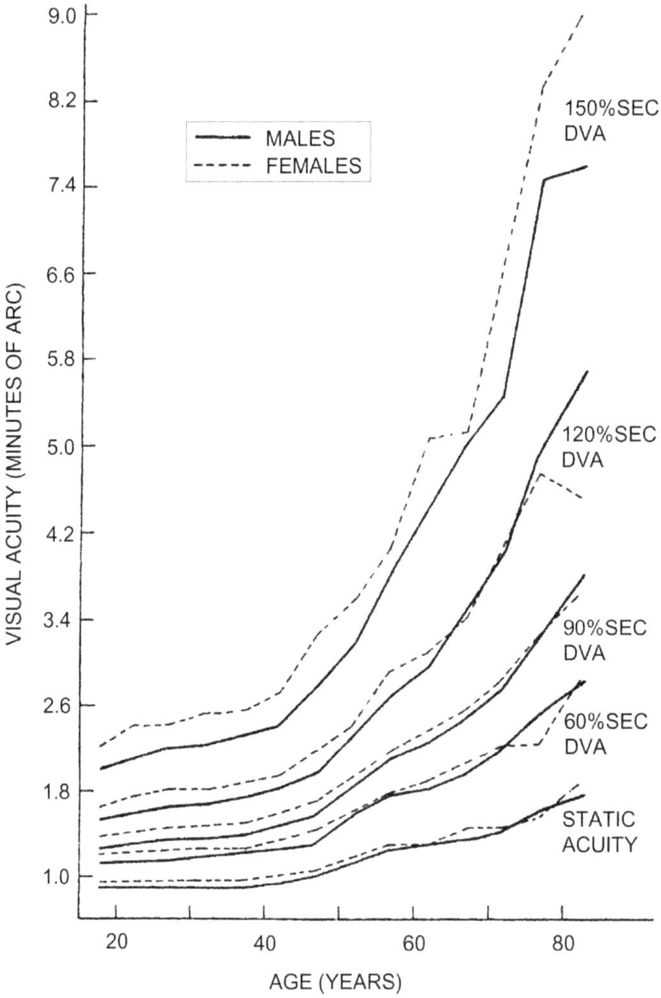

Figure 4-4. Dynamic visual acuity as a function of age and angular speed of the moving target, relative to static visual acuity (from Burg, 1966, with permission from the American Psychological Association).

Thus, for 40 years old drivers, acuity for a target moving at 120 degrees/second (so that it would take that Landolt ring 3 seconds to complete a full circle around the observer's head) was about 6/12 relative to static acuity of 6/6. However, for 80 years old drivers, the average dynamic visual acuity for a target moving at that speed was 6/30 relative to 6/8 for a static target. There is also physiological support for this age-related effect. Sharp and Sylvester (1978) found that young people could accurately track targets at velocities up to 30 degrees/sec, whereas older drivers began to have problems when the target velocity exceeded 10 degrees/sec.

The implication of the third conclusion is that a small deterioration in static acuity for a young driver may not have very severe implications for his or her dynamic acuity. But the same small deterioration in static acuity for an older driver – one that would still qualify that driver to drive – may be associated with a severe deterioration in dynamic visual acuity, and one that is arguably much more relevant to driving. Similar very large age-related deteriorations in dynamic acuity relative to static acuity were obtained in a later study on 890 Indiana drivers (Shinar, 1977).

Given the above considerations, all that remains now is to actually demonstrate that dynamic visual acuity is relevant to driving safety and crash involvement or at least more relevant than static visual acuity. This in fact was demonstrated by Burg (1968) and Shinar (1977) on California and Indiana drivers, respectively. With the very large number of drivers involved in both studies, even a small effect of little practical significance can be statistically significant. And in fact the correlations between dynamic visual acuity and crashes – while they were statistically significant and higher than the correlations between static visual acuity and crashes – were still very low: on the order of $r = 0.1$ in both studies. Not surprisingly dynamic visual acuity correlates better with intermediate measures of performance that are associated with driving skills or safety. Thus, Long and Kearns (1996) obtained correlations ranging from $r = .30$ to $r = .72$ (depending on the specific signs, and speed of movement) between sign identification thresholds and dynamic visual acuity. In contrast to these strong relations, static visual acuity did not correlate significantly with the identification thresholds of any of the signs. Finally, Wilkins *et al.* (2013) in a driving simulator study on young drivers found a correlation of $r = 0.61$ between performance on a dynamic visual acuity test and hazard perception score.

Another problem encountered with testing dynamic visual acuity is that it is very susceptible to practice. Unlike static acuity tests that are relatively unaffected by practice, dynamic visual test performance improves with repeated administration of the test (Shinar and Schieber, 1991). The more times people take the test the better their performance. The reason is that dynamic visual acuity depends on the optical and retinal properties of the eye, as well as on the motor coordination of the eye muscles that control the eye movements in order to retain the image of the target on the fovea. The faster the target moves, the more difficult it is for the eye to track it in such a manner that its position on the fovea remains constant. When the image location is not constant it appears smeared, and resolving details (such as the location of the gap in a Landolt Ring) becomes more difficult. This motor aspect of dynamic visual acuity can be improved through practice (like most motor behaviors). Because all of the findings relating dynamic visual acuity to crashes were based on performance in the first administration of this test, there is a real practical concern that people who might otherwise fail this test could practice at it before the critical licensing test, and then pass the test – without necessarily improving their dynamic visual performance in real driving situations. They would simply become "test-wise." This is the same phenomenon we see in intelligence or psychometric tests: people improve their performance even though it is clear that they do not increase their intelligence. Thus, the use of dynamic visual acuity for licensing will remain a "complicated issue." As long as there are no standard techniques that can provide a stable performance measure this visual function will most likely remain outside the battery of vision testing for licensing.

Color vision

The ability to distinguish among colors, colloquially known as color vision, is routinely tested in many licensing bureaus around the world. While total insensitivity to color is quite rare, color deficiency, especially the inability to distinguish between red and green is quite common among males (affecting 7-8 percent of adult males), but not among females where it is quite rare (0.4 percent) (Montgomery, 2005). Given this particular gender-specific deficiency of red-green confusion, one would think that it would be very dangerous to drive anywhere where traffic signal lights exist. It turns out that this is not the case, because in most places the placement of the lights is uniform (red-amber-green, from top to bottom), and color deficient people can rely on that information to determine the signal color. Also in many places the traditional "green" has been replaced by a more bluish light with which very few people have a problem. Consequently, in general, color deficient people are not over-involved in crashes (Verriest *et al.*, 1980; Vingrys and Cole, 1988), even though it has been shown that the reaction time of color deficient drivers to red lights is longer than that of color-normal people (Atchison *et al.*, 2003). However, a focused examination of involvement in particular crashes has shown that people with reduced sensitivity to red (protan color defect) are not over-involved in crashes in general, but they are over-involved in rear-end crashes, presumably because they may have some difficulty in sensing brake lights in time (Verriest *et al.*, 1980).

Notwithstanding the lack of evidence to demonstrate that there is a significant relationship between color vision and crash involvement, many jurisdictions require at least a gross ability to distinguish among green, amber, and red, especially for commercial drivers (e.g., FMCSA, 2001).

Motion detection

Motion detection is a critical skill that enables us to maintain safe distance from other moving vehicles or pedestrians. There are at least two types of motion that are important to detect: movement directly in front of us, as when a car ahead is slowing down or speeding away from us (movement-in-depth, or "looming"), and movement across our visual field, as when a car on a crossroad accelerates or decelerates as it nears an intersection ahead of us (angular motion). The visual cues that we have to rely on to detect these kinds of movements are the minute changes in object size for the vehicle moving ahead of us, and the minute changes in angular location of the vehicle moving across our visual field on a crossroad. How sensitive are we to these changes? And if some people are less sensitive than others, are they more likely to be involved in crashes – especially the kind that involve collisions with other moving vehicles?

This measure of visual performance has not been studied extensively, and no standardized tests exist for this measure. Nonetheless, early tests of this visual performance measure by Henderson and Burg (1974) and by Shinar (1977) indicated large individual differences in this ability, and they are mostly age-related. As with dynamic visual acuity, the rate of deterioration accelerates with age. Shinar (1977) found that while drivers 16-40 years old can detect a change in movement-in-depth of about 0.10 degrees/sec, drivers 80 years old and older could only detect changes that were approximately 0.5 degrees/sec. Hoffmann (1968) and Hoffman and Mortimer (1994) studied driver's ability to detect closure and obtained a threshold for motion detection of 0.17 degrees/sec. Thus, only when an approaching or a receding car is close enough to create a change that is greater than 0.17 degrees/sec in its retinal size can we perceive that we are closing in on it or distancing ourselves from it.

When our threshold for detecting movement-in-depth is translated to car following situations or overtaking situations, it turns out that when the relative speed between us and the car ahead of us is high we can first detect the change in our relative speed at fairly small distances. The specific relationship between relative speed and the distance at which we can detect the change in headway, or the time-to-collision, before we can respond to that change have been calculated by Hoffman and Mortimer (1996). For example, when we approach a slower vehicle at 20 km/hr (relative to its speed) we can detect that we are closing in on that vehicle while we are about 8 seconds away from it. On the other hand, if our relative speed is a very high, say 100 km/hr – as when we approach a very slow-moving vehicle on a highway – we first notice the change in the headway when we are only about 4 seconds away from it. Given that this is a highly unexpected situation, the actual recognition of this fact may leave us with less than 2 seconds to respond (see Chapter 5). The importance of sensitivity to movement-in-depth was demonstrated in a simulator study in which drivers were instructed to maintain a 2 seconds headway from the car ahead. At a random point, the lead car with its brake lights deactivated, braked suddenly. In this situation the brake reaction time of the following drivers was directly related to their sensitivity; the more sensitive they were the shorter their braking reaction time ($r = 0.46$) (Wilkins *et al.*, 2013). To offset our insensitivity to movement-in-depth, very slow-moving vehicles are required to have additional cues – such as flashing tail lights – that signal their very low speed to drivers coming up from behind them. A further aggravation of the problem is that our sensitivity to a looming car decreases with age, so that as we age we become less and less sensitive to the relative speed between us and the car ahead, or to the time we have to clear an intersection when another car is approaching it from the left or right (Poulter and Wann, 2013).

The threshold for detection of angular motion and movement-in-depth should be particularly relevant to night driving when often the only cues we have to tell us that we are driving into a slower moving vehicle is the rate at which the rear lights of the car ahead seem to spread apart. Similarly at night in the absence of streetlights, the only indication that we have if a vehicle on a crossroad is about to cross our path, or moving, or stopped, or slowing down, is the rate of the perceived angular movement of its lights. These theoretical considerations were validated in Shinar's (1977) analysis of the visual performance and crash histories of 890 drivers. The crash analyses showed that movement detection threshold was the best predictor – of all vision measures used, including static acuity (daytime, nighttime, and with glare), dynamic visual acuity, and visual field – of nighttime crash involvement for drivers 55 years old and older. A more recent analysis of the relationship between self-reported violations and crashes among older Florida drivers also yielded weak but statistically significant relationships with violations and crashes. However, this study did not seem to control for other variables that also correlated with crashes and violations such as the drivers' mental state (Smither *et al.*, 2012). Still, in a well-controlled laboratory setting motion detection sensitivity has been linked to the ability to detect road hazards (Lacherez *et al.*, 2014; Wilkins *et al.*, 2013), and in a simulation environment reduced motion detection sensitivity has also been associated with increased brake reaction time to the sudden deceleration of a lead vehicle (Wilkins *et al.*, 2013).

Unfortunately, as a practical test of vision, this measure has the same problem as dynamic visual acuity: it is strongly affected by practice. Apparently, people can learn to recognize test-specific cues to motion that may or may not transfer to motion detection in the real world. The silver lining in this practice effect is that it may actually help in improving the associated driving skills such as reaction to slowing vehicles (Wilkins *et al.*, 2013).

Contrast sensitivity

The main effect of glare is to reduce the contrast in the visual environment. Contrast is the relative brightness of adjacent objects. We need a minimal amount of contrast to detect a target, no matter how much light we have and how big the target is. For example,

Figure 4-5. The effects of reduced contrast on the ability to detect a child crossing the road (with permission from Ginsburg, 2003).

even in bright sunlight it may be impossible to read white letters on a white paper, but we can read the same writing on a black paper by the light of a single candle. We experience reduced contrast at night when the reflectance of light from dark obstacles on the road is very similar to the reflectance of the road pavement. We also experience reduced contrast in broad daylight when we drive directly into the sun, especially if our windshield is covered with dust. In both cases the objects may be as large as cars or trucks (much larger than needed for our visual acuity), but they reflect the same amount of light into our eyes as their surroundings. At night, both the object and the background are dark and reflect very little light back to our eyes, and in the daytime under glare, both the cars on the road and the roadway environment reflect too much light. The effect of a reduction in contrast – or in contrast sensitivity – on the ability to perceive a child crossing the road is dramatically illustrated in Figure 4-5 (from Ginsburg, 2003).

Given the fact that most crashes involve collisions with objects that are much larger than the minimal details we can see, over 50 years ago Schmidt (1961) argued that contrast sensitivity is much more relevant to safe driving than visual acuity, because the ability to distinguish large targets from their low-contrast background is much more relevant to safe driving needs than the ability to distinguish small details against a high contrast background. Interestingly, in the study by Emerson *et al.* (2012) mentioned above, age and contrast sensitivity were the best predictors of driving cessation, relative to all the off road predictors that were evaluated (including visual acuity, useful field of view (UFOV), field dependence, and various tests of perceptual motor skills). These findings imply that drivers are sensitive to their deterioration in contrast sensitivity and to its relevance to the confidence they have in their driving.

Because our ability to detect a target depends both on its luminance and its contrast, our general ability to detect low contrast objects is particularly poor at night. Many of the nighttime crashes are with parked vehicles, slower moving vehicles, pedestrians and bicyclists. All of these objects are much larger than our acuity levels for high contrast targets. However, these objects typically present a very low contrast against the dark road and dark sky background. In contrast to these objects, posted signs and lane delineation are high-contrast targets – and purposefully made to be so by highway engineers. The problem then arises, that we are misled by the delineators into the impression that we see well enough to drive at relatively high speed, because the cues necessary for vehicle guidance are clearly visible. But, unfortunately, many of the potential hazards – such as pedestrians walking along or crossing the road – are not. To make things worse, we are unaware of the *selective* deterioration of our vision for low-contrast targets relative to high contrast delineation (Leibowitz, Owens, and Tyrrell, 1998). Also, when we attempt to resolve the details of a moving target – as in a task requiring dynamic visual acuity – we need even more contrast, especially as we age (Wood and Owens, 2005).

In 1961 when Schmidt argued that contrast sensitivity is much more important for safe driving than acuity for high contrast targets, there were no simple easy-to-administer tests of contrast sensitivity, and the issue was largely theoretical. Since then several tests of contrast sensitivity, presented in charts that can be projected or hung on the wall, or on computer screens have been developed (e.g., Dorr *et al.*, 2013; Ginsburg, 1984; Pelli, Robson, and Wilkins, 1988), and their use has spread. With the aid of the Pelli-Robson test, Rubin *et al.* (1994) discovered that older drivers with low contrast sensitivity were more likely to report visual problems in both daytime and nighttime driving.

Compared to other measures of visual performance, contrast sensitivity is quite promising, especially when its validity is tested relative to performance on driving-related visual tasks. Thus, Evans and Ginsburg (1985) tested younger and older drivers (with average ages of 25 and 67, respectively) who had nearly identical static daytime (photopic) acuity of 6/6 or slightly better. Despite their similar acuity, the older drivers had significantly poorer contrast sensitivity, and did significantly worse at a visual discriminating task of highway signs that were projected in a movie taken from the perspective of an approaching driver. Nearly identical findings on the relationships between acuity, contrast sensitivity, and age on signs legibility distance were obtained by Kline *et al.* (1990). More recent results obtained on sign recognition in a controlled driving environment by Wood and Owens (2005) also demonstrated the superiority of contrast sensitivity over static acuity in either high or low levels of luminance. Wood and Owens obtained an unusually high correlation of $r = 0.43$ between the number of signs recognized at night with very dim headlights and performance on a contrast sensitivity test. Taken together, the three studies showed that on the one hand visual acuity is probably of little relevance to driving performance, and on the other hand contrast sensitivity can be critical for adequate performance of driving-related visual tasks. Interestingly, it appears that drivers may be sufficiently aware of their reduced contrast sensitivity, as they often limit their driving in terms of distance traveled and number of trips (Sandlin, McGwin, and Owsley, 2013). Still, much more research is needed to isolate the effects of contrast sensitivity from other confounding impairments.

Unfortunately, as with other measures of visual functions, empirical evidence for relationship between contrast sensitivity and actual driving behavior or crash involvement – especially when some potential confounding variables are controlled for – is quite weak (Charlton *et al.*, 2004; Green *et al.*, 2013). When a relationship is obtained it is mostly in older drivers who often suffer from cataracts that directly reduce contrast sensitivity (Wood *et al.*, 2012) as well as from a host of other visual and attentional problems (Decina and Staplin, 1993; Owsley *et al.*, 1998, 2001; see also Chapter 7), and when some of these confounding factors are controlled for the association between contrast sensitivity and crashes disappears.

While we have still not devised ways of improving contrast sensitivity, it is possible to improve or enhance the contrast of many targets in the visual field. We commonly do this with retroreflective markers that delineate the roadway and with retroreflective signs that significantly increase both detection and readability distances (Chrysler, Carlson, and Hawkins, 2003). We can also increase the conspicuity of vehicles in marginal weather conditions by using daytime running lights (DRL). Experimental research has demonstrated that daytime running lights make vehicles visible from greater distances, and epidemiological research has demonstrated that mandatory daytime running lights – especially in the winter in northern countries – reduces the number of collisions (Cairney and Styles, 2003; Commandeur, 2004; Elvik, 1996; Rumar, 2003). Crash analysis also indicates that DRL is effective in reducing daylight, dawn, and dusk fatalities (Sivak and Schoettle, 2011). Elvik *et al.* (2009) performed a meta-analysis of 25 studies conducted in 10 different countries on the effects of DRL on cars and found significant reduction in crashes ranging from six percent for multi-vehicle daylight collisions to 24 percent for collisions with pedestrians. Furthermore, they concluded that DRL is also quite cost-effective. Nonetheless, the mandatory use of DRL in all vehicles (as currently required in Canada and all EU countries) also has a drawback. Cavallo and Pinto (2012) embedded motorcycles with DRL in traffic scenes in which all the vehicles either had or did not have DRL. They found that the DRL of the other motor vehicles reduced the conspicuity and detectability of the motorcycles (who prior to the current EU regulation had the benefit of being almost the only vehicles with DRL. Jenness, Jenkins, and Zador (2011) using actual fatal crash data from the U.S. and Canada – with U.S. having no mandatory DRL laws while Canada does – reached a similar conclusion concerning the fatal effects of mandatory DRL on motorcyclists. Elvik *et al.* (2009) on the basis of their meta-analysis reached mixed conclusions, depending on the type of crash. In short, DRL is not good news for all road users.

Stereopsis and monocular vision

Driving involves movement in a three-dimensional space, and one of the primary cues to perceiving depth comes from the use of the two eyes. The cues that are provided by the two eyes (binocular cues) include retinal disparity and convergence. Retinal disparity is the slight difference in the image projected on the two retinas, due to the different angle from which each eye "sees" the same object – the closer the object the greater the disparity between the two perspectives. Convergence is the extent that the two eyes point (converge) toward each other – the closer the object the greater the convergence. Thus, it has often been argued that depth vision, or stereopsis, is needed for safe driving. However, this argument is quite simplistic, lacks the proper theoretical basis, and – based on empirical evidence – false.

From a theoretical perspective, the driving environment provides the driver with multiple cues to depth and distance that do not necessitate binocular vision. However this is true only during the daylight hours. At night many of these cues are missing because in general we have very few visual stimuli. Thus, many people know that it is very difficult to estimate the distance of a light source at night. However, that statement also implies that at night the binocular vision, once we look farther than a few meters away, does not aid us that much. This is because our two eyes are only 5-8 millimeters apart and objects further than a few meters away produce very small differences in retinal disparity or in the degree of convergence. How all of this relates to the depth perception in driving is briefly explained below.

In driving most of the information that is critical for depth perception is at a distance that is disproportionately greater than the distance between the two eyes (over 6 meters versus 6-8 millimeters). At such distances binocular cues to depth perception become irrelevant, and monocular cues are used instead. These monocular cues to depth perception were first identified by Leonardo da Vinci who recommended their use as guidelines for artists on how to represent the depth of a three-dimensional world on a two dimensional canvas (da Vinci, 1970), and were later used by the Gestalt psychologists to explain depth perception. These cues include relative size (the appearance of farther objects as smaller), linear perspective (the optical convergence of all receding parallel lines, such as the convergence of railroad tracks in the distance), occlusion (occluded objects are farther than occluding objects), shadowing (the direction of the shadow relative to the source of light), object height (objects that are farther away being higher), and aerial perspective (the hazier appearance of objects and less color distinction the farther they are). Indeed, with such a plethora of cues, the little empirical research that has been done in this area indicates that stereopsis is not a critical requirement for safe driving. However, because the most common cause of loss of stereopsis is the loss of an eye, the issue is further complicated by a reduced field of view (see discussion below). While people with a restricted field of view are not necessarily monocular, monocular people always have a restricted field of view. Thus, a test of stereopsis, almost by definition, is confounded with a restricted visual field.

Although monocular vision does not preclude driving in general, many countries restrict commercial driving to people with binocular vision (e.g., Australia, see Horton and Chakman, 2002; U.S., see FMCSA, 2001). Critical reviews of research that compared the crash rates of monocular drivers with that of binocular drivers have for the most part concluded that monocular drivers are no worse than binocular drivers (Bartow, 1982; North, 1985; Owsley and McGwin, 1999). In one study that was conducted on California heavy vehicle drivers, Rogers, Ratz, and Janke (1987) did find that monocular drivers had more crashes than binocular drivers, but the latter tended to under-report their crashes. This anomaly was due to the fact that monocular California drivers did not drive outside of California, because they did not comply with the Federal vision requirement of binocular vision. The binocular drivers did drive outside of California, but their California license records did not include their out-of-state crashes.

A direct test of the importance of stereopsis was conducted by McKnight, Shinar, and Hilburn (1991). In their study they recruited 40 binocular and 40 monocular professional heavy vehicle truck drivers, matched in age and driving experience, and gave them a battery of vision tests and various driving tasks. Comparisons between the two groups revealed – as expected – that the monocular drivers did worse on some of the vision tests. These included the expected deficiency in-depth perception (a test of stereopsis in which no binocular cues are present), and the total extent of the visual field. However, the monocular drivers also had slightly poorer visual acuity under low nighttime illumination, visual acuity in the presence of glare, and contrast sensitivity. While the total field of view of the monocular drivers was obviously smaller than that of the binocular drivers, the field of view in the individual functioning eyes were essentially the same. The monocular drivers also performed as well as the binocular drivers on the standard visual acuity test, dynamic visual acuity, and glare recovery time. Most important were the findings on the driving performance measures. Within both groups there were large individual differences on most measures. As a group the monocular drivers performed worse than the binocular drivers only in the daytime and nighttime sign reading task. The sign reading distance correlated with performance on the stereopsis test, so that the ones who were poorer in their stereopsis could read the signs from shorter distances. On all the other driving-related tasks – visual search behavior, lane keeping, clearance judgment, gap judgment, and hazard perception – the two groups did not differ significantly from each other.

One argument that could be made in response to the findings of McKnight *et al.* (1991) is that monocular people with long experience in driving with one eye have developed various compensatory mechanisms to cope with the loss of stereopsis. While this argument does not negate the irrelevance of monocular cues to depth perception, it would suggest that time is needed to develop compensatory skills. To address such potential criticism, Troutbeck and Wood (1994), conducted an experimental study of driving skills using drivers with normal binocular vision. They compared their driving with both eyes to their driving with the occlusion of one eye. Yet they too did not find any significant deterioration in performance when driving with one eye. Thus, the weight of the evidence suggests that monocularity and lack of stereopsis are not necessarily a hindrance to safe driving. Despite these findings, there is some indication that the loss of an eye at adulthood does cause a small percentage of the drivers to lose confidence in their driving ability to the point of giving it up (Kondo *et al.*, 2013). Thus, while the lack of binocular vision is not critical for driving safety, its sudden loss may be – at least temporarily and at least for some people – a subjective barrier to continued driving.

Visual field

In many situations a crash is the end result of a series of events that began somewhere off the driver's direct line of sight. This is so, because most of the driver's fixations are directed at the road ahead, while emerging risks – such as a pedestrian who darts out into the road and a vehicle entering from a crossroad or an alley – start at some point away from the center of the visual field. Consequently, it is not surprising that the most common visual requirement after a minimal threshold of visual acuity is a significant field of view.

The most common test of the field of view is to present a target (such as a spot of light) somewhere off the center of the visual field while the person is looking straight ahead. The test is conducted separately for each eye. A young healthy person without any visual deficiencies can typically detect such a target as far as 90 degrees off to the right with the right eye, and 90 degrees off to the left with the left eye, giving him or her a visual field that subtends a total of 180 degrees in the horizontal meridian. However, exactly how much of a visual field is needed is not clear, and this is reflected in the different licensing requirements. For example, in the U.S. only 36 states have some minimum required visual field, and these minimum levels range all the way from a narrow visual cone of 20 degrees to a large field of 150 degrees (Peli, 2002).

As with many other tests of visual performance, the relationship between visual field and crashes has been quite elusive so far. Many early studies were unable to establish any significant correlations between restricted visual field and crash involvement (see Shinar, 1977). One possibility that was considered was the fact that these studies used relatively small sample sizes, and in a representative sample of the driving population, severe restrictions of the visual field are quite rare. However, even with very large samples the results, for the most part, have not supported the importance of visual field – at least as it was clinically measured. Burg in his study of 17,000 California drivers (1967, 1968) found a very weak relationship between crashes and visual field – even weaker than between static visual acuity and crashes. Using an even larger sample of 52,000 North Carolina drivers, Council and Allen (1974) concluded that the "overall 2-year retrospective accident experience of those with limited visual fields (140 degrees or less) does not differ from drivers with 'normal' fields of view (greater than 160 degrees)." Other, more recent studies also failed to find significant relationships between the extent of the visual field and crashes (Ball *et al.*, 1993; Decina and Staplin, 1993; Hennessy, 1995; Owsley *et al.*, 1998; Woolnough *et al.*, 2013). Studies that have directly examined the relationship between visual field and driving performance have also failed to see a significant relationship between loss of visual field and poor performance. Racette and Casson (2005) evaluated the driving performance of patients with visual field problems and failed to find a significant association between moderate and severe visual field defects and on-road driving performance, as evaluated by a specially trained occupational therapist. As did McKnight *et al.* (1991) in their study on monocular drivers, Racette and Casson also found that a large proportion of their monocular drivers performed quite safely behind the wheel. Silveira *et al.* (2007) also failed to find a significant relationship between visual field and on-road driving performance of 100 senior Australian drivers as assessed by a team consisting of a driving instructor, an orthoptist (a professional who detects, diagnoses and treats motoric aspects of the eye such as nystagmus, amblyopia, and binocular vision), and an occupational therapist.

The most compelling evidence for the relevance of visual field to traffic safety comes from a study by Johnson and Keltner (1983) who measured the visual field of 10,000 California drivers (or as they labeled it, "20,000 eyes") when they reported for their periodic re-licensing. In their study, Johnson and Keltner controlled for exposure and found the searched for relationship, but only for people with very severe visual field restrictions *in both eyes*. However, monocular drivers with a normal field in the functioning eye, and drivers with a field loss in only one eye were not over-involved in crashes. Other studies that examined driving behavior of people with very severe field loss (that can be due to retinitis pigmentosis – a disease that progressively destroys the retinal cells from the periphery toward the fovea, or hemianopia – loss of vision in one side of the visual field of both eyes due to stroke) also found deficiencies in these people's driving behavior (Szlyk *et al.*, 1992; Szlyk, Brigell, and Seiple, 1993). Huisingh *et al.* (2015) also demonstrated a positive relationship between severe visual field loss and at-fault crash involvement of older drivers in Alabama. In their study they limited the visual field examination to the area most relevant to driving (60 degrees to each side, 15 degrees above, and 30 degrees below the direction of the gaze). They found that the critical region of visual field loss that is related to at-fault collisions is the lower left part of the visual field, and drivers with deficiencies in that region were 40 percent more likely to have an at-fault collision. This finding corresponds with the common finding that older people are especially over-involved in intersection collisions involving a left turn (see Chapter 7). It would be interesting to test if in a country where you drive on the left (such as the United Kingdom and Australia) the relevant impairment would be on the lower right side of the visual field. Thus, excluding severe loss in the parts of the visual field that correspond to specific types of collisions, the weight of the evidence suggests that minor or moderate loss of the visual field is not a significant risk factor for crash involvement.

Night vision and the implications of a dual vision system

In addition to the different functions of various parts of our retina, it appears that we also have two types of visual systems, mediated by different parts of the brain: focal and ambient. Focal vision enables us to detect and identify objects while ambient vision enables us to orient ourselves in space. Thus, the ambient vision, telling us where we are, provides us with visual guidance, is most effective in the peripheral field of view, and therefore relies mostly on the rods that can function at low contrast levels. Focal vision, telling us what we see ahead of us, is critical for object recognition, functions mostly at the central field of view, and therefore relies mostly on the cones that require mid- to high contrast (Schieber, Schlorholtz, and McCall, 2009). The fact that two independent visual systems are responsible for different safety-related visual needs is very important because enhancing one but not the other can actually compromise safety. Thus, in the absence of this awareness of the dual system, the common wisdom is that improvements in road delineation can help drivers perceive the direction of the road better and therefore assist them in safely maintaining the car within the lane, and therefore improve safety. This assumption is inherent in the thinking of both researchers (e.g., Horberry, Anderson, and Regan, 2006; McKnight, McKnight, and Tippetts, 1998) and highway engineers (e.g., the *U.S. Manual of Uniform Traffic Control Devices*, 2009). This is despite the fact that the negative implications of the dual system for night driving had already been pointed out by Leibowitz and Owens (1977) 40 years ago.

The danger of selectively enhancing the visual cues for the ambient vision was first demonstrated by Kallberg in 1993, who found that the enhancement of road delineation with raised reflectors in Finnish rural winding roads actually increased the number of accidents on these roads. Elvik *et al.* (2009) performed a meta-analysis on the results of 27 studies that evaluated the impact of various means of enhancing road delineation and concluded that there is no evidence that these treatments reduce crashes, but they do increase speeds.

In an attempt to analyze the effects of enhanced delineation in a controlled manner we (Sharfi and Shinar, 2014) did a driving simulation study where drivers were exposed to the same road segments in clear daylight without enhanced delineation, in daylight but with fog with and without the enhanced delineation, and at night with and without the enhanced delineation. The results were consistent with both theory and past findings. In general, the delineation enhancement caused drivers to drive faster and have almost twice as many collisions with obstacles on the road. Less expected but possibly just as disturbing was the drivers' lack of awareness of these effects. The drivers liked the enhancements, felt they reduced their stress, and were not aware of having more crashes with them.

Distributed Visual Attention

Vision, as described so far, appears to be a very passive system, in the sense that stimuli impinge on our eyes, and we respond to the excitation that they evoke in the retina. Dynamic visual acuity involved some active involvement but only as far as tracking a moving target.

But there is a lot more to vision than (sensitivity to a stimulus that) meets the eye. We have essentially two mechanisms to distribute our visual attention beyond the narrow 5-degree field that is projected on our fovea. The first mechanism involves an increase in awareness of objects or events in the peripheral visual field *while we are attending to events in the center of the field*, and the second mechanism (which is linked to the first) involves moving our eyes from fixating on one area of the visual field to fixating on another area. The first mechanism, of distributed visual attention is most commonly referred to as the "useful field of view" (Ball and Owsley, 1991), but has also been called by other names, such as the "functional field of view" (Crundall, Underwood, and Chapman, 1999) and the "effective visual field" (Shinar and Schieber, 1991).

The repeated (and frustrating) inability to find strong relationships between individual differences in visual performance and their crash involvement has led many researchers to the conclusion that while individual differences in vision in terms that have been discussed so far may be important, the way we distribute our attention and divide it between events in the central field of view and the periphery is probably much more important. This is because driving does not simply require sensitivity to events in the central or peripheral field of view, but it demands sensitivity to peripheral events *at the same time* that we look ahead and respond to events in the center of the visual field, such as changes in the behavior of cars and signals ahead. In a series of innovative studies focusing on our ability to effectively distribute our attention across the visual field, Ball and Owsley (Ball and Owsley, 1991; 1993; Ball *et al.*, 1991; Owsley, 1994; Owsley *et al.*, 1991, 1994, Owsley, Ball, and McGwin, 1999) demonstrated that having a retinal intactness needed to detect objects in the peripheral field may be a necessary condition for adequate processing of stimuli in different areas of the visual field, but it is not a sufficient condition. Sufficiency is met by a higher-order process of division of attention between centrally occurring events and peripheral ones.

Useful field of view (UFOV)

To test the concept of distributed visual attention Ball and Owsley developed a battery of tests that compare performance on a visual task that is presented to the fovea (in which an observer typically has to identify a silhouette of a car or truck that is briefly flashed in the center of the visual field) under three levels of peripheral task difficulty. In the simplest task the observer is required to perform the central task without any peripheral distractions. The performance measure here is one of information processing time, based on the shortest presentations in which the observer was able to distinguish between the silhouette of a car and a truck. In the second and more difficult task, the subject has to perform the same task, but now he or she also has to detect a peripheral target (car) that is briefly projected simultaneously in any one of 24 locations 10-30 degrees away from the central target. Task difficulty is controlled by the distance of the peripheral target from the center of the visual field and by its duration. The third and most difficult task is similar to the second, except that the visual field is not empty but cluttered with triangles that create a visually noisy environment. Various studies have demonstrated that visual noise lengthens processing time and slows reaction time (McCarthy and Donchin, 1981). A composite score based on the three tests is then derived and it is termed the UFOV. This term is somewhat misleading because what the test actually measures is visual information processing speed without distraction, with divided attention, and with selective attention.

UFOV and driving performance of older drivers

Simpler, PC-based UFOV tests have also been used to assess the UFOV's validity relative to driving-related performance measures that should theoretically be directly linked to performance on this test. For example, Broman *et al.* (2004) showed that older people with reduced UFOV are more likely to bump into obstacles than those without such a reduction, even after controlling for impairments measured in the traditional measure of visual field. Bowers *et al.* (2013), measured the UFOV of 47 elderly drivers who were evaluated on an on-road 45-minute drive in the Boston area. They found that of all vision and cognitive tests used, the UFOV was the best predictor of performance on an on-road driving evaluation. The UFOV score was able to identify 93 percent of the drivers judged unfit to drive, and correctly assess 72 percent of those considered fit to drive. While this seems to be a very good result, it also means that if this criterion were used for licensing of older drivers, approximately 30 percent of those who are fit to drive would be denied a license. Still, in comparison, on the same sample static visual acuity had essentially zero predictive power. Wood and her associates (Wood *et al.*, 2010; Wood and Troutbeck, 1992) in a direct evaluation of the UFOV found that its scores correlated with driving performance of elderly drivers on a closed track. Using a different measure that also involves an effective visual field, Crundall *et al.* (1999) asked young novice drivers, young experienced drivers, and young non-drivers to view video clips taken from a driver's perspective and point out whenever they saw a hazard. While they performed this visual search task for hazards, the participants were also asked to respond to a brief light that was flashed on the screen in one of four locations: 4.4 degrees above or below the center of the screen or 6.8 degrees to the right or left of the center of the screen. They found that when the scene was complex and demanding (i.e., it contained a hazard) detection of the peripheral targets was poorer than when the scene was devoid of any potential hazards. Thus, they were able to demonstrate the relation between the demands of a central task and performance on a peripheral task; though not necessarily with the specific measures generated by Ball and Owsley's UFOV test. Crundall and his associates also measured the deviation of each target light from the location of the observer's fixation at the moment the light appeared. This was their measure of the peripheral distance of the peripheral target from the observer's line of sight. As expected, target detection was poorer as the extent of the deviation increased, especially when this deviation was 7.0 degrees or more; that is, when the target was definitely outside the area covered by the high-resolution fovea.

UFOV as a predictor of crash involvement

Although the UFOV may be an important skill at all ages (e.g., Wilkins *et al.*, 2013, showed that it correlated with hazard perception ability of young drivers) its predictive validity has been tested most intensively on older drivers. In several tests that they conducted on older drivers Ball and Owsley were able to demonstrate that the UFOV distinguishes between crash-free and crash-involved drivers when other visual tests do not (as found in the many studies reviewed above), and when performance on other visual functions is statistically controlled for (e.g., Owsley *et al.*, 1991; Sims *et al.*, 1998). For example, in their 1991 study of 53 older drivers Owsley *et al.* found that none of the vision tests they considered (including visual acuity, contrast sensitivity, stereo acuity, glare resistance, color discrimination, and visual field) correlated significantly with self-reported accidents. Performance on these tests did, however, relate to measures of "eye health" (including ratings of the ocular media, acuity, peripheral vision, and presence or absence of various eye diseases such as glaucoma, cataracts, age-related macular degeneration, and diabetic retinopathy). Performance on the UFOV did correlate with some of the basic visual functions, as well as with the observer's "mental status"; a score based on performance on a battery of cognitive tests, including abstraction, short-term visual and verbal memory, comprehension, reading, writing, and drawing. Most interesting were the relationships among all of these visual and cognitive skills and accidents. In testing these relationships, Ball and Owsley distinguished between intersection accidents and all accidents. They argued that UFOV should be more closely associated with intersection accidents because these accidents are more likely to involve lack of awareness of peripheral stimuli (crossing vehicles and pedestrians). As they hypothesized, both the UFOV and the mental status scores correlated significantly with the number of accidents ($r = 0.36$ and $r = 0.34$, respectively), and especially with intersection accidents ($r = 0.41$ and $r = 0.46$). Thus, while eye health and traditional tests of vision did not correlate with accident involvement, the UFOV and the mental status of a person did: demonstrating the importance of both the higher-order mental functions, and the combined performance on a visual task that depends on them.

In several later studies Ball and Owsley demonstrated the repeated validity of the UFOV in distinguishing among crash-free and crash-involved older drivers. In a study on a much larger sample of 294 older drivers, Ball and her associates (1993) obtained similar findings, but though the vision and mental tests also correlated slightly with accident frequency, only the UFOV distinguished significantly between crash-free and crash-involved drivers: the older drivers with "substantial shrinkage" in the UFOV were six times more likely to be involved in crashes than those without such shrinkage. In a later study Owsley *et al.* (1998) followed up the crash involvement of these same subjects to determine the prospective or predictive validity of the UFOV. They discovered that those who were originally diagnosed with a significant loss in the UFOV were 2.2 times more likely to be involved in a crash in the following three years than those that had adequate UFOV. Thus, although the effect was not as dramatic as in the retrospective post hoc analysis, an over-involvement at twice the rate of those without significant loss in UFOV is still much better than the relationship obtained between crash involvement and any of the strictly visual measures. Recently, Ball and her associates (Edwards *et al.*, 2005) devised a simpler and shorter PC-based UFOV test that can be used with either a touch screen or a mouse. Performance on these new versions correlates quite well with the original test ($r = 0.66$ and $r = 0.75$ for the touch screen and the mouse, respectively).

In contrast to the studies conducted by Ball, Owsley, and their associates, the results of UFOV validation studies conducted by others were less encouraging. Two large-scale studies on normative samples of older drivers that evaluated the UFOV and a similar test yielded disappointing results. The first study (Brown *et al.*, 1993) was sponsored by a large U.S. insurance company and involved the testing of 1,475 drivers 50 years old or older. The study assessed the correlations between crash involvement and various visual tests including acuity, stereopsis, color vision, contrast sensitivity, and UFOV. The results showed that of these tests only contrast sensitivity and UFOV were significantly associated with crash involvement. However, the correlations of both with crashes were quite low: $r = 0.11$ for contrast sensitivity and $r = 0.05$ for UFOV. This very low correlation means that the UFOV could account for only a quarter of one percent of all the variance in the crashes. The second study was conducted by Hennessy (1995), on over 11,000 California drivers, ages 20-92, who reported for re-licensing. The test used was not the UFOV, but a conceptually similar test that required the subjects to divide their attention between a central task (counting the number of flashes of a light that flickered in the center of the field) and a peripheral task that required them to detect briefly flashing lights that appeared in the periphery. Although the test was more predictive of high-crash involvement than the passive field of view test, its levels of sensitivity (the ability to correctly identify a crash-involved driver) was only 53 percent, and its level of specificity (the ability to correctly determine that a driver is not crash-involved) was only 58 percent. In terms of the complement of specificity – false alarms – these results mean that using this test for screening would falsely identify 42 percent of the applicants as high-crash risk! Clearly such percentages make the test useless for licensing decisions, unless accompanied by other, more powerful tests.

The most extensive (and most recent) evaluation of the UFOV's relationship to crash risk was conducted by Ball, Owsley, and their colleagues (Friedman *et al.*, 2013) and it involved the testing of a population-based sample of 2,000 independently living, 70+ years old Alabama drivers. In their analyses they examined the relationship between the drivers' police crash record adjusted for the estimated exposure in terms of miles driven and their performance on three potentially predictive tests, including their latest version of the UFOV. To their acknowledged surprise the UFOV did not correlate significantly with the crash rates. The odds ratios (before and after adjustments for confounding variables like age, sex, race, education, contrast sensitivity, visual acuity, MMSE, and number of comorbid medical conditions) was not significantly different from 1.0. Although the authors offered some reasons why this study did not confirm their previous findings, the issue on the validity of the UFOV remains open.

When considered relative to other visual performance measures, the weight of the evidence indicates that UFOV is possibly the best measure that relates visual/cognitive performance to older drivers' crash involvement. However, even if its predictive validity were to be raised, there still remains a practical matter of what to do with people who perform poorly on this test. Because driving is a key to independent living in many countries (see Chapter 7 on older drivers) this is a critical issue that must be considered before a measure is used as a licensing criterion. According to Ball and Owsley (Ball *et al.*, 1988, 1991; Ball and Owsley, 1993; Owsley, 2013), training can actually improve the UFOV, and there is some evidence that cognitive training of older adults can reduce crash involvement (Ball *et al.*, 2010). However, the link between improvement in UFOV and crash reduction needs further study.

Visual Search and Eye Movements

The nature of eye movements

The rapid decline in our visual acuity for objects that are projected immediately outside the center of our visual field would be a severe handicap to our vision, were it not for the compensatory mechanism of eye movements. The high resolution in the foveal area actually serves as a very efficient means of directing our attention and focusing it on specific areas of the visual scene around us. In order to effectively view a larger area, we must move the eyes so that these other areas are also projected to the central – foveal – part of the retina. This process of scanning the visual field is established through effective eye movements. Eye movements are in fact necessary to resolve the details of a moving target, as needed for dynamic visual acuity. However, the type of eye movement that is best for dynamic visual acuity – a smooth pursuit movement that tracks a moving target – is not the typical manner in which our eyes move. More typically our two eyes move in a synchronized manner in a series of jumps (called saccades) separated by short stops (called fixations). The saccades are very quick – on the order of 10-50 milliseconds – while the fixations are significantly longer – on the order of 100-500 milliseconds. It is during the fixations that we gather most of the information from our visual environment in general, and in driving in particular (Velichkovsky *et al.*, 2002).

The direction of our visual gaze is a most important tool for understanding attention. This is because we gather most of our visual information during the fixations, and because to resolve details we need foveal vision. This is even imbedded in our language in the figure of speech "look here" when we want to direct a person's attention to a specific object. Thus, our visual system becomes a critical mechanism in selecting objects for attention. The selection process is reflected in the eye movements and the objects on which we fixate.

But how do we decide where to focus our attention? This has been the subject of extensive research in driving and in other contexts. The process by which we select information to attend is governed by both internal and external forces. External stimuli that attract visual attention include objects that are conspicuous in their field, contours of objects, and in general locations with a high amount of information in the strict information-theory sense of the word (Macworth and Morandi, 1967). In addition, external non-visual and peripheral visual stimuli can attract our fixations such as a sudden noise or a flash of light that are localized off the center of the visual field. The internal forces that direct our fixations are just as important. Our expectations as to where important information may be govern this process, and these expectations are based on our memory, previous experiences, knowledge of the particular environment and rules that apply to it, and instructions that may have been given to us. For example, in reading English we know that the text is written from left to right, and therefore our saccadic movements and fixations proceed from left to right. However, when reading Hebrew or Arabic where the text is written from right to left, the visual fixations also proceed from right to left. In the context of driving we do not have explicit rules that determine the order of fixations. Therefore, by studying eye movements and fixations of different drivers in different environments, we can understand what information is sought and used by the drivers, in what order, and sometimes even how.

Eye movements in driving

Although the driving environment is not as rigidly structured as text (in Hebrew or English), there are still some constancies that dictate the visual search process in driving. For example, exits and road signs are typically on the right and not on the left, and that is where drivers search for them. Thus, when a road exit is from the left lane (right lane in England, Australia, and Japan), unless warned well in advance we are likely to miss it. The same applies to traffic signs. In an interesting demonstration of the latter issue, Borowsky noticed a Tel Aviv, Israel street guidance sign placed on the left curb instead of on the right. In a controlled experiment he did some photo editing to place the sign on either side of the street in several pictures of the street as viewed by approaching drivers. He then exposed the pictures for brief durations to experienced and novice drivers. As hypothesized, experienced drivers were much more likely to fixate the signs and recall them when they appeared in their expected (right) location than when they appeared in the unexpected (left) location. In contrast, novice drivers were equally likely to fixate the signs and remember them when they were placed at either location; so much so that they performed better than the experienced drivers when the sign was on the unexpected left side (Borowsky, Shinar, and Parmet, 2008). Martens, in two driving simulation studies also showed how expectancy and experience govern drivers' visual search. In her first study with a more abstract task (Martens, 2004) she presented the drivers with distractors and targets that appeared on a simulated road. When the participants knew when a target or a distractor would appear, they fixated less on the distractors, whereas when their appearance was unpredictable they fixated equally on both. In her second study (Martens and Fox, 2007) 12 drivers drove through the same road segment 24 times over a period of five successive days, assuring over-familiarity with the road. As hypothesized, over the course of the repeated exposures they spent less and less time fixating the signs along the road while at the same time improving their recollection of the signs. Then, on the final drive before an intersection a "priority road" sign was changed to a "yield" sign. Although the drivers glanced quickly at the sign, only two drivers (less than 20 percent) slowed down in response to it and most drivers did not notice a change in the sign. This shows that even when repeated exposure does not radically change the search pattern, the attention to and processing of the unexpected information may suffer critically.

In the context of driver information processing, the first studies that recorded driver eye movements in actual on-road driving were conducted by Rockwell and his students in the 1960s. In their studies they fitted drivers with special helmets that had one camera pointing out at the road scene ahead of the driver, and another camera that photographed the driver's eye movements. They were then able to calibrate the location of the driver's gaze relative to objects on the road and in the car. The results of Rockwell's early studies have been replicated more recently with new technology that does not require the driver to wear devices that might affect the visual glance behavior (e.g., Victor, 2000), and his early findings have proven to be very stable.

Some of Rockwell's early seminal findings are presented in Figure 4-6, that depicts the percent of time a driver spends looking at different locations under various instructions to either attend to all signs (Trial 1), to attend only to signs relevant to the designated route (Trial 2), and under no particular instructions to attend to any signs (Trial 3). The distributions of fixations on the left three panels were obtained in open road driving, and those on the right panels were obtained in response to the same instructions but while following another vehicle.

To comprehend the data in Figure 4-6, consider first the schematic drawing of the straight roadway as seen from the driver's perspective. The point at which all roadway lane delineations converge is termed the "focus of expansion," indicating the imaginary point on the horizon where all parallel lines in the Z-axis (away from the driver) converge (as implied in the depth cue of "linear perspective"). The markings on the X- and Y-axes indicate relative deviations – in degrees – from that point. The fixations themselves are indicated by numbers or dots inside the figure: a number indicating the percent of time the driver looked at that location and a dot indicating that the driver fixated at that location at least once but the total amount of fixation time at that location was less than one percent.

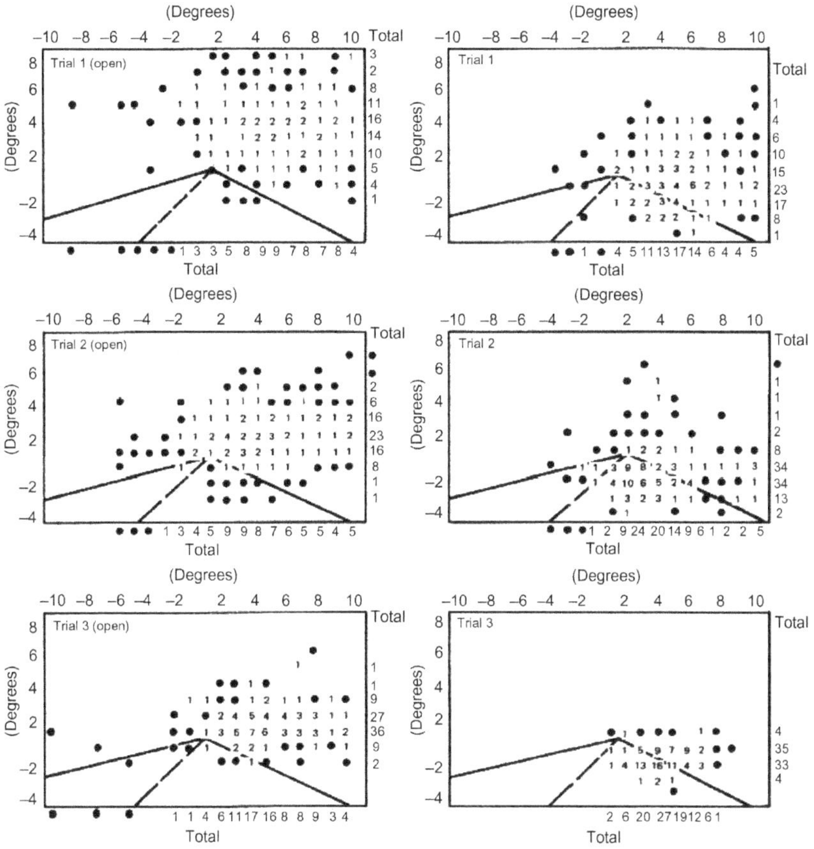

Figure 4-6. Distributions of a driver's fixations on the open road (left panels) and when following another vehicle (right panels), when asked to read all highway signs (Trial 1), when asked to read only signs pertaining to the designated route (Trial 2), and when not required to read any signs (Trial 3). Numbers indicate percent time in that area, and a black dot indicates <1.0 percent (from Mourant, Rockwell, and Rackoff, 1969).

The most important conclusion that can be drawn from these distributions of eye movements is that the driver's visual search pattern is – as in other situations – greatly determined by both the task that he or she has (i.e., internally driven search) and the demands of the dynamic visual environment (i.e., externally driven search). Furthermore, the specific pattern reflects the importance of various stimuli in the visual environment. When asked to regard all signs (Trial 1) the driver's fixations are concentrated around an area that is above and to the right of the road surface – where most signs are placed. In contrast, when the task does not require the driver to pay particular attention to the signs, the fixations are more concentrated and closer to the road. The introduction of a lead vehicle that the driver now has to follow requires constant monitoring of the location of that vehicle in order to be able to rapidly respond to a change in that vehicle's speed. This externally driven search causes the driver to shift the fixations to the driving lane. When the driver has to simultaneously engage in both sign reading and car following the visual fixations are distributed on the road as well as off and above the road to the right. Also note that when not engaged in car following and not instructed to pay particular attention to signs, the driver concentrates most of the fixations close to the focus of expansion. Fixations at that point provide the driver with the maximum advance warning to any obstacles or significant information that may be on the road. However, when engaged in car following, the fixations gravitated down – meaning closer – to the location of the car ahead.

A similar pattern of visual fixations was obtained in a rudimentary fixed-base driving simulator by Crundall, Shenton, and Underwood (2004). When their drivers were asked to follow a vehicle ahead, the spread of fixations was slightly reduced and fixation durations increased slightly (by approximately 10 percent), relative to driving on an open road. The task of following another vehicle was so demanding, in fact, that when the road was clear of distracting pedestrians, drivers spent 40 percent less time looking at the rear-view mirror, and 60 percent less time looking at the speedometer. Yet, despite spending less time on the mirrors and more time on the road, the restricted range of fixations when following a vehicle was also associated with more failures to detect pedestrians; by a fourfold increase in accidents that required the drivers to yield right of way, and by a twofold increase in right-of-way violations. Together these results show how focused attention can be very demanding, to the point of reducing the effective or useful field of view, and resulting in a phenomenon known as "tunnel vision" (Rogé *et al.*, 2004).

Another conclusion that emerges from Mourant *et al.*'s (1969) results, that is somewhat difficult to perceive from Figure 4-6, is the relative importance of different areas in the drivers' visual field, based on the percent of time that the drivers actually fixated on them. This is provided in Table 4-1. Perhaps the most significant information in this table is that a significant portion of the time – from 15 to 27 percent of the time – the driver is not looking at the road scene at all! This is despite the fact that the drivers in this study were well aware of being in a study – and were therefore on their "best" behavior – and that their visual fixations were being recorded (they were told that the purpose was to calibrate the system). Presumably some of that time (but definitely not all of it) was devoted to checking the instrument panel and the mirrors. If we add to that the times that the eyes were fixated on the road but the driver's attention was elsewhere (as when thinking about a paper that still has to be written), we have an early indication that even under fairly demanding experimental conditions, the driver has some spare attentional capacity; one that today seems to be siphoned by in-vehicles infotainment systems, including cell phones.

The situation is completely different when we approach an information-demanding situation such as a curve in the road. Here the location of the lane changes continuously and we must make continuous steering corrections to remain within our lane. In this case, the peripheral cues are no longer sufficient and we now have to attend directly to the lane markers that delineate the lane for us (Chattington *et al.*, 2007; Land and Horwood, 1995; Lehtonen, Lappi, and Summala, 2012; Lehtonen *et al.*, 2013, 2014;

Table 4-1. The percent of time a driver fixates on various objects on the visual scene ahead, in car following and open road driving, when instructed to read all signs (Trial 1), when instructed to read only signs pertaining to the designated route (Trial 2), and when not instructed to read any signs (Trial 3) (from Mourant *et al.*, 1969).

Category	**Open Road**			**Car following**		
	Trial 1	**Trial 2**	**Trial 3**	**Trial 1**	**Trial 2**	**Trial 3**
Looking ahead	50.4	54.2	58.3	31.2	32.8	30.7
Lead car and other vehicles	–	–	–	38.8	40.4	44.3
Vehicles	5.0	4.0	6.7	–	–	–
Road and lane markers	2.2	2.3	2.0	2.2	4.3	1.8
Road signs	7.5	6.2	5.4	4.9	4.3	2.5
Bridges	8.0	8.1	7.1	5.8	5.0	5.4
Out of view	26.9	25.2	20.5	17.1	13.2	15.3

Shinar, McDowell, and Rockwell, 1977). The effect of the curving road on our visual fixations is illustrated schematically in Figure 4-7. This figure depicts the sequence of visual fixations of two drivers as they drive over the same route that consists of a short left curve followed by a long right curve, and then immediately followed by a very short left curve. This sequence of curves is presented in Figure 4-7(a). Figures 4-7(b) and (c) show the saccadic eye movements in the horizontal meridian of two drivers, superimposed on this road geometry. The bottom graph depicts the saccadic eye movements of one of the drivers in the vertical meridian.

The most important parts of this figure are in panels (b) and (c) that demonstrate the similarity of the lateral eye movements of the two drivers. The vertical segments of the eye tracking line represent the very fast saccadic movements, which are essentially instantaneous on the time scale in this figure. The horizontal segments represent the fixations, when the drivers are actually absorbing the information, and the length of each segment indicates the duration of the fixation. The pattern is quite similar for both drivers: they both seem to track the road with their visual fixations, by fixating ahead, and then back (closer to the car), again further ahead and again closer to the car, and so on. This back-and-forth pattern indicates the driver's need to first attend to the location of the road ahead – which changes continuously – and then verify that the car has remained within the lane. Another interesting aspect of the horizontal fixation pattern is that the back-and-forth pattern of saccadic movements and fixations begins before the driver actually enters the curve, demonstrating the predictive role of the visual fixations in preparing the driver for events ahead.

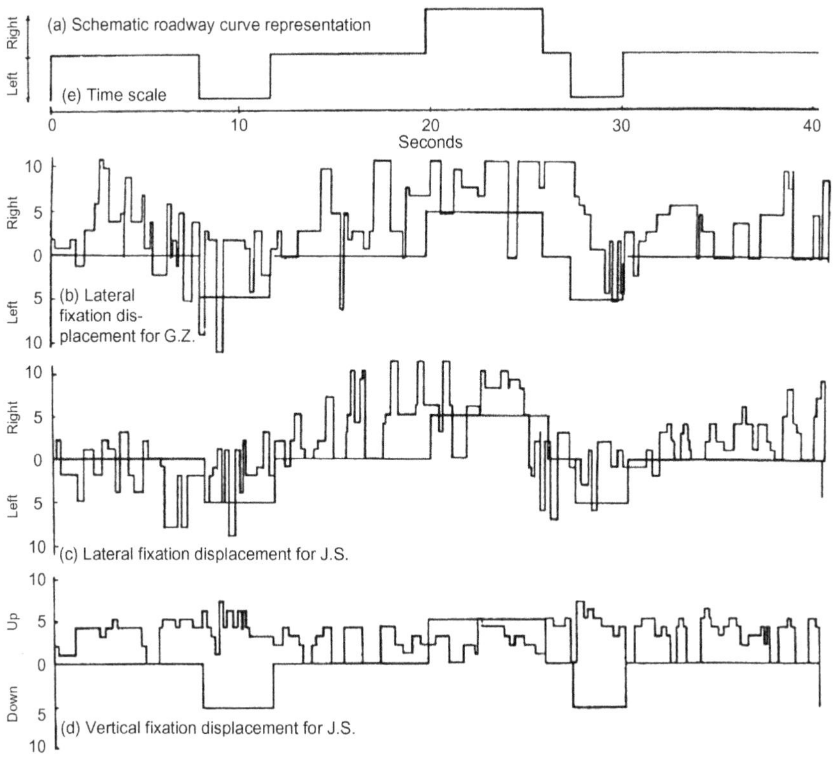

Figure 4-7. Panel (a), the top panel, is a schematic representation of a roadway segment with a left-right-left curve sequence. Panels (b) and (c) show the lateral fixation patterns of two typical drivers superimposed on the schematic roadway representation. Panel (d), the bottom panel, shows the vertical fixation pattern of the second driver (from Shinar *et al.*, 1977, reprinted with permission from the Human Factors and Ergonomics Society).

In accordance with this pattern of visual search behavior, Donges (1978), nearly 40 years ago, developed a two-level quantitative model of driver steering behavior. According to this model steering behavior is managed at an upper planning "guidance level" and at a lower operational "stabilization" level. The guidance level is to plan the instantaneous and future steering actions based on the upcoming road geometry, and the stabilization level is needed to correct deviations from the planned route using a closed-loop feedback from the relative position of the car on the road. Two decades later, Land and Horwood (1995) demonstrated in a simulator study using the occlusion technique that indeed the fixations farther ahead are used to estimate the road curvature and plan the steering while the fixations closer to the car are needed to provide the driver with feedback on the car's position within the lane. More recently Lehtonen and his colleagues (2013) replicated these results, and noted that the division between the two types is determined by the geometry of the road and the driver's cognitive load: the greater the load the nearer the look-ahead fixations, suggesting that drivers allocate fewer resources to the planning of the vehicle control and more to just keeping it on the road. However, with experience – probably because the driving itself requires less attention – drivers spend more time looking farther ahead allowing them to better plan their trajectory (Lehtonen *et al.*, 2012; 2013; 2014). In fact, Lehtonen and his colleagues (2012) demonstrated in real-road driving that drivers tend to fixate as far down the road as they can ("the occlusion point" – the end point of the unobstructed road ahead) so that they can maximize their planning time. This is also probably why chevron signs ahead of and inside a curve are so useful to approaching drivers. Wu *et al.* (2013), in a simulator study showed that these signs are useful in directing the drivers' fixations and attention to the road edges near the signs, and in reducing their speed inside the curve, and consequently in reducing the drivers' stress.

In the years since Rockwell's original studies, eye movement research has provided us with many insights concerning how different road users allocate their attention in various situations. For example it has been found that child pedestrians restrict their visual search closer to their intended crossing path than adult pedestrians (Tapiro *et al.*, 2013). Visual scanning behavior has also revealed that sleepiness can be predicted from eye movements (Ahlstrom *et al.*, 2013), and that sleepiness makes a driver more susceptible to distraction (Anderson and Horne, 2013; Taylor *et al.*, 2013); that the quality of bicycle paths affects the riders' visual scanning of their environments (Vansteenkiste *et al.*, 2014); that at night – and even more so in the rain – we narrow the dispersion of our scanning relative to daytime (Crundall *et al.*, 2004); that the number of fixations on highway signs increase as the amount of information in the sign increases – and that correspondingly less time is devoted to looking at the road ahead (Liu, Sun, and Rong, 2011); that minimal brain damage that does not preclude getting a driver license increases the frequency of long glances (>1.5 seconds) at in-vehicle distractors (Haikonen *et al.*, 1998); and that alcohol impairs the natural eye movements and fixation patterns (Moser, Heide, and Kömpf, 1998; Moskowitz, Ziedman, and Sharma, 1976). Research has also utilized eye movement analyses to examine the differences between novice, experienced drivers, and older drivers in scanning intersections (Konstantopoulos, Chapman, and Crundall, 2010; Scott *et al.*, 2013), and railroad crossings (Young *et al.*, 2015) prior to crossing them; difficulties in hazard perception and hazard anticipation of young drivers relative to experienced and professional drivers (Borowsky and Oron-Gilad, 2013; Taylor *et al.*, 2013); the relative risk of various sources of distraction such as in-vehicle systems and billboards (Horrey, Wickens, and Consalus, 2006; Jin *et al.*, 2014; Taylor *et al.*, 2013); and the potential benefits of different training programs for hazard detection (Samuel *et al.*, 2013). Eye movement analyses have even proven useful in assessing cognitive distractions such as talking on a cell phone (Birrell and Fowkes, 2014). To illustrate, Harbluk *et al.* (2007) found that responding to questions on the cell phone significantly diminished the extent of saccadic movements to potential hazards, reduced glances to the rear-view mirror, and increased fixations straight ahead. Thus, the reduction in the scanning activity reflected a regression toward "tunnel vision" where processing of external driving-relevant information is impaired. Furthermore, it appears that the reduction in visual search becomes more pronounced as the difficulty of the (non-visual) task increases (Reimer *et al.*, 2010). The effects of distraction on visual scanning are discussed in more detail in Chapter 13.

Because visual scanning is closely linked to visual attention and crash involvement, assessing visual scanning behavior is a very powerful tool in the assessment of task load in the context of current and emerging in-vehicle information systems (Victor, Harbluk, and Engström, 2005). Our understanding of the relationship between fixations and attention has enabled researchers such as Muñoz *et al.* (2015) and Horrey *et al.* (2006) to provide good quantitative models validated by experimental results on the interaction of in-vehicle tasks and the driving task. For example, Horry and his colleagues, in two experiments in a driving simulator demonstrated a strong negative relationship between the percent of the time the drivers fixated the outside world and the frequency of the in-vehicle task (reading seven-digit phone numbers presented on a dashboard screen), a strong negative relationship between the total fixation time on the outside world and the vehicle's lane position variability, a strong negative relationship between the total fixation time on the in-vehicle display and the brake reaction time to unexpected hazards, and a strong positive relationship between the frequency of wind gusts and the time fixated on the outside world. These relationships between driving performance, driving and non-driving task difficulty and priority manifest themselves in visual scanning behavior that can then be used as a valid intervening variable.

Concluding Comments

Given the ubiquity of vision testing for licensing, and the public's ready acceptance of the importance of vision for driving, it is surprising how little scientific and empirical evidence exists to support the relationship between individual differences in the intuitively or theoretically relevant visual skills and crash involvement.

The elusiveness of such relationships and explanations for our inability to find them in crash data was offered in a review of the state of the art in this area by Westlake (2000): "It is difficult to establish the relation between visual impairment and crash rates because visually impaired drivers tend to restrict their driving habits and change their behaviour to compensate for their visual loss. Crashes are fortunately rare events with multiple causes, and the effects of a driver's visual impairment are dwarfed by other factors such as the annual mileage driven, the driver's age, inattention, intoxication, and speeding. Furthermore, it is unsurprising that it is difficult to predict crash rates from measures of static visual acuity and the peripheral visual field since these indices do not reflect the visual, perceptual, and cognitive complexity of the driving task."

When visual skills are studied in relation to measures of driving performance, rather than in relation to crash involvement, the results are more encouraging. The overwhelming evidence of empirical studies indicates that individual differences in basic visual functions that are theoretically relevant to the visual needs for safe driving are at best moderately related to various measures of driving performance. This has been demonstrated for visual acuity and contrast sensitivity. However, all of the studies demonstrating these relationships were artificial in the sense that the drivers were aware of their participation in a study, drove in a simulator or on a closed road with no other traffic, and typically drove at a predetermined speed. Given these problems, Owsley, Wood, and McGuinn (2015) suggested that the gold standard for evaluating drivers suspected of suffering from medical or age-related impairment be the judgment of a Certified Driving Rehabilitation Specialist. As a precaution they recommend that these clinicians – and policy makers who set vision standards – understand the different methods (as detailed in Chapter 2) on which the various findings and conclusions are based so that they can make a better professional judgment.

Thus, in contrast to the driving performance studies, attempts to relate visual performance to crash involvement in actual driving have been spectacularly unsuccessful. When correlations were obtained, they were very low: typically accounting for less than four percent of the variance in crash involvement. The most likely reason for this is that driving – as stated by Westlake (2000) and argued in Chapter 3 – is not a passive process but one in which the driver has very much control over where, when, and how he or she drives. This is particularly true of older drivers who are also more likely to have visual impairments. Thus, it is most likely that the reason visual impairments are barely reflected in crash involvement is due to drivers' self-regulation and restriction of their driving to fewer trips, shorter trips, and trips in low risk situations (such as daytime fair weather driving only, driving in non-rush hours, driving only on familiar routes, etc.). This is true at least on the basis of drivers' self-reports of their driving habits (Stutts, 1998; West *et al.*, 2003). In summary, given Westlake's (2000) assessment above and the recommendation from leading researchers like Ball and Owsley to use experts judgments as a gold standard of driving safety, we must conclude that as of now, vision-based screenings are not highly valid predictors of crash involvement. Drivers' selective exposure are better guides to safe driving than the test scores that we have so far designed (see more in Chapter 7 on older drivers).

Current research – both in the areas of vision and in the area of crash causation – suggests that significant relationships between vision and driving safety are mediated by the driver's attention (or lack of it). Research on the UFOV and on drivers' eye movements have provided insights into the limitations of visual attention and into the interaction between vision and attention. Together these studies are telling us that higher-order processes that govern the distribution of attention and visual search may be much more critical to safe driving than purely sensory-based criteria such as visual acuity – at least once some minimal threshold level is achieved.

References

Adekoya, B. J., J. F. A. Owoeye, F. G. Adepoju and A. I. Ajaiyeoba (2009). Visual function survey of commercial intercity vehicle drivers in Ilorin, Nigeria. *Canadian J. Ophthal.*, *44*, 261-264.

Ahlstrom, C., M. Nyström, K. Holmqvist, C. Fors, D. Sandberg, A. Anund, G. Kecklund and T. Åkerstedt (2013). Fit-for-duty test for estimation of drivers' sleepiness level: Eye movements improve the sleep/wake predictor. *Transport. Res. C*, *26*, 20-32.

Allen, M. J., B. S. Abrams, A. P. Ginsburg and L. Weintraub (2001). *Forensic Aspects of Vision and Highway Safety*. Lawyers and Judges Publishing Co, Tucson, AZ.

Anderson, C. and J. A. Horne (2013). Driving drowsy also worsens driver distraction. *Sleep. Med.*, *14*, 466-468.

Anstey, K. J., M. S. Horswill, J. M. Wood and C. Hatherly (2012). The role of cognitive and visual abilities as predictors in the multifactorial model of driving safety. *Accid. Anal. Prev.*, *45*, 766-774.

Atchison, D. A., C. A. Pedersen, S. J. Dain and J. M. Wood (2003). Traffic signal color recognition is a problem for both protan and deutan color-vision deficients. *Hum. Fact.*, *45*(3), 495-503.

Birrell, S. A. and M. Fowkes (2014). Glance behaviours when using an in-vehicle smart driving aid: A real-world, on-road driving study. *Transport. Res. F.*, *22*, 113-125.

Ball, K. and C. Owsley (1991). Identifying correlates of accident involvement for the older driver. *Hum. Fact.*, *33*, 583-595.

Ball, K. and C. Owsley (1993). The useful field of view test: A new technique for evaluating age related declines in visual function. *J. Am. Ophthalmol. Ass.*, *64*, 71-80.

Ball, K., B. Beard, D. Roenker, R. Miller and D. Griggs (1988). Age and visual search: Expanding the useful field of view. *J. Opt. Soc. Am. A.*, *5*, 2210-2219.

Ball, K., J. D. Edwards, L. A. Ross and G. McGwin Jr. (2010). Cognitive training decreases motor vehicle collision involvement of older drivers. *J. Am. Geriatr. Soc.*, *58*(11), 2107-2113.

Ball, K., D. Roenker, J. Bruni, C. Owsley, M. Sloane, D. Ball and K. O'Connor (1991). Driving and visual search: Expanding the useful field of view. *Invest. Ophthalmol. Vis. Sci. Suppl.*, *32*, 1041.

Ball, K., C. Owsley, M. E. Sloane, D. L. Roenker and J. R. Bruni (1993). Visual attention problems as a predictor of vehicle crashes in the older driver. *Invest. Ophthalmol. Vis. Sci.*, *34*, 3110-3123.

Bartow, P. (1982). The monocular driver: A review of distant visual acuity risk analysis data. Report submitted by Bartow Associates to the Federal Highway Administration. U.S. Department of Transportation, Washington, DC.

Borowsky, A. and T. Oron-Gilad (2013). Exploring the effects of driving experience on hazard awareness and risk perception via real-time hazard identification, hazard classification, and rating tasks. *Accid. Anal. Prev.*, *59*, 548-565.

Borowsky, A., D. Shinar and Y. Parmet, (2008). The relation between driving experience and recognition of road signs relative to their locations. *Hum. Fact.*, *50*, 173-182.

Bowers, A. R., R. J. Anastasio, S. S. Sheldon, M. G. O'Connor, A. M. Hollis, P. D. Howe and T. S. Horowitz (2013). Can we improve clinical prediction of at-risk older drivers? *Accid. Anal. Prev.*, *59*, 537-547.

Broman, A. T., S. K. West, B. Munoz, K. Bandeen-Roche, G. S. Rubin and K. A. Turano (2004). Divided visual attention as a predictor of bumping while walking: The Salisbury eye evaluation. *Invest. Ophthalmol. Vis. Sci.*, *45*(9), 2955-2960.

Brown, J., K. Greaney, J. Mitchel and W. S. Lee (1993). *Predicting Accidents and Insurance Claims Among Older Drivers*. ITT Hartford Insurance Group, Southington, CT.

Bullough, J. D., E. T. Donnell and M. S. Rea (2013). To illuminate or not to illuminate: Roadway lighting as it affects traffic safety at intersections. *Accid. Anal. Prev.*, *53*, 65–77.

Burg, A. (1966). Visual acuity as measured by dynamic and static tests: A comparative evaluation. *J. Appl. Psychol.*, *50*(6), 460-466.

Burg, A. (1967). The relationship between vision test scores and driving record: General findings. Report No. 67-24. Department of Engineering, University of California, Los Angeles, CA.

Burg, A. (1968). Lateral visual field as related to age and sex. *J. Appl. Psychol.*, *52*, 10-15.

Cairney, P. and T. Styles (2003). Review of the literature on daytime running lights (DRL). Australian Transport Safety Bureau Report CR-218. AARB Transport Research, Victoria, AU.

Cavallo, V. and M. Pinto (2012). Are car daytime running lights detrimental to motorcycle conspicuity? *Accid. Anal. Prev.*, *49*, 78-85.

Chattington, M., M. Wilson, D. Ashford and D. E. Marple-Horvat (2007). Eye-steering coordination in natural driving. *Exp. Brain Res.*, *180*(1), 1-14.

Charlton, J., S. Koppel, M. O'Hare, D. Andrea, G. Smith, B. Khodr, J. Langford, M. Odell and B. Fildes (2004). Influence of chronic illness on crash involvement of motor vehicle drivers. Report No. 213. Accident Research Center, Monash University, Clayton Victoria, AU.

Chrysler, S. T., P. J. Carlson and H. G. Hawkins (2003). Nighttime legibility of traffic signs as a function of font, color, and retroreflective sheeting. Proceedings of the Transportation Research Board Annual Meeting. National Academies, Washington DC.

Chun, J., I. Lee, G. Park, J. Seo, S. Choi and S. H. Han (2013). Efficacy of haptic blind spot warnings applied through a steering wheel or a seatbelt. *Transport. Res. F*, *21*, 231-241.

Commandeur, J. (2004). State of the art with respect to implementation of daytime running lights. SWOV Institute for Road Safety Research Report No. R-2003-28. SWOV. Leidcshendam, Netherlands.

Cornsweet, T. N. (1970). *Visual Perception*. Academic Press, New York, NY.

Council, F. M. and J. A. Allen Jr. (1974). A study of the visual field of North Carolina drivers and their relationship to accidents. University of North Carolina, Highway Safety Research Center, Chapel Hill, NC.

Cross, J. M., G. McGwin Jr., G. S. Rubin, K. K. Ball, S. K. West, D. L. Roenker. (2009). Visual and medical risk factors for motor vehicle collision involvement among older drivers. *Br. J. Ophthalmol.*, *93*, 400-404.

Crundall, D., G. Underwood and P. Chapman (1999). Driving experience and the functional field of view. *Perception*, *28*, 1075-1087.

Crundall, D., C. Shenton and G. Underwood (2004). Eye movements during intentional car following. *Perception*, *33*, 975-986.

Da Vinci, L. (1970). *The Notebooks of Leonardo da Vinci* (Vol. 1), Dover.

Davison, P. A. (1985). Inter-relationships between British drivers' visual abilities, age and road accident histories. *Ophthalmic. Physiol. Opt.*, *5*, 195-204.

Decina, L. E. and L. Staplin (1993). Retrospective evaluation of alternative vision screening criteria for older and younger drivers. *Accid. Anal. Prev.*, *25*(3), 267-275.

DfT (2005). Vision and Driving (No. 2). Report No. 504592. UK Department of Transport, London. http://www.dft.gov.uk/stellent/groups/dft_rdsafety/documents/pdf/dft_rdsafety_pdf_504592.pdf

Donges, E. (1978). A two-level model of driver steering behavior. *Hum. Fact.*, *20*, 691-707.

Dorr, M., L. A. Lesmes, Z.-L. Lu and P. I. Bex (2013). Rapid and reliable assessment of the contrast sensitivity function on an iPad. *Invest. Ophthalmol. Vis. Sci.*, *54*, 7266–7273.

Edwards, J. D., D. E. Vance, V. G. Wadley, G. M. Cissell, D. L. Roenker and K. K. Ball (2005). Reliability and validity of useful field of view test scores as administered by personal computer. *J. Clinic. Exp. Neuropsychol.*, *27*(5), 529-543.

EEC (1991). Annex III, Minimum standards of physical and mental fitness for driving a power driven vehicle, *Offic. J. Euro. Comm.*, No. L237, *24*, 20-21.

Elvik, R. (1996). A meta-analysis of studies concerning the safety effects of daytime running lights on cars. *Accid. Anal. Prev.*, *28*(6), 685-694.

Elvik, R., A. Høye, T. Vaa and M. Sorensen (2009). *The Handbook of Road Traffic Safety Measures, 2nd ed.* Emerald, Bingley, UK.

Emerson, J. L., A. M. Johnson, J. D. Dawson, E. Y. Uc, S. W. Anderson and M. Rizzo (2012). Predictors of driving outcomes in advancing age. *Psychol. Aging*, *27*, 550-559.

Evans, D. W. and A. P. Ginsburg (1985). Contrast sensitivity predicts age-related differences in highway sign discriminability. *Hum. Fact.*, *27*(6), 637-642.

FMCSA (2001). Visual requirements for commercial motor vehicle drivers. Federal Motor Carrier Safety Administration, Publication No. FMCSA-MCRT-1-007. US Department of Transportation, Washington, DC.

Friedman, C., G. McGwin Jr., K. K. Ball and C. Owsley (2013). Association between higher order visual processing abilities and a history of motor vehicle collision involvement by drivers ages 70 and over. *Invest. Ophthalmol. Vis. Sci.*, *54*(1), 778.

Ginsburg, A. (1984). A new contrast sensitivity vision test chart. *Am. J. Optom. Physiol. Opt.*, *61*, 403-407.

Ginsburg, A. P. (2003). Contrast sensitivity and functional vision. In: *Functional Vision* (M. Packer, I. H. Fine and R. S. Hoffman eds.). pp. 5-15. Lippincott, Williams & Wilkins, Philadelphia, PA.

Green, K. A., G. McGwin Jr. and C. Owsley (2013). Associations between visual, hearing, and dual sensory impairments and history of motor vehicle collision involvement by older drivers. *Am. J. Geriatr. Soc.*, *61*, 252-257.

Gresset, J. A. and F. M. Meyer (1994). Risk of accidents among elderly car drivers with visual acuity equal to 6/12 or 6/15 and lack of binocular vision. Ophthalmic Physiol. Opt., *14*(1), 33-37.

Gruber, N., U. P. Mosimann, R. M. Müri and T. Nef (2013). Vision and night driving abilities of elderly drivers. *Traffic Inj. Prev.*, *14*, 477-485

Haikonen, S., A. S. Wikman, H. Kalska, H. Summala, M. Hietanen, T. Nieminen and J. Vilkki (1998). Neuropsychological correlates of duration of glances at secondary tasks while driving. *Appl. Neuropsychol.*, *5*(1), 24-32.

Harbluk, J. L., Y. I. Noy, P. L. Trbovich and M. Eizenman (2007). An on-road assessment of cognitive distraction: Impacts on drivers' visual behavior and braking performance. *Accid. Anal. Prev.*, *39*(2), 372-379.

Heiman, G. W. (2000). *Basic Statistics for the Behavioral Sciences*. Houghton Mifflin Co., Boston, MA.

Henderson, R. L. and A. Burg (1974). Vision and audition in driving. Report No. TM (L)-5297/000/00. Systems Technology Corporation, Santa Monica, CA.

Hennessy, D. F. (1995). Vision testing of renewal applicants: Crashes predicted when compensation for impairment is inadequate. Report No. RSS-95-152. California Department of Motor Vehicles, Sacramento, CA.

Higgins, K. E. and J. M. Wood (2005). Predicting components of closed road driving performance from vision tests. *Optom. Vis. Sci.*, *82*(8), 647-656.

Higgins, K. E., J. Wood and A. Tait (1998). Vision and driving: Selective effect of optical blur on different driving tasks. *Hum. Fact.*, *41*(2), 224-232.

Hoffmann, E. R. (1968). Detection of velocity changes in car-following. Proceedings of the 4th Conference of the Australian Road Research Board, pp. 821-837.

Hoffman, E. R. and R. G. Mortimer (1994). Drivers' estimation of time to collision. *Accid. Anal. Prev.*, *26*, 511-520.

Hoffman, E. R. and R. G. Mortimer (1996). Scaling of relative velocity between vehicles. *Accid. Anal. Prev.*, *28*(4), 415-421.

Hofstetter, H. W. (1976). Visual acuity and highway accidents. *J. Am. Optom. Assoc.*, *47*, 893-997.

Horberry, T., J. Anderson and M. A. Regan (2006). The possible safety benefits of enhanced road markings: A driving simulator evaluation. *Transport. Res. F*, *9*, 77-87.

Horrey, W. J., C. D. Wickens and K. Pl. Consalus (2006). Modeling drivers' visual attention allocation while interacting with in-vehicle technologies. *J. Exp. Psychol. Appl.*, *12*(2), 67-78.

Horton, P. and J. Chakman (2002). Optometrists association Australia position statement on driver vision standards. *Clin. Exp. Optom.*, *85*(4), 241-245.

Huisingh, C., G. McGwin Jr, J. Wood and C. Owsley (2015). The driving visual field and a history of motor vehicle collision involvement in older drivers: A population-based examination. *Invest. Ophthalmol. Vis. Sci.*, *56*, 132-138.

Jenness, J. W., F. Jenkins and P. Zador (2011). Motorcycle conspicuity and the effect of fleet DRL: Analysis of two-vehicle fatal crashes in Canada and the United States 2001-2007. NHTSA Report HS-811 505, U.S. Department of Transportation, Washington, DC.

Jin, L., H. Xian,Y. Jiang Q. Niu, M. Xu and D. Yang (2014). Research on evaluation model for secondary task driving safety based on driver eye movements. In: *Advances in Mechanical Engineering*. Article ID 624561, 8 pp.

Johnson, C. A. and J. L. Keltner (1983). Incidence of visual field loss in 20,000 eyes and its relationship to driving performance. *Arch. Ophthalmol.*, *101*, 371-375.

Kallberg, V. (1993). Reflector posts — Signs or danger? Transportation Research Record, No. 1403. Transportation Research Board of the National Academies, Washington, DC.

Kline, D. W., T. J. B. Kline, J. L. Fozard, W. Kosnic, F. Schieber and R. Sekular (1992). Vision, aging and driving: The problems of older drivers. *J. Gerontol. Psychol. Sci.*, *47*, 27-34.

Kline, T. J., L. A. Ghali, D. W. Kline and S. Brown (1990). Visibility distance of highway signs among young, middle-aged and older observers: Icons are better than text. *Hum. Fact.*, *32*, 609-619.

Kondo, T., W. T. Tillman, T. L. Schwartz, J. V. Linberg and V. Odom (2013). Health related quality of life after surgical removal of an eye. *Ophthalmol. Plast. Reconstr. Surg.*, *29*(1), 51-56

Konstantopoulos, P., P. Chapman and D. Crundall (2010). 'Driver's visual attention as a function of driving experience and visibility. Using a driving simulator to explore drivers' eye movements in day, night and rain driving. *Accid. Anal. Prev.*, *42*, 827-834.

Lacherez, P., S. Au and J. M. Wood (2014). Visual motion perception predicts driving hazard perception ability. *Acta Opthalmol.*, *92*, 88-93.

Land, M. and J. Horwood (1995). Which parts of the road guide steering? *Nature*, *377*, 339-340.

Lamble, D., H. Summala, L. Hyvarinen (2002). Driving performance of drivers with impaired central visual field acuity. *Accid. Anal. Prev.*, *34*(5), 711-716.

Lehtonen, E., O. Lappi, I. Koirikivi and H. Summala (2014). Effect of driving experience on anticipatory look-ahead fixations in real curve driving. *Accid. Anal. Prev.*, *70*, 195-208.

Lehtonen, E., O. Lappi, H. Kotkanen and H. Summala (2013). Look-ahead fixations in curve driving, *Ergonomics*, *56*(1), 34-44,

Lehtonen, E., O. Lappi and H. Summala (2012). Anticipatory eye movements when approaching a curve on a rural road depend on working memory load. *Transport. Res. F.*, *15*(3), 369-377.

Leibowitz, H. W. and D. A. Owens (1977). Nighttime driving accidents and selective visual degradation. *Science*, *197*, 422-423.

Leibowitz, H. W., D. A. Owens and R. A. Tyrrell (1998). The assured clear distance ahead rule: Implications for nighttime traffic. *Accid. Anal. Prev.*, *30*, 93-99.

Linksz, A. (1952). *Physiology of the Eye*. Grune & Stratton, Inc., New York, NY.

Liu, B., L. Sun and J. Rong (2011). Driver's visual cognition behaviors of traffic signs based on eye movement parameters. *J. Transport. Syst. Eng. Inf. Tech.*, *11*, 22-27.

Long, G. M. and D. F. Kearns (1996). Visibility of text and icon highway signs under dynamic viewing conditions. *Hum. Fact.*, *38*, 690-701.

Macworth, N. H. and A. J. Morandi (1967). The gaze selects informative details within pictures. *Percept. Psychophys.*, *2*, 547-552.

Martens, M. H. (2004). Stimuli fixation and manual response as a function of Expectancies. *Hum. Fact.*, *46*, 410-423.

Martens, M. H. and M. R. Fox (2007). Do familiarity and expectations change perception? Drivers' glances and response to changes. *Transport. Res. F*, *10*(6), 476-492.

Mashige, K. P. (2010). Night vision and glare vision thresholds and recovery time in myopic and hyperopic eyes. *Afr. Vision Eye Health*, *69*(3), 132-139.

McCarthy, G. and E. Donchin (1981). A metric for thought: A comparison of P300 latency and reaction time. *Science*, *211*(4477), 77-80.

McKnight, S. A., A. J. McKnight and A. S. Tippetts (1998). The effect of lane line width and contrast upon lanekeeping. *Accid. Anal. Prev.*, *30*(5), 617-624.

McKnight, A. J., D. Shinar and B. Hilburn (1991). The visual and driving performance of monocular and binocular heavy-duty truck drivers. *Accid. Anal. Prev.*, *23*(4), 225-237.

Montgomery, G. (2005). Color blindness: More prevalent among males. Howard Hughes Medical Institute, Chevy Chase, MD. http://www.hhmi.org/senses/b130.html

Moser, A., W. Heide and D. Kömpf (1998). The effect of oral ethanol consumption on eye movements in healthy volunteers. *J. Neurol.*, *245*, 542-550.

Moskowitz, H., K., Ziedman and S. Sharma (1976). Visual search behavior while viewing driving scenes under the influence of alcohol and marihuana. *Hum Fact.*, *18*, 417-431.

Mourant, R. R., T. H. Rockwell and N. J. Rackoff (1969). Drivers' eye movements and visual workload. *High. Res. Rec.*, *No. 292*, 1-10.

Muñoz, M., J. Lee, B. Reimer, B. Mehler and T. Victor (2015). Analysis of drivers'head and eye movement correspondence: Predicting drivers'glance location using head rotation data. In Proceedings of the 8th International Driving Symposium on Human Factors in Driver Assessment, Training, and Vehicle Design. Snowbird, UT.

National Eye Institute (2004). Statistics and data: Prevalence of blindness data. U.S. National Institutes of Health, National Eye Institute, Bethesda, MD. http://www.nei.nih.gov/eyedata/pbd_tables.asp

NHTSA (2003). A Physician's guide to assessing and counseling older drivers. National Highway Traffic Safety Administration Report DOT HS 809 647. U.S. Department of Transportation, Washington DC. http://www.nhtsa.dot.gov/people/injury/olddrive/OlderDriversBook

NHTSA (2013). Traffic safety facts 2011. National Highway Traffic Safety Administration Report DOT HS 811 754. U.S. Department of Transportation, Washington, DC.

North, R. V. (1985). The relationship between the extent of visual field and driving performance: A review. *Ophthalmic. Physiol. Opt.*, *5*, 205-210.

Osterberg, G. (1935). Topography of the layer of rods and cones in the human retina. *Acta. Ophthalmol.*, *6*, 1-103

Owsley, C. (1994). Vision and driving in the elderly. *Optom. Vis. Sci. 71*, 727-735.

Owsley, C. (2013). Visual processing speed. *Vis. Res. 90*, 52-56.

Owsley, C., K. Ball and G. McGwin Jr. (1999). Vision impairment and driving. *Sur. Ophthalmol.*, *43*(6), 535-550.

Owsley, C., K. Ball, G. McGwin Jr., M. E. Sloane, D. L. Roenker, M. F. White and E. T. Overley (1998). Visual processing impairment and risk of motor vehicle crash among older adults. *JAMA*, *279*(4), 1083-1088.

Owsley, C., B. Stalvey, J. Wells, M. E. Sloane and G. McGwin Jr. (2001). Visual risk factors for crash involvement in older drivers with cataract. *Arch. Ophthalmol.*, *119*(6), 881-887.

Owsley, C., K. Ball, M. E. Sloane, D. L. Roenker and J. R. Bruni (1991). Visual/cognitive correlates of vehicle accidents in older drivers. *Psychol. Aging.*, *6*, 403-415.

Owsley, C., K. Ball, M. E. Sloane, E. T. Overley and M. F. Whiter (1994). Predicting vehicle crashes in the elderly: Who is at risk? *Gerontologist.*, *34* (Special issue), 61.

Owsley, C. and G. McGwin (1999). Vision impairment and driving. *Sur. Ophthalmol.*, *43*(6), 535-550.

Owsley, C., J. M. Wood and G. McGuinn (2015). A road map for interpreting the literature on vision and driving. *Surv. Ophthalmol.*, *60*, 250-252.

Pegrum, B. V. (1972). The application of certain traffic management techniques and their effect on road safety. In: Proceedings of the National Road Safety Symposium, pp. 277-286. Dept of Shipping and Transport, Perth, Western Australia (as cited by Retting et al., 2003).

Peli, E. (2002). Low vision driving in the USA: Who, where, when, and why. *CE Optom.*, *5*(2), 54-58.

Pelli, D. G., J. G. Robson and A. J. Wilkins (1988). The design of a new chart for measuring contrast sensitivity. *Clin. Vis. Sci.*, *2*, 187-199.

Polus, A. and A. Katz (1978). An analysis of nighttime pedestrian accidents at specially illuminated crosswalks. *Accid. Anal. Prev.*, *10*, 223-228.

Poulter, D. R. and J. P. Wann (2013). Errors in motion processing amongst older drivers may increase accident risk. *Accid. Anal. Prev.*, *57*, 150-156.

Pulling, N. H., E. Wolf, S. P. Sturgis, D. R. Vaillancourt and J. J. Dolliver (1980). Headlight glare resistance and driver age. *Hum. Fact.*, *22*(1), 103-112.

Racette, L. and E. J. Casson (2005). The impact of visual field loss on driving performance: Evidence from on-road driving assessments. *Optom. Vis. Sci.*, *82*(8), 668-674.

Reimer, B., B. Mehler, Y. Wang and J. F. Coughlin (2010). The impact of systematic variation of cognitive demand on driver's visual attention across multiple age groups. *Proceedings of the Human Factors and Ergonomics Society*, *54*, 2052-2056.

Rogé J., P. Thierry, E. Lambilliotte, F. Spitzenstetter, D. Giselbrecht and A. Muzet (2004). Influence of age, speed and duration of monotonous driving task in traffic on the driver's useful visual field. *Vision Res.*, *44*, 2737-2744.

Rogers, P. N., M. Ratz and M. K. Janke (1987). Accident and conviction rates of visually impaired heavy-vehicle operators. Report No. CAL-DMV-RSS-87-11. California Department of Motor Vehicles, Sacramento, CA.

Rubin, G. S., E. S. Ng, K. Bandeen-Roche, P. M. Keyl, E. E. Freeman and S. K. West (2007). A prospective, population-based study of the role of visual impairment in motor vehicle crashes among older drivers: The SEE study. *Invest. Ophthalmol. Vis. Sci.*, *48*, 1483-1491.

Rubin, G. S., K. B. Roche, P. Prasada-Rao and L. P. Fried (1994). Visual impairment and disability in older adults. *Clin. Vis. Sci. 71*, 750-756.

Rumar, K. (2003). Functional requirements for daytime running lights. UMTRI Report 2003-11. Transportation Research Institute, University of Michigan, Ann Arbor, MI.

Samuel S., T., Zafian, A. Borowsky, M. R. E. Romoser and D. L. Fisher (2013). Can young drivers learn to anticipate hidden hazards: A driving simulation study.

Sandlin, D., G. McGwin and C. Owsley (2013). Association between vision impairment and driving exposure in older adults aged 70 years and over: A population-based examination. *Acta Ophthalmol.*, 1-6.

Schieber, F. (1994). High priority research and development needs for maintaining the safety and mobility of older drivers. *Exp. Aging. Res.*, *20*, 35-43.

Schieber, F., B. Schlorholtz and R. McCall (2009). Visual requirements of vehicular guidance. In: *Human Factors in Visual and Cognitive Performance in Driving* (C. Castro ed.). CRC Press, Taylor and Francis, Boca Raton, FL.

Schmidt, I. (1961). Are meaningful night vision tests for drivers feasible? *Am. J. Optom. Arch. Am. Acad. Optom.*, *38*, 295-348.

Scott, H., L. Hall, D. Litchfield and D. Westwood (2013). Visual information search in simulated junction negotiation: Gaze transitions of young novice, young experienced and older experienced drivers. *J. Safety Res.*, *45*, 111-116.

Sharp, J. A. and T. O. Sylvester (1978). Effects of age on horizontal smooth pursuit. Investigative *Ophthalmol. Vis. Sci.*, *17*, 465-468.

Shinar, D. (1977). Driver visual limitations, diagnosis, and treatment. Final Report on National Highway Traffic Safety Administration Contract No. DOT HS 5 1275. U.S. Department of Transportation, Washington, DC.

Shinar, D. (1978). *Psychology on the Road: The Human Factor in Traffic Safety*. Wiley and Sons, New York, NY.

Shinar, D., E. D. McDowell and T. H. Rockwell (1977). Eye movements in curve negotiation. *Hum. Fact.*, *19*, 63-72.

Sharfi, T. and D. Shinar (2014). Enhancement of road delineation can reduce safety, *J. Safety Res.*, *49*, 61-68.

Shinar, D. and F. Schieber (1991). Visual requirements for safety and mobility of older drivers. *Hum. Fact.*, *33*(5), 507-519.

Silveira, S., N. Jolly, R. Heard, N. J. Clunas and L. Kay (2007). Current licensing authority standards for peripheral visual field and safe on-road senior aged automobile driving performance. *Clin. Exp. Ophthalmol.*, *35*, 612-620.

Sims, R. V., G. McGwin Jr., R. M. Allman, K. Ball and C. Owsley (2000). Exploratory study of incident vehicle crashes among older drivers. *J. Gerontol. A Biol. Sci. Med. Sci.*, *55*(1), M22-27.

Sims, R. V., C. Owsley, R. M. Allman, K. Ball and T. M. Smoot (1998). A preliminary assessment of the medical and functional factors associated with vehicle crashes by older adults. *J Am. Geriatr. Soc.*, *46*(5), 556-561.

Sivak, M. (1981). Human factors and highway-accident causation: Some theoretical considerations. *Accid. Anal. Prev.*, *13*, 61-64.

Sivak, M. (1996). The information that drivers use: Is it indeed 90 percent visual. *Perception*, *25*, 1081-1089.

Sivak, M. and P. L. Olson (1982). Nighttime legibility of traffic signs: Conditions eliminating the effects of driver age and disability glare. *Accid. Anal. Prev.*, *14*(2), 87-93.

Sivak, M., P. L. Olson and L. A. Pastalan (1981). Effect of driver age on nighttime legibility of highway signs. *Hum. Fact.*, *23*, 59-64.

Sivak, M. and B. Schoettle (2011). Benefits of Daytime Running Lights. Report No. UMTRI-2011-6. University of Michigan Transportation Research Institute, Ann Arbor, MI.

Smither, J. A.-A., M. C. Gentzlera and R. S. Kennedy (2012). Movement-in-depth, cognitive impairment, and crash risk. *Work.*, *41*, 5386-5388.

Sojourner, R. S. and J. F. Antin (1990). The effects of a simulated headsup display speedometer on perceptual task performance. *Hum. Fact*, *32*, 329-339.

Stutts, J. C. (1998). Do older drivers with visual and cognitive impairments drive less? *J. Am. Ger. Soc.*, *46*(7), 854-861.

Szlyk, J. P., K. R. Alexander, K. Severing and G. A. Fishman (1992). Assessment of driving performance in patients with retinitis pigmentosa. *Arch. Ophthalmol.*, *110*, 1709-1713.

Szlyk, J. P., M. Brigell and W. Seiple (1993). Effects of age and hemianopic visual field loss on driving. *Optom. Vis. Sci.*, *70*, 1031-1037.

Tapiro, H., A. Meir, Y. Parmet and T. Oron-Gilad (2013). Visual search strategies of child-pedestrians in road crossing tasks. In D. de Waard (ed.), *Proceedings of the Human Factors and Ergonomics Society Europe*.

Taylor, T., A. K. Pradhan, G. Divekar, M. Romoser, J. Muttart, R. Gomez, A. Pollatsek and D. L. Fisher (2013). The view from the road: The contribution of on-road glance-monitoring technologies to understanding driver behavior. *Accid. Anal. Prev.*, *58*, 175-186.

Troutbeck, R. and J. M. Wood (1994). Effect of restriction of vision on driving performance. *J. Transport. Eng.*, *120*(5), 737-752.

van den Berg, T. J. T. P., L. J. (René) van Rijn, R. Kaper-Bongers, D. J. Vonhoff, H. J. Völker-Dieben and G. Grabner (2009). Disability glare in the aging eye. Assessment and impact on driving. *J. Opt.*, *2*, 112-118.

Pieter Vansteenkiste, P., L. Zeuwts, G. Cardon, R. Philippaerts and M. Lenoi (2014). The implications of low quality bicycle paths on gaze behavior of cyclists: A field test. *Transport. Res. F*, *23*, 81-87.

Velichkovsky, B. M., S. M. Dornhoefer, M. Kopf, J. Helmert and M. Joos (2002). Change detection and occlusion modes in road-traffic scenarios. *Transport. Res. F*, *5*, 99-109.

Verriest, G., O. Naubauer, M. Marre and A. Uvijls (1980). New investigations concerning the relationships between congenital colour vision defects and road traffic security. *Inter. Ophthalmol.*, *2*, 887-889.

Victor, T. (2000). A technical platform for driver inattention research. Volvo Technical Report for Project NUTEK Dnr 1P21-99-4131. Volvo, Goteborg, Sweden.

Victor, T. W., J. L. Harbluk and J. A. Engström (2005). Sensitivity of eye-movement measures to in-vehicle task difficulty. *Transport. Res. F.*, *8*(2), 167-190.

Vingrys, A. J. and B. L. Cole (1988). Are colour vision standards justified in the transport industry? *Ophthalmol. Physiol. Optics*, *8*, 257-274.

von Hebenstreit, B. (1984). Visual acuity and traffic accidents. *Klin. Monatsbl. Augenheilkd.*, *185*, 86-90. (as reported by Babizhayev, 2003).

West, C. G., G. Gildengorin, G. Haegerstrom-Portnoy, L. A. Lott, M. E. Schneck and J. A. Brabyn (2003). Vision and driving self-restriction in older adults. *J. Am. Geriatr. Soc.*, *51*(10), 1348-1355.

Westlake, W. (2000). Another look at visual standards and driving. *Br. Med. J.*, *321*, 972-973.

Wilkins, L., R. Gray, J. Gaska and M. Winterbottom (2013). Motion perception and driving: Predicting performance through testing and shortening braking reaction times through training. *Invest. Opthalmol. Vis. Sci.*, *54*, 8364-8374.

Wood, J., A. Chaparro, T., Carberry and B. S. Chu (2010). Effect of simulated visual impairment on nighttime driving performance. *Optom. Vis. Sci.*, *87*, 379-386.

Wood, J. M., A. Chaparro, P. Lacherez and L. Hickson (2012). Useful field of view predicts driving in the presence of distracters. *Optom. Vis. Sci.*, *89*, 373-381.

Wood, J. M., M. S. Horswill, P. F. Lacherez and K. J. Anstey (2013). Evaluation of screening tests for predicting older driver performance and safety assessed by an on-road test. *Accid. Anal. Prev.*, *50*, 1161-1168.

Wood, J. M. and D. A. Owens (2005). Standard measures of visual acuity do not predict drivers' recognition performance under day or night conditions. *Optom. Vis. Sci.*, *82*(8), 698-705.

Wood, J. M. and R. Troutbeck (1992). Effect of restriction of the binocular visual field on driving performance. *Ophthalmic. Physiol. Opt.*, *12*, 291-298.

Wood, J. M., R. A. Tyrrell, A. Chaparro, R. P. Marszalek, T. P. Carberry and B. S. Chu (2012). Even moderate visual impairments degrade drivers' ability to see pedestrians at night. *Invest. Ophthalmol. Vis. Sci.*, *53*, 2586-2592.

Woolnough, A., D. Salim, S. C. Marshall, K. Weegard, M. M. Porter, M. J. J. Rapoport, M. Man-Son-Hing, M. Bédard, I. Gélinas, N. Korner-Bitensky, B. Mazer, G. Naglie, H. Tuokko and B. Vrkljanb (2013). Determining the validity of the AMA guide: A historical cohort analysis of the assessment of driving related skills and crash rate among older drivers. *Accid. Anal. Prev.*, *61*, 311-316.

Wu, Y., X. Zhao, J. Rong and J. Ma (2013). Effects of chevron alignment signs on driver eye movements, driving performance, and stress. *Transport. Res. Record J. Transport. Res. Board*, *2365*(1), 10-16.

Young, M. S., L. Flood, S. Blakeney and S. Taylor (2012). Driving blind: The effects of vision on driving safety and performance. In: *Contemporary Ergonomics and Human Factors 2012* (M. Anderson ed.). Taylor and Francis, London.

Young, K. L., M. G. Lenné, V. Beanland, P. M. Salmon and N. A. Stanton (2015). Where do novice and experienced drivers direct their attention on approach to urban rail level crossings? *Accid. Anal. Prev.*, *77*, 1-11.

Zaidel, D. M. and I. Hocherman (1986). License renewal for older drivers: The effects of medical and vision tests. *J. Safety Res.*, *17*(3), 111-116.

5

Driver Information Processing: Attention, Perception, Reaction Time, and Comprehension

> "Another cultural activity we frequently engaged in was looking the wrong way before attempting to cross streets." (American Humorist Dave Barry, commenting on his family trip to London, in the *World According to Dave Barry*, 1994).

Driving is easy. It is so easy, that much of the time we do it we are barely aware of the information we take in (encode), process, and respond to. On our way to work we may be listening to the radio while we stop and then proceed through traffic signs and signals, we change lanes, and in response to cars ahead we slow down and speed up, engage the brake and the gas pedal, and use turn signals. Yet we do all of these things while we are barely aware of many of the driving-related stimuli and our responses to them. The fact that we can do all of that and still listen to the radio, eat, talk on the phone, check our appearance in the mirror, and even glance at a book, a newspaper, or a map while we drive, is an indication that most of the time the driving task does not require our total and undivided attention. In fact, by the time we arrive at our destination, we have absolutely no idea what were the specific cars and signals to which we responded so efficiently. Yet, occasionally, while we are allocating minimal attention to it, we are surprised by an unexpected event. When that happens, if we do not respond appropriately and in time, a crash occurs (see Figure 3-4).

In this chapter, I try to illustrate how the component processes of the information-processing model presented in Chapter 3 apply to our abilities to handle the driving requirements, and how they affect the way we drive. The driving task involves both conscious and unconscious processes, automated and controlled processes, and various biases that are based on our expectations, as they evolve through multiple experiences with the roadway traffic system.

The complete array of stimuli that impinge on our senses is simply too large for us to process fully. So the first stage in the process is one of selective attention: deciding what to attend to and what to ignore. This decision is governed by a combination of cues from the external stimuli (such as the flashing lights of a police car) as well as by our expectations (such as directing our gaze up to search for signal lights or to the right to search for a stop sign when we approach urban intersections). Most of the time these external and internal cues serve us well, but at other times they fail us. Next, we make some decisions as to the meaning of the stimuli to which we attend: their information value. For example, simply absorbing the graphics of a sign is useless. Sensing the lines of the sign is useless. The sign is useful only if we can interpret its meaning. Another critical decision is whether or not the objects and road ahead constitute a hazard that must be closely attended to or not. Next, we must decide how to react to the information. That decision, too, is based both on the external information (such as a yellow signal light in the approach to an intersection) and on our needs and driving style (such as if we are in a hurry or generally aggressive, respectively). Finally, at the end of this process we perform an overt control action that affects our vehicle. Once we act, the situation changes, and once again we must respond to the new situation, applying the same process.

In the context of safety, the two most common actions that a driver must execute quickly in response to a sudden emergency situation include steering away from the obstacle (when an escape route is available), and braking so as to stop in time to avoid a collision. The time it takes to perform all the component processes that lead up to these actions is known as perception reaction time (PRT), or simply reaction time.

A significant percentage of all crashes are attributed to delayed recognition of the imminent danger (see Chapter 18). This means that either the critical event or object was not recognized at all before the crash or the PRT was delayed to such an extent that by the time the driver responded to the situation it was too late. In this chapter, we discuss the impact of the attention and decision processes on the PRT, how we allocate our attention, how we visually search for the most relevant pieces of information, and how we are able to perceive hazards. We then focus on some specific situations that require very specific information processing capabilities such as maintaining a safe headway and passing other vehicles. Finally, we discuss the issues of comprehension of various symbols to which we have to attend: signs on the road and symbols in the car.

Allocation of Attention: Selective and Divided Attention

Information processing levels: Looking, attending, acting, and recalling

Eye movement research has been most beneficial in providing us with an idea where and to what extent drivers attend to various objects in and out of their cars. A driver's objects of fixation are the first clue that we have to what drivers attend to, and how much time they devote to different objects. However, it is possible to look and not see. The eyes are always fixated on one object or another, but our mind may be fixated elsewhere; on a place, an object, or concept that is not even in the visual field. Because of the limits on our processing capabilities, we may be attending to non-visual stimuli (such as a cell phone) at the cost of processing information from our eyes. Therefore, it is important to try and relate fixations to actual conscious processing.

Two different approaches have been used to determine the actual amount of visual information needed to perceive the driving scene. One approach, originally employed by John Senders 50 years ago (Senders *et al.*, 1966) involves visual occlusion of the view ahead. This is typically accomplished by having an occlusion device or a shutter mounted on the driver's head that mask the driver's visual field for different short durations, typically controlled by the experimenter. (For an interesting demonstration of John Senders' original device used on the highway see http://www.youtube.com/watch?v=kOguslSPpqo). Various organizations rely on this technique to specify the maximal time that the view can be exposed (Total Shutter Open Time – TSOT) for determining whether or not an in-vehicle information system that involves visual/manual distraction (such as texting and entering a destination on a navigation system) can be considered safe to use while driving (see Chapter 13 for discussion of the occlusion findings for in-vehicle distractions). We can use Backs *et al.*'s (2003) study to illustrate one use of the occlusion method for assessing the changing roadway demands. In their study, using a driving simulator, they had people drive on a winding road, with curves of different radii (the smaller the radius, the sharper the curve), and on some of the trials the visual scene was occluded (replaced by a blank screen). However, the driver could activate the view by pressing a button on the steering wheel. Each time the driver pressed the button the road scene was projected for 0.5 seconds (maximal time for a single fixation). By looking at the total number of times the drivers pressed the button in different segments of the road, Backs and his associates knew how much time the drivers needed to "see" the road. The study revealed that as the curves got sharper – requiring more corrective steering – the drivers activated the view of the scene more often. Thus a direct relationship between the visual information load and the time needed to view the roadway was established. Indirectly, the study also demonstrated the redundancy in information that is available when the visual scene does not change much (as on a sparsely populated straight road), and the drivers' capacity to direct their attention away from the road, regardless of where their fixations may rest. Another effective use of this technique was made by Ghazizadeh *et al.* (2013) who used the occlusion technique to quantify the time needed to read and write text messages while driving. Using the International Standards Organization (ISO) 16673 guidelines of alternating exposures and occlusions of 1.5 seconds each in a simulator environment, they found – as expected – that the exposure time needed is longer for writing than for reading, and increases with text length. More interesting perhaps was their finding that "ambient text," or text around the message box, did not increase the reading time suggesting that drivers were able to effectively filter out this text as noise.

The second approach to determine the actual amount of visual information needed to perceive the driving scene is to directly observe the driver's visual fixations. Luoma (1988, 1991) did this to study of the relationship between visual fixations and perception and recall of the objects in the driving scene. In his first study Luoma measured drivers' visual fixations while driving in the real world, and asked them to report on the signs and road markings they had just passed immediately after passing them. He then assessed the relationship between the visual fixations and the immediate recall abilities of different objects along the 50-kilometer drive. The results are listed in Table 5-1 in terms of percent of the times that drivers fixated and not fixated and recalled and not recalled the different objects.

The data in Table 5-1 are quite revealing. First, objects that are important to the driving task were both fixated foveally and recalled. This was true for the 80 km/hr speed limit

Table 5-1. Percent of time that drivers fixated on various objects as they approached them and percent of time that they were able to recall these objects immediately after passing them (from Luoma, 1988, with permission from Elsevier).

Target	**Fixated**		**Not Fixated**	
	Recalled	**Not recalled**	**Recalled**	**Not recalled**
Speed limit 80 km sign	100	0	0	0
Game crossing sign	60	0	7	33
Lane marking for right turn	93	7	0	0
Lane marking for left turn	7	0	0	93
No separate lanes	38	8	54	0
Intersection w/o pedestrian crossing	47	7	33	13
Pedestrian crossing ahead	8	54	0	38
Pedestrian crossing sign	0	21	0	79
Crosswalk lines	29	50	7	14
Roadside billboards (2)	20	23	0	57
Houses along the street (2)	0	0	0	100

sign and for the lane marking dedicating a lane for right turn (requiring the driver to shift the car away from the right lane in order to continue straight). Traffic control information that was not very relevant were generally neither fixated nor recalled (these included the game crossing sign and – unfortunately – the pedestrian crossing sign), or fixated but not recalled ("pedestrian crossing ahead" sign and crosswalk lines). Finally, objects that were not part of the traffic control system such as houses and roadside advertisements were either totally ignored in the visual scanning (houses) or equally likely to be recalled or not recalled even when they were fixated (roadside billboards). Interestingly, some driving-relevant objects – such as all the pedestrian crossing signs – were fixated but often not recalled. Thus, these results indicate that the level of processing seems to be a very efficient one that corresponds to the perceived relevance to the driving task. It progresses from not fixating at all, to fixating and not recalling, and to fixating and recalling. For most of the objects, in the absence of direct foveal fixations, there was also no recall. The only two exceptions were the correct recall without fixations of the "no separate lane markings" and "intersection" sign. It is possible that these changes in the road were so obvious that the drivers simply guessed that they were preceded by a sign (unlike many other signs such as "animal crossing").

In general there were extremely large differences in the recall of different signs. The speed limit sign was recalled by all drivers, whereas the "Pedestrian Crossing Ahead" sign was recalled by only eight percent of the drivers. Also the average time the drivers fixated the speed limit sign was approximately 50 percent longer than the time they fixated the animal crossing sign: 0.64 seconds versus 0.41 seconds. Most important, there is a relationship between fixations and recall. Signs that were not fixated were hardly ever recalled, whereas signs that were fixated could have been recalled or not. We can conclude from this that fixating an object is almost a necessary (but not sufficient) condition for processing the information in it. Once fixated, the level of processing of the sign depends on other factors. The most important of these factors is probably the perceived importance of the sign for the driver.

In his second study, Luoma (1991a, 1991b) addressed the issue of whether we may still respond to some of the signs without necessarily being able to recall them. In other words, can information be processed at a level that involves an appropriate response, without necessarily being stored in memory? Our current understanding of human information processing (see Figure 3-3) would suggest that this is possible. The study design was similar, except that in this study Luoma recorded three additional measures of behavioral responses: (1) slowing down in response to a lower posted speed sign (from 90 km/hr to 60 km/hr), (2) looking to the right after passing a sign indicating a T intersection with a minor road to the right ahead, and (3) looking right and left after passing a "game crossing" sign. With respect to the speed signs, as in the first study, 92 percent of the drivers fixated them and were able to recall them. Seventy five percent of these drivers also slowed down. With respect to the side road, 92 percent of the drivers fixated the sign, but only 79 percent recalled it correctly, and 79 percent scanned the side road itself. With respect to the game crossing 95 percent of the drivers fixated it, but only 80 percent were able to recall it, and only 28 percent actually scanned the sides of the road (presumably looking for animals). Looking at all the eight theoretically possible combinations of fixations, recall, and behavioral response, for the speed limit and the side road the most common combination was that of fixating the sign, responding appropriately, and correctly recalling it (71 percent for the speed limit and 66 percent for the side road). For the animal crossing the most common combination was fixating, not making any visual scanning response, but correctly recalling it (51 percent). Taken together, Luoma's two studies demonstrate the different levels of processing that are possible, and the relationship between the level of processing and the perceived importance of the information. Most notable in both studies is the finding that whenever the object was not fixated it was almost never recalled or responded to appropriately.

As measures of information processing load, the two techniques – occlusion and eye fixations – do not yield the same information. The occlusion technique forces the driver to allocate all of his or her information processing capacity to the road ahead for a brief time, during which we do not know exactly what information is picked. In contrast, with eye fixation data we know exactly where the driver was looking and for how long, but we do not know how much of the attentional capacity was actually devoted to the area of the focal point. In a direct comparison of the two techniques Ranney *et al.* (2013) studied the time to process the visual information to perform different distracting tasks (radio tuning, destination entry, 7-digit phone dialing, and 10-digit phone dialing). They found that despite the differences in the methods, the two approaches yield comparable results that lead to similar conclusions: that all of the above tasks demanded more time than allowed for safe driving, based on NHTSA guidelines (see Chapter 13). Perez, Hulse, and Angell (2013) reviewed the occlusion studies of the past decade and interviewed experts (people who have used the technique), and also concluded that the thresholds used in both methods, though not identical, are correlated. The specific recommendations for visual/manual distracting tasks with the two approaches are discussed in Chapter 13.

Levels of processing

As Backs' study demonstrates, we do not need to pay constant attention to the visual world in order to drive through it, and as Luoma's (1988, 1991) studies show, a significant percent of the time our visual fixations do not reflect the information that we are processing. Information may be totally unattended, or it may be only partially processed, responded to, and then quickly disappear from consciousness.

In the studies by Backs and his associates, and by Luoma, the drivers were aware of their participation in a driving study. But do these results apply to drivers who are not aware that they are part of an experiment? The answer is yes, and this was demonstrated in a series of studies in which unsuspecting drivers were stopped immediately after passing a traffic sign and asked to recall the last sign they passed. The results of the first study of this kind (Johansson and Rumar, 1966) were quite surprising: drivers who were stopped by an officer 700 yards after passing a sign were asked to recall the last sign they passed. Sign recall varied from as low as 17 percent for a sign of "pedestrian crossing 300 meters ahead" to as high as 78 percent for a "50 km/hr speed limit begins 300 meters ahead."

These low recall probabilities were unexpected given the relatively low perceptual demands of that road section and their significant information for the driving task. Furthermore, the actual percent of recall depended not on the visual characteristics of the different signs (such as size and contrast) but on their content. A subsequent study by Johansson and Backlund (1970) essentially replicated the same findings.

Several variables could have confounded or moderated the poor recall of the signs in Johansson's studies. The distance at which the drivers were stopped may have been too large, and the stress involved in being stopped by a police officer may have interfered with the information in memory. Indeed, Syvanen (1968) showed that the presence of uniformed police officers interfered with sign recall. In an attempt to correct for these factors, we (Shinar and Drory, 1983) stopped drivers, on a moderately traveled road in Israel, much closer to the sign (200 meters rather than 700 meters after the sign), and used less threatening staff to stop the drivers. We also limited the study to free-moving cars that were not following another vehicle, to eliminate the possibility that the drivers' attention might have been appropriately focused on a vehicle ahead. Despite all of these changes, overall recall levels were actually lower than in the Finnish studies. As in the previous studies there were great variations in recall for the different signs, but the essential results were quite similar except that recall performance did not appear to be related to the importance of the signs; at least if we assume that importance is judged in Israel in the same way that it is judged in Finland. The results are summarized in Table 5-2. Less than four percent of the drivers correctly recalled the "Stop Ahead" sign and only seven percent correctly recalled the "General Warning" sign. However, the percentages for the same signs were significantly higher – 18 and 17 percent – at night. Performance was also much better when the drivers were presented with a page containing icons of all standard signs, and were simply asked to point to the last one they passed. As in many other situations recognition performance is much better than recall performance (Wickens, Gordon, and Liu, 2004). Further studies in other countries utilizing the same method, did not yield significantly better results (e.g., Milosevic and Gajic, 1986). Direct support for the selective processing of

Table 5-2. Percent of signs recalled and recognized by drivers immediately after passing them, during the day and during the night (based on data from Shinar and Drory, 1983).

	Lighting Conditions	Portable Signs		Permanent Signs	
		Stop ahead	Side road	Winding road	General warning
Recall percent	Day	3.8	5.2	7.8	6.9
	Night	18.2	14.9	18.9	16.9
Recognition percent	Day	10.6	6.6	13.0	9.4
	Night	21.0	19.0	20.7	20.1

different signs was obtained by Costa *et al.* (2014). In their study they recorded visual fixations and tested sign recall at the end of an 8.34-kilometer drive. They found that only 25 percent of the signs were fixated, or looked at, and less than seven percent of the signs were correctly recalled. Here too, importance of the sign seemed to be a major determinant of the looking behavior and the recall, as the speed limit signs were the most frequently fixated and recalled.

Despite the extra measures taken in Shinar and Drory's study and in Johansson's studies to improve recall, and the on road performance of drivers who were aware of participating in a study in Costa's experiment, all three studies obtained much lower recall levels than those obtained by Luoma under experimental conditions. The principal differences between Luoma's studies and the other three studies were in the drivers' task and role: in Luoma's studies the drivers' task was to recall the signs immediately after passing them, and in their roles as subjects in the experiment they were aware of their participation in a sign recall study and were therefore predisposed and cued to attend to the signs and store them in memory long enough to be able to report them immediately after passing each one. In an attempt to address these disparities, Luoma (1993) conducted two more experiments. In one experiment, he compared the responses of volunteer "alert" drivers who were alert to the general nature of the study (to study looking behavior), and passing drivers who were unaware of being observed. Unbeknown to the "alert" drivers, he also measured speed change in response to the sign. As they approached a turn on a rural road, one-third of the drivers encountered a "game crossing" sign, one-third of the drivers encountered a "40 km/hr speed limit" sign, and one-third of the drivers encountered no sign at all. Though the two groups of drivers approached the curve at similar speeds, as expected, the alert volunteer drivers slowed more as they approached the curve, regardless of a presence or absence of a sign. But the most significant difference between the two groups was in response to the reduced speed limit sign: the alert drivers slowed down by an average of 5.5 km/hr, whereas the passing drivers slowed down by an average of only 2 km/hr. Almost all of the alert drivers fixated both signs, but the significant slowing was only in response to the speed limit sign.

The second experiment was conducted with alert drivers only and involved the same signs. Half the drivers were exposed to the animal crossing sign while the other half were exposed to the 40 km/hr speed limit sign. In both sign conditions, half of the drivers were asked to recall the last sign they passed immediately after passing it and half were asked to recall it after being told to stop at a bus stop 670 meters beyond the sign (approximately the same distance used by Johansson). Depending on their speed, this condition involved a delay in recall of approximately 55 seconds. Nearly all drivers fixated both signs, but recall of the speed sign was nearly perfect (94 percent) regardless of the delay in recall, whereas the recall of the animal crossing sign was lower and greatly affected by the delay: 71 percent correctly recalled it immediately after passing it versus 31 percent after the longer delay. Also, drivers hardly slowed down in response to the game crossing sign – regardless of whether they recalled it or not. In contrast, drivers slowed significantly in response to the speed limit sign, *except* when they were not able to recall it immediately.

Luoma's carefully controlled studies, therefore suggest that the poor sign recall obtained by Johansson (1966, 1970) by Shinar and Drory (1983), and by Costa *et al.* (2014) is not an indication of lack of attention, but only an indication that the information does not get processed any further, or is not retained in memory any longer than is necessary to take the proper action. More direct support for this conclusion is provided in a study by Strayer and Drews (2006) who had drivers drive a simulator that contained various objects on or off the road. During the drive the eye movement behavior was tracked. Immediately following the drive, the experimenter showed the drivers pictures of objects that either were or were not included in the driving scene, and asked them to decide if the object was or was not present in their drive. The average recognition level they obtained – of 20 percent – was similar to the recognition levels obtained by Johansson and by Shinar and Drory. More interesting, though, was the fact that 60 percent of the objects were fixated by the drivers. Thus, while driving the drivers fixated their gaze on three times as many objects as they were able to recall, indicating that the information was initially attended to, but was then immediately removed from the short-term memory before it was stored in long-term memory. These findings are similar to those of Costa *et al.* (2014) who also found that the percent of signs fixated along the drive was approximately 3.5 times the percent of signs recalled at the end of the drive. The large difference between the percent of signs fixated in Strayer and Drews' study and in Costa *et al.*'s study is most likely due to the fact that the real world scene is much more crowded with visual details than a simulated drive. These findings are consistent with our knowledge of human information processing, that posits that large amounts of data are focused on and stored in a very short-term sensory memory (for 1-2 seconds) and only some of that data is selected for further processing.

If we now attempt to summarize the results of the different studies on sign perception and recall, the most obvious conclusion is that different methods yield widely different results. The most likely factor that distinguishes among the different methods is that they utilize different skills. When we are not actively searching for a specific target, such as a sign, the likelihood of perceiving it is based on what is called "object conspicuity"; the extent to which the sign is visually prominent in the visual scene. Object conspicuity depends on physical and visual attributes such as the object size, contrast with the surrounding, and location in the visual field.

An object may be visually conspicuous, but not necessarily command our attention if it is not relevant to our task. A different kind of conspicuity is "search conspicuity," which is the degree to which an object can be found when a person actively searches for it; that is, its perceived relevance. Thus, a stop sign is important for all approaching drivers, and should therefore have high object conspicuity and high search conspicuity. This is not the case for route guidance or street signs that are only needed by people who are specifically searching for them (Martens, 2000). For these signs it is enough to have high search conspicuity. The poor recall performance of unsuspecting drivers in the studies by Johansson and Rumar (1966), Johansson and Backlund (1970), Shinar and Drory (1983), Strayer and Drews (2006), and Costa *et al.* (2014) all reflect low object conspicuity for most signs. The various levels of importance or relevance of different signs were reflected in Costa *et al.*'s observed range of fixations across all drivers; from a low of less than five percent for the warning signs of "uneven road" and "animals" to a high of over 35 percent for the prohibition sign of "no overtaking," the warning sign of "roundabout ahead" and "road works," and the information sign of "no through road for vehicles." Thus, signs that were not immediately perceived as important were not processed at a higher level. This distinction between object and search conspicuity probably also accounts for many motorcycle collisions, as motorcycles in traffic have poor object conspicuity despite the fact that they have high search conspicuity (see Chapter 16).

Controlled (top-down) and automated (bottom-up) processes in driving

One way we manage to perform complex skills, such as driving, is by automating some of our actions. The distinction between automated and controlled processes was originally proposed and demonstrated by Schneider and Shiffrin (1977). Automatic behavior is one that is highly practiced, fairly effortless, has a fixed sequence of stimulus-response chain, is not limited by short-term memory, uninfluenced by most environmental variations, and – once initiated – not under direct control of the operator. In contrast, controlled behavior is quite demanding because it requires full attention, is limited by short-term memory, and can be modified in response to environmental variations. The distinction can be applied to the difference between driving on a non-congested divided highway, in which our responses to various events are nearly automated, and entering that highway in congested traffic. In the first case our attentional capacities can be freed to engage in various other tasks, whereas in the latter case we are fully attentive to the driving environment, and make multiple discrete responses to the changes as they occur. The danger or "trick" is not to be lulled into an automated mode, and thus miss critical events that may lead to a crash. We suffer from this automated process, when we miss an exit that we usually do not use (because we were not attentive to the typically irrelevant the exit sign), but we can suffer from it much more if a car traveling on the highway ahead of us brakes suddenly and unexpectedly.

So how automated is our driving? One way to address this question is to study the mental load that is experienced by drivers with different amounts of experience, and in driving in environments with different complexities. This was done by Patten *et al.* (2006) who had drivers drive a predetermined course in the town of Linkoping, Sweden, while responding to lights that were occasionally projected onto the left side of the windshield. This peripheral target detection task constituted a secondary task for the assessment of workload. In their study they had two groups of drivers: highly experienced professional drivers with an average annual driving of 47,000 kilometers, and who were very familiar with the town. The less experienced group consisted of non-professional drivers with an average annual exposure of 10,000 kilometers who were unfamiliar with the town. To avoid confounding effects of vehicle control, none of the drivers were novice drivers. The complexity of the drive was manipulated by driving in different traffic densities with various vehicle handling requirements. The advantage of the experienced drivers over the less experienced drivers was clear-cut: their reaction times to the peripheral targets were on the average 0.25 seconds shorter than the reaction times of the less experienced drivers. The complexity of the drive was also reflected in the mental load, with reaction times to the peripheral target in the most demanding situations being 0.13 seconds longer than in the least demanding situation. Together the results suggest that the more demanding the driving task and traffic environment, the less "spare attention capacity" we have for non-driving tasks. Also, the more experienced we are the more we can automate various aspects of the driving task, and hence have more spare capacity for non-driving tasks. This of course has significant implications for the impact of driving distractions (as discussed in detail in Chapter 13).

The results from the sign recall studies reviewed above imply that we do not fully attend to many of the signs along the road, and that we adopt an automated driving mode much of the time. However, in a variation on the standard design of the sign perception studies, Summala and Näätänen (1974) told drivers in the beginning of the drive that their task will be to report every sign that they passed as they drove a 257-kilometer route. In this case the drivers perceived and reported nearly all 881 signs that they passed, missing less than two percent. Most interesting, though, was a comment made by the researchers that the drivers found the driving task under that condition much more fatiguing than otherwise. Thus, attention is effortful (Kahneman, 1973), and unless required to do so, we tend not to pay any more attention to the road and the driving task than we feel is required.

One highly practiced driving task (more in Europe than in the U.S.) is that of shifting gears. In fact, shifting gears has been used by many researchers as a prime example of an automated behavior (e.g., Anderson, 1995; Baddeley, 1990, Michon, 1985). Rather than accept this assumption at face value, we (Shinar, Meir, and Ben-Shoham, 1998) studied it by having drivers drive in busy Tel Aviv streets and report to the experimenter sitting next to them whenever they saw a "SLOW – CHILDREN" sign or a "NO STOPPING" sign. In this study, each driver drove his or her own car. Half the drivers were relatively inexperienced (with less than 2 years of licensed driving experience) and half had over 5 years of experience. Within each group half were males and half were females, and half had an automatic transmission car and half had a manual transmission car. The main hypothesis was that shifting gears would be less automatic for the novice drivers than for the experienced drivers, and that the former will therefore have less attention capacity to devote to the signs. The results, reproduced in Figure 5-1, bore this out.

As can be immediately seen from this figure, Novice drivers in general detected fewer of the signs than the more experienced drivers. More interesting, though, was the fact that there was a large and significant difference in the percent of signs detected by novice drivers driving an automatic transmission car than a manual transmission car. Novice drivers driving manual transmission cars detected 65 percent of the signs while novice drivers driving automatic cars detected 78 percent of the signs. This means that the expression "as automatic as shifting gears" does not apply to novice drivers. These results also illustrate how a task that has no visual component (shifting gears) can still demand a significant amount of the central processing capacity, leaving less for all other processing needs – including those stemming from visual inputs. With practice, the task does become much more automatic, as indicated by the sign detection

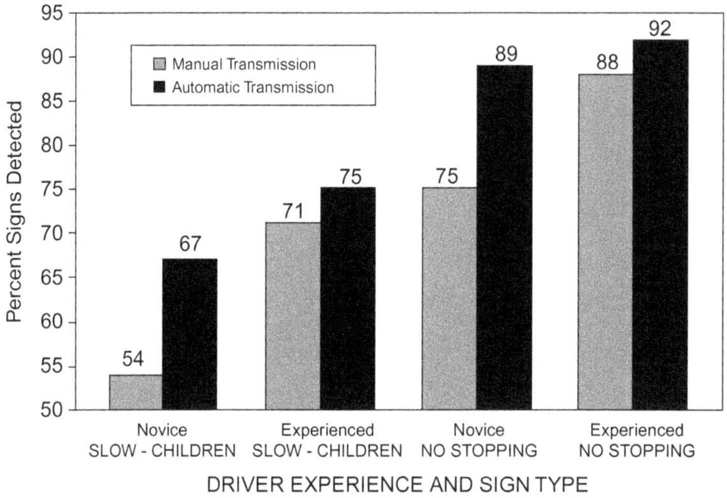

Figure 5-1. The percent of signs detected along an urban route by novice and experienced drivers, driving their own manual transmission or automatic transmission cars (from Shinar *et al.*, 1998, reprinted with permission from the Human Factors and Ergonomics Society).

performance of the more experienced drivers, who were not significantly affected by the shifting of gears. Interestingly (at least for some people), there was no gender effect, indicating that men were not any better than women at time sharing their driving with the sign detection task, and vice versa. Independent support for the gradual and partial automation of the gear shifting process comes from a study by Groeger and Clegg (1997) who found that on the one hand, as would be expected with an automated process, gear changing by experienced drivers did not suffer from time sharing the driving with a secondary task. On the other hand, another aspect of automatic behavior – a very low variance in the time to perform the component tasks – was not borne out in the same study. Interestingly, Selander, Bolin, and Falkmer (2011), found that older drivers – the most experienced drivers alive – have more difficulties with manual gears than with automatic transmission. Thus, it appears that as we age, there seem to be a reversal in the automation process and increasing number of activities require controlled actions (see Chapter 7).

In the light of this study on gear shifting we can again reflect on Luoma's findings. They demonstrate how automatic processing can be sufficient, so that even at low unconscious levels of processing we can still respond appropriately to signs, and thus there is often no need to utilize all or most of our attentional resources for a task that does not demand it. When the task changes – and drivers are aware of the requirement to identify signs along their path – then we revert to attention demanding controlled behavior and our performance improves dramatically. In this case we discover that all the signs had high search conspicuity.

Taken together the eye movement studies and the sign recall and response studies indicate that as drivers we are – for the most part – quite efficient in the use of our limited information processing resources. Fixating an object is a critical and often (but not always) a necessary condition for further processing, and once fixated the level of processing can proceed to the extent needed for the driving task. A sign of a change in speed limit is important (even if only because of the fear of enforcement) until it is replaced by another sign, and so it is likely to be fixated, attended, responded to, and remembered for a long time. In contrast, roadside scenery will or will not be processed and will or will not be retained depending on the attention allocated to subsequent objects and events. In an analogous manner, we may pass the same shoe repair store every day on a daily drive, and never realize it, even when we actually need it. With specific reference to road signs, their information typically supplements information that is already available directly to our senses. But when the visual environment is degraded – as at night or in fog – their significance for safe driving may be critical, and they are then much more likely to be fixated and attended.

A demonstration of the gradual process of automation in various driving tasks is provided in two studies by Charlton and Starkey (2011, 2013). In the first study experienced drivers drove in a simulator through the same 24-kilometer rural road, with geometry and signs identical to a real New Zealand rural road (but with different traffic on each drive). Unlike most studies in a driving simulator, here the drivers drove the same road twice a week for up to 12 weeks. As expected, learning took place over the 12 weeks and it was manifested in a reduction of speed variability and lane position variability on the one hand, and decreased subjective difficulty on the other hand. In other words more and more aspects of the driving became automated. Even the ability to detect a specified car along the way (a VW beetle) improved with practice. Interestingly, when unfamiliar segments were introduced on some sessions their perceived difficulty was much higher. Thus, much of the automation was specific to the specific road – a process we identify with roadway familiarity when we say we can drive that road "in our sleep" or in the authors' own words "driving without awareness." On the basis of these results they suggested that the skilled task of driving involves two processes: a conscious operating process and a mostly unconscious monitoring process. The latter involves a rapid comparison of each situation relative to stored schemas. As we drive again and again over the same road, we develop a more and more comprehensive and stable schema of that road, thus necessitating less and less attention to the multiple external stimuli. In their second study they tested that notion by predicting that experience would contribute to a reduction in "change blindness: our blindness to unexpected but large changes in the external situation" (Simons and Rensink, 2005). At different sessions the drivers had to detect either a VW Beetle, a change in the buildings alongside the road, and – toward the final session – drive on an unfamiliar road. As predicted, the repeated exposure to the same road reduced the perceived difficulty of the segments with the VW and the change in buildings, but not the perceived difficulty of the new road. Thus, they demonstrated another aspect of the flexibility we have in shifting among automated and controlled process according to the level of familiarity we have with the driving task and the driving environment.

Perception Reaction Time and Brake Reaction Time

It should be clear by now that it takes time to "see and respond." The expression "to stop on a dime" is just that: an expression. The time it takes from the moment a sound wave reaches our eardrum, or a light ray impinges on our retina, until we initiate a response to that stimulus is known as perception reaction time (PRT). In driving, the time that passes from the moment a stimulus – such as a brake light or a stop light – appears until we actually reach the brake pedal is known as brake reaction time (BRT).

The relevance of brake reaction time to safety

In driving PRT is a critical component in any emergency maneuver, such as the ones that often precede a crash. This becomes evident if we consider the distance that a vehicle requires to come to a complete stop from the moment that an imminent danger appears. The total stopping distance (TSD) – from the moment a stimulus impinges on our sensory system until the car comes to a full stop can be calculated from the following equation (AASHTO, 1994):

$$X_s = t_{PRT} \cdot v + \frac{v^2}{2(d + G \cdot g)}$$

where

X_s = stopping distance (m);
t_{PRT} = driver perception reaction time (PRT) (sec);
v = approach speed (m/sec);
d = typical deceleration rate for stopping on level pavement (m/sec^2);
G = grade of approach lanes (percent/100); and
g = acceleration of gravity (9.82 m/sec^2).

This equation assumes that the driver brakes with maximal force to take full advantage of the pavement's coefficient of friction and that there is no delay between the application of the brakes, and the reaction of the vehicle braking system to the brake application. Because neither assumption is always justified, the actual stopping distance is somewhat longer than the one calculated.

The coefficient of friction (f) is a function of many factors, but mostly the conditions of the vehicle tires and the pavement, the vehicle speed, and whether the road is wet or dry. Assuming good tires and pavement, on the basis of multiple measures on different roads, AASHTO (1994) recommends the use of different coefficients of friction for different speeds, as specified in Table 5-3.

Table 5-3. Coefficients of frictions (f) based on actual measurements for vehicles braking from different speeds on wet and dry pavements. d is the deceleration rate on level pavement (= f x 9.82 m/s^2) (from AASHTO, 1994).

On Dry Pavements		**On Wet Pavements**		**Design Approach**
d (m/sec^2)	**f**	**d (m/sec^2)**	**f**	**Speed (km/hr)**
6.58	0.67	3.93	0.40	30
6.48	0.66	3.73	0.38	40
6.38	0.65	3.44	0.35	50
6.28	0.64	3.24	0.33	60
6.19	0.63	3.04	0.31	70
6.09	0.62	2.95	0.30	80
6.09	0.62	2.95	0.30	90
5.99	0.61	2.85	0.29	100
5.99	0.61	2.75	0.28	110
5.99	0.61	2.75	0.28	120

Thus, all else being the same, the longer the BRT, the greater the speed, and the lesser the coefficient of friction, the greater the stopping time and consequently the longer the stopping distance. The wild card in the Stopping Distance equation is the PRT: the time it takes to perceive an event, analyze its meaning, decide on the response to it, and then initiate the desired response. Because PRT depends on all the components in the human component processing chain, and these in turn are affected by the driver's vehicle and environment, it is highly variable. It can be affected by various driver conditions, such as poor vision, fatigue, distraction, specific illnesses, uncertainty, and intoxication; by environmental conditions, such as visibility and visual clutter; by vehicular conditions such as brake and gas pedal-specific locations and heights; and by factors related to the interaction among the driver, environmental, and vehicular conditions.

An illustration of the implication of a conservative reaction time of 2.5 seconds, for stopping distances is provided in Table 5-4 (from Leibowitz, Owens, and Tyrrell, 1998). As speed increases from 40 km/hr to 105 km/hr, the distance covered in the 2.5 seconds that it takes the driver to reach the brake pedal more than doubles from nearly 30 meters to over 70 meters. The total stopping distance is affected by the friction with the road, and at these two speeds stopping distance more than triples from 38 meters to 138 meters on a dry road and more than quintuples from 46 meters to 221 meters on a wet road.

Table 5-4. Total stopping distances from different speeds assuming a braking reaction time of 2.5 seconds (from Leibowitz *et al.*, 1998, with permission from Elsevier).

Speed			P & R Distance (m@2.5s)	Braking Distance (m)	Total Stopping Distance (m) – Dry Road*	Total Stopping Distance (m) – Wet Road**
m/h	km/hr	m/s				
25	40	11.3	28.2	9.8	38.0	45.7
35	56	15.5	38.2	19.2	58.0	76.2
45	72	20.1	50.2	32.0	82.2	121.9
55	88	24.7	61.8	47.5	109.3	167.6
65	105	29.0	72.5	65.8	138.3	221.0

*Assuming f = 0.65 (for car/light truck).
**Assuming f = 0.29-0.38 (for heavy truck).

Reaction times in laboratory experiments, driving simulators, and on the road

Under optimal laboratory conditions, PRT can be quite short, typically less than 0.5 seconds, and as short as 0.1 seconds. Optimal conditions imply that there is a single stimulus requiring a single response (known as simple reaction time), a very high expectancy of the event by the responder (minimal uncertainty), a very compatible relationship between the stimulus and the response, and a very conspicuous target. For example, responding to the onset of the brake lights of the car ahead after detecting that a traffic signal ahead has turned red involves a situation of high expectancy and a fairly conspicuous target. Braking in response to the same brake lights (meaning the same brightness, the same distance, and the same place in our visual field) when the lead car driver brakes in response to a pothole in the middle of the freeway, is a response under very low level of expectancy. Braking in response to the same lead car's braking, but when its brake lights are not operative requires sensitivity to a different visual cue – the sudden change in the retinal size of the vehicle – and one that is of fairly low conspicuity.

Expectancy can be both temporal (when it is related to when we expect the light to come on), and spatial (when it is related to where one of several possible events can occur). As one might expect, reaction times to expected (i.e., anticipated) stimuli are much shorter than reaction times to unexpected stimuli. Compatibility is a measure of the "naturalness" of the relationship between a stimulus (such as a brake light) and a response (such as moving the foot from the accelerator pedal to the brake pedal). Often, we actually measure compatibility in terms of PRT. Thus, pressing a key in response to its vibration underneath a finger is a very compatible relationship that can elicit a PRT of less than .02 seconds. Pressing a key in response to a light is less compatible (approximately 0.2 seconds) and pressing a key in response to a number flashed on a screen is still less compatible (0.4 seconds) (Fitts and Posner, 1967). In the context of driving, an example of a simple reaction time task with high stimulus-response compatibility is that of a steering correction in response to a wind gust. Such reactions are very quick and the relationship is highly compatible, because the stimulus (wind gust) affects the same organ with which the driver responds (the hand that is holding the steering wheel). Consequently, such reaction times are typically about 0.5 seconds (Wierwille, Casali, and Repa, 1983). On the other hand pressing the brake pedal in response to the sound of a horn is much less compatible, and typically takes much longer, as discussed below.

We can now examine how driver reaction times vary along these two continua – compatibility and expectancy. The data in Figure 5-2 illustrate very quick reaction times that were obtained under near optimal conditions. In this study by Warshawsky-Livne and Shinar (2002), drivers sat behind a full-size mockup of the rear end of a passenger vehicle, with their foot on the accelerator pedal. The instructions to the subjects were to "brake as quickly as possible when the brake lights of the car in front come on." The average PRTs – the time from the onset of the brake light until the initial movement of the foot off the accelerator pedal – for 10 trials are indicated by the top three lines in Figure 5-2, each line representing the PRTs under a different level of temporal uncertainty. The quickest reaction times, averaging 0.36 seconds were obtained in the condition when the brake lights always came on 2 seconds after the experimenter signaled the start of a new trial. The middle line, with an average PRT of 0.39 seconds was obtained when the brake lights appeared at any time 2-10 seconds after the warning. The third line with an average PRT of 0.43 seconds was obtained when the brake light either appeared 2-10 seconds after the warning, or did not appear at all (and another trial was started about 20 seconds later). Note that in many respects these conditions still involve greater expectancy than drivers have on the road because in this study the driver had no other task to do other than brake, did not have to attend to anything other than the brake lights of the car ahead, did not have to share that attention with any other driving task, and was totally focused on an experimental task. Note also, that because the task is such a simple one, there is essentially no learning involved, and the first reaction times are just as quick as the last ones. Finally, the results also show that the movement times (MTs) from the accelerator pedal to the brake pedal are much shorter than the PRTs, and almost unaffected by the level of uncertainty, reflecting the automatic nature of the braking process once the decision to brake has been made. A similar finding was obtained in an instrumented vehicle on a controlled road course by Ruscio, Ciceri, and Biassoni (2015). In their study variations in the level of expectancy to an in-vehicle hazard warning device yielded significant variations in perception reaction time but no differences in the movement time from the gas pedal to the brake pedal. Most interesting was the similarity between the two studies – conducted in different countries, with different stimuli, and in different settings – in the movement and reaction times. The average movement time on the closed track was 0.18 s and the average PRT was 0.44 s – latencies very similar to the ones obtained by Warshawsky-Livne and Shinar (2002) in the sterile laboratory environment.

In general, as we move away from the sterile laboratory environment to a more complex one such as a driving simulator, or an experimental study on the road, or a naturalistic road study we can expect PRTs and BRTs to increase. And they do. In a review of

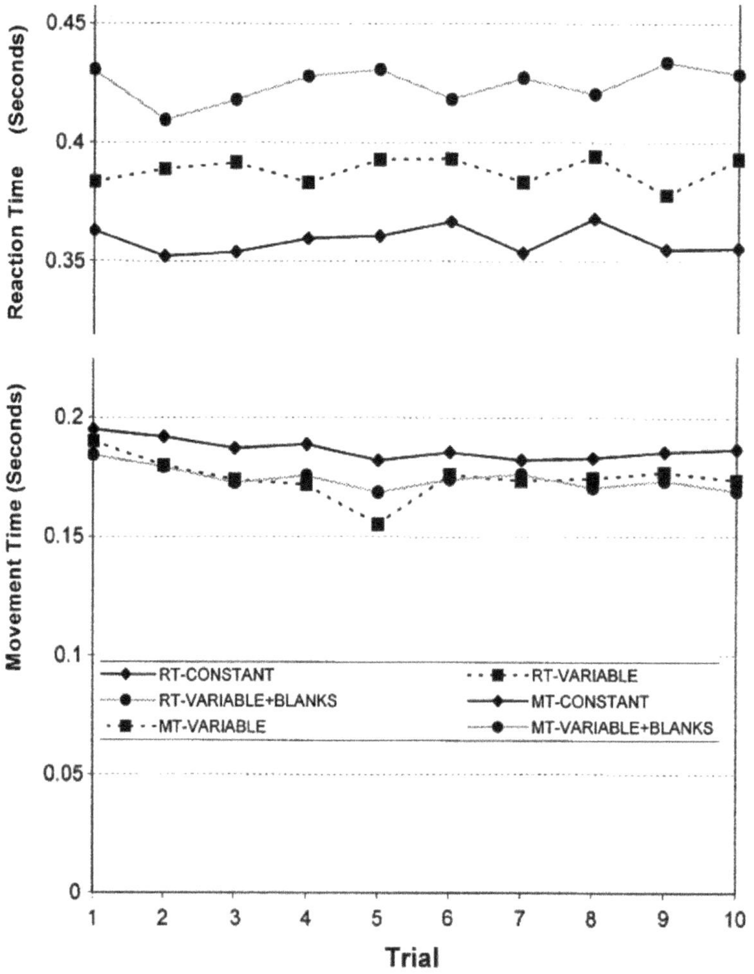

Figure 5-2. Perception reaction times (PRTs) and foot movement times (MTs) to a brake light, in a laboratory situation. PRTs are from the onset of the brake light to the initial release of the accelerator pedal. MTs are from the accelerator pedal to the brake pedal. Total braking reaction time is the sum of PRT and MT (from Warshawsky-Livne and Shinar, 2002, with permission from Elsevier).

over 30 studies of BRTs, Green (2000) noted that mean times varied from a short 0.42 seconds (when drivers in a simulator responded to an expected light while exposed to carbon monoxide; Wright and Shephard, 1978) to a high of 1.95 seconds (for older drivers responding to an unexpected stop by a police officer; Summala and Koivisto, 1990).

In a situation somewhat analogous to the Warshawsky-Livne and Shinar study, but this time on a real road, Summala, Lamble, and Laakso (1998) had drivers steer a car on a closed road section while the car's speed was controlled by an experimenter. The driver was asked to keep his or her foot on the brake pedal at all times and to brake as quickly as possible in response to the braking of a lead car. Two of the independent variables in this study were the speed of the two cars (30 or 60 km/hr) and the gap between the cars (15 or 30 meters in the slow speed and 30 or 60 meters at the high speed). The results yielded an average BRT that was slightly under 0.5 seconds and essentially the same in all four conditions. However, when the drivers also had to attend to a changing display inside the vehicle, then the farther away the visual angle of the display (the lower it was in the car relative to the position of the car outside) the slower the BRT was. Thus, when the drivers had to divide their attention and visual fixations between the car ahead and a display in the car, BRTs increased to as much as 5 seconds (when the vehicles were moving at the fastest speed, the lead car was 60 meters ahead, and the changing display was at the bottom of the dashboard).

The effect a distracting task might have on BRT is critical, as distracted driving increases due to ever-increasing in-vehicle sources of distractions such as cell phones, navigation systems, TV, and internet. Bellinger *et al.* (2009) and Berg and Dessecker (2013) studied BRTs in a partial and rudimentary simulator akin to the one used by Warshawsky-Livne and Shinar (2002). They compared the drivers' braking RT and MT when not distracted at all (control condition) to those observed while distracted by music at two different levels of volume, and while engaged in a cell phone conversation (either with or without music). They found that relative to the control condition conversing on the cell phones – either while listening to music or not – increased reaction times significantly by approximately 50 msec. However, in what they interpreted as an attempted compensation, MT was significantly faster when distracted than when not. Unfortunately that reduction was less than 20 msec; far less than needed for total compensation. Berg and Dessecker also measured the force of the braking and found that in the presence of the cell phone distraction, drivers applied significantly more force, thus adding another dimension to the compensatory effort or sense of urgency. (See Chapter 13 for a more detailed discussion of the effects of distraction on reaction times).

These studies – in the laboratory, the simulator, and on the road – demonstrate that reaction times can be quite fast under optimal non-driving conditions, but can increase by as much as tenfold when the conditions become more complex and the attention load increases. In driving, PRT is of lesser concern than actual driving response time: the time it takes to initiate some driving response. The most important driving responses – at least from the perspective of crash avoidance – are braking and steering. In the case of steering, the hand is typically already on the wheel, but this is not necessarily the case in braking, when the foot is typically on the accelerator pedal. Fortunately, various studies have demonstrated that unlike PRT, movement time is not affected by the event uncertainty (Fitts, 1954; Olson and Sivak, 1986; Warshawsky-Livne and Shinar, 2002; see the bottom three lines in Figure 5-2). Movement time is affected by physical features of the vehicle control devices, such as the relative locations of the accelerator and gas pedals, but that effect is quite small in relation to in-vehicle PRT (Hoffmann, 1991; Morrison, Swope, and Halcomb, 1986). Because movement is not involved, steering reaction times are typically shorter by approximately 0.3 seconds than BRTs (Green, 2000).

An interesting demonstration of the range of BRTs in response to increasingly demanding stimuli and increasingly complex actual driving contexts was provided already in 1938. In this study drivers either sat in a non-moving vehicle or drove a vehicle and had to brake in response to various events. The various events, or stimuli, and the average brake times are reproduced in Table 5-5 (as reported by Matson *et al.*, 1955). The conditions listed in the table progressed from those involving minimal uncertainty and maximal compatibility to those involving significant uncertainty and low compatibility. The shortest average reaction times were obtained when the car was standing and the driver had the foot on the brake pedal while he was anticipating an audible sound. Average reaction time in this condition was approximately a quarter of a second; even shorter than that obtained in the laboratory by Warshawsky-Livne and Shinar. Note that since the driver already had the foot on the brake, no movement time was involved in this

Table 5-5. Drivers' average brake reaction times in response to different stimuli as a function of signal quality, driver status (standing or moving) and expectancy. Note that the reaction times increase as the driving situation becomes more complex and the event uncertainty increases (from Matson, Smith, and Hurd, 1955, as cited by Shinar, 1978, with permission from McGraw Hill).

Car Movement	Stimulus	Starting Foot Position	Reaction Time (Seconds)
Standing	Audible	Brake pedal	0.24
Standing	Bright light	Brake pedal	0.26
Standing	Stop light	Brake pedal	0.36
Standing	Audible	Accelerator	0.42
Standing	Bright light	Accelerator	0.44
Moving – normal road conditions	Audible	Accelerator	0.46
Standing	Stop light	Accelerator	0.52
Moving – test conditions	Stop light	Accelerator	0.68
Moving – normal road conditions	Stop light	Accelerator	0.82
Moving – test conditions	None – stop light hidden	Accelerator	1.34
Moving – normal road conditions	None – stop light hidden	Accelerator	1.65

very short BRT. Also note that the reaction time to an audible signal is slightly shorter than to a bright light on the dashboard. This is because the number of synapses through which the signal has to travel is fewer for sounds than for lights. The significant increments begin when the driver also has to move the foot from the accelerator to the brake pedal and when the stimulus is a more realistic one imbedded in the environment. The next significant increase is when the driver actually has to perform the task while driving – in other words while the information load is greater and the reaction time task must be shared with the additional demands of a driving task. Finally, when the stimulus is also unexpected and appears suddenly behind some view obstruction, then reaction time is the longest, reaching an average of over 1.5 seconds. As old as these findings are, they are still valid. Unlike our vehicles, which have gone through extensive and significant transformations, our information processing capabilities have not changed at all in the course of the past century.

The next issue that must be considered is that PRT and BRT are not the same for everyone or even for the same person on repeated occasions. From the perspective of safety, this variation is critical. A highway design feature (such as the timing of a traffic signal) that is based on the average BRT, is likely to put many people at risk: essentially all the people who on any occasion might be slower than the average. Thus, if reaction times are distributed symmetrically around the average, the timing would be inappropriate for nearly 50 percent of the drivers!

In an attempt to consider that variability, and to identify different components of BRT that can be affected by it, McGee *et al.* (1983) reviewed the literature on individual differences in reaction times. Their summary of reaction times is reproduced in Table 5-6. In accordance with all information processing models (see Chapter 3), the total BRT was decomposed into perception, decision, and brake activation, and the perception phase was further decomposed into the physiological latency of the nerve conduction of the stimulus, the redirection of the eyes to fixate on it, the fixation duration that is needed to absorb the information, and the time it takes to recognize the meaning of the stimulus. Each of the columns in Table 5-6 represents a different percentile: the first indicating the response times of the 50th percentile (meaning that 50 percent of the population of drivers would be able to respond within that time) and the last one represents the 99th percentile (which means that nearly all, save one percent of the drivers, would be able to respond within that time). For design purposes, we usually consider it necessary to accommodate at least 85 percent of the road users (85th percentile), and possibly 95 percent of them (95th percentile). Note, though, that the total BRTs in Table 5-6 assume a purely serial process in which none of the component processes overlap. This is an assumption that is not necessarily warranted.

Using the data in Table 5-6, we can now see how for various considerations and applications BRT can vary from as little as 1.8 seconds to accommodate 50 percent of the drivers in simple undemanding situations to as much as 4.6 seconds to accommodate almost all drivers in complex and demanding situations. Some specific data elements within the table are also noteworthy. First, the time it takes to move the eyes and to

Table 5-6. Brake reaction times to unexpected roadway hazards based on the component times for different proportions of the populations, from the 50th to the 99th percentiles. Based on data from different sources (from McGee *et al.*, 1983).

	Percentile of Drivers					
Element	**50th**	**75th**	**85th**	**90th**	**95th**	**99th**
1. Perception						
a. Latency	0.24	0.27	0.31	0.33	0.35	0.45
b. Eye movement	0.09	0.09	0.09	0.09	0.09	0.09
c. Fixation	0.20	0.20	0.20	0.20	0.20	0.20
d. Recognition	0.40	0.45	0.50	0.55	0.60	0.65
2. Decision	0.50	0.75	0.85	0.90	0.95	1.00
3. Brake Reaction	0.85	1.11	1.24	1.42	1.63	2.16
Total A (1a-d + 2 + 3)	2.3	2.9	3.2	3.5	3.8	4.6
Total B (1c, d + 2 + 3)	2.0	2.5	2.8	3.1	3.4	4.1
Total C (1a-d + 3)	1.8	2.1	2.3	2.6	2.9	3.6

fixate the target is fairly constant for all people, and also a relatively small component in the total BRT. The more significant components are the recognition and decision times, and the most significant component is the BRT. Thus, most of the time is taken by the mental processes and not by the more automated physiological processes.

Ruscio *et al.* (2015) directly measured the component times involved in BRT using an instrumented vehicle and an eye movement tracking system. The drivers drove on a closed track and responded to (mostly) in-vehicle alerts with various levels of expectancy. Their results are presented in Table 5-7. Note that Ruscio *et al.*'s empirically obtained times are shorter than McGee *et al.*'s estimates based on their early literature review. Direct comparisons are hard to make as the definitions of the various components were not identical and the critical stimuli used were varied in each study and in general different. What can be appreciated from looking at the two studies is the multiple processes that are involved in the braking response and the range and variability of the durations involved in each process. However, we can note that in general the total BRTs in the earlier study are much longer than the ones measured in the study by Ruscio *et al.* (2015), thereby demonstrating that BRT is very far from being constant and that it depends on a myriad of factors, each with its own variance.

Table 5-7. Components of the brake reaction times to hazards with various levels of expectancy, from the 25th to 75th percentiles (based on data from Ruscio *et al.*, 2015).

Brake Response Components	**Component Times**				**Cumulative Mean Times**
	25th Percentile	**50th Percentile**	**75th Percentile**	**Mean**	
Gaze RT	.15	.19	.24	.21	.21
Initiate accelerator release	.09	.14	.18	.14	.35
Complete accelerator release	.07	.08	.10	.09	.44
MT to brake pedal	.13	.19	.21	.18	.62
T to complete brake depression	.51	.59	.68	.59	1.21

We can get an appreciation for the variability in actual total BRTs of drivers in a naturalistic setting from the results of an early field study by Johansson and Rumar (1971). In their study, drivers were stopped and notified that somewhere down the road within the next 10 kilometers they will hear a klaxon (an electrically operated horn), and when they do they should as quickly as possible tap the brakes. The horn was placed 5 kilometers down the road and when the driver passed it, his car triggered the horn and started a timer. An observer then stopped the timer as soon as he saw the car's brake lights come on. The results are plotted in Figure 5-3. The figure contains two distributions of reaction times. The narrow distribution with the very short reaction times is that of the experimenter. Because the experimenter had his own reaction time to the brake lights of the truck, his reaction times had to be deducted from the results of the drivers' recorded BRT data. Repeated tests of the experimenter's reaction times yielded a highly stable mean reaction time of 0.244 seconds (with a standard deviation of 0.016 seconds). These results are quite similar to those obtained for simple reaction time to highly expected stimuli in the studies quoted above. The wide distribution to the right of the experimenter's reaction time is that of the drivers' BRTs to the sound of the klaxon *after* the correction for the lag in the experimenter's reaction time. If we look closely at the values of this distribution, we note that the BRTs varied from a very short 0.3 seconds to 2.0 seconds, with a median BRT of 0.66 seconds. As realistic as the situation was, we must note that these drivers knew that they are participating in a study and therefore were probably relatively alert and expecting the sound of the horn. So we now turn to the effects of expectancy.

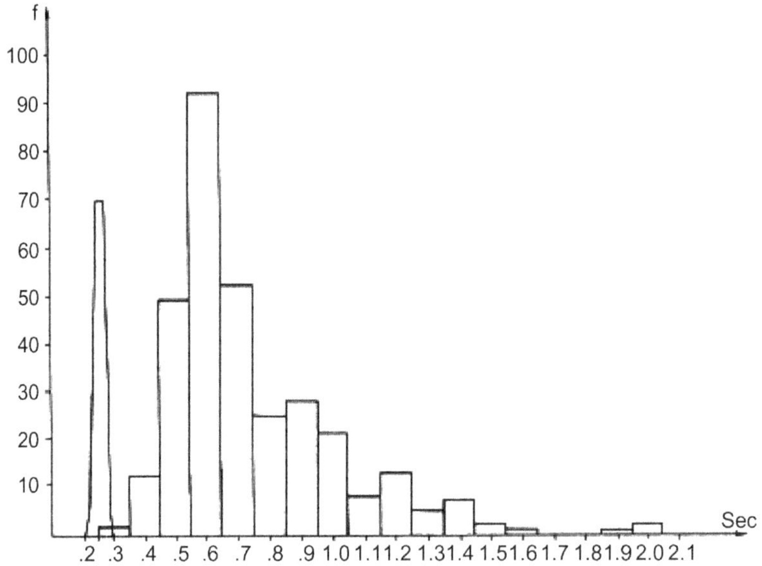

Figure 5-3. Distribution of driver brake reaction times to a loud horn. The narrow distribution on the left is of the experimenter's reaction times. The drivers' reaction times are the true BRTs, *after* subtraction of the experimenter's mean reaction time (from Johansson and Rumar, 1971, with permission from the Human Factors and Ergonomics Society).

Expectancy and brake reaction time

The study by Warshawsky-Livne and Shinar (Figure 5-2) demonstrated the effects of expectancy in strictly controlled laboratory situations. But the effects of expectancy are just as strong in driving in the real world where the range in the levels of expectancy is much larger, as shown in Table 5-5. Green (2000), after analyzing the various factors that influence BRT, concluded that the most significant one is expectancy. Expectancy can affect the reaction time by a factor of 2. When expectancy is maximal, and the nature, the location, and the time of the signal are nearly certain (as when responding to a red light following the yellow phase), BRT is 0.70-0.75 seconds. When the signal is a common one but unexpected (such as the sudden braking of a car ahead), the BRT increases to about 1.25 seconds, and when the stimulus is both rare and unexpected (such as an obstacle on the road) the BRT further increases to about 1.75 seconds. Such effects have been documented by more than one study, and the remainder of this section is devoted to more detailed descriptions of some of the more frequently cited studies that quantified the effects of expectancy.

In the study by Johansson and Rumar described above, the drivers were informed in advance of the stimulus (fog horn) and had a rough idea as to when to expect it. To adjust the distribution for the effects of uncertainty Johansson and Rumar (1971) conducted a second experiment. In that experiment they measured the reaction times of a small group of five drivers using the same method as for the larger sample. Then they installed a buzzer in their cars that went off at unexpected times, with intervals between two consecutive signals sometimes lasting more than a week. To stop the buzzer the drivers had to tap their brakes. For this group the median unexpected BRT was 0.73 seconds and the BRT to the expected signal was 0.54 seconds. The ratio between the two – 1.35 – is Johansson and Rumar's recommended adjustment for expectancy.

A direct test of the effects of uncertainty on BRT in the real world was done by Olson and Sivak (1986). In an experimental setting it is quite difficult to manipulate expectancy because drivers know that their behavior is being monitored. To create an unexpected situation, Olson and Sivak recruited 49 young drivers to participate in a study of "driving performance." The drivers were informed that their behavior would be studied in a test site "a few miles away." While they drove to the test site they were told that they could become accustomed to the car. Thus, as far as the drivers were concerned they were not being monitored until they got to the "test site." Unbeknown to them, an experimenter placed a yellow piece of foam rubber, 15 centimeters high and 91 centimeters wide, on the left side of the driver's lane just after a crest in the road, creating a situation where the obstacle suddenly came into the driver's view when it was only 46 meters in front of the car. Although the obstacle was soft and presented no danger to the driver, it was quite an alarming surprise, so it can be assumed that the drivers reacted to it as fast as they could. This constituted the condition with minimal expectancy or "surprise." Following that trial the drivers had a few more trials in which they had to respond as soon as they saw this obstacle. Although the specific location of the obstacle was varied from trial to trial, the drivers were prepared for it, so in this condition the drivers were assumed to be "alerted." Finally in the condition with the highest level of readiness (labeled "brake") a red light facing the driver was attached to the hood of the driver's car (simulating a very close brake light), and whenever the experimenter turned the light on, the driver had to tap the brake light as quickly as possible. In this condition there was no uncertainty at all concerning the location of the stimulus, only temporal uncertainty as to when it would be turned on. Olson and Sivak's (1986) results are plotted in three graphs – one for each condition – in Figure 5-4.

As can be seen from the cumulative distributions of reaction times, the BRT is plotted on the X-axis, and the percent of trials in which the drivers responded within each BRT is plotted on the Y-axis. It is quite obvious that the lower the expectancy, the slower the reaction time. Thus, if we look at the 50th percentile of responses, we see that in the surprise condition the BRT was 1.1 seconds, in the alerted condition it was 0.7 seconds, and in the brake condition it was 0.6 seconds. A similar relationship is obtained if we look at the 85th percentile with reaction times of 1.3, 0.9, and 0.7 seconds, respectively. Thus, the difference between maximal alertness and maximal surprise – within the constraints of this study is twofold, just as concluded by Green (2000). Two other findings are worth noting here. First, the range of BRTs is quite large: from 0.5 seconds to 1.5 seconds in the alerted condition and from 0.02 seconds to 0.9 seconds in the brake condition. Second, in the unalerted condition, one of the drivers was not able to respond before he hit the obstacle, hence the data points for the 49 drivers end at 98 percentile rather than 100. Although it is only one person, in reality the situation where an obstacle suddenly

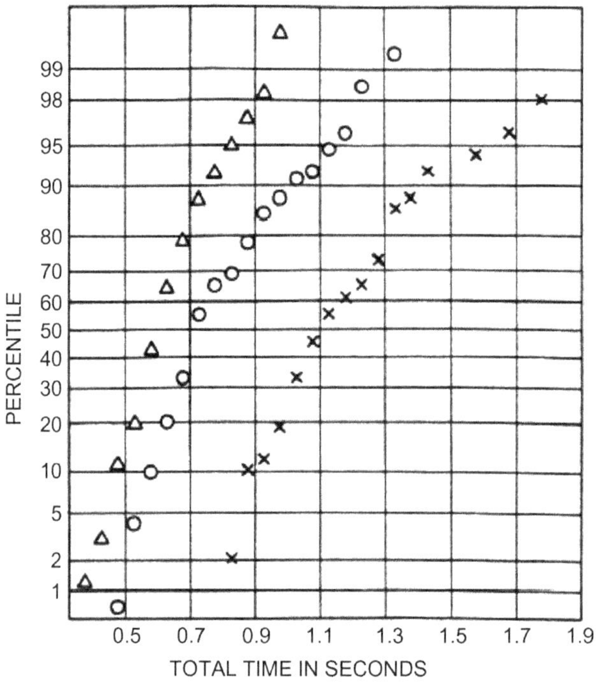

Figure 5-4. Cumulative brake reaction time distributions of young drivers to a high-contrast obstacle on the road under three levels of expectancy: x = "unalerted," o = "surprise," and Δ = "brake." See text for explanation (from Olson and Sivak, 1986, reprinted with permission from the Human Factors and Ergonomics Society).

appears before a driver without giving him or her sufficient time to respond is not all that rare – especially in collisions with children who dart into the road (see Chapter 20), or in night time collisions with pedestrians or stopped and slow-moving vehicles, when visibility is curtailed by our headlights.

Motorcyclists, who in general pay more attention to the road and to the road surface (as any small obstacle can flip their two-wheel vehicle) are also susceptible to the effects of expectancy. In a road study conducted on a campus road in Malaysia, Davoodi *et al.* (2012) measured motorcyclists' BRT to expected (a light activated by the side of the road) and unexpected (a road block in the middle of the lane) targets. They obtained mean BRT of 0.71 seconds to the expected target and mean BRT of 1.25 seconds to the unexpected target. The disparity in the 85th percentile BRTs was even greater: 1.01 seconds versus 2.12. It is possible that the disparity would have been even greater had the two targets been identical. Instead, the unexpected road block consisted of a huge yellow canvas with two large "STOP" signs on it, stretched across the complete lane and flanked by bright cones. Thus the unexpected target had a much higher level of conspicuity. In summary, these results again demonstrate the very large effect that expectancy has on our reaction time: essentially doubling it from a situation of nearly complete certainty to one of nearly total uncertainty.

One challenge facing highway engineers is to either allow for the effects of low expectancy in the system design or to increase drivers' expectancy to otherwise unexpected situations. Thus, drivers who expect to exit a highway tend to negotiate their vehicles to the right lane where the exit ramp is typically located. Occasionally, due to various constraints the exit ramp departs from the left (fast) lane. In such situations, to prevent last minute surprises, the road designers place warning signs to that effect much earlier up the stream of traffic. A different way of increasing expectancy for unexpected events is to employ forward collision warning systems. It appears that drivers' BRTs to vehicles slowing ahead – at least in a simulator environment – is greatly reduced (by as much as fifty percent) in the presence of such warning systems (Aust, Engström, and Viström, 2013).

Although less critical for safety, the effects of uncertainty and expectancy are not limited to braking RT, but to other reactions as well. For example, Li *et al.* (2014) showed that the presence of a countdown timer that indicates the time left before the signal light turns green reduces the driver's delay to the start of the acceleration from the stopped position to an average of 1.48 seconds from 2.12 seconds without the timer (actually both PRTs are somewhat shorter as the data were based on the actual starts of the cars).

Age and gender differences in brake reaction time

To establish a standardized measure of BRT, the American Automobile Association developed a BRT kit that includes a test light box with green and red lamps, and two foot pedals mimicking the accelerator and brake pedals. Using that device on a sample of over 1,400 people, the AAA (1952) noted that average RT increases monotonically from 0.44 seconds for the 20 years old to 0.52 for the 70+ years old. A later study by the AAA (1966) showed that on the average women were slightly slower than men (by a mean difference of 0.08 seconds), but with a very large overlap between the two groups. A more recent test of BRTs in a sample of 124 male and 272 female drivers ranging in age from 15(!) to 91 years with a similar device was conducted by Dickerson and her associates (2008). Temporal uncertainty was relatively small, as the red light appeared 2, 3, or 4 seconds after the onset of the green light on each trial. They found that the average brake RT was 0.46 seconds (with a standard deviation of 0.1 second) for males, and 0.52 seconds (SD = 0.16 seconds) for females. Thus, different studies examining a similar BRT, conducted 40 years apart obtained similar results. Although the average brake RT increased with age, reaching 0.54 seconds and 0.58 seconds for the 65+ years old male and female participants, respectively, Dickerson and her colleagues noted that most of the increase was due to a few slow older drivers than to a shift in the modal times. This can be seen in Figure 5-5, where it is also apparent that the modal and median brake RTs for drivers of all ages are approximately 0.5 seconds. The age-related increase in individual differences are important because as in all aspects of perceptual motor skills (see Chapter 4 on vision and Chapter 8 on older drivers) aging is often characterized more by greater variations among people than by a steady decline in the mode of all people. Consequently, chronological age is a dubious criterion for any licensing decision, except for indicating that a test may be in order. Dickerson *et al.*'s findings are also similar to those of Hollis *et al.* (2013) who tested the BRTs of 88 drivers ranging in age from

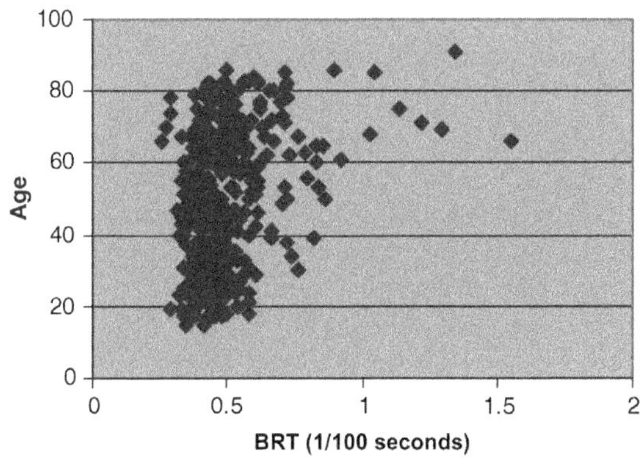

Figure 5-5. Brake reaction times for 396 drivers ranging in age from 15 to 91 (from Dickerson *et al.*, 2008, with permission of Taylor & Francis LLC (http://www.tandfonline.com)).

80 to 97 (58 males and 30 females), using the same AAA brake reaction timer. They obtained average brake RT of 0.60 seconds; only slightly higher than the times obtained by Dickerson *et al.* who pooled the RT data for all drivers 65 years old or older.

Driver reaction time in more complex situations

All of the situations considered till now were of the kind in which once the stimulus (e.g., brake lights of a lead vehicle, red light of a traffic signal, obstacle on the road) was recognized, the decision was an almost reflexive one of braking. This situation is often labeled "simple reaction time" in the sense that there is only one stimulus that has to be dealt with (e.g., a stop light) and only one appropriate response (e.g., braking). Many situations confront the drivers with a dilemma as to which stimulus to attend to and what is the most appropriate response (known as "choice-reaction time"), and resolving this dilemma – a decision process – typically increases reaction time.

Yellow light dilemma

A classic situation of this kind is the response to a yellow signal light following the green phase. When the driver is either quite far from the signalized intersection or very close to it, the decision is obvious: to brake in the former and accelerate in the latter. However, there is a zone where the decision is not trivial and the driver is presented with what has been labeled as the "amber light dilemma" or "yellow light dilemma" (e.g., Allen, 1995), where both braking and acceleration responses are observed. The significance of this dilemma is that (1) some drivers may decide to "beat" the red light and cross the intersection after the light has turned red and (2) some drivers who decide to stop may be rear-ended by the drivers behind them who decide to accelerate in order to beat the red light. Note that it is most likely that drivers entering this zone are already focused on the signal light, and they can be assumed to be in a high state of expectancy. Thus, whatever delay we observe in their reaction time is due to the uncertainty of the best decision, and not to the uncertainty with respect to the appearance of the stimulus. Zhang, Fu, and Hu (2014) reviewed the BRTs obtained in the dilemma zone (from the moment the light turned yellow until the brake lights came on) in nine field observation studies of a total of 40 intersections in different countries, spanning 50 years of research. They found that mean reaction times varied from a mean of 0.72 seconds to 1.30 seconds, while the 85th percentile in the different studies varied from an average of 0.92 seconds to 1.90 seconds. BRTs in the yellow light dilemma zone obtained by Diew and Kai (2001) – but not covered in Zhang *et al.*'s review – fell within these ranges for both mean BRTs and the 85th percentiles. Furthermore, for the drivers who braked in response to the light, the closer they were to the intersection the shorter their BRTs were – indicating a decrease in the dilemma or in the difficulty of making the decision. Thus, for the braking drivers who were within 2-4 seconds of the intersection when the light turned yellow, BRTs for many drivers were less than 0.6 seconds. Still, as Zhang *et al.* note these values are significantly above the standard 1.0 second BRT assumed for signal phasing design purpose.

Liu, Chang, and Yu (2011) identified multiple driver, traffic, and design factors that contribute to the large variance in the BRT, but a detailed discussion of these factors is beyond the scope of this book. As an illustration consider the observational study conducted in the U.S., on unaware drivers by Wortman and Matthias (1983) in eight different signalized intersections. The average BRT was 1.30 seconds and the 85th percentile was 1.8 seconds. Their data for each of the intersections are provided in Table 5-8. The results for the different intersections reveal something that is not obvious from the data averaged across all intersections: the high variability in BRT among the intersections, from an average BRT of 1.09 seconds to an average BRT of 1.55 seconds. With some exceptions of traffic- and intersection design-based variables, it is very hard on the basis of the observational data to determine what factors accounted for the variability among the sites. For example, an easy to assess variable of day versus night did not seem to affect BRT. On the other hand, psychological variables like expectancy may play a very significant role here. Regardless of the underlying factors responsible for the variance, if we want to accommodate most drivers (i.e., the 85th percentile), then we have to allow for a BRTs of up to 2.1 seconds, and possibly more if more intersections are considered.

Reaction time to different stimuli

When the BRT of the same general population is measured in response to a variety of stimuli, the range is expected to increase even more; and it does. This is illustrated in the BRTs to a variety of traffic control devices, as measured in Melbourne Australia by Triggs and Harris (1982), and reproduced in Table 5-9. Here too, the motorists were not aware of being measured. Triggs and Harris only provide the 85th percentile responses, and their range is significantly higher than the range observed above for the yellow traffic light: from a short 85th percentile BRT of 1.26 seconds in response to the braking of a car ahead in a car following situation, to a BRT nearly three times as long of 3.6 seconds in response to a barely visible amphometer (a pair of black hoses laid on the road,

Table 5-8. Brake reaction times of unsuspecting drivers to the change of a traffic signal light from green to yellow in the approach to different intersections in the same general geographic area (from Wortman and Matthias, 1983).

Intersection Approach	**Driver Response Time to Onset of Yellow Light**		
	Average time	**Standard deviation**	**85% Time**
University Drive	1.28	0.82	2.0
Southern Ave. (day)	1.49	0.62	1.9
Southern Ave. (night)	1.43	0.73	2.0
U.S. 60	1.38	0.60	2.1
First Ave.	1.24	0.51	1.8
Sixth Street	1.55	0.70	2.0
Broadway Blvd. (day)	1.16	0.48	1.5
Broadway Blvd. (night)	1.09	0.44	1.5
All approaches	1.30	0.60	1.8

used to measure the speeds of passing cars). Clearly visibility and expectancy are principal factors that affect the BRTs here.

The great variability in PRTs and BRTs makes the design of highway traffic systems quite complicated. While it is obvious that we must accommodate more than the average driver, can we accommodate all drivers? Not only would accommodating the 100th percentile be impractical, but it may also be counterproductive. This is easily illustrated in the timing of the duration of the yellow light in traffic signals. Using the data from Wortman and Matthias, the longest *average* BRTs were 1.55 seconds at Sixth Street and the standard deviation of the BRT was 0.7 seconds. If we make a simplifying assumption that the distribution of reaction times is symmetric around the mean (even though it really is not – see Figure 5-3), then in order to allow for 98 percent of the population we have to consider a BRT of 3.35 seconds. This is actually fairly close to the 3.0 seconds duration of the yellow phase in most traffic signals worldwide (e.g., Diew and Kai, 2001). Ostensibly, the longer the duration of the yellow phase, the more opportunity there is for the slow responders to respond in time and avoid entering the intersection after the red phase has started. Unfortunately, we tend to adapt to design changes, by allowing for the longer yellow light and taking chances hoping that we will be able to cross the intersection without violating the signals and risking a crash with the cross traffic. To reduce such risk-taking it would actually make sense to shorten the yellow phase. Hence the yellow light dilemma: any

Table 5-9. Brake reaction time of unsuspecting drivers to various traffic control devices and roadway situations in Australia: 85th Percentile in seconds (from Triggs and Harris, 1982, with permission from Monash University).

85th % BRT (Seconds)	**Roadway Situation**
3.00	C.R.B. "Roadworks Ahead" sign
1.50	Protruding vehicle with tire change
1.50	Lighted vehicle under repair at night
2.80	Parked police vehicle
3.40	Amphometer: Beaconsfield
3.60	Amphometer: Dandenong North
3.60	Amphometer: Gisborne
2.54	Amphometer: Tynong
1.50	Railway crossing: night (general pop.)
1.50	Railway crossing: night (rally drivers)
2.53	Railway crossing: day
1.26	Car following

duration that we select is going to be inadequate for some of the drivers: either the fast ones and high risk-takers when the duration is long or the slow ones and low risk-takers when the duration is short.

Still, given the critical role that reaction time plays in emergency crash-avoidance situations, we must make some design decision concerning BRTs. This has in fact been done and different reaction times are commonly assumed for various design considerations, such as train crossing warnings, no passing zones, and traffic signals. For example, for the purpose of keeping a safe headway – the temporal equivalent of the gap between cars traveling in the same direction – the assumed reaction time to the slowing of the lead car is 2.0 seconds, and the resultant recommendation is to keep a separation of 2 seconds, known as the "two-seconds rule" (U.S. National Safety Council, 1992). For intersection clearance, the American Association of State Highway Safety Traffic Officials (AASHTO, 1994, 2001) assumes a 2.5 seconds reaction time that a driver would need in order to stop in time and avoid a collision with another vehicle in the cross traffic of an intersection or with a train when approaching a railroad crossing.

Hazard perception: Situation awareness for lurking dangers

Up to this point the discussion concerning PRTs and BRTs was limited to highly conspicuous and fairly simple stimuli such as brake lights, traffic signal lights, or a loud horn. Unfortunately, to drive safely we must often detect stimuli that are not very obvious and not as easily defined. A significant class of such stimuli is hazards: stimuli that pose a threat that can materialize into an accident. Most hazardous situations are *potential* or dormant in the sense that they are schemas that can lead to an accident but generally do not. However, a few are active or *materialized* hazards in the sense that barring an avoidance response of one kind or another, they will result in an accident. For example a truck parked before a pedestrian crossing is a potential hazard because it blocks the view of a potential pedestrian. If in fact, a pedestrian is starting to cross the road at that location the potential hazard turns into a materialized hazard. Hazard perception can be defined as the detection of hazards in the context of driving or situation awareness (see Chapter 3) for dangerous situations in the traffic environment. Once they detect a hazard, drivers often tend to reduce their speed and direct their attention to it by reallocating some of their processing capacities; for example, by slowing their rate of conversation with passengers (Charlton, 2009). Because the cues for hazard perception are often subtle and slow to emerge, hazard perception skills may be linked to various visual skills. Thus, Lacherez, Au, and Wood (2014) found that hazard PRT can be predicted from performance on motion perception tests. This relationship is just one example of the inseparable link between vision, perception, information processing, and safe driving.

Hazard perception is typically measured by presenting a person with either still photographs or video clips of driving scenes as viewed from an approaching vehicle and asking the person to identify the potential hazards in these scenes. Typical potential hazards include a pedestrian walking along the road, a signalized intersection, or an obscured intersection preceded by a sign. Actual materialized hazards include braking of a car ahead, a pedestrian crossing the road, or a turning truck that blocks the view of another vehicle about to enter the driver's path (Borowsky and Oron-Gilad, 2013; Pollatsek *et al.*, 2006). Either reaction times or the number of correct identifications are then used as measures of hazard perception ability (Borowsky, Shinar, and Oron-Gilad, 2010; Borowsky and Oron-Gilad, 2013; Crundall *et al.*, 2012; Scialfa *et al.*, 2013; Vlakveld, 2011, 2014). As noted above, the cues we utilize to detect hazards are often very subtle, and hazard perception is a learned skill reflected in heightened situation awareness. Thus, though the correlation between the crash histories of different road segments and hazardous ratings of these sites based on video clips of those segments viewed from the driver's perspective at site is low, it is still significantly better for experienced drivers than for novice drivers (Price and Glynn, 2000).

Hazard perception and experience

Given the acquired nature of hazard perception, it is not surprising that experienced drivers are able to identify hazards – and more importantly situations of potential hazards – more easily and react to them faster than novice drivers (Borowsky *et al.*, 2010; Borowsky and Oron-Gilad, 2013; Crundall, 2016). Part of this skill acquisition is reflected in the change in patterns of saccadic eye movements that comes with experience (Borowsky *et al.*, 2010; Vlakveld, 2011, see also Chapter 4). Thus, an experienced driver is more likely to identify a hazard, and to identify it earlier than a novice driver. For example, an experienced driver would identify a child walking along the street as a potential hazard, anticipate the child's darting into the street, and be ready to react to the child's actual jumping into the street. In contrast, an inexperienced driver in the same situation would be less likely to recognize the impending potential hazard, and recognize the hazardous situation only once that hazard materializes and the child is actually in his or her path. In such situations the cues to which we must respond are not always as obvious as the brake lights of a car ahead of us, and the response that is desirable is not always necessarily a reflexive braking action.

A striking demonstration of the association between an indirect measure of hazard perception and experience in driving was provided in an early study by Helander (1976). In his study novice and experienced drivers drove an instrumented vehicle while their GSR (galvanic skin response – a measure of skin conductivity that correlates with tension – typically used for lie detection) was measured. He found that experienced drivers braked slightly and their GSR increased as they approached an intersection but not when they drove on a narrow bridge. In contrast, novice drivers braked slightly and their GSR increased markedly when they traversed the narrow bridge but not when they approached the intersection. Obviously an intersection can be a host to impending collisions with other vehicles or pedestrians, while a narrow bridge poses no such danger.

One illustration of the complexity of situations involving hazards – and the very different hazard perception times that they yield in comparison to other PRTs – is provided in a study conducted in the United Kingdom on relatively inexperienced drivers, most of them 17-18 years old (DfT, 1995). These young drivers were given a hazard perception test that consisted of a sequence of videotaped driving scenes with situations such as car emerging from the side, a stray dog on the curb, pedestrians crossing the road, a van with an open door parked in a curve with oncoming traffic, etc. The average perception recognition time to the hazards was 7.38 seconds; 5.7 times longer than reaction times to brake lights or traffic signal lights. One interesting aspect of the study was that training to recognize hazards (other than the ones encountered in the video test) resulted in a small but statistically significant reduction of the hazard perception time to 6.85 seconds – which is still much longer than PRTs to simple stimuli.

Except when it comes to older drivers, hazard perception skill, or the lack of it, has been consistently linked to driving experience: In the search for the underlying reasons for young/novice drivers' heightened crash risk, many recent studies have shown that novice drivers are much poorer than experienced drivers in hazard perception (Borowsky and Oron-Gilad, 2013; Borowsky *et al.*, 2010, 2012; Crundall *et al.*, 2010, 2012; McKenna and Crick, 1994; Vlakveld, 2011, 2014; Wetton *et al.*, 2010). Consequently, the issue is further discussed in Chapter 6 on young drivers. There are some data to indicate that older drivers also suffer from a somewhat poorer hazard perception ability (Wetton *et al.*, 2010; Wood *et al.*, 2013) but this is not borne out by all studies (Borowsky *et al.*, 2010). Interestingly, motorcyclists, who by the nature of their task must be much more attuned to the road ahead and to potential roadway hazards, are in fact better at hazard perception (Hosking, Liu, and Bayly, 2010).

The underlying reasons for the novice drivers' poorer hazard perception are not quite clear yet. Some research suggests that it is because they have a higher threshold for danger (meaning lack of appreciation of the danger) inherent in hazardous situations (Wallis and Horswill, 2007). This may be due to their impoverished bank of past experiences involving such situations. Other research suggests that it is due to their lower awareness of potential hazards that would otherwise guide their fixation patterns to focus on them (Borowsky *et al.*, 2010, 2012; Vlakveld, 2011).

Because of its criticality to safe driving, various training approaches have been developed with differing amount of success in improving hazard perception of novice drivers. Most of the training effects have been typically demonstrated in a driving simulator (Borowsky *et al.*, 2010; Crundall *et al.*, 2010; Pollatsek, *et al.*, 2006; Samuel *et al.*, 2013; Weiss *et al.*, 2013). But two studies have demonstrated its validity on the road as well. The first study by Taylor *et al.* (2011) showed significant improvements on an open road. The second study, by Horswill, Hill, and Wetton (2015) showed that young drivers who took a hazard perception test as a part of the Queensland, Australia licensing procedure, were 25 percent more likely to have a crash within a year after licensing if they failed the test. Also, it appears that even highly experienced drivers can benefit from such training (Horswill, Taylor *et al.*, 2013). However, as it has been studied mostly in the context of inexperience of novice drivers, it is further discussed in Chapter 6 on young drivers.

Judgments of Gaps, Clearances, and Headways

The ability to judge gaps in traffic is essential to driving. We need to judge gaps between vehicles when we cross an intersection, in order to decide if we have sufficient time to cross it. We need to judge a gap between us and opposing traffic when we wish to pass a slower-moving vehicle, in order to decide if we can complete the pass before the oncoming traffic arrives. These are not easy judgments to make and our ability to make them develops over time and experience behind the wheel (Leung and Starmer, 2005). We also need to judge the gap between ourselves and the car ahead of us, in order to maintain a safe headway. Headway is the distance between the front of a lead car and the front of a following vehicle (though some times it refers to the inter-vehicle distance: the gap between the rear end of the lead vehicle and the front end of the following vehicle). It can be expressed either in units of distance or in units of time. Time headways refer to the time it would take the following vehicle to reach the location of the lead vehicle if the following vehicle were to maintain its momentary speed. This is the time that a following driver has to respond to the braking of a lead vehicle in order to avoid hitting it. I will focus on this last situation, as illustrative of the processes and times involved. Interestingly, there is very little relationship between the ability to verbalize the gaps, by stating how many meters or feet or seconds separate us from a crossing car or a car ahead of us, and the ability to make the correct decision in terms of waiting or proceeding to pass (Lee, 1976).

Gap judgment between approaching cars is also a frequent task that pedestrians must perform before deciding whether or not to cross a street. This skill is still undeveloped in young children, and is moderately impaired in older people (Dommes *et al.*, 2014), and it is discussed in some detail in Chapter 15 on pedestrians.

Maintaining a safe distance from the car ahead is one of the most regularly performed tasks in driving. In fact, the law in most countries assumes that drivers are capable of that judgment, and failure to keep a sufficient time headway is often cited as a violation of traffic laws (e.g., in Israel). Legally, the term "sufficient" in this context is typically 2 seconds or at least 1 second. However, it can be much longer. For example the Maryland Driver's Manual recommends a following distance of at least 3-4 seconds and even more in stop-and-go traffic (MMVA, 2015).

As with speed, the admonition to maintain safe headways is often displayed on overhead programmable signs, on roadside signs, and on the rear bumper stickers of cars (in bumper stickers such as "If you can read this you are too close"). Most of the time we are able to maintain headways that enable us to avoid rear-end collisions. When we fail, the driver ahead of us cannot compensate for that failure, and we then have a rear-end crash. In general, rear-end crashes are much less severe than head-on, side- or single vehicle crashes, mostly because the speed differential is low and the energy of the impact can be greatly dissipated by the front and rear of the two cars rather than by the more vulnerable sides. Thus, though they constitute only a small percent of all fatal crashes (e.g., six percent of all fatal collisions in the U.S.), these crashes are relatively frequent in comparison to all other types of crashes, constituting approximately 30 percent of all crashes (NHTSA, 2012). Though not all rear-end crashes are due to failure to maintain a safe headway to the car ahead, and some of these crashes are with a parked or stopped vehicle, arguably most of the crashes involve insufficient headway.

When we drive behind another vehicle in traffic, we do not maintain a fixed distance or time to the car ahead. Instead, we oscillate between some minimal safe headway that we try not to go under, and a headway that we consider neither too far nor too close. These two extremes define our range of comfortable headways (Ohta, 1994). To avoid colliding with a vehicle ahead of us, we therefore have to maintain a time headway that is longer than our BRT in that situation. Based on studies of BRTs, a commonly recommended headway is 2 seconds, and a method that is commonly recommended to drivers in order to apply that rule is to wait until the lead vehicle crosses a definable point (such as a roadside post) and then count two seconds (e.g., "twenty one, twenty two") if we pass the definable point before we finish our counting then our gap is too short. This is known as the 2-seconds rule. In Germany the recommended minimum distance between cars is "half the speedometer," meaning that drivers should keep a gap that is in meters half the value of the speed in km/hr (Vogel, 2003). For example at motorway speeds of 130 km/hr the recommended gap should be 65 meters. In terms of time headway, this rule of thumb is equivalent to 1.8 seconds. In contrast to these recommendations, in real driving when drivers are unaware of being monitored typical headways are much shorter than the recommended two seconds. In fact, headways of 1 second or less are typical of fast rush hour traffic, at least in the U.S. (e.g., Chen, 1996; Evans & Wasielewski, 1983) and Israel (Blum and Shinar, 2005), and headways of 1.1-1.7 seconds seem to cover much of the range at which drivers feel comfortable when they follow another vehicle (Ohta, 1994; Brackstone, Waterson, and McDonald, 2009).

In a series of studies that we conducted in Israel we looked at drivers' choices of safe and comfortable headways, their ability to verbally and non-verbally estimate headways, the relationship between the headways drivers keep and their skills, their ability to improve their judgments, and the potential for feedback devices as learning tools to increase headways. The following is a brief description of these studies and the results from these and other studies.

Drivers' estimation of minimum safe headways and comfortable headways

In the first study (Taieb-Maimon and Shinar, 2001), experienced drivers with Snellen visual acuity of 6/9 or better were asked to drive on a four lane divided highway behind a lead vehicle. An experimenter that drove the lead vehicle adjusted its speed in a random fashion from 50 to 100 km/hr. At each speed, the driver in the following car was asked to follow the lead car by keeping a "minimal safe distance at which he or she would still be able to stop in time should the driver of the lead car break suddenly." Once the drivers reached that headway they were asked to estimate that gap – either in terms of meters, car-lengths, or seconds. Then the drivers were asked to slow down so that the gap widened significantly. They were then asked to follow the lead vehicle at what they considered a "comfortable" distance. Once this procedure was completed the lead driver selected another speed and the whole sequence was repeated.

The first issue was to determine the drivers' minimum safe headways, and how they adjust them as they increase the speed. The findings were a mix of good and bad news. The good news is that as speed increased, drivers increased the distance headway, as can be seen from Figure 5-6 (left panel). Better still, their increase was nearly exactly in accordance with the rate of the speed increase, so that the *time* headway remained almost the same at all speeds (right panel). Similar findings showing that time headway errors remained relatively constant across different speeds were obtained by Risto and Martens (2013) in a simulation environment. The bad news is that the time headways that the drivers selected were quite short – 0.66 seconds on the average. This headway is much shorter than the 85th percentile of BRTs in response to a lead car's brake lights in real driving, such as the 1.26 BRT obtained by Triggs and Harris (1982). In fact, in our study nearly all drivers (93 percent) maintained a minimum time headway of less than 1.0 second (i.e., less than half the headway recommended by driving manuals); none of them maintained headways greater than 1.4 seconds; and the highest-risk driver kept an unnerving headway of 0.25 seconds. Obviously, this driver either had unrealistic faith in his own reaction time or (justified) faith that the lead driver in this experiment will not brake suddenly.

If drivers are able to adjust their headways in order to keep the same safety margin at all speeds, why do they keep them so short? One possibility is that they underestimate the actual headway. Some support for that was found when we analyzed their verbal

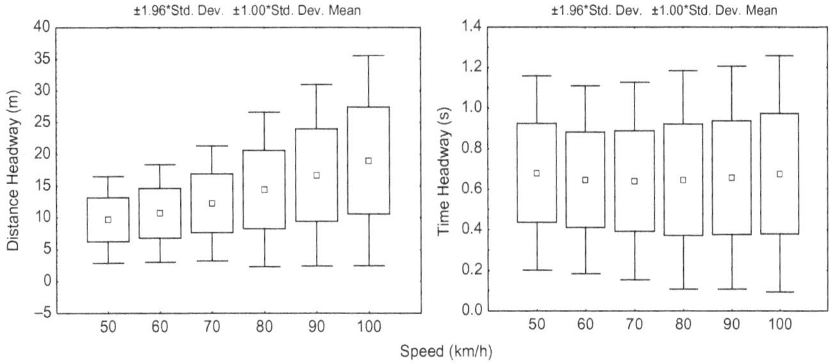

Figure 5-6. Mean, ±1 standard deviation, and ±1.98 standard deviations of distance headways (left panel) and time headways (right panel) kept by drivers who were asked to maintain a "minimum safe headway" (derived from data from Taieb-Maimon and Shinar, 2001).

estimates of their headways. All drivers invariably overestimated their headways, by an average of 0.24 seconds when using car lengths, by an average of 0.32 seconds when using meters, and by an average of 1.6 seconds(!) when estimating it in seconds. Risto and Martens (2013) also found that headway estimation accuracy differed between distance headway estimation and time headway estimation. Thus, in our study, it seems that when drivers directly estimated the time headway between them and the car ahead, they actually believed that they were maintaining a two-second gap. Another reason for the short headways may be due to the drivers' reliance on time-to-collision (TTC) – the time it would take to collide with the lead car given the speed differential. When two cars travel at the exact same speed, even if their headway is extremely short, the TTC equals infinity. In fact, most of the time we drive behind another car – regardless of the headway – we do not collide. That is because it is rare for the car ahead to brake suddenly and unexpectedly, especially at high speeds on motorways. Thus, our previous experience reinforces us that we should have no fear of collision even at short headways (Evans, 2004). Paradoxically, there may be times when we maintain short headways to feel safer. This may be the case in fog, when drivers reduce their headways in order to see the vehicle ahead – even at the cost of reducing their safety margins (Broughton, Switzer, and Scott, 2007). This also appears to be the case when the density of the oncoming traffic increases as drivers may feel safer sticking closer to the vehicle ahead and thus reducing their field of view and eliminating much of the oncoming traffic from their vision (Duan, Zhizhong, and Salvendy, 2013) (though Brackstone *et al.*, 2009 did not find an effect of traffic flow on time headways). Regardless of the explanation, the fact is that drivers feel comfortable – or at least safe – with headways that are significantly less than recommended, and probably less than they can manage in case of an emergency.

Several researchers have found that experienced drivers cognizant of their skills engage in riskier behaviors than inexperienced drivers, including shorter headways

(Van Winsum and Heino, 1996). Sayer *et al.* (1997) found that older drivers keep longer headways than younger drivers even though BRTs in response to the braking of a lead car do not seem to vary as a function of either driving experience (Summala *et al.*, 1998) or age (Warshawsky-Livne and Shinar, 2002).

There was a possibility, in our study, that the shorter headways were maintained by those who had faster reaction times. Therefore, we examined the PRT in optimal laboratory conditions to see how well it related to the headways the drivers kept on the road. The results were disappointing. The correlation between the two measures was essentially zero. Not only that, but for 7 of the 30 people who participated in the study the average PRT under optimal conditions was actually longer than the minimum time headway they kept on the road. For these drivers, were that car ahead to stop suddenly, the likelihood of colliding with it was very high. However, this lack of correlation between the headways drivers keep and their BRT should be investigated further, since at least one study found a positive correlation between the two, showing that those who keep short headways have quicker reaction times (Van Winsum and Brouwer, 1997).

Given the fact that (1) drivers can adjust their headway to maintain the same time headway at different speed, but (2) select headways that are too short to be safe, and then (3) verbally over-estimate their headways, the next issue is whether we can aid or train drivers to improve their headways. Various driver aids have been proposed to help drivers maintain a safe headway. For example, in the U.S. novice drivers are taught to allow for one car-length between them and the car ahead for every 10 mph in their speed (e.g., *Maryland Drivers' Handbook*, 1998; National Safety Council, 1992). In Europe novice drivers are taught to use the "2-second rule" mentioned above. In France, motorways have dashed shoulder striping designed to encourage drivers to keep two line segments between themselves and the car ahead. For uninitiated drivers and tourists there are also road-side signs that instruct drivers to keep two line segments between themselves and the car ahead. A similar approach is used in Spain, where chevron lines are painted in the lane. However all of these approaches are flawed: how well can we estimate car lengths and be able to position them virtually between us and a car ahead? How well can we estimate two seconds using the two-seconds method? The answer is: very poorly. Also the road markings in France and roadside signs in Spain are designed relative to the speed limit. But what is the optimal number of 'dashes' or spaces between segments or chevrons for drivers exceeding the speed limit or traveling below it? This approach, by the way, unintentionally promotes shorter headways for speeding drivers, because their time headways between segments is shorter. The most effective aids to keeping safe distance are in the realm of advance driver assistance systems (ADAS). Adaptive cruise control and headway collision warning systems that slow the car and warn the driver, respectively, when the time-to-collision falls below a critical level are very effective means of reducing rear-end collisions due to insufficient gaps. These systems are discussed in more detail in Chapter 19 on Crash Countermeasures).

In the discussion above and in the following sections the roadway features were not mentioned as a relevant variable. But they are. Although evaluations of the spatial distance between us and the car ahead should be relatively independent of the scenery surrounding us, it stands to reason that time headway – that takes speed into account – would be affected by the features of the peripheral visual environment; that is, the road delineation and off-road scenery. Indeed, it turns out that drivers maintain greater headways in tunnels than on the open road (Yeung and Wong, 2014), indicating that the rapid optic flow of the close tunnel walls creates a heightened sense of speed. For more in depth discussion of headways and means of improving it see Shinar and Shaham (2003) and Vashitz, Shinar, and Blum (2008).

Can we learn to improve on-the-road headway estimation

One method to improve headway judgments would be to have in-vehicle headway-o-meters (just as we have speedometers). The belief that minimum headways can be regulated and enforced rests on the assumption that drivers are capable of either directly perceiving or correctly estimating their headways. We do not make that assumption with respect to speed and that is why we have speedometers in our cars. The research on drivers' headway judgments shows that we are incapable of this task too, and need some kind of an aid.

Therefore, in the next study (Ben-Yaacov, Maltz, and Shinar, 2002), using drivers with at least 5 years of driving experience, we evaluated the potential benefits of a dashboard-mounted, laser-based device that continuously monitored the distance to the car ahead and after adjusting for the speed of the car in which it was installed provided the driver with time headway in real time. In this study, when the time headway decreased to 1.0 second it alerted the driver (via a tone). The drivers were instructed to drive as quickly as possible, while staying in the right lane of a freeway, and obeying the posted speed limit (100 km/hr). Whenever the drivers reached a slower car (a lead vehicle), they were told to maintain a headway of at least 1 second until permitted by the experimenter to pass. The lead drivers were unaware of being in the study. After a 10 kilometers practice period without any feedback, the drivers continued to drive without feedback for an additional 20 kilometers in which all headway data were recorded (unbeknown to them), then with headway feedback for 70 kilometers, and finally for an additional 20 kilometers in which the instructions were the same, the headways were monitored, but no feedback was provided. The purpose of the first no-feedback phase was to obtain a baseline of the drivers' actual headways when they believe that their headways are at least 1 second. The instruction to maintain headways of at least 1.0 seconds should not have prevented drivers from using headways that were actually shorter than 1.0 seconds, because the previous studies already demonstrated that drivers significantly overestimate their headways. The purpose of the second phase with the feedback was to test the effects of feedback on improving headways in the sense that drivers will be less inclined to keep headways that are less than 1.0 seconds. The purpose of the third – no feedback – phase was to see whether in the process of receiving feedback the drivers actually acquired an ability to better estimate their headways and apply it to their driving behavior even in the absence of feedback from an external measurement device. Some learning was expected because the second phase provided drivers with the two classical necessary conditions for learning and improvement: practice and feedback (e.g., Baddeley, Hitch, and Bower, 1974).

The headways from the three phases of the drive are presented in Figure 5-7. Even with the instruction to avoid headways less than one second, the typical headways were 0.4-0.8 seconds, and when drivers followed another vehicle (before they were permitted to pass), nearly half the time (42.2 percent) they maintained headways of less than 0.8 seconds. In contrast to this dangerous pattern, the introduction of feedback caused a dramatic shift in car following behavior. The percent of time with headways less than 0.8 seconds dropped from over 40 percent to 3.5 percent. Even after the feedback was removed, during the final 20 kilometers, the drivers maintained that safe behavior and drove with headways less than 0.8 seconds only 6.5 percent of the time. Thus, in the process of receiving feedback, the drivers must have internalized some critical cues that enabled them to judge 1 second headways fairly accurately, so that they performed nearly as well once the external feedback was removed.

The most surprising finding of the Ben-Yaacov *et al.* (2002) study was the result of an afterthought. Several months after the study officially ended, we wondered: how long can drivers retain that accurate headway estimation skill? As it turned out, all of the subjects were still available and willing to participate in one more drive. The delayed drive took place 6 months after the original study, and its results are plotted along those of the original results in Figure 5-7. The performance after a 6-month retention period is essentially identical to that obtained immediately after feedback, with the modal – most common – headway being in the desirable range of 0.8-1.2 seconds. This is consistent with Taieb-Maimon's (2007) finding (using the data from the first headway study

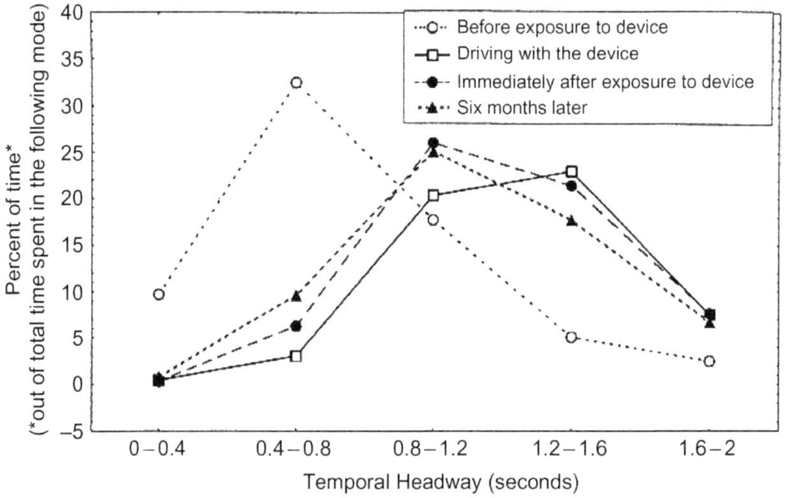

Figure 5-7. Percent of time drivers maintain different headways, with and without feedback from an electronic headway display device (from Ben-Yaacov *et al.*, 2002, reprinted with permission from the Human Factors and Ergonomics Society).

discussed above) that the learning of time headway is very rapid and nearly complete after four trials with feedback.

With these results in mind we can now state, with a significant amount of confidence, that (1) in the absence of feedback, drivers tend to keep headways that are significantly shorter than the recommended safe headways, and often shorter than their BRT, (2) they over-estimate their headways, so that they may actually believe that they are safer than they are, (3) with objective feedback, drivers are able to learn to estimate their time headways fairly accurately, and (4) once that learning occurs, it can be retained for long periods, at least as long as 6 months.

Drivers can and are inclined to improve their headways

There still remains one sticky issue. That issue relates to the difference between best performance and typical behavior: just because drivers can be trained to correctly perceive time headways, will they then be inclined to adopt them and make them a part of their typical driving behavior or habits? To answer that question we conducted one more study (Shinar and Schechtman, 2002); a field operational test (FOT) in which we installed headway monitoring and recording devices in the personal vehicles of 29 men and 14 women. The drivers ranged in age from 25 to 60, had at least 5 years of driving experience, and drove their car to and from work on a daily basis. The drivers were aware that a headway measuring device was installed in their vehicles, but were also told that the display unit will be installed a few weeks later. After approximately 3 weeks the display unit – that provided the driver with a continuous feedback of the time headway – was installed on the dashboards. The drivers were also told that the unit will sound a tone (whose volume the drivers could attenuate, but not totally eliminate), whenever their headway decreased to less than 1.0 second. Importantly, in this study the drivers were not given any instructions or incentives to maintain safe headways. The results of this study in terms of the percent of the time that drivers kept different headways in the 2 weeks before they received feedback and in the 2 weeks while they received feedback are displayed in Figure 5-8.

The first thing we can see from the results in Figure 5-8 is that with or without feedback, when the drivers were in a car-following mode, they were much more likely to keep safe headways (greater than 1.2 seconds) than unsafe headways (equal to or less than 0.8 seconds). Nonetheless, the feedback had a strong positive effect of reducing the percent of time spent at short headways from over 20 percent to under 15 percent, and at increasing the percent of time they maintained safe headways (greater than 1.2 seconds) from 57 percent to nearly 65 percent. This is important because the only motivation the drivers had to increase their headways was intrinsic: the desire to increase their own safety. No incentives for long headways or penalties for short headways were given, and the drivers were assured that the data would be used for statistical purposes only. Also, in this study the total number of driving hours was such that drivers drove according to their own preferences, rather than according to some experimental protocol as in the previous studies.

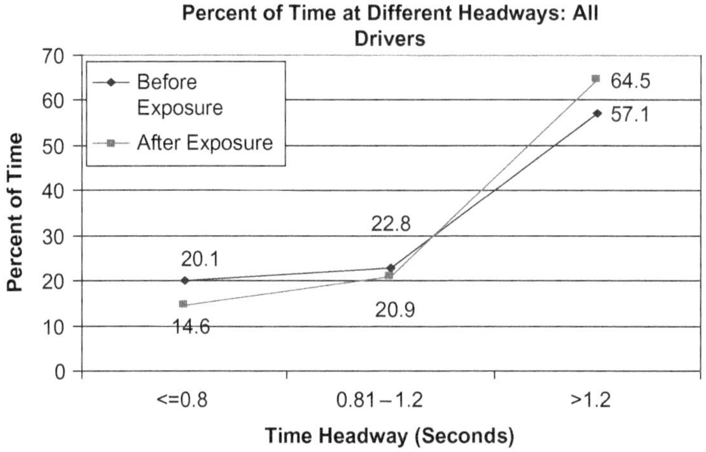

Figure 5-8. Percent of time that drivers keep various headways with and without feedback, without any external incentive to maintain safe headways (derived from Shinar and Schechtman data, 2002).

Because of the many hours of data, it was possible to examine the effects of the headway feedback under different driving conditions such as night versus day, and city (slow speed) driving versus highway (high speed driving). The effects of the feedback were consistently the same in all conditions: an approximately 25 percent reduction in the dangerously short headways (nearly identical to Ervin *et al.*'s finding of 26 percent reductions in headways <1.0 second), and an approximately 15 percent increase in the safe long headways.

As often done in behavioral research, we also analyzed the effects of gender and age. In all three studies (Taieb-Maimon and Shinar, Ben-Yaacov *et al.*, and Shinar and Schechtman), there were no consistent significant differences between males and females and no differences between the younger and older drivers. This indicates, that men and women do not differ in the perceptual-cognitive skills that are needed to estimate headways, and that age or driving experience is not a relevant issue – at least as long as all drivers are neither young novice drivers nor older than 60 years old.

At least five more recent studies have confirmed the benefits of headway feedback on the maintenance of safe headways. Three naturalistic driving studies by Ervin *et al.* (2005), Young *et al.* (2007), and Merrikhpour, Donmez, and Battista (2014) found that headway feedback caused drivers to increase their time headways (though Ervin and his colleagues also noted that the occasional false alarms frustrated some of the drivers). Furthermore, it seems that even experienced professional drivers can benefit from this feedback. Bao *et al.* (2012) in a naturalistic driving study on heavy truck drivers found that providing drivers with time headway feedback caused these drivers to increase their headways by 0.20 seconds in rain and by 0.28 seconds in dense traffic. Though these durations may seem very short, for a car traveling at 100 km/hr they reflect an increase of approximately 1.5 and 2 average car lengths, respectively. In England, Birrell, Fowkes, and Jennings (2014) fitted cars with a smart driving aid that among other things provided drivers with headway feedback, so that an initial warning (amber light) was displayed when the headway decreased below 2 seconds, and another warning (red light) was displayed whenever it decreased below 1.5 seconds. Forty experienced drivers drove a 45.5-kilometer route consisting of a motorway, urban, and inter-urban road, once with the system and once without it. The results showed that compared to driving without the system, mean headway increased to 2.3 seconds from 2.05 seconds and the time spent traveling closer than 1.5 seconds to the vehicle in front decreased by approximately two-thirds (from 6.6 percent to 2.3 percent). Merrikhpour and her colleagues further noted that the feedback is particularly effective for those drivers that are prone to keep shorter, riskier, headways.

In summary, the evidence is overwhelming that our natural ability to estimate time headways is quite deficient and that augmented feedback that serves as a forward collision warning is most helpful *and* appreciated. There is, however, one fly in that ointment. In their extensive on-road study that spanned 5 years, Ervin *et al.* also noted that "while incidents were found during manual driving in which the forward collision warning may have contributed to a timely driver response to an emerging rear-end crash conflict, the frequency or magnitude of such conflicts were unaffected by the forward collision warning presence." Thus, the magnitude of the safety benefit – number of crashes prevented – remains to be determined.

One cautionary note should be inserted here before we jump to the conclusion that feedback is the complete answer to maintaining safe headways. Some drivers try to avoid following another vehicle altogether. In a study we (Bar-Gera and Shinar, 2005) conducted on unsuspecting drivers on the open road, a lead car would appear in front of a vehicle and then adjust its speed to be either at, above, or below that of the following driver. It turns out that approximately 50 percent of the following drivers overtook the lead car even when it was traveling slightly faster than the following driver's average speed. It therefore appears that many (possibly most?) drivers do not like to find themselves following another car, and in order to avoid it they are willing to increase their speed, pass it, and then resume their previous lower speed (!). Thus, keeping a safe headway is not always a driver's goal. Not having to worry about it is a sufficient incentive to increase the speed and pass a lead car.

Comprehension of Information: Road Signs and In-Vehicle Displays

As we process inputs from the road ahead, before we can select a response we must analyze the meaning of the objects we perceive. To ease the task, vehicle manufacturers and highway engineers often resort to using symbols or icons for in-vehicle displays and highway signs and markings, respectively. To benefit from this we have to compare the data we extract from the display (such as a geometric shape of an octagon, with an outstretched white palm on a red background) with information stored in memory (the coded images of all traffic signs) in order to identify the meaning of the image (as the standard code for a stop sign), and to decide on an appropriate response (stop).

One simple method to convey accurate information would be to provide detailed text messages. For some applications this may not be very practical because it may take too long to read the text. For instance in the case of road signs, in order to read the text from a sufficient distance with a visual acuity of 6/12, some signs would also have to be quite large. Inside the car the problem may be even greater. Just think of the size of a dashboard, in which all the information – that is currently presented in small icons – is presented in text. There is also a language problem in multi-lingual driving populations; and in today's environment the driving population in many countries is quite multilingual because the indigenous populations are often multilingual (e.g., Canada, Switzerland, Israel), and because international travel allows people of most countries to drive in most other countries. But the primary reason for using symbols – in and out of the car – is that they are much faster to read and comprehend. But this is where the problem is: They are not always comprehended. So reading text takes too long, and "reading" symbols may be erroneous, and the benefits and shortcomings of each must be weighed against each other for every application.

To ease the decision, there are some rules concerning the proper use of icons. Coded symbols – or icons – should be preferred to text either in the car or on the road whenever any of the following conditions apply: (1) quick and accurate recognition of a message is necessary, (2) the information includes visual or spatial concepts, (3) the driver will be performing a visual search of alternatives (e.g., motorist services information), (4) the amount of space on the display is limited and presenting the information textually will take up more space than is available, and (5) an icon already exists and has a generally accepted meaning (Campbell, Hoffmeisterm, *et al.*, 2004; Campbell, Richman, *et al.*, 2004). In accordance with these principles one interesting study, conducted on mostly non-driving young Taiwanese students, Chi, Dewi, and Chen (2012) showed that similarities in shape and function (akin to spatial and conceptual compatibility) were the most common dimensions for coding similarities among various in-vehicle icons. In summary, the general guiding rule for improved comprehension of icons is that the representations conform to "user-centered design principles," and these are not specific to roadway signs or in-vehicle displays but rather to all iconic representations in just about all domains (e.g., Gatsou, Politis, and Zevgolis, 2012; Campbell *et al.*, 2004).

Comprehension of road signs

Road signs are the language that road designers use to communicate with road users. Unfortunately, some critical information is often lost in this process, and miscommunications occur. Most of us study the sign code in use in our country just once: prior to the licensing test. We then drive for several decades, during which time we forget signs that we do not encounter frequently, while never learning in a systematic manner new signs that are introduced into the sign code. The risk to safety is greatest when we misinterpret signs without being aware of it. To minimize such risks with new signs, many countries have a systematic process of designing alternative codes and then testing their comprehension on naïve drivers in a controlled environment, before a final design is adopted. Typical measures of comprehension include the identification distance, and verbal reports of the meaning of the sign or the action that it requires (Yang, Shurbutt, and Phillips, 2013). However, these recommended procedures are not religiously adhered to by all jurisdictions. For example, a survey of British motorists in London and Glasgow conducted by the British Royal Automobile Club Foundation in 2001 found that many quite common signs (such as "ending of a dual carriageway") are either not recognized or misinterpreted by the overwhelming majority of the motorists surveyed (BBC, 2001).

As our world shrinks toward a global village, and as more and more of us crisscross this "village," variations in signing among countries, poor sign design, and different levels of familiarity with signs used in different countries all contribute further to reduced communications among drivers. Unfortunately, there does not seem to be a standard that applies to all countries (despite the existence of a European system and what some call "international signs"). To reduce some of the confusions in sign comprehension, representatives of 18 European countries met in Vienna in 1968 and agreed on a "standardized" set of highway signs (EMCT 1974). These signs were eventually ratified by 73 countries, though additional countries may use the standardized set, or at least parts of it. Notable non-signatory countries that do use some of the standardized signs are the U.S. and China. Since the Vienna Convention on Road Traffic many signs have been modified and many signs have been added. Consequently, there is a UNECE Group of Experts on Road Signs and Signals (WP.1/GE1) that is currently working on updating and harmonizing current roadway signs (Pronin, 2014). These experts from around the globe are in essence trying to create an international language common to all road users, based on road signs design and symbols, As an integral part of the roadway environment such signs can contribute significantly to "self-explanatory" roads (see Chapter 19), by providing the road users with "an environment that can be easily understood and safely operated by all its users" (UNECE, 2010, p. iii).

Even within a country there are variations that do not seem to conform to any standard. An extreme example of the problem is provided by Bowman (1993) who noted that in the U.S. there were over 340 "traffic control devices" (including signs, road markings, and signals) that are in use and are consistent with accepted traffic engineering principles, but are not included in the U.S. Federal *Manual on Uniform Traffic Control Devices* (MUTCD, 2003). And the situation may be much worse now, more than 20 years after Bowman's review. Furthermore, there are comprehension problems even with the signs that are included in the MUTCD. Dewar and his associates (Dewar *et al.*, 1997) evaluated the comprehension of 85 symbols included in the MUTCD, and found that while comprehension was as high as 99 percent for some of the symbols, 12 percent of the symbols in their survey were understood by fewer than 40 percent of the drivers. Several studies have shown that despite high levels of comprehension of the more familiar signs, there are significant differences in sign comprehension among different signs and different drivers (see Shinar *et al.*, 2003, for a review).

There are also individual differences in sign comprehension, and different "types" of drivers may be differentially familiar with different signs. For example, older drivers seem to have more difficulties in comprehending "way finding" signs (such as bus, train, or gas stations) than younger ones (Dewar *et al.*, 1997), especially if they have some cognitive impairments (Scialfa *et al.*, 2008). Cultural differences also contribute to individual differences in sign comprehension. A poignant example is provided by Dudek *et al.* (1996) who surveyed international tourists in Florida and found that the question mark symbol ("?") used to designate "tourist information" was not understood as such by most of them. This is quite a problem, considering that this sign was designed to aid this very specific population. Lest we conclude that this problem is unique to Florida tourists, in a much earlier study with Canadian students, Dewar, Ells, and Cooper (1977), also obtained extreme variability in sign comprehension, and one of the signs that was misunderstood by all respondents was the European "tourist information" sign.

To simultaneously study the effects of some of the variables that may be related to sign comprehension, we (Shinar *et al.*, 2003) conducted an international survey of sign comprehension of five groups of drivers: (1) novice drivers within the first year of licensure, (2) tourists who were licensed in another country, (3) older drivers, 65 + years old, (4) problem drivers with multiple traffic offenses, and (5) university students with at least 2 years of licensed driving experience. The survey was conducted on the same groups of drivers in Canada, Finland, Israel, and Poland. All respondents were presented with the same 31 signs, shown in Figure 5-9, and defined in Table 5-10. These signs were selected so that approximately half of them were common to all four countries in the study and the rest were signs unique to the different participating countries. The findings of this study illuminated the large differences between countries and different groups of drivers. This is illustrated in the partial results presented in Figure 5-10. Two findings stand out. First, there are large differences among the countries, with average percent of signs correctly identified in different countries ranging from a low of under 45 percent to over 65 percent. Second, there are significant differences among the groups, with the elderly drivers doing worse than most other drivers (except in Poland). As expected, comprehension levels for the local signs were much higher than for the non-local signs: 78 percent versus 32 percent. The high error rate for the unfamiliar non-local signs is most likely indicative of poor coding. Although our study was conducted in only four countries, other studies on sign comprehension that have been conducted in Nigeria (Makinde and Oluwasegunfunmi, 2014), Turkey (Kirmizioglu and Tuydes-Yaman, 2012), India (Mukhopadhyay *et al.*, 2013), and in some countries in the Persian Gulf (Bahrain, Kuwait, Oman, Qatar, and United Arab Emirates) (Al-Madani and Al-Janahi, 2002), with different varieties of traffic warning and regulatory signs, yielded even lower comprehension levels, with a high variability among the different signs.

But what is an acceptable level of comprehension? According to the International Standards Organization (ISO, 2002), signs should have a comprehension level of at least 67 percent in their intended population. The American National Standards Institute (ANSI) is much stricter and has a criterion of 85 percent accuracy. Relative to these criteria, after reviewing 11 studies on sign comprehension Zhang and Chan (2013) concluded that "lack of traffic sign comprehension is a serious problem in many countries."

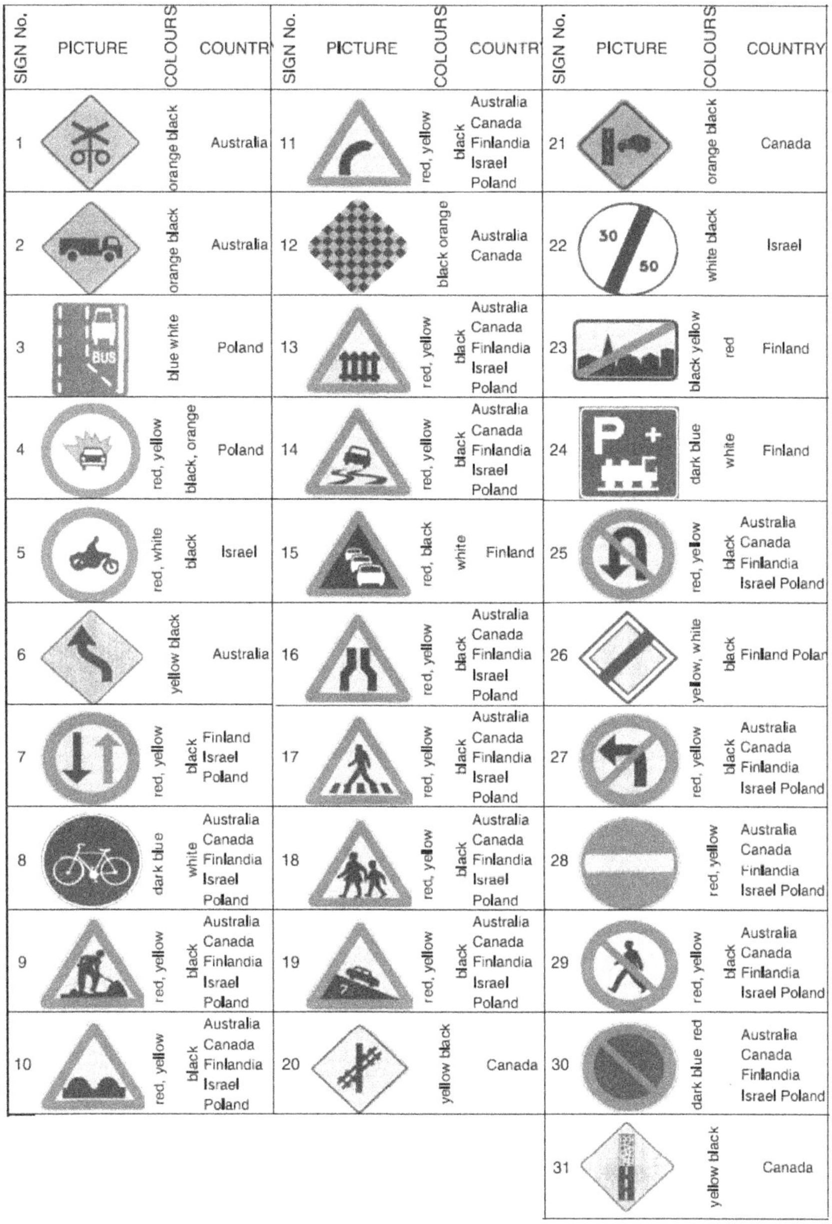

Figure 5-9. Signs used in an international sign comprehension study. The actual colors and the countries using the sign are indicated for each sign. For the meaning of each sign refer to Table 5-10 (from Shinar *et al.*, 2003, with permission from Taylor & Francis Group, Ltd.).

Table 5-10. The meaning of each sign in Figure 5-9, that was used in the international sign comprehension study (from Shinar *et al.*, 2003, with permission from Taylor Francis Group, Ltd.).

Sign number	Sign meaning
1	Railroad crossing with lights
2	Truck crossing
3	Bus lane begins
4	No entry for vehicles carrying explosives
5	No entry for motorcycles/mopeds
6	Reverse turn (left then right)
7	Priority for oncoming traffic
8	Bicycle path
9	Road works
10	Bumps on road
11	Right curve
12	Termination of road
13	Railroad crossing ahead
14	Slippery road
15	Congestion
16	Road Narrows
17	Pedestrian crossing ahead
18	Children crossing ahead
19	Steep hill ahead
20	Diagonal railroad crossing ahead
21	Truck entrance

Table 5-10. (*Continued*)

Sign number	Sign meaning
22	End speed limit (trucks 30 km/hr, cars 50 km/hr)
23	End built up area
24	Parking for public transport
25	No U turn
26	End priority road
27	No left turn
28	No entry
29	No entry for pedestrians
30	No parking
31	Pavement ends

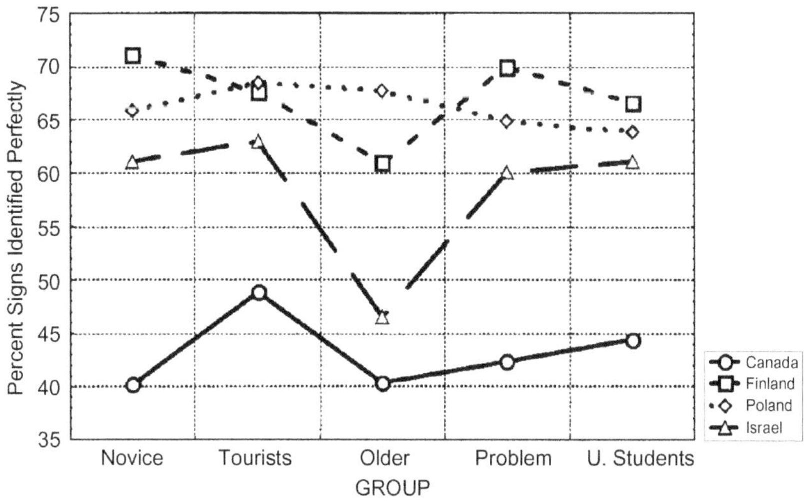

Figure 5-10. Percent of signs identified perfectly by different driver groups in different countries (from Shinar *et al.*, 2003, with permission from Taylor & Francis Group, Ltd.).

A most disturbing finding in the Shinar *et al.* (2003) study was the small but significant 2-5 percent of the signs that were interpreted to mean the opposite of their true meaning. This is a serious error that can lead to crashes. For example, sign # 7 is typically posted on narrow roads or bridges and indicates that oncoming traffic has priority. Obviously, the opposite interpretation can lead to a head-on collision. Errors of this type were not evenly distributed across all signs. The most problematic signs in this respect were # 2, #5, and #22, with 10, 21, and 26 percent errors of this type, respectively. A particularly problematic sign was #22 "End of posted speed limits of 50 km/hr for cars and 30 km/hr for trucks," and the distributions of responses to this sign are presented in Figure 5-11. This sign is used only in Israel, but even in Israel 28 percent of the respondents (40 out of 250) gave it the opposite meaning, believing that the prescribed speed limits start at that point rather than end there. Interestingly, in Finland and Poland this sign was often misinterpreted, but hardly anyone assigned it the opposite-than-intended meaning.

When we measured the processing time involved in sign comprehension by having the subjects press a button as soon as they identified the meaning of the sign we (Ben-Bassat and Shinar, 2015) found that the average sign identification time of both young and old drivers of the incorrectly identified signs was significantly longer than the identification time of the correctly identified signs: 2.27 seconds versus 1.39 seconds for the young drivers, and 4.86 seconds versus 2.93 seconds for the older drivers. In contrast, signs that were given the opposite than intended meaning were (mis)identified just as quickly as the signs that were correctly identified (1.84 seconds and 3.31 seconds, for the young and old drivers, respectively). These results show the double jeopardy of poor signing. Misidentified signs compromise safety by taking more time from the driving task and

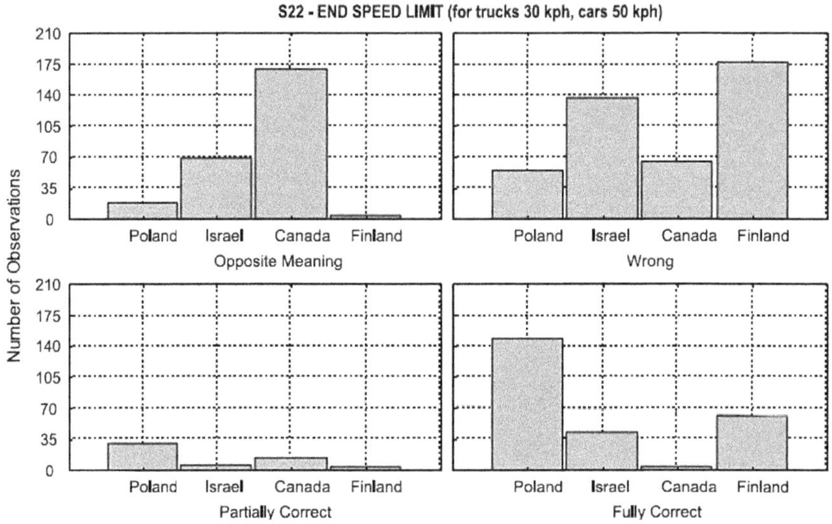

Figure 5-11. Levels of comprehension in different countries for sign number 22 (end of reduced differential speed limit for trucks and cars) (from Shinar *et al.*, 2003, with permission from Taylor & Francis Group, Ltd.).

leading drivers to make incorrect decisions. But signs that are interpreted as opposite of their intended meaning mislead the drivers who seem to respond to them as quickly as they do to signs that they identify correctly, indicating that in these infrequent cases the drivers are sure, but wrong. This finding of opposite than intended meanings is not unique. Kirmizioglu and Tuydes-Yaman (2012) conducted a similar study and obtained similar results with Turkish drivers. In fact, the common sign used in both studies (#7 – Priority for Oncoming Traffic) yielded an opposite than intended answer from nearly 50 percent of the Turkish respondents.

The results of the sign comprehension studies demonstrate a significant problem, but they do not identify the underlying source of the problem or its solution. To address both issues, we (Ben-Bassat and Shinar, 2006) hypothesized that signs that are not well comprehended are more likely to violate basic ergonomic principles of symbol design than signs that are well comprehended. To test this hypothesis, we examined the relationship between sign comprehension and its compliance with three ergonomic principles: familiarity, compliance with existing standards, and compatibility with the message it conveys. The same signs used in the previous studies (Figure 5-9) were presented to drivers who wrote their meaning and then rated their (1) degree of familiarity with each sign, (2) the extent to which it conforms to sign standards (e.g., a rectangular shape for warning signs, a red color for prohibition), and (3) the degree of compatibility with the message it conveys (e.g., an arrow turning to the right indicating a right turn, a silhouette of a man with a shovel indicating work zone). A group of ergonomics experts also rated the signs on the same three dimensions. The results supported the hypothesis and demonstrated the importance of these factors for sign comprehension. All three variables correlated with the likelihood of sign comprehension. The probability of comprehension had correlations of $r = 0.89$ with the ranking of familiarity, $r = 0.88$ with standardization, and $r = 0.76$ with compatibility. Despite the fact that the three dimensions also correlated well with each other, when considered simultaneously, in a linear regression analysis, they had a correlation of $r = 0.90$ with comprehension, thereby accounting for over 80 percent in sign comprehension variance. As an illustration, the relationship between familiarity and comprehension is provided in Figure 5-12, where each data point represents one of the 30 signs. As can be seen from this figure, the greater the average familiarity rating, the greater the percent of respondents that correctly identified the sign. In a similar study – but with mostly different signs – conducted on UK, German, and Polish drivers Jamson and Mrozek (2016) obtained similar results especially with respect to the criticality of standardization and physical and spatial compatibility. Unfortunately, though they acknowledged the importance of familiarity, they did not evaluate it.

The least understood signs – that were in fact misunderstood by all respondents – were signs #12 and #26 and the most understood signs – that were perfectly understood by all respondents – were signs #9 and #25 (see Figure 5-9 and Table 5-10). Even a casual look at these four signs would confirm this for most readers of this book. As noted above, there was quite a lot of overlap in the correlations of the three factors, suggesting that in the absence of one, the others may compensate. This is particularly important, because it implies that when familiarity cannot be relied upon (e.g., with a new sign), the designer should consider the compliance of a sign with existing standards and

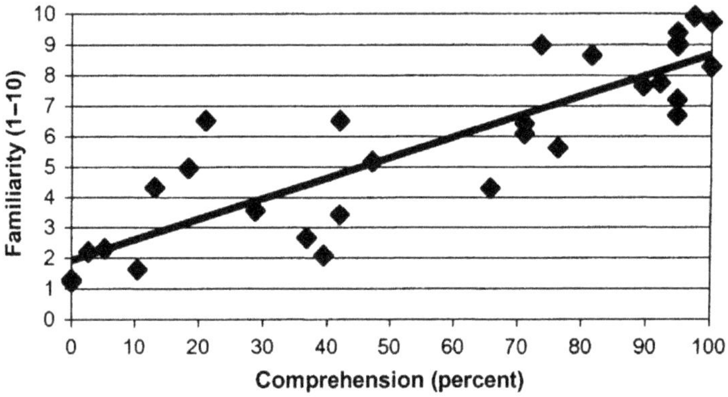

Figure 5-12. The relationship between the likelihood of comprehending a sign and its degree of familiarity (from Ben-Bassat and Shinar, 2006, with permission from the Human Factors and Ergonomics Society).

the compatibility of its content with the message it attempts to convey. A more recent study by Ou and Liu (2012) conducted on Vietnamese and Taiwanese 19-29 years old males and females also found that conceptual compatibility (which they termed "semantic closeness") and familiarity correlated highly with sign comprehension, though the correlations were different for the Taiwanese drivers (0.88 and 0.71, for compatibility and familiarity, respectively) and the Vietnamese drivers (0.80 and 0.42 for the compatibility and familiarity, respectively). In a study similar to ours (Ben-Bassat and Shinar, 2006), but on a smaller set of signs used in India, Mukhopadhyay *et al.* (2013) obtained significant correlations between comprehension and familiarity ($r = 0.55$), compatibility ($r = 0.80$), and standardization ($r = 0.72$). Ng and Chan (2008) in a similar study (but on different signs) in Hong Kong found that comprehension correlated strongly with familiarity (but not with "sign concreteness, simplicity, and meaningfulness"), Thus, despite cultural differences, and differences in the specific signs evaluated, the validity of these three ergonomic principles for predicting sign comprehension is quite high and quite useful for advance evaluations of sign design.

Given the above findings, when familiarity cannot be assumed but the drivers can read and understand the country's official language, it is probably better to have a text sign. Text signs are also more likely to be comprehended better by older drivers with mild cognitive impairments (Scialfa *et al.*, 2008). Although this seems to harken back to the days before standard symbols were developed, even now the U.S. Manual of Traffic Control Devices (MUTCD) recommends supplementing a symbolic sign with text when the symbol is new or unfamiliar (Federal Highway Administration, 2009). Examples that should therefore benefit from the use of text are signs #1, #4, #12, #20, and #22 in Figure 5-9.

To provide an empirical test of this hypothesis we (Shinar and Vogelzang, 2013) used the same set of signs in a study that compared symbol, text, and symbol + text signs.

Indeed we found that these signs scored low on both familiarity and on comprehension. In general the correlation between familiarity and comprehension in this study was r = 0.65, indicating again that comprehension of symbolic signs systematically increases with increasing familiarity. In the case of some signs this may be critical safety-wise; such as with railroad crossing signs (as in signs #1 and #4). As might be expected, misunderstandings disappear completely when text is used instead of or in addition to the symbol. In this case the correlation between familiarity and comprehension is essentially zero (r = 0.03 for text only and r = 0.14 for symbol + text), and the comprehension level is near-perfect. The data from sign #20 ("End of Priority Road") provide an interesting case of this conclusion. This sign complies with the convention and it is included in Israel's sign code book (i.e., standard). But it is essentially non-existent on Israeli roads as all intersections have signals, stop signs, or yield signs, making the use of this sign redundant. Thus, although it complies with the standard, because familiarity with the sign was extremely low it's comprehension level was very poor in all of our studies on Israeli drivers (Ben Bassat and Shinar, 2006; Shinar *et al.*, 2003; Shinar and Vogelzang, 2013), but not for the European Polish or Finnish drivers who are quite familiar with this sign (Shinar *et al.*, 2003)

As a final comment on this issue, one might suppose that sign comprehension in general and symbol-sign comprehension specifically would be better when the signs are presented in their natural context; that is, as part of the road scene. This, in fact, has been demonstrated on the comprehension of pictorial symbols selected from non-traffic domains such as workplace and public areas (Vukelich and Whitaker, 1993; Wolff and Wogalter, 1998). These findings cast a doubt on the ecological validity of the road signs studies reviewed above. To test the issue directly we (Ben-Bassat and Shinar, 2015) compared symbol-sign comprehension when the signs were presented alone and when they were presented in their natural environment. We found that the natural environment does not add to the comprehension, and if anything it slows down comprehension time, probably due to the added time needed to move the gaze and fixate the sign (that is rarely in the center of the driver's visual field). We account for this surprising finding by noting that unlike the case for drivers' comprehension of road signs, other signs evaluated on the general public are not systematically learned, the public is never tested on them, and many of the signs may be totally unfamiliar to the general population. Thus, in the case of road signs where the level of familiarity for most signs is very high and sign conventions are common around much of the world, the context has no added benefits.

Road markings

Road markings, like signs, should conform to the same ergonomic principles if they are to be easily understood. But symbolic or text messages painted on the road should also be adjusted to be viewed from the driver's perspective. This is illustrated in Figure 5-13, where the letter "C" that is painted on the road is distorted (left panel) so that it appears proportional to the approaching driver (right panel). The same rule is applied with messages such as "SLOW" or "STOP" are painted on the road pavement to supplement the message in a less conspicuous standard sign.

Figure 5-13. The letter C indicating Central London is painted on the road surface in a distorted shape (as can be seen from the curb), so that it will appear undistorted from the perspective of the approaching driver (photos by author).

Finally, a note of caution

Many of the differences in signing practices among countries are more subtle, but critical to safety. For example, in the U.S. the absence of a Stop or Yield sign implies the driver has right-of-way (because crossing traffic is assumed to have one of these signs), whereas in Europe, the absence of a sign implies that cross traffic coming from the right has the right-of-way (unless the driver's road is signed as a primary road – sign #26 in Figure 5-9, but without the central black diagonal line), and therefore drivers should yield to it even in the absence of a sign (Summala, 1998). Another difference is in the use of alternative signs to convey the same meaning. For example, speed limit signs have a specific posted speed on them that is understood in the same manner by all drivers. On the other hand, the sign indicating 'built-up area' (the same as sign 23 in Figure 5-9 but without the diagonal line) indicates that the driver is entering an urban area with a speed limit that is typically 50 km/hr. Because the speed limit is not explicitly displayed, this sign induces negligible speed reductions compared the standard speed limit sign. This is not because the drivers do not know the speed limit implication of the "built up area" sign, as speed reductions are the same for both signs when a police car is present close by (Lajunen, Hakkarainen, and Summala, 1996).

In-vehicle symbol comprehension

Rapid comprehension of symbols within the vehicle can be even more critical than comprehension of road signs because extracting that information also involves moving the eyes away from the road. Thus, slow comprehension of and long fixations on in-vehicle symbols can contribute to driver distraction (see Chapter 13). To minimize that possibility it is important to design symbols that meet the ergonomic principles stated above, and then assess not only the comprehension of the symbols but also the time needed to respond to them.

An early extensive study that evaluated various designs for common in-vehicle displays was conducted by Heard (1974) on 2,593 drivers in four different countries, and his symbols and results are presented in Figure 5-14. Although this study is more than 40 years old, and it evaluated only 15 functions its findings are instructive and relevant to the multiple functions that did not even exist at the time of the Heard study. For this reason, it is worthwhile to consider its main findings and conclusions. In this study three alternative designs for each symbol were presented to drivers and in each case the drivers had to identify the meaning of the symbol. The percentage of correct responses for each symbol varied greatly – from the near-perfect identification of Version B of the open trunk

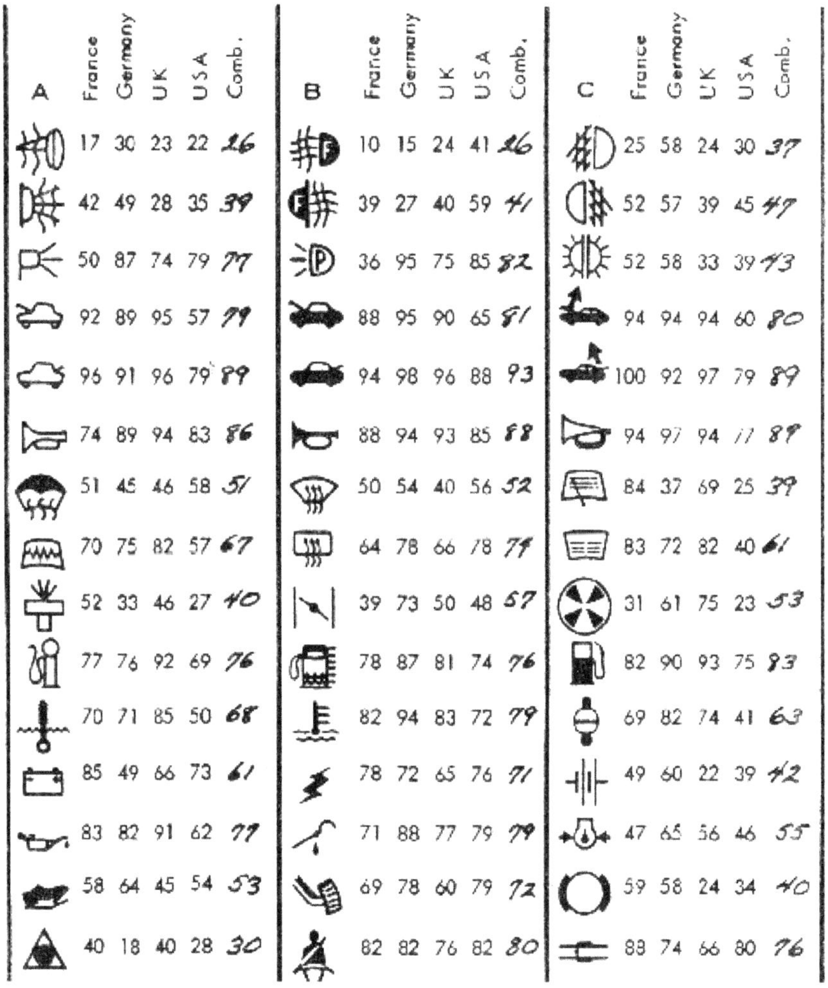

Figure 5-14. Percent correct identifications of alternative designs of different in-vehicle symbols by drivers in France, Germany, the United Kingdom, and the U.S. (from Heard, 1974, reprinted with permission from SAE International).

lid indicator to the dismally poor recognition of Version A of the seatbelt icon. A complicating factor in these results – similar to the one observed in the international sign recognition study by Shinar *et al.* (2003) – was the large differences between respondents in different countries. Thus, Version C of the front defogger (with the image of a windshield filled with horizontal lines) was the most recognized version for the French drivers, but the least recognized version for the American drivers. Recall that this study was conducted in the early 1970s. At that time there was very little standardization in icon design and the automotive industry was not as multi-national as it is today. There were significantly fewer imported cars in both Europe and the U.S. Consequently, the French were almost exclusively familiar with French cars and the American drivers were almost exclusively familiar with American cars. Even today when the choice of vehicles is nearly the same on all continents, and many drivers have experience in driving in different countries, we still find differences in preference and comprehension between drivers from different countries (Young *et al.*, 2012).

Good design not only increases comprehension, but also reduces the time it takes to comprehend the meaning of the sign. In Heard's study the correlation between the percentage of drivers who correctly identified the symbol and the time it took to identify it was quite high with $r = 0.78$. McCormack (1974) replicated Heard's study with Canadian drivers, and got results that were quite similar to those obtained by Heard for the American drivers.

As new functions are introduced to cars, new symbols have to be designed. The flashing red triangle, indicating a disabled or slow-moving vehicle, did not exist 40 years ago, and consequently an evaluation of its meaning yielded very low comprehension levels of less than 10 percent in 1970 (Jack, Hurd, and Pew, 1970 in Green, 1993). Today, with the same symbol used in just about all cars in all countries, it is likely to yield close to 100 percent correct identification everywhere. Thus, totally unfamiliar icons with little or no compatibility with the concept they represent, can become easily comprehended over time even if they violate the principle of compatibility, as long as they are standardized and become familiar through common use and repeated encounters (Ben-Bassat and Shinar, 2006).

The challenge to symbol comprehension remains as new vehicles introduce new safety features with new displays. The advent of cheap and sensitive computing and sensing devices has brought a whole slew of new features into new car models. Because the motoring public has also become more safety conscious, many of these devices are safety-related warning systems. However, to be effectively used drivers must know if these systems are operative or not. Such systems include airbags, safety belts, adaptive cruise controls, electronic stability control, lane deviation warnings, fatigue alerts, and collision warnings when the vehicle approaches an obstacle in any direction. Obviously, these warnings must somehow be displayed. But how? For simplification, let us focus on visual displays (though various auditory alarms are also used). Chi and Dewi (2014) asked experienced drivers and non-drivers to match 82 currently used displays on schematic drawings of a car's dashboard, center-stack, and steering wheel with their functions. Not surprisingly they found that word displays were generally better understood (i.e., better matched with their functions) than iconic displays where the icon was either image-related or concept-related. Surprisingly, comprehension was not significantly poorer for the non-drivers than for the experienced drivers, though for all types of displays the average comprehension levels were lower for the non-drivers. They therefore suggested that displays consisting of simple English words would be preferable to images, whenever comprehension of English can be assumed (an assumption that seems to be more appropriate with every passing decade).

The situation is different with new functions for which there is no standard icon. Figure 5-15 illustrates four different options for icons designed to represent forward collision avoidance warning systems. To assess these alternative symbols, Campbell *et al.* (2004) asked 77 American drivers to simply indicate what they think the symbol means. The percentages of drivers who interpreted the symbol perfectly (1) or at least adequately (2) are presented to the right of the symbols. It is easy to see that the least comprehended symbol was the first one, the one being proposed by the International Standards Organization. The best understood symbol was the third one that includes the icons of two cars facing each other. It is important to remember that at the time these symbols were evaluated, neither the symbols nor the systems behind them were standard. However, the one with the image of the two cars is apparently the most compatible with the concept, and would therefore be easier to understand if adopted by the auto industry, as it did with the flashing red triangle. The study also evaluated 6 side collision warnings and 7 lane departure collision warnings. When the same symbols were evaluated in Germany, Japan, and Sweden, using the same methodology, then unlike Green's findings obtained almost 40 years earlier, this time the results were similar and comparable to the results obtained in the U.S. This is most likely a reflection of the fact that we have in fact become one large global village.

Icon*		1	2
1_1		8%	15%
2_1		8%	26%
3_2		13%	32%
4_2		3%	8%

Figure 5-15. The percentages of drivers who understood either perfectly (1), or adequately (2), the meaning of each of four alternative forward collision avoidance warning systems (from Campbell *et al.*, 2004, reprinted with permission from SAE International).

In addition to new systems that need some representation on the dashboard, older systems have also gotten a face lift. Heating and cooling systems have morphed into climate control systems, radio and tape systems have evolved into complex sound systems that are linked to the radio, the compact disc player, the navigation system, and the telephone. And each of these subsystems now requires several controls and displays. As a consequence today's car panels look more and more like those of the cockpits of commercial air planes with hard and "soft" controls and displays. In addition, the plethora of cell phone applications that are designed to use while driving (such as navigation systems) bring additional control and display panels. But because these devices are small they create more difficulties for the driver (Quaresma and Gonçalves, 2014). The challenge now becomes one of how to effectively design these control and display interfaces in a manner that would minimize their distraction away from events occurring on the road. The optimal solution appears to be in a combination of standard, compatible, and familiar icons, commonly used text abbreviations (e.g., CD for compact disc player, A/C for air conditioning, vol for sound volume), and numbers (e.g., to indicate radio channels, volume levels, temperature) (Young *et al.*, 2012). Finally, when there are several alternative designs that seem to conform to the above ergonomic principles of design a controlled simulation study may have to be conducted (c.f. Rakauskas *et al.*, 2010 for alternative fuel economy displays).

Concluding Comments

When cars were slow and their operation was mostly manual, driving may have been a moderately easy manual task. In today's cars and on today's highways, driving is mostly an information processing task. Human information processing is the black box that mediates between the observable stimuli we absorb as we drive and the observable responses we make to stay safely on the road. The purpose of this chapter was to illustrate the role of the component mechanisms involved in the information processing chain, how they interact, and how they affect our behavior. Models of human information processing have greatly facilitated both our understanding of the process and its implications for safe highway and vehicle design. By designing roadway features and vehicle displays in such a way that they can rapidly satisfy the driver's information needs, we can provide drivers with better and timelier information.

As technology relieves us of more and more tasks, it is important to note that even when the driver is not controlling a certain function (such as speed while driving with a cruise control), he or she still retain the role of monitoring the vehicle's behavior and its environment. This changing role also implies a change in the functions the driver performs, and the need to understand how they are affected by basic information processing capabilities and limitations. In fact relieving the driver of continuous monitoring implies that in a case of emergency we must recruit our processing capacities to comprehend the situation and respond to it even faster than before. Understanding how human information processing works enables us to derive rules for improving everything from reaction time to hazards to quick comprehension of external and in-vehicle messages delivered via various icons.

Finally this chapter provided multiple examples to illustrate our flexibility in processing information, and how the processing changes in response to various external contingencies (such as different signals to which the driver must respond) as well as internal ones (such as the level of experience we bring to the driving task, and the level of expectancy we have for various events). Furthermore, these external and internal factors not only affect the speed of the different functions in the information processing sequence, but they can actually change the functions themselves, as we progress from controlled behavior to automated behavior.

Given all we know about driver information processing, we must realize that the simple act of driving is actually very complex.

References

AAA (1952). Age and complex reaction time. Report No. 41. Traffic Engineering and Safety Department, American Automobile Association, Washington, DC.

AAA (1966). Reaction time as related to age. Report No. 69. Traffic Engineering and Safety Departmetn, American Automobile Association, Washington, DC.

AASHTO (1994). A policy on geometric design of highway and streets (metric units edition). American Association of State Highway and Transportation Officials, Washington, DC.

AASHTO (2001). A policy on geometric design for streets and highways. American Association of State Highway and Transportation Officials, Washington, DC.

Al-Madani, H. and Al-Janahi, A. R. (2002). Assessment of drivers' comprehension of traffic signs based on their traffic, personal and social characteristics. *Transport. Res. F*, *5*(1), 63-76.

Allen, M. J. (1995). Yellow signal light timing and the dilemma zone. *J. Am. Optom. Assn.*, *66*(2):77-78.

Anderson, J. R. (1995). *Learning and Memory: An Integrated Approach*. Wiley, New York, NY.

Aust, M. L., J. Engström and M. Viström (2013). Effects of forward collision warning and repeated event exposure on emergency braking. *Transport. Res. F*, *18*, 34-46.

Backs, R. W., J. K. Lenneman, J. A. Wetzel and P. Green (2003). Cardiac measures of driver workload during simulated driving with and without visual occlusion. *Hum. Fact.*, *45*(4), 525-538.

Baddeley, A. D. (1990). *Human Memory: Theory and Practice*. Erlbaum, London.

Baddeley, A. D., G. Hitch and G. H. Bower (1974). *The Psychology of Learning and Motivation*. Academic Press, New York, NY.

Bao, S., D. J. LeBlanc, J. R. Sayer and C. Flannagan (2012). Heavy-truck drivers' following behavior with intervention of an integrated in-vehicle crash warning system: A field evaluation. Hum. Fact., *54*, 687-697.

Bar-Gera, H. and D. Shinar (2005). The tendency of drivers to pass other vehicles. Transport. Res. F., *8*, 429-439.

Barry, D. (1994). *The World According to Dave Barry*, p. 75. Wings Books, San Antonio, TX.

BBC (2001). Road signs baffle British Drivers. *BBC News*, April 20.

Bellinger, D. B., B. M. Budde, M. Mahida, G. B. Richardson and W. P. Berg (2009). Effect of cellular telephone conversation and music volume on braking response time. *Transport. Res. F*, *6*, 441-451.

Berg, W. P. and D. J. Dessecker (2013). Evidence of unconscious motor adaptation to cognitive and auditory distraction. *Adap. Behav.*, *21*, 346-355.

Ben-Bassat, T. and D. Shinar (2006). Ergonomic guidelines for traffic signs design increase signs comprehension. *Hum. Fact.*, *48*(1), 182-195.

Ben-Bassat, T. and D. Shinar (2015). The effect of context and drivers' age on highway traffic signs comprehension, in press. *Transport. Res. F*, *33*, 117-127.

Ben-Yaacov, A., M. Maltz and D. Shinar (2002). Effects of an in-Vehicle collision avoidance warning system on short and long-term driving performance. *Hum. Fact.*, *44*, 335-342.

Birrell, S. A., M. Fowkes and P. A. Jennings (2014). Effect of using an in-vehicle smart driving aid on real-world driver performance. *IEEE Transact. Intell. Transport. Syst.*, *15*(4), 1801-1810.

Blum, Y. and D. Shinar (2005). Travel speeds and headways in an urban freeway. Traffic Transport., (Tnua VeTachbura), July 2-8. (Hebrew).

Borowsky, A. and T. Oron-Gilad (2013). Exploring the effects of driving experience on hazard awareness and risk perception via real-time hazard identification, hazard classification, and rating tasks. *Accid. Anal. Prev.*, *50*, 548-565.

Borowsky, A., T. Oron-Gilad, A. Meir and Y. Parmet (2012). Drivers' perception of vulnerable road users: A hazard perception approach. *Accid. Anal. Prev.*, *44*, 160-166.

Borowsky, A., D. Shinar and T. Oron-Gilad (2010). Age, skill, and hazard perception in driving. *Accid. Anal. Prev.*, *42*, 1240-1249.

Bowman, B. L. (1993). Supplemental advance warning devices (No. Project 20-5 FY 1989). In NCHRP Synthesis of Highway Practice, Issue No. 186. Transportation Research Board, Washington, D.C.

Brackstone, M., B. Waterson and M. McDonald (2009). Determinants of following headway in congested traffic. *Transport. Res. F*, *12*, 131-142.

Broughton, K. L. M., F. Switzer and D. Scott (2007). Car following decisions under three visibility conditions and two speeds tested with a driving simulator. *Accid. Anal. Prev.*, *39*, 106-116.

Campbell, J. L., D. H. Hoffmeister, R. J. Kiefer, D. J. Selke, P. Green and J. B. Richman (2004). Comprehension testing of active safety symbols. SAE Paper No. 2004-01-0450. Society of Automotive Engineers, Detroit, MI.

Campbell, J. L., B. J. Richman, C. Carney and J. D. Lee (2004). In-vehicle display icons and other information elements, Volume 1: Guidelines. Report No. FHWA-RD-03-065. U.S. Department of Transportation, Washington, DC.

Charlton, S. G. (2009). Driving while conversing: Cell phones that distract and passengers who react. *Accid. Anal. Prev.*, *41*, 160-173.

Charlton, S. G. and N. J. Starkey (2011). Driving without awareness: The effects of practice and automaticity on attention and driving. *Transport. Res. F, 14*, 456-471.

Charlton, S. G. and N. J. Starkey (2013). Driving on familiar roads: Automaticity and inattention blindness. *Transport. Res. F, 19*, 121-133.

Chen, S. K. (1996). Estimation of car-following safety: Application to the design of intelligent cruise control. Ph.D. Dissertation. Massachusetts Institute of Technology, Cambridge, MA.

Chi, C. F. and R. S. Dewi (2014). Matching performance of vehicle icons in graphical and textual formats. *Appl. Ergon., 45*(4), 904-916.

Chi, C. F., R. S. Dewi and S.-C. Chen (2012). Ergonomic evaluation of icons for dashboard. In *Ergonomics in Asia* (Shih and Liang eds.), pp. 149-154. CRC Press, Taylor & Francis, London.

Costa, M., A. Simone, V. Vignali, C. Lantieri, A. Bucchi and G. Dondi (2014). Looking behavior for vertical road signs. *Transport. Res. F, 23*,147-155.

Crundall, D. (2016). Hazard prediction discriminates between novice and experienced drivers. *Accid. Anal. Prev., 86*, 47-58.

Crundall, D., B. Andrews, E. van Loon and P. Chapman (2010). Commentary training improves responsiveness to hazards in a driving simulator. *Accid. Anal. Prev., 42*, 2117-2124.

Crundall, D., P. Chapman, S. Trawley, L. Collins, E. van Loon, B. Andrews and G. Underwood (2012). Some hazards are more attractive than others: Drivers of varying experience respond differently to different types of hazard. *Accid. Anal. Prev., 45*, 600-609.

Davoodi, S. R., H. Hamid, M. Pazhouhanfar and J. W. Muttart (2012). Motorcyclist perception response time in stopping sight distance situations. Safety Sci., *50*, 371-377.

Dewar, R. E., J. G. Ells, and P. J. Cooper (1977). Evaluation of roadway guide signs at a large airport. *Transport Engineer, 47*(6), 19-23.

Dewar, R., D. Kline, F. Scheiber, and A. Swanson (1997). Symbol signing design for older drivers. Report No. FHWA-RD-94-069. U.S. Department of Transportation, Washington, DC.

Dickerson, A. E., T. Reistetter, M. Parnell, S. Robinson, K. Stone and K. Whitley (2008). Standardizing the RT-2S brake reaction time tester. *Phys. Occup. Ther. Geriatr., 27*, 96-106.

DfT (1995). The effects of hazard perception training. United Kingdom Department for Transport, London.

Diew, D. Y. and G. P. Kai (2001). Perception-braking response time of unalerted drivers at signalized intersections. *ITE J. Web, 19*, 73-76.

Dommes, A., V. Cavallo, J.-P. Dubuisson, I. Tournier and F. Vienne (2014). Crossing a two-way street: Comparison of young and old pedestrians. *J. Safety. Res., 50*, 27-34.

Duan, J., L. Zhizhong and G. Salvendy (2013). Risk illusions in car following: Is a smaller headway always perceived as more dangerous? Safety Sci., *53*, 25-33.

Dudek, C., R. Huchingson, N. Trout, and D. Chester (1996). International tourist guidance needs and understanding of selected guide signs in Florida. *Trans. Res. Rec.*, (1550), 37-47.

Ervin, R., J. Sayer, D. LeBlanc, S. Bogard, M. L. Mefford, M. Hagan, Z. Bareket and C. Winkler (2005). Automotive collision avoidance system field operational test: Methodology and results (Report No. DOT HS 809 900). National Highway Traffic Safety Administration, Washington, DC.

Evans, L. (2004). *Traffic Safety*. Science Serving Society, Bloomfield Hills, MI.

Evans, L. and P. Wasielewski (1983). Risky driving related to driver and vehicle characteristics. *Accid. Anal. Prev.*, *15*, 121-136.

Federal Highway Administration (2009). Manual on uniform traffic control devices. U.S. Department of Transportation, Washington, DC. http://mutcd.fhwa.dot.gov/pdfs/2009/pdf_index.htm

Fitts, P. M. (1954). The information capacity of the human motor system in controlling the amplitude of movement. *J. Exp. Psychol.*, *47*, 381-391.

Fitts, P. M. and M. I. Posner (1967). *Human Performance*. Brooks/Cole, Belmont, CA.

Gatsou, C., A. Politis and D. Zevgolis (2012). The importance of mobile interface icons on user interaction. *Int. J. Compt. Sci. Appl.*, *9*, 92-107.

Ghazizadeh, M., J. D. Lee, Y. Peng and L. N. Boyle (2013). Assessing text reading and text entry while driving using the visual occlusion technique. Proccedings of the Seventh International Driving Symposium on Human Factors in Driver Assessment, Training, and Vehicle Design, pp. 128-134.

Green, P. (1993). Symbols for controls and displays. In: *Automotive Ergonomics* (B. Peacock and W. Karwowski eds.), pp. 237-268. Taylor and Francis, London.

Green, M. (2000). "How long does it take to stop?" Methodological analysis of driver perception-brake times. *Transport. Hum. Fact.*, *2*(3), 195-216.

Groeger, J. A. and B. A. Clegg (1997). Automaticity and driving: Time to change gear conceptually. In: *Traffic and Transport Psychology: Theory and Application* (J. A. Rothengatter and E. Carbonell Vaya eds.), pp. 137-146. Elsevier, Amsterdam.

Heard, E. A. (1974). Symbol study – 1972. SAE paper No. 740304. Society of Automotive Engineers, Warrendale, PA. as cited by Green (1993).

Helander, M. (1976). Vehicle control and driving experience: A psychophysiological approach. Proceedings of the Humand Factors and Ergonomics Society Annual Meeting, **20**, 335-339. College Park, MD.

Hoffmann, E. R. (1991). Accelerator-to-brake movement times. *Ergonomics*, *34*(3), 277-287.

Hollis, A. M., A. K. W. Lee, L. R. Kapust, L. K. Phillips, J. Wolkin and M. G. O'Connor (2013). The driving competence of 90-year-old drivers: From a hospital-based driving clinic. *Traffic. Inj. Prev.*, *14*, 782-790.

Horswill, M. S., A. Hill and M. Wetton (2015). Can a video-based hazard perception test used for driver licensing predict crash involvement? *Accid. Anal. Prev.*, *82*, 213-219.

Horswill, M. S., K. Taylor, S. Newnam, M. Wetton and A. Hill (2013). Even highly experienced drivers benefit from a brief hazard perception training intervention. *Accid. Anal. Prv.*, *52*, 100-110.

Hosking, S. G., C. C. Liu and M. Bayly (2010). The visual search patterns and hazard responses of experienced and inexperienced motorcycle riders. *Accid. Anal. Prev.*, *42*, 196-202.

ISO (2002). Graphical symbols – Safety colours and safety signs, in Part 1: Design principles for safety signs in workplaces and public areas (ISO 3846). Switzerland.

Jamson, S. and M. Mrozek (2016). Is three the magic number? The role of ergonomic principles in cross country comprehension of road traffic signs. *Ergonomics*, *8*, 1-30.

Johansson, G. and F. Backlund (1970). Drivers and road signs. *Ergonomics*, *13*, 749-759.

Johansson, G. and K. Rumar (1966). Drivers and road signs: A preliminary investigation of the capacity of car drivers to get information from road signs. *Ergonomics*, *9*, 57-62.

Johansson, G. and K. Rumar (1971). Drivers brake reaction times. *Hum. Fact.*, *13*, 23-27.

Kahneman, D. (1973). *Attention and Effort*. Prentice Hall, Englewood Cliffs, NJ.

Kirmizioglu, K. and H. Tuydes-Yaman (2012). Comprehensibility of traffic signs among urban drivers in Turkey. *Accid. Anal. Prev.*, *45*, 131-141.

Lacherez, P., S. Au and J. M. Wood (2014). Visual motion perception predicts driving hazard perception ability. *Acta. Ophthalmol. (Copenh)*, *92*, 88-93.

Lajunen, T., P. Hakkarainen and H. Summala (1996). The ergonomics of road signs: Explicit and embedded speed limits. *Ergonomics*, *39*, 1069-1083.

Lee, D. N. (1976). A theory of visual control of braking based on information about time-to-collision. *Perception*, *5*, 437-459.

Leibowitz, H. W., D. A. Owens and R. A. Tyrrell (1998). The assured clear distance ahead rule: Implications for nighttime traffic. *Accid. Anal. Prev.*, *30*, 93-99.

Leung, S. and G. Starmer (2005). Gap acceptance and risk taking by young and mature drivers, both sober and alcohol-intoxicated, in a simulated driving task. *Accid. Anal. Prev.*, *37*, 1056-1065.

Li, Z., J. Zhang, J. Rong, J. Ma and Z. Guo (2014). Measurement and comparative analysis of driver's perception–reaction time to green phase at the intersections with and without a countdown timer. *Transport. Res. F*, *22*, 50-62.

Liu, Y., G. L. Chang and J. Yu (2011). Empirical study of driver responses during the yellow signal phase at six maryland intersections. *J. Transport. Eng.*, *138*(1), 31-42.

Luoma, J. (1988). Drivers' eye fixations and perceptions. In: Vision in Vehicles: *II* (A. G. Gale ed.). Elsevier, Oxford.

Luoma, J. (1991a). Perception of highway traffic signs: Interaction of eye fixations, recalls and reactions. In: Vision in Vehicles: *III* (A. G. Gale ed.). Elsevier, Oxford.

Luoma, J. (1991b). Evaluation of validity of two research methods for studying perception of road signs. University of Michigan Transportation research Center Report No. UMTRI-9 1-15. University of Michigan, Ann Arbor, MI.

Luoma, J. (1993). Effects of delay on recall of road signs: An evaluation of the validity of recall method. In: *Vision in Vehicles: IV* (A. G. Gale ed.). Elsevier, Oxford.

Makinde, O. O. and V. Oluwasegunfunmi (2014). Comprehension of traffic control devices amongst urban drivers-a study of Ado-Ekiti, Ekiti State, Nigeria. *European J. Eng. Technol.*, *2*(1), 9-19.

Martens, M. H. (2000). Assessing road sign perception: A methodological review. *Transport. Hum. Fact.*, *2*(4), 347-357.

Maryland Department of Transportation (1998). *Maryland Driver's Handbook*. Maryland Department of Transportation, Glen Burnie, MD.
Matson, T. M., W. S. Smith and F. W. Hurd (1955). *Traffic Engineering*. McGraw-Hill, New York, NY.
McCormack, P. D. (1974). Identification of symbols and its influence on training for motor vehicle controls. SAE Paper No. 740995. Society of Automotive Engineers, Warrendale, PA, as cited by Green (1993).
McGee, H. W., K. G. Hooper, W. E. Hughes and W. Benson (1983). Highway design and operations standards affected by driver characterstics. Volume II of Federal Highway Administration Report FHWA-RD-83-015. U.S. Department of Transportation, Washington, DC.
McKenna, F. P. and J. L. Crick (1994). Hazard perception in drivers: A methodology for testing and training. Department of Transport, TRL CR313, Transport and Road Research Laboratory. Crowthorne, Berkshire, CA, as cited in DfT (1995).
Merrikhpour, M., B. Donmez and V. Battista (2014). A field operational trial evaluating a feedback–reward system on speeding and tailgating behaviors. Transport. Res. F., *27*, 56-68.
Michon, J. A. (1985). A critical review of driver behavior models: What do we know, what should we do? In: *Human Behavior and Traffic Safety* (L. Evans and R. Schwing eds.), pp. 485-520. Plenum Press, New York, NY.
Milosevic, S. and R. Gajic (1986). Presentation factors and driver characteristics affecting road-sign registration. *Ergonomics*, *29*(6), 807-815.
MMVA (2015). *Maryland Driver's Manual*. Maryland Motor Vehicle Administration. http://www.mva.maryland.gov/_resources/docs/DL-002.pdf
Morrison, R. W., J. G. Swope and C. G. Halcomb (1986). Movement time and brake pedal placement. *Hum. Fact.*, *28*, 241-246.
Mukhopadhyay, P., J. Kaur, L. Kaur, A. Arvind, M. Kajabaje, J. Mann, ... S. Chakravarty (2013). Ergonomic design analysis of some road signs in India. *Info. Design J.*, *20*(3), 220-227.
MUTCD (2003). *Manual on Uniform Traffic Control Devices*. Edition 2003 (including Revision 1 dated November 2004). U.S. Department of Transportation, Washington, DC. http://mutcd.fhwa.dot.gov/pdfs/2003r1/pdf-index.htm
National Safety Council (1992). *Defensive Driving* Course [Course guide]. Author, Itasca, IL.
Ng, A. W. Y. and A. H. S. Chan (2008). The effects of driver factors and sign design features on the comprehensibility of traffic signs. *J. Safety Res.*, *39*, 321-328.
NHTSA (2012). Traffic safety facts 2011. Report No. DOT-HS-811-754. U.S. Department of Transportation, Washington, DC.
Ohta, H. (1994). Distance Headway behavior between vehicles from the viewpoint of proxemics. *IATSS Res.*, *18*, 6-14.
Olson, P. L. and M. Sivak (1986). Perception-response time to unexpected roadway hazards. *Hum. Fact.*, *28*, 91-96.
Ou, Y.-K. And Y.-C. Liu (2012). Effects of sign design features and training on comprehension of traffic signs in Taiwanese and Vietnamese user groups. *Int. J. Ind. Ergonom.*, *42*, 1-7.

Patten, C. J. D., A. Kircher, J. Ostlund, L. Nilsson and O. Svenson (2006). Driver experience and cognitive workload in different traffic environments. *Accid. Anal. Prev.*, *38*(5), 887-894.

Perez, M., M. Hulse and L. Angell (2013). Support for NHTSA visual-manual guidelines: Expert review of the visual occlusion method and how it compares to driver eye-glance behavior. NHTSA Report No. DOT HS 811 763. U.S. Department of Transportation, Washington, DC.

Pollatsek, P., V. Narayanaan, A. Pradhan and D. L. Fisher (2006). Using eye movements to evaluate a PC-based risk awareness and perception training program on a drivng simulator. *Hum. Fact.*, *48*, 447-464.

Price, J. M. and S. I. Glynn (2000). The relationship between crash rates and drivers's hazard assessments using the Connecticut photolog. Proceedings of the IEA2000/HFES 2000 Congress, pp. 26-266.

Pronin, M. (2014). Analysis of the convention on road signs and signals of 1968 and the European agreement supplementing the convention, Parts I and II. Prepared for the UNECE Secretariat (August).

Quaresma, M. and R. Gonçalves (2014). Usability analysis of smartphone applications for drivers. In: *Design, User Experience, and Usability. Theories, Methods, and Tools for Designing the User Experience* (pp. 352-362). Springer International Publishing, Berkeley, CA.

Rakauskas, M. E., J. S. Graving, M. P. Manser and J. W. Jenness (2010). Determining the accuracy and acceptance of using driver interface display components and fuel economy information types. Proceedings of the Human Factors and Ergonomics Society 54th Annual Meeting.

Ranney, T. A., G. H. S. Baldwin, L. A. Smith, J. Martin and E. N. Mazzae (2013). Driver behavior driving during visual-manual secondary task performance: Occlusion method versus simulated driving. U.S. NHTSA Report DOT HS 811. National Highway Traffic Safety Administration, Washington, DC.

Risto, M. and M. H. Martens (2013). Time and space: The difference between following time headway and distance headway instructions. *Transport. Res. F*, *17*, 45-51.

Ruscio, D., M. R. Ciceri and F. Biassoni (2015). How does a collision warning system shape driver's brake response time? The influence of expectancy and automation complacency on real-life emergency braking. Accid. Anal. Prev., *77*, 72-81.

Samuel, S., T. Zafian, A. Borowsky, M. R. E. Romoser and D. L. Fisher (2013). Can young drivers learn to anticipate hidden hazards: A driving simulator study. Proceedings of the Seventh International Driving Symposium on Human Factors in Driver Assessment, Training, and Vehicle Design, pp. 355-361. Bolton Landing, NY.

Sayer, J. R., M. L. Mefford, P. S. Fancher and R. E. Ervin (1997). An experimental design for studying how driver characteristics influence headway control. IEEE Conference on Intelligent Transportation Systems.

Schneider, W. and R. M. Shiffrin (1977). Controlled and automatic human information processing: I. Detection, search and attention. *Psychol. Rev.*, *84*(1), 1-66.

Scialfa, C. T., D. Borkenhagen, J. Lyon and M. Deschênes (2013). A comparison of static and dynamic hazard perception tests. Accid. Anal. Prev., *45*, 600-609.

Scialfa, C., P. Spadafora, M. Klein, A. Lesnik, L. Dial and A. Heinrich (2008). Iconic sign comprehension in older adults: The role of cognitive impairment and text enhancement. *Can. J. Aging*, *27*(3), 253-265.

Selander, H., I. Bolin and T. Falkmer (2011). Does automatic transmission improve driving behavior in older drivers? *Gerontology*, *58*(2), 181-187.

Senders, J. W., A. B. Kristofferson, and W. Levison (1966). *An investigation of automobile driver information processing*. Cambridge, MA: Bolt, Beranek and Newman.

Shinar, D. (1978). *Psychology on the Road: The Human Factor in Traffic Safety*. Wiley and Sons, New York, NY.

Shinar, D., R. E. Dewar, H. Summala and L. Zakowska (2003). Traffic sign symbol comprehension: A cross-cultural study. *Ergonomics*, *46*(15), 1549-1565.

Shinar, D. and A. Drory (1983). Sign registration in daytime and nighttime driving. *Hum. Fact.*, *25*, 117-122.

Shinar, D., M. Meir and I. Ben-Shoham (1998). How automatic is manual gear shifting? *Hum. Fact.*, *40*, 647-654.

Shinar, D. and E. Schechtman (2002). Headway feedback improves inter-vehicular distance: A field study. *Hum. Fact.*, *44*(3), 474-481.

Shinar, D. and M. Shaham (2003). Benefits of a moving point-of-light (POL) as a means to maintaining safe headways in tunnels. Proceedings of the 3rd Driving Simulation Conference – North America, October 10, Dearborn, MI.

Shinar, D. and M. Vogelzang (2013). Comprehension of traffic signs with symbolic versus text displays. Transport. Res. F., *18*, 72-82.

Simons, D. J. and R. A. Rensink (2005). Change blindness: Past, present, and future. *Trends. Cogn. Sci.*, *9*, 16-20.

Strayer, D. L. and F. A. Drews (2006). Multi-tasking in the Automobile. In: *Attention: From Theory to Practice* (A. Kramer, D. Wiegmann and A. Kirlik eds.). Oxford University Press, Oxford, England.

Summala, H. (1998). American drivers in Europe: Different signing policy may cause safety problems at uncontrolled intersections. *Accid. Anal. Prev.*, *30*(2), 285-289

Summala, H. and I. Koivisto (1990). Unalerted drivers' brake reaction times: Older drivers compensate their slower reaction times by driving more slowly. In: *Driving Behaviour in a Social Context* (T. Benjamin ed.), pp. 680-683. Paradigme, Caen, France.

Summala, H., D. Lamble and M. Laakso (1998). Driving experience and perception of the lead car's braking when looking at in-car targets. *Accid. Anal. Prev.*, *30*(4), 401-407.

Summala, H. and R. Näätänen (1974). Perception of highway traffic signs and motivation. *J. Safety Res.*, *6*, 150-153.

Syvanen, M. (1968). Effect of police supervision on the perception of traffic signs and driving habits. Report from Talja, No. 6, Helsinki, Finland. As reported by Martens (2000).

Taieb-Maimon, M. (2007). Learning headway estimation in driving. *Hum. Fact.*, *49*, 734-744.

Taieb-Maimon, M. and D. Shinar (2001). Minimum and comfortable driving headways: Reality versus perception. *Hum. Fact.*, *43*(1), 159-172.

Taylor, T., K. Masserang, A. Pradhan, G. Divekar, S. Samuel, J. Muttart, A. Pollatsek and D. Fisher (2011). Long-term effects of hazard anticipation trainng on noive drivers measured on the open road. Proceedings of the Sixth International Driving Symposium on Human Factors in Driver Assessment, Training and Vehicle Design. Olympic Valley, Lake Tahoe, CA.

Triggs, T. J. and W. G. Harris (1982). Reaction time of drivers to road stimuli. Department of Psychology Human Factors Report No. HFR-12. Monash University, Clayton, Australia.

UNECE (2010). Consolidated Resolution on Road Signs and Signals (R.E.2). United Nations Economic Commission for Europe, Inland Transport Committee. Geneva. http://www.unece.org/index.php?id=17582&L=0

Van Winsum, W. and W. Brouwer (1997). Time headway in car-following and operational performance during unexpected braking. *Percept. Mot. Skills*, *84*(3), 1247-1257.

Van Winsum, W. and A. Heino (1996). Choice of time-headway in car-following and the role of time-to-collision information in braking. *Ergonomics*, *39*, 579-592.

Vashitz, G., D. Shinar and Y. Blum (2008). In-vehicle information systems to improve traffic safety in Rrad tunnels. *Transport. Res. F*, *11*, 61-74.

Vlakveld, W. P. (2011). Hazard anticipation of young novice drivers. Doctoral dissertation. SWOV Institute of Road Safety Research, Leidschendam, the Netherlands. http://www.swov.nl/rapport/Proefschriften/Willem_Vlakveld.pdf

Vlakveld, W. P. (2014). A comparative study of two desktop hazard perception tasks suitable for mass testing in which scores are not ba/sed on response latencies. *Transport. Res. F*, *22*, 218-231.

Vogel, K. (2003). A comparison of headway and time-to-collision as safety indicators. *Accid. Anal. Prev.*, *35*, 427-433.

Vukelich, M. and L. A. Whitaker (1993, October). The effects of context on the comprehension of graphic symbols. In Proceedings of the Human Factors and Ergonomics Society Annual Meeting, **37**(8), 511-515.

Wallis, T. S. and M. S. Horswill (2007). Using fuzzy signal detection theory to determine why experienced and trained drivers respond faster than novices in a hazard perception test. *Accid. Anal. Prev.*, *39*(6), 1177-1185.

Warshawsky-Livne, L. and D. Shinar (2002). Effects of uncertainty, transmission type, and driver age and gender on brake reaction and movement time. *J. Safety Res.*, *33*, 117-128.

Weiss, T., T. Petzoldt, M. Bannert and J. Krems (2013). Calibration as side effect? Computer-based learning in driver education and the adequacy of driving-task-related self-assessments. *Transport. Res. F*, *17*, 63-74.

Wetton, M. A., M. S. Horswill, C. Hatherly, J. M. Wood, N. A. Pachana and K. J. Anstey (2010). The development and validation of two complementary measures of drivers' hazard perception ability. Accid. Anal. Prev., *42*, 1232-1239.

Wickens, C. D., S. E. Gordon and Y. Liu (2004). *An Introduction to Human Factors Engineering*. Pearson Prentice Hall, Upper Saddle River, NJ.

Wierwille, W. W., J. G. Casali and B. S. Repa (1983). Driver steering reaction time to abrupt-onset crosswinds, as measured in a moving-base driving simulator. *Hum. Fact.*, *25*(1), 103-116.

Wolff, J. S. and M. S. Wogalter (1998). Comprehension of pictorial symbols: Effects of context and test method. *Hum. Fact.*, *40*(2), 173-186.

Wood, J. M., M. S. Horswill, P. F. Lacherez and K. J. Anstey (2013). Evaluation of screening tests for predicting older driver performance and safety assessed by an on-road test. Accid. Anal. Prev., *50*, 1161-1168.

Wortman, R. H. and J. S. Matthias (1983). Evaluation of driver behavior at signalized intersections. *Transport. Res. Rec.*, *904*, 10-20.

Wright, G. R. and R. J. Shephard (1978). Brake reaction time—Effects of age, sex, and carbon monoxide. *Arch. Envir. Health*, *33*, 141-150.

Yang, C. Y. D., J. Shurbutt and B. Phillips (2013). Why drivers do whtat they do. *Public Roads*, *76*(4), 11.

Yeung, J. S. and Y. D. Wong (2014). The effect of road tunnel environment on car following behavior. Accid. Anal. Prev., *70*, 100-109.

Young, K. L., M. A. Regan, T. J. Triggs, N. Tomasevic, K. Stephan and E. Mitsopoulos (2007). Impact on car driving performance of a following distance warning system: Findings from the Australian Transport Accident Commission SafeCar Project. *J. Int. Transport. Syst.*, *11*, 121-131.

Young, K. L., C. M. Rudin-Brown, M. G. Lenné and A. R. Williamson (2012). The implications of cross-regional differences for the design of In-vehicle Information Systems: A comparison of Australian and Chinese drivers. *Appl. Ergon.*, *43*, 564-573.

Zhang, T. and A. H. Chan (2013). Traffic sign comprehension: A review of influential factors and future directions for research. In Proceedings of the International Multi-Conference of Engineers and Computer Scientists (IMECS) (Vol. 2). March 13-15, Hong Kong.

Zhang, Y., C. Fu and L. Hu (2014). Yellow light dilemma zone researches: A review. *J. Traffic Transport. Eng.* (English Edition), *1*(5), 338-352.

6

Young and Novice Drivers

"What a shame that youth is wasted on the young." (attributed to George Bernard Shaw and Oscar Wilde).

"But we age unevenly. More slowly in society than in our skull." (John Updike, From the introduction of "Olinger Stories." Vintage Books, 1968).

"But Uri has no driver license. He had three lessons and stopped. 'It is not right. It is not right that something so dangerous should be so boring.'" (from the novel Fontanella by Meir Shalev, p. 112).

Uri is a fictional character. He is fictional not only because he is a character in a novel, but also because young – particularly young male – drivers do not view the driving task as boring. Instead, they view it as an exciting rite of passage into adulthood and independence. Consequently, most young people of licensing age seek driving rather than shun it. An analysis of focus group discussions with teenage drivers in Denmark revealed that in addition to the benefits of mobility, they view driving as a way to attract attention, achieve status, and control a powerful machine (Moller, 2004). Beirness *et al.* (2004) sampled 1,221 younger (6-19 years old) and older (45-54 years old) Canadian drivers, and found that the younger drivers are three times as likely as older drivers to take driving risks "just for fun," six times as likely to receive tickets for moving vehicle violations (relative to the amount of kilometers they drive), significantly more likely to speed, and more likely to speed through traffic lights especially before they turn red. They are also by far the most likely to text or send email while driving, and not surprisingly the most involved in using a cell phone in a crash or near-crash, especially for texting (NHTSA, 2015). Using GPS technology, Porter and Whitton (2002), also found that compared to middle aged (30-64 years old) and older (65 + years old) drivers young (20-29 years old) drivers drove faster, decelerated and accelerated more abruptly, were less likely to come to a full stop at stop signs, followed other cars more closely, and were less likely to signal before turning.

Unfortunately, in terms of safety, young drivers have several strikes against them: they are inexperienced in the driving task and have problems with risk perception; they are high risk takers in their lifestyle (not just in driving) and immature; they often drive at high-risk conditions such as at night, when tired, and sometimes – when returning from parties – under the influence of alcohol and other drugs; and they are susceptible to peer pressures to assume more risk from their passengers/friends (Masten, 2004). In fact, an analysis of the U.S. national fatal motor-vehicle crash data bank (the Fatal Analysis Reporting System) revealed that among young drivers, the highest risk group for a fatal crash were male drivers traveling with young (16-20 years old) passengers (Ouimet *et al.*, 2010). To make things worse, most teen drivers consider themselves "safe drivers" (89 percent in one American survey of 3,574 teen drivers by Liberty Mutual Group and SADD, as cited by Hedlund and Compton, 2005). Interestingly, it appears that these tendencies are associated with a high crash risk almost exclusively in males. Begg and Langley (2004) found that the risky driving factors – such as low levels of self-control and "harm avoidance," aggressive behavior, and cannabis use, that typify all young Australian drivers (15 and 18 years old in their study) predicted subsequent risky behaviors (at ages 21 and 26) of males only and not of females. Very few females were persistent risky drivers. These findings are consistent with the over-involvement of young male drivers relative to female drivers in crashes (see Figure 6-2).

The Magnitude of the Young Driver Problem

If a picture is worth a thousand words, then Figure 6-1 probably says it: Traffic crashes are by far the single greatest killer of persons aged 15-24 in the 23 industrialized countries whose statistics were collated by the World Health Organization, accounting for 35 percent of all deaths in that age group (OECD, 2006).

From a slightly different perspective, young drivers – especially young male drivers (Maycock, 2002; Ouimet *et al.*, 2010) – constitute the age group with highest crash involvement. This is true when we look at their likelihood to be involved in accidents relative to their prevalence in the population of all drivers (Figure 6-2), and more so for males than for females. It is also true when we adjust for their exposure and look at their crash likelihood per miles or kilometers of driving, In this case we get a U-shaped function where the teen drivers and elderly drivers are the highest risk groups, but teen drivers are by far the highest of all groups, with an involvement rate that is three times that of a mature experience driver (Figure 6-3(a)) (Cicchino and McCartt, 2014). When fatalities rather than crash involvements are measured we get the U-shaped function that is reproduced in Figure 6-3(b). Here, the resilience of the young driver and the frailty of the older driver put the latter at a higher risk. The age-related U-shape functions are not

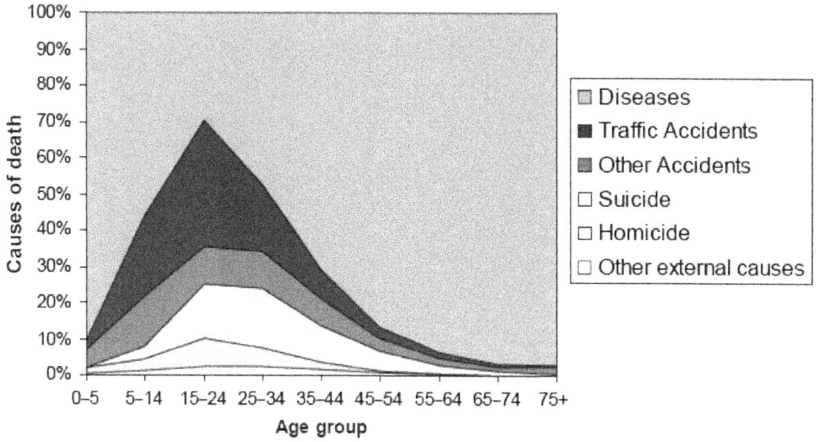

Figure 6-1. Causes of death for people at different ages for different countries in the Organization of Economic Cooperation and Development (OECD) countries (from OECD, 2006, reprinted with permission from OECD). *Source*: Aggregated data from the WHO Mortality database: WHO Statistical Information System (WHOSIS). http://www3.who.int/whosis.

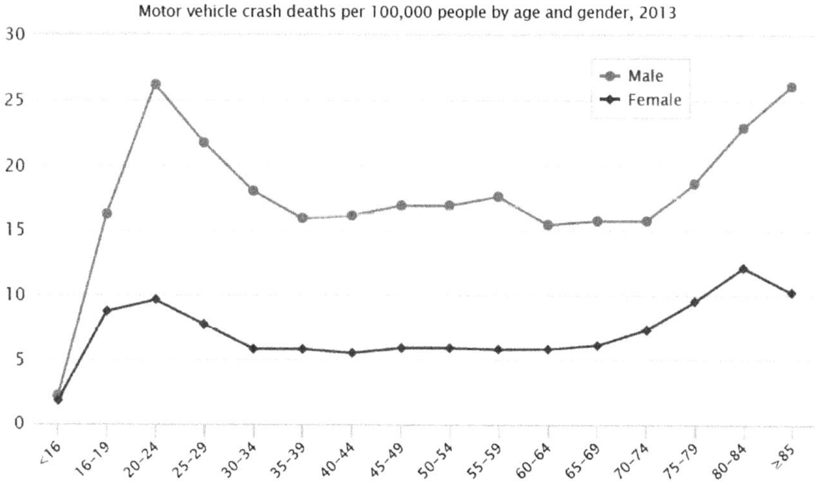

Figure 6-2. Driver involvement in fatal crashes relative to their frequency in the driver population (per 100,000 licensed drivers) (from U.S. data for 2013, IIHS, 2015, based on analysis of NHTSA FARS data).

unique to the U.S., and with variations in the absolute values they are common to all OECD countries (see examples in Chapter 7). Figure 6-3 also reflects the significant achievements that have been achieved in reducing teen (and older driver) death rates per distance traveled over the past two decades. This has been achieved, at least in part by

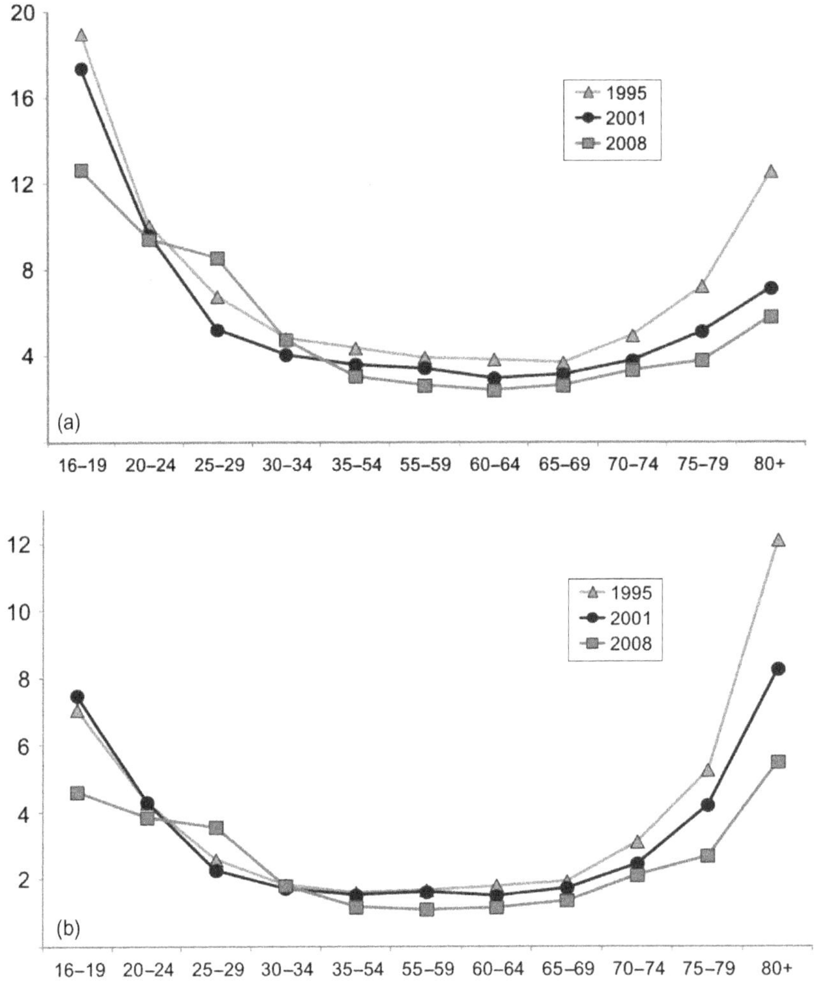

Figure 6-3 (a) U.S. national police-reported passenger vehicle driver crash involvements per 100 million vehicle miles traveled, by age groups, 1995, 2001, and 2008 (Cicchino and McCartt, 2014). (b) U.S. driver fatality rates per 100 million vehicle miles in 1995, 2001, and 2008 (from Cicchino and McCartt, 2014, with permission from Elsevier).

improvements in young driver training and use of restraints (as described below) and in providing better protection and aids for older drivers (as described in the next chapter).

Young drivers are also over-involved as victims in their crashes. Relative to their numbers in the population, drivers under 24 years old are 2-4 times as likely to be killed in an accident as other drivers: twice as likely in Australia, Canada, Iceland, Ireland, New Zealand, Poland, Portugal, Spain, and the U.S.; three times as likely in Austria, Great Britain, Belgium, Denmark, Finland, France, and the Netherlands; and four times as likely in Germany (OECD, 2006). Furthermore, they are especially over-represented in single-vehicle crashes. These are the crashes that are most closely associated with risky driving such as speeding, nighttime, fatigue, and alcohol impaired driving (OECD, 2006). Some of these elevated crash rates may be due to driving in riskier environments and situations (such as at night, tired, and intoxicated) or driving more dangerous cars (such as smaller cars and older cars that provide less protection; Williams *et al.*, 2006). But these effects – especially the vehicle factors – are probably very small compared to the drivers' own contribution to their increased risk.

Figure 6-2 also shows that men are much more involved in crashes than women, and their over-involvement relative to females remains even after adjusting for the fact that they drive more miles than women. While there is no difference between men and women in their cognitive and perceptual-motor skills, there is a difference in their attitudes toward driving. Men in general – and young men in particular – are less motivated to comply with traffic laws, see them as significantly less important than other laws, and consequently are more likely to violate them. Young males also have more confidence in their driving than women and therefore perceive less risk in violating traffic laws than women (Yagil, 1998). Thus, while the over-involvement of young drivers in general, may not be exclusively due to their risk taking behaviors, the difference between young male drivers and young female drivers is probably greatly influenced by their differential risk taking behaviors.

Sources of the Problem: Inexperience and Immaturity

To understand the root causes of their crash involvement, we must be able to untangle the relative contribution of the two handicapping factors that afflict all young drivers: youth that is associated with immaturity and high risk taking behaviors, and inexperience that is associated with inadequate driving skills. Because in today's western society almost all people receive their license as soon as they are legally permitted, it would appear to be impossible to separate the age factor from the experience factor. Fortunately, this is not quite the case. Using national databases from large motorized countries, it is still possible to find novice drivers at different ages, and thus it is possible to compare the crash involvements of novice drivers who first obtain their license at different ages. This was done by Cooper, Pinili, and Chen (1995) who analyzed the crash involvement of 140,000 British Columbia, Canada drivers. Their analysis focused on the first 3 years of driving. They separated the crashes into those that occurred within the first year of licensure, the second year of licensure, and the third year of licensure. Furthermore, they distinguished between crashes in which the drivers were charged with a violation (culpable crashes) and crashes in which they were not charged (non-culpable crashes). The results for the culpable crashes are displayed in Figure 6-4.

In this figure the accident likelihoods per driver are noted for each age group by calculating the ratio of the total number of crashes in each age group relative to the number of drivers in that group. The top (lightest) line is restricted to drivers who are in their first year of driving, the second line represents the drivers in their second year of driving, and the bottom (bold) line represents the drivers in their third year of driving. Although the data are quite noisy, the pattern is obvious: novice drivers – at least those who are under 35 years old – have significantly more crashes in their first year of driving than in their second and third years, which are not significantly different from each other.

Cooper *et al.* (1995), did not stop there, but went on to determine how the first-year accidents differ from the total number of crashes (for all years) for each age group. The results, presented in Figure 6-5, were striking. When looking only at culpable crashes, drivers in their first year are very different from the population of all drivers. Note that the two lines in Figure 6-5 coincide for the 16-year-old drivers, simply because that is the minimal licensing age in British Columbia, and therefore the two curves represent the same population.

In contrast to these results, a plot of the crash involvement for non-culpable drivers did not reveal any difference between the first year drivers and the more experienced drivers. In fact, the age effect alone was very small and crashes decreased with age in a very

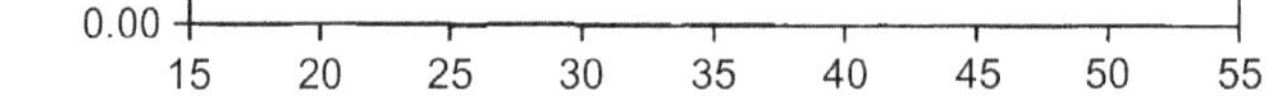

Figure 6-4. Culpable claim-related accident involvement in the first 3 years of license (from Cooper *et al.*, 1995, reprinted with permission from Elsevier).

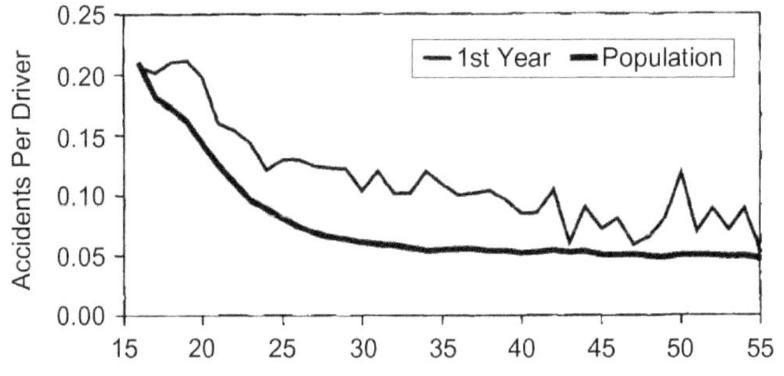

Figure 6-5. Culpable claim-related accident involvements: first year novice drivers versus general population (from Cooper *et al.*, 1995, reprinted with permission from Elsevier).

linear fashion from roughly 0.10 crashes per driver per year at the age of 16 to roughly 0.05 crashes per driver per year at the age of 55, regardless of years of driving.

Thus, it appears that both age and experience play a role in the risk of *causing* an accident, at least on the basis of police-cited culpability. Based on these Canadian data the effects of age are much more gradual and extend at least to age 35, whereas the effects of experience are much greater and are almost exclusively limited to the first year of driving.

In another study of the relative contribution of age and experience, Maycock and his associates analyzed the data from extensive surveys of British Motorists (Maycock, Lockwood, and Lester, 1991; Forsyth, Maycock, and Sexton, 1995) instead of using police records. They noted that police-reported crashes suffer from several shortcomings. They are limited to injury and fatal crashes, and their average frequency per driver is very small; roughly 0.01 accidents per driver per year according to their estimates. Also, the police data have no information on exposure in terms of miles driven, or years of driving experience. Other studies have also shown that in some respects self-reports of crashes are more complete and less biased than crashes documented by police (e.g., McGwin, Owsley, and Ball, 1998). Consequently, in both studies they resorted to using nationwide surveys with questionnaires on self-reported crash data. In the first study (Maycock *et al.*, 1991) the data base consisted of "just over 18,500" completed questionnaires, constituting a response rate of approximately 75-80 percent of all drivers surveyed. From these data the researchers were able to derive fairly detailed functions relating crash rates to age (as an indicator of maturity) and experience (as an indicator of skill). These functions are reproduced in Figure 6-6.

In this figure, drivers are grouped according to the age at which they were first licensed, and then each plot indicates the accident rate of each group (cohort) over the years of experience that they accumulated. The very sharp drop in the accident rate that is apparent for each group in the initial phase of driving provides an estimate of the role of experience, and the decreasing levels of the starting points of successive curves provide an estimate of the effect of age (characterized by the dashed line). While it is quite obvious that age – or maturation – effects persist well into the 50s, they are greatest in the teenage years and early 20s. More important, at all ages the effect of experience – or actually lack of it – plays a much greater role than age per-se in crash involvement.

One other significant bit of information that should be noted for the data in Figure 6-6 is that they represent people who reported driving approximately the same amount: about 7,500 miles/year. This is important because the relationship between the amount of driving and the crash involvement is not a linear one. Drivers who drive very few miles per year have a much greater crash rate per mile than drivers who drive many miles each year (Forsyth *et al.*, 1995; Hakamies-Blomqvist, Raitanen, and O'Neill, 2002; Langford, Methorst, and Hakamies-Blomqvist, 2006). One explanation for this is that drivers who drive many miles, drive more of them on inter-urban and limited-access divided highways (freeways, as they are known in the U.S., and motorways, as they are known in Europe), and these are generally safer roads with lower crash rates.

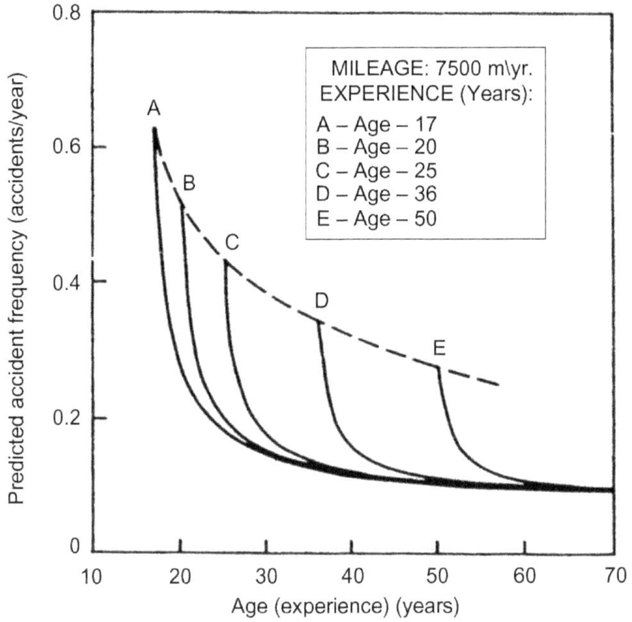

Figure 6-6. The estimated effects of age and driving on accident liability. Each function is for a cohort of drivers that received their license at a given age (from Maycock *et al.*, 1991, reprinted with permission from TRL).

In the second study, by Forsyth *et al.* (1995), a different sampling strategy was used. A cohort of over 7,000 drivers who passed their driving tests in England on a given day were followed up with questionnaires 1, 2, and 3 years after they were first licensed. Although the sample was different, the sampling technique was different, and the study included many other predictor variables, it essentially confirmed the results and the statistical model presented in the earlier study. Interestingly, they also found that even in their first years accident frequencies do not increase linearly with either the reported frequency of driving or the number of miles driven, and in fact each additional mile is associated with a lower likelihood of an accident. The most plausible explanation for this is that each additional time a novice driver ventures into the road, and each additional mile that he or she drives has the benefit of the previous experience, and the driver is thus less crash liable.

One shortcoming of the Maycock *et al.* (1991) and the Forsyth *et al.* (1995) studies was that experience was measured in months of driving rather than the more commonly accepted measure of exposure: miles or kilometers of driving. However, in an analysis of data collected in the Netherlands approximately 10 years later, and using accidents per billion kilometers driven, Vlakveld (2004) obtained a very similar pattern of results, which are presented in Figure 6-7. Another advantage of the Vlakveld results as presented in Figure 6-7 is that the line plots are of actual empirical crash data rather than of smoothed functions derived from a data-based model.

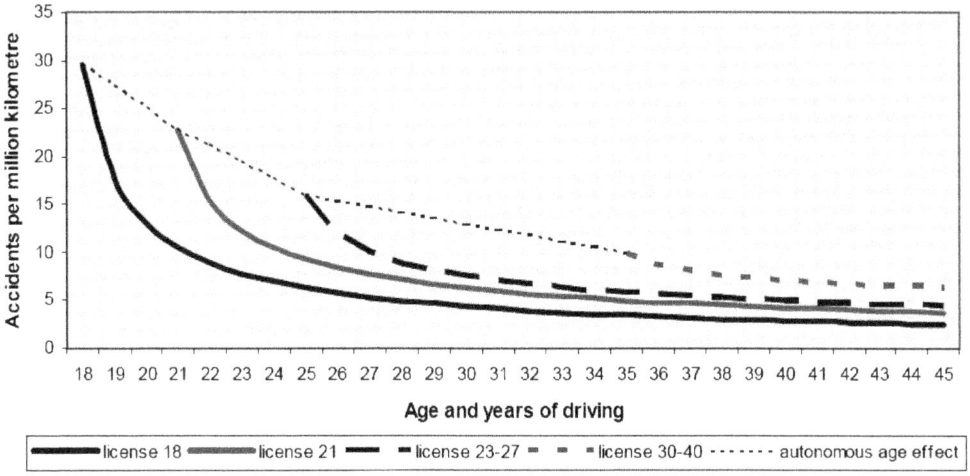

Figure 6-7. The effects of age and experience on crash involvement (accidents per billion kilometers driven) in the Netherlands (from Vlakveld, 2004, reproduced with permission from the Office of Public Sector Information, the United Kingdom).

Vlakveld's data corroborate Maycock's elegant functions, with one slight exception. People who start driving at a later age never achieve the low crash rates that people who start driving in their teens eventually achieve. Therefore, before we rush to postpone the licensure age till people are more mature, we should acknowledge the benefit of early skill acquisition (though this benefit of an early start may be an artifact of survival of the fittest – the most dangerous young drivers may have already perished in crashes at a young age).

Although the results presented by Maycock and by Vlakveld look very similar, it is important to stress the distinction between the two rates of crashes they used. In a study discussed below in some detail McCartt, Shabanova, and Leaf (2003) found that when they analyzed self-reported crash rates of young drivers relative to time since licensure, the higher the grade point average of the student and the greater the number of parental restrictions (e.g., no drinking and driving, no recreational driving, nighttime curfew), the greater the time delay until the first crash. In contrast, when the reported crash rates were analyzed relative to the number of miles driven, none of these factors played a part. Thus, McCartt's findings, too, suggest that lack of actual driving experience is a much more significant cause of the very high-crash risk for 16- and 17-year-old novice drivers than their age or lack of maturity.

The accumulation of driver experience

There is very little one can do about age, except to take comfort that at least in the domain of driving safety for the first 40-50 years aging is a good thing. An obvious, though impractical, solution would be to allow driving only when the age effects dissipate significantly, roughly at age 35-40. A more practical approach would be to delay full licensure (allowing unsupervised driving in all conditions) as much as possible beyond the age of 16 (McCartt *et al.*, 2009). But the issue of experience – the more important issue – is different. Here the traffic safety community can intervene, at least if we regard "experience" as equivalent to the acquisition of safe and defensive driving skills and habits. An approach that addresses both maturity and experience, labeled graduated driver licensing (GDL), has become the current standard in many countries, and is described in detail further below.

Let's look now at experience. Assuming that our novice driver survives the first year of driving, it is unlikely that at the anniversary of his or her first year of driving, the novice driver wakes up as a significantly safer driver. Experience builds up during the first year. But at what rate of progress? A simple way to consider this would be to look at the crash rate of novice drivers on a much finer scale: by small increments in the miles driven or by months instead of by years. Several researchers in different countries have done this, and the results are amazingly similar: all showing that crash involvement is the greatest immediately after licensure, and declines rapidly thereafter (Gregersen *et al.*, 2000, in Sweden; Laberge-Nadeau, 1997, and Mayhew, Simpson, and Pak, 2003, in Canada; McCartt *et al.*, 2003, in the U.S.; and Sagberg, 1998, in Norway).

Given the significance of these results and their implications for licensing and driver training, it is worthwhile to look at the often cited in-depth study by McCartt *et al.* (2003), in some detail. McCartt and her coworkers tracked the driving behavior of 911 (54 percent male) students from five northeastern states in the U.S. from their first year in high school till their last year. All of the survey participants received their license sometime after the first interview and prior to the last interview. Following an initial written survey, phone interviews were conducted every 6 months in the fall and spring over a three-year period. The researchers obtained personal and demographic information, the date of licensure, the amount of driving, and information on moving traffic violations and crashes in which the students were involved over the past 6 months (since the last interview). As might be expected, the initial amount of driving was quite low, averaging approximately 200 miles per month in the first month after obtaining the license. It then increased gradually to approximately 500 miles per month by the end of the first year, after which it leveled off. Also, as might be expected, males reported driving more miles than females, by an approximately constant 40 percent. Thus, assuming that the miles driven on the road are a measure of exposure to crash risk, the amount of exposure to crash risk increased over time. In fact they more than doubled within the first year.

Yet, despite the very low exposure in the beginning of their driving careers, the young drivers' crash involvement rate was the highest in the very first month of driving, when both males and females averaged almost one crash per every 4,000 miles, as illustrated in Figure 6-8. Thereafter the decline was very rapid so that after 5 months the crash rate was approximately 1 per every 20,000 miles. This is a drop by a factor of 5(!). McCartt and her colleagues also examined the likelihood of experiencing the "first" crash as a function of the miles driven since licensure. Here too, the results are striking. One out of ten young drivers had their first crash within the first 500 miles, one out of five had it before completing 2,000 miles, and one driver out of four had his or her first crash before completing 2,500 miles of driving.

The results were similar, but even more dramatic when the crash rate was calculated relative to the number of reported miles driven. These findings are presented in Figure 6-9. The first 250 miles are by far the most dangerous, with one crash per nearly 3,000 miles, or one crash for every 12 drivers. The crash risk then declines very rapidly within the first 1,000 miles, and seems to level off at about one crash per 20,000 miles after the driver has had about 3,000 miles of driving experience. Again, a drop in the crash rate by a factor of approximately 6-7.

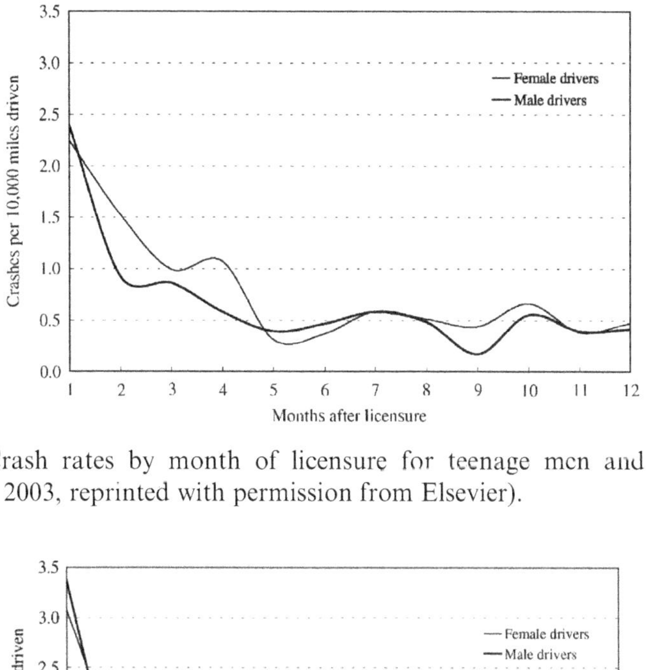

Figure 6-8. Crash rates by month of licensure for teenage men and women (from McCartt *et al.*, 2003, reprinted with permission from Elsevier).

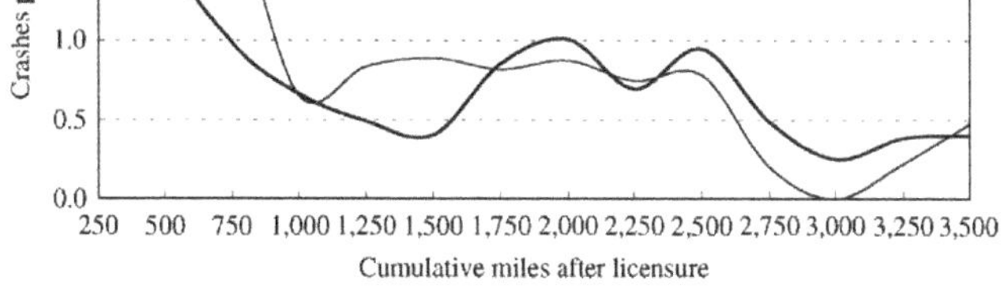

Figure 6-9. Crash rates by cumulative miles driven by teenage males and females after licensure (from McCartt *et al.*, 2003, reprinted with permission from Elsevier).

These results indicate, as McCartt and her coworkers argue, that the principal factor responsible for the novice drivers' high-crash risk is lack of experience and not lack of maturity. The overwhelming majority of crashes are in the very first 3 months, and the crash rate declines in a very consistent manner over this time. It is hard to argue that maturity changes that rapidly and that it occurs so systematically after obtaining the license. This kind of conclusion, which is very consistent with those of the previous studies reviewed above (Cooper *et al.*, 1995; Forsyth *et al.*, 1995; Maycock *et al.*, 1991; Vlakveld, 2004) can give us hope that all that is now left to do is to find a way of providing novice drivers with the experience-based skills that are needed for safe driving before they get into the high-risk situations where these skills are put to the test.

But the new drivers adopt many risk taking behaviors. In McCartt *et al.*'s study the manifestation of risk taking – as reflected in citations for moving traffic violations – increased with time and was much higher for the male drivers than for the female drivers. Furthermore, whereas within the first 1,500 miles the difference was small, after that the females' citation rate essentially leveled off while the males' rate kept increasing. Thus, by the end of their first 1,500 miles males were approximately 25 percent more likely to have received a citation for a violation, and by the time they had driven 3,500 miles males (or should they be called boys?) were 125 percent more likely than females to receive a traffic citation.

The rapid decrease in crash rate in the first months of driving is not unique to the U.S. teenage drivers. A very similar pattern was obtained in an analysis of the crash rates of Nova Scotia, Canada drivers as shown in Figure 6-10 (Mayhew *et al.*, 2003). Of added interest in the Canadian data is the very large difference in crashes between the

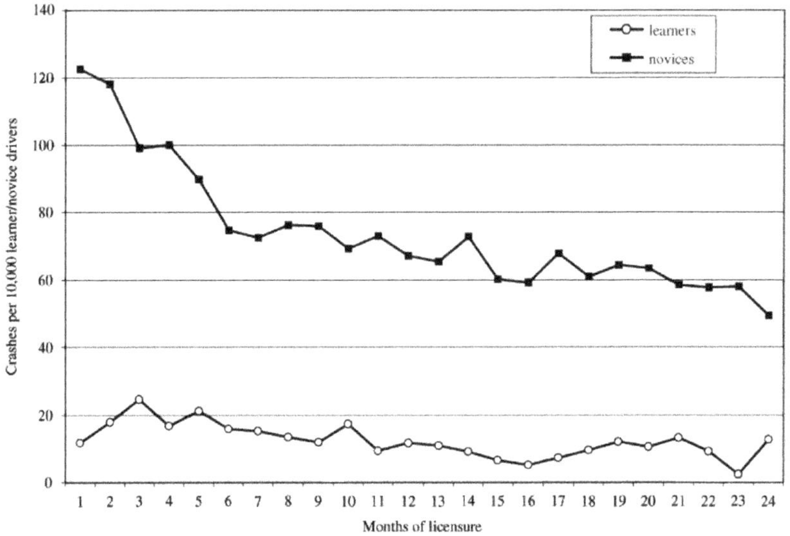

Figure 6-10. Crash rates of learners and novice drivers in Nova Scotia, Canada (from Mayhew *et al.*, 2003, reprinted with permission from Elsevier).

pre-licensure learners and the licensed new drivers. The learners, who must be supervised by an adult (typically a parent), have very low and relatively stable crash rates as long as they drive as "learners." However, as soon as they start driving unsupervised, their crash rate jumps by over 10-fold. It then decreases, at first sharply (during the first 6 months) and then gradually over the next year. Yet, in the course of their first 2 years of unsupervised driving the young drivers never reach the low crash rates levels that they maintained before they were licensed.

In summary, it appears that age (especially during the teenage years) and experience have independent effects on driving behavior and driving safety, and must both be considered in any attempt to promote safe driving. The weight of the evidence from multiple studies that addressed both issues suggests that experience is the more important of the two factors (see also a review by McCartt *et al.*, 2009).

Causes of Novice Drivers' Crashes

In an article titled "Young novice drivers: Careless or clueless?" McKnight and McKnight (2003) attempted to uncover the specific crash causes through which inexperience manifests itself. They did this by analyzing the content of the narratives of police accident reports of 16- to 19-year-old drivers in California and Maryland. The weight of the evidence presented so far suggests that lack of maturity (related to carelessness) is not the prime culprit. But simply stating that the problem is one of lack of experience (being clueless) is problematic too, because it does not point to the specific experience-related deficiencies. Their results were most interesting. The specific behaviors that contributed to the 2,128 crashes they analyzed, and the frequencies of the different behaviors are listed in Table 6-1. The percentages in this table are based on a total of 2,774 specific instances of "deficient behaviors" that they identified, indicating that in approximately 30 percent of the crashes more than one specific behavior contributed to the crash. Therefore, the total percent of crash-related behaviors in the table exceeds 100 percent.

The frequencies in this table reveal that the principal deficiencies of the young drivers lie in their inadequate visual scanning for potential obstacles (33.6 percent) – ahead of them (19.1 percent), to their side (14.2 percent) or behind them (9.4 percent) – and inattention to the driving task in general (23 percent).

The conclusions that McKnight and McKnight (2003) reached are based on post hoc clinical evaluations of reported crashes. As such, they can be challenged, though a more recent analysis of a better controlled set of U.S. teen crash data obtained similar findings (Curry *et al.*, 2011). But a more recent study, relying on the analysis of video clips from in-vehicle data recorders, reached very similar conclusions. In this study, Carney *et al.* (2015) analyzed video clips of 1,691 moderate-to-severe crashes of vehicles driven by 16- to 19-year-old drivers in naturalistic driving settings. Using a scheme similar to the one used by Treat *et al.* (1979) (see Chapter 18), and relying on the images of the scene, the direction of the driver's gaze and his/her pre-crash behavior the researchers coded drivers' failures as either recognition errors, decision errors, or performance errors. Recognition errors – defined as inadequate surveillance or engaging in extraneous behaviors – were the most common, accounting for 70 percent of the crashes. Closely followed in terms of their frequency were inadequate decisions that accounted for 60 percent of the crashes. Interestingly, recognition errors were much more common in collisions with another vehicle (89 percent), while decision errors were much more common in single-vehicle crashes (80 percent). Thus, the two different methods, one relying on post-crash police reports (McKnight and McKnight, 2003; Treat *et al.*, 1979) and one relying on objective recording of 6 seconds leading up to the crash (Carney *et al.*, 2015) yielded fairly similar conclusions despite the differences in methodology, geography, driver samples, and the more than 30 years' worth of improvements in vehicles and roadways.

A casual comparison between these crash "causes" and those presented for the general driving population (see Chapter 18) reveals that the causes of crashes of young drivers are quite similar to those of the driving population at large, leading both McKnight and McKnight and Carney *et al.* to conclude that most of the non-fatal crashes involve a human failure on the part of the driver, and that the most common failures are those associated with recognizing the imminent danger. In McKnight and McKnight's words: "the overwhelming majority of non-fatal accidents appears to result from failure to employ routine safe operating practices and failure to recognize the danger in doing so rather than what might be viewed as thrill-seeking or other forms of deliberate risk taking. Only a very small minority of accidents involved what could be termed deliberately risky behavior, such as operating at very high speeds or engaging in what was characterized as reckless driving (p. 924)." While the latter were not totally absent – with high speed relative to conditions contributing to 21 percent of the crashes, and inadequate space accounting for another 10 percent of the crashes – they are definitely less common than the skill-related deficiencies. Given that competent safe driving involves approximately 1,500(!) different perceptual-motor tasks that novice drivers have to master (McKnight and Adams, 1970), it is not surprising that in the first 3 months of driving they are not that accomplished at the task.

There is another objective indication that one of the problems novice drivers have is in their allocation of attention and ability to detect relevant stimuli in time. In our study on the interference of shifting gears with sign detection (Shinar, Meir, and Ben-Shoham, 1998, see Chapter 5 and Figure 5-1), we found that novice drivers detected significantly fewer traffic signs when they drove a manual transmission car than when they drove an automatic transmission car, whereas experienced drivers' sign detection was essentially unaffected by shifting gears. In addition, regardless of the type of transmission, the driving task itself was much more challenging for the novice drivers, and consequently they detected fewer signs than the experienced drivers.

Underlying some of the difficulties novice and experienced drivers have is poor behavioral adaptation to the changing driving environment. Experienced drivers adapt to changes in the environmental demands covertly by adjusting the allocation of their information processing resources, and overtly by adjusting their speed. Novice drivers are

Table 6-1. Percent of teen driver crashes attributable to deficiencies in specific driving behaviors of the teenage drivers involved (from McKnight and McKnight, 2003, reprinted with permission from Elsevier).

Percent of crashes attributable to deficiencies in specific driving behaviors					
Behavior	**Percentage**	**Behavior**	**Percentage**	**Behavior**	**Percentage**
Basic control	***8.0***	***Search ahead***	***19.1***	***Adjusting speed***	***20.8***
Lane keeping	2.6	Distance	3.1	Traffic/road conditions	8.7
Turning path	1.3	Roadsides	4.3	Curves	6.1
Braking	1.3	Before left turns	4.8	Slick surface	2.3
Turning speed	0.7	Car ahead	3.1	Slick curves	1.5
Other	2.1	Left-turning vehicle	2.9	High speed	0.7
Traffic controls	***5.6***	Next lane	0.9	Other	1.5
Traffic lights	1.7	***Search to the side***	***14.2***	***Maintaining space***	***9.8***
Stop signs	1.3	Intersection: burdened	7.7	Following distance	5.8
Lane use	1.5	Intersection: privileged	5.5	Crossing and entering	1.4
Passing	0.6	Sight obstructed	0.8	Side clearance	1.3
Other	0.5	Other	0.2	Overtaking	1.1
Attention	***23.0***	***Search to the rear***	***9.4***	Other	0.2
Maintaining attention	18.6	Slowing	3.0	Signals	***1.2***
Avoiding distractions	3.8	Backing	2.1	Interpreting signals	0.8
Attention sharing	0.07	Periodically	2.1	Signaling intent	0.3
Driver-vehicle	***6.3***	Changing lanes	1.5	Signaling presence	0.1
Alcohol impairment	2.4	Other	0.7	Emergencies	***9.4***
Fatigue	1.7	Other search	***0.9***	Swerving	5.6
Vehicle	1.5			Skid recov	1.4
Other	0.7			Braking	1.0
				Tire failure	0.7
				Brake fail.	0.7

much less adept at this. For example Mueller and Trick (2012) had inexperienced and experienced drivers drive in clear and simulated fog conditions. All the drivers in both groups were under 35 years old to minimize the effects of age as a confounding variable. They found that although the experienced drivers drove faster than the novice drivers in clear visibility, they adjusted their speed more than the novice drivers when driving in fog. Rudin-Brown, Edquist, and Lenné (2014) had drivers drive through different urban environments with varying complexity (and attentional demands). The simplest environment was a relatively empty suburban street, the more complex was a builtup area, and the most complex was a builtup area with cars parked along the two sides of the street. They found that all drivers decreased their speed as the complexity increased. In the simplest condition all drivers drove at about the same speed, but as complexity increased the less experienced drivers lowered their speed less than the experienced drivers. This was despite the fact that all drivers with all levels of experience reported similar increases in subjective workload as the road complexity increased. Thus, it appears that inexperienced drivers are much less sensitive to the adjustments they must make in response to the changing situation, even while they are aware of the added demands.

Additional evidence for the inadequate information processing skills of novice drivers comes from eye movement research (Borowsky, Shinar, and Oron-Gilad, 2010; Lehtonen *et al.*, 2014; Mourant and Rockwell, 1972; Underwood *et al.*, 2002). Underwood *et al.* (2002) presented novice and experienced drivers with video clips of the road videotaped from the driver's perspective. The novice drivers with less than a month of post-license experience were much less active in their visual search, and focused significantly less on critical items like other cars (ahead, in the adjacent lanes, and parked) than the experienced drivers who were approximately a year older with an average of 4.5 years of driving experience. In our own driving laboratory (Borowsky *et al.*, 2010), we tracked the eye movements of novice drivers (17-18 years old, with an average of 2.7 months of driving experience), experienced drivers (22-30 years old, with 7.3 years of driving experience), and older drivers (65-72) as they viewed video clips containing actual and potential hazards. While the scanning and hazard detection rates of mature and older drivers were similar, the visual scanning of the novice drivers was different and much less effective, causing them to miss many targets and potentially dangerous situations. For example, when approaching a side road, the mature and older drivers scanned the merging road on the right for approaching vehicles, while the novice drivers tended to fixate ahead only. Lehtonen *et al.* (2014) measured the fixations of novice drivers with less than 5,000 kilometers of driving experience and experienced drivers with more than 20,000 kilometers or driving experience as they drove on a winding rural road. They found that the experienced drivers spent much more time looking ahead into the curves where they could find information relevant to "trajectory planning." In contrast novice drivers spent more time looking at the road immediately ahead of the car so as facilitate their steering. Lehtonen's findings were similar to those obtained in a pioneering study, more than 40 years earlier, by Mourant and Rockwell (1972). Mourant and Rockwell compared the visual search patterns of novice drivers ("with almost complete lack of driving experience") with experienced drivers (with at least 8,000 miles/year for the last five years). They found that the novice drivers tended to focus their fixations closer in front of the vehicle and more to the right (where the lane marker was) as if to ensure that they stay in the middle of the road. These kinds of findings suggest that novice drivers' information processing is not as efficient as that of experienced drivers, and consequently their ability to detect and respond in time to hazards on the road should be impaired. Hazard perception studies, in fact, confirm this as described in detail below.

Hazard perception

Hazard perception is one of the few skills that consistently correlate with crash involvement (Horswill and McKenna, 2004). It has both attentional and perceptual components and therefore it is more deficient in young novice drivers whose attentional skills, visual search control, and situation awareness of the road are less developed than that of experienced drivers. Romer *et al.* (2014) proposed a general model of the attentional failures that may lead to failure to attend and respond to hazards. This model is reproduced in Figure 6-11. Among the "stable conditions" that lead to failure to attend to the driving task is incomplete maturation of attention skills, and among the "stable influences" that lead to failure to

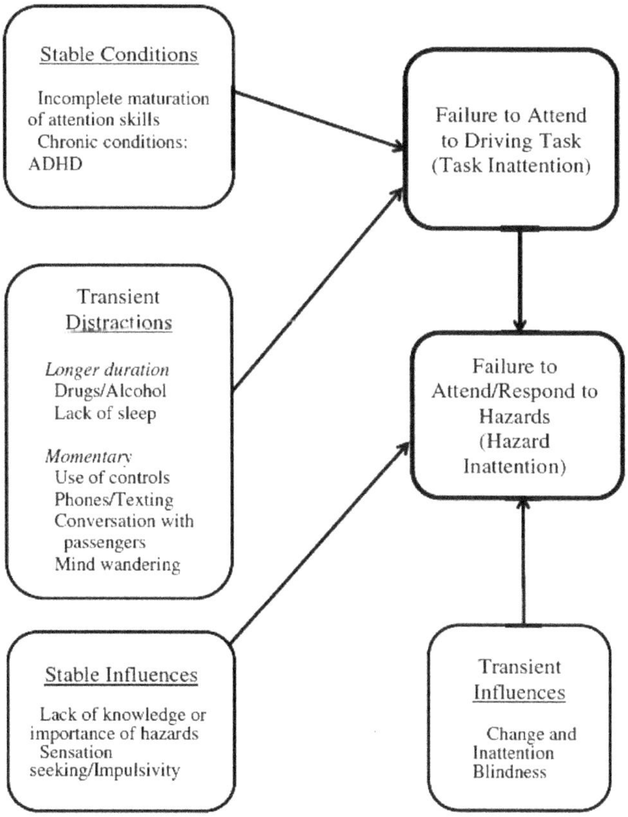

Figure 6-11. Model of sources of attention failures in novice drivers (from Romer *et al.*, 2014, reprinted with permission from Elsevier).

attend and respond to the hazards are lack of appreciation for the hazards and sensation-seeking. All of these factors are very salient in young novice drivers. A formal analysis (based on signal detection theory and fuzzy logic) led Wallis and Horswill (2007) to also conclude that the young drivers' poor hazard perception is due to a high threshold (i.e., lack of appreciation) for danger before they consider a situation hazardous.

Intersections, which are high-crash risk locations for all drives, present novice drivers with a very demanding situation of potential information overload. In intersections the most obvious sources of potential hazards are the cross roads on which other cars could be approaching. Therefore, a prerequisite to good hazard perception would be proper scanning to the right and left of the intersection. Unfortunately, young novice drivers are not good at this. As noted above, Borowsky *et al.* (2010) found that novice drivers were less likely than experienced drivers to fixate side roads and more likely to look only straight ahead as they approached T intersections, thereby exposing themselves to potential collisions with cross traffic. Fisher (2008), in a driving simulator study, found that newly licensed drivers were up to three times more likely to glance away from the road for more than two seconds than experienced drivers. Scott *et al.* (2013) demonstrated in a driving simulator that novice drivers (with an average of 6.6 months of licensed driving) were much less systematic than young-experienced drivers (with an average of 6.8 years of experience) in their eye movements and fixation patterns before making a right turn into an intersection. Borowsky and Oron-Gilad (2013) presented drivers with short video clips containing potential and materialized hazards, and found that novice drivers were less likely to fixate potential hazards (such as a signalized intersection, or a pedestrian standing on a pedestrian island, or a pedestrian walking along the side of the road) than experienced and professional drivers. In addition, when asked to overtly categorize the different video clips, their categorizations relied more on "materialized hazards" (such as braking of a lead car or a pedestrian crossing the road) than on "potential hazards." Mueller and Trick (2012) found that in a driving simulator novice drivers had longer reaction times to hazards than experienced drivers, and only the novice drivers had collisions with the hazards (e.g., a car that emerged from a driveway).

Similarly, in Australia, Whelan and his associates (2004) demonstrated that novice drivers are much slower than experienced drivers to detect hazards that lay ahead (presented in pictures of the road photographed from the driver's perspective), and that with increased driving exposure their performance improves. Pradhan *et al.* (2005) evaluated the hazard perception of novice drivers with less than 6 months of driving experience by having them drive through 16 scenarios containing some hazards, and checking to see whether or not they visually attended to each hazard. They then compared their performance with that of experienced mature (19-29 years old) and old (60-74 years old) drivers. Their findings were similar to those of Borowsky *et al.* (2010) noted above. Their novice drivers failed to fixate the hazards much more frequently than the other drivers, fixating them on only 35 percent of the encounters, compared to 50 percent for the young-experienced drivers and 66 percent for the older experienced drivers. Most recently, Crundall (2016), using a variant of a hazard perception test containing video clips of emerging hazards showed in three experiments that novice drivers were significantly poorer at hazard prediction than experienced drivers.

In summary, nearly all studies that examined novice young drivers' hazard perception found that it was worse than that of older experienced drivers. Still, as always the case in behavioral research, not all studies have been able to demonstrate this (e.g., Underwood, Ngai, and Underwood, 2013) and some studies have shown that this deficiency may be restricted to specific types of hazards (e.g., Crundall *et al.*, 2012). Nonetheless, hazard perception tests are gradually being integrated into the licensing system in some countries (e.g., the United Kingdom and Australia). A most recent evaluation of their predictive power was conducted by Horswill, Hill, and Wetton (2015) in Queensland, Australia where a video-based hazard perception test is administered as part of the GDL process, just prior to the last phase of the restricted license, after the driver has already been driving (mostly supervised) for at least 22.5 months. Their study included over 33,000 young drivers who were administered the HP test. The test itself consisted of video clips shot from the perspective of a moving driver, and the role of the person tested was to indicate with the mouse whenever they saw a road-user who could create a traffic conflict. Following a year of driving, the self-reported crash records of those who passed the test were compared to those who failed, and the relative risk of a crash for those who passed the text was 25 percent lower than for those who failed it. Such a finding on such a large sample provides a strong argument for both training in hazard perception and testing for it as a part of the licensing process.

Managing Experience: Driver Education, Graduated Licensing, and Training in Hazard Perception

The primary implication from the consistent and persistent crash statistics that show the over-involvement of young novice drivers is that we need to identify interventions that would address the issues with which the novice young driver apparently fails to deal effectively. The times and opportunities for interventions that are already employed by government and non-government institutions to improve the safety of road users, are quite varied: from kindergarten education programs for child pedestrians, through elementary school programs for bicycling and pedestrian safety, through high school driver education programs, through various pre-licensing driver training programs, through the licensing tests of new drivers, and lately through post-licensing training and monitoring and post-licensing tests. Leaving the issue of pedestrians and bicyclists to a separate discussion (Chapters 15 and 17), safety-oriented interventions for young drivers that have been applied and extensively studied include driver education and training on specific skills, and provisional licensing with various restrictions such as nighttime restrictions, restrictions on carrying passengers, and zero tolerance for alcohol. A comprehensive approach that combines some or all of latter restrictions in an incremental fashion, the Graduated Driver Licensing (GDL) program, is rapidly gaining ground and is being incorporated into the licensing program in most countries of the western world. Various variations of the GDL that have been implemented (especially in North America) have also been evaluated. The following sections discuss in more details driver education programs, the GDL, and training in hazard perception.

Driver Education and Driver Training

Driver education is a structured program that is designed to provide the future driver with knowledge, attitudes, and skills that are necessary to safely operate a vehicle in traffic. These can be quite comprehensive as illustrated by the specific objectives listed by the British Royal Society for the Prevention of Accidents (RoSPA, 2002). According to RoSPA the goals of driver education, training, testing, and licensing are to:

1. Instill in young people the right attitudes toward road safety and safe driving.
2. Guide learner drivers to take a more structured approach to learning.
3. Prepare them for their driving career and not just to pass a test.
4. Raise the standard of tuition offered by driving instructors.
5. Improve the driving test in the light of better understanding about what needs to be examined and effective ways to do it.
6. Focus on the immediate post-test period for novice drivers.
7. Enhance the status of advanced motoring qualifications.

Interestingly the first goal is to shape the young person's attitude. This is important because a basic requirement for safe driving is to adjust to the notion of being part of a system (the traffic system), and that may be radically opposed to the rebellious, sensation-seeking, independent, risk taking attitudes that characterize many young people at the time they start to drive. Thus, driver education and training must address both the acquisition of fairly complex vehicle control skills and the necessary attitudinal changes that govern the desired driving style. Of the two, the former is probably easier. For example, even with the rudimentary simulators available over 40 years ago, Lucas, Heimstra, and Speigel (1973) demonstrated how training people to improve their distance estimation can improve passing behavior.

The actual education and training that drivers receive varies immensely from one jurisdiction to another: from no formal education in some places to highly structured education in others. In a review of the driver education and training that was required in 26 different countries (mostly western European countries), Groot *et al.* (2001) identified six different models of driver education and training. Ranging from the most formal and structured to the least structured, they are:

1. Theory and practical training at a driving school is necessary, with 1-54 theory lessons, and 8-40 practical lessons.
2. Theory and practical training at a driving school without any obligations. The average number of theory lessons is 5-25 hours, and the average number of practical lessons is 25-35 hours.
3. Theory and practical training must begin at a driving school, followed by training with a non-professional driver. Typically, there are some restrictions – such as age and number of years with license – that apply to the non-professional trainer.
4. Theory and practical training must begin at a driving school, followed by training with a non-professional supervisor, obliged to report regularly to the driving school.

5. Training with a non-professional supervisor, without the involvement of a driving school.
6. Training at a driving school with a non-professional supervisor, followed by a non-accompanied internship.

To make things a little more confusing, some countries allow more than one model, and it is up to the student (or the parents) to select the most convenient one.

In addition to the diversity in the approach to driver education, there is also a great diversity in the material content. The time allocated to learning different content areas and the time spent in different traffic environments in different countries is provided in Tables 6-2 and 6-3 (from Groot *et al.*, 2001). The immediate and unmistakable impression from the entries in both tables is that there are very significant differences in the emphasis that different countries place on different aspects of driving. This great variation is also a testimony to the disconcerting state of knowledge concerning the importance and benefits of different aspects of driver education and training at the turn of this century.

The concept of driving education itself is not new. The first driver education program was developed in 1916, and the first high school behind-the-wheel training was given by Neuhart in 1930 (Warner, 1972). In 1955, the first mandated high school driver education was initiated in Michigan (Engstrom *et al.*, 2003). Similar programs started to proliferate in the U.S., typically requiring 6 hours of behind-the-wheel instruction and 30 hours of classroom instruction. Initial evaluations of these programs seemed to suggest that they are quite effective in reducing teenagers' violation and crash rates, and insurance companies quickly jumped on the band wagon and encouraged participation in the programs by offering discounts on the insurance premiums for young novice drivers. However, as pointed out in a comprehensive "Driver Education Evaluation Program," submitted to the U.S. Congress by the National Highway Traffic Safety Administration (NHTSA, 1975), most of the early evaluation studies were methodologically flawed. In general, these studies were based on comparisons between young drivers who were offered or volunteered to participate in driver education programs and young drivers who did not volunteer to participate in these relatively expensive programs. Thus, there was a host of confounding variables that also distinguished between the two groups including motivation, personality and attitudes toward safety, socio-economic status, exposure, and demographic characteristics (see Shinar, 1978, for a review of the earlier studies).

To resolve the issue and provide a better evaluation of driver education, in 1978 the NHTSA initiated the most comprehensive experimental study to date of driver education. The 3-year study became known as the DeKalb County Study after the Atlanta, Georgia suburb in which it was done. The study is briefly described below, and more information about it can be found in the original report by Stock and his associates (1983) as well as in more recent comprehensive reviews of driver education (Engstrom *et al*, 2003; Mayhew and Simpson, 1996; NHTSA, 1994). The study had two significant and critical advantages over all of the previous studies: its sample was very large – 16,338 students from 24 high schools – and its design was experimental rather than observational in the sense that students were *randomly* assigned to one of three groups. The three groups were:

1. *Safe Performance Curriculum (SPC)*. This was a deluxe version of driver education and training. It consisted of a total of 70 hours of training, including 32 hours of classroom instruction, 16 hours of simulator training, 16 hours of closed course driving, 3.5 hours of training in evasive maneuvers, and 3.5 hours in on-the-road driving.
2. *Pre-Driver Licensing (PDL)*. This was a bare-bone minimalist version of driver education and it consisted of a total of 20 hours that included classroom, simulator, closed road training, and open road training accompanied by parents. It was designed to provide the student with the minimal skills and knowledge needed to pass the driving test.
3. *Control*. This group received no formal training. Instead the students were expected to be taught, either by their parents or a by a driver instructor, before passing the test.

The large sample provided statistical robustness to the findings, and the random assignment ruled out the potential confounding variables that plagued the earlier studies.

The results of the DeKalb evaluation were succinctly summarized in NHTSA's report to congress (1994): "Analysis at the random assignment level (includes all students, licensed or not) showed no significant differences between the mean number of crashes or convictions for students who received training (both SPC and PDL combined) compared to students who did not receive training during their first two years of driving." Looking only at those who were licensed, the students who received training initially had fewer crashes and violations, but by the end of the first year (for crashes) and 18 months (for violations) there were no significant differences among the three groups. Thus, the report concludes, "In summary, for all practical purposes, there was no significant reduction in crashes or traffic violations for those students who received training compared to students who received no formal training."

Because of these dismal conclusions, driver education lost much of its glamour and essentially went out of fashion. Still, there were occasional attempts to revive it and evaluate it. Vernick *et al.* (1999) analyzed the results of nine studies of driver education programs (including the DeKalb study) that they considered adequately designed, and still concluded that "there is no convincing evidence that high school driver education reduces motor-vehicle crash involvement rates for young drivers, either at the individual or community level. In fact, by providing an opportunity for early licensure, there is evidence that these courses are associated with higher crash involvement rates for young drivers." Mayhew and Simpson (2002) following a critical review of the existing research reached a similar conclusion. More recently Lonero and Mayhew (2010) conducted a detailed and extensive review of 17 driver education evaluation studies performed in the U.S. and in other countries between 1978 and 2007. Though they refrained from explicitly stating their own conclusion concerning the effectiveness of driver education they did note that "reviewers of the evaluation literature have typically concluded that

Table 6-2. Compulsory number of hours spent on select topics in the theory training in 20 different countries (*100 means that the subject is treated on a compulsory basis, but the exact number of hours is unknown. Original table included "documents," "loading," "first aid" and "environmental friendly driving") (from Groot *et al.*, 2001).

Country	Traff. Regul.	Driver	Road	Behav. to others	Vehic. Equip	Vehic. Tech.	Drugs, Med., Alcohol	Emergency Handling	Bad Weather Cond.
A	4	2	4	4	1	4	2	1	2
ALG									
B									
CH		*100	*100	*100	*100	*100	*100		*100
D	9	1.5	1	3	1.5	2	2	1	1.5
DK									
E									
EST	12	7	4	4	1	3	1	2	2
F									
FIN	5	1	2	2	1	1	1	1	2
GB									
GR	2		3	2.5	2	5	1	1.5	1
H	10	2	2	3	2	4	0.5	0.5	1
HR	11	1	2	4	1	1	1	1	2
IL									
LV	44	1	1	1.5	0.5	2	1	0.5	0.5
MAR									
N									
NI									
P	*100	*100	*100	*100			*100		*100

Table 6-3. Average number of hours spent in driving in different traffic environments as part of the practical training in 20 different countries (*100 means that the subject is treated on a compulsory basis, but the exact number of hours is unknown) (Groot *et al.*, 2001).

Country	Residential Areas	Inside Builtup Areas	Outside Builtup Areas	Motorways	Other Locations
A					
ALG		5	5		*100
B					
CH		*100	*100	*100	*100
D	4	10	6	4	3
DK					
E					
EST	5	10	6		
F					
FIN	6	6	1	4	4
GB					
GR	6	6		3	
H	1	13	4	*100	
HR	4	10	4	2	2
IL		*100	*100	*100	
LV		13	3		
MAR					
N	*100	*100	*100	*100	*100
NI					
P	*100	*100	*100	*100	*100

beginner driver education has yet to demonstrate clear success in improving safety of new drivers" (p. 38). However, they do suggest that programs that have a better grounding in theory, evaluations consisting of more relevant (intermediate) measures of effectiveness, and better evaluation study designs may yield different conclusions. A review of more recent evaluations of traditional driving education programs by Beanland and her associates (2013) also concluded that "traditional driver training programs have not reduced young drivers' crash risk." Allowing for the typical qualified scientific jargon, these two recent reviews of possibly all the evaluation studies that have been conducted and published in the open literature provide a very damning verdict for driver education.

One reason why driver education has failed to meet its proponents' expectations is that almost invariably taking this program is linked to incentives that may offset its benefits. The most common incentive is a significant reduction in the otherwise very high insurance premium costs. Hirsch and Maag (2006) argued that the insurance benefits can actually backfire by (1) increasing young drivers' exposure, because their cost of car ownership and licensure is reduced and (2) increasing their "moral hazard"; a careless attitude toward safety and crash avoidance. Some support for their argument was provided in a survey that they conducted of nearly 1,804 Canadian novice drivers. They found that those drivers who ranked the importance of the insurance discount as high were not only more needy of the monetary savings, but were also more likely to commit moving traffic violations, and had more tolerant attitudes toward speeding and other risk taking behaviors. Another incentive that has backfired is to lure novice drivers to take a formal driver education course with a shortened supervised driving period. As might have been expected from Maycock *et al.*'s (1991) model that shows the benefits of delays in licensing (Figure. 6-6), the net effect can be negative. In Canada a 6-month supervised driving requirement was reduced to 3 months for those who completed an approved driver education program, and consequently drivers who opted for that option were eligible for a full license much earlier than those who did not. Consequently, one evaluation study on Canadian drivers, discussed in more details below (Wiggins, 2005), revealed that teenagers who took the driver education course and were then given a shorter period of supervised driving actually had higher rates of violations and crashes.

Still, the possibility remains that if formal driver education is properly directed it may be beneficial. At the very least it seems to increase the likelihood of passing the driving test (Nyberg, Gregersen, and Wiklund, 2007). There is also some evidence that training with a properly designed driving simulator program may transfer to safer driving. Hirsch and Bellavance (2016) compared the post-licensing performance of 2,187 Quebec, Canada young drivers who received six hours of driving in a simulator with an age- and gender-matched group who received the equivalent on-road hours of training. In their on-road examination the simulator-trained drivers obtained higher scores, and in their first 2 years of unsupervised driving they had fewer violations than the drivers who had not trained with the simulator. However, no difference was found between the two groups in their crash involvement. While these findings may be unique to the specific simulator training program and the relative amounts of on-road and simulated driving, they do demonstrate that driver education and training may be improved to actually provide us with safer young drivers. For example, a consistently demonstrated benefit of safety-oriented training is the case of training in hazard perception (see below).

A less optimistic view is that it is a bit naïve to expect driver education to significantly affect driver safety. After all, the primary motivation of the students is to obtain the driver license and its concomitant mobility and independence, and not to increase their safety. The schools – at least in some cases – are also primarily concerned with their success as measured in the percent of their students who pass the licensing test. Thus, the driving forces behind the administration and the implementation of driver education may be very different than the safety community's desires to use it to increase safety. Perhaps an alignment of goals of all participants may change the program impact. In fact, this kind of thinking would suggest that the Swedish "insight training" and "risk assessment" approach may be much more fruitful than the traditional mix of knowledge and vehicle handling. This, however, still has to be convincingly demonstrated (Beanland, Goode, Salmon, and Lenne, 2013).

Graduated Driver Licensing (GDL): Integrating Driver Education, Training, and Licensing

Pre GDL programs

Over the past three decades more and more jurisdictions around the world adopted what has been generically labeled as "graduated driver licensing," or in short GDL. The basic philosophy behind this approach is to gradually – by stages – introduce the novice driver to the driving environment, minimizing the risks involved at each stage, and building on good driving habits acquired in the previous states. In discussing the evolution of the GDL, Simpson (2003) distinguishes between the GDL and three other approaches to licensing: conventional, probationary, and provisional, each having its own strengths and shortcomings, as described below.

The conventional approach consists of three phases. The first phase is to require that the candidate pass a written test and a vision test, the second phase is supervised driving, and the final phase is a behind-the-wheel test that – once passed – qualifies the person to drive without any limitations. This approach does not recognize the complexities of skills needed for driving under a myriad of circumstances, and ignores the young driver's attitude toward driving. It only evaluates driving performance, and cannot assess the driver's typical behavior. It licenses drivers before that behavior has been shaped by better understanding of the driving task and the driving environment. The over-involvement of young novice drivers in crashes is a strong incentive to abandon this approach in favor of others.

The probationary approach adds a period – immediately after the licensing – in which it takes fewer violations demerit points to lose a license. Examples include zero tolerance for alcohol, and the requirement for fewer violations or violation-free record. The assumption behind this approach is that young drivers *consciously* commit high-risk behaviors. Thus, the primary force behind this approach is motivation through deterrence. However, if some violations are committed because of errors or inexperience rather than volition (as McKnight and McKnight, 2003, demonstrated), then suspending a license only further reduces the young driver's exposure and consequently reduces his or her chances to improve. Several evaluations of the probationary licensing approach have not shown that it is effective in crash reduction (Simpson, 2003).

The provisional licensing approach differs from the probationary approach in that its underlying assumption is that the novice driver's over-involvement in crashes is primarily due to lack of skills in handling high risk situations. Consequently, it limits the novice driver's exposure to such situations. A common example is the curfew on night driving and restrictions on carrying passengers in the first few months after licensing. Unfortunately, the few evaluations that have been conducted on provisional licensing programs have not provided consistent results that would indicate a significant benefit in crash reduction (Simpson, 2003).

Characteristics of the GDL

GDL combines most of the elements of all of the three licensing approaches. The fundamental objective of GDL is to "provide new drivers with the opportunity to gain driving experience under conditions that minimize risk" (Simpson, 2003). Thus, a good GDL will enhance skill acquisition by providing the drivers with many driving experiences, yet ensure that this exposure is controlled in such a way that high risk situations are only gradually introduced once the driver has mastered (or at least has become quite familiar) with less risky situations. This is not easy to accomplish. It is achieved, to some extent, through a core ingredient that is common to all GDL programs: a post-licensing supervised learning phase. A schematic representation of a "good" GDL program – on the basis of cumulative experimental evidence and expert opinion is provided in Figure 6-12 (Mayhew, Williams, and Pashley, 2014).

To qualify as a GDL a licensing program will generally incorporate at least two concepts: distributed learning over time and a progression from simple to complex skills (Waller, 2003). The implementation of these concepts typically involves the following components:

1. A learner stage in which the young driver is expected to learn the basic vehicle handling skills and basic rules of the road. At this stage driving is supervised by either a trained instructor or an experienced licensed driver. Before, during, or at the end of this phase the learner will also be given a vision test (see Chapter 4).
2. A written test and a driving test administered by the state. The written test assesses knowledge of rules of the road and various aspects of prudent driver behavior, while the driving test assesses the candidate's ability to handle a vehicle (but not necessarily in traffic).
3. A provisional license stage which has various restrictions on the license. Often this stage is also supervised, but this time the supervision is not by a licensed instructor but by a licensed experienced driver, most often a parent. A key assumption and goal of this phase is that in addition to honing the basic driving skills, the young driver will also adopt some of the more mature attitudes of the parent. This seems to be a valid

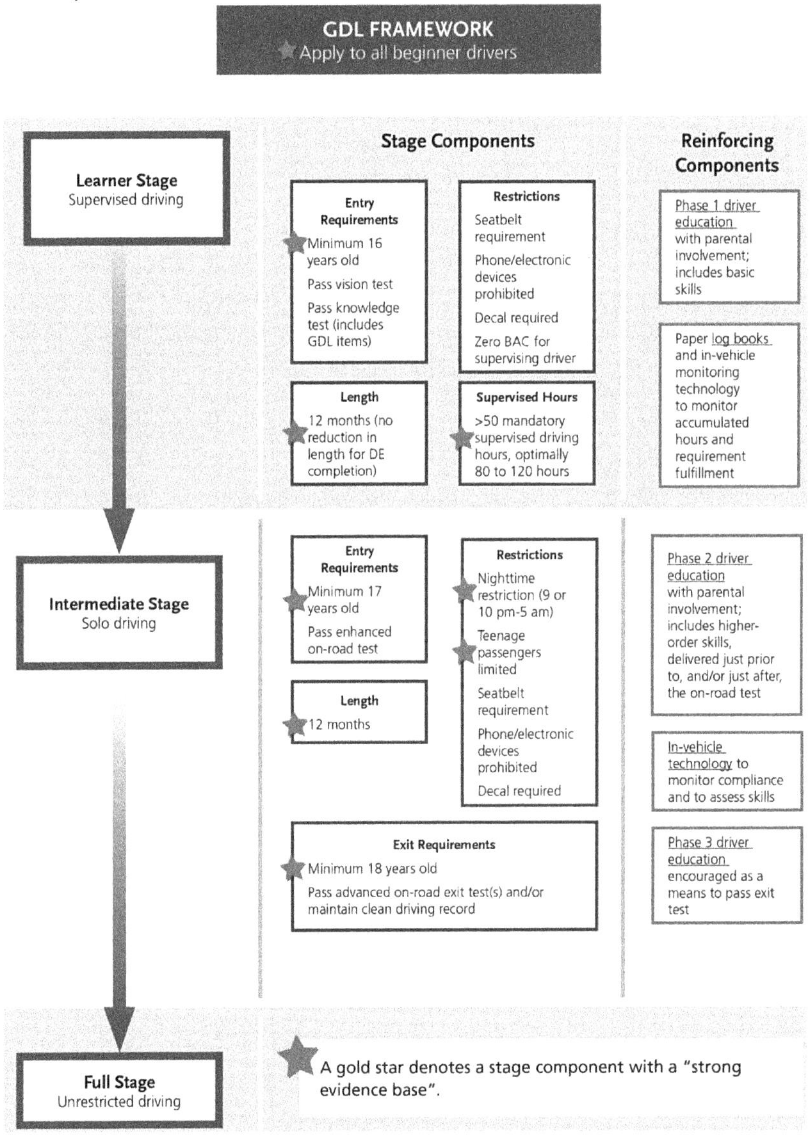

Figure 6-12. A schematic representation of a "good" GDL program (from Mayhew *et al.*, 2014, with permission from the Traffic Injury Research Foundation).

assumption. An analysis of the videoed conversations between parents and their teen drivers during this stage in a naturalistic driving study indeed showed that most of the conversations were driving related (61 percent) and the most common of these comments were about vehicle handling and operation (53 percent) (Goodwin *et al.*, 2014). This phase may also have additional restrictions designed to reduce the young driver's exposure to proven high-risk situations. Situations that have been identified as such

include carrying passengers in the car (Chen *et al.*, 2000; Howard, 2004; Keall, Frith, and Patterson, 2004; Preusser, Ferguson, and Williams, 1998), driving after drinking (Hyman, 1968), and driving at night (Preusser *et al.*, 1984).
4. A full license, which may be granted either automatically after the time limit of the provisional license has passed, or after the supervisor signs a statement of completion of the required supervised hours, or after an additional driving test.

The first GDL program was introduced in New Zealand in 1987. Since then there has been a gradual adoption of the GDL in North America where by 2011 all Canadian provinces and all U.S. states had some form of GDL. Australia, New Zealand and many European countries also have GDL programs in place (Hinchcliff *et al.*, 2010; Masten, Foss, and Marshall, 2011). The specific components for each stage – especially stages 1 and 3 – vary widely among jurisdictions, but there are converging data to indicate which aspects are critical and which may be superfluous. Based on the evaluation research up to the early 2000s, the Traffic Injury Research Foundation of Canada and the Insurance Institute of Highway Safety of the U.S. have formulated a list of practices that should be included in each of the two critical phases (IIHS, 2003). These recommendations include a 6-month learner phase with a minimum of 30-50 hours of certified driving with a supervisor and an intermediate phase (phase 3) that extends at least till the age of 18. In this phase driving should be initially supervised and then followed by restricted nighttime driving and no more than one passenger in the absence of an adult supervisor in the car.

The GDL is the most significant change in driver education and training in the past 50 years, and the obvious question that needs to be answered, is how beneficial is it? Like the driver education programs promoted 50 years ago it was designed with the notion that minimal handling skills are not sufficient for safe driving, and both programs stressed training with a supervised instructor. However, the GDL also recognizes that when the new driver passes the "test" (phase 2) he or she is not yet prepared to deal with all the complexities of driving. But does the remediation, in the form of additional supervised driving and limits on the driving to lower-risk situations, really help? Extensive amount of research designed to answer this question has shown that it is effective, but with a large caveat, as will be described below.

Evaluations of the GDL

As part of an early comprehensive review of the evolution of the GDL, Simpson (2003) and Mayhew, Simpson, and Singhal (2005) summarized the results of 13 studies that evaluated different GDL programs in different states in the U.S., and five studies that evaluated the GDL in different provinces in Canada. Two conclusions emerged from this review: (1) all the evaluation studies showed that the program is effective to some extent and (2) the degree of effectiveness varies tremendously – from 2 to 60 percent. These conclusions raise two questions: what makes the GDL effective and why the huge differences?

The variability in effectiveness among the programs can be attributed to at least two factors: the differences among the programs (as one would expect) and the statistical techniques used for the evaluations (as one would probably not suspect). Some indication of the contribution of the latter is provided by the very many different measures of effectiveness such as absolute number of crashes and injuries, per capita crash and injury rates, and per licensed drivers crash and injury rates. One of the most important distinctions that should be made is between the crash rates per driver and the crash rates per capita in the relevant age group. When the program's impact is evaluated on the raw number of crashes or the crashes per capita, part of the effect may due to the GDL's impact on the driver but part of the effect is simply due to the fact that GDL effectively delays licensing and reduces exposure. Consequently, fewer drivers in the youngest age groups are exposed to crashes and the reduction in the crash rate per capita is simply due to the spurious increase in the denominator. In the U.S., for example, the first GDL program was introduced in Florida in 1996, and by 2003 it was part of the licensing program in 46 states and the District of Columbia. This was reflected in the parallel decrease in the percent of 16-year-old drivers who were licensed – that dropped from 43 percent in 1995 to 31 percent in 2003 – and a decrease in per capita crash rates from 3.5 to 2.3 crashes per million 16-year-old people between 1995 and 2003. Unfortunately, the rates of fatal crashes or fatalities *per number of drivers* did not change at all over that period (Williams, Ferguson, and Wells, 2005). Nonetheless, the results of the studies reviewed by Simpson (2003) and Mayhew *et al.* (2005) that used per driver crash rates also yielded large GDL effects indicating that there are program effects on the drivers themselves (though even with respect to drivers-based rates, once the GDL is implemented, the 16-year-old drivers drive unsupervised for fewer months at that age).

To highlight the complexities and potential of the GDL, two of the studies reviewed by Simpson (2003) and Mayhew *et al.* (2005) are described below in some detail. The first study by Masten and Hagge (2004) provides a good illustration of the benefits and the complexities involved in teasing out valid measures of effectiveness. Their analyses focused on the impact of different components of the California GDL program on teen crashes that resulted in injuries or fatalities. They used time-series analysis, which is a technique to test for deviations from a trend over time. With this technique certain known confounding effects that are not under experimental control can be eliminated (e.g., seasonal effects), and a test is then done to see if a particular variable, such as a GDL component (whose time of introduction is known to the researchers) has a significant effect, in a sense that it changes the temporal trend. To rule out extraneous effects from other confounding variables they compared the crashes of 15- to 17-year-old drivers who participated in the GDL with crashes of older drivers 24-55 years old, over the same time period. The "bottom line" of their findings was that they did not find a significant overall effect of the GDL on injury and fatal crashes. However, they did obtain statistically significant positive (albeit, in their opinion, small) effects of the nighttime curfew (9 percent drop in nighttime injury/fatality crashes), and the passenger restrictions (14 percent drop in injury/fatality crashes).

These findings of Masten and Hagge (2004) raise as many questions as they answer. First, the size of the curfew effect must be evaluated in the context of the specific restriction in California, which only prohibited driving between midnight and 5 am. However, even without GDL only 5 percent of the young drivers' crashes occur within those hours, and most nighttime crashes occur earlier. Second, the effectiveness of the passenger restrictions was probably underestimated because the California law did not totally ban carrying any passengers, but only prohibited carrying passengers under the age of 20, and that restriction is waived if one of the passengers is 25 years old or older. Third, there is an apparent inconsistency between the absence of an overall effect and the presence of passenger and nighttime restriction effects. The authors attribute this paradox to the different statistical methods used to assess the overall effect (which involved a comparison to an older control group), and the methods used to assess the individual component effects in which only young drivers were used. Finally, a paradoxical finding is the lack of effect for the increased supervised learner phase from one month to 6 months. The explanation for this comes from an earlier investigation of the California licensing process that revealed that this requirement for prolonged supervision did not postpone the actual licensing age, but simply caused teenagers to apply earlier for their learner permit in order to still qualify for their license at the minimum age of 16.

The Masten and Hagge (2004) study illustrates all of the complexities that an evaluation of a GDL entails. It underscores the point that the benefits of GDL and its components can therefore not be judged on the basis of one study, as well controlled as it is, but on the basis of the weight of the evidence. And on that basis GDL is a qualified success.

The second study, by Wiggins (2005), evaluated the GDL program enacted in British Columbia, Canada. Wiggens had a very large database that enabled her to make some very detailed analyses: the driving records of 45,822 drivers who participated in a newly enacted GDL program (labeled GLP – Graduated License Program) and 67,086 young drivers who obtained their license just before the GLP went into effect (labeled Pre-GLP). The GDL program has an extended "learner" period of 6 months, with a 3 months discount for those taking the approved driver education program. During the learner period all the driving is supervised by an older licensed person. This phase ends with a road test, and is followed by an additional 18 months of a "novice" license, when supervision is not required but various restrictions still apply. Passing a second road test after that phase qualifies the driver as a fully licensed driver. Based on surveys, it appears that compliance with the license restrictions was very high (with a 3.4 percent self-reported rate of breaches per learner-years at the learner phase, and 11.8 percent at the novice phase). A comparison of the crash rates between those who had the GDL program and a matched group (by age and gender and the time they obtained their full license) showed that the GDL was beneficial at the learner stage, where the GDL drivers had a 10 percent lower crash involvement rate, but not at the novice driver stage where the two groups had the same crash rates, suggesting that the learner stage restrictions are more important than the novice stage restrictions. Figure 6-13 shows the crash rates of the two driver groups from the time each driver got his or her learner permit. As can be seen in that figure, during the supervised learner phase both groups had near zero crashes. However, as soon as this phase ended – sooner for the Non-GDL drivers than for the GDL drivers – the crash rate jumped from near zero to approximately 40 crashes per 1,000 months per driver; i.e., nearly one crash per two years of driving. When the crash rates were plotted relative to the time of obtaining the novice driver license (Figure 6-14), the near identity of crash involvement of the two groups became apparent.

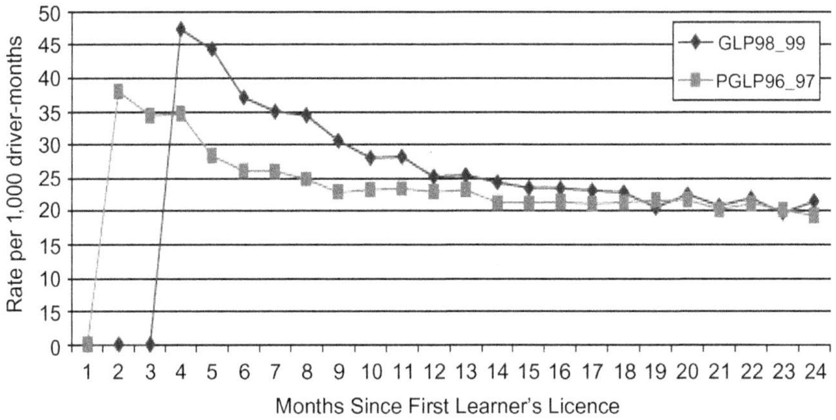

Figure 6-13. The effect of time since first obtaining a *learner permit* on crash rates for GDL drivers (GLP) and non-GDL drivers (PGL) (from Wiggins, 2005, with permission from the Insurance Corporation of British Columbia).

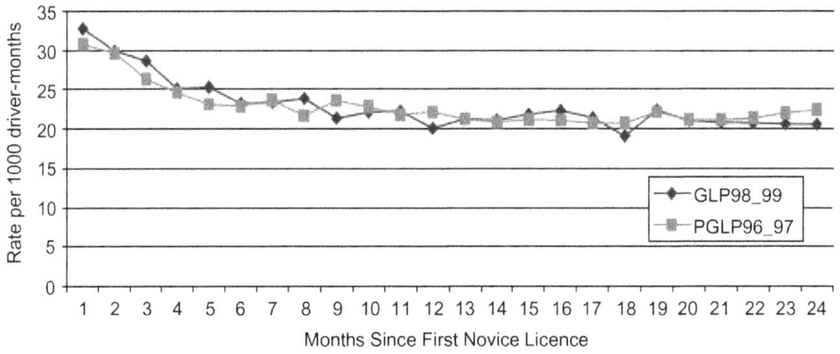

Figure 6-14. The effect of time since first obtaining a *driver license* on crash rates for GDL drivers (GLP) and non-GDL drivers (PGL) (from Wiggins, 2005, with permission from the Insurance Corporation of British Columbia).

Wiggins' evaluation also provided some more insight into the benefits – or lack of benefits – of driver education. The British Columbia GDL included a formal driver education program as an option. Those who elected to take this option, were then allowed a learning period of only 3 months instead of 6. Interestingly, the combination of a shortened learner phase with structured driver education actually resulted in a significantly higher crash rate than that of those who retained the learner license for the full duration instead of taking the course. This is illustrated in Figure 6-15 where the crash rate is presented relative to the date the driver obtained the learner permit. It can be seen that drivers who took the driver education program and presented a declaration of completion of the course demonstrated a sharp increase in their crash rate 3 months after obtaining the learner permit – presumably at the time they were eligible for the probationary license without the parental supervision. Those who did not take the driver education course, demonstrated a similar pattern – but the increase in their crash rate started only on the seventh month – when they first became eligible for the license.

It is hard to tell from Figure 6-15, whether or not the difference between the two groups persisted after full licensing, and if so for how long. To determine that, Wiggins provided the crash rate of the two groups from the time each driver received the license itself. These data are plotted in Figure 6-16, where it is obvious that driver education – when combined with the shortened supervised period – actually had a negative net effect.

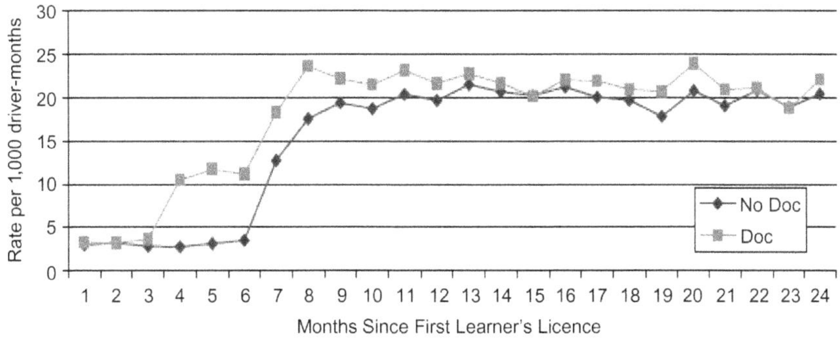

Figure 6-15. Crash rates as a function of time since obtaining a *learner permit*, of GDL drivers who took driver education and were eligible for a 3-month learning period (Doc), and GDL drivers who did not take driver education and completed 6 months of supervised learning period (from Wiggins, 2005, with permission from the Insurance Corporation of British Columbia).

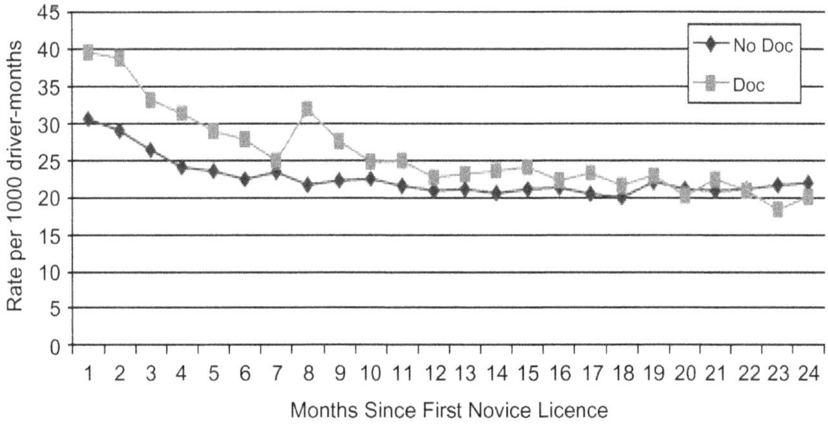

Figure 6-16. The crash rates as a function of time since obtaining a *driver license*, of GDL drivers who took driver education and were eligible for a 3-month learning period (Doc) and GDL drivers who did not take driver education and completed at least 6 months of supervised learning period (age- and gender-adjusted) (from Wiggins, 2005, with permission from the Insurance Corporation of British Columbia).

Wiggins' analysis demonstrated that drivers who completed their approved driver education program actually had a *higher* risk of violations and a *higher* risk of crashes. During the first year of the novice driver phase the crash risk of drivers who completed the driver education course was actually 26 percent higher (per years-driving) than that of young drivers who did not take the approved driver education course. Over a 2-year period it was still 18 percent higher. Consequently, if driver education is beneficial, it does not offset the benefits of added supervised driving and should not replace it.

It is important to stress that Wiggins' detailed analyses do not demonstrate that driver education is a bad thing as much as they demonstrate the difficulty of evaluating it. This is so for two reasons. First, unlike the GDL evaluation where the GDL and non-GDL programs applied equally to all potential drivers, and thus the samples were comparable, in the case of the driver education, because the drivers elected to choose it, all the potential confounding variables that existed in the early driver education evaluation studies existed here too. Second, driver education may have been useful, but either in aspects not immediately reflected in crash rates – such as better knowledge of the different road markings and signs – or not enough to counterbalance 3 months of supervised driving.

As more and more jurisdictions adopted the GDL, more and more evaluation studies surfaced. In a comprehensive review of the studies published between 2007 and 2010 on GDL effectiveness, Williams and Shults (2010), concluded that "it is clear from the entire body of evaluations to date that there are strong crash-reduction effects in the populations specifically addressed by GDL" (p. 79); that is, mostly the 16-year-old drivers. However, Williams and Shults also acknowledged that the long-term effects when these drivers turn 18 are quite controversial. In a later review Williams, Tefft, and Grabowski (2012) essentially reiterated the same conclusions, stating that "GDL, especially the systems that are most comprehensive, reduces all types of crashes in the age groups directly affected by the rules. In particular, all GDL evaluations indicate that 16-year-old driver crash rates have been sharply reduced." In the U.S. three independent reviews, using different methodologies concluded that for 16-year-old drivers, the comprehensive GDL programs are quite effective. Using quarterly fatality data from all 50 states Masten *et al.* (2011) did a time-series analyses comparing states with strong GDL programs (with restrictions of night time driving and of carrying passengers) with states that had no GDL programs and found a difference in crash rates of 16-year-old drivers of 26 percent. McCartt *et al.* (2010) did a Poisson regression analysis on the fatality rates of different age groups and found that 16-year-old drivers had on the average a 41 percent lower fatality rate in states that had "good" licensing programs than in states that had "poor" licensing laws (see Table 6-4 for definitions of program quality). Zhu *et al.* (2013) did a meta-analysis of all crashes in 11 U.S. states and one Canadian province and obtained a 22 percent reduction in all 16 years old crashes. These impressive reductions must, however, be weighed against the typical sharp increase in crash and fatality rates that occur once all the restrictions are lifted (in the U.S. it is by the age of 18). For example, in parallel with the fatality reductions for 16-year-old drivers, Masten *et al.* found a 12 percent increase in the rate of fatal crashes for 18-year-old drivers, and Zhu et al. and McCartt et al. essentially found no remaining significant positive effects of GDL for this age group.

Table 6-4. The U.S. Insurance Institute for Highway Safety's criteria for defining the quality of the GDL program (from McCartt *et al.*, 2010, with permission from Taylor and Francis, LLC, http://www.tandfonline.com.).

		Points[a]
Learner's phase		
Minimum permit age	16 or older	1 point
	Less than 16	0 points
Permit holding period	6 or more months	2 points
	3-5 months	1 point
	Less than 3 months	0 points
Required practice hours	30 or more hours	1 point
	Less than 30 hours	0 points
Intermediate phase		
Restriction on night driving	10 pm or earlier	2 points
	After 10 pm	1 point
	No restriction	0 points
Restriction on underage passengers	Zero or 1 passenger	2 points
	2 passengers	1 point
	3 or more passengers or no restriction	0 points
Duration of night driving restriction	12 months or more from minimum licensing age	1 point
	Less than 12 months	0 points
Duration of passenger restriction	12 months or more from minimum licensing age	1 point
	Less than 12 months	0 points

Table 6-4. (*Continued*)

		Points[a]
Graduated licensing rating[b]	Points	
Good	6 or more points	
Fair	4-5 points	
Marginal	2-3 points	
Poor	Less than 2 points	

[a]Where completion of driver education changes a requirement, point values are determined for the driver education track.
[b]Regardless of point totals, no state is rated above marginal if intermediate licensing age is younger than 16 or if night driving and passenger restrictions are both lifted before age 161/2.

All of the crash and injury rates used in the evaluations above referred to crashes per capita or per driver. However, it remains to be determined if the reduced rates are due to fewer crashes per mile driven or to fewer crashes in absolute numbers. This is because with the GDL part of the reduced exposure may be in terms of fewer miles driven. In a quest to resolve this issue, Zhu *et al.* (2015) compared the U.S. fatality rates (per capita) relative to the annual average miles driven by 16- to 18-year-old drivers before their states instituted a GDL program with the ratio after the institution of GDL. As did other studies reported above, they found that the 16-year-old drivers had fewer fatal crashes per person-year, but those who participated in the GDL also drove fewer miles. Consequently they concluded that the net effect of the GDL on fatal crashes is about half of the total reduction, the remaining half being due to less driving. For the 17 and 18 years old there were no GDL effects on fatal crashes per miles driven. Thus, this study confirms the previous evaluations that the GDL does reduce crash risk (at least fatal crashes) but the reduction is short lived and limited to the first year of driving only. Considering that the first year of license is the most dangerous one this is still a very significant benefit.

Importance of the number of GDL components

An evaluation of the GDL as a function of the number of its components was made by Baker, Chen, and Li (2006). In their analyses they compared the fatality rates of drivers exposed to various GDL programs with the fatality rates of drivers not exposed to any GDL. Their data base was quite extensive – all young driver fatalities in 43 U.S. states, from 1994 to 2004, grouped into quarterly-annual periods, totaling 1,480 state quarters. Their principal findings are displayed in Figure 6-17, where the fatal crash involvement rates are plotted separately for three age groups, as a function of the comprehensiveness of the GDL program in effect. Note that "fatal crash involvement rate" is the number of fatal crashes with drivers in that age group per 100,000 person-years of people in that age group. Thus,

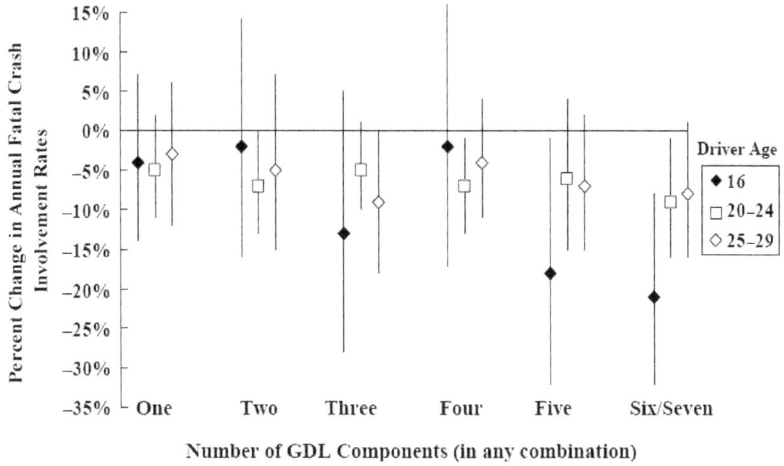

Figure 6-17. Percent change in annual fatal crash involvement rate in relation to number of GDL program components, compared to state quarters with none of the seven components, for drivers age 16, 20-24, and 25-29; U.S., 1994-2004. Vertical lines represent 95-percent confidence limits (from Baker *et al.*, 2006).

the fatality rates refer to all fatal crashes involving young drivers, regardless of who was killed in the crash. The comprehensiveness of the GDL programs was based on the number of GDL components out of the following seven: minimum age for learner permit, mandatory waiting period, minimum hours of supervised driving, minimum entry age for intermediate stage, minimum age for full licensing, nighttime restriction, and passenger restriction.

The results were quite convincing: with overall effectiveness being 11 percent reduction in crash fatality rates for 16-year-old drivers. The most compelling finding was that the number of components was critical so that only states with five or more components had statistically significant reductions, with impressive rates of 18-21 percent. Note that the number of components was immaterial for the two older driver groups, because the drivers in these groups were not covered in any of the GDL programs. In terms of the most effective components, the authors concluded that the most beneficial components were age requirements plus 3 or more months of waiting before the intermediate stage, nighttime driving restriction, and either supervised driving of at least 30 hours or a passenger restriction. A recent meta-analysis of the effectiveness of 14 evaluation studies conducted in the U.S. (Masten *et al.*, 2015) was also unable to determine which are the most important components, but was able to show that as a whole the GDL is effective; with significant relative risk reductions per driver for the 16- and 17-year-old drivers but not for the older ones.

Importance of specific GDL components

If GDL is effective – at least during the supervisory phase – then how important are the specific requirements of night curfew, passenger limits, and zero tolerance for alcohol? The relative contribution of different restrictions of the GDL is hard to assess because all the GDL evaluation studies are observational in their design rather than experimental. In no state or country is a GDL program assigned on a random basis to some of the drivers while non-GDL programs are assigned to others, as should be done in a well-controlled experimental study. Thus all of the evaluations have to rely on differences over time (before and after the implementation of the GDL, or before and after implementation of various GDL-like restrictions), or on differences between GDL states and non-GDL (control) states. As in the early evaluations of the driver education program, this allows for a host of confounding variables to affect the results. Recently, however, using sophisticated statistical techniques to disaggregate the effects of various components of the GDL, we have gained some understanding as to which of the GDL components are more effective and which ones are less effective, but with the insights that we gain from these analyses we also see the difficulty of arriving at solid estimates for the effects.

An interesting way of estimating the effectiveness of the GDL was devised by the U.S. Insurance Institute of Highway Safety (McCartt *et al.*, 2010). It categorized the various GDL programs on the basis of their quality as good, adequate, marginal, and poor – as defined in Table 6-4 above. The parameters for the evaluation are (1) the minimum permit age at which a teenager can begin driving, (2) the duration of the learner (supervised) period, (3) the number of supervised driving hours, and (4) the post-licensing restrictions in terms of night driving, and prohibitions on transporting teen passengers during the intermediate licensing period. Using quarterly insurance claims and U.S. crash fatality data for the years 1996-2007, they calculated the risk reductions as a function of changes in these parameters. Although they demonstrated that each of these restrictions can reduce the fatality rate of the 16- to 17-year-old drivers by some amount, the greatest benefits come from combining them. For example, for 16-year-old drivers their model estimates of the fatality rates of states with "good" laws was 41 percent lower than for states with "poor" GDL laws, and for states with "fair" GDL laws it was 18 percent lower than for states with "poor" GDL laws. Going out a bit on a limb, the IIHS also published an online calculator that estimates for each of the U.S. states the expected benefits (or loss) when any of the five GDL components is enhanced (or compromised), relative to its present GDL program (www.iihs.org/gdl).

The most recent analysis of the existing literature on the benefits of each of the components, by Senserrick and Williams (2015), is fairly consistent with the conclusions of McCartt *et al.* (2010), but suggests that for maximal effects the learning phase should be extended to 12 months (implying a recommended provisional license at a minimum age of 17), that greater benefits are attained with 80 supervised hours, and that the benefits of the night driving restrictions increase as the start time for "night" is moved to an earlier hour. Senserrick and Williams also observe that the benefits of a GDL program increase when it includes zero or lower-than-standard tolerance for alcohol, and when the licensing or post-licensing test includes a hazard perception test. They also note that additional issues – the formal requirements of the supervisor in the supervised phase, the nature of the license tests, the minimal duration of the provisional period, and restrictions on mobile phone use – have been discussed in the literature but no conclusions based on robust evaluations can be drawn at this stage.

In their 2010 study reported above, McCartt *et al.* also estimated the benefits of the individual GDL components in terms of the percent reductions of fatality rates. Their estimates in terms of percent reduction in fatal crash rates involving 15- to 17-year-old drivers are reproduced in Table 6-5. Note that these effects are quite large: 21 percent reduction when no teen passengers are allowed, 20 percent when with a driving curfew

Table 6-5. Estimated percentage changes in fatal crash rates (per 100,000 teen agers) for 15- to 17-year-old drivers associated with specific GDL components (from McCartt *et al.*, 2010, with permission from Taylor and Francis, LLC, (http://www.tandfonline.com).

GDL Component	Percentage Change
Delaying age of licensure	
1 month	−1
6 months	−7
1 year	−13
Restriction on teen passengers vs. no restriction or 2 + teen passengers	
None allowed	−21
1 allowed	−7
Night driving restriction	
8 pm	−20
9 pm	−18
10 pm	−16
11 pm	−14
Midnight	−12
1 am	−9
Delaying age of permit	
1 month	−1
6 months	−7
1 year	−13

beginning at 8 pm, and 13 percent when either the licensing age or the permit age are delayed by 1 year. Fell, Todd, and Voas (2011) used the U.S. Fatal Analysis Reporting System and implementation of GDL laws on a state-by-state level and found that nighttime curfew reduced 16- to 17-year-old drivers' involvement in fatal crashes by 10 percent, and the passenger restriction rules reduced their rate of crashes with teen passengers by nine percent. Though these findings are positive they may only reflect the reduced exposure of the teen drivers to these restrictive conditions. If this is the case, then no long-term effects of these restrictions should be expected. Unfortunately, Fell and his associates did not examine these longer term effects (and also unfortunately, with the few exceptions noted below, neither did most other studies).

It is also interesting to note that McCartt *et al.* (2010) did not obtain a significant effect of increasing the length of the learner period beyond one month or setting a minimum number of supervised hours (above 30). This is despite the fact that these two factors are included in their model. Ehsani, Bingham, and Shope (2013a) evaluated the specific effects of learner license duration and required hours of supervision by studying the change in 16- to 17-year-old fatal crash rates in states that introduced these specific components independently of others. They found that the pooled effect in all the states studied was not statistically significant and the effects of the minimal learner/supervised phase duration of 6 months were very modest – a 7 percent drop). Thus, this study in effect corroborated McCartt *et al.*'s (2010) model suggesting that these two specific components are less important than the others. One possibility for the lack of effect of the number of supervision hours is that it is simply not observed by the parents. O'Brien *et al.* (2013), after failing to find a reduction in injury and fatal crashes that could be attributed to the state's requirement of 30 hours of supervision, decided to probe further and interviewed parents in five states that required a certain minimum of hours of supervised driving and found that in four of them most parents were not able to state the required number of hours, and in one state – Maryland, which was the only state that required that the parents keep a log book of the hours – a little over half of the parents knew the number of hours. In a review of European studies of the effects of parental supervision on post-licensing crash statistics Simons-Morton and Ouimet (2006) concluded the findings are inconclusive. However, none of the studies reviewed was based on randomized assignment, and the supervision was a part of different GDL programs, of different lengths and controls. Consequently it was difficult to arrive at a conclusion concerning "supervision" in the generic sense. In summary, this component could be significant, if only it were actually observed by the parents and the number of supervised hours was extensive (as it was in a Swedish study that obtained significant effects following an average of 120 hours of parental supervision – probably much beyond the tolerance of most American parents).

In an interesting evaluation of the parental supervisory and guidance role Lotan and her colleagues (Taubman-Ben-Ari and Lotan, 2011; Toledo *et al.*, 2012) compared the crash involvement of two groups of young drivers in Israel. Both groups operated under the Israeli modified GDL program that required that no driving be done without parental supervision in the first 3 months of license. However, the drivers in the treatment group were part of a volunteer program that included face-to-face 45-minute meetings of safety experts with the parents and the novice drivers. In the meeting they provided the family with best practices of safe driving and also gave the parents and teen drivers tips on how to deal with in-vehicle parent-teen dynamics. In the study by Toledo *et al.* there were 44,454 drivers in the treatment group and 86,111 drivers in the matched control group. As found in other studies mentioned above, during the 3 months of parental supervision both groups were involved in very few crashes. Also as found elsewhere, crash rates increased immediately after that stage. However, the rate of injury crashes (per 1,000 drivers) was nearly 13 percent lower in the treatment group. A difference that was both statistically and practically highly significant. Furthermore, this study demonstrated that parental supervision can be highly effective for a long time (in this case up to 13 months post-licensing) even if the intervention itself is very short and administered only once at the start of a short parentally supervised phase. Interviews conducted by Taubman-Ben-Ari and Lotan also showed that the teen drivers who participated in the parental discussions also had more favorable attitudes toward the supervisory phase. Thus, both studies demonstrated that it is the quality of the supervision and not its quantity that counts, something that is of great practical importance for jurisdictions and parents with low tolerance for long-term chaperoning.

In summary, the weight of the evidence from the different studies suggests that to be effective, a GDL program has to incorporate many of the safety-critical restrictions, the most effective being age limits plus a significant initial learning period of supervised driving, nighttime restriction and teen-passenger prohibition. Despite its frequent reported violations, zero tolerance for alcohol – as well as other laws targeted at reducing underage drinking (Fell *et al.*, 2016) – also seems to be effective in crash reduction, and so – to a lesser extent – is the restriction on passengers (Engstrom *et al.*, 2003). Alcohol restriction does not feature in the evaluations done of U.S. GDL programs, simply because all U.S. states have zero tolerance for all drivers under 21 years old. In the U.S. where all states and the District of Columbia now have some form of GDL, Williams, McCartt, and Sims (2016) note that over the past 20 years nearly all states have upgraded their DGL to include more of the proven GDL components.

In what is possibly the most extensive evaluation of the merits of the different GDL components, Masten, Foss, and Marshall (2013), examined the fatal crash involvement of 16- to 17-year-old drivers as a function of the program in which they were involved in all U.S. states from 1986 to 2007. For their dependent measure they used population based crash rates rather than driver based rates (i.e., per capita versus per driver). Thus, their reported benefits did include the effects of reduced exposure (see discussion above). By correlating the crash rates with the different GDL programs relative to their components on a quarterly basis they were able to tease out the relative benefits of each component. Thus, with 22 years, four quarters per year, and 51 jurisdictions (50 states plus Washington, DC) worth of data they had a total of 4,488 individual crash rates on which to evaluate the GDL – a sufficient sample size by any standard. They found that the effectiveness of the different components varied, and was, in general, greater for the 16-year-old drivers than for the 17 years old. The most effective components were (1) a minimum learner permit (supervised driving) period of 9-12 months and (2) restrictions to carrying one teen passenger for 6 months or more. After adjusting for some confounding variables these two components yielded average reductions of 21 percent and 15 percent, respectively, relative to no learner phase and no passenger restrictions. For the other components, though not all of the effects were significant, the optimal levels for reducing fatal crash rates of 16-year-old drivers were (a) disallowing learner driving until age 16, (b) disallowing intermediate licensure until age 16½ to 17, and (c) a nighttime driving restriction starting at 10 pm or earlier.

Even a casual comparison of the findings and recommendations of the two multi-state extensive studies of McCartt *et al.* (2010) and Masten, Foss, and Marshall (2013), shows that the benefits attributed to the different components are very different in the two studies. This difference highlights the very significant effects that the different methodologies yield. Each one has its flaws and fails to correct for different confounding factors. Thus, we are left with the conclusion that the GDL is effective in crash reductions of young people, but a definite determination of the specific contributions from the different components remains elusive.

The explanations for the effects of the different components vary. The explanation for the effects of night curfew and zero tolerance for alcohol are simple: these restrictions remove the young and inexperienced driver from these high-risk, high-crash situations. The effects of alcohol on the crash involvement of young drivers are greater than would be expected by their additive effects alone. Peck *et al.* (2008) showed that the relative risk of crashes of drivers under 21 with positive BACs is greater than that of older drivers. The explanation for the effect of passenger restrictions is a little more complicated. First, it is probably because young drivers are more likely to be distracted by young passengers because they are not yet able to divide their attention efficiently. Second, young drivers seek the approval of their passenger friends, and these passengers – being young with the same needs to prove their independence – are often likely to challenge (explicitly or implicitly) the driver to more "daring" driving. Thus, young passengers are likely to cause young drivers to assume riskier behaviors. This has also been demonstrated for specific behaviors such as speed and headway maintenance, where it has been found that young drivers drive faster and keep shorter headways in the presence of young – especially male – passengers (Simons-Morton, Lerner, and Singer, 2005).

Teen passengers compromise safety of young drivers

The negative effects of passengers – probably due to all the reasons mentioned above – can be quite dramatic. This was demonstrated by Howard (2004) in Australia, and by Chen *et al.* (2000), Williams (2003), and Fell *et al.* (2011) in the U.S. Chen *et al.* (2000) and Williams (2003) analyzed the relationship between the presence of passengers and the likelihood of a crash (per 1,000 trips) using data from the U.S. Nationwide Personal Transportation Survey and the US Fatal Analysis Reporting System. Their results revealed that the risk of fatal injuries in a crash increases proportionately with the number of passengers, as illustrated in Figure 6-18 from Williams (2003). Note that the fatality risk per trip for first-year drivers with three or more passengers is four times that of the same drivers without passengers. For mature, more experienced drivers, there is no effect of passengers on the crash risk, and possibly even a positive one for older drivers

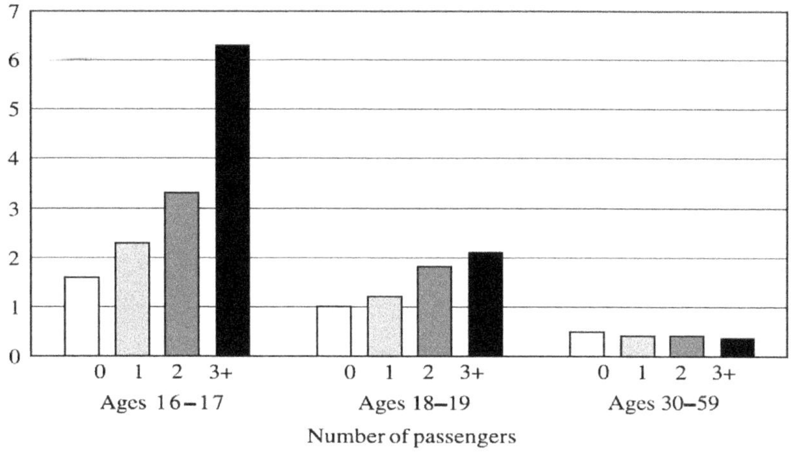

Figure 6-18. Crash likelihood (per 1,000 trips) and the number of passengers for different driver age groups (from Williams, 2003, with permission from Elsevier).

(see Chapter 7). Thus, the presence of young passengers is a significant risk factor for young novice drivers and when restrictions on passengers are imposed, teen drivers' crash rates diminish (Williams *et al.*, 2005).

Supervision has a positive but temporary benefit

One recurring finding in all studies that examined the benefits of GDL is that crashes during the supervised driving phase itself are very rare (Baughan and Simpson, 2002; Mayhew *et al.*, 2003; Wiggins, 2005; Williams *et al.*, 1997. Note also Figures 6-11 and 6-13). This can be attributed to at least three factors: first, during that phase the novice drivers' exposure is limited to relatively safe conditions; second, their behavior is closely monitored by an experienced adult who can prevent them from getting into dangerous situations; and third, the mature supervising passenger – unlike teenage passengers – acts as a restraining motivational force, who as a parent can also suspend their driving privileges. Unfortunately, all of these factors evaporate as soon as the supervised stage ends, and consequently the crash rates catapult precipitously. The additional restrictions that are often maintained even after the end of the supervised phase – nighttime curfew, zero tolerance for alcohol, and no teen passengers – do address some of the exposure and motivational issues, but apparently not enough and not all of them. One aspect that may not be sufficiently addressed during the supervised phase is the acquisition of safe behavior or habits as distinct from safe performance. As long as supervision is there, the novice driver is "performing" a task as required, but once the supervision disappears the driver switches from best/desired performance to "typical teen" behavior. Direct evidence of the adult supervisors' restraining effects on their children's behavior (rather than just crash outcome) was provided from a naturalistic driving study of 42 American teen agers, whose driving was monitored for 18 months, beginning 3 weeks after they received their provisional license. Risky driving was defined quantitatively on the basis of extreme g-forces from braking, accelerating, and making hard right and left turns. In this rather small-scale study but with detailed objective measures Simons-Morton et al. (2011) found that the teen drivers' risky driving was 67 percent lower and crash/near crash rates were 75 percent lower in the presence of adult (supervising?) passengers. It is likely that what the supervision does is suppress the "typical" teen behavior which is governed by multiple competing needs in which safety is just one, and probably not a dominant one (see also Chapter 9). In addition, parents can also use this time to provide their children with advice on how to drive safely. When such tips are given driving improves and remains better even when the supervision phase ends (Chung *et al.*, 2014; Toledo *et al.*, 2012).

Long-term effects of GDL: The jury is still out

With these concerns in mind, some well-controlled recent studies that have focused on the longer term effects of GDL (beyond the age of 18) have come up with very disappointing results. One such large scale study by Males (2013) evaluated the California GDL program effectiveness by studying the crash histories of California drivers up to the age of 25 and compared those drivers that were exposed to the GDL with those who received their license before the GDL program went into effect. Although all previous studies that tracked drivers' crash histories noted the jump in crashes as soon as the program ended, most often these studies did not examine the longer term effects. When the study period extended till the age of 25 Males noted that "the 16-25 age group subjected to GDL suffered significant net increases of 5% in drivers' fatal crash involvements and 7% in traffic fatalities compared to the control group not exposed to GDL. Declines in fatalities and fatal crashes among the 16- to 17-year-old age group were more than offset by larger increases in fatalities and fatal crashes among ages 18-25" (p. 23). Indeed Males too found that under age 18 the GDL group had lower fatality rate, but thereafter – from age 18 till 25 – their rates were consistently and significantly higher. But why? Why should the GDL – that helps drivers bypass the greater risks of immaturity – have such long lasting negative effects? Males suggests that the reason is experience, or rather the lack of it. He argues that the GDL in effect deprives the young drivers of important experiences for which they must make up in later years. However, if this is the case, then why should their overall crash rates be higher rather than just the same? Males does not provide an answer to this issue, but the empirical findings remain and so is the need for more and better studies that would tease out the positive aspects of the GDL while eliminating the negative ones. Though the Males study is the most extreme in its negative findings, there are other studies that either failed to find an effect of the GDL in the post GDL program or found a negative one. For example, Vanlaar *et al.* (2009) examined the GDL effects in 46 U.S. states plus the District of Columbia and 11 Canadian jurisdictions. Using a meta-analysis approach they found that the night restriction during the post-supervisory phase actually increased the relative fatality rates of the 19-year-old drivers. Ehsani, Bingham, and Shope (2013b) evaluated the effects of GDL in three states on the crash rates of minor crashes. While there was a modest positive effect on the drivers under 18 years old, this was not the case for the 18-year-old drivers. For these drivers there was a small positive effect in Maryland (7 percent), a small negative effect in Michigan (4 percent), and no effect in Florida. In summary, it is still not clear that the immediate positive effects of the GDL transcend the period in which the restrictions are in effect.

Out-of-the-vehicle extended supervision: A potential enhancement of GDL

Can the effects of supervision be extended without a supervisor in the car? Obviously, at some point a parent would like a relief from this obligation. One solution to this dilemma is to replace the parent's actual presence in the car with a remote monitoring system. With current technology it is possible to install monitoring devices that track and transmit a vehicle's location and various high-risk driver behaviors (such as speed, rapid accelerations and decelerations, and sharp steering movements). This allows parents at home to monitor their children's driving. This partial supervision retains two functions of live supervision: deterrence from high-risk behaviors and provision of corrective feedback. Given the consistent finding that supervision is effective while it lasts, the deterrence of the electronic monitor can inhibit the novice driver from engaging in risky behaviors that he or she (mostly he) might otherwise be tempted to commit. Initial ongoing evaluations of such systems in Israel and the U.S. suggest that they may be very effective (Farah *et al.*, 2013; 2014; Lotan and Toledo, 2006; McGehee *et al.*, 2007). In a direct evaluation of this concept, Farah et al. (2013; 2014) provided families with in-vehicle data recorders (IVDRs) that record whenever the driver applies excessive g force (i.e., rapid acceleration, hard braking, and abrupt steering), and also provided the parents with training on "vigilant care." This training consisted of supporting the parents in checking the secure website where they could track their child's driving behavior, and guiding them with how to provide feedback and set goals when the behavior is risky. Initial results of this approach were quite promising, yielding a drop of nearly 30 percent in risky driving events compared to a matched control group of new drivers who received no feedback at all. An unintended benefit of the program was a 23 percent drop in the parents' risky behaviors. Finally, it is noteworthy that when asked, parents in general indicated that they would like to have such monitoring systems (Guttman and Lotan, 2011).

Parents as role models: For better and for worse

The GDL restriction on teen passengers is well supported by crash data, and sociologically oriented studies that show that teen drivers who perceived their friends to be risky drivers also report higher risky driving behaviors than those who do not perceive their friends to be high risk takers. And since young drivers in general are high risk takers, the restrictions remove one source of negative social pressure. However, less studied, but perhaps just as important are the risk taking tendencies of the supervising parents. We tend to mellow as we age, and thus we tend to associate being an adult with being a responsible adult, but is that always the case? The evidence is mounting that young drivers who perceived their parents as risky drivers tend to imitate them.

Parents are our earliest and possibly longest lasting role models in many situations, including driving. Thus, it is perhaps not surprising that risky driving of young drivers is correlated with risky driving of their parents (Prato *et al.*, 2010), and the amount of distracted driving of adolescents is correlated with their perception of distracted driving of their parents (Carter *et al.*, 2014). In fact it may not even be the actual driving style that is imitated as much as the novice driver's perception of this parents' driving behavior (Taubman-Ben-Ari and Katz – Ben-Ami, 2012; Carter *et al.*, 2014). This generalized modeling of our behavior after our parents also tends to be gender-specific. Scott-Parker *et al.* (2014) surveyed Australian drivers at the start of the solo driving period (immediately after the end of the supervised period) and asked them, among other questions, how risky their parents were during their provisional license phase, how much did they base their driving during the solo phase on their mother's/father's/friends' driving, and several questions that assessed their own risky driving. As found by other studies, they obtained a positive relationship between the perceived riskiness of friends, the extent of patterning behavior after them, and the reported level of risk driving. More interesting though, they discovered that young male drivers were more influenced by their fathers in terms of patterning their behavior after them and being more risky when the fathers were perceived as more risky. The same relationship was obtained for young female drivers and their mothers, though this relationship failed to reach statistical significance. The implication of this kind of finding is that we cannot assume that parents are good role models, but that instead we should find ways to make them so. Similarly, Miller and Taubman-Ben-Ari (2010), found that after 1 year of driving post-supervision, young male drivers' reported level of anger correlated significantly with that of their fathers ($r = .33$) and young female drivers' level of reported anxiety correlated with that of their mothers ($r = .47$).

One recently developed and evaluated approach to post-licensing parental supervision is that of parental training in "vigilant care" (Shimshoni *et al.*, 2015): "a flexible attitude by which parents continuously adjust their levels of involvement to the alarm signs they detect. The lowest level of vigilant care is that of open attention. At this level, parents foster trust, dialogue, and openness, and establish positive and non-intrusive contacts with people in the child's environment .... So long as no alarming signs are detected, parents should stay mostly at this level .... However, if such signs appear, parents should move to the level of focused attention. At this point they start checking and asking the child specifically about the what, when, where, and with whom concerning his or her activities .... If the child refuses to collaborate or supplies unreliable information, or if there are other signs that he or she is probably involved in problematic activities, the parents move to active protection; that is, they take actual steps to reduce the risk" (pp. 70–71). Thus vigilant care is a level of parental involvement in the child's life that varies according to the overt signs of risk and danger. Shimshoni and her colleagues (2015) tested the benefits of this approach on young (17-22 years old), novice (<1.5 months of license), male drivers. The drivers' risk taking behaviors was assessed with specially developed in-vehicle data recorders (IVDR) that provided feedback to the drivers and their parents on the level of aggression in their driving, based on extreme accelerations and decelerations, sudden lane changes, lateral speeds in curves, and speed (Lotan and Toldeo, 2006; Prato *et al.*, 2010). The effectiveness of vigilant care was compared to three other conditions: no feedback, individual feedback (parents and young drivers received feedback of their own driving, but not of the other), and family feedback (parents and drivers received feedback of everyone's driving). The primary measure of performance was the rate of "risky events" per hour of driving. As shown in Figure 6-19, the rate of events was low and similar for all four groups of drivers as long as they were chaperoned according to the GDL regulations (before Month 0 in Figure 6-19). Once they were allowed to drive without in-car supervision by their parents the four groups diverged quickly and significantly. The Vigilant Care group retained their low level of negative events for the 5 months of follow-up, while the "No feedback" group immediately increased their risky driving to twice that of the vigilant care group. The two feedback groups had slightly higher levels of negative events, but well below that of the no feedback group. While the rise in events of the no feedback group is consistent with all the other data that shows rapid dissipation of the GDL program once the chaperoning phase ends, the sustained benefits of the vigilant care demonstrate a welcome solution to the issue. To be effective on a large scale, however, high levels of sustained commitment on the part of the parents are required, and this seems to be a problem in all studies that attempt to recruit participants for in-vehicle monitoring.

One effective way to sustain parental involvement is the "Checkpoints" program developed by Simons-Morton and his associates (e.g., Simons-Morton, Hartos, *et al.*, 2006; Simons-Morton and Ouimet, 2006). This is the most widely evaluated parent-directed teen driving intervention (Curry *et al.*, 2015) in which the parent and novice teen driver sign a parent-teen driving agreement that strictly limits teen driving under specific high-risk conditions, such as at night and with teen passengers, and gradually allows more driving privileges as teens gain driving experience and show responsible driving behavior. During the life of the program the parents get quarterly leaflets that discuss the dangers

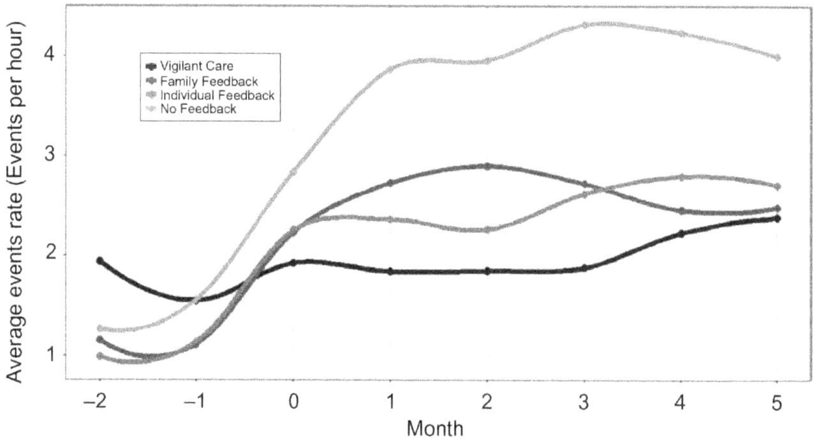

Figure 6-19. Young drivers' average aggressive driving events rate as a function of time before and after the end of the GDL supervisory phase and as a function of the feedback they received (from Shimshoni *et al.*, 2015, with permission from Elsevier).

or risky driving and stress the importance of limiting risky driving situations. In their evaluation studies, Simons-Morton and his associates showed that teens who participated in that program reported fewer risky behaviors and fewer violations than teens who did not. Summarizing the results obtained in a state-wide (Connecticut) evaluation study Simons-Morton *et al.* (2006a) conclude that "it is possible through passive persuasion methods to increase and maintain parent-imposed driving limits." This conclusion, of course, assumes that the self-reports were valid, and that greater social desirability on the part of the participants did not bias their answers.

Program acceptance

A related issue for a program to be successful, and for its extension with parental supervision, is its acceptance by the young drivers and their parents. This is much more important in the case of GDL than in the case of driver education, because the burden of providing the added supervision falls directly on the parents' shoulders. This is not an easy task – for neither the teen driver nor the more mature parent. From the perspective of the parents, it means a few more months of chauffeuring their children before they are finally freed of that burden, and from the perspective of the novice drivers it means another flashpoint for conflict with the parent at the critical age when they are trying to prove their independence. Given these two concerns – that may unite both the teen driver and the driver's parents – it is interesting that the few studies that have evaluated the acceptance of the GDL have very consistently reported positive attitudes toward it from both sides of the car. Williams, Nelson, and Leaf (2002) queried parents in California and found that nearly 80 percent of parents and students participating in the GDL supported it, and nearly all of them reported that their children complied with the requirement of 50 hours of supervised driving (of which 10 were at night). Similarly, Williams *et al.* (1998) found that over 90 percent of parents surveyed in five east coast U.S. states supported a minimum period of supervised driving and over 80 percent supported nighttime restrictions of the GDL. Ferguson *et al.* (2001), contacted some of the same parents whose children at the time of the first interview did not yet have a driver license. In the second interview, after most of their children were already licensed, these parents were even more supportive of the supervision and nighttime restrictions of the GDL program, even though by that time they had all been personally inconvenienced by these restrictions.

One means of improving compliance with the various restrictions during the restricted-license phase is to clarify the exact meaning of the restrictions for both drivers and parents. This is not a trivial issue. Hartos *et al.* (2004) interviewed 24 pairs of parents and their children who were novice drivers. At the time of the interview all teens had had their Maryland provisional license for 2-4 months. They found that teenage drivers – in an obviously self-serving manner – tend to report driving rules and consequences that are less strict than those reported by their parents. They also noted that this applies to other family rules, not just those related to driving. Although the sample was small, it yielded 72 different driving rules, including the need to request permission to drive and to report the destination, and limits on passengers, night driving, weather, and distance.

Unfortunately in only half the cases (37 out of 72) there was a match between the perception of the young driver and the perception of the parent, and even then the match was often not perfect. The variations and ambiguity in the rules was mostly in their interpretation. For example, there were significant differences on what hours constitute "night driving" and what are the specific limits on passengers. Given the similarity of these findings to their previous findings regarding other teen behaviors (with a much larger sample), the authors concluded that "parenting regarding teen driving is not different than that for other teen behaviors, such as substance abuse and sexual activity. Parents have rules but these rules are not understood as such by teens." As negative as this conclusion sounds, the reality may actually be worse, because teen drivers often admit to violating the rules – even as lax as they perceive them. This problem with setting parental rules may be the reason why studies that queried parents about the GDL and their acceptance of it, generally found that in the U.S. parents are quite supportive of the program even to the point of postponing the licensing age and taking a short parental course on safe and proper driving (Williams and Shults, 2010). A similar conclusion regarding the parental role in their children's safe driving was expressed in a survey of parents of young drivers in Israel with respect to the installation of in-vehicle data recorders that would provide parents with information about their children's aggressive behaviors. Still, a significant minority of the parents thought that providing parents with such information would erode the child-parent relationship in general, and trust in particular (Guttman and Lotan, 2011).

New Directions in Driver Education and Training

The analyses of crash rates of drivers as they mature and gain experience, the benefits of a prolonged supervised graduated driver training, and the hazard detection and attentional deficiencies that young drivers exhibit, all indicate the need for a better driver training program. The insights gained from these studies are now being put to use in the development of new driver education and training programs, and some of these efforts are described below.

Expanding the goals of driver education (GDE)

The dismal results of past evaluation studies of driver education led the US National Transportation Safety Board to conclude in 2005 that although "driver education has been available since the 1930s and, intuitively, should improve driving safety, in fact little consensus exists on the benefits of driver education and training, what it should entail, and how it should be delivered" (NTSB, 2005). There is obviously a need for a new approach to driver education. The GDL, as comprehensive as it may be, still must rely on some driver education. While it has provided insights into the importance of the component phases in the training, it has not specified the specific contents that the novice driver must learn and internalize.

One promising approach has been proposed by some European researchers (Hatakka *et al.*, 2002) based on the hierarchical model of the driving task (see Chapter 3, Figure 3-1). This approach suggests that we look beyond training of specific driving skills and into higher-order determinants of safe driving. These determinants are described as a hierarchy where specific behaviors of vehicle control are governed by driving in traffic, which in turn is managed within the goals and context of driving, which in turn are responsive to a yet higher-order level of goals and skills for living in general. Within this hierarchy a person applies a set of skills that interact with various aspects of driving that can increase or decrease risk. Drivers can adjust their risk by evaluating the perceived hazards relative to their perceived skills. This hierarchy of skills and the implications of each level in the hierarchy for the needed skills, risk assessment aspects, and self-assessment aspects are described in Table 6-6. It can be readily apparent, that traditional driver training and education has focused almost

Table 6-6. The goals for driver education (GDE) model proposed by Hatakka *et al.* (2002), to address issues beyond vehicle control in the process of driver education (derived from an extended table by Hatakka *et al.*, 2002).

	Knowledge and Skill	**Risk Increasing Aspects**	**Self-Assessment**
Goals for life and skill for living	Lifestyle, age group, culture, social position, etc. vs. driving behavior	Sensation-seeking Risk acceptance Group norms Peer pressure	Introspective Competence Own preconditions Impulse control
Goals and context of driving	Modal choice Choice of time Role of motives Route planning	Alcohol, fatigue Low friction Rush hours Young passengers	Own motives Influencing choices Self-critical thinking
Driving in traffic	Traffic rules Co-operation Hazard perception Automation	Disobeying rules Close-following Low friction Vulnerable road users	Calibration of driving skills Own driving style
Vehicle control	Car functioning Protective systems Vehicle control Physical laws	No seatbelts Breakdown of vehicle systems Worn-out tires	Calibration of car control skills

exclusively on the lower left cells in this 12-cell matrix. The GDL addresses the remaining cells by implicitly assuming that driving with an adult during the supervisory phase will result in modeling some of those safety-oriented goals, and in providing the novice driver with better self-assessment. However, the new GDE approach to driver education is to make the process explicit.

In many respects, the GDE approach enhances an earlier approach of "insight training" developed in Sweden in 1994.The insight training focused more on the risks of driving in traffic, the causes of young driver crashes, and understanding defensive driving, than on vehicle control and rules of the road. With this approach, for example, students became more appreciative of their skill limitations than students who trained at skid handling. Thus, the insight training produced an appreciation of the risks and driver's limitations without the unwarranted increase in confidence that the skill training yielded (Gregersen, 1996). The few studies that have evaluated insight training have provided some support for its effectiveness especially in reducing over-confidence (Carstensen, 2002; Engstrom *et al.*, 2003; Senserrick, 2002; Senserrick and Swinburne, 2001). One recent example is the evaluation conducted on novice New Zealand drivers (most of them still in the supervisory phase of licensing) by Isler, Starkey, and Sheppard (2011). They found that this kind of training in higher-order functions that included perceptual, motivational, and insight aspects of driving, yielded better driving performance. The performance was based on judgments by "professional driver assessors" in terms of better visual search, less risky driving, better hazard perception, and lower confidence in their driving, than either no training or traditional training in vehicular control. In summary, the GDE and its predecessor the insight training have received very limited and methodologically flawed evaluations that failed to demonstrate long-term effects on crash involvement, though they have demonstrated short-term effects on driving confidence (Beanland *et al.*, 2013).

A controlled study that directly compares the GDL and GDE is difficult to conduct because the two are applied in different countries with different cultures. In the U.S. and Canada, where GDL is part of the licensing system in all jurisdictions, there is no requirement for a formal pre-licensing training by a licensed instructor. The GDL components are generally built on different amounts of parental supervised driving, and consequently the additional formal restrictions imposed by the GDL may be most effective. In Europe, where some minimum number of on-the-road and in class hours are a requisite for initial licensing (see Tables 6-2 and 6-3), the added value of the GDL may be less, and the enhancement of the formal instruction is both more practical and possibly more beneficial. Yet, despite the promotion of the GDE in Europe, a recent analysis of the Spanish driver education curriculum, relative to the GDE framework revealed that most of the instruction and training is still focused on the traditional domains of knowledge and skills related to vehicle control and navigation (Molina, García-Ros, and Keskinen, 2014).

Training in hazard perception

Another approach that is gaining supporters – in Europe, Australia, Israel, and the U.S. – is the focused training in hazard perception. The rationale behind the approach is that the majority of crashes are due to attentional-perceptual shortcomings, and that novice drivers are particularly poor at the task of attending to and perceiving the hazards that can lead to crashes (Brown and Groeger, 1988; McKnight and McKnight, 2000; Whelan *et al.*, 2004). This shortcoming is consistent with the results of several studies that have repeatedly demonstrated that novice drivers are poor at scanning their environment for potential hazards (e.g., Borowsky *et al.*, 2010; Borowsky and Oron-Gilad, 2013; Falkmer and Gregersen, 2005; Mourant and Rockwell, 1972; Pradhan *et al.*, 2005). Consequently, several attempts have been made to develop programs that train young drivers to identify hazards on the road and correctly perceive the risks they pose.

But first we need to define some basic concepts. A hazard is anything on the road that has a significant potential to lead to a crash unless the driver takes some action such as changing speed, turning around the obstacle, or both. While some hazards are obvious to all (e.g., a big barrel in the middle of the road, or a slow moving pedestrian crossing the road), others are more difficult to perceive (such as a child playing with a ball on the sidewalk). One theoretical framework for hazard perception, proposed by Horswill and McKenna (2004) is situation awareness for dangerous situations (see Figure 3-7). Unlike the novice driver who is often a passive receiver of information, the experienced driver utilizes his or her schemata to seek information that can be cues to hazards. The relationship between hazard perception and driving was formalized in a qualitative model by Deery (1999). According to Deery, once a hazard is perceived, the driver has to assess the risk that it poses. The risk is the likelihood that the hazard will result in a negative outcome, weighted by the magnitude or cost of that outcome. In the case of a child playing ball on the curb by the side of the road, the risk is the product of the "cost" of a collision with the child and the likelihood that the child will dart into the street. The adjustment in behavior the driver makes is a function of the perceived risk and the driver's self-assessment of skill. Thus, a skilled driver may perceive the risk as greater than a novice driver, who may be totally oblivious to the danger inherent in that situation. On the other hand, the skilled driver probably also has a better self-assessment of his or her ability to handle the situation, and may decide to respond only if the child (or the child's ball) actually starts moving toward the road. Thus, the observable behavior of the driver will depend on the risk level that the driver assumes coupled with the skill of handling the vehicle.

Another potential theoretical framework is the one proposed half a century ago by Surry (1968) for coping with industrial hazards. According to Surry, the process of hazard perception and hazard control can be divided into two phases: in the first phase danger is built up and in the second phase danger is released. During the time that elapses within each phase the human operator can intervene to disrupt the process in which the danger builds up, or to disrupt the danger release process. The two phases and the options for the human intervention are illustrated in Figure 6-20. The information processing activities within each phase are also listed in the figure and they correspond closely to the typical information processing stages and functions discussed in Chapter 3. The model illustrates how a potential accident can be avoided by proper intervention at each stage within each phase. If the operator intervenes appropriately at any stage

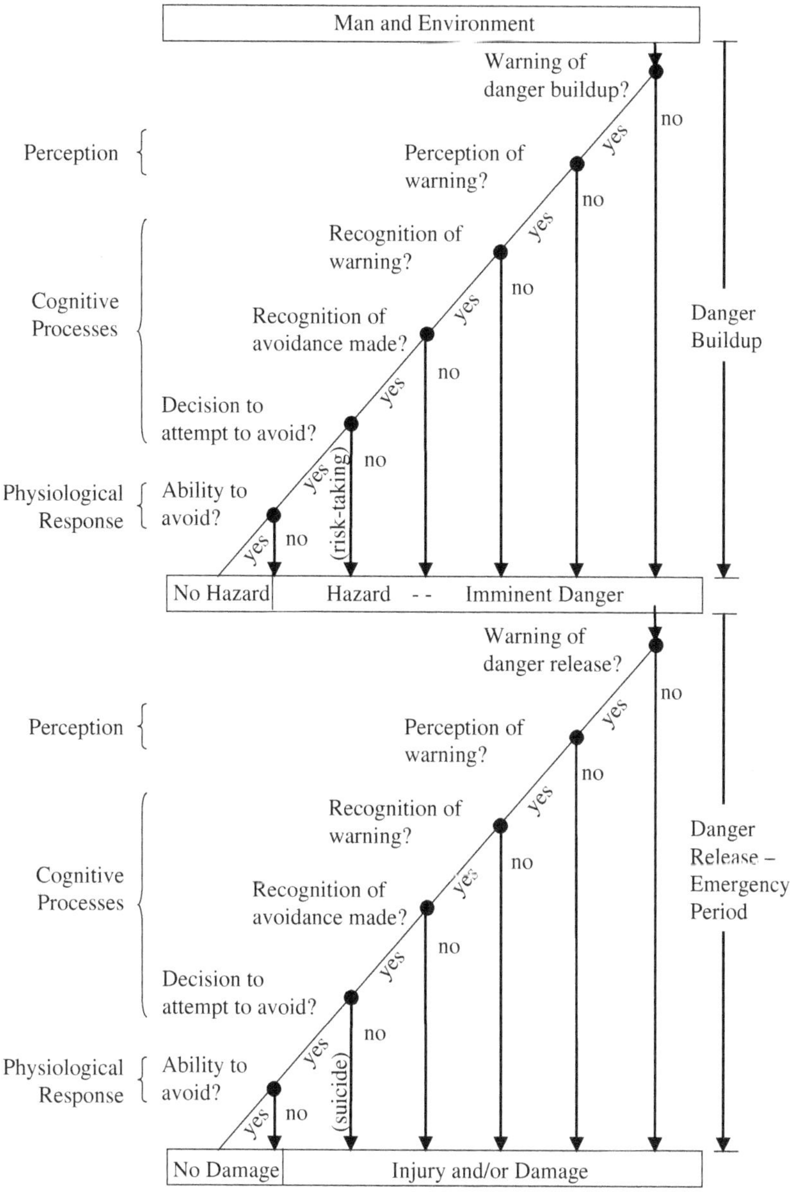

Figure 6-20. Surry's model of human factors in hazard detection and control (from Surry, 1968, with permission of the author).

during both phases the accident is avoided. Only when the operator fails at all stages does the accident occur. A very appealing aspect of this model is that it can provide insights to multiple ways of coping with hazards and multiple approaches to training in hazard perception and control. For example, an analysis of the crash files in the German

In-Depth Accident Study indicates that the danger release phase in 60 percent of rear-end crashes is over 1 second, enough time for intelligent in-vehicle active head restraint system to intervene to either prevent the crash or reduce its impact (Bogenrieder, Fehring, and Bachmann, 2009)

We can illustrate the application of the model to a typical hazard perception problem used in a study by Borowsky (Borowsky *et al.*, 2010). The purpose of the study was to see how beginning novice and experienced drivers respond to dangerous situations. In one of the staged situations that they created a driver driving on a suburban street encounters a teenager skateboarding on the road next to the curb traveling in the same direction as our approaching driver. The danger in this situation is the potential collision that might occur when the skate boarder reaches a parked car that is blocking his path. At that time he might instinctively try to maneuver around it by moving to the left, thereby merging into the path of the car that is coming up from behind. The danger build-up phase is the time from the appearance of the skate boarder and the parked car in the driver's field of view until the boarder veers into the vehicle path. The danger release phase is the time that elapses from the moment the boarder changes path and enters a collision course with the driver until they either collide or the driver manages to avoid the collision. An experienced driver should be able to recognize the potential danger almost at the start of the danger build-up. Once the danger is recognized an experienced driver would most likely select an appropriate action that might include honking, or slowing down.

The skate boarder's response would enable the driver to decide on the proper action – proceed at the same speed or wait for the boarder to pass the parked car, or pass the boarder by moving into the opposing lane, etc. If the driver is a novice driver who does not perceive the potential danger in time, or does not make an appropriate response, then we enter the danger release phase. The time involved in this phase is typically much shorter and therefore the driver must recognize the signs of the danger release very quickly in order to respond appropriately. If that happens, quick avoidance maneuvers may still prevent the collision. An interesting demonstration of this difference between the novice and the experienced driver in detecting the hazard build-up was provided by Helander (1976) who measured drivers' physiological stress (electrodermal response) while they drove. Novice drivers' electrodermal response amplitude increased significantly when they approached a narrowing in the road, but not when they approached an intersection; while experienced drivers showed increase in strain in response to the intersection but not in response to the road narrowing. Thus the benefits of experience were manifested both in the ease of handling a road narrowing and in heightened awareness of the potential hazards at intersections.

In summary, the weight of the evidence from earlier research (systematically reviewed by Deery, 1999), and current research reviewed above indicates that novice drivers are poorer than experienced drivers in hazard perception. Hazard perception, like any other skill, improves with practice. Novice drivers are slower to perceive hazards both on and near the road. Their visual scan pattern is less extensive, less efficient, and involves fewer fixations on objects further up the road. They check their mirrors less frequently, and are more likely to miss hazards altogether. Even when they perceived hazards, they under-estimate the risks they pose, while at the same time they over-estimate their skill relative to experienced drivers. These shortcomings are then likely to lead to a dangerous situation of accepting high risks while driving with poor skills. Experience helps drivers accumulate more schemata and more scripts to better and sooner recognize hazards, and to respond to them quicker. This also reduces the experienced driver's stress in driving, because the driver is proactive, more relaxed, and less loaded in terms of the information processing requirements. The higher attention load that novice drivers experience, relative to experienced drivers, also makes it more difficult for them to allocate attention to non-driving tasks such as talking on the phone (Olsen, Simons-Morton, and Lee, 2006).

The challenge that remains is to demonstrate a significant correlation between hazard perception skills and crash involvement. To begin with, there is still some confusion as to how to measure hazard perception, and different tests of risk perception – even in response to the same hazardous situations – do not yield similar responses (Farrand and McKenna, 2001). In the absence of agreed-upon standards for what constitute roadway hazards and how risk perception should be measured, it is not surprising that it is hard to obtain high correlations between hazard perception skills and experience. A case in point is the study by Sagberg and Bjornskau (2006) who administered a video-based test of hazard perception to novice Norwegian drivers who had to identify hazards as quickly as they perceived them. The researchers very appropriately reasoned that if poor hazard perception is a key factor in the over-involvement of novice drivers in crashes within their first few months of driving, then it should be reflected in their reaction times to hazards in the hazard perception test. They compared the perception reaction times of drivers with varying amounts of driving experience – 1, 5, and 9 months after licensing – and failed to find significant differences in the reaction times among the groups, though the small differences that were obtained were in the expected direction.

Training in hazard and risk perception involves early identification of hazardous situations, a quick assessment of the risk levels they create, and quick and appropriate responses to the risk. Different techniques to train novice drivers in hazard perception have been tried. One technique is "commentary driving" in which the novice driver makes running commentary on hazards and risks along the road while the instructor corrects and adds comments (Marek and Sten, 1997). There is some indication of the effectiveness of this technique (Spolander, 1990). Another approach is supplementing the driving instruction with video clips of hazards on the road and providing interactive PC instruction in hazard detection (Deery, 1999; McKenna and Crick, 1997). A third approach is to use hazard perception tests to both test and train young drivers in hazard perception (Ferguson, 2003).

Testing novice drivers in hazard perception can be a practical tool to screening drivers prior to full licensing for two reasons. First, in the absence of training hazard perception tests seem to be quite reliable and provide a stable estimate of this skill (Scialfa, Pereverseff, and Borkenhagen, 2014). Second, hazard detection can be improved by training. This is important for both safety and practical reasons, as it is unlikely that a skill that cannot be improved will serve to deny license simply because it is a statistically significant predictor of some safe driving measures. (To wit, some of the significantly relevant measures of visual performance discussed in Chapter 4 are impractical for licensing criteria, at least in part, because they cannot be improved significantly.) Thus, despite the maturation processes that are involved in hazard perception, several studies have demonstrated that just like other skills, training that focuses on improving the various components of hazard perception can improve hazard detection (Crundall *et al.*, 2010; Fisher, 2008; McMahon and O'Reilly, 2000; Meir, Borowsky, and Oron-Gilad, 2014; Petzoldt *et al.*, 2013; Wang, Zhang, and Salvendy, 2010; Weiss *et al.*, 2013). Part of the improvement is due to more effective visual search behavior. Zafian *et al.* (2014) showed that following hazard perception training, drivers in a simulator directed more fixations to the hazards, especially in complex dynamic situations. Chen and Mourant (2012) trained novice 18- to 20-year-old drivers in a hazard detection video game and then gave them a hazard detection task in a driving simulation. They found that compared to a matched group of drivers the trained drivers detected more hazards, had fewer false alarms, and developed a more active visual scanning pattern, which is more appropriate for early detection of hazards.

Consequently, some licensing agencies already require novice drivers to train in hazard perception and pass tests of hazard perception prior to receiving an unrestricted driver license (e.g., in Australia, Norway, Sweden, and the United Kingdom; Crundall *et al.*, 2012). Furthermore given the common computer-based training and evaluation methods, adding hazard perception to the driver training battery does not involve any significant cost to the licensing agency.

The most convincing validation of the value in hazard perception training was just provided in a recently completed large study on 5,251 novice California drivers (Thomas *et al.*, 2016). All participants who agreed to participate in the study, immediately after completing their driving tests, took a computer-based hazard perception test. Half of the participants then took the Risk Awareness and Perception Training (RAPT) developed by Fisher and his colleagues (e.g., Fisher *et al.*, 2002; Fisher, 2008; Fisher *et al.*, 2010). The two groups were then tracked for a year, and each driver's crash and violation data were obtained from the relevant state authorities. After 1 year of driving no effect of the RAPT was obtained for the female drivers, but the males who received the RAPT had a statistically significant lower crash rate than the males in the comparison group (by 24 percent). The puzzling effect of the RAPT on the males only may be due to their greater exposure both in terms of total distance driven and in driving at high risk situations (e.g., at night and after drinking). The greater exposure would then give these drivers more of an opportunity to benefit from better hazard detection skills. However, in the absence of exposure data this remains a speculation. Nonetheless, considering that the RAPT requires less than 30 minutes this is definitely a worthwhile early training investment.

In summary, multiple studies, on different driver groups, in different parts of the world, and with different methods have demonstrated the benefits of hazard perception training (and evaluation) (Horswill, 2016). So far it is arguably the most consistently demonstrated and cost-beneficial safety-oriented driver training tool that we currently have.

Can there be too much training?

In most perceptual-motor skills, over-learning – learning to perform beyond some required criterion – is considered a good thing. The benefits of added training can also be demonstrated in driving performance. For example, Dorn and Barker (2005) compared the performance of two highly experienced groups of drivers – with approximately 17 years of licensed driving – on a variety of driving simulation tasks. One group consisted of regular drivers and the other group consisted of police officers who received special police driving training. As might be expected, the police officers performed better on most driving tasks. However, it is important to note that this comparison was of driving performance rather than driving behavior (as defined in Chapter 2), and all subjects tried to maximize their performance.

Interestingly, when it comes to typical driving behavior (rather than best driving performance), the situation is quite different. Going to the extreme, Williams and O'Neill (1974) compared the crash and speeding violation rates of drivers registered as race drivers in three states in the U.S., relative to those of the rest of the driving population in those states. Despite their assumed higher skills at vehicle control and navigation among speeding cars, in all three states the race drivers had significantly more traffic violations and in one of the three states, they were also involved in more crashes. These results underscore the interplay between risk taking and skills. To have a safety benefit, the drivers' skills must exceed their confidence and their risk taking.

It is almost unavoidable to separate self-confidence and skill. As we teach drivers to become more skillful, we also inadvertently give them more confidence. From the perspective of risk homeostasis theory, the drivers adjust their behavior relative to their perceived new abilities. However, often the new abilities do not justify such an adjustment. This has been demonstrated in skid training. In Scandinavian countries where snow and frozen roads are quite common for much of the year, knowledge about how to avoid skidding and how to get out of a skid (when avoidance fails) is considered by many an essential skill. Thus, it is not surprising that in 1979 Norway instituted a two-phase new driver training program, in which the second phase consisted of skid training. An extensive evaluation of the program effectiveness was conducted by Glad (1988) who found that the immediate effect of the program was a 17 percent *increase* in young male crashes in general, and a 23 percent increase in crashes on slippery roads in particular. Interestingly, women, who were required to take the same training did not have higher crash rates (but not lower either).

A similar two-phase system was introduced in Finland in 1990, but the skid training differed slightly because it emphasized the hazard perception of slippery roads rather than the vehicle handling skills needed to handle skidding. Thus, the main idea was not to teach drivers to handle their car skillfully in slippery conditions but rather how to detect a slippery road and how to be more aware of the possible dangers of slippery conditions. Despite the differential emphasis, in an evaluation of the program Katila *et al.* (2004) noted, that "the priority given to anticipatory skills over maneuvering skills in slippery driving courses has generally been quite clear to instructors but not to students. The students themselves often consider both skills to be equally important (p. 544)." When the crash data of new drivers who took the new curriculum with the skid training was compared to that of new drivers with the old curriculum – without skid training – the skid-trained drivers were found to have higher crash rates (per driver) than the non-skid trained drivers. However, the drivers trained at skid training also had more confidence in their driving and were less afraid to drive on slippery roads. When the odds of having a crash on a slippery road relative to a non-slippery road were compared between the two groups, male drivers who were given skid training were approximately 50 percent more likely to have a crash on a slippery road (Odds ratio = 1.46). Finally, a more recent but small study that compared the citations and crash rates of young American drivers who received skid training post-licensing with a matched sample of drivers that did not, also failed to find any benefits of the skid training (Farmer and Wells, 2015).

The conclusion from these four studies is that the relationship between training, skills, and safety is complicated. It is mediated by driving attitudes, style, and self-confidence. That last variable – confidence – can be influenced by the trainer, but to a much lesser extent than the skill that the trainer imparts.

Concluding Comments

The significant over-involvement of young and novice drivers in crashes has stimulated a significant body of research aimed at understanding the roots of the problem and means of coping with it. In the past half century we have learned that experience is a much more significant factor than maturity – at least for people who begin driving at age 16. We have also identified some of the key skills that need to be acquired in the process of driver education and training and the deficient behaviors that are most common in novice driver crashes. One realization that has sunk in is that driving, especially driving in traffic and in high risk situations is quite a complex skill that cannot be acquired very rapidly. This understanding led to GDL programs whose benefits immediately post-licensing have been quite significant. Recent research on GDL's effectiveness has also identified the relative benefits of its components (pre-license learner period, post-license supervision, night driving restrictions, no-young-passenger rule). Unfortunately, the gain in crash reduction for the young licensees is typically offset by a sharp rise in violations and crashes once all the restrictions are lifted. What remains to do now is to identify the mechanisms by which the gains can be sustained into the older more experienced – and safer – phase of driving. An approach based on the hierarchical nature of safe driving behavior (Goals of Driving Education) is theoretically very appealing, but still has to be adopted (and evaluated) on a large scale. Teaching hazard perception, and higher-order driving skills appear to be promising strategies for the earlier phase, and remote monitoring appears to be a promising strategy for the latter phase of learning. As a note of caution, the sweeping generalizations about "young drivers" should be qualified by demonstrated individual differences. As an example, one of the more interesting individual differences is the differential levels of cortisol – a neurobiological marker of stress – that have been found to be related to involvement in crashes and near crashes (Ouimet *et al.*, 2014). Such findings can eventually be used to develop individually tailored effective programs of driver education and training.

Finally, in addressing traffic safety problems, we typically try to address potential remediation in all three major components of the driver-vehicle-environment system. In the case of young drivers, having located the problem in the driver, we seem to have exclusively focused on how to fix him (and to a lesser extent, her). Thus, a refreshing supplementary approach has been suggested by the U.S. Insurance Institute for Highway Safety (IIHS, 2014). Given the over-involvement of young drivers in crashes, and given the fact that they tend to drive older used cars (because they are cheaper), the IIHS recommends that these drivers should steer clear of "high horsepower" cars, try to drive bigger/heavier cars, make sure the car has electronic stability control (see Chapter 20), and has the best safety ratings possible. On the basis of their crashworthiness ratings, the IIHS then provides a list of their "best choices" and "good choices" of car models sold in the U.S. With a list of 56 cars in the first category, and 39 in the second, the safety-conscious parent has a lot of options to choose from. All that remains to do is to market this to the young drivers who are naturally attracted to sexier cars like "muscle cars," sports cars, and SUVs.

References

Baker, S. P., L.-H. Chen and G. Li (2006). National evaluation of graduated driver licensing. National Highway Traffic Safety Administration Report DOT HS 810 614. U.S. Department of Transportation, Washington, DC.

Baughan, C. and H. Simpson (2002). *Graduated licensing: A review of some current systems.* TRL Research Report 529. Transport Research Laboratory, Crawthorn, UK.

Beanland, V., N. Goode, P. M. Salmon and M. G. Lenne (2013). Is there a case for driver training? A review of the efficacy of pre- and post-licence driver training. *Safety Sci.*, *51*, 127-137.

Begg, D. J. and J. D. Langley (2004). Identifying predictors of persistent non-alcohol or drug-related risky driving behaviours among a cohort of young adults. *Accid. Anal. Prev.*, *36*(6) 1067-1071.

Beirness, D. J., D. R. Mayhew, H. M. Simpson and K. Desmond (2004). The road safety monitor: Young drivers. *Traffic Inj. Prev.*, *5*(3), 237-240.

Bogenrieder, R., M. Fehring and R. Bachmann (2009, June). Pre-Safe® in rear-end collision situations. In: The 21st International Technical Conference on the Enhanced Safety of Vehicles Conference (ESV), Stuttgart, Germany.

Borowsky, A. and T. Oron-Gilad (2013). Exploring the effects of driving experience on hazard awareness and risk perception via real-time hazard identification, hazard classification, and rating tasks. *Accid. Anal. Prev.*, *59*, 548-565.

Borowsky, A., D. Shinar and T. Oron-Gilad (2010). Age, skill, and hazard perception in driving. *Accid. Anal. Prev.*, *42*, 1240-1249.

Brown, I. D. and J. A. Groeger (1988). Risk perception and decision taking during the transition between novice and experienced driver status. *Ergonomics*, *31*, 585-597.
Carney, C., D. McGehee, K. Harland, M. Weiss and M. Raby (2015). Using naturalistic driving data to assess the prevalence of environmental factors and driver behaviors in teen driver crashes. AAA Foundation for Traffic Safety, Washington, DC.
Carstensen, G. (2002). The effect on accident risk of a change in driver education in Denmark. *Accid. Anal. Prev.*, *34*, 111-121.
Carter, P. M., C. R. Bingham, J. S. Zakrajsek, J. T. Shope and T. B. Sayer (2014). Social norms and risk perception: Predictors of distracted driving behavior among novice adolescent drivers. *J. Adolesc. Health*, *54*(5), S32-S41.
Chen, N. and R. R. Mourant (2012, June). A hazard perception training game for novice drivers. In IEEE 8th International Conference on Information Science and Digital Content Technology (ICIDT), 1, pp. 28-31.
Chen, L., S. P. Baker, E. R. Braver and G. Li (2000). Carrying passengers as a risk factor for crashes fatal to 16- and 17-year-old drivers. *J. Am. Med. Assoc.*, *283*, 1578-1582.
Chung, E. K., B. Choe, J. E. Lee, J. L. Lee and Y. W. Sohn (2014). Effects of an adult passenger on young adult drivers' driving speed: Roles of an adult passenger's presence and driving tips from the passenger. *Accid. Anal. Prev.*, *67*, 14-20.
Cicchino, J. B. and A. T. McCartt (2014). Trends in older driver crash involvement rates and survivability in the United States: An update. *Accid. Anal. Prev.*, *72*, 44-54.
Cooper, P. J., M. Pinili and W. Chen (1995). An examination of the crash involvement rates of novice drivers age 16-55. *Accid. Anal. Prev.*, *27*, 89-104.
Crundall, D. (2016). Hazard prediction discriminates between novice and experienced drivers. *Accid. Anal. Prev.*, *86*, 47-58.
Crundall, D., B. Andrews, E. Van Loon and P. Chapman (2010). Commentary training improves responsiveness to hazards in a driving simulator. *Accid. Anal. Prev.*, *42*, 2117-2124.
Crundall, D., P. Chapman, S. Trawley, L. Collins, E. van Loon, B. Andrews and G. Underwood (2012). Some hazards are more attractive than others: Drivers of varying experience respond differently to different types of hazard. *Accid. Anal. Prev.*, *45*, 600-609.
Curry, A. E., J. Hafetz, M. J. Kallan, F. K. Winston and D. R. Durbin (2011). Prevalence of teen driver errors leading to serious motor vehicle crashes. *Accid. Anal. Prev.*, *43*(4), 1285-1290.
Curry, A. E., C. Peek-Asa, C. J. Hamann and J. H. Mirman (2015). Effectiveness of parent-focused interventions to increase teen driver safety: A critical review. *J. Adolesc. Health*, *57*(1), S6-S14.
Deery, H. A. (1999). Hazard and risk perception among young novice drivers. *J. Safety Res.*, *30*(4), 225-236.
Dorn, L. and D. Barker (2005). The effects of driver training on simulated driving performance. *Accid. Anal. Prev.*, *37*, 63-69.
Ehsani, J. P., C. R., Bingham and J. T. Shope (2013a). The effect of the learner license graduated driver licensing components on teen drivers' crashes. *Accid. Anal. Prev.*, *59*, 327-336.

Ehsani, J. P., C. R. Bingham and J. T. Shope (2013b). Graduated driver licensing for new drivers: Effects of three states' policies on crash rates among teenagers. *Am. J. Prev. Med.*, *45*, 9-18.

Engstrom, I., N. P. Gregersen, K. Hernetkoski, E. Keskinen and A. Nyberg (2003). Young novice drivers, driver education and training: Literature review. VTI Rapport 491A. VTI Swedish National Road and Transport Research Institute, Stockholm, Sweden.

Falkmer, T. and N. P. Gregersen (2005). A comparison of eye movement behavior of inexperienced and experienced drivers in real traffic environments. *Optom. Vis. Sci.*, *82*, 732-739.

Farah, H., O. Musicant, Y. Shimshoni, T. Toledo, E. Grimberg, H. Omer and T. Lotan (2013). The first year of driving: Can an in-vehicle data recorder and parental involvement make it safer? *Trans. Res. Rec.*, No. 2327, 26-34.

Farah, H., O. Musicant, Y. Shimshoni, T. Toledo, E. Grimberg, H. Omer and T. Lotan (2014). Can providing feedback on driving behavior and training on parental vigilant care affect male teen drivers and their parents? *Accid. Anal. Prev.*, *69*, 62-70.

Farmer, C. M. and J. K. Wells (2015). Crash and citation records of young drivers with skid avoidance training. Insurance Institute for Highway Safety, Arlington, VA.

Farrand P. and F. P. McKenna (2001). Risk perception in novice drivers: The relationship between questionnaires measures and response latency. *Trans. Res. F*, *4*, 201-212.

Fell, J. C., M. Scherer, S. Thomas and R. B. Voas (2016). Assessing the impact of twenty underage drinking laws. *J. Stud. Alcohol Drugs*, *77*(2), 249-260.

Fell, J. C., M. Todd and R. B. Voas (2011). A national evaluation of the nighttime and passenger restriction components of graduated driver licensing. *J. Safety Res.*, *42*, 283-290.

Ferguson, S. A. (2003). Other high-risk factors for young drivers – How graduated licensing does, doesn't, or could address them. *J. Safety Res.*, *34*, 71-77.

Ferguson, S. A., A. F. Williams, W. A. Leaf, D. F. Preusser and C. M. Farmer (2001). Views of parents of teenagers about graduated licensing after experience with the laws. *J. Crash Prev. Inj. Control*, *2*, 221-227.

Fisher, D. (2008). Evaluation of PC-based novice driver risk awareness. National Highway Traffic Safety Administration Report No. DOT HS 810 926. U.S. Department of Transportation, Washington, DC.

Fisher, D. L., N. E. Laurie, R. Glaser, K. Connerney, A. Pollatsek and S. A. Duffy (2002). The use of an advanced driving simulator to evaluate the effects of training and experience on drivers' behavior in risky traffic scenarios. *Hum. Fact.*, *44*, 287-302.

Fisher, D. L., F. D. Thomas, A. K. Pradhan, A. Pollatsek, R. D. Blomberg and I. Reagan (2010). Development and evaluation of a PC-based attention maintenance training program National Highway Traffic Safety Administration Report No. DOT HS 811 252. U.S. Department of Transportation, Washington, DC.

Forsyth, E., G. Maycock and B. Sexton (1995). Cohort study of learner and novice drivers: Part 3, accidents, offences, and driving experience in the first three years of driving. Research Report 111. Transport Research Laboratory, Crowthorne, England.

Glad, A. (1988). Fase 2 i föreropplaringen. Effekt på ulykkes risikoen. Rapport 0015, Transportökonomisk institutt, Oslo (in Norwegian). As reported by Katila *et al.* (2004).

Goodwin, A. H., R. D. Foss, L. H. Margolis and S. Harrell (2014). Parent comments and instruction during the first four months of supervised driving: An opportunity missed? *Accid. Anal. Prev.*, *69*, 15-22.

Gregersen, N. P. (1996). Young drivers' overestimation of their own skill – An experiment on the relation between training strategy and skill. *Accid. Anal. Prev.*, *28*, 243-250.

Gregersen, N. P., H. Y. Berg, I. Engstrom, S. Nolen, A. Nyberg and P. A. Rimmo (2000). Sixteen years age limit for learner drivers in Sweden – an evaluation of safety effects. *Accid. Anal. Prev.*, *32*, 25-35.

Groot, H. A. M., D. Vandenberghe, G. Van Aerschot and E. Bekiaris (2001). Survey of existing methodologies and driver instructor needs. Commision Internationale des Examines de Conduite (CIECA), GRD1-1999-10024, Deliverable No 1.2. Brussels, Belgium.

Guttman, N. and T. Lotan (2011). Spying or steering? Views of parents of young novice drivers on the use and ethics of driver-monitoring technologies. *Accid. Anal. Prev.*, *43*, 412-420.

Hakamies-Blomqvist, L., T. Raitanen and D. O'Neill (2002). Driver ageing does not cause higher accident rates per km. *Transportation Res. F*, *5*, 271-274.

Hartos, J. L., T. Shattuck, B. G. Simons-Morton and K. H. Beck (2004). An in-depth look at parents imposed driving rules: Their strengths and weaknesses. *J. Safety Res.*, *35*, 547-555.

Hatakka, M., E. Keskinen, N. P. Gregersen, A. Glad and K. Hernetkoski (2002). From control of the vehicle to personal self control; broadening the perspectives to driver education. *Transport. Res. F*, *5*(3), 201-216.

Hedlund, J. and R. Compton (2005). Graduated driver licensing research in 2004 and 2005. *J. Safety Res.*, *36*(2), 109-119.

Helander, M. (1976). Vehicle control and driving experience: A pyschophysiological approach. *Proceedings of the 6th Congress of the International Ergonomics Association*. College Park, MD.

Hinchcliff, R., R. Q. Ivers, R. Poulos and T. Senserrick (2010). Utilization of research in policymaking for graduated driver licensing. *Am. J. Public Health*, *100*, 2052-2058.

Hirsch, P. and F. Bellavance (2016). Pilot project to validate the transfer of training of driving skills learned on a high fidelity driving simulator to on-road driving. CIRRELT 2016-16. Interuniversity Research Centre on Enterprise Networks, Logistics, and Transportation. Montreal, Canada.

Hirsch P. and U. Magg (2006). A profile of adolescents who attend driver education for the insurance discount: Are insurers rewarding bad risks? *Insur. Risk Manage.*, *73*(4), 499-524.

Horswill, M. S. (2016). Hazard perception in driving. *Curr. Dir. Psych. Sci.*, *25*(6), 425-430.

Horswill, M. S., A. Hill and M. Wetton (2015). Can a video-based hazard perception test used for driver licensing predict crash involvement? *Accid. Anal. Prev.*, *82*, 213-219.

Horswill, M. S. and F. P. McKenna (2004). Driver's hazard perception ability: Situation awareness on the road. In: *A Cognitive Approach to Situation Awareness* (S. Banbury and S. Tremblay eds.). pp. 155-175. Ashgate, Aldershot.

Howard, E. (2004). Victoria's experience and young driver safety issues. Presentation at the Young Driver Safety Forum, December, VicRoads, Canberra, Australia.

Hyman, M. M. (1968). Accident vulnerability and blood alcohol concentrations of drivers by demographic characteristics. *Quart. J. Stud. Alcohol Suppl.*, *4*, 34-57.

IIHS (2003). Graduated licensing: A blueprint for North America. Insurance Institute for Highway Safety, Arlington, VA.

IIHS (2014). Vehicles for teens. Insurance Institute for Highway Safety. Status Report (Special Issue) **49**(5), Arlington, VA.

IIHS (2015).Older drivers: 2013. Insurance Institute for Highway Safety, Arlington, VA.

Isler, R. B., N. J. Starkey and P. Sheppard (2011). Effects of higher-order driving skill training on young, inexperienced drivers' on-road driving performance. *Accid. Anal. Prev.*, *43*, 1818-1827.

Katila, A., E. Keskinen M. Hatakka and S. Laapotti (2004). Does increased confidence among novice drivers imply a decrease in safety? The effects of skid training on slippery road accidents. *Accid. Anal. Prev.*, *36*, 543-550.

Keall, M. D., W. J. Frith and T. L. Patterson (2004). The influence of alcohol, age and number of passengers on the night-time risk of driver fatal injury in New Zealand. *Accid. Anal. Prev.*, *36*, 49-61.

Laberge-Nadeau, C. (1997). New drivers: First year of driving experience and their crash rates. Proceedings of the Conference on Traffic Safety on Two Continents. Linkoping, Sweden, pp. 147-164.

Langford, J. R. Methorst and L. Hakamies-Blomqvist (2006). Older drivers do not have a high crash risk – A replication of low mileage bias. *Accid. Anal. Prev.*, *38*, 574-578.

Lehtonen, E., O. Lappi, I. Koirikivi and H. Summala (2014). Effect of driving experience on anticipatory look-ahead fixations in real curve driving. *Accid. Anal. Prev.*, *70*, 195-208.

Lonero, L. and D. Mayhew (2010). Large-scale evaluation of driver education review of the literature on driver education evaluation 2010 update. AAA Foundation for Traffic Safety, Washington, DC.

Lotan, T. and T. Toledo (2006). An in-vehicle data recorder for evaluation of driving behavior and safety. Transportation Research Board Annual Meeting, Paper No. 061607. The National Academies, Washington, DC, January 2006.

Lucas, R., N. Heimstra and D. Speigel (1973). Part-task simulation training of drivers' passing judgments. *Hum. Fact.*, *15*, 269-274.

Males, M. A. (2013). California's graduated driver licensing ten years later: Effects on motor vehicle fatalities and crashes through age 25. *Californian J. Health Promot.*, *11*, 23-35.

Marek, J., and T. Sten (1997). Traffic environment and the driver. *Driver Behavior and Training in International Perspective*. Charles C. Thomas Publisher, Springfield, IL.

Masten, S. V. (2004). Teenage driver risks and interventions. Research Report No. 207. Department of Motor Vehicles, Sacramento, CA.

Masten, S. V., R. D. Foss, and S. W. Marshall (2011). Graduated driver licensing and fatal crashes involving 16-to 19-year-old drivers. *JAMA*, *306*, 1098-1103.
Masten, S. V. and R. A. Hagge (2004). Evaluation of California's graduated driver licensing program. *J. Safety Res.*, *35*, 523-535.
Masten, S. V., R. D. Foss, and S. W. Marshall (2013). Graduated driver licensing program component calibrations and their association with fatal crash involvement. *Accid. Anal. Prev.*, *57*, 105-113.
Masten, S. V., F. D. Thomas, K. T. Korbelak, R. C. Peck and R. D. Blomberg (2015). Meta-analysis of graduated driver licensing laws. National Highway Traffic Safety Administration. Report No. DOT HS 812 211. U.S. Department of Transportation, Washington, DC.
Maycock, G. (2002). Novice driver accidents and the driving test. TRL Research Report 527. Transport Research Laboratory, Crowthorne, Berkshire.
Maycock, G., C. R. Lockwood and J. F. Lester (1991). The accident liability of car drivers. TRL Research Report 315. Transport and Road Research Laboratory, Crowthorne, England.
Mayhew, D. R. and H. M. Simpson (1996). Effectiveness and role of driver education and training in a graduated licensing system. Traffic Injury Research Foundation, Ottawa, Canada.
Mayhew, D. R. and H. M. Simpson (2002). The safety value of driver education and training. *Inj. Prev.*, *8*(Suppl. 2), ii3-ii8.
Mayhew, D. R., H. M. Simpson and A. Pak (2003). Changes in collision rates among novice drivers during the first months of driving. *Accid. Anal. Prev.*, *35*, 683-691.
Mayhew, D. R., H. M. Simpson and D. Singhal (2005). Best practices for Graduated Driver Licensing in Canada. Traffic Injury Research Foundation, Ottawa, CA.
Mayhew, D., A. Williams and C. Pashley (2014). A new GDL framework: Evidence base to integrate novice driver strategies. Traffic Injury Research Foundation, Ottawa, Canada.
McCartt, A. T., D. R. Mayhew, K. A. Braitman, S. A. Ferguson, and H. M. Simpson (2009). Effects of age and experience on young driver crashes: Review of recent literature. *Traffic Inj. Prev.*, *10*, 209-219.
McCartt, A. T., V. I. Shabanova and W. A. Leaf (2003). Driving experience, crashes and traffic citations of teenage beginning drivers. *Accid. Anal. Prev.*, *35*, 311-320.
McCartt, A. T., E. R. Teoh, M. Fields, K. A. Braitman, and L. A. Hellinga (2010). Graduated licensing laws and fatal crashes of teenage drivers: A national study. *Traffic Inj. Prev.*, *11*, 240-248.
McGehee, D. V., M. R. Raby, C. Carney, J. D. Lee and M. L. Reyes (2007). Extending parental mentoring using an event-triggered video intervention in rural teen drivers. *J. Safety Res.*, *38*, 215-227.
McGwin, G. Jr., C. Owsley and K. Ball (1998). Identifying crash involvement among older drivers: Agreement between self report and state records. *Accid. Anal. Prev.*, *30*, 781-791.
McKenna, F. P. and J. Crick (1997). Hazard perception in drivers: A methodology for testing and training. Transport Research Laboratory, Crowthorne, England.
McKnight, A. J. and B. D. Adams (1970). Driver education task analysis. Volume I: Task descriptions. Human Resources Research Organization, Alexandria, VA.

McKnight, A. J. and A. S. McKnight (2000). The behavioral contributors to highway crashes of youthful drivers. *Proceedings of the 44th annual conference of the Association for the Advancement of Automotive Medicine*, pp. 321-346. Association for the Advancement of Automotive Medicine, Des Plaines, IL.

McKnight, A. J. and A. S. McKnight (2003). Young novice drivers: Careless or clueless? *Accid. Anal. Prev.*, *35*, 921-925.

McMahon, K. and D. O'Reilly (2000). Evaluation of road safety education and novice driver safety measures in Great Britain. Proceedings of the International Cooperation on Theories and Concepts in Traffic Safety (ICTCT) Practice Workshop of 2000 in Corfu, Greece. www.ictct.org

Meir, A., A. Borowsky and T. Oron-Gilad (2014). Formation and Evaluation of Act and Anticipate Hazard Perception Training (AAHPT) intervention for young-novice drivers. *Traffic Inj. Prev.*, *15*, 172-180.

Miller, G. and O. Taubman-Ben-Ari (2010). Driving styles among young novice drivers—The contribution of parental driving styles and personal characteristics. *Accid. Anal. Prev.*, *42*, 558-570.

Molina, J. G., R. García-Ros, and E. Keskinen (2014). Implementation of the driver training curriculum in Spain: An analysis based on the Goals for Driver Education (GDE) framework. *Trans. Res. F*, *26*, 28-37.

Moller, M. (2004). An explorative study of the relationship between lifestyle and driving behavior among young drivers. *Accid. Anal. Prev.*, *36*(6), 1081-1088.

Mourant, R. R. and T. H. Rockwell (1972). Strategies of visual search by novice and experienced drivers. *Hum. Fact.*, *14*, 325-335.

Mueller, A. S. and L. M. Trick (2012). Driving in fog: The effects of driving experience and visibility on speed compensation and hazard avoidance. *Accid. Anal. Prev.*, *48*, 472-479.

NHTSA (1975). The Driver Education Evaluation Program (DEEP): A report to the Congress. U.S. Department of Transportation, Washington, DC.

NHTSA (1994). Research agenda for an improved novice driver education program – Report to congress. National Highway Traffic Safety Administration Report DOT-HS-808-161. U.S. Department of Transportation, Washington, DC.

NHTSA (2015). Young drivers report the highest level of phone involvement in crash or near-crash incidences. Traffic Safety Facts – Research Note. Report No. DOT-HS-811-611. U.S. Department of Transportation, Washington, DC.

NTSB (2005). National transportation safety board public forum on driver education and training, October, 28-29, 2003. Report of the Proceedings NTSB/RP-05-01 PB 2005-917003. Notation 633A. NTSB, Washington, DC.

Nyberg, A., N. P. Gregersen and M. Wiklund (2007). Practicing in relation to the outcome of the driving test. *Accid. Anal. Prev.*, *39*(1), 159-168.

O'Brien, N. P., R. D. Foss, A. H. Goodwin, and S. V. Masten (2013). Supervised hours requirements in graduated driver licensing: Effectiveness and parental awareness. *Accid. Anal. Prev.*, *50*, 330-335.

OECD (2006). Young drivers: The road to safety. Organization of Economic Cooperation and Development and the European Conference of Ministers of Transport Report ITRD. OECD Publishing, Paris, France.

Olsen, E. C., B. G. Simons-Morton, and S. E. Lee (2006). Novice teen and experienced adult drivers on the smart road intersection: does six months of experience matter? In *Proceedings of the Human Factors and Ergonomics Society Annual Meeting* (Vol. 50(22), pp. 2383-2387). Sage.

Ouimet, M. C., T. G. Brown, F. Guo, S. G. Klauer, B. G. Simons-Morton, Y. Fang, S. E. Lee, C. Gianoulakis and T. A. Dingus (2014). Higher crash and near-crash rates in teenaged drivers with lower cortisol response: An 18-month longitudinal, naturalistic study. *JAMA Pediatr*, *168*, 517-522.

Ouimet, M. C., B. G. Simons-Morton, P. L. Zador, N. D. Lerner, M. Freedman, G. D. Duncan, and J. Wang (2010). Using the US National Household Travel Survey to estimate the impact of passenger characteristics on young drivers' relative risk of fatal crash involvement. *Accid. Anal. Prev.*, *42*, 689-694.

Peck, R. C., M. A. Gebers, R. B. Voas, and E. Romano (2008). The relationship between blood alcohol concentration (BAC), age, and crash risk. *J. Safety Res.*, *39*, 311-319.

Petzoldt, T., T. Weiß, T. Franke, J. F. Krems, and M. Bannert (2013). Can driver education be improved by computer based training of cognitive skills? *Accid. Anal. Prev.*, *50*, 1185-1192.

Porter, M. and M. J. Whitton (2002). Assessment of driving with the global positioning system and video technology in young, middle-aged, and older drivers. *J. Gerontol. Med. Sci.*, *57A*(9), M578-M582.

Pradhan, A. K., K. R. Hammel, R. DeRamus, A. Pollatsek, D. A. Noyce and D. L. Fisher (2005). Using eye movements to evaluate effects of driver age on risk perception in a driving simulator. *Hum. Fact.*, *47*(4), 840-852.

Prato, C. G., T. Toledo, T. Lotan, and O. Taubman-Ben-Ari (2010). Modelling the behavior of novice young drivers during the first year after licensure. *Accid. Anal. Prev.*, *42*, 480-486.

Preusser, D. F., S. A. Ferguson and A. F. Williams (1998). The effect of teenage passengers on the fatal crash risk of teenage drivers. *Accid. Anal. Prev.*, *30*, 217-222.

Preusser, D. F., A. F. Williams, P. L. Zador and R. D. Blomberg (1984). The effect of curfew laws on motor vehicle crashes. *Law and Policy*, *6*, 115-128.

Romer, D., Y.-C. Lee, C. C. McDonald, and F. K. Winston (2014). Adolescence, attention allocation, and driving safety. *J. Adolesc. Health*, *54*, S6-S15.

RoSPA (2002). Young and novice drivers education and training. Royal Society for the Prevention of Accidents (RoSPA), London, England.

Rudin-Brown, C. M., J. Edquist, and M. G. Lenné (2014). Effects of driving experience and sensation-seeking on drivers' adaptation to road environment complexity. *Safety Sci.*, *62*, 121-129.

Sagberg, F. (1998). Month-by-month changes in accident risk among novice drives. Paper presented in the 24th International Congress of Applied Psychology, San Francisco, CA, 9-14 August (as cited by Groeger, 2000).

Sagberg, F. and T. Bjornskau (2006). Hazard perception and driving experience among novice drivers. *Accid. Anal. Prev.*, *38*, 407-414.

Scialfa, C. T., R. S. Pereverseff, and D. Borkenhagen (2014). Short-term reliability of a brief hazard perception test. *Accid. Anal. Prev.*, *73*, 41-46.

Scott, H., L. Hall, D. Litchfield, and D. Westwood (2013). Visual information search in simulated junction negotiation: Gaze transitions of young novice, young experienced and older experienced drivers. *J. Safety Res.*, *45*, 111-116.

Scott-Parker, B., B. Watson, M. J. King, and M. K. Hyde (2014). Young novice drivers and the risky behaviours of parents and friends during the provisional (intermediate) license phase: A brief report. *Accid. Anal. Prev. 69*, 51-55.

Senserrick, T. M. (2002). Training young drivers: Can it work? Developing Safer Drivers and Riders Conference Proceedings, pp. 71-79. Australian College of Road Safety, Mawson ACT, Australia.

Senserrick, T. M. and G. C. Swinburne (2001). Evaluation of an insight driver training program for young drivers. Report 186. Monash University Accident Research Center, Victoria, Australia.

Senserrick, T. M. and A. F. Williams (2015). Summary of literature on the effective components of graduated driver licensing systems. Austroads Report AP-R476-15. Austroads, Sydney, Australia.

Shalev, M. (2002). Fontanella. Am Oved, Ltd., Tel Aviv. (Quote from p. 112) (Hebrew).

Shimshoni, Y., H. Farah, T. Lotan, E. Grimberg, O. Dritter, O. Musicant, T. Toledo, and H. Omer (2015). Effects of parental vigilant care and feedback on novice driver risk. *J. Adolesc.*, *38*, 69-80.

Shinar, D. (1978). *Psychology on the Road: The Human Factor in Traffic Safety*. Wiley and Sons, New York, NY.

Shinar, D., M. Meir and I. Ben-Shoham (1998). How automatic is manual gear shifting? *Hum. Fact.*, *40*, 647-654.

Simons-Morton, B., N. Lerner and J. Singer (2005). The observed effects of teenage passengers on the risky driving behavior of teenage drivers. *Accid. Anal. Prev.*, *37*, 973-982.

Simons-Morton, B. G., J. L. Hartos, W. A. Leaf, and D. F. Preusser (2006). The effects of the checkpoints program on parent-imposed driving limits and crash outcomes among Connecticut novice teen drivers at 6-months post-licensure. *J. Safety Res.*, *37*(1), 9-15.

Simons-Morton, B. and M. C. Ouimet (2006). Parent involvement in novice teen driving: A review of the literature. *Inj. Prev.*, *12*(Suppl. 1), i30-i37.

Simons-Morton, B. G., M. C. Ouimet, Z. Zhang, S. E. Klauer, S. E. Lee, J. Wang, R. Chen, P. Albert and T. A. Dingus (2011). The effect of passengers and risk-taking friends on risky driving and crashes/near crashes among novice teenagers. *J. Adolesc. Health*, *49*, 587-593.

Simpson, H. M. (2003). The evolution and effectiveness of graduated licensing. *J. Safety Res.*, *34*, 25-34.

Spolander, K. (1990). Effects of commentary driving—A study on young male drivers. VTI Rapport 359. Swedish Road and Transport Research Institute, Linköping, Sweden.

Stock, J. R., J. K. Weaver, H. W. Ray, J. R. Brink and M. G. Sadoff (1983). Evaluation of safe performance secondary school driver education curriculum demonstration project. National Highway Traffic Safety Administration Report DOT HS 806 568. U.S. Department of Transportation, Washington, DC.

Surry, J. (1968). Industrial accident research: A human engineering appraisal. Department of Industrial Engineering, University of Toronto, and Occupational Health and Safety Division, Ontario Ministry of Labor, Toronto, Ontario.

Taubman-Ben-Ari, O. and L. Katz-Ben-Ami (2012). The contribution of family climate for road safety and social environment to the reported driving behaviour of young drivers. *Accid. Anal. Prev.*, *47*, 1-10.

Taubman-Ben-Ari, O. and T. Lotan (2011). The contribution of a novel intervention to enhance safe driving among young drivers in Israel. *Accid. Anal. Prev.*, *43*(1), 352-359.

Thomas, F. D.,, S. L. Rilea, R. D. Blomberg, R. C. Peck and K. T. Korbelak (2016). Evaluation of the safety benefits of the risk awareness and perception training program for novice teen drivers. National Highway Traffic Safety Administration Report No. DOT HS 812 235. U.S. Department of Transportation, Washington, DC.

Toledo, T., T. Lotan, O. Taubman-Ben-Ari, and E. Grimberg (2012). Evaluation of a program to enhance young drivers' safety in Israel. *Accid. Anal. Prev.*, *45*, 705-710.

Treat, J. R., N. S. Tumbas, S. T. McDonald, D. Shinar, R. D. Hume, R. E. Mayer, R. L. Stansifer and N. J. Castellan (1979). Tri-level study of the causes of traffic accidents: Final report. Volume I: Causal factor tabulations and assessments. National Highway Traffic Safety Administration. Report No. DOT HS 805 085. U.S. Department of Transportation, Washington, DC.

Underwood, G., P. Chapman, K. Bowden and D. Crundall (2002). Visual search while driving: Skill and awareness during inspection of the scene. *Transport. Res. F*, *5*, 87-97.

Underwood, G., A. Ngai and J. Underwood (2013). Driving experience and situation awareness in hazard detection. *Safety Sci.*, *56*, 29-35.

Vanlaar, W., D. Mayhew, K. Marcoux, G. Wets, T. Brijs and J. Shope (2009). An evaluation of graduated driver licensing programs in North America using a meta-analytic approach. *Accid. Anal. Prev. 41*(5), 1104-1111.

Vernick, J. S., L. Guohua, S. Ogaitis, E. J. MacKenzie, S. P. Baker and A. C. Gielen (1999). Effects of high school driver education in motor vehicle crashes, violations, and licensure. *Am. J. Prev. Med.*, *16*, 40-46.

Vlakveld, W. P. (2004). New policy proposals for novice drivers in the Netherlands. Fourteenth Seminar of the Behavioural Research in Road Safety. Department for Transport, London (as cited by OECD, 2006).

Waller, P. F. (2003). The genesis of GDL. *J. Safety Res.*, *34*, 17-23.

Wallis, T. S. and M. S. Horswill (2007). Using fuzzy signal detection theory to determine why experienced and trained drivers respond faster than novices in a hazard perception test. *Accid. Anal. Prev.*, *39*, 1177-1185.

Wang, Y., W. Zhang and G. Salvendy (2010). Effects of a simulation-based training intervention on novice drivers' hazard handling performance. *Traffic Inj. Prev.*, *11*, 16-24.

Warner, W. L. (1972). A brief history of driver education. *J. Traffic Safety Educ.*, *19*, 13, 15.

Weiss, T., T. Petzoldt, M. Bannert and J. Krems (2013). Calibration as side effect? Computer-based learning in driver education and the adequacy of driving-task-related self-assessments. *Trans. Res. F*, *17*, 63-74.

Whelan, M., T. Senserrick, J. Groeger, T. Triggs and S. Hosking (2004). Learner driver experience project, Report No. 221. Monash University Accident Research Center, Clayton, Victoria, Australia.

Wiggins, S. (2005). Graduated licensing program: Interim evaluation report – Year 3. Insurance Corporation of British Columbia, British Columbia, Canada. http://www.icbc.com/Library/glp_eval.html

Williams, A. F. (2003). Teen drivers: Patterns of risk. *J. Safety Res.*, *34*, 5-15.

Williams, A. F., S. A. Ferguson, W. A. Leaf and D. F. Preusser (1998). Views of parents of teenagers about graduated licensing systems. *J. Safety Res.*, *29*, 1-7.

Williams, A. F., S. A. Ferguson and J. K. Wells (2005). Sixteen-years-old drivers in fatal crashes, United States, 2003. *Traffic Inj. Prev.*, *6*, 202-206.

Williams, A. F., W. A. Leaf, B. G. Simons-Morton and J. L. Hartos (2006). Vehicles driven by teenagers in their first year of licensure. *Traffic Inj. Prev.*, *7*(1), 23-30.

Williams, A. F., A. T. McCartt, and L. B. Sims (2016). History and current status of state graduated driver licensing (GDL) laws in the United States. *J. Safety Res.*, *56*, 9-15.

Williams, A. F., L. A. Nelson, and W. A. Leaf (2002). Responses of teenagers and their parents to California's graduated licensing system. *Accid. Anal. Prev.*, *34*, 835-842.

Williams A. F. and B. O'Neill (1974). On-the-road driving records of licensed race drivers. *Accid. Anal. Prev.*, *6*, 263-270.

Williams, A. F., D. F. Preusser, S. A. Ferguson and R. G. Ulmer (1997). Analysis of the fatal crash involvements of 15-year old drivers. *J. Safety Res.*, *28*(1), 49-54.

Williams, A. F. and R. A. Shults (2010). Graduated driver licensing research, 2007-present: A review and commentary. *J. Safety Res.*, *41*, 77-84.

Williams, A. F., B. C. Tefft, and J. G. Grabowski (2012). Graduated driver licensing research, 2010-Present. *J. Safety Res.*, *43*, 195-203.

Yagil, D. (1998). Gender and age-related differences in attitudes towards traffic laws and traffic violations. *Transport. Res. F*, *1*, 123-135.

Zafian, T., S. Samuel, A. Borowsky, and D. L. Fisher (2014). Can young drivers be trained to better anticipate hazards in complex driving scenarios? A driving simulator study. Proceedings of the Transportation Research Board 93rd Annual Meeting (No. 14-4615). Transportation Research Board, Washington, DC.

Zhu, M., P. Cummings, H. Chu, J. H. Coben and G. Li (2013). Graduated driver licensing and motor vehicle crashes involving teenage drivers: An exploratory age-stratified meta-analysis. *Inj. Prev.* *19*, 49-57.

Zhu, M., P. Cummings, S. Zhao, J. H. Coben and G. S. Smith (2015). The association of graduated driver licensing with miles driven and fatal crash rates per miles driven among adolescents. *Inj. Prev.*, *21*, e21-e27.

7

Older Drivers

"My father quit driving when he was 25 .... He was always the navigator, and once, when he was 95 and she (mother) was 88 and still driving, he said to me, 'Do you want to know the secret of a long life?' 'I guess so', I said, knowing it probably would be something bizarre."

"No left turns," he said.

"What?" I asked.

"No left turns," he repeated. "Several years ago, your mother and I read an article that said most accidents that old people are in happen when they turn left in front of oncoming traffic. As you get older, your eyesight worsens, and you can lose your depth perception, it said. So your mother and I decided never again to make a left turn."

"What?" I said again. "No left turns," he said. "Think about it. Three rights are the same as a left, and that's a lot safer. So we always make three rights."

"You're kidding!" I said, and I turned to my mother for support. "No," she said, "your father is right. We make three rights. It works."

But then she added: "Except when your father loses count."

I was driving at the time, and I almost drove off the road as I started laughing. "Loses count?" I asked. "Yes," my father admitted, "that sometimes happens. But it's not a problem. You just make seven rights, and you're okay again."

I couldn't resist. "Do you ever go for 11?" I asked.

"No," he said. "If we miss it at seven, we just come home and call it a bad day. Besides, nothing in life is so important it can't be put off another day or another week."

"My mother was never in an accident, but one evening she handed me her car keys and said she had decided to quit driving. That was in 1999, when she was 90. She lived four more years, until 2003." (Michael Gartner, President of NBC News. *USA Today*, June 15, 2006).

"Clearly, the older road user is the customer of the future." (AARP, Public Policy Institute, 2009).

"Today's older drivers are not only less likely to be involved in crashes than prior generations, they are less likely to be killed or seriously injured if they do crash." (Insurance Institute for Highway Safety, February 2, 2014).

Problem Identification: Demographic Trends, Mobility, and Safety

The older driver "vision" embraced by the U.S. National Highway Traffic Safety Administration (NHTSA, 2003) is to have "a transportation system that offers safe mobility to all people and allows older people to remain independent and to age in place ... to extend safe driving and to offer other and convenient and affordable transportation options when driving and walking options must be curtailed." This is quite a challenge for an agency focusing on safety. Older driver – typically defined as 65+ years old – issues are unique because they involve the following seven, often contradictory, features:

1. It is the fastest growing age group in the population of developed countries. As more and more of the post-World War II baby boomers exceed that age, the percentage that will retain their license past age 65 is expected to approach 100 percent in the Western world (OECD, 2001; DfT, 2001). In the U.S., in 2013 they already constituted 14 percent of the total population, compared to 12 percent in 2004, and over that decade there was a 27 percent increase in the number of older drivers roaming the U.S. roads (NHTSA, 2015)
2. Life expectancy increases and quality of life – in the sense of being "disability-free" – in later years is constantly improving (Hakamies-Blomqvist, Siren, and Davidse, 2004).
3. The political and economic clout of older people is increasing. In addition to the increase in numbers, older people are wealthier than they were (Coughlin and D'Ambrosio, 2012).
4. Driving in most western society is the key to continued mobility, which in turn makes it the key to maintaining independence and socially active life.
5. Aging is a process accompanied by impairments in various driving-related functions, including vision, cognition, and motor capabilities.
6. While average performance in most functions deteriorates with age, individual differences increase significantly so that chronological age is not a very valid indicator

of a specific individual's performance. This makes chronological age a questionable decision criterion for license restrictions or remedial training (Midwinter, 2005).

7. The public image of the older driver, as a menace on the road may be incorrect given recent data on older drivers that show that "contrary to popular belief the older driver segment of the population is not a significant risk to others" (NHTSA, 2003, p. 2).

Demographic trends

Since the beginning of mass production of automobiles at the beginning of the 20th century, life expectancy in the Western world has increased by 28 years. The declining birth rates in the western world coupled with the increase in life expectancy makes older people in general, and older drivers in particular, the fastest growing driver age group in the population. In the beginning of this century, in the U.S. there were approximately 15 million people 65 years old and older and they constituted approximately 12 percent of the population. By 2030 their number is expected to double to 30 million and they will constitute approximately 20 percent of the U.S. population (NHTSA, 2003). This shift in the make-up of the population is dramatically illustrated in the age pyramids for 1960, 1990, and (the estimated figures for) 2020, reproduced Figure 7-1. In the top panel, the post-World War II baby boomers are the bars of the 15-24 years old (that follow the low birth rates in the decade immediately preceding them). By the year 2020 the baby boomers will be 75 years old, and they and the next two generations that followed them will constitute the top three bars in the bottom panel of Figure 7-1. Note how big these bars are relative to those of the same age groups in 1960. This trend is expected to continue, so that by 2030 the age distribution will be almost uniform, with nearly as many people over 80 years old as 60-64 years old (Dellinger, 2012) (For a dynamic visualization of the change in the population age, see http://www.census.gov/popclock/).

Medical breakthroughs and healthier lifestyles have not only added years to people's lives but also health. The older people of today are much healthier than their cohorts of yester year. In the U.S. the percentage of disabled people among the 65+ years old keeps shrinking at a rate of approximately 1.3 percent per year (Hakamies-Blomqvist *et al.*, 2004). As a result of these factors, the political and economic leverage of older people is also increasing. In the U.S. where people over 65 constitute 14 percent of the population, they control more than 40 percent of the disposable income, and their resources are expected to keep increasing (Coughlin and D'Ambrosio, 2012). Also, as a consequence of staying healthy longer, the percent of licensed drivers 65+ years old, out of the total licensed population, is constantly increasing. For example, in the U.S. in the mid-1960 they constituted approximately five percent, but by 2030 they are expected to exceed 20 percent (Meyer, 2009), and this too is an under-estimate as it does not take into consideration the emergence of assistive technologies that will make driving easier for the older people, and autonomous vehicles that will make human vehicle control superfluous. Also, relative to the number of people alive in their age group, the percent of 65+ years old drivers is significantly higher now than it was in the previous decade. For example, in 1983 approximately half of the 65+ years old people were driving in the U.S., whereas 25 years later the percent rose to approximately 80 percent. And though

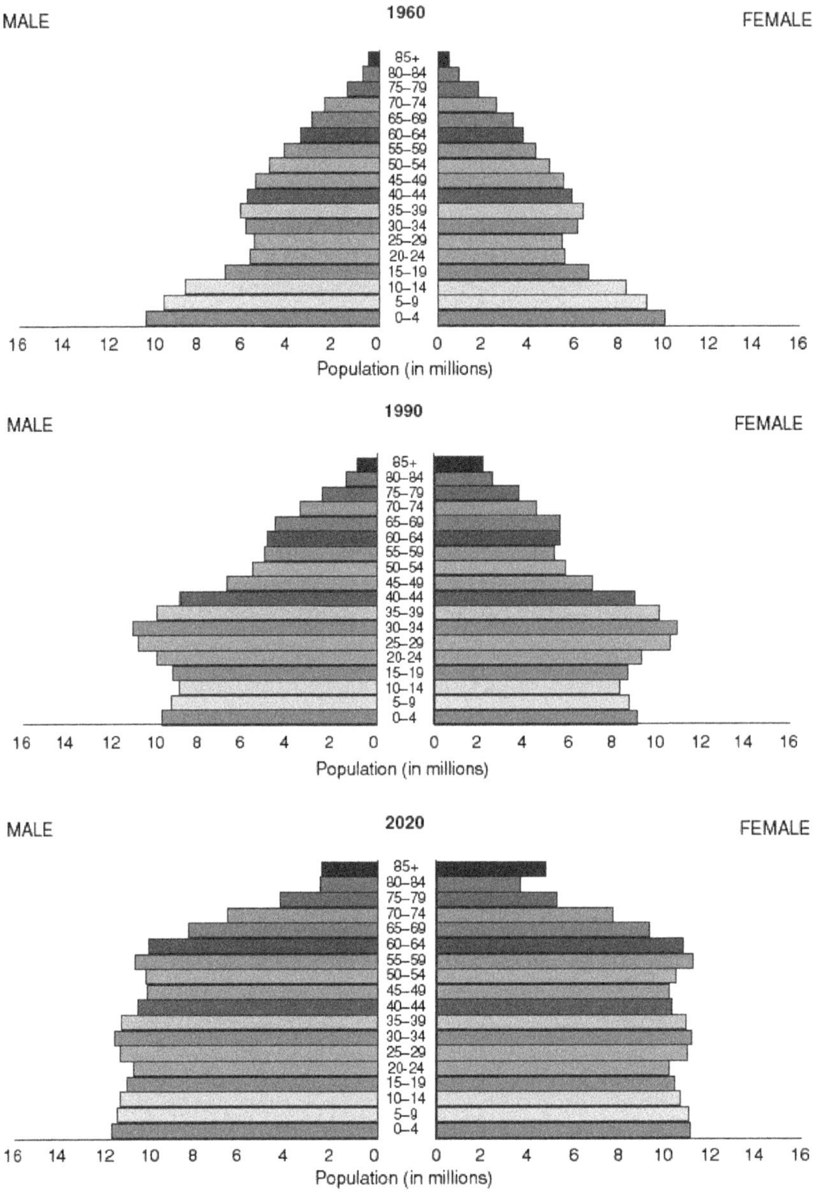

Figure 7-1. U.S. population age distributions in 1960, 1990, and the projected population for 2020, based on the U.S. Census Bureau data (from the Committee for Conference on Transportation in an Aging Society, 2005).

the specific percentages varied across countries, the trend seemed to be the same worldwide (Sivak and Schoettle, 2011).

Mobility patterns

The degree of dependence on the private vehicle of older people is remarkably similar to that of younger people. However, their driving pattern differs significantly: they rarely drink and drive, they do not drive to work, they tend to drive at off-peak hours and in the daytime, they do not speed, etc. Travel behavior for a representative sample of a whole country is practically impossible to measure directly, and therefore data are based on extrapolations from limited surveys. The most recent U.S. National Household Transportation Surveys were conducted by the U.S. Department of Transportation, in 2001, and 2009. The 2001 survey included 60,000 individuals from 26,000 households, and the 2009 survey included approximately 300,000 people from 150,000 households. The results presented below are based on these surveys (Collia, Sharp, and Giesbrecht, 2003; Memmot, 2006; Santos *et al.*, 2011).

In general, as people age they take fewer and fewer short (daily) and long (50+ miles) trips. Men take more trips than women, but the age-related pattern is the same for both genders: with people 75+ years old taking approximately 55 percent fewer trips than people 55-64 years old, as illustrated in Figure 7-2. The time they spend in their cars and their annual mileage decline consistently after age 40; with people 65+ years spending less than an hour per day (in both surveys). Interestingly though the annual mileage of 35-55 years old remained the same in 2001 and 2009, the annual mileage for the older people increased in 2009 by about seven percent for all older people, but by 21 percent

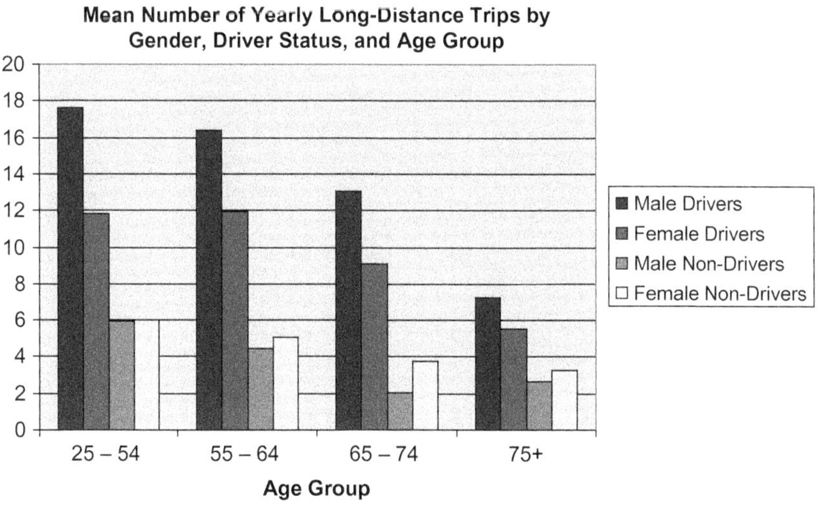

Figure 7-2. Number of long-distance trips drivers and non-drivers take as a function of age (based on U.S. 2001 data, from Memmot, 2006).

for women. The license itself is a key determinant, with people who drive taking approximately 50 percent more trips than people who don't. More interesting, and relevant to our concerns, is the mode of transportation that people use. Regardless of age, in the U.S. almost 90 percent of all trips are conducted by a personal vehicle, and most of the remaining trips are done by air. Thus, older people – whether they drive or not – continue to rely on the personal car for their primary mode of transportation.

When they do ride in a car, older people, just like younger ones, are more likely to drive than be driven, though as they age the percent of driving decreases from 70 percent for older drivers under 75 years old to approximately 55 percent for drivers 85+ years old. In parallel, the percent of trips taken with someone else driving a car increases from approximately 20 percent at age 65-74 to 25 percent at age 85+. Interestingly, the percent of walking trips and trips with a taxi or public transportation remain relatively constant at about 9 percent and 1-2 percent, respectively.

What changes significantly over time are the times-of-day that people drive and the purpose of their trips. This is true both for long trips and short daily trips. At all ages, most of the long-distance trips are for pleasure, but their proportion relative to other trip purposes increases with age, while the proportions of work-related trips – as might be expected – declines with age. Personal and social trips – both long and short-distance – increase with age, as illustrated for long-distance trips in Figure 7-3. Interestingly the latter survey showed an increase of 70 percent (from 6.2 percent to 10.6 percent) in the percent of work-related trips, suggesting that more 65+ years old people are now staying in the workforce.

In addition to taking fewer trips, older people also limit the times they drive to mostly late morning and early afternoon hours. This is most significant because these are the low-congestion good visibility hours. The number of trips during rush hours and night decline in a very consistent manner over the years as illustrated in Figure 7-4. This pattern reflects both a lesser need to drive at these hours, and a preference for picking low-risk times when problems of poor night vision and slowed cognitive processes are minimized. And when the older drivers eventually decide to cease driving altogether, age and diminishing contrast sensitivity appear to be the primary determinants of that decision (Emerson *et al.*, 2012) Thus, we have here our first indication of one of the best means of dealing with the aging process: self-regulation.

Safety of older drivers

Older drivers are the least involved in crashes. Older drivers are the most involved in crashes. Despite the apparent contradiction, both statements are true and require clarifications. From a public health perspective the number of injuries and fatalities suffered by older people is not a significant problem compared to the number of injuries and fatalities of other age groups. They constitute a very small part of the total number of fatalities in the U.S. and relative to their frequency in the population, they are the least involved (safest?) of all age groups, as can be seen in Figure 7-5 (NHTSA, 2015).

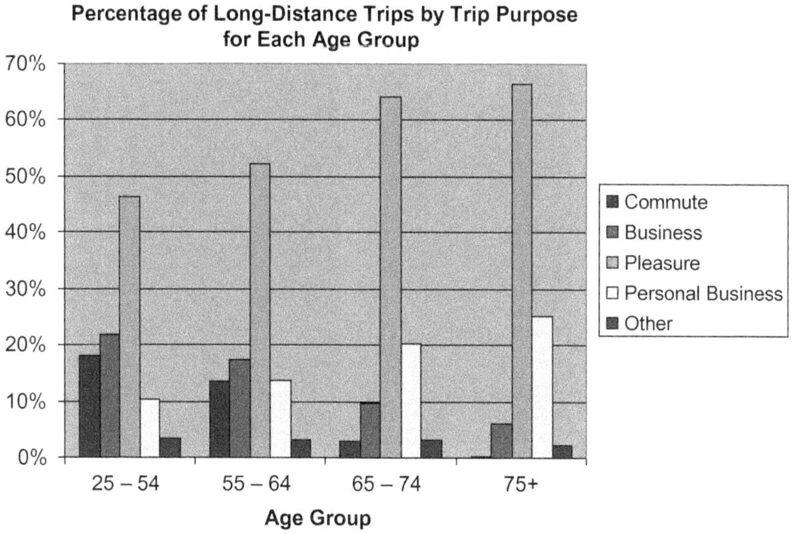

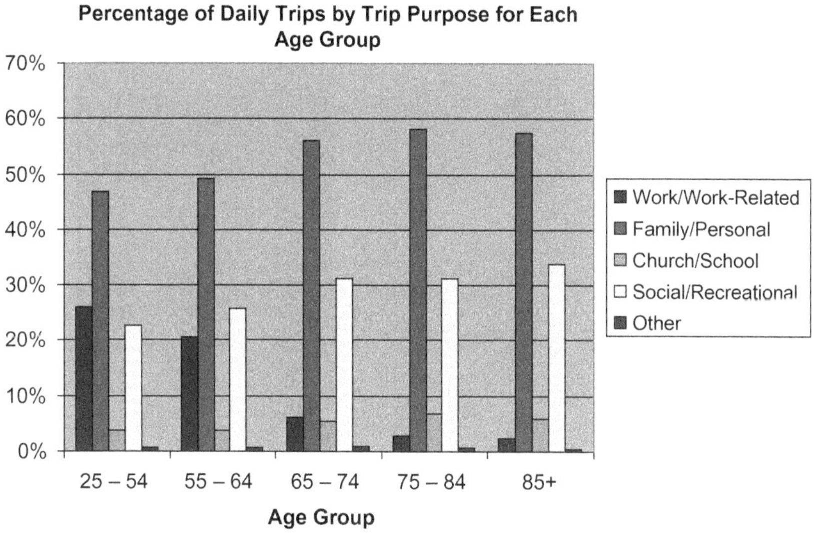

Figure 7-3. Percent of daily trips and long-distance trips that are taken for different purposes as a function of age (from Memmot, 2006).

Nonetheless, probably because of their growing numbers in the population and because they continue with an active life into later years than before, their share of the total number of traffic fatalities is slowly but consistently increasing in the developed countries. Thus, in the EU countries in 2012 they exceeded 30 percent, whereas in 2000 they were 23 percent. In Japan, where in 2012 the 65+ years old people constituted 30 percent of the population, they accounted for 55 percent of all road traffic fatalities! (OECD, 2014).

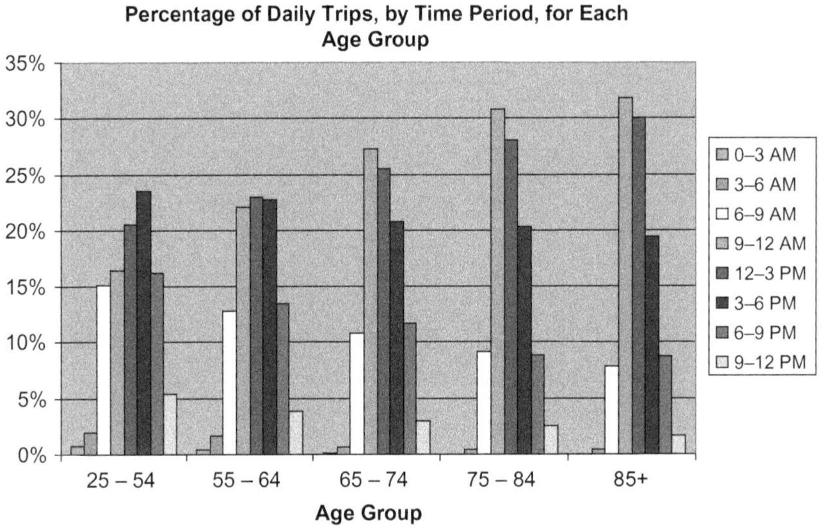

Figure 7-4. The percent of daily trips at different times of the day and night as a function of age (from Memmot, 2006).

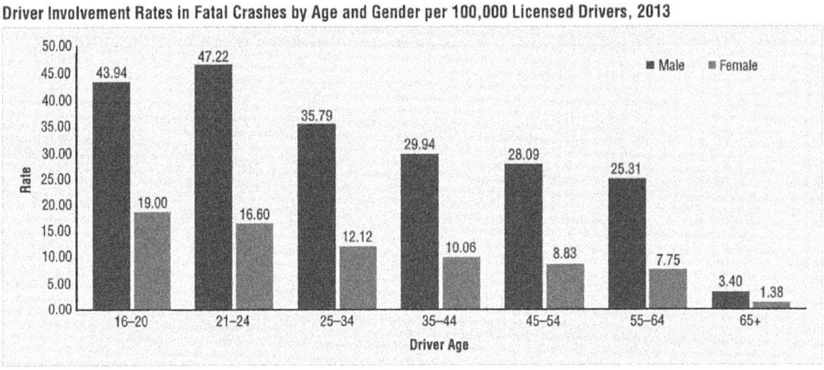

Figure 7-5. Driver involvement rate in fatal crashes by age and gender per 100,000 licensed drivers (based on FARS, 2013 data, from NHTSA, 2015).

Of course, this pattern of traffic fatalities is not adjusted for exposure. To adjust for exposure we have to first realize that older drivers are also a very small group of the driving population – smaller in fact than any other age group (see Figure 7-1). If we adjust the injuries and fatalities for the number of people in each age group, and look at injuries and fatalities per 10,000 people (Figure 7-6(a) in Finland and Sweden), we find that older people still have the lowest injury and fatality rates. This is generally true in most countries, and Figure 7-6(a) illustrates it for Finland and Sweden. However, unlike people in younger age groups, many older people do not drive. Therefore, the risk of driving for older people can be better estimated if we base their crash involvement rate on the number of licensed drivers instead of the number of people. But when we do that we again see a similar pattern (Figure 7-5 for the U.S. and Figure 7-6(b) for Sweden). However, when we examine the rates for the Finnish drivers in Figure 7-6(b) we now begin to see a U-shaped curve. While the young drivers still have the highest injury rates, after the age of 65 the injury rates of the Finnish drivers begin to increase with increasing age (Figure 7-6(b)). When we measure safety in terms of fatalities, older drivers because of their frailty are at even higher risk. Thus, recent U.S. data show that relative to their

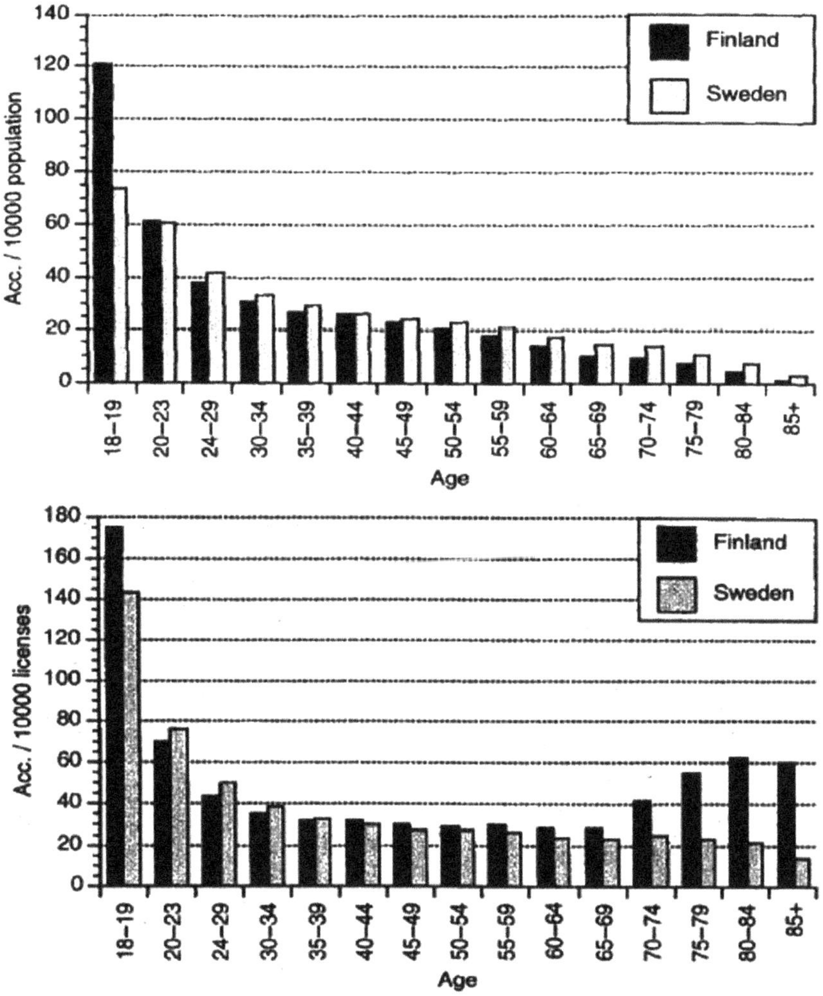

Figure 7-6. Accident rates in Finland with its strict relicensing procedures for older drivers, and in Sweden with its very lax procedures; calculated relative to the number of people (a – top panel) and relative to the number of licensed drivers (b – bottom panel) (from Hakamies-Blomqvist *et al.*, 1995, with permission from Elsevier).

number in the population the very old (85+ years old) drivers are equally at risk as the young 20-24 years old drivers. This is true for both males and females, though females are consistently at lower risk than males at all age groups (IIHS, 2015; see Figure 6-2).

But there is one more aspect of exposure that needs to be controlled: the amount of driving that people do. It is a reasonable assumption that the more kilometers a person drives, the more that person exposes himself or herself to the risk of a crash. This is because we assume that for a given person, his or her skill and driving style do not change over distance and therefore every kilometer of driving should increase the risk of a crash by a roughly constant amount. This in fact is the case (with some reservations detailed below), and it is easy to demonstrate that miles or kilometers of driving are the best predictor of crash risk (Evans, 2004). Getting back to the older drivers, as illustrated in Figure 7-2 they actually drive less than younger people, and often reduce their driving in response to age-related medical conditions such as glaucoma (McGwin *et al.*, 2004), cataracts, angina pectoris, and diabetes (Parmentier *et al.*, 2005). If we then calculate the injury rate relative to the exposure in terms of miles or kilometers driven, we get the alarming pattern that shows that relative to the amount of driving, the older drivers are the highest risk group of all drivers 30 years old or older (see Figure 6-3(a)). Finally, when we limit the injuries only to the fatal ones, the picture gets even worse. The fatality rate begins to increase at the age of about 70, and it is higher than for any other age group for drivers 80+ years old (Figure 6-3(b)) (Cicchino and McCartt, 2014). These differences between crash risk, injury risk and fatality risk are at the core of the older driver safety problem: not their crash risk but their likelihood to be severely injured or killed once a crash occurs.

To summarize so far, older people are not a significant problem from a societal public health perspective (even though the number of fatalities in the 65+ years old group is expected to double relative to the number in the beginning of the millennium; Lyman, *et al.*, 2002). They are also not at a very high risk to themselves in general because many of them do not drive, and the ones that do drive much less than younger drivers. However, once they get behind the wheel, for every unit of distance that they drive they are much more dangerous than drivers in any other age group – and they mostly endanger themselves and their passengers (Braver and Trempel, 2004). The U-shaped curve for crash and injury rates relative to exposure in terms of miles driven has been reported by different researchers using different data bases (Dellinger *et al.*, 2004; Evans, 1991, 2004; NHTSA, 2003), but not by all. For example, even with the often used data bases maintained by the U.S. National Highway Traffic Safety Administration, not all studies found an increase in crash rates for older drivers. Thus, Kweon and Kockelman (2003), found that young drivers (under 20 years old) have much higher crash rates than older drivers, and drivers over 60+ years old have the same or lower crash and fatality rates as drivers 20-60 years old (except for higher fatality rates for old women driving mini-vans). The reason for some of the discrepancies between studies stems from the different number of moderating variables used in the calculations, and more importantly from the different sources for estimation of the exposure.

The underlying factors that account for high per mile injury risks of older drivers are very different than those at work in the case of the young drivers at the other extreme of the U-shaped curve. Young drivers are inexperienced but overly confident, they drive at high risk times such as at night, and they drive under high-risk conditions such as when fatigued or intoxicated (see Chapter 6). Older drivers, in contrast, are the most experienced drivers in the whole driving population, they restrict their driving to low-risk times (daytime) and situations (non-rush hours), and they generally do not drive when they are fatigued or intoxicated. What the older drivers suffer from is the aging process that affects many of their driving-related skills and capabilities including vision, slowed information processing and reduced abilities to distribute their attention effectively, and morbidity that affects driving. This includes eye diseases, dementia, and increased likelihood of sudden incapacitation due to stroke and heart failure – the two most frequent causes of death among older people – see Table 1-1.

Before we examine the impact of the specific potential impairments that afflict older persons and their implications for their driving safety, we should examine the crash and injury data more closely. Several recent studies have done this and they not only provide some explanations for the increase in crash and injury rates, but they actually question the conclusion that older drivers are over-involved in crashes.

Detailed examination of older drivers' crash involvement – The role of exposure

In the western world most of the people get a license when they reach the minimum licensing age and keep it for as long as they can, typically until aging effects start seriously affecting their performance. The process of "de-licensing," losing the license either because it was revoked or voluntarily or involuntarily not renewed, is highly variable. It depends on many factors such as a person's self-perceptions of the need for the license, confidence in continued driving, and licensing procedures. For example, people who remain active in the workforce, people living in rural areas, and people who live alone are much more dependent on driving for their mobility and hence are likely to hang on to their license longer (Stutts, 2005). License renewals also vary immensely among different jurisdictions. For example in the U.S., some states allow license renewal by mail for all applicants, while others require a medical (specifically vision) check for older drivers. The time-to-expiration of the license also varies from as low as 1 year (in Israel for drivers over 80 years old) to as much as 10 years (in Florida and Sweden for all ages).

Licensing practices can have significant and complex effects on the crash and injury rates. This was demonstrated in the study briefly mentioned above by Hakamies-Blomqvist, Johansson, and Lundberg (1995) when they compared the relicensing practices and crash involvement of older people in the neighboring Scandinavian countries Finland and Sweden. They noted that the different requirements for license renewal for older drivers that exist in the two countries may also be a factor in older people's decision to apply for the license renewal, and they hypothesized that in countries that have more severe medical and legal screening criteria older people are more likely to reconsider applying for the license renewal. To test this hypothesis and its impact on safety they compared the crash rates of older people and older drivers in Finland and Sweden: two countries that have a similar culture, climate, roadway infrastructure, and demographics. The two countries, however, differ markedly in their license renewal requirements for older drivers. In Sweden the license is renewed every 10 years and all an applicant has to do is send the licensing bureau an updated picture, and then pick up the new license. In Finland, the license expires at the age of 70 at which time the applicant has to obtain a medical clean bill of health and two testimonials that the applicant has kept up his or her driving skills by continuous driving. This process has to be repeated every 5 years, and more frequently after age 80. This process leads to increasing disparity in the proportion of drivers in each age group in the two countries. For example, Blomqvist *et al.* note that of all the persons who had a license at age 65-69, by the time they turned 70-79 only 49 percent of the people retained the license in Finland compared to 71 percent in Sweden. Incidentally, the latter rate is identical to the renewal rate reported for older drivers in Victoria, Australia, who are referred for license re-evaluation (Di Stefano and Macdonald, 2003). The difference in the relicensing rates between Sweden and Finland can be explained by the hurdles placed on Finnish applicants. These hurdles probably catalyze a self-selection process in which only those who feel a great need to drive and are likely to drive more kilometers, actually make the effort to renew their license. Indirect support for drivers' determination to keep their license comes from a study conducted in Israel where license renewal after age 65 is contingent on strict medical screening. Zaidel and Hocherman (1986) tracked the re-application process of approximately 10,000 65-year-old Israeli drivers and discovered, that of those who persisted in their efforts to retain the license, not a single one was denied!

When Hakamies-Blonqvist and her associates looked at the accident rates per 10,000 people in the two countries they observed the same trends in both countries and same decline with age that has been found in other countries such as the U.S. (Committee for Conference on Transportation in an Aging Society, 2005). This is illustrated in the top panel of Figure 7-6. In fact, beginning at age 24-29 the rate was slightly lower in Finland. The picture changed dramatically when the crash rates were calculated per 10,000 drivers rather than people, as can be seen in bottom panel of Figure 7-6. With this measure of exposure, the crash rates started to diverge at age 70, with Finnish drivers having much higher crash rates. These results lead to the paradoxical conclusion that strict licensing procedures actually lead to more crashes per driver! In fact what these data show is that when the crash rates are calculated per drivers, and many of the drivers in one country hardly drive (Sweden) while in the other country they drive a lot (Finland), the crash rates will be higher for those who drive greater distances and under less forgiving situations. This finding is hardly surprising. The real implication of these results – and the one drawn by its authors – is that the number of licensed drivers is not an acceptable exposure measure for crash risk, unless the groups compared are treated exactly alike in the relicensing renewal process.

The findings of Hakamies-Blomqvist and her colleagues (1995) in Scandinavia were replicated on the other side of the globe, in Australia, by Langford *et al.* (2004a, 2004b). They compared the crash rates of older drivers in Melbourne and Sydney – two large Australian metropolitan areas belonging to different states with different licensing procedures. In Melbourne there is no mandatory assessment for older drivers' license renewal whereas in Sydney there is one from age 80. Their analyses showed that the 80+ years old drivers in Sydney had statistically higher crash rates per driver, per time spent on the road, and nearly significant higher rates per distance driven.

Confounding and biasing factors in assessing older drivers' crash involvement

Analyses of crash involvement based on police-reported accident data suffer from three biases, all overstating the involvement of the older drivers: a "frailty bias," a "driving context" bias, and a "low-mileage bias." To truly appreciate the involvement of older drivers in crashes a correction must be made for all three. Several attempts have been made to adjust for these biases, and their results are reported below.

Adjusting for frailty bias

A "frailty bias" (Fontaine, 2003; Hakamies-Blomqvist, Raitanen, and ONeill, 2002; Langford, Methorst, and Hakamies-Blomqvist, 2006; Tay, 2006) is introduced into the data whenever an analysis of older driver crash involvement is based on police accident reports. Once a crash occurs, the likelihood of fatality in an injury crash with a given impact increases with age: first slowly at age 50, and then rapidly after age 70. This effect is dramatically demonstrated in Figure 7-7 that displays the likelihood of fatality *given* an injury crash for belted and unbelted vehicle occupants as a function of age. Clearly, age-related frailty is a very significant factor, increasing the likelihood of fatality for an unbelted 75+ years old driver relative to that of a 16-year-old driver by a factor of 8! Using a different approach, Bédard *et al.* (2002) analyzed the likelihood of drivers' death given involvement in single-vehicle multiple-occupants fatal crashes. They found that the likelihood of dying in the crash increased with age so that the odds ratio of dying in crash for 80+ years old drivers relative to 40- to 49-year-old drivers was an alarming 5.0.

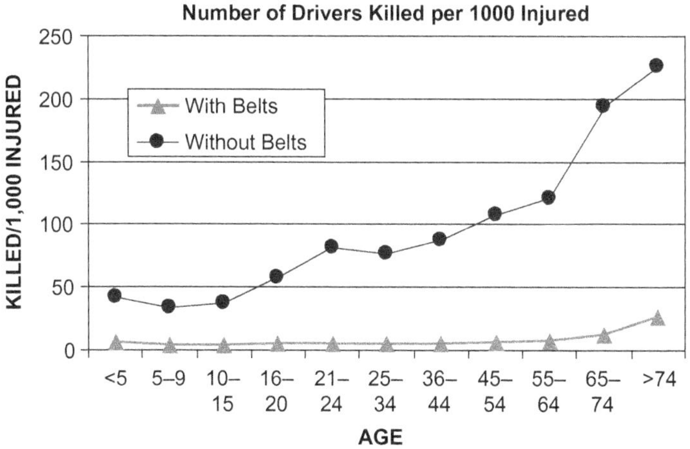

Figure 7-7. Fatality/injury ratios for vehicle occupants using and not using seat belts as a function of age (from NHTSA, 2005).

So what is the source of this biasing factor? For practical reasons the likelihood that the police will file an accident report increases with the levels of injuries incurred. For example in many jurisdictions the police only reports injury accidents. But, because of the greater frailty of older drivers the police are more likely to report an accident with a given physical impact and amount of property damage, when an older driver is involved than when a young driver is involved. This is because with identical impact forces the older driver may suffer serious injuries or be killed, while the young driver may only suffer a few bruises. Furthermore, the frailty bias extends beyond the accident itself because older drivers are also more likely to have post-crash complications as a result of other medical conditions that may affect their likelihood of recovery. Li, Braver, and Chen (2003) analyzed U.S. crash and travel data and used deaths per crash as an estimate of frailty. They found that the number of deaths per crashes starts to increase after age sixty, so that by the time the drivers are over 80 years old their death rates are four times as high as they are before age 60. Based on their analyses they concluded that "80–85% of the deaths per vehicle miles traveled in frontal, side, and rear impacts among drivers ages 60–74 could be explained by fragility. Among the oldest drivers, relative contribution estimates for the role of fragility were about 60% for frontal and side impacts and about 90% for rear impacts" (p. 233). Other studies (Eberhard, 1996; Eberhard and Trilling, 2001) also indicate that after age 70 frailty is the principal contributor to older driver fatalities.

Adjusting for context bias

The "context bias" is the tendency of older drivers to drive on different roads and at different times than younger drivers. Older drivers drive more in urban areas (and less on motorways or freeways) and more in the daytime than at night where the likelihood of a conflict with a pedestrian or another driver is much greater. To adjust for these differences in exposure, Keall and Frith (2004) combined detailed data from the New Zealand Travel Survey conducted in 1997-1998 with crash data from the 2 years. They found that older drivers actually had lower annual crash rates per distance traveled than all other drivers on motorways, and elevated crash rates on all other roads, especially minor and major urban roads. After adjusting for frailty, they found that older drivers' daytime crash risks increased after the age of 65, reaching levels similar to those of 25-year-old drivers by age 85+. On the other hand, the older drivers' nighttime crash rates risks were as low as those of any age group 35+ years old (younger drivers had, as expected much higher crash rates). Thus, it appears that older drivers become truly high risk only when they get to the age of 85+; an age when very few people still drive.

Adjusting for low-mileage bias

The third bias, the "low-mileage" bias stems from a the failure to correct for the amount of driving that *each* driver does – as opposed to the total amount of driving for a given age group. This has been pointed out in several, methodologically different, independent studies done on different driving populations in different countries. The first to challenge the interpretation of the U-curve on the basis of the low-mileage bias was Janke (1991). Although, on a population-wide basis as the total vehicle miles increases the number of crashes increase, the extrapolation to individual drivers is not a simple direct one. In fact, though drivers who drive more miles – due to sheer exposure – are more likely to be involved in a crash, the relationship between the number of miles a person drives and the likelihood of a crash is not linear: the likelihood *per mile* actually decreases with increasing mileage. Consequently, drivers who drive only a little are much more crash-prone *per unit distance* than drivers who drive a lot (Evans, 2004). Therefore, argued Janke, to correctly evaluate older drivers' crash risk per mile driven, an adjustment has to be made for the "low-mileage bias." This means that older drivers should not be compared as a group to all of the rest of the drivers, but only to drivers in other age groups who drive the same amount; that is, low-mileage drivers.

The low-mileage effect has since been demonstrated empirically on Finnish data by Hakamies-Blomqvist *et al.* (2002), on French data by Fontaine (2003), and on Dutch data by Langford *et al.* (2006). All three studies demonstrated that while traditional analyses yield the U-shaped crash involvement curves with over-involvement of older drivers, once the older drivers are matched to younger drivers who drive the same amount, the age effect disappears. The first two studies by Hakamies-Blomqvist *et al.* and by Fontaine were based on relatively small sample sizes (1,080 and 903 drivers) that necessitated pooling all drivers 65+ years old into a single group. Langford's study is the most recent and it is based on the largest sample, and so we examine it in some detail.

Langford *et al.* (2006) studied travel survey data obtained from over 47,000 Dutch drivers. This provided them with much larger samples than in the previous studies, and because they relied on self-reports rather than on police reports the data were less prone to "frailty bias" (though to some extent it still exists because younger drivers are more likely to omit slight crashes that for older drivers are more traumatizing). For the purpose of their analyses they divided the drivers into three groups according to the amount of driving they reported for the last year: low mileage of 3,000 km or less, medium mileage of 3,000-14,000 kilometers and high-mileage drivers who reported driving over 14,000 kilometers last year. As expected the crash rate per kilometer decreased as the drivers reported driving more, so that the overall crash rate per km of driving for the low-mileage group was six times the crash rate of the high-mileage group. This justified the stratification of the drivers according to their amount of driving before any age-related conclusions can be drawn. Once Langford plotted the data separately for the three groups of drivers, the age-related over-involvement in crashes not only disappeared for all but the very low-mileage groups, but high-mileage older drivers actually had lower crash rates than their younger comparable group. This finding is displayed in Figure 7-8. Furthermore, even the apparent increase in fatalities per million km noted for the older low-mileage group is not statistically significant from the rates for the lower age groups with the same exposure. The average number of crashes per million km of travel for this group is 50. However this group consists of only 98 drivers who drove less than 3,000 kilometer per year, and thus the standard error for that average is very high. In fact it is so high that at 95 percent level of confidence the actual rate of crashes per million km for the 75+ years old drivers could be anywhere from a low of 18 to a high of 83 crashes per million kilometer of travel. In a later analyses, addressing the issue of the unreliability of self-reports as a data source for distance traveled (raised by Staplin, Gish, and Joyce, 2008), Langford *et al.* (2008) then used odometer readings as a more reliable source and obtained similar results for the medium and high mileage groups but not for the low mileage group that was definitely worse than the younger comparable group (Figure 7-9). Thus, the weight of the evidence lends support to Langston *et al.*'s conclusions. The difference in the numerical values of the two figures suggests that self-reported travel distance is not only unreliable (especially for young drivers), but it seems to also be an over-estimate of actual driving distance (NRSA, 2015) (Figure 7-9).

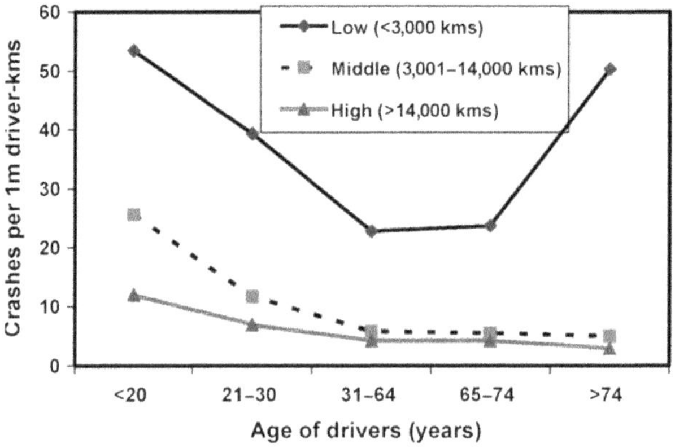

Figure 7-8. Crashes per million kilometer of driving as a function of age, plotted separately for groups with different amounts of driving. Based on self-reported data from 47,502 Dutch drivers (from Langford *et al.*, 2006, with permission from Elsevier).

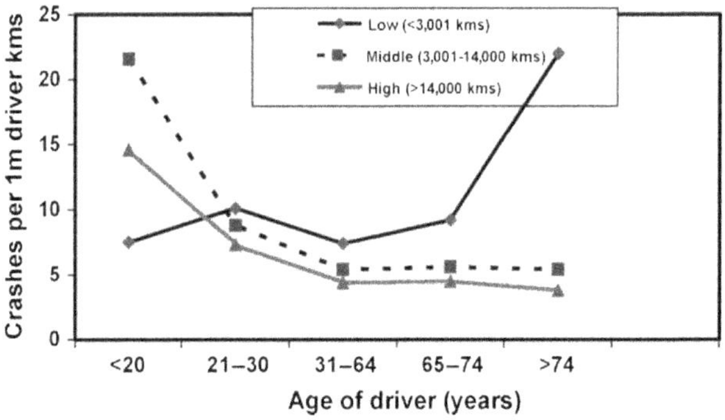

Figure 7-9. Crashes per million kilometer of driving as a function of age, based on the same crash data in Figure 7-8, but using odometer readings for kilometers of driving, rather than self-reports (from Langford *et al.*, 2008, with permission from Elsevier).

Going even further, Hakamies-Blomqvist and her associates (2005) argue that older drivers are actually under-involved in crashes relative to their exposure, and that as their proportion in the total population increases, their crash involvement actually decreases. This argument may be a special case of Smeed's Law (discussed in Chapter 1) that states that as a country becomes more motorized the rate of crashes per vehicle decreases. Hakamies-Blomqvist and her associates tested the analogous hypothesis that as the number of elderly drivers increases (i.e., the numbers of cars driven by elderly drivers increase) the crash rate per driver will decrease. Using the Swedish police-reported crash data for the years 1983-1999, they calculated the observed risk that a license holder is involved in a road accident separately for drivers 18-64 years old and for drivers 65-84 years old. The risk of crash involvement is the ratio between the number of passenger car drivers involved in police-reported road accidents in an age category and the number of license holders in that age category. Their results are presented in the left panel of Figure 7-10. Each data point in these lines in these graphs is the risk of being involved in a crash relative to the number of licensed drivers in that age group at that year. The most obvious effect in these graphs is that for all years the risk level of the older drivers is below that of the younger drivers.

It may be argued that the reason that the risk is lower for older drivers is because many of the licensed older drivers do not actually drive any more, and thus we are spuriously inflating the denominator for that group. To control for that, the authors recalculated the risks using only the number of "active drivers" – drivers who reported driving within the past year (rather than all licensed drivers). The risk levels measured this way are presented in the right panel of Figure 7-10 and they are very similar to those in the left panel. The difference between the risk levels of the younger drivers and those of the older drivers may be expressed as the ratio of the two, also known as the relative risk. Figure 7-11 shows the relative risk of the two groups of active drivers.

Two things are patently obvious in Figure 7-11: (1) in all 16 years studied the relative risk is less than one, meaning that the crash risk is lower for the older drivers and (2) over the years the relative safety of the "newer" older drivers actually increases. This last finding is very significant because it reflects improvement in driving of different

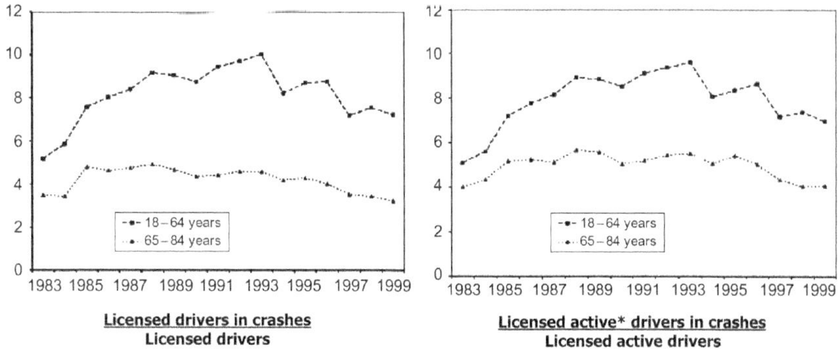

Figure 7-10. Observed risk that a license holder is involved in a road accident (i.e., the ratio between the number of passenger car drivers involved in police-reported road accidents and the number of license holders, in thousands) for passenger car drivers in Sweden from 1983 to 1999, partitioned into the age groups 18-64 (top curves) and 65-84 years (lower curves). Left panel is for all license holders. Right panel is for license holders who report actively driving (from Hakamies-Blomqvist, Wiklund, and Henriksson, 2005, with permission from Elsevier).

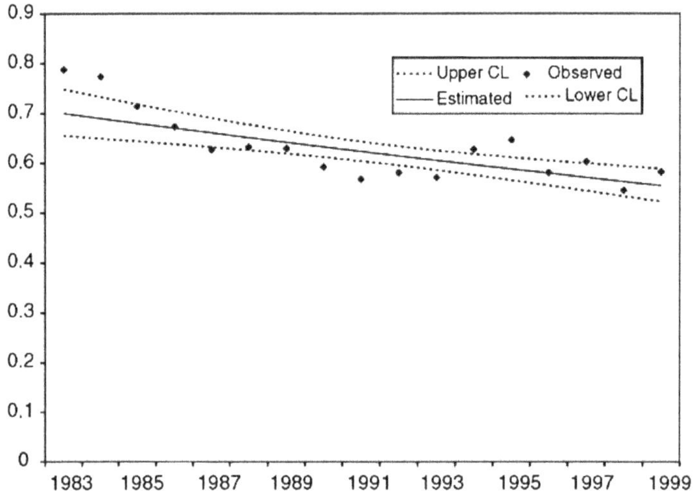

Figure 7-11. Risk of being involved in a passenger car accident of a 65- to 84-year-old driver relative to 18- to 64-year-old driver in Sweden from 1983 to 1999. Diamonds indicate the observed relative risks, the solid line is the estimated best linear approximation, and the dotted lines are the 95 percent confidence interval around the mean (from Hakamies-Blomqvist *et al.*, 2005, with permission from Elsevier).

populations. Those who reached their 70s in 1983 were not as safe as those who reached that age in 1999. It is likely that this trend still continues as over the past 15 years the safety features of cars and roads have improved, as have the health and safe driving habits of the elderly population. Furthermore, the proportion of older drivers who grew up throughout their adult life with a car has also increased since 1999.

Crash Culpability and Age-Related Impairments

A major reason for the recent realization that older drivers are not unsafe drivers is that they restrict their driving to low-risk situations, places, and conditions. Unfortunately, when they do get involved in crashes, they are more likely to be culpable than younger driver. But we have to remember that the determination of culpability is typically a subjective assessment. As such the assessor may be biased. For example police, who are often the primary source for that type of information, are often accused of an a priori bias to blame the very young and the very old drivers for their crashes. Still, there are data from various sources to support the claim that older drivers are more often than not the culpable drivers in their crashes. This has been demonstrated in analyses conducted on crash data in various countries – including the U.S., Canada, Sweden, and Australia – of police reports (Hakamies-Blomqvist, 1993; Langford *et al.*, 2005; Williams and Shabanova, 2003), insurance claims files (Braver and Trempel, 2004, Cooper 1990), coroner reports (Langford *et al.*, 2005), and independent "data coders" (Langford *et al.*, 2005). For example, Langford *et al.* using sub-samples of Australian fatality data found that the police assessments in fatal crashes were very similar to assessments made independently by coroners and by trained data coders (though it appears that they too had to rely on the police reports).

Older drivers' impairments and crash causes

In order to understand when and how drivers should restrict themselves it is necessary to understand the age-related driving-related impairments that affect older people. With this understanding we can then design an environment that is more compatible with their impairments. A summary of these impairments and their relation to driving is presented in Table 7-1 (from Langford *et al.*, 2005).

Table 7-1. Age-related impairments and their associated driving problems (from Langford *et al.*, 2005, with permission from Austroads).

Age-Related Impairments	Driving Problems
Increased reaction time. Difficulty dividing attention between tasks.	Difficulty driving in unfamiliar or congested areas.
Deteriorating vision, particularly at night.	Difficulty seeing pedestrians and other objects at night, reading signs. Difficulty with wet weather driving.
Difficulty judging speed and distance.	Failure to perceive conflicting vehicles. Accidents at intersections.
Difficulty perceiving and analyzing situations.	Failure to comply with Give Way signs, traffic signals and railway crossing signals. Slow to appreciate hazards.
Difficulty turning head, reduced peripheral vision.	Failure to notice obstacles while maneuvering. Failure to observe traffic behind when merging and changing lanes.
More prone to fatigue.	Get tired on long journeys, run-off road single-vehicle crashes.
General effects of ageing.	Worries over inability to cope with a breakdown, driving to unfamiliar places, at night, in heavy traffic.
Some impairments vary in severity from day to day. Tiredness, symptoms of dementia.	Concern over fitness to drive.

The causes of older driver crashes are quite similar to those of the general population – with a few exceptions. Langford and his associates (2005) analyzed 182 fatal Australian accidents in which the older driver was judged solely culpable for the accident and their findings are summarized in Table 7-2. The principal cause of most crashes, accounting for 44 percent of them, was an attentional-perceptual failure. The next in prevalence was a decision-judgment error, accounting for 14.2 percent of the crashes. These two types of errors were also the most prevalent in independent analyses of representative samples of crashes studied in England and in the U.S. in the 1970s. However, these early studies included crashes of all types and drivers of all ages, and the older drivers in those samples were a distinct minority (see Chapter 18). Older drivers differ from younger drivers in the high frequency of accidents attributed to pre-crash black-outs. These are most likely associated with age-related medical conditions such as cardio-vascular and neurovascular diseases, which are quite rare among younger people (see Table 1-1).

A less scientific approach to older driver crash causes is provided by an analysis of German police reports. Note that police cite drivers not for errors or failures but for traffic law violations. With this caveat in mind, the results summarized in Figure 7-12, are still quite interesting. According to these conclusions older drivers (65+ years old) are more culpable than younger drivers in crashes involving turning, backing up, yielding right-of-way, and "wrongdoing towards pedestrians," but less involved in crashes due to insufficient headways, excessive speed, and alcohol intoxication (Otte *et al.*, 2013). In the U.S., older drivers (and older pedestrians) are also the least involved in alcohol-related fatal crashes (NHTSA, 2015). These differences emphasize the shortcomings (and advantages) of older drivers: they are less likely to engage in risky driving (e.g., DWI), less likely to speed and drive aggressively and less likely to commit intentional violations. On the other hand, they are more likely to commit unintended errors due to perceptual and cognitive deficiencies. More important, these conclusions are corroborated by an in-depth analysis on a smaller sample (169 elderly and 817 non-elderly) of drivers – using the German In-Depth Accident Study (GIDAS). The GIDAS data show that the elderly drivers are more likely to fail in perceiving all the relevant information and in handling the vehicle (i.e., the initial and final stages in the information processing sequence), while the younger drivers were more likely to misjudge the situation and purposely plan an inappropriate action (such as speeding) (i.e., fail in the central stage of the information processing sequence).

The most common type of an older driver crash is a collision with another vehicle in an intersection. This can be seen in Table 7-2 for Australian data and has been replicated in other countries as well. For example, Clarke *et al.* (2010) obtained similar results in an analysis of over 2,000 crashes of older drivers in the United Kingdom. Their analyses showed the most common type of an older driver crash was when involving a "right of way violation," most often from colliding with an oncoming vehicle while making a right turn at an intersection (which would be equivalent to a left turn in countries where driving is on the right). Further analyses of these crashes revealed that the most common

Table 7-2. Causes of 182 Australian fatal crashes in which the older driver was judged solely culpable (from Langford *et al.*, 2005, with permission from Austroads).

All Crashes		**Number of Crashes per Crash Type**				**Cause**
		Two-vehicle		**Single-vehicle**		
Percent	**No.**	**Non-intersection**	**Intersection**	**Non-intersection**	**Intersection**	
27.5	50	12	35	3	0	Not see other road user
12.1	22	0	22	0	0	Not see signal
15.4	28	8	1	15	4	Blackout pre-crash
8.2	15	2	11	2	0	Misjudged speed
4.4	8	1	1	6	0	Not see other condition
6.0	11	4	0	6	1	Misjudged other
0.5	1	0	0	1	0	Excessive speed
2.2	4	0	0	4	0	Asleep/fatigue
6.0	11	3	1	6	1	Error at controls
0.5	1	0	1	0	0	Alcohol
17.0	31	8	6	17	0	Other
100.0	182	38	78	60	6	Total

errors the drivers made involved inefficient visual search (54 percent) and poor judgment of the approach speed of the other vehicles (21 percent). Oxley *et al.* (2006) who investigated over 400 crashes of older drivers (65+ years old) that occurred in 62 intersections in Australasia (New Zealand, Queensland, Tasmania, and Victoria) found that older drivers were significantly over-involved in crashes at these sites, and their crashes were

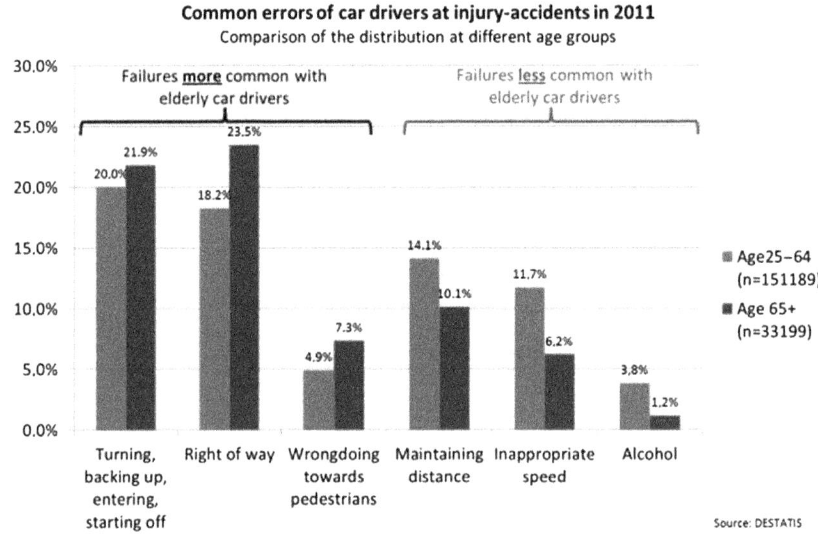

Figure 7-12. The violations committed by older and younger German drivers in injury crashes (from Otte *et al.*, 2013, with permission from the author).

characterized by a small number of specific site characteristics. The site characteristics that were most commonly associated with the older driver crashes were lack of separate controls for protected turns at signalized intersections, and limited sight distance at turns against opposing traffic (right turns in these countries), especially sight distances that provided less than 2.5 seconds reaction time to other traffic. In short, these were locations requiring effective visual search, good judgment of the time to arrival of the approaching vehicles, (i.e., time and distance judgments), and possibly quick response time.

Accordingly, the older driver impairments that have received most of the attention from researchers are those associated with vision, cognition, and medical conditions. The following is a brief review of the age-related impairments in these domains and their potential impact on driving safety.

Vision

Our visual system – the primary source of driving-related sensory inputs – begins to deteriorate in our forties, but different parts of it deteriorate at different rates (Shinar, 1977; Shinar and Schieber, 1991; also see Chapter 4). Some of that deterioration is simply age-related (such as loss of accommodation that requires reading glasses or multi-focal corrective lenses) and some is from age-related diseases (such as macular degeneration that leads to blindness). Age-related patterns for six different driving-related visual functions are presented in Figure 7-13 (Shinar and Schieber, 1991), where they are grouped into (corrected) static acuity functions that deteriorate rather late and

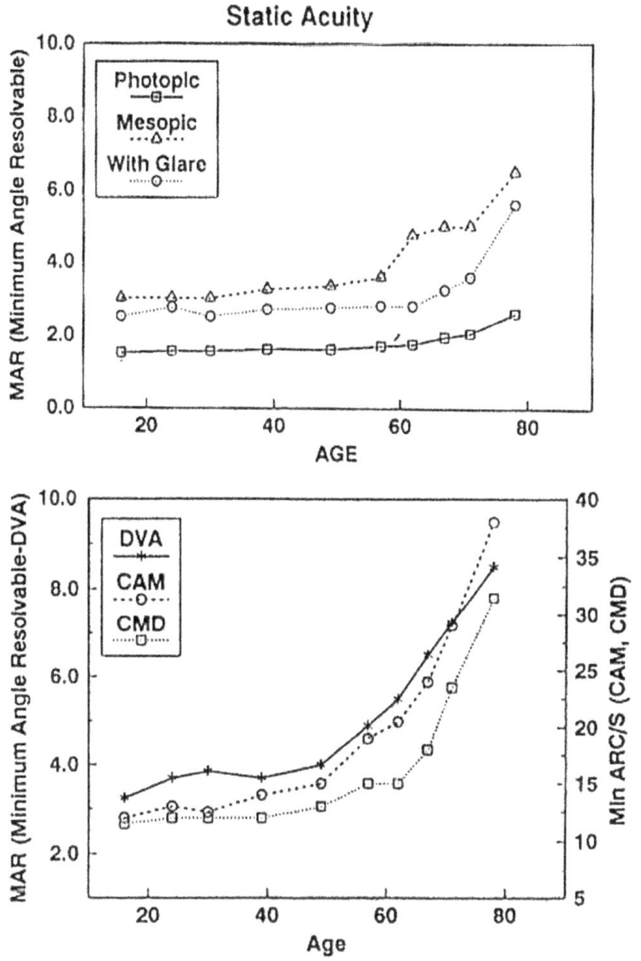

Figure 7-13. Age-related deterioration (a) in static acuity under optimal (photopic), low illumination (Mesopic), and glare conditions and (b) in dynamic visual acuity, ability to detect motion across the visual field (Central Angular Motion – CAM), and forward motion (Central Movement in Depth – CMD) (from Shinar and Schieber, 1991, data from Shinar, 1977).

by moderate amount, and more complex functions that involve combinations of skills (such as dynamic visual acuity) or a combination of sensory sensitivities with decision making (such as the detection of movement). As can be seen from the six individual functions, the least affected by age is (corrected) static acuity under optimal daytime illumination; mostly *because* we can correct it with glasses. Greater deteriorations that start at an earlier age can be observed for the other visual skills, all of which are more relevant to driving than static visual acuity. Unfortunately, for licensing purposes only static acuity is universally measured, and implicitly and incorrectly assumed to be a good surrogate of the other driving-related functions. The fallacy of this assumption is illustrated in different studies. For example, Sayer and Mefford (2004) found that the detection distance of a pedestrian at a work zone at night is approximately half as far for older (64-75 years old) drivers as for young (21-30 years old) drivers, despite their very similar visual acuity (when measured under conditions of optimal illumination and contrast). Also, higher order visual functions are more closely associated with crash involvement among the elderly than simple acuity tests (Green, McGwin, and Owsley, 2013; Raghuram and Lakshminarayanan, 2006; Shinar, 1977; Staplin *et al.*, 2013).

The number of visual functions that are at least theoretically relevant to driving is large, and many of them are described in Chapter 4. Table 7-3 summarizes the age-related deteriorations in various driving-related visual functions. Despite the specific deteriorations in driving-related skills noted in the table, very few of these functions are demonstrably and consistently related to driving performance and even less to crash involvement. The research in most of these areas is reviewed in Chapter 4. For the present discussion it is important to note that because of other difficulties and various co-morbidity problems, older drivers already adjust their exposure to allow for many of their visual deficiencies – even when they are not specifically aware of their visual problems. For example, as glare sensitivity increases, older driver refrain as much as possible from driving at night, and when they do they often project the problem to other drivers who drive with their high beams or other cars with brighter headlights – when in fact there is no evidence for either. Thus, drivers suffering from night myopia and increase in glare sensitivity typically restrict all or most of their driving to daylight hours.

It is important to note that the driving implications listed in Table 7-3 are not specified in terms of crashes. This is because it is very difficult to obtain a consistent relationship between any specific visual function and crash involvement. This may be because research is very limited or non-existent (e.g., glare recovery and accommodation); or research findings are inconsistent (e.g., visual field) or repeated findings on large samples show a significant effect, but its magnitude is negligible (daytime acuity, visual field, color vision).

Unlike some other impairments (such as some types of dementia), in the case of vision drivers are typically aware of their limitations and can compensate for them, as illustrated by the following two studies. In the first study, West and her associates (2003) assessed the visual performance on an extensive battery of vision tests and interviewed 629 55+ years old adults. They found that those who reported that they restricted their driving because of visual reasons differed from those who did not in several of their visual functions. Furthermore, they noted that "older adults with early changes in spatial vision function and depth perception appear to recognize their limitations and restrict their driving even if they do not acknowledge the visual impairment as the cause for restriction" (p. 1348). In the second study McGregor and Chaparro (2005) surveyed 195 low-vision and unimpaired older adults (with a mean age of 79) and had them complete

Table 7-3. Age-related changes in various driving-related visual functions (adapted from Meyer, 2004).

Ability	**Major Changes**	**Implications for Driving**	**Selected References**
Visual acuity (ability to resolve small details when viewed from a distance).	Decline of visual acuity (myopia, near sightedness). Can be partly corrected with lenses.	Need for corrective lenses while driving	Anderson and Palmore (1974); Charman (1997); Kline *et al.* (1992); Kosnick *et al.* (1988); Reuben, Silliman, and Traines (1988); Shinar and Schieber (1991); Wood (2002)
Dynamic visual acuity (ability to observe the direction and speed of a moving object correctly).	Decline in dynamic visual acuity	Difficulty in determining rate of approach and time to collision of moving objects	Charman (1997); Sekuler, Kline, and Dismukes (1982); Shinar and Schieber (1991); Wist, Schrauf, and Ehrenstein (2000); Wood (2002)
Focusing on near objects (ability to resolve small details in a near object – – far sightedness, or Presbyopia when related to age).	Difficulty to focus on near objects, due to the loss of elasticity in the lens of the eye. Can be corrected with reading glasses or bifocal lenses.	Need for bifocal lenses or reading glasses to see in-vehicle displays or to locate smaller controls	Bruckner (1967); Kline *et al.* (1992)
Contrast sensitivity (ability to detect changes in the lightness of a surface).	Decline in contrast sensitivity	Difficulty in detecting objects or changes in the road that appear as changes in shading	Charman (1997); Fozard (1990); Owsley, Sekuler, and Siemsen (1983); Owsley and McGwin (1999); Shinar and Schieber (1991)
Night vision (ability to see in poor lighting conditions).	Cataracts and senile meiosis limit the amount of light that reaches the receptors	Difficulty in seeing objects in dim lighting (at night, in tunnels, or garages)	Charman (1997); Charness and Bosman (1992), Kline *et al.* (1992), Shinar and Schieber (1991)

Table 7-3. (*Continued*)

Ability	**Major Changes**	**Implications for Driving**	**Selected References**
Disability glare (amount of luminance required to produce disability glare).	Less luminance is required to produce disability glare	Difficulty in night driving and in changing levels of illumination	Babizhayev (2003); Charman (1997); Olson (1988); Olson and Sivak (1984); Sanders *et al.* (1990)
Glare recovery (time required to regain night vision after exposure to bright light).	Increased susceptibility to glare and slower recovery from glare	Difficulty in night driving and driving in changing levels of illumination	Charman (1997); Charness and Bosman (1992); Pulling *et al.* (1980); Sloane, Owlsey, and Alvarez (1988); Wolf (1960)
Peripheral vision (angular width of field of view in which motion information is perceived)	Decrease in size of horizontal peripheral visual field	Late detection of events that develop in the periphery, such as approaching cars	Burg (1968); Charman (1997); Keltner and Johnson (1987); Owsley and McGwin (1999); Retchin *et al.* (1988); Wood (2002)
Useful field of view (width of visual field over which information can be acquired in a quick glance).	Decline in spatial and peripheral vision	Difficulty in detecting events that develop at the sides of the visual field (merging cars etc.)	Charman (1997); Haegerstrom-Portnoy, Scheck, and Brabyn (1999); Owsley and McGwin (1999); Sekuler, Bennett, and Mamelak (2000)
Color vision (differential perception of light with different wave lengths).	Loss of sensitivity to shorter wavelengths resulting in reduced ability to discriminate blues, greens and violets	Responses to color coded displays may be affected	Botwinick (1984); Charman (1997); Wood (2002)
Visual scan (speed and efficiency of movement of fixations in the visual field).	Slowing of visual scan	Difficulty to take in complex traffic situations	Maltz and Shinar (1999); Pradhan *et al.* (2003).

a questionnaire that contained questions about their perceived visual problems. They found that the majority of adults in both groups reported problems with static and dynamic acuity, peripheral vision, glare, illumination, night driving, and contrast sensitivity. Despite these self-reported visual deficiencies, 78 percent of the participants reported that they continue to drive, including 57 percent of the low-vision people. This simple finding illuminates at once the prevalence of visual problems of elderly people, the importance of driving to their life, and their ability to reconcile the two without necessarily being over-involved in crashes.

To justify visual performance criteria for licensing it is necessary to demonstrate their relationship to crash involvement. This is very difficult. The blind cannot drive but the self-aware nearly-legally-blind (with 20/100 or 6/30 acuity) apparently can. We can illustrate this with one theoretically critical, driving-related, much-studied function: horizontal visual field. The visual field shrinks with age in a consistent manner. Most young drivers under the age of 25 have an ability to detect a target that is as far as 90 degree from the direction of their gaze, yielding a binocular visual field of 180 degrees. However, by age sixty the average visual field of licensed drivers is down to 160 degrees, and by age 80 it is down to 140 degrees (Burg, 1968). It is also likely that among the oldest people the average extent is even less because many of them have quit driving. In many countries the licensing screening tests include a test of the visual field, and in most instances to obtain an unrestricted license a person must have a field of at least 120 degrees. Yet, the data to support this requirement are at best very questionable. Council and Allen (1974) were not able to find any significant relationship between visual field and crashes with a sample of 52,000 North Carolina drivers. More recent studies on smaller samples, that specifically focused on older drivers also failed to obtain significant relationships (Ball *et al.*, 1993; Decina and Staplin, 1993; Hennessy, 1995; Owsley, McGwin, and Ball, 1998). Sometimes conflicting results are obtained within the same study. Burg (1974) measured the visual field of 17,000 California drivers. He found a very small negative (as expected) correlation between the extent of the visual field and crashes, but a *positive* correlation with violations: meaning that people with larger visual field actually had more violations. Johnson and Keltner (1983) tested 10,000 drivers and found the looked-for relationship, but only for people with very severe visual field impairments in both eyes. Finally, in an even more extreme evaluation of the importance of visual field, McKnight, Shinar, and Hilburn (1991) did not find significant differences between normally sighted and monocular drivers in various driving tasks. Taken together, even for this intuitively highly relevant function there is no conclusive evidence on the relationship between visual field and crashes. If we accept that the absence of a relationship is due to self-restrictions, then the practical implication is that drivers can do a better job of self-regulation than formal licensing tests.

On the basis of current research there seem to be two possible exceptions to the generalization that drivers can adjust to their limitations by self-regulation of their driving. The first concerns contrast sensitivity and the second concerns the useful or effective field of view (in which peripheral target detection is measured in the presence of attentional load in the center of the field). The weight of the evidence – reviewed in Chapter 4 – suggests that they are both moderately associated with crash involvement. Furthermore, with respect to the attentional field of view, such as the Useful Field of View (UFOV), West *et al.*'s (2003) results also indicate that drivers with impaired attentional field did not report any self-restrictions. This insensitivity may be the underlying reason why this measure is associated with over-involvement in crashes.

Cognitive impairments

Cognitive performance also deteriorates with age. We often measure cognitive performance through reaction time, and older people typically (but not always; e.g., Olson and Sivak, 1986) have slower reaction times than younger people (e.g., Warshawsky-Livne and Shinar, 2002), especially in complex tasks such as on-the-road obstacle detection and sign identification (Ben-Bassat and Shinar, 2015). Two studies conducted in our laboratory on sign comprehension illustrate this quite well. In the first study (Shinar *et al.*, 2003), as part of a larger international study, different groups of 50 drivers each were shown pictures of various standard road signs and asked to identify their meaning. The older drivers (over 60 years old) consistently identified correctly fewer signs than young novice drivers, students, and even repeat violators. This is despite their more extensive experience in driving on different roads. In the second study (Ben-Bassat and Shinar, 2015), we tested 50 young (22-30 years old) drivers and 50 old (65+ years old) drivers. However, this time we tested sign comprehension under two conditions: as before when the sign was presented against a blank background, and in the context of the traffic scene. For example, in the second condition, a "Stop" sign would be seen in the foreground of an intersection and a "Curve ahead" sign would be seen in the foreground of a curving road. The expectation was that older drivers would again be poorer in sign identification, but that their relative deficiency would be less when the signs are presented in their natural context. On the other hand, with the signs in their natural context, the sign image was significantly smaller, and more time would be needed to visually locate the sign and fixate it, and consequently reaction time would be longer. The results, presented in Table 7-4, only partially bore this out.

As in the first study, the younger drivers demonstrated superior levels of comprehension, and they needed significantly less time to comprehend the signs' meaning and respond. Interestingly, the presence of the context did not facilitate comprehension, but it did significantly delay the time needed to identify the signs, and much more for the older drivers than for the younger ones. These results, demonstrate the slower pace of information acquisition and processing of older drivers, especially in the complex road environment. Two striking differences between the younger and older drivers, that are not very visible from the data in Table 7-4, are presented in Figure 7-14. First, there is nearly no overlap between the comprehension times of the young drivers and those of the older drivers. The average times for the young drivers are 1.73 seconds and 1.55 seconds, with and without context; and the average times for the older drivers are 3.79 seconds and 3.31 seconds with and without context; that is, the older drivers' responses were approximately twice as long as those of the young drivers. Second, and this is a recurring critical characteristic of older people, the variance in comprehension times – represented by the spread of the data points around the regression lines – is minimal for the young drivers, but

Table 7-4. Sign comprehension (a) and sign comprehension time (b) for younger and older drivers (from Ben-Bassat and Shinar, 2015, with permission from Elsevier).

	Young Drivers		**Old Drivers**	
	In context	**Without context**	**In context**	**Without context**
a. Percent Signs Comprehended				
Fully correct	76	76	68	67
Fully or partially correct	82	81	76	76
Wrong	14	15	19	19
Opposite meaning	4	4	5	4
b. Sign Comprehension Times (Seconds)				
Fully correct	1.53	1.36	3.25	2.76
Fully or partially correct	1.59	1.39	3.35	2.93
Wrong	2.43	2.27	5.70	4.86
Opposite meaning	2.13	1.84	3.31	3.31

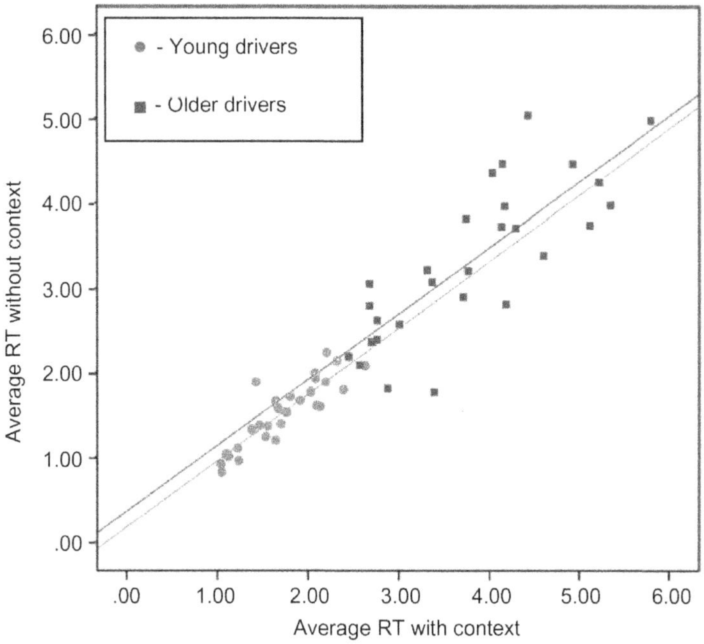

Figure 7-14. Mean response time of young and old drivers to 28 traffic signs presented with and without their context (from Ben-Bassat and Shinar, 2015, with permission from Elsevier).

quite large for the older drivers. This variance, again, should serve to warn us not to lump all biologically/chronologically older drivers into one bin.

Two deficiencies that have been fairly consistently associated with crash involvement among the elderly are their effective visual field and their mental status. The relationship between these two measures and crash involvement in older adults is illustrated in Figure 7-15 (Ball and Owsley, 1991). In this schematic representation between various deficiencies and crash involvement, each of these predictor or independent variables is based on performance in several measures. Eye health is based on a clinical ophthalmic exam that checks, among other things, for central and peripheral vision, cataracts, macular degeneration, diabetic retinopathy, and glaucoma. The different diseases affect different visual functions, with varying relevance to the visual needs for driving. For example, glaucoma affects two important driving-related functions: visual field and contrast sensitivity (Hawkins *et al.*, 2003; Szlyk *et al.*, 2005), and cataracts reduce glare resistance (Babizhayev, 2004). The visual function includes performance on tests of visual acuity, contrast sensitivity, glare resistance, color discrimination, visual field, and stereo acuity. The UFOV, described in detail in Chapter 4, is essentially a test that measures a person's ability to detect peripheral targets while simultaneously occupied in a visual task that requires attention to the central field. Mental status refers to scores on the Mattis Organic Mental Status Syndrome Examination which measures a variety of mental abilities including abstraction, short-term verbal and visual memory, comprehension, reading, and writing.

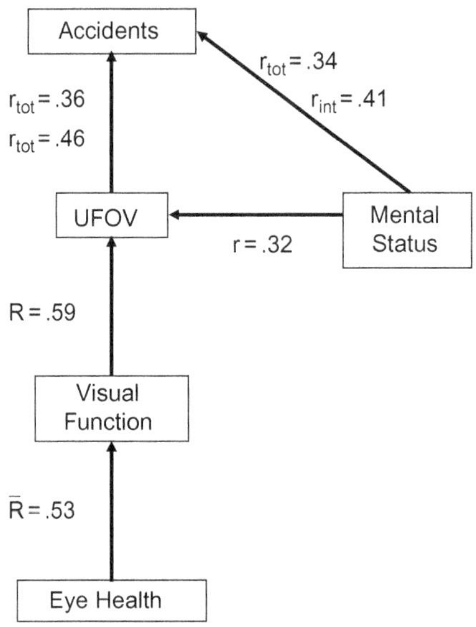

Figure 7-15. A predictive model of accidents in general (tot) and intersection accidents in particular (int) based on the results of a correlations obtained on a sample of 53 older drivers (from Ball and Owsley, 1991, with permission from the Human Factors and Ergonomics Society).

The numbers in the block diagram in Figure 7-15 are the correlations among various sets of tests, and between different tests and crash involvement. As can be seen from this diagram, both the UFOV and the driver's mental status correlated significantly with accidents: drivers performing badly on either or both of these measures had more accidents than those who performed well. Eye health correlated significantly with visual function, but not with the UFOV or accidents. Visual function correlated significantly with UFOV but not with accidents. The implication from this model is that a person's UFOV and mental status affect his or her likelihood to be involved in accidents. It also appears that the UFOV is mediated by both visual abilities and mental abilities because both are positively correlated with it. Part of the validity of this model also rests on the higher correlations obtained for intersection accidents to which older drivers are especially prone (Abdel-Aty, Chen, and Schott, 1998; Clarke *et al.*, 2010; Hauer, 1988; Mayhew, Simpson, and Ferguson, 2006; Ryan, Legge, and Rosman, 1998). Despite the model's sound theoretical reasoning and some empirical support from Ball and Owsley's studies (Ball and Owsley, 1991; Ball *et al.*, 2002; Owsley and McGwin, 1999), tests of the association between various tests of the effective visual field (including the UFOV) and crash involvement of older drivers by other researchers have been generally disappointing (see Chapter 4). Recently in a well-controlled study on a large population-based sample of 70+ years old drivers that adjusted for various confounding factors, even Owsley and Ball failed to find a significant relationship between the UFOV and crash involvement (Friedman *et al.*, 2013). Also, in the few studies, where statistically significant associations between the UFOV and crash involvement were obtained, the odds ratios have been approximately 2-3; that is, indicating that on average people with poor UFOV are on the average 2-3 times as likely to be involved in crashes as people with good UFOV. This is good enough to show that crash-involved older drivers as a group have poorer UFOV, but not good enough to serve as a screening tool, because it would also deny a license to too many safe drivers (as demonstrated by Langford, 2008).

The findings above indicate that a major age-related deficit is in the interaction between gathering visual information and processing its meaning. This was demonstrated quite effectively in a study by Wikman and Summala (2005), who had drivers of various ages drive 350 kilometers on the open highway and motorway near Helsinki, Finland, while having to perform a visual scanning task of a set of numbers presented at random locations on a rudimentary touch screen located in front of the dashboard. While driving, the drivers had to press the numbers on the screen in a numeric order (1, 2, 3, etc.) as quickly as they could. This test was very similar to the standardized Trails Test. In the Trails test a subject is required to point in numerical sequence (to 1, then 2, then 3, ... 15) to numbers that are randomly located on a sheet of paper, and performance is then measured by the highest number reached in a fixed time allotted, or the time it took to locate all 15 numbers (see Choca *et al.*, 1997, for test description). The Trails test (Especially version B) – a popular test for visual-cognitive functioning – has been repeatedly shown to correlate well with older drivers' safety-related measures such as hazard perception (Anstey *et al.*, 2012), and crash involvement (Betz and Fisher, 2009; Emerson *et al.*, 2012; Friedman *et al.*, 2013). Going back to Wikman and Summala they found that their number location task was much more distracting for the older, 57-73 years old, drivers than for the younger ones, and that the older drivers spent more time looking at the numbers screen than the younger drivers. The actual strategy of attending to the screen varied among drivers – with some preferring multiple short fixations and others preferring fewer but longer looks. These results are displayed in Figure 7-16, where the number of glances is plotted against the mean glance durations.

Note that in this figure, the older drivers' data points gravitate toward the top-right corner while the younger drivers' data points tend to gravitate toward the lower-left corner. Also important is the fact that a few of the older drivers need less time to extract and process the information from the display than some of the younger drivers. This is another manifestation of the increasing individual differences with age – with some older people functioning as well as very young people, while others deteriorate giving the impression that the group as a whole deteriorates. This was also evident in the analysis of the number of long – greater than 2 seconds – glances that drivers spent gazing at the display. While such long glances were rare for the young drivers, they were quite common for the older drivers. This is very significant because at the average speed of over 100 km/h that the drivers drove on the motorway, in the span of 2 seconds a driver travels over 55 meters.

Finally, Wikman and Summala also noted that although the distracting task was visual, the glance durations and frequencies and the vehicle lateral control performance were much more related to the drivers' cognitive capabilities (as measured by the Trails Test) than to their visual acuity and contrast sensitivity. Thus, these findings

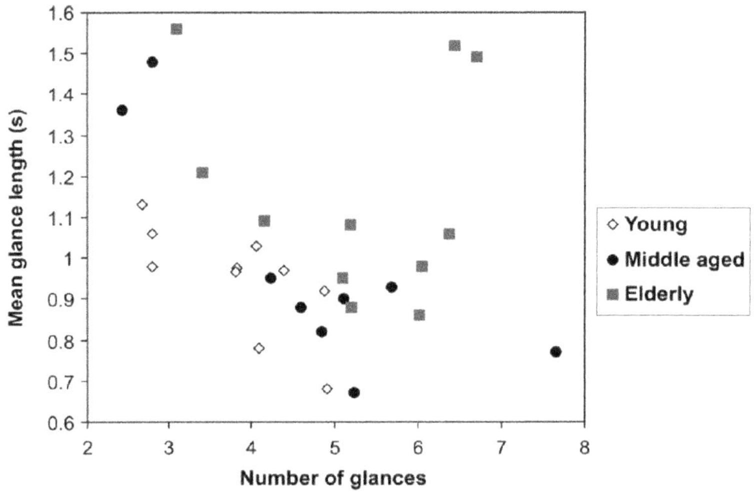

Figure 7-16. Number and durations of glances of drivers of different ages spent looking at a dashboard mounted display of digits that drivers had to scan while driving on an open road. Young drivers = 20-24 years old, middle aged drivers = 26-44 years old, and elderly = 57-73 years old (from Wikman and Summala, 2005, with permission from the American Academy of Optometry).

demonstrate the importance of the cognitive aspects of the task over its visual demands. In fact, Cuenen *et al.* (2015) used the UFOV as a measure of cognitive capacity and demonstrated that among older drivers, the effects of both visual and cognitive distractions on driver performance in a simulator were moderated by the drivers' cognitive capacity.

Complementary findings were obtained by Aksan *et al.* (2013), who had middle aged and older (65+ years old) drivers drive an instrumented vehicle while required to identify traffic signs and restaurant signs along their way. Although all the drivers were healthy, as might have been expected the older drivers performed worse than the younger ones on nearly all sensory, motor, and cognitive measures. On the road the older drivers drove slightly slower but still committed more driving errors (mostly in lane observance and use of the turn signals – as judged by driving instructors) and missed more restaurant signs than the younger drivers. Interestingly, though, they identified as many traffic signs as the younger groups, suggesting that they are still able to make judicious allocation of their reduced capacities. So while they may miss a good restaurant, they will probably not miss a critical traffic sign – a small price to pay for continued mobility.

Medical conditions and diseases

The potential effects of various medical conditions on driving and crash involvements have been studied by many researchers. Because the prevalence of these conditions is generally very low in younger drivers, their effects have been studied mostly on older drivers. Thus, there is a widespread recognition that there are different groups of older drivers, and the at-risk groups must be identified on the basis of driving-related medical conditions. Some of the age-related diseases – including heart failure and stroke – typically involve sudden death or loss of consciousness. Other illnesses, such as glaucoma can result in sudden loss of vision. All of these conditions, to say the least, compromise safe driving. Other conditions, such as cataracts merely degrade the person's level of functioning and make the person more vulnerable to glare, and the critical issue is whether or not a threshold level can be determined, above which the person is at risk while driving. The need for a performance threshold is critical, because the mere presence of a medical condition is not indicative of its risk to driving. For example, as noted above, cataracts reduce tolerance to glare and contrast sensitivity, but medication can improve performance on these functions, even though the medical condition is still there (Babizhayev, 2004). Furthermore, cataract surgery has been shown to be an effective intervention to improve driving performance, with the improvement in contrast sensitivity being the best predictor of the improvement in driving (Wood and Carberry, 2006). Other conditions, such as Parkinson's disease, affect driving control more subtly by making drivers more dependent on external cues than internal cues to guide and control their driving (Stolwyk *et al.*, 2005).

Even after controlling for the amount of driving and other effects of age, crash-involved drivers with specific conditions such as non-medicated diabetes, and a history of stroke and myocardial infraction, are more likely to be culpable in their crashes than people not suffering from these conditions (Sagberg, 2006). Other diseases that have been associated with slight to moderate increased crash risk include dementia, epilepsy, multiple sclerosis, psychiatric disorders (considered as a group), schizophrenia, sleep apnea, and cataracts (Charlton *et al.*, 2004). However, a statistically significant effect does not automatically imply a need for license restriction relative to that condition. This is because in most cases the size of the effect is quite small, implying that applying this criterion would prevent many drivers who are not at increased risk to lose their license, and hence their mobility and independence.

Despite the qualification above, most countries have medical and health requirements for licensing. These are requirements whose relevance increases with advancing age. For example, the 2009 U.S. household transportation survey revealed that the percent of disabled people essentially doubles for those 80+ years old relative to the 70-79 years old people (41.3 percent versus 22.6 percent in 2009). Consequently it is not surprising that the National Highway Traffic Safety Administration and the American Medical Association (AMA, 2005; Dobbs, 2005) provide guidelines to physicians that direct their attention to medical conditions that may result in driving-related functional impairments. These include eye conditions that can impair visual acuity such as cataracts, diabetic retinopathy, keratoconus, macular degeneration, nystagmus, and use of telescopic lens; conditions that can restrict the visual field such as glaucoma, hemianopia, monocular vision, ptosis, and retinitis pigmentosa. Because there is no compelling direct epidemiological evidence that any of the conditions are over-involved in crashes the recommendations – very appropriately – typically stress that these conditions should preclude or limit driving only to the extent that they actually impair the relevant function, such as visual acuity and visual field in the above examples.

The guidelines also provide recommendations for various cardio-vascular diseases, cerebrovascular diseases, neurological diseases, psychiatric diseases, metabolic diseases, musculoskeletal disabilities, peripheral vascular diseases, renal diseases, respiratory diseases, and effects of anesthesia surgery and medications. Most of the recommendations are based on medical analyses and not on crash and driving-related data. Therefore, despite some of the very specific recommendations, the empirical support for over-involvement of most of the specific diseases in crashes is non-existent. In fact, a recent extensive study conducted in Canada as part of an extensive Canadian research project – the Canadian Driving Research Initiative for Vehicular Safety in the Elderly (CanDRIVE; c.f. Marshall *et al.*, 2013) – on a cohort of 1,230 70+ years old drivers failed to obtain any consistent associations between the formal "Assessment of Driving-Related Skills" based on the AMA recommendations and crash involvement (Woolnough *et al.*, 2013). An even blunter refutation of the value of medical screening was expressed by one of the leading researchers in this area who argued that "medical screening of older drivers is not evidence based" (O'Neill, 2012). Again the fault is not in the validity of the symptoms, as much as in the drivers' abilities to compensate for them in their choice of actual driving times, places, and style.

The one disease that has been most consistently associated with impaired driving is dementia, especially the Alzheimer's type (Drachman and Swearer, 1993; Dubinsky *et al.*, 1992). Although it is most noticeably characterized by failures in short-term memory, it also disrupts motion perception – a critical requirement for driving (Rizzo and Nawror, 1998). The disease is characterized by mental impairments in six domains that include memory and at least one other cognitive function: general cognition (such as measured by the Mini-Mental State Examination and clinical assessment), attention and concentration (such as measured by the Trails A and B Tests, visual tracking, attention switching, and letter-cancellation), visuospatial skills (such as measured by picture completion and figure-ground tests), "executive functions" (such as measured by mazes, Stroop Color-Word test, and word fluency), and language (such as measured by verbal IQ and comprehension) (Reger *et al.*, 2004). In its initial stages it is often hard to diagnose, because the gradual loss of memory is often attributed to the aging process itself.

There is a significant body of evidence that people suffering from Alzheimer's disease are at increased crash risk (Drachman and Swearer, 1993; Morris, 1997), possibly because unlike many other diseases, the patients often deny their symptoms and refrain from adjusting their driving. Because the disease is progressive, the mere diagnosis of dementia should not preclude driving. Instead, the disease should only trigger an evaluation of the person's actual driving ability (AMA, 2005). In an attempt to provide better guidelines for driving, Reger *et al.* (2004) reviewed 27 different studies that evaluated the effects of Alzheimer's disease on driving performance. The driving performance measures varied greatly among the studies, but could be grouped into three types: naturalistic on-road tests, non-road tests such as simulators, and care-giver's reports. The technique used – meta-analysis – is a statistical procedure that combines data from different compatible studies into the equivalence of one large data set, thereby enabling the researcher to discover effects that may exist in several small studies, but are not statistically significant in any of them (because of the small number of participants in each study). Their results showed that only the performance on the visuomotor tests was consistently related to impaired driving as evaluated by all three types of tests (on-road, off-road, and care-giver's opinion). However, performance on all six Alzheimer's domains were significantly (though moderately) associated with the more objective on-road and off-road driving performance. With these findings in mind, and given the fact that studies that do not obtain significant effects are less likely to be published, the authors conclusion seem appropriately cautious: "neuropsychological testing makes a significant contribution to predicting driving ability. However, they do not indicate at what level of impairment a specific patient is unfit to drive." In conclusion, despite the extensive research, there appears to be "no commonly utilized method of assessing dementia severity in relation to driving, no consensus on the specific types of assessments that should be applied to older drivers with cognitive impairment, and no gold standard for determining driving fitness" (Carr and O'Neill, 2015, p. 1613).

Finally, some older drivers have more difficulty in moving, especially in turning their head and upper body (Dukic and Broberg, 2012). Thus, Isler, Parsonson, and Hansson, (1997) found that drivers 70+ years old, especially males, have approximately 30 percent loss in head rotation relative to drivers under 30 years old. Coupled with their reduced field of view, these drivers have a smaller effective field of view and more blind areas around them. This, in turn, interferes with their ability to scan all parts of the road when changing lanes and turning, especially when making left turns at un-signalized intersections – the two driving situations in which older drivers are particularly prone to accidents (Langford *et al.*, 2005; Preusser *et al.*, 1998; Romoser *et al.*, 2013).

Because of the tenuous relationships between specific medical conditions and crashes, the physician is urged to exercise judgment rather than indiscriminately recommend cessation of driving whenever a person has a condition that may impair some driving-related functions. In England in a report published by the Department for Transport, Spencer (2003) recommends that the decision whether or not a person with a known medical condition should be allowed to continue driving should be based on assessing (1) the exposure to risk (for example, the amount of driving that is undertaken), (2) the probability of impairment or incapacity while at the wheel, (3) the probability of an accident resulting from impairment or incapacity, and (4) the likely outcome of an accident. The first of these considerations – the exposure to risk – is particularly elusive to evaluate. For example, McGwin *et al.* (2004) found that – after adjusting for differences in visual acuity, demographic characteristics and other medical conditions – drivers diagnosed with glaucoma adjust their driving accordingly by avoiding as much as they can driving in high-risk situations such as at night, in the rain, in fog, and in rush hours, and consequently – perhaps not unexpectedly – are not over-involved in crashes relative to control drivers. Unfortunately, the data needed to make the assessments relative to driving are unavailable to the physician; most often because they are unknown.

Driving style

As mentioned above, as drivers age and as their post-work lifestyles change, they also change their driving patterns: driving less in general, and in high-risk situations in particular. In addition, older drivers tend to drive in a more careful manner. Porter and Whitton (2002) had drivers of different ages drive their own cars the same 30-mile route, while being tracked with a global positioning system installed in their cars. They were then able to demonstrate that older (65+ years old) drivers drive more slowly, accelerate and decelerate more gradually, commit fewer violations and maintain longer headways than younger drivers. Horberry *et al.* (2004) conducted an observational study of 6,480 Australian drivers while they drove and also found that older-looking drivers drove more slowly than younger looking drivers. It is possible that progress toward the safety of older drivers, may be made if their driving behavior assessment were adjusted to their needs, social context, beliefs and awareness, so that their strategic, tactical, and operational decisions can be more compatible with their skills and limitations (Lindstrom-Forneri *et al.*, 2010). Also, the clinical assessment and recommendation should be expanded to include the viability of transportation alternatives (Carr and O’Neill, 2015).

Solutions to Safety and Mobility of Older People

It should be quite obvious that as a group, older drivers are not a public health problem, and once the crash data are adjusted for their exposure and driving habits they are not over-involved in crashes. Nonetheless, it appears that when they do get involved in a crash, they are more likely to be culpable than younger drivers. There are several alternative ways to assist older drivers avoid dangerous driving situations in which they are likely to cause a crash. These include relicensing tests, a laissez-faire approach that relies on self-regulation, and educating and training drivers to understand their difficulties and learn to cope with them. Although many jurisdictions have age-based reassessments and relicensing tests for older drivers after the age of 70 or 75 (Charlton *et al.*, 2002), only the last two approaches – education and training – seem beneficial.

Screening functionally deficient drivers

There is some evidence that some tests – even easily administered ones – can distinguish high-risk drivers from safe drivers; especially when the determination is based on driving behavior in a simulator or on the road (Vanlaar *et al.*, 2014; Wood *et al.*, 2013). However, based on the current state of knowledge there is very little justification for implementing age-based licensing screening criteria. This is true because:

1. The measures we currently have that are related to driving performance do not necessarily distinguish between safe and unsafe drivers when safety is measured in terms of crash involvement (e.g., Camp, 2013; Hennessy and Janke, 2005; Langford, 2008).
2. Even for the very old drivers (80+) passing and failing rates on driving performance tests do not seem to be age-related. Furthermore, those who pass driving performance tests and those who fail them do not differ significantly in their physical and mental abilities (based on commonly used screening tests) (Charlton *et al.*, 2002).
3. When research demonstrates an effect of a given diagnostic test on driving performance, the discriminability is too gross to be useful for licensing. For example, Wood *et al.* (2013) showed that a battery of previously validated tests can discriminate between good and poor drivers (based on a driving test). However, even this extended battery missed 20 percent of the poor drivers (sensitivity = 80 percent); and more disconcerting, it failed 27 percent of the good drivers (specificity = 73 percent). Thus, implementation of this objective battery in licensing would deny license to about a quarter of the fit drivers.
4. Older drivers are not over-involved in crashes once the data are properly adjusted for differences in relicensing procedures, low-mileage bias, and frailty bias (Fontaine, 2003; Hakamies-Blomqvist *et al.*, 2004; Keall and Frith, 2004; Langford *et al.*, 2006; Langford *et al.*, 2004a, 2004b; Langford, 2008).
5. Even if tough relicensing screening criteria are employed it seems that those people who need or greatly desire to continue driving will manage to obtain the license (Zaidel and Hocherman, 1986).

6. From a purely societal cost-benefit perspective, the net effect on crashes will be negligible (Tay, 2006).

But we can always speculate that if we had good screening tools, then a relicensing process would be appropriate. It appears that even in that case, there is no justification for retesting. Torpey (1986) used crash data from Victoria, Australia, and applied some cost estimates to calculate the benefit-to-cost ratios for vision testing and medical examinations. For her calculations she assumed that (1) impaired vision and medical conditions are responsible for 0.3 percent of the crashes of 75+ years old drivers, (2) the administration of a medical and vision test would yield 50 percent improvement, and (3) the benefit would be identical if the tests were conducted on an annual basis or a tri-annual basis. With these assumptions, she found that the benefit-to-cost ratios are all significantly below 1.0 – meaning than the cost would be greater than the benefit. In fact the benefit/cost was 0.11 and 0.20 for annual vision and medical examinations, respectively, and 0.33 and 0.60 for tri-annual examinations. Even this dismal prognosis is optimistic given the fact that 50 percent effectiveness of the exams in screening out ineligible applicants is overly optimistic relative to Zaidel and Hocherman's findings (1986).

However, there is some evidence that older drivers' performance in on-road evaluations and cognitive screening tests correlates with their performance in driving simulations (Casutt *et al.*, 2014). Thus, one would presume that a hierarchical screening method based on such evaluations would also correlate with crash involvement. This kind of reasoning was probably behind California's three-tier system – where drivers are screened with progressively more complex assessment tools, culminating with an on-road examination and a provision of educational materials to help drivers be aware of and cope with their limitations. Unfortunately this presumption is not supported by the empirical evidence. Camp (2013) found no difference in post-screening crash involvement between the treatment group and the control group in the 2 years following renewal. As Camp cynically notes, the only practically significant difference was in the additional aggravations, delays, and restrictions the treatment group experienced in order to receive the license. This is despite the fact that the restrictions obviously reduced the treatment group's exposure.

Finally, in addition to all of the above in a theoretical discussion of the rationale for screening drivers on the basis of their crash risk, Hakamies-Blomqvist (2006) argues that in order to make a valid choice between "a certain bad outcome (mobility loss)" and a "low-probability bad outcome (accident)" we need valid data on the risk that an *individual* driver poses (with a combination of impairments, skills, driving strategies, and driving needs, as they fluctuate over time), relative to the risk level society considers acceptable. To date, we have the data for neither. In summary, the substantial amount of evidence gathered from different driving populations, and using different analytical techniques, all support Langford *et al.*'s (2004a) conclusion that "mandatory license retesting schemes of the type evaluated have no demonstrable road safety benefits overall."

In lieu of age-based screening, some researchers recommend age-based referral by physicians. These referrals should be based on the combined findings of few select behavioral, visual, and mental measures that do seem to correlate with driving performance (AMA, 2005; Charlton *et al.*, 2002). However, given the weak relationships between these measures and actual crash experience, the validity of this approach is also questionable (Nakagawa, Park, and Kumagai, 2013; O'Neill, 2012). Moreover, given the dilemma involved in "turning in" a patient who comes in for help, the ethical justification is also questionable (Rapoport *et al.*, 2007).

Another interesting alternative is the recruitment of family members to identify high crash risk. An interesting step in this direction was taken by Nakagawa *et al.* (2013) who developed a short, 14-item questionnaire – the Everyday Behavior Questionnaire – that consists of everyday non-driving behaviors that may be indicative of driving-related impairments. An initial evaluation of this questionnaire showed that it had a low but significant correlation with crash involvement (as recalled by the close family members). This approach has a some potential because close family members (1) actually get to observe the older driver in their family *after* he or she has already made the compensatory behaviors to compensate for his or her perceived limitations and (2) are assumed to have the health and welfare of the older driver as their primary concern. There are also various organizations that provide family members with guidance on how to evaluate and discuss this issue with an older family member. A very active organization in the U.S. is the American Association for Retired Persons (AARP) that has an online seminar at www.aarp.org/wntt.

Self-regulation and self-selection

It is apparent that self-regulation for people who retain their license is at least as effective as formal licensing tests. This was inadvertently demonstrated by Hennessy and Janke (2005) in their study on California drivers. They found that "compared to elder renewal license applicants who were assessed as somewhat functionally limited, elder renewals assessed as extremely functionally limited were more likely to fail a structured road test, but less likely to have been crash involved in the last three years." The paradoxical implications are similar to those from Hakamies-Blomqvist *et al.*'s (1995) study: people that are most likely to be relicensed may be more dangerous on the road than those whose license would most likely be revoked. Of course, the reason for this seeming paradox is that in the driving tests the two groups had to perform the same drives, whereas in real life the less functional people tend to restrict themselves to the point that they are actually less at risk.

Self-restriction is typically based on a combination of medical impairments, functional deteriorations, changes in lifestyle, and poor driving experience. Hakamies-Blomqvist and Wahlström (1998) queried 3,069 Finnish licensed drivers who did not renew their license at age 70 why they did not, and 3,073 drivers who did renew their license at age 70 why they decided to continue driving. They found that the most frequently cited reason men gave for not renewing their license was deterioration in health – but not because it was recommended by their physicians. In fact, less than seven percent reported that they received such professional advice. In contrast the most frequently cited reason for not renewing the license by women was that they had already stopped driving, mostly because they either did not need a car or found it too expensive. In general, reported health was best among those still driving and poorest among those who stopped driving before turning 65. Thus, at least for elderly men there is a strong association between perceived health and driving cessation. Thus, even if the effect is indirect, it seems that self-perceived health is a dominant determinant in the decision to continue or quit driving.

Three studies conducted in Australia and one conducted in Canada obtained similar results that support the relative adequacy of self-restrictions. In the first study, Keeffe *et al.* (2002) measured the visual acuity and interviewed a representative sample of 2,308 40+ years old people from the Melbourne area. They found that among the 92 percent who still drove, 2.6 percent had corrected visual acuity that was less than required for licensing (i.e., less than 6/12). In that subset of 46 drivers, those who were 65+ years old were more likely to report that they restricted their driving at night, at rush hours, and in city in general, but not in bad weather and not in long trips. In the second study, Charlton *et al.* (2003) interviewed 656 55+ years old drivers, and found that self-restriction – and stopping to drive altogether – was age related and associated with the person's overall health rating in general, and vision and arthritis in particular. Although her sample was a convenience sample and not representative of the adult population (it was based on people who responded to ads), the similarity of her findings to those of Keeffe *et al.* (2002) lends them a measure of validity. Interestingly most of the older people in her study who changed their driving habits attributed it to non-medical reasons, such as a change in their residence or employment. Charlton *et al.* (2003) also found that the most common situations that older drivers tended to avoid included night driving (25 percent), driving on wet roads at night (26 percent) and driving in busy traffic (22 percent).

While macro analyses indicate that self-restriction is currently the most effective criterion we have for maintaining the safety of older people (except in the case of people suffering from dementia), more detailed analyses indicate that people do not necessarily have a valid appreciation of the specific situations in which they are at risk, and thus self-regulation is still far from optimal. In the third Australian study Baldock *et al.* (2006) evaluated the fitness to drive of older drivers based on the number and type of errors they committed in an on-road test administered by a specially trained occupational therapist. They then compared the drivers' performance to their self-reported driving habits and attitudes. Despite the drivers' avoidance of risky driving situations – such as at night in the rain – or difficult driving tasks – such as parallel parking, in general poorer performance on the driving test was not strongly related to overall avoidance of difficult driving situations. On the other hand, drivers with poorer abilities did report avoiding specific driving situations in which they had low confidence *and* were able to avoid (such as parallel parking and driving at peak hours). Interestingly, one of the "barriers" to self-regulation was the people's lifestyles: they persisted in driving in risky situations in order to not compromise their lifestyle.

The fourth study, by Tuokko and her colleagues (2013), was conducted on a cohort of the 928 70+ years old participants in the CanDRIVE study. They examined the associations among various reported attitudes, perceptions, and health, and beliefs about driving. Using previously developed questionnaires to measure older drivers' day- and night-driving comfort scales (Myers, Paradis, and Blanchard, 2008) they found that driving comfort and perceived driving abilities correlated significantly with various measures of health and visual symptoms. However, though the correlations were statistically significant (because of the large sample size) they were quite low, explaining no more than approximately 10 percent of the variance; hence of no practical significance. More interesting was the finding that within this older driver sample, the older the drivers were the less comfortable they were about their driving (both day and night), and the more they reported that they were less likely to continue driving.

Older drivers, like drivers in general, tend to overrate their competence (Horswill *et al.*, 2013). Freund and her associates (2005) had drivers rate their own driving skill and performance and then compared their self-ratings to their performance in a fixed-base driving simulator. They found that approximately fifty percent of the older people who considered themselves better than the average driver of their age actually had unsafe driving performance, and drivers who considered themselves to be at least "slightly better" than the average driver their age were more than four times more likely to be unsafe as drives who rated themselves as "the same" or "a little worse" than other drivers. These types of results suggest that improved driver awareness of their limitations might make them safe drivers. To this end some structured self-awareness kits have been developed, most notably the Roadwise Review described below.

Driver education, structured self-assessment, and training

Between the time older drivers first get their license and the time that they start experiencing various medical symptoms and driving-related functional impairments, their driving environment – vehicles, roadways, traffic control systems, laws – can change dramatically. For example, older drivers comprehend significantly fewer signs than younger drivers, even when they drive approximately the same amount. Furthermore, the difference is most noticeable in the infrequently occurring signs, suggesting that older drivers' memory may be the culprit (Ben-Bassat and Shinar, 2015). Similarly poorer comprehension levels were obtained in samples of older drivers in Finland (Shinar *et al.*, 2003).

The first step in the process of adjusting to driving in later life is acknowledgment of a potential problem. Because many people are reluctant to consult with their physician for fear that the physician might be obliged to refer them to the licensing authorities, self-assessment techniques have been developed to enable people to assess their functional limitations in the comfort and privacy of their own home. One of the more popular self-assessment tools is the PC-based battery developed by Staplin (Staplin *et al.*, 2003; Staplin and Dinh-Zarr, 2006), and distributed by the American Automobile Association. The commercial version of the program – Roadwise Review (AAA, 2005) – assesses driving-related functions including leg strength and general mobility, head and neck flexibility, high-contrast and low-contrast visual acuity, short-term (working) memory, speed of processing visual information, and visual search efficiency. All of these functions have been related to driving behavior (see Chapter 4), and therefore one would expect performance on these measures to correlate with on road driving measures, such as self-reported driving problems, violations, and crashes. Unfortunately, that is not the case. At least two such evaluations have been published and both failed to find the expected correlations (Bédard *et al.*, 2011; Scialfa *et al.*, 2010). These frustrating results again reflect the difference between the deteriorations in some selected skills, and people's abilities to compensate for them on the road by reducing their exposure to high-risk situations and adopting cautious driving habits (e.g., no left turns). For example, Trick, Toxopeus, and Wilson (2010) found that people with poor vision and reduced Useful Field of View compensated for these weaknesses by reducing their speed in visibility-challenging situations (such as fog) in a driving simulator. Charlton *et al.* (2013) found that older people tend to reduce their involvement in distracting activities when faced with crossing non-signalized intersections (that are complex in the sense that they require good and fast gap judgments), and Molnar *et al.* (2014) found that the amount of self-regulation varies across a range of specific situations. In short, older drivers tend to regulate their driving in reaction to their self-perceived limits, but the validity of these perceptions is questionable. Still, at least one component test of this battery – a computerized Maze Test, a test of visual-spatial capabilities that is an effective indicator of mild dementia – has proven to correlate moderately with prospective crash involvement of older drivers (Staplin *et al.*, 2013)

There are also remedial programs that focus on specific older driver problems. For example, to compensate for potential forgetting of signs and rules of the road, "refresher" courses for older drivers are offered by various organizations. Thus, the American Automobile Association has a driver safety program that is endorsed by some insurance companies that reduce the insurance premiums of older drivers who take the course. However, to date no evaluation of the effectiveness of such programs has been published. Another program is the Ontario, Canada mandatory Group Education Session that is compulsory for all 80-year-old drivers wishing to renew their license. This 90-minute session covers updates on traffic rules and signs, the strengths of older drivers, physical changes related to aging and how these changes affect driving, the effects of medications on driving, good practices to maintain driving fitness, driving situations that are high risk for seniors, ways to reduce collision risk, the importance of self-awareness, and alternatives to driving. Using a time series analysis that compared drivers' safety before and after the course, Vanlaar *et al.* (2016) demonstrated that the program is effective in reducing collisions and convictions. However, the average effect was very small, and when analyzed separately the analyses revealed a positive effect on those who failed the test at the end of the course, and a *negative* effect on those who passed it. This is a perplexing outcome that is hard to explain and it may reflect the effects of other confounding variables that differentiated the two groups.

Another approach has been to focus on improving the performance on specific driving-related skills. Ball and her associates (2002) conducted a large-scale study on 2,832 elderly people, 65-94 years old in which they trained subgroups in memory tasks, reasoning tasks, or speeded processing of information. After 11 months, they gave the subjects an additional "booster" training session. In a later follow-up 2 years after the start of the study they found significant improvements in all three domains. However, the improvements were limited to the specific tasks that were practiced and were not generalized to daily functions that involved those skills. In a subsequent study (Roenker *et al.*, 2003) they focused on the utility of training people to improve their UFOV, relative to four hours of training in a driving simulator, as a means to improve driving performance in an on-road driving test. As in their first study, training in speeded processing improved the UFOV, and the improvement lasted for 18 months. They also found that training in both the speeded processing and the simulated driving improved performance in the on-road driving task, as rated by the trained examiners using a detailed scoring technique. More significant perhaps was the finding that training at speeded processing resulted in fewer on-road dangerous maneouvers – defined as maneouvers in which either the driving instructor had to take control of the car or the other vehicles had to alter their courses in order to avoid a collision. Rogé, Ndiaye, and Vienne (2014) trained older drivers (63-78 years old) in a simulator by exposing them to various targets and then giving them feedback. This realistic task was designed to improve UFOV. Following this training both the UFOV improved as well as the ability to detect pedestrians as measured in terms of the distance of the pedestrian when first detected. Though this is supposed to be a demonstration of the utility of specific training to improve UFOV, there is a logical problem here. The farther the pedestrian is detected the closer he or she is to the center of the visual field. Therefore, it is hard to explain why training in UFOV helped detect targets close to the center of the visual field. A more appropriate test would have been to see if a peripherally presented pedestrian is more likely to be detected following such training.

Training in hazard perception may also be effective. Horswill *et al.* (2010) demonstrated in a small study with 24 older drivers, that those who received training with a video of a drive containing various hazards improved their hazard perception by responding to hazards faster than those who did not receive the training. Furthermore, when the hazard perception time was tested after one and 3 months after the training (Horswill *et al.*, 2015) there was no decay in the response, indicating that the short training with video clips has a long-term effectiveness. Still, before it can be concluded that hazard perception training is effective on older drivers, it must be validated on a larger sample in real road driving. Training with video clips and then testing with similar clips has very limited ecological validity.

In summary, various programs exist to help older drivers adjust to driving at their age, and the little data that are available seem to suggest that though the improvements are not necessarily reflected in reduced crash rates, learning does occur and the skills do improve.

Designing vehicles and in-vehicle technologies to assist the older drivers

The advent of in-vehicle driver and infrastructure-based assistance technologies has made the resort to technology the leading strategy for safety improvements.

And while older drivers are the ones most likely to benefit from these assistance systems, they are also the ones most likely to suffer from its potential negative effects (Eby *et al.*, 2009). Fortunately, empirical studies in general demonstrate a positive net value and several vehicle control functions have already been incorporated into new safety standards, such as electronic stability control and back up cameras.

Automobile manufacturers have always "segmented" their potential markets and tried to produce different models to accommodate different drivers. Thus, vehicles for older drivers have traditionally focused on physical comfort, such as facilitating the entering and exiting of the vehicle (especially with the high SUVs), and reaching for the seat belts. In fact, Ford Motor Co. has developed a "Third Age Suit" which simulates the specific age-related problems such as restricted movements and reduced muscular strength to sensitize its engineers to this significant portion of the buying public (Bhise, 2012). This seems to be a prudent decision as older drivers are much more likely to report problems in entering and exiting cars (Herriotts, 2005; Shaw *et al.*, 2010). The Massachusetts Institute of Technology AgeLab has developed its own version of a suit that simulates the aging process (AGNES – Age Gain Now Empathy System) that replicates what it might be like to be in a 75-year-old body, including the reduced dexterity, flexibility, motor, and visual abilities associated with aging. Together with a car that monitors various driver behaviors and acquires context-sensitive information on the driver, environment, and vehicle (the AwareCar) the AgeLab researchers can now better evaluate the difficulties that older drivers have with various vehicle features, as well as the benefits of new innovative systems designed to minimize these problems (MIT, 2014; Yang and Coughlin, 2014). Such evaluations are critical for the safety of older people, as new technologies often involve changing behaviors, and these are particularly difficult for older people. However, even simple things – like the driving with an automatic gear shift instead of a manual one, helps older drivers focus more on the road and commit fewer errors (Selander, Bolin, and Falkmer, 2012), and fewer collisions (Piersma and de Waard, 2014).

With the plethora of optional electronic information and advanced driver assistance systems (ADAS) and with the evolvement of the autonomous vehicle, particular attention is also being paid to accommodating older drivers' visual and cognitive deteriorating performance. Contrary to some stereotypes, older drivers actually appreciate and embrace these assistive devices, provided they are properly trained to understand how they function and how to use them (Reimer, 2014). For example, the lane departure warning and side blind zone alerts that are being incorporated into more and more cars, are beneficial for all drivers, but especially to older drivers whose peripheral vision deteriorates, and for whom turning the head is a significant effort (Meyer, 2009). To ease the driving task, dashboard displays can be better designed, by reducing clutter and increasing contrast, which in turn reduce the durations of visual glances at the display and away from the road (Kim *et al.*, 2011). With 30+ years of driving experience without new assistive devices, depending on the particular in-vehicle aid, relearning to drive with the new aids may be a challenge to the older driver (Yang and Coughlin, 2014). Because new support systems are being added to new cars at an increasing rate, we have very little information on their adequacy for older drivers. For example, an enhancement that is now available on several cars is a head-up display (HUD), where critical information (such as speed) is projected on the windshield at optical infinity. This display can enable older people to maintain accommodation and stay visually focused on the road ahead. The HUD may be linked not only to the vehicle data, but also to the roadway transmitted data. Caird, Chisholm, and Lockhart (2008) in a driving simulator used a HUD to project the status of a signal light ahead of the intersection. They found that both young (18-24 years old) drivers and older (65+ years old) drivers responded to the advance HUD warning with slower approach speeds when the signal light turned yellow, and both groups stopped more often with the HUD warning than without of it. However, the younger drivers spent a greater percent of their fixations on the HUD than the older drivers. This and other research suggests that for optimal use of the HUD, drivers have to learn new strategies of information gathering and selective and divided attention (Oh and Ji, 2016).

Navigation systems

One of the difficulties that are amplified with age is orientation in unknown environments. Navigation aids are designed to reduce that stress by providing the drivers with timely directions for travel to designated destinations. But these systems can also be visually and cognitively distracting. Summarizing the empirical literature on the topic, Eby *et al.* (2009) concluded that it has both positive and negative effects. On the one hand older drivers tend to use the route guidance systems frequently, report only minimal distraction from it (but more than young drivers), use them to increase their range of driving to new places, and report a sense of greater safety, confidence, and relaxation when using it. On the other hand it takes them longer to learn to use the systems, they need more time to read the displays, and they are more likely to use them with a co-navigator than young drivers.

One approach to reduce visual distraction and the need to accommodate the eyes to proximal navigation displays on the dashboard is General Motors' totally voice-based online driver-aid and navigation system – "OnStar" – where a single push of a button connects the driver with an operator who can provide assistance with anything from route guidance directions to directory assistance. Older people are assumed to benefit from such systems because they are more distracted by cellular phones which require dialing, and navigation systems that require manual inputs and substantial visual attention. Also, because the systems are linked to airbag deployment, in case of a crash, they send a help signal that can direct emergency services to the exact vehicle location, an attractive feature noted by some older drivers (Zhan *et al.*, 2013).

A promising approach to improve the navigation systems is to augment them with "user friendly" and driving relevant information, so that needed information would be quick to pick up. For example, identifying street names on the road is difficult and is one of the few tasks that actually require good visual acuity. But reading street names on a navigation display is very time consuming, and providing the driver with distance information assumes (falsely – see Chapter 5) that drivers are able to estimate distances accurately. To circumvent these problems, May, Ross, and Osman (2005), tested the benefits of supplementing the navigation system's visual display with auditory messages relating the desired maneuver to conspicuous landmarks such as "turn right after the Texaco petrol station" instead of a message of "turn right in 500 feet." Using actual driving in traffic, in Leicester, England, May and his colleagues found the auditory landmark information superior to the distance information in every measure of performance and preference that they tested, both for the younger drivers (21-40 years old) and the older drivers (55+ years old). With the auditory landmark information, both younger and older drivers, but especially older drivers needed fewer glances at the display, spent less time looking at the display while moving, felt as confident or more confident in the maneuvers they made, and in general had a positive attitude toward the landmark system. Most important, both younger and older drivers made significantly fewer navigation errors, at no cost to the mental load (measured with the subjective NASA-TLX scale). Figure 7-17 is an illustration of the effects of the Landmark and distance warnings prior to a maneuver on the total time the drivers spent looking at the navigation system while driving. As can be seen from the graphs in this figure, the total time the drivers looked at the navigation display, and therefore the total time of being distracted from attending to the road, was much less with the landmark information (left panel) than with the distance information (right panel). The specific amount of time varied for the different maneuvers, possibly as a function of the conspicuity of the landmarks available and the varying traffic and road demands. Systems sensitive to drivers' needs and older driver limitations, such as the Landmark, are a very positive step in the right direction. Still, vehicle navigation systems can be significantly improved by simplifying the presentation of the needed information, and by eliminating unnecessary information that overwhelms the older driver (Emmerson *et al.*, 2013).

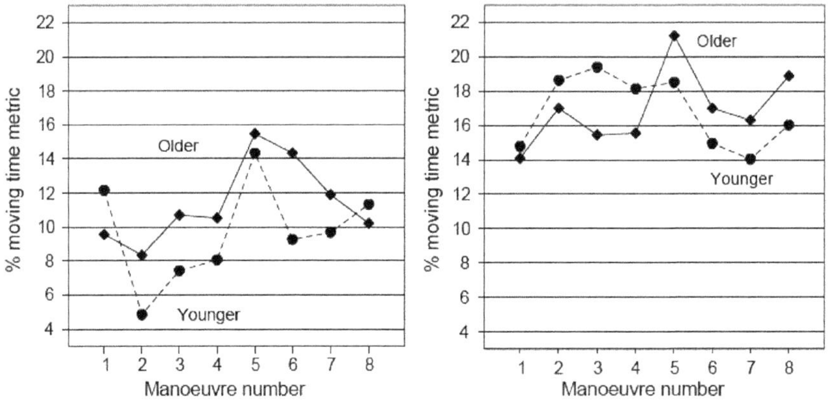

Figure 7-17. The percentage moving time spent glancing to the display during approach to a maneuver, according to age and information. Results for using landmarks are shown in the left panel, and those using distance in the right panel (from May *et al.*, 2005, with permission from Elsevier).

Hazard perception aids

One relevant skill that deteriorates with age is hazard perception (Bromberg *et al.*, 2012). What makes this situation even worse is that there appears to be no relationship between older drivers' rating of their hazard perception ability and their performance on a validated hazard perception test (Horswill *et al.*, 2013). This means that while this critical defensive driving skill deteriorates, many drivers remain oblivious to it. Two approaches have been tested and validated to counter this impairment. The first approach already discussed above is training in hazard perception. The second, more innovative approach was tested by Schall et al. (2012), who presented drivers with age-related cognitive deficiencies with an augmented reality cueing system that alerted them to potential hazards (a pedestrian, an emerging vehicle, a road warning sign of deer or pedestrian crossing). The cue in each case was a rhombus-shaped frame, displayed on the driving simulator screen around the potential hazard that increased in size as the driver approached it. In reality, such a system would be a head-up display. Their study demonstrated that the cues aided the drivers in detecting the hazard targets (most likely by increasing their visual conspicuity) *and* did not have a distracting effect from the rest of the driving task. These kinds of visual enhancements of actual hazards are already implementable, as systems to detect hazards in the form of vehicles, pedestrians, motorcycles and bicycles are already available (e.g., MobilEye®). However, identification of potential hazards remains a technological challenge (see Chapter 5 for the distinction between actual and potential hazards).

Night vision systems

These systems are designed to compensate for the poor nighttime visibility, and as such should be especially useful for older drivers. They typically provide the driver with an infrared based view of the road ahead and thus make the road geometry and obstacles on the road that are beyond the reach of the vehicle's headlights visible. Thus, such systems can compensate for older drivers reduced contrast sensitivity, and poor mesopic acuity (see Figure 4-3). Eby et al. (2009), based on their literature review concluded that these systems are a promising new technology, though their distracting effects need further evaluation.

CarFit

Older drivers can also be aided at the personal rather than system level, by assisting them in making their own needed adjustments to their cars. While this adjustment cannot directly help in visual and cognitive functions, it can improve posture and reach of the pedals and steering wheel through seat and steering adjustments. It can also increase visual field and reduce blind areas through mirror adjustments. After vision, restricted movement is the most common complaint of older people (Yee, 1985). One such program – "CarFit" – that was jointly developed by several major U.S. organizations concerned with mobility of the elderly (American Society on Aging, American Association of Retired Persons, American Occupational Therapy Association, and American Automobile Association), has received a significant amount of attention from both occupational therapists and researchers. Gaines *et al.* (2011) evaluated the program by comparing driving behavior and vehicle adjustments made by elderly people living in retirement communities in Canada, who received the intervention (N = 83) with those who did not (N = 112). Repeated evaluations up to 6 months post-treatment, based on self-reports did not reveal any benefits of the program to either reported comfort level or driving habits. Because implementation of the CarFit recommendations was voluntary and based on self-selection it was hard to conclude that the program is not effective, but it was certainly impossible to conclude that it was. Still, probably because of its intuitive appeal, the program is spreading in the U.S., Canada, Australia, and New Zealand (Craik *et al.*, 2015)

When all of the above issues and improvements are considered, one can imagine a new transformed vehicle: an older driver vehicle. It was in fact this kind of thinking that led Eby and Molnar (2012) to recommend the design of "older driver vehicle." Thus, just as the Ford Mustang was created specifically for the young drivers more than half a century ago, an older driver vehicle might attract the same people – now in their seventies. Although this approach is consistent with the market segmentation approach, Eby and Molnar concede that marketing these vehicles may be challenging, especially as getting the full benefits of some of the systems may involve training.

It is impossible to under-estimate the value the new advance driver assistance systems – such as automatic emergency braking, lane departure warning and lane keeping support, forward collision warning, and automatic emergency braking – for older drivers. These are exactly the kinds of aids these drivers need to remain behind the wheel as their visual, perceptual, and information processing abilities begin to deteriorate. Note that most of these systems compensate for error-causing deteriorations much more than they address risky driving. As illustrated in Figure 7-12, these are exactly the kinds of errors responsible for most of the older drivers' crashes. Thus, the rapid integration of these systems into new models may change earlier dire projections about the expected rise in older driver fatalities (Lyman, *et al.*, 2002). More importantly they will enable them to continue to enjoy independent living much longer (until they move into the autonomous vehicle).

Environmental treatments

Perhaps the most cost-effective approach to enhancing older driver mobility without sacrificing their safety is to make their driving environment beyond the shell of their car compatible with their limitations. This approach has been embraced by the U.S. Federal Highway Administration in its *Highway Design Handbook for Older Drivers and Pedestrians* (Staplin *et al.*, 2001), and the more recent *Handbook for Designing Roadways for the Aging Population* (Brewer, Murillo, and Pate, 2014). In these two volumes much of the research that has focused on specific difficulties of older drivers (and pedestrians) is applied to environmental design. This includes research on the older driver reduced nighttime vision (nighttime myopia and contrast sensitivity), poorer visual search behavior, reduced visual field, especially the effective visual field (e.g., UFOV), and slowed information processing rates (as measured by longer reaction times). One of the benefits of improving the environment for the older road users (both drivers and pedestrians), is that typically (but not always – roundabouts are such an exception) everyone – including young drivers – benefits. The more recent publication, by Brewer *et al.* (2014) describes treatments for 51 proven and promising traffic control and design elements distributed among five categories: Intersections, Interchanges, Roadway

Segments, Construction/Work Zones, and Highway-Rail Grade Crossings. Because of the older drivers' (and pedestrians') proven over-involvement in intersection collisions (e.g., Clarke *et al.*, 2010; Hauer, 1988), nearly half of the recommended treatments focus on intersections, especially for accommodating left turns, where older drivers seem to have most of their difficulties. To illustrate, to reduce confusion when making left turns at signalized intersections with protected/permissive left turn, a text message with the image of a filled green circle should be added next to the signal stating LEFT TURN YIELD ON GREEN. To accommodate the older driver's reduced visual acuity and contrast sensitivity increased letter sizes and retroreflective materials should be used for street names, and to accommodate the older driver's slower information processing rate and heightened frailty, specifications for roundabouts are provided as an alternative to intersections. Complementary comprehensive guidelines for accommodating older road users – again, both drivers and pedestrians – in urban environments are provided in the American Association of Retired Persons' guide, Planning Complete Streets of Aging America (AARP, 2009). This publication emphasizes the role of local and state planning agencies in designing multimodal accommodations for older road users.

To counteract reduced contrast sensitivity, reduced low-illumination acuity, and increase in glare sensitivity, the most effective countermeasure is increasing over-head fixed illumination. Street lighting provide a dual benefit, because they (a) increase the overall ambient illumination and make nighttime driving visually similar to daytime driving and (b) reduce the glare from oncoming traffic. The importance of the increase in overall level of illumination is supported by the consistent drop in nighttime crashes whenever street lights are installed, especially at junctions, intersections, access roads, and tunnels (European Commission, 2003; Staplin *et al.*, 2001). The glare reduction stems from the fact that our sensitivity to glare is determined in part by the level of illumination to which our eyes are adapted. When the ambient illumination is high, we adapt to a high level, and the *relative* amount of additional light from glare sources such as the headlamps of oncoming traffic is reduced. Of course, this accentuates the difficulties we have when we exit the lit environment and enter darker streets to which our eyes are not adjusted.

Another domain in which environmental treatments are essential for older drivers is intersection design. Because older drivers have more difficulty in judging safe gaps (Oxley *et al.*, 2006), the less uncertainty there is at an intersection, the easier it is for the older driver to handle. Thus, uncontrolled intersections, intersections with four-way stop signs, and intersections allowing right turn on red (RTOR) are more difficult for older drivers. For example, RTOR increases traffic flow and saves time and gas. However, the right turning traffic must yield to cross-traffic, and this requires head turning and good judgments of the speeds of approaching vehicles. In a comparison of the behaviors of drivers of different ages, Staplin *et al.* (1997) measured differences in drivers' RTOR behavior as a function of driver age and right-turn lane channelization. One hundred subjects divided across three age groups were observed as they drove their own vehicles around test routes consisting of local streets. They found that 25-45 years old drivers made a RTOR nearly 80 percent of the time when they had the chance to do so, compared with less than 36 percent of drivers 65-74 years old, and only 15 percent of the drivers who were 75+ years old. This reluctance is quite appropriate, because older drivers are also more likely than younger drivers to collide with other vehicles while turning in intersections, especially turning left (or right in countries where they drive on the left) (Austin and Faigin, 2003; McGwin and Brown, 1999; Zhang *et al.*, 2000). The reason for this age-related problem is that scanning the extended visual field that is necessary to make these turns in intersections is more difficult for many older drivers who also suffer from muscular-skeletal problems such as arthritis. Joint flexibility, an essential component in turning the head and the body, declines by approximately 25 percent in older adults due to arthritis, calcification of cartilage, and joint deterioration (Smith and Sethi, 1975). This difficulty further exacerbates their risk on merging ramps, when attempting to change lanes, and when turning in skewed intersections (Staplin *et al.*, 2001). Another potential cause of difficulty in safely crossing intersections is that the older drivers have difficulty inhibiting their "prepotent goal of monitoring the vehicle's intended path of travel," and consequently they fail to scan for potential hazards away from their intended path of travel (Romoser *et al.*, 2013). Some support for this hypothesis is provided in an on-road study by Dukic and Broberg (2012), who measured drivers' eye movements while driving on a 20 kilometer course containing rural and urban intersections. They found that all the drivers directed most of their fixations to the road straight ahead. However, the younger drivers (35-55 years old) even though they approached the intersections at higher speeds than the older drivers (75+ years old), spent more time fixating the road areas to the left and right of the intersections, from which crossing vehicles might come.

The seemingly obvious solution is to provide protected left turns – typically indicated by a separate green light with an arrow indicating the permitted direction of travel (Oxley *et al.*, 2006). However, it appears that older drivers also have difficulties comprehending the meaning of the signal designation, and slight variations in signal design can have a significant effect on their comprehension. For example, Williams, Ardekani, and Asante (1992), in a survey of 894 drivers in Texas found that a circular green light was less understood than a green arrow, even when the former was accompanied by an auxiliary sign indicating the intended direction. On the other hand, a circular green light is more visible, especially in glare.

Concluding Comments

Since the beginning of mass production of cars, life expectancy, motorization, and dependence on the private car have increased significantly. The generation that experienced all of these changes in the most direct manner is today's older drivers. For them, and for most of us today, driving, mobility, and independence are so interrelated that they are essentially synonymous. But as much as we may try to deny it the aging process is still there, and it is the older drivers who are most aware of it, and – so far at least – the most qualified to adjust to it. They most often decide how to adjust their driving habits, restrict their driving times and places, and – eventually – give up the keys. In parallel, research has made most significant strides in understanding the driving-related limitations of older drivers, the vehicle and environmental changes that must be made to accommodate them, and – to a much lesser extent – how to help them improve their skills, or at least make them more compatible with their driving needs.

The challenge now is to keep improving the older driver's environment and to keep the older person safe and mobile in or out of the car. As concluded in the recent ElderSafe EU project "elderly safety and mobility should be balanced equally in the development of an elderly transport safety strategy. Thus, maintaining the mobility of elderly who quit or are forced to cease driving will be a key policy priority in the (near) future" (Polders *et al.*, 2015, p. 9). The exploding plethora of advance driver assistance devices (ADAS) that can keep the elderly behind the wheel, coupled with alternative transportation options and services may be just the prescription that they need.

References

AAA (2005). Roadwise review: A tool to help seniors drive safely longer. American Automobile Association, Washington, DC. www.aaapublicaffairs.com

AARP (2009). Planning complete streets for an aging America. AARP Public Policy Institute, Washington, DC.

Abdel-Aty, M. A., C. L. Chen and J. R. Schott (1998). An assessment of the effect of driver age on traffic accident involvement using loglinear models. *Accid. Anal. Prev.*, *30*, 851-861.

Aksan, N., J. D. Dawson, J. L. Emerson, L. Yu, E. Y. Uc, S. W. Anderson and M. Rizzo (2013). Naturalistic distraction and driving safety in older drivers. *Hum. Fact.*, *55*, 841-853.

AMA (2005). Physicians' guide to assessing and counseling older drivers. American Medical Association, Washington, DC.

Anderson, D. and E. Palmore (1974). Longitudinal evaluation of ocular function. In: *Normal Aging: II. Reports from the Duke Longitudinal Studies, 1970-1973* (E. Palmore Ed.), pp. 166-230. Butterworth, London.

Anstey, K. J., M. S. Horswill, J. M. Wood and C. Hatherly (2012). The role of cognitive and visual abilities as predictors in the multifactorial model of driving safety. *Accid. Anal. Prev.*, *45*, 766-774.

Austin, R. A. and B. M. Faigin (2003). Effect of vehicle and crash factors on older occupants. *J. Safety Res.*, *34*, 441-452.

Babizhayev, M. A. (2003). Glare disability and driving safety. *Ophthalmol. Res.*, *35*, 19-25.

Babizhayev, M. A. (2004). Rejuvenation of visual functions in older adult drivers and drivers with cataract during a short-term administration of *N*-acetylcarnosine lubricant eye drops. *Rejuvenation Res.*, *7*(3), 186-198.

Baldock, M. R. J., J. L. Mathias, A. J. McLean and A. Berndt (2006). Self-regulation of driving and its relationship to driving ability among older adults. *Accid. Anal. Prev.*, *38*(5), 1038-1045.

Ball, K., C. Owsley, M. E. Sloane, D. L. Roenker and J. R. Bruni (1993). Visual attention problems as a predictor of vehicle crashes in older drivers. *Invest. Ophthalmol. Vis. Sci.*, *34*(11), 3110-3123.

Ball, K., D. B. Berch, K. F. Helmers, J. B. Jobe, M. D. Leveck, M. Marsiske, J. N. Morris, G. W. Rebok, D. M. Smith, S. L. Tennstedt, F. W. Unverzagt and

S. L. Willis (2002). Effects of cognitive training interventions with older adults: A randomized trial. *J. Am. Med. Assn.*, *288*, 2271-2281.

Ball, K. and C. Owsley (1991). Identifying correlates of accident involvement of the older driver. *Hum Fact.*, *33*(5), 583-595.

Bédard, M., G. H. Guyatt, M. J. Stones and J. P. Hirdes (2002) The independent contribution of driver, crash, and vehicle characteristics to driver fatalities. *Accid. Anal. Prev.*, *34*, 717-727.

Bédard, M., J. Riendeau, B. Weaver and A. Clarkson (2011). Roadwise review has limited congruence with actual driving performance of aging drivers. *Accid. Anal. Prev.*, *43*(6), 2209-2214.

Ben-Bassat, T. and D. Shinar (2015). Effect of context and drivers' age on highway traffic sign comprehension. *Trans. Res. F*, *33*, 117-127.

Betz, M. E. and J. Fisher (2009). The trail-making test B and driver screening in the emergency department. *Traffic Inj Prev.*, *10*, 415-420.

Bhise, V. D. (2012). *Ergonomics in the Automotive Design Process*. CRC Press, Taylor and Francis, Boca Raton, FL.

Botwinick, J. (1984). *Aging and Behavior: A Comprehensive Integration of Research Findings*. Springer, New York.

Braver, E. R. and R. E. Trempel (2004). Are older drivers actually at higher risk of involvement in collisions resulting in deaths or non-fatal injuries among their passengers and other road users? *Inj. Prev.*, *10*, 27-32.

Brewer, M., D. Murillo and A. Pate (2014). Handbook for designing roadways for the aging population. Report No. FHWA-SA-14-015. U.S. Department of Transportation, Washington, DC.

Bromberg, S., T. Oron-Gilad, A. Ronen, A. Borowsky and Y. Parmet (2012). The perception of pedestrians from the perspective of elderly experienced and experienced drivers. *Accid. Anal. Prev.*, *44*, 48-55.

Bruckner, R. (1967). Longitudinal research on the eye. *Gerontologia Clinica*, *9*, 87-95.

Burg, A. (1968). Lateral visual field as related to age and sex. *J. Appl. Psychol.*, *52*, 10-15.

Burg, A. (1974). Visual degradation in relation to specific accident types. University of California Report No. UCLA-ENG-7419. University of California, Institute of Transportation and Traffic Engineering, Los Angeles, CA.

Caird, J. K., S. L. Chisholm and J. Lockhart (2008). Do in-vehicle advanced signs enhance older and younger drivers' intersection performance? Driving simulation and eye movement results. *Int. J. Hum. Comp. Stud.*, *66*(3), 132-144.

Camp, B. J. (2013). The overall program effects of California's 3-tier assessment system pilot on crashes and mobility among senior drivers. *J. Safety Res.*, *47*, 1-8.

Carr, D. B. and D. O'Neill (2015). Mobility and safety issues in drivers with dementia. *Int. Psychogeriatr.*, *27*(10), 1613-1622.

Casutt, G., M. Martin, M. Keller and L. Jäncke (2014). The relation between performance in on-road driving, cognitive screening and driving simulator in older healthy drivers. *Trans. Res. F*, *22*, 232-244.

Charlton, J. L., M. Catchlove, M., Scully, S. Koppel and S. Newstead (2013). Older driver distraction: A naturalistic study of behaviour at intersections. *Accid. Anal. Prev.*, *58*, 271-278.

Charlton, J. L., B. N. Fildes, S. N. Koppel, D. J. Andrea, S. V. Newstead, P. E. Oxley and N. J. Pronk (2002). Evaluation of a referral assessment tool for assessing older and functionally impaired drivers. VicRoads, Melbourne, Australia.

Charlton, J. L., S. Koppel, M. O'Hare, D. Andrea, G. Smith, B. Khodr, J. Langford, M. Odell and B. Fildes (2004). Influence of chronic illness on crash involvement of motor vehicle drivers. Monash University Accident Research Report No. 213. Monash University Accident Research Center, Clayton, Victoria, Australia.

Charlton, J. L., J. A. Oxley, B. N. Fildes, P. E. Oxley, S. V. Newstead, M. A. O'Hare and S. N. Koppel (2003). An investigation of self-regulatory behaviours of older drivers. Monash University Accident Research Centre, Clayton, Victoria, Australia.

Charman, W. N. (1997).Vision and driving: A literature review and commentary. *Ophthalmol. Physiol. Opt.*, *17*(5), 371-391.

Charness, N. and E. Bosman (1992). Human factors and age. In: *Handbook of Aging and Cognition* (F. I. M. Craik & T. A. Salthouse eds.), pp. 495-552. Erlbaum, Hillsdale, NJ.

Choca, J. P., L. Laatsch, L. Wetzel and A. Agresti (1997). The Halstead category test: A fifty-year perspective. *Neuropsychol. Rev.*, *7*(2), 61-75.

Cicchino, J. B. and A. T. McCartt (2014). Trends in older driver crash involvement rates and survivability in the United States: An update. *Accid. Anal. Prev.*, *72*, 44-54.

Clarke, D. D., P. Ward, C. Bartle and W. Truman (2010). Older drivers' road traffic crashes in the UK. *Accid. Anal. Prev.*, *42*(4), 1018-1024.

Collia, D. V., J. Sharp and L. Giesbrecht (2003). The 2001 national household travel survey: A look into the travel patterns of older Americans. *J. Safe. Res.*, *34*, 461-470.

Committee for Conference on Transportation in an Aging Society (2005). Safe mobility for older Americans. Transportation Research Board, Washington DC.

Cooper, P. (1990). Differences in accident characteristics among elderly drivers and between elderly and middle aged drivers. *Accid. Anal. Prev.*, *22*, 499-508.

Coughlin, J. F. (2002). How will we get there from here? Strategies to keep an older America moving. Presented at the National Conference on Aging and Mobility, Scottsdale, AZ, March 25.

Coughlin, J. F. and L. A. D'Ambrosio (eds) (2012). *Aging America and Transportation: Personal Choices and Public Policy*. Springer, New York, NY.

Council, F. M. and J. A. Jr. Allen (1974). A study of the visual field of North Carolina drivers and their relationship to accidents. University of North Carolina, Highway Safety Research Center, Chapel Hill, NC.

Craik, J., E. Stern, J. Lapointe, N. McCarthy and E. S. Davis (2015). CarFit Canada: Lessons learned from an international collaboration. *World Fed. Occup. Therap. Bull.*, *71*(1), 22-25.

Cuenen, A., E. M. Jongen, T. Brijs, K. Brijs, M. Lutin, K. Van Vlierden and G. Wets (2015). Does attention capacity moderate the effect of driver distraction in older drivers? *Accid. Anal. Prev.*, *77*, 12-20.

Decina, L. E. and L. Staplin (1993). Retrospective evaluation of alternative vision screening criteria for older and younger drivers. *Accid. Anal. Prev.*, *25*(3), 267-275.

Dellinger, A. (2012) Describing the older adult population. In (Coughlin and D'Ambrosio, eds.) *Aging America and Transportation: Personal Choices and Public Policy*. Springer, New York, NY.

Dellinger, A., M. Kresnow, D. White and M. Sehgal (2004). Risk to self versus risk to others: How do older drivers compare to others on the road? *Am. J. Prev. Med.*, *26*(3), 217-221.

DfT (2001). Forecasting older driver accidents and casualties. Road Safety Research Report No. 23. UK Department for Transport, London.

Di Stefano, M. and W. Macdonald (2003). Assessment of older drivers: Relationships among on-road errors, medical conditions and test outcomes. *J. Safety Res.*, *34*, 415-429.

Dobbs, B. M. (2005). Medical conditions and driving: A review of the scientific literature (1960-2000). National Highway Traffic Safety Administration Report DOT HS 809 690. U.S. Department of Transportation, Washington, DC.

Drachman, D. A. and J. M. Swearer (1993). Driving and Alzheimer's disease: The risk of crashes. [published erratum appears in Neurology, 1994, 44, 4]. *Neurology*, *43*, 2448-2456.

Dubinsky, R. M., A. Williamson, C. S. Gray and S. L. Glatt (1992). Driving in Alzheimer's disease. [see comments in Journal of the American Geriatric Society, 1993, 41, 889-891]. *J. Am. Geriatr. Soc.*, *40*, 1112-1116.

Dukic, T. and T. Broberg (2012). Older drivers' visual search behaviour at intersections. *Trans. Res. F*, *15*(4), 462-470.

Eberhard, J. (1996). Safe mobility for senior citizens. *Inter. Assn. Traffic Safety Services Res.*, *20*(1), 29-37.

Eberhard, J. and D. Trilling (2001). The graying of America safe mobility for life — Developing a national agenda. http://wwwnrd.nhtsa.dot.gov/pdf/nrd-50/ciren/2001/1201nhtsa.pdf. October 12, 2004.

Eby, D. W. and L. J. Molnar (2012). Has the time come for an older driver vehicle? University of Michigan Transportation Research Institute Report UMTRI-2012-5. Ann Arbor, MI.

Eby, D. W., L. J. Molnar and P. S. Kartje (2009). *Maintaining safe mobility in an aging society*. CRC Press, New York, NY.

Emerson, J. L., A. M. Johnson, J. D. Dawson, E. Uc, S. W. Anderson and M. Rizzo (2012). Predictors of driving outcomes in advancing age. *Psychol. Aging*, *27*, 550-559.

Emmerson, C., W. Guo, P. Blythe, A. Namdeo and S. Edwards (2013). Fork in the road: In-vehicle navigation systems and older drivers. *Trans. Res. F*, *21*, 173-180.

European Commission (2003). Road Safety and Environmental Benefit-Cost and Cost-effectiveness Analysis for Use in Decision Making (ROSEBUD). WP-1: Screening of efficiency assessment experiences. European Union, Brussels.

Evans, L. (1991). *Traffic Safety and the Driver*. Van Nostrand Reinhold, New York, NY.

Evans, L. (2004). *Traffic Safety*. Science Serving Society, Inc., Bloomfield Hills, MI.

Fontaine, H. (2003). Age des conducteurs de voiture et accidents de la route: Quel risqué pour les seniors? (Driver age and road traffic accidents: What is the risk for seniors?). *Recherche-Transports-Securite*, *79-80*,107-120 (as cited by Langford *et al.*, 2006).

Fozard, J. (1990). Vision and hearing in aging. In: *Handbook of the Psychology of Aging* (J. E. Birren & K. W. Schaie eds.), *3rd ed.*, pp. 150-170. Academic Press, San Diego, CA.

Freund, B., L. A. Colgrove, B. L. Burke and R. McLeod (2005). Self-rated driving performance among elderly drivers referred for driving evaluation. *Accid. Anal. Prev.*, *37*, 613-618.

Friedman, C., G. McGwin, K. K. Ball and C. Owsley (2013). Association between higher order visual processing abilities and a history of motor vehicle collision involvement by drivers ages 70 and over. *Invest. Ophthalmol. Vis. Sci.*, *54*(1), 778-782.

Gaines, J. M., K. L. Burke, K. A. Marx, M. Wagner and J. M. Parrish (2011). Enhancing older driver safety: A driving survey and evaluation of the CarFit program. *J. Safety Res.*, *42*(5), 351-358.

Green, K. A., G. McGwin and C. Owsley (2013). Associations between visual, hearing, and dual sensory impairments and history of motor vehicle collision involvement of older drivers. *J. Am. Geriatr. Soc.*, *61*(2), 252-257.

Haegerstrom-Portnoy, G., M. E. Scheck, and J. A. Brabyn (1999). Seeing into old age: Vision function beyond acuity. *Opt. and Vis. Sci*, *76*, 141-158.

Hakamies-Blomqvist, L. E. (1993). Fatal accidents of older drivers. *Accid. Anal. Prev.*, *25*, 19-27.

Hakamies-Blomqvist, L. (2006). Are there safe and unsafe drivers? *Transport. Res. F*, *9*, 347-352.

Hakamies-Blomqvist, L., K. Johansson and C. Lundberg (1995). Driver licenses as a measure of older driver exposure: A methodological note. *Accid. Anal. Prev.*, *27*(6), 853-857.

Hakamies-Blomqvist, L., T. Raitanen and D. O'Neill (2002). Driver ageing does not cause higher accident rates per km. *Transport. Res. Part F*, *5*, 271-274.

Hakamies-Blomqvist, L., A. Siren and R. Davidsc (2004). Older drivers – A review. VTI Report No. 497A.2004. Swedish National Road and Transport Research Institute, Linkoping, Sweden.

Hakamies-Blomqvist, L. and B. Wahlström (1998). Why do older drivers give up driving? *Accid. Anal. Prev.*, *30*, 305-310.

Hakamies-Blomqvist, L., M. Wiklund and P. Henriksson (2005). Predicting older drivers' accident involvement – Smeed's law revisited. *Accid. Anal. Prev.*, *37*, 675-680.

Hauer, E. (1988). The safety of older persons at intersections. In Transportation in an Aging Society: Improving Mobility and Safety for Older Persons—Volume 2: Special Report 218, pp. 194-252. Transportation Research Board, Washington, DC.

Hawkins, A. S., J. P. Szlyk, Z. Ardickas, A. Ziba, K. R. Alexander and J. T. Wilensky (2003). Comparison of contrast sensitivity, visual acuity, and Humphrey visual field testing in patients with glaucoma. *J. Glaucoma*, *12*(2), 134-138.

Hennessy, D. F. (1995). Vision testing of renewal applicants: Crashes predicted when compensation for impairment is inadequate. Report No. 152. California Department of Motor Vehicles. Sacramento, CA.

Hennessy, D. F. and M. K. Janke (2005). Clearing a road to driving fitness by better assessing driver wellness: California's three-tier driving-centered assessment system. Report No. CAL-DMV-RSS-05-215. California Department of Motor Vehicles, Sacramento, CA.

Herriotts, P. (2005). Identification of vehicle design requirement for older drivers. *Appl. Ergon.*, *36*, 255-262

Horberry, T., L. Hartley, K. Gobetti, F. Walker, B. Johnson, S. Gersbach and J. Ludlow (2004). Speed choice by drivers: The issue of driving too slowly. *Ergonomics*, *47*, 1561-1570.

Horswill, M. S., E. K. Falconer, N. A. Pachana, M. Wetton and A. Hill (2015). The longer-term effects of a brief hazard perception training intervention in older drivers. *Psychol. Aging*, *30*(1), 62.

Horswill, M. S., C. N. Kemala, M. Wetton, C. T. Scialfa and N. A. Pachana (2010). Improving older drivers' hazard perception ability. *Psychol. Aging*, *25*, 464-469.

Horswill, M. S., K. Sullivan, J. K. Lurie-Beck and S. Smith (2013). How realistic are older drivers' ratings of their driving ability? *Accid. Anal. Prev.*, *50*, 130-137.

IIHS (2015). Older drivers: 2013. Insurance Institute for Highway Safety, Arlington, VA.

Isler, R. B., B. S. Parsonson and G. J., Hansson (1997). Age related effects of restricted head movements on the useful field of view of drivers. *Accid. Anal. Prev.*, *29*(6), 793-801.

Janke, M. (1991). Accidents, mileage and the exaggeration of risk. *Accid. Anal. Prev.*, *23*(2/3), 183-188.

Johnson, C. A. and J. L. Keltner (1983). Incidence of visual field loss in 20,000 eyes and its relationship to driving performance. *Arch. Ophthalmol.*, *101*, 371-375.

Keall, M. D. and W. J. Frith (2004). Older driver crash rates in relation to type and quantity of travel. *Traffic Inj. Prev.*, *5*, 26-36.

Keeffe, J. E., C. F. Jin, L. M. Weih, C. A. McCarty and H. R. Taylor (2002). Vision impairment and older drivers: Who is driving? *Br. J. Ophthalmol.*, *86*, 1118-1121.

Keltner, J. L. and C. A. Johnson (1987). Visual function, driving safety and the elderly. *Ophthalmology*, *94*, 1180-1188.

Kim, S. J., A. K. Dey, J. Lee and J. Forlizzi (2011). Usability of car dashboard displays for elder drivers. Proceedings of CHI 2011, pp. 493-502, Vancouver, Canada, May 7-12.

Kline, D. W., T. J. B. Kline, J. L. Fozard, W. Kosnick, F. Schieber, and R. Sekuler (1992). Vision, aging, and driving: The problems of older drivers. *J. Gerontology*, *47*, 27-34.

Kosnick, W., L. Winslow, D. Kline, K. Rasinski, and R. Sekuler (1988). Vision changes in daily life throughout adulthood. *J. Gerontology*, *43*, 63-70.

Kweon, Y.-J. and K. M. Kockelman (2003). Overall injury risks to different drivers: Combining exposure, frequency and severity models. *Accid. Anal. Prev.*, *35*, 441-450.

Langford, J. (2008). Usefulness of off-road screening tests to licensing authorities when assessing older driver fitness to drive. *Traffic Inj. Prev.*, *9*(4), 328-335.

Langford, J., D. Andrea, B. Fildes, T. Williams and M. Hull (2005). Assessing responsibility for older drivers' crashes. Austroads Publication No. AP-R265/05. Austroads, Inc., Canberra, Australia.

Langford, J., M. Fitzharris, S. Koppel and S. Newstead (2004a). Effectiveness of mandatory license testing for older drivers in reducing crash risk among urban older Australian drivers. *Traffic Inj. Prev.*, *5*, 326-335.

Langford, J., M. P. Fitzharris, S. V. Newstead and S. Koppel (2004b). Some consequences of different older driver licensing procedures in Australia. *Accid. Anal. Prev.*, *36*, 993-1001.

Langford, J., S. Koppel, D. McCarthy and S. Srinivasan (2008). In defence of the 'low-mileage bias'. *Accid. Anal. Prev.*, *40*, 1996-1999.

Langford, J., R. Methorst and L. Hakamies-Blomqvist (2006). Older drivers do not have a high crash risk – A replication of low mileage bias. *Accid. Anal. Prev.*, *38*, 574-578.

Li, G., E. R. Braver and L. Chen (2003). Fragility versus excessive crash involvement as determinants of high death rates per vehicle-mile of travel among older drivers. *Accid. Anal. Prev.*, *35*, 227-235.

Lindstrom-Forneri, W., H. A. Tuokko, D. Garrett and F. Molnar (2010). Driving as an everyday competence: A model of driving competence and behavior. *Clin. Gerontol*, *33*(4), 283-297.

Lyman, S., S. A. Ferguson, E. R. Braver and A. F. Williams (2002). Older driver involvement in police reported crashes and fatal crashes: Trends and projections. *Traffic Inj. Prev.*, *8*, 116-120.

Maltz, M. and D. Shinar (1999). Eye movements of younger and older drivers. *Hum. Fact.*, *41*, 15-25.

Marshall, S. C., M. Man-Son-Hing, M. Bedard, J. Charlton, S. Gagnon, I. Gélinas, S. Koppel, N. Korner-Bitensky, J. Langfordc, B. Mazere, A. Myers, G. Naglieg, J. Polgar, M. M. Porterk, M. Rapoport, H. Tuokkom, B. Vrkljann and A. Woolnough (2013). Protocol for Candrive II/Ozcandrive, a multicentre prospective older driver cohort study. *Accid. Anal. Prev.*, *61*, 245-252.

May, A., T. Ross and Z. Osman (2005). The design of next generation in-vehicle navigation systems for the older driver. *Interact. Comput.*, *17*, 643-659.

Mayhew, D. R., H. M. Simpson and S. A. Ferguson (2006). Collisions involving senior drivers: High-risk conditions and locations. *Traffic Inj. Prev.*, *7*, 117-124.

McGregor, L. N. and A. Chaparro (2005). Visual difficulties reported by low-vision and nonimpaired older adult drivers. *Hum. Fact.*, *47*(3), 469-478.

McGwin, G. and D. B. Brown (1999). Characteristics of traffic crashes among young, middle-aged, and older drivers. *Accid. Anal. Prev.*, *31*, 181-198.

McGwin, G. Jr, A. Mays, W. Joiner, D. K. DeCarlo, S. McNeal and C. Owsley (2004). Is glaucoma associated with motor vehicle collision involvement and driving avoidance? *Invest. Ophthalmol. Vis. Sci.*, *45*(11), 3934-3939.

McKnight, A. J., D. Shinar and B. Hilburn (1991). The visual and driving performance of monocular and binocular heavy-duty truck drivers. *Accid. Anal. Prev.*, *23*(4), 225-237.

Memmot, J. L. (2006). Overall travel patterns of older Americans. Presentation to the Transportation Research Board Committee on the Safe Mobility for Older Persons. Transportation Research Board Annual Meeting, Washington, DC, January.

Meyer, J. (2004). Personal vehicle transportation. In: *Technology for Adaptive Aging* (R. Pew and S. Van Hemel, eds.), pp. 253-281. National Research Council, Board on Behavioral, Cognitive and Sensory Sciences, Division of Behavioral and Social Sciences and Education. The National Academies Press, Washington, DC.

Meyer, J. (2009). Designing in-vehicle technologies for older drivers. *The Bridge*. National Academy of Engineering, Washington DC.
Midwinter, E. (2005). How many people are there in the third age? *Aging Soc.*, *25*, 9-18.
MIT (2014). http://agelab.mit.edu/agnes-age-gain-now-empathy-system
Molnar, L. J., J. L. Charlton, D. W. Eby, J. Langford, S. Koppel, G. E. Kolenic and S. Marshall (2014). Factors affecting self-regulatory driving practices among older adults. *Traffic Inj. Prev.*, *15*(3), 262-272.
Morris, J. C. (1997). Alzheimer disease and driving: Clinical, research and public policy. *Alzheimer Dis. Assoc. Disord.*, *11*(Suppl. 1), 1-83.
Myers, A. M., J. Paradis and R. A. Blanchard (2008). Conceptualizing and measuring confidence in older drivers: Development of the day and night driving comfort scales. *Arch. Phys. Med. Rehab.*, *89*, 630-640.
Nakagawa, Y., K. Park and Y. Kumagai (2013). Elderly drivers' everyday behavior as a predictor of crash involvement—Questionnaire responses by drivers' family members. *Accid. Anal. Prev.*, *50*, 397-404.
NHTSA (2003). Safe mobility for a maturing society: Challenges and opportunities. National Highway Traffic Safety Administration, U.S. Dept of Transportation, Washington, DC.
NHTSA (2005). Traffic safety facts 2004. National Highway Traffic Safety Administration. Report No. DOT HS 809 919. U.S. Dept of Transportation, Washington, DC.
NHTSA (2015). Traffic safety facts – 2013 data. Older population. Report No. DOT HS 812 899. U.S. Dept. of Transportation, Washington, DC.
NRSA (2015). Trends in road safety – 2014. Israel's National Road Safety Authority. Jerusalem, Israel.
OECD (2001). Aging and transport: Mobility needs and safety issues. Organization for Economic Cooperation and Development (OECD), Paris.
Oh, H. J. and Y. G. Ji (2016). Effects of superimposition of a head-up display on driving performance and glance behavior in the elderly. *Int. J. Hum. Comput. Interact.*, *32*(2), 143-154.
OECD (2014). Road Safety Annual Report 2014. International Transport Forum, OECD, Paris.
Olson, P. (1988). Problems of nighttime visibility and glare for older drivers. In Society for Automotive Engineers, Effects of Aging on Driver Performance (SP-762). Warrendale, PA, pp. 53-60.
Olson, P. L. and Sivak, M. (1984). Glare from automobile rear-vision mirrors. *Hum. Fact.*, *26*, 269-282.
Olson, P. and M. Sivak (1986). Perception-response time to unexpected roadway hazards. *Hum. Fact.*, *28*(1), 91-96.
O'Neill, D. (2012). Medical screening of older drivers is not evidence based. *Br. Med. J.*, *345*, e6371.
Otte, D., M. Jänsch, B. Pund and K. Duntsch (2013). Accident causation factor analysis of traffic accidents on the example of elderly car drivers using the causation analysis tool ACAS. Paper 13-0491 The 23rd International Technical Conference on the Enhanced Safety of Vehicles (ESV) Seoul, Republic of Korea, May 27-30.
Owsley, C. and G. McGwin (1999). Visual impairment and driving. *Surv. Ophthalmol.*, *43*(6), 535-550.

Owsley, C., G. McGwin Jr, and K. Ball (1998). Vision impairment, eye disease, and injurious motor vehicle crashes in the elderly. *Ophthalmic Epid.*, *5*(2), 101-113.

Owsley, C., Sekuler, R. and Siemsen, D. (1983). Contrast sensitivity throughout adulthood. *Vis. Res.*, *23*, 689-699.

Oxley, J., B. Fildes, B. Corben and J. Langford (2006). Intersection design for older drivers. *Transport. Res. F*, *9*(5), 335-346.

Parmentier, G., J.-F. Chastang, H. Nabi, M. Chiron, S. Lafont and E. Lagarde (2005). Road mobility and the risk of road traffic accident as a driver: The impact of medical conditions and life events. *Accid. Anal. Prev.*, *37*, 1121-1134.

Piersma, D. and D. de Waard (2014). Shifting from manual to automatic gear when growing old: Good advice? Results from a driving simulator study. In D. de Waard, K. Brookhuis, R. Wiczorek, F. di Nocera, R. Brouwer, P. Barham, C. Weikert, A. Kluge, W. Gerbino and A. Toffetti (eds.). Proceedings of the Human Factors and Ergonomics Society Europe Chapter 2013 Annual Conference. ISSN 2333-4959 (online). http://hfeseurope.org

Polders, E., T. Brijs, E. Vlahogianni, E. Papadimitriou, G. Yannis, F. Leopold, C. Durso and K. Diamandouros (2015). ElderSafe: Risks and countermeasures for road traffic of elderly in Europe. Report No. MOVE/C4/2014-244. European Commission, Brussels, BE. http://ec.europa.eu/transport/road_safety/pdf/studies/eldersafe_final_report.pdf

Porter, M. and M. J. Whitton (2002). Assessment of driving with the global positioning system and video technology in young, middle-aged, and older drivers. *J. Gerontol. Med. Sci.*, *57A*(9), M578-M582.

Pradhan, A. K., K. R. Hammel, R. DeRamus, A. Pollatsek, D. A. Noyce and D. L. Fisher (2003). *Proceedings of the Annual 2003 Meeting of the U.S. Transportation Research Board.* National Academies Press, Washington, DC.

Preusser, D. R., A. F. Williams, S. A. Ferguson, R. G. Ulmer and H. B. Weinstein (1998). Fatal crash risk for older drivers at intersections. *Accid. Anal. Prev.*, *30*(2), 155-159.

Pulling, N. H., S. P. Wolf, D. R. Sturgis, D. R. Vaillancourt, and J. J. Dolliver (1980). Headlight glare resistance and driver age. *Hum. Fact.*, *22*, 103-112.

Raghuram, A. and V. Lakshminarayanan (2006). Motion perception tasks as potential correlates to driving difficulty in the elderly. *J. Modern Opt.*, *53*(9), 1343-1362.

Rapoport, M. J., N. Herrmann, F. J. Molnar, M. Man-Son-Hing, S. C. Marshall, K. Shulman and G. Naglie (2007). Sharing the responsibility for assessing the risk of the driver with dementia. *Canad. Med. Assoc. J.*, *177*(6), 599-601.

Reger, M. A., R. K. Welsh, G. S. Watshon, B. Cholerton, L. D. Baker and S. Craft (2004). The relationship between neuropsycholgical functioning and driving ability in dementia: A meta-analysis. *Neuropsychology*, *18*(1), 85-93.

Reimer, B. (2014). Driver assistance systems and the transition to automated vehicles: A path to increase older adult safety and mobility? *Public Policy Aging Rep.*, *24*(1), 27-31.

Retchin, S. M., Cox, J., Fox, M., & Irvin, L. (1988). Performance-based measurements among elderly drivers and non-drivers. *J. Amer. Geriatrics Soc.*, *36*, 813-819.

Reuben, D. B., R. A. Silliman, and M. Traines (1988). The aging driver medicine, policy, and ethics. *J. Amer. Geriatrics Soc.*, *36*(12), 1135-1142.

Rizzo, M. and M. Nawror (1998). Perception of movement and shape in Alzheimer's diseases. *Brain*, *121*, 2259-2270.

Roenker, D. L., G. M. Cissell, K. K. Ball, V. G. Wadley and J. D. Edwards (2003). Speed-of-processing and driving simulator training result in improved driving performance. *Hum. Fact.*, *45*(2), 218-233.

Rogé, J., D. Ndiaye and F. Vienne (2014). Useful visual field training: A way to improve elderly car drivers' ability to detect vulnerable road users. *Trans. Res. F*, *26*, 246-257.

Romoser, M. R., A. Pollatsek, D. L. Fisher and C. C. Williams (2013). Comparing the glance patterns of older versus younger experienced drivers: Scanning for hazards while approaching and entering the intersection. *Trans. Res. F*, *16*, 104-116.

Ryan, G. A., M. Legge and D. Rosman (1998). Age related changes in drivers' crash risk and crash type. *Accid. Anal. Prev.*, *30*, 379-387.

Sagberg, F. (2006). Driver health and crash involvement: A case-control study. *Accid. Anal. Prev.*, *38*, 28-34.

Sanders, M., B. Shaw, B. Nicholson, and J. Merritt (1990). *Evaluation of glare from center-high-mounted stop lights. National Highway Traffic Safety Administration.* U. S. Department of Transportation, Washington, D.C.

Santos, A., N. McGuckin, H. Y. Nakamoto, D. Gray and S. Liss (2011). Summary of travel trends: 2009 national household travel survey. Report FHWA-PL-11-022. U.S. Department of Transportation, Washington, DC.

Sayer, J. R. and M. L. Mefford (2004). High visibility safety apparel and nighttime conspicuity of pedestrians in work zones. *J. Safety Res.*, *35*, 537-546.

Schall, M. C., M. L. Rusch, J. D. Lee, J. D. Dawson, G. Thomas, N. Aksan and M. Rizzo (2012). Augmented reality cues and elderly driver hazard perception. *Hum. Fact.*, *55*, 643-658.

Scialfa, C., J. Ference, J. Boone, R. Tay and C. Hudson (2010). Predicting older adults' driving difficulties using the Roadwise Review. *J. Gerontol. Psych. Sci. Soc. Behav.*, *65*(4), 434-437.

Sekuler, A. B., P. J. Bennett, and M. Mamelak (2000). Effects of aging on the useful field of view. *Exp. Aging Res.*, *26*, 103-120.

Sekuler, R., D. Kline, and K. Dismukes (1982). Aging and visual function of military pilots: A review. *Aviation, Space and Environmental Medicine*, *53*(8), 747-758.

Selander, H., I. Bolin and T. Falkmer (2012). Does automatic transmission improve driving behavior in older drivers? *Gerontology*, *58*(2), 181-187.

Shaw, L., J. M. Polgar, B. Vrkljan and J. Jacobson (2010). Seniors' perceptions of vehicle safety risks and needs. *Am. J. Occup. Ther.*, *64*(2), 215-224.

Shinar, D. (1977). Driver visual limitations diagnosis and treatment. U.S. Department of Transportation Report No. DOT-HS-5-1275. U.S. Department of Transportation, Washington, DC.

Shinar, D., R. E. Dewar, H. Summala and L. Zakowska (2003). Traffic sign symbol comprehension: A cross-cultural study. *Ergonomics*, *46*(15), 1549-1565.

Shinar, D. and F. Schieber (1991). Visual requirements for safety and mobility of older drivers. *Hum. Fact.*, *33*, 507-520.

Sivak, M. and B. Schoettle (2011). Recent changes in the age composition of drivers in 15 countries. Report UMTRI-2011-43. University of Michigan, Ann Arbor, MI.

Sloane, M. E., Owlsey, C. and Alvarez, S. L. (1988). Aging, senile miosis and spatial contrast sensitivity at low luminance. *Vis. Res.*, *28*, 1235-1246.

Smith, B. H. and P. K. Sethi (1975). Aging and the nervous system. *Geriatrics*, *30*, 109-115.

Spencer, M. B. (2003). The role of risk analysis in the evaluation of fitness to drive. Road Safety Research Report No. 40. Department of Transport, London.

Staplin, L., D. Harkey, K. Lococo and M. Tarawneh (1997). Intersection geometric design and operational guidelines for older drivers and pedestrians, Volume I: Final report. Publication No. FHWA-RD-96-132. Federal Highway Administration, U.S. Department of Transportation, Washington, DC.

Staplin, L. and T. B. Dinh-Zarr (2006). Promoting rehabilitation of safe driving abilities through computer-based clinical and personal screening techniques. *Topics Geriatr. Rehab.*, *22*, 129-138.

Staplin, L., K. W. Gish and J. Joyce (2008). 'Low mileage bias' and related policy implications—A cautionary note. *Accid. Anal. Prev.*, *40*, 1249-1252.

Staplin, L., K. W. Gish, K. H. Lococo, J. J. Joyce and K. J. Sifrit (2013). The maze test: A significant predictor of older driver crash risk. *Accid. Anal. Prev.*, *50*, 483-489.

Staplin, L., K. Lococo, S. Byington and D. Harkey (2001). Highway design handbook for older drivers and pedestrians. Federal Highway Administration Report FHWA-RD-01-103. U.S. Department of Transportation, Washington, DC.

Staplin, L., K. Lococo, K. Gish and L. Decina (2003). Model driver screening and evaluation program: Final technical report: Volume IIII: Maryland Pilot Older Driver Study, DOT HS 809 583. U.S. Dept. of Transportation, Washington, DC.

Stolwyk, R. J., T. J. Triggs, J. L. Charlton, R. Iansek and J. L. Bradshaw (2005). Impact of internal versus external cueing on driving performance in people with Parkinson's disease. *Mov. Disord.*, *20*(7), 846-857.

Stutts, J. C. (2005). Improving the safety of older road users – A synthesis of highway practices. NCHRP Synthesis 348. Transportation Research Board, National Academies of Sciences, Washington, DC.

Szlyk, J. P., C. Mahler, W. Seiple, E. Deepak and J. T. Wilensky (2005). Driving performance of glaucoma patients correlates with peripheral visual field loss. *J. Glaucoma*, *14*(2), 145-150.

Tay, R. (2006). Ageing drivers: Storm in a teacup? *Accid. Anal. Prev.*, *38*, 112-121.

Torpey, S. (1986). License retesting of older drivers. Victoria Road Traffic Authority, Hawthorn, Australia.

Tuokko, H., A. Myers, A. Jouka, S. Marshall, M. Man-Son-Hing, M. M. Porter, M. Bédard, I. Gélinas, N. Korner-Bitensky, B. Mazer, G. Naglie, M. Rapoport, B. Vrkljan (2013). Associations between age, gender, psychosocial and health characteristics in the Candrive II study cohort. *Accid. Anal. Prev.*, *61*, 257-271.

Trick, L. M., R. Toxopeus and D. Wilson (2010). The effects of visibility conditions, traffic density, and navigational challenge on speed compensation and driving performance in older adults. *Accid. Anal. Prev.*, *42*(6), 1661-1671.

Vanlaar, W., M. M. Hing, R. Robertson, D. Mayhew and D. Carr (2016). An evaluation of Ontario's Group Education Session (GES) for license renewal of seniors aged 80 and above. *J. Safety Res.*, *56*, 33-39.

Vanlaar, W. A. McKiernan, H. McAteer, R. Robertson, D. Mayhew, D. Carr, S. Brown and E. Holmes (2014). A meta-analysis of cognitive screening tools for drivers aged 80 and over. Traffic Injury Research Foundation, Ottawa, Canada.

Warshawsky-Livne, L. and D. Shinar (2002). Effects of uncertainty, transmission type, driver age, and gender on brake reaction and movement time. *J. Safety Res.*, *33*, 117-128.

West, C. G., G. Gildengo, G. Haegerstrom-Portnoy, L. A. Lott, M. E. Schneck and J. A. Brabyn (2003). Vision and driving self-restriction in older adults. *J. Am. Geriatr. Soc.*, *51*(10), 1348.

Wikman, A.-S. and H. Summala (2005). Aging and time-sharing in highway driving. *Optom. Vis. Sci.*, *82*, 716-723.

Williams, C., S. Ardekani and S. Asante (1992). Motorist understanding of left-turn signal indications and auxiliary signs. Transportation Research Record, No. 1376, pp. 57-63. Transportation Research Board, Washington, DC.

Williams, A. F. and V. I. Shabanova (2003). Responsibility of drivers, by age and gender, for motor-vehicle crash deaths. *J. Safety Res.*, *34*, 527-531.

Wist, E. R., M. Schrauf, and W. H. Ehrenstein (2000). Dynamic vision based on motion-contrast: changes with age in adults. *Exp. Brain Res.*, *134*, 295-300.

Wolf, E. W. (1960). Glare and age. *Arch. Ophthal.*, *64*, 502-514.

Wood, J. M. (2002). Aging, driving and vision. *Clin. Exp. Optom.*, *85*(4), 214-220. *Br. J. Ophthalmol.* 2006;90;1277-1280; originally published online July 6, 2006.

Wood, J. M. and T. P. Carberry (2006). Bilateral cataract surgery and driving performance. *Br. J. Opthalmol.*, *90*, 1277-1280.

Wood, J. M., M. S. Horswill, P. F. Lacherez and K. J. Anstey (2013). Evaluation of screening tests for predicting older driver performance and safety assessed by an on-road test. *Accid. Anal. Prev.*, *50*, 1161-1168.

Woolnough, A., D. Salim, S. C. Marshall, K. Weegard, M. M. Porter, M. J. Rapoport, M. Man-Son-Hing, M. Bédard, I. Gélinas, N. Korner-Bitensky, B. Mazer, G. Naglie, H. Tuokko, B. Vrkljan (2013). Determining the validity of the AMA guide: A historical cohortanalysis of the assessment of driving related skills and crash rate among older drivers. *Accid. Anal. Prev.*, *61*, 311-316.

Yang, J. and J. F. Coughlin (2014). In-vehicle technology for self-driving cars: Advantages and challenges for aging drivers. *Int. J. Auto. Technol.*, *15*(2), 333-340.

Yee, D. (1985). A survey of the traffic safety needs and problems of drivers age 55 and over. Needs and problems of older drivers: Survey results and recommendations. American Automobile Association Foundation for Traffic Safety, Washington, DC.

Zaidel, D. M. and I. Hocherman (1986). License renewal for older drivers: The effects of medical and vision tests. *J. Safety Res.*, *17*(3), 111-116.

Zhan, J., M. M. Porter, J. Polgar and B. Vrkljan (2013). Older drivers' opinions of criteria that inform the cars they buy: A focus group study. *Accid. Anal. Prev.*, *61*, 281-287.

Zhang, J., J. Lindsay, K. Clarke, G. Robbins and Y. Mao (2000). Factors affecting the severity of motor vehicle traffic crashes involving elderly drivers in Ontario. *Accid. Anal. Prev.*, *32*, 117-125.

PART C
DRIVING STYLE

8

Speed and Safety

> "Connecticut imposed the first maximum speed limit in the U.S. of 8 mph (13 km/h) in cities in 1901." (TRB, 1998, p. 1).
>
> "Speed regulations and speed limits denote a restraint upon the freedom of the speed in which he (the driver) desires to travel. Therefore limits or restraints should be imposed only to the extent that their use will facilitate traffic flow or decrease a traffic hazard. Public acceptance is a prerequisite to effective public obedience to traffic regulations. If regulations are imposed only where and when they are necessary, the driver will more readily accept the need for them." (*Traffic Engineering Handbook*, Institute of Traffic Engineers, 1965).
>
> "Excess and inappropriate speed is at the core of the road safety problem. The majority of accidents is directly or indirectly related to speed .... Speed affects accident risk .... Speed affects injury severity." (DaCoTA Project, 2012).

Speeding is logically related to mobility and subjectively related – for many people at least – to pleasure. Unlike the dangers of drinking and driving and the benefits of seat belts, about which there is a near-consensus, people's perceptions of the relationship between speed and crashes are quite varied. In an analysis of annual U.S. survey of Americans' health maintenance habits that we conducted over 15 years ago (Shinar, Schechtman, and Compton, 1999) we found that from 1985 to 1995 the self-reported use of seat belts increased dramatically, drinking and driving decreased consistently (though to a lesser degree), but the percent of people who said that they exceeded the speed limit actually increased (Figure 8-1). Sadly – in the case of speeding – this trend in the U.S.

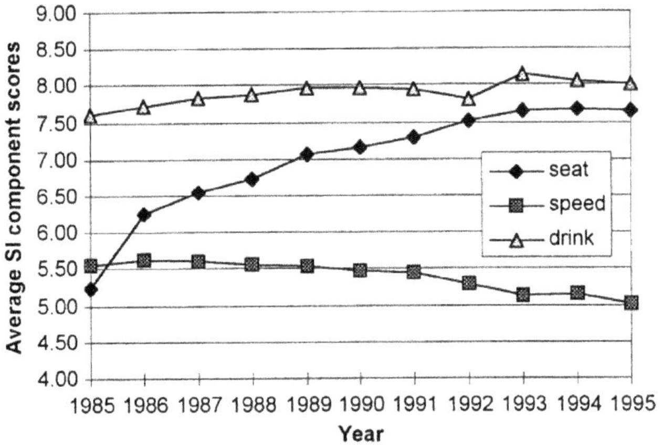

Figure 8-1. Seat belt use, refraining from drinking and driving, and obeying the speed limits in the U.S. 1985-1995. The Safety Index (SI) component score is derived from the product of average extent to which people report observing the rule and experts' rating of the importance of the rule for health. The maximum possible score then depends on experts' rating of the importance of the behavior. The maximum score for seat belt use is 9.16, for refraining from drinking and driving it is 9.03, and for observing the speed limit it is 7.65 (from Shinar et al., 1999, with permission from Elsevier).

has continued into the first decade of the 21st century, where the involvement of drinking and driving and non-use of seat belts in fatalities decreased monotonically from 1985 to 2010, while the involvement of speeding in traffic fatalities remained at a relatively constant 30-35 percent (GHSA, 2012; NHTSA, 2015). This is particularly alarming as speed is possibly the most over-involved single factor in severe traffic crashes. At the same time, in a particularly insightful book on the state of traffic safety policy, Johnston, Muir, and Howard (2014) argue convincingly that speed moderation is the most difficult issue of all. One possible reason for this difficulty is the schism between the beliefs people have about the dangers of speeding and their own acknowledged speeding. In a 2011 survey of a random sample of 16+ years old Americans, the American Automobile Association Foundation for Traffic Safety (AAAF, 2012) found that although speeding by over 15 mph (24 km/hr) above the speed limit on the highway was considered completely unacceptable by 50 percent of the drivers, 68 percent acknowledged doing it at least once in the past 30 days, and speeding by more than 15 mph (24 km/hr) above the speed limit on residential streets was considered completely unacceptable by 78 percent of the drivers, yet 30 percent acknowledged doing it at least once in the past 30 days.

The difference between speeding and the other dangerous driving behaviors reflects a very complex relationship between speeding and safety, and between the motives that govern our speed and the motives that govern other aspects of our driving behavior. This chapter will focus on three speed issues: how we select speed, its relationship to safety, and speeding countermeasures.

Variables Affecting Speed Choice

Whether advertising caters to the consumers' needs or shapes them, one thing is certain: advertising exposes us to a lot of speeding cars, typically without addressing the consequences of speed. Despite the fact that in interviews and surveys people stress the importance of safety in the choice of the cars they drive, marketing gurus – in general – believe otherwise. This is revealed in content analyses of advertisements and commercials for new cars that often depict unsafe driving, especially speeding. Shin *et al.* (2005) analyzed 250 car and truck commercials aired in North America and found that 25 percent of them contained speeding sequences (compared to 12 percent that contained some safety promotion). Ferguson, Hardy, and Williams (2003) evaluated the content of 561 car commercials that aired in the U.S. in 1998 and found that approximately 50 percent included performance in their theme, and half of those showed speed as one of the attractive attributes. In contrast, a safety theme appeared in only 8 percent of the commercials, and as a primary theme in only two percent. Schonfeld and her associates (2005) analyzed a sample of 380 car advertisements published in the period 1999-2004 in Australia and found that approximately 50 percent of them stressed performance as a primary theme, and one-quarter of the performance themes focused on speed. In contrast, safety appeared as a primary theme in less than 15 percent of the advertisements. More recently Watson and her colleagues (2010) analyzed the content of 200 Canadian television and print advertisements of cars and found that 27 percent of the television advertisements featured unsafe or aggressive driving and an additional 22 percent demonstrated or discussed speed. Thus, it appears that the emphasis on speed has not declined significantly since the beginning of this century. Summarizing the literature on the relationship between the media content and risk taking, Fischer *et al.* (2011) concluded that risk-glorification, including speeding, is a common theme in much of the media, and – to the extent that the media has an effect on our behavior – it has detrimental effects on risk taking inclinations. Interestingly, at the end of the last century in a pan-European survey of drivers' attitudes toward risky driving, approximately 50 percent of the drivers favored banning car advertisements that stressed speed (47 percent), requiring manufacturers to restrict maximum speed by installing speed limiters (54 percent), and requiring manufacturers to install a device that would assist the driver in not exceeding the speed limit (57 percent) (SARTRE 4, 1998).

If drivers look for speed and acceleration in their choice of cars, then one would assume that many drivers also intend to speed. But the car we drive is only one of many factors that influence our speed choice at any time. According to the American Association of State Highway and Transportation Officials the most important variables or conditions that determine drivers' speeds are the physical characteristics of the road and roadside interference, the weather, other vehicles, and the speed limit (AASHTO, 2001). But the actual list may be much longer. The World Health Organization (WHO, 2004) lists a total of 32 variables that presumably affect drivers' choice of speed, and even these are qualified as "examples" only. The list, reproduced in Table 8-1 includes seven road-related factors, four vehicle factors, three traffic factors, seven environmental factors, and eleven driver factors. To evaluate the relative contribution of each factor would

Table 8-1. Example of factors that affect drivers' choice of speed (from WHO, 2004, with permission from the World Health Organization).

Road and Vehicle Factors	**Traffic and Environment Factors**	**Driver-Related Factors**
Road	**Traffic**	Age
Width	Density	Gender
Gradient	Composition	Reaction time
Alignment	Prevailing speed	Attitudes
Surroundings	**Environment**	Thrill-seeking
Layout	Weather	Risk acceptance
Markings	Surface condition	Hazard perception
Surface quality	Natural light	Alcohol level
Vehicle	Road lighting	Ownership of vehicle
Type	Signs	Circumstances of journey
Power/weight ratio	Speed limit	Occupancy of vehicle
Maximum speed	Enforcement	
Comfort		

require an enormous data set that would include some variations in all 32 variables. There is also empirical support for the multiple determinants. An analysis of the European 22-country SARTRE survey of representative samples of approximately 1,000 drivers in each country revealed that the inclination to speed is associated with psychological variables such as perception of norms (others' speed) and the enjoyment of the speed; demographic variables such as age, gender, and amount of driving; environmental variables such as the type of road; and vehicle variables such as engine size (Yannis *et al.*, 2013). Fortunately, some of these variables are often correlated. For example high-speed roads are generally wide, with good markings, good signage, lighting, and higher levels of speed enforcement. Therefore, it is nearly impossible to evaluate all of these variables independently of each other.

The remainder of this section will focus on driver-related variables that have been studied in the context of speed choice. It should be clear however, that because drivers do not typically have full control of their speed, in the absence of road, vehicle, and traffic related variables, the driver variables can explain only a small portion of the choice of actual speeds observed on the road. In fact, on high-speed roads speed and speed variance are to a very large extent determined by the traffic flow regime; being low in congested traffic and high in light traffic (Golob, Recker, and Alvarez, 2004). Also, it appears that when drivers slowdown in response to marginal weather, such as fog or variable message advisory signs once they pass the signs and the weather changes, they tend to compensate for the lost time by increasing their speed to levels above those that they maintained before they felt forced to slow down (Boyle and Mannering, 2004). This tendency to compensate for lost time may be familiar to most readers too.

Driver-related variables that affect speed choice

Like many other behaviors, our choice of speed – to the extent that we can control it – is governed by who we are (in terms of individual differences) and what we want (in terms of motivating factors).

Individual differences

The most commonly studied individual differences are age and gender, and speeding and aggressive driving appear to be defining characteristics of both. In general, men tend to speed more than women, and young drivers tend to speed more than older drivers (NHTSA, 2012b; see also Chapter 6). As part of a national U.S. survey of the health and safety-related behaviors of the American adult population, we (Shinar, Schechtman, and Compton, 2001) analyzed the proportions of licensed drivers that reported that they drive within the speed limits "all the time." The results are summarized in Figure 8-2. As expected, fewer men report that they observe the speed limits than women (36 percent versus 45 percent), and fewer younger drivers report that they observe them than older drivers (28 percent of those 25 and under, 42 percent of those 26-50, and 52 percent of those over 50 years old). Other studies have also confirmed that young drivers are more likely to speed than mature drivers and that older drivers are more likely to drive slower than mature drivers (Horberry *et al.*, 2004; Porter and Whitton, 2002), and that men are more likely to speed than women (Jonah, Thiessen, and Au-Yeung, 2001). One explanation for the over-involvement of young men in speeding is that they experience greater peer pressure to speed (Conner, Smith, and McMillan, 2003). Consequently, males and young drivers also receive more citations for speeding violations, but this cannot be used as conclusive evidence of their over-involvement in speeding because men drive more miles – especially on highways – than women, and therefore their exposure to speed enforcement is much greater. In addition, when they speed men may be more likely to receive a citation than women, and young drivers may be more likely to be cited for it than older drivers, because of potential age and gender biases of arresting officers (Evans, 2004).

Surprisingly, as can be seen in Figure 8-2, observing the speed limit is inversely related to education and income. In our analysis the drivers who were more educated and more affluent were more likely to report that they speed than the less educated and poorer

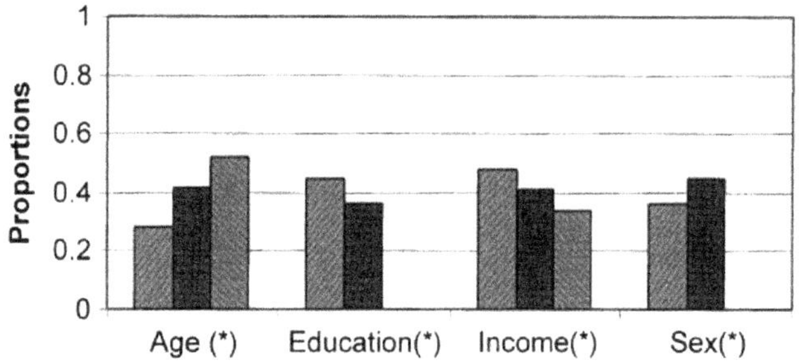

Figure 8-2. The proportion of U.S. drivers reporting that they drive within the speed limits "all the time" as a function of age, education, income, and gender. Levels within each category are: age: 18-25, 26-50, 51+. Education: < high school, high school +. Household income: ≤15,000, 15,001-35,000, 35,001+; Gender: M, F. Data are based on 1993-1994 surveys. (*) All differences were statistically significant at $\alpha = 0.05$ (from Shinar *et al.*, 2001, with permission from Elsevier).

respondents. These results, which have been replicated in a U.S. national survey on reported speeding behavior (Schroeder, Kostyniuk, and Mack, 2013) are in sharp contrast to avoiding drinking and driving and using seat belts where the relationship was direct: the higher the income and education the more likely were the people to use their belts "all the time" and to "never drink and drive." The speeding responses were surprising also because it is the better educated people who are more exposed to media coverage and public information campaigns on speeding and safety. The most plausible explanations for these unexpected relationships were that (1) as the level of education increases, people become more familiar with conflicting arguments and data about the relationship between speed and crashes and (2) in the absence of a strong belief about the impact of speeding on safety, the financial penalties that are typically levied on speed violators are less deterring for people with high income (Finland being an exception – see below).

Another characteristic that distinguishes among people in their proclivity to speeding is personality. Sensation seeking is one personality trait that has been associated with speeding as well as with aggressive driving and drinking and driving (see Chapters 9 and 11). Drivers who score high on the Zuckerman's Sensation Seeking Scale are more likely to report that they drive at excessive speeds in the absence of speed limits (Jonah *et al.*, 2001), and more likely to receive speeding citations (Whissell and Bigelow, 2003). Similarly, Husted *et al.* (2006) found a positive relationship between the amount of speeding and the amount of gambling that young drivers report. Thus, in many ways speeding can be considered as just one more manifestation of thrill-seeking and risk taking.

Motivational factors

The theory of planned behavior (Ajzen, 1991, see also Chapter 3) would suggest that speeding – just like any other behavior – is the end product of intentions and the amount of behavioral control over their execution. But what is the relative impact of the different components on the speed we finally choose? De Pelsmacker and Janssens (2007) attempted to answer that question by administering a questionnaire addressing the various components of the model to 333 Belgian drivers. A key measure in the questionnaire was the assessment of the end behavior – speeding. For this measure they asked drivers to respond to various questions related to their likelihood of speeding in a specific situation. Speeding was defined relative to the speed limit; for example driving over 60 km/hr in a 50 km/hr zone. Using a statistical technique known as structural equation modeling (SEM) they were able to determine the correlations among the various components of the theory of reasoned behavior, and their results are summarized in Figure 8-3. As can be seen from that figure, speeding behavior was greatly influenced by the intention to speed, but just as much by the habit of speeding; with correlations of 0.47 and 0.50, respectively. This means that much of our speeding behavior is habitual, essentially involving no conscious decision. We can appreciate the important role of habit in speed selection when we hear the fairly common statement from drivers who use cruise control in highway driving, that it helps them maintain the speed limit. Without it they would be driving at a different speed not by overt choice but because of an unconscious habit.

In De Pelsmacker and Janssens' study the conscious component of the speed choice – the intention to speed – was determined primarily by a person's attitude toward speeding and much less by his or her attitude toward speed limits. The attitude toward speeding, in turn, was affected by a host of norms including the subjective norm (what I think people think they should do), the normative norm (what I believe people actually do), the descriptive norm (what I see people around me do), the personal norm (what I think I should do according to my own moral values), and the driver's personal identity

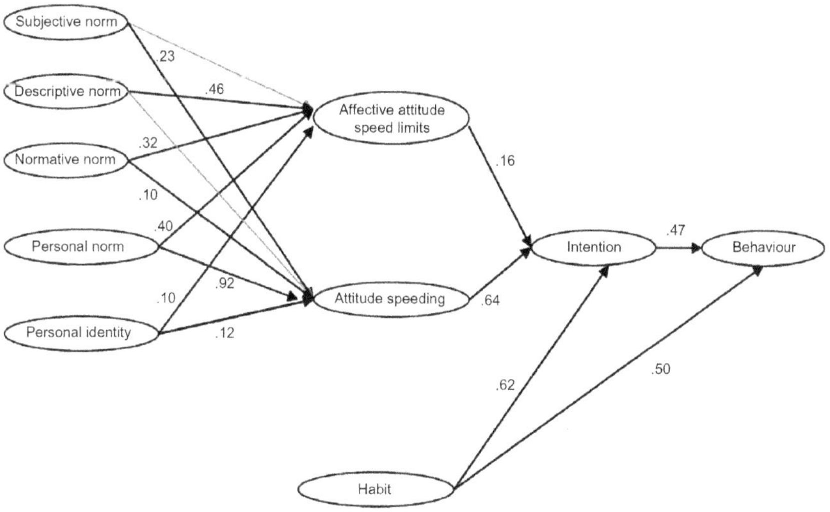

Figure 8-3. A model of speed choice behavior based on the theory of planned behavior. The strengths of the associations between the relevant concepts are based on structural equation modeling. Total effects of all model constructs R = 0.79 (from De Pelsmacker and Janssens, 2007, with permission from Elsevier).

(my sense of own driving skills). The relevance of these norms has also been shown by other studies. For example, Groeger and Chapman (1997) used an animated interactive driving environment that allowed drivers to violate the laws. As they "drove" they occasionally encountered variable message signs that stated the percent of drivers who were not speeding or tailgating at that road section. They found that the messages were effective in reducing speed and tailgating, but only where the driver could actually see that the majority of the drivers were not speeding or tailgating. Although these versions of subjective and normative norms had significant effects on the attitude toward speeding in De Pelsmacker and Janssens' study (as can be seen from the correlations in Figure 8-3) the drivers' personal norms had by far the greatest influence on their attitude toward speeding. But the personal norms also affected the drivers' feelings about speed limits in general. Together all these variables accounted for nearly 65 percent of the variance in the declared speeding behaviors.

Additional indirect support for the importance of a "personal norm" concerning speed comes from studies by Lewis-Evans, De Waard, and Brookhuis (2011) and Scott-Parker *et al.* (2013). In Lewis-Evans' study drivers in a driving simulator were required to drive at different speeds below and above their preferred speed, and at each speed rate their subjective level of task difficulty, risk, and level of effort. The results indicated that the ratings on these measures were not monotonically related to the driving speed, but rather relatively constant until the requested speed exceeded the preferred speed by a certain amount. The authors interpreted this finding as proof for a threshold effect, whereby stress and effort are unaffected by speed until it exceeds the driver's personal norm. This notion is conceptually similar to the "comfort zone" that has been found in drivers' choice of headways – another measure of risk taking in driving (see Chapter 5) – and to the notion that processing load becomes an issue only when it exceeds the driver's capability, as in Fuller's model (see Chapter 3). In Scott-Parker *et al.*'s study 378 novice drivers completed questionnaires relating to their speeding behavior on the one hand and their personal characteristics and internalization of various social values (derived from a Social Learning Theory) on the other hand. Applying hierarchical regression to the data they demonstrated that these two factors accounted for over 40 percent of the variance in reported speeding behaviors. Thus, though couched in different terms, personal norms again seem to play an important role in speeding.

In De Pelsmacker and Janssens' analysis, in more than 50 percent of the scenarios, the drivers' choice of speed was determined by their reported habits and intentions to speed ($R^2 = 0.62$). This may be an overestimate because this conclusion is based purely on people's responses to hypothetical situations. Also, the situations apparently did not include any constraints on the driver's control of his or her behavior, other than those indirectly implied in the descriptions of the situations (e.g., "a suburban, residential street"). But there is also observational empirical support for the role of habit in speed choice. Haglund and Åberg (2002) were able to measure the speeds of the same drivers on two different road sections with different speed limits and on different days, and found relatively high correlations of 0.5-0.8 between speeds at different times and different locations. These correlations do not imply that people ignored the different speed limits (even though the majority of the drivers violated them in both sections), but that people were moderately consistent in the sense that they retained their speed relative to the speed of the other drivers.

Direct impact of the environmental constraints was found by Lawton and her associates (1997). They presented drivers with various scenarios and asked them to select the speed at which they would drive through them. Based on the respondents' answers they concluded that most drivers based their decisions on the type of road and their perceptions of the amount of speeding that is "acceptable" in that environment. Finally, if people enjoy driving fast, then the knowledge that they are better drivers than the average driver also enables them to feel that they can drive above the average perceived traffic speed and still feel safe (Walton and Bathurst, 1998). Together, these disparate findings show that most of the concepts invoked in the theory of planned behavior are relevant to a person's speed choice.

So how do drivers make their choices in concrete situations? To what extent are they affected by various potential competing needs and constraints? To partially address these issues we conducted roadside interviews of 225 Israeli drivers. The interviews were conducted at gas stations along three types of inter-urban roads with three different speed limits: narrow winding two-lane roads without hard shoulders with a speed limit of 80 km/hr, improved two-lane roads with hard shoulders posted at 90 km/hr, and four-lane limited-access divided highways posted at 100 km/hr. At each site the drivers were asked about the speed that they usually maintain on that road, the speed they select when driving with their family, the speed they would choose if their sole goal was to save on fuel and vehicle wear-and-tear, the speed they consider safe, and the speed they would choose if there were no enforcement at all on the road – the one they would select to maximize pleasure or enjoy the "fun" of driving. Finally they were tested on their knowledge of the actual speed limit on that road. The results, plotted separately for each road type, are displayed in Figure 8-4. The first thing to note is that in general, on all choice dimensions, peoples' choices are primarily affected by the roadway, with roadways posted at and designed for slower speeds generating lower speed choices. The second thing to note is that different motives lead to different speed choices. The desire for fun motivates people to drive at the highest speeds, while frugality and safety motivate them to drive at the lowest speeds. Interestingly, the drivers' perceptions of the "safe" speed were sensitive to the nature of the road, but on the roads with the lower speed limits the perceived safe speed was slightly higher than the legal speed. This is despite the fact that nearly all drivers on all roads correctly identified the legal speed limit. Finally, the actual speed drivers report driving on the road seems to be a compromise among the various motives, road design constraints, and enforcement, though it does seem – at least in the Israeli driving culture – to be much closer to the "fun" speed than to the "safe" speed. It is also noteworthy that the reported "usual speeds" correspond quite closely to the speeds that have been actually observed on a nationally representative sample of the Israeli roads (Gitelman, Pishahov, and Chen, 2012; NRSA, 2014), lending the subjective reports some ecological validity.

It is prudent to question the generalizability of results of our study to the results obtained in other surveys of other drivers in other parts of the world. In New Zealand, Ahie, Charlton, and Starsky (2015) conducted a similar survey next to roads of different

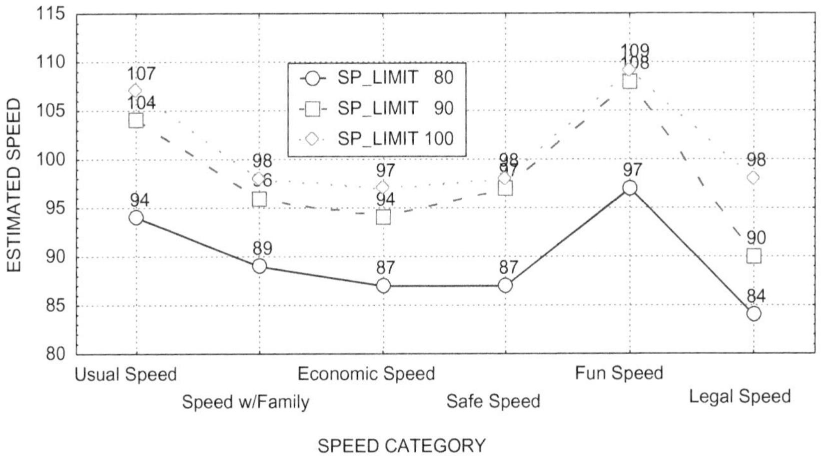

Figure 8-4. Average speed that drivers report they would select to maximize different goals relative to their actual speed and to the speed limit, on roads with 80, 90, and 100 km/hr posted speed limits (from Shinar, 2001).

speed limits and obtained strikingly similar results. Mean reported driving speed was close to the actual speed limit (actually a bit lower), and close to the drivers' reported "usual" driving speed, which was slightly higher than the "economic" and "safe" speeds but significantly lower that the "fun" speed. Schechtman, Bar-Gera, and Musicant (2016) conducted repeated surveys of drivers in the vicinity of newly installed speed cameras in Israel and found that the percent of drivers who report driving within their perceived speed limit gradually crept up from 82 percent in 2010 to 93 percent in 2013, and correspondingly the percent reporting exceeding the (perceived) speed limit decreased from 38 percent in 2010 to 11 percent in 2013. In the U.S., in a 2011 national survey, most drivers reported that they drive at their perceived safe speed (Schroeder *et al.*, 2013). However, drivers (and people in general) are notorious in their inconsistencies. In the same survey four out of five drivers agreed with the statements that "Driving at or near the speed limit makes it easier to avoid dangerous situations," "Driving at or near the speed limit reduces my chances of an accident," and that the speed limit should be enforced "all the time" or "often." Yet 70 percent felt that "Speed cameras are used to generate revenue," and only 55 percent felt that they "are used to prevent accidents."

Speed choice and design speed

In my on road survey above there was a strong correspondence between the posted speed limit on a road and the "design speed" of the road. The design speed is the speed at which a car can drive safely on the road. Often the design speed may not be obvious to the driver. This is because actual design considerations extend beyond the road's most visible characteristics such as its width, geometry, and quality of the road pavement, and into considerations of the shoulders' quality, sight distance, super-elevation in curves, lane markings, presence or absence of turning lanes, and presence or absence of intersections (Woolridge *et al.*, 2003). In addition, though not obvious to a passing driver, where pedestrians are likely to walk on or cross the road the speed limit is set much lower than its design suggests. When the actual design speeds or the posted speed limits are significantly lower than the perceived design speeds, we have a problem. The problem is that drivers do not perceive all the risks that the engineers see, and thus – barring visible enforcement – they tend to exceed the speed limit. McCoy *et al.* (1993) studied road sections in Nebraska and found that sites with perceived "reasonable" speed limits were safer than those with limits 5-10 mph (8-16 km/hr) below the perceived "reasonable" levels. Fitzpatrick *et al.* (2003) surveyed U.S. data and found that in curves, for example, unless they have very small radii the actual driving speeds are typically above the design speeds. One way to discover the drivers' "reasonable" speed limit and to ensure a good correspondence between the speed limit and drivers' natural speed choice is to use the traffic engineers' traditional rule of thumb for determination of speed limits: use the 85th percentile of the current speed distribution for existing roads (ITE, 2004), and the road "design" speed for new roads (Knowles *et al.*, 1997).

Speed and Crashes

Speeding is cited as one of the primary global culprits for traffic fatalities (WHO, 2013; World Bank, 2009). For example, in the U.S., according to the National Highway Traffic Safety Administration, from 2001 till 2014, speeding has accounted for a fairly stable estimate of 28-32 percent of all traffic fatalities, its involvement is consistently lower among female drivers than male drivers, and it decreases as a function of age from nearly 40 percent for male drivers under 25 years old to less than 10 percent for males 75 years old or more (NHTSA, 2012a, 2014, 2015).

The positive relationship between speed and crashes is axiomatic for many people in the traffic safety community. That axiom is encapsulated in the slogan "speed kills" and in sweeping generalizations such as "in highly motorized countries excessive and inappropriate speed is a major cause of around one in three of all fatal and serious crashes" (WHO, 2004). Speed is also listed as one of the manifestations of "aggressive driving" by the U.S. National Highway Traffic Safety Administration (NHTSA) (Martinez, 1997) and safety interest groups such as Advocates of Highway and Auto Safety (Snyder, 1997). Grass roots movements specifically targeting speeding have also emerged (e.g., Citizens against Speed and Aggressive Driving) (Shiekh, 1997). Yet a continued decline in U.S. traffic fatalities despite repeal of the 55-mph National Maximum Speed Limit (NMSL) serves to raise public doubts on the relevance of speed to crashes. Many drivers consider themselves safe drivers though they acknowledge that they often exceed the speed limits, and national respectable media front page captions like "Fewer dying despite faster speed limits" (*USA Today*, 1997) and "Safe at any speed" (*Wall Street Journal*, July 7, 2006) further erode this axiom.

To evaluate the validity of this "axiom" we resort to empirical research that attempts to study the *causal* relationship between speed and crashes. Three problems come up in attempting to do this. First, in referring to speed as a predictor variable and crashes as a predicted variable, we assume that speed is the independent variable of interest and that safety is the dependent variable of interest, in the sense that the former affects the latter, and is not just correlated with it. Optimally, to demonstrate that speed is the independent variable behind changes in crashes, it should be under the experimenter's control. But it rarely is. For crashes to be a true dependent variable, a causal relationship has to exist, and it can never be unequivocally justified. Second, both crashes and speed can be defined in many ways. For example we can study the effects of mean traffic speed, individuals' speed, variability in traffic speed, or percent of drivers exceeding a design speed. The effects can be studied on all crashes or injury crashes or fatal crashes, and within each category we can selectively focus on either injuries or crashes of all severities, or only injury crashes, all types of crashes or only single-vehicle crashes, etc. Therefore, we must be careful in our definitions of "speed" and "crashes" because the relationship is not the same for all. Finally we have to distinguish between the effects of speed on the likelihood of a crash, and the effects of speed on injury severity *given* a crash.

Definitions: Speed, safety, and intervening variables

At least two aspects of crashes should be considered as separate dependent measures of the effects of speed: crash probability (or incidence) and crash severity (given crash occurrence). In studying the effect of speed these two measures may not be highly correlated, because speed-related crashes are not evenly distributed across all severities. They tend to be more severe in the sense that they are more often associated with severe injuries and fatalities than with other types of crashes. In addition, the relationship between crash probability and speed is more complex, and speed-related crashes are not necessarily associated with high speeds. This last statement may seem counterintuitive, but it is easy to support it with an example. Driving slowly in congested urban traffic is associated with many fender benders but very few severe crashes; whereas driving fast on expressways is associated with very few fender benders but with a small but significant number of severe and fatal crashes. On the basis of these two situations, if we examine the relationship between speed and all crashes (combining all severities) we find that speed is paradoxically inversely related to crashes. But this is an artifact, as more crashes occur at low speeds than at high speeds. However, if only severe crashes are examined, the relationship between speed and crashes is direct: the higher the speed the higher the injury and fatality toll.

In discussing speed, we have to first distinguish between speed limits (prescribed speed) and travel speeds (drivers' speed). The two overlap only in the presence of at least one of the following: intense enforcement, speed calming devices such as bumps, or reduced visibility such as in fog or in curves. Whereas speed limit is a single value, driving speed can be the speed of a single crash-involved vehicle or some statistical attribute of the prevailing traffic speed distribution. Three such statistics have been used in evaluating the effects of speed: average travel speed, 85th percentile of the speed distribution, and some measure of the dispersion or variance in travel speeds.

In addition to the difficulty of integrating results obtained with the various speed measures mentioned above, there is also a problem with the validity of the speed measures themselves. It is nearly impossible to obtain an objective measure of the true pre-crash speeds of crash-involved vehicles. This is because crashes are not planned, and consequently speeds must be estimated post hoc by various subjective and objective techniques all having a limited validity. There are a few exceptions to the post hoc estimations. Four published studies used objective measures of impact speed. In the first study (West and Dunn, 1971) pre-crash speeds of approximately one-fourth of the crash-involved vehicles were determined with a high degree of certainty from data obtained from speed detectors embedded in a section of an Indiana rural state highway with a 55-mph (89 km/hr) speed limit. In the second study Pasanen and Salmivaara (1993), using a video camera specifically calibrated to measure speed, recorded 18 intersection collisions in Helsinki, 11 of which involved pedestrians. In the third study, a naturalistic driving study, Klauer *et al.* (2006) installed video cameras and other recording instruments on 100 cars whose movements were tracked around-the-clock for 12-13 months. In the course of this year and approximately two million miles that these cars traveled they were involved in 69 crashes, only 12 of which were severe enough to be reported to the police, and none were fatal. The fourth, most recent study was also a naturalistic driving study by Dingus *et al.* (2016), but this one tracked over 3,000 drivers who accumulated over 1,500 crashes over a period of 1–2 years. In this study excessive speed (relative to the speed limit or conditions) was noted in less than three percent of the control episodes, but relative to control situations with the same drivers it had a significant odds ratio of 12.8, meaning that speeding increased the odds of a crash by a factor of nearly 13! (see Chapter 18 for a more detailed description of this study and its results). Thus, such studies are very few and have either very little data or are extremely costly.

All other studies rely on drivers' estimates, police officers' estimates, or estimates of accident reconstruction experts based on tire markings and crash deformation data for calculating the speeds of crash-involved vehicles. For studies relating traffic-flow speeds to crashes, the actual speed of the traffic stream at the place and time of the crash is usually not known; instead, it is typically extrapolated from traffic-flow measures taken before or after the crash (e.g., Solomon, 1964).

The reasons drivers drive at different speeds and the environments in which they drive also affect the relationship between speed and crashes. For example, driving slowly in congestion is done for a different reason than driving slowly on an open freeway. A slow driver on the freeway may be a cognitively impaired elderly driver, whereas a slow driver on a congested urban street may be a highly capable driver hampered by traffic. In the most quoted early study on the relationship between speed and the likelihood of a crash, Solomon (1964) found that drivers who drove either significantly above *or* below the prevailing average traffic speed were more likely to have crashes than drivers who drove at speeds close to the average (Solomon, 1964). However, most crash-involved slow drivers were turning at the time of the crash; and when turning vehicles were removed from the analysis only those driving at speeds significantly above the traffic speed remained over-involved in crashes (Fildes and Lee, 1993).

Finally, in aggregating crash data from different roads and different times to evaluate the effect of speed as a single independent variable, one assumes (at least implicitly) that "all other things remain equal." In fact, this is never the case. In real life, driving speed is highly correlated with at least four types of confounding variables (Bowie and Walz, 1994): (1) other crash-related driver behaviors such as drinking, not using safety belts (Evans, 1996), and other types of aggressive driving (in fact, speeding is often considered as a subcategory of aggressive driving); (2) crash-related individual differences in variables such as age and gender; (3) road design (e.g., speed-related crashes are over-represented on curves), road conditions, traffic conditions, and speed limits; and (4) vehicular variables such as type of vehicle, engine power, and steering and brake performance.

Some theoretical issues – And a theoretical quagmire

There are at least three theoretical approaches or models of driver behavior that can and have been used to account for the relationship between speed and crashes. Each model views the driver and the traffic environment from a different perspective, and each leads to somewhat different conclusions – all of which have received some empirical support. Two of the models – the information processing and the risk homeostasis – have been described in some detail in Chapter 3, and the third one – the traffic conflict model will be described in some detail below.

Information processing approach

From a very simplistic point of view it appears that as speed increases, the time to react to emerging dangers is shortened, and the likelihood of successfully coping with the imminent crash situation decreases. Also, even after a driver reacts by braking, the braking distance of the vehicle is proportional to the square of the pre-braking speed. Therefore, the distance traveled until the vehicle comes to a complete stop increases as a function of the square of the speed, and the likelihood of a collision increases in a corresponding fashion. But reality is much more complicated. From the perspective of the driver as a limited capacity information processor unexpected events dramatically increase the amount of information that must be processed in a very short time. Such events include a car weaving in the lane, an obstacle in the travel lane, a curve with short sight distance, merging vehicles, a pedestrian jumping into the road, a car emerging from a hidden driveway, etc. In addition, at a critical moment some of the driver's capacity may be directed to other attention-demanding factors such as radio broadcasts, cellular phone conversations, and other distractions from within or outside the car. Consequently, at some speed the increase in the information load can make the driver more likely to fail to process and respond fast enough to all the information, and possibly have a crash. Also, because some highway design codes are based on assumed speed and driver response times (e.g., for reading signs) and assumed sight distance to potential obstacles (e.g., railroad crossings), information overload and lapses in attention are more critical the faster the driver is going. Finally, as speed increases, each of the driving tasks becomes more difficult – detection of obstacles, recognition of impending danger, decision making, and response selection – and that difficulty contributes to the increase in crash risk (Kallberg and Luoma, 1996). All of these considerations lead to the conclusion that "speed kills."

To complicate things a little, we must also acknowledge that drivers can – at least for a short time – increase their overall processing capacity. An increase in speed, therefore, constitutes an increase in stress but if drivers can adjust to it by recruiting additional capacities allocated to non-driving tasks – such as putting down the cell phone when the traffic demands increase – then it may not involve an increase in strain.

Stress is the external load that can be objectively measured, and strain is the load that is experienced by the person being stressed. The increase in stress with increasing speed is obvious, but the increase in strain must be demonstrated empirically. This was done by Liu and Lee (2006) who monitored volunteer drivers' heart rate while they drove an instrumented vehicle in urban streets and on a motorway in Taiwan. Heart rate is a common physiological measure of physical strain. Though it is much less sensitive to mental strain, it can also be used to measure mental strain, especially if it is not confounded with physical activity. Typically, heart rate increases the more stressed we feel; that is, the greater the workload (Casali and Wierwille, 1983; Wilson, 1993). By measuring the difference between the resting heart rate and the heart rate while driving Liu and Lee determined the strain experienced by drivers in different conditions. The relationship between the heart rate and speed was not statistically significant in the urban streets where most of the time speed was determined by the traffic and the streets. However, on the motorway where drivers had more control of their speed, heart rate increased linearly with speed, with a correlation of $r = 0.63$, as can be seen from Figure 8-5.

Is there an optimal speed level at which we feel the most comfortable and least stressed? Liu and Lee's data would suggest that the lower the speed the less stressed we would be. Yet, in the absence of any restrictions, most of us in a given environment drive at a speed

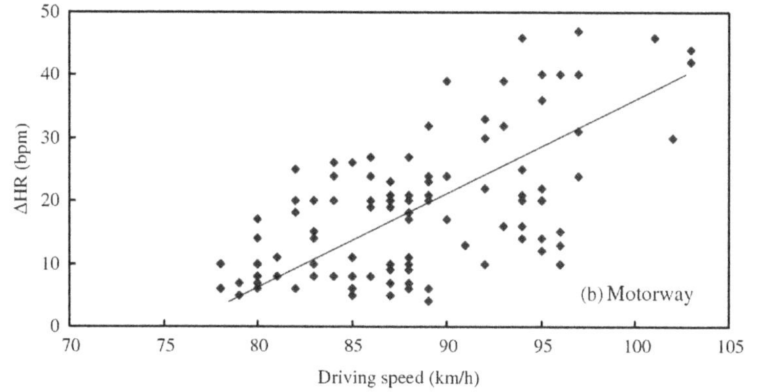

Figure 8-5. The relationship between driving speed on a motorway and increase in heart rate (ΔHR is the individually measured difference between driving heart rate and resting heart rate) (from Liu and Lee, 2006, with permission from Elsevier).

that seems the most comfortable to us. Recarte and Nunes (2002) argued that at that speed we need to allocate minimal attention to speed control, and deviations from such speed – either up or down – require us to allocate more resources to the speed control task, and consequently increase the task load. To test this hypothesis they designed a very interesting experiment. In their study drivers were required to drive on a motorway near Madrid where the posted speed limit is 120 km/hr. For half the distance the drivers had their speedometer concealed and on half the route it was visible. Within each condition, half of the time the drivers were not given any speed instructions and half of the time they were asked to restrict their speed to 90-100 km/hr. Finally, within each of the resulting four conditions they either drove without any distractions or while required to perform a distracting mental task.

The findings confirmed Recarte and Nunes' hypothesis. When the drivers could not see the speedometer and were not restricted in their speed, their speed averaged about 107 km/hr, and was unaffected by whether or not they had to perform the additional distracting task. When their view of the speedometer was restored they increased their speed to an average of 115 km/hr, again regardless of the mental task. However, when they were asked to restrict their speed to 90-100 km/hr they actually drove faster when they had to time-share the driving with the distracting task (102.2 km/h) than when they did not have the distracting task (99.5 km/hr). This speed difference demonstrates that as we change our speed the information processing demands are affected by both an increase in the rate of the visual inputs with the increasing speed, and the additional demands of speed monitoring and control. Another indication of the effort invested in speed control was the consistent reduction in speed variability (by an average of 2.5 km/hr standard deviations) whenever speed was restricted. This means that there is an optimal speed at which the driving task load is minimized. Most likely, that speed is different for different drivers and changes as a function of the road, the traffic situation, and the state of alertness of the driver. To some extent cruise control is used to that end too: to relieve the driver of the role of monitoring his or her own speed.

In addition to being counterintuitive, Recarte and Nunes' results contradict the findings of many studies that have found that drivers typically reduce their speed when performing distracting phone tasks (see Chapter 13). For example, Liu and Lee (2006) found that their drivers significantly reduced their speed by an average of 6 percent when they had to engage in a phone task, and in our driving simulator we (Tractinsky, Ram, and Shinar, 2013) obtained a speed reduction of two percent when the drivers were engaged in a cell phone conversation. Thus, Recarte and Nunes' results – if they can be replicated – do not invalidate the information processing model, but only indicate that the act of speed monitoring by itself demands some processing capacity, relative to self-selected comfortable speed.

Traffic conflict approach

This approach considers the traffic stream and roadway system as the sources of potential conflicts to which a driver responds. The load on the driver increases as a function of increasing disparities in speed in the traffic stream because of the different behaviors and speeds of the other drivers and vehicles. If all traffic moves in unobstructed lanes on divided highways at the same speed, then there is no uncertainty about the movement of the other vehicles, the differences in driving speeds approach zero, and the potential for conflicts among vehicles does not increase with increasing speeds. However, this is not the case and vehicle speeds are best represented by a distribution of speeds rather than a single speed. Different speeds involve passing maneuvers that can be viewed as potential conflicts. The number of such conflicts increases the more a driver deviates from the median traffic speed. Therefore, the more a driver deviates from the median traffic speed, the more conflicts he or she is likely to encounter (Hauer, 1971). This logic leads to the conclusion that it is not speed that kills but the deviation from the median or average traffic speeds that kills. It also implies that crash rates will be higher on roads with low median speeds but with a wide range of speeds (e.g., two-lane rural roads) than on roads with high median speeds but a narrower range of speeds (e.g., expressways), and that both slow drivers and speeding drivers will be over-involved in crashes. Navon (2003) showed that the number of conflicts increases as the average speed decreases, thereby providing a rationale for the findings that high-speed roads have fewer crashes than low-speed roads.

Risk-homeostasis motivational approach

The risk homeostasis model assumes that (a) drivers are not passive information processors who merely react to conflicts but are active in the sense that they have motives that affect their driving style and (b) a primary motive of drivers is to maintain a subjectively acceptable level of risk (see Chapter 3 for more details). This approach has intuitive appeal because most drivers "feel" that they adjust their speed in response to the changing demands of the highway and the traffic. If this adjustment in speed is appropriate, there should be no correlation between speed and crashes. If the adjustment is insufficient, crashes should increase with speed. By the same token, if the adjustment to a perceived danger is excessive, then crash probability may actually decrease. The question then becomes not one about the relationship between speed and crashes, but one about the correspondences between actual risk, perceived risk, and driver actions. This means that increasing speed per se is not a dangerous behavior but that an inappropriate excessive speed – stemming from misperception of the situational demands and lack of appreciation of the car and the driver's own handling capabilities – may be dangerous. This approach can lead to different predictions concerning the relationship between speed and crashes, but because most drivers' perceptions of the road and traffic ahead are fairly accurate, the model should predict that under most circumstances the voluntary increase in speed of most drivers would not necessarily increase crash risk. There is some empirical support for the risk-homeostasis theory. Mackay (1985) found that British drivers of newer and heavier cars drove at higher speeds than drivers of older and lighter cars (except for sports cars, which are the fastest), but speeds of belted and unbelted drivers did not differ (this study was conducted in 1982, before the use of seat belts was made mandatory). Rumar *et al.* (1976) found that drivers with studded tires drove faster than drivers without such tires on road curves in icy conditions but not in dry conditions, indicating that drivers adjust their speed according to their perceived safety or vehicle-handling capability. On the other hand, O'Day and Flora (1982) analyzed data from the U.S. National Crash Severity Study (NCSS) and found – in contrast to the prediction of the risk homeostasis hypothesis – that restrained occupants had lower impact speeds than unrestrained occupants, indicating that they drive at slower speeds.

With these apparently conflicting empirical findings, and models that can account for all of them, it is no wonder that the issue of the relationship between speed and safety is hotly debated and one on which the motoring public is divided. Of the three major safety issues – seat belt use, drinking and driving, and speeding – the reported tendency to obey speed limits is the lowest. In fact, in North America the tendency to observe the speed limit actually decreased in the last decades of the past century (see Figure 8-1).

A related motivational approach to speed choice was recently suggested by Schmidt-Daffy (2014), based on Kahneman and Tversky's (1979) Prospect Balancing Theory. According to this theory, in the context of driving, on an almost continuous basis a driver must decide between two prospects: increasing or decreasing his or her speed. That decision is based on the driver's bounded rationality (see Chapter 3). Consequently, that decision is not necessarily aligned with the true costs, benefits, and probabilities associated with the two decisions. Interestingly, Schmidt-Daffy argues that because of the nature of subjective gains and losses, this weighting should typically yield a "cautious speed choice." A small speed selection study in a driving simulator supported this model and it suggests that knowledge of the driver's perceptions and motivational criteria may be useful for road safety plans.

Speed and crash involvement

The most naïve way to consider the role of speed in crash causation is to simply look at national crash statistics. For example, the U.S. Fatal Analysis Reporting System (FARS) data indicate that "driving too fast for conditions or in excess of posted speed limit" is a "contributing factor" in 28-32 percent of all fatal crashes (NHTSA, 2012, 2015). However, crash data must be interpreted with caution because they do not include an exposure measure. In this case the exposure measure should be the percentage of drivers in the traffic stream where these crashes occurred who "exceed the speed limit or drive too fast for conditions" without being involved in a crash. Most traffic speed surveys indicate that in the absence of significant restrictions, and depending on the country or state 50 percent or more of the drivers exceed the speed limit (Haglund and Åberg, 2002; McKenna, 2005; Yannis *et al.*, 2013), and on high-speed limited-access roads (expressways or motorways) the percent exceeding the speed limits is even higher, exceeding 70 percent in the U.S. and Israel (NHTSA, 2012b; NRSA, 2014). For this reason, to evaluate accurately the contribution of speed to crashes, it is important to control for spurious effects either through well-designed correlational analyses of crash and travel data or through detailed cause-and-effect analyses of individual crashes. A third approach is the quasi-experimental design in which crash data are analyzed relative to changes in speed limits. The findings from studies relying on all three approaches are reviewed below, though unfortunately, none of these careful approaches is common.

Correlational studies of speed and crashes

Because of lack of controls for confounding variables, the results of correlational studies are often inconsistent with each other (Imprialou *et al.*, 2016). A good way to demonstrate the difficulty in directly testing the relationship between speed and crashes is to cite three studies that attempted to do that. The first is a comprehensive analysis of the correlation between fatality rates and speeds on various road systems in the U.S. during the 55-mph (89 km/hr) national maximum speed limit era. The correlations between fatality rates and percentage of drivers exceeding 65 mph (105 km/hr) were r = 0.33 for the expressways, r = 0.25 for rural arterial roads, and not significantly different from zero for rural collectors, urban arterials, and urban expressways. Furthermore, there were no significant correlations between fatality rates and the percentage exceeding 55 mph or 85th percentile speeds for any of the road types (TRB, 1984). The second analysis was more detailed and focused on crashes in the state of Virginia. This analysis failed to find any significant relationship between average speed and crash rates (Garber and Gadiraju, 1988). In the third study Liu and Popoff (1996) compared average speeds in seven sections of 100 km/hr roads in Saskatchewan, Canada, between 1969 and 1982 and 1983 and 1995. Their measure of speed dispersion was the speed differential between the 15th and the 85th percentile speeds (which roughly corresponds to two standard deviations). In three sections the average speed decreased, the speed range narrowed, and the crash rates declined. In two sections the average speed remained relatively constant, the speed range narrowed, and the crash rates declined. In one section the average speed increased, the speed range narrowed, and the crash rate declined. In one section both the average speed and the speed range decreased but the crash rate increased. In contrast to these mixed results, on the basis of regressions derived from nine speed surveys on Saskatchewan provincial highways conducted since 1969, Liu and Popoff concluded that the number of traffic casualties is linearly highly related to the average speed, and the number of injuries per km driven is linearly related to their measure of speed dispersion (r = 0.94). This mixed bag of results is probably due to the small range of average speeds observed (only 100-105 km/hr), the relatively small number of observations, and the absence of control over many other time-dependent factors. In summary, these three studies can be used as support for both the existence and the absence of a relationship between speed and crashes depending on the speed measures and conditions, the study design, and the crash statistics used.

Perhaps the best approach to this issue is to consider the evidence from a chronological perspective and attempt to integrate the data as they accumulated. The benchmark study of the relationship between speed and crash involvement and between speed and crash severity was conducted in the U.S. by Solomon in 1964. A critical component of Solomon's study was the inclusion of the speed of the traffic stream as a potential mediating factor, and the inclusion of all three aspects of speed – average speed of the traffic stream, speed dispersion, and reported speed of crash-involved vehicles. Because Solomon's study was the first and to date arguably the most detailed and comprehensive study of this nature, it is worth describing some of its essential design features before discussing its findings and conclusions.

Solomon (1964) analyzed the crash experience of 10,000 driver-vehicle units that had been involved in crashes between 1954 and 1958 on 1,000 kilometers of rural two- and four-lane highways consisting of 35 sections in 11 states. Roadway characteristics varied widely among these sections, as did speed limits [45-70 mph (73-113 km/hr) for passenger cars in the daytime] and design speeds [35-70 mph (56-113 km/hr)]. Traffic speed measurements at each of the sites were made during 1957 and 1958. Solomon also calculated the exposure of the vehicles traveling at different speeds by multiplying the number of vehicles measured at each speed in each road section by the length of the section, and then summing the data from all 35 sections. Finally, he defined crash involvement (his dependent variable) as the number of crashes per 100 million vehicle-miles (161 million vehicle-km).

When he first analyzed the data in terms of crash involvement relative to the average traffic speed he obtained an asymmetrical U-shaped curve in which the crash rate was lowest at the average traffic speed of approximately 60 mph for the daytime crashes and 70 mph for the nighttime crashes. Above and – even more so – *below* these average speeds the crash rates increased at a rapidly accelerating rate. These results are reproduced in the left panel of Figure 8-6. Note that the crash rate is plotted on a logarithmic scale, so the rate of increase relative to the minimum point would appear much steeper if the scale were linear. This was a curious result that seemed to suggest that up till average daytime traffic speed of approximately 60 mph (97 km/hr), crash rates decrease as speed increases – at least on rural roads.

Solomon then examined the relationship between the crash rate and the *difference* between the pre-impact speed of the crash-involved vehicles and the average traffic speed at each crash site. Once again he obtained U-shaped functions reproduced in the right panel of Figure 8-6 for daytime and nighttime crashes. The patterns were similar to those obtained for the vehicle speed (in the left panel), with nighttime crash rates being significantly higher.

An explanation of this phenomenon in terms of traffic conflicts was offered seven years later by Hauer (1971). He demonstrated mathematically that the number of vehicle encounters (in terms of passing or being passed) is a U-shaped curve with a minimum for vehicles traveling at the median traffic speed. Speeds greater than the median traffic speed involve more active passing maneuvers, and speeds below the median traffic speed involve more passive (being passed by others) passing maneuvers. If we now make the reasonable assumption that the speed distribution is not symmetric around the average but is negatively skewed (with a longer tail for slower-moving vehicles), then the average traffic speed is lower than the median. In that case the 55-65 mph at which crash rates were the lowest would correspond to the 5-10 mph minimum points above the average speed difference in Figure 8-6(b), confirming Hauer's (1971) theoretical derivation. Interestingly, the relative speeds at which the crash rates started increasing most substantially (approximately 30 km/hr above the average speed), correspond to the point beyond which time-to-collision diminishes rapidly leaving drivers very little time to stop before colliding with very slow-moving vehicles, such as vehicles slowing down to turn off the road (Hoffman and Mortimer, 1996).

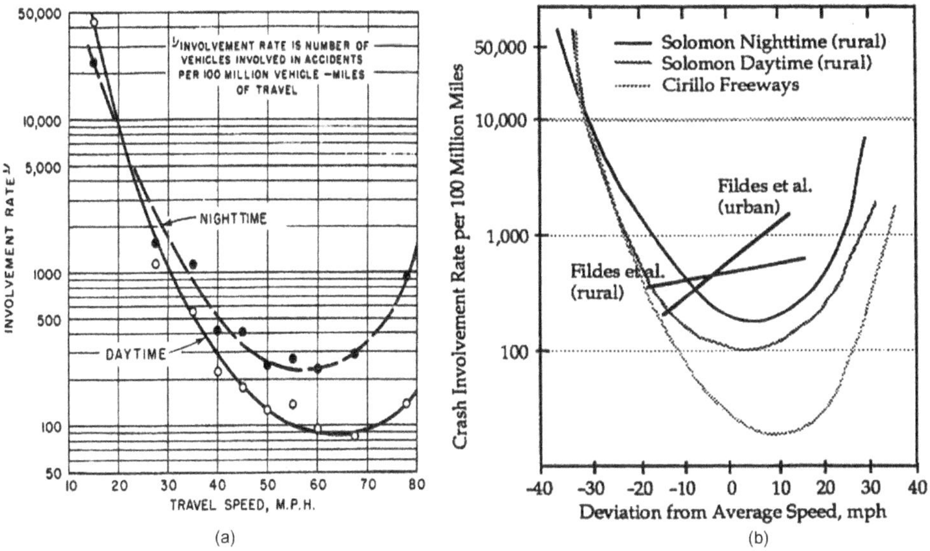

Figure 8-6. Daytime and nighttime crash involvement rates (crashes per 100 million vehicle miles, on logarithmic scale) (a) in relation to the average traffic travel speed (left panel) and (b) as a function of deviation from the average traffic speeds (from Cirillo, 1968; Fildes, Rumbold, and Leening, 1991; Solomon, 1964).

The patterns presented in Figure 8-6 led Solomon to conclude that "regardless of the average speed on a main rural highway, the greater the driver's deviation from this average speed, the greater his chance of being involved in an accident" (p. 16). Furthermore, in light of the higher rates at the lower vehicle speeds and the negative end of the speed differences, he further concluded that "low speed drivers are more likely to be involved in accidents than relatively high speed drivers" (p. 9). Solomon's findings from the predominantly rural highways of the late 1950s were generalized to interstate highway (motorway) crashes by Cirillo (1968). Although her data were limited to daytime rear-end, angle, and same-direction sideswipe collisions, they yielded a very similar pattern as can be seen in the same figure super-imposed on Solomon's data (in the right panel), though with a much lower overall crash rate.

With such controversial results, it is not surprising that Solomon's study and conclusions have been re-examined and critiqued by many researchers (Fildes and Lee, 1993; Imprialou *et al.*, 2016; Knowles *et al.*, 1997; Stuster, Coffman, and Warren, 1998). In their subsequent studies and analyses, these researchers raised and attempted to address four valid and critical shortcomings of this first comprehensive study: (1) the speed flow measures were not from the same times as the crashes. The speed data were collected in 1957 and 1958, whereas the crash data were collected from 1954 to 1958. (2) The speed data from turning vehicles were eliminated from the analysis of the average speeds, but turning-related crashes were not. (3) The pre-crash speeds of the crash-involved vehicles were obtained primarily from self-reports of the drivers, and these were probably biased downward because, as "Stannard's Law" states "drivers tend to explain their traffic accidents by reporting circumstances of lowest culpability compatible with credibility" (Aronoff, 1971). (4) The roads, traffic control devices, and vehicles are all from the 1950s and may not be relevant to today's environment.

Solomon's conclusions are also questionable because they rest on two assumptions that are probably not warranted. First, he makes the subtle substitution of a cause-and-effect relationship for the observed association between the speed deviation from the average traffic speed and crash involvement. Not only was speed deviation not manipulated in the study (as would be desirable for any independent variable), but the contribution of speed deviation per se to crash involvement was never demonstrated by comparing roads of similar physical geometry with different speed ranges. Second, speed varies as a function of many factors, an important one being the design speed of the highway. In his analysis Solomon did not control for the design speed of the various road sections. Drivers tend to adjust their speed to design speed, and when different routes with different design speeds (e.g., rural collector roads and expressways) are entered into the same equation, it can be shown that crash rates decrease with increasing average speed (Garber and Gadiraju, 1988; Navon, 2003).

Lave (1985) focused directly on the contribution of speed dispersion to crashes. Using the data from 48 U.S. states, he showed that for most road types, speed dispersion is positively related to crash rates, and when it is statistically controlled (so that its effects are statistically removed), the correlations between crash involvement and various measures of speed – including deviations from the average speed, percentage of vehicles exceeding 55 mph (89 km/hr), percentage exceeding 65 mph (105 km/hr), and 85th percentile speed – essentially disappear. Rodriguez (1990) used data from all 50 states and analyzed the contributions of average speed and speed dispersion to fatality rates (per vehicle miles) for each year from 1981 to 1985, and also obtained a significant relationship between crash rates and speed dispersion (for 4 of the 5 years), but no significant relationship between crash rates and average speed. In short, several different studies seem to support the variance hypothesis, and the similarity of their data to Hauer's theoretical derivation is quite good as can be seen in Figure 8-7. However, all of these analyses were unable to disaggregate slowing vehicles from slow-moving vehicles; an important distinction because drivers who slow down (to turn, to avoid another car, to obey a sign) are very different from drivers who continually drive at slow speeds.

Solomon was aware of the difference between slow-moving vehicles and vehicles that were slowing down to negotiate some maneuver. Conceptually the difference is very significant: the former suggests that slow-moving *drivers and vehicles* are dangerous, whereas the latter suggests that *situations and maneuvers* requiring slowing down are dangerous. A typical situation that requires slowing down is turning to enter or leave the highway. In Solomon's sample of roadways, with the exception of one segment of limited-access road, all segments had entrances and intersections. Solomon calculated that even if one-half of the crashes occurred at intersections and the data for these vehicles

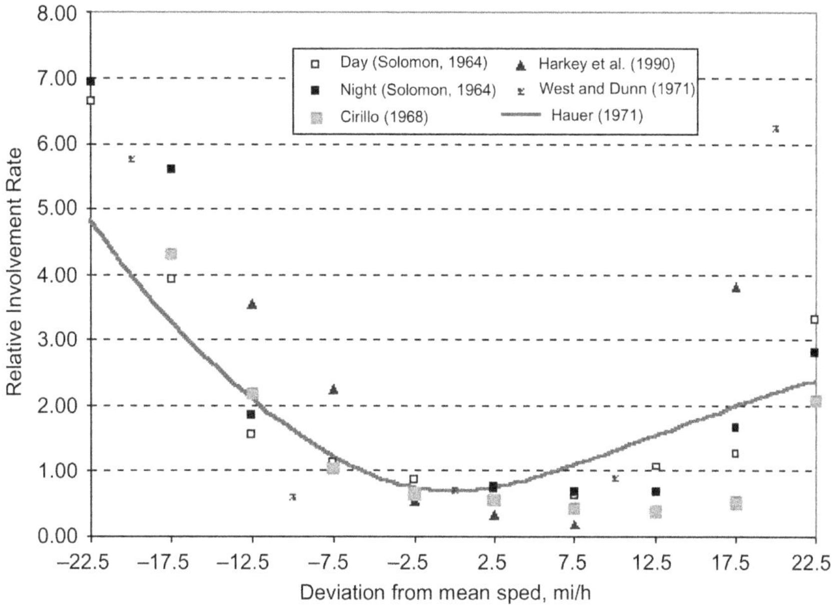

Figure 8-7. Crash involvement rates for empirical data from four different studies and overtaking rate from Hauer (1971) as a function of deviation from the mean speed (from Stuster *et al.*, 1998).

were eliminated from the analysis, the portion of the curve for low speeds in Figure 8-6 would be reduced by a fraction of a logarithmic unit. But what if more than one-half of the crashes were at intersections? And what if some of the rear-end crashes were due to vehicles suddenly slowing down in response to an emergency (such as another vehicle unexpectedly entering from a side road)? In an attempt to validate Solomon's U-shaped curve, a research team of the North Carolina Research Institute examined 200 crashes in which they were able to obtain accurate impact speeds (from physical reconstructions of the crashes), and compared them to the speeds of the cars that preceded or followed the crash vehicle (as measured by buried speed detection loops). While they did in fact replicate the U-shaped curve, they found that 44 percent of the crashes involved some kind of maneuver, and were therefore associated with slowing rather than slow-moving vehicles. When these crashes were removed from the data, the rate of increase of the function below the mean travel speed was much lower than that of Solomon's (RTI, 1970).

If it is not speed that kills but "variance kills," then presumably it is because the variance reflects the potential for inter-vehicle conflicts: the greater the variance the more conflicts. However, accounting for Solomon's, Cirillo's, Rodriguez's, and Lave's findings in terms of Hauer's (1971) and Navon's (2003) theoretical analyses of the potential for inter-vehicle conflicts is somewhat problematic. This is because maneuvers that are most likely to be involved in passing and overtaking account for a very small percentage of all maneuvers for crash-involved vehicles in the U.S. (e.g., merging/changing lanes = 3.7 percent, passing other vehicle = 1.2 percent; NHTSA, 2006). Furthermore, an analysis of the crash characteristics of fatal crashes indicates that most of them involve a single vehicle only (approximately 60 percent in the U.S.; NHTSA, 2006, 2015), and for those crashes that are judged as "speed related" nearly 70 percent are single vehicle crashes (Bowie and Walz, 1994). These statistics cast more doubt on the role of speed deviation and slow-moving vehicles. Solomon also calculated the crash involvements for different crash types as a function of speed and found that whereas the percent of single-vehicle crashes increased with travel speed, the percent of rear-end and angle crashes decreased with travel speed. Thus, Solomon's own findings and analyses also point to the likely roles that being stopped or entering and leaving the highway have in low-speed crashes.

Still we cannot rush to conclude that inter-vehicle conflicts are not a significant crash-causing factor. This is because in accident data bases crashes are typically coded as "single vehicle" if the crash-involved vehicle does not come in actual contact with another vehicle. However, often a single-vehicle crash, such as "run off the road," may be the end result of an attempt to avoid a collision with another vehicle that entered the driver's path. This information, which is often contained in crash narratives, is based primarily on the driver's (or occupants') report and is usually not available in the digitally coded crash data. In Indiana University's classic study of the causes of accidents (Treat *et al.*, 1977, see also Chapter 18), such crashes were coded as involving a "phantom vehicle." In their representative sample of crashes, such events were relatively rare and were cited as a probable factor in 3.8 percent of *all* crashes, including multiple-vehicle crashes. Their involvement may be greater in single-vehicle fatal crashes, but reports of their involvement would be rarer since very often the involved driver is killed.

To address the issue of the role of slow versus turning vehicles, West and Dunn (1971) collected crash and speed data on rural roads in Indiana and conducted separate analyses of the total data set and of crashes that did not involve turning vehicles. The difference between the two crash rate curves was dramatic: removing the turning vehicles reduced the over-all crash rate, and significantly flattened the U-shaped curve. Cowley (1987) addressed the same issue by using Solomon's data and involvement rates separately for six types of collisions. In these analyses he replicated the complete U-shaped curves only for nighttime head-on collisions. Predictably, crash rates increased with speed for single-vehicle run-off-the-road crashes and decreased with speed for rear-end crashes. However, angle collisions, "single vehicle struck object" crashes, and daytime-only head-on collisions decreased with increasing speed, suggesting that there is something to the argument that slow or slowing vehicles are over-involved in crashes – without necessarily shedding light on *why* this is so. These findings also mean that the results of any analysis on the relationship between speed and crashes will depend heavily on the specific mix of various roadway characteristics and travel patterns that existed in the data set. Thus, for example, Fildes *et al.* (1991) attempted to replicate Solomon's findings for rural highways and urban highways in Australia using a different method, and failed to obtain the U-shaped curve at all. In their study they measured the speed of drivers in traffic in two urban and two rural roads, posted at 60 and 100 km/hr, respectively. When they asked their drivers about their accident history in the past 5 years they found that the slower drivers were involved in fewer crashes than the faster ones, especially on the higher-speed rural roads. Their findings are super imposed over Solomon's data in Figure 8-6(b). A detailed discussion about the relationship between road type, speed, and crashes is available in Shinar (1998).

Given this array of different and probably confusing results, we can try to explain the U-shaped curve as follows: in a two-car following situation, slowing vehicles are more likely to be struck than fast vehicles because when they slow down, drivers behind them are often not immediately aware of the speed change, and thus slowing down reduces the headways of cars behind them. This may create imminent crash situations because of lapses in attention of following drivers, slowed responses of the following drivers, or misperception of the reduced gap by the following drivers. Lapses in attention (variously labeled as inattention, distraction, or improper lookout – see Chapter 13) are the most common human causes of traffic crashes (Dingus *et al.*, 2016; Evans, 1991; Sabey and Staughton, 1975; Shinar, 1978). Thus, the more and more often a driver has to slow down and the more rapid the deceleration, the more he or she are likely to be hit. Correspondingly, the faster the following driver is moving, given momentary lapses in attention, the more likely he or she are to fail to respond in time to an emerging collision situation.

Two studies conducted in Adelaide, Australia, in urban 60 km/hr zones focused on the effect of speed on urban crashes, and both obtained a positive power relationship between speed and crash probability. To rule out as many non-speed factors as possible, both studies used the case control method, in which for every injury crash the speeds of non-crashing control vehicles moving at "free travel speeds" were measured at the same sites, on the same days of the week, the same times-of-day, and under the same weather conditions. In addition, drivers with alcohol or drivers who were involved in illegal maneuvers were excluded from the studies. Although the case control method is a correlational-type study, it is a much more controlled one because every attempt is made to match crash and non-crash vehicles in terms of the driving situation. In the first study, Moore, Dolinis, and Woodward (1995) compared the speeds of 45 crash vehicles and 450 control vehicles, and found that crash involvement increased exponentially with increasing speeds above 55-64 km/hr, so that for drivers traveling at speeds greater than 85 km/hr the probability of a crash was almost 40 times as high as that of a vehicle traveling at 55-64 km/hr. The second and more extensive study by Kloeden, McLean, Moore, and Ponte (1997) compared the speeds of 151 crash vehicles with the speeds of 604 non-crash vehicles and obtained similar results. Injury rates were relatively constant below the speed limit of 60 km/hr, but increased exponentially so that for vehicles traveling at 85 km/hr the relative risk was 57(!).

In summary, with the exception of one small study (Pasanen and Salmivaara, 1993; with speed data on only 18 urban intersection collisions, 11 of which were with pedestrians), none of the observational/correlational studies that have been reviewed were able to measure or to empirically or statistically control for all the potential factors that mediate speed and crash probability. Therefore, any conclusion based on these studies must rest on the bulk of the evidence rather than on the results of a single study or series of a few studies. And the bulk of the evidence indicates that (a) speed is a significant contributing factor to crashes; (b) specific types of crashes, such as "run-off-the-road" crashes, are definitely associated with high speeds; (c) cars with pre-crash speeds that are significantly above the modal or average travel speed are over-involved in crashes; (d) cars with pre-crash speeds that are significantly below the modal or average travel speed also tend to be over-involved in crashes, though the data for this are much less conclusive (Aarts and Schagen, 2006); and (e) at least part of the over-involvement of slow vehicles is due to forced slowing down such as for turning, crossing intersections, and avoiding obstacles, rather than to traveling at a slow speed.

Causal analyses of crashes

The observational data and correlational studies of the relationship between speed and crashes cannot reveal the underlying causes of this relationship. Older drivers may not be able to respond to all emerging dangers even at low speeds because of age-related and medical impairments, whereas young drivers may be able to respond in time at these speeds. In contrast, mature drivers may have a better appreciation of their limitations and adjust speed accordingly, whereas young drivers may be oblivious to their vehicle-handling limitations as well as the handling limitations of the vehicle and may therefore travel at a speed too high to respond in time to a change in the roadway or the behavior of the traffic ahead. Causal analyses of individual crashes are useful in taking all these factors into consideration. Despite their subjective nature, causal analyses performed by different investigators at different times and places consistently show that excessive speed is a factor in at least 10 percent of all crashes.

The role of speeding as a direct crash cause was probably first analyzed in a detailed and comprehensive manner by Treat *et al.* (1977). In this study, described in detail in Chapter 18, a representative sample of more than 2,000 police-reported crashes was analyzed by crash investigators at the crash sites, and 420 of them were further analyzed by multidisciplinary teams. A cause was defined as an event or action whose absence would have prevented the crash, all other things being equal. Furthermore, a human cause was cited if the causal behavior was a deviation from the normal or expected behavior of the average driver. Thus, speed would not be cited in a crash of a speeding vehicle unless the speed deviated from the speed expected at that site under the conditions that prevailed and the crash would not have occurred had the speed been as expected. With this approach to causation, the study estimated excessive speed to be a definite cause in 7-8 percent of the crashes and a probable cause in an additional 13-16 percent of the crashes.

Clinical post hoc causal analysis becomes much more difficult and expensive for large data files. However, it is possible to integrate several files to obtain more reliable estimates of the role of speed in crash causation. This was done by Bowie and Walz (1994), who combined the comprehensive census of all fatal U.S. crashes with 1 year of data from all police-reported crashes from six states that have a common crash coding scheme, and the 420 crashes analyzed in depth by Treat *et al.* (1977). Although they were based on different data sets, times, and data collection methods, the three sources yielded similar estimates, with "excessive speed" being involved in approximately 12 percent of all crashes and more than 30 percent of the fatal crashes. Similar results were obtained by Liu (1997), who analyzed the Saskatchewan, Canada, crash data files for 1990-1995. He defined a speed-related crash as one in which the police crash report noted that the driver was both "exceeding the speed limit *and* driving too fast for conditions." Although this definition may appear conservative, it is appropriate because police reports are not as reliable as professional in-depth crash investigations. Liu found that speed was a causal factor in 9-11 percent of all crashes and in 12-15 percent of all injury and fatal crashes.

In summary, studies using clinical causal assessment are unanimous in their conclusions about the contribution of speed to crashes: excessive speed (not necessarily in relation to the speed limit) definitely contributes to a small but significant percentage of all crashes and to a higher percentage of the more severe and fatal crashes. However, these analyses, too, have shortcomings: (a) their assessment methodology is "soft," being based on post-hoc clinical judgments and (b) they do not adjust for exposure. Thus, if exposure data showed that the percentage of speeders in the traffic stream is greater than the percent of speeders in crashes, it could be argued – at least theoretically – that speeding is actually a mitigating factor rather than an exacerbating factor in crash involvement.

Quasi-experimental studies: Changes in crash experience as a function of changes in speed management

When actual speed data are not available, a speed management or regulation technique is often used to assess the relationship between speed and safety. It is then assumed that speed covaries with the speed assumed by the management technique. The best approach to evaluate the net effect of the change is to do a quasi-experimental study design. Instead of assigning the treatment to some sites and then comparing the changes relative to a matched control sample (as we would in a truly experimental design) we find sites where the treatment has already been applied and compare the effects obtained there to similar sites where the treatment has not been applied. The net effect is reflected by the changes in the treatment sites *relative* to changes in the control sites. The difficult part in this approach is to find truly comparable sites. The approaches that have been tried and evaluated include setting and posting speed limits, speed enforcement, and speed calming through traffic engineering (e.g., sequencing traffic lights) and roadway design (e.g., road bumps, traffic circles, and rumble strips). It then remains to be demonstrated that these techniques affect speed, and that crash reductions associated with the speed reductions are actually due to the reduced speeds. Most of the evaluations of this type examined the effects of changes in speed limits and changes in enforcement.

Changing speed limits

This is the most common (and cheapest) technique to regulate speed. Studies that evaluated changes in crashes and injuries in conjunction with changes (or introduction) of speed limits have generally supported the notion that increases in speed limits without other concurrent changes are associated with increases in crashes, and decreases, or setting of speed limits where none existed, are associated with crash and injury reductions (NHTSA, 1992; Rock, 1995; Summala, 1985; TRB, 1984). Elvik, Christensen, and Amundsen (2004) reviewed 51 studies conducted in different parts of the world between 1970 and 2004 and concluded that for every change of 10 km/hr in the speed limit there is a change of roughly 2.5 km/hr in the actual average speed; enough to produce noticeable and meaningful changes in injuries and fatalities as predicted by the power model presented later in this chapter.

In the U.S. the imposition of the National Maximum Speed Limit (NMSL) in 1974, its later relaxation in 1987 that increased the NMSL in rural interstate roads (motorways) to 65 mph, and its eventual total repeal in 1995, provided researchers with a naturalistic study in which the effects of the changes in the speed limits on speeds and crashes could be studied. First, it is important to note that before the NMSL existed, most interstate highways had speeds (and speed limits) above 55 mph, and the NMSL was instituted as an economic gas-saving measure. However, it was the (relatively) unexpected significant reductions in traffic fatalities that sustained the NMSL before it was relaxed and repealed. Based on two independent extensive analyses of the effects of the changes at both the national and state levels, Grabowski and Morrisey (2007) and Kockelman (2006) concluded that the increase in the speed limits on the high-speed roads was associated with "a less-than-equivalent increase in average vehicle speed: a 10 mph speed limit increase, for example, corresponds to average speeds around 3 mi/h higher" (Kockelman, 2006). But the effects of the increase on fatalities were much greater: the increase in fatalities on the high-speed roads was estimated at 24 percent (Kockelman, 2006) and the increase in fatalities on rural high-speed roads was 36-37 percent (Grabowski and Morrisey, 2007). Thus, while the increase in the average speed may appear to have been small, its implications for fatality rates are enormous. How small changes in speeds can result in large increases in fatalities is explained a little later below.

One possibility that should not be ignored is that changes in speed limits on some roads will change driving patterns in such a way as to either increase or decrease the use of other roads, and consequently affect the crash risk on other roads (Lave and Elias, 1994, 1997). Grabowski and Morrisey investigated this spillover effect directly in their analyses of U.S. crashes following the repeal of the NMSL, and did not find any support for this hypothesis. The increase in fatality rates on the high-speed roads was not accompanied by a decrease in fatalities in the slower rural roads.

Stuster *et al.* (1998) reviewed 19 studies conducted in seven different countries and noted that in six of the eight studies that evaluated the effect of a decrease in the speed limits, there was a significant drop in crashes or fatalities, and in eight of the 11 studies that evaluated the effects of an increase in the speed limit there was an increase in crashes, injuries, or fatalities. The one exception to this pattern was in one study conducted in 40 U.S. states where there was actually a small (3-5 percent) decrease in fatalities in 14 states that raised the speed limits (Lave and Elias, 1994). Still, with 14 out of 19 studies showing a significant effect in the expected direction, and with only one study showing an effect in the other direction, the weight of the evidence indicates that speed limit changes are accompanied by corresponding changes in actual speeds, in injuries, and in crashes.

However, all of these studies suffer from the shortcomings of poor control of potentially confounding variables such as changes in traffic patterns as a consequence of speed limit changes, spillover effects of crashes to adjacent roads, changes in road service levels, and the concurrent introduction of other safety-related variables including increased enforcement, increased use of safety belts, reduction in drinking and driving, and vehicle-based safety improvements. For example, when speed limits are lowered, they are typically accompanied by increased enforcement and public information campaigns (e.g., Nilsson,

1990), which affect the test sites, but not the control sites. The difficulties in controlling for all confounding variables are so great as to sometimes yield opposite conclusions *from the same data*, depending on the measure of crash involvement used and the factors other than speed limits that are included in the analyses (Lave, 1985, 1989; Lave and Elias, 1994; Lund and Rauch, 1992; Zador and Lund, 1991).

Speed enforcement

This is a common speed management technique and there is ample evidence that drivers respond to perceived enforcement by adjusting their behavior, most notably by reducing their speed (Shinar and McKnight, 1985). The effect of enforcement is typically maximal at the site of the perceived enforcement, but halo effects – an extension of the effect beyond the immediate time and location of the officer or the camera – are common. Thus, we (Shinar and Stiebel, 1986) showed that compliance with the speed limit was highest near the conspicuous police vehicles and diminished with increasing distance. Furthermore, the distance-halo effect was greater for a moving than for a stationary police vehicle, presumably because the moving vehicle could be perceived as more threatening even when it was already out of sight. A halo effect in time – where drivers' speeds remain suppressed after the enforcement is removed – was obtained by Holland and Conner (1996). In their study the time-halo effect lasted up to 9 weeks for speed enforcement coupled with signs stating "Police Speed Check Area." Vaa (1997) demonstrated that massive enforcement, with a daily average of nine hours of police presence, can yield speed reductions that last up to 8 weeks. Interestingly, Vaa noted that speed reductions varied by time of day, with morning peak-period speeders being the most resistant to change. This could have been due to pressure to get to work on time or the drivers' knowledge that enforcement is more difficult (and therefore perceived as less threatening) in high-density, peak-period traffic. Automated speed enforcement can also be quite effective, as long as it is sufficiently conspicuous to the drivers. Elvik (1997) conducted a meta-analysis of studies that evaluated automated speed enforcement in several countries including England, Germany, Sweden, Norway, Australia, and the Netherlands. His analysis of the combined effects of these studies showed that automated enforcement yielded an average 17 percent reduction in injury crashes. The effects appear to be greatest at high-crash locations, though some of the observed changes could be due to the statistical phenomenon of regression toward the mean (Hauer *et al.*, 2002) and others could be due to the "migration" of risky behaviors and their attendant crashes to other locations (Lave and Elias, 1994, 1997).

Changes in road design

Perhaps the most enduring and cost-effective speed management approach is through road design. This has been demonstrated with various "traffic calming techniques" that are employed primarily in urban high pedestrian concentration areas. Elvik *et al.* (2009) conducted a meta-analysis of the results obtained in 28 studies conducted between 1962 and 1996. Nearly all studies yielded consistent crash reductions following the modifications. The modifications included speed bumps (with documented reductions in all crashes of 7-41 percent), rumble strips ahead of junctions (yielding 30-33 percent reduction in junction accidents), and speed zones (16-27 percent). Interestingly, one study on raised intersections actually resulted in a small increase of five percent in injury accidents and 13 percent in property-damage-only accidents. However, these effects were not statistically significant and the study did not include matched control sites. Because speed calming techniques are typically implemented in areas with high pedestrian traffic, a detailed discussion of the effectiveness of these techniques is provided in Chapter 15 on pedestrian safety.

Speed and crash severity

When his son got a driver's license, a Carnegie-Mellon University physics professor glued a note with this reminder on the car's dashboard: $E = 1/2mv^2$. The son got the message and remembers it to this day, 31 years later (J. Engler, personal communication, 2016). The relationship between speed at impact and severity of injury is intuitively obvious. The faster a vehicle is moving prior to contact with another vehicle or a stationary object, the greater the impact force and the greater the injury. However, what the equation highlights – and many people do not know – is that the force of the impact is proportional to the *square* of the velocity, and consequently the expected effect on injury should also increase exponentially. Nonetheless, the actual effect on injury should be demonstrated empirically. This is because the power of the impact may be mitigated by various shock-absorbing behaviors and devices that occupants may adopt (e.g., use of safety belts) and the various shock-absorbing design features of the various car makes and models.

Crash severity can be defined in at least two ways. The first measure defines the physical severity of the impact speed or Delta-V. Delta-V, typically denoted by Δv, is the change in velocity of a vehicle's occupant compartment during the collision phase of a motor vehicle crash (Day and Hargens, 1985). In the case of a collision with a fixed object Δv is the same as the speed at impact because the velocity at the end of the crash phase is zero. The second definition of severity is in terms of the injuries to the vehicle occupants or other crash-involved people. Injury severity is described in various ways, with scales of different sensitivities ranging from a gross three-level scale (fatal, injury, or property-damage-only crash) to more refined ones, such as the Abbreviated Injury Scale (AIS) of the Association for Advancement of Automotive Medicine in which injury levels vary on a seven-levels scale, from 0 for property damage only to six for an unsurvivable injury or death at the scene.

In his 1964 report Solomon also studied the relationship between speed and severity using two measures of crash severity: (a) injury rates expressed as the number of people injured relative to the number of crash-involved vehicles and (b) property damage cost per crash-involved vehicle. His results showed very clearly that both measures of severity increased as a power function of the travel speed, demonstrating that the higher the speed, the greater the increase in cost; both in terms of injuries and in terms of property damage. Solomon also calculated fatality rates in a similar manner. With a total of 253 fatalities, Solomon found that the odds of a fatality given a crash accelerated with speed from a low of approximately 1-2 fatalities for every 100 crashes at speeds less than 55 mph (89 km/hr) to a high of more than 20 fatalities for every 100 crashes for speeds of 70 mph (113 km/hr) and above.

Further analyses on U.S. and European data have all confirmed the very strong associations between speed and injury severity. Bowie and Walz (1994) analyzed U.S. national data and showed that while speed is cited as a crash cause in 10.2 percent of property-damage-only crashes, and in 14.6 percent of crashes with minor (non-incapacitating) injuries, it is cited in 34.2 percent of all fatal crashes. More objective analyses that do not rely on possibly biased clinical assessments of the role of speed have also demonstrated the relationship in a much more direct manner, as discussed below.

In an analysis of the National Analysis Sampling System (NASS, 1998) data, Joksch (1993) found a consistent relationship between the fatality risk for a driver in car-car collisions and ΔV. His analysis revealed that the risk of fatality is closely related to ΔV^4 (i.e., to the fourth power). By fitting curves to crash data with known and estimated ΔVs and by using different assumptions for the estimated ΔV, Joksch obtained similar functions with exponents ranging from 3.9 to 4.1 for all types of crashes, and not just car-car. This led Joksch to conclude that "the findings are somewhat robust against changes in the assumptions" and that "the exponent 4 may reasonably reflect the relation between the fatality risk and Delta-V. Even if not precise, it may be useful as a rule of thumb" (p. 104). Later analyses of fatality risk by NHTSA (2005) confirmed these conclusions. The similarity of the Joksch's fatality risk for drivers in car-car collisions and NHTSA's fatality risk for all occupants in all crashes is illustrated in Figure 8-8.

The most extensive analysis of the relationship between ΔV and crash severity was conducted by Elvik (2009, 2013a). For their meta-analysis in 2009 they included the data from 115 published studies, containing 526 results of injuries at specific speeds. Because

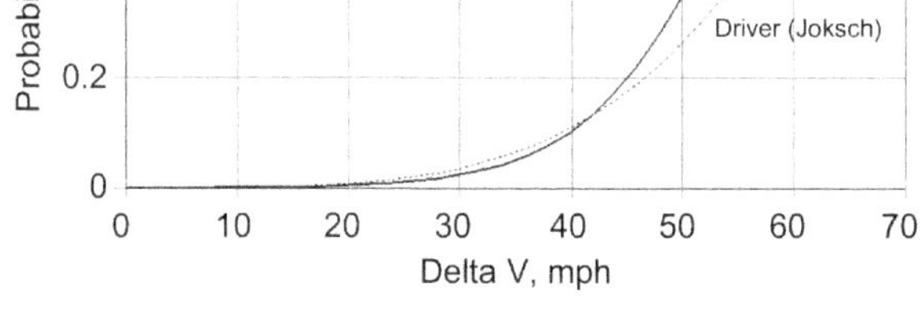

Figure 8-8. The relationship between risk of fatal injury and Delta-V for drivers in car-car collisions (Joksch, 1993) and for all vehicle occupants in all crash types (NHTSA, 2005). (For practical purposes Delta-V is a good approximation of the impact speed).

the initial impact speed is also highly relevant to the level of injury, for his 2013 analysis Elvik decomposed the data into crashes on rural versus urban roads. The estimated exponent values (α) for different measures of injuries on the two types or roads are provided in Table 8-2. As can be seen in the table, the more serious the injury the greater the value of **α**, and consequently the effect of the speed change. Also note that because of the prevailing speeds, **α** is significantly greater on inter-urban roads than on urban and residential roads. For example, **α** is more than 50 percent higher on rural roads for fatalities and fatal crashes. This is because due to the power function small changes in speed at higher impact speeds (typical of inter-urban travel) have significantly larger effects than changes by the same amount at low speeds (typical of urban travel). However, even in urban centers speed reduction is an effective safety measure. For example, in Oslo, Norway, the speed limit on arterial roads was temporarily reduced from 80 km/hr to 60 km/hr in order to reduce air pollution, and a positive by-product was a reduction in injury accidents by 25-35 percent (depending on

Table 8-2. The value of **α** in the power function $\text{Accidents}_{\text{after}} = \text{accidents}_{\text{before}} (\text{speed}_{\text{after}}/\text{speed}_{\text{before}})^{\alpha}$, in rural and urban roads (from Elvik, 2013a, with permission of Elsevier).

Accident or Injury Severity	**Summary Estimates of Exponents by Traffic Environment**			
	Rural roads/freeways		**Urban/residential roads**	
	Best estimate	**95% confidence interval**	**Best estimate**	**95% confidence interval**
Fatal accidents	4.1	(2.9, 5.3)	2.6	(0.3, 4.9)
Fatalities	4.6	(4.0, 5.2)	3.0	(−0.5, 6.5)
Serious injury accidents	2.6	(−2.7, 7.9)	1.5	(0.9, 2.1)
Seriously injured road users	3.5	(0.5, 5.5)	2.0	(0.8, 3.2)
Slight injury accidents	1.1	(0.0, 2.2)	1.0	(0.6, 1.4
Slightly injured road uses	1.4	(0.5, 2.3)	1.1	(0.9, 1.3)
Injury accidents – all	1.6	(0.9, 2.3)	1.2	(0.7, 1.7)
Injured road users – all	2.2	(1.8, 2.6)	1.4	(0.4, 2.4)[a]
Property-damage-only accident	1.5	(0.1, 2.9)	0.8	(0.1, 1.5)

[a]Confidence interval specified informally.

the method of evaluation used) (Elvik, 2013b). When combined for all roads – rural and urban – the effects on fatalities, injuries, and injury crashes are illustrated in Figure 8-9.

To further appreciate the significance of these power functions for injury and injury control, consider the two tables prepared by Hauer and Bonneson (2006), reproduced in Table 8-3, using the data prepared by Elvik *et al.* (2004). The cell entries in these tables are the best estimates of the increase or decrease in risk, with changes in average speed. The left table is for injury accidents with an estimated $\alpha = 1.5$ and the right table is for fatal accidents with $\alpha = 3.6$. As an example, consider an increase in average traffic speed of 3 mph (5 km/hr) from a prevailing speed of 60 mph (96 km/hr). Such a change would result in an increase in injury accidents by a factor 1.15, and an increase in fatal accidents by a factor of 1.27. These increases by 15 and 27 percent, respectively, are very significant considering the relatively small change in average traffic speed that triggers them. Note also how closely these estimates are to Kockelman's (2006) observed 24 percent increase in fatalities for a 3 mph increase in average speed.

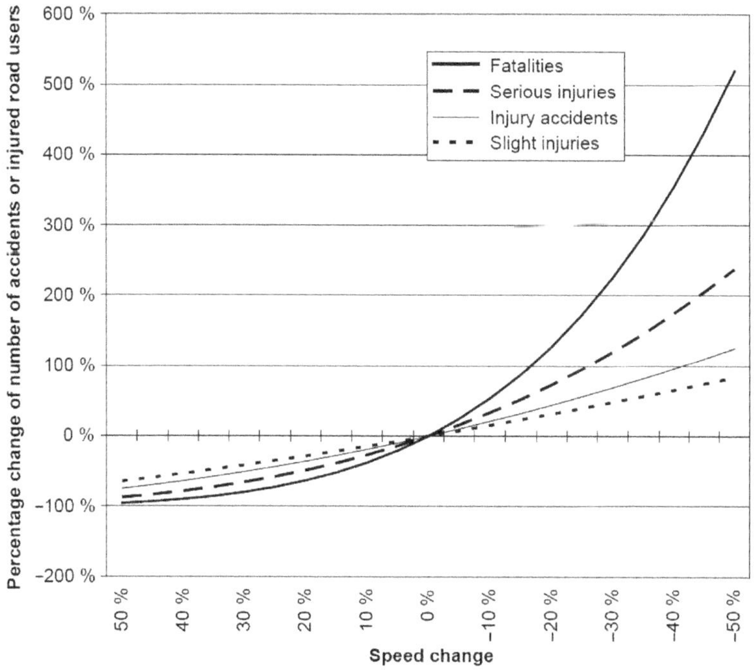

Figure 8-9. The effects of speed reductions or increases on injuries and accidents, as derived from the power functions. Combined for all roads: $\alpha = 4.5$ for fatalities, $\alpha = 3.5$ for serious injuries, $\alpha = 1.6$ for injury accidents, and $\alpha = 1.4$ for slight injuries (from Elvik *et al.*, 2009, with permission from Emerald Publishing).

Table 8-3. The change in relative risk of injury accidents and fatal accidents as a result of small increases and decreases in average traffic speeds for various prevailing speeds (from Hauer and Bonneson, 2006).

Injury Crashes	$\bar{v}_0$ **[mph]**						**Fatal Crashes**	$\bar{v}_0$ **[mph]**					
$\bar{v}_1 - \bar{v}_0$ **[mph]**	**30**	**40**	**50**	**60**	**70**	**80**	$\bar{v}_1 - \bar{v}_0$ **[mph]**	**30**	**40**	**50**	**60**	**70**	**80**
−5	0.57	0.66	0.71	0.75	0.78	0.81	−5	0.22	0.36	0.48	0.58	0.67	0.75
−4	0.64	0.72	0.77	0.80	0.83	0.85	−4	0.36	0.48	0.58	0.66	0.73	0.80
−3	0.73	0.79	0.83	0.85	0.87	0.88	−3	0.51	0.61	0.68	0.74	0.80	0.85
−2	0.81	0.86	0.88	0.90	0.91	0.92	−2	0.66	0.73	0.79	0.83	0.86	0.90
−1	0.90	0.93	0.94	0.95	0.96	0.96	−1	0.83	0.86	0.89	0.91	0.93	0.95
0	1.00	1.00	1.00	1.00	1.00	1.00	0	1.00	1.00	1.00	1.00	1.00	1.00
1	1.10	1.07	1.06	1.05	1.04	1.04	1	1.18	1.14	1.11	1.09	1.07	1.05
2	1.20	1.15	1.12	1.10	1.09	1.08	2	1.38	1.28	1.22	1.18	1.14	1.10
3	1.31	1.22	1.18	1.15	1.13	1.12	3	1.59	1.43	1.34	1.27	1.21	1.16
4	1.43	1.30	1.24	1.20	1.18	1.16	4	1.81	1.59	1.46	1.36	1.28	1.21
5	1.54	1.38	1.30	1.26	1.22	1.20	5	2.04	1.75	1.58	1.46	1.36	1.27

Concluding remarks on speed and crashes

The controversy and most of the research about the relationship between speed and crashes has evolved around three questions: what is the relationship between the absolute speed of a vehicle and its crash likelihood? What is the relationship between the deviation of a vehicle speed from the prevailing traffic speed and its crash likelihood? What is the relationship between the physical severity of impact in a crash and the injury severity of the occupants?

There is ample, but not unequivocal, evidence to indicate that on a given road, crash involvement rates of individual vehicles rise with increasing speeds. On urban streets there appears to be a strong relationship between crash rates and the absolute speed of crash-involved vehicles. However, this conclusion is based mainly on small data sets. When data from different road types are pooled together crash rates do not appear to increase with average road speed. This absence of effect has been termed "ecological fallacy" (Kockelman, 2006), that occurs when conclusions are drawn about disaggregate relationships – that may each exhibit a different pattern – from analyses of aggregate data that mask confounding variables. In the present case the confounding variables are the road design speed and enforcement levels that affect drivers' speed choices.

Variance is important. The absolute speed deviation of crash-involved vehicles from the average traffic speed appears to be positively related to crash probability, especially for rural arterial highways and motorways. This is not necessarily true for rural collector roads and urban streets, for which there are insufficient data to demonstrate such a relationship. The principal factor that accounts for the effects of speed deviation is not the conflict of a fast moving vehicle with a slow moving one, but the requirement to slow down to make turns and to enter and exit high-speed roads. Still, even when the effects of turning vehicles are removed from the data, some effects of speed deviation, especially at the extreme ends, remain, and they are most likely due to increased exposure to conflicts. But a cautionary note is needed here. The evidence for the relevance of speed dispersion in the traffic stream and the increased risk of slow-moving vehicles comes from correlational analyses that include slowing vehicles (rather than only slow-moving vehicles). When slowing vehicles are removed from the data, the over-involvement of the remaining slow-moving vehicles is greatly diminished. Furthermore, because the conclusions are not based on cause-and-effect analyses they cannot be used to suggest that if the same slow-moving drivers were to increase their speeds, their crash probability would be reduced.

With respect to the relationship between crash speeds and injuries, the data are unequivocal: the risk of injuries and fatalities increases as a function of impact speed or Delta-V. The many studies conducted on this relationship almost without exception indicate that the relationship is one of a power function in which a linear increase in speed is associated with an exponential increase in the likelihood of injury, especially a severe one. This power coefficient or exponent increases with injury severity so that the risk of fatality per million kilometers is raised to the fourth power of the average speed change. This means that small reductions in average speed can yield very high savings in lives – and vice versa.

Speeding Countermeasures

"Everywhere, speed limits are widely flouted" (Allsop, 1995). In urban and residential areas where speed limits in many European countries are set at 30 km/hr (to protect the vulnerable pedestrians) more than 50 percent of the drivers exceed the speed limits (McKenna, 2005), and in select study locations speeding violations exceed 90 percent (Haglund and Åberg, 2002). In Europe, across countries the percent of drivers exceeding the speed limit in urban roads ranges from a low of approximately 20 percent (the Czech Republic and Switzerland) to 80 percent (Poland) (ETSC, 2011). In a recent Norwegian survey 23 percent of the drivers thought that it was acceptable to drive at speeds of 100 mph (160 km/hr)(!) on rural roads when there were no other cars or pedestrians around (Iversen and Rundmo, 2004). Driving at speeds that exceed the posted speed limits is a world-wide phenomenon (NHTSA, 2012b; NRSA, 2014). For example, in the 22-country SARTRE survey 51-60 percent of the respondents in the different countries reported exceeding the speed limit on motorways (Yannis *et al.*, 2013). Given the rampant violation of speed limits and the implied approval of speeding as normative behavior, multiple efforts have been directed at educating the public about the risks of speeding, changing drivers' attitudes toward speeding, encouraging drivers to reduce their speeds, and ultimately at enforcing speed limits. This discussion will focus primarily on approaches to reduce speeds on inter-urban roads where the prevailing speeds and speed limits are high. Countermeasures to reduce speeds in urban streets and residential neighborhoods, where speed limits are set at 50 km/hr or less are discussed in Chapter 15 in the context of pedestrian safety.

Organizational/policy approaches

Setting speed limits

At the national level every country legislates speed limits in accordance with several criteria including the road design speed (quality of shoulders, lane width, divided versus undivided, etc.), the land use (such as residential, commercial, school, urban, rural), and the purpose of the road (such as motorway, main road, urban street, etc.). In general, the speed limit is a political decision that is a compromise between maximal safety (0 km/hr) and maximal mobility (no limit). Thus in urban areas, for the safety of pedestrians most countries set the speed limit at 50 km/hr, with even lower limits in high-risk areas such as hospitals and school zones. In inter-urban areas most EU countries set a speed limit of 130 km/hr for freeways and motorways (Germany – the land of Porsche, BMW, Mercedes and Audi – excepted), with lower limits on lower service-level roads, especially rural undivided two-lane roads (OECD, 2014). Even in Germany, a poll conducted in 2015 showed that the majority of Germans for the first time ever support a maximum speed limit on roads where there is no limit – but only if it were set at 150 km/hr. However, half of the older German drivers support the EU 130 km/hr limit (ETSC, 2015a). Nonetheless, the German federal transport minister – "reclining on the bonnet of his BMW" – ruled out an end to unlimited speeds on the motorways, despite the fact that the fatality rates on the German motorways per kilometers driven are higher than those of the Nordic countries, the Netherlands, the United Kingdom, France, and Austria (ETSC, 2015b).

When drivers can perceive the criteria used to set speed limits and their relevance, they also perceive the speed limit as "reasonable" and half the battle is already won. However, what is "reasonable" differs among different road users. Most drivers tend to base their judgment of "reasonable" on subjective risk rather than on objective risk, and the former is based on biased bounded rationality and not on objective rationality. For this reason alone speed choice needs to be regulated by speed limits (Elvik, 2010). Elvik (2010) also lists five additional reasons for setting speed limits: (1) Drivers tend to ignore or minimize the importance of the impact of speed that they do not readily perceived, such as the environmental effects in terms of increased pollution and energy consumption. (2) Drivers misperceive the correlation between speed and travel time, overestimating the benefits of small increases in high speeds and underestimating the benefits of small increases in low speeds. (3) Drivers underestimate the effect of speeds on crash probability and severity; because they do not think of the impact of speed on kinetic energy. (4) Drivers underestimate impact speed when a crash is unavoidable, but braking can reduce injury. (5) Drivers' estimates of "safe speeds" are quite heterogeneous, and therefore contribute to speed variance, a factor that is linked to increase in crash risk. For these reasons and because of the issues discussed below, the determination of safe speed, and consequently the speed limit, is better left to the professional road designer and authorities than to the driver.

In a survey of Swedish drivers Johansson-Stenman and Martinsson (2005) found that younger drivers and drivers of newer cars generally favor higher speed limits than older drivers and drivers of older cars. Thus, there is probably a significant self-serving component in the concept of reasonableness. Furthermore, not all of the criteria that make a speed limit reasonable to the highway designer are self-evident to the passing driver, and some of them may conflict with others. All of these considerations make legislation a necessary component in speed management, but far from a sufficient one. Setting speed limits is also a hotly debated political issue (ETSC, 2015a, 2015b), at least in part because they do not automatically generate a corresponding change in traffic speeds and crash rates, and it is not always clear when such changes will have the desired safety benefit (McCoy *et al.*, 1993).

In general, changes are applied where they are already perceived as reasonable – at least to some of the road users. A case in point is a pilot project conducted in Edmonton, Canada (El-Basyouny and El-Bassiouni, 2013). In this project the city of Edmonton decided to reduce urban injuries by lowering the speed limits from 50 km/hr to 40 km/hr in six residential areas. Pre- and post-change surveys of the residents of these communities showed that the change resulted in a reduction in the residents' concerns for safety issues in their communities, a reduction in perceived speeding, and an increase in the perceived safety. These findings indicate that when applied judiciously, speed limit reductions are acceptable to the motoring public. Thus, it is no surprise that changing the speed limits, in general, results in significant speed changes and significant changes in crashes and injuries.

Reductions in speed limits are typically accompanied by increased enforcement. However, across the various levels and types of enforcement applied, there is a strong relationship between the change in the speed limit and the change in speed, as summarized by Elvik *et al.* (2009) and reproduced in Figure 8-10, where it can be seen that a change in the speed limit by 10 km/hr leads to a predicted change in the average speed of approximately 2.5 km/hr. Given the discussion above, such a change is likely to have a very significant impact on injuries. As an illustration, in 2001 Belgium lowered the speed limits from 90 km/hr to 70 km/hr in many select inter-urban high-risk locations. The effect of this change – after controlling for trend effects with a comparison set of sections where the speed limit has not been changed – was a five percent decrease in the rate of all crashes, and a 33 percent(!) reduction in severe injury and fatal crashes (De Pauw *et al.*, 2014). A sample of the effects of changes in speed limits – lowering or raising them – is provided in Table 8-4. Though somewhat dated with data from the 1980s, the resulting changes in average traffic speeds and fatalities are still relevant and quite consistent with the relationships observed between speed and fatalities from other

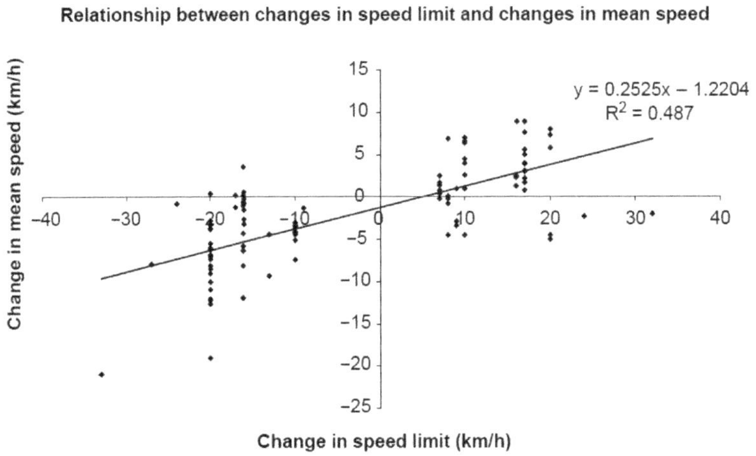

Figure 8-10. The relationship between changes in speed limits and changes in speed, on the basis of 51 independent studies (from Elvik *et al.*, 2009, p. 448, with permission from Emerald Publishing).

Table 8-4. Effects of speed limit changes on speeds and on fatalities (from European Transport Safety Council, 1995, cited with permission from the World Health Organization).

Year	Country	Type of Road	Speed Limit Change	Change in Speed	Reduction in Fatalities
1985	Switzerland	Motorways	130 km/hr to 120 km/hr	5 km/hr *decrease* in mean speeds	12%
1985	Switzerland	Rural roads	100 km/hr to 80 km/hr	10 km/hr *decrease* in mean speeds	6%
1985	Denmark	Roads in built-up areas	60 km/hr to 50 km/hr	3-4 km/hr *decrease* in mean speeds	24%
1987	U.S.	Interstate highways	55 mph (89 km/hr) to 65 mph (105 km/hr)	2-4 mph (3.2-6.4 km/hr) *increase* in mean speeds	19-34% *increase*
1989	Sweden	Motorways	110 km/hr to 90 km/hr	14.4 km/hr *decrease* in median speeds	21%

more recent data sources described above. It is important to note that in most of these cases, in addition to the "reasonablencss" used to justify the change, when the speed limit was lowered the change was accompanied by enhanced enforcement.

Given the quite conclusive data on the safety benefits of lowering speed limits, one has to remember that such policy initiatives are still a hard sell. By and large, most law makers try to cater to their constituents and their supporters, and the latter are not always sympathetic to restrictions on their individual freedom – as speed is often thought of. Thus, in the U.S., in the face of all the data, and despite the national agenda to reduce speeding and lower traffic deaths, when the a national maximum speed limit of 55 mph was repealed, most states raised the maximum speed limit on rural freeways – to as high as 85 mph (137 km/hr) in Texas and 80 mph (129 km/hr) in Idaho, Wyoming, and Utah (IIHS, 2014). This is a lamentable far cry from the 55 mph (88 km/hr) national maximum speed limit imposed in 1974 following the oil embargo.

A potential alternative to fixed speed limit reductions is a dynamic approach of changing the speed limit. A dynamic speed limit system is one where the speed limit is regulated and changed according to time of day, conditions of driving, congestion, etc. The advent of electronic speed limit signs, interactive navigation systems, and Intelligent Speed Adaptation (ISA) make such systems a practical possibility. The sensitivity of such systems to local and temporal circumstances is that they can optimize safety and credibility of the speed limit (Van Nes, Brandenburg, and Twisk, 2010), thus leading to greater compliance than with static traditional limits. Assuming – as most of the previous studies indicate – that speed variance is one source of collisions, Van Nes and her colleagues tested the effects of a dynamic speed limit system on intra- and inter-driver speed variance on Dutch drivers in a driving simulator. The dynamic system presented reduced speed limits in the presence of fog and in the presence of heavy traffic (on a two-lane road). As hypothesized, homogeneity of speed increased with the dynamic speed limits, and more so with the more sophisticated system where the speed limits were displayed in the vehicle. As expected, and possibly because of this, drivers had more confidence and gave greater credibility to the dynamic systems (and more to the more sophisticated in-vehicle one). This last finding is consistent with previous results obtained by Goldenbeld and van Schagen (2007) on data collected in the Netherlands. They found that the credibility of various road segments all having the same speed limit of 60 km/hr varied widely, with the perceived safe speed greatly dependent on visual characteristics of the site. Thus, dynamic speed limits tackle the issue of "selling" speed limits to the drivers by making them more reasonable or credible. Although the findings from this simulator study are very suggestive, they still have to be confirmed on the road and the impact of variable speed limit signs on crash reductions still has to be demonstrated.

Administrative actions

A common penalty for violating traffic laws is to charge the driver with demerit points; a system in which a driver's licensing authority issues demerits or penalty points to drivers on conviction for road traffic offenses. This approach is now common in the Western world and most OECD countries have them. The specifics of each program vary widely, and that may account for differing opinions about the program's effectiveness. To be effective the system should (1) have a good relationship between points charged and crash risk, (2) be limited to serious offences only, (3) be transparent and comprehensible in order to gain public knowledge and acceptance, (4) provide for means of recuperating points through remedial courses, (5) be accompanied by consistent enforcement, and (6) have a deterrence of loss of license for serious offenders and recidivists (ETSC, 2008). In most countries the most common point offence is speeding as it is widespread, the most commonly reported violation, and consistently related to crash risk. According to the European Transport Safety Council (ETSC, 2008) when consistent with the above criteria, the approach is very effective in reducing speeding and crashes as evidenced by case studies in Australia, Denmark and Spain.

An interesting novel approach to reduce speeding is to rely more on the carrot than on the stick; to provide an incentive to maintain the desired speed rather than penalize for exceeding it. In an empirical test of this approach Reagan and his associates (Reagan *et al.*, 2013; Reagan and Bliss, 2013b) equipped eight cars with an intelligent speed adaptation system (ISA – see Chapter 19) that detects and notifies the driver whenever he or she exceeds the speed limit. The system was set to provide a warning whenever the speed limit was exceeded by 5 mph or more. One group of drivers received information feedback whenever they exceeded the speed limit and another group received an incentive feedback in the form of deduction of a fixed sum from a maximal total bonus whenever they exceeded the speed limit by 5 mph or more. The result showed a clear-cut advantage of the bonus system. In the presence of the feedback only drivers drove at the same speeds as drivers in a control group who received neither; driving within the speed limit approximately 70 percent of the time. However, the addition of the monetary incentive increased that percentage to 80 percent (Reagan *et al.*, 2013). The authors argue that such a system may be practical too. For example, insurance companies could provide non-speeding drivers with reductions in the insurance premiums. Still, there was one drawback to this approach. Drivers in the incentive conditions reported higher levels of subjective mental demand, temporal demand, frustration, and effort (Reagan and Bliss, 2013). Thus, once again it appears that there is a cost to driving at speeds outside our comfort zone.

Behavioral approaches

Education

Educating the motoring public about the dangers of speeding has been difficult, as reflected by the common violation of the speed limits. In the study we conducted in Israel (Figure 8-4, Shinar, 2001), there were very few drivers who did not know the speed limits on the roads in which they were driving. What many drivers do not appreciate are the effects of speed on vehicle control and crash involvement and the effects of speed on injury severity (TRB, 1998). Most driver training manuals try to address the first issue by displaying stopping distance charts that illustrate the increase in stopping distance as a function of the increase in speeds. Although the stopping distance is a power function of the speed, most people quickly forget the stopping distances (to the extent that they ever knew them), and the power function that relates speed to impact force and injury severity is generally ignored in the teaching materials. This is a potentially fatal handicap. For example, when driving at a speed of 50 km/hr given a reaction time of 1.0 second and abrupt braking, a driver can stop before hitting an obstacle (child?) detected 35 meters ahead. However at a speed of 80 km/hr the car would hit that obstacle at a speed of over 60 km/hr, enough to potentially kill a pedestrian (see Chapter 15).

There are, however, special educational programs that are designed to increase "speed awareness" of licensed drivers; mostly through classroom presentations, discussions, and demonstrations. These courses do cover the relationships between speed and crash likelihood and severity, as well as additional topics such as the purpose and rationale for speed limits, the penalties in violating them, the driver's responsibility for speed choice, likelihood of being detected by various enforcement techniques, and safe driving tips. Speed awareness programs for drivers convicted for speeding violations are apparently quite common in the United Kingdom and several studies have evaluated their effectiveness (Fylan *et al.*, 2006; McKenna, 2005). As expected, most of the studies show that drivers who attend the courses state that they are less inclined to violate the speed limits after the completion of the course than before it. In a few studies that tracked the drivers' actual behavior, drivers who attended the courses also had lower re-arrest rates than drivers who did not attend these courses (Fylan *et al.*, 2006). Unfortunately, most of these studies were not conducted by objective researchers, but by the course organizers, with vested interest in proving the effectiveness of their courses. Also, the studies may suffer from sampling bias, so that those who need them the most – and are the most resistant to change – may not take them.

Therefore, if attitudes toward speeding are to be changed, we need to focus on the emotional and behavioral components of the attitude toward speeding rather than on the cognitive component. To change the emotional component from feeling comfort, pleasure, and thrill to feeling discomfort, tension, and fear is not easy. Every time we speed we tend to experience the former and not the latter. The most common method of changing our feelings about speeding is through negative advertising campaigns in which speeding is associated with negative consequences: a crash or arrest. But the most common way of changing our behavioral inclination and actual behavior is through enforcement in high-speed roads, and through traffic calming in low-speed – residential – zones.

Enforcement

The primary role of speed enforcement is the same as that of all other speed management techniques: deterrence. Although some drivers believe that the police are out there to get them, the police officers, in general, are more interested in preventing speeding than in catching speeders. Enforcement of speed limits appears to be the most common type of traffic law enforcement. As the police develop ever more sophisticated means of apprehending violators, the motoring public develops ever more sophisticated means of countering these efforts. This engages the police and the motoring public in a cat-and-mouse game. And in this game the 'mouse' driving the car is not helpless. If the majority of drivers violate the speed limits, they are very hard to enforce. The police then have no recourse but to allow most drivers to violate the speed limits with impunity, while focusing on the extreme speeders. A major problem with this approach is that it reinforces the notion that violations of traffic laws are an acceptable norm. In the U.S. during the last years of the national 55 mph speed limit, the public greatly ignored the speed limits and the police had to allow for a large tolerance. On motorways with high design speeds, laws limiting the maximum speed to 55 mph cause drivers to question the reasonableness of the speed limit, and consequently violate it in masses. This is the situation in Israel where most divided inter-urban highways have a maximum speed limit of 90 km/hr. Approximately 50 percent of the drivers exceed it in many locations, and the police officially announce that they do not enforce it until it has been exceeded by at least 10 km/hr. An alternative way to deal with this problem is to raise the speed limit and then allow very little tolerance. This method makes the job much easier for the police, reduces the number of "criminals on the road," and improves the consistency of the enforcement, making it a much more effective deterrent. The potential risk of this approach is that raising the speed limit is a one-time act that may be embraced by many drivers as a license to increase their speed, while stricter and more visible enforcement requires a sustained organizational effort that may be hard to implement especially in the face of initial strong public resistance.

In general, the rules to effective enforcement are the same as the rules of schedules of reinforcement formulated by B.F. Skinner on the basis of observations of pigeons and rats: the more consistent and intense (i.e., everywhere and visible) the enforcement, the greater the rate of compliance; the more immediate the feedback (i.e., the citation or arrest) the greater its effectiveness. These principles have been demonstrated repeatedly in many studies (e.g., De Waard and Rooijers, 1994; Shinar and McKnight, 1985). One contested issue concerns the severity of the penalty, or typically the amount of the fine. To be effective, according to behavioral theory the fine should be meaningful enough to deter the driver from committing the violation. In most countries the fines for specific offences, including speeding are fixed. However, it is obvious that the same fixed fine is not equally meaningful (or painful) to a pauper and a prince (at least a rich prince). To make it psychologically equivalent, Finland links the amount of the penalty to the violator's income on the basis of a concept of "day-fine": the person's earning in a day of work. Thus, a penalty that is equivalent to X number of days in jail equals a person's earning in so many days, based on his reported income for the previous year (Wikipedia, 2015). The amount of earning of course, differs, and consequently so does the fine. This has generated some extra-ordinary speeding fines for the very rich, exceeding 100,000(!) Euros (e.g., Pinsker, 2015). Interestingly, this concept of justice is not new. Already in 1748 Montesquieu, the French philosopher, wondered "cannot pecuniary penalties be proportionate to fortunes?" Though income-based fines may be perceived as fair by many, the application of this concept in Finland has generated extreme rage among the rich, and it's effectiveness in terms of highway safety remains to be tested.

The halo effects of enforcement – both in time and in place – also follow the psychological laws of schedules of reinforcement. Bracket and his associates demonstrated that a variable schedule of speed enforcement has longer lasting effects than a fixed schedule of daily enforcement that is abruptly terminated (Brackett and Beecher, 1980; Brackett and Edwards, 1977). The duration of the halo effect has been estimated to be at least 2 weeks

(Talebpour and Mahmassani, 2014), indicating that for enforcement to be perceived as consistent and persistent it need not be in the same place every day.

An interesting issue concerns the punitive effects of enforcement. Does an arrest or citation serve as a deterrent to future violations? The answer appears to be yes. Redelmeier, Tibshirani, and Evans (2003) studied the violation histories of 8,975 Canadian licensed drivers involved in fatal crashes. They discovered that the risk of a fatal crash within a month of citation for a violation was 35 percent lower than within a month with no citations for violations. This effect of citations declined with time, so that after 3-4 months it dissipated completely. They also found that the effect was greater when the citation was accompanied by penalty points. These results then indicate that actual convictions have a deterring effect and a safety benefit for their recipients – even though they are probably the last to acknowledge it.

When enforcement is conspicuous, it is quite effective but highly localized. Drivers tend to respond to the visible (or perceived) presence of enforcement by slowing down, but once drivers pass the officer, they tend to resume their speed. The effectiveness of enforcement is directly related to its perceived threat, which in turn is mostly affected by the likelihood of arrest (Shinar and McKnight, 1985). That is why, to maximize enforcement the driver has to see many police cars (that actually seem to enforce the speed limits). One effective method to increase the perceived presence is to use a mix of marked and unmarked police vehicles, and make sure through mass media, that the motoring public is aware of the presence of both. This has been shown to be a most effective strategy in the U.S. (Shinar and McKnight, 1985) and in Australia (Diamantopoulou and Cameron, 2002). Although the effects of enforcement on crash reduction are indirect, quasi-experimental studies that compared crash and injury rates before and after intensive enforcement with the change in crashes and injuries over the same time period in control sites, generally report significant reductions in crashes, especially serious injury and fatal crashes (Bjørnskau and Elvik, 1992; Goldenbeld and Schagen, 2005). More details about enforcement effects on crash and injury reductions are discussed in Chapter 19.

We have three measures with which we can evaluate the direct effects of speed enforcement on speed: (1) the extent of the speed reduction, (2) the spatial halo in terms of the distance at which speeds are still depressed, and (3) the temporal halo in terms of the duration of the speed reductions following the removal of the visible enforcement. Various paradigms of enforcement have been evaluated to determine the most effective strategy to maximize the effects on all three measures. A detailed discussion of the relative benefits of each is beyond the scope of this discussion, but is available elsewhere (Shinar and McKnight, 1985). This discussion will only briefly note the benefits of stationary and moving police enforcement, and the benefits of automated and programmable enforcement.

Moving versus stationary enforcement

One means of increasing a driver's exposure to the police officer is by having the officer drive the car rather than park it. While this increases the duration of exposure for those exposed, it reduces the total number of drivers exposed to the enforcement. Still, for those drivers who do pass by the officer, it is important to see how effective each strategy is in reducing speed, and how far does it extend beyond the passing point. We measured this in a study that we conducted in Israel on an inter-urban divided highway posted at 90 km/hr (Shinar and Stiebel, 1986). A total of 541 drivers who exceeded the speed limit by 2 km/hr or more before they were within sight of the officer were recorded, and their speeds were then measured again immediately before reaching the officer (when they reached or were close to their lowest speed), and then 4 kilometers down the road beyond the officer, when they were no longer in sight of the police vehicle. The responses of the speeding drivers to the two modes of visible enforcement were quite different. Prior to seeing the police the average speed was approximately 11.5 km/hr above the speed limit. In the presence of a parked police vehicle drivers reduced their speed to 4 km/hr below the speed limit, whereas when the police vehicle was moving they reduced their speed to within 0.5 km of the speed limit. But the greatest effect of the type of enforcement was in the halo effect 4 km after passing the police. At that point the drivers exposed to the moving police were still proceeding within the speed limit (actually 1 km/hr below it). But the drivers who passed the stationary police had by that point increased their speed to 4 km/hr above the speed limit. Thus, the stationary enforcement is more effective at the specific location, but the moving enforcement has a greater halo effect. Apparently drivers perceive the stationary police officer as more threatening (that is why he is there – to enforce the traffic code), but consider the moving officer as more likely to come up behind them after they had already passed him. In either case, an important conclusion is that some residual halo effect of localized enforcement remains even after four km. Therefore the deployment of enforcement should be well advertised and often even advertised by signs in the immediate vicinity of the enforcement activity.

Automated enforcement

A more cost-efficient way to enforce speed limits is through automated enforcement using speed cameras. Contrary to some motorists' beliefs, their primary purpose is not to catch violators but to regulate and increase speed compliance. In fact the installation of such cameras, without advance signing is not recommended because speeding drivers may detect them suddenly and then brake abruptly causing rear-end crashes (Kang, 2002). As a way of increasing their effectiveness "dummy" camera boxes are installed in multiple locations, and actual cameras are then rotated among them, so drivers perceive a higher density of automatic enforcement than there actually is. In general these cameras are placed in the vicinity of high-crash locations. However, in Victoria, Australia, and parts of Korea they are designed to cover complete roadway networks, in order to produce system-wide compliance with speed limits. An alternative low-tech approach is to place dummy cardboard cutouts of uniformed police along the roadway. This manipulation has been tried with some success in Belgium (ETSC, 2015c).

Evaluations of the effectiveness of speed cameras in speed reductions have been unequivocal: they work (TRB, 2011). In addition to speed reductions, they quite consistently result in crash and injury reductions (for reviews see Li, Graham, and Majumdar, 2013;

Pilkington and Kinra, 2005; WHO, 2004). Reductions in crashes have been recorded both at the specific sites and system-wide. For example, Pilkington and Kinra (2005) reviewed 14 observational studies that compared crash frequencies before and after installation of the cameras. They reported wide ranges of effectiveness: drops of 5-69 percent for crashes, 12-65 percent for injuries, and 17-71 percent for fatalities. Furthermore, there seemed to be no habituation response to the cameras and the effects remained for as long as the evaluations were carried out (3-4 years after installation in some cases). A formal evaluation by Elvik and his associates Elvik *et al.* (2009) based on meta-analysis of 16 studies from nine different countries, published between 1993 and 2008 essentially confirmed these findings, as summarized in Table 8-5. All the studies included in their analysis of the effects of fixed cameras included a comparison group, and the effect size has been adjusted for various potential confounding factors (see Chapter 2). A more recent qualitative analysis of 35 studies meeting strict methodological inclusion criterion by the Cochrane Review Collaboration (Wilson *et al.*, 2010) concluded that speed cameras are effective in both speed reductions and crash and injury reductions. Specifically, they noted that average speed reductions were 1-15 percent, and the percent of speeding vehicles dropped by 14-65 percent. Most important, in the 28 studies that measured the effects on crashes, injury and fatal crashes were reduced by 11-44 percent.

One explanation for the very large differences in effectiveness among studies is the heterogeneity in the evaluation methodologies, the context, and the locations in which the different studies were done (Wilson *et al.*, 2010). Thus, differences in the pre-camera speeds, geometric features of the road, crash experience, and users may have been responsible for the large differences in measured effectiveness. Also, more than half of the studies evaluated by Wilson *et al.* did not have control sites. Therefore, it is likely that some of the observed effects were due to other interventions and not necessarily the cameras. Finally, when measured, the effects seemed to encompass the extensive vicinity of the camera sites as well. This could be because the cameras had large halo effects or because the effects attributed to the cameras were at least in part due to other confounding factors. Of these two explanations the first is less likely because camera locations are well advertised and drivers slowdown in these specific locations. Thus, while the weight of the evidence indicates that speed cameras are effective safety devices, their exact contribution remains to be assessed in better controlled studies.

Perhaps the largest scale deployment and best known example of the effectiveness of automated speed enforcement and speed cameras is the national speed enforcement initiated by President Chirac in France. In July 2002 President Chirac announced that reducing road casualties is one of the top priorities of his next term. At that time France's fatality rate per 100,000 people was significantly higher than the average for the OECD countries, and nearly twice as high as that of Sweden (a leader in road safety – see Chapter 1). Recognizing that excessive speed was ubiquitous (60 percent of recorded speeds were above the speed limit), the program focused on massive automated speed enforcement and increased penalties for traffic violations – thereby fulfilling three key ingredients for effective enforcement: high visibility, high likelihood of apprehension, and immediate and significant penalties (citations were sent to violators within 8 days,

Table 8-5. Effects of speed cameras on accidents, with estimates derived from meta-analysis of 16 well-controlled studies (from Elvik *et al.*, 2009., p. 891, with permission from Emerald Publishing).

Characteristics of Enforcement	**Percentage Change in the Number of Accidents**		
	Accident severity	**Best estimate**	**95% confidence interval**
Fixed (visible) speed cameras			
All	Unspecified		
	Without control for publication bias:	−24	(−29; −19)
	With control for publication bias:	−16	(−23; −8)
All	Fatal accidents	−39	(−60; −7)
Less than doubled enforcement	Unspecified severity	−17	(−28; −5)
More than doubled enforcement	Unspecified severity	−35	(−51; −15)
New type of enforcement	Unspecified severity	−24	(−29; −19)
Mobile (hidden) speed cameras			
All	Injury accidents	−10	(−22; +4)
All	Fatal accidents	−16	(−33; +5)
Section control			
All	Injury accidents	−30	(−61; +25)

and fines and points increased relative to the excess speed). Between 2003 and 2010 over 2,750 cameras were installed and activated (approximately two-thirds in fixed locations and one third in marked and unmarked police cruisers). The initiative and the programs were widely publicized and consequently over that period the percent of drivers exceeding the speed limit by 10 km/hr or more dropped from 27 to 10 percent. Based on time series analysis that controlled for some potential confounding factors traffic fatalities per 100,000 people fell by a relatively stable 21 percent (Carnis and Blais, 2013; ONISR, 2010), bringing France to the median EU level in 2010 of 63 deaths per million inhabitants (Jost and Allsop, 2014).

Section control

Section control refers to the use of cameras to control the speed along a segment of the road, and not just at a specific point where a camera is located. Two approaches have been applied and evaluated. The first is the use of "*section cameras*" where *average* speed is enforced on a given road segment based on the time difference in passing two cameras at the two ends of the segment. Obviously, this approach is most appropriate for limited-access roads and motorways and is not appropriate for urban streets. Høye (2014) evaluated this technique at 14 Norwegian sites (eight of which were in tunnels), and even after controlling for various confounding factors, she obtained a remarkable 49-54 percent reduction in the number of severely injured or killed occupants. Soole, Watson, and Fleiter (2013) reviewed 26 independent assessments of this technique, conducted in six different countries (Australia, Austria, France, Italy, Netherlands, and the United Kingdom). Generalizing across all studies, the method was effective in just about all the measures examined: increased rate of compliance with speed limits, reductions in average and 85th percentile speeds, reduced speed variability between vehicles, and – most important – reductions in crash rates, especially fatal and serious injury crashes. The technique has some other unique benefits that are not obtained by traditional spot checks. In the authors' won words: "the approach has been shown to improve traffic flow, reduce vehicle emissions and has also been associated with high levels of public acceptance. Average speed enforcement offers a greater network-wide approach to managing speeds that reduces the impact of time and distance-halo effects associated with other automated speed enforcement approaches." Thus, with the possible exception of intelligent speed adaptation (ISA – see Chapter 19; ETSC, 2013), section cameras may be as close to panacea for speed control as we can possibly get.

The second approach to section control is that of "speed corridors." In speed corridors a limited number of cameras are regularly moved along a certain road section to prevent habituation to fixed camera locations. This approach can complement section cameras as it is most appropriate for urban settings and low-speed zones. An evaluation of this technique by Hu and McCartt (2015) demonstrated that it is quite effective in both speed and crash reductions. In their study they evaluated the effects of speed cameras installed in one county in the state of Maryland, with crashes in two nearby counties in Virginia. Using logistic regression they found that the cameras were associated with a 59 percent reduction in exceeding the speed limit by 10+ mph, and with a 39 percent reduction in the likelihood of an incapacitating injury or fatal crash. This is huge positive effect considering that the cameras were limited to zones of 35 mph or less. Two other aspects of this study were noteworthy. First, that the effect of the automatic speed enforcement was evaluated 7 years after the cameras were installed; that is, after a lengthy period of adaptation. Second, that the speed enforcement over a whole corridor rather than at fixed spots sent the drivers a message that a speed camera may be in use anywhere along the road segment, and not just in one or several specific locations, thus negating the tendency to speed up between camera locations. Interestingly, Hu and McCartt also surveyed local residents about the cameras. They discovered that nearly all of them were aware of the cameras and most of them supported the automated enforcement despite the fact that most of them had either received a camera-generated ticket or knew someone who did. Thus, it seems that in the proper context (and culture?) automated enforcement may be quite acceptable.

Yet, despite their cost-effectiveness in speed management (or perhaps because of it), speed cameras generate significant public resistance, to the point of an effective outcry. Thus, in England in 2007 – exactly because of their efficiency in detecting speeding drivers – more than 28,000 people signed a Downing Street petition calling for speed cameras to be scrapped (Kirkup and Millward, 2007), and consequently the number of speed cameras in the United Kingdom was reduced from its high of 6,000 in 2007. In the U.S. 2011 survey most respondents felt that "Speed cameras are used to generate revenue" (70 percent), rather than "to prevent accidents" (55 percent). Yet, approximately 85 percent of the respondents felt that they are useful in "school zones" or "where there have been many accidents" (Schroeder *et al.*, 2013).

How much enforcement?

The review so far should have been quite convincing that speed enforcement is effective in speed reduction and injury reduction. Yet how much enforcement is needed to achieve a predetermined goal? One laudable attempt to quantify this has been made by Elvik (2011). In his analysis Elvik fitted crash modification functions to 12 different studies that evaluated the effectiveness of various enforcement levels. A crash modification function is a mathematical formula that expresses the amount of benefit (e.g., percent reduction in injuries) that can be gained from a given type and amount of effort (e.g., level of enforcement). It quickly became apparent that each study yielded a different – and often inexplicable – function. Therefore, Elvik pooled data from similar conditions to reduce the variance, and on the basis of 11 studies and 16 data points, generated a best-fitting crash modification function that related the relative increase in enforcement to the expected reduction in crashes. This relationship was quite stable and linear for increases in effort up to doubling the original one, yielding a 20 percent reduction in crashes when the enforcement effort is doubled. Further increases in enforcement were also accompanied by further crash reductions but the noise in the data points around the fitted function was probably too large for making robust quantitative estimates.

How does enforcement compare to speed calming through roadway design?

One study in which direct comparisons were made between speed cameras and engineering approaches to speed reductions concluded that speed cameras are less effective in crash reductions than either speed bumps or a variety of horizontal treatments of the roadway such as narrowing, mini-roundabouts, chicanes, and speed activated signs (Hirst, Mountain, and Maher, 2005; Mountain, Hirst, and Maher, 2005). In this study on 149 30 mph sites in England, the researchers compared the speeds before and after the implementation of the treatment. Unfortunately, here too no comparisons were made with control sites that were not modified. Also, even if the researchers' conclusions are accepted at face value, they do not imply that wherever speed cameras are placed they should be replaced by road pavement modifications. This is because often the intervention of choice is dictated by external considerations, such as environmental considerations and public acceptance. For example, speed cameras are appropriate for all posted speed limits, whereas road bumps and narrowing are only appropriate in low speed zones.

Environmental approaches

The environmental approaches cover a whole range from redesigning the road to fit driver behavior, to the posting of advisory signs to change driver behavior to accommodate the current road design speeds. As one might suspect, the latter is the least expensive, though probably the least efficient (e.g., Daniels *et al.*, 2010). Environmental approaches labeled traffic calming – using speed bumps, rumble strips, replacing intersections with roundabouts, and lane narrowing at cross walks – have all been effective to various degrees at speed reductions. One interesting study that compared 20 different environmental treatments in the same driving environment and on the same drivers was conducted in a driving simulator by Jamson, Lai, and Jamson (2010). Because the ambient driving environment was controlled, and all drivers experienced all treatments, Jamson and her associates were able to evaluate the relative effectiveness of the different treatments. Thus, they found that various alerting treatments had more impact on speed than others, particularly in an urban environment. Rumble strips, pedestrian refuges, and variable (i.e., programmable) advisory speed signs were some of the more effective speed reduction techniques. As most of these treatments are geared to reduce speeds in order to prevent and reduce injuries to pedestrians crossing the road, they are discussed in more detail in the context of pedestrian safety (Chapter 15).

Perceptual countermeasures

Early theoretical analysis on how we perceive motion led Gibson (1979) to suggest that our sense of speed is governed primarily by the rate of the optical flow of images on the periphery of our retina. Thus, driving down a straight road in the middle of the desert with very few objects alongside the road would produce very little peripheral movement. In contrast, driving down a road with the same geometry but bounded by trees on the two shoulders should produce a greater flow of stimuli across the retinas and consequently a greater sense of speed. This had led some researchers to propose that one way to counteract inappropriate speed cues is to artificially create cues that would enhance drivers' sense of their speed. The basic idea behind this approach is to create on-the-road visual illusions. The most commonly applied perceptual modification has been to paint stripes across the roads with diminishing distance between them. That way, a driver proceeding at a constant speed would actually perceive speed cues that suggest that his or her speed is increasing – because the stripes would traverse the driver's retina at an increasing rate. The approach was first tried successfully both in a simulator and on the road by Denton (1971, 1973) in the United Kingdom, and later on roads in the U.S. (Shinar, McDowell, and Rockwell, 1977), Australia (Fildes and Jarvis, 1994; Godley, Triggs, and Fildes, 2000), and New Zealand (Charlton, 2004). Manser and Hancock

(2007) demonstrated a similar slowing effect in a simulated tunnel whose walls were painted with vertical strips that became progressively thinner. In our early studies we also tried and demonstrated the effectiveness of other perceptual modifications such as painting a herringbone illusion in the approach to the curve, and widening the edge lines in the apex of a curve so that the road would seem narrower from the driver's perspective. Despite promising results, this approach has not been widely implemented nor evaluated for long-term benefits.

Public information and highway signs

Public information campaigns

Social marketing of anti-speeding is very common, and is typically done by arousing fear. A typical commercial would show a speeding driver and a resulting crash or arrest by police. There is lack of agreement among researchers about the benefits of 'fear appeals' in general, and not just for driving (e.g., to counteract smoking, drug use, etc.). There is, however, evidence – both empirical and theoretical – that fear appeals are more effective when accompanied by a practical fear-relief strategy. The theoretical argument is that when fear is aroused a person seeks a way to reduce it. To do so a commercial has to first demonstrate the association between a practiced but undesirable behavior (speed) and a negative consequence (crash), and then offer the viewer an alternative behavior that is easy to accomplish (drive within the speed limit). This simple paradigm is not always easy to apply. For example, telling a smoker to simply stop smoking is not an alternative behavior that is easy to accomplish. Hence, anti-smoking commercials often include coping strategies that are presumably manageable. Rossiter and Thoronton (2004) applied this approach to anti-speeding by first exposing college students to two types of anti-speeding commercials: with and without a relief component. Without the relief component the speeding driver ends up in a crash, whereas with the relief component the commercial also demonstrates how at slower speed the driver would have responded in time and the crash would have been prevented. They then exposed the subjects to video driving segments where drivers selected the speeds. The results were instructive: while women reduced their speed in response to exposure to both types of commercials, men were positively and consistently affected only by the fear-relief commercials. One explanation for the difference is that women were able to identify the relief solution even when it was not presented to them, while men needed the extra conviction. This may be simply due to men's greater reluctance to obey speed limits.

In the real world, public information campaigns are relatively ineffective in shaping drivers' speeds, unless they are accompanied by visible enforcement. The effectiveness of enforcement, in turn, can be significantly increased when it is accompanied by timely and concrete public information campaigns that also stress the presence and penalties associated with enforcement (Holland and Conner, 1996; Shinar and McKnight, 1985). Thus, the combined impact of public information campaigns and enforcement is significantly greater than the impact of the sum of the two.

Speed limit signs

Speed limit signs are used in two contexts: along highways to indicate road speed limits, and at entry to curves or otherwise dangerous locations to indicate very local – often advisory – speed limits. In general, by themselves without enforcement signs are not an effective means of controlling speed. That is because most drivers perceive roadway signs as supplementary cues to the cues they perceive directly from the road. Consequently, simply posting a speed sign with a speed that is lower than the prevailing speeds is not effective (Charlton, 2004; Holland and Conner, 1996; Shinar, Rockwell, and Malecki, 1980). Given these disappointing findings, why not eliminate most of the speed signs and reduce the visual clutter? The reason is that when the roadway cues are insufficient to judge the appropriate speed the signs are very useful. This is the case in conditions of reduced visibility such as fog and night. Under these conditions the signs can become the primary cues for the drivers' speed choice (Drory and Shinar, 1982).

Graphic representational speed signs

Some signs, however, may be more effective than others. Charlton (2004) evaluated different advisory signs that preceded curves and noted that all signs were effective when they preceded very sharp curves. However where the needed speed reduction was less severe, only signs that contained a "strong perceptual component" in addition to the recommended speed limit were effective in reducing people's speeds. These signs included chevron markings on posts just prior to the curve, a diamond sign with a drawing representing the sharpness of the curve, and transverse lines painted on the road with diminishing distance as they approached the curve. These results suggest that signs that comply with good ergonomic principles of compatibility (see Chapter 5) have more credibility than text-only signs.

Variable message signs

The emergence of the intelligent transportation systems has made it possible to provide drivers with more timely information, including information related to speed. Traditional fixed signs such as "Slippery Road" have little effect on driver behavior because they are not sensitive to the prevailing conditions, and therefore do not have much credibility and face validity. They fail the test of "reasonableness." However, variable message signs are appropriately much more believable, and drivers do respond to them by reducing their speed. As part of her doctoral work, Rämä (Luoma *et al.*, 2000; Rämä, 2001; Rämä and Kulmala, 2000) evaluated the effects of variable message signs that displayed recommended (reduced) speed and a "slippery road sign." She found that drivers reduced their speed in response to the weather conditions even without the signs, but the reductions were greater with the signs. In interviews drivers reported that the signs also caused them to focus their attention on the road, adjust their speed, reduce overtaking, and increase headways. Finally, drivers reported that the signs also made them more comfortable. Thus, variable message signs that accurately convey timely information are a very useful speed calming device. Though their effects are highly local, they can be applied where the risk of excessive speeding is greatest.

Speed feedback indicators
As an attempt to raise speed awareness, and assuming that drivers' speeds may creep beyond their intended levels, speed feedback indicators are often placed by the side of the road. They provide approaching drivers with an electronic digital display of their own speed. Evaluations of these displays have generally concluded that they have limited effects in reducing both the average speed and speed variability (Casey and Lund, 1990; Hamalainen and Hassel, 1990; NCHRP, 2008; Perrillo, 1997; Pesti and McCoy, 2002), but no temporal halo effect once they are removed. These dynamic displays are especially useful in the vicinity of reasonable low-speed zones. Lee *et al.* (2006) evaluated the effectiveness of such displays in school zones in South Korea, and found that they are quite effective in reducing the mean speeds, the 85th percentile, and the number of speeding drivers. An interesting variation on this approach was tried in the United Kingdom. The variation involved adding the vehicle's license plate number to the display, so that drivers might be "shamed" or fear apprehension. According to a brief report in a trade magazine almost half the drivers who drove above the speed limit slowed down in response to this display (Auto Express News, 2006).

A slightly different variation on the feedback signs was evaluated by Wrapson, Harré, and Murrell (2006). In their study they tested the effects of three different speed signs on a busy two-lane road with a posted 50 km/hr speed limit. The sign either contained (1) a message that the average speed at the site is 50 km/hr (or 53 km/hr, or 54 km/hr), or (2) a warning that "your" speed is being monitored, or (3) both messages. The rationale behind the three versions can be deduced from the theory of planned behavior, as illustrated in Figure 8-3. The information about the average speed was meant to convey a "normative" norm and the information on monitoring was meant to reduce the driver's "perceived behavioral control" over the speed choice. The dependent variable for sign effectiveness was the percent of drivers exceeding the 60 km/hr limit. The results showed that the independent variable with the greatest effect on the percent of speeding drivers was the traffic volume: the higher it was the more the drivers were likely to ignore the signs. However in the low volume condition all three signs reduced the percent of speeders. These results suggest that in the presence of other traffic the drivers get direct descriptive norm and do not have to rely (or believe) the normative norm as presented on the sign. Also, in heavy traffic it is very difficult to enforce a speed limit when most of the drivers are violating it.

The most recent evaluation of speed feedback signs, involved not only information feedback but also mild chastisement in the case of speed limit violation or positive reinforcement in the case of speed limit compliance. In this study, conducted on two lanes of a residential section of Berlin, Germany, Gehlert, Schulze, and Schlag (2012) placed three versions of a dynamic speed display by the sides of the road. In the first version, only the drivers' speeds were displayed in yellow against a black background just below the message YOUR SPEED. In the second version the feedback speed was in green when the driver drove at or below the speed limit and in red when the driver exceeded it. The third, most innovative version, did not display the driver's speed, but instead flashed the word SLOW in red in the case of a speed violation, and the word THANK YOU in the case of speed compliance. As this was a residential street with a 30 km/hr speed limit, above the digital feedback there was a picture of a pretty smiling girl, to indicate the rationale for the low speed; i.e., there are children on the road here. The results were quite consistent with the researchers' hypothesis: speed reductions were observed for all three versions, but the effects were greatest with verbal feedback and least with the single-color speed feedback. Of the different measures of speed compliance, the greatest effects were observed for the reduction in the percent of drivers exceeding the speed limit: they were 10 percent, for the digital feedback only, 21 percent, for the colored digital display, and 29 percent for the verbal message. However, this large and significant effect was obtained for one lane and not for the other. A closer examination of the two lanes revealed the possible reasons. In the affected lane, there were on-street parking for cars and so there was a potential for a child to suddenly emerge from between two parked cars (one of the most common causes of driver-pedestrian collisions, see Chapter 15). In contrast on the other lane there were no on-street parking and a traffic light that was visible ahead probably had a large effect on the approaching speeds (especially on their variance). Thus, the feedback effect on the affected lane also had the benefit of reasonableness.

In summary sign information may be helpful when it is believable and perceived as justifiable. Otherwise the signs lose their credibility, and we end up fooling some of the people some of the time – and not for very long. Also, dynamic feedback cannot serve as a sole solution, and its effects are likely to be moderated by other variables such as the context, the infrastructure, and the traffic. Unfortunately when we adjust our speed relative to that of the rest of the traffic, we are likely to misperceive the other drivers as going faster, because – due to the nature of the traffic perturbations – a driver going at the average speed spends more time being overtaken than passing others (Redelmeier and Tibshirani, 1999, 2000). Fortunately, the perception of the other traffic is not a sufficiently strong motivator for many people. Otherwise drivers would continuously increase their speed to keep up with those around them.

Vehicles

In-vehicle systems to regulate speeding belong to one of two categories: governors that actually limit the vehicle speed (also known as speed limiters) and advisory systems that only advise and/or record whenever the speed limit is exceeded. In addition the system can be very dumb with a fixed speed limit, or smart and adaptive by adjusting for the posted speed limit as the driver moves on different roads (relying on a global positioning system – GPS), or even adjusting for the recommended speed based on the driving conditions (Regan, Young, and Haworth, 2003 2005). In the European Union all heavy vehicles are required to have speed limiters, but their impact on safety – given the possibility that this may increase the traffic speed variance – is yet to be determined. However, as far as perceptions go, they do seem to be effective safety devices. In a survey of North American, European, and Australian fleets 56 percent of the responding fleet safety managers stated that the speed limiters were either "successful" or "very successful" in reducing crashes. However, this survey had only seven percent response rate and thus it must be considered as exploratory (TRB, 2008). A more recent evaluation by Hickman *et al.* (2012) relied on analysis of actual truck crash data documented by 20 commercial truck fleets in the U.S. Their analysis compared the crash likelihood of trucks with and without speed limiters. With a data base of nearly 15,866 crashes they first determined for each crash whether it was "speed-limiter-relevant" or not and then compared the rate of relevant crashes (per truck) between those trucks who had a speed-limiting device and those that did not. The benefits of the speed limiters were dramatic: across all crashes the speed-limiter-equipped truck had 23 percent more crashes per truck, but for the smaller subset of speed-limiter-relevant crashes they had 45 percent less. Whether or not similar savings would apply to smaller privately owned vehicles is debatable, because both the driver and the vehicle characteristics and driving conditions are quite different.

Various variations of intelligent speed adaptation systems, in which the in-vehicle systems are constantly adjusted according to the local speed limits have been evaluated in Australia, Denmark, Finland, Japan, and the United Kingdom. Cost-benefit evaluations of such systems show that they can be quite effective. For example, Carsten and Tate (2000) estimated that the installation of a fixed speed limiter on all vehicles would reduce non-urban injury crashes by 31 percent and pedestrian injuries in urban areas by 21 percent. Interestingly, contrary to the prediction of the risk homeostasis theory, despite the fact that the systems slowed the drivers slightly the drivers did not increase their other risky behaviors such as running red lights. Regan *et al.* (2005) evaluated the effects of various in-vehicle advisory systems including an intelligent speed adaptation system that warned the driver whenever he or she exceeded the posted speed limit by 2 kilometers or more, and a forward distance warning that warned the driver whenever he or she got too close to the vehicle ahead. The effects of both systems were to reduce the average travel speed, and more importantly to reduce the frequency of the high speeders, reducing the 85th speed percentile by 2.7 km/hr, and reducing the time spent at driving over 10 km/hr above the speed limit by over 50 percent. Unfortunately, as with many novel systems, the benefits of the system disappeared when the feedback was removed. Also, in general, drivers seem to be quite accepting of advisory systems, but do not like (surprise, surprise) the limiters. These two findings suggest that the installation of such systems as permanent equipment on all vehicles (rather than just on trucking fleets, where the fuel and engine savings are the primary motivation) may be quite problematic, and eventually unacceptable.

An interesting approach to convey the dangers of speed, and hopefully reduce speeding was offered by Owens, Helmers, and Sivak (1993), who argued that drivers underestimate the risk of injury at high speeds. They therefore suggested that drivers be provided with an "E-meter": a display of the kinetic energy at each speed. Turbell (Rumar, 1999) went a step further and designed a speedometer display in which the distance between speed increments is proportional to the impact force (i.e., the square of the speed) rather than the speed itself. This design is displayed in the left panel of Figure 8-11 next to a standard display on the right. The elegance of this perceptual modification is that as humans it counteracts our general tendency to minimize marginal fixed values. Thus in general, most drivers would consider the change in speed from 30 km/hr to 40 km/hr as more significant than the change from 90 km/hr to 100 km/hr, because percent wise the first change is a speed increase of 33 percent while the latter is only an 11 percent

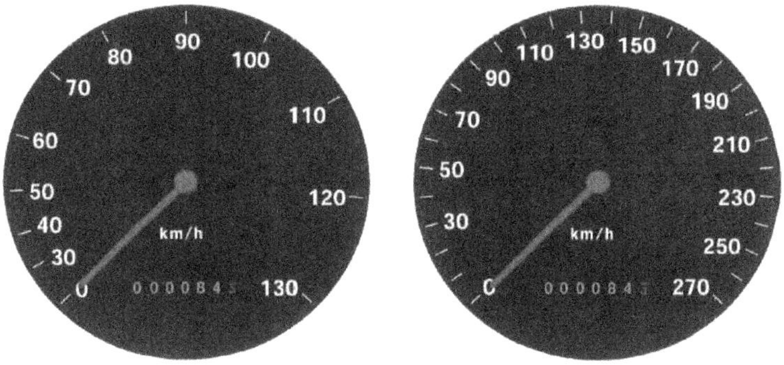

Figure 8-11. A speedometer proposed by Turbell scaled according to kinetic energy (impact force) (left) and a conventional speedometer scaled according to speed (right) (from Rumar, 1999, with permission from VTI).

increase in speed. However, in terms of the kinetic energy, or impact force, the increase at the high speed is three times as much (ΔV^2 = 700 km/hr versus 1,900 km/hr). Ward and Beusmans (1998) conducted an exploratory study to determine the effects of a rudimentary kinetic energy display on drivers' speed choice in a simulator and found that it significantly reduced both the proportion of times the drivers spent at high speeds and their average speed. These encouraging results imply that with appropriate representation of relevant information drivers will be inclined to reduce their speed, and hence reduce their risk. Given that in the driving simulator environment there is no real risk of injuries, one can only speculate that in the actual world this display would be an even more effective voluntary speed reduction device. However, there are many variables that operate in the real world, and so the critical tests still need to be done.

Combined approach: Speed management

The abundance of approaches to manage speed and the amount of existing research in this area can be overwhelming. It is evident that the goal to safety is not to just reduce speed but to develop a comprehensive "speed management" program. Most countries and jurisdictions have such programs. A U.S. "speed management and enforcement" study team reviewed strategies employed in several European countries (Germany, Netherlands, Sweden), Australia, and the U.S. and concluded that to be effective a "speed management plan should emphasize unity of purpose and objective, and foster coordination and cooperation. In particular, a coordinated approach to tactical planning of enforcement operations within an overall deterrence strategy appears to offer the greatest potential for achieving one of the key objectives of any speed management plan: a reduction in inappropriate speeds and speed-related crashes." This view, formulated 20 years ago is still valid today. Furthermore, according to this team, this strategic approach can be implemented only if it fulfills the following requirements (Coleman and Paniati, 1995):

- The speed-related safety problem must be clearly identified and effectively communicated to everyone involved, especially the public.
- Quantitative goals for the program should be established and revised as needed.
- The strategy or methods selected for implementation must have the potential for solving the problem.
- Engineering, enforcement, and educational speed management techniques must be integrated and coordinated. No single technique can effectively accomplish the goals of the program.
- The plan must be fair and reasonable to the majority of road users, for example, speed limits should be viewed as reasonable to the majority of drivers and be consistent for similar roadway and traffic conditions.
- Implementation must be augmented with a continuous ongoing evaluation program to monitor and determine the effectiveness of the management techniques.
- The plan must be flexible and change when safety conditions merit.
- The road safety community must work with legislators to insure that the necessary legislation is enacted and revised as needed to accomplish the speed management goals.
- Through each phase of the program, all participants must be kept informed and involved, especially the public.

Concluding Comments

Speed is a problem and speeding is possibly the most ubiquitous safety-related violation of the criminal code. Speeding is a positive experience for most drivers, and it can alleviate an otherwise boring driving activity. Yet the empirical fact is that speeding is associated with crashes, especially more severe ones. It is also undeniable that as impact speeds increase, fatalities rise in an exponential manner. Consequently, speed limits and speed limit enforcement have a most significant impact on injury and fatality rates. Even relatively small changes in average traffic speeds – especially at high speeds – can lead to significant reductions in crashes, especially severe and fatal crashes.

The only thing that has to be done is to reduce speeds. This can be achieved with a combined program that includes establishing reasonable enforceable limits (e.g., 85th percentile), aggressive and consistent enforcement, public information campaigns stressing the enforcement and coupled with public education on the relationship between speeds and road fatalities (TRB, 2011). What is lacking – in most countries – is the political will to do it. This will only be achieved once the value of safety dominates the multiple other values that motivate us to speed: both at the political level and at the individual level.

References

AAAF (2012). 2011 Traffic safety culture index. AAA Traffic Safety Foundation, Washington, DC. http://www.aaafoundation.org/pdf/2011TSCIndex.pdf

Aarts, L. and I. van Schagen (2006). Driving speed and the risk of road crashes: A review. *Accid. Anal. Prev.*, *38*, 215-224.

AASHTO (2001). A policy on geometric design of highways and streets. American Association of State Highway and Transportation Officials, Washington, DC.

Ahie, L. M., S. G. Charlton and N. J. Starsky (2015). The role of preferences in speed choice. *Trans. Res. F*, *30*, 66-73.

Ajzen, I. (1991). The theory of planned behavior. *Org. Behav. Hum. Dec. Proc.*, *50*, 179-211.

Allsop, R. E. (ed.) (1995). Reducing traffic injuries from inappropriate speed. European Transport Safety Council, Brussels, Belgium.

Aronoff, C. J. (1971). Stannard Baker, traffic safety pioneer, retires from NU Traffic Institute. *Northwestern University News*, August 27.

Auto Express News (2006). Speeders' plates in lights. http://www.autoexpress.co.uk/news/autoexpressnews/202483/speeders_plates_in_lights.html. August 31.

El-Basyouny, K. and M. Y. El-Bassiouni (2013). Modeling and analyzing traffic safety perceptions: An application to the speed limit reduction pilot project in Edmonton, Alberta. *Accid. Anal. Prev.*, *51*, 156-167.

Bjørnskau, T. and R. Elvik (1992). Can road traffic law enforcement permanently reduce the number of accidents? *Accid. Anal. Prev.*, *24*, 507-520.

Bowie, N. N. and M. Walz (1994). Data analysis of the speed-related crash issue. *Auto Traffic Safety*, *1*(2), 31-38.

Boyle, L. N. and F. Mannering (2004). Impact of traveler advisory systems on driving speed: Some new evidence. *Transport. Res. C*, *12*, 57-72.

Brackett, R. Q. and G. P. Beecher (1980). Longitudinal evaluation of speed control strategies. Texas Transportation Institute, Texas A&M University, College Station, TX.

Brackett, R. Q., and M. L. Edwards (1977). Comparative evaluation of speed control strategies. Texas Transportation Institute, Texas A&M University, College Station, TX.

Carsten, O. and F. Tate (2000). External vehicle speed control, Final report: Integration. Institute for Transport Studies, University of Leeds, UK. As cited by Regan *et al.* (2003).

Carnis L. and E. Blais (2013). An assessment of the safety effects of the French speed cameras program. *Accid. Anal. Prev.*, *51*, 301-309.

Casali, J. G. and W. W. Wierwille (1983). A comparison of rating scale, secondary-task, physiological, and primary-task workload estimation techniques in a simulated flight task emphasizing communications load. *Hum. Fact.*, *25*(6), 623– 641.

Casey, S. M. and A. K. Lund (1990). The effects of mobile roadside speedometers on traffic speeds. Insurance Institute for Highway Safety, Arlington, VA.

Charlton, S. G. (2004). Perceptual and attentional effects on drivers' speed selection at curves. *Accid. Anal. Prev.*, *36*, 877-884.

Cirillo, J. A. (1968). Interstate system accident research: Study II, interim report II. *Public Roads*, *35*, 71-75.

Coleman, J. A. and J. F. Paniati (1995). FHWA study tour for speed management and enforcement technology. FHWA, U.S. Department of Transportation, Washington, DC.

Conner, M., N. Smith and B. McMillan (2003). Examining normative pressure in the theory of planned behaviour: Impact of gender and passengers on intentions to break the speed limit. *Curr. Psychol.*, *22*(3), 252-263.

Cowley, J. E. (1987). The relationship between speed and accidents: A literature review. J .E. Cowley and Associates, Melbourne, Australia.

DaCoTA (2012). Speed and speed management, Deliverable 4.8s of the EC FP7 project DaCoTA.

Daniels, S., J. Vanrie, A. Dreesenb, and T. Brijs (2010). Additional road markings as an indication of speed limits: Results of a field experiment and a driving simulator study. *Accid. Anal. Prev.*, *42*, 953-960.

Day, T. D. and R. L. Hargens (1985). Differences between EDCRASH and CRASH3. SAE Paper No. 850253, February.

De Pauw, E., S. Daniels, M. Thierie, T. Brijs (2014). Safety effects of reducing the speed limit from 90 km/h to 70 km/h. *Accid. Anal. Prev.*, *62*, 426-431.

De Pelsmacker, P. and W. Janssens (2007). The effect of norms, attitudes and habits on speeding behavior: Scale development and model building and estimation. *Accid. Anal. Prev.*, *39*, 6-15.

De Waard, D. and T. Rooijers (1994). An experimental study to evaluate the effectiveness of different methods and intensities of law enforcement on driving speed on motorways. *Accid. Anal. Prev.*, *26*(6), 751-765.

Denton, F. F. (1971). The influence of visual pattern on perceived speed. Transport and Road Research Laboratory, Report LR409. Crowthorne, England.

Denton, F. F. (1973). The influence of visual pattern on perceived speed at Newbridge MB Midlothian. Transport and Road Research Laboratory, Report LR531. Crowthorne, England.

Diamantopoulou, K. and M. Cameron (2002). An evaluation of the effectiveness of overt and covert speed enforcement achieved through mobile radar operations. MUARC Report 187. Monash University Accident Research Center, Clayon, Victoria, Australia.

Dingus, T. A., F. Guo, S. E. Lee, J. Antin, M. Perez, M. Buchanan-King and J. Hankey (2016). Driver crash risk factors and prevalence evaluation using naturalistic driving data. Proc. National Acad. Sci. 201513271. doi:10.1073/pnas.1513271113. Retrieved from www.pnas.org.

Drory, A. and D. Shinar (1982). The effects of roadway environment and fatigue on sign perception. *J. Safety Res.*, *13*, 25–32.

Elvik, R. (1997). Effects on accidents of automatic speed enforcement in Norway. Presented at 76th Annual Meeting of the Transportation Research Board, Washington, DC.

Elvik, R. (2009). The power model of the relationship between speed and road safety. Update and new estimates. Report No. 1034. Institute of Transport Economics, Oslo.

Elvik, R. (2010). A restatement of the case for speed limits. *Transp. Policy*, *17*, 196-204.

Elvik, R. (2011). Developing an accident modification function for speed enforcement. *Safety Sci.*, *49*(6), 920-925.

Elvik, R. (2013a). A re-parameterisation of the power model of the relationship between the speed of traffic and the number of accidents and accident victims. *Accid. Anal. Prev.*, *50*, 854-860.

Elvik, R. (2013b). A before–after study of the effects on safety of environmental speed limits in the city of Oslo, Norway. *Safety Sci.*, *55*, 10-16.

Elvik, R., P. Christensen and A. Amundsen (2004). Speed and road accidents: An evaluation of the power model. TOI Report No. 740/2004. Institute of Transport Economics, Norway.

Elvik, R., A. Høye, T. Vaa and M. Sørensen (2009). *The Handbook of Road Safety Measures* (2nd ed.). Emerald Publishing, Bingley, UK.

ETSC (2008). Speed fact sheet: combatting speed through penalty point systems. European Transport Safety Council, Brussels, Belgium.

ETSC (2011). 2010 road safety target outcome. 5th Road Safety PIN Report. European Transport Safety Council, Brussels, Belgium.

ETSC (2013). Intelligent speed assistance – Frequently asked questions. European Transport Safety Council, Brussels, Belgium.

ETSC (2015a). Speed limits on the German motorways in the spotlight again. European Transport Safety Council, Brussels, Belgium. http://etsc.eu/speed-limits-on-german-motorways-in-the-spotlight-again/

ETSC (2015b). German Minister rules out end to unlimited motorway speeds. European Transport Safety Council, Brussels, Belgium. http://etsc.eu/german-minister-rules-out-end-to-unlimited-motorway-speeds/

ETSC (2015c). Dummy police can cut speeding. European Transport Safety Council, Brussels, Belgium. http://etsc.eu/dummy-police-can-cut-speeding/

European Transport Safety Council (1995). Reducing injuries from excess and inappropriate speed. Working Party on Road Infrastructure, Brussels, Belgium. As cited by WHO (2004).

Evans, L. (1991). *Traffic Safety and the Driver*. Van Nostrad Reinhold, New York, NY.

Evans, L. (1996). Safety-belt effectiveness: The influence of crash severity and selective recruitment. *Accid. Anal. Prev.*, *28*, 423-433.

Evans, L. (2004). *Traffic Safety*. Science Serving Society, Bloomfield Hills, MI.

Ferguson, S. A., A. P. Hardy and A. F. Williams (2003). Content analysis of television advertising for cars and minivans: 1983–1998. *Accid. Anal. Prev.*, *35*, 825-831.

Fildes, B. N. and J. R. Jarvis (1994). Perceptual countermeasures: Literature review. Report CR4/94 to the Federal Office of Road Safety, Australia.

Fildes, B. N. and S. J. Lee (1993). The speed review: Road environment, speed limits, enforcement, and crashes. CR 127 (FORS), CR 3/93 (RSB). Road and Traffic Authority of New South Wales, Australia, September.

Fildes, B. N., G. Rumbold and A. Leening (1991). Speed behavior and drivers' attitude to speeding. Report 16. Monash University Accident Research Center, Monash, Victoria, Australia, June.

Fischer, P., E. Vingilis, T. Greitemeyer, and C. Vogrincic (2011). Risk-taking and the media. *Risk Analysis*, *31*, 699-705.

Fitzpatrick, K., P. Carlson, M. Brewer, and M. D. Wooldridge (2003). Design speed, operating speed, and posted speed limit practices. *Proceedings of the*

Transportation Research Board 82nd Annual Meeting. TRB Paper No. 03-272. Transportation Research Board, Washington DC.

Fylan, F., S. Hempel, B. Grunfeld, M. Conner and R. Lawton (2006). Effective interventions for speeding motorists. Road Safety Research Report No. 66. Department for Transport, London.

Garber, N. J. and R. Gadiraju (1988). Speed variance and its influence on accidents. University of Virginia, Charlottesville.

Gehlert, T., C. Schulze, and B. Schlag (2012). Evaluation of different types of dynamic speed display signs. *Trans. Res. F, 15*, 667-675.

GHSA (2012). Speeding and aggressive driving: Survey of the states. Governors Highway Safety Association, Washington, DC.

Gibson, J. J. (1979). *The Ecological Approach to Visual Perception*. Houghton Mifflin, Boston, MA.

Gitelman, V., F. Pishahov, and S. Chen (2012). National survey of speeds in Israel 2012. National Road Safety Authority, Jerusalem, Israel (in Hebrew).

Godley, S. T., T. J. Triggs and B. N. Fildes (2000). Speed reduction mechanisms of transverse lines. *Transport. Hum. Fact.*, *2*(4), 297-312.

Goldenbeld, C. and I. van Schagen (2005). The effects of speed enforcement with mobile radar on speed and accidents: An evaluation study on rural roads in the Dutch province Friesland. *Accid. Anal. Prev.*, *37*, 1135-1144.

Goldenbeld, C. and I. van Schagen (2007). The credibility of speed limits on 80km/h rural roads: The effects of road and person (ality) characteristics. *Accid. Anal. Prev.*, *39*(6), 1121-1130.

Golob, T. F., W. W. Recker and V. M. Alvarez (2004). Freeway safety as a function of traffic flow. *Accid. Anal. Prev.*, *36*, 933-946.

Grabowski, D. C. and M. A. Morrisey (2007). Systemwide implications of the repeal of the national maximum speed limit. *Accid. Anal. Prev.*, *39*, 180-189.

Groeger, J. A. and P. R. Chapman (1997). Normative influences on decisions to offend. *Appl. Psychol.*, *46*(3), 265-286.

Haglund, M. and L. Åberg (2002). Stability in drivers' speed choice. *Transport. Res. F*, *5*, 177-188.

Hamalainen, V. and S. O. Hassel (1990). The giant speed-indicating display in police traffic control. Report No. HS-040 655. Central Organization for Traffic Safety, Helsinki, Finland. as cited by Stuster *et al.* (1998).

Hauer, E. (1971). Accidents, overtaking, and speed control. *Accid. Anal. Prev.*, *3*(1), 1-13.

Hauer, E. and J. Bonneson (2006). An empirical examination of the relationship between speed and road accidents based on data by Elvik, Christensen and Amundsen. Report Prepared for Project NCHRP 17-25.

Hauer, E., D. W. Harwood, F. M. Council and M. S. Griffith (2002). Estimating safety by the empirical Bayes method: A tutorial. *Transport. Res. Rec.*, **No. 1784**, 126-131.

Hirst, W. M., L. J. Mountain and M. J. Maher (2005). Are speed enforcement cameras more effective than other speed management measures? An evaluation of the relationship between speed and accident reductions. *Accid. Anal. Prev.*, *37*, 731-741.

Hoffman, E. R. and R. G. Mortimer (1996). Scaling of relative velocity between vehicles. *Accid. Anal. Prev.*, *28*(4), 415-421.

Holland, C. A. and M. T. Conner (1996). Exceeding the speed limit: An evaluation of the effectiveness of a police intervention. *Accid. Anal. Prev.*, *28*, 587-597.

Horberry, T., L. Hartley, K. Gobetti, F. Walker, B. Johnson, S. Gersbach and J. Ludlow (2004). Speed choice by drivers: The issue of driving too slowly. *Ergonomics*, *47*, 1561-1570.

Høye, A. (2014). Evaluation of the crash effects of section control (English Summary). TØI Report 1339/2014, Institute of Transport Economics, Oslo, Norway.

Hu, W. and A. T. McCartt (2015). Effects of automated speed enforcement in Montgomery County, Maryland on vehicle speeds, public opinion, and crashes. Insurance Institute for Highway Safety, Arlington, VA.

Husted, D. S., M. S. Gold, K. Frost-Pineda, M. A. Ferguson, M. C. K. Yang and N. A. Shapira (2006). Is speeding a form of gambling in adolescents? *J. Gambl. Stud.*, *22*, 209-219.

IIHS (2014). Going up: States keep raising speed limits. *Status Rep.*, *49*(6), 7.

Imprialou, M. I. M., M. Quddus, D. E. Pitfield, and D. Lord (2016). Re-visiting crash–speed relationships: A new perspective in crash modelling. *Accid. Anal. Prev.*, *86*, 173-185.

ITE (2004). Speed zoning information: A case of "majority rule." Institute of Transportation Engineers, Washington DC.

Iversen, H. and T. Rundmo (2004). Attitudes towards traffic safety, driving behaviour and accident involvement among the Norwegian public. *Ergonomics*, *47*(5), 555-572.

Jamson, S., F. Lai, and H. Jamson (2010). Driving simulators for robust comparisons: A case study evaluating road safety engineering treatments. *Accid. Anal. Prev.*, *42*(3), 961-971.

Johansson-Stenman, O. and P. Martinsson (2005). Anyone for higher speed limits? – Self-interested and adaptive political preferences. *Public Choice*, *122*, 319-331.

Johnston, I., C. Muir, and E. W. Howard (2014). *Eliminating Serious Injury and Death from Road Transport: A Crisis of Complacency*. CRC Press, Taylor and Francis, Boca Raton, FL.

Joksch, H. C. (1993). Velocity change and fatality risk in a crash. *Accid. Anal. Prev.*, *25*, 103-104.

Jonah, B. A., R. Thiessen and E. Au-Yeung (2001). Sensation seeking, risky driving and behavioural adaptation. *Accid. Anal. Prev.*, *33*, 679–684.

Jost, G. and R. Allsop (2014). Ranking EU progress in road safety: 8th road safety performance index report. European Transport Safety Council (ETSC), Brussels, BE.

Kallberg, V. P. and J. Luoma (1996). Speed kills – Or does it and why? *Proc., Conference of Road Safety in Europe, Birmingham*, United Kingdom, pp. 129-149, September 9-11.

Kahneman, D. and A. Tversky (1979). Prospect theory: an analysis of decisions under risk. *Econometrica*, *47* (2), 263–291.

Kang, J.-G. (2002). Changes of speed and safety by automated speed enforcement systems. *IATSS Res.*, *26*(2), 38-44.

Kirkup, J. and D. Millward (2007). Anger as fines from speed cameras soar. *The Telegraph*, December 4.

Klauer, S. G., T. A. Dingus, V. L. Neale, J. D. Sudweeks and D. J. Ramsey (2006). The impact of driver inattention on near-crash/crash risk: An Analysis using the 100-car naturalistic driving study data. National Highway Traffic Safety Administration Report No. DOT HS 810 594. U.S. Department of Transportation, Washington, DC.

Kloeden, C. N., A. J. McLean, V. M. Moore and G. Ponte (1997). Traveling speed and the risk of crash involvement. Technical Report. NHMRC Road Accident Research Unit, The University of Adelaide, Australia.

Knowles, V., B. Persaud, M. Parker and G. Wilde (1997). Safety, speed and speed management: A Canadian review. Final Report, Contract T8080-5-6858. Transport Canada.

Kockelman, K. (2006). Safety impacts and other implications of raised speed limits on high-speed roads. NCHRP Contractor Final Report on project 17-23. Transportation Research Board of the National Academies, Washington, DC.

Lave, C. (1985). Speeding, coordination, and the 55-mph limit. *Am. Econ. Rev.*, *75*, 1159-1164.

Lave, C. (1989). Speeding, coordination, and the 55-mph limit: Reply. *Am. Econ. Rev.*, *79*, 926-931.

Lave, C. and P. Elias (1994). Did the 65 mph speed limit save lives? *Accid. Anal. Prev.*, *26*(1), 49-62.

Lave, C. and P. Elias (1997). Resource allocation in public policy: The effects of the 65 mph speed limit. *Econ. Inq.*, *35*(3), 614–620.

Lawton, R., D. Parker, S. G. Stradling and A. S. R. Manstead (1997). Self-reported attitude towards speeding and its possible consequences in five different road contexts. *J. Comm. Appl. Soc. Psychol.*, *7*(2), 153-155.

Lee, C., S. Lee, B. Choi, and Y. Oh (2006). Effectiveness of speed-monitoring displays in speed reduction in school zones. *Trans. Res. Rec. J. Trans. Res. Board*, **No. 1973**, 27-35.

Lewis-Evans, B., D., De Waard, and K. A. Brookhuis (2011). Speed maintenance under cognitive load – Implications for theories of driver behaviour. *Accid. Anal. Prev.*, *43*(4), 1497-1507.

Li, H., D. J. Graham, and A. Majumdar (2013). The impacts of speed cameras on road accidents: An application of propensity score matching methods. *Accid. Anal. Prev.*, *60*, 148-157.

Liu, B.-S. and Y.-H. Lee (2006). In-vehicle workload assessment: effects of traffic situations and cellular telephone use. *J. Safety Res.*, *37*, 99-105.

Liu, G. X. (1997). Identification and analysis of speed related accidents on highways. Proc., Canadian Multidisciplinary Road Safety Conference X, Toronto, Ontario, Canada, June 8-11.

Liu, G. X. and A. Popoff (1996). Provincial wide travel speed and traffic safety study in Saskatchewan. Faculty of Engineering, University of Regina, Regina, Saskatchewan, Canada.

Lund, A. K. and W. J. Rauch (1992). On the contrary! A comment on Lave and Elias's question, "Did the 65 mph Speed Limit Save Lives?" Insurance Institute for Highway Safety, Arlington, VA.

Luoma, J., P. Rämä, M. Penttinen and V. Anttila (2000). Effects of variable message signs for slippery road conditions on reported driver behaviour. *Transport. Res. F*, *3*, 75-84.

Mackay, M. (1985). Seat belt use under voluntary and mandatory conditions and its effects on casualties. In: *Human Behavior and Traffic Safety* (L. Evans and R. C. Schwing eds.), pp. 259-277. Plenum Press, New York, NY.

Manser, M. P. and P. A. Hancock (2007). The influence of perceptual speed regulation on speed perception, choice, and control: Tunnel wall characteristics and influences. *Accid. Anal. Prev.*, *39*(1), 69-78.

Martinez, F. (1997). Statement before the subcommittee on surface transportation, committee on transportation and infrastructure, U.S. House of Representatives, July 17.

McCoy, P. T., B. A. Moen, G. Pesti and M. Mourssavi (1993). Evaluation of lower speed limits on urban highways. Research Report TRP-02-26-92. University of Nebraska, Lincoln. Cited by Knowles *et al.* (1997).

McKenna, F. P. (2005). What shall we do about speeding education? In: *Traffic and Transport Psychology* (G. Underwood ed.). Elsevier, Oxford.

Moore, V. M., J. Dolinis and A. J. Woodward (1995). Vehicle speed and risk of a severe crash. *Epidemiology*, *6*, 258-262.

Mountain, L. J., W. M. Hirst and M. J. Maher (2005). Are speed enforcement cameras more effective than other speed management measures? The impact of speed management schemes on 30 mph roads. *Accid. Anal. Prev.*, *37*, 742-754.

NASS (1998). Data from the 1995 crashworthiness data system. National Highway Traffic Safety Administration, U.S. Department of Transportation, Washington, DC.

Navon, D. (2003). The paradox of driving speed: Two adverse effects on highway accident rate. *Accid. Anal. Prev.*, *35*, 361-367.

NCHRP (2008). Guidelines for selection of speed reduction treatments at high-speed intersections. NCHRP Report 3-74. Transportation Research Board, Washington, DC.

NHTSA (1992). Report to congress on the effects of the 65 mph speed limit through 1990. U.S. Department of Transportation. Washington, DC.

NHTSA (2005). Tire pressure monitoring system. FMVSS No. 138. Final Regulatory Impact Analysis, U.S. Department of Transportation, Washington, DC, March 2005 (from Hauer, 2006).

NHTSA (2006). Traffic safety facts 2005 – Early edition. National Highway Traffic Safety Administration Report DOT HS 810 631. U.S. Department of Transportation, Washington, DC.

NHTSA (2012a). Traffic safety facts: Speeding. 2010 data. National Highway Traffic Safety Administration Report DOT HS 811 636. U.S. Department of Transportation, Washington, DC.

NHTSA (2012b). Traffic tech: National traffic speed survey II: 2009. National Highway Traffic Safety Administration Report DOT HS 811 647. U.S. Department of Transportation, Washington, DC.

NHTSA (2014). Traffic safety facts: Speeding. 2012 Data. National Highway Traffic Safety Administration Report DOT HS 812 021. U.S. Department of Transportation, Washington, DC.

NHTSA (2015). Traffic safety facts: 2014 crash data key findings. National Highway Traffic Safety Administration Report DOT HS 812 219. U.S. Department of Transportation, Washington, DC.

Nilsson, G. (1990). Reduction in the speed limit from 110 km/h to 90 km/h during summer 1989: Effects on personal injury accidents, injured, and speeds. VTI Report 358A. Swedish Road and Traffic Research Institute, Sweden. Cited by Knowles *et al.* (1997).

NRSA (2014). National survey of driving speeds in Israel 2013, Israel's National Road Safety Authority. Jerusalem, Israel (in Hebrew).

O'Day, J. and J. Flora (1982). Alternative Measures of restraint system effectiveness: Interaction with crash severity factors. SAE Technical Paper Series No. 820798. Warren dale, PA.

OECD (2014). Road safety annual report 2014. International Transport Forum (ITF), IRTAD, Paris, France.

ONISR (2010). Bilan de la Sécurité Routière du 1er Semestre 2010 en Données Provisoires: Premiers Chiffres. (Observatoire National Interministériel de Sécurité Routière). As cited by TRB (2011).

Owens, D., G. Helmers and M. Sivak (1993). Intelligent vehicle highway systems: A call for user-centred design. *Ergonomics*, *36*, 363-369.

Pasanen, E. and H. Salmivaara (1993). Driving speeds and pedestrian safety in the city of Helsinki. *Traffic Eng. Control*, *34*(6), 308-310.

Perrillo, K. V. (1997). Effectiveness of speed trailer on low-speed urban roadway. Master Thesis, Texas A&M University, College Station, TX. As cited by Stuster *et al.* (1998).

Pesti, G. and P. T. McCoy (2002). Effect of speed monitoring displays on entry ramp speeds at rural freeway interchanges. *Proceedings of the 81st Annual Meeting of the Transportation Research Board.* Transportation Research Board, Washington, DC.

Pilkington, P. and S. Kinra (2005). Effectiveness of speed cameras in preventing road traffic collisions and related casualties: Systematic review. *Br. Med. J.*, *330*, 331-334.

Pinsker, J. (2015). Finland, home of the $103,000 speeding ticket. *Atlantic.com.* http://www.theatlantic.com/business/archive/2015/03/finland-home-of-the-103000-speeding-ticket/387484/. March 12, 2015.

Porter, M. and M. J. Whitton (2002). Assessment of driving with the global positioning system and video technology in young, middle-aged, and older drivers. *J. Gerontol. Med. Sci.*, *57A*(9), M578-M582.

Rämä, P. (2001). Effects of weather-controlled variable message signing on driver behaviour. Doctoral dissertation, Helsinki University of Technology. VTT Publication 447. VTT- Technical Research Center of Finland, Helsinki.

Rämä, P. and R. Kulmala (2000). Effects of variable message signs for slippery road conditions on driving speed and headways. *Transport. Res. F*, *3*, 85-94.

Recarte, M. A. and L. Nunes (2002). Mental load and loss of control over speed in real driving. Towards a theory of attentional speed control. *Transport. Res. F*, *5*, 111122.

Redelmeier, D. A. and R. J. Tibshirani (1999). Why cars in the next lane seem to go faster. *Nature*, *401*, 35.

Redelmeier, D. A. and R. J. Tibshirani (2000). Are those other drivers really going faster? *Chance*, *13*(3), 8-14.

Redelmeier, D. A., R. J. Tibshirani and L. Evans (2003). Traffic-law enforcement and risk of death from motor-vehicle crashes: Case-crossover study. *Lancet*, *361*, 2177-2182.

Reagan, I. J. and J. P. Bliss (2013). Perceived mental workload, trust, and acceptance resulting from exposure to advisory and incentive based intelligent speed adaptation systems. *Transport. Res. F*, *21*, 14-29.

Reagan, I. J., J. P. Bliss, R. Van Houten, and B. W. Hilton (2013). The effects of external motivation and real-time automated feedback on speeding behavior in a naturalistic setting. *Hum. Fact.*, *55*, 218-230.

Regan, M. A., K. Young and N. Haworth (2003). A review of literature and trials of intelligent speed adaptation devices for light and heavy vehicles. Austroads Publication No. AP-R237/03. Austroads, Sydney, Australia.

Regan, M. A., K. Young, T. Triggs, N. tomasevic and E. Mitsopoulos (2005). Effects on driving performance of in-vehicle intelligent transport systems: Final results of the Australian TAC safecar project. Monash University Accident Research Center, Clayton, AU.

Rock, S. M. (1995). Impact of the 65 mph speed limit on accidents, deaths, and injuries in Illinois. *Accid. Anal. Prev.*, *27*, 207-214.

Rodriguez, R. J. (1990). Speed, speed dispersion, and the highway fatality rate. *Southern Econ. J.*, 349-356.

Rossiter, J. R. and J. Thornton (2004). Fear-pattern analysis supports the fear-drive model for antispeeding road-safety TV ads. *Psychol. Market.*, *21*(11), 945-960.

RTI (1970). Speed and accidents. Vols. I & II. Research Triangle Institute (RTI), North Carolina. As cited by Aarts and Schagen (2006).

Rumar, K. (1999). Speed – A sensitive matter for drivers. *Nordic Road Transport. Res.*, *No. 1*, 20-22.

Rumar, K., U. Bergrund, P. Jernberg and U. Ytterbom (1976). Driver reaction to a technical safety measure – studded tires. *Hum. Fact.*, *18*, 443-454.

Sabey, B. E. and G. C. Staughton (1975). Interacting role of road environment, vehicle, and road user in accidents. Presented at the 5th International Association for Accident and Traffic Medicine, London, September.

SARTRE 4 (1998). The attitude and behavior of European car drivers to road safety. http://www.attitudes-roadsafety.eu/index.php?eID=tx_nawsecuredl&u=0&file=uploads/media/Part_1_Report_on_principal_results_01.pdf&t=1451049730&hash=6976bb618f1c86b608275987757343fd

Schechtman, E., H. Bar-Gera, and O. Musicant (2016). Driver views on speed and enforcement. *Accid. Anal. Prev.*, *89*, 9-21.

Schmidt-Daffy, M. (2014). Prospect balancing theory: Bounded rationality of drivers' speed choice. *Accid. Anal. Prev.*, *63*, 49-64.

Schonfeld, C., D. Steinhardt and M. Sheehan (2005). A content analysis of Australian motor vehicle advertising: Effects of the 2002 voluntary code on restricting the use of unsafe driving themes. Paper presented at the Australian Road Safety Research Conference. Center for Accident Research and Road Safety, Queensland University of Technology, Queensland, AU.

Schroeder, P., L. Kostyniuk, and M. Mack (2013). 2011 national survey of speeding attitudes and behaviors. National Highway Traffic Safety Administration. Report No. DOT HS 811 865. U.S. Department of Transportation, Washington, DC.

Scott-Parker, B., M. K. Hyd, B. Watson and M. B. King (2013). Speeding by young novice drivers: What can personal characteristics and psychosocial theory add to our understanding? *Accid. Anal. Prev.*, *50*, 242-250.

Shiekh, L. (1997). Statement before the subcommittee on surface transportation. Committee on Transportation and Infrastructure, U.S. House of Representatives, July 17.

Shin, P. C., D. Hallett, M. L. Chipman, C. Tator and J. T. Granton (2005). Unsafe driving in North American automobile commercials. *J. Pub. Health*, *27*(4), 318-325.

Shinar, D. (1978). *Psychology on the Road: The Human Factor in Traffic Safety*. Wiley, New York, NY.

Shinar, D. (1998). Speed and crashes: A controversial topic and an elusive relationship. In: Managing Speed: A Review of Current Practice for Setting and Enforcing Speed Limits. National Research Council, Transportation Research Board Special Report 254. National Academy Press, Washington, DC.

Shinar, D. (2001). Driving speed relative to the speed limit and relative to the perception of safe, enjoyable, and economical speed. *Proceedings of the Conference on Traffic Safety on Three Continents. Moscow Russia*, September 19-21.

Shinar, D., E. D. McDowell, and T. H. Rockwell (1977). Eye movements in curve negotiation. *Hum. Fact.*, *19*, 63-72

Shinar, D. and A. J. McKnight (1985). The effects of enforcement and public information on compliance. In: *Human Behavior and Traffic Safety* (L. Evans and R. C. Schwing eds.), pp. 385-419. Plenum Press, New York, NY.

Shinar, D., T. H. Rockwell and J. Malecki (1980). The effects of changes in driver perception on rural curve negotiation. *Ergonomics*, *23*, 263-275.

Shinar, D., E. Schechtman and R. P. Compton (1999). Trends in safe driving behaviors and in relation to trends in health maintenance behaviors in the U.S.A.: 1985-1995. *Accid. Anal. Prev.*, *31*, 497-503.

Shinar, D., E. Schechtman and R. P. Compton (2001) Self-reports of safe driving behaviors in relationship to sex, age, education and income in the US adult driving population. *Accid. Anal. Prev.*, *33* (1), 111–116.

Shinar, D. and J. Stiebel (1986). The effectiveness of stationary versus moving police vehicle on compliance with speed limit. *Hum. Fact.*, *28*, 365-371.

Snyder, D. (1997). Statement before the subcommittee on surface transportation. Committee on Transportation and Infrastructure, U.S. House of Representatives, July 17.

Solomon, D. (1964). Accidents on main rural highways related to speed, driver, and vehicle. Bureau of Public Roads, U.S. Department of Commerce, July.

Soole, D. W., B. C. Watson, and J. J. Fleiter (2013). Effects of average speed enforcement on speed compliance and crashes: A review of the literature. *Accid. Anal. Prev.*, *54*, 46-56.

Stuster, J., Z. Coffman and D. Warren (1998). Synthesis of safety research related to speed. Federal Highway Administration Report FHWA-RD-98-154. U.S. Department of Transportation, Washington, DC.

Summala, H. (1985). Modeling driver behaviour: A pessimistic prediction? In: *Human Behavior and Traffic Safety* (L. Evans and R. C. Schwing eds.), pp. 43-65. General Motors Research Laboratories, Plenum Press, New York, NY.

Tractinsky, N., E. S. Ram, and D. Shinar (2013). To call or not to call—That is the question (while driving). *Accid. Anal. Prev.*, *56*, 59-70.

TRB (1984). Special report 204: 55: A decade of experience. National Research Council, Washington, DC.

TRB (1998). Managing speed: A review of current practice for setting and enforcing speed limits. National Research Council, Transportation Research Board Special Report 254. National Academy Press, Washington, DC.

TRB (2011). Special report 300: Achieving traffic safety goals in the United States: Lessons from other nations. National Research Council, Washington, DC.

Talebpour, A., and H. S. Mahmassani (2014). Effectiveness of innovative speed-enforcement techniques in Illinois. Federal Highway Administration, Research Report No. FHWA-ICT-14-006. U.S. Department of Transportation, Washington, DC.

TRB (2008). Safety impacts of speed limiter device installations on commercial trucks and buses A Synthesis of Safety Practice. CTBSSP Synthesis 16. Transportation Research Board, Washington, DC.

Treat, J. R., N. S. Tumbas, S. T. McDonald, D. Shinar, R. D. Hume, R. E. Mayer, R. L. Stansifer and N. J. Castellan (1977). Tri-level study of the causes of traffic accidents. Volume I: Causal Factor Tabulations and Assessment. DOT-HS-805-085. NHTSA, U.S. Department of Transportation.

USA Today (1997). Fewer dying despite faster speed limits. July 14.

Vaa, T. (1997). Increased police enforcement effects on speed. *Accid. Anal. Prev.*, *29*, 373-385.

Van Nes, N., S. Brandenburg, and D. Twisk (2010). Improving homogeneity by dynamic speed limit systems. *Accid. Anal. Prev.*, *42*(3), 944-952.

Walton, D. and J. Bathurst (1998). An exploration of the perceptions of the average driver's speed compared to perceived driver safety and driving skills. *Accid. Anal. Prev.*, *30*(6), 821–830.

Ward, N. J. and J. Beusmans (1998). Simulation of accident risk displays in motorway driving with traffic. *Ergonomics*, *41*(10), 1478-1499.

Watson, L., A. M. Lavack, C. Rudin-Brown, P. Burns, and J. H. Mintz (2010). Message content in Canadian automotive advertising: A role for regulation? *Can. Public Pol.*, *36*(Suppl. 1), S49-S67.

West, L. B., Jr. and J. W. Dunn (1971). Accidents, speed deviation and speed limits. *Traffic Eng.*, *41*(10), 52-55.

Whissell, R. W. and B. J. Bigelow (2003). The speeding attitude scale and the role of sensation seeking in profiling young drivers at risk. *Risk Anal.*, *23*, 811–820.

WHO (2004). World report on road traffic injury prevention. Edited by M. Peden *et al.* World Health Organization, Geneva. http://whqlibdoc.who.int/publications/2004/9241562609.pdf

WHO (2013). Global status report on road safety: Supporting a decade of action. World Health Organization, Geneva, Switzerland.

Wikipedia (2015). Day-fine. https://en.wikipedia.org/wiki/Day-fine

Wilson C., C. Willis, J. K. Hendrikz, R. Le Brocque, and N. Bellamy (2010). Speed cameras for the prevention of road traffic injuries and deaths. *Cochrane Database Syst. Rev.*, (11):CD004607.

Wilson, G. F. (1993). Air-to-ground training missions: A psychophysiological workload analysis. *Ergonomics*, *36*, 1071– 1087.

Woolridge, M. D., K. Fitzpatrick, D. W. Harwood, I. B. Potts, L. Elefteriadou and D. J. Torbic (2003). Geometric design consistency on high-speed rural two-lane roadways. NCHRP, Report 502. Transportation Research Board, Washington, DC.

World Bank (2009). *Confronting Death on Wheels: Making Roads Safe in Europe and Central Asia*. World Bank, Washington, DC.

Wrapson, W., N. Harré and P. Murrell (2006). Reductions in driver speed using posted feedback of speeding information: Social comparison or implied surveillance? *Accid. Anal. Prev.*, *38* (6), 1119-1126.

Yannis, G., G. Louca, S. Vardaki, and G. Kanellaidis (2013). Why do drivers exceed speed limits. *Eur. Transport Res. Rev.*, *5*(3), 165-177.

Zador, P. L. and A. K. Lund (1991). Comments on "Did the 65 mph Speed Limit Save 3,113 Lives?" by Charles A. Lave. Insurance Institute for Highway Safety, Arlington, VA.

9

Personality and Aggressive Driving

> "Man drives as he lives. If his personal life is marked by caution, tolerance, foresight, and consideration for others, then he would drive in the same manner. If his personal life is devoid of these desirable characteristics then his driving will have a much higher accident rate than the stable companion." (Tillman and Hobbs, 1949, p. 329).

Aggressive driving is a worldwide problem (Jovanović *et al.*, 2011). It captured the attention of the safety community and the general public at the end of the previous century, and has since remained a great public concern, so much so that in the U.S. over 50 percent of the motoring public considers it a very serious threat to their personal safety (AAAF, 2012). One official early estimate was that it is a factor in about two-thirds of all U.S. traffic fatalities (Martinez, 1997). However, its real extent is not known as different agencies have different definitions for aggressive driving. Most intriguing is the issue of whether it reflects a stable personality characteristic (or several characteristics) or whether it is a response to a particular driving situation, or both. Multi-national comparisons in driving behaviors including aggressive traffic violations indicate that some stable characteristics are involved in aggressive driving (Lajunen and Parker, 2001; Özkan *et al.*, 2006). In this chapter, I try to address this intricate issue so that effective countermeasures can be developed to deal with it.

The idea that we maintain some consistency in our behavior, in the sense that we behave similarly in different situations is at the root of the concept of personality: a hypothetical concept that defines a cluster of stable traits that distinguish among people and allows us to some extent to understand and predict how different people will respond to the same situation. Psychologists over the years have identified a variety of such traits that are of interest here including risk-taking, sensation-seeking, introversion-extroversion, locus-of-control, field dependence and independence, gender identity, and – of course – aggression. Once such stable characteristics can be demonstrated, we can think of them as aspects or components of personality. Different studies using multi-variate analyses techniques have also demonstrated that different driving styles are associated with different personality characteristics and motivations (e.g., Taubman – Ben-Ari and Yehiel, 2012). Given the complexity of driving behavior and the changing context within which it occurs, it is remarkable that such basic context-free characteristics have been associated even to a moderate degree with over-involvement in driving violations and crashes. To drive safely we have to adjust to the rules and norms of the traffic system. If some of our basic personality traits are incompatible with prevailing social norms, then they should be manifest in the context of driving. Therefore, social maladjustment should be related to driving maladjustment – and it is.

Social Maladjustment and Driving Behavior

In 1949, two Canadian psychiatrists published a landmark study in which they examined the social behavior of two groups of (male) taxi drivers: 96 high-accident drivers with four or more accidents on their record and 100 accident-free drivers. They focused on the encounters that these drivers had with various social and correctional agencies. The results, reproduced in Table 9-1 were striking. The high-accident drivers were seven times more likely than the accident-free drivers to have been involved with at least one such agency, especially adult courts and credit bureaus. The researchers' conclusion – stated in anachronistic, gender-biased terms – was that "man drives as he lives." People bring with them to the driver seat all the characteristics and behaviors that they exhibit outside the car. Therefore, people who repeatedly violate society's norms and rules of behavior are more likely to violate the norms that govern the traffic systems and are therefore more likely to have accidents.

Table 9-1. "Man drives as he lives." High-accident taxi drivers are much more likely to be involved in various social agencies than accident-free drivers. Cell entries are the percent of high-accident drivers and accident-free drivers involved with various social agencies (adapted from Tillman and Hobbs, 1949).

Taxi Drivers	**Adult Court**	**Juvenile Court**	**Public Health**	**Social Service**	**Credit Bureau**	**At Least 1 Agency**
High-accident	34	17	14	18	34	66
Accident-free	1	1	0	1	6	9

Lest one thinks of Tillman and Hobbs' finding as a dramatic aberration, more than 50 years later, across the Atlantic, Broughton (2007) corroborated the same general inescapable conclusion that traffic violations on the road are closely associated with social maladjustment off the road. For his analysis, Broughton studied the relationship between citations for traffic violations and non-motoring offenses committed on a sample of over 52,000 English drivers during the period 1999-2003. The most common non-motoring specific offenses were theft, violence against a person, drug offenses, criminal damage, burglary, fraud and forgery, robbery, and sexual offenses. The most common traffic violations were speeding, driving without proper insurance, driving without a proper license, driving under the influence of alcohol or drugs, disobeying traffic signs and directions, driving while suspended, and careless or reckless driving. Driving offenses were subdivided into serious violations (dangerous driving, drinking and driving, and driving while disqualified) and "other" offenses. Almost regardless of how he analyzed the data, Broughton found a very strong and very dramatic relationship between the two types of offenses. For example, people who committed 4-8 non-motoring offenses were cited for, on average, 21 times as many serious motoring violations, and 4 times as many "other motoring offenses" as those having non-motoring offenses. The relationship was different for men and women and is illustrated in Figure 9-1 for different frequencies of non-motoring offenses. The only (unexplainable) exception to this relationship was obtained for speeding violations, where non-motoring violations actually decreased with increasing citations for speeding. This may be due to the fact that speeding is a socially acceptable violation and is directly related to education and income: higher income and more educated drivers are more likely to speed (Shinar *et al.*, 2001). The problem is further exacerbated by the finding that even before they are old

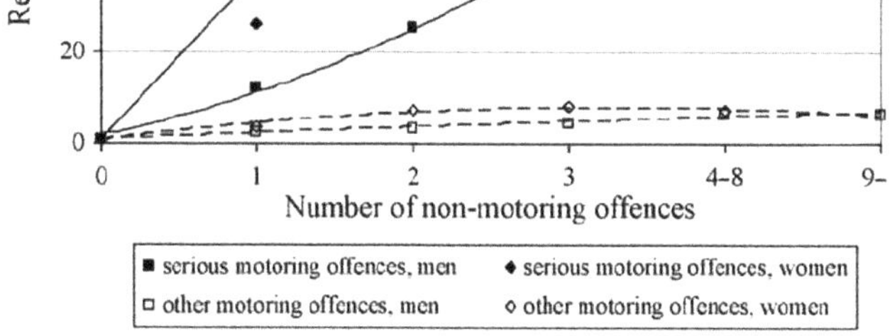

Figure 9-1. Relative number of citations for motoring offenses for people arrested for non-motoring offenses. The relative number is the relative risk of "serious" and "other" motoring offenses: (number committing a motoring offense of a given type/number not committing any motoring offense of that type) (from Broughton, 2007, with permission from Elsevier).

enough to start driving (in England), 11- to 16-year-old boys who manifest higher levels of social deviancy, also report more positive attitudes toward driving violations (Waylen and McKenna, 2008). Another possibly related finding of the link between social maladjustment and crash involvement is that of Staplin and Gish (2005). They found that the odds ratio of truck drivers of being involved in two or more crashes increases with the number of times they change jobs over a given time period. Of course, it is hard to determine the chain of causality, because involvement in multiple crashes could also lead to being fired from a job.

In general, various studies have been able to document the significant associations between various maladjustments and mental disorders and over-involvement in crashes. One particular aspect and increasingly common form of social maladjustment, attention-deficit hyperactivity disorder (ADHD) has been repeatedly linked to crash involvement (Jerome, Segal, and Habinski, 2006), even in delivery motorcycle drivers (motoboys) who use a motorcycle to deliver people and goods (Kieling *et al.*, 2011)

Aggressive Driving

One area of concern – and the focus of this chapter – is the relationship between driver's personality and his or her aggressive driving behaviors. The model presented in Figure 9-2 is one conceptual approach to describe the relationship between the two (Shinar, 1998). Different aspects of this model have been partially validated in several studies on the effects of age, gender, anonymity, and time pressure (O'Brien, Tay, and Watson, 2004; Lee and LaVoie, 2014); disposition toward anger (Danaf, Abou-Zeid, and Kaysi, 2015; Haje and Symbaluk, 2014; Zhang and Chan, 2016); sense of control (Stephens and Ohtsuka, 2014); cross-cultural differences (Sârbescu, Stanojević, and Jovanović, 2014); and road works (Walker and Calvert, 2015). Although this model is framed within concepts formulated long ago by Dollard *et al.* (1939), it is very consistent with Ajzen's (1991, 2011) theory of planned behavior (see Chapter 3).

In the remainder of this chapter, I shall focus on the relationship between personality and aggressive driving and illustrate how the various other factors that appear in the model above intervene to affect the resulting observable aggressive behavior. While it makes sense to describe all the factors from top to bottom, we must first define our dependent measure of behavior that appears at the bottom of the model: aggressive driving.

Aggression, frustration, and aggressive driving

To the extent that art is a reflection of reality, then it appears that aggressive driving even predated the motor-vehicle (see Figure 9-3). Aggressive driving was explicitly stated as a significant traffic safety problem nearly 50 years ago in a short monogram published in England and titled "Aggression on the Road'" (Parry, 1968). At about the same time,

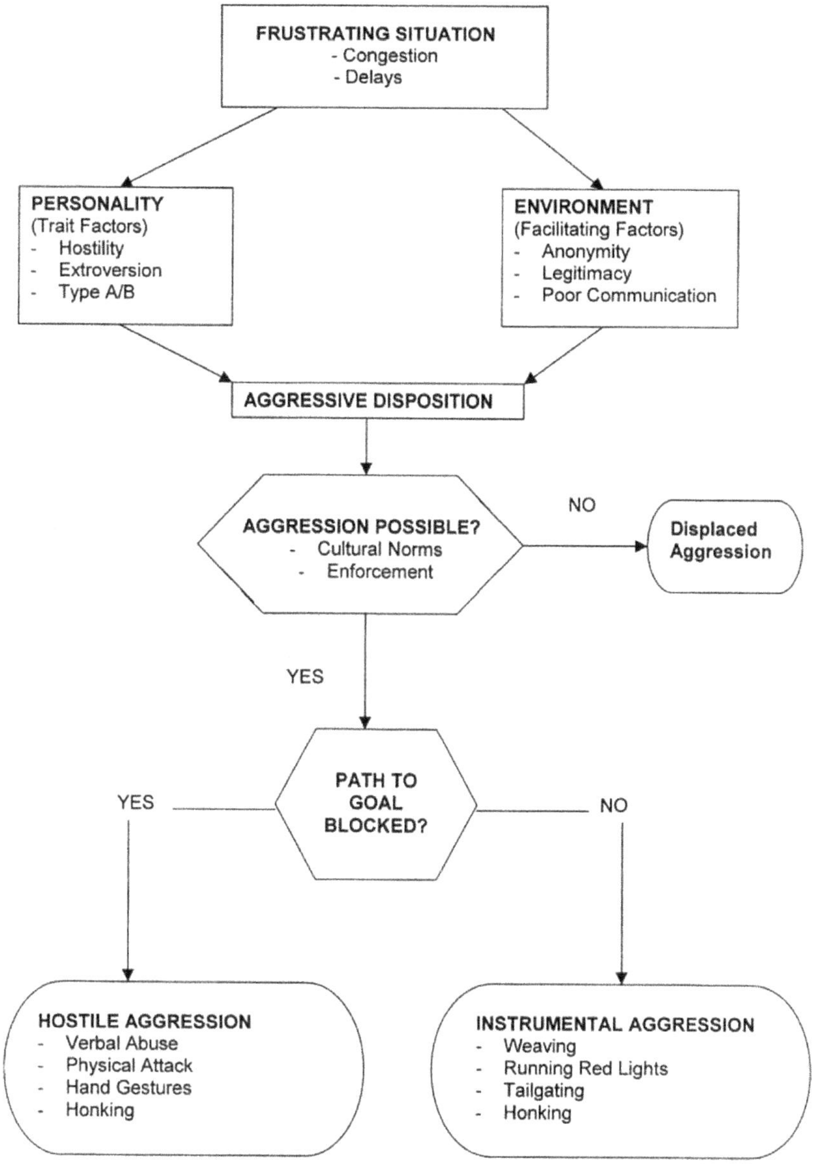

Figure 9-2. A proposed model to illustrate the interaction between personality characteristics, situational variables, and overt behaviors of aggressive driving (reprinted from Shinar, 1998, with permission from Elsevier).

Whitlock argued that aggression is the reason for 85 percent of all crashes, at least in Great Britain (Whitlock, 1971). However, the public interest in aggressive driving gained widespread interest only in the past two decades. In a survey of a representative sample of American drivers conducted slightly more than 10 years ago, 37 percent identified

Figure 9-3. Aggressive driving is not a new phenomenon (from Les Deux Carrosses by Claude Guillot, 1707).

"aggressive drivers" as the greatest threat to safety on the road – on par with distracted drivers and above all other potential threats (Mason-Dixon, 2005). Similarly, alarming high frequencies of drivers concerned with aggressive driving were obtained in other earlier American and Canadian surveys (AAA Foundation for Traffic Safety, 1997; NHTSA, 1998; Smart, Mann, and Stoduto, 2003; Tasca, 2000). Interestingly, only 16 percent of the Mason-Dixon (2005) sample admitted to engaging in aggressive driving themselves.

An international survey of driver opinions on aggressive driving was conducted by Gallup in 2003, covering representative samples of drivers in 23 different countries. In this survey, 75 percent of the American drivers and 80 percent of the European and Australian drivers believed that "the aggressiveness of drivers has increased over the past few years."

A major flaw in these surveys is that aggressive driving is either not well-defined or defined differently in different surveys. So having defined personality, we must now define aggressive driving. Although we know it when we see it, it is difficult to define in legally operational terms. Thus, in the U.S. by 2012 only 15 states had addressed aggressive driving in their legislature (GHSA, 2014). A practical approach is to build on the abundant psychological research in the area of aggression and see how it can be applied to the driving context. This can be done within the context of a "frustration-aggression" model proposed three quarters of a century ago in 1939 by Dollard and his associates (Dollard *et al.*, 1939), on the basis of their work with laboratory rats. They defined aggression as a "sequence of behavior, the goal-response to which is the injury of the person toward whom it is directed"' (p. 9), and postulated (and demonstrated very convincingly) that "aggression is always a consequence of frustration" (p. 2). Interestingly, though their experimental work was done with rats, already in 1939 Dollard and his associates chose to illustrate the frustration-aggression model in the context of driving. In their example, they used the behavior of a hypothetical college student who is stopped and berated by a police officer (the frustration source) in front of his girlfriend. Once he drove away, according to Dollard *et al.*, the student "grated the gears frequently in shifting, refused to let other cars pass him, and made insulting comments about every policeman who came in sight" (p. 12). This link of aggression to frustration is very important, because it also implies that aggressive behaviors do not happen in a vacuum. Instead, they are instigated by a frustrating situation, behavior, or event. The critical role of frustration is also acknowledged in the Merriam Webster dictionary where aggression is defined as "hostile, injurious or destructive behaviour especially when caused by frustration."

Measures of aggressive driving and road rage

With these concepts of aggression in mind we can now define and distinguish between the terms "aggressive driving" and "road rage." In this discussion – as implied by the model in Figure 9-2 – aggressive driving is defined as a syndrome of frustration-driven instrumental behaviors which are manifested in (a) inconsiderateness toward or annoyance of other drivers (tailgating, flashing lights, and honking at other drivers) and (b) deliberate dangerous driving to save time at the expense of others (purposefully running red lights and stop signs, obstructing path of others, weaving). We can also distinguish it from road rage which I define as a hostile (versus instrumental) behavior that is purposefully directed at other road users. Road rage can manifest itself in either driving behaviors (e.g., purposefully slowing in front of a following vehicle or purposefully hitting another vehicle) or non-driving behaviors (e.g., physically attacking someone, such as a driver of another vehicle). Road rage can also be directed at pedestrians, in the form of "assault with a vehicle" (that at least in one study accounted for approximately one percent of 5,000 pedestrian crashes; Hunter, Stutts, and Pein, 1977). Note that according to these definitions, neither aggressive driving nor road rage include speeding, because speeding – by itself – is not a behavior that is either directed at or inconveniences other drivers. The exclusion of speeding from aggressive driving is important because many studies of aggressive driving include speeding in the cluster of relevant behaviors while others do not. Thus, comparisons among studies are often hampered by their different – and hard to disaggregate – clusters of behaviors, especially when speeding is included in the definition. For example, Ulleberg (2004) reviewed the evidence on the effects of aggressive driving on crash risk and noted that the most dominant aggressive driving behaviors that increase crash risk are excessive speeding, tailgating, failure to yield the right of way for other road users, and red light running. More recently Paleti, Eluru, and Bhat (2010) analyzed the extensive data base of the U.S. National Motor Vehicle Crash Causation Study that includes nearly 7,000 injury crashes that occurred in 2005-2007. While they demonstrated the extensive role of aggressive driving in crashes, their definition too included speeding (the primary human behavior contributor in crashes) and consequently their estimate of the role of their "aggressive driving indicator" was not helpful in determining the role of aggressive driving in crashes.

Aggressive behavior can assume one of two general forms, listed at the bottom of the model in Figure 9-2: instrumental or hostile (Baron and Byrne, 1994). In the context of driving, instrumental behavior includes all of the driving behaviors that the aggressor assumes will help him or her move ahead and overcome the frustrating obstacle. Typical behaviors can be honking the horn at other road users blocking the road, weaving in and out of traffic, "cutting" in front of other drivers, and running red lights. Interestingly, the perception of an instrumental action may not be valid. In a quantitative analysis of simulated traffic conflicts, Habtemichael and Santos (2014) demonstrated that when reduction in travel time is the measure of the benefit of aggressive driving behaviors such as tailgating, weaving, and speeding, and crashes are the penalties, the odds ratios are definitely against aggressive driving. In their simulation, for both low and high congestion, the odds of the crashes were multiplied by a factor of 3-6, whereas the benefits were a saving of a measly 1-2 percent in travel time. This, incidentally, makes the risk-compensation hypothesis as an explanation for aggressive driving very questionable.

Hostile behaviors are actions that make us feel better without necessarily solving the problem. They are a means to vent anger and are more consistent with Dollard *et al.*'s (1939) original definition. They are actually aimed at hurting the person or thing that is frustrating us. In the context of driving, in extreme situations they fall under the category of road rage. Obviously, the dichotomy is not always clear-cut: honking the horn at a pedestrian or another driver may be both an instrumental and a hostile expression of aggression. In one interesting small study Lennon and Watson (2011) interviewed 30 drivers to determine the immediate motives behind their aggressive driving. Not surprisingly, they did not mention generalized aggression as a trait, but they did present it as a response to other inconsiderate drivers. The authors then classified their motivation as either "teaching them a lesson" or "justified retaliation." Obviously, both can lead to either instrumental or hostile actions.

Two techniques have been used to measure aggressive driving: observations and questionnaire-based self-reports. Obviously, observations of specific aggressive behaviors are more valid and objective than self-reports, but they are more difficult to conduct. Consequently, we must rely on both behavioral observations and questionnaires to understand aggressive driving.

Questionnaire-based measures of aggressive driving

The rationale behind traffic laws and regulations is that the transportation system is just that: a system. Its tolerance – from the perspective of expected driver behavior – is defined by the list of traffic violations or infringements. It is also implicitly assumed that drivers who commit many traffic violations are more likely to be involved in crashes than those who do not. This assumption has partial validity from studies that examined the relationship between violations and crashes (Barraclough *et al.*, 2016; de Winter and Dodou, 2016), though the strength of the relationship varies as a function of the violations studied (Cooper, 1997), and intervening variables such as rate of information processing (Fergenson, 1971).

From this assumed relationship between violations and crashes, it is only a small step to hypothesize that drivers who by their own admission commit many violations and unsafe driving actions should be over-involved in crashes. To test this, Reason and his associates (Reason, 1990; Reason *et al.*, 1990) developed the Driver Behavior Questionnaire (DBQ), as a tool for validating the theory of planned behavior (see Chapter 3). This questionnaire has been widely used as a stable indicator of driving behavior patterns and has been validated as such in on drivers in different countries such as France (Guého, Granie, and Abric, 2014), Denmark (Martinussen *et al.*, 2013), and China (Qu *et al.*, 2014). In a meta-analysis of 174 studies that used the DBQ, De Winter and Dodu (2010) obtained low but statistically significant correlations between DBQ errors and crashes ($r = 0.10$), and between DBQ violations and crashes ($r = 0.13$). Nonetheless, while the questionnaire as a whole may be a valid measure for actual violations, one study that tested the validity of specific reported violations (e.g., speed) relative to actual violations of the same type in simulated driving did not obtain a significant association between the two (Oppenheim *et al.*, 2015).

A version of the questionnaire, modified for American drivers by Reimer *et al.* (2005), is reproduced in Table 9-2. It consists of statements that the driver responds to by giving a score ranging from 0 to 5, where 0 indicates that the person very rarely engages in this behavior and 5 indicates that the person engages in this behavior nearly all the time. Evaluations of the DBQ have generally yielded a three-factor structure. These factors represent three types of questions in the questionnaire, indicative of three types of driving-related inappropriate behaviors:

1. Errors (E) – the results of failures of planned actions to achieve their intended consequence. Errors may result in potentially dangerous outcomes, such as crashes.
2. Violations (V) – deliberate deviations from behaviors that are considered necessary for safe driving. Aggressive behaviors are a subset of violations.
3. Lapses (L) – attention and memory failures which can cause embarrassment but are unlikely to have an impact on driving safety.

These behaviors indeed tend to cluster in the sense that people's aberrant behaviors are not randomly distributed across all three types but tend to fall into one or two specific categories. This has been demonstrated in factor analyses by Reason as well as by others (e.g., Lawton *et al.*, 1997; Özkan *et al.*, 2006a). Several large-scale surveys of drivers have validated the questionnaire by showing that the three types of items indeed represent different aspects of information processing and individual tendencies. Thus, men commit more violations – but not errors and lapses – than women (Özkan and Lajunen, *et al.*, 2006; Reimer *et al.*, 2005; Stradling and Meadows, 2000); violations and errors are more closely associated with accidents (Elliott, Baughan, and Sexton, 2007; Parker *et al.*, 1995); and older drivers' over-involvement in accidents is associated with high scores on the errors and lapses subscales (Parker *et al.*, 2000). Further research has revealed that violations have an emotional component that makes drivers "feel good" about committing them, and

Table 9-2. Reason's driver behavior questionnaire (adapted for U.S. drivers) with statements identifying errors (E), lapses (L), and violations (V). The items are rated from 0 (rarely) to 5 (nearly always) (reprinted from Reimer *et al.*, 2005, with permission from Elsevier).

#	Type	Measures
1	E	Try to pass another car that is signaling a left turn.
2	L	Select the wrong turn lane when approaching an intersection.
3	E	Fail to "Stop" or "Yield" at a sign, almost hitting a car that has right of way.
4	L	Misread signs and miss your exit.
5	E	Fail to notice pedestrians crossing when turning onto a side street.
6	V	Drive very close to a car in front of you as a signal that they should go faster or get out of the way.
7	L	Forget where you parked your car in a parking lot.
8	E	When preparing to turn from a side road onto a main road, you pay too much attention to the traffic on the main road so that you nearly hit the car in front of you.
9	L	When you backup, you hit something that you did not observe before but was there.
10	V	Pass through an intersection even though you know that the traffic light has turned yellow and may go red.
11	E	When making a turn, you almost hit a cyclist or pedestrian who has come up on your right side.
12	V	Ignore speed limits late at night or very early in the morning.
13	L	Forget that your lights are on high beam until another driver flashes his headlights at you.
14	E	Fail to check your rear-view mirror before pulling out and changing lanes.
15	V	Have a strong dislike of a particular type of driver, and indicate your dislike by any means that you can.
16	V	Become impatient with a slow driver in the left lane and pass on the right.
17	E	Underestimate the speed of an oncoming vehicle when passing.
18	L	Switch on one thing, for example, the headlights, when you meant to switch on something else, for example, the windshield wipers.
19	E	Brake too quickly on a slippery road, or turn your steering wheel in the wrong direction while skidding.
20	L	You intend to drive to destination A, but you "wake up" to find yourself on the road to destination B, perhaps because B is your more usual destination.
21	V	Drive even though you realize that your blood alcohol may be over the legal limit.
22	V	Get involved in spontaneous, spur-of-the-moment, races with other drivers.
23	L	Realize that you cannot clearly remember the road you were just driving on.
24	V	You get angry at the behavior of another driver and you chase that driver so that you can give him/her a piece of your mind.

that the thrill of taking the risks involved in the violations is a sufficient motivator to engage in them (DfT, 2004).

The original DBQ is now a quarter of a century old, and the driving environment with new intelligent assistive devices and infotainment systems (technologies designed to inform and entertain drivers) have given rise to new risky behaviors. Consequently, despite its repeated validation, it may be time to revise the questionnaire. At least two recent revisions have been offered. The first is in the form of a new 35-item DBQ that was developed on French drivers by Guého *et al.*, 2014. For their scale they did an internet based survey and ended up with responses from 525 French passenger car drivers (202 men and 320 women) ranging in age from 18 to 79. Their factor analysis yielded a six-factor structure containing the following six factors: "dangerous errors," "inattention errors," "inexperience errors," "ordinary violations," "aggressive violations," and "positive behaviors." The most recent and extensive revision is that of Cordazzo, Scialfa, and Ross (2016), who created a new questionnaire containing 65 items that they administered to 3,295 (1,568 males and 1,727 females) Canadian drivers, ranging in age from under 19 to over 80. Their factor analysis yielded a four-factor structure that consisted of inattention errors, age-related problems, distraction and hurry, and aggressive violations. Together these factors accounted for a significant percent of the variance among the drivers in explaining reported at-fault collisions and police citations. Though useful for today's driving, the authors themselves point out some limitations of their study that necessitate further development of the scale.

Like all questionnaires that purport to reflect stable characteristics, it is important to determine just how stable or how consistent is a person's score over time. Özkan *et al.* (2006b) administered the DBQ to 622 drivers and found that over a 3-year period the test-retest reliability of the scale scores was only $r = 0.61$. This is a fairly low level of reliability and it means that the DBQ can vary significantly over time, as one would expect given the findings that violations tend to diminish with age while lapses tend to increase with age. With a shorter – 3-month – test-retest interval the reliability appears to be slightly higher (Parker *et al.*, 1995), and with a 1 week interval the test-retest reliability is higher still ($r > .81$ as obtained by Li *et al.*, 2004, in China!). The utility of the DBQ, and its close relationship to scales of driver violence and vengeance (Li *et al.*, 2004) has also prompted the development of a Motorcycle Rider Behavior Questionnaire (Elliott *et al.*, 2007), in order to better understand the causes of motorcycle crashes (see Chapter 16). However, some long-term stability can even be found in driving violations record. Summala, Rajalin, and Radun (2014) examined the violations records of drivers identified 24 years earlier (!) as either "risky" or not. Risky drivers were those originally stopped by the police for risky driving, and the non-risky drivers were those who approached the same locations immediately after the police completed their citations of the risky drivers. They found that even after a quarter of a century, the two groups still differed in their violations records. Based on their self-reports, the "risky" drivers drive faster and overtake others more frequently than the control group drivers. This finding demonstrates that even at the most overt level aggressive driving can be a personality trait.

A questionnaire designed to measure driving aggression more directly was developed by James and Nahl (2000), and it is reproduced in Table 9-3. The scale consists of 17 statements, ranging from very mild expressions of aggression to very extreme ones. As in Reason's questionnaire, the respondent's task is to state the extent to which these

Table 9-3. A scale for measuring aggressive driving tendencies developed by James and Nahl (2000), and the percent of American drivers who agree with each item (reprinted from Wells-Parker et al., 2002, with permission from Elsevier).

Item	**Valid Responses (Unweighted Percent)**			
	Never	**Rarely**	**Sometimes**	**Often**
Say bad things to yourself about another driver (**SAYBAD**)	15	23	40	22
Complain/yell about another driver to your passenger (**COMPLAIN**)	26	22	39	13
Give other drivers dirty looks (**DIRTY LOOK**)	42	17	32	8
Honk/yell at someone through window (**HONK**)	62	18	17	3
Obscene gestures at other driver (**OBSCENE**)	84	9	6	1
Think about physically hurting other driver (**THINK HURT**)	89	5	4	1
Follow /chase other driver in anger (**CHASE**)	97	3	<0.05	0
Make sudden or threatening driving moves (**THREAT**)	95	4	1	≤0.01
Tailgate others to force move (**TAILGATE**)	87	7	6	≤0.1
Speed past other car/rev engine to show displeasure (**SPEED**)	87	8	6	<0.05
Keep someone from entering lane from anger (**KEEP OUT**)	81	12	6	1
Deliberately prevent other driver from passing (**PREVENT PASS**)	91	5	3	≤0.05
Try to cut another car off road (**CUT OFF ROAD**)	98	1	<0.05	≤0.01
Get out of car to argue with another driver (**ARGUE**)	98	2	<0.05	≤0.01
Deliberately hit another car (**HIT CAR**)	99	<0.05	<0.01	0
Get out of the car to hurt other driver (**HURT**)	99	<0.05	<0.01	0
Carry weapon if needed for driving incident (**WEAPON**)	96	1	2	1

statements apply to him or her. Wells-Parker and her associates (2002) tested the relationship between the inclination toward aggressive driving as measured by this scale, and crash involvement as reported by the drivers. Their sample consisted of 1,382 drivers, representative of the U.S. driver population in age, gender, income, and education. The percent of drivers that agreed with each statement at different levels of frequency is presented next to each item in Table 9-3. As can be seen from the table, most drivers occasionally mutter to themselves or to a passenger next to them unflattering comments about other drivers, and give other drivers dirty looks. However, very few drivers actually engage in overt aggressive driving that can directly lead to a crash, such as make a sudden or threatening driving maneuver, chase another driver in anger, try to cut another driver off the road, or deliberately hit another car.

When Parker *et al.* (2002) tried to relate these behaviors to crash involvement they concluded that there is no relationship between the mild expressions of annoyance and crash involvement. But the few people who tend to engage in actual confrontations with other drivers that frustrate them were involved in significantly more crashes (even after controlling for various confounding factors such as exposure, gender, age, and education). Furthermore, the few drivers who manifested this tendency toward extreme aggressive driving, also reported habitual speeding, and frequent driving after drinking. Thus, these results suggest that aggressive driving in milder forms is common to most drivers – and is dictated more by frustrating situations than by stable personality traits. Only extreme personality characteristics associated with aggression are therefore associated with individual differences in crash involvements.

Behavioral observable measures of aggressive driving

As indicated by the model in Figure 9-2 various behaviors that satisfy the definitions of aggressive driving can actually be observed. These have included – and will be discussed below in the context of specific studies – instrumental behaviors such as honking, weaving and cutting across multiple lanes, tailgating, and passing on the shoulders. Hostile aggressive behaviors that are observable include honking, cursing, and obscene gestures. As with questionnaire-based measures, observable measures also seem to be correlated, as illustrated by the results of a study by Shinar (1998), reproduced in Table 9-4, in which drivers' path was blocked by a car stopped in traffic in front of a green light. The

Table 9-4. The association between mean honking delay, type of honking behavior, and exhibition of visible signs of impatience (cursing and/or making hand gestures) (reprinted from Shinar, 1998, with permission from Elsevier).

	People Who Responded with:		
Manifested aggression in:	A single short honk (n = 51)	Repeated honks (n = 34)	Continuous honking (n = 42)
Honking delay	4.1 seconds	2.9 seconds	2.4 seconds
Visible impatience	15.7%	16.8%	62.9%

data indicate that the drivers who were the quickest to show their impatience by honking, also tended to honk continuously, or "lean" on their horn, and were also much more likely to express their hostility by gestures or by cursing the impeding driver. Ellison *et al.* (1995) using a similar technique to elicit aggressive responses from drivers also obtained significant correlations between the delay in honking, the frequency of honking, and the duration of honking.

Frustrating situations – Catalysts for aggressive driving

Although some drivers may be aggressive even in the absence of an apparent reason, Lajunen, Parker, and Stradling (1998) who surveyed 270 Finnish drivers, and Ward, Waterman, and Joint (1999) who surveyed 362 UK drivers, both found that drivers were more likely to report aggressive traffic violations when their progress was impeded; i.e., when they were frustrated. Dukes *et al.* (2001) provided undergraduate students with vignettes of aggressive and frustrating driving situations (a driver shifting in and out of lane nearly hitting the student's car, and a slow driver impeding the progress of a student's car, respectively). Using structural equation modeling they showed that these situations created feelings of anger and an inclination to retaliate against the offending driver. Roidl, Frehse, and Höger (2014) used a simulated driving task to show how frustrating situations, such as a slow car ahead of the driver, a construction zone, and an obstacle on the street, elicited feelings of anger and aggressive driving behaviors such as rapid accelerations and high speed once the impeding obstacle was passed.

Perhaps the primary reason for impedance of movement is congestion. The rapid increase in traffic density on the roads in the past few decades invariably leads to congestion and delays in driving. In the U.S. between 1983 and 2003, the increase in congestion in the largest metropolitan areas, resulted in a three-fold increase in the annual hours of delays in traffic from approximately 20 to slightly over 60 hours per person (Schrank and Lomax, 2005). But congestion is not the only reason for delays in traffic. Other reasons can include red lights, closure of travel lanes for maintenance, obstruction of travel lanes by disabled vehicles, and even impeded progress due to slow drivers. Smart *et al.* (2004) found that reports of aggressive driving and road rage were significantly associated with urban density and stressful driving conditions, and Van Rooy (2006) found that congestion, and even anticipation of congestion lead to feelings of anxiety and anger, which in turn can lead to driving aggression. Furthermore, aggression is only one way of coping with congestion. Hennessy and Wiesenthal (1997) found that in congested highway driving, typical of rush hour traffic, people report that they resort to one of three types of behaviors: direct coping behaviors through strategic planning (such as seeking preplanned routes and listening to radio traffic reports), "time facilitation behaviors" that help distract the driver from the driving task (such as listening to music or the radio), and – at the immediate control level – aggressive behaviors (such as tailgating, swearing and yelling at other drivers, and horn honking). While the incidence of aggressive behaviors increases during congestion, Hennessy and Wiesenthal (1997) found that these behaviors still ranked behind both direct coping behaviors and time facilitation behaviors.

In a series of studies conducted in Israel, we examined the effects of congestion and obstructions to movement, and in general demonstrated how they promote aggressive behaviors. These studies and others, suggest that the recent awareness of an increase in aggressive driving is probably not due so much to changes in drivers' personalities but to changes in congestion that create more delays and frustrations that are then manifested in more aggressive behaviors. This argument is illustrated in Figure 9-4, where actual densities of vehicles on U.S. highways from 1980 to 1995 are plotted over time. Overlaid on these real data are hypothetical distributions of the threshold of aggression of the driving population. The threshold is the amount of frustration that is needed to elicit overt aggressive behaviors. Let us assume – as drawn in Figure 9-4 – that the three distributions are identical in their means and variance. However, as the density of traffic (i.e., congestion) increases, it triggers aggressive behavior in more and more people, simply because the level of frustration increases to the point where it exceeds the threshold of a greater proportion of the driving population. What we witness then is simply an increase in the level of on-road societal frustration that exceeds the threshold of overt aggressive behavior of more and more people. Although the data in Figure 9-4 only go as far as 1995, the congestion – as measured by vehicles per roadway miles – has only increased since then, aggravating the problem and supposedly leading to more aggressive driving.

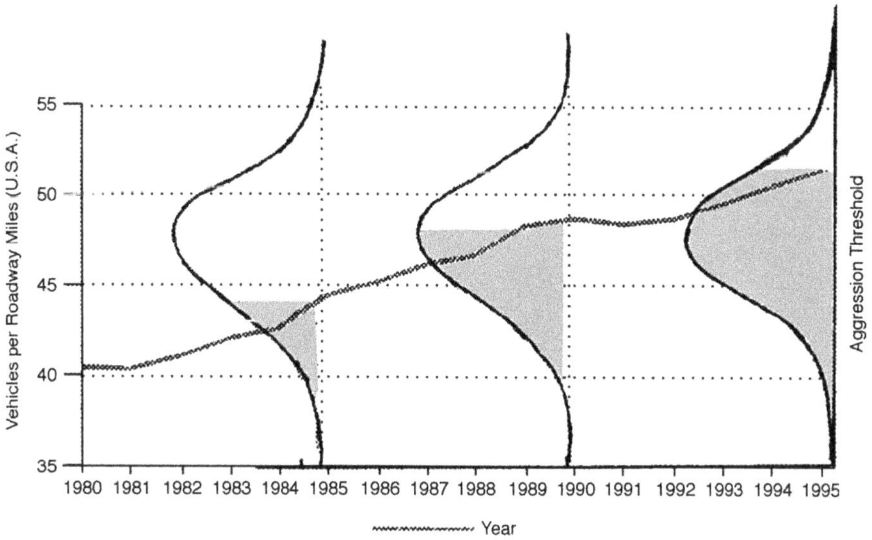

Figure 9-4. A proposed relationship between traffic density and the number of people showing aggressive driving. The monotonic function reflects actual increase in traffic density in the U.S. over time. The three identical normal distributions are hypothetical distributions of the threshold of aggression that remains the same over time. As congestion increases it exceeds the aggression threshold of more and more people (reprinted from Shinar, 1998, with permission from Elsevier).

There is empirical support for this argument. In one study (Shinar and Compton, 2004) we observed over 2000 aggressive driving behaviors at different locations in Israel in the course of 72 hours of observations. The aggressive behaviors that were recorded ranged from mild ones (honking, and cutting across a single lane) to severe ones (cutting across multiple lanes and passing on the shoulders). When we plotted the relationship between the number of aggressive actions and the traffic volume at each of the locations at the times that the behaviors were observed, we obtained a highly linear relationship with a correlation of $r = 0.90$. These data are plotted in Figure 9-5, and show that while the prevalence of observable aggressive actions increased with congestion, the *rate* of increase remained the same. This means that congestion per-se does not seem to significantly affect the *likelihood* of aggressive driving for a given driver (as Figure 9-4 would suggest if congestion is a frustrating event), and the increase in the number of aggressive acts observed at greater traffic densities for the most part simply reflects the increase in the number of cars on the road. Obviously to the passing driver – who actually observes more conflicts and more aggressive driving than on a relatively empty road – this seems to be an increase in aggressive driving. In a less controlled study in California, Sarkar, Marineau *et al.* (2001) also noted that the number of calls that motorists made to the police to complain of aggressive driving correlated with the level of congestion on the road, but they too suggested that the effect could be explained by different levels of average daily traffic volumes in the different roads.

As the definition of aggression suggests, the likelihood of aggression should increase when the source of delay or impedance is unjustified, illegitimate, or unclear. We often experience this kind of frustration when we are stuck in a traffic jam without knowing the reason for the delay – until we pass the cause of the delay (e.g., a lane closure because of traffic or because of road work) sometime later. A more rigorous demonstration of the importance of these factors is provided by a series of studies we conducted in Israel, which are briefly described below.

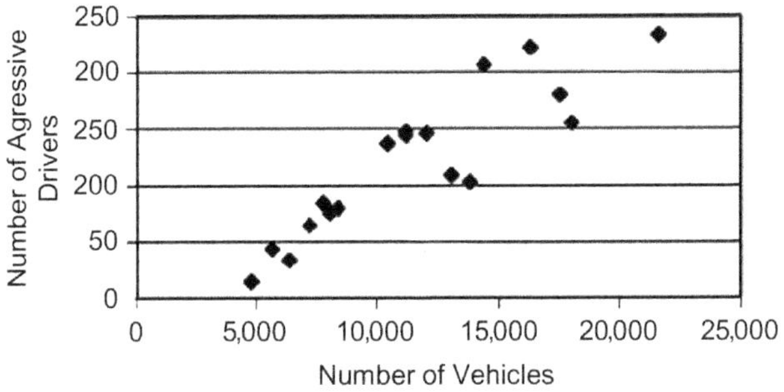

Figure 9-5. Number of drivers observed making aggressive behaviors (honking, cutting across lanes, and passing on the shoulders) as a function of the number of vehicles driving by at these hours. Each data point represents a 2-hour observation period from one of 6 locations each observed at three different times (reprinted from Shinar and Compton, 2004, with permission from Elsevier).

To test the effects of frustration caused by delays, we first tested the aggressive behavior in response to situations that differed in the amount of delay that they caused. In the first study, we observed the number of drivers who ran a red light as a function of the duration of the green and red light phase (the two are not complementary because the total cycle time also varies among intersections). Ten intersections with green-phase durations varying from 10 to 50 seconds were observed for 100 light cycles each. The results, illustrated in Figure 9-6 demonstrate that the shorter the green phase, the more drivers tended to run the red light rather than wait for another cycle. An inverse, but not as systematic effect of the duration of the red phase was also found, with more drivers running the red light when the red phase was long than when it was short. Of course the explanation of the light duration in terms of 'frustration' rests on the assumption that the drivers running the lights knew that the green phase was short and the red phase was long; a relatively safe assumption given the frequent waiting in queues, and the high likelihood that most of the drivers on these streets were local drivers.

But the duration of the traffic signal light is only an indirect measure of delay. To assess the effects of delay at the signal more directly, in a follow-up study we observed forty traffic lights with varying durations, half in a fast-paced city (Tel Aviv) and half in a slow-paced city (Beer Sheva). Each signal was observed for 100 cycles during the daytime hours and 100 cycles during the night hours, yielding a total of 80,000 traffic light cycle observations. In this study the delay of each driver that ran the red light was measured directly in terms of the time that the driver waited in the queue of cars prior to crossing the red light. A total of 226 drivers entered the intersection after the light change (all within 1-3 seconds) and the number who entered as a function of the time they waited in the queue is plotted in Figure 9-7. The correlation between the number of cars that entered the intersection after the light changed and the waiting time was

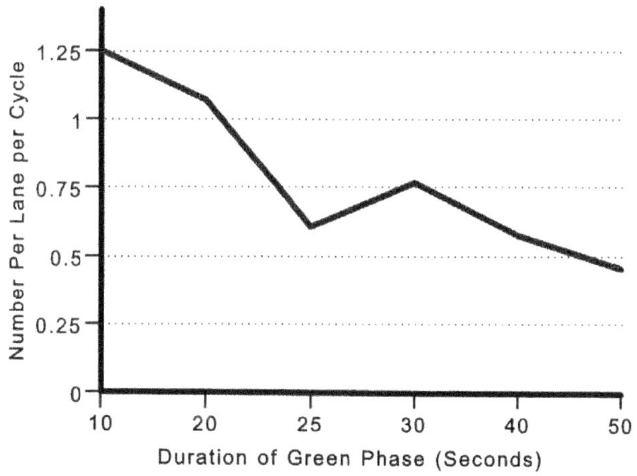

Figure 9-6. Number of drivers who run the red light per lane per cycle as a function of the duration of the green phase (reprinted from Shinar, 1998, with permission from Elsevier).

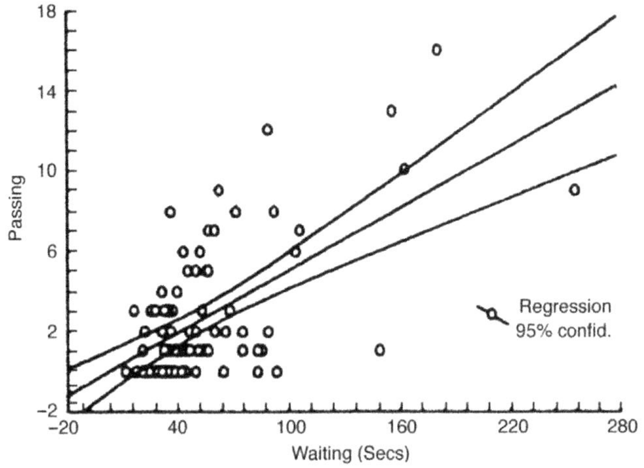

Figure 9-7. The relationship between the number of cars passing through the red light at signalized intersections and their waiting time in the queue; r = 0.60 (reprinted from Shinar, 1998, with permission from Elsevier).

0.60. Interestingly, the correlation between the number of cars that entered after the light change and the observer's subjective rating of the congestion at the intersection at the time was even higher: 0.75. Although it is possible that the observer's perceived congestion was also influenced by the measurement of the delay times, it may be that the drivers' sense of delay was more closely related to the observer's rating than to the actual time. An even stronger relationship between red light running and waiting time at the traffic signal was obtained in a later study where we observed 3600 traffic light cycles in 12 urban intersections. In that study the linear correlation between the likelihood of running the red light and the number of cars in the queue in front of the driver was a very high r = 0.91 (Shinar, Bourla, and Kaufman, 2004). Hamdar, Mahmassani, and Chen (2008) in an observational study in the Washington DC area also found that the propensity toward aggressive driving in an intersection is directly related to the delays it involves.

To directly affect frustration we needed to find a way to manipulate the delay, rather than rely on the observed delay. For this we conducted several studies that employed a technique originally developed by Doob and Gross (1968). In this method a confederate driver pulls in front of another car and drives up to a signalized intersection immediately after the light turns red. Then when the light turns green the confederate driver remains stationary and records the behavior of the driver that is being detained behind the confederate. In the first study of this kind we manipulated the delay at two signalized intersections: one with a long green phase of 35 seconds, and one with a short green phase of only 10 seconds. Time pressure was studied indirectly by observing the drivers' behavior during daily rush hours versus during weekend hours. The results of this study, shown in Figure 9-8, validated the interpretation of the previous findings by showing that delaying drivers at a short green light is more frustrating than delaying them at a long green light;

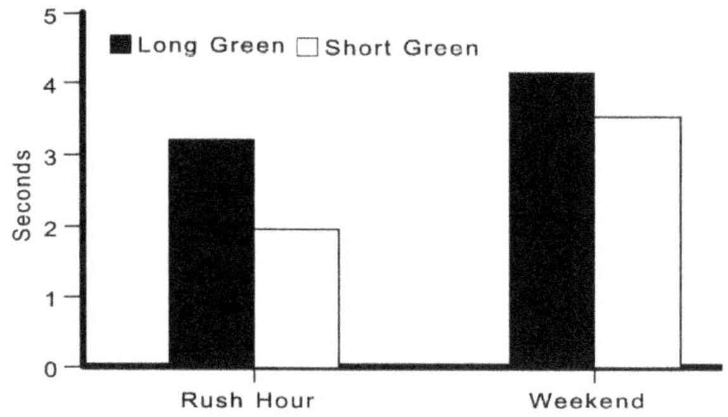

Figure 9-8. The effects of green light duration and traffic congestion/pressure, on honking delay after the light turns green and the lead car fails to start moving (reprinted from Shinar, 1998, with permission from Elsevier).

causing drivers to honk sooner after the light change than when the green phase is long. This study also showed that the frustration in response to the same event is greater during weekday rush hours than during weekend hours, and the importance of this finding relative to the value of time is discussed further below.

To validate the results of this study, a much larger one was conducted at multiple intersections. This time the confederate driver drove from one intersection to another, covering a total of 15 different intersections with a short green phase (10 seconds or less) and 15 different intersections with a long green phase (30 seconds or more). A total of 240 trials were run under various conditions that were assumed to create different levels of expected stress and frustration. As before, when the confederate driver failed to move drivers waited a shorter time before they honked at intersections with a short green phase than at intersections with a long green phase (3.0 s versus 3.7 s). Also, as found in many other studies, younger drivers were more aggressive and impatient and honked sooner than older looking drivers.

There is one study – by Lajunen, Parker, and Summala (1999) – that looked for but failed to find the anticipated relationship between congestion and aggressive behavior. However, Lajunen *et al.* did not conduct empirical observations of either congestion or aggressive driving. Instead, for surrogates of congestion they used national data of traffic density (vehicles per kilometers of roadway) in England (with greatest density of 62.9), the Netherlands (with density of 48.9), and Finland (with the lowest density of 28.1 vehicles per kilometer), and drivers answers in response to questions about their experiences in congestion. To evaluate aggression they used national violations statistics and drivers' responses to the DBQ (see Table 9-2). Their results did not show any significant differences in aggressive driving that were consistently related to their measures of congestion exposure. Aside from the significant methodological difference in the approach – of directly studying causality versus surmising causality from association (see Chapter 2) – it is possible that the reason the level of reported aggression was similar is because all three countries are highly industrialized, and as such most of their drivers drive in and reside in similarly congested urban centers, regardless of the national statistics of traffic densities.

The value of time – An intervening variable in the effects of congestion on aggression

One common finding in all the empirical studies quoted above is that the measured level of aggression was differentially affected by the value of time. This was demonstrated in our studies in three different ways. (1) The pace of life: under the same traffic signal conditions, drivers were more likely to run the red lights in the fast-paced city of Tel Aviv than in the slow-paced city of Beer Sheva. Furthermore, the disparity increased as the waiting time increased, to the point that in the fast-paced city, the long delays resulted in 2.5 times as many red light crossings as in the slow-paced city (see Figure 9-9). (2) Day of week: as mentioned above drivers were more impatient and honked sooner during weekdays' work hours than during weekends (3.1 versus 3.6 seconds). (3) Time of day: running the red light was twice as common during the daytime hours as during the night, despite the fact that enforcement was much lighter at night. Wiesenthal, Hennessy, and Totten (2003) also discovered that drivers were more likely to express mild aggression when they were under time pressure than when they were not.

Kinnear *et al.* (2015) attempted to assess directly the relationship between time pressure, frustration, and overtaking behavior. They exposed 183 UK drivers to video clips with various levels of traffic conditions and asked them to imagine how frustrating each situation is and whether or not they would attempt to overtake the vehicle ahead. They found that participants who were told that they were "under some time pressure as they were running late for an appointment" expressed a consistently higher level of frustration than those who were told that they were ""under no time pressure." And while the correlation between the level of frustration and the inclination to overtake was positive ($r = 0.64$), it was probably lower than would have been expected had it not been constrained by the actual possibility of overtaking in the different conditions.

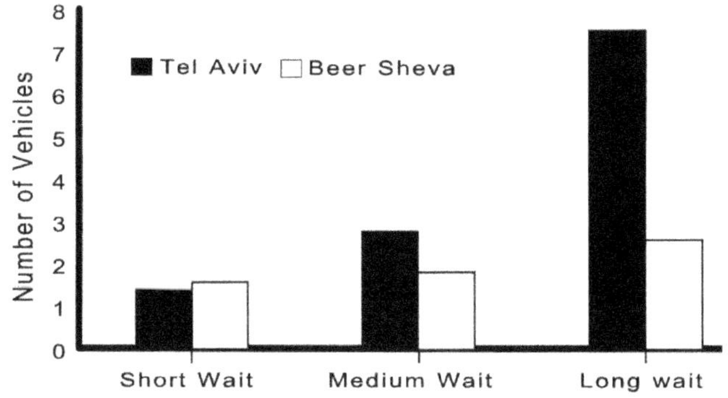

Figure 9-9. Effects of waiting time for signal change in a fast-paced city (Tel Aviv) and a slow-paced city (Beer Sheva) on the frequency of running red lights (number of vehicles running red lights per cycle per lane) (reprinted from Shinar, 1998, with permission from Elsevier).

Personality and Aggressive Driving

Psychologists have focused primarily on who is the aggressive driver? Why does he or she behave that way? And how is this behavior related to more basic measures of personality that extend to multiple domains, and not just driving? Obviously, not all drivers react to a frustrating event in the same manner, and the differences among the drivers – given the same situation – are attributed to their personality.

Driving aggression, violations, and accidents have been linked to many personality characteristics that will not be described here, but should at least be mentioned. Long before the concept of driving aggression came into vogue, Schuman *et al.* (1967) found that high-crash and high-violation male drivers scored higher on a measure of impulsivity than those with low numbers of crashes and violations. As described above, Tillman and Hobbs (1949), and Lawton *et al.* (1997) demonstrated that over-involvement in crashes and violations are related to social maladjustment. Yu, Evans, and Perfetti (2004) demonstrated significant relationships between aggressive driving behaviors and more stable characteristics such as depression and alcohol problems. Dula *et al.* (2010) administered various personality and driving behavior questionnaires to over 1,000 U.S. drivers and found that people with high trait anxiety were more likely to be involved in crashes and more likely to engage in aggressive behaviors. Lalloo, Sheiham, and Nazroo (2003) found that hyperactive children – as pedestrians – are almost twice as likely to be involved in serious accidents as age- and gender-matched non-hyperactive children. Castellà and Pérez (2004) gave 792 drivers a questionnaire that assessed their sensitivity to reward and punishment and found that people who were highly sensitive to punishment and insensitive to rewards (as a personality trait) tended to drive within the law, whereas those who were very sensitive to rewards and insensitive to punishment tended to commit many violations. This result is interesting because it exemplifies one of the difficulties of promoting safety: risky behavior behind the wheel is very rewarding to people most of the time, and punishment for it – in terms of a traffic ticket or an accident – is typically rare. Cavaiola *et al.* (2003) found that drivers involved in alcohol-related accidents score higher than control drivers on the psychopathic deviate and over-controlled hostility subscales of the commonly used Minnesota multiphasic personality inventory (MMPI) test. Butters *et al.* (2005) found that drivers who reported that they frequently engage in severe aggressive driving are more likely to have alcohol and drug history than those who do not. Gidron, Gal, and Desevilya (2003), Lajunen and Summala (1995), and Montag and Comrey (1987) found that aggressive driving behaviors and violations are related to "externality" of the locus-of-control; the tendency to attribute many events to external factors beyond the person's control. Finally, on a macro level Sivak (1983) showed that homicide rates (reflecting the prevalence of homicidal tendencies?) in the 50 U.S. states correlated positively with the traffic fatality rates (reflecting the rates of aggressive driving?).

Despite these and similar findings, a wide-sweeping generalization that personality determines driving behavior is too simplified, as the model in Figure 9-2 implies. People do not always behave in strict accordance with their personal tendencies – or personality – but rather in accordance with their personal tendencies and needs *and* the specific situational demands and constraints. Thus, we distinguish between "trait" and "state" tendencies. Trait tendencies are relatively stable and pervasive and are associated with what we call personality, and state tendencies are transient and contingent on specific environmental conditions and temporary needs of the person. Finally, stable traits and transient states may also interact so that someone who has a stable personality tendency toward risk-taking may also be more sensitive to specific situations that will elicit risk-taking behaviors. In light of all of these complications, it is not surprising that personality traits – as measured by personality inventories and tests – rarely explain more than 25 percent of the variance in individuals' social behavior (Argyle, 1983).

The low to moderate associations between personality traits and driving behavior are generally too small to be practical in predicting the specific behaviors of individual drivers, let alone their likelihood of causing accidents. Consequently, in most of the western world they are used more as tools of research or as supplemental information on drivers who have already demonstrated excessive high-risk driving (in terms of violations or crash involvement) than as effective general screening tools for licensing or license renewal. Exceptions to this generalization are four European countries that have adopted the use of "psycho-technical" tests for licensing. However, according to Lajunen (2002) the decision appears to be more a function of political expediency than of a scientifically valid decision making process. In contrast, the countries with the best traffic safety records (such as Australia, England, the Scandinavian countries, France, and the Netherlands) have not adopted this approach.

In summary, observable behavior – though it is affected by stable personality characteristics – is much more complex than the simple manifestations of personality. Still, personality traits may account for the observed correlations among various seemingly disparate on-road behaviors. For example, Golias and Karlaftis (2002) in an extensive survey of over 20,000 drivers in 19 countries found that questionnaire-based measures of individuals' risk-taking tendencies are correlated with both speeding and "general recklessness" in driving. This implies (as Golias and Karlaftis believe) that risk-taking tendencies may be an underlying factor common to both, regardless of the specific culture in which the drivers drive. Similarly, their findings suggest that a basic "law abiding tendency" may underlie the significant correlation between the use of seat belts and refraining from driving after drinking (which are not related to speeding and general recklessness). Some support for an underlying characteristic that affects both use of belts and drinking and driving also comes from a survey of U.S. nationally representative sample where the use of safety belts and refraining from drinking and driving were highly correlated, but speeding habits were not systematically associated with drinking and driving habits (Schechtman, Shinar, and Compton, 1999).

Also, as noted in the discussion above and implied by the model in Figure 9-2, the relative importance of personality in accounting for and predicting behavior varies drastically across situations. Thus, when coming up to a line of cars stopped at a red traffic light in mid-day downtown traffic all drivers stop and wait for it to turn green before proceeding, and individual differences in personalities have no bearing on this uniform behavior. In this case, personality is a very poor – essentially useless – predictor of behavior. However, let us assume a situation in which the light changes to green and one of the cars – for some unknown reason (or because it is part of the research described above) – is delayed in starting to move. In this situation we observe different responses of the drivers behind the stopped car, indicating various levels of aggression toward the stalled driver. In this situation it is quite safe to assume that the observed responses are associated with stable personality characteristics of aggression.

The discussion below will focus on the relevance of some of the personality-type characteristics that have been linked to crash involvement. Personality concepts that have been studied in the context of driving include accident proneness, risk-taking and sensation-seeking, aggression, gender and masculinity-femininity, and perceptual style. Although each of these concepts is described separately, it is important to note that various specific personality characteristics are interrelated. For example, Malta, Blanchard, and Freidenberg (2005) demonstrated that aggressive drivers can be characterized by multiple distinct medical disorders such as oppositional defiant disorder, alcohol and substance use disorders, conduct disorder, attention-deficit/hyperactivity disorder, and intermittent explosive disorder. There are also other personality traits that have been linked to driving and will not be discussed here. These include extraversion (the tendency to attend to external events rather than focus internally) (Smith and Kirkham, 1981) and externally-oriented locus-of-control (the tendency not to assume responsibility for events that happen to a person) (Mayer and Treat, 1977).

The first challenge is to determine whether or not there is a pervasive personality characteristic that makes people accident prone in general, a characteristic that has been labeled just that – accident proneness.

Accident proneness – Is there such a thing?

The most appealing – and least useful and least valid – personality characteristic that has been sought as a culprit in over-involvement in crashes is "accident proneness" (Shaw and Sichel, 1971). Simply stated this trait implies that some people have a pre-existing tendency to be involved in accidents. The concept was originally suggested nearly a 100 years ago in a study of the frequencies of industrial accidents. As a part of this study, Greenwood (Greenwood and Woods, 1919; Greenwood and Yule, 1920) tracked the industrial accidents of women working in a munitions factory and noticed that most of the accidents happened to very few women, while the majority of workers had no accidents at all. This early report led to a frantic search for the discovery of factors that would help identify these "accident prone" people in advance. In retrospect the search was quite naïve and based on both ignorance of statistical properties of rare events and psychological theory.

From the statistical perspective, accidents – including traffic accidents – by their nature are rare events. As such in a given period most people do not experience them. When aggregated over a short period of time (such as a year) they are distributed in such a manner – known as a Poisson distribution – in which very few people may have three accidents or more, a few have two accidents, and more people have one accident. However, the overwhelming majority of people have no accidents at all. We can all verify this for ourselves if we simply consider the accident experience over the past year of all the people we know personally. Despite the apparent concentration of accidents within a small sub-sample, this is still a random distribution of rare events. Thus, and this has been empirically demonstrated, if we were to remove these people from the population at risk (work force in a factory or drivers on the road), we would not significantly reduce future accidents of the population. It would only change the people that will have them. In fact, in the context of driving, Forbes (1939) demonstrated that when the high-accident drivers of one period are not removed from the driving population at one period, they are not the same drivers who are over-involved in accidents in another period. More recent studies have also demonstrated the independence of violators and accident-involved drivers at different time periods (e.g., Elliott *et al.*, 2000). Nonetheless, the issue has apparently not died. In a recent statistical analysis Blasco, Prieto, and Cornejo (2003) demonstrated that individuals have different a priori probabilities of having an accident (suggesting proneness), and once an accident happens to an individual, his or her probability of having another accident changes (suggesting dependency between crashes). Similar conclusions were reached by Visser *et al.* (2007) who reviewed 79 studies that reported crash frequencies. But because of severe methodological discrepancies in definitions of both "accident proneness" and the measure of crashes or injuries used, they narrowed their analysis to 15 studies that used samples of the general population. When they compared the rates of repeat accidents in that sample, they found that "there were more individuals with repetitive injuries than would be expected by chance alone." Thus both Blasco *et al.* (2003) and Visser *et al.* (2007) found some statistical support for the concept. But what does it mean? What characterizes accident prone people, other than the post hoc empirically demonstrated over-involvement in repeated crashes? What is the psychological trait behind the statistical phenomenon?

Psychologically and semantically the concept of accident proneness is also problematic. This is because its definition is tautological. It identifies accident prone people not on the basis of some independently measured characteristic but on the basis of their accident experience itself: as those who have had multiple accidents. This is a circuitous definition that does nothing to advance our understanding of why these people have these accidents. Still, as Evans (2004) points out, while accident proneness as a psychological characteristic that identifies people may not be valid, there may be other characteristics that make some people more prone than others to having an accident. This was demonstrated by Häkkinen (1979) who obtained significant associations between personality and information processing characteristics of Finnish bus and streetcar drivers and their likelihood to be involved in multiple crashes. The search for these accident-disposing characteristics is the focus of the remainder of this chapter.

Anger, aggression, and aggressive driving

If we accept Tillman and Hobbs' (1949) conclusion that "man drives as he lives," and that aggressive behavior in driving is simply one manifestation of aggression, then we should be able to relate a trait of generalized aggression to driving aggression. The first question here is whether or not there is a stable characteristic of anger or its expression through aggression that can serve to predict aggressive driving. In fact, as implied in the aggressive model presented above, Lajunen and Parker (2001) demonstrated on a sample of 270 British drivers that generalized aggressiveness correlates with driving aggression. Different questionnaires have been developed to measure driving anger, and they all correlate significantly with the more basic trait of generalized anger (Sullman and Stephens, 2013). Deffenbacher's Driving Anger Scale (Deffenbacher *et al.*, 2002; Stephens and Sullman, 2014) and a similar scale labeled Propensity toward Angry Driving (PAD) (Dahlen and Ragan, 2004) suggest that people do differ from each other significantly on such a trait. Thus, after controlling for the confounding effects of gender, miles driven per week, and trait anger on a sample of 232 students, Dahlen and Ragan showed that PAD still correlated significantly with moving tickets, minor accidents, aggressive driving, risky driving, and maladaptive driving and anger expression. Interestingly, it did not predict major accidents, but that may have been due to their relative rarity in the small sample of subjects evaluated. In a later study Dahlen *et al.* (2012) administered various questionnaires to 308 American license renewal applicants and found that drivers who were high on driving anger and low on agreeableness reported driving more aggressively and had more traffic citations and crashes than those who scored low on anger and high on agreeableness. Nesbit and Conger (2012) classified drivers as either low or high in aggressive driving based on Deffenbacher's driving anger scale and found that the high-driving aggression drivers scored higher on various trait anger scales. Kovácsová, Rošková, and Lajunen (2014), using a sample of 612 Slovak and Czech drivers, found that anger did not relate to directly to reported expressive aggression on the road, but did correlate with driving anger, which in turn correlated with aggressive "warnings" such as the use of flashing lights. Using a much larger sample of 7,423 Norwegian drivers Assum (1997) found that drivers who showed little concern or regard for other drivers (based on their answers to questionnaires), and were therefore labeled by him as "inconsiderate" were – based on their own responses to a second questionnaire distributed 2 years later – 2.6 times more likely to become involved in a collision within a 2-year period after answering the questionnaire (even after adjusting for the kilometers driven) than "considerate drivers."

Perhaps the most direct relationship between general aggression and driving aggression was demonstrated by Van Rooy and his associates (2006). They compared the responses of 322 drivers to a general aggression questionnaire and three different driving aggression questionnaires, and found that they are all highly interrelated, as illustrated in Figure 9-10. In fact the correlation between the general trait of aggression and the combined factor of driving aggression (which they labeled "road rage"), is essentially the same as the correlations among the three independent measures of driving aggression. Therefore, as Van Rooy and his partners concluded, aggressive driving is simply one mode in which a basic trait of aggression manifests itself, again substantiating Tillman and Hobbs's half-century-old conclusion that we drive as we live.

Using a similar structural equation modeling, Björklund (2008) found that anger (or irritation, as she labeled it) is a common response to three types of behaviors by other drivers: impeding one's progress by driving slower than called for (as predicted

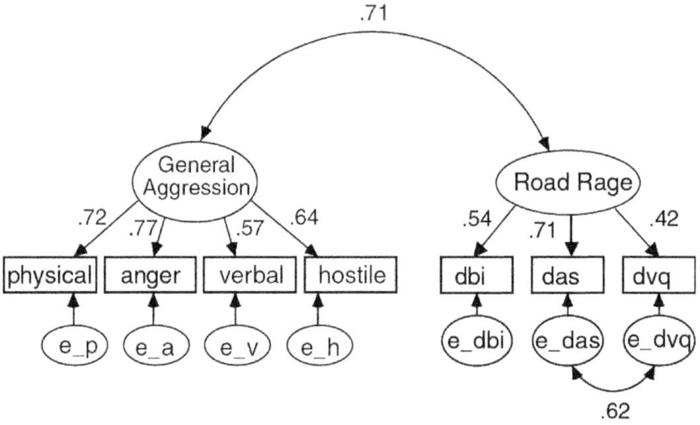

Figure 9-10. The factor loadings (correlations between the communal factor and the individual variables) of general aggression and driving aggression (labeled as "road rage") based on three different questionnaires: Driving Anger Scale (das), Driver Vengeance Questionnaire (dvq), and Driver Behavior Inventory (dbi), and among subscales of these questionnaires (from Van Rooy, Rotton, and Burns, 2006, with permission from John Wiley and Sons).

from the model in Figure 9-2), driving recklessly, and direct expressions of hostility. However, not all behaviors that stimulate anger, elicit aggressive reactions from the angered drivers. Thus, at least as far as Swedish drivers are concerned, tailgating, not dimming lights when driving toward you, backing up without looking first, and cutting in front to "steal" a parking spot are very likely to generate an aggressive reaction, while speeding and weaving in order to move quicker do not. In Israel, Taubman – Ben-Ari and Yehiel (2012) conducted a factor analysis of the responses of a heterogeneous sample of Israeli drivers to multiple personality and driving style questions and found that reckless driving behaviors and anger were associated with high levels of extraversion and thrill-seeking and low levels of "agreeableness" and conscientiousness. In Serbia, Jovanović *et al.* (2011) used regression analyses on data from 400 drivers to examine the relationship between personality factors, driving anger, and aggressive driving. They obtained results similar to those of Taubman – Ben-Ari and Yehiel (2012) noting that "neuroticism, agreeableness, and conscientiousness predicted driving-related anger and aggression … (and that) the relationship between neuroticism and aggressive driving is mediated by the driver's anger." Haje and Symbaluk (2014) administered multiple questionnaires including Deffenbacher's Driving Anger Questionnaire to 298 Canadian students and also found a moderate and significant correlation between driving anger and aggressive driving. Finally, in an interesting meta-analysis of the results of 26 different studies published between 1990 and 2003, Nesbit, Conger, and Conger (2007) found that anger is associated with aggressive driving, and it is irrelevant whether or not the anger was a reflection of a stable personality trait or a temporary state-induced one. The conclusion that emerges from all of these studies is that while the specific forms of aggressive behaviors that trigger an aggressive driving response may be culturally specific, the general pattern is the same: personality traits and transient states that measure anger and aggression are also associated with various aspects of aggressive driving.

A shortcoming of the above studies is that they are essentially correlational in nature and not experimental. Thus, the claim for cause (anger) and effect (aggressive driving) is based on a theoretical model rather than on empirical demonstration. However, there have been a few demonstrations in simulated driving environments that show that emotions created in the laboratory can affect driving. Thus, emotionally charged conversations can be more disruptive to driving than neutral ones (Shinar, Tractinsky, and Compton, 2005); Roidl *et al.* (2013, 2014). Donkor, Burnett, and Sharples (2014) confronted their drivers in a driving simulator with frustrating situations (such as an obstacle on the road) and found that these situations indeed generated feelings of anger and aggressive driving. In another simulator study we (Abdu, Shinar, and Meiran, 2012) induced anger by asking drivers to recall personal events that made them angry, and describe them in detail. Following this exercise the drivers had to drive in heavy urban traffic for 12 kilometers. As expected, drivers crossed many more yellow lights after anger induction than after the recall of emotionally neutral events.

Finally in a quasi-experimental study, conducted on the road in actual driving, Johnson and McKnight (2009) recruited drivers who previously scored either high or low on the Driver Anger Scale, and had them drive a preselected route containing construction work and related congestion on arterial roads and on an Interstate (high-speed limited access) highway. Half the drivers in each group received advance warning about the expected construction-related delays and half did not. Unbeknown to the drivers their driving behavior was being monitored through a camera positioned behind the front license plate and recording of the gas and brake pedals. The results showed that high-anger drivers drove significantly more aggressively when they received no warning than when they did, while low-anger drivers responded in the opposite manner, though their level of aggression (in the presence of warning) was relatively low – at nearly the same level as that of the high-anger drivers when they received the warning. Thus, though anger was not *experimentally* manipulated, congestion warning was and the outcome clearly showed the interaction of the personality factor (anger) with the environmental factor (congestion with and without warning).

The plethora of studies with different methodologies all showing a relationship between anger and driving aggression, and a recent meta-analysis of 51 studies that examined the relationship between anger and aggressive driving (Zhang and Chan, 2016), provide a very strong support for this part of the aggressive driving model presented in Figure 9-2. However, it is also important to acknowledge the multiple factors that mediate between anger or other personality traits and overt expressions of aggressive driving. For example, in an interesting study using content analysis of driving logs and responses to various questionnaires, Millar (2007) showed that a trait known as "public consciousness" can moderate the impact of anger. In his study, 125 American undergraduate students kept driving logs and filled out the driving anger scale and a "public consciousness" questionnaire. The driving logs were rated by two independent raters in terms of their

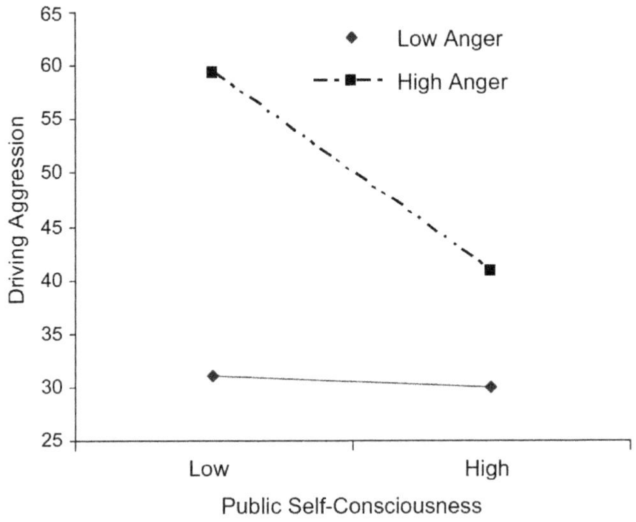

Figure 9-11. The association of driving anger and driving aggression at low self-consciousness (one SD below the mean) and high self-consciousness (one SD above the mean) (from Millar, 2007; with permission from Elsevier).

driving aggression. The results, partially reproduced in Figure 9-11, revealed that in general drivers with high-anger levels were more aggressive than drivers with low anger. Furthermore, those who were low in driving anger were low in driving aggression, irrespective of their public consciousness level. However, and this is the important part, drivers who scored high on anger drove more aggressively if they also scored low on public consciousness. In other words, the effects of Anger on driving aggression are mediated by public consciousness. Another characteristic that interacts with anger in its effects on aggressive driving is the "illusion of control" bias (Stephens and Ohtsuka, 2014). These results demonstrate the interactions among various attributes, all making up this complex concept we call personality, and that in its interactions with the environment determines the eventual level of overt aggression.

If we wish to reduce aggression, it is important to know how it develops. In an interesting study of the possible source of aggression Bianchi and Summala (2004) assessed the driving behavior of 174 parent-child pairs, who independently filled out Reason's (1990) DBQ, and answered questions about their driving exposure, life style, number of accidents they had, and tickets they received for moving violations in the past 3 years. They found that after controlling for age, life style, and exposure, there still remained moderate associations between the parents and their children in their errors and violations scores on the DBQ, but not in the scores on attention lapses. Furthermore, it appeared that fathers influenced both their sons and daughters, while mothers influenced their daughters more than their sons. The correlations obtained between parents and their children are provided in Table 9-5. They demonstrate that aggressive driving may be an imitated behavior that children – especially males – copy from their parents – especially their fathers. It also implies that these behaviors are part of a larger network of associations that novice drivers acquire, probably long before they start driving, making such behaviors all the more resilient and harder to change. Miller and Taubman – Ben-Ari (2010), using self-reports of parents and their children also found that young drivers, a year after getting their license tend to adopt their parents' driving styles.

Table 9-5. Correlations between parents and children on the different factors in the Driver Behavior Questionnaire (reprinted from Bianchi and Summala, 2004, with permission from Elsevier).

DBQ Factor	Father-Son	Father-Daughter	Mother-Son	Mother-Daughter	Parent-Child
Errors	.39*	.31*	.48*	.36*	.37**
Ordinary violations	.32*	.62**	n.s.	.32*	.33**
Aggressive violations	n.s.	.52**	n.s.	n.s.	.21**
Lapses	n.s.	n.s.	.56*	n.s.	.20**
N	41	54	19	60	174

Note: n.s. = not statistically significant; * = $p < .05$; ** = $p < .01$.

Risk-taking and driving safety

An appealing concept in the search for a trait that would explain over-involvement in crashes and violations is that of "risk-taking," the assumption being that some people tend to take greater risks than others, and this behavior should generalize to various domains, including driving. Turner, McClure, and Pirozzo (2004) examined this issue directly and reviewed the scientific evidence for such a relationship. They restricted their evaluation to studies that measured actual objective data – rather than self-reports – of accidents, and either questionnaire-based or behavior-based assessments of risk-taking behaviors. They uncovered three studies that used relevant driving behaviors: not using seat belts, drinking and driving, driving without a license, and speeding. These behaviors were considered to be indicators of risk-taking in the context of driving. The first study they reviewed (by Perneger and Smith, 1991), was a comprehensive analysis based on the U.S. Fatal Analysis Reporting System, in which these behaviors were extracted directly from the crash reports. The authors compared their prevalence in the drivers that were cited for being at fault in the crash to their prevalence among drivers not cited for being at fault in their crashes. They found that all of these factors were strong predictors of being at fault. However, as Turner *et al.* (2004) note, the presence of these factors could have also influenced the attribution of fault by the crash investigators. The second study by Rajalin (1994) used the Finnish Fatal Accident Information Data Base, and avoided this potential confounding by comparing the violations histories of the fatal crash drivers with a random sample of drivers sampled from the driver registration files. They discovered that the crash involved drivers were more likely to have previous risk-taking violations such as driving under the influence of alcohol, speeding, and driving without a license. Using a similar case-control technique of comparing crash involved with crash free drivers Crutcher *et al.* (1994) focused on teenage drivers in Georgia, U.S. For their study they developed a driving behavior questionnaire on which they compared the two groups. As hypothesized, the crash involved drivers were more likely to report speeding, illegal passing, and taking risks while driving. Using a different approach Iversen and Rundmo (2004) also demonstrated a fairly strong association between attitudes toward violations and risky driving behavior of Norwegian drivers and their culpability in crashes. Together all of these independent analyses of disparate data bases in different parts of the world demonstrate that there is a moderate and consistent relationship between various aspects of risk-taking tendencies and crash involvement. This, among others, is one of the justifications used for the demerit point system in the enforcement of speed and other traffic laws (see Chapter 8).

Risk-taking, as a stable personality characteristic that affects driver behavior has also been examined. Musselwhite (2006) analyzed the responses of 1,555 British motorists to a 16-item questionnaire, and on the basis of cluster analysis (a statistical technique that groups individuals with similar patterns of answers into homogeneous groups) identified four distinct types of risk-taking approaches that distinguish among drivers: (1) those who take an occasional risk unintentionally, (2) those who assume a risk in response to a stressful situation or when being in a hurry, (3) those who take calculated risks when the conditions allow it (e.g. late at night), and (4) those who repeatedly take risks "for their own sake." As might be expected, the repeat risk takers tended to be the youngest of the four groups and the unintentional risk takers were the oldest of the four groups. This result is consistent with results obtained with the DBQ that show that younger drivers tend to commit more violations, whereas older drivers tend to commit more lapses and errors. It is therefore not surprising that scores on tests that measure anger and sensation-seeking tendencies correlate quite highly with scores on the DBQ, and especially on the DBQ violations subscale (Schwebel *et al.*, 2006). One problem with drivers who intentionally engage in driving-related risk-taking behaviors – such as speeding, racing, tailgating, overtaking on the right, running red lights, chasing other drivers out of anger, and driving after drinking beyond the legal BAC limit – is that they do not have an increased concern of being involved in accidents, and therefore may be unaware of the safety implications of their risky behavior (McKenna and Horswill, 2006). The reason for such apparent indifference to the risks involved may be that these drivers do not view the overall risk of a crash as significant to begin with, and therefore even multiple increases in the risk still make it seem insignificant (Yates and Chua, 2002).

There is evidence that risk-taking is a general characteristic that is manifested on the road in multiple specific high-risk behaviors. Beck, Wang, and Mitchell (2006) queried over 2,000 American drivers about their beliefs, dispositions, and habits related to driving. Out of this sample they identified 305 drivers that they labeled aggressive drivers and 1,715 drivers that they labeled non-aggressive. Aggressive drivers were those who responded "yes" to the question "In the last month have you ever: driven aggressively yourself, driven 20 mph over the speed limit, run a stop sign or traffic light, or driven after having a few drinks?" The non-aggressive drivers were those who responded "no" to this question. The aggressive drivers differed significantly from non-aggressive drivers in their attitudes toward various other high-risk driving behaviors listed in Table 9-6. In addition, as might be expected, they also found that the aggressive drivers were generally more tolerant toward drinking and driving and believed that they were less likely to be apprehended by police for driving while intoxicated (DWI) than the non-aggressive drivers. Only 26 percent of the aggressive drivers – who had all confessed to DWI – felt that they were "almost certainly likely" to be stopped by the police for DWI. Of the non-aggressive drivers, who had apparently never or hardly ever been stopped for DWI, 33 percent felt that they were "almost certainly likely" to be stopped for DWI. This result reflects both the power of avoidance learning and the actual low levels of DWI enforcement. It is likely that the aggressive drivers have actually been positively reinforced for DWI each time they drove and were not apprehended (which is typically the overwhelming majority of times they drove while intoxicated), while the non-aggressive drivers who did not commit DWI, were therefore more likely to believe in the deterrence of enforcement. The implication from this finding, suggested

Table 9-6. Difference in percent admitting to various safety-related behaviors among self-described aggressive drivers and self-described non-aggressive drivers (reprinted from Beck *et al.*, 2006, with permission from Elsevier).

Driving Behaviors	**Aggressive Drivers**	**Non-Aggressive Drivers**
	%, (n = 305)	**%, (n = 1715)**
Used a cell phone in last month	70.5	45.7*
Driven while drowsy – last month	40.3	15.5*
Had an encounter with an aggressive driver – last month	69.5	45.0*
Driven when they know they've had too much to drink – last month	13.4	0.5*
Got a ticket or citation – last month	13.4	2.4*
Wear seat belts when you drive (always/nearly always)	88.5	97.7*
Drive a car (every day)	89.2	79.3*

Note: * Difference is statistically significant at $p < .001$.

by Beck and his associates and implied by the model in figure 9-2, is that visible intense enforcement may be much more effective in suppressing risk-taking behaviors than information campaigns.

Sensation-seeking and driving

People differ in the degree that they actively seek excitement, or sensations, in their life. According to Zuckerman, sensation-seeking is "a trait defined by the seeking of varied, novel, complex, and intense sensations and experiences and the willingness to take physical, social, legal, and financial risks for the sake of such experiences" (1994, p. 27). To determine the role of sensation-seeking in everyday behavior, Zuckerman and his associates (1964) developed a Sensation Seeking Scale (SSS) in which a person is presented with 40 pairs of statements, and has to select one statement of each pair as the most appropriate for him or her. For example in one such pair one has to choose between "I like wild and uninhibited parties" and "I prefer quiet parties with good conversations." The SSS has a very high 3-week test-retest reliability of $r = 0.94$ (Zuckerman, 1994), suggesting that it taps a fairly stable personality characteristic. Like other personality inventories it is sensitive to gender and age, showing that younger people and men are greater "sensation seekers" than older people and women (Arnett, Offer, and Fine, 1997; Zuckerman, 1994). Despite the fact that none of the statements in the SSS refer to driving behavior, SSS scores have been systematically linked to self-reported and objective measures of driving behaviors and crash involvement.

Jonah (1997) reviewed 40 studies that examined the relationship between the SSS and driver behavior and noted that whenever correlations were reported, they were all significant with magnitudes in the range of 0.30-0.40, leading him to conclude that "sensation seeking is moderately related to risky driving." In his review Jonah focused on the relationship between SSS scores and three types of pre-meditated risky driving behaviors: drinking and driving, speeding, and non-use of seat belts. Thirteen of the 18 studies that examined the relationship between SSS and DWI found that higher SSS scores were associated with higher frequencies of DWI – either reported or convicted. The fifteen studies that examined the relationship between SSS scores and other risky driving behaviors – mostly speeding, but also racing, following too closely, and non-use of seat belts – all found significant associations between the two types of measures. Finally, 6 out of 11 studies that examined violations and 7 out of the 12 studies that examined accident involvement also obtained significant relationships between SSS scores and violations and crashes, respectively.

The validity of SS as a personality trait associated with driving style and crash involvement is enhanced by the fact that these studies were conducted on a myriad of drivers from different cultures and countries including Canada, Finland, Great Britain, the Netherlands, Norway, Sweden, and the U.S. One extreme negative side effect of sensation-seeking was demonstrated in a German simulation study where high sensation seekers were almost three times as likely to fall asleep at the wheel as low sensation seekers (Karrer *et al.*, 2004). Apparently for these people the absence of sufficient stimulation (as in a monotonous simulator drive) quickly induces underload. An intriguing aspect of sensation-seeking is that it may be – at least in part – genetically linked (Jonah, 1997; Zuckerman, 1994). If this is the case, then it may be possible to identify high sensation-seeking drivers in advance and treat them differentially in the driver training and licensing process.

One operational measure of sensation-seeking is driving significantly above the speed limit. Blows *et al.* (2005), interviewed nearly 22,000 New Zealand drivers on their driving behavior, their violations history, and their crash history in the past 12 months. They found that those who reported that they frequently drove over 20 km/hr over the speed limit or frequently raced for excitement had an odds ratio of approximately 2.5 (relative to those who never did), to be involved in an injury accident.

Possibly the latest development in the concept of sensation-seeking, is the development of a children's version of SSS (Morrongiello and Lasenby, 2006), that may eventually prove useful in predicting – and possibly controlling – future crash risks of today's children.

For some applications some personality scales appear to be more relevant than others. In an interesting comparison of the relevance of three personality characteristics – sensation-seeking, anger/hostility, and conscientiousness – Schwebel *et al.* (2006) found that none of these traits correlated significantly with various aggressive behaviors in a virtual environment. However, sensation-seeking was the most closely associated with self-reported violations. Similar findings were obtained by Rowden *et al.* (2011), who analyzed the responses of 247 Government employees in Queensland, Australia, to several previously validated personality inventories and the DBQ. They found that the subscales of aggression and thrill-seeking of the Driving Stress Inventory were significant predictors of violations in the DBQ.

Gender and gender identity: Masculinity and femininity

In general, men are more likely to exhibit overt aggressive behaviors than women (e.g., Berkowitz, 1993; Aniţei *et al.*, 2014). This is also apparent in driving where gender is a great divide among drivers in their driving style, driving violations, and crash involvement. It is a truism that men differ from women, and this also appears to be true in terms of their driving behavior and crash involvement – especially among the young/novice drivers (see Chapter 6). In general men are more involved in accidents than women (even after adjusting for their greater amount of driving), and are more likely to be culpable for their crashes than women. Also, men are killed mostly while driving or motorcycling while women are killed mostly as pedestrians. For example, in the EU in 2011 the average male fatality rate was 95 per million inhabitants while the average female fatality rate was approximately one-third at 28 per million inhabitants. It is therefore not surprising that men are more likely to speed, drink and drive, and use their phones while driving (ETSC, 2013). So in the realm of traffic safety too "vive la difference" is in favor of women.

As might be expected from the relationship between aggression in general and aggression on the road, this difference extends to the world of driving. Aggressive driving – especially in its more extreme forms – is much more common among males – especially young males – than among females. This has been noted in both self-reports (Smart *et al.*, 2004) as well as in observational studies (Shinar, 1998; Shinar and Compton, 2004). Furthermore, the more aggressive the behavior the greater the gender and age gaps appear to be (Dahlen and Ragan, 2004; Shinar and Compton, 2004). Thus, Shinar and Compton found that men and younger drivers are slightly more likely to honk than women and older drivers (with an odds ratio of 1.7 for both men and young drivers relative to women and older drivers), but they are much more likely to cut across multiple lanes or pass on the shoulder than women or older drivers (with an Odds Ratio of 3.6, for men and 2.3 for younger drivers, respectively). González-Iglesias, Gómez-Fraguela, and Luengo-Martín (2012) in a survey of over 500 Spanish drivers noted that after control for the amount of driving males still reported greater number of fines and accidents, and were more prone to violating traffic regulations. Interestingly, in the extensive Gallup survey of 13,673 drivers in 23 countries, male drivers and young drivers were also more likely to report being the victims of aggressive driving than female drivers (60 percent versus 56 percent) and older drivers (66 percent for drivers 18-24 versus 49 percent for drivers 55+) (EOS Gallup Europe, 2003).

If men differ from women in multiple manifestations of behavior that are not directly related to the biological differences between the genders, then perhaps the difference between men and women is not so much a gender issue, but a reflection of difference in masculine-like behaviors versus feminine-like behaviors. Recent findings indeed support this notion that the gender effect is probably more an effect of a "masculinity-femininity" trait than that of gender itself. This radical diversion from the classic males versus females approach was first suggested by Bem in 1974. Bem (1974, 1981) suggested that we could distinguish between people on the basis of "gender role" or "gender identity," which are the shared expectations that society has for the behaviors of men and women. These are essentially the stereotypes we hold for men and women. For example, that men are more invested in their work role and women in their domestic roles, men are more instrumental and women are more expressive, men are more concerned with justice and women are more concerned with care.

Bem then developed a Sex-Role Inventory, which is a masculinity-femininity scale that is based on people's self-reports of their views relative to the above terms. In general men will identify more with masculinity and females will identify more with femininity. The scale has four dimensions and based on their dominance on each dimension people can be typed as primarily masculine, feminine, androgynous, and undifferentiated. It turns out that indeed many behaviors are better predicted by gender-role than by gender.

To determine the relevance of gender role to driving Özkan and Lajunen (2006) administered the Driving Behavior Questionnaire and the Bem Sex-Role Inventory to 354 undergraduate Turkish students. This is a questionnaire that defines a person's gender-role type on the basis of the person's identification with a list of traits that are differentially perceived as "male" or "female" characteristics. They found that both accidents and violations increased with increasing levels of "masculinity," and the worst safety record belonged to those who were high on the "masculinity" scale and low on the "femininity" scale. Although these results need validation in other cultures, they are intriguing in the sense that they suggest that the causal variable behind the gender difference in crash and violation risk is actually a personality trait that can be phrased in terms of "masculinity" and "femininity." Nielsen *et al.* (2015), surveyed workers in two male-dominated occupations (slaughterhouse and ambulance service providers) and even within these restricted populations they found that high identification with male roles was associated with more safety violations. In our driving simulator Oppenheim *et al.* (2015) compared the driving performance of four groups of drivers who were first typed as belonging to one of four sex-role stereotypes. Although gender identity was better than gender as a predictor of speeding and other violations, the results did not conform to the expected relationships. The worst violators were the undifferentiated drivers rather than the high masculinity drivers, while high masculinity, high femininity, an androgynous drivers did not differ from each other in their speeding violations. Thus, it appears that the relevance of the gender-role concept to actual driving still needs more validation research.

The Driving Environment: Annonymity of Others and Legitimacy of Their Behavior

The driving environment is the context within which most of the driving is conducted. This environment contains both relatively stable physical features and highly variable traffic features. We noted that real and perceived delays, such as congestion, can induce aggressive driving. But congestion is not the only environmental variable that affects aggression. Hamdar *et al.* (2008) studied 10 major signalized intersections in Washington, DC, and concluded that multiple features of the intersection and its traffic behavior can actually be analyzed to provide a quantitative model of its Aggressiveness Propensity Index. As we did in our studies (Shinar, 1998), and in accordance with the model presented in Figure 9-2, they too found that this propensity is fueled by congestion, duration of the red and yellow phases of the traffic signals, and the presence or absence of a red light camera (i.e., the presence of enforcement).

Perception of the environment also involves psychological dimensions. Two such variables that have been studied are the anonymity of the other drivers and the perceived legitimacy of their behavior. The very limited means of communication among drivers (through honking or flashing lights) and drivers' anonymity behind the tinted windows can increase driver frustration and facilitate aggressive behavior, respectively. However, if the frustrating event is perceived as legitimate, then it may not elicit any aggression.

According to Tyler (2006) "legitimacy is a psychological property of an authority, institution, or social arrangement that leads those connected to it to believe that it is appropriate, proper, and just." Thus, blocking a roadway in the middle of the rush hour may be frustrating, but if the reason for it – for example, extricating crash victims or moving accident-involved vehicles – is considered legitimate, then the frustration will most likely not lead to aggression. Similarly a pedestrian who steps off the curb to cross the street may irritate and frustrate an approaching driver, but the driver's response will probably depend on whether the crossing is done in a designated legitimate pedestrian crossing or if it is done in an illegitimate place such as mid-block. This in fact was demonstrated in a study (Shinar, 2000) in which an experimenter acted as a pedestrian who stepped off the curb whenever an approaching car reached a critical point at which the driver would have to stop in order to allow the pedestrian to cross. As expected, the driver was much more likely to slow down or even come to a complete stop when the pedestrian attempted to cross at a marked pedestrian crossing than in a mid-block location. Further support for the role of "legitimacy" comes from a study by Johnson and McKnight (2009). In actual driving in the Washington, DC area they used programmable variable message signs to drivers about congestion ahead, and found that indeed in the presence of the warning the frequency of aggressive driving behaviors was significantly reduced. Unfortunately, all too often frustrating congestion is inexplicable: we approach it, drive through it at a snail's pace, and then emerge from it to a clear road without ever seeing the reason for the slow-down.

The role of anonymity was elegantly demonstrated by Ellison and her associates (1995). To frustrate an unsuspecting driver and elicit an aggressive response they used Doob and Gross' (1968) method of having a confederate driver drive up to a signal during the red (stop) phase, and then remain there when the light turned green and observe and record the behavior of the driver that was now stuck behind her. Ellison *et al.*'s variation on this method was to impede the movement only of drivers of convertible vehicles (either passenger cars or sport utility vehicles) and record the impeded drivers' reactions as a function of whether the top of their vehicle was up (anonymous condition – hiding the driver from view) or down (identifiable condition – exposing the driver to view by other road users). As they predicted, all three horn honking measures of aggression that they used – reaction time to honk from the moment the light turned green, duration of the first honking, and frequency of honking – indicated that drivers were more aggressive in the anonymous condition than in the identifiable condition. This is illustrated in Table 9-7.

Table 9-7. Horn honking behavior (in seconds) of a driver of a convertible vehicle stuck behind a car that does not begin to move when the light turns green (from Ellison *et al.*, 1995, with permission from Select Press, Inc.).

Honking	**Anonymous – Top up**	**Identifiable – Top down**
Latency	6.39 seconds	9.26 seconds
Duration	.47 seconds	.27 seconds
Frequency	1.83	1.24

In summary, three situational factors interact with the driver's personality to reduce or increase overt aggression:

- Level of frustration – the greater it is the greater the frustration and the more aggressive the response (Dollard *et al.* 1939).

- Penalty for aggressive behavior – the greater the penalty and the greater likelihood of being penalized, the lower the likelihood of overt aggression (though it could be displaced to another form, time, and location) (Dollard *et al.*, 1939).
- Arbitrariness or legitimacy of the frustrator – aggression will be greater when the frustrator is perceived as unfair or inappropriate (Buss, 1963). Brown and Hernnstein (1975) stated it best by saying that aggression is instigated by "illegitimate (behavior that results in) disappointment of legitimate expectations" (p. 274). In this definition "legitimate'" is synonymous with "fair" or "appropriate." This definition implies that we have norms about what is fair, legitimate and appropriate versus what is not. Aggression is directed toward another person only when his or her behavior is considered illegitimate, unfair, contrary to the norm, or contrary to the expected behavior.

The role of legitimacy was also demonstrated by McGarva, Ramsey, and Shear (2006) using Ellison's technique. In their study an experimenter either drove well under the speed limit or remained stopped in an intersection after the light turned green. In half the trials the driver was either engaged in a "mock cell-phone conversation" that included hand gestures and head movements, and in half he was just looking straight ahead with both hands on the steering wheel. As would be predicted by the aggression-frustration model, following drivers were much more annoyed with the driver who was apparently engaged in a cell phone conversation than with the driver who was not. Honking at the intersection was quicker when the driver appeared engaged in the cell phone task, and visible signs of annoyance were greater – especially by female drivers, who seemed to be much less tolerant of the frustrating driver than male drivers. Indirectly this is also a reflection of the perceived illegitimacy of using cell phones while driving (see Chapter 13).

Aggressive Disposition: Personality Meets the Environment

To see how a personality trait of aggression and the environment interact to create an aggressive disposition, let us consider a hypothetical situation in light of the simple model proposed in Figure 9-2. Using this model we start by considering the interaction between the driver's personality and the driving environment. First, note that the driving environment has two elements that facilitate the expression of aggression: (1) very restricted means of communication among frustrating and frustrated drivers and (2) reduced threat of retaliation from other drivers because the car provides the aggressive driver a shield and anonymity.

The interaction between the personality characteristics of aggression and the environmental conditions that may elicit it was demonstrated in studies by Hennessy and Wiesenthal (1997) and by Deffenbacher and his associates (2003). Hennessy and Wiesenthal administered several personality questionnaires focusing on aggression and stress to 40 Canadian drivers and then interviewed them over a cellular phone while they drove in real traffic in high and low congestion conditions. The driving interview consisted of asking the drivers to respond to questionnaires that assessed "state stress" and "trait stress." "State" questions focus on a person's response in a particular situation (in this case the reaction to traffic congestion), whereas "trait" questionnaires focus on stable behavioral tendencies that are assumed to exist across a variety of situations – in short, measures of personality. They found that, in general, drivers reported being twice as stressed during high congestion than during low congestion, and reported that they engaged in twice as many aggressive behaviors in the high congestion condition than in the non-congested condition. Aggressive behaviors included horn honking at other cars, tailgating, flashing lights, making hand gestures, and swearing at other drivers. The most interesting result was the interaction between the driver's trait-stress level and the congestion condition on the driver's state stress level, as illustrated in Table 9-8. Drivers scoring high on the trait-stress test reported state stress levels that were nearly twice as high as the low-trait stress drivers, at both levels of congestion. Thus, the results showed how the personal stable dispositions of high trait stress, served to heighten the experience of strain (state stress) in response to stressful situations (congestion).

Table 9-8. State stress scores of high and low-trait stress drivers in conditions of high and low congestion (derived from graphed results of Hennessy and Wiesenthal, 1997).

	Low Trait Stress	**High Trait Stress**
Low Congestion	21	40
High congestion	38	72

In the second study Deffenbacher and his associates (2003) studied the driving behavior of two distinct groups of drivers who were identified as being low or high on a Driving Anger Scale (Deffenbacher, Oetting, and Lynch, 1994). They found that university students with high anger and aggression scores reported more aggressive and risky driving and more driving violations in their daily driving than students with low anger and aggression scores. Furthermore, when these students were given a simulated driving task, there was no difference in their behavior in non-frustrating driving situations, but there was a significant difference between them in frustrating situations (such as being stuck behind a slow moving driver). The high anger and high aggression students expressed more anger, maintained shorter headways and time-to-collision, and were twice as likely to have an accident in these situations as the low aggression drivers. Together both studies demonstrate the complex interaction between personality and the manifestation of aggression, and demonstrate not only that people react differently to the same situations, but also what stable personality factors underlie some of these differences.

Feasibility of Aggression

Once a driver is disposed to commit a traffic violation or act aggressively, he or she must still consider the outcomes of this behavior. Much of our aggressive behavior is governed by norms that are dictated by our culture, and other behaviors are held in check for fear of retaliation. In the case of driving the retaliation may be either from other drivers, from a camera, or from a police officer. For example, honking the horn may be acceptable in a noisy metropolis like New York, but not in a quiet residential suburb twenty miles away.

Culture and aggressive driving

Culture is an important variable that mediates the decision whether or not to act aggressively. "Each driver is an individual influenced by the social environment consisting of other road users, general social norms, traffic-related rules of conduct, and their representations, (and) at the same time each driver is also part of this collective, and thus influences others" (Zaidel, 1992, p. 585). The prevailing driving culture, in a sense, is the sum total of the rules of etiquette on the road. Given the large variations in cultures among different countries we should expect some differences in the driving style of drivers in different countries, including in levels of aggressive driving. Furthermore, culture is a multi-level concept. At the highest macro level it can describe the behavior of homo-sapiens as a species, and at the micro levels it can describe variations in behaviors among different environments within small geographical regions, indoors and outdoors, while walking and while driving.

To begin, drivers' perceptions of aggression differ in different countries. For example, in the EOS Gallup (2003) survey of drivers in 23 countries, 66 percent of the American drivers and 65 percent of the Russian drivers felt that they have been "the subject of aggressive behaviors from other drivers," compared to only 48 percent of the EU drivers and 26 percent of the Japanese drivers. The same survey also revealed significant differences between drivers in different countries in what they consider irritating behaviors. This is shown in Figure 9-12, which lists the percent of drivers who were "very irritated" by various aggressive behaviors. Drivers in all countries reacted in a similar fashion in response to drivers who used the shoulders to pass other cars in a sudden congested situation, but drivers' reactions varied significantly in response to other behaviors. For example Japanese drivers were much more tolerant than Australian drivers to other drivers driving on an open inside lane, and then in the last minute cutting across lanes into the congested exit lane. They were also much more tolerant toward drivers who drive on the inside (passing) lane when the outside lane is free. On the other hand the Japanese drivers were the least tolerant of all nations to double parking, while the Australians were the most tolerant.

In short the level of tolerance toward different manifestations of driver aggression change across cultures, and hence it is likely that aggressive behaviors that are acceptable in one culture are not acceptable in another. Consequently, while the cause-and-effect relationship between the norms and the behaviors is hard to prove, the association is probably there. For example, in a comparison between the level of aggressive driving – as measured by drivers' responses to the DBQ – in Finland, the Netherlands, and England, Lajunen *et al.* (1999) found that the Finns are four times as likely to commit aggressive violations as the Dutch, while the Brits were three times as likely to commit them as the Dutch. Unfortunately in that study the proportion of the male drivers – who consistently get higher ratings of aggression in the DBQ – was significantly different in the three

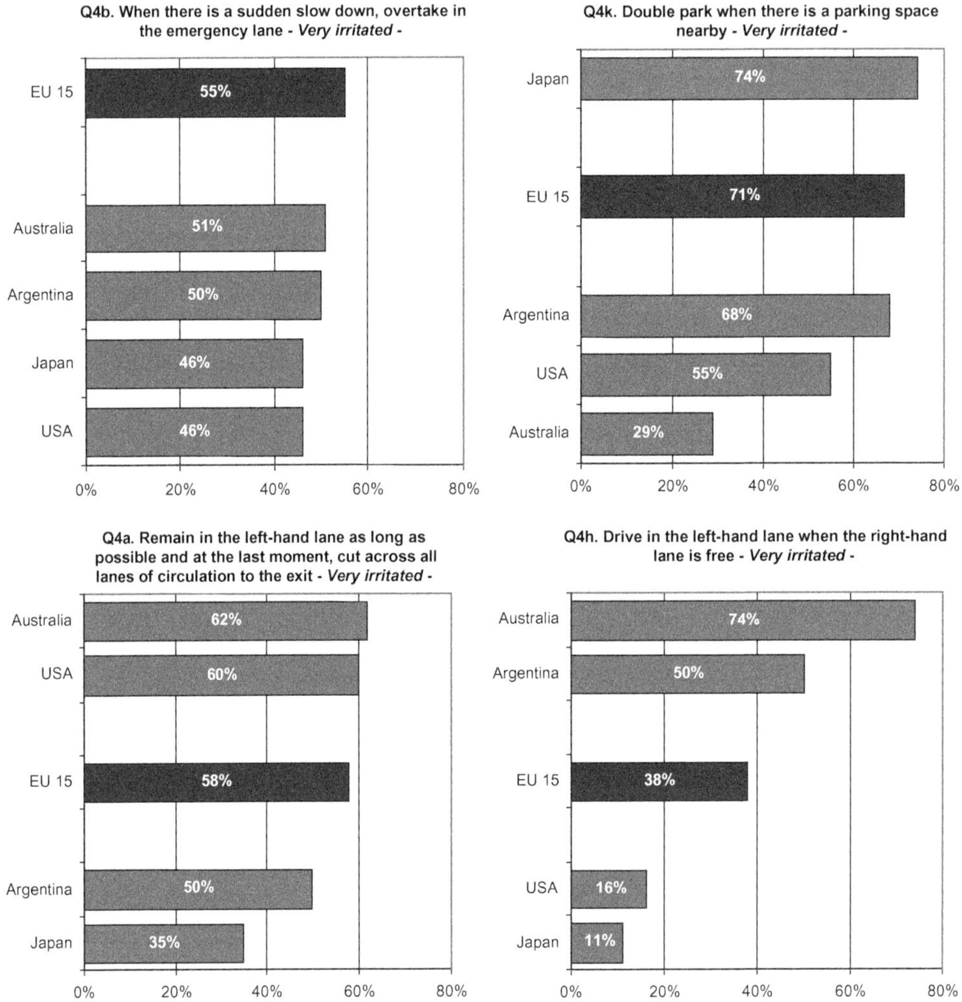

Figure 9-12. Percent of drivers in different countries who consider various aggressive behaviors "very irritating." Clockwise from top left: driving in the fast lane as long as possible and then at the last minute cutting across lanes to exit; driving in the inside (passing) lane when the outside lane is free; using the emergency lane to overtake other vehicles in case of a sudden congestion; double parking when there is a parking space nearby (from EOS Gallup, 2003).

countries: over 70 percent of the Dutch sample, compared to 46 percent of Finnish sample and 52 percent of the British sample. Thus, it is likely that had the proportion of males been identical, the differences would have been even greater.

One cultural norm that seems to prevail almost everywhere is the accommodation of handicapped people. It is most conspicuous when we search for a spot in a parking lot, and no matter how filled it is, most able drivers will not consider parking in a designated handicapped person parking space (though to further enforce this norm, in most countries this violation is heavily penalized). For a direct test of this hypothesis, we conducted a study (Shinar, 2000) in which a pedestrian stepped off the curb just as an approaching driver reached a critical point where he or she would have to slow down or stop in order to allow the pedestrian to cross. In a total of 400 attempted crossings, half were in a pedestrian crossing at an intersection and half were on the same street but mid-block. At each location in 100 attempts the pedestrian was not handicapped and in 100 attempts the same pedestrian wearing the same clothes leaned on crutches, imitating a handicapped person. The results showed that at the intersection (where all drivers are supposed to yield by law) as expected nearly all drivers yielded to the handicapped person, compared to approximately two-thirds who yielded to the non-handicapped person. But the difference in the accommodation of the two types of pedestrians was much greater in the mid-block location. There approximately two-thirds of the drivers still yielded to the handicapped person – despite the illegitimacy of the crossing – but very few yielded to the non-handicapped person.

Driving and Safety culture can also be a relatively local phenomenon, restricted to a community or an organization (Caird and Kline, 2004). To demonstrate these micro--level differences we measured honking behavior in response to blocking the path by a confederate driver in three intersections located in different places in Israel – all within 25 kilometers of each other: a high-income residential community, a low-income residential section of a town nearby, and an industrial section of the same town (that at night turned into a very active pub and disco center, attracting mostly young people). The same delaying technique was employed at all places during the daytime rush hours and again at night in the industrial area that turned into a pub center. The effects of the delay on honking and other aggressive signs of impatience are displayed in Table 9-9. In the low socio-economic location drivers demonstrated their impatience with the shortest honking delays and with the greatest frequency of visible gestures. In the pubs zone (at night) people were actually most courteous, waiting the longest before they honked their horns and showing over signs of impatience much less often.

Table 9-9. Honking delays and frequency of visible signs of impatience of drivers blocked by a confederate driver at a green light in an urban industrial zone, a low socio-economic part of town, a high socio-economic residential area, and a center of pubs (reprinted from Shinar, 1998, with permission from Elsevier).

Measure of Aggression	**Industrial Zone (n = 30)**	**Low Soc-Econ Zone (n = 40)**	**Hi Soc-Econ Zone (N = 29)**	**Pubs Zone (n = 28)**
Honking delay	2.7 seconds	2.3 seconds	3.6 seconds	4.6 seconds
Visibly impatient	59%	70%	45%	43%

It is also interesting to compare the differences in the honking delays between those obtained in Israel and those obtained by Ellison *et al.* (1995) in Maryland, U.S. (see Table 9-7). In this and in other studies that we conducted in Israel mean honking delay was always significantly shorter than in the U.S. (based on Ellison *et al.*'s 1995 single study), confirming the subjective impressions of many American visitors to Israel.

Environmental effects also extend to an even smaller microcosm: that of the car itself. The presence of a passenger in the car can also make a difference. Two very dramatic effects of the presence of an adult driver next to a novice young driver, as part of the graduated driver licensing, are (1) the near-zero rate of violations and accidents that persist as long as the novice driver is accompanied by the supervising (responsible) adult and (2) the drastic and immediate increase in violations and accidents as soon as that phase expires (see Chapter 6). Even when the passenger is not a supervising parent, the adult passenger seems to have a calming effect on the driver. In the large-scale observational study that we conducted in Israel (Shinar and Compton, 2004) we found that the odds of aggressive driving were significantly lower with a passenger next to the driver than when the driver was alone in the car. Whether the passenger's presence inhibits aggression or whether it provides the driver with an attractive distraction to frustrating situations (as suggested by Hennessy and Wiesenthal, 1997), is an open question, but one that is less important than the effect itself.

Another environmental factor is the presence of enforcement: it can eliminate or at least reduce overt aggressive driving. It is needed when the prevailing culture and local norms either tolerate aggressive driving or are not sufficiently compelling to suppress it. Most drivers will be reluctant to engage in aggressive driving acts in the presence of a police officer, especially when these behaviors also constitute driving violations. Two studies have been conducted to evaluate the potential of enforcement campaigns specifically targeted at aggressive driving. In the first study McCartt *et al.* (2001) evaluated a campaign of combined public information and enforcement in the city of Milwaukee, Wisconsin. The 6-months campaign consisted of a series of 3-week enforcement and publicity "sub-theme" campaigns, each initiated by a press conference by one of the participating police agencies, and each focusing on a specific traffic offense commonly associated with aggressive driving. Each theme was also tagged with a catchy phrase. For example, the campaign to encourage the use of flashers or turn signals was entitled the "Flasher Patrol," and the weaving, cutting in and out of traffic, and speeding was labeled "Basket Patrol." (Note that this program included speeding enforcement). In addition to speed, the program targeted tailgating, ramp meter violations, high occupancy vehicle (HOV) lane violations, stopping in an intersection causing traffic "gridlock," running a red light or a stop sign, failing to use a turn signal, failing to yield right of way, shouting, beeping, flashing lights or making hand gestures, and weaving and cutting in and out of traffic. The intensity of the program was reflected in drivers' raised awareness of being ticketed for running a red light and driving through a stop sign. This was probably a product of both the media campaign and a 55 percent increase in non-speed aggressive driving citations, most of which were for failure to obey signs and following too closely. The evaluation of the campaign's effectiveness consisted of tracking violation and accident records in Milwaukee (the campaign site) and in areas not exposed to the campaign (as comparison sites). Comparisons of behaviors, citations, and accidents in the 6 months preceding the campaign and in the 6 months during the campaign justified the intensive efforts: accidents in the 6-month period of the program dropped by 12.3 percent in the target area, compared to only 2.2 percent in the comparison area. Red light running declined at the targeted intersections from 6.5 percent during the pre-program period to 4.9 percent during the mid-program period, while it increased at the comparison intersections from 2.9 percent to 12.7 percent.

The Milwaukee program was as close to exemplary as one can be in terms of its intensity, focus, coverage, and combined use of enforcement and information dissemination. This is not necessarily the case for all enforcement programs. Stuster (2004) conducted two studies that evaluated the effects of intensive media campaigns against aggressive driving coupled with increased enforcements in Indiana and Arizona, and failed to find any reductions in aggressive driving violations. The enforcement at both locations focused on similar behaviors as in Milwaukee; that is, speeding, failure to obey traffic controls/devices, failure to yield, improper or unsafe lane changes, and following too closely. However, in both sites, most of the tickets were issued for speeding. In his evaluation Stuster compared the driving speeds and crash experience in the two sites immediately before the start of the program with those obtained during the program. The results were quite disappointing with both sites exhibiting essentially no change in average speed and an actual perplexing increase in crashes relative to matched control zones.

With two studies yielding different results it is difficult to assess the role of enforcement in suppressing aggressive driving. Still it appears that the approach is effective when the amount and combination of the public information and enforcement is appropriate. From driver survey data collected at the Indiana study it appears that the drivers were not as aware of the program as they were in Milwaukee. This means that to be effective, such combined efforts must be extremely well planned and tracked in terms of their dissemination and awareness by the motoring public.

Displaced aggression

Based on the model in Figure 9-2, and our current understanding of social behavior, if aggressive driving is suppressed at this stage – after an aggressive disposition has emerged – then it does not just disappear. Instead, it is most likely to resurface in the form of displaced aggression: off the road and toward innocent victims, such as the person's family or friends. Dollard *et al.*'s (1939) example of the driver who is being berated by a police officer is also fortuitous because it demonstrates that when we cannot directly confront the source of our frustration, we tend to direct our aggression elsewhere; in Dollard *et al.*'s example it is at other people and even at the car by "grating the gears." In Ellison *et al.*'s (1995) study it was by "gunning" the engine. This means that a negative side effect of enforcement – the principal means of suppressing aggression on the road – is that it may elicit aggressive responses elsewhere, where their effects may be just as significant.

Concluding Comments

Though there are indications that in frustrating situations people with heightened trait aggression will drive more aggressively, focusing on the aberrant driver to deal with aggressive driving is probably not the best tactic. An alternative approach to punishing the aggressive driver, and one that is more consistent with treating driver behavior as part of the driver-vehicle-roadway system, is to identify situations in which aggressive driving emerges and then determine how to eliminate or change these situations. Removing a select group of drivers (i.e., aggressive drivers) from the driving population is only one partial solution – and definitely not the most effective one. It is not effective because on the one hand it is very difficult to deny license to people on the basis of their personality characteristics (and we should hope that it remains this way), and on the other hand it is impractical (frustrating?) to wait until people with deviant personalities accumulate sufficient numbers of violations and accidents. An alternative approach – which is definitely more difficult – is to (1) consider aggression in the specific context in which it occurs, (2) identify the variables that determine the extent to which the personality characteristic of aggression manifests itself in driving, and (3) relative to that context consider the means of dealing with it. This approach has been validated in one study that found that novice drivers in Estonia who received a short intervention that sensitized them to their personal risk factors had fewer crashes following the intervention than a matched control group of novice drivers that received no such intervention. There are also indications that the clinical approach of treating the aggressive driver with cognitive, relaxation, and behavioral anger-reduction interventions may be effective in reducing aggression in specific cases (Deffenbacher, 2016). Still, because aggression is most often the consequence of frustration, the optimal strategy is to determine the sources of the frustration and remove them. This is much easier said than done, but in the long run, and at least in some contexts, it may be the most effective.

References

AAA Foundation for Traffic Safety (1997). Aggressive driving: Three studies. AAA Foundation for Traffic Safety, Washington, DC.

AAAF (2012). 2011 traffic safety culture index. AAA Traffic Safety Foundation.

Abdu, R., D. Shinar and N. Meiran (2012). Situational (state) anger and driving. *Trans. Res. F*, *15*(5), 575-580.

Ajzen, I. (1991). The theory of planned behavior. *Org. Behav. Hum. Dec. Pro.*, *50*, 179-211.

Ajzen, I. (2011). The theory of planned behaviour: Reactions and reflections (Editorial). *Psychol. Health*, *26*, 1113-1127.

Aniţei, M., C. Chraif, V. Burtaverde and T. Mihăilă (2014). The big five personality factors in the prediction of aggressive driving behavior among Romanian youngsters. *Int. J. Traffic Transport. Psychol.*, 2(1), 7-22.

Argyle, M. (1983). *The Psychology of Interpersonal Behaviour*. Penguin Books, Harmondsworth.

Arnett, J. J., D. Offer and M. A. Fine (1997). Reckless driving in adolescence: 'State' and 'trait' factors. *Accid. Anal. Prev.*, *29*(1), 57-63.

Assum, T. (1997). Attitudes and road accident risk. *Accid. Anal. Prev.*, *29*(2), 153-159.

Baron, R. A. and D. Byrne (1994). *Social Psychology* (7th ed.). Allyn and Bacon, Boston, MA.

Barraclough, P., A. Af Wåhlberg, J. Freeman, B. Watson and A. Watson (2016). Predicting crashes using traffic offences. A meta-analysis that examines potential bias between self-report and archival data. *PLoS One*, *11*(4), e0153390.

Beck, K. H., M. Q. Wang and M. M. Mitchell (2006). Concerns, dispositions and behaviors of aggressive drivers: What do self-identified aggressive drivers believe about traffic safety? *J. Safety Res.*, *37*, 159-165.

Bem, S. L. (1974). The measurement of psychological androgyny. *J. Clin. Consult. Psychol.*, *42*, 155-162.

Bem, S. L. (1981). Gender schema theory: A cognitive account of sex typing. *Psychol. Rev.*, *88*(4), 354.

Berkowitz, L. (1993). *Aggression: Its Causes, Consequences, and Control.* McGraw-Hill, New York, NY.

Bianchi, A. and H. Summala (2004). The "genetics" of driving behavior: Parents' driving style predicts their children's driving style. *Accid. Anal. Prev.*, *36*, 655-669.

Björklund, G. M. (2008). Driver irritation and aggressive behaviour. *Accid. Anal. Prev.*, *40*(3), 1069-1077.

Blasco, R. D., J. M. Prieto and J. M. Cornejo (2003). Accident probability after accident occurrence. *Safety. Sci.*, *41*(6), 481-501.

Blows, S., S. Ameratunga, R. Q. Ivers, S. K. Lo and R. Norton (2005). Risky driving habits and motor vehicle driver injury. *Accid. Anal. Prev.*, *37*, 619-624.

Broughton, J. (2007). The correlation between motoring and other types of offence. *Accid. Anal. Prev.*, *39*, 274-283.

Brown R. and R. J. Herrnstein. (1975). Moral reasoning and conduct. In: *Psychology*. Little, Brown, & Co., Boston, MA.

Buss, A. H. (1963). Physical aggression in relation to different frustrations. *J. Person. Social Psychol.*, *67*, 1-7.

Butters, J. E., R. G. Smart, R. E. Mann and M. Asbridge (2005). Illicit drug use, alcohol use and problem drinking among infrequent and frequent road ragers. *Drug Alcohol Depend.*, *80*, 169-175.

Caird, J. K. and T. J. Kline (2004). The relationship between organizational and individual variables to on-the-job driver accidents and accident-free kilometers. *Ergonomics*, *47*(15), 1598-1613.

Castellà, J. and J. Pérez (2004). Sensitivity to punishment and sensitivity to reward and traffic violations. *Accid. Anal. Prev.*, *36*, 947-952.

Cavaiola, A. A., D. B. Strohmetz, J. M. Wolf and N. J. Lavender (2003). Comparison of DWI offenders with non-DWI individuals on the MMPI-2 and the Michigan Alcoholism Screening Test. *Addict. Behav.*, *28*, 971-977.

Cooper, P. J. (1997). The relationship between speeding behaviour (as measured by violation convictions) and crash involvement. *J. Safety Res.*, *28*(2), 83-95.

Cordazzo, S. T., C. T. Scialfa, and R. J. Ross (2016). Modernization of the driver behaviour questionnaire. *Accid. Anal. Prev.*, *87*, 83-91.

Crutcher, J. C., G. Black, P. Campbell, J. D. Smith and K. Toomey (1994). Risky driving behaviors among teenagers – Gwinnett County, Georgia, 1993. *Morbid. Mortal. Week. Report*, *43*(22), 405-409 (reprinted in 1994 in the *J. Am. Med. Assoc.*, **272**(11), 844-845).

Dahlen, E. R., B. D. Edwards, T. Tubré, M. J. Zyphur, and C. R. Warren (2012). Taking a look behind the wheel: An investigation into the personality predictors of aggressive driving. *Accid. Anal. Prev.*, *45*, 1-9.

Dahlen, E. R. and K. M. Ragan (2004). Validation of the propensity for angry driving scale. *J. Safety Res.*, *35*, 557-563.

Danaf, M., M. Abou-Zeid, and I. Kaysi (2015). Modeling anger and aggressive driving behavior in a dynamic choice–latent variable model. *Accid. Anal. Prev.*, *75*, 105-118.

De Winter, J. C. F. and D. Dodou (2010). The driver behaviour questionnaire as a predictor of accidents: A meta-analysis. *J. Safety Res.*, *41*(6), 463-470.

de Winter, J. C. and D. Dodou (2016). National correlates of self-reported traffic violations across 41 countries. *Pers. Individ. Dif.*, *98*, 145-152.

Deffenbacher, J. L. (2016). A review of interventions for the reduction of driving anger. *Trans. Res. F*, *42*, 411-421.

Deffenbacher, J. L., E. R. Oetting and R. S. Lynch (1994). Development of a driving anger scale. *Psychol. Reports*, *74*, 83-91.

Deffenbacher, J. L., D. M. Deffenbacher, R. S. Lynch and T. L. Richards (2003). Anger, aggression, and risky behavior: A comparison of high and low anger drivers. *Behav. Res. Ther.*, *41*, 701-718.

Deffenbacher, J. D., R. S. Lynch, E. R. Oetting, and R. C. Swaim (2002). The driving anger expression inventory: A measure of how people express their anger on the road. *Behav. Res. Ther.*, *40*, 717-737.

DFT (2004). The attitudinal determinants of driving violations. Road Safety Research Report No. 13. Department for Transport, London.

Dollard, J., L. W. Doob, N. P. Miller, O. H. Mowrer and R. R. Sears (1939). *Frustration and Aggression*. Yale University Press, New Haven, CT.

Donkor, R. A.,. G. A. Burnett, and S. Sharples (2014). Measuring the emotional validity of driving simulators. *Adv. Transport. Stud. Int. J.*, 51-64.

Doob, A. N. and A. E. Gross (1968). Status of frustrator as an inhibitor of horn-honking responses. *J. Soc. Psychol.*, *76*, 213-218.

Dukes, R. L., S. L. Clayton, L. T. Jenkins, T. L. Miller, and S. E. Rodgers (2001). Effects of aggressive driving and driver characteristics on road rage. *Soc. Sci. J.*, *38*(2), 323-331.

Dula, C. S., C. L. Adams, M. T. Miesner, and R. L. Leonard (2010). Examining relationships between anxiety and dangerous driving. *Accid. Anal. Prev.*, *42*(6), 2050-2056.

Elliott, M. A., C. J. Baughan and B. F. Sexton (2007). Errors and violations in relation to motorcyclists' crash risk. *Accid. Anal. Prev.*, *39*(3), 491-499.

Elliott, M. R., P. F. Waller, T. E. Raghunathan, J. T. Shope and R. J. A. Little (2000). Persistence of violation and crash behavior over time. *J. Safety Res.*, *31*(4), 229-242.

Ellison, P. A., J. M. Govern, H. L. Petri and M. H. Figler (1995) Anonymity and aggressive driving behaviour: A field study. *J. Soc. Behav. Person.*, *10*(1), 265-272.

EOS Gallup Europe (2003). Aggressive behaviour behind the wheel. EOS Gallup Europe, Wavre, Belgium.

ETSC (2013). Risk on the roads: A male problem? The role of gender in road safety. PIN Flash Report 25. European Transport Safety Council, Brussels, Belgium.

Evans, L. (2004). *Traffic Safety*. Science Serving Society, Bloomfield Hills, MI.

Fergenson, P. E. (1971). The relationship between information processing and driving accident and violation record. *Hum. Fact. 13*(2), 173-176.

Forbes, T. W. (1939). The normal automobile driver as a traffic problem. *J. General Psychol.*, *20*, 471-474.

GHSA (2014). Aggressive driving laws. Governors Highway Safety Administration. Washington, DC. http://www.ghsa.org/html/stateinfo/laws/aggressivedriving_laws.html

Gidron, Y., R. Gal and H. S. Desevilya (2003). Internal locus of control moderates the effects of road-hostility on recalled driving behavior. *Transport. Res. F*, *6*, 109-116.

Golias, I. and M. G. Karlaftis (2002). An international comparative study of self-reported driver behavior. *Transport. Res. F*, *4*, 243-256.

González-Iglesias, B., J. A. Gómez-Fraguela, and M. Á. Luengo-Martín (2012). Driving anger and traffic violations: Gender differences. *Transport. Res. F*, *15*(4), 404-412.

Greenwood, M. and H. M. Woods (1919). A report on the incidence of industrial accidents upon individuals, with special reference to multiple accidents. Report No. 4. Industrial Fatigue Research Board, London.

Greenwood, M. and U. Yule (1920). An inquiry into the nature of frequency distributions representative of multiple happenings with particular reference to the occurrence of multiple attacks of disease or of repeated accidents. *J. Royal Stat. Soc.*, *83*(2), 255-279.

Guého, L., M. A. Granie, and J. C. Abric (2014). French validation of a new version of the Driver Behavior Questionnaire (DBQ) for drivers of all ages and level of experiences. *Accid. Anal. Prev.*, *63*, 41-48.

Habtemichael, F. G., and L. de Picado Santos (2014). Crash risk evaluation of aggressive driving on motorways: Microscopic traffic simulation approach. *Transport. Res. F.*, *23*, 101-112.

Haje, B. E. and D. G. Symbaluk (2014). Personal and social determinants of aggressive and dangerous driving. *Can. J. Family Youth*, *6*(1), 59-88.

Häkkinen, S. (1979). Traffic accidents and professional driver characteristics – A followup study. *Accid. Anal. Prev.*, *11*(1), 7-18.

Hamdar, S. H., H. S. Mahmassani, and R. B. Chen(2008). Aggressiveness propensity index for driving behavior at signalized intersections. *Accid. Anal. Prev.*, *40*(1), 315-326.

Hennessy, D. A. and D. L. Wiesenthal (1997). The relationship between traffic congestion, driver stress, and direct versus indirect coping behaviors. *Ergonomics*, *40*, 348-361.

Hunter, W. W., J. C. Stutts and W. E. Pein (1977). Pedestrian crash types: A 1990's informational guide. Federal Highway Administration Report FHWA-RD-96-163. U.S. Department of Transportation, Washington, DC.

Iversen, H. and T. Rundmo (2004). Attitudes towards traffic safety, driving behaviour and accident involvement among the Norwegian public. *Ergonomics*, *47*(5), 555-572.

James, L. and N. Nahl (2000). *Road Rage and Aggressive Driving*. Prometheus, Amherst, NY.

Jerome, L., A. Segal and L. Habinski (2006). What we know about ADHD and driving risk: A literature review. Meta-analysis and critique. *J. Can. Acad. Child Adolesc. Psychiatry*, *15*, 105-125.

Johnson, M. B. and S. McKnight (2009). Warning drivers about potential congestion as a means to reduce frustration-driven aggressive driving. *Traffic Inj. Prev.*, *10*(4), 354-360.

Jonah, B. A. (1997). Sensation seeking and risky driving: A review and synthesis of the literature. *Accid. Anal. Prev.*, *29*, 651-665.

Jovanović, D., K. Lipovac, P. Stanojević, and D. Stanojević (2011). The effects of personality traits on driving-related anger and aggressive behaviour in traffic among Serbian drivers. *Transport. Res. F.*, *14*(1), 43-53.

Karrer, K., T. Vöhringer-Kuhnt, T. Baumgarten, and S. Briest (2004). The role of individual differences in driver fatigue prediction. International Conference on Traffic and Transport Psychology. Nottingham.

Kieling, R. R., C. M. Szobot, B. Matte, R. S. Coelho, C. Kieling, F. Pechansky, and L. A. Rohde (2011). Mental disorders and delivery motorcycle drivers (motoboys): A dangerous association. *Eur. Psychiatry*, *26*(1), 23-27.

Kinnear, N., S. Helman, C. Wallbank, and G. Grayson (2015). An experimental study of factors associated with driver frustration and overtaking intentions. *Accid. Anal. Prev.*, *79*, 221-230.

Kovácsová, N., E. Rošková, and T. Lajunen (2014). Forgivingness, anger, and hostility in aggressive driving. *Accid. Anal. Prev.*, *62*, 303-308.

Lajunen, T. (2002). Psycho-technical driver assessment: A useful tool for detecting bad drivers or complete waste of money? Uluslararasi Trafik ve Yol Güvenligi Kongresi ve Fuari, Ankara, Turkey.

Lajunen, T., and D. Parker (2001). Are aggressive people aggressive drivers? A study of the relationship between self-reported general aggressiveness, driver anger and aggressive driving. *Accid. Anal. Behav.*, *33*(2), 243-255.

Lajunen, T. and H. Summala (1995). Driving experience, personality, and skill, and safety-motive dimensions in drivers' self-assessments. *Person. Individual Differ.*, *19*(3), 307-318.

Lajunen, T., D. Parker and S. G. Stradling (1998). Dimensions of driver anger, aggressive and highway code violations and their mediation by safety orientation in UK drivers. *Transport. Res. F*, *1*, 107-121.

Lajunen, T., D. Parker and H. Summala (1999). Does traffic congestion increase driver aggression? *Transport. Res. F*, *2*, 225-236.

Lalloo, R., A. Sheiham and J. Y. Nazroo (2003). Behavioural characteristics and accidents: Findings from the Health Survey for England, 1997. *Accid. Anal. Prev.*, *35*, 661-667.

Lawton, R., D. Parker, S. G. Stradling and A. S. R. Manstead (1997). Predicting road traffic accidents: The role of social deviance and violations. *Br. J. Psychol.*, *88*(2), 249-262.

Lee, Y. C. and N. LaVoie (2014, September). Relationship between frustration justification and vehicle control behaviors – A simulator study. Proceedings of the Human Factors and Ergonomics Society Annual Meeting, **58**(1), 2235-2239. Sage Publications.

Lennon, A., and B. Watson (2011). "Teaching them a lesson?" A qualitative exploration of underlying motivations for driver aggression. *Accid. Anal. Prev.*, *43*(6), 2200-2208.

Li, F., C. Li, Y. Long, C. Zhan and D. A. Hennessy (2004). Reliability and validity of aggressive driving measures in China. *Traffic Inj. Prev.*, *5*, 349-355.

Malta, L. S., E. B. Blanchard and B. M. Freidenberg (2005). Psychiatric and behavioral problems in aggressive drivers. *Behav. Res. Ther.*, *43*, 1467-1484.

Martinez, R. (1997). Statement of the Honorable Ricardo Martinez, M. D., Administrator, National Highway Traffic Safety Administration, before the US House of Representatives, Committee on Transportation and Infrastructure, Subcommittee on Surface Transportation. Washington, DC, July 17.

Martinussen, L. M., T. Lajunen, M. Møller, and T. Özkan (2013). Short and user-friendly: The development and validation of the Mini-DBQ. *Accid. Anal. Prev.*, *50*, 1259-1265.

Mason-Dixon (2005). *Drive for Life: Annual National Driver Survey*. Mason-Dixon Polling and Research, Inc., Washington, DC.

Mayer, R. E. and J. R. Treat (1977). Psychological, social, and cognitive characteristics of high-risk drivers: A pilot study. *Accid. Anal. Prev.*, *9*, 1-8.

McCartt, A. T., W. A. Leaf, T. L. Witkowski and M. G. Solomon (2001). Evaluation of the Aggression Suppression Program, Milwaukee, Wisconsin. National Highway Traffic Safety Administration Report DOT HS 809 395. U.S. Department of Transportation, Washington, DC.

McGarva, A. R., M. Ramsey, and S. A. Shear (2006). Effects of driver cell-phone use on driver aggression. *J. Social Psychol.*, *146*(2), 133-146.

McKenna, F. P. and M. S. Horswill (2006). Risk-taking from the participant's perspective: The case of driving and accident risk. *Health Psychol.*, *25*(2), 163-170.

Millar, M. (2007). The influence of public self-consciousness and anger on aggressive driving. *Person. Ind. Diff.*, *43*(8), 2116-2126.

Miller, G. and O. Taubman-Ben-Ari (2010). Driving styles among young novice drivers — The contribution of parental driving styles and personal characteristics. *Accid. Anal. Prev.*, *42*(2), 558-570.

Montag, I. and A. L. Comrey (1987). Internality and externality as correlates of involvement in fatal driving accidents. *J. Appl. Psychol.*, *72*, 339-343.

Morrongiello, B. A. and J. Lasenby (2006). Finding the daredevils: Development of a sensation seeking scale for children that is relevant to physical risk taking. *Accid. Anal. Prev.*, *38*(6), 1101-1106.

Musselwhite, C. (2006). Attitudes towards vehicle driving behaviour: Categorising and contextualising risk. *Accid. Anal. Prev.*, *38*, 324-334.

Nesbit, S. M. and J. C. Conger (2012). Predicting aggressive driving behavior from anger and negative cognitions. *Transport. Res. F.*, *15*(6), 710-718.

Nesbit, S. M., J. C. Conger, and A. J. Conger (2007). A quantitative review of the relationship between anger and aggressive driving. *Aggress. Violent Behav.*, *12*(2), 156-176.

NHTSA (1998). Aggressive drivers view traffic differently Capital Beltway focus groups find. Traffic Tech. Number 175. US Department of Transportation, Washington, DC.

Nielsen, K. J., C. D. Hansen, L. Bloksgaard, A. D. Christensen, S. Q. Jensen, and M. Kyed (2015). The impact of masculinity on safety oversights, safety priority and safety violations in two male-dominated occupations. *Safety Sci.*, *76*, 82-89.

O'Brien, S. R., R. S. Tay, and B. C. Watson (2004). Situational factors contributing to the expression of aggression on the roads. *IATSS Res.*, *28*(1), 101-107.

Oppenheim, I., T. Oron-Gilad, Y. Parmet, and D. Shinar (2015). Drivers' personality and violation tendency: Use of simulated driving scenarios to mimic the DBQ violations. Proceedings of the Road Safety and Simulation Conference, Orlando, FL, October 7.

Özkan, T. and T. Lajunen (2006). Why are there sex differences in risky driving? The relationship between sex and gender-role on aggressive driving, traffic offences, and accident involvement among young Turkish drivers. *Aggress. Behav.*, *31*, 547-558.

Özkan, T., T. Lajunen, J. E. Chliaoutakis, D. Parker, and H. Summala (2006a). Cross-cultural differences in driving behaviours: A comparison of six countries. *Transport. Res. F.*, *9*(3), 227-242.

Özkan, T. O., T. Lajunen and H. Summala (2006b) Driver behaviour questionnaire: A follow-up study. *Accid. Anal. Prev.*, *38*, 386-395.

Paleti, R., N. Eluru, and C. R. Bhat (2010). Examining the influence of aggressive driving behavior on driver injury severity in traffic crashes. *Accid. Anal. Prev.*, *42*, 1839-1854.

Parker, D., L. McDonald, P. Rabbitt and P. Sutcliffe (2000). Elderly drivers and their accidents: The aging driver questionnaire. *Accid. Anal. Prev.*, *32*, 751-759.

Parker, D., J. T. Reason, A. S. R. Manstead and S. G. Stradling (1995). Driving errors, driving violations and accident involvement. *Ergonomics*, *38*, 1036-1048.

Parry, M. H. (1968). *Aggression on the Road.* Tavistock, London.

Perneger, T. and G. S. Smith (1991). The driver's role in fatal two-car crashes: A paired "case—control" study. *Am. J. Epidemiol.*, *134* (10), 1138-1145.

Qu, W., Y. Ge, C. Jiang, F. Du, and K. Zhang (2014). The Dula dangerous driving index in China: An investigation of reliability and validity. *Accid. Anal. Prev.*, *64*, 62-68.

Rajalin, S. (1994). The connection between risky driving and involvement in fatal accidents. *Accid. Anal. Prev.*, *26*(5), 555-562.

Reason, J. T. (1990). *Human Error*. Cambridge University Press, New York, NY.

Reason, J. T., A. Manstead, S. Stradling, J. Baxter and K. Campbell (1990). Errors and violations on the roads: A real distinction? *Ergonomics*, *33* (10/11), 1315-1332.

Reimer, B. L., A. D'Ambrosio, J. Gilbert, J. F. Coughlin, J. Biederman, C. Surman, R. Fried and M. Aleardi (2005). Behavior differences in drivers with attention deficit hyperactivity disorder: The driving behavior questionnaire. *Accid. Anal. Prev.*, *37*, 996-1004.

Roidl, E., B. Frehse, and R. Höger (2014). Emotional states of drivers and the impact on speed, acceleration and traffic violations — A simulator study. *Accid. Anal. Prev.*, *70*, 282-292.

Roidl, E., F. W. Siebert, M. Oehl, and R. Höger (2013). Introducing a multivariate model for predicting driving performance: The role of driving anger and personal characteristics. *J. Safety Res.*, *47*, 47-56.

Rowden, P., G. Matthews, B. Watson, and H. Biggs (2011). The relative impact of work-related stress, life stress and driving environment stress on driving outcomes. *Accid. Anal. Prev.*, *43*(4), 1332-1340.

Sârbescu, P., P. Stanojević, and D. Jovanović (2014). A cross-cultural analysis of aggressive driving: Evidence from Serbia and Romania. *Transport. Res. F.*, *24*, 210-217.

Sarkar, S., A. Marineau, M. Emami, M. Khatib and K. Wallace (2001). Spatial and temporal analyses of the variations in aggressive driving and road. Paper presented at the 80th annual meeting of the Transportation Research Board, National Academies of Science, Washington, DC, January.

Schechtman, E., D. Shinar and R. P. Compton (1999). The relationship between drinking habits and safe driving behaviors. *Transport. Res. F*, *2*, 16-26.

Schrank, D. and T. Lomax (2005). The 2005 urban mobility report. Texas Transportation Institute, Texas A & M University, College Station, TX.

Schuman, S. H., D. C. Pelz, N. J. Ehrlich and M. L. Seltzer (1967). Young male drivers: Impulse expression, accidents and violations. *J. Am. Med. Assoc.*, *200*, 1026-1030.

Schwebel, D. C., J. Severson, K. K. Ball and M. Rizzo (2006). Individual difference factors in risky driving: The roles of anger/hostility, conscientiousness, and sensation-seeking. *Accid. Anal. Prev.*, *38*(4), 801-810.

Shaw, L. and H. Sichel (1971). *Accident Proneness*. Pergamon Press, Oxford, UK.

Shinar, D. (1998). Aggressive driving: The contribution of the drivers and the situation. *Transport. Res. F*, *1*, 137-160.

Shinar, D. (2000). Driver accommodation of pedestrians and perception of legitimacy. Paper presented at the Conference on Road Safety in Three Continents. Pretoria, South Africa, September 20.

Shinar, D., M. Bourla and L. Kaufman (2004). Synchronization of traffic signals as a means of reducing red light running. *Hum. Fact.*, *46*(2), 367-372.

Shinar, D. and R. Compton (2004). Aggressive driving: An observational study of driver, vehicle, and situational variables. *Accid. Anal. Prev.*, *36*, 429-437.

Shinar, D., E. Schechtman, and R. Compton (2001). Self-reports of safe driving behaviors in relationship to sex, age, education and income in the US adult driving population. *Accid. Anal. Prev.*, *33*(1), 111-116.

Shinar, D., N. Tractinsky and R. P. Compton (2005). Effects of practice, age, and task demands, on interference from a phone task while driving. *Accid. Anal. Prev.*, *37*, 315-326.

Sivak, M. (1983). Society's aggression level as a predictor of traffic fatality rate. *J. Safety Res.*, *14*, 93-99.

Smart, R. G., R. E. Mann and G. Stoduto (2003). The prevalence of road rage: Estimates from Ontario. *Can. J. Public Health*, *94*(4), 247-250.

Smart, R. G., G. Stoduto, R. E. Mann and E. M. Adlaf (2004). Road rage experience and behavior: Vehicle, exposure, and driver factors. *Traffic Inj. Prev.*, *5*, 343-348.

Smith, D. I. and R. W. Kirkham (1981). Relationship between some personality characteristics and driving records. *Br. J. Soc. Psychol.*, *20*, 229-231.

Staplin, L. and K. W. Gish (2005). Job change rate as a crash predictor for interstate truck drivers. *Accid. Anal. Prev.*, *37*, 1035-1039.

Stephens, A. N. and K. Ohtsuka (2014). Cognitive biases in aggressive drivers: Does illusion of control drive us off the road? *Person. Ind. Diff.*, *68*, 124-129.

Stephens, A. N. and M. J. Sullman (2014). Development of a short form of the driving anger expression inventory. *Accid. Anal. Prev.*, *72*, 169-176.

Stradling, S. G. and M. L. Meadows (2000). Highway code and aggressive violations in UK Drivers. Global web conference on aggressive driving issues. As cited by Reimer *et al.* (2005).

Stuster, J. (2004). Aggressive driving enforcement: Evaluation of two demonstration programs. National Highway Traffic Administration Report DOT HS 809 707. U.S. Department of Transportation, Washington, DC.

Sullman, M. J. and A. N. Stephens (2013). A comparison of the driving anger scale and the propensity for angry driving scale. *Accid. Anal. Prev.*, *58*, 88-96.

Summala, H., S. Rajalin, and I. Radun (2014). Risky driving and recorded driving offences: A 24-year follow-up study. *Accid. Anal. Prev.*, *73*, 27-33.

Tasca, L. (2000). A review of the literature on aggressive driving research. Ontario Advisory Group on Safe Driving Secretariat, Road User Safety Branch. Ontario Ministry of Transportation, Canada.

Taubman-Ben-Ari, O. and D. Yehiel (2012). Driving styles and their associations with personality and motivation. *Accid. Anal. Prev.*, *45*, 416-422.

Tillman, W. A. and G. E. Hobbs (1949). The accident-prone automobile driver. *Am. J. Psychiatry*, *106*, 321-332.

Turner, C., R. McClure and S. Pirozzo (2004). Injury and risk-taking behavior—A systematic review. *Accid. Anal. Behav.*, *36*, 93-101.

Tyler, T. R. (2006). Psychological perspectives on legitimacy and legitimation. *Ann. Rev. Psychol.*, *57*, 375-400.

Ulleberg, P. (2004). Aggressive driving: A literature review. TOI Report 709. Nordic Road and Transport Research, Norway.

Van Rooy, D. L. (2006). Effects of automobile commute characteristics on affect and job candidate evaluations: A field experiment. *Environ. Behav.*, *38*(5), 626-655.

Van Rooy, D. L., J. Rotton and T. M. Burns (2006). Convergent, discriminant, and predictive validity of aggressive driving inventories: They drive as they live. *Aggress. Behav.*, *32*, 89-98.

Visser, E., Y. J. Pijl, R. P. Stolk, J. Neeleman and J. G. M. Rosmalen (2007). Accident proneness, does it exist? A review and meta-analysis. *Accid. Anal. Prev.*, *39*(3), 556-564.

Walker, G. and M. Calvert (2015). Driver behaviour at roadworks. *Appl. Ergon.*, *51*, 18-29.

Ward, N. J., M. Waterman and M. Joint (1999). The psychology of driver aggression in relation to traffic events: A summary of a survey study. Invited presentation at the Scottish Road Safety Council Annual Seminar, October 27-28.

Waylen, A. E. and F. P. McKenna (2008). Risky attitudes towards road use in pre-drivers. *Accid. Anal. Prev.*, *40*(3), 905-911.

Wells-Parker, E., J. Ceminsky, V. Hallberg, R. W. Snow, G. Dunaway, S. Guiling, M. Williams and B. Anderson (2002). An exploratory study of the relationship between road rage and crash experience in a representative sample of US drivers. *Accid. Anal. Prev.*, *34*, 271-278.

Whitlock, F. A. (1971). *Death on the Road.* Tavistock, London.

Wiesenthal, D. L., D. A. Hennessy and B. Totten (2003). The influence of music on mild driver aggression. *Transport. Res. F*, *6*(2), 125-134.

Yates, J. F. and H. F. Chua (2002). Proceedings of the 16th International Council of Accidents Drugs and Driving, Montreal, CA, August 4-9.

Yu, J., P. C. Evans and L. Perfetti (2004). Road aggression among drinking drivers: Alcohol and non-alcohol effects on aggressive driving and road rage. *J. Criminal Justice*, *32*, 421-430.

Zaidel, D. M. (1992). A modeling perspective on the culture of driving. *Accid. Anal. Prev.*, *24*(6), 585-597.

Zhang, T. and A. H. Chan (2016). The association between driving anger and driving outcomes: A meta-analysis of evidence from the past twenty years. *Accid. Anal. Prev.*, *90*, 50-62.

Zuckerman, M. (1994). *Behavioral Expressions and Biosocial Bases of Sensation Seeking.* University of Cambridge Press, Cambridge, UK.

Zuckerman, M., I. Kolin, L. Price and I. Zoob (1964). Development of a sensation seeking scale. *J. Consul. Psychol.*, *28*, 477-492.

10

Use of Occupant Restraints

"The incident occurred around 10:25 p.m. in Northwest. A sport utility vehicle hit a small sedan, injuring the driver and another passenger. A second passenger was ejected from the Honda Civic and killed." (Washington Post – Express, November 14, 2006, p. 11).

"I was on my way to give a lecture on 'accident causation'. I had just started to make a right turn at an intersection after the signal light turned green, when a car in the opposing lane came and struck me head-on off-center. I was protected by my seat belt, and unfortunately – in this very specific situation – by an airbag. The bag exploded and hurled my hand that was turning the steering wheel into my left eye breaking the orbital bone. My wife, protected only by a seat belt, suffered minor bruises typical of belt injuries, but was otherwise spared." (Personal experience from a crash on March 24, 2006, in Melbourne Australia).

The most significant achievements in traffic injury prevention and reductions over the past half century are probably in protecting the vehicle occupants. For example, in the U. S., seat belts and child safety seats are estimated to have saved over 12,000 occupants, and frontal air bags have saved over 2,000 more lives each year for the past few years (NHTSA, 2013), totaling over 300,000 lives saved between 1975 and 2012 (NHTSA, 2014b). This reduction in fatalities was brought about by better understanding of the mechanism of injury in traffic crashes, the forces that operate in a crash, and development of means to attenuate these forces by the time they reach the vehicle occupants. Therefore, in order to appreciate the benefits and directions of future injury reductions we have to describe the injury process. We then discuss the three approaches that have been applied to reducing occupants injuries: active restraint systems where the occupant has to actively engage them in order to enjoy their benefits (such as belts), passive restraint systems that operate independently of the occupant's actions (such as headrests and air bags), and vehicle design changes that improve its crashworthiness. Because this book is concerned with behavior and safety, the main focus of discussion here is not about the mechanics of these systems, but about the human role in maximizing their benefits – and the human has a role in all of the systems. The special case of motorcycle rider protection with helmets is discussed separately in Chapter 16.

The Mechanism of Injury

As any crash reconstruction specialist can verify, crashes are complicated. Consider a "simple" head-on collision between two vehicles. Following the initial high-force impact one or both cars may rotate and in the process hit each other again, or hit other objects, or be hit by other cars, or slide into a ditch by the side of the road and roll over, or any combination of the above. Thus, a crash is not a single event but a process that evolves over time, albeit a very short time. But even a "simple" crash with a driver alone in a car striking a single stationary object is complex. That is because from the perspective of the occupants what we call a crash actually involves three or four collisions (Peterson *et al.*, 1999).

The first collision occurs when the vehicle strikes an object. At this stage some of the kinetic energy that is released by the rapid deceleration is absorbed by the crushing of the vehicle body and energy absorbing components in the vehicle (such as the bumpers). This collision stops the vehicle, but not its occupants. As the vehicle becomes crushed, if the driver and occupants are not restrained, they continue to move through inertia until they strike an obstacle. The second collision occurs when the driver crashes into the interior of the now stopped car. If the driver is not restrained, then the second collision occurs almost at the same speed of the first collision. The third collision occurs when the driver's body is stopped by the car's interior, but the internal organs still move within the body, until they strike an obstacle, as when the lungs strike the ribcage or the brain tissues strike the skull. The fourth collision, which may or may not occur, is the collision between the driver and loose objects (or passengers) in the car that may fly and strike the driver.

The basic scientific principle behind all injury protection devices is that of gradual force reduction or "ride-down" of force; that is, the reduction in kinetic energy. The maximum force or deceleration that a healthy young person can sustain is about 30G (where G is the gravitational constant = 9.8 m/s^2). Because the force of impact is proportional to the *square* of the speed divided by the stopping distance, the greater the stopping distance the lower the force. Now, let's assume a car is extremely sturdy, and upon striking the object in the first collision it is not deformed at all. In that case, the full force of the first collision is transferred to the second collision. An unrestrained or unprotected occupant is then propelled at the original travel speed into the car's interior where the second collision occurs. If we assume that the distance between the driver and the steering wheel is about 30 centimeters, then this is the distance that the driver has to decelerate. It can then be shown, that at a speed of approximately 30 km/hr the impact force is close to 30G. If, on the other hand, the car can absorb some of the impact through a shock absorbing bumper and a collapsible frame, and we also assume that the driver is belted, then the driver's forward motion is slowed by the seat belt. In this way the distance in which the driver "travels" while decelerating until reaching a complete stop increases significantly, and the driver has a much greater "ride-down" distance. For example, for a car traveling at the same speed as before, this distance may be now approximately 60 centimeters, and the resulting impact force is halved to less than 15 G (Peterson *et al.*, 1999). Using the belts allows the driver to take advantage of the "ride-down" potential, by not allowing him or her to keep moving at the previous speed. Another benefit of the belts is that they prevent ejection out of the car, a significant source of driver injuries and fatalities. There are less obvious design changes that increase the crashworthiness of the car, like moving the front wheels back so that much of the energy is absorbed before it reaches the wheels. Not all of these advantages are utilized in all collisions. For example, incompatibility in bumper heights between vehicles can essentially eliminate the absorption benefit of a car's bumper in a collision with a truck whose bumper height is above that of the car. That is why the U.S. Federal government is considering requiring low guards below the standard bumper of a single-unit truck to reduce injuries in underride collisions when a striking passenger vehicle goes under the truck (IIHS, 2015a).

So what is the role of the driver and other occupants in mitigating the consequences of a crash? Actually their role is quite crucial. First, they must take advantage of the best restraint systems that will keep them in their seats when a crash occurs. Second, the driver must not "compensate" for these benefits by engaging in high-risk behaviors that can increase the likelihood of a crash or the impact speed if a crash occurs. If we now recall the risk homeostasis hypothesis (see Chapter 3), this means that drivers must be convinced not to increase their speed because their car can help them survive high-speed crashes that were unsurvivable 40 years ago. Unfortunately, not everyone takes advantage of all the restraint systems available, and some occupants who do, still don't get all the expected benefits. Who these drivers and occupants are, why they behave this way and what can we do about it is the focus of this chapter.

Active Restraints – Seat Belts and Whistles

Active restraints are occupant restraints that are effective only if the driver activates them. The prime example of an active restraint is the seat belt. Passive restraints are those that operate automatically, such as air bags. By far the greatest contributor to injury reduction in the past few decades is the occupants' use of seat belts. The current retracting three-point seat belt provides much more protection than the early fixed lap belts. But despite their proven effectiveness, some drivers and passengers are still reluctant to use them.

The effectiveness of seat belts

Multiple independent analyses of seat belt effectiveness, using crash data from different countries, and different statistical methods have all yielded quite similar results, reducing fatalities and injuries by approximately 40-50 percent, as detailed in Table 10-1 (WHO, 2004). However, the exact numbers in the table should be considered as potentially inflated estimates because they are based on police reports, and these are known to inflate the percent of belt use. This is because drivers – when they can get away with it – will report to the officer that they had their belt on (Li, Kim, and Nitz, 1999). Consequently, as the injury severity decreases, the amount of over-estimation of belt use is most likely to increase.

Table 10-1. The effectiveness of belts in preventing fatalities and reducing injuries (from WHO, 2004, with permission from the World Health Organization).

Year	Reference	Injury Reducing Effect (%)		
		Fatal collisions	Moderate and severe injuries	All severities
1976	Griffith *et al.*	41		
1984	Hobbs and Mills		65	
1986	Department of Transportation, U.S.			40-50
1987	Malliaris and Digges	50 (drivers) 40 (front-seat passengers)		
1987	Evans	41		
1987	Campbell	65 (drivers) 54 (front-seat passengers)	51-52 (drivers) 43-44 (front-seat passengers)	
1996	National Highway Traffic Safety Administration, U.S.		48	
1996	Cooperative Crash Injury Study, UK (unpublished)		53	
2003	Cummings *et al.*	61		
	Effectiveness range	40-65	43-65	40-50

The most rigorous method to evaluate the contribution of belts to fatality reduction was developed by Evans (1986). With this method, known as the "double pair comparison" method, Evans first identified all fatal crashes involving cars with multiple occupants (where the driver was not necessarily the one who was killed). He then compared the fatality likelihood for drivers with and without belts relative to the likelihood of fatality of the other occupant with and without belts. The beauty of this approach is that there is no need for exposure measure, and hence no need to be concerned about exposure bias. Using the U.S. national Fatal Analysis Reporting System which documents every fatal crash in the U.S., Evans estimated that the combined lap + shoulder belts prevent approximately 43 percent of all driver fatalities: 34 percent from the reduction is in interior impact reduction and an additional nine percent is from the prevention of ejection. As might be expected, the effectiveness of the belts depends to a large extent on the separation between the occupant and the vehicle's frame, the impact absorption capability of the frame relative to the direction and location of impact, and the likelihood of ejection for each crash type. Thus, the overall injury reduction potential from belts is the product of the relative frequency of each crash type and the fatality prevention effectiveness of the belts for each crash type. These two factors were graphically illustrated by Evans (1990) and they are reproduced in Figure 10-1. The greatest effectiveness of the belts in reduction of driver fatalities is in rear-end and front-end collisions, which are the lowest and highest in fatalities. Also, the belts are more effective in protecting the driver in side impacts from the passenger side than from the driver side, where the separation between the driver and the vehicle interior is the smallest.

Depending on their age, the type of vehicle and type of crash, passengers can benefit from belts even more than drivers. Figure 10-2 depicts the risk of fatality of an unrestrained passenger relative to a restrained passenger as a function of the vehicle type and the passenger's age. It is based on all U.S. 1998-2002 single-vehicle fatal crashes as

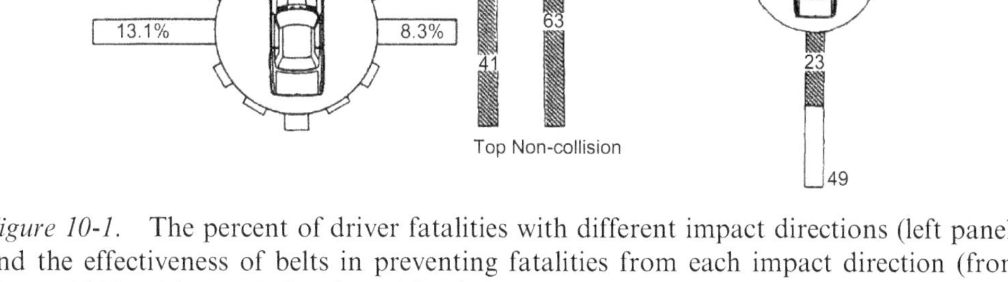

Figure 10-1. The percent of driver fatalities with different impact directions (left panel) and the effectiveness of belts in preventing fatalities from each impact direction (from Evans, 1990, with permission from Elsevier).

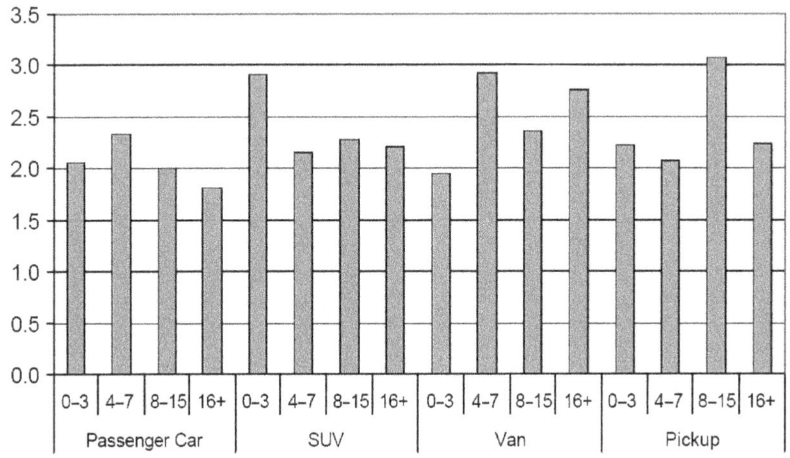

Figure 10-2. Relative risk of fatality of unrestrained passengers (relative to restrained passengers) in a single-vehicle fatal crash, by vehicle body type and age of passenger (from Starnes, 2005).

recorded in the national Fatal Analysis Reporting System (Starnes, 2005). In this figure, a relative risk of 2.0 is equivalent to 50 percent effectiveness in fatality reduction. As can be seen, for all ages and all vehicle types the relative risk of an unrestrained passenger ranges from a low of 1.7 for an adult passenger in a car to a high of 3.1 (approximately 67 percent reduction in fatalities) for a teen passenger in a pickup truck. However, these estimates are probably less accurate than Evans' because confounding variables such as the driving style (more risky when occupants are not belted) may inflate the estimates. Also – as noted above and by Starnes (2005) – the belt use data are determined by the police who often depend on the occupants reports and therefore may be over-reported for survivors. A similar analysis of the relative effectiveness of restraints for passengers in multi-vehicle crashes yielded an overall lower level of effectiveness ranging from the lowest relative risks for passengers of cars (RR 1.6-1.8) to the highest for passengers of sport utility vehicles, the vehicles most likely to roll over in a crash (from RR 3.1 for adult passengers to 5.4 for infants and toddlers). Finally, a recent analysis of the effectiveness of seat belts and air bags on injury and fatalities of medium/heavy truck drivers in the U.S. and China, by Hu and Blower (2013), yielded levels of effectiveness similar to those obtained by Evans for belts, but slightly lower levels of effectiveness for air bags.

Since their introduction, seat belts have gone through several improvements, beginning with the introduction of the three-point system (lap and shoulder belts), through retractable belts, and on to equipping the belts with pretensioners and load limiters. Pretensioners retract the seat belt to remove excess slack almost instantly upon sensing that the vehicle has crashed. Load limiters allow the belt to "give" or yield when forces on the belt rise above a predetermined level. In the U.S. though not required by law, they have become standard equipment in the front seats on all new cars and light trucks, and have been estimated by the National Highway Safety Administration to reduce driver and front-seat passenger fatalities by an additional 13 percent (Kahane, 2010). Overall, current estimates of the World Health Organization and NHTSA are that seat belts reduce the risk of a fatal injury by 40-50 percent for drivers and front-seat occupants, and by 25-75 percent for rear seat occupants (WHO, 2013), and the risk of moderate-to-critical injury by 65 percent (NHTSA, 2015b). In the EU, where 12,345 vehicle occupants were killed in crashes in 2012, Jost, Allsop, and Cesi (2014) estimate that seat belts saved the lives of 8,600 vehicle occupants; that is, reduced fatalities by 41 percent. They also estimated that had all crash-involved occupants used their seat belt an additional four percent would have been saved. The additional percent is relatively small because in the EU and affiliated countries seat belt use is generally quite high. In 2012, 10 of the EU and affiliated countries reported rates of 95+ percent for front-seat occupants. However, in Italy where the front seat use rate was relatively low at 70 percent, it was estimated that had all front-seat occupants used the belts, fatalities would have been reduced by 27 percent (Jost *et al.*, 2014).

Measuring seat belt use

Given the proven effectiveness of seat belts, it is a matter of national interest in every country to measure seat belt use in order to track changes in use rates as a function of various efforts to increase usage. But measuring use rates is not as simple as it may seem. Two approaches are typically used: direct observations and driver surveys and interviews. The first is nominally more objective but it is subjective in the sense that it depends on the abilities of the observers to determine whether or not a seat belt is used. This is relatively easy when a driver is stopped at a stop light on a spring day in broad daylight with the window open, and use of belts is recorded for front-seat occupants only. But it is much more difficult at night, in inclement weather (when the windows are closed), when the drivers are driving by at high speeds, and when we want to assess belt use in rear seats. To retain maximal validity of the observations, these measures are typically used in visually comfortable circumstances, and therefore extrapolations from these samples of observations to national estimates are problematic. The few studies that have evaluated the relationship between these moderating variables – such as day versus night and front seat versus rear seat – have shown that seat belt use rates are lower at night (Chaudhary, Alonge, and Preusser, 2005, Chaudhary and Preusser, 2006) and in the rear seats (Jost *et al.*, 2014; Glassbrenner and Ye, 2006; NRSA, 2015; Shimamura, Yarmazaki, and Fujita, 2005).

To obtain information that is difficult to see directly we resort to questionnaires and driver interviews. Here, the amount and type of information is limited only by the creativity of the researcher and the impatience of the driver. But here the problem is reporting bias – people generally want to portray themselves in a socially desirable manner, and consequently their responses typically over-estimate their actual use rates (Parada *et al.*, 2001; Samples, 2004; Streff and Wagenaar, 1989).

A few studies have measured the discrepancy directly by both observing and interviewing drivers. These studies have provided us with some insights about the magnitude of the discrepancies between the two types of measures and ways to compensate for these discrepancies. The standard approach is to unobtrusively observe and identify drivers and then query them about their belt use, without their knowledge that they were or will be observed. The ratio of the percent of drivers who report that they "always" use the seat belt relative to the percent who are observed wearing their seat belts is the estimate of over-reporting. Different studies have found discrepancies ranging from 4 to 20 percent, and over-reporting by a factor of 1.2 to 2.0 (Streff and Wagenaar, 1989), and even higher in populations of low belt users (such as Hispanics in the state of Texas; Parada *et al.*, 2001). Dee (1998) compared 126 self-reports from different U.S. cities in different years with observational seat belt use data from the same cities and years and found a strong relationship between the two measures (correlation $r = 0.81$), but an over-estimate of the self-reports by approximately 10 percent.

Another approach is to interview a representative sample of drivers in a given geographical region, and then observe belt use in the same region. The difference in the percent of the sample who state that they always use belts and the percent of belt users out of the total number of observations is another indicator of the discrepancy. This approach is even more problematic because it does not provide a direct comparison of specific individuals' responses with their behavior. This creates a conceptual problem: how can we ascertain the frequency of belt use for those observed wearing belts, so that we can relate it to the frequencies obtained in the interview sample. When the interviews are done by phone another bias – an age bias – is introduced. Telephone interviews tend to under-sample young drivers (who are harder to reach and less cooperative), and young drivers are less likely than older drivers to wear the seat belts. Consequently, this adds to the over-estimation bias (Streff and Wagenaar, 1989).

To have a better understanding of the relationships between the estimates obtained with different methods Streff and Wagenaar (1989) conducted a study in which they first observed Michigan drivers on the road and then stopped them for a brief interview. Two interview questions addressed the frequency of belt use. One question was "How often do you use your seat belt?" and the other was "Out of your last ten trips in a car how many times did you use the seat belt when one was available?" Several findings of this research were important and interesting. First, there was a relatively high correlation ($r = 0.71$) between the percent of drivers observed wearing a seat belt and the degree to which they stated that they do (on the "always – never" scale), but a much lower one with the subjective scale of "number of trips with belts" ($r = 0.28$). Second, estimates based on both subjective reports, over-stated the frequency of belt use. Only 45.2 percent of the people who reported that they always used a seat belt were actually observed wearing their seat belt. The over-reporting was even worse relative to the "number of times belts were used in the past": only 33 percent of those who said that they used it in all of their last 10 trips were observed with belts (28 percent for those reporting 9 out of 10, and 13 percent for those reporting 8 out of 10). The relationships between the objective observations and the subjective responses are illustrated in Figure 10-3, which also shows that the actual percent observed using belts is significantly smaller than the percent stating that they "always" use belts, or reported that they used the belts on all ten last trips. However, in reality the gap may be even larger. This is because it is highly likely that in this particular comparison the people stopped and interviewed on the road

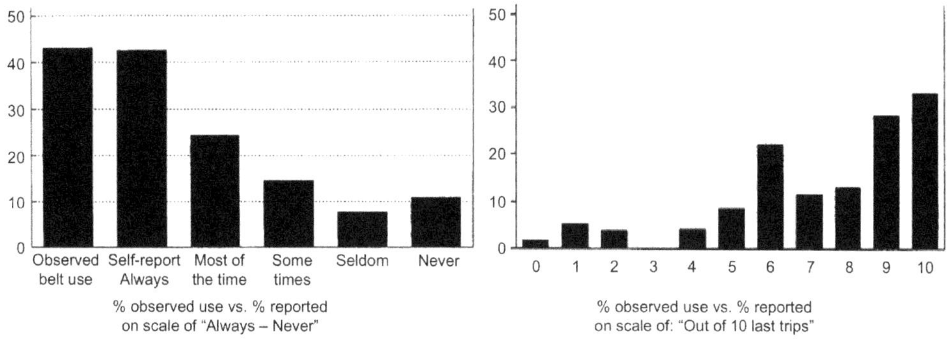

Figure 10-3. Percent of observed belt use relative to two subjective (reported) scales of estimated belt use (from Streff and Wagenaar, 1989, with permission from Elsevier).

were probably quite cognizant of a potential discrepancy between their answer "always" and their actual behavior a few minutes prior to being stopped, and they were therefore probably more honest in their responses than people would otherwise be when the interview is conducted over the phone at their home, an environment that is totally detached from actual driving.

One other data source in Streff and Wagenaar's study were telephone interviews with an independent probability sample of Michigan drivers. When they compared the percent who answered that they always used their seat belts with the percent that were observed using the seat belt they obtained a nine percent "over-reporting": with 56 percent reporting they used the belts "all the time" compared to only 47 percent of the drivers observed belted in traffic. However, estimates of over-reporting based on this method are even more questionable. In addition to the age bias mentioned above, presumably some of those observed wearing seat belts are people who would respond that they wear their seat belts "some of the time" or "sometimes," as indicated in the left panel of Figure 10-3. Thus, this method also yields an under-estimate of the gap, though it is impossible to determine its size. Results using this method become perplexing when the observed rates are actually the same or higher than the percent who report that they always use their belts. This, in fact was the case in a study by Samples (2004) when she compared the U.S. national estimates based on the observational study National Occupant Protection Use Survey (NOPUS) with the interview-based results of the Behavioral Risk Factors Surveillance System (BRFSS). She found that the 2002 national estimate based on the NOPUS was 79.4 percent while the "always" estimate from the BRFSS was 77.3 percent.

A more recent analysis that compared self-reports to observational data was conducted by Ibrahimova, Shults, and Beck (2011). They compared two U.S.-wide 2008 national data bases and found a near perfect correlation between the two methods, $r = .98$. Furthermore, the absolute use levels themselves were extremely similar, and in 38 states the use rate based on self-reports was actually lower than the observed rates. To account for these differences between their results and the earlier smaller scale studies, Ibrahimova and his associates suggest that as the belt use rose over the years, the differences between the observed and reported rates diminished because the social desirability of belt use spread from the verbal reports to the actual use. If this explanation is true, then for countries reporting high belt use (e.g., the Czech Republic, France, Germany, Israel, Netherlands, and Sweden all have more than 95 percent belt use in the front seats; Jost *et al.*, 2014) self-reports may provide sufficient estimates of belt use rates.

Users and non-users of seat belts

Despite their effectiveness, in the absence of laws that require seat belts, meaningful sanctions for not wearing seat belts, and consistent enforcement, some people still do not buckle up. Different study methods, and studies conducted in different countries consistently identify the same characteristics of non-users. The two most common methods used to identify characteristics that distinguish between users and non-users of seat belts have been surveys or interviews and observations. Observations are more objective, but they reveal very little about the driver (gender, apparent age, and some measure of socio-economic status based on the car value). Surveys and interviews can probe a whole host of variables, but because of social desirability they yield higher percentages of seat belt use than direct observations (Parada *et al.*, 2001; Streff and Wagenaar, 1989). Other, indirect, techniques have also been used. For example, in a study we conducted at 400 sites in the state of Ohio seat belt observations were conducted on a regular basis. User characteristics were then extrapolated from a different data base that provided socio-economic and demographic information of the people living within the proximity of these sites.

Despite the different methods and locations of the studies, the results are remarkably consistent and demonstrate that the use of seat belts is consistent with a cluster of socio-economic-demographic characteristics and attitudes toward high-risk behaviors. Specifically, the results of various studies conducted in different countries around the globe (Australia, France, Kuwait, the United Kingdom, U.S.) show that:

1. Older drivers are more likely to wear their seat belts than young drivers (Chaudhary, Solomon, and Cosgrove, 2004; Chaudhary and Northrup, 2004; Lerner *et al.*, 2001; Pickrell, Choi, and Shova, 2016; Shinar, 1993; Shinar, Schechtman, and Compton, 2001; Vivoda, Eby, and Kostyniuk, 2004).
2. Married drivers, especially with children at home, are more likely to use their belts than unmarried drivers (Chaudhary and Northrup; 2004; Lerner *et al.*, 2001; Shinar, 1993).
3. Women are more likely to wear their belts than men (Chaudhary and Northrup, 2004; Fernandez *et al.*, 2006; Koushki and Bustan, 2006; Lerner *et al.*, 2001; Shinar, 1993; Shinar *et al.*, 2001; Vivoda *et al.*, 2004; Williams, Wells, and Farmer, 2002).
4. People with of higher socio-economic status are more likely to use seat belts than people of lower socio-economic status, based on education (Shinar, 1993; Shinar *et al.*, 2001), home value (Shinar, 1993), blue versus white collar occupation (Shinar, 1993), and income (Chaudhary *et al.*, 2004; Chaudhary and Northrup, 2004; Lerner *et al.*, 2001; Shinar *et al.*, 2001).

5. Owners of newer and more expensive cars are more likely to buckle up than owners of older and less expensive cars (Colgan *et al.*, 2004).
6. Whites are more likely to use belts than blacks (Lerner *et al.*, 2001; Shinar, 1993; Vivoda *et al.*, 2004) or Hispanics (Parada *et al.*, 2001).
7. People who drive passenger cars are more likely to wear belts than drivers of trucks (including pickup trucks) (Bergoffen *et al.*, 2005; Besel, Dennis, and Drake, 2001; Chaudhary and Northrup, 2004; Glassbrenner and Ye, 2006; Vivoda *et al.*, 2004).
8. People who drink moderately and refrain from drinking and driving are more likely to use belts than people who engage in excessive drinking or drinking and driving (Fernandez *et al.*, 2006; Li *et al.*, 1999; Shinar, 1993).
9. Non-smokers are more likely to use belts than smokers (Koushki and Bustan, 2006).
10. Low-accident drivers and accident-free drivers are more likely to use seat belts than high accident drivers (Koushki and Bustan, 2006).

Earlier research is consistent with the above statements and has been reviewed elsewhere (Shinar, 1993). Together these findings indicate that people who are at the lower rungs of the socio-economic scale, and drivers who are inclined to engage in other high-risk behaviors (such as young males, and people who smoke and drink) are more likely to drive unbelted than others. If we make the reasonable assumption that most people most of the times have control over the use or non-use of their seat belts, then these results suggest that knowledge, peer behavior, and attitudes toward risk taking are the prime determinants of seat belt use. Research that examined the relevance of some of these factors is described below.

Why people don't use belts

Having read so far, the intelligent reader who had not been using seat belts should now be convinced of their effectiveness and use them consistently from now on. Regrettably this is a very naïve expectation. In fact, in their survey of 1,467 (mostly) Kuwaiti students Koushki and Bustan (2006) noted that 99 percent of the respondents believed that seat belts reduce severe injuries yet only 18 percent of the men and 64 percent of the women reported using them all the time. (A similar phenomenon exists with respect to the use of cell phones while driving, see Chapter 13). So knowledge alone is not a sufficient motivator. When people's knowledge conflicts with other components of their attitude – the emotions and behavioral tendencies – they will subvert the former in order to behave according to the latter. Thus, people will rationalize that belts are uncomfortable and interfere with their movements in the vehicle (Bergoffen *et al.*, 2005) or that their a priori risk of injury is negligible and further reductions are therefore meaningless (see Figure 3-11). Also, like most behaviors, attitudes toward seat belt use may be tied to other attitudes. Noting that previous studies have shown that Arabs living in Israel are more fatalistic than (mostly secular) Jews in Israel, Omari and Baron-Epel (2013), surveyed 380 Arabs after they were observed transporting children in their cars. Among other questions the drivers were also rated on their fatalistic beliefs that all events are determined by fate or God, based on their responses to statements related to crash risk and to using child safety belts. They then used logistic regression to show that drivers with fatalistic beliefs are significantly less likely (by 20 percent) to harness their children than those not having such beliefs.

Behavioral intentions are also often moderated by external situations. People who tend to speed and drive aggressively do not do that all the time, but only when the situation "allows" it. The same appears to be with respect to use of belts. Chaudhary and Northrup (2004) analyzed drivers' responses to the 1998-2000 U.S. National Motor Vehicle Occupant Safety Survey and found that while the frequency of belt use was associated with some of the demographic variables listed above, it was often moderated by attitudinal variables, such as fatalism, the perceived likelihood of being ticketed, and the perceived effectiveness of belts, which often interacted among themselves. For example, perceived risk of being stopped for not wearing a seat belt, by itself was only moderately associated with the percent of people who used seat belts "always." However in conjunction with the perceived effectiveness of the belts, it was highly relevant: 82 percent of the drivers who were classified as "high" on both the risk of ticketing and the perceived effectiveness used belts "'always," compared to only 57 percent of the drivers classified as "low" on both variables.

Most of the people who do not wear belts all the time, still wear them occasionally, and it appears that their decision to use their belts is determined by the situation. They use the belts only when the situation appears to demand it, but in the absence of enforcement or pressure from a family member they suppress the risk of a crash, and recruit various unconscious defense mechanisms to justify their behavior (such as rationalization, repression, and fatalism) (Brittle and Cosgrove, 2005).

Belt use rates and expected impact on national crash statistics

With belt use rates exceeding 80 percent in most of the Western world, one may wonder why safety organizations and advocates keep harping on the issue. The reason is twofold: selective recruiting and behavioral adaptation. The "selective recruitment" argument is that the involvement of those who do not use their belts in crashes, injuries, and fatalities is much higher than that of the average driver. This is because – as pointed above – non-use of seat belts is associated with various other high-risk behaviors. Thus, habitual non-users are much more likely to be involved in crashes than users, and consequently their potential impact on fatality reduction is much greater. The argument of behavioral adaptation is the same as risk homeostasis. When people start using their belts, they are likely to feel safer, which in turn may be an incentive for some to assume greater risk.

The presence of both factors was very elegantly demonstrated in an experimental study by Janssen (1994). In his study he conducted two experiments in which he had two groups of drivers: habitual users and habitual non-users of seat belts. The drivers' task was to drive an instrumented vehicle 105 kilometers on a Dutch freeway. In the first study the non-users were divided into two groups: those who were required to drive with the seat belts and those who were not required to – and did not – use the seat belts.

An analysis of the speed profiles of the three groups of drivers showed that the habitual non-users, regardless of whether they had the seat belts on or not during the experiment, drove faster than the habitual belt users, thereby demonstrating the selective recruitment effect: non-users are more dangerous drivers. In the second experiment half the non-users were given a significant incentive to use their belts whenever and wherever they drove in the following year, and half of the habitual users were given a significant incentive if they would not be involved in any crash in which they would be culpable during the following year. The other halves of the two groups were not given any specific instructions. All drivers were then asked to return for a drive in the instrumented vehicle three more times in the course of the following year. The rationale behind the second experiment was that the habitual non-users of belts who were given the incentive to use belts would compensate for wearing them by increasing their speed of driving. The rationale for urging half the belt users to drive more safely was that they would actually reduce their speed relative to the belt users who were not given such incentive. The results, using various measures of risky driving, indicated that with successive visits the "beginning wearers" (those who habitually did not use belts, but were given an incentive to do so) kept their obligation, but behaved in a progressively risky manner that included increasing their speed, maintaining shorter headways to cars ahead of them in traffic, and braking more abruptly. Thus, the second experiment demonstrated the gradual adaptation of compensatory behavior in response to the "forced" use of belts. The habitual wearers did not change their behavior even when getting the incentive to drive more carefully, possibly because they were already driving slower and in a safer manner.

One direct estimate of the nature and impact of the "selective recruitment" process on the expected impact of belt use, relative to the prevailing belt use levels was made by Nakahara *et al.* (2006) in Japan. In their study they used several different sources of mortality data and compared them to police recorded belt use data for the years 1979-2001. With such a wide range of years they were able to obtain mortality data for widely different levels of belt use: from 13.4 percent for front occupants in 1979 to 84.9 percent in 2003. The results of their best fit mathematical models are presented in Figure 10-4. While the mathematical modeling itself was quite complicated, the results are very simple to grasp: regardless of the data source, the risk of a potentially fatal crash per unbelted person in the driving population remains relatively stable (and low) until the belt use rate exceeds a very high level of 80-90 percent. This, according to Nakahara and his associates, is because when belt use rate is low, both safe and unsafe drivers contribute to the risk. As use rate increases, the first to use the belts, are the drivers who are otherwise law-abiding safe drivers, while the ones to resist use and disregard belt use laws are the high-risk drivers such as the young and impaired drivers (O'Neill, 2009). As more and more of them use belts, the proportion of the unsafe drivers – who tend to speed, drive while impaired, and drive aggressively – among the non-users increases. Consequently, with an increasing proportion of unsafe drivers in the non-users group the risk of fatality in that group increases. Furthermore, the benefits of belts are greater at night than in daytime driving: their impact on fatality reductions begins to show up at lower rates, and escalate to higher levels than in daytime crashes. This is because nighttime driving is more closely associated with high-risk driving due to fatigue, reduced visibility, and driving while impaired. Thus, it is only when the small segment of

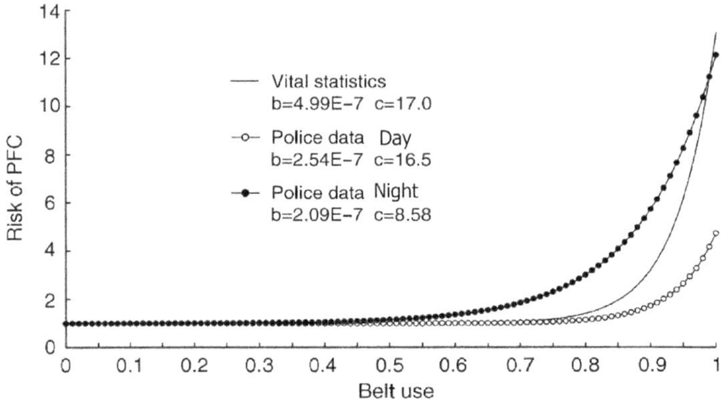

Figure 10-4. The risk of a potentially fatal crash for persons who *begin* to use their seat belts when the population belt use rate reaches a given level. The different functions are based on three different Japanese mortality data sources: vital statistics, police daytime fatalities, and police nighttime fatalities (from Nakahara *et al.*, 2006, with permission from Elsevier).

the high-risk driving population begins to use their seat belts that we are likely to see very large reductions in fatalities as a consequence.

Nakahara *et al.*'s findings support the selective recruitment hypothesis, but did not provide evidence for the claimed characteristics of the high-risk drivers. A direct demonstration of the selective recruitment effects on high-risk drivers was provided by Dee (1998). Dee used data from the U.S. Centers of Disease Control monthly Behavioral Risk Factors Surveillance System to examine the demographic and behavioral characteristics of the respondents who answered that they "always" used seat belts. His analysis focused on 16 cities that introduced seat belt laws during a 7-year period and for which there were monthly surveys of various demographics, behaviors, and belt use data. He then examined the change in the percent of respondents who reported that they "always used belts" immediately following the introduction of a belt law in their state. Based on these self-reports he found that the impact of the introduction and enforcement of the laws on belt use rates was significantly smaller on young drivers, males, and heavy drinkers than on older drivers, females, and non- or moderate drinkers. In short, the use of seat belts in response to the laws was much lower among the high-risk drivers than among the low risk drivers. In this context, it is important to note that Streff and Wagenaar (1989) found that the amount of over-reporting was unaffected by the existence of belt laws, so the validity of the self-reports in Dee's study was probably unaffected by the change in the laws.

How to increase belt use

Increasing belt use is relatively easy when the use levels are low, but it gets more and more difficult as the general use levels increase. Because people's motives for not using belts vary widely, different people respond to different incentives. Consequently, a wide variety of approaches has to be adopted to reach different segments of the driving population.

Belt use laws and use rate

Belt use laws exist in most countries today, and the difference between them is in the exceptions that they allow and the penalties that are attached to non-use. In 2013 the World Health Organization reported that 111 countries (covering nearly 70 percent of the world population) have comprehensive seat belt laws for all vehicle occupants (WHO, 2013). However, the use rate varies widely among countries. For example in the IRTAD (mostly European countries) the rate for 2012-2013 belt use in the front seats ranges from as high as over 95 percent (Czech Republic, Germany, Israel, Japan, New Zealand, and Sweden – topping the list with 98 percent observed use rate) to under 70 percent (Italy, Korea, Argentina, and Cambodia – at the bottom with only 16 percent). The use rates of the rear seat passengers are much lower, ranging from a high of over 95 percent in Germany and Australia to a low of under 15 percent in Malaysia, Italy, Korea, and Serbia (OECD, 2014). In the U.S. where seat belt laws are enacted and enforced at the state level, the use rate in 2013 also varied significantly; from as high as 97 percent (in Alabama, California, and Oregon) to under 80 percent (Arkansas, Massachusetts, Montana, Nebraska, New Hampshire, North Dakota, Virginia, and South Dakota – at the bottom of the list with 69 percent) (NHTSA, 2014a). The accuracy of reporting also varies widely, depending on the prevailing culture and method of data collection. For example, in China, that has a national seat belt law requirement; there are apparently wide variations in results reported in different studies. Some of these discrepancies may be due to "covert non-compliance"; defeating the system while making it appear to an outside observer as if the belt is buckled (Fleiter *et al.*, 2009). Two examples from pictures taken in Boston, U.S. and Beijing are shown in Figure 10-5. In Greece where use rate is among the lower of European countries I have actually seen specially designed buckles that fit into the belt latch so as to disarm the alarm/reminder without actually engaging the seat belt.

Regardless of the figures, the trend is positive. In a recent analysis of 1,891 moderate-to-severe crashes of 16- to 19-year-old U.S. drivers, that were videotaped by DriveCam® (a camera system that records the view outside and inside the car), Carney *et al.* (2015) found that in 93 percent of the crashes the driver was wearing a seatbelt. This is a very positive finding as it is much higher than the average rate in the U.S., and it is for an otherwise high-risk group. Most importantly, these drivers will affect the average use rate for many years to come.

Seat belt laws: Primary and secondary

Perhaps the most interesting variation in seat belt laws in the U.S. is the distinction between primary belt laws and secondary belt laws. A primary belt law is a law in the traditional sense: a motorist can be stopped and ticketed/fined for not using a seat belt. A secondary belt law requires that a motorist first be stopped for another violation, and then and only then – in addition to the violation for which he or she was stopped – be cited for not using a seat belt. In the U.S., where legislating the use of seat belts is still a hotly debated issue of individual freedom versus public health, With national seat belt

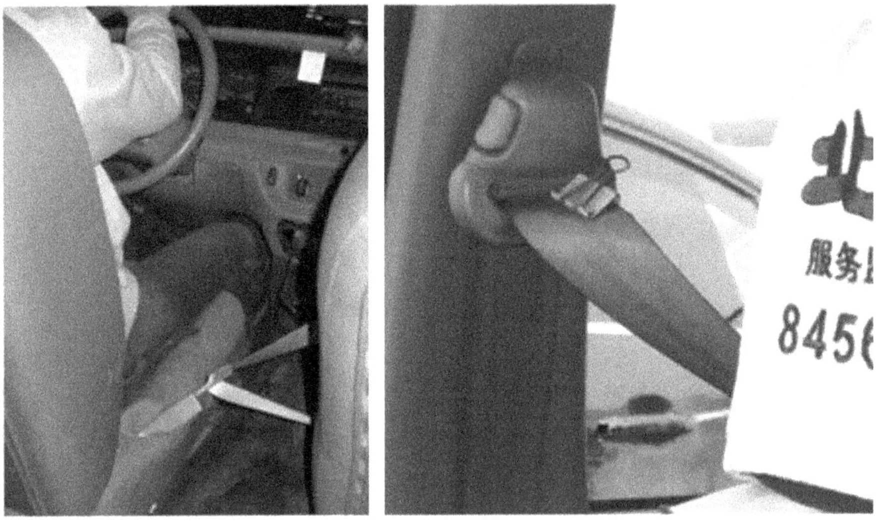

Figure 10-5. Defeating seat belt use requirements. Disarming the belt reminder by a Boston taxi driver (April, 2012), and defeating the retracting system allowing the belt to just lie on the driver's lap of a Beijing taxi driver so that he appears to be buckled (October, 2008). (Pictures by the author).

use rate of 87 percent, as of 2014 only 30 states (plus the District of Columbia) had a primary law, 19 states had a secondary law, and one state (New Hampshire) had no uniform seat belt law (NHTSA, 2015a). However, the trend over time is positive: from no laws, to secondary laws, to primary laws. Various studies that have compared the two laws have demonstrated the obvious benefit of primary laws. In 2014 the national average daytime observed belt use rate was 87 percent for front-seat occupants. However, in primary law states the average was 90 percent while in secondary law states the average was 79 percent (NHTSA, 2015a; Pickrell and Choi, 2015). Dee (1998) and Majumdar, Noland, and Ochieng (2004) found that even secondary laws increase belt use relative to no belt laws, but the change from secondary to primary laws – as expected – yields a further increase in belt use. Dinh-Zarr *et al.* (2001) and Shults *et al.* (2004) reviewed the effects of belt laws on use rates and noted that in all of the 15 studies that they reviewed the introduction of the law was followed by an increase in belt use: by 12-18 percent based on self-reports, and by 17-39 percent based on observations. The increase in belt use was also associated with a median drop of five percent in crash fatalities. Farmer and Williams (2005) analyzed the fatality trends in states that changed from secondary belt laws to primary belt laws and compared them to the trends in states that retained their secondary law. After adjusting for time trends and several potential economic factors, they concluded that primary laws further reduce the annual driver death rates by an average of seven percent. Primary seat belt laws have one added significant benefit: they are most effective for teen drivers. In an analysis that combined the FARS data and CDC national surveys of seat belt use among high-school students in grades 9-12 (i.e., mostly 16-19 years old) for 1991-2005, Carpenter and Stehr (2008) found that teen use rate increased by 45-80 percent and fatalities decreased by eight percent in states enacting primary seat belt laws. Furthermore, they found no evidence for "selective recruitment hypothesis" that states that the various safety measures are adopted mostly by lower risk drivers to begin with. In summary, primary seat belt laws are a very effective policy toward increasing seat belt use and reducing fatalities and injuries, especially in the highest risk group of young drivers. It is therefore not surprising that the U.S. National Highway Safety Administration gives primary seat belt enforcement their highest countermeasure rating of five stars (Goodwin *et al.*, 2015)

One caveat in the estimation of the effectiveness of belt laws is that they are typically passed when there is already significant public support for it. Laws rarely create norms; they typically reflect and reinforce them. In the case of belt laws this support often follows long public information campaigns and endorsements of belt use and belt laws by motoring and health organizations. Dee (1998), in the study mentioned above, found that immediately prior to the introduction of the laws there is a strong contemporaneous increase in belt use, and consequently effects that are attributed to the law itself are usually inflated. However, it is also likely that in the absence of the law, these "contemporaneous" changes in seat belt use would not have occurred to the same extent.

When belt laws contain exceptions that waive the requirement to use belts for certain sub-populations or situations, as might be expected, use rate and overall impact on fatalities diminish. For example, the state of Indiana has a primary seat belt law that exempts drivers and occupants of pickup trucks. Consequently, according to an analysis conducted by Besel *et al.* (2001) in these vehicles both the belt use rate is lower (by 50 percent!) and the number of fatalities is higher than would be expected relative to states who do not have this exemption.

Enforcement

Enforcement of primary belt laws, coupled with extensive media coverage, appears to be the most effective way of rapidly increasing seat belt use. This is clearly illustrated in the Finnish experience (WHO, 2004). Laws requiring the installation of belts in 1971 had minimal effect on use rates, but successive laws coupled with enforcement of belt use requirements, fines, and on-the-spot fines and accompanying media all had marked immediate effects, raising seat belt use in non-urban areas to over 90 percent. Dinh-Zarr *et al.* (2001) reviewed 15 studies that evaluated the effects of enhanced enforcement targeted at seat belt use, and found that the median increase in belt use as a result of the enforcement was 16 percent. However, their data also illustrate the limits of enforcement: beyond a certain level of use, it is very difficult to achieve additional gains through enforcement. Typically, once use rates reach levels of 80-90 percent, the remaining hardcore non-users (who already violate many other traffic laws) do not seem to be intimidated by tough laws and tough enforcement.

Two key variables determine enforcement's effectiveness: the perceived risk of being arrested and the magnitude of the penalty associated with the arrest. Their importance has been discussed in some detail in the context of speed enforcement (Chapter 8), and their relevance is the same with respect to belts. Chaudhary *et al.* (2004) found that the percent of drivers who reported that they "always" used seat belts increased linearly with the subjective level of perceived risk of being arrested for not wearing belts. Although this relationship was confounded with age and with the number of kilometers people drove – older drivers and drivers who drove few kilometers used their belts more often – even within each age group and driving exposure group there was a positive relationship between the perceived risk and the reported likelihood of wearing belts. When media and enforcement campaigns were introduced, the perceived risk increased slightly from 3.5 to 3.6 (on a five-point scale) and the reported use rate increased from 72 percent to 76 percent.

The role of enforcement as it specifically relates to seat belt use can be gleamed from the differences in seat belt use during the day and at night. Obviously, enforcing seat belt laws is much more difficult at night, and indeed, belt use rates are typically lower at night than during the day. To see the potential impact of nighttime enforcement, the police in Reading, PA advertised that they will begin to enforce seat belt laws at night with the use of nighttime vision equipment. The effectiveness of this threat was evaluated by measuring actual seat belt use before and after the enforcement campaign in the city of Reading, PA, as well as in another city, Bethlehem, that had similar demographics but was outside the range of the Reading media (Chaudhary *et al.*, 2005). As expected, belt use rates were generally lower at night than at daylight hours (but not on the more major roads), and the effect of the media + nighttime enforcement was followed by an increase in belt use in the test city of Reading but not in the comparison city of Bethlehem. However, the changes were relatively small: from an average of 50 percent use to 56 percent use. One explanation for the rather small effect is related to the low belt use in general. Pennsylvania only had a secondary belt law which meant that an officer could not arrest a driver for not wearing belt, but only for another offense. Thus the change in enforcement was probably not perceived as very threatening. When a similar evaluation was conducted on belt use across the whole state of Connecticut – a primary seat belt law state – the results were much more pronounced. The effect of the media campaign and the nighttime enforcement campaign was to increase seat belt use from 79 to 81 percent during the day and from 67 percent to 74 percent at night (Chaudhary *et al.*, 2006).

The combined effects of changing from secondary law to primary law, and massive enforcement of the law were examined as a case study in the state of Kentucky. Costich and Slavova (2015) examined the trends in both seat belt use rates and crashes relative to the change in the law in 2007. During the decade of 2003-2012, the number of citations more than doubled, the number of convictions nearly tripled, and the number of crash fatalities dropped by 24 percent. But these changes were not gradual; it was mostly between 2006 (before the law and the increased enforcement) and 2007 (when the law was passed and enacted). In that 1 year the number of citations nearly tripled and the number of convictions more than tripled, and these changes were sustained over time. Furthermore, over the 10-year period, there was a strong positive linear association between the safety belt nonuse conviction rate and the observed safety belt use, and a strong negative association between the safety belt nonuse conviction rate and the number of unbelted motor vehicle crash fatalities.

Incentive programs
One would assume that the greatest incentive to use belts is the nearly 50 percent reduction in the risk of being killed in a crash. Obviously, this is not an effective incentive for many drivers (see Figure 3-11). Given that, it is not surprising that various incentive programs have been unsuccessful (Bergoffen *et al.*, 2005). However, incentives tailored to specific sub-populations of non-users may be the best means of increasing belt use beyond the 80-90 percent levels. To be effective, these incentives should focus on relevant reference groups that non-users may want to imitate, and focus on mild negative impacts of non-use (getting a ticket) rather than extreme ones (death at the wheel), and on positive effects (such as pleasing a spouse or children, relieve worry of being stopped, exercising control) (Brittle and Cosgrove, 2005). To evaluate the effectiveness of an incentive program requires precise identification of the target groups, means of reaching them, and incentives to which they may be responsive. Once this is accomplished it is necessary to ensure that an appropriate experimental design is planned to test the effectiveness of this approach. All of these requirements still remain to be accomplished.

A quite successful incentive program that combines intensive high-visibility enforcement and public information campaigns, conducted annually in the U.S. around Memorial Day (end of May) since 2003 is the "Click-it or Ticket" campaign. The two components of the campaign are increased enforcement of safety belt use and massive advertisement of the campaign in all media venues (including digital) essentially letting the motoring public know that if they don't "click-it" (i.e., the seat belt buckle) they will be ticketed. The role of the media in this campaign is to enhance the high-visibility increased enforcement. Surveys that compare public awareness of the need to buckle up and the seat belt increased enforcement all show an immediate rise in awareness in the wake of the campaign (Hinch, Solomon, and Tison, 2014), and in actual belt use, though not as consistently in all years in all states (Morgan, 2015).

In-vehicle seat belt reminders
Most cars have subtle icons and tones – that appear when the car is started – to remind the driver to fasten the seat belts. However, as stated, these reminders are subtle. They typically consist of an initial auditory signal and a seat belt icon that flashes periodically for the first few minutes of the drive (or until the driver buckles the seat belt). Thus, they are probably effective for those who "forget" but not necessarily for those who consciously refuse to fasten their belts. This segment of the driving public may be quite big. In a national survey of U.S. drivers conducted by Eby *et al.* (2004) nearly 25 percent of the drivers who do not use belts consistently reported that it is because they forget and it is not their habit. If these answers are valid, then a reminder should be very effective for this group of drivers. Williams *et al.* (2002) observed drivers who drove into Ford service centers in 1998-2002 model cars that either had or did not have belt reminders, and found that 76 percent of the drivers of cars with the reminders had their belts on, compared to 71 percent of the drivers of cars that did not have the reminders. This effect, though small, was statistically significant. However, it was partially confounded by the model year, because all of the 1998 and 1999 models had no reminders and all of the 2002 models had reminders and, as noted above, people who drive newer cars are more likely to use belts (Colgran *et al.*, 2004). As use rate increased significantly over the past

decade, and because the rate is still low in the rear seats, the push now is to have seat belt reminders for all seating positions in the car (ETSC, 2013; SWOV, 2014), and indeed many cars already do. An incentive for the auto industry to have seat belt reminders in all car seating positions is that they are now part of the EuroNCAP (see below), vehicle safety criteria and its inclusion helps automakers achieve the highly desirable five-star safety rating (SWOV, 2014).

The reminder approach is analogous to the proverb that "you can bring a horse to the water, but you can't make him drink." One possible reason for the low level of effectiveness is that the reminder, which is typically a low-volume chime, is not very conspicuous. In Eby *et al.*'s (2004) study, the respondents who cited forgetfulness or lack of habit as reason for not wearing a seat belt regularly estimated that for them the most effective reminder would be a voice message, followed by a buzzer, followed by a seat vibrator (!), followed by a flashing light, and – at the very bottom of the list – a chime. Thus, it seems that in order to not irritate the driver, the auto industry (purposefully?) chose the least alerting and potentially the least effective reminder they could get away with, without annoying their customers.

Reminders can be much more effective when they become annoying to the point of actually interfering with the driving. Early belt reminder systems were also linked to the ignition so that the driver could not start the car unless the belt was buckled. While this interlock was quite effective in inducing the use of belts (Robertson, 1975), a public outcry led to its repeal. Current safety regulations in most countries require an auditory prompt that is activated with the vehicle startup functions if the driver has not buckled up before starting the car (e.g., in the U.S. FMVSS 208). A shortcoming of this rule is that it is oblivious to drivers' belt use habits.

A good reminder system should be one that is compatible with drivers' habits; that is, one that would conform to good human factors/ergonomics principles. An effective alarm should therefore appear only when it is truly relevant. Thus, reminders in new cars are "smart" in the sense that they do not engage before the car achieves a certain speed and travel distance threshold (SWOV, 2014), and thus, for example, do not engage while negotiating in parking lots. To maximize their use and acceptance the European Commission recommends that they should (1) target part-time users, that is, people who understand the value of a seat belt but sometimes do not use it; (2) not affect the drivability of the vehicle; (3) consist of a combination of visual and sound signals; (4) operate in a progressive manner; and (4) be expanded to the rear seats (EC, 2015).

One very systematic research effort to develop a system that would be both effective and sensitive to the drivers' needs and habits was made by Van Houten, Malenfant, and their associates in a series of four studies that focused on drivers' pattern of seat belt use, and their response to different alerting and interlocking systems. In their first study (Van Houten *et al.*, 2005) they conducted a behavioral analysis of drivers' seat belt use relative to the initial driving actions: ignition and shifting into gear. Based on their observations and driver interviews they concluded that drivers who do not buckle up would tend to do so if fastening the seat belt would decrease the startup operations rather than slow them down. They therefore suggested interlock system that is linked to the gearbox, so that unless the driver buckles up, the car cannot be shifted into the drive gear for a few seconds. In this study on five drivers a 5-20 second delay was very effective in inducing all drivers to regularly use their belts. However once the interlock system was removed the belt use frequency dropped to the pre-system levels. In a follow-up study Van Houten and Malenfant (2006) evaluated the system on 101 U.S. and Canadian commercial drivers, and the gearshift release delay was set at a fixed 8 seconds. The results were quite impressive. For the U.S. drivers, seat belt use increased from 47 to 68 percent and for the Canadian drivers it increased from 54 to 75 percent. These are very significant changes, and they seem to be effective on the very group that has been resistant to belt laws and to the intensive media and enforcement campaigns. However, again, once the interlock was removed, the use rate dropped significantly, though – at least for the brief duration of the post-treatment phase – it remained above the pre-treatment baseline condition. Thus alerting and annoying systems may be effective but they need to operate for a long time before they change drivers' habits.

In their third study on 800 U.S. and 800 Canadian drivers, Malenfant and Van Houten (2008) observed belt use as drivers left work, service stations, and parking lots. They found that more than 50 percent of the drivers fastened the belt only prior to shifting the car into gear. They therefore concluded that to be more effective the belt alarm should be sounded after some delay. On the basis of the ignition-seatbelt latencies that they observed, they recommended a delay of 30 seconds after the gear engagement. If applied in this manner, they argued, the reminder would be more effective as it would be much less frequent (and therefore not annoying to drivers who buckle up) and more salient (appearing alone and only to those not belted), applicable to only 1 percent who buckle after 30 seconds and those who don't buckle up at all. In their fourth study on 101 commercial U.S. and Canadian drivers, Van Houten *et al.* (2010) tested the impact of belt interlocking systems with various post ignition delays. They found that an 8-second delay in the ability to shift into gear (or 16 seconds for the more resistant drivers) resulted in a 40 percent belt use increase for the U.S. drivers and a 37 percent increased use for the Canadian drivers. Furthermore, once the seatbelt was fastened the drivers tended to leave it that way for the remainder of the trip. In their fifth study Van Houten, Reagan, and Hilton (2014) evaluated the effectiveness and drivers' acceptance of two engineering interventions to promote seat belt use. The first system was the previously described belt-gear interlock that prevented moving for 8s or until the belt was fastened, and the second system applied a counterforce that pushed against the accelerator pedal of unbelted drivers as soon as their vehicle speed exceeded 20 mile per hour. Unbelted drivers could still continue to drive and exceed 20mph by pressing harder than the counterforce but doing so required focused attention and physical effort. The first system was evaluated on 131 commercial fleet vehicles in Michigan (with an unknown exact number of drivers), and the second one was evaluated on 20 university students. They found that both systems increased seat belt use (to from 81 percent to 96 percent and from 56 percent to 99.7 percent, respectively). Furthermore, the second system, the more effective one, also received higher acceptance ratings. Thus, while both systems seem to have significant merit, because they were conducted on very different populations, for different experimental durations, and in different environments, the actual potential benefit on a nationwide basis remains to be studied. In summary, Van Houten and Malenfant's studies offer ergonomically designed, technically and socially feasible solutions to making belt use a standard habit-based practice, either through elimination of annoyance from unwanted and irrelevant alarms or through engineering interlocks that would make it impossible to drive "normally" without being belted. And though the engineering solution may be more effective, its implementation involves industry and user acceptance – a concept that is becoming more and more relevant as new technologies keep emerging (Regan, Horberry, and Stevens, 2014, see Chapter 19)

Seat belt use in the rear seats: Frequencies and implications

Because of the difficulty of observation, data on adult seat belt use in the rear seats is much more limited. In general, seat belt use is slightly lower for front-seat passengers than for drivers (Glassbrenner and Ye, 2006; NRSA, 2015; Pickrell and Choi, 2015), and significantly lower for rear seat passengers than for front-seat passengers (Boyle and Vanderwolf, 2004; Colgan *et al.*, 2004; Jost *et al.*, 2014; NRSA, 2015; OECD, 2014). For example, Olukoga and Noah (2005) note that in South Africa in 2002 seat belt use averaged 81 percent for drivers, 50 percent for front-seat passengers, and less than eight percent for rear seat passengers. In Japan the rear seat belt use at the turn of this century was estimated at 20-30 percent (Shimamura *et al.*, 2005) In Israel, where seat belt use is among the highest in the world, in 2013 it was 97 percent for drivers, 95 percent for front-seat passengers, and 72 percent for rear seat passengers (NRSA, 2015). In the EU in 26 countries that measured the use rate according to the strict criteria developed by the EU, in 2012 the front-seat use rate was 88 percent and the rear seat use rate was 74 percent (Jost *et al.*, 2014). While these rates may seem low, the good news is that use rates have been steadily increasing in all countries.

The importance of using seat belts in the rear is not only for the safety of the rear seat passengers themselves, but also because their non-use compromises the safety of the driver and the front-seat passengers. This is because in frontal collisions, when not belted, the rear passengers are propelled forward and can injure the front-seat passengers (collision number 4, above). In an analysis of Japanese front and rear crashes, Shimamura *et al.* (2005) estimated that – as for front-seat passengers – belted rear seat occupants reduce their risk of being killed or fatally injured by 45 percent. In addition, if all unbelted rear seat passengers were to be belted, the number of killed or seriously injured drivers would be reduced by 25 percent, and the number of seriously injured or killed front-seat passengers would be reduced by 28 percent. Cummings and Rivara (2004) evaluated the effects of unrestrained occupants on restrained occupants in various seating locations, using the U.S. Fatality Analysis Reporting System and obtained very similar effects: an average increase of 15-22 percent in the risk of fatality, depending on the seating locations of the restrained and unrestrained occupants. The effects are even greater when all injuries – not just fatalities or seriously injuries – are considered. MacLennan *et al.* (2004) used the U.S. National Automotive Sampling System data base and concluded that exposure to unbelted occupants increased the overall risk of injury by 40 percent. In short, buckling up in the rear seats is effective in injury reduction for all car occupants. Therefore, it is in the driver's best personal interest to have others buckle up.

Child protection and restraints

Most vehicle interiors are designed for adult occupants. So seat belts anchors are placed where they optimize adult passenger protection. The same is true of leg room and headrests. But children are also frequent passengers. According to one estimate, in the U.S. 0- to 10-year-old children constitute approximately 30 percent of rear seat occupants (Ebel and Grossman, 2003). Although they may sit in the front seat too, in general, even when not restrained, children are much more protected from injury sitting in the rear seats than sitting in the front where – in the event of a collision – their likelihood of being ejected or hitting a hard surface is much greater (Berg *et al.*, 2000; Durbin *et al.*, 2005; Starnes, 2005; Williams and Zador, 1977). Fortunately, both observational studies and crash analysis indicate that young children are more likely to sit in the rear seat than in the front seat. Ferguson, Wells, and Williams (2000) systematically observed children's sitting positions in three American cities and found that 24 percent of the children in cars with air bags were sitting in the front seat, compared to 38 percent in vehicles without air bags. Interestingly, a similar percentage for sitting in the front seat in urban areas was recorded in a small study conducted in North Dakota 10 years later (Huseth-Zosel, 2012). Fatal crash data analysis is consistent with the observational data showing that young children are essentially 2-4 times as likely to sit in the rear seat as in the front seat (Corneli, Cook, and Dean, 2000; Durbin *et al.*, 2005). But being restrained helps decrease death and injuries significantly more (Berg *et al.*, 2000; Corneli *et al.*, 2000; Durbin *et al.*, 2005; Tyroch *et al.*, 2000), especially in the front seat where the risk of fatality without a restraint may be nearly 10 times as high as the risk with restraints (Halman, Chipman, Parkin, and Wright, 2002). In high-income countries such as countries in North America, Europe, and Australasia, parents are highly sensitive to the benefits of child safety seats, and child restraint use is typically over 85 percent. In contrast, in low-income countries, the use of child restraints is "rare" (WHO, 2004). In fact, in high-income countries, at least based on seat belt use, people seem to be more concerned about the safety of their children than about their own. In general, though, children are much more likely to be restrained when they ride with drivers who are belted than when they ride with unbelted drivers (Ebel *et al.*, 2003; Halman *et al.*, 2002; Pickrell *et al.*, 2016). The few parents that do not restrain their infants and toddlers in safety seats are typically of lower socio-economic strata, and the non-use is probably because of their lifestyle (they do not use seat belts) and cost of the safety seat (Agran, Anderson, and Winn, 2004).

In most countries – and all U.S. states – young children are required by law to be restrained in child safety seats. But children grow, and optimal design of their restraints changes with the child's size, especially his or her height. To accommodate these changes various restraint systems have been designed, and they are typically grouped into four categories as described in Table 10-2 and illustrated in Figure 10-6. Both the U.S. and the Europe Union have recommended child seat standards (NHTSA, 2005 and ISOFIX for the EU; UNECE, 2013).

Table 10-2. Safety seats for children of different age groups (based on NHTSA, 2002, recommendations).

Type	**Child size**	**Characteristics**	**Warnings**
Infant	For children weighing up to 9-10 kg and up to 66-74 cm tall.	Infants outgrow this seat when they exceed the weight maximum or when their heads are <2.5 cm below the top. Faces rearward only. Comes with or without base; portable, inexpensive, and can be used as baby carrier.	Never use a rear-facing seat in a front seat where there is an airbag. Harness straps should be flat and snug on the child. Seat needs to be secured tightly with the safety belt or LATCH restraint system.
Convertible	For infants and toddlers weighing 9-18 kg and up to 102 cm tall (some are designed for bigger children).	Faces rearward for infants and forward for toddlers. Accommodates a larger age range. Child needs to be removed from the seat to exit the automobile.	For infants <1 year old but > than 9 kg. Select a seat with high enough rear-facing weight limit. Never use a rear-facing seat in a front seat with an airbag. Harness straps should be flat and snug on the child. Seat needs to be tightly secured with the safety belt or LATCH restraint system.
Forward facing/ combination	For children weighing 14-18 kg; height limits vary from 127 to 145 cm.	Forward-facing seats can only face forward. Combination seats have a removable harness system to allow later use as a booster seat.	Harness straps should be flat and snug on the child; harness system should not be used past the seat's weight limit; convertible seat needs to be secured tightly to the automobile with the safety belt or LATCH restraint system.
Booster seat	When child no longer fits in child safety seat but is not big enough for safety belt.	Used with an adult lap and shoulder belt. Seat is not attached to the automobile.	Should only be used in a seating position where there is a shoulder and lap belt. High-back seats and backless seats are good in most situations. If the back of the automobile seat or headrest is below the ears of the child, use a high-back booster.

LATCH = Lower Anchors and Tethers for Children.

Figure 10-6. Child restraints for different ages. (a) Infant rear-facing only (for children under 9 kilograms), (b) Convertible for infants and toddlers (for children under 18 kilograms), (c) Forward only (for children 9-18 kilograms), (d) Booster seat (for bigger children less than 145 centimeters tall) (from NHTSA, 2002).

Use and misuse of child safety seats

The use of child safety seats is much more common where infants and toddlers are concerned than where older children are concerned. Colgan and her colleagues (2004) observed the restraint use of rear seat passengers and estimated their approximate age (based on appearance). Their observations of over 1,000 passengers in six different locations in the U.K. revealed that while 95 percent of the babies were restrained only 76 percent of the older children less than 14 years old were belted (but still in greater numbers than the adults, of whom only 61 percent were belted). Eby *et al.* (2005) observed 1,764 4- to 8-year-old children in passenger cars in Michigan and noted that only 13 percent were in a safety seat or booster seat, an additional 43 percent used the car's seat belts, and the remaining 44 percent were not restrained at all. Decina and Lococo (2004) observed 5,527 children riding cars in six U.S. states and found that although virtually all infants and 90 percent of children aged 1-3 were restrained in child safety seats, only 37 percent of children aged 4-8 were in child safety seats or booster seats. The remainder used either the vehicle seat belt alone or no restraint at all. In a carefully controlled observational study Ebel and her colleagues (2003) observed 2,880 children in the states of Washington and Oregon as they were picked up by the parents from kindergarten and elementary schools. They briefly interviewed the parents and measured their children's height and weight. Relative to these dimensions they then determined whether or not the children were properly restrained. As in the other studies they found that proper restraint use was very high for small children but very low for older children. At one extreme, 80 percent of those needing a child seat were properly restrained and at the other extreme only 55 percent of those who could use the vehicle seat belts were properly restrained. Also, only 17 percent of those who needed a booster seat used one. A closer examination revealed that the percent of properly restrained children decreased systematically from the age of 1 to 6 and then started to increase as more and more children reached the seat belt-recommended minimum height.

The increase in the appropriate use of booster seats has been frustratingly slow. The U.S. National Highway Traffic Administration has been conducting an annual probability-based national survey of the use of booster seats since 2006. An analysis of the 2011 survey by Greenwell (2015) revealed a basic difference in the actualized benefits of the child safety seats and boosters. Whereas the use rate of child safety seats was very high, the percent of misuse of the seats was equally high at 59 percent. In contrast, booster seat use rates were much lower, but the percent of misuse was correspondingly lower at 20 percent. But use rates have been increasing. In the 2013 and 2015 surveys among the 4- to 7-year-old children the use rate of booster seats peaked at 46 percent of all children (compared to 41 percent in 2006) in 2013 and then dropped slightly to 44.5 percent in 2015 (Li, Pickrell, and Shova, 2016). However, in and of itself this is not an indication about the safety of the remaining 54 percent. In addition to those using booster seats, another 20 percent were using child car seats, and 24 percent were restrained by the vehicle's safety belt only. Thus (allowing for rounding errors) only nine percent were not restrained at all (Pickrell and Choi, 2014).

Crash data also reflect the low use rates of booster seats. Durbin *et al.* (2005), analyzed restraint use by children in over 11,000 crashes in 15 U.S. states. They found that while over 80 percent of the 9- to 15-year-old children used lap and shoulder belts, and 90 percent of the children under 4 years old were restrained in child safety seats, only 24 percent of the 4- to 8-year-old children were using booster seats.

Unlike belts, where proper adjustment is typically minimal to none, safety seats are much more complicated. To maximize their potential they have to be properly secured to the vehicle seat, and the children have to be properly secured in them. Although various safety organizations and popular health journals publish reliable information on the effectiveness and proper use of child restraints (e.g., Biagioli, 2005; IIHS, 2014; NHTSA, 2002), parents often misperceive the task of fitting child restraints as an easy one, and perhaps as a result, only a small percentage of parents actually refer to professionals or professional literature in the area (Lennon, 2006). To make things worse, the information that is most accessible to the consumers is often flawed. Ross and her colleagues (2002) contacted 158 manufacturers and 101 organizations involved in child safety seats in the U.S. and reviewed 401 instructional and educational items. They concluded that "many of the evaluated items do not contain all the basic information required from a resource on child passenger safety; the information most often missing was the importance of rear seating for children 12 and under. Some of the evaluated materials were factually inaccurate, providing incorrect guidelines for rear-facing infants." (p. 8). In Japan Nakahara, Ichikawa, and Wakai (2007) reviewed issues of "the three top-selling monthly baby and maternity magazines" published over a course of 1 year (2003) and noted that less than two percent of the pages addressed infant protection, and more than two-thirds of these were advertisements. Worse still, "some information was misleading and even incorrect: specifically related to when to start using a forward-facing seat, what products are attachable to the child safety seat, and the reuse of a child safety seat."

Insufficient information and inaccurate information cannot but lead to poor knowledge on why, when, and how to use child safety seats (Winston and Erkoboni, 2006).

Decina, Lococo, and Doyle (2006) observed drivers transporting 1,351 0- to 5-year-old children in seven U.S. states and found that many parents were unaware of the existence and importance of the tethers when securing the seat to the vehicle. Only 55 percent of parents used the top tether of the LATCH system. The two most common reasons given for not using the upper tether were "I didn't know how to use it," and "I didn't think it was important to use." Thus, there appears to be a communication failure between the manufacturers that abide by the regulatory requirements and the parents that are willing to invest as much as needed in their children's safety. The situation is even worse with respect to booster seats. Morris *et al.* (2000) examined the positioning of 164 belts of booster seats conducted in "child safety seat clinics" by safety professionals. They observed that 20 percent of the commonly used seats were misused (compared to 68 percent of the seats belonging to a less common type of booster seat – a "shield" booster seat designed to use with lap belts only). Together these findings show that the most significant problem in the use of safety seats is not lack of motivation on the part of the parents, but lack of information, education, and training for parents who actually desire it. Significant progress in this area has been made by the Insurance Institute for Highway Safety (IIHS, 2014). Realizing the problems of fitting the seat in the car and the child in the seat, the Insurance Institute created a rating system on which they rate the adequacy of different booster seats. Their system is not based on crash testing but on how well three-point lap and shoulder belts fit a child-size test dummy seated in the booster. The evaluation is done under four conditions spanning the range of safety belt configurations in passenger vehicles. Thus, according to their 2014 evaluations of 41 models, 27 were rated as "best bet" meaning that the belts are well positioned in all types of vehicles. Things got even better in 2015, when 20 out of 23 models evaluated were rated as "best bet" and the additional three were still considered "good bets" (IIHS, 2015b). Interestingly, in both evaluations there was no relation between price and safety, and seats with backs were not necessarily better than those without backs. So in this case cheaper can be better or at least as safe or safer.

Effectiveness of child restraints

Though being restrained with standard belts is better than not being restrained at all, child restraints that are specifically designed for the dimensions of children are much more effective in injury reduction.

Effectiveness of infant and child seats

According to the U.S. National Highway Traffic Safety Administration, based on the national Fatal Analysis Reporting System (FARS), child restraints are 71 percent effective in reducing fatalities of infants (under 1 year old), and 54 percent effective in reducing fatalities in children 1-4 years old (NHTSA, 1996). Analyses conducted by Starnes (2005) and by Elliott *et al.* (2006) also show similar reductions. Canadian data, cited by the World Health Organization (WHO, 2004) indicate that forward-facing child safety seats reduce serious injuries by 60 percent and rearward facing child safety seats reduce serious injuries by a remarkable 92 percent.

Effectiveness of booster seats

Unlike infant, convertible, and combination seats for younger children, the effectiveness of booster seats for older children is somewhat variable. Their benefits relative to the absence of restraints is not in question, but their benefits relative to the standard seat belts vary as a function of their fit and proper use. The problem seems to be centered on the *proper* use of the booster seats. Improper use is either premature "graduation" to booster seats, immature graduation out of the booster seat, or failure to use the belt (Sivinski, 2010). For maximum effectiveness, the factory installed lap belt has to be low across the abdomen or above the thigh, and the shoulder belt has to cross the chest and rest on the collar bone (and not on the neck). Obviously, the smaller (and younger) they are, the less compatible the adult restraint systems are for children, and the greater the benefits of specially designed restraints. Booster seats raise the child's sitting height and are designed for children until they reach a height of 145 centimeters or – better still – a sitting height of 74 centimeters (Ehiri *et al.*, 2006). At this height, which children typically reach when they are 10-11 years old, they outgrow the child safety seats (Biagioli, 2005; NHTSA, 2002).

Even when not used in an optimal fashion, crash analyses typically show that children in booster seats have lower injury risks than children in seat belts. Using parental reports on clinically significant injuries to their children in insurance claims, Durbin, Elliott, and Winston (2003) found that using belt-positioning booster seats reduced the odds of injury of 4- to 7-year-old children by 59 percent compared to seat belts alone. Winston *et al.* (2000) analyzed crash data from 13,853 insurance claims of crashes involving children. Although 98 percent of the 2-5 years old children were restrained, 40 percent of them were restrained in seat belts instead of booster seats, with increasing frequency as a function of age, so that over 80 percent of the 5 years old were restrained by seat belts. Based on their very large sample, they estimated the relative risk of "serious injury" from seat belts relative to child safety seats and booster seats at 4.0 for children 2-3 years old and 2.4 for children 4-5 years old. Their definition of serious injury was based on the Abbreviated Injury Scale (AIS) score of AIS > 2, an injury that may require major hospitalization and long-term disability. In other words, the use of belts without a booster seat can more than double the risk of serious injury to young children. In a later recent study, the same team (Durbin *et al.*, 2005) analyzed a probability sample of 11,506 insurance-reported crashes involving 17,980 children under 16 years old, and found that the probability of injury was greatly reduced with restraints. The difference between proper restraints and improper restraints was statistically significant, but quite small as can be seen from Figure 10-7. Although the risk is presented in absolute terms rather than relative terms, the reductions in relative risk are similar to the ones in their previous study. In addition, as the figure shows, the use of restraints – even when not appropriate – can reduce injuries to near zero levels. Focusing only on 4- to 8-year-old children, Sivinski (2010), analyzed documented child injuries in the U.S. Crashworthiness Data System (CDS) for the 10 years period 1998-2008 and found that booster seats reduced injuries by an average of 14 percent (relative to belts only), mostly due to an 11 percent reduction in fatalities and severe disabling injuries.

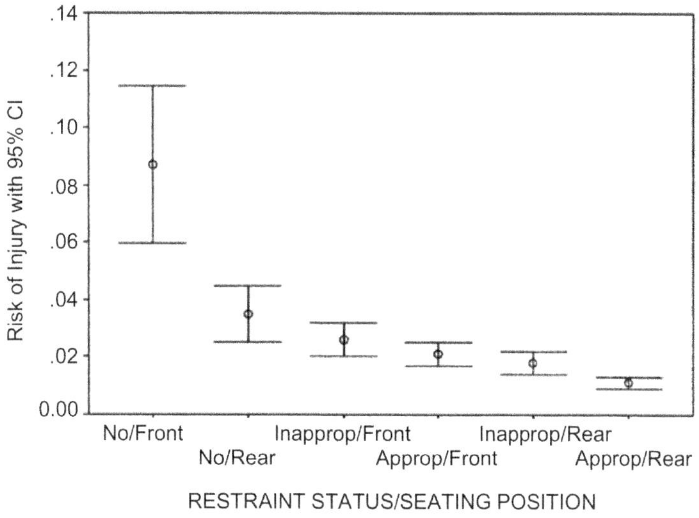

Figure 10-7. The risk of injury without restraints, with inappropriate restraints, and with appropriate restraints. Inappropriate restraints were belts for 4- to 8-year-old children and lap belt only or shoulder belt only for 9- to 15-year-old children (from Durbin *et al.*, 2005, with permission of the American Academy of Pediatrics).

Given the relatively small added absolute benefit of booster seats over seat belts, it is not surprising that at least one study failed to show that they have added benefits at all. Levitt (2005) analyzed all fatal crashes involving children in the U.S. in 1975-2003 and concluded that "child safety seats, in actual practice, are no better than seat belts at reducing fatalities among children aged 2-6." However, as Levitt himself noted, actual practice of use of safety (mostly booster) seats is not necessarily "proper use" of the seats, and benefits of booster seats that may not be evident in fatality data may show up in injury data, as demonstrated by the studies of Durbin and Winston.

How to increase use of child restraints

Booster seat use can be increased if we could better understand who are the non-users, why they do not use them, and how to counter their reasons. The research reviewed above indicates that legislation requiring the use of seat belts and infant seats has been extremely effective in increasing their use rate. So one key ingredient in the process of increasing booster seat use is legislation: specific legislation that would require children under 145 centimeters to be restrained in a booster seat. In the U.S. all 50 states require that children up till the age of four be in a child seat. But very few states (and not many countries) have specific child restraint requirements beyond that age; including states with primary belt laws. In a survey of parents in Michigan, where a primary belt law did not exist at the time, 60 percent of the parents who either do not use booster seats or use them only occasionally said they would be more likely to use them regularly if the law required it, and nearly 70 percent of those using them occasionally said they did so because the law required it (Bingham *et al.*, 2006). However, the law alone is not a sufficient requirement. Ebel and her colleagues (2003) asked parents who were observed harnessing their children in booster seats why they did so. Not surprisingly the most common answer was "safety" (61 percent). However, 12 percent of the parents cited "child comfort and visibility." Given children's restlessness and constant need for stimulation this may serve as a good incentive to promote booster seats. The primary reason given for not using a booster seat when one was called for was that the child "was too big for a car seat" (56 percent). Only a small percent of the respondents (8 percent) responded that they "had not heard" of booster seats. Ramsey, Simpson, and Rivara (2000), also received similar reasons for non-use of booster seats, but also noted that more than 50 percent of the parents who were observed not using it said that they did own a booster seat. Thus, an initial goal should be to increase booster seat availability and ownership to parents of children who outgrow their child safety seats.

As part of a deeper probe into the reasons parents do not use booster seats for their children, Winston and Erkoboni (2006) conducted multiple focus groups and discovered that the primary barrier to use of booster seats were lack of education and (paradoxically) fear of injury, especially among parents of lower socio-economic status. A different and very interesting inquiry into the reasons for use and non-use of booster seats was made by Bracchitta (2006), who interviewed 151 parents who had at least one 4- to 8-year-old child. Her approach to the issue was to see if the theory of planned behavior (see Chapter 3) could provide an adequate explanation of booster seat use and reveal the reasons for non-use. She questioned the parents about their frequency of use of seat belts and measured the correlation between this reported behavior and their intentions to use booster seats, their perceived sense of control over the use of booster seats, their attitudes toward booster seats, and their subjective norms on the subject. Her analyses revealed that the single best predictor of booster seat use was the parent's intention to do so ($r = 0.87$). In turn, the intention to use booster seats, correlated highly with the attitude toward these seats ($r = 0.77$). Neither behavioral control nor subjective norms had any additional effects on the intention. Thus, it appeared from the results that attempts to increase booster seat use should focus on making parents commit themselves to buying a seat and to intending to use it. This, in turn, can be accomplished by shaping their attitudes; not necessarily an easy task. It is also interesting to note that the norms of their environment were not related to the parents' use of booster seats, and as Bracchitta suggested "it seems that others' expectations (such as those of friends and family) do not necessarily influence the intention to use booster seats, nor do other parents' use of booster seats influence the intention to use the seats. Overall, the use of booster seats seems to be a highly individualized decision" (p. 282). Behavioral control did not seem to be a significant determinant of use in Bracchitta's study, though this may be an artifact of the sample in which nearly 75 percent reported an income of $75,000 or more (10 years ago!), and nearly 75 percent were college graduates.

Although explanations given by parents may not perfectly reflect the real reasons for use and non-use of booster seats, they do indicate a very large gap in parents' knowledge about child protection at the transition phase from child seats to seat belts. The little research that has been done in this area suggests that we need to address parents' attitudes and knowledge about booster seats. In terms of attitudes, it may be possible to reach the children directly and affect their attitudes by providing visually attractive booster seats and luring them with the ability to see better out of the car. We also need to better understand what information parents lack, what salient motives govern their decisions, and how to transfer that knowledge and relevant incentives to them. With respect to the attitude, Will (2005), argues that the most common reason that parents do not use child safety seats or use them incorrectly is what she labels an "immunity fallacy": a belief that the risk of traffic injury to their children is negligible. Therefore, she argues, the focus of education campaigns should not be on information about their use but on the risk involved when they are not used. Lennon (2006) conducted an extensive review of the child protection literature and concluded that "while almost all parents know when to use infant restraints and most know when to move their children into forward-facing child restraint systems, there is a gap in understanding about what the next stage should be and when it should occur." Regardless of the source of the obstacle to use, coping with that problem should not be insurmountable because the relevant age group can be easily reached through the public education system. Also if we consider Pickrell and Choi's findings (2014, 2015) we can conclude that to improve effectiveness of restraints in child safety seats requires post-purchase training or instructions, whereas to improve booster seats' effectiveness requires greater market penetration.

Passive Restraints and Protection

Passive protection devices are devices that reduce injury while the driver remains passive. It is commonly and mistakenly assumed that this also means that their safety benefits are unrelated to driver behavior. In this section, I will briefly review several passive protection systems and emphasize the driver's role in maximizing their benefits.

Seat location

Drivers do not have a choice of where to sit, but passengers do. In the case of a crash sitting in the rear seat is safer than sitting in the front seat. This is particularly true for small children in rear-facing infant seats that can be struck by an expanding airbag. Moving children, especially younger 0- to 4-year-old children, to the rear seat has been associated with dramatic reductions in child fatalities in the U.S. (Nichols, Glassbrenner, and Compton, 2005). Obviously, having parents move their very young children to the back seat – away from direct eye contact – is not an easy thing to accomplish and requires very active cooperation on their part.

Head restraints

All cars and nearly all vehicles today come with headrests that actually serve as restraints attached to the back of the seat. The most important role of the headrest is to protect the driver from whiplash; a neck injury due to forceful, rapid back-and-forth movement of the neck that occurs during a rear-end crash. But a one-size-fits-all solution for head-dress is problematic because car occupants differ in their sitting height. For example in the civilian adult U.S. population the median sitting height of men is 87 cm and the median sitting height of women is 82 centimeters. But the variations around these two medians are quite significant. The 5th to 95th percentile range for men is 80-93 centimeters, and the equivalent range for women is 75-88 centimeters (Sanders and McCormick, 1993). Thus, to accommodate 90 percent of the drivers the height of the seat and headrest must adjust to fit heights from 75 to 93 centimeters (and even more if we wish to adjust for most older drivers too). For a perfect fit the head restraint should be no less than 9 centimeters below the top of the occupant's head, and almost touching it from behind (IIHS, 1999; Winston *et al.*, 2005). Although most headrests are adjustable, drivers (let alone passengers) rarely adjust them. Winston *et al.*, measured the location of head restraints relative to 4,287 drivers' heads in Oregon, and found that only seven percent of the restraints were "optimally positioned." This was despite the fact that 75 percent of the drivers correctly identified the role of the head restraint as a safety device. Because drivers rarely adjust their adjustable head restraints, paradoxically fixed head restraints were three times as likely to be properly positioned as the adjustable ones. To counteract the drivers' lack of action in this area, new U.S. regulations that went into effect in 2010 require that head restraints be raised and closer to the back of the occupants' head. Consequently, an evaluation of head restraints by the U.S. Insurance Institute for Highway Safety (IIHS) rated 95 percent of the 2015 year models head restraints as "good," whereas in 2005 only nine percent were rated as "good." On the basis of insurance claims, the IIHS linked 11 percent reductions in injuries in rear-end crashes to the good head restraints (IIHS, 2015c). There are a few vehicles that have "intelligent" headrests that move forward in rear-end collisions (e.g., Toyota and Mercedes), making the headrest an effective active safety device rather than a passive one (Bogenrieder *et al.*, 2009). But until such technology-based solutions are implemented in all cars on the road, a simple solution to this problem is to have dealers check and adjust the headrests when people buy their cars or bring them to be serviced.

Air bags

When they were first introduced as safety devices, air bags were probably the most controversial safety feature in our cars (Farmer, 2006; Meyer, 2006). However, the public loved them and the automotive industry kept adding more and more of them into each car (with seven quickly becoming a standard in the United Kingdom and eight in some current car models), to protect drivers and passengers from both frontal and side impacts. Driver air bags were mandated by the U.S. Congress in 1984, and both driver and front passenger air bags are now installed in nearly all new cars worldwide. An air bag is deployed when the vehicle experiences a rapid deceleration that would be associated with a collision with a hard surface. Typically, the threshold for detonating (yes, that is what happens) the gas inside the bag is a delta-v of approximately 16 km/hr (Evans, 2004). The bag then inflates at such a high speed that it reaches its full size, close to the occupant's head and torso, before the occupant has had a chance to move forward significantly. In order to protect children (and other short occupants) who may be sitting much closer to the front to the car, the air bags in cars produced since 1998 are "depowered." Although originally designed to be used in lieu of belts, they are now considered supplementary to the belts (in fact the imprint on the cover of the steering wheel and the dashboard in front of the bag was originally the initials SRS – Supplementary Restraint System). Fortunately, most drivers are aware of this and in a national survey of U.S. drivers 95 percent of the respondents knew that they should still use their safety belt even though they have an air bag. The perceptions of the air bag's utility were mixed: although slightly more than half of the respondents were concerned about the safety of the air bags, over 80 percent of the respondents stated that they would like to have driver and passenger air bags in their next car (Boyle and Vanderwolf, 2005). In this context, it is interesting to speculate why many drivers are willing to spend significantly more money in order to have an air bag in their car with an added fatality reduction benefit of approximately 5-10 percent and still not wear their seat belts all the time in order to reduce their risk of being killed in a crash by approximately 45 percent. Obviously, the answer lies in the behavioral adaptations that we are or are not willing to make. This is further discussed below in the context of the "offset hypothesis."

Almost since its introduction the effectiveness of the air bag has been questioned, let alone its cost-effectiveness. Kent, Viano, and Crandall (2005) wrote an extensive review of the various evaluations that were conducted on different versions in its evolution. Early projections were that it alone (without belts) would reduce fatalities in frontal impacts by as much as 57 percent, but as data accumulated the estimates were revised downward to 22-29 percent for frontal collisions and 12-14 percent in all crashes (Kent *et al.*, 2005). The NHTSA currently estimates that when combined with seat belts frontal air bags reduce the likelihood of fatality by 11 percent, and without seat belts they reduce it by 14 percent (NHTSA, 2015b). With respect to injury reduction, the benefits are less clear-cut and some, on the basis of analyses of early U.S. crash data (Evans, 2004; McGwin *et al.*, 2003) questioned their effectiveness at all. By now, both their effectiveness and cost-effectiveness are an accepted fact. In the U.S. alone, since their introduction in 1987 and until 2012 (inclusive) frontal air bags saved nearly 40,000 lives (NHTSA, 2014b). A remarkable benefit from a bag of hot air.

The eagerness of the motoring public to have air bag equipped cars has also stimulated the addition of side air bags. Most cars marketed in the Western world now have side torso and side head air bags that are intended to protect drivers and passengers from side impact: where the distance between the occupant and the vehicle body is minimal and where there is only the vehicle frame to absorb some of the impact. The bags are therefore designed to attenuate and distribute the forces from the intruding side of the vehicle. Braver and Kyrychenko (2004) analyzed their effectiveness in reducing driver fatalities in crashes where the vehicle is struck on the driver's side using the U.S. Fatal Analysis Reporting System data and found (after adjustment for various confounding variables) that the risk of fatality was nearly halved (risk ratio = 0.55) when the driver was protected by head and torso air bags, and reduced by approximately 10 percent (risk ratio = 0.89) when the vehicle was equipped with torso-only air bags. In a more recent analysis, the U.S. National Highway Traffic

Safety Administration estimated the joint effect of head and torso air bags at 31 percent fatality reduction (Kahane, 2014).

Even when they do reduce injury levels, air bags can also cause injuries that would not have happened otherwise (Jernigan, Rath, and Duma, 2005; see also preface to this chapter). As crash data accumulated it turned out that air bags actually increased the risk to children and older people who were struck by it as it inflated. Consequently, a second generation of air bags was designed to inflate to lower pressure levels. This issue was addressed at both the engineering and behavioral levels. In terms of engineering, cars manufactured after 1997 have "depowered" air bags, and analyses of crash fatalities in the U.S. indicate that the remedy has been effective. On the basis of data from the U.S. Fatal Analysis Reporting System of all 1990-2002 fatal crashes, Olson, Cummings, and Rivara (2006) concluded that – after adjusting for seat position, restraint use, age, sex, and vehicle and crash characteristics – the relative risk of fatality for children under 6 years old dropped from a high of RR = 1.66 to RR = 1.10. This means that at the new level (that was not statistically significantly different from 1.0) there is essentially no increase in fatality risk associated with the air bag. This was achieved while the fatality risk to all occupants from second generation (depowered) air bags remained essentially the same (from RR = 0.90 for first generation to RR = 0.89 for second generation), and essentially the same for 13- to 49-year-old adults (with a change in relative risk from 0.92 to 0.93). On the basis of its own analysis of the U.S. fatality data, the U.S. National Highway Traffic Safety Administration concluded that the depowered air bags "undid the harm wrought by the first generation of air bags for child passengers up to age 10, while preserving the life-saving benefits of those air bags for pre-teens age 11-12 years." For the 0-12 years old children fatalities with the depowered air bags were 45 percent lower than with the original air bags and fatalities caused by air bags decreased by 83 percent. The fatality risk of drivers and right-front passengers (13+ years old) in frontal crashes remained unchanged (Kahane, 2006). The depowered air bags also reduce specific injuries such as eye injuries (Duma *et al.*, 2005), though surprisingly they do not seem to reduce skin injuries (Rath *et al.*, 2005). Another issue worth addressing in future air bag design is that of multiple impacts. Approximately 30 percent of all crashes involve multiple impacts, but the air bag is effective in mitigating the forces of the one – usually the first – impact only (Fay, Sferco, and Frampton, 2001). To their credit, automobile manufacturers have kept on improving the air bags. Newer air bags (called "advanced," "smart," or "multi-stage") now sense the weight of the occupant in the passenger seat and his/her seating position to adjust the deployment power.

However, the impact of engineering changes in new cars is relatively slow at the societal level (depending on the average age of the vehicles in the country), and an alternative or supplementary approach is needed to provide a short-term remedy. This can be accomplished by a rapid behavioral change. This was done in the U.S. in the beginning of 1996, when the National Highway Traffic Safety Administration and other organizations initiated massive media and education campaigns to move children to the rear seat. The campaign was quite effective, yielding a 16 percent reduction in the deaths of young children in the first year (Nichols *et al.*, 2005). The change in frequency of children deaths in the front seat relative to the pre-campaign level of 1992 is shown in Figure 10-8. It is

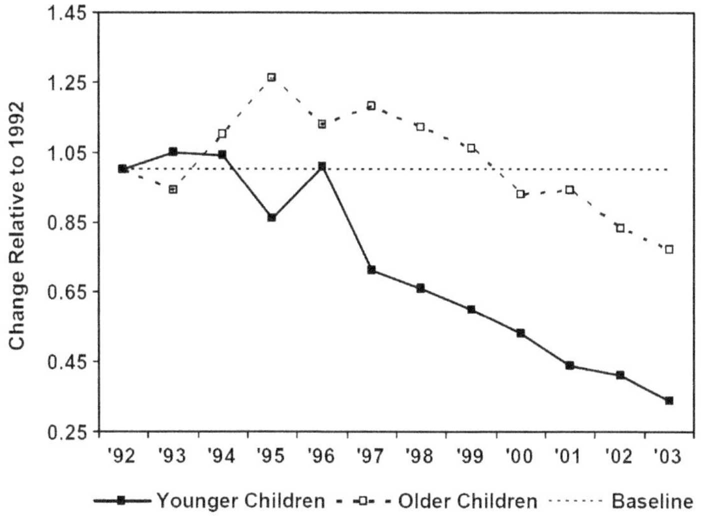

Figure 10-8. Change in front-seat fatalities relative to 1992 levels, younger children (0-3) versus older children (4-12) (from Nichols *et al.*, 2005, with permission from Elsevier).

quite clear that up until the start of the campaign the rate remained essentially the same, with random variations. But immediately after the campaign the rate dropped sharply and the drop continued since then. Obviously, with time the reduction in the number of children fatalities in the front seat was also due to the depowered air bags whose frequencies in the U.S. vehicle fleet is still increasing.

It should be obvious by now, that air bags are not totally passive. To begin, it is recommended that in cars equipped with air bags, the children sit in the back, even with the depowered air bags. When children are sitting in the front it is recommended that the passenger-side air bag be deactivated. But there is another more subtle issue. If air bags reduce the risk of injuries, then we should also witness a drop in injury rates of people who purchase cars with air bags relative to the time before they had them. Winston, Maheshri, and Mannering (2006) tested this hypothesis directly by analyzing 1,307 drivers' self-reports about their crashes and driving in the years 1992-1996, before air bags became mandatory in 1998. At that time purchasing an air bag was a voluntary issue, and – given their cost – a person had to be quite safety conscious to insist on having an air bag in his or her new car. During this 5-year period 271 of the drivers switched cars from one without an air bag to one with an air bag and 270 switched from one with an air bag to one without one. On the basis of the interview data the authors were able to ascertain that the safety conscious drivers were more likely than other drivers to acquire air bags and antilock brakes, but the presence of the air bag had no significant effect on collisions or injuries. Winston *et al.* concluded that people compensate for such a safety feature by adopting a more dangerous and reckless driving style, thereby maintaining the same level of risk. This behavior, that economists term "risk offset hypothesis," is the very same behavior that we described as risk "homeostasis hypothesis" (see Chapter 3). Whether the offset is such that the risk remains exactly the same or whether the drivers "offset" too much or too little varies across situations. But the important thing to consider is that drivers adapt their behavior to changes in their environment, and "passive" protection' systems – at least ones of whose presence and function drivers are aware – will typically not meet their designer's safety expectations. Obviously, once the safety device – the air bag in this case – is mandatory in all vehicles, its benefits may be greater than when it was purchased by choice by a non-representative sample of safety-oriented consumers. However, this has to be empirically demonstrated.

Crashworthiness

Crashworthiness is a measure of the vehicle's ability to absorb the energy of impact or intrusion in a crash. Today's vehicle are designed to absorb as much of the crash energy as possible, rather than remain undamaged and transfer the full impact to the occupants. Crashes of old cars often had minimal damage to the cars but were often fatal to their occupants. In contrast, in today's cars we often see a person "walk out of a total wreck." The features that increase a vehicle's crashworthiness are the design of its frame or "cage," the shock absorbing properties of the bumpers, the design of the interiors and the padding, the collapsible steering wheel and breakaway rear view mirrors, etc. In performing their ordained duties in a crash, the effectiveness of these features can be truly argued to be totally independent of the driver behavior. Also, because the driver is not visibly aware of these properties and has no role in their adjustment, it is unlikely that there is any significant behavioral adaptation or risk compensation involved. Because a detailed description of crashworthiness is outside the scope of this book on human behavior, the following paragraphs only briefly describe how crashworthiness is defined, measured, and evaluated for different vehicles.

Crashworthiness is typically evaluated in contrived crash testing where a car is crashed into an obstacle (or vice versa). Most tests today are done with sophisticated "crash dummies" that mimic many of the body's bio-mechanics and have sensors that measure impact forces and directions on multiple body parts. Using data previously obtained from crash tests with human cadavers, the impact registered by these sensors is then translated to expected human body tissue injuries.

Ecological validity of crash testing

Because crash testing is done using one or very few specific crash types (such as a specific type of frontal collision and a specific type of side collision), the validity of the results and the crashworthiness rating has to be evaluated against injuries in real-world crashes. One such evaluation of the European crashworthiness ratings (described below) was done by Lie and Tingvall (2002). In their study they examined the likelihood of injuries and fatalities in police-reported two-vehicle collisions in Sweden, that occurred in the period 1994-2000, for which data on the vehicle make, model, and weight were available. Their measure of risk was the frequency of crashes in which occupants of a given car make-model suffered serious injuries or were killed, relative to the frequency of crashes in which the occupants of the other car were seriously injured or killed. With this measure of relative risk of serious injury or fatality, vehicles with NCAP (see below) two-star ratings obtained a risk of 0.89, vehicles with three-star ratings had a risk of 0.75, and vehicles with four-star ratings had a risk of 0.70. On the basis of some further calculations, Lie and Tingvall concluded that vehicles with four-star ratings reduced the risk of serious injury or fatality in real life by over 30 percent relative to two-star rated or non-rated vehicles.

In the U.S. the National Highway Traffic Safety Administration conducts tests of crashworthiness using a different procedure than the European one (detailed below) and its validity was evaluated by Kahane, Hackney, and Berkowitz (1994). For their analysis they examined 396 fatal two-car collisions in which both vehicles were identical or very similar to cars tested for their crashworthiness. They found that in these collisions, the car with the better crashworthiness rating had (depending on the disparity in the rating) a 15-25 percent lower risk of fatal injury. Farmer (2005) used crash data to compare the injury and fatality risk of people in collisions involving cars with different crashworthiness ratings, as measured by the U.S. Insurance Institute for Highway Safety (that uses a procedure similar to the European one), and also found that in general fatality risk was the highest for poorly rated vehicles, and then progressively smaller for vehicles with marginal, acceptable, or good ratings. In head-on two-car collisions the estimated odds of driver fatality was approximately 74 percent lower for the good vehicle than for the poor vehicle. Thus, on the basis of these three evaluations of crashworthiness, as rated by three different organizations – using varying procedures in different facilities – we can conclude that there is a consistent relationship between the reactions of dummies in a test facility and the injuries to human occupants in real-world crashes.

But tests conducted at different testing facilities on the same vehicles do not necessarily yield the same results. First, like people, not all dummies are the same. Second, the specific testing procedures vary among different testing organizations. Three key differences in testing procedures are the impact speeds (or delta-V), the direction and location of the impact, and the nature of the obstacle that impacts the car. Thus, it is best to think of the results of tests conducted in different facilities on the same vehicle make and model, as complementary rather than comparable (or, in some cases, conflicting).

Frontal collisions

The most common test is that of frontal collision. Beyond that common label differences abound. For example, the U.S. National Highway Traffic Safety Administration's New Car Assessment Program (NCAP) simulates a frontal collision by crashing a car into a fixed barrier that extends the full width of the front of the car, at a speed of 35 mph (56.3 km/hr). This simulates a head-on collision of two cars of similar size and weight moving toward each other on the exact same path. The occupants are two dummies representing an average-sized adult in driver and front passenger seats and secured with the vehicle's seat belts. Instruments measure the force of impact to each dummy's head, neck, chest, pelvis, legs, and feet, and the rating is then published on a scale of 1-5 stars where one star indicates a risk of serious injury to the head and chest of either passenger of 45+ percent and five stars indicate a chance of injury to the head or chest of less than 10 percent. A serious injury is one requiring immediate hospitalization and may be life threatening.

A different approach is used by the U.S. Insurance Institute for Highway Safety (IIHS) and the European New Car Assessment Program (EuroNCAP). In their simulations of frontal collision the crash barrier only extends into 40 percent of the vehicle's width from the driver side and the impact speed is 40 mph (64.4 km/hr). Because of the partial overlap, the force is distributed over a smaller area, and the impact severity in the affected area (the driver's in this case) is therefore greater, but the injury severity in the passenger area is likely to be less. The rationale for the partial overlap is that most frontal collisions do not involved the full overlap of the two cars (who are supposed to be traveling in non-overlapping lanes), but some degree of overlap that is typically less than 100 percent. These two differences in speed and impact overlap imply that high ratings with full frontal collision testing do not necessarily predict high ratings with the higher speed frontal-offset testing, and consequently the relative rankings of different car models are likely to be different with the two tests. Therefore the tests should be considered independently.

In their discussion of the difference between the different testing procedures the insurance institute (IIHS, 2007) notes that the two test types – the offset and the full-width – actually complement each other. "Crashing the full width of a vehicle into a rigid barrier maximizes energy absorption so that the integrity of the occupant compartment, or safety cage, can be maintained well in all but very high-speed crashes. Full-width rigid-barrier tests produce high occupant compartment decelerations, so they're especially demanding of restraint systems. In offset tests, only one side of a vehicle's front end, not the full width, hits the barrier so that a smaller area of the structure must manage the crash energy. This means the front end on the struck side crushes more than in a full-width test, and intrusion into the occupant compartment is more likely. The bottom line is that full-width tests are especially demanding of restraints but less demanding of structure, while the reverse is true in offsets."

But do the two tests cover all types of frontal collisions? Obviously not. In an in-depth analysis of a representative sample of 53 frontal collisions involving 61 belted fatalities in Sweden, Lindquist, Hall, and Björnstig (2004) determined that slightly fewer than 50 percent of all fatalities and slightly more than 50 percent of all fatal crashes involved less than 30 percent overlap. The difference between 30 percent and 40 percent is quite meaningful, because with 30 percent overlap the impact does not involve the drive train as an active load path, whereas with 40 percent the drive train absorbs a significant portion of the impact, and its crash absorption properties become highly relevant to the occupants' injuries. In Lindquist *et al.*'s (2004) representative sample of Swedish fatal crashes only 23 percent of all frontal collision fatalities and 25 percent of fatal collisions involved loadings on the drive train similar to that used by the IIHS, EuroNCAP, and NCAP. The typical frontal collision, with less than 30 percent overlap is currently not being evaluated and seems to involve vehicle areas with very little energy absorption structures. Given the importance of the ratings to consumer decisions, it seems reasonable to believe that if these partial overlap frontal crashes were to be included in the standard testing for crashworthiness, the manufacturers would invest more efforts in reducing injuries from these types of collisions.

Side impacts

Side impacts are very different from frontal collisions, because the impacted vehicle absorbs all of the energy on its side, where absorption and the distance to the occupant are the smallest. A simulated impact of this type is assumed to represent an intersection-type collision.

In the NHTSA crash test a 3,015-pound barrier is moved into a standing vehicle at a speed of 38.5 mph (62 km/hr). To simulate the bumper of a car, the moving barrier is covered with crushable material. The vehicle occupants are crash test dummies buckled in the driver and rear passenger seats (both on the side of the impacting vehicle). The injury ratings are indicators of a serious injury (requiring hospitalization and life threatening), but are based on injuries to the chest only (not the head). A poor rating of one star indicates a chance of serious injury greater than 25 percent, and the best – five-star rating – indicates a chance of serious injury of five percent or less. Because the same size barrier is moved into the sides of all vehicles, for side impacts comparisons may be made between vehicles of different sizes. Here too, the IIHS and EuroNCAP are similar to each other but differ from NHTSA's NCAP. While the construction and weight of the crashing car is similar, it is driven at a lower speed of 30-31 mph (48-50 km/hr). Also, because females and children are more sensitive to injuries, the IIHS uses dummies that represent a small (5th percentile) female in the driver seat and a 12-year-old adolescent in the rear seat. The EuroNCAP also uses a restrained child dummy in the rear seat. One significant difference between adults and children is the position of the head: the head of the child passenger is in the window area where people's heads are more vulnerable to being struck by the front end of a striking vehicle in a real-world side impact.

Other tests of crashworthiness

In addition to these two tests, the NHTSA also tests vehicles for roll-over stability, the IIHS also tests for head restraints, and the EuroNCAP also tests crashworthiness for a side impact with a pole. More detailed information about all of the testing procedures is available at the websites of these organizations (IIHS: http://www.iihs.org/ratings/protocols/default.html; EuroNCAP: http://www.euroncap.com/content/test_procedures/downloads.php?area_ID=3; NHTSA: http://www.nhtsa.dot.gov/cars/testing/ncap/BASC2006/pages/CrashTestRatings.htm).

Concluding Comments

Occupant protection is solely concerned with injury prevention and reduction, and not with crash prevention. In fact, the best occupant protection is probably a viable crash prevention system. Though new crash avoidance systems are being integrated into new vehicles at an accelerating rate it is still prudent for divers to drive defensively as saving lives and injuries depends greatly on the various measures of occupant protection. Two goals of this chapter were to demonstrate the effectiveness of the different occupant protection devices and the role that the driver plays in maximizing their potential. The distinction between passive and active restraints is somewhat artificial because the driver can either aid or interfere with the effective deployment of both kinds. Exceptions to this generalization are vehicle features that are designed to maximize its crashworthiness. As crash tests become more and more sophisticated and representative of different types of crash impacts, and as demands for safety increase, it is likely that we will have safer and safer vehicles, aiding the drivers, and in spite of (some of) the drivers.

References

Agran, P. F., C. L. Anderson and D. G. Winn (2004). Violators of a child passenger safety law. *Pediatrics*, *114*(1), 109-115.

Berg, M. D., L. Cook, H. M. Corneli, D. D. Vernon and J. M. Dean (2000). Effect of seating position and restraint use on injuries to children in motor vehicle crashes. *Pediatrics*, *105*, 831-835.

Bergoffen, G., R. R. Knipling, S. A. Tidwell, J. B. Short, G. P. Krueger, R. E. Inderbitzen, G. Reagle and D. C. Murray (2005). *Commercial Motor Vehicle Driver Safety Belt Usage*. Transportation Research Board, National Academies, Washington, DC.

Besel, R. R., C. S. Dennis and M. L. Drake (2001). *Pickup Truck Occupant Safety Belt Usage*. Center for Advancement of Transportation Safety, Purdue University, West Lafayette, IN.

Biagioli, F. (2005). Child safety seat counseling: three keys to safety. *Am. Fam. Physician*, *72*(3), 473-478.

Bingham, C. R., D. W. Eby, H. M. Hockanson and A. I. Greenspan (2006). Factors influencing the use of booster seats: A state-wide survey of parents. *Accid. Anal. Prev.*, *38*, 1028-1037.

Bogenrieder, R., W. Eberle, R. Justen, H. Roehm, G. Villino, A. Wagner and M. Woldrich (2009). U.S. Patent No. 7,597,170. U.S. Patent and Trademark Office, Washington, DC.

Boyle, J. M. and P. Vanderwolf (2004). 2003 motor vehicle occupant safety survey. Volume 2: Safety belt report. NHTSA Report DOT HS 809 789. U.S. Department of Transportation, Washington, DC.

Boyle, J. M. and P. Vanderwolf (2005). 2003 motor vehicle occupant safety survey. Volume 3: Air bags report. NHTSA Report DOT HS 809 856. U.S. Department of Transportation, Washington, DC.

Bracchitta, K. M. (2006). Factors influencing parental use of booster seats for their children. *J. Clin. Psychol. Med. Settings*, *13*(3), 273-284.

Braver, E. R. and S. Y. Kyrychenko (2004). Efficacy of side air bags in reducing driver deaths in driver-side collisions. *Am. J. Epidemiol.*, *159*(6), 556-564.

Brittle, C. and M. Cosgrove (2005). Unconscious motivators and situational safety belt use: Literature review and results from an expert panel meeting. Final report on NHTSA project DTNH-22-04-P-05230 submitted to the U.S. Department of Transportation, Washington, DC.

Carney, C., D. McGehee, K. Harland, M. Weiss, and M. Raby (2015). *Using Naturalistic Driving Data to Assess the Prevalence of Environmental Factors and Driver Behaviors in Teen Driver Crashes.* AAA Foundation for Traffic Safety, Washington, DC.

Carpenter, C. S. and M. Stehr (2008). The effects of mandatory seatbelt laws on seatbelt use, motor vehicle fatalities, and crash-related injuries among youths. *J. Health Econ.*, *27*(3), 642-662.

Chaudhary, N. K., M. Alonge, and D. F. Preusser (2005). Evaluation of the Reading, PA nighttime safety belt enforcement campaign: September 2004. *J. Safety Res.*, *36*, 321-326.

Chaudhary, N. K. and V. S. Northrup (2004). Predictive models of safety belt use: A regression analysis of MVOSS data. *Traffic Inj. Prev.*, *5*, 137-143.

Chaudhary, N. K. and D. F. Preusser (2006). Connecticut nighttime safety belt use. *J. Safety Res.*, *37*, 353-358.

Chaudhary, N. K., M. G. Solomon and L. A. Cosgrove (2004). The relationship between perceived risk of being ticketed and self-reported seat belt use. *J. Safety Res.*, *35*, 383-390.

Colgan, F., A. Gospel, J. Petrie, J. Adams, P. Heywood and M. White (2004). Does rear seat belt use vary according to socioeconomic status? *J. Epidemiol. Community Health*, *58*, 929-930.

Corneli, H. M., L. J. Cook and J. M. Dean (2000). Adults and children in severe motor vehicle crashes: A matched-pairs study. *Ann. Emerg. Med.*, *36*(4), 340-345.

Costich, J. F. and S. S. Slavova (2015). Using enforcement and adjudication data to assess the impact of a primary safety belt law. *Traffic Inj. Prev.*, *16*(7), 664-668.

Cummings, P. and F. P. Rivara (2004). Car occupant death according to the restraint use of other occupants: A matched cohort study. *J. Am. Med. Assoc.*, *291*, 343-349.

Decina, L. E. and K. H. Lococo (2004). Misuse of child restraints. National Highway Traffic Safety Administration. Report No. DOT HS 809 671. U.S. Department of Transportation, Washington, DC, January 2004.

Decina, L. E., K. H. Lococo and C. T. Doyle (2006). Child restraint use survey: LATCH use and misuse. NHTSA Report No. DOT HS 810 679. U.S. Department of Transportation, Washington, DC.

Dee, T. S. (1998). Reconsidering the effects of seat belt laws and their enforcement status. *Accid. Anal. Prev.*, *30*(1), 1-10.

Dinh-Zarr, T. B., D. A. Sleet, R. A. Shults, S. Zaza, R. W. Elder, J. L. Nichols, R. S. Thompson and D. M. Sosin (2001). Reviews of evidence regarding interventions to increase the use of safety belts. *Am. J. Prev. Med.*, *21*(4S), 48-65.

Duma, S. M., A. L. Rath, M. V. Jernigan, J. D. Stitzel PhD and I. P. Herring (2005). The effects of depowered air bags on eye injuries in frontal automobile crashes. *Am. J. Emerg. Med.*, *23*, 13-19.

Durbin, D. R., I. G. Chen, R. Smith, M. R. Elliott and F. K. Winston (2005). Effects of seating position and appropriate restraint use on the risk of injury to children in motor vehicle crashes. *Pediatrics, 115*(3), e305-e309.

Durbin, D. R., M. R. Elliott and F. K. Winston (2003). Belt-positioning booster seats and reduction in risk of injury among children in vehicle crashes. *JAMA, 289*(21), 2835-2840.

EC (2015). Seat belt reminders. *Mobility and Transport, Road Safety*. European Commission, Brussels, Belgium. http://ec.europa.eu/transport/road_safety/specialist/knowledge/esave/esafety_measures_known_safety_effects/seat_belt_reminders_en.htm

Ebel, B. E. and D. C. Grossman (2003). Crash proof kids? An overview of current motor vehicle child occupant safety strategies. *Curr. Probl. Pediatr. Adolesc. Health Care, 33*, 38-55.

Ebel, B. E., T. D. Koepsell, E. E. Bennett and F. P. Rivara (2003). Too small for a seatbelt: Predictors of booster seat use by child passengers. *Pediatrics, 111*(4), 323-327.

Eby, D. W., C. R. Bingham, J. M. Vivoda and T. Ragunathan (2005). Use of booster seats by Michigan children 4–8 years of age. *Accid. Anal. Prev., 37*, 1153-1161.

Eby, D. W., L. J. Molnar, L. P. Kostyniuk, J. T. Shope and L. L. Miller (2004). Developing an optimal in-vehicle safety belt promotion system. Transportation Research Institute Report UMTRI 2004-29. University of Michigan, Ann Arbor, MI.

Elliott, M. R., M. J. Kallan, D. R. Durbin, and F. K. Winston (2006). Effectiveness of child safety seats vs seat belts in reducing risk for death in children in passenger vehicle crashes. *Arch. Pediatr. Adolesc. Med., 160*(6), 617-621.

Ehiri, J., W. King, H. O. D. Ejere and P. Mouzon (2006). Effects of Interventions to increase use of booster seats in motor vehicles for 4-8 year olds. American Automobile Association for Traffic Safety, Washington, DC.

ETSC (2013). Back on track to reach the EU road safety target? 7th Road Safety PIN Report. European Transport Safety Council, Brussels, Belgium.

Evans, L. (1986). Double pair comparison – A new method to determine how occupant characteristics affect fatality risk in traffic crashes. *Accid. Anal. Prev., 18*(3), 217-227.

Evans, L. (1990). Restraint effectiveness, occupant ejection from cars, and fatality reductions. *Accid. Anal. Prev., 22*(2), 167-175.

Evans, L. (2004). *Traffic Safety*. Science Serving Society, Inc, Bloomfield Hills, MI.

Farmer, C. (2005). Relationships of frontal offset crash test results to real-world driver fatality rates. *Traffic Inj. Prev., 6*, 31-37.

Farmer, C. M. (2006). Another look at Meyer and Finney's 'who wants air bags?' *Chance, 19*(4), 15-22.

Farmer, C. M. and A. F. Williams (2005). Effect on fatality risk of changing from secondary to primary seat belt enforcement. *J. Safety Res., 36*, 189-194.

Fay, P. A., R. Sferco and R. Frampton (2001). Multiple impact crashes – Consequences for occupant protection measures. Proceedings of the 2001 IRCOBI Conference on the Biomechanics of Impact, Isle of Man, UK, 10-12 October.

Ferguson, S. A., J. K. Wells, and A. F. Williams (2000). Child seating position and restraint use in three states. *Inj. Prev., 6*(1), 24-28.

Fernandez, W. G., S. D. Mehta, T. Coles, J. A. Feldman, P. Mitchell and J. Olshaker (2006). Self-reported safety belt use among emergency department patients in Boston, Massachusetts. *BMC Pub. Health, 6*, 111-121.

Fleiter, J. J., L. Gao, C. Qiu, and K. Shi (2009). Availability, functionality, and use of seat belts in Beijing taxis prior to thc 2008 Beijing Olympic Games. *Accid. Anal. Prev.*, *41*(2), 342-344.

Glassbrenner, D. and J. Ye (2006). Seat belt use in 2006 – Overall results. NHTSA Report DOT HS 810 677.

Goodwin, A., L. Thomas, B. Kirley, W. Hall, N. O'Brien and K. Hill (2015). Countermeasures that work: A highway safety countermeasures guide for State Highway Safety Offices. 8th edition. NHTSA Report No. DOT HS 812 202. U.S. Department of Transportation, Washington, DC.

Greenwell, N. K. (2015). Results of the National Child Restraint Use Special Study (NCRUSS). NHTSA Report No. DOT HS 812 142. U.S. Department of Transportation, Washington, DC.

Halman, S. I., M. Chipman, P. C. Parkin and J. G. Wright (2002). Are seat belts as effective in school age children as in adults? A prospective crash study. *Br. Med. J.*, *324*, 1123-1125.

Hinch, M., M. Solomon, and J. Tison (2014). The click it or ticket evaluation, 2012. National Highway Traffic Safety Administration, Report DOT HS 811 989. U.S. Department of Transportation, Washington, DC.

Hu, J. and D. Blower (2013). Estimation of seatbelt and frontal-airbag effectiveness in trucks: U.S. and Chinese perspectives. Report No. UMTRI-2013-2. University of Michigan Transportation Research Institute, Ann Arbor, MI.

Huseth-Zosel, A. L. (2012). Front versus rear seat placement of children aged 12 or younger within vehicles: A rural/urban comparison in North Dakota. *Traffic Inj. Prev.*, *13*(4), 388-392.

Ibrahimova, A., R. A. Shults and L. F. Beck (2011). Comparison of 2008 national and state-level self-reported and observed seatbelt use estimates. *Inj. Prev.*, *17*(3), 201-203.

IIHS (1999). Neck injuries in rear-end crashes. Status Report Special Issuc (Insurance Institute for Highway Safety), 34, pp. 1-11.

IIHS (2007). Frontal offset crash test details, ratings criteria, Crash test verification. Insurance Institute for Highway Safety, Arlington, VA. http://www.iihs.org/ratings/frontal_test_info.html

IIHS (2014). Safe seats: Record 27 new boosters earn highest IIHS rating. *Status Report*, **49**(9). Insurance Institute for Highway Safety, Arlington, VA. http://www.iihs.org/iihs/sr/statusreport/article/49/9/1

IIHS (2015a). Rear underride guard mandate may extend to more trucks under NHTSA proposal. *Status Report*, **50**(9). Insurance Institute for Highway Safety, Arlington, VA.

IIHS (2015b). Shop with confidence: more BEST BET boosters make buying one easier. *Status Report*, **50**(9). Insurance Institute for Highway Safety, Arlington, VA.

IIHS (2015c). Good head restraints linked to 11 percent reductioOn in injuries in rear-end crashes. *Status Report*, **50**(9). Insurance Institute for Highway Safety, Arlington, VA.

Janssen, W. (1994). Seat-belt wearing and driving behavior: an instrumented-vehicle study. *Accid. Anal. Prev.*, *26*(2), 249-261.

Jernigan, M. V., A. L. Rath and S. M. Duma (2005). Severe upper extremity injuries in frontal automobile crashes: the effects of depowered air bags. *Am. J. Emerg. Med.*, *23*, 99-105.

Jost, G., R. Allsop and A. Cesi (2014). Ranking EU progress on car occupant safety. PIN Flash Report 27, ETSC. European Transport Safety Council, Brussels, Belgium.

Kahane, C. J. (2006). An evaluation of the 1998-1999 redesign of frontal air bags. NHTSA Report DOT HS 810 685. U.S. Department of Transportation, Washington, DC.

Kahane, C. J. (2010). Effectiveness of pretensioners and load limiters for enhancing fatality reduction by seat belts. NHTSA Report DOT HS 811 835. U.S. Department of Transportation, Washington, DC.

Kahane, C. J. (2014). Updated estimates of fatality reduction by curtain and side air bags in side impacts and preliminary analyses of rollover curtains. NHTSA Report No. DOT HS 811 882. U.S. Department of Transportation, Washington, DC.

Kahane, C. J., R. J. Hackney and A. M. Berkowitz (1994). Correlation of vehicle performance in the new car assessment program with fatality risk in actual head on collisions. Proceedings of the Experimental Safety Vehicle (ESV) Conference. Paper no. 94-S8-O-11, Vol. 2, pp. 1388-1404. Munich.

Kent, R., D. C. Viano and J. Crandall (2005). The field performance of frontal air bags: A review of the literature. *Traffic Inj. Prev.*, *6*, 1-23.

Koushki, P. A. and B. Bustan (2006). Smoking, belt use, and road accidents of youth in Kuwait. *Safety Sci.*, *44*, 733-746.

Lennon, A. (2006). Issues of child occupant protection: A literature review. *J. Aust. Coll. Road Safety*, *17*(2), 38-45.

Lerner, E. B., D. V. Jehle, A. J. Billittier IV, R. M. Moscati, C. M. Connery and G. Stiller (2001). The influence of demographic factors on seatbelt use by adults injured in motor vehicle crashes. *Accid. Anal. Prev.*, *33* (5), 659-662.

Levitt, S. D. (2005). Evidence that child safety seats are no more effective than seat belts in reducing fatalities for children aged two and up. University of Chicago Department of Economics, Initiative on Chicago Price Theory, and American Bar Foundation, July.

Li, H. R., T. M. Pickrell, and K. C. Shova (2016). The 2015 National Survey of the Use of Booster Seats. NHTSA report no. dot HS 812 309. U.S. Department of Transportation, Washington, DC.

Li, L., K. Kim and L. Nitz (1999). Predictors of safety belt use among crash-involved drivers and front seat passengers: Adjusting for over-reporting. *Accid. Anal. Prev.*, *31*, 631-638.

Lie, A. and C. Tingvall (2002). How do euro NCAP results correlate with real-life injury risks? A paired comparison study of car-to-car crashes. *Traffic Inj. Prev.*, *3*, 288-293.

Lindquist, M., A. Hall and U. Björnstig (2004). Car structural characteristics of fatal frontal crashes in Sweden. *Inter. J. Crashworthiness*, *9*(6), 587-997.

MacLennan, P. A., G. McGwin Jr., J. Metzger, S. G. Moran and L. W. Rue III (2004). Risk of injury for occupants of motor vehicle collisions from unbelted occupants. *Inj. Prev.*, *10*, 363-367.

Majumdar, A., R. B. Noland and W. Y. Ochieng (2004). A spatial and temporal analysis of safety-belt usage and safety-belt laws. *Accid. Anal. Prev.*, *36*, 551-560.

Malenfant, J. E. and R. VanHouten (2008). Observations of how drivers fasten their seatbelts in relation to various startup tasks. *Accid. Anal. Prev.*, *40*(1), 309-314.

McGwin, G. Jr., J. Metzger, J. Alonso, L. Rue and W. III. Loring (2003). The association between occupant restraint systems and risk of injury in frontal motor vehicle collisions. *J. Trauma Inj. Infection Critic. Care.*, *54*(6), 1182-1187.

Meyer, M. (2006). Commentary on "another look at Meyer and Finney's 'who wants air bags?'". *Chance*, *19*(4), 23.

Morgan, M. A. (2015). Analyzing seat belt usage from accident data: An evaluation of click it or ticket enforcement campaigns in Ohio. *Int. J. Police Sci. Management*, *17*(1), 32-39.

Morris, S. D., K. B. Arbogast, D. R. Durbin and F. K. Winston (2000). Misuse of booster seats. *Inj. Prev.*, *6*, 281-284.

Nakahara, S. M. Ichikawa and S. Wakai (2007). Magazine information on safety belt use for pregnant women and young children. *Accid. Anal. Prev.*, *39*(2), 356-363.

Nakahara, S., T. Kawamura, M. Ichikawa and S. Wakai (2006). Mathematical models assuming selective recruitment fitted to data for driver mortality and seat belt use in Japan. *Accid. Anal. Prev.*, *38*, 175-184.

NHTSA (1996). Revised estimates of child restraint effectiveness. National Center for Statistics and Analysis, Research Note. U.S. Department of Transportation, Washington, DC.

NHTSA (2002). Types of child safety seats. Report DOT HS 809 230. U.S. Department of Transportation, Washington, DC.

NHTSA (2005). Child restraint systems. Federal Motor Vehicle Safety Standards. 49 CFR Parts 571 Docket No. NHTSA-2005-21245 RIN 2127-AJ44. U.S. Department of Transportation, Washington, DC.

NHTSA (2013). Lives saved in 2012 by restraint use and minimum drinking age laws. Traffic Safety Facts Report No. DOT HS 811 851. U.S. Department of Transportation, Washington, DC.

NHTSA (2014a). Seat belt use in 2013 – Use in the States and Territories. Report DOT HS 812 030. U.S. Department of Transportation, Washington, DC.

NHTSA (2014b). Traffic safety facts. Occupant Protection. Report DOT HS 811 892. U.S. Department of Transportation, Washington, DC.

NHTSA (2015a). Seat belt use in 2014 – Use rates in the states and territories. Report DOT HS 812 149. U.S. Department of Transportation, Washington, DC.

NHTSA (2015b). Occupant protection. Traffic safety facts 2013 data. Report DOT HS 812 153. U.S. Department of Transportation, Washington, DC.

Nichols, J. L., D. Glassbrenner, and R. P. Compton (2005). The impact of a nationwide effort to reduce airbag-related deaths among children: An examination of fatality trends among younger and older age groups. *J. Safety Res.*, *36*, 309-320.

NRSA (2015). Trends in road safety in Israel: 2014. 'Israel's National Road Safety Authority, Jerusalem, Israel.

OECD (2014). Road Safety Annual Report 2014. International Transport Forum (ITF), IRTAD, Paris, France.

Olson, C. M., P. Cummings and F. P. Rivara (2006). Association of first- and second-generation air bags with front occupant death in car crashes: A matched cohort study. *Am. J. Epidemiol.*, *164*(2), 161-169.

Olukoga, A. and M. Noah (2005). The use of seat belt by motor vehicle occupants in South Africa. *Traffic Inj. Prev.*, *6*, 398-400.

Omari, K. and O. Baron-Epel (2013). Low rates of child restraint system use in cars may be due to fatalistic beliefs and other factors. *Transport. Res. F.*, *16*, 53-59.

O'Neill, B. (2009). Preventing passenger vehicle occupant injuries by vehicle design—A historical perspective from IIHS. *Traffic Inj. Prev.*, *10*(2), 113-126.

Parada, M. A., L. D. Cohn, E. Gonzalez, T. Byrd and M. Cortes (2001). The validity of self-reported seatbelt use: Hispanic and non-Hispanic drivers in El Paso. *Accid. Anal. Prev.*, *33*, 139-143.

Peterson, T. D., B. T. Jolly, J. W. Runge and R. C. Hunt (1999). Motor vehicle safety: Current concepts and challenges for emergency physicians. *Annals Emerg. Med.*, *34*(3), 385-393.

Pickrell, T. M. and E. H. Choi (2014). The 2013 national survey of the use of booster seats. National Highway Traffic Safety Administration Report No. DOT HS 812 037. U.S. Department of Transportation, Washington, DC.

Pickrell, T. M. and E. H. Choi (2015). Seat belt use in 2014—Overall results. Traffic Safety Facts Research Note. National Highway Traffic Safety Administration Report No. DOT HS 812 113. U.S. Department of Transportation, Washington, DC.

Pickrell, T. M., E.-H. Choi and K. C. Shova (2016). Occupant restraint use in 2014: Results from the NOPUS controlled intersection study. National Highway Traffic Safety Administration Report No. DOT HS 812 244. U.S. Department of Transportation, Washington, DC.

Ramsey, A., E. Simpson and F. P. Rivara (2000). Booster seat use and reasons for non-use. *Pediatrics*, *106*(2), 20-25.

Rath, A. L., M. V. Jernigan, J. D. Stitzel and S. M. Duma (2005). The effects of depowered air bags on skin injuries in frontal automobile crashes. *Plast. Reconstruct. Surg.*, *115*(2), 428-435.

Regan, M. A., T. Horberry and A. Stevens (2014). *Driver Acceptance of New Technology: Theory, Measurement, and Optimisation.* Ashgate, Oxon, UK.

Robertson, L. S. (1975). Safety belt use in automobiles with starter-interlock and buzzer-light reminder systems. *Am. J. Pub. Health*, *65*, 1319-1325.

Ross, J. B., S. S. Gallagher, J. Hudson and C. Miara (2002). Seated for safety – Child passenger safety educational materials in the United States: Content, availability, accuracy, and appropriateness. American Automobile Association Foundation for Traffic Safety, Washington, DC.

Samples, A. M. B. (2004). Validity of self-reported data on seat belt use: The behavioral risk factor surveillance system. Ph.D. dissertation submitted to East Tennessee State University, Tennessee.

Sanders, M. S. and E. J. McCormick (1993). *Human Factors in Engineering and Design* (7th ed.). McGraw-Hill, New York, NY.

Shimamura, M., M. Yarmazaki and G. Fujita (2005). Method to evaluate the effect of safety belt use by rear seat passengers on the injury severity of front seat occupants. *Accid. Anal. Prev.*, *37*, 5-17.

Shinar, D. (1993). Demographic and socioeconomic correlates of safety belt use. *Accid. Anal. Prev.*, *25*(6), 745-755.

Shinar, D., E. Schechtman and R. P. Compton (2001). Self-reports of safe driving behaviors in relationship to sex, age, education and income in the U.S. adult driving population. *Accid. Anal. Prev.*, *33*, 111-116.

Shults, R. A., J. L. Nichols, T. B. Dinh-Zarr, D. A. Sleet, and R. W. Elder (2004). Effectiveness of primary enforcement safety belt laws and enhanced enforcement of safety belt laws: A summary of the guide to community preventive services systematic reviews. *J. Safety Res.*, *35*, 189-196.

Sivinski, R. (2010). Booster seat effectiveness estimates based on CDS and state data. NHTSA Report DOT HS 811 338. U.S. Department of Transportation, Washington, DC.

Starnes, M. (2005). Child passenger fatalities and injuries. Based on restraint use, vehicle type, seat position, and number of vehicles in the crash. NHTSA Report DOT HS 809 784. U.S. Department of Transportation, Washington, DC.

Streff, F. M. and A. C. Wagenaar (1989). Are there really shortcuts? Estimating seat belt use with self-report measures. *Accid. Anal. Prev.*, *21*(6), 509-516.

SWOV (2014). Seat belt reminders. Fact Sheet. https://www.swov.nl/rapport/Factsheets/UK/FS_Seatbelt_reminders.pdf

Tyroch, A. H., K. L. Kaups, L. P. Sue and S. O'Donnell-Nichol (2000). Pediatric restraint use in motor vehicles collisions. *Arch. Surg.*, *135*(10), 1173-1176.

UNECE (2013). Uniform provisions concerning the approval of enhanced child restraint systems used on board of motor vehicles (ECRS). Addendum: 128: Regulation: 129. Geneva, Switzerland. E/ECE/324/Rev.2/Add.128 – E/ECE/TRANS/505/Rev.2/Add.128.

Van Houten, R. and J. E. L. Malenfant (2006). Breaking the 92% seat belt use barrier-Phase 2: The effect of a seatbelt-gearshift delay on the seat belt use of service vehicle drivers who regularly make a large number of short daily trips. Center for Education and Research in Safety, Western Michigan University, Kalamazoo, MI.

Van Houten, R., J. E. L. Malenfant, J. Austin and A. Lebbon (2005). The effects of a seatbelt-gearshift delay prompt on the seatbelt use of motorists who do not regularly wear seatbelts. *J. Appl. Behav. Anal.*, *38*, 195-203.

Van Houten, R., J. E. Malenfant, I. Reagan, K. Sifrit, R. Compton, and J. Tenenbaum (2010). Increasing seat belt use in service vehicle drivers with a gearshift delay. *J. App. Behav. Anal.*, *43*(3), 369-380.

Van Houten, R., I. J. Reagan, and B. W. Hilton (2014). Increasing seat belt use: Two field experiments to test engineering-based behavioral interventions. *Transport. Res. F.*, *23*, 133-146.

Vivoda, J. M., D. W. Eby and L. P. Kostyniuk (2004). Differences in safety belt use by race. *Accid. Anal. Prev.*, *36*, 1105-1109.

WHO (2004). World report on road traffic injury prevention. Edited by M. Peden *et al.* World Health Organization, Geneva. http://www.who.int/world-health-day/2004/infomaterials/world_report/en/index.html; http://whqlibdoc.who.int/publications/2004/9241562609.pdf

WHO (2013). Global status report on road safety: Supporting a decade of action. World Health Organization, Geneva, Switzerland.

Will, K. E. (2005). Child passenger safety and the immunity fallacy: Why what we are doing is not working. *Accid. Anal. Prev.*, *37*(5), 947-955.

Williams, A. F., J. K. Wells and C. M. Farmer (2002). Effectiveness of Ford's belt reminder system in increasing seat belt use. *Inj. Prev.*, *8*, 293-296.

Williams, A. F. and P. Zador (1977). Injuries to children in automobiles in relation to seating location and restraint use. *Accid. Anal. Prev.*, *9*(1), 69-76.

Winston, C., V. Maheshri and F. Mannering (2006). An exploration of the offset hypothesis using disaggregate data: The case of air bags and antilock brakes. *J. Risk Uncertainty*, *32*, 83-99.

Winston, F. K., D. R. Durbin, M. J. Kallan and E. K. Moll (2000). The danger of premature graduation to seat belts for young children. *Pediatrics*, *105*(6), 1179-1183.

Winston, F. K. and D. C. Erkoboni (2006). Identifying information that promotes belt-positioning booster use Volume I: Summary and Findings. National Highway Traffic Safety Administration Report No. DOT HS 811 018.

Winston, F. K., D. C. Erkoboni, A. L. Young, B. T. Ragel, E. Su, C. N. Mann and E. H. Frank (2005). Assessing automobile head restraint positioning in Portland Oregon. *Inj. Prev.*, *11*, 97-101.

PART D
DRIVER TEMPORARY IMPAIRMENTS

11

Alcohol and Driving

"It provokes the desire, but it takes away the performance."
(Shakespeare, Macbeth, Act 2, Scene 3).

"Transport mishaps related to alcohol impairment are not new. It was common knowledge in the pre-industrial age that drunkards were at increased risk when riding horses or driving horse drawn vehicles, but to a limited extent a good horse could share the responsibility for safe transport with an incompetent driver, compensate for human impairment, and plod homeward in relative safety. The advent of the horseless carriage brought the era of forgiving transportation to an end." (Ogden and Moskowitz, 2004).

DRIVE HAMMERED, GET NAILED.
A popular public message on roadside billboards against drinking and driving.

Shakespeare was correct: alcohol has a lure, but it also has a cost. Mixing alcohol and driving makes for a terrible cocktail. Drinking and driving, or as it is commonly labeled driving under the influence (DUI) or driving while intoxicated (DWI), is probably the single greatest contributor to road deaths in the Western world. In fact, in the U.S. it is of such concern that it is included in many health and life-expectancy indicators. Because of its prominence as a cause of death, and concerted efforts to combat it, over the past four decades there have been significant reductions in the frequency of drinking and driving in the U.S. This is reflected in both self-reported annual national surveys of drivers (Shinar, Schechtman, and Compton, 1999), and in the drops of the share of alcohol in traffic fatality statistics; from 51 percent of all traffic fatalities in 1989 to 31 percent of all traffic fatalities in 2013 (NHTSA, 2015a) and from 0.45 fatalities per 100 million vehicle-miles in 2005 to 0.33 in 2014 (NHTSA, 2015c). In the EU, the situation is slightly better with alcohol impairment (defined there as BAC $\geq$ .05) accounting for approximately 25 percent of traffic fatalities (Mercier-Guyon, 2014).

The direct reason for the marked improvement is simple: fewer and fewer people drink and drive. The most direct evidence of the positive change is in nationally representative roadside sobriety checkpoints (Berning, Compton, and Wochinger, 2015). In these checks, alcohol at any level dropped from 36 percent of all weekend night drivers in 1973 to 8 percent in 2013-2014. The change in the prevalence of alcohol above the legal limit of .08 percent in that period dropped by 80 percent: from 7.5 percent to 1.5 percent (Berning *et al.*, 2015). There are probably multiple reasons for this positive behavioral change, but at least two are the emergence and impact of grass-roots citizen groups against drinking and driving (such as MADD – Mothers Against Drunk Driving), and the proliferation of effective laws and severe penalties.

The efforts to combat drinking and driving did not occur in a scientific vacuum. There is probably no area related to driving safety that has received more attention from researchers than that of drinking and driving. In fact, the body of scientific knowledge in this area is so extensive relative to the efforts actually made to reduce the problem that in a conference of leading highway safety researchers 10 years ago none of the participants identified research in this area as one of the top priorities. Not because it is not important, but because progress in this area was perceived as being impeded mostly by insufficient implementation of the knowledge that already exists due to political lack of will, and not for lack of knowledge (Hedlund, 2006).

Part of the problem, at least, is that drinking is a socially common and acceptable behavior in most parts of the world (save some Moslem countries). Worldwide, the average 15+ years old person consumes 6.2 liters of pure alcohol per year, which amount to 13.5 grams of alcohol per day (WHO, 2014). This is roughly equivalent to a can of beer per day (depending on the strength of the beer). The variability around that figure is very high, with some countries being very low (e.g., Israel = 2.8 l/yr), some being quite high (e.g., U.S.= 9.2), and some being very high (e.g., Russia = 15.1) (WHO, 2014). Europe is by far the heaviest drinking region in the world with most countries reporting more than 15 liters of pure alcohol per year per person (based on 2003-2005 data. WHO, 2010). Consequently, in this social climate absolute prohibition is not a viable countermeasure to DWI.

To understand the nature of the DWI problem and its countermeasures, it is necessary to first discuss the process by which alcohol affects various human functions, and the effects it has on driving and driving-related skills. I then address the impact of drinking on crashes, and the various countermeasures that have been used to reduce the problem.

Alcohol Absorption, Elimination and Blood Alcohol Concentration (BAC)

Alcohol, also known as the "wet drug" is a psychoactive drug. It is usually ingested in a drink (though thanks to technology it does not have to be a liquid anymore; AWOL, 2006). The alcohol in our drinks – ethanol or ethyl alcohol – is one of a family of compounds classified as alcohol. It is a colorless liquid that mixes in other fluids to form a homogenous liquid. Alcohol is absorbed in the blood stream very quickly because it does not have to be digested, and it passes quickly into the blood stream through the stomach walls (approximately 20 percent) and the walls of the small intestines (80 percent). It then spreads through the vascular system to rapidly reach the various tissues, including the nerve centers in the brain where it exerts its effects on multiple perceptual, cognitive, memory, and motor functions – all critical for safe driving (Ogden and Moskowitz, 2004). Because it spreads through the vascular system, its highest concentrations are in the blood-rich tissues of the brain, the liver, and the muscles. The rate of absorption of alcohol into the blood system is slowed down if we combine its intake with food, because the presence of food in the digestive tract slows its absorption. The elimination of alcohol from the body is a much slower process. Minute portions are eliminated through our breath, sweat, and urine, but most of the alcohol is eliminated slowly through metabolism in the liver.

The standard measure of alcohol in the blood is expressed in terms of percent of milligrams of alcohol per milliliter of blood. Although this is a ratio of weight per volume, we still think of this ratio as dimensionless because blood and alcohol weigh almost the same: 1 milliliter of water weighs 1.00 gram and 1 milliliter of blood weighs 1.05 grams. Thus, we typically express the amount of alcohol as percent Blood Alcohol Concentration (BAC). A concentration of 1 gram alcohol per 1 milliliter of blood would then yield BAC = 100 percent, and 1 milligram of alcohol (one thousandth of a gram) per 1 milliliter of blood would yield a BAC = 0.1 percent. A detailed description of the BAC measure and factors that affect it is provided by Brick (2006).

With this notation in mind, we can now quantify the rate of absorption and elimination of various amounts of alcohol. Figure 11-1 (based on data by Wilkinson *et al.*, 1977) presents the BAC reached at different times after drinking alcohol, when it is consumed all at once on an empty stomach. Several things should be noted in this figure. First, as can be seen from the multiple graphs in this figure, the peak alcohol level reached and the time it takes the body to dispose of it are directly related to the amount of alcohol consumed. Second, alcohol absorption is much quicker than its metabolism or elimination. The elimination is relatively slow and averages 0.017 percent per hour (NHTSA, 1994); being slightly faster for an experienced drinker and slightly slower for an inexperienced one. Thus, a person who reaches a BAC = 0.05 percent needs more than 3 hours to get the alcohol out of his or her system. Third, peak BAC level is reached approximately 30-60 minutes after drinking. This means that a person, who stops at a bar for a few drinks, may actually have a higher BAC – and therefore be more intoxicated – sometime after he or she has started driving than at the time he or she left the bar and

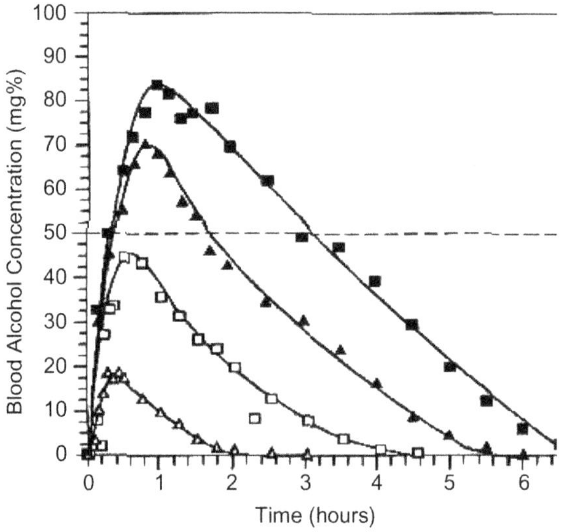

Figure 11-1. The rates of absorption and elimination, and the peak levels of BAC reached after drinking 1 (lowest curve), 2 (second curve), 3, and 4 drinks. The curves are based on drinking the whole quantity at once, on an empty stomach, by a male of average weight (from Boggan, 2005, based on data from Wilkinson *et al.*, 1977, with kind permission from Springer Science and Business Media).

entered the car. This also means that a person may feel quite "fine" getting into the car, and then may deteriorate without being aware of this.

Not apparent from Figure 11-1 are two other important facts. First, the peak BAC will be lower if a person consumes these drinks while eating (as in a restaurant), and over a long period. This is because the food slows the absorption process and the duration of the drinking period allows for some of the alcohol to be eliminated even though more alcohol is still being consumed. Second, the individual differences in the rates of absorption and elimination are quite significant, especially in the elimination (Christoforou, Karlaftis, and Yannis, 2013). This also means that the absolute levels of BAC at different times in the curves in Figure 11-1 can be misleading because the elimination process can be slightly faster for some people, but significantly slower for others (Boggan, 2005). Gender is also an important factor. In general, the same amount of alcohol ingested by a man and a woman of equal weight will result in a higher BAC in the woman than in the man. This is because the effect of the alcohol is a function of its dilution in the blood, and while water is 58 percent of an average man's weight, it is only 49 percent of an average woman's weight.

As a matter of procedure the measurement of a driver's BAC is most often not based on direct measurement of the blood content. Instead drivers are asked to blow into a portable breath tester and their lung air is analyzed. Because the breath alcohol concentration is highly correlated with the level of alcohol in the arterial and venous blood

(Linderg *et al.*, 2007), and is proportional to the BAC by a factor of 2.2727 (Vanlaar, 2005), the breath alcohol content can be easily converted into blood alcohol concentration. For example, a breath alcohol concentration of 0.22 mg alcohol per liter of exhaled air is equivalent to 0.5 g/l in the blood, or 0.05 percent BAC. Although this relationship is a statistically reliable one, it is a bit problematic when used to assess levels at or near the legal threshold (Schechtman and Shinar, 2011. See Enforcement section below).

Alcohol Effects on Driving, on Driving-Related Tasks, and on Subjective Sensations

Alcohol effects on cognitive and psychomotor functioning

Alcohol affects just about every capacity that we have, and performance deteriorations have been documented for just about every perceptual, attentional, decision, memory, and psychomotor task that has been evaluated. In fact, alcohol effects are so pervasive and consistent that the World Health Organization recommends that alcohol-related impairment serve as a benchmark for other impairments (Willette and Walsh, 1983). As might be expected, in general there is a direct dose-response relationship so that the amount of impairment is directly related to the amount of alcohol that enters the blood. The impairing effects can be demonstrated at very low alcohol levels and as the amount of alcohol in the blood rises, the number of functions that are impaired and degree of impairment increases (Moskowitz and Fiorentino, 2000; Moskowitz and Robinson, 1988; Ogden and Moskowitz, 2004).

The literature on the effects of alcohol on driving and driving-related functions is very extensive and the findings are very consistent: alcohol in almost any amount impairs driving or driving-related skills. In a review of the literature, Moskowitz and Robinson (1988) analyzed the results of 177 studies that examined the effects of low levels of alcohol (BAC levels of 0.10 percent or less) on driving-related functions and behaviors. They summarized their results in terms of the likelihood of impairment as a function of the BAC for nine different driving-related categories that are listed in Figure 11-2: reaction time, tracking, vigilance, divided attention, information processing, visual function, perception, psychomotor skills, and driving skill. Several aspects of their findings are significant. First and most obvious, as the BAC level increases the likelihood of finding impairment increases. This is true for all functions studied. Second, at BAC = 0.10 percent all the studies reviewed (100 percent of the studies in each category evaluated) indicated that all aspects of driving behaviors are impaired. Third, there are differences among the functions in their sensitivity to alcohol. The most sensitive function – producing impairment at the lowest levels of BAC – was divided attention. Approximately 50 percent of the studies demonstrate impairment in divided attention at BAC < 0.05 percent. The next most sensitive function was tracking, with similar percentages showing impairment at BAC = 0.05 percent. These findings are quite significant for safe driving because tracking and divided attention are inherent in just about all driving tasks, and inattention or distraction is involved in roughly 50 percent of all crashes (see Chapters

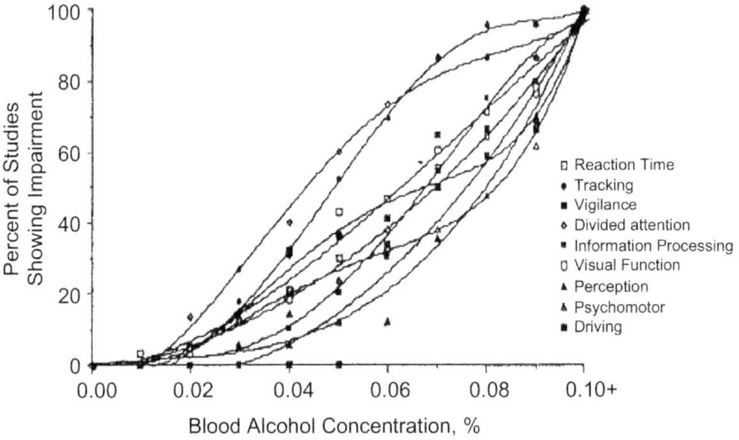

Figure 11-2. The percent of studies showing impairment from alcohol at different BACs for different categories of driving-related behaviors (from Moskowitz and Robinson, 1988).

13, 18). The least sensitive function was vigilance, with very few studies showing impairment below BAC = 0.08 percent.

The most important conclusion reached by Moskowitz and Robinson on the basis of their results was that "there is no lower threshold level below which impairment does not exist for alcohol" (p. vii). Thus, though some people may be more affected by small concentrations than others, this conclusion implies that as a national policy there is no safe level of alcohol for driving.

In a later review of the literature, Moskowitz and Fiorentino (2000) reviewed 112 studies spanning the period of 1981-1997. Table 11-1 provides a summary of the skills, functions, and tasks that were evaluated, the BAC levels at which they were evaluated, and the number of studies that evaluated each function. Although the categorization is not identical to the functions listed in the earlier study, there is a significant overlap between the two.

With a total of 556 BAC levels studied in the 112 studies, it was possible to determine quite accurately the statistical likelihood of impairments for different functions at different BACs. The results of this evaluation are summarized in Table 11-2, and several of the findings are worth dwelling on. First, even at the lowest levels tested (below 0.01 percent BAC) there are impairments in vehicular control and divided attention performance – skills that are critical for safe driving. Not only are impairments first detected at that level, but they are detected by more than 50 percent of the studies that evaluated performance at that low level. Second, the depressant effects of alcohol – manifest in the sensation of drowsiness – are also detected by at least 50 percent of the studies at the low BAC levels of 0.01-0.02 percent. Vigilance – measured in terms of the ability to detect supra-threshold but relatively rare events (such as an obstacle on a high-speed road) – is

Table 11-1. Behavioral areas and tasks, as identified by Moskowitz and Fiorentino (2000), that have been evaluated in for the effects of different BAC levels on driving-related skills.

Behavioral Areas and Tasks, by Articles and Bac Levels			
Domain	**Tasks**	**Number of Articles**	**Number of BAC Levels**
Aftereffects	Testing measured residual alcohol effects on a drinker's performance following a drinking session and the drinker's return to zero BAC. Various tasks from all other domains were used.	12	25
Cognitive tasks	Digit symbol substitution, mathematical and verbal reasoning, memory, pattern recognition, visual backward masking, card sorting.	31	145
Critical flicker fusion	Determination of the lowest frequency at which a flickering on-off light appears to be constant.	7	18
Divided attention	Simultaneous performance of two or more tasks such as tracking, visual search, number monitoring, and detection of auditory stimuli.	18	52
Driving skills	Actual driving, simulated driving, simulated flight, motorcycle simulator.	25	50
Perception	Detection of visual and/or auditory stimuli, time estimation, traffic hazard perception, anticipation time.	12	35
Psychomotor tasks	Finger tapping, body balance, hand steadiness, drill press operation, assembly of electronic parts.	18	57
Reaction time – Choice	Choice reaction time, choice reaction time with auditory distraction.	15	37
Reaction time – Simple	Single known stimulus with a single response.	5	20

Table 11-1. (Continued)

Behavioral Areas and Tasks, by Articles and Bac Levels			
Domain	**Tasks**	**Number of Articles**	**Number of BAC Levels**
Tracking	Pursuit tracking, compensatory tracking, critical tracking.	11	23
Vigilance	Vigilance.	9	18
Visual functions	Contrast sensitivity, depth perception, smooth pursuit, saccadic peak velocity, saccadic latency, saccadic inaccuracy, nystagmus, etc.	19	63
Drowsiness	Multiple sleep latency test, repeated test of sustained wakefulness.	6	13
Total		112	556

Note: Many articles covered more than one behavioral area.

impaired at BAC of 0.03-0.04 percent. Finally, most studies that evaluated more complex performance (such as tracking), and cognitive tasks (such as memory and decision making), found impairments at BAC levels of 0.05 percent and above. In fact, no function that was investigated was immune to BAC at all levels. In the authors' own words: "This review of the literature provides strong evidence that impairment of some driving-related skills begins with any departure from zero BAC. By 0.050 g/dl (BAC = 0.05 percent) the majority of studies reported impairment by alcohol. By BACs of 0.080 g/dl 94 percent of the studies reviewed reported impairment" (p. 14). The least sensitive function – critical flicker fusion (the rate at which a flickering light is first perceived as continuous) – is probably the least relevant for driving. In summary, this updated review also showed that there is no critical level of alcohol below which cognition and information processing are not impaired. Instead, it is more likely that the lowest level at which statistically significant impairment is first detected is a function of the study method; especially sample size and sensitivity of the performance measures used.

For the benefit of the driving population, simpler and qualitative versions of the increasing impairment of alcohol with increasing BACs have been published by various traffic safety organizations. Table 11-3 is one such summary published by the U.S. National Highway Traffic Safety Administration (2005). It is noteworthy that the association between the effects of various BAC levels of alcohol on driving performance measures is probably quite conservative, as deteriorations in these functions have been shown at levels lower than those indicated in Table 11-3. For example, deterioration in the ability to maintain lane position has been noted at levels significantly lower than 0.10 percent (e.g., Lenné *et al.*, 2010).

Table 11-2. Effects of different BAC levels on performance of various skills; in terms of the lowest BAC level that yielded significant effects, and the level at which at least 50 percent of the studies obtained a significant effect. The summary is based on 109 studies of 112 reviewed (from Moskowitz and Fiorentino, 2000).

BAC (mg/ml)	Function First Impaired at that BAC Level	BAC Level at which 50 percent of Tests Indicated Consistent Impairment
0.100	Critical flicker fusion	Simple reaction time, critical flicker fusion
0.060–0.069		Cognitive tasks, psychomotor skills, choice reaction time
0.050–0.059		Tracking
0.040–0.049	Simple reaction time	Perception, visual functions
0.030–0.039	Vigilance, perception	Vigilance
0.020–0.029	Choice reaction time, visual functions	
0.010–0.019	Drowsiness, psychomotor skills, cognitive tasks, tracking	Drowsiness
0.001–0.009	Driving, flying, divided attention	Driving, flying, divided attention

In addition to the multiple deleterious effects noted above, alcohol also impairs our ability to deal with otherwise insignificant distractions. This was demonstrated in a simulated driving task by Harrison and Fillmore (2011). Driving performance measured in terms of lane position variability, speed, reckless driving actions, and performance on a secondary task of sober drivers was unaffected by a minor distraction task, but was impaired when the same task was given to drivers with BAC levels of .08-.09 percent.

Alcohol effects on subjective feelings of "drunkenness" and impairment

All of the studies reviewed above have focused on the effects of alcohol on perceptual, cognitive, and motor functioning. Possibly not less important are the effects of alcohol on mood and subjective feelings of intoxication. The interaction between the two aspects – skills and feelings – is critical and dangerous. This is because many of the driving-related functions are impaired at levels at which people still feel quite fine. Thus, an insidious effect of alcohol is that at a BAC level that in most countries a person is considered "intoxicated" and unfit to drive (BAC = 0.05 percent), many people are not aware of being impaired or intoxicated (Shinar and Waisel, 2005).

Table 11-3. Qualitative guide of the effects of different levels of BAC on driving (NHTSA, 2005).

BAC	**Typical Effects**	**Predictable Effects on Driving**
.02%	Some loss of judgment Relaxation Slight body warmth Altered mood	Decline in visual functions (rapid tracking of a moving target) Decline in ability to perform two tasks at the same time (divided attention)
.05%	Exaggerated behavior May have loss of small-muscle control (e.g., focusing your eyes) Impaired judgment Usually good feeling Lowered alertness Release of inhibition	Reduced coordination Reduced ability to track moving objects Difficulty steering Reduced response to emergency driving situations
.08%	Muscle coordination becomes poor (e.g., balance, speech, vision, reaction time, and hearing) Harder to detect danger Judgment, self-control, reasoning, and memory are impaired	Concentration Short-term memory loss Speed control Reduced information processing capability (e.g., signal detection, visual search) Impaired perception
.10%	Clear deterioration of reaction time and control Slurred speech, poor coordination, and slowed thinking	Reduced ability to maintain lane position and brake appropriately
.15%	Far less muscle control than normal Vomiting may occur (unless this level is reached slowly or a person has developed a tolerance for alcohol) Major loss of balance	Substantial impairment in vehicle control, attention to driving task, and in necessary visual and auditory information processing

Notes: Information in this table shows the BAC level at which the effect is usually first observed, and has been gathered from a variety of sources including the National Highway Traffic Safety Administration, the National Institute on Alcohol Abuse and Alcoholism, the American Medical Association, the National Commission Against Drunk Driving, and www.webMD.com

Driving-related cognitive and psychomotor functions of most people are quite impaired before they are acutely intoxicated and feel "drunk." In a review of the literature that existed nearly half a century ago, a committee sponsored by the American Medical Association noted that approximately 50 percent of the people feel "drunk" only when their BAC exceeds 0.10 percent (Committee on Medicolegal Problems, 1970). Possibly due to the widespread education and public information campaigns that have been conducted since then, people are now more sensitive to the effects of alcohol. In our survey and BAC tests of over 500 Israeli pub patrons (Shinar, 2004), we found that the median number of drinks people felt they needed to get drunk was 3.5 (meaning that 50 percent of the drinkers feel they are not drunk if they drink less than 3.5 drinks), but the median number of drinks they felt they could drink before their driving was impaired was only 2.3. Nonetheless, 41 percent of the people exiting the pubs with BAC $\geq$ 0.05 percent (the threshold for alcohol impairment in Israel) intended to drive home (or to another pub) by themselves. Thus, with low and moderate amounts of alcohol that can already impair driving, many people still feel sober and quite able to drive safely, and act on it by getting behind the wheel. In fact, in our survey 21 percent of the pub patrons who actually felt drunk still drove away. To make things worse, when they drive, alcohol-impaired people tend to drive faster than when they are not alcohol impaired (Ronen *et al.*, 2004), and have poorer lateral control of their vehicle within the lane (Jongen, Vermeeren, van der Sluiszen, *et al.*, 2017). In summary, the discrepancy between our capabilities and our sensations makes the latter a very dangerous guide for responsible drinking limits.

Scope of the Problem: Role of Alcohol in Crashes

The ubiquitous living style in the Western world involves driving to socialize (at pubs, bars, and restaurants), and drinking as a part of socializing. And then we drive home (or to another pub). This combination of driving and drinking is a deadly mix. Though in chemical terms alcohol is a solution, in traffic safety it is a problem – and a most significant one. Although over the past several decades the prevalence of alcohol in the blood of weekend night drivers has been decreasing consistently, it is still significant and the prevalence of alcohol in severe crashes is intolerable. In 2013 and 2014, approximately 31 percent of all traffic fatalities in the U.S. involved alcohol-impaired driving (BAC $\geq$ 0.08) – exactly the same percent as 10 years earlier in 2004 (NHTSA, 2015a, 2015b). This makes drinking and driving the biggest behavioral safety issue on American roadways. The situation in Europe is not that much better. The specific definitions of the DWI crash statistics vary across countries but the big picture is the same. Based on 2002 data, 28 percent of the fatally injured drivers in Sweden had positive BACs; 14 percent of the people killed in traffic accidents in Germany were alcohol-related fatalities; 15 percent of the drivers involved in fatal accidents in France had BAC > 0.05 percent. These statistics of the proportion of alcohol-related fatal crashes out of all fatal crashes have remained quite stable since the mid-1990s (Sweedler *et al.*, 2004), and make drinking and driving the principal traffic safety concern in the Western world.

Despite the statistics listed above, the specific percentages of crashes that are attributed to alcohol are actually hard to assess for two reasons: first, the intervening variable between alcohol and the crash – that is, the direct human behavior that led to the crash – is not typically known. One noteworthy exception is a study by Dubois *et al.* (2015). In an analysis of all the U.S. Fatal Analysis Reporting System (FARS) crashes from 1991 to 2008 in which the drivers were tested for alcohol (and at least one other drug) they examined the added risk of an unsafe driving action (UDA) for drivers with low alcohol levels (BAC < 0.10). They found a significant effect of BAC with the likelihood of a UDA increasing at a rate of approximately 10 percent for each unit of .01 BAC. Unfortunately, they did not analyze the role of alcohol in the specific UDAs to determine the crash-related behaviors that are the most susceptible to alcohol impairment.

The second difficulty in assessing specific percentages of crashes attributable to alcohol is that the procedures for assessing the presence of alcohol in drivers vary greatly, and even when the same procedure is systematically applied to all crashes above a given severity level (as it is in many U.S. and Australian jurisdictions), assessing the causal role of alcohol remains tenuous. For example, in Israel up to the beginning of this century blood alcohol of crash-involved drivers was rarely measured, and consequently the national statistics listed alcohol involvement in only 1-2 percent of the injury and fatal crashes. However, as the awareness of the potential role of alcohol involvement in crashes began to sink in, and BAC tests became more and more common in fatal crashes, the official involvement levels increased from 1.9 percent of the fatalities in 2000, to 8 percent in 2007. This prompted a six-fold increase in roadside sobriety tests from 24 per 1,000 in the population in 2007 to 122 per 1,000 in 2010, accompanied by a decrease in fatalities to 3.7 percent (NRSA, 2013). In contrast, in the U.S., where BAC is routinely obtained in all injury and fatal crashes, it is estimated that 21 percent of the drivers involved in fatal crashes in 2014 were legally impaired at BAC > .08 percent (NHTSA, 2015c). The gap between the U.S. and Israel is actually more than the apparent 8.4-fold, the U.S. data refer to drivers with BAC ≥0.08 percent alcohol whereas in Israel the legal threshold for impairment is only 0.05 percent. It is also possible that the more accurate the data collection on DWI, the worse the statistics. Goldberg (2000) analyzed European crash statistics and found that in all countries where the police data indicate that alcohol is involved in less than 10 percent of the injury crashes – Belgium, Italy, Luxemburg, the Netherlands, and Sweden – the general level of alcohol consumption is not significantly different than that found in countries reporting more DWI crashes, leading him to conclude that lower rates of DWI crashes are more likely due to lower levels of alcohol data collection rather than to lower rates of DWI.

Another problem in interpreting alcohol-related crash statistics is that often, when alcohol is not directly measured, its involvement is derived from the type of crash. Thus, nighttime single-vehicle run-off-the-road crashes are often used as surrogates for alcohol-related crashes. This is because there is a strong association between the time and type of crash and the involvement of alcohol; with alcohol being involved in three times as many nighttime crashes as in daytime crashes (NHTSA, 2004b). However, this process of imputation is subject to both errors of omission because it does not include alcohol-related daytime and multi-vehicle collisions, and errors of commission because not all nighttime single-vehicle run-off-the-road crashes are due to alcohol. Many of these crashes are due to fatigue and falling asleep at the wheel, or to inadequate visibility of the roadway geometry. Consequently, even after the exclusion of nighttime visibility problems there is not a one-to-one correspondence between alcohol involvement and single-vehicle run-off-the-road nighttime crashes (Owens and Sivak, 1996).

Characteristics of drivers who drive while intoxicated

Fifty years ago, a common assumption held by many people (including judges adjudicating DWI cases) about a driver apprehended for DWI was that "there but for the grace of God go I." The intervening years have yielded overwhelming evidence that this is not the case. At least not for all of us. Although many drivers arrested for DWI will deny they have an alcohol problem and consider themselves "social drinkers," the truth is often different. In surveys of convicted DWI drivers conducted in Sweden and the U.S., approximately 10 years apart, 60 percent of the Swedish drivers and 70 percent of the American drivers were alcohol-dependent or alcohol abusers (based on the medical DSM – Diagnostic and Statistical Manual) (Bjerre, 2003; Hingson *et al.*, 2002). In an analysis of the blood of Luxemburg drivers suspected of DWI, 88 percent had confirmed alcohol in their blood, and 30 percent were probably chronic alcohol abusers based on a biological marker test (Appenzeller *et al.*, 2005). This realization has also resonated with the European Union whose licensing regulations forbid the issuance of a license to people who are alcohol-dependent. However, the license may be renewed after a period of abstinence and subject to an "authorized medical opinion and regular medical checkups" (Gómez-Talegón and Alvarez, 2006, p. 202). And while historically alcohol dependency was based on clinical judgments and subjective responses to questionnaires – and therefore highly subject to bias – new techniques involving biological markers that identify alcohol dependence are now quite accurate (Brinkmann *et al.*, 2002; Appenzeller *et al.*, 2005).

So who are the drivers involved in DWI accidents? Epidemiologic and crash data indicate that younger, male, single people are more likely to be involved in DWI incidents than older, female, married people (Chou *et al.*, 2006).

It also appears that many of the people arrested for DWI differ from the general driving population in several aspects of their personality. Cavaiola *et al.* (2003) administered the Minnesota Multi-Phasic Personality Inventory (MMPI-2) – one of the more common structured tests of personality – and the Michigan Alcoholism Screening Test (MAST) – a test that identifies various drinking-related problems and symptoms of alcoholism – to three groups of drivers consisting of those arrested for the first time for DWI, those arrested for repeat DWI offenses and a control group. Although the groups differed in their average age (the control drivers being the youngest and the repeat offenders being the oldest), the researchers noted that the personality and alcoholism scales – designed to measure stable traits – were relatively insensitive to age differences. The main finding of the study was that the two DWI groups differed significantly from the control group in their personality makeup, but not from each other. This would imply that many of the first-time offenders were also candidates for a repeat offense. In terms of their personality, the DWI drivers were more defensive (rather than frank and self-critical), were more likely to have alcohol problems or "potential for alcohol problems," had more psychopathic deviance symptoms, and had more hostility and aggression than the control drivers. Such extensive differences suggest that for many of the DWI offenders a traditional "treatment" consisting of sanctions may be quite ineffective. A similar relationship between aggression and alcohol abuse is apparent when the drivers are sampled from alcohol abuse and treatment centers. Yu, Evans, and Perfetti (2004) obtained significant correlations between alcohol abuse, violence, arrests for impaired driving, and measures of aggressive driving and road rage behavior.

Perhaps not surprisingly, people with alcohol abuse history are also likely to have more violations and collisions than people without such history. Macdonald *et al.* (2004) confirmed this when they compared the violations and crash records of drivers who voluntarily sought help for alcohol problems from the Center for Addiction and Mental Health in Toronto, Canada, with the violations and crash records of a non-patient sample of drivers matched in age and gender. The patients had approximately 30 percent more moving traffic violations and 100 percent more collisions than the control sample. Scott-Parker *et al.* (2014) obtained similar results when they surveyed young drivers: those who reported drinking and driving were also more likely to report other risky behaviors and more crashes and violations than those who did not report drinking and driving. Similarly people involved in severe road rage incidents often have alcohol problems (Butters *et al.*, 2005).

Driving while impaired by alcohol is often associated with binge drinking – drinking five or more drinks in a single session. In a U.S. study that tracked the prevalence of drinking and driving over a 10-year period (1993-2002; with over 100,000 annual phone interviews), 80 percent of the people who reported driving while impaired also reported that they engaged in binge drinking (Quinlan *et al.*, 2005). This is important because in the same survey, based on the respondents' self-reports, people who engaged in binge drinking were over 13 times(!) more likely to drive while intoxicated than people who did not engage in it. One possible reason for this greater tendency to drive while intoxicated is that these people have an acute tolerance to the subjective effects of intoxication, but not to its behavioral effects. Thus, these people are less sensitive to the feelings that accompany impairment, and are therefore more likely to drive while impaired (Marczinski and Fillmore, 2009).

As a final note – and warning to DWI drivers: alcohol can kill you off the road as well. The mortality rate of people apprehended for drunken driving is significantly greater than that of their age-gender matched cohorts (Skurtveit *et al.*, 2002).

The crash risks of drinking and driving

The acid test for the effects of alcohol on driving is the crash involvement. The best-known study of the risk of crashes as a function of alcohol impairment – known as the Grand Rapids study – was published by Borkenstein *et al.* in 1964. This study established the relative risk associated with drinking and driving on the basis of empirical crash and non-crash data. The relative risk was determined by comparing the measured BAC of 5,985 crash-involved drivers with the measured BAC of a control group of 7,590 drivers.

By simply knowing the BAC levels involved in the crash sample, we cannot assess the risk. For example, if half the drivers in the crash sample have BAC > 0.08 percent that does not imply that it is risky to have that much alcohol in the blood. To reach such a conclusion, we need an exposure measure; a measure that we can obtain from the control sample. If in the control sample, we find that only a small percentage of the drivers have BAC > 0.08 percent, then we can state that having BAC > .0.08 percent increases the risk of a crash. To determine a quantitative measure of the relative risk, it was necessary to select some criterion relative to which the risk can be evaluated. The obvious criterion is, of course, zero BAC. The relative risk was then determined by first calculating the ratio of the number of crash-involved drivers with a given BAC over the number of crash-involved drivers with zero BAC. Then dividing that ratio by the ratio of the equivalent frequencies in the control sample. Stated formally, the relative risk of being involved in a crash with a given level of alcohol, relative to the risk of being involved in a crash with zero alcohol, is:

$$RR_{(BAC=i)} = [M_{(BAC=i\%)}/N_{(BAC=0\%)}]/[K_{(BAC=i\%)}/L_{(BAC=0\%)}]$$

where RR is the relative risk; M is the frequency of crash-involved drivers with BAC = i percent; N is the frequency of crash-involved drivers with BAC =0 percent, K is the frequency of non-crash involved drivers with BAC = i percent; and L is the frequency of non-crash involved drivers with BAC = 0 percent.

In this formula, by definition, the relative risk of a crash of a driver with zero BAC is 1.0, and the relative risk at all other BACs depend on relative frequencies of those BACs in the crash and control samples. Using this formula, Borkenstein *et al.* found that the relative risk increases as an exponential function of the BAC, as can be seen in the lower line in Figure 11-3.

Later re-analyses of Borkenstein *et al.*'s data and other studies conducted since then in different parts of the world have generally confirmed the major findings of Borkenstein and his associates. All the studies showed an exponential increase in crash and injury risk as a function of BAC, especially the risk of fatal and severe injuries (Hurst, 1985; Traynor, 2005). This exponential increase was apparent at least up to levels of 0.20 percent BAC (McLean, Holubowycz, and Sandow (1980) in Australia; Zador, Krawchuk, and Voas (2000) in the U.S.; and Maycock (1997) in England). In France, a comparison between drivers injured in alcohol-related crashes and non-injury patients matched for age and gender showed that the injured drivers were four times as likely to have BAC levels of 0.05 percent or higher (the legal limit in France) than the matched control patients (Mura *et al.*, 2003). In Sweden, an analysis of the blood of 920 fatally injured drivers revealed that 22 percent had alcohol with a median level exceeding 0.15 percent BAC (Holmgren, Holmgren, and Ahlner, 2005).

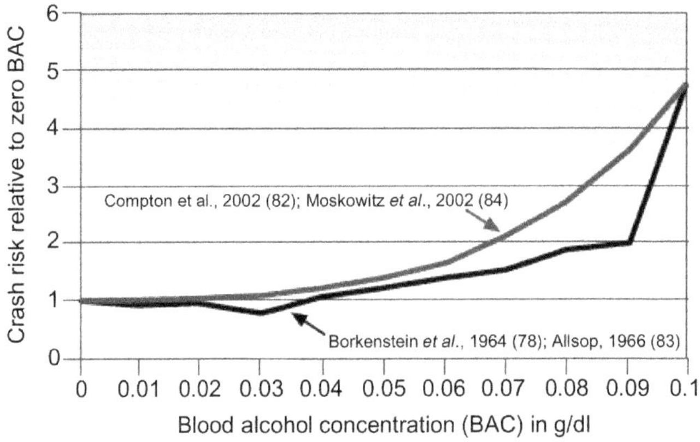

Figure 11-3. The crash risk with BAC > 0 relative to no alcohol, based on Borkenstein *et al.*'s (1964) data, and on the adjusted data from Moskowitz *et al.* (2002) and Compton *et al.*'s (2002) data for BAC levels equal to or less than 0.1%.

Despite the overwhelming evidence for the strong relationship between crash involvement and BAC, all of these data do not necessarily imply cause-and-effect relationship. The causal link is supplied by the experimental research on the relationship between alcohol consumption and impairments in driving-related functions (as reviewed above), and by additional in-depth analyses of the crash data. In these additional analyses, Borkenstein *et al.* showed that when the crashes of the culpable and non-culpable drivers were analyzed separately the relative risk of the culpable drivers increased at an even higher rate, while the relative risk of the non-culpable drivers remained close to 1.0 at all BAC levels. Later analysis of Borkenstein *et al.*'s data and the data from two other (much smaller) studies also showed a higher crash risk for the culpable drivers than for the non-culpable drivers (Hurst, 1973).

But there remained some unanswered questions. The Grand Rapids study was done nearly 50 years ago and there were several significant reasons for doing another comprehensive study to assess the crash risk associated with alcohol. First, although the crash and control samples were quite large, they were not matched on several critical factors, including the time and location of the accident and the direction of travel of the drivers. The control drivers were drivers who happened to drive through 200 sites that were randomly sampled from a pool of 2,000 sites in the same general area that had one or more accidents in the past three years. The control drivers were stopped at the time and day-of-week that the accidents occurred at these sites but *not* at the specific locations and times where the *study* crash-involved drivers had their accidents. Second, although data on some variables associated with alcohol consumption were collected – such as age, gender, drinking practices and education – these data were not considered in the determination of the final relationship between BAC and crash risk (Moskowitz *et al.*, 2002). These shortcomings can be quite significant because it is possible that better matching on these variables would have yielded more control drivers with alcohol in their blood. For example, control drivers traveling in the direction away from a bar are more likely to have alcohol in their blood than drivers traveling toward the same bar, and control drivers sampled during the day are less likely to have alcohol in their blood than drivers sampled at night, when most alcohol-related crashes occur. Third, both the techniques for measuring BAC and the statistical analysis procedures have become more sophisticated and accurate over the past four decades. Fourth, data on many confounding variables that are now known to be relevant to alcohol abuse and crash involvement were either not collected at the time or – as noted above – were not utilized in determining the crash risk. Fifth, it is also possible that over that period changes in driving and/or drinking patterns and improvements in vehicle and roadways may have changed the nature of the relationship. For example, in Japan the relative risk of death due to alcohol-impaired driving for passenger car drivers was 5.5 in 1986 but it rose to 8.0 in 2001 (Hitosugi *et al.*, 2003). This of course may have been due to either changes in the driving environment or to higher BACs consumed by drivers in 2001 than in 1986. Sixth and last, as can be seen in Figure 11-3 in the original study there was a slight dip in the curve at low alcohol levels, suggesting that with low amounts of alcohol, the crash risk is actually less than without any alcohol. Various explanations for this – potentially spurious – effect have been offered including that it was an artifact of an inadequate statistical analysis (Hurst, Harte, and Frith, 1994) or that it was due to fatigue of the control drivers (Corfitsen, 2003). But these explanations were post-hoc, and the results as presented still flew in the face of most of the experimental data that has accumulated since then that showed that alcohol at nearly all levels impairs performance in a dose-related manner (Moskowitz and Fiorentino, 2000; Moskowitz and Robinson, 1988).

In light of these considerations, in 1997-1999 the U.S. National Highway Traffic Safety Administration conducted an alcohol crash risk study (Blomberg *et al.*, 2004; Compton *et al.*, 2002). The study was conducted in Florida and California and included 4,919 crash-involved drivers and 10,066 matched control drivers. For every crash-involved driver, two matched control drivers were sampled. To match the two groups as closely as possible, for each crash-involved driver the two control drivers were sampled from the traffic stream of drivers traveling on the same road at the same location at the same day of the week, at the same time, and in the same direction a week after the crash.

The NHTSA study also had two unique features that were not included in the Grand Rapids study. One was an intense effort to locate every crash-involved hit-and-run driver. This was important because hit-and-run drivers constituted a significant 12 percent of the crash-involved drivers, and the 16 percent of these drivers that were apprehended within a short time of the crash had much higher BACs than the crash-involved drivers who did not try to escape the accident scene. This implied that the absence of their data in Borkenstein *et al.*'s study created an under-estimate of the effects of alcohol. Therefore, in the new study BAC levels for all hit-and-run drivers were estimated using the BAC frequency distribution obtained from those who were caught (Moskowitz *et al.*, 2002). The second feature of the new study was the derivation of an estimated BAC for the drivers who refused to take the breath test. This was done by using passive alcohol sensors, which provide an estimate of the BAC on the basis of the air 15 centimeter away from the driver's face. Typically these sensors are imbedded in the arresting officer's flashlight, and they can be unobtrusively activated while the officer shines the light in the driver's face. This technology was not available at the time of Borkenstein *et al.*'s 1964 study.

In summary, to obtain the BAC-related crash risk, it was necessary to adjust for three types of confounding variables that co-varied with alcohol consumption: (1) driver age, gender, and socio-economic and other demographic variables that do not have a direct causal relationship to alcohol but are associated with drinking and driving, (2) BAC refusals, and (3) BAC of hit-and-run drivers. The regression function that resulted after controlling for these factors is depicted in the upper curve in Figure 11-4. Interestingly, without these adjustments, the raw data of the new study also had a dip in the function yielding relative risks slightly less than 1.0 for BAC of 0.01-0.04 percent. However, in the final model, after adjusting for the above confounding variables, there is a continuous increase in the crash risk that becomes statistically significant at levels of 0.04 percent BAC and above. Thus, once the statistical biases are controlled for, and despite other improvements in the driver-vehicle-roadway system, it appears that the relationship between alcohol ingestion and crash involvement is just as stable and ominous as demonstrated by Borkenstein *et al.* half a century ago.

The impact of the adjustments for the demographic covariates, the missing data, and the hit-and-run drivers is most noticeable at higher BACs, because these biasing factors – especially the BACs of the non-cooperative drivers – play a much greater role at the

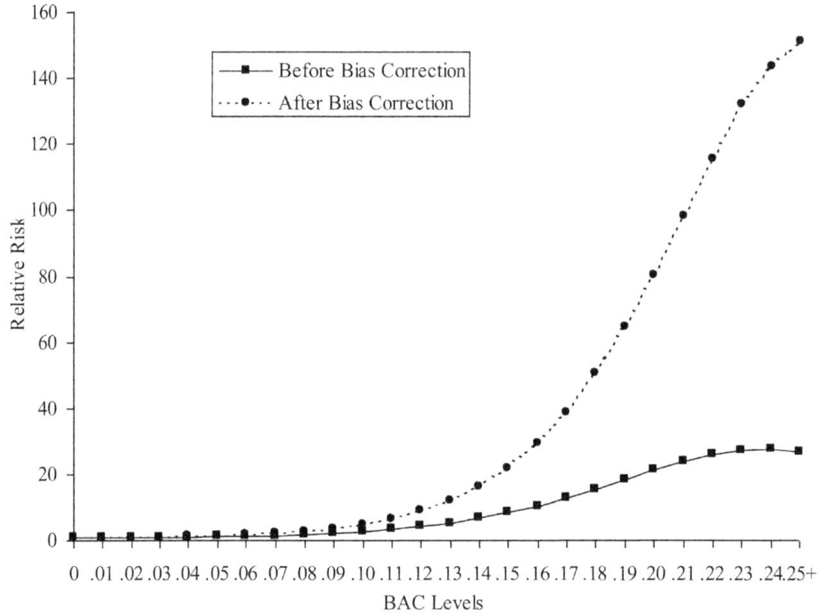

Figure 11-4. Alcohol-related crash risk as a function of BAC at levels of up to 0.25%, before and after adjustment for bias from covariates, refusals, and hit-and-run crash drivers (from Compton *et al.*, 2002).

higher BACs. To illustrate, 82 percent of the crash-involved drivers had no alcohol in their blood, and only 3.2 percent of the crash-involved drivers had BACs > 0.20 percent. In contrast, of the hit-and-run drivers that were apprehended only 31 percent had no alcohol in their blood, and 22 percent – seven times as many – had BACs > 0.20 percent.

Thus, at higher BACs the unadjusted and adjusted curves diverge significantly, and the exponential and very dangerous nature of the relationship between drinking and crash risk becomes more dramatic as illustrated in Figure 11-4 and Table 11-4. After adjustment, with a BAC of 0.25 percent (there were very few drivers with higher levels), the relative crash risk is over 150 times that of a driver with zero BAC! Of course, with that much alcohol in their blood, most drivers may not even be able to walk to the car, open its door, and start it; let alone make it home safely.

Perhaps the largest epidemiological study of crash risk from alcohol (and drugs – see Chapter 12) is the European study best known by its acronym DRUID (Driving Under the Influence of Drugs, Alcohol and Medicine). In that study (Hels *et al.*, 2011), alcohol and drug tests were conducted on 3,602 seriously injured (MAIS > 2) or killed drivers, and on a non-crash control sample of 37,749 drivers in the same countries (Belgium, Denmark, Finland, Italy, Lithuania, Netherlands, Norway, Portugal, and Sweden). Probably because of large differences among the countries in the sampling, data collection, and drug/alcohol testing procedures, the calculated risks differed widely among the countries. Nonetheless, in terms of the alcohol crash risk the results were quite consistent in showing the exponential rise of injury or fatality risk as a function of alcohol concentration. However, the variability among the countries was extremely large. For example, for low alcohol levels (<0.05 percent) the age- and gender-adjusted odds ratio for the pooled data set was 1.18. And because of the large variance among the countries, alcohol at that level did not constitute a statistically significant increased risk for injury. The risks varied from as low as 0.56 (in Italy) to 6.55 (in Finland); that is, from actually reducing injury risk to multiplying it by more than six-fold. For the pooled data the relative risks were 3.6 for 0.05 ≤ BAC < 0.08, 13.4 for 0.08 ≤ BAC < 0.12, and 62.8 for BAC ≥ 0.12. The pooled average relative risks for getting killed in a crash were 8.0, 45.9, 35.7, and 500.0, respectively. Thus, at each alcohol concentration the risk of fatality was actually higher than the risk of serious injury. Also, the risk of fatality was higher for alcohol concentrations of .05 < BAC < .08 than at 0.08 ≤ BAC ≤ 0.12, which is definitely counterintuitive. Such results and the large differences among countries make the interpretation of the European findings a bit difficult.

To reassess the role of alcohol (and other drugs – see Chapter 12) in crash risk, with a more robust set of data, in 2013-2014 NHTSA conducted a new crash risk study, using the exact case-control methodology of their previous study, but with a slightly smaller sample and in only one location (Virginia Beach, VA) (Compton and Berning, 2015). Thus, although the data were obtained in only one location in the U.S., the methodology – and therefore the results – were much more robust and reliable than those of the European DRUID study. The new study included 3,887 crash-involved drivers and 7,397 control drivers. The results of this study – where odds ratios are adjusted for age and gender – are

Table 11-4. Crash risk as a function of BAC based on the Grand Rapids raw data, the NHTSA raw data, and the NHTSA 1997-1999 study after adjustment for biases (from Compton *et al.*, 2002), and the NHTSA 2013-2014 survey (from Compton and Berning, 2015).

<table>
<tr><th rowspan="2">BAC Level</th><th rowspan="2">Grand Rapids (1964)</th><th colspan="3">NHTSA (1997-1999)</th><th></th></tr>
<tr><th>No covariates</th><th>Non-reactive demographic covariates</th><th>Final adjusted estimate</th><th>NHTSA (2013-2014)</th></tr>
<tr><td>.00</td><td>1.00</td><td>1.00</td><td>1.00</td><td>1.00</td><td>1.00</td></tr>
<tr><td>.01</td><td>0.92</td><td>0.91</td><td>0.94</td><td>1.03</td><td>0.54</td></tr>
<tr><td>.02</td><td>0.96</td><td>0.87</td><td>0.92</td><td>1.03</td><td>0.85</td></tr>
<tr><td>.03</td><td>0.80</td><td>0.87</td><td>0.94</td><td>1.06</td><td>1.20</td></tr>
<tr><td>.04</td><td>1.08</td><td>0.92</td><td>1.00</td><td>1.18</td><td>1.60</td></tr>
<tr><td>.05</td><td>1.21</td><td>1.00</td><td>1.10</td><td>1.38</td><td>2.07</td></tr>
<tr><td>.06</td><td>1.41</td><td>1.13</td><td>1.25</td><td>1.63</td><td>2.61</td></tr>
<tr><td>.07</td><td>1.52</td><td>1.32</td><td>1.46</td><td>2.09</td><td>3.22</td></tr>
<tr><td>.08</td><td>1.88</td><td>1.57</td><td>1.74</td><td>2.69</td><td>3.93</td></tr>
<tr><td>.09</td><td>1.95</td><td>1.92</td><td>2.12</td><td>3.54</td><td>4.73</td></tr>
<tr><td>.10</td><td rowspan="2">5.93</td><td>2.37</td><td>2.62</td><td>4.79</td><td>5.64</td></tr>
<tr><td>.11</td><td>2.98</td><td>3.28</td><td>6.41</td><td>6.67</td></tr>
<tr><td>.12</td><td rowspan="2">4.94</td><td>3.77</td><td>4.14</td><td>8.90</td><td>7.82</td></tr>
<tr><td>.13</td><td>4.78</td><td>5.23</td><td>12.60</td><td>9.11</td></tr>
<tr><td>.14</td><td rowspan="2">10.44</td><td>6.05</td><td>6.60</td><td>16.36</td><td>10.56</td></tr>
<tr><td>.15</td><td>7.61</td><td>8.31</td><td>22.10</td><td>12.18</td></tr>
<tr><td>.16</td><td rowspan="10">21.38</td><td>9.48</td><td>10.35</td><td>29.48</td><td>13.97</td></tr>
<tr><td>.17</td><td>11.64</td><td>12.74</td><td>39.05</td><td>15.96</td></tr>
<tr><td>.18</td><td>14.00</td><td>15.43</td><td>50.99</td><td>18.17</td></tr>
<tr><td>.19</td><td>16.45</td><td>18.31</td><td>65.32</td><td>20.60</td></tr>
<tr><td>.20</td><td>18.78</td><td>21.20</td><td>81.79</td><td rowspan="2"></td></tr>
<tr><td>.21</td><td>20.74</td><td>23.85</td><td>99.78</td></tr>
<tr><td>.22</td><td>22.07</td><td>25.99</td><td>117.72</td><td rowspan="4">23.29</td></tr>
<tr><td>.23</td><td>22.51</td><td>27.30</td><td>134.26</td></tr>
<tr><td>.24</td><td>21.92</td><td>27.55</td><td>146.90</td></tr>
<tr><td>.25+</td><td>20.29</td><td>26.60</td><td>153.68</td></tr>
</table>

presented in the last column of Table 11-4. These results provide slightly higher crash risk estimates than the previous studies, but are similar in showing the exponential rise in crash risk as a function of BAC. At BAC > .05 the crash risk doubles relative to no alcohol, and at BAC > .08 the crash risk is four-fold. Yet, because no adjustment was made for hit-and-run crashes, the estimates at the higher BAC levels are lower than the adjusted ones from the previous NHTSA study. Interestingly, the counterintuitive "dip" in crash risk for very low alcohol levels (0.01-0.02) reappeared.

An even steeper exponential function of the fatality risk was obtained in a study on New Zealand drivers. In this study, Keall, Frith, and Patterson (2005) matched the crash drivers with control drivers driving in the same geographical areas at the same times. In their study, relative to the risk of a crash with no alcohol, the risk with BAC = 0.05 percent was six times the risk of zero alcohol, and the risk with BAC = 0.08 percent was 17. At least part of the higher risks in the New Zealand study could be attributed to the use of different measures of risk: crash risk in the U.S. study and fatality risk in New Zealand. Aside from differences in the populations, culture, and roads (New Zealand's roads are notoriously narrow and winding), fatality risk is likely to be higher than crash risk because alcohol-related crashes typically occur at higher speeds and with greater severity than non-alcohol crashes. The best fitting exponential function based on Keall *et al.*'s data indicated that the fatality risk doubles for every increase of 0.02 percent BAC. However, because their study was based on a sample of only 103 fatally injured drivers (compared to over 5,000 injuries in the U.S. study) its estimates must be treated with some caution. Finally, Elvik *et al.* (2009) summarized the results of multiple studies from the U.S., Norway, the Netherlands, New Zealand, and Sweden and arrived at similar crash risk estimates.

Moderation of alcohol effects by crash and driver characteristics

The effects of alcohol on crash likelihood and injury severity are also moderated by specific crash and driver characteristics. Effects that have been studied include those of the impact speed and driver characteristics such as age, skill, and experience in alcohol consumption.

Fatality risk as a function of crash impact speed

The higher impact of alcohol on fatalities and severe injuries is due not only to the type of crash involved (nighttime, high speed, single vehicle), but apparently also to the reduced survivability of an alcohol-impaired driver relative to a sober driver for crashes with the same impact force. This was demonstrated by Waller *et al.* (1986), when they compared the proportions of alcohol impaired and sober drivers killed in crashes of similar types and similar impact velocities (as measured by the deformation of the vehicles). Their study was based on evaluations of the injuries of over 1.3 million U.S. drivers in crashes. Figure 11-5 shows the proportion of drivers killed as a function of the physical impact of the crash, the crash type, and whether or not the driver had been drinking. As expected, regardless of alcohol involvement, as crash severity increased, so did the probability of being killed. However, and perhaps less predictable, the *rate* of increase in the likelihood of being killed is much greater for the alcohol involved drivers; reaching

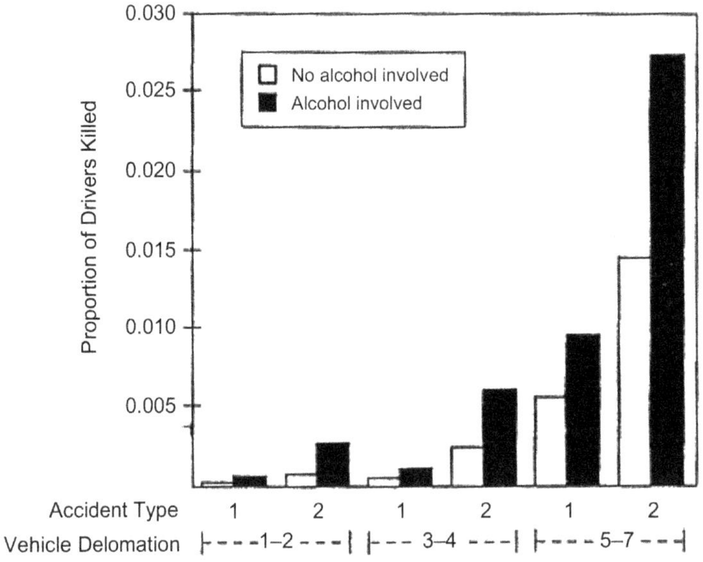

Figure 11-5. Estimated proportion of drivers killed as a function of vehicle deformation, crash type, and driver alcohol consumption. Solid bars indicate alcohol involved drivers. Type 1 accident is angle, rear-end, or other single vehicle; type 2 is overturn, head-on, or hit fixed-object. Vehicle deformation is rated on a 7-point scale with 1 being the least damage and 7 being the most (from Waller *et al.*, 1986, with permission from the American Medical Association).

probabilities that are twice as high for alcohol involved drivers as for sober drivers for the most severe head-on, overturn, and hit-fixed-object crashes. In a more recent analysis, Bédard *et al.* (2002) evaluated the driver fatality risk in single-vehicle fatal crashes that occurred in the U.S. from 1975 to 1998 and involved at least two vehicle occupants (thus, the driver was not necessarily the person who was killed). They found that after controlling for driver age and gender, drivers with BAC > 0.20 percent were more likely to die in the crash than drivers with no alcohol, and drivers with BAC > 0.30 percent were more than three times as likely to die in a crash than drivers with no alcohol in their blood. Together, these two studies demonstrate that alcohol not only increases the likelihood of a crash, but also the severity of injuries once the crash occurs.

Risk by age

In general, younger drivers are at greater risk of injury in alcohol-related crashes than older drivers. Keall, Frith, and Patterson (2004), in the study mentioned above, also analyzed their data separately for different age groups and found that young drivers are more susceptible to alcohol effects than older more experienced drivers. At all BAC levels the fatality risk of drivers 15-19 years old was five times as high as it was for 30+ years old adults, and the risk of 20-29 years old adults was three times as high. Furthermore, as noted above, for every age group, the risk doubled for every 0.02 percent increase in BAC, as illustrated in Figure 11-6 (from Keall *et al.*, 2004, as presented

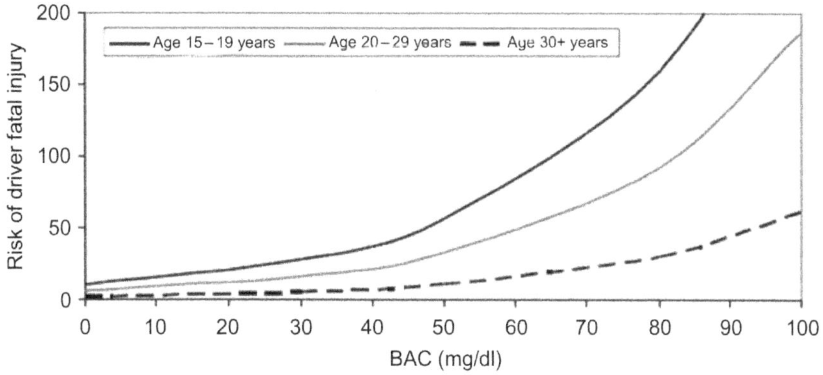

Figure 11-6. The risk of fatal injury as a function of BAC (in mg/dl) for different age groups, relative to 30+ years old sober drivers in New Zealand (from Keall *et al.*, 2004, with permission from Elsevier).

in OECD, 2006). Blomberg *et al.* (2004) also found that the crash risk of young drivers was higher than that of older drivers, though as the BAC levels got higher and higher, the age-related differences diminished – with the risk becoming extremely but equally high for drivers of all ages. Similar findings were obtained in the U.S. by Preusser (2002) and by Peck *et al.* (2008). For example, in Peck *et al.*'s study, the relative crash risk for drivers under 21 increased from 1.0 at 0.0 percent BAC quite rapidly to 2.6 at 0.05 percent, and then to 39.2 at BAC ≥ 0.08 percent. In contrast, at the same BAC levels the relative risk for adults 21+ years old did not increase above 1.0 until the BAC was greater than 0.05 percent and reached "only" 6.6 at BAC ≥ 0.08 percent. These findings indicate that the effects of alcohol and young age are synergistic. The young drivers' inexperience in both driving skills and in coping with alcohol makes them much more susceptible to crashes than older drivers. It is also likely that young drivers who drink and drive are higher risk takers as the DWI threshold for young drivers in both countries (under 20 in New Zealand) is 0.0 percent BAC. These findings, obtained at two ends of the world provide strong support for zero tolerance for alcohol for young drivers.

Driving skill

Because alcohol impairs the cognitive driving-related functions, and because many components of driving are automated (and hence we are able to do many of them with minimal attention), it is reasonable to assume that more experienced and skilled drivers for whom driving is more automated would also be less impaired by alcohol. There is some support for this from at least two studies. In the first study, Harrison and Fillmore (2005) trained drivers to drive in a simulator, and then dosed them with alcohol (to 0.08 percent BAC) or with a placebo. As they hypothesized, driving performance was worse with alcohol than with the placebo, but drivers who had better vehicle control before the dosing were less affected by the alcohol than drivers with poor vehicle control. In the second study, Freydier *et al.* (2014) evaluated driving performance of novice drivers with less than 2 months of driving experience and experienced drivers with 3+ years of experience. Part of the driving task, in a fixed base simulator was to follow a lead car at a fixed distance. The drivers in both groups were "social drinkers" who did not drink more than two glasses of alcohol chiefly in a social context. All drivers performed the driving task with 0, 0.02, and 0.05 percent BAC. Here too, the degree of impairment from alcohol was moderated by experience. Novice drivers significantly reduced their headways when under the effect of 0.05 percent BAC, whereas experienced drivers maintained very similar headways – which were longer than the novice drivers' reduced headways – under all conditions. It is possible, however, that the shorter headways were a reflection of greater risk taking under alcohol than greater skill impairment. Thus, until more evidence accumulates, it is probably premature to assume that better drivers can handle drinking and driving significantly better than novice drivers.

Risk by drinking frequency

We all know some people who can "handle" their alcohol better than others. One contributor to that ability is the amount of practice people have at exercising this "skill"; that is the frequency with which these people regularly drink. At least part of that skill is due to the fact that experienced drinkers are more efficient at eliminating alcohol from their blood. There is also some direct empirical support for this belief that people who are used to drinking are less affected by it. It comes from a reanalysis of the Grand Rapids data by Hurst (1973). Hurst analyzed the crash likelihood as a function of BAC separately for different groups of drivers who reported different frequencies of drinking, and his results are shown in Figure 11-7. In this figure, each line represents a different

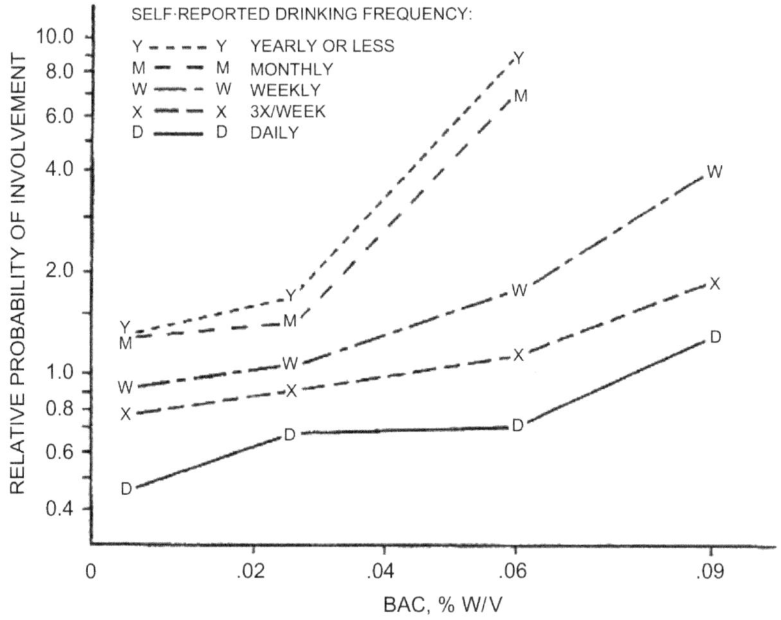

Figure 11-7. The relative risk of a crash as a function of BAC, for drivers with varying frequencies of drinking (from Hurst, 1973, based on a reanalysis of Borkenstein *et al.*'s data, with permission from Elsevier).

reported frequency of drinking. In addition to the increase in crash risk with increasing BACs, we can see that the risk of a crash is inversely related to the frequency of drinking: the more often a person drinks, the less he or she is likely to be involved in a crash at each BAC level. At one extreme end are daily imbibers who at all BAC levels measured in Borkenstein *et al.*'s study were actually below or at the risk level of the randomly sampled sober drivers. At the other extreme end are the very infrequent drinkers, who seem to be impaired by even the smallest amounts of alcohol. Lest this conclusion be interpreted as an endorsement of frequent drinking, it is important to consider that the data from the very frequent drinkers are based on very small samples in the control group – probably because the control drivers were not sampled at the same times and places as the crash-involved drivers. Also, in a controlled study using a driving simulator and a divided attention test, Moskowitz *et al.* (2000) failed to find consistent differences in the amount of impairment from alcohol between light drinkers, moderate drinkers, and heavy drinkers (a categorization based on their reported frequency and quantity of drinking). Although Moskowitz *et al.*'s study was based on an artificial simulator and divided attention tasks, it had the advantage that the driving experience of different groups of drinkers was essentially the same, whereas in naturalistic observational studies drinking experience is typically correlated with age, and therefore with driving experience. Thus, in Hurst's reanalysis of Borkenstein *et al.*'s study, part of the effect of drinking experience may be attributed to age and driving experience which are confounded. Finally, one should remember that frequent and heavy drinking have an undeniable negative effects on health and longevity.

Combining alcohol with (other) drugs

One complication in the assessment of DWI in naturalistic driving is the tendency of alcohol-impaired drivers to combine alcohol with other drugs. The impact of these combinations on performance – discussed in detail in Chapter 12 – is greatly determined by the dose levels and the nature of the other drugs. The issue is mentioned here because the frequency of such combinations, though it is probably culture-specific, is not negligible. For example, in a random stratified sample of the U.S. drivers on weekend nights, Voas, Lacey, Jones, Scherer, and Compton (2013), using a saliva test, found that approximately 27 percent of the drivers with BAC > 0.05 percent had a trace of some illegal drugs in their system, mostly marijuana. In contrast, only 10 percent of the unimpaired drivers had any detectible drugs in their saliva. Although these results were published in 2013, the data were collected in 2007, and since then drug use – especially marijuana and especially in the U.S. where it is undergoing decriminalization – has increased significantly.

DWI Countermeasures

The list of recommended and tried strategies to reduce DWI is very long. Typically it takes a concerted effort involving different agencies and delivery mechanisms to have a significant impact on DWI. No single technique has proven to be effective, and no single strategy is applied in a vacuum. Instead, there are two or more activities at play that affect the outcome, and it is not always easy to disaggregate the contributions of the individual components. A comprehensive summary of the effectiveness and costs of implementation of different behavioral and regulatory DWI countermeasures is available in NHTSA's Countermeasures that Work (Goodwin *et al.*, 2015). The strategies to deal with DWI are grouped below into legislative actions, motivational/media approaches, enforcement efforts, actions directed at repeat offenders, and post-drinking techniques to reduce impairment.

Legislation – BAC levels, zero tolerance and minimum legal drinking age laws

There are multiple effective legislative approaches to reduce drinking and driving. In the U.S., an independent Task Force on Community Preventive Services (2001) reviewed the extensive literature in this area and came up with several recommendations including minimum drinking age, reducing the BAC threshold and zero BAC tolerance for young drivers. By now most of the recommendations have been adopted by all states in the U.S. However, a recent analysis by Fell *et al.* (2016) revealed that very few states have adapted *all* the effective laws targeted at drinking and driving of young drivers – the highest risk age group (see Chapter 6). These and some additional approaches as well as the research supporting them are described below.

Maximum allowable blood alcohol concentration (BAC) for drivers
All or nearly all countries specify maximum legal limits of BAC for driving. These "per se" laws imply that a driver who has more alcohol in his or her blood than the allowed level is considered alcohol-impaired, regardless of whether or not a behavioral impairment is demonstrable. The introduction of such laws – when they are adequately advertised and enforced – is an effective DWI countermeasure. This was demonstrated quite early, in 1966 and 1967 – two and three years after the publication of Borkenstein *et al.*'s study – when Australia and the United Kingdom, respectively, established per se laws making it illegal to drive with BAC of 0.05 percent or more (Australia) and 0.08 percent or more (U.K.). To illustrate the effect of the law in the United Kingdom, in the 21 months prior to its introduction in September 1967, the associated number of fatalities and serious injuries on weekend nights in England and Wales was quite stable around 1,200. Following the law there was an immediate and dramatic drop of 66 percent in injuries and fatalities (Ross, 1988). However, it is important to point out that these data only show an association between the law and injuries and not a *causal* link between the two. Also, such dramatic changes are due in part to the extensive media coverage that preceded the law and the massive enforcement that followed it. Thus, in effect we see here the effects of a confluence of three strategies: public media campaigns that precede the law, the law change, and the enforcement that follows it. Yet even under these linked efforts fatalities and injuries began to increase gradually shortly after the passage of the law, until they leveled off at about 900 two years after the passage of the law.

But legislation only provides a foundation upon which other actions can be taken. When media coverage and enforcement are low, the mere introduction of BAC limits is not as effective, and Canada's passage of BAC = 0.08 percent limit in 1969 is a case in point (Evans, 1991).

Per se laws provide law enforcement authorities with a powerful tool, because they do not require any other overt symptoms (that are not always easy to detect at night on the road by an officer). Table 11-5 shows the per se BAC limits in many of countries. Given our knowledge of the effects of various BACs, and the fact that almost any measurable amount of alcohol is detrimental to some driving-related functions, it may be surprising that most countries are willing to tolerate any BAC greater than 0.0. This is because the legal threshold level is a political decision based on a compromise between what the public and alcohol industry will bear and what the safety community desires, and not a strictly safety-based decision. Nonetheless, the worldwide trend is to lower the BAC

Table 11-5. The legal percent Blood Alcohol Concentrations (BAC) for non-commercial adult drivers in 83 countries (from drinkdriving.org, and OECD, 2014).

BAC	**Countries**
Zero	Armenia, Azerbaijan, Czech Republic, Hungary, Jordan, Kyrgyzstan, Romania, Slovak Republic, Uzbekistan (9 countries)
0.01%	Albania (1)
0.02%	Columbia, Estonia*, Norway, Poland, Serbia, Sudan, Sweden (7)
0.03%	Chile, China, Georgia*, India, Japan, Moldova, Russia*, Turkmenistan (8)
0.04%	Belarus, Lithuania* (2)
0.05%	Argentina, Australia, Austria, Belgium, Bosnia Herzegovina, Bulgaria, Costa Rica, Croatia, Cyprus, Denmark, Finland, France, Germany, Greece, Iceland, Israel, Italy, Latvia, Macedonia, Monaco, Namibia, Netherlands, New Zealand, Peru*, Portugal*, Slovenia, South Africa, South Korea, Spain, Swaziland*, Switzerland, Taiwan, Thailand, Turkey, Yugoslavia (36)
0.08%	Belize, Brazil, Canada, Ecuador, Fiji, Ghana, Ireland, Jamaica, Luxembourg, Malaysia, Malta, Mauritius, Puerto Rico, Singapore, Tanzania, Uganda, United Kingdom, USA, Zimbabwe (19)
Note	Over 75 percent (i.e., 63) of the 82 applicable countries have a BAC limit $\leq$ 0.05% (not counting countries with religiously mandated zero limits such as Bahrain, Mali, Pakistan, Saudi Arabia, and the United Arab Emirates).

Note: Not all data come from official government documents. Some are from secondary sources (noted by an *). Many countries have lower limits for professional drivers, young drivers, and inexperienced drivers.

thresholds. For example, since the publication of the first edition of this book in 2007, New Zealand lowered its level from 0.08 to 0.05 percent, Chile lowered its threshold from 0.05 to 0.03 percent, and Serbia lowered its level from 0.03 to 0.02 percent. In addition, because young and novice drivers are the highest risk group of drivers (see Chapter 6), many countries have zero tolerance laws (0.0 BAC level) for young and novice drivers (e.g., 18 EU countries, Israel, New Zealand, U.S.). Also, because professional drivers have added responsibility, they are limited to 0.0-0.02 BAC in 18 EU countries (Mercier-Guyon, 2014). In 2011, the European Parliament initiated an effort towards an EU-wide harmonized BAC level, with zero tolerance for novice and professional drivers (ETSC, 2012). In fact, the European Transport Safety Commission (2012) has gone even further in recommending zero alcohol tolerance for all drivers.

In general, when sufficiently publicized and enforced, lowering the BAC legal threshold is accompanied by a significant lowering of alcohol-related crashes. This has been quite effectively demonstrated in the U.S. in an evaluation of the effects of lowering the BAC from 0.10 to 0.08 percent. Based on an analysis of the effects obtained in 19 jurisdictions on nighttime crashes Bernat, Dunsmuir, and Wagenaar (2004) concluded that the law had a net effect of reducing single-vehicle nighttime fatal crashes by 5.2 percent. An independent evaluation of the BAC change in a nearly identical set of U.S. states was conducted by Tippetts *et al.* (2005). However, they used a more directly related measure of effectiveness: the numbers of drivers with BACs greater than zero who were killed in a crash. Using this measure, Tippetts and his colleagues were able to both include multi-vehicle alcohol-related crashes and exclude single-vehicle crashes that were not alcohol-related from being considered as relevant crashes. In separate analyses for each jurisdiction, Tippets *et al.* obtained statistically significant reductions in the number of people killed with alcohol in their blood in nine of the 19 jurisdictions. When summed across all jurisdictions, the overall effect was significant in both the statistical sense and the practical sense: yielding an average 15 percent reduction in fatalities. Their detailed analyses also showed that the magnitude of the effect was generally higher in states that had frequent sobriety checkpoints and administrative license revocation laws (see below). In short, in states that had more intensive enforcement. In Japan, according to Hitosugi *et al.* (2003) lowering the legal BAC threshold in 2002 from 0.025 to 0.015 percent was followed with a 5 percent reduction in all traffic fatalities – an impressive reduction, especially given the very low threshold already in effect. Still, it should be noted that most drivers involved in alcohol-related crashes have BAC levels that are far higher than the legal limit. For example, in the U.S. as late as 2003, 84 percent of the drivers involved in alcohol-related fatal crashes had BAC above 0.08 percent and 50 percent of the drivers had BAC of 0.16+ percent – twice the legal limit – or higher (NHTSA, 2004b).

Still, lowering BAC is not always followed by the expected decline in alcohol-related crashes. An evaluation of a change in the limit in Denmark from 0.08 to 0.05 percent showed that although people were aware of the change, and reported appropriate changes in their drinking and driving habits, there was no drop in alcohol-related crashes. In fact, the institution of the law was actually followed by an increase in the proportion of fatal alcohol-related crashes; though the alcohol levels involved were a little lower than before the change (Bernhoft and Behrnsdorff, 2003). In a parallel fashion, raising the BAC level does not necessarily imply an increase in DWI-related crashes. A case in point was provided in Germany (Vollrath, Krüger, and Lobmann, 2005). Following the reunification of the East and the West in 1993, the legal BAC in East Germany was raised from the stringent zero tolerance (BAC = 0.0 percent) to the legal limit in West Germany of BAC = 0.08 percent. An analysis of the effects of the change on the East German drivers' drinking and driving habits and on their alcohol-related crashes, relative to the changes and trends over that period in West Germany revealed that the effects were negligible. No discernible effects were observed in the trends in alcohol-related crashes, and the number of drivers who drove under the influence of alcohol did not change. The only significant effect of the change was that the BAC levels of those driving after drinking increased, especially among the young drivers. In attempting to interpret these results, Vollrath *et al.* (2005) suggest that this is quite consistent with everything else we know about the difficult problem of reducing DWI. In their own words, "it seems that legal changes play a secondary role in preventing DUI incidents. BAC limits are a necessary prerequisite for the police and society to be able to act against DUI episodes. However, whether drivers accept these BAC limits depends on other factors like the prevailing social attitudes and the activity of the police" (p. 392). The obvious implication of this statement is that the previous 0.0 percent BAC limit in East Germany was not consistently enforced, and the law in many cases was irrelevant.

Zero Tolerance for young and novice drivers, and minimum drinking age laws

Despite pressures from the alcohol beverage industry, some countries have set the BAC at 0.0 percent (see Table 11-5). Also, as mentioned above, many countries with BAC thresholds greater than zero have "zero tolerance," or essentially a BAC = 0.0 percent for special subpopulations – particularly young and novice drivers (e.g., U.S., Israel, and many EU countries; Mercier-Guyon, 2014). Independently setting minimum drinking age at an age that is older than the minimum licensing age is also an effective approach to reducing teen drunk driving. In the U.S., in the wake of an act of Congress encouraging all states to set 21 as a minimum legal drinking age, the minimum legal drinking age was raised to 21 in all states by 1987. The impact of this law on both teenage drinking and young driver crashes was quite conclusive. Wagenaar and Toomey (2002) reviewed 241(!) empirical evaluations of the impact of this change and found that of the studies meeting their requirements for methodological and analytical robustness, 58 percent found a reduction in crashes following the raising of the drinking age, and none found an increase in crashes. Considering the various methods employed, and the various specific provisions, levels of enforcement, and socio-demographic characteristics involved, and the different measures used to evaluate the law's impact, we can state unequivocally that raising the minimum legal drinking age reduces alcohol consumption by young drivers and decreases their involvement in drinking and driving crashes. In the U.S., minimum drinking age laws were estimated by the National Highway Traffic Safety Administration to have saved 4,669 lives in the seven years period 2006-2012 (NHTSA, 2012, 2013a). However, the effectiveness of such laws is a function of the complete system involved. For example, Ferguson and Williams (2002) compared the level of awareness of the zero tolerance laws in three states in the U.S. and found, as they expected, that in the state where the laws were most difficult to enforce the awareness of the law among young drivers was the lowest, and the perceived likelihood of being arrested and having the license suspended was the lowest. The enforceability of the law depends not only on the police, but also on the community. The more the community is involved in preventing the sale and distribution of alcohol to under-age users, the more effective the laws (Dent, Grube, and Biglan, 2005). Finally, the impact of the law also depends on the procedures and measures used to evaluate it. Carpenter (2004), using self-reports from a large U.S. survey and quantitative modeling techniques, concluded that zero tolerance laws are effective in reducing "heavy episodic drinking" (meaning five or more drinks in one sitting) among males by 13 percent, but do not show conclusive reductions in drunk driving incidents.

Administrative sanctions: license revocation and vehicle impoundment
Another legislative approach is to sanction administrative license revocation (ALR) when a person is arrested for DWI. These laws enable immediate suspension of the driver license without going through arduous, costly, and time-consuming court procedures. This provides for a better contingency between crime and punishment: both by increasing the certainty of a penalty, and by making that penalty immediate. There is voluminous psychological research to show that the contingency between behavior and its consequences, known as Thorondike's Law of Effect, is critical to any behavior modification (Watson, 1997). Bernat *et al.* (2004) in their evaluation of the effect of lowering the BAC from 0.10 to 0.08% noted that ALR produced a further drop of 10.8 percent in single-vehicle nighttime fatal crashes. In general, ALR and vehicle impoundment are among the most effective DWI countermeasures – especially when accompanied by media campaigns to raise awareness to their implementation (Canadian Center on Substance Abuse, 2014; Goodwin *et al.*, 2015). Their effectiveness is most likely due to the combined immediacy of the action and the perceived severity: immediate denial of independent mobility.

The magnitude of the penalty for DWI
Contrary to many legislators' knee jerk response to DWI, increasing the penalties for drinking and driving does not produce the desired consistent effects. From a utility theory perspective, the perceived "cost" of DWI should be the product of the probability of arrest and the magnitude of the punishment. In this theoretical model for the rational decision maker the two are interchangeable. This formulation provides legislators with an attractive solution: instead of increasing the probability of arrest (through more intensive enforcement efforts), they increase the penalties, hoping to raise the negative utility of risky driving. However, utility theory was developed in the context of economics as a means to define the behavior of the "rational man." In reality, it does not seem to work that well, especially for low probability events. When the perceived likelihood of being apprehended for DWI is very low people tend to perceive it as being essentially zero, and then the size of the penalty is irrelevant (otherwise people would refrain from DWI simply because the penalty of a crash – and possible death – would be enough of a deterrent). In general, most of us are much more sensitive to the likelihood of arrest than to the magnitude of the punishment (Shinar and McKnight, 1986). Thus, not surprisingly, an evaluation of the effects of significant increases in the penalties for DWI in Australia showed that it did not result in a decrease in nighttime single-vehicle accidents, but actually in an increase in these crashes, though a slightly smaller one than the

increase in all types of crashes following the change in the law (Briscoe, 2004). Despite this evidence, the frustrating toll of DWI on innocent victims has led some prosecutors to charge DWI drivers with murder, and at least in one case – in the state of New York – to get a conviction of second degree murder for a repeat DWI offender (Simon, 2008). If not the punishment itself, then hopefully the extensive media coverage of this singular sentence may help.

Cognitive and motivational approaches to discourage DWI

Highway safety knowledge is now part of the information explosion, with driving safety messages vying for the driver's attention and competing with other – mostly commercial – messages. This section describes some of the current approaches to using public information to inform drivers about the dangers of drinking and driving and to motivate them to modify their behavior with regards to drinking and driving.

Informing the motoring public of their BAC

A recurring phenomenon in many research programs and surveys is the (surprising?) finding that many drivers are not aware of the DWI laws and BAC limits in their country (Shinar and Waisel, 2005), lack an understanding of the concept of BAC, and – in case they are familiar with the laws and the concept of BAC – do not know how to translate that information to personal guidelines in terms of the amount of alcohol they can consume before they become legally intoxicated (Johnson and Voas, 2004; Shinar and Waisel, 2005). To ameliorate this, many driver licensing manuals and safety brochures provide brief descriptions of how alcohol affects our behavior, the concept and relevance of BAC to driving, and a table of approximate average BAC levels reached by people of different weights after drinking various amounts of alcohol. Because there are many additional factors that can affect the BAC – including the duration of drinking, the amount of food eaten in conjunction with drinking, and the time that elapsed since drinking – these charts are only approximations. Furthermore, the charts differ for men and women. The same amount of alcohol ingested by a man and a woman of the same weight will result in a higher BAC in the woman than in the man. As noted above, this is because the effect of the alcohol is a function of its dilution in the blood and water, and women's bodies – in general – have less water than men (49 percent versus 58 percent). Table 11-6 is a BAC chart for men. To estimate the BAC for women, the cell entries in the chart should be multiplied by a factor of 1.18 (i.e., the ratio of 58/49).

Despite the fact that most drivers had probably seen such a chart at one time or another (typically when preparing for their licensure), the level of knowledge exhibited by licensed drivers is very low. Consequently many safety programs advocate educating the drivers about alcohol. The need for such education is underscored by the consistent finding that most – especially young college-age – drivers believe they can drink much more than they actually can before they reach the legal limit, and only a small proportion of drivers actually appreciate how little they should drink before they reach the legal limit. This has been repeatedly demonstrated in countries as far apart geographically and

Table 11-6. BAC estimation chart for men of different weights as a function of the number of drinks. One drink equals roughly one shot of whisky, or one 12oz. glass of beer, or one 5oz. glass of wine. To obtain the equivalent BAC estimate for women multiply the BAC by 1.18 (with permission from Virginia Tech, Alcohol Abuse Prevention Center, 2006. http://www.alcohol.vt.edu/Students/alcoholEffects/index.htm).

Drinks	**Weight in Pounds (1 lb = 0.44 kilogram)**								
	100	**120**	**140**	**160**	**180**	**200**	**220**	**240**	
0	.00	.00	.00	.00	.00	.00	.00	.00	Only safe driving limit
1	.04	.03	.03	.02	.02	.02	.02	.02	Driving skills impaired
2	.08	.06	.05	.05	.04	.04	.03	.03	
3	.11	.09	.08	.07	.06	.06	.05	.05	
4	.15	.12	.11	.09	.08	.08	.07	.06	
5	.19	.16	.13	.12	.11	.09	.09	.08	
6	.23	.19	.16	.14	.13	.11	.10	.09	Legally intoxicated
7	.26	.22	.19	.16	.15	.13	.12	.11	
8	.30	.25	.21	.19	.17	.15	.14	.13	
9	.34	.28	.24	.21	.19	.17	.15	.14	
10	.38	.31	.27	.23	.21	.19	.17	.16	Possible death

culturally as Israel (Shinar and Waisel, 2005) and New Zealand (Kypri and Stephenson, 2005), and most EU countries (SARTRE 4, 2012).

Overcoming drivers' ignorance about their limits is not as easy as it may seem, and the benefits of a few programs that have attempted this are not obvious. It appears that even when drivers have information on their BAC, especially if they are over the legal limit, they tend to discount the accuracy of that information, and instead rely more on their subjective perception of intoxication. Because drinking gives a person a sense of confidence, people who drive after drinking tend to feel that they are not as impaired as they actually are (Johnson and Voas, 2004).

It is only when drivers are provided with timely, valid, and individually tailored knowledge – such as when they take a breath test just before leaving a bar – *and* that knowledge is combined with massive DWI enforcement – such as frequent sobriety checkpoints – that intoxicated drivers actually heed that information. This was tested in

Melbourne Australia in the midst of a high-visibility safety enforcement campaign, consisting of intense graphic media campaigns and massive enforcement including frequent random breath testing. In that context, Haworth, Vulcan, and Bowland (1997) found that 16 percent of the people who intended to drive away from the bar and had test results of BAC > 0.05 percent changed their mind about driving. This is a significant effect, but given the immediate high risk of being apprehended for DWI, it is definitely not overwhelming considering that over 80 percent of the people with BAC > .05 percent still intended to drive.

Public Information (PI) dissemination campaigns
Public Information campaigns, delivered through print, audio, video, and roadside signs, are ubiquitous. In the field of traffic safety, PI campaigns addressing seat belts and alcohol are part of the media landscape. In the U.S., warnings against drinking and driving are even printed on all containers of alcoholic beverages, stating that "consumption of alcoholic beverages impairs your ability to drive a car and operate machinery, and may cause health problems." Yet many people who drink alcohol seem to be unaware of this message (HHS, 1997).

To be effective, media campaigns must penetrate the influx of information that is constantly bombarded at us, and then – somehow – make us change our attitudes and behaviors. Elder *et al.* (2004) proposed a model – reproduced in Figure 11-8 – that describes the mechanisms through which PI campaigns can affect drinking and driving behaviors and crashes. The first challenge that has to be addressed is to attract our attention. This can be achieved with humor (as done in billboards in New Zealand), gory images (as done in TV commercials in Victoria Australia), good graphics (as done in posters in England), and puns (as done in commercials in the U.S.). All of these approaches seem to work quite well. The next step – which is the first in Elder *et al.*'s model – is to raise our awareness with respect to the topic presented. Content wise, all PI messages can be classified as belonging to one of two domains: (1) containing information about the enforcement and/or legal consequences of a violation, and/or (2) containing information about personal health consequences. All too often, evaluations of the effectiveness of PI campaigns stop at this level by showing that a significant percent of the population has seen the message, and that a smaller percent actually remembers it (HHS, 1997). However, to claim on that basis that the approach is effective is quite presumptuous and probably quite naïve. Message recall and measures of attitude change are only weakly associated with observable behavioral changes (Wilde, 1995).

The next process in the model is that of internalizing the message: memorizing the information, changing attitudes in accordance with the new information, and changing behavioral dispositions. This is the critical phase because it involves an attitude change. Attitudes are hypothetical constructs consisting of a set of beliefs about a topic, feelings about that topic, and a behavioral tendency toward that topic (Krech, Crutchfield, and Ballachey, 1962). Building on Elder's model, Yadav and Kobayashi (2015) proposed a similar model in which legislation and enforcement serve as the basis for the mass media campaigns. The media's role is to promote behavioral change through emotive and informational advertisements that should transform the existing attitudes. A strong

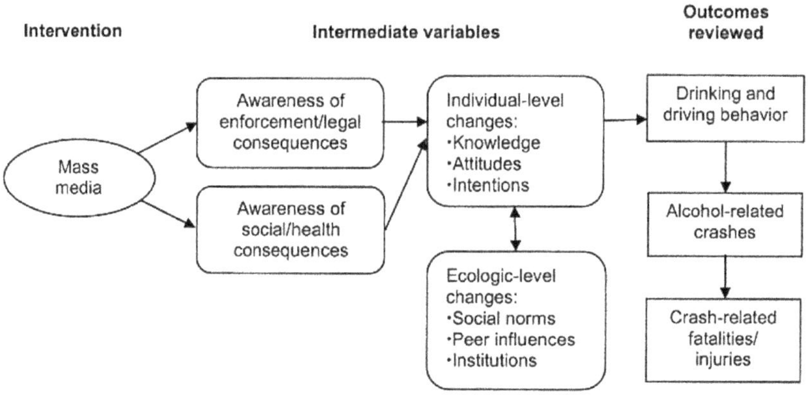

Figure 11-8. A conceptual model of the process by which mass media can affect an individual's knowledge, attitudes, on-road behavior, and ultimately crashes and injuries (from Elder *et al.*, 2004, with permission from Elsevier).

attitude about a topic (such as drinking and driving for people who like to drink on social occasions) involves a consistent relationship among the three components, and any attempt to change the attitude must address all components. And this is where many PI campaigns fail. Providing new knowledge and showing scary graphics at best create an unstable attitude because the new knowledge gained from the information and new feelings aroused by the graphics are inconsistent with the previous feelings (drinking makes me feel good), subjective knowledge (I can handle my alcohol), and current behavioral tendencies (to drink and drive – in that order). At worst such messages motivate a person to avoid exposure to the messages altogether, or to foster disbelief in their content. Thus, an effective campaign must also offer practical alternative behavioral strategies to the potential DWI driver. To make the driver adopt new behavioral tendencies is quite difficult. Even proclamations of intent to change behavior are insufficient proof of an attitude change and a program's effectiveness, because these intentions may not materialize at the right time – that is, after drinking. This, for example, has been the case in Victim Impact Panels, as described below in the context of prevention of recidivism (Shinar and Compton, 1995).

If many people are exposed to the same message and internalize it in the same manner, then we witness a change in the social norms. The new social norms, in turn, exert a strong influence on individuals' tendencies to conform to these norms. Such a normative social upheaval has in fact happened in the area of drinking and driving. A few decades ago it was socially acceptable to drink and then be helped into the car and drive (or attempt to drive) away. Now, in most motorized countries, it is not. At least part of the change in the social norms has been due to grass-roots movements such as Mothers Against Drunk Driving (MADD) and Students Against Drunk Driving (SADD) in the U.S. In an interesting comparison between attitudes towards alcohol-impaired drivers and drivers who texted prior to their accidents, Atchley, Hadlock and Lane (2012) presented college students with different crash scenarios and asked them to rate the drivers' responsibility for each crash and also decide on a fitting fine/jail sentence. In each scenario, the driver's behavior prior to the crash was specified as either being attentive, drinking, talking on the phone, or texting. They found that while the level of responsibility for the crash assigned to the driver was highest for texting, the recommended sentences were more severe for the alcohol-impaired drivers. This was interpreted as an indication that there is a "disconnect between knowledge of how risky the behavior is, and the willingness to find people at fault for violating rules against it" and that "compared to data from the 1970s, the results show that anti-drunk driving campaigns have changed how younger drivers view drunk driving, but that norms have not yet changed for distracted driving." This is good news and bad news: it shows that converging efforts to change social norms and behavior (e.g., towards drinking and driving) can be successful but that it takes time for people to internalize the knowledge in order to change their attitudes (e.g., texting).

Changes in individual and social norms are not the ultimate goal of safety campaigns. These changes are only intermediate variables that must exist to move on to the desired outcome measures: changes in on-road behaviors and consequently a reduction in relevant crashes and injuries. Therefore, the acid test of any safety PI campaign is whether it changes behavior and reduces relevant crashes or not. So are PI campaigns effective in changing our behavior? It turns out that this simple question is quite difficult to answer. This is because most PI campaigns are not conducted in a vacuum, but rather in conjunction with other programs – most notably intensified enforcement. Two systematic reviews of the literature attempted to assess the benefits of DWI-related PI campaigns, one by Elder *et al.* (2004), and a more recent one by Yadav and Kobayashi (2015).

Elder and his colleagues uncovered eight different scientifically sound evaluation studies – conducted in Australia, New Zealand, and the U.S. – that met their criteria for inclusion: they all had objective outcome data in terms of crashes and all had some control for exposure to rule out the effects of some extraneous confounding variables (such as a general downward trend in crashes over time, or changes in the law immediately before or during a campaign). A critical component common to all of these campaigns was that the enforcement level in the area of coverage was quite high and essentially the same before the campaign and during the campaign. Thus, any reduction in alcohol-related crashes could be attributed to the effects of the PI campaign, and not to an increase in enforcement. But, and this is an important "but," because the enforcement levels were already "quite high" the warning about the legal and arrest consequences were justifiably perceived as credible. In the PI campaigns that focused on the personal and social consequences of drinking and driving, the enforcement was not always constant. The best known of these public information safety campaigns – conducted in Victoria, Australia – relied on very graphic and often gruesome short video segments of actual crash victims and crash scenes. However, the campaigns also involved massive increases in enforcements including sobriety checkpoints.

When the outcome measures from the eight studies were combined, they showed a significant decrease in crashes relative to the period before the campaign: the median number of accidents of all types decreased by 13 percent, and injury crashes decreased by 10 percent. In three of the sites, it was also possible to evaluate the benefit-cost ratio, and in all three cases it was quite positive with the societal benefits substantially exceeding the costs involved. Despite these positive findings, the conclusions from this evaluation are still quite tenuous. The number of evaluations were quite small, there were some confounding factors that were not controlled for, the content of the messages differed greatly, and the range of crash reductions varied from zero to 16 percent for the fatal crashes (with only two evaluations), and from 6 to 18 percent for injury crashes. Elder *et al.* (2004), aware of these and other shortcomings, also noted that the eight studies they reviewed evaluated a highly select sample of PI campaigns, in the sense that they were all very well designed, their message style and content were pre-tested to maximize their effectiveness, and the length and frequency of audience exposure were maximized.

Yadav and Kobayashi (2015) also screened the available research and eventually summarized the effects of 19 independent studies that met their inclusion criteria (including three that were included in Elder's study), spanning a period of 30 years (1983-2013). Media activities included advertisements in newspaper, radio, broadcast and cable television, cinema, billboards, posters, banners, stickers, with a combination of paid and earned media. In some of the studies, an enforcement campaign coincided with the media campaign. The enforcement activities included interventions such as speed cameras, compulsory breath testing, sobriety checkpoints, and patrols. Summing the results of these studies that varied markedly in terms of their quality, Yadav and Kobayashi noted that although the median effects on alcohol-related crashes showed reductions of 15.1 percent for campaigns without enforcement and 8.6 percent for campaigns with concomitant enforcement, the "summary effects calculated from seven studies (that used the same measures) showed no evidence of media campaigns reducing the risk of alcohol-related injuries or fatalities." But because the review included both well designed and poorly designed studies, this summary conclusion may not be relevant to all well-planned and well-executed campaigns, and to all methodologically robust evaluation designs.

Very often, as both Elder *et al.* and Yadav and Kobayashi noted, because of lack of expertise and shortage of funding, media campaigns are not very well designed. This results in an inadequate implementation of a potentially good program. Not surprisingly, the evaluation is then quite negative. To avoid such a pitfall, Elder and his associates argue that "it is incumbent upon planners to assess whether they have adequate resources and a supportive environment to implement an effective mass media campaign. If not, the campaign should not be undertaken" (p. 64). This is good advice but one that is hard to follow considering the eagerness to "do something" with whatever means are available. Consequently most PI campaigns are launched without the necessary planning, and their scopes are based almost exclusively on the funds available – funds that typically do not allow for the added cost of an evaluation (often perceived by action-oriented program people as money wasted). But when this advice is followed, and DWI enforcement is intense, a well-designed PI campaign is likely to reduce DWI crashes and be cost-effective.

Elder *et al.*'s and Yadav and Kobayashi's models can also be used to promote social marketing as a means to combat drinking and driving. Social marketing involves the use of marketing strategies to promote public health programs (Janssen *et al.*, 2013). It relies on the basic notion that a consumer – in this case a potential drinking driver – can be enticed to choose between alternatives – drunk driving versus not driving after drinking (or not drinking before driving). To make the latter alternative more attractive, Rothschild, Mastin, and Miller (2006) conducted several focus groups of people who were known to drink and drive in order to determine why they drove after drinking. The researchers discovered that most people were aware that they were impaired but still chose to drive because they felt they did not have a practical and viable alternative. At the end of a night of drinking they were reluctant to leave their car at the bar, and/or did not have enough money for a cab (having spent it all on drinks), and/or liked to drink while they drove, and/or did not like riding in an unkempt taxi. The socially attractive and economically viable alternative that Rothschild and his associates developed consisted of a community organized service of drivers in upscale cars who drove the bar patrons both to the bar and from the bar (when they were called). The drinkers paid for the round-trip cost in advance and could continue to drink on the ride home. Although the program did not eliminate all the drinking and driving events in the community, the number of rides taken was quite high and the reported number of drinking-driving events decreased significantly, especially in the younger 21-34-years-old target group. Thus, in addition to its specific contribution, this program demonstrated the utility of a systematic community effort that is consistent with both community safety and individuals' "needs" to drink. But as appealing as it sounds – it works well in marketing coffee and laundry detergents – social marketing as a structured approach to behavioral change has not quite proven itself yet in reducing irresponsible drinking in general and in driving in particular (Jenssen *et al.*, 2013).

Alternative transportation programs

As in smoking campaigns, it is not enough to scare people about the hazards of DWI. An effective program that subscribes to the philosophy of social marketing should also provide an alternative or a solution. One such solution is the provision of alternative transportation either home or even to another drinking establishment. Various alternative transportation programs have been tried and evaluated, including the use of personal vehicles (with an extra driver to drive the impaired person's car home), limousines (for larger parties), taxis, buses, trolleys that operate all night, tow and ride services, and even scooters. Evaluations of the different programs are complicated and the ones conducted to date have been deficient in one way or another (Decina *et al.*, 2009). However, the concept is good and its implementation in a specific location should be evaluated relative to its practicality which in turn hinges on the cost, availability, and convenience.

Designated driver program

This is another solution to provide transportation to an impaired driver, but one that requires advance planning. As originally conceived the designated driver is one person in a group of people who participate in drinking, who (1) is a priori designated to drive everyone back from the bar or pub, and (2) must abstain from drinking any alcohol while the group is socializing (Ditter *et al.*, 2005). This approach is widely promoted by traffic safety organizations in the U.S., Europe, Australia and some other countries such as Israel. Many alcoholic establishments encourage the concept by offering designated drivers free non-alcoholic drinks as an incentive.

The approach has quite a lot of appeal to different interest groups because it is not expensive to implement, it does not require a major behavioral change, it is consistent with current social norms, and it is typically supported by the beverage industry (because it implicitly sanctions drinking more by the other party members). Despite the promotion and appeal of the program, evaluations of information campaigns to promote the concept have failed to yield a consistent increase in the use of designated drivers (Ditter *et al.*, 2005) or noticeable reductions in alcohol-related crashes (European Union, 2002). One problem is that the designated driver is defined differently by different people. Furthermore, the designated driver, as it is practiced is often quite different from the definition above. All too often that person is not designated in advance, does not agree to refrain from drinking before getting together for the social event, and sometimes even drinks with everyone – but simply drinks less (Ditter *et al.*, 2005; Watson and Watson, 2014). This may be the result of many young drivers' inability to decide as to whether to volunteer to be the designated driver or to join others in persuading someone else to assume that role (European Union, 2002). In one study conducted on college students in California the average BAC level of designated drivers leaving the bar with friends was 0.07 (Timmerman *et al.*, 2003) – a level at which they would be considered legally intoxicated in most countries around the globe (see note at bottom of Table 11-5), but not in the U.S.

Watson and Watson (2014) conducted an evaluation of an Australian designated driver program using a before-after, treatment-control design in two areas of Queensland, Australia. The already existing media-based program, known as "Skipper," was intensely advertised and promoted in one area (treatment) and not in another demographically similar area (the comparison/control area). The several dependent measures of the program effectiveness were all based on self-reports of the people surveyed in the two areas, before the start of the promotion and at two follow-up periods. Despite – or perhaps because – of the careful study design, the researchers found that even though awareness of the Skipper program in the intervention area was very high (rising from 6 percent of the people surveyed to over 70 percent), no significant changes were obtained for any of the key behavioral measures. Relative to the comparison sites there were no differences between before and after the promotion of the program, in the reported incidence of drinking and driving, in the number of positive BAC breath tests, and in the proportion of alcohol-related crashes between the baseline period and the two follow-up periods.

Perhaps the most optimistic summation of the designated driver program was the one provided in the concluding remarks on the impact of the Belgian designated driver program (known in Europe as "Bob") in 2001-2002. "On the one hand, we have a very successful prevention campaign and on the other hand, the number of alcohol tests is decreasing and the number of intoxicated drivers is increasing. Unfortunately, there is no positive effect on the number of accidents. This goes to prove once again that prevention and repression have to go hand in hand. When there is little risk of getting caught (objective and subjective risk), a prevention campaign, no matter how good it may be, cannot be effective. To bring about real change in behavior, deterrence is necessary" (European Union, 2002, p. 16). Thus, despite the extensive publicity of designated driver programs in Belgium, France, Greece, and The Netherlands; despite all the survey findings that show that the "Bob" designated driver campaigns are very well received; and despite the evaluation report's conclusion that the Bob campaigns "make people aware of the dangers of drink driving" (European Union, 2002, p. 43); despite all of these positive indications, in the absence of enforcement these programs fail the crucial test of efficacy as formulated in Elder *et al.*'s model: that of reducing DWI and reducing DWI-related crashes.

Server training

Approximately 40-60 percent of the people arrested for DWI or involved in alcohol-related crashes, do so shortly after they drank too much (usually beer) in a bar, a pub, or a restaurant, rather than after leaving a private residence. This finding has been repeatedly obtained in surveys and studies conducted in the U.S. (McKnight, 1991; O'Donnell, 1985), in Canada (Single and McKenzie, 1989), and in Australia (Stockwell, 1994). Thus, a rational approach to address a significant portion of the DWI issue would be to train pub and bar tenders to detect when a patron is intoxicated and then refuse to sell any more alcohol to that patron. Although this may create a conflict of interests – after all, the goal of a bartender is to sell as much alcohol as possible – owners of bars generally support such programs, possibly in part because in many jurisdictions it is also illegal to serve alcohol to an intoxicated patron. Various training programs have been developed, and several studies of their effectiveness in producing "responsible" serving have been conducted. The results of these studies provide conflicting evidence of their effectiveness, at best. A cautious conclusion that was reached in a report to the U.S. congress in 1997 stated that "evidence suggests that short-term effects of training are modest, and little is known about the long-term effects" (HHS, 1997, p. 12).

There are at least two inter-related reasons for the absence of a clear effect of these programs. One is that it is hard to change bartenders' reluctance to abstain from serving alcohol, even when the motivation is there. The other reason is that the relevant laws are not adequate. In an analysis of 23 "server" laws in different states in the U.S., Mosher *et al.* (2002) identified five necessary components in effective "responsible serving" laws: program requirements, administrative requirements, provisions for enforcement of the law, penalties for lack of compliance with the law, and benefits for participation in training programs. They then noted that almost all states that had such laws were weak in at least one of these components, thereby weakening the effectiveness of the law. These findings are consistent with the conclusions reached 10 years earlier by McKnight (1991) who found that server training was effective in terms of improving the servers' ability to detect and suggest to intoxicated patrons that they should not drink any more, but the effect on actual service if the patron desired it – and the patrons most often did – was essentially nil. The critical element that appears to tip the effectiveness of a server training program is the presence of effective enforcement. When it is there, the likelihood of its effectiveness is much greater than when it is missing (Graham *et al.*, 2014; McKnight and Streff, 1993; Stockwell, 2001).

Even when enforcement is present, it is still only one incentive. Liang, Sloan, and Stout (2004) interviewed 862 bartenders and waiters from a (relatively) representative sample of 545 U.S. bars and taverns in order to determine what incentives actually motivate them to serve responsibly. As expected, the main problem with the various programs is that they have to effectively counteract the monetary incentives that come from the patrons' tips – often the main source of income for waiters and bartenders. In general, they found that employees earned a higher pay when they served people in a manner that may lead to DWI, and did not get any pay incentives when they behaved in ways that would decrease the likelihood of DWI. Still, the employees were more likely to serve responsibly if they perceived that the likelihood of being sued by the owner was high. Thus, owner involvement in the process is critical. But this too is a problem, because the owners have essentially the same conflict of interests as the servers. Interestingly, while the owners in the study were concerned with legal liability, the servers were not. For them, the legal liability was not an effective deterrent, indicating that it was conceptually too far removed from their concerns during work. In summary, for server training to be effective it must be coupled with both legal implications and direct enforcement either by a law enforcement agency (and these are usually preoccupied with other issues) or by the bar owner. Consequently, as Godwin *et al.* (2015) concluded following their review of the literature, if these programs "are not intensive and are not supported, they are unlikely to result in greater refusals of service to intoxicated patrons" (pp. 1-51).

Enforcement

In the choice between the carrot and the stick, in the realm of reducing impaired driving the preference for the stick is ubiquitous. Even in the context of motivational approaches – such as media campaigns, designated driver, and server training – the need to accompany them with visible and sustained enforcement is repeatedly noted. After reviewing the "priority recommendations" of structured evaluation reports of impaired driver programs in 38 states in the U.S., Johnson (2004) concluded that the top recommendation in all states included "increasing the deterrence effect by prioritizing enforcement efforts and enhancing the arrest, prosecution, and adjudication process." This recommendation is quite consistent with the numerous studies that have demonstrated that DWI-targeted enforcement can reduce crashes by an average 3–12 percent, depending on the type of crash. Fortunately, the effects are greater on more severe crashes (Elvik, Mysen, and Vaa, 1997).

The problem with enforcement is that when it is exercised in the absence of media and other motivational approaches, it changes behavior without changing drivers' attitude. While some may consider that irrelevant to highway safety, this is not so. A behavioral change that is made solely because of an external incentive (and massive enforcement is certainly an effective external incentive) can always be justified without necessitating a change in attitude, and thus without generating cognitive dissonance. Cognitive dissonance is the situation when one of the components of an attitude is inconsistent with the others (Festinger, 1957, 1964). For example, if I believe that drinking three glasses of wine does not impair my driving skill (others' perhaps yes, but not mine), and I like to drink, then absent enforcement I will drink and drive. This makes the belief, emotion, and behavioral disposition consistent with each other. However, if enforcement is present then I can always justify refraining from DWI because of it, without having to change my attitude about drinking and driving. In that case once the enforcement is removed I have no reason to refrain from DWI. Thus, enforcement that is not accompanied by an attitude change is a Sisyphean effort: endless, effortful, and in the long-run ineffective because it does not lead to new habits.

There is another problem with enforcement. It is often difficult. Because penalties for DWI are often harsh, drivers apprehended for DWI will often contest the charge with the aid of very skillful lawyers who will often argue that the measurement of BAC based on alcohol breath testing is not accurate. This often leads the police to cite alcohol when the measured breath alcohol concentration (BrAC) is much higher than the legal threshold. A typical case in point is the status quo in Israel. In one detailed study we (Schechtman and Shinar, 2011) obtained a high correlation of 0.91 between BAC and BrAC levels in typical field conditions. Still, at the standard Israeli threshold for DWI of BAC =.05 percent, the measured equivalent of 240 mg/l, did include a few misses (3 percent) and quite a few false alarms (38 percent). To reduce the false alarms – cases where a person's BrAC was above the limit but the actual BAC was not – to 1 percent the breath alcohol threshold had to be raised to over 300 mg/l. Then in a precedent-setting court ruling, the judges added their own safety margin on top of that raising it to 400 mg/l. This level is equivalent to an average BAC of nearly 0.1 percent – twice the nominal legal limit! In the U.S. too, although the per se BAC level is 0.08 percent, the actual BAC levels of most people arrested for DWI are significantly higher (Stuster, 2006), and more than half of the drivers involved in alcohol-related fatal crashes have BACs of 0.15 percent or higher (NHTSA, 2015).

From the perspective of safety, the primary purpose of enforcement is deterrence. An effective enforcement program should deter drivers from committing violations, rather than apprehend drivers after committing them. There are two types of deterrence – specific and general – each requiring a different approach. Let us consider general deterrence first, and then discuss specific deterrence as it is applied to repeat DWI offenders.

General deterrence and the perceived risk of arrest

In the context of drinking and driving, general deterrence is aimed at dissuading all drivers from DWI, and the general tactic used to achieve that involves creating an impression that anyone on the road can be stopped and arrested if he or she is under the influence of alcohol. From the driver's perspective, the perceived risk of DWI is the product of the likelihood of being stopped and arrested and the penalty involved. As noted above, ample research exists to demonstrate that the two are not equivalent, and that a perceived high likelihood of arrest is much more effective than a high penalty. The perceived likelihood of an arrest, in turn, depends on the perceived level of enforcement in terms of the probability of being stopped. This is so important that according to the World Health Organization (2004) within the wider issue of public health "the only consistently effective strategy for dealing with the problem of excess alcohol is to increase the perceived risk of being caught. Such a perception is considered a better deterrent than the severity or the swiftness of the penalty" (p. 83). Unfortunately in most countries – Australia and the Nordic countries being conspicuous exceptions – both the actual and the perceived level of DWI enforcement are quite low (WHO, 2004). In Israel, for example, repeated bi-annual surveys of people exiting pubs showed that their perceived risk of being arrested for DWI was very low and even lower than their perceived risk of having an alcohol-related crash (Shinar and Waisel, 2005).

The perceived probability of arrest can be affected not only by the level of enforcement itself, but also by the intensity of public information that alerts the drivers to the increased enforcement (Shinar and McKnight, 1986). That is why safety departments typically advertise the increase in DWI enforcement on holiday nights. This combined effect of enforcement and media coverage can be quite significant and can increase the perceived risk of apprehension for DWI; and can consequently lead to a drop in DWI-related crashes (Voas, Holder, and Gruenewald, 1997).

DWI Cues and the Standardized Field Sobriety Test (SFST)
Given the wide array of psychomotor and cognitive functions affected by alcohol it was only natural that attempts would be made to provide police officers with a useful behavioral field tool to assess alcohol impairment. Two such tools have been developed: the DWI Cues guidelines and the Standardized Field Sobriety Test (SFST).

The DWI Cues guidelines were developed by the U.S. National Highway Traffic Safety Administration to assist officers in detecting alcohol-impaired driving. The guidelines provide a list of driving behaviors that can be observed by an officer, with associated probabilities that drivers exhibiting these cues are impaired. The original list, developed by Harris (1980), was based on interviewing officers and recording the cues noted by officers in 643 events in which the officers noted various DWI cues exhibited by alcohol-impaired drivers. After the adoption of the 0.08 percent BAC limit by all states, the U.S. National Highway Traffic Safety Administration developed a new version of the DWI detection guide; one that would be applicable to detecting the new lower BAC limits (NHTSA, 2006a). This guide, reproduced in Table 11-7, is based on observations made by officers in the course of over 12,000 enforcement stops. The driving behaviors were manifest in problems with (1) maintaining proper lane position, (2) speed and braking, (3) vigilance, and (4) judgments. The list also contains "Post-Stop Cues" that an officer can observe once the driver has stopped. These include difficulty with the vehicle controls, difficulty exiting the vehicle, fumbling with the license and/or registration, and repeating the officer's questions or comments. Finally, once the driver is ordered to step out of the car the officer can observe additional cues, including swaying, unsteadiness, or balance problems, leaning on the vehicle for balance, slurred speech, slowed responses to questions, giving incorrect information, and odor of alcohol. By being alert to the presence of these cues an officer can have a fairly good indication of the driver's impairment even before administering the formal SFST. In contrast to the high probabilities of DWI associated with these behaviors, the probability of stopping a driver who is DWI in a random nighttime sobriety check in the U.S. is approximately 0.03. This checklist should however be taken with a grain of salt, as not all of these tell-tale cues are supported by

Table 11-7. Estimated probabilities of DWI for drivers exhibiting different symptoms while driving, after being stopped, and after stepping out of their cars (from NHTSA, 2006a).

Category	**Behaviors**	***p*(DWI)**
Problems maintaining proper lane position	Weaving, weaving across lane lines, straddling a lane line, swerving, turning with a wide radius, drifting, almost striking a vehicle or other object	.50-.75
Speed and braking problems	Stopping problems (too far, too short, or too jerky), accelerating or decelerating for no apparent reason, varying speed, slow speed (10+ mph under limit)	.45-.70
Vigilance problems	Driving in opposing lanes or wrong way on one-way, slow response to traffic signals, slow or failure to respond to officer's signals, stopping in lane for no apparent reason, driving without headlights at night, failure to signal or signal inconsistent with action	.55-.65
Judgment problems	Following too closely, improper/unsafe lane change, illegal or improper turn (too fast, jerky, sharp, etc.), driving on other than the designated roadway, stopping inappropriately in response to officer, inappropriate or unusual behavior (throwing, arguing, etc.), appearing to be impaired	.35-.90
Post-stop cues	Difficulty with motor vehicle controls, difficulty exiting the vehicle, fumbling with driver's license or registration, repeating questions or comments, swaying, unsteady, or balance problems, leaning on the vehicle or other object, slurred speech, slow to respond to officer/officer must repeat, provides incorrect information, changes answers, odor of alcoholic beverage from the driver	>.85

Notes: Weaving + any other cue $p > .65$; any 2 cues $p > .50$.
Probability of DWI based on random traffic enforcement stops at night is $p = .03$.

scientific research. For example, the typical reaction of drivers to alcohol is not to reduce speed (as the table suggests) but to increase speed; see for example, Lenné *et al.*, 2010; Ronen *et al.*, 2008, 2010.

The second tool officers have is the Standard Field Sobriety Test (SFST). This test was developed in the 1970s for the U.S. National Highway Traffic Safety Administration (Burns and Moskowitz, 1974; Tharp, Burns, and Moskowitz, 1981). The goal was to evaluate and standardize a small group of behavioral tests that would correlate significantly with BAC, and could be administered by police officers on the road. The first evaluation of such a battery considered a wide variety of behavioral tests that past research and the experience of officers suggested might be useful (such as touching the finger to the nose, maze tracing, and counting backwards). After reviewing and evaluating many variations of various tests, the researchers proposed a battery of three tests that best distinguished between sober and impaired people (with BAC = 0.10 percent or higher). The battery consisted of three tests – walk-and-turn, one-leg-stand, and horizontal gaze nystagmus (HGN) – which are briefly described below.

The walk-and-turn test is a test of divided attention in which a person must listen to and follow instructions and then perform the task of taking nine steps forward, heel-to-toe, then turn on one foot and return to the starting position while walking in the same manner. The test has eight indicators of impairment: the suspect cannot keep balance while listening to the instructions, begins before the instructions are finished, stops while walking to regain balance, does not touch heel-to-toe, steps off the line, uses arms to balance, makes an improper turn, or takes an incorrect number of steps. The validation study by Burns and Moskowitz indicated that 68 percent of individuals who exhibit two or more of these performance indicators have a BAC of 0.10 percent or greater.

The one-leg-stand, is also considered a test of divided attention in which the person is instructed to stand with one foot approximately six inches off the ground and count aloud by thousands (One thousand-one, one thousand-two, etc.) until told to put the foot down. The suspect is timed for 30 seconds. The test has four indicators of impairment: swaying while balancing, using arms to balance, hopping to maintain balance, and putting the foot down. Past research showed that 65 percent of individuals who exhibit two or more such indicators in the performance of the test have a BAC of 0.10 percent of greater.

The horizontal gaze nystagmus (HGN) is an involuntary jerking of the eye which occurs naturally when the gaze is directed to the edge of a person's visual field. Under normal circumstances, nystagmus occurs when the eyes' rotation is greater than 45 degrees off the forward direction. However, when a person is impaired by alcohol, nystagmus is exaggerated and occurs at lesser angles. An alcohol-impaired person will also often have difficulty smoothly tracking a moving object (Citek, Ball, and Rutledge, 2003). In the HGN test, the officer moves an object, like a pen, from side to side in front of the suspect who is told to fixate that object. The officer then monitors the movement of the eyes to detect the break in the smooth movement. There are three possible indicators of impairment in each eye: Inability to follow a moving object smoothly, distinct jerking when the eye is at maximum deviation, and angle of onset of jerking that is less than 45 degrees off center. The last indicator – the angle of onset of jerking – is inversely correlated with the BAC. If, when counting the performance in each eye separately, there are four or more clues the suspect likely has a BAC of 0.10 percent or greater. The early validation research indicated that this test allows proper classification of approximately 77 percent of suspects. Since its original development and validation, the HGN has been validated for BAC limits of 0.08 percent too (Stuster, 2006; Stuster and Burns, 1998). In this validation study, 298 California drivers stopped for suspected DWI were administered a breath alcohol test and the HGN. The officers were requested to score the performance on the three SFST components, and also to estimate the suspects' BACs. When the test scores were correlated with the measured BACs the correlations were all positive and quite good (though far from excellent). They were $r = 0.45$ for the one-leg-stand, $r = 0.61$ for the walk-and-turn, and $r = 0.65$ for the horizontal gaze nystagmus. When the combined score of all three tests was used the correlation increased slightly to $r = 0.69$. Other analyses also indicated that the battery was quite useful at determining impairment relative to the 0.08 criterion. The officers correctly identified 98 percent of the 214 impaired drivers (with BAC $\geq$ .08 percent), and correctly identified as unimpaired 71 percent of the drivers with BAC $<$ 0.08 percent. The total error rate (for both false positives and incorrect rejections) was only 9.4 percent.

As good as these results are they do contain some caveats. First, the sensitivity of the officers is obviously influenced by the amount of alcohol that this particular sample had. The task is obviously easier the more intoxicated the drivers. In this particular sample, the mean measured BAC was 0.12 percent. This value is similar to the BAC observed in other studies of DWI arrests, but it does make the task much easier than with a sample of people who drink smaller quantities. Second, because of a statistical property of the correlation coefficient, a correlation of 0.69 means that the three tests together account for less than 50 percent of the variance in the BACs (100×0.69^2). Thus, half of the differences in BACs are not accounted for by the SFST. Third, while the walk-and-turn and the one-leg-stand have some face validity – we expect drunk drivers to stumble and have difficulties in balancing themselves – they are actually poorer predictors of alcohol impairment than the HGN. HGN which has little face validity for most people (and most judges) is actually the best predictor, and there is scientific evidence for its sensitivity to alcohol impairment even at low BACs (Citek *et al.*, 2003; Lehti, 1976; Wilkinson, Kime, and Purnell, 1974). Furthermore, the HGN is quite robust to small variations in testing procedure (such as the distance and height at which the pointer is held, and the speed of its movement) (Burns, 2003), which makes it particularly attractive for use under field conditions. Thus, the addition of the two behavioral tests adds very little to the total explanatory variance in BAC. Adding the walk-and-turn and the one-leg-stand tests to the HGN only accounts for an additional 5 percent of the variance. Elimination of these time-consuming tests would hardly detract from the validity of the test; though it might increase courtroom time to convince the judges that ocular behavior is a relevant indictor of a person's driving ability.

Breath testing: checkpoints, random breath testing, and compulsory breath testing

One means of deterring DWI and removing drunk drivers from the road is through sobriety checkpoints. In this method, police pick a high-risk location (in terms of expected prevalence of DWI) and stop all vehicles or a random sample of vehicles to evaluate their drivers for impairment and the presence of alcohol. The process is progressive so that drivers who do not appear impaired are immediately waived on and drivers who appear impaired are further tested, and if they are alcohol impaired they are detained and – depending on the situation – are either arrested or driven home.

Various evaluations have shown that checkpoints are an effective means of reducing DWI and DWI-related crashes (Elder *et al.*, 2002; Fell *et al.*, 2003), and even more so when they are publicized (Bergen *et al.*, 2014). Unfortunately, many enforcement agencies consider the process too cumbersome and expensive and instead of reducing the effort involved in each checkpoint, refrain from doing them at altogether; even though sobriety checkpoints staffed by a skeleton crew of officers can be almost as effective as full blown ones (Fell *et al.*, 2003; Fell, Lacey, and Voas, 2004). To encourage states to conduct sobriety checkpoints, the U.S. National Highway Traffic Safety Administration developed specific guidelines for implementation of effective "low staffing checkpoints" (NHTSA, 2006b).

A rough indication of the potential effectiveness of sobriety checkpoints is provided in Figure 11-9, which shows the U.K. trends, between 1967 and 2001, in driver fatalities for drivers with BAC > 0.08 percent and number of breath tests administered (Sweedler *et al.*, 2004). Although such trends are affected by many other variables, the relationship between the two trends is quite obvious. Between 1968 and 1975, the percent alcohol-related deaths doubled from approximately 17 to 35 percent. It then started to decrease at a very slow rate, and jumped again in 1983, prompting the introduction of evidential breath testing in police stations and a sharp increase in roadside breath tests. The increase in roadside breath testing was almost immediately mirrored in a decrease in BAC-related fatalities. The inverse relationship between the two continued until 1990, after which further increases in the testing, from approximately 600,000 per year to 800,000 per year seemed to have no further benefits. Thus, to the extent that these two curves reflect a causal relationship (and this is by no means certain), they show both the benefits and the limits of roadside testing. Bergen *et al.* (2014) summarized the results of

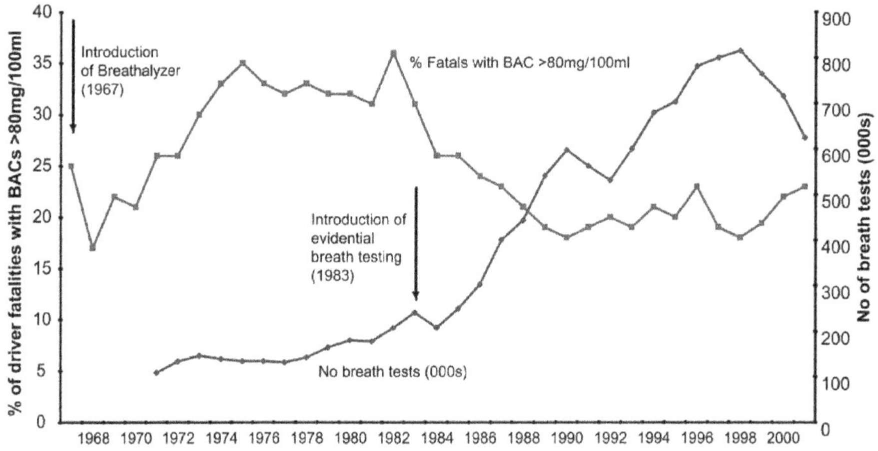

Figure 11-9. United Kingdom trends in percent fatalities of drivers with BAC > 0.08% (the legal limit in the United Kingdom at the time) relative to all accident fatalities, and the number of roadside breath tests conducted each year (from Sweedler *et al.*, 2004, with permission from Taylor and Francis Group, LLC., http://www.taylorandfrancis.com).

15 publicized checkpoint evaluation studies; all except one (in New Zealand) conducted in different locations in the U.S. They found that that the checkpoints led to a statistically significant median reduction of 9 percent in alcohol-related fatal crashes, and their conclusion was quite decisive: "The number of studies, magnitude of effect, and consistency of findings indicate strong evidence of the effectiveness of publicized sobriety checkpoint programs in reducing alcohol involved crash fatalities."

The prevalence of roadside breath testing varies greatly among countries. For example, in the EU on the basis of self-reports collected in 2004 the percent of drivers reported being checked at least once in the past three years varied from a low of 4 percent in Italy to a high of 64 percent in Finland. In general, the countries with the better safety records report greater frequencies of random breath testing (ETSC, 2008).

A variation on the theme of checkpoints is the compulsory breath testing (CBT) used in New Zealand. In this procedure, highly visible and advertised enforcement involves actually breath testing every driver that is stopped at the checkpoint. To make it efficient, the breath testing is a three-step process: first alcohol is detected with a passive screening "sniffing" device, then if alcohol is detected the level is measured with a screening device, and if it exceeds the legal limit (equivalent to 0.08 percent at the time, and zero tolerance for youth), then an evidentiary breath test is given. This procedure was applied extensively in large parts of New Zealand and its effectiveness in reducing night-time crashes (as a surrogate measure of alcohol-related crashes) was demonstrated by Miller, Blewden, and Zhang (2004) who concluded that the CBT reduced nighttime crashes by 22 percent. When coupled with extensive media campaigns and a conspicuous "booze bus," the night-time crash reductions exceeded 50 percent. While these results are quite remarkable in and of themselves, they are even more noteworthy because additional cost/benefit analysis showed that they are cost-effective with societal benefit/cost ratios of 14-26, depending on whether or not CBT was accompanied by the public information campaign and the "booze bus." Even when considering only the costs to the government the program was effective because, the authors concluded, "the government saved more than it spent on the program, especially with booze buses" (i.e., moving breath testing facilities).

Another variation of the checkpoint approach is random breath testing (RBT), introduced in Victoria, Australia in 1983. This technique involved stopping motorists for breath tests at random during the high alcohol use hours. This is a practical consideration, because driving under the influence of alcohol is not evenly distributed across all days of the week and hours of the day. For example, in an extensive roadside survey in Belgium, the percent of drivers with BAC > .05 percent (the legal limit in Belgium) was 7.7 percent on weekend nights, 3.0 percent on weekend days and weekday nights, and 1.8 percent on weekdays (Vanlaar, 2005). In the Australian study, the RBT was conducted from 4 pm to 6 am on the following day on weekdays, and over longer periods – starting earlier and ending later – on the weekends. The massive RBT resulted in an immediate drop in injury crashes at these times, a drop that accelerated even more following the introduction of graphically disturbing advertisements on the effects of crashes, labeled by the press as "commercials of death." Figure 11-10 depicts the monthly toll of injury and fatal crashes in Victoria Australia between January 1983 and

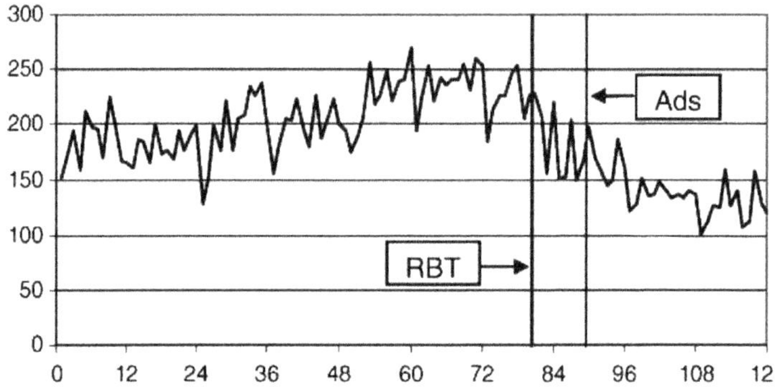

Figure 11-10. Injury crashes during "high-alcohol" drinking hours in Australia, per month from January 1983 to December 1992. Random Breath Testing was introduced in July 1989 and graphic and disturbing advertisements depicting traffic injuries – labeled by the press as "commercials of death" – were added in December 1989 (from Tay, 2005, with permission from Elsevier).

December 1992. Multiple analyses of these data have generally shown that the overall drop in crashes following the introduction of the RBT and the commercials is quite stable and robust, though the relative contributions of the enforcement and the advertising could not be separated from these data (Tay, 2005).

One cautionary note about breath testing as a DWI countermeasure is that some drivers refuse to have their breath tested. In the U.S., the refusal rates vary greatly among states, but seem to average around 20 percent (Namuswe, Coleman, and Berning, 2014). This is a very high percentage, and to discourage refusals, in some jurisdictions refusal is tantamount to admission of DWI.

As technology improves, the ability of police officers to obtain drivers' BAC improves. Portable breath testing devices are now accurate enough to be admissible as evidentiary evidence in court in some jurisdictions. Also, new technology of alcohol sensors – known as passive alcohol sensors – enables detecting alcohol in the air of the car near the driver without requiring the driver to actively blow into the device. These devices are typically installed in an officer's flashlight so that an alcohol reading can be obtained while an officer shines the light into the driver's face. Although they are likely to miss some intoxicated drivers, their likelihood to falsely indicate intoxication is low. According to an early evaluation study of their effectiveness in field conditions (Farmer *et al.*, 1999), they can correctly identify as impaired 75 percent of the drivers with BAC at or above 0.10 percent, and 70 percent of the drivers with BAC at or above 0.08 percent. When the evaluation is conducted under well controlled laboratory conditions, the percent of correct identifications is even higher. An analysis of the data in the large-scale crash risk study reported above (Blomberg *et al.*, 2004; Compton *et al.*, 2002; Moskowitz *et al.*, 2002) that compared the BAC levels obtained with passive alcohol sensors with BAC levels obtained with portable breath testers yielded a correlation of $r = 0.88$, and 73 percent correct identifications of crash-involved drivers with BAC at or above 0.08 percent (Voas, Romano, and Peck, 2006). While these levels of accuracy may be insufficient to convict a person of DWI, they are sufficient to provide the officer with a much better "feel" for a driver's state of intoxication, before a breath test is given. Passive alcohol sensors have in fact been used as quick screeners in New Zealand's compulsory breath testing program.

Economic disincentives to drinking

The economic approach involves regulated pricing and taxation of alcoholic beverages. This approach has a dual benefit: it adds money to the public coffers and it discourages people from spending too much money on alcohol. However, the relationship between pricing and consumption is not the same for all products. Economists describe that relationship in terms of price elasticity, or the sensitivity of consumption to the price of the item. For example, elasticity = −1.0 when a given percent increase in the price of a commodity results in a decrease in consumption of the same percent. Thus, if alcohol had −1.0 of elasticity, then doubling the price of an alcoholic drink would reduce its consumption by 50 percent. The elasticity of different alcoholic drinks has been estimated in different countries and on the basis of 73 such estimates. Evans (2004) notes that the average elasticity of beer is −0.41, the average elasticity of wine is −0.76, and the average elasticity of liquor is −0.78. Thus, taxing beer – the drink that is most relevant to DWI – will probably not be as effective in reducing its consumption as hoped because its elasticity is moderate (and much lower than that of hard liquor). Still, these estimates indicate that raising the price or the tax on alcoholic beverages may be a more effective strategy to cut their consumption than various prohibitions and enforcement actions. Reduction in consumption, in turn, should yield a reduction in DWI (Howat *et al.*, 2004). According to one estimate, increasing the price of alcoholic beverages in the U.S. by 10 percent should decrease DWI by 7 percent for men and 8 percent for women (Babor, Caetano, and Casswell, 2003). Unfortunately, as appealing as this approach might be for health and safety reasons, for obvious and different reasons, both industry and government are reluctant to increase the price of alcohol in order to reduce consumption. A related approach is to limit access to alcohol. Thus, some countries ban the sale of alcohol at petrol/gas stations, and some countries ban or restrict the advertising of alcoholic drinks (WHO, 2014).

Specific deterrence: prevention of recidivism and treatment of repeat offenders

Specific deterrence is aimed at specific groups and involves a myriad of tactics, depending on the group. In the context of DWI, specific deterrence is directed most often at repeat offenders and young drivers, typically under the legal minimum drinking age.

DWI is not a random event that is likely to involve all drivers to the same extent. Teetotalers are obviously immune to it. It is likely to happen more to people who drink regularly. Thus, it is not surprising that despite the severe penalties for DWI in most places, a significant proportion of the drivers arrested for DWI are repeat offenders. The exact proportion varies as a function of the prevailing laws, the specific definitions used for DWI, the place, and the time. In the U.S., approximately one-third of all drivers arrested or convicted of DWI have a previous DWI conviction (NHTSA, 2004a). In terms of crash involvement, the estimated numbers are much lower, with repeat DWI offenders constituting approximately 8 percent of the fatal DWI crashes, and 1-2 percent of all fatal crashes (Jones and Lacey, 2000). DeJong and Hingson (1998) state this in a more dramatic manner: "In a given year, if every driver who had been arrested the year before for alcohol-impaired driving could be kept off the road, less than 5 percent of alcohol-related traffic fatalities would be prevented." However, it is important to realize that many drivers that are impaired by alcohol and arrested are eventually charged with a lesser violation, such as reckless driving and thus the reported rates of recidivism are typically an under-estimate of the actual rates.

Although in absolute terms, these percentages are low, they are significant and offer a specific target group for focused law enforcement, adjudication and therapy. From the perspective of adjudication, this is the only group that judges can address. But no matter how effective the courts may be in removing the high-risk repeat offender from the road, as indicated above the overall impact on crashes will be small. Because the courts typically deal most severely only with the "high-risk" drivers (such as repeat offenders), they have a very limited role in affecting the overall phenomenon of DWI (Woodall *et al.*, 2004).

Despite the above concerns, there has been significant research on the effectiveness of different means of dealing with repeat offenders in the hope of preventing or at least reducing recidivism. The range of options, including sanctions and psychological interventions, is large and so is the range of costs involved.

There is one methodological caveat in most of the research in this area. Because these programs involve actual actions by the relevant authorities, it is typically difficult to design evaluation studies according to rigorous experimental design principles. The principle that most often gets compromised is the randomization of subjects. For example, to correctly evaluate a treatment – such as Victim Impact Panels (discussed below) – it is necessary to insure that the treatment group is identical to the control group that is not receiving that treatment. Unfortunately, this is rarely the case. Different judges and different types of drivers may be involved, and the control group may receive other treatments. Furthermore, there is "attrition" of subjects, because some cannot be tracked; and it is likely that these are the ones that are least responsive to the program. Thus, when a statistically significant effect is reported, it should be treated with caution because of the many potentially confounding variables that may be involved. Because of these artifacts, when a treatment strategy is "shown" to be effective, most often the estimated impact is spuriously high.

License suspension or revocation

License suspension is one of the more common penalties for drivers convicted of DWI. For example, in the U.S. most states have administrative license suspension for DWI offenders even before the case is brought to trial. The rationale for this is twofold: it is perceived as a severe penalty, and while the license is suspended the potentially drunk driver is off the road – at least in theory. It is that qualification that makes the approach problematic. Apparently, many drivers consider license suspension a penalty that is too severe to bear, and they resume their driving while their license is suspended. This was demonstrated by McCartt, Geary, and Berning (2003), who had surveillance professionals unobtrusively observe drivers whose license was suspended for six months for DWI. They conducted the study in two locations: Milwaukee, Wisconsin (rated as the "drunkest city in America" by Forbes Magazine; Ewalt, 2006) and Bergen County, New Jersey. A total of 93 suspended drivers were unobtrusively observed for eight hours while their license was suspended. Despite some significant differences between the drivers in the two locations, in both locations driving while suspended was rampant: 53 percent of the New Jersey drivers and 22 percent of the Milwaukee drivers were observed driving while suspended. The situation was even worse when the percentages were calculated only relative to the people who actually traveled while they were being observed. Of those who traveled, 88 percent of the Milwaukee drivers and 36 percent of the New Jersey drivers actually drove. Focus groups of suspended drivers revealed that they occasionally drive despite the suspension because they perceive the punishment as being too harsh and because they perceive the likelihood of being apprehended as being quite low. Thus, in the absence of a means of tagging these drivers so that they can be easily apprehended by police, this approach has significant limitations. This is especially so because quite often, these violators have a host of other law infractions, so one more penalty – and one that is not rigorously enforced – hardly provides the intended deterrence. In light of such findings, it is not surprising that in an earlier study De Young, Peck, and Helander (1997) estimated that nearly 10 percent of the California drivers on the road at any one time were driving without a valid license, and drivers whose license was suspended were over-involved in fatal crashes by a factor of nearly four.

Victim Impact Panels (VIP)

This approach, developed and promoted by Mothers Against Drunk Driving (MADD), requires convicted DWI drivers to attend a session in which they have to listen to a panel of DWI victims: people injured by drunk drivers and families of people killed or handicapped by drunk drivers. The rationale of the approach is that drivers who drink and drive rarely think of the consequences that their actions have on the victims. The VIP is designed to sensitize these drivers to the other road users and empathize with them. The VIP panelists present their personal stories, essentially forcing the drivers attending the session to realize the huge suffering they have caused, so that they might identify with it enough to refrain from drinking and driving in the future. The VIP do seem to have an immediate emotional effect on the people attending these sessions; an effect that is often coupled with declarations to never drink and drive again. However, to expect a one-time emotional appeal – that occurs in a situation totally removed from the drunk driving situation – to have a long-lasting effect on habits acquired in the course of many years, may be quite unrealistic. Also, at least one study (Jackson, 2009) failed to even show a significant change in the participants' feelings of shame, empathy, or guilt. And without a change in the emotions it is hard to conceptualize how an emotional appeal helps at all. Though some evaluations sponsored by MADD have shown a positive effect on recidivism (as reported by Wheeler *et al.*, 2004), the better controlled and independent evaluations of the effects of VIP on repeat offenses have failed to demonstrate its effectiveness either in terms of the participants' alcohol consumption and drinking and driving behavior, or in their recidivism rates (C'de Baca *et al.*, 2000; Polacsek *et al.*, 2001;

Shinar and Compton, 1995; Wheeler *et al.*, 2004). Polacsek *et al.* and Wheeler's findings, in particular, are important because unlike the other studies their evaluations were based on a random assignment of drivers to the treatment and control groups, and thus they were free of many potentially confounding variables. A study by Rojek, Coverdill, and Fors (2003) that was unable to control all potentially confounding variables experimentally attempted to do so statistically and did demonstrate a large positive effect of VIP on repeat DWI apprehensions. However, in this study the VIP group and the Control group were drawn from two different periods – one before the VIP was ordered by the judges and one after it became standard procedure – and it remained possible that the effect was due to some extraneous difference in the two periods of DWI enforcements. Summarizing the studies to date, Miller *et al.* (2015) also concluded that there is "no effect of such programs on reducing recidivism in DUI offenders" (p. 27).

Vehicle-based programs: vehicle impoundment, forfeiture and registration cancellation, and alcohol ignition interlock systems

Driving without a valid license – especially while a license is suspended – is a widespread phenomenon in many countries. People can still physically drive without a license. However, driving without a car is impossible. As an extreme step in the fight against DWI many states in the U.S. and some other countries (e.g., New Zealand, Israel) also have vehicle impoundment laws. Although presumably a driver can drive another car, such a car is not readily accessible to many convicted offenders, and consequently these sanctions seem to be quite effective in reducing recidivism (Voas *et al.*, 2004). However, vehicle impoundment and holding in special lots may not always be cost-effective because it involves costs that vehicle owners may decide not to pay. Instead they just leave their car in a guarded impoundment lot, while the cost of its storage increases. A much less costly procedure is to impound the vehicle registration plate. However, even this procedure requires a mechanism to collect the license plates, and is problematic when a car is also in use by other than the DWI offender. In jurisdictions, where the law allows the officer to remove the plate at the time of the DWI arrest, this approach has reduced recidivism (Voas *et al.*, 2004).

When education, licensing and driving regulations, and even traditional enforcement and adjudication fail, we often turn to technology. Over the past half century various devices – called Alcohol Ignition Interlock Devices – have been suggested as a means of preventing recidivism. These devices are essentially impairment testers that are connected to the ignition system. They consist of four components: (1) a sensor that detects alcohol in the breath sample at levels greater than the criterion level, and prevents the ignition if the BAC level exceeds that level (2) a retest feature that requires periodic testing once the car has been started, (3) a temper-detection component, and (4) a data logger that records the BAC levels, times of test, etc. (Marques, 2009). The devices are typically installed – following a court order – in the vehicles of people convicted of DWI. Once installed, in order to start the car the driver must first pass a sobriety test. Many of the early devices consisted of performance tests, such as memory, reaction time, and signal detection tests that were designed to determine if the driver is *behaviorally* fit to drive. Unfortunately no test or battery of tests could be found that had both sufficiently high sensitivity (to detect impairment when the driver was alcohol impaired) and specificity (to determine unimpairment when the driver was not alcohol impaired). With the advent of per se laws that made a driver legally impaired on the basis of blood alcohol level alone, the ignition interlock devices began to rely exclusively on breath tests. The tests themselves require the driver to blow into a device, and on the basis of the amount of alcohol in the exhaled air a BAC is determined. To prevent friends from "helping the driver" start the car and drive away, the devices also require repeated blowing during the drive.

Alcohol ignition interlock devices have been successfully installed, and interlock programs have been implemented in Australia, Canada, Sweden, and the U.S. The U.S. National Highway Traffic Safety Administration has also published a toolkit and guidelines on how to install a successful interlock program (Casanova-Powell *et al.*, 2015; Mayer, 2014; NHTSA 2013b), and their use has been increasing in an exponential manner (Marques, 2009). An unexpected obstacle to the use of the interlock device as a condition of retaining the license following a DWI conviction was discovered in Sweden (Forsman and Gustafsson, 2016). There, drivers convicted of DWI are given the option of a 1-2 years license suspension or driving with an alcohol interlock device during that time. In addition to the costs involved, some drivers refused the option because of the shame involved in being branded an alcoholic. In a follow-up of these drivers most of them reported that despite the significant loss in their quality of life as a result of the license suspension they were satisfied in their decision. This finding may provide a clue concerning the powerful effect of shaming and how it can be exploited to deter DWI; at least in a culture like Sweden's.

Several studies have addressed the effectiveness of these devices in preventing recidivism. In this context, an important distinction should be made between the effectiveness of a *device* in correctly detecting alcohol impairment (with very small percent of misses and false alarms), and the effectiveness of a *program* that incorporates the use of such a device. The latter depends on the local laws, the judges' inclination to consistently apply the law, the adequacy of enforcement and monitoring of the installation and maintenance of the interlock device, and – most important – what percent of the people assigned to an interlock treatment actually install it in their car and only drive that car. Zador *et al.*, (2011) found – not surprisingly – that adherence to the interlock program is greater when the assigned drivers are closely monitored by the administrative agency that manages the program. Obviously, from the perspective of traffic safety, what is most important is the effectiveness of the total program and not that of the device. Beirness and Marques (2004) reviewed the evaluations conducted on 11 different programs (in Sweden, in two provinces in Canada, and in seven states in the U.S.), and Elder *et al.* (2011) reviewed four more recent ones. Both groups of researchers noted that all programs were very effective in reducing recidivism. Sprattler (2009) in a review of the various programs and their evaluations also concluded that ignition interlock programs are generally effective. In the most recent evaluation, Marques (2013) found that the program reduced recidivism by over 60 percent.

As an illustration, in one of the more extensive evaluations, conducted on Canadian data, Marques, Voas, and Tippetts (2003) tracked the recidivism rates of 1982 DWI offenders who had an interlock device installed in their cars, and compared their recidivism to that of 17,857 DWI offenders who had their license suspended. Their main findings are plotted in Figure 11-11, and they show a definite advantage to the interlock approach. License suspension – even during the suspension period – did not prevent some drivers from repeat DWI arrests. In fact by the end of one year of license suspension, nearly 2 percent of the drivers had been re-arrested for a repeat DWI offense; a small percent of the ones actually driving. In contrast, the interlock – as long as it remained installed – was essentially 100 percent effective, with nearly zero recidivism. Unfortunately, once the interlock and the suspension phases ended, recidivism recurred at essentially the same rate for both groups. On the basis of these findings, Marques and his colleagues recommended that the period of interlock installation be extended; a rational appeal given the fact that – unlike license suspension – the device does not prevent sober driving. Marques and Voas (2008) also noted that most of the post-interlock recidivism was committed by the drivers with the highest rates of failed BAC tests. Thus, the device may have long-term benefits in mitigating DWI, but not on the hard core drinkers who even with the device repeatedly tried to drive. These general findings – of a strong effect while the device is employed, and the dissipation following its removal, indicate that in term of the mechanism involved, the interlock forces the driver to desist from DWI, but does not lead to any changes in the underlying attitude concerning DWI nor to a new behavioral change to safer, alcohol-free driving. This conclusion is underscored by a more recent evaluation of the interlock program effectiveness based on the records of 33,446 first-time, impaired-driving offenders in Florida (Voas, Tippetts, and Grosz, 2013). They found that while the drivers were on the program the recidivism rate was

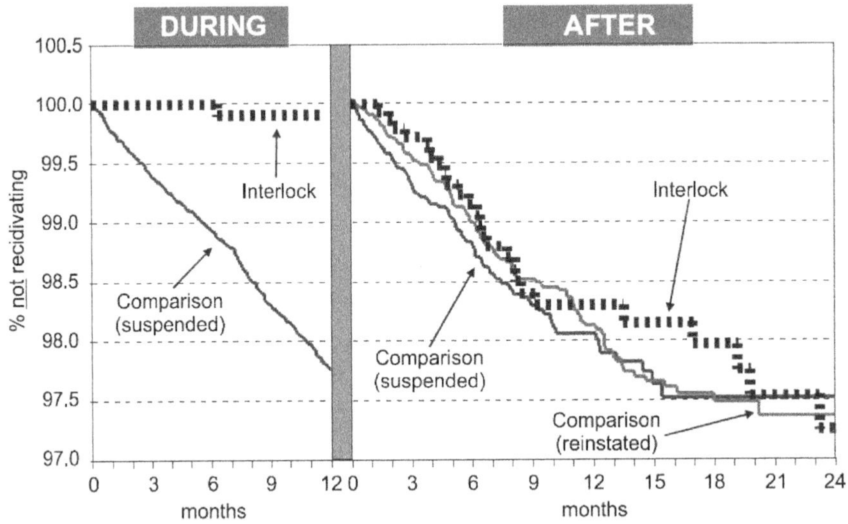

Figure 11-11. The cumulative effects of installing alcohol ignition interlocks versus a 12-months license suspension on the likelihood of NOT incurring a repeat DWI offense. The comparison group is further divided into those who received their license at the end of the suspension period and those who did not (from Marques *et al.*, 2003, with permission from Blackwell Publishing).

nearly zero (0.4 percent). But once the program ended the recidivism rate quintupled and was similar to that of drivers with revoked license.

There is one exception to the general assessment that the interlocks work only as long as they are installed (Westat, 2007). In this evaluation of an alcohol interlock program in Maryland multiple DWI-convicted drivers were randomly assigned to either an interlock program that lasted two years or to a control program. The evaluation demonstrated consistent effects of the interlock program (regardless of whether or not the assigned drivers actually complied with the restriction) both while it was required (first two years) and for a 2-year post-interlock period, on both violations and crashes. For example, while the interlock restriction was in effect there was a 44 percent reduction in all crashes, and a 73 percent reduction in the risk of an alcohol-related crash. In the following two years, although the risk of alcohol-related crashes increased there was still a 44 percent reduction in the risk of alcohol-related crashes, relative to the pre-program rate. In the most recent evaluation to date, Kaufman and Wiebe (2016) compared the alcohol involved fatal crash rates of 18 U.S. states that mandate interlocks for all DWI convictions with the comparable rates in 32 states with less stringent laws. After controlling for state and year effects the average adjusted rate for states with the universal interlock laws was 15 percent lower than the rate in the states with the less stringent laws. To provide some concrete perspective, the authors also noted that this effect was comparable to that of lives saved by frontal air bags.

A more comprehensive approach to the problem is to combine the installation of an alcohol interlock device with some type of treatment for the person's alcohol problem. An evaluation of the effectiveness of the interlock device coupled with a counseling and periodic medical evaluations of drivers convicted of DWI in Sweden (Bjerre, 2005) showed that the program was very effective in reducing dangerous alcohol drinking habits (based on a reduction in biological markers for alcoholism), and in the number of drivers with "dangerous or harmful alcohol habits." More important from the perspective of traffic safety, recidivism dropped from 5 percent to zero, and rate of involvement in injury crashes dropped seven fold, from 2.2 percent per year before enrolling in the program to 0.3 percent afterwards. Despite the apparent success of the program, interpreting these data is difficult for at least two reasons. First, the program was voluntary and those involved in it were more motivated to change their drinking and driving habits than those who refused (and had their license suspended) and those in jurisdictions not having the program. Second, drivers convicted of DWI who did not complete the program or refused to participate in the program and had their license revoked, or were not in the jurisdictions with the program, all had significantly lower crash rates during that period than before. Thus, either by itself or in comparison to other treatments, these results do not provide unequivocal support for the Swedish interlock program. Still, records obtained from the interlock devices showed a significant number of attempts to start the car with BAC > 0.02 percent (the legal limit in Sweden), and in these cases at least a presumably intoxicated driver was kept off the road.

In sum, although all studies that have evaluated alcohol interlock programs found that it was effective in reducing recidivism, with very few exceptions (e.g., Beck *et al.*, 1999) they all suffered from non-random assignment of drivers to the interlock and non-interlock conditions. Thus, until more studies control for the sampling bias the approach can be considered promising, but in need of better controlled evaluations. Still, given the consistent findings and the severity of the DWI issue, the European Parliament has initiated an EU policy that would require installation of alcohol interlocks in "all new types of commercial passenger and goods transport vehicles and to the vehicles of road users who already have committed more than one drink-driving conviction" (ETSC, 2012, p. 12). In the U.S. by the end of 2014, 24 states required the installation of alcohol interlock devices before a driver convicted of DWI can regain his or her licenses (MADD, 2015), and the U.S. Congress is now considering "Alisa's Law" that would require alcohol interlock devices for all convicted drunk drivers (U.S. Congress, 2014). Such moves are also likely to be supported by the public, as a recent survey of the AAA Traffic Safety Foundation found that the majority of adult Americans strongly support interlocks even for first-time DWI offenders (AAAF, 2012). Also, given the contingent nature of the interlocks' effects it is recommended to use them as part of a systems approach that combines them with other treatments (NCDC, 2012).

The lingering problem of DWI and the rapid evolvement of in-vehicle technologies has prompted a new U.S. cooperative effort involving the NHTSA and 17 of the world's leading automakers: Driver Alcohol Detection System for Safety (DADSS). To make the potential alcohol interlock solution more palatable to the general motoring public, this cooperative project is searching for effective passive sensors involving a non-invasive technology that would detect the presence of alcohol without requiring the driver to perform any active task, and would automatically lock the ignition when alcohol is detected. The program is currently evaluating various technological approaches for their reliability, validity, and practicality (Zaouk *et al.*, 2015), and initial demonstrations are quite promising (Associated Press, 2011). Two potential directions are passive breath testers that would detect alcohol in the natural breath exhaled by the driver, and a touch sensor on the steering wheel that would detect alcohol in the skin surface (Smouse, 2015). Though, still in early stages of development, in the quest to reconcile poor human decision making with driving safety we are likely to see such systems before the end of the decade: essentially letting the car decide if we are or are not fit to drive. Another step in this direction is a smart phone application, that when coupled with an accelerometer and an orientation sensor, can recognize erratic maneuvers consistent with the kinds made by impaired drivers. Initial evaluations of two independent efforts at developing such apps are very promising (Dai, Teng, Bai, *et al.*, 2010; Nassi, Rokach, and Elovici, 2016).

Court Monitoring

Court Monitoring is an approach developed by the grass-roots organizations MADD and SADD. It involves the attendance of a MADD or SADD volunteer in court whenever DWI cases are adjudicated. The rules for the monitor's courtroom behavior and interactions with the judge are always very specific: the monitor is instructed to make his or her presence known to the judge and prosecuting and defense attorneys, and then refrain from making any statements, from asking questions, from raising objections, or from interfering with the proceedings in any way while the case is in progress. Once sentencing is done, it is recommended that the monitor discuss cases with the judge and sensitize him or her to the citizen group's interest, concern, and satisfaction (or dissatisfaction) with the way the case was handled. Thus, when the court disposition does not appear to be consistent with the law, the monitor is encouraged to question and discuss it with the judge after the case is closed. In this discussion, the court monitor is assumed to have an educational role: one that would impact future cases. Thus, the court monitor is in a combined role of an educator, watchdog and concerned citizen – judging the performance of both the judge and the prosecuting attorney. In the U.S., where judges and prosecuting attorneys are elected officials, the monitor may have a significant influence on their re-election.

The goal of the court monitors is to verify that drivers accused of DWI will be prosecuted, convicted, and punished to the fullest extent of the law. Thus, in the context of specific deterrence, the court monitor can enhance the probability of a conviction and the magnitude of the penalty; albeit it is the less important component in the deterrence equation. In that limited role, court monitors appear to be quite effective. In a comparison of judgments and sentences of 397 DWI cases monitored by a MADD volunteer and 9,137 non-monitored cases in the state of Maine, monitored judges were more likely to find the DWI driver guilty, and handed out more severe penalties. The monitored cases were half as likely to be dismissed by the judge, and of the non-dismissed cases the likelihood of conviction when the monitor was present was 0.92 versus 0.87 when no monitor was present. When they convicted the drivers, the monitored judges meted out jail sentences that were 50 percent longer than non-monitored judges (averaging 31 days versus 20 days) (Shinar, 1992). The impact of the court monitors was greatest in cases adjudicating repeat offenders, as illustrated in Figure 11-12. For example, the

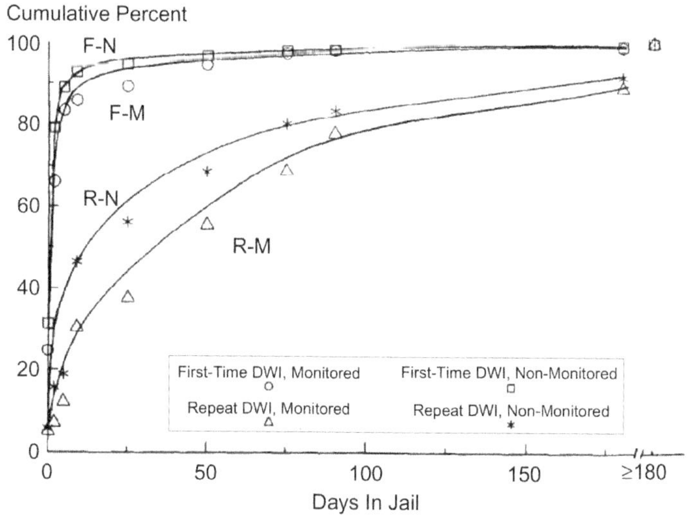

Figure 11-12. The effects of court monitoring on the sentencing of first-time DWI drivers and repeat offenders in terms of the days sentenced to jail (from Shinar, 1992, with permission from Elsevier).

figure shows that in the case of first-time offenders over 50 percent of the offenders did not receive a jail sentence at all, regardless of monitoring. In the case of repeat offenders, the situation is quite different. The median length of jail sentence was 10 days when the case was not monitored and 26 days when it was. Although in the study the monitoring cases were not randomly selected (as would have been desirable), a comparison between the monitored cases and the non-monitored cases revealed that they were almost identical in all the potential confounding variables that could be assessed: in the drivers' mean age, percent males, mean BAC, and mean number of previous DWI arrests. Thus, the study showed quite conclusively that the presence of a court monitor forced judges to respond to their sensitivities and in effect made the laws and the arrests more relevant to the driving population. Still, as court monitoring is managed differently in different places (Frattaroli *et al.*, 2006), it is difficult to conclude that all programs labeled as such are equally effective. Unfortunately, though court monitoring programs are still practiced, there is a lack of well-designed evaluations of these programs (Kromm *et al.*, 2009).

Psychological and Psychiatric Treatment

Given the prevalence of alcohol-dependent people among the drivers arrested for DWI or involved in DWI crashes, it is not surprising that one approach to deal with the problem is through forced psychological and psychiatric treatment. Although expensive, there is evidence that such programs are effective, and possibly more effective than traditional punitive approaches. In fact, in the absence of treating the alcohol problem itself, many people are resistant to change even with certain, severe, and swift punishment (Yu, Evans, and Clark, 2006).

The most extensive evaluation of the benefits of treatment was conducted by Wells-Parker and her associates in 1995. In a meta-analysis of 215 studies on various ways of dealing with convicted DWI offenders, they found that treatment and rehabilitation for alcohol abuse reduce DWI recidivism and involvement in re-occurrence of DWI-related crashes by 8-9 percent. Though this reduction may not seem very large, it was still greater than the effects achieved by conventional punitive measures such as fines and license suspensions. In a more recent evaluation on a small sample of 176 patients undergoing psychiatric treatment for alcohol problems, Gómez-Talegón and Alvarez (2006) found that the prevalence of traffic offenses in the year following initiation of a treatment was 4.3 percent compared to 15.9 in the year before treatment.

Forced psychological treatment is rarely meted out in court without additional actions, such as court monitored probation, continuous supervision (sometimes through electronic surveillance), and requirements for sobriety at all times. Although these comprehensive approaches are both expensive and complex to administer, they can be very effective; yielding as much as 50 percent reduction in repeat DWI offenses (Lapham *et al.*, 2006).

Psychological treatment can also be combined with arrest, and then it can be provided within the confines of a prison – a highly structured and controlled environment (to use an understatement). An evaluation of a combined prison-treatment program in New Mexico, USA, showed that drivers receiving this treatment had 40 percent fewer re-arrests than the control drivers who were cited for DWI but not assigned to the jail + treatment program (Woodall *et al.*, 2004). Given the heterogeneity of the control group (that also included drivers whose cases were dismissed), it was hard to conclude what was the cause for the reductions. To get a better understanding of the relevance of the treatment and the jail sentence, Delaney *et al.* (2005), reanalyzed the same data while statistically controlling for confounding factors that might affect the judges' sentence. For example, in New Mexico they noted that judges tended to be much more severe in their sentencing of Hispanic and Native American offenders than in their sentencing of white drivers. The data analysis was therefore statistically adjusted for this variable, as well as for the driver's gender and number of prior arrests. Still, even after adjustment for differences in these factors the likelihood of re-arrest for DWI was lower for the group that was convicted and sentenced to jail + treatment than for drivers who were convicted and only sentenced to jail, or convicted and not sentenced to jail, or not convicted at all. Thus, the benefits of the treatment were significant; especially because the worst approach appeared to be either not convicting the driver or convicting and sentencing the driver to a jail term without treatment. These last two groups did not differ from each other in their rates of recidivism.

Finally, when treatment is voluntary, and not a result of a DWI conviction it also appears to help. Macdonald *et al.* (2004), in the study mentioned above, found that patients who voluntarily checked themselves to an addiction treatment center reduced their relative collision risk by over 50 percent. However, it is possible that the mere intention to act on the problem (by volunteering to be in the program) may have contributed more to this outcome than the actual participation. This, of course, can only be tested by assigning the treatment only to a random sample of the drivers who volunteer to participate in it.

Secure Continuous Remote Alcohol Monitoring (SCRAM)

A fairly recent technological approach has been to require convicted DWI offenders to wear a monitoring anklet that continuously measures the alcohol evaporated from the blood through the skin, thus obtaining transdermal alcohol concentration. This measure is not as accurate as direct BAC monitoring and its response to alcohol ingestion is slow. However, for those sentenced to abstain totally it is an effective monitoring and deterrence system. In an evaluation of this program, the recidivism rates of drivers sentenced to wear the SCRAM in the states of Wisconsin and Nebraska were compared to a control group of convicted DWI offenders who were sentenced to be monitored in a traditional manner (e.g., to report for periodic alcohol checks) but not sentenced to wear the device. The SCRAM, in both states was effective in postponing the time to recidivate. In both Wisconsin and Nebraska less than 2 percent recidivated while wearing the device. However, paradoxically the total rate of recidivism was actually slightly higher for those wearing the device than for those not wearing it. This is most likely due not to a negative effect of the SCRAM but to a sampling bias as offenders sentenced to wearing the SCRAM were probably those considered by the judges as more likely to recidivate anyway (Tison *et al.*, 2015).

Counteracting the effects of alcohol with caffeine

For many drivers, the ultimate fantasy solution to DWI lies in the equivalent of a "morning-after pill": a magical after-the-fact solution. Unfortunately no such pill exists as yet for alcohol intoxication, though one substance that has limited positive counter effects is caffeine. Theoretically, this is a sensible approach because caffeine is a central nervous system stimulant while alcohol is a depressant. However, a review of early studies on the effects of caffeine after drinking yielded mixed results and the authors of the review, Fudin and Nicastro (1988), concluded that combining the two yields both antagonistic and synergistic effects, depending on the dosages and the particular task used to evaluate the effects.

Two studies by Burns and Moskowitz (1990) showed that caffeine can counteract some – but not all – impairing effects of alcohol. Moser, Heide, and Kömpf (1998) demonstrated that alcohol affects the efficiency of the visual search in a dose-response manner. The Burns and Moskowitz studies showed that caffeine mitigated the impairing effects of alcohol on visual search, tracking, and reaction time, but appeared to have little or no effect on divided attention (that involved a visual search task for targets while tracking a moving cursor on the screen) and on visual backward masking (in which a brief exposure of letters was followed by a screen of "broken letter pieces"). Furthermore, the dose-response relationship is not a simple one. Caffeine seemed to be most effective when both the caffeine levels and BAC were low (BAC = 0.05 percent). At higher BACs (0.10 percent) caffeine had either no effect or sometimes even a synergistic effect, amplifying the impairments from alcohol. More recent studies appear to support the same conclusions. For example, Mackay, Tiplady, and Scholey (2002) found that caffeine partially counteracted the impairing effects of alcohol on a short-term memory task (Digit Symbol Substitution Test), but not on the error rate in one of the two choice reaction time tasks. Marsden and Leach (2000) evaluated the effects of alcohol and caffeine on the performance of naval navigation tasks, and found that alcohol impairment was reduced by caffeine as measured in a visual search task and in solving of maritime navigation problems, but not in terms of the time needed to locate an item on a navigation chart.

In some respects, the use of a stimulant to counteract the depressant effects of alcohol may actually be counter-productive. This is because the stimulant may create euphoric subjective feelings and subjectively enhanced perceptions of well-being, without affecting the actual functioning. This was discovered by Ferreira *et al.* (2006) when they used an energy drink to counteract low and moderate amounts of alcohol. They found that although the energy drink reduced the alcohol effects of headache, weakness, and dry mouth (thus enhancing sensations of well-being), it did not improve motor-coordination or visual reaction time. In contrast, Ligouri and Robinson (2001) found that ingesting caffeine with alcohol (with doses equivalent to two and four 6-ounces cups of coffee) did not affect any of the alcohol-related subjective feelings (such as the sensations of confusion, dizziness, high, jitteriness, "drug effect," and alertness). Furthermore, as expected, objective performance was impaired by alcohol. Caffeine, however, had mixed effects. It did not produce any improvement in body sway and choice reaction time, but it did reduce the brake latency time – though not to the unimpaired level (i.e., with placebo).

Also, as noted by Burns and Moskowitz (1990), the higher caffeine dose did not improve performance relative to the lower dosc, and in the case of choice reaction time it actually increased it. Thus, based on the cumulative evidence attempting to counteract the behavioral effects of alcohol by ingesting caffeine can be quite risky: it can provide a subjective sensation of improvement – which explains why people who combine the two are more likely to drive when intoxicated (Woolsey *et al.*, 2014) – while having no or even negative effects on actual driving-related performance. In short, it will make a sleepy drunk driver a jittery drunk driver; but a drunk and impaired driver nonetheless.

Concluding Comments

The effects of alcohol on driving, the extent and context in which alcohol is mixed with driving, and a wide range of methods to reduce drinking and driving have all had several profound effects on the drinking and driving phenomenon. They have contributed to an extensive amount of empirical research on these topics, to better knowledge about the effects of alcohol on driving and driving-related functions, to heightened public awareness of the dangers of drinking and driving, to change in the social norms concerning the acceptability of drinking and driving, and finally to significant reductions in drinking and driving. However, the reductions have not been as significant as one might expect given the extent of the phenomenon. One reason – that escapes many researchers – is that most of the models we have to explain, predict, and change driver behavior do not apply here. A conspicuous example of this is the irrelevance of the theory of planned behavior. A driver's planned behavior may be rational and reasonable before he or she drinks, but because alcohol has a detrimental effect on our decision making capability, once drunk the same driver will change his or her plans to be more consistent with his or her subjective feelings as they are right after the last drink and just before heading to the car. Simple countermeasures in the form of increased enforcement and more consistent and severe punishments – in addition to being costly – are typically effective, but much less than desired. It seems that the only way to drastically reduce DWI is to combine multiple approaches – including education, public information campaigns, and intense and visible enforcement – with new technologies and strategies that target specific populations of drivers. Thus, the combined efforts to reduce DWI in the EU has produced a greater decline in alcohol-related fatalities than in any other type of road deaths. Over the decade of 2001 to 2010, alcohol-related deaths dropped in the EU by 56 percent, while the general drop in traffic fatalities was 47 percent (ETSC, 2012). A similar, but slightly lower reduction occurred in the U.S. where alcohol was once involved in 50 percent of the fatal crashes and now it is involved in about a third of them.

References

AAAF (2012). *2011 Traffic Safety Culture Index*. American Automobile Association Foundation for Traffic Safety. Washington, DC. https://www.aaafoundation.org/sites/default/files/2011TSCI.pdf

Appenzeller, B. M. R., S. Schneider, M. Yegles, A. Maul and R. Wennig (2005). Drugs and chronic alcohol abuse in drivers. *Forensic Sci. Int.*, *155*, 83-90.

Associated Press (2011). In future cars might decide if driver is drunk. January 28. http://www.cbsnews.com/news/in-future-cars-might-decide-if-driver-is-drunk/

Atchley, P., C. Hadlock and S. Lane (2012). Stuck in the 70s: The role of social norms in distracted driving. *Accid. Anal. Prev.*, *48*, 279-284.

AWOL (2006). Alcohol without liquid. www.awol.com. Accessed June 25, 2006.

Babor, T., R. Caetano and S. Casswell (2003). *Alcohol, No Ordinary Commodity: Research and Public Policy*. Oxford University Press, Oxford, England. (as cited by Howat *et al.*, 2004).

Beck, K., W. Rauch, E. Baker and A. Williams (1999). Effects of ignition interlock license restrictions on drivers with multiple alcohol offenses: A random trial in Maryland. *Am. J. Pub. Health*, *89*, 1696–1700.

Bédard, M., G. H. Guyatt, M. J. Stones and J. P. Hirdes (2002). The independent contribution of driver, crash, and vehicle characteristics to driver fatalities. *Accid. Anal. Prev.*, *34*, 717-727.

Beirness, D. J. and P. R. Marques (2004). Alcohol ignition interlock programs. *Traffic Inj. Prev.*, *5*, 299-308.

Bergen, G., A. Pitan, S. Qu, R. A. Shults, S. K. Chattopadhyay, R. W. Elder and J. M. Clymer (2014). Publicized sobriety checkpoint programs: A Community Guide systematic review. *Am. J. Prev. Med.*, *46*(5), 529-539.

Bernat, D. H., W. T. M. Dunsmuir and A. C. Wagenaar (2004). Effects of lowering the legal BAC to 0.08 on single-vehicle-nighttime fatal traffic crashes in 19 jurisdictions. *Accid. Anal. Prev.*, *36*, 1089-1097.

Bernhoft, I. M. and I. Behrensdorff (2003). Effect of lowering the alcohol limit in Denmark. *Accid. Anal. Prev.*, *35*, 515-535.

Berning, A., R. Compton and K. Wochinger (2015). *Results of the 2013–2014 National Roadside Survey of Alcohol and Drug Use by Drivers*. National Highway Traffic Safety Administration, Traffic Safety Facts, Research Note DOT HS 812 118. U.S. Department of Transportation, Washington, DC.

Bjerre, B. (2003). An evaluation of the Swedish Ignition Interlock program. *Traffic Inj. Prev.*, *4*, 98–104.

Bjerre, B. (2005). Primary and secondary prevention of drink driving by the use of alcolock device and program: Swedish experiences. *Accid. Anal. Prev.*, *37*, 1145-1152.

Blomberg, R. D., R. C. Peck, H. Moskowitz, M. Burns and D. Fiorentino (2004). Crash risk of alcohol involved driving. Final report on Contract No. DTNH22-94-C-05001 to the National Highway Traffic Safety Administration. Dunlop and Associates, Inc., Stamford, CT.

Boggan, W. (2005). *Alcohol, Chemistry, and You*. Chemcases.com. Kennesaw State University, Kennesaw, GA. http://chemcases.com/alcohol/index.htm. Accessed July 11, 2006.

Borkenstein, R. F., R. F. Crowther, R. P. Shumate, W. B. Ziel and R. Zylman (1964). *The Role of the Drinking Driver in Traffic Crashes*. Department of Police Administration, Indiana University, Indiana, USA.

Brick, J. (2006). Standardization of alcohol calculations in research. *Alcohol. Clin. Exp. Res.*, *30*(8), 1276-1287.

Brinkmann, B., J. Beike, H. Köhler, A. Heinecke and T. Bajanowski (2002). Incidence of alcohol dependence among drunken drivers. *Drug Alcohol Depend.*, *66*, 7-10.

Briscoe, S. (2004). Raising the bar: Can increased statutory penalties deter drink-drivers? *Accid. Anal. Prev.*, *36*, 919-929.

Burns, M. (2003). The robustness of the horizontal gaze nystagmus (HGN) test. Final report submitted to the National Highway Traffic Safety Administration under contract DTNH22-98D-55079. Southern California Research Institute, Los Angeles, CA.

Burns, M. and H. Moskowitz (1974). Psychophysical Tests for DWI Arrest. NHTSA Report DOT-HS-802-424. U.S. Department of Transportation, Washington, DC.

Burns, M. and H. Moskowitz (1990). Two experiments on alcohol-caffeine interaction. *Alcohol Drugs Driving*, *6*(1), 303-315.

Butters, J. E., R. G. Smart, R. E. Mann and M. Asbridge (2005). Illicit drug use, alcohol use and problem drinking among infrequent and frequent road ragers. *Drug Alcohol Depend.*, *80*, 169-175.

C'de Baca, J., S. C. Lapham, S. Paine and B. J. Skipper (2000). Victim impact panels: Who is sentenced to attend? Does attendance affect recidivism of first-time DWI offenders? *Alcohol.: Clin. Exp. Res.*, 24 (9), 1420–1426.

Canadian Center on Substance Abuse (2014). Administrative sanctions for low blood alcohol concentration drivers. Policy Brief. www.ccsa.ca.

Carpenter, C. (2004). How do zero tolerance drunk driving laws work? *J. Health Econ.*, *23*(1), 61-83.

Casanova-Powell, T., J. Hedlund, W. Leaf and J. Tison (2015, May). Evaluation of state ignition interlock programs: Interlock use analyses from 28 States, 2006–2011. NHTSA Report No. DOT HS 812 145. National Highway Traffic Safety Administration, U.S. Department of Transportation, Washington, DC.

Cavaiola, A. A., D. B. Strohmetz, J. M. Wolf and N. J. Lavender (2003). Comparison of DWI offenders with non-DWI individuals on the MMPI-2 and the Michigan Alcoholism Screening Test. *Addict. Behav.*, *28*, 971-977.

Christoforou, Z., M. G. Karlaftis and G. Yannis (2013). Reaction times of young alcohol-impaired drivers. *Accid. Anal. Prev.*, *61*, 54-62.

Citek, K., B. Ball and D. A. Rutledge (2003). Nystagmus testing in intoxicated individuals. *Optom.*, *74*(11), 695-710.

Committee on Medicolegal Problems (1970). *Alcohol and the impaired driver: A manual on the medicolegal aspects of chemical tests for intoxication (Committee Chairman R. S. Fisher)*. American Medical Association, Chicago, IL.

Compton, R. P. and A. Berning (2015). Drug and alcohol crash risk. National Highway Traffic Safety Administration, Traffic Safety Facts, Research Note DOT HS 812 117. U.S. Department of Transportation, Washington, DC.

Compton, R. P., R. D. Blomberg, H. Moskowitz, M. Burns, R. C. Peck and D. Fiorentino (2002). Crash risk of alcohol impaired driving. Proceedings of the 16th International Conference on Alcohol, Drugs and Traffic Safety (D. R. Mayhew and C. Dussault, eds.), Montreal, 4–9 August 2002. Montréal, Société de l'assurance automobile du Québec, 2002, pp. 39–44. http://www.saaq.gouv.qc.ca/t2002/actes/pdf/(06a).pdf. Accessed November 17, 2003.

Corfitsen, M. T. (2003). Tiredness! A natural explanation to The Grand Rapids "DIP". *Accid. Anal. Prev.*, *35*, 401-406.

Dai, J., J. Teng, X. Bai, Z. Shen and D. Xuan (2010, March). Mobile phone based drunk driving detection. In *Pervasive computing technologies for healthcare* (PervasiveHealth), Fourth International Conference on-NO PERMISSIONS (pp. 1-8). IEEE.

Decina, L. E., R. Foss, M. E. Tucker, A. Goodwin and J. Sohn (2009). Alternative transportation programs: A countermeasure for reducing impaired driving. NHTSA Report DOT HS 811 188. U.S. Department of Transportation, Washington, DC.

DeJong, W. and R. Hingson (1998). Strategies to reduce driving under the influence of alcohol. *Ann. Rev. Pub. Health*, *19*, 359–378.

Delaney, H. D., S. J. Kunitz, H. Zhao, W. G. Woodall, V. Weserberg, E. Rogers and D. R. Wheeler (2005). Variations in jail sentences and the probability of re-arrest for driving while intoxicated. *Traffic Inj. Prev.*, *6*, 106-109.

Dent, C. W., J. W. Grube and A. Biglan (2005). Community level alcohol availability and enforcement of possession laws as predictors of youth drinking. *Prev. Med.*, *40*, 355-362.

De Young, D. J., R. C. Peck and C. J. Helander (1997). Estimating the exposure and fatal crash rates of suspended/revoked and unlicensed drivers in California. *Accid. Anal. Prev.*, *29*(1), 17-23.

Ditter, S. M., R. W. Elder, R. A. Shults, D. A. Sleet, R. P. Compton and J. L. Nichols (2005). Effectiveness of designated driver programs for reducing alcohol-impaired driving: A systematic review. *Am. J. Prev. Med.*, *28*(5S), 280-287.

Drinkdriving.org. International BAC (blood alcohol concentration) Limits. Accessed January 3, 2015. http://www.drinkdriving.org/worldwide_drink_driving_limits.php

Dubois, S., N. Mullen, B. Weaver and M. Bédard (2015). The combined effects of alcohol and cannabis on driving: Impact on crash risk. *Forensic Sci. Int.*, *248*, 94-100.

Elder, R. W., R. A. Shults, D. A. Sleet, J. L. Nichols, R. S. Thompson and W. Rajab (2004). Effectiveness of mass media campaigns for reducing drinking and driving. *Am. J. Prev. Med.*, *27*(1), 57-65.

Elder, R. W., R. A. Shults, D. A. Sleet, J. L. Nichols, S. Zaza and R. S. Thompson (2002). Effectiveness of sobriety checkpoints for reducing alcohol-involved crashes. *Traffic Inj. Prev.*, *3*, 266-274.

Elder, R. W., R. Voas, D. Beirness, R. A. Shults, D. A. Sleet, J. L. Nichols and R. Compton (2011). Effectiveness of ignition interlocks for preventing alcohol-impaired driving and alcohol-related crashes: A Community Guide systematic review. *Am.. J. Prev. Med.*, *40*(3), 362-376.

Elliott, M. and J. Broughton (2004). How methods and levels of police affect road casualty rates. TRL Report PR SE/924/04. Transport Research Laboratory, Crowthorne, England.

Elvik, R., A. Høye, T. Vaa and M. Sørensen (2009). *The Handbook of Road Safety Measures* (2nd ed.), pp. 65-66. Emerald, Bingley, UK.

Elvik, R., A. B. Mysen and T. Vaa (1997). *Trafikksikkerhetshandbok*. Institute of Transport Economics, Oslo, Norway. (as cited by Elliott and Broughton (2004).

ETSC (2008). *Drink driving in the EU and road traffic law enforcement. ETSC Fact Sheet*. European Transport Safety Council, Brussels, Belgium.

ETSC (2012). *Drink Driving: Towards Zero Tolerance.* European Transport Safety Council, Brussels, Belgium.

European Union (2002). "Euro Bob": European designated driver campaign against drinking and driving 2001-2002. Final report. http://europe.eu.int/comm/transport/road/roadsafety/behaviour/campaigns/doc/eurobob_2001_2002.pdf

Evans, L. (1991). *Traffic Safety and the Driver.* Van Nostrand Reinhold, New York, NY.

Evans, L. (2004). *Traffic Safety.* Science Serving Society, Bloomfield Hills, MI.

Ewalt, D. M. (2006). America's drunkest cities. Forbes Special Report. *Forbes Magazine,* August 22.

Farmer, C. M., J. K. Wells, S. A. Ferguson and R. B. Voas (1999). Field evaluation of the PAS III passive alcohol sensor. *J. Crash Prev. Inj. Control, 1*(1), 55-64.

Fell, J. C., S. A. Ferguson, A. F. Williams and M. Fields (2003). Why are sobriety checkpoints not widely adopted as an enforcement strategy in the United States? *Accid. Anal. Prev., 35,* 897-902.

Fell, J. C., J. H. Lacey and R. B. Voas (2004). Sobriety checkpoints: Evidence of effectiveness is strong, but use is limited. *Traffic Inj. Prev., 5*(3), 220-227.

Fell, J. C., M. Scherer, S. Thomas and R. B. Voas (2016). Assessing the impact of twenty underage drinking laws. *J. Stud. Alcohol Drugs, 77*(2), 249-260.

Ferguson, S. A. and A. F. Williams (2002). Awareness of zero tolerance laws in three states. *J. Safe. Res., 33,* 293-299.

Ferreira, S. E., M. T. de Mello, S. Pompeia and M. L. O. de Souza-Formigoni (2006). Effects of energy drink ingestion on alcohol intoxication. *Alcohol. Clin. Exp. Res., 30,* 598-605.

Festinger, L. (1957). *A Theory of Cognitive Dissonance.* Stanford University Press, Palo Alto, CA.

Festinger, L. (1964). *Conflict, Decision, and Dissonance.* Stanford University Press, Palo Alto, CA.

Forsman, Å. and S. Gustafsson (2016). Participation rates in a voluntary alcohol interlock program for drink drivers in Sweden. 21st International Council on Alcohol, Drugs and Traffic Safety Conference T2016, Gramado, Brazil, October 16–19, 2016.

Frattaroli, S., V. T. Kuhn, D. M. Bishai, J. S. Mair and A. C. Gielen (2006). Advocacy and the judicial system: Process results from a two state evaluation of MADD's court monitoring program. The 134th Annual Meeting & Exposition (November 4–8, 2006) of APHA. Boston, MA.

Freydier, C., C. Berthelon, M. Bastien-Toniazzo and G. Gineyt (2014). Divided attention in young drivers under the influence of alcohol. *J. Safety Res., 49,* 13-18.

Fudin, R. and R. Nicastro (1988). Can caffeine antagonize alcohol-induced performance decrements in humans? *Percept. Mot. Sk., 67*(2), 375-391.

Goldberg, F. (2000). How accurate are statistics concerning unlicensed and drunk driving. Paper presented at the International Conference of Alcohol and Drugs Traffic Safety. Stockholm, May.

Gómez-Talegón, M. T. and F. J. Alvarez (2006). Road traffic accidents among alcohol-dependent patients: The effect of treatment. *Accid. Anal. Prev., 38,* 201-207.

Goodwin, A., L. Thomas, B. Kirley, W. Hall, N. O'Brien and K. Hill (2015). Countermeasures that work: A highway safety countermeasures guide for State

Highway Safety Offices. 8th edition. NHTSA Report No. DOT HS 812 202. U.S. Department of Transportation, Washington, DC.

Graham, K., P. Miller, T. Chikritzhs, M. A. Bellis, J. D. Clapp, K. Hughes, T. L. Toomey and S. Wells (2014). Reducing intoxication among bar patrons: Some lessons from prevention of drinking and driving. *Addiction*, *109*(5), 693-698.

Harris, D. H. (1980). Visual detection of driving while intoxicated. *Hum. Fact.*, *22*(6), 725-732.

Harrison, E. L. R. and M. T. Fillmore (2005). Are bad drivers more impaired by alcohol? Sober driving precision predicts impairment from alcohol in a simulated driving task. *Accid. Anal. Prev.*, *36*, 882-889.

Harrison, E. L. R. and M. T. Fillmore (2011). Alcohol and distraction interact to impair driving performance. *Drug Alcohol Depend.*, *117*(1), 31-37.

Haworth, N., P. Vulcan and L. Bowland (1997). The potential of public breath testing to reduce drunk driving. Proceedings of the 14th International Conference on Alcohol, Drugs and Traffic Safety (C. Mercier-Guyon, ed.), pp. 989–993. ICADTS, Annecy, France.

Hedlund, J. (2006). *Traffic Safety Issues of the Future: A Long Range Research Agenda.* AAA Foundation for Traffic Safety. Washington, DC. http://www.aaafoundation.org/pdf/FuturesReport.pdf. Accessed July 10, 2006.

Hels, T., I. M. Bernhoft, A. Lyckegaard, S. Houwing, M. Hagenzieker, S. A. Legrand, … A. Verstraete (2011). Risk of injury by driving with alcohol and other drugs DRUID Driving under the Influence of Drugs. Alcohol and Medicines, D2. 3.5.

HHS (1997). *Prevention of alcohol problems. 9th Special Report to the U.S. Congress and Alcohol and Health.* U.S. Department of Health and Human Services, Rockville, Maryland.

Hingson, R., T. Heeren, S. Levenson, A. Jamanka and R. Voas (2002). Age of drinking onset, driving after drinking, and involvement in alcohol related motor-vehicle crashes. *Accid. Anal. Prev.*, *34*(1), 85–92.

Hitosugi, M., Y. Sorimachi, A. Kurosu, T. Nagai and S. Tokudome (2003). Risk of death due to alcohol impaired driving in Japan. *Lancet*, *361*, 1132.

Holmgren, P., A. Holmgren and J. Ahlner (2005). Alcohol and drugs in drivers fatally injured in traffic accidents in Sweden during the years 2000–2002. *Forensic Sci. Int.*, *151*, 11-17.

Howat, P., D. Sleet, R. Elder and B. Maycock (2004). Preventing alcohol-related traffic injury: A health promotion approach. *Traffic Inj. Prev.*, *5*, 208-219.

Hurst, P. M. (1973). Epidemiological aspects of alcohol in driver crashes and citations. *J. Safe. Res.*, *5*, 130-148.

Hurst, P. M. (1985). Blood alcohol limits and deterrence: Is there a rational basis for choice? *Alcohol Drugs Driving*, *1*(1-2), 121-130.

Hurst, P. M., D. Harte and W. J. Frith (1994). The Grand Rapids dip revisited. *Accid. Anal. Prev.*, *26*, 647–654.

Jackson, A. L. (2009). The impact of restorative justice on the development of guilt, shame, and empathy among participants in a victim impact training program. *Victims and Offenders*, *4*(1), 1-24.

Janssen, M. M., J. J. P. Mathijssen, M. J. H. Van Bon-Martens, H. A. M. Van Oers and H. F. L. Garretsen (2013). Effectiveness of alcohol prevention interventions based on the principles of social marketing: A systematic review. *Substance Abuse Treatment Prevention and Policy*, *8*(18), 1-11.

Johnson, D. W. (2004). Impaired driving program assessments: A summary of recommendations (1991 to 2003). National Highway Traffic Safety Administration. Report DOT HS 809 815. U.S. Department of Transportation, Washington, DC.

Johnson, M. B. and R. B. Voas (2004). Potential risks of providing drinking drivers with BAC information. *Traffic Inj. Prev.*, *5*, 42–49.

Jones, R. K. and J. H. Lacey (2000). State of knowledge of alcohol impaired driving: Research on repeat DWI offenders. Report to NHTSA Contract No. DTNH22-98-C-05109. U.S. Department of Transportation, Washington, DC.

Jongen, S., A. Vermeeren, N. N. J. J. van der Sluiszen, M. B. Schumacher, E. L. Theunissen, K. P. C. Kuypers, ... J. G. Ramaekers (2017). A pooled analysis of on-the-road highway driving studies in actual traffic measuring standard deviation of lateral position (ie, "weaving") while driving at a blood alcohol concentration of 0.5 g/L. *Psychopharmacology*, *234*(5), 837-844.

Kaufman, E. J. and D. J. Wiebe (2016). Impact of state ignition interlock laws on alcohol-involved crash deaths in the United States. *Am. J. Pub. Health*, *106*(5), 865-871.

Keall, M. D., W. J. Frith and T. L. Patterson (2004). The influence of alcohol, age and number of passengers on the night-time risk of driver fatal injury in New Zealand. *Accid. Anal. Prev.*, *36*, 49-61.

Keall, M. D., W. J. Frith and T. L. Patterson (2005). The contribution of alcohol to night time crash risk and other risks of night driving. *Accid. Anal. Prev.*, *37*, 49-61.

Krech, D., R. S. Crutchfield and E. L. Ballachey (1962). *Individual in Society: A Textbook of Social Psychology*. Kogakusha, Tokyo.

Kromm, J. N., S. Frattaroli, J. S. Vernick and S. P. Teret, (2009). Public health advocacy in the courts: Opportunities for public health professionals. *Pub. Health Rep.*, *124*(6), 889-894.

Kypri, K. and S. Stephenson (2005). Drink-driving and perceptions of legally permissible alcohol use. *Traffic Inj. Prev.*, *6*, 219-224.

Lapham, S. C., L. R. Kapitula, J. C'de Baca and G. P. McMillan (2006). Impaired-driving recidivism among repeat offenders following an intensive court-based intervention. *Accid. Anal. Prev.*, 38, 1F62-169.

Lehti, H. M. J. (1976). The effects of blood alcohol concentration on the onset of gaze nystagmus. *Blutalkohol*, *13*, 411-414.

Lenné, M. G., P. M. Dietze, T. J. Triggs, S. Walmsley, B. Murphy and J. R. Redman (2010). The effects of cannabis and alcohol on simulated arterial driving: Influences of driving experience and task demand. *Accid. Anal. Prev.*, *42*(3), 859-866.

Liang, L., F. A. Sloan and E. M. Stout (2004). Precaution, compensation, and threats of sanction: The case of alcohol servers. *Int. Rev. Law Econ.*, *24*, 49-70.

Ligouri, A. and J. H. Robinson (2001). Caffeine antagonism of alcohol-induced driving impairment. *Drug Alcohol Depend.*, *63*, 123-129.

Lindberg, L., S. Brauer, P. Wollmer, L. Goldberg, A. W. Jones and S. G. Olsson (2007). Breath alcohol concentration determined with a new analyzer using free

exhalation predicts almost precisely the arterial blood concentration. *Forensic Sci. Int.*, *168*, 200-207.
Macdonald, S., R. E. Mann, M. Chipman and K. Anglin-Bodrug (2004). Collisions and traffic violations of alcohol, cannabis and cocaine abuse clients before and after treatment. *Accid. Anal. Prev.*, *36*, 795-800.
Marques, P. R. (2009). The alcohol ignition interlock and other technologies for the prediction and control of impaired drivers. In: *Drugs Driving and Traffic Safety* (J. C. Verster, ed.), pp. 457-476. Verlag, Switzerland.
Marques, P. R. (2013). Technologies to monitor the behavior of alcohol-involved drivers. Transportation Research Circular E-C174 (Countermeasures to Address Impaired Driving Offenders: Toward an Integrated Model), 54-79. U.S. Transportation Research Board, Washington, DC.
Marques, P. R. and R. B. Voas (2008). Alcohol Interlock Program Features Survey. Unpublished Survey Results from the Interlock Working Group of the International Council of Alcohol Drugs and Traffic Safety. Unpublished report cited by Sprattler (2009).
Marques, P. R., R. B. Voas and A. S. Tippetts (2003). Behavioral measures of drinking: Patterns from the Alcohol Interlock Record. *Addict.*, *98*, (Suppl 2), 13-19.
Marsden, G. and J. Leach (2000). Effects of alcohol and caffeine on maritime navigational skills. *Ergonomics*, *43*(1), 17-26.
Maycock, G. (1997). Drinking and driving in Great Britain—A review. TRL Report 232. Transport Research Laboratory, Crowthorne, UK.
Mayer, R. (2014). Ignition interlocks – What you need to know: A toolkit for policymakers, highway safety professionals, and advocates (2nd ed.). NHTSA Report DOT HS 811 883. U.S. Department of Transportation, Washington, DC.
McCartt, A. T., L. L. Geary and A. Berning (2003). Observational study of the extent of driving while suspended for alcohol impaired driving. *Inj. Prev.*, *9*, 133–137.
Mackay, M., B. Tiplady and A. B. Scholey (2002). Interactions between alcohol and caffeine in relation to psychomotor speed and accuracy. *Hum. Psychopharmacol. Clin. Exp.*, *17*(3), 151-156.
MADD (2015). *2015 Report to the Nation.* Mothers Against Drunk Driving. Irvin, TX.
Marczinski, C. A. and M. T. Fillmore (2009). Acute alcohol tolerance on subjective intoxication and simulated driving performance in Binge drinkers. *Psychol. Addict. Behav.*, *23*, 238-247.
McKnight, A. J. (1991). Factors influencing the effectiveness of server intervention education. *J. Stud. Alcohol*, *52*(5), 389-397.
McKnight, A. J. and F. M. Streff (1993). The effect of enforcement upon service of alcohol to intoxicated patrons of bars and restaurants. In: *Alcohol, Drugs, and Traffic Safety-T92.* Proceedings of the 12th International Conference on Alcohol, Drugs, and Traffic Safety. Cologne, Germany Verlag TUV Rheinland, 1993, pp. 1296-1302.
McLean, A. J., O. T. Holubowycz and B. L. Sandow (1980). *Alcohol and Crashes: Identification of Relevant Factors in This Association. Road Accident Research Unit.* University of Adelaide, Adelaide, Australia.
Mercier-Guyon, C. (2014).Alcohol and drugs and traffic safety. Presented at Edmonton's 6th International Conference on Urban Traffic Safety (April 28-May 2), Edmonton, Canada.

Miller, T., M. Blewden and J. Zhang (2004). Cost savings from a sustained compulsory breath testing and media campaign in New Zealand. *Accid. Anal. Prev., 36*, 783-794.

Miller, P. G., A. Curtis, A. Sønderlund, A. Day and N. Droste (2015). Effectiveness of interventions for convicted DUI offenders in reducing recidivism: a systematic review of the peer-reviewed scientific literature. *Amer. J. Drug and Alcohol Abuse., 41*(1), 16-29.

Moser, A., W. Heide and D. Kömpf (1998). The effect of oral ethanol consumption on eye movements in healthy volunteers. *J. Neurol., 245*, 542-550.

Mosher, J. F., T. L. Toomey, C. Goodman, E. Harwood and A. C. Wagenaar (2002). State laws mandating or promoting training programs for alcohol servers and establishment managers: an assessment of statutory and administrative procedures. *J. Pub. Health Policy, 23*(1), 90-113.

Moskowitz, H., R. D. Blomberg, M. Burns, D. Fiorentino and R. C. Peck (2002). Methodological issues in epidemiological studies of alcohol crash risk. Proceedings of the 16th International Conference on Alcohol, Drugs and Traffic Safety (D. R. Mayhew and C. Dussault, eds.), pp. 45–50. Montreal, 4–9 August 2002. Montreal, Canada. Société de l'assurance automobile du Québec, 2002.. http://www.saaq.gouv.qc.ca/t2002/actes/pdf/(06a).pdf. Accessed November 17, 2003.

Moskowitz, H., M. Burns, D. Fiorentino, A. Smiley and P. Zador (2000). Driver characteristics and impairment at various BACs. National Highway Traffic Safety Administration. Report DOT HS 809 075. U.S. Department of Transportation, Washington, DC.

Moskowitz, H. and D. Fiorentino (2000). A review of the literature on the effects of low doses of alcohol on driving-related skills. NHTSA Report DOT HS 809 028. U.S. Department of Transportation, Washington, DC.

Moskowitz, H. and C. D. Robinson (1988). Effects of low doses of alcohol on driving-related skills: A review of the evidence. NHTSA Report DOT HS 807 280. U.S. Department of Transportation, Washington, DC.

Mura, P., P. Kintz, B. Ludes, J. M. Gaulier, P. Marquet, S. Martin-Dupont, F. Vincent, A. Kaddour, J. P. Goullé, J. Nouveah, M. Moulsma, S. Tilhet-Coartet and O. Pourrat (2003). Comparison of the prevalence of alcohol, cannabis and other drugs between 900 injured drivers and 900 control subjects: Results of a French collaborative study. *Forensic Sci. Int., 133*, 79-85.

Namuswe, E. S., H. L. Coleman and A. Berning (2014). Breath test refusal rates in the United States – 2011 update. Research Note. NHTSA Report No. DOT HS 811 881. U.S. Department of Transportation, Washington, DC.

Nassi, B., L. Rokach and Y. Elovici (2016). Virtual Breathalyzer. *arXiv preprint arXiv:1612.05083.*

NCDC (2012). *Ignition Interlock Device Guidelines for DWI Courts.* National Center for DWI Courts, Alexandria, Virginia.

NHTSA (1994). Computing a BAC estimate. Office of Program Development and Evaluation, National Highway Traffic Safety Administration. U.S. Department of Transportation, Washington, DC. http://www.nhtsa.dot.gov/people/injury/alcohol/bacreport.html. Accessed July 7, 2006.

NHTSA (2004a). Repeat intoxicated driver laws. Traffic safety facts – Laws. U.S. Department of Transportation, Washington, DC. http://www.nhtsa.dot.gov/people/injury/new-fact-sheet03/RepeatIntoxicated.pdf. Accessed June 27, 2006.

NHTSA (2004b). Traffic Safety Facts 2003 Data: Alcohol. National Highway Traffic Safety Administration Report DOT HS 809 761. U.S. Department of Transportation, Washington, DC. http://www-nrd.nhtsa.dot.gov/pdf/nrd-30/NCSA/TSF2003/809761.pdf

NHTSA (2005). The ABCs of BAC. NHTSA Document DOT HS 809 844. U.S. Department of Transportation, Washington, DC. http://www.nhtsa.dot.gov/people/injury/alcohol/stopimpaired/ABCsBACWeb/page2.htm. Accessed July 7, 2006.

NHTSA (2006a). DWI detection Guide. National Highway Traffic Safety Administration. U.S. Department of Transportation, Washington, DC. http://www.nhtsa.dot.gov/people/injury/alcohol/dwi/dwihtml/guide.htm. Accessed July 10, 2006.

NHTSA (2006b). Low staffing sobriety checkpoints. National Highway Traffic Safety Administration Report DOT HS 810 590. U.S. Department of Transportation, Washington, DC.

NHTSA (2012). Lives saved in 2010 by restraint use and minimum drinking age laws. Traffic Safety Facts. NHTSA Report DOT HS 811 580. U.S. Department of Transportation, Washington, DC.

NHTSA (2013a). Lives saved in 2012 by restraint use and minimum drinking age laws. Traffic Safety Facts. NHTSA Report DOT HS 811 851. U.S. Department of Transportation, Washington, DC.

NHTSA (2013b). Model guideline for state ignition interlock programs. NHTSA Report DOT HS 811 859. U.S. Department of Transportation, Washington, DC.

NHTSA (2015a). State alcohol-impaired-driving estimates. Traffic Safety Facts, 2013 Data. NHTSA DOT HS 812 188. U.S. Department of Transportation, Washington, DC.

NHTSA (2015b). Traffic Safety Facts: 2014 crash data key findings. National Highway Traffic Safety Administration Report DOT HS 812 219. U.S. Department of Transportation, Washington, DC.

NHTSA (2015c). Alcohol impaired driving: 2014 data. NHTSA Traffic Safety Facts Report DOT HS 812 231. U.S. Department of Transportation, Washington, DC.

NRSA (2013). *Trends in Highway Safety in Israel 2012*. Israel National Road Safety Authority, Jerusalem, Israel.

O'Donnell, M. A. (1985). Research on drinking locations of alcohol-impaired drivers: Implications for prevention policies. *J. Pub. Health Policy*, *6*(4), 510-525.

OECD (2006). *Young drivers risks and effective countermeasures*. European Conference of Ministers of Transport, Joint OECD/ECMT Transport Research Center.

OECD (2014). *Road Safety Annual Report 2014*. International Transport Forum (ITF), IRTAD, Paris, France.

Ogden, E. J. D. and H. Moskowitz (2004). Effects of alcohol and other drugs on driver performance. *Traffic Inj. Prev.*, *5*(3), 185-198.

Owens, D. A. and M. Sivak (1996). Differentiation of visibility and alcohol as contributors to twilight road fatalities. *Hum. Fact.*, *38*(4), 680-689.

Peck, R. C., M. A. Gebers, R. B. Voas and E. Romano (2008). The relationship between blood alcohol concentration (BAC), age, and crash risk. *J. Safety Res.*, *39*(3), 311-319.

Polacsek, M., E. M. Rogers, W. G. Woodall, H. Delaney, D. Wheeler and N. Rao (2001). MADD victim impact panels and stages-of-change in drunk-driving prevention. *J. Stud. Alcohol*, *62*(3), 344-350.

Preusser, D. F. (2002, August). BAC and fatal crash risk. Proceedings of the 16th International Conference on Alcohol, Drugs and Traffic Safety (pp. 4-9). Montréal, Québec, Canada.

Quinlan, K. P., R. D. Brewer, P. Siegel, D. A. Sleet, A. H. Mokdad, R. A. Shults and N. Flowers (2005). Alcohol-impaired driving among U.S. adults, 1993–2002. *Am. J. Prev. Med.*, *28*(4), 346-350.

Rojek, D. G., J. E. Coverdill and S. W. Fors (2003). The effect of victim impact panels on DUI rearrest rates: A five-year follow-up. *Criminology*, *41*, 1319-1340.

Ronen, A., H. S. Chassidim, P. Gershon, Y. Parmet, A. Rabinovich, R. Bar-Hamburger, Y. Cassuto and D. Shinar (2010). The effect of alcohol, THC and their combination on perceived effects, willingness to drive and performance of driving and non-driving tasks. *Accid. Anal. Prev.*, *42*(6), 1855-1865.

Ronen, A., P. Gershon, H. Drobiner, A. Rabinovich, R. Bar-Hamburger, R. Mechoulam, Y. Cassuto and D. Shinar (2008). Effects of THC on driving performance, physiological state and subjective feelings relative to alcohol. *Accid. Anal. Prev.*, *40*(3), 926-934.

Ronen, A., Y. Moed, R. Gertner, T. Oron-Gilad, Y. Cassuto and D. Shinar (2004). Subjective feeling, performance and physiological strain while driving under alcohol intoxication. Proceedings of the 17th International Conference on Alcohol, Drugs and Traffic Safety. Glasgow, UK.

Ross, H. L. (1988). Deterrence-based policies in Britain, Canada, and Australia. In: *Social Control of the Drinking Driver* (M. D. Laurence, J. R. Snortum and F. E. Zimring, eds.), pp. 64-78. University of Chicago Press, Chicago, IL. (as cited by Evans, 1991).

Rothschild, M. L., B. Mastin and T. W. Miller (2006). Reducing alcohol-impaired driving crashes through the use of social marketing. *Accid. Anal. Prev.*, *38*, 1218-1230.

SARTRE 4 (2012). *European road users' risk perception and mobility*. European Commission, Brussels, Belgium.

Schechtman, E. and D. Shinar (2011). An analysis of alcohol breath tests results with portable and desktop breath testers as surrogates of blood alcohol levels. *Accid. Anal. Prev.*, *43*(6), 2188-2194.

Scott-Parker, B., B. Watson, M. J. King and M. K. Hyde (2014). "I drove after drinking alcohol" and other risky driving behaviours reported by young novice drivers. *Accid. Anal. Prev.*, *70*, 65-73.

Shinar, D. (1992). Impact of court monitoring on the adjudication of driving while intoxicated (DWI). *Accid. Anal. Prev.*, *24*(2), 167-179.

Shinar, D. (2004). Drinking and driving by pub patrons in Israel: A 10 year study of changing patterns. Proceedings of the 17th International Conference on Alcohol and Drugs in Traffic Safety. Glasgow, Scotland, August 8-13.

Shinar, D. and R. P. Compton (1995). Victim impact panels: Their impact on DWI recidivism. *Alcohol Drugs Driving*, *11*, 73–87.

Shinar, D. and A. J. McKnight (1986). The combined effects of enforcement and public information campaigns on compliance. In: *Human Behavior and Traffic Safety* (L. Evans and R. Schwing, eds.). Plenum Press, New York.

Shinar, D., E. Schechtman and R. P. Compton (1999). Trends in safe driving behaviors and in relation to trends in health maintenance behaviors in the USA: 1985–1995. *Accid. Anal. Prev.*, *31*, 497-503.

Shinar, D. and S. Waisel (2005). Drinking and driving of pub patrons in 2005. Final report to the National Authority for Highway Safety, Israel Ministry of Transportation. Ben Gurion University, Beer Sheva, Israel. (in Hebrew).

Simon, B. (2008). DWI deaths: Is it murder? CBS News 60 Minutes. December 31, 2008. http://www.cbsnews.com/news/dwi-deaths-is-it-murder/. Accessed September 25, 2014.

Single, E. and D. McKenzie (1989). The contribution of licensed establishments to impaired driving in Ontario. Report prepared for the Liquor License Board of Ontario, March.

Skurtveit, S., A. S. Christophersen, M. Grung and J. Mørland (2002). Increased mortality among previously apprehended drunken and drugged drivers. *Drug Alcohol Depend.*, *68*, 143-150.

Smouse, R. (2015). New car tech could stop drunken drivers. USA Today, July 7.

Sprattler, K. (2009). Ignition interlocks – What you need to know: A toolkit for policymakers. Highway Safety Professionals, and Advocates. NHTSA Report DOT HS 811 246. U.S. Department of Transportation, Washington, DC.

Stockwell, T. (1994). Informant Questionnaire for the WHO Project on Public Drinking, Australia.

Stockwell, T. (2001). Responsible alcohol service: Lessons from evaluations of server training and policing initiatives. *Drug Alcohol Rev.*, *20*(3), 257-265.

Stuster, J. (2006). Validation of the standardized field sobriety test battery at 0.08% blood alcohol concentration. *Hum. Fact.*, *48*(3), 608-614.

Stuster, J. and M. Burns (1998). Validation of the standardized field sobriety test battery at BACs below 0.10 percent. NHTSA Report DOT HS 808 839. U.S. Department of Transportation, Washington, DC.

Sweedler, B. M., M. B. Biecheler, H. Laurell, G. Kroj, M. Lerner, M. P. M. Mathijssen, D. Mayhew and R. J. Tunbridge (2004). Worldwide trends in alcohol and drug impaired driving. *Traffic Inj. Prev.*, *5*, 175-184.

Task Force on Community Preventive Services (2001). Recommendations to reduce injuries to motor vehicle occupants: Increasing child safety seat use, increasing safety belt use, and reducing alcohol-impaired driving. *Am. J. Prev. Med.*, *21*(4S), 16–22.

Tay, R. (2005). Drink driving enforcement and publicity campaigns: Are the policy recommendations sensitive to model specification? *Accid. Anal. Prev.*, *37*, 259-266.

Tharp, V., M. Burns and H. Moskowitz (1981). Development and field test of psychophysical tests for DWI arrest. NHTSA Report DOT-HS-805-865. U.S. Department of Transportation, Washington, DC.

Timmerman, M., E. Geller, K. Glindemann and A. Fournier (2003). Do the designated drivers of college students stay sober? *J. Safe. Res.*, *34*, 127–133.

Tippetts, A. S., R. B. Voas, J. C. Fell and J. L. Nichols (2005). A meta-analysis of .08 BAC laws in 19 jurisdictions in the United States. *Accid. Anal. Prev.*, *37*, 149-161.

Tison, J., J. L. Nichols, T. Casanova-Powell and N. K. Chaudhary (2015). Comparative study and evaluation of SCRAM use, recidivism rates, and characteristics.

NHTSA Report No. DOT HS 812 143. U.S. Department of Transportation, Washington, DC.

Traynor, T. L. (2005). The impact of driver alcohol use on crash severity: A crash specific analysis. *Transportation Res. E*, *41*, 421-437.

U.S. Congress (2014). H.R.5025 – Alisa's Law of 2014. SEC. 2. Use of ignition interlock devices to prevent repeat intoxicated driving. https://www.congress.gov/bill/113th-congress/house-bill/5025/text

Vanlaar, W. (2005). Drink driving in Belgium: Results from the third and improved roadside survey. *Accid. Anal. Prev.*, *37*, 391-397.

Voas, R. B., J. C. Fell, A. S. McKnight and B. M. Sweedler (2004). Controlling impaired driving through vehicle programs: An overview. *Traffic Inj. Prev.*, *5*, 292-298.

Voas, R. B., H. D. Holder and P. J. Gruenewald (1997). The effect of drinking and driving interventions on alcohol-involved traffic crashes within a comprehensive community trial. *Addict.*, *92*, S221-S236.

Voas, R. B., J. H. Lacey, K. Jones, M. Scherer and R. Compton (2013). Drinking drivers and drug use on weekend nights in the United States. *Drug Alcohol Depend.*, *130*(1), 215-221.

Voas, R. B., E. Romano and R. Peck (2006). Validity of the passive alcohol sensor for estimating BACs in DWI-enforcement operations. *J. Stud. Alcohol*, *67*(5), 714-721.

Voas, R. B., A. S. Tippetts and M. Grosz (2013, August). Recidivism following interlock: Any evidence of change? 20th International Conf. Alcohol Drugs and Traffic Safety (T2013). Brisbane, Queensland, Australia.

Vollrath, M., H. P. Krüger and R. Lobmann (2005). Driving under the influence of alcohol in Germany and the effect of relaxing the BAC law. *Transportation Res. E*, *41*, 377-393.

Wagenaar, A. C. and T. L. Toomey (2002). Effects of minimum drinking age laws: Review and analyses of the literature from 1960 to 2000. *J. Stud. Alcohol Suppl.*, *14*, 206-225.

Waller, P. F., J. R. Stewart, A. R. Hansen, J. C. Stutts, C. L. Popkin and E. A. Rodgman (1986). The potentiating effects of alcohol on driver injury. *J. Am. Med. Assn.*, *256*(11), 1461-1466.

Watson, J. B. (1997). *Behaviorism*. Transaction Publishers, Somerset, NJ. (Originally published by W. W. Norton in 1924).

Watson, A. and B. Watson (2014). An outcome evaluation of the 'Skipper' designated driver program. *Accid. Anal. Prev.*, *66*, 27-35.

Wells-Parker, E., R. Bangert-Drowns, R. McMillen and M. Williams (1995). Final results from a meta-analysis of remedial interventions with drink/drive offenders. *Addict.*, *90*(7), 907–926.

Westat (2007). Field test of ignition interlock devices. Draft Technical Report CONTRACT NO. DTNH22-97-C-05121 for the National Highway Traffic Safety Administration, U.S. Department of Transportation.

Wheeler, D. R., E. M. Rogers, J. S. Tonigan and W. G. Woodall (2004). Effectiveness of customized Victim Impact Panels on first-time DWI offender inmates. *Accid. Anal. Prev.*, *36*, 29-35.

WHO (2004). *World report on road traffic injury prevention*. World Health Organization, Geneva.

WHO (2010) *European Status Report on Alcohol and Health 2010*: World Health Organization, Geneva.

WHO (2014). *Global Status Report on Alcohol and Health 2014*. World Health Organization, Geneva.

Wilde, G. J. (1995). Effects of mass media communications on health and safety habits: An overview of issues and evidence. *Addict.*, *88*, 985-995.

Wilkinson, I. M. S., R. Kime and M. Purnell (1974). Alcohol and human eye movement. *Brain*, *97*, 785-792.

Wilkinson, P. K., A. J. Sedman, E. Sakmar, R. H. Erhart, D. J. Weidler and J. G. Wagner (1977). Pharmacokinetics of alcohol after oral administration in the fasting state. *J. Pharmacokinet. Biopharm.*, *5*, 207-224.

Willette, R. E. and J. M. Walsh (1983). *Drugs, driving, and traffic safety*. World Health Organization Publication No. 78. World Health Organization, Geneva.

Woodall, W. G., S. J. Kunitz, H. Zhao and D. R. Wheeler (2004). The prevention paradox, traffic safety, and driving-while-intoxicated treatment. *Am. J. Prev. Med.*, *27*(2), 106-111.

Woolsey, C. L., B. H. Jacobson, R. D. Williams Jr., A. E. Barry, R. T. Davidson, M. W. Evans Jr. and N. C. Beck (2014). A comparison of the combined-use of alcohol & energy drinks to alcohol-only on high-risk drinking and driving behaviors. *Subst. Use Misuse*. Posted online on September 30, 2014.

Yadav, R. P. and M. Kobayashi (2015). A systematic review: Effectiveness of mass media campaigns for reducing alcohol-impaired driving and alcohol-related crashes. *BMC Pub. Health*, *15*(1), 1.

Yu, J., P. C. Evans and L. P. Clark (2006). Alcohol addiction and perceived sanction risks: Deterring drinking drivers. *J. Criminal Justice*, *34*, 165-174.

Yu, J., P. C. Evans and L. Perfetti (2004). Road aggression among drinking drivers: Alcohol and non-alcohol effects on aggressive driving and road rage. *J. Criminal Justice*, *32*, 421-430.

Zador, P. L., E. M. Ahlin, W. J. Rauch, J. M. Howard and G. D. Duncan (2011). The effects of closer monitoring on driver compliance with interlock restrictions. *Accid. Anal. Prev.*, *43*, 1960–1967.

Zador, P. L., S. A. Krawchuk and R. B. Voas (2000). Relative risk of fatal crash involvement by BAC, age and gender. NHTSA Report DOT HS 809050. U.S. Department of Transportation, Washington, DC.

Zaouk, A. K., M. Wills, E. Traube and R. Strassburger (2015). Driver Alcohol Detection System For Safety (DADSS) – A status update. 24th International Tech. Conf. on the Enhanced Safety of Vehicles (ESV). Paper No. 15-0276. Gothenburg, Sweden.

12

Drugs and Driving

"You know I smoked a lot of grass.
Oh Lord! I popped a lot of pills.
But I've never touched nothin'
That my spirit couldn't kill." (Steppenwolf – The Pusher).

"With a tendency to stare zombie-like and run into stationary objects, a new species of impaired motorist is hitting the roads: the Ambien driver .... Ambien, the nation's best-selling prescription sleeping pill, is showing up with regularity as a factor in traffic arrests, sometimes involving drivers who later say they were sleep-driving and have no memory of taking the wheel after taking the drug .... The behavior can include driving in the wrong direction or slamming into light poles or parked vehicles, as well as seeming oblivious to the arresting officers, according to a presentation last month at a meeting of forensic scientists." (New York Times, March 8, 2006).

"Scientists need to conduct more research to know how much of a drug impairs a person's driving ability." (NIDA – U.S. National Institute on Drug Abuse, 2015).

Our 21st century society is a society of heavy drug users. As we age, we become heavily dependent on medicinal drugs, and before we get to that stage many of us turn to drugs to cope with the stress of life, and still before that we "experiment" with illegal drugs. In addition, our supermarkets and pharmacies are laden with non-prescription drugs. Many of these drugs are psychoactive and affect our psychological and motor functioning, and consequently many may have implications for our ability to drive while under their influence. The research on drugs and driving is ample and growing. At the time of this writing, a quick electronic search through the technical and scientific literature (e.g., www.scholar.google.com) yielded over 900 articles with both terms "drugs" and "driving" in the title, and over 1.3 million (!) reports with both terms anywhere in the text.

Despite the numerous studies on the effects of drugs on driving-related skills, on driving, and on crashes; and in contrast to the role of alcohol in driving and highway safety, we are amazingly ignorant of the role of drugs other than alcohol in driving and safety. There are two general reasons for this. The first is that compared to other drugs, alcohol is a very simple drug. It spreads quite quickly and evenly throughout the different body tissues so that blood alcohol levels correspond very well to concentrations of alcohol in the brain, and consequently the relationship between alcohol intake, blood alcohol concentration, and impairment is quite reliable and straight forward (Moskowitz, 2002). This is not the case with other drugs. Different sampling techniques and different residuals of the same drug have very different implications for the presence of drug impairment. For example, marijuana (with the active ingredient THC) is absorbed in fatty tissues and is then released back into the blood and urine as a metabolite that has no psychoactive effects (THC-COOH). Therefore, the detection of THC in the blood is indicative of recent ingestion, but the detection of marijuana metabolites in the urine or the blood only indicates that marijuana has been used – but the use could be as long as a few weeks ago. Thus, while elevated THC levels in the blood have been associated with increased crash risk, elevated levels of THC in the urine have not (Hartman and Huestis, 2013). The second reason is that alcohol is a singular drug with specific repeatedly demonstrated effects, while other "drugs" is a generic category that includes different drugs that have different effects. These drugs are not evenly absorbed in all body tissues, or even in the same brain centers; they do not necessarily have the same or similar physiological and behavioral effects; and they often do not exhibit a direct dose-response relationship. Finally, to make things worse, drugs other than alcohol are often taken in combination (also in combination with alcohol) and depending on the specific drugs, the specific doses, and the user's past experience with the drugs, they have joint effects that may be additive, synergistic, or antagonistic, and generally very difficult to predict.

Drug Definitions and Drug Categories

When we discuss drugs and driving, we typically think of illicit drugs. Prescription drugs undergo extensive tests of their side effects before they are approved for human use, and when they are, they are often accompanied by warnings such as not to drive within several hours of their ingestion (e.g., Ambien). This is obviously not the case for illicit drugs and controlled drugs that are abused for their psychological effects. The prescription drugs that are commonly abused for their psychological effects include opioids and marijuana (prescribed to treat pain), stimulants (prescribed for narcolepsy and Attention Deficit Hyperactivity Disorder), and depressants (prescribed for anxiety and sleep disorders). People afflicted by any of these conditions, may actually drive better when using their prescribed drugs (Barkley *et al.*, 2005). This chapter will focus on illegal and abused psychoactive drugs, and not on the effects of legally prescribed drugs. Information on the driving-related effects of legally prescribed drugs has been published by the American Medical Association (AMA, 2003), the U.S. National Highway Traffic Safety Administration (NHTSA, 2005), and the International Council on Accidents Drugs and Traffic Safety (ICADTS, 2006).

Short of saying that all drugs are bad (and even that statement is not true), it is impossible to have a general discussion on uniform drug effects. This is because different drugs have different pharmacological properties that cause different physiological and physical signs and symptoms, and consequently have different effects on attitudes and behavior in general and on driving-related attitudes and behaviors in particular. On the other hand, it is nearly impossible and (fortunately) unnecessary to discuss each drug separately. If we allow ourselves some generalizations, we can discuss the effects of drugs in terms of drug types or drug categories. The U.S. National Institute of Drug Abuse (NIDA) classifies the illicit drugs into seven major drug categories on the basis of their effects on the central nervous system. These classes and sample drugs within each class are listed in Table 12-1, and the following sections of this chapter focus on each in turn.

This chapter will first review the evidence for the involvement of drugs in driving and crashes in general, and then for each of the above categories consider the effects of drugs in that category on human behavior and mood, their effects on driving-related skills, their effects on actual driving behavior, and the evidence for their effects on crash risk. The

Table 12-1. The U.S. National Institute of Drug Abuse classification of drug categories, and the more common drugs in each category (NIDA, 2006a).

NIDA Drug Category	Drugs in Category
1. Cannabinoids	Marijuana, Hashish
2. CNS[a] depressants	Barbiturates, Benzodiazepines, GHB, Methaqualone
3. Dissociative anesthetics	PCP, Ketamine
4. Hallucinogens	Mescaline, Psilocybin, LSD
5. Opioids and morphine derivatives	Fentanyl, Codeine, Heroin, Morphine, Opium, Methadone, Oxycodone, HCL
6. CNS[a] stimulants	Amphetamines, Methamphetamines, Cocaine, MDMA, Methylphenidate, Nicotine
7. Other compounds	Inhalants, Anabolic steroids

[a]CNS – Central Nervous System.

final section will address the existing and potential countermeasures to combat drugged driving, or – as it is commonly known – driving under the influence of drugs (DUID).

Drug Effects Relative to Alcohol Effects

One useful approach to the evaluation of drug impairments is to compare them to alcohol impairments, about which we already know very much. To do this in a scientifically valid manner, performance of people under the effects of different levels of alcohol concentrations and specific drug doses must be compared. A first step in this direction was recently made by Jongen *et al.* (2016) in the Netherlands. Jongen and his associates reviewed 179 experimental studies that evaluated the effects of alcohol on various psychomotor tasks and found that performance on two types of tasks were consistently affected by BAC = 0.05 percent, the most common legal threshold for DWI: a cued reaction time task and a divided attention test consisting of a primary tracking task and a secondary visual search task. The argument then is that these tasks can serve as standardized criteria for evaluating drug-related driving impairment. Thus, drugs and drug levels that would affect performance on these tasks would be considered detrimental to safe driving. This, of course, does not mean that drugs that do not affect performance on these tasks are safe as they may affect other driving-related functions not covered by these two tasks.

When making comparisons with alcohol impairment, given the large individual differences in responses to alcohol and drugs, it is best to conduct the evaluation on the same subjects with the same tasks, such as the ones recommended by Jongen *et al.* (2016) (using within-subject experimental designs – see Chapter 2). This has been done in studies by Hindmarch, Kerr, and Sherwood (1991), and a summary of the results of such studies on the effects of prescription drugs that may be abused has been provided by Gier (1997).

Gier (1997) summarized a series of studies in which he compared the effects of different dose levels of different prescription drugs on actual driving behaviors to the effects of different BAC levels. Whenever the drug effects were equivalent to those obtained with BAC of 0.1% mg/ml or more, he suggested that the drugs taken at these dose levels cause "severe impairment." On the basis of such multiple evaluations, Gier derived "decision support tables" for physicians. In these tables, he lists the least impairing drugs within each drug category, along with some "general" signs of impaired driving to which a patient taking the drugs should be sensitized. The examples he provides include hypnotic drugs that supposedly have no impairing effects after 10 hours (or a full night's sleep). The recommended hypnotic depressants are temazepam 10 milligrams, tormetazepam 1 milligram, and zolpidem 10 milligrams, and the non-benzodiazepine tranquilizer buspirone 10 milligrams. Recommended antidepressants are fluoxetine 20 milligrams, moclobemide 200 milligrams, and paroxetine 20 milligrams. Recommended "new generation" antihistamines are cetirizine 10 milligrams, ebastine 20 milligrams, loratidine 10 milligrams, terfenadine 60 milligrams, and fexofenadine 60 milligrams. Gier's tables obviously are not exhaustive because they only pertain to prescription drugs, and – unfortunately – do not list drugs and dose levels for which significant impairments have been found. Note also that the BAC threshold of 0.1 percent is quite liberal, because most countries currently have BAC thresholds of 0.05 percent or lower for assuming alcohol-impaired driving (see Table 11-5).

In an earlier study, Hindmarch *et al.* (1991) conducted a meta-analysis of the existing drug studies to determine the effects of different drugs on various psychomotor and cognitive functions, relative to the impairing effects of alcohol. Next, they conducted their own experimental study in which they evaluated the effects of a placebo and four dose levels of alcohol on 18 young volunteers, using several tasks, including choice reaction time, compensatory tracking, critical flicker fusion, and short-term memory. Finally, they compared the effects that they obtained at the different BAC levels on the different tasks with the effects obtained in the published drug evaluation studies that used similar performance tasks. With this approach, they were able to categorize the effects of each drug that had been evaluated in past research on each type of performance measure as being either neutral (when performance was equivalent to that obtained in the placebo condition), negative (when performance was worse), and positive when performance was better.

A discussion of the detailed results of Hindmarch *et al.*'s (1991) study is beyond the scope of this book, but three general conclusions that can be drawn from their findings are worth noting here. First, some drugs can have a positive effect on performance – at least in the short run. Examples are nicotine and caffeine that typically improve performance relative to placebo. This is particularly important because in most experimental drug and alcohol studies subjects are instructed not to smoke or drink coffee for several hours before the experiment. In contrast, in real-life people often smoke and drink coffee which can – at least to some extent – counteract the effects of a depressant. The consistently positive effects of caffeine on fatigue and its more complex effects on alcohol intoxication are discussed in Chapters 14 and 11, respectively. Second, as expected Hindmarch *et al.* obtained a dose-response relationship between alcohol and performance, and performance with alcohol was never significantly better than that with placebo. Third, alcohol – especially at the higher BAC levels – impaired performance on all tasks and nearly all measures. This makes the task of distinguishing between alcohol impairment and drug impairment on the basis of observable behavior quite difficult, and has significant implications for techniques designed to detect and identify drug impairment on the basis of behavioral tests (as discussed below in the context of countermeasures).

Drugs and alcohol do share one commonality: their abuse and impact extend well beyond driving. Drivers apprehended for alcohol-impaired driving and drivers apprehended for drug-impaired driving both have a much shorter life expectancy than age-matched and gender-matched drivers who do not have a DWI or DUID arrest record. Skurtveit and her colleagues in Norway found that compared to the rest of the age-matched driving population, the death risk of 20-39-years-old drivers within a seven year period after their arrest for drug-impaired driving was 18 times higher for men and 28 higher for women. The most common reasons for the early death of these drivers were drug poisoning or overdose, suicide, and accidents. The worst outcome was for heroin-impaired drivers where 30 percent died within 8 years – 40 times the rate of the age-matched normal population (Skurtveit *et al.*, 2002a). In a later study, the same team obtained a similar effect for abused medicinal drugs that can impair driving – mostly depressants (Hausken, Skurtveit, and Christophersen, 2005). This is a clear indication that drugged driving is to a large extent a reflection of a self-destructive lifestyle that extends well beyond the driving situation – and hence one that is very difficult to eradicate. This conclusion is also supported by another study by the same team that found that driving under the influence of drugs is different than driving under the influence of alcohol in the sense that most of those arrested for drug abuse were repeat offenders with a history of drug abuse (Skurtveit, Abotnes, and Christophersen, 2002b).

The Prevalence of Drugs in Driving and Crashes

A high prevalence of drugs in the driving population is quite disturbing from the perspective of public health. However, from the perspective of highway safety the critical issue is the *relative* prevalence of drugs among crash-involved drivers; relative, that is, to the prevalence of drugs in the driving population. For example, if a high prevalence of drugs in crash-involved drivers is matched with an equally high prevalence of drugs in the driving population then drugs are not over-involved in crashes and do not increase crash risks. Thus, to understand the impact of drugs on both human behavior and crash involvement, it is important to study their prevalence in both the crash and the driving populations. To date, there have been only a few small-scale and a few large-scale partially controlled studies that have demonstrated that some drugs increase crash risk, and these studies are discussed below in relation to specific drug categories.

Prevalence of drugs in the driving population

Perhaps the biggest controversy surrounding drugs and driving is not one about their effects, but about their actual prevalence in the driving population. By far, the most common drug found in impaired drivers is alcohol. In fact, even in surveys and studies that focus on the prevalence of drugs in driving and crashes, drugs – when they are used – are most often used in conjunction with alcohol. This of course makes it difficult to assess non-alcohol drug-impaired driving independently of alcohol-impaired driving.

The estimates of drugs' involvement in driving vary as a function of time, place, and the method by which the estimate is derived. In most places, the number of arrests for driving under the influence of drugs (DUID) is very small relative to alcohol-related, or driving while intoxicated (DWI) arrests. However, that number could be small either because drug-impaired driving is not that common, or because police – for various reasons discussed below – are not capable of detecting drugged driving or are not inclined to arrest drivers for DUID. Based on the current evidence, both biasing effects are true: the prevalence of drugged driving is higher than it appears from police arrests, but lower than it appears from driver surveys and random on-road testing. One of the difficulties in assessing drug prevalence from police arrest data is that police in different countries place different emphasis on this problem. Even within a relatively homogenous group – such as the Scandinavian countries – significant differences in the attitudes of police officers toward the problem of drugs and driving may mask actual differences or similarities (Christophersen *et al.*, 1999).

The widely different prevalence rates from different countries and sub-populations of drivers range from as low as 2 percent for the general driving population in the Netherlands, to as high as 30 percent for young drivers exiting dance music events in the U.S. A 2000 survey of 961 Dutch drivers, who were stopped in different localities and different times and given a saliva test, revealed that only two percent (mostly 22-44-years-old males) had amphetamine, methamphetamine, benzodiazepines, cannabis, cocaine, or opiates in their system (Behrensdorff and Steentoft, 2003). In Australia, Starmer *et al.* (1997) tested (at the end of 1992) the saliva of 494 truck drivers, 199 bus drivers, and 995 car drivers randomly sampled in rest areas and truck stop stations on rural roads. Of all three groups, truck drivers – perhaps not surprisingly given their long distance driving – were the most likely to use drugs, especially stimulants. Sixteen percent of the truck drivers had taken legal stimulants (excluding coffee) and an additional 5 percent used illicit stimulants. Among bus drivers, the rates were 3 and 1 percent, and among car drivers the rates were 2 and 1 percent. The truck drivers also had definite opinions about the "best 'stay-awake' pills" indicating regular use of these drugs while driving. The drugs used included phentermine (trade name Duromine – 23 percent), ephedrine (26 percent), diethylpropion (trade name Tenuate Dosapan – 7 percent), and methylamphetamine ("speed" – 7 percent). Illegal depressants were not detected in any of the drivers, and legal ones were detected in 2 percent of the truck and bus drivers and 4 percent of the car drivers.

In the recently completed European project "Driving Under the Influence of Drugs Alcohol and Medicine" (DRUID) (Schulze *et al.*, 2012), large variations in drug use were found among six countries (Belgium, Denmark, Finland, Italy, Lithuania, and the Netherlands) that assessed crash risks from drugs. Use of stimulants varied from 1 to 7 percent, marijuana from 1 to 10 percent, illegal opiates from less than .5 to 3 percent, and benzodiazepines from 0 to 10 percent, Furthermore, the prevalence of the different drugs also varied among countries. Stimulants were most popular in Belgium and the Netherlands, marijuana in Belgium, illicit opiates in Italy, and benzodiazepines in Finland. When such surveys are conducted in conjunction with a survey on alcohol use, they are often limited to weekend nights, which make comparisons among surveys nearly impossible. When surveys are conducted on all days at all hours a totally different picture emerges. Thus, in 2008-2009 Gjerde *et al.* (2013a) conducted an all-days all-hours roadside survey of 9,410 drivers in Norway and found that 4.8 percent of them had psychoactive substances in their saliva; whereas only 0.3 percent had alcohol. Obviously the results would be different if sampling were limited to nights and weekends. Also, most of the psychoactive substances were medicinal drugs (3.2 percent) and only 1.5 percent were illegal drugs. This is because unlike alcohol which is consumed primarily on nights and weekends, drugs – especially medicinal drugs – are taken on all days at all hours.

In the U.S., a national all-days all-times roadside survey sponsored by the NHTSA in 2007 revealed that 11 percent of the daytime drivers had some potentially impairing drugs in their blood such as stimulants, sedatives, antidepressants, marijuana, and narcotic analgesics (including prescription), and 14.4 percent had some drug at night (Compton and Berning, 2009). Because these values are based on actual testing of samples obtained on the road, they are probably more trustworthy than estimates based on self-reports that are subject to all types of biases. Thus, the drug prevalence surveys show that the DUID problem, unlike the DWI problem, is – mostly because of medicinal drugs – also a daytime issue (Lacey, Kelly-Baker, Berning, *et al.*, 2016).

In an earlier evaluation, based on self-reports in the 1996 U.S. National Household Survey on Drug Abuse (SAMHSA, 1998), 28 percent of all active drivers reported that they drove at least once within the past 12 months within two hours after taking drugs or drinking alcohol. Twenty-three percent reported driving after drinking alcohol, 4 percent drove after drinking and taking drugs, but only 1 percent drove after taking drugs only. Driving after drug use was more common among young drivers (13 percent of those under 21 versus 5 percent of those 21 or more), and more common for male drivers than female drivers (7 percent versus 4 percent). In a 2002 U.S. national survey of drug use, approximately 15 percent of the people 17-25 years old reported driving under the influence of an illicit drug (DHHS, 2003). Marijuana was the most frequently abused illicit drug taken before driving. Of the total sample of drivers, 3.7 percent drove after taking marijuana, compared to 1 percent or less who drove after taking each of these drug types: cocaine, tranquilizers, stimulants, and sedatives.

The most recent, direct and objective estimate of the prevalence of drugs in driving in the U.S. was obtained in a comprehensive national representative roadside survey conducted in 2013-2014 (Berning, Compton, and Wochinger, 2015). The survey was conducted during both weekday daytime hours and weekend nights, and the presence of drugs was assessed by either oral fluids, blood samples, or both. It was conducted in 300 locations where a total of 9,455 drivers were tested for alcohol and drugs in their system. As before, in contrast to alcohol use, drug use – both illegal drugs and medications – was just as prevalent in the weekday daytime hours as in the weekend night hours; being present in 22.5 percent of the drivers at any one time. Illegal drugs were detected in 15.1 percent of the drivers (compared to 12.4 percent in a 2007 survey).

Though Berning *et al.*'s initial report did not specify the prevalence of specific drugs, estimates from a crash risk study conducted at about the same time in Virginia (Compton and Berning, 2015; discussed below in more detail) did provide these data (though not for the whole country). The crash risk study collected crash and control data on all days of the week and all hours of the day. In the control sample 8.8 percent of the drivers had one or more illegal drugs in their system. This is a much lower percentage than in the national roadside survey, even though the data were collected less than one year apart. The most common was marijuana (6.1 percent) followed by stimulants (3.6 percent) and narcotic analgesics (3.0 percent).

The findings above demonstrate that as might be expected – and as is the case for alcohol – the prevalence also depends on the times and locations in which the surveys are done. Degenhardt *et al.* (2006) interviewed drivers while they attended nightclubs in Victoria, Australia, and found that approximately one in 10 drivers stated they intended to either drive or be driven away from the nightclub while under the influence of alcohol (10 percent), cannabis (11 percent), and/or methamphetamine (8 percent). In total, over 20 percent of the people driving away from these nightclubs were presumably under the influence of an illegal drug. In California and Maryland, U.S.A., Furr-Holden *et al.* (2006) interviewed, gave alcohol breath tests, and took saliva samples from 240 people (71 percent of whom were 25 years old or younger) just before they drove away from electronic music dance events. They found that while 38 percent had neither drugs nor alcohol in their system, 16 percent had drugs and alcohol, and an additional 14 percent had drugs only in their system. Thus, in this environment 30 percent of the drivers were under the influence of drugs (primarily marijuana). In a driving simulation study, Ronen *et al.* (2010) queried their subjects after driving while under the influence of marijuana and found that they were equally willing to drive, even for non-essential purpose, after placebo, alcohol, marijuana, and marijuana + alcohol intake. It also appears that there is a link between alcohol and drug use among drivers. Voas *et al.* (2013) in a national roadside survey conducted in the U.S. in 2007 found illegal drugs in 10.5 percent of the non-drinking drivers, but in 26-33 percent of the drivers with illegal levels of breath alcohol.

In the following sections, the estimates for drugs in arrested drivers and in crash-involved drivers span over 20 years. Though it is impossible to provide quantitative estimates on the effect of the time of the study, it is fair to assume that relative to today's more permissive society and laws, estimates of drug use in older studies is an underestimate relative to today's driving population.

Prevalence of drugs in drivers arrested for impaired driving

Compared to the prevalence of drugs in the general driving population, the prevalence of drugs in drivers stopped for impaired driving is generally higher, indicating that drugs in general increase crash risk. The specific percentages of impaired drivers with drugs differ as a function of time, place, and the method used to measure drug presence. Reported rates range from a low of 7 percent to a high of 30 percent. Studies conducted in the Scandinavian countries on drivers stopped for impaired driving showed that a high percentage had drugs in their blood. Christophersen *et al.* (1990) tested blood samples of 270 Norwegian drivers suspected of DWI/DUID, and found that 20 percent of the drivers with either no alcohol or BAC < 0.05 percent had illicit drugs in their blood at concentrations which the researchers judged were high enough to impair driving. In a later evaluation of 3,343 Norwegian drivers, Skurtveit *et al.* (2002b) found that approximately 30 percent of the drivers stopped for suspected drug impairment had benzodiazepine depressants in their blood, most of whom were drug abusers. Lillsunde *et al.* (1996) analyzed the blood of 298 Finnish drivers suspected of DWI/DUID in 1979, and 332 Finnish drivers suspected of DWI/DUID in 1993. They found that the prevalence of drug-impaired drivers in this population increased significantly in the interim 14 years, from 7.0 to 27 percent. Augsburger *et al.* (2005) analyzed the blood of 440 drivers suspected of driving under the influence of drugs (DUID) in Switzerland, during a 2-year period ranging from 2002 to 2003. Even though all the drivers were suspected of driving under the influence of drugs other than alcohol, over 45 percent of them had alcohol in their blood, often with other drugs. The most commonly detected substance in the blood of these drivers was THC (in 53 percent of the drivers), followed by ethanol (46 percent), benzodiazepines (13 percent), cocaine (13 percent), amphetamines (9 percent), opiates (9 percent), and methadone (7 percent).

All of these findings indicate that in the context of driving safety drug abuse is a lesser problem than alcohol abuse, but one that goes relatively undetected. In one of the earlier studies on this topic, Tunbridge and Rowe (1999) offered several reasons why the incidence of convictions for DUID is much smaller than the prevalence of the phenomenon. These reasons include absence of accurate on-the-road screening devices; inability of police officers to identify drug impairment (in the absence of alcohol impairment); and an increase in testing for DWI, which paradoxically lowers the testing rates for other drugs. The rationale for the last reason is that the improvement in alcohol detection has caused most police officers to lose whatever skills they may have had in identifying impairments that are not obvious when drivers pass the breathalyzer tests. Notable exceptions are the aggressive specialized police training programs to identify drugs, such as ones developed in the U.S. (CCSA, 2015; Schechtman and Shinar, 2005; Shinar and Schechtman, 2005), Italy (Zancaner *et al.* 1997), the Scandinavian countries, and England (Tunbridge and Rowe, 1999). Unfortunately these programs rest on shaky scientific basis and are limited to a very small portion of the police traffic enforcement personnel. For example, in 2015 the Canadian Center for Substance Abuse estimated that there is a need to triple the number of police officers who are trained as Drug Recognition Experts (DREs – see below) relative to the existing 600 (CCSA, 2015).

Prevalence of drugs in crash-involved drivers

Drug presence in crash-involved drivers has been estimated from a low of 8 percent to a high of 51 percent. It varies among cultures and over time. Two studies based on data from the end of the last century are illustrative. In Spain, Alvarez *et al.* (1997) analyzed the blood of two samples of fatally injured drivers (collected in 1992-1995) and found illegal drugs in 8 and 10 percent of the samples, respectively. The most common drugs were cocaine (in 45 percent of the drivers with illegal drugs) and opiates (in 28 and 30 percent of the drivers with illegal drugs). Cannabis was less common (9 and 14 percent), and amphetamines were even less common (8 and 9 percent). In the United Kingdom, Tunbridge and Rowe (1999) found that the incidence of illicit drugs among road fatalities more than doubled from less than 10 percent in the 1980s to 24 percent in the late 1990s. In contrast, the number of drivers prosecuted for DUID in the United Kingdom, at least as of 1997, was quite low relative to the numbers prosecuted for DWI: 2,000 versus 100,000.

Still, compared to the prevalence of drugs in the driving population, the percent of crash-involved drivers with drugs is remarkably high. Six independent studies conducted on different crash-involved populations in North America obtained similar results. In Canada, toxicological evaluations of fatally injured drivers in Ontario revealed that

44 percent of the drivers had drugs in their blood (Woodall *et al.*, 2015). Crouch *et al.* (1993) analyzed all truck crashes with fatally injured drivers that occurred in eight U.S. states over the course of one year. They found one or more drugs in 67 percent of the 168 drivers (including prescription drugs), and one or more psychoactive drugs and/or alcohol in the blood of 33 percent of the drivers. Walsh *et al.* (2005) examined the blood of 121 drivers admitted to a trauma center following an accident and found that 66 percent of these drivers tested positive for alcohol and/or drugs; with 26 percent having only one drug and no alcohol, 15 percent having only alcohol, 16 percent having alcohol and one or more drugs, and 9 percent having multiple drugs. The U.S. National Highway Traffic Safety Administration (NHTSA, 2010a) analyzed the prevalence of drugs in all fatally injured drivers who were tested for the presence of drugs in the years 2005-2009. Their results showed that the prevalence of drugs in these five years increased from 28 to 33 percent. A later analysis of the presence of drugs in *all drivers* involved in fatal crashes and tested for drugs in the U.S. in the years 2008-2012 showed that drug presence in these drivers increased from 26 to 32 percent (Berning and Smithers, 2014).

A unique study of the prevalence of drugs in U.S. fatal crashes was done by Wilson, Stimpson, and Pagán (2014). The study was unique because it also provided information on trends in drug use. The analysis was done on the U.S. national Fatal Analysis Reporting System (FARS) data for the years 1993-2010. The FARS data base is a census of all fatal crashes that occur in the U.S., and it provides detailed crash information and information on all persons involved in the crash. It is compiled from several authoritative sources, including police, medical examiners, emergency medical technicians, and hospital providers. In short, it is the most comprehensive and uniform data source on fatal crashes that occur in the U.S. During that period, of the nearly 1 million drivers involved in fatal crashes, only 30 percent were suspected of DUID and tested for drugs, and of those only 21 percent tested positive; that is, were found to have drugs in their blood and/or urine. In other words, though 21 percent of the tested drivers had drugs in their system, only six percent *of all drivers* tested positive for drugs. Of course, this is an underestimate as we do not know how many of the non-tested drivers had drugs in their system, and it is very unlikely that none had. Still, by observing changes over time within the tested population, Wilson and his colleagues demonstrated that the use of drugs is like fashion: it can change radically over time. Overall, despite the steady reduction in fatal crashes over this period, the number of drivers tested for drugs increased by nearly 50 percent, making it difficult to estimate the actual number of drivers with drugs at any one year. Still there were interesting changes over time within the group that tested positive for drugs: the percent of drivers with single drugs decreased systematically while the percent of drivers with multiple drugs increased (from 32.6 to 45.8 percent). The presence of marijuana increased systematically till 2004 and then it leveled off, while the presence of cocaine and methamphetamine declined after 2005. Of the prescription drugs, the presence of diazepam (a depressant) declined, while the presence of alprazolam (also a depressant), hydrocodone (opioid), and oxycodone (opioid) increased.

However, in all six studies because of partial testing for drugs and in the absence of population exposure data, these findings could either mean that drugs are over-involved in crashes or that we have a lot of drugged drivers in the general population. A strong indication that the latter explanation is closer to the truth is Walsh *et al.*'s (2005) finding of similar percentages of alcohol and drugs in trauma patients admitted for reasons other than traffic injuries. Also, in the absence of exposure data the mere presence of drugs does not necessarily imply that the driver was drug-impaired and that the drug was causally involved in the crash.

Drugs and crash risk

The epidemiological approach to obtaining a valid estimate of the crash risk of drugged driving is to compare the proportion of crash-involved drivers with drugs in their system to the proportion of drivers in the driving population having drugs in their system. When the driver characteristics and the context of the two samples are matched, the study is known as a case-control design, which is the current gold standard for epidemiological assessment of alcohol or drug involvement. Many such studies have been conducted for alcohol (see Chapter 11) and they have quite conclusively demonstrated that crash risk increases exponentially with BAC level. The number of studies that have focused on other drugs is much smaller, their results are less uniform, and consequently drawing conclusions from them is more complicated (e.g., because of multiple drug use).

One of the earlier attempts to pool data to provide risk assessment of different drugs is that of Jones, Shinar, and Walsh (2003). In their study, they assessed relative crash risk of various drugs by pooling data from different studies, conducted in different parts of the world, and using different drug detection methods. They then tried to match data from crash-involved drivers with data obtained from the driving populations in the same countries and close to the same time. Admittedly, this is a far cry from a matched case-control study such as Blomberg *et al.*'s (2005) carefully designed and controlled study on alcohol crash risk. However, this is still better than having no exposure data at all. The importance of the minimal control in terms of gross matching in time (year of data collection) and place (country) is underscored in their findings of the different drugs found in fatally injured drivers in North America compared to other parts of the world (Europe, Australia, and New Zealand). Their findings are displayed in Figure 12-1. Given the variety of methods and countries, these data should be viewed with extreme caution. Still, even with this caveat in mind, three phenomena are striking in that figure. First, drug use in general is much more common in the driving population of North America than elsewhere. Second, it is obvious that in North America marijuana, at 15 percent, is by far the most common drug found in fatally injured drivers, followed by cocaine and benzodiazepines, which were found in 5-6 percent of the fatally injured drivers. The picture is not as clear in the other countries, where no particular drug appears to be dominant. Third, the prevalence of any one type of drug is much lower than the prevalence of alcohol.

To determine if drug impairment was a causal factor in these crashes, Jones *et al.* evaluated the risk of these fatal injuries due to taking the drugs. The risk was obtained either directly from studies that included a causal analysis (that directly evaluated the cause of the crash), and indirectly by attempting to relate crash involvement of drugs to their prevalence in the driving population. Both methods are extremely error prone: the first

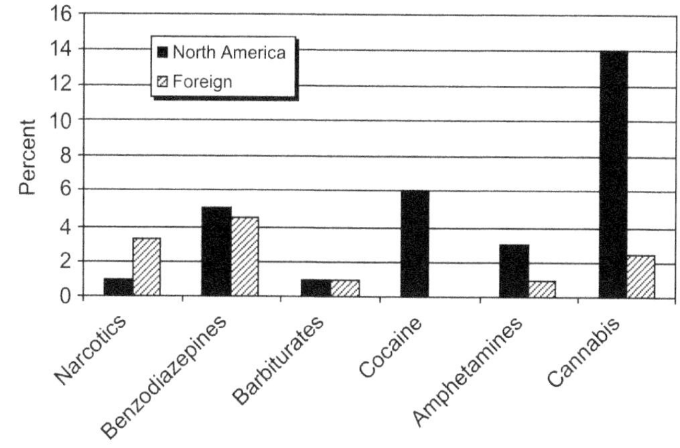

Figure 12-1. The percent of fatally injured drivers with various drugs in their blood, averaged separately for data from North America and for data from other countries (from Jones *et al.*, 2003).

because of its clinical speculative process, and the second because the exposure data are not taken from the same populations of drivers driving the same roads at the same times, and the design is therefore not of case-control. Nonetheless, for as good as they are, the data are presented in Figure 12-2. In this figure, "single studies" refers to studies that assessed the risk directly and "separate studies" refers to data in which the fatality rates were adjusted for the rates in the population of that country. From these data, it appears that cannabis and possibly narcotics and benzodiazepines increase the fatality risk, while stimulants – especially stimulants other than cocaine – may actually decrease it.

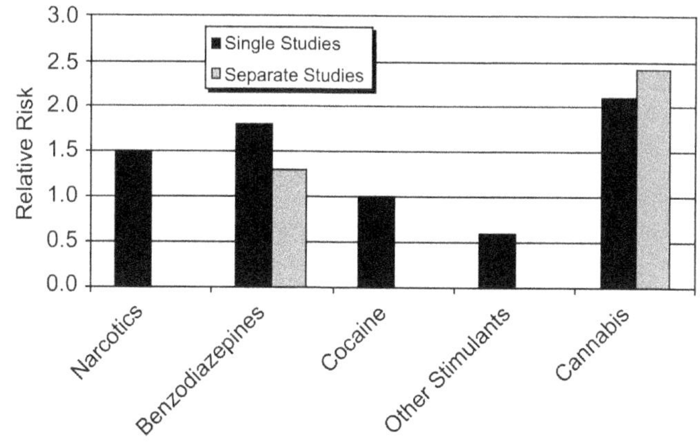

Figure 12-2. The relative crash risk posed by various drugs averaged across all studies reviewed by Jones *et al.* (2003).

Studies on the crash risk of drugs are complicated and expensive as they require valid and reliable drug data from crash-involved and appropriate control drivers. Movig *et al.* (2004) attempted to provide a relatively appropriate control sample for drug crash risk. In this study, the blood of 110 Dutch crash-involved drivers checked into a hospital was tested for drugs and alcohol, and compared to that obtained from a random sample of 816 drivers pulled from the traffic stream in the course of roadside checks. The control drivers were matched in their gender (not surprisingly 74 percent males) to the crash-involved drivers, and roughly matched in age. The percent of drivers with alcohol and/or drugs amongst the two groups are presented in Figure 12-3. First, and most obvious, is the finding that drugs and/or alcohol are three times as common in the crash-involved group as in the control group (40 percent versus 14 percent). Second, when only one drug was detected, it did not appear to increase the risk of crash involvement. In fact, the prevalence was slightly higher in the control group (9.7 percent) than in the crash-involved group (8.2 percent). Third, over-involvement in crashes was associated primarily with alcohol and not with drugs. In the absence of alcohol, drugs seemed to increase the risk of a crash (fourfold) only when several drugs were taken in combination.

When Movig *et al.* (2004) examined the relative risk of crash with specific classes of drugs they found that only one drug type – benzodiazepine depressants – significantly increased the risk of a crash. The odds ratios (OR – which reflect the relative crash risk) are presented in Table 12-2. For all other drug categories that they examined, the effect was not statistically significant (as indicated by confidence levels that extend to less than 1.0). This, by the way, is in stark contrast to alcohol, where at all levels above 0.05 percent BAC alcohol significantly increased the crash risk.

More recent analyses of drug-related crash risk were conducted by Gjerde *et al.*, (2011, 2013b) in Norway. In their 2013 study, they did a case-control analysis in which they compared the incidence of alcohol and 17 psychoactive substances (including medicinal drugs) in a sample of 508 fatally injured drivers whose blood was tested for the presence

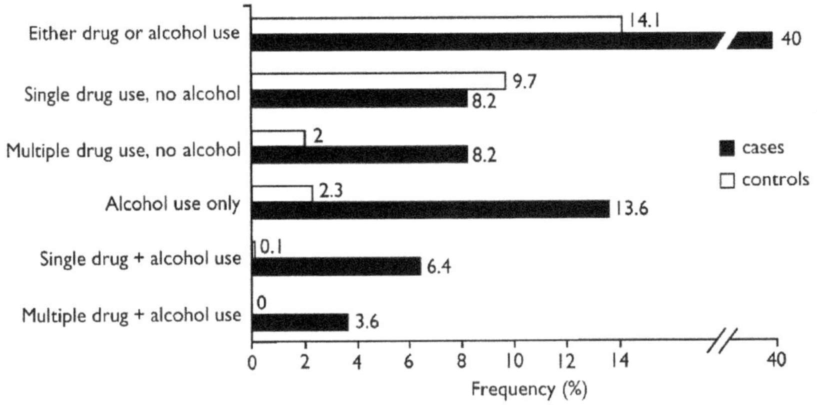

Figure 12-3. Alcohol and drugs in crash-involved and control drivers in the Netherlands (from Movig *et al.*, 2004, with permission from Elsevier).

Table 12-2. Risk of injury in a crash associated with current use of alcohol and drugs in real driving in the Netherlands (in terms of odds ratios and their 95 percent confidence intervals) (from Movig *et al.*, 2004, with permission from Elsevier).

Substance	**Odds Ratio**	**95% C.I.**
Amphetamines	2.10	0.66-6.73
Benzodiazepines	5.05	1.82-14.04
Cannabis	1.22	0.55-2.73
Cocaine	2.04	0.69-6.09
Opiates	2.35	0.87-6.32
BAC <0.05%	1.00	–
BAC 0.05-0.079%	5.46	1.28-23.22
BAC ≥0.08%	15.5	7.09-33.90
Multiple drugs versus no drug	6.05	2.60-14.10
Drug-alcohol combination versus no drug	112.22	14.10-893

of alcohol and drugs, with the incidence of the same drugs in a random sample of 9,261 drivers that were pulled from the traffic stream and provided oral fluids in the same geographical areas at about the same periods. The crash cases spanned an eight-year period (2003-2010) and the control drivers were sampled over a period of one year 2007-2008. To assess the impact of the different drugs, the researchers conducted the same logistic regression analysis separately on all crashes and on single vehicle crashes. The rationale for the separate analysis of the single vehicle crashes is that the issue of culpability becomes moot, as there is no other driver (though in rare cases the fault could be another driver that initiated the imminent crash, or an environmental condition, or a vehicular malfunction). The rationale for the analysis of all crashes, according to the authors, is to enable comparisons to similar analyses reported by other researchers in other countries (such as Movig *et al.*, 2004). The data for both single vehicle crashes and all crashes are presented in Table 12-3. Though the odds ratios are adjusted for age, gender, time of day, and season, the impact of the different periods of testing in the crash and control sample remains a troubling unknown.

There are a few noteworthy conclusions that can be drawn from these data on the adjusted odds ratios. First, of all drugs evaluated, alcohol in the amounts consumed by Norwegian drivers (in this study, it was any concentration of BAC ≥.02 percent) is by far the biggest culprit, and much more so when it is combined with any of the drugs tested. The adjusted odd ratio (comparable to the relative risk – see Chapter 2)

Table 12-3. Adjusted odds ratios for fatal injury in a single car crashes in Norway for alcohol, various drugs, and their combinations. (from Gjerde *et al.*, 2013b. With permission from Elsevier).

	Single Vehicle Fatalities (N = 204)		**All Fatalities (N = 508)**	
Substance(s)	Adj. OR[c]	95% C.I.	Adj. OR[c]	95% C.I.
Any substance	80.3	53.8-119.8	34.6	26.1-45.9
Two or more substances	120.5	57.8-251.6	85.0	46.3-156.1
Alcohol	405.0	203.9-804.7	199.5	112.6-353.2
Alcohol only[a]	221.6	110.7-443.5	124.6	69.1-224.9
Alcohol + drug(s)	889.1	101.3-7806.7	602.2	76.1-4764.0
Psychoactive medicinal drugs	28.0	16.7-46.9	16.1	11.1-23.3
Two or more medicinal drugs[a]	24.8	2.4-261.1	28.8	7.3-113.6
Only a single medicinal drug[a]	9.3	4.5-19.4	6.0	3.7-9.8
Benzodiazepines	38.7	21.5-69.7	25.5	16.4-39.8
Only benzodiazepines[a]	11.7	4.7-29.1	8.8	4.7-16.5
Diazepam	31.7	14.7-68.2	18.9	10.2-35.0
Only diazepam[a]	10.5	3.1-35.2	6.4	2.5-16.7
Zopiclone	4.1	1.1-15.1	5.8	3.0-11.3
Only zopiclone	1.0	0.1-8.9	2.1	0.8-5.4
Illegal drug(s)	24.8	14.3-43.1	21.4	13.8-33.2
THC	9.6	4.9-18.9	8.9	5.2-15.4
Only THC[a]	2.3	0.7-7.2	1.9	08.-4.6
Amphetamines	90.2	38.8-210.1	76.9	38.7-152.9
Only amphetamines[a]	15.9	1.7-152.5	41.6	12.6-137.1
Only amphetamines + benzo[a]	247.9	56.6-1085.2	98.2	24.9-386.9

Adj. OR[c] Odds Ratio adjusted for time period, region, season, road type, gender, and age group.
[a]No other drugs or alcohol.

for a single vehicle crash for alcohol alone is 221, and the risk is quadrupled when it is combined with another drug (OR = 889), making it possibly a full-proof suicide. In fact, the researchers themselves note that in some of these cases suicide may be the underlying cause. For most drugs, the risk from multi-drug use is higher than from single-drug use. Thus, when two or more substances other than alcohol are combined the risk of a single vehicle crash is still very high at OR = 120, and when amphetamine (a stimulant) is combined with benzodiazepine (a depressant) the risk of a single vehicle crash skyrockets from OR = 16 for amphetamine alone to OR = 248 for both. Some medicinal drugs – especially benzodiazepines – pose a greater risk factor than some illegal drugs, such as marijuana. When used alone the most dangerous illegal drug was amphetamine/methamphetamine, producing an elevated single vehicle crash risk of OR = 16. Comparisons of the single vehicle crashes to all crashes yield some puzzling results. As might be expected, in most cases (though not all) the ORs were higher for the single vehicle crashes than for the total sample of crashes. A conspicuous exception is amphetamine. Its effects on single vehicle fatalities were much smaller than on all fatalities combined. One possible reason is the very small numbers of cases with specific drugs. For example, the odds ratios for even the most common combinations of two substances – amphetamine/methamphetamine + benzodiazepine – were based on only 11 "cases" and 2 "controls." These small numbers may also account for some very large differences in the ORs of this study that was based on a total of 508 fatalities, and the ORs in Gjerde *et al.*'s 2011 study that was based on 204 fatalities.

A more comprehensive, but less controlled study of the odds ratios for different drugs was conducted within the EU study DRUID: Driving Under the Influence of Drugs Alcohol and Medicine (Hels *et al.*, 2011). In this study, data on the risk of being seriously injured or killed in an accident while testing positive for a given substance was calculated as the ratio between the odds for a driver of being seriously injured/killed in an accident while testing positive for a given substance and the odds of being seriously injured/killed while testing negative. Data were collected in Belgium, Denmark, Finland, Italy, Lithuania, and the Netherlands. The driver samples included 2,490 seriously injured and 1,112 killed drug-positive drivers, and 15,832 and 21,917 drivers stopped and tested at the roadside that constituted the two respective control groups. The control sample was based on random roadside surveys conducted in the same countries. When pooled across the six countries amphetamines, cocaine, and benzodiazepines showed heightened risk, while cannabis and opiates did not (see Table 12-4). Note that whenever the lower level of the confidence interval is less than 1.0, the effect of the drug is not statistically significant. One problem with the results of the pooled data in the six countries is the huge variability in the odds ratios obtained for the different drugs in the different countries. An examination of the methods in the six studies revealed that at least part of the reason is the large random and systematic errors in the sampling of the data in the different countries (Houwing *et al.*, 2013).

In the U.S., an attempt to maximize sample size in a case-control design was made by Li, Brady, and Chen (2013) by comparing drug involvement in the data of the 2007

Table 12-4. Serious injury/fatal crash risk from various drugs evaluated in the DRUID program (Hels *et al.*, 2011).

Substance	Adjusted Odds Ratio	Confidence Interval
All drugs	2.35	(1.72-3.21)
Amphetamine	8.35	(3.91-17.83)
Cocaine	3.30	(1.40-7.79)
Cannabis	1.38	(0.88-2.17)
Opiates (Illicit)	2.47	(0.50-12.10)
Benzodiazepines	1.99	(1.36-2.91)

FARS data set with drug involvement in the national roadside survey that was conducted in the same year. To improve the matching, the FARS data was limited to those crashes that occurred at the same months and hours that the roadside survey was conducted. This sampling procedure yielded a total of 737 drivers involved in fatal crashes at those hours and 7,719 control drivers. Although the study was defined as case-controlled, because the authors only had aggregate exposure data the matching is limited only to the hours of data collection and not to the specific locations, direction of travel, or the specific driver characteristics as was the case in the Compton and Berning's (2015) study reported below. Nonetheless, given the large sample size the matching is relatively adequate. Across all drug categories, the prevalence of drugs in the crash sample was higher than in the control sample. For drugs alone, across all the drugs tested (marijuana, depressants, stimulants, and narcotics), the odds ratio was OR = 2.22. However, when combined with alcohol it jumped to OR = 23.24. This is consistent with the recurrent findings that alcohol is by far a higher risk factor for a fatal crash than the other drugs typically evaluated.

To synthesize the results of different studies on the effects of specific drugs on the risk of crash injuries and fatalities, Elvik (2013) surveyed the literature (including Movig *et al.*'s study above) on the crash risk of different drugs. He pooled the data from the different studies using a meta-analysis that included 66 studies, of which 47 studies were published between 2000 and 2011, that together yielded 264 estimates of the crash risk of different drugs. Because a recurrent problem in assessing drug effects is that drivers often have multiple drugs in their system (e.g., alcohol and cannabis), Elvik included in his analysis only the single-drug data. Selected findings from his analyses are reproduced in Table 12-5. In these analyses, the largest effects were of amphetamines (including cocaine) and the smallest and non-significant effects were of cannabis. As might have been expected, in the absence of synergistic effects from other drugs the risks of the specific drugs evaluated were lower than those obtained in most studies cited above, where there was often potential confounding from other drugs.

Table 12-5. Odds Ratios of risk of crash involvement for different drugs based on meta-analyses. Numbers in bold are significant at .05. Data on additional drugs, where the odds ratio is based on a single estimate, and estimates for property damage accidents are not included though they are presented in the original study (from Elvik, 2013. With permission from Elsevier).

Drug	Crash Severity	Number of Estimates	Odds Ratio	Confidence Interval
Amphetamine	Fatal	8	**5.61**	2.74-11.49
	Injury	2	**6.19**	3.46-11.06
Antidepressants	Injury	20	**1.39**	1.17-1.70
Benzodiazepines	Fatal	10	**2.30**	1.59-3.32
	Injury	51	**1.65**	1.40-1.82
Cannabis	Fatal	10	1.31	0.01-1.88
	Injury	15	1.26	0.99, 1.60
Cocaine	Fatal	4	**2.96**	1.18-7.38
	Injury	3	1.66	0.91-3.02
Opiates	Fatal	7	**2.13**	1.23-3.72
	Injury	18	**1.94**	1.51-2.50

Finally, in the most recent, and very comprehensive and rigorous crash risk survey conducted for the U.S. NHTSA, with 3,000 crash-involved drivers and 6,000 matched control drivers, only alcohol yielded a significant odds ratio for crash risk. After adjustments for age, gender, race and alcohol concentration, none of the remaining odds ratios was significantly different than one; with THC OR = 1.00 (95% CI = .83, 1.22), Antidepressants OR = .86 (.56, 1.33), Narcotic analgesics OR = 1.17 (.87, 1.56), Sedatives OR = 1.19 (.86, 1.64), Stimulants OR = .92 (.70, 1.19), Illegal drugs OR = .99 (.84, 1.18), and Medications OR = 1.02 (.83, 1.26). It should be noted, however, that unlike some of the studies that found significant drug-related impairments, all the crashes in the U.S. study were relatively minor and the study did not include motorway driving.

Drug effects based on culpability assessments

Another approach to assess the role of drugs is to look at culpability: the driver's responsibility for causing the crash. In the absence of exposure data, the odds of culpability is calculated by examining the ratio of drivers judged culpable for a crash over the number of drivers not judged as culpable. For example, if all the drivers with a given drug are selected, and 75 percent of them are judged as culpable (and 25 percent are not) then the odds of culpability are 3.0. The shortcoming of this approach is that the culpability assessment is subjective, and may be influenced by the presence of the drug and not by its impairing effect. However, if there is a comparable population of drug-free crash-involved drivers, then the *ratio* of the odds of culpability of each group can be calculated, to determine the likelihood of culpability for the drug. This ratio is then an odds ratio of culpability. Assuming that the biasing factors in judging culpability are similar, the *relative* odds ratio of the two culpability ratios is less biased than the odds of culpability calculated for the drugged drivers only. Using both culpability analysis and a case-control design on a sample of approximately 3,400 fatally injured drivers in Australia, Drummer *et al.* (2004) calculated both the odds of culpability and the odds ratios for alcohol and various drugs. Half the drivers in his sample were alcohol and drug-free (control sample) and half the drivers had alcohol and/or either drugs in their blood. The calculated odds of culpability odds ratios and their confidence intervals are presented in Table 12-6. Not surprisingly, given the differences in time, country, and method of analysis, these odds ratios are quite different from those obtained at about the same time by Movig *et al.* (2004). Still, some commonalities are noteworthy. As a group, drugs other than alcohol are significantly less involved in crashes than alcohol. When they are over-involved, they are most often taken in combination with alcohol, or

Table 12-6. The relative risk of culpability in a crash with different drugs, based on culpability ratios calculated from Australian fatal crash data. Numbers in bold are statistically significant (from Drummer *et al.*, 2004, with permission from Elsevier).

Drug/Alcohol	**Percent of Sample**	**Culpability Odds Ratio**	**95% C.I.**
Drug/alcohol free	50.1	1.0	
All drugs (including with alcohol)	26.7	**1.7**	1.3-2.2
Drugs only	14.2	**1.8**	1.3-2.4
THC only	1.7	2.7	1.0-7.0
THC only (>5 ng/ml)	1.4	**6.6**	1.5-28
THC + BAC (.01% gram) versus BAC alone	1.3	**2.9**	1.1-7.7
Stimulants	1.6	2.27	0.9-5.6
Benzodiazepines	1.0	1.27	0.5-3.3
Opiates	1.7	1.41	0.7-2.9

as a combination of multiple drugs. The studies disagree on the relative importance of specific drug types. For example, THC was not significantly over-involved in Movig *et al.*'s study but was in Drummer *et al.'s* study; benzodiazepines had a high odds ratio in Movig *et al.*'s study but did not contribute significantly to culpability in Drummer *et al.*'s study. The potential reasons for the discrepancies are many. In addition to actual true differences in times and locations, the differences are most likely due to the methodological differences in calculating the odds ratios (based on frequencies alone and based on prevalence of culpability), and the use of two different types of data bases: injured drivers versus drivers killed.

Methodological concerns about drugs and driving research

Drug-driving research can be based on either naturalistic observations or on experimental manipulation. But rigorous control and true cause-and-effect relationships can only be achieved by the experimental paradigm. However, applying this paradigm poses several problems that are unique to drugs research. These problems or questions do not have textbook answers, and every experimental approach used has advantages and disadvantages that should be remembered when conclusions are drawn. Seven such questions are:

1. Who should serve as participants or subjects in the studies? For high ecological validity, the subjects should be representative of the driving population that is most likely to be impaired by the drugs. In the case of prescription (legal) drugs, patients who are prescribed the drugs and the ones who abuse them may represent different populations; the former population tends to be older with co-morbidity, while the latter population tends to be younger without co-morbidity. Consequently, the effects of a drug on the two groups may be quite different. Furthermore, the typical "healthy volunteers" often recruited for experimental studies are different from both groups because they are not "adapted" to the drugs, and are not representative of the actual drug-taking patients or abusers. In contrast, research that relies on clinical patients, for both treatment and control groups, deprives the control group of the drug's benefits, which may outweigh its negative side-effects. For example, what are the effects of opiates when used medicinally as pain killers? In most countries, the use of opiates precludes driving. But no country prohibits driving while in pain. Thus, the relevant question is "are people suffering from severe pain better drivers while they are in pain – when it is difficult to attend to anything but the pain – or while they are drugged and pain-free?" Finally, in many studies the subjects are typically young males while the actual patient population may consist of mostly elderly people or middle-aged females (Clayton, 1976).
2. Do and can experimental and epidemiological research methods answer the same questions? Experimental studies typically administer drugs and then look for an effect relative to a placebo condition. Their typical hypothesis is that *given drug ingestion* impairment will follow. Epidemiological studies are typically based on drivers stopped for suspected DWI/DUID impairment. Thus, they ask a very different question: *given observed impairment* is there a detectable drug plasma concentration? These are two different issues based upon two unrelated conditional probabilities.

Also, epidemiological studies of drug impairment – unlike alcohol impairment studies – typically have no exposure data against which over-involvement of a drug can be evaluated. Thus, in these studies the conclusion of cause and effect often rests on the fact that a person with a drug in his or her blood or urine either died or was injured (in crash analysis) or was impaired (in impaired driving studies). What is needed is a control group, such as drivers of same age and sex who are sampled from the traffic stream at the same day of the week, time, and place. Also, while experimental studies document impairments on carefully structured measures and scales, epidemiological studies cannot identify the specific driving behaviors that were impaired by the drug(s), the extent of the impairment, and the relationship of these two aspects to the cause of the crash.

3. How is the impairment related to dose levels? Laboratory-based research often shows a dose-response relationship, based on the dose levels administered. Unfortunately the dose administered to drivers in crashes or stopped in traffic is unknown, and – unlike alcohol – impairment from most drugs is very poorly correlated with blood plasma levels. This is because, unlike alcohol that tends to distribute evenly in different body tissues, other drugs are unevenly distributed in different tissues, and direct measures of the concentrations in critical brain tissues cannot be easily (or ethically) obtained (Ogden and Moskowitz, 2004).
4. Which is more relevant to crash risk analysis: acute or chronic drug administration? Some studies are based on chronic drug use (with multiple administrations over several days) while others report the effects of a single acute dose of the drug. The difference is critical because in the case of some drugs chronic administration results in drug conditioning or adaptation: a decrease in the effects with repeated administrations. For example, regular use of alcohol and some other depressants increases the users' resistance to these drugs' impairing effects, and consequently regular users can perform better with the drugs than occasional users (see Figure 11-7 for the case of alcohol). On the other hand, with other drugs, the impairing effects of repeated use *increase* over time because residuals of the metabolites from the previous administrations remain in the tissues and may continue to affect performance.
5. What drug-dose levels should be tested? The dose levels used in experimental studies are not always relevant to drug abuse on the road. The typical therapeutic dose levels of prescription drugs may be far lower than those used by drug abusers, and the human responses to the two levels are often quite different. With medicinal drugs, most of the research is done with therapeutic levels, and the control group often consists of people matched in age and sex, but without the same symptoms that prompt the prescription of that drug. In that case, there is always a possibility that while the treatment group may perform worse than the control group, the treatment group's performance may actually be even worse without the drug (e.g., for antipsychotic drugs and antidepressants; Cremona, 1986).
6. How does the drug evaluated interact with alcohol and other drugs? The interaction of drugs with alcohol is critical to the evaluation of drug effects. In experimental studies, the effects can be separated, but in epidemiological studies most drivers stopped for impaired driving that have a specific drug in their system also tend to have alcohol and/or additional drugs in their blood. Unfortunately, even in experimental studies, the interactions between different drug-dose levels and different alcohol

concentrations are rarely studied. Also in experimental studies, subjects are typically instructed not to smoke or drink coffee for several hours before the evaluation, whereas in real-life people also drink coffee and smoke, and caffeine and nicotine actually help sustain performance on driving-related tasks such as vigilance (Koelega, 1989).

7. Can impairment in a laboratory task be generalized to driving impairment; and if so, then what are the most appropriate measures of driving-related impairments? It is very difficult to extrapolate findings on impairments in driving-related skills to actual driving impairments. This is illustrated by the findings of Vermeeren and O'Hanlon (1998). In their study on the effects of one drug (fexofenadine), they found that performance on a critical tracking task was impaired with the drug, while the conceptually similar lane positioning in actual road driving was not. The researchers explained the discrepancy by arguing that the tracking task involved high frequency corrections while the driving task required low frequency corrections. The drug, they argued, increases the general level of responsiveness – an effect that is beneficial for the low-response-rate driving task, but not for the already demanding tracking task. However, the authors acknowledged that this was an unexpected effect, and therefore their explanation is speculative and post-hoc. Thus, the issue of transfer of behavior from laboratory driving-related skills to actual driving remains unresolved.

Effects of Specific Types of Drugs on Driving-Related Behaviors and Crashes

This section provides a brief discussion of the various driving and safety-related aspects of the drugs in each of the seven NIDA drug categories. The review of each drug category covers the principal drugs in that category, the evidence that is available about dose-response relationships, the psychoactive, physiological and physical effects of the drugs, the durations of these effects, and the existing evidence for the drug's role in crash involvement. More detailed information on each of these aspects is available in Couper and Logan (2004), Jones *et al.* (2003), Shinar (2006), and a special issue of the journal Forensic Science Review dedicated to studies of the effects of drugs on human performance and behavior (Farrell, 2003). Additional current information is available at the U.S. National Institute on Drug and Alcohol Abuse website (NIDA, 2016).

Scientific proof for the role of drugs in crash involvement requires that the following three statements be true. (1) The drug should have demonstrable effects on driving-related skills. This requires an experimental investigation in which the drug can be causally linked to the impairment. It also involves demonstrating that the magnitude of the effect is related to the dose given and the amount of the drug in critical brain tissues. (2) The presence of the drug should be reliably measured in the driving and crash populations, in a manner similar to the way that its presence is assessed in controlled laboratory settings. (3) The drug should be statistically or clinically associated with crash involvement. This means that its prevalence should be higher in crash-involved drivers than in matched drivers from the general driving population, or that its prevalence should be higher in drivers judged culpable of crashes than in crash-involved matched drivers not judged as culpable in their crashes. Unfortunately, confirming all three statements has been quite difficult for most drugs as discussed below.

Cannabinoids: Delta-9-Tetrahydrocannabinol (THC), marijuana, and hashish

Cannabinoids are compounds that can be extracted from the cannabis sativa plant (marijuana) or the cannabis indica plant (hashish – Arabic word meaning grass), or produced synthetically, or produced in the body after ingestion and metabolism of cannabis, or even occur naturally within the body or brain (Solowij, 1998). The primary psychoactive cannabinoid is Delta-9-Tetrahydrocannabinol (THC). In this text, the drug will most often be labeled THC, but occasionally the other terms will be used, especially in describing specific studies that refer to specific sources of the THC (e.g., marijuana).

Because of the time it takes to reach the blood stream, the effects of THC are quicker and greater when it is smoked (e.g., in marijuana cigarettes) than when it is taken orally, with time-to-peak levels in the brain being 7-8 minutes versus an hour, respectively. The psychoactive effects peak within 10-30 minutes and disappear after an hour or two, though traces of THC metabolites that by themselves have no psychoactive properties (such as THC-COOH) can be detected in the urine for as long as a month following ingestion (Chesher, 1995). Unlike alcohol, THC does not distribute evenly in all tissues, and its rate of absorption and elimination is different for experienced and inexperienced users. Therefore, the method of measurement greatly affects the implications for impairment and the estimated time of ingestion. Although the subjective level of "high" experienced by subjects in well-controlled studies is quite highly correlated with the THC level in the blood serum (Robbe, 1994), it is difficult to establish a relationship between a person's THC blood or plasma concentration and performance impairing effects. Still, a moderate relationship between performance on eye-hand coordination and THC has been found (NHTSA, 2005; Shinar and Schechtman, 2005).

The most commonly noted effects of THC or marijuana include sensations of confusion, anxiety, euphoria, and sleepiness. Physiologically, THC raises the heart rate. Because cannabinoids receptors are concentrated in several distinct regions of the brain – the cerebellum, hippocampus, basal ganglia, and cortex – the effects of THC are quite varied. It impairs cognitive functions that result in slowed thinking and reaction time, impaired memory and learning, difficulties in sustaining and shifting attention, and difficulties in problem solving. It also impairs motor functions leading to loss of coordination, and to impaired balance. Interestingly, while THC does not have a large effect on sensory functions, it does impair cortex-mediated higher-order perceptual functions, resulting in distorted time and distance perception (Laberge and Ward, 2004; NHTSA, 2005; NIDA, 2006b). However, in experimental situations subjects can often "pull themselves together" to concentrate on simple tasks for brief periods of time, thus making it difficult to generalize from laboratory findings to real life (NHTSA, 2005; NIDA, 2005).

While this applies to behavioral effects, it does not apply to physiological effects. Schechtman and Shinar (2005) found that in a carefully controlled experimental environment cannabis quite consistently slowed pupil reaction to light, increased pupil size (both in the light and in the dark), increased pulse rate, and impaired ocular convergence (of the two eyes toward a close object). Unlike alcohol, marijuana did not produce nystagmus or affect any of the common balance tests, such as the one-leg-stand, finger-to-nose, and walk-and-turn.

THC effects on driving-related skills

To really understand the effects of THC on driving, we must turn to experimental studies. The experimental paradigm enables us to control for the effects of potentially confounding variables, and to systematically vary the drug (marijuana) dose and observe its effects.

If marijuana actually impairs driving-related skills, then – unlike performance in naturalistic driving – poor performance on such skills should be measurable in laboratory or otherwise controlled situations. Indeed, as described below, impairments have been found. Fortunately, many of the studies that evaluated the effects of THC also evaluated the effects of alcohol, so the THC impairment can be compared to alcohol impairment. The number of studies that examined this issue is quite large and a very useful meta-analysis from 197 study results on alcohol and 60 study results on cannabis was conducted by Berghaus, Schultz, and Szegedi (1998a). Some of the results of the meta-analysis are reproduced here in Table 12-7. The reader who is interested in more detailed findings is referred to some of the individual studies (e.g., Bech, Rafaelsen, and Rafaelsen, 1973; Chait and Perry, 1994; Heishman, Stitzer, and Bigelow, 1988, 1989, 1990; Moskowitz, 1984; Perez-Reyes *et al.*, 1988; Rafaelsen, Christup, and Bech, 1973) as well as to more recent review by Ramaekers *et al.* (2004). In this table, the specific experimental tasks are grouped into cognitive and psychomotor functions. It is important to note that the number of results that show an impairment for each function is not necessarily independent because most studies provide results on more than one function, and often a study will report several results – with different dependent measures – all related to the same function (e.g., reaction time tasks are usually measured in terms of time and errors).

The results summarized in Table 12-7 show both the similarity of THC and alcohol-related impairments, and their difference. They are similar in that at some level of drug dose, both affect a wide variety of functions. But they are dissimilar in that the level of blood alcohol needed to show impairment is nearly the same in all studies, with the median approximately 0.07 percent – slightly above the per se threshold in most European countries and slightly below the threshold in the U.S. and the United Kingdom. In contrast, the range of THC concentrations needed to affect the various functions is quite large, with some functions – the inter-related functions of tracking, psychomotor behavior, and driving/simulator performance – being impaired at low THC levels, while others – such as information processing and visual functions – being impaired at much higher levels. This is important because the uniformity of impairment with alcohol provides a rationale for setting specific BAC limits, while the

Table 12-7. Rank order of functions impaired after smoking cannabis based on median THC plasma concentration, number of results available, and number of results from alcohol studies and corresponding median alcohol BACs (from results reported by Berghaus *et al.*, 1998a, as cited by Ward and Dye, 1999).

Driving-Related Functions	**Rank**	**Total Number of Results ≤15 ng/ml**	**Median THC Concentration (ng/ml plasma)**	**Total Number of Results with Alcohol**	**Median % BAC**
Tracking	1	79	6	88	0.070
Psychomotor	2	28	8	145	0.073
Driving/ simulator	3	139	9	74	0.064
Attention	4	76	13	122	0.078
Divided attention	5	39	13	116	0.068
Encoding/ decoding	6	78	14	57	0.068
Reaction time	7	10	15	108	0.077
Visual function	8	41	≥15	213	0.069
All Functions		**490**	**11**	**923**	**0.073**
Automatic processes		119	10		
Control processes		107	11		

lack of such uniformity for THC concentrations makes it very difficult to determine safe driving threshold levels for THC. Still, to the extent that a simple averaging is appropriate, Berghaus, Krüger, and Vollrath's (1998b) findings imply that it is possible to set a THC concentration threshold level. In the present case, it would appear that the effects of 11 ng/ml plasma are roughly equivalent to 0.07 percent BAC.

In another analysis of the effects of THC on performance, Berghaus *et al.* (1998b) conducted an extensive review of 87 findings on the effects of THC dosing on various driving-related psychomotor tasks. They then summarized their results in terms of the percent of results that showed significant impairments with different dose levels and at

Table 12-8. Percent of results showing THC-related impairments as a function of THC dose, means of administration, and time after smoking or taking orally (from results by Berghaus *et al.*, 1998b, as summarized by Ramaekers *et al.*, 2004).

THC-Dose (milligram)	**Time after Smoking (h)**							
	<1		1-2		2-3		3-4	
	Impaired (%)	# of Tests	Impaired (%)	# of Tests	Impaired (%)	# of Tests	Impaired (%)	# of Tests
Route of THC administration: smoking								
<9	61	271	36	33	(30)	10	(0)	10
9-18	53	193	38	48	(38)	8	(0)	6
≥18	64	64	36	28	(40)	10	(53)	15
Overall	58	528	37	109	36	28	26	31
Route of THC administration: oral								
<9	(33)	3	14	49	27	37	(8)	13
9-18	(0)	3	39	41	42	45	(18)	17
≥18	(0)	3	60	45	(40)	15	(33)	15
Overall	(11)	9	37	135	36	97	20	45

different times after drug administration. This summary is reproduced in Table 12-8. As can be seen, when inhaled, the effect of cannabis peaks within the first hour, and diminishes afterwards. When eaten (digested), the effect is delayed by about 1-2 hours. The dose-response relationship is not very consistent, and even under careful experimental conditions within the first hour of smoking and with a high dose of over 18 ng/ml THC, 40 percent of the results failed to demonstrate impaired performance. Obviously, these results reflect a mix of psychomotor tasks, some very sensitive to THC and some not. The most sensitive tasks, the ones that show the greatest and most consistent impairments, are ones involving attention, tracking, reaction time, learning and short-term memory. Thus, recall for information learned after cannabis ingestion is greatly impaired, while recall of information in long-term memory is not impaired (Ramaekers *et al.*, 2004).

THC effects on driving performance in a simulator

Several simulator and on-road studies have compared driving performance of cannabis-dosed drivers with that of drivers under the influence of either placebo or alcohol. Early studies in driving simulators failed to show significant effects of marijuana on vehicle control (e.g., Crancer *et al.*, 1969). However, this could have been due to the unrealistic car dynamics in early non-interactive simulators (Smiley, 1999). Later studies, with either simulated or actual driving, demonstrated few significant impairments while drivers were under the influence of marijuana, such as poorer lateral control (Ramaekers, Robbe, and O'Hanlon, 2000; Robbe, 1994), and greater compensatory headways with a high dose of THC (Smiley, Moskowitz, and Zeidman, 1981). Summarizing the results of various studies, Ramaekers *et al.* (2004) concluded that "the effects of THC on lateral position variability were moderate and comparable to that of an alcohol dose producing a BAC of about 0.05 g/dl, the legal limit for driving under the influence in most European countries. However, its combination with a low dose of alcohol (i.e., BAC < 0.05 g/dl) produced severe performance impairment in the Road Tracking Test, and to lesser extents also in the Car-Following and City-Driving Test. There was no significant interaction between alcohol and THC, indicating that the effects were additive" (p. 115).

More recent studies of simulated driving have demonstrated significant dose-related impairments from THC. In a study conducted in our driving laboratory (Ronen *et al.*, 2008), we used a large-screen fixed based simulator, and gave recreational marijuana users low tar and low nicotine cigarettes injected with either 13 milligrams or 17 milligrams of synthesized THC. In a within-subject design, on each session the participants smoked a cigarette and drank a glass of juice. The cigarettes and drink contents varied so that in effect the drivers ingested either one of the THC doses (with no alcohol in the drink), or 0.05 percent BAC (with no THC in the cigarette), or control (drinking orange juice alone) or placebo (drinking orange juice and smoking a THC-free cigarette). The researchers then evaluated the driving performance, heart rate, and the subjective measure of stress using the NASA TLX. During the drive, the drivers also had to engage in a secondary task: pressing a button in response to an occasional light that appeared on the dashboard. The results clearly showed that THC affected driving in a dose-dependent manner: reaction time to the secondary task was similarly slowed by the alcohol and low THC level, but more by the higher THC level. Relative to the control and placebo conditions, when driving under the influence of alcohol, drivers increased their speed but when driving under the influence of THC they decreased their speed; and more so at the higher level. Lane position variability increased under alcohol, but more so under the THC conditions. Subjectively, the participants felt that they exerted more effort and experienced more discomfort when driving under the influence of THC (especially at the higher dose), but felt sleepier after driving with alcohol. Heart rate increased markedly after smoking THC and only slightly after drinking alcohol. Interestingly, after 24 hours there were no residual effects of THC on any of the measures. In a follow-up study, we (Ronen *et al.*, 2010) examined the interaction effects of smoking and drinking. In this study, the participants either had alcohol alone (at BAC = 0.05 percent), THC alone (at 13 milligrams), neither, or both. This time, in a manner consistent with crash risk studies, the greatest impairment was observed when alcohol was combined with THC. In addition to replicating the results of the previous study, this study also demonstrated that the greatest impairments – on just about all objective and subjective measures – were obtained when THC was combined with alcohol. An interesting finding of this study was that even under the three impairing conditions the drivers stated they would be willing to drive some distance even when it is not urgent (e.g., driving to a friend or a party), though a shorter distance than in the control and placebo conditions.

At about the same time, in Australia, Lenné *et al.* (2010) also looked at the independent and combined effects of alcohol and marijuana on simulated driving. Using either 19 milligrams THC (equivalent to Ronen *et al.*'s, 2008, high level) or a very high level of 38 milligrams THC, they obtained similar effects: mean speed increased slightly with alcohol and decreased slightly with marijuana; speed variability and lane position variability increased with both; and the RT on a secondary sign detection task was unaffected by alcohol but increased slightly with marijuana. Possibly as an indication of the sensed impairment, when instructed to keep a fixed headway from the car ahead, the drivers' headways were unaffected by alcohol, but both mean headway and headway variability increased with increasing levels of THC. In the U.S., Hartman *et al.* (2015) examined the effects of alcohol and THC on lane position variability on 17 drivers who drove in the National Advanced Driving Simulator – probably the most advanced driving simulator in the world. They found that both alcohol and THC degraded lateral control in a dose-related manner. However, the combination of alcohol and marijuana yielded results that were inconsistent with other studies. Hartman and her colleagues found that the effects on lateral control are additive, while the other studies obtained synergistic effects. For example, Downey *et al.* (2013) found that even at the low level of 0.05 percent BAC the impairing effects of THC were exacerbated. It is also important to note that measures that supposedly reflect the same skill – such as lateral control when measured via the standard deviation of lane position (SDLP) and lane departures per minute (LD) – do not necessarily yield the same results. Hartman *et al.* found that the former (SDLP) is more sensitive and shows the degrading effects of THC, while the latter (LD) was only affected by alcohol; at least with the levels of THC used.

In summary, cannabis produces significant impairments in controlled experimental studies, but these effects are not as consistent as those of alcohol. They dissipate quickly after one hour, so that several hours after ingestion they are no longer significant, even though cannabinoid metabolites can be detected (especially in the urine) for several weeks after ingestion. Furthermore, as long as drivers feel "high" they also feel impaired and try to compensate for it, albeit not always sufficiently or successfully (Ronen *et al.*, 2008). Heart rate, balance, and nystagmus may be significant cues for distinguishing between alcohol impairment and marijuana impairment: heart rate increases in response to cannabis but not in response to alcohol, while loss of balance and nystagmus are consistent responses to alcohol but not to cannabis. Of the behavioral measures studied, marijuana seems to effect the encoding of information and its short-term storage. It has been found that marijuana impairs short-term memory for digit span (forward and backward) and time estimation. While alcohol causes an underestimate of time, marijuana causes an over-estimate of time, and consequently an under-production of temporal periods in time-production tasks. Impairments in tracking and reaction time have also been noted, but in a much less consistent manner than with alcohol impairment. In simulated driving, drivers drive slower and tend to maintain longer headways when under the effects of marijuana, but their vehicle control and processing of visual information – as manifested in reaction time to secondary signal or sign detection task – are impaired.

THC effects on actual driving

Studies of actual driving under the influence of marijuana have used both closed courses and open road scenarios. In the first such reported study, Klonoff (1974) dosed different subjects with either a placebo, low-dose THC (4.9 milligrams) or high-dose THC (8.4 milligrams) and studied their driving in both closed course and city driving. The drivers' performance was evaluated by driving examiners sitting next to them. The examiners recorded the drivers' behavior on 11 standard measures that are used in actual driving tests. In the closed course, there were significant differences between the placebo and marijuana groups in three of the eight maneuvers: the slalom and driving through the two tunnels. In the city-driving portion of the evaluation, only the high dose subjects showed significant impairments. In addition to these mixed results and questionable interpretation of the results, Klonoff noted that some marijuana-dosed drivers performed as well as the placebo-dosed drivers, and some actually performed better than expected under the influence of marijuana. He therefore concluded that "the effect of marijuana on driving is not uniform for all subjects, however, but is in fact bidirectional … (suggesting that it is) dependent both on the subject's capacity to compensate and on the dose of marijuana" (p. 323).

Lamers and Ramaekers (2001) also used professional instructors to rate their drivers' performance while they drove through city streets. However, their study was a within-subject design, and thus all drivers received all combinations of drugs, including placebo, alcohol (0.05 percent BAC), THC (100 micrograms/kg body weight), and alcohol + THC. They found no differences in the rated performance of the drivers under the different conditions, but this could be attributed to the low alcohol and drug levels used. More interesting, they found that despite the "double-blind" nature of the study – meaning that neither the instructors nor the drivers were told what dosing they received on each drive – the drivers generally correctly identified if they were truly dosed or not. This means that even at levels sufficient to feel the drug "high" no significant effects on performance were observed. When the drivers were under the THC-only condition, they evaluated their performance as significantly worse than under the placebo, the alcohol, and the alcohol + THC conditions. Thus, the study confirmed the hypothesis that, unlike alcohol, marijuana actually enhances the perception of impairment rather than mitigate it. Two on-road studies conducted by Robbe and O'Hanlon (Hindrik, Robbe, and O'Hanlon, 1999; Robbe and O'Hanlon, 1993) also revealed that when driving under the influence of marijuana drivers are aware of their impairment, whereas when driving under the influence of alcohol they are not. Thus, when the experimental task allows it, they tend to compensate for their perceived impairment by decreasing speed and by refraining from passing other cars. Nonetheless, these researchers found a dose-dependent deterioration in lane-tracking performance (both in the variability of the lateral position and in total time outside the lane); a deficiency that was exacerbated when the drivers were impaired by both THC and alcohol. Similar compensatory behaviors as well as THC-related impairments have also been observed in simulated driving (Ronen *et al.*, 2008, 2010).

THC in impaired drivers and in crash involvement
Perhaps the most striking effect of marijuana, already noted above, is that (unlike alcohol), people who have smoked marijuana are much more aware of their potential limitations, consider their performance to be poorer than those impaired by alcohol, and exert much more effort to compensate for it (Robbe, 1994; Ronen *et al.*, 2010; Smiley, 1999; Ward and Dye, 1999). It is therefore surprising that most regular marijuana users and many occasional users report driving after smoking marijuana (Terry and Wright, 2005). This is probably one of the reasons that THC is the most commonly detected drug other than alcohol in the blood of drivers stopped for impaired driving. Several studies that tested the blood for the presence of drugs have been conducted in different countries, including Canada (Dussault *et al.* (2002), France (Mura *et al.*, 2003), Norway (Bjorneboe *et al.*, 1990; Gjerde *et al.*, 2013a Gjerde and Kinn, 1991), Sweden (Holmgren, Loch, and Schuberth, 1985), The Netherlands (Neuteboom and Zweipfenning, 1984), the U.S. (Bédard, Dubois, and Weaver, 2007; Compton and Berning, 2015; Sutton and Paegle, 1992), and (using a slightly different approach) Italy (Zancaner *et al.*, 1997). Together, these studies indicate that relative to other illicit drugs, marijuana is quite common among drivers suspected of drug-impaired driving, but the actual prevalence varies quite widely from 2 to 40 percent, depending on the year, the country, and the driver age distributions (Ward and Dye, 1999).

There is abundance but inconsistent evidence to indicate a significant involvement of marijuana in crash victims. For example, Crouch *et al.* (1993) analyzed all truck crashes with fatally injured drivers in eight U.S. states over the course of one year and found cannabinoids (without alcohol) in 13 percent of the drivers. Ward and Dye (1999) summarized the results of 20 epidemiological studies of cannabis involvement in crashes and found that, depending on the study, cannabis was detected in as few as 2.5 percent of the crash-involved drivers and in as many as 38 percent of the crash-involved drivers. These wide differences are due to multiple differences among the studies including cultural differences in different countries (U.S., Jamaica, and Australia), differences in the years when the data were collected (from 1982 to 1998), differences in the threshold criterion for detection of drug presence (i.e., THC in the blood or saliva that does not last for a long time, versus THC-COOH, a metabolite in the urine or blood that can last for weeks; well beyond any psychological effects of THC), and differences in the type of drivers sampled (all fatalities versus injured drivers only versus fatally injured young males). In addition, Ward and Dye noted that in most of these studies 50 percent or more of the victims also had significant amounts of alcohol in their blood. A partial summary of the findings of some of the studies they reviewed is reproduced in Table 12-9. On the basis of these studies, Ward and Dye concluded that "there is no standard experimental paradigm, no consistency in reporting format, dose administration or detection method. In short, the research strategy to evaluate the effect of cannabis has been piecemeal. Consequently, firm and reliable conclusions cannot be drawn" (p. 3).

The frustrations expressed by Ward and Dye stem from at least two major difficulties in the interpretation of these epidemiological data. The first is the issue of confounding variables of alcohol and age. Across all studies, in approximately 80 percent of the cases where THC was detected, alcohol was also found. Also, marijuana is primarily used by

Table 12-9. Selected findings from epidemiological studies of cannabis detection in accident involved drivers (from Ward and Dye, 1999; citing Robbe, 1994, and not included in the Reference section here).

Years	Country	Case	% THC Detected	Authors (Cited by Robbe, 1994)
–	U.S.	Injured	9.5	Terhune, 1982
–	Australia	Injured	7.7	Chester and Starmer, 1983
–	Tasmania	Injured	10.8	McLean *et al.*, 1987
1985-1986	U.S.	Injured	31.7	Soderstrom *et al.*, 1988
1994	Australia	Injured	7.1	Hunter *et al.*, 1998
1978-1979	Canada	Fatal	3.7	Cimbura *et al.*, 1980, 1982
1982-1984	Canada	Fatal	10.9	Cimbura *et al.*, 1990
1978-1979	U.S.	Fatal	5.9	Owens, 1981
1978-1981	U.S.	Fatal	7.8	Mason and McBay, 1984
1985	U.S.	Fatal	15.9	Garriott *et al.*, 1986
1983-1984	Tasmania	Fatal	9.5	McLean *et al.*, 1987
1985-1988	U.S.	Fatal	19	Budd *et al.*, 1989
1990-1991	U.S.	Fatal	4.2	Terhune *et al.*, 1992
1989-1990	Australia	Fatal	4.1	Gerostamoulos and Drummer, 1993
1990-1991	U.S.	Injured	2.7	Soderstrom *et al.*, 1995
1990-1991	Canada	Fatal	3.5	Mercer and Jeffery, 1995
1990-1993	Australia	Fatal	11	Drummer, 1995

young males, who are over-represented in fatal crashes and are associated with socially high-risk-taking behaviors, even without smoking marijuana (Smiley, 1999). Therefore, as with alcohol, to assess the crash risk of cannabinoids the prevalence of THC in equivalent driving populations (i.e., similarly alcohol impaired and of the same age, gender, country, time) is needed. The second difficulty in interpreting these data is that no exposure data exist for any of the epidemiological studies listed in Table 12-9. The few roadside surveys of THC in drivers that have been conducted have yielded fairly low rates: 4 percent in Canada in 1974, 2.9 percent in France in 2001-2003 (Laumon *et al.*, 2005), 1.2 percent in Italy in 1982, and only 0.6 percent (based on the less sensitive saliva test) in Germany in 1992–1994. The only data base that is at least somewhat relevant to the epidemiological crash data is a Canadian driver survey conducted in 1974. When the data from this survey were compared to the Canadian 1978-1979 fatality analysis, it appeared that cannabis was not over-involved in fatal crashes. In fact, when the exposure data were refined to match for age and gender it appeared that, if anything, marijuana was actually under-involved in traffic crashes (Ward and Dye, 1999).

Seven more recent case-control studies have assessed the crash risk of marijuana and also failed to demonstrate a consistent increase in crash risk in the presence of cannabis. In the first study, conducted on drivers in Canada, Dussault *et al.* (2002) compared the presence of cannabis in 354 crash-involved drivers to its presence in a sample of 9,792 drivers sampled from the traffic stream. They found that cannabis was over-involved in fatalities with an odds ratio of 2.2. however, the interpretation of this finding is difficult because (a) the over-involvement ratios for crash risk were higher by an order of magnitude for drivers who had both cannabis and alcohol (with BAC = .08+ percent); OR = 80.5; and (b) a culpability analysis of the crash-involved drivers only failed to yield a significant odds ratio for cannabis. In the second study conducted in the Netherlands, Movig *et al.* (2004) controlled for exposure by randomly sampling drivers from the traffic stream. Despite the fact that the control drivers were not sampled from the same locations and times as the crash-involved sample – and they were therefore probably less likely to be risky drivers – the researchers did not find that marijuana was associated with increased crash risk. In the third study, Mura *et al.* (2003), compared the presence of THC in the blood of accident-involved injured drivers in French trauma centers, and a control sample of people attending the same units "for non-traumatic reasons," matched for age and gender. They obtained a significant odds ratio of 2.5 only for the younger drivers (under 27 years old). In the fourth study, Blows *et al.* (2005) compared 588 crash-involved drivers in New Zealand to a random sample of 571 drivers. Instead of matching the control drivers in the sampling process, they statistically controlled for some of the potential confounding factors such as age, gender, education, ethnicity, number of passengers, and time of day. They found that drivers who reported smoking marijuana within three hours of the crash yielded an odds ratio for crash involvement of 3.9 (compared to control drivers who reported not smoking within three hours of being sampled). However, after controlling for other risk factors such as BAC, belt use, speed, and sleepiness score, the odds ratio dropped to 0.8, and THC was no longer associated with a statistically significant increased crash risk. The fifth study by Gadegbeku, Amoros, and the SAM group (2010) was conducted on French drivers involved in fatal crashes as part of the European DRUID study of alcohol and drug involvement in traffic crashes. Using a culpability analysis on 4,946 drivers culpable for their fatal crashes and 1,986 non-culpable drivers in fatal crashes, they found an odds ratio of 1.89 for marijuana based on blood THC > 1 ng/ml. Thus, on the basis of their analysis – even after adjusting for age, sex, and alcohol presence – marijuana doubles the risk of a fatal crash. The sixth study was a case-control study of 204 fatally injured drivers and 10,540 drivers sampled at the same times and places in a roadside survey in Norway (Gjerde *et al.*, 2011). In this study, THC had a significant risk ratio only when it was combined with other drugs (including alcohol) (OR = 9), but not when it was the only drug found in the body. The last study was a similar analysis by Gjerde *et al.* (2013b) that was based on a larger sample of Norwegian fatal crashes sampled over an eight-year period. In that analysis too, the adjusted odds ratio for fatality was not significant when the driver had only THC and no other substance in the blood, but as before it was greater and statistically significant when combined with other drugs (OR = 8.9, see Table 12-3).

A meta-analysis of nine high- and medium-quality studies published between 1982 and 2007, comprising a total of 49,411 drivers that were tested for the presence of alcohol and drugs, was performed by Asbridge, Hayden, and Cartwright (2012). To eliminate the possible spurious effects of alcohol or other drugs, Asbridge and his colleagues considered only crashes with drivers who had either no drugs at all or THC only. The studies involved both case-control and culpability analysis. Across all studies marijuana was over-involved in crashes with an OR = 1.92; that is, marijuana essentially doubled the risk of a crash. Interestingly, the odds ratio based on the case-control analysis was greater than the odds ratio based on the culpability analysis: OR = 2.79 versus OR = 1.65, though both were significantly greater than zero. In general, the odds ratios were also greater for high-quality studies than for medium-quality studies (OR = 2.21 versus 1.78), and for fatal crashes than for non-fatal crashes (OR = 2.10 versus 1.74). A graphical summary of the odds ratios obtained for each of the nine studies included in their analysis is reproduced in Figure 12-4. In this figure, the horizontal lines that extend from each OR level are the 95 percent confidence limits, and whenever the line crosses the 1.0 level, the effect is not significant. Thus, although the odds ratio based on the total number of drivers from all nine studies was significant, in three of the nine studies the odds ratios were not significantly different from zero. As expected, when the sample of

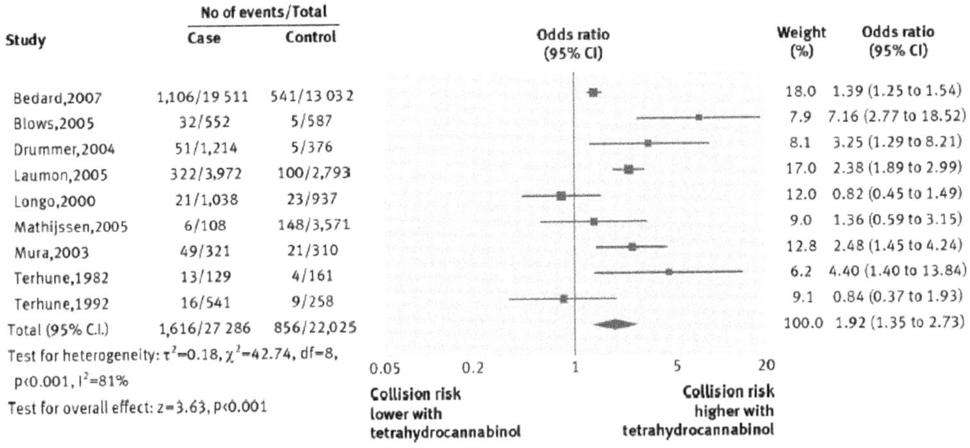

Figure 12-4. Meta-analysis of nine observational studies investigating the association between acute cannabis consumption and motor vehicle crashes (from Asbridge *et al.*, 2012. With permission from BMJ).

marijuana-impaired drivers included also those who had alcohol in their blood, the odds ratios were significantly higher.

Two recent studies conducted in the U.S. obtained somewhat different results and conclusions concerning the crash risk from marijuana. A study by Li *et al.* (2013), described above, evaluated the risk of various drugs using 2007 U.S. FARS data for the crashes, and linking it to the national roadside survey conducted in the same year. However, because the crash data did not have consistent reliable measures of all drugs, their analysis did not enable them to adjust the odds ratios by biasing factors such as driver's age, gender, and crash location. Furthermore, it is not clear from their report whether the drugged cases included only those with the drug evaluated (in this case marijuana) or also those with alcohol and other drugs. The second study, sponsored by the National Highway Traffic Safety Administration (Compton and Berning 2015; Lacey *et al.*, 2016), is possibly the most carefully designed and comprehensive epidemiological study to date. It was a case-control study that compared the presence of drugs in the drivers of all police-reported crashes in Virginia Beach, VA, during 2010-2011 with the presence of drugs in the comparable driving population. A total of 3,095 crash-involved drivers were identified and tested for the presence of drugs and alcohol in their blood or saliva. For each driver, two control drivers were selected from the traffic stream in the same locations, traveling in the same direction, and at the same time of day exactly a week after the crash. In this most recent and carefully controlled study, the odds ratio for marijuana was not significant; neither in the crude measure nor after adjusting for age and gender (OR = 1.05).

Taken together, these results, summarized in Table 12-10, indicate that THC, to the extent that it is associated with increased crash risk, is probably not the only cause of the THC-involved crashes, but a correlate of other risk-taking factors that go hand-in-hand with smoking marijuana. Although it is unlikely that frequent marijuana smokers are aware of all the studies quoted above, it is interesting that at least one study that investigated users' perceptions of the dangers of smoking and driving found that approximately 75 percent of the males and 50 percent of the females felt that marijuana smoking impairs their driving, but over 90 percent of the females and 100 percent of the males felt that when marijuana is combined with alcohol driving is impaired (Lenné *et al.*, 2001).

A somewhat different approach to crash risk from marijuana was taken by Dubois *et al.* (2015). Their analysis included all the crashes in the U.S. Fatal Analysis Reporting System in 1991-2008, in which the drivers were tested for alcohol and THC. The unique aspect of their study was that they examined the added risk of an unsafe driving action (UDA) for 20+ years old drivers with low alcohol levels (BAC <.10), with any amount of THC, or with both. Though they found a significant effect on UDA of BAC alone, the risk of a UDA did not increase when alcohol was combined with THC. It did increase slightly, by approximately 16 percent, with THC alone. Thus, these results provide a direct link between fatal crashes and the role of alcohol in increasing UDAs, but they do not support a strong link between fatal crashes and UDAs for drivers with marijuana in their blood. It is important to stress though, that these are not the crash risks that increase but the likelihood of an unsafe driving action preceding the crash.

Table 12-10. Odds ratios of crash risk from different recent large-scale studies for drivers with cannabis in their system relative to drug-free drivers.

Authors (year)	**Sample Sizes (Place) Crash + Control**	**Adjusted Odds Ratio**[a]
Blows *et al.* (2005)	588 + 571 (New Zealand)	0.8, n.s.
Dussault *et al.* (2002)	354 + 11,574 (Canada)	2.2, $p < .05$[b]
Movig *et al.* (2004)	110 + 816 (The Netherlands)	1.2, n.s.
Mura *et al.* (2003)	900 + 900 (France)	2.5, $p < .05$[c]
Hels *et al.* (2011)	3,602 + 37,749 (9 EU Countries)	1.39, 1.33, n.s.
Gjerde *et al.* (2011)	204, 10,540 (Norway)	0.9, n.s.
Asbridge *et al.* (2012)	27,286 + 22,025 (diff. countries)	1.92, $p < .05$
Gjerde *et al.* (2013b)	508 + 9,261 (Norway)	1.9, n.s.
Li *et al.* (2013)	737 + 7,719 (U.S)	1.83, $p < .05$[d]
Compton and Berning (2015); Lacey *et al.* (2016)	3,095 + 6,190 (VA, U.S.)	1.05, n.s.

[a]Adjusted for different factors in different studies.
[b]But a culpability analysis did not yield a significant OR.
[c]For THC > 1 ng/ml, and only for the younger (<27 years old) drivers.
[d]Based on FARS 2007 crash data. Crude OR, without adjustments for age, gender.

As noted above, to circumvent the lack of exposure data, some studies have looked at culpability. A review of the results of several culpability studies was conducted by Ramaekers *et al.* (2004), and their results are summarized in Table 12-11. Note that in this case the odds ratio is the percent of culpable crash drivers with detectable levels of THC relative to the percent of non-culpable drivers with THC. Needless to say, the judgment of culpability should be made by people who are "blind" to the presence or absence of the drug.

One culpability study that has systematically implicated THC in crashes was conducted by Laumon *et al.* (2005) in France. It compared the frequencies of various THC levels in 6,766 culpable drivers with the THC levels of 3,006 non-culpable drivers; all involved in fatal crashes in France in the years 2001-2003. After adjusting for the presence of alcohol, they found that THC more than doubled the relative risk of a crash (yielding an odds ratio = 2.4), and that there was a definite dose-response relationship: with the odds

Table 12-11. Culpability analysis of the Odds Ratios of being involved in a fatal or injury crash while under the influence of alcohol, cannabis, or both (based on nine studies reviewed by Ramaekers *et al.*, 2004, with permission from Elsevier).

Drug	**No. of Studies (Publication Dates)**	**Odds Ratios**	**95% Confidence Intervals**	**Statistical Significance**
Drug-free		1.0		
Alcohol	7 (1982-2003)	3.2-6.8	1.1-9.4 – 4.3-11.1	All
THC-COOH	6 (1982-2001)	0.2-2.1	0.2-1.5 – 0.7-6.6	None
THC (ng/ml)	2 (1998-2003)	0.4-6.6	<0.1-2.1 – 1.5-28.0	Only if THC >5 ng/ml
Alc. + THC or THC-COOH	5 (1985-2001)	3.5-11.5	1.2-11.4 – 4.6-36.7	All

ratio increasing from 1.9 for THC concentrations <1 ng/ml blood to 4.7 for THC ≥ 5 ng/ml blood. However, as in Blows *et al.*'s (2005) study, after further adjustments for driver age, type of vehicle, and time of crash, the odds ratios decreased, but they were still significantly greater than 1.0 as long as the THC concentration was >1 ng/ml. Thus, even this study suggests that the association between THC and crash risk is both slight and limited to high dose levels.

Given the inconsistencies in test results for THC, another approach is to rely on survey-based self-reports of drivers. Asbridge, Poulin, and Donato (2005) did that with a sample of 6,087 high-school drivers who were asked to report on their crash experience, citations for moving violations, and driving while under the influence of marijuana. Using a logistic regression to determine the variables that were significantly associated with their crash involvement, the researchers found that the best predictors of crash involvement were driver gender, experience (meaning exposure), driving under the influence of cannabis, and driving under the influence of alcohol. Unfortunately, because no data were available on other high-risk behaviors, it is impossible to determine if the increased crash risk was due to the use of cannabis or to proclivity for other high-risk behaviors by the same individuals. The potential role of other high-risk behaviors is reinforced by a finding that drivers treated for marijuana addiction have more traffic violations than age-gender-matched control drivers (Macdonald *et al.*, 2004).

In conclusion, the myriad of inconsistent results on the effects of cannabis on both behavior and crash involvement show that we still lack sufficient data on the levels of cannabinoids that compromise driving, or how to measure them in a dose-response related manner. Even if we focus on the studies that did show a relationship between THC, driving impairment, and crash involvement, to conclude that the relationship is causal still requires a large leap of faith. The mere presence of cannabinoids in impaired drivers is only testimony to presence of a substance and not to its effect, and proof of association is not proof of causality. This is particularly true in the case of THC whose metabolites can be detected days and weeks after its psychological effects have worn off. Furthermore, over 100 THC metabolites have been detected in the blood following ingestion of THC, but so far only one has been associated with impairment (11-OH-THC) (Berning *et al.*, 2015). Also, as noted above, when THC or cannabinoids were found in the blood of crash-involved drivers, the drivers were more likely than not to also have alcohol, whose impairing effects overshadow those of marijuana. Thus, given our state of knowledge it appears that THC impairs driving but the impairment is not as significant as alcohol, and it is manifested mostly when the dose levels are high.

The bottom line now is that we still do not have a definitive bottom line concerning the role of cannabis in crash risk. Three studies that summarized the results of multiple individual studies of crash analysis have generally converged on an odds ratio of approximately 2.0 or less; meaning that marijuana at the levels smoked by drivers essentially doubles the risk of a crash. To put it in perspective, an odds ratio of 2 is equivalent to blood alcohol concentration of BAC = 0.05 percent (Compton and Berning, 2015); which is slightly below the critical level in the U.S., Canada, and the United Kingdom. Hartman and Huestis (2013) did a qualitative review of the findings of 10 epidemiologic studies conducted in six different countries and concluded that marijuana roughly doubles the risk of a crash. Lending support to this estimate is their observation that when examined, blood THC concentration was strongly related to culpability. On the other hand, Elvik's (2013) meta-analysis of 10 results of fatal crashes and 15 results of injury crashes did not yield a significant elevated crash risk from cannabis alone (see Table 12-5). In his analysis, cannabis had a significantly elevated crash risk only on property damage crashes, and this too was fairly low at 1.48 (with a confidence interval of 1.28-1.72). Asbridge *et al.* (2012) summarized the net THC effects (i.e., comparing crash involvement with THC only versus without any drugs or alcohol) of nine studies published between 1982 and 2007, and found that the crash risk from THC was significant in seven of the nine studies, and greater for fatal collisions and case-control studies. Averaged across all studies the odds ratio was 1.9, suggesting that marijuana consumption before driving, when not confounded with the effects of alcohol, doubles the crash risk. Finally, the quagmire remains: the recent and extensive European DRUID study and the American NHTSA study failed to demonstrate an added crash risk for marijuana, while the most recently reported meta-analysis, based on 21 observational studies yielded an over-involvement average adjusted Odds Ratio for serious injuries of 1.86 (Rogeberg and Elvik, 2016).

Legalization of marijuana

If marijuana is a significant crash risk, then one reason for added concern is the trend to legalize marijuana. In the U.S., the commercialization of medical marijuana in Colorado in 2009 led to an increase in the presence of THC with alcohol in fatal crashes without an increase in the presence of alcohol alone (Salomonsen-Sautel *et al.*, 2014). Note, however, it is likely that the commercialization of marijuana also increased the prevalence of THC of drivers not involved in fatal crashes (i.e., in the traffic stream), and consequently the increased presence alone is not indicative of a heightened risk or causality. Going a step beyond Colorado, California decriminalized the possession of small amounts of Marijuana in the beginning of 2011. An evaluation of the effects of the change in the law on the prevalence of THC in the blood of both drivers in the traffic stream and in the blood of those involved in fatal crashes by Pollini *et al.* (2015) yielded paradoxical findings. On the one hand, there was an increase in the prevalence of THC in fatal crashes, but on the other hand there was no increase in the prevalence of THC in the driving population. Perplexed, the authors suggested that the discrepant results are due to biases in "surveillance and testing methods."

In short, more carefully controlled epidemiological studies are needed before a firm conclusion can be drawn. While the data on marijuana effects on driving-related skills is fairly conclusive, the weight of the evidence indicates that smoking marijuana prior to driving is either not a significant crash risk factor, or a relatively minor one – especially in comparison to alcohol. (This contradiction between the crash indicators and the crash outcome measures is similar to the one for the effects of cognitive distraction from talking on the phone on driving and on crash risk. See Chapter 13). The explanation probably lies in (1) partial compensation for impairment in actual driving, and (2) confounding of the THC effect with other drugs (especially alcohol). It is also possible that given the relatively small increases in crash risk the impact of legalization may be very minor relative to the crash risk from other concomitant crash factors such as alcohol and fatigue.

CNS depressants

Central Nervous System depressants, often referred to as sedatives and tranquilizers, are drugs that slow normal brain functions. The most common drugs in that category include barbiturates, benzodiazepines, antihistamines, methaqualone, and gamma-hydroxybutyrate (GHB). Although depressants are often prescribed as a treatment for anxiety and sleep disorders, it is the drowsiness and calmness that they cause that leads to their abuse, and to potential danger in the context of driving. As drugs of abuse they are known by the names of barbs, reds, and yellows (for barbiturates), as candy and downers (for benzodiazepines), and as ludes and quads (for methaqualone). Impairing effects of depressants typically peak at 2-3 hours after ingestion, and they can last up to 6 hours after drug administration. After that (or in the following morning) there are typically few or no impairments (Ghoneim, Mewaldt, and Thatcher, 1975). However, as long as the sedating effect persists it may impair driving-related functions. Within a short time of taking the drug, there seems to be a direct relationship between the drug blood level and the likelihood of impairment (Bramness, Skurtveit, and Mørland, 2002), but over longer periods, unlike alcohol, the dose-response relationship is much more complicated, making the drug/plasma level an unreliable correlate of impairment (Ellinwood and Heatherly, 1985). Physiological and physical symptoms of impairment – at least as evaluated on alprazolam (a benzodiazepine) – include problems with ocular convergence, an increase in pulse rate, a drop in temperature, horizontal gaze nystagmus, and poor coordination as reflected in the walk-and-turn test (Schechtman and Shinar, 2005). In that respect, the effects of CNS depressants are similar to alcohol; the most commonly abused depressant.

According to NIDA (2006b), the psychoactive effects of depressants such as benzodiazepines include reduced anxiety, feeling of well-being, lowered inhibitions, slowed pulse and breathing, lowered blood pressure, poor concentration, and fatigue. In the case of barbiturates, they include sedation, drowsiness, depression, unusual excitement, and irritability. Benzodiazepines produce sedation, and drowsiness, or dizziness. GHB produces drowsiness, nausea or vomiting, and headache. Methaqualone can produce euphoria and depression, poor reflexes, and slurred speech.

Depressant effects on driving-related skills

Because of their use as prescription drugs, benzodiazepines, barbiturates, and antihistamines have all been tested extensively to determine their potential harmful effects on driving and driving-related skills. In an early review of 101 studies, McNair (1973) concluded that "mild tranquilizers have little effect on human performance, or ... little is known about their effect on human performance, or both." Since then, there have been many studies that have documented impaired human performance due to such drugs, but the results are still quite inconsistent. Some of the reasons for inconsistencies are large individual differences in personality and motivation (McNair, 1973), use of different evaluation procedures (short-term versus long term, treatment-control groups versus crossover sampling, group testing versus individual testing), use of different dependent measures of performance, absence of a clear dose-response relationship, and different intervals between drug administration and impairment testing (same evening versus following morning). Finally, even though all of these drugs affect the same neurotransmitter (gammaaminobutyric acid – GABA), their specific effects and side effects vary significantly (NIDA, 2006b). For example, Hindmarch *et al.* (1991) found that the benzodiazepines Lorazepam and Nitrazepam impair performance on a wide variety of tasks, such as tracking, short-term memory, and reaction time, while clobazam does not impair performance on such tasks and even improves performance on other tasks (such as critical flicker fusion). Even greater differences in effects exist among different classes of sedatives such as benzodiazepines and barbiturates. Most of the studies that have been conducted in this area focused on benzodiazepines, and therefore so will this section.

As long as the sedating effect of benzodiazepines persists, depressants can impair steering, lane positioning, and reaction time skills (Hindmarch, 1988). Benzodiazepines are distinguished from each other primarily in terms of the duration of their effects. Long half-life benzodiazepines (such as flurazepam, nitrazepam, flunitrazepam, and diazepam) sustain their effects – and their side effects – for more than nine hours. Short half-life benzodiazepines (such as triazolam and loprazolam) typically reach peak effects within the first 2-3 hours.

Clayton (1976) reviewed 35 studies that examined the effects of different depressants (barbiturates, non-barbiturates, tranquilizers, and antidepressants) on various skills.

After grouping the effects into sensory/perceptual, cognitive, and motor functions, it appeared that most drugs did not produce significant impairments on most of the tasks. However, some effects were discernible. Of the sensory/perceptual functions, critical flicker fusion and dynamic visual acuity were impaired by several of the drugs whereas static acuity, depth perception, and visual search were relatively immune to the drugs tested. Of the cognitive skills, one short-term memory task (Digit Symbol Substitution Test) and a response competition test (Stroop color-word test) were the most impaired, while mental arithmetic and digit span (which is also a short-term memory task) were relatively unaffected. Of the motor tasks, the most commonly tested and the one that was most significantly impaired was tracking. However, in Clayton's review for every finding of a significant drug effect there were four statistically non-significant effects, indicating that most of the studies failed to find significant impairing effects. Furthermore, in many cases a significant effect was obtained for a one drug in one study, but not for another drug (also a CNS depressant) in another study. Given this myriad of results it is not surprising that Clayton concluded that "differences that exist in the methodology, task, drug doses, and subjects used make it extremely difficult to reach any firm conclusions as to the practical effects, upon the driving performance of patients, of any prescribed psychotropic drug" (p. 250).

Experimental studies of drug effects and literature reviews conducted since Clayton's review in 1976 have not clarified the picture by much. In a comprehensive review of the impairing effects of benzodiazepines, Wittenborn (1979) also concluded that their effects vary among the different types of benzodiazepines. When impairment was found it was most likely to be with higher doses, and within 2-6 hours of drug administration. After that period the drug effects on behavior tended to dissipate. These conclusions are generally supported by Johnson and Chernik's (1982) review of 52 studies on the effects of benzodiazepines on next-day performance. However, they concluded that with sufficiently high dose levels all benzodiazepines that are taken at night impair next-day performance, and the impairment is greater for long-life hypnotics.

Wittenborn (1979) also reviewed the literature on the negative effects of benzodiazepines and noted that many of the effects observed were drug specific. In general, though, he concluded that benzodiazepines impair the speed of simple repetitive acts, impair learning and immediate memory, but "there is relatively little indication that well-established higher mental faculties are adversely involved." Based on the studies he reviewed, the most impaired functions seem to be critical flicker fusion (significantly impaired in 5 out of 5 studies), followed by learning and memory (4 out of 4), manipulative tasks (2 out of 2), time estimation (2 out of 2), digit symbol substitution (6 out of 10), letter cancellation (4 out of 9), card sorting (3 out of 7), and tapping (3 out of 8). The least affected were spatial skills, auditory perception, reaction time, visual coordination, arithmetic, pursuit rotor tracking, and symbol copying. Koelega (1989) reviewed 26 studies that focused on the effects of different benzodiazepines on vigilance and found that with young (non-patient) volunteers, vigilance is relatively sensitive to benzodiazepine impairment, causing people to miss more signals and respond more slowly to ones that they see. Kunsman *et al.* (1992a) also studied and reviewed the effects of benzodiazepines and found that they tend to impair simple and choice reaction time, which is slowed by therapeutic doses as long as the testing is done within 1-3 hours of the ingestion. However, continued repeated administrations eventually cause resistance (adaptation) to the impairing effects. They consistently impair performance on Digit Symbol Substitution Tests, but here too, with repeated administrations (typical of medical prescriptions) these effects tend to disappear, indicating an adaptation effect. Critical Flicker Fusion, tracking performance, divided attention, visual scanning, and simple arithmetic are also impaired within 1-4 hours of the drug administration.

Although 20 years old, probably the most extensive summary of the relevant side-effects of benzodiazepines to date is that of Berghaus and Grass (1997), who summarized the results of over 500 experimental studies that related performance on driving-related psychomotor and perceptual tasks to benzodiazepine impairment. Most experiments had multiple results – as there were often several dependent measures on which the drug effects were measured. They found a clear-cut nearly linear relationship between the serum concentration and the percent of studies that obtained a significant effect, for both the short-acting triazolam (based on 1,253 results of experimental tests), and for the long-acting nitrazepam (based on 531 results of experimental tests). It is important to note, though, that multiple effects were not independent results of independent studies. Similar relationships were obtained for other benzodiazepines such as temazepam, flunitrazepam, flurazepam, alprazolam, bromazepam, diazepam, oxazepam, and lorazepam. One exception was clobazam for which significant effects were obtained only at exceedingly high serum level of 400 ng/ml. Berghaus and Grass also found that the percent of studies obtaining an impairment was much higher (by approximately 30 percent) when the serum concentration was measured during the absorption phase (e.g., less than 3 hours after administration for diazepam), than when it was measured during the elimination phase (after 5 or more hours after administration for diazepam). This effect is similar to that obtained for alcohol, but it is much stronger with benzodiazepines, where the percent studies that found an impairment during the elimination phase was approximately half of the percent that found it during the absorption phase. In summary, despite significant differences among the individual benzodiazepines, they generally impair performance on most performance tasks, in particular those that tap visual encoding of information (such as attention, vigilance, visual search, peak saccadic velocity, and critical flicker fusion), and short-term memory (as measured in digit symbol substitution, memory scan, recognition memory, and serial subtraction tasks).

Under tightly controlled experimental conditions, Schechtman and Shinar (2005) found that alprazolam produced effects similar to those of alcohol: nystagmus, poor performance on all balance tests (one-leg-stand, finger-to-nose test, and walk-and-turn test), slowed reaction to light, and poor ocular convergence to nearby objects. Therefore, it is not surprising that in driving, depressants, especially benzodiazepines, have effects that are quite similar to those of alcohol. This was empirically demonstrated by Bramness *et al.* (2002) in Norway, where physicians routinely examine drivers suspected of drug-impaired driving. For the purpose of their evaluation, they compared the percent of drivers judged to be clinically impaired (based on the clinical evaluations and several formal tests given by the physicians) who had only benzodiazepine in their blood with the percent of clinically impaired drivers who had only alcohol in their blood. The percent of

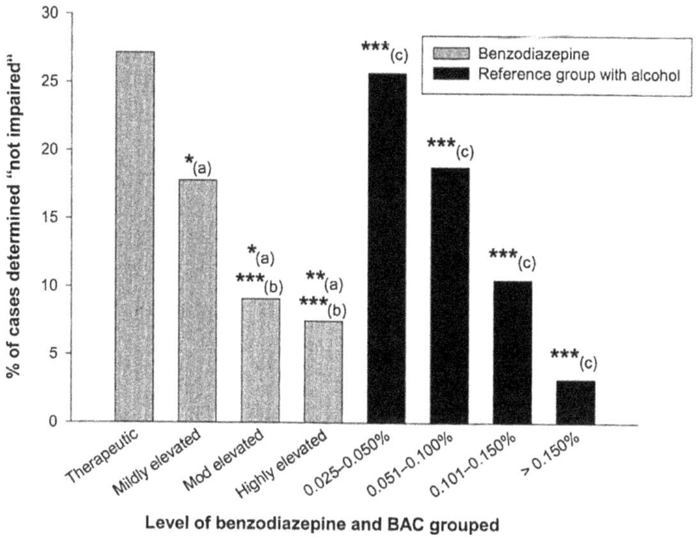

Figure 12-5. The percent of drivers judged unimpaired as a function of the blood benzodiazepine concentration (N = 818) or BAC (N = 10,759). Drivers had only benzodiazepine or only alcohol in their blood. In the benzodiazepine group, there were significant differences in the percent judged as "not impaired" between the therapeutic and the mildly, moderately and highly elevated blood concentration levels (a), and between the mildly elevated and the moderately elevated and the highly elevated (b). In the alcohol, there were significant differences between all groups (c). $^{*}p = 0.05$, $^{**}p = 0.01$, and $^{***}p = 0.001$ (from Bramness *et al.*, 2002, with permission from Elsevier).

drivers judged impaired increased in a very orderly fashion as a function of both the drug and the alcohol blood concentrations, as illustrated in Figure 12-5. Because the study samples were quite large – 818 drug-impaired drivers and 14,215 alcohol impaired drivers – their results are quite robust and the differences seen in the graph are highly significant, despite the subjective nature of clinical evaluations. It is important to note, however, that there are non-sedative depressants (anxiolytics such as buspirone, Clobazam, and temazepam) that do not seem to impair performance on any of the driving-related functions that have been studied.

Only two studies (Mintzer *et al.*, 1997; Pickworth *et al.*, 1997) were found who evaluated the effects of depressants on performance without the interactions of alcohol. Both used different amounts of pentobarbital, and the results of both suggest that barbiturates affect psychomotor functions in ways similar to that of alcohol and benzodiazepines.

Although alcohol is a depressant, when alcohol is combined with other CNS depressants the results are not always additive or synergistic and may even be antagonistic. Linnoila (1973) studied the effects of impairment from combinations of alcohol (0.5 g/kg) and several depressants including nitrazepam (5 or 10 milligrams), diazepam (10 milligrams), ethinamate (0.5 g), and bromvaletone (0.6 g) and found that in the absence of alcohol, only nitrazepam showed some impairments (slowed reaction time, high error rates in choice reaction time task, and increase in tracking errors). Furthermore, when combined with alcohol people impaired by nitrazepam actually improved their performance (i.e., quickened their choice reaction time) when they also ingested alcohol.

Hindmarch and Gudgeon (1982) administered a short half-life diazepine (loprazolam, <10 hours) and a long half-life diazepine (flurazepam, > 40 hours) together with alcohol (2 shots of vodka ~0.5 ml/kg), and compared the effects to those with alcohol alone and to placebo. To allow for adaptation effects, drug and alcohol administration was conducted every evening for three nights, and testing was done on the fourth morning. The subjects were 12 female volunteers in a crossover design. No significant differences between the alcohol alone and the alcohol with either drug were found on any of the extensive battery of sensori-motor, cognitive, and driving tasks. The only marginally significant effect was a greater subjective sense of drowsiness and fatigue following flurazepam. Later studies (Lister and File, 1983; Roache *et al.*, 1993; and Starmer and Bird, 1984) also yielded inconsistent results suggesting the individual differences among drugs and among people make simple conclusions quite inappropriate.

One class of antidepressants that has yielded consistent findings is antihistamines. While most early antihistamines (known as first generation) had been shown to impair driving-related skills, a review of 130 experimental studies revealed that only one-fifth of them found impaired performance with second generation antihistamines, and only 10 percent of the studies that evaluated actual driving performance obtained drug-related impairments (Moskowitz and Wilkinson, 2003).

Depressants' effects on crash involvement

The significance of benzodiazepines for driving is due to the fact that they are also used during the day by healthy people before stressful events (as an anxiolytic – anxiety reducing drug). Although they are rarely used as recreational drugs, their abuse and misuse among patients seeking their psychotropic effects is high (Kunsman *et al.*, 1992b). In their review of the literature, Kunsman *et al.* (1992a) note that several studies found increase in crash rates attributed to hypnotic benzodiazepines. More recent studies also indicate that people taking benzodiazepines – especially long-term anxiolytic ones – are over-involved in crashes.

The complexity of the impairing effects of depressants was highlighted in an early extensive epidemiological study by Barbone *et al.* (1998). They analyzed the crash involvement of 40,400 people who had benzodiazepine prescriptions at any time during a three-year period (1992-1995). In their sample, 19,386 were involved in a "first road accident" during that period, and 916 of them were users of benzodiazepines at the time. The researchers' principal findings and conclusions were that users of benzodiazepines were slightly more likely to have a crash than non-users of benzodiazepines (with an average odds ratio of OR = 1.62), and crash risk was dose-related. Also, the risk associated with benzodiazepine increased dramatically when the driver also used alcohol (with an odds ratio of 8.15 for those with positive BAC). On the other hand, no over-involvement was obtained for hypnotic benzodiazepines. This could have been because these drugs are taken mostly at night before going to sleep whereas anxiety reducing benzodiazepines are typically taken during the day, often before driving. Nonetheless, very similar findings were obtained in large American and Canadian cohort studies (Hemmelgarn *et al.*, 1997; Ray, Fought, and Decker, 1992). But, as is often the case with drug impairment studies, several studies conducted in different countries – using different study designs – failed to find an increase in crash risk for users of benzodiazepines and sedating antihistamines (Drummer *et al.*, 2004; French Benzodiazepine/Driving Collaboration Group, 1993; Leveille *et al.*, 1994).

The most recent analyses of the crash risk of depressants indicate that it does increase crash risk by a small amount. In his quantitative analysis of the crash risk of benzodiazepines alone without any other drugs, using meta-analysis of 51 injury data points and 10 fatal data points, Elvik (2013) obtained low but significant odds ratios of 1.65 and 2.30 for the over-involvement in crash injuries and fatal injuries, respectively (Table 12-5). Somewhat greater risk of benzodiazepines was obtained in the DRUID study where the odds ratio was 1.99 (see Table 12-4, Hels *et al.*, 2011). Li *et al.* (2013), in the study quoted above, used FARS data for drug prevalence in crashes and the NHTSA sponsored roadside survey for exposure (Compton and Berning, 2009; Lacey *et al.*, 2009). They obtained a significant crude OR = 4.83. However, this odds ratio was not adjusted for any confounding variables and is most likely spuriously high. The most extreme estimate was obtained by Gjerde *et al.* (2013b) in the study quoted above where the risk for fatality from benzodiazepines alone was OR = 11.7 for single vehicle crashes and OR = 8.8 for all crashes (Table 10-3).

In summary, crash analyses seem to indicate that depressants such as benzodiazepines may interfere with driving, to the point of increasing crash likelihood, but the increased crash rate obtained in most studies is not very high and the effects vary significantly among specific drugs, countries, and study designs and controls. Studies involving crash analysis generally show a slight but significant crash risk. However, these studies are correlational in nature and not experimental, and they are susceptible to confounding effects from many uncontrolled variables that probably co-vary with the use or non-use of drugs, and often the odds ratios are not adjusted for them.

Dissociative anesthetics

Dissociative drugs, originally developed as general anesthetics for surgery, are labeled as such because they distort perceptions of sight and sound and produce feelings of detachment – dissociation – from the environment and from oneself. Drugs in that category include PCP (phencyclidine) (also known by street names as "angel dust" and "love boat"), and ketamine (also known as "cat" "valiums," and "special K"). Dissociative anesthetics should not be confused with hallucinogens because they do not produce the profound distortions of reality that hallucinogens cause. Dissociative drugs act by altering distribution of the neurotransmitter glutamate throughout the brain. Glutamate is involved in perception of pain, responses to the environment, and memory (NIDA,

2001, 2006b). The effects of PCP and ketamines are very similar, and because PCP is the more commonly abused of the two, most of the research has been done on it.

The onset of PCP effects is very rapid when smoked or injected (1-5 minutes) and delayed when snorted or orally ingested (30 minutes), with a gradual decline of major effects over 4-6 hours. However, complete recovery to the "normal" state may take up to 24 hours (NHTSA, 2004). Physiological effects include increase in heart rate and blood pressure, profuse sweating, numbness of extremities, and nystagmus. The range of psychological effects of these drugs is very large and includes numbness, nausea or vomiting, panic, agitation, aggression, violence, loss of appetite, depression, euphoria, calmness, feelings of strength and invulnerability, lethargy, disorientation, loss of coordination, and distinct changes in body awareness (NHTSA, 2004; NIDA 2006b).

Dissociative anesthetics, driving, and crash involvement
Direct scientific evaluations of the effects of these drugs on driving and driving-related skills are still lacking. A complicating factor in the assessment of the effects of dissociative anesthetics is that there is no direct correlation between their concentration in the blood and behavioral or physical impairments (at least for PCP; NHTSA, 2004). Their prevalence in impaired driving is probably small, and in one study conducted on drivers arrested for impaired driving in the Washington DC area over 20 years ago PCP was found in 9 percent of the impaired drivers, compared to 39 percent who had cannabinoids in their system (Sutton and Paegle, 1992). Thus, while theoretically the effects of these drugs on driving should be quite dangerous, empirical research to indicate that the problem exists is still needed.

Hallucinogens

Hallucinogens are drugs that cause profound distortions in a person's perceptions of reality, to the extent that people see images, hear sounds, and feel sensations that seem real but do not exist. They cause their effects by disrupting the interaction of nerve cells and the neurotransmitter serotonin (NIDA, 2001). The best known and most commonly abused drug in that category is LSD (an abbreviation of the German words for "lysergic acid diethylamide"). It is also known by street names such as "acid" and "yellow sunshine." Other abused hallucinogens include mescaline and psilocybin, also known as "buttons" and "purple passion," respectively (NIDA, 2006a).

The effects of LSD are unpredictable and depend on the dose ingested, the user's personality, mood, expectations, and the surroundings. Following intravenous injection, the onset of LSD effects is approximately 10 minutes, and following oral ingestion onset of the first effects is approximately 20-30 minutes, peaking at 2-4 hours and gradually diminishing over 6-8 hours. The physiological effects of hallucinogens include increased body temperature, increased heart rate and blood pressure, dilated pupils, sweating, dry mouth, sleeplessness, numbness, weakness, and tremors. The psychological effects include hallucinations, enhanced color perception, altered mental state, thought disorders, temporary psychosis, delusions, body image changes, and impaired perceptions of depth, time, and space. Users may feel several emotions at once or swing rapidly from one emotion to another. "Bad trips" may consist of severe, terrifying thoughts and feelings, fear of losing control, and despair (NHTSA, 2004; NIDA, 2006b).

Hallucinogens, driving, and crash involvement
The potential danger of hallucinogens is obvious, but the prevalence of hallucinogens in driving and crashes appears to be very rare. In Colorado, among a group of 242 drivers suspected of DUID, LSD was found in the urine of only one driver (NHTSA, 2004). In the Netherlands, Neuteboom and Zweipfenning (1984) analyzed 38,203 cases of Dutch drivers stopped for impaired driving and based on the judgments of "medical officers" (which, in turn, were based mostly on drivers' admissions), they noted that 9.7 percent of these drivers had used drugs before driving. Of these, 8.2 percent used "non-medical drugs," and of these, only one person used LSD. Thus, out of nearly 40,000 drivers stopped for impaired driving only one driver had a positive identification of LSD, making the use of LSD among car drivers almost non-existent. Even though the true percentages may be higher than documented, it appears that in the context of driving, hallucinogen impairment is probably very rare, and people who take hallucinogens prefer their virtual "trips" to actual road trips.

Narcotic analgesics – Opioids and Morphine Derivatives

Narcotic analgesics are extremely addictive and include morphine (known on the street as monkey and white stuff) and morphine derivatives such as heroin (known as brown sugar, dope, junk, and smack) and opium (known as big O, and black stuff), codeine (known as cody), and fentanyl (known as china white, tango, and friend). All of these drugs bind to opioid receptors that are located principally in the brain and gastrointestinal tract. They are medicinally prescribed for pain relief, and they are abused for their psychological effects of euphoria (known as a "rush") and feelings of well-being. The physiological effects include sweating, fixed and constricted pupils, lowered pulse rate and blood pressure, diminished reflexes, flushing of the face (due to dilation of subcutaneous blood vessels), and depressed consciousness, which in large doses may lead to unconsciousness, coma, and death (NIDA, 2006b). The psychological effects – in addition to the euphoria or "rush" – include sedation, drowsiness, nausea, and confusion. There is a drug-dose relationship, but because people develop tolerance to the drugs, interpretation of blood or plasma concentrations are extremely difficult. Peak plasma morphine concentrations occur within an hour of oral administration, and within 5 minutes following intravenous injection. The onset of psychological effects is generally within 15-60 minutes and the effects may last 4-6 hours. Following heroin use, the intense euphoria lasts from 45 seconds to several minutes, peak effects last 1-2 hours, and the overall effects wear off in 3-5 hours, depending on dose (NHTSA, 2004).

Opioids, driving and crash involvement
In therapeutic doses, given for pain control (e.g., fentanyl) or for drug addiction (methadone), opioids do not seem to impair driving-related psychomotor skills (Galski, Williams, and Ehle, 2000; Sabatowski *et al.*, 2003) or affect driving to the extent that

they increase crash risk. Lenné *et al.* (2000) reviewed 17 published studies that examined the relationship between opioid ingestion and performance on driving-related skills, simulated driving, and actual driving, and found that "in the main these studies have shown few effects of the opioids on driving." Studies that compared performance of morphine-administered cancer patients to control groups in driving-related tasks typically do not find significant differences between the two groups in vigilance, concentration, motor reactions, or divided attention (Fishbain *et al.*, 2003; Kress and Kraft, 2005; NHTSA, 2004), though the drug does slow down reaction time and increases critical flicker fusion threshold (Hindmarch *et al.*, 1991; NHTSA, 2004). In simulated driving, Lenné *et al.* (2003) failed to find any impairment in driving skills in heroin patients on methadone, LAAM, or buprenorphine (all opioid pharmacotherapeutic drugs) relative to control subjects. The prevalence of narcotics in the driving population appears to be quite low (Behrensdorff and Steentoft, 2003; Jonasson *et al.*, 2000), and when they are present they do not seem to be significantly over-involved in crashes (Compton and Berning, 2015; Drummer *et al.*, 2004; Hels *et al.*, 2011; Lacey *et al.*, 2016; Laumon *et al.*, 2005; Movig *et al.*, 2004; see Tables 12-2 and 12-4), or in culpability analysis of fatal crashes (Gadegbeku *et al.*, 2010).

There are three exceptions to this generalization. One is Skurtveit *et al.*'s (2002a) finding in which 19 percent of all 20-39-years-old Norwegian drivers who were stopped for suspected DUID in 1992 and confirmed to have a drug other than alcohol had heroin in their blood. Though this number appears high, it still constitutes only 1.9 percent of all drivers stopped for impaired driving in Norway. The other exception is Elvik's (2013) meta-analyses of 7 fatal accident data sets and 18 injury accident data sets. His analyses yielded significant odds ratios of OR = 2.13 and OR = 1.94 for the two crash types (Table 12-5). While Skurtveit *et al.*'s study lacked many controls, Elvik's analysis is more difficult to discount as it is based on case-control studies, cohort studies, and culpability studies. Li *et al.* (2013), in the study quoted above, used FARS data for drug prevalence in crashes and the NHTSA sponsored roadside survey (Compton and Berning, 2009; Lacey *et al.*, 2009) for exposure. They obtained a significant crude OR = 3.03. However, this odds ratio was not adjusted for any confounding variables and is most likely spuriously high.

In summary, it appears that opiates are not very common in crash-involved victims, and yield relatively low – but sometimes statistically significant – crash risks, especially when compared to alcohol and depressants.

CNS stimulants

The basic mechanisms by which stimulants affect the central nervous system differ among the different stimulant drugs. However, their physiological, psychological, and behavioral effects are similar so that they can be grouped into a single category. Common stimulants include amphetamine (also known as "bennies," "speed," "uppers"), methamphetamine (also known as "speed," "meth," and "choke"), cocaine (also known as "coke," "crack"), 3,4-methylenedioxy-methamphetamine (MDMA, also known as "ecstasy"), and nicotine

Caffeine is also a stimulant but it is discussed in Chapter 14 in the context of fatigue countermeasures. The onset and duration of effects vary greatly across the drugs, the means of administration (smoking, sniffing, or injecting), and individual levels of tolerance to the drug. For example, a "hit" of smoked crack (cocaine) or snorting of cocaine produce an almost immediate intense experience and will typically produce effects lasting 5-15 minutes in the former and 15-30 minutes in the latter. In contrast, the effects of methamphetamine can last 6-8 hours (NIDA, 2002, 2004, 2006b).

Physiological effects that are common to all stimulants include increased or irregular heart rate, raised blood pressure, and faster metabolism. There are also significant variations among drugs. Amphetamine symptoms include rapid breathing or tremors and loss of coordination. Cocaine symptoms include increased temperature or chest pain, increase in light sensitivity and body temperature, dilated pupils, constriction of peripheral blood vessels, rapid speech, dyskinesia (impairment of voluntary movements; tics), nausea, and vomiting. MDMA can lead to hyperthermia.

Psychological effects include feelings of exhilaration, sense of increased energy and mental alertness, nervousness, and insomnia. There are also drug-specific psychological effects. Amphetamine causes delirium, panic, paranoia, impulsive behavior, and aggression. Cocaine causes headaches, panic attacks, and nausea. MDMA causes mild hallucinogenic effects, increased tactile sensitivity, impaired learning and memory, and empathic feelings. Methamphetamine elicits aggression, violence, and psychotic behavior, and is also associated with impaired learning and memory (NHTSA, 2004; NIDA, 2006b). This wide range of effects is further complicated by significant psychological changes over the course of time after administration. For example, in the case of cocaine the initial positive feelings of euphoria, excitation, feelings of well-being, general arousal, increased sexual excitement, increased alertness, mental clarity, increased talkativeness, and motor restlessness are followed by dysphoria (emotional discomfort, feeling of malaise), depression, agitation, nervousness, drug craving, fatigue, and insomnia. In addition, high doses of cocaine can induce a pattern of psychosis with confused and disoriented behavior, delusions, hallucinations, irritability, fear, paranoia, antisocial behavior, and aggression (NHTSA, 2004; NIDA, 2004, 2006b).

Stimulants in driving and crash involvement

While some stimulants, such as coffee, may be an effective fatigue countermeasure, when abused and taken for their psychoactive effects they may or may not constitute a crash risk (Jones *et al.*, 2003). Thus, drivers treated for cocaine addiction have more traffic violations than age-gender-matched control drivers (Macdonald *et al.*, 2004), and cocaine has been associated with speeding, losing vehicle control, causing collisions, turning in front of other vehicles, high-risk behaviors, aggressive driving, and inattentive driving. However, this guilt by association may be an artifact of these drivers' tendencies for high-risk behaviors rather than a result of the cocaine. When it comes to direct evidence for crash risk the results are not consistent. Five independent studies using different analysis techniques failed to find a significant crash risk for amphetamines or cocaine. Movig *et al.* (2004) in their study of crash risk in the Netherlands did not find that drivers who had taken either amphetamines or cocaine were over-involved in crashes (Tables 12-2). Laumon *et al.*

(2005), in their extensive analysis of drivers involved in fatal crashes, and after adjusting for various covariates, failed to find increased crash rates for drivers with either amphetamines or cocaine in their blood. Drummer *et al.* (2004), in their analysis of crash culpability in three states in Australia, failed to obtain a significant increase in crash risk for the complete sample of drivers (Table 12-6). Gadegbeku *et al.* (2010) in a culpability analysis of French drivers in fatal crashes failed to find significant odds ratios for either amphetamines or cocaine. Finally, the most recent, extensive, and comprehensive U.S. study on the crash risk from various drugs failed to obtain a significant effect of any of the drugs tested, including stimulants such as amphetamines and cocaine, either before or after adjustment for age, gender, and alcohol in the blood (Compton *et al.*, 2015; Lacey *et al.*, 2016).

In contrast to the above studies, five studies did find that stimulants increase crash risk. Elvik (2013) on the basis of eight fatal studies and two injury studies (including the three studies quoted above) found that amphetamines increased the crash risk more than any other drug studied with OR = 5.61, and cocaine yielding OR = 2.96 (see Table 12-5). Similar findings were obtained from the pooled data in the European DRUID study where amphetamine use yielded a significant odds ratio of OR = 8.35 and cocaine yielded a significant odds ratio of OR = 3.30 (Hels *et al.*, 2011, Table 12-4). Li *et al.* (2013) in the study quoted above used FARS data for drug prevalence in crashes and the NHTSA sponsored roadside survey (Compton and Berning, 2009; Lacey *et al.*, 2009) for exposure data. They obtained a significant crude OR = 3.57. However, this odds ratio was not adjusted for any confounding variables and is most likely spuriously high. Gjerde *et al.* (2013) in their analysis of Norwegian fatal crashes found that amphetamines when taken alone increased the fatality risk in single vehicle crashes to OR = 15.9, and in all crashes to 41.6(!) (Table 12-3). Laumon *et al.* (2005) who failed to obtain an increase in fatality risk for their complete data set found an amphetamine effect on truck drivers only. Truckers with amphetamines in their blood had a crash risk that was nearly nine times higher than that of truckers without drugs in their blood. However, this last finding should be treated with caution because truckers often take amphetamines to counteract the effects of fatigue, and consequently many of these crashes could have been caused more by fatigue than by the impairing effects of the drugs.

In summary, despite the multiple studies that evaluated the effects of stimulants in general and amphetamines and cocaine in particular on crash risk, there is no consensus in the conclusions. This is due either to the fact that reactions to stimulants vary greatly among drivers, specific drugs, and doses, or to inadequate study designs. More careful controls and study designs must be evaluated before we can conclude that stimulants increase crash risk.

Inhalants

Inhalants are volatile substances that produce chemical vapors that can be inhaled to induce a psychoactive, or mind-altering, effect. The common characteristic of these substances is not in their chemistry or pharmacological effects but in their mode of ingestion: almost always by inhalation. There are three general categories of inhalants that are abused for their psychoactive effects: volatile solvents, that are liquids that vaporize at room temperatures (including paint thinners, gasoline, and glue); aerosols, which are sprays of solvents and propellants (such as spray paint, and deodorants); and gases, that are mostly medical anesthetics (such as ether, chloroform, and nitrous oxide). Inhalants are very rapidly absorbed into the blood stream, and reach the brain within seconds. However, because their effects often last only a few minutes, abusers tend to inhale repeatedly (NIDA, 2005). The psychological effects of inhalants are a rapid high that resembles alcohol intoxication with initial excitation, euphoria, and floating sensations followed by reduced ability to concentrate, slowed reaction time, drowsiness, disinhibition, lightheadedness, agitation, and even hallucinations (NHTSA, 2004; NIDA, 2005). There is no consistent dose-response relationship, though when the levels are high (over 9 mg/l) people are typically visibly impaired (NHTSA, 2004).

Inhalants, driving, and crash involvement
There are no experimental studies that examined the relationship between administration of inhalants and impairments in driving skills or driving. Neither have any crash risk studies been found.

Drugged Driving Countermeasures

It is very difficult to deal with a problem whose magnitude is hotly debated, and whose characteristics are so diverse. To date, efforts to reduce DUID have focused on the administrative and policy actions that set criteria for defining drugged driving or driving under the influence of drugs, and on the identification and removal of drugged drivers off the road; with very limited success – at least so far.

Legislation dealing with driving under the influence of drugs (DUID)

Given the complexity of the DUID, it is no wonder that the laws and regulations concerning drugged driving are often vague and vary widely across countries and jurisdictions. As a first step, a country has to define the drugs to which DUID applies. In general, in most countries this includes either all illegal drugs (e.g., Belgium, Denmark, Germany, Israel) or a list of specific drugs (e.g., Australia) (OECD, 2010). Next a country has to define the criteria by which a person is judged as "impaired." In the U.S., following a detailed analysis of the laws in each of the states, Walsh (2009) identified three approaches to the issue:

1. Statutes that require drugs to render a driver "**incapable**" of driving safely; for example, Alabama, Kansas, Nevada, Vermont.
2. Statutes requiring that the drug impair the driver's ability to operate safely or require a driver to be "**under the influence** or affected by an intoxicating drug"; for example, Florida, Indiana, South Carolina.
3. "**Per se**" statutes that make it a criminal offense to have a drug or metabolite in one's body/body fluids while operating a motor vehicle (often referred to as "zero tolerance" laws) (e.g., Arizona, Illinois, Michigan, Pennsylvania, Virginia, Wisconsin).

The first two types of statutes are the more prevalent in the U.S. and possibly in the world). With these laws, the burden of proof of DUID is much greater than in states and countries that have per se laws. In jurisdictions where proof of incapacity or impairment are required, Drug Recognition Experts' (DREs) evaluations – as flawed and contested as they are – are often used in support of the case for DUID *when there is evidence of drug in the blood.* But because of the much greater difficulties in enforcing DUID than DWI, and the complexities of DUID assessment it is difficult to identify, prosecute, or convict drugged drivers. (Berning and Smithers, 2014; Walsh, 2009).

Drug per se laws are not synonymous with alcohol per se laws. Whereas the latter set an empirically based threshold of alcohol concentration, in the case of drugs, where no simple dose-response relationships exist the laws typically involve "zero tolerance"; that is, any detectable level of the listed drugs is proof of impairment (NHTSA, 2010b). Although such a simple solution to a complex problem is tempting, it is definitely not relevant to medicinal drugs that are either taken over the counter or prescribed (OECD, 2010). As a part of the EU project DRUID mentioned above some efforts have already been made to harmonize pan-European regulations for DUID by stimulants. This included agreement on several driving performance measures and the consensus that a drug shall be considered impairing if it produces performance decrements equivalent to alcohol at BAC = .05 percent (the most common threshold for DWI in Europe) (Ramaekers *et al.*, 2012). However, a recent evaluation of the impact of per se drug laws in the U.S. where 30 states had such laws at the time of the analysis (2013) did not reveal any significant effect on traffic fatalities (Anderson and Rees, 2015).

Once laws are established for specific drugs the next issue is how to enforce them. An emerging deterrence approach of on-road random drug testing for amphetamine, methamphetamine, and cannabis (specifically THC) has been approved in Victoria, Australia (Boorman and Owens, 2009), though the effectiveness of this approach for DUID still has to be proven.

Finally, the law must set the penalties for DUID. These are typically the same as for DUI, as the laws typically combine the two under one provision of impairment by alcohol and/or other drugs. Consequently, when alcohol is detected at or above the critical level drivers are rarely further tested for or charged with DUID. This of course complicates any objective assessment of the risk of drugs on the basis of police-reported crash data.

On-road drug detection and identification: The Drug Evaluation and Classification Program (DECP)

Perhaps it is a testament to the state of the art in this area that the major effort in countering drugged driving, or DUID, is in developing reliable and valid methods to detect it. We still do not have reliable and valid instruments for the detection and identification of drugs that law enforcement officers can apply within their settings. An extensive evaluation conducted in Europe and the U.S. of various devices intended to measure drugs in saliva under field conditions (Rosita-2) failed to find one that would meet the desired sensitivity levels >90 percent (and coupled with high specificity). Consequently, at least as of 10 years ago the Rosita-2 project team concluded that "no device was considered to be reliable enough in order to be recommended for roadside screening of drivers" (Verstraete and Rues, 2006).

Perhaps the best known and arguably the most comprehensive approach to the problem was initiated by the California Highway Patrol, when, in the early 1980s, its officers repeatedly encountered visibly impaired drivers who often failed the standard field sobriety test (SFST) – a test based on behavioral measures developed for assessment of alcohol impairment (see Chapter 11) – yet did not have any alcohol in their breath or blood.

The program that was developed to detect and identify certain types of drugs, known as the Drug Evaluation and Classification Program (DECP), was based on the best available knowledge at the time. Its implementation was formalized in a structured curriculum that involved training police officers to become Drug Recognition Experts (DREs). Using the DECP, DREs conduct a 12-step procedure that culminates in an assessment of whether or not a person is drug-impaired, and if so what is or are the impairing drug categories. The 12 steps include:

1. Breath-alcohol test, given to measure blood alcohol concentration (BAC).
2. Interview of the arresting officer. To determine if any drugs paraphernalia were in the car or any street names of drugs were mentioned by the driver.
3. Preliminary examination, consisting of the observations of general physical appearance, use of corrective lenses, and appearance of the eyes.
4. Examination of the eyes, including tests for horizontal and vertical gaze nystagmus and lack of convergence.
5. Divided attention psychophysical tests. Four tests that measure motor control, balance, and the ability to count and estimate time. The tests include (a) walk-and-turn test, in which the subject has to walk heel-to-toe along a line, nine steps in each direction; (b) one-leg-stand test, in which the subject has to stand on one leg, keep both arms at the sides of the body, and count for 30 seconds, and then repeat the process while standing on the other leg; (c) Romberg balance test, in which the subject has to stand straight with the eyes closed for an estimated 30 seconds; and (d) finger-to-nose test, in which the subject has to touch the nose with a finger six times while the eyes are closed and the two hands are outstretched to the sides.
6. Vital signs examination. Tests of pulse rate, blood pressure, and temperature.
7. Dark room examination. Measurements of the pupil size under different light conditions (in normal room light, in darkness, and with direct light into the eye) and the reaction of the pupils to light.
8. Examination of muscle tone.
9. Examination of skin surface for injection sites.
10. Interview, suspect's statements, and other observations. Based on an initial impression of drug-related impairment, the DRE interviews the suspect about his or her drug use.

11. Opinion of the officers as to whether or not the subject was drug-impaired, and if so, what were the likely drug categories causing the impairment. The officers' protocol allows them to list two categories (of the NIDA 7; see Table 12-1), and the conclusion is considered valid if one of them is identified in the toxicological evaluation.
12. Toxicological evaluation. Samples of urine or blood are collected and sent to a certified toxicological laboratory to obtain admissible scientific evidence to substantiate the DRE's opinions.

The seven distinct drug categories that the DREs are trained to identify are the same as the NIDA drug categories listed in Table 12-1: CNS stimulants, CNS depressants, narcotic/analgesics, phencyclidine (PCP), cannabis, hallucinogens, and inhalants. Presumably the drugs in each category have enough in common in terms of their observable physical signs and symptoms, that using the above procedure the DRE should be able to (1) positively identify drug-related impairment from drugs in each category and (2) distinguish among the categories in their impairing effects.

Over the past 30 years, the program gained acceptance by various law enforcement agencies, so that by the end of 2015, over 7,000 law enforcement officers from all 50 states in the U.S. had participated in it. The program has also been implemented in Canada where there are approximately 600 trained and certified DREs. The program has not (yet?) been implemented in other countries, though police officers from other countries such as Australia, England, Germany, Norway, and Sweden have been certified as DREs (CCSA, 2015; Shinar and Schechtman, 2005). Early evaluations of the program yielded positive indications of its validity in assessing drug-related impairments and its effectiveness in convicting drivers arrested for DUID (Adler and Burns, 1994).

Unfortunately, the early evaluations of the DECP validity were plagued with various analytical shortcomings and methodological problems, and an issue that had remained essentially unresolved was the scientific basis for the interpretation of physiological, behavioral, and vital signs symptoms. An example of seemingly supportive evidence is a study by Smith *et al.* (2002). In this study, DREs (that we will label as study DREs) evaluated drug impairment solely on the basis of 70 forms previously filled out by other DREs for apprehended suspects. The forms contained all of the recorded observations of physiological and behavioral signs and symptoms but did not include any information supplied by the arresting officer or the interview with the suspect. Obviously, they also did not contain the original DRE's conclusions and the results of the toxicological test. In short, the information on which the study DREs had to base their conclusions was that obtained in steps 3-9. The study DREs were told that in all of these cases, the original DREs' conclusions were corroborated by toxicology tests. For their evaluation, Smith *et al.* looked at the percent of cases in which the evaluation on the basis of the signs and symptoms matched the original conclusions. They obtained relatively high agreements: 80 percent for cannabis, 69 percent for depressants, 94 percent for narcotic analgesics, and 66 percent for no drugs. However, as an estimate of the scientific validity of the signs and symptoms, these seemingly high numbers are quite misleading. First, the sample is not random, because it represents the actual distributions of drugs in the population arrested for drugged driving, and therefore simply knowing the likelihood of different drugs in the street (with which the study DREs were quite familiar) would already yield identification percentages higher than chance. Second, the sample only represented the cases in which the original assessment was corroborated by the toxicology findings, and forms where the observed signs and symptoms and the original DRE conclusions were not supported by the toxicology tests were eliminated. This biased the sample only to definitive cases in which the recorded signs and symptoms were consistent with both the DRE guidelines and the toxicology results. Third, as human judges our observations are often guided by our hypotheses and preconceptions, and in the original assessments the DREs *had* the benefits of the interview with the arresting officer and the suspect's confession to guide them in the way they recorded their observations – most likely emphasizing symptoms consistent with their hypothesis, and de-emphasizing or ignoring symptoms that are inconsistent with it. All of these biases have statistical implications that yield spuriously high estimates of validity.

Two studies were conducted by Porath-Waller and her colleagues (Porath-Waller, Beirness, and Beasley, 2009; Porath-Waller and Beirness, 2010) to assess the validity of the specific signs and symptoms recorded by the DREs. Both studies examined at the validity of the recorded signs and symptoms in predicting specific drug impairments. In the first study, they only included 742 single-drug cases having only one of the four more popular drug categories (stimulants, depressants, marijuana, and narcotic analgesics) and 56 no drug cases. The number of cases of each drug was an approximate match of their relative frequency in the arrested DUID drivers. In the second study, they used 692 drug-impaired cases and 127 no-drug cases to evaluate the predictive validity of three popular drug combinations: central nervous system (CNS) stimulants with cannabis, CNS stimulants with narcotic analgesics, and cannabis with alcohol. The first study yielded 81 percent accuracy in distinguishing among the four types of impairments on the basis of nine clinical signs symptoms. The second study yielded 75 percent correct classifications of the three drug combinations on the basis of 11 clinical signs and symptoms. These levels of correct classifications are most likely greatly over-inflated for two principal reasons: (1) both studies included only cases in which the DRE conclusion was consistent with the blood test, thus excluding more difficult cases, and (2) only the more popular select individual drugs and drug combinations were evaluated, and the predictive validity was not adjusted for a-priori probabilities of the presence of these drugs and drug combinations in the driving population.

To provide an unbiased rigorous assessment of the scientific basis of the DECP, the U.S. National Highway Traffic Safety Administration and the U.S. National Institute of Drug Abuse conducted an extensive study that involved the administration of four drugs representing four drug categories to drug users who volunteered to participate in the study. The drugs selected for the study included a narcotic analgesic (codeine), a depressant (alprazolam), a stimulant (d-amphetamine sulfate), and marijuana. In a double-blind design (in which neither the subjects nor the experimenters knew which drug – if any – had been administered on each trial), certified and experienced DREs performed an evaluation of drug impairment without the benefit of any information other than observable signs and symptoms. Thus, they were deprived of the benefits of prior information from an arresting officer, and the benefits of an interview with the suspect (Steps 2 and 10 – that often elicit a confession). The officers' conclusions were based solely on observable signs and symptoms, on systematically measured vital signs, and on the standardized sobriety tests of motor coordination. The DREs were told that the subjects could be impaired by a drug belonging to any of five drug categories (the above four and dissociative drugs), a combination of drugs from these categories, or no drugs at all. In reality, only single drugs were used (making the identification much simpler), and on any given trial the subject had – with equal likelihood – either a high dose of a given drug, a low dose of a drug, or a placebo.

The data collected in the NHTSA-NIDA study has been analyzed and reported by Heishman, Singleton, and Crouch (1998), by Shinar and Schechtman (2005), and by Schechtman and Shinar (2005). The last two analyses are reported below in some detail. With a total of 300 evaluations, the DREs were able to detect drug impairment at better-than-chance levels. Their overall sensitivity (correct detection of impairments) was 72 percent, but their specificity (correct identification of no impairment) was only 43 percent. This means that in 57 percent of the evaluations the DREs falsely identified drug impairment; clearly a level that is too high to be acceptable for enforcement purposes. In addition, the associations between drug ingestion and identification of the specific impairing drug category – reflected in the Phi Coefficients – were not very high, as indicated in Table 12-12.

As these data clearly show, drug detection and identification performance varied widely among the four drugs. While impairment was noted nearly 50 percent of the times when the subject received cannabis, alprazolam, or codeine, it was detected only 10 percent of the times when the impairing drug was the stimulant amphetamine. However, the most disturbing aspect of the evaluation was not the moderate levels of correct identifications (sensitivity) but the alarmingly high rates of false identifications (false alarms) that were about 50 percent for the better-detected drugs. It is most likely that the DREs based their evaluations in part on their past experience in which suspects brought to their

Table 12-12. The DREs' performance in detecting drug impairment and correctly identifying the drug category, on the basis of a physical examination only (from Shinar and Schechtman, 2005, with permission from Elsevier).

Drug	Chi Square	% Sensitivity	% Specificity	% False Alarms	% Misses	Phi Correlation
Cannabis	5.86*	49	69	31	51	0.14 (0.02-0.26)
Alprazolam	16.24**	47	80	20	53	0.23 (0.11-0.36)
Codeine	5.58*	45	72	28	55	0.14 (0.02-0.26)
Amphetamine	0.02	10	91	9	90	0.01 (0.11-0.12)

*$p < 0.05$.
**$p < 0.001$.

attention were already most likely impaired by a drug. Thus, the same experience that helped them in the Smith *et al.* (2002) study and Porath-Waller studies (2009, 2010) may have inappropriately biased their judgments in this study where a-priori the likelihood of no drug impairment at all was one-third.

A closer inspection of the data uncovered some of the reasons for the DREs' poor performance. The underlying difficulty common to all DREs was their inability to simultaneously integrate the results of all of their observations into a coherent pattern, a difficulty that has also been noted by Porath-Waller *et al.* (2009). With over 50 different measures of performance based on steps 3-9 alone, it is nearly inhuman to correctly and optimally integrate such a large multidimensional data set in short-term memory. Furthermore, given the large variations in human responses to different drugs, it is likely that there are no iron-clad sets of mutually exhaustive symptoms that are always indicative of the various drugs. It is also important to note that this study too suffers from one of the shortcomings of the Porath-Waller studies noted above, and that is the inclusion of only five drug categories in the instructions to the DREs, thus increasing the probability of chance-guessing correctly. With all seven drug categories the DREs' performance would have most likely been even worse.

One method to deal with this human information processing limitation is to resort to computer-assisted decision models. In medical diagnostic systems, such models integrate scientific data, theory, and observations into a coherent scheme in which a physician is guided to obtain specific measurements and observations, and then enter the results into the computer. The computer then provides the physician with alternative plausible diagnosis, often with attendant probability of each. Using a similar approach, we (Schechtman and Shinar, 2005) evaluated the potential of a computer-assisted diagnostic system on the data collected in the NIDA-NHTSA study. Obviously, this model was restricted to the observations recorded by the DREs in accordance with the DECP protocol. Yet, even with this limitation, using the same data set recorded by the DREs to reach their conclusions, the computer model performed significantly better than the DREs. The results of this evaluation are presented in Table 12-13, where the DREs' performance is compared to that of the best fitting logistic regression model. Perhaps the best summary measure, by which to evaluate the two approaches is the uncertainty coefficient (Uc Coeff). This measure – whose values can range from 0.0 to 1.0 – indicates the amount of uncertainty that is reduced by the logistic model and by the DREs. Looking at this measure, it is clear that the logistic regression model provides a higher level of validity for the correct identification of cannabis, depressant (alprazolam), and stimulant (amphetamine). In the case of codeine, the abilities of both the DREs and the model are essentially no better than chance. The Phi Coefficients are the correlations between the correct diagnoses and the ones made by the model or DRE. They too reflect the superiority of the formal models, and they too indicate that in the case of the narcotic codeine, neither approach is valid. Both the Uncertainty Coefficient and the Phi Coefficient are based on the frequencies of correct identifications of the drug's presence (sensitivity), correct identifications of no drug impairment (specificity), incorrect identification of drug impairment (false alarms or false positives) and incorrect decisions of no impairment (misses or false negatives). The frequencies in these cells underscore the danger of relying on just one of these statistics rather than simultaneously considering all of them. In summary, this

Table 12-13. A comparison between the diagnostic power of formal logistic regression models and DREs' conclusions based observations of physical signs and symptoms recorded by DREs (from Schechtman and Shinar, 2005, with permission from Elsevier).

Drug	**Model versus DRE**	**Sensitivity**	**Specificity**	**False Alarms**	**Misses**	**Phi Coef.**	**Uc Coef.**
Cannabis	Model	63	91	9	37	0.57	0.25
	DRE	49	69	31	51	0.14	0.02
Alprazolam	Model	67	91	9	33	0.61	0.29
	DRE	47	80	20	53	0.23	0.05
Codeine	Model	21	89	11	79	0.13	0.01
	DRE	45	72	28	55	0.14	0.02
Amphetamine	Model	67	92	8	33	0.62	0.30
	DRE	10	91	9	90	0.01	0.00

analysis leads to three important conclusions. First, it shows that when simultaneously evaluating multiple signs and symptoms, a formal computer-based model is better than the frail human mind. Second, the information already noted and recorded in the DECP is quite useful in detecting impairments from some drug categories, such as cannabis, depressants, and stimulants. Third, even when recording all of the data as specified by the DECP, for some drug impairments – such as codeine – these signs and symptoms are simply not sufficiently valid to arrive at a conclusion that is better than chance.

The formal model has one other benefit that is quite critical for application of the DECP, and that is the ability to adjust the model to arrive at different tradeoffs between the two types of errors: misses and false alarms. As modeled above, the regression models minimized all errors. However, for law enforcement purposes, it is much more important to miss some drug-impaired drivers (and thus accept a high level of misses), than to arrest unimpaired drivers (and accept a high level of false alarms). This is because criminal conviction must be rest on evidence that is "beyond reasonable doubt," and obviously an estimate that is associated with a high level of false alarms fails this test.

To estimate the practical utility of the DECP with a formal logistic regression model, Schechtman and Shinar set the false alarm rate to 5 percent and then empirically determined the rates for sensitivity, and misses (specificity is the complement of false alarms, and therefore 95 percent). The results are presented in Table 12-14, and they show that – as expected – when false alarms are kept to a low level, the rates of "misses" increase

Table 12-14. The ability to identify cannabis, depressants, narcotic analgesics, and stimulants with a formal logistic regression model, using signs and symptoms recorded by DREs according to the DECP, when the false alarm level is set to 5 percent (and specificity is set to 95 percent) (from Schechtman and Shinar, 2005, with permission from Elsevier).

Drug	Sensitivity	Specificity	False Alarms	Misses	Phi Correlations	Uncertainty Coefficients
Cannabis	58.7	94.8	5.2	41.3	0.60	0.28
Alprazolam	60.9	94.8	5.2	39.1	0.62	0.30
Codeine	12.8	94.8	5.2	87.2	0.13	0.01
Amphetamine	54.2	94.8	5.2	45.8	0.56	0.24

dramatically, and the sensitivity rates decrease just as dramatically. Thus, the sensitivity of the DECP data for identifying cannabis and depressants (with alprazolam) decreases from approximately 90 percent to approximately 60 percent. With these data we can now safely say that the DECP is a useful tool for the detection of drug impairment, and for identification of impairments caused by cannabis, some stimulants and some depressants. For cannabis identification, the significant predictors were enlarged pupil, raised pulse rate, and lack of convergence. For depressant (alprazolam) impairment, the significant predictors were horizontal gaze nystagmus, slowed pupil reaction, and lack of convergence. For stimulant (amphetamine) impairment, the significant predictors were raised pulse rate and blood pressure, and for the narcotic/analgesic (codeine) impairment, the only significant predictor – of very limited validity – was constricted pupil.

It is very important to emphasize that the results of our analyses are not indicative of the diagnostic value of the complete 12-step DECP and the DRE evaluation procedures but only of the diagnostic value of the physical signs and symptoms collected by the DREs as part of the DECP protocol. This is because in reality, the likelihood of different drugs is not the same, and the DRE is aware of these likelihoods and uses that information to his or her advantage. Also in reality, the DRE has the benefit of other evidence and indicators based on the interview with the arresting officer and the interview with the suspect. Finally, in reality the DRE often elicits a confession from the driver. Therefore, all the indications are that the complete program is much more valid than the conclusions based on the restricted data set of signs and symptoms. Still, the latter are critical to accepting or rejecting the scientific basis for the approach, and as such it is quite lacking. What has to be done to improve the situation is to reconsider the extensive amount of information that has accumulated in this area since the program was initially designed, to focus on the more prevalent and risk elevating drugs, and for these drugs to either find existing physical and behavioral signs symptoms and tests, or to conduct controlled studies to identify such measures. Another interesting possibility is to expand the scope of the tests beyond observable signs and symptoms to neurophysiological measures (Gevins, Smith, and McEvoy, 2002).

Finally, there is growing evidence that the SFST that was originally used to detect alcohol impairment may serve as a good screening device for some other drugs as well, such as cannabis (Papafotiou, Carter, and Stough, 2005; Bosker *et al.*, 2012), some types of amphetamines such as MDMA (Downey *et al.*, 2012), and potentially many drugs belonging to the four categories of depressants, stimulants, narcotic analgesics, and cannabis. This broad range of sensitivities was revealed by analyzing 2,142 DECP assessments that were made in Canada, where different aspects of the horizontal gaze nystagmus test correlated significantly with the presence of depressants, failure of the One-Leg-Stand test correlated with presence of depressants, stimulants, narcotic analgesics, and cannabis, and inability to keep balance while listening to the instructions of the Walk-and-Turn test correlated with the presence of depressants, stimulants, and narcotic analgesics (Porath-Waller and Beirness, 2014). Thus, we come to a full circle where failing the SFST and having no or very low BAC may be somewhat indicative of impairment from many illegal drugs – the initial indications that California Highway Patrol discovered over 50 years ago. However, at least for now the levels of specificity and sensitivity are too low to warrant arrest on the basis of such evidence alone in the absence of overt impaired behavior.

Enforcement of DUID

The main limiting factor of enforcement is the very low rate of arrests for DUID, which at least in part stems from the difficulties in assessing drug impairment. Various devices have been developed and evaluated, with the search for instruments that would have high detection rates, low false alarm rates, be non-invasive, practical, and inexpensive (Walsh *et al.*, 2007). In general, these devices can test for drugs and their metabolites in the blood, saliva, urine, sweat, and hair. One of the problems encountered is the delay in the appearance of these tell-tale signs: from several minutes (blood and saliva), to hours and days (urine and sweat), to weeks and months (hair). Obviously, the longer the delay the less likely the person is still impaired by the drug, and the less relevant the test for evaluating DUID.

One thing is known – in the absence of a consistent and high probability of arrest for driving under the influence of drugs, increasing the penalties associated with driving under the influence of drugs will likely have a very small effect. This was demonstrated, at least conceptually, in an Australian survey of drivers apprehended for driving under the influence of cannabis. In this study, Jones *et al.* (2006) asked different groups of drivers how likely they were to refrain from driving after smoking marijuana given different combinations of the likelihood of being caught and severity of the penalties. As has been argued in Chapter 11 in the context of DWI, the drivers were much less likely to repeat the offense and much more sensitive to increases in the risk of apprehension than to increases in the severity of the punishment. This is very problematic because it means that increasing the penalties for DUID will most likely have a very limited effect, but increasing the risk of apprehension is very difficult, costly, and still not very reliable.

Treatment for drug addiction

A comprehensive approach to the problem of DUID may require treatment for drug addiction. This is particularly true if most people who drive after taking drugs are regular drug users. In an evaluation of such an approach, Macdonald *et al.* (2004) examined the number of traffic violations and crashes of drivers who were treated in addiction clinics for alcohol abuse, cannabis abuse, and cocaine abuse and compared them to the number of violations and crashes of a control group of drivers matched in age, gender and geographical area. Although they found that the number of traffic violations was lower in the five year post-treatment period than in the preceding period, the same applied to the control group (where the critical dates were matched to those of the treatment group). To test the effect of the treatment, they compared the reductions in violations and crashes of each treatment group relative to the reductions in the control group. The results were disappointing. None of the treatments yielded significant reductions in violations, and only the cocaine treatment group had significantly lower crashes in the post-treatment period than the control group. However, even that finding had a dubious implication, because a close examination revealed that it was primarily due to an *increase* in crashes in the control group in the post-treatment period, rather than a decrease in crashes of the treatment group. Thus, even an expensive treatment program may not have a significant payoff – at least in terms of increasing traffic safety.

Education and public information campaigns

Limited research has been directed at evaluating the effectiveness of educational programs and campaigns to reduce drugged driving. Holmes, Vanlaar, and Robertson (2014) were able to identify only six studies that evaluated four education programs and three studies that evaluated public campaigns. The programs varied in their scope and comprehensiveness from a one-day awareness raising program (Prevent Alcohol and Risk Related Trauma in Youth – PARTY) to multiple sessions over three years involving education, exposure to trauma victims and facilities, discussions, and group activities (Alcohol and Substance Abuse Prevention ASAP, Life Skills Training – LST, Alcohol Drugs Driving and You – ADDY). All programs are directed at young teens mostly before licensing age. In general these programs were effective in increasing knowledge and improving attitudes toward drug use and drugged driving. One program was also significantly associated with slightly fewer driving violations (LST), and participants in the PARTY program had slightly fewer trauma injuries than their matched control group. All in all, these programs indicated that early education and experiences in relevant life skills can be effective tools in later driving behavior. Still, though these programs have been in use for over 20 years, a crash-based measure of effectiveness remains unknown.

The effectiveness of public information campaigns on drugged driving has been evaluated on three different campaigns in Canada, Scotland, and the United Kingdom. Unfortunately, the three evaluations reviewed by Holmes *et al.*'s (2014) were quite limited in their scope, and on their basis the best that Holmes *et al.* (2014) could conclude about these campaigns was that "some evidence suggests that media and awareness campaigns are effective in reaching the target audience and raising awareness about drugged driving issues, but are less effective at increasing knowledge and understanding." Unfortunately none of the evaluation measures included concrete indicators of behavioral changes, but given the very limited effects on knowledge and understanding there may be none.

Concluding Comments

The significance of driving under the influence of drugs is very difficult to assess. The name "drugs" covers a whole slew of different substances, with widely differing pharmacological properties and a large array of psychological and behavioral effects. Even when drugs are categorized according to some common properties in terms of their effects or chemical properties, it is still difficult to assess their potential impact on driving. Furthermore, at this stage about all that we can say about the "drug problem" in traffic safety is that it is much smaller than that of alcohol and driving, and much more difficult to detect, assess, and treat than driving under the influence of alcohol.

The issue of drug assessment was addressed in a sobering (no pun intended) statement by Moskowitz (2006) who said that "we're not arguing that there is no scientific relationship between drug level at the CNS sites and resulting behavior. Many experimental studies with marijuana show that if you increase the dose you get a perfectly unimodal drug/dose curve of increasing impairment. The problem is with our ability to measure drug concentrations at CNS receptor sites. Until new technology permits us to peer into drug levels in the brain, I suggest there are intrinsic limits to the knowledge that can be obtained using correlation of traffic collisions with blood samples or with any other body fluid samples… I suggest that researchers studying the traffic safety effects of drugs with epidemiological techniques have to re-examine their goals. At this point in history, I cannot conceive how curves, such as the Grand Rapids BAC versus accident probability curves, can be generated for drugs. There is a great deal of information being generated by current epidemiological and experimental studies. What is necessary is to consider what analyses would accomplish the task of providing society with the information it needs for public drug policies, given the limitations of existing studies." In short, nine years after Moskowitz made that statement the U.S. National Institute on Drug Abuse is echoing it by stating that more research is needed (NIDA, 2015).

Several recent studies on the effects of various drugs on crash risk have not yielded consistent results. All of these studies have suffered from one or more methodological shortcomings, making comparisons quite difficulties. Only once specific drugs are consistently associated with significantly higher crash risks can we develop new and scientifically more valid tests that can be administered by law enforcement officers. Because of the complexity of the drug issue, the differences between drugs, and the ethical and practical constraints on drugs-related crash-risk studies, this is a very tall order. In fact, given these difficulties, the critical studies or tests may never be done, and we might just have to live with tentative conclusions based on partial and potentially biased data.

References

Adler, A. V. and M. Burns (1994). Drug Recognition Expert (DRE) validation study. Final Report to Arizona Governor's Office of Highway Safety. Southern California Research Institute, Santa Monica, CA.

Alvarez, F. J., M. Sancho, J. Vega, M. C. Del Rio, M. A. Rams and D. Queipo (1997). Drugs other than alcohol (medicines and illicit drugs) in people involved in fatal road accidents in Spain. In: *Alcohol, Drugs and Traffic Safety – T'97* (C. Mercier-Guyon, ed.), Volume II, pp. 677-681. CERT, Annecy, France.

AMA (2003). Physician's guide to Assessing and Counseling Older Drivers. Jointly published by the U.S. Department of Transportation as NHTSA Report No. DOT HS 809 647 and by the American Medical Association, Washington, DC.

Anderson, D. M. and D. I. Rees (2015). Per se drugged driving laws and traffic fatalities. *Int. Rev. Law and Econ.*, *42*, 122-134,

Asbridge, M., J. A. Hayden and J. L. Cartwright (2012). Acute cannabis consumption and motor vehicle collision risk: Systematic review of observational studies and meta-analysis. *Brit. Med. J.*, *344*(e536), 1-9.

Asbridge, M., C. Poulin and A. Donato (2005). Motor vehicle collision risk and driving under the influence of cannabis: Evidence from adolescents in Atlantic Canada. *Accid. Anal. Prev.*, *37*, 1025-1034.

Augsburger, M., N. Donze, A. Ménétrey, C. Brossard, F. Sporkert, C. Giroud and P. Mangin (2005). Concentration of drugs in blood of suspected impaired drivers. *Forensic Sci. Int.*, *153*, 11-15.

Barbone, F., A. D. McMahon, P. G. Davey, A. D. Morris, I. C. Reid, D. G. McDevitt and T. M. MacDonald (1998). Association of road-traffic accidents with benzodiazepine use. *Lancet*, *352*(9137), 1331-1336.

Barkley, R. A., K. R. Murphy, T. O'Connell and D. F. Connor (2005). Effects of two doses of methylphenidate on simulator driving performance in adults with attention deficit hyperactivity disorder. *J. Safe. Res.*, *36*, 121-131.

Bech, P., L. Rafaelsen and O. J. Rafaelsen (1973). Cannabis and alcohol: Effects on estimation of time and distance. *Psychopharmacol.*, *32* (4), 373-381.

Bédard, M., S. Dubois and B. Weaver (2007). The impact of cannabis on driving. *Canadian J. Pub. Health*, *98*, 6-11.

Behrensdorff, I. and A. Steentoft (2003). Medicinal and illegal drugs among Danish car drivers. *Accid. Anal. Prev.*, *35*, 851-860.

Berghaus, G. and H. Grass (1997). Concentration-effect relationship with benzodiazepine therapy. Proceedings of the 14th International Conference on Accidents Drugs and Traffic Safety (ICADTS – T97), pp. 705-709. Centre dEtudes et de Recherches en Medecine du Trafic (CERMT), Annecy, France.

Berghaus, G., H. P. Krüger and M. Vollrath (1998b). Beeinträchtigung fahrrelevanter leistungen nach rauchen von cannabis und alcoholconsum. Eine vergleichende metaanalyse experimenteller studien. In: *Cannabis im Straßenverkehr* (G. Berghaus and H. P. Krüger, eds.), pp. 99–111. Gustav Fisher Verlag, Stuttgart. (as cited by Ramaekers *et al.*, 2004).

Berghaus, G., E. Schultz and A. Szegedi (1998a). Cannabis und fahrtû chtigkeit. Ergebnisse der experimentelle forschung. In: *Cannabis im Straßenverkehr* (G. Berghaus and H. P. Kr̂uger, eds.), pp. 73–97. Gustav Fisher Verlag, Stuttgart. (as cited by Ramaekers *et al.*, 2004).

Berning, A., R. Compton and K. Wochinger (2015). *Results of the 2013–2014 National Roadside Survey of Alcohol and Drug Use by Drivers*. National Highway Traffic Safety Administration, Traffic Safety Facts, Research Note DOT HS 812 118. U. S. Department of Transportation, Washington, DC.

Berning, A. and D. D. Smithers (2014). Understanding the limitations of drug test information, reporting, and testing practices in fatal crashes. Traffic Safety Facts Research Note DOT HS 812 072. U.S. Department of Transportation, Washington, DC.

Blomberg, R. A., R. C. Peck, H. Moskowitz, M. Burns and D. Fiorentino (2005). *Crash Risk of Alcohol Involved Driving: A Case-Control Study*. Dunlap and Associates Inc., Stamford, CN. (Also published by ICADTS on www.icadts.org).

Blows, S., R. Q. Ivers, J. Connor, S. Ameratunga, M. Woodward and R. Norton (2005). Marijuana use and car crash injury. *Addict.*, *100*(5), 605-611.

Boorman, M. and K. Owens (2009). The Victorian legislative framework for the random testing drivers at the roadside for the presence of illicit drugs: An evaluation of the characteristics of drivers detected from 2004 to 2006. *Traffic Inj. Prev.*, *10*(1), 16-22.

Bosker, W. M., E. L. Theunissen, S. Conen, K. P. C. Kuypers, W. K. Jeffery, H. C. Walls, G. F. Kauert, S. W. Toennes, M. R. Moeller and J. G. Ramaekers (2012). A placebo-controlled study to assess Standardized Field Sobriety Tests performance during alcohol and cannabis intoxication in heavy cannabis users and accuracy of point of collection testing devices for detecting THC in oral fluid. *Psychopharmacol.*, *223*, 439–446.

Bramness, J. G., S. Skurtveit and J. Mørland (2002). Clinical impairment of benzodiazepines – Relation between benzodiazepine concentrations and impairment in apprehended drivers. *Drug Alcohol Depend.*, *68*, 131-141.

CCSA (2015). Drug evaluation and classification program. Policy Brief. Canadian Center on Substance Abuse, Ottawa, CA.

Chait, L. D. and J. L. Perry (1994). Acute and residual effects of alcohol and marijuana, alone and in combination, on mood and performance. *Psychopharmacol.*, *115*(3), 340-349.

Chesher, G. B. (1995). Cannabis and road safety: An outline of the research studies to examine the effects of cannabis on driving skills and on actual driving performance. In Road Safety Committee, Parliament of Victoria (Eds.) Inquiry into the effects of drugs (other than alcohol) on road and safety in Victoria. Government Printer, North Melbourne.

Christophersen, A. S., G. Ceder, J. Kristinsson, P. Lillsund and A. Steentoft (1999). Drugged driving in the Nordic countries – A comparative study between five countries. *Forensic Sci. Int.*, *106*, 173-190.

Christophersen, A. S., H. Gjerde, A. Bjornebone, J. Sakshaug and J. Morland (1990). Screening for drug use among Norwegian drivers suspected of driving under influence of alcohol or drugs. *Forensic Sci. Int.*, *45*(1-2), 5-14.

Clayton, A. B. (1976). The effects of psychotropic drugs upon driving-related skills. *Hum. Fact.*, *18*(3), 241-252.

Compton, R. P. and A. Berning (2009). *Results of the 2007 National Roadside Survey of Alcohol and Drug Use by Drivers*. Traffic Safety Facts. Research Note DOT HS 811 175. U.S. Department of Transportation, Washington, DC.

Compton, R. P. and A. Berning (2015). Drug and alcohol crash risk. NHTSA Traffic Safety Facts Research Note DOT HS 812 117. U.S. Department of Transportation, Washington, DC.

Couper, F. J. and B. K. Logan (2004). Drugs and human performance fact sheets. National Highway Traffic Safety Administration Report No. DOT HS 809 725. U.S. Department of Transportation, Washington, DC. http://www.nhtsa.dot.gov/people/injury/research/job185drugs/drugs_web.pdf

Crancer, A. Jr., J. M. Dille, J. C. Delay, J. F. Wallace and M. D. Haykin (1969). Comparison of the effects of marijuana and alcohol on simulated driving performance. *Science*, *164*(881), 851-854.

Cremona, A. (1986). Mad drivers: Psychiatric illness and driving performance. *Br. J. Hospital Med.*, *35* (3), 193-195.

Crouch, D. J., M. M. Birky, S. W. Gust, D. E. Rollins, J. M. Walsh, J. V. Moulden, K. E. Quinlan and R. W. Beckel (1993). The prevalence of drugs and alcohol in fatally injured truck drivers. *J. Forensic Sci.*, *38*(6), 1342-1353.

Degenhardt, L., P. Dillon, C. Duff and J. Ross (2006). Driving, drug use behaviour and risk perceptions of nightclub attendees in Victoria, Australia. *Int. J. Drug Policy*, *17*, 41-46.

DHHS (2003). *Results from the 2002 National Survey on Drug Use and Health: National Findings*. Substance Abuse and Mental Health Services Administration, DHHS (Publication No. SMA 03-3836). U.S. Department of Health and Human Services, Rockville, MD.

Downey, L. A., R. King, K. Papafotiou, P. Swann, E. Ogden, M. Boorman and C. Stough (2013). The effects of cannabis and alcohol on simulated driving: Influences of dose and experience. *Accid. Anal. Prev.*, *50*, 879-886.

Downey, L. A., R. King, K. Papafotiou, P. Swann, E. Ogden and C. Stough (2012). Examining the effect of dl-3,4-methylenedioxymethamphetamine (MDMA) and methamphetamine on the standardized field sobriety tests. *Forensic Sci. Int.*, *220*, e33–e36.

Drummer, O. H. (1995). Drugs and accident risk in fatally-injured drivers. Proceedings of the 13th International Conference on Alcohol, Drugs and Traffic Safety (C. N. Kloeden and A. J. McLean, eds.), pp. 426-429. Adelaide, Australia.

Drummer, O. H., J. Gerostamoulos, H. Batziris, M. Chu, J. Caplehorn, M. D. Robertson and P. Swann (2004). The involvement of drugs in drivers of motor vehicles killed in Australian road traffic crashes. *Accid. Anal. Prev.*, *36*, 239-248.

Dubois, S., N. Mullen, B. Weaver and M. Bédard (2015). The combined effects of alcohol and cannabis on driving: Impact on crash risk. *Forensic Sci. Int.*, *248*, 94-100.

Dussault, C., M. Brault, J. Bouchard and A. M. Lemire (2002). The contribution of alcohol and other drugs among fatally injured drivers in Quebec: Some preliminary results. Proceedings of the 16th International Conference on Alcohol, Drugs and Traffic Safety T2002, pp. 423–430. Montreal, Canada.

Ellinwood, E. H. and D. G. Heatherly (1985). Benzodiazepines, the popular minor tranquilizer: Dynamics of effect on driving skills. *Accid. Anal. Prev.*, *17*(4), 283-290.

Elvik, R. (2013). Risk of road accident associated with the use of drugs: A systematic review and meta-analysis of evidence from epidemiological studies. *Accid. Anal. Prev.*, *60*, 254-267.

Farrell, L. J. (2003). The effects of drugs on human performance and behavior (ed.). Special issue of *Forensic Sci. Rev.*, **15**(1), 1-74.

Fishbain, D. A., R. B. Cutler, H. L. Rosomoff and R. S. Rosomoff (2003). Are opioid dependent/tolerant patients impaired in driving-related skills? A structured evidence-based review. *J. Pain Symptom Management*, *25*, 559–577.

French Benzodiazepine/Driving Collaboration Group (1993). Are benzodiazepines a risk factor for road accidents? *Drug Alcohol Depend.*, *33*(1), 19-22.

Furr-Holden, D., R. B. Voas, T. Kelley-Baker and B. Miller (2006). Drug and alcohol-impaired driving among electronic music dance event attendees. *Drug Alcohol Depend.*, *85*, 83-86.

Gadegbeku, B., E. Amoros and the SAM group (2010). Responsibility study: Main illicit psychoactive substances among car drivers involved in fatal road crashes in France. DRUID project, WP2, Task 2.3.3, Deliverable 2.3.2. Project No. TREN-05-FP6TR-S07.61320-518404-DRUID. EU, Brussels.

Galski, T., J. B. Williams and H. T. Ehle (2000). Effects of opioids on driving ability. *J. Pain Symptom Management*, *19*(3), 200-208.

Gevins, A., M. E. Smith and L. K. McEvoy (2002). Tracking the cognitive pharmacodynamics of psychoactive substances with combinations of behavioral and neurophysiological measures. *Neuropsychopharmacol.*, *26*(1), 27-39.

Ghoneim, M. M., S. P. Mewaldt and J. W. Thatcher (1975). The effect of diazepam and fentanyl on mental, psychomotor and electroencephalographic functions and their rate of recovery. *Psychopharmacol.*, *44*(1), 61-66.

Gier de, J. J. (1997). Decision support tables for psychotropic medicines. In: *Alcohol, Drugs and Traffic Safety – T'97* (C. Mercier-Guyon, ed.), Volume III, pp. 1275-1282. CERT, Annecy, France.

Gjerde, H., A. S. Christophersen, P. T. Normann, T. Assum, E. L. Øiestad and J. Mørland (2013a). Norwegian roadside survey of alcohol and drug use by drivers (2008–2009). *Traffic Inj. Prev.*, *14*(5), 443-452.

Gjerde, H., A. S. Christophersen, P. T. Normann and J. Mørland (2013b). Associations between substance use among car and van drivers in Norway and fatal injury in road traffic accidents: A case-control study. *Trans. Res. F.*, *17*, 134-144.

Gjerde, H. and G. Kinn (1991). Impairment in drivers due to cannabis in combination with other drugs. *Forensic Sci. Int.*, *50*(1), 57-60.

Gjerde, H., P. T. Normann, A. S. Christophersen, S. O. Samuelsen and J. Mørland (2011). Alcohol, psychoactive drugs and fatal road traffic accidents in Norway: A case–control study. *Accid. Anal. Prev.*, *43*(3), 1197-1203.

Hartman, R. L. and M. A. Huestis (2013). Cannabis effects on driving skills. *Clinical Chemistry*, *59*, 478-492.

Holmes, E., W. Vanlaar and R. Robertson (2014). The problem of youth drugged driving and approaches to prevention: A systematic literature review. Canadian Center on Substance Abuse, Ottawa, Canada.

Hartman, R. L., T. L. Brown, G. Milavetz, A. Spurgin, R. S. Pierce, D. A. Gorelick, G. Gaffney and M. A. Huestis (2015). Cannabis effects on driving lateral control with and without alcohol. *Drug Alcohol Depend.*, *154*, 25-37.

Hausken, A. M., S. Skurtveit and A. S. Christophersen (2005). Mortality among subjects previously apprehended for driving under the influence of traffic-hazardous medicinal drugs. *Drug Alcohol Depend.*, *79*, 423-429.

Heishman, S. J., M. A. Huestis, J. E. Henningfield and E. J. Cone (1990). Acute and residual effects of marijuana: Profiles of plasma THC levels, physiological, subjective, and performance measures. *Pharmacol. Biochemic. Behav.*, *37*(3), 561-565.

Heishman, S. J., E. G. Singleton and D. J. Crouch (1998). Laboratory validation study of drug evaluation and classification program: alprazolam, D-amphetamine, codeine, and marijuana. *J. Analytic. Toxicol.*, *22*, 503–514.

Heishman, S. J., M. L. Stitzer and G. E. Bigelow (1988). Alcohol and marijuana: Comparative dose effect profiles in humans. *Pharmacol. Biochemic. Behav.*, *31*(3), 649-655.

Heishman, S. J., M. L. Stitzer and J. E. Yingling (1989). Effects of tetrahydrocannabinol content on marijuana smoking behavior, subjective reports, and performance. *Pharmacol. Biochemic. Behav.*, *34*(1), 173-179.

Hels, T. I., M. Bernhoft, A. Lyckegaard, S. Houwing, M. Hagenzieker, S.-A. Legrand, C. Isalberti, T. Van der Linden and A. Verstraete (2011). Risk of injury by driving with alcohol and other drugs. DRUID project, WP2, Deliverable 2.3.5. Project No. TREN-05-FP6TR-S07.61320-518404-DRUID. EU, Brussels.

Hemmelgarn, B., S. Suissa, A. Huang, J. F. Bolvin and G. Pinard (1997). Benzodiazepine use and risk of motor vehicle crash in the elderly. *J. Amer. Med. Assn.*, *278*, 27-31.

Hindmarch, I. (1988). The psychopharmacological approach: Effects of psychotropic drugs on car handling. *Int. Clin. Psychopharmacol.*, *3*(Suppl 1), 73-79.

Hindmarch, I. and A. C. Gudgeon (1982). Loprazolam (HR158) and flurazepam with ethanol compared on tests of psychomotor ability. *Eur. J. Clin. Pharmacol.*, *23*(6), 509-512.

Hindmarch, I., J. S. Kerr and N. Sherwood (1991). The effects of alcohol and other drugs on psychomotor performance and cognitive function. *Alcohol Alcohol.*, *26* (1), 71-79.

Hindrik, W., J. Robbe and J. F. O'Hanlon (1999). Marijuana, Alcohol, and Actual Driving Performance. National Highway Traffic Safety Administration, Report No. DOT HS 808 939. U.S. Department of Transportation, Washington, DC.

Holmgren, P., E. Loch and J. Schuberth (1985). Drugs in motorists traveling Swedish roads: On-the-road-detection of intoxicated drivers and screening for drugs in these offenders. *Forensic Sci. Int.*, *27*(1), 57-65.

Houwing, S., M. Hagenzieker, R. P. M. Mathijssen, S.-N. Legrand, A. G. Verstraete, T. Hels, I. M. Bernhoft, K. W. Simonsen, P. Lillsunde, D. Favretto, S. D. Ferraraf, M. Caplinskiene, K. L. L. Movig and K. A. Brookhuis (2013). Random and systematic errors in case–control studies calculating the injury risk of driving under the influence of psychoactive substances. *Accid. Anal. Prev.*, *52*, 144-153.

Hunter, C. E., R. J. Lokan, M. C. Longo, J. M. White and M. A. White (1998). *The Prevalence and Role of Alcohol, Cannabinoids, Benzodiazepines and Stimulants in*

Non-Fatal Crashes. Forensic Science, Department for Administrative and Information Services, Adelaide, Southern Australia.

ICADTS (2006). *Categorization System for Medicinal Drugs Affecting Driving Performance*. International Council on Accidents Drugs and Driving. http://www.icadts.org/reports/medicinaldrugs1.pdf

Johnson, L. C. and D. A. Chernik (1982). Sedative-hypnotics and human performance. *Psychopharmacol.*, *76*, 101-113.

Jonasson, U., B. Jonasson, T. Saldeen and F. Thuen (2000). The prevalence of analgesics containing dextropropoxyphene or codeine in individuals suspected of driving under the influence of drugs. *Forensic Sci. Int.*, *112*, 163-169.

Jones, C. N., W. Donnelly, D. Swift and D. Weatherburn (2006). Preventing cannabis users from driving under the influence of cannabis. *Accid. Anal. Prev.*, *38*(5), 854-861.

Jones, R. K., D. Shinar and J. M. Walsh (2003). State of knowledge of drug impaired driving. National Highway Traffic Safety Administration Report DOT HS 809 642. U.S. Department of Transportation, Washington DC.

Jongen, A., E. F. P. M. Vuurman, J. G. Ramaekers and A. Vermeeren (2016). The sensitivity of laboratory tests assessing driving related skills to dose-related impairment of alcohol: A literature review. *Accid. Anal. Prev.*, *89*, 31-48.

Klonoff, H. (1974). Marijuana and driving in real-life situations. *Science*, *186*, 317-332.

Koelega, H. S. (1989). Benzodiazepines and vigilance performance: A review. *Psychopharmacol. (Berl)*, *98*(2), 145-156.

Kress, H. G. and B. Kraft (2005). Opioid medication and driving ability. *Eur. J. Pain*, *9*, 141-144.

Kunsman, G. W., J. E. Manno, B. R. Manno, C. M. Kunsman and M. A. Przekop (1992a). The use of microcomputer-based psychomotor tests for the evaluation of benzodiazepine effects on human performance: A review with emphasis on temazepam. *Br. J. Clin. Pharmacol.*, *34*(4), 289-301.

Kunsman, G. W., J. E. Manno, M. A. Przekop, B. R. Manno and C. M. Kunsman (1992b). The effects of temazepam and ethanol on human psychomotor performance. *Eur. J. Clin. Pharmacol.*, *43*(6), 603-611.

Laberge, J. C. and N. J. Ward (2004). Research note: Cannabis and driving – Research needs and issues for transportation policy. *J. Drug Issues*, Fall, 971-989.

Lacey, J. H., T. Kelley-Baker, A. Berning, E. Romano, A. Ramirez, J. Yao, C. Moore, K. Brainard, K. Carr, K. Pell and R. Compton (2016). Drug and alcohol crash risk: A case-control study. NHTSA Report No. DOT HS 812 355. U.S. Department of Transportation, Washington, DC.

Lacey, J. H., T. Kelley-Baker, D. Furr-Holden, R. Voas, C. Moore, K. Brainard, A. S. Tippetts, E. Romano, P. Torres and A. Berning (2009). *2007 National Roadside Survey of Alcohol and Drug Use by Drivers: Methodology*. National Highway Traffic Safety Administration, Report DOT HS 811 237. US Department of Transportation, Washington, DC.

Lamers, C. T. and J. G. Ramaekers (2001). Visual search and urban driving under the influence of marijuana and alcohol. *Hum. Psychopharmacol. Clin. Exp.*, *16*(5), 393-401.

Laumon, B., B. Gadegbeku, J. L. Martin, M. B. Biecheler and the SAM Group (2005). Cannabis intoxication and fatal road crashes in France: Population based case-control study. *Br. Med. J.*, *331*, 1371-1376.

Lenné, M. G., P. Dietze, G. Rumbold, J. R. Redman and T. J. Triggs (2000). Opioid dependence and driving ability: A review in the context of proposed legislative change in Victoria. *Drugs Alcohol Rev.*, *19*(4), 427-429.

Lenné, M. G., P. Dietze, G. R. Rumbold, J. R. Redman and T. J. Triggs (2003). The effects of the opioid pharmacotherapies methadone, LAAM and buprenorphine, alone and in combination with alcohol, on simulated driving. *Drug Alcohol Depend.*, *72*, 271-278.

Lenné, M. G., P. M. Dietze, T. J. Triggs. S. Walmsley, B. Murphy and J. R. Redmand (2010). The effects of cannabis and alcohol on simulated arterial driving: Influences of driving experience and task demand. *Accid. Anal., Prev.*, *42*, 859-866.

Lenné, M. G., C. Fry, P. Dietze and G. Rumbold (2001). Attitudes and experiences of people who use cannabis and drive: Implications for drugs and driving legislation in Victoria, Australia. *Drug. Education Prev. Policy*, *8*(4), 307-313.

Leveille, S. G., D. M. Buchner, T. D. Koepsell, L. W. McCloskey, M. W. Woof and E. H. Wagner (1994). Psychoactive medications and injurious motor vehicle collisions involving older drivers. *Epidemiol.*, *5*(6), 591-598.

Li, G., J. E. Brady and Q. Chen (2013). Drug use and fatal motor vehicle crashes: A case-control study. *Accid. Anal. Prev.*, *60*, 205-210.

Lillsunde, P., T. Korte, L. Michelson, M. Portman, J. Pikkarainen and T. Seppala (1996). Drugs usage of drivers suspected of driving under the influence of alcohol and/or drugs. A study of one week's samples in 1979 and 1993 in Finland. *Forensic Sci. Int.*, *77*(1-2), 119-129.

Linnoila, M. (1973). Effects of diazepam, chlordiazepoxide, thioridazine, haloperidole, flupenthixole and alcohol on psychomotor skills related to driving. *Ann. Med. Exp. Biol. Fenn.*, *51*(3), 125-132.

Lister, R. G. and S. E. File (1983). Performance impairment and increased anxiety resulting from the combination of alcohol and lorazepam. *J. Clin. Psychopharmacol.*, *3*(2), 66-71.

Macdonald, S., R. E. Mann, M. Chipman and K. Anglin-Bodrug (2004). Collisions and traffic violations of alcohol, cannabis and cocaine abuse clients before and after treatment. *Accid. Anal. Prev.*, *36*, 795-800.

McNair, D. M. (1973). Anti anxiety drugs and human performance. *Arch. Gen. Psychiatry.*, *29*(5), 611-617.

Mintzer, M. Z., J. Guarino, T. Kirk, J. D. Roache and R. R. Griffiths (1997). Ethanol and pentobarbital: Comparison of behavioral and subjective effects in sedative drug abusers. *Exp. Clin. Psychopharmacol.*, *5*(3), 203.

Moskowitz, H. (1984). Attention tasks as skills performance measures of drug effects. *Br. J. Clin. Pharmacol.*, *18* (Suppl 1), 51S-61S.

Moskowitz, H. (2002). Alcohol and drugs. In: *Human Factors in Traffic Safety* (R. E. Dewar and P. Olson, eds.), pp. 177-207. Lawyers & Judges Publishing, Tucson, AZ.

Moskowitz, H. (2006). Further methodological issues in epidemiological studies of alcohol driving. Proceedings of the Transportation Research Board Annual Meeting January 20-23. Transportation Research Board, Washington, DC.

Moskowitz, H. and C. J. Wilkinson (2003). Antihistamines and driving-related behavior: A review of the evidence for impairment by first- versus second-generation H1-antagonists. National Highway Traffic Safety Administration. U.S. Department of Transportation, Washington, DC.

Movig, K. L. L., M. P. M. Mathijssen, P. H. A. Nagel, T. van Egmond, J. J. de Gier, H. G. M. Leufkens and A. C. G. Egberts (2004). Psychoactive substance use and the risk of motor vehicle accidents. *Accid. Anal. Prev.*, *36*, 631-636.

Mura, P., P. Kintz, B. Ludes, J. Gaulier and P. Marquet (2003). Comparison of the prevalence of alcohol, cannabis and other drugs between 900 injured drivers and 900 control subjects: Results of a French collaborative study. *Forensic Sci. Int.*, *133*(1-2), 79–85.

Neuteboom, W. and P. G. Zweipfenning (1984). Driving and the combined use of drugs and alcohol in The Netherlands. *Forensic Sci. Int.*, *25*(2), 93-104.

NHTSA (2004). Drugs and human performance fact sheets. National Highway Traffic Safety Administration Report DOT HS 809 725. U.S. Department of Transportation, Washington, DC.

NHTSA (2005). Medical conditions and driving: A review of the literature (1960-2000). National Highway Traffic Safety Administration Report DOT HS 809 690. U.S. Department of Transportation, Washington, DC.

NHTSA (2010a). Drug involvement of fatally injured drivers. National Highway Traffic Safety Administration Report DOT HS 811 415. U.S. Department of Transportation, Washington, DC.

NHTSA (2010b). Drug per se laws: A review of their use in the states. National Highway Traffic Safety Administration Report, Traffic Tech. Number 393. U.S. Department of Transportation, Washington, DC.

NIDA (2001). Hallucinogens and dissociative drugs. Research Report. U.S. National Institute of Drug Abuse, Rockville, MD.

NIDA (2002). Methamphetamine abuse and addiction. Research Report Series. U.S. National Institute of Drug Abuse, Rockville, MD.

NIDA (2004). Cocaine abuse and addiction. Research Report Series. U.S. National Institute of Drug Abuse, Rockville, MD.

NIDA (2005). Inhalant abuse. Research Report. U.S. National Institute of Drug Abuse, Rockville, MD.

NIDA (2006a). Commonly abused drugs chart. U.S. National Institute of Drug Abuse, Rockville, MD. http://www.nida.nih.gov/DrugPages/DrugsofAbuse.html

NIDA (2006b). Drugs of abuse information. U.S. National Institute of Drug Abuse, Rockville, MD. http://www.nida.nih.gov/DrugPages.html

NIDA (2016). DrugFacts: Drugged driving. http://www.drugabuse.gov/publications/drugfacts/drugged-driving

OECD (2010). Drugs and driving: Detection and deterrence. Joint Transport Research Center of the OECD and the International Transport Forum. Paris, France.

Ogden, E. J. D. and H. Moskowitz (2004). Effects of alcohol and other drugs on driver performance. *Traffic Inj. Prev.*, *5*, 185-198.

Papafotiou, K., J. D. Carter and C. Stough (2005). An evaluation of the sensitivity of the Standardised Field Sobriety Tests (SFSTs) to detect impairment due to marijuana intoxication. *Psychopharmacology*, *180*, 107-114.

Perez-Reyes, M., R. E. Hicks, J. Bumberry, A. R. Jeffcoat and C. E. Cook (1988). Interaction between marihuana and ethanol: Effects on psychomotor performance. *Alcohol Clin. Exp. Res.*, *12*(2), 268-276.

Pickworth, W. B., M. S. Rohrer and R. V. Fant (1997). Effects of abused drugs on psychomotor performance. *Exp. Clin. Psychopharmacol.*, *5*(3), 235-241.

Pollini, R. A., E. Romano, M. B. Johnson and J. H. Lacey (2015). The impact of marijuana decriminalization on California drivers. *Drug Alcohol Depend.*, *150*, 135-140.

Porath-Waller, A. J. and D. J. Beirness (2010). Simplifying the process for identifying drug combinations by drug recognition experts. *Traffic Inj. Prev.*, *11*(5), 453-459.

Porath-Waller, A. J. and D. J. Beirness (2014). An examination of the validity of the standardized field sobriety test in detecting drug impairment using data from the drug evaluation and classification program. *Traffic Inj. Prev.*, *15*(2), 125-131.

Porath-Waller, A. J., D. J. Beirness and E. E., Beasley (2009). Toward a more parsimonious approach to drug recognition expert evaluations. *Traffic Inj. Prev.*, *10*(6), 513-518.

Rafaelsen, L., H. Christup and P. Bech (1973). Effects of cannabis and alcohol on psychological tests. *Nature*, *242*, 117-118.

Ramaekers, J. G., G. Berghaus, M. van Laar and O. H. Drummer (2004). Dose related risk of motor vehicle crashes after cannabis use. *Drug Alcohol Depend.*, *73*, 109-119.

Ramaekers, J. G., K. P. C. Kuypers, W. M. Bosker, K. A. Brookhuis, J. A. Veldstra, R. Simons, M. Martens, M. Hjälmdahl, Å. Forsman and A. Knoche (2012). Effects of stimulant drugs on actual and simulated driving: Perspectives from four experimental studies conducted as part of the DRUID research consortium (Commentary). *Psychopharmacol.*, 1-6.

Ramaekers, J. G., H. W. J. Robbe and J. F. O'Hanlon (2000). Marijuana, alcohol and actual driving performance. *Hum. Psychopharmacol. Clin. Exp.*, *15*, 551–558.

Ray, W. A., R. L. Fought and M. D. Decker (1992). Psychoactive drugs and the risk of injurious motor vehicle crashes in elderly drivers. *Am. J. Epidemiol.*, *136*(7), 873-883.

Roache, J. D., D. R. Cherek, R. H. Bennett, J. C. Schenkler and K. A. Cowan (1993). Differential effects of triazolam and ethanol on awareness, memory and psychomotor performance. *J. Clin. Pharmacol.*, *13*(1), 3-15.

Robbe, H. W. J. (1994). *Influence of Marijuana on Driving*. University of Limburg, Maastricht, The Netherlands.

Robbe, H. and J. O'Hanlon (1993). *Marijuana and actual driving performance*. National Highway Traffic Safety Administration Report DOT HS 808 078. U.S. Department of Transportation, Washington DC.

Rogeberg, O. and R. Elvik (2016). The effects of cannabis intoxication on motor vehicle collision revisited and revised. *Addiction*, in press.

Ronen, A., P. Gershon, H. Drobiner, A. Rabinovich, R. Bar-Hamburger, R. Mechoulam, Y. Cassuto and D. Shinar (2008). Effects of THC on driving performance, physiological state and subjective feelings relative to alcohol. *Accid. Anal. Prev.*, *40*, 926-934.

Ronen, A., H. Schwartz Chassidim, P. Gershon, Y. Parmet, A. Rabinovich, R. Bar-Hamburger, Y. Cassuto and D. Shinar (2010). The effect of alcohol, THC and their combination on perceived effects, willingness to drive and performance of driving and non-driving tasks. *Acci. Anal. Prev.*, *42*, 1855-1865.

Sabatowski, R., S. Schwalen, K. Rettig, K. W. Herberg, S. M. Kasper and L. Radbruch (2003). Driving ability under long-term treatment with transdermal fentanyl. *J. Pain Symptom Management*, *25*, 38-47.

Salomonsen-Sautel, S., S. J. Min, J. T. Sakai, C. Thurstone and C. Hopfer (2014). Trends in fatal motor vehicle crashes before and after marijuana commercialization in Colorado. *Drug Alcohol Depend.*, *140*, 137-144.

SAMHSA (1998). National Survey on Drug Use and Health. Substance Abuse and Mental Health Services Administration (SAMHSA), Office of Applied Studies, National Survey on Drug Use and Health. U.S. Department of Health and Human Services, Washington DC. http://www.samhsa.gov.

Schechtman, E. and D. Shinar (2005). Modeling drug detection and diagnosis with the 'drug evaluation and classification program'. *Accid. Anal. Prev.*, *37*(5), 852–861.

Shinar, D. (2006). Drug effects and their significance for traffic safety. Proceedings of a Symposium on Drugs and Traffic (Woods Hole, MA, June 20-21, 2005). Transportation Research Circular, No. E-C096, May. Transportation Research Board, Washington, DC.

Shinar, D. and E. Schechtman (2005). Drug identification performance on the basis of observable signs and symptoms. *Accid. Anal. Prev.*, *37*(5), 843–851.

Skurtveit, S., B. Abotnes and A. S. Christophersen (2002b). Drugged drivers in Norway with benzodiazepine detections. *Forensic Sci. Int.*, *125*, 75-82.

Skurtveit, S., A. S. Christophersen, M. Grung and J. Mørland (2002a). Increased mortality among previously apprehended drunken and drugged drivers. *Drug Alcohol Depend.*, *68*, 143-150.

Smiley, A. (1999). Marijuana: On road and driving simulator studies. In: *The Health Effects of Cannabis* (H. Kalant, W. A. Corrgall, W. Hall and R. G. Smart, eds.). Centre for Addiction and Mental Health, Toronto, Ontario M5S 2S1, Canada.

Smiley, A. M., H. Moskowitz and K. Zeidman (1981). Driving simulator studies of marijuana alone and in combination with alcohol. Proceedings of the 25th Conference of the American Association for Automotive Medicine, pp. 107-116.

Smith, J. A., C. E. Hayes, R. L. Yolton, D. A. Rutledge and K. Citek (2002). Drug recognition expert evaluations made using limited data. *Forensic Sci. Int.*, *130*, 167-173.

Soderstrom, C. A., P. C. Dischinger, T. J. Kerns and A. L. Trifillis (1995). Marijuana and other drug use among automobile and motorcycle drivers treated at a trauma center. *Accid. Anal. Prev.*, *27*(1), 131-135.

Solowij, N. (1998). Cannabis and Cognitive Functioning. Cambridge University Press, Cambridge, UK.

Starmer, G. A. and D. K. Bird (1984). Investigation of drug-ethanol interactions. *Br. J. Clin. Pharmacol.*, *18*(Suppl 1), 27S-35S.

Starmer, G. A., T. Bock, J. Harris, D. J. Mascord, J. Nelson, B. Tattam and R. Zeleny (1997). Drug usage by Australian drivers. In: *Alcohol, Drugs and Traffic Safety – T'97* (C. Mercier-Guyon, ed.), Volume III, pp. 1135-1141. CERT, Annecy, France.

Sutton, L. R. and I. Paegle (1992). The drug impaired driver. Detection and forensic specimen analysis. *Blutalkohol*, *29*(2), 134-138.

Terry, P. and K. A. Wright (2005). Self-reported driving behaviour and attitudes towards driving under the influence of cannabis among three different user groups in England. *Addict. Behav.*, *30*, 619-626.

Tunbridge, R. and D. Rowe (1999). Roadside identification of drug impaired drivers in Great Britain. Paper presented in the International Conference on Traffic Safety in Two Continents. Sept. 20-22, Malmo, Sweden.

Vermeeren, A. and J. F. O'Hanlon (1998). Fexofenadine's effects, alone and with alcohol, on actual driving and psychomotor performance. *J. Allergy Clin. Immunol.*, *101*, 306-311.

Verstraete, A. G. and E. Raes (2006). Rosita-2 Project Final Report. Ghent University, Belgium. http://www.rosita.org/docs/Rosita2%20Final%20report%20May2006.pdf

Voas, R. B., J. H. Lacey, K. Jones, M. Scherer and R. Compton (2013). Drinking drivers and drug use on weekend nights in the United States. *Drug Alcohol Depend.*, *130*(1), 215-221.

Walsh, J. M. (2009). A state-by-state analysis of laws dealing with driving under the influence of drugs. NHTSA Report No. HS-811 236. U.S. Dept. Transportation, Washington, DC.

Walsh, J. M., L. A. Cangianelli, J. V. Moulden and N.-H. Park (2007). Rosita 2 Project. Final Report U.S. Sites.

Walsh, J. M., R. Flegel, R. Atkins, L. A. Cangianelli, C. Cooper, C. Welsh and T. J. Kerns (2005). Drug and alcohol use among drivers admitted to a Level-1 trauma center. *Accid. Anal. Prev.*, *37*, 894-901.

Ward, N. J. and L. Dye (1999). *Cannabis and Driving: A review of the literature and commentary (ISSN 1468-9138)*. Department of the Environment, Transport and the Regions, London, UK. http://www.roads.dft.gov.uk/roadsafety/cannabis/index.htm

Wilson, F. A., J. P. Stimpson and J. A. Pagán (2014). Fatal crashes from drivers testing positive for drugs in the US, 1993-2010. *Pub. Health Rep.*, *129*(4), 342-350.

Wittenborn, J. R. (1979). Effects of benzodiazepines on psychomotor performance. *Br. J. Clin. Pharmacol.*, *7*(Suppl 1), 61S-67S.

Woodall, K. L., B. L. C. Chow, A. Lauwers and C. Cass (2015). Toxicological findings in fatal motor vehicle collisions in Ontario, Canada: A one-year study. *J. Forensic Sciences*, *60*, 669–674.

Zancaner, S., R. Giorgetti, C. Dal Pozzo, G. Molinari, R. Snenghi and S. Ferrara (1997). Driving under the influence of drugs. Correlation between clinical signs and type of intoxication. In: *Alcohol, Drugs and Traffic Safety T'97*, Volume II. International Council on Alcohol, Drugs and Traffic Safety, Annecy, France.

13

Distraction and Inattention

"A grave problem that developed in New Hampshire... now has all the motor-vehicle commissioners of the eastern states in a wax. It's whether radios should be allowed on cars. Some states don't want to permit them at all – say they distract the driver and disturb the peace... The commissioner (of Massachusetts) thinks the things should be shut off while you are driving... The whole problem is getting very complex, but the upshot is that you'll probably be allowed to take your radio anywhere, with possibly some restriction on the times when you can play it." (Nicholas Trott in 1930, as cited by Goodman *et al.*, 1997).

"Keep your mind on your drivin'/Keep your hands on the wheel/Keep your snoopy eyes on the road ahead/We're havin' fun sittin' in the back seat/Kissin' and a'huggin' with Fred." (Refrain from "Seven Little Girls Sitting in the Backseat" released by Paul Evans, 1959).

"Distracted driving" was chosen as the 'word of the year' for 2009 by Webster's New World Dictionary. (https://www.youtube.com/watch?v=2IIu_wdAPcE)

"A dramatic fall in traffic accidents this week has been directly linked to the three-day disruption in BlackBerry services. In Dubai, traffic accidents fell 20 per cent from average rates on the days BlackBerry users were unable to use its messaging service. In Abu Dhabi, the number of accidents this week fell 40 per cent and there were no fatal accidents." (The National, October 15, 2011).

As the traffic demands fluctuate over time, so does the amount of resources that are necessary for safe driving. Blumenthal's model (Chapter 3) provides an intuitively appealing and simple function that links the driving demands with the attention allocated to them. If we allocated all of our attentional capacities to the driving and adjusted our speed and exposure to various driving situations in such a way that the demands never exceed our maximum available resources for processing the traffic and roadway information, then we could eliminate all the accidents that are due to inattention and "delayed recognition." Unfortunately, this patently simple suggestion is not as easy to apply as it sounds. When the driving demands are low, when the roadway is monotonous, and when we are fatigued, it is actually very difficult to devote all of our attention to the driving task. We then seek to occupy ourselves with non-driving tasks. This was dramatically illustrated in several studies conducted in the 1970s and 1980s that revealed that drivers' abilities to recall road signs they had just passed was unexpectedly low: from under 50 percent to as low as 5 percent, depending on the "relevance" of the sign and the study methodology (see Chapter 5, and Martens, 2000). To gain some insight into the process, Summala and Näätänen (1974) had drivers drive in naturalistic traffic conditions and report *all* signs as they encountered them. With this specific instruction, cueing the drivers in advance to attend to and report the signs, the drivers were able to correctly report over 98 percent of the signs they encountered. However, the researchers noted that the drivers invariably commented that driving while attending to all signs was "extremely fatiguing" (or "difficult," using Fuller's 2002 term). We can empathize with this fatiguing effect if we compare how tired we feel at the end of a long drive in congested stop-and-go traffic versus a drive lasting just as long on a divided highway in fair weather with little traffic. In the former case, we must allocate nearly all of our attention to changing traffic signals, weaving drivers, and stop-and-go traffic, whereas in the latter case we can relax and allocate much of our attention to non-driving tasks such as listening to music.

Distraction versus inattention, internal distraction, and mind-wondering

In the absence of distractions within the car or outside of it, we often occupy our mind with what we may term "internal distraction" or "mind wondering" as when we are occupied with non-driving issues such as thoughts about school, job, home, or relationships. The two types of distractions are often labeled "inattention" and "distraction," where distraction may be considered a subset of inattention, or conceptually different from it (Regan, Hallett, and Gordon, 2011). In the EU SafetyNet crash data base, for the purpose of assigning crash causes distraction is assigned whenever "the performance of a task is suspended because the person's attention was caught by something else or the attention has shifted," and inattention is cited whenever the driver is suffering from "low vigilance due to loss of focus" (Talbot, Fagerlind, and Morris, 2013). The problem with this distinction is that it lumps fatigue and inattention into the same category. Therefore, for our purposes we will define distraction as the direction of attention to an object, event, or task away from the driving task. Inattention is then relegated to mind-wandering and direction of attention to internal (to the driver) distractions.

Martens and Brouwer (2013) demonstrated that inattention as an internal distraction can be just as harmful to driving performance as external distractions. In their study, they asked participants to recall a crime event and try to think of the motive of the crime while driving in a simulator. When they compared the driving performance of these drivers to that of participants occupied with a listening and remembering task, they found that performance of both groups of drivers was impaired relative to drivers in the control group that were not distracted at all. Savage, Potter, and Tatler (2013) also demonstrated poorer hazard detection when participants were preoccupied with solving a riddle than when not. Another interesting demonstration of the effects of inattention (or non-specific distraction, or mind-wandering) was provided by Yanko and Spalek (2014), who showed that in a simulated drive drivers' brake reaction times were longer, their speeds were higher, and their headways were shorter when they acknowledged that their minds were wandering than when their minds were focused on the driving task. Thus, these experimental studies provide support to Treat *et al.*'s (1979) pooling of inattention, internal distraction, and external distraction into a common category of delayed recognition (of safety-critical events) (see Chapter 18 on crash causation).

Consequently, we can conclude that distraction is not necessarily the fault of an external (or internal) stimulus that attracts our attention. It is just as likely to be the end result of our own needs to seek stimulation when the driving task is not very demanding. We are active information gatherers and not just recipients of information that happens to impinge on our senses. Thus, we can initiate turning the radio on, call a friend on a cell phone, visually search the environment in areas that have no relevant information for driving, eat or drink while we drive, or even glance at a newspaper. The list is endless but the consequence is the same: the driving task receives only a part of our attentional resources.

One way to reduce the effort involved in driving (or in any task) is to estimate the amount of attention that is required and then allocate to the driving a portion of our capacity that is somewhere between the minimum required and the maximum we have. According to Navon and Gopher (1979), in order to minimize our effort the typical strategy we assume is to pick a level above the minimum required but as close to it as we can judge sufficient. The problem we encounter in driving is our inability to anticipate many of the rapid changes in the amount required – as when a driver ahead of us suddenly and unexpectedly brakes. This was demonstrated in a carefully controlled study in a driving simulator by Marciano and Yeshurun (2015), in which they manipulated the amount of perceptual load from the roadway and from its adjacent areas. The load from the roadway was governed by the density of the traffic and the load from the adjacent roadside areas was controlled by the numbers of pedestrians, parked cars, and buildings. The effects of the two types of information/distraction sources was tested by observing the driver's reaction to the sudden braking of a lead car and the sudden entry of a car or a pedestrian from a side road or the curb, respectively. They found that the perceptual load from the road itself affected mostly the driving speed, being approximately 40 percent higher when the load was low. In contrast, the perceptual load from the roadside affected mostly collisions and reaction times (RT) to the critical events. The proportions of collisions were higher and RT were longer for peripheral events when the level of peripheral load was high than when it was low. Thus, drivers distribute their attention in accordance with the driving demands, but are then surprised by unexpected events that originate in the less attended regions of the visual field.

Scope of the problem

Because of different definitions and different research methods, the proportion of crashes due to distraction is hard to pinpoint. Using the Fatal Analysis Reporting System (FARS) that is a census of all fatal crashes in the U.S., the official statistic is that in 2014 distracted driving was involved in 10 percent of all fatalities (NHTSA, 2015a). In contrast, an analysis of the EU SafetyNet data base of 1,005 fatal crashes from six European countries (Finland, Germany, Italy, Netherlands, Sweden, and the United Kingdom), assigned inattention and distraction as the crash cause in 32 percent of the crashes (21 percent distraction and 14 percent inattention; Talbot *et al.*, 2013). In general, different studies cite significantly higher rates when all – not just fatal – crashes are included; from a "low" of 20 percent of all crashes (Hendricks, Fell, and Freedman, 2001), through 39-51 percent (Treat *et al.* 1979 – for the different phases of the Indiana University study when "improper lookout," "inattention," and "internal distractions" at the "probable" level are combined), to a high of 80 percent (Klauer *et al.*, 2006 – when drowsiness is included) of all crashes. The recent attention of the media to driver distraction – mostly from cell phones and their associated applications – and the dramatic accident stories related to cell phone use are probably also responsible for claims that "31 percent of the drivers consider using the cell phone while driving as "the most aggravating" aspect of other drivers' behavior" (Mason-Dixon, 2005). In the first complex and large-scale study of naturalistic driving behavior, the motor and visual behaviors of drivers in 100 instrumented cars were tracked and recorded by various systems for a period of 12 to 13 months, yielding 43,000 hours of data collected over approximately 2 million vehicle miles (Neale *et al.*, 2005). During this time, the drivers were involved in 69 crashes (mostly very minor) in which their visual scanning behavior was available. An examination of the visual glances immediately before the crashes indicated that visual inattention *and* fatigue were involved in nearly 80 percent of the crashes. Furthermore, of the various specific sources of distraction that were observed, "wireless devices" (primarily cell phones) were the most common – though they still constituted only a third of all the distracting events.

Distraction may also be a factor in the severity of crashes. Bunn *et al.* (2005) assessed the association between various human factors and crash severity in commercial trucks. In their study, they compared the frequencies in which different causes were attributed to crashes in which the commercial vehicle driver died versus the relative frequencies of causes involved in crashes in which the driver was non-fatally injured. After adjustment for driver age and use of seat belts, they found that drivers who were "distracted/inattentive" were 3.2 times as likely to die in a fatal crash as drivers that were only injured. Though this finding is interesting it should not be accepted at face value. This is because (1) it is theoretically difficult to understand why inattention-related crashes would be more severe, unless they involved other factors like high-speed highway driving in which case inattention is just a confound factor, and (2) the causal assessment of "distracted/inattentive" was made by "the investigating officer" and it is likely that in the case of fatal crashes, in the absence of brake marks or another conspicuous crash cause, the assessment of distraction or inattention is made by a default (the same criticism applies to the obtained over-involvement in fatal crashes attributed to fatigue/fell asleep, though here – at least for commercial drivers – the driver's log book can be used to corroborate hours of driving).

Defining Inattention and Distraction

Part of the difficulty of assessing the risks of distraction is that different researchers use different definitions for the term. If inattention is synonymous with distraction then it may account for over fifty percent of all crashes (Treat *et al.*, 1979). But if distraction is limited to external identifiable sources that attract our attention away from the driving task then the problem is smaller; and it is still smaller if it is limited to attention to in-vehicle devices such as a radio, a cell phone, or a navigation system. Pettitt, Burnett, and Stevens (2005) reviewed the many ways that distraction has been defined in the literature and suggested that distraction occurs when: (1) a driver is delayed in the recognition of information necessary to safely maintain the lateral and longitudinal control of the vehicle, (2) due to some event, activity, object or person, within or outside the vehicle, that (3) compels or tends to induce the driver's shifting attention away from fundamental driving tasks, by (4) compromising the driver's auditory, biomechanical, cognitive or visual faculties, or combinations thereof. A much more concise definition that essentially covers all four components, is the one proposed by the International Standards Organization: distraction is "attention given to a non-driving-related activity, typically to the detriment of driving performance" (ISO, 2004). A similar definition has been proposed by a US-EU Bi-lateral ITS Task Force (2010) of six leading researchers. According to them "Driver distraction is the diversion of attention from activities critical for safe driving to a competing activity." This definition is also the one adopted by the World Health Organization (WHO, 2011). Note that according to all three definitions the source of distraction is not specified and it could be external (to an object in or out of the car) or internal (to mind-wandering and thoughts unrelated to driving). It would be useful to keep this definition in mind when evaluating some of the research below, especially the findings from naturalistic driving studies (NDS) that often only consider distraction when the eyes are directed away from the road.

Sources and Types of Distraction

Although smart cell phones seem to get most of the press coverage as a dangerous source of distraction and a potential cause of accidents, they are definitely not the only source and possibly not the most common source of distraction (Stutts *et al.*, 2003, 2005). Still, in the Mason-Dixon survey (2005) mentioned above, 37 percent of American drivers considered distracted drivers the greatest threat to safety on the road (on par with aggressive drivers, and much more than fatigued or alcohol-impaired drivers). Yet in the same survey, 74 percent of the drivers admitted to engaging in one form or another of distracting behavior at least once in the past six months.

In their seminal study of crash causation, Treat *et al.* (1979) distinguished among three types of distractions, all leading to delayed recognition of an impending crash: (1) internal distractions, which are caused by directing attention to objects or events in the car (such as children, radio); (2) external distractions, which are due to being distracted by objects or events outside the vehicle (such as billboards, street signs, pedestrians); and

(3) inattention, which was a situation where the source of the distraction was internal to the driver (such as daydreaming or preoccupation with non-driving thoughts), so that even if the driver's gaze was directed at the road, the attention was internally directed. In current jargon, we call this last form cognitive distraction. On occasion inattention due to cognitive distraction can actually be observed. For example, in some two-vehicle intersection collisions studied by Treat *et al.* (1979) one of the drivers testified that he or she saw the other driver looking directly at them, while the other driver claimed that he or she did not see the other car at all until they collided. In this chapter, the discussion will be limited to the first two types of distractions; that is, distraction due to an identifiable source either outside or inside the vehicle. These sources of distraction can cause visual, manual, or cognitive distractions, or any combination of these types of distraction, as discussed below. Some aspects of inattention that are not due to distraction are discussed in Chapters 5 and 18.

Different study methods yield different findings

The relative frequencies of different sources of distraction in driving have been investigated using three different methods: direct observations, driver surveys, and post-crash analyses and interviews. Each of the different techniques has unique advantages and disadvantages. The driver surveys enable collecting subjective information from a large and nationally representative sample of drivers. On the other hand, the observational technique yields behavioral data that are much more objective and easy to analyze and interpret than the data from subjective responses. Immediate post-crash interviews can yield much more detailed data tied to objective events than phone surveys, and can provide insights to causes of distraction that objective video recordings cannot. In addition to these differences, it is important to remember that empirical studies are always conducted within a certain culture and time. This is important because the rapid dissemination of potentially distracting in-vehicle information systems makes comparisons between studies conducted in different years and on different continents difficult to interpret. Thus, the different techniques differ significantly in their data (objective observations versus subjective responses), their representativeness of the driving population (a convenience sample versus a representative sample), the size of the sample (e.g., under 100 drivers versus over 500 drivers), and the year and location of data collection. These are all significant differences that can account for differences in the types of distracting activities noted, their frequencies, and the estimated amount of time they consume.

The advent of naturalistic driving studies in which the driver's view of the road and his or her visual and manual behavior are continuously monitored also enables us to distinguish among the three essential aspects of workload – and consequently the three different loci of distraction in the driver's information processing and handling sequence (see Chapter 3): visual (where the driver glances away from the road ahead), motor (where the driver is occupied with non-driving motor tasks such as dialing a number or entering text), and cognitive (where the mind is occupied with a non-driving task such as talking and/or listening to a passenger or a caller) (Fitch *et al.*, 2013). Thus, as the song "Seven Little Girls" (above) implies, all three are important and relevant to safe driving.

A brief summary of some of the findings of three methodologically different studies of distracted driving conducted in the U.S., and one study of crash-involved drivers conducted in Australia, is provided below to highlight both the similarities and differences in the findings.

Direct observations

Using the observation approach, Stutts and her associates (2003, 2005) used a convenience sample of drivers from North Carolina and Philadelphia, who agreed to have video cameras installed in their vehicles and record events inside and outside their own vehicles. The cameras were attached to the windshield just below the inside rear-view mirror and they recorded the road, the driver's face, and the vehicle interior in the cars of 70 drivers. Ten hours of driving were recorded in each car. The final data set consisted of a representative sample of 207 hours of video data (3 hours from almost all drivers). While the data that was recorded was objective, coding the data was a subjective process, and the two data coders involved in the process repeatedly consulted with each other to minimize inter-observer variability.

The principal results of the study are reproduced in Table 13-1, which lists the main categories of distracting activities, the percent of drivers engaged in these activities (for any duration during the three hours of coded video data), the percent of time the drivers engaged in these activities while the vehicle was moving, and the "adjusted percent of time in a distracting activity while the vehicle was moving," which consisted of the ratio of the first two variables. This ratio reflects the percent of time drivers are engaged in an activity, *given* that they do it at all. Thus, the percent of time spent smoking while moving was only 1.5, because only 7 percent of the drivers smoked at all. On the other hand, the ones who did engage in it did it 21 percent of the time that they were actually moving. In contrast, conversing with a passenger occupied nearly as much total time (19.9 percent) by those engaged in it, but that was because 11 times as many drivers were seen conversing with a passenger as were seen smoking (77 percent). Thus, the total time of distraction due to conversing with a passenger was 15 percent (compared to 1.5 percent for smoking). Note that of all the sources of distraction coded, the duration of distraction from using the cell phone was relatively low (total of 1.3 percent of the time). The researchers also noted that this percent was quite similar to that observed when the vehicle was not moving (1.4 percent), indicating that the drivers did not distinguish between the risk levels involved in using the cell phone in the two situations. In this context it is important to note that the data were collected in 2000-2001. This estimate would probably be much higher in today's culture and ubiquitous use of cell phones. Since the time of this study the number of cell phone subscriptions in the U.S. more than tripled, so that by the beginning of 2014 ninety percent of American adults had at least one cell phone (Pew Research, 2014). In contrast, the number of people smoking probably declined a little, and the number of passengers in cars probably remained unchanged.

Perhaps the most important conclusion from the data in Table 13-1 is that not a single driver allocated all of his or her attention to the driving task all the time. Everyone engaged in some form of distraction some of the time. The most common

Table 13-1. Percent of time drivers engaged in different distracting activities, percent of drivers engaging in these activities, and the adjusted percent of time for each activity (percent of time only for those engaging in the activity) (from Stutts *et al.*, 2003, with permission from the AAA Foundation for Traffic Safety).

Potential Distraction	**% of Total Time While Vehicle Moving**[a]	**% of Drivers Engaging in Activity**	**Adjusted % of Total Time While Vehicle Moving**[b]
Using cell phone (includes talking, dialing, answering)	1.30	34.3	3.8
Eating, drinking, spilling	1.45	71.4	2.0
Preparing to eat or drink	3.16	58.6	5.4
Manipulating audio controls	1.35	91.4	1.5
Smoking (includes lighting and extinguishing)	1.55	7.1	21.1
Reading or writing	0.67	40.0	1.8
Grooming	0.28	45.7	0.6
Other occupants:			
Baby distraction	0.38	8.6	4.4
Child distraction	0.29	12.9	2.2
Adult distraction	0.27	22.9	1.2
Conversing	15.32	77.1	19.9
Internal distraction[c]	3.78	100.0	3.8
External distraction	1.62	85.7	1.9
TOTAL:			
Without conversing	16.10	–	49.7
With conversing	31.42		69.6

[a]Based on total sample of 70 drivers.

[b]Adjusted to reflect the percentage of drivers engaging in that activity; that is, (% of total time while vehicle moving)/(proportion of drivers engaging in that activity). Also represents percentage of total time assuming *all* drivers engaged in the activity.

[c]All categories except for falling object and insect, etc. in vehicle, which were recorded as events without an associated duration.

activities – engaged in by three quarters of the drivers or more are eating and drinking-related activities, manipulating audio controls, conversing with a passenger, and being distracted by something within the vehicle. However, the durations of these activities vary greatly, and consequently the total time that a driver is distracted is very much activity-related.

Surveys

While the observational method provides concrete objective data, it does not provide much by way of explanation. Interviews and driver questionnaires can probe deeper to understand the relationships between attitudes (that are not observable) and behaviors (that are). To obtain that information the U.S. National Highway Traffic Safety Administration (NHTSA) surveyed in 2002 a representative sample of 4,010 drivers (Royal, 2003) and, 10 years later, in 2012 a representative sample of 6,016 drivers (Schroeder, Meyers, and Kostyniuk, 2013). In these surveys, the drivers were asked to check the frequencies in which they were engaged in various pre-selected distracting activities. In the 2002 survey, the drivers were also asked whether or not they think each of these behaviors endanger driving. The main results of both surveys are reproduced in Table 13-2. Perhaps the most striking patterns in these results are that (1) nearly all of us engage in various distracting activities while we drive, and (2) the frequencies of engagement in different distracting activities changed over the decade. From Royal's survey, we can also conclude that (1) we are sensitive to the impairing effects that these activities have on driving safety, and (2) the more common an activity is (in driving) the less likely it is to be considered dangerous. This last relationship is indeed very strong: the correlation between the percent engaging in each activity and the percent who think that it makes driving "much more dangerous" was $r = -0.77$ (as one increases the other decreases) and if the last behavior "telematics" is taken out of the calculation the correlation increases to $r = -0.91$ ("telematics" is problematic because many people are unfamiliar with its features or implications). While it is hard to determine a cause-and-effect relationship here, it seems that as a behavior becomes more common it becomes more acceptable; and as it becomes more acceptable people tend to consider it less dangerous simply because "we all do it." In support of this argument is the study's finding that those who engaged in specific distracting activities were less likely to think that these activities are dangerous. Still, this association may be either a result of responsible decision making or the defensive property of rationalization.

Comparisons between the studies by Stutts and her colleagues and by Royal are difficult to make even though they were conducted at about the same time. To begin with, Stutts *et al.* had a relatively small, non-representative sample. More importantly it is impossible to compare the observed use rate with the reported rate. The one similarity between the two studies is in the ranking of the distracting behaviors in terms of their prevalence. On the other hand, comparisons between the two NHTSA surveys are easy and they reflect the cultural and technological shift in the sources of distraction over the decade. Some activities remained equally practiced, like talking to a passenger, eating/drinking, and changing radio stations. Other habits – all cell phone and communications related – have changed dramatically. Making or accepting phone calls increased from about 25 percent to 40 percent, while the use of email and text messaging, that were not even

Table 13-2. The percent of drivers engaging in different distracting activities *more than rarely or never* and the percent of drivers who think that these activities make driving "much more dangerous" (from Royal, 2003, and Schroeder *et al.*, 2013).

Activity	**Royal (2003)**		**Schroeder *et al.* (2013)**
	% Engaged	**% Saying it makes driving much more dangerous**	**% Engaged**
Talking with other passengers	81	4	80
Eat or drink	49	17	47
Changing radio stations or looking for CDs or tapes	66	18	68[a]
Making outgoing calls on a cell phone	25	48	40[b]
Taking incoming calls on a cell phone	26	44	40[b]
Dealing with children riding in the rear seat	24	40	36
Reading a map or directions while driving	12	55	
Personal grooming	8	61	9
Reading printed material	4	80	1
Responding to a beeper or pager[a]	3	43	
Using wireless remote Internet access	2	63	
Using telematics (navigation and crash avoidance)	2	23	
Read e-mails or text messages			14
Send text messages or e-mails			10
Change CDs, DVDs, or tapes			25

[a]Adjust car radio.
[b]Make or accept phone calls.

included in the first survey, were now engaged by 10 percent or more of the drivers. Finally, the change in technology has caused some sources to simply disappear; for example, reading maps and responding to a beeper/pager.

In a survey of a representative sample of American Drivers conducted over 10 years ago by Mason-Dixon (2005) 1,100 drivers were interviewed by phone and asked to indicate whether or not they had participated in a list of activities "in the past six months." As in the NHTSA surveys (Royal, 2003; Schroeder *et al.*, 2013), the sources of distraction were defined in advance and therefore some potentially distracting activities that drivers may have engaged in did not appear in the data. This means that the components of distracted driving are quite different in the different studies. For example, the Mason-Dixon survey did not include conversing with a passenger and smoking – two highly time-consuming behaviors for the drivers who engage in them. The distracting activities queried in the survey included eating (52 percent of the respondents acknowledged doing it at least once in the past 6 months), using a cell phone (43 percent), reading (17 percent), had a "romantic moment" (10 percent), groomed themselves (8 percent), adjusted a DVD player (6 percent), consulted a navigation system (5 percent), used a PDA (3 percent), and even watched a video (2 percent)! As one might suspect, young drivers were much more involved in some of the distracting behaviors than older drivers. For example, 73 percent of the young drivers stated they ate at least once while driving in the past 6 months, 65 percent said they talked on the cell phone, and 25 percent read emails. Because of differences in study methods, framing of the questions, and the year of data collection it is impossible to use the frequencies noted in the different studies in order to quantitatively determine the trend. Still, it is interesting to note that the percent of drivers who stated that they used the phone in this survey is approximately twice as high as in the direct observations conducted in 2001. However, all of the interview-based surveys suffer from the flawed memory of the respondents, whereas the observations are based on actual recorded use, but – in the case of the Stutts *et al.* survey – only over a three hour period of driving. Therefore, it is best to consider the data from each study on its own.

Post-crash interview

The post-crash interview technique was used by McEvoy, Stevenson, and Woodward (2007) on a sample of 1,367 crash-injured drivers who were admitted to a hospital in Perth, Australia, between mid-2002 and mid-2004. In their interviews, 32 percent of the drivers reported being distracted just prior to the crash, and in 14 percent of the crashes a distraction was a considered (by the drivers) to be a contributing cause. The primary sources of distraction were conversations with other passengers (11 percent), lack of concentration (11 percent), and external distractions (9 percent). Thus, the principal source of crash-causing distraction in this study – conversing with a passenger – was also the most prevalent type of distraction in driving in general (according to Stutts *et al.*'s, 2003, video recordings and the two NHTSA surveys; Royal, 2003; Schroeder *et al.*, 2013), but one not considered at all in the Mason-Dixon survey. Given the common occurrence of conversations with passengers, it is likely that this event is not over-involved in crashes. It is also very likely that drivers are likely to attribute the crash cause to conversing with passengers – whether in fact it is or it is not – because when they can, people tend to attribute negative events to others rather accept responsibility (as formulated by Attribution Theory – e.g., Ho *et al.*, 2000).

In summary, the different studies, despite their many significant methodological differences, times, and locations demonstrate that distraction is very much a part of our driving behavior. In part, it is something that we succumb to (when the distracting event is externally driven such as a phone ring or a conspicuous event off the road), and in part, it is something that we seek (such as conversing with a passenger, talking on the phone, or adjusting the audio controls). This makes the driving task only a part of the driver information processing activity, and one that may be compromised, to the point of losing control, when the attentional resources allocated to the driving task are insufficient relative to the task demands.

We typically observe the distraction effect on the driver's overt behavior. And while this approach is practical – as driver behavior is what we desire to understand, predict, and affect – these studies do not tell us how distraction affects our cognitive processes. An interesting attempt to study this directly was made by Young, Salmon, and Cornelissen (2013) who had drivers drive in an urban section of Melbourne, Australia, and continuously report what they saw and did. Distraction was manipulated experimentally with a peripheral light detection task. Analyses of the verbal protocols showed that in general drivers uttered slightly fewer words when distracted than when not. This was not surprising. However, there was also a difference in *what* the drivers reported under the two conditions. When not distracted, information elements associated with scanning the environment and observing other road users were more prominent; for example, words like "checking" "looking," "cars," "behind," "front," "ahead," and "coming" as they related to the surrounding roadway and traffic. In contrast, when the drivers were distracted, they reported more concepts related to vehicle control tasks, such as "speed," "lane," "light," and "slowing." Thus, the visual distraction task reduced the visual elements that the drivers observed (or at least reported). This is highly significant considering the critical role that hazard detection has in safe driving.

The remainder of this chapter will consider the knowledge we have gained about the extent of distraction in driving from various potential sources, the driving impairments that different distracting activities pose, and the crash risk due to these distractions.

Distraction Effects of Various Sources

Given the prevalence of distractions in driving, and given the irrefutable evidence for their negative effects on driving and driving-related functions, it would be reasonable to assume that distraction would feature as one of the principal factors in crashes. The Indiana University study of crash causation (Treat *et al.*, 1979) indeed found that overall improper allocation of attention accounted for nearly 50 percent of all crashes, while distraction from attending to an event or object inside the vehicle (labeled internal distraction) accounted for 9 percent of all crashes (at a subjective level of confidence of

80 percent); and this is long before the days of cell phones, internet, and navigation devices! (see Chapter 18).

Are all sources of distraction – visual and non-visual – equally distracting? Are they all equally dangerous? There is a significant body of theory and new empirical research on the effects of various sources of distraction on driving safety. The overwhelming conclusion of that research is that non-driving tasks can and do pose significant threats to safety and are implicated in crashes, especially when they include visual distraction. However, as suggested above and will become apparent below, it is almost impossible to avoid all distractions. Therefore, the critical task is to evaluate the different risks associated with different types and sources of distraction. In evaluating the potential distraction from various sources, it is beneficial to consider Wickens' (1984, 2008) multiple resource model of attention (see Chapter 3), as it provides good predictions concerning the expected interference of various tasks depending on their input and output modalities and locus of processing demands. In brief, the greater the competition for the same resources, the greater the expected interference between them, and the greater the impact on performance. For example, as most of driving is based on visual inputs, one should expect reading or sending text messages that also require visual attention to be more detrimental to driving than talking on the phone that involves primarily cognitive resources.

Unfortunately, there is no single metric that is accepted by all researchers to evaluate distractions, though Strayer and his associates (2015b) have made an ambitious initial effort in scaling cognitive distraction. Therefore, it is often impossible to evaluate the relative risks of different sources of distraction examined in different studies. We have a plethora of study methods – from basic laboratory tasks and rudimentary simulators, through moving-base simulators and instrumented vehicles on closed and open road, to observational naturalistic driving studies and crash analyses. Obviously, different methods also lend themselves to different measures of the effects of distraction including reaction time to unexpected events, steering and speed control, performance on secondary tasks, glance behavior, and crash rates.

There has been one notable attempt to develop an industry standard that could serve as both a measure of distraction and a criterion for distinguishing between safe and unsafe distracting activities. The measure proposed by the American Society of Automotive Engineers (Green, 1999; SAE, 2000) is based on the time it takes a person to perform the distracting task as a sole task (without driving). This measure produced the "15-second rule" that implies that if an activity requires more than 15 seconds to complete in the absence of any competing activities (including driving) then it is not safe to perform that activity while driving. The concept was developed by Green (1999) as a means of evaluating various navigation systems before they are implemented in actual vehicles. Though 15 seconds may seem like a long time to attend to the non-driving scene, note that it includes not just visual attention but manual and cognitive attention as well.

Despite its intuitive appeal as a simple tool for dealing with the complex distraction problem, the validity of the approach is questionable. In a study conducted on the road with experienced drivers used to operate the phone and a navigation system while driving, Christoph, Van Nes, and Knapper (2013) found that after excluding phone conversations per se, 48 percent of the interactions with the phone and 40 percent of the interactions with the navigation system took longer than 15 seconds. Of course, these findings are specific to the designs of the phone and navigation systems installed in their study. Another study that evaluated the 15-second rule obtained very low correlations between the time taken to complete various distracting tasks while standing and while driving. The tasks included entering the destination on different navigation systems, tuning the radio, dialing familiar and unfamiliar phone numbers on a mobile phone, and adjusting the heating, fan, and air-conditioning controls. In fact, some tasks, surprisingly, took longer to complete in isolation than while driving (Tijerina *et al.*, 2000). As an alternative, Salvucci *et al.* (2005) developed a computer-based "expert system" that evaluates the distraction potential of proposed in-vehicle systems by incorporating a quantitative cognitive model of the different processing mechanisms and time involved in attention, perception, decision times, and response selection and execution. This theory-based attempt is interesting but may not be valid given the emerging questionable role of cognitive distraction in crash involvement (e.g., Fitch *et al.*, 2013; Shinar, 2015). Nonetheless, with proper frequency distributions of these functions under various driving situations and task demands, this approach may provide a useful evaluation tool.

The remainder of this section is devoted to evaluating the distraction from some of the sources listed above. Though documented in simulator studies where even singing can affect some driving-related measures (Hughes, Rudin-Brown, and Young, 2013), the effects of such activities will not be discussed here. Cell phones have been the most talked-about and studied source of distraction in the past decade and they therefore merit a separate and more detailed discussion.

For all types of distractions, the effects on driving performance and crash risk are very much dependent on their timing in relation to the rapidly changing dynamics of the immediate driving situation and the resulting demands placed on the driver. In a naturalistic driving task, it is impossible to control the driving demands, the changes in attention allocation, and the timing of a distracting event. Therefore, most of the research has been conducted in experimental settings. This enables the researcher to better understand the relative impairments caused by different distracting activities, at the cost of compromising ecological validity. However, as will be seen below, the crash risk associated with various laboratory-proven distractions is not always consistent with the expectations from these studies and with the crash risk obtained from NDS. The differences in the findings highlight the differences between simulation studies and NDS as described in Chapter 2 on research methods.

One note of caution. All the research and discussion of distraction assumes simultaneous demands of a driving and a non-driving task. However, there is a well-known phenomenon, known as the psychological refractory period, according to which stimulus processing persists beyond its initial presentation and physical duration. Thus, a stimulus that is presented and ends immediately before another one – typically by less than one second – can still be distracting. In a somewhat crude attempt to verify this effect with an in-vehicle driver distraction task, Hibberd, Jamson, and Carsten (2010), showed that a reactions to the braking of a lead car are slowed by simple in-vehicle reaction time tasks that precede the braking of the lead car by as much as approximately half a second. Although this was demonstrated with a very basic simulator (where the headway and speeds of the two cars were kept constant, and the response to the lead car's braking was artificial) the consistency of the effect with different distracting stimuli and different responses is indicative of the strength of this phenomenon and the realization that it should be taken into account. A related effect has been documented by Borowsky *et al.* (2015), where drivers in a simulator were distracted by an in-vehicle visual task that followed immediately after a cue to the location of a road hazard. When such a distraction existed the drivers needed more time to fixate on the on-road hazards and consequently missed more of them.

Music

Listening to music is possibly the most common activity we engage in while driving. In fact, we listen to music in our cars (when driving unaccompanied) more than anywhere else; and twice as much as when we are home (Sloboda, ONeill, and Ivaldi, 2001). As the quote at the top of this chapter suggests, its introduction into the vehicle was accompanied by some concerns. Some justification for that concern comes from drivers' own reports that listening to music while driving influences their rhythm of driving and concentration as well as "charging their perceptions of relaxation and stimulation" (Brodsky, 2002, citing Oblad, 2000). But music can be both a source of stimulation in an otherwise monotonous and fatigue-inducing drive, and a source of distraction and a potential crash risk factor. Factors that enhance the attention capturing aspects of music, such as high volume and complexity, are probably the ones that are most distracting (Brodsky, 2002). Although there is no direct evidence that loud music affects driving performance, it does seem to increase drivers' mental load even in non-demanding driving situations; and in the case of monotonous driving it can to some extent help in sustained attention (Ünal, Steg, and Epstude, 2012).

One particular aspect of music that was investigated in detail at least in one study is music tempo. For this study, Brodsky (2002) recruited Israeli drivers who stated that they listened to music all or most of the times they drove. He then had them drive in a rudimentary PC-based simulator in an environment consisting of urban streets and motorways, as they would in their normal driving. The drivers performed the drive under four different conditions: without any music or with instrumental music that was either slow (with a tempo of 56-65 beats per minutes), medium (94-112 BPM), or fast (132 BPM). The results were quite dramatic and internally consistent. Music affected all measures of driving safety. In general, the faster the music tempo the worse was the driving; with more lane departures, more red light violations, and more accidents. The data are summarized in Table 13-3, where it can also be seen that drivers tended to increase their speed in accordance with the increase in tempo, and that they were aware of it. Furthermore, this increase in tempo and driving speed correlated with the increase in mental load as reflected by the lower heart rate variability.

Table 13-3. The effects of music tempo on driving safety (average speed, perceived speed, accidents, lane departures, and red light running per trial) and mental load (heart rate variability) (reprinted from Brodsky, 2002, with permission from Elsevier).

	Actual Speed	**Perceived Speed**	**Crashes**	**Lane Departures**	**Red Light Crossings**	**Heart Rate Variability**
No music	145	92	.07	2.43	.61	3.4
Slow tempo	141	94	.14	3.36	.72	2.9
Med. tempo	143	95	.14	4.68	.79	2.7
Fast tempo	147	102	.36	6.50	1.21	2.9

In a follow-up study, Brodsky and Slor (2013) evaluated the effect of instrumental musical selections that were "structurally designed to generate moderate levels of perceptual complexity" relative to driving without any music, and relative to driving with the drivers' preferred music (mostly dance, trans, techno, middle-Eastern, and rock; which they brought with them to the study). The 85 Israeli participants were all young novice drivers licensed for less than a year. The experimental task was to drive an instrumented vehicle for approximately 45 minutes on a 40 kilometers route consisting of urban, interurban, and high-speed roads. Using instrumented dual-control cars, a certified driving instructor sat next to the driver and evaluated the driver on various safety-related skills. A smart in-vehicle data recorder provided an automated rating of the level of aggressiveness of each driver (based on sudden accelerations and decelerations and rapid swerving). Each participant drove and was evaluated under the three music conditions. The results showed that while the drivers' preferred music had a positive effect on the drivers' mood, it also resulted in poorer evaluations of the driving by both the driving instructors and the automated system than driving without music. In contrast, the specially designed music either did not impair driving or for some measures, such as searching the scene ahead, adjusting speed, and maintaining safe headways, it even made it better than in the control condition.

In summary, the nature of the music may be a major determinant of whether it is distracting or not. Compared to the cognitive demands of a phone conversation, it seems to have minimal effects on driving performance, even when the volume is fairly high at 78 dBA (Bellinger *et al.*, 2009). Furthermore, even when it is distracting music may have a silver lining. Wiesenthal, Hennessy, and Totten (2003) found that drivers (when they were not in a hurry or under time stress) were less likely to express mild aggressive driving behaviors when they listened to music on their way to and from school or work than when they were not allowed to turn their radio on.

Roadside signs and billboards

Roadside commercial billboards are *designed* to attract attention, and as such they should constitute a source of distraction. Rockwell's early studies of drivers' eye movements and glance behavior indeed showed that a significant number of fixations and a significant portion of our looking behavior are directed toward objects off the road. In his research, Rockwell found that in real driving only 60 percent of the drivers' fixations were directed toward the road, the traffic, and the highway signs, while 20-27 percent of the looks were directed at objects off the road, including billboards (Mourant, Rockwell, and Rackoff, 1969). Later studies, by Hughes and Cole (1984) and by Smiley and her associates (Beijer, Smiley, and Eizenman, 2004; Smiley, Smahel, and Eizenman, 2004), documented specifically drivers' glances at roadside commercial signs – including electronic (digital dynamic) billboards – and showed that despite the glances toward the signs, driving performance did not seem to be significantly affected. Luoma (1988) had his drivers drive a route of 50 kilometers in Finland, while recording their visual fixation patterns. He found that drivers' fixations on roadside advertisements were much longer than their fixations on pedestrian road markings and speed limit signs. This suggests that the drivers needed (and spent) much more time to process the information in the advertisements.

The cost associated with the diversion of attention from the road is unclear. For example, in a controlled simulator study in England, Young *et al.* (2009) found that roadside advertisements resulted in an increase in lane excursions, though without a significant increase in visual fixations away from the road. In the U.S., several states evaluated the safety before and after the installation of electronic information displays and failed to find a significant change in any of the safety measures (Farbry *et al.*, 2001).

To understand this apparent paradox, we conducted an on-road study (Shinar, Peleg, and Segev, 2003) in which 16 experienced drivers drove an instrumented car on an urban route that included a huge billboard – with a picture of an attractive topless male model – that covered the whole side of a nine-story building. The route included driving toward the billboard so that it was quite visible and conspicuous, and driving on the same road from the other direction, from which the billboard was not visible. A miniature camera installed immediately below the inside mirror – of which the drivers were not aware – recorded the drivers' looking behavior. The drivers looking behavior is summarized in Table 13-4. Note that the time drivers spent looking at the road and the traffic was essentially unaffected by the presence or absence of the sign in their field of view. But when driving toward the sign, the drivers looked in its direction (to the right of the road) 23 percent of the time, while when driving from the other direction they looked to the right of the road only 10 percent of the time. It seems that what the sign did to the drivers' attention was attract their *spare* capacity away from other less conspicuous and less attractive objects that were not related to the driving task and were *off* the road. Thus, drivers were able to allocate a significant amount of their attention to the sign but they did not do that at the expense of the attention that they allocated to monitoring the road and the traffic.

Table 13-4. Percent of time drivers spent looking at the road ahead and to the right and left of the road, in the presence and absence of giant billboard on right (from Shinar *et al.*, 2003).

Direction of Travel	**% Looks to the Right**	**% Looks at the Road**	**% Looks to the Left**
Facing the billboard on right[a]	23	68	10
Not facing the billboard	10	71	19
AVERAGE[a]	16.5	69.5	14.5

[a]Numbers in this row do not sum up to 100% because of rounding.

Smiley *et al.*'s (2004) Canadian studies focused specifically on the effects of video signs. These are more likely to attract drivers' attention because (1) our eyes are instinctively attracted to change, (2) their contrast relative to their background (especially at night) is much greater than that of reflective signs, and (3) these signs are inherently more interesting because their content changes continuously. Still, Smiley found that her drivers spent 69-76 percent of their time looking at the road and traffic; a percentage that is nearly identical to what we observed with the Israeli drivers and the oversized reflective billboard.

In a different context, Birrell and Fowkes (2014) noted that drivers provided with a smartphone application that provided online information on short headways and lane departures spent an average of 4.3 percent of the driving time looking at the device, but these looks did not detract from the time spent looking at the road ahead or the mirrors. With and without the system, approximately 48 percent of the glances were directed at the center of the road. The tradeoff was in glances off the road: 31 percent of the glances without the system versus 22 percent of the glances with it. The time and number of glances looking at the mirrors and in-vehicle equipment remained the same. Thus, this in-vehicle distraction apparently used up only spare visual processing capacity.

There is however one well-designed large-scale study that had demonstrated the crash risk from roadside advertisements. The study was a natural experiment that was conducted on Israel's most congested suburban freeway that cuts across the metropolis of Tel Aviv. The section that was studied is a 26 kilometer divided highway with 4-5 lanes in each direction and 18 interchanges for exiting and entering the road. In a fortuitous sequence of events in response to safety and environmental concerns, a court-order decreed that all the billboards be covered for a year while the risk they pose is being evaluated. At the end of that year, in the absence of new evidence, the signs were once again exposed. This created a situation with three treatment periods: uncovered signs in 2006-2007, covered signs in 2008-July 2009, and uncovered signs in September 2009-2012. In addition, it was possible to identify treatment and control segments: segments where there were billboards (8), and segments without billboards (6), respectively. Analyses that compared the crash rates in both types of segments and in the three study periods showed large and statistically significant effects of the signs on all types of crashes. The initial removal of the signs resulted in 35-45 percent drop in injury crashes (depending on the specific crash measure used), and the reinstatement of the signs was accompanied by an increase of 40-50 percent in injury crashes (Gitelman *et al.*, 2014). In their quest to explain these dramatic changes in crash rates (compared to previous studies with much smaller effects), Gitelman and her colleagues note that unlike many other studies, in this study the road provided a possibly unique combination of high speeds, urban environment, high-volume multi-exit highway, with a high density of potentially distracting signs, and a detailed high-quality data base of all crashes. Thus, in this environment of multiple potential distractors when drivers must make frequent emergency decisions in response to unexpected events (other drivers entering the driver's lane, switching lanes and braking), the added workload imposed by the luring signs was just too much to handle simultaneously with the driving-related workload. Therefore, it is possible that the keyword in explaining the effects of billboards is moderation. When they are few and far apart – as evaluated in previous studies – their distracting effects can be overcome by the drivers. However, when they are many and in high density they can create a serious safety hazard on high-volume roads with multiple driver maneuvers. This kind of reasoning led the Dutch Institute for Road Safety to limit the number of roadway signs in certain locations rather than eliminate them totally (SWOV, 2009).

Taken together the distractibility of roadway signs (including those conveying driving-related information) is probably affected by a host of factors that include traffic characteristics, sign visual and ergonomic characteristics, sign placement, signage density, and driver characteristics. It also appears that because signs are not surprising or unpredictable to the drivers, most of the time the drivers are able to divide their attention between the signs and the driving task sufficiently well. In order to determine the particular characteristics that may compromise safety due to signs distraction better controlled studies have to be done. The one conclusion that can be made now is that the greater the amount of information in the sign the longer the drivers will need to process that information; and the more complex the driving situation the more attention the driver has to devote to it. When the demands from both exceed a certain – currently unknown – threshold, safety is compromised. This is true for both commercial signs (as in Luoma's 1988 study), and for highway guidance signs (McNees and Messer, 1981).

One issue that has only recently been explored is the location of the sign. A primary determinant of a sign's – or any object's – distracting potential is its conspicuity: "the property of an object that causes it to attract attention or to be readily located by search" (Hughes and Cole, 1984). Because drivers tend to concentrate their fixations slightly below the focus of expansion (the optical "end of the road") (Mourant and Rockwell, 1972), one would suppose that a sign is less likely to attract the driver's attention the farther it is from the line of sight directly ahead. The answer of course is a little more complicated, as discovered by Crundall, Van Loon, and Underwood (2006). In their study, they examined the visual fixations of drivers as they viewed video clips of driving segments photographed from a dashboard-mounted camera that faced the direction of travel. Some of the clips contained advertisements placed off the road at street level (such as on the sidings of bus stop shelters) and some contained "raised level advertisements" placed on poles or street lights 3 meters above the roadway. The pattern of the results was quite complex, but the conclusion that emerged from them was simple: street level advertisements that were closer to the drivers' line of sight were more distracting than raised advertisements that were farther from the drivers' line of sight, as measured by the amount of time the drivers gazed at them.

Not all signs are created equal. The advent of new digital technology has prompted a sharp increase in digital signs with changeable messages and dynamic scenes. The distraction potential of such signs and billboards is much greater than that of static signs because of phototropism (the tendency of the eye to be drawn toward objects that are brighter than their surroundings), their motion (or apparent motion), and because their content changes providing the drivers with a new message every few seconds. Their potential for compromising safety is based on such theoretical underpinnings as well as on the results of experimental studies by independent researchers – but not by research sponsored by advertising agencies (surprise, surprise) (see Wachtel, 2009, for an extensive review of the research). For example, digital billboards attract more and longer fixations than static billboards (Dukic *et al.*, 2013), and these longer fixations away from the road have been linked to crash risk. Driven by safety concerns, several countries and jurisdictions within countries (e.g., states and cities in Australia and the U.S.) have developed specific guidelines that restrict the use of this form of advertisement (Wachtel, 2009). Given the difficulty of eradicating these signs, Wachtel (2011) suggests four ways to at least limit their distraction potential: control the lighting at nighttime, lengthen the dwell time of messages, simplify the message by limiting the number and types of words and symbols, and prohibit message sequencing across several still images.

Eating and drinking

Eating and drinking are among the most common non-driving tasks, with 50-70 percent of the drivers doing it (Mason-Dixon, 2005; Royal, 2003; Schroeder *et al.*, 2013; Stutts *et al.*, 2003). Despite its prevalence, it has not received nearly as much attention as the distraction from other in-vehicle activities such as using cell phones and navigation systems. Two studies have addressed this source of distraction. In the first study, Jenness *et al.* (2002) found eating (specifically a cheeseburger) to be as distracting as entering a number in a voice-activated cell phone during a simulated drive. In the second study by Young *et al.* (2008), also in a simulator, drivers were presented with an unexpected pedestrian while eating (specifically opening a sealed snack and a water bottle). Despite the difficult manual task, eating did not affect driving performance, though the drivers felt more overloaded. Thus, as it appears now, eating/drinking is not a high-risk distracting activity. This may be because eating is mostly a manual task and not a visual one and one that is primarily user-paced. Even when the situation is contrived to combine the activity with a critical driving maneuver as was done in Young *et al.*'s study, the greater load experienced by the drivers did not exceed a threshold that impaired driving. To be more definitive, because "eating" actually describes a wide range of behaviors, different eating-related activities should be studied separately to determine if any of them compromise driving safety.

Children and pets

Little researched but often experienced and reported in surveys (e.g., Royal, 2003; Schroeder *et al.*, 2013; Stutts *et al.*, 2003) is the distraction caused by pets and children. At least one survey (albeit, based on an internet convenience sample) suggests that interacting with child passengers is the most frequently reported distracting event that results in crashes (Lansdown, 2012). Their restless behavior and demand for instant attention and gratification has been a source of anguish for many parents. Approximately 24 percent of American adult drivers report that they have to deal with their kids while driving (Beirness, 2005). An acknowledgment of the load that children place on their parents while driving was provided in a survey of over 36,000 Canadian drivers of whom approximately 60 percent stated that interacting with children is "very harmful to driving" (Laberge-Nadeau, 2003. See Table 13-6). Indirect evidence for the added load from children was supplied by Roney *et al.* (2013) in a survey of 539 parents (78 percent females, as might have been expected) recruited from large pediatric care practices in Connecticut. Overall, 92 percent of the drivers reported that they used their cell phones while driving. However, the percent that reported using it when driving their children was significantly lower for all uses: talking on the phone, texting, and surfing the internet.

The most direct evidence of the distractibility from children comes from a very recent study conducted on a Finnish fatal crash data set (Maasalo *et al.*, 2016). The data included the conclusions of multi-disciplinary teams that conducted an in-depth clinical crash analysis of each crash. A total of 1,828 licensed drivers of private passenger cars, of parental age 26-47 years old), that were not speeding, alcohol-impaired, or unbelted, were obtained from fatal crashes that occurred over 15 years (1988-2012). The results were interesting in that they showed a significant effect of child presence for the female drivers but not for the male drivers, as shown in Table 13-5. When no passengers are present at all, the culpability rates of the male and female drivers are nearly identical at about 50 percent. The differences between the genders emerge and are pronounced when there is a child under 18 years old, and especially when the child is very young. With children under 5 years old, women drivers were more than twice as culpable as men drivers (65 percent versus 27 percent). The gap is slightly smaller for older children but still there until they reach maturity at 18; or at least become mature enough not to disrupt their mother while driving. The data in Table 13-5 included all the crashes in which there could also be adult passengers with the children. When Maasalo and his associates looked only at the crashes in which there were only children passengers, the number of cases was much smaller but the gap was essentially the same. Mothers with children 0-4 years old were culpable in 68 percent of the crashes, while fathers with 0-4 years old children were culpable in only 29 percent of the crashes. This statistically significant Gender × Child presence interaction is interesting. Although the authors are careful in their interpretation of the findings, they do believe that the significant gender-child-age

Table 13-5. Number of male and female drivers culpable in fatal crashes, as a function of the presence of children in the car, and the percent culpable within each gender (in parenthesis) (from Maasalo *et al.*, 2016, reprinted by permission of Taylor & Francis LLC, http:// www.tandfonline.com).

Passenger(s) Age	Male Drivers		Female Drivers	
	Culpable (%)	Non-culpable	Culpable (%)	Non-culpable
No passenger	189 (50)	187	110 (54)	93
18 years	103 (44)	131	47 (52)	43
0-17 years	78 (34)	146	76 (61)	48
0-4 years	27 (27)	72	38 (65)	16
5-9 years	34 (34)	66	32 (64)	18
10-17 years	35 (37)	59	32 (56)	25

association may be causally linked. Because potential confounding factors such as speeding and alcohol impairment were controlled-for in the sample selection process, and because culpability was assessed by professional multi-disciplinary teams, it is indeed possible that the relationship is causal. In that case, it remains to determine whether it is because men are less attentive to their children or because they can multi-task better when driving. This finding is also interesting in light of Laberge-Nadeau's (2003) finding, that men and women were equally likely to consider distraction from children as "very harmful to driving".

An increasingly common method of reducing distraction from children in the backseat is to occupy them with video games or with watching movies on a fixed TV screen or a nomadic device. This seems to be an effective way of keeping them occupied and the soundtrack does not seem to distract driving any more than a regular radio program (Hatfield and Chamberlain, 2008).

As far as pets are concerned recent media has raised some concerns about the safety – of both pets and humans – when they ride in cars (Huisingh *et al.*, 2016). Two studies by Owsley and her colleagues investigated the effects of driving with pets on the crash involvement of older drivers. In the first one, a retrospective study, Blunck *et al.* (2013) studied the relationship between riding with pets and crash involvement in 691 older independently living drivers who owned a pet and either did or did not drive with their pet. There were no statistically significant differences in vision, cognitive functioning, or morbidity between the two groups, and – to the relief of pet owners – there were no differences in crash rates between the two groups; though, the small group of 15 drivers who always drove with their pets had nearly twice as many collisions as those who never did. The second study by Huisingh *et al.* (2016) was a prospective study on the same population of drivers, and its objective was to validate the findings from the first study. In this study, the crash rates of 70+ years old drivers who had a pet were tracked *after* they filled out the questionnaires regarding their driving habits with their pets. The results of this study were quite similar to those of the first. Crash rates of drivers who have ever driven with a pet were similar to those who never drove with their pet. But this time the drivers who reported always or sometimes driving with their pet did not differ significantly in their crash rates from those who never drove with a pet. Also, there were no significant differences in the crash rates between those reporting having a pet frequently ride in the front of the vehicle and those who did not drive with a pet in the front. Thus, to the relief of pet owners, current data suggest that pets are not a risk factor in distracted driving; even to older drivers (who are more susceptible to distractions than younger drivers).

Sex (NOT gender)

Among young drivers' risk-taking behaviors is having sex while driving. In a recent attempt to quantify this activity and determine its impact on driving, Struckman-Johnson and her colleagues (2014, 2015) queried 706 students about their experience in this dual task. Surprisingly (or not) 33 percent of the males and 9 percent of the females had engaged in sex while driving as drivers, while 9 percent of the men and 29 percent of the women reported that they had engaged in sex as passengers. This reversal in percentages may either reflect the fact that when riding together men are more often the drivers, or that women are more likely to use their brains when driving. Again, as with some other risky behaviors where there is a disconnect between attitudes and behaviors, most respondents (78 percent) felt that it should be illegal.

Distraction from Cell Phones

Is there a problem, and if so then how big is it?

At the turn of this century, in his 2001 testimony to the U.S. Congress the executive director of the U.S. National Highway Traffic Safety Administration (NHTSA) stated that "our problem now is to understand a new set of distractions associated with an ever-growing array of new in-vehicle electronic devices, referred to as "telematics," rapidly being developed by the electronics and automobile industries. The devices that are receiving NHTSA's main attention are cell phones, route navigation systems, on-board computers that deliver personalized Internet-based information, and other multifunction systems... (However) studies have shown that cell phones often reduce emergency response times and actually save lives. In many respects, these new technologies may make it easier for people to drive more safely. For a number of years, policymakers have been weighing the benefits of wireless technology in cars against the growing evidence of their potential to increase driver distraction and the risks to highway safety" (NHTSA, 2001). For better or worse, the use of cell phones – especially among young drivers and especially for texting – has been increasing since then. In the U.S., on the basis of their annual probability-based observational survey (NOPUS – National Occupant Protection Use Survey), NHTSA estimates that "visible manipulation of hand held devices," which includes texting – increased ten-fold in the decade between 2004 and 2015 (from 0.2 percent to 2.2 percent) in the general driving population, to 15-fold (from 0.3 percent to 4.9 percent) among drivers under 25 years old (NHTSA, 2015b, 2016a). Drivers' self-reports present an even more disturbing picture. According to a national survey conducted by the AAA Traffic Safety Foundation in 2014, 27 percent of the drivers admitted to sending a text message or email "while driving in the past month" (AAAF, 2015). Thus, if visual-manual distraction from cell phones is a problem, it is a rapidly growing one, especially in the highest risk segment of the driving population.

Depending on one's perspective cell phones are the biggest telecommunications bane or boon of this century. Their penetration has been very rapid both in terms of global spread and in terms of rate of proliferation. To cite two examples, in Taiwan by April 2002 there were slightly more registered cell phone accounts than people; including infants and children (Liu and Lee, 2006). In the U.S., the number of cell phone users roughly equaled the population size at the end of 2013 (IIHS, 2014). In the most recent U.S. national survey of cell phone use while driving, close to 50 percent of drivers under 25 years old reported that they have sent text messages or emails while driving. Furthermore, approximately 70 percent of these drivers reported that they did so without bothering to pull over to the side of the road, hand the phone to a passenger, or use voice command (NHTSA, 2015c). In short, one thing is certain, despite numerous articles, warnings, and prohibitions, the use of a cell phone while driving is on the increase.

Innovative in-vehicle technologies, collectively known as in-vehicle information systems (IVIS) are part of broader class known as Intelligent Transportation Systems (ITS). They increase the scope of activities drivers can perform while driving. They increase drivers' communication capabilities, entertainment options, and potential safety benefits (e-safety). The most ubiquitous manifestation of the new technologies is the in-vehicle cellular phone and the use of portable/nomadic cellular phones while driving. As the number of people with cell phones increases, so does the number of people who use them while driving. The data to support this conclusion comes from many and different sources. In a nationally representative telephone survey conducted by the U.S. AAA Foundation for Traffic Safety in 2009 over two-thirds of the respondents admitted to talking on the phone while driving at least once "in the past 30 days" (AAAF, 2009), and that level has remained substantially unchanged as of 2014 (AAAF, 2015). Already at the beginning of this century, in a survey conducted on over 1,000 professional drivers in Denmark in the spring of 2003, 99 percent(!) of the drivers admitted to using cell phones while driving, and nearly 40 percent of them used the phone daily for 15 minutes or more (Troglauer, Hels, and Christens, 2006). In a survey of the employees of one Spanish university 10 years ago, over 60 percent reported using the phone while driving, mostly for conversing, but also for sending and receiving text messages (Gras *et al.*, 2007), and a random poll of Finnish mobile phone owners "who drive regularly or at least occasionally" revealed that 81 percent of them use their phone while driving "at least occasionally" (Pöysti, Rajalin, and Summala, 2005). In a 2008 internet survey of 1,057 New Zealand drivers, 36 percent reported talking on their cell phone at least once in the past week, and the more a person reported talking the less risky he or she considered that activity (Hallett, Lambert, and Regan, 2011).

Probably the most objective estimate of cell phone use while driving comes from naturalistic driving studies (NDS), where the drivers' actual use of the phone in the course of their regular driving is tracked over time. In such a study on 204 drivers in Victoria, Australia, who prior to recruitment reported using the phone while driving "at least once a day," Fitch *et al.* (2013) found that on the average these drivers used their cell phones 10.6 percent of the time their "vehicle was in operation," though not necessarily moving. A complication that is rarely mentioned in the context of phone use, is that it often entails the need to write something on a piece of paper (Green, George, and Jacob, 2004), making the conversation much more than just cognitively distracting. An interesting finding from the Troglauer *et al.* (2006) survey was that only 6 percent of the drivers experienced a dangerous situation as a result of their phone use, but 66 percent experienced a dangerous situation as a result of other drivers' phone use. This pattern is, of course, consistent with people's tendencies to consider themselves better than others in most domains.

Drivers perceptions of cell phones: hazardous – but they still use them

The use of the phone while driving is a conscious decision that appears to be mediated by safety concerns. All the surveys mentioned above show that the amount of use is highly age-related, with both the frequency of use and the duration of the talks declining with age. In addition, the Finnish survey by Pöysti *et al.* (2005) found that the frequency of phone use was also lower among females, among those who drive less, and among retired people (who are also older drivers), leading the researchers to conclude that the "potential risks of mobile phones are being controlled at many levels, by strategic as well as tactical decisions and, consequently, phone-related accidents have not increased in line with the use of the mobile phones." A similar phenomenon has been pointed out by Hancock and Sawyer (2015) relative to the rise in phone use in the U.S. and the concomitant drop in crashes. Lerner and Boyd (2005) also found that drivers report that they use their phone in a very consistent inverse relation to the perceived hazard of the situation ($r = -0.98$!). But do they really? A nationally representative telephone survey conducted in the U.S. at the end of 2010 (Tison, Chaudhary, and Cosgrove, 2011) demonstrated that people are also quite inconsistent in their responses. In the survey, as drivers more than half the respondents believed that using a cell phone or sending a text message made no difference in their driving performance. Yet when asked about their feelings as passengers 90 percent said they would feel "very unsafe" if the driver was talking on the phone or texting. In the same survey older drivers were less likely to use the phone to talk or to text than younger drivers: with less than 1 percent of the 55+ years old texting "regularly," versus over 15 percent of the 16-35 years old drivers. This large difference suggests that the problem is at least partially age-related (AAAF, 2009). Also, while attitudes and concerns about phone use have changed slightly for the better, the reported use actually increased; with 77 percent of drivers saying they were likely to answer a call (and 41 percent to initiate it), and 10 percent stating they were likely to read text messages (and 6 percent to write one). As in previous surveys young males were more likely to use the phone than older people, especially older women. And the situation is only getting worse. In the most recent U.S. nationally representative survey over 75 percent of all drivers reported that they answer the phone while driving and 40 percent reported that they initiate calls as well. Over 50 percent felt that it makes no difference to their driving, and only approximately 20 percent reported that they slow down when engaged in a phone call. As before, the worst violators and the ones who feel that their driving is the least affected by the phone use are the young drivers, under the age of 25 (NHTSA, 2015c).

However, in all of the above studies the estimates were based on drivers' self-reports rather than on actual observed use. Actual use reveals a different and more complex pattern. Stutts *et al.* (2003) reported that drivers were more likely to read and write, manipulate vehicle controls, attend to an external distraction, reach for objects inside their vehicle, dial a cell phone, carry on a cell phone conversation, and perform grooming activities when their vehicle was stopped. But some distracting activities were not more frequent when stopped than when moving. These included eating and drinking, manipulating music controls, smoking, attending to a baby or a child, and conversing with passengers. With respect to cell phones, those who used cell phones were also more likely to use them when the car was stopped rather than moving, but on the other hand, they were twice as likely to use them when the weather was bad than when it was good, and slightly more likely to use them in moderate and heavy traffic than in light traffic. Thus, the actual use of cell phones while driving reveals a different set of strategies than the stated use: drivers are not as risk-aversive as they claim and their use pattern is much less consistent than reported.

Using a cell phone while driving is not a constant uniform activity. It is made up of several different attention demanding activities. Making a call, reaching for the phone to answer a call, listening, talking, and terminating a call are all different activities that probably demand different amounts of attention and levels of information processing. Therefore, they are likely to have differential distracting effects. In fact, even the ringing of the phone can be distracting enough to increase crash risk when it coincides with the appearance of unexpected hazards – at least in contrived situations in a driving simulator (Holland and Rathod, 2013). Dialing and responding to a call are more distracting and dangerous because they also involve visual distraction in redirection of the visual gaze away from the roadway, and manual distraction in removing the hand(s) from the steering wheel. Fortunately, relative to the conversation time they are short. In their study using videotaped recordings, Stutts *et al.* (2003, 2005) found that placing a call required an average of 12.9 seconds, while retrieving a phone from the time it started ringing – required an average of 7.9 seconds. The conversations themselves averaged 90 seconds, but their duration was highly variable: from as little as 1-2 seconds to as long as 20 minutes. In contrast, in a recent analysis of 1,691 videotaped crashes of teen U.S. drivers, that occurred in 2007-2013, Carney *et al.* (2015) noted that the average eyes-off-the-road time while operating or looking at the phone was 4.1 seconds, compared to 0.9 seconds while talking or listening.

Though more than 10 years old, the most extensive study of the perceived effects of cell phones was conducted by Laberge-Nadeau and her associates (2003) on 36,078(!) drivers registered in Quebec, Canada. All of these drivers answered a detailed questionnaire, and gave permission to examine their cell phone use records. As part of the questionnaire the respondents noted how harmful different activities are. The perceived dangers of cell phone use relative to other potential sources of distraction are indicated in Table 13-6 that lists the percent of respondents who thought that different activities are "very harmful to driving." The table reveals a very large difference between the percent of drivers who consider listening to the radio or talking to passengers as very dangerous (1-3 percent) and the percent of drivers who consider talking on the cell phone as very dangerous (36-76 percent). This is despite the fact that all of these tasks are auditory and vocal. Both users and non-users, men and women, considered the phone much more distracting than listening to radio or talking to passengers. One important variable that was related to whether or not talking on the cell phone was perceived as dangerous was whether or not the person had a cell phone. Ninety-five percent of the men and 87 percent of the women who had cell phones reported using them while driving, and a smaller proportion of those owning a cell phone considered them dangerous than of those not owning a cell phone. Given today's culture, it is probably best to use only the data from those who owned a phone. Also, of the different cell phone-related functions, significantly more people considered dialing as a "very harmful" activity compared to just talking on the cell phone. Given these and similar more recent findings (e.g., Lansdown, 2012) it is remarkable that 50 percent of the men who had cell phones and 27 percent of the women who had cell phones reported using them "often or very often while driving." This means that a significant proportion of those who used their cell phone while driving rationalized it by not considering it so dangerous. But it also means that a significant

Table 13-6. Percent of men and women who have and do not have cell phone who consider different activities "very harmful to driving" (from Laberge-Nadeau *et al.*, 2003, with permission from Elsevier).

Distracting Activity	**Men**		**Women**	
	With phone	**W/o phone**	**With phone**	**W/o phone**
Taking care of children	62	53	64	65
Talking with passengers	2	3	3	3
Listening to radio/cd/tape	1	1	1	1
Talking on cell phone	36	70	50	76
Dialing on cell phone	68	84	77	85

proportion of those who used them also acknowledged that the practice was very harmful to driving, though the temptation is too great to resist (think of how we sprint from the bathroom to answer a phone). This is hard to reconcile with the Risk Homeostasis Theory, unless the same people also compensate for the added perceived hazard.

Determinants of the decision to use the cell phone

Self-reports and observational surveys reviewed above repeatedly find that older drivers limit their phone use while driving more than young drivers, indicating that some kind of self-control is being exercised. Still, in light of the dismally small effect of deterrence, laws, and public information campaigns, it is interesting to examine the determinants of using the phone, in the hope that manipulating them can affect behavior. Walsh *et al.* (2008) attempted to do just that by presenting drivers with different driving scenarios and then asking them to decide whether they would be likely to use the phone to talk and to text under these conditions, and Waddell and Wiener (2014) conducted an internet survey on drivers' inclination to respond to and initiate text messaging and phone calls. Using the theory of planned behavior (TPB – see Chapter 3) as a theoretical framework, they assessed the extent to which the driver's attitudes toward driving and using the phone, subjective norms, and perceived behavioral control determine the intention to combine the phone tasks with driving. Both groups of researchers found that the drivers' attitudes and subjective norms correlated significantly with the intention, suggesting that social pressure is a significant factor especially in reading text messages and responding to phone calls. Both studies also found that age was also a significant predictor, showing that younger drivers were more likely to use the phone. There is some evidence that drivers also adjust their phone use in accordance with the situational demands; using it less when the driving demands increase (Liang, Horrey, and Hoffman, 2015) and using it more while stopped, and when driving at high speeds (Metz, Landau, and Just, 2014). However, this exercise of good judgment may not include young drivers who are the most prone to using their phone while driving (Tractinsky, Ram, and Shinar, 2013).

When directly asked why they use the phone, as part of an Israeli survey of a nationally representative sample of drivers, the most popular reasons given were because: "it is a work tool" (21 percent), "my job expects me to be available at all times" (20 percent), "so as not to waste time" (11 percent), "it is almost the only time I have to make phone calls" (10 percent), and "I need it for emergency situations" (10 percent) (Tomer-Fishman, 2010). Thus, it seems that people will resort to functional reasons when directly asked why they use the phone, but deeper psychological factors may actually govern this behavior.

The concern that young drivers – with less driving experience and greater propensity for risk taking – are the most likely to use the phone while driving, prompted us to study this in a driving simulator (Tractinsky *et al.*, 2013). In the study, young (<20 years old), mature (24-30 years old), and older (65+ years old) drivers had to drive in three different environments: a mostly straight two-lane rural road without any traffic, a four-lane road with heavy traffic, and a two-lane winding road. These three road segments ranged from the easiest to the most difficult, on the basis of the average speed, the speed variance, and the subjective workload (as assessed in a prior experiment). At different unexpected times the hands-free phone rang and the driver had to decide whether to answer it or not. Also, during the drives the drivers were given the option to initiate telephone calls by dialing any 10-digit number of their choice. The "conversation" consisted of three simple arithmetic exercises (as in McKnight and McKnight, 1993; and Shinar *et al.*, 2005). The drivers were paid for each call they completed successfully but were penalized heavily for each accident. The results, reproduced in part in Table 13-7 were striking. The Novice drivers were the highest risk-taking group, answering all calls and initiating as many calls as possible in all driving conditions. In contrast, the older drivers were the most risk-averse and both initiated and answered fewer calls than the other two groups. As expected, the likelihood of making or answering a call decreased with increased road complexity. A similar effect was noted in naturalistic driving, where drivers were more likely to engage in a phone task when stopped in traffic than when actually driving (Metz *et al.*, 2014; Tivesten and Dozza, 2015). Also, answering an incoming call was apparently more compelling (or considered less disruptive) than initiating a call, as the percent of answered calls was higher than the percent of calls initiated (out of all possible opportunities). Thus, despite the fact that an incoming call is oblivious to the driving situation, people tend to answer it. In contrast, when making calls drivers – but not young drivers – seem to be a little more judicious. As in other simulator studies

Table 13-7. Percentage of calls answered and initiated as a function of the driver age and road complexity (Tractinsky *et al.*, 2013, with permission from Elsevier).

	Road Condition			**Overall (%)**
	Easy (%)	**Heavy traffic (%)**	**Winding (%)**	
Incoming (answered) calls				
Young	100	100	100	100
Experienced	100	100	100	100
Elderly	94	83	44	74
Overall	98	94	81	91
Outgoing (initiated) calls				
Young	83	100	100	94
Experienced	77	94	83	85
Elderly	50	55	50	51
Overall	70	83	77	77

(e.g., Engström, Johansson, and Östlund, 2005; Törnros and Bolling, 2005; Yannis *et al.*, 2010) speed was slightly but consistently lower when talking on the phone, highest for the novice drivers and lowest for the older drivers, and highest on the easy road and lowest on the winding road. The older drivers, in addition to responding and initiating fewer calls, when they did respond they allowed the phone to ring longer, and when allowed to call they waited longer than the novice and the mature drivers before initiating the call. This was true especially in the winding road when the older drivers' average time to respond and to initiate a call was nearly twice as long as that of the young and mature drivers.

The higher risk that the young drivers assumed in our study did come with a price tag: most of the accidents during the incoming and outgoing calls were caused by the young drivers while engaged in the phone tasks. To make things worse, the novice drivers were not aware of the risks of the phone tasks, and they rated the driving task as less difficult than the experienced mature drivers. Similar conclusions were reached by Lerner, Singer, and Huey (2008), who asked drivers to rate their willingness to engage in different distracting tasks while actually driving in different scenarios. Although the drivers did not actually performed these tasks, the researchers found that only older drivers (60+ years old) were differentially sensitive to engaging in a phone conversation, whereas all other drivers did not attribute much risk to any of the phone tasks and were quite willing to dial, pick up a phone, and converse while driving in most scenarios. Finally, the added sensitivity of older drivers to the risk is also supported by Fitch and Hanowski's (2011) naturalistic study finding that although professional truck drivers tend to use their phones while driving more than drivers of passenger vehicles, they adjust their phone use to the driving demands. Consequently, in demanding situations they actually use the phone less than non-professional drivers.

A somewhat similar study, though more artificial than ours, was conducted by Pouyakian *et al.* (2013). In their experiment, drivers watched video scenes of driving while sitting in a driving simulator and had to decide whether or not to answer a phone when it rang. The researchers varied the driving demands by changing the headway to a lead car and by changing the speed. They found that the percent decisions to answer calls decreased as headway decreased and as speed increased. Interestingly, in their study the experienced older drivers (28-35 years old) had greater answering rates than the younger drivers (23-28 years old), though with such a small age range the effect may only be due to driving experience and skill. One difficulty in comparing the two studies is that Pouyakian *et al.'s* "drivers" did not actually drive the car and there were no incentives to answer the phone and no penalties for crashes (which did not happen). Multiple variables that are often not studied or controlled affect the tendency to call or answer a call. In our pilot studies, we found that the reward/penalty scheme has a large effect on the decisions to answer or initiate calls. Zhou *et al.* (2009) applied the theory of planned behavior (see Chapter 3) to evaluate the determinants of phone use and to understand why young drivers use the phone despite its perceived hazard. They found that the attitude toward its use, subjective norms concerning use, and especially the perceived behavioral control over its use determined actual use to a large extent. In a follow-up study (Zhou *et al.*, 2012) on more experienced drivers (>1 year of driving), they also found that the theory of planned behavior could account for the drivers' choice of compensatory behaviors to offset the perceived risk: including letting the caller know that they are driving and to limiting the conversation time.

Cell phones' effects on driving performance

Although phone conversations may be short, and occupy a small fraction of the driving time, they may pose a higher risk than some other distractions such as listening to the radio or talking to a passenger. This is in part because in the case of incoming calls, the driver has no control of the timing of the distraction. If a call arrives when the driving task is easy or the attention allocated to the roadway is much more than needed, then the risk is minimal. On the other hand, if a call arrives when the attention needed suddenly increases the driver may be unprepared for that and unable to cope. This was demonstrated in a nicely controlled study by Hancock, Lesch, and Simmons (2003), where drivers drove 48 times in an instrumented vehicle on a test track that contained a traffic light. On one half of the trials the drive was not interrupted at all and the light remained green throughout the drive. In the remaining half of the trials, on one-third of the occasions, the light turned red just as the driver approached it, on one-third of the trials the in-vehicle phone rang and the driver had to attend to a number flashed on its screen, and on one-third of the trials the light changed to red immediately after the phone rang (0.5-1.0 seconds). The duration of this interval is of critical importance because during that interval the driver had enough time to direct his or her gaze toward the phone but not enough time to process the phone information and redirect the eyes toward the road and the traffic light (see eye movements discussion in Chapter 4). Thus, it was not surprising that when the phone task was combined with the light change, drivers' brake reaction times to the light change were either delayed (from an average reaction time of 0.52 seconds to an average reaction time of 0.71 seconds), or – in 5 to 20 percent of the trials – the drivers did not respond to the light change at all, and drove through the red light. Interestingly, both the delayed brake reaction times and the total misses of the light change were almost exclusively limited to the older drivers (55-65 years old). Younger (25-36 years old) drivers rarely missed the red light, reinforcing the notion that young drivers are better able to divide their attention among multiple inputs than older drivers. A direct demonstration of this age effect was made by McPhee *et al.* (2004) who showed that older (56-71 years old) drivers' sign recognition performance was significantly more impaired when they were required to simultaneously listen to auditory messages, than that of younger (17-33 years old) drivers, especially when the signs were imbedded in a highly cluttered road scene. Similarly, using two tasks unrelated to driving (programming a video cassette recorder and tracking) Monk, Boehm-Davis, and Trafton (2004a) demonstrated that the effects of a subsidiary task on a primary task were much greater with older people (55-69 years old) than with younger people (17-26 years old). However, youth is not a guarantee against the dangers of distraction. Horrey, Wickens, and Consalus (2006) found that young (19-37 years old) drivers' brake reaction times to unexpected hazards were significantly affected by a subsidiary task of reading phone numbers from a dashboard display.

Even when the critical driving-related information that must be attended to is not transient, a cell phone conversation may still be disruptive. Strayer and Drews (2007) observed 1,748 drivers as they approached intersections with STOP signs, and noted whether or not they stopped and whether or not they were using their phone as they approached the intersection. They found that 75 percent of the drivers who were on the phone did not stop at the STOP sign, compared to 19 percent of those of were not on the phone. The ratio of these two numbers – the relative risk of RR = 3.95 – indicates that people conversing on the phone were four times as likely to fail to stop at an intersection as people not on the phone. Although some of this difference may be due to distracted attention from the phone task, it is also possible that cell phone users are higher risk takers and generally more likely to violate traffic laws. Support for this comes from a survey conducted by Response Insurance that found that people who use cell phones while they drive were also more likely to preoccupy their mind with everyday issues while they drive, such as thinking about their relationships, their jobs, and what to eat (Online Auto Insurance News, 2003). Pöysti *et al.* (2005) also found that people who tend to use the phone while driving are generally younger drivers and lower in their safety motivation than people who do not tend to use their phone. Thus, as in aggressive driving (see Chapter 9), the consequences of cell phone use may be a product of the cell phone user's general risk-taking tendencies as much as a direct effect of the cell phone.

One issue that must be considered is the relative importance that the drivers attach to the driving and the distraction tasks. In most studies, the instructions are not specific; giving the drivers the impression that the distracting task and the driving task are equally important. But, argue Levy, Pashler, and Boer (2006), in real driving drivers know that the driving is more important than the distraction task, and therefore the distracting effects should be less. To test for this, they had drivers follow another vehicle in a rudimentary simulator. Occasionally the lead car braked, and the drivers had to brake in response to its brake lights. On some of the trials, the drivers were also presented with an auditory tone to which they had to respond by pushing a button with their right hand. The auditory tone could appear either simultaneously with the brake lights, 0.15 seconds before the brake lights, or 0.15 seconds after the brake lights. The drivers were also instructed to consider the driving task as the primary task, to the point of aborting any response to the tone as the driver would be expected to do in "real-life." Despite these specific instructions, when the two stimuli were presented (even when the tone followed the brake lights) most drivers attempted to respond to the tone, so that consequently most drivers occasionally totally failed to respond to the brake lights of the lead car. When they did respond to the brake lights the responses were significantly delayed relative to the trials in which the tone was not presented. A similar phenomenon was noted by Meyer (2006). In his study, drivers were given a phone task while driving, but were told that if at any time the driving task became very challenging they could press a button that would signal their phone partner that the connection is still there, but that they would continue in a few seconds when the traffic conditions allow it. Meyer found that very few people used that option. Instead, most drivers most of the time preferred to continue both tasks even at the cost of compromising their driving performance and risking their safety. This could be either because the phone call was so compelling that people refused to interrupt it, or because pressing the button was perceived as a greater distraction than just continuing with the conversation. In either case, people demonstrate some resistance to interrupting their cell phone conversations.

Effects on visual performance

The demands of driving are mostly in the processing of visual information. In contrast, the demands of a cell phone – except for the manipulation involved in dialing and answering – are mostly in processing auditory information. Nonetheless, as discussed above, when the demands imposed by the two tasks are high, interference can and does occur between the two sources.

Several studies have demonstrated the degradation of visual performance from an auditory phone task. In a well-controlled laboratory study, Barkana *et al.* (2004) examined people's visual field while they were engaged in a distracting hands-free phone task and when they were not. The standard visual field test required the subject to gaze straight ahead, while 100 points of lights distributed across the visual field of 135 degrees in the horizontal plane were projected sequentially in a random sequence. The phone task consisted of a structured conversation in which a technician sitting in another room asked all participants the same set of questions, trying to maintain the same pace. In general, both with and without the phone task the participants detected nearly all points. However, with the phone task they missed nearly three times as many points as without it (an average of 2.6 percent versus an average of 1.0 percent), and the time needed to detect and respond to the lights also increased by a small but statistically significant 15 percent. The missed points were equally frequent within the para-foveal (near central) field of 30 degrees as they were beyond it, suggesting that the reduced attention is equally distributed across the visual field, rather than assuming the effect of "tunnel vision." One of the interesting observations made by Barkana and his associates was that despite the relatively homogenous group of subjects and despite the near perfect performance of all subjects in the absence of the phone task, the effects of the cell phones on the individual's visual field varied widely across subjects with some experiencing "minimal" degradation and others performing quite "poorly." This observation should serve as a warning against sweeping generalizations on the effects of cell phones on our attention. Obviously different people have different attention capacity. While Barkana *et al.*'s study only evaluated the effects of a phone task on the passive clinical field of view, Atchley and Dressel (2004) demonstrated that a phone task also significantly reduces the functional field of view; the ability to attend to peripheral targets while being engaged in a task involving the center of the visual field. Two studies measured the responses to a peripheral visual target while driving with and without a distracting phone task. In both studies, the detection task consisted of pressing a button in response to a light that appeared on the left side of the windshield slightly above the dashboard. In the first study, Patten *et al.* (2004) had 40 professional drivers drive on a Swedish motorway in three conditions: when not engaged in a phone task, while engaged in a simple phone task requiring the repetition of digits, and while engaged in a complex phone task involving single digit calculations and memory. They found that both the probability of detecting the lights and the reaction times to the lights increased when the drivers had the cell phone task; with a 45 percent increase in reaction time while conducting the complex phone task relative to driving without a phone task. In the second study, Törnros and Bolling (2005) used an advanced moving-base driving simulator with a difficult phone task (similar to the one used by Patten *et al.*, 2004). They found that both dialing and "conversing" on the phone increased the reaction times to the targets, and the likelihood of missing some of the targets.

The problem is further compounded because a phone task also affects the visual search process itself. Sodhi *et al.* (2002a) and Harbluk *et al.* (2007) monitored eye movements of drivers in real driving and found that a phone task suppressed drivers' visual search pattern, reducing the frequency of glances to the side of the road and to the vehicle instruments. Jin *et al.* (2014) measured eye movements in a driving simulator and obtained similar suppressive effects of the dispersion of the visual fixations. Engström *et al.* (2005) also found in both a simulated drive and in an instrumented car on the road that cognitive load increased gaze concentration, while a visual peripheral task increased the variability in lane position, and Reimer *et al* (2010) found that the greater the difficulty of the non-driving cognitive task, the greater the reduction in the eye movements.

After reviewing over 125 studies, McCartt, Hellinga, and Braitman (2006a) noted that as of the end of 2005 not a single study was conducted on people driving their own cars. To see how drivers perform in their own cars with their own phones, we conducted such a study in a naturalistic setting in Israel. For this study, we recruited drivers who already had a hands-free phone system in their car and reported that they used their cell phones while driving. They then drove their own cars in an urban route, while pointing out whenever they detected either a "CHILDREN CROSSING" or a "NO PARKING" sign. The route was divided into three segments, each containing a total of 16 signs (approximately half of each kind). In one segment, the drive was conducted without any distraction, in another segment the drivers had to engage in a phone conversation with an experimenter, and in another segment they had to perform a math operations task in response to questions presented over the phone. The math operations task was similar to one used in other studies (e.g., McKnight and McKnight, 1993) where the driver was presented with a succession of single digit numbers that they had to add to, subtract from, divide by, or multiply with the result of the last operation. Thus, the two phone tasks varied in their cognitive demands, the math operations being much more demanding, but much less similar to a real phone conversation. The main results of the study,

Table 13-8. Percent of signs missed by drivers when not engaged in a cell phone task, when engaged in a cell phone conversation, and when engaged with a cell phone math task (from Shinar, 2006).

Driver Age	**Phone Task**		
	None	**Conversation**	**Math task**
Younger (25–55)	11	18	28
Older (60–85)	25	37	48

presented in Table 13-8, were clear cut: though younger drivers detected more signs than older drivers, both younger and older drivers were equally affected by the auditory-vocal phone task. When the cognitive demands of the phone task were sufficiently high, and the drivers were old, they missed nearly 50 percent of the signs that they were supposed to detect. Another indication of the greater difficulty of the phone task for the older drivers was the fact that the pace at which the two groups performed the math operations was nearly the same when they did so without driving (0.6 and 1.1 seconds per operation for the young and old, respectively), but slowed down much more for the older drivers when they had to do it in the context of driving (2.1 and 5.0 seconds, respectively). Thus, this study validated the earlier findings of the better controlled, but less realistic, laboratory studies that showed that visual performance can be significantly impaired by a cell phone conversation.

Effects on speed
If drivers are aware of their information processing limits, then task overload should induce them to compensate for it in some manner. Given that a person is already aware of the demands of the traffic environment when a secondary task – cell phone conversation, navigation system alert, or even a conversation with a passenger – is added, a driver can adjust to the added demand by reducing the rate at which the driving-related information must be processed. This in fact is what we do when we slow down. When we slow down we decrease the rate of the information flow. It appears that drivers employ this strategy when they are distracted. This compensatory response has been found in simulated driving (Burns *et al.*, 2002; Lansdown, Brook-Carter, and Kersloot, 2004; Shinar *et al.*, 2005; Strayer and Drews, 2004; Waugh *et al.*, 2000), in real-world driving (Liu and Lee, 2006; Yannis *et al.*, 2010), and in a survey of drivers (Gras *et al.*, 2007). The compensation is at least in part a conscious decision. For example, Liu and Lee (2006) found that drivers reduced their speed by approximately 6 percent when engaged in a computational task delivered over the phone relative to their speed without any phone distractions. Similarly, Lansdown *et al.* (2004) noted 8 percent reduction in speed when their drivers in a simulator had to engage in a secondary task involving short term memory.

But the actual speed reduction does not necessarily indicate a safer compensatory behavior. It is possible that drivers reduce their speed simply because they do not pay attention to it, and unconsciously reduce the pressure on the accelerator pedal. Support for this hypothesis comes from a study by Hatfield and Murphy (2007) who observed that pedestrians crossing the street while talking on the phone took more time to cross the street than pedestrians crossing it while not talking on the phone. Obviously, it is hard to argue that slower walking in this case is indicative of safer compensatory behavior. The critical issue for drivers is whether the amount of speed reduction compensates adequately for the added task load. The answer to that appears to be no. These compensations are not always made (Recarte and Nunes, 2002), and when they are they may be insufficient (Caird *et al.*, 2008). In most studies where both the driving speed and other driving or driving-related performance measures were obtained, performance still deteriorated in conjunction with the phone task despite the observed speed reductions (Shinar *et al.*, 2005; Strayer and Drews, 2004).

Effects on headway

When we increase the headway between ourselves and the car ahead of us, we increase the time to respond to sudden and unexpected events, such as an unexpected stopping or slowing of the car ahead. There are less data on the effects of cell phone distraction on driving headways, but the little data that exist suggest that here too drivers attempt to compensate for the distraction. Strayer and Drews (2004) found that drivers engaged in a hands-free conversation with an experimenter while driving in a simulator, maintained longer headways than when the driving was not disrupted by a phone conversation; and this was true for both young and old drivers. In their study, drivers were required to follow a lead vehicle that braked intermittently. The drivers' task was to brake whenever the lead car braked, and then resume their speed whenever the lead car accelerated. The driving performance results are reproduced in Table 13-9. As can be seen in this table, both younger and older drivers, had longer brake reaction times in response to the braking of a lead car, both maintained longer headways (following distance) when involved in a phone conversation, and both needed longer time to recover their original speed (1/2 recovery time) once the lead car resumed its speed. The small changes in speed in response to the added demands of the phone task were not statistically significant for either group, but regardless of the phone task the older drivers drove significantly slower than the younger drivers.

In a car following study of driving on a closed track, Ranney and his associates (2005) asked drivers to follow a lead car at a "close but safe" distance while they were required to perform a secondary target detection task in response to randomly appearing lights on the windshield, and while they were engaged in receiving and responding to emails. They too found that drivers increased their headways when they performed the secondary task, the email task, or both tasks relative to the control condition in which they could concentrate only on their driving. One possible reason for the relatively consistent effects on speed and the less consistent effects on headways may be that drivers are quite accurate in judging speeds (Shinar and Ronen, 2007) but generally poor in judging gaps

Table 13-9. Average driving performance (and standard errors) in a driving simulator when the drivers only have to drive (Single Task) and when they have to time-share the driving with a cell phone task (Dual Task) (from Strayer and Drews, 2004, with permission of the Human Factors and Ergonomics Society).

	Younger Adults		**Older Adults**	
	Single task	**Dual task**	**Single task**	**Dual task**
Brake onset time (millisecond)	780 (49)	912 (83)	912 (49)	1086 (83)
Following distance (meter)	22.7 (3)	26.4 (2)	37.1 (3)	40.7 (2)
Driving speed (mph)	63.3 (2)	62.1 (1)	52.4 (2)	53.7 (1)
½ Recovery time (second)	4.6 (0.4)	5.9 (0.4)	6.4 (0.4)	7.0 (0.4)

(Brown, Tickner, and Simmonds, 1969; Taieb and Shinar, 2001). Another problem with headways is that they are often highly correlated with speed, and after inclusion of speed as a variable in relation to cell phone use, headway may no longer remain a significant factor (Yannis *et al.*, 2010).

Brake reaction times and lateral control

As would be expected, vehicle control, in general, deteriorates when people are required to engage in a cell phone task. Horrey and Wickens (2006) and Caird *et al.* (2008) conducted meta-analyses (a statistical technique that combines data from different studies that use similar measures) of 23 and 33 studies, respectively, that examined the effects of cell phones on various driving performance measures. Both groups of researchers concluded that the effects of a phone task are much more pronounced on reaction time tasks (such as responses to visual targets or obstacles) than on vehicle lane keeping measures. Multiple studies have demonstrated that brake reaction times are significantly slower when drivers are engaged in a phone task. Consequently, when they do brake drivers brake much harder while engaged on the phone, thereby leaving other drivers less time to respond (Alm and Nilsson, 1995; Lamble *et al.*, 1999; Lee *et al.*, 2002; Levy *et al.*, 2006; Strayer, Drews, and Johnston, 2003).

One of the more consistent effects of cell phone distraction is that of increased variability in lane position and an increase in steering deviations. Lateral control is especially compromised by the dialing activity, as has been demonstrated in a simulator (Brookhuis, de Vries, and Waard, 1991; Törnros and Bolling, 2005). This is because the dialing actually requires redirection of the visual gaze away from the road and the removal of at least one hand off the wheel. Therefore, as might be expected, this risk can be reduced with voice dialing (e.g., Apple's Siri®. Graham and Carter, 2001; Shutko *et al.*, 2009; Yager, 2013). Another approach is the one adopted by GM in some of their cars with their OnStar© system. This system eliminates some of the potential in-vehicle distractions by providing the driver through the push of a single readily accessible button immediate access to a live person who can find and dial phone numbers, provide navigation information, and in essence serve as a resource for just about any information the driver needs (GM, 2006). However, even the phone task itself may be sufficiently absorbing as to impair steering, at least initially (Shinar *et al.*, 2005).

Cell phone effects on subjective mental load

Although drivers are often not aware of the impairing effects of time-sharing driving with other tasks in general and with a cell phone in particular, they do feel that the dual task is more demanding and their subjective ratings of the mental load typically increase when a phone task or a mental computational task is added to the driving. This has been confirmed by higher scores on various subjective scales of mental load such as the NASA-TLX and the Subjective Workload Assessment Task (SWAT) (Alm and Nilsson, 1995; Brookhuis *et al.*, 1991; Fairclough *et al.*, 1991; Lansdown *et al.*, 2004; Matthews, Legg, and Charlton, 2003; Parkes, Fairclough, and Ashby, 1993; Rakauskas, Gugerty, and Ward, 2004; Waugh *et al.*, 2000). Interestingly, while time-sharing the two tasks, performance on the phone task suffers too. Thus, the increase in the load also reduces the effectiveness of drivers' ability to handle the phone task or other secondary tasks relative to their performance level on these tasks when they are not driving (Lansdown *et al.*, 2004; Parkes, 1991; Shinar, 2006).

The ecological validity of experimental cell phone studies

The experimental studies reviewed above almost invariably suffer from one or more of the following shortcomings: (1) they used a "one shot" approach; (2) they mislabeled the phone task as "conversation" when in fact it is not; (3) they used a phone task that was paced by the experimenter; and (4) they often did not distinguish between types of users such as younger versus older drivers. The "one shot" approach involves administering the phone task for one trial or one block of trials only. This approach does not allow for learning effects. Because learning involves the process of automation of many controlled actions, it frees attention resources that can be allocated to other tasks. When drivers in an experiment drive with the cell phone only once – typically with an unfamiliar vehicle or a laboratory simulator – they do not have the opportunity to learn or automate any of their actions. In real driving, our behavior is greatly influenced by learning and much of our driving is automated freeing us to engage in other tasks (as discussed in Chapters 5 and 7).

The use of the term "cell phone conversation" has often been misleading because in many studies (including some of my own) the cell phone task had little or no resemblance to actual conversations. Perhaps the first misuse of the term was made by McKnight and McKnight (1993). Using a rudimentary driving simulation they gave their subjects two distracting phone tasks: a conversation with an experimenter which they termed "casual conversation" and a mathematical computational task which they termed "intense conversation." The effects of the conversation on driving were much smaller than those of the math computations but the conclusions were framed in terms of detrimental effects of phone "conversation." Other early studies have also reported very small, if any, effects of actual conversation on driving behavior relative to computational and memory tasks (e.g., Alm and Nilsson, 1995). Other studies that used computational tasks, memory tasks (Parkes, 1991), backward counting (Olsson and Burns, 2000) and logical reasoning tasks further misused (and abused) the term "conversation" either in the text (Patten *et al.*, 2004; Törnros and Bolling, 2005) or even in the title (Atchley and Dressel, 2004; Burns, Parkes, and Lansdown, 2003). Another euphemism for a structured paced phone task has been the use of the term "talking" (Waugh *et al.*, 2000). A common feature of all of these mislabeled tasks is that their attentional demands are purposefully high and likely to cause interference, something that cannot so readily be assumed for a true conversation. Even when the phone task was a true possible conversation, it could vary from "inconsequential" (McKnight and McKnight, 1993; Shinar, 2006) to "topics that are of interest to the drivers" (Strayer and Drews, 2004; Strayer *et al.*, 2003), to "emotionally challenging conversations" (Shinar *et al.*, 2005).

As an illustration, consider the study by Patten *et al.* (2004) with hand-held and hands-free phone. In their study, drivers drove on a Motorway in Sweden and were required to perform two different phone tasks (that Patten *et al.* mislabeled as "conversations"). The "complex conversation" consisted of adding single digit numbers at a fixed pace, and the "simple conversation" required that the drivers merely repeat single digit numbers presented over the phone at the same rate. As expected the hands-free and hand-held phones slowed detection reaction time to peripheral targets to the same degree. However, the nature of the phone task had a significant effect on the responses to the peripheral targets. Relative to the control condition, in which drivers were not involved with a phone task, the simple phone task increased detection reaction time by 12 percent and the complex task increased it by 45 percent.

An interesting validation of the difference between the artificial cognitive task and an actual conversation was provided in a simulation study by Leung *et al.* (2012), who showed that the effects of the cognitive task are similar to the effects of alcohol impairment at BAC = .07, whereas the effects of the natural conversation are equivalent to BAC = .04 – a level that is typically not associated with a statistically significant crash risk, and is below the legal threshold for impairment in most countries.

The issue of pacing is a difficult one to handle. To assure that all subjects in a study are exposed to the exact same conditions of distraction, an artificial experimenter-paced task must be contrived. However, a true conversation – on the phone or with a passenger – is at least partially paced by the driver who can at any time decide whether or not to speak, and even whether or not to pay attention at all. When an experiment employs a real conversation as the distracting task it is difficult to assume that all subjects are equally "loaded" by the phone task (as defined in Chapter 3 – in terms of the attention load imposed by the task). Thus, for the sake of rigorous experimental control a paced task is preferable, but for the sake of ecological validity a partially paced task is preferred.

The final issue is that of individual differences. It is well known that experienced drivers can handle distractions better than novice or old drivers (see Chapters 7 and 8). But many studies only have one relatively homogeneous group from which the results are generalized to all drivers. This requires that studies either have several age groups (as did Hancock *et al.*, 2003), or limit their conclusions to a specific driver category such as older or younger drivers (as did Strayer and Drews, 2004). Also, in most studies experience during the study itself is a parameter (a fixed measure), as the participants typically perform the experimental task only once. Thus, if there is a potentially positive learning effect it is not addressed in these studies. One exception to this paradigm of a single test session is an early study by Brookhuis *et al.* (1991) where 12 volunteer drivers of different ages drove in an instrumented car in real traffic every weekday for three weeks, for a total of 15 drives over the same 13 kilometers route. As expected, over this period the mental workload as measured by the heart beats decreased. In addition performance on the arithmetic phone task improved, and the variability in lane position in the motorway section decreased. A simulator study on the distracting effects of manipulating an MP3 player also showed that with repeated trials, driving performance in all the driving conditions improved. Though visual distraction was greater when manipulating the MP3 player than when not, over a sequence of seven sessions the difference between the two conditions decreased significantly (Chisholm, Caird, and Lockhart, 2008).

In an attempt to control for all of the issues of learning, nature of the "conversation," driver age, and driving difficulty, we conducted a simulator study that manipulated these factors (Shinar *et al.*, 2005). In this study, we sampled drivers from three age groups – young/novice drivers (18 years old), experienced drivers (30-33 years old), and older drivers (60-71 years old). The drivers were required to drive in a driving simulator at three levels of difficulty, with three levels of distraction. The driving task was easiest when drivers were requested to drive at 50 mph and most difficult when they were requested to drive at 65 mph. The three levels of distraction consisted of no distraction, an "emotionally charged conversation," and a computational task. Emotional conversations tend to create higher workload, and result in lower situation awareness (Jeon, Walker, and Gable, 2014), more driving errors (Abdu, Shinar, and Meiran, 2012; Briggs, Hole, and Land, 2011), and less effective glance behavior and visual search (Briggs *et al.*, 2011; Stephens *et al.*, 2013). For the emotionally charged conversation, the experimenter first interviewed the driver about his or her interests, hobbies, job, and/or studies and then used that information to challenge the driver on his attitudes and activities in these areas. The one feature of the study that had not been incorporated into any of the previous studies, except for Brookhuis *et al.*'s (1991) study, was the learning process. Therefore, in our experiment each driver drove five times over the course of two weeks. As predicted, the interference from the emotionally charged conversation was much less than from the computational task, and the interference diminished over practice so that on some measures driving performance after five days was the same with and without the phone task. In parallel, drivers also experienced a decrease in the subjective workload over time. The diminishing effects of the mathematical computation distraction task on vehicle control with practice are illustrated on one measure of performance – steering control – in Figure 13-1. It is quite obvious from this figure that vehicle steering control – while performing the difficult phone task – is initially poor for all drivers, and significantly worse for the older drivers than for the younger ones. However, with practice all groups improve so that by the fifth day of driving the older drivers perform as well as the younger drivers. It is important to note that the improvement in driving while performing the phone task was not at the expense of worsening performance on the phone (math operations) task. In fact, performance on the math operations task reflected a similar pattern, as seen in Figure 13-2. All groups of drivers made more errors initially than they did with practice, with the youngest drivers making the most mistakes. However, as for the driving task, by the fifth day all groups performed at the same level of accuracy.

The results of this study should not be misinterpreted to indicate that with enough practice using a phone while driving is inconsequential to safety. For one thing, we do not know how much practice is needed to achieve such a stage, if it is achievable at all. Second, while talking on the phone may help us learn to combine the two tasks, we may get killed or injured in the process. Finally, the danger of conducting a phone conversation while driving is not constant, but depends on the timing of the driving events and

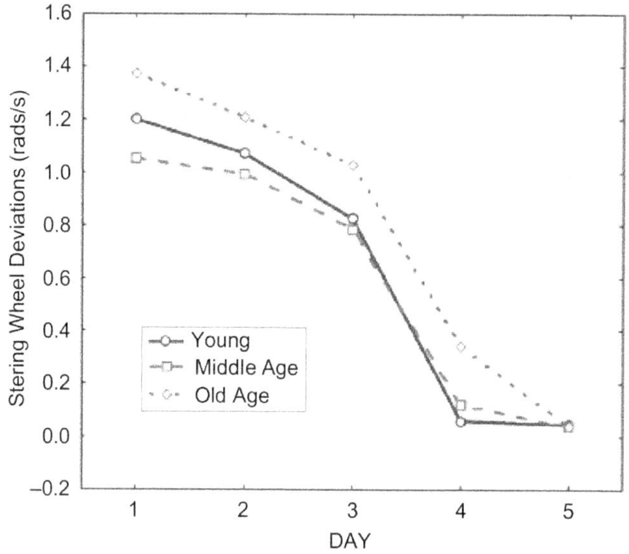

Figure 13-1. The effects interference from a phone task as a function of practice for three driver age groups, on steering wheel deviations – a measure of vehicle control – when required to maintain a speed of 65 mph (from Shinar *et al.*, 2005, with permission from Elsevier).

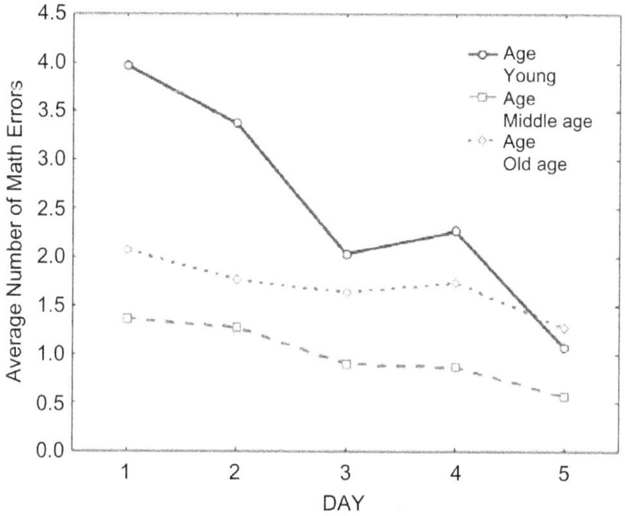

Figure 13-2. The effects of practice on the performance of the computational phone task, for three driver age groups (from Shinar *et al.*, 2005, with permission from Elsevier).

the phone conversation (Hancock *et al.*, 2003), and unexpected events are still likely to pose a greater hazard to drivers who are distracted by the phone (or another source) than to drivers who are alertly monitoring the road and traffic.

But our study too had its own ecological validity problem. It was conducted in a simulator and not in a naturalistic real driving environment. Still, even in a simulated driving task Cooper and Strayer (2008) failed to obtain the effects of practice, especially when their drivers were transferred to a new scenario. However, their results were somewhat paradoxical as they appeared to suggest that practice actually degrades performance as measured by brake reaction time and speed compliance on the one hand, while it reduces crash likelihood on the other hand. Our more recent study on sign detection (described above) that was conducted in a real driving environment showed that a demanding phone task can significantly impair visual detection of targets. Thus, it would appear that though practice improves performance, it is still possible to show impairments from cell phone use in well-controlled simulator studies as well as in real-world driving.

Cell phones and crash risk – where the picture gets complicated

The increased focus on the crash risk of cell phones is justifiably driven by two concerns: (1) the overall increase of cell phones in general and their use while driving in particular, and (2) their documented and consistently demonstrated effects on driving performance. Given the steady increase in cell phone ownership and use while driving, the role of cell phones in crashes varies in different analyses. Yet, relative to the extensive media coverage of the issue it still remains surprisingly low. For instance, in the U.S. an analysis of the NHTSA Crash Worthiness data conducted on injury crashes occurring during the years 1995-1999 indicated that the distraction due to a cell phone was associated with the cause of 1.5 percent of the crashes. An analysis of crash data from the state of Pennsylvania for the years 1999-2000 revealed an involvement in 5.2 percent of the crashes (as reported by Stutts *et al.*, 2003).

One problem with the earlier estimates is that the police whose input is the basis of all national crash data did not have a category for checking distraction from cell phones. In 2005, 21 U.S. states had a code for cell phone use in their police crash reports, and the data from these states indicate that cell phones were a causal factor in less than one percent of all crashes. This is a very small percent. Furthermore, relative to their reported and observed use, these studies actually show under-involvement of cell phones in crashes! However, these findings are quite unreliable (NCSL, 2005), as police do not necessarily check the cell phone providers' records for actual phone use, and surviving drivers may be reluctant to admit cell phone use, especially if they know it is illegal. Later estimates did not provide a consistent level of crash risk from cell phone distraction. Thus, while in 2010 the U.S. National Safety Council estimated that phone-related distractions were responsible for 28 percent of all crashes (NSC, 2010), The U.S. National Highway Traffic Safety Administration estimated that in 2014 distraction of any kind was a causal factor in 18 percent of all police-reported crashes and in 10 percent of fatal crashes. Of these 10 percent, cell phone was identified as the distractor in 13 percent (NHTSA, 2016b); that is, cell phone was the causal factor in only 1.3 percent of fatal crashes. Obviously this is more than a small discrepancy that can be dismissed by the difference in the years. However, this average masks the fact that involvement is not uniformly distributed across all ages. The involvement of cell phones in fatal crashes is twice as high for drivers under 20 years old than for the rest of the driving population, and it is relevant to only one sixth of one percent for drivers 70+ years old (NHTSA, 2012a). These figures are consistent with young drivers' self-reports on crash involvement while using their cell phones (NHTSA, 2012b) and somewhat consistent with the findings of the NHTSA-sponsored 2012 national survey of drivers where only 4 percent of those who were involved in a crash in the past year reported that they were using their cell phone at the time of the crash: 1.6 percent talking, 1.6 percent sending text, and 1.0 percent reading text (Schroeder *et al.*, 2013).

To assess the actual risk of cell phones more carefully controlled studies are needed. Here we find that the estimates are quite methodology-bound; that is, the research method influences the estimated involvement to a large degree. Three epidemiological studies of the relative risk of crashes with cell phones have been often-cited and they are reviewed below. While each of the studies can be faulted for various methodological limitations, the fact that they all indicate over-involvement suggests that increased crash risk is a real phenomenon. On the other hand, estimates derived from naturalistic studies present a more complicated picture.

Epidemiological studies

The first comprehensive epidemiological study was conducted by Redelmeier and Tibshirani (1997) on crash-involved drivers in the Toronto, Canada area. In their study they examined the phone use of 699 crash-involved drivers who had a cell phone registered in their name. Using the phone company's billing records they recorded the exact time and date of all calls that transpired during the week preceding each driver's crash. They then calculated the risk of a crash with a phone relative to the risk without a phone by comparing the probability that the drivers used the phone at the same time of the crash but on a day previous to the crash with the probability of using the phone at the time of the crash itself. For the control period they considered several alternatives including the previous day, the previous same day of the week, and the preceding workday. The "time" used for the analysis varied from the five minutes that immediately preceded the police-recorded time of the crash to the 16-20 minutes before the crash. The results showed that the relative crash risk increased systematically from 1.3 (30 percent above the risk without a phone call) 15 minutes before the crash to 4.8 (nearly five times as high as without a phone call) 1-5 minutes before the crash. Furthermore, the relative crash risk did not differ significantly between male and female drivers, among different age and experience groups, and between hand-held and hands-free phones. There were some trends that suggested that young drivers are more at risk than older drivers, and that the risk decreases with experience in using the cell phones. However, possibly because of the (relatively) small sample size for these detailed analyses, these trends were not statistically significant. Still, the difference between those who have been using a cell phone for a year or less (relative risk, RR = 7.8) and those who reported using it for 5-6 years (RR = 2.8) is consistent with the findings that risk decreases with practice (Brookhuis *et al.* 1991; Shinar *et al.*, 2005). One other interesting finding was that 39 percent of the drivers used their cell phone to make a call immediately after the crash, suggesting that the phone cell may be a very useful post-crash life-sustaining device (see Chapter 18).

The second study, already mentioned above, was conducted by Laberge-Nadeau and her associates (2003) in Quebec Canada, where 41 percent of the male drivers and 25 percent of the female drivers had cell phones at the time. All of these drivers gave permission to examine their cell phone use records. To evaluate the crash risk associated with cell phone use the researchers compared the risk of a crash for those who reported that they used their phone while driving with the risk of a crash for those who reported that they did not use the phone while driving. They found that the relative risk of having a crash (both injury crashes and property damage-only crashes) in any given year was 38 percent higher for those who used their cell phones while driving than for those who did not. Furthermore, there was a dose-response relationship between the frequency of cell phone use and the relative risk of a crash, with the heaviest users having crash rates approximately 100 percent higher than the rare users, who did not differ significantly from the non-users. On the basis of these analyses, Laberge-Nadeau and her associates concluded that cell phone users have a higher rate of collisions than drivers who do not use their cell phone while driving. However, they stopped short of concluding that the use of the cell phone per se increases the risk of collision. This could not be claimed because after they controlled for other known crash risk factors – such as the number of kilometers driven, the driver's age, amount of night driving, and level of education – the remaining increase in risk (for all crashes combined) from cell phone use dropped from an average of 38 percent to 10 percent for men and to 21 percent for women. These percentages were still statistically significantly higher than chance variations (because of the very large sample), but in terms of practical considerations they are not very much higher than chance. Thus, much of the apparent crash risk involved in the use of cell phone was probably due to the fact that the cell phone users were higher-risk drivers in general, being younger, driving more miles, driving more at night, and being less educated.

The third study, by McEvoy *et al.* (2005), was an epidemiological survey conducted on crash-involved Australian drivers. Using hospital admittance records they identified 456 crash-injured drivers who had a cell phone. With the drivers' consent, they checked the phone companies' records to determine whether or not each of these drivers was using the cell phone within the ten minutes period that preceded the crash. This information provided the researchers with the odds of the number of crashes with associated cell phone use relative to the number of crashes unrelated to cell phone use. To adjust for the frequency of use in actual driving, the researchers then calculated the odds of using the cell phones while driving in a similar circumstance. To do that they identified an identical time a day before the crash, three days before the crash, and seven days before the date and time of the crash and determined for each of these time "windows" the number of drivers who were driving and using the phone and the number of drivers who were driving and not using the phone. The ratio of these two odds – the odds ratio – is a direct measure of the over- or under-involvement of cell phones in injury accidents. The findings were remarkably similar to those reported by Redelmeier and Tibshirani (1997) eight years before. The odds ratio was OR = 4.1, indicating that the use of a cell phone while driving creates a fourfold increase in the risk of a crash. More detailed analysis also showed that the increase in risk is approximately the same for hand-held and hands-free phone (OR = 4.9 versus OR = 3.8, respectively; and the difference was not statistically significant), giving strong epidemiological support to the laboratory and on-road experimental research that has compared the two modes of phone use.

In summary, the three studies quite conclusively demonstrate that using a cell phone while driving is associated with an increased crash risk. The increase appears to be small when the analysis is the crudest (Laberge-Nadeau *et al.*, 2003), but it is quite high with an average of a fourfold increase when the analysis of the risk in both the crash situation and the control situation is based on the same drivers and is therefore less affected by confounding variables (McEvoy *et al.*, 2005; Redelmeier and Tibshirani, 1997).

Alternative analysis and alternative estimates

The relative risk estimates of the epidemiological studies have been questioned on three different grounds: (1) on the basis of a reanalysis of the data and analyses of other data (Young, 2012, 2013), (2) because the dramatic increase in cell phone use while driving has not been reflected in a parallel increase in crash rates (Farmer, Braitman, and Lund, 2010), and (3) because NDS studies failed to show that the act of talking on the phone is associated with either crashes or safety-critical events (Fitch *et al.*, 2013). Young found in a GPS tracked sample of 439 cars in the Puget Sound area of the state of Washington that given driving in one period (equivalent to the crash period in the epidemiological studies), the likelihood of driving in the matching control period was only one fourth that of the first period. This would require a correction in the Relative Risk of a distraction-related crash or injury from approximately 4.0 to 1.0, as in one-fourth of the control periods the people were not even driving. This adjustment essentially nullifies any effect of the cell phone. Also, in an interesting approach to the issue Bhargava and Pathanya (2013) studied the use rates and crash rates in a U.S. region where the cost of calling or receiving a call dropped at 9 pm. Although the use rate after 9 pm went up by 7.2 percent, the crash rate did not increase significantly. Thus, it seems that the effects obtained by Redelmeier and Tibshirani (1997) and by McEvoy *et al.* (2005) may be methodology-bound and converging evidence from different approaches may not support their conclusions. Finally, there is one other weakness to these studies. While the phone records are very accurate with respect to the time a call is initiated and terminated, the time of the crash is not that accurate as it depends on the time that someone notifies the police. Given that the first thing people do after a crash is call a spouse, parent, or friend, it is also likely that in many of the cell phone-related crashes the phone was actually used *after* the crash and not before it. This possibility is underscored by Chung and Chang's (2015) finding in Korea that the police crash reported times differed from that of the vehicles' factory-installed EDRs (in-vehicle Event Data Recorders, or "black boxes") by an average of 29 minutes.

In an attempt to provide a summary quantitative assessment of the crash risk of cell phone conversations, Elvik (2011) conducted meta-analyses of 11 studies that analyzed crash data, and Caird *et al.* (2014) synthesized the results of four naturalistic driving studies that examined the effect of phone use on safety-critical events and crashes. In Elvik's analysis, the distraction from the phone conversation was analyzed for the whole activity: from dialing/picking up the phone, through the conversation, and until hanging up. Thus, it did not distinguish among the visual, cognitive, and manual distractions. In his analysis, he distinguished between two types of studies: ones (five studies) where the phone use was known and the timing of the crashes and the phone conversations were clearly established, and ones (six studies) where the phone use was unknown so they could only distinguished between drivers who had a phone and those who did not, and thus a direct link between engaging in a phone task and the crash could not be established. This is important because in these between-subjects studies drivers who have a phone and in general talk while driving may be involved in other high-risk driving behaviors as well. This in fact was the artifact in Laberge-Nadeau *et al.*'s study. To define the impact of the phone use, Elvik used the Odds Ratio. His meta-analysis revealed that the average odds ratio for the studies where the use of the phone was unknown was small at OR = 1.28 and not statistically significant. In contrast the odd ratio for the studies where the phone use was known was OR = 2.86 (with a confidence interval of 1.72-4.75) and statistically significant. Thus, summing across all published – relatively reliable – available data Elvik concluded that using a cell phone is associated with nearly three times the risk of a crash relative to driving without engaging in a phone activity.

To determine the locus of the interference in the sequence of actions during phone tasks, naturalistic driving studies (NDS) document crashes and safety-critical events in relation to the specific phone tasks the drivers were involved in immediately preceding or at the time of the crash. In these "case cross-over" studies, behavior at the time of a crash or near-crash is coded relative to phone use, and then this odds of phone use to no-phone use is compared to the odds at a different "control" period to provide the odds ratio. Caird *et al.* (2014) examined four naturalistic driving studies that have done that; all conducted by researchers at the Virginia Technical Institute. All the studies provided odds ratios for the complete phone calls as well as for their components. In all of these, the conversation itself – and the cognitive load associated with it – did not increase the risk significantly. This finding is very much at odds with the conclusion that prevailed until the results of these studies were published, and for that matter it is also at odds with the conclusion stated in the previous edition of this book. This means that the cognitive load posed by just talking on the phone is not enough to increase crash risk; a most significant conclusion relative to our proclivity for on-road time-sharing of the driving with talking on the phone.

However, the visual/manual activities involved in the phone call – looking at the phone, dialing, picking it up, and putting it down – did elevate the crash or near-crash risk. These studies obtained average elevated odds ratios for these visual/manual distractions of OR = 2.79 (with a confidence interval of 1.6–4.9) for drivers in their personal cars (Klauer *et al.*, 2006), OR = 5.93 (4.6–7.7) for commercial motor-vehicle drivers (Olson *et al.*, 2009), OR = 3.51 (2.9–4.3), for bus and truck drivers (Hickman and Hanowski,

2012), and OR = 3.34 (1.76-6.35) for passenger car drivers (Fitch *et al.*, 2013). In a fifth naturalistic driving study of teen drivers, Klauer *et al.* (2014) obtained OR = 8.32 for dialing and OR = 7.05 for reaching for the cell phone, Common to all of these studies, was the pooling of real crashes with "safety critical events," which were essentially situations judged by the researchers as near-crashes. This was done because the number of actual crashes was quite small. However, the most recent analyses of the distraction from various cell-phone-related activities was based on newly released SHRP2 data (see Chapter 2) that contained close to 1,000 non-trivial crashes. A trivial crash was one without any physical damage or bodily harm such as a "tire strike." With a data set that large, there was no need to combine real crashes with near-crashes. Two examinations of the driver activities at the time of each crash relative to the same driver's activities in a sample of non-crash episodes yielded high statistically significant odds ratios of OR = 4.96 for "manipulating a cell phone" (Kidd and McCartt, 2015, with a sample of 845 crashes), and OR = 12.2 for dialing on a hand-held cell phone (Dingus *et al.*, 2016, with a sample of 905 crashes). However, the conversation itself yielded odds ratios of approximately 2.0 in both studies. Furthermore, after adjusting for some confounding variables Kidd and McCartt noted that their conversation OR was no longer significant. Similarly, when Young (2017) made some adjustments for potential biases in Dingus et al.'s results the odds ratio for the conversation itself was also no longer significant. Thus, across the board all the naturalistic data studies demonstrate a very high crash risk from the visual/manual engagement involved in phone conversations, but not from the cognitive load of the conversation itself.

Hands-free versus hand-held: it is all in our heads

In an attempt to reduce the dangers of cell phone, several countries and jurisdictions have instituted laws to control their use (41 U.S. states and the District of Columbia – McCartt, Kidd, and Teoh, 2014; Australia, Austria, Germany, Greece, India, Israel, Italy, Japan, Netherlands, Norway, Poland, Russia, U.K. – http://www.cellular-news.com/car_bans/). In rare cases, the prohibition is total, involving all cell phone use (e.g., Indiana, Massachusetts, New York, North Carolina). The most common prohibition is to allow hands-free phones and ban the use of hand-held phones (e.g., Australia, Denmark, Israel, Arizona, California, Connecticut, Hawaii, Kansas, Minnesota, Mississippi, Montana, Nebraska, Ohio, Pennsylvania, Rhode Island, Virginia, Vermont, Washington, and the District of Columbia). In the U.S. some of the more limited restrictions, apply only to young and novice drivers and to school bus drivers. Currently, according to the World Health Organization, 139 countries prohibit the use of hand-held cell phones, and 31 countries prohibit the use of both hand-held and hands-free phones while driving (WHO, 2015). In other words most countries now have some restriction on using the phone while driving. The restrictions are facilitated by the fact that there is public support for laws that restrict phone use, and even among users of cell phones.

Drivers are also sensitive to the different loads imposed by different phone-related tasks. In a survey of 237 drivers who owned a cell phone, Wogalter and Mayhorn (2005) found that not all phone-related activities are perceived as equally dangerous. Their results, partially reproduced in Table 13-10, show that nearly all drivers (90 percent) believed that pressing the buttons on the phone (as in dialing) can "cause an accident." Note that this survey was conducted before there were any empirical data, such as the NDS findings, to support this. In general, as could be expected, heavier phone users were less likely than light users to perceive using the cell phone as dangerous. Perhaps the most interesting aspect of Wogalter and Mayhorn's finding is the low percentage of drivers who considered the use of a hands-free phone as dangerous – 19 percent regardless of the amount of phone use (versus 50 percent for hand-held phone). White, Eiser, and Harris (2004) also questioned people about their perceived risk of various activities and found that using a hand-held phone while driving was considered very dangerous; dangerous as reading a map while driving, and just slightly less dangerous than shaving or applying makeup. In contrast, using a hands-free cell phone was considered almost risk-free, even less than sneezing. How valid are these beliefs and what is their basis? Obviously, based on the earlier crash research reviewed above these perceptions are quite invalid. Using a hands-free phone may reduce some of the subjective physical load but not the objective mental load (Burns *et al.*, 2002; Matthews *et al.*, 2003). Furthermore, as the findings of the recent naturalistic studies demonstrate the hands-free phone is really not hands-free as it does not relieve its user from the visual/manual load involved in handling the phone prior to and after the conversation.

The similarity in the cognitive load of hands-free and hand-held load in terms of driving performance and crash involvement has led most researchers to conclude that the culprit is the cognitive load imposed by the conversation. This is the cognitive demand on our limited resources of attention, a demand that is the same with a hand-held and a hands-free phone.

Table 13-10. Proportion of cell phone owning drivers who believe that a phone-related activity can "cause an accident" (with standard deviations in parentheses) (from Wogalter and Mayhorn, 2005, with permission of the Human Factors and Ergonomics Society).

Operator Action Statements	**Amount of Cellular Phone Usage**		
	Lower	**Higher**	**Mean**
Pressing buttons on the cellular phone	.90 (.32)	.92 (.30)	.91
Answering the cellular phone	.74 (.46)*	.58 (.50)	.66
Talking on the cellular phone	.57 (.50)*	.42 (.49)	.50
Using a hands-free cellular phone	.19 (.38)	.19 (.39)	.19
Mean	.60	.53	

Notes: Ratings are based on yes/no responses coded as 1 and 0, respectively. Higher scores indicate participants' increasing beliefs that an operator action might cause an accident. Amount of cellular phone use was split at the median of 60 minutes (lower: n = 107; higher: n = 130).
*p < .001.

This has been repeatedly demonstrated in the crash studies reviewed above (Redelmeier and Tibshirani, 1997; and McEvoy *et al.*, 2005) and in multiple experimental studies (Mazzae *et al.*, 2004; Patten *et al.*, 2004; Strayer and Drews, 2007; Strayer *et al.*, 2005, 2015a; Strayer and Johnston, 2001). All of these studies have repeatedly shown that hand-held and hands-free phones are equally distracting and harmful to vehicle control and various driving tasks, including braking reactions in response to emergencies.

There is one particularly interesting study on the difference between hand-held and hands-free phones. This study was conducted by Matthews *et al.* (2003) on a sample of 13 New Zealand drivers who drove on a rural road while performing a phone task. The phone task involved listening to and repeating words presented at the rate of one every two seconds. The interference from the phone was evaluated in terms of the intelligibility of the words (based on the correctness of the repeated words) and the subjective mental task load that the drivers felt in performing the phone task. There were three types of phones: a hand-held phone, a hands-free phone with an external speaker, and a hands-free phone with a personal (ear-based) speaker. The subjective task load was evaluated with measure originally developed by U.S. National Air and Space Administration (NASA-TLX) in which people evaluate the subjective load they experience in terms of the mental demands, physical demands, temporal demands, performance, effort and frustration they feel in the process of performing the combined driving and phone task. Matthews *et al.* found that relative to the control condition when the drivers did not have a phone task, all three phone types caused an increase in the task load. Perhaps less obvious and more interesting and relevant to our immediate concern were the differences they found in the subjective workload among the three phone types. The differences were manifested in two dimensions only: the subjective physical demands and the frustration. The frustration was the greatest with the speaker-based hands-free phone and it was associated with its poorer sound quality. But the physical demands were experienced as greater with the hand-held phone than with either one of the hands-free phones. In an earlier study with a driving simulator, Burns *et al.* (2002) also found that the subjectively experienced task load is greater with a hand-held phone than with a hands-free phone. These findings may explain why drivers think that a hands-free phone is safe. It simply *feels* less demanding. These findings also demonstrate that our subjective feeling of task load is not always consistent with our performance, and in the case of cell phones and driving this disparity creates a dangerous situation.

In at least one study, however, drivers rated the hands-free and hand-held phones as equally demanding, for both dialing and for conversing. Törnros and Bolling (2005) had drivers drive through 70 kilometers of urban and rural environments in an advance driving simulator while performing two phone tasks: a paced serial addition task (patterned after Brookhuis *et al.*, 1991), which they termed "conversation," and a dialing task in which the driver had to dial a number displayed on the phone. One group of drivers used a hands-free phone while another group used a hand-held phone. Objective mental load was assessed by measuring reaction time to a peripheral target that appeared on the screen, and subjective load was assessed by asking the subjects to rate the subjective mental load at the end of the drive. All the analyses indicated that the detrimental effects of the hands-free phone were equivalent to those of the hand-held phone. Reaction time to the peripheral stimulus increased by 0.16 seconds when the subjects conversed on the phone and by an average of 0.27 seconds when they dialed a number. Conversing on the phone resulted in an increase of 13 percent in the number of peripheral targets missed, and dialing increased the misses by 24 percent. In both modes, conversation did not affect the lateral control of the vehicle, while dialing disrupted it; but again to the same extent with both phone modes. In general the phone task was associated with speed reductions by an average of 2-4 km/hr in all but the hands-free conversation task; where speed was unaffected. Also, in contrast to the other studies, the rated effort with the hand-held and hands-free phones was essentially the same. One possibility for this result is that the drivers only rated the difficulty of conversing and dialing together, and dialing with a hands-free may be more demanding because the driver has to direct the gaze further away from the road to the fixed-base phone. Still, the subjective sensations were not a good reflection of actual impairments. Thus, most of the drivers were unaware of their poorer lateral control or their speed reductions, leading to the disturbing conclusion that although drivers may feel the stress of the added task, they are oblivious to its detrimental effects on their driving.

Given the general absence of significant differences between hand-held and hands-free phone on driving performance and on crash involvement, and given the perception of many drivers that conversing with hands-free phones is less demanding, it is interesting to note that using a hands-free phone may create a paradoxical effect of misleading drivers who install hands-free phone to use the phone more readily than drivers who do not have a speaker phone. This was corroborated by Gras *et al.* (2007) who found that drivers who have hands-free phones use them while driving significantly more often than those who do not. Consequently the current trend to limit the use of cell phones by selectively prohibiting hand-held phones is probably counterproductive because these laws mislead drivers to believe that hands-free phones are safe – when in fact they are not. In addition, their impact even on the use of hand-held phone is inconsistent with indications that after an initial decline, in some jurisdictions use rate goes up again (McCartt *et al.*, 2006b; McCartt and Hellinga, 2007), or they are replaced by texting (Goodwin, OBrien, and Foss, 2012).

In conclusion, we are left with seemingly two inconsistent sets of findings: (1) similar detrimental effects of conversations with hands-free and hand-held devices on driving performance measures and crash involvement, and (2) NDS studies that show that the talking/listening phase – the one associated with only cognitive load – is not associated with increased crash risk. This means that we should perhaps revise our thinking about the distracting effect of conversing with hand-held or hands-free phone, altogether. The similarity in the distractibility of the two types of phones is probably not due to the common cognitive task but to the fact that both still involve visual and manual distractions associated with initiating and terminating a call. The mere act of holding the phone in one hand is not a sufficient manual distraction to interfere with the driving to the level of increasing the likelihood of a crash. This conclusion does not negate the fact that time-sharing of driving with a purely cognitive distracting task does not impair driving; only that the impairment is such that in actual driving with real conversations drivers can compensate for it enough so that it does not increase crash risk.

Nature of the phone task and the role of cognitive load

In assessing the distraction from phone use, we have already distinguished among three sources of potential distraction: visual distraction, cognitive distraction, and manual distraction; that is, the distraction caused by redirection of the visual gaze to enter a number or type a message, the distraction caused by cognitive preoccupation with the phone conversation or content of a message, and the distraction caused by the needed manual manipulation involved in dialing, keying data, and picking up or moving the phone, respectively. In most conversations (but not in texting), the visual and manual manipulations take a small fraction of the total time. Consequently, and also because it is often difficult to distinguish among the three phases (e.g., in the epidemiological studies) most studies have focused on the impairing effects of the cognitive distraction.

The focus on cognitive overload and cognitive distraction can also be traced to the similarity in the effects of hands-free and hand-held phones (Caird *et al.*, 2008). Also, experimental studies have provided further support for this by showing a dose-response relationship between the difficulty of the conversation and the complexity of the drive on the one hand and the impaired driving performance on the other hand (McKnight and McKnight, 1993; Shinar *et al.*, 2005). In addition, research with functional MRI has demonstrated that responding to simple statements while "driving" on a winding road presented on a small screen in the MRI machine impairs not only the driving performance, but also the brain activity. When listening to the messages while driving the activation of the parietal lobe (that is associated with spatial processing that is critical for driving) decreased by 37 percent compared to the activity level when driving undisturbed (Just, Keller, and Cynkar, 2008).

Probably the most comprehensive study of the cognitive load imposed by different distracting tasks was done by Strayer and his associates (2015b) where drivers were given seven different potentially distracting tasks in three situations: when performed alone, when performed while driving in a driving simulator, and when performed while driving on the road. A unique feature of the tasks was that they were primarily cognitive in their demands. Cognitive load was measured using subjective reports (NASA-TLX), physiological data (P300 of the EEG-based Evoked Response Potential), secondary task performance (detection reaction time), and driving performance (brake reaction time, following distance, and glances to the sides at cross-roads and pedestrian crossings). A unified measure of cognitive load was then calculated in terms of average standard score from all the above measures. Using this derived measure of cognitive load, Strayer *et al.* were able to rank-order the seven tasks they evaluated. Figure 13-3 illustrates the composite cognitive workload from each of the tasks used in the study. In this figure the control situation of driving without any additional task is listed as "single" and receives a score of 1. Relative to this situation the added cognitive load increases gradually with listening to the radio, listening to an excerpt from an audio book, a casual conversation with a passenger, talking to a family member on a hand-held phone, the same but talking on a hands-free phone, communicating (e.g., emailing) via a simulated speech-based system, and the most difficult task of simultaneously solving math problems while performing a memory task (OSPAN).

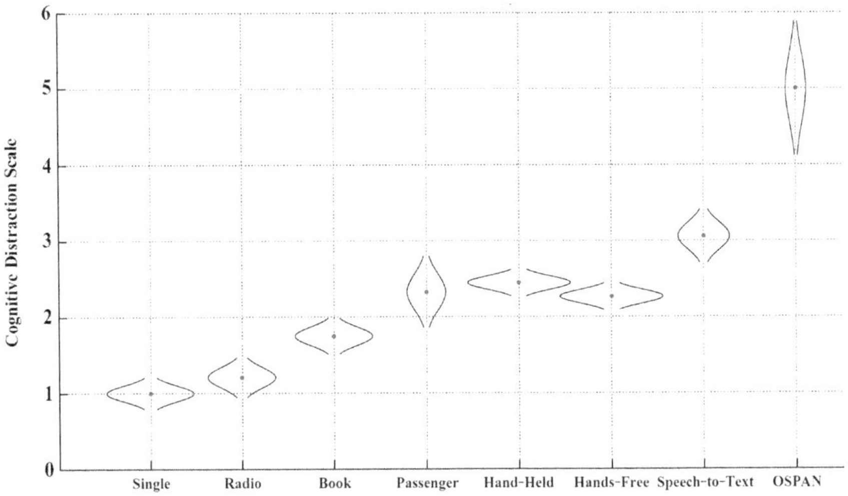

Figure 13-3. Cognitive distraction from seven tasks relative to driving without an additional task ("Single"). The distraction scale is a composite of standardized scores on physical, secondary, subjective, and physiological measures of workload. Circles indicate the point estimate for each condition, and the cat eyes indicate the 95 percent confidence intervals normally distributed around the respective point estimates (from Strayer *et al.*, 2015b, with permission from Sage Publishing).

The findings are interesting in several respects. First, listening to the radio is no more demanding than driving without any (external) distractions. This validates the use of "radio" as a benchmark against which some studies have assessed the distraction from various sources. Second, listening to a book is slightly more distracting probably because the driver has to attend to it continuously in order not to miss significant information. Third, listening to a passenger, and talking on the phone – hand-held or hands-free – are equally distracting and not much more demanding than listening to an audio book. Fourth, the conversation through an automated speech-to-text system may not be the solution to the risks of texting as it was cognitively more demanding than all other tasks except for the artificial and very difficult OSPAN.

Strayer *et al.*'s (2015b) findings are important because they are based on more than just one experiment and one (or very few measures) of load, and because they involve (almost) purely cognitive tasks that are compared to each other in the same setting and on the same drivers. As expected, their findings support previous findings that hands-free and hand-held conversations are equally distracting, but surprisingly they also show that neither task is more distracting than conversing with a passenger. Also unexpected is the finding that audio communication with a text-to-voice interface is actually much more demanding than a phone conversation. Though this could be an artifact of the novelty of the system it is also important to note that in this study the system was error-free; something to which current systems can only aspire. Also, in an earlier study Lee *et al.* (2001) also concluded that speech-based email can have a very high cognitive load.

While Strayer *et al.*'s analyses do provide a scale of distraction they do not provide a benchmark of the level of distraction that significantly increases crash risk beyond a critical threshold. Thus, the issue of how dangerous is this information overload remains unresolved.

As important as Strayer *et al.*'s study is toward the scaling of cognitive load and cognitive distraction it is important to note that it provides no indication of the relationship between the index level of different distractors and crash risk. Also, it has been challenged on various levels. The process of using the different measures and combining them involves some unwarranted methodological and psychometric assumptions (Shinar, 2015), it ignores drivers' compensatory behaviors (Young, 2015), and its relation to cognitive overload in actual driving, that is, its ecological validity, has also been challenged on various grounds (Caird, 2015; Fisher, 2015; Hancock and Sawyer, 2015). Despite these criticisms, it remains the first systematic attempt to scale some of the common distracting tasks that have been studied in the context of driving. In short, the main challenge in Strayer *et al.*'s study is to determine the extent to which it can be validly generalized to actual driving with all of its inherent complexities (Lee and Boyle, 2015).

Cell phones' effects relative to other impairing situations

The very consistent findings of the impairing effects of cell phones – from both experimentally controlled studies as well as epidemiological crash analyses and NDS – make its comparison to other sources of impairment very appealing. It is appealing because it may help us better understand the risk if we can compare it to the crash risk for acknowledged sources of impairment (such as alcohol and fatigue) or to other potential sources of distraction with which we seem to be quite comfortable (such as listening to music or talking to passengers).

Cell phone distraction relative to alcohol impairment

The most extensively studied source of driving impairment is alcohol (see Chapter 11). Research on the effects of alcohol shows a very robust relationship between blood alcohol concentrations and interference with driving tasks and crash involvement. Consequently, almost all countries have restrictions on drinking and driving that are specified in terms of specific blood alcohol levels. Therefore, it is interesting to compare the cell phone effects to the effects of alcohol at a specific threshold level. Two studies – one in England and one in the U.S. – have done this. Both studies compared the effects of a cell phone task to alcohol impairment at BAC = 0.08 percent, the legal threshold in England and in the U.S.

In the first study, Burns *et al.* (2002) had British drivers drive a fixed-base simulator under various road conditions at a desired speed of 60 mph. The drivers were either impaired by alcohol, distracted by a hands-free or a hand-held phone conversation with an experimenter, or unimpaired and undistracted (the control condition). Both the cell phone task and the alcohol impaired driving, but the specific effects were quite different.

First, when unimpaired and not on the phone drivers were able to maintain a steady speed quite close to the desired 60 mph. When on the phone the drivers compensated for its distraction by slowing down by approximately 2 mph. In contrast, when alcohol-impaired the drivers speeded up by approximately 1.5 mph. Second, reaction time to warning signs was impaired by both alcohol and conversation (relative to the control condition), but the effect was much greater when conversing on the phone than when impaired by alcohol. Third, when the drivers were alcohol-impaired they did not rate the mental effort of the drive as greater than in the control condition, while when they talked on the phone they rated the mental load as significantly higher. This pattern of results suggests that while using a cell phone driver performance is impaired, but drivers are aware of the impairment and – at least partially – compensate for it. In contrast, alcohol impairment is more insidious because drivers are often oblivious to it and make no attempts to compensate for it.

The second study was conducted on American drivers by Strayer and Drews (2007). In their study, drivers in fixed-base simulator responded to the braking of a lead car while engaged in a (real) phone conversation. In one session, they drove while under the influence of 0.08 percent BAC and in another session they drove without alcohol. In each session, in one segment of the drive they drove while conversing with a hands-free phone, in one segment they conversed on a hand-held phone, and one segment they were not distracted by a phone task. To control for learning effects, the order of the sessions and segments was counterbalanced across subjects. The results of the study showed that both the cell phone conversation and the alcohol degraded performance relative to the control condition. The average performance levels on each of the measures without any alcohol and phone distraction (baseline), with alcohol impairment, and with cell phone distraction are presented in Table 13-11 (because there were no significant differences in performance between the hands-free and hand-held phone, only the average performance of the two phone modes is presented in the table).

It is clear from Strayer and Drews' (2006) results that both alcohol and conversing on the phone impair driving performance, but again the specific effects are quite different. For example, while under the influence of alcohol the drivers assumed greater risks by maintaining shorter safety margins; in terms of both shorter headways to the car ahead and in terms of shorter time-to-collision (from the moment they braked in response to the lead car's braking). On the other hand, the distraction from the cell phone affected their attention level which significantly delayed the brake reaction time (to the braking of the lead car), relative to the control and alcohol condition.

In conclusion, the two studies indicate that driving is impaired by both distraction from a cell phone and by alcohol. Although Strayer and Drews (2006) conclude from these results that "driving performance was more impaired when drivers were conversing on a cell phone than when these same drivers were intoxicated at .08%," it is very hard to draw such conclusion because there is no logical scale on which performance on the different measures in Table 13-11 can be combined. Consequently, all that we can say on the basis of the experimental evidence is that both alcohol and phones impair driving, that the former increases risk-taking behaviors while the latter decreases attention

Table 13-11. Driver performance in simulator when under the influence of 0.08% BAC and when talking on a cell phone, relative to driving without alcohol and without a phone conversation (from Strayer and Drews, 2007, with permission from Oxford University Press).

	Alcohol	**Baseline**	**Cell Phone**
Total accidents	0	0	3
Brake reaction time (milliseconds)	779 (33)	777 (33)	849 (36)
Maximum braking force	69.8 (3.7)	56.7 (2.6)	55.5 (3.0)
Speed (mph)	52.8 (2.0)	55.5 (0.7)	53.8 (1.3)
Mean following distance (meters)	26.0 (1.7)	27.4 (1.3)	28.4 (1.7)
SD following distance (meters)	10.3 (0.6)	9.5 (0.5)	11.8 (0.8)
Time-to-collision (seconds)	8.0 (0.4)	8.5 (0.3)	8.1 (0.4)
Time-to-collision < 4 seconds	3.0 (0.7)	1.5 (0.3)	1.9 (0.5)

to the driving, and the inattention due to phone distraction can slow reaction time to critical on-road effects more than alcohol intoxication at the legal threshold level of 0.08 percent BAC.

Cell phone distraction relative to distraction from passengers

Comparing cell phone effects to passengers' effects is complicated, because neither task has a simple and uniform effect. Therefore it is not surprising that some of the research suggests that cell phone conversations are more disruptive to driving than conversations with passengers (Drews, Pasaputhi, and Strayer, 2008); some research suggests that they may be even less disruptive (Horrey and Wickens, 2006); and some research indicates that they are roughly equally disruptive (Strayer *et al.*, 2015b). Even within individual studies not all measures reflect the same pattern. For example, Waugh *et al.* (2000) found that their drivers slowed down more while engaged in a phone task than while conversing with a passenger, even though the drivers' self-reported subjective workload was essentially the same in the two conditions. One argument for the greater distraction from a cell phone than from a passenger is that the person on the other end of the line (admittedly an anachronistic term) is not aware of the traffic situation and therefore does not modulate the pace of information relative to the driving demands. In contrast, the person on the other side of the car is not only aware of the situation, but can assist the driver with another pair of eyes. Though some research that examined this issue directly failed to confirm this hypothesis (Amado and Ulupinar, 2005; Gugerty, Rakauskas, and Brooks, 2004), other research did. Charlton (2009) and Drews *et al.* (2008) found that passengers in a driving simulator modulated their conversation relative to the demands of the drive and suppressed the conversation in the presence of road hazards. Occasionally, they even pointed out the hazard to the drivers. Drews *et al.* (2008) also noted more references to the traffic situation in the conversation with a passenger than with a remote conversant. Consequently, compared to a having a partner on a cell phone, with in-vehicle partners engaged in the same general conversation the drivers had faster reaction times to hazards, lower approach speeds, and better avoidance of road hazards. An even more direct test of the source of interference was done by Gaspar *et al.* (2014). In their study, they compared driving and conversations under four conditions: (1) when the driver in a simulator drove alone and did not converse with anyone (2) when the driver conversed with a passenger in the car, (3) when the driver conversed on a cell phone, and (4) when the conversant on the cell phone had a videophone in which he viewed the road and the driver's face on a video screen in real time. They found that collision rates with merging cars were highest when conversing on the cell phone, and lower and similar when the conversant was either a passenger or had the benefits of the video. Also, like Drews *et al.* (2008) the conversations were modulated, the utterances were shorter, and more references were made to the traffic when the conversant was either a passenger or had the benefit of the video scene. Nonetheless, passengers can still be distracting. In a simulator study where hazards were only briefly displayed, White and Caird (2010) found that the more attractive and extroversive the passenger the more he or she are likely to cause the driver to miss sudden brief hazards. Thus, it appears that passengers can have either a distracting or a supporting effect in the car, depending on the role they assume. Together these results indicate that passengers may be less disruptive to driving than a cell phone conversant, but depending on their characteristics and the dynamics between them and the driver they can also be more disruptive. Finally, in real outdoor driving Crundall *et al.* (2005) also found that relative to driving while conversing on the phone or talking to a blindfolded passenger, driving with a passenger who was not blindfolded resulted in fewer utterances, especially in the most demanding urban environment.

One reason for the inconsistent findings may be the different phone and non-phone tasks involved. As noted above, often the so called phone conversations are not true conversations but demanding experimenter-paced information processing tasks, that disrupt driving much more than naturalistic conversations (e.g., McKnight and McKnight, 1993; Shinar *et al.*, 2005) such as those that are likely to be conducted with passengers. In fact, in naturalistic driving situations the presence of passengers generally (with the exception of young drivers with young passengers – see Chapter 6) has a positive effect on driving behavior (Shinar and Compton, 2004) and crash involvement (Klauer *et al.*, 2006; Olson *et al.*, 2009).

Another reason for the inconsistent findings is the mediating effect of the driver's age. Bédard and Mayers (2004) analyzed the U.S. crash fatality data (FARS) and found that in general the presence of passengers was a significant risk of an unsafe action that led to the crash, and that the relative risk increased as the number of passengers increased: from $RR = 1.32$ with one passenger to $RR = 2.15$ with 3+ passengers. In contrast, for drivers 65+ years old the presence of passengers actually decreased the likelihood of an unsafe act, and thus they had a "protective" effect rather than a disruptive effect. Chen *et al.* (2000), also using the FARS data and some other data, compared the rate of fatal crashes/per 10 million trips and obtained similar results. For drivers 16 and 27 years old, there was a significant increase in relative risk from passengers; a risk that rose from 1.4 for one passengers to approximately 3 for 3+ passengers. But for drivers 30-59 years old passenger presence actually reduced the relative risk by 20-40 percent regardless of the number of passengers. Thus, we can conclude that passengers per se are not a threatening distraction, but the nature of the interaction with the passengers (which is often age-related) may be.

When the phone tasks are identical to the conversations conducted with a passenger, the differences tend to disappear. An example of the effects of the two modes of controlled distraction is provided by Burns *et al.* (2003). In their study, they required drivers to respond to specific warning signs by flashing their lights. While they drove they were asked to perform various in-vehicle tasks (such as adjusting fan, radio, changing compact disks, etc.), or conduct a hands-free cell phone conversation, or converse with the experimenter who acted as a passenger sitting next to them. Relative to the control condition – driving without any distraction task – all distracting tasks interfered equally with the driving, causing greater variance in speed, lane position, and time headways. However, significant differences between the tasks were manifest in the reaction times to the warning signs. Average reaction times were shortest in the control condition (0.9 seconds), longer for the in-vehicle tasks (1.35 seconds) and conversations with passenger condition (1.3 seconds), and longest in the hands-free cell phone condition (1.45 seconds). A similar pattern was obtained in the drivers' ranking of their mental load: being highest with the cell phone and lowest in the control condition. Collet *et al.* (2009) also found that when driving on a "private track" that resembled a winding rural road their drivers' reaction time and physiological stress levels increased in a similar manner to a remote phone conversation as to a passenger engaging the drivers in the same conversations.

Lastly, in an interesting study unrelated to driving, Monk *et al.* (2004b) contrived situations where either a single collaborator talked on the phone while standing or sitting next to a commuter, or two collaborators talked to each other face-to-face while standing or sitting next to a commuter. The contents and voice levels of the conversations were identical. Immediately after each of these short conversations, an experimenter approached the unsuspecting commuter and asked him or her to rate the level of intrusiveness and annoyance of the conversation. Even though the loudness of the voice was controlled to be the same in both situations, the commuters rated the phone conversations as significantly more noticeable, intrusive, and loud. Interestingly people were not annoyed by the ring tone, only by the conversation. This is despite the fact that the total volume of the phone conversations was about half of the face-to-face conversations in which the commuters could hear – and possibly ignore – both speakers. Why cell phones conversations are more annoying and disruptive is not clear from this research, but this work does suggest that the problem is a general one that transcends driving.

In summary, the jury is still out on the relative degree of interference of the two sources. The one systematic meta-analysis of the few existing studies that examined conversations with passengers (with a total of five conditions) and the many studies that examined effects of a phone task on similar measures (with a total of 23 comparable conditions) did not find a significant difference between the two (Horrey and Wickens, 2006).

Distraction from Other In-Vehicle Technologies/Applications

The common denominator of all cell phone conversation-related distractions is that except for the brief dialing and termination of a call, the source of the distraction is exclusively auditory/cognitive. But other systems can also involve other senses, especially vision. This is true of navigation systems, text messaging, and surfing the internet. Östlund *et al.* (2006) compared the nature of the interference from artificial visual and auditory tasks and found that although both impair driving visually demanding tasks – as expected – have greater detrimental effects. In their study – conducted in an advanced moving-base simulator and on the road – they noted that both types of distractions caused drivers to reduce their speed to compensate for the added information load, but visual distraction was significantly more disruptive to maintaining good lateral control of the vehicle in the lane. Other studies, reported below, have tried to assess the effects of more realistic distractions such as the kinds stemming from navigation systems and text messaging. The impact of these and other smartphone activities is particularly important as by mid-2015, at least in the U.S., the respondents in an ATT survey stated that *while driving* they: text (reported by 61 percent), email (33 percent), surf the net (28 percent), use Facebook (27 percent), snap a selfie/photo (17 percent), use Twitter (14 percent), use Instagram (14 percent), shoot a video (12 percent), use Snapchat (11 percent), and engage in video chat (10 percent) (PR Newswire, 2015).

Navigation systems

Navigation systems are commonplace in many new cars, and increasingly popular in dash board-mounted versions on older cars. They are more complex to operate while driving than cell phones because they can involve not only cognitive distraction but also visual distraction for significant periods of time, such as when entering a destination and when looking at the map. Consequently it is not difficult to demonstrate impairment in vehicle control when it is combined with navigation-related activities (Blanco *et al.*, 2006; Tijerina *et al.*, 2000; Tijerina, Parmer, and Goodman, 1998; Tsimhoni, Smith, and Green, 2004). Unfortunately, at least one British survey suggests that approximately 10 percent of the drivers who have such systems, enter their destination after starting to drive, and of those, approximately 50 percent set their destination while actually driving, and admitting to being distracted by the system (Computerworld, 2006).

A notable effort to provide some ecological validity to assessing the severity of interference has been the above mentioned 15-second rule proposed by the American Society of Automotive Engineers (SAE, 2000). Tsimhoni *et al.* (2004) attempted to apply this rule when they compared three different methods of entering a destination. They found that speaking the address with the aid of a voice-based recognition system required an average of 15 seconds, using a character based recognition system (where the driver had to spell the individual characters) required 41 seconds, and using a manual keyboard required 86 seconds. This sixfold difference between the fastest and the slowest system was also reflected in the drivers' lateral control of the (simulator) car that was 60 percent poorer with the keyboard entry than with the voice systems (based on the standard deviation of the vehicle's lateral position).

As one might expect, there are also age-related differences in the effects of the various systems on vehicle control. Tsimhoni *et al.* (2004) found that the interference with vehicle control while entering data through a voice recognition system was similar for old and young drivers, but entering data manually was much more difficult for older than for younger drivers. Older drivers required three times as much time to enter the destination with a keyboard while driving than while parked, whereas younger drivers only needed twice as long. In an early study on this subject, Tijerina *et al.* (1998) obtained similar results in actual driving on a closed track and also concluded that voice-based data entry systems are a viable alternative to manual destination entry, especially for older drivers.

Unlike many other cell phone uses, it can be argued that phone-based navigation systems are beneficial and possibly even promote safety (by preventing distraction from outside while searching for an address or cues for directions). As a case in point, in California – where talking on a cell phone while driving is prohibited – a driver was cited for using the navigation application. The conviction was overturned by a court (Wald, 2014), but the issue remains. Can an in-vehicle navigation system be considered a driving aid while a similar phone-based system is a distraction? A similar concern is also raised with the advent of head-up displays that provide information (such as speed) on the windshield, overlapping the view of the road ahead and possibly obstructing the view of some objects (Williams, 2015).

Text messaging

Written electronic correspondence has infiltrated our driving environment to the same extent as other more traditional behaviors, such as eating and talking on the phone. The popularity of text messaging, especially among younger people, and the advent of phone-based email systems indicate that their use while driving may become as commonplace as talking on cell phones in the very near future. Already in 2002, as many as 30 percent of the drivers surveyed in Australia reported text messaging while driving (Young, Regan, and Hammer, 2003). According to a Nielsen survey, in the U.S. by the second quarter of 2008 texting surpassed talking on the phone (Kiley, 2008), A year later in a survey sponsored by the AAA Traffic Safety Foundation more than one-fifth of the drivers reported reading or writing text messages while driving within the past 30 days. Another U.S. national survey conducted in 2010 revealed that among heavy text users, more than 50 percent would rather get a text message than a voice call (Smith, 2011). In a 2012 nationally representative survey, 14 percent of the drivers reported they text or send email while driving (Schroeder *et al.*, 2013). In Athens, Greece, Yannis *et al.* (2014) found that over 90 percent of the students who participated in a driving simulation study texted "quite often" or "often" or "always" while driving.

Unlike talking on the phone, text messaging is predominantly a young driver activity. In a 2012 phone survey of over 2,600 16-18-years-old drivers, University of Michigan researchers found that one-quarter of the drivers either read or wrote at least one text message every time they drove (UMTRI, 2012). In fact, in the AAAF nationally representative survey conducted in 2009 close to 20 percent of the teen drivers reported that they do it "fairly often," compared to 55+ years old drivers who barely do it at all. It should therefore not be surprising that a 2011 survey of a representative sample of 8,505 U.S. high school students found that 45 percent of them have texted at least once in the past 30 days (Olsen, Shults, and Eaton, 2013). Furthermore, this was not an isolated risky behavior. Compared to the students who had not texted in the past 30 days, these students were more likely to have not always used their seat belts, ridden with an alcohol-impaired driver, and drink and drive themselves. This clustering of risky behaviors enabled Schroeder *et al.* (2013) to classify drivers as either distraction-prone or distraction-averse, and note that the distraction-prone drivers tended to be younger, more affluent, and more educated than the distraction-averse drivers. As expected, the distraction-prone drivers were more likely to use their cell phone, text, and email. What makes things worse, is that it is very likely that as this young generation ages – and possibly even before – texting will spread to older age groups, as it has for talking on the phone where the use level is relatively high and constant, and already exceeds 70 percent for all drivers under 55 years old (AAAF, 2009). In Schroeder *et al.*'s (2013) survey of the U.S. drivers, approximately 70 percent of the 16-44 years old drives admitted to "ever" text messaging. After age 45 the percent started to decrease from approximately 50 percent to 33 percent for drivers 65+ years old. Finally, the latest U.S. statistics indicate that texting while driving is increasing and that this behavior, that is most common to young drivers, is indeed spreading to other age groups. Approximately 25 percent of drivers at all age groups feel that texting or emailing does not affect their driving at all, and only 36 percent of the men and 25 percent of the women acknowledge that they slow down when they text (NHTSA, 2015c). Nonetheless, there is a significant and worrisome disconnect between the behavioral tendencies and the feelings and beliefs toward texting. In the above cited AAAF survey 94 percent of the drivers felt it was unacceptable to text a message (or email) while driving and 87 percent of the drivers felt it was a serious threat to their personal safety. Thus, the findings of these surveys cast a serious doubt on the potential utility of repeated campaigns about the dangers of texting. Such campaigns will probably not contribute much to eliminating this behavior.

What does seem to partially determine the texting-while-driving behavior of young drivers is their stated intention to do so, which in turn is partially determined by their attitudes toward that behavior and their subjective norms. This was demonstrated in a survey of Australian students who filled out extensive questionnaires based on the Theory of Planned Behavior (TPB – see Chapter 9) containing questions about their intentions, attitudes, subjective norm (of people important to them, as they perceive it), group norm (of their friends, as they perceive it) perceived behavioral control, and their moral norms concerning reading and sending text messages while driving. A week later the same students were asked to respond to two more items: how many times did they send and read text messages within the past week. The results showed that on all of the above measures there were high correlations ($0.75 < r < 0.95$) between sending and reading text messages, indicating that those who read also write. The findings also provided partial support for the validity of the TPB, by showing that the reported behavior was moderately well predicted by the stated intentions to text; $r = .48$ and $r = .49$ for sending and reading, respectively, In turn, the stated intentions to text were moderately well predicted by group norms, and subjective norms.

But norms can be changed. An interesting approach to establish the norms that drivers have was used by Atchley, Hadlock, and Lane (2012) who presented drivers with written descriptions of accidents and asked them to decide on the punishment the drivers deserved in each scenario. For one group of respondents the drivers were described as "attentive," for another group they were described as "had been drinking," for a third group the driver was described as "talking on the phone," and for a fourth group the driver was presented as "engaged in texting." The respondents – students at two U.S. mid-western universities – judged the drivers as most responsible when they were texting but assigned the harshest punishments in terms of jail time and fines to those who had been drinking. Thus, it seems that unlike driving while drinking where the norms have been internalized, in the case of texting the attitude is more permissive. All of these findings are consistent and useful in pointing at the direction that is needed to change this behavior: a change in attitudes and social norms. Easy to write, but not easy to accomplish. In the case of drinking and driving the process is still evolving and in the case of texting – despite public education campaigns and banning laws, it has barely begun.

Theoretically, text messaging should be more distracting than aural communications. This is because, in addition to taxing our limited central processing capacity, text messaging also involves visual and manual distraction. On the other hand, compared to talking on the phone texting does not command the temporal urgency that aural communications do, and drivers may postpone attending to them to times when the driving demands allow it. Studies that have investigated the effects of texting on driving performance have generally found that they are quite distracting. Caird *et al.* (2014) synthesized the results of 22 experimental studies that evaluated the effects of texting on various driving behaviors and concluded that all the behavioral measures they studied were significantly degraded in one or more studies. Of the seven measures they assessed, the ones that were most often adversely affected by sending text were reaction time, lateral control, longitudinal control, speed variance, eye movements, and subjective workload. On the other hand, some compensatory behaviors were also consistently observed in the form of lower average speed and longer headways. Yannis *et al.* (2014) also noted that texting while driving in a simulator was accompanied by speed reduction, though not enough to compensate for an increase in crashes. Of course, the length of the text is an important variable. Peng, Boyle, and Lee (2014) found that sending a message even four-characters-long can already increase lane position variability and speed variability. Perhaps most significant – especially with respect to the role of visual distraction – Fitch *et al.* (2013)

found that the average total time off-the-road while texting was an alarming 23.3 seconds, compared to the visual distraction time involved in the initiation and ending of a cell phone conversation which was only 1.3-2.5 seconds.

Jamson *et al.* (2004) studied the driving performance of drivers in a fixed-base simulator while they were presented with and had to respond to what the researchers termed "speech based e-mail" messages. The messages were all linguistic reasoning questions involving the alphabetical sequence of letters, such as "P is not preceded by F," and the driver had to respond in terms of "true" or "false" ("true" in this example). The messages were preceded by a warning tone and an image of an envelope displayed on an in-vehicle screen. In one condition – driver-controlled – the drivers pressed a button mounted on the steering wheel whenever they were ready to accept the message, thus they could pace the presentation relative to the driving demands. In the other condition – system-controlled – the message was automatically presented two seconds after the warning tone. The driving task required following another vehicle, and the driving situation varied from a relatively undemanding open road to crossing a signalized intersection that required stopping. The effects of the competing driving demands and the two email systems were quite consistent across a variety of measures: when the drivers were engaged in the email task and the lead car braked the minimum time-to-collision and the time headway were shorter, reflecting a delayed response. In fact, when engaged with the email the time-to-collision was roughly halved. However, the drivers did apply some compensatory mechanisms to handle the email task: they took more time to respond to the email questions while driving than while stopped, and they maintained longer headways to the lead car when responding to the email than when not. Interestingly, it made no difference whether the message presentation was driver-controlled or system-controlled, indicating that either the drivers made no adjustment for the driving demands or that the driving demands were not sufficiently high.

Extrapolating Jamson *et al.*'s (2004) results to actual email correspondence is quite problematic. This is because despite labeling the task as "e-mail" it was much more similar to a cell phone task: the messages were all auditory, and therefore no text had to be read or entered. But, as noted above, Strayer *et al.* (2015b) found that the workload induced by texting when interfaced with a text-to-speech system was actually very high in comparison to talking on the phone. In that respect a study by Ranney, Harbluk, and Noy (2005) was much more similar to real email text. In one of their study conditions a typed message appeared on a commercial dashboard-mounted display, much like the display of an in-vehicle radio. They too found that text messaging interfered with the driver's vehicle control on a closed driving course, even though their drivers also partially compensated for this by increasing their headways when required to engage in the email task.

A much more ecologically valid simulation study of the effects of text messaging was conducted in simulated driving in Australia by Hosking, Young, and Regan (2006). In their study they focused on the high-risk group that uses text messaging the most: young drivers. Their subjects were 18-21 years old drivers with 6 months or less of driving experience (while still in the probationary phase of the graduated licensing system). Although these participants were not yet skilled in driving, they were very skilled in text messaging. Their task was to drive in a fixed-base simulator as close as possible to the speed limit, and respond to text messages whenever they appeared on their cell phone. The messages were programmed to appear while the drivers encountered eight specific demanding driving situations that included (1) a change in the traffic signal from green to red when the driver was less than 100 meters away, (2-4) car following behind a vehicle that cut into the driver's lane either 50 or 33 or 29 meters ahead of his or her car, (5) a pedestrian that emerged from a narrow space between parked cars and entered the road when the driver was 80 meters away, (6-7) a requirement to change lanes as indicated by a sign on the side of the road, and (8) a vehicle turning into the road and crossing the driver's path from a side road 84 meters away. Driving behavior and direction of gaze were recorded in these situations both when distracted by text messaging and when not distracted.

The results of the driving simulation study demonstrated clearly the negative effects of text messaging on driving safety. As expected, the text messaging required redirection of the visual fixations, and the extent of this was quite dramatic. When not distracted by text messaging the drivers looked at the road approximately 90 percent of the time, but when distracted by text messaging they looked at the road only 60 percent of the time. The effect of text messaging in terms of proportion of time the drivers' gaze was off the road is shown in Figure 13-4 for the eight driving situations. The figure reveals a very similar effect of messaging, almost regardless of the specific driving demands. When not engaged in text messaging the drivers' eyes were directed *off* the road ahead approximately 10 percent of the time, but when engaged in sending a text message that proportion increased to 40 percent; a fourfold difference! Thus, on the average for every 30 second episode of text messaging approximately 12 seconds were spent with the eyes directed off the road. This very large increase in total glance duration off the road was due to the fact that while text messaging the drivers made more and longer off-road glances. The fact that there are hardly any differences among the different conditions – despite obvious differences in the urgency and risks that they pose – is an acute indication of how compelling the distraction from text messaging can be.

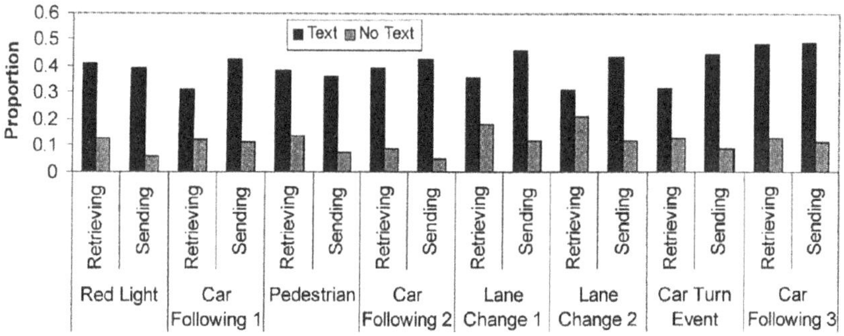

Figure 13-4. The average proportion of time drivers spent looking *away* from the road in eight different driving situations, while engaged or not engaged in a text messaging task (from Hosking *et al.*, 2006, with permission from Monash University Accident Research Center).

Given the effects of text messaging on visual and manual distraction it is not surprising that vehicle control in responding to the environmental contingencies deteriorates accordingly. The greatest consistent impairment that Hosking *et al.* (2006) noted was in maintaining lane position. Lane position variability increased by 70 percent, and – more importantly – the number of lane excursions increased by 28 percent relative to the same situations without text messaging. The only silver lining in the results of the study was that all twenty drivers participating in the study felt that sending messages impaired their driving and 19 out of the twenty drivers acknowledged that receiving messages impaired their driving too. To compensate for this they increased their headways when text messaging relative to the same condition without text messaging. This compensatory behavior, however, was irrelevant to their inability to cope with the emerging pedestrian or the signal light change. Unfortunately the researchers did not measure the drivers' reaction time to the light change and the pedestrian and therefore the extent to which text messaging affected hazard detection could not be assessed. Hosking *et al.* (2006) did note however, that the drivers did not reduce their speed while text messaging, though this could have been due at least in part to the fact that they were specifically instructed to stay as close as possible to the posted speed limit.

It is important to note that we can be equally visually distracted by other driving and non-driving tasks. Thus, we can compare email and text messaging to other – more traditional – driving and non-driving visual tasks such as changing a radio station, checking the rear-view mirror or checking the odometer. Sodhi, Reimer, and Llamazares (2002b) measured drivers' visual glance behavior in actual driving and found that while their drivers engaged in these tasks, they time-shared their fixations between the road and the task. While they performed these tasks they fixated on the distracting device nearly 50 percent of the time. However, the maximum glance duration away from the road never exceeded two seconds, and the total time used for the tasks themselves was relatively short: from 21 seconds to change a radio station, to 20 seconds to check the rear-view mirror, and to 9 seconds to check the odometer.

The most alarming conclusions on the effects of text messaging come not from controlled experimental studies, but from naturalistic driving studies. In these studies, comparisons of crash and near-crash (safety-critical) events with random events have shown that texting is far more prevalent in the safety-critical events than in the control events. Texting multiplies the relative crash and near-crash risk significantly; by at least twice (Fitch *et al.*, 2013), or by as much as 23 times (Olson *et al.*, 2009), or possibly even 164 times (Hickman and Hanowski, 2012). Although the number of texting events in each of these studies is small, together these results provide fairly conclusive evidence that visual/manual distraction from texting is a significant – and possibly very high – crash risk factor. The most definitive (to date) estimate of the increase in crash risk comes from the analyses of the 945 real crashes documented in the SHRP2 data (Dingus *et al.*, 2016). Although texting was involved in less than 2 percent of the normal driving episodes, its odds ratio was 6.1; i.e., a six-fold increase in the likelihood of a crash.

One way to cope with the visual/manual distraction in texting is to simply eliminate it. Arguing that Email and text messaging do not necessarily have to be mostly visually based, and that they can be transmitted with voice-based systems, does not seem to solve the problem. Ranney *et al.* (2005), Tsimhoni *et al.* (2004), and Tijerina *et al.* (1998) have shown that auditory navigation systems are less distracting than visual ones, but Strayer *et al.* (2015a, 2015b) have found that a speech-to-text interface is still cognitively quite demanding and in fact actually much more cognitively demanding (and potentially distracting) than a hand-held or hands-free phone conversation (2015b). Furthermore, they also found that in controlled actual on-road driving some residual cognitive distraction effects persisted for as long as 18 seconds after the termination of the auditory task (2015a). This is a remarkably long time considering that the drive was in a 25 mph (40 km/hr) zone, the text messages themselves were quite short and emotionally neutral, and that at that speed the drivers covered a distance of approximately 200 meters – nearly double the length of an (American or European) football field. In short, Strayer's findings suggest that texting either by writing or by dictating is a significant source of cognitive distraction and one that does not terminate with the task itself. Incidentally, the distracting effects differed significantly among the different systems that are available, and – as could be expected – were generally related to the ease of operation and design features of the specific systems (Strayer *et al.*, 2015a). Eliminating texting while driving through education is an uphill battle: the most frequent texters are teen drivers who already acknowledge that it is dangerous. Thus, as suggested above, informative messages will have little effect on their behavior, though emotional ones might.

Other potential distractors

The increasing time we spend in the car and the many crash avoidance safety features lure many drivers to engage in more and more activities while driving. The classic radio and radio-CD combinations have given way to complex "infotainment systems" with multiple soft controls and displays. Consequently they often require more extensive glances for adjustments. In an evaluation of two such systems both featuring touch screens, AM/FM radio, CD/DVD/MP3 player, and other functions, Perez *et al.* (2015) observed the amount of visual distraction these systems elicit. In a naturalistic driving task, with nearly 700 hours of driving obtained from 17 participants they found that the most common but least distracting was volume adjustment; with an average glance duration of 0.2 second. The most distracting was the interaction with the navigation system, with average glance duration of 2.4 seconds. Furthermore, the 85th percentile of glance durations while interacting with the navigation systems was 3.1 seconds; well above the NHTSA recommended limit of 2 seconds.

The latest distractors include surfing on the internet or watching TV directly from the navigation monitor installed in cars (already available in Japan and Israel, but not legal in many other countries; Dawson, 2013), or by attaching trays to the steering wheel(!) from which the driver can eat or work on a laptop while driving (cf., "steering wheel trays" in www.google.com). Needless to say, all of these activities involve a heavy dose of visual and manual distraction from the driving task. In addition new technologies such as Google Glass may make reading text and watching videos even more common, despite evidence that they retain the negative aspects of distraction, especially when the drivers tend to superimpose their view on the natural (driving) line of sight (Sawyer *et al.*, 2014). Thus, the risks keep growing and short of reliable autonomous vehicles, potential restrictive technologies, a cultural/normative change, and a sensible modicum of self-control, the solution is not in sight.

Countermeasures to phone distraction

The range of potential countermeasures to engaging in phone-based tasks includes public education and information, legislation and enforcement, and technological solutions. In fact, to be most effective, countermeasures should be developed within a systems approach: viewing distraction as an activity that is enabled, encouraged, or suppressed by multiple stake holders and technologies. The stake holders involved are at different levels beginning with government and legislature, through companies and organizations, and ending with drivers and passengers. All of these can effect on-road phone distraction. In fact, according to Young and Salmon (2015), the combined and coordinated action of all of these actors will have a greater effect than the sum of the effects of the individual components; and hence the system approach.

Policy and regulatory interventions

At the legislative and policy level, though there seems to be no country that totally bans the use of cell phones while driving, many jurisdictions limit their use to hands-free devices, and ban texting. Banning texting while driving is an easy action, as the overwhelming majority of drivers support it (Schroeder *et al.*, 2013). In the U.S., the primary action in curbing distracted driving has been legislative: 41 states and the District of Columbia have laws that limit the use of cell phones while driving (McCartt *et al.*, 2014), and 44 states ban texting while driving (GHSA, 2015). In Europe, France, Germany, Greece, Italy, Poland, Portugal, Russia, Spain, and the U.K. ban texting while driving. Given the consistent findings on the effects of texting on both driving performance measures and crash involvement, there is more support for these laws than for laws that ban talking on the phone. While banning may be an easy approach, it is not an easy fix. The effectiveness of banning laws is at best dubious. Abouk and Adams (2013) studied the fatal crash rates in states that introduced texting bans and found that though there was a small immediate drop in crashes, the effect lasted only a few months. In a review of the effectiveness of such laws in terms of the reductions in either texting or in crashes, as evaluated in 11 peer-reviewed studies, McCartt *et al.* (2014) concluded that it is "unclear" that the laws were having their desired effect. Furthermore, an evaluation of the change over time in North Carolina showed that in a two-year period following the restrictions on teenagers phone use, there were no significant decreases in overall phone use and possibly even a dangerous shift from talking on the phone to texting (Goodwin *et al.*, 2012). Following recent analyses of the relationship between text banning laws in the U.S. and changes in crash statistics, Harding (2013) and Cheng (2012) concluded that these laws are ineffective as they do not reduce cell phone-related crashes. Two possible reasons for the limited effect (if any) are that enforcement is lax and that teens who are the principal texters are more likely to violate traffic laws in general than adult drivers, and that in general – as multiple surveys indicate – much of the public is willing to violate them. Given these dismal results, it is not surprising that despite the increase of hands-free systems, the U.S. annual observational surveys have shown that the percent of drivers seen holding their phone to their ear while driving has remained fairly constant at around 6 percent for males and 4 percent for females over the past decade (NHTSA, 2015b). One interesting finding in this consistently discovered lack of effect of banning hand-held phones and texting is that of Lim and Chi (2013). They analyzed the U.S. fatal crash data for young (14-20 years old) drivers in relation to banning laws. They found that while laws that ban hand-held phone use by teen drivers are ineffective, laws that target all drivers are effective in reducing teen fatal crashes. A very likely reason for this is that enforcement of an age-related ban is much more difficult than uniform enforcement, which in turn, may still leave the officers biased in enforcing it more on young drivers than on older ones. Other studies have also shown a link between the law and its enforcement on crashes. Ferdinand *et al.* (2014) analyzed the FARS 2000-2010 data to test for differences in fatalities between states where texting is a primary offense and states where it is a secondary offense; that is, those that enable arrest for texting and those that enable it only if the driver is stopped for another (primary) offense. They found that the states where texting was a primary offense experienced a significant 3 percent reduction in traffic fatalities in all age groups. Where the law was restricted to young drivers, its greatest impact was on 15-21 years old drivers. Furthermore, Secondarily enforced restrictions were not associated with any reduction in fatalities. In conclusion, banning can work as long as it a primary offense that is rigorously enforced.

One possible reason for the small or no effect of laws and regulations than ban the use of hand-held phones or texting while driving is that the level of enforcement of the different programs is quite low. As with speed control, enforcement is the key to effective regulations. To test the effects of high-visibility enforcement accompanied by media campaigns, Chaudhary *et al.* (2015) studied its impact on drivers' awareness, observed use of hand-held phones while driving, and crash data in the states of California and Delaware. Although comparisons of crash data before and during the enforcement periods did not show an effect on crashes, the campaigns did increase driver awareness and observed use dropped in both sites by over 30 percent. These findings and others (Cosgrove, Chaudhary, and Reagan, 2011) suggest that high-visibility enforcement is effective in controlling behavior but as noted above, the change from hand-held to hands-free phones does not necessarily increase distraction to the level needed to increase crash involvement.

Technological interventions

Perhaps the most promising countermeasures are the new technologies that detect degraded driving performance and compensate for it. In the domain of distracted driving initial research suggests that tracking the driver's eye movements and using data mining techniques to analyze it can provide the vehicle with indicators of distraction on which it might be able to act (Liang, Reyes, and Lee, 2007). Eye movement metrics are also the basis for the U.S. NHTSA recommended guidelines for assessment of distraction (NHTSA, 2014). Roughly, their guidelines recommend that in-vehicle devices be designed so that they cannot be used by the driver unless 85 percent of the glances away from the road or the mean glance duration away from the road are less than 2.0 seconds, and the total glance time is less than 12.0 seconds (NHTSA, 2012c). Thus, based on empirical data, this standard allows for dialing a phone number with many interfaces, but does not allow texting. A major shortcoming of this type of standard, however, is that it does not consider nomadic devices whose interface is typically poorer than that of built-in (ergonomically designed) devices. Yet, with the rapidly evolving in-vehicle technologies, more complex vehicle based detection and mitigation systems are being developed and protocols for their evaluation are being introduced (Lee *et al.*, 2013). For example, Köhler *et al.* (2014) evaluated a "telephone manager" that automatically detects stressful driving situations such as crossing an intersection. When such situations occur incoming phone calls are suppressed. They were able to demonstrate that compared to the situations when the driver answered a call while crossing an intersection, the suppression reduced the subjectively reported mental workload. Perhaps, even more significant was the fact that the drivers actually liked the suppression system.

Another technological approach to curtailing in-vehicle distractions is to rely on sensors that detect the use of potentially distracting devices, and disable them in risky situations. Various phone applications (apps) already exist but they all assume acceptance of the limiting intervention. Interventions and limiting mechanisms that are not acceptable to drivers will most likely not sell well and consequently have limited market penetration. For example, even when the client is a safety oriented organization that prohibits texting while driving, its drivers may simply bypass the system by using personal cell phones. In an interesting small-scale evaluation of the viability of various in-vehicle safety systems, Albert and her colleagues (2015) conducted structured interviews of 26 experts in safety, policy, social marketing, psychology, and technology. The experts evaluated a variety of distraction-limiting applications in terms of their perceived effectiveness and in terms of their acceptability. Acceptability was defined in terms of "willingness to use" and in terms of "expected public support." The systems included text prevention, call limitation, voice control, in-vehicle data recorders (IVDR), collision warnings and head-up displays. The findings were quite interesting. The systems that were perceived as being potentially the most effective – call limitation, texting prevention, and IVDR – were perceived as having low social support potential: both in terms of personal intention to use and in terms of public acceptance. The potentially less effective systems – head-up display and voice control – actually received higher social support ratings. The only distraction countermeasure that was perceived as both highly effective and had high support rating was the collision warning system. In summary, this study showed that even among experts when it comes to evaluating personal and public attitudes toward the use of distraction-limiting devices, in terms of acceptability convenience trumps safety. Safety is important, people realize when it is compromised, but the desire to read and text messages overrides it.

A more comprehensive approach that relies on technology-based feedback was proposed by Donmez, Boyle, and Lee (2008). They suggest that we distinguish among four feedback strategies on a temporal basis: (1) immediate or concurrent feedback that provides the driver with feedback on the vehicle behavior relative to the driving context in either a warning mode or a control mode. This feedback operates on the scale of milliseconds and can mitigate distraction effects in real time. (2) Delayed feedback that operates on the scale of seconds. This may be effective in the case of cognitive overload, but at the cost of compromising immediate corrective actions. (3) Retrospective feedback that is provided at the end of the trip, giving drivers an appreciation of the risks they incurred while driving, in the hope that this may shape their future driving. (4) Cumulative feedback that is a "comprehensive summary of past driving performance and driver behavior." Donmez and her associates argue that the more immediate the feedback, the greater its momentary and immediate impact. However, the more delayed and comprehensive the feedback the greater its instrumental value in shaping long term driving behavior. Their argument seems to be valid because both immediate concurrent technologies designed to reduce distraction effects and delayed comprehensive feedback affect driving as expected: the concurrent one in reducing driving errors while it is operative, and the delayed one in shaping driver behavior in ways that reduce crash involvement (e.g., McGehee *et al.*, 2007).

Concluding Comments

Driver inattention and distraction are not new phenomena. They have been identified as one of the more common causes of crashes for a long time, though in the early research most of the inattention and distraction was not due to in-vehicle sources. The burst of novel in-vehicle technologies in the this century has ushered in many safety devices, but has also brought new in-vehicle sources of distraction in the form of entertainment, navigation, information, and communications systems. Their potential detriment to safety is a good reason to focus on their contribution to driver inattention and distraction, and on the potential methods to deal with their effects. The emergence and use of these technologies has also caused an unprecedented interest in distracted driving: by both the media and the driving safety research community. This was driven mostly by the exponential increase in the spread of in-vehicle telecommunication systems: notably the smartphone with its multiple applications.

The amount of attention that we allocate to the driving task varies over time as a function of the task demands and our psychological and physical state. Our rate of information processing is limited, and so is our capacity to divide our attention among many tasks. Most often we adjust the level of attention that we allocate to the driving task, so that it is above the minimum required; a strategy that is both safe and non-taxing. The distractions from the driving task can be both external (such as passengers, billboards, music, and cell phones) and internal (such as mind-wandering, and preoccupation with thoughts). For safe driving we must always remember that as long as we are behind the wheel, our primary task is driving. And this is not always the case. When we allow the non-driving tasks to capture our attention to the point of becoming oblivious to road and traffic related events we compromise safety, and enter the state colloquially known as distracted driving.

The level and type of distraction, and therefore the crash risk of various sources of distraction such as music, commercial and road signs, eating and drinking, conversations with passengers, and even dealing with children and pets – have all been studied. But the most studied of all, and the most hotly debated has been the use of cell phones and telecommunication devices. Many of the early studies focused on, and showed that hand-held and hands-free phones are equally risky. This led to the conclusion that the culprit is the added cognitive load and the resulting cognitive distraction. More recent studies – particularly naturalistic driving studies – have been able to disaggregate the phone activity into its manual/visual distraction components (such as dialing, picking the phone up, texting, and putting it down) and the purely cognitive component of listening and talking. These studies effectively demonstrated that the culprit responsible for the elevated crash risk is the visual/manual distraction. This is welcome news to the increasing number of drivers who talk on their phone while driving. It also implies that improved integration of these systems with the car – that is, better ergonomics in system design – can reduce the risk from time-sharing the phone and the driving tasks.

Because we are prone to distractions while driving, and because we also seek distractions while driving, it is likely that the cell phone is here to stay in our motor-vehicles. In a way, the cell phone controversy is reminiscent of the controversy surrounding the use of a radio in the 1930s. Given this conclusion, the most promising behavioral approach to reduce the harmful distraction from the new distracting devices and applications is to transform the cultural norms in a way that we have been transforming the drinking and driving culture, to the point where in most circles such behavior ranges from uncool to downright stupid and unacceptable. In parallel, we should seek to refine and regulate the technologies that will limit proven inherently dangerous activities, such as texting, surfing the net, and entering navigation data while driving. A systems approach consisting of a combination of public support, highly reliable and publicly acceptable technology, and proper regulations is probably the best way to proceed.

References

AAAF (2009). *Safety Culture: Text Messaging and Cell Phone Use while Driving*. AAA Foundation for Traffic Safety, Washington, DC.

AAAF (2015). *2014 Traffic Safety Culture Index*. AAA Foundation for Traffic Safety, Washington, DC.

Abdu, R., D. Shinar and N. Meiran (2012). Situational (state) anger and driving. *Transportation Res. F, 15*(5), 575-580.

Abouk, R. and S. Adams (2013). Texting bans and fatal accidents on roadways: Do they work? Or do drivers just react to announcements of bans? *Amer. Econ. J: App. Econ., 5*(2), 179-199.

Albert, G., O. Musicant and T. Lotan (2015). A "Safety Suit" for smartphone apps: What do the experts say? 4th International Distraction and Inattention Conference. Sydney, Australia.

Alm, H. and L. Nilsson (1995). The effects of a mobile telephone task on driver behaviour in a car following situation. *Accid. Anal. Prev.*, *27*(5), 707–715.

Amado, S. and P. Ulupınar (2005). The effects of conversation on attention and peripheral detection: Is talking with a passenger and talking on the cell phone different? *Transportation Res. F*, *8*(6), 383-395.

Atchley, P. and J. Dressel (2004). Conversation limits the functional field of view. *Hum. Fact.*, *46*, 664-673.

Atchley, P., C. Hadlock and S. Lane (2012). Stuck in the 70s: The role of social norms in distracted driving. *Accid. Anal. Prev.*, *48*, 279-284.

Barkana, Y., D. Zadok, Y. Morad and I. Avni (2004). Visual field attention is reduced by concomitant hands-free conversation on a cellular telephone. *Am. J. Ophthalmol.*, *138*, 347-353.

Bédard, M. and J. R. Meyers (2004). The influence of older drivers involved in fatal crashes. *Experimental Aging Res.*, *30*, 205–215.

Beirness, D. J. (2005). Distracted driving: The role of survey research. Paper presented at the International Conference on Distracted Driving, Toronto, Canada, October 2-5.

Beijer, D., A. Smiley and M. Eizenman (2004). Observed driver glance behavior at roadside advertising signs. *Transportation Res. Record*, *1899*, 96-103.

Bellinger, D. B., B. M. Budde, M. Machida, G. B. Richardson and W. P. Berg (2009). The effect of cellular telephone conversation and music listening on response time in braking. *Transportation Res. F*, *12*(6), 441-451.

Bhargava, S. and V. S. Pathanya (2013). Driving under the (cellular) influence. *Amer. Econ. J.: Econ. Policy*, *5*, 92-125.

Birrell, S. A. and M. Fowkes (2014). Glance behaviours when using an in-vehicle smart driving aid: A real-world, on-road driving study. *Transportation Res. F*, *22*, 113-125.

Blanco, M., W. J. Biever, J. P. Gallagher and T. A. Dingus (2006). The impact of secondary task cognitive processing demand on driving Performance. *Accid. Anal. Prev.*, *38*(5), 895-906.

Blunck, H., C. Owsley, P. A. Maclennan and G. McGwin (2013). Driving with pets as a risk factor for motor vehicle collisions among older drivers. *Accid. Anal. Prev.*, *58*, 70-74.

Borowsky, A., W. J. Horrey, Y. Liang, A. Garabet, L. Simmons and D. L. Fisher (2015). The effects of momentary visual disruption on hazard anticipation and awareness in driving. *Traffic Inj. Prev.*, *16*(2), 133-139.

Briggs, G. F., G. J. Hole and M. F. Land (2011). Emotionally involving telephone conversations lead to driver error and visual tunnelling. *Transportation Res. F*, *14*(4), 313-323.

Brodsky, W. (2002). The effects of music tempo on simulated driving performance and vehicular control. *Transportation Res. F*, *4*, 219-241.

Brodsky, W. and Z. Slor (2013). Background music as a risk factor for distraction among young-novice drivers. *Accid. Anal. Prev.*, *59*, 382-393.

Brookhuis, K. A., G. de Vries and D. Waard (1991). The effects of mobile telephoning on driving performance. *Accid. Anal. Prev.*, *23*(4), 309–316.

Brown, I. D., A. H. Tickner and D. C. V. Simmonds (1969). Interference between concurrent tasks of driving and telephoning. *J. Appl. Psychol.*, *53*(5), 419–424.

Bunn, T. L., S. Slavova, T. W. Struttmann and S. R. Browning (2005). Sleepiness/fatigue and distraction/inattention as factors for fatal versus nonfatal commercial motor vehicle driver injuries. *Accid. Anal. Prev.*, *37*, 862–869.

Burns, P. C., A. Parkes, S. Burton, R. K. Smith and D. Burch (2002). How dangerous is driving with a mobile phone? Benchmarking the impairment to alcohol. TRL Report 547. Transport Research Laboratory, Berkshire, UK.

Burns, P. C., A. M. Parkes and T. C. Lansdown (2003). Conversations in cars: The relative hazards of mobile phones. International Ergonomics Association Annual Conference.

Caird, J. K. (2015). On the effects of listening and talking to humans and devices on driving. *Hum, Fact.*, *57*(8), 1325-1327.

Caird, J. K., K. A. Johnston, C. R. Willness and M. Asbridge (2014). The use of meta-analysis or research synthesis to combine driving simulation or naturalistic study results on driver distraction. *J. Safety Res.*, *49*, 91-96.

Caird, J. K., C. R. Willness, P. Steel and C. Scialfa (2008). A meta-analysis of the effects of cell phones on driver performance. *Accid. Anal. Prev.*, *40*(4), 1282-1293.

Carney, C., D. McGehee, K. Harland, M. Weiss and M. Raby (2015). *Using Naturalistic Driving Data to Assess the Prevalence of Environmental Factors and Driver Behaviors in Teen Driver Crashes.* AAA Foundation for Traffic Safety, Washington, DC.

Charlton, S. G. (2009). Driving while conversing: Cell phones that distract and passengers who react. *Accid. Anal. Prev.*, *41*(1), 160-173.

Chaudhary, N. K., J. Connolly, J. Tison, M. Solomon and K. Elliott (2015). Evaluation of the NHTSA distracted driving high-visibility enforcement demonstration projects in California and Delaware. NHTSA Report No. DOT HS 812 108. U.S. Department of Transportation, Washington, DC.

Chen, L.-H., S. P. Baker, E. R. Braver and G. Li (2000). Carrying passengers as a risk factor for crashes fatal to 16- and 17-year-old drivers. *JAMA*, *283*, 1578–1582.

Cheng, C. (2012). *The Effect of Cell Phone Bans on Driver Behavior, Accidents, and Casualties.* Texas A&M University, Department of Economics, College Station, Texas.

Chisholm, S. L., J. K. Caird and J. Lockhart (2008). The effects of practice with MP3 players on driving performance. *Accid. Anal. Prev.*, *40*(2), 704-713.

Christoph, M., N. Van Nes and A. Knapper (2013). Naturalistic driving observations of manual and visual-manual interactions with navigation systems and mobile phones while driving. *Transportation Res. Record*, *2365*(1), 31-38.

Chung, Y. and I. Chang (2015). How accurate is accident data in road safety research? An application of vehicle black box data regarding pedestrian-to-taxi accidents in Korea. *Accid. Anal. Prev.*, *84*, 1-8.

Computerworld (2006). In-car navigation systems can be dangerous, report warns, February 22. http://computerworld.com/printthis/2006/0,4814,108871,00.html

Collet, C., A. Clarion, M. Morel, A. Chapon and C. Petit (2009). Physiological and behavioural changes associated to the management of secondary tasks while driving. *Appl. Ergonom.*, *40*(6), 1041-1046.

Cooper, J. M. and D. L. Strayer (2008). Effects of simulator practice and real-world experience on cell-phone-related driver distraction. *Hum. Fact.*, *50*(6), 893-902.

Cosgrove, L., N. Chaudhary and I. Reagan (2011). Four high-visibility enforcement demonstration waves in Connecticut and New York reduce hand-held phone use. Traffic Safety Facts, NHTSA Report No. DOT HS 811 845. U.S. Department of Transportation, Washington, DC.

Crundall, D., M. Bains, P. Chapman and G. Underwood (2005). Regulating conversation during driving: a problem for mobile telephones? *Transportation Res. F, 8*(3), 197-211.

Crundall, D., E. Van Loon and G. Underwood (2006). Attraction and distraction of attention with roadside advertisements. *Accid. Anal. Prev., 38*(4), 671-677.

Dawson, C. (2013). In Japan television viewing doesn't have to take a back seat. Wall Street Journal, April 23.

Dingus, T. A., F. Guo, S. E. Lee, J. Antin, M. Perez, M. Buchanan-King and J. Hankey (2016). Driver crash risk factors and prevalence evaluation using naturalistic driving data. Proc. National Acad. Sci. 201513271. Retrieved from www.pnas.org/cgi. doi:10.1073/pnas.1513271113.

Donmez, B., L. Boyle and J. D. Lee (2008). Designing feedback to mitigate distraction. In: *Driver distraction: Theory, effects, and mitigation* (K. Young, J. D. Lee and M. A. Regan eds.). CRC Press. Taylor and Francis, London.

Drews, F. A., M. Pasaputhi and D. L. Strayer (2008). Passenger and cell phone conversations in simulated driving. *J. Exp. Psych: App., 14*, 392-400.

Dukic, T., C. Ahlstrom, C. Patten, C. Kettwich and K. Kircher (2013). Effects of electronic billboards on driver distraction. *Traffic Inj. Prev., 14*(5), 469-476.

Elvik, R. (2011). Effects of mobile phone use on accident risk. *Transportation Res. Record: J. Transportation Res. Board, 2236*, 20-26.

Engström, J., E. Johansson and J. Östlund (2005). Effects of visual and cognitive load in real and simulated motorway driving. *Transportation Res. F, 8*(2), 97-120.

Fairclough, S. H., M. C. Ashby, T. Ross and A. M. Parkes (1991). Effects of hands free telephone use on driving behaviour. Proceedings of the ISATA Conference. Florence, Italy.

Farbry, J., K. Wochinger, T. Shafer, N. Owens and A. Nedzesky (2001). Research review of potential safety effects of electronic billboards on driver attention and distraction. Final report submitted to the Office or Real Estate Services, U.S. Federal Highway Administration. McLean, VA.

Farmer, C. M., K. A. Braitman and A. K. Lund (2010). Cell phone use while driving and attributable crash risk. *Traffic Inj. Prev., 11*(5), 466-470.

Ferdinand, A. O., N. Menachemi, B. Sen, J. L. Blackburn, M. Morrisey and L. Nelson (2014). Impact of texting laws on motor vehicular fatalities in the United States. *Amer. J. Pub. Health, 104*(8), 1370-1377.

Fisher, D. L. (2015). Cognitive distraction in the wild next steps—Addressing a not-so-humdrum conundrum. *Hum. Fact., 57*(8), 1331-1333.

Fitch, G. M., & R. J. Hanowski (2011). The risk of a safety-critical event associated with mobile device use as a function of driving task demands. Proceedings of the 2nd International Conference on Driver Distraction and Inattention (pp. 5-7), Gothenburg, SE.

Fitch, G. A., S. A. Soccolich, F. Guo, J. McClafferty, Y. Fang, R. L. Olson, M. A. Perez, R. J. Hanowski, J. M. Hankey and T. A. Dingus (2013). The impact of hand-held and hands-free cell phone use on driving performance and safety-critical event risk. NHTSA Report No. DOT HS 811 757. U.S. Department of Transportation, Washington, DC.

Gaspar, J. G., W. N. Street, M. B. Windsor, R. Carbonari, H. Kaczmarski, A. F. Kramer and K. E. Mathewson (2014). Providing views of the driving scene to drivers' conversation partners mitigates cell-phone-related distraction. *Psychol. Sci.*, *25*(12), 2136-2146.

GHSA (2015). *Distracted Driving Laws.* Governors Highway Safety Association, Washington, DC. http://www.ghsa.org/html/stateinfo/laws/cellphone_laws.html

Gitelman, V., D. Zaidel, E. Duba and R. Zilberstein (2014). The effects of advertising signs on crashes in Ayalon Highway: Comparisons between three periods – with, without, and again with signs. Final Report to Israel's National Road Safety Authority. Jerusalem, Israel. (in Hebrew).

GM (2006). OnStar by GM. http://www.onstar.com/us_english/jsp/plans/index.jsp?seo=GOO_telematics

Goodman, M., F. D. Bent, L. Tijerina, W. Wiewille, N. Lerner and D. Benel (1997). An investigation of the safety implications of wireless communications in vehicles. National Highway Traffic Safety Administration Report DOT HS 808-635. U.S. Department of Transportation, Washington, DC. www.nhtsa.dot.gov:80/people/injury/research/wireless/

Goodwin, A. H., N. P. O'Brien and R. D. Foss (2012). Effect of North Carolina's restriction on teenage driver cell phone use two years after implementation. *Accid. Anal. Prev.*, *48*, 363-367.

Graham, R. and C. Carter (2001). Voice dialing can reduce the interference between concurrent tasks of driving and phoning. *Int. J. Vehicle Control*, *26*(1), 30-47.

Gras, M. E., M. Cunill, M. J. M. Sullman, M. Planes, M. Aymerich and S. Font-Mayolas (2007). Mobile phone use while driving in a sample of Spanish university workers. *Accid. Anal. Prev.*, *39*(2), 347-355.

Green, P. A. (1999). The 15-second rule for driver information systems. Intelligent Transportation Society of America, Annal Conference Proceedings.

Green, P., J. George and R. Jacob (2004). *What constitutes a typical cell phone call. UMTRI-2003-38*. University of Michigan Transportation Research Institute, Ann Arbor, MI.

Gugerty, L., M. Rakauskas and J. Brooks (2004). Effects of remote and in-person verbal interactions on verbalization rates and attention to dynamic spatial scenes. *Accid. Anal. Prev.*, *36*, 1029-1043.

Hallett, C., A. Lambert and M. A. Regan (2011). Cell phone conversing while driving in New Zealand: Prevalence, risk perception and legislation. *Accid. Anal. Prev.*, *43*(3), 862-869.

Hancock, P. A., M. Lesch and L. Simmons (2003). The distraction effects of phone use during a crucial driving maneuver. *Accid. Anal. Prev.*, *35*, 501–514.

Hancock, P. A. and B. D. Sawyer (2015). Judging thieves of attention commentary on "Assessing Cognitive Distraction in the Automobile," by Strayer, Turrill, Cooper, Coleman, Medeiros-Ward, and Biondi (2015). *Hum. Fact.*, *57*(8), 1339-1342.

Harbluk, J. L., Y. I. Noy, P. L. Trbovich and M. Eizenman (2007). An on-road assessment of cognitive distraction: Impacts on drivers' visual behavior and braking performance. *Accid. Anal. Prev.*, *39*, 372-379.

Harding, C. J. (2013). Failure of state texting-while-driving laws. *Pitt. J. Tech. Law. Policy*, *13*, 1-17.

Hatfield, J. and T. Chamberlain (2008). The effect of audio materials from a rear-seat audiovisual entertainment system or from radio on simulated driving. *Transportation Res. F*, *11*(1), 52-60.

Hatfield, J. and S. Murphy (2007). The effects of mobile phone use on pedestrian crossing behaviour at signalised and unsignalised intersections. *Accid. Anal. Prev.*, *39*(1), 197-205.

Hendricks, D. L., J. C. Fell and M. Freedman (2001). The relative frequency of unsafe driving acts in serious injury accidents. Final report submitted to NHTSA under contract No. DOT NH 22 94 C 05020. Veridian Engineering, Buffalo, NY.

Hibberd, D. L., S. L. Jamson and O. M. Carsten (2010). Managing in-vehicle distractions: Evidence from the psychological refractory period paradigm. Proceedings of the 2nd International Conference on Automotive User Interfaces and Interactive Vehicular Applications (pp. 4-11). ACM, Pittsburgh, PA.

Hickman, J. S. and R. J. Hanowski (2012). An assessment of commercial motor vehicle driver distraction using naturalistic driving data. *Traffic Inj. Prev.*, *13*(6), 612-619.

Ho, R., G. Davidson, M. Van Dyke and M. Agar-Wison (2000). The impact of motor vehicle accidents on the psychological well-being of at-fault drivers and related passengers. *J. Health Psychol.*, *5*(1), 33-51.

Holland, C. and V. Rathod (2013). Influence of personal mobile phone ringing and usual intention to answer on driver error. *Accid. Anal. Prev.*, *50*, 793-800.

Horrey, W. J. and C. D. Wickens (2006). Examining the impact of cell phone conversations on driving using meta-analytic techniques. *Hum. Fact.*, *48*(1), 196-205.

Horrey, W. J., C. D. Wickens and K. P. Consalus (2006). Modeling drivers' visual attention allocation while interacting with in-vehicle technologies. *J. Exp. Psych: App.*, *12*(2), 67-78.

Hosking, S., K. Young and M. Regan (2006). The effects of text messaging on young novice driver performance. Monash University Accident Research Center Report No. 246. Monash University, Clayton, Victoria, AU.

Hughes, P. K. and B. L. Cole (1984). Search and attention conspicuity of road traffic control devices. *Australian Road Res.*, *9*(3), 322-329.

Hughes, G. M., C. M. Rudin-Brown and K. L. Young (2013). A simulator study of the effects of singing on driving performance. *Accid. Anal. Prev.*, *50*, 787-792.

Huisingh, C., E. B. Levitan, M. R. Irvin, C. Owsley and G. McGwin (2016). Driving with pets and motor vehicle collision involvement among older drivers: A prospective population-based study. *Accid. Anal. Prev.*, *88*, 169-174.

IIHS (2014). *Distracted driving*. Insurance Institute of Highway Safety, Arlington, VA. http://www.iihs.org/iihs/topics/t/distracted-driving/qanda

ISO (2004). Road vehicles – Ergonomic aspects of transport information and control systems – Occlusion method to assess visual distraction due to the use of in-vehicle systems. ISO TC 22/SC 13 N 763 R.

Jamson, A. H., S. J. Westerman, G. R. J. Hockey and O. M. J. Carsten (2004). Speech-based e-mail and driver behavior: Effects of an in-vehicle message system interface. *Hum. Fact.*, *46*(4), 625-939.

Jenness, J. W., R. J. Lattanzio, M. O'Toole and N. Taylor (2002). Voice-activated dialing or eating a cheeseburger: Which is more distracting during simulated driving? Proceedings of the Human Factors and Ergonomics Society 46th Annual Meeting, Pittsburgh, PA.

Jeon, M., B. N. Walker and T. M. Gable (2014). Anger effects on driver situation awareness and driving performance. *Presence: Teleop. Virtual Environ,*, *23*(1), 71-89.

Jin, L., H. Xian, Y. Jiang, Q. Niu, M. Xu and D. Yang (2014). Research on evaluation model for secondary task driving safety based on driver eye movements. *Adv. Mech. Eng.*, *2014*, 1-8.

Just, M. A., T. A. Keller and J. Cynkar (2008). A decrease in brain activation associated with driving when listening to someone speak. *Brain Res.*, *1205*, 70-80.

Kidd, D. G. and McCartt, A. T. (2015). The relevance of crash type and severity when estimating crash risk using the SHRP2 naturalistic driving data. International Driver Distraction and Inattention Conference. Sydney, Australia. November.

Kiley, D. (2008). Texting surpasses calling among cell phone subscribers. Bloomberg Business, September 23. http://www.bloomberg.com/bw/stories/2008-09-23/texting-surpasses-calling-among-cell-phone-subscribers

Klauer, S. G., T. A. Dingus, V. L. Neale, J. D. Sudweeks and D. J. Ramsey (2006). The impact of driver inattention on near-crash/crash risk: An analysis using the 100-car naturalistic driving study data. National Highway Traffic Safety Administration Report No. DOT HS 810 594. U.S. Department of Transportation, Washington, DC.

Klauer, S. G., F. Guo, B. G. Simons-Morton, M. C. Ouimet, S. E. Lee and T. A. Dingus (2014). Distracted driving and risk of road crashes among novice and experienced drivers. *New England J. Med.*, *370*(1), 54-59.

Köhler, L., K. Bengler, C. Mergl, K. Maier and M. Wimmer (2014). Validation of a Telephone Manager for stressful driving situations. Proceedings of the Human Factors and Ergonomics Society Europe Chapter 2014 Annual Conference. Lisbon, Portugal.

Laberge-Nadeau, C., U. Maag, F. Bellavance, S. D. Lapierre, D. Desjardins, S. Messier and A. Säıdi (2003). Wireless telephones and the risk of road crashes. *Accid. Anal. Prev.*, *35*, 649–660.

Lamble, D., T. Kauranen, M. Laakso and H. Summala (1999). Cognitive load and detection thresholds in car following situations: Safety implications for using mobile (cellular) telephones while driving. *Accid. Anal. Prev.*, *31*, 617–623.

Lansdown, T. C. (2012). Individual differences and propensity to engage with in-vehicle distractions–A self-report survey. *Transportation Res. F*, *15*(1), 1-8.

Lansdown, T. C., N. Brook-Carter and T. Kersloot (2004). Distraction from multiple in-vehicle secondary tasks: Vehicle performance and mental workload implications. *Ergonomics*, *47*(1), 91–104.

Lee, J. D., B. Caven, S. Haake and T. L. Brown (2001). Speech-based interaction with in-vehicle computers: The effect of speech-based e-mail on drivers' attention to the roadway. *Hum. Fact.*, *43*(4), 631-640.

Lee, J. D., D. V. McGehee, T. L. Brown and M. L. Reyes (2002). Collision warning timing, driver distraction and driver response to imminent rear-end collisions in a high-fidelity driving simulator. *Hum. Fact.*, *44*(2), 314-334.

Lee, J. D., J. Moeckli, T. L. Brown, S. C. Roberts, C. Schwarz, L. Yekhshatyan, E. Nadler, Y. Liang, T. Victor, D. Marshall and C. Davis (2013). Distraction detection and mitigation through driver feedback. National Highway Traffic Safety Administration Report No. DOT HS 811 547A. U.S. Department of Transportation, Washington, DC.

Lerner, N. and S. Boyd (2005). On-road study of willingness to engage in distracting tasks. National Highway Traffic Safety Administration Report DOT HS 809 863. U.S. Department of Transportation, Washington, DC.

Lerner, N., J. Singer and R. Huey (2008). Driver strategies for engaging in distracting tasks using in-vehicle technologies. National Highway Traffic Safety Administration Report No. DOT HS 810 919. U.S. Department of Transportation, Washington, DC.

Leung, S., R. J. Croft, M. I. Jackson, M. E. Howard and R. J. Mckenzie (2012). A comparison of the effect of mobile phone use and alcohol consumption on driving simulation performance. *Traffic Inj. Prev.*, *13*(6), 566-574.

Levy, J., H. Pashler and E. Boer (2006). Central interference in driving. Is there any stopping the psychological refractory period? *Psychol. Sci.*, *17*(3), 228–235.

Liang, Y., W. J. Horrey and J. D. Hoffman (2015). Reading text while driving: Understanding drivers' strategic and tactical adaptation to distraction. *Hum. Fact.*, *57*(2), 347-359.

Liang, Y., M. L. Reyes and J. D. Lee (2007). Real-time detection of driver cognitive distraction using support vector machines. *IEEE Trans. ITS*, *8*(2), 340-350.

Lim, S. H. and J. Chi (2013). Are cell phone laws in the US effective in reducing fatal crashes involving young drivers? *Transport Policy*, *27*, 158-163.

Liu, B.-S. and Y.-H. Lee (2006). In-vehicle workload assessment: Effects of traffic situations and cellular telephone use. *J. Safe. Res.*, *37*, 99-105.

Luoma, J. (1988). Drivers' eye fixations and perceptions. In: *Vision in Vehicles: VI* (A. G. Gale, M. H. Freeman, C. M. Hasleman, P. Smith and S. P. Taylor, eds.). North Holland Press, Elsevier Science Publishers, New York, NY.

Maasalo, I., E. Lehtonen, J. Pekkanen and H. Summala (2016). Child passengers and driver culpability in fatal crashes by driver gender. *Traffic Inj. Prev.*, *17*(5), 447-453.

Marciano, H. and Y. Yeshurun (2015). Perceptual load in different regions of the visual scene and its relevance for driving. *Hum. Fact.*, *57*, 701-716.

Martens, M. H. (2000). Assessing road sign perception: A methodological review. *Transportation Hum. Fact.*, *2*(4), 347-357.

Martens, M. H. and R. F. Brouwer (2013). Measuring being lost in thought: An exploratory driving simulator study. *Transportation Res. F*, *20*, 17-28.

Mason-Dixon (2005). Drive for life: Annual national driver survey. Conducted by the Mason-Dixon Polling and Research Inc. for the National Highway Traffic Safety Administration, U.S. Department of Transportation, June 2005.

Matthews, R., S. Legg and S. Charlton (2003). The effect of cell phone type on drivers subjective workload during concurrent driving and conversing. *Accid. Anal. Prev.*, *35*, 451–457.

Mazzae, E. N., T. A. Ranney, G. S. Watson and J. A. Wightman (2004). Hand-held or hands-free? The effects of wireless phone interface type on phone task performance and driver performance. Proceedings of the 48th Annual Meeting of the Human Factors and Ergonomics Society (pp. 2218-2221).

McCartt, A. T. and L. A. Hellinga (2007). Longer-term effects of Washington, DC, law on drivers' hand-held cell phone use. *Traffic Inj. Prev.*, *8*(2), 199-204.

McCartt, A. T., L. A. Hellinga and K. A. Braitman (2006a). Cell phones and driving: Review of research. *Traffic Inj. Prev.*, *7*, 89-106.

McCartt, A. T., L. A. Hellinga and L. L. Geary (2006b). Effects of Washington, D.C. Law on drivers' hand-held cell phone use. *Traffic Inj. Prev.*, *7*, 1-6.

McCartt, A. T., D. G. Kidd and E. R. Teoh (2014). Driver cellphone and texting bans in the United States: Evidence of effectiveness. *Annals Adv. Automotive Med.*, *58*, 99-114.

McEvoy, S. P., M. R. Stevenson, A. T. McCartt, M. Woodward, C. Haworth, P. Palamara and R. Cercarelli (2005). Role of mobile phones in motor vehicle crashes resulting in hospital attendance: A case-crossover study. *Br. Med. J.*, *331*, 428-430.

McEvoy, S. P., M. R. Stevenson and M. Woodward (2007). The prevalence of, and factors associated with, serious crashes involving a distracting activity. *Accid. Anal. Prev.*, *39*(3), 475-482.

McGehee, D. V., M. Raby, C. Carney, J. D. Lee and M. L. Reyes (2007). Extending parental mentoring using and event-triggered video intervention in rural teen drivers. *J. Safety Res.*, *38*, 215–227

McKnight, A. J. and A. S. McKnight (1993). The effect of cellular phone use upon driver attention. *Accid. Anal. Prev.*, *25*(3), 259–265.

McNees, R. W. and C. J. Messer (1981) Evaluating urban freeway guide signing. Federal Highway Administration Report No. FHWA/TX-81/5 + 220-3. U.S. Department of Transportation, Washington, DC.

McPhee, L. C., C. T. Scialfa, W. M. G. Dennis, W. M. G. Ho and J. K. Caird (2004). Age differences in visual search for traffic signs during a simulated conversation. *Hum. Fact.*, *46*(4), 674-685.

Metz, B., A. Landau and M. Just (2014). Frequency of secondary tasks in driving–Results from naturalistic driving data. *Safety Sci.*, *68*, 195-203.

Meyer, J. (2006). Helping drivers limit distraction: Some lessons from a failed idea. Ben Gurion University of the Negev, Israel. Unpublished manuscript.

Monk, C. A., D. A. Boehm-Davis and J. G. Trafton (2004a). Recovering from interruptions: Implications for driver distraction research. *Hum. Fact.*, *46*(4), 650-663.

Monk, A., J. Carroll, S. Parker and M. Blythe (2004b). Why are mobile phones annoying? *Behav. Inform. Technol.*, *23*(1), 33-41.

Mourant, R. R. and T. H. Rockwell (1972). Strategies of visual search by novice and experienced drivers. *Hum. Fact.*, *14*, 325–335.

Mourant, R. R., T. H. Rockwell and N. J. Rackoff (1969). Drivers' eye movements and visual workload. *Highway Res. Record*, *292*, 1-10.

Navon, D. and D. Gopher (1979). On the economy of the human-processing systems. *Psychol. Rev.*, *86*(3), 214-255.

NCSL (2005). *Cell phones and highway safety: 2005 State legislative update.* National Conference of State Legislators, Washington, DC.
Neale, V. L., T. A. Dingus, S. G. Klauer, J. Sudweeks and M. Goodman (2005). An overview of the 100-car naturalistic study and findings. Experimental Safety Vehicles (ESV) conference Paper Number 05-0400, Washington, DC.
NHTSA (2001). Statement of L. Robert Shelton, Executive Director, National Highway Traffic Safety Administration, before the Subcommittee on Highways and Transit, Committee on Transportation and Infrastructure, U.S. House of Representatives, May 9.
NHTSA (2012a). Distracted Driving 2010. Traffic Safety Facts, National Highway Traffic Safety Administration Report DOT HS 811 650. U.S. Department of Transportation, Washington, DC.
NHTSA (2012b). Young drivers report the highest level of phone involvement in crash or near-crash incidences. Traffic Safety Facts, National Highway Traffic Safety Administration Report DOT HS 811 611. U.S. Department of Transportation, Washington, DC.
NHTSA (2012c). Visual-manual NHTSA driver distraction guidelines for in-vehicle electronic devices. National Highway Traffic Safety Administration Docket No. NHTSA-2010-0053. U.S. Department of Transportation, Washington, DC.
NHTSA (2014). Visual-manual NHTSA driver distraction guidelines for in-vehicle electronic devices. Federal Register. 09/16/2014.
NHTSA (2015a). Traffic Safety Facts: 2014 Crash data key findings. National Highway Traffic Safety Administration Report DOT HS 812 219. U.S. Department of Transportation, Washington, DC.
NHTSA (2015b). Driver electronic device use in 2013. Traffic Safety Facts, National Highway Traffic Safety Administration Report DOT HS 812 114. U.S. Department of Transportation, Washington, DC.
NHTSA (2015c). Young drivers report the highest level of phone involvement in crash or near-crash incidences. Traffic Safety Facts – Research Note. Report No. DOT-HS-811-611. U.S. Department of Transportation, Washington, DC.
NHTSA (2016a). Driver electronic device use in 2015. Traffic Safety Facts, National Highway Traffic Safety Administration Report DOT HS 812 326. U.S. Department of Transportation, Washington, DC.
NHTSA (2016b). Distracted Driving 2014. Traffic Safety Facts, National Highway Traffic Safety Administration Report DOT HS 812 260. U.S. Department of Transportation, Washington, DC.
NSC (2010). Understanding the distracted brain: Why driving while using hands-free cell phones is risky behavior. U.S. National Safety Council White Paper. March. https://www.fnal.gov/pub/traffic_safety/files/NSC%20White%20Paper%20-%20Distracted%20Driving%203-10.pdf
Oblad, C. (2000). On using music – The car as a concert hall. In: *Proceedings of the 6th International Conference on Music Perception and Cognition.* (C. Woods, G. Luck, R. Brochard, F. Seddon and J. A. Sloboda, eds.) Keele University, Staffordshire, UK (as cited in Brodsky, 2000).
Olsen, E. O., R. A. Shults and D. K. Eaton (2013). Texting while driving and other risky motor vehicle behaviors among US high school students. *Pediatrics*, *131*(6), e1708-1715.

Olson, R., R. Hanowski, J. Hickman and J. Bocanegra (2009). Driver distraction in commercial vehicle operations (Rep. No. FMCSA-RRR-09-042). Federal Motor Carrier Safety Administration, U.S. Department of Transportation, Washington, DC.

Olsson, S. and P. C. Burns (2000). *Measuring driver visual distraction with a peripheral detection task*. Driver Distraction Internet Forum, National Highway Traffic Safety Administration, U.S. Department of Transportation, Washington, DC.

Online Auto Insurance News (2003). Even when not on the phone cell phone users are more distracted when driving. Press release. Meridian, CT, July 1.

Östlund, J., L. Nilsson, J. Törnros and Å. Forsman (2006). Effects of cognitive and visual load in real and simulated driving. VTI Report 533A for the EC Project HASTE. Swedish National Road and Transport Institute (VTI), Linköping, Sweden.

Parkes, A. (1991). Drivers business decision making ability whilst using carphones. In: *Proceedings of the Ergonomics Society Annual Conference* (E. J. Lovesey, ed.), pp. 427-432. Taylor and Francis, London.

Parkes, A. M., S. H. Fairclough and M. C. Ashby (1993). Carphone use and motorway driving. In: *Contemporary Ergonomics 1993* (E. J. Lovesey, ed.). Taylor and Francis, London.

Patten, C. J. D., A. Kircher, J. Ostlund and L. Nilsson (2004). Using mobile telephones: Cognitive workload and attention resource allocation. *Accid. Anal. Prev.*, *36*, 341–350.

Peng, Y., L. N. Boyle and J. D. Lee (2014). Reading, typing, and driving: How interactions with in-vehicle systems degrade driving performance. *Transportation Res. F*, *27*, 182-191.

Perez, M. A., L. S. Angell and J. M. Hankey (2015). Assessment of naturalistic use patterns of advanced infotainment systems. *Hum. Fact.*, *57*, 674-688.

Pettitt, M., G. Burnett and A. Stevens (2005). Defining driver distraction. Paper presented at World Congress on Intelligent Transport Systems, San Francisco, November.

Pew Research (2014). Mobile Technology Fact Sheet. http://www.pewinternet.org/fact-sheets/mobile-technology-fact-sheet/

Pouyakian, M., H. A. Mahabadi, S. M. Yazdi, E. Hajizadeh and A. Nahvi (2013). Impact of headway distance and car speed on drivers' decisions to answer an incoming call. *Traffic Inj. Prev.*, *14*(7), 749-755.

Pöysti, L., S. Rajalin and H. Summala (2005). Factors influencing the use of cellular (mobile) phone during driving and hazards while using it. *Accid. Anal. Prev.*, *37*, 47–51.

PR Newswire (May 19, 2015). Smartphone use while driving grows beyond texting to social media, web surfing, selfies, video chatting. http://www.prnewswire.com/news-releases/smartphone-use-while-driving-grows-beyond-texting–to-social-media-web-surfing-selfies-video-chatting-300085207.html

Rakauskas, M. E., L. J. Gugerty and N. J. Ward (2004). Effects of naturalistic cell phone conversations on driving performance. *J. Safe. Res.*, *35*, 453-464.

Ranney, T. A., J. L. Harbluk and Y. I. Noy (2005). Effects of voice technology on test track driving performance: Implications for driver distraction. *Hum. Fact.*, *47*(2), 439-454.

Recarte, M. A. and L. Nunes (2002). Mental load and loss of control over speed in real driving. Towards a theory of attentional speed control. *Transportation Res. F, 5*, 111–122.

Redelmeier, D. A. and R. J. Tibshirani (1997). Association between cell phones calls and motor vehicle collisions. *New England J. Med., 336*(2), 453–458.

Regan, M. A., C. Hallett and C. P. Gordon (2011). Driver distraction and driver inattention: Definition, relationship and taxonomy. *Accid. Anal. Prev., 43*(5), 1771-1781.

Reimer, B., B. Mehler, Y. Wang and J. F. Coughlin (2010). The impact of systematic variation of cognitive demand on driver's visual attention across multiple age groups. *Proc. Human Fact. Ergonom. Soc., 54*, 2052-2056.

Roney, L., P. Violano, G. Klaus, R. Lofthouse and J. Dziura (2013). Distracted driving behaviors of adults while children are in the car. *J. Trauma Acute Care Surg., 75*(4), S290-S295.

Royal, D. (2003). National survey of distracted and drowsy driving: Attitudes and behaviors 2002. National Highway Traffic Safety Administration, Report No. DOT HS 809 566. U.S. Department of Transportation, Washington, DC.

SAE (2000). SAE Recommended Practice: Navigation and route guidance function accessibility while driving (SAE 2364), January 20.

Salvucci, D. D., M. Zuber, E. Beregovaia and D. Markley (2005). Distract-R: Rapid prototyping and evaluation of in-vehicle interfaces. CHI (Computer Human Interface) Annual Conference, Portland, OR, April 2-7.

Savage, S. W., D. D. Potter and B. W. Tatler (2013). Does preoccupation impair hazard perception? A simultaneous EEG and Eye Tracking study. *Transportation Res. F, 17*, 52-62.

Sawyer, B. D., V. S. Finomore, A. A. Calvo and P. A. Hancock (2014). Google glass a driver distraction cause or cure? *Hum. Fact., 56*, 1307-1321.

Schroeder, P., M. Meyers and L. Kostyniuk (2013). National survey on distracted driving attitudes and behaviors – 2012. National Highway Traffic Safety Administration Report No. DOT HS 811 729. U.S. Department of Transportation, Washington, DC.

Shinar, D. (2006). *Driving, cell phones, and sign detection in a naturalistic setting*. Ben Gurion University of the Negev, Israel. Unpublished report.

Shinar, D. (2015). Cognitive workload ≠ crash risk: Rejoinder to study by Strayer et al. (2015). *Hum. Fact., 57*(8), 1328–1330.

Shinar, D. and R. Compton (2004). Aggressive driving: An observational study of driver, vehicle, and situational variables. *Accid. Anal. Prev., 36*, 429-437.

Shinar, D., G. Peleg and A. Segev (2003). *The effects of oversized billboards in an urban area on drivers' looking behavior*. Ben Gurion University of the Negev, Israel. Unpublished study.

Shinar, D. and A. Ronen (2007). Validation of speed perception and production in STI-SIM single screen simulator. Proceedings of the International Conference on Road Safety and Simulation, Rome, November 7-9.

Shinar, D., N. Tractinsky and R. P. Compton (2005). Effects of practice, age, and task demands, on interference from a phone task while driving. *Accid. Anal. Prev., 37*, 315-326.

Shutko, J., K. Mayer, E. Laansoo and L. Tijerina (2009). Driver workload effects of cell phone, music player, and text messaging tasks with the Ford SYNC voice interface versus handheld visual-manual interfaces. SAE Technical Paper No. 2009-01-0786. Society of Automotive Engineers, Detroit, Michigan.

Sloboda, J. A., S. A. O'Neill and A. Ivaldi (2001). Functions of music in everyday life: An exploratory study using the experience sampling method. *Music. Scient.*, *5*, 9-32.

Smiley, A., T. Smahel and M. Eizenman (2004). Impact of video advertising on driver fixation patterns. *Transportation Res. Record*, *1899*, 76-83.

Smith, A. (2011). *Americans and Text Messaging*. Pew Research Center, Washington, DC.

Sodhi, M., B. Reimer, J. L. Cohen, E. Vastenburg, R. Kaars and S. Kirschenbaum (2002a). On road driver eye movement tracking using head-mounted devices. Proceedings of ETRA 2002: Eye Tracking Research and Applications Symposium (pp. 61-68).

Sodhi, M., B. Reimer and I. Llamazares (2002b). Glance analysis of driver eye movements to evaluate distraction. *Behav. Res. Methods Instruments Computers*, *34*(4), 529-538.

Stephens, A. N., S. L. Trawley, R. Madigan and J. A. Groeger (2013). Drivers display anger-congruent attention to potential traffic hazards. *App. Cog. Psych.*, *27*(2), 178-189.

Strayer, D. S., J. M. Cooper, J. Turrill, R. R. Coleman and R. J. Hopman (2015a). *The smartphone and the driver's cognitive workload: A comparison of Apple, Google, and Microsoft's intelligent personal assistants.* AAA Foundation for Traffic Safety, Washington, DC.

Strayer, D. L. and F. A. Drews (2004). Profiles in driver distraction: Effects of cell phone conversations on younger and older drivers. *Hum. Fact.*, *46*(4), 640-649.

Strayer, D. L. and F. A. Drews (2007). Multi-tasking in the Automobile. In: *Attention: From Theory to Practice* (A. F. Kramer, D. A. Wiegmann and A. Kirlik, eds.). Oxford University Press, Oxford, England.

Strayer, D. L., F. A. Drews, D. J. Crouch and W. A. Johnston (2005). Why do cell phone conversations interfere with driving? In W. R. Walker and D. Herrmann (Eds.) *Cognitive Technology: Transforming Thought and Society*. McFarland & Company Inc., Jefferson, NC.

Strayer, D. L., F. A. Drews and W. A. Johnston (2003). Cell phone-induced failures of visual attention during simulated driving. *J. Exp. Psychol. Appl.*, *9*, 23–32.

Strayer, D. L. and W. A. Johnston (2001). Driven to distraction: Dual-task studies of simulated driving and conversing on a cellular phone. *Psychol. Sci.*, *12*, 462-466.

Strayer, D. L., J. Turrill, J. M. Cooper, J. R. Coleman and N. Medeiros-Ward (2015b). Assessing cognitive distraction in the automobile. *Hum. Fact.*, *75*, 1300-1324.

Struckman-Johnson, C., S. Gaster and D. Struckman-Johnson (2014). A preliminary study of sexual activity as a distraction for young drivers. *Accid. Anal. Prev.*, *71*, 120-128.

Struckman-Johnson, C., S. Gaster and D. Struckman-Johnson (2015). Corrigendum to 'A preliminary study of sexual activity as a distraction for young drivers'. *Accid. Anal. Prev.*, *74*, 368.

Stutts, J., J. Feaganes, D. Reinfurt, E. Rodgman, C. Hamlett, K. Gish and L. Staplin (2005). Driver's exposure to distractions in their natural driving environment. *Accid. Anal. Prev.*, *37*, 1093-1101.

Stutts, J., J. Feaganes, E. Rodgman, C. Hamlett, T. Meadows, D. Reinfurt, K. Gish, M. Mercandante and L. Staplin (2003). *Distractions in Everyday Driving*. AAA Foundation for Traffic Safety, Washington, DC.

Summala, H. and R. Näätänen (1974). Perception of highway traffic signs and motivation. *J. Safe. Res.*, *6*, 150-154.

SWOV (2009). *Roadside Advertising and Information*. SWOV Fact Sheet. SWOV, Leidschendam, The Netherlands.

Taieb, M. and D. Shinar (2001) Minimum and comfortable driving headways: Reality vs perception. *Hum. Fact.*, *43*, 159-172.

Talbot, R., H. Fagerlind and A. Morris (2013). Exploring inattention and distraction in the SafetyNet Accident Causation Database. *Accid. Anal. Prev.*, *60*, 445-455.

Tijerina, L., S. Johnston, E. Parmer, M. D. Winterbottom and M. Goodman (2000). Driver distraction with wireless telecommunications and route guidance systems. National Highway Traffic Safety Administration Report No. DOT HS 809-069. U.S. Department of Transportation, Washington, DC.

Tijerina, L., E. Parmer and M. J. Goodman (1998). Driver workload assessment route guidance system destination entry while driving: A test track study. Proceedings of the 5th ITS World Congress.

Tison, J., N. Chaudhary and L. Cosgrove (2011). National phone survey on distracted driving attitudes and behaviors. National Highway Traffic Safety Administration Report No. DOT HS 811 555. U.S. Department of Transportation, Washington, DC.

Tivesten, E. and M. Dozza (2015). Driving context influences drivers' decision to engage in visual–manual phone tasks: Evidence from a naturalistic driving study. *J. Safety Res.*, *53*, 87-96.

Tomer-Fishman, T. (2010). *Driver distraction due to use of electronic communications*. National Road Safety Authority Report, Jerusalem, Israel. (in Hebrew).

Törnros, J. E. B. and A. K. Bolling (2005). Mobile phone use Effects of handheld and handsfree phones on driving performance. *Accid. Anal. Prev.*, *37*, 902–909

Tractinsky, N., E. S. Ram and D. Shinar (2013). To call or not to call—that is the question (while driving). *Accid. Anal. Prev.*, *56*, 59-70.

Treat, J. R., N. S. Tumbas, S. T. McDonald, D. Shinar, R. D. Hume, R. E. Mayer, R. L. Stansifer and N. J. Castellan (1979). Tri-level study of the causes of traffic accidents: Final report. Volume I: Causal factor tabulations and assessments. National Highway Traffic Safety Administration Report No. DOT HS 805 085. U.S. Department of Transportation, Washington, DC.

Troglauer, T., T. Hels and P. F. Christens (2006). Extent and variations in mobile phone use among drivers of heavy vehicles in Denmark. *Accid. Anal. Prev.*, *38*(1), 105-1111.

Tsimhoni, O., D. Smith and P. Green (2004). Address entry while driving: Speech recognition versus a touch-screen keyboard. *Hum. Fact.*, *46*(4), 600-610.

UMTRI (2012). University of Michigan Transportation Research Institute, Press release November 27, 2012. http://www.ns.umich.edu/new/releases/21000-driver-distraction-do-as-i-say-not-as-i-do-or-what-you-think-i-do

Ünal, A. B., L. Steg and K. Epstude (2012). The influence of music on mental effort and driving performance. *Accid. Anal. Prev.*, *48*, 271-278.

US-EU Bi-lateral ITS Task Force (2010). Expert group on driver distraction: Definition and research needs. April 28, Berlin, Germany.

Wachtel, J. (2009). Safety impacts of the emerging digital display technology for outdoor advertising signs. Final report for NCHRP Project 20-7 (256). Veridian Group, Berkeley, California.

Wachtel, J. (2011). Digital billboards, distracted drivers. *Planning*, *77*(3), 25-27.

Waddell, L. P. and K. K. Wiener (2014). What's driving illegal mobile phone use? Psychosocial influences on drivers' intentions to use hand-held mobile phones. *Transportation Res. F*, *22*, 1-11.

Wald, M. L. (2014). Agency aims to regulate map aids in vehicles. New York Times, June 15. http://www.nytimes.com/2014/06/16/business/agency-aims-to-regulate-map-aids-in-vehicles.html?_r=1

Walsh, S. P., K. M. White, M. K. Hyde and B. Watson (2008). Dialling and driving: Factors influencing intentions to use a mobile phone while driving. *Accid. Anal., Prev.*, *40*(6), 1893-1900.

Waugh, J. D., M. M. Glumm, P. W. Kilduff, R. A. Tauson, C. C. Smyth and R. S. Pillalamarri (2000). Cognitive workload while driving and talking on a cellular phone or to a passenger. Proceedings of the Human Factors and Ergonomics Society Meeting.

White, C. B. and J. K. Caird (2010). The blind date: The effects of change blindness, passenger conversation and gender on looked-but-failed-to-see (LBFTS) errors. *Accid. Anal. Prev.*, *42*, 1822-1830.

White, M. P., J. R. Eiser and P. R. Harris (2004). Risk perceptions of mobile phone use while driving. *Risk Anal.*, *24*(2), 323-334.

WHO (2011). *Mobile phone use: A growing problem of driver distraction.* World Health Organization, Geneva, Switzerland.

WHO (2015). *Global status report on road safety 2015: Supporting a decade of action.* World Health Organization, Geneva, Switzerland.

Wickens, C. D. (1984). Processing resources in attention. In: *Varieties of Attention* (R. Parasuraman and R. Davies, eds.), pp. 63–101. Academic Press, New York, NY.

Wickens, C. D. (2008). Multiple resources and mental workload. *Hum. Fact.*, *50*(3), 449-455.

Wiesenthal, D. L., D. A. Hennessy and B. Totten (2003). The influence of music on mild driver aggression. *Transportation Res. F*, *6*(2), 125-134.

Williams, S. (2015). As head-up displays become common, distraction becomes an issue. New York Times, September 10.

Wogalter, M. S. and C. B. Mayhorn (2005). Perceptions of driver distraction by cellular phone users and nonusers. *Hum. Fact.*, *47*(2), 455-467.

Yager, C. (2013). An evaluation of the effectiveness of voice-to-text programs at reducing incidences of distracted driving. Texas A&M Transportation Institute Report No. SWUTC/13/600451-00011-1. College Station, TX.

Yanko, M. R. and T. M. Spalek (2014). Driving with the wandering mind the effect that mind-wandering has on driving performance. *Hum. Fact.*, *56*(2), 260-269.

Yannis, G., A. Laiou, P. Papantoniou and C. Christoforou (2014). Impact of texting on young drivers' behavior and safety on urban and rural roads through a simulation experiment. *J. Safety Res.*, *49*, 25.e1.

Yannis, G., E. Papadimitriou, X. Karekla and E. Kontodima (2010). Mobile phone use by young drivers: Effects on traffic speed and headways. *Transportation Plan. Technol.*, *33*(4), 385-394.

Young, K., M. Regan and M. Hammer (2003). Driver distraction: A review of the literature. Monash University Accident Research Center (MUARC), Report No. 206. Clayton, Victoria, AU.

Young, K. L. and P. M. Salmon (2015). Sharing the responsibility for driver distraction across road transport systems: A systems approach to the management of distracted driving. *Accid. Anal. Prev.*, *74*, 350-359.

Young, K. L., P. M. Salmon and M. Cornelissen (2013). Missing links? The effects of distraction on driver situation awareness. *Safety Sci.*, *56*, 36-43.

Young, M. S., J. M. Mahfoud, N. A. Stanton, P. M. Salmon, D. P. Jenkins and G. H. Walker (2009). Conflicts of interest: The implications of roadside advertising for driver attention. *Transportation Res. F*, *12*(5), 381-388.

Young, M. S., J. M. Mahfoud, G. H. Walker, D. P. Jenkins and N. A. Stanton (2008). Crash dieting: The effects of eating and drinking on driving performance. *Accid. Anal. Prev.*, *40*(1), 142-148.

Young, R. A. (2012). Cell phone use and crash risk. *Epidemiology*, *23*(1), 116-118.

Young, R. A. (2013). Cell phone conversation and automobile crashes: Relative risk is Near 1, Not 4. Proceedings of the 3rd International Conference on Driver Distraction and Inattention, September 4-6, 2013, Gothenburg, Sweden (No. 68-P).

Young, R. A. (2015). Driver compensation impairment or improvement? *Hum. Fact.*, *57*(8), 1334-1338.

Young, R. (2017). Removing biases from crash odds ratio estimates of secondary tasks: A new analysis of the SHRP 2 Naturalistic Driving Study Data. SAE Technical Paper No. 2017-01-1380. SAE, NY.

Zhou, R., P.-L. P. Rau, W. Zhang and D. Zhang (2012). Mobile phone use while driving: Predicting drivers' answering intentions and compensatory decisions. *Safety Sci.*, *50*(1), 138-149.

Zhou, R., C. Wu, P.-L. P. Rau and W. Zhang (2009). Young driving learners' intention to use a handheld or hands-free mobile phone when driving. *Transportation Res. F*, *12*, 208–217.

14

Fatigue and Driving

DROVE TOO LONG
DRIVER SNOOZING
WHAT HAPPENED NEXT
IS NOT AMUSING
Burma Shave
(Staggered roadside signs posted on U.S. Interstate roads in the 1940s and 1950s).

The Concept of Driver Fatigue

Defining fatigue

Although we all know it when we feel it, fatigue is not that easy to define. It is a hypothetical concept that cannot be directly observed. As such it is often defined as "a biological drive for recuperative rest" (Williamson *et al.*, 2011). In more practical terms, nearly 70 years ago, Bartley and Chute (1947, as cited by Brown, 1982) attempted to define fatigue by a list of what it is and what it isn't. This list of identifying features is reproduced in Table 14-1.

In short, according to Brown (1982) it is a "subjective experience of tiredness and unwillingness to continue working." The obvious shortcoming of this definition is that it is based on purely subjective experiences and therefore very difficult to study in a scientific manner. Unfortunately not much has changed in this respect over the past half century, and there is still no agreed-upon definition of fatigue among researchers (Åhsberg and

Table 14-1. Inclusion and exclusion criteria for fatigue offered by Bartley and Chute (1947) (as cited by Brown, 1982).

What Fatigue Is	**What Fatigue Is Not**
It is always directly experienced – impairment is not necessarily so	It is not identical to impairment – one can be fatigued and not show impairment and vice versa
It is a personal experience related to a person's self-evaluation and present and past experiences	It cannot be measured by impairment
It is cumulative	It does not depend crucially on energy expenditure
It results from a conflict – when a person cannot escape an undesirable situation	It is not the same as boredom – though the latter can contribute to it
Its onset and recovery may be sudden (unlike impairment)	It is not limited to specific body parts – it is generalized

Gamberale, 1998; Belz, Robinson, and Casali, 2004; Di Milia *et al.*, 2011; Williamson *et al.*, 2011; Phillips, 2015).

If we consider fatigue as a causal factor in impaired performance and crashes then we can relate it to three general observable and measurable independent variables that affect it and three dependent kinds of outcomes. The independent variables that are associated with and likely to cause fatigue are: the length of time a person has been awake, the time-of-day (see circadian rhythm below), and task characteristics (such as a monotonous drive) (Williamson *et al.*, 2011). In terms of outcome measures, Åhsberg and Gamberale (1998) on the basis of an extensive review of the scientific literature noted that the deteriorations (dependent variables) can be defined in terms of three dimensions: bodily changes (such as reductions in physiological potentials and neuron-muscular capabilities), performance changes (such as output, reaction time, and disinclination to continue working), and subjective sensations (such as feelings of tiredness, weariness, lack of motivation, and sleepiness). A noble attempt to include all these factors in the definition of fatigue was made by Phillips (2015), who provides both a very lengthy comprehensive definition as well as concluding that the origin of fatigue is exertion in one form or another (mental or physical).

To provide a practical tool to measure fatigue, Åhsberg and Gamberale (1998) compiled all the different aspects of fatigue, and conducted statistical analyses to identify its independent dimensions. They came up with 25 descriptors of fatigue that could be mapped into five dimensions: Lack of energy, Physical exertion, Physical discomfort, Lack of motivation, and Sleepiness. The expressions were then incorporated into an inventory – the Swedish Occupational Fatigue Inventory (SOFI) – that can be used to identify the subjective level of fatigue a person experiences on each one of these dimensions (Åhsberg and Gamberale, 1998; Åhsberg, Gamberale, and Kjellberg, 1997; Gutierrez *et al.*, 2005). As expected, prolonged physical work is reflected mostly in physical exertion and physical discomfort, and prolonged mental work – like driving – results mostly in lack of energy, lack of motivation, and sleepiness (Desmond, Hancock, and Monette, 1998).

An alternative to defining fatigue in terms of subjective experience is to define it in terms of some observable, measurable, and conceptually related variables such as sleep deprivation or time-on-task. Sleep deprivation – typically when carried to extreme, such as continuous wakefulness for more than 24 hours (Barger *et al.*, 2005; Peters *et al.*, 1999) – is associated with deteriorations in driver performance and an increase in accidents. In fact, some researchers use fatigue and sleepiness interchangeably (Connor *et al.*, 2001; Williamson *et al.*, 2001). Still another approach is to define fatigue in terms of its *expected* measurable consequences. These include impairments in physiological functioning, such as an increase in heart rate variability (Oron-Gilad, Ronen, and Shinar, 2008) and long eye-closures (Knipling, 1998; Verwey and Zaidel, 1999); or changes in performance, such as slowed information processing, increased reaction time, reduced vigilance, and lapses in attention (NHTSA, 1998; Thiffault *et al.*, 2003; Verwey and Zaidel, 1999). Perhaps the most commonly used fatigue-related performance measures are attention-related measures such as "vigilance" – an impairment in an operator's ability to detect small changes or targets in an otherwise uneventful situation (Dinges, 1995; Wierwille *et al.*, 1994; Williamson *et al.*, 2001).

For our purposes, here we will define fatigue as a state of mind that a driver equates with sleepiness, tiredness, drowsiness, and lack of energy that is associated with some measure of decrease in performance or a physiological indicator of reduced arousal. It is significant that this definition dissociates fatigue from lack of sleep, though it is often correlated with it. Sleep and "sleepiness" – the tendency to fall asleep – are complex phenomena that depend on the interaction of many variables in addition to the lack of sleep (Johns, 2000; Ogilvie, 2001). Thus, with this definition a person may experience fatigue that is a result of a monotonous driving task even after a full night sleep and it can be documented as such if it is accompanied by some deterioration in driving performance. This definition is similar to the one offered by Thiffault and Bergeron (2003) who define fatigue as a general term that relates to the deterioration in both physiological and psychological processes that results in a decreased capacity to perform a given task, along with the subjective states which are associated with decreased performance. This definition also implies that the subjective, physiological, and behavioral aspects of fatigue are correlated. This is often the case but not always. In fact, in one field study that tracked the appearance, the manners, and the subjective ratings of fatigue of nine truck drivers over a 5-6 day work trip, Belz *et al.* (2004) failed to find practically significant correlations between the drivers' subjective level of "sleepiness" (using the Karolinska Institute 9-level sleepiness scale; Akerstedt and Gillberg, 1990), their reaction times to a prompt to report their sleepiness, the ratings of drowsiness by external observers (based on observations of the drivers' faces as they were recorded during the drive), headways, and time-to-collision with vehicles in front (that were automatically calculated and recorded). This means that we must be cautious when we assume a driver is fatigued based on a single measure – either objective or subjective.

The dissociation of fatigue from lack of sleep (within limits) creates an apparent paradox: fatigue is not the same as lack of sleep, yet taking a short nap is probably the most effective way of counteracting fatigue. This is because taking a nap also relieves the driver from the fatiguing driving task. In fact, in an interesting study, Philip *et al.* (2003) evaluated the driving behavior of drivers who pulled into a rest stop while they were on a long-distance trip on a motorway linking Sweden and Portugal. The evaluation was based on their vehicle control as they drove a relatively primitive simulator that was set up at the rest stop. Relative to a control group who had not been driving prior to the simulated drive, the lateral vehicle control of the drivers on the long simulated trip was very poor. Using statistical regression to determine which variables were specifically associated with the performance deterioration, Philip and his associates found that hours of sleep and hours since waking up were not significant predictors of performance while hours of driving was a significant factor: the more hours drivers had spent on the road prior to pulling into the rest stop, the poorer their performance was. In a later study, Philip and his associates (2006) had drivers drive a 200-kilometer route in the evening (6 to 7:30 pm) and late at night (2:00 to 3:30 am). Just prior to the night drive they either drank half a cup of coffee (200mg caffeine), or a placebo, or had a 30-minute nap. The results showed that after the placebo drink drivers crossed the lane markers 3.7 times as often as after drinking coffee, and 2.9 times as often as after taking a nap. In addition, the drivers' subjective ratings of sleepiness were also lower with the coffee and with the nap than with the placebo – even though the sleepiness ratings during the night drive – for all three night conditions – were higher than the sleepiness ratings during the evening drive.

Finally, not all drivers' performance deteriorates at the same rate in response to prolonged driving. Some drivers may drive longer before they experience subjective and objective symptoms of fatigue than others. Interestingly, the subjective level of fatigue at which drivers' performance deteriorates appears to be the same, but different drivers can tolerate different amounts of driving before they reach that level. This was demonstrated in a driving simulation study by Nilsson, Nelson, and Carlson (1997) where drivers were asked to drive as long as they possibly could. (Parenthetically, it should be noted that one of the significant differences between real world driving and driving in a simulation is that fatigue onset begins much earlier in a simulator than in real driving.) Although different drivers quit at different times anywhere from 90 to 240 minutes, their subjective ratings of their fatigue were quite the same at the time they felt they could not continue to drive. This was true both for generalized subjective evaluation of fatigue such as "feeling drowsy" as well as for specific symptoms such as "sore feet" and "tired eyes." One possible source of the individual differences may be the amount of attention drivers need to allocate to manage the driving task. In our driving simulation studies, we found that when driving on a monotonous route professional truck drivers despite having similar subjective and physiological reactions from fatigue are able to better maintain their lane position even when fatigued. Also, in our simulated fatigue-inducing drives most non-professional drivers fell asleep after about 90 minutes, while most professional truck drivers could continue beyond two hours. This finding has both theoretical implications for defining fatigue as well as practical implications for designing fatigue countermeasures. We turn first to the theoretical issues and conclude with the applications issues.

Fatigue and driving – a theoretical framework

The primary effect of fatigue on driver behavior is in the attentional domain: from the decreased sampling of information (part but not all due to eyelid closing), to the partial and slowed processing of stimuli that impinge on our sensory systems. One simple hypothesis is that fatigue lowers our overall level of attention. This is an appealing argument and it is supported by evidence that allocating attentional resources to a task – or simply stated paying attention – is an effort (Kahneman, 1973). Fatigue makes us reluctant to expend the effort needed for a task. In terms of Blumenthal's (1968) model (see Chapter 3), it would imply that because the overall level of attention is lowered, we are more likely to encounter situations where the allocation falls short of the demands. Kahneman's model and other resource theories, such as Wickens' (see Chapter 3) would then predict that any additional cognitive load imposed on an already fatigued driver would further impair his or her performance. However, as we will show below the opposite is true: in a state of fatigue, performance can actually improve when the driver is provided with stimulation either from the roadway or from additional cognitive tasks. This is something most drivers intuitively feel as they seek to counteract fatigue by turning on the music or asking a passenger to talk to them. Empirical research, discussed below, also demonstrates that loading the fatigued driver with added stimulation and tasks can actually improve performance (Desmond and Matthews, 1997; Gershon *et al.*, 2009a; Oron-Gilad *et al.*, 2008; Takayama and Nass, 2008; Verwey and Zaidel, 1999). These paradoxical experiences and findings necessitate an alternative theory that would relate the effects of fatigue to human performance.

A model that is consistent with the fatigued driving data has been proposed by Desmond and Matthews (1997). According to them fatigue does not lower the amount of attention available, but rather "disrupts matching of effort to task demands, such that the fatigued driver fails to regulate effort effectively when the task appears easy." The emphasis in this dynamic approach is on the process of regulation and not so much on the fixed decrease in attention. Thus, according to Desmond and Matthews "fatigue reduces the range or efficiency of strategies available for regulation of effort" (p. 516). In two studies that they conducted they showed that fatigue impaired vehicle lateral control while driving on easy, straight, and monotonous road sections, but not when driving on more demanding winding road sections.

In general, as the task demands increase we are typically able to exert more effort and allocate more attention to the task (Kahneman, 1973). However, when our attention decreases below some threshold level, according to Desmond and her associates, we lapse into complacency and fail to allocate the necessary amounts of our resources. Interestingly, this theory and the findings that support it also imply that many of the driver aids that are being introduced into cars – aids that are designed to ease the driving task by decreasing the driving demands and attention overload – can also induce monotony and fatigue and thus be counter-productive (Desmond *et al.*, 1998). An alternative to the notion of complacency (a concept that does not fit well into any theoretical framework) has been offered by Verwey and Zaidel (1999). According to them, fatigue increases the rates of "micro sleep" periods. Micro sleeps are periods of sleep lasting from a few seconds to one minute. An interesting and dangerous aspect of micro sleeps is that people who experience them are usually unaware of them, and believe to have been awake the whole time. Thus, the effect of fatigue is not a general lowering of attention, but brief lapses in attention that occur with increasing frequency. Empirical evidence that shows increases in long eye-closures and head nodding lend credence to this explanation. When the micro sleeps are rare and far between, their effects are negligible. However, as they become more frequent they increase the likelihood of failing to respond to critical cues and, consequently, going off the road and having a crash (Verwey and Zaidel, 1999). When the driving task becomes more demanding, and the change in demands can be anticipated – such as when entering a curve or overtaking a vehicle – then drivers are able to fight drowsiness and temporarily reduce the number of micro sleeps.

An interesting approach to resolve the two conflicting explanations was offered by Oron-Gilad *et al.*, (2002, 2008). Oron-Gilad suggests that we should distinguish between decision-making (and motoric/physical) fatigue and attentional-perceptual fatigue. Dynamic models, according to which drivers adjust their attention allocation, are more appropriate for perceptual tasks while capacity models are more appropriate for decision-making tasks. The distinction between the two types of fatigue also has empirical support. Desmond *et al.* (1998) found that a drive in a simulator produced a significantly higher level of physical fatigue when it was completely controlled by the driver than a drive over the same route in which the vehicle speed and trajectory were under system control. On the other hand, perceptual fatigue symptoms were similar for both conditions. Brown (1982) reviews the literature on fatigue and also concludes that unlike attention and vigilance, vehicle control skills, which are largely automated, are essentially unaffected by fatigue. Jackson *et al.* (2013) reached the same conclusions but based them on direct experimental evidence. They conducted a simulation study where drivers on one day drove in the morning after a night of normal sleep and on another day they drove after 27 hours of sleep deprivation. After comparing the driving performance (and performance on some neuropsychological tests) they found that after sleep deprivation lateral position variability, speed variability, and reaction time in a vigilance task increased. From the results on the neuropsychological tests, they then concluded that that fatigue from sleep deprivation does not affect the processing speed and executive functions but does lower the vigilance. Another, less direct support for this notion comes from a study by Lisper, Laurell, and Van Loon (1986), where in a long monotonous drive on a closed road segment drivers had to maintain the car as much as possible in the center of the lane while performing a subsidiary reaction time task. The younger and less experienced drivers, for whom lane keeping is less automated, had less difficulty in staying awake than experienced drivers, probably because it was more challenging for them.

In the Lewinian tradition (Lewin, 1943), Oron-Gilad further suggests that driving performance is a function of two sets of variables: driver states – that can be defined on a continuum of "fitness to drive," and situational demands – that can be defined on a continuum of the rate of information flow or situational uncertainty that the driver must resolve. The approach is similar to Blumenthal's (see Chapter 3), except that it specifically attributes the attention allocation to the driver's state. Driver performance can then be defined relative to these two categories in the manner depicted in Figure 14-1.

There are three regions in Figure 14-1; each reflecting a different condition of driver performance. When the situational demands are high (e.g., complex traffic situation in high-speed travel) and the driver is not very fit to drive (e.g., the driver is a novice driver or impaired), the driver experiences an overload. When the situation is not demanding (e.g., driving on a straight empty road) and the driver is quite fit (e.g., highly experienced) the driver experiences an underload. Between these two extreme situations, there is a zone of optimal performance. With this representation in mind it is easy to understand Lisper *et al.*'s (1986) results. The novice "low-fitness" drivers who were challenged by the task were performing within their optimal range and were therefore less fatigued than the skilled drivers who were under-loaded with the exact same task.

Oron-Gilad's representation has two very positive attributes. First, it is parsimonious because it helps organize all the research data in terms of two concepts. Second, it points toward practical means of addressing the information overload and underload (fatigue) problem. This is illustrated in Figure 14-2. Whereas an overloaded driver in a demanding situation has little immediate recourse (other than escaping the situation) short of miraculously improving his or her performance by becoming more skilled and "fit," a fatigued driver's performance can be improved by loading the driver with additional tasks that

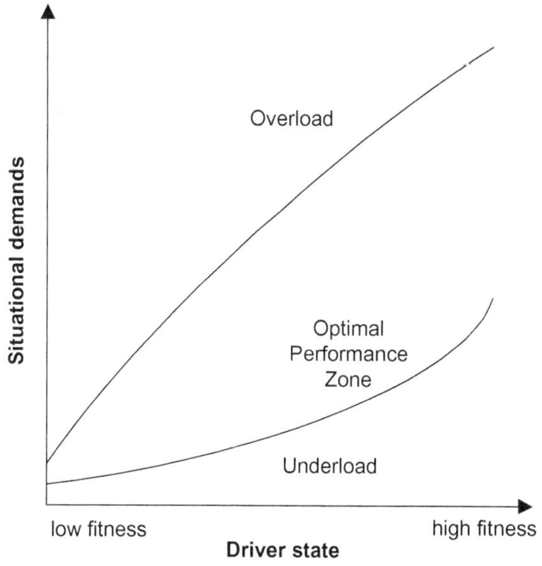

Figure 14-1. The relationship between the driver state, the situational demands, and driver performance (from Oron-Gilad *et al.*, 2002, 2008).

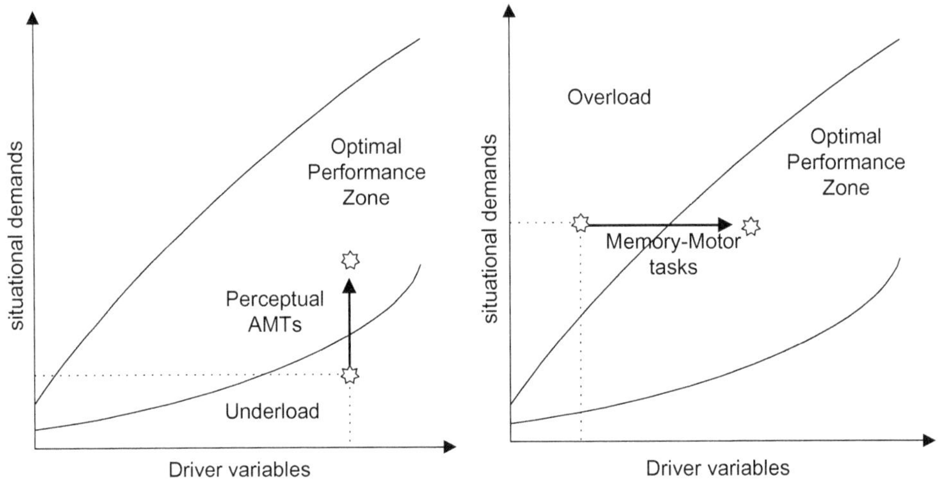

Figure 14-2. A theoretical framework to illustrate drivers' adjustment to underload (a) by increasing stimulation with Alertness Maintaining Tasks (AMTs), and to overload (b) by allocating more capacity (based on Oron-Gilad *et al.*, 2002, 2008).

do not interfere with the driving task itself. Examples of this approach are discussed below in the context of fatigue countermeasures.

Measuring the Effects of Fatigue

Because of the complexity of the concept, different aspects and effects of fatigue – subjective, physiological, and performance – have been studied extensively and often independently. Perhaps the first studies to document the effects of fatigue on human performance in complex tasks were those performed by British psychologists on the effects of fatigue on pilots and radar operators in World War II. Mackworth (1948) demonstrated that a monotonous task such as monitoring a radar screen causes reductions in signal detection after only half an hour, long before the operator is aware of it. Bartlett (1948, as cited by Brown, 1997) noticed that fatigued bomber crews lose their ability to handle their task as a whole and start responding to individual components of their task.

In the context of driving, the effects of fatigue on performance extend to more and more functions as the degree of fatigue increases, culminating in total non-responsiveness when a person falls asleep. In a meta-analysis of the effects of fatigue from sleep deprivation, Pilcher and Huffcutt (1996) concluded that sleep deprivation, particularly partial sleep deprivation, has a substantial effect on mood and various cognitive functions and to a lesser extent on motor performance. Peters *et al.* (1999) had drivers drive in a simulator for a relatively short trip of 20 miles after continuous wakefulness of 9, 12, 36, and 60(!) hours. They did not find significant effects at the ends of the shorter periods, but after 36 hours of wakefulness the drivers had more crashes, greater variance in their lane positions, and more lane excursions. While the sensation of fatigue is also related to many of its objective manifestations, the effects are insidious because drivers – though they are usually aware of becoming drowsy – are often unaware of just how impaired they are relative to their performance and physiological indicators of fatigue (Brown, 1997).

Subjective symptoms of fatigue and sleepiness

Most drivers sense the onset of fatigue before they fall asleep. The internal cues vary and may be idiosyncratic, but they are apparently quite consistent and congruent with electroencephalogram (EEG) measures of sleepiness (Horne and Baulk, 2004). However, the process of falling asleep is actually quite complicated and seems to be captured only by a combination of behavioral, physiological, and subjective indicators (Ogilvie, 2001). Thus, Howard *et al.* (2014) found that the frequency of signs of sleepiness increased in tandem with the increase in physiological, driving performance, and subjective measures of sleepiness. In their survey of military truck drivers, Oron-Gilad and Shinar (2000) asked the drivers about their experience with different fatigue-related symptoms and found that some symptoms and changes in perceptions and behavior were common to many drivers, while others were quite idiosyncratic, as shown in Table 14-2.

A slightly different set of reported symptoms that drivers listed as "first sign(s) of drowsiness" while driving was obtained by Nguyen, Jauregui, and Dinges (1998). In their survey, the five most common harbingers of drowsiness were involuntary eyelid closures (35 percent), inattention (24 percent), yawning (16 percent), inability to stay in lane (16 percent), feeling of "disengagement from the environment" (12 percent), and feeling tired (12 percent). Involuntary eyelid closure has in fact been used as a metric for fatigue in driving, and several attempts have been made to use this measure. The most common measure PERCLOS is the percent of time the eyelid closes 80 percent or more. Cameras using image processing technology have been used to automatically detect PERCLOS and alert professional truck drivers; unfortunately with very limited success (Hanowski *et al.*, 2008).

Structured scales of subjective sensations

Perhaps the best reflection of the meaning of fatigue is the way it is measured in subjective ratings. One of the more popular subjective measures of fatigue is the Swedish Occupational Fatigue Inventory (SOFI), described above. In a validation of this scale, Åhsberg, Gamberale, and Gustafsson (2000) demonstrated that the ratings on its five subscales differ significantly between tasks that involve mostly mental fatigue (such as a vigilance task and a proof reading task) and tasks that involve primarily physical fatigue (such as a cycling task and an endurance task). Her results are reproduced in Figure 14-3. As can be seen in the figure, the combined ratings for all the tasks (CR10) were quite similar. However, the vigilance and proof reading tasks had their greatest effects on

Table 14-2. Fatigue-related subjective symptoms and perceptual/behavioral changes that drivers report "feeling frequently" when experiencing fatigue (from Oron-Gilad and Shinar, 2000, with permission from Elsevier).

Subjective Symptoms and Perceptions	Percent Experiencing Frequently
Subjective symptoms	
Feeling physical discomfort	41
Feeling bored	28
Feeling sleepy and less concentrated	23
Subjective Perceptual/Behavioral Changes	
Slower perceived reaction times	17
Seeing blurred and out of focus	17
Discovering an object on the road too late	15
Difficulties in speed estimation	14
Reduced attention to road signs	12
Slowing down without a particular reason	12
Difficulties in estimating headways	11
Drifting from the lane	11
Crossing a traffic light without noticing its color	7
Crossing a stop sign without slowing or stopping	2
Drifting off the road shoulder	1

the subjective dimensions of lack of energy, lack of motivation, and sleepiness, while the two physical tasks had their greatest effects on the dimensions of physical exertion and physical discomfort. Just as interesting was the fact that these researchers failed to obtain any consistent relationships between the subjective sensations and the physiological measures of blood pressure, heart rate, heart rate variability, and muscle activity. This dissociation between the subjective measures of fatigue and objective measures, especially in driving, is unfortunately quite common (Belz *et al.*, 2004).

Other frequently used subjective measures of fatigue are sleepiness scales such as the seven-level Stanford Sleepiness Scale (SSS – Hoddes, Dement, and Zarcone, 1972),

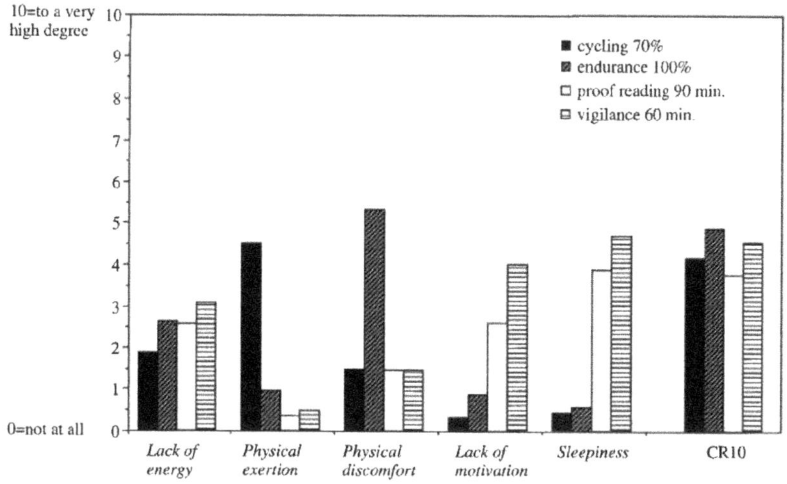

Figure 14-3. Subjects' ratings of their fatigue on the five SOFI scales and the average ratings on a combined scale of fatigue (CR10), following performance of two physically demanding tasks and two mentally demanding tasks (from Åhsberg *et al.*, 2000, with permission from Taylor and Francis, Ltd. http://www.informaworld.com).

the Epworth Sleepiness Scale (ESS – Johns, 1992) and the Karolinska Sleepiness Scale (KSS – Gillberg, Kecklund, and Akerstedt, 1994; Horne and Reyner, 1995; Otmani, Rogé, and Muzet, 2005). The scales are all similar in the sense that they ask the person to grade his or her sensation of sleepiness on some unidimensional ordinal or interval scale (or a score of the sum of scores on individual items that are added up in the case of the Epworth Sleepiness Scale) that allows statistical analysis. Table 14-3 illustrates a modified (Horne and Reyner, 1995) KSS and the Stanford Sleepiness Scale.

Otmani *et al.* (2005) used this scale, among other measures to assess the fatigue of professional drivers who drove for 90 minutes in a simulator; once in the afternoon (2 to 4 PM) and once late at night (11 PM to 1 AM). All drivers had their regular night sleep the night before the drive. While they drove their driving performance was monitored, and every 10 minutes they were prompted to rate their sleepiness on the KSS. The sleepiness ratings for the younger and older drivers are presented in Figure 14-4, where the data from the afternoon sessions and the night sessions are combined. The results show a steady increase in the subjective sensation of sleepiness almost immediately, and definitely after 30 minutes of driving. Also interesting is that the younger drivers felt sleepier than the older drivers. These results are consistent with the typical findings that younger drivers are more involved in fatigue-related crashes, and generally suffer from more sleep debt (National Sleep Foundation, 2002). As might have been expected sleepiness was greater during the night session than during the afternoon session.

Because subjective sleepiness correlates well with other measures of fatigue, it can be used to develop predictors of driver fatigue. For example, Ahlstrom *et al.* (2013)

Table 14-3. The Karolinska Sleepiness Scale with Horne and Reyner's (1995) verbal labels, and the Stanford Sleepiness Scale.

Karolinska Sleepiness Scale (KSS)		**Stanford Sleepiness Scale (SSS)**	
Rank	**Verbal label**	**Rank**	**Degree of sleepiness**
1	Extremely alert	1	Feeling active, vital, alert, or wide awake
2	Very alert	2	Functioning at high levels, but not fully alert
3	Alert	3	Awake, but relaxed; responsive but not fully alert
4	Rather alert	4	Somewhat foggy, let down
5	Neither alert nor sleepy	5	Foggy, losing interest in remaining awake; slowed down
6	Some signs of sleepiness	6	Sleepy, woozy, fighting sleep; prefer to lie down
7	Sleepy – but no difficulty remaining awake	7	No longer fighting sleep, sleep onset soon; having dream-like thoughts
8	Sleepy. Some effort to keep alert	X	Asleep
9	Extremely sleepy, fighting sleep		

developed a fitness-for-duty test in which the KSS is the criterion measure of fatigue, and its prediction is based on performance on a variety of eye-movement measures. Once these objective measures can be easily obtained – preferably in real time on the road – they can serve as fatigue sensors/alarms for the driver. Currently, however, with a correlation of $r = 0.74$ that they obtained the expected false alarm rates and miss rates are too high to provide a valid alerting system for the individual driver.

Objective measures – correlates of fatigue

It is very appealing to define fatigue in terms of sleeplessness, because it makes fatigue an objectively measured concept that can be quantified in terms of hours of sleep, hours-awake, or time-on-task. We also know that sleep deprivation is a very significant factor in the sensation of fatigue. In fact, being one of the few easy to measure and quantify

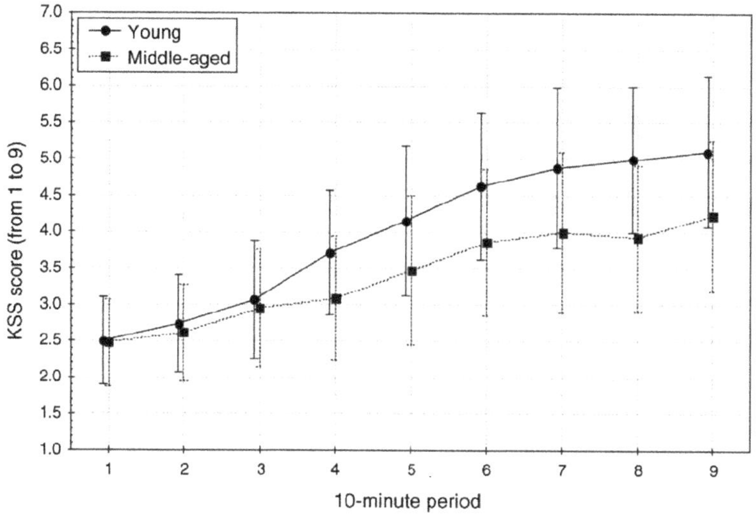

Figure 14-4. Subjective sleepiness of Young (average age 32) and middle aged (49 years old) professional male drivers as a function of time-on-task (from Otmani *et al.*, 2005, with permission from Elsevier).

aspects of fatigue, most licensing agencies regulate long-distance commercial driving in terms of this variable. For example, the Federal Motor Carrier Safety Administration of the U.S. Department of Transportation specifies that commercial drivers, among other limitations "may drive a maximum of 11 hours after 10 consecutive hours off duty... (and) may not drive after 60/70 hours on duty in 7/8 consecutive days. A driver may restart a 7/8 consecutive day period after taking 34 or more consecutive hours off duty" (FMCSA, 2005). More stringent limitations on the number of consecutive driving hours and off duty hours are imposed on commercial drivers in most Western countries including Canada, Australia, the United Kingdom, and the European Union.

Sleep deprivation

For many people (including sleep experts), sleep deprivation is almost synonymous with fatigue and sleepiness. It is certainly a key variable that affects fatigue. One of the effects of sleep deprivation is the loss of ability to effectively divide attention between a central task and a peripheral target detection task. Figure 14-5 shows some of the results of a study by Rogé and her associates (2003). In this study, drivers in a driving simulator had to drive behind a lead vehicle on a very monotonous road, either after a full night's sleep or after a sleepless night. In parallel they had to perform a central target detection task (involving a change in color of a spot on the rear of the lead car) and a peripheral target detection task in which they had to respond to a light that appeared briefly in one of several locations away from the center of the visual field (see Figure 14-8). As can be seen from Figure 14-5, detection of the peripheral target – in all locations – suffered equally as a result of sleep deprivation.

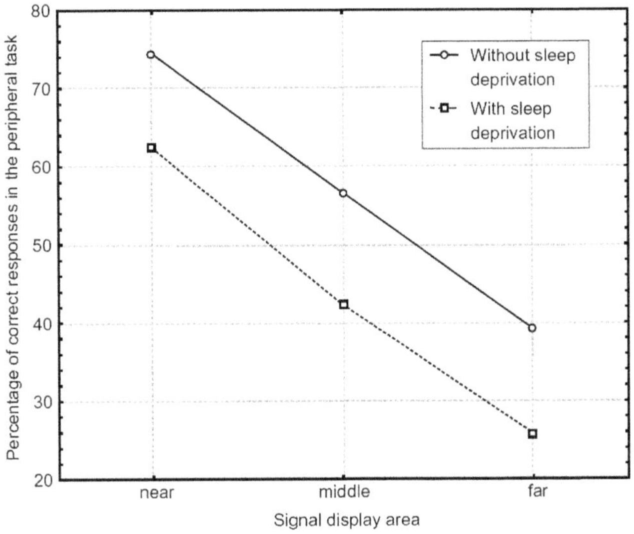

Figure 14-5. Percent of correct responses in the peripheral task as a function of sleep deprivation (without sleep deprivation versus sleep deprivation) and of signal display area (near versus middle versus far) (from Rogé *et al.*, 2003, with permission from Elsevier).

Circadian rhythm

A significant shortcoming of the mandated hours-of-operation limits is that they do not necessarily coincide with our natural cycle of wakefulness. As we all experience, our level of arousal or wakefulness varies over the time-of-day. Most people experience a slight drop in their wakefulness in the early afternoon hours (from approximately 2:00 PM to 4:00 PM) and a most significant drop in early morning hours (from approximately 2:00 AM to 6:00 AM). This extensively studied cyclic change is known as the circadian rhythm and it is depicted in Figure 14-6. Fortunately for most of us, we are asleep during those hours of the night (and fortunately for some Europeans, the afternoon hours correspond to their siesta period). However, if we happen to drive at these hours we are more likely to experience fatigue than at other hours, as in fact many drivers report (Feyer and Williamson, 1995). Altering the circadian cycle is difficult, especially as we get older. Thus, because older drivers have more difficulty in altering this cycle, they are more prone to early afternoon single-vehicle crashes (Pack *et al.*, 1995). The problem is further aggravated for older professional drivers who have less control over their driving hours (Di Milia *et al.*, 2011). Direct evidence for the effect of the circadian rhythm on driving-related skills has also been obtained under controlled laboratory conditions. Williamson *et al.* (2001) tested drivers repeatedly over a period of 24 hours and found that the speed of performance on several tasks varied according to the drivers' circadian rhythms. This included tasks involving simple reaction time, divided attention, short-term memory and vigilance. Interestingly accuracy on these tasks and visual search behavior seemed to be unaffected by the circadian rhythm.

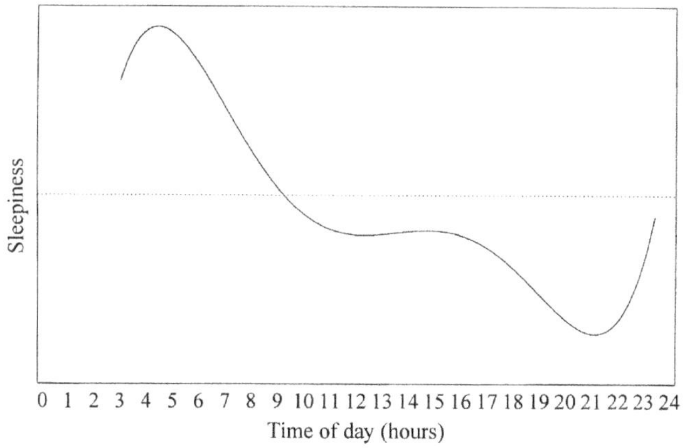

Figure 14-6. The circadian rhythm. Sleepiness is greatest between 2 AM and 6 AM, and increases slightly in the early afternoon between 2 PM and 4 PM (from Broughton, 1994, with permission from the American Psychological Association).

The interaction between the circadian rhythm and the time of driving is critical, especially for commercial long-distance drivers who tend to do much of their driving at night (Feyer and Williamson, 1995). However, even for the general driver population, time-of-day is one of the most consistent factors in the prevalence of crashes attributed to falling asleep at the wheel (Horne and Reyner, 1995; Pack *et al.*, 1995; Sagberg, 1999). This is demonstrated in Figure 14-7 where the numbers of crashes attributed by the police to "driver falling asleep" in North Carolina for four different age groups are plotted against the time-of-day (Pack *et al.*, 1995). For all age groups, peak crash involvement is in the two troughs of the circadian rhythm. The change with age is that young drivers' crashes are primarily at night, while older drivers as they age tend to have more and more of their falling asleep crashes in the afternoon hours. Obviously, a mediating factor in the absolute crash frequencies is the exposure: young drivers drive more at night, whereas older drivers drive more in the afternoon and refrain from night driving. As clear-cut as the data in Figure 14-7 are, it is important to note that falling asleep as a crash cause is quite difficult to assess, especially in severe and fatal crashes. This is because police officers often attribute causation on the basis of circumstantial evidence (such as no sign of braking or any other avoidance maneuvers) or the type of the crash (such as single-vehicle, run-off-the-road, high-speed) rather than on the basis of direct indicators. In the present study, the researchers tried to control for this type of bias by looking at the pattern of crashes that were not judged by the police to be due to falling asleep: in these crashes the pattern did not mirror the circadian rhythm, giving some support to the validity of the police assessment of falling asleep and to the relevance of the circadian rhythm to these crashes. However, another confounding factor that the analysis could not address is that late night crashes are also associated with longer periods of wakefulness. A third potentially confounding factor that is associated with late night driving is alcohol impairment. To control for this, Bruno (2004) examined the single-vehicle crashes in Texas, after deleting the cases where alcohol was noted as a probable or possible cause. As expected from the circadian rhythm hypothesis, fatigue-related crashes of

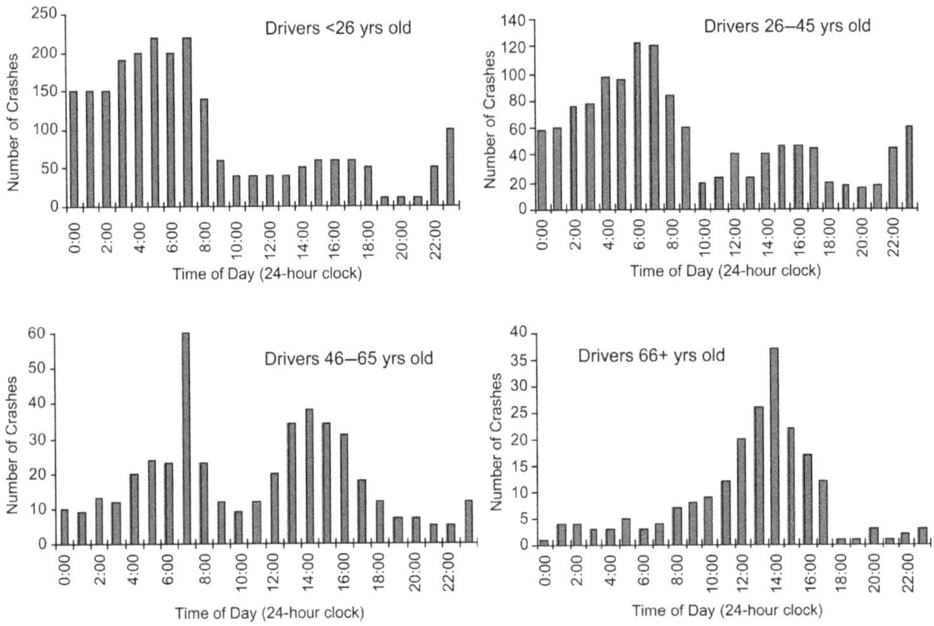

Figure 14-7. Time of occurrence of crashes for drivers of different ages in which the crashes were attributed by the police to the driver being asleep and in which alcohol was not judged to have been involved (data from Pack *et al.*, 1995, with permission from Elsevier; NHTSA, 1998).

drivers 18-45 years old peaked at 2-3 AM, while those of 65+ years old drivers peaked at 2-3 PM. Similar results were obtained for crashes of older drivers in the U.K., whose crashes peaked between 12 and 4 pm (Clarke *et al.*, 2010).

Time-on-task (e.g., hours of driving)

Because the driving task itself is fatiguing, several studies have focused on the effects of time-on-task on the subjective sensations of fatigue and on driving performance, as illustrated above in Otmani *et al.*'s (2005) and Rogé *et al.*'s (2003) studies. In another study, Van der Hulst, Meijman, and Rothengatter (2001) had drivers drive in a simulator on a monotonous rural road for approximately 30 minutes, then drive for 75 minutes on a demanding urban route, and finally drive another 30 minutes on the rural road. When they compared performance on the first rural drive with performance on the second rural drive they found that drivers' sensations of sleepiness, fatigue, aversion to driving, mental effort, and subjective sense of their performance quality were all intercorrelated and affected by the demanding intervening drive. Some but not all of the driving measures were also affected by the time-on-task. Lateral vehicle control was impaired by the time-on-task, but hazard detection was not. This led Van der Hulst and her colleagues to conclude that drivers are able to judiciously allocate their capacities to the higher-priority tasks. Oron-Gilad and Ronen (2007) also found that drivers are able to apply a flexible strategy when fatigued. In their simulated driving task, the manifestation of the deterioration with time-on-task depended greatly on the context of the drive. Thus, on straight roads drivers tended to cope with their fatigue by tolerating less control of their lane position, whereas on a winding road – where lateral control is much more demanding – the drivers kept control of the lane position but relaxed their control of the speed.

One of the effects of increasing time-on-task is to reduce the sensitivity to peripheral targets, probably due to the added effort required to process the information straight ahead. Rogé *et al.* (2003), in the same study mentioned above in the context of the effects of time-of-day, demonstrated this effect in a driving simulator in which drivers were required to follow another vehicle for one hour. During the drive, the drivers had to attend to both a central stimulus consisting of a circle superimposed on the lead car that occasionally changed its color, and to a peripheral stimulus that could appear 4-16 degrees away from the center of the driver's visual field. Rogé and her associates then measured performance separately for the first half-hour and the second half-hour, and separately for the peripheral targets that were either "near" (4 degrees from the center of the visual field), or in the "middle" (8 degrees from the center of the visual field), or "far" (12 and 16 degrees from the center of the visual field). The potential locations of the central and peripheral targets are illustrated in Figure 14-8.

The effects of time-on-task were evaluated by comparing driving performance in the second half of the drive with performance in the first half of the drive. Even after half an hour of a simulated monotonous drive there were deteriorations in performance as can be seen from Figure 14-9. Detection deteriorated more for targets farther away from the center of the visual field than for the peripheral targets that were close to the center of the visual filed. This phenomenon – narrowing of the visual field – is often labeled "tunnel vision" and was also demonstrated in early driving eye-movement data (Rockwell, 1972).

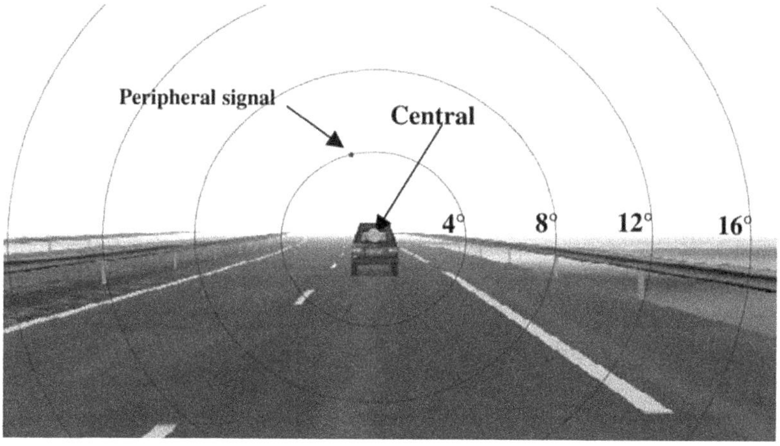

Figure 14-8. The visual view of the road in the simulated drive with overlay of the locations of the central and the peripheral targets (from Rogé *et al.*, 2003, with permission from Elsevier).

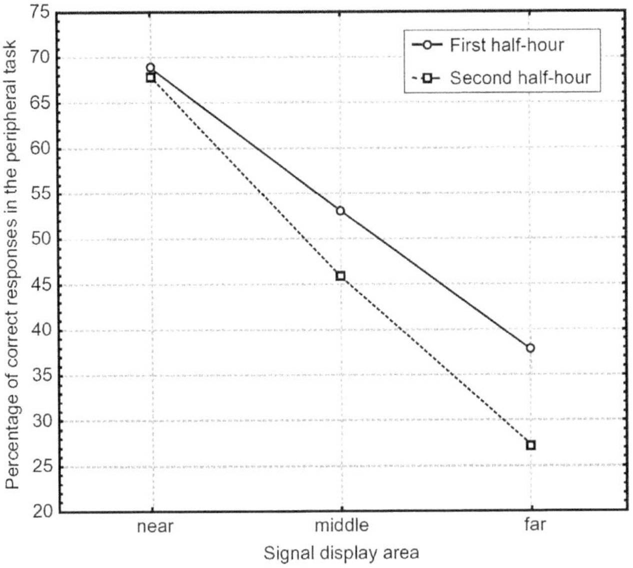

Figure 14-9. Percentage of correct responses in the peripheral task as a function of driving time (first half-hour versus second half-hour) and location of the peripheral target (near versus middle versus far from the center of the visual field) (from Rogé *et al.*, 2003, with permission from Elsevier).

Thus, Rogé's results demonstrate the effects of different aspects of fatigue. Sleep deprivation causes a generalized reduction in attention as manifest in a uniform reduction in target detection everywhere in the field (Figure 14-5). Time-on-task, in contrast, is associated with a selective reduction in attention, in which the deterioration is in direct relation to the deviation of the targets from the center of the visual field. The two situations correspond to state fatigue that is independent of the specific task a person is involved in, and task-induced fatigue that is caused by the characteristics of the task itself.

Distance-driven

Given the strong effects of time-on-task on the subjective sensations of fatigue and the deterioration in performance, we would also expect a relationship between the total number of miles or kilometers a person travels and their likelihood of being involved in a fatigue-related crash. This is because it is most likely that those who drive more kilometers also drive longer trips. Such a relationship has indeed been found, but it is not a linear one. According to Sagberg's (1999) survey of Norwegian drivers, it is a strong log-linear relationship ($R^2 = 0.84$): initially there is a sharp increase in fatigue-related crash frequency as a function of distance-driven and then the frequency of crashes levels off at a stable level. The leveling off in the rate is most probably due to the fact that the people who drive the most miles are most likely to be professional drivers, and are more likely to better manage their fatigue and driving, as we found in our simulation studies of fatigued driving.

Physiological indicators of fatigue

Three physiological correlates of fatigue in driving have been studied quite extensively: heart rate and heart rate variability (HRV), blinking behavior, and electroencephalogram (EEG) recordings from the skull (Borghini *et al.*, 2014).

EEG

The EEG is considered by sleep researchers to be the most important indicator of wakefulness and sleepiness, and specific frequencies of the EEG have been associated with different levels of wakefulness and sleepiness. A distinction is typically made among four ranges of frequencies (Andreassi, 2000; Nguyen *et al.*, 1998):

1. Delta waves (0.5-4 Hz) – appear during the deepest stage of sleep or in brain tumors. Very rare in a wakeful condition.
2. Theta waves (5-7 Hz) – occur in the early stages of sleep and when occupied by a cognitive task.
3. Alpha waves (8-12 Hz) – are characteristic of an awake-relaxed state. They are an early indication of drowsiness. They disappear when a person is suddenly tasked with a cognitive task. As much as 10 percent of the population does not exhibit alpha waves at all.
4. Beta waves (13-25 Hz) – are common in alert condition, when performing a cognitive or physical task.

Because increases in alpha and theta waves indicate increasing sleepiness, they are also likely to indicate lapses in attention (Dinges, 1995). For example, in the study by Otmani *et al.* (2005), the increasing subjective levels of sleepiness, based on the KSS (see Figure 14-4), were also accompanied by an increase in the alpha waves, especially in light traffic that is associated with greater fatigue, as seen in Figure 14-10.

Kecklund and Akerstedt (1993) also found an increase in alpha and theta waves as a function of fatigue among truck drivers, and Lal *et al.* (2003) found significant increases in the rates of delta waves (0-4 Hz), theta waves (4-8 Hz), and alpha waves (8-13 Hz) in extreme fatigue. Lal and his associates then developed an algorithm, based on a combination of these indicators that can serve a trigger for automatic detection of fatigue – at least in a simulated drive.

Blink behavior and droopy eyelids

As we become drowsy or sleepy, our blinking behavior changes. In states of relaxed wakefulness, we blink regularly at the rate of 15-20 per minute, and the blink durations are brief on the order of 200-400 milliseconds (Andreassi, 2000). When we are occupied with demanding cognitive tasks, the blink frequency can drop to as low as three blinks per minute (Svensson, 2004). When fatigued, blink rate increases, blink duration increases, and the amplitude of the eye opening decreases. Furthermore, the blinks themselves are much slower and are characterized more by drooping of the eyelids rather than rapid full closures. Using oculogram recordings to derive measures of eye blink

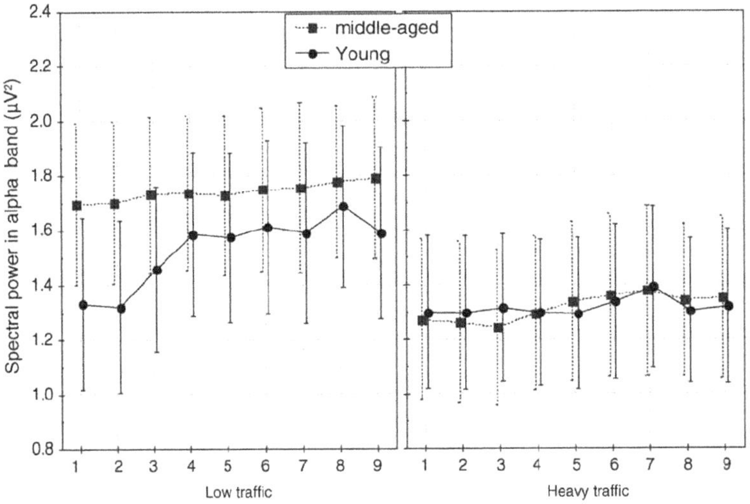

Figure 14-10. The increase in alpha power for younger and older drivers in light and heavy traffic as a function of time-on-task. The increase in alpha power was statistically significant only in the more monotonous light traffic condition (from Otmani *et al.*, 2005, with permission from Elsevier).

behavior, Svensson (2004) was able to achieve a high association between eye blink durations, blink intervals, and drivers' subjective KSS ratings of sleepiness while driving in a simulator. However, as she notes, a practical limitation of these measures is that they must be calibrated individually to each driver's idiosyncratic eye blink behavior when the person is not fatigued.

Still, the potential promise of blinking behavior as a fatigue indicator was revealed in a comprehensive study that evaluated various physiological measures on the same subjects performing the same task. Wierwille and his colleagues (1994; Knipling, 1998) kept their subjects awake for 42 hours, and every two hours gave them a vigilance task – with an assumption that vigilance is an important component in driving. In parallel, they measured the subjects' EEG, the changes in head position (nodding), and various aspects of blinking. They further distinguished between the rapid full closure of the eyelid – that characterizes blinking in a state of wakefulness – and the slow incomplete closure that characterizes fatigue. They discovered that of nine different metrics, the measure they labeled PERCLOS P80 – the percent of the time the eyelid dropped to 80 percent of full closure – was the one that most consistently correlated with the deterioration of vigilance performance over the 42 hours of testing. The correlations between PERCLOS P80 and vigilance for the individual subjects ranged from $r = 0.67$ to $r = 0.97$. Measuring PERCLOS in real driving for four hours, Lin *et al.* (2012) found that PERCLOS doubled over the drive from 6.1 percent at the start of the drive to 12.2 percent at the end. These findings make the PERCLOS the current leading single physiological correlate of driver fatigue.

There have been several attempts to automate recordings of PERCLOS (Ayoub, Grace, and Steinfeld, 2003), and significant progress has been made in the past decade (Blanco *et al.*, 2009), but to be sufficiently reliable and cost-effective to install in vehicles to provide online valid warnings will probably take a few more years. Some of the interesting work in this area is dedicated to developing an application that could utilize the smart phone camera (Kong *et al.*, 2015). However, some complications still have to be overcome to make this a practical real-time indicator of fatigue. In addition to the need for individual calibration mentioned above, to make it sufficiently valid, and not elicit too many false alarms the threshold for the percent of time the eyes must be 80 percent shut must be quite high. Unfortunately, this means that all too often drowsiness is detected too late. Another limitation is that some people may experience fatigue-related diminished mental capacity while their eyes remain open (Svensson, 2004). Finally, because of individual differences the correlation between vigilance performance and PERCLOS is not sufficiently high for all drivers (Knipling, 1998). Nonetheless, fatigue detection systems based on a combination of PERCLOS and other eye tracking metrics, such as head movements, can increase the system's reliability (Xie, Xie, and Zhu, 2012).

Multi-dimensional measurement of fatigue

Given the complexity of the concept of fatigue and the myriad of measures employed to quantify it, it is now obvious that no single measure – subjective, physiological, or behavioral – is enough to capture it completely. Thus, most studies on fatigue include more than one measure, and some researchers have attempted to combine the different measures into a multi-dimensional indicator of fatigue (Belz *et al.*, 2004; Kircher, Uddman, and Sandin, 2002). However, this solution to the problem is often problematic by itself. It is a problem because the different measures do not necessarily behave in a similar fashion, and then we are faced with a complicated multi-dimensional phenomenon. This was illustrated by Belz *et al.* (2004) who were not able to show any convincingly strong relationships among an array of behavioral driving measures, drivers' subjective ratings, and evaluations of fatigue based on viewing of videos of the drivers' faces as they drove. For example, the correlation between the observers' ratings of drowsiness and the drivers' own ratings of their sleepiness (based on the KSS) was $r = 0.28$, and the correlation between the observers' ratings and the reaction time to targets was $r = 0.33$. With sufficiently large samples, these relationships can be statistically significant. However, they are too weak to be of practical significance.

Variables associated with fatigued driving

Many fatigue studies have examined the effects of fatigue separately on drivers of different ages and in different driving environments. Age and driving context appear to be quite closely linked to the fatigue-related crashes, and their link to fatigue merits a closer look.

Age
Most studies on fatigue and driving show that young drivers are significantly more susceptible to falling asleep while driving than mature and older drivers. They are also more often implicated in crashes associated with fatigue, drowsiness, and falling asleep. This is a consistent finding that has been replicated in surveys conducted in different countries such as Canada (Beirness, Simpson, and Desmond, 2005), Israel (Oron-Gilad and Shinar, 2000), Norway (Nordbakke, 2004), and the U.S. Some of the young drivers' over-involvement in fatigue-related crashes is probably due to their insufficient sleep (burning the candle at both ends), and the fact that they often drive late at night when alcohol impairment is also a factor. However, even when alcohol is ruled out young drivers are still over-represented in fatigue-related crashes (Pack *et al.*, 1995). Also, even when the sleeping conditions are the same, young drivers still report feeling sleepier at the wheel than older experienced drivers (Otmani *et al.*, 2005). The reasons for this are not totally clear, but one possibility is that the driving task is more demanding for young and inexperienced drivers than for mature experienced drivers and consequently they exert more effort in the process of driving and get fatigued more quickly.

Driving context
The context in which the driving is conducted has a significant effect on the likelihood of falling asleep or feeling drowsy. For example, in one U.S. survey drivers reported that their drowsiness increased after drinking alcohol, when they drove at night (especially after midnight; that is, during the dip in the circadian rhythm), when the road was straight, and when there was very little or no traffic (Nguyen *et al.*, 1998). Unfortunately, if we stop to consider these situations, then we quickly realize that a worst-case scenario – driving at night, after drinking, on an empty and monotonous road – is quite a common combination, especially for young drivers at the end of "a night on the town." In contrast, the same drivers felt that some situations actually decreased their drowsiness (or increased their alertness). These situations included driving while being in a hurry, when they had to go to the bathroom, and driving under demanding conditions such as in high winds, on a bumpy road, and in heavy traffic. This means that to some extent highway design can be an effective mean to counteract potential drowsiness and fatigue, by increasing the situational demands on otherwise under-loaded drivers. Most drivers would also readily admit that it is much easier to fall asleep on a long straight freeway than on a winding mountain road. This is quite consistent with Oron-Gilad's model above.

Individual differences in sleepiness
Individual differences in the context of fatigue have not been explored much, but they have been noted by some researchers (e.g., Matthews and Desmond, 1998; Thiffault and Bergeron, 2002) and they complicate the development of countermeasures. A start in this direction was made by Verwey and Zaidel (1999) who – on the basis of answers to a questionnaire – divided their drivers into two groups: "high drowsiness" drivers and "low drowsiness" drivers. When they had all the subjects drive in a simulator they found that the high drowsiness drivers were three times more likely than the low drowsiness drivers to fall asleep while driving in the simulator (69 percent versus 23 percent), and

twice as likely to have an accident "due to drowsiness" (15 percent versus 8 percent). Furthermore, the high drowsiness drivers were also more likely to use all of the cognitive countermeasures that the researchers made available to them to counter fatigue. Individual differences may also play a part in self-selection of drivers. Thus, Lucidi *et al.* (2006) in their study of fatigue-related coping behaviors of young drivers noted that those drivers who reported driving more at night were less concerned about having sleepiness related crashes. Sharwood *et al.* (2011) reviewed the literature on fatigue in heavy vehicle drivers, and found that in seven of the 11 studies they reviewed there was an increase in crash risk for drivers with high scores on the Epworth Sleepiness Scale, with odd ratios ranging from $OR = 1.91$ to $OR = 2.98$; that is, an increase in relative risk (relative to drivers without sleepiness tendencies) of 100-200 percent.

A more rigorous approach to defining drivers in terms of their inclination for sleepiness was taken by Drake *et al.* (2010) who used a physiological assessment tool of sleepiness: the multiple sleep latency test (MSLT). In this test, after monitoring a person during a full night sleep, the time from the start of a nap session until the appearance of the first signs of sleep is noted as the level of sleepiness. In their study, Drake and his associates categorized drivers as either excessively sleepy ($MSLT \leq 5min$), moderately sleepy ($5min < MSLT \leq 10min$), or alert ($MSLT > 10min$). They then examined the 10-year crash history of 618 drivers from the official Michigan state accident records, yielding a total of 551 crashes; with half the sample having no crashes at all. Using several measures of crash involvement, they consistently found that the higher the MSLT the lower the crash rate. For example, they found that the prevalence of accidents was 59 percent among the excessively sleepy drivers, 53 percent for the moderately sleepy driver, and 47 percent for the alert drivers. Thus, the excessively sleepy drivers had a relative risk of $RR = 1.26$ relative to the alert driver. Though statistically significant, this over-involvement of 26 percent is not very high. As known from other studies, fatigue is more involved in high-speed severe crashes, and indeed for severe injury crashes only the rates were 4.3 percent and 0.6 percent, respectively. At these levels of involvement the relative risk was $RR = 7.17$; that is, over 600 percent increase. However, it should be noted that the relation between sleepiness and crashes is moderated by multiple other factors, such as actual sleeping and driving patterns, times, roads, and conditions of driving, that were not controlled in this study.

Scope of the Drowsy Driving Problem

Significance of the problem

Surveys of drivers repeatedly show that drowsy driving and actually falling asleep at the wheel are not rare phenomena, with approximately 10 to nearly 40 percent of drivers reporting that they have fallen asleep behind the wheel at least once in the past year. In Norway, 11 percent of private vehicle drivers have reported falling asleep within the past year (Nordbakke, 2004). In a 2012 nationally representative survey of active drivers in the U.S., almost half the drivers reported falling asleep or nodding off at least once in their lifetime, and 10 percent reported falling asleep or nodding off within the past month (Lindsay and Tefft, 2012). The frequency of falling asleep at the wheel is not the same for all: young drivers are the most susceptible and older drivers are the least susceptible (15 percent for drivers under 25 years old and 4 percent for drivers 75+), and males reported it twice as frequently as females. In Canada, one out of every 5-7 drivers reported "nodding off or falling asleep" at least once within the past year (Beirness *et al.*, 2005; Vanlaar *et al.*, 2007). In Australia in a representative sample of the drivers in New South Wales who have reported feeling sleepy at the wheel, 70 percent reported that they continued to drive while "feeling sleepy" (Watling *et al.*, 2015). As might be expected, the situation is worse for professional long-distance truck drivers who drive longer distances and more at night, with over 25 percent admitting to falling asleep while driving at least once within the past year (McCartt *et al.*, 2000). In Israel, Oron-Gilad and Shinar (2000) surveyed military truck drivers and noted that 37 percent reported falling asleep while driving at least once in the past year. Furthermore, these high percentages that are quite alarming by themselves are probably conservative estimates because admitting to falling asleep, especially for professional drivers is probably a bit compromising.

Crash involvement

Relative contribution of fatigue to crashes

Because of the vague terminology used, because fatigue is over-involved in severe and fatal crashes, and because valid assessments of fatigue are difficult to make (especially in fatal crashes), the contribution of fatigue to crashes and fatalities is hard to assess. Estimates vary from as low as 1-4 percent of fatalities (in the U.S., Knipling and Wang, 1995; NHTSA, 2005, 2011, 2015; Stutts *et al.*, 2006), to 10-15 percent (in England, Maycock, 1995; in Finland, Summala and Mikkola, 1994; in the U.S., Stutts *et al.*, 2006), to 16-20 percent (in different countries, MacLean, Davies, and Thiele, 2003; in the U.S., Tefft, 2012), and to as high as 30-40 percent (in the U.S., Leger, 1994; Smith *et al.*, 2005). A testament to the difficulty of estimating the scope of the problem is that the variance among the estimates is greater between different surveys in the same country at approximately the same time than between countries at different times. In the largest U.S. National Large Truck Crash Causation Study (LTCCS) that analyzed in-depth a representative sample of 963 crashes involving 1,123 large trucks, falling asleep at the wheel was judged as the "critical reason" for 13 percent of all single-vehicle crashes (Starnes, 2006). Given that falling asleep is the most extreme form of fatigue, fatigue must have been involved in at least and probably more than 13 percent of these crashes. Furthermore, the problem is probably bigger because not every instance of falling asleep at the wheel is a terminal event, and for every fatigue-related fatality there are probably a few more fatigue-related injuries.

Even when the terminology is specific, the range is quite large. Connor *et al.* (2001) conducted a meta-analysis of 18 cross-sectional and one case-control study to assess the contribution of fatigue to crashes. An interesting aspect of their review was that they did not rely on the crash investigators' assessments of fatigue as a cause of the crash, thereby eliminating one bias. Instead, they identified a crash as fatigue-related whenever any of the "commonly used measures of fatigue and its likely determinants" were mentioned in the accident file. These included "sleepiness at the time of the crash, usual daytime sleepiness, acute sleep deprivation, chronic sleep deprivation, sleep fragmentation, shift work or other circadian rhythm disturbance, time-on-task (driving), snoring and sleep disorders." The most commonly noted disorder was "obstructive sleep apnea"; noted in 14 of the 19 studies. (Obstructive sleep apnea is a breathing disorder in which breathing stops or becomes shallow frequently for a few seconds (but up to a few minutes) while a person is asleep. Ellen *et al.* (2006) conducted a meta-analysis of 40 studies that examined the relationship between sleep apnea and crash involvement and found that for non-commercial drivers, sleep apnea was associated with a 2-3-fold increase in the relative crash risk compared to control groups. However, no consistent relationship was obtained for commercial drivers.) Using this approach, Connor *et al.* (2001) obtained estimates for fatigue involvement in crashes ranging from 1-3 percent in the U.S., to 25 percent in Victoria Australia; a 10-fold increase from the lowest to the highest. A more interesting statistic is the *over-involvement* of fatigue in crashes – the extent to which fatigued drivers are more likely to be involved in a crash relative to a matched population of non-fatigued drivers. Across all studies, Connor *et al.* (2001) obtained a range of odds ratios of $OR = 0.6$ (essentially no over-involvement, and a possible under-involvement) to $OR = 10.9$ (a greater than 10-fold increase). When they looked at what they considered were the best three studies with "moderately robust design," the over-involvement odds ratios were 2.6 (Wu and Yan-go, 1996), 3.4 (Young *et al.*, 1997), and 7.2 (Terán-Santos, Jiménez-Gómez, and Cordero-Guevara, 1999; the only case-control study). In sum, fatigue is a significant factor in highway crashes, but its exact contribution to crash statistics is hard to assess and still quite unknown.

Regardless of its absolute contribution to crashes, it is also important to note that fatigue is a greater contributor to fatal crashes than to less severe crashes. Using a similar approach in which fatigue involvement is based only on fatigue-related crash characteristics, and using crash data from New South Wales, Australia, Fell (1994) found that fatigue accounted for 6 percent of all crashes, but 15 percent of all fatal crashes, and 30 percent of all fatal crashes on rural roads. Thus, although the specific estimates should be taken with many grains of salt, the trend is obvious: fatigue seems to be more common in more severe and fatal crashes, especially ones on (relatively empty and poorly lit) dark rural roads ((Maycock, 1995; Smith *et al.*, 2005); that is, at night with low traffic demands.

Urban fatigue-related crashes – though less frequent – are still of concern. These crashes may be more closely associated with shift work and long work hours (Fell and Black, 1997). One of the more interesting studies to document this detrimental effect of shift work and sleeplessness was conducted by Barger and her associates (2005). In their study, they surveyed 2,737 medical residents who filled out a total of 17,003 monthly reports in which they detailed their crash and near-crash involvements along with their hours of work. When the two types of data were linked, a remarkable relationship was obtained: the likelihood of a crash was 2.5 times as high after working an extended shift (longer than 24 hours – which is quite common in that work environment) than after a regular shift. Of course, crash involvement is only one manifestation of impaired cognitive processes, and one must wonder how well these fatigued physicians function in their medical decision-making profession… A less dramatic finding, though methodologically better controlled, was obtained by Lee *et al.* (2016). In their study, 16 night-shift workers drove for two hours on a closed course either after a full night sleep, or after a night shift. While driving after a full night sleep was essentially uneventful, in the fatigued condition six of the 16 drivers had a near crash and 11 of the 16 drivers could not complete the drive for safety reasons. In short, driving after a sleepless night roughly doubled the risk of a crash.

Characteristics of fatigue-related crashes

The characteristics of fatigue-related crashes are quite uniform: as indicated above, they tend to peak around early morning hours and 3 pm, which are also the hours of circadian lows (see Figures 14-6 and 14-7 for U.S. data), with early morning hours being characteristic of 18-45 years old drivers and afternoon crashes being characteristic of older drivers (Pack *et al.*, 1995). Similar findings were obtained by Sagberg (1999) who surveyed 9,200 Norwegian drivers with insurance-reported crashes. Based on the drivers' own reports, fatigue was a contributing factor to nearly 4 percent of the crashes in which the drivers admitted they were at fault. The characteristics of these crashes were similar to those noted above for the British, American, and Australian fatigue-related crashes: fatigue was much more prevalent in nighttime accidents (18.6 percent of crashes between midnight and 6 am), in single-vehicle running-off-the-road accidents (8.3 percent), in accidents after driving more than 150 km on one trip (8.1 percent), and in personal injury accidents (7.3 percent). When they ran off the road, drivers tended to go off to the right of the road much more than into the opposing traffic lanes on their left (40 percent versus 16 percent); probably due to the crown of the road that leads to drifting to the right when the grip on the steering wheel is relaxed (or left in U.K. and similar countries), and the fact that when crossing the left lane markers – in the absence of opposing traffic – the driver has more time to recover vehicle control before going off the road.

The prevalence of "run-off-the-road" crashes relative to other types of crashes is striking and is shown in Figure 14-11 from Sagberg's (1999) survey of Norwegian drivers. The likelihood of running off the road is twice as high as the average for all types of accidents (including running-off-the-road). In contrast, the likelihoods of head-on and intersection collisions are nearly half as high as the average. Despite the large sample, Sagberg's findings should be treated with caution because (1) the sample consists of crash-involved drivers who filed a report with the insurance company and not a representative sample of all drivers, and (2) the results are based on the drivers' own admissions with all the biases that attend them (see Chapter 2). Still, these results are corroborated by similar findings from an analysis of police-reported crashes a continent away in North Carolina, U.S. (Stutts *et al.*, 2006).

Perhaps the best indicators of fatigue-related crashes are the ones that were identified by Stutts and her associates (2006), using logistic regression models. They first used one data set to identify variables in police reports that would improve the prediction of fatigue-related crashes, and then validated these models on a different data set. In this particular case, the model was developed on the North Carolina crash data files from

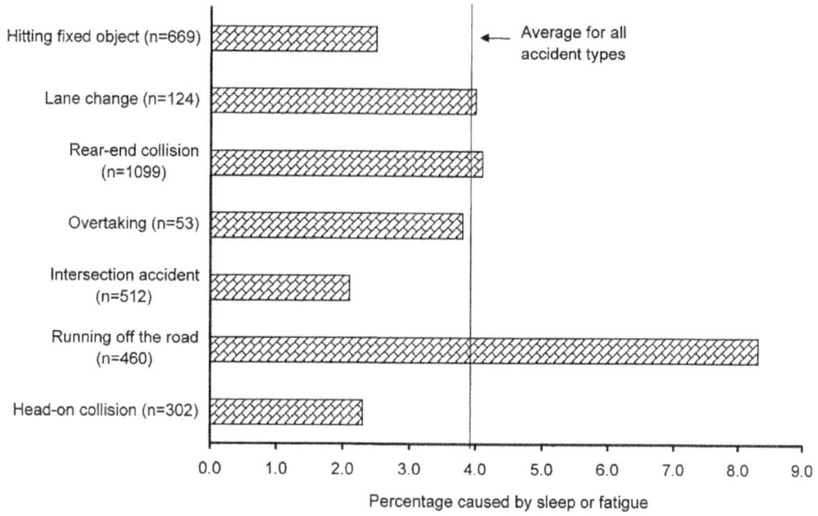

Figure 14-11. The incidence of various types of crashes caused by sleep or fatigue in Norway (from Sagberg, 1999, with permission from Elsevier).

1998, and then validated on the 1999 police crash data files from the same state. The model they developed yielded a sensitivity of 82 percent and a specificity of 87 percent. This means that the model correctly identified fatigue (assuming that the police assessment was correct) in over 80 percent of the crashes that were identified by the police as fatigue-related, and correctly identified nearly 90 percent of the non-fatigue-related crashes as such. With such a high level of validity, it is likely that the variables identified as critical in the prediction and identification of fatigue-related crashes are indeed indicative of such crashes. Of the 21 police-reported variables in the model, the ones with greatest predictive power (on the basis of their unadjusted odds ratios) were: running-off-the-road, hitting a parked vehicle, being cited for a reckless driving violation (this may be idiosyncratic to North Carolina), crash occurring in marginal weather conditions (fog, smoke, smog, or dust), driving alone, crash occurring away from an intersection, alcohol not involved (this may be an artifact because presence of alcohol would typically result in citing alcohol rather than fatigue as a cause even if fatigue was a factor), occurring during darkness, and involving a severe injury or fatality. Thus, Stutts *et al.*'s analysis substantiated many of the previous conclusions about the factors that are closely associated with fatigued driving. One caveat in the validity of this list is that it is quite similar to the causes of alcohol-related crashes. In fact, nighttime, single-vehicle, run-off-the-road crashes are often used as surrogates to impute alcohol-related crashes.

Driver impairment: fatigue versus alcohol

Given the poor – or at least inconsistent – definition of fatigue, and the wide range of estimates of its impact on crashes, some attempts have been made to relate impairment from fatigue to alcohol impairment. The advantage of alcohol impairment as a reference or benchmark is that it has a commonly accepted criterion of impairment – the relative concentration of ethanol in the blood; typically expressed as the ratio of mg ethanol/ml blood (see Chapter 11). Furthermore, alcohol is a depressant and as such it causes sleepiness. For example, in one survey of professional truck drivers 63 percent of the respondents reported that alcohol makes them sleepy (Oron-Gilad and Shinar, 2000).

Williamson *et al.* (2001) studied and compared the performance of Australian professional truck drivers and non-professional drivers when they were sleep deprived and when they were alcohol impaired. When they were sleep deprived, the drivers were tested at 15 regular intervals over a 27-hour period, and in the alcohol condition the drivers were tested at BAC levels of 0.025 percent, 0.05 percent, 0.075 percent, and 0.10 percent. Testing involved eight perceptual-cognitive-motor tests and a subjective evaluation of fatigue using visual analog scales for different dimensions of fatigue. In general, Williamson and her associates found that while alcohol impaired performance on all tests, fatigue-impaired performance in a much more selective manner, and – unlike alcohol – did not affect the speed and accuracy of visual search or logical reasoning. The subjective sensations of fatigue in terms of "tiredness" "muzzy headedness" and "drowsiness" were similarly affected by both alcohol and sleep deprivation. The ratings for muzzy headedness and drowsiness are reproduced in Figure 14-12. Note that subjective fatigue – regardless of the word used – increased monotonically with increasing alcohol levels and with increasing hours of sleep deprivation. All three aspects of fatigue reached their maximum levels after approximately 23 hours of sleeplessness. (The apparent slightly greater effect of the hours of sleeplessness on the non-professional drivers than on the professional truck drivers was marginally statistically significant only for the "drowsiness" assessment). Thus, it can be concluded that sensation-wise both groups of drivers were similarly affected by alcohol and sleep deprivation. In terms of calibrating the magnitude of the effect of sleep deprivation relative to alcohol, 14-16 hours of sleep deprivation (S9-S10 in Figure 14-12) felt essentially the same as 0.10 percent BAC (A5 in Figure 14-12), and additional hours of sleep deprivation felt much worse. Relative to the subjective drowsiness at BAC = 0.05 percent, there was a significant difference between the regular and professional drivers. Regular drivers reached that level after only 4 hours, while professional drivers could drive for approximately 18 hours before feeling that drowsy.

In terms of performance, only some of the abilities impaired by alcohol were also affected by sleep deprivation; but to a lesser extent and less consistently than by alcohol. This was true even after 27 hours of sleep deprivation. The abilities that were not consistently affected by sleep deprivation included simple reaction time and symbol-digit memory task. Still, several performance measures followed a similar pattern for both alcohol impairment and fatigue. These included performance on a vigilance task, the likelihood of missing signals in a simple reaction time task, and time-sharing a simple reaction time task with tracking. The effects of alcohol and sleep deprivation on vigilance are illustrated in Figure 14-13. The vigilance task used by Williamson and her colleagues was very similar to the original "clock" test used by Mackworth in his classic 1948 study. In this task, the drivers observed a circle of 24 equally spaced dots that were lit in

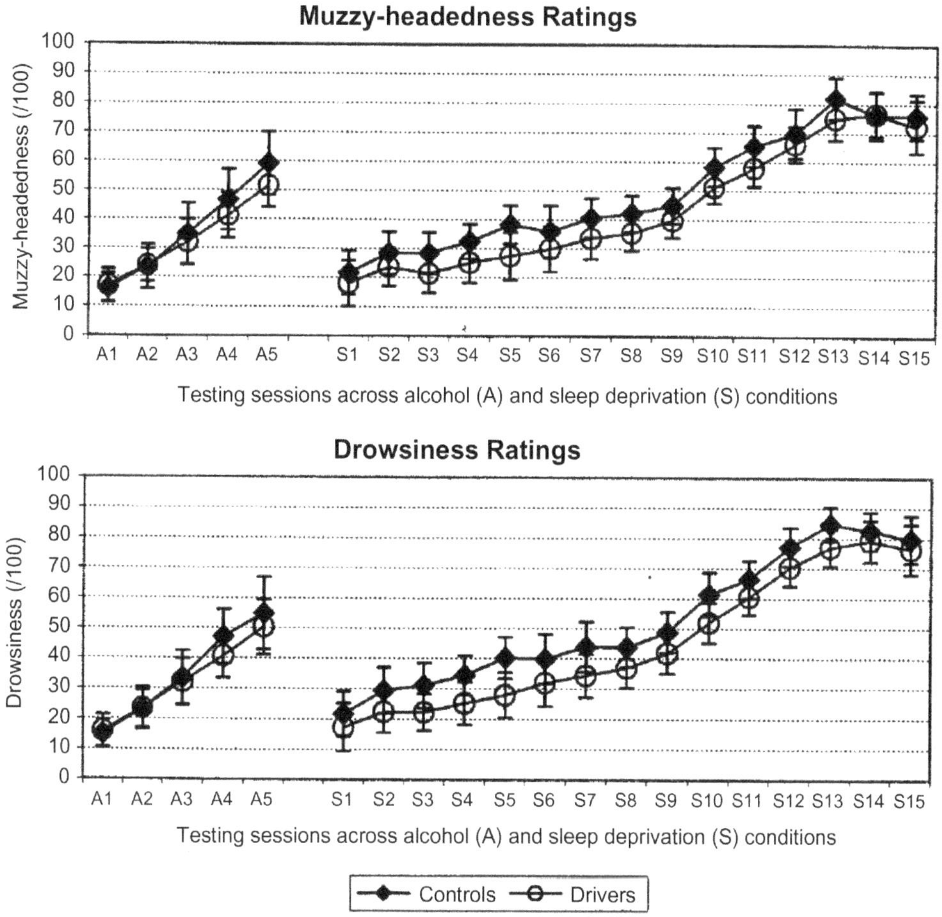

Figure 14-12. Effects of alcohol and fatigue on subjective feelings of "tiredness" "muzzy-headedness" and "drowsiness" for professional truck drivers (Drivers) and non-professional drivers (Controls). Alcohol levels vary from 0.00 percent BAC (A1) to 0.10 percent BAC (A5). Fatigue varies from 2 (S1) to 27 (S15) hours of sleeplessness (S15) (time from waking up in the morning) (from Williamson *et al.*, 2001, with permission from Elsevier).

succession at a constant rate. Occasionally, a dot would be skipped and the light would jump a dot in the sequence. The subject's task was to respond to that by pushing a button as quickly as possible. The three graphs in Figure 14-13 show the performance in terms of the subjects' reaction time, number of correct detections, and number of false alarms (pressing the button when no dot had been skipped). Note that in this task there are essentially no differences between the control drivers and the professional drivers. More important, while the effects of alcohol impairment and sleep deprivation are apparent for each of the three measures, the magnitude of the effects, their onset, and the point at which they level off vary across the three measures. Nonetheless, the effect is

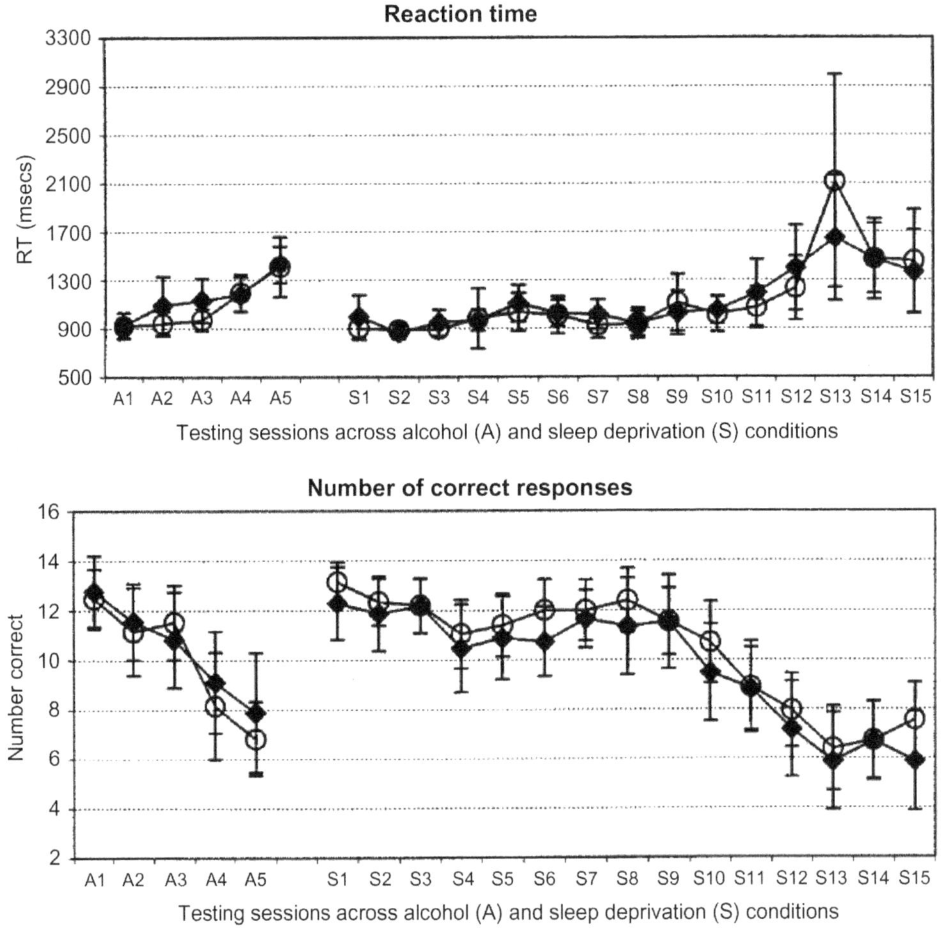

Figure 14-13. The effects of alcohol and fatigue on vigilance in terms of the reaction times to signals and the number of signals detected in a vigilance task. Alcohol levels vary from 0.00 percent BAC to 0.10 percent BAC. Fatigue varies from 2 to 27 hours of sleeplessness. Open circles represent truck drivers and filled diamonds represent control drivers (from Williamson *et al.*, 2001, with permission from Elsevier).

clear-cut, with a performance decrement at approximately 20-22 hours of sleep deprivation (S12-S13 in the charts) being equivalent to that induced by 0.10 percent BAC.

Some interesting conclusions can be drawn from Williamson *et al.*'s study. First, unlike the effects of sleep deprivation on the subjective measures, performance did not deteriorate in a nice linear manner as a function of hours of sleep deprivation. Instead – and this was characteristic of all the performance measures that were affected by the sleep deprivation – subjects were able to control their performance quite well for a while (despite reporting increasing tiredness and drowsiness), and then they deteriorated quite rapidly. Second, it is also interesting to note that the pattern of effects observed for both the subjective and objective measures of fatigue is quite independent of the non-linear function of the circadian rhythm. Finally, and possibly the most interesting implication from these findings, the parallel effects of alcohol and fatigue are either very alarming or suspicious.

If in fact the subjective effects of 14-16 hours of fatigue (periods S9-S10 in the graphs) are equivalent to the felt impairments of alcohol at 0.10 percent BAC, then they are quite alarming because in today's society many people drive after being awake for more than 14 hours, and even after being awake for 18 hours. Given Williamson's results, it means that they are impaired at a level equivalent to 0.10 percent BAC – beyond the threshold of just about all countries! On the other hand, these findings cast doubts on the validity of this equivalency because it implies that many people going out for an evening of dinner and a movie after a full day's work should be feeling as tired and function as impaired as after consuming a significant amount of alcohol – an amount that in most of the world would consider them legally intoxicated and unfit to drive. Thus, despite the meticulous study design and the orderly relationships obtained in this attempt to calibrate the effects of fatigue, the conclusions that can be drawn from this study still need further confirmation in real, or at least simulated, driving.

Fatigue Countermeasures

Fatigue countermeasures – like most safety treatments – can be categorized in terms of the system component that they address: the roadway and driving environment (such as rumble stripes, edge markings, and rest stops), the vehicle (such as in-vehicle monitoring and alerting devices) and the driver (such as education, sleep management, and self-induced stimulation). Stutts (2000) summarized the benefits of different approaches, based on the opinions of highway safety experts and the literature existing up till the beginning of this millennium, and her conclusions are consistent with more recent findings and recommendations presented below.

Driver-behavioral countermeasures to fatigue

In spite of drivers' awareness of their risk of falling asleep at the wheel, and despite knowledge of the significance of stopping for a short nap to counteract fatigue, most drivers continue driving after they are already aware of being sleepy. And as has been noted in many surveys and a few in-vehicle monitoring studies, some even continue after they doze off momentarily (Nordbakke, 2004). For obvious reasons, very few drivers continue to drive after they fall asleep and sleep for more than a few seconds. To counteract fatigue, drivers resort to various behavioral techniques that they believe will help them stay awake and sufficiently aroused. These techniques and the scientific support (or absence of support) for their effectiveness are briefly reviewed below.

Management of sleep, napping, and driving

Because performance deteriorates with increasing time-on-task and improves with increasing hours of sleep (up to a point), driving time and hours of sleep are useful in regulation of driving to minimize fatigue. Understanding how and at what rate these two variables – and sleep-related impairments such as sleep apnea – affect driving has been instrumental in regulating hours of operation, time-on-task, and screening of professional drivers (Smiley, 1998). Indeed most countries regulate commercial drivers' exposure by limiting the total number of hours allowed for continuous driving and the minimum hours of sleep required between driving sessions. Though the complete set of rules is usually quite complicated, the core criteria are the limits on the hours of continuous driving and the rest periods between them. For example, the rules in the U.S. since 2011 specify a maximum of 11 hours of continuous driving with a minimum of a 10 hours rest period between driving sessions. In addition, a driver may not drive for more than 8 hours without taking a break of at least 30 minutes (Goel, 2014). In Canada, the maximum allowed driving time in one day is 13 hours (and even 15 hours below the 60 degree latitude). Still different criteria are used by the various EU countries (Parkes, Gillan, and Cynk, 2009). Because the empirical data on fatigue and safety is quite incomplete with respect to all the relevant factors, the limits on fatigued driving are a compromise between the trucking lobby and the safety community. Also, it is important to remember that even if the limits are in some sense "reasonable," they still only apply to commercial drivers, leaving the majority of drivers on the road unregulated relative to fatigued driving. In this respect, both in terms of cultural norms and official regulations the safety community has done a much better job in restricting driving while impaired by alcohol than in restricting driving while impaired by fatigue.

According to sleep experts, the number one fatigue countermeasure is careful scheduling of sleep and driving duties (e.g., avoiding night duty and starting the day early). The second choice is behavioral sleep management such as taking breaks to nap briefly on long drives (Åkerstedt, 1995); a strategy that is recommended for night-shift operators as well (Bonnefond *et al.*, 2004). Interestingly, a meta-analysis of 12 studies on the effects of naps on performance shows that short naps – lasting 10-20 minutes are generally better than longer naps (Driskell and Mullen, 2005). This is because when we sleep for more than 20 minutes we descend into the deeper stages of sleep, and waking up from insufficient deep sleep results in "sleep inertia" (Bruck and Pisani, 1999). Napping before a night drive is also beneficial. Macchi *et al.* (2002) found that night driving after an afternoon nap caused drivers to feel less sleepy, to perform better on reaction time tasks, and to have an EEG spectrum indicative of alertness (less activity in the alpha and theta range) than when they spent the afternoon in non-driving sedentary activities.

But what about all the behavioral techniques that we as drivers use, such as increasing the volume of the radio, opening a window, or talking to a passenger? According to a survey of 283 researchers, educators, medical health professionals, transportation safety experts, and human factors specialists from around the world, whose work or interest were related to fatigue and driving, "there exists little if any scientific proof of what behaviors are effective (or ineffective) countermeasures to drowsiness while driving. A review of the scientific data available for this study also indicated that most people, regardless of their occupation, level of education, and any other demographic characteristics, agree that there is no substitute for sleep" (Nguyen *et al.*, 1998).

Given these expert opinions and data-based conclusions it is not surprising that the top 10 recommended behavioral strategies for coping with sleepiness while driving in Nguyen's study, reproduced in Table 14-4, focused mostly on sleep. In fact, the top four recommended strategies all involve sleep. In contrast, in the same survey, activities such as eating a snack, chewing gum, listening to the radio or CD, playing mind games, driving barefoot, and talking to oneself were not considered effective by most of the experts. In general, the sleep experts gave significantly lower ratings to all the activities that did not involve actual sleep.

Drivers seem to appreciate the importance of sleep to counteract fatigue, but their actual behavior indicates that they belie that. Feyer and Williamson (1995) surveyed Australian commercial long-distance drivers, and found that only one-third reported that they use sleep to manage their fatigue at least "sometimes." At least one reason given for not doing this is that often appropriate rest areas are just not available. While the evidence

Table 14-4. Experts' top 10 behavioral fatigue coping strategies (with effectiveness rated on a scale of 1-4 where 1 = "will definitely not increase alertness," 2 = will probably not increase alertness; 3 = will probably increase alertness; and 4 = will definitely increase alertness) (from Nguyen *et al.*, 1998, with permission from the AAA Foundation for Traffic Safety).

Rank	**Behavior**	**Mean Effectiveness**
1	Letting someone else drive for 1-2 hours while you sleep in the passenger seat before driving again	3.68
2	Pulling off road to take a 30-45 minute nap	3.57
3	Pulling off road to take a nap for >1 hour	3.52
4	Pulling off road to take a 10-20 minute nap	3.41
5	Pulling off road to exercise for 10 minutes	3.37
6	Pulling off road to consume caffeinated beverage	3.32
7	Pulling of road to walk for 10 minutes	3.29
8	Conversing with someone in vehicle	3.24
9	Consuming caffeinated beverage while driving	3.19
10	Stopping by rest area to wash face with cold water	3.16

for Neguyen et al.'s (1998) recommendations is quite dated, most sleep researchers still support these conclusions. However, more recent research on fatigue and driving validates some of the drivers' non-sleep strategies, as described below.

Drivers' behavioral strategies

Either because of their reluctance to stop or because of their inability to find a good rest area, most drivers have strong beliefs in the utility of other (personal experience-based) approaches. In a 1994 survey of 1,000 drivers in the state of New York, the drivers picked the following as their seven most recommended strategies for coping with drowsy driving (McCartt *et al.*, 1996): stopping and getting out of the car, napping, changing drivers, listening to the radio, conversing, consuming beverages or snacks (including those with caffeine), and (yes) slapping the face.

Yet, drivers do not necessarily adopt even their own recommended fatigue coping strategies. When we compared truck drivers' opinions about the effectiveness of different strategies and the extent of using these strategies we (Gershon *et al.*, 2011; Oron-Gilad and Shinar, 2000) found that in general there is a correspondence between the two, but there are also some notable differences between the two. The results of the comparisons based on a survey of 100 professional drivers and 90 non-professional drives are presented in Table 14-5. It contains the ratings for frequency of usage and perceived effectiveness of 16 previously stated strategies (Oron-Gilad *et al.*, 2001). Interestingly, the correlations between usage and effectiveness vary greatly among the behaviors and between the two groups. In general, the correlations were higher for the professional drivers, ranging from $r = 0.42$ for listening to the radio and washing the face to $r = 0.90$ for smoking; and ranging from $r = 0.18$ for listening to the radio to $r = 0.87$ for shelling and eating sunflower seeds for the non-professional drivers. A striking difference between the two groups was that the professional drivers – who also reported driving longer distances and driving at night more frequently – engaged more in activities that required planning for prolonged driving and counteracting fatigue by stopping for a nap or to exercise, taking and drinking coffee, and taking water to wash their face. In contrast, non-professional drivers tend to limit their coping strategies to tactical/operational measures (Gershon *et al.*, 2011). Thus, acts like opening a window or listening to the radio that are easy to accomplish are the most often practiced; and they are perceived as relatively effective by both groups. More interesting, perhaps, in Gershon *et al.*'s, study are the differences between perceived effectiveness and actual practice. The largest discrepancies are between the perceived effectiveness and actual practice of a short nap and exercise. In both cases, these activities are perceived as highly effective but little practiced, possibly because professional drivers are often on tight time schedules and possibly because safe stopping and resting areas are not always available.

As can be seen in Table 14-5, one of the methods frequently used and perceived as very effective by professional drivers is stopping for exercise. Other driver surveys conducted in different parts of the world have all yielded similar results – listing very similar activities with slight variations in frequencies (Beirness *et al.*, 2005, in Canada; Lucidi *et al.*, 2006, in Italy; McCartt *et al.*, 1996, in New York; Verwey and Zaidel, 1999, in the Netherlands). A recent study conducted on 1,518 Australian drivers who have

Table 14-5. Activities used by professional and non-professional drivers in terms of their frequency of use and perceived effectiveness. Rankings are based on a Likert scale of 1-5. For usage 1 = never and 5 = always; for perceived effectiveness 1 = least and 5 = most. Significant differences between professional and non-professional drivers are noted by: *** for $p < .001$, ** for $p < .01$, * for $p < .05$ (from Gershon *et al.*, 2011. With permission from Elsevier).

	Usage			Perceived Effectiveness		
Coping-Behavior	**Professional**	**Non-professional**	**Total**	**Professional**	**Non-professional**	**Total**
Stop for short nap	***2.07	1.51	1.79	***2.96	1.77	2.37
Opening the window	3.46	3.42	3.44	3.25	3.22	3.24
Listening to the radio	4.19	4.33	4.26	3.39	3.47	3.43
Drinking coffee	***3.47	2.74	3.11	**3.23	2.72	2.98
Drinking energy drink	1.25	1.28	1.27	1.34	1.28	1.31
Shelling and eating sunflower seeds	***1.87	1.26	1.57	***2.13	1.46	1.80
Smoking	**1.91	1.37	1.64	**1.68	1.34	1.51
Talking on the cellular phone	1.95	***2.68	2.32	2.13	***2.81	2.47
Eating salty snacks	1.79	1.67	1.73	*2.03	1.78	1.91
Eating chocolate snacks	2.05	1.90	1.98	2.33	2.08	2.21
Talking with passenger	3.13	**3.73	3.43	3.06	***3.68	3.37

Table 14-5. (*Continued*)

	Usage			Perceived Effectiveness		
Coping-Behavior	**Professional**	**Non-professional**	**Total**	**Professional**	**Non-professional**	**Total**
Driving barefoot	1.12	1.34	1.23	1.26	1.28	1.27
Stopping for exercise	***1.79	1.37	1.58	***2.22	1.61	1.92
Washing the face	***2.92	2.4	2.66	**3.38	2.9	3.14
Change seat position	1.99	2.12	2.06	2.06	2.06	2.06
Watching the view	***2.73	1.89	2.31	***2.43	1.71	2.07
Thinking personal thoughts	***2.34	1.57	1.96	***2.21	1.54	1.88

"experienced sleepiness while driving" also found that the most common countermeasures – employed by approximately 35 percent of all drivers – were turning up the radio volume and/or opening the window (Watling *et al.*, 2015). In a direct test of the effectiveness of this strategy, Watling, Smith, and Horswill (2014) had drivers drive for two hours in a driving simulator and then take a 15-minute break that consisted of either a 10-minute walk or a 15-minute opportunity to rest. Following the break they were required to drive for another hour. The results were interesting because the physiological (EEG), psychological (Karolinska Sleepiness Scale) and behavioral (Hazard Perception Test) indicators of fatigue differed significantly. As expected, both the nap and the active break reduced subjective sleepiness, but the physiological EEG indicator was positively affected only by the nap. The authors – relying on the EEG as their "gold" standard suggest that subjective fatigue is a potentially dangerous erroneous perception, However, it is possible that because hazard perception was unaffected by either the nap or the exercise a critical level of fatigue, to the extent that it elevates crash risk, was not really achieved.

Adapting driving behavior to the existing conditions

As in other contexts, drivers adapt themselves to the conditions under which they drive. Thus, for example, we noted in the previous chapter that when distracted by cell phones drivers typically tend to reduce their speed and sometimes increase their headways. Some of that adaptation is evident in fatigue too. Within limits, and before sleepiness turns into actual sleep, drivers may be able to adjust their driving. Van der Hulst *et al.* (2001) found that with prolonged time-on-task in a driving simulator, drivers increased their headways to the car ahead. This enabled them to retain the same level of hazard avoidance skill, despite their deteriorating vehicle control. Also, when the conditions allow it – for example, on straight monotonous roads – drivers tend to increase their speed to combat fatigue, a perfectly rational approach to cope with underload (see Figure 14-2a).

Another strategy that drivers adopt is to allow themselves to deteriorate selectively in a way that is perceived as the least harmful. Fatigue-related performance-based symptoms of fatigue are then a function of the specific driver/environment relationship (Thiffault and Bergeron, 2003). This was clearly demonstrated by Oron-Gilad and Ronen (2007) in a study conducted in a driving simulator. Their drivers drove for up to two hours (or until they actually fell asleep at the wheel) on a roadway that contained three types of segments: a relatively empty and straight 4-lane divided highway, a relatively straight 2-lane road, and a winding 2-lane rural road with some very sharp curves. After approximately one hour, there was evidence of impaired driving, but it assumed a different form in each of the different road types: on the straight roads the drivers lost some of the lateral control of the vehicle (as evident in more steering wheel corrections), especially in the four-lane road (where there was also greater variance in lane position). In contrast, on the winding road the only significant change was in the speed: that actually increased toward the end of the prolonged drive (by an average of 12 percent). Thus, when the road was straight and visibility ahead was good, the drivers could afford to relax their lane position, but when the road was curvy and the visibility ahead was limited, the drivers were able to retain the accuracy of their steering and position in the lane at the cost of neglecting to maintain the required speed.

Cognitive loading

Among the techniques that drivers commonly resort to in order to combat fatigue are several whose role is to either increase the stimulation (such as playing music) or increase the cognitive load (such as conversing with a passenger). Increasing speed – as noted in Oron-Gilad and Ronen's (2007) study – actually increases both. According to the dynamic models of attention that define fatigue in driving as a situation with attention or information underload (Oron-Gilad *et al.*, 2002, 2008; see Figures 14-1 and 14-2) this approach should be quite effective.

To apply this coping strategy, it is necessary to find cognitive tasks that at once challenge the driver and are relatively insensitive to fatigue. One clue to such tasks can be obtained from Williamson *et al.*'s (2001) study that compared the effects of fatigue from sleep deprivation with the effects of alcohol impairment. As noted above, they found that their more cognitively complex tasks – such as a memory task and a logical-reasoning task – were affected by alcohol but not by sleep deprivation. This may imply that these higher functions are not as susceptible to fatigue as lower, more automated tasks. This is also consistent with the theoretical understanding of the nature of fatigue that is characterized by under-stimulation. A challenging cognitive task can then actually alleviate fatigue because it increases the driver's stimulation.

This type of reasoning was the rationale for an innovative study by Verwey and Zaidel (1999). In their study, twenty-six 25-49-years-old drivers drove a monotonous rural road for over two hours in a fixed-base driving simulator. The drivers were tested at night, after being awake all day: once in a control condition – in which the drivers only had to perform the driving task – and once in a "gamebox" condition – in which the drivers were provided with an option to play several different games while they drove. The drivers were preselected into two groups as either "low drowsiness" drivers or "high drowsiness" drivers on the basis of responses to questions concerning their tendency to get drowsy, tired, or sleepy when driving at night. Driving difficulty was manipulated by three shifts of driving, which correspond to increasing hours of sleeplessness and lower levels of circadian arousal: 23:00-01:15, 01:30-3:45, and 04:00-6:15.

At the heart of the study was the "gamebox." This device allowed the drivers to choose one of 12 games that were not overly difficult and did not interfere with the driving. There were three types of games: games involving "measuring time, distance, and speed; auditory tasks analogues to known games such as the card game '21' or the computer game Tetris; and activities based on recording and playing back the driver's own voice" (p. 202). The drivers could start playing the games at any time, could select any game they wanted, and could change games at any time. With this approach, the gamebox had positive effects on both performance and subjective feelings. Without the gamebox as the drive progressed, the level of drowsiness increased. However, when the gamebox was an option the drivers consistently felt less drowsy, as can be seen in Figure 14-14.

Similar effects of the gamebox were obtained for driver performance. The number of accidents and the number of times the drivers crossed the lane marker or drove off the road increased as the difficulty of the drive progressed from the first to the third shift. However, the number of such incidents was consistently smaller when the drivers could use the gamebox than when they did not have it, as can be seen in Table 14-6.

Interestingly, the drivers in Verwey and Zaidel's study were quite good at deciding when they needed the gamebox. The "high drowsiness" drivers used the gamebox much more than the "low drowsiness" drivers. Also, the "high drowsiness" drivers started using the gamebox quite frequently already in the first (late evening) shift, whereas the "low drowsiness" drivers made little use of the gamebox in the first two shifts, but used it as much as the "high drowsiness" drivers in the third (early morning) shift. This pattern of use reinforces the notion that people, in general, are sensitive to their state of fatigue, and given a viable option to cope with it they will use it.

The possibilities raised by the findings of Verwey and Zaidel prompted Oron-Gilad *et al.* (2008) and Gershon *et al.* (2009a) in Israel and Takayama and Nass (2008) in the U.S. to pursue this line of research and investigate the relative effectiveness of different

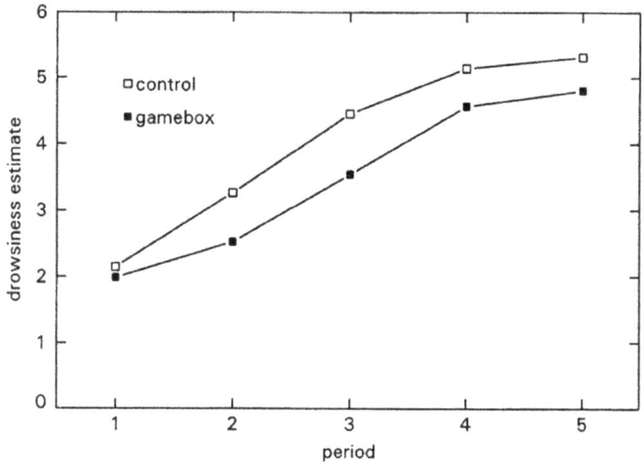

Figure 14-14. Subjective drowsiness ratings during the 2:15 hours' drive. Drowsiness ratings are on a scale of 0-6 where 0 = Fully alert and 6 = Very Sleepy (from Verwey and Zaidel, 1999, with permission from Elsevier).

Table 14-6. Number of drivers who had an accident and number of times the drivers went off the road or crossed a lane marker in each shift with and without the gamebox (from Verwey and Zaidel, 1999, with permission from Elsevier).

	Number of Drivers Who Had an Accident		**Number of Drivers Who Went off the Road or Crossed the Lane Marker**	
	Control	**Gamebox**	**Control**	**Gamebox**
Shift 1	0	0	4	7
Shift 2	2	0	13	2
Shift 3	4	2	31	12
Total	6	2	48	21

cognitive tasks, and how receptive would drivers be to such tasks. All three studies confirmed Verwey and Zaidel's general finding that such tasks may be beneficial, and also re-affirmed Belz *et al.*'s (2004) findings that not all measures of fatigue are affected in the same way.

Oron-Gilad's study was a simulator study in which professional truck drivers drove a monotonous route and on different days received a secondary cognitive task (termed Alertness Maintaining Task – AMT) to perform while they drove. She used three different tasks – each loading a different mechanism of the driver's information processing: a perceptual task (choice reaction time), a short-term memory task (patterned after the game "Simon"), and a long-term memory task (trivia quiz). Performance in these conditions was compared to performance under two different control conditions: one in which the drivers had no distractions at all, and one in which the drivers could listen to music (for which the drivers brought their own favorite music). In terms of driving performance, the only measure that was consistently affected relative to both control conditions was the speed: it was lower when the drivers performed the memory task than in the control conditions or with the other AMT's. In both control conditions (No AMT and music), there was essentially no change in speed between the beginning and the end of the driving session. The trivia and the choice reaction time tasks also failed to yield a significant change in speed. The drop in the speed with the memory AMT suggests that the task may have been quite difficult. Subjectively, too, drivers considered the memory task the most demanding of the three cognitive tasks. Despite its effectiveness, the memory task was the least appealing, and the trivia game the most appealing. In fact 60 percent of the drivers said they would be interested in having such a game in their vehicle to counteract fatigue.

The most direct and dramatic effect of the different cognitive tasks was reflected in the physiological measure of heart rate variability (HRV). As noted above, under stressful/wakeful conditions the variability is quite low, and as we relax or get fatigued it increases. To quantify the magnitude of the fatigue effects on HRV, a baseline HRV is arbitrarily and conveniently set at 100 in the beginning of the drive, the changes in HRV are then noted in terms of percent change relative to that level. Prior to the drive the drivers were restful and their HRV was approximately 75 percent higher than at the start of the drive. In the absence of an AMT, as the drive progressed HRV increased so that by the end of the 58 kilometer drive HRV in the basic control condition – without a gamebox or music – increased by an average of 250 percent. Relative to this control condition, all the alertness maintaining tasks produced a significantly lower HRV. The most effective tasks were the trivia game and the memory task, which yielded HRVs that did not differ significantly from the 100 percent level at the beginning of the drive. In other words, based on the HRV, with either the trivia or short-term memory game the drivers were as alert and awake at the end of the drive as they were when they started it. Music tended to have a slight effect, yielding an increase of 160 percent, but the HRVs with the trivia game and the memory task were significantly lower than with music. The average HRV's in the final segment of the drive are displayed in Figure 14-15.

In a follow-up to Oron-Gilad *et al.*'s study, we (Gershon *et al.*, 2009a) conducted a driving simulator study in which drivers drove for 140 minutes on a two-lane mostly straight rural road, with a few curves, low traffic density, and desert scenery. This was a sufficiently long monotonous drive to induce fatigue symptoms. For this study, the trivia game was improved to make it more user-friendly and appealing. The game consisted of five different themes, including movies, sports, current events, general knowledge, and cuisine, and the driver could choose and switch from one to another. The questions progressed from easy to difficult – based on a pilot study – and following each answer the driver received feedback. After two incorrect responses, the theme was switched. In this

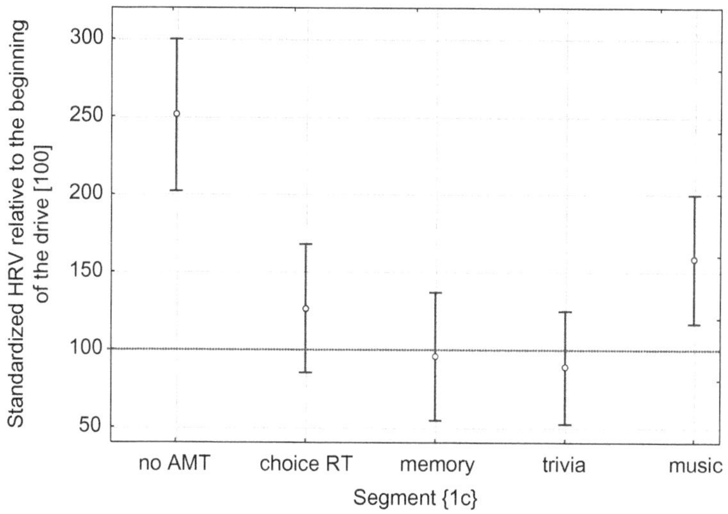

Figure 14-15. The effects of different cognitive tasks on heart rate variability at the end of a 58 km drive, relative to HRV = 100 at the beginning of the drive (Rest). The higher the HRV the more restful and sleepy the driver is (from Oron-Gilad *et al.*, 2002, 2008).

manner, drivers nearly always got positive feedback. Each driver drove three sessions on similar roads: an adaptation session, a control session without any distractions, and a treatment session that included the option to play the trivia game for 20 minutes at two points along the drive: after 60 minutes of driving and after 100 minutes of driving. The effects of the cognitive game were immediate and consistent on all measures of performance. Compared to the control drive and to the segments immediately before and after the addition of the trivia game, when engaged in the game the drivers' HRV was smaller, their lane position variability was less, steering wheel corrections were smaller, and subjective ratings on the SOFI measures of "lack of motivation" and "sleepiness" were lower.

Takayama and Nass (2008) also evaluated the benefits of cognitive loading in a simulated drive. Their drivers were composed of two groups: 40 drivers who scored very high on the Epworth Sleepiness scale and 40 drivers who scored very low on the ESS. While they drove they had to either "listen and try to learn each phrase" in a prerecorded (Swedish) language learning course, or to "listen carefully, repeat, and try to learn each phrase." The driving route for half the participants in each group was mostly straight without any traffic, and for the other half it was a "varied course, consisting of the same number of turns as in the monotonous course but incorporating heavy traffic with aggressive drivers and crowded streets with people and dogs crossing, more towns and cities, and more intersections." Driving safety performance was based on a single composite measure that included road edge excursions, center line crossings, accidents, and signal lights violations. The results showed that for the drowsy drivers increasing the task load, either by the demand to repeat the phrases or by making the driving more difficult, increased driving safety. Thus, paradoxically the drowsy drivers benefitted rather than suffered from the more complex drive. This finding is also consistent with the fact that drowsiness increases the propensity to become distracted (Anderson and Horne, 2013), and the desire to seek a cognitive increase in the load as an intuitive countermeasure to fatigue.

Two related observations are also important in the context of cognitive load as an antidote to driving fatigue. Schömig *et al.* (2015) conducted a driving simulation study in which drivers first drove "manually" (i.e., with full control of the car) on a high-speed road. Fatigue was assessed by monitoring the rate and duration of eye blinks. When, based on monitoring of eye blinks, the driver reached a predetermined level of fatigue, the continued drive was either the same as before, fully automated with the vehicle controlling both lateral position and vehicle speed, or manual but with a cognitive task consisting of a quiz task. The results showed that following the initial manual phase, in the continued manual driving and automated driving drowsiness continued to increase while in the manual driving + cognitive task drowsiness leveled off at the lower level. Thus, the concern for the pitfalls of automated driving (see Chapter 19) is also illustrated here, where automated driving aggravated fatigue symptoms. The second observation is that the effects of cognitive load on fatigued driving are similar to their effects in studies on distracted driving (Chapter 12). Both simulator and on-road studies show that in distracted driving too cognitive loading causes drivers to slow down (e.g., Strayer *et al.*, 2015), and distractions from cell phones reduce the crash risk of drowsy drivers in naturalistic driving (Young, 2013).

In summary, all the studies that increased cognitive load on fatigued drivers (Gershon *et al.*, 2009a; Oron-Gilad *et al.*, 2002, 2008; Takayama and Nass, 2008; Schömig *et al.*, 2015; Verwey and Zaidel, 1999; Young, 2013) demonstrated both the potential effectiveness and the practical utility of mental tasks or games as a means to alleviate (or at least postpone) the effects of fatigue. The challenge now is to refine these to the point where they could become an attractive application that can be easily used while driving and feeling fatigued. While Oron-Gilad demonstrated the utility of the "trivia" game, there are probably large individual differences in drivers' preferences in general and even in the choice of content area and difficulty of the questions of a trivia game in particular. In the development of such games, it is important to realize that some information processing tasks can be performed at such a low level of consciousness, that drivers can perform them automatically without increasing their low alertness level. This, for example, was discovered in an attempt to apply a simple reaction time task to the requirements of driving a train; a decidedly monotonous task. Intermittently a light would come on and the train engineer would have to press a button to deactivate it, or else an alarm would go off. It turned out that the engineers could do the task while being nearly asleep (Bonnefond *et al.*, 2004) – giving a concrete demonstration that there are some things that we can do in our sleep.

Other alertness maintaining activities: manual dexterity/mastication secondary task

In our early study on the techniques drivers use to combat fatigue (Oron-Gilad and Shinar, 2000), we noted that a few drivers resorted to shelling and eating sunflower seeds and this activity was noted by the few who used it as extremely efficient (Table 14-5). To validate its effectiveness, Gershon, Shinar, and Ronen (2009b) conducted a simulation study where 23-30 years old drivers drove for 2 hours on a relatively monotonous road with a few shallow curves and very light traffic. In different sessions, the drivers had either an energy drink, a placebo drink (glucose-free, caffeine-free, and taurine-free), or a bag of unshelled sunflower seeds that they could shell and eat (labeled MD/MT – manual dexterity/mastication task). All drivers reported that they occasionally shell and eat sunflower seeds (a common snack in Israel). The results were striking. After two hours of driving, subjective fatigue – as measured by the SOFI (the difference between the subjective fatigue at the end of the drive and the start of the drive) – was greatest in the control/placebo condition, less after drinking the energy drink, and the least after the shelling/chewing of the sunflower seeds (Figure 14-16). Unlike coffee and energy drinks (see also Figure 14-17), the shelling/chewing effect persisted as long as the driver kept doing it. Also, unlike coffee and energy drinks the effects were immediate and ended immediately when the driver stopped shelling/chewing. Thus, this is a countermeasure that works immediately and leaves no after-effects (except for gaining a few calories). The effects on the standard performance measures such as lane position variability and reaction time to unexpected stimuli were harder to evaluate with shelling/chewing because the activity itself required one-handed manual actions. Therefore, future studies pursuing this countermeasure should include a control condition with driving with one hand.

Chemical stimulants: caffeine and others

Stimulants of the central nervous system – such as caffeine, taurine, and amphetamines – are often used to counteract the effects of fatigue. As noted in many surveys of driver coping behaviors, one of the more common approaches to counteract fatigue is to ingest a stimulant, especially caffeine; typically in the form of coffee (Lucidi *et al.*, 2006; Nguyen *et al.*, 1998).

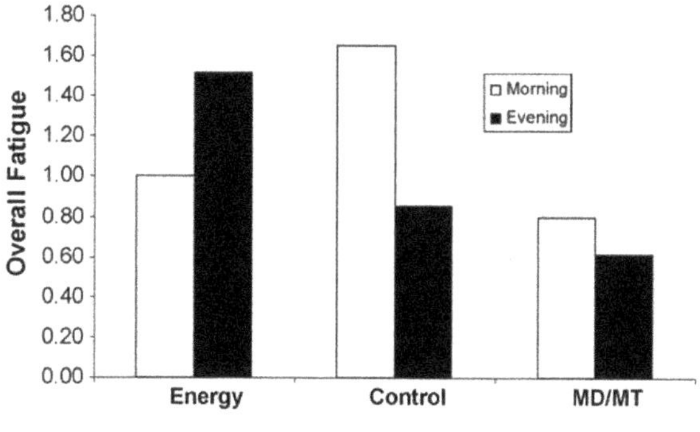

Figure 14-16. Overall fatigue based on the after/before SOFI score, after a two-hour drive for drivers after drinking an energy drink, a placebo (control), and after shelling and chewing sunflower seeds (MD/MT), on a morning (after a night's sleep) and evening drive. The lower the score the greater the fatigue mitigation effect (Gershon *et al.*, 2009b, with permission from Elsevier).

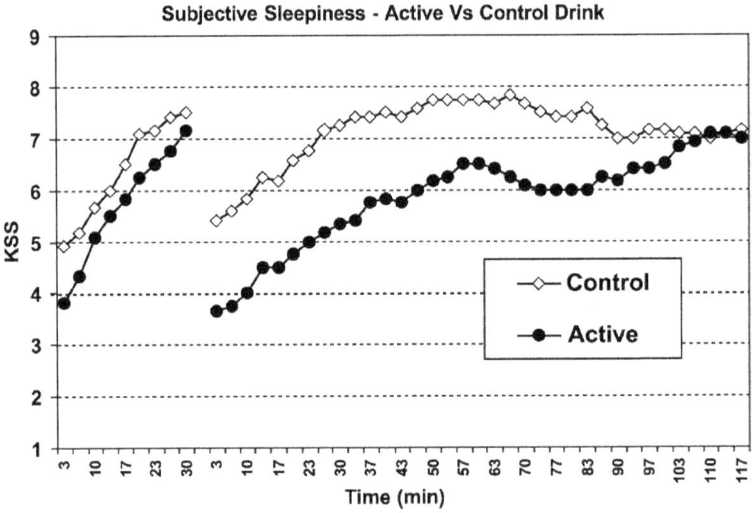

Figure 14-17. Average fatigue rating on the Karolinska Sleepiness Scale during the warm-up period and the test period in the placebo (Control) and Active (Energy drink) conditions (from Reyner and Horne, 2002, with permission from Elsevier).

Caffeine has non-specific stimulant effects on attention and alertness, in the sense that it affects multiple capacities. Furthermore, unlike many illegal drugs it has a self-limiting effect in the sense that users do not desire to increase the amount they drink the more they drink. In fact, at low doses increases in caffeine improve performance but at high doses caffeine actually impairs performance. At high doses, users tend to feel anxiety and tension which cause them to abstain from further use (Bonnefond *et al.*, 2004; Smith, 2002). This self-limiting nature also means that caffeine has a very low addictive potential (Lorist and Tops, 2003).

In their reviews of the many documented effects of caffeine, Lorist and Tops (2003), and Smith (2002) list improvements in attention, in visual search, in vigilance, and in driving performance. They also review the evidence for the specific physiological effects of caffeine on event-related brain potentials, all indicating an enhancement in information processing, especially in fatigued people. Horne and Reyner in three separate studies (Horne and Reyner, 1996; Reyner and Horne, 1997, 2002) also demonstrated that caffeine is an effective countermeasure to fatigue in simulated driving, and Philip *et al.* (2006) demonstrated its effectiveness in real driving. However, some incremental effects of fatigue on physiological functioning (electroencephalogram) and accidents, even after drinking coffee have been noted in simulated driving (Eoh, Chung, and Kim, 2005).

Drinking coffee is most effective when it is combined with a short nap, especially if the caffeine is ingested just before a 20-30 minutes nap (Reyner and Horne, 1997). This is because the caffeine takes approximately 30 minutes to be absorbed in the blood stream. Thus, resuming driving after the coffee + nap synchronizes and maximizes the effects of both. One caveat in this strategy is that the amount of caffeine in coffee is highly variable (Nehlig, 1999). This can undermine the typical recommendation to drivers to drink "two cups of coffee"; a recommendation that is based on the assumption that these cups contain a total of about 150 milligrams caffeine. But drivers cannot discern the amount of caffeine in their coffee because it is not detectable by color, taste, or smell.

In recent years, more potent legal stimulants have been introduced in the form of "energy drinks." In addition to caffeine, these products also contain taurine and sugar. The research that has been conducted on the effects of these drinks has shown them to be at least as effective as caffeine in terms of improvements in vehicle control and reduced sensations of fatigue (Reyner and Horne, 2002; Ronen *et al.*, 2014). In Reyner and Horne's study, subjects drove twice on a monotonous road in a simulator while rating their subjective sensation of fatigue on the Karolinska Sleepiness Scale approximately every three and a half minutes. On each drive, the first 30 minutes were a warm-up, and the next two hours were the test period. Between the warm-up and the test period, the subjects drank a sweet drink that was either an energy drink or a placebo (control) drink and waited 30 minutes to allow for the absorption of the drink. The effects of the energy drink on the subjective level of sleepiness (Figure 14-17) and on the frequency of crossing the lane markers (Figure 14-18) were quite distinctive. During the warm-up, prior to drinking the energy drink, both the sensation of sleepiness and the driving quality were similar in the two conditions. But during the main phase there was a noticeable difference between the two drinks in the feeling of sleepiness and the driving performance. Immediately, from the start of the main phase (30 minutes after the ingestion of the drink) drivers were much less fatigued when they had the energy drink. However, over time, the energy drink effects wore off, so that after approximately 100 minutes the drivers felt just as sleepy as in the control condition. Overall, the results are quite similar to those obtained by Gershon *et al.* (2009b) with the SOFI (Figure 14-16). In that study too, at the end of the drive the energy drink's effects wore off and the rated

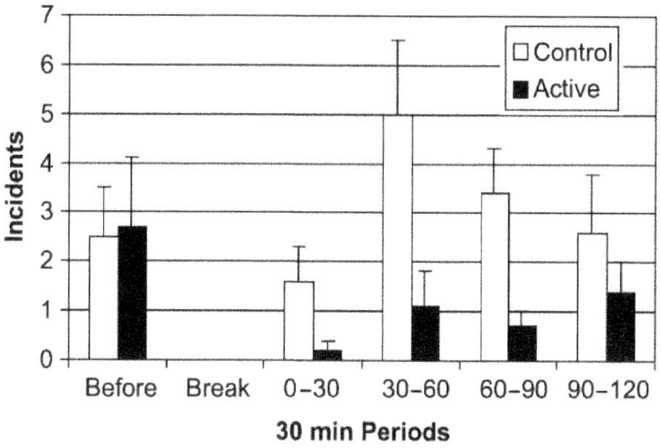

Figure 14-18. Frequencies of incidents involving crossing the lane markers during the warm-up period and the test period in the placebo (Control) and Active (Energy drink) conditions (from Reyner and Horne, 2002, with permission from Elsevier).

level of fatigue was the same as in the control condition. The behavioral effects in Reyner and Horne's study were also quite large and persisted for as long as 90 minutes, after which the difference between the two conditions was not statistically significant. Interestingly, in the control condition lane crossing incidents were most noticeable 30-60 minutes after the break and *decreased* systematically thereafter. The reason for this remained unexplained. Thus, these results have both positive and negative implications: on the positive side, coffee and energy drinks can counteract the effects of fatigue; but on the negative side drivers should know that these effects are temporary, lasting – at least in a simulator – only about an hour. A possibility that has yet to be examined is whether or not there is a rebound effect to the stimulant so that eventually performance may actually be worse with it than without it.

Another stimulant used to counter fatigue is amphetamine. It is much less common than coffee or energy drinks, probably because it is a controlled substance. However, it has been used and proven to be effective in a variety of tasks as a means to enhance performance following sleep deprivation. For example, in World War II soldiers used it following sleepless nights of military activities (Bonnefond *et al.*, 2004). In the context of driving, its use – especially by commercial drivers – has been reported. For example, Mabbott and Hartley (1999), in a survey of Australian truck drivers, found that 28 percent used stimulant drugs other than caffeine, and of those drivers approximately one-third used them on every trip. This approach of "better life through chemistry" should serve more to highlight a problem of prolonged driving than to offer a solution, because it obviously has its shortcomings in terms of overall driver health.

In-vehicle alerting systems

There are at least two strong arguments to be made for harnessing technology to counteract fatigue: both in detecting it and in coping with it. First, drivers – especially professional drivers – are often under pressure to drive and reach their destination by a certain time, regardless of their condition. Second, because fatigue impairs cognitive processes drivers can be impaired before they feel fatigued. Even if they feel fatigued, drivers are often unaware of quite how impaired they are (Brown, 1997). Having an independent assessment provided by a "computer" can give a driver the needed incentive and rationale to stop and take a break. However, there are also limits to the utility of this approach, because the reliability and validity of these systems are still quite low. If a system is designed to alert the driver when early signs of fatigue are detected the false alarm rates may be too high, and drivers may develop "cry wolf" tendencies to ignore the alarms and continue to drive – even when the alarm is appropriate. In contrast, if the system fails to detect a true state of fatigue (resulting in a "miss") the driver may continue driving under the false impression that he or she is not as fatigue-impaired as he or she feels.

The devices that have been developed can be classified as either devices that monitor the driver or devices that monitor the vehicle and the road. An advantage of the driver monitoring devices is that they can tap directly to a behavioral measure of fatigue. Their drawback is that they must be individually calibrated to the driver. The advantage of the vehicle monitoring devices is that once installed in a car, they are adequate for all drivers. Their drawback is that their measures are more removed from the driver, indifferent to individual differences in driving style, and therefore more removed from the actual driver fatigue.

With these concerns in mind, different devices, based on different observable fatigue indicators, have been developed. Driver monitoring approaches include devices that monitor the driver's face to detect eyelid closure, head nodding, and even yawning (Abtahi, Hariri, and Shirmohammadi, 2011, 2014; Sanap *et al.*, 2015). Vehicle monitoring devices include steering wheel movements (Lawoyin, Fei, and Bai, 2015), and lane excursions (Golz *et al.*, 2010). For example, Golz *et al.* (2010), using a driving simulator, evaluated the validity of two technologies that measured PERCLOS and lane deviations, relative to subjective rating on the KSS. They found that while these devices provide reliable indicators of fatigue on a gross time scale (>30 minutes), they "fail to give a valid prediction of subjective fatigue as well as of driving performance on an individual level." Four years later, in 2014 Dawson and his colleagues conducted a meticulous review of the published literature in this area and concluded that "none of the current technologies met all the proposed fatigue risk management system regulatory criteria for a legally and scientifically defensible device. Further, none were sufficiently well validated to provide a comprehensive solution to managing fatigue-related risk at the individual level in real time" (p. 141).

One detailed study sponsored by the U.S. Department of Transportation evaluated the effectiveness and practicality of four different devices that are either already available on the market or at the time of the evaluation 10 years ago were at various stages of marketing (Carroll, 2005; Dinges *et al.*, 2005). The evaluation included two driver-based devices and two vehicle-based devices:

1. SleepWatch – a device containing an activity recorder (Actigraph©) worn around the wrist. It monitors the wrist movements, and with the aid of an algorithm records the rest and activity patterns, discerning between sleep and wakefulness. With a press of a button, it gives the driver a numeric estimate of "performance readiness" on a scale of 0-100.
2. Co-Pilot – a dashboard-mounted device that monitors the driver's face and records eyelid closures using the percent of time the eye is closed (PERCLOS) as a trigger to alert the driver.
3. SafeTRAC© – consisting of a lane monitoring camera that records and analyzes the vehicle position in the lane, providing drivers with feedback whenever they drift or cross the lane marker.
4. Power Center Steering System – consisting of a hydraulic device that reduces the physical demands of driving by stabilizing the steering in response to disturbances such as cross-winds. The corrections, which can actually be felt by the driver, lessen the need for manual steering corrections.

The data collected from that study was possibly the most detailed and extensive in this area to date. With a high sampling rate of 1 Hz, the automated systems yielded over five million data elements over the one month testing period. In addition to the fatigue monitoring devices, the drivers maintained daily activity logs, performed a psychomotor vigilance task twice a day (once mid-trip and once at the end of the trip for that day), and filled out subjective fatigue questionnaires twice a day (before and after the second vigilance task). The conclusions of the study were that the eyelid monitoring and feedback system was effective in reducing fatigue as reflected in slight reductions in eyelid closures and lower subjective ratings of fatigue. However, a follow-up study (Blanco *et al.*, 2009) on 48,000 heavy truck driving hours yielded only marginally positive results, indicating that more developmental work is still needed. In addition, the results of the vigilance tests and the lane deviation records did not show that the systems were effective. The sleep monitoring system did not seem to have the desired effect because there was no increase in sleep time when the drivers were given feedback – either as measured by the device or as recorded in the drivers' log books. Interestingly, despite these results the drivers liked the fatigue training course and the fatigue monitoring devices, especially the vehicle-based lane tracking and self-correcting steering control systems.

The dearth of positive findings from this extensive study and its follow-up is quite disappointing. Furthermore, even the few positive effects (on eyelid closure and subjective ratings) are hard to interpret because the experimental design of the study was such that when the countermeasures were applied they were all applied at the same time. Thus, although it is likely that changes in eyelid closures were due to eyelid closure feedback, the change in subjective ratings can be attributed to that particular system, or to any other system, or to any combination of the four systems tested. In summary, it is likely that more than anything else these results reflect more on the state of the art of in-vehicle fatigue countermeasures than on the concept involved. As such repeated studies with newer technologies will probably yield greater effects.

Despite the lack of supportive high-quality evaluation research, some devices are actually available for purchase as options on new cars. These include Mercedes' "Attention Assist" that monitors the driver's steering behavior, Volvo's "Alert Control and Lane Departure Warning," Volkswagen's "Driver Alert System" that is based on steering wheel movements and lane deviations. To date, all of these devices fall quite short of their goals in preventing fatigued driving. Consequently, the intelligent integration of the multiple inputs that is necessary to counteract the various strategies drivers adopt to cope with fatigue is still a few years away (Bowman *et al.*, 2012; EC, 2015).

In the search for new automatic fatigue detection systems, the stress should be on the word "system." Simple solutions, such as measures of the deterioration in steering skills (as suggested by Brown, 1997) cannot be sufficiently reliable in the context of varying roadways and traffic conditions. To be reliable and valid, such devices should be able to integrate several data inputs – from the driver, the car, and the road – and use them with different algorithms in different driving conditions (Bowman *et al.*, 2012). This complex challenge is based on our multivariate methods of measuring fatigue – in subjective, behavioral, and physiological terms – as well as on the vehicle's behavior (e.g., lane excursions). Such a system should allow for drivers' abilities to adjust their fatigued driving in accordance with the tolerance allowed by the road and task (Oron-Gilad *et al.*, 2001; Van der Hulst *et al.*, 2001). One such complex multi-sensor approach that combines physiological, behavioral, and vehicle-roadway information was evaluated in a multi-year European Union study, with the very appropriate acronym AWAKE (System for effective Assessment of driver vigilance and Warning According to traffic risk Estimation) (EC, 2004). It considered the integration of information from the immediate environment (traffic and time-to-collision as sensed from within the vehicle), the vehicle (speed, lateral position in lane, steering wheel angle), and the driver (visual gaze, eyelid, and grip on the steering wheel). Figure 14-19, from Hermann (2004), is a schematic illustration of this approach. Unfortunately, in summarizing this effort Wright *et al.* (2007) concluded that "no single method exists that is commonly accepted to detect driver fatigue in an operational context... Devices based on physiological measures were too intrusive, (and) devices based on physical measures are not sufficiently sensitive." There is some hope for devices measuring eye activity, but in general, the best strategy was to

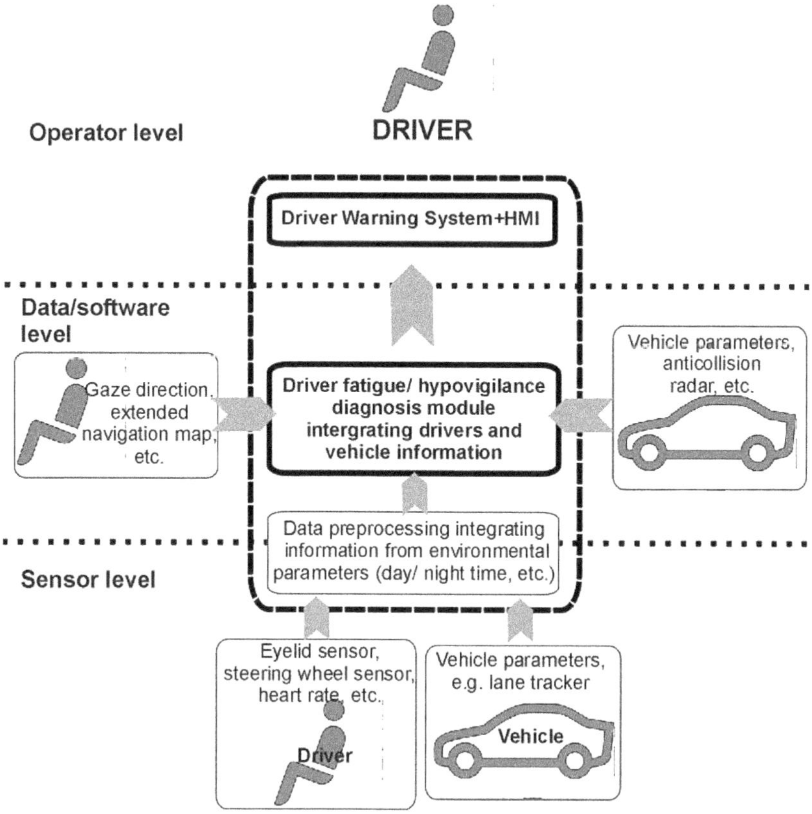

Figure 14-19. Potential components that should be integrated to provide drivers with a reliable and valid fatigue detection and alerting system (from Hermann, 2004, with permission from the author and IOS Press).

focus on system-based devices that integrate information from all three sources, as illustrated in Figure 14-19.

Finally, there is one additional complication that is common to many human-machine systems: driver adaptation. Some early research has indicated that drivers' response to fatigue detection systems is to simply rely on their warnings as alerting devices, and instead of heeding the warning by taking the recommended break or nap, the drivers continue to drive (Vincent, Noy, and Laing, 1998). In summary, quoting the European Commission, "currently, no single method exists that is commonly accepted to detect driver fatigue" (EC, 2015).

Environmental countermeasures

Perhaps the most direct environmental treatment for fatigued and sleepy driving is to provide drivers with strategically located rest areas. Drivers, especially long-distance professional drivers often state that they would stop to rest when fatigued if a rest area existed (McCartt *et al.*, 1996). In one U.S. observational survey of 1,630 rest area users, 48 percent of the passenger car drivers and 62 percent of the truck drivers used the stop for resting or stretching (Stutts, 2000). In Norway, the recommendation is that a major rest area be built every 45 km on national highways, and a minor one every 15 km (Elvik *et al.*, 2009). In Australia rest areas have also been used to introduce motorists to "driver reviver programs" – campaigns that encourage drivers to take rest breaks during long drives. However, the direct safety benefits of the campaigns, and for that matter, of rest stops in general are still to be determined. Some research has shown that drivers who use rest stops have lower crash risks than those who do not (Cummings *et al.*, 2001), but this may be a defining characteristic of the drivers as much as it is of the rest stops. Still the little research that exists on this topic suggests that rest areas are beneficial. Ronen, Oron-Gilad, and Gershon (2014) compared driving performance of 15 professional truck drivers who drove for two and a half hours under three conditions in a driving simulator. In one condition (control), they only received a sweet placebo drink at the start of the monotonous drive. In the second condition, they received an actual energy drink, and in the third condition they received the energy drink and in addition were provided with a roadside rest area after driving for approximately 100 minutes. There they could rest for 10 minutes. The differences between the three groups in their vehicular lateral control were large and in the expected direction. Figure 14-20 illustrates the effects of time-on-task in terms of the variability of lane position: the greater the vehicle control the lesser the variability. As expected, the energy drink had an almost-immediate effect enabling drivers to maintain good control of the vehicle position for the first 80 minutes. However, after about an hour and a half, its effects wore off, the level of control deteriorated, and the driving with and without the energy drink was about the same. Very similar effects following ingestion of the same energy drink (Red Bull®) were obtained by Mets *et al.* (2011), using a very similar simulator (STI_SIM®). In their study too, a short rest period for only 10 minutes enabled the drivers to retain their position in the center of the lane as well as with the energy drink before the rest. Thus, the rest prevented the deterioration in driving performance.

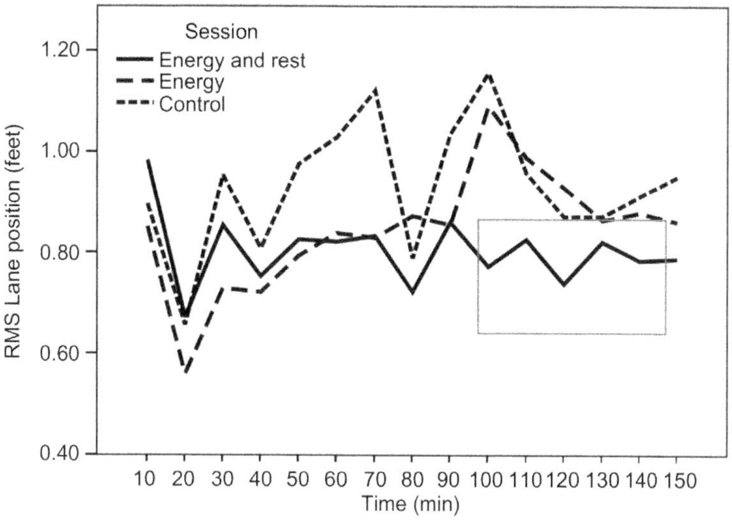

Figure 14-20. Lane position deviation over a 150-minute drive, with no countermeasures (Control), after drinking an energy drink at the beginning of the drive (Energy), and after drinking an energy drink and resting for 10 minutes after 100 minutes of driving (from Ronen *et al.*, 2014, with permission from Elsevier).

A less direct, but apparently quite effective means of combating fatigue through roadway treatment is the milling of rumble strips along road shoulders and lane dividers. These are typically placed on high-speed, relatively straight segments of rural motorways. Syntheses of reports on the effectiveness of such rumble strips show that they are remarkably effective in reducing drive-off-the-road crashes by 30-50 percent (Garder and Alexander, 1995; National Sleep Foundation, 1997), and possibly by as much as 70 percent (Perrillo, 1998). Thus, they are a relatively low-cost solution with a potentially high benefit-to-cost ratio. Although this treatment is not a fatigue-specific countermeasure (it could be just as effective for distracted driving), in one survey of New York long-haul truck drivers, 56 percent of the drivers said that rumble strips had alerted them when they felt drowsy (McCartt *et al.*, 2000). Rumble strips also appear to be effective in or next to the barrier lane markers between opposing lanes on two-lane rural roads. Persaud, Retting, and Lyon (2004) found a 14 percent reduction in all crashes in road segments totaling over 335 kilometer, and an even more impressive 25 percent reduction in frontal and side-swipe injury collisions between cars traveling in opposing directions. Sometimes even a fresh coat of paint helps. Räsänen (2005) studied the effect of painting and marking the centerlines of a curve in a rural road in Finland, and found that the variance of lane position of cars traveling in the curve decreased from 123 to 78 centimeters, and after adding the rumble strips they decreased farther to 58 centimeters.

Concluding Comments

Driving while fatigued or sleepy is a significant highway safety problem that is further aggravated by an absence of a good operational definition. It is also a complex phenomenon because it is manifested in behavioral, subjective, and physiological changes that are not always correlated with each other. Despite these difficulties various approaches have been developed to detect, control and attenuate fatigued driving. From a behavioral perspective many driver coping behaviors are useless, but some are not, and drivers need to understand the difference between the two. Most effective in this respect is an intake of caffeine followed by a short nap while the body absorbs the drink. Coffee and energy drinks by themselves are also effective (once 15-30 minutes are allowed to digest them), but their effects are temporary. Less traditional strategies such as engaging in cognitively demanding tasks/games and shelling and chewing sunflower seeds appear to be quite promising. Most of the recent work and some of the recent progress has been in the development of in-vehicle fatigue monitoring systems. Because of the complexity of fatigue and its effects, we now understanding that a device that measures a single symptom – be it physiological, behavioral, or an aspect of vehicle behavior – is inadequate. Current efforts must now focus on the systems approach: using complicated algorithms that combine multiple indicators. Though none of these systems are quite reliable yet, they are constantly improving. Finally, infrastructure-based systems, such as rest stops and rumble stripes appear to be effective and desirable by the motoring public. What remains to be done now is improve these approaches so that they can better accommodate the large individual differences in fatigue indicators and coping styles.

References

Abtahi, S., B. Hariri and S. Shirmohammadi (2011). Driver drowsiness monitoring based on yawning detection. Proc. IEEE International Instrumentation and Measurement Technology Conference, Binjiang, Hangzhou, China, May 10-12.

Abtahi, S., M. Omidyeganeh, S. Shirmohammadi and B. Hariri (2014). YawDD: A yawning detection dataset. Proceeding MMSys '14 Proceedings of the 5th ACM Multimedia Systems Conference, pp. 24-28. ACM, New York, NY.

Ahlstrom, C., M. Nyström, K. Holmqvist, C. Fors, D. Sandberg, A. Anund, G. Kecklund and T. Åkerstedt (2013). Fit-for-duty test for estimation of drivers' sleepiness level: Eye movements improve the sleep/wake predictor. *Trans. Res. C: Emerg. Technol.*, *26*, 20-32.

Åhsberg, E. and F. Gamberale (1998). Perceived fatigue during physical work: An experimental evaluation of a fatigue inventory. *Int. J. Indust. Ergonomics*, *21*, 117-131.

Åhsberg, E., F. Gamberale and K. Gustafsson (2000). Perceived fatigue after mental work: An experimental evaluation of a fatigue inventory. *Ergonomics*, *43*(2), 252-268.

Åhsberg, E., F. Gamberale and A. Kjellberg (1997). Perceived quality of fatigue during different occupational tasks: Development of a questionnaire. *Int. J. Indust. Ergonomics*, *20*, 121-135.

Åkerstedt, T. (1995). Work hours, sleepiness and accidents Introduction and summary. *J. Sleep Res.*, *4*(s2), 1-3.
Akerstedt, T. and M. Gillberg (1990). Subjective and objective sleepiness in the active individual. *Int. J. Neuroscience*, *52*, 29-37.
Anderson, C. and J. A. Horne (2013). Driving drowsy also worsens driver distraction. *Sleep Med.*, *14*, 466-468.
Andreassi, J. (2000). *Psychophysiology: Human Behavior and Physiological Response.* Lawrence Erlbaum Associates, Publishers, London.
Ayoub, E. M., R. Grace and A. Steinfeld (2003). A user-centered drowsy-driver detection and warning system. ACM, 1-58113-728-1 03/0006 5.00.
Barger, L. K., B. E. Cade, N. T. Ayas, J. W. Cronin, B. Rosner, F. E. Speizer and C. A. Czeisler (2005). Extended work shifts and the risk of motor vehicle crashes among interns. *New England J. Med.*, *352*, 125-134.
Bartlett, F. C. (1948). A note on early signs of skill fatigue. Air Ministry Flying Personnel Research Committee Report No. 703. Ministry of Defence, London. (as cited By Brown, 1982).
Bartley, S. H. and E. Chute (1947). *Fatigue and Impairment in Man.* McGraw-Hill Book Co., New York, NY.
Beirness, D. J., H. M. Simpson and K. Desmond (2005). *The Road Safety Monitor 2004: Drowsy Driving.* Traffic Injury Research Foundation, Ottawa, Ontario, Canada.
Belz, S. M., G. S. Robinson and J. G. Casali (2004). Temporal separation and self-rating of alertness as indicators of driver fatigue in commercial motor vehicle operators. *Hum. Fact.*, *46*(1), 154-169.
Blanco, M. J., L. Bocanegra, J. F. Morgan, G. M. Fitch, A. Medina, R. L. Olson, R. J. Hanowski, B. Daily and R. P. Zimmermann (2009). Assessment of a drowsy driver warning system for heavy-vehicle drivers. NHTSA Report HS 811 117. U. S. Department of Transportation, Washington, DC.
Blumenthal, M. (1968). Dimensions of the traffic safety problem. *Traffic Safe. Res. Rev.*, *12*, 7-12.
Bonnefond, A., P. Tassi, J. Rogé and A. Muzet (2004). A critical review of techniques aiming at enhancing and sustaining worker's alertness during the night shift. *Indust. Health*, *42*, 1-14.
Borghini, G., L. Astolfi, G. Vecchiato, D. Mattia and F. Babiloni (2014). Measuring neurophysiological signals in aircraft pilots and car drivers for the assessment of mental workload, fatigue and drowsiness. *Neuroscience Biobehav. Rev.*, *44*, 58-75.
Bowman, D., R. J. Hanowski, A. Alden, S. Gupta, D. Wiegand, S. Baker, L. M. Stanley and W. Wierwille (2012). Development and assessment of a driver drowsiness monitoring system. Federal Motor Carrier Safety Administration, Report No. FMCSA-RRR-12-008. U.S. Department of Transportation, Washington, DC.
Broughton, R. (1994). Important underemphasized aspects of sleep onset. In: *Sleep Onset: Normal and Abnormal Processes* (R. D. Oglive and J. R. Harsh eds.), p. 25. American Psychological Association, Washington, DC. (as cited by Driskell and Mullen, 2005).
Brown, I. D. (1982). Driver fatigue. *Endeavour*, *6*(2), 83-90.
Brown, I. D. (1997). Prospects for technological countermeasures against driver fatigue. *Accid. Anal. Prev.*, *29*, 525-531.

Bruck, D. and D. L. Pisani (1999). The effects of sleep inertia on decision-making performance. *J. Sleep Res.*, *8*(2), 95-103.
Bruno, G. A. (2004). Temporal patterns of single-vehicle accidents in Texas due to driver fatigue or sleep during 1975–1994 [M.P.H. thesis]. The University of Texas School of Public Health, Houston, TX. (As reported by Smolensky *et al.*, 2011).
Carroll, R. J. (2005). Pilot test of fatigue management technologies. FMCSA Report FMCSA-RT-04-009. U.S. Department of Transportation, Washington, DC.
Clarke, D. D., P. Ward, C. Bartle and W. Truman (2010). Older drivers' road traffic crashes in the UK. *Accid. Anal. Prev.*, *42*(4), 1018-1024.
Connor, J., G. Whitlock, R. Norton and R. Jackson (2001). The role of driver sleepiness in car crashes: A systematic review of epidemiological studies. *Accid. Anal. Prev.*, *33*, 31-41.
Cummings, P., T. D. Koepsell, J. M. Moffat and F. P. Rivara (2001). Drowsiness, counter-measures to drowsiness, and the risk of a motor vehicle crash. *Inj. Prev.*, *7*, 194-199.
Dawson, D., A. K. Searle and J. L. Paterson (2014). Look before you (s) leep: Evaluating the use of fatigue detection technologies within a fatigue risk management system for the road transport industry. *Sleep Med. Rev.*, *18*(2), 141-152.
Desmond, P. A., P. A. Hancock and J. L. Monette (1998). Fatigue and automation-induced impairments in simulated driving performance. *Transportation Res. Record*, **1628**, 8-14.
Desmond, P. A. and G. Matthews (1997). Implications of task-induced fatigue effects of in-vehicle countermeasures to driver fatigue. *Accid. Anal. Prev.*, *29*, 515-523.
Di Milia, L., M. H., Smolensky, G. Costa, H. D. Howarth, M. M. Ohayon and P. Philip (2011). Demographic factors, fatigue, and driving accidents: An examination of the published literature. *Accid. Anal. Prev.*, *43*(2), 516-532.
Dinges, D. F. (1995). An overview of sleepiness and accidents. *J. Sleep Res.*, *4*(S-2), 4-14.
Dinges, D. F., G. Maislin, R. M. Brewster, G. P. Krueger and R. J. Carroll (2005). Pilot test of fatigue management technologies. *Transportation Res. Record*, **1922**, 175-182.
Drake, C., T. Roehrs, N. Breslau, E. Johnson, C. Jefferson, H. Scofield and T. Roth (2010). The 10-year risk of verified motor vehicle crashes in relation to physiologic sleepiness. *Sleep*, *33*(6), 745.
Driskell, J. E. and B. Mullen (2005). The efficacy of naps as a fatigue countermeasure: A meta-analytic integration. *Hum. Fact.*, *47*, 360-377.
EC (2015). In-vehicle detection and warning devices. http://ec.europa.eu/transport/road_safety/specialist/knowledge/fatique/countermeasures/in_vehicle_detection_and_warning_devices_en.htm#_In-vehicle_detection_and
Ellen, R. L., S. C. Marshall, M. Palayew, F. J. Molnar and K. G. Wilson (2006). Systematic review of motor vehicle crash risk in persons with sleep apnea. *J. Clin. Sleep Med.*, *2*, 193-200.
Elvik, R., A. Høye, T. Vaa and M. Sørensen (2009). *The Handbook of Road Safety Measures* (2nd ed.). Emerald, Bingley, UK.
Eoh, H. J., M. K. Chung and S. H. Kim (2005). Electroencephalographic study of drowsiness in simulated driving with sleep deprivation. *Int. J. Indust. Ergonomics*, *35*, 307-320.

European Commission (2004). AWAKE – System for effective assessment of driver vigilance and warning according to traffic risk estimation. http://www.awake-eu.org/. Accessed June 23, 2006.

Fell, J. (1994). Safety update: Problem definition and counter measure. Summary: fatigue. New South Wales Road Safety Bureau, RUS No. 5. (As reported by Sagberg, 1999).

Fell, D. L. and B. Black (1997). Driver fatigue in the city. *Accid. Anal. Prev., 29*(4), 463-469.

Feyer, A. M. and A. M. Williamson (1995). The influence of operational conditions on driver fatigue in the long distance road transport industry in Australia. *Int. J. Indust. Ergonomics, 15*, 229-235.

FMCSA (2005). Hours of service regulations effective. Federal Motor Carrier Safety Administration 49CFR, Part 395. October 1, 2005. U.S. Department of Transportation, Washington, DC. http://www.fmcsa.dot.gov/rules-regulations/topics/hos/hos-2005.htm

Garder, P. and J. Alexander (1995). Fatigue related accidents and continuous shoulder rumble strips. Proceedings of the Transportation Research Board's 74th Annual Meeting. January 22-28. National Academies, Washington, DC.

Gershon, P., A. Ronen, T. Oron-Gilad and D. Shinar (2009a). The effects of an interactive cognitive task (ICT) in suppressing fatigue symptoms in driving. *Transportation Res. F., 12*(1), 21-28.

Gershon, P., P. Shinar, T. Oron-Gilad, Y. Parmet and A. Ronen (2011). Usage and perceived effectiveness of fatigue countermeasures for professional and nonprofessional drivers. *Accid. Anal. Prev., 43*(3), 797-803.

Gershon, P., D. Shinar and A. Ronen (2009b). Evaluation of experience-based fatigue countermeasures. *Accid. Anal. Prev., 41*(5), 969-975.

Gillberg, M., G. Kecklund and T. Akerstedt (1994). Relations between performance and subjective ratings of sleepiness during a night awake. *Sleep, 17*(3), 236-241.

Goel, A. (2014). Hours of service regulations in the United States and the 2013 rule change. *Transp. Policy, 33*, 48-55.

Golz, M., D. Sommer, U. Trutschel, B. Sirois and D. Edwards (2010). Evaluation of fatigue monitoring technologies. *Somnologie, 14*(3), 187-199.

Gutierrez, J. L. G., B. M. Jimenez, E. G. Hernandez and A. L. Lopez (2005). Spanish version of the Swedish Occupational Fatigue Inventory (SOFI): Factorial replication, reliability and validity. *Int. J. Indust. Ergonomics, 35*, 737-746.

Hanowski, R. J., M. Blanco, A. Nakata, J. S. Hickman, W. A. Schaudt, M. C. Fumero, R. L. Olson, J. Jermeland, M. Greening, G. T. Holbrook, R. R. Knipling and P. Madison (2008). The drowsy driver warning system field operational test: Data collection methods. NHTSA Report DOT HS 811 035. U.S. Department of Transportation, Washington, DC.

Hermann, S.(2004). Driver monitoring – New challenges for smart sensor-based systems. In: *Wearable eHealth Systems for Personalised Health Management* (A. Lymberis and D. De Rossi eds.), pp. 103-110. IOS Press, Amsterdam.

Hoddes, E., W. C. Dement and V. Zarcone (1972). The history and use of The Stanford Sleepiness Scale [abstract]. *Psychophysiol., 9*(2), 150.

Horne, J. A. and S. D. Baulk (2004). Awareness of sleepiness when driving. *Psychophysiol.*, *41*(1), 161.
Horne, J. A. and L. A. Reyner (1995). Sleep related vehicle accidents. *Br. Med. J.*, *310*, 565-567.
Horne, J. A. and L. A. Reyner (1996). Counteracting driver sleepiness: Effects of napping, caffeine, and placebo. *Psychophysiol.*, *33*, 306-309.
Howard, M. E., M. L. Jackson, D. Berlowitz, F. O'Donoghue, P. Swann, J. Westlake and J. L. Pierce (2014). Specific sleepiness symptoms are indicators of performance impairment during sleep deprivation. *Accid. Anal. Prev.*, *62*, 1-8.
Van der Hulst, M., T. Meijman and T. Rothengatter (2001). Maintaining task-set under fatigue: A study of time-on-task effects in simulated driving. *Transportation Res. F*, *4*, 103-108.
Jackson, M. L., R. J. Croft, G. A. Kennedy, K. Owens and M. E. Howard (2013). Cognitive components of simulated driving performance: Sleep loss effects and predictors. *Accid. Anal. Prev.*, *50*, 438-444.
Johns, M. W. (1992). Reliability and factor analysis of the Epworth Sleepiness Scale. *Sleep*, *15*(4), 376-381.
Johns, M. W. (2000). A sleep physiologist's view of the drowsy driver. *Transportation Res. F*, *3*, 241-249.
Kahneman, D. (1973). *Attention and Effort*. Prentice Hall, Englewood Cliffs, NJ.
Kecklund, G. and T. Akerstedt (1993). Sleepiness in long distance truck driving: An ambulatory EEG study of night driving. *Ergonomics*, *36*, 1007-1017.
Kircher, A., M. Uddman and J. Sandin (2002). Vehicle control and drowsiness. Swedish National Road and Transport Research Institute (VTI), Linkoping, Sweden. (as cited by Svensson, 2004).
Knipling, R. (1998). PERCLOS: A valid psychophysiological measure of alertness as measured by psychomotor vigilance. Report FHWA-FMCRT-89-006. U.S. Department of Transportation, Washington, DC.
Knipling, R. R. and J. S. Wang (1995). Revised estimates of the US drowsy driver crash problem size based on general estimates system case reviews. Association for the Advancement of Automotive Medicine, 39th Annual Proceedings.
Kong, W., L. Zhou, Y. Wang, J. Zhang, J. Liu and S. Gao (2015). A system of driving fatigue detection based on machine vision and its application on smart device. *J. Sensors*, Hindawi Publishing Corp. Article ID 548602, 1-11.
Lal, S. K. L., A. Craig, P. Boord, L. Kirkup and H. Nguyen (2003). Development of an algorithm for an EEG-based driver fatigue countermeasure. *J. Safe. Res.*, *34*, 321-328.
Lawoyin, S., D.-Y. Fei and O. Bai (2015). Accelerometer-based steering-wheel movement monitoring for drowsy driving detection. *Proc. Inst. Mech. Eng. Part D: J. Automobile Eng.*, *229*(2), 163-173.
Lee, M. L., M. E. Howard, W. J. Horrey, Y. Liang, C. Anderson, M. S. Shreeve, C. S. O'Brian and C. A. Czeisler (2016). High risk of near-crash driving events following night-shift work. *Proc. Natl. Acad. Sci.*, *113*(1), 176-181.
Leger, D. (1994). The cost of sleep-related accidents: A report for the National Commission on Sleep Disorders Research. *Sleep*, *17*, 84-93.
Lewin, K. (1943). Defining the 'field at a given time'. *Psych. Rev.*, *50*(3), 292.

Lin, S. T., Y. Y. Tan, P. Y. Chua, L. K. Tey and C. H. Ang (2012). PERCLOS threshold for drowsiness detection during real driving. *J. Vision, 12*, 546.

Lindsay, L. S. and B. C. Tefft (2012). *2012 Traffic Safety Culture Index: Motorists Admit to Driving Drowsy*. AAA Foundation for Traffic Safety, Washington, DC.

Lisper, H. O., H. Laurell and J. Van Loon (1986). Relation between time to falling asleep behind the wheel on a closed track and changes in subsidiary reaction time during prolonged driving on a motorway. *Ergonomics, 29*, 445-453.

Lorist, M. M. and M. Tops (2003). Caffeine, fatigue, and cognition. *Brain Cognition, 53*, 82-94.

Lucidi, F., P. M. Russo, L. Mallia, A. Devoto, M. Lauriola and C. Violani (2006). Sleep-related car crashes: Risk perception and decision-making processes in young drivers. *Accid. Anal. Prev., 38*, 302-309.

Mabbott, N. A. and L. R. Hartley (1999). Patterns of stimulant drug use on Western Australian heavy transport routes. *Transportation Res. F, 2*, 115-130.

Macchi, M. M., Z. Boulosa, T. Ranney, L. Simmons and S. S. Campbell (2002). Effects of an afternoon nap on nighttime alertness and performance in long-haul drivers. *Accid. Anal. Prev., 34*, 825-834.

Mackworth, N. H. (1948). The breakdown of vigilance during prolonged visual search. *Quarterly J. Exp. Psychol., 1*, 6-21.

MacLean, A. W., D. R. T. Davies and K. Thiele (2003). The hazards and prevention of driving while sleepy. *Sleep Med. Rev., 7*(6), 507-521.

Matthews, G. and P. A. Desmond (1998). Personality and multiple dimensions of task-induced fatigue: A study of simulated driving. *Pers. Indiv. Diff., 25*, 443-458.

Maycock, G. (1995). Driver sleepiness as a factor in car and HGV accidents. Transport Research Laboratory Report 169. Crowthorne, Berkshire, UK.

McCartt, A. T., S. A. Ribner, A. I. Pack and M. C. Hammer (1996). The scope and nature of the drowsy driving problem in New York State. *Accid. Anal. Prev., 28*, 511-517.

McCartt, A. T., J. W. Rohrbaugh, M. C. Hammer and S. Z. Fuller (2000). Factors associated with falling asleep at the wheel among long-distance truck drivers. *Accid. Anal. Prev., 32*, 493-504.

Mets, M. A., S. Ketzer, C. Blom, M. H. Van Gerven, G. M. Van Willigenburg, B. Olivier and J. C. Verster (2011). Positive effects of Red Bull® energy drink on driving performance during prolonged driving. *Psychopharmacol., 214*(3), 737-745.

National Sleep Foundation (1997). Survey: Sleepiness in America. National Sleep Foundation, Washington, DC.

National Sleep Foundation (2002). *Adolescent Sleep Needs and Patterns: Research Report and Resource Guide*. National Sleep Foundation, Washington DC.

Nehlig, A. (1999). Are we dependent upon coffee and caffeine? A review on human and animal data. *Neuroscience Behav. Rev., 23*, 563-576.

Nguyen, L. T., B. Jauregui and D. F. Dinges (1998). *Changing Behaviors to Prevent Drowsy Driving and Promote Traffic Safety: Review of Proven, Promising, and Unproven Techniques*. American Automobile Association Foundation for Traffic Safety, Washington, DC.

NHTSA (1998). Drowsy driving and automobile crashes. A report of an Expert Panel on Driver Fatigue and Sleepiness, Report DOT HS 808 707. U.S. Department of Transportation, Washington, DC.

NHTSA (2005). Drowsy driving. NHTSA notes. *Annals Emerg. Med.*, *45*(4), 433-434.
NHTSA (2011). Drowsy driving: A brief statistical summary. Traffic Safety Facts Report HS 811 449. U.S. Department of Transportation, Washington, DC.
NHTSA (2015). Traffic Safety Facts: 2014 Crash data key findings. National Highway Traffic Safety Administration Report DOT HS 812 219. U.S. Department of Transportation, Washington, DC.
Nilsson, T., T. M. Nelson and D. Carlson (1997). Development of fatigue symptoms during simulated driving. *Accid. Anal. Prev.*, *29*(4), 479-488.
Nordbakke, S. (2004). Driver fatigue and falling asleep – Experience, knowledge and conduct among private drivers and professional drivers. TOI Report 706/2004. TOI (Institute of Transport Economics), Oslo, Norway.
Ogilvie, R. D. (2001). The process of falling asleep. *Sleep Med. Rev.*, *5*(3), 247-270.
Oron-Gilad, T. and A. Ronen (2007). Road characteristics and driver fatigue: A simulator study. *Traffic Inj. Prev.*, *8*, 281-289.
Oron-Gilad, T., A. Ronen, Y. Cassuto and D. Shinar (2002). Alertness maintaining tasks while driving. Proceedings of the Human Factors and Ergonomics Society Conference, Baltimore, MD.
Oron-Gilad, T., A. Ronen and D. Shinar (2008). Alertness maintaining tasks (AMTs) while driving. *Accid. Anal. Prev.*, *40*(3), 851-860.
Oron-Gilad, T., A. Ronen, D. Shinar and Y. Cassuto (2001). Fatigue of professional truck drivers in simulated driving: A preliminary study. Proceedings of Traffic Safety on Three Continents, International Conference in Moscow, Russia, September 19-21.
Oron-Gilad, T. and D. Shinar (2000). Driver fatigue among military truck drivers. *Transportation Res. F*, *3*, 195-209.
Otmani, S., J. Rogé and A. Muzet (2005). Sleepiness in professional drivers: Effect of age and time of day. *Accid. Anal. Prev.*, *37*, 930-937.
Pack, A. I., A. M. Pack, E. Rodgman, A. Cucchiara, D. F. Dinges and C. W. Schwab (1995). Characteristics of crashes attributed to the driver having fallen asleep. *Accid. Anal. Prev.*, *27*(6), 769-775.
Parkes, A., W. Gillan and S. Cynk (2009). The relationship between driver fatigue and rules limiting hours of driving and work. Transport Research Laboratory report PPR413, Crawthorne, U.K.
Perrillo, K. (1998). *The Effectiveness and Use of Continuous Rumble Strips*. Federal Highway Administration, U.S. Department of Transportation, Washington, DC. Online Posting June 23, 2006. http://safety.fhwa.dot.gov/fourthlevel/pdf/continuousrumble.pdf
Persaud, B. N., R. A. Retting and C. A. Lyon (2004). Crash reduction following installation of centerline rumble strips on rural two-lane roads. *Accid. Anal. Prev.*, *36*, 1073-1079.
Peters, R. D., E. Wagner, E. Alicandri, J. E. Fox., M. L. Thomas, D. R. Thorne, H. C. Sing and S. M. Balwinski (1999). Effects of partial and total sleep deprivation on driving performance. *Pub. Roads*, *62*(4), 2-8.
Philip, P., J. Taillard, E. Klein, P. Sagaspe, A. Charles, W. L. Davies, C. Guilleminault and B. Bioulac (2003). Effect of fatigue on performance measured by a driving simulator in automobile drivers. *J. Psychosomatic Res.*, *55*, 197-200.

Philip, P., J. Taillard, N. Moore, S. Delord, C. Valtat, P. Sagaspe and B. Bioulac (2006). The effects of coffee and napping on nighttime highway driving: A randomized trial. *Annals Internal Med., 144*, 705-711.

Phillips, R. O. (2015). A review of definitions of fatigue–And a step towards a whole definition. *Transportation Res. F, 29*, 48-56.

Pilcher, J. J. and A. I. Huffcutt (1996). Effects of sleep deprivation on performance: A meta-analysis. *Sleep, 19*, 318-326.

Räsänen, M. (2005). Effects of a rumble strip barrier line on lane keeping in a curve. *Accid. Anal. Prev., 37*, 575-581.

Reyner, L. A. and J. A. Horne (1997). Suppression of sleepiness in drivers: Combination of caffeine with a short nap. *Psychophysiol., 34*, 721-725.

Reyner, L. A. and J. A. Horne (2002). Efficacy of a 'functional energy drink' in counteracting driver sleepiness. *Physiol. Behav., 75*, 331-335.

Rockwell, T. H. (1972). Eye movement analysis of visual information acquisition in driving. Paper presented at the Australia Research Board.

Rogé, J., T. Pebayle, S. El Hannachi and A. Muzet (2003). Effect of sleep deprivation and driving duration on the useful visual field in younger and older subjects during simulator driving. *Vision Res., 43*, 1465-1472.

Ronen, A., T. Oron-Gilad and P. Gershon (2014). The combination of short rest and energy drink consumption as fatigue countermeasures during a prolonged drive of professional truck drivers. *J. Safety Res., 49*, 39-41e1.

Sagberg, F. (1999). Road accidents caused by drivers falling asleep. *Accid. Anal. Prev., 31*, 639-649.

Sanap, G., S. Lagad, K. Lohar and P. Lokhande (2015). A review on vision-based real-time driver fatigue detection system for efficient vehicle control. International Journal of Advance Foundation and Research in Computer (IJAFRC), 2, Special Issue (NCRTIT 2015), January 2015, pp. 135-140.

Schömig, N., V. Hargutt, A. Neukum, L. Petermann-Stock and I. Othersen (2015). The interaction between highly automated driving and the development of drowsiness. *Procedia Manufacturing, 3*, 6652-6659.

Sharwood, L. N., J. Elkington, M. Stevenson and K. K. Wong (2011), Investigating the role of fatigue, sleep and sleep disorders in commercial vehicle crashes: A systematic review. *J. Australasian College Road Safety, 22*(3), 24-30.

Smiley, A. (1998). Fatigue management: Lessons from research. In: *Managing Fatigue in Transportation* (L. Hartley ed.), pp. 1-23. Elsevier, Oxford, UK.

Smith, A. (2002). Effects of caffeine on human behavior. *Food Chemical Toxicol., 40*, 1243-1255.

Smith, S. B., W. Baron, K. Gay and G. Ritter (2005). Intelligent transportation systems and truck parking. Report No. FMCSA-RT—05-001. U.S. Department of Transportation, Washington DC.

Smolensky, M. H., L. Di Milia, M. M. Ohayon and P. Philip (2011). Sleep disorders, medical conditions, and road accident risk. *Accid. Anal. Prev., 43*(2), 533-548.

Starnes (2006). Large truck crash causation study: an overview. Federal Highway Administration Report DOT HS 810 646. U.S. Department of Transportation. Washington, DC.

Strayer, D. L., J. Turrill, J. M. Cooper, J. R. Coleman and N. Medeiros-Ward (2015). Assessing cognitive distraction in the automobile. *Hum. Fact.*, *75*, 1300–1324.

Stutts, J. C. (2000). Sleep deprivation countermeasures of motorist safety. NCHRP Synthesis 287. Transportation Research Board, Washington, DC.

Stutts, J. C., S. V. Masten, C. A. Martel and L. Thomas (2006). Predicting daytime and nighttime drowsy driving crashes based on crash and driver interview data. Highway Safety Research Center Final report to NHTSA. University of North Carolina, Chapel Hill, NC.

Summala, H. and T. Mikkola (1994). Fatal accidents among car and truck drivers: Effects of fatigue, age, and alcohol consumption. *Hum. Fact.*, *36*, 315-326.

Svensson, U. (2004). Blink behavior based drowsiness detection – Method development and validation. Linkoping University Report LiU-IMT-EX-04-369. Linkoping University, Linkoping, Sweden.

Takayama, L. and C. Nass (2008). Assessing the effectiveness of interactive media in improving drowsy driver safety. *Hum. Fact.*, *50*(5), 772-781.

Tefft, B. C. (2012). Prevalence of motor vehicle crashes involving drowsy drivers, United States, 1999–2008. *Accid. Anal. Prev.*, *45*, 180-186.

Terán-Santos, J., A. Jiménez-Gómez and J. Cordero-Guevara (1999). The association between sleep apnoea and the risk of traffic accidents. *New England J. Med.*, *340*, 847-851.

Thiffault, P. and J. Bergeron (2002). Fatigue and individual differences in monotonous simulated driving. *Pers. Indiv. Diff.*, *33*, 1-18.

Thiffault, P. and J. Bergeron (2003). Monotony of road environment and driver fatigue: A simulator study. *Accid. Anal. Prev.*, *35*, 381-391.

Vanlaar, W., H. Simpson, D. Mayhew and R. Robertson (2007). *Fatigue and drowsy driving*. Traffic Injury Research Foundation, Ottawa, Ontario, Canada.

Verwey, W. B. and D. M. Zaidel (1999). Preventing drowsiness accidents by an alertness maintenance device. *Accid. Anal. Prev.*, *31*, 199-211.

Vincent, A., I. Noy and A. Laing (1998). Behavioural adaptation to fatigue warning systems. Paper Number 98-S2-P-2 1. Proceedings of the 16th International Technical Conference on the Enhanced Safety of Vehicles. Windsor, Canada. http://www-nrd.nhtsa.dot.gov/pdf/nrd-01/Esv/esv16/98S2P21.PDF

Watling, C. N., A. Kerry, A. Armstrong and I. Radun (2015). Examining signs of driver sleepiness, usage of sleepiness countermeasures and the associations with sleepy driving behaviours and individual factors. *Accid. Anal. Prev.*, *85*, 22-29.

Watling, C. N., S. S. Smith and M. S. Horswill (2014). Stop and revive? The effectiveness of nap and active rest breaks for reducing driver sleepiness. *Psychophysiology*, *51*(11), 1131-1138.

Wierwille, W. W., L. A. Ellsworth, S. S. Wreggit, R. J. Fairbanks and C. L. Kirn (1994). Research on vehicle based driver status/performance monitoring: Development, validation, and refinement of algorithms for detection of driver drowsiness. National Highway Traffic Safety Administration Report DOT HS 808 247. U.S. Department of Transportation, Washington, DC.

Williamson, A. M., A. M. Feyer, R. P. Mattick, R. Friswell and S. Finlay-Brown (2001). Developing measures of fatigue using an alcohol comparison to validate the effects of fatigue on performance. *Accid. Anal. Prev.*, *33*, 313-326.

Williamson, A., D. A. Lombardi, S. Folkard, J. Stutts, T. K. Courtney and J. L. Connor (2011). The link between fatigue and safety. *Accid. Anal. Prev.*, *43*(2), 498-515.
Wright, N. A., B. M. Stone, T. J. Horberry and N. Reed (2007) *A review of in-vehicle sleepiness detection devices.* Published project Report 157. TRL Ltd., Crowthorne, U.K. http://www.trl.co.uk/store/report_detail.asp?srid=6171&pid=211. Accessed January 29, 2008.
Wu, H. and F. Yan-Go (1996). Self-reported automobile accidents involving patients with obstructive sleep apnoea. *Neurology*, *46*, 1254-1257.
Xie, J. F., M. Xie and W. Zhu (2012, December). Driver fatigue detection based on head gesture and PERCLOS. 2012 International Conference on Wavelet Active Media Technology and Information Processing (ICWAMTIP), pp. 128-131. IEEE.
Young, R. A. (2013). Drowsy driving increases severity of safety-critical events and is decreased by cell phone conversation. Proceedings of 3rd International Conference on Driver Distraction and Inattention, September 4-6, Gothenburg, Sweden.
Young, T., J. Blustein, L. Finn and M. Palta (1997). Sleep-disordered breathing and motor vehicle accidents in a population-based sample of employed adults. *Sleep*, *20*, 608-613.

PART E
VULNERABLE ROAD USERS

15

PEDESTRIANS

"The pedestrian is a humble man, who has been pushed around first by a man on horseback, then by a man in a carriage, and now by others in cars and trucks." (Bird, 1969).

"Walking is such a basic way of travelling that one tends to forget its importance. Walking can be seen as the lubricating oil of the transport system." (Methorst, 2010b).

Pedestrians, motorcyclists, and bicyclists are often grouped together under the label of "vulnerable road users" (VRUs). This is because – once they are involved in a crash – they have two distinct disadvantages: (1) they are totally exposed, having no shield at all to protect them in case of a collision (except for the helmets that are worn by cyclists and motorcyclists), and (2) the difference in mass between them and cars or trucks with which they may collide is very large – and not in their favor. These two factors make their likelihood of being seriously injured or killed in collisions much higher than that of vehicle occupants. But pedestrians and bicyclists share other critical features that distinguish them from vehicle occupants, especially drivers. They comprise a much more heterogeneous group in the sense that their age range is greater; their range of cognitive, motor, and visual skills is greater; their movement in traffic is less regulated and more variable; and their compliance with traffic laws and safety regulations is much more variable. All of these differences make them – especially pedestrians – much more difficult to protect. Thus, in many respects pedestrian safety is much more complicated than occupant safety.

As the level of motorization increases, one would suppose that the amount of walking would decrease. This is not true. Motorization changes the nature of walking, essentially reducing door-to-door walking, while increasing the amount of walking between different modes of travel, making walking an integral part of multimodal mobility. The amount of walking varies markedly in different countries – and not necessarily in an inverse relation to the level of motorization. For example, walking constitutes only 9 percent of the mobility time in the U.S. but 45 Percent in Switzerland, 35 percent in Spain, 24 percent in the UK, and 22 percent in the Netherlands and Finland (DaCoTA, 2012). In the developed world for most adults, walking is definitely not the most common mode of mobility. In a survey of mobility patterns in 28 European Union countries, only 14 percent of the respondents noted walking as the most frequent mode of daily travel (trailing car and public transport as the two most common modes); and this percent ranged from a high of 25 percent in Spain and Bulgaria to a low of 4 percent in the Netherlands (EU, 2014). Yet even in the Netherlands an average Dutch person walks approximately 200-250 kilometers per year, which is 600-700 meters per day, or roughly 15 minutes per day (Methorst, 2010a).

This chapter first looks at the crash risk of pedestrians and the scope of the problem. We then focus on pedestrian safety issues including the characteristics of pedestrian crashes, the causes of these crashes in terms of the behaviors and conditions that immediately precede them, and some of the key approaches to pedestrian crash prevention and injury reduction.

Scope of the Problem: Pedestrian Crash and Injury Risk

Motor-vehicle crashes with pedestrians constitute a relatively small proportion of all crashes, at least in the industrialized world. However, because of their vulnerability the injury and fatality risks of pedestrians are much greater. Worldwide, of the 1.2 million traffic fatalities, 400,000 are pedestrians, and more than half of these occur in low-income countries (Naci, Chisholm, and Baker, 2009). Yet even in the EU countries, on the average, relative to their exposure (in terms of distance traveled) pedestrians are 6.7 times more likely to be killed in a traffic accident than vehicle occupants (WHO, 2004). The extent of the problem may actually be greater as some pedestrian accidents do not involve a motorized vehicle and may occur off the road and are therefore not included in official police accident data bases (Turner, Roozenburg, and Francis, 2006). Consequently, because national statistics are based primarily on police reports, and pedestrian (and bicyclist) crashes are under-reported, the problem is probably much greater than it appears in official statistics. This issue was highlighted by Karsch *et al.* (2012) in their review of pedestrian accident research when they concluded that "methods should be sought to link or combine data from police reports, hospitals, emergency rooms, and other medical sources. If necessary, surveys or other sampling methods could be used to estimate crashes and injuries that do not appear on official records."

As is true for all road users, pedestrians seem to be much more at risk in the less developed countries than in the more developed ones. The data in Figure 15-1 represent the percent of pedestrian fatalities out of all traffic fatalities in 44 countries (mostly for the years 2002

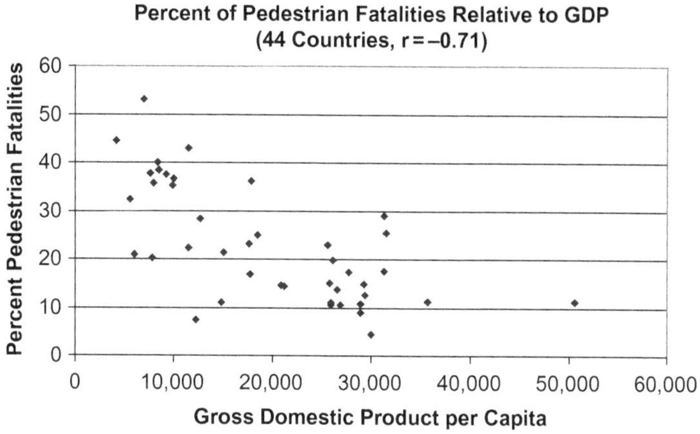

Figure 15-1. The relationship between the percent of pedestrian fatalities (out of all traffic fatalities) and the gross domestic product per capita (based on data collated by Link, 2006).

and 2003) as a function of the gross domestic product per person. The countries vary widely in terms of this measure of affluence; with a range of nearly 20-fold from the poorest in this particular list (Brazil) to the richest (Luxemburg). It is patently obvious that there is a relationship between the two measures; and it is a relatively strong one with a correlation of $r = 0.71$. In poor countries, pedestrians constitute more than 35 percent of all fatalities (53 percent in Romania and 45 percent in Georgia and Ukraine), whereas in the richer countries they tend to constitute 15 percent or less (4.5 percent in Iceland, 9 percent in the Netherlands, and approximately 10-11 percent in Finland, New Zealand Norway, Sweden, and the U.S.). A similar but weaker relationship between percent pedestrian fatalities and the level of motorization exists within the IRTAD (i.e., developed) countries where the percent pedestrian fatalities varies from a low of about 10 percent for the highly motorized countries such as Netherlands, New Zealand, and the U.S. to a high of over 30 percent for the less motorized countries such as Israel (34 percent), and S. Korea (39 percent) (IRTAD, 2013). But no single variable can explain all the variance in the rate of pedestrian fatalities, and they must be attributed to multiple factors such as socioeconomic, infrastructure, urbanization, and climate.

Motorization is a measure of the number of vehicles per number of people in population (see Chapter 1), and it is obviously correlated with the average income level ($r = 0.82$ for the data set in Figure 15-1). This relationship between motorization and pedestrian injuries is true when comparisons are made among countries and when comparisons are made for a given country over a period of time. For example, in the mid-1940s, pedestrian fatalities constituted approximately 35 percent of all traffic fatalities in the U.S. and nearly 55 percent of all traffic fatalities in the United Kingdom. By 2003, they were approximately 10 percent in the U.S. and 20 percent in the United Kingdom (Evans, 2004). But there are also conspicuous deviations from that rule. In Israel, with over US $37,000 per capita income in 2014, pedestrians constitute approximately 35 percent of all traffic accident fatalities. In contrast, in Slovakia with a much lower per capita GDP of under US $16,000 in 2014 the percentage was only 18 (EC, 2015). The reasons for the differences within a given level of affluence are not clear, but the variability itself suggests that countries with the same level of per capita income may improve their pedestrian safety by learning from each other. In the EU countries, where there is a significant sharing and cross-pollination of safety ideas among countries, pedestrian fatalities have decreased by 41 percent in the decade of 2002-2012 (Adminaite, Allsop, and Jost, 2015).

The reasons for the inverse relationship between the risk of being killed as pedestrians and the level of motorization and affluence may be the same ones provided in Chapter 1 as an explanation of Smeed's Law concerning the more general relationship between fatalities per number of vehicles and number of vehicles per size of population. Specifically, as motorization and affluence increase more and more people learn to respect the right of vehicles on the roadway and how and where to cross the road properly (beginning with children who receive formal safety education). In parallel, the state provides better separations between vehicles and pedestrians by constructing pedestrian pavements, marked and signalized pedestrian crossings, and dedicated pedestrian overpasses and underpasses. Also, pedestrian exposure decreases as motorization increases; for longer distances people tend to walk less and less and drive more and more. For example, in the U.S. pedestrian trips constitute nearly 40 percent of all trips less than one mile. But overall, walking is estimated to be only 1-4 percent of all trips (Fitzpatrick *et al.*, 2006). Sadly, the relationship between wealth and pedestrian safety remains even at the micro level. Studies in various communities in the U.S. and Canada have shown that children from poorer families (who tend to live in poorer communities) are at much higher crash risk as pedestrians than children from richer families (Laflamme and Diderichsen, 2000; Rivara, 1990).

Pedestrian injuries are not evenly distributed on all roads. As one would expect, they are concentrated mostly in urban areas, where the densities of both pedestrians and motor vehicles are highest, and the likelihood of a conflict is greatest. Thus, in the U.S., pedestrian fatalities constitute 14 percent of all traffic fatalities, and 73 percent of these occur in urban areas (NHTSA, 2015). In the EU countries too – with the exception of Latvia and Lithuania – most pedestrian fatalities are in urban areas (Adminaite *et al.*, 2015).

Pedestrian Crash Risk, Behavior, and Causes of Crashes

Most readers of this book probably tend to see themselves more in the driver's role than in the pedestrian's role. In fact, during our adult years most of our mobility is motorized and consequently we rarely think of ourselves as pedestrians. We typically think of pedestrians as people who are unable to drive; either because they are not yet old enough to drive, or because they are too old to continue driving. But in fact, we are all pedestrians from the moment we are able to walk independently. As drivers we all know and – most of us most of the time – observe the rules of the road as they relate to observing the rights of other drivers, but we seem to be much more casual about observing the few rights of pedestrians. Furthermore, as pedestrians we are much more relaxed about observing the traffic rules and regulations. Thus, when drivers' disregard for pedestrians and pedestrians' disregard of traffic rules combine, we have the potential for a driver-pedestrian conflict and a crash. For example, as drivers we want to ensure that we are seen by other motorists and rely on our headlights for our own visibility. Yet as pedestrians or bicyclists we often move without being adequately visible to drivers (Hagel *et al.*, 2007). Consequently, the reasons for pedestrian (and bicycle) crashes are somewhat different from the reasons or causes of crashes in general.

Pedestrian crash risk

To estimate the risk of a crash, we need to evaluate the crash data against an exposure measure, such as the number of pedestrians in the population, the distance they walk, the number of hours they spend walking, or the number of times they attempt to cross a street. The first measure, the number of pedestrians, is relatively easy to obtain if we assume that everyone in the population census – except for the very young and very old – is a pedestrian. Therefore, within a wide range of ages, the approximation is good enough. Obtaining the other pedestrian-specific measures of exposure is much more complicated and most often it is simply not available. This is important because researchers frequently argue that these difficult-to-obtain measures are the most appropriate ones to use. For example, Fontaine and Gourlet (1997) suggest that the most appropriate measure of exposure for older pedestrians is the number of roads crossed. The difference between the validity of this measure and the number of people in the population is that people of different ages make different number of walking trips involving different number of crossings. Thus, older pedestrians may walk very little, and may try to plan their routes in ways that minimize street crossings, while younger people may select the walking route that is the shortest (often involving mid-block crossing), walk more in busy urban areas, and be indifferent to the need to cross streets when they plan their trips.

One very detailed analysis of pedestrian crash, injury, and fatality risk that considered the different exposure measures was conducted by Keall (1995). Though somewhat dated, the patterns of crash risk obtained in his analyses are still relevant. For his analyses, he combined travel exposure data from the 1989-1990 New Zealand Travel Survey with pedestrian accident data from the New Zealand national Traffic Accident Report files for the period 1988-1991. The travel survey data for children 5-9 years old were obtained from interviews with the parents or other adults in the same household. The pedestrian casualty data as a function of the pedestrian age are plotted in Figure 15-2. If we look first at the absolute numbers of pedestrians injured or killed as a function of age and gender we see the expected high numbers of young (5-19 years old) pedestrians. We also see that more males than females are injured or killed.

But while we may assume that the proportion of males and females walking the streets and roads of New Zealand is similar across all age groups (except the oldest where there are more females), we cannot assume that the population size is the same for all age groups. After adjusting for the population size for each gender at each age group, we get the pedestrian crash risk per person that is displayed in Figure 15-3. This graph illustrates

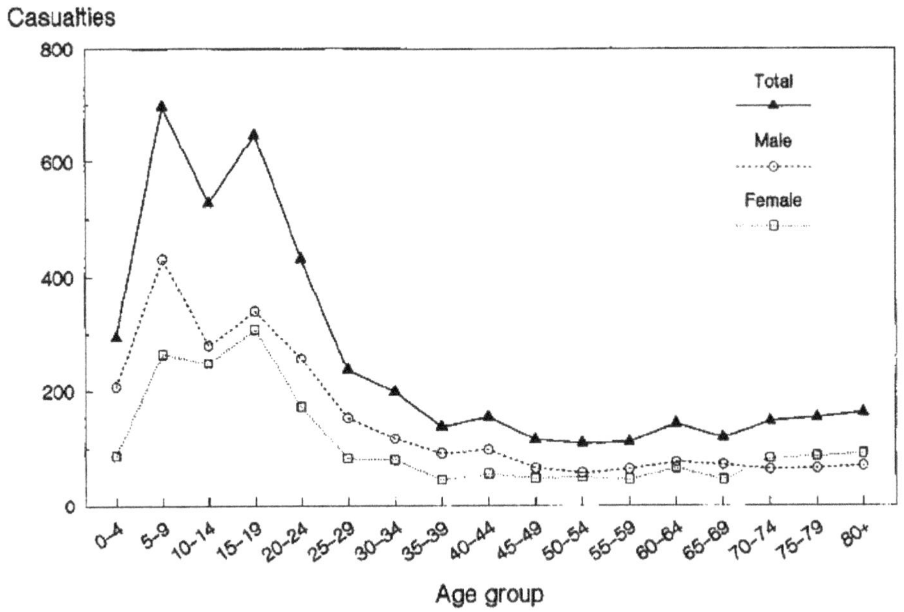

Figure 15-2. Number of injured or killed pedestrians in New Zealand, 1988-1991 as a function of age and gender (from Keall, 1995, with permission from Elsevier).

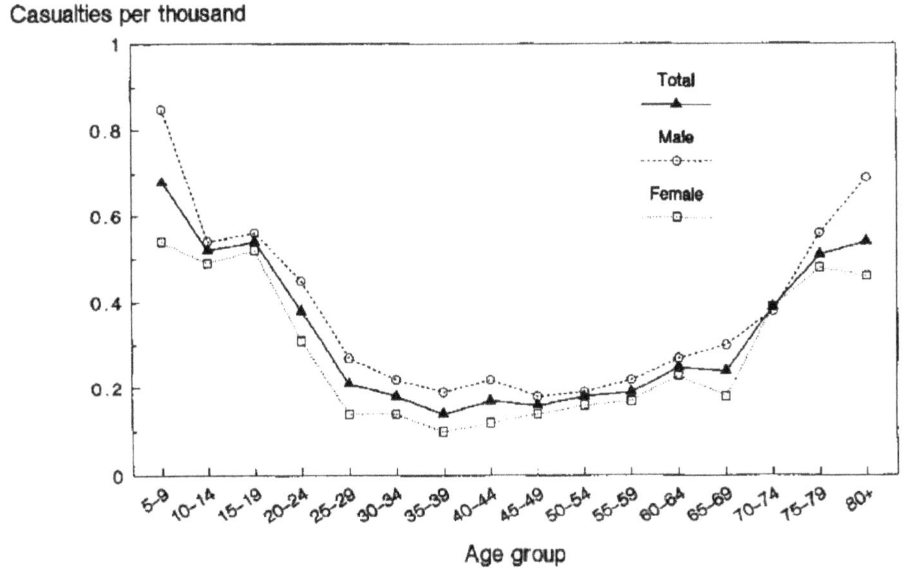

Figure 15-3. New Zealand pedestrian casualty rate as a function of gender and age per thousands of people (from Keall, 1995, with permission from Elsevier).

that the young (under 25 years old) but also the old (70+ years old) are at much greater risk to be injured or killed as pedestrians, with males more at risk than females, especially at the two extremes of the age range. Similar gender- and age-related patterns exist in more recent U.S. and E.U. pedestrian fatality data (Zegeer and Bushell, 2012).

For true exposure to crash risk, we need a measure that is actually related to the amount or distance of walking that a person does. The decision to walk is most often based on the distance we have to traverse; and consequently in a highly motorized country like the U.S. approximately three quarters of the pedestrian trips are half a mile or less (NPTS, 1995). However, the actual amount of walking varies for different age groups, so we should examine the injury rates per kilometers or hours of walking by age group. This is depicted in Figure 15-4. The general shape of this curve – a U-shaped curve – is similar to the rate per population, but it is more extreme at the two ends and flatter in the middle. This is because despite the fact that the very young and the very old tend to spend a greater percent of their total travel time walking (approximately 25 percent of the travel time for 10-19 years old and as much as 35 percent of the time for the 75+ years old), the total amount of time they spend walking is less than people in the 25-70 working-age group. A similar relationship of age-related increase of fatality rate per distance traveled is reported for Swedish data by Öström and Eriksson (2001).

Another biasing factor in the injury rate data is that as people reduce their walking time and distance, they should also reduce the time that they spend crossing streets – the actual exposure to conflicts with motorized vehicles. Therefore, an even more direct measure of exposure to traffic and crash risk is the number of crossings that people do. Keall (1995) was able to calculate the pedestrian casualty rate relative to their estimated number of crossings, and his results are displayed in Figure 15-5. Using this measure of

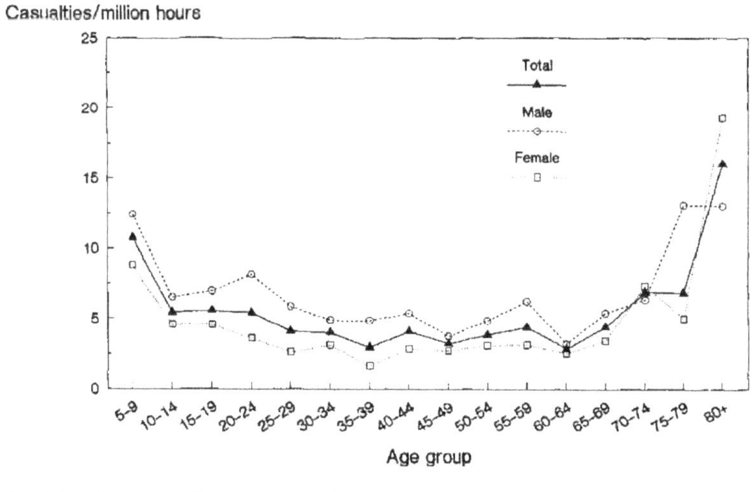

Figure 15-4. The New Zealand pedestrian casualty rate as a function of gender and age per estimated million hours of walking (from Keall, 1995, with permission from Elsevier).

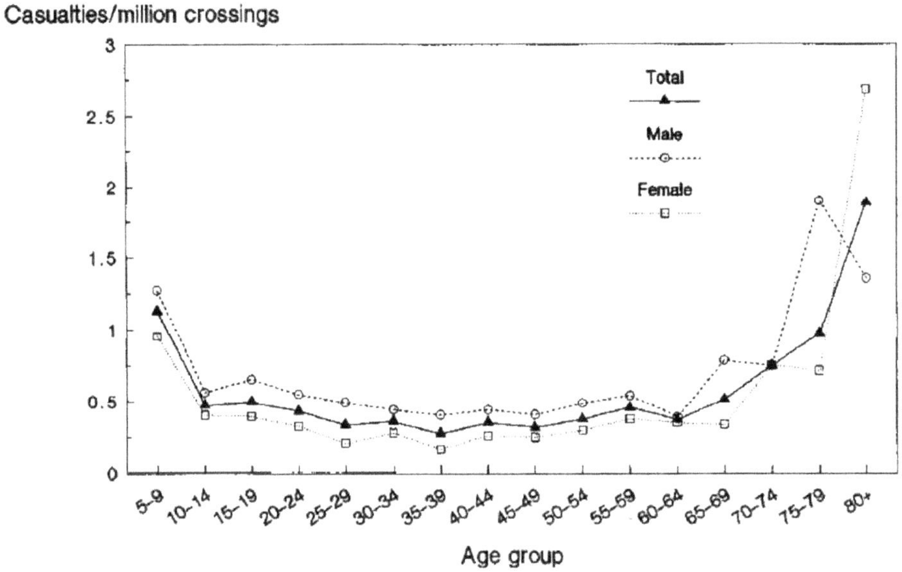

Figure 15-5. The New Zealand pedestrian casualty rate as a function of gender and age per estimated million crossings (from Keall, 1995, with permission from Elsevier).

exposure, the risk of the oldest, 80+ years old, pedestrians is clearly much greater than that of all other pedestrians. In fact the risk of injury to an 80+ years old woman is nearly 10-fold that of a 35-39-years-old woman.

Finally, although we call all pedestrians "vulnerable road users," an age-sensitive aspect of vulnerability is frailty. Older people are more frail, and when injured are less likely to survive – either the injury itself or the post-crash treatment. This is reflected in the casualty rates, but it is even more pronounced when the analysis is conducted separately on severe and fatal crashes. Keall (1995), therefore, also conducted separate analyses of fatality and severe injury rates and the results of these analyses are plotted in Figure 15-6. These analyses further differentiated the older pedestrians from the rest of the pedestrian population. In addition, the analyses showed that the very young who are over-involved in casualties are not over-involved in fatalities. Given an injury, children and adolescents remain quite resilient and are as likely to survive the impact as young and mature adults. In fact, even among the older pedestrians, those under 80 years old seem to survive their injury crashes as well as the younger people. The role of frailty is most apparent (on the average) for those who are already 80 years old or older, and then their risk of getting killed is quadrupled!

The synergistic effects of age and frailty on crash outcome are directly demonstrated by the results of a study by Henary, Ivarsson, and Crandall (2006). They compared the injury severity of pedestrians hit by cars at different speeds and found that the likelihood of older pedestrians (60+ years old) to be seriously injured or killed was significantly greater than that of younger ones (19-50). This was true at all impact speeds, for all vehicle body types,

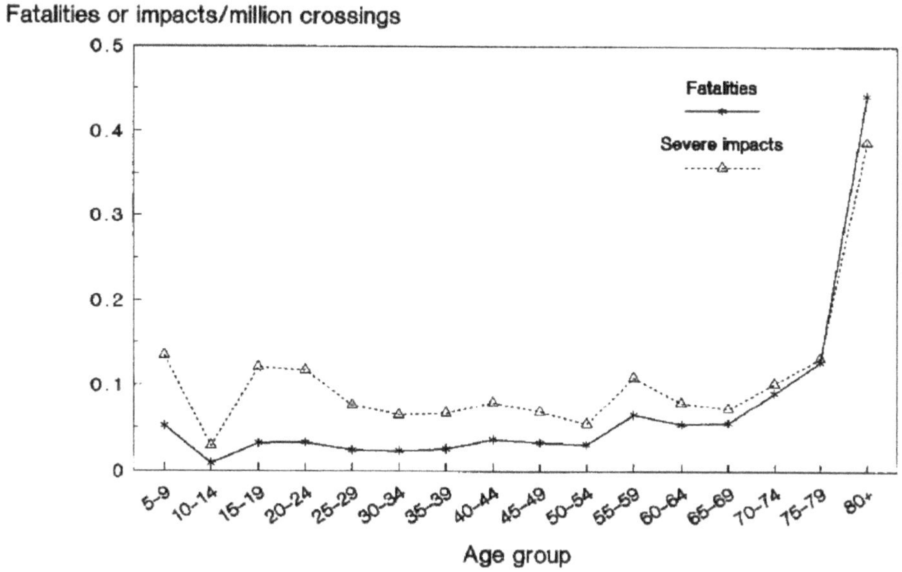

Figure 15-6. The New Zealand pedestrian rates of severe injuries and fatalities per million crossings (from Keall, 1995, with permission from Elsevier).

for both male and female pedestrians and for pedestrians of different weights and heights. Other data – from Denmark, Germany, and the Netherlands – also show that relative to the distance walked 64+ years old pedestrians are 4-5 times as likely to be killed while crossing the street as pedestrians under 64 years old; and British data suggest they may be even 7 times as likely to be killed (Dunbar, Holland, and Maylor, 2004). Finally, a recent analysis of fatality rates by age for 27 EU countries showed that children under 15 years old are the safest at 3.4 deaths/million in population. It doubles for adults under 50; increases to 13 deaths/million for adults 50-65 years old; and reaches 28 deaths/million for adults 65+ years old (Adminaite *et al.*, 2015). Frailty is also a significant contributor to older driver fatalities (see Chapter 7), but older pedestrians suffer from double jeopardy: they are more likely to be involved in a crash (while older drivers are not), and once involved, the severity of their injuries is likely to be greater than that of younger people. This is also discussed below in the context of the effects of vehicle speed.

There is one exposure measure that Keall (1995) did not consider, and it is probably the one that is most relevant to crash risk. This is the time spent crossing streets, or the time of actual exposure. Obviously, it is not just the number of crossings that matter, but the total time a pedestrian is in the street being exposed to traffic. The time it takes to cross the street varies widely among different age groups. One does not need to be a scientist to observe that younger people walk faster than older people, but objective empirical data do support that conclusion (see data in Table 15-1). Thus, it is very likely that one more contributor to the over-involvement of older pedestrian in injury and fatal crashes is due to the fact that each crossing takes them longer than it takes younger people. Pedestrian crossing speeds are important for the design of traffic control systems and

Table 15-1. Average and 15th percentile street crossing speeds (in meters/second) at signalized intersections for younger and older pedestrians in various situations (from Knoblauch *et al.*, 1996).

	Average		**15th percentile**	
	Younger	**Older**	**Younger**	**Older**
All pedestrians	1.51	1.25	1.25	0.97
Gender				
Males	1.56	1.31	1.30	1.02
Females	1.46	1.19	1.20	0.93
Road width				
Narrow (<13.1 m)	1.44	1.15	1.19	0.91
Wide (15.7+ m)	1.57	1.35	1.30	1.06
Temperature				
Cold (<6.1 centigrade)	1.60	1.34	1.31	1.02
Warm (>14.5 cent.)	1.48	1.24	1.25	0.96
Signal at start of walk				
WALK	1.46	1.20	1.21	0.94
Steady DON'T WALK	1.60	1.36	1.32	1.06

they are affected not only by our age but also by a host of environmental, medical, and psychological factors, as discussed below.

Pedestrian street crossing behavior and crossing speed

Crossing the street involves a complex set of sequential behaviors that begin with the decision to cross. Despite the standard recommendation to stop-look-cross, adults often plan their crossing strategy as they approach the road. Consequently, they may select the crossing location and speed of approach so that they will not have to stop at the edge of a curb. Thus, children are faced with a discrepancy between doing what they are taught and doing what they observe (Routledge, Repetto-Write, and Howarth, 1976). Geruschat, Hassan, and Turano (2003) observed the behavior and the visual fixation patterns of mature adults as they approached the street and crossed it and identified three distinct stages in the process: (1) the approach phase when the pedestrian visually monitors the crossing "decision elements"; mostly traffic signals in signalized intersections and approaching vehicles in non-signalized intersections, (2) the waiting phase when a similar pattern continues with more fixations on cars, and (3) the crossing phase when they look straight ahead or fixate on potential danger zones. While this combined walking and looking strategy may serve most adults well, it may be inappropriate for older people, as discussed below. These decisions are governed primarily by road type, traffic flow, and traffic control, but individual differences in risk taking also play a critical role, especially in mid-block (non-intersection) crossings (Papadimitriou, Lassarre, and Yannis, 2016).

From the perspective of the design engineer, the most important aspect of pedestrian behavior is the street crossing speed. As people age their walking speed decreases and they need more time to cross the road. Unlike car drivers, whose speed is directly related to the likelihood and severity of a crash, in the case of pedestrians, when colliding with a motor vehicle, the impact speed is not related to their walking speed. In fact, their slow speed is an impediment as it only increases their exposure to injury. It is therefore important to know at what speeds people cross streets, and what variables affect these speeds.

For traffic system design, it would be very convenient to have a single value that defines a street crossing speed that accommodates all pedestrians. Crossing speed is important for many system parameters, the most important one being the timing of pedestrian traffic signals relative to the road width. The prevailing design standard assumes a crossing speed of 1.2 m/s (MUTCD, 2015; NYDOT, 2015). Obviously, this single value does not typify or accommodate all pedestrians. The most commonly and consistently observed deviations from this value are age- and gender-related; with older people walking slower than younger people, and women walking slower than men (Jain, Gupta, and Rastogi, 2014). Other factors that have shown to affect crossing speed include the location of the crossing (at or away from a crosswalk), the signal phase (WALK or DON'T WALK), the width of the roadway, the number of lanes, the amount of traffic, whether or not there is a median island, and whether crossing alone or in a group. In fact, almost any factor studied seems to be significantly associated with the crossing speed. This is illustrated in Table 15-1 from Knoblauch, Pietrucha, and Nitzburg (1996). In their study, they unobtrusively observed and measured the crossing times of 7,129 adults in 16 signal-controlled intersections in four urban areas in the U.S. In addition to their crossing time, each pedestrian was identified as "older" or "younger" depending on whether he or she looked 65+ years old or under 65 years old.

The observed variations were not negligible. Mean crossing speeds ranged from a speedy 1.65 m/s for "younger" pedestrians crossing outside the crosswalk to a slow pace of 1.17 m/s for older pedestrians at narrow streets with long signal cycles. Women were consistently slower than men and older people were consistently slower than younger people. Note that the design speed of 1.2 m/s is slower than most of the specific average speeds in this table. This is because average speed is not a very relevant measure for design purposes. For design purposes, we would like to accommodate most of the population and not just the hypothetical average person and those walking at a faster than average pace. A common benchmark in highway design is to accommodate at least 85 percent of the population – known as the 85th percentile – or in this case the walking speed of all but the slowest 15 percent (15th percentile). The walking speeds for the 15th percentile men and women young and old are reproduced in the right two columns of Table 15-1. Thus, in order to accommodate 85 percent of the pedestrians in all of these situations we would have to design our system to accommodate a walking speed of no more than 0.90 m/s. Although the difference between 1.2 and 0.9 seems small, it translates to significant differences in the duration of pedestrian walk cycles and signal timing. To allow for such variations, the U.S. Manual on Uniform Traffic Control Devices (MUTCD, 2015) recommends that the standard should allow slower pace in the case of "pedestrian facilities serving nursing homes, elementary schools, or medical facilities. When determining the proper walking speed for crossing an intersection, project designers should consider pedestrians who may be disabled, or are age 65 years or older, and 14 years and younger... using a slower walking speed such as 0.8 to 1.1 m/s" (Section 18.7.1.2). Of course, the more people we want to accommodate, the slower the threshold speed that we must assume. Finally, because of the many variables that affect walking speeds the results of different studies in different countries vary slightly. For example, Griffiths, Hunt, and Marlow (1984) conducted observations on 20,000 pedestrians at 26 sites in the United Kingdom and obtained higher mean speeds than those observed by Knoblauch *et al.* (1996), but with similar patterns; with the "young" walking at a mean speed of 1.72 m/s, the "middle age" walking at a mean speed of 1.47 m/s, and the "elderly" at a speed of 1.16 m/s. If the British design standards were to be based on British data, would an American tourist have more difficulty crossing the streets of London (in addition to the difficulties he or she already encounters in properly scanning the road for approaching vehicles from the unexpected direction)?

One of the difficulties in setting a walking speed standard for older pedestrians – the ones with the highest severe injury risk while crossing streets – is that many of them also have medical conditions that further restrict their movement. In fact, Dunbar *et al.* (2004), after reviewing the literature on the various variables that affect walking speed, concluded that the largest reductions in walking speed are due to illnesses, and not to age. For example, Shumway-Cook and Woollacott (2000) had three different groups of people walk for 3 minutes at their preferred speed. The young adults (50 years old or less) walked at a mean speed of 1.7 m/s, the healthy old adults (average age of 75 years old) walked at 1.2 m/s, and the old adults with balance problems (average age 85 years old) walked at the very slow speed of 0.47 m/s. Given a design walking speed of 1.2 m/s, this means that many older pedestrians cannot safely cross signalized intersections. In fact, Asher and her colleagues (2012) found that based on measurements of "normal walking speed" for a distance of "8 feet," 84 percent of the men and 93 percent of the women in the United Kingdom are impaired in the sense that they walk at a slower pace. Of course, as a group the infirm were also older than the healthy adults, but there was a significant overlap in the ages of the two groups. These significant differences among people translate to very significant – and often expensive – adjustments that must be made for such special populations to allow them to cross the street safely.

Environmental factors also affect the speed at which pedestrians cross the road. Within their physical limitations, people can increase their speed when they perceive urgency or a greater-than-usual risk. Thus, as shown in Table 15-1, Knoblauch *et al.* (1996) found that pedestrians walked faster when they had a red light than when they had a green light (most likely because they felt protected from crossing cars), and when they crossed wide roads than when they crossed narrow roads. Bowman and Vecellio (1995) observed pedestrian walking speeds at various urban locations and noted that they walked faster when they crossed the road at mid-block than at controlled intersections; and more quickly at intersections with two-way streets with left turning cars than at undivided roads. Thus, when they perceive the risk of exposure as high pedestrians tend to adjust by minimizing their crossing time. Also, pedestrians often take a calculated risk when they deliberately cross in front of a vehicle assuming that it will slow down or stop to let them pass, especially when they are in a crowd (Yang *et al.*, 2006). Finally, it appears that the longer they wait to cross, the shorter the gap that pedestrians (and drivers) accept (Lobjois, Benguigui, and Cavallo, 2013), and consequently, the denser the traffic the more risks the pedestrians assume when they cross. More disturbing is Sun *et al.*'s (2015) finding in a naturalistic traffic environment in Beijing, China, that when the approaching car is traveling at high speeds (>65 km/hr) at a distance of 50 meters pedestrians underestimate the driver's stopping distance, thus putting themselves at an even greater risk, falsely believing that in case they decide to cross the street the driver can stop in time.

Driver-pedestrian communications

According to Snyder and Knoblauch (1971) to avoid a collision, pedestrians and drivers have to be aware of each other and to communicate with each other – at least partially. This interaction between the approaching driver and the crossing pedestrian requires both of them to perform at least six sequential processes: (1) select the path of movement; (2) visually scan the relevant scene for the potential or actual presence of the other; (3) detect the other and assess his or her relative location; (4) evaluate the intention of the other; (5) decide on the proper course of action; and (5) make the proper response to avoid a collision. If either the driver or the pedestrian performs *all* of these processes appropriately, a collision between them is avoided. However, if *both* fail to adequately perform any *one* of these processes then they are likely to collide. While it is a routine matter for drivers to visually search their environment for other traffic and potential obstacles (see Chapter 4), this is not the case for pedestrians. When pedestrians cross the street they must adjust their situation awareness. They have to change their direction of movement, attention, and visual search pattern whenever they change their walking path from the curb to the road. Consequently, many crashes occur because drivers fail to detect the (relatively) low-visibility pedestrian or because pedestrians fail to make the proper adjustments in these critical tasks, as in entering the roadway while engaged in a phone task.

The complicated time-based sequence of interactions between the driver and the pedestrian is not a purely theoretical one. Katz, Zaidel, and Elgrishi (1975) designed an experimental study in which pedestrians stepped off the curb and into the road as if intending to cross the street as an unsuspecting driver approached them. In two locations the crossing was marked and in two it was not. On half the trials the pedestrian looked right and left to make eye contact with the driver and on half the trials pedestrian stepped off the curb without looking to the sides. The two variables that had the greatest impact on the drivers' inclinations to slow down were their approach speed and the type of crossing (legal or not). More interesting, though, was the finding that drivers were more likely to slow down when the pedestrians did not look at them and did not establish eye contact than when they did. In this condition, the pedestrians entrapped the drivers to assume total responsibility for the pedestrian's safety. Thus, when the drivers were unable to communicate their dominance or right-of-way to the pedestrians, they had no recourse but to give them right-of-way. This finding should not be interpreted as a recommendation to cross the street without regard to the traffic. It simply means that communication is important, and in its absence – given sufficient warning time – it appears that drivers are inclined to accommodate crossing pedestrians. But when the time gap between the car and the pedestrian is too small or when the driver fails to detect the pedestrian this inclination is of little comfort, and a "dart-out" crash is most likely to occur (as described below). To avoid such a collision, the pedestrian must assume responsibility before entering the path of the approaching vehicle. Also, it is important to point out that in Katz *et al.*'s study not all drivers slowed down significantly when the pedestrian did not look at them.

Because the quality of communication between drivers and crossing pedestrians is quite poor – depending on body language and a horn – they have to assume some common norms. These include pedestrian's right-of-way at signalized intersections and the driver's right-of-way in mid-block unmarked crossing (i.e., jaywalking). In an empirical investigation on how pedestrians and drivers treat this issue, we observed 800 crossings of a confederate pedestrian in front of cars. Half the crossings were at an urban marked non-signalized intersection and half were mid-block (approximately 150 meters from that intersection). At each location on half of the trials the pedestrian hobbled on crutches and on half of the trials the (same) pedestrian was not handicapped. An ordinal measure of "driver aggression" based on the driver's giving right-of-way or not was derived, ranging from 1 (driver coming to a full stop to allow the pedestrian to cross) to 3 (driver not slowing down, not giving right-of-way, and making aggressive gestures with hands or horn). The results displayed in Figure 15-7 showed that there was a shared cultural (and legal) norm to yield to pedestrians at marked crossing and not mid-block, but that drivers also respected patently handicapped pedestrians and tended to allow them to cross mid-block too (though not as much as in the crossings). In fact, in this particular Israeli environment the level of yielding to handicapped pedestrians in mid-block was approximately the same as to non-handicapped pedestrians at the marked crossing.

In a more recent study, conducted in four non-signalized crosswalks of four-lane roads in Beijing, China, Zhuang and Wu (2014) demonstrated that pedestrian hand gestures are an effective method to both draw the drivers' attention to a waiting pedestrian and to actually yield to the pedestrian in a marked crossing. In their study, they noted that in the absence of any of the selected gestures, the drivers yielded to the pedestrian by slowing down or stopping in only 3.6 percent of the attempted crossings. In contrast, with the most effective gesture – where the pedestrian looked at the driver and raised his left hand to a bent 90-degree level – the drivers yielded in 12.9 percent of the cases. Despite the relative effectiveness of the hand gestures, these low levels of accommodating the pedestrian are disheartening, especially considering the Chinese regulations that require the drivers to yield.

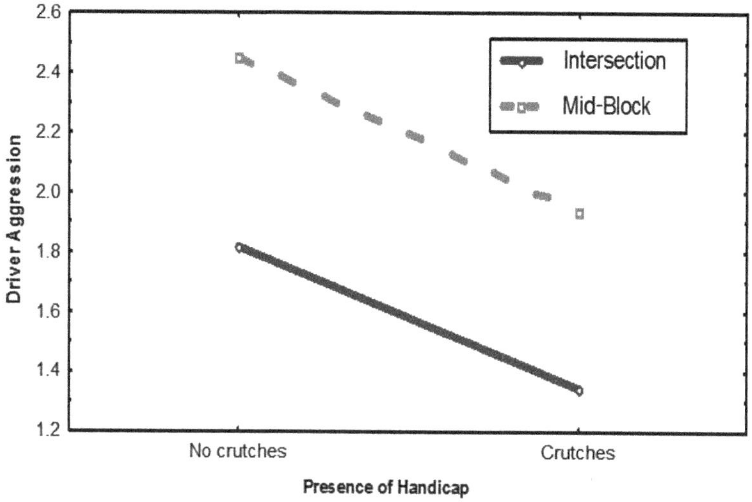

Figure 15-7. Level of accommodating pedestrians when crossing at a marked crossing and mid-block, and when appearing to be handicapped and not (Shinar, 2000).

The most interesting behavioral intervention that has been evaluated is the use of a smile. In a novel approach, Guéguen *et al.* (2016), noting that smiles facilitate social interactions, tested the effect of smiling on drivers' behavior as they approached pedestrian crosswalks. In two experiments conducted in Western France, they found that drivers were more likely to stop and yield to a pedestrian (a young researcher dressed in jeans and T-shirt), when the latter smiled at the approaching driver than when he or she did not. Furthermore, in both experiments, the percent of drivers yielding was greater when the pedestrian was of the opposite sex than of the same sex. In their third experiment, an unsmiling pedestrian waited to cross, and after a car stopped to let the pedestrian cross he or she either acknowledged the yielding with a smile or not. Again, when the pedestrian smiled, the driver behaved differently: in this case driving away at a slower speed. Also, in this experiment too, the departure speed was lower when the driver and the experimenter were of the opposite sex than when they were of the same sex. Thus, as in other interactions, smiling helps! At least in France.

Causes of pedestrian crashes

In the first comprehensive study of the causes of pedestrian accidents, Snyder and Knoblauch (1971) analyzed 2,157 pedestrian accidents. The accidents were sampled from 13 major U.S. cities, and in each case the surviving participants were interviewed, the scene was investigated, and the police record was obtained. The analysis showed that in 55 percent of the accidents, it was the pedestrian's action that was primarily responsible for the accident. The most common cause – characterizing 34 percent of all crashes – was the pedestrian's "darting out" from a mid-block location into the street; too late for the car to stop. The other principal crash causes were "intersection dashes" (9 percent) that were the same as dart outs, except that they occurred at intersections; "vehicle turn/merge with attention conflict" (7 percent) which was characterized by a collision in which the driver was making a turn and attending to traffic in one direction, while the pedestrian was in an unattended location; and "multiple-threats" (3 percent) which were situations in which the pedestrian was struck by a car after another car stopped to allow him or her to cross, and in the process created a view obstruction for the car that eventually hit the pedestrian. Thus, either darting out or dashing out to the traffic accounted for nearly half of all pedestrian crashes. In these situations, the pedestrians failed to perform the first of the five sequential tasks mentioned above. The frequencies of failures in the different processes, as recorded by Snyder and Knoblauch (1971), are presented in Table 15-2. As can be seen from this table, the total number of times that all the factors were cited is nearly twice the number of accidents. This is because most accidents are caused by more than one factor. For example, the pedestrian chooses an improper path

Table 15-2. Frequency of pedestrian accident causes, in term of failures in the driver-pedestrian interaction sequence (based on 2,157 pedestrian crashes; derived from Snyder and Knoblauch, 1971).

Factor Group	**Number of Times Selected**	**Percent of Factors Selected**	**Percent of Crashes Selected**
Pedestrian course	1,206	30.6	55.9
Pedestrian search	1,166	29.4	54.1
Pedestrian detection	238	6.0	11.0
Pedestrian evaluation	158	4.0	7.3
Pedestrian decision	17	0.4	0.8
Pedestrian action	19	0.5	0.9
Driver course	181	4.6	8.4
Driver search	510	12.9	23.6
Driver detection	292	7.4	13.5
Driver evaluation	82	2.1	3.8
Driver control-action	75	1.9	3.5
Driver and pedestrian interaction	9	0.2	0.4
Total	3,953	100.0	–

(such as darting out from between two parked cars) *and* the driver fails to detect the pedestrian in time. Thus, for the collision to occur both behavioral failures and errors have to occur, and if either one of them does not occur, the collision is avoided. Next, note that 70 percent of the factors cited were pedestrian factors, and in approximately 55 percent of the accidents the pedestrian either chose an improper path or failed to properly search for the presence of an approaching vehicle, or both. In contrast, driver failures were much less common and constituted only 30 percent of the factors cited, with improper search and failure to detect the pedestrian accounting for 24 and 14 percent of the collisions, respectively. Thus, for both drivers and pedestrians the rates of failures in detection were similar around 11-13 percent. But pedestrians, much more than drivers failed to even look for the other before attempting to cross.

Perhaps the greatest shortcoming of Snyder and Knoblauch's (1971) study is that it is old. It is based on a culture, roadways, cars, and safety systems that existed half a century ago when the motorization level was much lower and the safety culture less developed. To test the relevance of their findings to our current driver-vehicle-environment-pedestrian system, the U.S. Federal Highway Administration commissioned a second, more recent, study. In this study, Hunter *et al.* (1995) examined the pre-crash factors of a random sample of 5,073 police reports of pedestrian crashes in five U.S. states. They then classified the crashes using the model and taxonomy developed by Snyder and Knoblauch. Although their sample size was approximately four times as large as that of Snyder and Knoblauch, their investigation relied exclusively on the police reports, and was compromised by the different police coding schemes. Therefore, they could not analyze the crashes at the same level of detail that Snyder and Knoblauch (1971) did. Still, within their data limitations, they concluded that in 66 percent of the accidents the pedestrian was at fault – either wholly or with the driver – compared to 55 percent of the crashes where the driver was at fault, either alone or with the pedestrian. Thus, in approximately two-thirds of the crashes, had the pedestrian performed all the perceptual-cognitive processing stages correctly the collision would not have happened, and in slightly more than 50 percent of the crashes had the driver done the same the collision would not have occurred. The most cited contributing factors for the pedestrians and the drivers are reproduced in Table 15-3. Environmental and vehicular factors were far less common. The environmental factors were cited as contributing factors (rather than primary factors), and were primarily related to reduced visibility, including "vision blockage" (in 10.6 percent of the collisions), dusk/darkness (3.2 percent), and sun glare (1.0 percent). No specific vehicle factor was cited in more than 0.5 percent of the crashes.

But Hunter *et al.*'s study is also somewhat dated. A more recent and more comprehensive analysis based on all U.S. fatal pedestrian crashes yields a similar picture but shows an even greater contribution of the pedestrians to their own demise. According to the U.S. Fatal Analysis Reporting System, in 2004 pedestrian factors contributed to the causes of 67 percent of all pedestrian fatalities, with "improper crossing of roadway or intersection" constituting 25 percent, "walking, playing, working, etc., in roadway" constituting 24 percent, "failure to yield right of way" constituting 16 percent, and being "not visible" and "darting or running into road" contributing another 11 percent each (NHTSA, 2005). The frequencies and percentages of the 12 primary causes are listed in Table 15-4.

Table 15-3. The primary pedestrian and driver causes of crashes (from Hunter *et al.*, 1995).

Rank Order	**Pedestrian Factors**		**Driver Factors**	
	Factor	**Percent**	**Factor**	**Percent**
1	Ran into road	15.0	Hit and run	16.2
2	Failed to yield	11.8	Failure to yield to pedestrian	15.0
3	Alcohol impaired	10.3	Improper backing	5.6
4	Stepped from between parked vehicles	7.1	Safe movement violation	4.8
5	Walk/run wrong direction	5.3	Exceed safe speed	4.4
6	Stepped into road	4.1	Inattention/distraction	4.2
7	Talking/standing in road	3.1	Reckless driving	3.4
8	Jaywalking	3.1	Alcohol impairment	3.1
9	Fail to obey signal	3.0	Fail to secure in "Park"	1.8
	Percent of all accidents	**66**	**Percent of all accidents**	**55**

These findings based on the national U.S. fatality data are also consistent with an even more recent evaluation of the causes of pedestrian crashes that was conducted in four U.S. cities: Chicago, Los Angeles, New York, and Phoenix (Kar and Gajula, 2008). In this study, the most common pedestrian cause was "improper crossing." The principal contributing causes on the part of the drivers were "failure to yield right of way" and "hit and run." Unfortunately, as with the previously cited NHTSA study, the level of inquiry into the crash causes was limited by the information available in the FARS and police reports. Consequently, the reasons for these behaviors are hard to assess. This makes it difficult to recommend the appropriate countermeasures to eliminate these behaviors.

Crash causation and pedestrian age

Pedestrian crash risk factors differ at different ages. In their analyses of the causes of 5,125 pedestrian crashes, Hunter *et al.* (1995) noted the factors associated with each age group, and they are listed in Table 15-5.

Table 15-4. The primary causes responsible for pedestrian fatalities in the U.S. Note that the sum of the numbers and percentages are greater than the "Total" numbers because more than one factor may have contributed to a given fatality. "None reported" implies that the pedestrian was not at fault (from NHTSA, 2005).

Factors	**Number**	**Percent**
Improper crossing of roadway or intersection	1,148	24.7
Walking, playing, working, etc., in roadway	1,119	24.1
Failure to yield right-of-way	727	15.7
Not visible	521	11.2
Darting or running into road	500	10.8
Inattentive (talking, eating, etc.)	122	2.6
Failure to obey traffic signs, signals, or officer	78	1.7
Physical impairment	48	1.0
Emotional (e.g., depression, angry, disturbed)	25	0.5
Ill, blackout	22	0.5
Getting on/off/in/out of transport vehicle	20	0.4
Non-motorist pushing vehicle	7	0.2
Other factors	156	3.4
None reported	1,416	30.5
Unknown	141	3.0
Total Pedestrians	**4,641**	**100.0**

Causes of child and teen pedestrian crashes

On the basis of the information in Table 15-5 and other findings, we can characterize the crash-causing behaviors of children and young teenagers as follows. The youngest pedestrians, 1-2 years old, rarely venture out into the street by themselves, and when they are involved in an accident they are more likely to be struck by cars backing up on driveways and on private property. In these situations, when the car has no rear facing camera or sensors, the driver simply cannot see the child who is totally obscured from view. These types of crashes are most typical of driveways that are not separated from

Table 15-5. The primary pedestrian crash causes for pedestrians at different ages (based on Hunter *et al.*, 1995).

Age	Primary Pedestrian Contributing Factors
0-9	Ran into street, ran from between parked vehicles, playing in street
10-14	Ran into street, ran from between parked vehicles, failed to obey signal, unsafe skateboard or rollerblade maneuvers, unsafe entering or exiting, safe movement violation
15-19	Failed to obey signal, unsafe skateboard maneuver, walking/running in wrong direction, leaning/clinging to vehicle
20-24	Alcohol impaired, walking/running in wrong direction, talking/standing in road, lying in road, jogging in road
25-44	Alcohol impaired, working on car in parking lot, talking/standing in road, lying in road
45-64	Jaywalking, lack of conspicuity, alcohol impaired
65+	Jaywalking, stepped into street, failed to yield

the children's play area (Roberts, Norton, and Jackson, 1995). Slightly older children, 3-9 years old, are more likely to collide with vehicles when they dart out into the traffic stream (often from between parked cars) because they do not yet have safe pedestrian skills. Young children under the age of 11 are also less effective in the manner they scan the road before crossing. Older children and adults spend more time fixating the peripheral areas of their visual field prior to crossing the street than children 7-10 years old (Tapiro *et al.*, 2013).

Ten to fourteen-years-old pedestrians also tend to dart out, but in their case the reason is that they do not yet have good street crossing habits, the traffic system is not yet fully internalized, and so they do not always apply safe pedestrian skills that they have already acquired but not yet turned into habits (Cross and Hall, 2005; Schieber and Vegega, 2002). According to independent analyses by Posner *et al.* (2002) in the U.S., and by Sentinella and Keigan (2005) in the United Kingdom, most of child pedestrian collisions occurred while the children were at play or "at leisure" rather than on the way to or from school; reinforcing the notion that preoccupation and lack of awareness of traffic have a significant role in their crashes. When they are hit in the process of crossing the road, Sentinella and Keigan noted that in approximately 25 percent of the child pedestrian collisions the child "crossed the road without looking both ways and/or crossed at an inappropriate location." In addition, Lalloo, Sheiham, and Nazroo (2003) found that children who suffer from hyperactivity and conduct disorder double their probability of being involved in a crash compared to normal children their age. In short, these findings indicate that children are either unable to properly focus their attention on traffic before crossing the road, or are unable to divide their attention between crossing the road and other behaviors (such as play) in which they are engaged at the time.

Older teenagers usually do have safe crossing skills, but they do not always apply them. Instead, while they seem to behave mostly in accordance with planned behavior it often involves high risk behaviors such as crossing against the light, skateboarding, talking on the phone, and running on the road. In an interesting essay on risk taking in adolescence, Steinberg (2004) argues that risk taking at this stage is not due to faulty risk perception, but rather to two incompatible biologically driven processes: the rapid increase in sensation seeking (and doing daring things) and insufficient development of "self-regulatory competence" which matures at a later stage. If this is correct, argues Steinberg, then to ensure the safety of adolescents we must accept that they are "*inherently* more likely than adults to take risks" and we should therefore focus more on harm reduction than on the prevention of risk-taking behaviors. This is a pessimistic view that – unfortunately – seems to be consistent with repeated failures to reduce teen crashes and young pedestrian crashes.

Adult pedestrian crashes, alcohol and inattention

Adult pedestrians seem to be plagued by the same problem that many adult drivers have: alcohol impairment. This is repeatedly found in different studies that measure the presence of alcohol. Snyder and Knoblauch (1971) found it in approximately 10 percent of the pedestrians (compared to 3 percent of the drivers) in their sample, and Hunter *et al.* (1995) recorded it as a primary cause of 20-45-years-old pedestrians' accidents. Öström and Eriksson (2001) found alcohol in the blood of 24 percent of pedestrian males killed in collisions with cars. Clayton and Colgan (2001) in two studies of pedestrian crashes in England found that 40 percent of the injured pedestrians who were measured for alcohol, had blood alcohol concentrations (BAC's) of 0.10 percent or higher. Even higher percentages of alcohol involvement (with BAC > 0.10 percent) were obtained in a North Carolina study of pedestrian crashes (Campbell *et al.*, 2004). In summary, alcohol intoxication among pedestrians is a significant problem in many countries, and the estimates based on the police crash data may be an underestimate of the actual magnitude of alcohol involvement because there is often a reluctance to measure alcohol in pedestrian crash victims. This means that drinking and walking may be as common or even more common – and as severe a problem or more severe – than drinking and driving. In fact, as drink-driving campaigns increase their effectiveness they may lead to a drink-walking problem. Thus, Clayton and Colgan (2001) noted that the decline in drink-driving crashes in the United Kingdom seems to be associated with a parallel increase in drinking-related pedestrian accidents.

As was the case for drinking and driving, to demonstrate causation rather than just a presence of a variable (such as alcohol), we need to show not only that it is present but also that it increases the risk of a crash. We do that epidemiologically by demonstrating that the proportion of people with a given level of alcohol in crashes is greater than the proportion of people with the same level of alcohol in an exposure sample of road users who are not involved in a crash. Several studies of this kind have been conducted in various countries and they clearly demonstrate the causal role of alcohol in driving (see Chapter 11). Unfortunately there is a dearth of comparable information on pedestrians. In one small-scale study, with a sample of only 31 injured pedestrians and 139 control pedestrians, BAC was measured for both groups. In this study, Clayton and Colgan (2001) found that the likelihood of a pedestrian injury accident increased in a manner similar to that obtained for drivers. Pedestrians with BAC's of 0.10-0.15 percent were 2.4 times more likely to be involved in a crash than pedestrians with lower BAC; and pedestrians with BAC > 0.20 percent were 24 times more likely to be involved in a crash than those with BAC < 0.01 percent. In a large Canadian study, an analysis of the fatality data base and serious injury data base revealed that for the period 2000-2010 thirty-eight percent of those tested for alcohol in their blood had .05 percent BAC or more (most of them were males) (Vanlaar *et al.*, 2013). Assuming that the 41 percent of the pedestrians not tested did not have alcohol in their blood, this still leaves 22 percent of the pedestrian victims under the influence of alcohol. Of course, in the absence of the prevalence of impaired pedestrians not crash involved, this does not allow us to estimate the over-involvement due to alcohol. Still it is unlikely that a similar percentage of the people walking the streets are under the influence of alcohol. These findings – though they should be corroborated by additional studies – raise the question of whether impaired drivers should be encouraged not to drive without a concomitant encouragement not to walk! Instead, they should always be transported by others.

One of the problems of drinking and walking is the general lack of public awareness of the risks involved. The fact that there are very few laws (and even less enforcement) prohibiting public inebriation also contributes to this misperception. In a study conducted in Australia, Lang and her associates (2003) interviewed 78 young adults (under 30 years old) as they exited a popular night spot. They asked the respondents to estimate the risk of various drinking and driving behaviors, and found that walking in public after drinking was considered significantly less dangerous than drunk driving, not wearing a seat belt, speeding, and driving when fatigued. These estimates were also validated behaviorally as many drivers said that on occasion when they felt too drunk to drive, they left their cars and walked.

Inattention and distraction

Pedestrian distractions may also be significant reasons for increased involvement of adult pedestrians in accidents. Hunter *et al.* (1995) cited "talking/standing in the road" as one of the primary reasons for the adult pedestrian accidents. It appears that – unlike the younger and older groups – adults cross roads without disrupting whatever activity they were engaged in, and consequently they are less attentive than needed to the traffic. Note that Hunter *et al.*'s analysis was based on crashes that occurred in the early 1990s, and in order to talk to someone people had to *be* with that person. This was before cell phones became ubiquitous. But while the detrimental effects of cell phone on attention and safety of drivers have been extensively documented (see Chapter 13), the impact of cell phones on pedestrian behavior and crash involvement is only now beginning to be explored, and the indications are that it may be just as problematic.

There is cause for concern about distractions from cell phones, as their use while walking and crossing streets is becoming commonplace. In a recent observational survey of nearly 35,000 high school students crossing the street in the vicinity of a school zone in 17 U.S. states, one out of five were distracted by an electronic device, with listening to music with headphones and texting being the most common (Ferguson *et al.*, 2013). Thompson *et al.* (2013) observed in 2012 the crossing behaviors of 1,102 pedestrians in 20 locations in Seattle, WA. They noted that 30 percent of all pedestrians were engaged in a cell phone distraction activity while crossing the street. When these pedestrians were compared to those who were not using the cell phone, they found that those who were text-messaging were four times as likely to fail to look to the right and left before crossing the street *and* took significantly longer to cross the street than those who were not distracted by a cell phone; thus increasing their risk even more. This is particularly disturbing as texting (which involves visual distraction) seems to be the most common teen distraction now (Ferguson *et al.*, 2013).

Hatfield and Murphy (2007) observed pedestrians while they crossed intersections in three Sydney, Australia, suburbs and recorded their walking speed and behavior. For every cell phone user that they observed, they also recorded the next non-cell phone user that crossed at the same location in the same direction (hence matching the control pedestrians in place and time), and the next non-user of the same gender and apparent age (thus obtaining a demographically matched control sample). Their sample consisted of 182 cell phone users and equal numbers of time-matched control pedestrians and demographically matched control pedestrians. They found that cell phone use had some significant negative effects – but only on women. In general, women using cell phones were less likely to look at traffic before starting to cross, less likely to wait for traffic to stop, and less likely to look at traffic while crossing. Surprisingly, and making things even worse, these behaviors were more likely in uncontrolled crossings than at signalized crossings where the pedestrians are presumably more protected. Specifically, when crossing an uncontrolled intersection 55 percent of the women without a phone looked at the traffic before crossing compared to only 28 percent of the women who were talking on the phone; 43 percent of the non-users waited for traffic to stop before crossing compared to only 15 percent of the phone users. And while and 25 percent of the non-users actually looked at the traffic while crossing, none (!) of the women talking on the phone did so. Also, as Thompson *et al.* (2013) noted in their study, both male and female phone users walked slower when crossing the street than non-phone users; exposing themselves to traffic for longer times and potentially increasing their crash risk. Summarizing the literature on the effect of pedestrian distraction, Scopatz and Zhou (2016) concluded that although there is evidence that cell phone-related distractions have a negative effect on pedestrian crossing behavior – to the point of failing to observe traffic while texting – there are no data to indicate increased crash risk. This may be either because distracted pedestrians adopt compensatory behaviors (such as not crossing against the light) or because the police crash reports are not sufficiently specific to analyze this. In short, as is often the case, we need more and better data. Incidentally, the distracting effect is greater on children's crossings, especially young children (Tapiro, Oron-Gilad, and Parmet, 2016).

To overcome both problems posed above, we can use controlled field studies and simulation studies. Schwebel *et al.* (2012) had undergraduate students cross a virtual street while either talking on the phone, texting, listening to music, or without any distractions. In general, the effects of the distraction were minor. In all distracted conditions, the pedestrians looked away from the road while crossing more than in the control condition but only texting and listening to music yielded significant increases in the number of virtual collisions with approaching cars. In fact, listening to music was the most disruptive distraction; a finding which is at odds with other data on the relative amount of cognitive distraction from music (Strayer *et al.*, 2015), and the absence of any visual distraction. In a different kind of study that we (Tractinsky and Shinar, 2008) conducted in our university, we placed bendable horizontal rods at different heights in peoples' path as they entered the university cafeteria and noted if they collided with them or not. There were no difference in the likelihood of collisions with these obstacles between those engaged in a phone conversation while walking and those not engaged in a cell phone conversation. In conclusion, based on the little data that are available, the actual distraction risk posed by cell phones to pedestrians may not be as high as it is for drivers. Nonetheless, this can be ascertained only with more ecologically valid empirical data.

Elderly pedestrians' limitations and crashes

Older people – much more than young adults – walk for the sake of walking and exercising. Thus, for them walking is not only a means to mobility, but also a form of exercise. Fortunately, they seem to choose their paths so that they cross fewer roads than younger people (Dunbar *et al.*, 2004). Yet, as shown above, once they venture out, for every kilometer they walk and every road they cross they are at a higher risk than any other age group. Hunter *et al.*'s (1995) analysis suggests that the older pedestrians' involvement in collisions is due primarily to a well-recognized risk-taking behavior: crossing the street in mid-block (jaywalking). Considering their good comprehension of the traffic system, slower gait, and greater frailty this is quite perplexing. In general, elderly people seem to prefer safer crossing situations, and – at least in hypothetical choice behavior situations – they are much more reluctant to cross the street away from intersections (Holland and Hill, 2007).

There seem to be five reasons for the very high crash risks of the elderly pedestrians, especially those over 75 years old. First, it is likely that when they cross the street in unprotected crossings (and do it more slowly than the younger pedestrians) they do so because walking to a safer controlled intersection may be too strenuous. Second, older people often fail to see approaching vehicles, either because of attentional lapses (Maltz and Shinar, 1999), or because of reduced contrast sensitivity (Schieber, 1992; Scialfa *et al.*, 1992; also see Chapter 4), or possibly because they fail to visually search for approaching vehicles while they cross the street. Also, older people tend to be concerned with falls, and tend to look down and ahead while walking (Avineri, Shinar and Susilo, 2012) and even before they begin to cross the street (Dommes *et al.*, 2015). Thus, coupled with their slow gait they may fail to notice an approaching car that was out of their visual field before they started crossing the street. In a survey of crash involved older pedestrians (average age of 75) in England, 63 percent reported that they failed to see the vehicle that hit them at all, or in time to take evasive action (Sheppard and Pattinson, 1986). Third, the cognitive abilities of older people to correctly estimate time gaps in traffic appear to be impaired relative to the abilities of younger people. In simulated street crossing situations, Oxley *et al.* (2005) and Cavallo and her colleagues (Dommes and Cavallo, 2011; Lobjois and Cavallo 2007, 2009) found that 70+ years old people have greater difficulty in judging the approach speed of traffic, and tend to rely on distance cues alone (as, incidentally, do children). Consequently, with slow approaching vehicles they miss many safe crossing opportunities, while with fast moving vehicles they sometimes decide to cross the street without a sufficient clearance (especially given their slower walking speed). Thus, while young pedestrians (20-30 year old) make the same small percent of unsafe decisions in the face of an approaching car, older pedestrians (61+ years old) make more and more unsafe decisions as the speed of the approaching car increases (Dommes and Cavallo, 2011). Investigations into the reasons for this failure show that they are associated with age-related functional declines in processing visual information (Langevin *et al.*, 2011; Dommes, Cavallo, and Oxley, 2013); especially estimation of time-to-arrival of a moving object (Dommes and Cavallo, 2011). Older persons do seem to compensate – at least in a simulation setting – for their slower gate by initiating the crossing sooner than younger people (Lobjois and Cavallo, 2009). However, older people may also tend to underestimate the time it would take them to cross the street (though older people with impairments actually overestimate this time and are therefore paradoxically safer) (Naveteur *et al.*, 2013). Still, in general, younger people are much better at estimating the available time gap when they cross streets. Fourth, because of their frailty, crashes at low impact speeds that may leave a younger person essentially unharmed can be very injurious to an older person who can break a hip just from losing balance and falling down. Fifth, once they find themselves on a collision course with a car, older people may be much slower to recognize the danger and successfully avoid it. Thus, with five age-specific handicaps crossing the street can be a very challenging task for older people.

Visibility and conspicuity in crash risk and crash causation

Most pedestrian crashes occur in daylight (Dunbar *et al.*, 2004; Hunter *et al.*, 1995; Snyder and Knoblauch, 1971). However, most pedestrian fatalities occur in the evening and night hours – that is, when it is dark (NHTSA, 2015). Also, once the crash frequencies are adjusted for exposure and vehicle flow, the rate of nighttime pedestrian crashes is greater than that of daytime crashes (Goodwin and Hutchinson, 1977). Unlike daytime accidents that are caused by a variety of factors, at night the pedestrians' low visibility appears to be the primary cause for their crashes. Thus, despite their lower exposure at night, daSilva, Smith, and Najm (2003) found that nearly 60 percent of the U.S. pedestrian crashes in which the pedestrian was walking straight along the roadway at a non-junction occurred at night.

Before discussing the factors involved in nighttime visibility, it is important to note that visibility and perceptual factors are also relevant during the daytime. Because relative to most other potential hazards on the road (i.e., cars and trucks) pedestrians are smaller and less expected, they are also more likely to be missed even by an alert driver. For example, Sanocki *et al.* (2015) demonstrated that spotting a pedestrian in traffic depended on the proximity of cars next to him/her. In their study they presented pictures of traffic scenes that could be either crowded with traffic or not, and with or without a vulnerable road user (VRU – a pedestrian, a bicyclist, or a motorcyclist). The scenes were presented very briefly for 250 milliseconds, and the observer had to decide whether or not each scene contained a VRU. In the uncrowded scene, the VRU was detected 77 percent of the time and in the crowded scene 59 percent of the time.

An indirect but interesting demonstration of the importance of visibility was provided by Sullivan and Flannagan (2001, 2002a, 2002b). They used the changeover to daylight saving time (DST) in order to obtain crash data for the same hours and locations, but at different levels of illumination immediately before and after the changeover in time. Using U.S. national fatality data from 1987 to 1997, they calculated the ratio of the number of fatalities in the twilight hour for the three weeks before the changeover (when it was still dark) by the number of fatalities in the same hour after changeover (when it was light). This method assured that the only difference between the two periods was in the amount of light. In terms of the activities (going to and from school or work) that might be responsible for crashes, the two conditions were matched. The effect of the daylight saving time was much greater in the evening twilight hours than in the morning changeover hours, and the results for the evening hours are presented in Figure 15-8. As can be seen in that figure, collisions of cars with pedestrians (or animals) were more than four times more likely in the darkness hours than in daylight, whereas collisions between vehicles were only 1.3 times more likely in the darkness than in daylight. A more detailed analysis revealed that the effect was greatest – with a dark/light ratio of 6.8 – on limited access roads

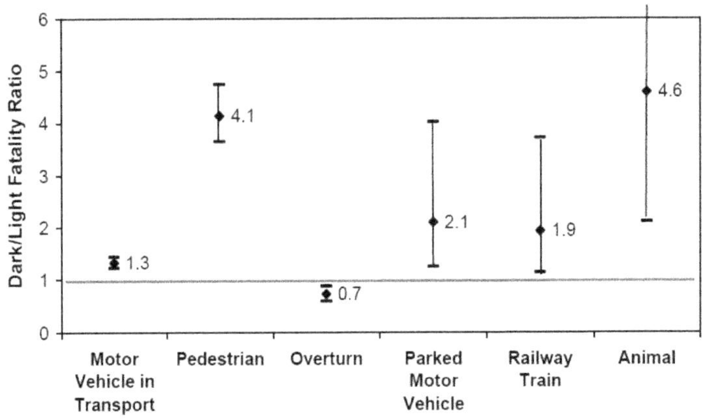

Figure 15-8. Dark/Light fatality ratios for different types of crashes (in terms of first harmful event). Bracketing lines indicate 95% confidence intervals around the ratios. A ratio > 1.0 indicates over-involvement of crashes in the dark. Data were compiled from evening daylight savings time transition periods of one hour before and one hour after twilight, for 3 weeks before and after spring and fall changeovers (from Sullivan and Flannagan, 2001, 2002a, with permission from the University of Michigan Transportation Research Institute).

(freeways and motorways), where pedestrians are least expected and cars are traveling at the highest speeds. In a corresponding manner, the impact of the time change was smallest on local roads (3.0) where pedestrians may be expected and traffic speeds are lower.

In a more recent analysis, Sullivan and Flannagan (2007) investigated whether some pedestrian groups were at a higher risk for visibility-related fatal crashes than others. They found that the risk of adults and elderly pedestrians increased nearly sevenfold in the transition from light to darkness, whereas the risk of children and teenagers (under 18 years old) increased by less than 50 percent. The reasons for lower risk levels for children could not be determined from the data, but the authors offer the reasonable suggestion that this may be due to parents' reluctance to let young children go out by themselves after dark. This explanation is plausible, but it should be verified by further breakdown of the data by annual or bi-annual age groups, and then seeing if there is a marked change at the 6-10-years-old stage. Finally, when the ratio of dark/light fatalities for adult pedestrians was examined relative to the vehicle speed, they obtained an accelerating function with dark/light fatality ratios reaching approximately 15 for speeds of 65 mph.

Nighttime pedestrian visibility: determining factors

In the absence of overhead street lighting, the visibility that is afforded by vehicle headlights, especially low beams, is very poor. Consequently a common nighttime experience shared by many drivers is passing very close to a pedestrian walking along the road, and not seeing the pedestrian until they are almost alongside of him or her. This happens because most of us under most free-flowing traffic situations over-drive the visibility distance afforded by our headlights; meaning that when we drive at night on a dark road we drive at such a speed that by the time we detect an obstacle – such as a pedestrian – it is too late for us to stop in time to avoid it. For example, when we drive with low beams and high expectancy we can detect a pedestrian at an average distance of about 35 meters. However, using conservative reaction time of 1.0 seconds and a dry road we need approximately 50 meters in order to detect the obstacle, apply the brakes, and come to a complete stop (Leibowitz and Owens, 1986). Furthermore, when the road is wet the total braking distance increases by roughly 50 percent (Leibowitz, Owens, and Tyrrell, 1998). The visibility is further reduced when we have to detect the pedestrian in the presence of the glare from opposing traffic. Unfortunately, the law does not recognize this discrepancy between our visual limitations and drivers' behavior. Within the general requirement that a driver operate the vehicle in a "safe" manner is the Assured Clear Distance Ahead (ACDA) rule that makes the driver responsible for avoiding a collision "with any obstacle that might appear along the vehicle's path" (Leibowitz *et al.*, 1998). As Leibowitz and his associates point out, this requires drivers to have an awareness of their visual limitations; something that most drivers do not have.

In fact, even when we look for a pedestrian and the pedestrian is in the lane we sometimes fail to see him or her. This has happened independently to Merrill Allen (Allen *et al.*, 1970), and to me while conducting research on nighttime pedestrian visibility. That means that even when we are aware of the possibility of an obstacle on the road, such as a pedestrian, and even when we are actively searching the road to detect that obstacle, there is still a good chance that by the time we detect it (or him or her) we will not have sufficient time to stop and avoid a collision. Why or how does that happen?

To understand what it takes to see the pedestrian, the first thing we must do is define visibility. Langham and Moberly (2003) reviewed 16 studies of pedestrian visibility and – surprise surprise – noted that it is defined differently in different studies. For our purposes, we can use their distinction between two aspects of an object's visibility: its conspicuity and its detectability. Conspicuity is the extent to which an object "stands out from its surrounding" and detectability is the "ease of detection when the observer is aware of the target location." The detectability of an object is primarily affected by physical variables such as illumination, reflectance, and contrast, whereas conspicuity is greatly affected by psychological variables, especially expectancy. The relevance of each of these variables to our ability to see a pedestrian at night is very briefly discussed below.

Visibility and illumination

To understand the problems of timely detection and identification of a pedestrian at night, we must briefly describe the processes involved on the part of the driver, and the pedestrian's contribution to these processes. Perhaps the first and the most intuitively obvious variable to consider is the amount of illumination that our headlights provide. The relationship between the illumination – the light falling on an object – and light intensity – the amount of light emitted by a headlamp, is dictated by an inverse power function: the amount of illumination decreases as a function of *square* of the distance between the headlights and the object. This means that for every doubling of the distance between the pedestrian and the car, the amount of light reaching the pedestrian is reduced by a factor of four. This also means that constant increases in the luminous intensity of the headlights add decreasing benefits in visibility distance, so that eventually huge amounts of luminous power have a negligible effect on the level of illumination (Roper and Howard, 1938). Therefore, there is a limit to our ability to improve detection distance by increasing the power of the headlights.

Another factor that affects the illumination of a pedestrian is the aim of the beams. Headlamps are carefully constructed chambers designed to maximize the light output in some directions (ahead and below the horizon), without exceeding some levels in other directions (to the left of the lane and above the horizon). This also means that the aim or misaim of the beams affects the illumination in any given part of the driver's forward field of view. In general, the higher the beams are aimed the greater the illumination. However, the higher the beams are aimed, the greater the glare that they produce for oncoming drivers. Thus, the trick is to maximize the intensity directed below the horizon while not exceeding certain limits for the intensity directed above the horizon (the eye level of approaching drivers). A difference in aim between 4 degrees above the horizon and 4 degrees below the horizon translates to approximately 40 percent reduction in pedestrian visibility distance (Bhise and Matle, 1989). Small deviations in headlight aim are critical because the farther away the object is from the driver, the closer it is to the visual horizon.

Visibility and luminance

The next variable to consider is the amount of light reflected back from the pedestrian to the approaching driver. This amount – known as luminance – is equivalent to the amount falling on the pedestrian multiplied by the reflectance; the proportion of the light that is reflected toward the driver's eyes. The reflectance is affected by the quality of the material that a pedestrian wears: with dark clothing reflecting very little light and light clothing reflecting more light. For example, dark winter coats reflect only 4-8 percent of the light falling on them (Bhise *et al.*, 1977). Typically people do not consider reflectance when they shop for clothes, or when they select clothes to wear outside. Consequently, most of us go out into a dark night – especially during the winter months – wearing clothes that reflect only a small percentage of the light. Various studies have corroborated this by showing that very few pedestrians wear conspicuous bright clothing. For example, Hagel *et al.* (2007) observed 563 pedestrians in Edmonton, Canada, and noted that approximately 30 percent of them wore clothing that would make them either "nearly impossible" or "difficult" to detect at night. In this context, it is important to note that because vehicle headlights direct more illumination toward the pavement rather than up (to avoid glare), pedestrians' lower body is much better illuminated than the torso or the head. Even though Hegel *et al.* conducted their observations during the summer months – when people typically wear light colored clothes – only 8 percent of the pedestrians wore white or brightly colored (orange, red, or yellow) pants, and none wore retroreflective strips on their legs.

Visibility and contrast

The pedestrian's visibility is further compromised by low contrast – the amount of light reflected from the pedestrian relative to the amount of light reflected from his or her immediate surroundings. High contrast is a key variable to making things "stand out" or become conspicuous. Our visual system (see Chapter 4) is sensitive to both overall illumination and contrast, so that to a certain extent one can compensate for one with the other. But in the present case, both are compromised. The contrast of a pedestrian is typically low because both the pedestrian and the pavement around him or her reflect very small percentages of the light falling on them. For example, Bhise *et al.* (1977) found that the reflectance from an asphalt road under a variety of conditions varies from a low of 6 percent to a high of 13 percent. This level of reflectance is very similar to the range of reflectance of pedestrians wearing a variety of clothing. Thus, in detecting a pedestrian from a sufficient distance the driver has to overcome both low luminance and low contrast.

Visibility and expectancy

Expectancy, in the context of pedestrian detection, is a psychological variable that represents the degree to which the driver anticipates a pedestrian on the road. To be detected, an unexpected object must be conspicuous to attract the drivers' fixation (and attention). In contrast, detecting an expected object involves a visual search that is directed at detecting the object's most salient features. If we also know what to look for and where to look, the process is much quicker because our visual fixation and attentional mechanisms are already directed at it (see Chapters 3 and 4 for a discussion on the difference between top-down and bottom-up processing and visual attention, respectively). Several studies have demonstrated the importance of expectancy for pedestrian detection. The effect was first quantified more than three quarters of a century ago by Roper and Howard (1938), who measured drivers' detection distance to an obstacle on the road when it was either expected or unexpected. With 46 drivers/observers they found that "the average driver perceives the unexpected obstacle only half as far away as from the expected one…all of them saw the unexpected obstacle at least 20 percent as far as the expected obstacle, whereas none saw it at more than 80 percent of the distance" (pp. 419-420). Thus, this seminal study showed that an unexpected pedestrian is likely to be detected at roughly half the distance as an expected one.

To see how driver expectancy (to encounter a pedestrian) and the pedestrian's clothing reflectance interact and affect the pedestrian's visibility distance, we conducted an experiment that manipulated both independent variables. In this study (Shinar, 1985), the subjects/observers sat next to an experimenter who drove at a constant speed with high beams. The subjects were told that the purpose of the study was to determine pedestrian visibility, and that their task was to press a button whenever they detected an object or a pedestrian along the road. After a short distance in which they practiced pressing the button several times, they were told that they will now be driven to the test site, but if they should happen to detect a pedestrian along the way they should practice the task by pressing the button as quickly as they could. After driving for about 15 minutes on a deserted road, they encountered a pedestrian (who was actually a confederate in the study). Their detection distance in this condition was considered the visibility distance with the least amount of expectancy. They then had to detect the pedestrian under several other conditions that constituted increasing levels of expectancy: (1) when they knew the experiment had started but the pedestrian could be anywhere along a 2-kilometers road, (2) when they knew where along the road the pedestrian is supposed to be, but not where in the lane he may be, and (3) when the car was stationary and the pedestrian walked away till he disappeared and then walked back till he reappeared. The two visibility distances with the stationary vehicle were not the same and the average of the two was considered the condition of maximum expectancy. All four conditions were conducted with four different groups of observers each having to detect a pedestrian with different clothing: dark khaki clothes (with 5 percent reflectance) (Group 1); light khaki clothing with 70 percent reflectance (G2); and dark khaki clothing with a retroreflective tag on the chest (facing the approaching driver) (G3). The fourth group of subjects was exposed to the pedestrian with the dark khaki clothes and the reflector, but they were instructed to push the button whenever they detected a bright object (the retroreflective tag) (G4). Thus, they were cued to respond to the reflector.

The results of this study, reproduced in part in Figure 15-9, showed that both variables had a significant effect. The bars in Figure 15-9 indicate the average detection distances of the four groups (G1-G4), under the four levels of expectancy (E1-E4). The most obvious effect in this figure is the increase in detection distance with the increase in expectancy. But note that the visibility distances and the size of the expectancy effect are greatest for groups 3 and 4 – the ones exposed to a pedestrian wearing a retroreflective tag. Furthermore, the observers in group 3 who were requested to respond when they thought that they saw a pedestrian – and not just a bright spot down the road – performed very poorly in the first

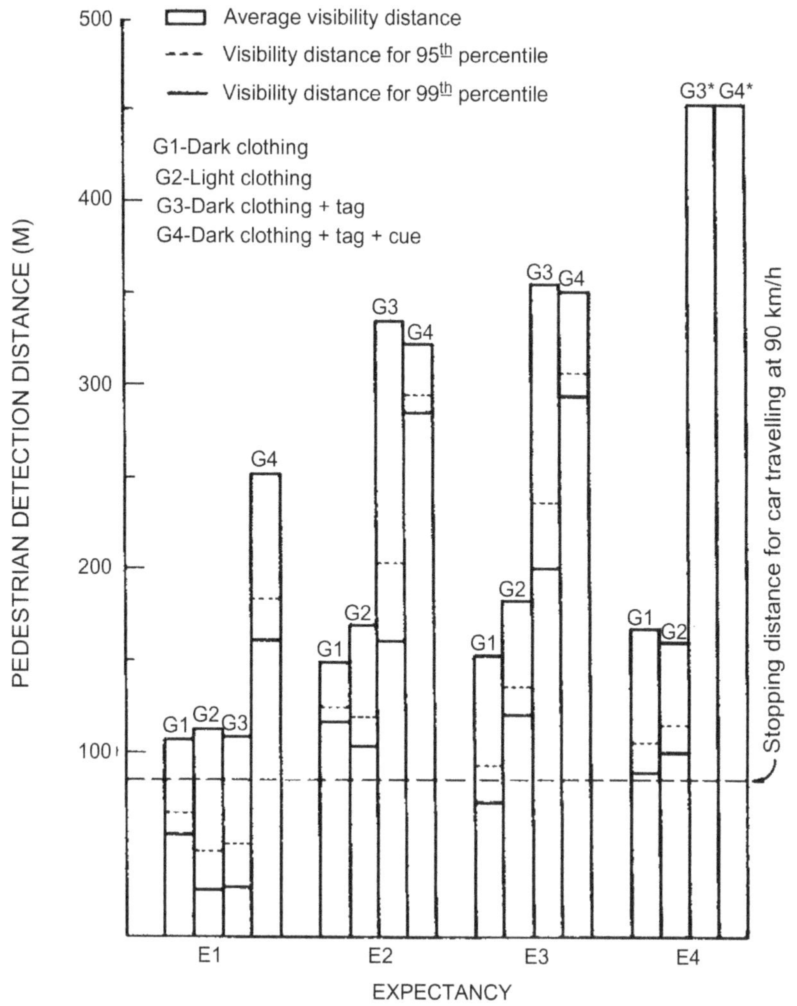

Figure 15-9. Average, 95th percentile, and 99th percentile pedestrian detection distances under varying levels of pedestrian conspicuity (G1-G4) and varying levels of driver expectancy (E1-E4) (see text for explanation). *In condition E4, detection distance for subjects in G3 and G4 was the maximum sight distance afforded by the road geometry (from Shinar, 1984, with permission from Taylor and Francis, Ltd.).

trial with minimum expectancy (E1-G3). This means that in the absence of an association between the tag and the pedestrian, the conspicuous tag was totally useless as a means of increasing pedestrian visibility distance. To be effective, the driver had to know that the retroreflective object is part of a pedestrian. The drivers in G4 had that knowledge and for them the visibility distance in the first trial was more than twice as high as for the drivers in the other groups. For the drivers in G3 this association was established only after the first trial, and consequently in the second trial (E2) their visibility distance was the same as that of the drivers in G4. Thus, high conspicuity does not necessarily imply recognition, and drivers are much less likely to brake in response to a bright spot somewhere in the dark (that could be a piece of glass on or off the road) until they actually realize it represents a real obstacle in their path (which they did in conditions E2-E4). Note also, that without the benefit of the tag (Groups G1-G2) average visibility distance increases with increasing levels of expectancy – from the lowest to the highest – by about fifty percent. This is significantly less than Roper and Howard's (1938) early finding, but the level of least expectancy here was still far from a totally unexpected situation. In this study the subjects knew the purpose of the study, they tried to do their best, and they were probably more alert than the "normal" driver driving alone at night on a deserted rural road.

The practical implications of these findings become apparent when these pedestrian detection distances are compared to the stopping distance of an approaching driver who is traveling at 90 km/hr; a fairly conservative speed for a rural or intercity road. For example, the dashed horizontal line in Figure 15-9 represents the stopping distance of an approaching driver, assuming a typical reaction time and vehicle braking distance. The line is below all bars, indicating that the average driver would be expected to be able to stop in time to avoid a collision with a pedestrian in all of these conditions. However, because the bar represents an average of a fairly symmetrical distribution, approximately half the subjects would detect the pedestrian at a shorter distance than the average. For this reason, each vertical bar is also marked by a dashed horizontal line, representing the detection distance of the 95th percentile of the sample, and a continuous line representing the 99th percentile of the detection distances. With this information in mind, we see that in more than 5 percent of all encounters with a relatively unexpected pedestrian – with either dark or light clothing – the driver would not be able to detect the pedestrian in time to stop.

Relying on the results of multiple studies of pedestrian detection distances, Leibowitz and Owens (1986) concluded that under dry road stopping conditions a driver proceeding at 90 km/hr would be unlikely to be able to stop in time even if the car has the high beams on and the pedestrian is wearing white clothes; let alone when the driver is proceeding with low beams and the pedestrian is clad in dark clothing. One small qualification to this conclusion is in order, however. These studies were conducted in the early 1980s and since then vehicle stopping distance has improved slightly due to the introduction of anti-lock brake systems (ABS) and electronic stability control (ESC), better asphalt, and better tires. However, driver vision and reaction time have not improved at all.

Expectancy is just as important in the daylight hours, when a pedestrian should be ostensibly visible. Borowsky and his colleagues (2012) showed drivers video clips of drives down urban and residential areas and asked them to note any hazard that they encountered. When analyzing the pedestrian detections, the researchers found that the pedestrians were much more likely to be detected in the residential areas where they were highly expected than in the sparsely populated urban areas where they were less expected.

Actual versus estimated visibility

In addition to their poor visibility, pedestrians further contribute to their own demise by failing to realize how poorly they are seen. This was first demonstrated by Allen *et al.*

(1970) and has since then been confirmed by others (Shinar, 1985; Tyrrell, Patton, and Brooks, 2004a; Tyrrell, Wood, and Carberry, 2004b). The discrepancy between the actual visibility distance and the distance from which a pedestrian believes that he or she can be seen by the approaching driver is shown in Figure 15-10 (from Shinar, 1985). In this study, participants performed two tasks. In one task, they sat next to a driver and had to indicate when they first detected a pedestrian down the road. In the other task, they were the pedestrians standing on the edge of the road and had to indicate when they believed that the approaching driver could first detect them. To see if pedestrians were sensitive to their differential visibility under different conditions of illumination, the actual and estimated visibility distances were evaluated in high beams and low beams, and with and without the glare from an opposing car.

As can be seen from the results, the pedestrians were, in general, sensitive to the lighting conditions; estimating their visibility as being the best when they had a retroreflective tag

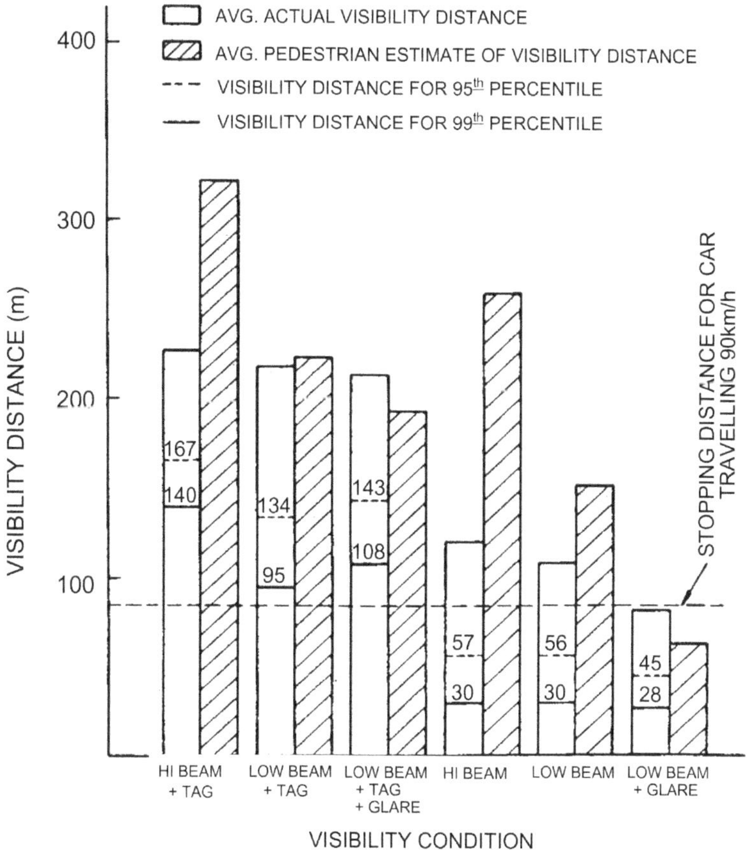

Figure 15-10. Actual pedestrian visibility distances and pedestrians' estimate of their visibility distance in high and low beams, with and without glare from an opposing car (from Shinar, 1985, with permission from the Human Factors and Ergonomics Society).

and the driver approached them with high beams, and estimating their visibility as being the poorest when the approaching driver faced the glare from the headlights of an oncoming car. However, in both high and low beams, when not wearing a tag, they felt that they could be seen from a distance that was greater by 50 percent or more than the distance from which *they themselves* as drivers were able to detect a pedestrian. This is quite disturbing, especially when we consider that these are the two most common situations in nighttime driver-pedestrian encounters. Also, as in the previous study, in these conditions, even with a driver that is expecting to see a pedestrian, the stopping distance would be too long to accommodate the short detection distance of many drivers. Similar effects of overestimation were obtained by Tyrrell and his associates (Tyrrell *et al.*, 2004a). Furthermore, this problem is exacerbated by the finding that the overestimation is insensitive to severe reductions in the headlight illumination levels (Borzendowski *et al.*, 2013). One small comfort in this disturbing phenomenon is that people can be trained to improve their visibility estimates (Tyrrell *et al.*, 2004b). However, reaching and training most pedestrians is a nearly impossible task.

The discrepancy between actual visibility and estimated pedestrian visibility is true for drivers too. In a somewhat similar study, Borzendowski *et al.* (2015), measured the recognition distance of a pedestrian either with or without a retroreflective vest. In their study, they first asked a group of drivers to estimate the distance at which they could see a pedestrian at night if he or she were standing next to a car facing the driver and providing a source of different amounts of glare: with either the parking lights on, the low beams with a filter to reduce their illumination, or the low beams without a filter. They further had to imagine, for each of the glare levels that the imaginary pedestrian was either wearing dark clothing or dark clothing with a retroreflective vest. As expected, the estimated visibility distance was greater with the retroreflective vest (by 40–80 percent). However, the estimates were unaffected by the strength of the glare source. Borzendowski *et al.* then had different observers, sitting as passengers in a car moving toward the glaring car, press a button as soon as they became "confident" that they saw "a person (not just a thing)" on the roadway or on the shoulder of the roadway ahead of them. As each participant took part in only one trial, the level of expectancy was similar to the lowest level in our study (E1). This time, as expected, the actual visibility distance decreased as the glare increased. However, regardless of the pedestrian's clothing and the level of glare, the average actual recognition distance was only one third (!) of the estimated recognition distance, measured by the different subjects in the first part of the study. Thus, while drivers may appreciate the effects of increased contrast due to a retroreflective vest, they are oblivious to the significant impairing effects of glare.

As a final comment on pedestrian visibility, it is interesting to point out that there is one group of pedestrians who are very sensitive to their visibility: road work crews. These people always wear retroreflective materials when out on the road, and whenever possible also put advance signs on the road to maximize the benefits of the effects of expectancy. With well-designed placing of the retroreflective stripes on their vest, the nighttime visibility of these people can be up to tripled relative to their visibility with dark work clothes (Sayer and Mefford, 2004).

Effects of vehicle speed and size, and the risk of being injured or killed

When a driver and a pedestrian are on a collision course, it is obvious that the pedestrian, as the most vulnerable road user is at a distinct disadvantage. Unlike car occupants, the pedestrian has no protective cage, airbag or seatbelts to absorb the impact. Also, unlike a bicyclist or a motorcyclist the pedestrian does not have a helmet. Therefore, the risk of fatality begins at relatively low impact speeds and increases dramatically with speed. This is demonstrated in Figure 15-11 that depicts the relationships observed in three different studies (as presented by Corben *et al.*, 2004). Similar relationships have been reported by Elvik, Christensen, and Amundsen (2004) and by Henary *et al.* (2006).

As can be seen from this figure, up until the speed of 20 km/hr the risk of serious injury is negligible. However, beyond that speed the risk of injury accelerates rapidly. At 50 km/hr there is a 50 percent chance of being killed, and fatal injury is near certain when the impact speed reaches 70 km/hr. These graphs are based on crashes involving all pedestrians, and obviously the curves shift to the left for older, more vulnerable, pedestrians (Henary *et al.*, 2006).

Although the curves in Figure 15-11 have been supported by multiple studies that analyzed pedestrian crash data, Rosén, Stigson, and Sander (2011) argue convincingly that they are biased. This is because in these and other early studies low speed collisions were

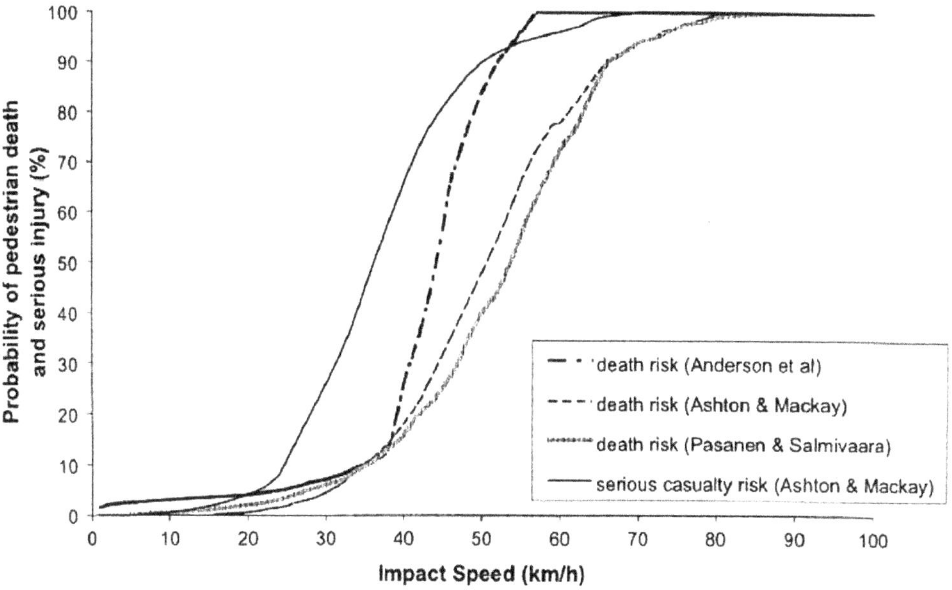

Figure 15-11. The probability of severe and fatal injuries to a pedestrian as a function of the impact speed (from Corben *et al.*, 2004, based on studies by Anderson *et al.*, 1997; Ashton and Mackay, 1979; and Pasanen and Salmivaara, 1993. Reprinted with permission from Monash University Accident Research Center).

often not recorded, and thus the fatality and severity risks appeared higher at the lower speeds than they actually were had none of the data been missing. After adjustment for that bias, Rosén and his colleagues found that the absolute risk levels are much lower in the more recent and more representative data. For example, the 50 percent fatality risk in the earlier studies is between 50 and 60 km/hr, whereas in the newer data it is nearly 80 km/hr. This could be comforting news, as it provides a greater margin of safety for pedestrians in slow urban traffic. However, for older pedestrians (60+ years old) the curve is shifted to the left and the 50 percent probability of fatality is still just below 50 km/hr (Davis, 2001).

In a more recent study, Tefft (2013) used the estimated impact speed as calculated in crash reconstructions of pedestrian crashes recorded in the U.S. National Automotive Sampling System (NASS). His severe injury and fatality risk functions, in relation to impact speed in a sample of 315 pedestrians aged 15+ years struck by a single forward-moving car or light truck model year 1989-1999, are reproduced in Figure 15-12. To account for multiple confounding variables, Tefft adjusted his data for pedestrian age, height, weight, body mass index, and type of striking vehicle. Furthermore, because the U.S. population has aged over the past decades (see Chapter 7) and because the proportions of sports utility vehicles (SUVs) and trucks have increased significantly (and these vehicles with their higher center of gravity are much more dangerous in collisions), Tefft standardized his data with respect to these variables relative to their frequencies in the U.S. in 2007-2009. Thus, after correcting for the sampling bias and for changing demographics and vehicle mix, the old and new risk curves are quite similar.

The risks at these relatively low speeds are significantly higher than the injury and fatality risks of vehicle occupants (see Chapter 8, Figure 8-8) and they have a very direct implication for pedestrian safety management: in areas where pedestrians are likely to cross the streets traffic speed should be significantly lower than in areas devoid of

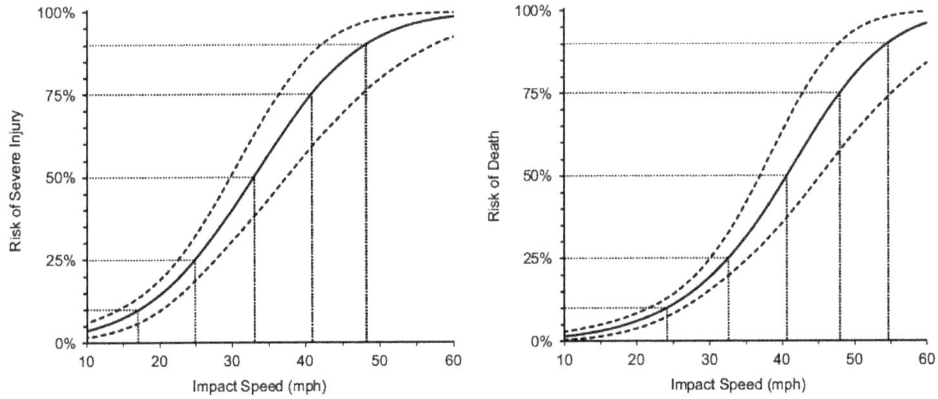

Figure 15-12. Pedestrian severe injury (AIS $\geq$ 4) and fatality risks as a function of speed in a sample of U.S. crashes, after adjustments for various confounding factors (see text) (from Tefft, 2013, with permission from Elsevier).

pedestrians. This is not only because of the pedestrians' greater vulnerability to injury from collisions, but also because pedestrians are often detected very late and the approaching driver does not have enough time to stop or even decelerate sufficiently to avoid a serious injury collision. This is why "dart-outs" identified in crash causation studies are such dangerous behaviors that often entrap the driver into a collision.

The force of impact is a function of the square of the velocity, but it is also a function of the energy mass, or the vehicle weight. For any given speed, the greater the mass of the vehicle the greater its force of impact at collision. Therefore, it should not be surprising that the severity of injury increases with the size of the vehicle, even after controlling for vehicle speed (Lefler and Gabler, 2004). The likelihood of fatality given a collision with a large van is three times as high as it is for a collision with a car, and the likelihood of fatality from a collision with a compact pickup truck is twice as high as the likelihood for a collision with a passenger car. Therefore, the increasing proportions of "sport utility vehicles" (SUV's) and pickup trucks further compromise pedestrian safety. In addition to their greater weight, these vehicles are also stiffer and "geometrically more blunt" than passenger cars and these features compound the danger that they pose to pedestrians (Lefler and Gabler, 2004).

Effects of culture on pedestrian safety

Social norms also play a significant role in the interactions between drivers and pedestrians. In general, both drivers and pedestrians are aware of the pedestrian's legal right-of-way in a pedestrian crossing (though the exact laws vary from one jurisdiction to another), and both know that mid-block crossing is dangerous and illegal. So it is not surprising that drivers are more likely to accommodate pedestrians at marked pedestrian crossings than in unmarked crossings (Katz *et al.*, 1975; Shinar, 2000). Relying on this formal norm, we tested the effects of the unwritten social norm of being more considerate toward handicapped people. As noted above and displayed in Figure 15-7 drivers were much more likely to allow the handicapped person to cross the street mid-block in the absence of a marked crossing, then to do the same for the physically fit pedestrian (Shinar, 2000). Similar effects were obtained by Guth *et al.* (2005) who had a pedestrian pose as a blind person intending to cross a street at four different marked pedestrian crossings. With the exception of a downtown crosswalk signal, drivers were much more likely to yield to the pedestrian when he had a long white cane or a guide dog than when he did not (also supporting Katz *et al.*'s, 1975, early findings on the role of driver-pedestrian communications).

Cultural norms also mediate the pedestrians' behavior. In a telephone survey conducted in four culturally different communities in Australia, Lam (2005) found that Chinese and Arabic speaking parents or caregivers perceived the road environment as significantly less hazardous for their 4-12-year-old children (as pedestrians) than Vietnamese and English-speaking parents. This was true even after adjusting for the age of child, the families' socioeconomic status, and the living environments of the respondents. Also, in a study conducted on Chinese pedestrians Yang *et al.* (2006) noted that the Chinese culture is such that despite attempts at enforcement, pedestrians often exploit gaps in traffic to cross during the DON'T WALK phase of a signal. The exceptions are older people who tend to respond to the law rather than to the gaps in traffic.

Countermeasures to Improve Pedestrian Safety

Pedestrian crash countermeasures range from policy statements proclaimed at the national level to specific behavior modifications, and modifications in vehicle and environmental designs. Unfortunately, as already noted, the level of effort directed at reducing pedestrian casualties is actually inversely related to the scope of the problem: with poor countries in which the pedestrians are a large proportion of traffic fatalities allocating fewer resources than rich countries where the problem is significantly smaller. Unlike programs designed to reduce vehicle occupants' injuries that are directed at modifying driver behavior, pedestrian safety programs must address behavioral modifications of both drivers and pedestrians, and consequently have to be more systems-oriented. It is also important to realize that the current trend toward sustainable mobility implies moving toward bicycling and walking and away from the use of the private car. One of the reasons the trend is not accelerating as much as it might is that it is not enough to stress the health, environmental, and economic benefits of walking. In an interesting analysis of the implications of walking and bicycling for policy-making, Pooley *et al.* (2013) concluded that perceptions of risk, constraints related to family responsibilities, and perception of the prevailing norms also have to be addressed.

At the international level, the World Health Organization has focused on five different specific pedestrian crash countermeasures including (1) reducing pedestrian exposure to motor-vehicle traffic, (2) reducing vehicle speeds, (3) improving visibility of pedestrians, (4) improving safety awareness and behavior of pedestrians and motorists, and (5) improving vehicle design for pedestrian injury reduction (WHO, 2013). These countermeasures and their effectiveness are described below within the framework of three general approaches that have been applied to improving pedestrian safety: organizational, behavioral, and engineering/design.

Organizational policy approach

Policy is the driving force of concrete actions. Following a survey of European practices to improve pedestrian safety, a team of U.S. experts recommended the creation of a "transportation policy (at national, State, and local levels) that addresses the safety and mobility of walking, biking, and other non-motorized modes so that these modes are given the highest priority in the road user hierarchy" (Fischer *et al.*, 2010).

Policies, in turn, should be backed by concrete goals. Just as goal setting is appropriate for setting target reductions in traffic fatalities in general, some jurisdictions have set specific goals for reducing pedestrian fatalities. For example, in the beginning of this century the U.K. Department for Transport set a goal of halving the total number of child deaths and injuries by 2010 relative to the 1994-1998 casualties (Christie *et al.*, 2004). While the goal does not affect the end result directly, it sets a standard against which all efforts are evaluated, and it heightens the motivation of everyone responsible for achieving that goal. The important role of goal setting in improving traffic safety is discussed in detail in Chapter 18. Goals can also be set for intermediate measures. For example, to enhance pedestrian mobility and safety the city of Lund, Sweden, has set goals for the year 2030 such as increasing the length of walkways by 30 percent, and increasing the proportion of safe crossings in the city by 100 percent. Tracking the change is then part of a regular performance evaluation program that measures progress toward these goals (Fischer *et al.*, 2010).

In a comprehensive review of pedestrian safety approaches and measures, Zegeer and Bushell (2012) note that Northern European nations emphasize walking as a mode of transportation and provide multiple incentives toward safe pedestrian mobility. These policy-based strategies include street hierarchy that gives walking top priority, urban land-use policies that promote walking and bicycling, pedestrian and traffic safety education in public schools, well-marked signing and detailed walking maps for tourists, providing safety islands in multi-lane roads, and shortening the length of pedestrian crossings through widening of the curbs at the crossing point. Some of these interventions are detailed below.

Given the relationship between injury risk and impact speed (see Figures 15-10 and 15-11), a very effective countermeasure – though unpalatable to some motorists – is speed limit reduction, especially in areas with high concentration of children. "Zone 30," referring to areas with 30 km/hr speed limits, and comparable "Zone 20" referring to 20 mph speed limits, that have become popular in Europe and in a few U.S. states are quite effective in pedestrian injury reductions. For example, in the U.K. urban speed limit reductions from 30 mph (48 km/hr) to 20 mph (32 km/hr) reduced child pedestrian casualties by 70 percent! (ETSC, 2005).

But there is an intransigent fly in the ointment. "Although there is agreement on the importance of walking for the functioning of the transport system, research on walking and pedestrians' quality needs has proved to be commercially unattractive. Providing for pedestrians is universally perceived to be a public task, thus needing governmental attention and funding" (Methorst, 2010b, p. 15). This awareness leads directly to the need for a systems-based approach to improve pedestrian safety and mobility. Furthermore, because the increasing proportion of older people is a significant issue in most countries, and because older people tend to walk as a form of exercise, public policies to provide for and promote safe walking must be set. To be effective, programs geared toward the safety of older pedestrians should also consider inputs from the public health field (Levi *et al.*, 2013). One example of embracing the system approach for improving pedestrian safety is the National Highway Traffic Administration's Pedestrian Safety Workshop that targets older pedestrians, as well as local transportation engineers, law enforcement officers, traffic safety educators, and relevant decision makers (Wagner, 2010). Unfortunately, such programs are relatively rare and some experts still feel that as far as pedestrian safety is concerned "system thinking is music of the future" (Methorst, 2010b).

Behavioral interventions

Education

Hunter *et al.*'s (1995) identification of the principal cause of child pedestrian crashes as "running into the street" (see Table 15-5) can serve as a measure of dangerous behavior and its reduction can be a goal for behavior modification. This can be achieved through an age-appropriate educational program, and there is evidence from at least one evaluation that this approach is effective. In this particular case, Hotz *et al.* (2004) evaluated the effects of a one-week "WalkSafe" program that was administered to 6,467 children enrolled in kindergarten through grade 5 in 16 schools in Florida. The program employed videos, formal educational curricula, workbooks, and outside simulation activities (e.g., crossing an imaginary road located on school grounds) to promote pedestrian safety among school-age children. The curriculum was structured in a hierarchical manner to allow for the different levels of cognitive development and pedestrian skills at the different ages. The program's effectiveness was evaluated by comparing the children's knowledge and actual street crossing behaviors immediately after the program and three months after the program to their knowledge and behavior prior to the program. The results were generally positive, showing a significant improvement in both knowledge and behavior immediately after the completion of the program. The percent of children who stopped at the curb before crossing increased from 12.5 percent before the program to 19.5 percent immediately after the program and the percent of children who were observed in mid-street dart outs decreased from 33.0 percent to 24.4 percent. However, after three months the effects were numerically smaller (17.3 percent and 28.5 percent, respectively) and no longer statistically significant. Thus, these results contain good and bad news. The good news is that the approach has an immediate behavioral impact; the bad news is that an intensive but short program cannot be expected to have a very lasting effect and a more sustained effort is necessary to sustain or improve the change.

Tailoring a program to the child's stage of development, as was done in the WalkSafe program is not easy. Researchers who addressed this problem over 40 years ago observed that young children, especially under the age of five, are simply not capable of making the cognitive judgments that the complex traffic system requires (Avery, 1974; Liss and Haith, 1970; Sandels, 1975; Zwahlen, 1974). And failure to realize this can lead to dangerously absurd results, as discovered by Pease and Preston (1967). They found that many young children who were taught a jingle to remind them of proper scanning before crossing ("Look to the Right Look to the Left" in England) believed that simply repeating the jingle protected them of the cars – regardless of how close or fast the cars were going. In short, didactic teaching of knowledge only is ineffective because children cannot generalize this learning to the real road environment (Schieber and Thompson, 1996).

The World Health Organization, in a comprehensive study titled World Report on Road Traffic Injury Prevention (WHO, 2004), reviews the impact of educational strategies to reduce pedestrian crashes and notes that "educational programmes use a variety of methods, frequently in combination. These approaches include talks, printed materials, films, multi-media kits, table-top models, mock-ups of intersections, songs and other forms of music." However, the report concludes, "overall, the effect of safety education of pedestrians on behavior varied considerably. Knowledge of pedestrian safety in children can translate into changed attitudes and even into appropriate forms of behavior, but there is uncertainty about the extent to which the observed behavioral changes persist over time. There is no evidence that observed behavior is causally related to the risk of occurrence of pedestrian injury. If it is, though, there is no reliable information about the size of the effect of pedestrian behavior on the frequency of pedestrian injuries. Reliable scientific information on the effectiveness of educational approaches to pedestrian safety in low-income and middle-income countries is lacking. Also needing more research is the effectiveness of educational approaches in all countries with elderly pedestrians" (p. 138).

With these kinds of concerns in mind, the Organization of Economic Cooperation and Development (OECD, 2004) recommends that educational efforts be tailored to the child's stage of development, and that the focus of responsibility for child road safety be shifted more toward drivers. "However well children may be educated and trained in road safety skills, they remain less able than adults to use their skills and knowledge consistently." Drivers, because they are licensed and regulated can be more easily trained to be on the lookout for pedestrians – especially children. This, in fact is part of the process of acquiring hazard perception skills. Training in proper visual search and detection – by both drivers and pedestrians – should therefore be a primary goal in safety education.

Adjusting child safety programs to the children's age also implies that below a certain age children are simply not capable of making the right decisions concerning safe street crossing. There is also a near-consensus that this critical age is about 9-10 years old (Percer, 2009; Meir, Parmet, and Oron-Gilad, 2013). Below that threshold age children cannot reliably (1) evaluate whether a specific crossing place should be defined as "safe" or "dangerous," (2) identify the presence of potentially dangerous traffic (relying primarily on distance cues and ignoring speed), and (3) integrate information from different elements and directions of the traffic environment into a holistic appreciation of the situation.

These arguments are well supported by empirical data. In a recent controlled simulation study in our driving laboratory Meir and her colleagues (Meir *et al.*, 2013) presented pedestrians with visual dynamic traffic scenes as observed from the edge of a curb, and asked them to decide as quickly as possible when it was safe to cross. Overall, they found that the younger children (7-9 years old) demonstrated a lower level of awareness of potential hazards than older children who were more hesitant and less likely to cross the street in marginal situations. In a later study in the same simulator environment, Meir, Oron-Gilad, and Parmet (2015a) demonstrated that children's hazard perception ability to detect partially obstructed hazards when standing at the curb and facing traffic was significantly poorer than that of adults. Similar findings were obtained in another study conducted in Israel by Rosenbloom *et al.* (2015), who developed their own pedestrian hazard perception test consisting of short video clips with actual and potential hazards. They found that although adults performed better than 7-10-years-old children, both groups benefitted from training at the task. These kinds of results led Israel's National Road Safety Authority to initiate an effective country-wide campaign with large banners posted near kindergartens and schools throughout the country proclaiming "KIDS UNDER 9 YEARS OLD DO NOT CROSS THE STREET ALONE."

Nonetheless, it appears that given the right approach even young children can improve their street crossing skills. In her most recent study, Meir and her colleagues (2015b) trained 7-9-years-old children to perceive hazards by showing them short videos of street views taken from the pedestrian's perspective and from a higher viewing angle of 3 meters. The higher angle significantly improved the visibility and perception of partially obstructed hazards. Following a structured training session with feedback, these children made significantly better street crossing decisions than a matched group of children who did not receive that training. Thus, while this study demonstrates that children do have an ability to improve hazard perception and street crossing decisions, given the right training approach, their decisions may still be quite inferior relative to those of skilled and practiced adults. Also, how well the findings from these simulation studies extend to the real world remains to be demonstrated.

Teaching pedestrians to wear high-reflectance clothing with biomotion cues

Daytime visibility distances are increased significantly when pedestrians wear fluorescent materials, and nighttime visibility increases when pedestrians wear retroreflective materials (Kwan and Mapstone, 2006). However, as demonstrated above these increased detection distances are not the same as recognition distances. To be recognized as pedestrians, it is important to provide the approaching driver with cues to the nature of the object behind the reflected light. This can be achieved when the reflective materials are attached to the pedestrian's clothing at the location of the joints. The natural movement that is generated by the walking gait of the pedestrian produces cues to biological motion or biomotion that appears to the observer as a moving pedestrian (Luoma and Penttinen, 1998). For an interesting demonstration of the effect see http://www.biomotionlab.ca/Demos/BMLwalker.html. Here, conspicuity is definitely a function of quality rather than quantity: a few reflecting light sources at the joints are much better than a whole reflecting vest. For example, in real driving on a test track, Tyrrell *et al.* (2009) found that drivers responded to the presence of a pedestrian wearing a reflecting vest at night at an average distance of a mere 9 meters, compared to over 213 meters when the pedestrian had reflectors placed at the ankles and wrists only. Thus, the biological motion cues multiplied the identification distance more twenty fold! These two distances are quite extreme (in both directions) and are most likely due to the experimenter's instructions not to respond "until they were confident that what they saw was a pedestrian." Consequently, while the vest did not provide an identity cue to the visible object, the biological motion cues most certainly did. As expected the benefit was slightly smaller for older drivers (61+ years old) than for younger ones (21-34 years old), but it still increased pedestrian's visibility to nearly 150 meters. Similar benefits of biomotion with retroreflective stripes around the wrist, elbows, ankles, knees, shoulders, and waist, were obtained on the same closed road circuit by Wood *et al.*, (2010, 2012). Interestingly, Tuttle, Sayer, and Buonarosa (2009) were not able to demonstrate differential benefits in terms of detection distance of vests worn by emergency road crews with and without retroreflective stripes on the elbows and end of the sleeves, even when the pedestrian walked in place, thus simulating biomotion. It appears that to be effective the biomotion markers must provide cues to more than just the hand movements. How effective these various visibility treatments are in reducing crash risk remains unknown as there are no empirical evaluations of the crash risk with the various treatments (Kwan and Mapstone, 2006). Probably because biomotion cues are more difficult to regulate, most EU countries now require vehicle occupants to wear high-visibility vests (with mostly yellow retroreflective material) when they exit their car if it is disabled on the road or highway (EC, 2007).

Enforcement

Enforcing traffic regulations on pedestrians is very difficult, because they (together with bicyclists) are an unregulated element in the user-roadway-vehicle system. Consequently, efforts are most often directed at the motorists, and most often at controlling their speed. Unfortunately, the most common approach to control driver behavior through the posting of regulatory roadside PEDESTRIAN CROSSING signs seem to have little or no effect on driver speeds (Klundt *et al.*, 2006).

Contrary to some regulators' opinions, a survey of 23 European countries revealed great public support for greater speed enforcement and more severe penalties for speeding (SARTRE, 2004). Similarly, an analysis of responses to the 2003-2004 British census survey indicates that "speeding cars" is the problem of greatest concern in residential neighborhoods (followed by "rubbish" and "parked cars"). Interestingly, the people most concerned with speeding are not the elderly but the ones in the 30-59 age range, possibly reflecting parental concerns (Poulter and McKenna, 2007). With such public support, speed management techniques can be quite effective almost regardless of the specific approach used – active police monitoring, speed cameras, or changes in roadway design. For example, speed cameras have yielded reductions in pedestrian injury crashes ranging from approximately 10-15 percent (Mountain, Hirst, and Maher, 2005), to as much as 39 percent for fatal crashes (Elvik *et al.*, 2009).

Environmental design

Several integrative approaches to improving pedestrian safety through better infrastructure designs have been developed. A model specifically tailored for intersection was developed by Carter *et al.* (2006) for the U.S. Federal Highway Administration. After evaluating the design features and pedestrian behaviors at 68 intersections in different U.S. cities, they derived a pedestrian "intersection safety index." The index score was based on objective and experts' ratings on different variables including type of intersection control (signal or stop sign), number of through lanes, 85th percentile vehicle speed, main street traffic volume, and area type. The process of intersection evaluation and the quantitative models that were derived eventually led to a user-friendly Pedestrian Safety Guide and a Countermeasure Selection System. Though they are too complex to describe here the guide along with other pedestrian safety information are accessible on the internet (http://pedbikesafe.org/PEDSAFE/index.cfm). Other comprehensive guidelines are provided in the publications of the U.S. Federal Highway Administration's "Highway Design Handbook for Older Drivers and Pedestrians" (Staplin *et al.*, 2001), and the more recent "Handbook for Designing Roadways for the Aging Population" (Brewer, Murillo, and Pate, 2014). For the urban environments, the American Association of Retired Persons has published Planning Complete Streets of Aging America (AARP, 2009), which emphasizes the role of local and state planning agencies in designing multimodal accommodations for older road users.

A review of best practices in leading countries in the EU led Fischer *et al.* (2010) to recommend the following design solutions for pedestrian safety: raised crosswalks at pedestrian crossings (applied at mid-block and roundabouts); passive detection of pedestrians in waiting areas and crosswalks to extend or cancel pedestrian phase; accessible pedestrian signals with confirmation lighting; crossing islands at pedestrian crossings, even on narrow roadway widths; and partial crossings at wide signalized intersections with wide medians (additional push buttons and pedestrian signals will be required). Although all of these are intuitively appealing, no empirically based statistical data were provided to demonstrate their effectiveness.

Given the cognitive limitations of children, and the physical and sensory limitations of older people, the most promising approach to pedestrian crash reduction is to try to accommodate these road users by treating their environment. Retting, Ferguson, and McCartt (2003) reviewed the effectiveness of various environmental design treatments and distinguished among four types of such strategies: (1) harmonizing the coexistence of motorized traffic with pedestrian traffic by ensuring low vehicle speeds (below the critical 40 km/hr – see Figures 15-10 and 15-11); (2) providing temporal separation of pedestrians and motor vehicles, typically through pedestrian crossing signals; (3) providing spatial separation by creating pedestrians-only zones and pedestrian overpasses and underpasses; and (4) enhancing the visibility of pedestrians. Each approach is effective, and each is applicable to slightly different set of circumstances, as described below.

Coexistence: shared-space approach and traffic calming

This approach includes speed or traffic "calming" through infrastructure design that inhibits drivers from exceeding very low speed limits, posted "green districts" that mandate low speeds, and "home zones" that encourage walking and cycling over driving and give priority on the road to pedestrians and cyclists. It is most appropriate to locations with dense pedestrian traffic. Hirst, Mountain, and Maher (2005) and Mountain *et al.* (2005) found that traffic calming through roadway design is more effective than automated enforcement techniques. In particular, infrastructure designs that are "child-centered" rather than driver-centered appear to be one of the features that distinguish countries with good child safety record from those with poor child safety record (OECD, 2004). Specific speed calming techniques that have been effectively used include roundabouts, speed bumps, lane narrowing, and curb extensions at intersections (effectively narrowing the road width). However, the implementation of this approach should be accompanied by a careful evaluation of pedestrians' – especially children's – behavior before and after the implementation, because children have been shown to behave more dangerously when they feel more protected (Morrongiello, Walpole, and Lasenby, 2007).

A very popular speed calming technique that implies coexistence of pedestrians with motorized traffic is the roundabout. In an extensive review of the literature on the effectiveness of different "speed calming" techniques designed to reduce vehicular speeds in the vicinity of pedestrians, Retting *et al.* (2003) found that converting intersections to roundabouts reduced collisions with pedestrians by approximately 75 percent – but only as long as the roundabouts were limited to a single lane. However, in a more recent analysis of the crash experience in Flanders, Belgium, de Brabander and Vereeck (2007) compared the crash experience in 95 roundabouts with 230 intersections and reached a different conclusion. Their results confirmed the overall crash-reduction benefits of roundabouts, but showed that as far as pedestrians were concerned the indiscriminant use of roundabouts is dangerous. Replacing unsignalized intersections with roundabouts on roads posted at the relatively slow speeds of 50 km/hr decreased pedestrian fatalities, but replacing signalized intersections with roundabouts appeared to be counterproductive. Thus, at least as far as pedestrian safety is concerned, coexistence in roundabouts is probably not a good alternative to temporal separation at intersections by signalization. This finding illustrates that coexistence must be very carefully planned and considered before it is implemented. Because in a pedestrian-vehicle conflict, it is "might" and not "right" that matters, a possible moderating variable may be the prevailing driving culture where the implementation is planned (e.g., the aggressiveness of drivers and pedestrians).

One way to increase the safety of roundabouts for pedestrians is to build them with guardrails that guide the pedestrians toward the marked crossings. In an analysis of the effectiveness of such crossings, Cohen *et al.* (2013) videoed over 11,000 pedestrian crossings at 10 roundabouts in Israel with and without guardrails, and noted that the channeling guardrails reduced illegal crossings by approximately 20-30 percent, depending on various other factors such as traffic density (greater density led to fewer violations). Similar findings were obtained by Zheng, Hall, and McDonald (2007) in London. Note that pedestrian guardrails are not a true barrier as much as they are a physical obstacle that can be overcome with minor inconvenience. Yet it is a "nudge" in the right direction to induce many people to comply with it.

Temporal separation

Retting *et al.* (2003) reviewed nine studies that evaluated various means of temporally separating pedestrians from traffic, and found that all had a positive effect on either pedestrian behavior (in terms of looking for approaching vehicles), or on vehicle--pedestrian conflicts, or on pedestrian crashes. Table 15-6 provides a summary of research on the effects of signalized pedestrian crossings on crashes in different contexts. This summary by Elvik *et al.* (2009) is based on 14 studies, conducted in five different countries, published between 1965 and 1986. It provides compelling evidence that signalization is not a good solution for all situations. While it is estimated to reduce mid-block pedestrian injury crashes by nearly 50 percent when it replaces an unmarked crossing,

Table 15-6. Summary of the effects of signalized crossings on pedestrian and vehicle crashes in different environments (from Elvik *et al.*, 2009, with permission from Emerald Publishing).

Accident Severity	**Percentage Change in the Number of Accidents**		
	Type of accidents affected	**Best estimate**	**95% confidence interval**
Signalized pedestrian crossing versus no crosswalk			
Injury accidents	Pedestrian accidents mid-block	−49	(−81; +35)
Injury accidents	Pedestrian accidents at junctions	−2	(−48; +84)
Signalized pedestrian crossing versus marked crosswalk			
Injury accidents	Pedestrian accidents	−27	(−59; +29)
Injury accidents	Vehicle accidents	+53	(−45; +309)
Injury accidents	All accidents	−23	(−56; +32)
Pelican crossing versus no crosswalk			
Injury accidents	Pedestrian accidents	−20	(−34; −2)
Injury accidents	Vehicle accidents	+3	(−22; +36)
Injury accidents	All accidents	−9	(−21; +5)
Pelican crossing versus marked crosswalk			
Injury accidents	Pedestrian accidents	+3	(−25; +42)
Injury accidents	Vehicle accidents	−23	(−35; −10)
Injury accidents	All accidents	−16	(−30; +1)

it is also estimated to increase vehicle crashes by the same amount when it is added to an existing marked crosswalk.

The most common way of temporally separating pedestrians from drivers is with pedestrian traffic signals. The critical issue here is the determination of the design walking speed. As noted above, the U.S. Department of Transportation Manual on Uniform Traffic Control Devices recommends that signal phasing should assume a 1.2. m/s pedestrian walking speed. However, the manual also acknowledges that in places with pedestrians who walk more slowly than the "normal" population, slower speeds should be assumed. Based on their review of the literature, Fitzpatrick *et al.* (2006) recommend that the normal design speed should be 1.1 m/s and the design speed in places used by older and less able pedestrians be further reduced to 0.9 m/s. Nonetheless, they too acknowledge that disabled pedestrians using various assistive devices have average walking speeds that are as slow as 0.6 m/s; needing twice the time allowed for a healthy adult.

A recent innovation in pedestrian signals is the addition of count-down signals (CDS) to the standard walk/don't walk signals. Typically, as the green "go" light comes on a digital display of the number of seconds left to cross safely comes on. Multiple surveys have shown that many pedestrians do not quite understand the meaning of the flashing DON'T WALK phase; erroneously believing that they will *not* have enough time to cross the street safely if they are already off the curb. Therefore, one explicit purpose of the CDS is to give pedestrians exact information on the time they have left to complete their crossing. The spread of CDS has been rapid (e.g., CityNews, 2013; Grynbaum, 2010), and surveys of both pedestrians and drivers indicate that the CDS is hugely popular and perceived as a good safety device. But is it?

Evaluations of the CDS have been conducted at two levels: how does it affect the pedestrians' behavior, and how does it affect their crash risk. And the findings have been mixed. In one of the earlier evaluations of CDS, Huang and Zegeer (2000) compared the behavior of pedestrians in Florida in intersections that had CDS with intersections that did not have it (i.e., with only a standard pedestrian signal consisting of a green WALK phase, a flashing red DON'T WALK phase, and a continuous red DON'T WALK phase). They found that the CDS had the beneficial effect of reducing the number of pedestrians that started running when the flashing DON'T WALK appeared, but had the detrimental effect of reducing compliance with the WALK phase. Most recently two studies in North America compared crash data before and after the installation of CDS. In one analysis of pedestrian accidents at 1,965 pedestrian crossings in Toronto, Canada, Richmond *et al.* (2014), after controlling for the baseline pedestrian crash rates, season, and year of signal installation, found that the CDS actually raised the rate of pedestrian accidents by 26 percent on the average, and even more (by 51 percent) for serious injuries and deaths. However, an evaluation of the CDS' effectiveness in Detroit, Michigan – only 370 highway kilometers away from Toronto – yielded totally different results. A time series analysis of 362 sites in which a standard signal was converted to a CDS showed that the CDS reduced pedestrian collisions to about one third of the pre-installation level (Huitema, Van Houten, and Manal, 2014). It is hard to reconcile the results of the two studies as they are both statistically sound and are based on large samples in similar cultures. When other earlier studies are considered, the Toronto study seems to be an outlier, as most previous studies suggest that the CDS is effective. Hopefully this is the case, as CDSs are spreading quickly throughout North America and Europe, and as far as China (Xiong *et al.*, 2014). One unintended consequence of the CDS is that drivers and motorcyclists seem to exploit that information to drive more aggressively and violate their red light (Chen *et al.*, 2015).

Spatial separation

Overpasses and underpasses are excellent means of separating cars and pedestrians. However, to be effective they must be used, and to be used their location must be planned very carefully, and their design should consider the pedestrians' needs and limitations (Campbell *et al.*, 2004). For example, if they are located too far from the pedestrians' preferred crossing location, or involve many stairs they will not be used by elderly pedestrians, who may continue to risk crossing the street at the traffic level. Also, while pedestrian crashes may decrease by as much as 90-80 percent in the immediate vicinity of overpasses and underpasses, non-pedestrian crashes may increase, though to a much lesser extent and with lesser severity (Retting *et al.*, 2003). Separation can also be facilitated by channeling pedestrians toward specific crossing areas by constructing rigid hard-to-penetrate barriers along the median of the road. Despite tell-tale evidence of pedestrians' attempts to break down such barriers – even with wire cutters and crowbars – these barriers are still quite effective in reducing pedestrian collisions. Also, because of the attempts to penetrate them, they are more effective if they permit some visibility of high risk-taking pedestrians who are determined to cross them (Retting *et al.*, 2003).

A simple, inexpensive means of increasing vehicle-pedestrian separation at signalized intersections is to move the Stop line further away from the intersection and from the path of the pedestrian crossings. Retting and Van Houten (2000) evaluated the effects of moving the stop line at four urban intersections in St. Petersburg, Florida, from 1 meter ahead of the zebra crossing to 6 meters ahead of the zebra crossing. They found that more than 50 percent of the drivers complied with the marking. More important, the line displacement significantly reduced the number of cars stopping inside the pedestrian crosswalk from 25 percent to a mere 7 percent. These results, however, may be location-specific because drivers in other cultures and places may not comply with such markings to the same extent that the Florida drivers – with a high proportion of elderly pedestrians – did.

Safe routes to school programs

This is an innovative program designed to increase the safety of children as they walk to and from school. It involves the identification of the potentially safest routes to schools from various commonly used locations and then improving the signage, and building sidewalks, bicycle lanes, and safe crossings along these routes. In an evaluation of such a program in the city of New York, DiMaggio and Li (2013) found that following its implementation, school-aged pedestrian injuries during the school-travel hours (7-9 am and 2-4 pm) along the tracts affected by the program decreased by 44 percent while the injury rates at the same times and for the same aged kids in areas unaffected by the program remained essentially unchanged. This is a remarkable decrease in crashes that is due both to the environmental improvements where kids tended to walk, as well as to their effect on inducing more kids to use these routes.

Enhancing visibility and conspicuity of pedestrian crossings
While we cannot dictate the use of high-visibility garments for pedestrians, municipal authorities can at least enhance the visibility of pedestrian crossings in order to alert drivers to the possible presence of pedestrians at these locations. However, pedestrian and driver behavior in response to these modifications are not easy to predict. Huang *et al.* (2000) observed the behavior of drivers and pedestrians before and after three different enhancements of pedestrian crossings. The three treatments that were evaluated included a regulatory overhead CROSSWALK sign directly above the crosswalk, brightly colored cones placed in the middle of the road at the pedestrian crossing with the message STATE LAW – YIELD TO PEDESTRIANS ON YOUR HALF OF THE ROAD, and a pedestrian activated overhead sign that flashed STOP FOR PEDESTRIANS IN CROSSWALK. While the cones and the overhead regulatory signs increased yielding behavior by approximately 15 percent, the pedestrian activated sign did not. However, when an automatic pedestrian detector is added to the push button system, the number of conflicts between pedestrians and drivers is reduced dramatically (Hughes *et al.*, 2001). Another possible improvement is in the form of an advance warning system consisting of a yield sign in front of the crosswalk markings. In a driving simulator this sign prompted drivers to direct their looks at the pedestrians earlier and to yield to them more often than when it was absent (Fisher and Garay-Vega, 2012). However, this demonstration still needs to be validated in the real world. In contrast to the inconsistent effects of these treatments in daylight, crosswalk illumination at night – that illuminates both the road and the crossing pedestrians – is very decidedly effective. The simple installation of intensive nighttime illumination above pedestrian crossings has shown to decrease pedestrian accidents – nearly half a century ago – by over 50 percent in Australia (Pegrum, 1972) and in Israel (Polus and Katz, 1978).

Some low-cost low-tech treatments can also be quite effective. One such low-cost treatment that has shown initial promise is the creation of a "gateway" in front of a marked pedestrian crossing. The gateway consists of upright bendable banners placed on the pavement in such a way as to narrow the lane just before the crossing. Presumably, this visual narrowing helps focus drivers on the crosswalk and slow them down so as not to run over the banners. In several crosswalks where the average yielding rates to pedestrians prior to their installation, they increased the yielding rates from as low as 7 percent to over 70 percent (Bennett, 2015). Another low-cost low-tech visibility enhancement technique is the painting of zigzag lines along the road just before pedestrian crossings, especially for mid-block crossings. These markings are quite popular in the United Kingdom and Europe but not in the U.S. Their purpose is to prevent parking along the road just before the crossing and in this manner both increase the pedestrian's visibility (that might otherwise be obstructed by a parked vehicle) and alert approaching drivers to the potential presence of pedestrians. Interestingly, it seems that though its meaning is not clear to many drivers (Mutabazi, 2010), it does seem to raise approaching motorists alertness and cause them to slow down (Dougald, 2010).

Paradoxical effects of marked pedestrian crossings
Interestingly, the ubiquitous marking of crosswalks by two lines or "zebra crossing" – the most common pedestrian "safety" device – does not seem to be an effective accident countermeasure, and may even be counterproductive. This is despite the fact that drivers are more likely to yield to pedestrians in marked and conspicuous crosswalks than when they cross the street in unmarked or less conspicuous crossings (Katz *et al.*, 1975; Shinar, 2000; Van Houten, 1992).

The apparent ineffectiveness of marked crosswalks was first demonstrated in a controversial study by Herms (1972). For his analysis, he identified 400 intersections in San Diego where at least one crossing was marked and at least one crossing was not marked. Thus, each intersection provided its own treatment and control sites. When he compared the crash experience in the unmarked crossings with the crash experience in the marked crossings he found no difference between the two. In his attempt to explain this perplexing result, he argued that it was due not to the marking of the crosswalks as to "the pedestrian's attitude and lack of caution when using the marked crosswalk." A simpler explanation could be that the marked crosswalks attracted more pedestrians and the higher number of pedestrian crashes in the crossing was simply because there were many more of them there. It is then still possible that the *rate* of pedestrian crashes (per number of crossings) in the marked crossing was smaller even though the absolute number was not. Consequently the finding may be an artifact of differential exposure levels. Indeed, in a study that controlled for the exposure (of both pedestrian crossings and vehicle volumes) in marked and unmarked crossings, Tobey, Shunamen, and Knoblauch (1983) found that marked crosswalks had fewer pedestrian accidents than unmarked ones. However, Zegeer *et al.*, (2004, 2005) controlled for traffic and pedestrian volumes and still failed to find a benefit for marked crossings at unsignalized intersections. In their study, they compared the crash experience in 1,000 marked crosswalks at unsignalized and unsigned intersections with the crash experience of a matched set of intersections without the marked crosswalks and found no difference between the two. Furthermore, on multi-lane high-volume roads marked crosswalks were associated with *higher* pedestrian crash rates. These dramatic findings are reproduced in Figure 15-13 where the crash rates for pedestrian crashes per million crossings are plotted for the various types of road crossings. The greatest difference in crash rate between the marked and unmarked crossing is on undivided high-volume multi-lane roads where the risk of a crash in a marked crossing is almost five times that of crossing in an unmarked area.

Leden, Gårder, and Johansson (2006) also reported an increase in crashes at marked crossing in Sweden, and they too suggested that it is due to the pedestrians' "false sense of security" in these locations. However, an in-depth analysis of the causes of the crashes in Zegeer *et al.*'s (2004, 2005) study revealed an unsuspected cause for the negative effect of the crossings: multiple-threats. A multiple-threat (already mentioned above) was the situation where a car in the right lane stopped to allow the pedestrian to cross, and while it was stopped another driver, who was driving in the left lane behind the stopped car (and therefore could not see the pedestrian who was partially or fully obscured by the stopped car) drove through the crossing and struck the pedestrian. Eighteen percent of the pedestrian crashes in marked crosswalks were classified as multiple-threat crashes

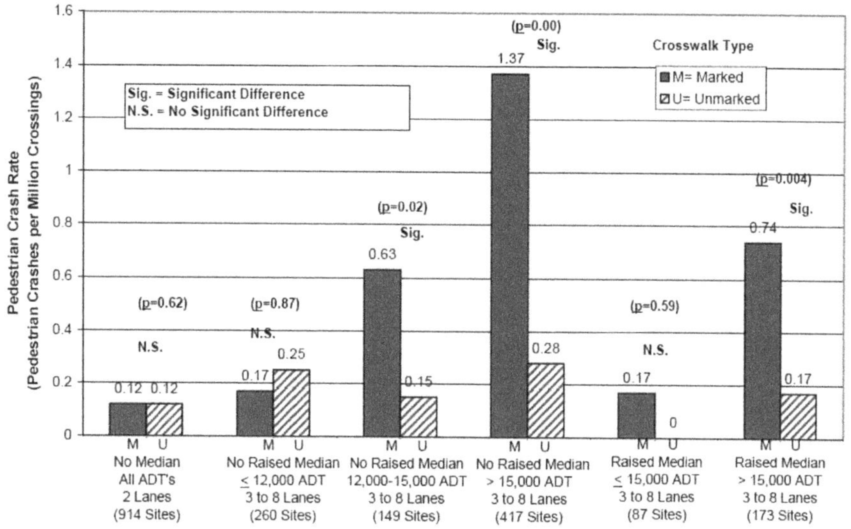

Figure 15-13. Pedestrian crash risk at marked and unmarked crossing for different road types (from Zegeer *et al.*, 2005).

while none of the pedestrian crashes in unmarked crosswalks was a multiple-threat crash. This also explains why the markings were particularly harmful in heavily traveled roads: these roads had multiple lanes and multiple opportunities for multiple-threats. Thus, a seemingly positive approach that was unsupported empirically was finally explained. This series of studies, spanning more than 30 years, can serve as a warning: crash countermeasures must be evaluated from a system's perspective before they are implemented, and once implemented their impact should be carefully monitored to verify their effectiveness. In the specific case of multiple-threats, where feasible, this problem can be eliminated by narrowing the vehicle paths with single lane entry to roundabouts and with curb extensions at intersections (Johnson, 2005).

Safety-in-numbers

Though not directly a design parameter, the number of pedestrians crossing the road together is related to controlled crossings. Safety-in-numbers is a phenomenon where the more pedestrians cross the street together, the lesser the risk *per pedestrian*. This effect has been found in several observational studies and is discussed by Elvik *et al.* (2009, pp. 58-59). The safety-in-numbers phenomenon can also account for some of the benefits of the environmental channeling designs. The channeling increases the pedestrians' visibility and conspicuity. On the flip side of this safety benefit is the fact that people who cross in the company of others tend to look more at the other people around them both before crossing and while crossing, and are more likely to cross during the pedestrian red light phase (Dommes *et al.*, 2015), as if they are assuming that they are more secure. The concept is discussed in much more detail in Chapter 17 in the context of bicyclists' safety.

Vehicle-based systems

Not all progress is good for all users. A case in point is the growth in hybrid electric vehicles (HEV) that rely on electricity at low (typically urban) speeds. At low speeds, the difference in the noise level between internal combustion engine (ICE) vehicles and HEV vehicles is the greatest. Consequently, the concern is that pedestrians who might otherwise hear the sound of an approaching standard ICE car miss the sound of an HEV, and expose themselves to a potential collision. This concern was validated in a study by Hanna (2009) who analyzed the NHTSA data on 77 and 3,578 pedestrians that were involved in crashes with HEVs and ICE vehicles, respectively. He found that the incidence rate of pedestrian crashes that probably occurred at very low speed such as when the vehicles were turning, slowing, stopping, backing up, or entering or leaving a parking space, was approximately twice as high with HEVs as with ICE vehicles. As a countermeasure, Japan, the U.S., and the European Union have all legislated a requirement that all HEVs be provided with acoustic vehicle alerting systems, which are already common on many HEVs. It now remains to test whether the warning-equipped HEVs are less of a crash risk to pedestrians than the models without them. A conceptually similar approach has been suggested for countering the relatively silent braking of cars with anti-lock braking systems (ABS) and electronic stability control (ESC). Here, the suggestion is to add a "screech" sound to the braking with ABS and ESC (see Chapter 19). The – yet untested – idea behind this patent is that the screech will provide pedestrians with previously available last minute alarm of an impending collision (Bunker, 2006).

Very few people think of vehicle modifications as a means to improve pedestrian safety. Indeed, the vehicle for the most part – unlike its driver – seems to be uninvolved. However, new ideas are emerging, but their implementation is complicated and their potential impact is hard to predict. For example, there are now obstacle detectors that are activated whenever a car's gear is switched into the reverse mode. Research on the effectiveness of cameras and/or sensors shows that they are very effective in preventing backover collisions with small objects, such as children that sometime play behind the cars in driveways (Kidd *et al.*, 2015; Mazzae *et al.*, 2008). Interestingly, in both controlled on road studies more collisions were avoided with the gear-linked camera than with the camera + audible sensor alert. Still, even with the camera system alone 42 percent of the drivers in Mazzae's study and 66 percent of the drivers in Kidd's study hit the stationary object while backing. These statistics may change as the market penetration of backup cameras increases because at least part of the reason drivers collided with the obstacles despite the presence of the camera is that the visual search involved in backing up is an acquired habit that needs changing when the camera view is added. Thus, it is likely that the benefits of such systems will actually be greater than observed in the controlled studies. In contrast, audible warning from sensors may prove less effective than in controlled studies because as these cheap systems become ubiquitous drivers may learn to ignore them, as many of us do for many alarms (e.g., consider most people's responses to a fire alarm or a burglar alarm emanating from a parked car). Weighing the costs and benefits of cameras in 2010 the U.S. NHTSA issued its plan to require a video system for improved rear-view visibility for all 2015 light vehicles (under 10,000 lbs of gross vehicle weight) (NHTSA, 2010). Another promising approach is utilizing current sensor technology to detect pedestrians ahead of the vehicle who are on a collision course, and applying the brake before the collision occurs. Such systems are already available for installment on existing vehicles, and their benefits in reducing fatalities and injuries are already demonstrable (Rosén *et al.*, 2010).

An approach with a potentially larger impact on pedestrian safety is intelligent speed adaptation (ISA). This is a systems approach to speed control in which short range transmitters send speed limit information to vehicles, and speed limiters within the vehicles then use that information to set maximum speed levels within these zones. Limited experimentation and computer simulation models indicate that the approach may be quite effective in reducing pedestrian casualties. One interesting aspect of ISA is that drivers who volunteered to use the system for over 6 months improved their driving by yielding the right-of-way to pedestrians more often than before (Ma and Andréasson, 2005). However, to date all users of such systems have done so voluntarily and disseminating these speed limiting devices to the rest of the driving population (where most of the problem may reside) is not easy.

There are also novel ideas to reduce pedestrian injuries by providing them with some impact protection. The European New Car Assessment Program (Euro-NCAP) now includes ratings of pedestrian protection based on the injuries sustained to the legs and head from the bumper, the bonnet, and the windshield. These ratings constitute important incentives to automobile manufacturers to improve the safety of their vehicles (see http://www.euroncap.com/en/vehicle-safety/the-ratings-explained/pedestrian-protection/). Possibly the most ambitious pedestrian protection device is Volvo's pedestrian airbag. It is deployed at speeds of 20-50 km/hr. When sensors in the front of the vehicle sense the pedestrian the hood near the windshield rises and an airbag emerges. This softens the impact with the hood and the would-be impact with the windshield that is now behind the airbag (see https://www.youtube.com/watch?v=NCjVS_-6hYs). Though demonstrable in crash testing, the actual benefits and the cost/benefit are still unknown.

Concluding Comments

Pedestrian crashes typically constitute a small proportion of the total number of crashes, but they are over-represented in the proportion of severe injuries and fatalities. Unfortunately they constitute a greater proportion of fatalities in poorer countries; countries that are also less likely to employ effective programs to prevent them.

Pedestrians are both poorly regulated to prevent them from being involved in a crash, and are vulnerable road users (VRUs) who are poorly protected to reduce their injuries once they are involved in a crash. There are a host of causes to pedestrian crashes, and many of them are age-related. Young children and elderly people are both over-involved in pedestrian fatalities – but for different reasons. Children lack many of the cognitive abilities needed to comprehend and cope with the traffic system and older people have reduced information processing, visual, and motor capabilities necessary for safe street crossings. Consequently, different behavioral and engineering approaches have been designed to address the problems of the two groups. Behavioral approaches focus on education and skill training (especially for children). Engineering approaches focus on environmental changes that are designed to improve pedestrians' visibility and reduce drivers' speeds, and more recently on vehicular improvements to avoid collisions with pedestrians, and lessen the injuries if a collision occurs. A notable engineering effort is the U.S. Federal Highway Administration's Highway Design Handbook for Older Drivers and Pedestrians (Staplin *et al.*, 2001). Increasing pedestrian conspicuity by having them wear more reflective clothing at night could prevent many pedestrian crashes, but has not really been sufficiently explored in the actual market. A singular exception is the use of reflectors on athletic shoes (mostly children). For better market penetration, perhaps safety specialists should work together with fashion designers.

Though both behavioral and environmental design approaches seem to be effective at reducing pedestrian crashes, their implementation often results in less-than-expected benefits, mostly due to system-wide adaptations to the new countermeasures. One single variable solution that does seem to be consistently effective is enhancement of the pedestrians' nighttime conspicuity with fixed illumination at and near pedestrian crossings. An innovative approach is the increased use of daylight saving time that seems to be quite effective at crash reduction during the twilight hours.

The increased focus on pedestrian safety in the developing world has led to investments in two seemingly incompatible countermeasures: separating pedestrians from motorized traffic and sharing the road with motorized traffic. The former is an approach of choice for high-speed high traffic volumes and the latter is the approach of choice for low speed high pedestrian volume areas such as residential and inner city streets. When judiciously applied both seem to work well.

Finally, to be effective, any approach to reduce pedestrian crashes and injuries must consider system implications. This has been aptly demonstrated in the use of marked pedestrian crossings. Although they increase the visibility distance of the crossing to the approaching drivers, who in turn tend to stop and yield the right-of-way, they create new dangers in multi-lane roads in the form of "multi-threats." One aspect of the traffic system that is important – but often ignored – is the culture in which we live. Perhaps more than in any other traffic safety domain, the nature of the interaction between drivers and pedestrians is very culture-specific. Therefore, an effective approach to the problem probably has to be tailored to each culture, or at least to ensure cultural similarities before programs developed in one country are implemented in another. One approach that has not been sufficiently explored is to sensitize both drivers and pedestrians – often the same people – to the limits of each other and the fallacies of both. These include driver's fallacies that pedestrians will not walk on the road or jump into the street from behind parked cars, and pedestrians' fallacies that drivers can see them from afar, and will yield to them if needed.

References

AARP (2009). *Planning Complete Streets for an Aging America.* AARP Public Policy Institute, Washington, DC.

Adminaite, D., R. Allsop and G. Jost (2015). Making walking and cycling on Europe's roads safer. PIN Flash Report 29. European Transport Safety Council (ETSC). Brussels, Belgium.

Allen, M. J., R. D. Hazlett, H. L. Tacker and B. V. Graham (1970). Actual pedestrian visibility and the pedestrians estimate of his own visibility. *Am. J. Optom. Archives Am. Academy Optom.*, *47*(1), 44-49.

Anderson, R., A. McLean, M. Farmer, B. Lee and C. Brooks (1997). Vehicle travel speeds and the incidence of fatal pedestrian crashes. *Accid. Anal. Prev.*, *29*(5), 667-674.

Asher, L., M. Aresu, E. Falaschetti and J. Mindell (2012). Most older pedestrians are unable to cross the road in time: A cross-sectional study. *Age and Ageing*, *41*(5), 690-694.

Ashton, S. J. and G. M. Mackay (1979). Some characteristics of the population who suffer trauma as pedestrians when hit by cars and some resulting implications. Proceedings of the IRCOBI International Conference, Gothenborg (as cited by Corben *et al.*, 2004).

Avery, G. C. (1974). The capacity of young children to cope with the traffic system: A review. Traffic Accident Research Unit, Department of Motor Transport, New South Wales, Australia.

Avineri, E., D. Shinar, D. and Y. O. Susilo (2012). Pedestrians' behaviour in cross walks: The effects of fear of falling and age. *Accid. Anal. Prev.*, *44*(1), 30-34.

Bennet, M. (2015). An examination of several variables influencing the efficacy of the gateway in street sign configuration on motorist yielding behavior. Dissertation paper 734. Western Michigan University.

Bhise, V. D., E. I. Farber, C. S. Saunby, G. M. Troeell, J. B. Walunas and A. Bernstein (1977). Modeling vision with headlights in a systems context. SAE Report 770238. Society of Automotive Engineering, Detroit, MI.

Bhise, V. D. and C. C. Matle (1989). Effects of headlamp aim and aiming variability on visual performance in night driving. *Transportation Res. Record*, 1247, 46-55.

Bird, A. D. (1969). How to plan for the pedestrian. The American City, July.

Borowsky, A., T. Oron-Gilad, A. Meir and Y. Parmet (2012). Drivers' perception of vulnerable road users: A hazard perception approach. *Accid. Anal. Prev.*, *44*(1), 160-166.

Borzendowski, S. A. W., R. L. Rosenberg, A. S. Sewall and R. A. Tyrrell (2013). Pedestrians' estimates of their own nighttime conspicuity are unaffected by severe reductions in headlight illumination. *J. Safety Res.*, *47*, 25-30.

Borzendowski, S. A. W., A. A. S. Sewall, P. J. Rosopa and R. A. Tyrrell (2015). Drivers' judgments of the effect of headlight glare on their ability to see pedestrians at night. *J. Safety Res*, *53*, 31-37.

Bowman, B. L. and R. L. Vecellio (1995). Pedestrian walking speeds and conflicts at urban median locations. *Transportation Res. Record*, *1438*, 67-73.

Brewer, M., D. Murillo and A. Pate (2014). Handbook for designing roadways for the aging population. Report No. FHWA-SA-14-015. U.S. Department of Transportation, Washington, DC.

Bunker, L. (2006). Screeching tires save lives. Press release, August 17. U.S. Trademark & Patent Office, Patent # 6,819,234.
Campbell, B. J., C. V. Zegeer, H. H. Huang and M. J. Cynecki (2004). A review of pedestrian safety research in the United States and abroad. Federal Highway Administration. Report FHWA-RD-03-042. U.S. Department of Transportation, Washington, DC.
Carter, D. L., W. W. Hunter, C. V. Zegeer, J. R. Stewart and H. F. Huang (2006). Pedestrian and bicyclist intersection safety indices: final report. Federal Highway Administration Report No. FHWA-HRT-06-125. U.S. Department of Transportation, Washington, DC.
Chen, P. L., C. W. Pai, R. C. Jou, W. Saleh and M. S. Kuo (2015). Exploring motorcycle red-light violation in response to pedestrian green signal countdown device. *Accid. Anal. Prev., 75*, 128-136.
Christie, N., S. Cairns, H. Ward and E. Towner (2004). Children's traffic safety: International lessons for the UK. Road Safety Research. Report No. 50. Department of Transport, London.
CityNews (2013). Pedestrian countdown signals cause more crashes: study. October 4, 2013. http://www.citynews.ca/2013/10/04/pedestrian-countdown-signals-cause-more-car-crashes-study-2/
Clayton, A. B. and M. A. Colgan (2001). Alcohol and pedestrians. DfT Report No. 20. Department for Transport, London.
Cohen, A., H. Bar-Gera, Y. Parmet and A. Ronen (2013). Guardrail influence on pedestrian crossing behavior at roundabouts. *Accid. Anal. Prev., 59*, 452-458.
Corben, B., T. Senserrick, M. Cameron and G. Rechnitzer (2004). Development of the visionary research model: Application to the car/pedestrian conflict. Accident Research Center. Report 229. Monash University, Clayton, Victoria, AU.
Cross, D. S. and M. R. Hall (2005). Child pedestrian safety: The role of behavioral science. *Med. J. Australia, 182*(7), 317-318.
DaCoTA (2012). Pedestrians and cyclists. Deliverable 4.81 of the EC FP7 project DaCoTA.
daSilva, M. P., J. D. Smith and W. G. Najm (2003). Analysis of pedestrian crashes. National Highway Traffic Safety Administration. Report DOT HS 809 585. U.S. Department of Transportation, Washington, DC.
Davis, G. A. (2001). Relating severity of pedestrian injury to impact speed in vehicle pedestrian crashes. *Transport Res. Record*, **1773**, 108-113. (as cited by Rosén *et al.*, 2011).
De Brabander, B. and L. Vereeck (2007). Safety effects of roundabouts in Flanders: Signal type, speed limits and vulnerable road users. *Accid. Anal. Prev., 39*(3), 591-599.
DiMaggio, C. and G. Li (2013). Effectiveness of a safe routes to school program in preventing school-aged pedestrian injury. *Pediatrics, 131*, 290-296.
Dommes, A. and V. Cavallo (2011). The role of perceptual, cognitive, and motor abilities in street-crossing decisions of young and older pedestrians. *Ophthalmic Physiol. Opt., 31*, 292-301.
Dommes, A., V. Cavallo and J. Oxley (2013). Functional declines as predictors of risky street-crossing decisions in older pedestrians. *Accid. Anal. Prev., 59*, 135-143.

Dommes, A., M. A. Granié, M. S. Cloutier, C. Coquelet and F. Huguenin-Richard (2015). Red light violations by adult pedestrians and other safety-related behaviors at signalized crosswalks. *Accid. Anal. Prev.*, *80*, 67-75.

Dougald, L. E. (2010). Best practices in traffic operations and safety: Phase II: Zig-zag pavement markings. Federal Highway Administration Report No. FHWA/VTRC 11-R9. U.S. Department of Transportation, Washington, DC.

Dunbar, G., C. A. Holland and E. A. Maylor (2004). Older pedestrians: A critical review of the literature. Road Safety Research. Report No. 37. Department for Transport, London.

EC (2007). Mandatory safety equipment for private passenger cars. http://ec.europa.eu/transport/road_safety/observatory/doc/safetyequip_car_rules.pdf. Accessed September 29, 2015.

EC (2015). Road safety in the European Union: Trends, statistics and main challenges. Brussels, Belgium. http://ec.europa.eu/transport/road_safety/pdf/vademecum_2015.pdf

Elvik, R., P. Christensen and A. Amundsen (2004). Speed and road accidents: An evaluation of the power model. TOI report 740/2004. Institute of Transport Economics, Oslo.

Elvik, R., A. Høye, T. Vaa and M. Sørensen (2009). *The Handbook of Road Safety Measures* (2nd ed.). Emerald, Bingley, UK.

ETSC (2005). Child safety in the UK. VOICE Fact Sheet, European Transport Safety Council.

EU (2014). Special Eurobarometer 422a "Quality of Transport". Brussels, BE.

Evans, L. (2004). *Traffic Safety*. Science Serving Society, Bloomfield Hills, MI.

Ferguson, R. W., Z. Xu, A. Green and K. M. Rosentha (2013). *Teens and Distraction: An In-Depth Look at Teens' Walking Behaviors*. Safe Kids Worldwide, Washington, DC.

Fischer, E. L., G. K. Rousseau, S. M. Turner, E. J. Blais, C. L. Engelhart, D. Henderson and C. V. Zegeer (2010). Pedestrian and bicyclist safety and mobility in Europe. FHWA Report No. FHWA-PL-10-010. Federal Highway Administration, U.S. Department of Transportation, Washington, DC.

Fisher, D. and L. Garay-Vega (2012). Advance yield markings and drivers' performance in response to multiple-threat scenarios at mid-block crosswalks. *Accid. Anal. Prev.*, *44*(1), 35-41.

Fitzpatrick, K., S. Turner, M. Brewer, P. Carlson, B. Ullman, N. Tront, E. S. Park, J. Whitacre, N. Lalani and D. Lord (2006). Improving pedestrian safety at unsignalized crossings. NCHRP Report 562. Transportation Research Board, National Academies, Washington, DC.

Fontaine, H. and Y. Gourlet (1997). Fatal pedestrian accidents in France: A typological analysis. *Accid. Anal. Prev.*, *29*, 303-312.

Geruschat, D. R., S. E. Hassan and K. A. Turano (2003). Gaze behavior while crossing complex intersections. *Optom. Vision Sci.*, *80*(7), 515-528.

Goodwin, P. B. and T. P. Hutchinson (1977). The risk of walking. *Transportation*, *6*, 217-230.

Griffiths, J. D., J. G. Hunt and M. Marlow (1984). Delays at pedestrian crossings: 1. Site observations and the interpretation of data. *Traffic Engineering Control*, *25*, 365-371.

Grynbaum, M. M. (2010). Deadliest for city's walkers: Male drivers, left turns. New York Times, August 16.

Guéguen, N., C. Eyssartier and S. Meineri (2016). A pedestrian's smile and drivers' behavior: When a smile increases careful driving. *J. Safety Res.*, *56*, 83-88.

Guth, D., D. Ashmead, R. Long, R. Wall and P. Ponchillia (2005). Blind and sighted pedestrians' judgments of gaps in traffic at roundabouts. *Hum. Fact.*, *47*(2), 314-331.

Hagel, B. E., A. Lamy, J. W. Rizkallah, K. L. Belton, G. S. Jhangri, N. Cherry and B. H. Row (2007). The prevalence and reliability of visibility aid and other risk factor data for uninjured cyclists and pedestrians in Edmonton, Alberta, Canada. *Accid. Anal. Prev.*, *39*(2), 284-289.

Hanna, R. (2009). *Incidence of pedestrian and bicyclist crashes by hybrid electric passenger vehicles*. National Highway Traffic Safety Administration Report No. HS-811 204. U.S. Department of Transportation, Washington, DC.

Hatfield, J. and S. Murphy (2007). The effects of mobile phone use on pedestrian crossing behaviour at signalised and unsignalised intersections. *Accid. Anal. Prev.*, *39*, 197-205.

Henary, B. Y., B. J. Ivarsson and J. R. Crandall (2006). The influence of age on the morbidity and mortality of pedestrian victims. *Traffic Inj. Prev.*, *7*, 182-190.

Herms, B. (1972). Pedestrian crosswalk study: Crashes in painted and unpainted crosswalks. *Transportation Res. Record*, **406**, 1-14. Transportation Research Board, Washington, DC.

Hirst, W. M., L. J. Mountain and M. J. Maher (2005). Are speed enforcement cameras more effective than other speed management measures? An evaluation of the relationship between speed and accident reductions. *Accid. Anal. Prev.*, *37*, 731-741.

Holland, C. and R. Hill (2007). The effect of age, gender and driver status on pedestrians' intentions to cross the road in risky situations. *Accid. Anal. Prev.*, *39*, 224-337.

Hotz, G. A., S. M. Cohn, A. Castelblanco, S. Colston, M. Thomas, A. Weiss, J. Nelson, R. Duncan and the Pediatric Pedestrian Injury Task Force (2004). WalkSafe: A school-based pedestrian safety intervention program. *Traffic Inj. Prev.*, *5*, 382-389.

Huang, H. and C. Zegeer (2000). The effects of pedestrian countdown signals in Lake Buena Vista. Tallahassee, Florida. Report to the Florida Department of Transportation.

Huang, H., C. Zegeer, R. Nassi and B. Fairfax (2000). The effects of innovative pedestrian signs at unsignalized locations: A tale of three treatments. Federal Highway Administration. Report FHWA-RD-00-098. U.S. Department of Transportation, Washington DC.

Hughes, R., H. Huang, C. Zegeer and M. Cynecki (2001). Evaluation of automated pedestrian detection at signalized intersections. Federal Highway Administration. Report FHWA-RD-00-097. U.S. Department of Transportation, Washington, DC.

Huitema, B. E., R. Van Houten and H. Manal (2014). Time-series intervention analysis of pedestrian countdown timer effects. *Accid. Anal. Prev.*, *72*, 23-31.

Hunter, W. W., J. C. Stutts, W. E. Pein and C. L. Cox (1995). Pedestrian and bicycle crash types of the early 1990's. Federal Highway Administration. Report FHWA-RD-95-193. U.S. Department of Transportation, Washington DC.

IRTAD (2013). Road Safety Annual Report 2013. International Traffic Safety Data and Analysis Group, International Transport Forum, OECD.

Jain, A., A. Gupta and R. Rastogi (2014). Pedestrian crossing behaviour analysis at intersections. *International J. Traffic and Trans. Eng.*, *4*(1), 103-116.

Johnson, R. S. (2005). Pedestrian safety impacts of curb extensions: A case study. Federal Highway Administration. Report FHWA-0R-DF-06-01. U.S. Department of Transportation, Washington DC.

Kar, K. and S. Gajulua (2008). Focusing on pedestrian safety. *Public Roads*, *71*(6), 1-10. Federal Highway Administration, U.S. Department of Transportation, Washington, DC.

Karsch, H. M., J. H. Hedlund, J. Tison and W. A. Leaf (2012). Review of studies on pedestrian and bicyclist safety, 1991-2007. National Highway Traffic Safety Administration Report No. DOT HS 811 614. U.S. Department of Transportation, Washington, DC.

Katz, A., D. Zaidel and A. Elgrishi (1975). An experimental study of driver and pedestrian interaction during the crossing conflict. *Hum. Fact.*, *17*(5), 514-527.

Keall, M. D. (1995). Pedestrian exposure to risk of road accident in New Zealand. *Accid. Anal. Prev.*, *27*(5), 729-740.

Kidd, D. G., B. K. Hagoski, T. G. Tucker and D. P. Chiang (2015). Effects of a rearview camera, parking sensor system, and the technologies combined on preventing a collision with an unexpected stationary or moving object. *Hum. Fact.*, *57*, 689-700.

Klundt, K., J. L. Brown, J. Richman and J. L. Campbell (2006). Human factors literature reviews on intersections, speed management, pedestrians and bicyclists, and visibility. Federal Highway Administration. Report FHWA-HRT-06-034. U.S. Department of Transportations, Washington, DC.

Knoblauch, R. L., M. T. Pietrucha and M. Nitzburg (1996). Field studies of pedestrian walking speed and start-up time. *Transportation Res. Record*, **1538**, 27-38.

Kwan, I. and J. Mapstone (2006). Interventions for increasing pedestrian and cyclist visibility for the prevention of death and injuries. The Cochrane Library, Issue 4. Wiley and Sons.

Laflamme, L. and F. Diderichsen (2000). Social differences in traffic injury risks in childhood and youth – A literature review and a research agenda. *Inj. Prev.*, *6*, 293-298.

Lalloo, R., A. Sheiham and J. Y. Nazroo (2003). Behavioural characteristics and accidents: Findings from the Health Survey for England, 1997. *Accid. Anal. Prev.*, *35*, 661-667.

Lam, L. T. (2005). Parental risk perceptions of childhood pedestrian road safety: A cross cultural comparison. *J. Safe. Res.*, *36*, 181-187.

Lang, C., R. Tay, B. Watson, C. Edmonston and E. O'Connor (2003). Drink walking: An examination of the related behaviour and attitudes of young people. 2003 Road Safety Research, Policing and Education Conference – From Research to Action: Conference Proceedings (pp. 164-169). New South Wales Roads and Traffic Authority, Sydney, AU.

Langevin, S., A. Dommes, V. Cavallo, J. Oxley and F. Vienne (2011). Cognitive, perceptual and motor decline as predictors of risky street-crossing decisions in older pedestrians. Driving Assessment 2011: 6th International Driving Symposium on Human Factors in Driver Assessment, Training, and Vehicle Design (pp. 409-416).

Langham, M. P. and N. J. Moberly (2003). Pedestrian conspicuity research: A review. *Ergonomics*, *46*(4), 345-363.

Leden, L., P. Gårder and C. Johansson (2006). Safe pedestrian crossings for children and elderly. *Accid. Anal. Prev.*, *38*, 289-294.

Lefler, D. E. and H. C. Gabler (2004). The fatality and injury risk of light truck impacts with pedestrians in the United States. *Accid. Anal. Prev.*, *36*, 295-304.

Leibowitz, H. W. and D. A. Owens (1986). We drive by night. Psychol. Today, January, 55-58.

Leibowitz, H. W., D. A. Owens and R. A. Tyrrell (1998). The assured clear distance ahead rule: Implications for nighttime traffic safety and the law. *Accid. Anal. Prev.*, *30*(1), 93-99.

Levi, S., D. M. De Leonardis, J. Antin and L. Angel (2013). Identifying countermeasure strategies to increase safety of older pedestrians. National Highway Traffic Safety Administration Report No. DOT HS 811 798. U.S. Dept. of Transportation, Washington, DC.

Link, D. (2006). Accident and population statistics from various countries. Data collated for the Israel National Road Safety Authority, Jerusalem, Israel.

Liss, P. H. and M. M. Haith (1970). The speed of visual processing in children and adults: Effects of backward and forward masking. *Percept. Psychophys.*, *8*, 396-398.

Lobjois, R., N. Benguigui and V. Cavallo (2013). The effects of age and traffic density on street-crossing behavior. *Accid. Anal. Prev.*, *53*, 166-175.

Lobjois, R. and V. Cavallo (2007). Age-related differences in street-crossing decisions: The effects of vehicle speed and time constraints on gap selection in an estimation task. *Accid. Anal. Prev.*, in press.

Lobjois, R. and V. Cavallo (2009). The effects of aging on street-crossing behavior: From estimation to actual crossing. *Accid. Anal. Prev.*, *41*(2), 259-267.

Luoma, J. and M. Penttinen (1998). Effects of experience with retroreflectors on recognition of nighttime pedestrians: Comparison of driver performance in Finland and Michigan. *Transportation Res. F*, *1*, 47-58.

Ma, X. and I. Andréasson (2005). Predicting the effect of various ISA penetration grades on pedestrian safety by simulation. *Accid. Anal. Prev.*, *37*, 1162-1169.

Maltz, M. and D. Shinar (1999). Eye movements of younger and older drivers. *Hum. Fact.*, *41*(1), 15-25.

Mazzae, E. N., F. Barickman, G. H. S. Baldwin and T. Ranney (2008). On-road study of drivers' use of rearview video systems. (ORSDURVS). NHTSA Report DOT HS 811 024. U.S. Department of Transportation, Washington, DC.

Meir, A., T. Oron-Gilad and Y. Parmet (2015a). Are child-pedestrians able to identify hazardous traffic situations? Measuring their abilities in a virtual reality environment. *Safety Sci.*, *80*, 33-40.

Meir, A., T. Oron-Gilad and Y. Parmet (2015b). Can child-pedestrians' hazard perception skills be enhanced? *Accid. Anal. Prev.*, *83*, 101-110.

Meir, A., Y. Parmet and T. Oron-Gilad (2013). Towards understanding child-pedestrians' hazard perception abilities in a mixed reality dynamic environment. *Transportation Res. F.*, *20*, 90-107.

Methorst, R. (2010a). Letselongevallen van voetgangers en fietsers. Rijkswaterstaat Dienst Verkeer en Scheepvaart, Delft, NL.

Methorst, R. (2010b). COST 358 – Pedestrian Quality Needs. PQN Final Report – introduction and conceptual framework. EC, Brussels, BE.

Morrongiello, B. A., B. Walpole and J. Lasenby (2007). Understanding children's injury-risk behavior: Wearing safety gear can lead to increased risk taking. *Accid. Anal. Prev.*, *39*(3), 618-623.

Mountain, L. J., W. M. Hirst and M. J. Maher (2005). Are speed enforcement cameras more effective than other speed management measures? The impact of speed management schemes on 30 mph roads. *Accid. Anal. Prev.*, *37*, 742-754.

Mutabazi, M. (2010). Sight obstruction at at-grade pedestrian crossings: A review of the understanding of the meaning of zigzag lines. *Safety Sci.*, *48*(3), 283-287.

MUTCD (2015). *Manual on Uniform Traffic Control Devices*. U.S. Department of Transportation, Washington, DC. http://mutcd.fhwa.dot.gov/

Naci, H., D. Chisholm and T. D. Baker (2009). Distribution of road traffic deaths by road user group: A global comparison. *Inj. Prev.*, *15*, 55-59.

Naveteur, J., J. Delzenne, P. Sockeel, E. Watelain and M. A. Dupuy (2013). Crosswalk time estimation and time perception: An experimental study among older female pedestrians. *Accid. Anal. Prev.*, *60*, 42-49.

NHTSA (2005). Traffic Safety Facts 2004. National Highway Traffic Safety Administration. Report DOT HS 809 919. U.S. Department of Transportation, Washington, DC.

NHTSA (2010). Notice of proposed rulemaking. 9 CFR Parts 571 and 585, Docket No. NHTSA-2010-0162, RIN 2127-AK43. NPRM 12032010. Federal Register. Washington, DC.

NHTSA (2015). Traffic Safety Facts: Pedestrians – 2013 data. National Highway Traffic Safety Administration. Report DOT HS 812 124. U.S. Department of Transportation, Washington DC.

NPTS (1995). 1995 Nationwide Personal Transportation Survey. Bureau of Transportation Statistics. U.S. Department of Transportation, Washington, DC. http://npts.ornl.gov/npts/1995/doc/NPTS_Booklet.pdf

NYDOT (2015). Highway design manual, Chapter 18, Pedestrian Facility Design. NY Dept. Transportation. https://www.dot.ny.gov/divisions/engineering/design/dqab/hdm/hdm-repository/chapt_18.pdf

OECD (2004). *Keeping Children Safe in Traffic*. Organisation for Economic Co-operation and Development, Paris.

Öström, M. and A. Eriksson (2001). Pedestrian fatalities and alcohol. *Accid. Anal. Prev.*, *33*, 173-180.

Oxley, J., B. Fildes, E. Ihsen, J. Charlton and R. Day (2005). Crossing roads safely: An experimental study of age differences in gap selection by pedestrians. *Accid. Anal. Prev.*, *37*(5), 962-971.

Papadimitriou, E., S. Lassarre, and G. Yannis (2016). Introducing human factors in pedestrian crossing behaviour models. *Trans. Res. F.*, *36*, 69-82.

Pasanen, E. and H. Salmivaara (1993). Driving speeds and pedestrian safety in the city of Helsinki. *Traffic Engineering Control*, *34*(6), 308-310.

Pease, K. and B. Preston (1967). Road safety education for young children. *Br. J. Educational Psychol.*, *37*, 305-313.

Pegrum, B. V. (1972). The application of certain traffic management techniques and their effect on road safety. Proceedings of the National Road Safety Symposium (pp. 277-286). Department of Shipping and Transport, Perth, Western Australia (as cited by Retting *et al.*, 2003).

Percer, J. (2009). Child pedestrian safety education: Applying learning and developmental theories to develop safe street-crossing behaviors. National Highway Traffic Safety Administration Report HS 811 190. U.S. Department of Transportation, Washington, DC.

Polus, A. and A. Katz (1978). An analysis of nighttime pedestrian accidents at specially illuminated crosswalks. *Accid. Anal. Prev.*, *10*, 223-228.

Pooley, C. G., D. Horton, G. Scheldeman, C. Mullen, T. Jones, M. Tight, A. Jopson and A. Chisholm (2013). Policies for promoting walking and cycling in England: A view from the street. *Transport Policy*, *27*, 66-72.

Posner, J. C., E. Liao, F. K. Winston, A. Cnaan, K. N. Shaw and D. R. Durbin (2002). Exposure to traffic among urban children injured as pedestrians. *Inj. Prev.*, *8*(3), 231-235.

Poulter, D. R. and F. P. McKenna (2007). Is speeding a "real" antisocial behavior? A comparison with other antisocial behaviors. *Accid. Anal. Prev.*, *39*, 384-389.

Retting, R. A., S. A. Ferguson and A. T. McCartt (2003). A review of evidence-based traffic engineering measures designed to reduce pedestrian–motor vehicle crashes. *Am. J. Pub. Health*, *93*(9), 1456–1463.

Retting, R. A. and R. Van Houten (2000). Safety benefits of advance stop lines at signalized intersections: Results of a field evaluation. *ITE J.*, *70*, 47-54.

Richmond, S. A., A. R. Willan, L. Rothman, A. Camden, R. Buliung, C. Macarthur and A. Howard (2014). The impact of pedestrian countdown signals on pedestrian-motor vehicle collisions: A reanalysis of data from a quasi-experimental study. *Inj. Prev.*, *20*(3), 155-158.

Rivara, F. P. (1990). Child pedestrian injuries in the United States. *AJDC*, *144*, 692-696.

Roberts, I., R. Norton and R. Jackson (1995). Driveway-related child pedestrian injuries: A case-control study. *Pediatrics*, *95*(3), 405-408.

Roper, V. J. and E. A. Howard (1938). Seeing with motor car headlamps. *Trans. Illum. Eng. Soc.*, *33*(5), 417-438.

Rosén, E., J. E. Källhammer, D. Eriksson, M. Nentwich, R. Fredriksson and K. Smith (2010). Pedestrian injury mitigation by autonomous braking. *Accid. Anal. Prev.*, *42*(6), 1949-1957.

Rosén, E., H. Stigson and U. Sander (2011). Literature review of pedestrian fatality risk as a function of car impact speed. *Accid. Anal. Prev.*, *43*(1), 25-33.

Rosenbloom, T., R. Mandel, Y. Rosner and E. Eldror (2015). Hazard perception test for pedestrians. *Accid. Anal. Prev.*, *79*, 160-169.

Routledge, D. A., R. Repetto-Write and C. I. Howarth (1976). The development of road crossing skill by child pedestrians. Proceedings of the International Conference on Pedestrian Safety. Michlol, Haifa, Israel.

Sandels, S. (1975). *Children in Traffic*. Elek Books, London.

Sanocki, T., M. Islam, J. K. Doyon and C. Lee (2015). Rapid scene perception with tragic consequences: Observers miss perceiving vulnerable road users, especially in crowded traffic scenes. *Atten. Percept. Psychophys.*, 1-11.

SARTRE (2004). European drivers and road risk, Part 1: Report on principal analyses, 49-71. Institut National de Recherche sur les Transports et leur Securite (INRETS), Arcueil, France.

Sayer, J. R. and M. L. Mefford (2004). High visibility safety apparel and nighttime conspicuity of pedestrians in work zones. *J. Safe. Res.*, *35*, 537-546.

Schieber, F. (1992). Aging and the senses. In: *Handbook of Mental Health and Aging*. (J. E. Birren, R. Sloan and G. Cohen eds.), pp. 251-306. Academic Press, New York.

Schieber, R. A. and N. J. Thompson (1996). Developmental risk factors for childhood pedestrian injuries. *Inj. Prev.*, *2*, 228-236.

Schieber, R. A. and M. E. Vegega (eds.) (2002). Reducing childhood pedestrian injuries: Summary of a multidisciplinary conference. *Inj. Prev.*, 8(Suppl 1): i1-i10.

Schwebel, D. C., D. Stavrinos, K. W. Byington, T. Davis, E. E. O'Neal and D. de Jong (2012). Distraction and pedestrian safety: How talking on the phone, texting, and listening to music impact crossing the street. *Accid. Anal. Prev.*, *45*, 266-271.

Scialfa, C. T., P. M. Garvey, R. A. Tyrrell and H. W. Leibowitz (1992). Age differences in dynamic contrast thresholds. *J. Gerontol. Psychologic. Sci.*, *47*, 172-175.

Scopatz, R. A. and Y. Zhou (2016). Effect of electronic device use on pedestrian safety: A literature review. National Highway Traffic Safety Administration Report No. DOT HS 812 256. U.S. Department of Transportation, Washington, DC.

Sentinella, J. and M. Keigan (2005). Young adolescent pedestrians' and cyclists' road deaths: Analysis of police accident files. Report TRL620. Transport Research Laboratory, Crowthorne, UK.

Sheppard, D. and M. Pattinson (1986). Interviews with elderly pedestrians involved in road crashes. TRRL report RR 98. Transportation Road Research Laboratory, Crowthorne, UK.

Shinar, D. (1984). Actual versus estimated nighttime pedestrian visibility. *Ergonomics*, *27*, 863-871.

Shinar, D. (1985). Effects of expectancy, clothing reflectance, and detection criteria on nighttime pedestrian visibility. *Hum. Fact.*, *27*, 327-334.

Shinar, D. (2000). Driver accommodation of pedestrians and perception of legitimacy. Paper presented at the Conference on Road Safety in Three Continents. September 20, Pretoria, South Africa.

Shumway-Cook, A. and M. Woollacott (2000). Attentional demands and postural control: The effect of sensory context. *J Gerontol. Series A*, *55A*(1), M10-M16.

Snyder, M. G. and R. L. Knoblauch (1971). Pedestrian safety: The identification of precipitating factors and possible countermeasures. National Highway Traffic Safety Administration. Report DOT FH-11-7312. U.S. Department of Transportation, Washington, DC.

Staplin, L., K. Lococo, S. Byington and D. Harkey (2001). Highway design handbook for older drivers and pedestrians. Federal Highway Administration. Report FHWA-RD-01-103. U.S. Department of Transportation, Washington, DC.

Steinberg, L. (2004). Risk taking in adolescence: What changes and why? *Annals New York Academy Sci.*, *1021*, 1-8.

Sullivan, J. M. and M. J. Flannagan (2001). Characteristics of pedestrian risk in darkness. Report UMTRI-2001-3. University of Michigan Transportation Research Institute, Ann Arbor, Michigan.
Sullivan, J. M. and M. J. Flannagan (2002a). Some characteristics of pedestrian risk in darkness. Paper presented at the 16th Biennial Symposium on Visibility and Simulation, June 2-4, Iowa City, Iowa.
Sullivan, J. M. and M. J. Flannagan (2002b). The role of ambient light level in fatal crashes: Inferences from daylight saving time transitions. *Accid. Anal. Prev.*, *34*(4), 487-498.
Sullivan, J. M. and M. J. Flannagan (2007). Determining the potential safety benefit of improved lighting in three pedestrian crash scenarios. *Accid. Anal. Prev.*, *39*(3), 638-647.
Sun, R., X. Zhuang, C. Wu, G. Zhao and K. Zhang (2015). The estimation of vehicle speed and stopping distance by pedestrians crossing streets in a naturalistic traffic environment. *Transportation Res. F*, *30*, 97-106.
Tapiro, H., A. Meir, Y. Parmet and T. Oron-Gilad (2013). Visual search strategies of child-pedestrians in road crossing tasks. Proceedings of the Annual Meeting of the Human Factors and Ergonomics Society – Europe.
Tapiro, H., T. Oron-Gilad and Y. Parmet (2016). Cell phone conversations and child pedestrian's crossing behavior: A simulator study. *Safety Science*, *89*, 36-44.
Tefft, B. C. (2013). Impact speed and a pedestrian's risk of severe injury or death. *Accid. Anal. Prev.*, *50*, 871-878.
Thompson, L. L., F. P. Rivara, R. C. Ayyagari and B. E. Ebel (2013). Impact of social and technological distraction on pedestrian crossing behaviour: An observational study. *Inj. Prev.*, *19*(4), 232-237.
Tobey, H. N., E. M. Shunamen and R. L. Knoblauch (1983). Pedestrian trip making characteristics and exposure measures. Federal Highway Administration. Report DTFH61-81-C-00020. U.S. Department of Transportation, Washington, DC.
Tractinsky, N. and D. Shinar (2008). Are we more likely to bump into things while speaking on a cell phone? CHI'08 Extended Abstracts on Human Factors in Computing Systems (pp. 2433-2442). ACM.
Turner, S. A., A. P. Roozenburg and T. Francis (2006). Predicting accident rates for cyclists and pedestrians. Land Transport New Zealand Research Report 289. 180 pp.
Tuttle, S. J., J. R. Sayer and M. L. Buonarosa (2009). The conspicuity of first-responder safety garments. *J. Safety Res.*, *40*(3), 191-196.
Tyrrell, R. A., C. W. Patton and J. O. Brooks (2004a). Educational interventions successfully reduce pedestrians' overestimates of their own nighttime visibility. *Hum. Fact.*, *46*(1), 170-182.
Tyrrell, R. A., J. M. Wood and T. P. Carberry (2004b). On-road measures of pedestrians' estimates of their own nighttime conspicuity. *J. Safe. Res.*, *35*, 483-490.
Tyrrell, R. A., J. M. Wood, A. Chaparro, T. P. Carberry, B. S. Chu and R. P. Marszalek (2009). Seeing pedestrians at night: Visual clutter does not mask biological motion. *Accid. Anal. Prev.*, *41*(3), 506-512.

Van Houten, R. (1992). The influence of signs prompting motorists to yield before marked crosswalks on motor vehicle-pedestrian conflicts at crosswalks with flashing amber. *Accid. Anal. Prev.*, *24*(3), 217-225.

Vanlaar, W., H. McAteer, S. Brown, S. R. McFaull and J. Crain (2013, August). Involvement of alcohol and drugs in crashes with vulnerable road users in Canada. 20th International Conference on Alcohol, Drugs and Traffic Safety (T2013), Brisbane, Australia.

Wagner, E. (2010). Watching out for senior walkers. *Public Roads*, *73*(5), 11.

WHO (2004). *World report on road traffic injury prevention* (M. Peden, R. Scurfield, D. Sleet et al., eds.). World Health Organization, Geneva. http://www.who.int/world-health-day/2004/infomaterials/world_report/en/index.html

WHO (2013). *Pedestrian safety: A road safety manual for decision-makers and practitioners*. World Health Organization, Geneva, Switzerland. http://www.who.int/roadsafety/projects/manuals/pedestrian/en/

Wood, J., A. Chaparro, T. Carberry and B. S. Chu (2010). Effect of simulated visual impairment on nighttime driving performance. *Optometry & Vis. Sci.*, *87*(6), 379-386.

Wood, J. M., R. A. Tyrrell, A. Chaparro, R. P. Marszalek, T. P. Carberry and B. S. Chu (2012). Even moderate visual impairments degrade drivers' ability to see pedestrians at night. *Invest. Opthal. & Visual Sci.*, *53*(6), 2586-2592.

Xiong, H., L. Xiong, X. Deng and W. Wang (2014). Evaluation of the impact of pedestrian countdown signals on crossing behavior. *Adv. Mech. Eng.*, 2014. Article ID 518295, 7 pages. http://dx.doi.org/10.1155/2014/518295

Yang, J., W. Deng, J. Wang, Q. Li and Z. Wang (2006). Modeling pedestrians road crossing behavior in traffic system micro-simulation in China. *Transportation Res. A*, *40*, 280-290.

Zegeer, C. V. and M. Bushell (2012). Pedestrian crash trends and potential countermeasures from around the world. *Accid. Anal. Prev.*, *44*(1), 3-11.

Zegeer, C. V., C. T. Esse, J. R. Stewart, H. H. Huang and P. A. Lagerwey (2004). Safety analysis of marked versus unmarked crosswalks in 30 cities. *ITE J.*, January, 34-41.

Zegeer, C. V., J. R. Stewart, H. H. Huang, P. A. Lagerwey, J. Feaganes and B. J. Campbell (2005). Safety effects of marked versus unmarked crosswalks at uncontrolled locations: Final report and recommended guidelines. Federal Highway Administration. Report FHWA-HRT-04-100. U.S. Department of Transportation, Washington, DC, CAROL TAN ESSE.

Zheng, P., R. Hall and M. McDonald (2007). Pedestrian behaviour and safety in the presence of guard railing. 2nd Institution of Engineering and Technology International Conference on System Safety, October 22-24, 2007. (as cited by Cohen *et al.*, 2013).

Zhuang, X. and C. Wu (2014). Pedestrian gestures increase driver yielding at uncontrolled mid-block road crossings. *Accid. Anal. Prev.*, *70*, 235-244.

Zwahlen, H. T. (1974). Distance judgment capabilities of children and adults in a pedestrian situation. Proceedings of the 3rd International Congress of Automotive Safety, San Francisco, CA.

16

Motorcyclists and Riders of Other Powered Two-Wheelers (PTWs)

"Steelers quarterback Ben Roethlisberger, who has said he dislikes wearing a motorcycle helmet, was seriously injured in a motorcycle crash and taken to a hospital Monday. Roethlisberger was riding a motorcycle known for its speed and power, a 2005 Suzuki Hayabusa. The 24-year-old has said in the past that he prefers not to wear a helmet when riding his motorcycle. He has pointed out that Pennsylvania's 35-year-old state law requiring helmets to be worn was amended to make helmets optional. At 11:15 am a silver Chrysler New Yorker traveling in the opposite direction took a left hand turn and collided with the motorcycle, and Roethlisberger was thrown from the bike. According to one witness Roethlisberger went over his handlebars, hit the windshield of the car, and then fell to the ground." (from various news reports including CNN and AP, June 12, 2006).

"Most of the challenges associated with PTWs relate to safety, while the majority of the opportunities relate to mobility… Safety professionals see the challenges, while transport professionals and PTW enthusiasts embrace the opportunities." (Narelle Haworth, 2012).

Motorcycles are fun. Motorcycles are dangerous. Motorcycles are so dangerous, that some people would consider motorcycle safety an oxymoron. Riding a motorcycle is akin to a ride in an amusement park – with all the death defying thrills, but with very few of the safety protections. Though motorcyclists – at least male motorcyclists – perceive themselves as more masculine, motorcycle riding is associated with significantly higher than normal rates of erectile dysfunction (Ochiai *et al.*, 2006).

Table 16-1 illustrates the risk of motorcycling relative to other modes of transportation. As can be seen from this table, riding a motorcycle is by far the most dangerous means of transportation. The risk of being killed in a motorcycle crash per kilometer of travel according to the World Health Organization (WHO, 2004) is nearly 20 times that of being killed in a car crash. The numbers vary among countries – from a "low" of 5 times per kilometer traveled to a high of 25 times per kilometers travel in the EU countries (Espié, Bekiaris, and Nikolaou, 2010). The numbers also vary among specific measures of risk, but the theme is the same: motorcycles are much more dangerous to their riders than cars are to their occupants. The U.S. safety data also damn the motorcycle. In 2013, the fatality rate per 100,000 registered vehicles was 56.8 for motorcyclists versus 13.83 for car occupants. Worse still, the fatality rate per 100 million miles traveled was 23.44 for motorcycle riders versus 1.29 for car occupants (or 37.71 versus 2.08 per 100 million kilometers traveled). In other words, kilometer per kilometer (or mile per mile) of exposure a rider was more than 18 times as likely to be killed on a motorcycle as in a

Table 16-1. Deaths per 100 million passenger-kilometers and per passenger-travel hours in European Union countries for the period 2001-2002 (from WHO *et al.* 2004, p. 75, reproduced with modifications from Koornstra, 2003, with permission from the World Health Organization).

	Deaths per 100 Million Passenger Kilometers[a]	**Deaths per 100 Million Passenger-Travel Hours**[b]
Roads (total)	0.95	28
Powered two-wheelers	13.8	440
Foot	6.4	75
Cycle	5.4	25
Car	0.7	25
Bus and coach	0.07	2
Ferry	0.25	16
Air (civil aviation)	0.035	8
Rail	0.035	2

[a]Passenger-kilometers is the total distance covered by all individuals traveling in that mode.
[b]Passenger-travel hours is the total time spent by all individuals traveling in that mode.

car. In that year, motorcycles made up only 3.12 percent of all registered vehicles in the United States and accounted for only 0.7 percent of all vehicle miles traveled. But motorcycle riders accounted for 14.27 percent of the total traffic fatalities (NHTSA, 2015c). Furthermore, the death rate for riders 50+ years old has been consistently increasing since 1989 (NHTSA, 2015b). In the European Union, the data are just as alarming. There the risk of being killed per kilometer traveled while riding a powered two wheeler (a category that includes mopeds and motorcycles) is estimated to be 20 times that of driving a car (Avenoso and Beckmann, 2005; EC, 2010; WHO, 2004). Furthermore, while the overall fatality rate per kilometers of travel for all modes of transportation combined has been constantly decreasing on both sides of the ocean, this has not been the case for PTW fatalities. In the EU countries, between 1996 and 2008 fatalities have actually steadily increased by about 15 percent (EC, 2010), though the rise is mostly due to fatalities from the heavier motorcycles than the light mopeds and scooters (EC, 2013). In the U.S., the rate has remained fairly constant since 2009 (NHTSA, 2015c).

Despite these alarming statistics, the number of registered motorcycles, the engine size of the average motorcycle, and the age of the average rider are all constantly and sharply increasing both in the U.S. and in Europe, with more and more older people buying bigger and bigger motorcycles (Huang and Preston, 2004; Ministerio del Interior Spain, 2007; Paulozzi, 2005; Shankar and Varghese, 2006). The unsettling trends in motorcycling fatalities and injuries are in sharp contrast to the steady decline in car-related fatalities, both in the U.S. and in Europe. In addition, the proportion of motorcycle fatalities relative to driver fatalities is on the rise in the Western world (Grzebieta, 2014; Haworth, 2012). If these trends continue, and current projections are that they will, then the incidence and rates of motorcycle fatalities will surely keep increasing.

The only silver lining in the discussion of motorcycle or powered two-wheel vehicle safety is that their numbers and use are still very very low. In the EU countries, their frequency of use is very far below that of the favorite means of transportation: the personal car. Based on an October 2014 survey of 500 adults in each of the 28 EU countries (Eurobarometer, 2014), 54 percent reported that the mode of transport they use most often is the car and only 2 percent reported they use a "motorbike or moped" most often (from 0 percent in Bulgaria, the Czech Republic, Finland, and Sweden to 7 percent in Italy and 9 percent in Greece). Across these countries the main users of PTWs are men, under 25 year old, and students. The primary reasons given for this choice are convenience and speed. Thus, in Europe at least, the PTW appears to be mostly a practical and inexpensive temporary solution to mobility.

Speed and Injury

Motorcyclists' vulnerability is somewhere between that of a car occupant who is protected by the shell of the car, the seatbelt, and air bags, and a pedestrian who is totally exposed. In an analysis of a weighted sample of 30,000 single-vehicle fixed-object collisions that occurred in the U.S. in the years 2000-2009, Bambach, Grzebieta, Olivier, and McIntosh (2011) evaluated the probability of fatality as a function of speed at impact with different objects. Based on logistic regression models, they provide risk curves for various types of single-vehicle collisions. Some of their curves are reproduced in Figure 16-1 and can be compared to those in Chapter 9 for car drivers and those in Chapter 15 for pedestrians. Although this is a laudable effort to quantify fatality risk of motorcycling as a function of speed, these functions should be treated with caution. To begin, the weighted sample is based on an actual sample of only 751 crashes, and the confidence limits around these curves are extremely wide. For example, at 175 km/hr the average probability of fatality from collision with a barrier is approximately 0.6, but the 90th percentile confidence limits are from under 0.4 to over 0.8. Also, an inexplicable finding in their analysis was that helmets reduce the probability of fatality – but only up to a speed of 145 km/hr. At higher speeds, helmet use is actually associated with a greater likelihood of fatality. Thus, the poor reliability of the average risk coupled with inexplicable findings indicate that more data (and possibly better data) are needed for truly reliable and valid risk functions.

Definition of a Motorcycle and a Powered Two-Wheeler (PTW)

The term motorcycle is often used to denote all motorized two-wheel motor vehicles, also known as powered two-wheelers (PTWs). We typically distinguish among four PTW categories on the basis of their engine size and design speed: heavy motorcycles

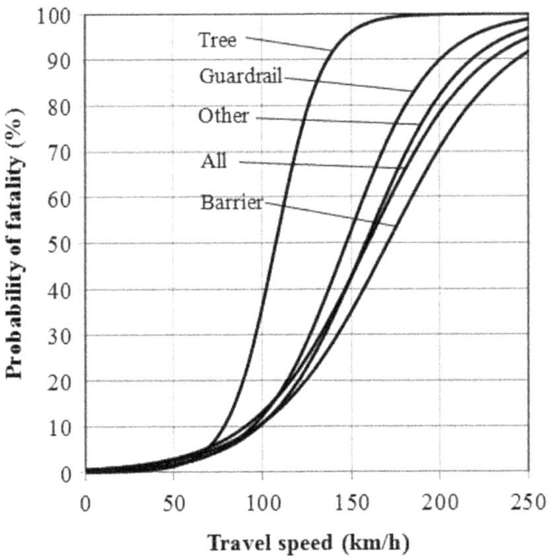

Figure 16-1. Fatality risk for motorcyclists infixed object collisions (from Bambach *et al.*, 2011). Reprinted by permission of the Southeastern Transportation Center, http://www.stc.utk.edu.

(over 125 cc engine), light motorcycles and scooters (under 125 cc engine displacement), mopeds (50 cc, with speed limit of 45 km/hr), and mofas (small mopeds with speed limit of 25 km/hr) (ACEM, 2004; EC, 2013; Otte, Jänsch, and Wiese, 2013). However, the different types of PTWs also differ in their actual speeds on the roads, purpose of use, conditions of use, geographic locations, and their users (Haworth, 2012). For example, among the full-size motorcycles, the Supersport motorcycles have the highest engine power/weight ratio, the highest accelerations and speeds and – not surprisingly – the highest rate of fatalities per registered vehicles (IIHS, 2011). We often think of motorcycles as dangerous and fun to ride on country roads, and of mopeds and scooters as inexpensive and practical to ride in congested urban traffic. Because they are used in different environments, and by people with different needs and skills, who operate them at different speeds, their safety is quite different. For example, Zambon and Hasselberg (2006b), using Swedish motorcycle crash injury data, showed that the risk of severe injury or fatality is higher for rural crashes (where the speed limit is >50 km/hr) than for urban crashes (where the speed limit is $\leq$50 km/hr), and it is also higher for motorcycles with engine size of 125 + cc than for motorcycles and mopeds with smaller engines. In general, the injury severity increases with the engine size and the design speed, and with the power/weight ratio of the PTW (Otte, Jänsch, and Wiese, 2014).

Despite the significant difference between the two types of PTWs, studies of PTW safety and PTW crash data do not always distinguish between the smaller and larger PTWs. For example, The U.S. Federal Highway Administration labels motorcycles as all two or three-wheeled motorized vehicles, including motorcycles, motor scooters, mopeds, motor-powered bicycles, and three-wheel motorcycles. In contrast, the European Union terminology restricts the term motorcycles to the heavy PTWs. Consequently, in comparing U.S. and European data on motorcycle safety we are often comparing "apples and oranges" (in U.S. data) with "oranges" alone (in EU data).

Characteristics and Primary Causes of PTW Crashes

Far less research has been devoted to the causes of PTW crashes than to the causes of crashes of passenger cars. Given the obvious differences between the vehicles, their users, and the road conditions in which the two types of vehicles are used, it is questionable – if not downright wrong – to extrapolate from one to the other. Therefore, to understand the causes of PTW crashes we must investigate them directly. Over the years, several studies have examined the causes of PTW crashes (ACEM, 2004; Clarke *et al.*, 2004, 2007; Haworth *et al.*, 1997; Hurt, Ouellet, and Thom, 1981; Newman and Webster, 1974; Otte *et al.*, 1998, 2014; Pedder, Hurt, and Otte, 1979; Vis, 1995; see also EC, 2013). Three studies stand out in their scope and detail. The first, known as the Hurt study, was conducted in Los Angeles California in the late 1970s (Hurt *et al.*, 1981). The second study, known as MAIDS (Motorcycle Accident In-Depth Study), was done at the turn of this century in Europe (ACEM, 2004). A common positive feature of both studies is that they combined the benefits of clinical causation analysis with statistical exposure analysis (see Chapter 18). Thus, the two studies have both statistical rigor and clinical insights. Because of the central role of the two studies in our understanding of PTW crash causation, they both warrant brief descriptions of their scope and methods. The third study, GIDAS (Otte *et al.*, 2014), analyzed and compared the crash causes of cars, light motorcycles, and heavy motorcycles in Germany, but did not have an exposure sample of drivers and riders that were not involved in crashes.

In-depth studies of PTW crashes: the Hurt, MAIDS, and GIDAS studies

The MAIDS (ACEM, 2004) was conducted in a coordinated effort by multi-disciplinary research teams in five European countries (France, Germany, Italy, the Netherlands, and Spain). The teams investigated and analyzed a total of 921 crashes involving two-wheeled motor vehicles during the years 1999-2000, all using the same investigative and reporting protocol. The accidents studied were those that occurred in five geographic regions – one region in each of the participating countries – and the analysis of each crash included a detailed reconstruction of the scene of the crash, a post-crash examination of the vehicles involved, interviews with the riders, drivers, and occupants, and reviews of crash-related medical records. Approximately 50 photographs were taken and approximately 2000(!) variables were coded for each crash. When data collection for a given case was completed, the team met to discuss it and to decide on the causal factors that contributed to the crash. In addition to the accident data, the MAIDS researchers also collected data on a random sample of 923 control PTW riders. This was done in order to determine if specific characteristics associated with accident vehicles and riders, were over- or under-involved in crashes relative to the control PTWs and riders. The control riders were sampled in equal numbers from the different regions by interviewing riders and inspecting their PTW in petrol stations in the same geographic regions. Thus, the control cases were not individually matched to the accident cases in terms of the exact times and places. However, the technique used in the study enabled the researchers to collect more detailed information than would have been practical had they attempted to stop riders in the traffic stream (as was done by Blomberg *et al.*, 2004, and Compton and Berning, 2015, in the case-control crash evaluation study for alcohol crash risks. See chapter 11).

The earlier study, by Hurt *et al.* (1981), used a similar approach with a similar sized sample of crashes, except that in this study the control group consisted of over 2,000 PTWs and they were sampled from the traffic stream at the same time-of-day, day-of-week, and environmental conditions as their matched crash cases. On the other hand, the amount of data obtained on each crash and control case was much less than in the MAIDS study, and the data collection was limited to one urban site (Los Angeles). Another significant difference between the two studies was the population of motorcycles. Over the past 40 years, motorcycles engine size increased significantly. Yet even in 1980, in the American exposure sample 75 percent of the motorcycles had engine displacement of 251 cc's or more; whereas in the European exposure sample, a quarter of a century later, 39 percent were mopeds with engine displacement of 50 cc's or less. Thus, although both studies examined powered two-wheelers, the vehicles studied (and most likely the riders too) were quite different. Despite these differences and the differences in time and place, it is interesting to compare the results of these two extensive studies in order to appreciate both the commonalities – that transcend time, PTW type, and culture – and differences in their findings.

The basic situation in which most of the PTW crashes occurred was quite similar in both studies. The majority of accidents occurred in daylight (75 percent in the Hurt study and 73 percent in MAIDS), and in clear weather (84 percent and 90 percent, respectively). The most common type of crash – characteristic of approximately three quarters of all crashes – was one involving a collision with another vehicle (75 percent in the Hurt study and 80 percent in MAIDS). It is not surprising that the most frequent vehicles with which the PTWs collided were passenger cars (65 percent in Los Angeles and 60 percent in the EU), and that approximately 50 percent of the crashes occurred at intersections – where conflicts with other vehicles are most likely to occur (67 percent in Los Angeles and 54 percent in the EU). In this context, it is important to note that both studies were based on representative samples of police-reported crashes, and neither study focused on fatal crashes. This is important because fatal crashes have slightly different characteristics than less severe crashes. For example, in the U.S. in 2005 forty-nine percent of the fatal crashes did not involve another motor vehicle, compared to 35 percent of the crashes that resulted in property damage only (NHTSA, 2005). The most common type of fatal motorcycle crash is a "run off the road" crash involving only the rider, often at night and with alcohol impairment (Preusser, Williams, and Ulmer, 1995). One reason for the difference between the two types of crashes is that fatal crashes are more typical of high speed rural riding than of low speed congested urban riding (ACEM, 2004).

The role of human, environmental, and vehicular factors in PTW crash causation

The most interesting aspects of the two studies and the GIDAS analysis are the causes of the crashes that they uncovered. Despite some differences in definitions and categorizations, it is possible and worthwhile to compare the Los Angeles data collected in the late 1970s with the European data collected in the early 2000s, and to a lesser extent with the German data collected mostly in the first decade of this century. The principal crash causes in the two studies are listed in Table 16-2. Note that in both studies only one principal cause was listed for each accident, though it is generally acknowledged that many (often most) crashes are caused by the joint occurrence of two or more events.

The results are strikingly – and surprisingly – similar, with the overwhelming majority of the crash causes being driver and/or rider failures. When the data distinguished between the two (ACEM, 2004; Hurt *et al.*, 1981), the main cause of the crashes was the behavior of the driver of the other vehicle, followed by the behavior of the PTW rider. Similar findings were obtained in a British motorcycle causation study where in accidents involving a collision with another vehicle, the motorcycle rider was culpable in less than 20 percent of the accidents (Clarke *et al.*, 2004). When the causes attributed to the rider and to the driver are combined, it is obvious that in nearly all crashes the predominant

Table 16-2. Principal causes of powered two-wheel crashes in the Los Angeles study (Hurt *et al.*, 1981), the European study (ACEM, 2004), and the German study (GIDAS, Otte *et al.*, 2013).

Primary Causal Factor	**Percent Cases – Hurt *et al.* (1981)**	**Percent Cases – ACEM (2004)**	**Percent Cases – GIDAS (2013)[a]**
Rider	41	37	91.4 (combined)
Driver of other vehicle	51	50	
Roadway defect	2	8	16.8
Vehicle defect	3	1	2.7
Others	3	4	
Total	100	100	

[a]In GIDAS all human causes were pooled, and the report combined both driver and rider errors. Also, a crash could be coded as due to a combination of human and other causes, hence the total percent causes exceeds 100.

cause is a human failure – accounting for approximately 90 percent of all crashes. This statistic is nearly identical to the one obtained in crash causation analyses of accidents of all motor vehicles (see Chapter 18), and in the more recent GIDAS analysis of PTW accidents in Germany (Otte *et al.*, 2014). Also, as in the case of crashes in general, environmental factors are more common than vehicular failures, the latter being quite rare as the principal cause of a crash.

Human Causes of PTW Crashes

A detailed breakdown of the specific human factors that precipitated the crashes in MAIDS is provided in Table 16-3. The causes are grouped into the four human information processing mechanisms used in information processing models of driver behavior (see Chapter 3).

The table reveals a very sharp distinction among the different potential human failures. By far, the most common cause of all crashes is the failure of the driver to attend to and perceive the PTW in time to avoid the crash. The implication is that in 37 percent of the crashes the PTW rider behaved appropriately (because only one cause is cited per crash) and the driver was both obliged to give the PTW the right-of-way and had sufficient time to do so. The primary role of the other driver in failing to give right-of-way has also been noted by other studies, more limited in their scope or depth (Clarke *et al.*, 2007; EC, 2013). The example of Roethlisberger at the beginning of this chapter is an

Table 16-3. Percent of primary crash-causing human errors attributed to the riders and the drivers in the MAIDS (ACEM, 2004).

Primary Human Failure	Percent Cases – Riders	Percent Cases – Drivers
Perception/attention	11.9	36.5
Comprehension	3.6	1.4
Decision	13.0	9.9
Reaction	5.5	0.2
Other	2.9	2.4
Total	37.1	50.4

apparent case in point. In MAIDS, the driver failed to notice the PTW approximately three times as often as the cyclist failed to see the car. In the Hurt study, the driver failed to see the cyclist twice as often as the cyclist failed to see the car. Furthermore, Hurt *et al.* (1981) found that in 65 percent of the crashes the rider had the right-of-way but the driver of the other vehicle failed to give it.

Two different, but interrelated reasons can account for drivers' failures to perceive the motorcyclist in time: inattention on the part of the driver to the traffic situation in general and to the rider in particular, and difficulty in perceiving the rider and PTW despite attention to the traffic. Given the smaller size of the PTW and its lower conspicuity, the latter explanation seems quite plausible. Support for the latter reason comes from several studies. A naturalistic driving study conducted in Japan found that drivers making a right turn (equivalent to a left turn in most countries) while a motorcyclist is approaching, concentrate their gaze on their projected turning pass once they initiate the turn, thus reducing the chance of detecting the motorcyclist as he or she approaches from the left (Uchida *et al.*, 2010). Clarke *et al.* (2004, 2007) analyzed 1,003 UK police reports of motorcycle accidents and also found that in a car-motorcycle collision the primary cause was the driver's failure to detect the rider in time (or at all). In general, in 81 percent of the right-of-way collisions, it was the driver who "looked but did not see" the rider and failed to give the right-of-way. Further analysis of these crashes showed that they were particularly characteristics of older drivers at T-junctions. Detecting the approaching rider in these intersections requires head movements – a trivial action for young drivers but a significant effort for older drivers. In contrast, in motorcycle crashes in bends or curves, the rider was most often at fault, the cause was attributed to "loss of control," and the rider was young and inexperienced (30 years old on the average with 5.3 years of riding experience).

Another indication that the problem is most likely a perceptual one and not a decision one – that is, due to failure in detection – comes from laboratory experiments by Crundall, Humphrey, and Clarke (2008). In their study, they presented viewers with pictures of traffic scenes that contained either an approaching car or an approaching motorcycle at the same distance from the viewer. When the pictures were presented briefly, for only 0.25 seconds, and the approaching vehicle was far the likelihood of detecting the car was approximately 50 percent greater than the likelihood of detecting the motorcycle. But when the pictures were presented for a longer duration and the viewer had to decide whether it is safe or not to pull out in front of the approaching vehicle there were no differences between motorcycles and cars that were at the same physical distance from the camera. Finally, in an in-depth analysis of the MAIDS data Comelli *et al.* (2008) calculated the odds ratio of a collision with another vehicle relative to various rider and motorcycle features. For the comparison group, the researchers noted the presence or absence of the same features in motorcycles in the traffic stream at the same time-of-day and locations as the crash-involved vehicles. They found that in crashes identified by the original MAIDS investigators as due to failures in the drivers' perception/attention the odds ratio of a crash was only 0.2 if the motorcyclist had bright clothing and a bright helmet. This suggested to the researchers that the bright colors increase the motorcyclists' conspicuity and therefore reduced their likelihood of not being detected by the driver. Unfortunately, the information about the helmet and clothing brightness and the assessment that poor perception/inattention were the causes of the crashes were based on subjective impressions of the investigators. More objective analyses of the role of conspicuity (see below) indicate that the issue is quite complex.

The impression that the motorcyclist is more attentive than the driver to the road and to potential hazards is supported by research. But this research also indicates that this orientation may have a cost in interacting with cars. In an interesting study, Muttart *et al.* (2011) fitted 32 drivers who also rode a motorcycle with eye tracking devices while they drove and rode on low-volumes open roads. Analyses of the eye movements showed that when they rode the motorcycle they directed more glances toward the pavement but were less likely to make last glances toward the direction of most threatening traffic before turning than when they drove the car. As riders they were also less likely to come to complete stops at stop signs when approaching intersections. The findings are especially telling because each participant served as both a rider and a driver, demonstrating an attitudinal shift in risk taking between the two roles, rather than reflecting different personal levels in risk taking. Additional information about riders' strategies in scanning their environment in different traffic scenarios comes from a small study conducted in real traffic on urban and inter-urban roads in Greece, but the study collected data on only three riders and thus it is only exploratory (Nathanael *et al.*, 2012).

The most recent motorcycle crash analysis study – based on the German In-depth Accident Study (GIDAS) – assessed and compared the human causes of crashes involving 163 riders of PTW < 125 cc, 177 riders of PTW > 125 cc, and 2,942 car drivers. All the crashes occurred in the 12-year period from 1999 to 2011 in the districts of Dresden and Hannover, Germany. The human causal category labels were somewhat different than those given above for the Hurt and MAIDS study but they reflect highly similar involvement of the different mechanisms involved in the human information processing and vehicle handling chain. The main results are summarized in Figure 16-2. Unlike the previous studies, the disaggregation of light and heavy PTWs indicates that their crash

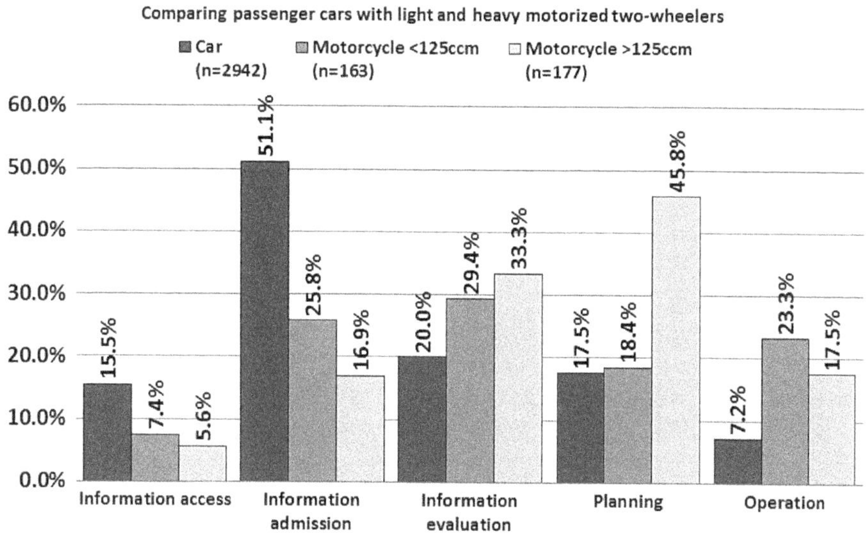

Figure 16-2. Percent involvement of the principal human causes of crashes of car drivers and PTW riders in the GIDAS 1999-2011 data (from Otte *et al.*, 2013, 2014, with permission of the author).

causes differ. In the case of smaller PTWs, most of the riders' failures were due to inattention (26 percent – labeled "information admission") and miscomprehension of the situation (29 percent – labeled "information evaluation"), whereas the riders of the heavy PTWs mostly made decision errors (33 percent – labeled "information evaluation") and poor "planning" mostly in speed choice (46 percent). In contrast, more than half of the drivers' failures (15.5 + 51.1 percent) were due to inattention and misperception (Otte *et al.*, 2013, 2014). Thus, all three studies highlight the primary role of the driver's recognition failures in detecting the cyclists.

Because of differences in the coding and assessment schemes of the Hurt study, the MAIDS study, and the GIDAS study, it is impossible to provide a table that directly compares the relative role of specific human causes in the three studies. Nonetheless, whenever comparisons can be made, they are noted in the discussion below. This is done with respect to failures in attention, problems with the rider conspicuity, the contribution of inadequate skills and reactions to imminent dangers, and the role of alcohol.

Inattention in crashes

Inattention is a commonly cited crash cause in all motor-vehicle accident analyses. The reason is that it is very difficult to continuously attend to all the relevant cues for prolonged periods of time. This general problem is discussed in detail in Chapter 3, and specifically as it relates to crashes in Chapter 18. Inattention is much more dangerous for PTW riders than for car drivers. In their analysis, Hurt *et al.* (1981) identified problems in the motorcyclist's attention in 40.9 percent of the crashes. Most often (in 21.9 percent of the crashes), the inattention could be attributed to a specific source of distraction (other traffic, 12.6 percent; non-traffic items, 5.1 percent; and distraction from the motorcycle itself, 4.2 percent). However, in 19 percent of the crashes the reason for the inattention could not be determined. Despite greater attention to the road that is needed for motorcycling than for driving, lack of attention for reasons such as pre-occupation or mind wandering is not rare because the riding and driving tasks typically do not demand all of our attention, and therefore we rarely devote all of our attentional capacity to the riding/driving task. Unfortunately, Hurt *et al.* did not report the frequencies of inattention on the part of the drivers of the non-PTW vehicles. However, a direct comparison between riders and drivers of the frequencies in which inattention was a cause of the crash could be made in MAIDS and in GIDAS. In MAIDS, inattention (including "distractions and stress") was noted for only 10.6 percent of the riders, but for 18.4 percent of the drivers. In the GIDAS analyses, inattention as a crash cause was attributed to 17 percent for the heavy PTWs and 26 percent for the lighter ones, but to 50 percent of the car drivers. In both studies, this is a difference of approximately 100 percent in the relative risk associated with this factor; and it indicates that riders, in general, are much more attentive to their riding than drivers of other (more stable) vehicles. This should not be surprising to anyone who has ridden a motorcycle, because riding requires much more attention to the road surface and to the traffic than driving.

Recently, Penumaka *et al.* (2014) conducted a more detailed analysis of 245 MAIDS collisions that did not involve mofas (motorized bikes with max speed of 25 km/hr), mechanical failures of the PTW, impairment of the rider, and primary or contributing cause consisting of a vehicle/environmental factor. In short, they analyzed the collisions that were strictly attributed to human errors and failures of unimpaired riders. They distinguished among attention/perception, comprehension, and execution errors and examined their nature and frequency in various collision configurations. Although the relative frequencies varied among the different collision configurations, in general they too found that drivers had mostly perception and comprehension failures while PTW riders typically made perception and execution failures. This analysis again highlights the poor visibility and low conspicuity of the riders on the one hand, and the potential in training riders in crash avoidance techniques; for example, in coordinated braking with both brakes.

An additional insight into the role of rider inattention in crash avoidance is provided by an analysis of the association between crash involvement and riders' responses to a Motorcycle Rider Behavior Questionnaire (MRBQ) that was developed by Elliott, Baughan, and Sexton (2007) to provide a tool for assessing rider behavior style. The questionnaire is patterned after and similar to Reason *et al.*'s (1990) Driver Behavior Questionnaire (see Chapter 9), but it includes items specific to motorcycle riding such as engaging in stunts, speeding in corners to the point of nearly losing control, and "lane splitting" (riding between two lanes). A factor analysis of the 43-item MRBQ revealed that the questions can be grouped into five independent dimensions: traffic errors, control errors, speed violations, performance of stunts, and use of safety equipment. Together these factors accounted for 41 percent of variance among the 8,666 British riders who completed the questionnaire. This factor structure is quite different from that obtained with drivers responding to the Driver Behavior Questionnaire, where the principal factors are violations, errors, and lapses (see Chapter 3). In their analysis of the relationship between self-reported crash frequencies and the answers of the motorcyclists to the MRBQ, Elliott *et al.* (2007) found that only "traffic errors" were significantly associated with crash frequencies. However, an examination of the items that make up the category of "traffic errors" reveals that it is a misnomer because items associated with that factor are actually statements about attention lapses. These include "Fail to notice that pedestrians are crossing when turning into a side street from a main road," "Not notice someone stepping out from behind a parked vehicle until it is nearly too late," "Not notice a pedestrian waiting to cross at a zebra crossing, or a pelican crossing that has just turned red," "Pull out on to a main road in front of a vehicle that you had not noticed, or whose speed you have misjudged," "Miss 'Give Way' signs and narrowly avoid colliding with traffic having the right of way," "Fail to notice or anticipate that another vehicle might pull out in front of you and have difficulty stopping," "Queuing to turn left on a main road, you pay such close attention to the main traffic that you nearly hit the vehicle in front," "Distracted or pre-occupied, you belatedly realise that the vehicle in front has slowed and you have to brake hard to avoid a collision," and "Attempt to overtake someone that you had not noticed to be signalling a right turn." Thus, although motorcycle riding is often associated with risk taking, risk taking may actually be less relevant to riders' crash involvement than inattention to the surrounding traffic.

Rider and cycle conspicuity

Difficulties in timely perception of the rider – even for an attentive driver – are typically due to the poor conspicuity of the PTW and its rider. For one thing, they are much smaller than cars and trucks, and consequently can sometimes be totally obscured by other vehicles or by blind areas in the driver's field of view. In the GIDAS analysis, this was the reason behind 15.5 percent of the collisions. For another thing, their form in the driver's field of view is less regular and less continuous – and not a simple box-like object as that of cars. Thus, the only means a rider has of increasing his or her conspicuity is by increasing his or her contrast relative to the background. This is typically done by turning on the headlights (DRL – Daytime Running Lights) or wearing bright highly reflective clothing and a helmet. Relative to these factors, Hurt *et al.* (1981) rated the conspicuity of the PTW as "low" or "completely inconspicuous" in 46.0 percent of the cases. In contrast, the "other vehicles" colliding with the PTWs – mostly cars and trucks that are larger, have a regular shape, and relatively uniform color – were rated as such in only 5.2 percent of the cases. Relative to riding with daytime running lights, the odds ratio of crash involvement for riding without daytime running lights was 3.4; meaning that riding without lights was more than three times as prevalent in the crash sample as it was in the exposure sample. Similar effects of DRL on the enhancement of conspicuity and improvement in detectability – especially at long distances – were obtained by Law *et al.* (2016). Returning to the Hurt study, even more striking was the effect of the rider's upper torso clothing. Only two riders (1.8 percent) in the accident sample had a "high visibility upper torso garment" compared to 30 percent in the exposure sample. Notably, helmet color did not differ significantly between the crash and the exposure samples. In addition to enabling earlier detection, DRL also seem to improve gap judgment in the sense that drivers intending to turn in front of an oncoming motorcycle are less likely to accept short gaps when the motorcycle has the lights on (Mitsopoulos-Rubens and Lenné, 2012).

In the MAIDS, the researchers examined the conspicuity of the PTWs and other vehicles against their background as viewed from the perspectives of the driver and rider, respectively. They found that the background had a "negative effect on conspicuity" of the PTW in 14.4 percent of the collisions, but had a "negative effect on conspicuity" of the "other vehicle" in only 5.6 percent of the crashes in which there were other vehicles in the riders' line of sight. Thus, conspicuity problems were much more prevalent for the crash-involved PTW riders than for the crash-involved cars and trucks drivers. In summary, although conducted over 20 years apart, on different rider and driver populations, using different measures of effectiveness, the results of both studies demonstrate the very important role of conspicuity – or its absence – in causing PTW crashes.

The lack of conspicuity is most critical in situations in which the car driver fails to yield the right-of-way to the motorcycle. In an analysis of 259 collisions in the Netherlands, Vis (1995) found that in 81 percent of the collisions the PTW had the right-of-way, yet in 50 percent of these collisions the car drivers claimed that they did not see the PTW at all, and in another 20 percent the drivers said that they saw the PTW when it was already too late to stop. This is in contrast to the PTW riders who said they saw the other vehicle in time in 70 percent of the cases... but still entered its path, knowing they had the right-of-way and assuming they had been seen. Hurt, Ouellet, and Thom (1981) also noted that in 51 percent of their crashes the precipitating accident factor was failure of the other drivers to yield right-of-way to the motorcyclists, presumably because they failed to see them. Finally, Clarke *et al.* (2004) noted that in 65 percent of the accidents involving a failure to yield right-of-way, the motorcyclists were not at fault, and the driver of the other vehicle failed to see the motorcycle that was in clear view. A typical example of such a collision is given in Box 16-1. This example is typical because most of these accidents occurred in uncontrolled + or T type intersections. It is also the same type of an accident cited in the beginning of this chapter (with Roethlisberger).

There is another, more subtle factor that affects the conspicuity of PTWs. That is their saliency or prevalence in the general traffic. It has been shown in many contexts that detection likelihood and detection distance are greatly influenced by expectancy. Thus, drivers can detect and respond to small targets such as pedestrians and on-road obstacles earlier and from much greater distances when they expect them than when they do not expect them (Olson and Sivak, 1986; Shinar, 1985; see also Chapter 15). With this reasoning in mind, Hancock *et al.* (1990) argued that PTWs have low cognitive conspicuity. Their rationale was that because there are significantly fewer motorcycles than cars in the traffic stream, they are much less expected to be there, and consequently much less likely to attract drivers' attention. Beanland, Lenné, and Underwood (2014), in a controlled laboratory simulation demonstrated that drivers detect motorcyclists from a greater distance when their prevalence on the road is high than when it is low, implying that prevalence generates expectation. Regardless of the underlying reason, this phenomenon of lower crash risk as prevalence increases, has been labeled "safety-in-numbers"

Box 16-1. An example of a driver failure to see a motorist in a "Right of Way Violation" accident (from Clarke *et al.*, 2004, with the permission of the Controller of HMSO and Queen's Printer for Scotland).

Story:

It was early in the afternoon on a fine spring day. The rider (M, 44) of a Honda CBR1000 motorcycle was traveling along an unclassified urban road at around the 30 mph limit. According to witnesses, he was not going above the speed limit and was displaying daytime lights. As he approached a junction ahead on the offside, he could see a Vauxhall Astra (2), driven by (F, 63) waiting to turn right at the give way line to travel in the same direction as him. As he got to within 20 meters of the junction mouth, the car driver began to emerge, making her right turn. The motorcyclist braked heavily and steered nearside in an effort to get his bike between the nearside kerb and the turning car before he hit it. However, he was unsuccessful in this, and he hit the nearside of the car as it turned, causing a severe injury to his right hand that required two operations and several months off work. The Astra driver claimed that she had looked left, but had simply not seen the motorcyclist, despite the fact that visibility was good and the rider was displaying lights. She was charged with driving without due care and attention.

Diagram:

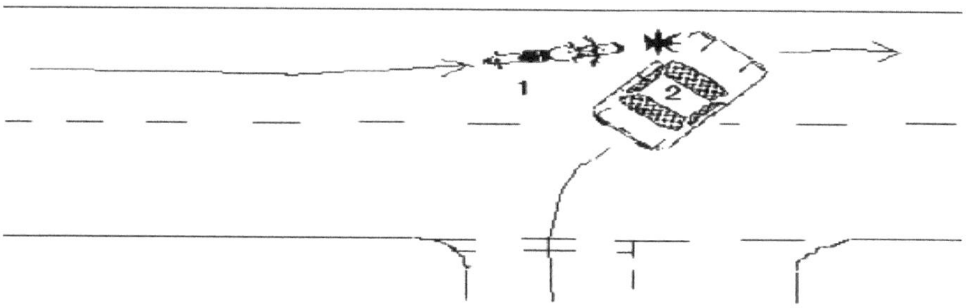

and has been repeatedly demonstrated in the context of pedestrian and bicycling safety (see Chapters 16 and 17). An interesting finding that supports the argument for the role of expectancy is that of Brooks and Guppy (1990) who found that drivers who are also motorcycle riders or have family or close friends that ride a motorcycle are more likely to observe motorcycles in traffic and less likely to collide with them.

The distinction between cognitive conspicuity and search conspicuity is important. In the context of seeing motorcycles in traffic, we define *attention or cognitive conspicuity* as the ability to detect a PTW when it is unexpected, and we define search conspicuity as the ability to detect a PTW while actively searching for it. Thus, in terms of information processing, attention conspicuity is a top-down process where the viewer's characteristics – such as expectancy and experience – come into play. In contrast, search conspicuity is a bottom-up process where the physical/visual features of the PTW and its environment – such as brightness, size, and contrast – come into play. In a study that directly demonstrated the difference between the two, we (Gershon, Ben-Asher, and Shinar, 2012; Gershon and Shinar, 2013, 2015) presented viewers with video clips of approaching traffic with and without approaching motorcyclists wearing different helmets. Half of the clips contained no motorcyclists and half contained a motorcyclist. The viewers tested for attention conspicuity viewed the short clips and at the end of each exposure just indicated what types of vehicles were in the scene. The viewers tested for search (or sensory) conspicuity viewed the same video clips but were instructed to look for a motorcycle and push a button as soon as they decided whether the scene contained one or not. As might be expected in the attention conspicuity experiment, the viewers were much less likely to detect the motorcycle, and this is shown in Table 16-4 in the most visually demanding situation: riding at dusk. Though there were large differences in the detection rates among the different helmets – with search conspicuity being the greatest for the white helmet – for all helmets search conspicuity was significantly higher than attention conspicuity. The novel helmet treatment of ABLS is discussed below.

One of the difficulties in raising a cyclist's conspicuity is that a major factor – that of the contrast with the environment is impossible to control. Thus, a white helmet may increase contrast at night against the dark sky, but a black helmet is much more effective against the bright blue daytime sky. In addition, objects and lights in the background also change constantly, and consequently so does the contrast. In our study, the most effective helmet treatment was the ABLS – an alternating blinking light system – and it is described below as a potential collision countermeasure. The evaluation of the ABLS was also a part of a recently completed EU study on motorcycle safety (2BESafe – www.2besafe.eu) with 14 participating countries. This study was dedicated in a large part to exploring ways to improving PTW's conspicuity (Rößger *et al.*, 2015b) and some of the findings of that study are described below in the context of crash countermeasures.

Table 16-4. Percent detections of motorcyclist when unexpected (attention conspicuity) and expected. ABLS is an alternating blinking light system (search conspicuity) at dusk (Gershon and Shinar, 2015).

Helmet Treatment	**Attention Conspicuity**	**Search Conspicuity**	**Difference in Detection**
Black	34	40	6
White	22	65	43
Reflective	17	43	27
ABLS	68	73	5

Rider skills and performance

Skilled performance is very critical in crash avoidance while riding a PTW. Hurt *et al.* (1981) noted that the median time available to avoid the crash in their 900 crashes was only 1.9 seconds. This is a very short time to detect the impending danger, decide on a proper course of action, and then execute it effectively. According to their crash reconstructions, in 43 percent of the crashes that had enough data, there was a "proper" evasive action. Yet, its execution was correct in only 24 percent of the times that it was attempted. Elliott *et al.* (2007) also found that control errors and speed violations (which reduce the time-to-collision) were significantly associated with the frequency of crashes in which the rider assumed at least some responsibility.

The most common error in the execution of evasive action in the Hurt *et al.* study (1981) was in the braking: failing to use both front and rear brakes, and relying on the rear brakes only. A related finding was the close association between riding experience – specifically with the crash motorcycle – and crash involvement. Inexperienced riders – with six months or less of riding experience on the specific motorcycle – constituted 57 percent of the crash-involved riders, compared to 40.4 percent of the exposure sample. An even more interesting observation was the difference between the crash and exposure samples in their "dirt bike experience"; an experience that challenges and hones a rider's vehicle handling skills. Only 29 percent of the crash sample had any such experience, compared to 63 percent of the exposure sample. In the MAIDS, the researchers noted a "reaction failure" whenever the rider or driver "failed to react to the dangerous condition, resulting in a continuation or faulty collision avoidance. For example, the PTW rider observes small objects on the roadway and decides to continue on the same path of travel. An accumulation of these small objects in the tyre of the PTW causes the PTW rider to lose control of the PTW and crash." Although reaction failures constituted only 5.7 percent of the primary crash causes, they were overwhelmingly attributed to the PTW riders and not to the drivers of the other vehicles: cited in 5.5 percent of the crashes that were attributed to rider action error versus 0.2 percent of the crashes that were attributed to the drivers of the other vehicles.

To get a better understanding of the role of experience, controlled studies are needed. In one such study in a simple simulator, Hosking, Liu, and Bayly (2010) sat riders with various levels of experience on a full-size motorcycle in front of a screen subtending 180° horizontally; essentially providing an unbounded view of the scene ahead. The riders' role was to push a button anytime they detected a hazard – defined as "a feature of the road or environment that has an immediate or potential threat to their personal safety." Although the researchers did not find a significant relationship between riding experience and visual behavior, the reaction times to the hazards were greatly related to experience, with riders inexperienced in both riding and driving being slowest and those experienced in both being fastest. Similar findings with video clips of street scenes with and without hazards were obtained by Underwood, Ngai, and Underwood (2013), who compared the performance of experienced riders with that of experienced drivers. They found that experienced riders did not detect significantly more hazards than experienced drivers, but they did respond faster to gradually evolving hazards, reflecting a better sense of anticipation of hazards. The experienced riders also responded much more often in general to situations that the experimenter did not define as hazard, again indicating a much greater sensitivity to potential hazards. Using a similar procedure, Bellet and Banet (2012) compared the hazard detection times of four groups of riders: two experienced groups made up of professional police PTW riders and non-professional experienced riders of the same age and an average of 13 years and 130,000 kilometers of riding experience, and two inexperienced drivers made up of young "novice" riders who had an average of 8 months of post-licensing riding experience, and "beginning" riders who had no post-licensing experience of riding on the open road. Both groups of experienced riders were significantly faster than the young and beginning riders at detecting hazards in the video clips. Between the two groups at each level of experience there were essentially no differences. However, in their assessment of the "situational criticality" of these hazards the novices performed as well as the experienced drivers and only the beginners underestimated their criticality and overestimated their ability to handle them. Thus, these studies demonstrate that experience is a gradual process with different cognitive skills and abilities acquired at different rates.

Alcohol and drugs

As with driving, so with riding a motorcycle, alcohol intoxication significantly impairs the ability of the rider to perceive hazards in time, make the right decisions on how to avoid them, and control the motorcycle effectively while making these avoidance maneuvers. Fortunately, possibly because the manual control of the motorcycle is more demanding than the control of a car, alcohol is not as prevalent in riding as it is in driving. In Hurt *et al.*'s study (1981), 2.1 percent of the riders had alcohol in their blood, with a median level of 0.12 percent BAC, compared to 3.4 percent of the drivers involved in the crash, who had a median of 0.16 percent BAC. However, when the comparisons were restricted to those considered "under the influence" of alcohol, the crash risk of alcohol became quite apparent. In the exposure population of riders, only 0.7 percent were considered under the influence, whereas among the crash-involved riders it was 4.2 percent. In the MAIDS, alcohol was present in 1.5 percent of the exposure sample, in 2.3 percent of the crash-involved drivers, and in 3.9 percent in the crash-involved riders. In short, both studies show that alcohol use is not that common among motorcycle riders, but when it is used it significantly increases crash risk, and especially the risk of fatality.

Other studies have also found that the prevalence of alcohol in riding is much lower than in driving, but when it is present it is associated with greater crash and injury severities just as it is in driving. In an analysis of all police-reported motorcycle crashes that occurred in Hawaii over a 10-year period, Kim, Boski, and Yamashita (2002) reported that alcohol impairment was noted in less than 3 percent of all crashes. In a more recent analysis of Swedish crashes, Zambon and Hasselberg (2006b) found that alcohol is a very strong determinant of injury severity; with the risk of severe injury or fatality being approximately three times as high when there is suspicion of alcohol involvement than when there is no such suspicion. The reason in part is that crash-involved alcohol-impaired riders are more likely to speed and are less likely to wear helmets than crash-involved riders who are not alcohol impaired (Kim *et al.*, 2002). However, even after controlling for the effects of speed, culpable crash-involved PTW riders are more likely to have alcohol in their blood than non-culpable crash-involved riders (Lardelli-Claret *et al.*, 2005).

The involvement of alcohol is pre-eminent in fatal crashes. In the Hurt study, alcohol was detected in the blood of more than one-third (37 percent) of the 54 riders who were killed in the crash and 23.5 percent of the fatally injured riders were judged "under the influence." More recent studies have shown that alcohol may even play a more dominant role in motorcycle crashes than in other motor-vehicle crashes (Lin and Kraus, 2009; NHTSA, 2013). For example, in the U.S. FARS data 30 percent of all fatally injured motorcycle riders had alcohol at BAC $\geq$ .08 g/dl (the threshold limit in the U.S.); a rate that was essentially unchanged relative to 10 years earlier (NHTSA, 2013). Also, because of the more complex control task in riding than in driving and because the rider is not as protected as the driver, the fatality risk is greater and rises much faster as the BAC level increases (Grzebieta, 2014).

In both the MAIDS and the Hurt *et al.* study (1981), less than one percent of the crash-involved riders admitted taking a drug prior to riding. However, the methodological limitations of both studies are such that specific quantitative estimates of the impact of various levels of alcohol and drugs on crash likelihood and crash severity cannot be drawn from them.

Gap perception

The small size of a motorcycle relative to the size of the car can affect not only its conspicuity but also drivers' perceptions of the gaps between them and approaching motorcycles. There are two underlying mechanisms that can lead drivers to perceive the gap between them and an approaching motorcycle (e.g., at an intersection) as greater than it is for an approaching car. First, the small size leads to lower angular velocity. Second, because of a perceptual phenomenon known as size-distance constancy, smaller objects are perceived as being farther away than similar objects that are *assumed* to have a similar size. Thus, Horswill *et al.* (2005) hypothesized that because smaller objects such as motorcycles are perceived as further away than larger objects such as cars, drivers expect them to reach the driver later than in fact they do. To test this hypothesis, Horswill and his associates exposed their subjects to brief presentations of video segments showing an approaching car or motorcycle, and asked the viewers to press a button when they believed the approaching vehicle would have reached them. In two separate studies with different durations of exposure, they indeed found that the expected arrival time of a motorcycle was significantly later than that of a car or a van. This finding, of course, has implications for both driver and rider training. For the driver, the implication is reminiscent of the mirror warning ("objects are closer than they appear"); namely that the motorcycle is closer and moving faster than it appears. For the riders, the implication is that they should maintain longer headways because drivers over-estimate the headways and clearance that they have.

Speed

Speed is generally associated with injury severity, but it also has a consistent effect on the likelihood of a crash. The MAIDS crash investigation teams concluded that in 8 percent of the crashes the motorcycle's speed contributed to the crash, compared to only 5 percent of the crashes in which the other vehicle's speed contributed to the crash. Lardelli-Claret *et al.* (2005) assessed the accident causes of all the PTW injury collisions that occurred in Spain from 1993 to 2002, that did not involve a pedestrian, and in which only one of the drivers or riders was considered culpable. With a total data base of 128,273 crash-involved mopeds and 62,005 crash-involved motorcycles, they calculated the crash risk of the culpable riders relative to that of the non-culpable riders. After adjusting for various confounding variables, they found that the factors that were most over-involved in culpable crashes were "inappropriate speed" (with an odds ratio of 13 for motorcycles and 10 for mopeds), and "excessive speed" (with an odds ratio of 7 for motorcycles and 6 for mopeds). The effects of speed in general are discussed in much more details in Chapter 8.

Who Are the Riders at Risk?

Motorcycling, especially with heavy motorcycles, unlike driving, must also be considered as part of social behavior. Riders tend to identify with other riders, and often form clubs. Though they may be benevolent, the ones that get most media exposure are the malevolent ones, like Hell's Angels, and their members may be aggressive to the point of being violently criminal (e.g., the fatal gang brawl in Waco Texas on May 17, 2015; Wikipedia, 2017). As such these groups may have different norms than other road users – norms that shape attitudes and create intentions that ultimately lead to violent unsocial behavior on the road, in accordance with the Theory of Planned Behavior (See Chapter 3). The cultural and social aspects of motorcycling safety have not received much attention and should be studied more (Huth, Füssl, and Risser, 2014; Njå and Nesvåg, 2007; Ratanavaraha and Jomnonkwao, 2013).

Two groups of riders are at greatest risk of a PTW crash: the young and inexperienced riders, and the "older" riders; "older" in this case being mature 40+ years old riders who are either inexperienced or returning to motorcycling after a long hiatus.

The young and inexperienced rider

In terms of rider characteristics, as in driving, it is the young rider who is greatly over-involved in crashes (EC, 2013; Huang and Preston, 2004; Hurt *et al.*, 1981; Lardelli-Claret *et al.*, 2005; Lin and Kraus, 2009; Mullin *et al.*, 2000; Zambon and Hasselberg, 2006a). In one crash-control study, Mullin *et al.* (2000) compared the characteristics of 490 riders who either died or were severely injured and hospitalized as a consequence of a crash that occurred between 6 am and midnight in the Auckland, NZ area, with the characteristics of

1,518 control riders sampled at the same time period from the same area. Only two of the variables they studied were significantly associated with over-involvement in crashes: the rider age and the rider's experience with the specific motorcycle with which he or she had the crash. Relative to their frequencies in the driving population, young drivers, under the age of 25, and drivers with less than 1,000 kilometers of riding experience in the specific motorcycle that they crashed were more than twice as likely to be involved in a crash as older drivers and drivers with more kilometers of experience, respectively. Interestingly, the youngest group of riders, 15-19 years old, was not significantly more involved in crashes than the 20-24 years old riders. Also, the amount of general experience in riding or driving was not related to the risk of a crash, and neither was gender. If these findings are accepted at face value, then they cast doubt on the relevance of training in general. This is because once the data are adjusted for age and experience with the specific motorcycle, additional riding experience (in all motorcycles) and driving experience do not seem to affect crash involvement. This discrepancy between motorcycle riding and car driving should be considered tentative because the partition into age and experience was based on fairly large categories.

With respect to the young riders, the central issue is whether the over-involvement is due to immaturity (age) or inexperience (skills). In driving, significant amount of research has demonstrated the role of both, with an indication that experience plays a greater role (see Chapter 6). Much less research has been dedicated to this issue in the case of motorcycle riding. Haworth and her associates (2005) report two related findings from their studies in Australia. In one study they found that inexperience (defined as either riding less than three days per week, or less than 100 kilometers per week, or riding less than three years) was not associated with increased crash risk, and in the second study they found that riders under 30 years old had double the crash rate (per license holders) of riders over 30 years old. Thus, when both results are considered together it appears that age is the culprit and not inexperience. However, in neither study was the other factor controlled, and most likely age and experience co-varied in both studies.

Only one study has focused directly on the relative contributions of young age and inexperience, and tried to statistically control the effects of both variables. In this study, Rutter and Quine (1996) first surveyed motorcycle owners in the United Kingdom and questioned them about their beliefs, perceptions, and behaviors related to riding. A year later they queried the same people about their motorcycle crash experience over the past year. A total of 1,304 riders completed both questionnaires, and the relationship between age, experience and reported crash involvement of this sample is presented in Table 16-5. Although the cell entries for the younger and less experienced riders are small (e.g., there were only nine 20-24-years-old riders with two years of riding experience or less), the results are consistent with those obtained for passenger car driving in showing that both age and experience are relevant: with young age being a greater contributor to crashes than inexperience. Thus, amongst the youngest group, 30-35 percent of the riders were involved in a crash within the year of the study regardless of their experience. In contrast, amongst the oldest group only 8-16 percent of the riders were involved in a crash. In fact, the inexperienced older riders were the least involved in crashes. Also, within each level of experience the younger the riders were the more likely they were to be

Table 16-5. Self-reported 1-year crash involvement of motorcycle riders in the U.K. as a function of age and experience (from Rutter and Quine, 1996, with permission from Elsevier).

Age	**<20 Years old**		**20-24 years old**		**55+ years old**	
Experience	P(crash)	N	P(crash)	N	P(crash)	N
≤2 Years	.30	30	.22	9	.08	12
3 Years	.35	23	.37	19	.16	25
4+ Years	.35	20	.13	100	.12	1066

involved in a crash. However, before embracing these results as conclusive support for the greater importance of age over experience, it is important to note three significant caveats in these data. First, because all the data are based on self-reports, riders who were fatally or severely injured (so as to become incapacitated) were not included in the sample. Second, there is a significant difference between self-reported crashes and police-recorded crashes, the latter including only more severe ones. Thus, these results are valid only with respect to non-injury and minor injury crashes. Third, the levels of experience were quite gross, with the first one being up to two years. In contrast, the extensive research on the role of experience in driving has consistently demonstrated that the critical period is less than one year, and even the first six months. Unfortunately, this level of resolution could not be achieved with this data base.

To understand what it is that makes the young rider over-involved in crashes, Rutter and Quine (1996) examined the riders' answers to a detailed questionnaire about their riding behaviors and attitudes toward riding. They found that riders who had one or more crashes within the study year were significantly more likely to engage in two types of behaviors that they termed "breaking laws and rules" and "carelessness." Breaking laws and rules included speeding, breaking traffic laws, breaking the Highway Code, and riding too close to other vehicles. Carelessness involved primarily riding too close to another vehicle (which was also part of breaking the law) and losing concentration. Finally, Rutter and Quine examined which of these variables was significantly associated with age, which with experience, and which with both. They found that all four behaviors associated with breaking laws and rules were significantly associated with age, but none were associated with experience. The young riders reported breaking the traffic laws, violating the Highway Code, speeding, and riding too close to other vehicles much more often than did the older riders. Furthermore, these behaviors were related – or in their words "predictable" – from the riders' reported beliefs and attitudes toward breaking the laws and rules of safe riding, and from their beliefs and attitudes toward "taking care." As they conclude in their own words: "beliefs play a mediating role between age and behaviour: though there are direct paths from youth to behaviour, the strongest paths are through beliefs, so that youth produces particular beliefs which in turn produce particular behaviours" (p. 21). In summary, though exclusively based on self-reports, this study very systematically demonstrated the crucial role of age (as distinct from experience) in motorcycle crashes, and further identified the relevant dangerous behaviors and attitudes associated with the young age. Based on their study it appears that the young riders' dangerous immaturity can be directly traced to their lack of respect of the rules of the road and lack of understanding of the limits of a motorcycle within a dynamic traffic system. This is also consistent with Bellet and Banet's (2012) finding that beginning riders under-estimate the risk involved in hazards that they perceive.

Relying on more objective data, Mullin *et al.* (2000) in the study briefly described above conducted a population-based case-controlled study where they compared the characteristics of crash-involved riders in Oakland, NZ, with non-crash-involved riders in the same area at the same places and times (non-residential public roads, between 6 am to midnight, in 1992-1995). Univariate analyses showed that both young age (25 years old and younger) and inexperience (less than five years of riding) contributed to over-involvement in crashes. However, when the analysis was adjusted for age and other potentially confounding variables, the effect of general riding experience disappeared and only the effect of experience with the specific motorcycle remained significant. The risk of a crash was nearly halved for riders with over 1,000 kilometers of experience with that specific motorcycle. In summary, their finding also demonstrated the joint effects of age and experience (though in the very strict sense of experience with the specific motorcycle involved).

In general and in driving youth is associated with greater risk taking and sensation seeking (Jonah, 1997). To the young rider, the motorcycle is also a means to experience thrills. Given the high cost of new powerful motorcycles today, it is likely that many people do not purchase a motorcycle as a means of cheap transportation, but as a transport mode that offers an ego trip, fun, and excitement. A common stereotype of the motorcycle rider is that of a young sensation-seeking male, and there are at least two empirical studies to support that stereotype. Horswill and Helman (2003) compared motorcycle riders with a matched group of non-motorcycling car drivers and found that the former chose faster speeds, overtook other cars more often, and pulled into smaller gaps in traffic than the latter. However, they did not maintain shorter headways to vehicles ahead, indicating that they are sensitive to the motorcycle's poorer stopping ability. Watson *et al.* (2007) analyzed the responses of 229 motorcyclists who answered questions about their intentions and behaviors when riding their motorcycle and found that unsafe behaviors were strongly correlated with sensation-seeking and rider aggression.

The "older" motorcycle rider

"Motorcycles are a symbol of youth that young people no longer particularly care for... According to the Motorcycle Industry Council, nowadays not even 4 percent of bikers are under 18. Roughly half are over 40, and more than a quarter is over 50" (Caldwell, 2006). This trend of older people riding heavy motorcycles, which emerged in the 1990s, was quickly followed by a new trend of increasing numbers of injuries and fatalities among older riders (Haworth and Mulvihill, 2005). "Older riders" – unlike older drivers – are typically defined as 40+ years old. The growth in PTW crashes has been attributed, in part to the increase in motorcycle license registrations in this age group

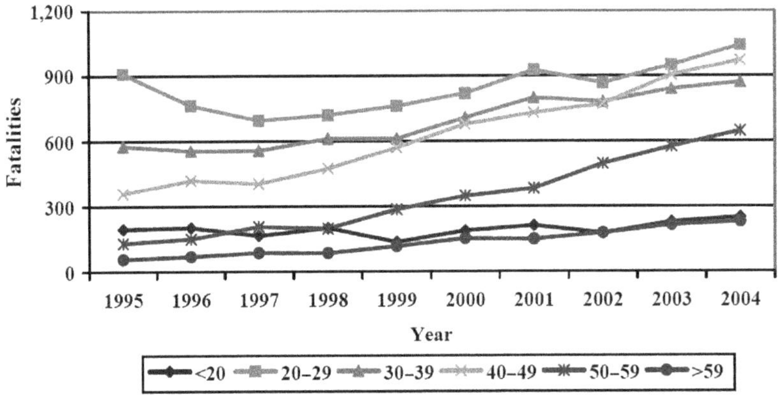

Figure 16-3. Changes in the number of motorcyclists' fatalities in the U.S. from 1988 to 2004 as a function of the rider's age (Shankar and Varghese, 2006).

and the increase in the number of heavy motorcycles (with engine sizes >1,000 cc) – especially those owned by older people. In the U.S. fatalities of cyclists less than 30 years old decreased systematically and dramatically from 1988 to 1998, and then remained relatively constant. In contrast, the number of fatalities among 40+ years old riders continuously increased over that period. These changes over time can be seen in Figure 16-3. Similar trends have been observed in Europe and England (Huang and Preston, 2004). For example, in their extensive analysis of motorcycle accident causes in Spain, Lardelli-Claret *et al.* (2005) found that both the very young and the old (over 65 years old) riders are approximately 50 percent more likely to be involved in a collision than a 35 years old rider.

However, the rate of increase in motorcyclist fatalities has been higher than the rate of increase in motorcycle registrations (Shankar and Varghese, 2006). The reasons behind the older riders' crashes are not yet fully understood, but it is reasonable to suppose that the greater perceptual skills (such as hazard detection – discussed below) and the greater vehicle control skills that are required for riding relative to driving, move age-related impairments to a much earlier phase in life. It seems quite clear that motorcycle riders – if they persist in riding into their later years – mirror the crash pattern of passenger cars drivers. The difference is that behind the motorcycle bars "old age" (and potential death from a crash) arrives much earlier than behind the wheel of a car.

The rider of lower socioeconomic status

As in driving a car, socio-economics seem to be associated with crash involvement. Riders from lower socioeconomic levels are over-involved in crashes, especially at their early stage of riding. The joint association of age and socioeconomic status with crash risk is illustrated in an analysis of crash data of Swedish motorcyclists, by Zambon and Hasselberg (2006a). Their results are shown in Figure 16-4 where it can be seen that the age-related decline in crash risk – from the age of 17 onward – is very marked

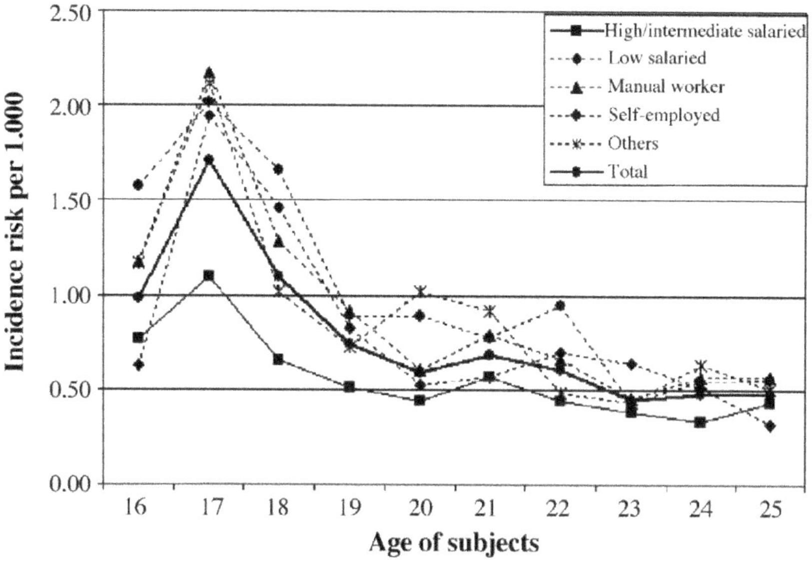

Figure 16-4. Risk of first injury or fatal crash (per 1,000 Swedish residents) in a motorcycle as a function of the rider age and socioeconomic status of the parents. Based on a cohort born in 1970-1971 and tracked from 1998 to 1995 (from Zambon and Hasselberg, 2006a, with permission from Elsevier).

for riders of all socioeconomic levels (because the minimum age for a light (<125 cc) motorcycle license is 16, the crash involvement is spuriously low for that age group because very few riders actually ride at that age for a whole year). However, up until their early twenties, the crash risk for riders from the upper socioeconomic levels is consistently lower than it is for riders from the lower socioeconomic levels. Of course, the socioeconomic class is only a surrogate measure of other measures that may directly affect riders' safety. In the authors' own words, "besides having safer driving behaviour, subjects from high socioeconomic positions could have access to better driving training, availability, and tendency to wear safer equipment, higher supervision given by the parents, as well as a greater familiarity with the vehicle, among other factors" (p. 5). To these factors, we can probably also add safer riding environments of the riders of higher socioeconomic level, and fewer kilometers ridden by the more affluent riders because they also have access to a car. This vague list of options does not shed much light on the issue of the personal characteristics that directly contribute to crash risk, but it does illustrate the potential role of variables that may indirectly affect riding safety.

Improving Motorcyle Rider Safety

As for other aspects of road safety, organizational actions in terms of strategic plans, policy, and regulations can have a significant impact on motorcycle rider safety. In Spain, for example, a strategic plan was formulated in 2007 following a 53 percent increase in the number of registered motorcycles between 2003 and 2006 (compared to 16 percent for cars) (Ministro del Interior, 2007). The plan had a shared vision of multiple offices and organizations and defined two concrete goals: (1) to reverse the rising trend of motorcycle fatalities and injuries, and (2) bring the number of fatalities down to 25 per 100,000 PTWs. To reach these goals, 36 different safety performance indices were defined (e.g., strengthening the safety components in the training and licensing tests, delaying licensing for heavy PTWs, improving vehicle stability, improving road conditions, special actions on accident hotspots, etc.). Follow-up indicators were then defined to measure the success of each measure and the program as a whole. A different approach was adopted by the Swedish Motorcycling Association (SMC, 2014); one that applies the Vision Zero approach (see Chapter 19) specifically to motorcyclists. This recommended program both accepts the cyclists' responsibilities (in terms of acquiring skills, enhancing his/her visibility, using protective equipment, reducing speed, and refraining from alcohol and drug use), and at the same time spells out the environmental and vehicular factors that should be addressed by the government and the vehicle makers.

Below are a select group of measures that have been addressed in the literature and adopted and evaluated by governments and various organizations.

Training and licensing requirements

It seems almost axiomatic that motorcycle riding is a more complex skill than car driving. Thus, according to Haworth and Mulvihill (2005), an optimal model of motorcycle training and licensing should consider granting a full motorcycle license as a "higher step," and one that follows a full driver license. Yet, following their review of existing training and licensing systems in various parts of the world, Haworth and Mulvihill (2005) note that "in most jurisdictions, the motorcycle licensing system is similar to that for car drivers, with similar stages (learner, provisional and full licence) and with similar minimum ages and duration for these stages." This may be the reason for its general ineffectiveness in reducing young-novice riders' crashes. In fact, according to Haworth and Mulvihill, the existing research "suggests that any safety benefits of motorcycle licensing and training probably result more from exposure reduction (a reduction in the total amount of riding) than from crash risk reduction." Nonetheless – even with very little scientific support for it – they suggest that best practices in motorcycle education, training, and licensing should include (1) compulsory training rather than voluntary, (2) an increased emphasis on "road-craft" (without reducing the time spent on vehicle control skills), (3) longer or more costly compulsory programs, and (4) hazard perception training. Possibly the best approach to accomplish all of these goals is through the graduated driver licensing systems that have been implemented mostly for driver licensing (see Chapter 7), but have also been implemented for motorcycle riding in the United Kingdom, Australia, New Zealand, and parts of the U.S. (and reviewed by Huang and Preston, 2004).

An acknowledgment of the different skills required for handling PTW is evidenced in the fact that nearly all countries require riders to obtain a special license to operate a PTW, especially motorcycles. Most countries further require some version of a training program. The research evidence suggests that rider education and strict licensing criteria may in fact decrease crash involvement. McGwin *et al.* (2004) conducted an evaluation of motorcyclists' mortality rates as a function of the various licensing requirements in different U.S. states and found that fatality rates were significantly lower in states that required a skill test for a motorcycle permit, required rider training, had a long-duration learner permit (over 190 days), and imposed three or more restrictions on riding during the learner period. However, as Baldi, Baer, and Cook (2005) demonstrated in their review of previous research in this area, the evidence for the effectiveness of these requirements is far from conclusive. According to them, one reason for the mixed results is the very large heterogeneity among the countries and states in their programs and requirements. To re-assess the benefits of rider training and licensing programs, they evaluated 47 U.S. states in terms of the extent to which they observe "best practices in rider education and licensing." A best practice system, according to Baldi *et al.*, is one which is cost-effective and includes those components that have been shown to be the most effective in reducing injuries and fatalities, without creating undue hardships on the applicants. Consequently, they argued that a successful program should not only reduce crashes but also be cost-effective.

In the absence of objective criteria, Baldi *et al.* (2005) used expert opinions and past research to determine the components of best practices for program administration, rider education, and licensing. Table 16-6 contains their list of 13 "best" practices.

Next, Baldi *et al.* (2005) assessed each of the 47 U.S. states that had state-legislated rider education programs in 2003, relative to whether or not they complied with each of the 13 individual practices. Depending on the level of compliance with the different practices each state was then rated as having a low "best practices" score, or a medium "best practices" score, or a high "best practices" score. Finally, these scores were compared to the motorcycle crash rates of each state. The results gave some support to the role of rider training and licensing in safety: the states scoring the highest on their best practices had the lowest rates of fatalities (1.21 per 100,000 residents in that state) and the states scoring the lowest had the highest rates of fatalities (1.45 per 100,000 residents), with those rated "medium" in terms of best practices, scoring in-between (1.25 per 100,000 residents). However, this relationship was partially confounded by exposure to risk: the best states also had the lowest per capita number of miles ridden and the worst states had the highest per capita number of miles ridden. Still, a regression function showed that the effects of the "best practices" on state motorcycle fatalities remained significant even after controlling for the effects of vehicle miles traveled, number of registered riders, and number of registered motorcycles. This support for Baldi's approach is still extremely tenuous, and much more research is needed before this comprehensive – and expensive – approach to rider education and licensing can be justified, especially in light of some of the findings presented below.

As noted above, the MAIDS (ACEM, 2004) and Hurt *et al.* (1981) comprehensive crash causation studies, and the more limited study by Mullin *et al.* (2000) showed that crash involvement is related not to the amount of experience a rider has with motorcycling in

Table 16-6. The components of best practices for motorcycle rider education and licensing according to Baldi *et al.* (2005) (with permission from Elsevier).

Program Administration	**Rider Education**	**Licensing**
Integration between rider education and licensing	Sound curricula	Graduated licensing system
An adequate, dedicated funding source	Effective training and delivery	Comprehensive and sound testing
Collection of rider training, licensing, and crash data	Outreach and information efforts	Comprehensive and sound procedures for obtaining and renewing a license
	Incentives for training	Incentives for licensing
	Regular program assessments and quality control	
	Instructor education and training	

general but to the amount of experience that riders have in the *specific* motorcycle with which they crashed. This complicates matters, because it means that (unlike car driving) the most effective training program should be conducted on the rider's own motorcycle. Furthermore, it is possible that with each new motorcycle, the rider has to progress through a new learning phase, during which he or she may be very vulnerable and may therefore needs new training. The high crash risk associated with new motorcycles (Paulozzi, 2005) is definitely suggestive of that, but more direct research still has to be conducted to address this issue and its implications for licensing and relicensing.

Other insights we can gain from crash research is that the two domains that should be stressed in rider training are comprehension of the traffic system within which the cyclists operate and understanding the limitations of their PTW and those of the other drivers around them. Rutter and Quine's (1996) results imply that young novice riders need to acquire a whole "mind-set" concerning the importance of operating within the limits of the systems, including the relevance of the traffic and highway laws, and how their violations can lead to crashes. Whether this can actually be done within a short training program is an open question. Summarizing the state of the art on practices and research in the U.S., Goodwin *et al.* (2015) conclude that both motorcycle rider licensing and training programs are common to most states, but their effectiveness in terms of crash reduction is marginal at best (rated as "one-star," meaning that "limited or no high-quality research exists"). Perhaps cynically, Goodwin *et al.* argue that "data suggests that having mandatory pre-license training for motorcyclists may reduce crashes and offenses by discouraging motorcycle riding, thus limiting exposure" (p. 5-22). A telling illustration is the recent research of Ivers *et al.* (2016). In a well-controlled study, they evaluated the effects of post-licensing coaching on novice motorcyclists who had passed their licensing test within the past 12 months. They were not able to find any differences in crash experience between the coached riders and a matched control group after 3 and 12 months. However, they did find that the coached riders were more confident in their riding and reported more speeding behaviors. Consequently, as with driving, some training can do more (and more damage) to affect attitudes and increase risk taking than to actually increase safety.

One specific area that seems to hold promise is that of training in hazard perception and in coping with hazards. Some of the research described above and other findings discussed immediately below indicate that this area seems to hold the most – as yet unfulfilled – promise.

Training in hazard perception and in responding to hazards

Because of the inherent instability of PTW, two skills that riders must acquire are acute hazard perception and quick appropriate responses to emerging hazards. Small objects on the road, potholes, pavement deformations, spaces between adjoining pavement segments, cracks in asphalt and concrete, oils spills, loose gravel, and puddles that may be inconsequential to car drivers can be life-threatening hazards to the motorcyclists, and must be avoided at all costs. A recent analysis of recorded events in a small-scale naturalistic riding study conducted on six novice motorcycle riders in France revealed that most of the safety critical events were associated poor hazard perception skills (Aupetit *et al.*, 2016). For example, as part of a motorcycle crash risk study conducted in Australia, Haworth *et al.* (1997) revisited the same sites where 206 motorcycles crashed and noticed that in 14 percent of the crashes unclean road and loose material on the road probably contributed significantly to the occurrence of the crash. Such factors are essentially non-existent in the causation of car crashes, and they emphasize the added mental effort and attention that motorcycle riders must allocate to the road immediately ahead of them. Consequently, it is reasonable to argue that in order to survive, experienced motorcyclists must develop the ability to detect, assess, and cope with such potential hazards. Indeed, the little evidence that has been gathered in this area seems to confirm this hypothesis. Horswill and Helman (2003) compared motorcyclists with non-motorcycling car drivers in a test of hazard perception and found that the motorcyclists detected road hazards faster than the car drivers. Armsby, Boyle, and Wright (1989) in a study on hazard perception, noted that car drivers who also rode (or had ridden) motorcycles were more sensitive to specific road hazards – especially when responding from a motorcyclist point of view – than drivers who did not ride motorcycles. Shahar *et al.* (2010) presented drivers and motorcyclists with vignettes of hazardous situations and asked them to rate their level of hazardousness. Drivers who were also motorcyclists rated the scenes as more hazardous, and when asked to assume a mind-set of either drivers or motorcyclists, both group when they were in the role of motorcyclists rated scenes as more dangerous than when they assumed the mind-set of drivers. These results indicate that licensed motorcyclists are more sensitive to hazards on the road, and especially so when they are asked to rate them *as* motorcyclists. It is interesting that non-cyclists too were more sensitive to the hazards when asked to assume a mind-set of a motorcyclist – even though they had no riding experience!

Given the different sources of risk in driving a car and in riding a PTW, do riders and drivers scan their environment differently? Two limited-scope studies addressed this question, and they yielded different findings. In the first study, Nagayama *et al.* (1980) examined the visual scanning behavior of three people who were experienced drivers and motorcyclists. The visual scan pattern was examined when they drove and rode in traffic on an actual road. The researchers found that the same people directed their visual fixations to points much closer on the road when they rode a motorcycle than when they drove a car, suggesting that they are heeding potential small obstacles and hazards (that cannot be discerned when looking further out toward the horizon). When riding a motorcycle, the riders directed approximately 30 percent of their fixations to the road pavement immediately ahead of them, whereas when driving a car they rarely looked at the pavement directly in front of them. In the second study, Tofield and Wann (2001) compared the scanning of different groups of riders and drivers in a simulator and obtained opposite results: the riders fixated farther ahead than the drivers. In the presence of other traffic, the car drivers fixated their gaze at an average headway distance of 2.1 seconds ahead while the motorcycle riders fixated their gaze at a distance of 3.0 seconds ahead. Although the results appear to contradict each other, the differences in their methods are such that comparing them is actually very difficult. Whereas Nagayama *et al.* used the same subjects in the car and on the motorcycle and conducted their evaluation in real-world conditions, Tofield and Wann used different groups of subjects who drove in a rudimentary simulator. Thus, there is no a priori reason to assume that the motorcycle riders in Tofield and Wann's study would not have behaved differently if they were actually riding a motorcycle. More than anything else, these different results are an indication of the close correspondence that must be observed between the study method and the conclusions that can be drawn from it. Nonetheless, briefly summarizing the state of the art on the effectiveness of rider training, Goodwin *et al.* (2015) believe the training in hazard perception may be effective.

Other vehicles can also constitute hazards that are unique to motorcycle riders. This is because car drivers detect other cars more easily than they detect motorcycles. A good rule of thumb for safe riding is that in interacting with cars and trucks it is much better for the motorcyclist to be safe than right. In Hurt *et al.*'s (1981) analysis of motorcycle crashes in California, they noted that one-third of the crashes involved an obstruction of the motorcyclist's and/or car driver's view of each other in critical moments immediately preceding the collision. Furthermore, the hazards posed by other vehicles are often compounded by the specific roadway environment. Thus, crash statistics show that roundabouts and intersections can increase the likelihood of failure to give right-of-way to the PTW, and traffic lights can increase the risk of rear-end collisions (when a lead car brakes abruptly) or of angle collisions with a car that runs the red lights (Haworth, Mulvihill, and Symmons, 2005).

To appropriately respond to an unexpected hazard a rider or driver has to disrupt a mostly automatic process of riding or driving, in order to perceive and assess an infrequent or rare event and then respond to it in a controlled (rather than automatic) and less practiced manner. A relatively simple model of risk perception and response has been offered by Grayson *et al.* (2003). According to their model, in order to cope with a potential danger the rider has to successfully perform the following four tasks: detect the hazard, appraise the threat (or risk) involved, select an appropriate action, and adequately implement that action. These functions are essentially the same information processing tasks involved in all driving as described in Chapter 3. However, the focus here is on the perception and responses to specific stimuli that constitute dangerous situations. In addition, the model has feedback loops among all four processes. For example, an incorrect or delayed appraisal of a marginally dangerous situation may actually increase the level of danger and change its perception as the rider gets closer to the hazard.

Most of the training and tests of hazard perception focus on the hazard detection aspect and ignore the response aspect. According to Haworth *et al.* (2005), hardly any attention has been directed to training riders on how to respond to hazards and dangerous situations. It is therefore not surprising that crash analyses indicate very limited and often inadequate use of the brakes in emergency pre-crash situations (e.g., ACEM, 2004; Hurt *et al.*, 1981; Penumaka *et al.*, 2014). Many riders typically respond to an emergency by deploying the rear brakes only, instead of using both front and rear brakes (a problem that does not exist in driving, where the brakes of all four wheels are linked to each other). This realization has prompted some motorcycle manufacturers to automatically link the front brakes to the rear brakes whenever the rider activates the latter. One preemptive approach that has been offered but not evaluated is for the motorcyclist to adopt a defensive riding strategy through the choice of lane positioning. This approach, recommended by Ouellet (1990), requires the rider to evaluate risk on a moment-by-moment basis and select the lane position that would maximize the distance between the PTW and other vehicles and minimize the opportunity for conflicts with potential danger sources. For example, staying to the right of a vehicle in the left lane because that vehicle might turn left without perceiving the motorcycle.

Comprehensive training in hazard perception and in coping with hazards is still at its infancy. Although no program specific to hazard perception for motorcycle riders has been developed (Haworth *et al.*, 2005), in the U.K. applicants for motorcycle license must pass a hazard perception test – but one that was designed for car drivers who, paradoxically, are not required to take it. Initial steps toward training in hazard perception and control have been made in Australia, with a recommendation that such a program combine class, simulation, and on-the-road training. However, an evaluation of such an operational program has still not been performed (Wallace, Haworth, and Regan, 2005). In Japan, training in a motorcycle simulator is part of the requirements for motorcycle licensing (Haworth *et al.*, 2005), but the benefits of this approach are still unproven.

Increasing MC and rider conspicuity

Given the unequivocal role of poor conspicuity as a cause for many PTW collisions, various means of increasing the conspicuity of PTW riders have been considered and evaluated. The most common method of increasing conspicuity has been to require daylight running lights (DRL). Early evaluations by Bragg, Dawson, and Jonah (1980), Hurt *et al.* (1981), Vaughan, Pettigrewm, and Lukin (1977) and more recent ones by Umar, Mackay, and Hills (1996) and Wells *et al.* (2004) all noted that the introduction of laws requiring PTWs to operate with daytime running lights is associated with significant crash reductions. The magnitude of the effect appears to be quite high: Umar *et al.* (1996) estimated the reduction at 27 percent of conspicuity-related PTW accidents in Malaysia, and Wells *et al.* (2004) estimated the reduction at 27 percent in New Zealand (after adjusting for the rider age, weather, alcohol consumption, and speed limit). However, an analysis of the MAIDS and Swedish crash data led Paine *et al.* (2005) to suggest that a more realistic estimate of the crash reduction benefits of daylight running lights is on the order of 12 percent. Estimating the exact magnitude of the effects of DRL is not easy. If all crashes are included, then one can argue that the effect is underestimated as single-vehicle crashes should not be affected by the DRL and should be excluded or be used as a control condition. On the other hand, some – and we do not know how many – of the single-vehicle crashes are the result of cyclists' attempts to avoid other vehicles, and thus when the effect is adjusted for these crashes, we have an over-estimate (Lin and Kraus, 2009).

To understand the factors that contribute to the conspicuity of motorcyclists, Hole, Tyrrell, and Langham (1996) conducted three controlled laboratory studies in which they presented subjects with slides of traffic scenes, some with motorcyclists and some without motorcyclists. The scenes could be of traffic in semi-rural settings, in urban traffic settings, and against varying amounts of visual clutter (in the form of other cars in the immediate vicinity). Conspicuity was measured in terms of the time it took the subjects to detect the motorcycle. They found, as expected, that reaction time increased as the distance to the motorcycle increased and that it was longer for smaller PTWs than for larger ones. This demonstrated the relevance of the optical size of the motorcycle to its visual conspicuity, and supported the notion that part of the reason for the poor detection of PTWs by drivers is due to their smaller size (relative to cars). The effects of other factors were also quite strong, but more complicated. Although, in general, the use of headlights and bright clothing reduced the detection times, the benefits of headlights and bright clothing depended greatly on the environmental conditions. Thus, contrary to expectations, headlights did not consistently improve conspicuity; they improved conspicuity more when the motorcycle was positioned next to parked cars than when it was positioned on an empty side of the street (where apparently their added value to conspicuity was insignificant) – and the benefits of the headlights increased with increasing distance. Hole *et al.*'s findings have been replicated by other more recent studies conducted in Israel, France, and Germany, and the most general conclusion that can be drawn from all of these studies is that the effectiveness of various conspicuity aids – especially clothing – depends more on the specific environment in which they are imbedded than on their reflectance or brightness properties per se (Cavallo and Pinto, 2015; Gershon *et al.*, 2012; Gershon and Shinar, 2013, 2015; Pinto, Cavallo, and Saint-Pierre, 2014; Rößger *et al.*, 2015a). This means that brightness contrast (with the background) may be much more important than the visual features of the motorcycle and rider by themselves. Unfortunately this conclusion, which is also supported by the results of Blackwell's basic research on vision (CIE, 1982) complicates the efforts to improve riders' safety through increased conspicuity, because we hardly ever have control of the background lighting and texture, and it often changes instantaneously. Thus, running headlights may be beneficial in marginal weather but not in the bright sun with reflections from other vehicles and obstacles, as demonstrated in an experimental study involving both real and simulated driving (Brooks *et al.*, 2005).

A more comprehensive approach to the role of conspicuity was adopted by Wells and her colleagues (2004) who compared the conspicuity of 463 crash-involved injured and killed riders to that of a control sample of 1,233 riders randomly selected from roadside survey sites in the Auckland, New Zealand area. After adjustment for rider age and alcohol consumption, they found that various treatments that enhanced conspicuity reduced the odds of crash risk. These treatments included wearing high visibility – retro-reflective or fluorescent – clothing (associated with a 37 percent reduction in injury crashes), wearing a white helmet (24 percent reduction relative to a black helmet; though yellow, orange, and blue helmets were not associated with significant reductions), and using daytime running headlight (associated with 27 percent crash reduction). The frontal color of the cyclist's clothing and the color of the motorcycle itself were not associated with significant crash reductions.

In summary, highly reflective helmets and clothing, and running daylights can all add significantly to a rider's conspicuity and significantly reduce his or her likelihood of being involved in a crash with another vehicle. However, the contributions of most treatments are highly variable and change with the visual environment of the rider. Also, riders are somewhat insensitive to the benefits of conspicuity enhancements. They must be educated about their insufficient conspicuity to car drivers, and about the means to enhance their conspicuity. Otherwise, they will continue to assume that they are as visible to car drivers as cars are to them, and further assume that they are being seen when in fact they are not.

A particular type of crash where conspicuity is of great importance is the collision with another vehicle when either one fails to give the right-of-way. As noted in the Hurt *et al.* study and in the MAIDS, in these cases drivers often report that they did not see the motorcycle at all or not in time. Thus, most conspicuity enhancements concern the frontal view of the rider as he or she would be seen by the driver. Because these types of crashes happen even with DRL, added means are being tested. Common to all of them is the search for a unique pattern of the lights that will distinguish the MC from other vehicles. Three different studies considered this in the context of the 2BESafe framework mentioned above. In one study, Rößger *et al.* (2015a) considered various configurations of lights on the handlebars, on the back of the handlebars mirrors and on the front fork (or along the side panels of scooters), and even on the helmet; all in addition to the existing center light. Their subjects were given pictures of traffic scenes and were instructed to focus on vehicles they should attend to if they plan to cross an intersection or pull out into the road. The focus of the study was on cognitive conspicuity as the subjects were not cued to look for motorcycles. They found that a T-shaped light configuration was more effective than none or others in attracting the observer's fixation to the PTW. Judgments of gaps in traffic also improved with the novel configuration, indicating that the lights improved the judgment of speed and distance. In France, Cavallo and her colleagues (Cavallo and Pinto, 2015; Pinto *et al.*, 2014) examined the benefits of different PTW light configurations in the presence of DRL on cars. This is important because the EU has issued a recent directive requiring all *cars* in EU countries to drive with DRL throughout the year. This raises the concern that once all vehicles drive with lights on, the PTWs will lose the relative advantage they had in their conspicuity. It is then hoped that a unique configuration of lights will re-enable the PTW to become more conspicuous against the background of other vehicles. Indeed, using a similar method of showing drivers pictures of traffic scenes with and without PTWs and in the presence of other vehicles with DRL or without it Cavallo and her colleagues demonstrated that motorcyclists with DRL were less detectable in the presence of traffic with DRL than without it. To overcome this, they evaluated the benefits of different motorcycle light colors and configurations. They found that replacing the single center white light – that is similar to other DRLs – with a yellow light was the most effective treatment followed by adding a light to the top of the helmet or adding two lights at the ends of the handlebars thus forming a triangle with the (slightly lower) headlight. Of the three alternative lighting systems, the only one that was (statistically) significantly better than the current white single headlight was its replacement with a yellow light of equal brightness. Because drivers also over-estimate the gap to an approaching motorcycle (relative to a car), Cavallo *et al.* (2015) reasoned that additional lights on the handlebars and on the helmet would increase the perceived size of an approaching motorcycle and thus affect its perceived distance. They indeed found in a driving simulator that with the additional lights drivers chose greater gaps when crossing an intersection in the presence of an approaching motorcycle.

The third study, in our university (Gershon and Shinar, 2013, 2015), used a different approach to attract attention and thereby increase attention conspicuity. We equipped the helmet of a motorcyclist with a short vertical rod with a light at the top and at the bottom. The two lights flashed on and off in an alternating fashion so as to create an apparent movement of a light source moving up and down. The idea behind the alternating blinking light system (ABLS) was to provide drivers with a visual cue that has strong attentional power (as flashing lights do) and is different from all the other potential lights that may be encountered on the road. The stimuli for the study consisted of video clips of approaching traffic either with or without the motorcycle. The motorcyclist either had a black helmet, a white helmet, a retroreflective helmet or a helmet with the ABLS. The evaluation of the treatment was based on the detection probability in video clips containing either the ABLS or the other treatments. The advantage of the ABLS over a white, black, or fluorescent helmet was remarkable as can be seen in Table 16-4. The ABLS doubled the probability of detecting a motorcycle when the viewers were not cued to look for it (i.e., in a test of attention conspicuity), and was also significantly better than all other treatments when the viewers were cued to look for a motorcyclist. An even greater effect, with an improved ABLS was obtained in a more recent study we conducted on bicycle conspicuity (see Chapter 17).

Effectiveness of helmets in injury and fatality reductions

The number one life-saving device for motorcycle riders is the helmet. Using the method originally developed by Evans (1986) to evaluate the benefits of seat belts (see chapter 10), the U.S. National Highway Traffic Safety Administration (NHTSA) estimates that – all other things being equal – the use of helmets reduces fatalities by 37 percent (Deutermann, 2004). That means that across all crashes, a rider wearing an approved helmet can reduce his or her risk of being killed in a crash by 37 percent. Due primarily to the continued progress in helmet design and energy-absorbing materials, that estimate is eight percent higher than the one made by NHTSA 15 years earlier (Mellor and StClair, 2005). Three years later, a Cochrane collaborative review of 61 studies concluded that the fatality risk reduction was actually 42 percent and the reduction in the risk for head injury was 69 percent (Liu *et al.*, 2008). These risk reductions translate to very large savings in lives. For example, in 2013 in the U.S. alone helmets saved the lives of 1,630 motorcyclists (NHTSA, 2015a, 2015b).

The simple reason for the marked effect of helmets on safety is that head injuries are the principal cause of death in motorcycle fatalities. In fact, the benefits of the helmet are limited to reducing head and face injuries only. Several studies have shown that there are no differences in the frequencies of injuries other than head and face between helmeted and non-helmeted riders. In a review of 13 U.S. studies that evaluated the effectiveness of helmets on injuries and hospitalization Lin and Kraus (2009) found that in all but one study (where no difference was found), head injury risk was much greater without a helmet. Furthermore, when they survive, helmeted riders have fewer traumatic brain injuries; a very significant issue, as in the U.S. the cost of treating riders with traumatic brain injury is 13 times higher than that of those not incurring it (Cook *et al.*, 2009). These conclusions on the effectiveness of helmets have also been generally supported in analyses based motorcyclist injuries from combined police and hospital reports (Kindelberger and Milani, 2015). Even with the helmets available two decades ago, NHTSA (1996) estimated that the cost of patient care of non-helmeted motorcyclists was 8 percent higher than for helmeted motorcyclists, reflecting the more severe injuries of surviving non-helmeted motorcyclists.

One would think that this alone should be a sufficient incentive to use a helmet. Unfortunately, this is not the case. In the U.S., where there are active and effective anti-helmet motorcyclist lobbying groups, in 2014 only 19 states (out of 50) and the District of Columbia had "universal helmet laws" requiring the use of a helmet by all riders. In these states – based on direct observations – 89 percent of the riders used "Department of Transportation compliant" helmets. In states that do not have universal helmet laws, only 48 percent of the riders were observed with Department of Transportation compliant helmets (NHTSA, 2015a). Worldwide, the situation is actually better. All OECD countries have universal helmet laws for motorcyclists (OECD, 2014), and worldwide 155 countries have them – covering 88 percent of the world population (WHO, 2013).

The empirical research on the benefits of helmets is quite conclusive, and the only differences among the different reports are in the specific percentages of lives saved and injuries mitigated. Three different approaches have been used to estimate the effectiveness of motorcycle helmets: (1) the epidemiological approach in which statistical methods are applied to large sets of crash data, and the relative contributions of various factors – including the use of helmets – are determined, (2) the quasi-experimental approach in which the change in frequencies and rates of injuries and fatalities following the introduction of helmet laws are compared to the frequencies and rates before the law change, and (3) the quasi-experimental approach in which change in injuries and fatalities following the *repeal* of helmet laws is evaluated (yes, some jurisdictions actually repeal them despite their proven effectiveness).

Epidemiological evaluations

The epidemiological approach was used by Keng (2005) who analyzed the data from 26,452 police-reported PTW crashes in Taiwan. Using a logistic regression analysis, he concluded that helmets reduce the probability of death from a motorcycle crash in Taiwan by 40 percent, and the likelihood of neck and head injuries – the most common cause of death in motorcycle crashes – by 53 percent. In Thailand, Nakahara *et al.* (2005) estimated that riders not wearing helmets increase their risk of fatality by a factor of 3.5 relative to those wearing them. In the U.S., Norvell and Cummings (2002) examined motorcycle crashes in which two riders were on the motorcycle, and either one of them or both were killed, thus ruling out confounding effects of motorcycle characteristics, speed, and crash characteristics. Using the U.S. data base of fatal crashes (Fatal Analysis Reporting System – FARS) they evaluated the survivability of 18,444 pairs of such riders for whom data were available on whether or not they were wearing their helmet at the time of the crash. After further controlling for the effects of seat position, rider age, and gender, they still found that wearing the helmet reduced the likelihood of a fatality by an average of 39 percent. Ouellet and Kasantikul (2006) examined the fatalities and injuries of riders involved in approximately 1,000 PTW crashes in the U.S. and Malaysia. Despite differences in culture, in motorcycle size (much heavier motorcycles in the U.S. versus high prevalence of mopeds in Malaysia), in the time of data collection (25 years difference), and types of helmets used (more thin-lined less energy absorbing in Malaysia), traffic situations, and probable speeds; despite all these differences the data from both countries showed that non-helmeted riders were two to three times more likely to be killed in the crash and three times more likely to be seriously injured. In short, different analytic approaches, conducted at different times, in different countries and cultures all showed that helmets are very significant life-saving devices in motorcycle crashes.

Quasi-experimental evaluation of the introduction (and repeal) of universal helmet laws

Mandatory helmet laws have been a very effective means of increasing helmet usage and rider safety. The most effective laws are known as universal helmet laws. These laws require that all motorcycle riders at all times wear a helmet, without any exceptions. A review of 21 studies that compared the impact of helmet laws – either when they are enacted or when they are repealed showed that in general when universal helmet laws are in effect usage rates go up and motorcycle deaths, head injuries, days of hospitalization, and medical costs decrease (Lin and Kraus, 2009). In contrast to the universal helmet laws are the limited (or state) helmet laws, which are often the result of a compromise between safety advocates and motorcycle riders' lobbyists. These laws require helmet use only for specific sub-groups such as riders under a certain age, riders in the learning phase, and riders with less than a year of experience. Whenever they are compared, the limited helmet laws are less effective in reducing deaths and injuries than the universal helmet laws (Ichikawa, Chadbunchachai, and Marui, 2003; Sosin and Sacks, 1992). However, even the universal helmet laws often yield less-than-expected benefits. The main reason for this is that even with the law, not all riders wear helmets, and among those who do, some wear "novelty" or "fake" helmets that are lighter, and have a hard shell but no energy-absorbing liner (Erhardt *et al.*, 2016; Ouellet and Kasantikul, 2006). As such they protect their riders mostly from the sun.

Compliance with the laws is greatly determined by the level of enforcement. In the U.S., helmet use in the late 1980s and early 1990s in states that had universal helmet laws was close to 100 percent. Since the beginning of this century use rate in these states has dropped to approximately 50 percent in 2005 (Glassbrenner and Ye, 2007), but has gone back up to 89 percent in 2014 (NHTSA, 2015a). In the case of helmets, enforcement is quite easy because the absence of a helmet is quite conspicuous – certainly more than the use or non-use of belts or cell phones. When strictly enforced use rates quickly increase to near full compliance. For example, in the 16 southern European Union countries where helmet use is required, over 90 percent of motorcyclists wear their helmets (Avenoso and Beckmann, 2005) and in Israel annual observational surveys repeatedly show that 98-100 percent of all riders wear a helmet, and nearly all of them wear a full helmet (NRSA, 2010).

Another reason for the less-than-expected benefits of helmet laws is that adding a helmet does not imply that "all other things remain the same." In fact, it has been argued that wearing a helmet by some riders who previously did not use it may provide an incentive to increase risk in other ways – such as speeding – in accordance with the risk-compensation hypothesis (Graham and Lee, 1986). Apparently, for many riders the need for a sense of freedom is greater than the need to live.

In the U.S., the conflict between those opposing helmet laws (mostly on the basis of infringement on individual rights) and those who demand helmet laws (mostly because it is a public health issue in which the public bears the brunt of the costs) has resulted in states enacting helmet laws, repealing helmet laws, reinstating helmet laws, and modifying helmet laws. These changes have also provided researchers with ample opportunities to examine the effects of helmet laws on motorcycle injuries and fatalities. In general, the weight of the evidence is quite conclusive: helmet laws work, and the more comprehensive they are, the more effective they are in reducing injuries and fatalities. Several evaluations of motorcycle fatalities and injury rates in different U.S. states, before and after adoption of helmet laws, show that the adoption of a helmet law is accompanied by an immediate increase in helmet use rates to nearly 100 percent and in a significant drop in serious injuries and fatalities. This has been shown for California (Kraus *et al.*, 1994), Maryland (Mitchell *et al.*, 2001), Texas (Fleming and Becker, 1992), and Washington (Mock *et al.*, 1995). Significant savings in lives (25 percent) have also been demonstrated in Spain following the introduction of mandatory universal helmet laws in 1992 (Ferrando *et al.*, 2000).

Quasi-experimental evaluation of the repeal of universal helmet laws

For various reasons, especially in motorized countries, safety improves over time (see Chapter 1). Thus, in many of the studies reviewed above attempts were made to control for confounding factors that would have accounted for the time-related improvements in safety that are not due to the passing of universal helmet laws. But invariably not all potential confounding factors can be controlled, and not all are even known. Therefore, in places where helmet laws are repealed or weakened and these changes are accompanied by an increase in injury and fatality rates, the argument for helmet laws is much more compelling. Muller (2004) evaluated the effect of Florida's repeal of the mandatory helmet law for riders who have a medical insurance for $10,000 or more, and estimated that the net effect of the weakening of the law – after controlling for trends in increase in travel miles and number of motorcycle registrations – was to increase rider fatalities by 21 percent. A more recent analysis of the effects of the weakening of the Florida Helmet laws, by Kyrychenko and McCartt (2006), yielded very similar conclusions. Preusser and his associates evaluated the repeal of universal helmet laws in Texas and Arkansas (Preusser, Hedlund, and Ulmer, 2000), and in Kentucky and Louisiana (Ulmer and Preusser, 2003) and found that in all four states helmet use dropped precipitously after the repeal of the law – from nearly 100 percent to 50-66 percent – and injuries and fatalities increased concurrently. Motorcyclist fatalities increased by over 20 percent in Arkansas, over 30 percent in Texas, 50 percent in Kentucky, and over 100 percent in Louisiana. Injuries also increased substantially in all states, as did the rates of fatalities per registered motorcycles. These significant changes in motorcycle safety are all the more amazing when it is realized that in all four states the helmet laws were not completely repealed, but replaced by laws that required young riders under 18 years old (Arkansas, Louisiana, Texas) or under 21 years old (Kentucky) only to wear helmets. Had helmet use requirements been totally suspended, the effect in each of these states would have been significantly greater. This is because the youngest riders are the highest risk riders and the ones most over-involved in crashes. Similar negative effects of repeal of helmet laws have been reported in other analyses conducted on the state of Arkansas (Bledsoe *et al.*, 2002), and the city of Miami Florida (Hotz *et al.*, 2002). Sass and Zimmerman (2000) conducted a panel study spanning 20 years that compared states with helmet laws to states without them, and showed that across all states helmet laws were effective in reducing motorcyclists' fatality rates by an average of approximately 30 percent. Thus, all of the studies that evaluated the benefits of universal helmet laws demonstrated their effectiveness in terms of compliance and in terms of injury and fatality reductions.

Comparisons between states with universal helmet laws and states without universal helmet laws

In terms of their impact on the use of helmets, universal helmet laws significantly raise their use by all age groups. A recent analysis by NHTSA of 2015 observational data showed that the use rate in states with universal helmet laws averaged 95 percent compared to 50 percent in states without it (NHTSA, 2016). In addition, analyses of the impact of this law on injuries should dispel any remaining doubts about the effectiveness of universal helmet laws. In the first analysis, conducted by U.S. National Highway Traffic Safety Administration (2006b), data from the Fatal Analysis Reporting System revealed that in 2005 sixty-five percent of the fatally injured motorcycle riders in states without universal helmet laws were not wearing a helmet, compared to only 14 percent in states with universal helmet laws. In the second analysis Coben, Steiner, and Miller (2007) compared the injury outcomes of 16,105 motorcyclists hospitalized for crash injuries in states with universal helmet laws with the outcomes of 9,689 riders hospitalized in states without such laws. On every measure examined, the outcome was significantly worse for the injured riders from the states without the universal helmet laws. Coben *et al.*'s main findings, summarized in Table 16-7, revealed that motorcyclists hospitalized from states without universal helmet laws are more likely to die during the hospitalization, are more likely to sustain severe traumatic brain injury, and are more likely to require care at long-term care facilities. To make the situation worse, motorcyclists in these states were more likely to lack adequate health insurance. Thus, in addition to the personal tragedy associated with lack of universal helmet laws, the states (and residents of these states) also pay a financial penalty for the high risk behavior of these riders. Yet, as mentioned above, despite the overwhelming evidence for its effectiveness, in 2015 only 19 states and the District of Columbia had universal helmet laws (NHTSA, 2016).

Comparisons of injured riders with different types of helmets and without helmets
Comparisons in motorcycle injuries and fatalities between riders who use and do not use helmets are often difficult, or at least difficult to interpret, because this variable and crash involvement are confounded with various other factors related to risky behaviors. These confounding variables can be partially controlled when a study limits its

Table 16-7. Average percent of riders with various outcomes out of all hospitalized riders following a motorcycle crash in 17 U.S. states with universal helmet laws and in 16 states without universal helmet laws (from Coben *et al.*, 2007, with permission from Elsevier).

The Percent of Riders Who:	States with Universal Helmet Laws (17)	States with No Helmet Laws or Partial Law (16)
Die in the hospital	1.80	2.52
Are referred to short-term facilities	4.01	2.43
Are referred to long-term facilities	8.82	10.92
Have principal diagnosis of intra-cranial injury	11.52	16.17

population to those already injured, and then examines the injury severity of those who wore helmets and those who did not. This comparison eliminates the confounding effects of other risky behaviors of non-users of helmets. Hundley *et al.* (2004) conducted such a comparison on the outcome of nearly 10,000 hospitalized injured motorcycle riders. They found that those who did not wear a helmet at the time of their crash were significantly more likely to have higher injury severity rating, were more likely to die as a result of the crash, accrued greater hospitalization charges, and (to spite) were less likely to have private insurance to cover their hospitalization costs. Thus Hundley *et al.*'s findings are very similar and complement those of Coben *et al.*'s (2007) in demonstrating the beneficial effects of helmets – both to their users and to the society at large.

But not all helmets are created equal. The U.S. Government has a helmet safety standard (NHTSA, 2011) that specifies minimum construction and performance requirements. But many riders prefer non-standard helmets, especially those known as "novelty" helmets. When evaluated in terms of their injury reduction potential they consistently perform worse. According to Erhardt *et al.* (2016), their use is based on the false assumption that standard full helmets, because of their size and weight, contribute to neck injuries. To test for this, Erhardt and her associates evaluated the injuries sustained by 7,051 injured California riders. They found that helmet type was strongly associated with head injuries but not with neck injuries. The most protective was a full-face helmet, less effective were half-helmet and open-face helmet, and the least effective were the novelty helmets that were associated with a relative risk of RR = 2.78 compared to the full-face helmet; that is, they were involved in nearly three times the rate of head injuries.

The weather: a confounding exposure variable that mediates the impact of universal helmet laws

The evaluation of helmet effectiveness via comparisons between states that have universal helmet laws and states that only have limited laws is a little problematic. This is because different states have different populations of riders and riding environments, regardless of their specific helmet laws. An important variable is the amount of riding, or kilometers of exposure – a variable that is greatly influenced by the weather. Branas and Knudson (2001) compared motorcycle fatality rates in states with universal helmet laws with the rates in states that did not have such laws, while statistically controlling for differences in average temperature, precipitation, population density, alcohol use, speeding, and engine size. After all of these variables were controlled for, the universal helmet law was still associated with a small numerical reduction in per capita fatality rates, but the small reduction was no longer statistically significant. This led Branas and Knudson to conclude that there is no sufficient evidence to show that universal helmet laws are effective. This conclusion was recently challenged by Morris (2006), who compared states with universal helmet laws to states without them and controlled for the effects of average temperature and precipitation – with the assumption that as the number of days of rain and the number of cold days increase the likelihood of venturing out in a motorcycle decreases. The temperature effect was quantified in terms of the amount of heating that was needed across all days of the year. Using a data base covering all U.S. states and a 10-year period (1993-2002), he indeed showed a very high correlation between injuries and fatalities and the amount of heating (r = –0.98 for both injuries and fatalities), and inches of precipitation ($r = -0.80$ for fatalities and $r = -0.77$ for injuries). More importantly, even after these two factors were controlled for, there remained a statistically significant positive effect of the universal helmet law, though its effect was smaller than that of the two weather variables. Although Morris does not quantify the percent reduction in the fatality rate due to the universal helmet law, it is important to note that all the states that did not have a universal law, still had specific helmet laws that presumably applied to the highest risk groups. Thus, even when the weather caveat is considered, universal helmet laws are an effective means of enforcing the use of helmets, and ultimately saving lives.

The negative side effects of helmets – none; and helmets can be further improved

Motorcycle riders often object to wearing safety helmets arguing that they are uncomfortable, potentially risky to neck (cervical cord) injuries (debunked above), and more importantly interfere with their ability to perceive impending danger by reducing their hearing and visual field. To counter the "discomfort" arguments helmets are constantly being improved in terms of their materials, ventilation, and thermal qualities. For example, Buyan *et al.* (2006) evaluated the discomforting effects of glare and heat from current motorcycle visors, with both heat-sensitive mannequins and humans, and based on their findings recommended the use of visors with infrared filtering properties. Bogerd and Brühwiler (2009) evaluated comfort in terms of heat loss of 27 different models of full-face motorcycle helmets, and found that the heat loss in the scalp section varied from 0 to 2 watts with the vents closed, and from nearly zero to 4 watts with the vents open. These are very significant differences in terms of thermal comfort. In a later study, Bogerd *et al.* (2014) sat 19 healthy males in front of a computer in a very warm climate chamber and assigned them various demanding cognitive tasks (visual vigilance, auditory vigilance, and letter cancelation), with and without a helmet. They found that, as expected, the helmet reduced comfort, and increased temperature perception but did not significantly affect performance on any of the cognitive tasks.

With respect to the potential risk for cervical cord injuries, a few studies examined the prevalence of such injuries in hospitalized riders who were and were not wearing helmets at the time of the crash. None of the studies found an increase in the risk to such injuries as a result of wearing a partial (open face) or a full-face helmet (e.g., O'Connor, 2005; Orsay *et al.*, 1994). In parallel, regulatory agencies such as NHTSA are constantly working to improve the standard with newer tests and better materials and performance requirements (NARA, 2015).

The concerns about the helmets' interference with vision and hearing were effectively rebuffed by McKnight and McKnight (1995), who conducted a well-controlled naturalistic experimental evaluation of the effects of helmets on hearing and seeing. In their study, 50 experienced riders rode their own motorcycles on a four lane highway (with traffic) at 30 and 50 mph, and upon hearing a horn from the experimenter driving behind them they were to switch lane. Half the riders participated in the "hearing" study and half in the "vision" study. The dependent measure for hearing was the decibel level of the sound to which the motorist responded; and the dependent measure for the interference with vision was the amount of head rotation the rider did prior to changing lanes. The cyclists rode under three conditions: without a helmet (not mandated by law at the time in Maryland), with a partial helmet, and with a full helmet. In the hearing study, the helmet had no effect on threshold decibel level, as can be seen in Figure 16-5a. The only effect on hearing was that of the speed; with higher speeds generating more turbulence and engine noise, and requiring a higher decibel level. For the vision study, it was noted that the partial helmet reduced the riders' static horizontal visual field by an average of 25 degrees, and the full helmet reduced the riders' horizontal visual field by an average of 18 degrees. To compensate for this loss in visual field, as can be seen in Figure 16-5b, the riders turned their heads the most when riding with the partial helmet and the least when wearing no helmet. Interestingly, though, the extent of the head movement did not fully compensate for the reduced visual field. Most important, however, the time needed to complete the visual check prior to switching lanes did not differ significantly among the three helmet conditions. Together these results led McKnight and McKnight to conclude that "wearing helmets does not restrict the ability to hear horn signals nor does it have an appreciable effect upon the likelihood of visually detecting a vehicle in an adjacent lane prior to initiating a lane change." Furthermore, it is possible that the effects of the helmets on head turning would have been even less had the helmets used in the study provided the riders with the U.S. Federally mandated minimum visual field of 105 degrees to each side (NHTSA, 2004). This requirement exceeds the actual visual field of most healthy young people (see Chapter 4), and the fact that in McKnight and McKnight's study the helmets reduced the actual visual field by approximately 20 degrees implies that they did not provide the optimal fit relative to the riders' eye position.

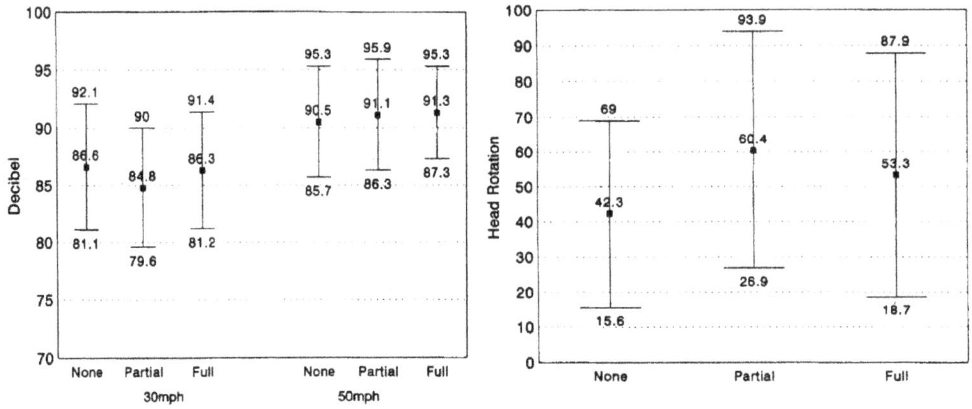

Figure 16-5. (a – left) Average hearing threshold (+1 s.d.) of motorcycle riders when riding their own motorcycles at 30 and 50 mph, without a helmet, with a partial helmet, and with a full helmet. (b – right) Average degrees of head rotation performed prior to changing lanes without a helmet, with a partial helmet, and with a full helmet (from McKnight and McKnight, 1995, with permission from Elsevier).

Given the proven effectiveness of helmets, the European Commission embarked on an effort to improve them in two respects: to increase usage by searching for ways of improving them from the perspective of the user, and in terms of their visibility to other drivers (COST 357, 2006). This collaborative multi-disciplinary effort labeled Accident Prevention Options with Motorcycle Helmets, evaluated changes in helmet design that would (1) minimize distraction from noise or thermal discomfort, maximize useful field of view, and provide the rider with necessary air exchange, and (2) maximize the conspicuity of the PTW-rider combination. The rationale for the former is that a more comfortable helmet would reduce stress-related impairments that might become significant over long rides. The rationale for the latter is that the helmet is generally the highest visible point of a rider-motorcycle unit and can be seen from all sides from the farthest distance. Some of the results of this project have been discussed above relative to improving riders' conspicuity (Cavallo and Pinto, 2015; Gershon *et al.*, 2012; Gershon and Shinar, 2013, 2015; Pinto *et al.*, 2014; Rößger *et al.*, 2015b), and relative to rider comfort (Bogerd and Brühwiler, 2009).

Vehicle and roadway improvements

Behavioral approaches to motorcycle safety can and should be supplemented by improvements to the PTWs and the roads. Two major safety concerns that should be and have been addressed by motorcycle manufacturers are the poor visibility of the motorcycles to drivers, and their poorly controlled and long braking distances (Bayly, Regan, and Hosking, 2006). The benefits of improved daylight running lights were discussed above and new motorcycles now have hardwired daytime running lights that are turned on whenever the engine is turned on. Improved braking and greater vehicle stability are currently being pursued by various manufacturers, but evaluation research on the effectiveness of various systems is still pending. In general, the introduction of intelligent transportation systems (ITS) has not benefited motorcycle safety as much as it has benefited car safety (Bayly *et al.*, 2006). Nonetheless, new safety systems are being developed and improved, including anti-lock braking systems (ABS) which prevent the wheels from locking up in hard braking, traction control systems (TCS), tire pressure monitoring systems (TPMS), and cooperative ITS – systems that communicate with other vehicles and with the roadway (ACEM, 2014). There is, however, a complicating issue that must be considered when it comes to the inclusion of new rider safety systems, and that is their acceptability by the riders. The issue is somewhat unique to motorcycling as a significant aspect of riding a motorcycle is the enjoyment and need for thrill. Systems that interfere with the riders' full control of the motorcycle – such as Intelligent Speed Adaptation – that warn riders of exceeding the speed limit or even limit their ability to do so are quite unpalatable to riders while advance warning systems – such as curve warning – are generally desired by riders (Huth, 2014).

Anti-lock Braking Systems (ABS)

ABS, as its name implies, prevents the wheels from locking up under hard braking. This can improve both braking distance and vehicle control. ABS is already operational on the more recent models, and just about all the analyses conducted to date have demonstrated its effectiveness in crash and injury reduction. The U.S. Insurance Institute for Highway Safety compared the involvement in fatal crashes of ABS-equipped motorcycles with identical models that do not have the ABS and found the former to be less involved by 31 percent (IIHS, 2014; Teoh, 2011). Analyses of crash data that compared ABS-equipped motorcycles with similar but non-ABS-equipped motorcycles in Italy, Spain, and Sweden indicated that it was associated with 34, and 42 percent reductions in severe and fatal crashes in Spain, and Sweden, respectively, and slightly less in Italy. The decrease in rear-end crashes – the crash type that is expected to be most affected by the ABS – was even greater: from 57 percent in Spain to 60 percent in Sweden (Rizzi *et al.*, 2015). These are huge effects from a single device. Given these and similar findings the European Parliament approved legislation that requires the installment of ABS on all new motorcycles over 125 cc from 2016, and similar requirements have been legislated in India, Japan (from 2018) and Taiwan (from 2019) (IIHS, 2016).

When coupled with a "combined braking system" that integrates the front and rear brake controls an additional small drop in crash risk is achieved (IIHS, 2013). The potential benefit of combined braking systems is illustrated in an analysis of the MAIDS data by Penumaka *et al.* (2014). They found that in those cases where the rider attempted to avoid the collision with a car, in 32.7 percent of the accidents, riders used their rear brake only; in 22.4 percent of the accidents riders used front brake only; and in 32.7 percent of the accidents, riders used both front and rear brakes (in 5 percent of the accidents the rider's evasive maneuver could not be ascertained). Also, in 41 percent of the collisions the hard braking resulted in wheel locking. Thus, it seems that most often, in the absence of advance braking systems, riders do not take full advantage of their braking power. Further good news about these systems is that when they are installed on the newer motorcycles, the riders do not adopt a risk-compensation strategy – or at least not one that negates all the benefits of the systems. More advanced braking systems such as autonomous emergency braking systems that are activated when a sensor detects an imminent collision with an object ahead are also being developed and at least one detailed analysis based on computer reconstruction of 212 motorcycle crashes in Australia, Italy, and Sweden indicates that such a system can significantly reduce impact speeds (Savino *et al.*, 2014).

As new advance rider assistance systems (ARAS) are being considered and developed a major issue is the rider's acceptance. In an interesting evaluation of alternative designs of curve warning systems, intersection support system, forward collision warning system, and lane change support system, Huth and Gelau (2013) found that rider acceptance in terms of intention to use the system depended mostly on the perceived social norm of fellow riders, and less on the interface design. Surprisingly, the perceived risk of riding without the system did not figure at all in the riders' intention to use the system. This could mean one of two things: that safety is not a prime concern for motorcycle riders or that those who said they would not activate such a system felt safer on their cycles than those who stated they would activate the system. A further analysis of the responses indicated that the latter is true. Thus, in order for riders to accept an ARAS, riders first have to be convinced that motorcycles are not safe. A more practical approach is to focus on the development of passive safety systems that do not require rider activation (as is the case with the ABS and the combined braking systems).

To improve motorcycle conspicuity – especially when it brakes – Tang, Tsai, and Lee (2006) evaluated the potential benefits of having the two rear signal lights flash simultaneously as long as the center brake light between them remains on. The rationale is that with only one brake lamp, it is often difficult to quickly detect braking – especially at night when the running red rear light is already on (A similar rationale led to the evaluation of alternative car stop lights, and resulted in the successful application of the center high-mounted stop lamp that is now a standard requirement of all cars in the U.S. and in many other countries). Although Tang *et al.*'s study design was quite rudimentary, employing a fairly primitive simulation, the effect was quite large: average reaction time of the "following" driver in response to the motorcycle brake lights was reduced by an average of 0.2 seconds. The use of the flashing lights was especially effective when the motorcycle's rear lights were in the driver's peripheral visual field. As expected, the simultaneous flashing of the signal lights did cause some confusion when the cyclist employed the turn signal (without the brakes), but in that case – relative to the standard lighting system – the reaction time was delayed by only 0.12 seconds. Considering that this is the first study of its kind, it appears that improvements in the motorcycle braking systems lights can improve their early detectability to following car drivers, and this line of research should therefore be continued.

Roadway design can also be tailored to enhance cyclists' safety. As long as motorcycles use the same lanes as cars and trucks – unlike bicycles that often have dedicated lanes – highway engineers have to consider how to best accommodate them with the other vehicles. A detailed discussion of infrastructure safety measures are outside the scope of this book, but many can be found in the ACEM's (2006) "Guidelines for PTW-Safer Road Design in Europe" (www.acem.eu). Some of these considerations have resulted in new "motorcycle-friendly" safety barriers that have been recently introduced in Portugal and France, and "forgiving roadsides" that can allow riders to get off the road without necessarily losing their balance or traction in Cyprus (Avenoso and Beckmann, 2005). In a few countries with high PTW volumes, Malaysia for example, separate motorcycle paths are built with consideration to providing the motorcyclists with adequate sight distance that allows them to stop safely in case of an obstacle (Davoodi *et al.*, 2012). Where space is not available, motorcycles in some cities have been allowed to use the public transportation lane ("bus" lane). Though this may make car drivers and motorcyclists feel better, it seems to be bad for safety. In London, for example, this resulted in higher motorcycle speeds and crash rates, and targeted speed enforcement was unable to mitigate either (York, Ball, and Hopkin, 2011).

Another, human-factors oriented, approach to integrating riders with the other traffic is to consider the lane width that a PTW requires. In general typical marked lane widths are 3-4 meters wide and they are designed to accommodate 4-wheeled vehicles. This often creates dangerous situations, whereby motorcycles pass cars by riding on the lane marker between cars in adjacent lanes (known by riders as lane splitting or lane sharing).

To assess the space needed to accommodate motorcycles, Hussain *et al.* (2005) recorded the actual paths of small and medium sized motorcycles (<150 cc) in Malaysian motorcycle lanes. They noted that while the actual average handlebar width of the motorcycles was approximately 0.8 meters, the operational width – the width of the motorcycle plus the buffer zone needed to comfortably pass another vehicle – was 1.3 meters. Consequently, with motorcycle lane widths less than 1.7 meters the riders tended to ride behind one another, while with larger lane widths, they tended to ride in parallel or pass each other. Therefore, to avoid weaving behavior between cars in adjacent lanes, roads that are heavily used by motorcycles, should be designed with special motorcycle lanes in mind; and these lanes should be either significantly narrower than 1.7 meters (to discourage passing and parallel riding) or significantly wider (to allow for safe passing and parallel riding). Dedicated motorcycle lanes are not common in the Western world, but with the increase in PTW in traffic, we may begin to see more and more of them. Until that happens we are likely to witness an increase in lane splitting as the preferred riders' tactic to defeating congestion. In fact, in California lane splitting is now legal under some circumstances (such as when the traffic moves at 30 mph or less) (Kane, 2013).

Concluding Comments

Motorcycles are inherently more dangerous than cars on the road: they are less stable and do not provide their riders with a protective shield. These facts are reflected in much higher crash and severe injury risk for motorcycles than for cars. Research into the causes of motorcycle crashes has revealed that the two principal issues behind motorcycle accidents are their poor visibility (relative to cars), and the often inadequate and inappropriate responses of the riders to rapidly emerging hazards. Various behavioral and technological approaches have been taken to address the visibility problem, and a few means have been developed to improve the handling of motorcycles in emergency braking situations. However, the greater societal awareness of the motorcycle safety problem is prompting the development and evaluation of behavioral, design and technological approaches to reduce their crash risk. An extreme approach, not likely to be adopted soon in most countries is to simply ban motorcycles from streets and roads used by other motor vehicle. As radical as it seems, this approach has been applied to all-terrain vehicles (ATVs, also known as "dune buggies"), and has been decreed in Guangzhou, China as of the beginning of 2007 (Johnson, 2006). An alternative approach is to accommodate motorcycle riders by providing them with dedicated lanes. If the current trends in urban congestion and in the numbers of motorcycle registrations continue, we are likely to see an increase in both solutions.

In terms of injury and fatality reductions, the motorcycle helmet is an impressively effective device, reducing fatalities by approximately 20 percent. Despite their proven effectiveness, their use rates in the U.S. are still much lower than could be achieved by proper legislation and relatively inexpensive enforcement. One obstacle to increasing their use is the cyclists' reason for using motorcycles – especially the high performance large engine types: the thrill of the ride. Their use rates may possibly be increased if they are perceived by riders as less discomforting and interfering. Research and development efforts are currently under way to improve their thermal comfort and reduce their interference with the rider's cognitive functioning as well as to improve their visibility. As long as the lure of riding a motorcycle is there, it is up to society to ensure that the riders are well protected – from their own risky behavior (with helmets) and from their lack of visibility to other road users. Given the extreme over-involvement of motorcycles in crashes and fatalities, it is obvious that much work is still left to be done on both fronts. As things look now, our arsenal of behavioral interventions is very limited and ineffective. This is underscored by the poor rating of – licensing, education, training, and communication programs in NHTSA's latest edition of Countermeasures that Work (Goodwin *et al.*, 2015). The direct implication of this is that future safety efforts should be focused more on vehicle and roadway improvement to accommodate poor riding, than on the improvement of riding behavior itself.

References

ACEM (2004). *MAIDS: In-Depth Investigations of Accidents Involving Powered Two-Wheelers.* Association de Constructeurs Européens de Motocycles (ACEM), Brussels, BG. http://MAIDS.acembike.org

ACEM (2006). Guidelines for PTW-Safer Road Design in Europe. Brussels, Belgium. http://www.enmotomasseguro.com/_Documentacion/Informes_Estadisticas/INFORMES%20Y%20ESTUDIOS/A%C3%91O%202006/guidelines%20for%20ptw-safer%20road%20design%20in%20europe.pdf

ACEM (2014). *The safe ride to the future: The motorcycle's industry commitment to road safety.* European Association of Motorcycle Manufacturers (ACEM), Brussels, BG. www.acembike.org

Armsby, P., A. J. Boyle and C. C. Wright (1989). Methods for assessing drivers' perception of specific hazards on the road. *Accid. Anal. Prev.*, *21*, 45-60.

Aupetit, S., V. Gallier, J. Riff, S. Espié and F. Delgehier (2016). Naturalistic study of the risky situations faced by novice riders. *Ergonomics*, *59*(8), 1109-1120.

Avenoso, A. and J. Beckmann (2005). The safety of vulnerable road users in the Southern, Eastern and Central European Countries (The "SEC Belt"). European Transport Safety Council, Brussels, Belgium.

Baldi, S., J. D. Baer and A. L. Cook (2005). Identifying best practices states in motorcycle rider education and licensing. *J. Safe. Res.*, *36*, 19-32.

Bambach, M. R., R. H. Grzebieta, J. Olivier and A. S. McIntosh (2011). Fatality risk for motorcyclists in fixed object collisions. *J. Trans. Safe. Secur.*, *3*(3), 222-235.

Bayly, M., M. Regan and S. Hosking (2006). Intelligent transport systems and motorcycle safety. Monash University Accident Research Center, Report 260. Monash University, Clayton, Victoria, Australia.

Beanland, V., M. G. Lenné and G. Underwood (2014). Safety in numbers: Target prevalence affects the detection of vehicles during simulated driving. *Atten. Percept. Psychophys.*, *76*(3), 805-813.

Bellet, T. and A. Banet (2012). Towards a conceptual model of motorcyclists' risk awareness: A comparative study of riding experience effect on hazard detection and situational criticality assessment. *Accid. Anal. Prev.*, *49*, 154-164.

Bledsoe, G. H., S. M. Schexnayder, M. J. Carey, W. N. Dobbins, W. D. Gibson, J. W. Hindman, T. Collins, B. H. Wallace, J. B. Cone and T. J. Ferrer (2002). The negative impact of the repeal of the Arkansas Motorcycle Helmet Law. *J. Trauma-Inj. Infect. Crit. Care*, *53*(6), 1078-1087.

Blomberg, R. D., R. C. Peck, H. Moskowitz, M. Burns and D. Fiorentino (2004). Crash risk of alcohol involved driving. Final report on Contract No. DTNH22-94-C-05001 to the National Highway Traffic Safety Administration. Dunlop and Associates, Inc., Stamford, CT.

Bogerd, C. P. and P. A. Brühwiler (2009). Heat loss variations of full-face motorcycle helmets. *Appl. Ergon.*, *40*(2), 161-164.

Bogerd, C. P., I. Walker, P. A. Brühwiler and R. M. Rossi (2014). The effect of a helmet on cognitive performance is, at worst, marginal: A controlled laboratory study. *Appl. Ergon.*, *45*(3), 671-676.

Bragg, B. W., N. E. Dawson and B. A. Jonah (1980). Profile of the accident involved motorcyclist in Canada. International Motorcycle Safety Conference, Washington, 3:1131-51. (as cited by Wells *et al.*, 2004).

Branas, C. C. and M. M. Knudson (2001). Helmet laws and motorcycle rider death rates. *Accid. Anal. Prev.*, *33*, 641-648.

Brooks, A. M., D. P. Chiang, T. A. Smith, J. W. Zellner, J. P. Peters and J. Compagne (2005). A driving simulator methodology for evaluating enhanced motorcycle conspicuity. 19th Annual Conference of Experimental Safety Vehicles. Paper 05-0259. U.S. Department of Transportation, Washington, DC.

Brooks, P. and A. Guppy (1990). Driver awareness and motorcycle accidents. Proceedings of the International Motorcycle Safety Conference, II, 10-27-10-56. (as cited by Huang and Preston, 2004).

Buyan, M., P. A. Brühwiler, A. Azens, G. Gustavsson, R. Karmhag and C. G. Granqvist (2006). Facial warming and tinted helmet visors. *Int. J. Ind. Ergon.*, *36*(1), 11-16.

Caldwell, C. (2006). Geezery rider. New York Times Magazine, October 29.

Cavallo, V. and M. Pinto (2015). Visual factors affecting motorcycle conspicuity: Effects of car daytime-running lights and motorcycle headlight design. In: *Increasing Motorcycle Conspicuity: Design and Assessment of Interventions to Enhance Rider Safety* (L. Rößger, M. G. Lenné and G. Underwood eds.). Ashgate, Farnham, England.

Cavallo, V., M. Ranchet, M. Pinto, S. Espié, F. Vienne and N. T. Dang (2015). Improving car drivers' perception of motorcycle motion through innovative headlight configurations. *Accid. Anal. Prev.*, *81*, 187-193.

CIE (1982). An analytical model for describing the influence of lighting parameters upon visual performance. CIE Publication No. 19/2.1. Commission Internationale de l'Eclairage (CIE), Vienna, Austria.

Clarke, D. D., P. Ward, C. Bartle and W. Truman (2004). In-depth study of motorcycle accidents. Road Safety Research. Report No. 54. Department for Transport, London.

Clarke, D. D., P. Ward, C. Bartle and W. Truman (2007). The role of motorcyclist and other driver behaviour in two types of serious accident in the UK. *Accid. Anal. Prev.*, *39*(5), 974-981.

Coben, J. H., C. A. Steiner and T. R. Miller (2007). Characteristics of motorcycle-related hospitalizations: Comparing states with different helmet laws. *Accid. Anal. Prev.*, *39*(1), 190-196.

Comelli, M., A. Morandi, D. Magazzù, M. Bottazzi and A. Marinoni (2008). Brightly coloured motorcycles and brightly coloured motorcycle helmets reduce the odds of a specific category of road accidents: A case-control study. *Biomed. Stat. Clin. Epid.*, *2*(1).

Compton, R. P. and A. Berning (2015). Drug and alcohol crash risk. National Highway Traffic Safety Administration, Traffic Safety Facts, Research Note DOT HS 812 117. U.S. Department of Transportation, Washington DC.

Cook, L. J., T. J. Kerns, C. A. Burch, A. Thomas and E. Bell (2009). Motorcycle helmet use and head and facial injuries: Crash outcomes in CODES-linked data. NHTSA Report No. HS-811 208. U.S. Department of Transportation, Washington, DC.

COST 357 (2006). *Accident prevention options with motorcycle helmets*. European Commission, Brussels, Belgium. http://www.cost357.org/index-e.shtml (accessed March 25, 2007)

Crundall, D., K. Humphrey and D. Clarke (2008). Perception and appraisal of approaching motorcycles at junctions. *Transportation Res. F*, *11*(3), 159-167.

Davoodi, S. R., H. Hamid, M. Pazhouhanfar and J. W. Muttart (2012). Motorcyclist perception response time in stopping sight distance situations. *Safety Sci.*, *50*, 371-377.

Deutermann, W. (2004). Motorcycle helmet effectiveness revisited. National Highway Traffic Safety Administration. Report DOT HS 809 715. U.S. Department of Transportation, Washington, DC.

EC (2010). Regulation on two- or three-wheel vehicles and quadricycles: Executive Summary. F1 558340 DT. European Commission, Brussels, Belgium.

EC (2013). DaCoTA (2012) Powered Two Wheelers, Deliverable 4.8n of the EC FP7 Project DaCoTA. European Commission, Brussels, Belgium.

Elliott, M. A., C. J. Baughan and B. F. Sexton (2007). Errors and violations in relation to motorcyclists' crash risk. *Accid. Anal. Prev.*, *39*(3), 491-499.

Erhardt, T., T. Rice, L. Troszak and M. Zhu (2016). Motorcycle helmet type and the risk of head injury and neck injury during motorcycle collisions in California. *Accid. Anal. Prev.*, *86*, 23-28.

Espié, S., E. Bekiaris and S. Nikolaou (2010). Naturalistic rider studies for the analysis of riders' behavior and safety: "2BESAFE". Proceedings of the Road Safety on Four Continents Conference (Vol. 15, pp. 194-199). Yas Island, Abu Dhabi.

Eurobarometer (2014). Special Eurobarometer 422a "Quality of Transport". Wave EB82.2 – TNS Opinion & Social. European Commission, Brussels, Belgium.

Evans, L. (1986). Double pair comparison – A new method to determine how occupant characteristics affect fatality risk in traffic crashes. *Accid. Anal. Prev.*, *18*(3), 217-227.

Ferrando, J., A. Plasència, M. Orós, C. Borrell and J. F. Kraus (2000). Impact of a helmet law on two wheel motor vehicle crash mortality in a southern European urban area. *Inj. Prev.*, *6*, 184-188.

Fleming, H. S. and E. R. Becker (1992). The impact of the Texas 1989 motorcycle helmet law on total and head-related fatalities, severe injuries, and overall injuries. *Med. Care, 30*, 832-845.

Gershon, P., N. Ben-Asher and D. Shinar (2012). Attention and search conspicuity of motorcycles as a function of their visual context. Accid. Anal. Prev., *44*(1), 97-103.

Gershon, P. and D. Shinar (2013). Increasing motorcycles attention and search conspicuity by using Alternating-Blinking Lights System (ABLS). *Accid. Anal. Prev., 50*, 801-810.

Gershon and Shinar (2015). Powered two-wheelers conspicuity: The effects of visual context and awareness. In: *Increasing Motorcycle Conspicuity: Design and Assessment of Interventions to Enhance Rider Safety* (L. Röβger, M. G. Lenné and G. Underwood eds.). Ashgate, Farnham, England.

Glassbrenner, D. and J. Ye (2007). Motorcycle helmet use in 2007 – Overall results. National Highway Traffic Safety Administration, Traffic Safety Facts, Research Note DOT HS 810 840. U.S. Department of Transportation, Washington DC.

Goodwin, A., L. Thomas, B. Kirley, W. Hall, N. O'Brien and K. Hill (2015). *Countermeasures that work: A highway safety countermeasures guide for State Highway Safety Offices*. 8th edition. NHTSA Report No. DOT HS 812 202. U.S. Department of Transportation, Washington, DC.

Graham, J. D. and Y. H. Lee (1986). Behavioral-response to safety regulation—the case of motorcycle helmet-wearing legislation. *Policy Sci., 19*(3), 253-273.

Grayson, G. B., G. Maycock, J. A. Groeger, S. M. Hammond and D. T. Field (2003). Risk, hazard perception and perceived control. Report TRL 560. Transport Research Laboratory, Crowthorne, U.K.

Grzebieta, R. (2014). Safety of motorcyclists. 6th International Annual Conference on Urban Traffic Safety. (April 28-May2). Edmonton, CA.

Hancock, P. A., G. Wulf, D. Thom and P. Fassnacht (1990). Driver workload during differing driving maneuvers. *Accid. Anal. Prev., 22*(3), 281-290.

Haworth, N. (2012). Powered two wheelers in a changing world—Challenges and opportunities. Accid. Anal. Prev., *44*(1), 12-18.

Haworth, N. and C. Mulvihill (2005). Review of motorcycle licensing and training. Monash University Accident Research Center. Report No. 240. Monash University, Clayton, Victoria, AU.

Haworth, N., C. Mulvihill and M. Symmons (2005). Hazard perception and responding by motorcyclists – Background and literature review. Monash University Accident Research Center. Report No. 235. Monash University, Clayton, Victoria, AU.

Haworth, N., R. Smith, L. Brumen and N. Pronk (1997). *Case control study of motorcycle crashes* (CR174). Federal Office of Road Safety, Canberra, AU.

Hole, G. J., L. Tyrrell and M. Langham (1996). Some factors affecting motorcyclists' conspicuity. *Ergonomics, 39*(7), 946-965.

Horswill, M. S. and S. Helman (2003). A behavioral comparison between motorcyclists and a matched group of non-motorcycling car drivers: Factors influencing accident risk. *Accid. Anal. Prev., 35*, 589-597.

Horswill, M. S., S. Helman, P. Ardiles and J. Wann (2005). Motorcycle Accident Risk Could Be Inflated by a Time to Arrival Illusion. *Optom. Vision Sci., 82*(8), 740-746.

Hosking, S. G., C. C. Liu and M. Bayly (2010). The visual search patterns and hazard responses of experienced and inexperienced motorcycle riders. *Accid. Anal. Prev., 42*(1), 196-202.

Hotz, G. A., S. M. Cohn, C. Popkin, P. Ekeh, R. Duncan, E. W. Johnson, F. Pernas and J. Selem (2002). The impact of a repealed motorcycle helmet law in Miami-Dade County. *J. Trauma-Inj. Infect. Crit. Care, 52*(3), 469-474.

Huang, B. and J. Preston (2004). A literature review of motorcycle collisions. Transport Studies Unit, Oxford University, Oxford, UK.

Hundley, J. C., P. D. Kilgo, R. Miller, M. C. Chang, R. A. Hensberry, J. W. Meredith and J. J. Hoth (2004). Non-helmeted motorcyclists: A burden to society? A study using the National Trauma Data Bank. *J. Trauma-Inj. Infect. Crit. Care, 57*(5), 944-949.

Hurt, H. H. Jr., J. V. Ouellet and D. R. Thom (1981). Motorcycle accident cause factors and identification of countermeasures: Volume I: Technical report. National Highway Traffic Safety Administration. Report DOT-HS-805-862. U.S. Department of Transportation, Washington, DC.

Hussain, H., R. S. Radin-Umar, M. S. Ahmad-Farhan and M. M. Dadang (2005). Key components of a motorcycle traffic system – A Study along the motorcycle path in Malaysia. *IATSS Res., 29*(1), 50-56.

Huth, V. (2014). Motorcycle riders' acceptance of advance rider assistance systems. Chapter 13. In: *Driver Acceptance of New Technology: Theory, Measurement and Optimisation* (P. Underwood ed.). Taylor and Francis.

Huth, V., E. Füssl and R. Risser (2014). Motorcycle riders' perceptions, attitudes and strategies: Findings from a focus group study. *Transportation Res. F, 25*, 74-85.

Huth, V. and C. Gelau (2013). Predicting the acceptance of advanced rider assistance systems. Accid. Anal. Prev., *50*, 51-58.

Ichikawa, M., W. Chadbunchachai and E. Marui (2003). Effect of the helmet act for motorcyclists in Thailand. *Accid. Anal. Prev., 35*(2), 183-189.

IIHS (2011). These machines are designed for the racetrack. *Status Rep., 42*(9), September 11. Insurance Institute for Highway Safety, Arlington, Virginia.

IIHS (2014). *New research adds to the evidence that motorcycle ABS prevents crashes.* Insurance Institute for Highway Safety, Arlington, Virginia.

IIHS (2016). India is latest to require motorcycle ABS; no action in the U.S. despite clear evidence. *Status Rep., 51*(5), May 24, p. 7. Insurance Institute for Highway Safety, Arlington, Virginia.

Ivers, R. Q., C. Sakashita, T. Senserrick, J. Elkington, S. Lo, S. Boufous and L. de Rome (2016). Does an on-road motorcycle coaching program reduce crashes in novice riders? A randomised control trial. *Accid. Anal. Prev., 86*, 40-46.

Johnson, T. (2006). Latest edict bans motorcycles. Seattle Times, Sunday December 10. http://seattletimes.nwsource.com/html/nationworld/2003470362_chinabikes10.html

Jonah, B. A. (1997). Sensation seeking and risky driving: a review and synthesis of the literature. *Accid. Anal. Prev., 29*, 651-665.

Kane, W. (2013). Motorcycle lane-splitting rules unveiled. San Francisco Chronicle. February 12.

Keng, S. H. (2005). Helmet use and motorcycle fatalities in Taiwan. *Accid. Anal. Prev., 37*(2), 349-355.

Kim, K., J. Boski and E. Yamashita (2002). Typology of motorcycle crashes. *Transportation Research Record*, No. 1818, paper No. 02-2885, 47-53.

Kindelberger, J. and J. A. Milani (2015). Crash Outcome Data Evaluation System (CODES): Program transition and promising practices. Report No. DOT HS 812 178. U.S. Department of Transportation, Washington, DC.

Koornstra, M. K. (ed.) (2003). Transport safety performance in the EU. European Transport Safety Council, Transport Accident Statistics Working Party, Brussels, Belgium. http://www.etsc.be/rep.htm. Accessed November 17, 2003.

Kraus, J. F., C. Peek, D. L. McArthur and A. Williams (1994). The effect of the 1992 California motorcycle helmet usage law on motorcycle crash fatalities and injuries. *JAMA*, *272*, 1506-1511.

Kyrychenko, S. Y. and A. T. McCartt (2006). Florida's weakened motorcycle helmet law: Effects on death rates in motorcycle crashes. *Traffic Inj. Prev.*, *7*, 55-60.

Lardelli-Claret, P., J. J. Jiménez-Moleón, J. de Dios Luna-del-Castillo, M. García-Martín, A. Bueno-Cavanillas and R. Gálvez-Vargas (2005). Driver dependent factors and the risk of causing a collision for two wheeled motor vehicles. *Inj. Prev.*, *11*, 225-231.

Law, T. H., M. Ghanbari, H. Hamid, A. Abdul-Halin and C. P. Ng (2016). Role of sensory and cognitive conspicuity in the prevention of collisions between motorcycles and trucks at T-intersections. *Accid. Anal. Prev.*, *96*, 64-70.

Lin, M. R. and J. F. Kraus (2009). A review of risk factors and patterns of motorcycle injuries. *Accid. Anal. Prev.*, *41*(4), 710-722.

Liu, B. C., R. Ivers, R. Norton, S. Blows and S. K. Lo (2008). Helmets for preventing injury in motorcycle riders. *Cochrane Database Syst. Rev.*, *1*. Art No.: CD004333.

McGwin, G. Jr., J. Whatley, J. Metzger, F. Valent, F. Barbone and L. W. III Rue (2004). The effect of state motorcycle licensing laws on motorcycle driver mortality rates. *J. Trauma-Inj. Infect. Crit. Care*, *56*(2), 415-419.

McKnight, A. J. and A. S. McKnight (1995). The effects of motorcycle helmets upon seeing and hearing. *Accid. Anal. Prev.*, *27*(4), 493-501.

Mellor, A. and V. StClaire (2005). Advanced motorcycle helmets. 19th ESV Conference, June, paper 05-0329. U.S. Department of Transportation, Washington, DC.

Ministerio del Interior (2007). Strategic plan for the road safety of motorcycles and mopeds. Direccion General de Traffico, Spain.

Mitchell, K. A., J. A. Kufera, M. F. Ballesteros, J. E. Smialek and P. C. Dischinger (2001). *Autopsy study of motorcyclist fatalities: The effect of the 1992 Maryland helmet use law.* Paper Presented at the International Motorcycle Safety Conference, Orlando, Florida.

Mitsopoulos-Rubens, E. and M. G. Lenné (2012). Issues in motorcycle sensory and cognitive conspicuity: The impact of motorcycle low-beam headlights and riding experience on drivers' decisions to turn across the path of a motorcycle. Accid. Anal. Prev., *49*, 86-95.

Mock, C. N., R. V. Maier, E. Boyle, S. Pilcher and F. P. Rivara (1995). Injury prevention strategies to promote helmet use decrease severe head injuries at a Level 1 trauma center. *J. Trauma*, *39*, 29-35.

Morris, C. C. (2006). Generalized linear regression analysis of association of universal helmet laws with motorcyclist fatality rates. *Accid. Anal. Prev.*, *38*, 142-147.

Muller, A. (2004). Florida's motorcycle helmet law repeal and fatality rates. *Am. J. Pub. Health, 94*(4), 556-558.

Mullin, B., R. Jackson, J. Langley and R. Norton (2000). Increasing age and experience: Are both protective against motorcycle injury? A case-control study. *Inj. Prev., 6*, 32-35.

Muttart, J. W., L. R. Peck, S. Guderian, W. Bartlett, L. P. Ton, C. Kauderer, D. L. Fisher and J. E. Manning (2011). Glancing and stopping behavior of motorcyclists and car drivers at intersections. *Transportation Res. Record, 2265*(1), 81-88.

Nagayama, Y., T. Morita, T. Miura, J. Watanabem and N. Murakami (1980). Motorcyclists' visual scanning pattern in comparison with automobile drivers'. Society of Automotive Engineers. (as cited by Haworth *et al.*, 2005).

Nakahara, S., W. Chadbunchachai, M. Ichikawa, N. Tipsuntornsak and S. Wakai (2005). Temporal distribution of motorcyclist injuries and risk of fatalities in relation to age, helmet use, and riding while intoxicated in Khon Kaen, Thailand. *Accid. Anal. Prev., 37*, 833-842.

NARA (2015). 49 CFR Part 571 Federal Motor Vehicle Safety Standards; Motorcycle Helmets. *Federal Register, 80*(98), 29458-29487. National Archives and Records Administration, Washington, DC.

Nathanael, D., E. Portouli, K. Gkikas and V. Papakostopoulos (2012). What does a motorcyclist look at while driving at urban arterials? *Work: A Journal of Prevention, Assessment and Rehabilitation, 41*, 4900-4906.

Newman, J. A. and G. D. Webster (1974). The mechanics of motorcycle accidents. Proceedings of the 18th Annual Conference of the American Association for Automotive Medicine, pp. 265-302.

NHTSA (1996). Benefits of safety belts and motorcycle helmets: Report to Congress. Based on Data from The Crash Outcome Data Evaluation System (CODES). National Highway Traffic Safety Administration. Report DOT HS 808 347. U.S. Department of Transportation, Washington, DC.

NHTSA (2004). Standard Number 571.218. Motorcycle Helmets. October 1, 2004 Edition. U.S. Department of Transportation, Washington, DC.

NHTSA (2005). Traffic Safety Facts 2004. National Highway Traffic Safety Administration. Report HS 809 919. U.S. Department of Transportation, Washington, DC.

NHTSA (2011). Federal Motor Vehicle Safety Standard No. 218: Motorcycle Helmets. U.S. Department of Transportation, Washington, DC.

NHTSA (2013). Motorcycles. Traffic Safety Facts, 2011 data. National Highway Traffic Safety Administration Report DOT HS 811 765. U.S. Department of Transportation, Washington, DC.

NHTSA (2015a). Lives Saved in 2013 by Restraint Use and Minimum Drinking Age Laws, Traffic Safety Facts. National Highway Traffic Safety Administration Report DOT HS 812 137. U.S. Department of Transportation, Washington, DC.

NHTSA (2015b). 2013 Crash overview. Data Webinar, January 15. National Highway Traffic Safety Administration, U.S. Department of Transportation, Washington, DC.

NHTSA (2015c). Traffic Safety Facts 2013. National Highway Traffic Safety Administration Report DOT HS 812 139. U.S. Department of Transportation, Washington, DC.

NHTSA (2016). Motorcycle helmet use in 2015—Overall results. Traffic Safety Facts. National Highway Traffic Safety Administration Report DOT HS 812 275. U.S. Department of Transportation, Washington, DC.

Njå, O. and S. M. Nesvåg (2007). Traffic behaviour among adolescents using mopeds and light motorcycles. J. Safety Res., *38*(4), 481-492.

Norvell, D. C. and P. Cummings (2002). Association of helmet use with death in motorcycle crashes: A matched-pair cohort study. *Am. J. Epidemiol.*, *156*(5), 483-487.

NRSA (2010). Behavior of PTW riders: Observations and interviews. The Israel National Road Safety Authority, Jerusalem, Israel.

Ochiai, A., Y. Naya, J. Soh, Y. Ishida, S. Ushijima, Y. Mizutani, A. Kawauchi and T. Miki (2006). Do motorcyclists have erectile dysfunction? A preliminary study. *Int. J. Impotence Res.*, *18*, 396-399.

O'Connor, P. J. (2005). Motorcycle helmets and spinal cord injury: Helmet usage and type. *Traffic Inj. Prev.*, *6*, 60-66.

OECD (2014). Road Safety Annual Report 2014. International Transport Forum (ITF), IRTAD, Paris, France.

Olson, P. L. and M. Sivak (1986). Perception-response time to unexpected roadway hazards. *Hum. Fact.*, *28*, 91–96.

Orsay, E. M., R. L. Muelleman, T. D. Peterson, D. H. Jurisic, J. B. Kosasih and P. Levy (1994). Motorcycle helmets and spinal injuries: Dispelling the myth. *Ann. Emerg. Med.*, *23*(4), 802-806.

Otte, D., M. Jänsch and B. Wiese (2013). Injury severity and causation factors of motorcyclists in traffic accidents in comparing drivers of motorcycle and all kinds of motorized two-wheelers. MFS Motorcycle Conference, October 16-20, Orlando, FL.

Otte, D., M. Jänsch and B. Wiese (2014). Influence parameter and accident factors in comparing light and heavy motorized-two-wheelers. Annual Conf. Int. Forum of Automotive Traffic Safety INFATS, Nov, 13-14. Chong Qing, China.

Otte, D., H. Willeke, B. Chinn, D. Doyle and E. Shuller (1998). Impact mechanisms of helmet protected heads in motorcycle accidents – accident study of COST 327. Safety – Environment – Future II, proceedings of the 1998 International Motorcycle Conference.

Ouellet, J. (1990). Environmental hazards in motorcycle accidents. 26th Annual Proceedings American Association for Automotive Medicine, October 4-6, 1982, Ontario, Canada.

Ouellet, J. V. and V. Kasantikul (2006). Motorcycle helmet effect on a per-crash basis in Thailand and the United States. *Traffic Inj. Prev.*, *7*, 49-54.

Paine, M., D. Paine, J. Haley and S. Cockfield (2005). Daytime running lights for motorcycles. Abstract ID 05-0178. Proceedings of the 19th Experimental Safety Vehicle Conference. U.S. Department of Transportation, Washington, DC.

Paulozzi, L. J. (2005). The role of sales of new motorcycles in a recent increase in motorcycle mortality rates. *J. Safe. Res.*, *36*, 361-364.

Pedder, J. B., J. R. Hurt and D. Otte (1979). Motorcycle accident impact conditions as a basis for motorcycle crash tests. Proceedings of the 12th NATO conference on Experimental Safety Vehicles.

Penumaka, A. P., G. Savino, N. Baldanzini and M. Pierini (2014). In-depth investigations of PTW-car accidents caused by human errors. Safety Sci., *68*, 212-221.

Pinto, M., V. Cavallo and G. Saint-Pierre (2014). Influence of front light configuration on the visual conspicuity of motorcycles. Accid. Anal. Prev., *62*, 230-237.

Preusser, D. F., J. H. Hedlund and R. G. Ulmer (2000). Evaluation of motorcycle helmet law repeal in Arkansas and Texas. National Highway Traffic Safety Administration. Report DTNH22-97-D-05018. U.S. Department of Transportation, Washington, DC.

Preusser, D. F., A. F. Williams and R. G. Ulmer (1995). Analysis of fatal motorcycle crashes: Crash typing. *Accid. Anal. Prev.*, *27*(6), 845-851.

Ratanavaraha, V. and S. Jomnonkwao (2013). Community participation and behavioral changes of helmet use in Thailand. *Transport Policy*, *25*, 111-118.

Reason, J. T., A. Manstead, S. Stradling, J. Baxter and K. Campbell (1990). Errors and violations on the roads: A real distinction? *Ergonomics*, *33*(10/11), 1315-1332.

Rizzi, M., J. Strandroth, A. Kullgren, C. Tingvall and B. Fildes (2015). Effectiveness of motorcycle antilock braking systems (ABS) in reducing crashes, the first cross-national study. *Traffic Inj. Prev.*, *16*(2), 177-183.

Röβger, L., J. Krzywinski, F. Muhlbauer and B. Schlag (2015a). Design studies on improved frontal light configurations for powered two-wheelers and testing in laboratory experiments. In: *Increasing Motorcycle Conspicuity: Design and Assessment of Interventions to Enhance Rider Safety* (L. Röβger, M. G. Lenné and G. Underwood eds.). Ashgate, Farnham, England.

Röβger, L., M. G. Lenné and G. Underwood (eds.). (2015b) *Increasing motorcycle conspicuity: Design and assessment of interventions to enhance rider safety*. Ashgate, Farnham, England.

Rutter, D. R. and L. Quine (1996). Age and experience in motorcycling safety. *Accid. Anal. Prev.*, *28*(1), 15-21.

Sass, T. R. and P. R. Zimmerman (2000). Motorcycle helmet laws and motorcyclist fatalities. *J. Regul. Econ.*, *18*(3), 195-215.

Savino, G., M. Rizzi, J. Brown, S. Piantini, L. Meredith, B. Albanese, M. Pierini and M. Fitzharris (2014). Further development of Motorcycle Autonomous Emergency Braking (MAEB), What can in-depth studies tell us? A multinational study. Traffic Inj. Prev., *15*(suppl 1), S165-S172.

Shahar, A., D. Poulter, D. Clarke and D. Crundall (2010). Motorcyclists' and car drivers' responses to hazards. *Transportation Res. F*, *13*(4), 243-254.

Shankar, U. and C. Varghese (2006). Recent trends in fatal motorcycle crashes: An update. National Highway Traffic Safety Administration. Report No. DOT HS 810 606. U.S. Department of Transportation, Washington, DC.

Shinar, D. (1985). Effects of expectancy, clothing reflectance, and detection criteria on nighttime pedestrian visibility. *Hum. Fact.*, *27*, 327-334.

SMC (2014). The motorcycle vision 2.0. Swedish Motorcyclists Association, Borlänge, Sweden.

Sosin, D. M. and J. J. Sacks (1992). Motorcycle helmet-use laws and head injury prevention. *JAMA*, *267*(12), 1649-1651.

Tang, K. H., L. C. Tsai and Y. H. Lee (2006). A human factors study on a modified stop lamp for motorcycles. *Int. J. Industrial Ergonomics*, *36*, 533-540.

Teoh, E. R. (2011). Effectiveness of antilock braking systems in reducing motorcycle fatal crash rates. Traffic Inj. Prev., *12*(2), 169-173.

Tofield, M. I. and J. P. Wann (2001). Do motorcyclists make better car drivers? Proceedings of Psychological Post-graduate Affairs Group conference. Glasgow, Scotland. (as cited by Haworth *et al.*, 2005).

Uchida, N., M. Kawakoshi, T. Tagawa and T. Mochida (2010). An investigation of factors contributing to major crash types in Japan based on naturalistic driving data. IATSS Res., *34*(1), 22-30.

Ulmer, R. G. and D. F. Preusser (2003). Evaluation of the repeal of motorcycle helmet laws in Kentucky and Louisiana. National Highway Traffic Safety Administration. Report DOT HS 809 530. U.S. Department of Transportation, Washington, DC.

Umar, B. S. R., M. G. Mackay and B. L. Hills (1996). Modelling of conspicuity-related motorcycle accidents in Seremban and Shah Alam, Malaysia. *Accid. Anal. Prev.*, *28*, 325-332.

Underwood, G., A. Ngai and J. Underwood (2013). Driving experience and situation awareness in hazard detection. *Safety Sci.*, *56*, 29-35.

Vaughan, R. G., K. Pettigrewm and J. Lukin (1977). *Motorcycle crashes: A level two study*. Traffic Accident Research Unit, Department of Motor Transport, New South Wales, Sydney. (as cited by Wells *et al.*, 2004).

Vis, A. (1995). De onveiligheid van motorrijden nader bekeken: een beschrijving van de aard en omvang van het problem. SWOV, Netherlands. (as cited by Brooks *et al.*, 2005).

Wallace, P., N. Haworth and M. Regan (2005). Best training methods for teaching hazard perception and responding by motorcyclists. Monash University Accident Research Center, Report 236. Monash University, Clayton, Victoria, AU.

Watson, B. C., D. J. Tunnicliff, K. M. White, C. C. Schonfeld and D. E. Wishart (2007). Psychological and social factors influencing, motorcycle rider intentions and behaviour. ATSB Research and Analysis Report. Road Safety Research Grant Report 2007-04. Australian Transport Safety Bureau.

Wells, S., B. Mullin, R. Norton, J. Langley, J. Conner, R. Lay-Yee and R. Jackson (2004). Motorcycle rider conspicuity and crash related injury: Case-control study. *Br. Med. J.*, *328*, 857-863.

WHO (2004). *World report on road traffic injury prevention* (M. Peden, R. Scurfield, D. Sleet et al., eds.). World Health Organization, Geneva. http://www.who.int/world-health-day/2004/infomaterials/world_report/en/index.html

WHO (2013). *Global status report on road safety: Supporting a decade of action*. World Health Organization, Geneva, Switzerland.

Wikipedia. (2017). 2015 Waco Shootout. https://en.wikipedia.org/wiki/2015_Waco_shootout

York, I., S. Ball and J. Hopkin (2011). Motorcycles in bus lanes – Monitoring of the second TfL trial. CPR1224, Transport Road laboratory, Crawthorne, England.

Zambon, F. and M. Hasselberg (2006a). Socioeconomic differences and motorcycle injuries: Age at risk and injury severity among young drivers. A Swedish nationwide cohort study. *Accid. Anal. Prev.*, *38*(6), 1183-1189.

Zambon, F. and M. Hasselberg (2006b). Factors affecting the severity of injuries among young motorcyclists—A Swedish nationwide cohort study. *Traffic Inj. Prev.*, *7*, 143-149.

17

Bicyclists

> "The bicycle is a vehicle for revolution. It can destroy the tyranny of the automobile as effectively as the printing press brought down despots of flesh and blood." (Daniel Behrman, 1973, The Man who Loved Bicycles).

> "Differences in bicycle use can be observed in bicycle culture, purpose of bicycle use, the position of the cyclist in traffic, and the measures that have been taken to make cycling safer... cycling is healthy, cycling is good for the environment if it takes the place of motorized journeys, cycling makes a contribution to the prevention of congestion because cyclists take up less space than (parked) cars, and cycling is cheaper than travel by passenger car or public transport... Nowadays, more and more governments, cities and villages, communities encourage their citizens to cycle... One important objection can be made against promoting cycling: it is rather dangerous." (Wegman, Zhang, and Dijkstra, 2012).

The bicycle may not be a vehicle for revolution, but bicycling – in increasing numbers – is revolutionizing our mobility patterns. In many ways, bicycling is an anomaly in the road traffic system. Bicyclists are not registered or licensed, and hence barely regulated, yet they are expected to ride on the road (and not on the curb) and obey the traffic rules (which they never learned formally, may not know, and on which they have never been tested). Also, typically health and safety go hand in hand – but this is not the case in bicycling. On the one hand, cycling is promoted as an economically viable environmentally friendly alternative to driving. It is a healthy activity that provides cardiovascular exercise in lieu of the sedentary stressed sitting position behind the wheel, and several studies have demonstrated that compared to non-cyclists cyclists have lower risk of morbidity and mortality from various causes including cancer and cardiovascular diseases (Oja *et al.*, 2011). On the other hand, cyclists are vulnerable road users who are not shielded by anything, except – sometimes – a light-weight helmet. And when they mix with the motorized traffic they provide a recipe for disaster; a crash in which they are the primary victims. In the Netherlands, for example, per kilometer of riding, bicyclists are approximately at five times the risk of a car driver of being injured, and for older cyclists the risk is approximately ten times as high (Wegman *et al.*, 2012). Nonetheless, because of its health benefits, reduced congestion, and reduced pollution the Dutch mortality data showed that the tradeoff is positive and bicycling should be encouraged (de Hartog *et al.*, 2010). However, a different analysis by Stipdonk and Reurings (2012) also on Dutch data, but one that considered only traffic injuries as an outcome, suggests that a modal shift from driving to cycling would result in a net increase in both fatalities and hospitalized casualties.

The challenge facing a societal trend toward cycling is how to manage the safety of these vulnerable road users while promoting their exposure. This, according to the past director of the Dutch Institute for Road Safety Research (SWOV), can be done (Wegman *et al.*, 2012). However, safely integrating the cyclists with the rest of the traffic system is a formidable task as Wegman notes that "a cyclist is vulnerable (in a crash), flexible (in behavior), unstable (may fall off the bike), inconspicuous (difficult to see), has differing abilities (due to a wide range of the cycling population), is conscious of effort (i.e., highly motivated to minimize energy expenditure), and sometimes seen as intruder in the traffic system, rather than as an integral part (of it)" (p. 20). Furthermore, though governments at both local and national levels often have both mobility goals and safety goals for cycling as a mode of transport, research that links cycling mobility and safety is scarce (Schepers *et al.*, 2015). This is critical because the behavioral, cultural, legal, and environmental factors that affect risk are intrinsically tied to the safety of cycling. A comprehensive treatment of the health and safety risks and benefits is provided in the OECD/ITF (2013) report.

Scope of Bicycling

Cycling trends over time have differed significantly among countries. In the western world especially in Europe cycling has been on the increase in the past several decades, both as an independent means of mobility and as a part of a multimodal system involving cycling and public transportation. Up until the 1970s worldwide bicycle sales were very similar to those of cars. However, the two trends diverged in the 1970s so that by 2007 bicycle sales nearly tripled those of car sales (Economist, 2008). Recently, the European Cyclists' Federation (ECF) developed a "Cycling Barometer" that ranks 27 EU countries in terms of five criteria measures of cycling behavior and attitudes. The five criteria are the (1) modal split of bicycling (percent cycling as a mode of transportation), (2) safety of cycling (fatalities per number of cyclists), (3) cycling tourism (number of tourism trips relative to the country's population), (4) bicycle market (sales per inhabitants), and (5) advocates (the number of individuals within ECF-affiliated groups relative to the country's population). Based on the combined score, in 2013-2015 the five leading bicycle-friendly countries were Denmark, closely followed by the Netherlands, Sweden, Finland, and Germany (ECF, 2016). In an EU survey of these countries, 23 percent of the respondents in Denmark and 36 percent of the respondents in the Netherlands reported that "on a typical day" bicycling is their most common mode of transport, and the primary reason for this choice was "convenience" (EC, 2014). By comparison, in Beijing, China, known for its bicycling density, 32 percent of the people report cycling as their main mode of daily transport. Even in the U.S. where the percent of people who use the bicycle to commute to work is very low, over the 8-year period from 2000 to 2008 this percent increased from 0.4 percent to 0.6 percent (Goodwin *et al.*, 2015). Though low in absolute numbers, this is still a 50 percent increase in less than a decade.

Figure 17-1 shows the share of bicycling out of all trips taken in 25 European countries relative to the Netherlands that has by far the highest bicycle riding share in the EU, with 31 percent reporting that their primary mode of transportation is the bicycle. In North America, the increase in cycling has been generally slower, and quite variable. In locations that are amenable to cycling, are congested by motorized traffic, and where cycling infrastructure is improving – such as Marine Co., CA, and New York, NY – the increase has been quite rapid. For example, in New York the number of cycling trips doubled over the five year period of 2007-2011 (Nabors *et al.*, 2012). In a 2012 survey of a nationally representative sample of 16+ years old U.S. residents 22 percent reported that they had ridden a bicycle in the past 30 days (Schroeder and Wilbur, 2013).

To promote bicycle safety through new and existing infrastructure, the U.S. Federal Highway Administration has produced Bicycle Road Safety Audit Guidelines and Prompt Lists (Nabors *et al.*, 2012) that provide planners and highway officials with principles of bicycle safety and guidelines on how to conduct cycling-oriented road safety audits (RSA). A RSA is a formal safety examination of a future roadway plan or an existing roadway that is conducted by an independent, experienced, and multidisciplinary RSA team. For example, design-wise a critical factor to consider in an RSA is

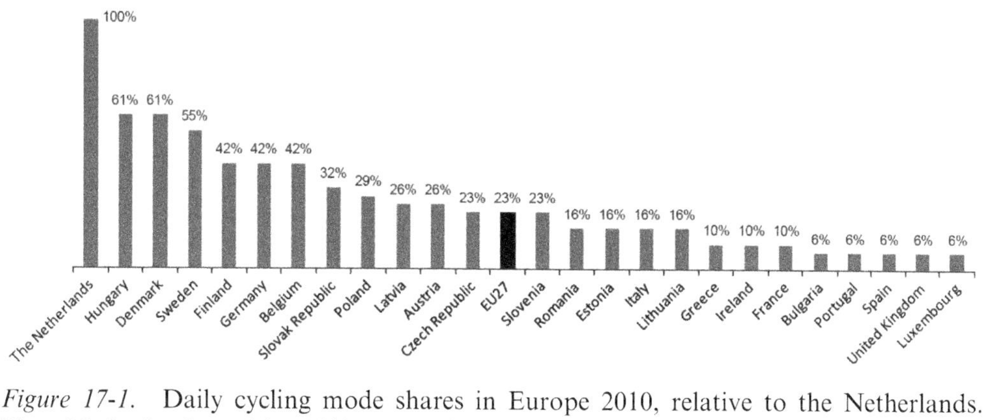

Figure 17-1. Daily cycling mode shares in Europe 2010, relative to the Netherlands. The Netherlands with 31% reporting that cycling is their main mode of transport = 100% (from OECD/ITF, 2013; data source: EC, 2011, with permission from the OECD, Paris).

the bicycle path/track width. Considering that the width of a bicycle at the handlebar is 0.75 meters, the recommended minimum operating width should be 1.2 meters, and even more to avoid hitting "linear obstacles" such as a wall. In intersections there is also a need to consider the longitudinal clearance – for example in the design of painted "bicycle boxes" – that is based on the length of a bicycle (about 1.8 meters for a regular bicycle) and number of bicycles expected to stop in parallel (Nabors *et al.*, 2012).

Studies that examined the causes for the prevalence of bicycling in the Netherlands in comparison to some other countries generally concluded that the main factor has been policies that promote its convenience and safety (Schepers *et al.*, 2017). In the far east, where bicycling has been the primary means of transportation for decades, the change is now reversing with a rapid increase in motorized traffic (including electric bicycles; e.g., in China). Even in the Western world the amount of bicycling varies greatly, from an average of 100 meters per person per day (Greece, Portugal, Spain, and the U.S.), to the EU average of about 0.5 kilometer per person per day, to the high of 1.6 kilometer per person per day in Denmark, and 2.6 kilometers per person per day in the Netherlands (Wegman *et al.*, 2012). The differences are due not only to the obvious differences in the geographical layouts of the different regions, but also to differences in economy, culture, policies, and infrastructure. All of these can and do affect people's mobility patterns.

Cycling as Part of a Multimodal Travel Pattern

Much of the travel behavior and safety of cyclists is considered within a multimodal frame of mind. This is because many cycling trips are in fact a part of a trip that combines several modes: bicycles with private cars and bicycles with public transportation modes like buses and trains. This is true not only for work related travel but also for sporting travel where the beginning and end of a trip is by a car (with a bike carrier). This is important because it seems that bicycling safety is closely linked to the modal split between bicycling and other means of transportation. In general, the greater the share of bicycling in a given area, the safer it is per cyclist (Schepers *et al.*, 2013; Wegman *et al.*, 2012). This is true for both bicycle-car collisions as well as for single bicycle crashes. The increase in the bicycle share of travel (either in terms of trips or in terms of kilometers of travel) is significantly less than the increase in the modal share. Various factors contribute to this phenomenon that is typically labeled "safety-in-numbers" and they are detailed further below.

Who are the cyclists? Not all cycling is the same, as cycling serves different needs for different people in different environments. One way to "type" cyclists was offered by Damant-Sirois and his associates (Damant-Sirois and El-Geneidy, 2015; Damant-Sirois, Grimsrud, and El-Geneidy, 2014) on the basis of a survey of over 2,000 18+ years old Montreal, Canada cyclists' stated cycling habits, motivation for, and barriers to cycling. Using cluster analysis, they identified four types of cyclists. The largest group (36 percent of the sample) consisted of "path-using cyclists." For these people the motivation for cycling is based on expediency of time, availability of infrastructure, enjoyment of cycling, and parental encouragement when they were children. The next two groups were "dedicated cyclists" (24 percent) and "fair weather utilitarians" (23 percent). Dedicated cyclists are motivated by time expediency, organizational support for cycling, and the enjoyment of riding, and they are not concerned at all by the availability or absence of infrastructure. The utilitarian riders adjust their riding to the weather conditions and the required effort, while the pleasure of riding is not a relevant consideration. The last group, "leisure cyclists" cycle because the enjoy cycling, identify themselves as cyclists, and do not ride for reasons of expediency. Whereas dedicated and path-using cyclists cycle primarily for utilitarian reasons such as commuting to and from work, most leisure cyclists rarely use their bicycles for that reason. The groups also differ in their socioeconomic strata, with leisure cyclists being more affluent. A critical implication of this typology is that to increase cycling as a mode of transport, one has to focus on the needs of the first three types of cyclists, and be aware that these needs are not uniform across all of them.

Issues of safety, convenience, and opinions of cycling in the relevant populations are all relevant to the decision to bicycle. Willis, Manaugh, and El-Geneidy (2013) conducted a different multi-variate analysis on data from a travel survey of McGill University commuters in Montreal, Canada. Of the nearly 5,000 responses to the survey only 268 (less than 5 percent) were cyclists (after all, this was in hilly cold-weather Montreal). Because the Damant-Sirois survey included cyclists everywhere in the Montreal area and the Willis survey included only McGill University commuters, it is hard to explain the similarities and differences between these studies. However, it is noteworthy that in their study on the smaller sample Willis and his colleagues were able to classify riders according to two types only: fair-weather cyclists and year-round cyclists (about one fourth of the total sample). Because their data base contained non-cyclist commuters they could compare the two groups in terms of their satisfaction with their commuting. Despite the effort and the weather of Montreal, and the longer distances of their commute, the cycling enthusiasts were much more satisfied with their commute than the transit riders and walkers. Poulos *et al.* (2015), on the basis of a survey of cyclists in New South Wales, Australia, distinguished between two groups of cyclists: those who ride mainly for pleasure and those who do it mainly for transport; that is, the "leisure" cyclists versus all the others. In addition to the obvious differences between these groups in the riding patterns, they also differed in many personal characteristics (transport cyclists were younger, traveled more days per week, and more in the city on rush hours). Interestingly, the rate of injuries and crashes was similar for the two groups, but the types and locations of the crashes differed.

Because the most frequent cyclist commuters are the dedicated and path-using cyclists, researchers' standard recommendation is to develop fast and direct routes that minimize the riders' exposure to extreme conditions. The implementation of this recommendation is obviously culture- and location-specific. Thus, in Montreal where the survey was conducted one solution (not necessarily the one recommended by the authors) would be to integrate cycling routes into the city's underground network of connecting tunnels. In contrast, in a city like Amsterdam the expeditious approach might be to implement the road functionality approach of Sustainable Safety (see *Safe system approach* below and Chapter 19).

SCOPE OF THE PROBLEM – CYCLING AND CRASHES

In the Western world, bicyclists constitute a very small but growing proportion of the people killed in traffic crashes. For example, in the U.S. over the past decade cyclists fatalities increased from 1.8 percent of all fatalities in 2005 and 2006 to 2.2 percent of all fatalities in 2014 (NHTSA, 2016). Though in absolute terms the difference may seem small, the relative increase is over 20 percent! In the EU where cycling is much more popular, bicycle fatalities constitute an average of 8 percent of all the road deaths (Adminaite, Allsop, and Jost, 2015). Figure 17-2 shows the percent of cycling fatalities relative to all traffic fatalities in 25 European countries and in the U.S. The most conspicuous element in this figure is the Dutch rate: 22 percent; nearly twice as high as the second-ranking country, Hungary. This high proportion is simply a reflection of the popularity of cycling in this country (see Figure 17-1), which actually has the lowest fatality rate per kilometer of bicycle riding. In fact, the distribution in Figure 17-2 closely parallels that of the percent of people who report cycling as their main mode of daily travel. The increase in bicycle use is also reflected in the increase in fatality and injury rates per population size. However, because of significant under-reporting (see below) the data on bicycle safety and bicyclists in terms of injuries and crashes are much sparser and less reliable.

Figure 17-3 shows the wide variation among the EU countries in the fatalities per million people in the population for different rider-age groups. When averaged across all ages, the rates range from a very low of less than 2 in Spain to over 10 in the Netherlands. Yet the Netherlands ranks highest on the "Cycling Barometer." This apparent contradiction is because the Netherlands has the highest percent of people who use the bicycle for their daily commute to work and other short-distance trips.

To truly appreciate the risk of cycling, the number of injured or killed should be expressed relative to the distance traveled. Unlike driving, reliable exposure measures

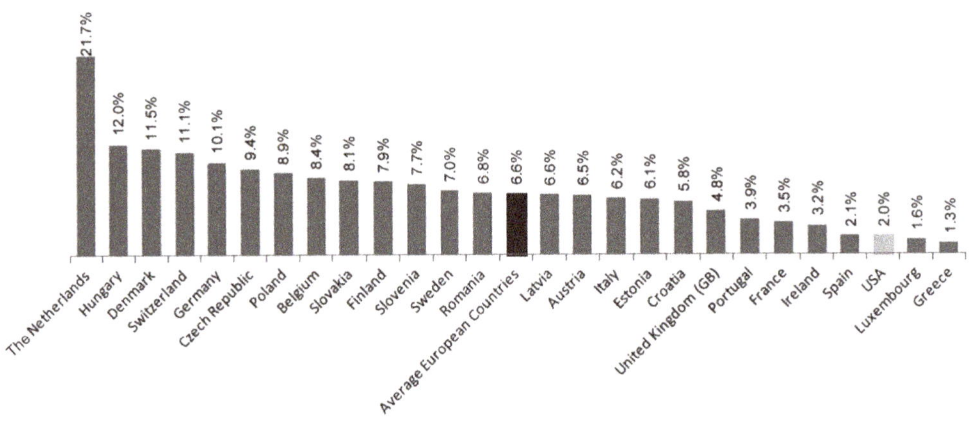

Figure 17-2. Percent of cycling fatalities of all traffic fatalities in Europe 2010 (from OECD/ITF, 2013; data source: EC, 2011, with permission from the OECD, Paris).

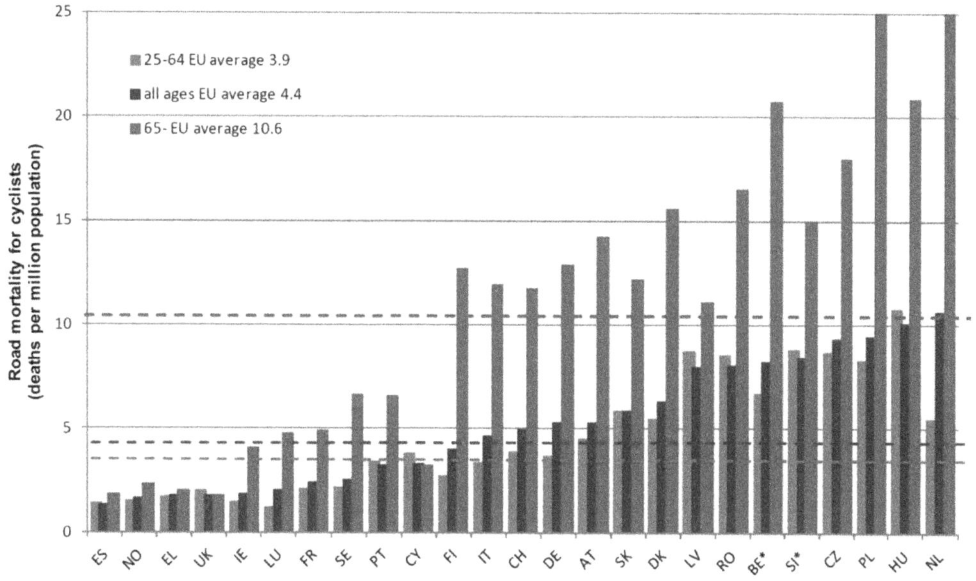

Figure 17-3. Cyclists fatality rates (per million people in the population) in different EU countries as function of age for mature adults and older riders (from Steriu, 2012a, with permission from the European Transport Safety Council, Brussels).

of cycling – especially kilometers-ridden – are not available for most countries. Vanparijs *et al.* (2015) conducted a literature search to identify cycling safety studies that included an exposure measure, and found only 20. Of these, the most relevant measure of distance cycled was available on only 12, and not all of them were able to distinguish between on-road and off-road cycling. Relative to kilometers-ridden, bicyclists are an especially high-risk group. In Australia their fatality risk is 4.5-18.6 higher than that of car occupants and their injury risk is 12.9-33.5 higher than that of car occupants (Garrard, Greaves, and Ellison, 2010). In Denmark and the Netherlands – the two countries with the highest "Cycling Barometer" scores (see Figure 17-1) in the EU – the fatality rate per billion km of travel in 2008-2010 was approximately 12.5 (Steriu, 2012a, 2012b) (compared to under 5.0 for all traffic deaths – see Chapter 1). In Rôhne County, France, Blaizot *et al.* (2013) used several different measures of crashes and injuries, and on all measures cycling was more dangerous relative to all other modes of travel except PTW. For example, using police-reported crashes of all injury severities, per 1 million kilometers the injury rates were 0.2 for car occupants, 0.6 for pedestrians, 1.2 for cyclists, and 4.5 for PTW riders. The true picture is even worse when we consider that cycling crashes are significantly under-reported by police (see below). It should also be noted that the countries that measure injuries and fatalities per kilometers of cycling are typically the most cycling-oriented countries. In these countries, cycling fatality risk relative to driving ranges from approximately 6 in Norway and the Netherlands to 14 in the United Kingdom (OECD/ITF, 2013). Also, once involved in a crash, bicyclists are 5.7 times more likely to be fatally injured than vehicle occupants (WHO, 2004). In short, relative to driving or riding in a car, bicycling is quite dangerous (though less than motorcycling).

Because the interaction between bicyclists and motorized traffic is somewhat different than the interaction between pedestrians and drivers, even as vulnerable road users they have a unique set of issues. On the one hand, they share the road with drivers, but on the other hand they do not move at the traffic speed, they do not have a license (and are therefore less controlled), and they do not adhere as much to the rules of the road. Consequently, they do have some unique risk factors that should be considered.

Age as a risk factor

Analyses of crash data from different countries do show some consistent risk factors in crash causation. The age-related risk level is striking, as can be seen above in Figure 17-3. As with pedestrians and car occupants, in nearly all EU countries the oldest riders (65+ years old) have significantly higher fatality rates (averaging 10.6) than the younger 25-64-years-old riders (averaging 3.9). This gap is the greatest for the Netherlands, where many people persist in riding into old age. There, relative to their numbers in the population, the older riders are at five times the risk of the younger riders. Not shown in this figure, but included in the Steriu (2012a) report is the significantly lower risk of young and very young riders; averaging 2.6 for 15-24-years-old riders and 1.5 for riders under the age of 15. Thus, it seems that the risk of being killed in a bicycle crash increases exponentially with age; a reflection of both the loss of agility and skills, and the gradually accelerating increase in frailty especially after the age of 70. This is very similar to the risk of the age-related pedestrian fatalities. In the U.S., the fatality risk is highest for the 55-59-years-old cyclists (4.86 per thousands in population; NHTSA, 2015). However, this also reflects the recent trend of mature adults to return to bicycling; once a transportation mode almost exclusive to children. In the five-years period of 2009-2013, relative to 2004-2008, the number of cyclists killed in the U.S. increased for the 45+ years old adults and decreased for the 21-44 years old (Goodwin *et al.*, 2015). Perhaps the most extreme over-involvement in fatalities of older riders is in Japan, where 63 percent of the fatally injured cyclists are 65-74 years old riders! (OECD/ITF, 2013). In contrast, the young riders (<25) are at a lower than average risk in the EU, and approximately at the average in the U.S. However, before we rush to conclude that young riders are safer riders than old ones, we should adjust these numbers by the different frailty levels of the two groups: older riders being much frailer. To do this, we should examine the ratio of killed/all injury levels. And because the data on non-fatal injuries are very unreliable for bicycling we cannot make that adjustment. When non-fatal injury data are available, the young riders emerge as a high crash risk group. In the U.S., the 15-24 years old riders have the highest injury rates per thousands in population (of over 300 versus 82 for the 55-59 years old; NHTSA, 2015). Also, in Spain Martinez-Ruiz *et al.* (2013) found a greater risk for collisions with a motor vehicle for 10-19 years old riders, but not for single vehicle crashes, and noted similar effects for New Zealand and the Netherlands.

Gender as a risk factor

The fatality risk is significantly higher for males than for females, at least in the Western world. This is true for all EU countries, where the gender gap ranges from 63-67 percent males and 37-34 percent females in Sweden, Denmark, Finland, and the Netherlands to 91-98 percent males and 9-2 percent females in Spain, Greece, Romania, and Israel. Again, the culprit for the gap – at least in part – is exposure: males are much more likely to ride the bicycle than females. For example, in the Netherlands, where males account for 63 percent of the fatalities, they also account for 52 percent of the travel kilometers. However, there are most likely true gender-related differences that make males more susceptible to crashes, and these include riding at high-risk hours (night), riding while impaired, riding at greater speeds, and riskier riding style. An interesting difference was revealed to us in the course of a study we conducted on rider education and training for children. Part of the program involved cycling in a closed environment consisting of streets, sidewalks, signals, and traffic signs, but no cars or pedestrians. We noticed that whereas most of the girls kept seeking the instructors' advice and approval on their correct safe riding behavior, many of the boys engaged in horseplay and daring illegal riding tricks whenever the instructors were not watching them. This kind of early pre-adolescent behavior may account for Johnson *et al.*'s (2011) finding in Melbourne, Australia that male cyclists violated the red traffic lights nearly twice as much as female cyclists.

Alcohol as a risk factor

As for driving, alcohol impairment is also a risk factor in bicycle crashes. In the U.S., in 2013 one-fifth of all cyclists killed in crashes had alcohol BAC >.08 mg/ml (Goodwin *et al.*, 2015; NHTSA, 2015). Possibly, some, or many of these may be the people who decided not to drive because they were impaired... In Germany, the problem has become sufficiently severe that the German Road Safety Council and other safety-oriented organizations are promoting the enactment of maximum BAC levels for cyclists (Adminaite *et al.*, 2015).

Climate as a risk factor

Climate is also an important factor. In the U.S. and Europe, most bicycle fatalities occur during the summer months, especially July-August, and the fewest occur during the cold winter months of November-March (OECD/ITF, 2013). This is obviously not due to the temperature itself as to the greater amount of riding in the summer: both because the weather is more amenable to riding and because there are more daylight hours (when more than half the fatalities happen).

UNDER-REPORTING OF BICYCLE CRASHES – A COMPLICATING FACTOR IN SCOPE APPRAISAL

Crash statistics on bicycles suffer from significant under-reporting as they are often not documented by the police (e.g., when a motor vehicle is not involved, such as when a cyclist hits a fixed object or falls, on or off the road) (Schepers, 2008, 2010). In fact, following a meta-analysis of the level of under-reporting of bicycle crashes in official state records of 19 countries relative to data from hospital admissions, Elvik and Mysen (1999) concluded that while there is a great variability among countries, of all the crash types, consistently the least reported are bicycle crashes, and in particular single vehicle bicycle injury crashes that "are very rarely reported in official road accident statistics" (0-8 percent in the various countries). This is a worldwide phenomenon (OECD/ITF, 2013) that greatly compromises our comprehension of the scope and our understanding of the nature, causes, characteristics – and ultimately – countermeasures to bicycle crashes. Even in the Netherlands, where cycling safety is a high national priority, based on hospital admissions records, approximately 75 percent of the serious injury bicycle crashes are single vehicle crashes, and thus not involving a motor vehicle (Schepers *et al.*, 2015). In Israel, based on hospital admissions in 2001-2007, only 30 percent of the bicycle crash victims were involved a bicycle-motor vehicle collision or conflict (Siman-Tov *et al.*, 2012) and therefore 70 percent of the crashes were not included in the official police reports.

Even when a motor vehicle is involved many of the collisions are not documented in police records. In a prospective study that tracked the cycling behavior and crashes of 1,087 adult commuter riders in Brussels, Belgium, over a period of one year, the police documented only 7 percent of the accidents, even though 19 percent involved a collision with a car (de Geus *et al.*, 2012). Even in a city where bicycling is more common than driving (Munster, Germany), hospital admission records contain twice as many injury bicycle crashes as the police records (Juhra *et al.*, 2012). An extreme example of the problem was documented in recent survey that we conducted on Israeli bicyclists where 80 percent of the riders reported an injury crash in the past year, but none of them were reported to the police! (Haworth, Shinar, and Oron-Gilad, 2014). Exceptions are fatal crashes. In part at least because the more severe the injury the more likely that it is due to a collision with a motor vehicle, and hence the more likely it is to be documented by the police (Schepers *et al.*, 2015). Table 17-1 lists the estimated levels of under-reporting of crashes of different severities for different types of road users in the U.K and in the Netherlands. Note that bicycling injuries are the most under-reported of all crash types in both the U.K and the Netherlands. In both countries, just slightly over 30 percent of the crashes with severely injured cyclists are documented by the police.

The problem of under-reporting of bicycle injury accidents is best illustrated in Figure 17-4 that plots the injury and fatal crash trends in the Netherlands from 2000 to 2009. In the case of cyclist fatalities, there is a small but constant difference between the number of police-recorded accidents and those obtained from the combined records of the police and hospital data. However, in the case of serious injuries (MAIS 2+) there is

Table 17-1. Percent of casualties reported by the police for different road users at different injury levels (from European Road Safety Observatory, 2008, as cited by Wegman *et al.*, 2012, with permission from Elsevier).

	U.K.			The Netherlands		
	Fatal	**Severe**	**Slight**	**Fatal**	**Hospitalized**	**Slight**
Car	100	89	77	96	92	33
Motorcycle	100	70	51	94	63	13
Bicycle	100	33	21	86	31	4
Pedestrian	100	85	67	90	56	20

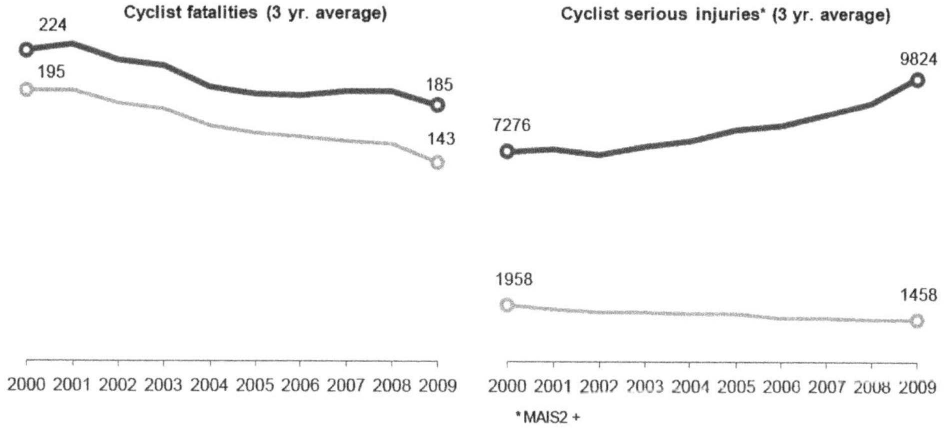

Figure 17-4. Actual versus police-registered number of fatalities (30 days) and serious injuries (MAIS 2+) in the Netherlands 2000-2009 (3 year rolling average) (from OECD/ITF, 2013, p. 106, with permission from the OECD, Paris).

a big difference: while the police data show a 26 percent *decrease* in injuries over the decade, the real number of injured cyclists actually *increases* by 35 percent!

The total amount of under-reporting is even greater than the studies above indicate. With the exception of the study by de Geus *et al.* (2012), the typically cited level of under-reporting is relative to hospital admissions. But cyclists also crash without reporting to the hospital. In a recent international survey of over 7,000 cyclists from 17 countries, we queried cyclists about their crashes in the past year (Shinar *et al.*, 2016), and whether or not they reported their most serious crash to the police. Across all countries, an average of only 9 percent of all of "the most serious" crashes were reported to the police, with a wide range among countries: from a minimum of less than 5 percent

(Israel, Croatia, and Greece) to a maximum of a 35 percent (Germany). Of the most severe crashes, resulting in hospital admission only 38 percent were reported to the police, and of those resulting in injury that required medical attention but not resulting in hospital admission only 13 percent were reported to the police. As might be expected collisions with motor vehicles, and serious injury crashes were more likely to be reported than other crash types and crashes resulting in less severe injuries. Interestingly, across all counties falling off the bicycle was the most common crash (approximately 50 percent of the most serious crashes reported), but it was the least reported to the police (less than 3 percent), while crashes with a motor vehicle accounted for 23 percent of the most serious accidents but as expected, at 25 percent they were the most likely to be reported.

Finally, in calculating bicycling crash rates the under-reporting of crashes causes an underestimate of the risk of bicycling. But there is another complicating factor: the denominator in the rate (e.g., number of cyclists, trips, or kilometers of cycling in the relevant group) is less reliable than the comparable rate for motorized traffic. Consequently, our estimated rates of injuries, and crashes, are both underestimates of the magnitude of the problem, and less reliable than our estimates for drivers and car occupants.

How can this significant under-reporting be overcome? As our study suggests, self-reporting may be the best option to document crashes that are not reported to the police or the hospital, and technology has now come to aid the process and makes it more reliable and valid. A new cell phone application, SafeVRU, that is now available in a few countries (Belgium, Denmark, Spain, and Sweden) may be the solution. SafeVRU (InDev, 2016) consists of a questionnaire to collect detailed crash information and a function for automatic detection of accidents based on movements registered by the cyclist's smartphone. Coupled with speed, exact time, and crash location, and when linked to other data bases (such as weather and roadway), the system can provide an excellent source of detailed data – objective and subjective – for both exposure and crashes.

Cyclists' Visibility

Being smaller than cars, bicycles and cyclists suffer from the same low visibility problems that motorcyclists and pedestrians have. Consequently, with respect to visibility at least, much of the research on and solutions to motorcyclists' visibility (Chapter 16) and pedestrian visibility (Chapter 15) is relevant and applicable to bicyclists. Because of its importance, however, cyclists' visibility is treated in a separate section below.

It is unfortunate but well established by research (e.g., Kwan and Mapstone, 2004; Wood *et al.*, 2009) that cyclists (and pedestrians and motorcyclists) are often first detected by drivers when it is already too late to avoid them. To improve their visibility, many cyclists try to find brighter lights or use flickering lights in the front and rear. However, in an evaluation of this enhancement researchers at the Netherlands Organisation for Applied Scientific Research (TNO) concluded that cyclists' detection (not even requiring the positive identification of a bicyclist, per se) is not improved by the added lights (Toet *et al.*, 2008). In fact, they concluded that the flickering lights are actually counterproductive for detectability. However, the poor visibility of cyclists to passing motorists is not pre-ordained, as there are various treatments (mostly reflective materials) that can make the cyclist more visible. Kwan and Mapstone (2004, 2009) reviewed the results of 10 studies that evaluated nighttime detection without any aids versus with various treatments such as bicycle lights, and cyclists' fluorescent and reflective materials, and found that just about all the treatments increased recognition distances and reduced recognition times. Note, though, that recognition distance is different from detection as the former involves the comprehension that the object is a bicycle, whereas the latter only implies detection of "something."

Visibility and detectability

Wood *et al.* (2012) evaluated the visibility of cyclists at night with various combinations of bicycle lights and clothing reflectance materials. In their study, they positioned a stationary dark-clothed cyclist facing the approaching driver and pedaling in place on the edge of a dark road adjacent to simulated glare-producing headlights of an oncoming car. The recognition distance at which approaching drivers could detect a person ahead was defined in terms of the distance at which the drivers became "confident that what they saw was a person." Although the drivers expected to see a person along the road, they had no specific expectation regarding the location of the cyclist. The test track was dark and the low beam headlights were the only light source available to detect the cyclist. Their results were surprising in the sense that detection likelihood and detection distance were unaffected by the bicycle light: either off, continuously on, or flashing. On the other hand, recognition distance was greatly affected by the cyclist's clothing, as illustrated in Figure 17-5. The likelihood of detecting the cyclist increased when he wore

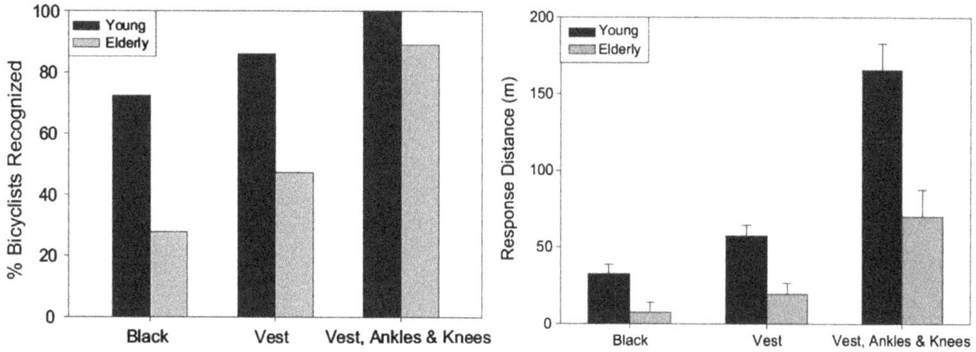

Figure 17-5. Recognition likelihood (left panel) and recognition distance (right panel) of cyclists with black clothing, with a fluorescent vest, and with a fluorescent vest and reflectors on the ankles and knees, by young (<35 years old) and elderly (>65 years old) drivers (from Wood *et al.*, 2012, with permission from Elsevier).

a yellow fluorescent vest with silver retroreflective material on the shoulders front and back, and increased even more when the retroreflective material was attached to the ankles and knees; that is, the only moving joints when a person is cycling. The range of detection percentages was very large: from less than 30 percent for elderly drivers approaching a black-clothed cyclist to 100 percent for young drivers approaching a bicyclist with the fluorescent vest and joint reflectors. In a similar fashion, the detection distances also ranged from a very low of 5 meters for older drivers approaching a black-clothed cyclist to high of 223 meters for younger drivers approaching the cycle with the vest and joint reflectors. The added advantage of the reflecting materials at the joint approximates the consistent advantage of pedestrians with biomotion lights or reflectors (see Chapter 15).

Compounding the problem of the poor nighttime visibility of bicyclists is the fact that bicyclists – like pedestrians – overestimate their visibility. Using a method similar to the one we employed earlier for pedestrian visibility, Wood and her associates (2013) had bicyclists with the same combinations of bicycle lights and clothing reflectance estimate the distance at which an oncoming driver would first detect them. As expected, the cyclists were sensitive to the benefits of their reflective clothing and the retroreflective stripes on their ankles and knees. However, across all conditions they greatly overestimated their visibility distance at approximately twice the actual visibility distances recorded with different observers in Woods *et al.*'s 2012 study. Interestingly, frequent cyclists were consistently more conservative in their estimates, possibly because of some close previous encounters they may have had with motorists. One shortcoming of this study is that unlike the Shinar (1984) study on pedestrian actual versus estimated visibility the bicyclists in this study were not the same people who served as drivers in the previous study and the two studies were not done at the same time, and therefore there may have been some differences in the ambient and vehicle illumination. Still these findings are consistent with those obtained for pedestrians and generally indicate that as pedestrians and bicyclists we overestimate our nighttime visibility believing that if we can see a car, its driver can see us. A potentially fatal false assumption.

One particular problem is the visibility of cyclists during the daytime and dusk hours. According to the International Transport Forum "Data showed that most crashes occur during daylight, but the rise in fatal crashes at dusk, both in absolute numbers and as a share of overall traffic fatalities, underscores the sensitive nature of this transition period. Better lighting (streets and bicycles) and better conspicuity by cyclists may help in reducing these numbers – as might raising motor vehicle driver awareness" (OECD/ITF, 2013, p. 153). Furthermore, the report states that "the share of fatal and serious injury crashes is relatively more elevated in low-light conditions in the early evening" (OECD/ITF, 2013, p. 158). Unfortunately improving cyclist visibility in daytime and dusk conditions is much more difficult than at night, as it calls for improving the visual search or sensorial conspicuity. The two studies reviewed by Kwan and Mapstone (2004) that evaluated the effects of fluorescent jackets compared to a dark jacket on daytime recognition distances found negligible effects on the recognition distance, despite the fact that theoretically fluorescent materials should be more effective in the daytime as they convert the ultra-violet rays from the sun to longer visible wavelengths. In addition, Wood *et al.* (2009) in a survey of Queensland, Australia, drivers and cyclists found that despite the cyclists' awareness of the benefits of reflecting materials and lights their actual use was low. This may be because of the cyclists' overestimation of their visibility distance to the approaching motorist by approximately 100 percent.

In an attempt to increase the cyclist's sensorial conspicuity, we searched for a unique cue that would be effective both at dusk and during the daytime. Partial biomotion cues such as the ones provided by Wood and her colleagues (2012) are not very effective because (a) they are partial and (b) the moving cues (attached to the knees and ankles) are close to the ground and thus likely to be obstructed by vehicular traffic. The cue we chose was one that relied on the Phi-phenomenon. The phi-phenomenon is an optical illusion that creates a perception of movement when adjacent discrete lights are illuminated in succession. We see this in digital billboards and in "moving" neon arrows. In our case, we first demonstrated the value of the phi-phenomenon for enhancing conspicuity by attaching a pair of alternating lights on top of a motorcycle helmet (see Chapter 16). To enhance the bicyclist's conspicuity we devised a system where one light was attached to the center of the handlebar and one to the helmet. When synchronized, the lights flashed in an alternating fashion at the rate of 2 Hz. When viewed from the distance, they appeared like a vertical movement of a light, going up and down between the rider's helmet and the bicycle's handlebar.

For the evaluation study, we first videotaped the bicyclist as he approached the camera, in daylight and in dusk. We then presented subjects with short video clips; half containing a bicyclist and half not containing a bicyclist. The study was divided into two experiments. The first experiment tested the cognitive conspicuity of the cyclist. Subjects viewed seventy-two 1.0 second video clips of traffic approaching the camera and then had to identify the various types of vehicles they saw by dragging schematic images of a car, a van, a motorcycle, a bicycle, or a bus to the relevant quadrant on an empty grid on the screen. Half the slides were videoed in the midday hours and half were videoed at dusk (just after the sun disappeared below the horizon). Within each set, half the clips had no cyclist, and half contained a cyclist. In the 36 clips containing a cyclist, he was either far (140 meters) or near (60 meters) the camera, and within each distance the cyclist either had no lights at all, a single blinking light on the handlebar, or the new Alternating Blinking Light System (ABLS). Most important is the fact that the drivers were not cued to detect a bicycle in the traffic. Thus, the detectability of the bicycle reflected its level of cognitive conspicuity. In the second experiment – with a different group of subjects – we evaluated the bicyclist's sensorial conspicuity by presenting the same video clips and instructed the subjects to press the <space> bar as soon as they either detected a bicyclist or decided the clip did not contain one.

In midday daylight conditions, the cyclists' conspicuity was significantly higher than at dusk. For the cognitive conspicuity experiment the cyclist was detected with the ABLS or without any lights approximately 60 percent of the time when he was far, and

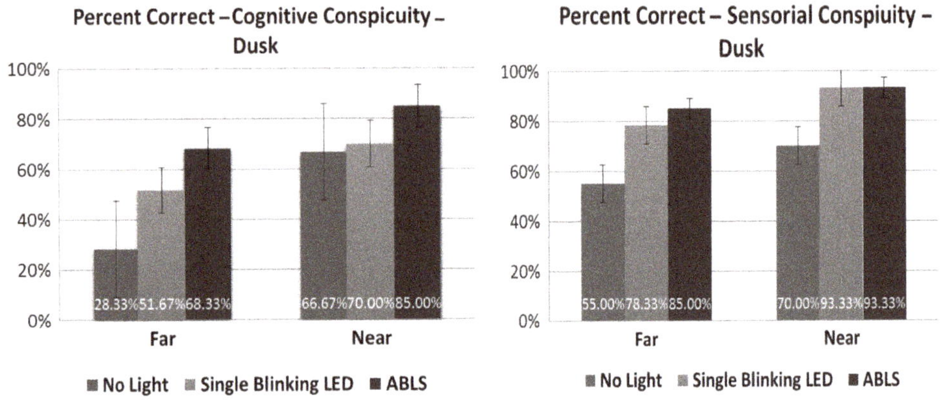

Figure 17-6. The effects of different cyclist lights on his cognitive (left) and sensorial (right) conspicuity at dusk. The ABLS creates the illusion of a vertically moving point of light between the helmet top and the handlebar (Shinar, 2014).

approximately 80 percent of the times when he was near. In the sensorial conspicuity experiment, the cyclist was detected approximately 95 percent of the times when he was far and 100 percent of the time when he was close. The effects of the ABLS on both cognitive and sensorial conspicuity were most consistent and noticeable in the dusk, and they are reproduced in Figure 17-6. The ABLS was very effective in attracting the viewers' attention to the cyclist – enhancing cognitive conspicuity – and enabling them to identify the object as a bicyclist on a bicycle; both when the cyclist was far and when he was near. When cued to search for a cyclist – sensorial conspicuity – performance was better in all conditions but the advantage of the ABLS was still there. Thus, this study showed that if we can provide a bicyclist a unique attention-attracting signature, his or her conspicuity and safety can be significantly improved.

Visibility and crash involvement

Although there is no direct objective evidence for the safety benefits of visibility aids in crash prevention or injury reduction (Kwan and Mapstone, 2009), there are a few survey-based and epidemiological studies that provide weak support for the positive effect of some visibility aids. Thornley *et al.* (2008) surveyed 2,469 cyclists who participated in the New Zealand 2006 "Lake Taupo Cycle Challenge" on their riding habits, biographical details, and crash experience. Their answers were subjected to regression analyses to determine the effects of various predictor variables such as use of helmet, front and back bicycle lights, and fluorescent clothing, on the frequency of injury crashes and on their severity in terms of the number of days-off-work. Relative risks were then adjusted to control for various confounding factors and intervening variables such as age, gender, off-road cycling, cycling in dark, average cycling speed, bike type, years of cycling experience, and exposure in terms of kilometers cycled per year. The results confirmed the expectations: increasing visibility was associated with reduced crash involvement and crash injury severity. The average adjusted relative risk of injury crash for riders who "always" wore fluorescent clothing compared to those who "never" wore fluorescent clothing was 0.73, and their relative rate of days-off-work was 0.23. Interestingly, "always using a back light while riding in the dark" was associated with significant crash reduction (RR = 0.83), but using a front light was not, suggesting that unlit cyclists are more vulnerable to cars approaching them from behind than to cars approaching them head-on. This, of course makes sense if we can assume that the riders typically rode in the same direction as the motor vehicles in their lane. In a more recent survey-based study of 2,590 Taupo riders involved in 48 collisions (out of a total of 290 crashes), Tin, Woodward, and Ameratunga (2013) found a 50 percent statistically significant reduction in nighttime crashes when riders reported that they "sometimes" used reflective materials at night. But paradoxically there was no significant reduction for those who reported "always" using reflective material at night. This inconsistency within the same survey is hard to explain unless it is due to differences between the two groups that were not adjusted for in the analysis. In addition, the same survey failed to obtain any significant benefits of wearing fluorescent colors or using front and rear lights in the dark. In a later analysis based on a longer follow-up period (median of 4.6 years) on 162 riders involved in 187 collisions with motor vehicles, Tin, Woodward, and Ameratunga (2014) used a composite index of visibility based on multiple visibility-enhancing devices, and failed to find a statistically significant effect. Hagel *et al.* (2014) examined the frequency of use of various visibility aids in crash-injured bicyclists hospitalized in the Edmonton and Calgary, Canada area. They compared the use of visibility aids of 278 collision-involved injured bicyclists with 2,125 non-collision crash-involved bicyclists. After controlling for the possible confounding effects of sex, type of bicycling (commuting versus recreational) and bicyclist speed, they found that clothing reflectance had a significant effect on the likelihood of collisions in both daytime and nighttime collisions. Daylight collisions were significantly less frequent for riders in upper-body white than black clothing (OR = 0.57), and in upper-body light-colored clothing than in dark-colored clothing (OR = 0.71). Nighttime collisions indicated that collision involvement was higher for riders with red/orange/yellow front upper-body clothing (OR = 4.11) and taillights (OR = 2.54). Finally, some indirect support for the role of visibility comes from an Australian survey where drivers were four times as likely as bicyclists to report visibility as a factor in their near-crash and crash experience with bicyclists (Wood *et al.*, 2009). In summary, the research to date is both methodologically weak and non-conclusive. It indicates that visibility is probably a factor in bicycle-automobile collisions, but the magnitude of the effect and the most beneficial visibility enhancement are still to be determined.

Cyclists-Drivers Interactions

As long as cyclists and drivers share the road – or parts of the road – they must adopt a safe strategy of interacting with each other. Ignoring one another is definitely not a good strategy. Simply obeying the rules of the road – for example, in yielding right-of-way – may make a cyclist right but seriously injured when he or she are not seen in time by the driver. It also appears that by taking some precautions, such as using a helmet, a cyclist cannot assume that "all else stays the same" in terms of the drivers' behaviors. For example, a recent study by Ian Walker (2007) in Bath, England, revealed that drivers leave a slightly smaller lateral safety clearance (by about 7 centimeters) when overtaking a helmeted cyclist than when overtaking a non-helmeted cyclist, as if assuming that the former is less likely to make an unexpected erratic deviation from his or her path. In addition, in the same study, the farther the rider was away from the road edge, the smaller the lateral safety margin left by the driver. From these findings, Walker concluded that drivers do not adjust their clearing distance from the bicyclist in order to maintain the same safety margin. In fact, they actually "follow the same path no matter where the cyclist is" (p. 422). The hypothesis that the helmet effect may have been due to the rider's perceived skill or experience was tested by Walker in a follow-up study. In that study the rider wore different outfits suggestive of different levels of experience (and therefore presumably also reliability and consistency in riding behavior). The only outfit that had a positive effect was a retroreflective vest with the large print "POLICE – CAMERA CYCLIST – MOVE OVER" (Walker, Garrard, and Jowitt, 2014). Thus, the hypothesis was not confirmed and once again the fear of the stick proved more effective than the lure of the carrot ("POLITE – PLEASE SLOW DOWN"). Also, the average gap of 1.17 meter that the drivers assumed in this study was much less than the legally prescribed 1.5 meter. Considering both studies together, it seems that the cyclist's appearance can affect the behavior of nearby drivers, though exactly how remains to be further explored.

The rider's gender also appears to affect motorists' overtaking behavior. Both Walker (2007) in England and Chuang *et al.* (2013) in China found that motor vehicle drivers tended to allow more lateral distance for female riders than for male riders. However, neither study analyzed whether this greater distance was due to the drivers' consideration for the female riders, or to the female riders' tendency to ride closer to the edge of the road and away from the motorized traffic.

Unlike car drivers, cyclists tend to adapt their behavior according to expediency rather than according to the rules. An interesting demonstration of this behavior was demonstrated in an elegant study by Bjørnskau (2014) who noted that in Norway when cyclists cross the road either from a pavement or from a bicycle (and pedestrian) track, they are supposed to yield to crossing traffic on the road. However, when pedestrians cross over the zebra crossings the cars must yield according to the law. This gives the bicyclists two legal options, to either stay on the bicycle and give way to the cars or dismount and have the right-of-way as a pedestrian. However, neither behavior is a good solution from the perspective of game theory. Instead, what cyclists do predominantly – as manifest in three different crossing locations at different times – is consistent with the game-theoretic solution: depending on the time and location of the observation, in 57 to 84 percent of the observation locations and times the cyclists crossed the street on their bicycles and forced drivers to yield. This led Bjørnskau to conclude – quite logically – that instead of wasting time on law enforcement, it may be more practical to reconsider the regulations and to accommodate the actual behavior to which both drivers and cyclists already tend to adhere.

Distracted cycling

Like drivers, cyclists – at least commuting cyclists – are not immune to distraction from cell phones. In an observational study carried out in the heavily cycled town of Groningen, Netherlands, de Waard, Westerhuis, and Lewis-Evans (2015) observed cyclists' cell phone use in six city locations and compared it to the results of a similar study five years earlier in 2008. Interestingly, they found that while the rate of phone use has not increased (being steady at approximately 3 percent of all cyclists), the nature of the phone task changed: from 79 percent talking and 21 percent involved in some sort of screen operation (most likely texting) in 2008 to 77 percent operating the screen and 23 percent talking in 2013. The good news is that despite the overall increase in cell phones, the percent of riders using the phone while riding did not increase. But the bad news is that of those using the phone the majority were now texting: a behavior involving visual distraction that is much more dangerous than cognitive distraction. This change parallels the increase in texting of drivers, especially young ones (see Chapter 13). De Ward and his colleagues also noted that cyclists using their phones tended ride farther away from the curb than those not using the phone. This is a rational behavior if the curb is perceived by the cyclist as a threat, but an irrational one considering the diminishing lateral distance from passing cars. In the U.S., where riding as a transport mode is much less common, in a national survey of 61+ years old adults 16 percent of those who reported riding a bike also reported they use an electronic device on at least half of their trips (Schroeder and Wilbur, 2013). However, in the U.S. most of the cycling is not commuting and therefore the interactions with motor-vehicle traffic are fewer, and consequently so are the risks.

To better understand how cyclists divide their attention between their phone and the road and traffic around them Ahlstrom, Kircher, and their colleagues (Ahlstrom *et al.*, 2016; Kircher *et al.*, 2015) in Sweden provided 22 16-25 years old cyclists who used their cell phones while riding with an instrumented bicycle that among other things recorded their riding speed and visual search behavior as they rode on a predetermined 1 kilometer trail adjacent to a road (left of the track), that crossed four intersections. While they rode, they were requested to engage in five phone distracting activities: answer and initiate a call, receive and send a text message, and check a newspaper headline on the internet. The effects of these tasks on the visual search was evaluated by measuring the number of glances and total glance durations in different areas of interest while performing these tasks relative to two control conditions: riding without any distractions and riding while listening to music on headphones. Glance direction was defined in terms of one of six areas of interest: ahead on the cycle track, the road ahead to the left of the cycle track, to the right into an intersecting road, over the shoulder to the back, to the phone, and to other areas. Figure 17-7 summarizes the frequency of glances and total durations of the glances directed at each of these areas of interest. It is patently obvious (and quite expected) that most of the visual attention is split between the cycle track ahead and the phone. Of the different phone tasks, the most demanding are texting (both sending and receiving) and internet search. In fact, when talking on the phone riders still fixate the cycle path more than the phone, but when engaged in texting and internet search most of the glances and longer glance durations are dedicated to the phone at the expense of the cycle track. Also, the time spent looking at the phone is

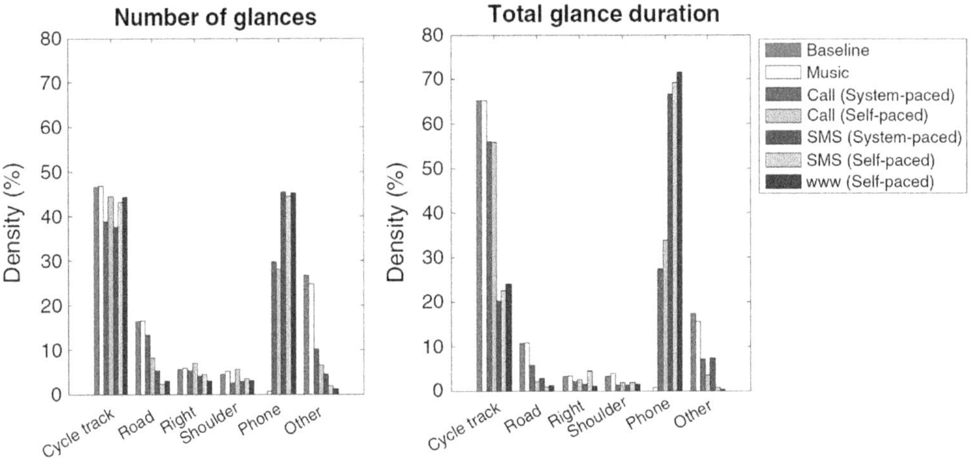

Figure 17-7. The number of glances and total glance duration spent on different areas of interest while cycling on a track adjacent to a road, and being engaged in different cell phone tasks. Systems-paced tasks are those initiated by the experimenter (receiving a call or a text message), and self-paced tasks are those initiated by the rider (placing a call, sending a text message, and searching the internet) (from Ahlstrom *et al.*, 2016, with permission from Elsevier).

primarily at the expense of time that would otherwise be spent on looking at the track. This was also reflected in the pattern of eye movements. Most of the saccadic movements were between the track and the phone. Interestingly, in the absence of a distracting task – during the control and music condition – the gaze shifted more to "other areas" and the road than to the right when approaching intersections. What does all of this mean? Most likely it means that in general cyclists are able to allocate their attention to different sources without compromising their safety. In fact, the researchers also note that "glances directed towards the phone did not lead to traffic relevant gaze targets being missed." In terms of speed adaptation, just as drivers tend to reduce their speeds when engaged with the cell phone (see Chapter 13) so did the cyclists. Relative to their speed in the absence of distraction, the cyclists tended to increase their speed while listening to music (though this may be function of the music tempo chosen: Brodsky, 2001) and to reduce their speed when either initiating or answering the phone to talk or to text. In addition, 20 percent of the cyclists stopped to read or answer a call and 30 percent stopped before initiating a call or sending a message (Kircher *et al.*, 2015). This pattern of glances and riding behaviors is quite similar to the patterns we observe in drivers. We found the same judicious shift of glances in response to billboard distraction in Tel Aviv, and the same slowing down in driving while engaging in a cell phone activity (see Chapter 13). However, note that the cyclists in Ahlstrom's and Kircher's studies constituted a very small biased sample, they were practiced in using the phone while cycling, and the test route was quite short. This general conclusion may not apply to all cyclists in all circumstances, and it only takes a rare diversion of attention exactly when an unexpected hazard appears to have a crash.

The impact of distraction on bicycling crash risk is difficult to determine. Self-reported survey data does implicate phone use with over-involvement in crashes. Goldenbeld *et al.* (2012) conducted an internet survey in the Netherlands in 2009, where he noted that the frequency of using cell phones either for listening to music or for talking and texting declined with age. On the average 77 percent of the young riders (<18 years old) reported using the phone, compared to 14 percent of the riders 50+ years old. More relevant to safety, phone use was associated with increased crash risk for all age groups, though the increase was smaller than typically reported for car drivers. The highest crash risk was recorded for teen cyclists who reported using the phone on each trip. Their risk relative to those who reported that they never listen to music or use the phone was 1.6; that is, 60 percent higher. However, for those who rarely listened to music or rarely used the phone there was no significant increase in crash risk.

Cycling and Crash Causation

Defining a crash cause is much more difficult for bicycle crashes than for motor vehicle and motorcycle crashes as there exist no in-depth multi-disciplinary large-scale crash causation studies analogous to the ones conducted on cars and motorcycles. Instead, crash analyses typically rely on police data that are more focused on traffic law violations, and are also notorious for under-reporting bicycle crashes and injuries; more than for cars, motorcycles, and pedestrians (NRSA, 2012; Wegman *et al.*, 2012). Thus, analyses based on police reports are plagued by shallowness and biases – both due more to the nature of the available information than to limits in the skill and insights of the researchers. We do know, though, that at least in the EU countries most cycling deaths are due to collisions with motorized vehicles, especially passenger cars, which accounted for 52 percent of all cyclist fatalities in 2008-2010. In contrast, crashes in which only the cyclist was involved accounted for only 13 percent (Steriu, 2012a).

An example is an investigation conducted by Bíl and his colleagues (2010) on police reports of motor vehicle-bicycle collisions involving Czech Republic drivers and adult cyclists severely injured or killed in collisions between 1995 and 2007. In most crashes, the fault was assigned to the drivers (62 percent of the fatal crashes and 57 percent of the severe-injury crashes). When they calculated the odds ratios of different factors responsible for the crash they found that they were the highest for speeding by the drivers ($OR = 8.27$ relative to the frequency of "denying right of way"), followed by the driver's "faulty driving style" ($OR = 4.52$). The cyclists in turn were cited much more often than the drivers for "denying right of way" and "faulty overtaking" ($OR = 3.3$ for each relative to drivers' denial of right-of-way). Thus, at least from the perspective of the police crash investigators and the analysis of Bíl and his colleagues, the main culprits for crash causation are the drivers' high speeds (that translate to high impact forces), and general carelessness. The cyclists' contributions are mostly in inappropriate riding style. These conclusions have to be qualified – as Bíl *et al.* themselves acknowledge – because they are based on investigations seeking law infractions, limited to crashes occurring only on public roads and involving cars only. It is obvious that a scientific investigation of a representative sample of all severe and fatal bicycle crashes would yield a totally different set of explanatory factors (as we see in motor vehicle crashes). Still, the findings are important because the majority of cyclist fatalities are from collisions with motor vehicles. However, such analyses also significantly under-report nighttime crashes and bias the frequencies of different cash types and crash causes, as crashes due to collision with a car are more likely during the daytime, whereas crashes from falls or collision with a fixed object are more likely during the night hours (Juhra *et al.*, 2012). In the U.S., according to the NHTSA, most fatal bicycle collisions with motor vehicles also occur in urban areas in non-intersections (NHTSA, 2015).

In a review of the percent of fatal and serious injury collisions with a motor vehicles and collisions with a fixed object in 12 European countries, collision with a motor vehicle was the most common type of fatal crash: from 63 percent in Austria to 92 percent in the United Kingdom and Croatia. The most common rider behavior at the time of the crash was moving straight forward. The frequencies of cyclists changing lanes or turning, slowing or stopping or overtaking were rare by comparison (OECD/ITF, 2013). These findings reinforce the critical role of the motorist as the one who either changes his or her path or fails to adjust his position to accommodate the cyclist.

The current choice method for the study of crash causation is naturalistic driving studies (see Chapter 2). An exploratory naturalistic cycling study was recently conducted on 16 Swedish cyclists in Gothenburg, Sweden (Dozza and Werneke, 2014). Although the sample was small, the results were interesting in the sense that they demonstrated the relative risk for a (minor) crash or a near-accident ("safety-critical-event") in different situations. These findings are interesting also because they are at odds relative to some findings by Bíl *et al.* For example, in the Bíl analysis the likelihood of a collision was not significantly different in an intersection or at a roundabout than on a straight road. Dozza and Werneke, however, found that that the risk in an intersection is four times that of a near-accident while cycling on a straight segment, and 12 times risker when the intersection also contained a visual obstruction in the rider's visual field. Given the small size of the study, its restriction to a small area, and absence of any severe-injury crashes, all that can be concluded from it is that the methodology is appropriate but a greater sample of observations must be collected in multiple locations with various infrastructures in order to reach valid conclusions on the relative likelihood of different factors that cause or contribute to bicycling crashes. Other conclusions about cyclists' crash involvement must be attributed to the specific characteristics of the user population, geography, climate, and infrastructure in which these limited scope studies were conducted. For example, in Dozza and Werneke's study only 30 percent of the conflicts were with motorized vehicles. Most of the conflicts were collisions with other vulnerable road users; primarily pedestrians and other cyclists, 29 percent and 16 percent, respectively. These kinds of conflicts were not even recorded by the Czech police, but that may be due to the prevalence of pedestrian and bicycle paths in Gothenburg.

There are other sources that indicate that in collisions with cars it is typically the car driver who is at fault for not yielding to the cyclist (e.g., Zaieg, 2009, in Israel). An analysis of the U.S. FARS data for the years 2005-2011 determined that 68 percent of the fatal crashes "involved no improper action on the part of the cyclist or had no record of an improper action." Where an improper action was noted, the most frequent ones were failure to yield right-of-way (23 percent), followed by failure to obey signs, signals, or a police officer (9 percent), and riding/playing in the roadway, not being visible, and improper crossing of an intersection (8 percent each). Similar conclusions were reached from an analysis of serious injury bicycle crashes in twelve European countries mentioned above (OECD/ITF, 2013). In summary, the one relatively consistent finding that emerges from all the studies is that culpability rests more on the drivers than on the cyclists. Notwithstanding the poor visibility of the cyclists, this is somewhat paradoxical. After all of the two of them – the riders and the drivers – it is the drivers who are more mature, tested on rules of the road, licensed, and in general better-regulated road users.

Crash Countermeasures – Improving Bicycling Safety

Before reviewing and assessing the efficacy of different approaches to the safeguarding of bicyclists, it must be acknowledged that proposed and proven countermeasures are typically based on small scale research limited to specific locations and cultures. Therefore, extreme care must be exercised in their blind application. In a European project on Best Practice to Promote Cycling and Walking, Dijkstra, Levelt, and Thomsen (1998) suggest that different facilities are most appropriate for countries with different proportions of urban trips conducted on bicycles. This means that research conducted on a given countermeasure in a given country may not apply to another country with a significantly different density of bicycling and road-use culture. By promoting the use of bicycles (for health, ecology, or economics), we increase exposure, and therefore without a concomitant effort to decrease conflicts with other vehicles, we are in essence promoting risk and injury. Therefore, a primary aim of all countermeasures should be to reduce the risk of conflicts with vehicles of greater speeds and larger mass; i.e., cars and trucks.

Policy and organizational approaches

More and more countries and jurisdictions either have or are developing comprehensive bicycling safety policies. Leading the way is Europe where over 60 percent of the countries have a policy of encouraging walking and cycling; compared to less than 40 percent of the south, central, and North American countries, and less than 10 percent of the African countries (WHO, 2013). An extensive review of such policies is provided in the OECD/ITF (2013) report. Described below is the general safe systems approach and some critical components of safe cycling policies.

The safe system approach

When bicycling becomes a major vehicle for mobility and the use rate (or potential use rate) is high, national policies are needed. These polices are especially effective when addressing all relevant factors that impact safety – an approach known as Safe System – which involves four basic principles: functionality, homogeneity, predictability, and forgiveness (OECD/ITF, 2013). A stellar example of this approach is the Netherlands, where fatality rate per kilometer of riding from bicycle crashes dropped by 80 percent over the past 30 years. Schepers *et al.* (2017) in a detailed description of the Dutch system attribute most of this improvement to a bicycle-friendly policy of "street hierarchy," an integral aspect of the Dutch "Sustainable Safety" system approach according to which the entire network of roads, vehicles, and road users are addressed (Wegman *et al.*, 2012). The street hierarchy is based on the principles of homogeneity and functionality. The *homogeneity* principle means that on a given travel route "differences in speed, direction and mass should not be too large; for example, a safe speed for mixing cyclists with motorized traffic is no higher than 30 km/h." This requirement is consistent with the finding of the Czech crash analysis that found that excess speed on the part of a car driver is the most likely cause of a fatal injury to the bicyclist (Bíl, Bílová, and Müller, 2010). It is also consistent with the results of an analysis conducted in North Carolina that showed how the injury severity of bicyclists involved in bicycle-car collisions increases exponentially with the speed limit at the crash site (see Figure 17-8). The *functionality* principle implies that the function of faster roads (mostly freeways) is to enhance traffic flows whereas "lower order roads" are designed to provide "access to origins and destinations." Thus, on high speed freeways bicyclists are not allowed at all, while in residential streets, bicycling is accommodated with separate lanes. These two principles are the antidote to the two greatest risk factors in cycling collisions with motorized traffic: speed difference and mass difference; the primary determinants of the kinetic energy at impact.

The *predictability* principle is a basic human factors/ergonomic principle. The road design, the signing, and other traffic control devices should be such that all users will understand the behavior expected of them. The U.S. Positive Guidance principles and the EU Self-Organizing roads are good road safety applications of this principle (see Chapter 19). Finally, the *forgiveness* principle states that if a crash is unavoidable, its severity should be minimized. This principle can be applied to impact-absorbing infrastructure, vehicle design, use of helmets, and immediate access to emergency medical services.

The safe system approach has been very successful at increasing road safety for all users. For cycling safety it means that policies should address both cyclists and drivers. However, it is important to stress that the specific application of the safe system

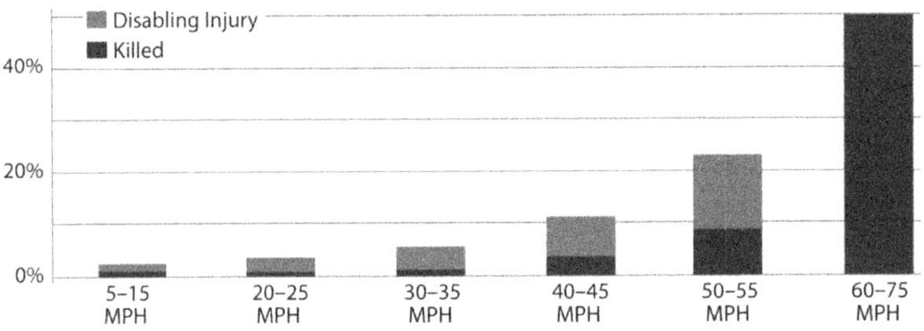

Figure 17-8. Percentage of bicyclists killed or seriously injured in bicycle-motor vehicle crashes by posted speed limit in North Carolina (as cited by Nabors *et al.*, 2012).

approach differs among countries as a function of the culture, the geography, the facilities available for the different road users, the modal split, the level of urbanization, and – of course – the strength of the political will and the funding. It also requires top-level coordination between cycling policies and other policies that may affect cycling safety (OECD/ITF, 2013). An extension of the safe system approach and an indirect way of encouraging cycling – though in and of itself not necessarily safe cycling – is to provide integrated trans-modal transportation and convenient bicycle paths and parking facilities next to train stations. Many European countries in fact do that (Fischer *et al.*, 2010).

Share-the-Road and the street hierarchy

At the lowest level of the street hierarchy is Share-the-road: a policy-driven design according to which a road pavement is designed to serve both motorized and non-motorized traffic, with priority given to the latter. This has an immediate implication for the legal and design speed. Such areas are sometimes known as home zones (from the Dutch term Woonerfs, meaning "home zones"). The assumption is that children may be playing in these streets, and therefore the speed limit there is 15 km/hr and motorists give way to pedestrians. Home zones and low speed zones are also common in cities in England, Germany, Sweden, and Switzerland (Fischer *et al.*, 2010). At the next level of the hierarchy the traffic is still mixed and the speed limit is 30 km/hr; the limit that is recommended for traffic calming. At still higher speeds of distributor roads where the speed limit is 50-70 km/hr, bicycles are provided with separate bicycle lanes or paths. Finally, at the highest level, consisting of roads with higher speed limits bicycles are not allowed. This policy of different levels of "sharing the road" has implications not only for the design of the infrastructure but also for comprehensive traffic education and training of both cyclists and motorists. It also requires traffic regulations that favor cyclists and pedestrians in the sense that in lower-level streets the motorist is almost always liable in a collision with a bicyclist. Perhaps the most important outcome of this policy is that it reduces the exposure of cyclists to fast moving motor vehicles. In the Netherlands, by 2008, 85 percent of the access roads in built up areas had a speed limit of 30 km/hr (Weijermars and Wegman, 2011). Alongside the impressive progress made in the Netherlands in road safety in general and bicycle safety in particular, one has to acknowledge that a key ingredient in the success of the program is political will and public support – two ingredients that are often hard to obtain.

The mere decision to adopt a share-the-road approach is not a guarantee of its success. The policy must be compatible with either existing social culture or a comprehensive strategy for behavioral change (including enforcement). As an example, in the U.S. the implementation of this policy by mere placing of verbal signs informing drivers to "SHARE THE ROAD" coupled with a standard bicycle warning sign (diamond-shaped sign with a schematic drawing of a bicycle on a yellow background) immediately below it on two rural road sections in Michigan had no significant effect on the average lateral safety margin that drivers ceded to the cyclists. The drivers were much more affected by a centerline rumble strip in the center of the road than by the bicyclists. Consequently, in the presence of the rumble strip the drivers left narrower lateral safety margins between themselves and the cyclists, though they did slow down somewhat (Kay *et al.*,

2014). However, before the plea to drivers to share the road by signing is dismissed, it should be noted that the sign used by Kay *et al.* may not have been the best possible one to convey the message that bicycles may use the middle of the lane and should be treated like all other vehicles. In an evaluation of different means of conveying that message, Hess and Peterson (2015) compared the standard SHARE THE ROAD + bicycle warning sign with a rectangular sign with a picture of a bicycle and underneath it the message "MAY USE FULL LANE." Using a web-based survey, they analyzed 1,824 responses and found that in "almost all cases" the explicit message was better understood as indicating that bicyclists may ride in the center of the lane and do not have to move to the right to yield to a passing motorized vehicle. These findings support the predictability principle: signs should be as ergonomically designed and as explicit as possible to improve comprehension (see Chapter 5). Still, to maximize the benefits of the regulation the other principles must be embraced as well.

If a given jurisdiction can in fact develop and implement a comprehensive plan for a modal shift in mobility from motorized vehicles to pedestrians and bicyclists (as the Dutch have done), then based on multiple analyses from different parts of the world, it is most likely that it will be accompanied by a decrease in pedestrian and cyclists injuries (see "safety-in-numbers" section below) (Elvik, 2009; Elvik and Bjørnskau, 2017; Fyhri *et al.*, 2016; Wegman *et al.*, 2012). At the turn of this century, the percent of bicycling and walking constituted less than 5 percent of all traffic in the U.S. and over 18 percent in the EU countries (Wei and Lovegrove, 2012). This means that such modal shifts are probably easier to accomplish in Europe than in North America. This disparity also supports Wegman's argument that the specific components in system safety are country/culture/geography specific.

Helmet laws

Many countries have helmet laws, most often requiring the use of helmets by children when riding on the road. However, unlike motorcycle helmets, not a single European country has universal bicycle helmet laws, and only a few countries have age-related laws, requiring helmet use for children under various ages; from 10 years old in Malta, 15-16 years old in Estonia, Croatia, Sweden, and Slovenia, to 18 years old in the Lithuania and the Czech Republic. In Spain, they are required for all ages, but only in urban areas (EC, 2015). Their effectiveness has been hotly debated as some have argued (and produced data to support their arguments) that the increased safety as measured by reduced numbers of injuries and/or fatalities is due to reduced cycling rather than to an increase in helmet use (Robinson, 1996). Most cross-sectional studies that compare injuries and fatalities between jurisdictions with helmet laws and those without them find that helmet laws reduce injuries. A recent example is the study by Meehan *et al.* (2013) that compared cycling fatalities of children 0-16 years old in states that that have helmet laws with cycling fatalities in states that do not. Using the U.S. Fatalities Analysis Reporting System (FARS) for their data source they found that both before adjustment for any confounding factors and after adjusting for differences in maximum legal blood alcohol limit, median household income, and age-based elderly licensure laws, the average incidence rate of fatalities in states with helmet laws was nearly 20 percent lower than in states without them. However, this study (and other studies like it) did not consider many other potentially confounding variables such as climate, amount of ridership, gender, and cycling infrastructure. These limitations, argue helmet law opponents, make such studies methodologically flawed, and their conclusions suspect. Notwithstanding these limitations other studies using epidemiological data have demonstrated the laws' effectiveness in terms of estimated number of head injuries averted by the introduction of the law (e.g., Scuffham *et al.*, 2000).

There are statistical methods that can effectively control for possible reduced exposure. A good example is the study by Walter *et al.* (2011) on the effects of the helmet law enacted in New South Wales, Australia, where helmet laws were introduced in 1991 for adults (>16 years old, in January 1) and then for children (<16 years old in July 1). To circumvent the exposure issue, Walter and his colleagues studied the ratio of head to limb injuries, correctly assuming that the helmet requirement would only affect the head injuries. They indeed found that the law and the observed increase in helmets were accompanied by a lower head/limb injury rate following the enactment of the law. Furthermore, they also found that that pedestrian head/limb injury rates remained unchanged after the law. Though Walter *et al.*'s results are quite strong, so is their assumption that the head/limb ratio of injuries is a valid exposure-free measure. To their credit, they address some possible arguments that would make this assumption – in the absence of supporting data on helmet use – questionable.

When head injuries are reduced, some people – and researchers – argue that the cost of good helmets may overweigh the benefits in head injury reductions (Robinson, 2007). Thus, even when the benefits of the helmets are no longer being questioned, there is a real issue of how to increase helmet use (in terms of percent of riders with helmets) without reducing the number of people who bicycle instead of using other modes of transportation. An analysis performed by Taylor and Scuffham on New Zealand injury, bicycling, and cost data indicated that helmets are cost-effective for the young users (5-12 years old) but not for the older ones (Taylor and Scuffham, 2002).

Perhaps the best argument for helmet laws is NHTSA's conclusion that they are by far the most effective of all cyclist-oriented means of increasing cycling safety. The NHTSA compendium on "Countermeasures that Work" gives children helmet laws a 5-star rating, and adult helmet laws a 4-star rating (Goodwin *et al.*, 2015).

Rideshare/bikeshare programs

Bikeshare (also known as rideshare) are cycle sharing programs that have sprouted in multiple cities throughout the worlds as a potential strategy to reduce urban – especially inner city – congestion and pollution. These programs are rapidly spreading throughout many cities; with over 800 programs and half a million bicycles worldwide (Fishman and Schepers, 2016). In these programs, people can use "city bikes" for commuting from one place to another in congested urban centers, as well as integrate them into multimodal transport, especially cycling and riding the bus or train. Bicycles and bicycle riding facilities are distributed throughout a city, and people can pick up a bicycle in one place and drop it off at another. As an incentive to use the bikes for commuting rather than for pleasure riding, the fee is graduated so that typically the first half hour is minimal (or free to subscribers) and after that it progresses exponentially. While these programs are quite effective in increasing urban cycling, they encapsulate the conflict between expanding bicycle use and increasing the use of helmets. The programs do not provide helmet protection, as most people do not want to be burdened with carrying a helmet on the one hand, or use a helmet worn by many (unknown!) others on the other hand.

The safety concern of the bikeshare programs has been addressed in an evaluation by Fishman and Schepers (2016), using the crash data obtained in selected North American, Australian, and European cities. They concluded that per kilometer of riding bikeshare is safer than riding one's own bike. In their analysis, the likelihood of being fatally injured while riding a bikeshare bicycle was approximately half of that with one's personal bicycle! This is despite the fact that the users are less familiar with the bike, and do not use helmets. As an explanation for this surprising finding, Fishman and Schepers suggest that it may be due to increased driver awareness and cautiousness around bikeshare users, an upright riding position and slower speed, and more positive attitudes on the part of the drivers as perceived by the bikeshare users compared to when these riders ride their own bikes (Fishman, Washington, and Haworth, 2012). However, this "benefit" may also be an artifact of confounding variables such as different locations, times, and routes where these bicycles are used. In designing these programs, city planners pick the locations and routes that are the most congested and where the likelihood of using the bikes is greatest. However, by doing so they reinforce the potential positive effects of "safety-in-numbers" that may also account for most of the safety benefits (see below). Admittedly, safety-in-numbers may be the intervening variable behind the drivers' increased awareness, though when evaluated at the same times and locations it should serve private bicycle cyclists and bikeshare cyclists equally.

The effects of bike-sharing on reducing car use are mixed. In user surveys conducted in Toronto, Montreal, Washington, DC, and St. Paul-Minneapolis, on the average 40 percent of the respondents reported that bike-sharing reduced their driving and none reported that it increased it. However, the range was enormous: from less than one percent in Washington, DC, to over 50 percent in Minnesota (Shaheen *et al.*, 2012, 2013). In his review of the literature prior to that study, Fishman *et al.* (2013) concluded that in general – based on evaluations conducted in cities in France, Ireland, the U.S., and China – the majority of bikeshare users switch to it from other modes of sustainable transportation such as public transportation and walking. Still, independent data indicate that in all of these cities, bikeshare programs have been accompanied by reductions in private car use. One exception was London where there was an increase in motor vehicle traffic, in part due to the trucks that keep balancing the distribution of bicycles (Fishman, Washington, and Haworth, 2014). In summary, while they do provide a partial solution to environmental, economic, and congestion problems, the safety benefits of bikeshare programs are equivocal as they pose a barrier to increased use of helmets.

Behavioral approaches

Safe cycling education

Perhaps the best and most thorough behavioral program to improve cyclists' behavior is that of the Netherlands, where bicycling safety education in elementary school is common and even theoretical tests on proper cycling behavior are part of many curricula. Some other countries such as England, Denmark, and Germany also have such programs, but to the extent that these programs have been evaluated, just as with driver education (see Chapter 6) they have not yielded consistent significant effects (Goodwin *et al.*, 2015; Schepers *et al.*, 2017; Wegman *et al.*, 2012); possibly because some of the safe behavior requirements involve perceptual-motor and information-processing skills that are beyond the children's capacity at the critical developmental stage. Being aware of the potential gap between the safe cycling requirements and the target audience (children) capabilities, to assist in program development the U.S. National Highway Administration published two reports *Child Pedestrian Safety Education: Applying Learning and Developmental Theories to Develop Safe Street-Crossing Behaviors* (Percer, 2009), and *Bicycle Safety Education for Children From a Developmental And Learning Perspective* (Ellis, 2014). However, their effectiveness is yet to be determined. Interestingly, only by the time they are eight years old, the visual search behavior – a critical indicator of skill – of children seems to mimic that of experienced adult cyclists: focusing farther ahead as they increase their speed and focusing more on the near pathway on narrow lanes (Vansteenkiste, Cardon, and Lenoir, 2015).

Still, there is a plethora of educational programs, in sharp contrast to the dearth of scientific evidence of their effectiveness or impact on cycling safety. Admittedly, there are many obstacles in designing a valid program evaluation study. Evaluations in terms of the ultimate safety criteria – crashes and injuries – are very costly. Because crashes are rare events the evaluation must either be based on a very large sample or on a long-term tracking, or both. Evaluations in terms of behavioral criteria, such as risky riding behaviors are more practical, but their relevance to injury reduction can be questioned, and to be objective they must be based on objective observations. A third approach is to measure changes in *reported* risky behaviors. This is the least expensive of the three options, but obviously the farthest removed from crash involvement. Nonetheless, using this approach Twisk and her colleagues (2014) evaluated the impact of five different short-term educational programs on risk taking behaviors while cycling. Three of the programs were cognitive – in the sense that they focused on improving the cyclists' "understanding and insight through information and demonstrations of the safety-critical features, such as braking/stopping distances, limitations in visual perception and reaction times, and the vulnerability of the human body." The other two programs stressed the negative emotions associated with crashes and aimed at generating fear of risky behaviors by showing videos of crashes and personal accounts of road victims (this is a very popular approach in media campaigns against speeding, drunk-driving, and non-use of seat belts). All the programs were relatively short lasting from two hours to one day, and all had a significant common feature: they were already being administered in the Netherlands on a regular basis and each of them was funded by policy makers "because of its assumed effectiveness." The evaluation consisted of asking the participants to fill out a pre-treatment questionnaire relating to their involvement in different risky cycling behaviors just before the program, and then again a month later. The criteria for program effectiveness was the reported change relative to the change in a control group who filled out the questionnaires on two occasions a month apart but did not take the course. The results showed a significant reduction in reported risky behaviors for three of the five programs: two cognitive programs and one emotional program. The details of these programs are not very important because even when there was a statistically significant improvement, it was not sufficiently large to be of practical significance. Or, in the authors' own words, they found "the impacts of all five programmes to be small. Practitioners expectations of the effects were higher than those actually found in the evaluation... These findings underscore the need for evidence-based interventions that are developed using thorough evaluation studies." So much for assuming – rather than testing for – effectiveness.

Increasing the use of helmets
Given their proven and accepted safety benefits, a major effort is often directed at encouraging cyclists to use helmets. Combined educational programs, attractive helmet design and marketing, and laws that make helmet use mandatory for children help achieve high rates of usage. Most countries are reluctant to impose universal mandatory helmet laws for cycling, though in a few countries – for example, Austria, Czech Republic, Estonia, Japan, Slovenia, and Sweden – it is mandatory for children below a certain age (Steriu, 2012b).

Use rate varies greatly by user and place. For example, in Israel an observational survey of "sport" cyclists on inter-urban roads and trails revealed that 93-96 percent of them wore a helmet (and nearly all of them wore riding outfits) (Gitelman, Pisachov, and Carmel, 2012). Thus, in addition to being safety-oriented, for these riders helmets may be part of the standard "cool" riding gear. However, in an observational survey conducted in Israel a year earlier in central urban and residential areas the use rate was only 11-21 percent (Gitelman, Pisachov, and Carmel, 2011). The striking exception to the lack of use of helmets was the very high use rate of small children (<4 years old), which were 53 percent in urban centers and 33 percent in residential areas. At this age, children are not yet exposed to formal safety education so obviously here the impact of parental control is the key. Even in countries that rank among the safest in the world, such as the Netherlands and Norway, use rate of helmets is low. In Norway, in 2014, it was 54 percent (Lajunen, 2016), and in cities in the Netherlands a helmeted cyclist is a very rare sight. Nonetheless, helmet use can be increased. In Australia where universal helmet laws have been in effect since 1991, a recent observational survey conducted in multiple urban, suburban, and rural locations in Queensland yielded extremely high use rates of 98 percent overall. The range was also quite small: varying from a "low" of 94 percent for children (across all locations and times) to a high of nearly 100 percent (99.0+ percent) for nearly all other users and conditions. Also, as expected, boys, being higher risk takers, had lower use rates than girls (Debnath *et al.*, 2016). How does one achieve such high use rates is unfortunately not revealed or even discussed in this study, thereby making its implications for other countries questionable.

To understand the reasons for helmet use or non-use, Lajunen (2016) interviewed 235 Norwegian 10-16 years old children and 106 of their parents about barriers and facilitators to helmet use. Previous studies have listed "not owning" one and "lack of awareness" of its benefits as primary reasons for not using a helmet. On the other hand, having friends or parents who use helmets increases the use of helmets. In Lajunen's survey, 44 percent of the children and 54 percent of the adults reported "always" wearing a helmet. Among children the greatest barriers to helmet use were the feeling that "it is uncomfortable to wear," "I would rather use a hat or a cap," "I don't need it because I'm not riding a bicycle where the motor vehicles are," "the helmet looks ridiculous," and "I just ride a bicycle close to home." For adults the barriers were similar but the strength of the association between these arguments and not wearing a helmet was much smaller. The best predictors of helmet use by children were that "it is a habit" and that they "feel safer with a bicycle helmet on." In contrast, among adults it was just that it was a "habit." Also interesting was that the best correlate of non-use among children was age: the older the child the less likely she or he were to wearing a helmet. Synthesizing all of these results, it seems that the multiple barriers that children cite make it a very difficult challenge for parents and educators. If these answers are valid, then the best strategy is to create helmet use part of a habit, and this is most easily done at a very early age when parental control is still effective.

Improving cyclists' visibility

Helmets – for enhanced bicyclist's visibility

The use of helmets is obviously based on safety concerns, control, and convenience. Thus, is it not surprising that helmet use on public roads is most common among children (e.g., in New Zealand; Scuffham *et al.*, 2000) where parental controls (often with age-related helmet wearing laws – e.g., in Israel) are prime determinants. Interestingly, while there is widespread support for compulsory use of helmets for children (e.g., 87 percent in the U.S. in 2012), there is much less support for making it compulsory for adults (e.g., 63 percent in the U.S. in 2012; with 46 percent reporting that they "never" use a helmet) (Schroeder and Wilbur, 2013). Making helmets look cool, probably helps, and having others around you wear helmets is probably also an incentive. Fortunately, to look cool most helmets have bright colors and some even have retroreflective materials. However, the cyclist's awareness of their poor visibility is simply not there, at least on the basis of the low number of cyclists that use various lights and materials to increase the bicycle's visibility (e.g., Hagel *et al.*, 2007).

Bicycle lights

In the beginning of this century, the EU made the use of daytime running lights on all cars in Europe mandatory. While there had been evidence for the contribution of DRL to crash reductions for cars, this act further decreased the visibility and conspicuity of bicycles. To enhance their conspicuity, many have argued that bicycles too should have DRL. In a large-scale experimental field study conducted in Odense, Denmark, by Madsen, Andersen, and Lahrmann (2013), 1,845 randomly selected volunteers had their bikes fitted with a new generation of lights that are automatically turned on whenever the bicycle wheels are turning. A fairly matched group of 2,000 control volunteers received these lights as a gift when the experiment ended a year later. Because of the acknowledged under-reporting of bicycle accidents by the police, the two groups were asked by bi-monthly emails to report any accidents in which they had been involved. An accident was defined as "an incident where you, riding your bicycle, have unwillingly been forced off your bike and/or crashed either by yourself or due to collision or near-collision with others; cars, trucks, vans, mopeds, other cyclists, pedestrians etc." The results supported the expected effect of the lights. Over the whole year, the incidence rate of personal injury accidents was 41 percent lower with the lights, and the incidence rate for all accidents was 33 percent lower. Interestingly the significant effects were limited to daytime hours. The absence of a safety effect of the lights at night is curious, but consistent with that found by Wood *et al.* (2012). Apparently the lights were more helpful in being seen by other road users than in seeing other road users. This argument is strengthened by the fact that the lights did not have a significant effect on single vehicle or falling crashes. Also, the authors note, it is possible that at night many of the riders in the control group still used their conventional bicycle lights.

These results and simple intuition have led many countries to require visibility enhancements for bicyclists. In Spain retroreflective equipment is compulsory for cyclists at night and outside urban areas. In Denmark, legislation requires all bicycles to have lamps and front, rear and wheel reflectors. In the Netherlands, all bicycle tire sidewalls must be provided with retroreflective elements (ETSC, 2006). However, legislating is one thing, enforcement and compliance is another, and effectiveness of the various devices is still another thing.

Increasing expectancy

Much of our visual behavior is governed by expectancies (see Chapter 4), which can either aid in detecting critical safety information (when they are met), or hinder it (when they are violated). A cycling-related example is provided in an early study by Summala and his colleagues (1996). In examining crash data in the Finnish city of Helsinki, they noticed that the most common type of a car-bicycle crash was an intersection collision where the driver intended to turn right and the cyclist was coming from the right on the main road. They then installed video cameras at two T intersections and monitored entering drivers' head movements and cyclists' approach to the intersection. As expected, they found that drivers turning right into the main road looked less frequently (and typically later) to the right to accommodate motor vehicle traffic coming from their left, and were therefore likely to miss or detect too late bicyclists coming from their right. Another situation that exemplifies the often-violated expectancy is that of bicyclists riding the wrong way in one-way streets, repeatedly surprising drivers. Though a false assumption by a driver is a known crash cause for motor vehicles, it is more common in car-bicycle interactions because bicyclists are more likely to violate the traffic laws (e.g., riding the wrong way in a one-way street). In a later analysis by the same researchers (Räsänen and Summala, 1998) they noted that in the intersection collisions only 11 percent of the drivers detected the cyclist before the collision, compared to 68 percent of the cyclists who detected the driver in time. Unfortunately, nearly all of these cyclists (92 percent) assumed that the drivers saw them and would give way to them as required by the local laws. These findings are very similar to the ones obtained in motorcycle collisions (see Chapter 16). In summary, our expectations govern both where to look and what we see (and this is where drivers often fail), and our assumptions (mostly on the part of the cyclists) govern what we do; sometimes with dire consequences. Thus, a most promising safety strategy would be to increase drivers' expectancies concerning the presence of cyclists on the road, and not necessarily where the rules-of-the-road dictate that they should be. The cyclists for their part should try to ride as much as possible according to the rules-of-the-road in order to improve their detectability in time.

Safety-in-numbers

In the context of cycling safety, the safety-in-numbers principle states that for any given number of motor vehicles on the road, the higher the volumes of cyclists on the road the lower their risk of collision. In general, multiple studies show that as the number/density of cyclists on the road increases, the crash risk per cyclist actually decreases (Elvik, 2009). According to Jacobsen (2003), who was the first to observe, study, and name this phenomenon, this finding is counter to the common experience that as the volume of road users increases – that is, as their exposure increases – so does their crash risk. Jacobsen was able to demonstrate the safety-in-numbers effect at the international, national, and local government levels by comparing different countries in Europe, by looking at trends over time in the Netherlands and the United Kingdom, and by comparing different Danish and California towns, respectively. The effect is illustrated in Figure 17-9 that plots the risk fatality relative to the percent of cycling and walking in the commute to work in 68 California municipalities. A convincing demonstration that the effect is in fact due primarily to the number or density of bicycles in traffic was provided in a controlled driving simulation study by Thompson, Savino, and Stevenson (2015). They developed a mathematical simulation known as agent-based modeling in which the effects of introducing more and more bicycles into a traffic system with a fixed

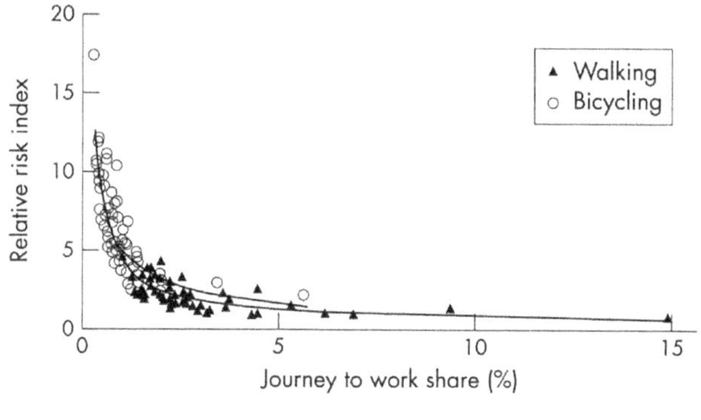

Figure 17-9. The risk of traffic injury per capita as a pedestrian and as a cyclist as a function of the percent of walking and cycling, respectively, that people engage in in their travel to work. Based on data from 68 California municipalities (Jacobsen, 2003, with permission from BMJ).

number of cars are evaluated on the interactions (i.e., collisions) between the bicycles and the cars. They found – as predicted – that as the number of bicycles increased – that is, as their density in the traffic increased the absolute number of collisions increased but the relative risk of collisions (per cyclists) decreased. Reversing the change by decreasing the number of bicycles resulted in an increase in the rate of collisions. International data from the past decade also show that the greater the bicycle travel per inhabitant per year, the lower the fatality rate per kilometers of riding (OECD/ITF, 2013). Most recently, Fyhri *et al.* (2016) demonstrated the effect by showing a correlation between bicycle crash rates and conflicts and seasonal changes in Norway, where cycling is much more common in the summer than in the winter months.

Jacobsen also suggested that the increased safety is not due to the changes in the cyclists' behavior as their numbers increase, as much as it is due to the drivers' adaptation to seeing many more cyclists. This hypothesis is consistent with the significant role of expectancy in obstacle detection (see Chapters 2 and 16 with respect to pedestrian detection). The expectancy effect on target detection is larger than the effect of many physical aspects of a stimulus. It states that a target that is expected is much more likely to be detected and is detected from a greater distance than one that is not expected. Still, it is difficult to test the expectancy hypothesis on the safety-in-numbers as the data are typically from naturalistic observations where there is very little control over confounding variables such as the improved infrastructure that often accompanies the greater use of cycling in specific locations and countries. To counter this specific argument, Schepers *et al.* (2011) statistically controlled for the bicycle facilities in Dutch intersections and found that the safety-in-numbers phenomenon remained. In another study Schepers (2012) found the safety-in-numbers effect even for crashes not involving motor vehicles, and both Jacobsen (2003) and Elvik and Bjørnskau (2017) found that it exists for pedestrian collisions as well, as can also be seen in Figure 17-9. Thus, it appears that expectancy is not the sole variable responsible for the "safety-in-numbers" effect. Instead, we must conclude that it is a product of multiple safety enhancements processes: the heightened visibility of the cyclists and the heighted expectancy of the motorists; "cumulative danger awareness" or "crowd sourcing" whereby the cyclists benefit from each other's detection and avoidance of obstacles; and the concomitant improvements in infrastructure that accompany the increasing use of bicycles (and that in turn attract more cyclists to the dedicated infrastructure). In this respect, safety-in-numbers is quite similar to Smeed's Law for all traffic fatalities (see Chapter 1).

Infrastructure design

In general, the increase in bicycle use in the Western world is most closely coupled with the investments jurisdictions make in the cycling infrastructure (Nabors *et al.*, 2012). Infrastructure treatments to promote bicycling differ in urban and non-urban environments. The relative emphasis on each should, of course, depend on the use levels and the crash risk in the two types of environments. In the EU countries, on the average 56 percent of the fatalities occur in urban areas. But the range is quite large; from over 60 percent urban in Romania, Denmark, Finland, Hungary, Italy, and Switzerland, to less than 40 percent in Latvia, Ireland, Spain, and Lithuania (Steriu, 2012a). To be most effective, the infrastructure modifications should be part of a system approach. To illustrate, they can take the form of comprehensive design of neighborhood street patterns in a manner that discourages through motor vehicle traffic and promotes walking and bicycling. Wei and Lovegrove (2012) demonstrated that some neighborhood street designs that achieve that (three-way offset, and fused grid networks) actually increase safety without compromising mobility and accessibility. At the micro level, where the street patterns already exist, infrastructure treatments can take one or two forms: separating bicycles from the motor vehicle traffic by providing bicyclists with separate tracks, trails, and stopping areas (boxes – see below) or by reducing the speed of cars when they share the same lanes, such as in intersections, by converting them to roundabouts.

Bicycle trails/tracks and paths/lanes

The effects of separating cyclists from the motorized traffic depend on the nature of the separation. Safety-wise the best are the bicycle trails or tracks that are physically separate from the surface of the motorized traffic. Bicycle crash rates (per kilometer ridden) are much lower there than on the road with the cars. This has been documented in the U.S. where less than half of one percent of the adults cycle to commute to work (Lusk *et al.*, 2013), and in the Netherlands where over 30 percent of the adult population use their bicycle as their main mode of transportation. However, not all bicycle trails are the same: wide and smooth surface trails allow the cyclists to distribute their visual search across their forward visual field much more evenly than narrow and rough ones where most of the visual fixations are directed toward the path itself (Vansteenkiste *et al.*, 2014), leaving the rider with less spare capacity to focus on potential approaching hazards. Marked bicycle paths and tracks that share the paved road are generally associated with only a slightly reduced risk; except for the two-way bicycle paths that actually increase the crash risk at intersections. There, motorists entering the priority road are likely to collide with cyclists coming from the right (the left in the United Kingdom, Japan, etc.) (Schepers *et al.*, 2011). This is a clear case of what Treat *et al.* (1979) in their classic analysis of the causes of traffic accidents labeled "false assumption" (see Chapter 18), where a driver does not expect crossing traffic in the near lane to approach from the right. To prevent such situations, the environmental design must conform to the users' expectations – or at the very least provide the users with ample warnings that their "normal" expectations do not apply in a specific situation.

To be safe bicycle paths must be wide enough to accommodate all the pedestrians and bicycle traffic that they are expected to carry. van der Horst *et al.* (2014) recorded the behavior of cyclists, pedestrians and moped riders in bicycle paths in two cities in the Netherlands. In Amsterdam by far the most common conflict was between cyclists and pedestrians in crossing areas. In Eindhoven, the most common conflict was between two bicyclists; mostly in intersections where one crosses another on the main thoroughfare. This information can then be used to redesign the specific high-risk conflict locations. One factor to consider is that the creation of bicycle tracks and lanes is also likely to create a modal shift: with more people using the bicycles. Dill (2009) conducted a naturalistic riding study that tracked 166 bicyclists over a 7-day period. The study, conducted in Portland, Oregon, yielded trip-routing data for nearly 2,000 trips. She found that nearly 50 percent of all the travel miles were on dedicated bicycle lanes or tracks, despite the fact that these dedicated lanes and tracks constituted only 8 percent of the roadway kilometers. Of course, it is hard to determine if the tracks and lanes were constructed on routes popular and attractive to riders, or if the riders changed their habits to use them. This is because the most popular reason given for choosing a bicycle route was that it minimized total distance, but the close second highest rated reason for choosing the bike lane or path was that it enabled the riders to avoid streets "with lots of vehicle traffic."

Intersection treatments

Intersections present drivers and cyclists with the greatest potential for conflicts, and hence with the greatest collision risk. The common theme to all intersection treatments is to increase the cyclist's visibility and conspicuity and minimize the number, area, and duration of conflicts. In an attempt to cover all the safety-relevant aspects, Carter *et al.* (2006) developed a bicycle "intersection safety index." The index score was based on objective and experts' ratings on 18 variables including presence of bicycle lane, main and cross street traffic volumes, number of through lanes, presence of on-street parking, main street speed limit, presence of traffic signal, and number of turn lanes. Final models were developed for different bicycle maneuvers (e.g., right turning) and also included behavioral data collected at the study sites. The process of intersection evaluation and the quantitative model that were derived eventually led to a user-friendly "Bicycle Safety Guide and Counter Measure Selection System" that is too complex to describe here but the guide along with other bike safety information is accessible on the internet (http://pedbikesafe.org/?/bikesafe).

In signalized intersections, one way to increase the drivers' awareness of the cyclists is through the creation of "bicycle boxes" – an area reserved for bicyclists between the stopping line for the motorized traffic and the pedestrian crossing just before the intersection. When the light turns green the cyclists are directly in front of the cars, are very conspicuous, and precede the cars in crossing the intersection. Evaluations of these boxes indicate that both cyclists and motorists like and respect them (Dill, Monsere, and McNeil, 2012). An alternative treatment is to provide cyclists with separate signals, where the onset of the cyclists' green light precedes the green light for cars. In both cases, the cyclists are given temporal priority in crossing the intersection ahead of the cars. These treatments are illustrated in Figure 17-10 (from Schepers *et al.*, 2017). To mitigate injury severity, speed bumps at cyclists' crossing are also employed.

An innovative approach to reduce red light running in intersections has been applied in China. Hypothesizing that many such violations are due to cyclists' impatience to wait and perspire under the sun until the light changes, sunshields were constructed over two bicycle paths in front of two intersections in the city of Hangzhou, China. As a result, the percent of riders violating the red light decreased slightly but consistently from 47 percent without the shade to 42 percent with the shade. Interestingly, the effect was observed on cloudy days as well as on sunny days and for electric bicycles as well as traditional bicycles (Zhang and Wu, 2013).

Figure 17-10. Bicycle box (left panel) and a pre-start green light for bicycles (right panel) to prevent conflicts with right turning vehicles in the Netherlands (from Schepers *et al.*, 2017, with permission from the author).

Roundabouts/circles

Converting intersections to roundabouts, while generally associated with crash and injury reduction for car occupants has not proven to benefit cyclists (Schepers *et al.*, 2014b; Wegman *et al.*, 2012; Wilke, Lieswyn, and Munro, 2014). Roundabouts are beneficial for cars because they force the drivers to reduce the speed when approaching the cross-road and, in the case of a collision it is typically an angle collision rather than a side collision between the front end and the (relatively soft) side of the other car. However, a collision between a car entering the roundabout and a bicyclist moving in it is can still be at a speed that is dangerous to the vulnerable cyclist. This is also by far the most common type of roundabout collision. For example, in an analysis of collisions in four Auckland, New Zealand cities Campbell, Jurisich, and Dunn (2006) found that 68 percent of the police-reported multi-lane roundabout collisions were of this type: an entering motorist colliding with a circulating cyclist. This has been shown repeatedly by many researchers in many countries (see Reynolds *et al.*, 2009; and Wilke *et al.*, 2014, for reviews). Furthermore, in a counterproductive move, some municipalities modify the traditional radial design of the circle and its arms with a tangential design that provides separate entry and exit lanes into the circle. While this can reduce the severity of collisions with vehicles in the circle (by reducing the impact angle), it also enables and entices the approaching drivers to enter the circle at higher speeds – a most detrimental situation for the cyclist circling inside the roundabout who is now more peripheral in the entering driver's visual filed and consequently often not detected in time. The two designs are illustrated in Figure 17-11.

To avoid such high-risk conflicts, the guiding principle for protecting cyclists at roundabouts should be speed reductions at the approach and inside the roundabout – to approximately 25-30 km/hr (Campbell *et al.*, 2006; Wilke *et al.*, 2014). This should be achieved not by enforcement but rather by careful design that includes narrowing entry lanes and preference of the radial design over the tangential design. This ergonomic

Figure 17-11. The design of a radial roundabout and its arms (left), and a tangential roundabout and its approaches (right) Photos by author.

approach automatically leads drivers to adopt the safe behavior without threat of punishment. Also, bicycle paths should end at the beginning of the approach segment so that just before the circle the approach arm should be too narrow to accommodate cyclist and cars next to each other.

In an attempt to synthesize the various infrastructure recommendations, the OECD International Transport Forum (2013) summarizes their recommendations in terms of problem definitions and infrastructure solutions for crashes and conflicts in various types of infrastructures. The recommended approach to road sections and signalized intersections is reproduced in Table 17-2.

Vehicle- and bicycle-based improvements

Not all progress is good for all users. A case in point is the growth in hybrid electric vehicles (HEV) that rely on electricity at low (typically urban) speeds. At low speeds, the difference in the noise level between internal combustion engine (ICE) vehicles and HEV is the greatest. Consequently, the concern is that unwary bicyclists (and pedestrians) who might otherwise hear the sound of an approaching ICE car miss the sound (and the car) and expose themselves to a potential collision. This concern was validated in a study by Hanna (2009) who analyzed the NHTSA data on 48 bicyclists that were involved in collisions with HEVs and 1,862 bicyclists that were involved in collisions with ICE vehicles. He found that the incidence rate of bicycle crashes that probably occurred at very low speed – such as when vehicles are turning, slowing, stopping, backing up, or entering or leaving a parking space – with HEVs was approximately 60 percent higher than that of collisions with ICE vehicles. As a countermeasure, Japan, the U.S., and the European Parliament have all introduced legislation requiring all HEV vehicles to have acoustic vehicle alerting systems, which are already common on many HEV cars. It now remains to test whether the warning-equipped HEV vehicles are less of a crash risk to bicyclists (and pedestrians) than the models without them.

Safety improvements in vehicles have been directed to both collision avoidance and injury reduction mechanisms: vehicle based forward collision warning systems and better crash absorption design for the cars, and helmets and visibility aids for bicycles.

Table 17-2. Select infrastructure solutions to various types of bicycle crashes in road sections and signalized intersections (from OECD/ITF, 2013, with permission from OECD).

Accident Problem	**Hypothesis**	**Possible Solutions**
Road sections		
Accidents with bicyclists being run over from behind	Speeds are too high	Speed reducing measures
		Narrowing of lanes with edge line
	Narrow, dense traffic	Bicycle lanes/bicycle and pedestrian path
	Darkness, moist weather	Road lighting
		Campaigns on the use of bicycle lights
	Road side parking	Prohibit parking/ stopping
Accidents with bicyclists hitting parked cars	Narrow roads	Markings (Parking lane)
		Prohibit parking
Accidents with bicyclists hitting pedestrians	Accidents concentrated	Refuge/verge
		Raised pedestrian crossing
	Wide street, accidents spread out	Center island
Signalized Intersections		
Turning cars hit bicyclists	Bicyclists are overlooked	Cross-junction bicycle markings
		Avoid pre-green for nearside turning vehicles

Table 17-2. (Continued)

Accident Problem	**Hypothesis**	**Possible Solutions**
Right-angle collisions in far end of big junctions	Insufficient clearance phase for slow bicyclists	Increase amber phase
Bicyclists turn offside in front of straight going traffic	No waiting area or signal for cyclists	Establish waiting area
		Separate signal/phase for bicyclists
Bicyclists cross on red	Long waiting time	Retime signal
Nearside turning cars/lorries hit straight going bicyclists	Not sufficient sight in mirrors	Staggered stop line for cars
		Remove verge
		Cut back bicycle track
	Sight OK, but insufficient orientation	Separate regulation
		Cut back bicycle track
		Pre-green stage for cyclists
		Avoid pre-green for nearside turning cars

Vehicle based advance warning systems

To compensate for the poor detection of bicyclists and their low conspicuity, electronic aids have been developed that can detect bicyclists on the road ahead and provide visual and auditory warnings when the time-to-collision drops below a predetermined threshold (typically 2s), giving the driver sufficient time to avoid a collision. Although these systems are already available in new cars and as after-market safety devices (e.g., MobilEye® C2-270) their benefits under real driving conditions remains to be quantified.

Vehicle design to reduce injury severity

Design changes to reduce injuries are quite problematic because while head injuries to pedestrians and bicyclists are the greatest threat in a collision, the impact point of the cyclist's head is higher than that of a pedestrian's head (Wegman *et al.*, 2012), and pedestrian injuries are much more common. One treatment that has been effective – for motorcyclists too – is the requirement for "side under-run protection" on heavy vehicles. These lowered beams or sides, protect cyclists from being under-run by trucks in case of a collision (Wegman *et al.*, 2012).

Bicycle helmets and bicycle equipment

Helmets

Although already discussed above, relative to helmet laws and improvements in visibility, it should be stated clearly that a properly designed and worn helmet provides by far the best protection against head and brain injury. However, the quantification of the level of protection remains hotly debated. One problem with the conclusions reached by different researchers is the highly variable quality of the different studies (Elvik, 2013). Still there have been a few attempts to arrive at a quantitative estimate based on the aggregate of these multiple studies, mostly in terms of the reduced risk to head and brain injury. One analysis by the Dutch SWOV estimates that a good helmet can reduce the risk of head and brain injury by up to 45 percent (Wegman *et al.*, 2012). Elvik (2013), on the basis of a meta-analysis of 23 independent estimates, after correcting for trend and publication bias (see Chapter 2), calculated an average effect of 50 percent reduction in head injuries and approximately 20 percent reduction in facial injuries – quite impressive for a single safety device that typically weighs less than 250 grams (less than half a pound).

Visibility enhancements

Elvik *et al.* (2009) on the basis of meta-analysis of different studies provide average estimates on the crash reduction potential of various bicyclist/bicycle systems. Their summary for the various systems is presented in Table 17-3. It is important to note here that these estimates are contaminated by multiple confounding factors, and thus should be considered as indicators of association and not as causal crash reduction factors. Also, these evaluations are conducted on existing systems only, and consequently the novel enhancements described above are not included in Elvik *et al.*'s analyses. The most effective of the components considered are the various visibility enhancements, especially the pedal reflectors for multi-vehicle nighttime collisions, and the taillights for rear-end nighttime collisions. It is probably not a coincidence that these are the two visibility enhancements that provide motorists with biomotion cues to the presence of the cyclist.

As might be expected, the braking systems also play a crucial role, with front + rear brakes being much more effective than rear brakes alone. This conclusion parallels the increase in motorcycle crash risk when the rear brakes alone are engaged (ACEM, 2004; Hurt, Ouellet, and Thom, 1981), and the benefits of the "combined braking system" that integrates the front and rear motorcycle brake controls (IIHS, 2014). In contrast, some bicycle components actually increase crash risk, such as high- or drop-handlebars and small wheels. However, it is most likely that the higher risks of the different handlebars and the small wheels are not due to the handlebars themselves but to the high-risk riding style and locations associated with these bars and wheels.

Table 17-3. Effects on potential accident rates of different types of equipment on bicycles (from Elvik *et al.*, 2009, p. 673, with permission from Emerald Publishing).

Type of Equipment	**Percentage Change in Potential Risk**		
	Types of accidents affected	**Best estimate**	**95% confidence Interval**
Reflectors and lamps			
Pedal reflectors	Multi-vehicle accidents in darkness	−75	(−85; −60)
Spoke reflectors	Multi-vehicle accidents in darkness	+9	(+1; +18)
Cyclist's ankle light	Multi-vehicle accidents in darkness	−22	(−35; −9)
Reflectors on cyclist's jacket	Multi-vehicle accidents in darkness	−10	(−15; −5)
Taillight (lit)	Rear-end collisions in darkness	−80	(−67; −90)
Brakes			
Brakes on front wheel versus back wheel	All bicycle accidents	−28	(−30; −26)
Brakes on both wheels versus back wheel	All bicycle accidents	−48	(−51; −46)
Rim brakes versus hub brakes	All bicycle accidents	−5	(−7; −3)
Hand brake versus pedal brakes	All bicycle accidents	−22	(−25; −20)
Synthetic brake blocks versus rubber	Bicycle accidents in dry weather	−20	(−25; −10))
	Bicycle accidents in wet weather	−40	(−50; −30)
Rubber brake blocks versus leather	Bicycle accidents in dry weather	−5	(−25; +5)
	Bicycle accidents in wet weather	+190	(+30; +250)

Table 17-3. (Continued)

Type of Equipment	**Percentage Change in Potential Risk**		
	Types of accidents affected	**Best estimate**	**95% confidence Interval**
Drop handlebars and gears			
Drop handlebars compared to standard handlebars	All bicyle accidents	+78	(+38; +129)
Bicycles with two to five gears compared with bicycles without gears	All bicyle accidents	−17	(−32; +1)
Bicycles with more than five gears Compared with bicycles without gears	All bicyle accidents	+62	(+25; +109)
Other			
High handlebars versus standard handlebars	Overturning accidents with bicycles	+55	(+40; +80)
Small wheels versus standard wheels	Overturning accidents with bicycles	+30	(+5; +55)
Distance markers	Multi-vehicle accidents involving bicycles	−7	(−10; −4)
Spoke protectors	All bicyle accidents	−37	(−74; +55)

E-Bikes: Electric Bicycles and Pedelecs

It is impossible to discuss bicycles and bicycling safety now without acknowledging the new kid on the block – the electric bicycle. There are generally two types of electrically assisted bicycles: pedelecs and electric bikes (or e-bikes). Pedelecs require pedaling to move, and power is supplied proportionally to the speed with maximum speed typically set at 25 km/hr. E-bikes, on the other hand, can move on power even when the pedals are not activated and their top speed is typically 25-32 km/hr. Still, because of their functional similarities, and the tendency to refer to all power-assisted bicycles as e-bikes, in this section I refer to both types as electric bicycles or e-bikes.

The use of e-bikes has witnessed an explosion all over the world (e.g., Schepers *et al.*, 2014c), but especially in China and the EU countries, where bicycling has always been a popular means of transport. In China, the number of e-bikes grew from 560,000 in 1998 to 120 million in 2010 (Yang, 2010). This is more than a 20-fold increase. In the Netherlands, in the four years between 2006 and 2009 their number quadrupled from 40,000 to 153,000. An important aspect of riding an electric bicycle, and probably a major contributor to their popularity – and danger – is that most countries do not regulate their use. In general, at this stage, policies to regulate e-bikes' use, or enforcement of existing regulations are quite far behind the sales and immersion of these vehicles in traffic. For example, as of 2014 in the U.S. very few states had comprehensive e-bike legislation, though 44 states officially impose a 20-30 mph (32-48 km/hr) limit on them. Twenty-eight states require an operator's license to ride an e-bike, and 37 states have a minimum age requirement (typically 16) (MacArthur and Kobel, 2015). Similar rider-age and speed restrictions have just been announced in Israel, though many doubt that these regulations can be effectively enforced. In Europe, the EU has issued the EN1519 standard that defines e-bike as a bicycle and limits their electric motor to 250w.

In general, so far, very few jurisdictions have addressed the safety issues related to e-bikes, such as proper location for riding them (on the road or on the curb), rider-age restrictions (e.g., 14 years old in the United Kingdom and Israel, and 16 in some U.S. states), helmet requirements, maximal speed or power, and registration and licensing requirements. In the U.S., there is one safety-related federal regulation (23 USC Section 217) that permits electric bicycles to be used on trails and pedestrian walkways that are built using federal funds where state or local regulations permit them (MacArthur and Kobel, 2015). An essential component of legislating and enforcement of e-bikes' regulations is their registration. In most places, like manual bicycles, they are not registered. In China, for example, some jurisdictions require it and some do not. Even when it is required, the majority of e-bike owners do not register them. For example, a survey of e-bike users in Nanjing, China (Guo *et al.*, 2015) where registration is required revealed that 70 percent of the owners did not register their e-bikes, and that these people were more likely to be males, young, less educated, and less affluent. The impact of registration on safety is not clear either. In the Nanjing study, the likelihood of being involved in an at-fault crash in the past three years did not differ significantly between the two groups (30 percent for the registered versus 37 percent for the non-registered) and even the small difference could be accounted for by difference in exposure. But because enforcement of the traffic rules is quite lax, it is hard to summarily conclude that registration is ineffective for safety. Instead, like other safety programs it must be evaluated as part of a larger safe system approach.

The e-bikes' user population is quite heterogeneous. It is especially characteristic of older people in European countries like the Netherlands who would like to extend their cycling days, and of younger people in China and South East Asia as an inexpensive means to upgrade their personal vehicles and still comply with bans on motorcycles in many polluted cities (Yang, 2010). In addition to their obvious benefits for current cyclists, these bicycles bring new cyclists into the roads, and significantly increase the range of cycle-based mobility up to 20 kilometers. Because of their higher speeds and because of their popularity among older riders, when these bicycles mix with pedestrians and traditional cycles on bike paths, trails, and sidewalks, they increase the potential for serious crashes and collisions. Consequently, it is not surprising that riders on e-bikes travel at higher speeds than those on manual bicycles (Dozza *et al.*, 2016), crashes with these bicycles are more severe than with classical bicycles (Hu *et al.*, 2014), and they are more likely to end in emergency room treatment (Schepers *et al.*, 2014c). E-bikes are also particularly worrisome when the users are young children: combining lack of experience with lack of knowledge of and respect for the rules of the road. Other conclusions about crash involvement with e-bikes must be attributed to the specific characteristics of the user population, geography, climate, and infrastructure in which these limited scope studies were conducted. To summarize with a disturbing anecdote, in my own residential community I quite frequently encounter young teen e-bikers riding at night, on unlit streets, without lights and helmets and in the wrong lane, while talking on their cell phone.

E-bikes and crashes

Very few studies have looked at the crash involvement of e-bikes. In one study, conducted in two Chinese cities, by Yao and Wu (2012), 603 e-bike riders filled out questionnaires about their riding behavior, safety attitudes, risk perception, and at-fault crash involvement. Although all the information was based on subjective reporting, males, people reporting aggressive behaviors, and riders without a driver license were more likely to be involved in at-fault crashes than women, less aggressive riders, and licensed drivers. These findings are not surprising and are quite consistent with those obtained for other road users; paraphrasing Tillman and Hobbs' conclusion from 1949 that "man rides as he lives."

Concluding Comments

Bicycling – and more recently cycling on electric bikes – is the most rapidly emerging trend in short-distance mobility. Bicycling is beneficial for health, economic, and environmental reasons, but it introduces safety issues, especially when it is combined with the motor vehicle traffic. In the developed world, the exponentially increasing growth in bicycle sales, especially in light of the flattening and possibly decreasing numbers of passenger cars (Sivak, 2014) requires both individuals and governments to adjust to this modal shift in terms of travel patterns and travel behavior on the one hand, and bicycling regulations and infrastructure on the other hand. The good news is that increased bicycling can be associated with greater safety, and the Netherlands is the stellar example of this. However, to achieve this success requires a comprehensive approach such as the Dutch safe system policy and implementation.

While separating the bicycle traffic from the motoring traffic is expensive and not always feasible, integrating the two is a tricky act. This is due to two primary factors. First, the difference between motor vehicles and bicycles in terms of speeds and mass has dire consequences in case of a collision. Second, while car drivers are trained, licensed, and regulated, bicyclists are not. Furthermore driving is age-restricted and bicycling is not. This means that we now have road users who do not understand the traffic systems with all its rules and norms, and in the case of young riders they do not even have the cognitive capacity to comprehend and adjust to it. Riding electric bicycles has brought these issues to the forefront, especially when children start riding them in traffic.

The current research on bicycling safety – while not as extensive as the research on cars and driving safety – has already identified the key issues, and the vehicle-, environmental- and human-related factors associated with crashes. This research has prompted manufacturers and riders to adopt various safety strategies. At the behavioral levels, poor visibility and non-compliance with traffic rules have been identified, and various strategies to increase the former and reduce the latter have been implemented. Furthermore, there are multiple ongoing research efforts to enhance visibility through rider use of various reflecting materials on the bicycles and on his or her clothing. In addition, new bicycle detection systems that alert drivers to bicycles near them are also being incorporated into new vehicle models. In terms of injury reduction, the most effective safety device is the bicycle helmet, but compulsory helmet laws are still few and compliance with them is even rarer. While policy, organizational, and infrastructure changes are slow and non-linear, safety improvements at the individual level are flooding the market. These include new vehicle systems that can detect riders and alert drivers to them, low bumper bars on truck to prevent under-ride in case of a collision, improved bicycle helmets and lights, and biomotion reflectors on clothing.

The current immediate research issues must go beyond the individual treatment of riders and drivers and into the system implications of integrating children and older people riding manual and electric bicycles, mixing (or not) with pedestrians and motorized vehicles, on shared roads and on dedicated paths and trails. This is a complex issue that needs immediate attention and solutions as the spread of bicycles, and especially electric bicycles is not slowing down or waiting of the safe solutions.

References

ACEM (2004). MAIDS: In-depth investigations of accidents involving powered two-wheelers. Association de Constructeurs Européens de Motocycles (ACEM), Brussels, BG. http://MAIDS.acembike.org

Adminaite, D., R. Allsop and G. Jost (2015). Making walking and cycling on Europe's roads safer. PIN Flash Report 29. European Transport Safety Council (ETSC). Brussels, Belgium.

Ahlstrom, C., K. Kircher, B. Thorslund and E. Adell (2016). Bicyclists' visual strategies when conducting self-paced vs. system-paced smartphone tasks in traffic. *Transportation Res. F, 41*, 204-216.

Behrman, D. (1973). *The man who loved bicycles.* Harper Magazine Press, New York, NY.

Bíl, M., M. Bílová and I. Müller (2010). Critical factors in fatal collisions of adult cyclists with automobiles. *Accid. Anal. Prev., 42*(6), 1632-1636.

Bjørnskau, T. (2014). The zebra crossing game – A game theoretic model to explain counter-rule interaction between cars and cyclists. Proceedings of the International Cycling Safety Conference. Goteborg, Sweden, 18-19 November.

Blaizot, S., F. Papon, M. M. Haddak and E. Amoros (2013). Injury incidence rates of cyclists compared to pedestrians, car occupants and powered two-wheeler riders, using a medical registry and mobility data, Rhône County, France. *Accid. Anal. Prev., 58*, 35-45.

Brodsky, W. (2001). The effects of music tempo on simulated driving performance and vehicular control. *Transportation Res. F, 4*(4), 219-241.

Campbell, D., I. Jurisich and R. C. M. Dunn (2006). Improved multi-lane roundabout designs for cyclists. Land Transport New Zealand.

Carter, D. L., W. W. Hunter, C. V. Zegeer, J. R. Stewart and H. F. Huang (2006). Pedestrian and bicyclist intersection safety indices: Final report. Federal Highway Administration Report No. FHWA-HRT-06-125. U.S. Department of Transportation, Washington, DC.

Chuang, K. H., C. C. Hsu, C. H. Lai, J. L. Doong and M. C. Jeng (2013). The use of a quasi-naturalistic riding method to investigate bicyclists' behaviors when motorists pass. *Accid. Anal. Prev., 56*, 32–41.

Damant-Sirois, G. and El-Geneidy, A. M. (2015). Who cycles more? Determining cycling frequency through a segmentation approach in Montreal, Canada. *Transportation Res. A, 77*, 113-125.

Damant-Sirois, G., M. Grimsrud and A. M. El-Geneidy (2014). What's your type: A multidimensional cyclist typology. *Transportation, 41*(6), 1153-1169.

Debnath, A. K., N. Haworth, A. Schramm and A. Williamson (2016). Observational study of compliance with Queensland bicycle helmet laws. *Accid. Anal. Prev., 97*, 146-152.

de Geus, B., G. Vandenbulcke, L. L. Panis, I. Thomas, B. Degraeuwe, E., Cumps, J. Aertsens, R. Torfs and R. Meeusen (2012). A prospective cohort study on minor accidents involving commuter cyclists in Belgium. *Accid. Anal. Prev., 45*, 683-693.

de Hartog, J. J., H. Boogaard, H. Nijland and G. Hoek (2010). Do the health benefits of cycling outweigh the risks? *Environ. Health Perspect., 118*, 1109-1116.

de Waard, D., F. Westerhuis and B. Lewis-Evans (2015). More screen operation than calling: The results of observing cyclists' behaviour while using mobile phones. *Accid. Anal. Prev., 76*, 42-48.

Dijkstra, A., P. Levelt and J. Thomsen (1998). *Best practice to promote cycling and walking (ADONIS): Research project for the EU Transport RTD programme.* Directorate General for Transport, Danish Road Directorate, Copenhagen, Denmark.

Dill, J. (2009). Bicycling for transportation and health: The role of infrastructure. *J. Public Health Policy, 30*, S95-S110.

Dill, J., C. M. Monsere and N. McNeil (2012). Evaluation of bike boxes at signalized intersections. *Accid. Anal. Prev., 44*(1), 126-134.

Dozza, M., G. F. B. Piccinini and J. Werneke (2016). Using naturalistic data to assess e-cyclist behavior. *Trans. Res. F, 41*, 217-226.
Dozza, M. and J. Werneke (2014). Introducing naturalistic cycling data: What factors influence bicyclists' safety in the real world? *Transportation Res. F, 24*, 83-91.
EC (2011). Eurobarometer Flash Report. Future of transport Analytical report. PLoS One, 1-67. http://ftp.infoeuropa.eurocid.pt/database/000046001-000047000/000046475.pdf
EC (2015). *Road safety in the European Union*. European Commission. Brussels, Belgium. http://ec.europa.eu/transport/road_safety/pdf/vademecum_2015.pdf
ECF (2016). ECF Cycling Barometer 2013-2015 Comparison. https://ecf.com/groups/ecf-cycling-barometer-2013-2015-comparison
Economist (The) Sept. 18, 2008. On your bike. http://www.economist.com/node/12270958
Ellis, J. (2014). Bicycle safety education for children from a developmental and learning perspective. NHTSA Report No. DOT HS 811 880. U.S. Department of Transportation, Washington, DC.
Elvik, R. (2009). The non-linearity of risk and the promotion of environmentally sustainable transport. *Accid. Anal. Prev., 41*, 849-855.
Elvik, R. (2013). Corrigendum to: "Publication bias and time-trend bias in meta-analysis of bicycle helmet efficacy: A re-analysis of Attewell, Glase and McFadden, 2001" [Accid. Anal. Prev. 43 (2011) 1245–1251]. *Accid. Anal. Prev., 60*, 245-253.
Elvik, R. and T. Bjørnskau (2017). Safety-in-numbers: A systematic review and meta-analysis of evidence. *Safety Sci., 92*, 274-282.
Elvik, R., A. Høye, T. Vaa and M. Sørensen (2009). *The Handbook of Road Safety Measures*. (2nd Ed.). Bingley: Emerald.
Elvik, R. and A. Mysen (1999). Incomplete accident reporting: Meta-analysis of studies made in 13 countries. *Transportation Res. Record*, **1665**, 133-140.
ETSC (2006). Conspicuity and Road Safety. ETSC Fact Sheet No. 9. European Transport Safety Commission, Brussels, Belgium.
Fischer, E. L., G. K. Rousseau, S. M. Turner, E. J. Blais, C. L. Engelhart, D. R. Henderson and C. V. Zegeer (2010). Pedestrian and bicyclist safety and mobility in Europe. Federal Highway Administration Report No. FHWA-PL-10-010. U.S. Department of Transportation, Washington, DC.
Fishman, E. and P. Schepers (2016). Global bike share: What the data tells us about road safety. *J. Safety Res., 56*, 41-45.
Fishman, E., S. Washington and N. Haworth (2012). Barriers and facilitators to public bicycle scheme use: A qualitative approach. *Transportation Res. F, 15*(6), 686-698.
Fishman, E., S. Washington and N. Haworth (2013). Bike share: A synthesis of the literature. *Transport Rev.*, 33(2), 148-165.
Fishman, E., S. Washington and N. Haworth (2014). Bike share's impact on car use: Evidence from the United States, Great Britain, and Australia. *Transportation Res. D, 31*, 13-20.
Fyhri, A., H. B. Sundfør, T. Bjørnskau and A. Laureshyn (2016). Safety in numbers for cyclists—conclusions from a multidisciplinary study of seasonal change in interplay and conflicts. *Accid. Anal. Prev.*, in press.

Garrard, J., Greaves, S. and Ellison, A., 2010. Cycling injuries in Australia: Road safety's blind spot? *J. Australasian College of Road Safety*, *21*, 37–43.
Gitelman, V., F. Pisachov and R. Carmel (2011). Helmet use by bicyclists: National observational survey 2010. Final Report for Israel's National Road Safety Authority, Jerusalem, Israel. (in Hebrew).
Gitelman, V., F. Pisachov and R. Carmel (2012). National observational survey of inter-urban cycling. Final Report for Israel's National Road Safety Authority, Jerusalem, Israel. (in Hebrew).
Goldenbeld, C., M. Houtenbos, E. Ehlers and D. De Waard (2012). The use and risk of portable electronic devices while cycling among different age groups. *J. Safety Res.*, *43*(1), 1-8.
Goodwin, A., L. Thomas, B. Kirley, W. Hall, N. O'Brien and K. Hill (2015). Countermeasures that work: A highway safety countermeasures guide for State Highway Safety Offices. 8th edition. NHTSA Report No. DOT HS 812 202. U.S. Department of Transportation, Washington, DC.
Guo, Y., Y. Wu, Z. Li and K. Chen (2015). Investigating the factors related to the registration of electric bicycle licenses in China. Transportation Research Board 94th Annual Meeting (Paper No. 15-5374), Washington, DC.
Hagel, B. E., A. Lamy, J. W. Rizkallah, K. L. Belton, G. S. Jhangri, N. Cherry and B. H. Row (2007). The prevalence and reliability of visibility aid and other risk factor data for uninjured cyclists and pedestrians in Edmonton, Alberta, Canada. *Accid. Anal. Prev.*, *39*(2), 284-289.
Hagel, B. E., N. T. R. Romanow, N. Morgunov, T. Embree, A. B. Couperthwaite, D. Voaklander and B. H. Rowe (2014). The relationship between visibility aid use and motor vehicle related injuries among bicyclists presenting to emergency departments. *Accid. Anal. Prev.*, *65*, 85-96.
Hanna, R. (2009). Incidence of pedestrian and bicyclist crashes by hybrid electric passenger vehicles. National Highway Traffic Safety Administration Report No. HS-811 204. U.S. Department of Transportation, Washington, DC.
Haworth, N., D. Shinar and T. Oron-Gilad (2014). Developing an international survey of bicycle and Helmet usage. Proceedings of the International Cycling Safety Conference. Goteborg, Sweden, 18-19 November.
Hess G. and M. N. Peterson (2015). "Bicycles may use full lane" signage communicates U.S. roadway rules and increases perception of safety. *PLoS ONE*, *10*(8), e0136973. doi:10.1371/journal
Hu, F., D. Lv, J. Zhu and J. Fang (2014). Related risk factors for injury severity of e-bike and bicycle crashes in Hefei. *Traffic Inj. Prev.*, *15* (3), 319–323.
Hurt, H. H. Jr., J. V. Ouellet and D. R. Thom (1981). Motorcycle accident cause factors and identification of countermeasures: Volume I: Technical report. National Highway Traffic Safety Administration. Report DOT-HS-805-862. U.S. Department of Transportation, Washington, DC.
IIHS (2014). *New research adds to the evidence that motorcycle ABS prevents crashes.* Insurance Institute for Highway Safety, Arlington, Virginia.
InDev (2016). Smartphone app "SafeVRU" to simplify self-reporting of accidents – Participants for study welcome. Newsletter from the InDev Project No. 2.

November. http://www.indev-project.eu/InDeV/EN/News/Newsletter/download/newsletter-02.pdf?__blob=publicationFile&v=2

Jacobsen, P. L. (2003). Safety-in-numbers: More walkers and bicyclists, safer walking and bicycling. *Inj. Prev.*, *9*(3), 205-209.

Johnson, M., S. Newstead, J. Charlton and J. Oxley (2011). Riding through red lights: The rate, characteristics and risk factors of non-compliant urban commuter cyclists. *Accid. Anal. Prev.*, *43*, 323–328.

Juhra, C., B. Wieskotter, K. Chu, L. Trost, U. Weiss, M. Messerschmidt, A. Malczyk, M. Heckwolf and M. Raschke (2012). Bicycle accidents—do we only see the tip of the iceberg? A prospective multi-centre study in a large German city combining medical and police data. *Injury*, *43*, 2026–2034.

Kay, J. J., P. T. Savolainen, T. J. Gates and T. K. Datta (2014). Driver behavior during bicycle passing maneuvers in response to a Share the Road sign treatment. *Accid. Anal. Prev.*, *70*, 92-99.

Kircher, K., C. Ahlstrom, L. Palmqvist and E. Adell (2015). Bicyclists' speed adaptation strategies when conducting self-paced vs. system-paced smartphone tasks in traffic. *Transportation Res. F*, *28*, 55-64.

Kwan, I. and J. Mapstone (2004). Visibility aids for pedestrians and cyclists: A systematic review of randomised controlled trials. *Accid. Anal. Prev.*, *36*, 305-312.

Kwan, I. and J. Mapstone (2009). *Interventions for increasing pedestrian and cyclist visibility for the prevention of death and injuries (Review)*. The Cochrane Collaboration, Wiley & Sons, Ltd.

Lajunen, T. (2016). Barriers and facilitators of bicycle helmet use among children and their parents. *Transportation Res. F*, *41*, 294-301.

Lusk, A. C., P. Morency, L. F. Miranda-Moreno, W. C. Willett and J. T. Dennerlein (2013). Bicycle guidelines and crash rates on cycle tracks in the united states. *Amer. J. Pub. Health*, *103*, 1240-1248.

MacArthur, J. and N. Kobel (2015). Regulations of E-bikes in the United States: A policy review. Transportation Research Board 94th Annual Meeting (No. 15-4235). Washington, DC.

Madsen, J. C. O., T. Andersen and H. S. Lahrmann (2013). Safety effects of permanent running lights for bicycles: A controlled experiment. *Accid. Anal. Prev.*, *50*, 820-829.

Martínez-Ruiz, V., P. Lardelli-Claret, E. Jiménez-Mejías, C. Amezcua-Prieto, J. J. Jiménez-Moleón and J. D. D. L. del Castillo (2013). Risk factors for causing road crashes involving cyclists: An application of a quasi-induced exposure method. *Accid. Anal. Prev.*, *51*, 228-237.

Meehan, W. P., L. K. Lee, C. M. Fischer and R. Mannix (2013). Bicycle helmet laws are associated with a lower fatality rate from bicycle–motor vehicle collisions. *J. Pediatrics*, *163*(3), 726-729.

Nabors, D., E. Goughnour, L. Thomas, W. DeSantis, M. Sawyer and K. Moriarty (2012). Bicycle road safety audit guidelines and prompt lists. Federal Highway Administration Report No. FHWA-SA-12-018. U.S. Department of Transportation, Washington, DC.

NHTSA (2015). *Bicyclists and other cyclists. NHTSA Traffic Safety Facts DOT HS 812 151*. U.S. Department of Transportation, Washington, DC.

NHTSA (2016). *Bicyclists and other cyclists. NHTSA Traffic Safety Facts DOT HS 812 282.* U.S. Department of Transportation, Washington, DC.

NRSA (2012). Trends in road safety in Israel: 2005-2011. Israel National Road Safety Authority. Jerusalem, Israel. (in Hebrew).

OECD/ITF (2013). Cycling, health and safety, OECD International Transport Forum Publishing/ITF. http://dx.doi.org/10.1787/9789282105955-en

Oja, P., S. Titze, A. Bauman, B. De Geus, P. Krenn, B. Reger-Nash and T. Kohlberger (2011). Health benefits of cycling: A systematic review. *Scandinavian J. Med. Sci. in Sports*, *21*(4), 496-509.

Percer, J. (2009). *Child pedestrian safety education: Applying learning and developmental theories to develop safe street-crossing behaviors.* NHTSA Report No. HS-811 190. U.S. Department of Transportation, Washington, DC.

Poulos, R. G., J. Hatfield, C. Rissel, L. K. Flack, S. Murphy, R. Grzebieta and A. S. McIntosh (2015). Characteristics, cycling patterns, and crash and injury experiences at baseline of a cohort of transport and recreational cyclists in New South Wales, Australia. *Acc. Anal. Prev.*, *78*, 155-164.

Räsänen, M., H. Summala (1998). Attention and expectation problems in bicycle–car collisions: An in-depth study. *Accid. Anal. Prev.*, *30*(5), 657-666.

Reynolds, C. C., M. A. Harris, K. Teschke, P. A. Cripton and M. Winters (2009). The impact of transportation infrastructure on bicycling injuries and crashes: A review of the literature. *Environ. Health*, *8*(1), 47-66.

Robinson, D. L. (1996). Head injuries and bicycle helmet laws. *Accid. Anal. Prev.*, *28*(4), 463-475.

Robinson, D. L. (2007). Bicycle helmet legislation: can we reach a consensus? *Accid. Anal. Prev.*, *39*(1), 86-93.

Schepers, P. (2008). De rol van infrastructuur bij enkelvoudige fietsongevallen (The Role of Infrastructure in Single-vehicle Bicycle Accidents). Rijkswaterstaat Dienst Verkeer en Scheepvaart, Delft. As reported by van-der Horst *et al.* (2014).

Schepers, P. (2010). Fiets-fietsongevallen: Botsingen tussen fietsers (Bicycle–Bicycle Accidents: Collisions Between Bicyclists). Rijkswaterstaat Dienst Verkeer en Scheepvaart, Delft. As reported by van-der Horst *et al.* (2014).

Schepers, J. P. (2012). Does more cycling also reduce the risk of single-bicycle crashes? *Inj. Prev.*, *18* (4), 240–245.

Schepers, P., N. Agerholm, E. Amoros, R. Benington, T. Bjørnskau, S. Dhondt and A. Niska (2015). An international review of the frequency of single-bicycle crashes (SBCs) and their relation to bicycle modal share. *Inj. Prev.*, *21*, e138-e143.

Schepers, J. P., E. Fishman, P. den Hertog, K. K. Wolt and A. L. Schwab (2014c). The safety of electrically assisted bicycles compared to classic bicycles. *Accid. Anal. Prev.*, *73*, 174-180.

Schepers, P., M. Hagenzieker, R. Methorst, B. Van Wee and F. Wegman (2014b). A conceptual framework for road safety and mobility applied to cycling safety. *Accid. Anal. Prev.*, *62*, 331-340.

Schepers, J. P., P. A. Kroeze, W. Sweers and J. C. Wüst (2011). Road factors and bicycle–motor vehicle crashes at unsignalized priority intersections. *Accid. Anal. Prev.*, *43*(3), 853-861.

Schepers, P., D. Twisk, E. Fishman, A. Fyhri and A. Jensen (2017). The Dutch road to a high level of cycling safety. *Safety Sci.*, *92*, 264–273.

Schroeder, P. and M. Wilbur (2013). 2012 National survey of bicyclist and pedestrian attitudes and behavior, volume 1: Summary report. NHTSA Report No. DOT HS 811 841 A. U.S. Department of Transportation, Washington, DC.

Scuffham, P., J. Alsop, C. Cryer and J. D. Langley (2000). Head injuries to bicyclists and the New Zealand bicycle helmet law. *Accid. Anal. Prev.*, *32*(4), 565-573.

Shaheen, S., A. Cohen and E. Martin (2013). Public bikesharing in North America: Early operator understanding and emerging trends. *Transportation Res. Record*, **2387**, 83-92.

Shaheen, S., A. Cohen, E. Martin and R. S. Finson (2012). Public bikesharing in North America: Early operator and user understanding, MTI Report 11-19. Mineta Transportation Institute, San José, CA.

Shinar, D. (1984). Actual versus estimated nighttime pedestrian visibility. *Ergonomics*, *27*, 863-871.

Shinar, D. (2014). Improving cyclists' conspicuity and visibility with an Alternating Flashing Light (AFL) System. International Cycling Safety Conference, November 18-19, Gothenburg, Sweden.

Shinar, D., P. Valero-Mora, M. van Strijp-Houtenbos, N. Haworth, A. Schramm, G. de Bruyne, V. Cavallo, J. Chliaoutakis, J. Dias, D. Dulf, A. Fyhri, A. Hursa, K. Kuklane, R. Ledesma, O. Mascarell, A. Morandi, M. Muser, D. Otte, M. Papadaki, A. Sajatovic, M. Saplioglu and G. Tzamalouka (2016). Under-reporting bicycle accidents to police in the COST TU1101 International Survey: Cross-country comparisons and associated factors. Proceedings of the International Cycling Safety Conference (ICSC), Bologna, November 3.

Siman-Tov, M., D. H. Jaffe, K. Peleg and Israel Trauma Group (2012). Bicycle injuries: A matter of mechanism and age. *Accid. Anal. Prev.*, *44*(1), 135-139.

Sivak, M. (2014). Has motorization in the US peaked? Part 5: Update through 2012. Report No. UMTRI-2014-11. University of Michigan Transportation Research Institute, Ann Arbor, MI.

Steriu, M. (2012a). Pedalling towards safety. European Transport Safety Council (ETSC), European Commission, Brussels, Belgium.

Steriu, M. (2012b). Raising the bar: Review of cycling safety policies in the European Union. European Transport Safety Council (ETSC), European Commission, Brussels, Belgium.

Stipdonk, H. and M. Reurings (2012). The effect on road safety of a modal shift from car to bicycle. *Traffic Inj. Prev.*, *13*(4), 412-421.

Summala, H., E. Pasanen, M. Räsänen and J. Sievänen (1996). Bicycle accidents and drivers' visual search at left and right turns. *Accid. Anal. Prev.*, *28*(2), 147-153.

Taylor, M. and P. Scuffham (2002). New Zealand bicycle helmet law—Do the costs outweigh the benefits? *Inj. Prev.*, *8*(4), 317–320.

Thompson, J., G. Savino and M. Stevenson (2015). Reconsidering the safety-in-numbers effect for vulnerable road users: An application of agent-based modeling. *Traffic Inj. Prev.*, *16*(2), 147-153.

Thornley, S. J., A. Woodward, J. D. Langley, S. N. Ameratunga and A. Rodgers (2008). Conspicuity and bicycle crashes: Preliminary findings of the Taupo Bicycle Study. *Inj. Prev.*, *14*(1), 11-18.

Tillman, W. A. and G. E. Hobbs (1949). The accident-prone automobile driver. *Am. J. Psychiatry*, *106*, 321-332.

Tin, S. T., A. Woodward and S. Ameratunga (2013). Incidence, risk, and protective factors of bicycle crashes: Findings from a prospective cohort study in New Zealand. *Prev. Med.*, *57*(3), 152-161.

Tin, S. T., A. Woodward and S. Ameratunga (2014). The role of conspicuity in preventing bicycle crashes involving a motor vehicle. *European J. Pub. Health*, cku117, 1-5.

Toet, A., J. Beintema, S. C. de Vries, N. van der Leden and J. W. W. M. Alferdinck (2008). Comparison of bicycle lighting forms. TNO Report No. TNO-DV 2008 C238, The Netherlands. (in Dutch, with English Abstract).

Treat, J. R., N. S. Tumbas, S. T. McDonald, D. Shinar, R. D. Hume, R. E. Mayer, R. L. Stansifer and N. J. Castellan (1979). Tri-level study of the causes of traffic accidents: final report. Volume I: Causal factor tabulations and assessments. National Highway Traffic Safety Administration. Report No. DOT HS 805 085. U.S. Department of Transportation, Washington, DC.

Twisk, D. A., W. P. Vlakveld, J. J. Commandeur, J. T. Shope and G. Kok (2014). Five road safety education programmes for young adolescent pedestrians and cyclists: A multi-programme evaluation in a field setting. *Accid. Anal. Prev.*, *66*, 55-61.

van der Horst, A. R. A., M. de Goede, S. de Hair-Buijssen and R. Methorst (2014). Traffic conflicts on bicycle paths: A systematic observation of behaviour from video. *Accid. Anal. Prev.*, *62*, 358-368.

Vanparijs, J., L. L. Panis, R. Meeusen and B. de Geus (2015). Exposure measurement in bicycle safety analysis: A review of the literature. *Accid. Anal. Prev.*, *84*, 9-19.

Vansteenkiste, P., G. Cardon and M. Lenoir (2015). Visual guidance during bicycle steering through narrow lanes: A study in children. *Accid. Anal. Prev.*, *78*, 8-13.

Vansteenkiste, P., L. Zeuwts, G. Cardon, R. Philippaerts and M. Lenoir (2014). The implications of low quality bicycle paths on gaze behavior of cyclists: A field test. *Transportation Res. F*, *23*, 81-87.

Walker, I. (2007). Drivers overtaking bicyclists: Objective data on the effects of riding position, helmet use, vehicle type and apparent gender. *Accid. Anal. Prev.*, *39*(2), 417-425.

Walker, I., I. Garrard and F. Jowitt (2014). The influence of a bicycle commuter's appearance on drivers' overtaking proximities: An on-road test of bicyclist stereotypes, high-visibility clothing and safety aids in the United Kingdom. *Accid. Anal. Prev.*, *64*, 69-77.

Walter, S. R., J. Olivier, T. Churches and R. Grzebieta (2011). The impact of compulsory cycle helmet legislation on cyclist head injuries in New South Wales, Australia. *Accid. Anal. Prev.*, *43*(6), 2064-2071.

Wegman, F., Zhang, F. and Dijkstra, A. (2012). How to make more cycling good for road safety? *Accid. Anal. Prev.*, *44*(1), 19-29.

Wei, V. F. and G. Lovegrove (2012). Sustainable road safety: A new (?) neighbourhood road pattern that saves VRU lives. *Accid. Anal. Prev.*, *44*(1), 140-148.

Weijermars, W. A. M. and F. C. M. Wegman (2011), Ten years of sustainable safety in the Netherlands. *Transportation Res. Record, 2213*, 1-6.

WHO (2004). World Report on Road Traffic Injury Prevention. Edited by M. Peden *et al.* World Health Organization, Geneva. http://whqlibdoc.who.int/publications/2004/9241562609.pdf

WHO (2013). *Global status report on road safety 2013: Supporting a decade of action.* World Health Organization, Geneva, Switzerland.

Wilke, A., J. Lieswyn and C. Munro (2014). *Assessment of the effectiveness of on-road bicycle lanes at roundabouts in Australia and New Zealand.* Austroads Report No. AP-R461/14, Sydney, Australia.

Willis, D. P., K. Manaugh and A. El-Geneidy (2013). Uniquely satisfied: Exploring cyclist satisfaction. *Transportation Res. F, 18*, 136-147.

Wood, J. M., P. F. Lacherez, R. P. Marszalek and M. J. King (2009). Drivers' and cyclists' experiences of sharing the road: Incidents, attitudes and perceptions of visibility. *Accid. Anal. Prev., 41*(4), 772-776.

Wood, J. M., R. A. Tyrrell, R. Marszalek, P. Lacherez and T. Carberry (2013). Bicyclists overestimate their own night-time conspicuity and underestimate the benefits of retro-reflective markers on the moveable joints. *Accid. Anal. Prev., 55*, 48-53.

Wood, J. M., R. A. Tyrrell, R. Marszalek, P. Lacherez, T. Carberry and B. S. Chu (2012). Using reflective clothing to enhance the conspicuity of bicyclists at night. *Accid. Anal. Prev., 45*, 726-730.

Yang, C. J. (2010). Launching strategy for electric vehicles: Lessons from China and Taiwan. *Technol. Forecast. Soc. Change, 77*(5), 831-834.

Yao, L. and C. Wu (2012). Traffic safety of e-bike riders in china: Safety attitudes, risk perception, and aberrant riding behaviors. Paper presented at the Transportation Research Board Annual Meeting, January. Washington, DC.

Zaieg, R. (2009). Bicyclists' injuries in traffic accidents. National Road Safety Authority, Jerusalem, Israel. (in Hebrew).

Zhang, Y. and C. Wu (2013). The effects of sunshields on red light running behavior of cyclists and electric bike riders. *Accid. Anal. Prev., 52*, 210-218.

PART F
CRASH CAUSATION AND COUNTERMEASURES

18

Accident/Crash Causation and Analysis

"Three baseball umpires were discussing their styles of refereeing. Says the first: I look at the ball and if it's a ball it's a ball, and if it's a strike it's a strike – and I call it as it is. The second umpire says: I look at the ball and if it's a ball it's a ball, and if it's a strike it's a strike – and I call it as I see it. The third umpire then says: I look at the ball and I call it a strike or a ball – but it ain't nothin' till I call it." Story told to the author by Patricia F. Waller.

"The government is very keen on amassing statistics – they collect them, add them, raise them to the nth power, take the cube root and prepare wonderful diagrams. But what you must never forget is that every one of those figures comes in the first instance from the village watchman, who just puts down what he damn pleases." (Sir Josiah Stamp, 1929).

"The epidemic of traffic accidents is not like that of cholera. There is no single agent in the form of the vibrio cholera ... nor is there a simple and decisive remedy .... This is why the search for causes may not hold the promise of unexpected discoveries leading to novel, cheap and effective interventions. Still, the quest for causes goes on ... (nonetheless) because our business is prevention, and because prevention requires the alteration of causes, only those causes that can be reasonably altered by a human action are of interest to us." (Hauer, 2016).

According to the online American Heritage Dictionary an accident is "An unexpected and undesirable event, especially one resulting in damage or harm: (such as) *car accidents on icy roads* ... an unforeseen incident ... (involving) lack of intention; chance." Similarly, the Oxford online dictionary defines an accident as "1. an unfortunate incident that happens unexpectedly and unintentionally; 2. an incident that happens by chance or without apparent cause; 3. chance."

If we were to accept these definitions, then the investigation of the causes of traffic accidents would be very short, very simple, and the same for all accidents, leading to one singular cause: chance. Fortunately, this is not the case. Traffic accidents are not accidents in the dictionary sense of the word. Most research in this area indicates that the causes of traffic crashes are not chance events, and therefore they can be investigated, identified, and – hopefully – provide us with insights on how to prevent future crashes.

The legal definition of "accident" according to the Merriam-Webster Legal Dictionary, allows for this as it defines accident as "an unexpected usually sudden event that occurs without intent or volition although sometimes through carelessness, unawareness, ignorance, or a combination of causes and that produces an unfortunate result (as an injury)." However, even this definition includes the term "unexpected."

If an accident cannot be anticipated or expected by anyone, then it is indeed due to chance or to forces beyond our understanding (Figure 18-1). In that case, the term "accident causation" is an oxymoron. Alternatively, if we accept the notion that traffic accidents are not chance events or acts of God, then they can be predicted and prevented. This rationale led the U.S. National Highway Traffic Safety Administration and the journal Nature to replace the term "accident" with the term "crash." With this approach we assume that if a person with some relevant expertise has at his or her disposal all of the necessary data immediately before an accident happens, he or she can foresee the accident. From the perspective of that expert the accident can or could have been avoided. The knowledge that is available to our mythical expert is what we seek in our attempts to understand the reasons or causes of accidents.

Drivers too, in general, believe that crashes are not chance events. In fact, drivers in different countries share similar perceptions concerning the causes of traffic accidents. This was demonstrated in a large-scale European Union project (SARTRE 3, 2004; Vanlaar and Yannis, 2006) conducted between September 2002 and April 2003. In the survey over 1,000 drivers in each of 23 participating countries were interviewed face-to-face and were presented with a list of fifteen factors and were asked "How often do you think each of the fifteen factors is the cause of traffic accidents?" Perhaps the most interesting finding was that the perceptions of the drivers in the 23 countries were quite similar. This enabled pooling the data of all 24,372 respondents into a single data base. From this data base, using a multi-dimensional analysis technique, the researchers were able to describe the responses in terms of two dimensions: perceived risk and perceived prevalence. The level of each of the 15 factors on these two dimensions is provided in Figure 18-2. It is obvious that the factors of greatest concern are the ones with a high score in on both dimensions; that is, the factors with the highest perceived risk and

Figure 18-1. A crash is not an accident; it is not a chance event; it is not an act of God (from Martin Perscheid, undated).

the highest perceived prevalence. These factors, in the upper right quadrant of Figure 18-2 include impairments from the use of chemical substances (drugs, alcohol, and medicines) and fatigue. It is important to keep in mind that these perceptions are very much time-dependent. For example, it is likely that the same survey conducted now – more than ten years since the original survey – would place the cell phone (hand-held or hands-free) much higher in both prevalence and perceived risk. In general, most drivers believe that the primary causes of crashes stem from the drivers' behaviors rather than from vehicular failures or environmental conditions. In this respect the drivers' perceptions are somewhat similar to the actual risks on the road from these factors as revealed by crash causation studies described below. When they differ, they indicate the need for better driver education programs.

For a more objective understanding of the causes of crashes, we must rely on methods other than drivers' opinions. Three general approaches have been extensively used to study accident causes: the retrospective clinical approach, the epidemiological/statistical approach, and the prospective naturalistic driving study (NDS) approach. The clinical approach is based on post hoc detailed analyses of all the events, behaviors, and conditions that preceded a crash in order to determine which specific event, behavior, condition or combination of events behaviors and conditions made the crash inevitable, or in other words caused it. The epidemiological approach involves searching crash data bases in order to determine if particular factors or variables are more prevalent in the crash

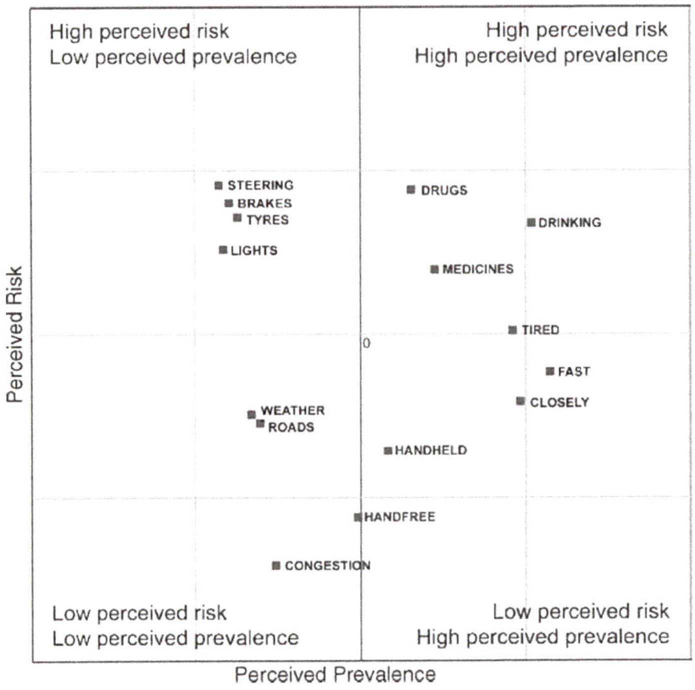

Figure 18-2. The perceived risk and perceived prevalence in traffic of 15 different factors. Rated by 24,372 drivers from 23 different countries; September 2002-April 2003. Ratings were on a scale of 1-6, 1 = never and 6 = always (from Vanlaar and Yannis, 2006, with permission from Elsevier).

data than in the normal driving population. The third – and newest – approach is that of the prospective naturalistic driving study in which drivers and vehicles are monitored continuously while they conduct their regular driving, so that when a crash happens all of the behaviors, events, and conditions that preceded it are available in an objective data format. The three approaches and the conclusions that can be drawn from them are discussed in detail below.

The Clinical Approach

The clinical approach is a post hoc analysis of the events and behaviors that transpired before the crash in the environment within which they occurred. As such it requires data extraction of past events and an educated interpretation of these data elements. The weakest links in the process of clinical crash causation analysis are the definitions of the data elements and their interpretation. The investigator in the role of the referee is omnipotent – but can easily be wrong, or at least at variance with someone else's interpretation. The example in Box 18-1, of the causes attributed by police and engineers to the same set of crashes, demonstrates that quite conclusively. Police officers are responsible for law

Box 18-1. Crash causes are in the eye of the beholder (from Gilutz, 1937).

AN INVESTIGATION and REPORT on FOUR YEARS' FATAL ACCIDENTS IN OXFORDSHIRE - by M.S. Gilutz. B.Sc. Eng.

Study analyzed the causes of 148 fatal accidents in Oxfordshire over a 4-year period.

Definition: A contributory factor is one that had it been removed, the accident would have been prevented.

Study background: According to the police "fewer than 1% of accidents are primarily due to road defects and that in only 3% of cases are road defects contributory to any degree."

Approach: It is probably correct to say that personal error is a contributory cause in every accident other than those due entirely to "Act of God." .... Unless we are to assume that the behavior of road users is capable of being perfected, there is little significance in this statement." .... There were 146 accidents with personal error but "that does not mean that the error was in the nature of gross carelessness or misbehavior. In many, indeed the error was such as any normal person might commit under the stress of circumstances or owing to momentary lack of attention."

In this analysis of 148 fatal accidents:

"Ordinary" road defects were contributory to 36% of the accidents'

"Major" road defects were contributory to another 17% of the accidents'

"Major and ordinary" road defects were contributory to 23% of the accidents

"Ordinary and/or major" road defects were contributory to 76% of the accidents

Major Road defect – fixing would require reconstruction: divided highway, bike lanes, by-passes for crossing rural roads, etc.

Ordinary Road defect – fixing would require better visibility, staggering of junctions, better radius or super-elevation in curves.

Source: Oxford: The Vincent Works, 1937.

enforcement and citation of drivers for their violations. Therefore, it is not surprising that in the eyes of the police officers who investigated the 148 Oxsfordshire fatal crashes essentially all crashes were due to the drivers' (or pedestrians') "personal errors." When civil engineers – whose role is to improve the road system – investigated the same crashes, in 76 percent of the cases they attributed the cause to the roadway! This is because the police cannot give a citation to a road or a sign, and the engineers cannot fix a driver or a pedestrian. Anderson (1976) made a similar argument 40 years ago.

One of the insidious, and hardly acknowledged, limitations of the post hoc clinical approach to crash causation assessment is that of hindsight bias. Hindsight bias was first identified and defined by Fischhoff (1975) as a tendency of people to increase the perceived likelihood of an outcome (such as a crash) when they know it (i.e., that a crash has in fact happened). Fischhoff demonstrated this in several experiments in which subjects were presented with scenarios (as diverse as the antecedents of the 1814 war between the British and the Gurkas of Nepal, and the description of a clinical case), that could have several outcomes. In different studies, different groups of subjects were presented with the same descriptions of the scenarios, but one group was not provided with an outcome, while the other groups were given different outcomes, including the true one (the one that actually happened). The subjects then had to assign their predicted probabilities to the different outcomes (that had to add to 1.0). The results clearly showed that all outcomes were overwhelmingly picked "predicted" by those who were also provided with them in advance. In contrast, the group that had to predict the outcome without being foretold of any outcome distributed their predictions much more evenly among the various options.

The hindsight bias is insidious also because not only are we not aware of it, but warning of its existence hardly affects or reduces it (Fischhoff, 1975). The implications of hindsight bias for crash reconstruction and causation were described by Dilich, Kopernik, and Goebelbecker (2004) who stated that in the process of assigning causes (and culpability) to a crash that has already happened "The situation that we clearly perceive, with the benefit of evidence, science and time, when looking backward into the past, is fundamentally different than the unexpected and risk-laden emergency that suddenly confronted the reactive driver, who had no second chance to respond differently, as s/he rapidly traveled forward and into an uncertain future." In evaluating the results of the different crash causes based on clinical judgments, it may be judicious to assume that the experts who generated these causes suffered from the same bias, and therefore the actual probabilities may be slightly lower than presented.

At its most sophisticated level the clinical approach consists of an in-depth multidisciplinary investigation. It involves experts from at least three disciplines – automotive engineering, crash reconstruction or highway engineering, and psychology. Each of these team members conducts an independent thorough investigation of the relevant issues in his or her area of expertise, and then jointly they piece together all the elements that led to the crash, and arrive at a conclusion concerning the cause or causes of the crash.

Unfortunately, even when the investigators are highly qualified in their respective disciplines collecting the data elements, making sense of them, and using them to understand the cause or causes of a crash is a subjective process. This is because crash reconstruction is akin to putting together a puzzle, with a few of the pieces missing. Often, some of the critical data elements – related to the vehicle, the environment, or the driver behavior and incapacities – do not survive the crash. For example, an assessment of vehicle behavior prior to the crash can be obtained from examinations of the vehicles and the roadway. Assessing the exact location of the impact and the pre-crash speeds and trajectories relies on the road markings left by the cars, and these are often quickly obliterated. The cars are removed from the scene, the road is cleaned of debris, and various objects that may have been involved in the crash are removed. In addition, anti-lock brakes that are available on most cars eliminate telltale skid marks that were once very useful to determine the pre-crash speeds. Information about the vehicle condition is also difficult to assess. This is because the vehicles are often towed and repaired before they can be examined in detailed, or because they are damaged to such an extent that the functioning levels of various systems (e.g., lights, brakes) is hard to assess. Finally, information about what the drivers were doing just prior to the crash is the most elusive. A driver's memory is often distorted quickly, events compressed in time are difficult to recall, and drivers are not objective observers of the crash. In fact, given enough time to collect their thoughts, drivers will often seek the least incriminating logically plausible explanation for why they had the crash (Baker and Fricke, 1986). Thus, a crash investigation team must contend with partial and biased information to arrive at the cause or causes of a crash.

The definition of a cause is also problematic. The analogy of the referees' call at the beginning of this chapter is not far-fetched. Crash investigators have an explicit or implicit theory of human behavior to which they attach the causes. Most often it is one version or another of the human information processing model discussed in Chapter 3. This means that most driver behaviors that lead to a crash will be considered as some kind of a failure in information processing: a delayed recognition of a hazard, a misperception of events, a poor decision based on misjudgment of the situation, the selection of an inappropriate avoidance maneuver, the improper execution of a correct maneuver – or any combination of the above. Thus, an inappropriate high speed for a curve may be considered a "misjudgment" error whenever the driver overestimates the speed at which the curve could be negotiated. However, an investigator approaching the situation from a motivational theory may label the same behavior as a "risk taking" behavior, implying volition to speed through the curve. The two approaches would then lead to two different results and different causes of crashes.

Because most clinical investigations of crash causation have assumed the information processing model and not the motivational model, most crash causes described below will be framed in terms of failures in information processing, though some references to motivational factors will occasionally be made as well.

Indiana University Tri-Level Study of Accident Causes

The first, and possibly the most thorough investigation of the causes of crashes, up till the recent emergence of naturalistic driving studies (see Chapter 2) was the Tri-Level Study of Accident Causes, conducted in the 1970s by a research team from Indiana University for the U.S. National Highway Traffic Safety Administration (NHTSA) (Treat *et al.*, 1979). In this study, an attempt was made to investigate all crashes within a single county. The study was therefore comprehensive in terms of the different types of crashes at all levels of severity. All the crashes studied were police-reported crashes. In fact, the police most often notified the research team about a crash as soon as they were notified. Once alerted, a special research vehicle would be sent to the crash site; hopefully before most of the crash scene evidence would be removed. After an on-site investigation of the crash, this team of two technicians would then assess the cause or causes of the crash. Over 2,000 crashes were analyzed in this fashion. In addition to their own analyses, the crash investigators also asked all surviving drivers involved if they would be willing to cooperate in a more thorough in-depth analysis, promising them complete confidentiality. Whenever such cooperation was assured, then within one week the crash scene would be investigated in detail by an accident reconstructionist who would also reconstruct the vehicle(s)' movements, the drivers would be interviewed and evaluated relative to their visual acuity and reaction time by a psychologist, and the vehicles would be examined by an automotive engineer who would disassemble all systems that may have been relevant to the crash. The team members would then meet to discuss their findings and arrive at a group decision concerning the cause or causes of the crash. A total of 420 crashes that occurred from 1971 to May 1975 were investigated in-depth in that manner.

Attribution of cause in the Indiana University study was limited to a previously developed detailed taxonomy of potential human failures, vehicle failures, and environmental problems. Human causes were further subdivided into direct and indirect. Direct causes were the actions and inactions that immediately preceded the crash and were responsible for making it inevitable. Indirect causes were human impairments that may have been responsible for the direct behaviors. The direct human causes included factors such as inattention, improper lookout, misjudgment, and inappropriate evasive maneuvers, whereas indirect causes that may have been responsible for these lapses and poorly performed actions included impairments from alcohol or drugs, fatigue, poor vision, lack of skill or unfamiliarity with the vehicle and/or the road. The theoretical relationship between the indirect causes and the direct causes is depicted in Figure 18-3 in terms of cause-and-effect. The direct human causes are presented in their original hierarchical scheme in Figure 18-4 and defined later below in Table 18-1. Although impairments that constitute the indirect causes can be crash risk factors, they do not appear to be a necessary condition for a failure in driver information processing and a crash (Shinar, Treat, and McDonald, 1983).

The study yielded several significant findings, which at the time were quite unexpected. First, the researchers discovered that in approximately 50 percent of the crashes more than one factor caused the crash. This means that in a crash caused by two or more factors, the absence of *any one* of the factors would have prevented the crash. This also means that quite often two factors or more had to occur at the same time for a crash to happen.

The most important finding of the study was the assessment of the relative role of the human, environmental, and vehicular causes. Although the study originally focused on the identification of vehicle defects that cause crashes (Joscelyn, Treat, and Miller, 1973; Lee and Fell, 1988), and the two principal investigators were – quite appropriately – a physicist and an automotive engineer, the crash analyses revealed that the overwhelming majority of the crashes were caused or at least precipitated by human errors. A much smaller proportion of the causes were environmental, and only a very small proportion of the causes were vehicular. Because the multi-disciplinary team members were aware

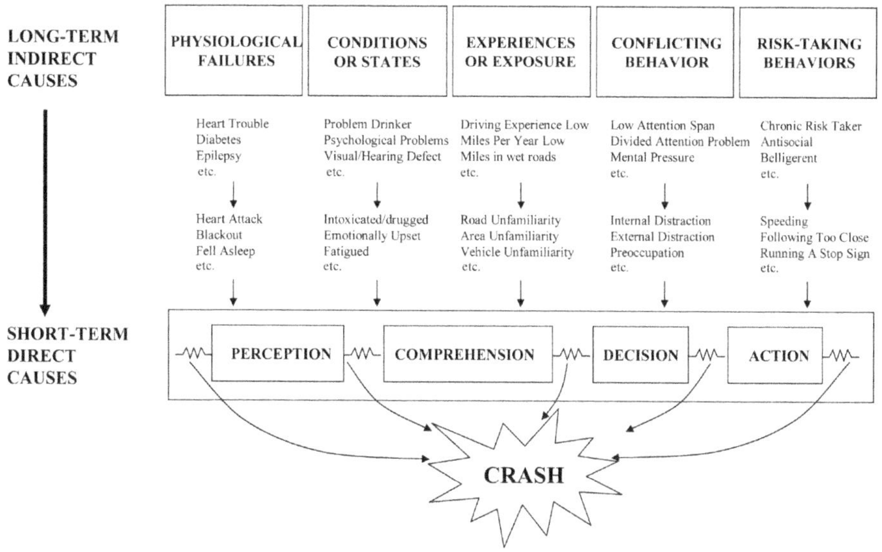

Figure 18-3. A theoretical cause-and-effect relationship between impairing driver conditions and direct human causes of crashes (from Lee and Fell, 1988).

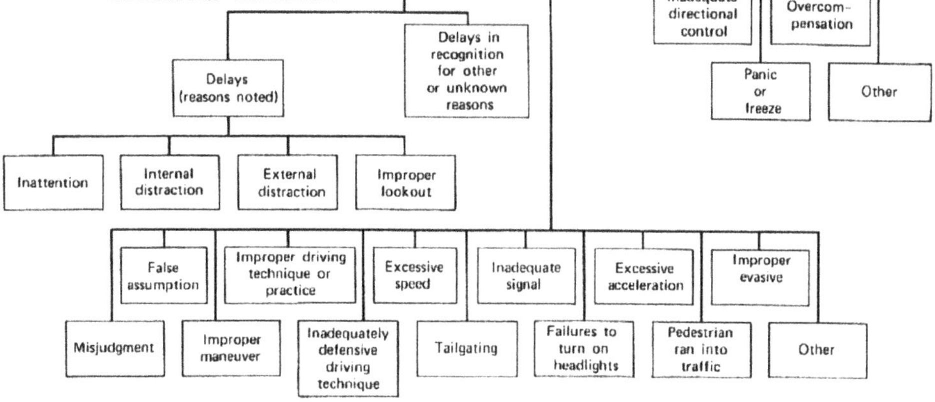

Figure 18-4. The hierarchical taxonomy of direct human causes of accidents in the Tri-Level Study of Accident Causes (from Treat *et al.*, 1979).

Table 18-1. Partial definitions of the ten most frequently cited human causes in the Tri-Level Study of Accidents (from Treat *et al.*, 1979).

Category	**Definition**
Improper lookout	Delayed recognition due to failure to perform an adequate visual search in a situation that requires a distinct visual surveillance (e.g., in intersections and pulling out of a parking space)
Excessive speed	Speed that is excessive relative to the traffic, roadway, and ambience conditions – regardless of the legal speed limit
Inattention	Delayed recognition due to preoccupation with irrelevant thoughts or wandering of the mind
Improper evasive action	Failing to take an emergency action that is apparent and within the capabilities of an adequately trained and alert driver (e.g., locking the brakes and as a result losing control of the car, in a situation where steering could have prevented the accident)
Internal distraction	Delayed recognition due to an attentional shift to an event, activity, object, or person within the vehicle
Improper driving technique	Engaging in an improper control of vehicle path or speed, in an habitual maneuver (e.g., cresting hills while driving in the center of the road)
Inadequately defensive driving technique	Unnecessarily placing the vehicle in a position where there is a foreseeable and substantial risk of collision if another driver performs contrary to normal expectorations, or failing to check that another driver is not engaged in such an unexpected action
False assumption	Taking action on the basis of an assumption that is not valid – even if it is based on the traffic system rules (e.g., pulling in front of a driver who is signaling a turn but does not in fact turn)
Improper maneuver	Willfully choosing a vehicle path that is wrong, since it increases the chance of a collision (e.g., turning from the wrong lane, driving the wrong way in a one-way street)
Overcompensation	Improper reactions to emergency situations that cause loss of control, such as overbraking or oversteering (e.g., oversteering back into the highway after going off into the road shoulder)

of the subjective nature of their conclusions, they also estimated the subjective probability that a factor was a cause in the crash (the probability that – with all other things being equal – had that factor not existed, the crash would have been avoided). For the statistical summary, the team assigned each factor a confidence level: "definite" whenever the average subjective probability that the factor was causal was equal to or greater than 0.95, and "probable" whenever the subjective probability was 0.8-0.95. This enabled them to arrive at conservative estimates (based on the cases considered "definite") and liberal estimates (based on the cases considered "probable") of the role of different causes. The relative contributions of the three main factors or causes at the probable and definite levels are depicted in Figure 18-5.

The most striking feature of the results depicted in Figure 18-5 is that both the on-site analyses and the in-depth analyses indicated that in the overwhelming majority of the crashes the cause (or one of the causes) was human. At the probable level of confidence based on the in-depth analysis, a human error was responsible for approximately

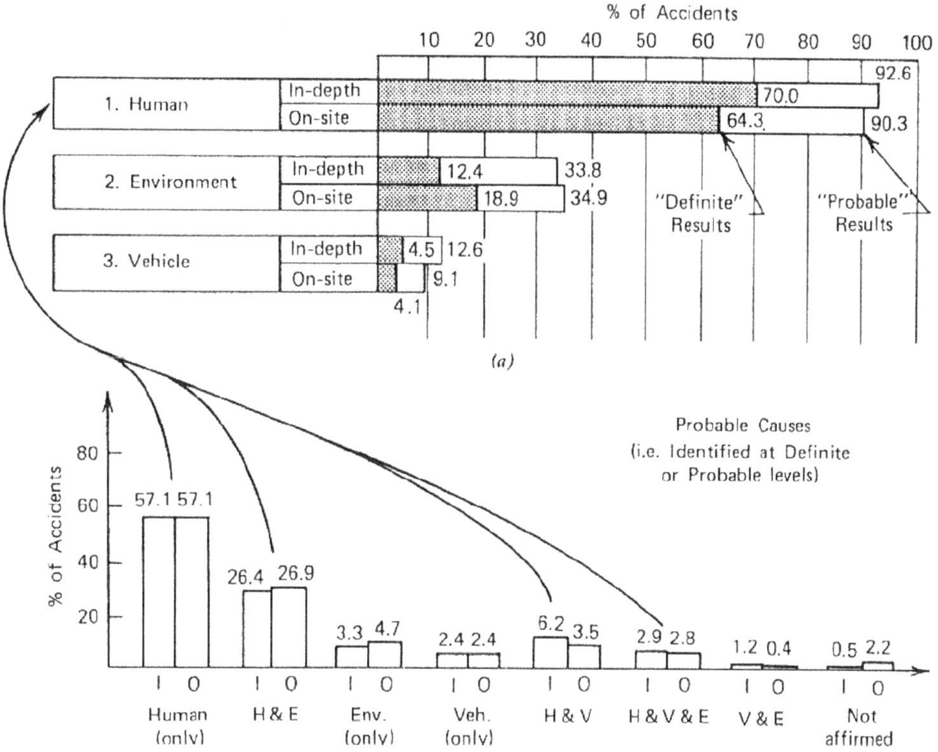

Figure 18-5. The percent of crashes caused by human, environment, and vehicle causes, at the probable and definite levels, based on the on-site and in-depth crash analyses, and (bottom) the relative proportions of combinations of these causes. Because crashes can have more than one cause, the totals add up to more than 100 percent (from Treat *et al.*, 1979).

93 percent of all crashes. Today, this sounds like a truism, but at the time it was surprising and shocking. Second, in nearly 60 percent of the crashes, the cause was strictly human, without any contribution from the environment or the vehicle. The remaining 30 percent of the crashes with a "human" cause consisted of crashes that occurred because there were both human and environmental defects (approximately 26 percent), human and vehicle factors (approximately 5 percent), and crashes in which all three factors were involved (approximately 3 percent). Third, the initial suspect and potential culprit – the vehicle – accounted for only 10 percent of all crashes, and in most of these crashes there were also non-vehicular factors involved. A vehicle defect alone accounted for only 2-3 percent of the crashes. Fourth, despite the fact that the causal assessment process is subjective, there was a remarkable similarity in the relative contributions of the three factors – human, environment, and vehicle – between the on-site team's conclusions that were based on 2,258 crashes and the in-depth team's conclusions that were based on the sub-sample of 420 crashes. Finally, the investigation into the human conditions and states revealed that in the overwhelming majority of the crashes (88 percent) no impairments in the drivers' state of mind – labeled impaired human conditions and states – could be identified at the probable or definite level by either the on-site team or the in-depth team. This means that most crashes occurred to "normal" people driving without any predisposing impairments or handicaps. When impairment was identified, it was most often (50 percent) alcohol-related. Although the taxonomy contained conditions such as drug impairment, fatigue, driver inexperience, driver being in a hurry, emotional upset, vehicle and roadway unfamiliarity, pressure from other drivers, and reduced vision, none of these factors was implicated in more than two percent of the crashes (Shinar, McDonald, and Treat, 1978).

Other studies of the role of human, environmental, and vehicular causes

Communication in the 1970s was very different than it is today. There were no faxes, no emails, no satellite or cellular telephones, and international flights and inter-continental phone conversations were quite expensive. Thus, it so happened that at the same time that the Indiana University researchers were collecting their data a similar study was being conducted in England, without the researchers involved in one knowing about the other. The British study was conducted by a team of the UK's Transport Road Research Laboratory, and it involved a similar process of post-hoc analyses of crashes in England. Its results were first presented in 1975 (Sabey and Staughton, 1975). Despite the different countries, the different vehicles (at the time the world was not a "small village": the overwhelming majority of most cars in both countries were locally manufactured), the different drivers and driving norms (driving on the right versus driving on the left), the different researchers, the different taxonomies and the slightly different definitions of causes; despite all of these differences, the results were remarkably similar as illustrated in a comparison made by Rumar (1985), and reproduced in Figure 18-6.

Overall, if we combine the percentages of all crashes involving a human factor, we can see from Figure 18-6 that the British team estimated that the human factor was the cause of 94 percent of the crashes, whereas the U.S. team estimated it at 93 percent.

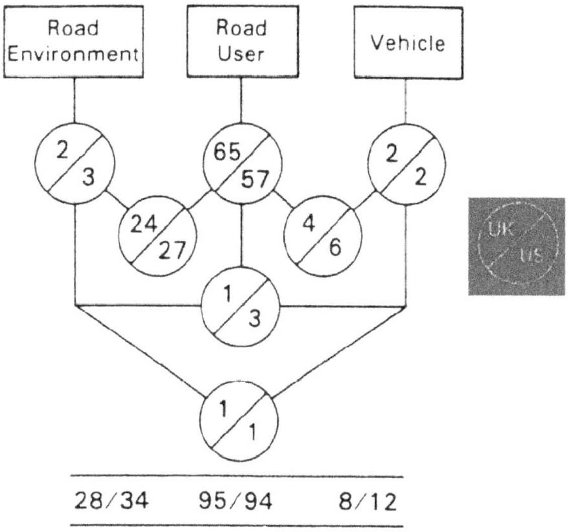

Figure 18-6. A comparison of the percent of crashes caused by human, environment, and vehicle defects or failures in England (upper number in each circle) and in the U.S. (lower number in each circle) (from Rumar, 1985, with kind permission of Springer Science and Business Media).

The environment was responsible for 28 percent of the crashes according to the British team and 34 percent of the crashes according to the U.S. team, and the vehicle was the cause of only 8 and 9 percent, respectively. Even at the level of the interactions, or joint effects, of the different causes the agreement is striking. Thus, the two research teams have provided us with an inadvertent demonstration of the reliability of the clinical approach to causal assessment. Also, as in the U.S. results, the British analysis also indicated that 30 percent of all crashes are due to a combination of causes – mostly human and environment (versus 36 percent in the U.S. data).

Despite the agreement between the U.S. study results and the British results, the validity of these conclusions today – 40 years after the U.S. and British data were collected – is questionable. In the past quarter century there have been great technological changes in vehicles, in roadway materials and crash-absorbing devices, and even in driver licensing and enforcement practices. So the question now is how relevant are these results to today's traffic safety issues. To answer this question the U.S. National Highway Traffic Safety Administration conducted another evaluation of crash causes approximately 25 years after the Indiana University study. In the new study, Hendricks, Fell, and Freedman (2001) analyzed 723 injury crashes that occurred between April 1996 and May 1997. The objective of the study was "to determine the specific driver behaviors and unsafe driving acts (UDA's) that lead to crashes and the situational, driver, and vehicle characteristics associated with these behaviors." (p. ii). The study method was somewhat different than that of the Indiana University Tri-Level study. Most of the information on the crashes was obtained from documents prepared by specially trained personnel that routinely investigate a representative sample of all U.S. police reported crashes (as a part of the crash investigations of NASS – the National Automotive Sampling System). Their level of expertise was somewhat similar to that of the on-site technicians in the Tri-Level study. For this study, to determine the human behaviors that preceded the crash, the study team created a detailed interview form that was used by the crash investigators to obtain the additional information that would otherwise not be collected. Figure 18-7 contains a comparison of the main results from the Hendricks *et al.* (2001) and the Tri-Level studies.

Given the significant differences in time, sampling strategy, and investigation approach, the similarity is very high. In both studies nearly all crashes were attributed to a human cause. The Tri-Level study attributed more causes to the environment and the vehicle and that is quite understandable for at least two reasons: (1) the depth of investigation involved and the expertise of the investigators enabled these researchers to ascertain the presence and involvement of environmental and vehicular causes that the UDA team was simply unable to uncover and (2) the UDA study emphasis was on the human failures, and the amount and quality of evidence collected on the environment and vehicles was therefore much lower. A more recent analysis of 248 passenger car accidents included in the German In-Depth Accident Study (GIDAS) showed that a human failure or error was responsible for 97 percent of the crashes, while the environment was cited in six percent and the vehicle was cited in two percent (Otte, Pund, and Jänsch, 2009). Thus, the Tri-Level study's main findings, concerning the relative role of the human, environment, and vehicle have withstood the test of time, and also the test of place.

In summary, the comparisons among the studies indicate both how stable and reliable the Tri-Level findings were, and how important the research methods are in influencing the results of the study. Again, if it's a "ball" but you can't see it, you are not likely to call it a "ball."

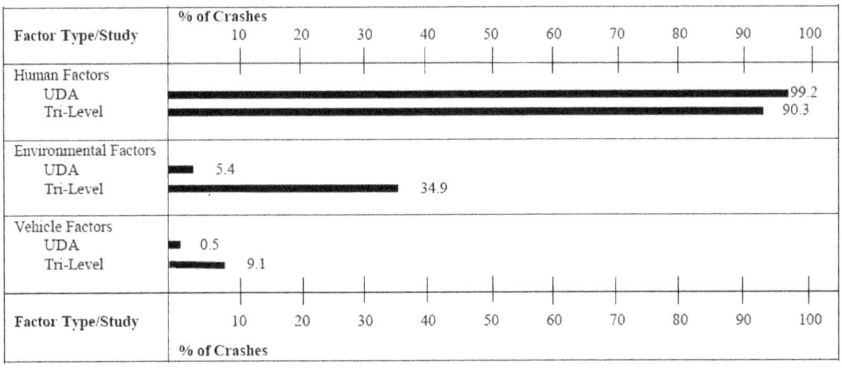

Figure 18-7. Human, environmental, and vehicular causes of crashes according to the Unsafe Driving Actions (UDA) study and the Indiana University Tri-Level study (from Hendricks *et al.*, 2001).

Specific human causes of crashes

All in-depth studies go beyond the gross classification of causes into human, environment and vehicle. In the Tri-Level study, the principal human direct causes of crashes – based on the in-depth analyses of 420 crashes –were recognition errors (responsible for 56 percent of the crashes at the definite and probable levels of confidence), followed by decision errors (responsible for 51 percent of the crashes at the definite and probable levels of confidence), followed by performance errors (responsible for 11 percent of the crashes at the definite and probable levels of confidence). Non-accident (e.g., suicide) and critical non-performance (e.g., loss of consciousness from a heart attack) accounted for less than two percent at the definite and probable levels. However, their rarity may be due as much to difficulty of assessment of these causes (the crashes are typically single vehicle, and the driver – for obvious reasons – cannot be interviewed), as to their actual low frequency. The 10 most frequently cited specific causes – within these general categories of information processing failures – are listed in Figure 18-8, and the definition for each of these causes is provided in Table 18-1.

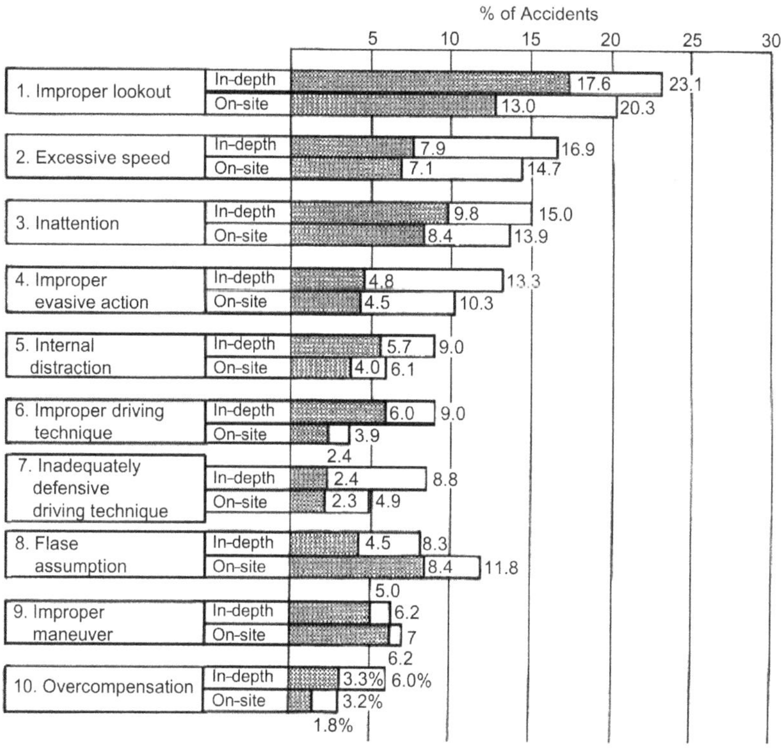

Figure 18-8. Percentages of crashes caused by specific human direct causes at the probable and definite levels of confidence, based on the on-site and in-depth investigations in the Indiana University Tri-Level study (from Treat *et al.*, 1979).

The most frequently cited single cause was "improper lookout" which alone accounted for over 20 percent of all crashes. The failure to adequately obtain the information necessary to avoid the accident was also manifest in the prevalence of inattention and internal distraction. Together these three factors demonstrate the critical role of the (visual) information gathering, and the inherent danger in its lapses. Interestingly, internal distraction – even before the days of cellular phones, navigation systems, and the internet – was already a significant factor in crash causation (see Chapter 13 for a detailed discussion about distraction). When all the attentional errors are combined (improper lookout, inattention, and internal and external distraction) it turns out that they account for nearly 50 percent of all crashes (47.9 percent) at the probable or certain level. This is not an aberration of the study method or a human failure unique to the Indiana drivers, as the study conducted in England by Sabey and Staughton (1975) revealed a nearly identical finding: "looked, but failed to see," "distraction," "failed to look," and "lack of attention" accounted for 28 percent of all "human errors contributing to accidents," and to as much as 48.7 percent of the crashes (the exact percentage is impossible to calculate given the way in which the data are presented). Even more astounding is Neyens and Boyle's (2007) finding, based on an analysis of the U.S. General Estimates System (a data base maintained by the U.S. National Highway Administration, consisting of a stratified sample of crashes that is weighted to represent national U.S. crash rates). Using young drivers' (16-19 years old) 2003 crash data, they found that the most common type of crash-causing distraction, accounting for 30 percent of all crashes was "cognitive": being "lost in thought" or "looking but not seeing." This estimate is very similar to the Treat *et al.*'s (1979) combined estimates for these two causes (27 percent at the "certain" and 38 percent at the probable level – see Figure 18-8). In contrast, distraction from the ubiquitous cell phone – something that did not exist in the 1970s – accounted for less than one percent of the 2003 teen crashes, a strikingly similar estimate to NHTSA' more recent estimate for drivers of all ages on the basis of the 2012 Fatal Analysis Reporting System (NHTSA, 2014). In the German GIDAS study too – where the causal taxonomy was also based on the human information processing model – distraction of all types, inattention, and "wrong focus of attention" accounted for 40 percent of the human factors (Otte *et al.*, 2009).

Among the 10 leading causes are also some decision errors such as improper driving technique, false assumption, improper maneuver, and speed. Whereas the first three are probably best understood in terms of failures in information processing, excessive speed probably has a strong motivational component and reflects the interaction between the motivational factors and the information processing factors that together lead to crashes. Finally, actual vehicle handling – often the most emphasized element in driver training programs – was the least involved of all human direct causes, and when it was involved it was primarily in a very specific situation of overcompensation in response to an emergency situation. This is a skill that is relatively rarely trained – and when it is taught, its benefits are at best dubious (see Chapter 19 on the negative effects of skid training).

The relevance of these more specific causes was also evaluated in the Unsafe Driving Actions study, and their results compared to those of the Tri-Level study are presented in Figure 18-9. Because of the slightly different definitions, only the more frequently cited

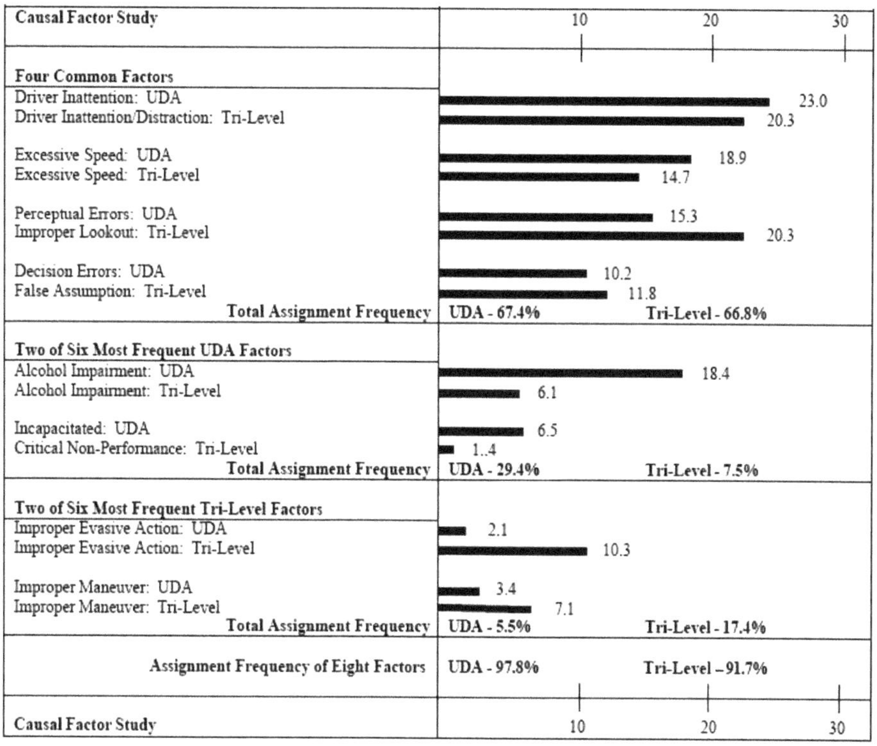

Figure 18-9. Comparisons of the six most frequently assigned UDA's with the Tri-Level causal factors (from Hendricks *et al.*, 2001).

factors are included in this figure. At this level of specificity the amount of agreement varies for different factors. For the most part, where there is a significant difference it is more likely due to the different methods and the different definitions employed rather than to significant changes in the actual causes. Thus, when the two definitions are not identical, one cannot expect to obtain a perfect overlap in the results. Still, the most commonly cited factors in the Tri-Level study – inattention/distraction, excessive speed, improper lookout, and false assumption – re-emerged a quarter of a century later in the UDA study with very similar frequencies. The two conspicuous disparities are alcohol caused crashes and improper evasive action. In the case of alcohol, the Tri-Level study reflects the involvement of alcohol in all crashes of all severities (including non-injury crashes), whereas the UDA study sample is biased towards the more severe crashes, and it is well known that alcohol involvement is greater in severe injury and fatal crashes (see Chapter 11). With respect to improper evasive action, it is possible that the less professional evaluation of the UDA causes made it more difficult to assess such failures, and the introduction of anti-lock brakes systems (ABS) actually reduced the frequencies of these types of causes.

In Germany, in GIDAS, decision errors (labeled "Wrong expectation," "Misjudgment of others or accident place," "Misjudgment of own vehicle" and "Decision error") accounted for a total of 34 percent of all human errors, somewhat less than recognition/attention errors (Otte *et al.*, 2009)

An interesting finding in the Indiana University study (as well as in other in-depth investigations) is the rarity of predisposing conditions or states that could account for the human direct causes. In the Indiana University study impairments in human conditions and states were involved in only 12.4 percent of the crashes investigated in-depth at the probable or certain level. The ten most commonly cited indirect causes, in descending order – involved in 1-3 percent of all crashes – were alcohol impairment (3.1 percent), drug impairment (2.1 percent), fatigue (1.7 percent), inexperience (1.4 percent), being in a hurry (1.2 percent), emotional upset (1.2 percent), vehicle unfamiliarity (1.0 percent), pressure from other drivers (0.7 percent), road area unfamiliarity (0.7 percent), and reduced vision (0.5 percent). In GIDAS, alcohol was involved in only four percent of the cases. These findings are in stark contrast to the crash causation model presented in Figure 18-3 that assumes that all direct human causes are due to some sort of driver impairment. Instead, it seems that most crashes are caused by people operating a vehicle when they are in their "normal" condition!

To summarize, the clinical approach to analyzing crashes and understanding their causes, despite its subjective nature, seems to yield fairly robust estimates of the relative frequencies of various human information processing failures. An advantage and a shortcoming of this approach is that it is theory and taxonomy bound. That is, the analyst must have some theory of driver behavior to guide him or her in the development of definitions of potential reasons or causes of crashes. The benefit of the theoretical underpinning is that when a cause is identified the causal relationship is supported by the theory; how that cause "operates" can be understood within the context of the theory. The shortcoming of this approach is that failures that were not previously identified as "potential" causes will not emerge from the data, no matter how frequently they occur! Thus, different multi-disciplinary teams using different taxonomies may arrive at different crash causes. This makes comparisons across studies difficult, but the information from each study is still useful at the local or national level. Other countries, such as Denmark, Finland, Germany, and Sweden have also created crash data bases relying on the multi-disciplinary in-depth approach to crash causation analysis (Larsen, 2004; Otte *et al.*, 2009). Even within the same crash data set, differences may exist when the team members change. For example, in Finland, the Ministry of Transport and Communications, supervises a multi-disciplinary crash investigation effort, initiated in 1968, in which approximately 500 crashes (mostly fatal) are investigated in-depth, and data are collected on 500 pre-defined variables. Each crash is investigated by a team consisting of a police officer, a vehicle specialist, a road specialist, and a physician. In some of the cases, a psychologist is also involved. The weakness of the approach, and consequently of the data base, was exposed by Keith and his associates (2005) who were impressed that "the presence or absence of a psychologist on the team could critically alter conclusions and interpretation of data" (p. 12). Nonetheless, the clinical approach, coupled with new in-vehicle data recorders (IVDRs), may eliminate some of these sources of errors, and make the approach much more objective and robust, as discussed below.

The U.S. National Motor Vehicle Crash Causation Survey (NMVCCS)

The NMVCCS is the most recent U.S. effort to assess crash causes using the clinical post-crash investigation methodology (NHTSA, 2008; Singh, 2015). Compared to the Tri-Level study it had some advantages and disadvantages. The first and foremost advantage is that it is relatively recent and much larger; based on 5,470 crashes that occurred over the three years 2005-2007. Thus, it can provide more reliable statistics on a new generation of drivers, cars, and infrastructures. Second, the sample is a weighted representative sample of all U.S. injury crashes, and thus it could reveal the frequencies of different causes at the U.S. national level. In the Tri-Level study the extrapolation to national estimates of various causes was quite tenuous as all its data came from a single county in one state (Monroe, Indiana), with an over-representation of young students. Thus, the NMVCCS was expected to yield results that are much more relevant to the current U.S. traffic system. The significant disadvantage of the NMVCCS was that its level of analysis was roughly similar to that of the on-site investigation of the Tri-Level study rather than its multi-disciplinary in-depth investigations. There is also one other significant difference between the two studies. The Tri-Level study used the term "cause" of an accident, assigned each of the causes in a crash a subjective probability, and considered multiple causes. The NMVCCS analyzed each crash by determining the final critical event that made the crash inevitable, and then determined the *single* critical reason for that critical event. Thus, in the NMVCCS each crash was assigned only one "cause," or to be more exact only one critical reason. Nonetheless, what makes the two studies relatively easy to compare is that the NMVCCS used a taxonomy and terminology for its critical reasons that was very similar to the Tri-Level study's crash causes.

The principal findings of the primary human, environmental, and vehicular critical reasons from the NMVCCS study were somewhat surprising. Once again, despite all the advances in safety, the driver contributed the overwhelming majority of the critical crash reasons: 94 percent of all crashes. The environment and vehicle were each held responsible in only two percent of the crashes, and the remaining two percent could not be determined. The high involvement of the drivers is nearly identical to that determined 30 years earlier in the Tri-Level study. The very low involvement of the environment and the vehicles can be attributed to three reasons. First, attribution of a critical reason to these factors required a more in-depth investigation than was feasible in the NMVCCS. Second, only one critical reason was assigned to each crash. Note that in the Tri-Level study, the environment alone was cited in only 3.3 percent of the crashes, and the vehicle alone was cited in only 2.4 percent of the crashes (Figure 18-5). Third, over the 30-year period that elapsed between the two studies the U.S. infrastructure and vehicle fleet has become much safer. For example, many roads were upgraded with more lighting, more hard shoulders, better guard rails, better asphalt, and safer designs (e.g., roundabouts). Safety-wise, cars have been practically transformed, with multiple airbags, retracting seat belts, and better crash-absorbing cages. In stark contrast, we the human operators have not changed at all (well, we do drink-and-drive less, and buckle-up more).

The critical reasons and their frequencies within each of the three system components are listed in Table 18-2. Even within each component the results are highly similar to

Table 18-2. The primary critical human, environmental, and vehicular critical reasons for crashes in the National Motor Vehicle Crash Causation Survey (out of 100 percent for each component) (from Singh, 2015).

	Driver		Environment		Vehicle	
	Reason	**%**	**Reason**	**%**	**Reason**	**%**
1	Recognition error	41	Slick roads	50	Tires/wheels	35
2	Decision error	33	Glare	17	Brake-related	22
3	Performance error	11	View obstructions	11	Steering/suspension/ transmission/engine	3
4	Non-performance error	7	Other highway-related conditions	9	Other/unknown	40
5	Other	8	Fog/rain/snow	4		
6			Other weather-related	4		
7			Signs/signals	3		
8			Road design	1		

those cited in the Tri-Level study. Driver recognition errors – which include inattention, distraction, and delayed perception – are cited almost as often as they were 40 years ago. This is particularly interesting in light of the multiple new distractions that we have now that did not exist then such as cell phones and navigation systems. The effects of the new in-vehicle and nomadic devices are reflected in the finding that approximately half (10.7 percent) of the recognition errors are due to internal distractions, a magnitude quite similar to that observed in the Tri-Level study, again indicating that while the objects of our distraction may have changed over the years, the need to seek non-driving stimulation is fairly constant. As in the Tri-Level study, here too external distractions were less common: only 3.8 percent of all human errors. The principal decision errors are selecting a speed that is either too high for the conditions or for a curve (13.3 percent out of 34.1 percent). Performance errors are still a very minor part of the failures, again indicating that the problem does not lie in poor vehicular control. Non-performance was due mostly to falling asleep, and their greater frequency here than in the Tri-Level study is probably due to the inclusion of more long-distance driving.

The term looked-but-failed-to-see has been used for a variety of recognition errors in which the driver claimed to have properly searched the visual environment but failed to perceive or in some other sense process the presence of the other vehicle or object. In an interesting analysis of French crash data Koustanaï *et al.* (2008) were able to distinguish between two types of this recognition failure: those occurring at the sensorial or perceptual stage where the drivers never really "saw" the other car, and those occurring at the decision-making stage in the information processing sequence where the other car was perceived but not in time to react properly and the failure was actually a recall failure when describing the crash. In these cases there was evidence that the driver actually perceived the threat as there were scuff marks or brake marks on the pavement, indicative of an attempt to avoid the crash. They further noted that the first type involved mostly crashes where the drivers were driving straight through an intersection or turning left to park their car, while the latter typically happened while the drivers were overtaking another vehicle or trying to find their way. The implication of this distinction between the two types of looked-but-failed-to-see is that different visual search strategies are involved in the two types of environments and training to improve the search should consider the two environments separately.

It is important to stress, that in all of the crash causation studies, the data reported here was based on the total sample of crashes, combining different crash types, vehicle types, crash severities, etc. However, the relative contributions of the different driver failures are not the same for all crash locations, times, and types. For example, in the NMVCCS study, an analysis limited to run-off-the-road crashes revealed that though human failures were responsible for over 96 percent of all crashes, the principle critical reasons were not recognition errors but performance errors (28 percent) such as "overcompensation" and "poor directional control" (Liu and Ye, 2011). This is another indication that countermeasures have to be tailored to specific crash types.

How normal are the human failures in crash causation assessments?

There is one issue that is generally overlooked in the interpretation of clinical crash assessments. This is the validity of our assumption of what constitutes a "normal" human, vehicle, and environment. We therefore often accept as givens a narrow unlit winding road, and a vehicle's curve handling capabilities. These assumptions may be valid relative to the current state of roadway design guidelines and vehicle technology. In this respect, we are conservative in faulting the vehicle or the environment. On the other hand our assumption concerning the driver's abilities are often unjustified. For example, we expect the driver to be alert and detect all information that is sensorially available. This may be a fair assumption at any one moment, but it is unrealistic for a total drive. We cannot attend to all the information all the time. Checking the rear-view mirror or attending to a roadway sign (either a guidance sign or a billboard) is normal driver behavior, and at times it can lead to a crash. And while crash investigators are familiar with the vehicle and infrastructure norms, they all too often have unrealistic expectations of the hapless crash-involved driver, assigning to the driver unlimited "brain power." Our assumptions then are much more similar to those of the police officers who investigated the causes of the Oxfordshire crashes in the 1930s than to those of the civil engineer who evaluated the same crashes (see Box 18-1). This was demonstrated in the example cited above when a psychologist was added to the Finnish in-depth team

(Keith *et al.*, 2005). Hauer, in a critique of the clinical assessment process, also noted that faulty road design – even if it conforms to the guidelines – can be as much to blame for some crashes, and addressing it would serve safety much better than lamenting the road users' failures (Hauer, 2016).

Validity of Police Assessment of Crash Causation Relative to the Multi-Disciplinary In-Depth Clinical Approach

Police accident reports are the most ubiquitous source of crash data on a national basis. They are generally the most comprehensive data base of crashes, and they contain – in addition to a coded description of the crash – various details about the drivers and the cars. They also contain information on violations related to the crash that were committed by the driver(s) and a short narrative of the officer's impression of how the crash happened. Given all this information, why not simply use the police reports to study the causes of crashes? This, in fact, is a common procedure in many countries. However, it is extremely naïve, biased, and nonproductive. To be a good data source for crash causation, the data have to be collected with that goal in mind. Assessment of culpability is not the same as assessment of causation, and the goal of the police investigation is to determine the former and not the latter. The police are responsible for law enforcement, and therefore their reports are a good source of violations committed by the drivers. In addition to their – justifiable – bias, the police typically do not have the resources (expertise, time, and money) to investigate crashes at the level done by a multi-disciplinary crash investigation team. This automatically means that less frequent, less expected, and more difficult to assess causes will often be missed.

In general, police accident reports are quite accurate in describing the observable details of the crash (drivers' id, time, location, etc.). Yet, even on these items there are errors. Chung and Chang (2015) analyzed 569 taxi-pedestrian collisions in Korea, and found significant differences between the vehicles' black box objective recordings and the police's manual recordings in the accident reports, averaging a deviation of 158 meters in the crash location and 29 minutes in the time of the crash. The use of the police reported violations should also be considered with some reservations. Often summary statistics of these violations are misrepresented as "reasons" for the crash or crash "causes." For example, Israel's National Traffic Police publishes an annual report that contains the "reasons for crashes." The most frequent reasons cited (in that order) are: deviation from lane, failure to maintain safe distance, failure to yield right of way, failure to stop at a stop sign, and failure to yield at a yield sign (Israel Police, 2001). Inattention – the most common cause of crashes according to in-depth investigations – does not appear as a cause because it is not a directly observable violation of the traffic code.

Police reports are probably the least valid when it comes to causal assessments. Two examples will suffice to illustrate the danger of relying on the police for crash causation. The first is the cause of rear-end crashes. In rear-end crashes, police typically cite the following driver with failure to maintain a safe distance. This may or may not be true, but it is easy to argue that the fact that a collision occurred implies – by definition –

that the following driver did not keep a safe distance. This argument is circular but seems to be accepted in court. Thus, the police typically cite that violation, and later cite that as the reason or cause for the crash. In fact there is a host of other potential reasons that could have been responsible for the crash: brake failure, undetectable slippery area of the road, an *unexpected* braking of the lead car, glare from the sun when the lead car slowed down, distraction at the time the lead car slowed down, faulty brake lights on the lead car (which typically serve as the first cue to braking), etc. Assessment of any of the above causes is more difficult, or more time-consuming, or more expensive, or more subjective, or all of the above. In addition, a very likely cause for rear-end collisions is momentary inattention, distraction, or improper lookout. Thus, the direct true causes may be other human factors, environmental factors, or vehicular factors.

Another example is a collision at a controlled intersection with a stop or yield sign. The police will almost automatically cite the driver facing the sign with "failure to stop" or "failure to give right-of-way." Other possible causes that will not appear on the police report are faded signs, glare from the sun, and view obstructions of the sign by foliage or other cars. The police do not issue tickets to the roadway or the cars. They issue tickets to drivers.

To provide a quantitative determination of the adequacy of police reports for cause assessment we (Shinar *et al.*, 1983) compared a subset of 207 Tri-Level cases to the police reports that were filed for the same crashes. In general, if we assume that the causes unearthed by the multi-disciplinary team are the true crash causes, then the police assessments, with two notable exceptions that are easy to assess – failure to yield right of way, and going through a stop sign – were very deficient. A frequent crash-related violation that is easy to document such as failure to yield right of way, is easy for the police to assess, but a less frequent cause, that is difficult to assess on the basis of objective evidence, such as fatigue, is very difficult for the police to assess. The adequacy of the police assessments relative to those of the Tri-Level study team for the "easy" to assess cause of failure to yield right-of-way and the difficult to assess cause of fatigue are provided in Table 18-3. As can be seen from this table, even though "fatigue" was a coded category on the police accident report it was cited in only one crash, and in that one case the Tri-Level team did not believe that fatigue was a causal factor.

It is important to note, that the tri-level team did not consider "failure to yield" a crash cause, but just a behavioral descriptor of the event immediately preceding the crash. The actual cause of failure to yield could have been an attention error, a decision error of misjudgment of time and distance, a performance error, or possibly an environmental view obstruction, or a vehicular failure. In any case, this frequent behavior was noted "correctly" (meaning in agreement with the Tri-Level team) by the police in a total of 198 of the 207 cases, or 95.7 percent of the cases (when it was present as well as when it was absent). Superficially, the results seem just as good for the identification of fatigue, where the agreement was in 98.6 percent of the cases. However, the ability of the police to detect fatigue when it was present (their sensitivity) was zero. In the two cases when the Tri-Level team identified fatigue as a cause the police failed to notice it. For this reason, the two measures of association listed below the % agreements – the Phi Coefficient and

Table 18-3. Probability of police assessment given the Tri-Level study assessment of fatigue and failure to yield right of way (numbers in parenthesis indicate number of cases) (adapted from Shinar *et al.*, 1983, with permission from Elsevier).

Police Cause Assessment	**Tri-Level Cause Assessment**					
	Fatigue			**Failure to yield right of way**		
	Present	**Absent**	**Total**	**Present**	**Absent**	**Total**
Present	0.0 (0)	0.005 (1)	(1)	0.97 (32)	0.05 (8)	(40)
Absent	1.0 (2)	0.995 (204)	(206)	0.03 (1)	0.95 (166)	(167)
Total	(2)	(205)	(207)	(33)	(174)	(207)
% Agreements	98.6			95.7		
Phi coefficient	0.007			0.86		
Contingency coeff.	0.007			0.65		

the Contingency Coefficient – are much better indicators of the police performance relative to the Tri-Level assessments. Similar results were obtained for other infrequent causes such as all vehicle causes, all environmental causes, and the human causes of driving too fast for conditions, and driving left of center (on a road without a marked median). The failures in human information processing – the most frequently cited causes by the Tri-Level team – were not even considered by the police, and so by default their sensitivity to these factors was zero (as quantified by the Phi and the contingency coefficients). In sum, this detailed comparison of police reports against in-depth analyses by professional crash investigation teams underscores the danger in using the police data as an alternative to more objective in-depth investigations that are not guided by the search for legal culpability.

An interesting distinction in this context was made by Reason *et al.* (1990) who argued that true traffic law violations are conscious deviations from normative behavior as coded in the traffic laws. In contrast, many police-coded violations are in fact unintentional acts, lapses in attention, or erroneous decisions. Using a questionnaire that they developed for the purpose of distinguishing between the two types of behaviors – the DBQ – Reason *et al.* demonstrated that violations, not errors, are associated with accident involvement. Thus, young drivers who are inclined to speed exemplify the assertion that intentional deviations from normative behavior are a major explanation for increased accident-involvement (see also Chapter 9). The distinction also defines the limits of law enforcement for traffic safety. Crashes due to errors cannot be eliminated by increased enforcement, and even total (unrealistic) enforcement that would eliminate all traffic law violations will not eliminate all human-caused crashes.

The Statistical/Epidemiological Approach to Crash Causation

The clinical approach is a theory-based approach. All of the studies cited above in the context of the clinical approach assumed that the highway traffic system can be considered as a closed-loop system in which the driver is the primary information processor, responding to inputs from the changing environment and controlling the vehicle in response. But is that enough? Is it possible that failures of attention are just a convenient theoretical concept that really has no relation to crashes?

To address that weakness of the clinical approach we go to the other extreme and look for theory-free "logical relationships" and "over involvement." The derivation of causality from logical relationships was formalized by the British philosopher John Stuart Mill, in his 1843 book *A System of Logic*. In it he proposed a set of five methods – or logical contingencies – that can enable us to draw conclusions about cause and effect. The first two methods, the "method of agreement" and "method of difference," specify the necessary and sufficient conditions for a causal relationship. Briefly stated, the method of agreement states that if a single common factor (e.g., alcohol intoxication) exists in all cases where a phenomenon occurs (e.g., crash), then we can attribute the phenomenon to that factor. This is a necessary condition. The method of difference states that if one set of circumstances (e.g., alcohol intoxication) leads to a given phenomenon (e.g., crashing vehicles) and another set of circumstances (e.g., driving sober) does not (e.g., non-crashing vehicles), and the sets differ only in a single factor (alcohol intoxication) that is present in the first set and not in the second set, then the phenomenon (crash) can be attributed to that factor. When both contingencies are satisfied, we get Mill's third method: "joint method of agreement and difference"; and we have the necessary and sufficient conditions to argue for causality.

The problem with Mill's argument is that our proof is based purely on induction – an extrapolation to the future on the basis of past events. Already a century before Mill presented his principles of causation, the Scottish philosopher David Hume, in his 1748 book *An Inquiry Concerning Human Understanding*, argued that while we cannot deny the concept of causation, we could never prove it sufficiently. This is because basing causation on induction, assumes that the future will resemble the past. This is something for which we have no proof. Inductions, as opposed to deductions, can only predict probability, but can never prove the thing they purport to prove. For example, in the absence of a theory to account for the planetary movements, just because the sun rose yesterday morning and two days ago and every morning for the past 2000 years, does not mean, necessarily, that it will rise tomorrow. In fact, absent the theory of planetary movements, an eclipse of the sun is a great surprise! The situation is even murkier if we now switch to human behavior and driving. Just because a drunk had a crash the last three times he or she stepped outside the bar, does not assure us that the same thing will happen the next time.

So we must resort to the epidemiological approach with statistical probabilities when we discuss causation. The epidemiological approach to crash causation builds on Mill's methods, but instead of requiring that the conditions be either totally absent or totally present in a particular set of data, we only look for over-presence or under-presence in our data. The data in this case are composed of two different data sets. One data set is the crash files, typically from the police reports, and the other one – used to provide "exposure" data – is from a non-crash file. The exposure data file should contain the frequencies of different potential crash "causes" in the "normal" or "relevant" driving population. Using the two data bases the basic argument behind an assessment of a cause is then as follows. If a particular behavior or phenomenon (e.g., speeding) is noted in the crash file at a certain frequency, and the frequency of the same behavior (speeding) can be obtained from the exposure file of the behavior of all drivers – driving the same roads at the same times as the drivers in the crash file – then all we have to do is compare the two frequencies. If the behavior is more common in the crash data file, we conclude that this behavior is associated with a *high risk* of crash involvement. If the frequencies in the two files are not statistically different from each other, then we cannot state that it is associated with a higher risk. If the behavior is actually more frequent in the exposure data file, then we can conclude that it actually suppresses the risk of a crash. A prime example of the application of this method is the relationship between crash risk and drivers' blood alcohol concentrations (see Chapter 11).

The distinction between association and causation is not a simple one. Even with all the safeguards proposed by Mill, a relationship between two variables (e.g., speeding and crashes) may reflect nothing more than a spurious or chance association, or the joint influence of a third variable on both. For this reason the epidemiological approach can reveal an increased risk but not necessarily a cause. For example, epidemiological analyses of crash data relative to population driving data invariably reveal that young novice drivers are over-involved in crashes (see Chapter 6). Yet, it is unlikely that there is something magical about the numbers 16-20, a defining characteristic age of most novice drivers. Thus, we look for underlying variables that could account for the over-involvement of 16-20 years old drivers in crashes. Two obvious candidates are "lack of maturity" and "inexperience." However, it is not easy to determine the contribution of each factor because age and driving experience typically co-vary, meaning that they generally increase in parallel. Still, careful statistical analyses that have controlled the effects of both have shown that both factors are involved (see Chapter 6).

In the context of medical causation, Sir Austin Bradford Hill, suggested in 1965 that to imply causation from the observation of association we should consider its (1) strength, (2) consistency, (3) specificity – the restriction to specific conditions, (4) temporality – the order of events, (5) dose-response relationship, (6) theoretical plausibility, and (7) coherence – the consistency with other related phenomena. Although these guidelines were presented in the context of medicine and epidemiology, it would be very useful to keep these necessary conditions for causality in mind when evaluating crash causation on the basis of statistical associations. Note also that the 6th principle invokes "theory."

Thus, whereas in theory-based clinical analyses we can feel comfortable in using the term "cause," in the context of epidemiological analysis it is more prudent to use the term risk. Only when Hill's (1965) sixth condition of "theoretical plausibility" is fulfilled we can use the term cause. Without the theoretical basis all we have is a statistical relationship, and not a true causal relationship. To determine a causal relationship between the two measures (e.g., crash involvement and speed) we need to rely on a theoretical framework that would describe how and why increasing speed should "cause" more crashes. The statistical approach would then serve to either validate the theory or invalidate it. But without the theory we have no basis for such a claim.

Using speed as a crash cause example was not done by chance. I picked it because speed is one behavior or human factor that can be (relatively easily) observed both in crash data and in traffic flow data. Environmental and vehicle factors can also be obtained in both types of data and are prime candidates for evaluation via the statistical approach. Other measures are more difficult. For example, alcohol involvement in crashes can be assessed if alcohol levels are obtained from the crash-involved drivers (not too difficult to do) and from the general traffic population (much more difficult since it requires random stopping of drivers to check for their alcohol levels – even if they did not commit any traffic violation). Still other behaviors are practically impossible to evaluate statistically. Unfortunately, the behaviors that fall into this category are the most frequent ones to emerge in the clinical evaluations: attentional, perceptual, and decision failures. They are difficult to ascertain in the crash data (and are typically absent in police crash reports), and almost impossible to determine from the traffic population data (for a rare exception see the discussion on distraction in Chapter 13).

Crash causes derived from epidemiological studies

With these limitations in mind, we can consider the role of various factors for which there is some theoretical basis to support their over involvement. The epidemiological approach, because it typically relies on existing data bases, does not account for all crash causes, or all factors that can account for all the crashes in a given data base. Instead, it seeks to determine the increased risk associated with specific variables. Thus, statistical crash risk analyses have demonstrated the contribution of inexperience and young age to increase in crash risk (Chapter 6), the increased risk of older drivers (relative to some exposure measures – Chapter 7), the increased crash risk of alcohol and some drugs (Chapters 10 and 11, respectively), the increased crash risk from distraction and fatigue (Chapters 13 and 14, respectively), and the reduced crash risk in bicycling due to safety-in-numbers (Chapter 17).

Because the epidemiological approach – or at least the statistical analysis that it involves – is theory-free it is prone to many misinterpretations. This can best be illustrated with the findings of a study that evaluated the increased crash risk due to a specific color of a car. In other words, does the color of a car affect the likelihood of its getting involved in a crash? Furness and his associates (2003) addressed that question by examining the data for 567 crash-involved vehicles in the Auckland region of New Zealand in which at least one of the occupants was either severely injured or killed. They compared the frequencies of different car colors in the crash sample to the frequencies of different car colors in an exposure sample of 588 vehicles traveling on the roads in the same region. The results of their analyses are summarized in Table 18-4.

Table 18-4. The association of car color with crash injury in Auckland, New Zealand (from Furness *et al.* 2003, with permission from BMJ Publishing Group Ltd.).

Car Color	No (%) of Cases (n = 567)	No (%) of Controls* (n = 588)	Univariate Odds Ratio	Multivariable Odds Ratio†
White	145 (25.6)	146 (25.9)	1	1
Yellow	31 (5.5)	15 (2.8)	2.0 (1.0 to 4.0)	0.8 (0.3 to 2.3)
Gray	52 (9.2)	61(10.0)	0.9 (0.6 to 1.5)	0.6 (0.3 to 1.3)
Black	36 (6.4)	34 (5.5)	1.2 (0.7 to 2.0)	2.0 (1.0 to 4.2)
Blue	91 (16.1)	96 (17.4)	0.9 (0.6 to 1.4)	0.9 (0.5 to 1.6)
Red	85 (15.0)	82 (13.3)	1.1 (0.7 to 1.8)	0.7 (0.4 to 1.4)
Green	42 (7.4)	44 (7.0)	1.1 (0.6 to 1.8)	1.8 (1.0 to 3.6)
Brown	55 (9.7)	49 (6.8)	1.4 (0.8 to 2.5)	2.1 (1.1 to 4.2)
Silver	30 (5.3)	61 (11.3)	0.5 (0.3 to 0.8)	0.4 (0.2 to 0.9)
P value			0.04	0.003

*Proportions of controls are adjusted for the cluster sampling design.
†Adjusted for driver's age, ethnicity, alcohol consumption in past 6 hours, seat belt use, vehicle speed, average driving time each week, driving license status, vehicle insurance status, and weather.

From the numbers in the second column of that table we can see that white cars were involved in more crashes than any other cars. Of course this does not mean that the color white increases the likelihood of a crash. To determine the risk involved in driving a white car, we have to compare the prevalence of each color in the crash-involved vehicles with the prevalence of each of the colors in the control/exposure population. The third column shows the prevalence of each color in the control population, and as might have been expected in that group too white is the predominant color. If we now examine the ratio of the two percentages or odds, we obtain the "odds ratio" in the fourth column. We then discover that white colored cars are neither over- nor under-involved in crashes. In fact, the ratio is almost exactly 1.0 (0.99), and therefore we conclude that having a white colored car does not increase the risk of a crash. However, the data in the same column indicate that yellow cars are associated with twice as many crashes as would be expected from their frequency on the road (Odds ratio = 2.0), and silver colored cars are half as likely to get involved in a crash relative to their prevalence on the Auckland roads.

We could stop there and try to explain these results, but we would immediately realize that there are many other variables that may be confounded (see Chapter 2) with the vehicle color. For example it is possible that young drivers are more likely to pick yellow colors and older drivers are more likely to pick silver colors; and these two groups have very different driving patterns and crash risks. We could also speculate that drivers of yellow cars tend to drive faster, be less likely to use seat belts, be more likely to drink-and-drive, and drive under different weather and lighting conditions than drivers of silver cars. To rule out these potential confounding effects, Furness and his associates (2003) did a multivariate analysis that statistically controlled for all of these factors. After taking into account all of these additional factors in the crash and driving populations the resulting odds ratios (listed in the right-most column) were quite different.

It now appears that yellow cars are neither under- or over-involved in crashes, but black, green, and brown cars are over-involved in crashes. Silver cars remain the only ones under-involved. However, there are still other potentially confounding variables. For example, is it possible that silver cars are driven mostly by woman (who are less involved in crashes than males)? Perhaps silver is a more popular color than black in recent cars, and therefore silver cars tend to be newer and safer? These kinds of arguments can go on ad-infinitum. Instead we could stop here – as Furness *et al.* (2003) did – and try to account for this effect. One intuitively appealing explanation would be that green, brown, and black cars are less conspicuous on the road (especially at night because of their low contrast against the dark sky), and hence their over-involvement in crashes. This is an appealing argument because there are many studies that demonstrate the importance of conspicuity and visibility for traffic safety. However, this is a post-factum explanation. To validate this explanation we would want to add two other variables to the list of factors already controlled for: time of crash (daytime versus nighttime) and type of collision (vehicle being hit versus vehicle hitting another vehicle or an obstacle). If these additional analyses were done, and the results would remain unchanged, then we could actually state with some moderate confidence, that dark-colored cars are more likely to be struck at night than light colored vehicles because of their low conspicuity. Unfortunately, Furness *et al.* did not conduct this analysis, and in their concluding remarks they appropriately wrote that "the possibility of residual confounding remains. The extent to which these results can be generalized to other settings is open to question" (p. 1456).

At a macro level, the epidemiological approach has also been used to link traffic safety with economic welfare. In a landmark study published in 1984, Partyka studied the relationship between U.S. traffic fatalities and three economic indicators of employment: the number of employed, unemployed, and people not in the labor force per 1,000 in the population. She found a near-perfect correspondence between these indicators and the number of fatalities for the 23-year period, 1960-1982; $r^2 = .89$, and $r^2 = 0.98$ when the oil embargo year (October 1973-March 1974) was added as a dummy variable. If this exceptional relationship is causal then the way to improve safety is to create unemployment! However, it is not difficult to conjecture some causal variables behind this relationship. Economic recession is associated with reduced leisure travel, commuting by public transport instead of the private car, driving less when not having to commute to work, reducing social nighttime activities associated with DWI, etc. Partyka, however, was careful not to make such claims, and stated that the "model describes the observed coinciding of changes among variables, but does not of itself imply cause and effect." Furthermore, she warned that "predictions are especially tenuous when based upon data beyond the range of the historical experience used to create the model." Indeed, when she attempted to validate the model seven years later (Partyka, 1991), the near-perfect relationship practically evaporated, as can be seen in Figure 18-10. Two factors that probably account for much of the discrepancy between the model and the actual much lower number of fatalities in 1983-1989 were the new behavioral norms of using seat belts and the decreasing number of DWI drivers.

Partyka's much cited studies provide a stellar case against causal assessments based on strictly correlational data. Nonetheless, relative to the specific relationship between economic welfare and traffic fatalities, other more recent studies suggest that indeed there is such a relationship, albeit not as strong as originally claimed by Partyka. Consequently the claim made by the OECD International Transport Form that "there is clear evidence that when economic growth declines, and particularly when unemployment increases, road safety improves" (OECD, 2015) is probably not warranted. In the developed world, since the 2008 recession the economy has recovered greatly and fortunately traffic fatalities have continued to decrease in most countries.

In conclusion, causality based on epidemiological associations is quite tenuous unless the associations tested (1) stem from a valid theory and (2) can be cross-validated on a different data set.

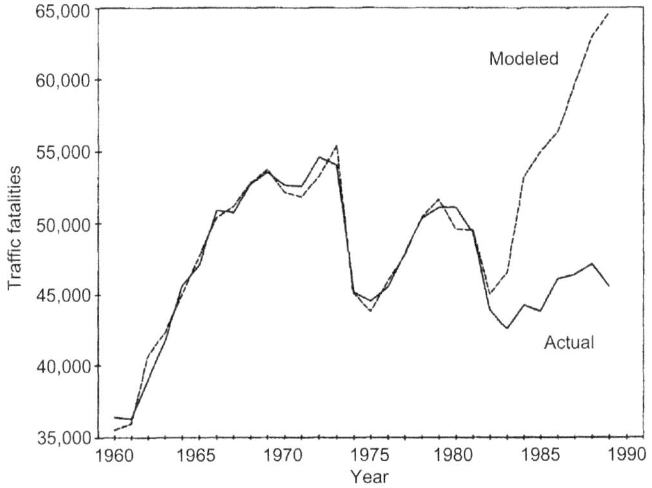

Figure 18-10. Actual number of U.S. traffic fatalities in the years 1960-1989, and the predicted model based on economic employment statistics (from Partyka, 1991, with permission from Elsevier).

The Naturalistic Driving Study (NDS) Approach: Prospective In-Vehicle Monitoring

A significant shortcoming of the clinical and the statistical approaches is that they are both based on retrospective data. All the information about events and behaviors that preceded the crash is collected or reconstructed after the crash has occurred and distortions, fading of events, conditions, and memory loss of these situations and behaviors have begun. This no longer has to be the case in all investigations. In the past two decades there has been a proliferation of various monitoring and recording devices that can be added to the infrastructure and the vehicles. Vehicles are now factory-equipped with online event data recorders (EDRs) that can record vehicle speed, acceleration, steering control movements, brake activation, and location (with a GPS). Typically, they record the last few seconds over and over, and in case of a crash, they stop and retain the data recorded in the final few seconds. This information can then be retrieved and analyzed to gain insights into the pre-crash vehicle and driver behaviors. In the case of a crash, for example, the impact speed derived from these EDRs appears to be just as accurate as a measure of crash severity as mathematically more complicated measures that are calculated post hoc (Gabauer and Gabler, 2008). This method of data collection, when it is retrieved from the drivers' normal driving activity is labeled "naturalistic," and studies based on such data are known as naturalistic driving studies (NDSs). For the purpose of in-depth crash investigations, the EDRs provide objective data that can be supplemented with in-vehicle video cameras that can record the environment and traffic around the vehicles, as well as drivers' head movements, eye movements, and manual activities. Finally, all of these data elements can be integrated and related to drivers' post-crash verbal reports. Together these data provide a complete crash reconstruction that is much more valid than previously available.

The NDS has one other advantage over the post hoc clinical approach. Like the epidemiological approach, the NDS can also provide us with exposure data – or the frequency of the various driver, environmental, and vehicular failures in non-crash control situations. Despite the high cost of such studies, they are proliferating worldwide. Some NDSs have been reviewed above in the context of crash causes involving vulnerable road users. The sections below focus on the evolvement of NDS, and crash causation findings that have emerged from them.

The U.S. "100-Car" study

The first large-scale attempt to use NDS to gain insight into naturalistic driver behavior and crash causation was initiated by the U.S. National Highway Traffic Safety Administration in the beginning of this century (Dingus *et al.*, 2006; Klauer *et al.*, 2006; Neale *et al.*, 2005). In this study 100 privately owned or leased cars were instrumented to record the driver activation of the pedals and steering, the vehicle lateral and longitudinal kinematics, headways to the car ahead and gaps from the cars behind the drivers. The cars were also equipped with a side obstacle detection system and a five-camera video system that recorded the vehicle environment as well as the driver's face and behavior. In the course of the study the researchers obtained nearly 43,000 hours of data from approximately two million miles of driving. Over this time and distance the 100 cars were involved in 69 crashes, 761 near-crashes, and 8,296 incidents. A crash was defined as any contact between the study vehicle and another vehicle, pedestrian, bicyclist, animal, or fixed object. A near-crash was a conflict that required a severe evasive maneuver to avoid a crash and an incident was defined as a conflict requiring an evasive action but "of a lesser magnitude" than a near-crash. Obviously, the definitions of the near-crash and the incident are subjective, but the data patterns for near-crashes and crashes seemed to be similar (Guo *et al.*, 2010).

As just stated, over the course of the two million miles of travels there were a total of only 69 crashes in the study, good news for safety but tough for data analysis. Of these, 35 percent were single vehicle crashes, 22 percent were collisions with a vehicle ahead, 17 percent were rear-end collisions, 13 percent were with a fixed object, and the remaining 13 percent of the crashes were with a parked vehicle, an animal, a vehicle turning in front of the car, or a vehicle in the adjacent lane. These situations also accounted for 87 percent of the near-crashes and 93 percent of the conflicts. Because actual crashes were quite few, most analyses also included the 761 near-crashes and 8,296 incidents observed in the data (Neale *et al.*, 2005).

Given the implication of driver inattention as a major human crash cause in clinical in-depth analyses, and the recent demonstration of the crash risk from cell-phone-related inattention (see Chapter 13), an interesting challenge in the 100-car study was to extract information on the causal roles of inattention and distraction from these data without resorting to the drivers' subjective reports. To this end the drivers' visual gazes were studied from the video images of the drivers' faces. The researchers considered four categories that constituted inattention: manifest fatigue, secondary task distraction (e.g., talking on the cell phone), driving-related inattention to the forward roadway scene at a critical time (e.g., looking at the mirrors), and non-specific eye glances (away from the road, but not towards a specific identifiable object). Together, these four types of inattention accounted for 78 percent of the crashes and 65 percent of the near-crashes. However, such episodes of inattention were also present in 73 percent of all randomly selected 6-second exposures of non-event driving that were used as baseline control data. Thus, while the crash data revealed that inattention was involved in most crashes, based on the exposure data, inattention was not over-involved in crashes or near-crashes, and it did not significantly increase the risk of a crash. The specific distributions of secondary task distractions, driving-related distractions, and manifest drowsiness in the three types of events – crashes, near-crashes, and baseline control epochs – are presented in Figure 18-11.

As can be seen from this figure, distractions from a secondary task were the most common type of inattention that caused crashes and near-crashes, but – and this is very important from an epidemiological perspective – they were just as frequent in the baseline epochs as in the crashes. Driving-related distractions were also just as frequent in the baseline epochs as in the crashes. Only drowsiness was significantly more frequent in the crash and near-crash events than in the baseline epochs, indicating that fatigue as

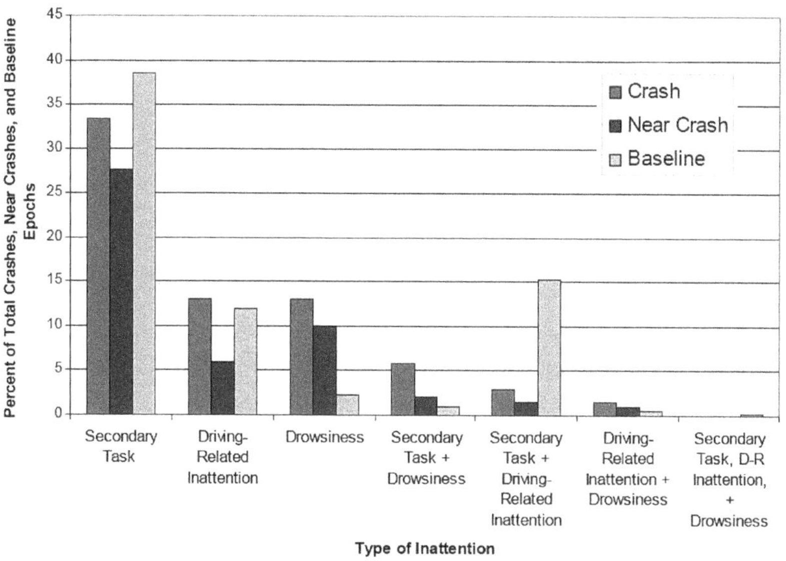

Figure 18-11. The percent of crashes and near-crashes in which three types of inattention were identified as a contributing factor in the 100-car study (N = 69 crashes, 761 near-crashes, and 19,827 baseline epochs) (from Klauer *et al.*, 2006).

measured by overt behavior does increase the crash and near-crash risk, approximately sixfold in the present study. These results reinforce several conclusions reached by prior studies. First, constant attention to the roadway is not normal behavior. Lapses in attention are very common – occurring in nearly 40 percent of the 6-second randomly selected driving episodes in the 100-car study. Second, drivers learn to time-share their attention to the roadway ahead with both driving-related tasks and non-driving tasks, so that the frequencies of these events are not greater in the crash and near-crash data than in the exposure data. Third, fatigue-induced inattention that is easy to observe from video is over-represented in crashes and near-crashes. In the present study it was judged to be a causal factor in over 12 percent of the crashes and near-crashes, but it was observed in the exposure data in less than three percent of the epochs.

Non-driving secondary task distractions are of particular interest because they can only have a negative effect on driving safety. Therefore it is important to note the relative danger of various types of such distractions. In the 100-car study by far the most frequent distraction was from a "wireless device" – a type of distraction that did not exist at the time of the Tri-Level and British studies, and was still a rarity at the time of the Hendricks *et al.* study at the end of the 20th century. However, in this study it was implicated in nearly 50 percent of all the distraction cases, mostly in near-crashes and incidents. Still, out of all crashes, distraction from a cell phone was implicated in only six crashes (9 percent); and in all of them it was while the driver was talking or listening, and not while engaged in dialing or otherwise manipulating information. In contrast, listening and talking on the phone was responsible for approximately 70 percent of all incidents. Such a discrepancy raises the issue of whether incidents are appropriate surrogates of crashes and whether the two can be combined into a single data base.

As noted above, the 100-car study, despite its many hours of recorded data only yielded 69 crashes. This makes it a very small crash causation study. Furthermore, even the 69 crashes documented in the study were not representative of crashes in police-reported files. Thus, a contact between a vehicle backing up in a parking space until it touched with the vehicle behind it would not be considered an "accident" by most drivers, would not be included in a police crash report, but did qualify as a crash in this study. On many occasions such an "accident" would not even qualify as an unexpected event, because in small parking spaces drivers often maximize their maneuvering space by making contact with the adjacent vehicles on purpose. Indeed, in the 100-car study most of the crashes were of very low impact and only 12 were sufficiently severe to be reported to the police. Consequently, the 100 car study should be viewed as a demonstration of proof-of-concept, rather than as a definitive crash causation study. Accepting this, the U.S. Congress agreed to fund a much larger (and much more costly) study, known as the SHRP2 NDS.

The U.S. SHRP2 naturalistic driving study

To be more useful as a crash causation study, a NDS with instrumented vehicles should involve significantly more vehicles, include more and a greater variety of driving situations, and – most importantly – combine the strength of the objective data from the naturalistic approach with the more detailed insights about causality itself that can still be obtained only from interviews with the drivers. A most significant step in this direction was taken by the U.S. Transportation Research Board in its second Strategic Highway Research Plan (SHRP2) (TRB, 2006).

In this ambitious SHRP2 study to obtain a significant number of crashes, continuous driving data were collected on an unprecedented scale. The study involved 3,147 drivers, from six different geographic locations in the continental U.S., who drove their own cars (3,370 mostly passenger cars, 2,000+ model years) for 12-24 months, for a total of approximately 80 million(!) kilometers (50 million miles), generating approximately five million trip files. Despite its huge exposure the study yielded a total of approximately 1,500 crashes, of which only 154 were severe enough to be "police reportable." Of the remaining crashes, 591 were "minor crashes," and 617 were "low risk tire strike." Installation of the data acquisition systems in the cars began in October 2010 and data collection ended in November 2013, yielding a total of 46,866 data months or 3,905 data years (Blatt *et al.*, 2015). In a parallel, data collection effort a Roadway Information Database (RID) study recorded slightly over 40,000 roadway kilometers in the same geographic areas. Thus, for assessment of crash causation each crash had detailed objective data on the behavior of the driver and the vehicle as well as on the roadway environment. For a better understanding of the digital data, the driver was also continuously monitored by four video cameras that recorded the scene ahead of the car, the driver's head, the dashboard and controls, and the scene behind the car. These video clips were then presented on a single screen so that data analysts could simultaneously consider all the information. An illustration of the combined video images is provided in Figure 2-6 (Chapter 2).

Although a comprehensive crash causation analyses using the complete data base of the SHRP2 NDS has not yet been made, the study has already yielded multiple technical reports on topics such driver inattention and visual search, the characteristics of roadway departures on curves, the effects of offset left-turn lanes, and more (SHRP2, 2015). The most recent SHRP2 NDS report that has been published to date is based on the analysis of 905 injury and property damage crashes (Dingus *et al.*, 2016). In this respect, this is the largest NDS-based crash causation analysis that relies solely on actual crashes of significant damage and injuries. The analysis of these crashes revealed that a human failure was involved in 87.7 percent of the crashes. Most of the failures – 74 percent – were due to driver performance or judgment errors. Sixty-eight percent of the crashes involved an observable distraction, and only six percent involved impairment. The total exceeds 100 percent for the simple reason, that as in the Tri-Level study many crashes involved more than one factor. The most common crash scenario involved an unimpaired driver, being distracted and committing an error (51 percent).

Comparing these data to those of the Tri-Level study 40 years earlier, one can only conclude that the more things change, the more they stay the same. The overwhelming majority of crashes involve a human cause/factor and in nearly all cases the driver is not observably impaired. It is important to note that impairment in the NDS was actually a subset of the impairments included in the Tri-Level study (that also included unfamiliarity with the vehicle or road, inexperience, pressure from other drivers, being in a hurry, and impaired vision). When as in the NDS only alcohol/drug impairment, drowsiness/ fatigue, and emotional upset are considered, the Tri-Level study has only 8.1 percent; quite similar to the NDS six percent. But there are differences between the two studies in the relative frequencies of distraction and judgment/performance errors. However, they are probably due to differences in the definitions and the methodology as much as they may be due to actual shifts in driving behavior and failures. For example, the highest risk "error" is failing to yield right-of-way. In the Tri-Level study this type of behavior would most often be considered as a recognition error associated with general inattention, improper lookout, or look-but-did-not-see.

Proceeding to more specific categories of crash causes, Dingus *et al* provide the odds ratios for the various categories that make up the three more general types of human failures. At this level of the more detailed analysis it is impossible to compare the results of the Tri-Level study with those of the NDS because the former did not have exposure data to calculate risk. The NDS odds ratios are presented in Table 18-5 along the prevalence in driving of the different specific failures. Without going into a discussion of each of type of impairment, error, or distraction, several general conclusions are worth mentioning. First, and fortunately, the prevalence of most of the failures in the general driving is quite low: from less than one tenth of one percent (for apparent inexperience with the vehicle or roadway, reading from a tablet, blind spot, right-of-way error, sudden/ improper braking, unsafe speeding in work zones, following too closely) to 1-2 percent.

Table 18-5. The odds ratios and baseline prevalence of specific observable driver impairments, performance errors, momentary judgment errors, and observable distractions in the SHRP2 NDS (from Dingus *et al.*, 2016).

	O.R. (95% CI)	**Baseline Prevalence**
*Observable impairment**		
Overall	5.2 (3.8-7.1)	1.92%
Drug/alcohol	35.9 (17.0-75.8)	0.08%
Drowsiness/fatigue	3.4 (2.3-5.1)	1.57%
Emotion (anger, sadness, crying, and/or emotional agitation)	9.8 (5.0-19.0)	0.22%
Driver performance error		
Overall	18.2 (14.8-22.3)	4.81%
Major error sub-categories (observed in crash and baseline events)		
Apparent inexperience with vehicle/roadway	204.5 (111.1-376.6)	0.07%
Blind spot error	55.1 (21.6-140.6)	0.05%
Improper turn	92.1 (68.8-123.4)	0.51%
Right-of-way error	936.1 (123.8-7078.3)	0.01%
Signal violation	28.3 (15.9-50.2)	0.19%
Stop/yield sign violation	7.4 (4.9-11.4)	1.05%
Wrong side of road	22.3 (12.0-41.5)	0.19%
Driving too slowly	2.3 (1.1-4.8)	0.97%
Sudden or improper braking/stopping	247.8 (53.1-1156.2)	0.01%
Failed to signal	2.5 (1.5-4.0)	2.27%
Driver momentary judgment error (speeding/aggressive driving)		
Overall Aggressive driving (general observed behavior)	11.1 (9.0-13.8) 34.8 (17.2-70.5)	4.22% 0.10%
Speeding (over limit and too fast for conditions	12.8 (10.1-16.2)	2.77%
Speeding/unsafe in work zone	14.2 (3.9-52.0)	0.05%
Illegal/Unsafe passing	14.4 (7.2-28.8)	0.18%

Table 18-5. (*Continued*)

	O.R. (95% CI)	**Baseline Prevalence**
Following too closely	13.5 (4.4-41.4)	0.07%
Intentional signal violation	15.3 (7.9-29.9)	0.19%
Intentional stop/yield sign violation	5.3 (3.4-8.4)	1.04%
*Observable distraction***		
Overall	2.0 (1.8-2.4)	51.93%
Major distraction sub-categories (observed in crash and baseline events)		
In-vehicle radio	1.9 (1.2-3.0)	2.21%
In-vehicle climate control	2.3 (1.1-5.0)	0.56%
In-vehicle device (other)	4.6 (2.9-7.4)	0.83%
Total in-vehicle device	2.5 (1.8-3.4)	3.53%
Cell browse	2.7(1.5-5.1)	0.73%
Cell dial (handheld)	12.2 (5.6-26.4)	0.14%
Cell reach	4.8 (2.7-8.4)	0.58%
Cell text(handheld)	6.1 (4.5-8.2)	1.91%
Cell talk (handheld)	2.2 (1.6-3.1)	3.24%
Total cell (handheld)	3.6 (2.9-4.5)	6.40%
Child rear seat	0.5 (0.1-1.9)	0.80%
Interaction with adult/teen passenger	1.4 (1.1-1.8)	14.58%
Reading/writing (includes tablet)	9.9 (3.6-26.9)	0.09%
Eating	1.8 (1.1-2.9)	1.90%
Drinking (non-alcohol)	1.8 (1.0-3.3)	1.22%
Personal hygiene	1.4 (0.8-2.5)	1.69%
Reaching for object (non-cell phone)	9.1 (6.5-12.6)	1.08%
Dancing in seat to music	1.0 (0.4-2.3)	1.10%
Extended glance duration to external object	7.1 (4.8-10.4)	0.93%

*Observable from 20-second pre-crash and baseline sample video segments.

**Observable from 6-second pre-crash and baseline sample video segments.

Exceptions – with high prevalence are two sources of distraction: using a cell phone (6.4 percent) and interacting with a passenger (14.6 percent). Second, the statistically-significant failures are associated with a wide range of odds ratios: from less than 2 (e.g., being distracted by eating, listening to the radio or by grooming) to over 100 (performance errors like being inexperienced with the vehicle or the road, failing to yield right-of-way, and sudden or improper braking). Third, the odds ratios and the prevalence levels are unrelated, indicating that while some behaviors are very dangerous with high odds ratios, they are quite rare in normal driving. Examples are use of alcohol/drugs, inexperience, blind spot error, failure to yield right-of-way, and sudden or improper braking. On the other hand, some failures – like interacting with a passenger – may have a low odds ratio, constituting a relatively low risk, but they are relatively common and therefore likely to be implicated in more crashes. Fourth, distraction – a crash cause that has received much more public, media, and research attention than any other potential crash cause in this decade – is definitely a significant crash cause, with an overall OR = 2.0. However, this risk level is based on an average that includes some fairly low risk activities such as eating, drinking, engaging in personal hygiene, and listening to the radio. Finally, it is interesting to note some similarities between the subjective opinions of road users, as reflected in the SARTRE study quoted above and the technologically based conclusions of the NDS. Fatigue and the use of drugs/alcohol are two examples. The risk perceptions of both are high in both studies, but the NDS provides a true and very different level of their actual prevalence.

Within the general class of distractions, the detailed, accurate, and high-sampling rate of data obtained from the video recordings of the NDS also enable fine distinctions among the risks of the various cell-phone activities. In general a handheld phone is riskier than a hands-free phone. But this is not due to holding it while talking (OR = 2.2). It is because of the other phone-related activities that involve visual distraction, or looking away from the road. These include dialing (OR = 12.2) texting (OR = 6.1) and reaching for the phone (OR = 4.8). A much more detailed discussion on the effects of cell phones on crash involvement, using the SHRP2 NDS data, is provided by Victor *et al.* (2015) but their analysis is based on a very partial set of the NDS data consisting of only 46 crashes (and 211 near-crash events), and 257 matched baseline events. Even though the number of crashes was 1/20th of the number in Dingus *et al.*'s analysis, and even though they mixed crashes with near-crashes, they arrived at similar conclusions that texting and handling the phone are risky, while talking and listening are not. (For a detailed discussion on the effects of distraction on driving and crashes see Chapter 13).

The SHRP2 NDS 2-petabyes of data should provide many more – and hopefully more insightful – conclusions concerning crash causation. The stated hope and expectation is that this large dataset will be a most useful tool for understanding driver behavior and its implications for safety improvements for at least 20 years. This is a questionable expectation given the advances in driver assistance technologies (see Chapter 19), their absence in most of the vehicles tracked in the SHRP2 NDS, and the rapid development and dissemination of multiple crash avoidance technologies that are leading us into the autonomous vehicles era.

In the wake of the SHRP2 NDS, other countries have also initiated similar NDSs. The largest current NDS is the European Union project UDRIVE (European naturalistic Driving and Riding for Infrastructure & Vehicle safety and Environment) (EU, 2016). This project involves 19 organizations from 14 different countries. Though this project is collecting data on a smaller sample of drivers, it also includes trucks and scooters, and examines pedestrian and bicyclists safety too. Other studies are underway in Australia, Japan, and Canada. The Canadian study is using the exact protocol of the SHRP2 NDS, so that eventually its data will be added to the SHRP2 data to constitute an even larger database for North America.

Though the NDS is presented as the gold standard for objective ecologically valid data, the use of this data is not straightforward. In calculating the crash risk from different activities or events, the exact definition of the activity (the numerator in the odds ratio) and the definition of the control sample (for the denominator) are not straightforward. For example, in Dingus et al.'s analysis of the crash risk of various distracting activities, they obtained an OR = 2.2 for talking on the phone. This finding is in stark contrast to the findings of other recent analyses – including NDS – that indicate that the conversation itself is not a significant crash risk. Young (2017) examined the case selection used by Dingus *et al.* (2016) and identified two case-selection biases that spuriously increased the OR: "video clip selection bias" and "driver behavior error bias." The first bias consisted of counting "talk" segments as those when the driver talked on the phone independently of whether or not he or she were engaged in other activities. However, for the non-talk segments, they only counted those in which the driver was not engaged in any distracting activity. The second bias was due to including segments with concomitant high-risk driver behaviors, whose high crash OR should also bias the estimate upward. After controlling for these two factors, the OR for talking on the phone decreased from 2.2 to 0.92; rendering the net action of talking on the phone a no-risk activity. But Young's reanalysis can also be challenged. For example, as he himself pointed out, just like Dingus *et al.* (2016) for the exposure sample he too relied on a stratified random sample of driving events for each driver rather than use a case-control design in which the exposure sample is based on events recorded on same time-of-day/day-of-week/location of event by each driver. What all this means is that while the different results presented by both Dingus *et al.* and by Young are correct, their interpretation differs, and it is the critical reader who has to decide which analysis is more appropriate for the conclusion drawn.

Caveat Emptor: Obvious But Wrong Implications from Studies of Crash Causation

The standard justification for crash causation studies is the "medical model": a cure cannot be discovered before the cause of the illness is identified. From there, it is a short leap of faith to the conclusion that the cure is to kill the agent or the pathogen. This works pretty well in medicine, but it does not in traffic safety (Hauer, 2016). There is no single germ or virus (cause) responsible for all traffic deaths. A traffic crash is the end-result of a host of factors that can be traced to events and actions that occurred a long time before the crash and to events and actions just seconds prior to it; and all of them were operative simultaneously at the time of the crash. Crash causation can identify these factors or individual contributors, but their identification is a function of our diagnostic tools and semantics. This chapter provided multiple examples of how the same objective events can lead to very different – yet equally valid – conclusions of the crash causes.

A tongue-in-cheek illustration of the fallacy of the post-hoc clinical approach was provided by Frank Haight the founder and first editor of the journal Accident Analysis and Prevention (Haight, 1973). Haight conjured a "traffic safety fable" according to which in an attempt to save money on the construction of a bridge, the railing was eliminated, despite some safety-related objections. After a few years' experience it turned out that a significant number of cars drove over the bridge, drowning their occupants. However, a very efficient rescue team was created that managed to quickly mark the locations of the car drownings, thereby enabling their retrievals – though failing to save any lives. Each of these cases was analyzed and the summary statistics indicated that driver errors were responsible for 88 percent of the crashes (the following factors were noted: alcohol, inattention, recklessness, driving too close to the edge, and miscellaneous). Roadway conditions were responsible for seven percent of the crashes (e.g., ice), and vehicle factors for an additional five percent. Because several of the fatalities were small children, this caused significant public indignation to "do something" about these crashes. "Since the problem had been shown statistically to be due primarily to bad driving, and especially the consumption of alcohol, the focus was on drivers." Various recommendations were made including more rigorous police enforcement and more severe punishments for these crash-causing behaviors. Eventually the "responsible authorities" issued a contract for an in-depth investigation of the crashes, utilizing advance mathematical and engineering techniques, and (surprisingly) the research team recommended that a railing be constructed. However, in the wake of another multi-vehicle crash, there was a huge public outcry do something "now," so building a railing was discarded as a solution that would take too much time. Instead a multi-faceted public information media campaign was launched to everyone's relief. Happily, this is a "fairy tale."

The fairy-tail lesson is relevant to many real crash analyses. The analyses often reveal the inappropriate behaviors that immediately preceded the crash and made it inevitable, but they do not necessarily identify the most appropriate countermeasure. This is especially true of infrastructure-based causes. We typically and easily identify a transient recent pothole, a slippery road or a faded STOP sign as infrastructure-based crash causes. But – Gilutz's insight in 1937 (Box 18-1) notwithstanding – we just as frequently fail to consider pre-existing factors such as poor designs (e.g., a bridge without a railing) that do not consider some human failures as an inevitable given. Hauer (2016) illustrates this with an example of the common design used to integrate bicycling and driving. Often the road pavement is marked with the right-most lane as a parking lane, the next one as a bicycle lane, and the left-most lane(s) as driving lane(s). A common consequence of this design is the cyclist being "doored" by a driver exiting a parked car. Linking the countermeasure to the immediate "causal" behaviors (driver inattentiveness or misjudgment that a bicyclist would not travel on his left), the typical regulator's response is to cite the driver for a violation. On the other hand, these types of crashes should have been foreseen and could have been prevented by having the cycling lane next to the curb and the parking lane to the left of it (as it is in some streets in Europe and Israel). This remediation would also protect the cyclist from the cars moving in traffic. In this particular case the standard taxonomy of crash causes – regardless of the study method – simply did not go back far enough in time to cite design failures as crash causes. Crash cause analysis is much more productive when design issues are considered, as was done in Amsterdam in response to drivers driving into the canals. Unlike Haight's fairy tale above these were real serious crashes. But as in Haight's imaginary tale the initial "cures" involved postings of signs along the canals and public media campaigns cautioning the drivers. However, with the Dutch approach of sustainable safety the real design cause was eventually recognized as lack of proper separation between the travel area and the waterway, and barriers were installed along the canal edges – solving the issue completely (F. Wegman, personal communication, 2015).

In summary, once the distinction between causes and countermeasures is recognized, and once the limitations of the definitions of causes is accepted, crash causation analysis can be quite useful. Comprehension of the crash causes in individual situations, or groups of situations, can indicate whether a potential countermeasure (a railing or change in location of a bicycle lane) would eliminate or reduce the effect of a specific cause (by preventing the car from going off the bridge in this case).

Concluding Comments

The attribution of a crash cause – no matter how objective the process – involves a very significant subjective element: either in defining the causal categories (in the clinical approach) or in selecting the variables of study (in the epidemiological approach), or in determining the data that are collected and the coding and reducing of the bits of data into meaningful categories (in the NDS approach). In the most subjective of these approaches – the clinical approach – a cause is whatever we explicitly define as such. Of the existing methods, the most promising approach is that of NDS supplemented by driver interviews. Unfortunately, this method is extremely expensive because it requires many hours of data collection and a complex data reduction process for every crash that is documented. However, the initial results from the SHRP2 NDS are a testimonial to its value: both in validation of insights already gained from previous studies, such as the predominant role of the human factors in crash causation; and in terms of the new and different insights that it generates, such as in the much more refined specification of the crash-causing distractions.

In contrast to a cause, a countermeasure can be defined by another –more objective – criterion: its effectiveness in crash prevention or its cost/benefit. This implies that while a cause can be identified as a 'human factor' the most practical solution might be sought elsewhere. In fact, we see this all the time: whenever a two-way two-lane road is upgraded to a multi-lane divided highway the number of crashes – especially head-on crashes "caused" by human failures in judgment or vehicle control – practically disappear. The cause was human, but the solution was in the infrastructure. In the same context of driver errors that cause crashes, Anderson (1976) noted the "nut behind the wheel myth" does not account for the "literally hundreds of documented studies which clearly indicate the value of environmental improvements in reducing accidents" (pp. 20-21). Finally, a specific behavior – such as inattention or distraction – may be responsible for many crashes, but paying constant attention to all the roadway information is not a part of normative driving behavior, and when it is forced on a driver it appears to be an extremely fatiguing task (Näätänen and Summala, 1976). The recurring identification of this factor in the 1970s (Treat *et al.*, 1979), at the end of the twentieth century (Hendricks *et al.*, 2001), and again now (Klauer *et al.*, 2006; Dingus *et al.*, 2016), simply demonstrates that most of the time the driving task is not sufficiently demanding to require full attention, and with or without high-tech in-vehicle infotainment devices drivers typically seek some distractions.

The ultimate benefit of crash causation analyses in general, and understanding of the human factors involved in crashes in particular, may be in directing our efforts to vehicular and environmental changes. These changes can either eliminate "crash-causing" behaviors or mitigate their effects. Punishing drivers for committing these behaviors, or simply accepting them as "human nature" will neither advance our knowledge nor improve traffic safety.

References

Anderson, H. S. (1976). Let's try to dispel some highway safety myths. *Traffic Eng.*, *46*, 20-23.

Baker, J. S. and L. B. Fricke (1986). *The Traffic-Accident Investigation Manual: At-Scene Investigation and Technical Follow-up.* Northwestern University Traffic Institute, Evanston, IL.

Blatt, A., J. Pierowicz, M. Flanigan, P. S. Lin, A. Kourtellis, P. Jovanis and M. Hoover (2015). Naturalistic driving study: Field data collection. Report No. SHRP 2 Safety Project S07 RW1. Transportation Research Board, Washington, DC.

Chung, Y. and I. Chang (2015). How accurate is accident data in road safety research? An application of vehicle black box data regarding pedestrian-to-taxi accidents in Korea. *Accid. Anal. Prev.*, *84*, 1-8.

Dilich, M., D. Kopernik and J. Goebelbecker (2004). Hindsight judgment of driver fault in traffic accident analysis: Misusing the science of accident reconstruction. Proceedings of the Transportation Research Board Annual Meeting. Transportation Research Board, Washington, DC.

Dingus, T. A., F. Guo, S. E. Lee, J. Antin, M. Perez, M. Buchanan-King and J. Hankey (2016). Driver crash risk factors and prevalence evaluation using naturalistic driving data. *Proc. National Acad. Sci.* www.pnas.org/cgi/doi/10.1073/pnas.1513271113

Dingus, T. A., V. L. Neale, S. G. Klauer, A. D. Petersen and R. J. Carroll (2006). The development of a naturalistic data collection system to perform critical incident analysis: An investigation of safety and fatigue issues in long-haul trucking. *Accid. Anal. Prev.*, *38*, 1127-1136.

EU (2016). UDRIVE: European Naturalist Driving Study. SWOV, Hague, the Netherlands. http://www.udrive.eu/index.php/about-udrive/overview

Fischhoff, B. (1975). Hindsight ≠ foresight: The effect of outcome knowledge on judgment under uncertainty. *J. Exp. Psychol. Hum. Percept. Perform.*, *1*, 288-299.

Furness, S., J. Connor, E. Robinson, R. Norton, S. Ameratunga and R. Jackson (2003). Car colour and risk of car crash injury: Population based case control study. *Br. Med. J.*, *327*(7429, Health Module), 1455-1456.

Gabauer, D. J. and H. C. Gabler (2008). Comparison of roadside crash injury metrics using event data recorders. *Accid. Anal. Prev.*, *40*(2), 548-558.

Gilutz, M. S. (1937). An investigation and report on four years' fatal accidents in Oxfordshire. The Vincent Works, Oxford, England.

Guo, F., S. Klauer, J. Hankey, and T. Dingus (2010). Near crashes as crash surrogate for naturalistic driving studies. *Trans. Res. Rec.*, No. 2147, 66-74.

Haight, F. A. (1973). A traffic safety fairy tale. *J. Safety Res.*, *5*, 226-228.

Hauer, E. (2016). An exemplum and its road safety morals. *Accid. Anal. Prev.*, *94*, 168-179.

Hendricks, D. L., J. C. Fell and M. Freedman (2001). The relative frequency of unsafe driving acts in serious injury accidents. Final report submitted to NHTSA under contract No. DOT NH 22 94 C 05020. Veridian Engineering, Buffalo, NY.

Hill, A. B. (1965). The environment and disease: Association or causation? *Proc. Royal Soc. Med.*, 295-300.

Israel Police (2001). Annual Report for 2000. Ministry of Internal Security, Jerusalem, Israel.

Joscelyn, K. B., J. R. Treat and D. A. Miller (1973). A study to determine the relationship between vehicle defects and crashes. Final report on U.S. Department of Transportation. Contract DOT HS 032 2 263. Institute for Research in Public Safety, Indiana University, Bloomington, IN.

Keith, K., M. Trentacoste, L. Depue, T. Granda, E. Huckaby, B. Ibarguen, B. Kantowitz, W. Lum and T. Wilson (2005). Roadway Human Factors and behavioral safety in Europe. Report FHWA-PL-05-005. Federal Highway Administration, U.S. Department of Transportation, Washington, DC.

Kennedy, P. (1998). *A Guide to Econometrics*. MIT Press, Cambridge, MA.

Klauer, S. G., T. A. Dingus, V. L. Neale, J. D. Sudweeks and D. J. Ramsey (2006). The impact of driver inattention on near-crash/crash risk: An analysis using the 100-car naturalistic driving study data. National Highway Traffic Safety Administration. Report DOT HS 810 594. U.S. Department of Transportation, Washington, DC.

Koustanaï, A., E. Boloix, P. Van Elslande, and C. Bastien (2008). Statistical analysis of "looked-but-failed-to-see" accidents: Highlighting the involvement of two distinct mechanisms. *Accid. Anal. Prev.*, *40*(2), 461-469.

Larsen, L. (2004). Methods of multi-disciplinary in-depth analysis of road traffic accidents. *J. Hazard Mater.*, *111*, 115-122.

Lee, S. N. and J. C. Fell (1988). An historical review of the National Highway Traffic Safety Administration field accident investigations activities. NHTSA Report No. DOT HS 807 293. U.S. Department of Transportation, Washington, DC.

Liu, C. and T. J. Ye (2011). Run-off-the-road crashes: An on-scene perspective. NHTSA report DO HS 811 500. U.S. Department of Transportation, Washington, DC.

Mill, J. S. (1843). A system of logic, as cited in Wikipedia, accessed December 2, 2005. http://en.wikipedia.org/wiki/Mill's_methods

Moskowitz, H. and R. K. Sarin (1983). Improving the consistency of conditional probability assessments for forecasting and decision making. *Management Science*, *29*(6), 735-749.

Näätänen, R. and H. Summala (1976). *Road user behavior and traffic accidents*. North-Holland, Amsterdam.

Neale, V., T. A. Dingus, S. G. Klauer, J. Sudweeks and M. Goodman (2005). An overview of the 100-car naturalistic study and findings. 19th International Technical Conference on the Enhanced Safety of Vehicles, June 6-9. www-nrd.nhtsa.dot.gov/pdf/nrd-12/100Car_ESV05summary.pdf

Neyens, D. M. and L. N. Boyle (2007). The effect of distractions on the crash types of teenage drivers. *Accid. Anal. Prev.*, *39*(1), 206-212.

NHTSA (2008). National motor vehicle crash causation survey: A Report to Congress. DOT HS 811 059. U.S. Department of Transportation, Washington, DC.

NHTSA (2014). Distracted driving 2012. Traffic Safety Facts, National Highway Traffic Safety Administration Report DOT HS 812 012. U.S. Department of Transportation, Washington, DC.

OECD (2015). Why does road safety improve when economic times are hard? International Transport Forum, Paris, France.

Otte, D., B. Pund, and M. Jänsch (2009). A new approach of accident causation analysis by seven steps ACASS. 21st ESV Conference, Paper No. 09-0245. Stuttgart, Germany, June 15-18.

Partyka, S. C. (1984). Simple models of fatality trends using employment and population data. *Accid. Anal. Prev.*, *16*(3), 211-222.

Partyka, S. C. (1991). Simple models of fatality trends revisited seven years later. *Accid. Anal. Prev.*, *23*(5), 423-430.

Reason, J. T., A. S. R. Manstead, S. G. Stradling, J. S. Baxter and K. Campbell (1990). Errors and violations on the roads: A real distinction? *Ergonomics*, *33*, 1315-1332.

Rumar, K. (1985). The role of perceptual and cognitive filters in observed behavior. In: *Human Behavior and Traffic Safety* (L. Evans and R. Schwing, eds.). Plenum Press, New York, NY.

Sabey, B. E. and G. C. Staughton (1975). Interacting roles of road, environment, and road user in accidents. Paper presented at the Fifth International Conference of the International Association for Accident and Traffic Medicine, and the 3rd International Conference on Drug Abuse of the International Council on Alcohol and Addiction, London, UK, September 1-5.

SARTRE 3 (2004). Project on social attitude to road risk in Europe. Report on European Drivers and Road Risk. INRETS, Acrueil, France. http://sartre.inrets.fr/english/pub-en.htm. Accessed on June 26, 2006.

Shinar, D., S. T. McDonald and J. R. Treat (1978). The interaction between driver mental and physical conditions and errors causing traffic accidents: An analytical approach. *J. Safety Res.*, *10*, 16-23.

Shinar, D., J. R. Treat and S. T. McDonald (1983). The validity of police reported accident data. *Accid. Anal. Prev.*, *15*(3), 175-191.

SHARP2 (2015). Strategic Highway Research Program 2 (SHRP 2) Safety Research Reports. Transportation Research Board, Washington, DC. http://www.trb.org/Publications/PubsSHRP2ResearchReportsSafety.aspx

Singh, S. (2015). Critical reasons for crashes investigated in the national motor vehicle crash causation survey. NHTSA Traffic Safety Facts Report No. DOT HS 812 115. US. Department of Transportation, Washington, DC.

Stamp, J. (1929). Some economic factors in modern life. King and Son, London (as cited by Moskowitz and Sarin, 1983).

TRB (2006). Strategic Highway Research Program (SHRP2): Safety. U.S. Transportation Research Board, Washington, DC. www.trb.org/SHRP@/SHRPII_safety.asp. Accessed April 1, 2007.

Treat, J. R., N. S. Tumbas, S. T. McDonald, D. Shinar, R. D. Hume, R. E. Mayer, R. L. Stansifer and N. J. Castellan (1979). Tri-level study of the causes of traffic accidents: Final report. Volume I: Causal factor tabulations and assessments. National Highway Traffic Safety Administration. Report No. DOT HS 805 085. U.S. Department of Transportation, Washington, DC.

Vanlaar, W. and G. Yannis (2006). Perception of road accident causes. *Accid. Anal. Prev.*, *38*, 155-161.

Victor, T., M. Dozza, J. Bärgman, C. N. Boda, J. Engström, C. Flannagan, J. D. Lee, and G. Markkula (2015). Analysis of naturalistic driving study data: Safer glances, driver inattention, and crash risk. NCHRP report No. SHRP 2 Report S2-S08A-RW-1. Transportation Research Board, Washington, DC.

Young, R. (2017). Removing biases from crash odds ratio estimates of secondary tasks: A new analysis of the SHRP 2 naturalistic driving study data. *SAE* Technical Paper No. 2017-01-1380. Society of Automotive Engineers, New York, NY.

19

Crash Countermeasures and Design of Safety

pan·a·cea
Pronunciation: \ˌpa-nə-ˈsē-ə\
Function: *noun*
Etymology: Latin, from Greek *panakeia,* from *panakEs* all-healing, from *pan-* + *akos* remedy: a remedy for all ills or difficulties: cure-all (Merriam Webster's dictionary online).

"In Greek mythology, Panaceia, or *Πανάκεια* (Latin Panacea), was the goddess of healing. She was the daughter of Asclepius, god of healing and medicine, and the granddaughter of Apollo, god of healing." (Wikipedia Online Encyclopedia, December 12, 2006).

"The history of public health may well be written as a record of successive redefinings of the unacceptable." (Sir Geoffrey Vickers, pioneer systems scientist, in a talk in the Harvard School of Public Health, 1957; Lancet, 1958).

There is no panacea in traffic safety. Safety is a multi-dimensional issue, and crashes are the outcome of multiple variables that interact at a specific place and time. Unfortunately, most of us do not think in terms of systems, but in terms of our interests and concerns. The public's cries for better roads and less congestion, the regulators' demands for safer cars, and the licensing and enforcement agencies' changing strategies for driver control are all going to fail without each other's involvement and a coordinated effort to improve safety. This is all because if there is one singular firm conclusion that can be drawn from all the research on driver behavior it is that drivers are extremely flexible and adaptive, so that changes in vehicles, roadways, and regulations will invariably result in changes in driver behavior as well. We typically exercise caution when our environment demands it (such as when driving on slippery roads) in order to maintain our safety margins in high-risk situations. Conversely, we can – and often do – take advantage of road and vehicle safety features by engaging in high (or at least higher) risk behaviors, and in the process sometimes throw caution to the wind. Given the greater safety of alternative means of transportation such as buses, trains and planes, ipso facto we are willing to assume some risk when we get behind the wheel, let alone behind a motorcycle's or a bicycle's handle bars.

The previous chapters focused on specific issues, and in their context considered the effectiveness of various countermeasures to crash risks such as young drivers' inappropriate attitudes and inadequate skills, visual impairments, older drivers' difficulties in information processing, speeding, aggressive driving, driving under the influence of alcohol or drugs, distracted driving, fatigued driving, low conspicuity of motorcyclists and bicyclists, and poor accommodation of pedestrians. The purpose of this chapter is to provide a more integrative approach and consider more general principles that are relevant to road safety. The underlying assumption behind all of these approaches is the same one explicitly stated in the Introduction of this book: that crashes are not accidents; they do not just happen. For this reason several researchers and organizations promote the use of the term crash instead of the term accident. This is a consciousness raising effort to consider crashes as probabilistic outcomes of various situations and behaviors, rather than as unexpected chance events. This can also be a good first step toward developing countermeasures. For this reason I have titled this chapter "Crash Countermeasures" rather than accident countermeasures. The different approaches to countermeasures will be discussed first in the context of the highway traffic system, and then in their applications through policy and organizational development, behavior modification, environmental design, and vehicle improvements. In the vehicle domain we are rapidly moving from providing the driver with crash prevention assistance systems to autonomous driving, at which point the concept of "traffic safety and human behavior" must be re-examined.

System Considerations in Highway Safety

The safe system approach to safety: Accommodating human error

Probably the two best known and successful comprehensive programs of traffic safety at the national level are the Swedish Zero Vision model (Johansson, 2009; Larsson, Dekker, and Tingvall, 2010), and the Dutch Sustainable Safety program (Wegman and Aarts, 2006; Wegman, Zhang, and Dijkstra, 2012). In both programs traffic safety is viewed as a system that consists of the traditional components of road users, infrastructure, and vehicles, but both introduce a unique system approach that focuses on the adaptation of the traffic context (i.e., mostly infrastructure) to the needs, capabilities, and failings of its human users. The safe system approach acknowledges the existence of driver errors, and strives to ensure that when they occur they will not lead to a severe injury or fatality. In other words, crashes can occur, but when they do the impact energy should remain below the threshold of a likely death or serious injury. As summarized by the International Transport Forum, the Safe System approach incorporates three central principles. "First, people make mistakes that can lead to road crashes. Second, the human body has a known, limited physical ability to tolerate crash forces before harm occurs. Third, while individuals have a responsibility to act with care and within traffic laws, a shared responsibility exists with those who design, build, manage and use roads and vehicles to prevent crashes resulting in serious injury or death and to provide post-crash care. Fourth, all parts of the system must be strengthened in combination to multiply their effects, and road users are still protected if one part fails ... (Furthermore) there is no single way for the adoption, establishment, and implementation of a Safe System .... The experiences of the pioneering countries show that each follows its own journey, shaped by the cultural, temporal and local context, but guided by the four underlying principles" (ITF, 2016, p. 12).

This approach to safety is not obvious or commonplace around the world. For example, only 47 countries that represent close to one billion people have urban speed management strategies that conform to "best practice," and only 34 countries representing 2.6 billion people have "best practice" drinking-and-driving laws (WHO, 2015).

The Dutch approach, known as Sustainable Safety, is based on five principles that are summarized in Table 19-1. In addition to these principles, Sustainable Safety has identified three factors as the principle contributors to crashes and crash severity: speed (in crashes), mass/protection (of/by vehicles), and physical vulnerability (of the road users). The goal of system safety is to apply the five principles to these sources of harm in a cost/effective manner that is ethical and politically feasible. As it has been applied in the Netherlands the emphasis has been on infrastructure design (Koornstra *et al.*, 2002), but consideration of human capacities and limitations are at the heart of the approach to the other components. The continuous reduction in traffic fatalities and the status of the Netherlands as one of the safest nations in the world (see Chapter 1) are a testament to the success of the approach.

Understanding driver behavior, driver sensory, cognitive, and motor skills and limitations, driver motives and driver attitudes is a key to improving highway safety. But, like a New York City apartment, it takes more than one key to open the door. The importance of behavior – of drivers', passengers', and pedestrians' – is in the context of the total traffic system; hence the need for a systems approach. This is not because we should focus on improving driving behavior, but because we should see the driver – in terms of his or her needs, limitations, and capacities – in the context of the total traffic system. By understanding these aspects of the road user (including drivers, cyclists, and pedestrians) we can also improve our roads and vehicles intelligently. The role of vehicle and environmental improvements in this context is to compensate for drivers'

Table 19-1. The five sustainable safety principles in the Dutch approach to Traffic Safety (adapted from Wegman and Aarts, 2006; Wegman *et al.*, 2012).

Sustainable Safety Principle	**Description**
Road functionality	Road functionality is defined in a hierarchy of through roads, distributor roads, or access roads
Homogeneity of vehicle mass and/or speed and direction	Correspondence between speed, direction and mass at medium and high speeds
Forgiveness toward the environment and road users	Injury mitigation through anticipation of road user errors and design of forgiving environment
Predictability of road course and road users behavior through self-organizing roads	Road environment that supports road users' expectations through consistency in road design
Awareness of the road users' state	The ability to assess the users' capabilities to handle the different driving tasks

shortcomings, as identified in crash analyses and in studies of driver behavior. As explicitly stated in a World Health Organization report, the role of the driver's environment (i.e., vehicle and infrastructure) is to "accommodate and compensate for human vulnerability and fallibility" (Peden *et al.*, 2004).

A first step in the development of a countermeasure is to identify the nature of the problem. There are two issues to consider in safety improvement through problem identification: (1) the relationship between the source of the problem and the solution and (2) the effects of changes in any component on the total system. The first issue implies that the source of a problem and the source of its solution do not necessarily have to be the same. This was illustrated in different parts of the book, especially in the discussion of crash causation. Treating "inattention" is exemplary in this respect. Various studies have indicated the significant role that inattention – especially in the form of visual distraction – plays in traffic crash causation (see Chapters 13 and 18). Inattention to the proper stimulus at the right time can be identified as a causal factor in as much as fifty percent or more of all traffic crashes (Treat *et al.*, 1979; Klauer *et al.*, 2006; Singh, 2015). The simplistic interpretation of this recurring finding is that we should somehow eradicate inattention. Unfortunately, all the theories and models of human behavior and all the empirical studies in this area and in the area of vigilance indicate that to do so for more than a short period is a nearly impossible task. We can encourage, motivate, and require drivers to be attentive, but we cannot compel and enforce attention. In contrived situations attention to specific stimuli, such as to highway signs, can be sustained for long times, but the effort is extremely tiring (Summala and Näätänen, 1974). If we approach inattention from a system's perspective then we can devise alternative approaches to deal with the problem. The sustainable safety approach to crash prevention allows for the possibility that road users will make mistakes and errors, and compensates for them. Thus, for example, to counter momentary critical inattention, we can develop roadway-based sensors that detect unusual conditions and alert the driver to their presence at critical moments, and/or provide in-vehicle crash avoidance warning systems, such as self-correcting lane position control, adaptive cruise control, autobraking, etc. These new safety devices and drivers' adaptation to them are discussed below.

When we change the roads or the vehicles to accommodate and compensate for driver limitations, we have to anticipate how the drivers will react to the change – for better or for worse. We often estimate the benefits of a safety device by implicitly assuming that all else will stay the same. But it rarely does. Providing drivers with better traction in snow and ice also causes drivers to increase their speed in these conditions (Fridestroem, 2001), teaching skid control increases drivers' risky behaviors (Gregersen, 1996; Katila *et al.*, 2004), painting pedestrian crossing lines on multi-lane roads encourages some drivers to stop for pedestrians but also obscures them from the view of drivers in adjacent lanes who then collide with them (Zegeer *et al.*, 2004, 2005), adding guardrails entices drivers to drive faster as the width of the shoulder is increased (Ben-Bassat and Shinar, 2011), and enhancing roadway delineation to improve nighttime visibility encourages drivers to increase their speed and increase the likelihood of crashes with low-contrast obstacles on the road (Kallberg, 1993; Sharfi and Shinar, 2014). In short, improving safety through changes in various system components is an ongoing process in which we must consider the system outcomes; particularly the driver's reactions to system "enhancements."

Using the safe system approach, and specifically vision zero, Fleisher, Wier, and Hunter (2016) developed a highly detailed matrix of crash countermeasures of proven "best practices" that are being used by eight large U.S. cities, London, Sweden, the Netherlands, and Australia. The countermeasures are divided into nine categories that include – among others – infrastructure, engineering, education, enforcement, policy, and vehicle technologies. While all of the recommended countermeasures are not covered in this book, many are discussed below and in the previous chapters.

Obstacles to increasing highway safety

Given the complexity of the highway traffic system, and the variability of driver behavior we have to acknowledge that improving safety is not an easy task. There are at least ten reasons that make improvements difficult, and they all pose problems that must be overcome.

1. The driver's crash risk every time he or she gets into a vehicle is very low (fortunately). In fact, because we rarely perceive a risk when we take a trip, psychologically the driver's subjective risk is essentially zero. Furthermore, the risk is even smaller per unit distance traveled – so at any one time, any action that is needed to

overcome it (such as attending to the road) has a certain cost and almost no risk reduction associated with it. Interestingly – perhaps because we perceive that we have control over our safety – we are not apprehensive of being in a crash as drivers, but other family members are worried when we take a long drive.

2. Safety often conflicts with other societal norms of mobility and personal needs of freedom, independence, and thrill. If we start restricting our driving to safe conditions we sacrifice some of that independence and freedom, and when we slow down we sacrifice some of the potential thrill of the drive.
3. Driving can satisfy other needs such as power, pleasure, and comfort. Automobile manufacturers advertise these sources of satisfaction, and people strive to experience them. Satisfaction of these needs can also compromise safety.
4. Lack of expertise of those in charge of safety. Highway traffic safety is still not a well-developed discipline and consequently worldwide there are only a handful of academic dedicated highway safety education programs. A recent review of existing academic programs in highway safety conducted for the U.S. National Academies concluded that "there are relatively few current offerings (of courses) within engineering programs (29 out of 117) and a comparable lack of coverage within public health programs (7 of 34) .... Highway safety is underrepresented in transportation curricula throughout the United States" (NCHRP, 2006, p. 17). Fortunately, the U.S. Transportation Research Board has taken initial steps in preparing a professional traffic safety workforce. These steps include a "Model Curriculum for Highway Safety Core Competencies" (TRB, 2010) and an introductory course of "Road Safety 101" based on these needed core competencies (HSRC, 2016).
5. There is often an absence of a central organization that has responsibility, authority, and accountability for highway safety. For example, in Israel a National Road Safety Authority is supposed to coordinate all safety-related activities, but it has no authority over safety-related activities of the Ministry of Education, the National Traffic Police, the Ministry of Transportation Licensing Administration, or the Ministry of Health. In the U.S. the National Highway Traffic Safety Administration was created in 1966 to improve traffic safety but the implementation of its recommended driver behavior improvement programs is determined by the 50 individual states. Such decentralized safety systems lead to multiple uncoordinated efforts without a structured quality control process. In particular, by dissociating responsibility, authority, and accountability from each other motivation to evaluate and improve performance quickly dissipates.
6. The Traffic system is enormous. It is large and complex in scope (all roads, all regions, all environments), in conditions (time-of-day, weather, familiarity), in the mix of vehicles (two-wheelers, cars, buses, and trucks), and in its users (young drivers, old drivers, and pedestrians and cyclists of all ages). Accommodating all users at all places under all conditions is often impossible and tradeoffs must be considered. For example, accommodating pedestrians and drivers in urban streets often involves compromising the safety or mobility or both of one or the other.
7. The preventive nature of safety often makes it difficult to show cost/effectiveness of specific programs. Crashes are rare events and no single treatment is effective in preventing all of them or in reducing all injuries. Consequently potentially effective

programs are difficult to demonstrate on a small-scale or a short-term basis – and most evaluation research is conducted on a small-scale short-term basis.

8. Because the driver is the controlling element in the road-vehicle-driver system, there is a tendency – especially on the part of authorities – to blame the driver for crashes that may in fact be due to other system failures. This tendency is amplified when the people who set traffic safety policies fail to recognize legitimate driver limitations.
9. Some of the research in highway safety is of questionable quality – some because researchers do not have the appropriate training, and some because of the constraints of the real world that make it difficult to carry out properly designed and properly controlled empirical studies. The problem is further aggravated when policy makers do not have the tools and background to distinguish among studies on the basis of their quality, and often the studies that show the greater effect of a program's effectiveness are the ones of poorer quality (e.g., Lund and Williams, 1985; Elvik *et al.*, 2009).
10. Some sound research findings are often ignored due to lack of political will. This is probably the greatest obstacle in the implementation of some safety features. Reluctance to enact primary belt laws and motorcycle helmet laws in all U.S. states are prime examples. Alcohol and seat belt interlocks that prevent starting the car if the driver is intoxicated or unbuckled, respectively, are technologically feasible yet the political will to require them in all cars is absent. These countermeasures exemplify the conflict between safety and other societal norms (in this case individual freedom).

With these obstacles in mind, the role of highway safety researchers and highway safety program specialists is to find the ways to implement valid research findings without compromising various other social values.

Safety performance indicators and the SUNflower pyramid

At the turn of this century researchers from the three leading countries in highway safety initiated a most interesting project, called SUNflower (SUN being the acronym of Sweden, United Kingdom, and the Netherlands). The project's aim was to "determine the underlying elements in the current policies and programmes of the SUN countries, which make them particularly effective in coping with the traffic safety problem, and thereby identify policy improvements most likely to produce casualty reductions in both SUN countries and other (European) countries" (Koornstra *et al.*, 2002). Two general conclusions emerged from this project: (1) all three countries had a centralized comprehensive approach to traffic safety that was defined by a global strategy related to similar policy areas, that led to actions and measurements of progress as a result of these actions and (2) the strategies and actions were country-specific depending on the problems and culture of each country. This approach to safety management is represented schematically as a pyramid in Figure 19-1. Briefly, this pyramid is a visualization of the components in Europe's transport safety policy plan (ECMT, 2002). At the base of the pyramid a country should have a safety vision and a policy-driven plan of programs designed to achieve it (e.g., increase seat belt use through enforcement). The second layer

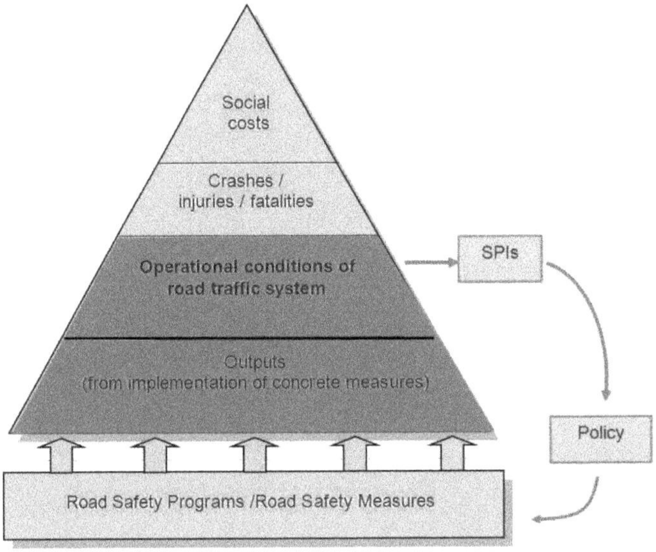

Figure 19-1. The SUNflower pyramid with Safety Performance Indicators (SPIs) (from Thomas *et al.*, 2009).

consists of the observable and measureable outputs from the implementation of these programs (e.g., police hours of enforcement, number of drivers ticketed, etc.). If these programs are effective, then their impact should be demonstrable in changes in the traffic system. These observable changes can be quantified in the third layer by defining safety performance indicators (SPIs), which are measures of direct impact (i.e., outcome) of these programs (e.g., increase in percent drivers/passengers using seat belts). Assuming that the policy and programs were well grounded in theory and data on the impact of SPIs on bottom-line measures of crashes and injuries, then at the next level of the pyramid, we should witness a change in traffic crashes and casualties. Finally, if these changes are significant then they should impact the quality of life and could be measured in savings in social costs.

The second and third tiers of the SUNflower pyramid are shaded for an important reason. These are the levels that traffic safety personnel can affect directly. They are responsible for the programs' outputs and for the objective measurement of the effects of these outputs on the SPIs. Determination of safety-relevant SPIs should be made by traffic safety experts and researchers familiar with the state of knowledge on traffic safety. If indeed traffic crashes and injuries are causally linked to these SPIs, then changes in their levels should affect changes in crashes. The theory-based and research-supported assumption that this indeed is the case is what drives safety policy and the programs that it generates. Because these relationships have been empirically validated, most of the crash and injury countermeasures focus on SPIs as output measures. Consequently, our programs are designed to improve safety through changes in traffic speeds, user behaviors, vehicle safety standards, and infrastructure design. And when we discuss countermeasures, this is where we look for their effects.

Haddon's model of crash prevention and injury reduction

The most quoted framework within which highway safety improvements can be addressed is known as Haddon's Matrix. This simple yet comprehensive and exhaustive matrix addresses crash prevention and injury reduction from the perspectives of the driver, vehicle, and environment, relative to three time periods: pre-crash, crash, and post-crash. The cells in the matrix contain the potential safety interventions as illustrated in Table 19-2. The specific actions that can be taken within each cell have changed significantly since the matrix was first introduced by Haddon over 40 years ago (Haddon, 1972), but the general principles have remained quite the same. To illustrate, half a century ago nearly all efforts in crash prevention efforts would have focused on the road user as the decision maker and controlling element in the roadway-user-vehicle system. Today, many driving functions that used to be exclusively human are relegated to or shared with the vehicle. These include speed control (with cruise control) maintaining

Table 19-2. A modified Haddon matrix of means of increasing safety in terms of crash prevention, injury prevention, and injury reduction in the broader context of the social environment.

ORGANIZATIONAL STRUCTURES

POLICIES

PHASE	GOAL	FACTORS AFFECTING SYSTEM COMPONENT		
		Road User	Vehicle	Environment
Pre-Crash	Crash Prevention	Licensing, education, enforcement	Inspection of brakes, lights, tires, Crash avoidance systems, alerting systems	Road design and layout, high-friction pavement, speed calming, pedestrian separation, safety policy and goals
Crash	Injury prevention and reduction of injury severity	Use of restraints, impairment	Occupant restraints, air bags, crash absorption, safety glass, padded interiors	Crash absorption barriers, breakaway poles, elimination of roadside objects, hard shoulders
Post-Crash	Injury treatment, life preservation	Medical treatment and evacuation	Ease of extraction, fire prevention	Rescue facilities, evacuation lanes and recognized traffic control procedures in congestion, treatment procedures

NORMS / VALUES

CULTURE

safe headways (with adaptive cruise control, forward collision warning, and hazard detection), and lane position control (with lane deviation warning, and lane keeping support). Other traditional driver responsibilities are in advanced stages of shifting to the vehicle or the infrastructure, such as in-vehicle fatigue monitoring and alertness maintaining devices (with new lane position detection systems). The automation of enforcement – with speed cameras, red light cameras, and intelligent speed adaptation – is another area where the role of the human (in this case, the law enforcement officer) is being replaced by the infrastructure.

All of these changes occurred because of two significant evolutionary processes. The first is the introduction of intelligent transportation systems (ITS) in the form of interactive in-vehicle and infrastructure-based systems that alert the driver to dangerous conditions and to the status of his or her vehicle. The second is the expansion of the environment beyond the immediate roadway and its structures to include the prevailing culture, and even the impact of alternative modes of transportation and organizational climate within which safety is treated. This is noted within the circle surrounding the original matrix; though in fact it is a third dimension – Non-Physical Context – that should be added to the original nine-cell matrix. The non-physical context includes the policies, organizational structures, and the prevailing social norms/culture/values. The importance of such variables to implementing potential countermeasures was already illustrated nearly 20 years ago by Runyan (1998) for dealing with inadvertent house fires and school violence by firearms. Runyan was also pragmatic in suggesting that the different potential solutions must be evaluated in terms of 'decision criteria' that included effectiveness, cost, freedom, equity, stigmatization, preferences, and feasibility.

The rest of this chapter is devoted to a discussion of safety measures that seem to be effective in improving traffic safety in each of the newly expanded domains listed in the modified Haddon matrix.

Policy and Organizational Changes

In every organization the person at the top of the hierarchy is believed to have the most significant effect on the organization's performance. The same applies to safety. It has been shown that industrial organizations committed to safety in their policy and actions have better safety climates and better safety records than organizations in which safety is relegated to people lower in the chain of control (Zohar, 1980, 2002). The same should apply to traffic safety. It is therefore not surprising that traffic safety is most advanced in countries where traffic safety is a national issue, with national goals and with a commitment to these goals at the highest levels. An effective national policy, according to the World Health Organization should address all "five pillars" of traffic safety: road safety management, safer roads and mobility, safer vehicles, safer road users, and effective post-crash response (note the partial overlap with Haddon's matrix). Worldwide this is a sore issue. Only 28 countries, representing a meager seven percent of the world's population, have adequate laws that address all five universally recognized risk factors: speed, drink-driving, non-use of helmets, non-use of seat-belts, and non-use of child restraints (WHO, 2013a).

To make road safety a national priority many organizations must be involved. An illustration of the various organizations and stakeholders that can and should have inputs to this effort is provided by the World Health Organization (Peden *et al.*, 2004) and reproduced in Figure 19-2.

In a manner consistent with the system approach, a strategic approach to safety that involves coordinated efforts of different organizations and professionals can address multiple issues in parallel and achieve greater effectiveness than possible with disparate well-intentioned but uncoordinated efforts. Currently, of the 192 member countries in the UN 167 countries have an agency that leads national road safety efforts (WHO, 2015). Such an agency can be effective in leading and coordinating various programs that affect different road users that are typically reached by different agencies. Table 19-3 illustrates one such approach and its potential impact.

Perhaps the most revealing aspect of the information in Table 19-3 is that specific actions and strategies (listed in the columns of the table) can affect multiple aspects of the highway safety problems (listed in the rows). With multiple effects of different approaches, the potential for impact is very high. This is demonstrated in Table 19-4, which contains estimates of the benefits realized in the United Kingdom from the implementation of policies that affect the roadways, the vehicles, and the road users. According to the UK

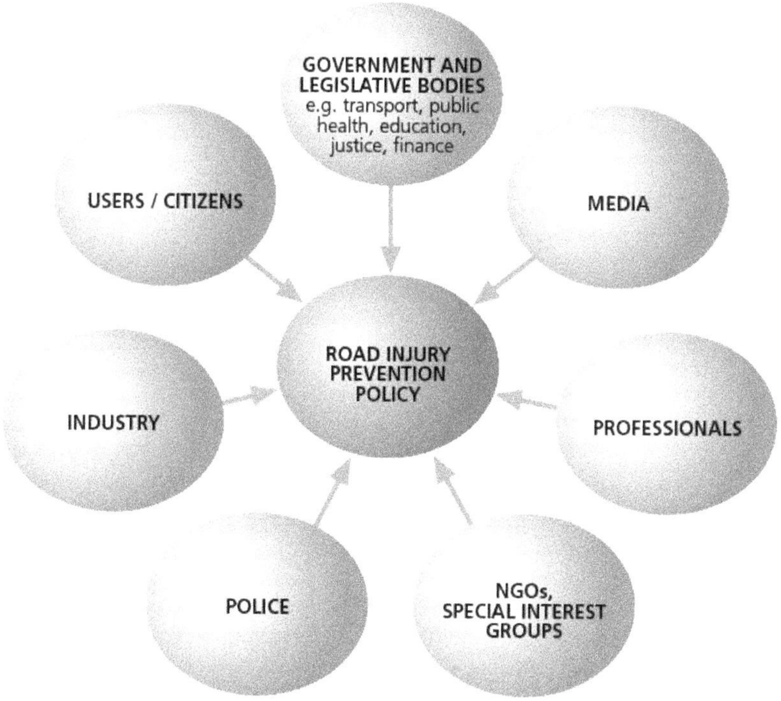

Figure 19-2. Key organizations that influence traffic safety policy development (from Peden *et al.*, 2004, with permission from the World Health Organization).

Table 19-3. Generic measures beneficial to specific road safety issues (from the Government of Western Australia, 2002, with permission of the Office of Road Safety, Department of the Premier and Cabinet, Western Australia).

Road Safety Issues	**Classes of Initiatives**						
	Better enforcement	**Public education**	**Lower speeds**	**Safer roads**	**Occupant protection**	**Safer modes of travel**	**Planning a safer system**
Drink-driving	√√	√√		√√	√√	√√	
Speeding	√√	√√		√√	√√	√	
No seat belt	√√	√√		√	√√	√	
Driver fatigue		√√		√√	√√		
Young drivers	√√	√√	√√	√√	√√	√	√√
Older drivers	√		√√	√√	√√	√	√√
Motorcycles	√√	√	√√	√√	√√	√	
Bicycles	√	√	√√	√√	√√	√	
Pedestrians	√	√	√√	√√	√√	??	√√
Heavy vehicles				√√	√√		
Drugs				√√	√√	√√	

√√ indicates greater potential impact than √.

data, the total impact of these measures has been a 35 percent reduction in serious injuries and fatalities on UK roads. Although the specific contributions of the various measures may be arguable, the total benefits are measurable, real, and quite impressive. Obviously, it is costly to attain these benefits, and therefore the specific programs should be evaluated in terms of their cost-effectiveness, so that the highest benefits/cost ratios can be achieved. Though some issues are outside the scope of cost-benefit analyses, such as basic human rights and fairness, in general cost-benefits analyses can and have been applied to setting highway safety program priorities (Elvik, 2001; Elvik *et al.*, 2009).

Table 19-4. Estimated percent reductions in serious injuries and fatalities from various policies enacted in the UK addressing the safety of vehicles, roadways, and users (modified from Broughton, Allsop, and Lynam, 2000 by Peden *et al.*, 2004, Table 4.3, with permission from WHO).

Policy	**Car Occupants**	**Pedestrians**	**Cyclists**	**Motorcyclists**	**Others**	**All Users**
New road safety engineering programs	6.0	13.7	4.3	6.0	6.0	7.7
Improved vehicle crash protection	10.0	15.0	–	–	–	8.6
Other vehicle safety improvements	5.4	2.0	3.2	8.0	3.0	4.6
Motorcycle and bicycle helmets	–	–	6.0	7.0	–	1.4
Improving safety of rural single carriageways	4.1	–	–	4.2	4.1	3.4
Reducing novice drivers' crash involvement	2.8	1.3	1.0	0.8	0.4	1.9
Additional measures for pedestrian and cyclist protection	–	6.0	4.0	–	–	1.2
Additional measures for speed reduction	5.0	5.0	5.0	5.0	5.0	5.0
Additional measures for child protection	–	6.9	0.6	–	–	1.7
Reducing casualties in drink-drive accidents	1.9	0.4	0.2	0.8	0.5	1.2
Reducing crashes during high-mileage work driving	2.1	0.9	1.2	1.9	1.9	1.9
Additional measures for improved driver behavior	1.0	1.0	1.0	1.0	1.0	1.0
Combined effect of all measures	33	42	24	30	19	35

Some policy changes can affect traffic safety inadvertently – for better or for worse. For example, the response of the U.S. Federal government to an energy crisis in 1974 was to set maximum national speed limits at 55 mph. The much greater-than-expected savings in traffic fatalities caused the government to retain that speed limit and encourage its enforcement for over 20 years – long after the energy crisis became a dim memory. Another example is setting the clock for daylight savings time in order to save energy. Because it changes the visibility (especially of pedestrians) in the morning and evening commutes to and from work, daylight savings time also yields a safety benefit (Sullivan and Flannagan, 2002), without increasing crashes during the transition period while the circadian rhythm is adjusted (Lahti *et al.*, 2010). In fact, a year-round change to daylight savings is estimated to reduce pedestrian fatalities in the U.S. by 13 percent and vehicle occupant fatalities by three percent (Coate and Markowitz, 2004).

Setting highway safety goals

The first commitment at the policy level must be to a goal that is acceptable and comprehensible to road users and relevant organizations. The importance of goal setting and the characteristics that make a goal an effective agent of change were extensively studied by Locke and his associates (Locke *et al.*, 1981; Locke and Latham, 1990, 2002). Their studies and those of others have demonstrated that setting difficult but realistic goals leads to better performance and achievements than setting easy goals, asking people to "do their best," or simply stating the desire for improvement without setting any goals. It appears that setting goals helps in focusing people's attention on the most relevant tasks, mobilizes organizational efforts, increases people's persistence, and motivates them to develop strategies toward their attainment. To attain maximal effectiveness the goals must be (1) stated in concrete measurable terms, (2) specific, (3) challenging but attainable, and (4) accepted by the people responsible for their achievement. In addition, (5) the people assigned to work toward the goals must have the required knowledge base and skills and (6) the process must be accompanied by feedback relative to the achievement of the goal.

In the context of highway safety, a commitment to a concrete and measurable goal sets in motion several different actions including: (1) the formulation of a comprehensive safety policy, program, and procedures to achieve the program, (2) coordination among agencies, (3) allocation of funds, (4) creation of incentive for creative thinking to examine new approaches, and (5) evaluation research to track advancements in safety.

There is ample evidence that setting challenging highway safety goals works. Elvik (1993) evaluated safety progress in 19 jurisdictions in Norway and divided them into those that had demanding concrete goals, those that formulated non-demanding concrete goals, and those that had goals that were not specified in concrete terms. Over the same approximate time period the greatest reductions in crashes per kilometers traveled were in the first group, smaller reductions were recorded in the second group, and crash rates remained essentially the same in the third group. At the national level, several countries have demonstrated the impact of fatality reduction goals. In the 1980s England, Denmark, Finland, the Netherlands, and Sweden set fatality reduction goals for 2000 ranging from 25 percent (the Netherlands) to 50 percent (Finland and Sweden), and achieved a reductions of 24 percent (the Netherlands) to 41 percent (Finland) (OECD, 2002). A more recent evaluation of the association between fatality reductions and setting of national road safety targets in 14 countries also confirmed the strong association between the goals and the outcomes, by showing that these countries achieved greater fatality reductions than matched comparison countries that did not set such goals (Wong *et al.*, 2006). Sensitive to the importance of goal-setting, the European Union and the World Health Organization regularly set 10-year goals in fatality reductions. The current goal, common to both is to halve traffic fatalities by 2020 relative to 2010 (WHO, 2015).

Defining the goal in understandable concrete terms is quite easy. In highway safety the simplest and easiest to understand goal is one that is stated in terms of a reduction in the absolute number or percent of serious injuries and fatalities by a certain target date. The most ambitious goal of this type is the one declared by the Swedish government and adopted by the Swedish Parliament in 1997 under the heading of "Vision Zero." According to this approach, "the goal is that no-one shall be killed or seriously injured as a consequence of accidents in road traffic. The design and function of the road transport system shall be adapted to meet the requirements that follow from Vision Zero." This approach may be the ultimate redefinition of "the unacceptable" (using Vickers' terminology at the top of this chapter). It constituted a radical departure from the standard approach that placed most of the blame and the responsibility on the narrow shoulders of the road users, and shifted the responsibility to counteract human failures to the big shoulders (and deep pockets) of the central government (Belin *et al.*, 2012). It also set a long-term goal of zero deaths, rather than the more common goals of a greater-than-zero number of deaths to which the state aspires, a goal that Johnston, Muir, and Howard (2014), decries as license to kill so many people. The starting point for designing the Swedish safe traffic system is making sure that the environment does not allow people to exceed the human tolerance for impact (Johansson, 2009). This, incidentally, allows for greater speeds (and impact speeds) for protected vehicle occupants than for unprotected pedestrians. Thus, in an environment that includes pedestrians, the roadway design should guide the driver (naturally) into driving at speeds less than 35 km/hr. In a complementary manner, where cars are allowed to move at high speeds, the roadway design should be such as to prevent head-on collisions, and collisions with vulnerable road users (especially bicyclists and pedestrians). This is achieved with limited access highways and separate bicycle/pedestrian paths or trails.

The Swedish parliamentary statement has several implications: (1) life is of paramount importance and cannot be traded off against other values such as pleasure or expediency (e.g., from speeding), (2) the responsibility for achieving this goal rests with the government (thus, faulting the driver is not an acceptable alternative), who is responsible for infrastructure design and vehicle safety standards, and (3) achieving this goal requires a system-wide approach (Elvik, 1999a; Fildes, 2001). Although the approach was unique when it was first adopted, it seems to be proving itself in the sense that Sweden is one of the world's leaders in highway safety. And though it was revolutionary when it was first announced, Vision Zero has caught on as more and more countries have embraced it. With some variations on the theme it has been embraced by various countries in Europe, several U.S. states (the U.S. Highway Governors Safety Association; Toward Zero Deaths, 2009), and municipalities (e.g., New York City). One approach to achieve such a goal is to transform an entrenched social norm according to which casualties are a necessary cost of transportation. The new alternative approach, promoted by "safety culture" advocates states that death on the road is simply not acceptable, and consequently government, organizations, and individuals must revise their behavior in terms of safety. More details about this high-level approach is provided by the U.S. AAA Foundation for Traffic Safety (AAAF, 2007, 2015), and the U.S. Transportation Research Board (TRB, 2015).

For safety goals to be measurable, they must have a target date: the date by which the goal is to be achieved. In this sense, Zero Vision and Safety Culture are lacking. A Notable – but more humble – goal that specifies a date is the UN's World Health Organization worldwide goal, that was presented as part of a strategic plan known as Decade of Action, to cut traffic fatalities by 50 percent between 2011 and 2020 (Bliss and Breen, 2012). The European Union has set the same goal for the EU countries. Currently, there are 28 EU member countries committed to this challenging goal. But given the progress achieved in the first 4 years of this decade, this goal may be realized only if efforts are increased (EC, 2015; ETSC, 2014a). Also, as stated above, to be effective a goal should be acceptable to those in charge of achieving it. This is not the case with the EU target. Although the target was endorsed by the European Parliament and the European Council, "the target is not binding on EU Member States and it is not in conflict with separate target setting by Member States on national level" (EC, 2015, p. 11).

Currently 126 countries have defined target fatality rates as a part of their national road safety strategy (WHO, 2015). Table 19-5 contains a sample of national goals and even a quick cursory look reveals that different country-specific goals relate to different traffic safety concepts. In contrast to easy-to-grasp goals such as absolute number of fatalities or percent reduction in fatalities, there are goals that are not as simple to comprehend and appreciate by the public. These goals are stated in terms of rates rather than in absolute numbers or percent reductions. For example China set its goal for 2015 in terms of percent reduction in fatalities per 100,000 vehicles (thereby allowing for an increase in absolute number of fatalities as motorization level increases). In Russia and Spain it was defined relative to the size of the population (which is equivalent to absolute numbers if the population size remains fairly stable). The U.S.'s goal for many years was stated in terms of fatalities per 100 million passenger vehicle miles. At the beginning of this century it was set at 1.0 for 2008 (NHTSA, 2003). But with a 1.08 fatalities per million vehicle miles in 2014 (NHTSA, 2016e), this goal still has to be met.

Because national goals are typically set for 5-10 year cycles, evaluation of progress toward the goals must be made at intermediate phases and in terms of intermediate

Table 19-5. A sample of countries that have a national safety policy with stated targets of fatality reductions (selected data from the Country Profiles in WHO, 2013a, except for the U.S. which is derived from the Country Profiles in IRTAD, 2015; and Israel which is derived from the NRSA 2015 annual report).

Country	Base Year	Target Year	Target Fatality Reduction
Australia	2011	2020	50%
Austria	2011	2020	30%
Bangladesh	2008	2023	50%
Belgium	2010	2020	50%
China	2011	2015	32% per 100,000 vehicles
Czech Republic	2002	2012	50%
Denmark	2007	2012	40%
European Union*	2011	2020	50%
Finland		2025	100 deaths/year
France		2012	<3,000 deaths/year
Greece		2020	<640 deaths/year
Iran	2011	2020	10% per year
Israel	2006	2015	510 to >300 fatalities (41%)
Japan	2011	2015	<3,000 deaths/year
Mexico	2011	2020	50%
The Netherlands	2010	2020	<500 deaths/year
New Zealand	2010	2020	Different (for specific groups/ performance Index measures)
Poland	2003	2013	50%

Table 19-5. (Continued)

Country	Base Year	Target Year	Target Fatality Reduction
Russia		2030	8 deaths per 100,000 pop.
South Africa	2010	2014	5% annually
Spain		2020	3.7 deaths per 100,000 pop.
Sweden	2007	2020	50%
United Kingdom	2005-2009	2020	37-46%
United States		2016	<1.02 fatalities per 100m vehicle miles

*Identical with the national goals of Belgium, Hungary, Italy, Luxembourg, Slovakia, Slovenia.

measures of performance, or intermediate variables. In road safety the relevant intermediate variables are SPIs (SPIs in Figure 19-1). For example, programs designed to increase safety through improvements in highway design should measure improvements in infrastructure; programs designed to reduce fatalities through behavioral changes (such as lower speeds and greater belt use), should be accompanied by periodic unobtrusive observations of behavioral changes (such as actual speeds and belt use rates); and programs affecting in-vehicle safety devices should evaluate dissemination of the devices, their proper use, and impact on expected driver behaviors.

Setting a goal for non-fatal injury reduction is much more complicated than for fatality reduction (see Chapter 1). It is hampered by significant differences among countries in terms of definitions, data quality, and under-reporting of injuries (especially, bicycling-related injuries) (EC, 2015). But initial effort in this direction has been made by EU bodies, with a similarly stated goal of 50 percent reductions in the 2010-2020 decade (ETSC, 2013).

The central role of the central government (but industry can and should join)

Though not explicitly stated in those words, the responsibility for most of the actions and the goals listed above is that of the national government. This, of course, is made explicit in the Swedish Vision Zero and the Dutch Sustainable Safety strategic plans. The formidable goal of reducing traffic fatalities through multiple coordinated efforts must be assumed by a central government, with whom the authority to make many of these changes resides (Bliss and Breen, 2012). Ultimately, the government should also be accountable for achieving that goal. Blaming irresponsible, reckless, aggressive, unskilled, etc. drivers, cyclists, and pedestrians is a poor excuse for lack of government leadership in this area. The World Health Organization (Peden *et al.*, 2004, p. 160) recommends that each country "identify a lead agency in government to guide the national road traffic safety effort, ... with the authority and responsibility to make decisions, control resources and coordinate efforts by all sectors of government – including those of health, transport, education and the police. This agency should have adequate finances to use for road safety, and should be publicly accountable for its actions." While a central organization responsible for safety exists in many countries, it is often devoid of the needed authority to implement its recommended safety programs. To assist in the creation of a coherent and effective safety policy, the World Health Organization has even published a practice and resource manual for strengthening road safety legislation (WHO, 2013b).

The highway traffic safety policies advocated by the World Health Organization (Peden *et al.*, 2004) are divided into three domains: institutional development, legislative policy and its enforcement, and making highway safety a public health issue. Given its central role in affecting highway safety, the government can directly affect and regulate road users' behavior, their infrastructure, and their vehicles, as illustrated by the specific actions listed in Table 19-6.

To have the desired impact, actions such as those recommended in Table 19-6 must be promoted and supported by other organizations such as local governments and communities, and non-governmental organizations such as foundations and civic groups

Table 19-6. Specific highway safety institutional actions to be taken by governments, as recommended by the World Health Organization (from Peden *et al.*, 2004, with permission from the World Health Organization).

Institutional Development
• Make road safety a political priority. • Appoint a lead agency for road safety, give it adequate resources, and make it publicly accountable. • Develop a multidisciplinary approach to road safety. • Set appropriate road safety targets, and establish national road safety plans to achieve them. • Support the creation of safety advocacy groups. • Create budgets for road safety and invest in demonstrably effective road safety activities.
Policy, legislation, and enforcement
• Enact and enforce occupant protection legislation including the use of seat-belts, child restraints, motorcycle helmets, and bicycle helmets.

• Enact and enforce legislation to prevent alcohol-impaired driving. • Set and enforce appropriate speed limits. • Set and enforce strong and uniform vehicle safety standards. • Ensure that all environmental and transportation project plans include a safety impact analysis. • Establish data collection and analyses systems and use them to improve safety. • Set appropriate road design standards that promote safety for all. • Manage infrastructure to promote safety for all. • Provide efficient, safe and affordable public transport services. • Encourage walking and the use of bicycles.
Public health policy and actions
• Include road safety in health promotion and disease prevention activities. • Set goals for the elimination of unacceptable health losses arising from road traffic crashes. • Systematically collect health-related data on the magnitude, characteristics, and consequences of road traffic crashes. • Support research on risk factors and on the development, implementation, monitoring and evaluation of effective interventions, including improved care. • Promote capacity building in all areas of road safety and the management of survivors of road traffic crashes. • Translate effective science-based information into policies and practices that protect vehicle occupants and vulnerable road users. • Strengthen pre-hospital and hospital care as well as rehabilitation services for all trauma victims. • Develop trauma care skills of medical personnel at the primary, district and tertiary health care levels. • Promote the further integration of health and safety concerns into transport policies and develop methods to facilitate this, such as integrated assessments. • Campaign for greater attention to road safety, based on the known health impact and costs.

committed to reducing deaths and injuries on the highways. Thus, the U.S. strategic transportation safety plan, though it fails to specify quantitative measurable goals, does include multiple cooperative efforts with state and local governments, the auto industry, and safety organizations (DOT, 2014). In addition to encouraging the central government to commit to the goals listed above, these organizations and individuals can also (1) address local safety problems and plan and push for local countermeasures and (2) encourage their constituents to drive in a safe manner consistent with the actions above.

Setting safety goals should not be limited to governments and safety organizations. The automotive industry can and should join. The best case for safety goal setting by the automotive industry is the one set by Volvo in 2016 by its CEO: "Our vision is that by 2020 no one should be killed or seriously injured in a new Volvo car." Working toward living up to that ambitious vision (paralleling Vision Zero) Volvo has been aggressive in installing various electronic safety devices consisting of sensors and activators designed to not only protect its vehicle occupants but also pedestrians in the paths of its cars (e.g., Ernberg, 2013; Valdes-Dapena, 2016).

Behavioral Approaches

Efforts to directly affect driver behavior are often the strategy of choice in many countries, especially the less affluent ones. This is because the immediate financial burden is the smallest and much of it is shouldered by the road users. Interventions in road users' behavior can be done almost from the cradle to the grave as specified in Table 19-7. Not all interventions are applicable to all road users at all stages in their lives, but the main modes of intervention – education and public information, training, licensing, enforcement, and adjudication – are all applicable to more than one type of user at one stage in his or her life. However, not all users can be reached and affected with equal ease. For example, school age pedestrians and bicyclists are easy to reach (through their schools) but very difficult to affect. This is because they are not regulated at all (i.e., they are not licensed), they are rarely subjected to the threat of enforcement or punishment, and the only means of affecting their behavior is through education. Older pedestrians are difficult to reach and even more difficult to educate. In fact, as Table 19-7 makes obvious, they are the most difficult to affect by any of the standard behavioral modification

Table 19-7. Behavioral approaches to affect road users' behaviors.

Age	**Road User**	**Means of Intervention**				
		Education + PI	**Training**	**Licensing**	**Enforcement**	**Adjudication**
0-3	**Parents**	√	√		√	√
4-15	**Pedestrians**	√				
	Bicyclists	√				
16-25	**Novice drivers**	√	√	√	√	√
26-64	**Mature drivers**	√			√	√
65+	**Older drivers**	√	√	√		
	Older Pedestrians	√				

approaches that we have at our arsenal. Consequently, to improve their safety we must turn to the other system components of safer roads and safer vehicles.

Previous chapters in this book focused on specific road user groups. Here, in an attempt to integrate the data in terms of the use of various interventions and countermeasures the focus will be on means of intervention. Still, it is important to remember that there is no panacea and no 'one size fits all' solution. One comprehensive compendium to behavioral countermeasures is the U.S. National Highway Traffic Safety Administration's "Countermeasures that Work." This practical manual was first published in 2005 and has since been updated several times, most recently in 2015 (8th edition, Goodwin *et al.*, 2015). The countermeasures are divided into topics similar to the ones covered in this book (alcohol, seatbelts, aggressive driving and speeding, distracted and fatigued driving, motorcycle safety, young drivers, older drivers, pedestrians, and bicyclists), and countermeasures that have been suggested, used, and/or evaluated are summarized in a tabular format. An example of such a summary table addressing the effectiveness, use, cost, and time needed for implementation of a graduated driver licensing program for novice drivers (discussed in detail in Chapter 6) is reproduced in Table 19-8.

In addition to the summary tables, the compendium also includes references to published studies and reviews from which the summary tables are derived. An important – and often overlooked – statement in the report is the following cautionary note on the estimated effectiveness of any program: "The effectiveness of any countermeasure can

Table 19-8. Summary evaluation of the Graduated Driving Licensing (GDL) programs according to the U.S. National Highway Traffic Safety Administration (from Goodwin *et al.*, 2015).

Countermeasure	**Effectiveness**	**Use**	**Cost**	**Time**
Graduated driver license – overall	☆☆☆☆☆	High	Low	Medium
1. Learner's permit length, supervised hours	☆☆☆☆☆	High	Low	Medium
2. Intermediate nighttime restrictions	☆☆☆☆☆	High	Low	Medium
3. Intermediate passenger restrictions	☆☆☆☆☆	High	Low	Medium
4. Belt use requirements	☆☆	Low	Low	Medium
5. Cell phone restrictions	☆☆	Medium	Low	Medium
6. Intermediate violation penalties	☆	High	Low	Medium

Five stars – Demonstrated to be effective by several high-quality evaluations with consistent results.
Four stars – Demonstrated to be effective in certain situations.
Three stars – Likely to be effective given balance of evidence from high-quality evaluations or other sources.
Two stars – Effectiveness still undetermined; different implementation methods produce different results.
One star – Limited or no high-quality evaluation evidence.

vary immensely from State to State or community to community. *What* is done is often less important than *how* it is done. The best countermeasure may have little effect if it is not implemented vigorously, publicized extensively, and funded satisfactorily. Evaluation studies generally examine and report on high-quality implementation because there is little interest in evaluating poor implementation. Also, the fact that a countermeasure is being evaluated usually gets the attention of those implementing it, so that it is likely to be done well. *The countermeasure effectiveness data presented in this guide probably show the maximum effect that can be realized with high-quality implementation*" (p. 2). The last highlighted sentence is probably true for all countermeasures described below, and not just the ones in the U.S. guidebook to countermeasures. Once a measure is implemented on a large scale its effectiveness will almost invariably be less than obtained in a small-scale demonstration study. Finally, in its introductory comments the report also states that "many countermeasures have not been evaluated well, or at all, as noted in the effectiveness data." This is unfortunately true of many traffic safety programs that persist and assume a life of their own in the absence of any evaluations that would indicate their effectiveness, let alone their cost-effectiveness.

Education and training

As in other areas, education should be a life-long process. At different stages in life we need to learn how to cope with the traffic system in different modes: first as dependent passengers (where the onus falls on our parents), then as pedestrians and bicyclists, and finally as drivers. At each mode we must learn different aspects of the system: from basic rules of the road – as young pedestrians and cyclists – to our vulnerabilities and perceptual and information processing limitations – as beginning drivers, and once again as elderly drivers.

We typically think of education in a formal school setting, and many countries have highway traffic safety education programs that progress from kindergarten to the end of high school, culminating in formal driver education. Educating children about the traffic system and how to behave safely when out in the street is the first venue for formal education in highway safety. It appears to be important in early childhood when children begin their independent movement in traffic. In the case of children, the risky behaviors are well known (mostly darting out into traffic), and the reasons for them are well understood (mostly lack of understanding of the traffic system and drivers' limitations). The little research that exists in this area indicates that teaching and training children to behave safely in the street is beneficial and that the learned behaviors can be transferred to the real traffic environment (Hotz *et al.*, 2004; Peden *et al.*, 2004. See also Chapter 15 for a more detailed discussion).

The benefits of safety education at later phases of adolescence are less obvious. Though there is a tendency to promote safety education as a critical element in achieving safety goals, there is no consistent evidence to demonstrate its effectiveness in changing road user behaviors and lowering crash rates. There are consistent relationships that show that crash rates (using various measures) tend to decline with increasing levels of *general* education expenditures and average level of education. However these are only associations and they tend to be confounded with other factors such as demographics and urbanization (O'Neill and Kyrychenko, 2006). The same applies to use of seat belts and refraining from drinking and driving that tend to be higher among people with higher levels of education than among drivers with lower levels of education (Shinar, Schechtman, and Compton, 2001).

Much attention and research has been devoted to the evaluation of formal driver education for novice drivers. Large-scale studies and extensive reviews of studies conducted throughout the world have been done and they are discussed in some details in Chapter 6. In brief, the conclusion of all of these evaluations – though disheartening – is unequivocal: there is no statistically reliable evidence that driver education – in any form that was evaluated – is beneficial to highway safety (Achara *et al.*, 2001; Mayhew and Simpson, 2002; NTSB, 2005; Thomas, Blomberg, and Fisher, 2012). Couching such a conclusion in more subtle academic terms Thomas *et al.* (2012), after a careful review of the literature in this area for the NHTSA, conclude that "driver education appears to do a good job in preparing students to pass state licensing examinations; the expectation that driver education by itself will lead to a decreased teen crash rate is unrealistic." Yet even the same reports that reach such conclusions are wary about dismissing the benefits of driver education. Thus, for example, Mayhew and Simpson (2002, p. 3) conclude that "the international literature provides little support for the hypothesis that formal driver instruction is an effective safety measure ... (but) education/training programs might prove to be effective in reducing collisions if they are more empirically based, addressing critical age and experience related factors." Thus, when it comes to driver education hope springs eternal. Consequently driver educators continue to argue for its inclusion (Robinson, 2002), and most governments – even in the face of overwhelming evidence to the contrary – continue to promote and support driver education. The best that can be said for policies promoting and funding driver education is that, at least as a means to increasing safety, they are faith-based and not evidence-based. Driver education may be important for teaching vehicle control and rules of the road to young drivers, but there is no evidence that *formal* school-based driver education has an added value for safety.

Education is probably valuable where there is evidence that unsafe behaviors are associated with ignorance rather than with ulterior motives. This, for example is the case in the use of child booster seats, where most parents are unaware or misinformed of their importance and proper use, and for adjustment of head rests in car seats where most drivers do not know the proper adjustment (see Chapter 10).

Education can also be useful through less formal channels, including media exposure and public education and information campaigns. For example, to educate the motoring public about the safety of their vehicles, the U.S. congress passed a law that requires automobile dealers to prominently display each vehicle's safety rating (based on crash tests conducted by the National Highway Traffic Safety Administration) on a label attached to the price sticker on the vehicle's window, just like its gas consumption (NHTSA, 2006a).

Actual practical training is limited in most countries to young drivers in preparation for their license and – with graduated driver licensing programs – to young drivers shortly after initial licensing. The benefits of training and the skills that need to be acquired at this stage are discussed in Chapter 6. However, some training programs are also available for training children to cross streets (see Chapter 15), and for training older drivers to adjust their driving to their limitations and even to improve their driving-related cognitive skills (see Chapter 7). Though the objectives of such programs are commendable there are no data to indicate that they are very effective. Finally, some types of training may actually be counterproductive. For example, various studies have shown that highly skilled drivers such as race drivers may be over-involved in crashes (Williams and O'Neill, 1974) and teaching advanced driving skills such as skid control may cause drivers to assume greater-than-appropriate risks (Katila *et al.*, 2004).

Public information campaigns

Public information campaigns through the media or by roadside signs are popular ways for many jurisdictions to promote traffic safety. But beyond the explicit demonstration of concern and show that the regulator is "doing something" about safety, how effective are they? Studies conducted in different countries have yielded mixed results. The measures of effectiveness have ranged from a change in the knowledge level, to a change in intended and actual behavior, and to the ultimate measure: reductions in crashes and injuries. To address the latter, Elvik *et al.* (2009) and Phillips, Ulleberg, and Vaa (2011) conducted meta-analyses that evaluated the effects of road safety campaigns on crashes. Phillips *et al.* evaluated 67 studies with 119 specific results that spanned the time period of 1975 to 2007, and were conducted in 12 different countries. In short, a very comprehensive evaluation. Though there were large differences among the studies in the reported effects, the aggregate data indicated that overall, media campaigns reduce crashes (of all types) by approximately nine percent. Analyses of the results as a function of the media used, the content, and the type of crashes affected revealed large and significant differences in effectiveness. Public information campaigns were more effective when they included personal communication. Road signs were more effective when their content included both information and emotional appeals, and when they were accompanied by enforcement. Interestingly, Phillips and his colleagues also concluded that the campaigns were effective when they addressed alcohol-related crashes, but not when they addressed speeding-related crashes. Elvik *et al.*'s (2009) meta-analysis covered 34 studies conducted in different countries and published between 1978 and 1999. They too found an average reduction of nine percent across all studies on all accident types. This is not surprising considering the large overlap in the studies that the two groups of researchers included in their analyses. More important though, Elvik *et al.* distinguished between campaigns accompanied by enforcement and campaigns not accompanied by enforcement, and found that campaigns not accompanied by enforcement were not effective at all. In the authors' own emphatic words "only those campaigns that are combined with enforcement were found to reduce accidents. Campaigns alone do not seem to have any effect at all" (p. 871). Also they too found that the only effective campaigns were those addressing drinking and driving (with an average of 14 percent reduction in all accidents), while campaigns addressing speeding and pedestrians were not effective at all. The U.S. positive experience with "high visibility enforcement campaigns" to discourage drinking and driving is a good example of how public information can be used to leverage the saliency of enforcement and reduce alcohol-related fatalities (NHTSA, 2007).

A common shortcoming of most public information campaigns is that they are not very strongly grounded in either the theory of human behavior or the empirical data related to the campaigns. Even a well-designed and theory-based campaign is not guaranteed to succeed. One such campaign to reduce speeding was conducted in Scotland. It was based on the Theory of Planned Behavior (TPB see Chapter 9) and its messages were designed to affect subjective norms, perceived behavioral control, and attitudes toward speeding. Consequently, according to the TPB changes in these factors should lead to changes in actual behavior. Unfortunately, in the "acid test" of actual changes in speeding the campaign failed (Stead *et al.*, 2005).

While it is easy to attach a number to average effectiveness of a campaign, (e.g., the nine percent reduction in all types of crashes, above), the validity of the number should always be questioned. One reason is that different campaigns focus on different issues, addressing different populations, and use different contents – without an equal balance on all of these variables. Thus, most of the campaigns evaluated by Elvik *et al.* and by Phillips *et al.* focused on drinking and driving, thus tainting the meaning of an "average" effect of a media campaign. Phillips *et al.* made one other interesting observation: that the campaigns were more effective when they focused on the risk of detection and apprehension than on the risk of a crash or injury. Thus, once again, we find that most of us are more sensitive to small but high-probability penalties (arrests) than to very high cost but low probability outcomes (crashes).

If after all of the above qualifications one still decides to try to affect behavior – or at least awareness and knowledge – through a public information campaign then it is essential that the campaign be based on valid knowledge of the relevant situation beforehand, and that it should be properly designed, implemented, and evaluated. A useful resource on public information campaign design is the European Commissions' series of guidelines for the design, implementation, and evaluation of road safety communication campaigns (EC, 2009a, 2009b, 2010).

Licensing and license suspension/revocation

The main impact of licensing on safety is probably not in filtering out the unfit to drive safely as it is in ensuring that those who are licensed to drive meet some minimal requirements in terms of their vision, their health, their knowledge of rules of the road, and their vehicle control skills. Nearly all young and old people – the two groups that are over-involved in crashes relative to their exposure – who are highly motivated to obtain or retain a driver license manage to get one (see Chapters 6 and 7). Furthermore, placing strict "health related" restrictions on license renewal for older drivers can paradoxically result in an increase in crashes per number of licensed drivers because this approach to licensing and license renewal eliminates the low-mileage low-crashes drivers from the driving population (Hakamies-Blomqvist, Johansson, and Lundberg, 1995, see Chapter 7).

The most common license-related systematic approach to discourage drivers from committing traffic law violations is through the Demerit Point System (DPS). This system, adopted by most of the western world countries, involves tracking drivers' violations records and "punishing" them progressively, by either giving them demerit points as they accumulate more and more violations, or deducting "good points" from an initial number of points (i.e., merit point system; e.g., Spain, France, Italy). The effectiveness of the system rests on the assumption that the points act as deterrents that may eventually result in license suspension. Based more on intuitive appeal than hard science, nearly all U.S. states and EU countries have one form or another of DPS. Indeed, a meta-analysis of 50 results obtained from different countries around the globe shows that the introduction of a DPS is associated with a 15-20 percent drop in accidents. Unfortunately the same analysis also indicates that this drop is temporary and dissipates within 18 months (Castillo-Manzano and Castro-Nuño, 2012). Still, on the basis of qualitative reviews and quantitative analyses of the existing research a standardized best practice version (labeled EU BestPoint) has been recommended by a consortium of 11 European research institutes and transport authorities. The system consists of four steps that are associated with increasing demerit (or decreasing merit) points: a warning letter, a driver improvement course (that focuses on attitudes and behaviors and not on knowledge and driving skills), license withdrawal (for 3-12 months), and a remediation course that must be taken and passed before the license is reissued. The violations recommended for demerit points are the ones that pose a crash risk and consist of the following 12 behaviors: speeding, driving under the influence of alcohol and/or drugs, not using occupant restraints, running red lights, dangerous overtaking, not keeping minimum headway, endangering pedestrians at pedestrian crossings, illegal use of mobile phones or other communication devices, violating railway crossing rules, driving the wrong way, and committing a hit-and-run accident (Klipp, Machata, and van Schagen, 2013). Although labeled as "best practice" only time (and program evaluation research) will tell if it is.

Short-term license suspension is also a problematic safety device. Short-term suspensions seem to keep some – but not all – suspended drivers off the road. Studies conducted in various countries have estimated that over 50 percent of these drivers continue to drive (DeYoung, 1999, estimated that 75 percent continue to drive; Knox and Silcock, 2003, estimated that the percentage is above 45 percent; Malenfant, Van Houten, and Jonah, 2002, 57 percent; Ross and Gonzales, 1988, 66 percent; Williams, Hagen, and McConnell, 1984, 65 percent). The principal reason for continued driving is that license suspension is hard to enforce, and can only be detected when a driver is stopped for another violation. One would then think that these drivers would be very cautious, but the reality is that they constitute a significant percent of the drivers stopped for various other violations (see Knox and Silcock, 2003, for a review), especially for driving while intoxicated (TRB, 2013). Drivers with suspended license are also over-represented in crashes, though most of the over-representation is confounded with these drivers' other high-risk characteristics (Blows *et al.*, 2005).

The effectiveness of long-term and permanent license revocation is even lower. This is because in addition to the low likelihood of being arrested for driving without a license, people who would otherwise refrain from driving for a short time – so as not to jeopardize their license renewal at the end of the suspension – feel that the punishment is unbearable and they have little left to lose. Thus, in a survey of 768 drivers who received life-time license revocation in Taiwan, Chang, Woo, and Tseng (2006) found that 23 percent of these drivers continued to drive almost the same as before, 60 percent drove significantly less than before, and only 17 percent gave up driving completely. Whether or not these proportions are representative of other countries is unknown, but they are consistent with the findings noted above for short-term license suspension. In Korea Kim, Myeong, and Kweon (2011) conducted a direct comparison between drivers whose license was revoked and drivers whose license was suspended after they appealed the original revocation sentence. They found that recidivism of both violations and crashes were higher for those whose license had been revoked than those whose license was suspended. However, they acknowledged that the two groups of drivers may have also differed in many respects related to driving and driving attitudes. This confounding is highly likely as these differences may have been the reason for commuting the revocation sentence. One strategy to counter the impression that driving without a license is hard to detect has been adopted in Israel, where a highly publicized special police unit actually conducts surveillance of drivers whose license has been suspended. However, the cost of such a draconian program is high and its impact is unknown and remains to be evaluated.

Given the less-than-expected effects of license suspension, several jurisdictions around the world impound vehicles or confiscate license plates after their owners have committed repeated or serious offences. The strategy seems to be more effective than license suspension in reducing crashes, though it does create various logistics problems (Cooper, Chira-Chavala, and Gillen, 2000; DeYoung, 2013; Voas *et al.*, 2004, see Chapter 11).

Enforcement

Enforcement is a means of last resort to change driver behavior. In a sense its importance is an indication of the failure of the driver education, training, and licensing process. It is a testimonial to the salience of motives other than safety. The legitimacy and appropriateness of enforcement rests on two assumptions. The first assumption is that driving is a privilege and not a right, and that it is an aspect of social behavior that has to conform to the rules of the system in which it takes place. As Evans (2003) phrased it, "driving is a public, not a private, activity. The privacy that is rightly sacrosanct for private activities should not apply to driving because of the enormous threat it poses to others .... The breakthrough that is required is an agreement that other drivers pose so great a threat to our lives that we have the right to enforce traffic laws effectively." Furthermore, in the context of driving even our own well-being is not a private affair because the costs of medical treatment for crash victims are rarely borne by them alone. So if society has to pay for the "damages," then society has the right to demand that drivers observe the traffic rules and regulations, that car occupants be restrained, and that motorcyclists wear helmets. The second assumption is that violations of traffic laws (which is what enforcement attempts to control) lead to crashes. The data on this relationship is quite clear: there are positive correlations between violations (frequencies and rates) and crashes (frequencies and rates). However, the associations are often complex and the correlations are quite low (De Winter and Dodou, 2010; DfT, 2004; Gebers and Peck, 2003).

There are many variations in enforcement strategies (see Chapter 8 in the context of speeding), and there is no single strategy that is optimal. However, to be effective in reducing high-risk behaviors an enforcement strategy must meet two basic requirements: (1) it has to be salient enough to be perceived as threatening (i.e., drivers committing a violation will most likely be stopped and arrested) and (2) the penalty associated with violating the traffic laws has to be certain and significant (i.e., once stopped the likelihood of receiving a significant punishment is very high). Furthermore, as discussed in the context of speed (Chapter 8), use of belts (Chapter 10), drinking and driving (Chapter 11), and distracted driving (Chapter 13) enforcement is most effective when combined with public information campaigns. The latter, in effect, increase its perceived presence. As long as enforcement is visibly present or perceived as present it is generally effective.

The effectiveness of enforcement can be measured in different ways, and when it is intensive and accompanied by media exposure its effectiveness can be demonstrated in a decrease in crashes, in injuries and fatalities (especially speed-related fatalities), in hospital admissions from motor vehicle crashes, and in reduced stay and costs of treatment of crash victims in the hospital (Davis *et al.*, 2006). Reviews of the many studies on enforcement effects on crash reductions have been published by Bjørnskau and Elvik (1992), by Elliott and Broughton (2004), and by Elvik *et al.* (2009). Elvik *et al.* (2009) conducted meta-analyses on the effects of speed enforcement on crashes, and found that enforcement with speed cameras reduces crashes by an average of 16 percent, and the effects are greater on fatal crashes than on less severe ones. Seat belt enforcement increased seat belt use rate by an average of 20 percent, and the size of the effect was inversely related to the initial use rate; with smaller effects where the initial use rate is already high.

Being labor-intensive, manual enforcement is often implemented in spurts of intense and high-visibility campaigns. In addition, manual enforcement is often culturally biased (e.g., in the U.S. it is reportedly biased against blacks who are both stopped and cited more often than white drivers; LaFraniere and Lehren, 2015). Also, the effects of enforcement are quite temporary – with a halo effect lasting no more than a few months. This was demonstrated in an interesting analysis by Redelmeier, Tibshirani, and Evans (2003), who analyzed the driving records of 8,975 drivers who died in a crash in Ontario, Canada over a period of 11 years. When they examined the relationship between the date of the fatal crash and the time interval to their last cited violation they found that the risk of the fatal crash was 35 percent lower in the month following a citation relative to the risk of death following a month of no citations. The reduced risk was less after 2 months, and essentially nonexistent after 3 months or more. This means that to be effective, enforcement must be sustained at a high frequency, an effort that may not be feasible for police forces at most jurisdictions.

Limits of enforcement

Enforcement cannot provide a remedy to all inappropriate and driving behaviors, and its effectiveness is limited by several factors:

1. Unless it is automated (as discussed in the context of infrastructure-based countermeasures) it is expensive.
2. Its effects are highly localized in terms of time and location, so that when it is removed the high-risk behaviors tend to increase to previous levels (Bjørnskau and Elvik, 1992).
3. To extend the effects to a larger area, it is paradoxically more effective when the locations of the enforcement activities are changed in a random fashion than when enforcement concentrates on high-violation locations (Bjørnskau and Elvik, 1992; Newstead, Cameron, and Leggett, 2001). However, this may be true only for intensive highly-visible enforcement that gives the drivers the sense that it could be anywhere, and not just in select expected places.
4. The impact of enforcement cannot be significantly increased by increasing the penalties for violations without a concomitant increase in enforcement activity. This is in sharp contrast to the classic economic utility theory which assumes that the likelihood of violation is a product of the likelihood of an arrest and the magnitude of the penalty. When it comes to enforcement the most important rule is to make it intensive and consistent, so that drivers will not consider it irrelevant. We all experience this effect when we deposit coins in a parking meter whenever we know that parking enforcement is intense, without even knowing the penalty for not paying.
5. To be equally effective to all road users, the risk of apprehension and cost of traffic violations should be the same for all road users. However, this is not easy to accomplish, because the same monitory fine has a different subjective cost (i.e., financial burden) for people with different incomes. The most extreme – and psychologically sound – example of attempting to make the punishment equally meaningful to all road users is implemented in Finland, where fines are tied to the violator's reported income level. This has resulted in a few headline-grabbing fines of over $100,000(!) for speeding (AP, 2002; BBC 2004). However, it is unlikely that Finland's high safety levels are due to these draconian measures. In fact, excessive penalties tend to boomerang because the police are less inclined to issue a citation (Bjørnskau and Elvik, 1992) and the drivers are more inclined to contest them.
6. Not all people are equally sensitive and responsive to enforcement. Some people are more sensitive to rewards and less sensitive to punishments, and such people are more likely to violate the law (e.g., because speeding is rewarding). Others are more sensitive to punishment than rewards and these people are more affected by enforcement (Castellà and Pérez, 2004).
7. Probably the weakest link in the deterrence value of enforcement is the gross inconsistencies among judges in meting different penalties for similar violations (Hessin and Kremnitzer, 1998) and the inability of the courts to follow up the extent of compliance with the penalties for various convictions. These two shortcomings undermine the perceived consistency of enforcement – and therefore much of its deterrent value.

Not all crashes can be traced to traffic law violations. According to Elvik *et al.* (2009) even if all road users respected all the traffic laws all the time, the expected reduction in fatalities would still be less than 50 percent (48 percent with a large confidence interval of 18-78 percent). This is because enforcement is an effective countermeasure to deliberate violations. But data from some of the countries leading in road safety indicate "that about (only) 30 percent of serious crashes are caused by deliberate violations and risk-taking behavior while the majority result from simple errors of perception and judgement by otherwise compliant persons" (ITF, 2016). If we acknowledge that no amount of enforcement is enough to ensure 100 percent compliance, the expected effect shrinks further.

Roadway and Environmental Modifications

To be effective environmental design should be user-centered; meaning that the design guidelines should accommodate the users rather than force the users to adjust to the design. The users in this case are drivers, motorcyclists, bicyclists, and pedestrians, and accommodating all of them is often a challenge. Fortunately, there are human factors guidelines for the design and analyses of roadway systems including curves, rural and urban roads, intersections and interchanges, sight distance and more (e.g., Campbell *et al.*, 2012) The general approach to the design of safe roads is to minimize the potential for going off the road and the potential for conflicts: conflicts among cars, bicycles, motorcycles, and pedestrians. We strive to do that by separating motorized vehicles from pedestrians (with overpasses, underpasses, and pedestrian-only streets), from bicycles (by providing cyclists with dedicated paths and trails), and from each other (by constructing divided highways). But separation, the desire to eliminate potential obstacles, and the construction of roadside barriers, all convey an unintended message to the driver: it is safe to increase the speed, reduce attention, and engage in non-driving tasks. Roadway designs to accommodate pedestrians and bicyclists were discussed in Chapters 15 and 17, and therefore the focus in this chapter will be on how we resolve these conflicting goals through driver-centered environmental design.

Crash modification factors

To evaluate the potential benefits of various treatments, crash modification factors (CMFs), have been calculated, based on crash experience. The CMF provides an estimate of the crashes that would be saved if a treatment is applied. There are several compendiums of CMFs, and they are typically country-specific, as the size of the effect can vary across countries with different driving cultures, vehicle mixes, and infrastructures. For some specific factors there are studies that compare the CMFs in different countries. An example is a comparative study by Elvik (2013) who reviewed the effects of replacing short-radius curves (i.e., short sharp curves) with long-radius (long and shallow) curves. By comparing data from eight different countries he was able to show that the inverse relationship between the curve radius and crash risk is similar in all countries except for the very sharp curves (with a radius of 50 meters or less) where the crash risks vary widely among the different countries (being highest in Germany and the U.S. and lowest in Norway and Portugal). Similarly, analysis of mostly U.S. data provides CMFs for various shoulder widths; essentially documenting the intuitive conclusions that increasing widths – on both divided and undivided roads – decreases crashes (Stamatiadis and Pigman, 2009).

There are compendiums of CMFs for a variety of treatments such as Elvik *et al.*'s *Handbook of Road Safety Measures* (2009), the *Road Safety Engineering Risk Assessment*, Part 6: *Crash Reduction Factors for Australia* (Turner *et al.*, 2010), and the *Highway Safety Manual*, Part D: *Crash Modification Factors* (AASHTO, 2010). As an example, according to these guides replacing narrow two-lane roads with divided highways with wide median strips or barriers between opposing traffic lanes reduces crash and injury likelihoods. Replacing rural arterial roads with high-speed divided highways reduces fatality risk relative to total distance traveled by about 45 percent while significantly cutting travel time. Replacing signalized intersections with modern roundabouts increases safety and under most conditions also improves traffic flow. Replacing intersections with overpasses and underpasses eliminates collisions with cross traffic and improves traffic flow. Providing passengers with bridges and underground crossings reduces jay walking and pedestrian injuries while it increases traffic flow. While the guides typically provide an exact numerical value for the percent in crash reductions, many of them also acknowledge that the confidence levels in most of the CMFs are low or at best medium (Turner *et al.*, 2010), as the average levels effectiveness are typically based on very few results and the variance is high. Also, many of these CMFs require costly changes in the infrastructure.

A significant shortcoming of CMFs is that they are most often univariate. For example, with respect to shoulder width, as stated above the greater the better. Yet, the CMFs do not consider the interactions between shoulder width and the presence or absence of guardrails and retroreflective delineators, the climate (how often is the road slippery), or the presence or absence of various lane departures avoidance systems in the prevailing traffic. Thus, as mentioned below (Ben-Bassat and Shinar, 2011) in a simulated environment, on roads with guardrails as shoulder width increased so did the drivers' speed, whereas when guardrails were not present, the shoulder width had no effect on speed. Given the strong relationship between speed and crashes it is likely that the CMF for shoulder width would be dependent on the presence or absence of guardrails.

As CMFs are often dependent on the context in which they were developed, transfer to other regions is risky unless an analysis is first made of the transferability of the findings. The Organization of Economic Cooperation and Development (OECD) has developed one such detailed guide (OECD, 2012) that should be carefully studied before CMFs are assumed to be valid in places and times other than those for which they were originally calculated.

But there are other, less obvious, and significantly less expensive environmental enhancements based on basic psychological principles that can assist drivers in avoiding crashes, and they are considered below.

Perceptual modifications: Affecting drivers' perception of the roadway

In an optimal roadway system there should be no need for signs, signals, and roadside barriers. This is because in an optimal system the roadway and its immediate environment will provide all the necessary information to the drivers. Regrettably this is often not the case. While highway designers have a bird's eye view of the road as they view it on their screens, drivers have a very limited – and sometimes perceptually misleading – perspective. In early studies conducted on crash data on rural curves in Ohio we noticed that the physical parameters of curvature have less to do with crash statistics at curves than the drivers' visual perspective of these curves (Shinar, 1977), and changes in the delineation system in the curves and immediately ahead of them, that affected the drivers' perceptions of the curve and the road leading into the curve, were effective in reducing driver speeds as they entered the curve (Shinar, Rockwell, and Malecki, 1980). For example, by painting a sequence of lines perpendicular to the road with decreasing spaces between adjacent lines it is possible to give drivers an enhanced sense of speed, which they then reduce to maintain their "desired" speed (Denton, 1973; Fildes and Jarvis, 1994; Godley, Triggs, and Fildes, 2000, 2004; Shinar *et al.*, 1980). Other modifications such as painting a herring-bone pattern that is supposed to induce a perception of road narrowing has also been shown to reduce drivers' speed (Shinar *et al.*, 1980) and variability in their lane position (Charlton, 2007). Perceptual modifications are more effective than instructional signs (such as speed advisory signs), because most drivers prefer to trust their direct sensory impressions than instructional and warning signs. Despite repeated demonstrations of the effectiveness of perceptual modifications in studies conducted in Australia, England, Japan, Sweden, and the U.S. (Fildes and Jarvis, 1994), the approach has not gained wide appeal; perhaps, because it implies "tricking" the drivers' perceptions.

In a very comprehensive experiment Jamson, Lai, and Jamson (2010) studied the effects of 20 different roadway treatments – consisting mostly signs, pavement markings, and rumble stripes – on speed reduction in various environments including a rural curve, a rural junction, a rural straight road, an entry to a village, a straight urban road, and an urban junction. The study was conducted in moving-base simulator on young male drives: the most hardcore speed violators. The most interesting finding was that nearly all treatments were effective to some extent in reducing the speed in all environments, except in the straight rural road section where pavement hatch markings in the center of the road actually resulted in increase in speed. These results fly in the face of some on-road research (described below) that too much signage is actually detrimental to safety. However, it is possible that in the simulator environment with a single exposure to each condition the adaptation that is common in real driving is missing and each cue can have an alerting and a speed-mitigating effect.

Designers, possibly aware of these perceptual problems often provide signs to enhance or supplement the drivers' perceptions of the roadway. The use of chevron markings posted inside sharp curves seems to be effective in the sense that drivers use them as indicators that a signed curve is sharper than it appears. Thus, Charlton (2007) in Australia, Jamson *et al.* (2010) in England, and Zhao *et al.* (2015) and Wu et al. (2016) in China found that in driving simulators drivers slow down more for curves when they are augmented by chevrons at the edge of the road than when they are not, and the chevrons' presence reduces the drivers' stress in sharp curves. Apparently because such signs are not overused, drivers tend to lend them credibility. An innovative addition to the chevrons was evaluated in France (Bordel *et al.*, 2012). Speed detectors were positioned just ahead of the curve, and whenever a driver exceeded the recommended entry speed into the curve two yellow beacons mounted on top of the chevrons started flashing. This interactive system was quite effective in reducing speed to the desired level. However, the long-term effects of such an interactive device should be evaluated to see if over time and in real driving drivers adapt to these warnings and ignore them, in which case the threshold for its activation should be adjusted. In two other on-road studies conducted in multiple locations in the U.S. the conspicuity and visibility of standard STOP signs were increased by either supplementing each sign with a flashing red beacon (FHWA, 2008a) or by using sheeting with higher retroreflectivity (FHWA, 2008b), respectively. The addition of the beacons reduced injury and fatal crashes by 10 percent, but the increase in retroreflectivity yielded inconsistent results; in essence not reducing accidents significantly. These results imply that many of the crashes at intersections are not due to poor visibility or conspicuity of the STOP sign but to the drivers' attitude and visual search behavior at these intersections; that is, the problem seems to be more of a driver's conscious violation than a driver's error.

A problem with many modern high-speed roads (with presumably good CMFs) is that they relieve the driver of so much of the driving task that their monotony actually induces fatigue and tends to induce what some have labeled "highway hypnosis" – driving without awareness (DWA) that is due to a tendency to become drowsy and fall asleep. DWA is assumed to be caused by the very high predictability, repetitiveness of visual cues, and a visual environment with minimal stimulation. These characteristics are salient when the roadway has very few signs, is relatively straight and much of the stimulation comes from repetitive and identical lane markers. This induces a state of DWA in which drivers fail to monitor their own behavior to the point where they steer their vehicle "subconsciously with their attention removed from the roadway such that they are also unaware of any impending hazards" (Belz, Robinson, and Casali, 2004). There is some scientific basis for this phenomenon. Cerezuela *et al.* (2004) showed that drowsiness as measured by changes in EEG was greater after driving for prolonged periods on motorways than on conventional roads. To counter this and other reasons for exceeding the lane boundaries, rumble strips along the shoulder markers and along the median striping on two-lane rural roads have been proposed, and in some locations installed. Charlton (2007) found that rumble strips on the center lines and edge lines before curves reduced drivers' entry speeds, and Persaud, Retting, and Lyon (2004) demonstrated that such rumble stripes etched in the median marker of two-lane rural roads significantly reduce crashes, especially head-on collisions with opposing traffic.

User-friendly road design

There are at least three formalized approaches to improve road safety by improving the communication between the road design and the road users. Two – positive guidance developed by the U.S. Federal Highway Administration and self-organizing roads developed in the EU – consist of general principles and selected applications. A third, more specific approach is that of using roundabouts or traffic circles. This traffic calming technique has spread rapidly in Europe and from there to the rest of the world. These approaches and a few other user-oriented designs are discussed below.

Positive guidance

To enhance veridical perceptions of the road, and to enable drivers to make correct control and guidance decisions quickly, the U.S. Federal Highway Administration proposed a set of rules for a user-centered design concept called "positive guidance": placing and designing roadway features in a way that maximizes the likelihood that drivers will respond with appropriate speed and route selection (Alexander and Lunenfeld, 1975; Lunenfeld and Alexander, 1990). Positive guidance is provided when "the information is presented unequivocally, unambiguously and with sufficient conspicuity to allow the driver to detect a hazard in a roadway environment that may be visually cluttered, recognize the hazard or its threat potential, select an appropriate speed and path, and initiate and complete the required maneuver safely" (Dewar, Olson, and Alexander, 2001, p. 34). Thus, positive guidance improves situation awareness. In the context of environmental design, the rules of positive guidance are most relevant to the guidance and navigation decisions that a driver makes. As the complexity of the environment increases, especially in urban settings, the driver begins to selectively attend to the available information. To be compatible with the driver's limited attentional capacity positive guidance implies that information placement should conform to the following rules of good ergonomics:

1. Primacy – Information on signs should be placed according to its importance to the driver, and in the case of possible information overload, less important information should be deleted altogether.
2. Spreading – When the total content requires too many words, the information should be spread over several successive signs.
3. Coding – Information should be coded according to ergonomic principles and conform to existing standards, driver experience and expectations, and population stereotypes (see Chapter 5).
4. Redundancy – There should be some redundant information, to ensure that in case one source is missed by the driver the other is not. For example, "no passing" information can be provided by both pavement markings and signs. Information for urban speed limits can be provided by signs indicating entry into an urban (or built up) zone and by additional specific speed limit signs (Lajunen, Hakkarainen, and Summala, 1996) The design of the highway itself should also contain some redundancy because drivers tend to pick up most of the information from the road itself. For example a wide multi-lane road is inconsistent with a low-speed limit, and if low speed is desired, then the road should contain various traffic calming features in addition to the speed limit signs.
5. Expectancy – All guidance and navigation information should conform to the drivers' expectancies (e.g., exits from right lanes). In general, drivers expect continuity in their driving (e.g., vehicle ahead will not brake abruptly), that very low probability events will not happen (e.g., pedestrians will not appear on a high-speed motorway), and that cyclic events will conform to temporal predictability (e.g., the longer a traffic

light has been green, the more likely it will turn red before the driver reaches it). The importance of expectancy in highway design cannot be over-emphasized, because unexpected events significantly increase driver reaction times (see Chapter 5). Even our visual acuity for signs with familiar words is better than our acuity for signs with unfamiliar or unexpected words or anagrams (Forbes, 1972). A common violation of this principle is the use of different town names for exits on motorways. Thus, a driver may be cued by signs to look for an exit to "Aurora" only to discover – too late – that the desired exit name was replaced by other names on the exit sign itself.

Self-organizing and self-explaining roads

A complementary approach to positive guidance that was developed in Europe is that of "self-organizing" or "self-explaining" roads. The basic concept here is that the roadway itself should provide the drivers with all the necessary cues concerning speed and steering. It has been shown that treatments consistent with that philosophy – such as road narrowing, introduction of curves and roundabouts, and conspicuous speed bumps – are more effective at speed reduction than speed control through signing and automated enforcement (Hirst, Mountain, and Maher, 2005; Mountain, Hirst, and Maher, 2005). In an interesting analysis on the relationship between the extent of "self-explanation" and situation awareness, Walker and his colleagues (2013) had a small sample of 12 drivers drive over 20 kilometers in the real world on a route consisting of various types of roads. While they drove they were instructed to provide real-time commentary on "why they were performing current actions, what information they were taking from the environment, how the vehicle is behaving and what actions they planned to take." In short, they were asked to provide verbal descriptions of the principal components of situation awareness (see Chapter 3). Content analysis (using semantic networks) of 27,225 words from the verbal output showed a strong compatibility between the road type and the drivers' situation awareness. Compatibility was high, meaning that the drivers were correctly aware of the situation and what it required of them, on motorways/freeways, and deteriorated as the roadway became increasingly minor and the amount of proper design diminished. Thus, this small study provides a critical link between the behavioral-cognitive theory of situation awareness and an empirically validated approach to roadway design.

Interestingly, the approach can sometimes contradict the traditional safety-oriented design principles of providing road users with greater safety margins (by increasing lane width and adding wide hard shoulders) and reducing the drivers' workload (by minimizing curves). For example, the desire to minimize curves is prompted by the fact that they increase the run-off-the-road crashes compared to straight segments (Elvik, 2013); especially by speeding and alcohol-impaired drivers driving on two-lane undivided roads (Najm, Schimek, and Smith, 2001; Neuman *et al.*, 2003). In that sense minimizing curves is a driver-centered design to the extreme because it accommodates even risky and impaired drivers. To combine the two approaches some creativity is necessary. For example, designing curves and narrowing lanes should be practiced only when it can be ensured that the approaching drivers have a good valid perception of the road with sufficient sight distance, that roadway features (such as perceptual treatments) induce drivers to adopt the proper curve entry speeds, and that any potential hazards can be detected and recognized well in advance. Similarly, the common assumption, embodied in standard guidelines (e.g., the *U.S. Manual on Uniform Traffic Control Devices*, FHWA, 2009) is that wider shoulder and guardrails increase safety. However, they also lead to a dangerous change in driver behavior. In a simulated driving study we (Ben-Bassat and Shinar, 2011) found that in the presence of guardrails, increasing the shoulder width caused drivers to perceive the road as safer and accordingly increase their speed. Similarly, in simulated tunnel driving Liu *et al.* (2016) found that as the shoulder width increased so did the drivers' speeds. Note that in a tunnel, the width of the shoulder is determined by the tunnel walls (that are akin to guardrails). Thus, the added safety margins that are provided by design, can actually nullify or at least mitigate some of the positive effects of the increase in the safety margin, providing one more example of the frustrating effects of risk compensation (See Chapter 3).

An interesting application of the self-organizing roads concept is the "2 + 1 roads" to prevent risky passing of slow-moving vehicles. The 2 + 1 roads are three-lane road segments in which every several kilometers the road will have two lanes in one direction and a single lane in the other direction. These designs are common in some European countries such as Denmark, Germany, Finland, and Sweden (but quite rare in the U.S. where nearly all major high-speed roads are at least two lanes in each direction). Signs along the 2 + 1 roads inform drivers of the distance to the next two-lane passing segment. By designing the passing segments fairly close to each other, this system encourages drivers to be patient and stay behind slow-moving vehicles rather than risk passing in the presence of oncoming traffic. The approach has proven itself and drivers tend to be very responsive to this design. It reduces risky passing behaviors, crashes and fatalities, while increasing traffic flow. In Germany, the crash rates on 2 + 1 roads are 36 percent lower than on conventional two-lane highways; in Finland 2 + 1 roads are estimated to have crash rates that are 22-46 percent lower than conventional two-lane highways; and Sweden has experienced a reduction of over 50 percent in fatal and injury accidents with the implementation of 2 + 1 roads with cable barriers along the median (2 + 1 roads without cable barriers were less effective) (Keith *et al.*, 2005; Potts, 2003). These results are impressive, but their effectiveness relative to crash rates on two-lane roads is somewhat misleading, because these are essentially three-lane roads. A more interesting evaluation is to compare them to four-lane divided highways, which are more expensive to build and maintain. Chae, Lee, and Cho (2013) did this in an analysis of the safety and economic benefits of 2 + 1 roads, and concluded that their cost\benefit ratio is better than that of four-lane roads. Yannis *et al.* (2015) in an extensive evaluation of various current infrastructure safety improvements list 2 + 1 roads as one of the recommended safety treatments, despite its high implementation cost.

To a great extent most roads are at least partially self-organizing and already provide positive guidance. Sign perception and registration studies show that most drivers do not process all of the information in roadway signs (Martens, 2000; Näätänen and Summala, 1976; Shinar and Drory, 1983, see Chapter 5), and instead rely on the actual road features for their control and guidance decisions. Furthermore, it can be argued that a good indication of failure of self-organizing roads and positive guidance is when the standard traffic control devices and road markings are insufficient to assure safe travel. In fact, there are situations where the direct perception of the road environment and communications with other road users are more effective and safer than dictating behavior through traffic control devices. A case in point is Persaud *et al.*'s (1997) finding that the replacement of traffic signals with multi-way stop signs in one-way streets in Philadelphia, PA, resulted in a 24 percent decrease in collisions. In this case intersection crossings based on drivers' own decisions proved safer than relinquishing the role of decision to traffic signals. Taking the same concept to extreme, a few small towns in Europe (Drachten in the Netherlands, Ejby in Denmark, Ipswich in England, and Ostende in Belgium) have replaced the traditional design that contains multiple traffic control devices with "shared space" design. This approach is applied to high-density urban centers, where through mutual agreement among motorists, cyclists, and pedestrians, nearly all traffic controls, light signals and signs are eliminated, and the flow of people and vehicles is governed almost exclusively by shared norms (e.g., pedestrians have right of way) and unobstructed visual communications. The latter also implies strict prohibition of parked vehicles that can pose view obstructions. The shared space design seems to be very popular with the town's people (Schulz, 2006), but not all and definitely not the majority of the elderly pedestrians (Gerlach *et al.*, 2009). Still, where appropriately applied it does seem to improve both traffic flow and safety (Edquist and Corben, 2012; Gerlach *et al.*, 2009).

Traffic calming with roundabouts

Traffic calming techniques through highway design changes appear to be the most effective means of slowing drivers, especially through the use of single-lane traffic roundabouts. Their effectiveness in crash reduction has been so great and consistent, that they are rapidly replacing uncontrolled and controlled intersections. Also, with only one traffic management rule (vehicles in the roundabout have the right-of-way), they are perhaps the most ubiquitous manifestation of positive guidance and self-organizing roads, and there is an abundance of research that demonstrates their crash reduction benefits (Elvik *et al.*, 2009; Flannery and Datta, 1996; Niederhauser, Collins, and Myers, 1997; Persaud *et al.*, 2001; Retting *et al.*, 2001; see also Chapter 15). Furthermore, their effectiveness is greater in reductions of severe and fatal crashes than in non-injury and slight injury crashes (Elvik *et al.*, 2009). Retting et al.'s (2001) evaluation of the effects of replacing signals and stop signs with single lane roundabouts at 24 U.S. intersections is a good example. Using an empiric Bayes procedure to estimate the magnitude of the effect of intersection conversions they found a 76 percent decrease in injury crashes and 90 percent decrease in incapacitating injury and fatal crashes. Furthermore, the safety benefits of roundabouts do not compromise mobility. In fact, roundabouts actually reduce delays compared to stop-controlled and signal-controlled intersections. Jacquemart (1998) measured the delay of traffic in eight stop-controlled and signal-controlled intersections before and after they were converted to roundabouts, and obtained 78 percent reduction in total delay (stopped delay plus move-up time in queue) in the morning peak periods, and 76 percent reductions in total delays in the afternoon peak periods after the intersections were converted to roundabouts.

There are several reasons for the effectiveness of roundabouts in crash and injury reductions:

1. They force drivers entering the roundabout to reduce their speed. This makes it easier to choose a gap to enter the circle, and in the case of a crash it reduces the impact speeds.
2. They eliminate all left turns (right turns in England, Australia, etc.) which often involve detecting and judging gaps to approaching oncoming traffic. This eliminates a maneuver that is particularly difficult for older drivers.
3. Their larger curb radius improves maneuverability.
4. They simplify the drivers' decision process by making it a one-way operation: yield-at-entry.
5. They reduce the number of inter-vehicle conflict points compared to a conventional four-leg intersection – from 32 vehicle-to-vehicle conflicts and 24 vehicle-to-pedestrian conflicts for a conventional four-leg intersection to eight vehicle-to-vehicle conflicts and eight vehicle-to-pedestrian conflicts for a roundabout with four one-lane entries.
6. When collisions do occur at roundabouts they are rear-end or merge-type crashes; both involving low speed and low impact with few (if any) injuries (Wallwork, 1993).
7. They improve pedestrian safety by providing pedestrians with shorter crossing distances, fewer possibilities for conflicts with vehicles, and lower vehicle speeds.

There is, however, one caveat in this apparent panacea: roundabouts may compromise the safety of older – especially visually impaired – pedestrians. These road users have difficulties in judging gaps from approaching vehicles (Lobjois and Cavallo, 2007), and so for them pedestrian signals are probably preferable. In addition, where roundabouts are not common, older drivers may not know how to negotiate them, and may be also slow to adjust to the novel system. Thus, the impact of roundabouts on older road users needs more investigation.

Enforcement as part of environmental traffic control

When the cues from the roadway itself are insufficient, we rely on enforcement. Enforcement can be part of the environmental approach to safety improvements in two respects: by embedding automated enforcement in the infrastructure and by enforcing the proper design and maintenance required of the local authorities.

Automated enforcement

Today's technology enables us to automate various aspects of traffic law enforcement. Red light cameras can detect, photograph, and record the license plate numbers of traffic light violators. Speed cameras can do the same for speed limit violators, and even headways between vehicles can be monitored and recorded – though not as reliably – to enforce safe headways (UK Speed Trap Guide, 2006). The obstacles to wide-area implementation of such devices are social, legal, and financial; and the latter is constantly diminishing. However, because much of the motoring public would like to have both safety and freedom, the high reliability and ease of installation of such systems make them unpalatable to many drivers and their elected representatives. Still, the trend appears to be one of increasing use of automated enforcement – especially red light cameras – and freeing police officers to deter other high-risk behaviors that are not easily detected by automated systems, such as impaired driving, aggressive driving, and distracted driving. In a review of evaluation studies of the effectiveness of automated enforcement Decina *et al.* (2006) concluded that both speed cameras and red light cameras not only reduce the frequencies of these violations, but are also effective in injury reductions.

The effects of speed cameras on speeds and crashes were evaluated in Australia, Canada, the Netherlands, New Zealand, the United Kingdom, and the effects of red light cameras on crashes and injuries were evaluated in Australia, Canada, Hong Kong, the Netherlands, Singapore, the United Kingdom, and the U.S. The results of most of the studies (and several meta-analyses conducted on multiple studies) showed that speed cameras are effective in both speed and crash reduction (Elvik *et al.*, 2009). It should be noted here, that typically both the existence and the locations of the cameras are well advertised in order to maximize their deterrence effect rather than – as some drivers believe – maximize the number of citations.

Unlike speed cameras, red light cameras are viewed by the public as a more legitimate safety device (Schechtman, Bar-Gera, and Musicant, 2016). They are probably also more acceptable to the motoring public because red light running is less acceptable than speeding. Most importantly they are effective in reducing red light violations – with up to 96 percent reduction in the frequency of this dangerous behavior when the yellow phase is extended by 1.0 seconds and the signal light is preceded by a warning sign of photo enforcement (Retting, Ferguson, and Farmer, 2008). It is therefore not surprising that in their review of studies conducted around the world, Decina *et al.* (2006) concluded that red light cameras are effective in injury reductions because they decrease the frequencies of the severe side collisions with cross traffic at the expense of an increase in less severe rear-end collisions. The increase in rear-end crashes is with following vehicles that do not respond fast enough to a sudden braking of the vehicle ahead (e.g., Ahmed and Abdel-Aty, 2015). However, the net effects of the interaction between the type of collision and the camera presence on crashes of different severities is still debatable because of the small number of crashes observed in many of the evaluation studies (De Pauw *et al.*, 2014; Høye, 2013; Lund, Kyrychenko, and Retting, 2009).

Enforcement of proper design and maintenance

Although not practiced very much, in some countries (e.g., Israel) the police may also issue citations against the local authority whenever it neglects to properly maintain the driving environment. This can include replacing of faded traffic signs, trimming of foliage that can obstruct the drivers' view, repairing potholes, and repainting road markings. With such a view of enforcement, the concept of traffic law violations can be extended to agencies responsible for the safety of our driving environment, thereby positively affecting many more road users. Unfortunately neither the public nor the law enforcement agencies see that as their role, and so a great potential to improve the driving environment is not realized.

Selective visual enhancement of roadway features

Under normal – daytime, dry road – conditions, the roadway geometry, the road signs and markings, and the traffic are quite visible. However, at night, in fog, and in the presence of glare the visual environment is degraded, and unless the driver accommodates to the new situation appropriately the risk of a crash increases. Three methods are used to increase legibility and visibility of signs, markings, and roadways: improving legibility and comprehension of signs through ergonomic design, increasing the ambient nighttime illumination (with street lighting and vehicle headlamps), and increasing the contrast of obstacles and sources of information (with choice of colors and by using retroreflective or fluorescent materials).

Improving sign legibility

Legibility and comprehensibility of information can be improved by careful selection of letter fonts and icons, respectively. With the world turning more and more into a global village, symbol signs are the most effective means of conveying language-independent highway information. Iconic – symbol – signs are a practical alternative to text signs when their icons are (1) familiar to the users (such as "no entry" signs), (2) their design is compatible with the content they represent (such as an arrow indicating a curve), and when they conform to standards the user is familiar with (such as a diagonal line across a symbol to indicate prohibition) (Ben-Bassat and Shinar, 2006). Under such conditions symbol signs can be perceived from twice as far as a comparable text message. However, some signs are perceived from three times as far, while others are perceived from only half as far (Jacobs, Johnston, and Cole, 1975). It turns out that the visibility of iconic signs depends on the degree that they use high spatial frequency contours (i.e., small details) to convey critical information, so that the greater the dependence on high frequencies, the shorter the legibility distance (Schieber 1998), and when the signs are modified to eliminate these small details their legibility distance is increased. Kline and Fuchs (1993) compared the visibility distance for signs that were presented as text, standard (American) symbols, or "improved" symbols as illustrated in Figure 19-3. The improved symbol signs retained the original general design (so that they remained familiar to the drivers) but maximized contour size, size of small details (gaps), and contour separation. The effects of these seemingly small changes were quite dramatic, especially for the older drivers. For drivers of all ages, standard symbol signs were identified from twice the distance as the text signs, and their "improved" symbol signs were identified from an additional 50 percent farther by middle-aged and older drivers.

When there is no icon that fulfills all three conditions listed above or when the message to convey is a name of a street or a town, text signs must be used. With text signs, the legibility – the distinctiveness of different letters of the alphabet – greatly depends on the font. Ergonomics guidelines provide specifications of the appropriate letter height (for drivers with 6/12 Snellen visual acuity), the optimal width-to-height ratio (3:5-1:1) and stroke width-to-letter-height ratio (1:6-1:8) (Sanders and McCormick, 1993). However, even within these specific recommendations variations in font can make a significant difference, especially for drivers with reduced vision, such as many of the older drivers.

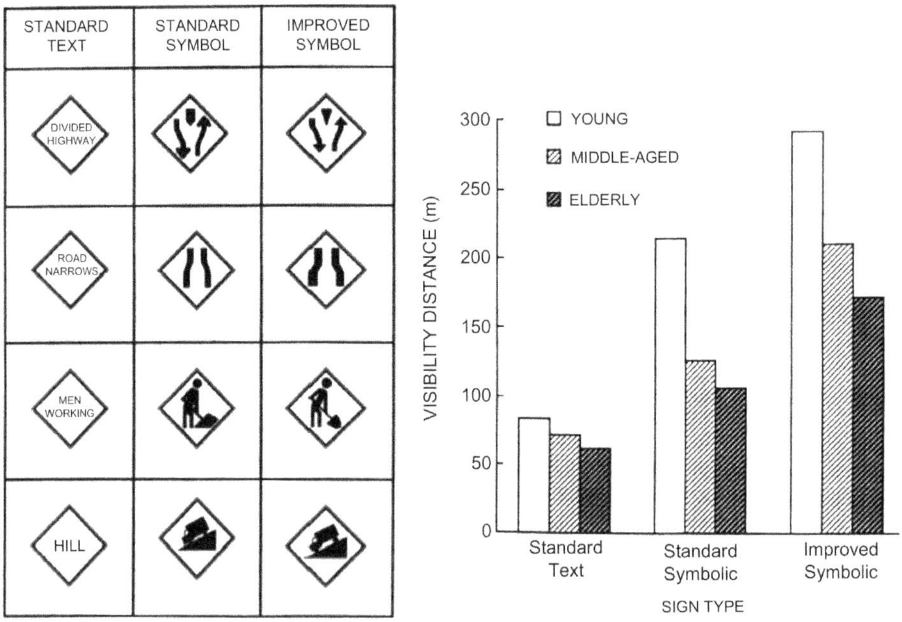

Figure 19-3. Text, standard symbol, and improved symbol signs (left panel) and their visibility distance by drivers of different ages (from Kline and Fuchs, 1993, with permission from the Human Factors and Ergonomics Society).

In the U.S. the standard highway sign font (known as Highway Gothic) remained unchanged for over 50 years (since 1949), until a new one – Clearview – was developed by a multidisciplinary team of traffic engineers, optics engineers, vision experts, type designers, graphic designers, and psychologists with expertise in perception (Garvey, Pietrucha, and Meeker, 1998). Clearview became the new U.S. Federal standard in the *Uniform Manual of Traffic Control Devices* in 2003, and it is illustrated alongside the highway gothic font in Figure 19-4. It differs from the Highway Gothic style in that (1) it uses both upper and lowercase letters, versus upper case letters only (that from a distance tend to appear like indistinguishable boxes), (2) the lowercase letters are taller and the interior shapes of the letters have greater spaces within them, and (3) the spacing between the lowercase letters is greater. Although the changes may appear very small, they had a significant effect on the legibility distance: daytime reading distance increased by five percent and nighttime reading distance increased by 17 percent (Garvey *et al.*, 1998). When tested for white-on-green (positive contrast) signs it yielded faster word recognition at longer distances, better letter legibility, and less of an overglow (a halo-like effect when a retroreflective sign is illuminated by a car's headlights, which is especially troublesome for older drivers) (Carlson, 2001; Garvey, Pietrucha, and Meeker, 1997; Garvey et al., 1998, 2016; Hawkins *et al.*, 1999; Holick and Carlson, 2003). Interestingly, when tested with black letters on white, yellow, or orange background (negative contrast) the Clearview font did not yield better performance than the Highway Gothic font

Typeface: Destination Legend: FHWA Standard Alphabet, Series E-modified

Typeface: Destination Legend: Clearview 5-W replaces FHWA Standard Alphabet, Series E-modified

Figure 19-4. The old Highway Gothic standard font (left panel) and the improved clearview font (right panel), with positive contrast (for the letters) and negative contrast (for the route numbers) (from FHWA, 2003).

(Holick *et al.*, 2006). However, in general with a positive contrast (white-on-green) the new font improves sign legibility, especially for older people (Garvey *et al.*, 2016).

Roadway illumination

The use of fixed-lighting for roadway illumination is commonplace on urban roads and streets where pedestrians are likely to share the road. Overhead illumination is also becoming more and more common on inter-urban roads. Without this illumination the visibility of the road surface and obstacles on it are greatly degraded, especially in the presence of glare from other cars, and especially for older people (Schieber and Kline, 1994, see Chapters 4 and 7). Multiple studies have repeatedly demonstrated that despite its (unintended) effects of raising speeds, roadway illumination is quite effective in crash reductions (EC, 2003). For example, overhead illumination of high-speed motorways in the Netherlands reduced injury crashes by approximately 50 percent (Wanvik, 2009). Interestingly the effects were more pronounced in good weather and on dry roads. A possible explanation is that illumination may compensate for the higher speeds in these conditions, whereas in marginal weather drivers slow down sufficiently so that the added illumination is less critical.

Contrast enhancement

The benefits of contrast enhancement are more controversial. The reason is that we cannot increase the contrast of all roadway elements (e.g., of an animal crossing the road at night), and the selective enhancement of fixed elements can actually be detrimental. To illustrate, a common safety treatment is that of increasing the nighttime conspicuity of the lane delineators, which enables the driver to perceive the roadway geometry farther ahead. However, this does not enhance the visibility of obstacles that may be on the road. This can create a very dangerous situation because (1) perception of detail and obstacle detection is governed by a different visual process than spatial orientation that is enhanced by the reflectorized lane delineators and (2) drivers are unaware that the visibility improvement from the high contrast delineation is selective (Leibowitz and Owens, 1977). Thus, if the driver in response to the increased visibility of the road geometry increases his or her speed, the net effect on crashes will be negative. Kallberg (1993) evaluated the effects of delineation reflector posts in Finland where in 22 pairs of similar rural road segments one road was equipped with the reflectorized posts along the edge and one was not. He found that in the presence of reflectorized posts drivers increased their speed, and nighttime injury crashes increased by 40-60 percent. In a fully controlled simulation study we selectively enhanced the visibility of lane markings of road segments without increasing the visibility of the road surface or obstacles on it. While the enhancement of the lane markings reduced drivers' lateral variability in the lane, it also induced drivers to increase their speeds and to have more crashes. Furthermore, post-experimental interviews showed that the drivers were not aware of the selective degradation in their performance (Sharfi and Shinar, 2014).

Traffic signals management

Traffic signals are one of the more common means of regulating traffic flows, especially in urban areas. One of the challenges in designing the change intervals from green to yellow to red is how to accommodate approaching drivers so that they will maximize the available green phase interval without driving through the red interval. This is where the yellow light and yellow light dilemma enter. The yellow (or amber) light dilemma is whether to stop before the intersection or accelerate through it when the light turns yellow. Obviously if the driver is very far he or she will slow down and stop; if the driver is very near he or she will just proceed to clear the intersection. But there is a certain distance at which the driver may do either, and that zone is termed the dilemma zone. Typically the yellow light duration is approximately 3 seconds. However, to minimize the range of indecision the yellow phase duration should depend on various factors such as the traffic approach speed, size of the intersection, and drivers' reaction time. The Institute of Transportation Engineers (ITE) recommends a formula in which the yellow light duration is based on the approaching driver's reaction time, the approach speed, and the rate of deceleration. In this formula the recommended assumed value for driver reaction time is 1.0 seconds, and the assumed deceleration rate is 3 m/s^2. Thus, the only true variable is the approach speed (ITE, 1999). However, driver reaction time is not constant and varies significantly among drivers and circumstances (see Chapter 5), and consequently there remains a zone at which some drivers approaching at a given speed may decide to stop while some – and occasionally right behind the stopping drivers – may decide to accelerate and proceed. While it is difficult to design the light to prevent such rear-end collisions, collisions with cross traffic from drivers who enter the intersection after the light has turned red, can be reduced by adding an "all red" phase. The importance of the all red phase can be appreciated in light of the fact that approximately 75 percent of all red light violations occur within the first second of the red phase (Retting, Williams, and Greene, 1998). The ITE also has recommendations for the duration of such a phase, and they are based on the width of the intersection and the traffic speed. However, often engineers simply use a fixed yellow phase duration (which approximates the ITE recommended duration for many urban intersections) for all intersections regardless of the traffic approach speeds and decelerations (e.g., 3 seconds in Israel). In general, timing the signal phasing according to the ITE recommendations is safer than timing the phases so that they do not provide for adequate clearance of the intersections. This has been shown both in terms of the frequencies of drivers running the red lights (Retting and Greene, 1997; Retting *et al.*, 2008), and in terms of injury crashes; especially with pedestrians and bicyclists (Retting, Chapline, and Williams, 2002).

Synchronization of the green cycle along travel routes is often used to improve traffic flow. But it also has an added safety benefit. In a study conducted in select Tel Aviv urban routes, we found that drivers are much less likely to run the red lights when the timing of the signals along the route is synchronized with the traffic speed than when it is not. Furthermore, the likelihood of running red lights increased as congestion increased, traffic speed deviated more and more from the design speed, and the signal timing became less and less relevant to the drivers along the route (Shinar, Bourla, and Kaufman, 2004).

Other environmental treatments

In an attempt to help safety agencies improve their funding decisions, the European Commission (EC, 2003) embarked on an ambitious project to estimate the Benefit/Cost ratios (B/C) of various safety measures on one common scale. The project – ROSEBUD (ROad Safety and Environmental Benefit-cost and cost-effectiveness analyses for Use in Decision-making) – reviewed each program that had been implemented and evaluated for its effectiveness and cost-effectiveness. To provide a basis for comparisons among programs, standard crash-related costs were assigned to each fatality (1.92 million Swiss Francs – CHF), serious injury (247, 000 CHF), slight injury (9,000 CHF), and property damage (28,000 CHF). Because the numerical values – for both the cost estimates and the benefits estimates – are sometimes based on questionable assumptions, a rough guideline is to consider a B/C ratio as poor when B/C < 1.0 or the cost "per life year saved" is greater than $20,000; good when the 3.0 > B/C > 1.0 or the cost per life year saved is $10,000-$20,000; and excellent when B/C > 3 or the cost per life year saved is <$10,000. The B/C ratios for selected environmental treatments are listed in Table 19-9.

The quantification of the benefit/cost ratios in Table 19-9 can be a useful guide to setting priorities and allocation of funds to improve safety. However, the application of this information is not so simple for the following reasons:

1. In most instances program evaluations are based on one or two demonstration studies only. When there is a single B/C estimate it is derived from a single study.
2. The costs involved in a given treatment may vary significantly among countries and therefore the B/C ratios would differ as well.
3. Many of the treatments have benefits other than safety (e.g., traffic flow) and the safety B/C ratio is therefore only one component of the benefits to be achieved. This, for example, was probably the case in the (expensive) construction of bypass roads in Norway and Sweden.

Table 19-9. Selected environmental treatments and their benefit/cost ratios in specific select evaluations (based on data from EC, 2003).

Treatment	**b/c Ratio**
Management of traffic interferences in Switzerland	0.09
Intelligent speed adaptation in the United Kingdom	>5.0
Intelligent speed adaptation devices in Sweden	1.37
Variable speed control sign in Finland	<1.0
Variable message signs in Sweden and Norway	1.13-1.45
Traffic surveillance and control system for an urban freeway in Israel	1.7-6.3
Safety audit – Denmark	1.46
Implementation of Road Safety Audits (RSA) in Germany	4.0-99
Winter maintenance of roads in Norway and Sweden	2.67-3.17
Securing of highway construction sites in Switzerland	7.0
Bicycle lanes in urban areas in Norway	9.74
Traffic calming: integrated area-wide urban speed reduction in the United Kingdom	0.36-9.72
Traffic calming: road narrowing and humps in residential areas in Germany	17
Traffic calming: roundabouts in Norway and Sweden	1.23-8.61
Black spot treatment program in Australia	4.10-5.10
Bypass roads in Norway and Sweden	0.84-0.88
Installing of road lights in Norway	7.23-9.25
Paving shoulders on rural two-lane roads in Australia	2.8

4. Similar (or similarly labeled) treatments can have widely different B/C ratios. Area-wide traffic calming is one such example, and implementation of road safety audits is another.
5. The B/C for the same treatment can vary over different road segments. This, for example, was the case in assessing the B/C of traffic surveillance in Israel's central

urban motorway. The benefits in the central high-congestion portions were much greater than the benefits in the farther outlying segments.

In summary, the EU report is more useful as a compendium of the results of slightly dated research on safety treatments, than as a standard or a guideline for deciding on which treatments to apply. Still, when different treatments are being considered their B/C values can help in preferring treatments that have yielded high B/C ratios over treatments that have yielded low ones.

Road safety audits and road assessment programs (RAPs)

Road safety audits

Road safety audits are formal procedures designed to assess the expected safety of planned and existing roads. Their goal is to examine the road from the perspective of its potential users (drivers, bicyclists, pedestrians), and then – once a road is considered safe and it is opened to the public – monitor the behavior of the users to see if they in fact behave as expected and if their safety is assured. Safety audits are increasing in popularity and they are recommended by the U.S. Federal Highway Administration (FHWA, 2014), the American Institute of Transportation Engineers (ITE, 2007), the European Union (ETSC, 2005), and Austroads of Australia (Morgan and Jordan, 2000). In fact, road safety audits are inherent in the Human Factors Guidelines for Road System (Campbell *et al.*, 2016). Good audits evaluate road safety relative to the principles of positive guidance and self-organizing roads (Vardaki, Papadimitriou, and Kopelias, 2014). The benefits of road safety audits go beyond the specific issues raised in the individual audits and the estimated crash reductions from their implementation. It is likely that the crash savings are under-estimated because even when no changes in design are recommended, as a result of the process the mere requirement of the audit raises the awareness of and attention to safety issues on the part of the planners, the designers, and the contractors.

Road assessment programs

Road assessment programs (RAPs) are not strictly crash countermeasures, but they are supplementary tools that provide a metric to measure the safety of the road system and progress in its improvement. There are now several such programs at various stages of development in the U.S. (usRAP), in Europe (euroRAP) and in Australia (ausRAP), and there is even an international program (iRAP). According to this program, the safety levels of individual road segments in a network of roads are defined in terms of their rates of fatality and serious injury crashes (either per road length or per total distance traveled by all cars). The RAP approach, like the NCAP system for cars (described below), rates each road segment in terms of its fatality/serious injury crash risk on a five-level risk category providing a five-level star rating system based on the inclusion of road safety features known to reduce crash likelihood and severity. Regional, state, and national goals can then be described in terms of the percent of inter-urban roads in each risk category, thereby providing an incentive to increase road-based safety features and evaluate progress relative to road improvements (Harwood *et al.*, 2008, 2010). Because investments designed to improve the RAP ratings may be high, the issue of cost/benefit is paramount. In this context, both the costs of construction and the value of life (most commonly defined in neutral terms as the value of statistical life – VSL), vary greatly among countries (Milligan *et al.*, 2014), and obviously impact relevant policy decisions.

Vehicle Safety and Design for Safety

Probably the most significant improvements in safety over the past decade have been in vehicles: vehicle crashworthiness and more recently crash avoidance systems. These systems, often labeled as e-Safety or ADAS (advanced driver assistance systems), rely on new sensing and control technologies that continuously monitor the driver and vehicle behavior, sense their driving environment (road and traffic) and merge the information from these various sources to identify imminent hazards and prevent them from materializing into crashes. These new safety systems coexist with the traditional approach to periodically test vehicles for their safety (and exhaust emissions), and improvements in design and materials to reduce crash injury. The latter are evaluated in standardized crash testing generically known as New Car Assessment Programs (NCAP).

Unlike the roadways where engineers are cognizant of the conflicting demands to reduce driver uncertainty by removing as many potential obstacles as possible (thus inadvertently enabling distracted driving and speeding), and by positive guidance and self-organizing roads guidelines (that often induce slow speeds), the situation in vehicle design is quite different. Here the emphasis appears to be on improving crashworthiness and crash avoidance by reducing the driver's *decision making* load and uncertainty as much as possible, while providing the driver with alternative targets for his or her attention: mostly in the form of expanded communications and entertainment systems.

Periodic motor vehicle inspections

Vehicles have always had safety features. Over the years these features have improved in their performance (e.g., tires and brakes) and in their variety (e.g., hazard and lane departure warning systems). So it is reasonable to expect that one of the primary prerequisites for safe driving be a safe vehicle, or at least one that performs according to the current safety standards. Consequently, to verify that all the vehicles on the road meet minimum safety standards, many countries have periodic motor vehicle inspections (PMVI's) as part of a proactive safety policy that is recommended by the World Health Organization (Peden *et al.*, 2004).

But are PMVIs relevant and effective? The answer is yes and (probably) no. Christensen and Elvik (2007) analyzed Norwegian crash data and found that technical defects in cars were associated with a small, but statistically significant increase in accident rate and that periodic inspections were effective in getting car owners to repair technical defects. However, the accident rate of inspected cars did not decline, but actually showed a weak tendency to increase. Similar findings have been obtained by other researchers in other parts of the world. Evaluations that compared crash rates before and after PMVIs, crash rates in jurisdictions with and without PMVIs, and crash rates as a function of the comprehensiveness of the PMVI have generally failed to demonstrate any safety benefits of the PMVIs (Christensen and Elvik, 2007; Fosser, 1992; Jarosiński, 2014; Leigh, 1994; Poitras and Sutter, 2002). The most likely explanation for this puzzling result is that of behavioral adaptation. Just as people increase risk-taking behavior in response to added safety features, they also adjust their driving habits to accommodate for their vehicle's idiosyncrasies and deficiencies (Christensen and Elvik, 2007; Poitras and Sutter, 2002). This explanation seems quite consistent with crash causation analyses that indicate that vehicle systems – by themselves, without human and environmental factors – are responsible for no more than 0.5-2 percent of crashes (Chapter 18). Another explanation is that defective vehicles are one more manifestation of lack of concern for safety on the part of some drivers, and the periodic inspection and repairs that follow it do very little to offset the high-risk driving of these people. One analysis has even shown that PMVIs have essentially no impact on the mechanical conditions of old vehicles – the ones that should be the most affected by them – as reflected by absence of benefits to the auto repair industry (Poitras and Sutter, 2002).

There have, however, been three studies – all conducted in New Zealand – that suggest that PMVIs are effective. In New Zealand annual PMVIs are conducted on vehicles that are less than 6 years old and bi-annual PMVIs are done on vehicles that are 6 years old or older. The rationale is that the rate of vehicle defects increases with increasing vehicle age. White (1986) examined the likelihood of a crash as a function of time since PMVI, and found – as he hypothesized – that crash probability increased with increasing time since the last PMVI. However, vehicle defects were noted in only 2.5 percent of vehicles less than 15 years old, and in approximately five percent of the vehicles that were 15 years old or older (of which there are not many vehicles). Furthermore the increase over time – regardless of vehicle age – was less than one percent. Blows *et al.* (2003) conducted a small-scale study in Auckland NZ where they compared the odds of inspection in nearly 600 crash-involved drivers and a control group of drivers sampled from the traffic stream. They found that the odds of no inspection within the past 6 month or no tire pressure check within the past 3 months were greater among the crash-involved drivers than among the control drivers. However, the confidence intervals around the obtained odds ratios of 3.08 for the PMVI and 1.89 for the tire pressure check had fairly large confidence intervals around them, indicating a potentially weak effect (1.87-5.05 and 1.16-3.08, respectively). In a more recent New Zealand study Keall and Newstead (2013) evaluated the benefits of the bi-annual inspections required for the 6+ years old cars and vans and found that the PMVI was associated with a small crash reduction.

The real justification for a PMVI should rest not on the savings in crashes but in the benefit/cost ratio. These programs are quite expensive as they cover whole populations of vehicles, and their benefits are actualized on very few vehicles. Even when the evaluations demonstrate crash reductions, the cost/benefit analyses repeatedly show that the crash reduction is not cost-effective: the total cost of the crashes prevented is significantly less than the cost of the inspections, even before including the management of the system (Elvik *et al.*, 2009; Keall and Newstead, 2013).

Given the weight of the evidence, one wonders why PMVI's exist and persist. Obviously, they do not serve the public safety or the public interest in a cost-effective manner. Sutter and Poitras (2002) analyzed this policy issue and concluded – that unlike many other policies that support special-interest groups (like the automotive or repair industry) – this policy supports neither public nor special-interest groups. Their conclusion was therefore that it remains in effect simply due to "political transactions costs" (A similar rationale appears to be the requirement for the use of running daylights in countries of lower latitudes such as Israel). Thus, while PMVI may be beneficial for emissions and vehicle licensing control, safety-wise it has not justified itself.

Vehicle safety standards and new car assessment programs (NCAP)

Safety standards and injury reductions
It may seem surprising, but the first vehicle safety standards were issued only in the late 1960s by the U.S. NHTSA and were applied in U.S. to vehicles manufactured after January 1, 1968. The standards were defined not in terms of specific design requirements but in terms of performance or functional requirements that would mitigate injuries in all three phases of Haddon's matrix: pre-crash, crash, and post-crash. For the next three decades safety was driven primarily through regulation, and only toward the end of the last century did the buying public start demanding it, and the automobile manufacturers started marketing it as part of the appeal of their cars (O'Neill, 2009).

Vehicle safety features have contributed greatly to crash and injury reductions, and the new and emerging technologies are expected to contribute even more. The estimated benefits – in terms of estimated number of lives saved in the U.S. in 2012 – of various standards associated with vehicle safety devices were calculated by Kahane (2015) and are provided in Table 19-10. According to the U.S. NHTSA in 2012 33,561 people were killed in traffic crashes and the estimated number of lives saved by all 14 safety standards was 27,621. In other words, if it were not for these safety technologies and the standards that required them the number of people killed would have been 61,182 or 82 percent higher. This of course assumes that the effects are additive (a shaky assumption) and that all else remains the same (also a shaky assumption given driver adaptation). Regardless of the absolute number of lives saved so far, the expected contribution of these systems is likely to increase as their penetration increases (with the removal of older vehicles, and with the expected increase in the use of seat belts). Note also that most of these systems are not patently visible to the driver, and thus their expected benefits are probably not reduced by any risk-compensation tendencies. On the other hand seat belts and electronic stability controls are, and therefore their net benefit in reducing fatalities may be lower because of driver adaptation. Seat belts alone, given their use levels in the U.S., were responsible for 25 percent reduction, frontal air bags saved an additional five percent, and electronic stability control (ESC) saved approximately two percent more. Note, however, that in 2012 seat belts were installed in nearly all vehicles running on the road and the average use rate

Table 19-10. Estimates of lives saved in the U.S. in 2012 by safety technologies required by U.S. Federal Motor Vehicle Safety Standards (FMVSS), 1960-2012 (from Kahane, 2015).

FMVSS and Associated Safety Technologies	**Car Occupants**	**LTV Occupants**	**Pedestrians Bicyclists Motorcyclists**	**Total**
105/135: Dual master cylinders and front disc brakes	217	201	65	480
108: Conspicuity tape for heavy trailers	90	70		161
126: Electronic stability control for cars and LTVs	500	824	38	1,362
201: Instrument panel improvements and head impact protection	778	573		1,350
203/204: Energy-absorbing steering assemblies	1,323	1,084		2,407
206: Improved door locks	486	641		1,127
208: Seat belts – all types, all seating positions15	7,169	8,316		15,485
208: Frontal air bags	1,738	1,193		2,930
212: Adhesive windshield bonding	177	95		271
213: Child safety seats	213	145		357
214: Side impact protection and curtain/side air bags	1,196	315		1,512
216: Roof crush resistance (eliminate true hardtops)	122			122
226: Curtains that deploy in rollovers	3	41		43
301: Fuel system integrity – rear impact upgrade	5	4		9
TOTAL	14,018	13,500	103	27,621

exceeded 85 percent. On the other hand ESC became compulsory only in 2012 cars, and thus most of the vehicles on the road did not have it yet.

Most of the early safety features were "passive" protection systems in the sense that they operated without any driver intervention. They included crash absorbing bumpers, energy-absorbing steering assemblies, improved door locks (that prevented doors from popping open during a crash and thus reducing the chance that the vehicle occupants would be ejected), side door beams to better protect passengers from side impacts, and adhesive bonding of the windshields. Also, these systems – even when not passive (as in the case of seat belts and child safety seats) – focused on the crash phase (in the Haddon matrix) and were therefore protective systems rather than preventive systems designed to prevent crashes. Of these, by far the most effective in terms of saving lives has been the three-point belt system; an active system that required the cooperation of the driver. Getting the drivers and passengers to cooperate through laws or persuasion was most difficult, because driver behavior was not a part of the vehicle safety system. It was the combined standard requiring the belts AND compliance on the part of the motoring public that made belts by far the most effective vehicle safety feature in terms of saving lives in the past several decades.

New car assessment programs (NCAP)

A direct test to measure compliance with safety requirements was to subject cars and occupants to standardized crash tests. These were first initiated by NHTSA in the late 1970s to evaluate the protection afforded by belts in different car models. This standardized early testing was the predecessor of the now ubiquitous NCAPs.

The NCAPs evaluate the injury protection provided by different model cars as tested in crashes with anatomically accurate instrumented dummies, and the crash prevention potential on the basis of the inclusion of various crash prevention systems. NCAPs – coupled with increasingly demanding safety standards and the public's growing demand for safety – have undoubtedly become the most significant incentives of the automobile manufacturers' scramble to improve the safety of their vehicles. The specific procedures vary slightly among the major NCAP evaluations (in the U.S. by NHTSA and the Insurance Institute of Highway Safety, in Europe by EuroNCAP, and in Australia by ANCAP). One common user-friendly feature is the 1-5-star ratings of various protections (frontal impact to driver and passenger, side impact). This feature acts as a significant incentive to all automakers as today's consumers are more and more concerned with the safety of their vehicles. In fact, because of the rush of manufacturers to excel in crash protection "virtually all new vehicles are five-star performers" in terms of occupant frontal crash protection (O'Neill, 2009). Over the years the system has expanded to include occupant protection from offset frontal crashes, side crashes, rear crashes, and most recently frontal collisions with pedestrians. Of course, the value of the tests relies on the assumption that they mimic real road crashes. This assumption has been validated by several studies. Kullgren, Lie, and Tingvall (2010) found a clear relationship between the risk of severe and fatal injuries and the star ratings based on the Euro NCAP, as can be seen in Figure 19-5. Paine *et al.* (2013) also found a similar relationship

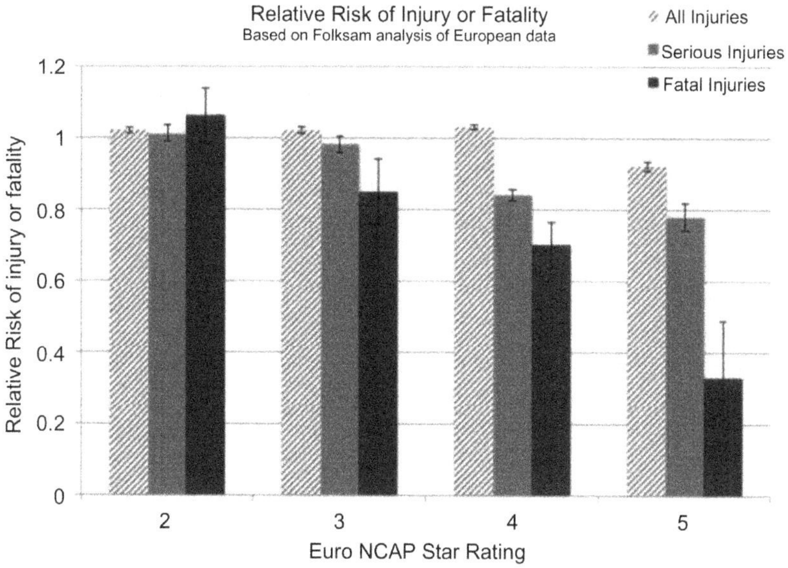

Figure 19-5. The relative risk of injury and fatality in crashes in Europe as a function of their Euro NCAP ratings (based on table data from Kullgren *et al.*, 2010, with permission of Taylor & Francis LLC, http://www.tandfonline.com).

between the ANCAP ratings and crash experience of cars marketed in Australia. According to their analysis an improvement in one star is equivalent to a 20-25 percent reduction in the risk of serious injury. Pastor (2013) obtained a significant correlation between the NCAP pedestrian protection score and pedestrian injury severity in real crashes. In short, good things happen when the safety of automobiles is coupled with effective marketing of vehicle safety that acknowledges the change in the safety culture.

This decade, in a strategic leap, the EuroNCAP expanded its evaluations and ratings to crash avoidance and driver assistance technologies evaluations (EuroNCAP, 2009; van Ratingen *et al.*, 2016). The first to be added were speed limiters, intelligent speed adaptation (ISA) systems, and collision mitigation systems based on collision warning and adaptive cruise control (ACC) with active braking. Currently the EuroNCAP ratings include the following proven systems: electronic stability control, seatbelt reminders, speed assistance, automatic emergency braking, and lane support systems (EuroNCAP, 2017). Given the desire of the auto industry to supply consumers with safe cars, this move should motivate the industry to incorporate these crash avoidance systems (pre-crash vehicle countermeasures in the Haddon matrix) as quickly as possible in as many models as possible.

E-Safety: Intelligent Safety Systems and In-Vehicle Technologies

The automotive industry was rather late in embracing digital technology, but once it did, it did it with alacrity. Intelligent transportation systems (ITS), vehicle informatics, vehicle telematics, advanced driver assistance systems (ADAS), and e-Safety systems are now integral parts of all new vehicles, and the number of such features seems to be increasing in an exponential manner. These new additions can be defined as either safety or "infotainment" (information + entertainment) systems. While the former are specifically designed to increase safety, the latter are designed to increase entertainment and information, presumably while minimizing additional crash risks. The distinction is not always clear-cut. For example, navigation systems are definitely time-relevant information systems, but some of the information they impart may enhance safety (e.g., prevailing speed limit and notifications of accidents or work zones ahead). Unfortunately, a by-product of infotainment systems (the cell phone with its many applications is the most ubiquitous one) is that they compromise safety by increasing driver distraction and inattention. (See Chapter 13 for a detailed discussion of infotainment systems relative to their distraction potential). One can only hope that the combined effects of both systems result in a net gain for safety.

Electronic safety systems – e-Safety

The new installed and emerging in-vehicle safety technologies, labeled e-Safety or advance driver assistance systems (ADAS), have focused more on crash prevention (the pre-crash phase in the Haddon matrix) than on the crash and the post-crash severity reduction and occupant treatment phases. Their development is grounded in consistently recurring crash-causing human errors. The goal of these systems is to effectively compensate for these driver errors because unlike the human controllers they are always alert, "monitoring the road ahead and never getting tired or distracted" (Lund, 2015).

In a major cooperative effort in 2006 the European Union initiated the project eIMPACT designed to "assesses the socio-economic effects of Intelligent Vehicle Safety Systems (IVSS), (and) their impact on traffic safety and efficiency." In addition to the European-wide estimated assessments of savings in money, crashes, and lives from different IVSS, it also developed a methodology that can be applied in any country to determine the costs/benefits associated with different systems so that it might directly impact national safety policy at the highest levels (Baum *et al.*, 2008). The project assessed the following 12 e-Safety systems: electronic stability control (ESC), full speed range adaptive cruise control (FSR), emergency braking (EBR), pre-crash protection for vulnerable road users (PCV), lane change assistant (LCA), lane keeping support (LKS), night vision warning (NIW), driver drowsiness monitoring (DDM), eCall – automatic alerts of emergency crews in case of an accident – (ECA), intersection safety (INS), wireless local danger warning (WLD), and speed alert (SPE). Some of these systems are discussed below. Using different assumptions concerning market penetration, the researchers provided high and low estimates for monetary and crash savings of the different systems. Table 19-11 summarizes the estimated fatalities, injuries, and crash savings from the different systems by 2020. In addition, the project also calculated the cost/benefit ratios for the different systems. In term of cost/effectiveness the best systems are EBR, ESC, and LCA. At the other end of the spectrum, PCV, NIW, and INS had cost\effective ratios less than 1.0; meaning that fiscally speaking they are not worth installing in all vehicles. But as our

Table 19-11. Estimated fatalities, injuries, and accidents prevented in 2020 in the EU countries with the different e-Safety systems. See text for definitions of abbreviations (from Baum *et al.*, 2008, with permission from the European Transport Safety Council, Brussels).

	Year 2020: Number of Avoided					
	Fatalities		**Injuries**		**Accidents**	
	Low	**High**	**Low**	**High**	**Low**	**High**
ESC	2,577	3,253	41.549	52,182	36,263	45,543
FSR	49	101	3,668	9,774	2,750	7,329
EBR	72	193	4,241	10,925	3,180	8,192
PCV	14	39	718	1,918	539	1,438
LCA	33	86	3,449	8,596	2,586	6,445
LKS	197	678	5,109	17,296	3,831	12,969
NIW	30	73	1,046	2,542	784	1,906
DDM	20	94	682	2,715	512	2,036
ECA	*1,199*		*severe: 8,398*		*0*	
			slight: −9,598			
INS	*803*		*63,700*		*47,764*	
WLD	29	66	989	1,906	742	1,429
SPE	753	1,076	24,643	34,887	18,478	26,159
Base	20,791		873,695		798,808	

technological capabilities advance, new safety systems are created and their impact must be evaluated. For example, a small-scale experimental study conducted in the U.S. demonstrated that adaptive headlights that swivel in response to the steering inputs, thereby providing illumination into curves as the car enter them (Reagan, Brumbelow, and Frischmann, 2015) do in fact increase target detection on the inside of curves. Currently, such systems are expensive and available on some high-end models only. But as further evidence demonstrates their crash reduction potential and as their price drops they may spread to more cars and eventually be included in the NCAP safety star ratings.

It is important to realize that the crash and injury savings in individual countries may differ significantly from the savings presented in Table 19-11, as the different countries differ in many relevant characteristics. Nonetheless, the eIMPACT method used to arrive at the estimates is probably valid for all countries, and can be used to arrive at country-specific adjustments. Bekhor *et al.* (2012), used the eIMPACT method to evaluate the safety potential of various e-Safety systems in Israel and found that the most effective in saving lives is ISA, closely followed by LDW. The potential impact of ECA is a good example of differences among countries. In sparsely populated upstate New York it was deemed effective as it reduced crash notification time significantly (Bachman and Preziotti, 2001), and in Finland it was estimated to reduce fatalities by 4-8 percent (Sihvola *et al.*, 2009). On the other hand, Israel being a small country with a dense road network and traffic would not benefit that much from ECA. ESC, the most effective system in Malone's study has been required in all new vehicles in Israel since 2011 and it was therefore not evaluated.

e-Safety, political will, and policy

In a perfectly rational system policy and actions would be driven exclusively by scientifically-determined cost/benefit considerations. But there is more to implementing IVSS than just cost/benefit. One way to classify the different systems is in terms of a dichotomy: those that improve vehicle and driver performance and those that impose limits on driver and vehicle performance. The former include e-call (ECA), electronic stability control (ESC), adaptive cruise control (ACC), hazard and lane keeping support (LKS), and all the other systems evaluated in eIMPACT with the exception of speed alert. The latter include seat belt interlocks, alcohol-ignition interlocks, and speed warning/monitoring/limiting devices such as Intelligent Speed Adaptation (ISA). Unfortunately, it is the latter, politically less palatable, systems that appear to contribute the most to crash prevention and injury reduction as can be seen in Figure 19-6, where

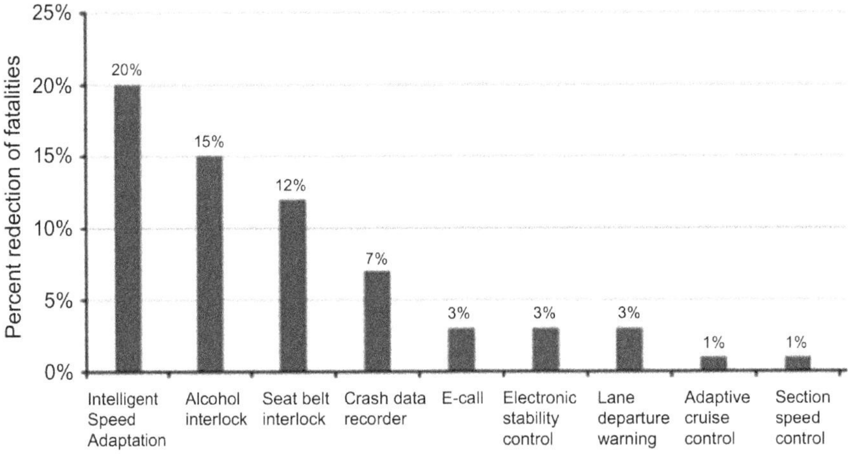

Figure 19-6. The maximum potential in traffic fatalities reductions by means of different intelligent transportation systems (ITS). Based on Norwegian data (from Elvik, 2014, with permission from the author).

the potential benefits in terms of lives saved are presented for Norway (from Elvik, 2014). Note that – at least for Norway – these three systems are 4-7 times as effective at saving lives as the top-ranked ESC in Table 19-11. Unfortunately, because these technologies actually impede the drivers, the political will to require their installation is simply not there. However cultural norms change and just as we have learned to accept the (annoying) seat belt reminders and ignition security codes, we may adjust our norms for these systems too; and safety-wise the sooner the better. Again, focusing on country-specific issues, alcohol interlocks will probably have a much lesser impact on crash fatalities in countries where drinking under the influence of alcohol is less of a problem.

As more and more e-Safety systems are being implemented in new cars, empirical on-the-road data accumulate and it becomes easier to establish their value. The electronic safety devices in Table 19-11 and Figure 19-6 are only partial lists of new and emerging systems. The complete list is as limited (or unlimited) as the creative imagination of innovators around the globe. The e-Safety systems described below are by necessity a biased sample that in my opinion illustrate some of the issues involved in integrating e-Safety into our cars. The three systems described below are all operational systems that are either currently installed or instantly implementable, and on which data-based evaluation analyses have already been conducted.

Autonomous emergency braking (EBR)
These systems are designed to engage in emergency braking situations whenever the car is traveling at a low speed (typically less than 50 km/hr) and its time-to-collision to the car ahead drops below a critical threshold. Initial studies that evaluated autobraking relied on either simulation or case studies; that is, artificial environments or small biased samples. Consequently, it was hard to extrapolate from them the real-life benefits of EBR. However, now such systems – under various different names – already exist in many new cars such as Fiat, Ford, Honda, Nissan, Subaru, Volkswagen, and Volvo models. And because the EBRs are typically offered as optional equipment, it is feasible to study their effects by comparing the crash involvement of cars that have them with otherwise identical cars that do not. Three studies have done that. Fildes *et al.* (2015) conducted a prospective meta-analysis in which six countries – Australia and five European countries – joined forces to abide by the same protocol for definitions and data collection procedures. The data sources in all countries were from naturalistic exposures; that is, police accident reports for 2009-2014. The meta-analysis was based on the combined data set of 279 rear-end crashes of cars with EBR and 3,050 cars without EBR. By looking at the ratios between being struck (irrelevant to EBR) and striking (relevant to EBR) collisions in the two groups, they calculated the odds ratios of front-end collisions for cars with EBR relative to cars without EBR in each country. When averaged across all countries, the EBR yielded an estimated 38 percent (with a 95 percent confidence interval of 18-53 percent) reduction in the relevant low-speed, rear-end crashes. In a study conducted in Sweden, Isaksson-Hellman and Lindman (2015) analyzed insurance claims filed in 2012-2014 for Volvo cars with and without the system and obtained 28 percent fewer claims for the EBR-equipped cars. In the third study Cicchino (2016) analyzed police-reported rear-end crashes from 22 states in the U.S. to determine the difference in striking rear-end crashes between the EBR cars and otherwise identical non-EBR cars. The results were strikingly

similar to those obtained by Fildes *et al.* (2015). The EBR cars were involved in 39 percent fewer striking rear-end injury crashes than the non-EBR cars (RR = 0.61, with a 95 percent confidence interval of 64-91 percent). Cicchino also found that cars that had a forward warning collision systems but no EDR were also less involved in striking rear-end crashes, but to a significantly lesser extent (23 percent, mostly in non-injury crashes). Together, the three studies demonstrate that EDR can yield impressive reductions in rear-end crashes, albeit these reductions are mostly in low-speed, minor-injury collisions. It is also important to realize that in their benefit/cost analysis, Baum *et al* (2008) estimate a roughly six fold benefit/cost ratio of EBR by 2020. In light of these findings, the NHTSA and 20 automakers representing more than 99 percent of the U.S. auto market agreed to make automatic emergency braking a standard feature on virtually all new cars no later than September 1, 2022 (NHTSA, 2016a). This is the culmination of one more gratifying science-to-policy process to benefit all motorists.

Sensors and backup cameras for rear visibility

A very dramatic type of crash is the rear-end crash with an obstacle too small or too low for the driver to see while backing up the car. These crashes are not very frequent, but when they occur they involve mostly toddlers and small children, often the driver's own. Many cars have sensors that detect the presence of a large object such as a wall or a car parked behind us, and they are very helpful while reversing the car into a parking spot – but just for that (IIHS, 2014a). However, their range is short, and even within that range they have many blind zones where small objects like stationary toddlers are most likely to be missed. To improve the detection of small "obstacles" many of these systems are now replaced or supplemented by "'backup" cameras that are typically installed just above the rear license plate. In an evaluation of the crash likelihood with these systems, the Insurance Institute of Highway Safety tested unsuspecting drivers' actual collisions with a moving or stationary "foam cut-out of a child-size crash test dummy." Even with the camera, while they were backing out of the garage 56 percent of the drivers hit the stationary dummy. But with the sensors only, the hit rate was 94 percent, and without either a camera or sensors all 100 percent of the drivers hit the dummy (IIHS, 2014b). These alarming crash rates were obtained when the drivers backed out of a parking garage never suspecting (i.e., with zero-level expectancy) that there could be a small object behind them. As a result of such dramatic high-publicity collisions with toddlers, and demonstration studies such as the one by the IIHS, the U.S. National Highway Traffic Safety Administration issued a new safety standard, to be implemented gradually with 100 percent compliance by May 1, 2018. According to this standard (NHTSA, 2014a, 2014b) all vehicles will be required to have a rear-facing camera and an associated display that will cover an area 10x20 feet (3.07x6.14 metres) behind the car. Interestingly, unlike all previously published safety standards that had a positive benefit/cost estimate, here the cost associated with installing the system on all new vehicles was significantly more than its expected benefits (translated to fiscal terms). This is a demonstration that where the public support exists, and the cost to the car buyer is not prohibitive, human-lives considerations can on occasion transcend the cold economic ones. As an added incentive to the industry to install such systems before they are required on all cars, the NHTSA also includes their presence as a factor in its NCAP.

One counter-intuitive finding regarding the rear visibility is the IIHS finding that the combination of the sensors with the camera yielded poorer detection than the camera alone. Although the report did not provide an explanation for this finding, the poorer detection may be due to poor driver adaptation to the system. It is possible that the drivers in the study had already been familiar with the sensor technology (as it is commonly installed on many vehicles), and when it missed a target (in this case the small dummy) they assumed wrongly that the area was clear and did not bother to check the camera view. Also, why did a few drivers miss the object despite the camera? Recall that drivers' habitual behavior to check behind their car is limited to turning their head and/or checking the mirrors, and not to look *down* at the display console. Regardless, even if these two explanations are unfounded, the findings highlight the need to carefully evaluate driver performance and adaptation to new systems independently of the systems' technical capabilities, *before* the benefits of the latter can be estimated.

Intelligent speed adaptation (ISA) and top-speed limiter (TSL)
This is a location-sensitive speed advisory, enforcement, or regulating system that relies on vehicle-to-infrastructure communications. As a vehicle travels on different streets and roads it receives relevant posted/enforced/advisory speed limits. Depending on the level of regulation, the system may be passive and limit itself to advisory information to the driver, or be active and actually intervene and limit the speed to the posted/legal speed limit. ISA constitutes a conceptual departure from traditional speed enforcement as it "shifts the provision of information on momentary speed compliance into the vehicle" (Carsten, 2012). With different levels of passive and active systems, speed control through ISA may be more effective than the highly touted French heavy handed (but effective) approach initiated in by President Chirac in 2002 (Carnis and Blais, 2013). ISA is particularly useful in urban environments, where manual speed enforcement is more difficult. Technologically, the systems are implementable right now and have been for a few years, but in practice they are a rarity. Various versions of ISA systems have been developed and evaluated since the beginning of this millenium and the conclusions of the different studies are quite unanimous: ISA is quite effective in speed and injury reductions, but its acceptability varies widely among countries, types of users, and nature of the system (passive versus active).

In the Norwegian evaluation summarized in Figure 19-6 an active ISA had the greatest life-saving potential of all e-Safety systems evaluated, while a fixed "top-speed limiter" (TSL) was estimated as the least effective (Vaa, Assum, and Elvik, 2014). However, because like many other e-Safety systems ISA is still not a part of an actual operational system, crash data on its effectiveness are missing. An exception is an early evaluation on the crash rates of drivers with and without an active ISA system in the city of Lund, Sweden (Várhelyi *et al.*, 2004). The active system was an ISA where the driver could override the speed limit, but as a disincentive he or she had to apply much more force to the accelerator pedal to exceed the speed limit. The ISA was installed in 284 vehicles and its crash potential was assessed by the odds ratio of the drivers' crash rates before and after the system was installed relative to the crash rates of a the "other drivers" driving in Lund at these times. The effect was quite pronounced: the odds ratio for the

ISA-equipped cars was OR = 0.51, indicating a roughly 50 percent crash reduction. Note that this system still enabled exceeding the speed limit, so the effect would have probably been greater had it prevented that. In fact, the ability to exceed the speed limit was differentially exploited by different driver populations: speed compliance was maximal among women and older drivers (the two physically weakest, low-risk groups) and least with young male drivers (the highest risk group). Unfortunately, as might have been expected acceptability of the system was low, and has remained low. In bi-annual surveys carried out in Norway since 1998 60-70 percent of the drivers do not agree that there "*should be a device in the car making it unpleasant to exceed speed limits.*"

As an indication of the huge cultural shift in norms that is needed to make ISA acceptable to the motoring public, Lahrmann *et al.* (2012) note the agonies of recruiting subjects for an ISA evaluation study in Jutland, Denmark. Early market analysis indicated that as many as 50 percent of the drivers would be "interested" or "very interested" in participating in the project. Yet when over 11,000 drivers were sent letters offering them free installation of ISA in their cars and a 30 percent discount in their insurance only 50 people (people, not percent!) signed up. Thus, "voting with their feet" less than one half of one percent of the drivers supported the system. In general, there is a much greater agreement about required installation of ISA in cars of drivers with either high crash rates or numerous speeding violations than in all cars (Vaa *et al.*, 2014), though this may just be a case of support for something that "does not affect me." The acceptability issue of ISA has also spilled over into a philosophical debate over "big brother" intervention of this type (e.g., Smids, 2016), and it is likely that much greater acceptability of such interventions will be needed before there is political will to legislate and enforce it.

In an innovative approach to the dilemma of an effective speed control measure and lukewarm acceptability, the Road Transport department of NSW, Australia developed an Android-based advisory ISA free application that drivers can download to their phones. The app contains the speed limits for nearly a quarter of a billion kilometers of NSW roads. It was launched in early 2014, and had over 81,000 downloads in the first 14 months (Wall *et al.*, 2015). As with air bags this rapid deployment and spread may eventually either make regulation unnecessary or sufficiently palatable for policy makers. As a start, the European Transport Safety Council recommends that passive ISA "that warns drivers of speed limits and assists the driver to adapt to the correct speed, should be introduced on all professional vehicles such as vans, lorries and buses as part of the EU's ongoing review of general vehicle safety rules, and, in time, for all new vehicle types" (ETSC, 2014b).

There is one other vehicle-based currently-operating speed control system: top-speed limiter (TSL). In a sense TSL is a "stupid" active speed adaptation system that is set at a fixed speed – typically at some threshold above the maximum inter-urban speed limit. Consequently, it is rarely activated anywhere except on motorways, that have the lowest crash rates to begin with. TSLs are already installed on heavy trucks and buses in many places, but they have "no meaningful effect when driving on urban and rural roads with lower speed limits" (ETSC, 2014b). It is therefore not surprising that system-wide they are rated among the least effective e-Safety devices.

Driver acceptance of and adaptation to new technologies

When new systems are introduced, their initial estimated benefits are typically based on (1) the scope of the problem they address, (2) the effectiveness demonstrated in one or several small studies, and (3) their expected market penetration. Such considerations are part of the eIMPACT process. However, the impact assessment that begins with the empirical results of a few studies is fraught with questionable assumptions. For example, it is probably wrong to assume that the impact demonstrated in initial studies will be the actual impact once the system becomes commonplace, as demonstrated by the CHMSL example below. In many instances the initial impact is likely to be greater than the eventual one because of a "novelty" effect – people's reactions are more extreme to new systems than to existing ones. The novelty effect, however, is only one response in a class of responses known as behavioral adaptation – changes in driver behavior that may undermine or enhance the potential benefits of the new systems.

Acceptance and acceptability
A determining factor in the success or failure of a system is driver acceptance. Driver acceptance of new systems is particularly critical now when the automobile is undergoing the most rapid changes ever in its design and functionality. There is a rapid shift in functions once reserved for the drivers (e.g., monitoring lane markers and other vehicles) to the vehicle, coupled with increasing number of non-driving functions that may now be performed by the driver while driving (e.g., various communication options). A critical issue the designer must face is whether the driver, the consumer, will embrace the technological change or reject it. "Good" systems that may improve safety may never get off the ground because of the public's non-acceptance (e.g., seat belt interlocks). This simple question has no simple answer as there are many definitions and methods of measurement of acceptance. To begin we should distinguish between acceptability and acceptance. Acceptability is a measure of people's likelihood to like/use a system before it is actually installed in their vehicle. Acceptance is the measure of people liking/using a system that already exists. Thus, acceptability is a measure of potential acceptance (Schade and Schlag, 2003). Acceptability is invariably measured in subjective terms of potential users (e.g., how much would people be *willing* to pay for a system?), whereas acceptance can be measured in both subjective terms and in objective quantifiable terms (e.g., what percent of the potential users actually buy the system at a given price?). Designers need to know acceptability in order to have some estimate of later, actual, acceptance. Extensive research and development work has gone into measuring different dimensions of acceptability and acceptance, and the interested reader can find much of it summarized in a comprehensive recent volume on Driver Acceptance of New Technology: Theory, Measurement, and Optimisation (Regan, Horberry, and Stevens, 2014). It is important to note that a product may get implemented even if its acceptability is low, as long as it can be regulated and enforced. An example is the installation of seat belt reminders that are now common in all vehicles, despite their reported annoyance (as a measure of acceptability). Another example of the difference between the two is the gap between willingness to participate in a study on ISA and actual participation in the study (see Lahrmann *et al.*, 2012).

Behavioral adaptation

While our personal cars are not yet autonomous, they do incorporate more and more components of the autonomous vehicle in the form of e-Safety systems. And as these are integrated into or added to the car we – as drivers – try to adapt to them by changing our driving style. The process is called behavioral adaptation. Behavioral adaptation, like acceptance, is sometimes hard to predict, and once a system is in place it is sometimes hard to even measure. Yet, small-scale naturalistic driving studies can aid in this prediction. For example, Morando, Victor, and Dozza (2016) studied driver glance behavior in response to adaptive cruise control with forward collision warning that displays and sounds an alarm whenever the car enters an imminent forward collision situation. They found that drivers adapt to the system by redirecting their glances to the forward visual field just prior to such warnings, as a consequence of the ACC's deceleration/braking, the looming of the image of the car ahead, and its brake lights. This is critical because in a review of the literature on the effects of ACC, de Winter *et al.* (2014) found that ACC reduces drivers' subjective workload, but if they are engaged in non-driving secondary tasks (such as using the cell phone) the system reduces their situation awareness. Thus the adaptive glance behavior can compensate, at least partially, for potential distracting activity.

An early poignant example of behavioral adaptation was provided by the introduction of studded tires over 20 years ago. This is a passive safety system in the sense that once installed in a vehicle the driver does not have to adjust his or her behavior to reap its benefits. But, apparently drivers do, and they do it in a counterproductive manner. Studded tires were designed to increase the friction on icy roads and reduce crashes due to skidding. Early estimates of the benefits of studded tires on icy roads were based on the assumption that drivers would not change their behavior once they replaced their tires. But drivers did. They quickly realized the better traction that they had, and – as some anticipated – increased their speed to take advantage of the greater safety; thereby negating some of the benefits of the studded tires. Consequently, the net effect of studded tires, based on a meta-analysis of multiple results, was quite small (Elvik, 1999b). However, because not all drivers switched to studded tires there was a possibility that the findings were contaminated by various driver/vehicle sampling biases. To account for these, Elvik and his associates (2013) compared the injury crash data over different periods of time in four Norwegian cities and statistically controlled for 25(!) variables including city, maximum temperature, specific holidays, and type and amount of precipitation. When all of these were accounted for, they found that overall studded tires did have a small safety benefit – about two percent crash reduction for approximately 20 percent increase in use, and five percent increase in crashes when the use was reduced by 25 percent. Following various straw-hat arguments to the contrary, Elvik *et al.* argued that though the study design was observational, the findings do indicate a cause-and-effect relationship, showing that injury crashes in Norway are affected in the expected direction by the use and non-use of studded tires. One possibility for the discrepancy in the conclusions that emerged from the initial 1999 evaluation and the recent one, is that the reduced rate of using studded tires was not uniform across all types of drivers, and only the die-hard risk-taking speeding drivers retained them, thereby leading to a spurious relationship.

Projected versus actual post-adaptation benefits of safety systems

The specific nature of behavioral adaptation to an individual component is hard to anticipate – let alone quantify. In her forward to a compendium of papers on behavioral adaptation and road safety Smiley (2013) concludes that "behavioral adaptation can be positive, neutral, or negative. If the third one, it can stymie our best efforts in designing safety countermeasures." Typically, if most of us subscribe to some version of risk-homeostasis in our lives we should expect that evaluations based on more drivers gaining more experience in using the system will yield lesser safety benefits than projected by early evaluations based on fewer drivers with less experience. But even when drivers do not consciously attempt to compensate for the added safety, other factors may intervene to reduce the effectiveness of a safety device once it is incorporated into the majority of vehicles on the road. Often these factors are hard to predict, and therefore it is difficult to adjust for their effects. Therefore, the full real benefits of potentially beneficial devices and systems can be assessed only after their actual implementation. Three examples are provided below. The first two examples of inflated expected benefits illustrate the difficulties of assessing the benefits of a given safety device in the absence of an ability to predict how the total traffic system will react to it: the center high-mounted stop lamp (CHMSL) and the anti-lock braking system (ABS). A third example where the optimistic prediction has been validated is that of the currently standard in-vehicle intelligent safety device known as the electronic stability control (ESC) or electronic stability program (ESP).

Center high-mounted stop lamp (CHMSL)

The CHMSL is a red light that is positioned in the center of the rear of the vehicle above the height of the two standard brake lights – most often on the top of the trunk lid or behind the rear windshield of passenger cars. The CHMSL was introduced in the U.S. as a requirement for new cars in 1986. Studies that preceded its required installation demonstrated that this single central rear light reduced "relevant" rear end crashes by 50 percent; or an estimated overall reduction in rear end collisions of 35 percent. Relevant rear end crashes were defined as those in which the driver attempted to brake in response a stopping or slowing vehicle ahead. However, 1 year after it was introduced the estimate of its effectiveness based on national U.S. crash data dropped to 8.5 percent. As the presence of the CHMSL in the traffic stream continuously increased (with more and more post 1986 vehicles coming into the market) repeated evaluations indicated that its safety benefits decreased in parallel. Finally, in 1989-1995 its effectiveness in the U.S. was down to 4.3 percent, which was considered its long-term stable effectiveness (Kahane, 2004). Given its very low cost, even at that level the CHMSL is still cost-beneficial. However, a more recent evaluation of the CHMSL conducted in Israel, showed that prior to controlling for various confounding factors the CHMSL effectiveness in preventing police-reported rear end collisions appeared to be approximately seven percent, but following adjustment for some potentially confounding variables more sensitive analyses showed that this reduction may be due to these potentially confounding factors that are unrelated to the CHMSL (Bar-Gera and Schechtman, 2005). Perhaps a critical shortcoming of the CHMSL was that it was not a technological innovation on the one hand, and it lacked a strong theoretical basis for its effectiveness on the other hand. Thus, whatever the underlying reasons for its initial effectiveness (novelty effect being one of them), they wore off after a few years. The EBR that addresses the same crash scenarios (and more) will most likely retain its effectiveness as it does not involve any behavioral adaptation. It will remain alert and responsive and not be distracted.

Anti-lock braking systems (ABS)

The four-wheel anti-lock braking system (ABS) is an electronic system that automatically detects whenever any of the four wheels begin to skid, and then releases the braking of that wheel until it rolls again at which time it reactivates the braking. Its expected benefits were based on the assumption that few drivers are sufficiently skilled to modulate their braking (by "pumping the brakes") in a manner that would maximize deceleration. Locking the brakes – as often happens in emergency braking (and detected by skid marks) – increases stopping distance and causes loss of steering control. When the front wheels lock the car continues in the same path but steering to avoid obstacles is lost. When the rear wheels lock the driver loses vehicle control. The ABS was therefore designed and expected to significantly reduce both problems. Early evaluations of stopping distance and steering control on test tracks were very impressive, especially on wet surfaces (where the coefficient of friction is greatly reduced) (Kahane, 1994). Following such demonstrations, ABS was first introduced in luxury cars in 1986 and then became standard equipment on most cars and light trucks. Its early marketing success, unfortunately, has not been matched by proven crash reduction benefits. Multiple crash analyses, employing various exposure measures in which the crash involvement of ABS-equipped vehicles was compared to the crash involvement of vehicles without ABS, have yielded fairly consistent results: ABS-equipped cars have fewer frontal impacts, especially on wet roads, but they have more run-off-the-road crashes, rollovers, collisions with fixed objects, and side impacts than non-ABS-equipped cars. Consequently, the net effect of the ABS on both crash reductions and fatalities has been essentially nil (Evans, 1998; Kahane, 2004), and possibly even negative (Wilde, 2013).

The question is why did ABS fail to prove itself as expected in real driving on real roads? Various explanations have been offered to account for the increase in single vehicle crashes. All of the explanations lay the responsibility (blame?) at the driver's feet (literally). Single vehicle crashes are often high-speed crashes, and there is some evidence that ABS encourages some drivers to compensate for the reduced risk by increasing their speed (Evans and Gerrish, 1996). An alternative explanation is that many drivers simply do not know how to adapt their braking behavior to ABS; where hard continuous braking is optimal rather than a pumping action (Kahane, 2004). This is because most drivers on the road today first learned to drive (and survive) with non-ABS brakes that required pumping action to avoid skidding. Some support for this hypothesis comes from the fact that more recent evaluations find lower rates of over-involvement in single vehicle crashes, and that these crashes are associated with DWI, where drivers have poor control of their actions (Harless and Hoffer, 2002). Most damningly European evaluations in real traffic in Germany and Norway have demonstrated that drivers compensate for the benefits of the ABS by driving more aggressively, with more extreme braking actions and shorter headways to vehicles ahead (Wilde, 2013). Whatever the explanation, the fact remains that the potential enhanced safety of the ABS was not realized.

Electronic stability control (ESC)

Electronic stability control systems (ESC) compare the vehicle's steering inputs relative to the vehicle actual attitude and detect and correct for situations of oversteering (when the steering input is greater than the change in the vehicle's attitude) and understeering (when the change in attitude is greater than the change in the steering) by activating the brake of the relevant wheel and by adjusting torque of the engine. Understeer and oversteer typically happen at high speeds and on wet or ice/snow-covered roads, when the driver makes a lateral change as in entering a curve or in abruptly changing lanes. For example, oversteering results in loss of control of the vehicle's rear end. Thus, oversteer in a left curve would cause the rear end of the vehicle to veer to the right. The ESC is designed to detect that and activate the front right brake so that the steering would correspond to the car's direction and that way the car would remain on the road.

Several studies have evaluated the crash reductions associated with ESC by calculating the odds of single vehicle crashes (that are supposed to be affected the most by ESC) relative to other types of crashes in ESC-equipped vehicles and non-ESC-equipped vehicles, and then looking at the ratio of the two odds (the odds ratio) to determine if the ESC changed the relative proportions significantly. The results obtained in studies in the U.S. (Bahouth, 2006; Dang, 2004; Farmer, 2004, 2006), in Sweden (Strandroth *et al.*, 2012; Tingvall *et al.*, 2003), and in Japan (Aga and Okada, 2003) were all quite positive. For example, Farmer (2004, 2006) found a seven percent reduction in overall crash involvement of ESC-equipped vehicles, a 34 percent reduction in fatal crashes, and a 41 percent reduction in single vehicle crashes. Dang (2004) found a 35 percent reduction in single vehicle passenger car crashes and a 30 percent reduction in fatal crashes. Even higher reductions (67 percent) in crashes were obtained when the analysis was restricted to sport utility vehicles (SUV's) – vehicles that are notorious for their susceptibility to rollovers. Analysis restricted to the most relevant crash-type loss-of-control – in Swedish crashes showed a reduction of 29 percent in injury crashes, beyond the reduction due to the use of studded tires (Strandroth *et al.*, 2012). These and similar very positive findings led the American Consumers Union to proclaim already in 2007 that the ESC is "the most important safety advance since the safety belt" (Consumer Union, 2007). The U.S. National Highway Traffic Safety Administration estimated in 2006 that once ESC is available on most vehicles it should result in 30 percent reductions of all U.S. single vehicle crashes and a savings of close to 10,000 lives annually (NHTSA, 2006b). Such proclamations and their dissemination were responsible for the ESC spread in new vehicles in Sweden from 15 percent to 90 percent in just 4 years (Krafft *et al.*, 2009), and from 22 percent in 2007 to 92 percent in 2011 in the U.S (NHTSA 2016c). Given the very high public support and market penetration, the U.S. NHTSA issued a safety standard that required all 2012 and newer cars and light trucks to be equipped with ESC, and already in 2012 alone it was estimated to have saved 1,362 lives on American roads (Kahane, 2015). Other countries, like Israel, were quicker to respond to the research findings and the motoring public's support and made the ESC a required standard feature on all new cars beginning in 2011. Once implemented, ESC has proven itself, though not as much as originally expected. In the U.S. NHTSA (2016c) estimated that in 2014, with nearly 40 percent of all vehicles being equipped with ESC it reduced vehicle occupant fatalities by approximately seven percent. Though a bit shaky, an extrapolation to 100 percent immersion brings the total to over 17 percent of all vehicle occupants (note: not all fatalities), a figure that is roughly consistent with the EU 2008 estimate in Table 19-11.

The success of the ESC both in terms of proven effectiveness and in terms of market penetration and rulemaking has made it an exemplary case for the effective dissemination and implementation of solid scientific results. Belin *et al.* (2014) translated this success story into a prescription of how to make good use of factual information. According to them the first stage in the process is to scientifically study the effects of the proposed device. This should be followed by (2) the dissemination of the findings in the media. Good media exposure will then (3) affect (safety-conscious) buyers' demands from their new vehicles. With enough of a demand (4) producers and importers will implement the system in their vehicles. Finally, when these steps are accomplished one can expect (5) agencies (like NCAP) and governments to incorporate the product into their vehicle safety ratings and their safety standards, respectively. The rapid immersion of multiple air bags in all cars today is another good example of this process.

Moving Ahead: From Driver Support Systems to Autonomous (Self-Driving) Vehicles

There is a new player in the road traffic system – the autonomous self-driving vehicle. And according to its proponents it is also the ultimate crash countermeasure.

To better understand the implications of the autonomous or self-driving vehicle we should regress a little more than 60 years ago. In 1951 Paul Fitts, created the Fitts' List that articulated tasks or functions that humans or machines were better at (which evolved into the acronym HABA-MABA: *humans* are better at/*machines* are better at), providing some guidance to designers or users of automation regarding appropriate functional allocation. Simply followed, tasks that humans are better at should be performed by humans and tasks that automation is better at should be performed by automation. It is interesting that many of the elements of the list still hold true to this day, even though technology has now progressed significantly and automation is nearly ubiquitous in myriad forms and purposes across different domains, applications, and industries.

The widespread use of automation has been accompanied by hundreds of studies of human-automation interaction published in the scientific literature. Although a thorough review is well beyond the scope of this chapter (see Parasuraman and Wickens, 2008, for a primer); two issues are relevant to the viability of the autonomous vehicle: (a) automation, depending on its type, can have a profound impact on the role of the human (in comparison with his or her role prior to automation) and (b) the outcome of automation, even in spite of overall benefits, can yield unintended (and sometimes adverse) consequences. Because automation can be involved at all stages of human information processing – from sensing through perceiving and decision making to control (see Figures 3-3 and 3-5) – its viability will depend on which functions along the process are actually performed better by the "machine." Indiscriminate application of all functions to the vehicle can lead to undesirable outcomes, and ultimately to crashes, as discussed later below in the context of two crashes in which the automated vehicles were culpable.

The verb to drive has meant different things at different times. When the first Ford Model T cars rolled off the production line in 1908, they did not have an electrical starter and starting the engine was a hard manual job with a serious risk of injury. The gear box (with two gears) was manual and a hand-operated throttle was the accelerator. The driver's hands served as the turn signals, braking and steering were not power-assisted. The air and fuel mixture delivered to the engine had to be continuously adjusted by the driver with a manual choke lever (until the engine warmed up sufficiently). Combine that with a hardly regulated poor infrastructure (gravel roads without edge lines, lane markers, hard shoulders, or traffic control devices) and you have driving as a complicated fully-attention-demanding task (with probably minimal tolerance for "distracted driving").

As more and more systems became automated and removed from the driver's control, the driving task changed gradually: from that of a car operator to that of a car controller. New manual functions and features were added (dimming lights, turning on wipers), and eventually became automated (ibid). Sensors were added to detect not only the condition of the engine and the car (e.g., to change gears, to adjust the fuel delivery for cruise control) but also to "see" and "feel" the environment; mostly road features like lane markers and other road users. Fast forwarding a few decades, we enter the current era with enough sensors (of the car's own behavior and position, and of the roadway and the traffic conditions) and control functions that can respond to these sensors, to make the human driver (almost) redundant and superfluous.

To better explore the ramification of automation, the U.S. National Highway Traffic Safety Administration (NHTSA, 2013) and the Society of Automotive Engineers (SAE, 2014) proposed similar five-category rating systems for automation – from non-automated with driver in full control but assisted with various warning systems (Level 1) to fully automated with the driver totally removed from the control loop and the vehicle in full control (Level 5). The categories are distinguished from each other by the level of automation and the required availability of the driver. Obviously, we are now somewhere in-between the two extremes, with partial automation in specific contexts. More important than where we are along the automation continuum is the fact that the new and emerging systems are – for the most part – much better than the human driver in their sensing, decision-making, and control abilities. In fact, the premise of the proponents of the autonomous vehicle is that the human driver is an imperfect sensor of the environment and a flawed controller of the vehicle, and therefore, can and should be replaced with a more reliable sensor and controller – the computer. Volvo's vision of zero deaths in their cars by 2020 is based on the rapid development of these proven e-Safety systems.

But there are many obstacles still to be overcome, and many of them are not technological but psychological, social, regulatory, and legal. First and foremost who is the driver? In a bold step the U.S. NHTSA stated in a February 4, 2016 letter sent to Google that "NHTSA will interpret 'driver' in the context of Google's described motor vehicle design as referring to the SDS (self-driving system), and not to any of the vehicle occupants. We agree with Google its SDV will not have a 'driver' in the traditional sense that vehicles have had drivers during the last more than 100 years. The trend toward computer-driven vehicles began with such features as anti-lock brakes, electronic stability control, and air bags, continuing today with automatic emergency braking, forward crash warning, and lane departure warnings, and continuing on toward vehicles with Google's SDV and potentially beyond. No human occupant of the SDV could meet the definition of 'driver' .... If no human occupant of the vehicle can actually drive the vehicle, it is more reasonable to identify the 'driver' as whatever (as opposed to whoever) *is* doing the driving. In this instance, an item of motor vehicle equipment, the SDS, is actually driving the vehicle" (NHTSA, 2016b). More recently NHTSA (2016d) issued a comprehensive "Automated Vehicle Policy Guidance" in which it states that "Today the automobile industry is on the cusp of a technological transformation that holds promise to catalyze an unprecedented advance in safety on U.S. roads and highways. The development of advanced automated vehicle safety technologies, including fully self-driving cars, may prove to be the greatest personal transportation revolution since the popularization of the personal automobile nearly a century ago." But this "revolution" also opens a Pandora's Box. What will the licensing requirements of the driver and the car be? What kind of "maladies" will disqualify it from driving? Under what weather conditions will it be drivable (e.g., when snow covers the lane and edge markers)? What level of protection from hackers will be there? How will it handle a computer "fatal error"? How will the automakers guarantee privacy of information when they know at every minute where every car is and what it does? How will the insurance be handled? How will today's drivers react to being deprived of the thrill of driving? How will the driver cope with the "fear of letting go"? Will an autonomous vehicle transport a minor without an adult in the car? And from what age? Some of these issue are addressed in the NHTSA document but this is still an initial and quite sketchy statement of the government's position on what it terms "Highly Automated Vehicles" (HAVs). The document lists 15 issues that will require a safety assessment, among them the human-machine interface or "approaches for communicating information to the driver, occupant and other road users."

Once (and if) all of the obstacles to the autonomous car can be overcome – for all driving environments, in all weather and traffic conditions – the car as we know it will be relegated to the scrap heap of technological history, or at least to amusement parks and dedicated special trails – just like go-carting and horse-riding.

Safety of the autonomous vehicle

Autonomous cars are now being developed by all major automakers, as well as by many hi-tech firms. This in itself is a testament to the transition of the car from a mechanical transportation device to an electronic device. The Google car project started in 2009, and Google cars can now be seen on the roads and streets of some locations in California, Texas, and the state of Washington. By the end of February 2016 they had logged nearly 1.5 million miles (2.4 million kilometer) of autonomous driving on public roads (Google, 2016).

Empirical studies are inconclusive
Two independent studies evaluated the safety of the self-driving – mostly Google – cars. In the first study, Schoettle and Sivak (2015) analyzed the crashes of three makes of autonomous vehicles (Google, Delphi, and Audi) traveling on the roads and streets of California. They found that in the 1.2 million miles traveled (nearly all in the Lexus Google car) there were a total of 11 crashes (up until September 2015); all occurring when the vehicle was either stopped (three crashes) or traveling at less than 5 mph (eight crashes). Only two of the crashes were injury crashes. After comparing these rates to a "weighted" sample of the U.S. police-reported crashes Schoettle and Sivak found that the autonomous vehicles averaged much lower crash rates and much lower injury rates than the conventional cars (1.9 versus 9.1 and 0.77 versus 3.99 crashes and injuries per million miles driven, respectively). Although the differences are patently huge, because of the limited exposure of the self-driving cars (with only 11 crashes of which none were fatal), neither difference was statistically significant. Thus, the most optimistic conclusion the authors could muster for their findings was that "we currently cannot rule out, with a reasonable level of confidence, the possibility that the actual rates for self-driving vehicles are lower than for conventional vehicles."

The second study, conducted by Blanco *et al.* (2016) from the Virginia Tech Transportation Institute used a different approach. The study, commissioned by Google, compared the cumulative exposure and crash experience of the Google cars with the driving and crash experience of both the national NHTSA data and the 1,000+ cars tracked in the recently completed SHRP2 naturalistic driving study (see Chapter 2 for a description of that study). Using the latter as a comparison group may not have the benefits of a nationally representative data base, but it eliminates the bias toward inclusion of only more severe crashes in the comparison (conventional) group. Thus, the data base for the self-driving cars was essentially the same as the one used in the UMTRI study (with the exclusion of the two limited-exposure Audi cars), with nearly identical exposure in terms of miles driven and identical total number of crashes in autonomous mode. However, the SHRP2 comparison data was obtained from 1,000+ cars and 3,500+ drivers driving in six different locations in six U.S. states with 1,000+ crashes. In this study, after adjusting the crash rates for the different levels of severities, the crash rates in automated driving were numerically lower at all crash severity levels, but – again – due to the very small number of crashes in self-driving mode the differences were not statistically significant.

In summary, on the basis of available crash data the jury is still out. Even if the current data were sufficient to demonstrate the relative safety of the self-driving cars, today's technology still limits their use to optimal conditions (e.g., excluding inclement weather and poorly delineated roads), and to relatively safe middle-aged drivers who can afford these cars. Consequently the findings are biased. Also, while it can be reliably determined if a crash occurred in an autonomous mode or not, it is not known how many (and what kind) of the miles are driven in a conventional manner.

In-depth crash analysis highlight the fallibility of self-driving cars

Some insights into the importance of the "human element" come from two crashes caused by autonomous vehicles; both demonstrating that there are no simple (or complex) algorithms that cover all potential crash situations. The first case with a Google car illustrates a failure in the decision making phase of the information processing leading to a critical false assumption, while the second crash with a Tesla car illustrates a failure in automated perception.

The Google car crash occurred on February 14, 2016, and it was the first documented crash in which the self-driving car was culpable (Google 2016). The crash happened when a Google car that had stopped to avoid an obstacle in the right turning lane attempted to get back to the thru lane. As it was turning into the center of the adjacent travel lane at 2 mph a bus traveling in that lane at 15 mph side-swiped the Google car causing minimal damage. Obviously, the Google car was culpable as it was the one encroaching on the bus's lane. Following a detailed analysis of why the collision happened, Google acknowledged that "our car had detected the approaching bus, but predicted that it would yield to us because we were ahead of it." Furthermore, Google notes that "our test driver, who had been watching the bus in the mirror, also expected the bus to slow or stop. And we can imagine the bus driver assumed we were going to stay put. Unfortunately, all these assumptions led us to the same spot in the lane at the same time." In this statement the company admitted that its car made the exact kind of error already noted more than 35 years earlier by Treat *et al.* (1979) as "false assumption" or "misjudgement" (see Table 18-4), that is typical of many human-caused crashes. Google also acknowledged this when it added that "this type of misunderstanding happens between human drivers on the road every day." The fix, according to Google, was to make "refinements to our software. Our cars will more deeply understand that buses and other large vehicles are less likely to yield to us than other types of vehicles, and we hope to handle situations like this more gracefully in the future" (Google, 2016). There are two interesting aspects in this response. First, note that Google humanizes its cars with the term "will more deeply understand." Second, Google then adds the bus size as a relevant factor in the decision making process, something most drivers do automatically in potential conflicts with buses or trucks.

But this collision highlights another problem: that of a traffic system containing both human and computerized drivers. If all cars were autonomous, and all shared the *exact* program and algorithms on how to deal with *every* contingency, this type of collision would not have happened. However, when one of the drivers is human, "certainty" about expected behavior no longer applies. Computer-human miscommunications can be just as – or more – common as human-human miscommunications. Resetting the computer values for re-entering the lane can only make it more "conservative" to the point of avoiding many human practical maneuvers that rely on subtle communications and accommodations among drivers. Of course, a legally appropriate but less practical algorithm would be one in which merging would be attempted if and only if other drivers with the right-of-way would not have to adjust their driving. But at certain times in certain parts of California this would mean the risk of running out of gas before that happened. Interestingly, the algorithm used by Google was apparently a good imitation of the heuristics used by human drivers. In fact, the test driver sitting in the Google car stated that he, too, expected the bus driver to slow down to let the Google car merge. One is now left to speculate if a human driver would have made the same decision, and if so, would he or she have aborted the merging maneuver in time.

The second crash had a much more tragic outcome. On May 7, 2016 a Tesla driver was killed while using the car's self-driving mode. Driving on a multi-lane road in Florida, the car struck at full speed an on-coming tractor-trailer that was making a left turn at an intersection in front of it. It appears that the car's systems failed to recognize the white side of the trailer as an obstacle, did not apply the brakes, and drove straight into the truck and under it. In its response Tesla acknowledged that the algorithm to detect obstacles and apply autobraking is still imperfect (Yadron and Tynan 2016). But even with the best algorithms for most situations, computers (and computer programmers) are fallible. They do make mistakes, and cannot anticipate *all* situations. Thus, harkening back to Fitts' (1951) list, Machines outperform us when it comes to detecting sub-threshold visual stimuli, but humans are generally better at interpreting the sensory signals that excite individual cones and rods in our retinas (see Chapter 4) and integrating them into meaningful percepts (such as the side of trailer). Thus, both the Google car and the Tesla car crashes would probably not have occurred with human drivers. A human driver of the Google car would have been able to judge whether or not the bus was slowing down and if it weren't he or she would have aborted the merging action. In the case of the Tesla driver human perception would definitely be able to detect and identify the very large obstacle in its path.

But the autonomous vehicle is moving ahead – literally and figuratively – at an increasing speed. Because their sensing and control systems are continuously improving state-of-the-art technological marvels that in general (but not always) can outperform the human, the projections are still rosy. Fagnant and Kockelman (2015) conducted an extensive analysis of the safety, ecological, economic, legal, and policy implications of the introduction of the autonomous vehicles to the U.S. transportation system. They concluded that in the U.S. alone a 10 percent market penetration would save 1,100 lives annually, a 50 percent penetration would save 9,600 lives, and a 90 percent penetration would save 21,700 lives; that is, approximately two-thirds of all U.S. traffic fatalities. The spread of the autonomous vehicles would also lead to equally impressive reductions in injury and property damage crashes, and consequently to significant economic savings of over $3,000 per car with the 90 percent penetrations. However, until that happens Fagnant and Kockelman also state that complicating issues such as the ones noted above must be resolved, and that the task is not easy.

Trust in and acceptance of the autonomous vehicle

General public acceptance of automated driving will depend on the public gaining trust in the various stakeholders that are involved in providing, promoting, accommodating, and regulating automatic driving. The three key institutions that are most relevant to developing public trust in automated driving are equipment/vehicle manufacturers, government, and academia. Our safety-related expectations from the manufacturers, given their acceptable profit motive and spotty history is moderated by our expectations from the government and academia to oversee them. We do expect the government to act as a regulator and a watchdog, as it currently does through its vehicle safety standards. While the creation of standards and oversight of their compliance has been quite effective historically, this may not be the case in the autonomous vehicles where technology is progressing in leaps and bounds while regulation dismally lags behind. The trust in academic research is probably there, but research is also agonizingly slow, and in the case of autonomous vehicles where there is a dearth of real-life safety data, it is often too little too late.

In addition to the conflicts of interests among the various institutions, there are subtle conflicts within us, the ultimate users of the autonomous vehicles. One such conflict, is "the social dilemma of autonomous vehicles" that was demonstrated by Bonnefon, Shariff, and Rahwan (2016) in a series of six surveys. In their surveys they presented respondents with a moral dilemma involved in a specific situation of an inevitable crash, in which a driver approaches a group of pedestrians crossing the road immediately in front of him or her. The essence of the driver's options were to either drive straight into the group or veer off the road and hit a wall. The first option would likely kill a number of pedestrians but spare the driver while the latter one would kill just one person – the driver. When asked for their preferred algorithm, most of the respondents opted for the utilitarian, socially desirable design option; namely minimizing the number of injured persons. However, when asked how likely they were to purchase a vehicle programmed to minimize total injuries versus a vehicle programmed to protect its occupants at all costs, they generally preferred the self-protective option. Furthermore, most respondents opposed any government regulatory role that would dictate the utilitarian algorithm. In short, their study demonstrated that we all want to increase overall safety, but not at the cost of our own.

The issue of public acceptance and acceptability was discussed above in the context of advanced driver assistance systems. The issue becomes critical when the new in-vehicle technologies are integrated into an autonomous vehicle. In an identical survey conducted in six countries (Australia, China, India, Japan, the United Kingdom, and U.S.) Schoettle and Sivak (2014a, 2014b, 2016) discovered that in all countries the majority of the respondents have heard of the autonomous vehicle, were concerned about riding in one (especially one without driver controls), but were still interested in having that technology in their cars. With this uneven level of acceptability it is very hard to see how and what kind of an autonomous vehicle would reach 50 percent market penetration, let alone higher levels.

Concluding Comments

A quick scan of the plethora of strategies and devices designed to increase traffic safety should make it obvious that safety is a complex issue for which there is no panacea or "magic bullet." Many stakeholders are involved in the delivery of safety, beginning with the government and safety-oriented organizations, all the way to individual researchers designing and evaluating new safety products and strategies, and ending with road users who must make instantaneous decisions on the road. Safety is maximized when all efforts are coordinated and safety systems are user-centered. Organization-wise, on a national basis, setting a difficult but achievable concrete goal for crash reduction is a key element in a crash countermeasure program.

Because crashes are caused by a variety of factors (that often have to occur simultaneously) safety improvements can only be achieved by multiple strategies – targeted at specific well defined problems. No single program can be optimal for all types of road users, environments, and crashes. On the other hand, many programs, safety-oriented behavioral management strategies, environmental designs, and technological innovations have contributed to consistent reductions in crash and injury rates over the past few decades.

The different successful (and unsuccessful) strategies reviewed in this final chapter also make it clear that safety does not have to come at the cost of mobility and other values. There are many safety measures that have zero, or minimal, effects on mobility and other cherished values. Vehicle improvements in crashworthiness and passenger protection have increased safety at no cost to mobility or to the pleasure of driving. Intelligent active crash prevention systems should also be effective crash countermeasures that do not reduce the "fun of driving" as long as they remain invisible to the driver until appropriately activated in – relatively rare – imminent crash situations. Safer highway designs – such as roundabouts – and "furniture" – such as break-away posts and signs, crash barriers, and rumble striping of lane delineators – should all reduce injuries and improve safety without affecting mobility and hopefully without negative behavioral adaptations.

Still we must accept the fact that life involves tradeoffs that force compromises. With today's systems many of these tradeoffs are very easy to accept. For example, modern seat belts are easy to use, quite comfortable and, as Evans (2004) points out, the 2 seconds it takes a driver to fasten a safety belt increases the duration of a typical 15-minute trip by 0.2 percent, a totally insignificant reduction in mobility, but one of very consequential magnitude. Other tradeoffs encounter greater resistance. For example, vehicle, environmental, and driver management techniques for speed control all explicitly require drivers to reduce their speed, and if speed is a desired value in driving then by definition it must be compromised. Yet even in speed control some approaches are quite acceptable to most drivers (e.g., environmental traffic calming) while others are not so acceptable (e.g., speed enforcement).

The challenge in the development and implementation of socially acceptable crash countermeasures is finding strategies that minimize the tradeoffs between safety and other driving-related values such as mobility and pleasure. This is where science, technology, and careful scientifically robust evaluations must converge. Many early safety countermeasures that are still with us could be viewed as based on common sense (Sivak, 2002). With limited technology and limited options, the introduction of safety "systems" was slow and often intuitive. However, as safety regulations, vehicles, and roads became more complex, and technological innovations flourished, common sense countermeasures gave way to science-based, empirically evaluated, and technology-based safety improvements. It is important that this trend continues, especially now with heightened public sensitivity to safety. Advances in technology and science – including the science of driver behavior – have provided us with many unconventional and new solutions to old problems such as vehicle control while braking, head-up displays to reduce visual in-vehicle distraction, and collapsible sign posts to reduce injury severity in crashes.

Finally, despite all the safety regulations, innovations in environmental design, improvements in-vehicle crashworthiness and adaptive vehicle technologies, it is – at least for now – the driver who remains the most adaptive and controlling element in the traffic system. Therefore, engineering-based solutions to increasing safety will remain relatively ineffective unless they take into account user acceptance and all the potential effects on behavior adaptation in response to these changes. To be most effective, engineering solutions should be user – pedestrian, cyclist, and driver – centered. Regulated and enforced user-friendly solutions designed to address driver limitations in an increasingly dense and complex driving environment are our best hope for improving traffic safety with high public acceptance.

But many of these issues and solutions will become moot, if or once the roads are dominated by autonomous vehicles. Self-driving cars were subjects for futurologists in the 1939 World's Fair, and the stuff of comic books and animated TV series (e.g., Batman, The Jetsons) before they actually appeared on our roads. But now they are and they are making fast inroads into the transportation system. We are now at the stage of partial automation with increasing numbers of advanced driver assistance systems that – depending on the specific system – operate some or most of the time. Complete automation implies an integration of ADAS to replace all driver sensing, decision-making, and motor functions that can operate all the time under all conditions. Eliminating most of the 90+ percent of crash-causing driver errors may be the Holy Grail of Safety that we seek. If the autonomous vehicles can achieve that, then the next step after making them legal, will be to make them mandatory, so that eventually a (human) driver's license will be a rare credential like a Latin professorship or a tugboat captain (Vella, 2016). If and when that happens this book will at best be (to quote from Edgar Allan Poe's The Raven) "a quaint and curious volume of forgotten lore."

References

AAA Foundation for Traffic Safety (2007). Improving traffic safety culture in the United States. Compendium of papers funded by the AAAF, Washington, DC.

AAAF (2015). 2014 traffic safety culture index. AAA Foundation for Traffic Safety, Washington, DC.

AASHTO (2010). Highway Safety Manual. American Association of State Highway and Transportation Officials. Washington, DC. http://www.highwaysafetymanual.org/Pages/default.aspx

Achara, S., B. Adeyemi, E. Dosekun, S. Kelleher, M. Lansley, I. Male, N. Muhialdin, L. Reynolds, I. Roberts, M. Smailbegovic and N. van der Spek (2001). Evidence based road safety: The driving standards agency's schools programme. *Lancet, 358*, 230-232.

Aga, M. and A. Okada (2003). Analysis of vehicle stability control (VSC)'s effectiveness from accident data. Enhanced Safety of Vehicles Conference, Paper #541, Nagoya, Japan.

Ahmed, M. M. and M. Abdel-Aty (2015). Evaluation and spatial analysis of automated red-light running enforcement cameras. *Transport. Res. C, 50*, 130-140.

Alexander, G. J. and H. Lunenfeld (1975). *Positive Guidance in Traffic Control.* FHWA, U.S. Department of Transportation, Washington, DC.

AP (2002). Exec gets 6-figure speeding ticket (Yikes!). Associated Press. Posted on April 14, 2002 1:42:15 PM PDT.

Bachman, L. R. and G. R. Preziotti (2001). Automated Collision Notification (ACN) Field Operational Test (FOT) evaluation report. National highway traffic safety administration. Report DOT- HS-809-304. U.S. Department of Transportation, Washington, DC.

Bahouth, G. (2006). Reductions in crash injury and fatalities due to vehicle stability control technology. SAE Technical Paper No. 2006-01-0925. Society of Automotive Engineers, New York.

Bar-Gera, H. and E. Schechtman (2005). The effect of Center High Mounted Stop Lamp (CHMSL) on rear-end accidents in Israel. *Accid. Anal. Prev., 37*, 531-536.

Baum, H., T. Geißler, U. Westerkamp and C. Vitale (2008). eIMPACT; Socio-economic impact assessment of stand-alone and co-operative intelligent vehicle safety systems (IVSS) in Europe, (Deliverable D6: Cost-benefit analyses for stand-alone and co-operative intelligent vehicle safety systems. TNO. Delft, Netherlands. http://www.eimpact.info/download/eIMPACT_D6_V2.0.pdf

BBC (2004). Finn's speed fine is a bit rich. *BBC News*. 2004/02/10 17:12:13 GMT http://news.bbc.co.uk/go/pr/fr/-/1/hi/business/3477285.stm

Bekhor, S., Y. Abramson, V. Gitelman and S. Shefer (2012). Overview of e-safety systems and their safety aspects. National Road Safety Authority, Jerusalem, Israel (Hebrew).

Belin, M. Å., P. Tillgren and E. Vedung (2012). Vision Zero – A road safety policy innovation. *Int. J. Inj. Control Safety Promot., 19*(2), 171-179.

Belin, M. Å., E. Vedung, K. Meleckidzedeck and C. Tingvall (2014). Carrots, sticks and sermons: State policy tools for influencing adoption and acceptance of new vehicle safety systems. In (M. A. Regan, T. Horberry and A. Stevens Eds.), *Driver Acceptance of New Technology*. 241-252. Ashgate, Farnham, England.

Belz, S. M., G. S. Robinson and J. G. Casali (2004). Temporal separation and self-rating of alertness as indicators of driver fatigue in commercial motor-vehicle operators. *Hum. Fact., 46*(1), 154-169.

Ben-Bassat, T. and D. Shinar (2006). Ergonomic guidelines for traffic signs design increase signs comprehension. *Hum. Fact., 48*(1), 182-195.

Ben-Bassat, T. and D. Shinar (2011). Effect of shoulder width, guardrail and roadway geometry on driver perception and behavior. *Accid. Anal. Prev.*, *43*(6), 2142-2152.

Bjørnskau, T. and R. Elvik (1992). Can road traffic law enforcement permanently reduce the number of accidents? *Accid. Anal. Prev.*, *24*, 507-520.

Blanco, M., J. Atwood, S. Russell, T. Trimble, J. Mcclafferty and M. Perez (2016). Automated vehicle crash rate comparison using naturalistic data. Final Report of the Virginia Tech Transportation Institute. https://vtechworks.lib.vt.edu/bitstream/handle/10919/64420/Automated%20Vehicle%20Crash%20Rate%20Comparison%20Using%20Naturalistic%20Data_Final%20Report_20160107.pdf?sequence=1&isAllowed=y

Bliss, T. and J. Breen (2012). Meeting the management challenges of the decade of action for road safety. *IATSS Res.*, *35*(2), 48-55.

Blows, S., R. Q. Ivers, J. Connor, S. Ameratunga and R. Norton (2003). Does periodic vehicle inspection reduce car crash injury? Evidence from the Auckland Car Crash Injury Study. *Aust. N Z J. Pub. Health*, *27*(6), 323-327 (with comments on p. 656).

Blows, S., R. Q. Ivers, J. Connor, S. Ameratunga, M. Woodward and R. Norton (2005). Unlicensed drivers and car crash injury. *Traffic Inj. Prev.*, *6*, 230-234.

Bonnefon, J.-F., A. Shariff and I. Rahwan (2016). The social dilemma of autonomous vehicles. *Science*, *352*(6293), 1573-1576.

Bordel, S., A. Somat, H. Barbeau, P. Subirats and M. L. Gallenne (2012). Design, implementation and assessment of innovative devices for road safety: An example from the SARI project. *Procedia Soc. Behav. Sci.*, *48*, 2464-2472.

Broughton, J., R. E. Allsop and D. A. Lynam (2000). The numerical context for setting national casualty reduction targets. TRL Report 382. Transport Research Laboratory, Crowthorne, England (as cited by Peden *et al.*, 2004).

Campbell, J. L., K. Kar, R. Y. Szymkowski and S. C. Tignor (2016). Applying the human factors guidelines for road systems (HFG) to the road safety audit (RSA) Process. Transportation Research Board 95th Annual Meeting, Washington, DC.

Campbell, J. L., M. G. Lichty, J. L. Brown, C. M. Richard, J. S. Graving (2012). Human factors guidelines for road systems. NCHRP Report 600. Transportation Research Board. Washington, DC.

Carlson, P. J. (2001). Evaluation of Clearview alphabet with microprismatic retroreflective sheeting. TTI Report 4049-1. Texas Transportation Institute, College Station, TX.

Carnis, L. and E. Blais (2013). An assessment of the safety effects of the French speed cameras program. *Accid. Anal. Prev.*, *51*, 301-309.

Carsten, O. (2012). Is intelligent speed adaptation ready for deployment? *Accid. Anal. Prev.*, *48*, 1-3.

Castellà, J. and J. Pérez (2004). Sensitivity to punishment and sensitivity to reward and traffic violations. *Accid. Anal. Prev.*, *36*, 947-952.

Castillo-Manzano, J. I. and M. Castro-Nuño (2012). Driving licenses based on points systems: Efficient road safety strategy or latest fashion in global transport policy? A worldwide meta-analysis. *Transport Policy*, *21*, 191-201.

Cerezuela, G. P., P. Tejero, M. Chóliz, M. Chisvert and M. J. Monteagudo (2004). Wertheim's hypothesis on 'highway hypnosis': Empirical evidence from a study on motorway and conventional road driving. *Accid. Anal. Prev.*, *36*, 1045-1054.

Cicchino, J. (2016). Effectiveness of forward collision warning systems with and without autonomous emergency braking in reducing police-reported crash rates. Insurance Institute for Highway Safety. Arlington, VA, January.

Chae, C. D., D. M. Lee and H. S. Cho (2013). Evaluation of 2 + 1 roads application to improve rural two-lane highway in Korea. *Int. J. Highway Eng.*, *15*(3), 85-92.

Chang, H. L., T. H. Woo and C. M. Tseng (2006). Is rigorous punishment effective? A case study of lifetime license revocation in Taiwan. *Accid. Anal. Prev.*, *38*, 269-276.

Charlton, S. G. (2007). The role of attention in horizontal curves: A comparison of advance warning, delineation, and road marking treatments. *Accid. Anal. Prev.*, *39*(5), 873-885.

Christensen, P. and R. Elvik (2007). Effects on accidents of periodic motor vehicle inspection in Norway. *Accid. Anal. Prev.*, *39*(1), 47-52.

Coate, D. and S. Markowitz (2004). The effects of daylight and daylight saving time on US pedestrian fatalities and motor vehicle occupant fatalities. *Accid. Anal. Prev.*, *36*, 351-357.

Consumer Union (2007). What's next in auto safety? Consumer Reports, 26-27. April issue. Consumer Union of U.S. Inc., Yonkers, NY.

Cooper, D., T. Chira-Chavala and D. Gillen (2000). Safety and other impacts of vehicle impound enforcement. Institute of Transportation Studies, Research Paper UCB-ITS-RR-2000-1. University of California, Berkeley, CA.

Dang, J. N. (2004). Preliminary results analyzing the effectiveness of electronic stability control (ESC) systems. NHTSA evaluation note. Report DOT HS 809-790. U.S. Department of Transportation, Washington, DC.

Davis, J. W., L. D. Bennink, D. R. Pepper, S. N. Parks, D. M. Lemaster and R. N. Townsend (2006). Aggressive traffic enforcement: A simple and effective injury prevention program. *J. Trauma Inj. Infect. Critic. Care*, *60*(5), 972-977.

De Pauw, E., S. Daniels, T. Brijs, E. Hermans and G. Wets (2014). To brake or to accelerate? Safety effects of combined speed and red light cameras. *J. Safety Res.*, *50*, 59-65.

De Winter, J. C. F. and D. Dodou (2010). The driver behaviour questionnaire as a predictor of accidents: A meta-analysis. *J. Safety Res.*, *41*(6), 463-470.

De Winter, J. C., R. Happee, M. H. Martens and N. A. Stanton (2014). Effects of adaptive cruise control and highly automated driving on workload and situation awareness: A review of the empirical evidence. *Transport. Res. F*, *27*, 196-217.

Decina, L. E., L. Thomas, R. Srinivasan and L. Staplin (2006). Automated enforcement: A compendium of worldwide evaluations of results. Final Report on Project NTS-01-5-05127 submitted to the National Highway Traffic Safety Administration. U.S. Department of Transportation, Washington, DC.

Denton, G. G. (1973). The influence of visual pattern on perceived speed at Newbridge MB Midlothian. TRRL Report No. LR531. Transport and Road Research Laboratory, Crowthorne, England.

Dewar, R. E., P. L. Olson and G. J. Alexander (2001). Perception and information processing. In: *Human Factors in Traffic Safety* (R. E. Dewar and P. L. Olson Eds.), Lawyers and Judges Publishing Co. Inc., Tucson, AZ.

DeYoung, D. J. (1999). An evaluation of the specific deterrent effects of vehicle impoundment on suspended, revoked, and unlicensed drivers in California. *Accid. Anal. Prev.*, *31*, 45-53.

DeYoung, D. J. (2013). Controlling the risk of impaired drivers through use of vehicle-based sanctions: Impoundment, forfeiture, and license plate sanctions. Transport. Res. E-Circular, E-C174, 20-31. Transportation Research Board, Washington, DC.

DfT (2004). The attitudinal determinants of driving violations. Road Safety Research Report No. 13. Department for Transport, London.

DOT (2014). Transportation for a new generation: Strategic Plan | fiscal years 2014-2018. U.S. Department of Transportation, Washington, DC. https://www.transportation.gov/sites/dot.gov/files/docs/2014-2018-strategic-plan_0.pdf

EC (2003). ROad safety and environmental benefit-cost and cost-effectiveness analyses for use in decision-making (ROSEBUD). European Commission Contract GTC2/2000/33020. Thematic Network funded by the European Commission, Directorate General for Energy and Transport. EU 5th framework programme. Brussels, Belgium.

EC (2009a). Evaluation tool for road safety campaigns. European Commission, Brussels, Belgium.

EC (2009b). Campaigns and awareness raising strategies in in traffic safety. Contract No TREN-05-FP6TR-S07.59641-019520-CAST. European Commission, Brussels, Belgium.

EC (2010). *Road Safety Communication Campaigns: Manual for Design, Implementation, and Evaluation*. European Commission, Brussels, Belgium.

EC (2015). *Interim Evaluation of the Policy Orientations on Road Safety 2011-2020*. European Commission, Brussels, Belgium.

ECMT (2002), Safety on roads: What's the vision? *European Council of Transport Ministers (ECMT)*. OECD, Paris.

Edquist, J. and B. Corben (2012). Potential application of Shared Space principles in urban road design: Effects on safety and amenity. *Report to the NRMA-ACT Road Safety Trust, MONASH University, Accident Research Centre.*

Elliott, M. and J. Broughton (2004). How methods and levels of police affect road casualty rates. TRL Report PR SE/924/04. Transport Research Laboratory, Crowthorne, England.

Elvik, R. (1993). Quantified road safety targets: A useful tool for policy making? *Accid. Anal. Prev.*, *25*(5), 569-583.

Elvik, R. (1999a). Can injury prevention efforts go too far? Reflections on some possible implications of Vision Zero for road accident fatalities. *Accid. Anal. Prev.*, *31*, 265-286.

Elvik, R. (1999b). The effects on accidents of studded tires and laws banning their use: A meta-analysis of evaluation studies. *Accid. Anal. Prev.*, *31*(1-2), 125-134.

Elvik, R. (2001). Cost-benefit analysis of road safety measures: Applicability and controversies. *Accid. Anal. Prev.*, *33*, 9-17.

Elvik, R. (2013). International transferability of accident modification functions for horizontal curves. *Accid. Anal. Prev.*, *59*, 487-496.

Elvik, R. (2014). The potential for ITS systems to improve road safety. Lecture given at a National Road Safety Authority Workshop, Tel Aviv, Israel, February 24.

Elvik, R., L. Fridstrøm, J. Kaminska and S. F. Meyer (2013). Effects on accidents of changes in the use of studded tyres in major cities in Norway: A long-term investigation. *Accid. Anal. Prev.*, *54*, 15-25.

Elvik, R., A. Høye, T. Vaa and M. Sørensen (2009). *Handbook or Road Safety Measures* (2nd ed). Emerald, Bingley, UK.

Ernberg, T. (2013). Volvo's vision 2020—'no death, no serious injury in a volvo car'. *Auto Tech Review*, *2*(5), 12-13.

ETSC (2005). ETSC fact sheet (no. 5): Road safety audit. European Transport Safety Council, Brussels, Belgium.

ETSC (2013). ETSC response to the European commission staff working document "First Milestone towards a Serious Injury Strategy." European Transport Safety Council, Brussels, BE. http://archive.etsc.eu/documents/ETSC_Response_to_EC_First_Milestone_Towards_an_Injury__Strategy_May_2013.pdf

ETSC (2014a). Ranking EU progress on road safety – 8th road safety performance index report. European Transport Safety Council, Brussels, Belgium.

ETSC (2014b). Intelligent Speed Assistance 'most effective' driver support system. ETSC News April 14. European Transport Safety Council, Brussels, Belgium. http://etsc.eu/intelligent-speed-assistance-most-effective-driver-support-system/

EuroNCAP (2009). Moving forward: 2010-2015 Strategic Roadmap. Brussels, Belgium. http://euroncap.blob.core.windows.net/media/1385/euro-ncap-moving-forward-strategic-roadmap-2010-2015-december-2009-0-0107f3c0-5f99-4e32-a6c6-c1e5be97aa84.pdf

EuroNCAP. (2017). The ratings explained. http://www.euroncap.com/en/vehicle-safety/the-ratings-explained/

Evans, L. (1998) Antilock brake systems and risk of different types of crashes in traffic. Proceedings of the Enhanced Safety Vehicles (ESV) Conference Paper No. 98-S2-O-12. Windsor.

Evans, L. (2003). A new traffic safety vision for the united states (editorial). *Am. J. Pub. Health*, *93*(9), 1384-1386.

Evans, L. (2004). *Traffic Safety*. Science Serving Society, Bloomfield Hill, MI.

Evans, L. and P. H. Gerrish (1996). Antilock brakes and risk of front and rear impact two-vehicle crashes. *Accid. Anal. Prev.*, *28*(3), 315-323.

Fagnant, D. J. and K. Kockelman (2015). Preparing a nation for autonomous vehicles: Opportunities, barriers and policy recommendations. *Transport. Res. A.*, *77*, 167-181.

Farmer, C. M. (2004). Effect of electronic stability control on automobile crash risk. *Traffic Inj. Prev.*, *5*, 317-325.

Farmer, C. M. (2006). Effects of electronic stability control: An update. *Traffic Inj. Prev.*, *7*(4), 319-324.

FHWA (2003). *Manual on Uniform Traffic Control Devices (MUTCD). Federal Highway Administration.* U.S. Department of Transportation, Washington DC. http://mutcd.fhwa.dot.gov/HTM/clearfont/cf-english4.htm#9

FHWA (2008a). Safety evaluations of flashing beacons at stop-controlled intersections. Report FHWA-HRT-08-048. U.S. Department of Transportation, Washington, DC.

FHWA (2008b). Safety evaluations of increasing retroflectivity of STOP signs. Report FHWA-HRT-08-047. U.S. Department of Transportation, Washington, DC.

FHWA (2009). Manual on uniform traffic control devices. http://mutcd.fhwa.dot.gov/

FHWA (2014) Safety: Road safety audits. U.S. Department of Transportation, Washington, DC. http://safety.fhwa.dot.gov/rsa/benefits/

Fildes, B. (2001). *Achieving the National Strategy Target – A Role for Vision Zero?* Monash University Accident Research Center, Clayton Victoria, AU.

Fildes, B. N. and J. R. Jarvis (1994). Perceptual countermeasures: Literature review. Report CR4/94 to the Federal Office of Road Safety, Australia.

Fildes, B., M. Keall, N. Bos, A. Lie, Y. Page, C. Pastor, L. Pennizi, M. Rizzi, P. Thomas and C. Tingvall (2015). Effectiveness of low speed autonomous emergency braking in real-world rear-end crashes. *Accid. Anal. Prev.*, *81*, 24-29.

Fitts, P. M. (1951). *Human Engineering for an Effective Air Navigation and Traffic Control System*. National Research Council, Washington, DC.

Flannery, A. and T. K. Datta (1996). Modern roundabouts and traffic crash experience in the United States. *Transport. Res. Record, No. 1553*, 103-109.

Fleisher, A., M. L. Wier and M. Hunter (2016). A vision for transportation safety: Framework for identifying best practice strategies to advance vision zero. *Transport. Res. Rec., No. 2582*, 72-86.

Forbes, T. W. (1972). *Human Factors in Highway Traffic Safety Research*. Wiley-Interscience, New York, NY.

Fosser, S. (1992). An experimental evaluation of the effects of periodic motor vehicle inspection on accident rates. *Accid. Anal. Prev.*, *24*, 599-612.

Fridestroem, L. (2001). The safety effect of studded tyres in Norway. Report No. TØI-RAP-493/2000. Norwegian Institute of Transport Economics (TØI), Oslo, Norway.

Garvey, P. M., M. J. Klena, W. Y. Eie, D. T. Meeker and M. T. Pietrucha (2016). Legibility of the clearview typeface and FHWA standard alphabets on negative- and positive-contrast signs. *Transport. Res. Rec., No. 2555*, 28-36.

Garvey, P. M., M. T. Pietrucha and D. Meeker (1997). Legibility of guide signs. *Transport. Res. Rec., No. 1605*, 73-79.

Garvey, P. H., M. T. Pietrucha and D. T. Meeker (1998). Clearer road signs ahead. *Ergon. Design, July*, 7-11.

Gebers, M. A. and R. C. Peck (2003). Using traffic conviction correlates to identify high accident-risk drivers. *Accid. Anal. Prev.*, *35*, 903-912.

Gerlach, J., R. Methorst, D. Boenke and J. Leven (2009). Sense and nonsense about Shared Space-For an objective view of a popular planning concept. Luettavissa: http://katana.hsrc.unc.edu/cms/downloads/Shared%20Space_short_german-Eng.pdf

Godley, S. T., T. J. Triggs and B. N. Fildes (2000). Speed reduction mechanisms of transverse lines. *Transport. Hum. Fact.*, *2*(4), 297-312.

Godley, S. T., T. J. Triggs and B. N. Fildes (2004). Perceptual lane width, wide perceptual road centre markings and driving speeds. *Ergonomics*, *47*(3), 237-256.

Goodwin, A., L. Thomas, B. Kirley, W. Hall, N. O'Brien and K. Hill (2015). Countermeasures that work: A highway safety countermeasures guide for State

Highway Safety Offices. 8th edition. NHTSA Report No. DOT HS 812 202. U.S. Department of Transportation, Washington, DC.

Google (2016). Google self-driving car project monthly report. February 2016. https://static.googleusercontent.com/media/www.google.com/iw//selfdrivingcar/files/reports/report-0216.pdf

Gregersen, N. P. (1996). Young drivers' overestimation of their own skill – An experiment on the relation between training strategy and skill. *Accid. Anal. Prev.*, *28*, 243-250.

Haddon, W. Jr. (1972). Reducing highway losses: A logical framework for categorizing highway safety phenomena and activity. *J. Trauma*, *12*, 193-207.

Hakamies-Blomqvist, L., K. Johansson and C. Lundberg (1995). Driver licenses as a measure of older driver exposure: A methodological note. *Accid. Anal. Prev.*, *27*(6), 853-857.

Harless, D. W. and G. E. Hoffer (2002). The antilock braking system anomaly: A drinking driver problem? *Accid. Anal. Prev.*, *34*, 333-341.

Harwood, D., K. Bauer, D. Gilmore, R. Souleyrette and Z. Hans (2010). Validation of US road assessment program star rating protocol: Application to safety management of US roads. *Transport. Res. Rec.*, *No.* (2147), 33-41.

Harwood, D. W., D. K. Gilmore D. J. Torbic, R. Souleyrette and Z. N. Hans (2008). usRAP. Pilot program: Phase II. AAA Foundation for Traffic Safety, Washington, DC.

Hawkins, H. G., M. D. Wooldridge, A. B. Kelly, D. L. Picha and F. K. Greene (1999). Legibility comparison of three freeway guide sign alphabets. Report FHWA/TX-99/1276-1F. Texas A&M University, College Station, TX.

Hessin, Y. and M. Kremnitzer (1998). Uniformity in penalties for traffic offences. *Mishpatim*, *18*, 2-32 (Hebrew).

Hirst, W. M., L. J. Mountain and M. J. Maher (2005). Are speed enforcement cameras more effective than other speed management measures? An evaluation of the relationship between speed and accident reductions. *Accid. Anal. Prev.*, *37*, 731-741.

Holick, A. J. and P. J. Carlson (2003). Nighttime guide design legibility for microprismatic Clearview legend on high intensity background. Federal Highway Administration. Report FHWA/TX-04/0-1796-4. U.S. Department of Transportation, Washington, DC.

Holick, A. J., S. T. Chrysler, E. S. Park and P. J. Carlson (2006). Evaluation of the clearview font for negative contrast traffic signs. Federal Highway Administration. Report FHWA/TX-06/0-4984-1. U.S. Department of Transportation, Washington, DC.

Hotz, G. A., S. M. Cohn, A. Castelblanco, S. Colston, M. Thomas, A. Weiss, J. Nelson, R. Duncan and the Pediatric Pedestrian Injury Task Force (2004). WalkSafe: A school-based pedestrian safety intervention program. *Traffic Inj. Prev.*, *5*, 382-389.

Høye, A. (2013). Still red light for red light cameras? An update. *Accid. Anal. Prev.*, *55*, 77-89.

HSRC (2016). *Road Safety 101*. Highway Safety Research Center, University of North Carolina, Chapel Hill, NC.

IIHS (2014a). Parking sensors help reduce property damage crashes. Status Report, **14** (2). Insurance Institute for Highway Safety, Arlington, VA.

IIHS (2014b). Preventing driveway tragedies: Rear cameras help drivers see behind them. Status Report, **14**(2). Insurance Institute for Highway Safety, Arlington, Virginia.

IRTAD (International Road Traffic and Accident Data) (2015). *Road Safety Annual Report*. International Transport Form, OECD, Paris, France.

Isaksson-Hellman, I. and M. Lindman (2015). Real-world performance of city safety based on Swedish insurance data. In 24th International Technical Conference on the Enhanced Safety of Vehicles (ESV). Vol. 8, Paper 15-0121. Göteburg, Sweden.

ITE (1999). *Traffic Engineering Handbook* (5th ed). Institute of Transportation Engineers, Washington, DC.

ITE (2007). Road safety audits.

ITF (2016). *Zero Road Deaths and Serious Injuries: Leading a Paradigm Shift to a Safe System*. OECD Publishing, Paris. doi:10.1787/9789282108055-en

Jacobs, R. J., A. W. Johnston and B. L. Cole (1975). The visibility of alphabetic and symbolic traffic signs. *Aust. Road Res.*, *5*, 68-86.

Jacquemart, G. (1998). Modern roundabout practice in the United States. Synthesis of Highway Practice 264. Transportation Research Board, Washington, DC.

Jamson, S., F., Lai and H. Jamson (2010). Driving simulators for robust comparisons: A case study evaluating road safety engineering treatments. *Accid. Anal. Prev.*, *42*(3), 961-971.

Jarosiński, W. (2014). Periodic technical inspections of vehicles and road traffic safety with the number of road accidents involving fatalities. *Eksploatacja i Niezawodność*, *16*(1).

Johansson, R. (2009). Vision Zero—Implementing a policy for traffic safety. *Safety Sci.*, *47*(6), 826-831.

Johnston, I. R., C. Muir and E. W. Howard (2014). *Eliminating Serious Injury and Death from Road Transport*. Taylor & Francis, CRC Press, London.

Kahane, C. J. (1994). Preliminary evaluation of the effectiveness of antilock brake systems for passenger cars. NHTSA Technical Report No. DOT HS 808 206. U.S. Department of Transportation, Washington, DC.

Kahane, C. J. (2004). Lives saved by the federal motor vehicle safety standards and other vehicle safety technologies, 1960-2002 – Passenger Cars and Light Trucks – With a review of 19 FMVSS and their effectiveness in reducing fatalities, injuries and crashes. National Highway Traffic Safety Administration. Report DOT HS 809 833. U.S. Department of Transportation, Washington, DC.

Kahane, C. J. (2015). Lives saved by vehicle safety technologies and associated Federal Motor Vehicle Safety Standards, 1960 to 2012 – Passenger cars and LTVs – With reviews of 26 FMVSS and the effectiveness of their associated safety technologies in reducing fatalities, injuries, and crashes. NHTSA Report No. DOT HS 812 069. U.S. Department of Transportation, Washington, DC.

Kallberg, V. P. (1993). Reflector posts – Signs of danger? *Transport. Res. Rec., No. 1403*, 57-66.

Katila, A., E. Keskinen, M. Hatakka and S. Laapotti (2004). Does increased confidence among novice drivers imply a decrease in safety? The effects of skid training on slippery road accidents. *Accid. Anal. Prev.*, *36*, 543-550.

Keall, M. D. and S. Newstead (2013). An evaluation of costs and benefits of a vehicle periodic inspection scheme with six-monthly inspections compared to annual inspections. *Accid. Anal. Prev.*, *58*, 81-87.

Keith, K., M. Terentacoste, L. Depue, T. Giranda, E. Huckaby, B. Ibarguen, B. Kantowitz, W. Lum and T. Wilson (2005). Roadway human factors and behavioral safety in Europe. Federal Highway Administration. Report FJWA-PS-05-005. U.S. Department of Transportation, Washington, DC.

Kim, K. S., M. H. Myeong and Y. J. Kweon (2011). Differences in traffic violations and at-fault crashes between license suspension and revocation. *Accid. Anal. Prev.*, *43*(3), 755-761.

Klauer, S. G., T. A. Dingus, V. L. Neale, J. D. Sudweeks and D. J. Ramsey (2006). The impact of driver inattention on near-crash/crash risk: An analysis using the 100-car naturalistic driving study data. National Highway Traffic Safety Administration. Report DOT HS 810 594. U.S. Department of Transportation, Washington, DC.

Kline, D. W. and P. Fuchs (1993). The visibility of symbolic highway signs can be increased among drivers of all ages. *Hum. Fact.*, *35*, 25-34.

Klipp, S., K. Machata and I. van Schagen (2013). The EU BestPoint project: Getting the best out of a demerit point system. In Australasian Road Safety Research Policing Education Conference, August 2013, Brisbane, Queensland, Australia.

Knox, D. and B. R. Silcock (2003). Research into unlicensed driving – Literature review. Road Safety Research Report No. 38. Department for Transport, London, England.

Koornstra, M., D. Lynam, G. Nilsson, P. Noordzij, H.-E. Pettersson and F. Wegman (2002). *SUNflower: A Comparative Study of the Development of Road Safety in Sweden, the United Kingdom, and the Netherlands*. SWOV Institute for Road Safety Research, Leidschendam, the Netherlands.

Krafft, M., A. Kullgren, A. Lie and C. Tingvall (2009). From 15% to 90% ESC penetration in new cars in 48 months-the Swedish experience. In 21st International Conference on the Enhanced Safety of Vehicles (ESV). Stuttgart, Germany.

Kullgren, A., A. Lie and C. Tingvall (2010). Comparison between Euro NCAP test results and real-world crash data. *Traffic Inj. Prev.*, *11*(6), 587-593.

LaFraniere, S. and A. W. Lehren (2015). The disproportionate risks of driving while black. *New York Times*, October 24. http://nyti.ms/1jFXsFJ

Lahrmann, H., N. Agerholm, N. Tradisauskas, T. Næss, J. Juhl and L. Harms (2012). Pay as you speed, ISA with incentives for not speeding: A case of test driver recruitment. *Accid. Anal. Prev.*, *48*, 10-16.

Lahti, T., E. Nysten, J. Haukka, P. Sulander and T. Partonen (2010). Daylight saving time transitions and road traffic accidents. *J. Env. Pub. Health*, *2010*, 1-3.

Lajunen, T., P. Hakkarainen and H. Summala (1996). The ergonomics of road signs: Explicit and embedded speed limits. *Ergonomics*, *39*(8), 1069-1083.

Larsson, P., S. W. Dekker and C. Tingvall (2010). The need for a systems theory approach to road safety. *Safety Sci.*, *48*(9), 1167-1174.

Leibowitz, H. W. and D. A. Owens (1977). Nighttime driving accidents and selective visual degradation. *Science*, *197*, 422-423.

Leigh, J. P. (1994). Non-random assignment, vehicle safety inspection laws and highway fatalities. *Pub. Choice*, *78*(304), 373-387.
Liu, S., J. Wang and T. Fu (2016). Effects of lane width, lane position and edge shoulder width on driving behavior in underground urban expressways: A driving simulator study. *Int. J. Env. Res. And Pub. Health*, *13*(10), 1010.
Lobjois, R. and V. Cavallo (2007). Age-related differences in street-crossing decisions: The effects of vehicle speed and time constraints on gap selection in an estimation task. *Accid. Anal. Prev.*, *39*(5), 934-943.
Locke, E. A. and G. P. Latham (1990). *A Theory of Goal-Setting and Task Performance*. Prentice-Hall, Englewood Cliffs, NJ.
Locke, E. A. and G. P. Latham (2002). Building a practically useful theory of goal setting and task motivation: A 35-year odyssey. *Am. Psychol.*, *57*, 705-717.
Locke, E. A., K. N. Shaw, L. M. Saari and G. P. Latham (1981). Goal setting and task performance: 1969-1980. *Psychol. Bull.*, *90*, 125-152.
Lund, A. and A. F. Williams (1985). A review of the literature evaluating the defensive driving course. *Accid. Anal. Prev.*, *17*, 449-460.
Lund, A. K. (2015). As cited in NHTSA (2015b).
Lund, A. K., S. Y. Kyrychenko and R. A. Retting (2009). Caution: A comment on Alena Erke's red light for red-light cameras? A meta-analysis of the effects of red-light cameras on crashes. *Accid. Anal. Prev.*, *41*(4), 895-896.
Lunenfeld, H. and G. J. Alexander (1990). A users' guide to positive guidance. Federal Highway Administration. Report FHWA-SA-90-017 (3rd ed.). U.S. Department of Transportation, Washington, DC.
Malenfant, J. E. L., R. Van Houten and B. Jonah (2002). A study to measure the incidence of driving under suspension in the Greater Moncton area. *Accid. Anal. Prev.*, *34*, 439-447.
Martens, M. H. (2000). Assessing road sign perception: A methodological review. *Transport. Hum. Fact.*, *2*(4), 347-357.
Mayhew, D. R. and H. M. Simpson (2002). The safety value of driver education and training. *Inj. Prev.*, Supplement II, *8*, ii3-ii7.
Milligan, C., A. Kopp, S. Dahdah and J. Montufar (2014). Value of a statistical life in road safety: A benefit-transfer function with risk-analysis guidance based on developing country data. *Accid. Anal. Prev.*, *71*, 236-247.
Morando, A., T. Victor and M. Dozza (2016). Drivers anticipate lead-vehicle conflicts during automated longitudinal control: Sensory cues capture driver attention and promote appropriate and timely responses. *Accid. Anal. Prev.*, *97*, 206-219.
Morgan, R. and P. Jordan (2000). The new Austroads road safety audit guidelines. In ITE 2000 Annual Meeting Compendium of Technical Papers.
Mountain, L. J., W. M. Hirst and M. J. Maher (2005). Are speed enforcement cameras more effective than other speed management measures? The impact of speed management schemes on 30 mph roads. *Accid. Anal. Prev.*, *37*, 742-754.
Näätänen, R. and H. Summala (1976). *Road-User Behavior and Traffic Accidents*. North-Holland, Amsterdam.
Najm, W. G., P. M. Schimek and D. L. Smith (2001). Definition of the light vehicle off-roadway crash problem for the intelligent vehicle initiative. *Transport. Res. Rec.*, *No. 1759*, 28-37.

NCHRP (2006). *Core Competency for Highway Safety Professionals. Research Results Digest 302.* National Cooperative Highway Research Program. Transportation Research Board, Washington, DC.

Neuman, T. R., R. PfeferSlack, K. L. Kennedy, K. Hardy, F. Council, H. McGee, L. Prothe and K. Eccles (2003). *NCHRP Report 500, Volume 6: A Guide for Addressing Run-Off-Road Collisions.* Transportation Research Board, Washington, DC.

Newstead, S. V., M. H. Cameron and M. W. Leggett (2001). The crash reduction effectiveness of a network-wide traffic police deployment system. *Accid. Anal. Prev.*, *33*, 393-406.

NHTSA (2003). Statement of Jeffrey W. Runge, M.D., Administrator, National Highway Traffic Safety Administration, before the Subcommittee of Transportation, Treasury and Independent Agencies of the Committee on Appropriations, United States House of Representatives, Washington, DC, April.

NHTSA (2006a). New Car Assessment Program (NCAP): Safety labeling. National Highway Traffic Safety Administration 49 CFR Part 575 [Docket No. NHTSA-2006-25772] RIN 2127-AJ76. U.S. Department of Transportation, Washington, DC.

NHTSA (2006b). PROPOSED FMVSS No. 126. Electronic Stability Control Systems: Preliminary regulatory impact analysis. U.S. Department of Transportation, Washington, DC.

NHTSA (2007). Evaluation of the national impaired driving High Visibility enforcement campaign 2003-2005. Report No. DOT-HS-810-789. U.S. Department of Transportation, Washington, DC.

NHTSA (2013). U.S. Department of Transportation Releases Policy on Automated Vehicle Development. NHTSA Press Release 14-13. U.S. Department of Transportation, Washington, DC. http://www.nhtsa.gov/About+NHTSA/Press+Releases/U.S.+Department+of+Transportation+Releases+Policy+on+Automated+Vehicle+Development

NHTSA (2014a). Federal motor-vehicle safety standards; rear visibility. 49 CFR Part 571. U.S. Federal Register, **79**(66), Rules and Regulations, 19178-19250, Washington, DC, April 7.

NHTSA (2014b). NHTSA announces final rule regarding rear visibility technology. Press Release, U.S. Department of Transportation, Washington, DC, March 31, 2014.

NHTSA (2016a). U.S. DOT and IIHS announce historic commitment of 20 automakers to make automatic emergency braking standard on new vehicles. http://www.nhtsa.gov/About+NHTSA/Press+Releases/nhtsa-iihs-commitment-on-aeb-03172016

NHTSA (2016b). Letter from NHTSA Chief Council, Paul Hemmersbaugh, to Google Director of the Self-Driving Project, Chris Urmson. February 4, 2016. http://isearch.nhtsa.gov/files/Google%20–%20compiled%20response%20to%2012%20Nov%20%2015%20interp%20request%20–%204%20Feb%2016%20final.htm

NHTSA (2016c). Estimating lives saved by electronic stability control, 2010-2014. NHTSA Research Note DOT HS 812 277. U.S. Department of Transportation, Washington, DC.

NHTSA (2016d). Federal automated vehicles policy: Accelerating the next revolution in roadway safety. 12507-091216-v9. U.S. Department of Transportation, Washington, DC.

NHTSA (2016e). Summary of motor vehicle crashes (Final). Traffic safety facts: 2014 Data, Report DOT HS 812 263. Department of Transportation, Washington, DC.

Niederhauser, M. E., B. A. Collins and E. J. Myers (1997). The use of roundabouts: Comparison of alternate design solutions. In: Compendium of Technical Papers for the 67th ITE Annual Meeting, Boston, MA. Institute of Transportation Engineers, Washington, DC.

NTSB (2005). National transportation safety board public forum on driver education and training. Report of the Proceedings NTSB/RP-05-01 PB 2005-917003. Notation 633A. National Transportation Safety Board, Washington, DC, October 28-29, 2003.

OECD (2002). *Safety on Roads. What Is the Vision?* Organisation for Economic Co-operation and Development, Paris.

OECD (2012). Sharing road safety: Developing an international framework for crash modification functions. *Organization of Economic Cooperation and Development.* OECD Publishing, Paris, France.

O'Neill, B. (2009). Preventing passenger vehicle occupant injuries by vehicle design—A historical perspective from IIHS. *Traffic Inj. Prev., 10*(2), 113-126.

O'Neill, B. and S. Y. Kyrychenko (2006). Use and misuse of motor-vehicle crash death rates in assessing highway-safety performance. *Traffic Inj. Prev., 7*(4), 307-318.

Paine, M., D. Paine, M. Case, J. Haley, C. Newland and S. Worde (2013). Trends with ANCAP safety ratings and real-world crash performance for vehicle models in Australia. ESV Paper 13-0390.

Parasuraman, R. and C. D. Wickens (2008). Humans: Still vital after all these years of automation. *Hum. Fact., 50*, 511-520.

Pastor, C. (2013). Correlation between pedestrian injury severity in real-life crashes and Euro NCAP pedestrian test results. 23rd Technical Conference on the Enhanced Safety of Vehicles (ESV). Seoul, Korea.

Peden, M., R. Scurfield, D. Sleet, D. Mohan, A. Hyder, E. Jarawan and C. Mathers (eds.) (2004). *World Report on Road Traffic Injury Prevenion.* World Health Organization, Geneva, Switzerland. www.who.int/world-health-day/2004/infomaterials/world_report/en/index.html

Persaud, B., E. Hauer, R. Retting, R. Vallurupalli and K. Mucsi (1997). Crash reductions related to traffic signal removal in Philadelphia. *Accid. Anal. Prev., 29*(6), 803-810.

Persaud, B., R. Retting, P. Garder and D. Lord (2001). Safety effect of roundabout conversions in the united states: Empirical Bayes observational before-after study. *Trans. Res. Rec. J. Trans. Res. Board, 1751*, 1-8.

Persaud, B. N., R. A. Retting and C. A. Lyon (2004). Crash reduction following installation of centerline rumble strips on rural two-lane roads. *Accid. Anal. Prev., 36*, 1073-1079.

Phillips, R. O., P. Ulleberg and T. Vaa (2011). Meta-analysis of the effect of road safety campaigns on accidents. *Accid. Anal. Prev., 43*(3), 1204-1218.

Poitras, M. and S. Sutter (2002). Policy ineffectiveness or offsetting behavior? An analysis of vehicle safety inspections. *Southern Econ. J.*, *68*(4), 922-934.

Potts, I. (2003). Application of 2 + 1 European roadway design. national cooperative highway research program. Research Results Digest, No. 275. Transportation Research Board, Washington, DC.

Reagan, I. J., M. Brumbelow and T. Frischmann (2015). On-road experiment to assess drivers' detection of roadside targets as a function of headlight system, target placement, and target reflectance. *Accid. Anal. Prev.*, *76*, 74-82.

Redelmeier, D. A., R. J. Tibshirani and L. Evans (2003). Traffic-law enforcement and risk of death from motor-vehicle crashes: Case-crossover study. *Lancet*, *361*(9376), 2177-2182.

Regan, M. A., T. Horberry and A. Stevens (Eds.) (2014). *Driver Acceptance of New Technology: Theory, Measurement and Optimisation.* Ashgate Publishing, Farnham, England.

Retting, R. A., J. F. Chapline and A. F. Williams (2002). Changes in crash risk following re-timing of traffic signal change interval. *Accid. Anal. Prev.*, *34*, 215-220.

Retting, R. A. and M. A. Greene (1997). Influence of traffic signal timing on red light running and potential vehicle conflicts at urban intersections. *Transport. Res. Rec., No. 1595*, 1-7.

Retting, R. A., A. F. Williams and M. A. Greene (1998). Red-light running and sensible countermeasures. Summary of research findings. *Transport. Res. Rec.*, No. *1640*, 23-26.

Retting, R. A., B. N. Persaud, P. E. Gardner and D. Lord (2001). Crash and injury reduction following installation of roundabouts in the United States. *Am. J. Public Health*, *91*, 628-631.

Retting, R. A., S. A. Ferguson and C. M. Farmer (2008). Reducing red light running through longer yellow signal timing and red light camera enforcement: Results of a field investigation. *Accid. Anal. Prev.*, *40*(1), 327-333.

Robinson, A. (2002). Discussion paper of "The safety value of driver education and training" by Mayhew and Simpson (2002). *Inj. Prev.* Supplement II, *8*, ii7-ii8.

Ross, H. L. and P. Gonzales (1988). Effects of license revocation on drunk-driving offenders. *Accid. Anal. Prev.*, *20*, 291-379.

Runyan, C. W. (1998). Using the Haddon matrix: Introducing the third dimension. *Inj. Prev.*, *4*, 302-307.

SAE (2014). Standard, S. A. E. (2014). J3 016, "Sae international taxonomy and definitions for terms related to on-road motor vehicle automated driving systems," levels of driving automation.

Sanders, M. S. and E. J. McCormick (1993). *Human Factors in Engineering and Design.* McGraw-Hill, New York, NY.

Schade, J. and B. Schlag (2003). Acceptability of urban transport pricing strategies. *Trans. Res. F.*, *6*(1), 45-61.

Schechtman, E., H. Bar-Gera and O. Musicant (2016). Driver views on speed and enforcement. *Accid. Anal. Prev.*, *89*, 9-21.

Schieber, F. (1998). Optimizing the legibility of symbol highway signs. In *Vision in Vehicles* 6., North Holland Publishing Co. Amsterdam, NL.

Schieber, F. and D. W. Kline (1994). Age differences in the legibility of symbol highway signs as a function of luminance and glare level: A preliminary report. Proceedings of the Human Factors and Ergonomics Society 38th Annual Meeting, pp. 133-136. Santa Monica, CA.

Schoettle, B. and M. Sivak (2014a). Public opinion about self-driving vehicles in China, India, Japan, the US, the UK, and Australia. UMTRI-2014-30. University of Michigan Transportation Research Institute, Ann Arbor, MI.

Schoettle, B. and M. Sivak (2014b). Motorists' preferences for different levels of vehicle automation: 2016. UMTRI Report SWT-2016-8. University of Michigan Transportation Res. Institute, Ann Arbor, MI.

Schoettle, B. and M. Sivak (2015). A preliminary analysis of real-world crashes involving self-driving vehicles. UMTRI-2015-34. University of Michigan Transportation Research Institute, Ann Arbor, MI.

Schulz, M. (2006). European cities do away with traffic signs. Spiegel Magazine, SPIEGELnet GmbH, Germany, September 16.

Sharfi, T. and D. Shinar (2014). Enhancement of road delineation can reduce safety. *J. Safety Res.*, *49*, 61-68.

Shinar, D. (1977). Curve perception and accidents on curves: An illusive curve phenomenon. *Zeitschrift fur Verkehrssichercheit (J. Traffic Safety)*, *23*, 16-21.

Shinar, D. and A. Drory (1983). Sign registration in daytime and nighttime driving. *Hum. Fact.*, *25*, 117-122.

Shinar, D., M. Bourla and L. Kaufman (2004). Synchronization of traffic signals as a means of reducing red-light running. *Hum. Fact.*, *46*, 367-372.

Shinar, D., T. H. Rockwell and J. Malecki (1980). The effects of changes in driver perception on rural curve negotiation. *Ergonomics*, *23*, 263-275.

Shinar, D., E. Schechtman and R. P. Compton (2001). Self-Reports of safe driving behaviors in relationship to sex, age, education and income in the U.S. adult driving population. *Accid. Anal. Prev.*, *33*, 111-116.

Sihvola, N., J. Luoma, A. Schirokoff, A. J. Salo and K. Karkola (2009). In-depth evaluation of the effects of an automatic emergency system on road fatalities. *Eur. Transp. Res. Rev.*, *1*, 99-105.

Singh, S. (2015). Critical reasons for crashes investigated in the national motor vehicle crash causation survey. NHTSA Traffic Safety Facts Report No. DOT HS 812 115. US. Department of Transportation, Washington, DC.

Sivak, M. (2002). How common sense fails us on the road: Contribution of bounded rationality to the annual worldwide toll of one million traffic fatalities. *Transport. Res. F*, *5*, 259-269.

Smids, J. (2016). The moral case for intelligent speed adaptation. *J. App. Philosophy*, *33*(2).

Smiley, A. (2013) Forward to Rudin-Brown, C. and S Jamson (Eds.) (2013). Behavioural adaptation and road safety: Theory, evidence and action. ix-x. CRC Press, Boca Raton, FL.

Stamatiadis, N. and J. Pigman (2009). Impact of shoulder width and median width on safety. NCHRP Report 633. National Academies Press, Washington, DC.

Stead, M., S. Tagg, A. M. MacKintosh and D. Eadie (2005). Development and evaluation of a mass media Theory of Planned Behaviour intervention to reduce speeding. *Health Ed. Res.*, *20*(1), 36-50.

Strandroth, J., M. Rizzi, M. Olai, A. Lie and C. Tingvall (2012). The effects of studded tires on fatal crashes with passenger cars and the benefits of electronic stability control (ESC) in Swedish winter driving. *Accid. Anal. Prev.*, *45*, 50-60.

Sullivan, J. M. and M. J. Flannagan (2002). The role of ambient light level in fatal crashes: Inferences from daylight saving time transitions. *Accid. Anal. Prev.*, *34*, 487-498.

Summala, H. and R. Näätänen (1974). Perception of highway traffic signs and motivation. *J. Safety Res.*, *6*, 150-153.

Sutter, D. and M. Poitras (2002). The political economy of automobile safety inspections. *Pub. Choice*, *113*(3-4), 367-387.

Thomas, F. D., III, R. D. Blomberg and D. L. Fisher (2012, April). A fresh look at driver education in America. NHTSA Report No. DOT HS 811 543. U.S. Department of Transportation, Washington, DC.

Thomas, P., G. Yannis, G. Duchamp, M. Vis, H. Jahi and E. Dupont (2009). Building the European Road Safety Observatory. SafetyNet final activity report. European Commission, Brussels, Belgium.

Tingvall, C., M. Krafft, A. Kullgren and A. Lie (2003). The effectiveness of esp (electronic stability programme) in reducing real life accidents. Enhanced Safety of Vehicles Conference, Paper #261. Nagoya, Japan.

TRB (2010). Model curriculum for highway safety core competencies. NCHRP Report 667. Transportation Research Board, Washington, DC.

TRB (2013). Countermeasures to address impaired driving offenders. A symposium August 15-16, 2011. TRB Circular E-C134. Transportation Research Board, Washington, DC.

TRB (2015). TRB 2nd national summit on roadway safety culture: Moving toward zero deaths through organizational transformation. Transportation Research Board, Washington, DC, November 5-6.

Treat, J. R., N. S. Tumbas, S. T. McDonald, D. Shinar, R. D. Hume, R. E. Mayer, R. L. Stansifer and N. J. Castellan (1979). Tri-level study of the causes of traffic accidents: Final report. Volume I: Causal factor tabulations and assessments. National Highway Traffic Safety Administration. Report No. DOT HS 805 085. U.S. Department of Transportation, Washington, DC.

Turner, B., K. Imberger, P. Roper, V. Pyta and J. McLean (2010). Road safety engineering risk assessment: Part 6: Crash reduction factors. Austroads Report No. AP-T151/10, Austroads Ltd., Sydney, Australia.

UK Speed Trap Guide (2006). Marom traffic law enforcement system. http://www.ukspeedtraps.co.uk/speed01.htm. February 13, 2007.

Vaa, T., T. Assum and R. Elvik (2014). Driver support systems: Estimating road safety effects at varying levels of implementation. TOI – Norwegian Institute of Transport Economics. Oslo, Norway.

Valdes-Dapena, P. (2016). Volvo promises deathproof cars by 2020. *CNN*, January 21, http://money.cnn.com/2016/01/20/luxury/volvo-no-death-crash-cars-2020/

van Ratingen, M., A., Williams, A. Lie, A., Seeck, P. Castaing, R. Kolke, G. Adriaenssens and A. Miller (2016). The European new car assessment programme: A historical review. *Chin. J. Traumatol*, *19*(2), 63-69.

Vardaki, S., E. Papadimitriou and P. Kopelias (2014). Road safety audit on a major freeway: Implementing safety improvements. *Eur. Transport. Res. Rev.*, *6*(4), 387-395.

Várhelyi, A., M. Hjälmdahl, C. Hydén and M. Draskóczy (2004). Effects of an active accelerator pedal on driver behaviour and traffic safety after long-term use in urban areas. *Accid. Anal. Prev.*, *36*(5), 729-737.

Vella, M. (2016). Why you shouldn't be allowed to drive. *Time*, *187*, No. 8, 25-29.

Voas, R. B., J. C. Fell, A. S. McKnight and B. Sweedler (2004). Controlling impaired driving through vehicle programs: An overview. *Traffic Inj. Prev.*, *5*(3), 292-298.

Vickers, G. (1958). What sets the goals of public health? *Lancet*, *271*(7021), 599-604. (Originally published as Vol. 1, Issue 7021).

Walker, G. H., N. A. Stanton and I. Chowdhury (2013). Self explaining roads and situation awareness. *Safety Sci.*, *56*, 18-28.

Wall, J., V. Vecovski, J. Costabile and M. Clifton (2015). Rapid deployment of intelligent speed adaptation in New South Wales: The story of Speed Adviser. In 1st Australasian Road Safety Conference. Gold Coast, Queensland, Australia, October.

Wallwork, M. J. (1993). Traffic calming. In: Traffic Safety Toolbox, pp. 235-245. Institute of Transportation Engineers, Washington, DC.

Wanvik, P. O. (2009). Effects of road lighting on motorways. *Traffic Inj. Prev.*, *10*(3), 279-289.

Wegman, F. and L. Aarts (2006). Advancing sustainable safety: National road safety exploration for 2005-2020. SWOV Institute for Road Safety Research, Leidschendam, Netherlands.

Wegman, F., F. Zhang and A. Dijkstra (2012). How to make more cycling good for road safety? *Accid. Anal. Prev.*,*44*(1), 19-29.

White, W. T. (1986). Does periodic motor vehicle inspection prevent crashes? *Accid. Anal. Prev.*, *18*(1), 51-62.

WHO (2013a). Global status report on road safety 2013: Supporting a decade of action. World Health Organization, Geneva, Switzerland.

WHO (2013b). Sterngthening Road Safety Legislation: A practice and resource manual for countries. World Health Organization, Geneva, Switzerland.

WHO (2015). Global status report on road safety 2015: Supporting a decade of action. World Health Organization, Geneva, Switzerland.

Wilde, G. J. (2013). Homeostasis drives behavioural adaptation. In (Rudin-Brown and Jamson Eds.), *Behavioural Adaptation and Road Safety*, pp. 61-86. CRC Press, Boca Raton, FL.

Williams, A. F. and B. O'Neill (1974). On-the-road driving records of licensed race drivers. *Accid. Anal. Prev.*, *6*, 263-270.

Williams, R. L., R. E. Hagen and E. J. McConnell (1984). A survey of suspension and revocation effects on the drink-driving offender. *Accid. Anal. Prev.*, *16*(5/6), 339-350.

Wong, S. C., N. N. Sze, H. F. Yip, B. P. Y. Loo, W. T. Hung and H. K. Lo (2006). Association between setting quantified road safety targets and road fatality reduction. *Accid. Anal. Prev.*, *38*, 997-1005.

Wu, Y., X. Zhao, C. Chen, J. He, J. Rong and J. Ma (2016). Modeling the influence of Chevron alignment sign on young male driver performance: A driving simulator study. *Accid. Anal. Prev.*, *95*, 479-480.

Yadron, D. and D. Tynan (2016). Tesla driver dies in first fatal crash while using the autopilot mode. *The Guardian*. https://www.theguardian.com/technology/2016/jun/30/tesla-autopilot-death-self-driving-car-elon-musk

Yannis, G., E. Papadimitriou, P. Evgenikos and A. Dragomanovits (2015). Good practices on cost–effective road infrastructure safety investments. *Int. J. Inj. Conrol Safety Promot.*, 1-15.

Zegeer, C. V., C. T. Esse, J. R. Stewart, H. H. Huang and P. A. Lagerwey (2004). Safety analysis of marked versus unmarked crosswalks in 30 cities. *ITE J.*, 34-41.

Zegeer, C. V., J. R. Stewart, H. H. Huang, P. A. Lagerwey, J. Feaganes and B. J. Campbell (2005). Safety effects of marked versus unmarked crosswalks at uncontrolled locations: Final report and recommended guidelines. Federal Highway Administration. Report FHWA-HRT-04-100. U.S. Department of Transportation, Washington, DC.

Zhao, X., Y. Wu, J. Rong and J. Ma (2015). The effect of chevron alignment signs on driver performance on horizontal curves with different roadway geometries. *Accid. Anal. Prev.*, *75*, 226-235.

Zohar, D. (1980). Safety climate in industrial organizations: Theoretical and applied implications. *J. Appl. Psychol.*, *65*(1), 96-102.

Zohar, D. (2002). The effects of leadership dimensions, safety climate, and assigned priorities on minor injuries in work groups. *J. Organ. Behav.*, *23*(1), 75-92.

Glossary of Acronyms

AAA	American Automobile Association
AAAF	AAA Foundation for Traffic Safety
AARP	American Association of Retired Persons
AASHTO	American Association of State Highway Safety Officials
ABLS	Alternating Blinking Light System
ABS	Anti-lock Braking System
ACC	Adaptive Cruise Control
ADAS	Advanced Driver Assistance System
AMA	American Medical Association
ANSI	American National Standards Institute
BAC	Blood Alcohol Concentration
BRT	Brake Reaction Time
CDC	(U.S.) Centers for Disease Control
CDS	Count-Down Signal
CHMSL	Center High-Mounted Stop Light
CMF	Crash Modification Factor
CNS	Central Nervous System
DALY	Disability Adjusted Life Year
DBQ	Driver Behavior Questionnaire
DECP	Drug Evaluation and Classification Program
DPS	Demerit Point System
DfT	(U.K.) Department for Transport
DOT	(U.S.) Department of Transportation
DRE	Drug Recognition Expert
DRL	Daylight Running Lights
DRUID	Driving Under the Influence of Drugs Alcohol and Medicines
DUID	Driving Under the Influence of Drugs
DWI	Driving While Intoxicated
EDR	Event Data Recorder
EC	European Commission
EEG	Encephalogram
ESC	Electronic Stability Control

ETSC	European Transport Safety Council
EU	European Union
FARS	Fatality Analysis Reporting System
FHWA	(U.S.) Federal Highway Administration
FMCSA	(U.S.) Federal Motor-Carrier Safety Administration
FOT	Field Operational Test
GDE	Goals for Driver Education
GDL	Graduated Driver Licensing
GDP	Gross Domestic Product
GHSA	(U.S.) Governors Highway Safety Association
GIDAS	German In-Depth Accident Study
HGN	Horizontal Gaze Nystagmus
HRV	Heart Rate Variability
HUD	Head-Up Display
ICADTS	International Council on Alcohol Drugs and Traffic Safety
IIHS	(U.S.) Insurance Institute for Highway Safety
ITF	International Transport Forum
IRTAD	International Road Traffic Accident Data
ISA	Intelligent Speed Adaptation
ISO	International Standards Organization
ITE	Institute of Transportation Engineers
ITS	Intelligent Transportation System
IVDR	In-Vehicle Data Recorder
KSS	Karolinska Sleepiness Scale
LATCH	Lower Anchors and Tethers for Children
MADD	Mothers against Drunk Driving
MAIDS	Motorcycle Accident In-Depth Study
MAIS	Maximum Abbreviated Injury Score
MUTCD	(U.S.) Manual of Uniform Traffic Control Devices
NCAP	New Car Assessment Program
NADS	(U.S.) National Advanced Driving Simulator
NASA-TLX	(U.S.) National Aeronautics and Space Administration Task Load Index
NASS	(U.S.) National Automotive Sampling System
NCSS	(U.S.) National Crash Severity Study
NDS	Naturalistic Driving Study
NHTSA	(U.S.) National Highway Traffic Safety Administration

NIDA	(U.S.) National Institute of Drug Abuse
NMVCCS	(U.S.) National Motor-Vehicle Crash Causation Survey
NRSA	(Israel) National Road Safety Authority
NSC	(U.S.) National Safety Council
NTSB	(U.S.) National Transportation Safety Board
OR	Odds Ratio
OECD	Organization of Economic Cooperation and Development
PI/E	Public Information and Education
PMVI	Periodic Motor Vehicle Inspection
PRT	Perception Reaction Time
PTW	Powered Two-Wheeler
RAP	Road Assessment Program
RAPT	Risk Awareness and Perception Training
RR	Relative Risk
RTOR	Right Turn On Red
SAE	Society of Automotive Engineers
SARTRE	Social Attitudes to Road Traffic Risk
SFST	Standardized Field Sobriety Test
SHRP	Strategic Highway Research Program
SOFI	Swedish Occupational Fatigue Inventory
SPI	Safety Performance Indicator
SSS	Sensation Seeking Scale *or* Stanford Sleepiness Scale
SWOV	(The Netherlands) Institute for Road Safety Research
THC	Tetra Hydro Cannabinol
TNO	(The Netherlands) Organization for Applied Scientific Research
TPB	Theory of Planned Behavior
TRB	(U.S.) Transportation Research Board
TTC	Time -to-Collision
UDA	Unsafe Driving Action
UFOV	Useful Field of View
UNECE	United Nations Economic Commission for Europe
VRU	Vulnerable Road User
WHO	World Health Organization

Author Index

Page Numbers in Italics Refer to References

Aarts, L. 416, *447*, 1086, 1088, *1174*
Abdel-Aty, M. 357, *377*, 1124, *1159*
Abdu, R. 66, *80*, 485, *502*, 750, *780*
Abdul-Halin, A. *978*
Åberg, L. 398, 408, 425, *450*
Abotnes, B. 642, *708*
Abouk, R. 776, *780*
Abou-Zeid, M. 462, *504*
Abrams, B. S. *34*, *178*
Abramson, Y. *1159*
Abric, J. C. 123, *127*, 467, *505*
Abtahi, S. 843, *848*
Achara, S. 1108, *1159*
Adams, B. D. 270, *320*
Adams, C. L. *504*
Adams, J. 22, *33*, *553*
Adams, S. 776, *780*
Adekoya, B. J. 146, *177*
Adell, E. *1028*, *1032*
Adepoju, F. G. *177*
Adeyemi, B. *1159*
Adlaf, E. M. *510*
Adler, A. V. 690, *699*
Adminaite, D. 864, 869, *915*, 988, 991, *1028*
Adriaenssens, G. *1173*
Aertsens, J. *1029*
Af Wåhlberg, A. 5, *34*, *503*
Aga, M. 1149, *1159*
Agar-Wison, M. *785*
Agerholm, N. *1033*, *1167*
Agran, P. F. 535, *552*
Agresti, A. *379*
Aharonson-Daniel, L. 49, *84*
Ahie, L. M. 399, *447*
Ahlin, E. M. *636*
Ahlner, J. 577, *628*
Ahlstrom, C. 175, *177*, *783*, 807, *848*, 1001, 1002, *1028*, *1032*
Ahmad, O. *83*
Ahmad-Farhan, M. S. *977*
Ahmed, M. M. 1124, *1159*
Åhsberg, E. 797–798, 799, 805, 807, *848*
Ajaiyeoba, A. I. *177*
Ajzen, I. 109, 111, *125*, 396, *447*, 462, *502*
Åkerstedt, T. *82*, *177*, 799, 807, 815, 828, *848*, *849*, *851*, *852*
Aksan, N. 359, *377*, *386*
Albanese, B. *981*
Albert, G. 778, *780*
Albert, P. *323*
Alden, A. *849*
Aleardi, M. *508*
Alexander, G. J. 1119, *1159*, *1161*, *1168*
Alexander, J. 107, *130*, 847, *851*
Alexander, K. R. *186*, *381*
Alferdinck, J. W. W. M. *1035*
Alicandri, E. *854*
Allen, M. J. 5, *34*, 141, *178*, 216, *247*, 887, 892–893, *915*
Allen Jr., J. A. 162, *179*, *379*
Allman, R. M. *185*
Allsop, R. 425, 437, *447*, *451*, 519, *556*, 864, *915*, 988, *1028*, 1097, *1160*
Alm, H. 747, 748, *781*
Alonge, M. 519, *553*
Alonso, J. *557*
Alsop, J. *1033*
Alvarez, F. J. 575, 620, *627*, 646, *699*
Alvarez, S. L. 352, *387*
Alvarez, V. M. 395, *450*
Amado, S. 765, *781*
Ameratunga, S. *503*, *700*, 999, *1034*, *1081*, *1160*

Amezcua-Prieto, C. *1032*
Amoros, E. 27, *34*, 49, *80*, 669, *702*, *1028*, *1033*
Amundsen, A. 417, *449*, 895, *917*
Anastasio, R. J. *178*
Andersen, T. 1013, *1032*
Anderson, B. *511*
Anderson, C. 175, *178*, 535, *552*, 838, *849*, *852*
Anderson, D. 351, *377*, 688, *699*
Anderson, H. S. 1043, 1080, *1080*
Anderson, J. 163, *181*, 199, *247*
Anderson, R. *84*, 895, *915*
Anderson, S. W. *180*, *377*, *380*
Andrea, D. *179*, *379*, *382*
Andreassi, J. 815, *849*
Andréasson, I. 913, *920*
Andrews, B. *249*, *316*
Ang, C. H. *853*
Angel, L. *920*
Angell, L. 194, *253*, *790*
Anglin-Bodrug, K. *630*, *705*
Anitei, M. 491, *502*
Anstey, K. J. 51, *80*, 145, *178*, *187*, *255*, *256*, 357, *377*, *388*
Antin, J. 138, *186*, *448*, *783*, *920*, *1080*
Anttila, V. *453*
Anund, A. *82*, *128*, *177*, *848*
Appenzeller, B. M. R. 575, *624*
Arbogast, K. B. *557*
Ardekani, S. 376, *388*
Ardickas, Z. *381*
Ardiles, P. *976*
Aresu, M. *915*
Argyle, M. 480, *502*
Armitage, C. J. 110, *126*
Armsby, P. 955, *973*
Armstrong, A. *856*
Arnett, J. J. 490, *503*
Aronoff, C. J. 412, *447*
Arvind, A. *252*
Asante, S. 376, *388*
Asbridge, M. *80*, *503*, *625*, 670, 672, 673, 674, *699*, *782*
Ashby, M. C. 747, *783*, *790*
Asher, L. 872, *915*
Ashford, D. *179*
Ashmead, D. *918*
Ashton, S. J. 91, 895
Assum, T. 483, *503*, *702*, 1143, *1173*
Astolfi, L. *849*
Atchison, D. A. 154, *178*
Atchley, P. 596, *624*, 743, 748, 771, *781*
Atkins, R. *709*
Atwood, J. *1160*
Au, S. 145, 220, *251*
Augros, X. *81*
Augsburger, M. 645, *699*
Aupetit, S. 955, *973*
Aust, M. L. 215, *247*
Austin, J. *559*
Austin, R. A. 376, *377*
Au-Yeung, E. 395, *451*
Avenoso, A. 929, 963, 971, *973*
Avery, G. C. 900, *915*
Avineri, E. 884, *915*
Avni, I. *781*
Ayas, N. T. *849*
Aymerich, M. *784*
Ayoub, E. M. 817, *849*
Ayyagari, R. C. *924*
Azens, A. *974*

Babiloni, F. *849*
Babizhayev, M. A. 352, 356, 359, *377*
Babor, T. 611, *624*
Bachman, L. R. 1140, *1159*
Bachmann, R. 310, *315*
Backlund, F. 195, 197, *251*
Backs, R. W. 191, *247*
Baddeley, A. D. 199, 228, *247*
Baer, J. D. 953, 954, *973*
Bahouth, G. 1149, *1159*
Bai, O. 843, *852*
Bai, X. 618, *626*
Bains, M. *783*
Bajanowski, T. *625*
Baker, E. *624*
Baker, J. S. 1045, *1080*
Baker, L. D. *385*
Baker, S. P. 292, 293, *315*, *316*, *324*, *782*, *849*

Baker, T. D. 862, *921*
Baldanzini, N. *980*
Baldi, S. 953, 954, *973*
Baldock, M. R. J. 366, *377*
Baldwin, G. H. S. 66, *83*, *253*, *920*
Balk, S. A. *83*
Ball, B. 606, *625*
Ball, D. *178*
Ball, K. 26, *36*, *38*, 162, 164, 167, 168, 177, *178*, *179*, *180*, *183*, *184*, *185*, 263, *320*, 353, 357, 368, *377*, 378, 381, *385*, *386*, *509*
Ball, S. 971, *982*
Ballachey, E. L. 595, *629*
Ballesteros, M. F. *978*
Balwinski, S. M. *854*
Bambach, M. R. 930, *973*
Bandeen-Roche, K. *178*, *184*
Banet, A. 944, 949, *974*
Bangert-Drowns, R. 620, *635*
Bannert, M. *255*, *322*, *324*
Bao, S. *129*, 230, *247*
Bar-Gera, H. 400, *455*
Barak, B. 47, *80*
Barbeau, H. *1160*
Barbone, F. 680, *699*, *978*
Bareket, Z. *250*
Barger, L. K. 799, 821, *849*
Bar-Gera, H. 61, 62, 73, *80*, 231, *248*, *916*, 1124, 1147, *1159*, *1171*
Bärgman, J. 75, *81*, *1083*
Bar-Hamburger, R. *633*, *707*
Barickman, F. *920*
Barkana, Y. 743, *781*
Barker, D. 313, *316*
Barkley, R. A. 639, *699*
Barnard, K. 5, *34*
Barnard, Y. *81*, 94, 120, *125*
Baron, W. *855*
Baron-Epel, O. *126*, 523, *558*
Barraclough, P. 466, *503*
Barry, A. E. *636*
Barry, D. 189, *248*
Bartle, C. *379*, *850*, *974*, *975*
Bartlett, F. C. 804, *849*
Bartlett, W. *979*
Bartley, S. H. 797, 798, *849*
Bartow, P. *178*, 260
Bastien, C. *1081*
Bastien-Toniazzo, M. *627*
Bathurst, J. 399, *457*
Battista, V. 230, *252*
Batziris, H. *701*
Bauer, K. *1165*
Baughan, C. 299, *315*, 467, *504*, 938, *975*
Baulk, S. D. 805, *852*
Baum, H. 1138, 1139, 1142, *1159*
Bauman, A. *1032*
Baumann, M. *81*
Baumgarten, T. *506*
Baxter, J. *131*, *508*, *981*, *1082*
Bayly, M. 221, *250*, 943, 969, *973*, *977*
Beanland, V. *187*, 281, 282, 307, *315*, 940, *973*
Beard, B. *178*
Beasley, E. E. 691, *707*
Beatty, J. 104, *129*
Bech, P. 661, *699*, *707*
Beck, K. *318*, 488, 489, *503*, 617, *624*
Beck, L. F. 521, *555*
Beck, N. C. *636*
Beckel, R. W. *701*
Becker, E. R. 964, *976*
Beckmann, J. 929, 963, 971, *973*
Bédard, M. *83*, *187*, 339, 368, *378*, *383*, *387*, *388*, 584, *624*, *626*, 667, *699*, *701*, 766, *781*
Beecher, G. P. 432, *447*
Begg, D. J. 258, *315*
Behrensdorff, I. 590, *624*, 643, 684, *699*
Behrman, D. 983, *1028*
Beijer, D. 727, *781*
Beike, J. *625*
Beintema, J. *1035*
Beirness, D. 257, *315*, 615, *624*, *626*, 691, 696, *707*, 731, *781*, 818, 820, 830, *849*
Bekhor, S. 1140, *1159*
Bekiaris, E. *318*, 928, *975*
Belin, M. Å. 1099, 1150, *1159*
Bell, E. *975*
Bellamy, N. *458*

Bellavance, F. 281, *318*, *786*
Bellet, T. 944, 949, *974*
Bellinger, D. B. 207, *248*, 726, *781*
Bellis, M. A. *628*
Belton, K. L. *918*, *1031*
Belz, S. M. 798, 799, 806, 817, 835, *849*, 1118, *1159*
Bem, S. L. 492, *503*
Ben-Asher, N. 942, *976*
Ben-Bassat, T. 238, 239, 240, 241, 244, *248*, 354, 355, 367, *378*, 1089, 1116, 1121, 1125, *1159*, *1160*
Benel, D. *784*
Bengler, K. *786*
Benguigui, N. 873, *920*
Benington, R. *1033*
Bennet, M. *915*
Bennett, E. E. *554*
Bennett, P. J. 352, *386*
Bennett, R. H. *707*
Bennink, L. D. *1161*
Ben-Shoham, I. 101, 199, *254*, 270, *323*
Benson, W. *83*, *252*
Bent, F. D. *784*
Ben-Yaacov, A. 227, 228, *248*
Berch, D. B. *377*
Beregovaia, E. *791*
Berg, H. Y. *318*
Berg, M. D. 535, *552*
Berg, W. P. 207, *248*, *781*
Bergen, G. 608, *624*
Bergeron, J. 799, 818, 833, *856*
Berghaus, G. 661, 662, 663, 678, *699*, *700*, *707*
Bergoffen, G. 523, 531, *552*
Bergrund, U. *455*
Berkowitz, A. M. 549, *556*
Berkowitz, L. 491, *503*
Berlowitz, D. *852*
Bernat, D. H. 590, 592, *624*
Berndt, A. *377*
Bernhoft, I. M. *82*, 590, *624*, *628*, *703*
Berning, A. 564, 581, 582, 610, 613, *624*, *625*, *630*, *631*, 644, 647, 654, 667, 671, 672, 674, 681, 684, 686, 688, *700*, *701*, *704*, 932, *975*
Berns, S. 7, *34*
Bernstein, A. *915*
Berthelon, C. *627*
Besel, R. R. 523, 529, *552*
Betz, M. E. 357, *378*
Beusmans, J. 445, *457*
Bex, P. I. *180*
Bhargava, S. 755, *781*
Bhat, C. R. 465, *508*
Bhise, V. D. 5, *34*, 370, *378*, 888, 889, *915*
Biagioli, F. 538, 540, *552*
Bianchi, A. 47, *80*, 486, 487, *503*
Biassoni, F. 205, *253*
Biecheler, M. B. *634*, *705*
Biederman, J. *508*
Biever, W. J. *781*
Bigelow, B. J. 396, *457*
Bigelow, G. E. 661, *703*
Biggs, H. *509*
Biglan, A. 592, *626*
Bijleveld, F. D. 6, *36*
Bíl, M. 1006, *1028*
Billittier IV, A. J. *556*
Bílová, M. 1006, *1028*
Bingham, C. R. 296, 300, *316*, *317*, 542, *552*, *554*
Bioulac, B. *854*, *855*
Bird, A. D. 861, *915*
Bird, D. K. 680, *708*
Birky, M. M. *701*
Birrell, S. A. 175, *178*, 231, *248*, 728, *781*
Bishai, D. M. *627*
Bittner Jr., A. C. 108
Bjerre, B. 575, 617, *624*
Björklund, G. M. 483, *503*
Bjornebone, A. *700*
Bjørnskau, T. 311, *322*, 433, *447*, 1000, 1008, 1016, *1028*, *1030*, *1033*, 1113, 1114, *1160*
Björnstig, U. 550, *556*
Black, B. 821, *851*
Black, G. *504*
Blackburn, J. L. *783*
Blais, E. 437, *447*, *917*, *1030*, 1143, *1160*
Blaizot, S. 989, *1028*
Blakeney, S. *187*

Blanchard, E. B. 481, *507*
Blanchard, R. A. 367, *384*
Blanco, M. 768, *781*, 817, 844, *849*, *851*, 1153, *1160*
Blasco, R. D. 482, *503*
Blatt, A. 1072, *1080*
Bledsoe, G. H. 964, *974*
Blewden, M. 609, *631*
Bliss, J. P. *131*, *455*
Bliss, T. 1100, 1102, *1160*
Bloksgaard, L. *508*
Blom, C. *853*
Blomberg, R. A. 648, *700*
Blomberg, R. D. *317*, *320*, *322*, *324*, 579, 585, 610, *624*, *625*, *631*, 932, *974*, 1108, *1173*
Blower, D. 518, *555*
Blows, S. 491, *503*, 663, 672, 673, *700*, *978*, 1111, 1133, *1160*
Blum, Y. 223, 227, *248*, *255*
Blumenthal, M. 100, 111, *125*, 801, *849*
Blunck, H. 732, *781*
Blustein, J. 821, 857
Blythe, M. *788*
Blythe, P. *380*
Bocanegra, J. *85*, *790*
Bocanegra, L. *849*
Bock, T. *708*
Boda, C. N. *1083*
Boehm-Davis, D. A. 741, *788*
Boenke, D. *1164*
Boer, E. *83*, 742, *787*
Bogard, S. *129*, *250*
Bogenrieder, R. 310, *315*, 544, *552*
Bogerd, C. P. 967, 969, *974*
Boggan, W. 566, *624*
Bolin, I. 200, *254*, 370, *386*
Bolling, A. K. 740, 744, 747, 748, 759, *793*
Boloix, E. *1081*
Bolvin, J. F. *703*
Bonnefon, J.-F. 1156, *1160*
Bonnefond, A. 828, 838, 840, 842, *849*
Bonneson, J. 423, 424, *450*
Boogaard, H. *1029*
Boone, J. *386*
Boord, P. *852*
Boorman, M. 688, *700*, *701*
Bord, S. *126*
Bordel, S. 1118, *1160*
Borghini, G. 815, *849*
Borkenhagen, D. *253*, 311, *322*
Borkenstein, R. F. 576, 577, 578, 579, 580, 586, 587, 588, *624*
Borowsky, A. 97, 106, 107, *125*, 170, 175, *178*, *184*, 220, 221, 222, *248*, *253*, 272, 274, 308, 310, 312, *315*, *321*, *325*, *378*, 725, *781*, 892, *915*
Borrell, C. *975*
Borzendowski, S. A. W. 894, *915*
Bos, N. *1164*
Bosker, W. M. 696, *700*, *707*
Boski, J. 944, *978*
Bosman, E. 351, 352, *379*
Bottazzi, M. *975*
Botwinick, J. 352, *378*
Bouchard, J. *701*
Boufous, S. *977*
Boulosa, Z. *853*
Bourla, M. 476, *509*, 1129, *1172*
Bowden, K. *324*
Bower, G. H. *247*
Bowers, A. R. 165, *178*
Bowie, N. N. 404, 414, 416, 421, *447*
Bowland, L. 595, *628*
Bowman, B. L. 233, *248*, 872, *915*
Bowman, D. 844, *849*
Boyd, S. 735, *787*
Boyle, A. J. 955, *973*
Boyle, E. *978*
Boyle, J. M. 534, 545, *552*
Boyle, L. 63, *80*, *250*, 395, *447*, 771, 778, *783*, *790*, 1054, *1082*
Brabyn, J. A. *186*, 352, *381*, *388*
Bracchitta, K. M. 542, *552*
Brackett, R. Q. 432, *447*
Brackstone, M. 224, 225, *248*
Braddy 92, *125*
Bradshaw, J. L. 359, *387*
Brady, J. E. 653, *705*
Bragg, B. W. 958, *974*
Brainard, K. *704*
Braitman, K. A. *320*, 744, 755, *783*, *788*

Bramness, J. G. 675, 678, 679, *700*
Branas, C. C. 966, *974*
Brandenburg, S. 429, *457*
Brauer, S. *629*
Brault, M. *701*
Braver, E. 116, *127*, *316*, 336, 340, 344, *378*, *383*, 545, *552*, *782*
Breen, J. 1100, 1102, *1160*
Breslau, N. *850*
Brewer, M. 374, *378*, *449*, 904, *915*
Brewer, R. D. *633*
Brewster, R. M. *850*
Brick, J. 565, *624*
Briest, S. *506*
Brigell, M. 162, *186*
Briggs, G. F. 750, *781*
Brijs, K. 110, *125*, *379*
Brijs, T. *125*, 300, *324*, *379*, *385*, *448*, *1161*
Brink, J. R. *323*
Brinkmann, B. 575, *625*
Briscoe, S. 593, *625*
Brittle, C. 524, 531, *553*
Broberg, T. 361, 376, *380*
Brodsky, W. 5, *34*, 725, 726, *781*, 1002, *1029*
Broman, A. T. 165, *178*
Bromberg, S. 373, *378*
Brook-Carter, N. 114, *129*, 745, *786*
Brookhuis, K. A. *82*, 104, 114, *125*, 398, *452*, *703*, *707*, 747, 749, 750, 754, 759, *781*
Brooks, A. M. 959, *974*
Brooks, C. *915*
Brooks, J. 765, *784*, 893, *924*
Brooks, P. 941, *974*
Brossard, C. *699*
Broughton, J. 27, *34*, 461, *503*, *626*, 1097, 1113, *1160*, *1162*
Broughton, K. L. M. 225, *248*
Broughton, P. 5, *34*
Broughton, R. 811, *849*
Brouwer, R. F. 712, *787*
Brouwer, W. 226, *255*
Brown, D. B. 376, *383*
Brown, I. D. 107, *125*, 308, *316*, 747, *782*, 797, 798, 802, 804, 805, 842, 844, *849*
Brown, J. 167, *178*, *919*, *981*, *1160*
Brown, R. 495, *503*
Brown, S. *182*, *388*
Brown, T. G. *322*
Brown, T. L. 82, *83*, *703*, *786*, *787*
Browning, S. R. *782*
Bruck, D. 828, *850*
Bruckner, R. 351, *378*
Brühning, E. 7, *34*
Brühwiler, P. A. 967, 969, *974*
Brumbelow, M. 1139, *1171*
Brumen, L. *976*
Bruni, J. *38*, *178*, *184*, *377*
Bruno, G. A. 811, *850*
Bucchi, A. 95, *126*, *249*
Buchanan-King, M. *448*, *783*, *1080*
Buchner, D. M. *705*
Budde, B. M. *248*, *781*
Bueno-Cavanillas, A. *978*
Buliung, R. *922*
Bullough, J. D. 150, *179*
Bumberry, J. *707*
Bunker, L. 912, *916*
Bunn, T. L. 714, *782*
Buonarosa, M. L. 903, *924*
Burch, C. A. *975*
Burch, D. *782*
Burg, A. 146, 151, 152, 153, 155, 162, *179*, *181*, 352, 353, *378*
Burke, B. L. *381*
Burke, K. L. *381*
Burnett, G. 66, *81*, 485, *504*, 715, *790*
Burns, M. 605, 606, 622, 623, *624*, *625*, *631*, *634*, 690, *699*, *700*, *974*
Burns, P. *457*, 745, 748, 758, 759, 763, 767, *782*, *790*
Burns, T. M. 484, *510*
Burtaverde, V. *502*
Burton, S. *782*
Bushell, M. 866, 899, *925*
Buss, A. H. 495, *503*
Bustan, B. 522, 523, *556*
Butters, J. E. 479, *503*, 576, *625*
Buyan, M. 967, *974*
Byers, J. C. 108
Byington, K. W. *923*

Byington, S. *387*, *923*
Byrd, T. *84*, *558*

Cacciabue, P. C. 5, *34*, 125, *126*
Cade, B. E. *849*
Caetano, R. 611, *624*
Caird, J. 6, *35*, 79, *80*, 371, *378*, 499, *503*, 745, 747, 750, 756, 761, 763, 766, 771, *782*, *788*, *794*
Cairney, P. 159, *179*
Cairns, S. *916*
Caldwell, C. 949, *974*
Caldwell, H. *80*
Calvert, M. 462, *510*
Calvo, A. A. *791*
Camden, A. *922*
Cameron, M. 433, *448*, *916*, 1114, *1169*
Camp, B. J. 363, 364, *378*
Campbell, B. J. 881, 908, *916*, *925*, *1175*
Campbell, D. 1019, 1020, *1029*
Campbell, J. L. 232, 245, *248*, *919*, 1115, 1131, *1160*
Campbell, K. 76, *80*, *131*, *508*, *981*, *1082*
Campbell, P. *504*
Campbell, S. S. *853*
Cangianelli, L. A. *709*
Caplehorn, J. *701*
Caplinskiene, M. *82*, *703*
Carberry, T. *187*, 359, *388*, 893, *924*, *925*, *1036*
Carbonari, R. *784*
Carciofo, R. *131*
Cardon, G. *186*, 1011, *1035*
Carey, M. J. *974*
Carlson, D. 800, *854*
Carlson, P. 158, *179*, *449*, 1126, *1160*, *1165*
Carmel, R. 1012, *1030*
Carney, C. *248*, 269, 270, *316*, *320*, 527, *553*, 736, *782*, *788*
Carnis, L. 437, *447*, 1143, *1160*
Carpenter, C. 528, *553*, 592, *625*
Carr, D. 361, 362, *378*, *387*, *388*
Carr, K. *704*
Carr, S. B. *86*
Carroll, J. *788*
Carroll, R. J. *81*, 843, *850*, *1080*
Carsten, O. 72, *81*, 94, *125*, *128*, 444, *447*, 725, *785*, *786*, *1160*
Carstensen, G. 307, *316*
Carter, C. 747, *784*
Carter, D. L. 903, *916*, 1018, *1029*
Carter, J. D. 696, *706*
Carter, P. M. 302, *316*
Cartwright, J. L. 670, *699*
Casali, J. G. 205, *255*, 405, *447*, 798, *849*, 1118, *1159*
Casanova-Powell, T. 615, *625*, *634*
Case, M. *1170*
Casey, S. M. 442, *447*
Cass, C. *709*
Casson, E. J. 162, *184*
Cassuto, Y. *633*, *707*, *854*
Casswell, S. 611, *624*
Castaing, P. *1173*
Castanier, C. 110, *126*
Castelblanco, A. *918*, *1165*
Castellà, J. 479, *503*, 1114, *1160*
Castellan, N. J. *324*, *457*, *793*, *1035*, *1083*, *1173*
Castillo-Manzano, J. I. 1111, *1160*
Castro, C. 5, *34*
Castro-Nuño, M. 1111, *1160*
Casutt, G. 364, *378*
Catchlove, M. *378*
Cavaiola, A. A. 479, *503*, 575, *625*
Cavallo, V. 159, *179*, *249*, 873, 885, *916*, *919*, *920*, 958, 959, 960, 969, *974*, *981*, *1034*, 1123, *1168*
Caven, B. *786*
C'de Baca, J. 613, *625*, *629*
Ceder, G. *700*
Ceminsky, J. *511*
Cercarelli, R. *788*
Cerezuela, G. P. 1118, *1160*
Cesi, A. 519, *556*
Cestac, J. 110, *126*
Chadbunchachai, W. 963, *977*, *979*
Chae, C. D. 1121, *1161*
Chait, L. D. 661, *700*
Chakman, J. 160, *181*
Chakravarty, S. *252*

Chamberlain, T. 732, *785*
Chan, A. H. 234, 240, *252*, *256*, 462, 485, *511*
Chang, G. L. 217, *251*
Chang, H. L. 1112, *1161*
Chang, I. 26, *34*, 755, *782*, 1060, *1080*
Chang, M. C. *977*
Chaparro, A. *187*, 350, *383*, *924*, *925*
Chapline, J. F. 1129, *1171*
Chapman, P. 107, *126*, *129*, 164, 175, *179*, *182*, *249*, *316*, *324*, 398, *450*, *783*
Chapon, A. *782*
Charles, A. *854*
Charlton, J. *83*, *84*, 158, *179*, 359, 360, 363, 365, 366, 368, *378*, *379*, *383*, *384*, *387*, *921*, *1031*
Charlton, S. 107, *126*, 201, 220, *248*, *249*, 399, 439, 441, *447*, 747, 765, *782*, *787*, 1117, 1118, *1161*
Charman, W. N. 351, 352, *379*
Charness, N. 351, 352, *379*
Chassidim, H. S. *633*
Chastang, J.-F. *385*
Chattington, M. 172, *179*
Chattopadhyay, S. K. *624*
Chaudhary, N. 519, 522, 523, 524, 529, 530, *553*, *634*, 735, 777, 782, *783*, *793*
Chaziris, A. *34*
Chen, C. 357, *377*, *1174*
Chen, I. G. *554*
Chen, K. *1031*
Chen, L. 285, 292, 298, *315*, *316*, 340, *383*, 766–767, *782*
Chen, N. 312, *316*
Chen, P. L. 908, *916*
Chen, Q. 653, *705*
Chen, R. *323*, 476, *505*
Chen, S. 399, *450*
Chen, S.-C. 232, *249*
Chen, S. K. 223, *249*
Chen, W. 261, *316*
Cheng, C. 776, *782*
Cherek, D. R. *707*
Chernik, D. A. 677, *707*
Cherry, E. C. 100, *126*
Cherry, N. *918*, *1031*
Chesher, G. B. 660, *700*
Chester, D. *249*
Chi, C. F. 232, 244, *249*
Chi, J. 777, *787*
Chiang, D. P. *919*, *974*
Chikritzhs, T. *628*
Chinn, B. *980*
Chipman, M. *132*, *456*, 535, *555*, *630*, *705*
Chira-Chavala, T. 1112, *1161*
Chiron, M. *385*
Chisholm, A. *922*
Chisholm, D. 862, *921*
Chisholm, S. L. 371, *378*, 750, *782*
Chisvert, M. *1160*
Chliaoutakis, J. *508*, *1034*
Cho, H. S. 1121, *1161*
Choca, J. P. 357, *379*
Choe, B. *316*
Choi, B. *452*
Choi, E. H. 522, 528, 534, 538, 543, *558*
Choi, S. *179*
Cholerton, B. *385*
Chóliz, M. *1160*
Chow, B. L. C. *709*
Chowdhury, I. *1174*
Chraif, C. *502*
Christ, R. C. 108
Christens, P. F. 734, *793*
Christensen, A. D. *508*
Christensen, P. 417, *449*, 895, *917*, 1132, 1133, *1161*
Christie, N. 899, *916*
Christoforou, C. *794*
Christoforou, Z. 566, *625*
Christoph, M. 724, *782*
Christophersen, A. S. *634*, 642, 643, 645, *700*, *702*, *703*, *708*
Christup, H. 661, *707*
Chrysler, S. T. 158, *179*, *1165*
Chu, B. S. *187*, *924*, *925*, *1036*
Chu, H. *325*
Chu, K. *1031*
Chu, M. *701*
Chua, H. F. 115, *133*, 488, *511*
Chua, P. Y. *853*
Chuang, K. H. 1000, *1029*

Chun, J. 138, *179*
Chung, E. K. 300, *316*
Chung, M. K. 840, *850*
Chung, Y. 26, *34*, 755, *782*, 1060, *1080*
Churches, T. *1035*
Chute, E. 797, 798, *849*
Cicchino, J. 1141, *1161*
Cicchino, J. B. 258, 260, *316*, 336, *379*
Ciceri, M. R. 205, *253*
Cirillo, J. A. 411, *447*
Cissell, G. M. *180*, *386*
Citek, K. 606, 607, *625*, *708*
Clapp, J. D. *628*
Clarion, A. *782*
Clark, L. P. 620, *636*
Clarke, D. 346, 357, 375, *379*, 812, *850*, 931, 933, 934, 935, 936, 940, 941, *974*, *975*, *981*
Clarke, K. *388*
Clarkson, A. *378*
Clayton, A. B. 657, 676, *701*, 881, 882, *916*
Clayton, S. L. *504*
Clegg, B. A. 200, *250*
Clifton, M. *1174*
Cloutier, M. S. *917*
Clunas, N. J. *185*
Clymer, J. M. *624*
Cnaan, A. *922*
Coate, D. 1098, *1161*
Coben, J. H. *325*, 965, 966, *975*
Cockfield, S. *980*
Coelho, R. S. *506*
Coffman, Z. 411, *456*
Cohen, A. 905, *916*, *1033*, *1034*
Cohen, J. L. *792*
Cohen, T. 59, *85*
Cohn, L. D. *84*, *558*
Cohn, S. M. *918*, *977*, *1165*
Cole, B. L. 154, *186*, 727, 729, *785*, 1125, *1166*
Coleman, H. L. 610, *631*
Coleman, J. A. 445, *447*
Coleman, J. R. *85*, *792*, *856*
Coleman, R. R. *792*
Coles, T. *554*
Colgan, F. 523, 534, 537, *553*
Colgan, M. A. 881, 882, *916*
Colgrove, L. A. *381*
Collet, C. 767, *782*
Collia, D. V. 331, *379*
Collins, B. A. 1122, *1170*
Collins, L. *249*, *316*
Collins, T. *974*
Colston, S. *918*, *1165*
Comelli, M. 936, *975*
Commandeur, J. 6, *36*, 159, *179*, *1035*
Compagne, J. *974*
Compton, R. 8, *38*, 114, 258, *318*, *364*, 391, 395, *456*, 474, 480, 485, 492, 500, *509*, 522, 543, *557*, *558*, *559*, 564, 578, *579*, 580, 581, 582, 587, 592, 596, 610, 614, *624*, *625*, *626*, *633*, *635*, 644, 654, 667, 671, 672, 674, 681, 684, 686, *700*, *701*, *704*, *709*, 766, *791*, 932, *975*, 1108, *1172*
Comrey, A. L. 479, *507*
Cone, E. J. *703*
Cone, J. B. *974*
Conen, S. *700*
Conger, A. J. 484, *508*
Conger, J. C. 483, 484, *508*
Conner, J. *982*
Conner, M. *130*, 395, 419, 440, 441, *448*, *450*, *451*
Connerney, K. *317*
Connery, C. M. *556*
Connolly, J. *782*
Connor, D. F. *699*
Connor, J. *700*, 799, 820, 821, *850*, 857, *1081*, *1160*
Consalus, K. P. 175, 741, *785*
Cook, A. L. 953, 954, *973*
Cook, C. E. *707*
Cook, L. 535, *552*, *553*, 961, *975*
Cooney, L. M. 26, *36*
Cooper, C. *709*
Cooper, D. 1112, *1161*
Cooper, J. M. *85*, 752, *782*, *792*, *856*
Cooper, P. 48, *81*, 234, *249*, 261, 262, 268, *316*, 344, *379*, 467, *503*
Coquelet, C. *917*
Corben, B. *385*, 895, *916*, 1122, *1162*

Cordazzo, S. T. 469, *503*
Cordero-Guevara, J. 821, *856*
Corfitsen, M. T. 579, *626*
Cornejo, J. M. 482, *503*
Corneli, H. M. 535, *552*, *553*
Cornelissen, M. 722, *795*
Cornsweet, T. N. 139, *179*
Cortes, M. *84*, *558*
Cosgrove, L. 522, *553*, 735, 777, *783*, *793*
Cosgrove, M. 524, 531, *553*
Costa, G. *850*
Costa, M. 95, *126*, 196, 197, *249*
Costabile, J. *1174*
Costandi, M. 88, *126*
Costich, J. F. 530, *553*
Coughlin, J. F. *184*, 328, 329, 370, *379*, *388*, *508*, *791*
Council, F. 76, *81*, 162, *179*, *379*, *450*, *1169*
Couper, F. J. 659, *701*
Couperthwaite, A. B. *1031*
Courtney, T. K. 857
Coverdill, J. E. 614, *633*
Cowan, K. A. *707*
Cowley, J. E. 414, *448*
Cox, C. L. *918*
Cox, J. *385*
Craft, S. *385*
Craig, A. *852*
Craik, J. 374, *379*
Crancer, A. Jr. 664, *701*
Crandall, J. 545, *556*, 868, *918*
Cremona, A. 658, *701*
Crick, J. 107, *130*, 221, *252*, 311, *320*
Cripton, P. A. *1033*
Croft, R. J. *787*, *852*
Cronin, J. W. *849*
Cross, D. S. 880, *916*
Cross, J. M. 145, *179*
Crouch, D. J. 647, 667, 692, *701*, *703*, *792*
Crowther, R. F. *624*
Crundall, D. 106, 107, *126*, *129*, *130*, 164, 165, 172, 175, *179*, *182*, 220, 221, 222, *249*, 274, 275, 312, *316*, *324*, 729, 766, *783*, 936, *975*, *981*
Crutcher, J. C. 488, *504*
Crutchfield, R. S. 595, *629*
Cryer, C. *1033*
Cucchiara, A. *854*
Cuenen, A. *125*, 359, *379*
Cummings, P. *325*, 534, 546, *553*, *557*, 846, *850*, 962, *980*
Cumps, E. *1029*
Cunill, M. *784*
Curry, A. E. 269, 303, *316*
Curtis, A. 614, *631*
Cutler, R. B. *702*
Cynecki, M. *916*, *918*
Cynk, S. 828, *854*
Cynkar, J. 761, *786*
Czeisler, C. A. *849*, *852*

Dadang, M. M. *977*
Dahdah, S. *1168*
Dahlen, E. R. 483, 492, *504*
Dai, J. 618, *626*
Daily, B. *849*
Dain, S. J. *178*
Dal Pozzo, C. *709*
Damant-Sirois, G. 986, *1029*
D'Ambrosio, L. A. 328, 329, *379*, *508*
Danaf, M. 462, *504*
Dang, J. N. 1149, *1161*
Dang, N. T. *974*
Daniels, S. 439, *448*, *1161*
daSilva, M. P. 885, *916*
Datta, T. K. *1032*, 1122, *1164*
Davey, P. G. *699*
Davidse, R. 328, *381*
Davidson, G. *785*
Davidson, R. T. *636*
Davies, D. R. T. 820, *853*
Davies, W. L. *854*
Da Vinci, L. 160, *179*
Davis, C. *787*
Davis, E. S. *379*
Davis, G. A. 896, *916*
Davis, J. W. 1113, *1161*
Davis, R. 7, *34*
Davis, T. *923*
Davison, P. A. 146, *179*
Davoodi, S. R. 214, *249*, 971, *975*

Dawson, C. 775, *783*
Dawson, D. 843, *850*
Dawson, J. D. *180*, *377*, *380*, *386*
Dawson, N. E. 958, *974*
Day, A. *631*
Day, R. *921*
Day, T. D. 420, *448*
Dean, J. M. 535, *552*, *553*
Debnath, A. K. 1012, *1029*
De Brabander, B. 905, *916*
de Bruyne, G. *1034*
DeCarlo, D. K. *383*
Decina, L. 158, 162, 353, *379*, *387*, 537, 539, *553*, 599, *626*, 1124, *1161*
Decker, M. D. 681, *707*
de Dios Luna-del-Castillo, J. *978*
Dee, T. S. 520, 526, 528, 529, *553*
Deepak, E. *387*
Deery, H. A. 308, 310, 311, *316*
Deffenbacher, D. M. *504*
Deffenbacher, J. D. 483, *504*
Deffenbacher, J. L. 495, 496, 502, *504*
Degenhardt, L. 644, *701*
De Geus, B. 992, 993, *1029*, *1032*, *1035*
de Gier, J. J. *706*
de Goede, M. *1035*
Degraeuwe, B. *1029*
de Hair-Buijssen, S. *1035*
de Hartog, J. J. 984, *1029*
de Jong, D. *923*
DeJong, W. 612, *626*
Dekker, S. W. 1086, *1167*
Delaney, H. 621, *626*, *633*
Delay, J. C. *701*
del Castillo, J. D. D. L. *1032*
De Leonardis, D. M. *920*
Delhomme, P. 110, *126*
Dellinger, A. 329, 336, *380*
Delord, S. *855*
Del Rio, M. C. *699*
Delzenne, J. 92
de Mello, M. T. *627*
Dement, W. C. 806, *851*
Deng, W. *925*
Deng, X. *925*
den Hertog, P. *1033*
Dennerlein, J. T. *1032*
Dennis, C. S. 523, *552*
Dennis, W. M. G. *788*
Dent, C. W. 592, *626*
Denton, F. F. 439, *448*
Denton, G. G. 121, *126*, 1117, *1161*
De Pauw, E. 427, *448*, 1124, *1161*
De Pelsmacker, P. 396, 397, *448*
de Picado Santos, L. 466, *505*
Depue, L. *82*, *129*, *1081*, *1167*
DeRamus, R. *322*, *385*
de Rome, L. *977*
Derriks, H. M. 25, *34*
DeSantis, W. *1032*
Deschênes, M. *253*
Desevilya, H. S. 479, *505*
Desjardins, D. *786*
Desmond, K. *315*, 818, *849*
Desmond, P. A. 799, 801, 802, 818, *850*, *853*
de Souza-Formigoni, M. L. O. *627*
Dessecker, D. J. 207, *248*
Deutermann, W. 961, *975*
Devlin, A. *83*
Devoto, A. *853*
De Vries, G. 114, *125*, 747, *781*
De Vries, S. C. *1035*
De Waard, D. 104, 114, *125*, 370, *385*, 398, 432, *448*, *452*, 1000, *1029*, *1031*
Dewar, R. 5, *34*, *37*, 233, 234, *249*, *254*, *386*, 1119, *1161*
Dewi, R. S. 232, 244, *249*
De Winter, J. C. 123, *126*, 466, 467, *504*, 1146, 1113, *1161*
Dey, A. K. *382*
De Young, D. J. 613, *626*, 1111, 1112, *1162*
Dhillon, P. K. 49, *81*
Dhondt, S. *1033*
Dial, L. *254*
Diamandouros, K. *385*
Diamantopoulou, K. 433, *448*
Dias, J. *1034*
Dickerson, A. E. 210, 216, *249*
Diderichsen, F. 864, *919*
Dietze, P. *629*, *705*

Diew, D. Y. 217, 218, *249*
Digges, K. H. 69, *81*
Dijkstra, A. 983, 1005, *1029*, *1035*, 1086, *1174*
Dilich, M. 1044, *1080*
Dill, J. 1017, 1018, *1029*
Dille, J. M. *701*
Dillon, K. M. 115, *126*
Dillon, P. *701*
DiMaggio, C. 908, *916*
Di Milia, L. 798, 810, *850*, *855*
Dinges, D. F. 799, 805, 843, *850*, *853*, *854*
Dingus, T. *1081*
Dingus, T. A. 74, 75, *81*, *82*, *83*, *127*, *129*, *322*, *323*, 403, 415, *448*, *452*, 757, 774, *781*, *783*, *786*, *789*, 1069, 1073, 1074, 1077, 1080, *1081*, *1082*, *1167*
Dinh-Zarr, T. B. 367, *387*, 528, 529, *553*, *559*
Dischinger, P. C. *708*, *978*
Dismukes, K. 351, *386*
Di Stefano, M. 338, *380*
Ditter, S. M. 599, 600, *626*
Divekar, G. *85*, *186*, *255*
Dobbins, W. N. *974*
Dobbs, B. M. 360, *380*
Dodou, D. 123, *126*, 466, 467, *504*, 1113, *1161*
Dolinis, J. 415, *453*
Dollard, J. 462, 464, 465, 466, 494, 495, 501, *504*
Dolliver, J. J. *184*, *385*
Dommes, A. 223, *249*, 884, 885, 911, *916*, *917*, *919*
Donato, A. 673, *699*
Donchin, E. 104, *127*, 165, *183*
Dondi, G. 95, *126*, *249*
Donges, E. 87, *126*, 174, *180*
Donkor, R. A. 66, *81*, 485, *504*
Donmez, B. 230, *252*, 778, *783*
Donnell, E. T. 150, *179*
Donnelly, W. *704*
Donovan, R. J. 114, *126*
Donze, N. *699*
Doob, A. N. 476, 494, *504*
Doob, L. W. *504*
Doong, J. L. *1029*
Dorn, L. 5, *34*, *39*, 313, *316*
Dornhoefer, S. M. *186*
Dorr, M. 158, *180*
Dosekun, E. *1159*
Dougald, L. E. 909, *917*
Downey, L. A. 665, 696, *701*
Doyle, C. T. 539, *553*
Doyle, D. *980*
Doyon, J. K. *922*
Dozza, M. 75, *81*, 739, *793*, 1004, 1026, *1029*, *1083*, 1146, *1168*
Drachman, D. A. 361, *380*
Dragomanovits, A. *1175*
Drake, C. 819, *850*
Drake, M. L. 523, *552*
Draskóczy, M. *1174*
Dreesenb, A. *448*
Dressel, J. 743, 748, *781*
Drews, F. A. 197, *254*, 742, 745, 746, 747, 748, 749, 759, 764, 765, 766, *783*, *792*
Driskell, J. E. 828, *850*
Dritter, O. *323*
Drobiner, H. *633*, *707*
Drory, A. 95, 195, 197, *254*, 441, *448*, 1121, *1172*
Droste, N. *631*
Drummer, O. H. 656, 668, 681, 684, 686, *701*, *707*
Du, F. *131*, *508*
Duan, J. 225, *249*
Duba, E. *784*
Dubinsky, R. M. 361, *380*
Dubois, S. 574, *626*, 667, 671, *699*, *701*
Dubuisson, J.-P. *249*
Duchamp, G. *1173*
Dudek, C. 234, *249*
Duff, C. *701*
Duffy, S. A. *317*
Dukes, R. L. 472, *504*
Dukic, T. 361, 376, *380*, 730, *783*
Dula, C. S. 479, *504*
Dulf, D. *1034*
Duma, S. M. 546, *553*, *555*, *558*
Dunaway, G. *511*
Dunbar, G. 868, 872, 884, 885, *917*

Duncan, G. D. *322*, *636*
Duncan, R. *918*, *977*, *1165*
Dunn, D. L. 115, *126*
Dunn, J. W. 403, 414, *457*
Dunn, R. C. M. 1019, *1029*
Dunsmuir, W. T. M. 590, *624*
Duntsch, K. *384*
Dupont, E. *1173*
Dupuy, M. A. *921*
Durbin, D. R. *316*, 535, 538, 540, 541, *554*, *557*, *560*, *922*
Durso, C. *385*
Dussault, C. 667, 669, 672, *701*
Dye, L. 662, 667, 668, 669, *709*
Dziura, J. *791*

Eadie, D. *1172*
Eaton, D. K. 770, *789*
Ebel, B. E. 535, 537, 542, *554*, *924*
Eberhard, J. 340, *380*
Eberle, W. *552*
Eby, D. W. 5, *35*, 370, 371, 373, 374, *380*, *384*, 522, 531, 532, 537, *552*, *554*, *559*
Eccles, K. *1169*
Edmonston, C. *919*
Edquist, J. 272, *322*, 1122, *1162*
Edwards, B. D. *504*
Edwards, D. *851*
Edwards, J. D. 167, *178*, *180*, *386*
Edwards, M. L. 432, *447*
Edwards, S. *380*
Eenink, R. 75
Efrat, K. 110, *126*
Egberts, A. C. G. *706*
Eggemeier, F. T. 103, *130*
Ehiri, J. 540, *554*
Ehle, H. T. 683, *702*
Ehlers, E. *1031*
Ehrenstein, W. H. 351, *388*
Ehrlich, N. J. *509*
Ehsani, J. P. 296, 300, *316*, *317*
Eie, W. Y. *1164*
Eiser, J. R. 758, *794*
Eizenman, M. *181*, 727, *781*, *785*, *792*
Ejere, H. O. D. *554*
Ekeh, P. *977*
El-Bassiouni, M. Y. 427, *447*
El-Basyouny, K. 427, *447*
Elder, R. *553*, *559*, 595, 596, 597, 598, 599, 601, 608, 615, *624*, *626*, *628*
Eldror, E. *922*
Elefteriadou, L. *458*
El-Geneidy, A. 986, 987, *1029*, *1036*
Elgrishi, A. 873, *919*
El Hannachi, S. *855*
Elias, P. 418, 419, *452*
Elias, W. 110, *126*
Elkington, J. *855*, *977*
Ellen, R. L. 821, *850*
Ellinwood, E. H. 675, *702*
Elliott, K. *782*
Elliott, M. A. 110, *126*, 467, 469, *504*, *626*, 938, 939, 943, *975*, 1113, *1162*
Elliott, M. R. 482, *504*, 539, 540, *554*
Ellis, J. 1011, *1030*
Ellison, A. 989, *1030*
Ellison, P. A. 472, 494, 500, 501, *505*
Ells, J. G. 234, *249*
Ellsworth, L. A. *856*
Elovici, Y. 618, *631*
Eluru, N. 465, *508*
Elvik, R. 5, 25, 78, 79, *81*, 108, 117, 121, *126*, 150, 159, 163, *180*, 417, 419, 421, 422, 423, 426, 427, 428, 433, 435, 436, 438, *447*, *448*, *449*, 583, 602, *626*, 654, 655, 674, 681, 686, *702*, *707*, 756, *783*, 846, *850*, 895, 903, *917*, 992, 1008, 1015, 1016, 1023, 1024, *1030*, 1091, 1096, 1098, 1099, 1109, 1113, 1114, 1115, 1120, 1122, 1124, 1132, 1133, 1134, 1140, 1141, 1143, 1146, *1160*, *1161*, *1162*, *1163*, *1173*
Elvik, R. A. 5, *35*
Emami, M. *509*
Embree, T. *1031*
Emerson, J. L. 147, 157, *180*, 332, 357, *377*, *380*
Emmerson, C. 372, *380*
Endsley, M. R. 105, 106, *127*
Engelhart, C. L. *917*, *1030*

Engström, J. 46, *86*, 176, *186*, 215, *247*, 277, 297, 307, *317*, *318*, 740, 744, *783*, *1083*
Eoh, H. J. 840, *850*
Epstude, K. 725, *793*
Erhardt, T. 963, 966, *975*
Erhart, R. H. *636*
Eriksson, A. 867, 881, *921*
Eriksson, D. *922*
Erke, A. 79, *81*
Erkoboni, D. C. 538, 542, *560*
Ernberg, T. 1105, *1163*
Ervin, R. 230, *250*, *253*
Espié, S. 928, *974*, *975*
Esse, C. T. *925*, *1175*
Eugensson, A. 8, *35*
Evans, D. W. 158, *180*
Evans, L. 5, 9, 22, *35*, 115, 116, 120, 121, *127*, 223, 225, *250*, 336, 341, *380*, 395, 404, 415, 433, *449*, *455*, 482, *505*, 517, 544, 545, *554*, 589, 611, *627*, 863, *917*, 961, *975*, 1112, 1113, 1148, 1157, *1163*, *1171*
Evans, P. C. 479, *511*, 576, 620, *636*
Evans Jr., M. W. *636*
Evgenikos, P. *34*, *1175*
Ewalt, D. M. 613, *627*
Ewing, M. *126*
Eyssartier, C. *918*

Fagerlind, H. 712, *793*
Fagnant, D. J. 1155, *1163*
Fahlquist, J. N. 16, *35*
Fahner, G. *80*, *81*
Faigin, B. M. 376, *377*
Fairbanks, R. J. *856*
Fairclough, S. H. 747, *783*, *790*
Fairfax, B. *918*
Falaschetti, E. *915*
Falconer, E. K. *382*
Falkmer, T. *128*, 200, *254*, 308, *317*, 370, *386*
Fallon, I. 4, *35*
Fancher, P. S. *253*
Fang, J. *1031*
Fang, Y. *81*, *127*, *322*, *783*
Fant, R. V. *707*
Farah, H. 71, *81*, 301, *317*, *323*
Farber, E. 5, *37*, *915*
Farbry, J. 727, *783*
Farmer, C. 116, *127*, 314, 317, 549, 522, 528, 544, *554*, *559*, 610, *627*, 755, *783*, 1124, 1149, *1163*, *1171*
Farmer, M. *915*
Farrand, P. 311, *317*
Farrell, L. J. 659, *702*
Fassnacht, P. *976*
Favretto, D. *82*, *703*
Fay, P. A. 546, *554*
Feaganes, J. *792*, *793*, *925*, *1175*
Fehring, M. 310, *315*
Fei, D.-Y. 843, *852*
Feldman, J. A. *554*
Fell, D. L. 821, *851*
Fell, J. 296, 297, 298, *317*, 588, 608, *627*, *634*, *635*, 714, *785*, 821, *851*, 1046, 1047, 1051, *1081*, *1174*
Ferdinand, A. O. 777, *783*
Ference, J. *386*
Fergenson, O. E. 123, *127*
Fergenson, P. E. 467, *505*
Ferguson, M. A. *451*
Ferguson, R. W. 883, *917*
Ferguson, S. A. 114, *127*, 285, 286, 304, 311, *317*, *320*, *322*, *325*, 357, *383*, *385*, 393, *449*, 535, *554*, 591, *627*, 904, *922*, 1124, *1171*
Fernandez, W. G. 522, 523, *554*
Ferrando, J. 964, *975*
Ferrara, S. *709*
Ferraraf, S. D. *82*, *703*
Ferreira, S. E. 622, *627*
Ferrer, T. J. *974*
Festinger, L. 602, *627*
Feyer, A. M. 810, 811, 829, *851*, *856*
Field, D. T. *976*
Fielder, L. J. *126*
Fields, M. *320*, *627*
Figler, M. H. *505*
Fildes, B. 66, *82*, 121, *127*, *179*, *379*, *382*, *385*, 403, 411, 414, 439, *449*, *450*, *921*, *981*, 1099, 1117, 1141, 1142, *1164*
File, S. E. 680, *705*

Fillmore, M. T. 571, 576, 585, *628*, *630*
Fine, M. A. 490, *503*
Finlay-Brown, S. *856*
Finn, L. 821, 857
Finomore, V. S. *791*
Finson, R. S. *1034*
Fiorentino, D. 567, 568, 569, 571, 579, *624*, *625*, *631*, *700*, *974*
Fischer, C. M. *1032*
Fischer, E. L. 898, *917*, 1007, *1030*
Fischer, P. 393, *449*
Fischhoff, B. 1044, *1081*
Fishbain, D. A. 684, *702*
Fishbein, M. 109, *125*
Fisher, D. 5, 6, *35*, *85*, *184*, *186*, *253*, *255*, 274, 312, *317*, *322*, *325*, *385*, *386*, 763, *781*, *783*, *909*, 917, *979*, 1108, *1173*
Fisher, J. 357, *378*
Fishman, E. 1009, 1010, *1030*, *1033*
Fishman, G. A. *186*
Fitch, G. A. 46, 75, *81*, 716, 724, 735, 755, 757, 771, 774, *783*
Fitch, G. M. 99, *127*, 740, *783*, *849*
Fitts, P. M. 58, *81*, 204, 207, *250*, 1155, *1164*
Fitzharris, M. *382*, *383*, *981*
Fitzpatrick, K. 401, *449*, *458*
Flack, L. K. *1033*
Flanigan, M. *1080*
Flannagan, C. *247*, *1083*
Flannagan, M. J. 886, 887, *924*, 1098, *1173*
Flannery, A. 1122, *1164*
Flegel, R. *709*
Fleisher, A. 1089, *1164*
Fleiter, J. J. 437, *456*, 527, *555*
Fleming, H. S. 964, *976*
Flood, L. *187*
Flora, J. 407, *454*
Flowers, N. *633*
Folkard, S. 857
Fontaine, H. 336, 341, 363, *380*, 865, *917*
Font-Mayolas, S. *784*
Forbes, T. W. 5, *35*, 482, *505*, 1120, *1164*
Forlizzi, J. *382*
Fors, C. *177*, *848*
Fors, S. W. 614, *633*
Forsb, C. *82*
Forsman, Å. 131, 615, *627*, *707*, *790*
Forsyth, E. 49, *81*, 263, 264, 268, *317*
Foss, R. 285, 297, 298, *318*, *320*, *321*, *626*, 760, *784*
Fosser, S. 1133, *1164*
Fought, R. L. 681, *707*
Fournier, A. *634*
Fowkes, M. 175, *178*, 231, *248*, 728, *781*
Fox, J. E. *854*
Fox, M. 170, *182*, *385*
Fozard, J. *182*, 351, *381*, *382*
Frampton, R. 546, *554*
Francis, T. 26, *39*, 862, *924*
Frank, E. H. *560*
Franke, T. *322*
Frattaroli, S. 620, *627*, *629*
Fredriksson, R. *922*
Freedman, M. *322*, 714, *785*, 1051, *1081*
Freeman, E. E. *184*
Freeman, J. *503*
Frehse, B. 472, *509*
Freidenberg, B. M. 481, *507*
Freund, B. 367, *381*
Freydier, C. 585, *627*
Fricke, L. B. 1045, *1080*
Fridestroem, L. 119, *127*, 1089, *1164*
Fridstrøm, L. *1163*
Fried, L. P. *184*
Fried, R. *508*
Friedman, C. 167, *180*, 357, *381*
Frischmann, T. 1139, *1171*
Friswell, R. *856*
Frith, W. J. 285, *319*, 340, 363, *382*, 579, 583, 584, *628*, *629*
Frost-Pineda, K. *451*
Fry, C. *705*
Fu, C. 217, *256*
Fu, T. *1168*
Fuchs, P. 1125, 1126, *1167*
Fudin, R. 622, *627*
Fujita, G. 519, *558*
Fuller, R. 5, *35*, 89, 108, 111, 112, 113, 120, *127*
Fuller, S. Z. *853*

Fumero, M. C. *851*
Furness, S. 1065, 1066, 1067, *1081*
Furr-Holden, D. 645, *702*, *704*
Füssl, E. 946, *977*
Fyhri, A. 1008, 1016, *1030*, *1033*, *1034*
Fylan, F. 431, *450*

Gabauer, D. J. 1069, *1081*
Gable, T. M. 750, *786*
Gabler, H. C. 897, *920*, 1069, *1081*
Gadegbeku, B. 669, 684, 686, *702*, *705*
Gadiraju, R. 409, 412, *450*
Gaffney, G. *703*
Gagnon, S. *383*
Gaines, J. M. 373, *381*
Gajic, R. 95, *130*, 195, *252*
Gajulua, S. 877, *919*
Gal, R. 479, *505*
Gallagher, J. P. *781*
Gallagher, S. S. *558*
Gallenne, M. L. *1160*
Galski, T. 683, *702*
Gálvez-Vargas, R. *978*
Gamberale, F. 797–798, 799, 805, *848*
Gao, L. *555*
Gao, S. *852*
Garabet, A. *781*
Garay-Vega, L. 909, *917*
Garber, N. J. 409, 412, *450*
García-Martín, M. *978*
García-Ros, R. 307, *321*
Garder, P. 847, *851*, *1170*
Gårder, P. 910, *920*
Gardner, J. W. 87, *127*
Gardner, P. E. *1171*
Garrard, I. 1000, *1035*
Garrard, J. 989, *1030*
Garretsen, H. F. L. *629*
Garrett, D. *383*
Garvey, P. H. 1126, *1164*
Garvey, P. M. *923*, 1126, 1127, *1164*
Gaska, J. *187*
Gaspar, J. G. 766, *784*
Gaster, S. *792*
Gates, T. J. *1032*
Gatsou, C. 232, *250*
Gaulier, J. *706*
Gaulier, J. M. *631*
Gay, K. *855*
Ge, Y. *131*, *508*
Geary, L. L. 613, *630*, *788*
Gebers, M. A. *322*, *632*, 1113, *1164*
Gehlert, T. 442, *450*
Geißler, T. *1159*
Gelau, C. 970, *977*
Gélinas, I. *187*, *383*, *387*, *388*
Geller, E. *634*
Gentzlera, M. C. *186*
George, J. 735, *784*
Gerlach, J. 1122, *1164*
Gerostamoulos, J. *701*
Gerrish, P. H. 1148, *1163*
Gersbach, S. *382*, *451*
Gershon, P. *633*, *707*, 801, 830, 831, 834, 836, 838, 839, 841, 846, *851*, *855*, 942, 958–959, 959, 960, 969, *976*
Gertner, R. *633*
Geruschat, D. R. 870, *917*
Gesser-Edelsburg, A. *126*
Gevins, A. 695, *702*
Ghali, L. A. *182*
Ghanbari, M. *978*
Ghazizadeh, M. 191, *250*
Ghoneim, M. M. 675, *702*
Gianoulakis, C. *322*
Gibson, J. J. 439, *450*
Gibson, W. D. *974*
Gidron, Y. 479, *505*
Gielen, A. C. 124, *127*, *324*, *627*
Gier de, J. J. 640, *702*
Giesbrecht, L. 331, *379*
Gilbert, J. *508*
Gildengo, G. *388*
Gildengorin, G. *186*
Gillan, W. 828, *854*
Gillberg, M. 799, 807, *849*, *851*
Gillen, D. 1112, *1161*
Gilmore, D. *1165*
Gilutz, M. S. 4, *35*, 1043, *1081*
Gineyt, G. *627*
Ginsburg, A. *34*, 156, 157, 158, *178*, *180*
Giorgetti, R. *709*

Giranda, T. *1167*
Girasek, D. C. 6, *35*
Giroud, C. *699*
Giselbrecht, D. *184*
Gish, K. *387*, *792*, *793*
Gish, K. W. 341, *387*, 462, *510*
Gitelman, V. 6, *36*, 399, *450*, 729, *784*, 1012, *1030*, *1159*
Gjerde, H. 643, 650, 652, 653, 667, 670, 672, 681, *700*, *702*
Gkikas, K. *979*
Gkikas, N. 5, *35*
Glad, A. 313, *318*
Glaser, R. *317*
Glassbrenner, D. 519, 523, 534, 543, *555*, *557*, 963, *976*
Glatt, S. L. *380*
Glindemann, K. *634*
Glumm, M. M. *794*
Glynn, S. I. 220, *253*
Gobetti, K. *382*, *451*
Godley, S. T. 66, *82*, 121, *127*, 439, *450*, 1117, *1164*
Goebelbecker, J. 1044, *1080*
Goel, A. 828, *851*
Gold, M. S. *451*
Goldberg, F. 574, *627*
Goldberg, L. *629*
Goldenbeld, C. 429, 433, *450*, 1002, *1031*
Golias, I. 480, *505*
Golob, T. F. 395, *450*
Golz, M. 843, *851*
Gomez, R. *85*, *186*
Gómez-Fraguela, J. A. 492, *505*
Gómez-Talegón, M. T. 575, 620, *627*
Gonçalves, R. 246, *253*
Gonzales, P. 1111, *1171*
Gonzalez, E. 84, *558*
González-Iglesias, B. 492, *505*
Goode, N. 282, *315*
Goodman, C. *631*
Goodman, M. *83*, 711, 768, *784*, *789*, *793*, *1082*
Goodwin, A. 529, *555*, 588, 592, *626*, *627*, 954, 956, 973, *976*, 985, 990, 991, 1009, 1011, *1031*, 1106, *1164*
Goodwin, A. H. 284, *318*, *321*, 760, 776, *784*
Goodwin, P. B. 885, *917*
Gopher, D. 104, *127*, 713, *788*
Gordon, C. P. 712, *791*
Gordon, S. E. 195, *255*
Gorelick, D. A. *703*
Gospel, A. *553*
Goughnour, E. *1032*
Goullé, J. P. *631*
Gourlet, Y. 865, *917*
Govern, J. M. *505*
Grabner, G. *186*
Grabowski, D. C. 418, *450*
Grabowski, J. G. 290, *325*
Grace, R. 817, *849*
Graham, B. V. *915*
Graham, D. J. 434, *452*
Graham, J. D. 963, *976*
Graham, K. 601, *628*
Graham, R. 747, *784*
Granada, T. *129*
Granda, T. *82*, *1081*
Granie, M. A. 123, *127*, 467, *505*
Granieé, M. A. *917*
Granqvist, C. G. *974*
Granton, J. T. *132*, *456*
Gras, M. E. 734, 745, 760, *784*
Grass, H. 678, *699*
Graving, J. S. *253*, *1160*
Gray, C. S. *380*
Gray, D. *386*
Gray, R. *187*
Grayson, G. *506*, 957, *976*
Greaney, K. *178*
Greaves, S. 989, *1030*
Green, A. *917*
Green, K. A. 145, 146, *180*, 350, *381*
Green, M. 206, 207, 212, *250*
Green, P. 125, *127*, 244, *247*, *248*, *250*, *723*, 735, 768, *784*, *793*
Greene, F. K. *1165*
Greene, M. A. 1128, 1129, *1171*
Greening, M. *851*
Greenspan, A. I. *552*
Greenwell, N. K. 538, *555*

Greenwood, M. 481, *505*
Gregersen, N. P. 266, 281, 307, 308, *317*, *318*, *321*, 1089, *1165*
Greitemeyer, T. *449*
Gresset, J. A. 147, *180*
Griffith, M. S. *450*
Griffiths, J. D. 872, *917*
Griffiths, R. R. *705*
Griggs, D. *178*
Grimberg, E. *81*, *317*, *323*, *324*
Grimsrud, M. 986, *1029*
Groeger, J. *325*
Groeger, J. A. 5, *36*, 200, *250*, 308, *316*, 398, *450*, *792*, *976*
Groot, H. A. M. 276, 277, 279, 280, *318*
Gross, A. E. 476, 494, *504*
Grossman, D. C. 535, *554*
Grosz, M. 616, *635*
Grube, J. W. 592, *626*
Gruber, N. 151, *180*
Gruenewald, P. J. 604, *635*
Grunfeld, B. *450*
Grung, M. *634*, *708*
Grynbaum, M. M. 907, *918*
Grzebieta, R. 75, *82*, *84*, 929, 930, 945, *973*, *976*, *1033*; *1035*
Guarino, J. *705*
Guderian, S. *979*
Gudgeon, A. C. 680, *703*
Guéguen, N. 875, *918*
Guého, L. 123, *127*, 467, 469, *505*
Gugerty, L. 747–748, 765, *784*, *790*
Guiling, S. *511*
Guilleminault, C. *854*
Guo, F. 74, 75, 78, *81*, *82*, *83*, *127*, *129*, *322*, *448*, *783*, *786*, 1070, *1080*, *1081*
Guo, W. *380*
Guo, Y. 1026, *1031*
Guo, Z. *251*
Guohua, L. *324*
Guppy, A. 941, *974*
Gupta, A. 871, *919*
Gupta, S. *849*
Gust, S. W. *701*
Gustafsson, K. 805, *848*
Gustafsson, S. 615, *627*
Gustavsson, G. *974*
Guth, D. 897, *918*
Gutierrez, J. L. G. 799, *851*
Guttman, N. 5, *36*, 301, 305, *318*
Guyatt, G. H. *378*, *624*

Haake, S. *786*
Habinski, L. 462, *506*
Habtemichael, F. G. 466, *505*
Hackney, R. J. 549, *556*
Haddak, M. M. *1028*
Haddon, W. Jr. 1093, *1165*
Hadlock, C. 596, *624*, 771, *781*
Haegerstrom-Portnoy, G. *186*, 352, *381*, *388*
Hafetz, J. *316*
Hagan, M. *250*
Hagel, B. E. 865, 889, *918*, 999, 1013, *1031*
Hagen, R. E. 1111, *1174*
Hagenzieker, M. 6, 7, *36*, *82*, *628*, *703*, *1033*
Hagge, R. A. 286, 287, *320*
Haglund, M. 398, 408, 425, *450*
Hagoski, B. K. *919*
Haight, F. A. 120, *127*, 1078, *1081*
Haikonen, S. 175, *180*
Haith, M. M. 900, *920*
Haje, B. E. 462, 484, *505*
Hajizadeh, E. *790*
Hakamies-Blomqvist, L. 91, *128*, 263, *318*, *319*, 328, 329, 335, 337, 338, 339, 341, 342, 343, 344, 363, 364, 365, *381*, *383*, 1111, *1165*
Hakkarainen, P. 242, *251*, 1119, *1167*
Hakkert, A. S. 6, *36*
Häkkinen, S. 482, *505*
Hakuli, S. *39*
Halcomb, C. G. 207, *252*
Haley, J. *980*, *1170*
Hall, A. 550, *556*
Hall, L. *185*, *323*
Hall, M. R. 880, *916*
Hall, R. 905, *925*
Hall, W. *555*, *627*, *976*, *1031*, *1164*
Hallberg, V. *511*
Hallett, C. 712, *784*, *791*, 2011

Hallett, D. *132*, *456*
Hallvig, D. 66, *82*
Halman, S. I. 535, *555*
Hamalainen, V. 442, *450*
Hamann, C. J. *316*
Hamdar, S. H. 476, 493, *505*
Hamid, H. *249*, *975*, *978*
Hamlett, C. *792*, *793*
Hammel, K. R. *322*, *385*
Hammer, M. 769, *795*, *853*
Hammond, S. M. *976*
Han, S. H. *179*
Hancock, P. A. 439, *453*, 735, 741, 749, 752, 763, *784*, *791*, 799, *850*, 940, *976*
Hane, M. *80*, *81*
Hankey, J. *81*, *82*, *127*, *448*, *783*, *790*, *1080*, *1081*
Hanna, R. 912, *918*, 1022, *1031*
Hanowski, R. *81*, *85*, *127*, 740, 756, 774, *783*, *785*, 790, 805, *849*, *851*
Hans, Z. *1165*
Hansen, A. R. *635*
Hansen, C. D. *508*
Hansson, G. J. 361, *382*
Happee, R. *129*, *1161*
Harbluk, J. L. 46, *86*, 175, 176, *181*, *186*, 744, 772, *785*, *790*
Harding, C. J. 776, *785*
Hardy, A. P. 114, *127*, 393, *449*
Hardy, K. *1169*
Hargens, R. L. 420, *448*
Hargutt, V. *855*
Hariri, B. 843, *848*
Harkey, D. *387*, *923*
Harland, K. *316*, *553*, *782*
Harless, D. W. 1148, *1165*
Harms, L. *1167*
Harré, N. 442, *458*
Harrell, S. *318*
Harris, D. H. 604, *628*
Harris, J. *708*
Harris, M. A. *1033*
Harris, P. R. 758, *794*
Harris, W. G. 217, 224, *255*
Harrison, E. L. R. 571, 585, *628*
Harte, D. 579, *628*
Hartley, L. *85*, *382*, *451*, 842
Hartman, R. L. 638, 665, 674, *702*, *703*
Hartos, J. L. 303, 304, *318*, *323*, *325*
Harwood, D. *450*, *458*, 1131, *1165*
Harwood, E. *631*
Hassan, S. E. 870, *917*
Hassel, S. O. 442, *450*
Hasselberg, M. 931, 944, 947, 951, *982*
Hatakka, M. 306, 307, *318*, *319*, *1166*
Hatfield, J. 732, 745, *785*, 883, *918*, *1033*
Hatherly, C. *178*, *255*, *377*
Hauer, E. 55, *82*, 357, 375, *381*, 407, 410, 413, 419, 423, 424, *450*, 1039, 1060, 1077, 1078, *1081*, *1170*
Haukka, J. *1167*
Haupt, J. 75, *85*
Hausken, A. M. 642, *703*
Haustein, S. 110
Haven, S. E. 4, *39*
Hawkins, A. S. 356, *381*
Hawkins, H. G. 158, *179*, 1126, *1165*
Haworth, C. *788*
Haworth, N. *84*, *455*, 595, *628*, 927, 929, 931, 950, 952, 955, 957, *976*, *982*, 992, 1010, *1029*, *1030*, *1031*, *1034*
Hayden, J. A. 670, *699*
Hayes, C. E. *708*
Haykin, M. D. *701*
Hazlett, R. D. *915*
He, J. *1174*
Heard, E. A. 243, *250*
Heard, R. *185*
Heatherly, D. G. 675, *702*
Heckwolf, M. *1031*
Hedlund, J. 21, *36*, 76, *82*, 258, *318*, 564, *625*, *628*, *919*, 964, *981*
Heeren, T. *628*
Heide, W. 175, *183*, 622, *631*
Heiman, G. W. 146, *181*
Heimstra, N. 276, *319*
Heinecke, A. *625*
Heino, A. 226, *255*
Heinrich, A. *254*
Heishman, S. J. 661, 692, *703*
Helander, C. J. 613, *626*
Helander, M. 221, *250*, 310, *318*

Helland, A. 66, *82*
Hellinga, L. A. *320*, 744, 760, *788*
Helman, S. *506*, 949, 955, *976*
Helmers, G. 444, *454*
Helmers, K. F. *377*
Helmert, J. *186*
Hels, T. *82*, 581, *628*, 653, 654, 672, 681, 684, 686, *703*, 734, *793*
Hemmelgarn, B. 681, *703*
Hempel, S. *450*
Henary, B. Y. 868, 895, *918*
Henderson, D. *917*, *1030*
Henderson, R. L. 155, *181*
Hendricks, D. L. 714, *785*, 1051, 1052, 1055, 1080, *1081*
Hendrikz, J. K. *458*
Hennessy, D. A. 472, 478, 495, 496, 500, *505*, *507*, *511*, 726, *794*
Hennessy, D. F. 162, 167, *181*, 353, 363, 365, *381*
Henningfield, J. E. *703*
Henriksson, P. 343, *381*
Hensberry, R. A. *977*
Herberg, K. W. *708*
Hermann, S. 125, *128*, 845, *851*
Hermans, E. *1161*
Herms, B. 910, *918*
Hernandez, E. G. *851*
Hernetkoski, K. *317*, *318*
Herrin, G. D. 98, *128*
Herring, I. P. *553*
Herriotts, P. 370, *382*
Herrmann, N. *385*
Herrnstein, R. J. 495, *503*
Hertz, E. 70, 73, *82*
Hess, G. 1008, *1031*
Hessin, Y. 1114, *1165*
Heywood, P. *553*
Hibberd, D. L. 725, *785*
Hickman, J. S. *85*, 756, 774, *785*, *790*, *851*
Hicks, R. E. *707*
Hickson, L. *187*
Hietanen, M. *180*
Higgins, K. E. 144, 146, *181*
Hilburn, B. 160, *183*, 353, *383*
Hill, A. 106, 222, *250*, 275, *318*, *382*, 1064, *1081*
Hill, K. *555*, *627*, *976*, *1031*, *1164*
Hill, R. 110, *128*, 884, *918*
Hill, S. G. 104, 108
Hills, B. L. 958, *982*
Hilton, B. W. *131*, *455*, 533, *559*
Hinch, M. 531, *555*
Hinchcliff, R. 285, *318*
Hindman, J. W. *974*
Hindmarch, I. 640, 641, 676, 680, 684, *703*
Hindrik, W. 666, *703*
Hing, M. M. *387*
Hingson, R. 575, 612, *626*, *628*
Hirdes, J. P. *378*, *624*
Hirsch, P. 281, *318*
Hirst, W. M. 438, *450*, *453*, 903, 904, *918*, *921*, 1120, *1165*, *1168*
Hitch, G. *247*
Hitosugi, M. 579, 590, *628*
Hjaldahl, M. *34*
Hjälmdahl, M. *125*, *126*, *707*, *1174*
Ho, C. 5, *36*
Ho, R. 722, *785*
Ho, W. M. G. *788*
Hobbs, G. E. 459, 460, 461, 479, 482, 483, *510*, 1027, *1034*
Hocherman, I. 147, *187*
Hockanson, H. M. *552*
Hockey, G. R. J. *128*, *786*
Hoddes, E. 806, *851*
Hoe, C. *84*, *85*
Hoek, G. *1029*
Hoffer, G. E. 1148, *1165*
Hoffman, E. R. 155, *181*, 410, *450*
Hoffman, J. 66, *82*, 738, *787*
Hoffmann, E. R. 155, *181*, 207, *250*
Hoffmeister, D. H. 232, *248*
Hofstetter, H. W. 146, *181*
Höger, R. 472, *509*
Holbrook, G. T. *851*
Holder, H. D. 604, *635*
Hole, G. J. 750, *781*, 958, *976*
Holick, A. J. 1126, 1127, *1165*
Holland, C. 110, *128*, 419, 440, 441, *451*, 736, *785*, 868, 884, *917*, *918*

Hollands, J. G. 99, *133*
Hollis, A. M. *178*, 215, *250*
Holmes, E. *86*, *388*, 697, *702*
Holmgren, A. 577, *628*
Holmgren, P. 577, *628*, 667, *703*
Holmqvist, K. *177*, *848*
Holubowycz, O. T. 577, *630*
Holweg, E. *129*
Homberg, V. 58, *85*
Hooper, K. G. *83*, *252*
Hoover, M. *1080*
Hopfer, C. *708*
Hopkin, J. 971, *982*
Hopman, R. J. *792*
Horberry, T. 5, *34*, *38*, 163, *181*, 362, *382*, 395, *451*, 534, *558*, 857, 1145, *1171*
Horne, J. A. 175, *178*, 805, 807, 808, 811, 838, 840, 841, *849*, *852*, *855*
Horowitz, T. S. *178*
Horrey, W. 6, *35*, 94, 99, 110, *128*, *133*, 175, 176, *181*, 738, 741, 747, 765, 768, *781*, *785*, *787*, *852*
Horswill, M. S. 106, 107, *128*, *130*, *178*, *187*, 222, *250*, *255*, *256*, 273, 274, 275, 308, 312, *318*, *319*, *324*, 367, 369, 373, *377*, *382*, *388*, 488, *507*, 832, *856*, 945, 949, 955, *976*
Horton, D. *922*
Horton, P. 160, *181*
Horwood, J. 172, 174, *182*
Hosking, S. 221, *250*, *325*, 772, 773, 774, *785*, 943, 969, *973*, *977*
Hoth, J. J. *977*
Hotz, G. A. 900, *918*, 964, *977*, 1107, *1165*
Houtenbos, M. *1031*
Houwing, S. 54, 72, *82*, *628*, 653, *703*
Howard, A. *922*
Howard, E. 285, 298, *319*
Howard, E. A. 888, 889–890, 892, *922*
Howard, E. W. 5, *36*, 392, *451*, 1099, *1166*
Howard, J. M. *636*
Howard, M. E. *787*, 805, *852*
Howarth, C. I. 97, *131*, 870, *922*
Howarth, H. D. *850*
Howat, P. 611, *628*
Howe, P. D. *178*
Høye, A. *81*, *180*, 437, *449*, *451*, *626*, *850*, *917*, *1030*, 1124, *1163*, *1165*
Hoye, T. V. *35*
Hsu, C. C. *1029*
Hu, F. 1026, *1031*
Hu, J. 518, *555*
Hu, L. 217, *256*
Hu, W. 437, *451*
Huang, A. *703*
Huang, B. 929, 946, 950, 952, *977*
Huang, H. 907, 909, *916*, *918*, *925*, *1029*, *1175*
Huchingson, R. *249*
Huckaby, E. *82*, *129*, *1081*, *1167*
Hudson, C. *386*
Hudson, J. *558*
Huestis, M. A. 638, 674, *702*, *703*
Huey, R. 740, *787*
Huffcutt, A. I. 804, *855*
Hughes, B. P. 89, *128*
Hughes, G. M. 724, *785*
Hughes, K. *628*
Hughes, P. K. 727, 729, *785*
Hughes, R. 909, *918*
Hughes, W. E. *83*, *129*, *252*
Huguenin-Richard, F. *917*
Huisingh, C. 162, *181*, 732, 733, *785*
Huitema, B. E. 907, *918*
Hull, M. *382*
Hulse, M. 194, *253*
Hume, R. D. *324*, *457*, *793*, *1035*, *1083*, *1173*
Humphrey, K. 936, *975*
Hundley, J. C. 966, *977*
Hung, W. T. *1174*
Hunt, J. G. *917*
Hunt, R. C. *558*
Hunter, C. E. 668, *703*
Hunter, M. 1089, *1164*
Hunter, W. W. 465, *506*, 877, 878, 880, 881, 882, 884, 885, 900, *916*, *918*, *1029*
Hurd, F. W. 208, *252*
Hursa, A. *1034*
Hurst, P. M. 577, 578, 579, 586, 587, *628*
Hurt, H. H. Jr. 931, 932, 933, 934, 935, 937, 939, 943, 944, 945, 946, 953, 956, 957, 958, *977*, 1023, *1031*

Hurt, J. R. 931, *980*
Huseth-Zosel, A. L. 535, *555*
Hussain, H. 972, *977*
Husted, D. S. 396, *451*
Hutchinson, T. P. 885, *917*
Huth, V. 946, 969, 970, *977*
Hyd, M. K. *456*
Hyde, M. K. *323*, *633*, *794*
Hydén, C. *1174*
Hyder, A. *84*, *85*, *1170*
Hyman, M. M. 285, *319*
Hyvarinen, L. 143, *182*

Iansek, R. 359, *387*
Iavecchia, H. P. 108
Ibarguen, B. *82*, *129*, *1081*, *1167*
Ibrahimova, A. 521, *555*
Ichikawa, M. *557*, 963, *977*, *979*
Ifver, J. *39*
Ihsen, E. *921*
Imberger, K. *1173*
Imprialou, M. I. M. 409, 411, *451*
Inderbitzen, R. E. *552*
Irvin, L. *385*
Irvin, M. R. *785*
Isaksson-Hellman, I. 1141, *1166*
Isalberti, C. *703*
Ishida, Y. *980*
Islam, M. *922*
Isler, R. B. 307, *319*, 361, *382*
Ivaldi, A. 725, *792*
Ivarsson, B. J. 868, *918*
Ivarsson, J. *35*
Ivers, R. *318*, *503*, *700*, 955, *977*, *978*, *1160*
Iversen, H. 110, 111, 425, *451*, 488, *506*

Jackson, A. L. 613, *628*
Jackson, M. I. *787*
Jackson, M. L. 802, *852*
Jackson, R. *850*, 879, *922*, *979*, *982*, *1081*
Jacob, R. 735, *784*
Jacobs, R. J. 1125, *1166*
Jacobsen, P. L. 1015, 1016, *1031*
Jacobson, B. H. *636*
Jacobson, J. *386*
Jacquemart, G. 1122, *1166*
Jaffe, D. H. *1034*
Jahi, H. *1173*
Jain, A. 871, *919*
Jamanka, A. *628*
James, L. 470, *506*
Jamson, A. H. 114, *128*, 772, *786*
Jamson, H. 67, 439, *451*, 1117, *1166*
Jamson, S. 5, *38*, 67, 72, *81*, 239, *251*, 439, *451*, 725, *785*, 1117, *1166*
Jäncke, L. *378*
Janke, M. 340, *382*
Janke, M. K. 160, *184*, 363, 365, *381*
Jänsch, M. *384*, 931, 934, 937, *980*, 1052, *1082*
Janssen, M. M. 599, *629*
Janssen, W. 90, *128*, 524, *555*
Janssens, W. 396, 397, *448*
Janstrup, K. H. 49, *82*
Jarawan, E. *1170*
Jarosinski, W. 1133, *1166*
Jarvis, J. R. 439, *449*, 1117, *1164*
Jauregui, B. 805, *853*
Jeffcoat, A. R. *707*
Jefferson, C. *850*
Jeffery, W. K. *700*
Jehle, D. V. *556*
Jeng, M. C. *1029*
Jenkins, D. P. *795*
Jenkins, F. 159, *181*
Jenkins, L. T. *504*
Jenness, J. W. 159, *181*, *253*, 730, *786*
Jennings, P. A. 231, *248*
Jensen, A. *1033*
Jensen, S. Q. *508*
Jenssenc, G. D. *82*
Jeon, M. 750, *786*
Jermeland, J. *851*
Jernberg, P. *455*
Jernigan, M. V. 546, *553*, *555*, *558*
Jerome, L. 462, *506*
Jhangri, G. S. *918*, *1031*
Ji, Y. G. 371, *384*
Jiang, C. *131*, *508*
Jiang, Y. *181*, *786*
Jimenez, B. M. *851*
Jiménez-Gómez, A. 821, *856*

Jiménez-Mejías, E. *1032*
Jiménez-Moleón, J. J. *978*, *1032*
Jin, C. F. *382*
Jin, L. 175, *181*, 744, *786*
Jobe, J. B. *377*
Johansson, C. 910, *920*
Johansson, E. 740, *783*
Johansson, G. 59, *82*, 194, 195, 197, 211, 212, *251*
Johansson, K. 337, *381*, 1111, *1165*
Johansson, R. 1086, 1099, *1166*
Johansson-Stenman, O. 427, *451*
Johns, M. W. 799, 807, *852*
Johnson, A. M. *180*, *380*
Johnson, B. *382*, *451*
Johnson, C. A. 162, *181*, 352, 353, *382*
Johnson, D. W. 602, *629*
Johnson, E. *850*, *977*
Johnson, L. C. 677, *707*
Johnson, M. 110, *128*, 485, 494, *506*, 593, 594, *629*, *707*, 991, *1031*
Johnson, R. S. *919*
Johnson, T. 972, *977*
Johnston, A. W. 1125, *1166*
Johnston, I. 5, *36*, 392, *451*, 1099, *1166*
Johnston, K. A. *80*, *782*
Johnston, S. *793*
Johnston, W. A. 747, 759, *792*
Joiner, W. *383*
Joint, M. 472, *511*
Joksch, H. C. 421, *451*
Jolly, B. T. *558*
Jolly, N. *185*
Jomnonkwao, S. 946, *981*
Jonah, B. 118, *128*, 395, 396, *451*, 490, 491, *506*, 949, 958, *974*, *977*, 1111, *1168*
Jonasson, B. *704*
Jonasson, U. 684, *704*
Jones, A. W. *629*
Jones, C. N. 696, *704*
Jones, K. 587, *635*, *709*
Jones, R. K. 612, *629*, 648, 649, 659, 685, *704*
Jones, T. *922*
Jongen, A. 640, *704*
Jongen, E. M. *379*
Jongen, S. 573, *629*
Joos, M. *186*
Jopson, A. *922*
Jordan, P. 1131, *1168*
Joscelyn, K. B. 1046, *1081*
Jost, G. 437, *451*, 519, 522, 534, *556*, 864, *915*, 988, *1028*
Jou, R. C. *916*
Jouka, A. *387*
Jovanis, P. *1080*
Jovanovic, D. 459, 462, 484, *506*, *509*
Jowitt, F. 1000, *1035*
Joyce, J. 341, *387*
Juhl, J. *1167*
Juhra, C. 992, 1004, *1031*
Jurisic, D. H. *980*
Jurisich, I. 1019, *1029*
Just, M. 738, 761, *786*, *788*
Justen, R. *552*

Kaars, R. *792*
Kaczmarski, H. *784*
Kaddour, A. *631*
Kahane, C. J. 70, 73, *82*, 120, *128*, 519, 546, 549, *556*, 1134, 1135, 1147, 1148, 1149, *1166*
Kahneman, D. 104, 108, 115, *129*, *132*, 199, *251*, 408, *451*, 801, *852*
Kai, G. P. 217, 218, *249*
Kajabaje, M. *252*
Kallan, M. J. *316*, *554*, *560*
Kallberg, V. 116, *129*, 163, *181*, 405, *451*, 1089, 1128, *1166*
Källhammer, J. E. *922*
Kalska, H. *180*
Kaminska, J. *1163*
Kane, W. 972, *977*
Kanellaidis, G. *458*
Kang, J.-G. 434, *451*
Kantowitz, B. *82*, *88*, *129*, *1081*, *1167*
Kaper-Bongers, R. *186*
Kapitula, L. R. *629*
Kaplan, S. *82*
Kapust, L. R. *250*
Kar, K. 877, *919*, *1160*

Karekla, X. *795*
Karkola, K. *1172*
Karlaftis, M. G. 480, *505*, 566, *625*
Karlssonc, J. G. *82*
Karmhag, R. *974*
Karrer, K. 491, *506*
Karsch, H. M. 862, *919*
Kartje, P. S. 5, *35*, *380*
Karwowski, W. 5, *38*
Kasantikul, V. 962, 963, *980*
Kasper, S. M. *708*
Katila, A. 307, *319*, 1089, 1109, *1166*
Katz, A. 150, *184*, 873, 897, 909, 910, *919*, *922*
Katz-Ben-Ami, L. 302, *324*
Katzourakis, D. 98, *129*
Kauderer, C. *979*
Kauert, G. F. *700*
Kaufman, E. J. 617, *629*
Kaufman, L. 476, *509*, 1129, *1172*
Kaups, K. L. *559*
Kaur, J. *252*
Kaur, L. *252*
Kauranen, T. *786*
Kawakoshi, M. *85*, *982*
Kawamura, T. *557*
Kawauchi, A. *980*
Kay, J. J. 1007, *1032*
Kay, L. *185*
Kaysi, I. 462, *504*
Keall, M. 285, *319*, 340, 363, *382*, 583, 584, 585, *629*, 865, 866, 867, 868, 869, *919*, 1133, 1134, *1164*, *1167*
Kearns, D. F. 153, *182*
Kecklund, G. *177*, 807, 815, *848*, *851*, *852*
Kecklundd, G. *82*
Keeffe, J. E. 366, *382*
Keigan, M. *34*, 880, *923*
Keith, K. 68, *82*, 101, *129*, 1056, 1060, *1081*, 1121, *1167*
Kelleher, S. *1159*
Keller, M. *378*
Keller, T. A. 761, *786*
Kelley-Baker, T. 644, *702*, *704*
Kelly, A. B. *1165*
Keltner, J. L. 162, *181*, 352, 353, *382*
Kemala, C. N. *128*, *382*
Keng, S. H. 962, *977*
Kennedy, G. A. *852*
Kennedy, K. L. *1169*
Kennedy, P. *1081*
Kennedy, R. S. *186*
Kent, R. 545, *556*
Kerns, T. J. *708*, *709*, *975*
Kerr, G. *80*
Kerr, J. S. 640, *703*
Kerry, A. *856*
Kersloot, T. 114, *129*, 745, *786*
Keskinen, E. 307, *317*, *318*, *319*, *321*, *1166*
Kettwich, C. *783*
Ketzer, S. *853*
Keyl, P. M. *184*
Khatib, M. *509*
Khodr, B. *179*, *379*
Kidd, D. G. 76, *82*, 757, *786*, *788*, 912, *919*
Kiefer, R. J. *248*
Kieling, C. *506*
Kieling, R. R. 462, *506*
Kilduff, P. W. *794*
Kiley, D. 769, *786*
Kilgo, P. D. *977*
Kim, K. 516, *556*, 944, 945, *978*, 1112, *1167*
Kim, S. H. 840, *850*
Kim, S. J. 370, *382*
Kime, R. *636*
Kindelberger, J. 961, *978*
King, M. B. *456*
King, M. J. *323*, *633*, *1036*
King, R. *701*
King, W. *554*
Kinn, G. 667, *702*
Kinnear, N. 478, *506*
Kinra, S. 435, *454*
Kintz, P. *631*, *706*
Kircher, A. *131*, *253*, *790*, 817, *852*
Kircher, K. 72, *81*, *783*, 1001, 1002, *1028*, *1032*
Kirk, T. *705*
Kirkham, R. W. 481, *510*
Kirkup, J. 438, *451*
Kirkup, L. *852*

Kirley, B. *555*, *627*, *976*, *1031*, *1164*
Kirmizioglu, K. 234, 239, *251*
Kirn, C. L. *856*
Kirschenbaum, S. *792*
Kjellberg, A. 799, *848*
Klauer, S. 46, 75, *81*, *82*, *83*, 98, 99, *129*, *322*, *323*, 403, *452*, 714, 756, 757, 766, *786*, *789*, 1069, 1071, 1080, *1081*, *1082*, 1088, *1167*
Klaus, G. *791*
Klee, H. 68, *83*
Klein, E. *854*
Klein, M. *254*
Klena, M. J. *1164*
Kline, D. 138, 158, *182*, *249*, 351, *382*, *386*, 1125, 1126, 1127, *1167*, *1172*
Kline, T. J. *182*, *382*, 499, *503*
Klipp, S. 1111, *1167*
Kloeden, C. N. 415, *452*
Klonoff, H. 666, *704*
Klundt, K. 909, *919*
Knapper, A. 724, *782*
Knipling, R. 78, *83*, *552*, 799, 816, 817, 820, *851*, *852*
Knoblauch, R. L. 870, 871, 872, 873, 875, 876, 877, 881, 885, 910, *919*, *923*, *924*
Knoche, A. *707*
Knowles, V. 401, 411, *452*
Knox, D. 1111, *1167*
Knudson, M. M. 966, *974*
Kobayashi, M. 595, 597, 598, 598, 599, *636*
Kobel, N. 1026, *1032*
Kockelman, K. 336, *382*, 418, 423, 424, *452*, 1155, *1163*
Koelega, H. S. 659, 677, *704*
Koepsell, T. D. *554*, *705*, *850*
Kohlberger, T. *1032*
Köhler, H. *625*
Köhler, L. 778, *786*
Koirikivi, I. *182*, *319*
Koivisto, I. 206, *254*
Kok, G. *1035*
Kolenic, G. E. *384*
Kolin, I. *511*
Kolke, R. *1173*
Kömpf, D. 175, *183*, 622, *631*
Kondo, T. 161, *182*
Kong, W. 817, *852*
Konstantopoulos, P. 107, *129*, 175, *182*
Kontodima, E. *795*
Koornstra, M. 928, *978*, 1087, 1091, *1167*
Kopelias, P. 1131, *1174*
Kopernik, D. 1044, *1080*
Kopf, M. *186*
Kopp, A. *1168*
Koppel, S. *179*, *378*, *379*, *382*, *383*, *384*
Korbelak, K. T. *320*, *324*
Korner-Bitensky, N. *187*, *383*, *387*, *388*
Korte, T. *705*
Kosasih, J. B. *980*
Kosnic, W. *182*
Kosnick, W. 351, *382*
Kostyniuk, L. 396, *456*, 522, *554*, *559*, 719, *791*
Kotkanen, H. *182*
Kourtellis, A. *1080*
Koushki, P. A. 522, 523, *556*
Koustanaï, A. 1059, *1081*
Kovácsová, N. 483, *506*
Krafft, M. *39*, 1149, *1167*, *1173*
Kraft, B. 684, *704*
Kramer, A. F. *784*
Kraus, J. F. *81*, 945, 947, 958, 961, 963, 964, *975*, *978*
Krawchuk, S. A. 577, *636*
Krech, D. 595, *629*
Kremnitzer, M. 1114, *1165*
Krems, J. 5, *34*, *255*, *322*, *324*
Krenn, P. *1032*
Kresnow, M. *380*
Kress, H. G. 684, *704*
Kristinsson, J. *700*
Kristofferson, A. B. *254*
Kroeze, P. A. *1033*
Kroj, G. *634*
Kromm, J. N. 620, *629*
Krueger, G. P. *552*, *850*
Krüger, H. P. 591, *635*, 662, *699*
Krzywinski, J. *981*
Kufera, J. A. *978*
Kuhn, V. T. *627*

Kuiken, M. 5, *39*
Kuklane, K. *1034*
Kullgren, A. *39*, *981*, 1136, 1137, *1167*, *1173*
Kulmala, R. 441, *454*
Kumagai, Y. 365, *384*
Kunitz, S. J. *626*, *636*
Kunsman, C. M. *704*
Kunsman, G. W. 677, 680, *704*
Kuo, M. S. *916*
Kuper, S. 9, *36*
Kurosu, A. *628*
Kuypers, K. P. C. *629*, *700*, *707*
Kwan, I. 902, 903, *919*, 994, 995, 996, 998, *1032*
Kweon, Y. J. 336, *382*, 1112, *1167*
Kyed, M. *508*
Kypri, K. 594, *629*
Kyrychenko, S. 15, *38*, 545, *552*, 964, *978*, 1108, 1124, *1168*, *1170*

Laakso, M. 206, *254*, *786*
Laansoo, E. *791*
Laapotti, S. 307, *319*, *1166*
Laatsch, L. *379*
Laberge, J. C. 660, *704*
Laberge-Nadeau, C. 266, *319*, 731, 732, 737, 754, 755, *786*
Lacey, J. H. 587, 612, *627*, *629*, *635*, 644, 671, 681, 684, 686, *704*, *707*, *709*
Lacherez, P. 145, 156, *182*, *187*, 220, *251*, *256*, *388*, *1036*
Laflamme, L. 864, *919*
Lafont, S. *385*
LaFraniere, S. 1113, *1167*
Lagad, S. *855*
Lagarde, E. *385*
Lagerwey, P. A. *925*, *1175*
Lahrmann, H. 1013, *1032*, 1144, 1145, *1167*
Lahti, T. 1098, *1167*
Lai, C. H. *1029*
Lai, F. 67, 94, *125*, 439, *451*, 1117, *1166*
Laing, A. 846, *856*
Laiou, A. *794*
Lajunen, T. *84*, *85*, 110, *130*, *131*, 242, *251*, 459, 467, 472, 477, 479, 480, 483, 492, 497, *506*, *507*, *508*, 1012, *1032*, 1119, *1167*
Lakshminarayanan, V. 350, *385*
Lal, S. K. L. 815, *852*
Lalloo, R. 479, *506*, 880, *919*
Lam, L. T. 897, *919*
Lambert, A. *784*, 2011
Lambilliotte, E. *184*
Lamble, D. 143, *182*, 206, *254*, 747, *786*
Lamers, C. T. 666, *704*
Lamy, A. *918*, *1031*
Land, M. 172, 174, *182*, 750, *781*
Landau, A. 738, *788*
Lane, S. 596, *624*, 771, *781*
Lang, C. 882, *919*
Langevin, S. 885, *919*
Langford, J. *179*, 263, *319*, 338, 339, 341, 342, 344, 345, 346, 347, 357, 362, 363, 364, *379*, *382*, *383*, *384*, *385*
Langfordc, J. *383*
Langham, M. 888, 958, *976*, *919*
Langley, J. 258, *315*, *979*, *982*, *1033*, *1034*
Lansdown, T. C. 114, *129*, 731, 737, 745, 747, 748, *782*, *786*
Lansley, M. *1159*
Lantieri, C. 95, *126*, *249*
Lapham, S. C. 620, *625*, *629*
Lapierre, S. D. *786*
Lapointe, J. *379*
Lappi, O. 172, *182*, *319*
Lardelli-Claret, P. 945, 946, 947, 950, *978*, *1032*
Larsen, L. 1056, *1081*
Larsson, P. 1086, *1167*
Lasenby, J. 491, *507*, 905, *921*
Lassarre, S. 871, *921*
Latham, G. P. 16, *36*, 1098, *1168*
Lattanzio, R. J. *786*
Lauer, A. R. 5, *36*
Laumon, B. 27, *34*, 49, *80*, 669, 672, 684, 685, 686, *705*
Laurell, H. *634*, 802, *853*
Laureshyn, A. *1030*
Laurie, N. E. *317*

Lauriola, M. *853*
Lauritsen, J. *82*
Lauwers, A. *709*
Lavack, A. M. *457*
Lave, C. 412, 418, 419, *452*
Lavender, N. J. *503*, *625*
LaVoie, N. 462, *507*
Law, T. H. 939, *978*
Lawoyin, S. 843, *852*
Lawton, R. *130*, 399, *450*, *452*, 467, 479, *507*
Lay-Yee, R. *982*
Leach, J. 622, *630*
Leaf, W. 27, *36*, 265, 304, *317*, *320*, *323*, *325*, *507*, *625*, *919*
Lebbon, A. *559*
LeBlanc, D. J. 93, *129*, *247*, *250*
Le Brocque, R. *458*
Leden, L. 910, *920*
Ledesma, R. *1034*
Lee, A. K. W. *250*
Lee, B. *915*
Lee, C. 442, *452*, *922*
Lee, D. M. 1121, *1161*
Lee, D. N. 222, *251*
Lee, I. *179*
Lee, J. D. 5, *35*, *38*, 63, 67, 75, *80*, *81*, *82*, *83*, *129*, *248*, *250*, *320*, *386*, 747, 762, 771, 777, 778, *783*, *786*, *787*, *788*, *790*, *1083*
Lee, J. E. *316*
Lee, J. L. *316*
Lee, Joonbum *183*
Lee, Joonhwan *382*
Lee, L. K. *1032*
Lee, M. L. 822, *852*
Lee, S. *452*
Lee, S. E. *83*, *129*, 311, *322*, *323*, *448*, *783*, *786*, *1080*
Lee, S. J. 403, 411, *449*
Lee, S. N. 1046, 1047, *1081*
Lee, W. S. *178*
Lee, Y. C. *322*, 462, *507*
Lee, Y. H. 104, *130*, 405, 406, *452*, 734, 745, *787*, 963, 971, *976*, *981*
Leening, A. 411, *449*
Lefler, D. E. 897, *920*
Leger, D. 820, *852*
Legg, S. 747, *787*
Legge, M. 357, *386*
Leggett, M. W. 1114, *1169*
Legrand, S. A. *628*, *703*
Legrand, S.-N. *82*, *703*
Lehren, A. W. 1113, *1167*
Lehti, H. M. J. 607, *629*
Lehtonen, E. 172, 174, 175, *182*, 272, *319*, *787*
Leibowitz, H. W. 157, 163, 203, 204, *251*, 887, 892, *920*, *923*, 1127, *1167*
Leigh, J. P. 1133, *1168*
Lemaster, D. M. *1161*
Lemire, A. M. *701*
Lenné, M. 5, *38*, *84*, *187*, *256*, 272, 282, *315*, *322*, 570, 605, *629*, 665, 671, 684, *705*, 940, *973*, *978*, *981*
Lenneman, J. K. *247*
Lennon, A. 466, *507*, 538, 543, *556*
Lenoi, M. *186*
Lenoir, M. 1011, *1035*
Leonard, R. L. *504*
Leopold, F. *385*
Lerner, E. B. 522, 523, *556*
Lerner, M. *634*
Lerner, N. *129*, 298, *322*, *323*, 735, 740, *784*, *787*
Lervågc, L.-E. *82*
Lesch, M. *784*
Lesmes, L. A. *180*
Lesnik, A. *254*
Lester, J. F. 27, *36*, 48, *83*, 263, *320*
Leufkens, H. G. M. *706*
Leung, S. 222, *251*, 749, *787*
Leveck, M. D. *377*
Leveille, S. G. 681, *705*
Levelt, P. 1005, *1029*
Leven, J. *1164*
Levenson, S. *628*
Levi, S. 899, *920*
Levison, W. *254*
Levitan, E. B. *785*
Levitt, S. D. 541, *556*
Levy, J. 742, 747, *787*

Levy, P. *980*
Lewin, K. 802, *852*
Lewis-Evans, B. 398, *452*, 1000, *1029*
Li, C. *507*
Li, F. 469, *507*
Li, G. 292, *315*, *316*, *325*, 340, *383*, 653, 671, 672, 681, 684, *705*, *782*, 908, *916*, 986
Li, H. 434, *452*, 538, *556*
Li, L. 516, 523, *556*
Li, Q. *925*
Li, Z. 215, *251*, *1031*
Liang, L. 602, *629*
Liang, Y. 738, 777, *781*, *787*, *852*
Liao, E. *922*
Lichty, M. G. *1160*
Lie, A. *35*, *39*, *132*, 548, 549, *556*, 1136, *1164*, *1167*, *1173*
Lieswyn, J. 1019, *1035*
Lightstone, A. S. *81*
Ligouri, A. 622, *629*
Lillsund, P. *700*
Lillsunde, P. *82*, 645, *703*, *705*
Lim, P. C. 106, *130*
Lim, S. H. 777, *787*
Lin, M. R. 945, 947, 958, 961, 963, *978*
Lin, P. S. *1080*
Lin, S. T. 816, *853*
Linberg, J. V. *182*
Lindberg, L. *629*
Lindman, M. 1141, *1166*
Lindquist, M. 550, *556*
Lindsay, J. *388*, 820, *853*
Lindstrom-Forneri, W. 362, *383*
Link, D. 22, *36*, 863, *920*
Linksz, A. 141, *182*
Linnoila, M. 679, *705*
Lipovac, K. *506*
Lisper, H. O. 802, 803, *853*
Liss, P. H. 900, *920*
Liss, S. *386*
Lister, R. G. 680, *705*
Litchfield, D. *185*, *323*
Little, R. J. A. *504*
Liu, B. C. 961, *978*
Liu, B. -H 175, *182*
Liu, B.-S. 104, *130*, 405, 406, *452*, 734, 745, *787*
Liu, C. 221, *250*, 943, *977*, 1059, *1081*
Liu, G. X. 409, 416, *452*
Liu, J. *852*
Liu, S. 1121, *1168*
Liu, Y. 13, *36*, 195, 217, 240, *251*, *252*, *255*
Llamazares, I. 774, *792*
Lo, H. K. *1174*
Lo, S. *503*, *977*, *978*
Lobjois, R. 873, 885, *920*, 1123, *1168*
Lobmann, R. 591, *635*
Loch, E. 667, *703*
Locke, E. A. 16, *36*, 1098, *1168*
Lockhart, J. 371, *378*, 750, *782*
Lockwood, C. R. 27, *36*, 48, *83*, 263, *320*
Lococo, K. *387*, 537, 539, *553*, *923*
Lofthouse, R. *791*
Logan, B. K. 659, *701*
Lohar, K. *855*
Lokan, R. J. *703*
Lokhande, P. *855*
Lomax, T. 472, *509*
Lombardi, D. A. 857
Lonero, L. 278, *319*
Long, G. M. 153, *182*
Long, R. *918*
Long, Y. *507*
Longo, M. C. *703*
Loo, B. P. Y. *1174*
Lopez, A. L. *851*
Lord, D. *451*, *1170*, *1171*
Lord, S. R. *80*
Loring, W. III. 557
Lorist, M. M. 840, *853*
Lotan, T. 47, 71, *81*, *84*, 296, 301, 302, 305, *317*, *318*, *319*, *322*, *323*, *324*, *780*
Lotsberg, G. 68, *83*
Lott, L. A. *186*, *388*
Lotz, F. *39*
Louca, G. *458*
Lovegrove, G. 1008, 1016, *1035*
Lu, Z.-L. *180*
Lucas, R. 276, *319*
Lucidi, F. 819, 830, 839, *853*
Ludes, B. *631*, *706*

Ludlow, J. *382*, *451*
Lüdtke, A. 34, *125*, *126*
Luengo-Martín, M. Á. 492, *505*
Lukin, J. 958, *982*
Lum, W. *82*, *129*, *1081*, *1167*
Lund, A. K. 116, *127*, 419, 442, *447*, *452*, *458*, 755, *783*, 1091, 1124, 1138, *1168*
Lundberg, C. 337, *381*, 1111, *1165*
Lunenfeld, H. 119, 1119, *1159*, *1168*
Luoma, J. 192, 193, 196, *251*, 405, 441, *451*, *453*, 727, *787*, 902, *920*, *1172*
Lurie-Beck, J. K. *382*
Lusk, A. C. 1017, *1032*
Lutin, M. *379*
Lv, D. *1031*
Lyckegaard, A. *628*, *703*
Lydersend, S. *82*
Lyman, S. 336, 374, *383*
Lynam, D. 1097, *1160*, *1167*
Lynch, R. S. 496, *504*
Lyon, C. A. 847, *854*, 1118, *1170*
Lyon, J. *253*

Ma, J. 175, *187*, *251*, *1174*, *1175*
Ma, X. 913, *920*
Maag, U. *786*
Maasalo, I. 731, 732, *787*
Mabbott, N. A. 842, *853*
Macarthur, C. *922*
MacArthur, J. 1026, *1032*
Macchi, M. M. 828, *853*
Macdonald, S. 576, 621, *630*, 673, 685, 697, *705*
MacDonald, T. M. *699*
Macdonald, W. 338, *380*
Machata, K. 1111, *1167*
Machida, M. *781*
Mack, M. 396, *456*
Mackay, G. M. 895, *915*
Mackay, M. G. 407, *453*, 622, *630*, 958, *982*
MacKenzie, E. J. *324*
MacKintosh, A. M. *1172*
Mackworth, N. H. 804, 824, *853*
MacLean, A. W. 820, *853*
MacLennan, P. A. 534, *556*, *781*
Macworth, N. H. 169, *182*
Madigan, R. *792*
Madison, P. *851*
Madsen, J. C. O. 1013, *1032*
Magazzù, D. *975*
Magg, U. 281, *318*
Mahabadi, H. A. *790*
Maher, M. J. 438, *450*, *453*, 903, 904, *918*, *921*, 1120, *1165*, *1168*
Maheshri, V. 547, *560*
Mahfoud, J. M. *795*
Mahida, M. *248*
Mahler, C. *387*
Mahmassani, H. S. 433, *457*, 476, *505*
Maier, K. *786*
Maier, R. V. *978*
Mair, J. S. *627*
Maislin, G. *850*
Majumdar, A. 434, *452*, 528, *556*
Mak, P. M. 25, *34*
Makinde, O. O. 234, *251*
Malczyk, A. *1031*
Male, I. *1159*
Malecki, J. 121, 441, *456*, 1117, *1172*
Malenfant, J. E. 532, 533, 534, *556*, *559*, 1111, *1168*
Males, M. A. 300, *319*
Mallia, L. *853*
Malta, L. S. 481, *507*
Maltz, M. 93, 102, *130*, 227, *248*, 352, *383*, 884, *920*
Mamelak, M. 352, *386*
Manal, H. 907, *918*
Manaugh, K. 987, *1036*
Mandel, R. *922*
Mangin, P. *699*
Mann, C. N. *560*
Mann, J. *252*
Mann, R. E. 464, *503*, *510*, *625*, *630*, *705*
Mannering, F. 395, *447*, 547, *560*
Manning, J. E. *979*
Mannix, R. *1032*
Manno, B. R. *704*
Manno, J. E. *704*
Manser, M. P. *253*, 439, *453*
Man-Son-Hing, M. *187*, *383*, *385*, *387*, *388*

Manstead, A. *131*, *452*, *507*, *508*, *981*, *1082*
Mao, Y. *388*
Mapstone, J. 902, 903, *919*, 994, 995, 996, 998, *1032*
Marciano, H. 713, *787*
Marcoux, K. 300, *324*
Marczinski, C. A. 576, *630*
Marek, J. 311, *319*
Margaritis, D. *86*
Margolis, L. H. *318*
Marineau, A. 474, *509*
Marinoni, A. *975*
Markkula, G. *1083*
Markley, D. *791*
Markowitz, S. 1098, *1161*
Marlow, M. 872, *917*
Marottoli, R. A. 26, *36*
Marple-Horvat, D. E. *179*
Marques, P. R. 614, 615, 616, *624*, *630*
Marquet, P. *631*, *706*
Marre, M. *186*
Marsden, G. 622, *630*
Marshall, D. *787*
Marshall, S. C. *187*, 360, *383*, *384*, *385*, *387*, *388*, *850*
Marshall, S. W. 285, 297, 298, *320*
Marsiske, M. *377*
Marszalek, R. *187*, *924*, *925*, *1036*
Martel, C. A. *856*
Martens, M. 95, *130*, 170, *182*, 197, 224, 225, *251*, *253*, *707*, 712, *787*, 1121, *1161*, *1168*
Martin, E. *1033*, *1034*
Martin, J. *253*
Martin, J.-L. 27, *34*, 49, *80*, *705*
Martin, M. *378*
Martin-Dupont, S. *631*
Martinez, F. 401, *453*
Martinez, R. 459, *507*
Martínez-Ruiz, V. 990, *1032*
Martinsson, P. 427, *451*
Martinussen, L. M. 123, *130*, 467, *507*
Marui, E. 963, *977*
Marx, K. A. *381*
Mascarell, O. *1034*
Mascord, D. J. *708*
Mashige, K. P. 150, *182*
Masserang, K. *255*
Masten, S. V. 258, 285, 286, 287, 290, 293, 297, 298, *319*, *320*, *321*, *856*
Mastin, B. 599, *633*
Mathers, C. *1170*
Mathewson, K. E. *784*
Mathias, J. L. *377*
Mathijssen, J. J. P. *629*
Mathijssen, M. P. M. *634*, *706*
Mathijssen, R. P. M. *82*, *703*
Matle, C. C. 888, *915*
Matson, T. M. 208, *252*
Matte, B. *506*
Matthews, G. *509*, 801, 818, *850*, *853*
Matthews, R. 747, 758, 759, *787*
Matthias, J. S. 217, 218, *256*
Mattia, D. *849*
Mattick, R. P. *856*
Maul, A. *624*
May, A. 372, *383*
Maycock, B. *628*
Maycock, G. 27, *36*, 48, 49, *81*, *83*, 258, 263, 264, 268, 281, *317*, *320*, 577, *630*, 820, 821, *853*, *976*
Mayer, K. *791*
Mayer, R. 615, *630*
Mayer, R. E. *324*, *457*, 481, *507*, *793*, *1035*, *1083*, *1173*
Mayhew, D. *86*, 266, 268, 277, 278, 283, 284, 285, 286, 299, 300, *315*, *319*, *320*, *324*, 357, *383*, *387*, *388*, *634*, *856*, 1108, *1168*
Mayhorn, C. B. 757, 758, *794*
Maylor, E. A. 868, *917*
Mays, A. *383*
Mazer, B. *187*, *387*, *388*
Mazere, B. *383*
Mazzaae, E. N. 66, *83*
Mazzae, E. N. *253*, 759, *788*, 912, *920*
McArthur, D. L. *978*
McAteer, H. *388*
McAteer, R. *86*
McCall, R. 163, *185*
McCarthy, D. *383*

McCarthy, G. 165, *183*
McCarthy, N. *379*
McCartt, A. T. 27, *36*, 76, *82*, 258, 260, 265, 266, 267, 269, 290, 291, 294, 295, 296, 297, 298, *316*, *320*, *325*, 336, *379*, 437, *451*, 500, *507*, 613, *630*, 744, 757, 760, 776, *786*, *788*, 820, 830, 846, 847, *853*, 904, *922*, 964, *978*
McCarty, C. A. *382*
McClafferty, J. *81*, *127*, *783*
Mcclafferty, J. *1160*
McCloskey, L. W. *705*
McClure, R. 487, *510*
McConnell, E. J. 1111, *1174*
McCormack, P. D. 244, *252*
McCormick, E. J. 544, *558*, 1125, *1171*
McCoy, P. T. 401, 427, 442, *453*, *454*
McDevitt, D. G. *699*
McDonald, C. C. *322*
McDonald, L. *508*
McDonald, M. 224, *248*, 905, *925*
McDonald, S. T. 26, *38*, *324*, *457*, *793*, *1035*, 1046, 1050, *1082*, *1083*, *1173*
McDowell, E. D. 173, *185*, 439, *456*
McEachan, R. R. C. 110, 111, *130*
McEvoy, L. K. 695, *702*
McEvoy, S. P. 721, 754, 755, 759, *788*
McGarva, A. R. 495, *507*
McGee, H. 59, *83*, *129*, 209, 210, *252*, *1169*
McGehee, D. 66, *82*, *83*, 301, *316*, *320*, *553*, 779, *782*, *787*, *788*
McGregor, L. N. 350, *383*
McGuckin, N. *386*
McGuinn, G. 177, *184*
McGwin Jr., G. 26, *36*, 145, 158, 160, 164, *178*, *179*, *180*, *181*, *183*, *184*, *185*, 263, *320*, 336, 350, 351, 352, 353, 357, 362, 376, *381*, *383*, *384*, *385*, 545, *556*, *557*, *781*, *785*, 953, *978*
McIntosh, A. S. 930, *973*, *1033*
McKenna, F. P. 106, 107, *130*, 221, *252*, 273, 308, 311, *317*, *319*, *320*, 408, 425, 431, *453*, 462, 488, *507*, *511*, 903, *922*
McKenzie, D. 601, *634*
Mckenzie, R. J. *787*
McKiernan, A. *388*
McKiernan, H. *86*
McKnight, A. J. 70, *83*, 121, 160, 163, *183*, 269, 270, 271, 283, 308, *320*, *321*, 353, *383*, 419, 432, 433, 440, *456*, 592, 601, *630*, *633*, 739, 744, 748, 761, 766, *788*, 967, 968, *978*
McKnight, A. S. 269, 270, 271, 283, 308, *321*, *635*, 739, 744, 748, 761, 766, *788*, 967, 968, *978*, *1174*
McKnight, S. 161, 163, *183*, 485, 494, *506*
McLaughlin, S. 75, *83*
McLean, A. *377*, 415, *452*, 577, *630*, *915*
McLean, J. *1173*
McLeod, R. *381*
McMahon, A. D. *699*
McMahon, K. 312, *321*
McMillan, B. 395, *448*
McMillan, G. P. *629*
McMillen, R. 620, *635*
McNair, D. M. 676, *705*
McNeal, S. *383*
McNees, R. W. 729, *788*
McNeil, N. 1018, *1029*
McPhee, L. C. 741, *788*
McRuer, D. T. 89, *130*
Meadows, M. L. 467, *510*
Meadows, T. *793*
Mechoulam, R. *633*, *707*
Medeiros-Ward, N. *85*, *792*, *856*
Medina, A. *849*
Meehan, W. P. 1008, *1032*
Meeker, D. 1126, *1164*
Meeusen, R. *1029*, *1035*
Mefford, M. L. *250*, *253*, 350, *386*, 894, *923*
Mehler, B. *183*, *184*, *791*
Mehta, S. D. *554*
Meijman, T. 812, *852*
Meineri, S. *918*
Meir, A. *125*, *186*, *248*, 312, *321*, 901, 902, *915*, *920*, *924*
Meir, M. 101, 199, *254*, 270, *323*
Meiran, N. *80*, 485, *502*, 750, *780*
Meleckidzedeck, K. *1159*
Mellor, A. 961, *978*

Memmot, J. L. 33, 331, 334, *383*
Menachemi, N. *783*
Ménétrey, A. *699*
Mercandante, M. *793*
Mercier-Guyon, C. 564, 590, 591, *630*
Meredith, J. W. *977*
Meredith, L. *981*
Mergl, C. *786*
Merrikhpour, M. 230, *252*
Merritt, J. 352, *386*
Messer, C. J. 729, *788*
Messerschmidt, M. *1031*
Messier, S. *786*
Methorst, R. 263, *319*, 339, *383*, 861, 862, 899, *920*, *1033*, *1035*, *1164*
Mets, M. A. 846, *853*
Metz, B. 738, 739, *788*
Metzger, J. *556*, *557*, *978*
Mewaldt, S. P. 675, *702*
Meyer, F. M. 147, *180*
Meyer, J. 329, 351, 370, *383*, *384*, 742, *788*
Meyer, M. 544, *557*
Meyer, S. F. *1163*
Meyers, J. R. 766, *781*
Meyers, M. 719, *791*
Miara, C. *558*
Michelson, L. *705*
Michon, J. A. 89, 90, 199, *252*
Midwinter, E. 329, *384*
Miesner, M. T. *504*
Mihaila, T. *502*
Miki, T. *980*
Mikkola, T. 820, *856*
Milani, J. A. 961, *978*
Milavetz, G. *703*
Mill, J. S. 1063, *1082*
Millar, M. 485, 486, *507*
Miller, A. *1173*
Miller, B. *702*
Miller, D. A. 1046, *1081*
Miller, G. 47, *83*, 302, *321*, 487, *507*
Miller, L. L. *554*
Miller, N. P. *504*
Miller, P. 614, *628*, *631*
Miller, R. *178*, *977*
Miller, T. L. *504*
Miller, T. R. 609, *631*, *975*
Miller, T. W. 599, *633*
Milligan, C. 1132, *1168*
Millward, D. 438, *451*
Milosevic, S. 95, *130*, 195, *252*
Min, S. J. *708*
Mindell, J. *915*
Mintz, J. H. *457*
Mintzer, M. Z. 679, *705*
Miranda-Moreno, L. F. *1032*
Mirman, J. H. *316*
Mitchel, J. *178*
Mitchell, K. A. 964, *978*
Mitchell, M. M. 488, *503*
Mitchell, P. *554*
Mitsopoulos, E. *256*, *455*
Mitsopoulos-Rubens, E. 940, *978*
Miura, T. *979*
Mizutani, Y. *980*
Moberly, N. J. 888, *919*
Mochida, T. *85*, *982*
Mock, C. N. 964, *978*
Moeckli, J. *787*
Moed, Y. *633*
Moeller, M. R. *700*
Moen, B. A. *453*
Moenc, T. *82*
Moffat, J. M. *850*
Mohan, D. *1170*
Mokdad, A. H. *633*
Molina, J. G. 307, *321*
Molinari, G. *709*
Moll, E. K. *560*
Møller, M. 110, *130*, 257, *321*, *507*
Molnar, F. *383*, *385*, *850*
Molnar, L. J. 5, *35*, 368, 374, *380*, *384*, *554*
Monette, J. L. 799, *850*
Monk, A. 767, *788*
Monk, C. A. 741, *788*
Monsere, C. M. 1018, *1029*
Montag, I. 479, *507*
Monteagudo, M. J. *1160*
Montgomery, G. 154, *183*
Montufar, J. *1168*
Moore, C. *704*

Moore, N. *855*
Moore, V. M. 415, *452*, *453*
Morad, Y. *781*
Moran, S. G. *556*
Morandi, A. 169, *182*, *975*, *1034*
Morando, A. 1146, *1168*
Morel, M. *782*
Morency, P. *1032*
Morgan, J. F. *849*
Morgan, M. A. 531, *557*
Morgan, R. 1131, *1168*
Morgunov, N. *1031*
Moriarty, K. *1032*
Morita, T. *979*
Mørland, J. 82, *634*, *700*, *702*, *708*
Morris, A. *86*, *699*, 712, *793*
Morris, C. C. 966, *978*
Morris, J. C. 361, *384*
Morris, J. N. *377*
Morris, S. D. 539, *557*
Morrisey, M. 418, *450*, *783*
Morrison, R. W. 207, *252*
Morrongiello, B. A. 491, *507*, 905, *921*
Mortimer, R. G. 155, *181*, 410, *450*
Moscati, R. M. *556*
Moser, A. 175, *183*, 622, *631*
Mosher, J. F. 601, *631*
Mosimann, U. P. *180*
Moskowitz, H. 175, *183*, 563, 565, 567, 568, 569, 571, 578, 579, 587, 605, 606, 610, 622, 623, *624*, *625*, *631*, *632*, *634*, 638, 658, 661, 664, 680, 698, *700*, *705*, *706*, *708*, *974*, *1082*
Moulden, J. V. *701*, *709*
Moulsma, M. *631*
Mountain, L. J. 438, *450*, *453*, 903, 904, 904–905, *918*, *921*, 1120, *1165*, *1168*
Mourant, R. R. 46, *83*, 107, *130*, 171, 172, 173, *183*, 272, 308, 312, *316*, *321*, 727, 729, *788*
Mourssavi, M. *453*
Mouzon, P. *554*
Movig, K. L. L. *82*, 650, 651, 656, 659, 672, 684, 685, *703*, *706*
Mowrer, O. H. *504*
Mrozek, M. 239, *251*
Mucsi, K. *1170*
Muelleman, R. L. *980*
Mueller, A. S. 272, 274, *321*
Muhialdin, N. *1159*
Muhlbauer, F. *981*
Muir, C. 5, *36*, 392, *451*, 1099, *1166*
Mukhopadhyay, P. 234, 240, *252*
Mullen, B. 828, *850*
Mullen, C. *922*
Mullen, N. 66, *83*, *626*, *701*
Muller, A. 964, *979*
Müller, I. 1006, *1028*
Mullin, B. 947, 949, 953, *979*, *982*
Mulvihill, C. 950, 952, 957, *976*
Munoz, B. *178*
Muñoz, M. 176, *183*
Munro, C. 1019, *1035*
Mura, P. 577, *631*, 667, 669, 672, *706*
Murakami, N. *979*
Müri, R. M. *180*
Murillo, D. 91, 374, *378*, 904
Murphy, B. *629*, *705*
Murphy, K. R. *699*
Murphy, S. 745, *785*, 883, *918*, *1033*
Murray, D. C. *552*
Murrell, P. 442, *458*
Muser, M. *1034*
Musicant, O. 71, *81*, *317*, *323*, 400, *455*, *780*, 1124, *1171*
Musselwhite, C. 488, *507*
Mutabazi, M. 909, *921*
Muttart, J. *85*, *186*, *255*
Muttart, J. W. *249*, 936, *975*, *979*
Muzet, A. *184*, 807, *849*, *854*, *855*
Myeong, M. H. 1112, *1167*
Myers, A. 367, *383*, *384*, *387*
Myers, E. J. 1122, *1170*
Mysen, A. 25, 602, *626*, 992, *1030*

Näätänen, R. 5, 23, *37*, 107, *130*, 199, *254*, 712, *793*, 1080, *1082*, 1088, 1121, *1168*, *1173*
Nabi, H. *385*
Nabors, D. 985, 986, 1006, 1016, *1032*
Naci, H. 862, *921*
Nadler, E. *787*

Nagai, T. *628*
Nagayama, Y. 956, *979*
Nagel, P. H. A. *706*
Naglie, G. *187*, *385*, *387*, *388*
Naglieg, G. *383*
Nahl, N. 470, *506*
Nahvi, A. *790*
Najm, W. G. 885, *916*, 1120, *1168*
Nakagawa, Y. 365, *384*
Nakahara, S. 525, 526, *557*, 962, *979*
Nakamoto, H. Y. *386*
Nakata, A. *851*
Namdeo, A. *380*
Namuswe, E. S. 610, *631*
Narayanaan, V. *253*
Nass, C. 801, 834, 837, 838, *856*
Næss, T. *1167*
Nassi, B. 618, *631*
Nassi, R. *918*
Nathanael, D. 936, *979*
Naubauer, O. *186*
Naveteur, J. 885, *921*
Navon, D. 407, 412, *453*, 713, *788*
Nawror, M. 361, *386*
Naya, Y. *980*
Nazroo, J. Y. 479, *506*, 880, *919*
Ndiaye, D. 369, *386*
Neal, V. L. 74, *83*
Neale, V. *81*, *129*, *452*, 714, *786*, *789*, 1069, 1070, *1080*, *1081*, *1082*, *1167*
Nedzesky, A. *783*
Neeleman, J. *510*
Nef, T. *180*
Nehlig, A. 841, *853*
Nelson, J. *708*, *918*, *1165*
Nelson, L. 304, *325*, *783*
Nelson, T. M. 800, *854*
Nentwich, M. *922*
Nesbit, S. M. 483, 484, *508*
Nesvåg, S. M. 946, *980*
Neuhardt, J. B. 98, *128*
Neukum, A. *855*
Neuman, T. R. 1120, *1169*
Neuteboom, W. 667, 683, *706*
Newland, C. *1170*
Newman, J. A. 931, *979*
Newnam, S. *250*
Newstead, S. *128*, *378*, *379*, *382*, 383, *1031*, 1114, 1133, 1134, *1167*, *1169*
Neyens, D. M. 1054, *1082*
Ng, A. W. Y. 240, *252*
Ng, C. P. *978*
Ng, E. S. *184*
Ngai, A. 275, *324*, 943, *982*
Nguyen, H. *852*
Nguyen, L. T. 805, 815, 818, 829, 839, *853*
Nicastro, R. 622, *627*
Nichols, J. L. 543, 546, 547, *553*, *557*, *559*, *626*, *634*
Nicholson, B. 352, *386*
Nicholson, R. N. 69, *81*
Niederhauser, M. E. 1122, *1170*
Nielsen, K. J. 493, *508*
Nieminen, T. *180*
Nijland, H. *1029*
Nikolaou, S. 928, *975*
Nilsson, G. 418, *454*, *1167*
Nilsson, L. *131*, *253*, 747, 748, *781*, *790*
Nilsson, T. 800, *854*
Niska, A. *1033*
Nitz, L. 516, *556*
Nitzburg, M. 871, *919*
Niu, Q. *181*, *786*
Njå, O. 946, *980*
Njord, J. 76, *84*
Noah, M. 534, *557*
Noland, R. B. 528, *556*
Nolen, S. *318*
Noordzij, P. *1167*
Nordbakke, S. 818, 819, 827, *854*
Normann, P. T. *702*
North, R. V. 160, *183*
Northrup, V. S. 522, 523, 524, *553*
Norton, R. *503*, *700*, *850*, 879, *922*, *978*, *979*, *982*, *1081*, *1160*
Norvell, D. C. 962, *980*
Nouveah, J. *631*
Noy, I. 846, *856*
Noy, Y. I. 5, *37*, *181*, 772, *785*, *790*
Noyce, D. A. *322*, *385*
Nunes, L. 114, 406, *454*, 745, *791*
Nyberg, A. 281, *317*, *318*, *321*

Nysten, E. *1167*
Nyström, M. *177*, *848*

Oblad, C. 725, *789*
O'Brian, C. S. *852*
O'Brien, N. 296, *321*, *555*, *627*, 760, *784*, *976*, *1031*, *1164*
O'Brien, S. R. 462, *508*
Ochiai, A. 928, *980*
Ochieng, W. Y. 528, *556*
O'Connell, T. *699*
O'Connor, E. *919*
O'Connor, K. *178*
O'Connor, M. G. *178*, *250*
O'Connor, P. J. 967, *980*
O'Day, J. 407, *454*
Odell, M. *179*, *379*
Odom, V. *182*
O'Donnel, R. D. 103, *130*
O'Donnell, M. A. 601, *632*
O'Donnell-Nichol, S. *559*
O'Donoghue, F. *852*
Oehl, M. *509*
Oetting, E. R. 496, *504*
Offer, D. 490, *503*
Ogaitis, S. *324*
Ogden, E. 563, 565, 567, *632*, 658, *701*, *706*
Ogilvie, R. D. 799, 805, *854*
Oh, H. J. 371, *384*
Oh, Y. *452*
O'Hanlon, J. 659, 664, 666, *703*, *707*, *709*
O'Hare, M. *179*, *379*
Ohayon, M. M. *850*, *855*
Ohta, H. 121, *130*, 223, 224, *252*
Ohtsuka, K. 462, 486, *510*
Øiestad, E. L. *702*
Oja, P. 984, *1032*
Okada, A. 1149, *1159*
Olai, M. *132*, *1173*
Olivier, B. *853*
Olivier, J. 930, *973*, *1035*
Olsen, E. C. 311, *322*
Olsen, E. O. 770, *789*
Olshaker, J. *554*
Olson, C. M. 546, *557*
Olson, P. 5, *34*, *37*, 148, *185*, 207, 213, 214, *252*, 352, 354, *384*, 940, *980*, 1119, *1161*
Olson, R. 75, *81*, *85*, *127*, 756, 766, 774, *790*, *783*, *849*, *851*
Olsson, S. *629*, 748, *790*
Olukoga, A. 534, *557*
Oluwasegunfunmi, V. 234, *251*
Omari, K. 523, *558*
Omer, H. *81*, *317*, *323*
Omidyeganeh, M. *848*
O'Neal, E. E. *923*
O'Neill, B. 15, *38*, 120, *130*, 313, *325*, 525, *558*, 1108, 1109, 1134, 1136, *1170*, *1174*
O'Neill, D. 4, *35*, 263, *318*, 339, 360, 361, 362, 365, *378*, *381*, *384*
O'Neill, S. A. 725, *792*
Oppenheim, I. 467, 493, *508*
O'Reilly, D. 312, *321*
Oron-Gilad, T. 106, 107, *125*, 175, *178*, *186*, 220, 221, *248*, 272, 274, 308, 312, *315*, *321*, *378*, *508*, *633*, 799, 801, 802, 804, 805, 806, 812, 818, 820, 824, 830, 833, 834, 837, 838, 846, *851*, *854*, *855*, 883, 901, 902, *915*, *920*, *924*, 992, *1031*
Orós, M. *975*
Orsay, E. M. 967, *980*
Osman, Z. 372, *383*
Osterberg, G. 140, *183*
Östlund, J. 92, *131*, *253*, 768, *783*, *790*
Öström, M. 867, 881, *921*
Othersen, I. *855*
Otmani, S. 807, 809, 812, 815, 816, 818, *854*
O'Toole, M. *786*
Otte, D. 346, 348, *384*, 931, 932, 934, 937, *980*, *1034*, 1052, 1054, 1056, *1082*
Ou, Y.-K. 240, *252*
Ouellet, J. 931, 957, 962, 963, *977*, *980*, 1023, *1031*
Ouimet, M. C. *83*, *129*, 258, 296, 303, 315, *322*, *323*, *786*
Ouschan, R. *126*
Overley, E. T. *183*, *184*

Owens, D. 144, 149, 157, 158, 163, *187*, 203, *251*, 444, *454*, 575, *632*, 887, 892, *920*, 1127, *1167*
Owens, K. 688, *700*, *852*
Owens, N. *783*
Owlsey, C. 352, *387*
Owoeye, J. F. A. *177*
Owsley, C. 26, *36*, *38*, 145, 146, 158, 160, 162, 164, 166, 167, 168, 177, *178*, *180*, *181*, *183*, *184*, *185*, 263, *320*, 350, 351, 352, 353, 357, *377*, *378*, *381*, *383*, *384*, *385*, *781*, *785*
Oxley, J. 347, 375, 376, *379*, *385*, 885, *916*, *919*, *921*, *1031*
Oxley, P. E. *379*
Özkan, T. 50, *84*, 110, *130*, *131*, 459, 467, 469, 492, *507*, *508*

Pachana, N. A. *128*, *255*, *382*
Pack, A. I. 810, 811, 812, 818, 822, *853*, *854*
Pack, A. M. *854*
Paegle, I. 667, 682, *708*
Pagán, J. A. 647, *709*
Page, Y. *1164*
Pai, C. W. *916*
Paine, D. *980*, *1170*
Paine, M. 958, *980*, 1136, *1170*
Paine, S. *625*
Pak, A. 266, *320*
Palamara, P. *788*
Palayew, M. *850*
Paleti, R. 465, *508*
Palmore, E. 351, *377*
Palmqvist, L. *1032*
Palta, M. 821, 857
Paniati, J. F. 445, *447*
Panis, L. L. *1029*, *1035*
Papadaki, M. *1034*
Papadimitriou, E. *34*, *385*, *795*, 871, *921*, 1131, *1174*, *1175*
Papafotiou, K. 696, *701*, *706*
Papakostopoulos, V. *979*
Papantoniou, P. *794*
Papon, F. *1028*
Parada, M. A. 51, *84*, 519, 520, 522, 523, *558*
Paradis, J. 367, *384*
Paran, F. 110, *126*
Parasuraman, R. 1150, *1170*
Park, E. S. *1165*
Park, G. *179*
Park, K. 365, *384*
Park, N.-H. *709*
Parker, D. 108, 110, *131*, *452*, 459, 467, 469, 472, 477, 483, *506*, *507*, *508*
Parker, M. *452*
Parker, S. *788*
Parkes, A. 747, 748, *782*, *783*, *790*, 828, *854*
Parkin, P. C. 535, *555*
Parks, S. N. *1161*
Parmentier, G. 336, *385*
Parmer, E. 768, *793*
Parmet, Y. 97, *125*, 170, *178*, *186*, *248*, *378*, *508*, *633*, *707*, *851*, 883, 901, 902, *915*, *916*, *920*, *924*
Parnell, M. *249*
Parrish, J. M. *381*
Parry, H. M. 5, *38*
Parry, M. H. 87, *131*, 462, *508*
Parsonson, B. S. 361, *382*
Partonen, T. *1167*
Partyka, S. C. 1067, 1068, *1082*
Pasanen, E. 415, *454*, 895, *921*, *1034*
Pasaputhi, M. 765, *783*
Pashler, H. 742, *787*
Pashley, C. 283, *320*
Pastalan, L. A. 148, *185*
Pastor, C. 1137, *1164*, *1170*
Pate, A. 374, *378*, 904, *915*
Paterson, J. L. *850*
Pathanya, V. S. 755, *781*
Patten, C. J. D. 103, 104, *131*, 198, *253*, 743, 744, 748, 749, 759, *783*, *790*
Patterson, T. L. 285, *319*, 583, 584, *629*
Pattinson, M. 884, *923*
Patton, C. W. 893, *924*
Paulozzi, L. J. 929, 954, *980*
Pazhouhanfar, M. *249*, *975*
Peacock, B. 5, *38*
Pease, K. 900, *921*
Pebayle, T. *855*

Pechansky, F. *506*
Peck, L. R. *979*
Peck, R. 611, *635*
Peck, R. C. 298, *320*, *322*, *324*, 585, 613, *624*, *625*, *626*, *631*, *632*, *700*, *974*, 1113, *1164*
Pedder, J. B. 931, *980*
Peden, M. 1088, 1095, 1097, 1103, 1107, 1132, *1170*
Pedersen, C. A. *178*
Peek, C. *978*
Peek-Asa, C. *81*, *316*
Pegrum, B. V. 150, *184*, 909, *921*
Pein, W. E. 465, *506*, *918*
Pekkanen, J. *787*
Peleg, G. 727, *791*
Peleg, K. 49, *84*, *1034*
Peli, E. 143, 162, *184*
Pell, K. *704*
Pelli, D. G. 158, *184*
Pelz, D. C. *509*
Peng, Y. *250*, 771, *790*
Pennizi, L. *1164*
Penttinen, M. *453*, 902, *920*
Penumaka, A. P. 938, 957, 970, *980*
Pepper, D. R. *1161*
Percer, J. 901, *922*, 1011, *1033*
Pereverseff, R. S. 311, *322*
Pérez, J. 479, *503*, 1114, *1160*
Perez, M. *81*, *127*, 194, *253*, *448*, 775, *783*, *790*, *1080*, *1160*
Perez, W. A. *129*
Perez-Reyes, M. 661, *707*
Perfetti, L. 479, *511*, 576, *636*
Pernas, F. *977*
Perneger, T. 487, *508*
Perrillo, K. 442, *454*, 847
Perry, J. L. 661, *700*
Persaud, B. *452*, 847, *854*, 1118, 1122, *1170*, *1171*
Pesti, G. 442, *453*, *454*
Petermann-Stock, L. *855*
Peters, J. P. *974*
Peters, R. D. 799, 804, *854*
Petersen, A. D. *81*, *1080*
Peterson, M. N. 1008, *1031*
Peterson, T. D. 514, 515, *558*, *980*
Petit, C. *782*
Petri, H. L. *505*
Petrie, J. *553*
Pettersson, H.-E. *1167*
Pettigrewm, K. 958, *982*
Pettitt, M. 715, *790*
Petzoldt, T. *255*, 312, *322*, *324*
PfeferSlack, R. *1169*
Philip, P. 800, 840, *850*, *854*, *855*
Philippaerts, R. *186*, *1035*
Phillips, B. 233, *256*
Phillips, L. K. *250*
Phillips, R. O. 79, *84*, 798, *855*, 1109, *1170*
Piantini, S. *981*
Piccinini, G. F. B. *1029*
Picha, D. L. *1165*
Pickrell, T. M. 522, 528, 534, 535, 538, 543, *556*, *558*
Pickworth, W. B. 679, *707*
Pierce, J. L. *852*
Pierce, R. S. *703*
Pierini, M. *980*, *981*
Pierowicz, J. *1080*
Piersma, D. 370, *385*
Pietrucha, M. T. 871, *919*, 1126, *1164*
Pigman, J. 1116, *1172*
Pijl, Y. J. *510*
Pikkarainen, J. *705*
Pilcher, J. J. 804, *855*
Pilcher, S. *978*
Pilkington, P. 435, *454*
Pillalamarri, R. S. *794*
Pinard, G. *703*
Pinili, M. 48, *81*, 261, *316*
Pinsker, J. 432, *454*
Pinto, M. 159, *179*, 958, 959, 960, 969, *974*, *981*
Pirozzo, S. 487, *510*
Pisachov, F. 1012, *1030*
Pisani, D. L. 828, *850*
Pishahov, F. 399, *450*
Pitan, A. *624*
Pitfield, D. E. *451*
Planes, M. *784*
Plasència, A. *975*

Pless, I. B. 50, *85*
Pocock, S. J. 53, *84*
Poitras, M. 1133, 1134, *1171*, *1173*
Polacsek, M. 613, 614, *633*
Polders, E. 377, *385*
Polgar, J. *383*, *386*, *388*
Politis, A. 232, *250*
Pollack, I. 104, *129*
Pollatsek, A. *85*, *186*, *255*, *317*, *322*, *385*, *386*
Pollatsek, P. 220, 222, *253*
Pollini, R. A. 675, *707*
Polus, A. 150, *184*, 909, *922*
Pompeia, S. *627*
Ponchillia, P. *918*
Ponte, G. 415, *452*
Pooley, C. G. 898, *922*
Popkin, C. *635*, *977*
Popoff, A. 409, *452*
Porath-Waller, A. J. 691, 693, 696, *707*
Porter, B. E. 5, *38*
Porter, M. *187*, 257, *322*, 362, *385*, *387*, *388*, 395, *454*
Porterk, M. M. *383*
Portman, M. *705*
Portouli, E. *979*
Posner, J. C. 880, *922*
Posner, M. I. 58, *81*, 204, *250*
Potter, D. D. 713, *791*
Potts, I. *458*, 1121, *1171*
Poulin, C. 673, *699*
Poulos, R. *318*, 987, *1033*
Poulter, D. R. 155, *184*, 903, *922*, *981*
Poulton, E. C. 124
Pourrat, O. *631*
Pouyakian, M. 740, *790*
Pöysti, L. 735, 742, *790*
Pradhan, A. *85*, *186*, *253*, *255*, 274, 308, *317*, *322*, 352, *385*
Prasada-Rao, P. *184*
Prato, C. G. 47, *82*, *84*, 302, *322*
Preston, B. 900, *921*
Preston, J. 929, 946, 950, 952, *977*
Preusser, D. F. 285, *317*, *322*, *323*, *325*, 519, *553*, 585, *633*, 933, 964, *981*, *982*
Preusser, D. R. 362, *385*
Preziotti, G. R. 1140, *1159*
Price, J. M. 220, *253*
Price, L. *511*
Prieto, J. M. 482, *503*
Pronin, M. 233, *253*
Pronk, N. *379*, *976*
Prothe, L. *1169*
Przekop, M. A. *704*
Pulling, N. H. 150, *184*, 352, *385*
Pund, B. *384*, 1052, *1082*
Purnell, M. *636*
Puvanachandra, P. *84*, *85*
Pyta, V. *1173*

Qiu, C. *555*
Qu, S. *624*
Qu, W. 123, *131*, 467, *508*
Quaresma, M. 246, *253*
Quddus, M. *451*
Queipo, D. *699*
Quine, L. 947, 948, 954, *981*
Quinlan, K. E. *701*
Quinlan, K. P. 576, *633*

Rabbitt, P. *508*
Rabinovich, A. *633*, *707*
Rabinovich, A. *707*
Raby, M. *316*, *320*, *553*, *782*, *788*
Racette, L. 162, *184*
Rackoff, N. J. 171, *183*, 727, *788*
Radbruch, L. *708*
Radin-Umar, R. S. *977*
Radun, I. 469, *510*, *856*
Raes, E. 689, *709*
Rafaelsen, L. 661, *699*, *707*
Rafaelsen, O. J. 661, *699*
Ragan, K. M. 483, 492, *504*
Ragel, B. T. *560*
Raghunathan, T. E. *504*
Raghuram, A. 350, *385*
Ragunathan, T. *554*
Rahwan, I. 1156, *1160*
Raitanen, T. 263, *318*, 339, *381*
Rajab, W. *626*
Rajalin, S. 469, 488, *508*, *510*, 735, *790*

Rakauskas, M. E. 246, *253*, 747–748, 765, *784*, *790*
Rakotonirainy, A. *84*
Ram, E. S. 406, *457*, 738, *793*
Rämä, P. 441, *453*, *454*
Ramaekers, J. G. *629*, 661, 663, 664, 666, 672, 673, 688, *700*, *704*, *707*
Ramirez, A. *704*
Rams, M. A. *699*
Ramsey, A. 542, *558*
Ramsey, D. J. *129*, *452*, *786*, *1081*, *1167*
Ramsey, M. 495, *507*
Ranchet, M. *974*
Ranney, T. 89, *131*, 194, *253*, 746, 772, 775, *788*, *790*, *853*, *920*
Rao, N. *633*
Rapoport, M. *187*, 365, *383*, *385*, *387*, *388*
Räsänen, M. 847, *855*, 1014, *1033*, *1034*
Raschke, M. *1031*
Rasinski, K. *382*
Rasmussen, J. 89, *131*
Rastogi, R. 871, *919*
Ratanavaraha, V. 946, *981*
Rath, A. L. 546, *553*, *555*, *558*
Rathod, V. 736, *785*
Ratz, M. 160, *184*
Rau, P.-L. P. *133*, *795*
Rauch, W. *624*
Rauch, W. J. 419, *452*, *636*
Ray, H. W. *323*
Ray, W. A. 681, *707*
Rea, M. S. 150, *179*
Reagan, I. 119, *131*, *317*, *455*, 533, *559*, 777, *783*, 1139, *1171*
Reagle, G. *552*
Reason, J. 122, 123, *131*, 467, 486, *508*, 938, *981*, 1062, *1082*
Rebok, G. W. *377*
Recarte, M. A. 114, 406, *454*, 745, *791*
Rechnitzer, G. *916*
Recker, W. W. 395, *450*
Redelmeier, D. A. 433, 443, *454*, *455*, 753, 755, 759, *791*, 1113, *1171*
Redman, J. R. *629*, *705*
Redmand, J. R. *705*
Redshaw, S. 5, *38*
Reed, N. 857
Reed, S. *86*
Rees, D. I. 688, *699*
Regan, M. 5, *38*, 75, *84*, 163, *181*, *256*, *455*, 534, *558*, 712, 769, *782*, *784*, *785*, *791*, *795*, 957, 969, *973*, *982*, 1145, *1171*, 2011
Reger, M. A. 361, *385*
Reger-Nash, B. *1032*
Reid, I. C. *699*
Reimer, B. 175, *183*, *184*, 370, *385*, 467, 468, *508*, 744, 774, *791*, *792*
Reinfurt, D. *792*, *793*
Reistetter, T. *249*
(René) van Rijn, L. J. *186*
Rensink, R. A. 201, *254*
Repa, B. S. 205, *255*
Repetto-Wright, R. 97, *131*, 870, *922*
Retchin, S. M. 352, *385*
Rettig, K. *708*
Retting, R. 847, *854*, 904, 905, 908, *922*, 1118, 1122, 1124, 1128, 1129, *1168*, *1170*, *1171*
Reuben, D. B. 351, *385*
Reurings, M. 984, *1034*
Reyes, M. L. *320*, 777, *787*, *788*
Reyner, L. A. 807, 808, 811, 840, 841, *852*, *855*
Reynolds, C. C. 1019, *1033*
Reynolds, L. *1159*
Ribner, S. A. *853*
Riccioli, C. *34*, *125*, *126*
Rice, T. *975*
Richard, C. M. *1160*
Richards, T. L. *504*
Richardson, G. B. *248*, *781*
Richman, B. J. 232, *248*
Richman, J. *248*, *919*
Richmond, S. A. 907, *922*
Riendeau, J. *378*
Rilea, S. L. *324*
Rimmo, P. A. *318*
Rissel, C. *1033*
Risser, R. 5, *34*, 946, *977*
Risto, M. 224, 225, *253*
Ritter, G. *855*

Rivara, F. P. 534, 542, 546, *553*, *554*, *557*, *558*, *850*, 864, *922*, *924*, *978*
Rizkallah, J. W. *918*, *1031*
Rizzi, M. *39*, *132*, 970, *981*, *1164*, *1173*
Rizzo, M. 5, *35*, *180*, 361, *377*, *380*, *386*, *509*
Roache, J. D. 680, *705*, *707*
Robbe, H. 660, 664, 666, 667, 668, *707*
Robbe, J. 666, *703*
Robbins, G. *388*
Roberts, I. 879, *922*, *1159*
Roberts, S. C. *787*
Robertson, D. *86*
Robertson, L. S. 120, *131*, 532, *558*
Robertson, M. D. *701*
Robertson, R. *387*, *388*, 697, *702*, *856*
Robinson, A. 1108, *1171*
Robinson, C. D. 567, 568, 579, *631*
Robinson, D. L. 1008, 1009, *1033*
Robinson, E. *1081*
Robinson, G. S. 798, *849*, 1118, *1159*
Robinson, J. H. 622, *629*
Robinson, S. *249*
Robson, J. G. 158, *184*
Roche, K. B. *184*
Rock, S. M. 417, *455*
Rockwell, T. H. 46, *83*, 107, 121, *130*, 171, 173, *183*, *185*, 272, 308, *321*, 439, 441, *456*, 727, 729, *788*, 813, *855*, 1117, *1172*
Rodgers, A. *1034*
Rodgers, S. E. *504*
Rodgman, E. *635*, *792*, *793*, *854*
Rodriguez, R. J. 412, *455*
Roehm, H. *552*
Roehrs, T. *850*
Roenker, D. L. *38*, *178*, *179*, *180*, *183*, *184*, 369, *377*, *386*
Rogé, J. 172, *184*, 369, *386*, 807, 809, 810, 812, 813, 814, *849*, *854*, *855*
Rogeberg, O. 674, *707*
Rogers, E. *626*, *633*, *635*
Rogers, P. N. 160, *184*
Rohde, L. A. *506*
Rohrbaugh, J. W. *853*
Rohrer, M. S. *707*
Roidl, E. 472, 485, *509*
Rojek, D. G. 614, *633*
Rokach, L. 618, *631*
Rollins, D. E. *701*
Romano, E. *322*, 611, *632*, *635*, *704*, *707*
Romanow, N. T. R. *1031*
Romer, D. 273, *322*
Romoser, M. *85*, *184*, *186*, *253*, 362, 376, *386*
Ronen, A. 51, 61, 65, *84*, *85*, *378*, 573, 605, *633*, 645, 664, 665, 666, 667, *707*, 746, *791*, 799, 812, 833, 839, 841, 846, 847, *851*, *854*, *855*, *916*
Roney, L. 731, *791*
Rong, J. 175, *182*, *187*, *251*, *1174*, *1175*
Rooijers, T. 432, *448*
Roozenburg, A. P. 26, *39*, 862, *924*
Roper, P. *1173*
Roper, V. J. 888, 889–890, 892, *922*
Rosén, E. 895, 910, *922*
Rosenberg, R. L. *915*
Rosenbloom, T. 902, *922*
Rosentha, K. M. *917*
Rößger, L. 5, *38*, 942, 959, 969, *981*
Rošková, E. 483, *506*
Rosmalen, J. G. M. *510*
Rosman, D. 27, *38*, 357, *386*
Rosner, B. *849*
Rosner, Y. *922*
Rosomoff, H. L. *702*
Rosomoff, R. S. *702*
Rosopa, P. J. *915*
Ross, H. L. 588, *633*, 1111, *1171*
Ross, J. 532, *558*, *701*
Ross, L. A. *178*
Ross, R. J. 469, *503*
Ross, T. 372, *383*, *783*
Rossi, R. M. *974*
Rossiter, J. R. 440, *455*
Rotenberg, E. 59, *85*
Roth, T. *850*
Rothengatter, T. 121, *131*, 812, *852*
Rothman, L. *922*
Rothschild, M. L. 599, *633*
Rotton, J. 484, *510*

Rouse, E. J. 69, *81*
Rousseau, G. K. *917*, *1030*
Routledge, D. A. 97, *131*, 870, *922*
Row, B. H. *918*, *1031*
Rowden, P. 491, *509*
Rowe, B. H. *1031*
Rowe, D. 646, *709*
Royal, D. 719, 720, 721, 730, 731, *791*
Rubin, G. S. 145, 158, *178*, *179*, *184*
Rudin-Brown, C. 5, *38*, *256*, 272, *322*, *457*, 724, *785*
Rue, L. *557*
Rue III, L. W. *556*, *978*
Ruiter, R. A. C. *125*
Rumar, K. 59, *82*, 159, *184*, 194, 197, 211, 212, *251*, 407, 444, 445, *455*, 1050, 1051, *1082*
Rumbold, G. 411, *449*, *705*
Rundmo, T. 110, 111, 425, *451*, 488, *506*
Runge, J. W. *558*
Runyan, C. W. 1094, *1171*
Rusch, M. L. *386*
Ruscio, D. 205, 210, 211, *253*
Russell, S. *1160*
Russo, P. M. *853*
Rutledge, D. A. 606, *625*, *708*
Rutter, D. R. 947, 948, 954, *981*
Ryan, G. A. 357, *386*

Saari, L. M. *1168*
Sabatowski, R. 683, *708*
Sabey, B. E. 415, *455*, 1050, 1054, *1082*
Sacks, J. J. 963, *981*
Sadoff, M. G. *323*
Sagaspe, P. *854*, *855*
Sagberg, F. 266, 311, *322*, 360, *386*, 811, 814, 822, 823, *855*
Sahami, S. 61, *84*
Säidi, A. *786*
Saint-Pierre, G. 959, *981*
Sajatovic, A. *1034*
Sakai, J. T. *708*
Sakashita, C. *977*
Sakmar, E. *636*
Sakshaug, J. *700*
Sakshaugc, K. *82*
Saldeen, T. *704*
Saleh, W. *916*
Salim, D. *187*, *388*
Salmivaara, H. 415, *454*, 895, *921*
Salmon, P. M. 6, *39*, *187*, 282, *315*, 722, 776, *795*
Salo, A. J. *1172*
Salomonsen-Sautel, S. 674, *708*
Salvendy, G. 225, *249*, 312, *324*
Salvucci, D. D. 724, *791*
Samples, A. M. B. 519, 521, *558*
Samuel, S. 175, *184*, 222, *253*, *255*, *325*
Samuelsen, S. O. *702*
Sanap, G. 843, *855*
Sancho, M. *699*
Sandberg, D. *177*, *848*
Sandels, S. 900, *922*
Sander, U. *922*
Sanders, M. 352, *386*, 544, *558*, 1125, *1171*
Sandin, J. 817, *852*
Sandlin, D. 158, *185*
Sandow, B. L. 577, *630*
Sanocki, T. 885, *922*
Santos, A. 331, *386*
Santos, J. A. 5, *35*
Saplioglu, M. *1034*
Sârbescu, P. 462, *509*
Sarin, R. K. *1082*
Sarkar, S. 474, *509*
Sass, T. R. 964, *981*
Saunby, C. S. *915*
Savage, S. W. 713, *791*
Savino, G. 970, *980*, *981*, 1015, *1034*
Savolainen, P. T. *1032*
Sawyer, B. D. 735, 763, 776, *784*, *791*
Sawyer, M. *1032*
Sayed, T. 61, *84*
Sayer, J. *129*, 226, *247*, *250*, *253*, 350, *386*, 894, 903, *923*, *924*
Sayer, T. B. *316*
Schade, J. 1145, *1171*
Schall, M. C. 373, *386*
Schaudt, W. A. *851*
Schechtman, E. 8, *38*, 71, 73, *80*, *85*, 229, 230, *254*, 391, 395, 400, *455*, *456*, 480, *509*, 522, *558*, 564, 567, 603, *633*, *634*,

646, 660, 661, 676, 678, 690, 692, 693, 694, 695, *708*, 1108, 1124, 1147, *1159*, *1171*, *1172*
Scheck, M. E. 352, *381*
Scheiber, F. *249*
Scheldeman, G. *922*
Schenkler, J. C. *707*
Schepers, J. P. 1016, 1017, 1025, 1026, *1033*
Schepers, P. 984, 992, 1005, 1009, 1010, 1011, 1018, 1019, *1030*, *1033*
Scherer, M. *317*, 587, *627*, *635*, *709*
Schexnayder, S. M. *974*
Schieber, F. 58, *85*, 145, 150, 153, 163, 164, *182*, *185*, 348, 349, 351, *382*, *386*, 884, *923*, 1125, 1127, *1171*, *1172*
Schieber, R. A. 880, 901, *923*
Schimek, P. M. 1120, *1168*
Schirokoff, A. *1172*
Schlag, B. 442, *450*, *981*, 1145, *1171*
Schlorholtz, B. 163, *185*
Schmidt, I. 157, *185*
Schmidt-Daffy, M. 108, *131*, 408, *455*
Schneck, M. E. *186*, *388*
Schneider, S. *624*
Schneider, W. 56, *84*, 101, *131*, 198, *253*
Schoettle, B. 159, *185*, 331, *386*, 1153, 1156, *1172*
Scholey, A. B. 622, *630*
Schömig, N. 838, *855*
Schonfeld, C. 114, *131*, 393, *455*, *982*
Schott, J. R. 357, *377*
Schramm, A. *1029*, *1034*
Schrank, D. 472, *509*
Schrauf, M. 351, *388*
Schroeder, P. 396, 400, 438, *456*, 719, 720, 721, 730, 731, 753, 770, 776, *791*, 985, 1001, 1013, *1033*
Schuberth, J. 667, *703*
Schultz, E. 661, *700*
Schulz, M. 1122, *1172*
Schulze, C. 442, *450*
Schumacher, M. B. *629*
Schuman, S. H. 479, *509*
Schwab, A. L. *1033*
Schwab, C. W. *854*
Schwalen, S. *708*
Schwartz, T. L. *182*
Schwartz Chassidim, H. *707*
Schwarz, C. *787*
Schwebel, D. C. 488, 491, *509*, 883, *923*
Schwing, R. C. 5, *35*
Scialfa, C. *80*, *128*, 220, 234, 240, *253*, *254*, 311, *322*, 368, *382*, 386, 469, *503*, 782, *788*, 884, *923*
Scofield, H. *850*
Scopatz, R. A. 883, *923*
Scott, D. 225, *248*
Scott, H. 175, *185*, 274, *323*
Scott-Parker, B. 302, *323*, 398, *456*, 576, *633*
Scuffham, P. 1009, 1013, *1033*, *1034*
Scully, M. *378*
Scurfield, R. *1170*
Searle, A. K. *850*
Sears, R. R. *504*
Sedman, A. J. *636*
Seeck, A. *1173*
Segal, A. 462, *506*
Segev, A. 727, *791*
Sehgal, M. *380*
Seidler, R. D. 58, *84*
Seiple, W. 162, *186*, *387*
Sekular, R. *182*
Sekuler, A. B. 352, *386*
Sekuler, R. 351, *382*, *385*, *386*
Selander, H. 200, *254*, 370, *386*
Selem, J. *977*
Selke, D. J. *248*
Seltzer, M. L. *509*
Sen, B. *783*
Senders, J. W. 191, *254*
Senserrick, T. *84*, 294, 307, *318*, *323*, *325*, *916*, *977*
Sentinella, J. 880, *923*
Seo, J. *179*
Seppala, T. *705*
Sethi, P. K. 376, *387*
Severing, K. *186*
Severson, J. *509*
Sewall, A. A. S. *915*
Sewall, A. S. *915*

Sexton, B. 49, *81*, 263, *317*, 467, *504*, 938, *975*
Sferco, R. 546, *554*
Shabanova, V. I. 27, *36*, 265, *320*, 344, *388*
Shafer, T. *783*
Shaham, M. 63, *85*, 227, *254*
Shahar, A. 955, *981*
Shaheen, S. 1010, *1033*, *1034*
Shalev, M. 257, *323*
Shankar, U. 929, 950, *981*
Shapira, N. A. *451*
Sharfi, T. 116, *132*, 164, *185*, 1089, 1128, *1172*
Shariff, A. 1156, *1160*
Sharma, S. 175, *183*
Sharp, J. 152, *185*, 331, *379*
Sharples, S. 66, *81*, 485, *504*
Sharwood, L. N. 819, *855*
Shattuck, T. *318*
Shaw, B. 352, *386*
Shaw, K. N. *922*, *1168*
Shaw, L. 370, *386*, 481, *509*
Shear, S. A. 495, *507*
Sheehan, M. 114, *131*, *455*
Shefer, S. *1159*
Sheiham, A. 479, *506*, 880, *919*
Sheldon, S. S. *178*
Shen, Z. 618, *626*
Shenton, C. 172, *179*
Shephard, R. J. 206, *256*
Sheppard, D. 884, *923*
Sheppard, E. 106, *130*
Sheppard, P. 307, *319*
Sherwood, N. 640, *703*
Shi, K. *555*
Shiekh, L. 401, *456*
Shiffrin, R. M. 56, *84*, 101, *131*, 198, *253*
Shiftan, Y. *126*
Shimamura, M. 519, 534, *558*
Shimshoni, Y. *81*, 302, 303, *317*, *323*
Shin, P. C. 114, *132*, 393, *456*
Shinar, D. 5, 8, 26, *38*, 44, 48, 51, 57, 58, 59, 60, 61, 62, 63, 65, 69, 70, 71, 77, *80*, *83*, *85*, *86*, 93, 95, 97, 101, 102, 106, 107, 114, 116, 121, *125*, *130*, *132*, 145, 146, 149, 151, 153, 155, 160, 162, 164, 170, 173, 174, *178*, *183*, *185*, 195, 197, 199, 200, 205, 206, 207, 208, 220, 223, 224, 225, 226, 227, 229, 230, 231, 234, 235, 236, 237, 238, 239, 240, 241, 244, *248*, *254*, *255*, 270, 272, 277, *315*, *323*, *324*, 348, 349, 350, 351, 352, 353, 354, 355, 367, *378*, *383*, *386*, *388*, 391, 392, 395, 396, 400, 406, 415, 419, 430, 432, 433, 434, 439, 440, 441, *448*, *456*, *457*, 461, 462, 463, 471, 473, 474, 475, 476, 477, 478, 480, 485, 492, 493, 494, 499, 500, *502*, *508*, *509*, 522, 523, *558*, 564, 567, 571, 573, 592, 593, 594, 596, 603, 604, 614, 619, *633*, *634*, 646, 648, 659, 660, 661, 676, 678, 690, 692, 693, 694, 695, *704*, *707*, *708*, 724, 727, 728, 738, 739, 744, 745, 746, 747, 748, 750, 751, 754, 761, 763, 766, *780*, *791*, *793*, 799, 805, 806, 818, 820, 824, 830, 838, 839, *851*, *854*, 874, 884, 890, 891, 893, 897, 910, *915*, *920*, *923*, *924*, 940, 942, 959, 960, 969, *976*, *981*, 992, 993, 996, 998, *1031*, *1034*, *1035*, 1046, 1050, 1061, 1062, *1082*, *1083*, 1089, 1108, 1116, 1117, 1121, 1125, 1128, 1129, *1159*, *1160*, *1172*, *1173*
Shirmohammadi, S. 843, *848*
Shoham, A. 110, *126*
Shope, J. 296, 300, *316*, *317*, *324*, *504*, *554*, *1035*
Short, J. B. *552*
Shova, K. C. 522, 538, *556*, *558*
Shreeve, M. S. *852*
Shu, C. C. *128*
Shuller, E. *980*
Shulman, K. *385*
Shults, R. A. 305, *325*, 521, 528, *553*, *555*, *559*, *624*, *626*, *633*, 770, *789*
Shumate, R. P. *624*
Shumway-Cook, A. 872, *923*
Shunamen, E. M. 910, *924*
Shurbutt, J. 233, *256*
Shutko, J. 747, *791*
Sichel, H. 481, *509*
Siebert, F. W. *509*
Siegel, P. *633*

Siemsen, D. 351, *385*
Sievänen, J. *1034*
Sifrit, K. *387*, *559*
Sihvola, N. 1140, *1172*
Silcock, B. R. 1111, *1167*
Silliman, R. A. *385*
Silveira, S. 162, *185*
Siman-Tov, M. 992, *1034*
Simmonds, D. C. V. 747, *782*
Simmons, L. *781*, *784*, *853*
Simon, B. 593, *634*
Simone, A. 95, *126*, *249*
Simons, D. J. 201, *254*
Simons, R. *707*
Simonsen, K. W. *82*, *703*
Simons-Morton, B. *83*, *129*, 296, 298, 300, 303, 304, 311, *318*, *322*, *323*, *325*, *786*
Simpson, E. 542, *558*
Simpson, H. 266, 277, 278, 282, 283, 285, 286, 299, *315*, *320*, *323*, 357, *383*, 818, *849*, 856, 1108, *1168*
Sims, L. B. 297, *325*
Sims, R. V. 146, 166, *185*
Sing, H. C. *854*
Singer, C. *39*
Singer, J. *129*, 298, *323*, 740, *787*
Singh, S. 13, *36*, 1057, 1058, *1083*, 1088, *1172*
Singhal, D. 285, *320*
Single, E. 601, *634*
Singleton, E. G. 692, *703*
Siren, A. 328, *381*
Sirois, B. *851*
Sivak, M. 15, 19, *38*, 108, *132*, 138, 146, 148, 159, *185*, 207, 213, 214, *252*, 331, 352, 354, *384*, *386*, 444, *454*, 479, *509*, 575, *632*, 940, *980*, 1027, *1034*, 1153, 1156, 1157, *1172*
Sivinski, R. 540, *559*
Skipper, B. J. *625*
Skurtveit, S. 576, *634*, 641, 642, 645, 684, *700*, *703*, *708*
Slavova, S. 530, *553*, *782*
Sleet, D. 124, *127*, *553*, *559*, *626*, *628*, *633*, *1170*
Sloan, F. A. 602, *629*
Sloane, M. *38*, *178*, *183*, *184*, 352, *377*, *387*
Sloboda, J. A. 725, *792*
Slor, Z. 726, *781*
Slørdala, L. *82*
Smahel, T. 727, *792*
Smailbegovic, M. *1159*
Smart, R. G. 464, 472, 492, *503*, *510*, *625*
Smeed, R. J. 22, *38*
Smialek, J. E. *978*
Smids, J. 1144, *1172*
Smiley, A. 6, *39*, 116, *132*, *631*, 664, 667, 668, *708*, 727, 728, *781*, *792*, 828, *855*, 1147, *1172*
Smith, A. 769, *792*, 840, 855
Smith, B. H. 376, *387*
Smith, D. 768, *793*
Smith, D. I. 481, *510*
Smith, D. L. 1120, *1168*
Smith, D. M. *377*
Smith, G. *179*, *325*, *379*, 487, *508*
Smith, I. 22, *39*
Smith, J. A. 690, 693, *708*
Smith, J. D. *504*, 885, *916*
Smith, K. *922*
Smith, L. A. *253*
Smith, M. E. 695, *702*
Smith, N. 395, *448*
Smith, R. *554*, *782*, *976*
Smith, S. B. 820, 821, *855*
Smith, S. S. *382*, 832, *856*
Smith, T. A. *974*
Smith, W. S. 208, *252*
Smither, J. A.-A. 156, *186*
Smithers, D. D. 647, 688, *700*
Smolensky, M. H. *850*, *855*
Smoot, T. M. *185*
Smouse, R. 618, *634*
Smyth, C. C. *794*
Snenghi, R. *709*
Snow, R. W. *511*
Snyder, D. 401, *456*
Snyder, M. G. 873, 875, 876, 877, 881, 885, *923*
Soccolich, S. A. *81*, *127*, *783*
Sockeel, P. *921*
Soderstrom, C. A. 668, *708*

Sodhi, M. 744, 774, *792*
Soh, J. *980*
Sohn, Y. W. *316*
Sohn, J. *626*
Sojourner, R. S. 138, *186*
Solomon, D. 403, 410, 411, *456*
Solomon, M. *507*, 522, 531, *553*, *555*, *782*
Solowij, N. 660, *708*
Somat, A. *1160*
Sommer, D. *851*
Sønderlund, A. *631*
Soole, D. W. 437, *456*
Sørensen, M. *35*, *81*, *180*, *449*, *626*, *850*, *917*, *1030*, *1163*
Sorimachi, Y. *628*
Sosin, D. M. *553*, 963, *981*
Souleyrette, R. *1165*
Spadafora, P. *254*
Spalek, T. M. 713, *794*
Speigel, D. 276, *319*
Speizer, F. E. *849*
Spence, C. 5, *36*
Spencer, M. B. 362, *387*
Spitzenstetter, F. *184*
Spolander, K. 311, *323*
Sporkert, F. *699*
Sprattler, K. 615, *634*
Spurgin, A. *703*
Srinivasan, R. *1161*
Srinivasan, S. *383*
Stalvey, B. *183*
Stamatiadis, N. 1116, *1172*
Stamp, J. 1039, *1083*
Stanley, L. M. *849*
Stanojevic, D. *506*
Stanojevic, P. 462, *506*, *509*
Stansifer, R. L. *324*, *457*, *793*, *1035*, *1083*, *1173*
Stanton, N. A. 5, 6, *39*, *187*, *795*, *1161*, *1174*
Staplin, L. 158, 162, 341, 350, 353, 367, 368, 374, 375, 376, *379*, *387*, 462, *510*, *792*, *793*, 904, 914, *923*, *1161*
Starkey, N. J. 107, *126*, 201, *249*, 307, *319*
Starmer, G. 222, *251*, 643, 680, *708*
Starnes 820, *855*
Starnes, M. 518, 535, 539, *559*
Starsky, N. J. 399, *447*
Staughton, G. C. 415, *455*, 1050, 1054, *1082*
Stavrinos, D. *923*
StClaire, V. 961, *978*
Stead, M. 1110, *1172*
Steel, P. *80*, *782*
Steentoft, A. 643, 684, *699*, *700*
Steg, L. 725, *793*
Stehr, M. 528, *553*
Steinberg, L. 881, *923*
Steiner, C. A. *975*
Steinfeld, A. 817, *849*
Steinhardt, D. 114, *131*, *455*
Stelmach, G. E. 58, *84*, *85*
Sten, T. 311, *319*
Stephan, K. *256*
Stephens, A. N. 462, 483, 486, *510*, 750, *792*
Stephenson, S. 594, *629*
Steriu, M. 989, 990, 1003, 1012, 1016, *1034*
Stern, E. *379*
Sternlund, S. *39*
Steudle, K. 76, *84*
Stevens, A. 5, *38*, 534, *558*, 715, *790*, 1145, *1171*
Stevenson, M. 721, *788*, *855*, 1015, *1034*
Stewart, J. R. *635*, *916*, *925*, *1029*, *1175*
Stiebel, J. 419, 434, *456*
Stigson, H. 895, *922*
Stiller, G. *556*
Stimpson, J. P. 647, *709*
Stipdonk, H. 984, *1034*
Stitzel, J. D. *553*, *558*
Stitzer, M. L. 661, *703*
Stock, J. R. 277, *323*
Stockwell, T. 601, *634*
Stoduto, G. 464, *510*
Stolk, R. P. *510*
Stolwyk, R. J. 359, *387*
Stone, B. M. 857
Stone, K. *249*
Stones, M. J. *378*, *624*
Stough, C. 696, *701*, *706*

Stout, E. M. 602, *629*
Stradling, S. G. *131*, *452*, 467, 472, 477, *506*, *507*, *508*, *510*, *981*, *1082*
Strandroth, J. 119, *132*, *981*, 1149, *1173*
Strassburger, R. *636*
Strayer, D. L. 46, *85*, 93, *129*, 197, *254*, 723, 742, 745, 746, 747, 748, 749, 752, 759, 761, 762, 764, 765, 772, 775, *782*, *783*, *792*, 838, *856*
Strayer, D. S. 759, 775, *792*
Street, W. N. *784*
Streff, F. M. 50, 519, 520, 521, 522, 526, *559*, 601, *630*
Strohmetz, D. B. *503*, *625*
Struckman-Johnson, C. 733, *792*
Struckman-Johnson, D. *792*
Struttmann, T. W. *782*
Stulginskas, J. V. 50, *85*
Sturgis, D. R. *385*
Sturgis, S. P. *184*
Stuster, J. 411, 413, 418, *456*, 501, *510*, 603, 606, *634*
Stutts, J. 177, *186*, 337, *387*, 465, *506*, *635*, 715, 717, 718, 721, 730, 731, 736, 752, *792*, *793*, 820, 822, 827, 846, *856*, 857, *918*
Styles, T. 159, *179*
Su, E. *560*
Subirats, P. *1160*
Subramanian, R. 13, *36*
Sudweeks, J. *83*, *789*, *1082*
Sudweeks, J. D. *129*, *452*, *786*, *1081*, *1167*
Sue, L. P. *559*
Suissa, S. *703*
Sulander, P. *1167*
Sullivan, J. M. 886, 887, *924*, 1098, *1173*
Sullivan, K. *382*
Sullman, M. 5, *39*, 483, *510*, *784*
Summala, H. 5, 23, *37*, 47, *80*, 107, 115, 121, *130*, 143, 172, *180*, *182*, 199, 206, 226, 242, *251*, *254*, *319*, 357, 358, *386*, *388*, 417, *457*, 469, 479, 486, 487, *503*, *506*, *508*, *510*, 712, 735, *786*, *787*, *790*, *793*, 820, *856*, 1014, *1033*, *1034*, 1080, *1082*, 1088, 1119, 1121, *1167*, *1168*, *1173*
Sun, L. 175, *182*
Sun, R. 873, *924*
Sundfør, H. B. *1030*
Surman, C. *508*
Surry, J. 308, 309, *324*
Susilo, D. 884, *915*
Susilo, Y. O. 884, *915*
Sutcliffe, P. *508*
Sutter, D. 1134, *1173*
Sutter, S. 1133, *1171*
Sutton, L. R. 667, 682, *708*
Svenson, O. *253*
Svensson, U. 815, 816, 817, *856*
Swaim, R. C. *504*
Swann, P. *701*, *852*
Swanson, A. *249*
Swearer, J. M. 361, *380*
Sweedler, B. 573, 608, *634*, *635*, *1174*
Sweers, W. *1033*
Swift, D. *704*
Swinburne, G. C. 307, *323*
Switzer, F. 225, *248*
Swope, J. G. 207, *252*
Sylvester, T. O. 152, *185*
Symbaluk, D. G. 462, 484, *505*
Symmons, M. 957, *976*
Syvanen, M. 195, *254*
Sze, N. N. *1174*
Szegedi, A. 661, *700*
Szlyk, J. P. 162, *186*, 356, *381*, *387*
Szobot, C. M. *506*
Szymkowski, R. Y. *1160*

Tacker, H. L. *915*
Tagawa, T. *85*, *982*
Tagg, S. *1172*
Taieb, M. 747, *793*
Taieb-Maimon, M. 62, *85*, 224, 225, 228, 230, *254*
Taillard, J. *854*, *855*
Tait, A. 144, *181*
Takayama, L. 801, 834, 837, 838, *856*
Talbot, R. 712, 714, *793*
Talebpour, A. 433, *457*
Tan, Y. Y. *853*
Tang, K. H. 971, *981*

Tapiro, H. 175, *186*, 880, 883, *924*
Tarawneh, M. *387*
Tasca, L. 464, *510*
Tassi, P. *849*
Tate, F. 444, *447*
Tatler, B. W. 713, *791*
Tator, C. *132*, *456*
Tattam, B. *708*
Taubman-Ben-Ari, O. 47, *83*, *84*, 296, 302, *321*, *322*, *324*, 460, 484, 487, *507*, *510*
Tauson, R. A. *794*
Tay, R. 339, 364, *386*, *387*, 462, *508*, 610, *634*, *919*
Taylor, D. H. 117, *132*
Taylor, H. R. *382*
Taylor, K. 222, *250*
Taylor, M. 1009, *1034*
Taylor, N. *130*, *786*
Taylor, S. *187*
Taylor, T. 71, *85*, 175, *186*, 222, *255*
Tecl, J. *34*
Tefft, B. C. 290, *325*, 820, *853*, 896, *924*
Tejero, P. *1160*
Tenenbaum, J. *559*
Teng, J. 618, *626*
Tennstedt, S. L. *377*
Teoh, E. R. *320*, 757, *788*, 970, *981*
Terán-Santos, J. 821, *856*
Terentacoste, M. *1167*
Teret, S. P. *629*
Terry, P. 667, *709*
Teschke, K. *1033*
Tey, L. K. *853*
Tharp, V. 605, *634*
Thatcher, J. W. 675, *702*
Theeuwes, J. R. 5, *39*
Theunissen, E. L. *629*, *700*
Thiele, K. 820, *853*
Thierie, M. *448*
Thierry, P. *184*
Thiessen, R. 395, *451*
Thiffault, P. 799, 818, 833, *856*
Thigthorsson, H. 119, *132*
Thom, D. 931, *976*, *977*, 1023, *1031*
Thomas, A. *975*
Thomas, F. D. 312, *317*, *320*, *324*, 1108, *1173*
Thomas, G. *386*
Thomas, I. *1029*
Thomas, L. *555*, *627*, *856*, *976*, *1031*, *1032*, *1161*, *1164*
Thomas, M. *854*, *918*, *1165*
Thomas, P. 1092, *1164*, *1173*
Thomas, S. *317*, *627*
Thompson, J. 1015, *1034*
Thompson, L. L. 883, *924*
Thompson, N. J. 901, *923*
Thompson, R. S. *553*, *626*
Thomsen, J. 1005, *1029*
Thorne, D. R. *854*
Thornley, S. J. 998, *1034*
Thornton, J. 440, *455*
Thorslund, B. *1028*
Thuen, F. *704*
Thurstone, C. *708*
Tibshirani, R. J. 433, 443, *454*, *455*, 753, 755, 759, *791*, 1113, *1171*
Tickner, A. H. 747, *782*
Tidwell, S. A. *552*
Tight, M. *922*
Tignor, S. C. *1160*
Tijerina, L. 724, 768, 769, 775, *784*, *791*, *793*
Tilhet-Coartet, S. *631*
Tillgren, P. *1159*
Tillman, W. A. 459, 460, 461, 479, 482, 483, *510*, 1027, *1034*
Tillman, W. T. *182*
Timmerman, M. 600, *634*
Tin, S. T. 999, *1034*
Tinetti, M. E. 26, *36*
Tingvall, C. 10, *35*, *39*, *132*, 548, 549, *556*, *981*, 1086, 1136, 1149, *1159*, *1164*, *1167*, *1173*
Tiplady, B. 622, *630*
Tippetts, A. S. 163, *183*, 590, 615, 616, *630*, *634*, *635*, *704*
Tipsuntornsak, N. *979*
Tison, J. 531, *555*, 621, *625*, *634*, 735, *782*, *793*, *919*
Titze, S. *1032*

Tivesten, E. 739, *793*
Tobey, H. N. 910, *924*
Todd, M. 296, *317*
Toennes, S. W. *700*
Toet, A. 994, *1035*
Tofield, M. I. 956, *982*
Tokudome, S. *628*
Toledo, T. 47, 71, *81*, *84*, 296, 300, 301, 302, *317*, *319*, *322*, *323*, *324*
Tomasevic, N. *256*, *455*
Tomer-Fishman, T. 738, *793*
Ton, L. P. *979*
Tonigan, J. S. *635*
Tontsch, A. *86*
Toomey, K. *504*
Toomey, T. L. 591, *628*, *631*, *635*
Toops, H. A. 4, *39*
Tops, M. 840, *853*
Torbic, D. J. *458*, *1165*
Torfs, R. *1029*
Törnros, J. *131*, 740, 744, 747, 748, 759, *790*, *793*
Torpey, S. 364, *387*
Torres, P. *704*
Totten, B. 478, *511*, 726, *794*
Touliou, K. *86*
Tournier, I. *249*
Towner, E. *916*
Townsend, R. N. *1161*
Toxopeus, R. 368, *387*
Tractinsky, N. 114, 406, *457*, 485, *509*, 738, 739, *791*, *793*, 884, *924*
Tradisauskas, N. *1167*
Trafton, J. G. 741, *788*
Traines, M. *385*
Traube, E. *636*
Trawley, S. *249*, *316*, *792*
Traynor, T. L. 577, *635*
Trbovich, P. L. *181*, *785*
Treat, J. R. 26, *38*, 269, 270, *324*, 414, 416, *457*, 481, *507*, 713, 714, 715, 716, 722, *793*, 1017, *1035*, 1045, 1046, 1047, 1048, 1049, 1050, 1053, 1054, 1080, *1081*, *1082*, *1083*, 1088, 1154, *1173*
Trempel, R. 116, *127*, 336, 344, *378*
Trentacoste, M. *82*, *129*, *1081*
Trick, L. 6, *35*, 272, 274, *321*, 368, *387*
Trifillis, A. L. *708*
Triggs, T. 66, *82*, 121, *127*, 217, 224, *255*, *256*, *325*, 359, *387*, 439, *450*, *455*, *629*, *705*, 1117, *1164*
Trilling, D. 340, *380*
Trimble, T. *1160*
Troeell, G. M. *915*
Troglauer, T. 734, 735, *793*
Trost, L. *1031*
Troszak, L. *975*
Trout, N. *249*
Troutbeck, R. 138, 161, 165, *186*, *187*
Truman, W. *379*, *850*, *974*, *975*
Trutschel, U. *851*
Tsai, L. C. 971, *981*
Tseng, C. M. 1112, *1161*
Tsimhoni, O. 768, 769, 775, *793*
Tubré, T. *504*
Tucker, M. E. *626*
Tucker, T. G. *919*
Tumbas, N. S. *324*, *457*, *793*, *1035*, *1083*, *1173*
Tunbridge, R. *634*, 646, *709*
Tunnicliff, D. J. *982*
Tuokko, H. *187*, 366, *383*, *387*, *388*
Tuokkom, H. *383*
Turano, K. A. *178*, 870, *917*
Türker, Ö. 51, *85*
Turner, B. 1116, *1173*
Turner, C. 487, *510*
Turner, S. A. 26, *39*, 862, *924*
Turner, S. M. *917*, *1030*
Turrill, J. *85*, *792*, *856*
Tuttle, S. J. 903, *924*
Tuydes-Yaman, H. 234, 239, *251*
Tversky, A. 108, 115, *132*, 408, *451*
Twisk, D. 75, *85*, 429, *457*, *1011*, *1033*, *1035*
Tyler, T. R. 493, *510*
Tynan, D. 1155, *1175*
Tyroch, A. H. 535, *559*
Tyrrell, L. 958, *976*
Tyrrell, R. A. 157, *187*, 203, *251*, 893, 894, 902, *915*, *920*, *923*, *924*, *925*, *1036*
Tzamalouka, G. *1034*

Uc, E. *180*, *377*, *380*
Uchida, N. 75, *85*, 935, *982*
Uddman, M. 817, *852*
Ulleberg, P. 465, *510*, 1109, *1170*
Ullenberg, P. 79, *84*
Ullman, G. L. *129*
Ulmer, R. G. *325*, *385*, 933, 964, *981*, *982*
Ulupinar, P. 765, *781*
Umar, B. S. R. 958, *982*
Ünal, A. B. 725, *793*
Underwood, G. 5, *38*, 107, *126*, 164, 172, *179*, *249*, 272, 275, *316*, *324*, 729, *783*, 940, 943, *973*, *981*, *982*
Underwood, J. 275, *324*, 943, *982*
Unverzagt, F. W. *377*
Ushijima, S. *980*
Utesch, F. *81*
Uvijls, A. *186*

Vaa, T. 5, 6, *39*, 79, *81*, *84*, 90, 123, *132*, *133*, *180*, 419, *449*, *457*, 602, *626*, *850*, *917*, *1030*, 1109, 1143, 1144, *1163*, *1170*, *1173*
Vaillancourt, D. R. *184*, *385*
Valdes-Dapena, P. 1105, *1173*
Valent, F. *978*
Valero-Mora, P. 75, *86*, *1034*
Vallurupalli, R. *1170*
Valtat, C. *855*
Van Aerschot, G. *318*
Van Bon-Martens, M. J. H. *629*
Vance, D. E. *180*
van den Berg, T. J. T. P. 151, *186*
Vandenberghe, D. *318*
Vandenbulcke, G. *1029*
van der Horst, A. R. A. 1017, *1035*
van der Horst, R. 5, *39*
Van der Hulst, M. 812, 833, 845, *852*
van der Leden, N. *1035*
Van der Linden, T. *703*
van der Sluiszen, N. N. J. J. 573, *629*
van der Spek, N. *1159*
Vanderwolf, P. 534, 545, *552*
Van Dyke, M. *785*
van Egmond, T. *706*
Van Elslande, P. *1081*
Van Gerven, M. H. *853*
Van Houten, R. *131*, *455*, 532, 533, 534, *556*, *559*, 907, 908, 910, *918*, *922*, *925*, 1111, *1168*
van Laar, M. *707*
Vanlaar, W. 79, *86*, 300, *324*, 363, 368, *387*, *388*, 567, 609, *635*, 697, *702*, 820, *856*, 1040, 1042, *1083*
Van Loon, E. *249*, *316*, 729, *783*
Van Loon, J. 802, *853*
Van Nes, N. 75, *85*, 429, *457*, 724, *782*
Van Oers, H. A. M. *629*
Vanparijs, J. 989, *1035*
van Ratingen, M. 1137, *1173*
Vanrie, J. *448*
Van Rooy, D. L. 472, 483, 484, *510*
van Schagen, I. 416, 429, 433, *447*, *450*, 1111, *1167*
Vansteenkiste, P. 175, *186*, 1011, 1017, *1035*
van Strijp-Houtenbos, M. *1034*
Van Vlierden, K. *379*
Van Wee, B. *1033*
Van Willigenburg, G. M. *853*
Van Winsum, W. 226, *255*
Vardaki, S. *458*, 1131, *1174*
Varghese, C. 929, 950, *981*
Várhelyi, A. 1143, *1174*
Vashitz, G. 227, *255*
Vastenburg, E. *792*
Vaughan, R. G. 958, *982*
Vecchiato, G. *849*
Vecellio, R. L. 872, *915*
Vecovski, V. *1174*
Vedung, E. *1159*
Vega, J. *699*
Vegega, M. E. 880, *923*
Veldstra, J. A. *707*
Velenis, E. *129*
Velichkovsky, B. M. 168, *186*
Vella, M. 1158, *1174*
Vereeck, L. 905, *916*
Vermeeren, A. 573, *629*, 659, *704*, *709*
Vernick, J. S. 278, *324*, *629*
Vernon, D. D. *552*
Verreault, R. 50, *85*

Verriest, G. 154, *186*
Verster, J. C. *853*
Verstraete, A. G. *82*, *628*, 689, *703*, *709*
Verwey, W. B. 799, 801, 802, 818, 830, 834, 835, 838, *856*
Viano, D. C. 545, *556*
Vickers, G. 1085, *1174*
Victor, T. 46, *86*, 102, 176, *186*, *133*, 170, *183*, *787*, 1076, *1083*, 1146, *1168*
Vienne, F. *249*, 369, *386*, *919*, *974*
Vignali, V. 95, *126*, *249*
Vilkki, J. *180*
Villino, G. *552*
Vincent, A. 846, *856*
Vincent, F. *631*
Vingilis, E. *449*
Vingrys, A. J. 154, *186*
Violani, C. *853*
Violano, P. *791*
Vis, A. 931, 940, *982*
Vis, M. *1173*
Visser, E. 482, *510*
Viström, M. 215, *247*
Vitale, C. *1159*
Vivoda, J. M. 522, 523, *554*, *559*
Vlahogianni, E. *385*
Vlakveld, W. P. 220, 221, 222, *255*, 264, 265, 268, *324*, *1035*
Voaklander, D. *1031*
Voas, R. 110, *128*, 296, *317*, *322*, 577, 587, 593, 594, 604, 611, 614, 615, 616, *626*, *627*, *628*, *629*, *630*, *632*, *634*, *635*, *636*, 645, *702*, *704*, *709*, 1112, *1174*
Vogel, K. 223, *255*
Vogelzang, M. 240, 241, *254*
Vogrincic, C. *449*
Vöhringer-Kuhnt, T. *506*
Völker-Dieben, H. J. *186*
Vollrath, M. 591, *635*, 662, *699*
von Hebenstreit, B. 151, *186*
Vonhoff, D. J. *186*
Vonsalus, K. P. 94, *128*
Vrkljan, B. *386*, *387*, *388*
Vrkljanb, B. *187*
Vrkljann, B. *383*
Vukelich, M. 241, *255*
Vulcan, P. 595, *628*
Vuurman, E. F. P. M. *704*

Waard, D. 747, *781*
Wachtel, J. 730, *794*
Waddell, L. P. 110, *133*, 738, *794*
Wadley, V. G. *180*, *386*
Wagenaar, A. C. 50, 519, 520, 521, 522, 526, *559*, 590, 591, *624*, *631*, *635*
Wagner, A. *552*
Wagner, E. *705*, *854*, *925*
Wagner, J. G. *636*
Wagner, M. *381*
Wahdea, M. *82*
Wählberg, A. 5, *39*
Wahlström, B. 365, *381*
Waisel, S. 571, 573, 593, 594, 604, *634*
Wakai, S. *557*, *979*
Wald, M. L. 769, *794*
Walker, B. N. 750, *786*
Walker, F. *382*, *451*
Walker, G. 6, *39*, 462, *510*, *795*, 1120, *1174*
Walker, I. *974*, 999, 1000, *1035*
Walker, L. 5, *34*
Wall, J. 1144, *1174*
Wall, R. *918*
Wallace, B. H. *974*
Wallace, J. F. *701*
Wallace, K. *509*
Wallace, P. 957, *982*
Wallbank, C. *506*
Waller, P. F. 283, *324*, *504*, 583, 584, *635*
Wallis, T. S. 222, *255*, 274, *324*
Walls, H. C. *700*
Wallwork, M. J. 1123, *1174*
Walmsley, S. *629*, *705*
Walpole, B. 905, *921*
Walsh, J. M. 567, *636*, 647, 648, 687, 688, 696, *701*, *704*, *709*
Walsh, S. P. 738, *794*
Walter, S. R. 1009, *1035*
Walton, D. 399, *457*
Walunas, J. B. *915*
Walz, M. 404, 414, 416, 421, *447*
Wang, J. *322*, *323*, 820, *852*, *925*, *1168*

Wang, M. Q. 488, *503*
Wang, W. *925*
Wang, Y. *184*, 312, *324*, *791*, *852*
Wang, Z. *925*
Wann, J. 155, *184*, 956, *976*, *982*
Wanvik, P. O. 1127, *1174*
Ward, H. *916*
Ward, N. *83*, 445, *457*, 472, *511*, 660, 662, 667, 668, 669, *704*, *709*, 747–748, *790*
Ward, P. *379*, *850*, *974*, *975*
Warner, W. L. 277, *324*
Warren, C. R. *504*
Warren, D. 411, *456*
Warshawsky-Livne, L. 44, 48, 57, *86*, 205, 206, 207, 226, *255*, 354, *388*
Washington, S. 1010, *1030*
Wasielewski, P. 223, *250*
Watanabem, J. *979*
Watelain, E. *921*
Waterman, M. 472, *511*
Waterson, B. 224, *248*
Watling, C. N. 820, 832, *856*
Watshon, G. S. *385*
Watson, A. *503*, 600, *635*
Watson, B. *84*, *323*, 437, *456*, 462, 466, *503*, *507*, 508, *509*, 600, *633*, *635*, *794*, *919*, 949, *982*
Watson, G. S. *788*
Watson, J. B. 592, *635*
Watson, L. 393, *457*
Waugh, J. D. 745, 748, 765, *794*
Waylen, A. E. 462, *511*
Weatherburn, D. *704*
Weaver, B. *378*, *626*, 667, *699*, *701*
Weaver, J. K. *323*
Webster, G. D. 931, *979*
Weegard, K. *187*, *388*
Wege, C. 102, *133*
Wegman, F. 983, 984, 986, 993, 1003, 1006, 1007, 1008, 1011, 1019, 1022, 1023, *1033*, *1035*, 1086, 1088, *1167*, *1174*
Wei, V. F. 1008, 1016, *1035*
Weidler, D. J. *636*
Weih, L. M. *382*
Weijermars, W. A. M. 1007, *1035*
Weinstein, H. B. *385*
Weintraub, L. *34*, *178*
Weir, D. H. 89, *130*
Weiß, T. *322*
Weiss, A. *918*, *1165*
Weiss, M. *316*, *553*, *782*
Weiss, T. *255*, 312, *324*
Weiss, U. *1031*
Wells, H. 5, *39*
Wells, J. *183*, 286, 314, *317*, *325*, 522, 535, *554*, *559*, *627*
Wells, S. *628*, 958, *982*
Wells-Parker, E. 470, 471, *511*, 620, *635*
Welsh, C. *709*
Welsh, R. *86*, *385*
Wenjun, C. 48, *81*
Wennig, R. *624*
Werneke, J. 1004, *1029*
Weserberg, V. *626*
West, C. G. 177, *186*, 350, 354, *388*
West, L. B. Jr. 403, 414, *457*
West, S. K. *178*, *179*, *184*
Westerhuis, F. 1000, *1029*
Westerkamp, U. *1159*
Westerman, S. J. *128*, *786*
Westina, A. A. *82*
Westlake, J. *852*
Westlake, W. 176, 177, *186*
Westwood, D. *185*, *323*
Wets, G. *125*, 300, *324*, *379*, *1161*
Wetton, M. 106, *128*, 221, 222, *250*, *255*, 275, *318*, *382*
Wetzel, J. A. *247*
Wetzel, L. *379*
Whatley, J. *978*
Wheeler, D. 613–614, *626*, *633*, *635*, *636*
Whelan, M. 274, 308, *325*
Whissell, R. W. 396, *457*
Whitaker, L. A. 241, *255*
White, C. B. 766, *794*
White, D. *380*
White, J. M. *703*
White, K. M. *794*, *982*
White, M. *553*
White, M. A. *703*
White, M. F. *183*

White, M. P. 758, *794*
White, W. T. 1133, *1174*
Whiter, M. F. *184*
Whitley, K. *249*
Whitlock, F. A. 463, *511*
Whitlock, G. *850*
Whitton, M. J. 257, *322*, 362, *385*, 395, *454*
Wickens, C. D. 94, 95, 99, *128*, *133*, 175, 195, *255*, 723, 741, 747, 765, 768, *785*, *794*, 1150, *1170*
Wiebe, D. J. 617, *629*
Wiegand, D. *849*
Wiener, K. K. 110, *133*, 738, *794*
Wier, M. L. 1089, *1164*
Wierwille, W. 205, *255*, 405, *447*, 799, 816, *849*, *856*
Wiese, B. 931, 934, 937, *980*
Wiesenthal, D. L. 472, 478, 495, 496, 500, *505*, *511*, 726, *794*
Wieskotter, B. *1031*
Wiewille, W. *784*
Wiggins, S. 281, 287, 288, 289, 299, *325*
Wightman, J. A. *788*
Wiklund, M. 281, *321*, 343, *381*
Wikman, A.-S. *180*, 357, 358, *388*
Wilbur, M. 985, 1001, 1013, *1033*
Wilde, G. 9, *39*, 89, 117, 118, *133*, *452*, 595, *636*, 1148, *1174*
Wilensky, J. T. *381*, *387*
Wilke, A. 1019, 1020, *1035*
Wilkins, A. J. 158, *184*
Wilkins, L. 153, 155, 156, 166, *187*
Wilkinson, C. J. 680, *706*
Wilkinson, I. M. S. *636*
Wilkinson, P. K. 565, 566, *636*
Will, K. E. 543, *559*
Will, S. 102, *133*
Willan, A. R. *922*
Willeke, H. *980*
Willett, W. C. *1032*
Willette, R. E. 567, *636*
Williams, A. 114, 120, *127*, 130, 261, 283, 285, 286, 290, 294, 297, 298, 299, 304, 305, *317*, *320*, *322*, *323*, *325*, 344, *383*, *385*, *388*, 393, *449*, 522, 528, 531, 535, *554*, *559*, *560*, *624*, *627*, 933, *978*, *981*, 1091, 1109, 1128, 1129, *1168*, *1171*, *1173*, *1174*
Williams, C. 376, *386*, *388*
Williams, J. B. 683, *702*
Williams, M. *511*, 620, *635*
Williams, R. L. 1111, *1174*
Williams, S. 769, *794*
Williams, T. *382*
Williams, A. F. 313, *325*, 591, *627*
Williams Jr., R. D. *636*
Williamson, A. *380*, 797, 798, 857
Williamson, A. M. 799, 810, 811, 824, 825, 826, 829, 833, *851*, *856*
Williamson, A. R. 84, *256*, 1029
Willis, C. *458*
Willis, D. P. 987, *1036*
Willis, S. L. *378*
Willness, C. R. *80*, *782*
Wills, M. *636*
Wilson, C. 435, *458*
Wilson, D. 368, *387*
Wilson, F. A. 647, *709*
Wilson, G. F. 405, *458*
Wilson, K. G. *850*
Wilson, M. *179*
Wilson, T. *82*, *129*, *1081*, *1167*
Wimmer, M. *786*
Windsor, M. B. *784*
Winkler, C. *250*
Winn, D. G. 535, *552*
Winner, H. 6, *39*
Winslow, L. *382*
Winston, C. 547, *560*
Winston, F. K. *316*, *322*, 538, 540, 542, 544, 547, *554*, *557*, *560*, *922*
Winterbottom, M. *187*, *793*
Winters, M. *1033*
Wishart, D. E. *982*
Wist, E. R. 351, *388*
Witkowski, T. L. *507*
Wittenborn, J. R. 677, *709*
Wochinger, K. 564, *624*, 644, *700*, *783*
Wogalter, M. S. 241, *256*, 757, 758, *794*
Woldrich, M. *552*
Wolf, E. *184*, 352, *388*

Wolf, J. M. *503*, *625*
Wolf, S. P. *385*
Wolff, J. S. 241, *256*
Wolkin, J. *250*
Wollmer, P. *629*
Wolt, K. K. *1033*
Wong, K. K. *855*
Wong, S. C. 1099, *1174*
Wong, Y. D. 227, *256*
Woo, T. H. 1112, *1161*
Wood, J. *80*, 138, 144, 145, 149, 157, 158, 161, 165, 177, *178*, *181*, *184*, *186*, *187*, 220, 221, *251*, *255*, *256*, 351, 352, 359, 363, *377*, *388*, 893, 903, *924*, *925*, 994, 995, 996, 997, 999, 1014, *1036*
Woodall, K. L. 647, *709*
Woodall, W. G. 612, 621, *626*, *633*, *635*, *636*
Woodman, T. T. 110, *126*
Woods, H. M. 481, *505*
Woodward, A. 415, *453*, 999, *1034*
Woodward, M. *700*, 721, *788*, *1160*
Woof, M. W. *705*
Wooldridge, M. D. *449*, *1165*
Woollacott, M. 872, *923*
Woolley, J. *84*
Woolnough, A. 147, 162, 360, *383*, *388*
Woolridge, M. D. 400, *458*
Woolsey, C. L. *636*
Worde, S. *1170*
Wortman, R. H. 217, 218, *256*
Wrapson, W. 442, *458*
Wreggit, S. S. *856*
Wright, C. C. 955, *973*
Wright, G. R. 206, *256*
Wright, J. G. 535, *555*
Wright, K. A. 667, *709*
Wright, N. A. 845, 857
Wu, C. *795*, 875, *924*, *925*, 1019, 1027, *1036*
Wu, H. 821, 857
Wu, Y. 175, *187*, *1031*, 1117, *1174*, *1175*
Wulf, G. *976*
Wüst, J. C. *1033*

Xian, H. *181*, *786*
Xie, J. F. 817, 857
Xie, M. 817, 857
Xiong, H. 908, *925*
Xiong, L. *925*
Xiong, Y. *131*
Xu, M. *181*, *786*
Xu, Z. *917*
Xuan, D. 618, *626*

Yadav, R. P. 595, 597, 598, 598, 599, *636*
Yadron, D. 1155, *1175*
Yager, C. 747, *794*
Yagil, D. 261, *325*
Yair, N. 61, *84*
Yamashita, E. 944, *978*
Yang, C. J. 1025, 1026, *1036*
Yang, C. Y. D. 233, *256*
Yang, D. *181*, *786*
Yang, J. 370, *388*, 873, 898, *925*
Yang, M. C. K. *451*
Yan-Go, F. 821, 857
Yanko, M. R. 713, *794*
Yannis, G. *34*, *385*, 394, 408, 426, *458*, 566, *625*, 740, 745, 747, 770, 771, *794*, *795*, 871, *921*, 1040, 1042, *1083*, 1121, *1173*, *1175*
Yao, J. *704*
Yao, L. 1027, *1036*
Yarmazaki, M. 519, *558*
Yates, J. F. 115, *133*, 488, *511*
Yazdi, S. M. *790*
Ye, J. 519, 523, 534, *555*, 963, *976*
Ye, T. J. 1059, *1081*
Yee, D. 373, *388*
Yegles, M. *624*
Yehiel, D. 460, 484, *510*
Yekhshatyan, L. *787*
Yeshurun, Y. 713, *787*
Yeung, J. S. 227, *256*
Yingling, J. E. *703*
Yip, H. F. *1174*
Yolton, R. L. *708*
York, I. 971, *982*
Young, A. L. *560*
Young, K. 5, *38*, *84*, 175, *187*, 230, 244, 246, *256*, 455, 722, 724, 776, *782*, *785*, *795*

Young, M. S. 143, 144, *187*, 727, 730, *795*
Young, R. 755, 757, 763, *795*, 838, 857, 1077, *1083*
Young, T. 821, 857
Ytterbom, U. *455*
Yu, J. 217, *251*, 479, *511*, 576, 620, *636*
Yu, L. *377*
Yule, U. 481, *505*

Zacklad, A. L. 108
Zadok, D. *781*
Zador, P. 159, *181*, *322*, 419, *458*, 535, *560*, 577, 615, *631*, *636*
Zafian, T. *184*, *253*, 312, *325*
Zaidel, D. 147, *187*, 497, *511*, *784*, 799, 801, 802, 818, 830, 834, 835, 838, *856*, 873, *919*
Zaieg, R. 1004, *1036*
Zakowska, L. *254*, *386*
Zakrajsek, J. S. *316*
Zambon, F. 931, 944, 947, 951, *982*
Zancaner, S. 646, 667, *709*
Zaouk, A. K. 608, *636*
Zarcone, V. 806, *851*
Zaza, S. *553*, *626*
Zegeer, C. 866, 899, 907, 910, 911, *916*, *917*, *918*, *925*, *1029*, *1030*, 1089, *1175*
Zeidman, K. 664, *708*
Zeleny, R. *708*
Zellner, J. W. *974*
Zeuwts, L. *186*, *1035*
Zevgolis, D. 232, *250*
Zhan, C. *507*
Zhan, J. 371, *388*
Zhang, D. *795*
Zhang, F. 983, *1035*, 1086, *1174*
Zhang, J. *251*, 376, *388*, 609, *631*, *852*
Zhang, K. *131*, *508*, *924*
Zhang, T. 234, *256*, 462, 485, *511*
Zhang, W. *133*, 312, *324*, *795*
Zhang, Y. 217, *256*, 1019, *1036*
Zhang, Z. *323*
Zhao, G. *924*
Zhao, H. *626*, *636*
Zhao, S. *325*
Zhao, W. *131*
Zhao, X. 175, *187*, 1117, *1174*, *1175*
Zheng, P. 905, *925*
Zhizhong, L. 225, *249*
Zhou, L. *852*
Zhou, R. 110, *133*, 740, *795*
Zhou, Y. 883, *923*
Zhu, J. *1031*
Zhu, M. 290, 292, *325*, *975*
Zhu, W. 817, 857
Zhuang, D. *133*
Zhuang, X. 875, *924*, *925*
Ziba, A. *381*
Ziedman, K. 175, *183*
Ziel, W. B. *624*
Zilberstein, R. *784*
Zimmerman, P. R. 964, *981*
Zimmermann, R. P. *849*
Zohar, D. 1094, *1175*
Zoob, I. *511*
Zuber, M. *791*
Zuckerman, M. 118, *133*, 490, 491, *511*
Zwahlen, H. T. 900, *925*
Zweipfenning, P. G. 667, 683, *706*
Zylman, R. *624*
Zyphur, M. J. *504*

Subject Index

Abbreviated Injury Scale (AIS), 420
ABS. *See* Anti-lock brake systems
ABW. *See* Advance Brake Warning
Acceptance, 16, 430, 690
  versus acceptability, 1145
Accident
  causes, 13, 261, 269–275, 345–348, 414, 864, 875, 879, 931, 933–934, 1040, 1041–1042, 1044, 1045–1052, 1064
  first, 3–4, 145–146, 262, 264, 267
  proneness, 47, 481–482
  See also Crash
Accidents
  versus other causes of death, 11, 13, 259, 337, 563, 573, 1049
  rates, 263, 335, 338, 462, 1024, 1132
  and violations, 47, 110, 123, 257, 261, 266, 268, 277, 278, 290, 313, 353, 362, 460, 466, 479, 487–488, 491, 500, 576, 697, 725, 823, 940, 954, 1061–1063, 1113, 1114
  See also Crashes
Acuity
  dynamic visual, 148, 151–154, 349–350, 353
  static visual, 146, 148, 150, 151–153, 156, 158, 348–350, 677
Adaptive Cruise Control (ACC), 102, 244, 760, 1089, 1093, 1137, 1140
Advance brake warning (ABW), 55, 57, 59
Advanced driver assistance systems (ADAS), 226, 370–371, 1132
Age, 215–216, 263, 345, 349, 351, 584–585, 818, 990–991
Age related
  frailty, 339
  impairments, 344–362
Aggression, 462–465
  and anger, 482–487, 496
  displaced, 463, 501
  feasibility of, 496–501
  and personality, 482–487
Aggressive behavior(s), 258, 472, 474
Aggressive driving, 393, 401, 459, 462
  and aggression, 463, 464, 482–483
  aggressive disposition, 495–496
  catalysts for, 472–477
  and congestion, 463, 473–474, 478
  and culture, 463, 497–501
  and displaced aggression, 501
  and driving environment, 493–495
  and feasibility of aggression, 496
  and frustration, 462–465
  and honking, 463, 465, 471–472, 474, 496
  measures of, 465–472, 576
  and personality, 479–493
  and running red light, 463, 465–466
  and social maladjustment, 460–462
Air bags, 117, 515, 544–548, 1144
Alcohol
  absorption and elimination, 565–567
  and cognitive functioning, 567–571
  and crashes, 573–587
  and drowsiness, 568, 824, 825, 1073
  and drunkenness, 571–573
  DUI, 563–564
  DWI countermeasures, 587–623
  effects on driving, and on subjective sensations, 567–573
  effects on driving skills, 585–586
  and fatigue, 823–827
  and Ignition Interlock, 614–618
  and server training, 601–602
  and social marketing, 599
  and vigilance, 640–642

Alertness maintaining task (AMT), 804, 835–836
Alternating blinking light system (ABLS), 942, 959, 997
Amber light dilemma. *See* Yellow light dilemma
American Association for Retired Persons (AARP), 365, 375
American Association of State Highway Safety Traffic Officials (AASHTO), 219, 393–394
American Automobile Association (AAA), 215–216, 367–368
American Automobile Association Foundation for Traffic Safety (AAAF), 392
American Heritage Dictionary, 1040
American Institute of Transportation Engineers (ITE), 1131
American Medical Association (AMA), 360, 639
American National Standards Institute (ANSI), 234–235
American Society of Automotive Engineers (SAE), 768
Amphetamine, 639, 651, 652, 654, 655, 684–685, 839
  See also Stimulants
"Angel dust". *See* Phencyclidine (PCP)
Anger, 482–487
Anonymity, 326, 350
Antidepressants, 655
Antihistamine, 640, 675–676, 680–681
  See also Depressants
Anti-lock brake systems (ABS), 102, 116, 892, 912, 969, 1055, 1147, 1148
Attention
  attention-deficit hyperactivity disorder (ADHD), 462
  controlled and automated processes in driving, 198–201
  divided, 191–201
  and information processing, 191–194
  information processing levels, 191–194
  selective, 191–201
  See also Distraction; Inattention
Automated enforcement, 434–437, 1123–1124
Automated processes, 101, 190, 198–201
  automation, 107
  autonomous emergency braking, 1141–1142
  autonomous vehicle, 32, 94, 329, 370, 1150–1156

BAC (blood alcohol concentration), 565–567
  and effects on driving, 567, 572
  and impairment, 571–573
  laws, 588–593
  legal limit, 577, 588, 590, 594
Backup camera, 1142–1143
Barbiturates, 639, 675–676
Bayes procedure, 1122
Behavioral adaptation, 115–117, 524, 1146
Behavioral research
  confounding variables, 43, 46–48
  control variables, 43, 44–45
  dependent variables, 43–44
  independent variables, 43–44
  intervening variables, 43, 45–46
  key concepts in, 43
  moderating variables, 43, 48
  validity and reliability, 48–52
  variables of interest, 43–48
Belt use laws, 527
Ben Gurion University, 63, 65
"Bennies". *See* Amphetamine
Benzodiazepines, 639, 643, 645–646, 648–657, 675–681
Beta waves, 815
"Between subjects" design, 53–54
Biasing factors in assessing older drivers' crash involvement, 339–344
Bicycle/bicycling, 23, 275, 861–862, 984–986
  accident rates, 1024–1025
  bicycle-based improvements, 1022
  crash countermeasures, 1005–1023
  and crashes, 988–991, 1003–1005
  helmets and equipment, 1022–1023

lights, 1013–1014
as part of multimodal travel pattern, 986–988
and societal trend, 984
trails/tracks and paths/lanes, 1017–1018
Bicyclists, 275, 983
cyclists-drivers interactions, 999–1003
cyclists' visibility, 994–999
under-reporting of bicycle crashes, 992–994
See also Motorcycles
Billboards, 101–102, 175, 727–730
Bio-motion, 902–903, 996, 997, 1023, 1028
Blink behavior, 815–817
Blood Alcohol Concentration (BAC), 565–567, 580, 588–591, 593–595, 689, 881
Blumenthal's model, 114, 712, 801
Booster seats, 536–539, 541–542, 1108
effectiveness, 540–541, 543
Brake reaction time (BRT), 56, 202–222, 747
age and gender differences, 215–216
in complex situations, 216–219
and expectancy, 212–215
and hazard perception, 220–222
and relevance to safety, 202–204
Braking, 44, 55–59, 69–71, 87, 91, 97–98, 112, 147, 190, 202–206, 216–217, 222, 226, 404, 525, 606–607, 746, 753, 764, 892, 912, 943, 969, 971, 1061, 1148, 1158
Breath alcohol concentration (BrAC), 566, 567, 603
Breath testing, 607–611
checkpoints, 607

Caffeine, 622–623, 839
Cameras
red light cameras, 1094, 1123–1124
section cameras, 437
speed cameras, 400, 434–435, 437–438, 1124
Cannabinoids, 639
compared to alcohol, 639, 661
and crashes, 660, 667, 668, 674, 682
and driving, 659, 660–666, 668–669, 674
effects, 660, 676
prevalence, 642, 645–648, 659
Cannabis, 651, 654, 655
Car following and headway, 60, 222–223
CarFit, 373–374
"Case control" design, 54, 648
Cell phone(s), 733–768
conversations, 404–405, 748
and mental load, 747–748
relative to alcohol, 763–765
relative to passengers, 765–768
Center High Mounted Stop Lamp (CHMSL), 55, 56, 69, 73, 971, 1147–1148
Child protection, 535, 542
Child restraints, 535, 538, 539–543
Child safety seat
effectiveness, 516–519
type of, 536
use of, 534, 535
Children safety, 731–733
CHMSL. *See* Center High Mounted Stop Lamp
Circadian rhythm, 810–812
Clearances judgment, 222–231
"Click-it or Ticket" campaign, 531
Climate as risk factor, 991
Clinical approach, 1041, 1042–1060, 1063
Clothing, 889, 890, 894, 958, 995, 999, 1028
Cluster analysis, 987
Cocaine, 639, 643–646, 648, 651, 654–655, 684–685, 697
See also Stimulants
Cocktail party phenomenon, 99–100
Coded symbols, 232
Codeine. *See* Narcotic analgesics
Coefficient of friction, 59–60, 119, 202
Cognitive
approaches to discourage DWI, 593–602

conspicuity, 941
dissonance, 602–603
functioning, alcohol effects on, 567–571
impairments, 354–359
load, 761–763, 833, 838
processes, 332
Collision, 7, 514
Commentary driving, 311
Compulsory breath testing (CBT), 607–611
Concurrent feedback, 778–779
Confounding variables, 46–48
Congestion, 473–474, 478, 493
Conspicuity
bicycle, 939–942
motorcycle rider, 939–942, 944, 958–961, 971
object, 197
pedestrian, 885–887, 891, 907, 914
search, 197–198
Contrast, and visibility, 889
Contrast sensitivity, 142–148, 156–159, 166–167, 176, 332, 351, 353, 356, 358–359, 374–375, 884
Controlled processes, 101, 190, 198–201
Cost-benefits analyses, 1096
Count-down signals (CDS), 907
Court monitoring, 618–620
Crash causation, 715–716, 1059–1060, 1077–1079
cycling and, 1003–1005
statistical/epidemiological approach to, 1063–1068
validity of police assessment, 1060–1062
Crash causes, 1003, 1043
from clinical studies, 659–660, 1042–1045, 1056, 1063, 1070
environmental, 933, 1046, 1050–1052
from epidemiological studies, 680, 753–755, 763, 962, 1063–1065, 1065–1068, 1070
human, 415, 934, 1046–1049, 1048–1049, 1050–1052, 1053–1056, 1070
NDS approach, 1069, 1072–1077
U.S. 100-car study, 1069–1072
vehicular, 1046–1047, 1050–1052
Crash culpability, 344
and cognitive impairments, 354–359
and driving style, 362
and medical conditions and diseases, 359–362
and older drivers, 345–348
and vision, 348–354
Crash(es), 4, 6–7, 22–24, 161, 339, 401, 548–549, 988, 1041
accidents vs., 6–7
analysis, 155–156, 159, 267, 414, 540, 657, 668–689, 681, 685–686, 715–716, 722–723, 752, 763, 905, 950, 957, 971, 1047, 1049, 1078, 1086, 1148
causal analyses of, 416–417
causes, 864–898, 875–878
countermeasures, 32, 564, 898, 911, 1005–1023, 1085–1158
crash modification factors (CMFs), 1115–1116
and drugs, 682–686
severity, 420–424, 714
and speed, 402–404, 408
statistics, 992
testing, 548–549
theoretical issues, 404–408
worthiness, 513–514, 548–551, 1157
See also Accidents
Cycling, 988
age as risk factor, 990–991
alcohol as risk factor, 991
climate as risk factor, 991
and crash causation, 1003–1005
gender as risk factor, 991
and multimodal travel pattern, 986–988
"Cycling Barometer", 984–985, 988–989

Dark adaptation, 149
"Dart-out" crash, 874
Daylight running lights (DRL), 158, 958
Daylight saving time (DST), 886

Decision making, 1132
hierarchical decision making, 90–94
Demerit Point System (DPS), 1111
Depressant
compared to alcohol, 658, 676, 679, 824
and crashes, 650, 658, 680–681
and driving, 479, 642, 645, 676
effects, 568, 622, 641, 676–681
prevalence, 576, 642–659, 944
See also Barbiturates; Benzodiazepine
Design speed, 400–401
Designated driver program, 599–601
Deterrence, 603–621
Diazepam, 652
Disability-adjusted life years (DALYs), 11
Dissociative anesthetics, 681–683, 687
See also Ketamine; Phencyclidine (PCP)
Distracted driving, 711
Distraction, 711–779, 882–884
and accident cause, 715, 1045–1050
from cell phone, 733–768
from email, 769
external, 715, 718, 721, 736, 1047
and headway, 746–747, 764, 767, 772
internal, 715, 718, 1046, 1048, 1054
and lateral control, 358, 747, 760, 768, 801, 833
from passengers, 717, 721, 737, 765
prevalence in driving, 642, 645
and reaction time, 747
sources of, 715–722, 780, 1076
and speed, 723, 725, 745, 764, 773
from text messaging, 768, 769–775
Drinking and driving, 564, 576, 730–731
countermeasures, 687
and court monitoring, 618–620
and crash risks, 576–583
deterrence of, 603, 611, 1114
economic disincentives to drinking, 611
frequency of, 586–587
ignition interlock, 614–618
license suspension, 614, 616, 620, 1110–1112
minimum drinking age laws, 591–592
psychological treatment, 620–621
vehicle impoundment, 614–618
victim impact panels, 596, 613–614
and Zero Tolerance laws, 590, 591, 687
See also Alcohol; Driving while intoxicated (DWI)
Driver Behavior Questionnaire (DBQ), 123, 467, 469, 477, 486, 497, 938
Driver education, 275, 367–369
and crash involvement, 278, 293
and driver training, 276–282, 305–314
and hazard perception, 281, 307–312, 955–957
Driver Education Evaluation Program (DEEP), 47, 277
Driver information processing. *See* Information processing
Driver licensing, 151, 275, 278, 282, 593, 952, 1051
Driver training, 87, 97, 266, 276–282, 305–314, 313, 430, 490, 780, 1054
Driving
Anger Questionnaire (DAP), 484
Experience, 45, 65, 143, 160, 199, 225–226, 229, 234, 263, 265, 267, 272, 283, 311, 365, 587, 773, 947, 1047, 1064
simulator, 49, 60–68, 64, 172, 191, 204–212, 367, 445, 587, 662, 744, 746, 750, 759, 809, 813, 833
skill, 91, 585–586
style, 362
Driving under influence (DUI), 563–564
Driving under the influence of drugs (DUID), 640, 641, 642, 642–643, 645, 687–688, 696
Driving Under the Influence of Drugs, Alcohol and Medicine (DRUID), 581, 643, 653
education and public information campaigns, 697–698
enforcement of DUID, 696
legislation dealing with, 687–688
See also Drugs and driving
Driving while intoxicated (DWI), 489, 563–564, 642–643

cognitive and motivational approaches to discourage DWI, 593–602
counteracting effects of alcohol with caffeine, 622–623
countermeasures, 587
cues, 604–607
enforcement, 602–603
general deterrence and perceived risk of arrest, 603–611
legislation, 588–593
prevention of recidivism and treatment, 611–621
repeat offenders, 575, 587, 611–621, 619, 642
See also Drinking and driving
Drowsiness. *See* Fatigue
Drug(s)
addiction, treatment for, 697
categories, 638–640, 659, 690, 694
combining alcohol with, 587
definition, 638–640
Drug Evaluation and Classification Program (DECP), 688–696
Drug Recognition Experts (DREs), 688, 689
effects, 52, 369, 622, 638, 658, 677, 698
prevalence, 335
and PTW crashes, 944–945
relative to alcohol effects, 330
See also under specific drugs and drug categories
Drugs and driving, 638–642
behaviors and crashes, 659–687
countermeasures, 687–698
and crash risk, 642, 683, 684
methodological concerns, 657–659
NIDA, 637
prevalence, 642–659
relative to alcohol, 567, 640–642, 642
treatment, 697
Dynamic visual acuity, 151–154, 349–350

Eating, 730–731
Education, 430–431
campaigns, 697–698
and training, 1107–1109
Electric bikes (e-bikes), 1023–1027
Electroencephalogram (EEG), 805, 815, 832, 840
Electronic stability control (ESC), 87, 102, 370, 892, 912, 1134–1135, 1138, 1140, 1147, 1149–1150
Enforcement, 529–530, 602–603, 903, 1112–1115
automated, 434–437, 1123–1124
and DWI, 489, 594, 598, 603
moving versus stationary, 433–434
as part of environmental traffic control, 1123–1124
speed, 431–433, 438
Environment(al), 1050–1052
approaches, 439–440
causes, 1050–1052
countermeasures, 846–847
design, 903–911
driving environment, 493–495
modifications, 1115–1132
and personality, 495–496
treatments, 374–376
Epidemiological approach, 962, 1041–1042, 1063–1068
Epworth Sleepiness Scale (ESS), 807
Ergonomic principles, 239–240
e-Safety, 1132, 1137, 1138
acceptance of and adaptation, 1145–1150
autonomous emergency braking, 1141–1142
eCall (ECA), 1138, 1140
ISA, 1143–1144
political will, and policy, 1140–1141
sensors and backup cameras, 1142–1143
TSL, 1143–1144
ESC. *See* Electronic stability control
Ethanol. *See* Alcohol
EuroNCAP, 3, 550, 913, 1136, 1137
European Cyclists' Federation (ECF), 984–985
European naturalistic Driving and Riding for Infrastructure & Vehicle safety and Environment (UDRIVE), 1077

European New Car Assessment Program (EuroNCAP), 3, 532, 550–551, 913, 1136–1137
European Transport Safety Council (ETSC), 430, 1144
Expectancy, 212–215, 1119–1120, 1142
increasing, 1014–1015
and reaction time, 212–215
and target detection, 166
and visibility, 889–892
Experience, 200, 275
Experimental design, 531, 844
Extraversion, 481
Eye movements, 168–169
in driving, 169–176
and fixations, 168
and saccades, 168
See also Visual search

Fatal Analysis Reporting System (FARS), 258, 296, 298, 487, 517–518, 539, 545, 546, 574, 647, 671, 714, 877, 962, 965, 1054
Fatigue, 797–801, 821
and alertness maintaining task (AMT), 834–835
and circadian rhythm, 810–812, 820–821, 827
and crashes, 805, 807, 811, 817, 820
detection, 815, 844, 912, 1154
and driving, 797–847
and heart rate variability (HRV), 104, 726, 799, 806, 815, 836
and music, 801, 833, 836
and rumble strips, 827, 847, 1118
subjective, 571–573, 799, 804–819, 812, 814, 824, 827, 835, 841, 843
symptoms of, 800, 802, 805, 833
and vigilance, 799, 802, 805, 824, 826, 844, 847
Federal Highway Administration (FHWA), 33, 240, 904, 914, 985–986, 1119, 1131
Federal Motor Carrier Safety Administration (FMCSA), 809
Federal Motor Vehicle Carrier Safety Administration (FMVCSA), 33
Fentanyl, 639, 683
Field operational test (FOT), 71–72, 229
"15-second rule", 723–724, 768–769
Fovea, 140, 153, 162, 164, 165, 166, 169
Frailty bias, 339
Frustration-aggression model, 464–465
Fuller's TCI model, 111–114

Gap judgment and perception, 222–231, 941–946
Gears, 90–91, 97, 101, 199–200, 270, 464–465
Gender
differences in brake reaction time, 215–216
and identity, 491–493
as risk factor, 991
German In-Depth Accident Study (GIDAS), 346, 932–933, 936, 1052
Glare, 148–151
Glaucoma, 359
Global positioning system (GPS), 443–444
Goals of driver education (GDE), 305–307
Google Car, 32, 1152–1153
Graduated driver licensing (GDL), 193, 198–199, 221, 275, 282–305, 356, 673, 740, 742, 1106
Grand Rapids Study, 576–577, 578–579

Haddon's Matrix, 1093–1094
Hallucinogens, 682–683
Halo effects, 419, 432–433
Hand-held phones, 757–760
Hands-free phones, 757–760
Hashish, 639, 660–674
Hazard perception, 220–222, 273–275, 307–312, 373, 832
Head restraints, 543–544
Head-up display (HUD), 371
Headway
cell phones effects on, 746–747
comfortable, 223, 224–227

estimation, 227–229
judgment, 222–231
and learning, 224, 228–229
minimum, 224–227
safe, 224–227
Heart rate variability (HRV), 104, 725, 726, 799, 815, 836, 837
Helmet laws, 1008–1009
Helmets, 961–969, 1012–1013, 1022–1023
Heroin, 639, 683
See also Narcotic analgesics
Highway hypnosis, 1118
Hindsight bias, 1043–1044
Honking, 310, 465, 466, 471, 472, 474, 477, 493, 494, 495, 496, 499, 500, 820
Horizontal gaze nystagmus (HGN), 606–607
Human information processing. *See* Information processing
Hurt study, 931–933
Hybrid electric vehicles (HEV), 912, 1022

Illumination, 148–151, 349–350, 888
See also Luminance
Inattention, 469, 712–713, 716, 882–884
of adult pedestrians, 881–882
in crashes, 937–939
distraction and, 715
errors, 469
Independent variables, 43–44, 57
In-depth crash analysis, 1154
In-depth study of crash causes
cars, 931–932
motorcycles, 932–933
pedestrians, 875, 910–911
Indiana University Tri-Level Study of Accident Causes, 1045–1050
Inexperience errors, 469
Infant seats, 541, 543
Information processing
approach, 404–406
and attention, 94–107, 191
automation, 198–201
controlled processes, 98–99, 190, 198–201
levels, 191–194
limited capacity, 95, 102, 404–405
load, 194
models, 94–107, 190
and speed, 102, 104–105, 189–190, 193–196
Infotainment systems, 1138
Inhalants, 686–687
Injury
mechanism, 514–515
pedestrian, 862–864
severity, 27, 420, 583, 931, 1006, 1022
Institute for Road Safety Research (SWOV), 33
Institute for Transport Economics (TOI), 33
Institute of Transportation Engineers (ITE), 1128
Insurance Institute for Highway Safety (IIHS), 33, 259, 285, 294, 315, 319, 336, 429, 451, 515, 538–539, 544, 550, 551, 555, 558, 734, 785, 931, 970, 1023, 1142–1143
Intelligent Speed Adaptation. *See* ISA (intelligent speed adaptation/ assistance)
Intelligent Speed Assistance. *See* ISA (intelligent speed adaptation/ assistance)
Intelligent transportation systems (ITS), 6, 441, 734, 969, 1094, 1137–1138, 1140
International Standards Organization (ISO), 191–192, 234–235, 715
International Transport Forum, 996–997
Intersection, 274, 1138
design for older drivers, 347, 356, 361–362, 375–376
safety index, 904, 1018
Intervening variables, 45–46, 402–404
In-vehicle crash avoidance warning (IVCAW), 102, 1089
In-vehicle data recorders (IVDRs), 301, 302–303, 778, 1056

In-vehicle icons or symbols, 232, 242–246
In-vehicle information systems (IVIS), 734
In-Vehicle Safety Systems (IVSS), 32, 778
ISA (intelligent speed adaptation/assistance), 429, 437, 913, 1137, 1140, 1143–1145
IVCAW. *See* In-vehicle crash avoidance warning

Karolinska Sleepiness Scale (KSS), 808, 832
Ketamine, 639, 681–682
  See also Dissociative anesthetics

Lane change assistant (LCA), 1138
Lane keeping support (LKS), 1138, 1140
Legibility, 148, 158, 1125–1127
Legislation, 588–593, 687–688
Legitimacy, 493–495, 1112–1113
License, 332, 365
  revocation, 592, 1110–1112
  suspension, 612–613, 615, 616, 1110–1112
Licensing, 282–305, 337–338, 952–955, 1110–1112
Life Skills Training (LST), 697
Limited-capacity model, 101, 102
Low-mileage bias, 339, 340–344
"Low vision" people, 143
Luminance, 888–889
  See also Illumination
Lysergic acid diethylamide (LSD), 639, 682
  See also Hallucinogens

MAIS. *See* Maximal Injury Severity Scale
Marijuana, 638, 639, 644, 660–675
  See also Cannabinoids
Masculinity and femininity, 491–493
Maximal Injury Severity Scale (MAIS), 10–12
Media, 393, 396, 529, 530, 588, 598, 946, 1109, 1110, 1113, 1150
Memory
  long-term (LTM), 88, 96, 105–106, 197, 663, 836
  sensory storage (SS), 95, 105
  short-term (STM), 88, 96, 105–106, 198, 361, 622, 641, 663, 665, 676, 677, 693, 745, 836
Mental fatigue, 805
Mental load, 104, 198–199, 747–748
  mental task load measurement, 102
  performance on secondary task, 103–104
  physiological indicators of stress, 104
  subjective scales, 104
  subsidiary task paradigm, 103
Mescaline, 639, 682
  mesopic acuity, 149, 150–151
Meta-analysis, 78–79, 300–301
Methadone, 639, 646, 683, 684
Methamphetamine, 639, 684–685
Methaqualone, 639, 675–676
3,4-Methylenedioxy-methamphetamine (MDMA), 639, 684–685
Methylphenidate, 639
Michigan Alcoholism Screening Test (MAST), 575–576
Mind-wondering, 712–713
Minnesota multiphasic personality inventory (MMPI), 479, 575–576
Mislabeled conversation, 749
Mobility, 257–258, 331–332, 363–376
Model
  of driver behavior, 87, 108–109, 117
  hierarchical, 92–94, 108, 305–306
  of human information processing, 95, 693–694, 934, 1056, 1061–1062
  integrative, 122–123
  motivational, 89, 114–122, 407–408, 1045
  risk homeostasis (Wilde's), 117–122, 404
  task difficulty model (Fuller's), 111
Moderating variables, 48
Monocular vision, 159–161
"Moral hazard", 281
Morphine, 639, 683–684
  See also Narcotic analgesics
Mothers Against Drunk Driving (MADD), 564, 596–597, 613–614
Motion detection, 142, 147–148, 154–156

Motorcycle Accident In-Depth Study (MAIDS), 931–940, 944, 945, 946, 958, 959, 970
Motorcycle Rider Behavior Questionnaire (MRBQ), 469, 938
Motorcycles, 927, 930–931, 949
  crash causes, 931–934
  and crash rate, 947, 953
  and fatality rate, 928, 964, 966, 967
  helmets, 961–969
  human causes of PTW crashes, 934–946
  licensing requirements, 952–955
  MC and rider conspicuity, 958–961
  rider safety, 951–972
  rider skills, 943–944
  riders at risk, 946–951
  and roadway improvements, 969–972
  speed and injury, 929–930
  training, 952–955, 955–957
Motorization, 862, 863–864
  and accidents, 22–24
  and Smeed's law, 22–24
Movement times (MTs), 58–59, 205
Multiple Sleep Latency Test (MSLT), 819
Music, 712, 725–726, 736, 763

NADS–National Advance Driving Simulator
Narcotic analgesics, 683–684, 686, 690, 691, 695, 696
  See also Codeine; Heroin; Morphine
NASA-TLX, 104, 372, 747, 759
National Advance Driving Simulator, 64
National Automotive Sampling System (NASS), 421, 896, 1052
National Highway Traffic Safety Administration (NHTSA), 6, 33, 47, 69, 70, 277, 328, 336, 373, 401, 516, 539, 546, 549, 570, 579, 604, 608, 639, 648, 691, 719, 733, 734, 864, 961, 965, 1040, 1041, 1051, 1069, 1090, 1106, 1108, 1149
National Institute of Drug Abuse (U. S.) (NIDA), 637, 639, 691–692
National Maximum Speed Limit (NMSL), 401, 418
National Occupant Protection Use Survey (NOPUS), 521, 734
National Road Safety Authority (Israel), 37, 384, 450, 454, 557, 632, 784, 793, 902, 920, 980, 1030, 1036, 1090, 1159, 1163, 1179
National Safety Council (U. S.), 15, 219, 226, 752
Naturalistic Driving Study (NDS), 72, 74–78, 715, 735, 756, 1041–1042, 1069
  UDRIVE, 75, 1077
  U.S. "100-Car" study, 1069–1072
  U.S. SHRP2 naturalistic driving study, 1072–1077
Navigation systems, 101, 207, 246, 371–372, 429, 715, 721, 723–724, 730, 745, 768–769, 775, 1138
New Car Assessment Program (NCAP), 549–550, 1132, 1136–1137
NHTSA. *See* National Highway Traffic Safety Administration
Nicotine, 639, 641, 659, 664
Night vision, 148, 163–164, 373, 1138
Novice drivers, 257–314
  See also Young drivers
Nystagmus, 162, 360, 606, 665, 678–679

Occupant protection
  active restraints, 515–543
  child protection and restraints, 535–543
  crashworthiness, 548–551
  mechanism of injury, 514–515
  See also Air bags; Booster seats; Head restraints; Infant seats; Safety seats; Seat belts
Odds ratio (OR) and relative risk (RR), 79
Offenders, treatment of repeat, 611–621
Older drivers, 328–376, 522
  and bias, 339–344
  and cognitive impairment, 354–359
  and crash causes, 345–348
  and crash involvement, 337–344

and culpability, 344–362
and demographic trends, 329–331
and driving style, 362
and environmental treatments, 374–376
and injuries, 332, 334–336, 339–340
and left turns, 327, 362, 375
and licensing, 337–339
and medical condition, 359–362
and mobility, 331–332
and safety and mobility, 363–376
and training, 367–369
and useful field of view, 352, 354, 368
and vehicle design, 369–374
and vision, 348–354
Older rider, 949–950
One-leg-stand, 606–607
On-road drug detection and identification, 688–696
OnStar© system, 371, 747
Opiates, 643, 646, 651, 654, 655, 656, 657, 684
Opioids, 638–639, 683–684
See also Narcotic analgesics
Opium, 639, 683
Organizational approaches, 426–430
policy and organizational changes, 898–900, 1094–1105
Organization of Economic Cooperation and Development (OECD), 258, 259, 901, 1116

Passenger(s)
and distraction, 717, 720–721, 737, 765–768
and graduated driver licensing, 266, 275, 282–305, 500, 1106, 1109
restriction rules, 296
and seat belts, 515–519, 534–535, 538–539, 543–547, 551
Passing, 287, 363, 407, 410, 413–414, 471, 497, 1121
Passive alcohol sensors, 610–611
Passive restraints, 543–548
Pedelecs, 1023–1027
Pedestrian(s), 861
and age, 865–869, 878–885
causes of crashes, 864–898
conspicuity, 885–887
crash and injury risk, 862–864
and crash countermeasures, 898–913, 1086–1088
and crash risk, 865–869
crossing, 869–873, 903, 910–911
crossing ahead sign, 193
culture effects on pedestrian safety, 897–898
distraction, 882–884
driver-pedestrian communications, 873–875
and fatalities, 863–869, 877, 879, 885, 886, 887, 898–899
handicapped, 874–875, 897
signals, 870–871, 904, 907
and speed, 869–873, 895–897
street crossing, 869–873
visibility, 885–887, 887–894
walking speed, 871–873, 883, 907
Percent of time the eye is closed (PERCLOS), 805, 843
Perception, 96, 493
Perception reaction time (PRT), 190, 202, 202–212
in complex situations, 216–219
and expectancy, 212–215
and hazard perception, 220–222
Perceptual countermeasures, 439–440
Perceptual modifications, 440, 444–445, 1117–1118
Periodic Motor Vehicle Inspection (PMVI), 1132–1134
Permanent storage. *See* Memory—long-term (LTM)
Personality, 459–501
and accident proneness, 481–482
and aggression, 462–465, 482–487
and aggressive driving, 459–501
anger, 482–487
and depression, 479
and environment, 495–496
and gender, 491–493
and impulsivity, 479

and locus of control, 460, 479, 481
and observable behavior, 480
and risk-taking, 487–490
and sensation-seeking, 490–491
and social maladjustment, 460–462
and stress, 488, 495–496
Phencyclidine (PCP), 639, 681–682, 690
See also Dissociative anesthetics
Point system, 488, 1111
Policy and organizational approaches, 426–430, 1005–1010
Positive guidance, 1119–1120, 1132
Powered two wheelers (PTW), 927–972
See also Motorcycles
Psilocybin, 639, 682
Public information (PI) campaigns, 440–443, 595–599, 697–698, 1109–1110

Random breath testing (RBT), 607–611
Rationality–bounded and unbounded, 108–109
Reaction time, 44, 204–212, 713
brake reaction time, 202–222
in complex situations, 216–219
to different stimuli, 217
distributions, 59
and expectancy, 212–215
individual differences in, 209, 395–396
and stopping distance, 202–204
and uncertainty, 204–205, 207–208, 212–215, 217
See also Perception reaction time
Rear-end collisions, 55–57, 112, 517
Rear visibility, 1142–1143
Recidivism, 611–621
Reckless driving, 111, 270, 461, 547–548, 823
Recognition errors, 270
Red light, 475–478, 488, 500–501, 726, 741, 872–873, 957, 1094, 1123–1124, 1128–1129, 1147–1148
Redundancy, 1119
Reliability, 48–52
of crash data, 25–27
Research methods, 41–79
"Restriction of range" effect, 146
Retina, 139–140
Retinitis pigmentosis, 162–163
Retroreflection, 148, 158, 375, 890, 893–894, 903, 995, 1013, 1126
Rideshare/bikeshare programs, 1009–1010
"Right of Way Violation" accident, 941
Right turn on red (RTOR), 375–376
Risk allostasis theory (RAT), 111–114
Risk Awareness and Perception Training (RAPT), 312
Risk homeostasis theory, 738
and speed, 117–122, 404, 407–408, 444, 515
Risk perception, 115, 258–259, 311, 881, 957
Risk-speed compensation model, 117
Risk taking, 487–490, 1045, 1047
Road assessment programs (RAPs), 1131–1132
Road markings, 241–242
Road rage, 465–472, 483
See also Aggressive driving
Road safety audits (RSA), 985–986, 1131
Road signs. *See* Signs
Roadway
design, 438–439, 970
illumination, 1127
modifications, 1115–1132
Roundabouts, 374–375, 904, 905, 1019–1021, 1116, 1122–1123, 1157
Rumble strips, 417, 827, 847–848, 1118, 1157

Safe system approach, 1005–1007, 1086–1089
Safety, 6–9, 30, 402–404, 1086
culture, 499
safety-critical-event, 1004
safety index (SI), 392
safety-in-numbers, 911, 1015–1016
safety performance indicators (SPIs), 1091–1093
Safety belts. *See* Seat belts

Safety seats, 535–539
Scotopic acuity, 149
Seat belts, 391–392, 515
  benefits of, 119, 391–392, 526, 961
  and child restraints, 535–537
  and crash statistics, 524–526
  effectiveness, 516–519
  effectiveness of child restraints, 539–543
  enforcement of, 529–530
  incentives, 531
  laws, 527–529
  in rear seats, 534–535
  reminders, 531–534
  use, 519–522, 526–534
  users and non-users of seat belts, 522–523
Secondary task, performance on, 103–104
Section control, 437–438
Sedatives, 675
Selective recruitment hypotheses, 524, 525–526, 529
Self-driving vehicles, 1150–1156
Self-explaining roads, 233, 1120–1122
Self-organizing roads, 1120–1122
Sensation-seeking, 490–491
  Sensation Seeking Scale (SSS), 490
Server training, 601–602
Sex-Role Inventory, 492
Share-the-road approach, 1007–1008
Short-term license suspension, 1111
Short-term memory (STM), 96
Short-term sensory storage (STSS), 95, 105
Significance
  practical, 54–55
  statistical, 54–55
Signs
  comprehension, 231–242
  conspicuity, 197, 729
  design, 233
  familiarity, 233, 239–240
  international comparisons, 233–234
  perception, 197, 199
  recall, 194–201
  recognition, 244
  registration, 199
  standardization, 231–232, 239–241
Simple reaction time, 42, 204, 216
"Simpson's Paradox", 21
Simulators, 51, 57, 361
Situation Awareness (SA), 100, 104–107
Size-distance constancy, 945
Sleep, 799
  apnea, 828
  deprivation, 799, 809–810
  individual differences in, 818–819
  management, 828–830
  scales, 806–807
  See also Fatigue
"Smeed's Law", 22–24, 864
Snellen acuity, 141, 143, 146
Sobriety checkpoints, 564, 590, 608
Social maladjustment, 460–462
Social marketing, 599
Social pressure, 738
Socioeconomic status, 522, 950–951
Speed, 393, 402–404
  and calming, 402, 417, 438–439, 905
  cameras, 400, 434, 438, 598, 1124
  cell phones effects on, 745
  choice, 393–401
  corridors, 437–438
  countermeasures, 425–446
  and crashes, 401–425
  design speed, 400–401, 426, 1007
  enforcement, 419
  and fatality risk with crash impact, 583–584
  feedback indicators, 442–443
  and individual differences, 395
  and injuries, 417–418
  intelligent speed adaptation, 444, 1130
  limit, 402, 425–426, 426–429
  limit signs, 196, 441
  management, 417, 445–446
  and motivation, 396–400
  of motorcycles, 946
  perception, 391, 399
  power law, 394, 404, 422, 430
  PTW crashes, 929–930, 946
  reasonable speed, 401

and risk-taking, 487–490
and safety, 391–446
severity, 420–424
variance, 425
Standardized Field Sobriety Test (SFST), 604–607, 689
Stanford Sleepiness Scale (SSS), 806–807, 808
"Stannard's Law", 412
Stationary enforcement, 433–434
Statistical methods, 285–286, 397, 1009, 1063–1068
Stereopsis, 159–161
Stimulants
compared to alcohol, 684–685
and crashes, 685–686
and driving, 685–686
effects, 685–686, 839–842
prevalence, 643–644
See also Amphetamine; Cocaine
"Stop Ahead" sign, 195–196
Stopping distance, 59, 119, 203–204, 430–431, 892, 894, 1148
"STOP" signs, 214, 354
Strain, 405
Street hierarchy, 1007–1008
Stress, 104, 405, 495–496
Structural equation modeling (SEM), 397, 483–484
Students Against Drunk Driving (SADD), 596–597
Study design, 52
between subjects, 53–54
experimental, 52–53
observational studies, 52–53
within subjects, 53–54
Subjective Workload Assessment Scale (SWAT), 104, 747
Subsidiary task paradigm, 103
SUNflower pyramid, 1091–1093
Supplementary Restraint System (SRS), 545
Surveys method, 719–721
"Sustainable Safety" system approach, 1006, 1087, 1089
Swedish Occupational Fatigue Inventory (SOFI), 799, 805
Task load, measuring, 102–104
Taurine, 839
Teen passengers, 298–299
Teen pedestrian crashes, 878–881
"Telematics", 719, 733
Temporal separation, 905–908
Texas Transportation Institute, 33
Text messaging, 769–775
THC (Tetra Hydro Cannabinol). *See* Marijuana
Theory
of driver behavior, 87–125
of human information processing, 95, 193, 693, 934, 1045, 1056, 1062
of planned behavior (TPB), 738, 740–741, 770–771, 946, 1110
of reasoned behavior, 109, 397
"Theory of Multiple Resources", 99
See also Model
Theta waves, 815
Thorondike's Law of Effect, 592
Time-series analysis, 286
Time-to-collision (TTC), 225
Tire pressure monitoring systems (TPMS), 969
Top-speed limiter (TSL), 1143–1144
Traffic calming techniques, 1122
and pedestrian safety, 419, 431, 439, 904–905, 1122–1123
Traffic conflicts approach, 406–407, 410
Traffic Injury Research Foundation (TIRF), 33, 285
Traffic signal
duration, 218–219, 475–476
management, 1128–1129
Training
and older drivers, 367–369
and pedestrians, 894, 901, 902, 914
and young drivers, 276–282
Tranquilizers, 675
Transport Research Laboratory (TRL), 33
Tri-Level study of accident causes, 1045–1050, 1057, 1073
Tunnel, 68, 139, 666
vision, 172, 175, 813

"Unbounded" rationality, 108
"Uncertainty", 44
Unconscious processes, 190, 201
Universal helmet laws, 961, 962–967, 1012
University of Michigan Transportation Research Institute (UMTRI), 33, 50–51
Useful field of view (UFOV), 26, 157, 164, 165–168, 172, 352, 354, 368, 969

Validity, 48–52
  of crash data, 25–27
  of police assessment, 1060–1062
  of simulation and simulators, 748–749
Vehicle design
  for older drivers, 369–374
  and safety, 70, 84, 514, 1132–1137
Victim Impact Panels (VIP), 612, 613–614
Vigilance, 799
  and distraction, 605
  and fatigue, 799, 826
Violations (V), 122, 123, 467
  and accidents, 47, 110, 123, 257, 261, 266, 281–282, 290, 461, 486–487, 490–493, 697, 823, 941, 1060–1062, 1112
  and impulsivity, 479
  and Reason's theory of aberrant behaviors, 122–123, 467
Visibility
  enhancements, 1023
  pedestrian, 885–887, 887–894
Vision, 138, 348–354
  color vision, 154
  and highway safety, 1086, 1089
  monocular, 159–161
  stereopsis, 159–161
  and visual search, 137–176
"Vision Zero" approach, 16, 952, 1099, 1100
Visual
  acuity, 138, 142–151
  field, 161–163, 353
  search, 168–176
  system, 138–142, 348–349, 889
  See also Dynamic visual acuity

Walk-and-turn test, 606–607
Walking, 220, 221, 606, 745, 861, 862, 865, 867, 871–872, 882–883, 1008
Workload, 77, 104, 198, 716
  subjective, 272, 747–748, 750, 765–766
World Health Organization (WHO), 11, 14, 17, 25, 31, 258, 259, 393–394, 428, 519, 529, 539, 567, 603, 715, 898, 901, 928, 1088, 1094, 1095, 1099, 1103–1104, 1132

Yellow light dilemma, 216–217, 1128
Young drivers, 221, 258, 337, 584–585
  and accidents, 258–265
  and alcohol, 584–585
  and crash causation, 269–275, 1054
  education and training, 276–282, 305–314
  and experience, 265–269
  and fatigue, 261, 271, 306
  GDL, 282–305
  and gender/sex, 259, 261, 266–269
  inexperience and immaturity, 261–269
  and risk perception, 258, 311
  and skill, 261, 265–266, 270, 276, 278, 306, 311–312
  and zero tolerance (for alcohol), 591–592
  See also Novice drivers
Young rider of PTW, 946–949

"Zebra crossing", 908, 910, 939, 1000
"Zero tolerance" laws, 687–688
  for young and novice drivers, 591-592
Zopiclone, 652